ST/ESA/STAT/SER.S/30

Department of Economic and Social Affairs
Statistics Division

Département des affaires économiques et sociales
Division de statistique

Statistical Yearbook 2009

Fifty-fourth issue

Data available as of December 2010

Annuaire statistique 2009

Cinquante-quatrième édition

Données disponibles en décembre 2010

United Nations | Nations Unies

New York, 2011

Department of Economic and Social Affairs

The Department of Economic and Social Affairs of the United Nations Secretariat is a vital interface between global policies in the economic, social and environmental spheres and national action. The Department works in three main interlinked areas: (i) it compiles, generates and analyses a wide range of economic, social and environmental data and information on which States Members of the United Nations draw to review common problems and to take stock of policy options; (ii) it facilitates the negotiations of Member States in many intergovernmental bodies on joint courses of action to address ongoing or emerging global challenges; and (iii) it advises interested Governments on the ways and means of translating policy frameworks developed in United Nations conferences and summits into programmes at the country level and, through technical assistance, helps build national capacities.

Note

The designations employed and the presentation of the material in this publication do not imply the expression of any opinion whatsoever on the part of the Secretariat of the United Nations concerning the legal status of any country, city or area, or of its authorities, or concerning the delimitation of its frontiers or boundaries.

In general, statistics contained in the present publication are those available to the United Nations Secretariat up to March 2010 and refer to 2009 or earlier. They therefore reflect the country nomenclature currently in use.

The term "country" as used in the text of this publication also refers, as appropriate, to territories or areas.

The designations "developed" and "developing" which appear in some tables are intended for statistical convenience and do not necessarily express a judgement about the stage reached by a particular country or area in the development process.

Symbols of United Nations documents are composed of capital letters combined with figures.

Département des affaires économiques et sociales

Le Département des affaires économiques et sociales du Secrétariat de l'Organisation des Nations Unies assure le lien essentiel entre les politiques adoptées au plan international dans les domaines économique, social et écologique et les mesures prises au plan national. Il mène ses activités dans trois grands domaines interdépendants : i) il compile, produit et analyse une grande variété de données et d'informations économiques, sociales et écologiques dont les États Membres de l'ONU tirent parti pour examiner les problèmes communs et faire le point sur les possibilités d'action; ii) il facilite les négociations que les États Membres mènent dans un grand nombre d'organes intergouvernementaux sur les moyens d'action à employer conjointement pour faire face aux problèmes mondiaux existants ou naissants; et iii) il aide les gouvernements intéressés à traduire les orientations politiques établies lors des conférences et sommets de l'ONU en programmes nationaux et contribue à renforcer les capacités des pays en leur apportant une assistance technique.

Note

Les appellations employées dans la présente publication et la pré-sentation des données qui y figurent n'impliquent, de la part du Secrétariat de l'Organisation des Nations Unies, aucune prise de position quant au statut juridique des pays, territoires, villes ou zones, ou de leurs autorités, ni quant au tracé de leurs frontières ou limites.

En règle générale, les statistiques contenues dans la présente publication sont celles dont disposait le Secrétariat de l'Organisation des Nations Unies jusqu'à mars 2010 et portent sur la période finissant en 2009. Elles reflètent donc la nomenclature des pays en vigueur à l'époque.

Le terme « pays », tel qu'il est utilisé dans la présente publication, peut également désigner des territoires ou des zones.

Les appellations « développées » et « en développement » qui figurent dans certains tableaux sont employées à des fins exclusivement statistiques et n'expriment pas nécessairement un jugement quant au niveau de développement atteint par tel pays ou telle région.

Les cotes des documents de l'Organisation des Nations Unies se composent de lettres majuscules et de chiffres.

ST/ESA/STAT/SER.S/30

UNITED NATIONS PUBLICATION
Sales No. B.10.XVII.1.H

ISBN 978-92-1061284-5
ISSN 0082-8459

ST/ESA/STAT/SER.S/30

PUBLICATION DES NATIONS UNIES
Numéro de vente : B.10.XVII.1.H

ISBN 978-92-1061284-5
ISSN 0082-8459

Preface

The 2009 United Nations *Statistical Yearbook* is the fifty-fourth issue of the publication, prepared by the Statistics Division of the Department of Economic and Social Affairs. Ever since the compilation of data for the *Statistical Yearbook* series was initiated in 1948, it has consistently provided a wide range of internationally available statistics on social and economic conditions and activities at the national, regional and world levels.

The tables include series covering from one to ten years, depending upon data availability (as of 31 December 2010) and space constraints. The ten-year tables generally cover the period up to 2008 or 2009.

The *Yearbook* tables are based on data which have been compiled by the Statistics Division mainly from official national and international sources as these are more authoritative and comprehensive, more generally available as time series and more comparable among countries than other sources. These sources include the United Nations Statistics Division in the fields of national accounts, industry, energy and international trade, the United Nations Statistics Division and Population Division in the field of demographic statistics, and over 20 offices of the United Nations system and international organizations in other specialized fields. In some cases, official sources have been supplemented by other sources and estimates, where these have been subjected to professional scrutiny and debate and are consistent with other independent sources.

The United Nations agencies and other international, national and specialized organizations which furnished data are listed under "Statistical sources and references" at the end of the *Yearbook*. Acknowledgement is gratefully made for their generous and valuable cooperation in continually providing data.

The 70 tables of the *Yearbook* are organized in four parts. The first part presents key world and regional aggregates and totals. In the other three parts, the subject matter is generally presented by countries or areas, with world and regional aggregates shown in some cases only. Parts two, three and four cover, respectively, population and social topics, national economic activity and international economic relations. Each chapter ends with brief technical notes on statistical sources and methods for the tables it includes.

The three annexes contain information on country and area nomenclature and the conversion coefficients and factors used in the various tables, and list those tables which were added to or omitted from the last issue of the *Yearbook*.

The *Statistical Yearbook* is prepared by the Statistical Dissemination Section, Statistical Services Branch of the Statistics Division, Department of Economic and Social Affairs of the United Nations Secretariat. The programme manager is Mary Jane

Préface

L'Annuaire statistique des Nations Unies 2009 est la cinquante-quatrième édition de cette publication, préparée par la Division de statistique du Département des affaires économiques et sociales. Depuis son instauration en 1948 comme outil de compilation des données statistiques internationales, l'*Annuaire statistique* s'efforce de constamment diffuser un large éventail de statistiques disponibles sur les activités et conditions économiques et sociales, aux niveaux national, régional et mondial.

Les tableaux présentent des séries qui couvrent d'un à dix ans, en fonction de la disponibilité des données (à la date du 31 décembre 2010) et des contraintes d'espace. Les tableaux décennaux couvrent généralement la période jusqu'à 2008 ou 2009.

Les tableaux de l'*Annuaire* sont construits essentiellement à partir des données compilées par la Division de statistique et provenant de sources officielles, nationales et internationales; c'est en effet la meilleure source si l'on veut des données fiables, complètes et comparables, et si l'on a besoin de séries chronologiques. Ces sources sont: la Division de statistique du Secrétariat de l'Organisation des Nations Unies pour ce qui concerne la comptabilité nationale, l'industrie, l'énergie et le commerce extérieur, la Division de statistique et la Division de la population du Secrétariat de l'Organisation des Nations Unies pour les statistiques démographiques; et plus de 20 bureaux du système des Nations Unies et d'organisations internationales pour les autres domaines spécialisés. Dans quelques cas, les données officielles sont complétées par des informations et des estimations provenant d'autres sources qui ont été examinées par des spécialistes et confirmées par des sources indépendantes.

Les institutions spécialisées des Nations Unies et les autres organisations internationales, nationales et spécialisées qui ont fourni des données sont énumérées dans la section "Sources statistiques et références" figurant à la fin de l'ouvrage. Les auteurs de l'*Annuaire statistique* les remercient de leur précieuse et généreuse collaboration.

Les 70 tableaux de l'*Annuaire* sont regroupés en quatre parties. La première partie présente les principaux agrégats et totaux aux niveaux mondial et régional. Dans les trios parties suivantes, les thèmes sont généralement présentés par pays ou régions. Les agrégats mondiaux ou régionaux ne sont indiqués que dans certains cas seulement. Les trois parties autres sont consacrées à la population et aux questions sociales (deuxième partie), à l'activité économique nationale (troisième partie) et aux relations économiques internationales (quatrième partie). Chaque chapitre termine par une brève note technique sur les sources et les méthodes statistiques utilisées pour les tableaux présentés.

Les trois annexes donnent des renseignements sur la nomenclature des pays et des zones, ainsi que sur les coefficients et facteurs de conversion employés dans les différents tableaux. Une liste des tableaux ajoutés et

Holupka and the chief editor is Jacob Assa. They are assisted by David Carter, Anuradha Chimata and Aida Diawara. Bogdan Dragovic developed the software.

Comments on the present *Yearbook* and its future evolution are welcome. They may be sent via e-mail to statistics@un.org or to the United Nations Statistics Division, Statistical Dissemination Section, New York, NY 10017, USA.

supprimés depuis la dernière édition de l'*Annuaire* y est également disponible.

L'*Annuaire statistique* est préparé par la Section de la diffusion statistique, Service des statistiques de services de la Division de statistique, Département des affaires économiques et sociales du Secrétariat de l'Organisation des Nations Unies. La responsable du programme est Mary Jane Holupka, et le rédacteur en chef est Jacob Assa. Ils sont secondés par David Carter, Anuradha Chimata et Aida Diawara. Bogdan Dragovic est chargé des logiciels.

Les observations sur la présente édition de l'*Annuaire* et les suggestions de modification pour l'avenir seront reçues avec intérêt. Elles peuvent être envoyées par message électronique à statistics@un.org, ou adressées à la Division de statistique des Nations Unies, Section de la diffusion statistique, New York, NY 10017 (États-Unis d'Amérique).

New features in this issue

One objective of the *Statistical Yearbook* is to provide updated information annually for most of the regular tables. In addition, the *Yearbook* team strives to improve the publication and add new and useful features whenever possible. Several such additions have been made to this issue of the *Statistical Yearbook.*

New data series

Table 63, Outbound tourism, now has an additional series – Departures.

Industrial commodities – value

For the first time, the *Statistical Yearbook* now presents data on the value (in millions of US dollars) of industrial commodities, in addition to the usual volume statistics. This applies to the following tables:

- Table 36: Beer production
- Table 37: Cigarette production
- Table 38: Footwear production (uppers of leather)
- Table 41: Cement production
- Table 42: Pesticide production
- Table 43: Pig iron and crude steel production
- Table 44: Aluminium production (unwrought)
- Table 45: Radio and television receiver production
- Table 46: Passenger car production
- Table 47: Refrigerator production (for household use)
- Table 48: Household washing and drying machine production

Statistical Yearbook web site

The *Statistical Yearbook* now has an online presence at a dedicated web site - http://unstats.un.org/unsd/syb. The site features information on the latest *Yearbook,* including its table of contents, regional groupings, subject index and country index, as well as PDF versions of recent *Yearbooks* free of charge. It also has links to the United Nations Publications web site for access to hard copies of the *Yearbook* and other publications.

Les nouveautés de la présente édition

Chaque année, un des objectifs de *l'Annuaire statistique* est de fournir une mise à jour des données dans les tableaux usuels. De plus, l'équipe de *l'Annuaire* tente d'améliorer la qualité de la publication en ajoutant des nouveautés utiles dans la mesure du possible. Ainsi, plusieurs de ces améliorations ont été apportées à cette édition de *l'Annuaire statistique.*

Nouvelles séries de données

Tableau 63, Tourisme à l'étranger, comporte maintenant une nouvelle série – Départs.

Statistiques industrielles par produit - valeur

Pour la première fois, l'*Annuaire statistique* présente la valeur des produits industriels en dollars des Etats-Unis, ainsi que par volume comme il est d'usage. Cela s'applique aux tableaux suivants:

- Tableaux 36 : Production de bière
- Tableaux 37 : Production de cigarettes
- Tableaux 38 : Chaussures à dessus en cuir naturel
- Tableaux 41 : Production de ciment
- Tableaux 42 : Production de pesticides
- Tableaux 43 : Production de fonte et acier brut
- Tableaux 44 : Production d'aluminium non travaillé
- Tableaux 45 : Production de récepteurs de radio et de télévision
- Tableaux 46 : Production de voitures de tourisme
- Tableaux 47 : Production de réfrigérateurs à usage domestique
- Tableaux 48 : Production de machines à laver et à sécher le linge, de type ménager

Site web de l'Annuaire statistique

L'*Annuaire statistique* est maintenant présent en ligne : http://unstats.un.org/unsd/syb. Le site met à disposition gratuitement des informations sur le dernier *Annuaire.* Il contient également la table des matières, les groupements régionaux, l'index général, l'index des pays et les versions PDF des *Annuaires* récents. On peut aussi y trouver les liens vers les sites des parutions des Nations Unies afin d'accéder aux versions papiers de l'*Annuaire* ou d'autres publications.

Contents

Table des matières

Part Three: Economic activity

Troisième partie: Activité économique

Part Four: International economic relations

Quatrième partie: Relations économiques internationales

** Asterisks preceding table names identify tables that were presented in previous issues of the *Statistical Yearbook* which are not contained in the present issue. These tables will be updated in future issues of the *Yearbook* when new data become available.

** Ce symbole indique les tableaux publiés dans les éditions précédentes de l'*Annuaire statistique* mais qui n'ont pas été repris dans la présente édition. Ces tableaux seront actualisés dans les futures livraisons de l'*Annuaire* à mesure que des données nouvelles deviendront disponibles.

Explanatory notes

In general, the statistics presented in the present publication are based on information available to the Statistics Division of the United Nations Secretariat up to 31 December 2010.

Units of measurement
The metric system of weights and measures has been employed throughout the *Statistical Yearbook*. For conversion coefficients and factors, see annex II.

Country notes and nomenclature
As a general rule, the data presented in the *Yearbook* relate to a given country or area within its present de facto boundaries. A complete list of countries and territories is presented in Annex I.

It should also be noted that unless otherwise indicated, for statistical purposes, the data for China exclude those for Hong Kong Special Administrative Region of China, Macao Special Administrative Region of China and Taiwan province of China.

Symbols and conventions used in the tables

. A point is used to indicate decimals.
- A hyphen between years, for example, 2008-2009, indicates the full period involved, including the beginning and end years.
/ A slash indicates a financial year, school year or crop year, for example 2008/09.
... Data not available or not applicable.
* Provisional or estimated figure.
# Marked break in series.
^0 Not zero but less than half of the unit used.

A space is used as a thousands separator, for example 1 000 is one thousand.

Details and percentages in the tables do not necessarily add to totals because of rounding.

Notes explicatives

En général, les statistiques qui figurent dans la présente publication sont fondées sur les informations dont disposait la Division de statistique du Secrétariat de l'ONU jusqu'à 31 décembre 2010.

Unités de mesure
Le système métrique de poids et mesures a été utilisé dans tout l'*Annuaire statistique*. On trouvera à l'annexe II les coefficients et facteurs de conversion.

Notes sur les pays et nomenclature
En règle générale, les données renvoient au pays ou zone en question dans ses frontières actuelles effectives. Une liste complète des pays et territoires figure à l'annexe I.

Il convient de noter aussi que sauf indication contraire, les données statistiques relatives à la China ne comprennent pas celles qui concernent la région administrative spéciale de Hong Kong, la région administrative spéciale de Macao et la province chinoise de Taiwan.

Signes et conventions employés dans les tableaux

. Les décimales sont précédées d'un point.
- Un tiret entre des années, par exemple "2008-2009", indique que la période est embrassée dans sa totalité, y compris la première et la dernière année.
/ Une barre oblique renvoie à un exercice financier, à une année scolaire ou à une campagne agricole, par exemple "2008/09".
... Données non disponibles ou non applicables.
* Chiffre provisoire ou estimatif.
# Discontinuité notable dans la série.
^0 Non nul mais inférieur à la moitié de l'unité employée.

Le séparateur utilisé pour les milliers est l'espace : par exemple, 1 000 correspond à un millier.

Les chiffres étant arrondis, les totaux ne correspondent pas toujours à la somme exacte des éléments ou pourcentages figurant dans les tableaux.

Introduction

The 2009 United Nations *Statistical Yearbook* is the fifty-fourth issue of this publication, prepared by the Statistics Division, Department of Economic and Social Affairs, of the United Nations Secretariat. The tables include series covering from one to ten years, depending upon data availability and space constraints. The tables generally cover the period up to 2008 or 2009. For the most part, the statistics presented are those which were available to the Statistics Division as of 31 December 2010.

Objective and content of the Statistical Yearbook

The main purpose of the *Statistical Yearbook* is to provide in a single volume a comprehensive compilation of internationally available statistics on social and economic conditions and activities, at world, regional and national levels, covering a ten-year period to the extent possible.

Most of the statistics presented in the *Yearbook* are extracted from more detailed, specialized databases prepared by the Statistics Division and by many other international statistical services. Thus, while the specialized databases concentrate on monitoring topics and trends in particular social and economic fields, the *Statistical Yearbook* tables aim to provide data for a more comprehensive, overall description of social and economic structures, conditions, changes and activities. The objective has been to collect, systematize, coordinate and present in a consistent way the most essential components of comparable statistical information which can give a broad picture of social and economic processes.

The content of the *Statistical Yearbook* is planned to serve a general readership. The *Yearbook* endeavours to provide information for various bodies of the United Nations system as well as for other international organizations, governments and non-governmental organizations, national statistical, economic and social policy bodies, scientific and educational institutions, libraries and the public. Data published in the *Statistical Yearbook* may also be of interest to companies and enterprises and to agencies engaged in market research. The *Statistical Yearbook* thus provides information on a wide range of social and economic issues which are of concern in the United Nations system and among the governments and peoples of the world. A particular value of the *Yearbook* is that it facilitates meaningful analysis of issues by systematizing and coordinating the data across many fields and shedding light on such interrelated issues as:

- General economic growth and related economic conditions;
- Progress towards the Millennium Development Goals;

Introduction

L'Annuaire statistique des Nations Unies 2009 est la cinquante-quatrième édition de cette publication, établi par la Division de statistique du Département des affaires économiques et sociales du Secrétariat de l'Organisation des Nations Unies. Les tableaux présentent des séries qui couvrent d'un à dix ans, en fonction de la disponibilité des données et des contraintes d'espace. Les tableaux couvrent généralement la période jusqu'à 2008 ou 2009. La majeure partie des statistiques présentées ici sont celles dont disposait la Division de statistique à la date du 31 décembre 2010.

Objectif et contenu de l'Annuaire statistique

Le principal objectif de *l'Annuaire statistique* est de fournir en un seul volume un inventaire complet de statistiques internationales concernant la situation et les activités sociales et économiques aux niveaux mondial, régional et national, sur une période s'étalant, dans la mesure du possible, sur dix ans.

La plupart des données qui figurent dans l'*Annuaire statistique* proviennent de bases de données spécialisées davantage détaillées, préparées par la Division de statistique et par bien d'autres services statistiques internationaux. Tandis que les bases de données spécialisées se concentrent sur le suivi de domaines socioéconomiques particuliers, les données de l'*Annuaire* sont présentées de telle sorte qu'elles fournissent une description globale et exhaustive des structures, conditions, transformations et activités socioéconomiques. On a cherché à recueillir, systématiser, coordonner et présenter de manière cohérente les principales informations statistiques comparables, de manière à dresser un tableau général des processus socioéconomiques.

Le contenu de l'*Annuaire statistique* a été élaboré en vue d'un lectorat large. Les renseignements fournis devraient ainsi pouvoir être utilisés par les divers organismes du système des Nations Unies, mais aussi par d'autres organisations internationales, les gouvernements et les organisations non gouvernementales, les organismes nationaux de statistique et de politique économique et sociale, les institutions scientifiques et les établissements d'enseignement, les bibliothèques et les particuliers. Les données publiées dans l'*Annuaire* peuvent également intéresser les sociétés et entreprises, et les organismes spécialisés dans les études de marché. L'*Annuaire* présente des informations sur un large éventail de questions socioéconomiques liées aux préoccupations actuelles du système des Nations Unies, des gouvernements et des peuples du monde entier. Une qualité particulière de l'*Annuaire* est de faciliter une analyse approfondie de ces questions en systématisant et en articulant les données d'un domaine/secteur à l'autre, et en apportant un éclairage sur des sujets interdépendants, tels que :

- La croissance économique générale, et les conditions économiques qui lui sont liées;

- Population by sex and rate of increase, surface area, density, population in urban and rural areas;
- Unemployment, inflation and prices;
- Energy production and consumption and the development of new energy sources;
- Expansion of trade;
- The financial situation of countries;
- Education, training and eradication of illiteracy;
- Improvement in general living conditions;
- Pollution and protection of the environment;
- Assistance provided to developing countries for social and economic development purposes.

Organization of the Yearbook

The 70 tables of the *Yearbook* are grouped into four broad parts:

- Part One: World and Region Summary (chapter I, tables 1-6);
- Part Two: Population and Social Statistics (chapters II-V: tables 7-16);
- Part Three: Economic Activity (chapters VI-XIV: tables 17-57);
- Part Four: International Economic Relations (chapters XV-XVIII: tables 58-70).

The more aggregated information shown in part one provides an overall picture of development at the world and region levels. More specific and detailed information for analysis concerning individual countries or areas is presented in the other three parts. Each of these parts is divided into chapters, by topic, and each chapter ends with a section on "Technical notes", which provides brief descriptions of major statistical concepts, definitions and classifications required for interpretation and analysis of the data. Information on the methodology used for the computation of the figures can be found in the publications on methodology of the United Nations and its agencies, listed in the section "Statistical sources and references" at the end of the *Yearbook*.

Part One, World and Region Summary, comprises six tables highlighting the principal trends in the world as well as in each of the regions and in the major economic and social sectors. It contains global totals of important aggregate statistics needed for the analysis of economic growth, the structure of the world economy, major changes in world population and expansion of external merchandise trade. The global totals are, as a rule, subdivided into major geographical areas.

Part Two, Population and Social Statistics, comprises ten tables which contain more detailed statistical series on population, gender, education and communication.

Of the 41 tables in Part Three, Economic Activity, 20 provide data on national accounts, interest rates, labour force, prices, energy, environment and science and technology; 21 tables

- Les progrès accomplis dans la réalisation des Objectifs du Millénaire pour le Développement;
- La population selon le sexe, taux d'accroissement, superficie et densité, population urbaine et rurale;
- Le chômage, l'inflation et les prix;
- La production et la consommation d'énergie et le développement de nouvelles sources d'énergie;
- L'expansion des échanges;
- La situation financière des pays;
- L'éducation, la formation et l'élimination de l'analphabétisme;
- L'amélioration des conditions de vie;
- La pollution et la protection de l'environnement;
- L'assistance aux pays en développement à des fins socioéconomiques.

Présentation de l'Annuaire

Les 70 tableaux de l'*Annuaire* sont groupés en quatre parties:

- La première partie : Aperçu mondial et régional (chapitre I, tableaux 1 à 6);
- La deuxième partie : Statistiques démographiques et sociales (chapitres II à V, tableaux 7 à 16);
- La troisième partie : Activité économique (chapitres VI à XIV, tableaux 17 à 57);
- La quatrième partie : Relations économiques internationales (chapitres XV à XVIII, tableaux 58 à 70).

Les valeurs les plus agrégées qui figurent dans la première partie donnent un tableau global du développement à l'échelon mondial et régional, tandis que les trois autres parties contiennent des renseignements plus précis et détaillés qui se prêtent mieux à une analyse par pays ou par zones. Chacune de ces trois parties est divisée en chapitres portant sur des sujets donnés, et chaque chapitre comprend une section intitulée "Notes techniques" où l'on trouve une brève description des principales notions, définitions et classifications statistiques nécessaires pour interpréter et analyser les données. Les méthodes de calcul utilisées sont décrites dans les publications se référant à la méthodologie des Nations Unies et de leurs organismes, énumérées à la fin de l'*Annuaire* dans la section "Sources et références statistiques".

La première partie, intitulée "Aperçu mondial et régional", comprend six tableaux présentant les principales tendances dans le monde et dans les régions ainsi que dans les principaux secteurs économiques et sociaux. Elle fournit des chiffres mondiaux pour les principaux agrégats statistiques nécessaires pour analyser la croissance économique, la structure de l'économie mondiale, les principaux changements dans la population mondiale et l'expansion du commerce extérieur de marchandises. En règle générale, les chiffres mondiaux sont répartis par grandes régions géographiques.

La deuxième partie, intitulée "Population et statistiques sociales", comporte dix tableaux où figurent des

provide data on production in the major branches of the economy (using, in general, the *International Standard Industrial Classification*, ISIC), namely agriculture, hunting, forestry and fishing, and manufacturing. Consumption data are combined with the production data in tables on specific commodities, where feasible.

Part Four, International Economic Relations, comprises 13 tables on international merchandise trade, international tourism and transport, international finance and development assistance.

A subject index and a country index (in English only) are provided at the end of the *Yearbook*.

Annexes and regional groupings of countries or areas

The annexes to the *Statistical Yearbook,* and the section "Explanatory notes" preceding the Introduction, provide additional essential information on the *Yearbook's* contents and presentation of data.

Annex I provides information on countries or areas covered in the *Yearbook* tables and on their arrangement in geographical regions and economic or other groupings. The geographical groupings shown in the *Yearbook* are generally based on continental regions unless otherwise indicated. However, strict consistency in this regard is impossible. A wide range of classifications is used for different purposes in the various international agencies and other sources of statistics for the *Yearbook*. These classifications vary in response to administrative and analytical requirements.

Similarly, there is no common agreement in the United Nations system concerning the terms "developed" and "developing" when referring to the stage of development reached by any given country or area, and its corresponding classification in one or the other grouping. The *Yearbook* thus refers more generally to "developed" or "developing" regions on the basis of conventional practice. Following this practice, "developed" regions or areas comprise Canada and the United States in Northern America, Japan in Asia, Australia and New Zealand in Oceania, and Europe, while all of Africa and the remainder of the Americas, Asia and Oceania comprise the "developing regions". These designations are intended for statistical convenience and do not necessarily express a judgement about the stage reached by a particular country or area in the development process.

Annex II provides detailed information on conversion coefficients and factors used in various tables, and annex III provides a list of tables added and omitted in the present edition of the *Yearbook*. Tables for which a sufficient amount of new data is not available are not being published in this *Yearbook*. Their titles nevertheless are still listed in the table of contents since it is planned that they will be published

séries plus détaillées concernant la population, la situation des femmes, l'éducation et la communication.

La troisième partie, intitulée "Activité économique", comporte 41 tableaux, 20 qui présentent des statistiques concernant les comptes nationaux, les taux d'intérêt, la population active, les prix, l'énergie, l'environnement, et la science et technologie; et 21 qui présentent des données sur la production des principales branches d'activité économique (en utilisant en général la *Classification internationale type, par industrie, de toutes les branches d'activité économique*): agriculture, chasse, sylviculture et pêche, et industries manufacturières. Les tableaux traitant de certains produits de base associent autant que possible les données relatives à la consommation aux valeurs concernant la production.

La quatrième partie, intitulée "Relations économiques internationales", comprend 13 tableaux relatifs au commerce international de marchandises, au tourisme et transport internationaux, aux finances internationales, et à l'aide au développement.

Un index de pays figure à la fin de l'*Annuaire*.

Annexes et groupements régionaux des pays et zones

Les annexes à l'*Annuaire statistique,* et la section intitulée "Notes explicatives" qui précède l'introduction, offrent d'importantes informations complémentaires quant à la teneur et à la présentation des données figurant dans le présent ouvrage.

L'annexe I donne des renseignements sur les pays ou zones couverts par les tableaux de l'*Annuaire* et sur leur regroupement en régions géographiques et groupements économiques ou autres. Sauf indication contraire, les groupements géographiques figurant dans l'*Annuaire* sont généralement fondés sur les régions continentales, mais une présentation absolument systématique est impossible à cet égard car les diverses institutions internationales et autres sources de statistiques employées pour la confection de l'*Annuaire* emploient, selon l'objet de l'exercice, des classifications fort différentes en réponse à diverses exigences d'ordre administratif ou analytique.

Il n'existe pas non plus dans le système des Nations Unies de définition commune des termes "développé" et "en développement" pour décrire le niveau atteint en la matière par un pays ou une zone donnés ni pour les classifier dans l'un ou l'autre de ces groupes. Ainsi, dans l'*Annuaire*, on s'en remet à l'usage pour qualifier les régions de "développées" ou "en développement". Selon cet usage, les régions ou zones développées sont le Canada et les Etats-Unis dans l'Amérique septentrionale, le Japon dans l'Asie, l'Australie et la Nouvelle-Zélande dans l'Océanie, et l'Europe, alors que toute l'Afrique et le reste des Amériques, l'Asie et l'Océanie constituent les régions en développement. Ces appellations sont utilisées pour plus de commodité dans la présentation des statistiques et n'impliquent pas nécessairement un jugement quant au stade de développement auquel est parvenu tel pays ou telle

in a later issue as new data are compiled by the collecting agency.

Data comparability, quality and relevance

The major challenge continuously facing the *Statistical Yearbook* is to present series which are as nearly comparable across countries as the available statistics permit. Considerable efforts have already been made among the international suppliers of data and by the staff of the *Statistical Yearbook* to ensure the compatibility of various series by coordinating time periods, base years, prices chosen for valuation, and so on. This is indispensable in relating various bodies of data to each other and in facilitating analysis across different sectors. Thus, for example, relating data on short-term interest rates to those on prices makes it possible to arrive at a general understanding about the inflation environment, and relating a country's data on tourism expenditure in other countries to those on its per capita GDP provides a gauge on that country's wealth status. In general, the data presented reflect the methodological recommendations of the United Nations Statistical Commission issued in various United Nations publications, and of other international bodies concerned with statistics. Publications containing these recommendations and guidelines are listed in the section "Statistical sources and references" at the end of the *Yearbook*. The use of international recommendations not only promotes international comparability of the data but also ensures a degree of compatibility regarding the underlying concepts, definitions and classifications relating to different series. However, much work remains to be done in this area and, for this reason, some tables can serve only as a first source of data, which require further adjustment before being used for more in-depth analytical studies. While on the whole, a significant degree of comparability has been achieved in international statistics, there will remain some limitations, for a variety of reasons.

One common cause of non-comparability of economic data is different valuations of statistical aggregates such as national income, wages and salaries, output of industries and so forth. Conversion of these and similar series originally expressed in national prices into a common currency, for example into United States dollars, through the use of exchange rates, is not always satisfactory owing to frequent wide fluctuations in market rates and differences between official rates and rates which would be indicated by unofficial markets or purchasing power parities. The use of different kinds of sources for obtaining data is another cause of incomparability. This is true, for example, in the case of employment and unemployment, where data are obtained from different sources, namely household and labour force sample zone.

L'annexe II fournit des renseignements sur les coefficients et facteurs de conversion employés dans les différents tableaux, et l'annexe III contient la liste de tableaux qui ont été ajoutés ou omis dans la présente édition de l'*Annuaire*. Les tableaux pour lesquels on ne dispose pas d'une quantité suffisante des données nouvelles, n'ont pas été publiés dans cet *Annuaire*. Comme ils seront repris dans une prochaine édition à mesure que des données nouvelles seront dépouillées par l'office statistique d'origine, ses titres figurent toujours dans la table des matières.

Comparabilité, qualité et pertinence des statistiques

Le défi majeur auquel l'*Annuaire Statistique* fait continuellement face est de présenter des séries aussi comparables entre les pays que la disponibilité des statistiques le permettent. Les sources internationales de données et les auteurs de l'*Annuaire* ont réalisé des efforts considérables pour faire en sorte que diverses séries soient compatibles, en harmonisant les périodes de référence, les années de base, les prix utilisés pour les évaluations, etc. Cette démarche est indispensable si l'on veut rapprocher divers ensembles de données, et faciliter l'analyse intersectorielle de l'économie. Ainsi, lier les données concernant les taux d'intérêt à court terme à celles des prix permet d'arriver à une compréhension globale de l'environnement de l'inflation; lier les données de dépenses touristiques d'un pays dans d'autres pays à celles de son PIB par tête fournit un indicateur de la richesse de ce pays. De façon générale, les données sont présentées selon les recommandations méthodologiques formulées par la Commission de statistique des Nations Unies, et par les autres entités internationales impliquées dans les statistiques. Les titres des publications contenant ces recommandations et leurs lignes directrices figurent à la fin de l'*Annuaire*, dans la section "Sources et références statistiques". Le respect des recommandations internationales tend non seulement à promouvoir la comparabilité internationale des données, mais elle assure également une certaine comparabilité entre les concepts, les définitions et classifications utilisés. Mais comme il reste encore beaucoup à faire dans ce domaine, les données présentées dans certains tableaux n'ont qu'une valeur indicative, et nécessiteront des ajustements plus poussés avant de pouvoir servir à des analyses approfondies. Bien que l'on soit parvenu, dans l'ensemble, à un degré de comparabilité appréciable en matière de statistiques internationales, diverses raisons expliquent que subsistent encore de nombreuses limitations.

Une cause commune de non comparabilité des données économiques réside dans la diversité des méthodes d'évaluation employées pour comptabiliser des agrégats tels que le revenu national, les salaires et traitements, la production des différentes branches d'activité industrielle, etc. Il n'est pas toujours satisfaisant de ramener la valeur

surveys, establishment censuses or surveys, official estimates, social insurance statistics and employment office statistics, which are not fully comparable in many cases. Non-comparability of data may also result from differences in the institutional patterns of countries. Certain variations in social and economic organization and institutions may have an impact on the comparability of the data even if the underlying concepts and definitions are identical. These and other causes of non-comparability of the data are briefly explained in the technical notes to each chapter.

A further set of challenges relate to timeliness, quality and relevance of the data contained in the *Yearbook*. Users generally demand the most up-to-date statistics. However, due to the different development stages of statistical capacity in different countries, data for the most recent years may only be available for a small number of countries. For a global print publication, therefore, a balance has to be struck between presenting the most updated information and satisfactory country coverage. Of course the United Nations Statistics Division's website offers greater flexibility in presenting continuously updated information and is therefore a useful complement to the annual print publication. Furthermore, as most of the information presented in this *Yearbook* is collected through specialized United Nations agencies and partners, the timeliness is continuously enhanced by improving the communication and data flow between countries and the specialized agencies on the one hand, and between the United Nations Statistics Division and the specialized agencies on the other. The development of new XML-based data transfer protocols will address this issue and is expected to make international data flows more efficient in the future.

Data quality at the international level is a function of the data quality at the national level. The United Nations Statistics Division in close cooperation with its partners among the UN agencies and the international statistical system continues to support countries' efforts to improve both the coverage and the quality of their data. Metadata, as for example reflected in the footnotes and technical notes of this publication, are an important service to the user to allow an informed assessment of the quality of the data. Given the wide variety of sources for the *Yearbook*, there is of course an equally wide variety of data formats and accompanying metadata. An important challenge for the United Nations Statistics Division and its partners for the future is to work further towards the standardization, or at least harmonization, of metadata.

The final challenge relates to maintaining the relevance of the series included in the *Yearbook*. As new policy concerns enter the developmental debate, the United Nations Statistics Division will need to

des séries de ce type—exprimée à l'origine en prix nationaux—à une monnaie commune (par exemple le dollar des États-Unis) car les taux de change du marché connaissent fréquemment de fortes fluctuations, et parce que les taux officiels ne coïncident pas avec ceux des marchés officieux ni avec les parités réelles de pouvoir d'achat. Le recours à des sources diverses pour la collecte des données est un autre facteur qui limite la comparabilité. C'est le cas, par exemple, des données d'emploi et de chômage, obtenues par des moyens aussi peu comparables que les sondages, le dépouillement des registres d'assurances sociales et les enquêtes auprès des entreprises. Dans certains cas, les données ne sont pas comparables en raison de différences entre les structures institutionnelles des pays. Des changements dans l'organisation et les institutions économiques et sociales peuvent affecter la comparabilité des données, même si les concepts et définitions sont fondamentalement identiques. Ces causes, et d'autres, de non comparabilité des données sont brièvement expliquées dans les notes techniques de chaque chapitre.

Un autre ensemble de défis à relever concerne la fraîcheur, la qualité et la pertinence des données présentées dans l'*Annuaire*. Les utilisateurs exigent généralement des données les plus récentes possibles. Toutefois, selon le niveau de développement de la capacité statistique des pays, les données pour les dernières années peuvent n'être disponibles que pour un nombre limité de pays. Dans le cadre d'une publication mondiale, un équilibre doit être trouvé entre la présentation de l'information la plus récente et une couverture géographique satisfaisante. Bien entendu, le site Internet de la Division de statistique des Nations Unies offre une plus grande flexibilité, puisqu'il propose une information actualisée au fil de l'eau, et constitue ainsi un complément utile à la publication papier annuelle. Par ailleurs, étant donné que la plupart des informations présentées dans cet *Annuaire* sont collectées parmi les agences spécialisées des Nations Unies et autres partenaires, la fraîcheur des données est continuellement améliorée, grâce à une meilleure communication et un meilleur échange de données entre les pays et les agences spécialisées d'une part, et entre la Division de statistique des Nations Unies et les agences spécialisées d'autre part. Le développement de nouveaux protocoles de transfert de données basés sur le langage XML devrait contribuer à rendre, à l'avenir, les échanges de données internationales encore plus efficaces.

La qualité des données au niveau international est fonction de la qualité des données au niveau national. La Division de statistique des Nations Unies, en étroite collaboration avec ses partenaires dans les agences de l'ONU et dans le système statistique international, continue de soutenir les efforts des pays pour améliorer à la fois la couverture et la qualité de leurs données. Des métadonnées, comme l'illustrent les notes de bas de page et les notes techniques de cette publication, constituent un important service fourni à l'utilisateur pour lui permettre d'évaluer de

introduce new series that describe concerns that have gained prominence as well as to prune data as they become outdated and continue to update the recurrent *Yearbook* series that still address those issues which are most pertinent. Often choosing the appropriate moment when the statistical information on new topics has matured sufficiently so as to be able to disseminate meaningful global data can be challenging. Furthermore, a balance has to continuously be found between the ever-increasing amount of information available for dissemination and the space limitations of the print version of the *Statistical Yearbook*. International comparability, data availability and data quality will remain the key criteria to guide the United Nations Statistics Division in its selection.

Needless to say, more can always be done to improve the *Statistical Yearbook*'s scope, coverage, design, metadata and timeliness. The *Yearbook* team continually strives to improve upon each of these aspects and to make its publication as responsive as possible to its users' needs and expectations, while at the same time focusing on a manageable body of data and metadata. Since data disseminated in digital form have clear advantages over those in print, as much of the *Yearbook* information as possible will continue to be included in the Statistics Division's online databases. Still, the *Statistical Yearbook* will continue to claim its rightful place among the products of the Statistics Division as a useful resource for a general understanding of the global social and economic situation.

manière avisée la qualité des données. Etant donné la grande variété des sources de *l'Annuaire*, il y a bien entendu une non moins grande variété de formats de données et de métadonnées associées. Un important défi que la Division de statistique des Nations Unies et ses partenaires doivent relever dans le futur est d'aboutir à la standardisation, ou au moins l'harmonisation, des métadonnées.

Le dernier défi concerne la constance de la pertinence des séries présentées dans *l'Annuaire*. Au fur et à mesure que de nouvelles préoccupations politiques pénètrent le débat lié au développement, la Division de statistique des Nations Unies doit introduire dans l'*Annuaire* de nouvelles séries qui leur sont liées, et, ce faisant, effectuer une coupe sombre parmi les données qui lui semblent dépassées, tout en s'assurant de continuer à actualiser les séries récurrentes de qui paraissent encore pertinentes. Souvent, choisir le moment idoine auquel les données statistiques sur de nouveaux thèmes sont suffisamment matures pour qu'elles puissent, au niveau mondial, être diffusées sans hésitation, est un défi en soi. Par ailleurs, un équilibre doit continuellement être trouvé entre le volume toujours croissant d'informations disponibles à la diffusion, et les contraintes d'espace de la version papier de l'*Annuaire statistique*. La comparabilité internationale, la disponibilité des données et leur qualité devront rester le principal critère à considérer par la Division de statistique des Nations Unies dans sa sélection.

Inutile de dire qu'il est toujours possible d'améliorer l'*Annuaire statistique* en ce qui concerne son champ, sa couverture, sa conception générale, ses métadonnées et sa mise à jour. L'équipe en charge de l'*Annuaire* s'évertue en permanence à améliorer chacun de ces aspects, et de faire en sorte que cette publication réponde au plus près aux besoins et aux attentes de ses utilisateurs, sans toutefois oublier de mettre l'accent sur un corpus gérable de données et de métadonnées. Puisqu'il est avéré que les données diffusées de manière digitale ont des avantages comparés à celles diffusées sur papier, autant d'informations de l'*Annuaire* que possible continueront d'être inclues dans les bases de données électroniques de la Division de statistique. L'*Annuaire statistique* garde toujours une place de choix parmi les produits de la Division de statistique comme une ressource utile pour une compréhension général de la situation sociale et économique globale.

Part One

World and region summary

Chapter I   World and region summary (tables 1-6)

This part of the *Statistical Yearbook* presents selected aggregate series on principal economic and social topics for the world as a whole and for the major regions. The topics include population and surface area, agricultural production, external trade, government financial reserves, and energy production and consumption. More detailed data on individual countries and areas are provided in the subsequent parts of the present *Yearbook*. These comprise Part Two: Population and Social Statistics; Part Three: Economic Activity; and Part Four: International Economic Relations.

Regional totals between series may be incomparable owing to differences in definitions of regions and lack of data for particular regional components. General information on regional groupings is provided in annex I of the *Yearbook*. Supplementary information on regional groupings used in specific series is provided, as necessary, in table footnotes and in the technical notes at the end of chapter I.

Première partie

Aperçu mondial et régional

Chapitre I   Aperçu mondial et régional (tableaux 1 à 6)

Cette partie de l'*Annuaire statistique* présente, pour le monde entier et ses principales subdivisions, un choix d'agrégats ayant trait à des questions économiques et sociales essentielles: population et superficie, production agricole, commerce extérieur, réserves financières publiques, et la production et la consommation d'énergie. Des statistiques plus détaillées pour divers pays ou zones figurent dans les parties ultérieures de l'*Annuaire*, c'est-à-dire dans les deuxième, troisième et quatrième parties intitulées respectivement: population et statistiques sociales, activités économiques et relations économiques internationales.

Les totaux régionaux peuvent être incomparables entre les séries en raison de différences dans la définition des régions et de l'absence de données sur tel ou tel élément régional. A l'annexe I de l'*Annuaire*, on trouvera des renseignements généraux sur les groupements régionaux. Des informations complémentaires sur les groupements régionaux pour certaines séries bien précises sont fournies, lorsqu'il y a lieu, dans les notes figurant au bas des tableaux et dans les notes techniques à la fin du chapitre I.

World statistics: selected series

Population, production, external trade and finance

Statistiques mondiales : séries principales

Population, production, commerce extérieur et finances

Series Séries	Unit or base Unité ou base	2000	2001	2002	2003	2004	2005	2006	2007	2008
Population • Population										
World population [1] Population mondial [1]	million	6 115	6 195	6 274	6 354	6 433	6 512	6 592	6 671	6 750
Output / production • Production										
Gross domestic product • Produit intérieur brut										
GDP at current prices PIB aux prix courants	billion US $ milliard $ E.-U.	32 089	31 869	33 186	37 292	41 975	45 424	49 178	55 277	60 820
GDP per capita PIB par habitant	US $ $ E.-U.	5 248	5 145	5 290	5 871	6 526	6 977	7 462	8 288	9 012
GDP real rates of growth Taux de l'accroissement réels	%	4.2	1.7	2.0	2.7	4.1	3.5	4.0	3.9	2.2
Agriculture, forestry and fishing production • Production agricole, forestière et de la pêche										
Index numbers - Indices										
All commodities[2] Tous produits[2]	1999-01 = 100	100	101	102	105	110	112	114	116	120
Food[2] Produits alimentaires[2]	1999-01 = 100	100	101	102	105	110	112	113	116	121
Quantities - Quantités										
Cereals[2] Céréales[2]	million t.	2 060	2 109	2 031	2 090	2 281	2 269	2 237	2 349	2 525
Meat[2] Viande[2]	million t.	233	236	243	247	253	259	266	271	278
Roundwood[2] Bois rond[2]	million m^3	3 430	3 332	3 360	3 413	3 478	3 559	3 533	3 551	3 410
Fish production[2] Production halieutique[2]	million t.	136	136	139	139	148	151	152	156	159
Industrial production • Production industrielle										
Quantities - Quantités										
Coal[2] Houille[2]	million t.	3 273	3 448	3 499	3 819	4 201	4 515	4 764	4 994	5 280
Lignite and brown coal[2] Lignite et charbon brun[2]	million t.	1 312	1 355	1 355	1 375	1 378	1 394	1 444	1 471	1 495
Crude petroleum[2] Pétrole brut[2]	million t.	3 351	3 358	3 324	3 462	3 566	3 609	3 617	3 604	3 635
Natural gas[2] Gaz naturel[2]	petajoules pétajoules	114 878	116 158	119 125	123 127	127 837	131 654	135 472	138 769	137 411
Electricity[3] Electricité[3]	billion kWh milliard kWh	15 482	15 578	16 188	16 788	17 554	18 343	19 057	19 909	20 496
Sugar, raw Sucre, brut	million t.	130	131	142	148	147	141	152	166	162
Woodpulp[2] Pâte de bois[2]	million t.	172	166	168	171	176	175	176	181	177
Sawnwood[2] Sciages[2]	million m^3	386	380	394	401	428	438	446	442	404

Series Séries	Unit or base Unité ou base	2000	2001	2002	2003	2004	2005	2006	2007	2008
External trade • Commerce extérieur										
Value - Valeur										
Imports, c.i.f. Importations c.a.f.	billion US $ milliard $ E.-U.	6 535	6 299	6 536	7 616	9 296	10 577	12 149	13 994	16 157
Exports, f.o.b. Exportations f.o.b.	billion US $ milliard $ E.-U.	6 365	6 118	6 409	7 459	9 075	10 348	11 970	13 800	15 926
Volume: index of exports - Volume: indice des exportations										
All commodities Tous produits	2000 = 100	100	99	103	109	122	133	147	157	165
Manufactures Manufacturés	2000 = 100	100	100	103	111	128	139	153	145	146
Unit value: index of exports[4] - Valeur unitaure: indice des exportations[4]										
All commodities Tous produits	2000 = 100	100	97	97	107	117	121	126	136	148
Manufactures Produits manufactures	2000 = 100	100	98	98	104	110	111	114	125	131
Finance • Finances										
International reserves minus gold[5] - Réserves internationales moins l'or[5]										
All countries[2] Tous les pays[2]	billion SDR milliard DTS	1 552.0	1 707.4	1 857.1	2 122.4	2 489.8	3 071.4	3 526.8	4 271.9	4 808.0
Position in IMF[2] Disponibilité au FMI[2]	billion SDR milliard DTS	61.7	71.5	89.8	98.8	86.6	40.8	26.3	21.7	38.7
Foreign exchange[2] Devises[2]	billion SDR milliard DTS	1 486.1	1 630.9	1 771.2	2 035.8	2 413.6	3 022.6	3 490.7	4 239.4	4 763.7
SDR (special drawing rights)[2] DTS (droits de triage spéc.)[2]	billion SDR milliard DTS	28.1	27.1	29.3	32.0	33.3	30.7	32.3	33.9	33.0

Source:
Databases of the Food and Agriculture Organization of the United Nations (FAO), Rome; the International Monetary Fund (IMF), Washington, D.C.; and the United Nations Statistics Division, New York.

Notes
1 Mid-year estimates.
2 As of December 2010.
3 Electricity generated by establishments for public or private use.
4 Indices computed in US dollars.
5 End of period.

Source:
Les bases de données de l'Organisation des Nations Unies pour l'alimentation et l'agriculture (FAO), Rome; du Fonds Monétaire International (FMI), Washington, D.C. ; et de la Division de statistique de l'Organisation de Nations Unies, New York.

Notes
1 Les estimations au milieu de l'année.
2 De décembre 2010.
3 L'électricité produite par des entreprises d'utilisation publique ou privée.
4 Indice calculé en dollars des Etats-Unis.
5 Fin de la période.

2 Population, rate of increase, birth and death rates, surface area and density

Population, taux d'accroissement, taux de natalité, taux de mortalité, superficie et densité

Major areas and regions Grandes régions	Mid-year population estimates (millions) Estimations de population au milieu de l'année (millions)							Annual rate of increase Taux d'accroissement annuel %	Crude birth rate Taux bruts de natalité (p.1 000)	Crude death rate Taux bruts de mortalité (p.1 000)	Surface area Superficie (000 km²)	Density[1] Densité[1]
	1950	1960	1970	1980	1990	2000	2008	2005 - 2010			2008	2008
World Monde	**2 529**	**3 023**	**3 686**	**4 438**	**5 291**	**6 115**	**6 750**	**1.2**	**20**	**8**	**136 127**	**50**
Africa Afrique	**227**	**285**	**367**	**482**	**639**	**820**	**987**	**2.3**	**36**	**12**	**30 312**	**33**
Eastern Africa Afrique orientale	65	82	108	144	193	253	311	2.6	40	13	6 361	49
Middle Africa Afrique centrale	26	32	41	54	73	98	123	2.6	43	16	6 613	19
Northern Africa Afrique du Nord	53	68	87	113	148	180	206	1.7	24	7	8 525	24
Southern Africa Afrique australe	16	20	26	33	42	51	57	1.0	23	15	2 675	21
Western Africa Afrique occidentale	68	84	106	139	183	238	291	2.5	40	14	6 138	47
Northern America[2] Amérique septentrionale[2]	**172**	**204**	**231**	**254**	**283**	**319**	**345**	**1.0**	**14**	**8**	**21 776**	**16**
Latin America and the Caribbean Amérique latine et Caraïbes	**167**	**220**	**287**	**363**	**442**	**521**	**576**	**1.1**	**19**	**6**	**20 546**	**28**
Caribbean Caraïbes	17	21	25	30	34	39	42	0.8	19	7	234	178
Central America Amérique centrale	38	51	70	92	112	135	150	1.2	21	5	2 480	60
South America Amérique du Sud	112	148	191	241	296	347	385	1.1	18	6	17 832	22
Asia Asie	**1 403**	**1 694**	**2 125**	**2 623**	**3 179**	**3 698**	**4 075**	**1.1**	**19**	**7**	**31 880**	**128**
Eastern Asia Asie orientale	660	779	972	1 159	1 337	1 472	1 547	0.6	13	7	11 763	131
South-central Asia Asie centrale et du Sud	516	627	783	991	1 251	1 518	1 729	1.5	24	8	10 791	160
South-eastern Asia Asie du Sud-est	176	220	283	356	440	517	576	1.2	19	7	4 495	128
Western Asia[3] Asie occidentale[3]	52	67	88	117	152	190	224	1.9	24	6	4 831	46
Europe[3] Europe[3]	**548**	**605**	**656**	**693**	**721**	**727**	**732**	**0.1**	**10**	**11**	**23 049**	**32**
Eastern Europe Europe orientale	220	254	276	295	310	304	294	-0.4	10	14	18 814	16
Northern Europe Europe septentrionale	78	82	87	90	92	94	98	0.5	12	10	1 810	54
Southern Europe Europe méridionale	108	117	127	138	143	145	152	0.5	10	10	1 317	116
Western Europe Europe occidentale	141	152	166	171	176	183	188	0.2	10	9	1 108	170

2 Population, rate of increase, birth and death rates, surface area and density *(continued)*
Population, taux d'accroissement, taux de natalité, taux de mortalité, superficie et densité *(suite)*

Major areas and regions Grandes régions	Mid-year population estimates (millions) Estimations de population au milieu de l'année (millions)							Annual rate of increase Taux d'accroissement annuel %	Crude birth rate Taux bruts de natalité (p.1 000)	Crude death rate Taux bruts de mortalité (p.1 000)	Surface area Superficie (000 km²)	Density[1] Densité[1]
	1950	1960	1970	1980	1990	2000	2008	2005 - 2010			2008	2008
Oceania[2] Océanie[2]	**12.8**	**15.9**	**19.6**	**22.9**	**26.9**	**31.2**	**34.9**	**1.3**	**17**	**7**	**8 564**	**4**
Australia and New Zealand Australie et Nouvelle-Zélande	10.1	12.6	15.5	17.8	20.5	23.0	25.3	1.0	13	7	8 012	3
Melanesia Mélanésie	2.3	2.7	3.4	4.3	5.5	7.0	8.4	2.2	30	8	541	16
Micronesia Micronésie	0.1	0.2	0.2	0.3	0.4	0.5	0.6	1.3	22	5	3	186
Polynesia Polynésie	0.2	0.3	0.4	0.5	0.5	0.6	0.7	0.8	22	5	8	83

Source:
United Nations Statistics Division, New York, *Demographic Yearbook 2008*.

Source:
Organisation des Nations Unies, Division de statistique, New York, *Annuaire démographique 2008*.

1 Population per square kilometre of surface area. Figures are merely the quotients of population divided by surface area and are not to be considered either as reflecting density in the urban sense or as indicating the supporting power of a territory's land and resources.

2 Hawaii, a state of the United States of America, is included in Northern America rather than Oceania.

3 The European portion of Turkey is included in Western Asia rather than Europe.

1 Nombre d'habitants au kilomètre carré. Il s'agit simplement du quotient du chiffre de la population divisé par celui de la superficie, il ne faut pas y voir d'indication de la densité au sens urbain du terme ni de l'effectif de population que les terres et les ressources du territoire sont capables de nourrir.

2 Hawaii, un Etat des Etats-Unis d'Amérique, est compris en Amérique septentrionale plutôt qu'en Océanie.

3 La partie européenne de la Turquie est comprise en Asie Occidentale plutôt qu'en Europe.

3 Index numbers of total agricultural and food production

1999 – 2001 = 100

Indices de la production agricole totale et de la production alimentaire

1999 – 2001 = 100

Region - Région	2000	2001	2002	2003	2004	2005	2006	2007	2008	2009
World Monde										
Agricultural – agricole	**100**	**101**	**102**	**105**	**110**	**112**	**114**	**116**	**120**	**121**
Food – alimentaire	**100**	**101**	**102**	**105**	**110**	**112**	**113**	**116**	**121**	**121**
Africa Afrique										
Agricultural – agricole	99	101	105	110	113	117	122	121	127	129
Food – alimentaire	99	101	105	111	114	118	124	122	128	131
Americas Amériques										
Agricultural – agricole	100	100	101	105	111	112	113	118	120	119
Food – alimentaire	100	100	101	106	110	111	113	119	121	120
Asia Asie										
Agricultural – agricole	100	102	104	107	111	116	119	123	126	128
Food – alimentaire	100	102	104	107	111	115	118	122	126	128
Europe Europe										
Agricultural – agricole	99	100	101	97	105	101	100	99	105	104
Food – alimentaire	99	100	101	97	105	101	100	99	105	104
Oceania Océanie										
Agricultural – agricole	98	102	91	100	97	103	92	94	99	98
Food – alimentaire	98	103	91	103	101	105	94	98	104	102

4 Index numbers of per capita agricultural and food production

1999 – 2001 = 100

Indices de la production agricole et de la production alimentaire par habitant

1999 – 2001 = 100

Region - Région	2000	2001	2002	2003	2004	2005	2006	2007	2008	2009
World Monde										
Agricultural – agricole	**100**	**100**	**100**	**101**	**104**	**105**	**105**	**107**	**109**	**108**
Food – alimentaire	**100**	**100**	**100**	**101**	**104**	**105**	**105**	**107**	**109**	**108**
Africa Afrique										
Agricultural – agricole	99	99	100	102	103	104	106	103	105	105
Food – alimentaire	99	99	100	103	104	105	107	104	106	106
Americas Amériques										
Agricultural – agricole	100	99	98	101	105	105	105	109	110	107
Food – alimentaire	100	99	98	102	105	105	105	109	111	108
Asia Asie										
Agricultural – agricole	100	100	101	103	106	109	110	113	115	115
Food – alimentaire	100	100	101	103	105	108	110	112	114	114
Europe Europe										
Agricultural – agricole	99	100	101	97	105	101	100	99	104	103
Food – alimentaire	99	100	101	97	105	101	100	99	105	104
Oceania Océanie										
Agricultural – agricole	98	101	89	96	92	96	85	85	88	86
Food – alimentaire	98	101	89	99	95	98	86	88	92	90

Source:
Food and Agriculture Organization of the United Nations (FAO), Rome, FAOSTAT data, last accessed September 2010.

Source:
Organisation des Nations Unies pour l'alimentation et l'agriculture (FAO), Rome, données FAOSTAT, dernier accès septembre 2010.

5 Production, trade and consumption of commercial energy

Thousand metric tons of oil equivalent and kilograms per capita

Production, commerce et consommation d'énergie commerciale

Milliers de tonnes d'équivalent pétrole et kilogrammes par habitant

Region	Year Année	Primary energy production – Production d'énergie primaire: Total Totale	Solids Solides	Liquids Liquides	Gas Gaz	Electricity Electricité	Changes in stocks Variations des stocks	Imports Importations	Exports Exportations
World	**2001**	**8 893 068**	**2 418 147**	**3 675 823**	**2 338 112**	**460 986**	**65 853**	**3 771 125**	**3 734 440**
	2002	**8 967 528**	**2 447 756**	**3 649 137**	**2 399 879**	**470 756**	**1 227**	**3 821 394**	**3 753 385**
	2003	**9 355 734**	**2 603 701**	**3 791 473**	**2 489 859**	**470 701**	**2 414**	**4 003 180**	**3 956 222**
	2004	**9 870 894**	**2 891 230**	**3 928 973**	**2 555 309**	**495 381**	**8 680**	**4 283 776**	**4 223 457**
	2005	**10 219 370**	**3 083 173**	**3 994 035**	**2 631 735**	**510 428**	**5 394**	**4 385 395**	**4 392 055**
	2006	**10 510 653**	**3 250 954**	**4 016 730**	**2 717 996**	**524 973**	**62 023**	**4 501 744**	**4 492 936**
	2007	**10 667 728**	**3 361 440**	**4 019 974**	**2 760 599**	**525 714**	**-603**	**4 616 603**	**4 508 391**
Africa	2001	664 912	126 867	409 941	120 010	8 094	944	78 299	445 224
	2002	669 932	125 034	406 815	129 382	8 701	481	76 869	442 568
	2003	713 948	129 465	440 341	135 640	8 503	1 684	83 637	478 876
	2004	767 719	131 589	482 572	144 550	9 008	-1 445	88 051	523 344
	2005	826 081	132 909	510 843	173 341	8 988	-547	98 018	565 541
	2006	853 027	132 754	518 810	191 989	9 474	1 077	97 507	593 654
	2007	857 608	134 185	524 729	189 090	9 603	-360	104 027	591 372
America, North	2001	2 138 145	614 675	664 621	729 890	128 959	67 975	874 524	431 199
	2002	2 121 605	592 892	674 311	716 127	138 275	-19 987	854 817	439 648
	2003	2 112 628	560 979	687 008	727 918	136 723	-9 056	902 430	459 009
	2004	2 132 755	590 011	684 653	717 308	140 783	381	961 933	476 523
	2005	2 119 134	601 043	665 043	709 479	143 568	-5 036	992 180	476 522
	2006	2 158 513	614 723	667 045	730 105	146 640	34 567	992 574	488 753
	2007	2 168 216	607 401	668 381	746 382	146 051	-15 814	1 010 013	509 951
America, South	2001	530 503	36 582	361 953	87 038	44 930	1 918	89 221	260 233
	2002	518 069	36 312	348 937	86 037	46 783	2 665	92 169	245 081
	2003	519 927	39 800	341 567	89 538	49 023	3 962	89 259	238 786
	2004	536 330	42 229	346 886	96 691	50 525	-735	103 167	261 443
	2005	561 211	46 620	362 478	98 645	53 468	732	93 729	270 510
	2006	571 244	51 170	360 025	103 914	56 136	-2 677	97 895	272 644
	2007	564 609	53 747	350 805	102 479	57 578	6 114	108 565	252 074
Asia	2001	3 257 840	1 096 548	1 525 275	536 077	99 939	-7 612	1 254 803	1 388 226
	2002	3 310 995	1 149 532	1 477 949	582 752	100 762	2 425	1 301 069	1 348 616
	2003	3 602 135	1 319 190	1 555 903	625 562	101 480	-2 717	1 374 191	1 455 243
	2004	3 983 408	1 572 786	1 632 765	664 544	113 312	-523	1 518 623	1 562 465
	2005	4 261 712	1 735 153	1 687 563	717 210	121 787	-2 989	1 545 645	1 651 099
	2006	4 480 559	1 886 983	1 709 436	754 597	129 544	1 993	1 622 458	1 712 135
	2007	4 625 554	1 989 634	1 704 189	801 463	130 268	6 236	1 727 459	1 708 710
Europe	2001	2 040 098	362 651	675 438	826 688	175 321	-3 141	1 438 641	1 043 980
	2002	2 081 227	357 336	705 570	846 106	172 215	13 660	1 459 560	1 105 655
	2003	2 142 971	366 277	733 658	871 993	171 044	8 305	1 515 758	1 153 112
	2004	2 182 141	359 496	752 392	892 715	177 538	10 552	1 573 230	1 224 058
	2005	2 172 467	362 394	741 517	889 897	178 658	14 501	1 614 329	1 244 586
	2006	2 167 574	360 499	735 404	892 561	179 110	28 357	1 647 397	1 241 011
	2007	2 152 622	356 795	743 625	874 074	178 129	-2 571	1 619 620	1 248 322
Oceania	2001	261 570	180 824	38 595	38 409	3 742	5 768	35 636	165 578
	2002	265 701	186 650	35 556	39 475	4 019	1 983	36 910	171 816
	2003	264 124	187 990	32 998	39 209	3 929	238	37 905	171 196
	2004	268 541	195 119	29 706	39 501	4 215	450	38 773	175 624
	2005	278 764	205 052	26 591	43 163	3 958	-1 266	41 495	183 797
	2006	279 736	204 826	26 011	44 831	4 068	-1 295	43 914	184 738
	2007	299 120	219 678	28 245	47 111	4 085	5 793	46 919	197 963

Source:
United Nations Statistics Division, New York, the energy statistics database, last accessed April 2010.

5 Production, trade and consumption of commercial energy *(continued)*

Thousand metric tons of oil equivalent and kilograms per capita

Production, commerce et consommation d'énergie commerciale *(suite)*

Milliers de tonnes d'équivalent pétrole et kilogrammes par habitant

Bunkers - Soutes			Consumption - Consommation							
Air Avion	Sea Maritime	Unallocated Nondistribué	Per capita Par habitant	Total Totale	Solids Solides	Liquids Liquides	Gas Gaz	Electricity Electricité	Year Année	Région
102 355	**140 599**	**400 046**	**1 345**	**8 220 900**	**2 411 966**	**3 025 223**	**2 321 929**	**461 783**	**2001**	**Monde**
105 418	**144 781**	**392 104**	**1 357**	**8 392 008**	**2 471 474**	**3 047 797**	**2 400 632**	**472 104**	**2002**	
108 028	**144 523**	**459 605**	**1 386**	**8 688 122**	**2 652 173**	**3 073 643**	**2 491 479**	**470 827**	**2003**	
114 253	**159 021**	**473 603**	**1 446**	**9 175 656**	**2 938 180**	**3 194 053**	**2 547 745**	**495 678**	**2004**	
121 272	**169 113**	**464 188**	**1 470**	**9 452 743**	**3 088 008**	**3 225 100**	**2 628 947**	**510 688**	**2005**	
124 118	**178 886**	**472 707**	**1 487**	**9 681 727**	**3 244 120**	**3 241 633**	**2 670 996**	**524 978**	**2006**	
128 558	**186 367**	**478 419**	**1 511**	**9 983 198**	**3 396 945**	**3 286 285**	**2 773 737**	**526 232**	**2007**	
4 811	6 845	24 829	325	260 559	95 542	98 040	58 586	8 390	2001	Afrique
4 781	5 894	19 920	333	273 156	92 537	104 344	67 367	8 908	2002	
4 674	7 105	25 924	332	279 322	96 225	106 347	68 101	8 650	2003	
4 510	6 072	24 601	345	298 688	103 438	113 533	72 541	9 176	2004	
5 067	6 405	29 909	358	317 724	102 078	117 824	88 675	9 147	2005	
5 072	5 660	21 427	355	323 644	103 176	122 058	88 769	9 642	2006	
5 428	5 569	26 188	354	333 439	107 068	126 769	89 614	9 988	2007	
21 658	24 658	59 746	4 902	2 407 433	574 327	1 000 473	703 745	128 889	2001	Amérique du Nord
21 122	28 104	48 731	4 951	2 458 803	581 542	1 005 321	733 393	138 546	2002	
20 588	23 867	63 629	4 899	2 457 022	572 717	1 021 593	726 080	136 632	2003	
20 935	29 377	65 192	4 938	2 502 280	588 343	1 054 862	718 280	140 796	2004	
21 596	30 487	54 138	4 952	2 533 609	596 472	1 074 851	718 719	143 567	2005	
20 509	32 522	55 685	4 874	2 519 050	590 117	1 063 026	719 369	146 538	2006	
21 343	35 158	46 144	4 927	2 581 447	596 552	1 075 976	762 435	146 485	2007	
2 557	5 446	31 352	904	318 219	19 453	167 376	86 420	44 970	2001	Amérique du Sud
3 332	5 663	37 708	884	315 789	18 841	164 457	85 685	46 806	2002	
3 487	5 190	40 576	876	317 185	20 293	158 541	89 477	48 874	2003	
4 443	5 512	24 724	937	344 111	20 888	175 894	96 762	50 566	2004	
4 532	6 124	24 752	936	348 290	21 597	174 353	98 681	53 659	2005	
4 895	5 966	27 708	956	360 603	21 696	178 460	104 007	56 440	2006	
4 193	5 205	30 987	974	374 600	22 903	191 019	102 768	57 911	2007	
27 692	54 658	229 936	760	2 819 742	1 207 760	976 991	534 403	100 587	2001	Asie
30 857	55 332	232 149	784	2 942 685	1 266 686	995 922	578 689	101 387	2002	
32 447	58 017	261 719	834	3 171 618	1 435 599	1 013 168	621 380	101 471	2003	
34 979	64 305	289 336	924	3 551 468	1 706 367	1 077 891	653 912	113 298	2004	
37 883	70 308	284 548	968	3 766 507	1 855 704	1 088 211	700 791	121 800	2005	
39 753	75 873	301 099	1 008	3 972 163	2 002 096	1 095 916	744 667	129 485	2006	
41 826	80 997	308 358	1 055	4 206 884	2 144 928	1 128 323	803 874	129 759	2007	
42 252	47 845	57 174	3 153	2 290 628	464 197	741 077	910 150	175 204	2001	Europe
42 483	48 627	56 316	3 134	2 274 046	460 680	735 031	905 898	172 437	2002	
43 451	49 207	69 846	3 209	2 334 808	475 944	730 191	957 402	171 272	2003	
45 958	52 523	72 856	3 226	2 349 424	466 984	727 780	977 033	177 627	2004	
48 363	54 524	73 099	3 221	2 351 723	456 266	724 224	992 678	178 556	2005	
50 255	57 436	67 072	3 242	2 370 840	470 615	737 174	984 246	178 805	2006	
51 546	58 171	67 007	3 207	2 349 768	469 994	719 194	982 577	178 003	2007	
3 385	1 146	-2 991	3 955	124 320	50 687	41 266	28 625	3 742	2001	Océanie
2 843	1 160	-2 721	3 996	127 530	51 188	42 721	29 601	4 019	2002	
3 380	1 136	-2 089	3 953	128 167	51 395	43 804	29 040	3 929	2003	
3 429	1 232	-3 106	3 942	129 685	52 160	44 092	29 218	4 215	2004	
3 831	1 265	-2 258	4 040	134 890	55 892	45 637	29 403	3 958	2005	
3 634	1 430	-284	3 991	135 427	56 419	45 000	29 939	4 068	2006	
4 222	1 267	-265	3 966	137 059	55 499	45 004	32 471	4 085	2007	

Source:
Organisation des Nations Unies, Division de statistique, New York, la base de données pour les statistiques de l'énergie, dernier accès avril 2010.

Total imports and exports: index numbers

Volume and unit value indices and terms of trade (2000 = 100)

Importations et exportations totales : indices

Indices du volume et de la valeur unitaire et termes de l'échange (2000 = 100)

Region	2001	2002	2003	2004	2005	2006	2007	2008	Région
Total									**Total**
Imports : Volume [1]	**100**	**104**	**111**	**124**	**133**	**144**	**152**	**154**	**Imp.: Volume [1]**
Imports : Unit value indices US $ [2]	**96**	**96**	**104**	**114**	**120**	**127**	**139**	**157**	**Imp.: Indices de la val. unit. en $ E.-U. [2]**
Exports : Volume [1]	**99**	**103**	**109**	**122**	**133**	**148**	**157**	**165**	**Exp.: Volume [1]**
Exports : Unit value indices US $ [2]	**97**	**97**	**107**	**117**	**121**	**126**	**136**	**148**	**Exp.: Indices de la val. unit. en $ E.-U. [2]**
Developed economies [3]									**Economies développées [3]**
Imports : Volume [1]	100	103	108	118	125	135	139	138	Imp.: Volume [1]
Imports : Unit value indices US $ [2]	96	96	106	116	122	128	140	157	Imp.: Indices de la val. unit. en $ E.-U. [2]
Exports : Volume [1]	99	102	104	113	118	128	134	136	Exp.: Volume [1]
Exports : Unit value indices US $ [2]	98	99	111	121	126	131	143	157	Exp.: Indices de la val. unit. en $ E.-U. [2]
Terms of trade [4]	102	103	104	104	104	102	102	100	Termes de l'échange [4]
North America									**Amérique du Nord**
Imports : Volume [1]	97	101	106	116	124	130	131	126	Imp.: Volume [1]
Imports : Unit value indices US $ [2]	96	94	97	103	111	116	121	135	Imp.: Indices de la val. unit. en $ E.-U. [2]
Exports : Volume [1]	94	91	92	97	104	113	119	123	Exp.: Volume [1]
Exports : Unit value indices US $ [2]	100	98	101	107	113	117	124	132	Exp.: Indices de la val. unit. en $ E.-U. [2]
Terms of trade [4]	103	104	104	104	102	101	102	98	Termes de l'échange [4]
Europe									**Europe**
Imports : Volume [1]	102	104	108	118	125	137	144	144	Imp.: Volume [1]
Imports : Unit value indices US $ [2]	97	99	114	127	130	137	152	169	Imp.: Indices de la val. unit. en $ E.-U. [2]
Exports : Volume [1]	103	107	109	118	123	135	140	141	Exp.: Volume [1]
Exports : Unit value indices US $ [2]	98	101	117	130	134	139	155	170	Exp.: Indices de la val. unit. en $ E.-U. [2]
Terms of trade [4]	100	102	103	102	103	101	102	101	Termes de l'échange [4]
Asia and the Pacific									**Asie et le Pacifique**
Imports : Volume [1,5]	103	103	111	121	126	133	131	135	Imp.: Volume [1,5]
Imports : Unit value indices US $ [2]	88	88	94	104	113	120	133	158	Imp.: Indices de la val. unit. en $ E.-U. [2]
Exports : Volume [1,5]	91	97	101	111	113	121	125	127	Exp.: Volume [1,5]
Exports : Unit value indices US $ [2]	94	91	98	108	115	117	124	141	Exp.: Indices de la val. unit. en $ E.-U. [2]
Terms of trade [4]	107	103	105	104	101	98	93	89	Termes de l'échange [4]
Africa									**Afrique**
Imports : Volume [1]	111	111	113	124	143	...	...	...	Imp.: Volume [1]
Imports : Unit value indices US $ [2]	94	94	113	131	137	...	...	...	Imp.: Indices de la val. unit. en $ E.-U. [2]
Exports : Volume [1]	101	101	108	128	172	198	224	311	Exp.: Volume [1]
Exports : Unit value indices US $ [2]	93	95	109	122	123	124	128	121	Exp.: Indices de la val. unit. en $ E.-U. [2]
Terms of trade [4]	99	101	97	93	90	...	...	...	Termes de l'échange [4]
Northern Africa									**Afrique du Nord**
Imports : Volume [1]	109	140	134	166	180	189	219	303	Imp.: Volume [1]
Imports : Unit value indices US $ [2]	93	76	83	87	95	99	109	116	Imp.: Indices de la val. unit. en $ E.-U. [2]
Exports : Volume [1]	102	98	122	152	207	241	261	345	Exp.: Volume [1]
Exports : Unit value indices US $ [2]	90	93	95	99	100	102	110	115	Exp.: Indices de la val. unit. en $ E.-U. [2]
Terms of trade [4]	96	122	114	114	105	104	100	99	Termes de l'échange [4]
Sub-Saharan Africa									**Afrique subsaharienne**
Exports : Volume [1]	100	102	100	113	145	165	195	286	Exp.: Volume [1]
Exports : Unit value indices US $ [2]	95	97	119	141	149	148	146	128	Exp.: Indices de la val. unit. en $ E.-U. [2]
Latin America and the Caribbean									**Amérique latine et Caraïbes**
Imports : Volume [1]	99	100	106	114	113	122	132	130	Imp.: Volume [1]
Imports : Unit value indices US $ [2]	99	91	90	101	121	134	148	183	Imp.: Indices de la val. unit. en $ E.-U. [2]
Exports : Volume [1]	102	102	105	119	135	149	161	170	Exp.: Volume [1]
Exports : Unit value indices US $ [2]	94	95	101	110	118	127	134	147	Exp.: Indices de la val. unit. en $ E.-U. [2]
Terms of trade [4]	95	104	113	108	97	95	90	80	Termes de l'échange [4]
Latin America									**Amérique latine**
Exports : Volume [1]	102	102	105	119	134	148	159	168	Exp.: Volume [1]
Exports : Unit value indices US $ [2]	94	95	101	110	118	127	134	148	Exp.: Indices de la val. unit. en $ E.-U. [2]
Western Asia									**Asie occidentale**
Imports : Volume [1]	97	107	115	135	151	162	183	192	Imp.: Volume [1]
Imports : Unit value indices US $ [2]	99	99	109	123	133	144	158	187	Imp.: Indices de la val. unit. en $ E.-U. [2]
Exports : Volume [1]	96	102	115	138	169	191	195	220	Exp.: Volume [1]
Exports : Unit value indices US $ [2]	97	96	105	117	126	131	145	170	Exp.: Indices de la val. unit. en $ E.-U. [2]
Terms of trade [4]	98	97	96	95	95	91	92	91	Termes de l'échange [4]

Total imports and exports: index numbers *(continued)*

Volume and unit value indices and terms of trade (2000 = 100)

Importations et exportations totales : indices *(suite)*

Indices du volume et de la valeur unitaire et termes de l'échange (2000 = 100)

Region	2001	2002	2003	2004	2005	2006	2007	2008	Région
Other Asia									**Autre Asie**
Imports : Volume [1]	98	111	128	154	173	193	210	...	Imp.: Volume [1]
Imports : Unit value indices US $ [2]	95	93	96	105	110	116	124	...	Imp.: Indices de la val. unit. en $ E.-U. [2]
Exports : Volume [1]	100	114	132	160	186	217	247	268	Exp.: Volume [1]
Exports : Unit value indices US $ [2]	94	90	93	99	101	105	109	116	Exp.: Indices de la val. unit. en $ E.-U. [2]
Terms of trade [4]	98	97	97	94	92	90	88	...	Termes de l'échange [4]
Eastern Asia									**Asie orientale**
Imports : Volume [1]	99	115	140	169	184	206	233	242	Imp.: Volume [1]
Imports : Unit value indices US $ [2]	94	91	95	104	109	115	120	136	Imp.: Indices de la val. unit. en $ E.-U. [2]
Exports : Volume [1]	101	118	145	179	212	255	300	326	Exp.: Volume [1]
Exports : Unit value indices US $ [2]	93	90	92	98	100	101	103	108	Exp.: Indices de la val. unit. en $ E.-U. [2]
Terms of trade [4]	99	99	97	94	91	87	86	80	Termes de l'échange [4]
Southern Asia									**Asie australe**
Imports : Volume [1]	105	111	123	141	175	216	204	341	Imp.: Volume [1]
Imports : Unit value indices US $ [2]	96	102	113	132	142	137	177	...	Imp.: Indices de la val. unit. en $ E.-U. [2]
Exports : Volume [1]	103	114	121	135	163	182	194	223	Exp.: Volume [1]
Exports : Unit value indices US $ [2]	94	92	105	119	126	141	153	166	Exp.: Indices de la val. unit. en $ E.-U. [2]
Terms of trade [4]	98	90	94	90	88	103	87	...	Termes de l'échange [4]
South-eastern Asia									**Asie du Sud-est**
Imports : Volume [1]	95	101	104	127	141	147	159	182	Imp.: Volume [1]
Imports : Unit value indices US $ [2]	97	95	98	101	110	120	125	138	Imp.: Indices de la val. unit. en $ E.-U. [2]
Exports : Volume [1]	96	106	111	134	150	166	177	192	Exp.: Volume [1]
Exports : Unit value indices US $ [2]	94	90	92	96	99	105	110	120	Exp.: Indices de la val. unit. en $ E.-U. [2]
Terms of trade [4]	96	94	94	95	89	88	88	87	Termes de l'échange [4]

Source:
United Nations Statistics Division, New York, trade statistics database, last accessed January 2010.

1 Volume indices are derived from value data and unit value indices. They are base-period weighted.

2 Regional aggregates are current-period weighted.

3 This classification is intended for statistical convenience and does not, necessarily, express a judgment about the stage reached by a particular country in the development process.

4 Unit value index of exports divided by unit value index of imports.

5 The correction of trade values for Japan (re-exports) in November 2008 led to significant changes in the volume index.

Source:
Organisation des Nations Unies, Division de statistique, New York, la base de données pour les statistiques du commerce extérieur, dernier accès janvier 2010.

1 Les indices du volume sont calculés à partir des chiffres de la valeur et des indices de valeur unitaire. Ils sont à coefficients de pondération correspondant à la période en base.

2 Les totaux régionaux sont à coefficients de pondération correspondant à la période en cours.

3 Cette classification est utilisée pour plus de commodité dans la présentation des statistiques et n'implique pas nécessairement un jugement quant au stage de développement auquel est parvenu un pays donné.

4 Indice de la valeur unitaire des exportations divisé par l'indice de la valeur unitaire des importations.

5 La correction en Novembre 2008 des valeurs de réexportations du Japon a conduit à des changements significatifs au niveau des indices de volume.

Technical notes: tables 1-6

Table 1: The series of world aggregates on population, output, production, external trade and finance have been compiled from statistical publications and databases of the United Nations and the specialized agencies and other institutions. The sources should be consulted for detailed information on compilation and coverage.

Table 2 presents estimates of population size, rates of population increase, crude birth and death rates, surface area and population density for the world and regions. Unless otherwise specified, all figures are estimates of the order of magnitude and are subject to a substantial margin of error.

The population estimates and rates presented in this table were prepared by the Population Division of the United Nations Secretariat and published in *World Population Prospects: The 2008 Revision.*

The average annual percentage rates of population growth were calculated by the Population Division of the United Nations Secretariat, using an exponential rate of increase formula.

Crude birth and crude death rates are expressed in terms of the average annual number of births and deaths respectively, per 1,000 mid-year population. These rates are estimated.

Surface area totals were obtained by summing the figures for the individual countries or areas.

Density is the number of persons in the 2008 total population per square kilometre of total surface area.

The scheme of regionalization used for the purpose of making these estimates is presented in annex I. Although some continental totals are given, and all can be derived, the basic scheme presents macro regions that are so drawn as to obtain greater homogeneity in sizes of population, types of demographic circumstances and accuracy of demographic statistics.

Tables 3-4: The index numbers in table 3 refer to agricultural production, which is defined to include both crop and livestock products. Seeds and feed are excluded. The index numbers of food refer to commodities which are considered edible and contain nutrients. Coffee, tea and other inedible commodities are excluded.

The index numbers of total agricultural and food production in table 3 are calculated by the Laspeyres formula with the base year period 1999-2001. The latter is provided in order to diminish the impact of annual fluctuations in agricultural output during base years on the indices for the period. Production quantities of each commodity are weighted by 1999-2001 average national producer prices and summed for each year. The index numbers are based on production data for a calendar year.

Index numbers for the world and regions are computed in a similar way to the country index numbers except that instead of using different commodity prices for each country

Notes techniques: tableaux 1 à 6

Tableau 1: Les séries d'agrégats mondiaux sur la population, la production, le commerce extérieur et les finances ont été établies à partir de publications statistiques et bases de données des Nations Unies et les institutions spécialisées et autres organismes. On doit se référer aux sources pour tous renseignements détaillés sur les méthodes de calcul et la portée des statistiques.

Le *Tableau 2* présente les estimations mondiales et régionales de la population, des taux d'accroissement de la population, des taux bruts de natalité et de mortalité, de la superficie et de la densité de population. Sauf indication contraire, tous les chiffres sont des estimations de l'ordre de grandeur et comportent une assez grande marge d'erreur.

Les estimations de la population et tous les taux présentés dans ce tableau ont été établis par la Division de la population du Secrétariat des Nations Unies et publiés dans "*World Population Prospects: The 2008 Revision*".

Les pourcentages annuels moyens de l'accroissement de la population ont été calculés par la Division de la population du Secrétariat des Nations Unies, sur la base d'une formule de taux d'accroissement exponentiel.

Les taux bruts de natalité et de mortalité sont exprimés, respectivement, sur la base du nombre annuel moyen de naissances et de décès par tranche de 1.000 habitants au milieu de l'année. Ces taux sont estimatifs.

On a déterminé les superficies totales en additionnant les chiffres correspondant aux différents pays ou régions.

La densité est le nombre de personnes de la population totale de 2008 par kilomètre carré de la superficie totale.

Le schéma de régionalisation utilisé aux fins de l'établissement de ces estimations est présenté dans l'annexe I. Bien que les totaux de certains continents soient donnés et que tous puissent être déterminés, le schéma de base présente les grandes régions qui sont établies de manière à obtenir une plus grande homogénéité en ce qui concerne l'ampleur des populations, les types de conditions démographiques et la précision des statistiques démographiques.

Tableaux 3-4: Les indices du tableau 3 se rapportent à la production agricole, qui est définie comme comprenant à la fois les produits de l'agriculture et de l'élevage. Les semences et les aliments pour les animaux sont exclus de cette définition. Les indices de la production alimentaire se rapportent aux produits considérés comme comestibles et contenant des éléments nutritifs. Le café, le thé et les produits non comestibles sont exclus.

Les indices de la production agricole et de la production alimentaire présentés au tableau 3 sont calculés selon la formule de Laspeyres avec les années 1999-2001 comme période de référence, cela afin de limiter l'incidence, sur les indices correspondant à la période considérée, des fluctuations annuelles de la production agricole enregistrée pendant les années de référence. Les chiffres de production de chaque

group, "international commodity prices" derived from the Gheary-Khamis formula are used for all country groupings. This method assigns a single "price" to each commodity.

The indexes in table 4 are calculated as a ratio between the index numbers of total agricultural and food production in table 3 described above and the corresponding index numbers of population.

For further information on the series presented in these tables, see the FAO *Statistical Yearbook* and http://faostat.fao.org.

Table 5: For a description of the series in table 5, see the technical notes to chapter XII.

Table 6: For a description of the series in table 6, see the technical notes to chapter XV. The composition of the regions is presented in table 58.

produit sont pondérés par les prix nationaux moyens à la production pour la période 1999-2001 et additionnés pour chaque année. Les indices sont fondés sur les données de production de l'année civile.

Les indices pour le monde et les régions sont calculés de la même façon que les indices par pays, mais au lieu d'appliquer des prix différents aux produits de base pour chaque groupe de pays, on a utilisé des "prix internationaux" établis d'après la formule de Gheary-Khamis pour tous les groupes de pays. Cette méthode attribue un seul "prix" à chaque produit de base.

Les indices du tableau 4 sont calculés comme ratio entre les indices de la production alimentaire et de la production agricole totale du tableau 3 décrits ci-dessus et les indices de population correspondants.

Pour tout renseignement complémentaire sur les séries présentées dans ces tableaux, voir l'*Annuaire Statistique de la FAO* et http://faostat.fao.org.

Tableau 5: On trouvera une description de la série de statistiques du tableau 5 dans les notes techniques du chapitre XII.

Tableau 6: On trouvera une description de la série de statistiques du tableau 6 dans les notes techniques du chapitre XV. La composition des régions est présentée au tableau 58.

Population by sex, rate of population increase, surface area and density

Population selon le sexe, taux d'accroissement de la population, superficie et densité

Country or area+ Pays ou zone+	Latest census Dernier recensement Date	Both sexes Les deux sexes	Men Hommes	Women Femmes	Mid-year estimates (thousands) Estimations au milieu de l'année (milliers) 2005	2008	Annual rate of increase Taux d'accroissement annuel % 2005-08	Surface area Superficie (km²) 2008	Density& Densité& 2008
Africa · Afrique									
Algeria Algérie	16 IV 2008	*34 452 759[1]	*17 428 500[1]	*17 024 259[1]	32 906[1]	*34 745[1]	1.8	2 381 741	15
Angola Angola	15 XII 1970	5 646 166	2 943 974	2 702 192	...	...	...	1 246 700	...
Benin Bénin	11 II 2002	6 769 914[1]	3 284 119[1]	3 485 795[1]	*7 395[2]	*8 225[2]	3.5	112 622	73
Botswana Botswana	17 VIII 2001	1 680 863	813 625	867 238	1 708[1]	1 755[1]	0.9	582 000	3
Burkina Faso Burkina Faso	9 XII 2006	14 196 259[1]	6 842 560[1]	7 353 699[1]	13 374[1]	14 731[1,2]	3.2	272 967	54
Burundi Burundi	16 VIII 1990	5 139 073	2 473 599	2 665 474	...	...	...	27 834	...
Cameroon Cameroun	10 IV 1987	10 493 655	...	...	...	...	...	475 442	...
Cape Verde Cap-Vert	16 VI 2000	436 863	211 479	225 384	475	500	1.7	4 033	124
Central African Rep. Rép. centrafricaine	8 XIII 2003	3 151 072	1 569 446	1 581 626	...	...	...	622 984	...
Chad Tchad	8 IV 1993	6 158 992	2 950 415	3 208 577	...	...	...	1 284 000	...
Comoros Comores	1 IX 2003	575 660[3]	...	...	...	...	...	2 235	...
Congo Congo	6 VI 1996	*2 600 000	...	...	3 488[2]	3 752[2]	2.4	342 000	11
Côte d'Ivoire Côte d'Ivoire	21 XI 1998	15 366 672	7 844 621	7 522 050	19 097	*20 807	2.9	322 463	65
Dem. Rep. of the Congo Rép. dém. du Congo	1 VII 1984	29 916 800	14 543 800	15 373 000	...	*68 076	...	2 344 858	29
Djibouti Djibouti	11 XII 1960	81 200	...	...	...	...	...	23 200	...
Egypt Egypte	21 XI 2006	72 798 031[4]	37 219 056[4]	35 578 975[4]	70 653	75 194	2.1	1 002 000	75
Equatorial Guinea Guinée équatoriale	1 II 2002	1 014 999	501 387	513 612	...	...	...	28 051	...
Eritrea Erythrée	9 V 1984	2 748 304	1 374 452	1 373 852	...	...	...	117 600	...
Ethiopia Ethiopie	28 V 2007	73 918 505[5]	37 296 657[5]	36 621 848[5]	73 044[6]	79 221[6]	2.7	1 104 300	72
Gabon Gabon	1 XII 2003	*1 269 000	...	...	1 313[7]	...	...	267 668	...
Gambia Gambie	15 IV 2003	*1 364 507	*676 726	*687 781	1 436	...	...	11 295	...
Ghana Ghana	26 III 2000	18 912 079	9 357 382	9 554 697	21 367	22 901	2.3	238 533	96
Guinea Guinée	1 XII 1996	7 156 406	3 497 979	3 658 427	...	10 183	...	245 857	41
Guinea-Bissau Guinée-Bissau	1 XII 1991	983 367	476 210	507 157	1 326[2]	...	...	36 125	...

7 Population by sex, rate of population increase, surface area and density *(continued)*
Population selon le sexe, taux d'accroissement de la population, superficie et densité *(suite)*

Country or area[+] Pays ou zone[+]	Latest census Dernier recensement Date	 Both sexes Les deux sexes	 Men Hommes	 Women Femmes	Mid-year estimates (thousands) Estimations au milieu de l'année (milliers) 2005	 2008	Annual rate of increase Taux d'accroissement annuel % 2005-08	Surface area Superficie (km²) 2008	Density[&] Densité[&] 2008
Kenya Kenya	24 VIII 1999	28 686 607	14 205 589	14 481 018	35 267	*38 300	2.7	580 367	66
Lesotho Lesotho	9 IV 2006	1 741 406	818 379	923 027	...	...	...	30 355	...
Liberia Libéria	21 III 2008	*3 489 072	*1 764 555	*1 724 517	...	...	...	111 369	...
Libyan Arab Jamah. Jamah. arabe libyenne	15 IV 2006	*5 657 692[8]	*2 934 452[8]	*2 723 240[8]	...	...	...	1 759 540	...
Madagascar Madagascar	1 VIII 1993	12 238 914	6 088 116	6 150 798	17 730	18 865	2.1	587 041	32
Malawi Malawi	8 VI 2008	*13 066 320	*6 365 771	*6 700 549	12 341[2]	13 630[2]	3.3	118 484	115
Mali Mali	1 IV 1998	9 926 219[9]	4 905 510[9]	5 020 709[9]	11 732[10]	*12 706[10]	2.7	1 240 192	10
Mauritania Mauritanie	1 XI 2000	2 548 157	1 240 414	1 307 743	2 906[2]	*3 160[2]	2.8	1 025 520	3
Mauritius Maurice	2 VII 2000	1 178 848[1]	583 756[1]	595 092[1]	1 243[1]	1 269[1]	0.7	1 969	644
Mayotte[1] Mayotte[1]	31 VII 2007	186 387	91 405	94 982	...	...	...	...	...
Morocco Maroc	1 IX 2004	29 680 069	14 640 662	15 039 407	30 172	31 177	1.1	446 550	70
Mozambique Mozambique	1 VIII 2007	*20 530 714	*9 787 135	*10 743 579	19 420[2]	20 854[2]	2.4	801 590	26
Namibia Namibie	27 VIII 2001	1 830 330	887 721[11]	942 572[11]	1 957[2]	2 065[2]	1.8	824 268	3
Niger Niger	20 V 2001	11 060 291[1]	5 516 588[1]	5 543 703[1]	12 628[1,2]	14 297[1,2]	4.1	1 267 000	11
Nigeria Nigéria	21 III 2006	*140 003 542	*71 709 859	*68 293 683	133 767[2]	...	...	923 768	...
Réunion Réunion	1 I 2006	781 962[1]	379 176[1]	402 786[1]	777[1]	*806[1,10]	1.2	2 513	321
Rwanda Rwanda	16 VIII 2002	8 128 553[1]	3 879 448[1]	4 249 105[1]	...	...	...	26 338	...
Saint Helena ex. dep. Sainte-Hélène sans dép.	10 II 2008	*4 255	*2 166	*2 089	...	4[12]	...	122	33
Ascension Ascension	8 III 1998	712[1]	458[1]	254[1]	...	1[1]	...	88	8
Tristan da Cunha Tristan da Cunha	31 XII 1988	296	139	157	...	...	...	98	...
Sao Tome and Principe Sao Tomé-et-Principe	25 VIII 2001	136 554	67 422	69 132	149	158	1.9	964	164
Senegal Sénégal	8 XII 2002	9 552 442	4 665 730	4 886 712	10 848[1]	*11 343[1]	1.5	196 722	58
Seychelles Seychelles	26 VIII 2002	81 755[1,13]	40 751[1,13]	41 004[1,13]	83[1]	87[1]	1.6	452	193
Sierra Leone Sierra Leone	4 XII 2004	4 976 871	2 420 218	2 556 653	...	...	...	71 740	...
Somalia Somalie	15 II 1987	7 114 431	3 741 664	3 372 767	...	...	...	637 657	...

7 Population by sex, rate of population increase, surface area and density *(continued)*

Population selon le sexe, taux d'accroissement de la population, superficie et densité *(suite)*

Country or area+ Pays ou zone+	Latest census Dernier recensement				Mid-year estimates (thousands) Estimations au milieu de l'année (milliers)		Annual rate of increase Taux d'accroissement annuel %	Surface area Superficie (km²)	Density& Densité&
	Date	Both sexes Les deux sexes	Men Hommes	Women Femmes	2005	2008	2005-08	2008	2008
South Africa Afrique du Sud	10 X 2001	44 819 778	21 434 041	23 385 737	47 335[14]	48 687[14]	0.9	1 221 037	40
Sudan Soudan	22 IV 2008	*39 154 490	*20 073 977	*19 080 513	35 397	*38 193	2.5	2 505 813	15
Swaziland Swaziland	11 V 2007	*1 018 449	*481 428	*537 021	1 126	...	...	17 364	...
Togo Togo	22 XI 1981	2 719 567	1 325 641	1 393 926	5 337	5 596	1.6	56 785	99
Tunisia Tunisie	28 IV 2004	9 910 872	4 965 435	4 945 437	10 029	10 329	1.0	163 610	63
Uganda Ouganda	12 IX 2002	24 442 084	11 929 803	12 512 281	26 741	29 593	3.4	241 550	123
United Rep. of Tanzania Rép.-Unie de Tanzanie	24 VIII 2002	*34 443 603	*16 829 861	*17 613 742	37 379	40 600	2.8	945 087	43
Western Sahara[15] Sahara occidental[15]	31 XII 1970	76 425	43 981	32 444	...	...	...	266 000	...
Zambia Zambie	25 X 2000	9 337 425	4 594 290	4 743 135	11 441[2]	12 526[2]	3.0	752 612	17
Zimbabwe Zimbabwe	17 VIII 2002	11 631 657	5 634 180	5 997 477	11 830[16]	12 150[16]	0.9	390 757	31
America, North · Amérique du Nord									
Anguilla Anguilla	9 V 2001	11 430[17]	5 628[17]	5 802[17]	14	15	4.1	91	170
Antigua and Barbuda Antigua-et-Barbuda	28 V 2001	76 886	36 107	40 779	83	...	...	442	...
Aruba Aruba	14 X 2000	90 506[1]	43 434[1]	47 072[1]	101[1]	105[1]	1.5	180	585
Bahamas Bahamas	1 V 2000	303 611	147 715	155 896	325	338	1.3	13 943	24
Barbados Barbade	1 V 2000	250 010	119 926	130 084	273	275	0.2	430	639
Belize Belize	12 V 2000	240 204	121 278	118 926	292	322	3.3	22 966	14
Bermuda Bermudes	20 V 2000	62 059[1,18]	29 802[1,18]	32 257[1,18]	64[1]	64[1]	0.3	54	1 181
British Virgin Islands Iles Vierges britanniques	21 V 2001	20 647	10 627	10 020	...	...	...	151	...
Canada Canada	16 V 2006	31 612 895[1,19]	15 475 970[1,19]	16 136 930[1,19]	32 245[1,20,21]	33 327[1,21,22]	1.1	...	3[1]
Cayman Islands Iles Caïmanes	10 X 1999	39 020[1,23]	19 033[1,23]	19 987[1,23]	52[1,24]	57[1,24]	2.8	264	216
Costa Rica Costa Rica	26 VI 2000	3 810 179[1]	1 902 614[1]	1 907 565[1]	4 266[1]	4 533[1,25]	2.0	51 100	89
Cuba Cuba	7 IX 2002	11 177 743[1]	5 597 233[1]	5 580 510[1]	11 243[1]	11 236[1]	0.0	109 886	102
Dominica Dominique	12 V 2001	69 625[18]	35 073[18]	34 552[18]	71	72	0.6	751	96
Dominican Republic Rép. dominicaine	18 X 2002	8 562 541[1]	4 265 215[1]	4 297 326[1]	9 226[2]	9 625[2]	1.4	48 671	198

7 Population by sex, rate of population increase, surface area and density *(continued)*
Population selon le sexe, taux d'accroissement de la population, superficie et densité *(suite)*

Country or area⁺ Pays ou zone⁺	Latest census Dernier recensement				Mid-year estimates (thousands) Estimations au milieu de l'année (milliers)		Annual rate of increase Taux d'accroissement annuel %	Surface area Superficie (km²)	Density& Densité&
	Date	Both sexes Les deux sexes	Men Hommes	Women Femmes	2005	2008	2005-08	2008	2008
El Salvador El Salvador	12 V 2007	5 744 113[1]	2 719 371[1]	3 024 742[1]	6 049[26]	6 125[26]	0.4	21 041[27]	291
Greenland Groenland	1 I 2008	56 462[1,28]	29 885[1,28]	26 577[1,28]	57[1,28]	56[1,28]	-0.4	2 166 086	^0
Grenada Grenade	25 V 2001	102 632	50 481	52 151	...	109	...	344	318
Guadeloupe Guadeloupe	1 I 2006	400 736[1,29]	188 720[1,29]	212 016[1,29]	446[1]	*403[1,10,29]	-3.4	1 705	236
Guatemala Guatemala	24 XI 2002	11 237 196[1]	5 496 839[1]	5 740 357[1]	12 701[14]	13 678[14]	2.5	108 889	126
Haiti Haïti	11 I 2003	8 373 750[1]	4 039 272[1]	4 334 478[1]	9 295[1,30]	...	...	27 750	...
Honduras Honduras	28 VII 2001	6 071 200	3 000 530	3 070 670	7 197[31]	7 707[31]	2.3	112 492	69
Jamaica [1] Jamaïque [1]	10 IX 2001	2 607 632[32]	1 283 548[32]	1 324 084[32]	2 650	2 687	...	...	...
Martinique Martinique	1 I 2006	397 732[1]	185 604[1]	212 128[1]	396[1,10]	400[1,10]	0.3	1 128	354
Mexico Mexique	17 X 2005	103 263 388[1]	50 249 955[1]	53 013 433[1]	103 947[1,2]	106 683[1,2]	0.9	1 964 375	54
Montserrat Montserrat	12 V 2001	4 491	2 418	2 073	5	5	0.6	102	48
Netherlands Antilles Antilles néerlandaises	29 I 2001	175 653[1]	82 521[1]	93 132[1]	184[1,10]	*197[1,10]	2.4	800	246
Nicaragua Nicaragua	4 VI 2005	5 142 098[1]	2 534 491[1]	2 607 607[1]	5 450[1]	5 669[1]	1.3	130 373	43
Panama Panama	16 V 2010	*3 322 576	*1 672 568	*1 650 008	3 228[33]	3 395[33]	1.7	75 417	45
Puerto Rico Porto Rico	1 IV 2000	3 808 610[1,34]	1 833 577[1,34]	1 975 033[1,34]	3 912[1,34]	3 954[1,34]	0.4	8 870	446
Saint Kitts and Nevis Saint-Kitts-et-Nevis	14 V 2001	45 841	22 784	23 057	*39	...	...	261	...
Saint Lucia Sainte-Lucie	22 V 2001	157 164	76 741	80 423	164	...	...	539[35]	...
Saint Pierre and Miquelon Saint-Pierre-et-Miquelon	19 I 2006	6 125	3 034	3 091	...	...	...	242	...
Saint Vincent-Grenadines Saint Vincent-Grenadines	14 V 2001	109 022[18]	55 456[18]	53 566[18]	104	...	...	389	...
Trinidad and Tobago Trinité-et-Tobago	15 V 2000	1 262 366	633 051	629 315	1 294[36]	1 309[36]	0.4	5 130	255
Turks and Caicos Islands Iles Turques et Caïques	10 IX 2001	19 886	9 897	9 989	31[1]	*37[1]	6.0	948[37]	39
United States Etats-Unis	1 IV 2000	281 421 906[1,38]	138 053 563[1,38]	143 368 343[1,38]	295 561[1,38]	304 060[1,38]	0.9	9 629 091	32
United States Virgin Is. Iles Vierges américaines	1 IV 2000	108 612[1,34]	51 864[1,34]	56 748[1,34]	110[1,34]	110[1,34]	0.1	347	317

Population by sex, rate of population increase, surface area and density *(continued)*
Population selon le sexe, taux d'accroissement de la population, superficie et densité *(suite)*

Country or area⁺ Pays ou zone⁺	Latest census Dernier recensement Date	 Both sexes Les deux sexes	 Men Hommes	 Women Femmes	Mid-year estimates (thousands) Estimations au milieu de l'année (milliers) 2005	 2008	Annual rate of increase Taux d'accroissement annuel % 2005-08	Surface area Superficie (km²) 2008	Density& Densité& 2008
America, South · Amérique du Sud									
Argentina Argentine	18 XI 2001	36 260 130	17 659 072	18 601 058	38 592	39 746	1.0	2 780 400	14
Bolivia (Plurinational State of) Bolivie (État plurinational de)	5 IX 2001	8 274 325	4 123 850	4 150 475	9 427	10 028	2.1	1 098 581	9
Brazil Brésil	1 VIII 2000	169 799 170[1,39]	83 576 015[1,39]	86 223 155[1,39]	183 383[39]	189 613[39]	1.1	8 514 877	22
Chile Chili	24 IV 2002	15 116 435	7 447 695	7 668 740	16 267	16 763	1.0	756 102	22
Colombia Colombie	22 V 2005	41 468 384	20 336 117	21 132 267	42 889[40]	44 450[40]	1.2	1 141 748	39
Ecuador Equateur	25 XI 2001	12 156 608[41]	6 018 353[41]	6 138 255[41]	13 215[2,41]	13 805[2,41]	1.5	256 369	54
Falkland Is. (Malvinas)[42] Iles Falkland (Malvinas)[42]	8 X 2006	2 955[43]	1 569[43]	1 386[43]	...	...	...	12 173	...
French Guiana Guyane française	1 I 2006	205 954[1]	101 930[1]	104 023[1]	*200[1]	*222[1,10]	3.4	83 534	3
Guyana Guyana	15 IX 2002	751 223	376 034	375 189	758	766	0.3	214 969	4
Paraguay Paraguay	28 VIII 2002	5 163 198	2 603 242	2 559 956	5 899[16]	6 230[16]	1.8	406 752	15
Peru Pérou	21 X 2007	27 412 157	13 622 640	13 789 517	27 811[14]	28 807[14]	1.2	1 285 216	22
Suriname Suriname	2 VIII 2004	492 829[1,44]	247 846[1,44,45]	244 618[1,44,45]	499[1]	517[1]	1.2	163 820	3
Uruguay Uruguay	1 VI 2004	3 241 003[46]	1 565 533[46]	1 675 470[46]	3 306[14]	3 334[14]	0.3	176 215	19
Venezuela (Boliv. Rep. of) Venezuela (Rép. boliv. du)	30 X 2001	23 054 210[47]	11 402 869[47]	11 651 341[47]	26 577	27 935	1.7	912 050	31
Asia · Asie									
Afghanistan Afghanistan	23 VI 1979	13 051 358[48]	6 712 377[48]	6 338 981[48]	...	...	...	652 090	...
Armenia Arménie	10 X 2001	3 002 594[49]	1 407 220[49]	1 595 374[49]	3 218[1]	3 234[1]	0.2	29 743	109
Azerbaijan Azerbaïdjan	13 IV 2009	*8 922 300[1]	...	...	8 392	8 680	1.1	86 600	100
Bahrain Bahreïn	7 IV 2001	650 604[1]	373 649[1]	276 955[1]	889	1 107	7.3	758	1 461
Bangladesh Bangladesh	22 I 2001	124 355 263[50]	64 091 508[50]	60 263 755[50]	138 600	*144 500	1.4	143 998	1 003
Bhutan Bhoutan	30 V 2005	634 982	333 595	301 387	...	671[51]	...	38 394	17
Brunei Darussalam Brunéi Darussalam	21 VIII 2001	*332 844	*168 974	*163 870	370	398	2.4	5 765	69
Cambodia Cambodge	3 III 2008	13 395 682	6 516 054	6 879 628	*13 661[52]	*14 509[52]	2.0	181 035	80
China[53] Chine[53]	1 XI 2000	1 242 612 226[1,54]	640 275 969[1,54]	602 336 257[1,54]	1 303 720[1,55]	...	...	9 596 961	...

7 Population by sex, rate of population increase, surface area and density *(continued)*
Population selon le sexe, taux d'accroissement de la population, superficie et densité *(suite)*

Country or area[+] Pays ou zone[+]	Latest census Dernier recensement Date	 Both sexes Les deux sexes	 Men Hommes	 Women Femmes	Mid-year estimates (thousands) Estimations au milieu de l'année (milliers) 2005	 2008	Annual rate of increase Taux d'accroissement annuel % 2005-08	Surface area Superficie (km²) 2008	Density[&] Densité[&] 2008
China, Hong Kong SAR Chine, Hong Kong RAS	14 VII 2006	6 864 346[1]	3 272 956[1]	3 591 390[1]	6 813[1]	6 978[1]	0.8	1 104	6 320
China, Macao SAR Chine, Macao RAS	19 VIII 2006	502 113[1]	245 167[1]	256 946[1]	473[1]	552[1]	5.1	30	18 705
Cyprus[1] Chypre[1]	1 X 2001	689 565[56,57]	338 497[56,57]	351 068[56,57]	758[57]	*793[57]	1.5	9 251	86
Georgia Géorgie	17 I 2002	4 355 673	2 049 786	2 305 887	4 361	4 384	0.2	69 700	63
India Inde	1 III 2001	1 028 610 328[58,59]	532 156 772[58,59]	496 453 556[58,59]	1 101 318[2,58]	1 150 196[2,58]	1.4	3 287 263	350
Indonesia Indonésie	30 VI 2000	206 264 595[60]	103 417 180[60]	102 847 415[60]	219 852[1]	228 523[1]	1.3	1 910 931	120
Iran (Islamic Rep. of) Iran (Rép. islamique d')	28 X 2006	70 495 782[1]	35 866 362[1]	34 629 420[1]	69 390[1,61]	72 584[1,61]	1.5	1 628 750[62]	45
Iraq Iraq	16 X 1997	19 184 543[63]	9 536 570[63]	9 647 973[63]	27 963	31 895	4.4	435 244	73
Israel Israël	4 XI 1995	5 548 523[1,64]	2 738 175[1,64]	2 810 348[1,64]	6 930[1,64]	7 309[1,64]	1.8	22 072	331
Japan Japon	1 X 2005	127 767 994[1,65]	62 348 977[1,65]	65 419 017[1,65]	127 773[1,65]	127 704[1,65]	0.0	377 930[66]	338
Jordan Jordanie	1 X 2004	5 103 639[67]	2 626 287[67]	2 477 352[67]	5 473[24,67]	5 850[24,67]	2.2	89 342	65
Kazakhstan Kazakhstan	26 II 1999	14 955 106[1]	7 202 954[1]	7 752 152[1]	15 147	15 674	1.1	2 724 900	6
Korea, Dem. P. R. Corée, R. p. dém. de	1 X 2008	24 052 231[1]	11 721 838[1]	12 330 393[1]	...	...	...	120 538	...
Korea, Republic of Corée, République de	1 XI 2005	47 278 951[1,68]	23 623 954[1,68]	23 654 997[1,68]	48 138[1]	48 607[1]	0.3	99 828	487
Kuwait Koweït	20 IV 2005	*2 213 403	*1 310 067	*903 336	2 245	2 496	3.5	17 818	140
Kyrgyzstan Kirghizistan	24 III 2009	*5 107 700	*2 489 200	*2 618 500	5 007	5 078	0.5	199 951	25
Lao People's Dem. Rep. Rép. dém. pop. lao	1 III 2005	5 621 982[1]	2 800 551[1]	2 821 431[1]	5 679[69]	*6 000[69]	1.8	236 800	25
Lebanon Liban	3 III 2007	3 759 134[70]	1 857 659[70]	1 901 475[70]	...	...	...	10 452	...
Malaysia Malaisie	5 VII 2000	23 274 690[1,71,72]	11 853 432[1,71,72]	11 421 258[1,71,72]	26 128[1,33]	27 729[1,33]	2.0	330 803	84
Maldives Maldives	21 III 2006	298 968	151 459	147 509	294	310	1.7	300	1 032
Mongolia Mongolie	5 I 2000	2 373 493	1 177 981	1 195 512	2 548	2 659	1.4	1 564 100	2
Myanmar Myanmar	31 III 1983	35 307 913	17 518 255	17 789 658	55 396	58 377	1.7	676 578	86
Nepal Népal	22 VI 2001	23 151 423[1,73]	11 563 921[1,73]	11 587 502[1,73]	25 343[1]	*26 967[1]	2.1	147 181	183
Occupied Palestinian Terr. Terr. palestinien occupé	1 XII 2007	*3 761 646[74]	*1 908 432[74]	*1 853 214[74]	3 508	3 826	2.9	6 020	635
Oman Oman	7 XII 2003	2 340 815	1 313 239	1 027 576	2 509	2 867	4.5	309 500	9

7 Population by sex, rate of population increase, surface area and density *(continued)*
Population selon le sexe, taux d'accroissement de la population, superficie et densité *(suite)*

Country or area[+] Pays ou zone[+]	Latest census Dernier recensement: Date	Latest census Dernier recensement: Both sexes Les deux sexes	Latest census Dernier recensement: Men Hommes	Latest census Dernier recensement: Women Femmes	Mid-year estimates (thousands) Estimations au milieu de l'année (milliers): 2005	Mid-year estimates (thousands) Estimations au milieu de l'année (milliers): 2008	Annual rate of increase Taux d'accroissement annuel %: 2005-08	Surface area Superficie (km²): 2008	Density[&] Densité[&]: 2008
Pakistan Pakistan	2 III 1998	130 579 571[75]	67 840 137[75]	62 739 434[75]	144 367[75,76]	162 370[75]	...	796 095	204
Philippines Philippines	1 VIII 2007	*88 574 614[1]	...	...	85 261[1,77]	90 457[1,77]	2.0	300 000	302
Qatar Qatar	16 III 2004	744 029	496 382	247 647	906	1 448	15.6	11 586	125
Saudi Arabia Arabie saoudite	15 IX 2004	22 678 262	12 557 240	10 121 022	23 119	*24 807	2.3	2 149 690	12
Singapore Singapour	30 VI 2000	4 017 700[78]	2 061 800[78]	1 955 900[78]	3 468	3 643[79]	1.6	710	5 131
Sri Lanka Sri Lanka	17 VII 2001	16 929 689[80]	8 425 607[80]	8 504 082[80]	19 644	20 216	1.0	65 610	308
Syrian Arab Republic Rép. arabe syrienne	22 IX 2004	*17 921 000[81]	*9 161 000[81]	*8 760 000[81]	18 138[81]	19 644[81]	2.7	185 180	106
Tajikistan Tadjikistan	20 I 2000	6 127 493	3 069 100	3 058 393	6 850	7 295	2.1	143 100	51
Thailand Thaïlande	1 IV 2000	60 617 200[1]	29 850 100[1]	30 767 100[1]	64 839[1,2]	66 480[1,2]	0.8	513 120	130
Timor-Leste Timor-Leste	11 VII 2004	*924 642	*467 757	*456 885	...	...	...	14 874	...
Turkey Turquie	31 XII 2008	71 517 100[1,82]	35 901 154[1,82]	35 615 946[1,82]	68 582[1,82]	71 079[1,82]	1.2	783 562	91
Turkmenistan Turkménistan	10 I 1995	4 483 251	2 225 331	2 257 920	...	...	...	488 100	...
United Arab Emirates Emirats arabes unis	5 XII 2005	4 106 427	2 806 141	1 300 286	4 041	4 765	5.5	83 600	57
Uzbekistan Ouzbékistan	12 I 1989	19 810 077[1]	9 784 156[1]	10 025 921[1]	...	...	...	447 400	...
Viet Nam Viet Nam	1 IV 1999	76 323 173	37 469 117	38 854 056	82 394	85 122	1.1	331 212	257
Yemen Yémen	16 XII 2004	19 685 161	10 036 953	9 648 208	20 283[24]	22 198[24]	3.0	527 968	42
Europe · Europe									
Åland Islands[83] Îles d'Åland[83]	31 XII 2000	25 776[1,28]	12 700[1,28]	13 076[1,28]	27[1,28]	27[1,28]	0.8	1 552	18
Albania Albanie	1 IV 2001	3 069 275	1 530 443	1 538 832	3 142	*3 182	0.4	28 748	111
Andorra Andorre	31 XII 2000	65 844[1,28]	34 268[1,28]	31 576[1,28]	79[1,28]	84[1,28]	2.2	468	179
Austria Autriche	15 V 2001	8 032 926[1]	3 889 189[1]	4 143 737[1]	8 225[1]	8 337[1]	0.4	83 871	99
Belarus Bélarus	16 II 1999	10 045 237[1]	4 717 621[1]	5 327 616[1]	9 775	9 681	-0.3	207 600	47
Belgium Belgique	1 X 2001	10 296 350[1]	5 035 446[1]	5 260 904[1]	10 473[1]	10 667[1,10]	0.6	30 528	349
Bosnia and Herzegovina Bosnie-Herzégovine	31 III 1991	4 377 033[1]	2 183 795[1]	2 193 238[1]	3 843	3 842	0.0	51 197	75
Bulgaria Bulgarie	1 III 2001	7 928 901[1]	3 862 465[1]	4 066 436[1]	7 740	7 623	-0.5	110 879	69

7 Population by sex, rate of population increase, surface area and density *(continued)*

Population selon le sexe, taux d'accroissement de la population, superficie et densité *(suite)*

Country or area[+] Pays ou zone[+]	Latest census Dernier recensement Date	Both sexes Les deux sexes	Men Hommes	Women Femmes	Mid-year estimates (thousands) Estimations au milieu de l'année (milliers) 2005	2008	Annual rate of increase Taux d'accroissement annuel % 2005-08	Surface area Superficie (km²) 2008	Density[&] Densité[&] 2008
Croatia Croatie	31 III 2001	4 437 460[1]	2 135 900[1]	2 301 560[1]	4 442[1]	4 435[1]	-0.1	56 594	78
Czech Republic[1] République tchèque[1]	1 III 2001	10 230 060	4 982 071	5 247 989	10 234	10 430	0.6	78 865	132
Denmark[84] Danemark[84]	1 I 2001	5 349 212[1,28]	2 644 319[1,28]	2 704 893[1,28]	5 416[1,28]	5 489[1,28]	0.4	43 094	127
Estonia Estonie	31 III 2000	1 370 052[1]	631 851[1]	738 201[1]	1 346	1 341	-0.1	45 227	30
Faeroe Islands Iles Féroé	1 I 2008	48 433[1,28]	25 174[1,28]	23 259[1,28]	48[1]	49[1]	0.2	1 393	35
Finland[85] Finlande[85]	31 XII 2000	5 181 115[1,28]	2 529 341[1,28]	2 651 774[1,28]	5 246[1,28]	5 313[1,28]	0.4	338 424	16
France[86] France[86]	1 I 2006	61 399 541[1,87]	29 714 539[1,87]	31 685 002[1,87]	61 181[1,87]	*62 277[1,87]	0.6	551 500	113
Germany Allemagne	28 III 2004	82 491 000[88,89,90,91]	40 330 000[88,89,90,91]	42 161 000[88,89,90,91]	82 464[1]	*82 127[1]	-0.1	357 114	230
Gibraltar Gibraltar	12 XI 2001	27 495[92]	13 644[92]	13 851[92]	29[93]	29[93]	0.6	6	4 881
Greece Grèce	18 III 2001	10 964 020[94]	5 427 682[94]	5 536 338[94]	11 104[95]	11 237[95]	0.4	131 957	85
Guernsey Guernesey	29 IV 2001	59 807[1]	29 138[1]	30 669[1]	...	62[96]	...	78	791
Holy See[97] Saint-Siège[97]	1 VII 2000	*798[28]	*529[28]	*269[28]	...	...	...	^0	...
Hungary Hongrie	1 II 2001	10 198 315	4 850 650	5 347 665	10 087	10 038	-0.2	93 028	108
Iceland Islande	1 VII 2000	281 154[1,28]	140 718[1,28]	140 436[1,28]	296[1,28]	319[1,28]	2.5	103 000	3
Ireland Irlande	23 IV 2006	4 239 848	2 121 171	2 118 677	4 131[98]	*4 422[98]	2.3	70 273	63
Isle of Man Ile de Man	23 IV 2006	80 058[1]	39 523[1]	40 535[1]	79[1,99]	82[1,99]	1.2	572	143
Italy Italie	21 X 2001	57 110 144	27 617 335	29 492 809	58 607	59 832	0.7	301 336	199
Jersey Jersey	11 III 2001	87 186[1]	42 484[1]	44 702[1]	88	...	...	116	...
Latvia Lettonie	31 III 2000	2 377 383[1]	1 094 964[1]	1 282 419[1]	2 301[1]	2 266[1]	-0.5	64 559	35
Liechtenstein Liechtenstein	5 XII 2000	33 307	16 420	16 887	35[1]	35[1]	0.7	160	222
Lithuania Lituanie	6 IV 2001	3 483 972[1]	1 629 148[1]	1 854 824[1]	3 414[1]	3 358[1]	-0.6	65 300[1]	51[1]
Luxembourg Luxembourg	15 II 2001	439 539[1]	216 541[1]	222 998[1]	465[1]	489[1]	1.6	2 586	189
Malta Malte	27 XI 2005	404 962[1]	200 819[1]	204 143[1]	404[1,100]	412[1,100]	0.7	316	1 304
Monaco Monaco	9 VI 2008	31 109[1]	15 076[1,101]	15 914[1,101]	...	...	...	2	...
Montenegro Monténégro	31 X 2003	620 145[1]	305 225[1]	314 920[1]	623[1]	629	0.3	13 812	46

7 Population by sex, rate of population increase, surface area and density *(continued)*

Population selon le sexe, taux d'accroissement de la population, superficie et densité *(suite)*

Country or area+ Pays ou zone+	Latest census Dernier recensement Date	 Both sexes Les deux sexes	 Men Hommes	 Women Femmes	Mid-year estimates (thousands) Estimations au milieu de l'année (milliers) 2005	 2008	Annual rate of increase Taux d'accroisse-ment annuel % 2005-08	Surface area Superficie (km²) 2008	Density& Densité& 2008
Netherlands Pays-Bas	1 I 2002	16 105 285[1,102]	7 971 967[1,102]	8 133 318[1,102]	16 320[1]	16 446[1]	0.3	37 354	440
Norway [103] Norvège [103]	3 XI 2001	4 520 947[1,9,28]	2 240 281[1,9,28]	2 280 666[1,9,28]	4 623[1,9]	4 768[1,9]	1.0	323 782[104]	15
Poland Pologne	20 V 2002	38 230 080[105]	18 516 403[105]	19 713 677[105]	38 161[105]	*38 116[105]	^0.0	312 685[106]	122
Portugal Portugal	12 III 2001	10 356 117	5 000 141	5 355 976	10 549[1]	10 622[1]	0.2	92 090	115
Republic of Moldova République de Moldova	5 X 2004	3 386 673[107]	1 629 689[107]	1 756 984[107]	3 595[1,107]	3 570[1,107]	-0.2	33 846	105
Romania Roumanie	18 III 2002	21 680 974[1]	10 568 741[1]	11 112 233[1]	21 624[1]	21 504[1]	-0.2	238 391	90
Russian Federation Fédération de Russie	9 X 2002	145 166 731[1]	67 605 133[1]	77 561 598[1]	143 114[1]	141 956[1]	-0.3	17 098 242	8
San Marino Saint-Marin	1 VII 2000	26 941[28]	13 185[28]	13 756[28]	31[28]	32[28]	1.6	61	531
Serbia Serbie	31 III 2002	7 498 001[1,108]	3 645 930[1,108]	3 852 071[1,108]	7 441[1,108]	7 350[1,108]	-0.4	88 361	83
Slovakia Slovaquie	25 V 2001	5 193 376	2 502 721	2 690 655	5 387[1]	5 407[1]	0.1	49 037	110
Slovenia Slovénie	31 III 2002	1 987 971[9]	971 203[9]	1 016 768[9]	2 001[1]	2 023[1]	0.4	20 273	100
Spain Espagne	1 XI 2001	40 847 371[109]	20 012 882[109]	20 834 489[109]	43 398[1]	45 593[1]	1.6	505 992	90
Svalbard and Jan Mayen Is. Svalbard et îles Jan Mayen	1 XI 1960	3 431[110]	2 545[110]	886[110]	2[111]	2[111]	0.7	62 422	0
Sweden Suède	31 XII 2003	8 975 670[1,28]	4 446 656[1,28]	4 529 014[1,28]	9 030[1,28]	9 220[1,28]	0.7	450 295	20
Switzerland Suisse	5 XII 2000	7 288 010	3 567 567	3 720 443	7 437[1]	7 648[1]	0.9	41 277[112]	185
TFYR of Macedonia L'ex-R.Y. Macédoine	31 X 2002	2 022 547[1]	1 015 377[1]	1 007 170[1]	2 037	2 047	0.2	25 713	80
Ukraine Ukraine	5 XII 2001	48 240 902	22 316 317	25 924 585	47 281[10]	46 373[10]	-0.6	603 500	77
United Kingdom Royaume-Uni	29 IV 2001	58 789 187[113]	28 579 867[113]	30 209 320[113]	60 238	*61 383	0.6	242 900	253
Oceania · Océanie									
American Samoa Samoa américaines	1 IV 2000	57 291[1,34]	29 264[1,34]	28 027[1,34]	62[1,34]	65[1,34]	1.6	199	327
Australia Australie	8 VIII 2006	20 061 646	9 896 500	10 165 146	20 395[1,14]	21 499[1,14]	1.8	7 692 024	3
Cook Islands [114] Iles Cook [114]	1 XII 2006	*19 569	*9 932	*9 637	22	22	0.9	236	94
Fiji Fidji	16 IX 2007	837 271	427 176	410 095	825	...	...	18 272	...
French Polynesia Polynésie française	20 VIII 2007	*259 596[1]	...	...	253	262	1.2	4 000	66
Guam Guam	1 IV 2000	154 805[1,34]	79 181[1,34]	75 624[1,34]	*169[1,34]	*176[1,34]	1.4	549	320

7 Population by sex, rate of population increase, surface area and density *(continued)*
Population selon le sexe, taux d'accroissement de la population, superficie et densité *(suite)*

Country or area⁺ Pays ou zone⁺	Latest census Dernier recensement: Date	Both sexes Les deux sexes	Men Hommes	Women Femmes	Mid-year estimates (thousands) Estimations au milieu de l'année (milliers): 2005	2008	Annual rate of increase Taux d'accroissement annuel % 2005-08	Surface area Superficie (km²) 2008	Density& Densité& 2008
Kiribati Kiribati	7 XII 2005	92 533	45 612	46 921	...	...	...	726[62,115]	...
Marshall Islands Iles Marshall	1 VI 1999	50 848	26 034	24 814	...	53[2]	...	181	294
Micronesia (Fed. States of) Micronésie (Etats féd. de)	1 IV 2000	107 008[1]	54 191[1]	52 817[1]	108[1]	108[1]	^0.0	702	154
Nauru Nauru	23 IX 2002	10 065	5 136	4 929	...	...	...	21	...
New Caledonia Nouvelle-Calédonie	31 VIII 2004	*230 789	*116 485	*114 304	234	242	1.1	18 575	13
New Zealand Nouvelle-Zélande	7 III 2006	4 143 282[116]	2 021 277[116]	2 122 005[116]	4 134[1,117]	4 269[1,117]	1.1	270 467	16
Niue Nioué	9 IX 2006	1 625	802	823	2	...	...	260	...
Norfolk Island Ile Norfolk	8 VIII 2006	2 523	1 218	1 305	...	...	...	36	...
Northern Mariana Islands Iles Mariannes du Nord	1 IV 2000	69 221	31 984	37 237	80	87	2.5	464	187
Palau Palaos	1 IV 2005	19 907[1]	10 699[1]	9 208[1]	...	21	...	459	47
Papua New Guinea Papouasie-Nvl-Guinée	9 VII 2000	5 190 786	2 691 744	2 499 042	...	...	...	462 840	...
Pitcairn Pitcairn	31 XII 1991	66	...	...	...	^0[24]	...	5	12
Samoa Samoa	5 XI 2006	*179 186	*92 961	*86 225	183	188	0.9	2 842	66
Solomon Islands Iles Salomon	21 XI 1999	409 042	211 381	197 661	471	507	2.4	28 896	18
Tokelau Tokélaou	19 X 2006	1 151	583	568	...	...	...	12	...
Tonga Tonga	30 XI 2006	101 991[1]	51 772[1]	50 219[1]	102[118]	...	...	747	...
Tuvalu Tuvalu	1 XI 2002	9 561	4 729	4 832	10	...	...	26	...
Vanuatu Vanuatu	16 XI 1999	186 678[1]	95 682[1]	90 996[1]	...	...	...	12 189	...
Wallis and Futuna Islands Iles Wallis et Futuna	21 VII 2008	*13 484	...	...	...	...	...	142	...

Source:
United Nations Statistics Division, New York, *Demographic Yearbook 2008* and the demographic statistics database.

Source:
Organisation des Nations Unies, Division de statistique, New York, *Annuaire démographique 2008* et la base de données pour les statistiques démographiques.

⁺ Unless otherwise indicated, figures refer to de facto (present-in-area) population for the present territory.

& Population per square kilometre of surface area in 2008. Figures are merely the quotients of population divided by surface area and are not to be considered either as reflecting density in the urban sense or as indicating the supporting power of a territory's land and resources.

⁺ Sauf indication contraire, les chiffres se rapportent à la population effectivement présente sur le territoire (population de fait), tel qu'il est actuellement défini.

& Nombre d'habitants au kilomètre carré en 2008. Il s'agit simplement du quotient du chiffre de la population divisé par celui de la superficie: il ne faut pas y voir d'indication de la densité au sens urbain du terme ni de l'effectif de population que les terres et les ressources du territoire sont capables de nourrir.

7 Population by sex, rate of population increase, surface area and density *(continued)*
Population selon le sexe, taux d'accroissement de la population, superficie et densité *(suite)*

1 De jure population.
2 Data for estimates refer to national projections.
3 Excluding Mayotte.
4 Excluding border population.
5 Total includes the estimated population of eight rural kebeles (21,410) in Elidar wereda (Affar Region).
6 Projections based on the 1994 population census.
7 Based on the results of the Gabonese Survey for the Evaluation and Tracking of Poverty.
8 As reported by the country. Reasons for discrepancy with other tables not ascertained.
9 Including residents temporarily outside the country.
10 Data refer to 1 January.
11 The number of males and/or females excludes persons whose sex is not stated (18 urban, 19 rural).
12 Data based on 2008 Population Census.
13 Data have not been adjusted for under-enumeration, estimated at 2.4 percent.
14 Mid-year estimates have been adjusted for under-enumeration, at latest census.
15 Comprising the Northern Region (former Saguia el Hamra) and Southern Region (former Rio de Oro).
16 Data are based on projections from 2002 Census.
17 Excluding persons who were not contacted at the time of the census.
18 Excluding the institutional population.
19 Because of rounding, totals are not in all cases the sum of the parts.
20 Final intercensal estimates.
21 Revised intercensal estimates adjusted for net under-coverage (including adjustment for incompletely enumerated Indian reserves).
22 Updated postcensal estimates.
23 Excluding 390 residents of institutions.
24 Data refer to 31 December.
25 Result of Household Multiple Purpose Survey.
26 Projections based on 2007 Population Census.
27 The total surface is 21040.79 square kilometers, without taking into account the last ruling of The Hague.
28 Population statistics are compiled from registers.
29 Excluding data for Saint Barthélémy and Saint Martin.
30 Projections produced by the Latin American and Caribbean Demographic Centre (CELADE) - Population Division of ECLAC.
31 Data are based on projections of the 2001 Population and Housing Census data.
32 Total represents population in private dwellings, the non-institutional population and persons found on the streets between the hours of 5 a.m. and 7 a.m. on September 26, 2001; the figures represent the census counts adjusted for under-coverage.
33 Data refer to projections based on the 2000 population census.
34 Including armed forces stationed in the area.
35 Refers to habitable area. Excludes St. Lucia's Forest Reserve.
36 Based on the results of the population census.
37 Including low water level for all islands (area to shoreline).
38 Excluding armed forces overseas and civilian citizens absent from the country for an extended period of time.
39 Data include persons in remote areas, military personnel outside the country, merchant seamen at sea, civilian seasonal workers outside the country, and other civilians outside the country, and exclude nomads, foreign military, civilian aliens temporarily in the country,

1 Population de droit.
2 Les données se réfèrent aux projections nationales.
3 Non compris Mayotte.
4 À l'exception de la population frontalière.
5 Le total comprend l'effectif estimé de la population de huit kebele ruraux (21,410 habitants) du woreda d'Elidar (région Afar).
6 Projections fondées sur le recensement de la population de 1994.
7 Sur base des résultats de l'enquête gabonaise sur l'évaluation et le suivi de la pauvreté.
8 Données comme déclarées par le pays. On ne sait pas comment s'explique la divergence entre ces chiffres et les chiffres correspondants indiqués ailleurs.
9 Y compris les nationaux se trouvant temporairement hors du pays.
10 Les données se réfèrent au 1er janvier.
11 Il n'est pas tenu compte dans le nombre d'hommes et de femmes des personnes dont le sexe n'est pas indiqué (18 en zone urbaine et 19 en zone rurale).
12 Données fondées sur le recensement de population de 2008.
13 Les données n'ont pas été ajustées pour compenser les lacunes du dénombrement, estimées à 2,4 p. 100.
14 Les estimations au milieu de l'année tiennent compte d'une ajustement destiné à compenser les lacunes du dénombrement lors du dernier recensement.
15 Comprend la région septentrionale (ancien Saguia-el-Hamra) et la région méridionale (ancien Rio de Oro).
16 Données fondées sur des projections tirées du recensement de 2002.
17 La population non comprend pas les personnes qui n'ont pas été contactées à l'heure du recensement.
18 Non compris la population dans les institutions.
19 Les chiffres étant arrondis, les totaux ne correspondent pas toujours rigoureusement à la somme des chiffres partiels.
20 Estimations inter censitaires definitives.
21 Estimations inter censitaires corrigées pour tenir en compte du sous dénombrement net (y compris les réservations en Inde incomplètement énumérées).
22 Estimations postcensitaires préliminaires.
23 À l'exclusion de 390 personnes en établissements de soins.
24 Les données se réfèrent au 31 décembre.
25 Les chiffres résultent d'enquêtes sur les ménages polyvalentes.
26 Projections fondées sur le recensement de la population de 2007.
27 La superficie totale est égale à 21040.79 km2, sans tenir compte de la dernière décision de la Haye.
28 Les statistiques de la population sont compilées à partir des registres.
29 Non compris les données pour Saint Barthélémy et Saint Martin.
30 Les données sont projections produits par le centre démographique de l'Amérique latine et les Caraïbes - Division de la population de la CEPALC.
31 Les données sont basées sur les projections du recensement de 2001 de la population et de l'habitat.
32 Le total représente la population vivant dans des logements privés et les personnes trouvées dans la rue entre 5 et 7 heures du matin le 26 septembre 2001, mais ne tient pas compte des personnes vivant dans des établissements; les chiffres sont ceux du recensement corrigés pour tenir compte du sous-dénombrement.
33 Les données se réfèrent aux projections basées sur le recensement de la population 2000.
34 Y compris les militaires en garnison sur le territoire.
35 S'applique à la zone habitable. Exclut la réserve forestière de Sainte-Lucie.
36 D'après les résultats du recensement de la population.
37 Incluent le niveau de basses eaux pour toutes les iles.
38 Non compris les militaires à l'étranger, et les civils hors du pays pendant une période prolongée.
39 Y compris les personnes dans des régions éloignées, le personnel militaire en dehors du pays, les marins marchands, les ouvriers saisonniers civils de couture en dehors du pays, et autres civils en dehors du pays, et non compris les nomades, les militaires étrangers, les étrangers civils temporairement

transients on ships and Indian jungle population.

40 Data have been adjusted on the basis of the Population Census of 2005.

41 Excluding nomadic Indian tribes.

42 A dispute exists between the governments of Argentina and the United Kingdom of Great Britain and Northern Ireland concerning sovereignty over the Falkland Islands (Malvinas).

43 Includes 477 persons present in the Falkland Islands in connection with the military garrison, but excludes all military personnel and their families.

44 The previous census was conducted only 16 months earlier (on 31 March 2003) but it was repeated because all of its data were destroyed in a fire before they could be fully processed, analyzed, and reported.

45 Figures for male and female population do not add up to the figure for total population, because they exclude 365 persons of unknown sex.

46 Data refer to resident population in Uruguay according to Census Phase 1, carried out between the months of June and July 2004.

47 Excluding Indian jungle population.

48 Excluding nomad population.

49 The methodology used for calculating the number of the de facto and de jure population in the 2001 census data differs as follows from the methodology used in previous censuses: the duration that defines a person as being "temporarily present" or "temporarily absent" is now under one year; the previously applied definition was for 6 months.

50 Data have not been adjusted for under-enumeration, estimated at 4.96 per cent.

51 Data refer to projections based on the 2005 population census.

52 Excluding foreign diplomatic personnel and their dependants. Data for estimates based on 1998 census result.

53 For statistical purposes, the data for China do not include those for the Hong Kong Special Administrative Region (Hong Kong SAR), Macao Special Administrative Region (Macao SAR) and Taiwan Province of China.

54 Data refer to the civilian population of 31 provinces, municipalities and autonomous regions.

55 Data for 2005 are estimated from the National Sample Survey of 1 per cent population.

56 Including all persons irrespective of citizenship, who at the time of the census resided in the country or intended to reside for a period of at least one year. No distinction is made between those present or absent at the time of census.

57 Data refer to government-controlled areas.

58 Including data for the Indian-held part of Jammu and Kashmir, the final status of which has not yet been determined.

59 Excluding Mao-Maram, Paomata and Purul sub-divisions of Senapati district of Manipur. The population of Manipur including the estimated population of the three sub-divisions of Senapati district is 2 291 125 (Males 1 161 173 and females 1 129 952).

60 The figure includes an estimated population of 459 557 persons in urban and 1 857 659 persons in rural areas that were not directly enumerated, and a population of 566 403 persons in urban and 1 717 578 persons in rural areas who declined to participate. Also included are 421 399 non permanent residents (the homeless, the crew of ships carrying national flag, boat/floating house people, remotely located tribesmen and refugees.)

61 Data refer to the Iranian Year which begins on 21 March and ends on 20 March of the following year.

62 Land area only.

dans le pays, les transiteurs sur des bateaux et les Indiens de la jungle.

40 Données ajustées sur la base du recensement de la population de 2005.

41 Non compris les tribus d'Indiens nomades.

42 La souveraineté sur les îles Falkland (Malvinas) fait l'objet d'un différend entre le Gouvernement argentin et le Gouvernement du Royaume-Uni de Grande-Bretagne et d'Irlande du Nord.

43 Comprend 477 personnes installées dans les îles Falkland du fait de la présence d'une garnison militaire, mais exclut tous les membres du personnel militaire et leurs familles.

44 Le recensement précédent a eu lieu seulement 16 mois auparavant (le 31 mars 2003), mais a dû être refait parce que toutes les données ont été détruites dans un incendie avant que l'on n'ait pu les traiter et les analyser.

45 Les chiffres relatifs à la population masculine et féminine ne correspondent pas au chiffre de la population totale, parce que l'on en a exclu 365 personnes de sexe inconnu.

46 Les données se rapportent à la population résidente en Uruguay d'après la phase 1 du recensement, qui a eu lieu entre juin et juillet 2004.

47 Non compris les Indiens de la jungle.

48 Non compris les nomades.

49 La méthode utilisée pour dénombrer la population présente et la population légale dans le contexte du recensement de 2001 diffère de celle qui a été appliquée lors des recensements antérieurs en ce que la durée considérée pour définir la "présence temporaire" ou "l'absence temporaire" était dorénavant fixée à "moins d'un an" alors qu'elle était de 6 mois auparavant.

50 Les données n'ont pas été ajustées pour compenser les lacunes du dénombrement, estimées à 4,96 p.100.

51 Les données se réfèrent aux projections basées sur le recensement de la population de 2005.

52 Non compris le personnel diplomatique étranger et les membres de leur famille les accompagnant. Les estimations se réfèrent aux des résultats 1998 de recensement.

53 Pour la présentation des statistiques, les données pour la Chine ne comprennent pas la Région Administrative Spéciale de Hong Kong (Hong Kong RAS), la Région Administrative Spéciale de Macao (Macao RAS) et la province de Taiwan.

54 Pour la population civile seulement de 31 provinces, municipalités et régions autonomes.

55 Les données pour 2005 ont été estimées à partir de l'enquête nationale qui a porté sur un échantillon de 1% de la population.

56 Les chiffres comprennent toute la population, quelle que soit la nationalité, qui à l'époque de recensement avait résidé dans le pays, ou avait l'intention de résider, pendant une période d'au moins un an. Il n'y a pas de distinction entre les personnes présentes ou absentes au moment du recensement. Les données se rapportent aux zones contrôlées par le Gouvernement.

57 Les données se rapportent aux zones contrôlées par le Gouvernement.

58 Y compris les données pour la partie du Jammu et du Cachemire occupée part l'Inde dont le statut définitif n'a pas encore été déterminé.

59 Non compris les subdivisions Mao-Maram Paomata et Purul du district de Senapati dans l'État du Manipur. Cet État compte 2 291 125 habitants (1 161 173 hommes et 1 129 952 femmes), y compris la population estimative des trois subdivisions du district de Senapati.

60 Y compris la population estimée a 459 557 personnes dans les zones urbaines et de 1 857 659 personnes dans les zones rurales qui n'ont pas été énumérées directement, aussi que 566 403 personnes qui non pas répondu dans les zones urbaines et de 1 717 578 personnes dans les zones rurales. Y compris 421 399 résidants non permanents (les sans abri, l'équipage des bateaux portant le pavillon national, les habitants des embarcations ou des maisons flottantes, les habitants des tribus isolées et les réfugiés.)

61 Les données concernent l'année iranienne, qui commence le 21 mars et se termine le 20 mars de l'année suivante.

62 La superficie des terres seulement.

63	Excluding the population in three autonomous provinces in the north of the country.	63	La population des trois provinces autonomes dans le nord du pays est exclue.
64	Including data for East Jerusalem and Israeli residents in certain other territories under occupation by Israeli military forces since June 1967.	64	Y compris les données pour Jérusalem-Est et les résidents israéliens dans certains autres territoires occupés depuis 1967 par les forces armées israéliennes.
65	Excluding diplomatic personnel outside the country and foreign military and civilian personnel and their dependants stationed in the area.	65	Non compris le personnel diplomatique hors du pays ni les militaires et agents civils étrangers en poste sur le territoire et les membres de leur famille les accompagnant.
66	Data refer to 1 October 2007.	66	Les données se réfèrent au 1er octobre 2007.
67	Excluding data for Jordanian territory under occupation since June 1967 by Israeli military forces. Excluding foreigners, including registered Palestinian refugees.	67	Non compris les données pour le territoire jordanien occupé depuis juin 1967 par les forces armées israéliennes. Non compris les étrangers, mais y compris les réfugiés de Palestine enregistrés.
68	Excluding usual residents not in country at time of census.	68	À l'exclusion des résidents habituels qui ne sont pas dans le pays au moment du recensement.
69	Based on the results of the 2005 Population and Housing Census.	69	Données fondées sur les résultats du recensement de la population et de l'habitat de 2005.
70	Based on the results of a household survey.	70	D'après les résultats d'une enquête de ménages.
71	Data have been adjusted for under-enumeration, at latest census.	71	Les données ont été ajustées pour compenser les lacunes du dénombrement lors du dernier recensement.
72	Excluding Malaysian citizens and permanent residents who were away or intended to be away from the country for more than six months. Excluding Malaysian military, naval and diplomatic personnel and their families outside the country, and tourists and businessmen who intended to be in Malaysia for less than six months.	72	Non compris les citoyens Malaisiens et les résidents permanents qui étaient ou qui ont prévu d'être hors du pays pour six mois ou plus. Non compris le personnel militaire Malaisien, le personnel naval ou diplomatique et leurs familles hors du pays, et les touristes et les hommes d'affaires qui avaient l'intention de rester en Malaisie moins de six mois.
73	Data including estimated population from household listing from Village Development Committees and Wards which could not be enumerated at the time of the census.	73	Les données incluent la population estimée par les listes des ménages des comités de développement des villages et des circonscriptions qui n'ont pas pu être énumérée au moment du recensement.
74	Data have been adjusted for under-enumeration, estimated at 2.70 per cent.	74	Les données ont été ajustées pour compenser les lacunes du dénombrement, estimées à 2,70 p. 100.
75	Excluding data for the Pakistan-held part of Jammu and Kashmir, the final status of which has not yet been determined.	75	Non compris les données pour le Jammu et Cachemire occupée par le Pakistan dont le statut définitif n'a pas encore été déterminé.
76	Data based on Population Demographic Survey. These estimates do not reflect completely accurately the actual population and vital events of the country.	76	D'après les résultats de l'Enquête démographique par sondage. Ces estimations ne dénotent pas d'une manière complètement ponctuelle la population actuelle et les statistiques de l'état civil du pays.
77	Data are based on projections of the 2000 Population and Housing Census data.	77	Les données sont basées sur les projections du recensement de 2000 de la population et de l'habitat.
78	Excluding transients afloat and non-locally domiciled military and civilian services personnel and their dependants.	78	Non compris les personnes de passage à bord de navires, ni les militaires et agents civils domiciliés hors du territoire et les membres de leur famille les accompagnant.
79	Data refer to resident population only.	79	Pour la population résidante seulement.
80	The Population and Housing Census 2001 did not cover the whole area of the country due to the security problems; the Census was complete in 18 districts only; in three districts it was not possible to conduct it; and in four districts it was partially conducted.	80	Le recensement de la population et de l'habitat en 2001 n' pas couvert la totalité du pays pour des problèmes de sécurité ; le recensement à été complété seulement en 18 districts ; dans 3 districts ça n'a pas été possible de conduire le recensement et dans 4 districts il a été partialement conduit.
81	Including Palestinian refugees.	81	Y compris les réfugiés de Palestine.
82	Data based on Address Based Population Registration System.	82	Les données sont basées sur le registre national de la population basé sur l'adresse.
83	Also included in Finland	83	Comprise aussi dans Finlande.
84	Excluding Faeroe Islands and Greenland shown separately, if available.	84	Non compris les Iles Féroe et le Gröenland, qui font l'objet de rubriques distinctes, si disponible.
85	Including Aland Islands.	85	Y compris les Îles d'Åland.
86	Excluding Overseas Departments, namely, French Guiana, Guadeloupe, Martinique and Reunion, shown separately.	86	Non compris les départements d'outre-mer, c'est-à-dire la Guyane française, la Guadeloupe, la Martinique et la Réunion, qui font l'objet de rubriques distinctes.
87	Excluding diplomatic personnel outside the country and including members of alien armed forces not living in military camps and foreign diplomatic personnel not living in embassies or consulates.	87	Non compris le personnel diplomatique hors du pays et y compris les militaires étrangers ne vivant pas dans des camps militaires et le personnel diplomatique étranger ne vivant pas dans les ambassades ou les consulats.
88	Excluding homeless persons.	88	Non compris les personnes sans domicile fixe.
89	Excluding foreign military personnel and foreign diplomatic and consular personnel and their family members in the country.	89	Non compris le personnel militaire étranger, le personnel diplomatique et consulaire étranger et les membres de leur famille se trouvant dans le pays.
90	Data of the microcensus - a 1% household sample survey - refer to a single reference week in spring (usually last week in April).	90	Les données du microrecensement (enquête sur les ménages, réalisée sur un échantillon de 1 %) concernent une seule semaine de référence au printemps (habituellement la dernière semaine d'avril).
91	Sample survey, de jure.	91	Enquête par sondage, Population de droit.

92 Excluding families of military personnel, visitors and transients.
93 Excluding military personnel, visitors and transients.
94 Including armed forces stationed outside the country, but excluding alien armed forces stationed in the area.
95 Excluding armed forces stationed outside the country, but including alien armed forces stationed in the area.
96 Data refer to 31 March.
97 Data refer to the Vatican City State.
98 Data refer to 15 April.
99 Data refer to 30 April.
100 Including civilian nationals temporarily outside the country.
101 Figures for male and female population do not add up to the figure for total population, because they exclude 119 persons of unknown sex.
102 Census results, based on compilation of continuous accounting and sample surveys.
103 Excluding Svalbard and Jan Mayen Island shown separately.
104 Mainland surface area.
105 Excluding civilian aliens within country, but including civilian nationals temporarily outside country.
106 Surface area includes inland waters as well as part of internal waters.
107 Excluding Transnistria and the municipality of Bender.
108 Excluding Kosovo and Metohia.
109 Excluding transients visitors.
110 Inhabited only during the winter season. Census data are for total population while estimates refer to Norwegian population only. Included also in the de jure population of Norway.
111 Data refer to 1 January. Data refer to Svalbard only.
112 Excluding state forests and communanzas (7.15 km2).
113 Counts for the 2001 Census are taken from "Key Statistics table 1 for the Urban/Rural classification: England and Wales" available on CD-ROM, based on the usually resident population.
114 Excluding Niue, shown separately, which is part of Cook Islands, but because of remoteness is administered separately.
115 Excluding 84 square km of uninhabited islands.
116 This data has been randomly rounded to protect confidentiality. Individual figures may not add up to totals, and values for the same data may vary in different tables.
117 Excluding diplomatic personnel and armed forces stationed outside country; also excluding alien armed forces within the country.
118 Data refer to national projections. Based on the results of the 1996 population census not necessarily mid-year estimated.

92 Non compris les familles des militaires, ni les visiteurs et transients.
93 Non compris les militaires, ni les visiteurs et transients.
94 Y compris les militaires nationaux hors du pays, mais non compris les militaires étrangers en garnison sur le territoire.
95 Non compris les militaires en garnison hors du pays, mais y compris les militaires étrangers en garnison sur le territoire.
96 Données se rapportent au 31 mars.
97 Les données se réfèrent à la Cité du Vatican.
98 Données se rapportent au 15 avril.
99 Données se rapportent au 30 avril.
100 Y compris les civils nationaux temporairement hors du pays.
101 Les chiffres relatifs à la population masculine et féminine ne correspondent pas au chiffre de la population totale, parce que l'on en a exclu 119 personnes de sexe inconnu.
102 Les résultats du recensement, d'après les résultats des dénombrements et enquêtes par sondage continue.
103 Non compris Svalbard et Jan Mayen qui font l'objet de rubriques distinctes.
104 La superficie du territoire continental.
105 Non compris les civils étrangers dans le pays, mais y compris les civils nationaux temporairement hors du pays.
106 Superficie comprends les eaux intérieures et une partie des eaux situées en deçà de la ligne de base de la mer.
107 Les données ne tiennent pas compte de l'information sur la Transnistria et la municipalité de Bender.
108 Non compris Kosovo et Metohia.
109 Non compris les visiteurs en transit.
110 N'est habitée pendant la saison d'hiver. Les données de recensement se rapportent à la population totale, mais les estimations ne concernent que la population norvégienne, comprise également dans la population de droit de la Norvège.
111 Données se raportent au 1 janvier. Données ne concernant que le Svalbard.
112 Non comprises les forêts domaniales et communanzas (7,15 km2).
113 Les chiffres du recensement de 2001 proviennent du tableau intitulé "Key Statistics table 1 for the Urban/Rural classification: England and Wales" disponible sur CD-ROM et sont fondés sur la notion de résidence habituelle.
114 Non compris Nioué, qui fait l'objet d'une rubrique distincte et qui fait partie des îles Cook, mais qui, en raison de son éloignement, est administrée séparément.
115 La superficie des terres seulement. Exclut des îles inhabitées d'une superficie de 84 kilomètres carrés.
116 Ces données ont été arrondies de façon aléatoire afin d'en préserver la confidentialité. La somme de certains chiffres peut ne pas correspondre aux totaux indiqués et les valeurs des mêmes données peuvent varier d'un tableau à un autre.
117 Non compris le personnel diplomatique et les militaires hors du pays; non compris également les militaires étrangers en garnison dans le pays.
118 Les données se réfèrent aux projections nationales. À partir des résultats du recensement de la population de 1996, pas nécessairement des estimations en milieu d'année.

Population in urban and rural areas, rates of growth and largest urban agglomeration population

Population urbaine, population rurale, taux d'accroissement et population de l'agglomération urbaine la plus peuplée

Region, country or area Région, pays ou zone	Year Année	Population estimates and projections / Estimations de la population et projections: Rural % Rurale %	Urban % Urbaine %	Annual growth rate (%) [1] / Taux d'accroissement annuel (%) [1]: Rural pop. Pop. rurale	Urban pop. Pop. urbaine	Population of largest urban agglomeration with 750 000 inhabitants or more in 2009 / Population de l'agglomération urbaine la plus peuplée avec 750 000 habitants ou plus en 2009: Number (000s) Nombre (000s)	% of urban % d'urbaine	% of total % de totale
World	**2005**	**51.4**	**48.6**	**0.5**	**1.9**	...	...	...
Monde	**2010**	**49.5**	**50.5**	**0.3**	**1.9**	...	...	...
Africa	**2005**	**62.1**	**37.9**	**1.6**	**3.4**	...	...	...
Afrique	**2010**	**60.0**	**40.0**	**1.5**	**3.3**	...	...	...
Algeria	2005	36.7	63.3	-0.3	2.5	2 512	12.1	7.6
Algérie	2010	33.5	66.5	-0.3	2.3	2 740	11.9	7.9
Angola	2005	46.0	54.0	0.6	4.3	3 533	39.4	21.3
Angola	2010	41.5	58.5	0.6	4.0	4 511	42.3	24.4
Benin	2005	60.0	40.0	2.5	4.2	720	22.9	9.2
Bénin	2010	58.0	42.0	2.1	4.0	815	21.9	9.1
Botswana	2005	42.7	57.3	-0.4	2.7	...	...	...
Botswana	2010	38.9	61.1	-0.6	2.3	...	...	...
Burkina Faso	2005	78.5	21.5	2.3	6.9	1 328	44.8	9.7
Burkina Faso	2010	74.3	25.7	1.9	6.2	1 777	45.4	11.3
Burundi	2005	90.5	9.5	2.6	5.8	...	...	...
Burundi	2010	89.0	11.0	1.6	4.9	...	...	...
Cameroon	2005	45.7	54.3	0.4	3.7	1 767	18.3	9.9
Cameroun	2010	41.6	58.4	0.2	3.3	2 053	18.3	10.5
Cape Verde	2005	42.6	57.4	-0.4	2.7	...	...	...
Cap-Vert	2010	38.9	61.1	-0.5	2.4	...	...	...
Central African Rep.	2005	61.9	38.1	1.6	2.3	...	...	...
Rép. centrafricaine	2010	61.1	38.9	1.3	2.5	...	...	...
Chad	2005	74.7	25.3	2.1	4.6	732	28.9	7.3
Tchad	2010	72.4	27.6	1.8	4.6	808	26.6	7.2
Comoros	2005	72.1	27.9	2.2	2.5	...	...	...
Comores	2010	71.8	28.2	1.8	2.8	...	...	...
Congo	2005	39.8	60.2	0.9	2.5	1 172	57.0	34.3
Congo	2010	37.9	62.1	1.2	3.0	1 292	56.9	35.1
Côte d'Ivoire	2005	53.2	46.8	0.8	3.8	3 564	39.5	18.5
Côte d'Ivoire	2010	49.4	50.6	0.8	3.7	4 009	38.2	19.0
Dem. Rep. of the Congo	2005	67.9	32.1	1.8	4.6	7 106	37.5	12.0
Rép. dém. du Congo	2010	64.8	35.2	1.6	4.5	8 401	36.8	12.7
Djibouti	2005	24.0	76.0	1.6	1.8	...	...	...
Djibouti	2010	23.8	76.2	1.1	1.8	...	...	...
Egypt	2005	57.0	43.0	1.7	2.0	10 565	31.8	13.7
Egypte	2010	56.6	43.4	1.3	2.1	10 902	30.3	13.1
Equatorial Guinea	2005	61.1	38.9	2.4	3.0	...	...	...
Guinée équatoriale	2010	60.3	39.7	1.9	3.1	...	...	...
Eritrea	2005	80.6	19.4	2.6	5.2	...	...	...
Erythrée	2010	78.4	21.6	2.1	5.2	...	...	...
Ethiopia	2005	84.1	15.9	2.4	3.5	2 633	22.1	3.5
Ethiopie	2010	83.3	16.7	2.2	3.8	2 863	21.0	3.5
Gabon	2005	16.4	83.6	-1.4	2.4	...	...	...
Gabon	2010	14.0	86.0	-0.8	2.1	...	...	...
Gambia	2005	46.1	53.9	0.8	4.3	...	...	...
Gambie	2010	41.9	58.1	0.7	3.7	...	...	...
Ghana	2005	52.2	47.8	0.6	3.6	1 985	19.0	9.1
Ghana	2010	48.5	51.5	0.5	3.4	2 269	18.8	9.5

8 Population in urban and rural areas, rates of growth and largest urban agglomeration population *(continued)*
Population urbaine, population rurale, taux d'accroissement et population de l'agglomération urbaine la plus peuplée *(suite)*

Region, country or area Région, pays ou zone	Year Année	Population estimates and projections / Estimations de la population et projections: Rural % Rurale %	Urban % Urbaine %	Annual growth rate (%) [1] / Taux d'accroissement annuel (%) [1]: Rural pop. Pop. rurale	Urban pop. Pop. urbaine	Population of largest urban agglomeration with 750 000 inhabitants or more in 2009 / Population de l'agglomération urbaine la plus peuplée avec 750 000 habitants ou plus en 2009: Number (000s) Nombre (000s)	% of urban % d'urbaine	% of total % de totale
Guinea	2005	67.0	33.0	1.5	3.6	1 411	46.4	15.3
Guinée	2010	64.6	35.4	1.9	4.3	1 597	45.5	15.9
Guinea-Bissau	2005	70.4	29.6	2.1	2.5	...	...	...
Guinée-Bissau	2010	70.0	30.0	2.0	3.0	...	...	...
Kenya	2005	79.3	20.7	2.3	4.0	2 814	37.9	7.9
Kenya	2010	77.8	22.2	2.1	4.2	3 375	38.8	8.5
Lesotho	2005	76.7	23.3	-0.1	3.8	...	...	...
Lesotho	2010	73.1	26.9	-0.3	3.4	...	...	...
Liberia	2005	53.9	46.1	3.5	4.9	1 202	78.3	36.1
Libéria	2010	52.2	47.8	1.8	3.4	882	47.0	22.3
Libyan Arab Jamah.	2005	23.0	77.0	1.2	2.2	1 059	23.2	17.9
Jamah. arabe libyenne	2010	22.1	77.9	0.8	2.1	1 095	22.0	17.1
Madagascar	2005	71.5	28.5	2.2	3.8	1 590	31.7	9.0
Madagascar	2010	69.8	30.2	1.9	3.9	1 816	31.0	9.3
Malawi	2005	82.7	17.3	2.2	5.4	662	28.0	4.8
Malawi	2010	80.2	19.8	2.1	5.3	821	27.9	5.4
Mali	2005	68.0	32.0	1.2	4.7	1 368	36.1	11.6
Mali	2010	64.1	35.9	1.1	4.4	1 628	35.7	12.5
Mauritania	2005	59.6	40.4	2.1	2.9	...	...	...
Mauritanie	2010	58.6	41.4	1.5	2.9	...	...	...
Mauritius [2]	2005	57.8	42.2	0.8	0.5	...	...	...
Maurice [2]	2010	58.2	41.8	0.5	0.8	...	...	...
Mayotte	2005	49.8	50.2	2.7	2.6	...	...	...
Mayotte	2010	49.9	50.1	2.2	2.5	...	...	...
Morocco	2005	44.8	55.2	-0.2	2.3	3 138	18.6	10.3
Maroc	2010	41.8	58.2	-0.3	2.2	3 245	17.6	10.1
Mozambique	2005	65.5	34.5	1.1	4.5	1 341	18.7	6.4
Mozambique	2010	61.6	38.4	0.8	4.0	1 589	18.4	6.9
Namibia	2005	64.9	35.1	1.0	3.5	...	...	...
Namibie	2010	62.0	38.0	0.7	3.3	...	...	...
Niger	2005	83.4	16.6	3.7	4.4	848	39.0	6.5
Niger	2010	82.9	17.1	3.5	4.7	1 004	38.7	6.6
Nigeria	2005	53.8	46.2	0.9	3.8	8 767	13.5	6.2
Nigéria	2010	50.2	49.8	0.7	3.5	10 203	13.4	6.6
Réunion	2005	7.6	92.4	-3.5	1.7	...	...	...
Réunion	2010	6.0	94.0	-2.6	1.4	...	...	...
Rwanda	2005	82.5	17.5	2.4	4.1	775	49.1	8.6
Rwanda	2010	81.1	18.9	2.3	4.4	909	49.0	9.1
Saint Helena [3]	2005	60.3	39.7	-1.4	-1.3	...	...	...
Sainte-Hélène [3]	2010	60.3	39.7	-0.9	-0.3	...	...	...
Sao Tome and Principe	2005	41.9	58.1	-0.5	3.0	...	...	...
Sao Tomé-et-Principe	2010	37.8	62.2	-0.4	2.8	...	...	...
Senegal	2005	58.9	41.1	2.2	3.2	2 434	52.4	21.6
Sénégal	2010	57.6	42.4	1.8	3.3	2 777	52.6	22.2
Seychelles	2005	47.1	52.9	-0.6	1.4	...	...	...
Seychelles	2010	44.7	55.3	-1.0	1.3	...	...	...
Sierra Leone	2005	63.2	36.8	2.2	3.5	785	41.7	15.4
Sierra Leone	2010	61.6	38.4	1.7	3.4	875	40.4	15.4
Somalia	2005	64.8	35.2	1.6	3.5	1 415	48.1	16.9
Somalie	2010	62.6	37.4	1.9	4.1	1 353	40.1	14.8
South Africa	2005	40.7	59.3	-0.2	1.8	3 263	11.4	6.8
Afrique du Sud	2010	38.3	61.7	-0.9	1.2	3 607	11.8	7.2

8 Population in urban and rural areas, rates of growth and largest urban agglomeration population *(continued)*
Population urbaine, population rurale, taux d'accroissement et population de l'agglomération urbaine la plus peuplée *(suite)*

Region, country or area Région, pays ou zone	Year Année	Population estimates and projections / Estimations de la population et projections: Rural % Rurale %	Urban % Urbaine %	Annual growth rate (%) [1] / Taux d'accroissement annuel (%) [1]: Rural pop. Pop. rurale	Urban pop. Pop. urbaine	Population of largest urban agglomeration with 750 000 inhabitants or more in 2009 / Population de l'agglomération urbaine la plus peuplée avec 750 000 habitants ou plus en 2009: Number (000s) Nombre (000s)	% of urban % d'urbaine	% of total % de totale
Sudan	2005	63.5	36.5	1.0	4.1	4 518	32.0	11.7
Soudan	2010	59.9	40.1	0.7	3.7	5 021	30.2	11.9
Swaziland	2005	78.1	21.9	1.5	0.8	...	...	...
Swaziland	2010	78.6	21.4	1.3	1.5	...	...	...
Togo	2005	60.1	39.9	1.3	4.2	1 310	54.7	21.9
Togo	2010	56.6	43.4	1.0	3.9	1 593	56.3	24.1
Tunisia	2005	34.7	65.3	-0.2	1.6	734	11.4	7.4
Tunisie	2010	32.7	67.3	-0.3	1.5	759	11.0	7.4
Uganda	2005	87.5	12.5	3.1	4.4	1 318	36.6	4.6
Ouganda	2010	86.7	13.3	3.0	4.8	1 535	35.8	4.7
United Rep. of Tanzania	2005	75.8	24.2	2.3	4.6	2 680	28.4	6.9
Rép.-Unie de Tanzanie	2010	73.6	26.4	2.2	4.7	3 207	28.3	7.3
Western Sahara	2005	19.2	80.8	2.6	4.0	...	...	...
Sahara occidental	2010	18.2	81.8	2.1	3.6	...	...	...
Zambia	2005	65.0	35.0	2.2	2.8	1 265	30.8	10.8
Zambie	2010	64.3	35.7	2.0	3.2	1 413	30.7	10.9
Zimbabwe	2005	64.1	35.9	-0.5	1.6	1 513	33.8	12.1
Zimbabwe	2010	61.7	38.3	1.2	3.4	1 606	34.0	12.8
Northern America	**2005**	**19.3**	**80.7**	**-0.6**	**1.3**	**...**	**...**	**...**
Amérique septentrionale	**2010**	**17.9**	**82.1**	**-0.6**	**1.2**	**...**	**...**	**...**
Bermuda	2005	0.0	100.0	0.0	0.3	...	...	...
Bermudes	2010	0.0	100.0	0.0	0.2	...	...	...
Canada	2005	19.9	80.1	0.5	1.1	5 035	19.5	15.6
Canada	2010	19.4	80.6	0.3	1.1	5 377	19.9	16.0
Greenland	2005	17.2	82.8	-1.6	0.4	...	...	...
Groenland	2010	15.8	84.2	-1.6	0.3	...	...	...
Saint Pierre and Miquelon	2005	10.1	89.9	-1.8	-0.2	...	...	...
Saint-Pierre-et-Miquelon	2010	9.4	90.6	-1.4	0.2	...	...	...
United States	2005	19.2	80.8	-0.7	1.3	18 727	7.7	6.2
Etats-Unis	2010	17.7	82.3	-0.7	1.2	19 300	7.5	6.1
Latin America and Caribbean	**2005**	**22.3**	**77.7**	**-0.7**	**1.6**	**...**	**...**	**...**
Amérique latine et Caraïbes	**2010**	**20.4**	**79.6**	**-0.6**	**1.4**	**...**	**...**	**...**
Anguilla	2005	0.0	100.0	0.0	2.5	...	...	...
Anguilla	2010	0.0	100.0	0.0	1.7	...	...	...
Antigua and Barbuda	2005	69.3	30.7	1.3	0.9	...	...	...
Antigua-et-Barbuda	2010	69.7	30.3	0.9	1.4	...	...	...
Argentina	2005	8.6	91.4	-1.5	1.2	12 551	35.5	32.4
Argentine	2010	7.6	92.4	-1.3	1.1	12 988	35.0	32.2
Aruba	2005	53.4	46.6	1.1	1.3	...	...	...
Aruba	2010	53.1	46.9	0.1	0.6	...	...	...
Bahamas	2005	16.9	83.1	0.0	1.5	...	...	...
Bahamas	2010	15.9	84.1	-0.2	1.4	...	...	...
Barbados	2005	58.7	41.3	-0.8	1.7	...	...	...
Barbade	2010	55.5	44.5	-1.0	1.7	...	...	...
Belize	2005	49.8	50.2	1.2	2.9	...	...	...
Belize	2010	47.8	52.2	0.9	2.7	...	...	...
Bolivia (Plurinational State of)	2005	35.8	64.2	0.4	2.5	1 524	25.9	16.6
Bolivie (État plurinational de)	2010	33.5	66.5	0.2	2.3	1 642	25.2	16.6
Brazil	2005	15.8	84.2	-2.2	1.5	18 647	11.9	10.0
Brésil	2010	13.5	86.5	-2.0	1.1	19 960	12.0	10.3
British Virgin Islands	2005	60.1	39.9	0.7	1.7	...	...	...
Iles Vierges britanniques	2010	59.0	41.0	0.3	1.8	...	...	...

8 Population in urban and rural areas, rates of growth and largest urban agglomeration population *(continued)*
Population urbaine, population rurale, taux d'accroissement et population de l'agglomération urbaine la plus peuplée *(suite)*

Region, country or area Région, pays ou zone	Year Année	Population estimates and projections Estimations de la population et projections				Population of largest urban agglomeration with 750 000 inhabitants or more in 2009 Population de l'agglomération urbaine la plus peuplée avec 750 000 habitants ou plus en 2009		
				Annual growth rate (%) [1] Taux d'accroissement annuel (%) [1]				
		Rural % Rurale %	Urban % Urbaine %	Rural pop. Pop. rurale	Urban pop. Pop. urbaine	Number (000s) Nombre (000s)	% of urban % d'urbaine	% of total % de totale
Cayman Islands	2005	0.0	100.0	0.0	1.5	...	...	...
Iles Caïmanes	2010	0.0	100.0	0.0	0.9	...	...	...
Chile	2005	12.4	87.6	-1.4	1.3	5 605	39.2	34.4
Chili	2010	11.0	89.0	-1.2	1.2	5 883	39.1	34.7
Colombia	2005	26.4	73.6	0.3	1.9	7 353	23.2	17.1
Colombie	2010	24.9	75.1	0.1	1.7	8 262	24.2	18.1
Costa Rica	2005	38.2	61.8	0.0	2.2	1 232	46.1	28.5
Costa Rica	2010	35.6	64.4	-0.2	2.1	1 416	48.4	30.9
Cuba	2005	24.4	75.6	0.3	-0.1	2 187	25.8	19.5
Cuba	2010	24.8	75.2	0.0	0.0	2 140	25.4	19.1
Dominica	2005	33.1	66.9	-0.5	-0.2	...	...	...
Dominique	2010	32.8	67.2	-0.5	0.3	...	...	...
Dominican Republic	2005	34.3	65.7	-0.7	2.4	1 981	31.6	20.8
Rép. dominicaine	2010	30.8	69.2	-0.8	2.1	2 138	30.9	21.2
Ecuador	2005	36.4	63.6	-0.9	2.1	2 386	28.7	18.3
Equateur	2010	33.1	66.9	-0.7	2.0	2 634	29.2	19.3
El Salvador	2005	38.4	61.6	-1.0	1.3	1 401	37.5	23.1
El Salvador	2010	35.7	64.3	-0.9	1.4	1 534	39.0	24.9
Falkland Is. (Malvinas)	2005	29.2	70.8	-1.6	1.2	...	...	...
Iles Falkland (Malvinas)	2010	26.4	73.6	-1.7	0.9	...	...	...
French Guiana	2005	24.4	75.6	2.1	2.9	...	...	...
Guyane française	2010	23.7	76.4	1.5	2.7	...	...	...
Grenada	2005	62.6	37.4	-0.3	1.4	...	...	...
Grenade	2010	60.7	39.3	-0.4	1.6	...	...	...
Guadeloupe	2005	1.6	98.4	0.4	0.5	...	...	...
Guadeloupe	2010	1.6	98.4	0.1	0.4	...	...	...
Guatemala	2005	52.8	47.2	1.6	3.4	984	16.4	7.7
Guatemala	2010	50.5	49.5	1.4	3.4	1 075	15.6	7.7
Guyana	2005	71.7	28.3	-0.1	0.1	...	...	...
Guyana	2010	71.4	28.6	-0.5	0.5	...	...	...
Haiti	2005	55.9	44.1	-1.5	4.9	2 171	52.3	23.1
Haïti	2010	47.9	52.1	-1.6	3.9	2 643	52.1	26.3
Honduras	2005	51.4	48.6	0.8	3.2	901	26.9	13.1
Honduras	2010	48.4	51.6	0.6	3.1	1 000	26.3	13.4
Jamaica	2005	48.0	52.0	0.5	0.5	...	...	...
Jamaïque	2010	48.0	52.0	0.2	0.6	...	...	...
Martinique	2005	10.7	89.3	0.9	0.3	...	...	...
Martinique	2010	11.0	89.0	0.4	0.2	...	...	...
Mexico	2005	23.7	76.3	-0.3	1.4	18 735	23.3	17.8
Mexique	2010	22.2	77.8	-0.5	1.2	19 319	22.7	17.6
Montserrat	2005	86.5	13.5	1.0	2.2	...	...	...
Montserrat	2010	85.7	14.3	0.6	2.4	...	...	...
Netherlands Antilles	2005	8.1	91.9	-1.9	1.8	...	...	...
Antilles néerlandaises	2010	6.8	93.2	-2.2	0.8	...	...	...
Nicaragua	2005	44.1	55.9	0.7	1.8	909	29.8	16.7
Nicaragua	2010	42.7	57.3	0.7	2.1	934	28.5	16.3
Panama	2005	29.2	70.8	-1.3	2.7	1 216	53.1	37.6
Panama	2010	25.2	74.8	-1.2	2.3	1 346	52.6	39.0
Paraguay	2005	41.5	58.5	0.3	2.8	1 762	51.0	29.8
Paraguay	2010	38.5	61.5	0.1	2.5	1 977	51.1	31.1
Peru	2005	25.0	75.0	-0.4	1.7	8 081	38.7	29.0
Pérou	2010	23.1	76.9	-0.5	1.6	8 769	39.3	30.1

8 Population in urban and rural areas, rates of growth and largest urban agglomeration population *(continued)*
Population urbaine, population rurale, taux d'accroissement et population de l'agglomération urbaine la plus peuplée *(suite)*

Region, country or area Région, pays ou zone	Year Année	Population estimates and projections / Estimations de la population et projections: Rural % Rurale %	Urban % Urbaine %	Annual growth rate (%) [1] / Taux d'accroissement annuel (%) [1]: Rural pop. Pop. rurale	Urban pop. Pop. urbaine	Population of largest urban agglomeration with 750 000 inhabitants or more in 2009 / Population de l'agglomération urbaine la plus peuplée avec 750 000 habitants ou plus en 2009: Number (000s) Nombre (000s)	% of urban % d'urbaine	% of total % de totale
Puerto Rico Porto Rico	2005	2.4	97.6	-12.8	0.7	2 601	68.1	66.5
	2010	1.2	98.8	-9.4	0.5	2 730	69.5	68.6
Saint Kitts and Nevis Saint-Kitts-et-Nevis	2005	67.8	32.2	1.2	1.4	...	...	...
	2010	67.6	32.4	0.9	1.9	...	...	...
Saint Lucia Sainte-Lucie	2005	72.4	27.6	0.9	1.3	...	...	...
	2010	72.0	28.0	0.7	1.6	...	...	...
Saint Vincent-Grenadines Saint Vincent-Grenadines	2005	52.9	47.1	-0.8	1.0	...	...	...
	2010	50.7	49.3	-1.0	1.0	...	...	...
Suriname Suriname	2005	32.8	67.2	-0.4	1.6	...	...	...
	2010	30.6	69.4	-0.6	1.5	...	...	...
Trinidad and Tobago Trinité-et-Tobago	2005	87.8	12.2	0.0	2.9	...	...	...
	2010	86.1	13.9	-0.1	3.0	...	...	...
Turks and Caicos Islands Iles Turques et Caïques	2005	10.3	89.7	-7.0	2.3	...	...	...
	2010	6.7	93.3	-6.1	1.6	...	...	...
United States Virgin Is. Iles Vierges américaines	2005	5.8	94.2	-4.1	0.2	...	...	...
	2010	4.7	95.3	-3.5	-0.1	...	...	...
Uruguay Uruguay	2005	8.1	91.9	-1.1	0.4	1 622	53.1	48.8
	2010	7.5	92.5	-1.1	0.5	1 633	52.6	48.6
Venezuela (Boliv. Rep. of) Venezuela (Rép. boliv. du)	2005	8.1	91.9	-2.2	2.0	2 929	11.9	11.0
	2010	6.6	93.4	-1.8	1.7	3 051	11.5	10.7
Asia **Asie**	**2005**	**60.2**	**39.8**	**0.3**	**2.3**	**...**	**...**	**...**
	2010	**57.8**	**42.2**	**0.2**	**2.2**	**...**	**...**	**...**
Afghanistan Afghanistan	2005	78.7	21.3	3.1	4.6	2 994	57.3	12.2
	2010	77.4	22.6	2.8	4.7	3 573	56.9	12.7
Armenia Arménie	2005	35.9	64.1	0.1	0.2	1 104	56.2	36.0
	2010	35.8	64.2	0.0	0.5	1 110	56.1	36.0
Azerbaijan Azerbaïdjan	2005	48.5	51.5	0.9	1.3	1 867	42.9	22.1
	2010	48.1	51.9	0.7	1.4	1 950	42.6	22.1
Bahrain Bahreïn	2005	11.6	88.4	1.7	2.1	...	...	...
	2010	11.4	88.6	1.2	1.9	...	...	...
Bangladesh Bangladesh	2005	74.3	25.7	0.8	3.2	12 555	31.9	8.2
	2010	71.9	28.1	0.5	3.1	14 251	31.9	8.8
Bhutan Bhoutan	2005	69.0	31.0	0.6	4.0	...	...	...
	2010	65.3	34.7	0.4	3.8	...	...	...
Brunei Darussalam Brunéi Darussalam	2005	26.5	73.5	0.2	2.5	...	...	...
	2010	24.3	75.7	0.0	2.2	...	...	...
Cambodia Cambodge	2005	81.2	18.8	1.3	3.0	1 354	52.0	9.8
	2010	79.9	20.1	1.2	3.2	1 519	51.8	10.3
China [4] Chine [4]	2005	57.5	42.5	-1.0	2.6	15 184	2.7	1.2
	2010	53.0	47.0	-1.0	2.3	16 344	2.6	1.2
China, Hong Kong SAR Chine, Hong Kong RAS	2005	0.0	100.0	0.0	0.5	6 883	100.0	100.0
	2010	0.0	100.0	0.0	0.9	7 022	100.0	100.0
China, Macao SAR Chine, Macao RAS	2005	0.0	100.0	0.0	2.3	...	...	...
	2010	0.0	100.0	0.0	0.8	...	...	...
Cyprus Chypre	2005	30.6	69.4	0.4	1.3	...	...	...
	2010	29.7	70.3	0.3	1.3	...	...	...
Georgia Géorgie	2005	47.5	52.5	-1.3	-1.0	1 093	46.7	24.5
	2010	47.3	52.7	-1.0	-0.4	1 115	49.7	26.2
India Inde	2005	71.3	28.7	1.1	2.3	19 493	6.0	1.7
	2010	70.0	30.0	0.8	2.4	21 720	6.1	1.8
Indonesia Indonésie	2005	57.0	43.1	0.7	1.7	8 795	9.3	4.0
	2010	55.7	44.3	0.4	1.7	9 121	9.0	4.0

8 Population in urban and rural areas, rates of growth and largest urban agglomeration population *(continued)*

Population urbaine, population rurale, taux d'accroissement et population de l'agglomération urbaine la plus peuplée *(suite)*

Region, country or area Région, pays ou zone	Year Année	Population estimates and projections / Estimations de la population et projections: Rural % Rurale %	Urban % Urbaine %	Annual growth rate (%)[1] / Taux d'accroissement annuel (%)[1]: Rural pop. Pop. rurale	Urban pop. Pop. urbaine	Population of largest urban agglomeration with 750 000 inhabitants or more in 2009 / Population de l'agglomération urbaine la plus peuplée avec 750 000 habitants ou plus en 2009: Number (000s) Nombre (000s)	% of urban % d'urbaine	% of total % de totale
Iran (Islamic Rep. of)	2005	32.4	67.6	-0.9	2.1	7 044	14.7	10.0
Iran (Rép. islamique d')	2010	29.2	70.8	-0.9	1.9	7 190	13.8	9.7
Iraq	2005	33.1	66.9	2.6	2.0	5 327	28.2	18.9
Iraq	2010	33.8	66.2	2.7	2.6	5 751	28.2	18.7
Israel	2005	8.3	91.7	1.3	1.7	3 012	49.1	45.0
Israël	2010	8.1	91.9	0.9	1.5	3 219	48.9	44.9
Japan	2005	34.0	66.0	-0.6	0.2	35 622	42.4	28.0
Japon	2010	33.2	66.8	-0.9	0.2	36 507	43.1	28.7
Jordan	2005	21.7	78.3	2.8	3.1	1 042	23.9	18.7
Jordanie	2010	21.5	78.5	1.0	1.6	1 088	22.0	17.2
Kazakhstan	2005	42.9	57.1	0.1	1.2	1 267	14.6	8.3
Kazakhstan	2010	41.5	58.5	-0.2	1.3	1 360	15.0	8.7
Korea, Dem. P. R.	2005	40.2	59.8	0.2	0.5	2 805	19.9	11.9
Corée, R. p. dém. de	2010	39.8	60.2	0.0	0.6	2 828	19.7	11.8
Korea, Republic of	2005	18.7	81.3	-1.4	0.8	9 825	25.4	20.7
Corée, République de	2010	17.0	83.0	-1.5	0.6	9 778	24.5	20.2
Kuwait	2005	1.7	98.3	1.3	2.5	1 888	71.2	69.9
Koweït	2010	1.6	98.4	0.9	2.1	2 230	75.9	74.7
Kyrgyzstan	2005	64.9	35.1	1.4	0.9	820	44.8	15.7
Kirghizistan	2010	65.5	34.5	1.1	1.3	854	45.0	15.6
Lao People's Dem. Rep.	2005	72.6	27.4	0.1	5.7	702	43.6	11.9
Rép. dém. pop. lao	2010	66.8	33.2	0.0	4.9	799	39.5	12.6
Lebanon	2005	13.4	86.6	-0.2	1.0	1 777	50.3	43.5
Liban	2010	12.8	87.2	-0.3	0.9	1 909	51.9	45.2
Malaysia	2005	32.4	67.6	-1.3	3.0	1 405	8.1	5.5
Malaisie	2010	27.8	72.2	-1.3	2.4	1 493	7.6	5.4
Maldives	2005	66.3	33.8	-0.6	4.9	...	...	...
Maldives	2010	59.9	40.1	-0.7	4.2	...	...	...
Mongolia	2005	40.5	59.5	-0.2	2.0	873	57.6	34.2
Mongolie	2010	38.0	62.0	-0.3	1.9	949	57.7	35.5
Myanmar	2005	69.6	30.4	-0.1	2.9	3 928	26.7	8.1
Myanmar	2010	66.4	33.6	-0.1	3.0	4 259	25.8	8.5
Nepal	2005	84.1	15.9	1.2	5.0	817	18.8	3.0
Népal	2010	81.4	18.6	1.0	4.7	990	18.7	3.4
Occupied Palestinian Terr.	2005	26.9	73.1	2.4	3.5	...	...	...
Terr. palestinien occupé	2010	25.9	74.1	1.9	3.2	...	...	...
Oman	2005	28.1	71.9	1.2	2.4	...	...	...
Oman	2010	27.0	73.0	1.0	2.3	...	...	...
Pakistan	2005	65.5	34.5	1.7	3.0	11 618	20.3	7.0
Pakistan	2010	64.1	35.9	1.6	3.1	12 817	19.9	7.1
Philippines	2005	51.9	48.1	1.5	2.1	10 761	26.2	12.6
Philippines	2010	51.1	48.9	1.1	2.3	11 449	25.6	12.4
Qatar	2005	4.6	95.4	8.8	10.7	...	...	...
Qatar	2010	4.2	95.8	-0.2	1.6	...	...	...
Saudi Arabia	2005	19.0	81.0	0.9	2.4	4 193	21.9	17.8
Arabie saoudite	2010	17.9	82.1	0.7	2.2	4 725	22.4	18.4
Singapore	2005	0.0	100.0	0.0	2.5	4 267	100.0	100.0
Singapour	2010	0.0	100.0	0.0	0.9	4 737	100.0	100.0
Sri Lanka	2005	85.3	14.7	1.0	0.3	...	...	...
Sri Lanka	2010	85.7	14.3	0.7	1.1	...	...	...
Syrian Arab Republic	2005	46.2	53.8	2.4	4.0	2 605	25.3	13.6
Rép. arabe syrienne	2010	44.3	55.7	0.7	2.5	2 985	24.6	13.6

8 Population in urban and rural areas, rates of growth and largest urban agglomeration population *(continued)*

Population urbaine, population rurale, taux d'accroissement et population de l'agglomération urbaine la plus peuplée *(suite)*

Region, country or area Région, pays ou zone	Year Année	Population estimates and projections Estimations de la population et projections		Annual growth rate (%) [1] Taux d'accroissement annuel (%) [1]		Population of largest urban agglomeration with 750 000 inhabitants or more in 2009 Population de l'agglomération urbaine la plus peuplée avec 750 000 habitants ou plus en 2009		
		Rural % Rurale %	Urban % Urbaine %	Rural pop. Pop. rurale	Urban pop. Pop. urbaine	Number (000s) Nombre (000s)	% of urban % d'urbaine	% of total % de totale
Tajikistan	2005	73.6	26.4	1.6	1.6	...	...	...
Tadjikistan	2010	73.7	26.3	1.7	2.2	...	...	...
Thailand	2005	67.7	32.3	0.2	1.7	6 614	31.0	10.0
Thaïlande	2010	66.0	34.0	-0.2	1.8	6 902	30.3	10.2
Timor-Leste	2005	73.9	26.1	2.8	4.8	...	...	...
Timor-Leste	2010	71.9	28.1	2.7	5.0	...	...	...
Turkey	2005	32.7	67.3	-0.3	1.9	9 710	20.3	13.6
Turquie	2010	30.4	69.6	-0.4	1.7	10 378	20.0	13.9
Turkmenistan	2005	52.7	47.3	0.5	2.2	...	...	...
Turkménistan	2010	50.5	49.5	0.3	2.2	...	...	...
United Arab Emirates	2005	17.7	82.3	0.7	3.3	1 264	37.6	30.9
Emirats arabes unis	2010	16.0	84.1	0.0	2.3	1 518	39.4	33.0
Uzbekistan	2005	63.3	36.7	1.2	0.9	2 169	22.5	8.2
Ouzbékistan	2010	63.8	36.2	1.0	1.4	2 201	22.1	8.0
Viet Nam	2005	72.7	27.3	0.3	3.3	5 264	22.9	6.3
Viet Nam	2010	69.6	30.4	0.1	3.0	5 976	22.8	6.8
Yemen	2005	71.1	28.9	2.0	4.8	1 801	29.6	8.6
Yémen	2010	68.2	31.8	1.8	4.6	2 229	30.3	9.5
Europe	**2005**	**28.3**	**71.7**	**-0.7**	**0.4**	**...**	**...**	**...**
Europe	**2010**	**27.2**	**72.8**	**-0.9**	**0.4**	**...**	**...**	**...**
Albania	2005	53.3	46.7	-1.7	2.5	...	...	...
Albanie	2010	48.1	51.9	-1.5	2.3	...	...	...
Andorra	2005	9.7	90.3	5.9	1.2	...	...	...
Andorre	2010	12.0	88.0	4.4	1.1	...	...	...
Austria	2005	33.5	66.5	-0.3	0.7	1 642	30.0	20.0
Autriche	2010	32.4	67.6	-0.6	0.6	1 693	30.1	20.2
Belarus	2005	27.8	72.2	-2.4	0.2	1 775	25.1	18.1
Bélarus	2010	25.3	74.7	-2.5	0.2	1 837	25.7	19.1
Belgium	2005	2.7	97.3	-0.6	0.6	1 840	18.2	17.7
Belgique	2010	2.6	97.4	-0.8	0.4	1 892	18.2	17.8
Bosnia and Herzegovina	2005	54.3	45.7	-1.2	1.1	...	...	...
Bosnie-Herzégovine	2010	51.4	48.6	-1.5	1.1	...	...	...
Bulgaria	2005	29.8	70.2	-1.5	-0.3	1 169	21.5	15.1
Bulgarie	2010	28.5	71.5	-1.6	-0.3	1 192	22.2	15.8
Channel Islands	2005	69.3	30.7	0.0	0.7	...	...	...
Iles Anglo-Normandes	2010	68.6	31.4	-0.2	0.8	...	...	...
Croatia	2005	43.5	56.5	-0.8	0.3	...	...	...
Croatie	2010	42.3	57.7	-1.0	0.4	...	...	...
Czech Republic	2005	26.5	73.5	0.4	0.4	1 164	15.5	11.4
République tchèque	2010	26.5	73.5	-0.2	0.3	1 162	15.2	11.2
Denmark	2005	14.1	85.9	-1.3	0.5	1 125	24.2	20.8
Danemark	2010	13.1	86.9	-1.3	0.4	1 174	24.8	21.5
Estonia	2005	30.6	69.4	-0.2	-0.1	...	...	...
Estonie	2010	30.5	69.5	-0.3	0.1	...	...	...
Faeroe Islands	2005	60.2	39.8	0.5	0.9	...	...	...
Iles Féroé	2010	59.7	40.3	0.4	0.9	...	...	...
Finland	2005	16.3	83.7	-1.4	0.7	1 067	24.3	20.3
Finlande	2010	14.9	85.1	-1.4	0.6	1 107	24.5	20.8
France	2005	18.4	81.6	-4.0	1.4	10 105	20.3	16.6
France	2010	14.7	85.3	-3.5	1.0	10 410	19.7	16.7
Germany	2005	26.6	73.4	-0.5	0.1	3 391	5.6	4.1
Allemagne	2010	26.2	73.8	-0.8	0.0	3 438	5.7	4.2

8

Population in urban and rural areas, rates of growth and largest urban agglomeration population *(continued)*
Population urbaine, population rurale, taux d'accroissement et population de l'agglomération urbaine la plus peuplée *(suite)*

Region, country or area Région, pays ou zone	Year Année	Population estimates and projections / Estimations de la population et projections: Rural % Rurale %	Urban % Urbaine %	Annual growth rate (%) [1] / Taux d'accroissement annuel (%) [1]: Rural pop. Pop. rurale	Urban pop. Pop. urbaine	Population of largest urban agglomeration with 750 000 inhabitants or more in 2009 / Population de l'agglomération urbaine la plus peuplée avec 750 000 habitants ou plus en 2009: Number (000s) Nombre (000s)	% of urban % d'urbaine	% of total % de totale
Gibraltar	2005	0.0	100.0	0.0	0.2	...	...	...
Gibraltar	2010	0.0	100.0	0.0	0.2	...	...	...
Greece	2005	39.6	60.4	-0.3	0.6	3 230	48.4	29.2
Grèce	2010	38.6	61.4	-0.6	0.6	3 252	47.6	29.1
Holy See [5]	2005	0.0	100.0	0.0	0.1	...	...	...
Saint-Siège [5]	2010	0.0	100.0	0.0	0.0	...	...	...
Hungary	2005	33.7	66.3	-1.3	0.3	1 698	25.4	16.9
Hongrie	2010	31.9	68.1	-1.4	0.3	1 705	25.2	17.1
Iceland	2005	7.1	92.9	0.7	2.3	...	...	...
Islande	2010	6.6	93.4	-0.1	1.5	...	...	...
Ireland	2005	39.5	60.5	1.1	2.3	1 037	41.0	24.8
Irlande	2010	38.1	61.9	0.4	1.8	1 084	39.0	24.0
Isle of Man	2005	48.8	51.2	0.3	-0.2	...	...	...
Ile de Man	2010	49.4	50.6	0.0	0.0	...	...	...
Italy	2005	32.4	67.6	0.0	0.7	3 352	8.5	5.7
Italie	2010	31.6	68.4	-0.6	0.5	3 357	8.2	5.6
Latvia	2005	32.0	68.0	-0.3	-0.5	...	...	...
Lettonie	2010	32.3	67.7	-0.4	-0.4	...	...	...
Liechtenstein	2005	85.4	14.6	0.9	0.4	...	...	...
Liechtenstein	2010	85.7	14.3	0.7	0.9	...	...	...
Lithuania	2005	33.4	66.6	-1.2	-0.9	...	...	...
Lituanie	2010	33.0	67.0	-1.1	-0.5	...	...	...
Luxembourg	2005	16.1	83.9	-0.5	1.5	...	...	...
Luxembourg	2010	14.8	85.2	-0.5	1.4	...	...	...
Malta	2005	6.4	93.6	-3.2	0.6	...	...	...
Malte	2010	5.3	94.7	-2.7	0.5	...	...	...
Monaco	2005	0.0	100.0	0.0	0.3	...	...	...
Monaco	2010	0.0	100.0	0.0	0.3	...	...	...
Montenegro	2005	38.2	61.8	0.2	-0.1	...	...	...
Monténégro	2010	38.5	61.5	-0.1	0.1	...	...	...
Netherlands	2005	19.8	80.2	-2.5	1.1	1 023	7.8	6.3
Pays-Bas	2010	17.1	82.9	-2.2	0.8	1 044	7.6	6.3
Norway [6]	2005	22.5	77.5	-0.9	1.4	818	22.8	17.7
Norvège [6]	2010	20.6	79.4	-1.0	1.2	875	23.0	18.2
Poland	2005	38.5	61.5	0.2	-0.3	1 693	7.2	4.4
Pologne	2010	39.0	61.0	-0.2	-0.1	1 710	7.4	4.5
Portugal	2005	42.4	57.6	-1.2	1.4	2 747	45.2	26.0
Portugal	2010	39.3	60.7	-1.5	1.0	2 808	43.6	26.2
Republic of Moldova	2005	56.8	43.2	-2.4	0.7	...	...	...
République de Moldova	2010	53.1	47.0	-2.1	0.9	...	...	...
Romania	2005	45.4	54.6	-1.7	0.6	1 931	16.3	8.9
Roumanie	2010	42.5	57.5	-1.7	0.6	1 933	16.0	9.1
Russian Federation	2005	27.1	72.9	-0.6	-0.3	10 418	10.0	7.3
Fédération de Russie	2010	26.8	73.2	-0.7	-0.2	10 523	10.2	7.5
San Marino	2005	6.0	94.0	0.6	0.9	...	...	...
Saint-Marin	2010	5.9	94.1	0.2	0.6	...	...	...
Serbia	2005	45.6	54.4	-0.7	0.6	1 116	20.8	11.3
Serbie	2010	43.9	56.1	-0.9	0.6	1 115	20.3	11.3
Slovakia	2005	44.4	55.6	0.4	-0.1	...	...	...
Slovaquie	2010	45.0	55.0	0.1	0.1	...	...	...
Slovenia	2005	49.8	50.2	0.5	-0.1	...	...	...
Slovénie	2010	50.5	49.5	0.2	0.2	...	...	...

8 Population in urban and rural areas, rates of growth and largest urban agglomeration population *(continued)*
Population urbaine, population rurale, taux d'accroissement et population de l'agglomération urbaine la plus peuplée *(suite)*

Region, country or area Région, pays ou zone	Year Année	Population estimates and projections / Estimations de la population et projections: Rural % Rurale %	Urban % Urbaine %	Annual growth rate (%)[1] / Taux d'accroissement annuel (%)[1]: Rural pop. Pop. rurale	Urban pop. Pop. urbaine	Population of largest urban agglomeration with 750 000 inhabitants or more in 2009 / Population de l'agglomération urbaine la plus peuplée avec 750 000 habitants ou plus en 2009: Number (000s) Nombre (000s)	% of urban % d'urbaine	% of total % de totale
Spain Espagne	2005	23.3	76.7	0.4	1.2	5 409	16.4	12.6
	2010	22.6	77.4	0.0	1.0	5 762	16.6	12.8
Sweden Suède	2005	15.7	84.3	0.0	0.6	1 248	16.3	13.8
	2010	15.3	84.7	-0.2	0.6	1 279	16.3	13.8
Switzerland Suisse	2005	26.7	73.3	0.2	0.5	1 114	20.4	15.0
	2010	26.4	73.6	-0.1	0.5	1 143	20.5	15.1
TFYR of Macedonia L'ex-R.Y. Macédoine	2005	40.9	59.1	0.0	0.2	...	...	...
	2010	40.7	59.3	-0.4	0.3	...	...	...
Ukraine Ukraine	2005	32.2	67.8	-1.3	-0.4	2 673	8.4	5.7
	2010	31.2	68.8	-1.5	-0.1	2 779	8.9	6.1
United Kingdom Royaume-Uni	2005	21.0	79.0	-0.1	0.7	8 506	17.9	14.1
	2010	20.4	79.6	-0.3	0.7	8 615	17.6	14.0
Oceania Océanie	**2005**	**29.7**	**70.3**	**1.4**	**1.3**	**...**	**...**	**...**
	2010	**29.8**	**70.2**	**1.2**	**1.2**	**...**	**...**	**...**
American Samoa Samoa américaines	2005	8.7	91.3	-2.6	2.1	...	...	...
	2010	7.0	93.0	-1.9	1.8	...	...	...
Australia[7] Australie[7]	2005	11.8	88.2	-0.6	1.3	4 260	23.7	20.9
	2010	10.9	89.1	-0.6	1.2	4 395	23.2	20.6
Cook Islands Iles Cook	2005	29.0	71.0	-2.3	2.0	...	...	...
	2010	24.7	75.3	-2.4	1.4	...	...	...
Fiji Fidji	2005	50.1	49.9	-0.2	1.4	...	...	...
	2010	48.1	51.9	-0.5	1.3	...	...	...
French Polynesia Polynésie française	2005	48.2	51.8	1.4	1.2	...	...	...
	2010	48.6	51.4	1.1	1.3	...	...	...
Guam Guam	2005	6.9	93.1	1.1	1.3	...	...	...
	2010	6.8	93.2	0.7	1.2	...	...	...
Kiribati Kiribati	2005	56.4	43.6	1.5	1.7	...	...	...
	2010	56.1	43.9	1.1	1.9	...	...	...
Marshall Islands Iles Marshall	2005	30.0	70.0	1.0	2.7	...	...	...
	2010	28.2	71.8	0.6	2.4	...	...	...
Micronesia (Fed. States of) Micronésie (Etats féd. de)	2005	77.7	22.3	0.2	0.6	...	...	...
	2010	77.3	22.7	0.3	1.3	...	...	...
Nauru Nauru	2005	0.0	100.0	0.0	0.3	...	...	...
	2010	0.0	100.0	0.0	0.6	...	...	...
New Caledonia Nouvelle-Calédonie	2005	42.0	58.0	1.8	1.3	...	...	...
	2010	42.6	57.4	1.3	1.4	...	...	...
New Zealand Nouvelle-Zélande	2005	13.9	86.1	0.7	1.0	1 189	33.6	28.9
	2010	13.8	86.2	0.4	0.9	1 360	37.0	31.9
Niue Nioué	2005	64.8	35.2	-3.4	-1.4	...	...	...
	2010	62.5	37.5	-3.4	-1.3	...	...	...
Northern Mariana Islands Iles Mariannes du Nord	2005	9.2	90.8	0.7	2.1	...	...	...
	2010	8.7	91.3	0.3	1.8	...	...	...
Palau Palaos	2005	22.3	77.7	-5.5	1.8	...	...	...
	2010	16.6	83.4	-4.7	1.4	...	...	...
Papua New Guinea Papouasie-Nvl-Guinée	2005	87.4	12.6	2.4	2.3	...	...	...
	2010	87.5	12.5	2.1	2.9	...	...	...
Pitcairn Pitcairn	2005	100.0	0.0	0.0	0.0	...	...	...
	2010	100.0	0.0	0.4	0.0	...	...	...
Samoa Samoa	2005	78.8	21.2	0.3	-1.0	...	...	...
	2010	79.8	20.2	0.3	0.0	...	...	...
Solomon Islands Iles Salomon	2005	83.0	17.0	2.1	4.3	...	...	...
	2010	81.4	18.6	1.7	4.3	...	...	...

8 Population in urban and rural areas, rates of growth and largest urban agglomeration population *(continued)*
Population urbaine, population rurale, taux d'accroissement et population de l'agglomération urbaine la plus peuplée *(suite)*

Region, country or area Région, pays ou zone	Year Année	Population estimates and projections / Estimations de la population et projections: Rural % Rurale %	Urban % Urbaine %	Annual growth rate (%) [1] / Taux d'accroissement annuel (%) [1]: Rural pop. Pop. rurale	Urban pop. Pop. urbaine	Population of largest urban agglomeration with 750 000 inhabitants or more in 2009 / Population de l'agglomération urbaine la plus peuplée avec 750 000 habitants ou plus en 2009: Number (000s) Nombre (000s)	% of urban % d'urbaine	% of total % de totale
Tokelau	2005	100.0	0.0	-0.1	0.0	...	...	...
Tokélaou	2010	100.0	0.0	-0.2	0.0	...	...	...
Tonga	2005	76.8	23.2	0.4	0.7	...	...	...
Tonga	2010	76.6	23.4	-0.1	0.8	...	...	...
Tuvalu	2005	51.9	48.1	-0.5	1.4	...	...	...
Tuvalu	2010	49.6	50.4	-0.6	1.4	...	...	...
Vanuatu	2005	76.5	23.5	2.0	4.3	...	...	...
Vanuatu	2010	74.4	25.6	1.7	4.2	...	...	...
Wallis and Futuna Islands	2005	100.0	0.0	0.7	0.0	...	...	...
Iles Wallis et Futuna	2010	100.0	0.0	0.7	0.0	...	...	...

Source:
United Nations Population Division, New York, *World Urbanization Prospects: The 2009 Revision.*

Source:
Organisation des Nations Unies, Division de statistique, New York, *"World Urbanization Prospects: The 2009 Revision."*

1 Annual rates of growth calculated for the periods 2005 - 2010 and 2010 - 2015.
2 Including Agalega, Rodrigues and Saint Brandon.
3 Including Ascension and Tristan da Cunha.
4 For statistical purposes, the data for China do not include those for the Hong Kong Special Administrative Region (Hong Kong SAR) and Macao Special Administrative Region (Macao SAR).
5 Data refer to the Vatican City State.
6 Including Svalbard and Jan Mayen Islands.
7 Including Christmas Island, Cocos (Keeling) Islands and Norfolk Island.

1 Ces taux d'accroissement annuel ont été calculés pour les périodes 2005 à 2010 et 2010 à 2015.
2 Y compris Agalega, Rodrigues et Saint Brandon.
3 Y compris Ascension et Tristan da Cunha.
4 Pour la présentation des statistiques, les données pour la Chine ne comprennent pas la Région Administrative Spéciale de Hong Kong (Hong Kong RAS) et la Région Administrative Spéciale de Macao (Macao RAS).
5 Les données se réfèrent à la Cité du Vatican.
6 Y compris îles Svalbard et Jan Mayen.
7 Y compris les îles Christmas, Cocos (Keeling) et Norfolk.

Technical notes: tables 7 and 8

Table 7 is based on detailed data on population and its growth and distribution published in the United Nations *Demographic Yearbook*. Only official national population estimates reported to the United Nations Statistics Division are included in this table. For a comprehensive description of methods of evaluation and the limitations of the data, consult the *Demographic Yearbook*.

Unless otherwise indicated, figures refer to de facto (present-in-area) population for the present territory; surface area estimates include inland waters.

Table 8: The statistics on population in urban and rural areas, rates of growth and largest urban agglomeration population of each country or area are estimates and projections published by the Population Division of the Department of Economic and Social Affairs of the United Nations Secretariat in the *World Urbanization Prospects: The 2009 Revision*. Because of national differences in the specific characteristics that distinguish urban from rural areas, there are no internationally agreed definitions of urban and rural. In most countries, the distinction is mainly based on size of locality. For the latest available census definition of urban areas in a particular country or area, reference should be made to the *Demographic Yearbook*.

An urban agglomeration comprises the city or town proper and also the suburban fringe or thickly settled territory lying outside, but adjacent to, its boundaries. The largest urban agglomerations refer to those inhabited by 750,000 people or more. Annual rates of change in urban and rural population are computed as average annual percentage changes using midyear population estimates.

Notes techniques : tableaux 7 et 8

Le *tableau 7* est fondé sur des données détaillées sur la population, sa croissance et sa distribution, publiées dans l'*Annuaire démographique* des Nations Unies. Le tableau inclut seulement des estimations officielles de la population qui ont été envoyées à la Division de Statistique des Nations Unies. Pour une description complète des méthodes d'évaluation et une indication des limites des données, voir l'*Annuaire démographique*.

Sauf indication contraire, les chiffres se rapportent à la population effectivement présente sur le territoire tel qu'il est actuellement défini; les estimations de superficie comprennent les étendues d'eau intérieures.

Le *tableau 8:* Les statistiques sur la population urbaine, la population rurale, les taux d'accroissement et population de l'agglomération urbaine la plus peuplée de chaque pays ou zone sont des estimations et projections publiées par la Division de la population du Département des affaires économiques et sociales du Secrétariat des Nations Unies dans "*World Urbanization Prospects: The 2009 Revision*." Il n'existe pas de définition reconnue à l'échelle internationale des zones urbaines et rurales parce que les caractéristiques retenues pour distinguer ces deux types de zone diffèrent d'un pays à un autre. Dans la plupart des pays, cette distinction est essentiellement une fonction de la taille des agglomérations. Pour la définition la plus récente des zones urbaines utilisée dans une région ou un pays donné, se reporter à l'*Annuaire démographique*.

L'agglomération urbaine comprend la ville proprement dite et ses faubourgs ou banlieues, et tout territoire à forte densité de population situé à sa périphérie. Les agglomérations urbaines les plus peuplées se rapportent à celles habitées par 750 000 personnes ou plus.

Les taux annuels de variation des populations urbaines et rurales se calculent sur la base de la variation annuelle moyenne en pourcentage déterminée à partir des estimations de la population au milieu de l'année.

Proportion of seats held by women in national parliament

Percentage, as of 31 January 2010

Proportion de sièges occupés par des femmes au parlement national

Pourcentage, données disponibles en 31 janvier 2010

Country or area Pays ou zone	1990	2002	2003	2004	2005	2006	2007	2008	2009	2010
Afghanistan Afghanistan	3.7	...	...	...	...	27.3	27.3	27.7	27.7	27.3
Albania Albanie	28.8	5.7	5.7	5.7	6.4	7.1	7.1	7.1	7.1	16.4
Algeria Algérie	2.4	3.4	6.2	6.2	6.2	6.2	6.2	7.7	7.7	7.7
Andorra Andorre	...	14.3	14.3	14.3	14.3	28.6	28.6	25.0	25.0	35.7
Angola Angola	14.5	15.5	15.5	15.5	15.0	15.0	15.0	15.0	37.3	38.6
Antigua and Barbuda Antigua-et-Barbuda	0.0	5.3	5.3	5.3	10.5	10.5	10.5	10.5	10.5	10.5
Argentina Argentine	6.3	30.7	30.7	30.7	33.7	36.2	35.0	40.0	40.0	38.5
Armenia Arménie	35.6	3.1	3.1	4.6	5.3	5.3	5.3	9.2	8.4	9.2
Australia Australie	6.1	25.3	25.3	25.3	24.7	24.7	24.7	26.7	26.7	27.3
Austria Autriche	11.5	26.8	33.9	33.9	33.9	33.9	32.2	32.8	27.3	27.9
Azerbaijan Azerbaïdjan	...	10.5	10.5	10.5	10.5	12.0	11.3	11.4	11.4	11.4
Bahamas Bahamas	4.1	15.0	20.0	20.0	20.0	20.0	20.0	12.2	12.2	12.2
Bahrain Bahreïn	...	...	0.0	0.0	0.0	0.0	2.5	2.5	2.5	2.5
Bangladesh Bangladesh	10.3	...	2.0	2.0	2.0	14.8[1]	...	...	6.3[2]	18.6
Barbados Barbade	3.7	10.7	10.7	13.3	13.3	13.3	13.3	10.0	10.0	10.0
Belarus Bélarus	...	10.3	10.3	10.3	29.4	29.1	29.1	29.1	31.8	31.8
Belgium Belgique	8.5	23.3	23.3	35.3	34.7	34.7	34.7	35.3	35.3	38.0
Belize Belize	0.0	6.9	6.9	3.3	6.7	6.7	6.7	3.3	0.0	0.0
Benin Bénin	2.9	6.0	6.0	7.2	7.2	7.2	7.2	10.8	10.8	10.8
Bhutan Bhoutan	2.0	9.3	9.3	9.3	9.3	9.3	2.7	2.7	8.5	8.5
Bolivia (Plurinational State of) Bolivie (État plurinational de)	9.2	11.5	18.5	18.5	19.2	16.9	16.9	16.9	16.9	22.3
Bosnia and Herzegovina Bosnie-Herzégovine	...	7.1	16.7	16.7	16.7	16.7	14.3	11.9	11.9	19.0
Botswana Botswana	5.0	17.0	17.0	17.0	11.1	11.1	11.1	11.1	11.1	7.9
Brazil Brésil	5.3	6.8	8.6	8.6	8.6	8.6	8.8	9.0	9.0	8.8
Bulgaria Bulgarie	21.0	26.3	26.3	26.3	26.3	22.1	22.1	21.7	21.7	20.8
Burkina Faso Burkina Faso	...	8.1	11.7	11.7	11.7	11.7	11.7	15.3	15.3	15.3
Burundi Burundi	...	19.5	18.4	18.4	18.4	30.5	30.5	30.5	30.5	31.4

Proportion of seats held by women in national parliament *(continued)*

Percentage, as of 31 January 2010

Proportion de sièges occupés par des femmes au parlement national *(suite)*

Pourcentage, données disponibles en 31 janvier 2010

Country or area Pays ou zone	1990	2002	2003	2004	2005	2006	2007	2008	2009	2010
Cambodia Cambodge	...	7.4	7.4	9.8	9.8	9.8	9.8	19.5	16.3	21.1
Cameroon Cameroun	14.4	5.6	8.9	8.9	8.9	8.9	8.9	13.9	13.9	13.9
Canada Canada	13.3	20.6	20.6	20.6	21.1	20.8	20.8	21.3	22.1	22.1
Cape Verde Cap-Vert	12.0	11.1	11.1	11.1	11.1	15.3	15.3	18.1	18.1	18.1
Central African Rep. Rép. centrafricaine	3.8	7.3	7.3	...	...	10.5	10.5	10.5	10.5	9.6
Chad Tchad	...	2.4	5.8	5.8	6.5	6.5	6.5	5.2	5.2	5.2
Chile Chili	...	12.5	12.5	12.5	12.5	15.0	15.0	15.0	15.0	14.2
China Chine	21.3	21.8	21.8	20.2	20.2	20.3	20.3	20.6	21.3	21.3
Colombia Colombie	4.5	11.8	12.0	12.0	12.0	12.1	8.4	8.4	8.4	8.4
Comoros Comores	0.0	...	...	...	3.0	3.0	3.0	3.0	3.0	3.0
Congo Congo	14.3	12.0	9.3	8.5	8.5	8.5	8.5	7.3	7.3	7.3
Costa Rica Costa Rica	10.5	19.3	35.1	35.1	35.1	35.1	38.6	36.8	36.8	36.8
Côte d'Ivoire Côte d'Ivoire	5.7	8.5	8.5	8.5	8.5	8.5	8.5	8.9	8.9	8.9
Croatia Croatie	...	20.5	20.5	17.8	21.7	21.7	21.7	20.9	20.9	23.5
Cuba Cuba	33.9	27.6	36.0	36.0	36.0	36.0	36.0	43.2	43.2	43.2
Cyprus Chypre	1.8	10.7	10.7	10.7	16.1	16.1	14.3	14.3	14.3	12.5
Czech Republic République tchèque	...	15.0	17.0	17.0	17.0	17.0	15.5	15.5	15.5	15.5
Dem. Rep. of the Congo Rép. dém. du Congo	5.4	...	...	12.0	12.0	12.0	8.4	8.4	8.4	8.4
Denmark Danemark	30.7	38.0	38.0	38.0	38.0	36.9	36.9	38.0	38.0	38.0
Djibouti Djibouti	0.0	0.0	10.8	10.8	10.8	10.8	10.8	13.8	13.8	13.8
Dominica Dominique	10.0	18.8	18.8	18.8	19.4	12.9	12.9	16.1	18.8	14.3
Dominican Republic Rép. dominicaine	7.5	16.1	17.3	17.3	17.3	17.3	19.7	19.7	19.7	19.7
Ecuador Equateur	4.5	14.6	16.0	16.0	16.0	16.0	25.0	25.0	27.6[3]	32.3
Egypt Egypte	3.9	2.4	2.4	2.4	2.9	2.0	2.0	1.8	1.8	1.8
El Salvador El Salvador	11.7	9.5	9.5	10.7	10.7	10.7	16.7	16.7	19.0	19.0
Equatorial Guinea Guinée équatoriale	13.3	5.0	5.0	5.0	18.0	18.0	18.0	18.0	6.0	10.0
Eritrea Erythrée	...	14.7	22.0	22.0	22.0	22.0	22.0	22.0	22.0	22.0
Estonia Estonie	...	17.8	17.8	18.8	18.8	18.8	18.8	20.8	20.8	22.8

Proportion of seats held by women in national parliament *(continued)*

Percentage, as of 31 January 2010

Proportion de sièges occupés par des femmes au parlement national *(suite)*

Pourcentage, données disponibles en 31 janvier 2010

Country or area Pays ou zone	1990	2002	2003	2004	2005	2006	2007	2008	2009	2010
Ethiopia Ethiopie	...	7.7	7.7	7.7	7.7	21.4	21.9	21.9	21.9	21.9
Fiji Fidji	...	5.7	5.7	5.7	8.5	8.5[4]	...	...	...	...
Finland Finlande	31.5	36.5	36.5	37.5	37.5	37.5	38.0	41.5	41.5	40.0
France France	6.9	10.9	12.2	12.2	12.2	12.2	12.2	18.2	18.2	18.9
Gabon Gabon	13.3	...	9.2	9.2	9.2	9.2	12.5	16.7	16.7	14.7
Gambia Gambie	7.8	...	13.2	13.2	13.2	13.2	9.4	9.4	9.4	7.5
Georgia Géorgie	...	7.2	7.2	7.2	9.4	9.4	9.4	9.4	6.0	5.1
Germany Allemagne	...	31.7	32.2	32.2	32.8	31.8	31.6	31.6	32.2	32.8
Ghana Ghana	...	9.0	9.0	9.0	10.9	10.9	10.9	10.9	7.9	8.3
Greece Grèce	6.7	8.7	8.7	8.7	14.0	13.0	13.0	14.7	14.7	17.3
Grenada Grenade	...	26.7	26.7	26.7	26.7	26.7	26.7	26.7	13.3	13.3
Guatemala Guatemala	7.0	8.8	8.8	8.2	8.2	8.2	8.2	12.0	12.0	12.0
Guinea Guinée	...	8.8	19.3	19.3	19.3	19.3	19.3	19.3[5]	...	...
Guinea-Bissau Guinée-Bissau	20.0	7.8	7.8	...	14.0	14.0	14.0	14.0	10.0	10.0
Guyana Guyana	36.9	20.0	20.0	20.0	30.8	30.8	29.0	29.0	30.0	30.0
Haiti Haïti	...	3.6	3.6	3.6	3.6	3.6	4.1	4.1	4.1	4.1
Honduras Honduras	10.2	9.4	5.5	5.5	5.5	23.4	23.4	23.4	23.4	18.0
Hungary Hongrie	20.7	8.3	9.8	9.8	9.1	9.1	10.4	11.1	11.1	11.1
Iceland Islande	20.6	34.9	34.9	30.2	30.2	33.3	33.3	33.3	33.3	42.9
India Inde	5.0	8.8	8.8	8.8	8.3	8.3	8.3	9.1	9.1	10.8
Indonesia Indonésie	12.4	8.0	8.0	8.0	11.3	11.3	11.3	11.6	11.6	18.0
Iran (Islamic Rep. of) Iran (Rép. islamique d')	1.5	3.4	4.1	4.1	4.1	4.1	4.1	4.1	2.8	2.8
Iraq Iraq	10.8	7.6	7.6	...	...	25.5	25.5	25.5	25.5	25.5
Ireland Irlande	7.8	12.0	13.3	13.3	13.3	13.3	13.3	13.3	13.3	13.9
Israel Israël	6.7	13.3	15.0	15.0	15.0	15.0	14.2	14.2	14.2	19.2
Italy Italie	12.9	9.8	11.5	11.5	11.5	11.5	17.3	17.3	21.3	21.3
Jamaica Jamaïque	5.0	13.3	11.7	11.7	11.7	11.7	11.7	13.3	13.3	13.3
Japan Japon	1.4	7.3	7.3	7.1	7.1	9.0	9.4	9.4	9.4	11.3

Proportion of seats held by women in national parliament *(continued)*

Percentage, as of 31 January 2010

Proportion de sièges occupés par des femmes au parlement national *(suite)*

Pourcentage, données disponibles en 31 janvier 2010

Country or area Pays ou zone	1990	2002	2003	2004	2005	2006	2007	2008	2009	2010
Jordan Jordanie	0.0	1.3	1.3	5.5	5.5	5.5	5.5	6.4	6.4	6.4
Kazakhstan Kazakhstan	...	10.4	10.4	10.4	10.4	10.4	10.4	15.9	15.9	17.8
Kenya Kenya	1.1	3.6	7.1	7.1	7.1	7.1	7.3	7.2[6]	9.8	9.8
Kiribati Kiribati	0.0	4.8	4.8	4.8	4.8	4.8	7.1	4.3	4.3	4.3
Korea, Dem. P. R. Corée, R. p. dém. de	21.1	20.1	20.1	...	20.1	20.1	20.1	20.1	20.1	15.6
Korea, Republic of Corée, République de	2.0	5.9	5.9	5.5	13.0	13.4	13.4	14.4	13.7	14.7
Kuwait Koweït	...	0.0	0.0	0.0	0.0	1.5[7]	1.5[8]	1.5[9]	3.1[10]	7.7
Kyrgyzstan Kirghizistan	...	10.0	10.0	10.0	10.0	0.0	0.0	25.6	25.6	25.6
Lao People's Dem. Rep. Rép. dém. pop. lao	6.3	21.2	22.9	22.9	22.9	22.9	25.2	25.2	25.2	25.2
Latvia Lettonie	...	17.0	21.0	21.0	21.0	21.0	19.0	20.0	20.0	22.0
Lebanon Liban	0.0	2.3	2.3	2.3	2.3	4.7	4.7	4.7	4.7	3.1
Lesotho Lesotho	...	3.8	11.7	11.7	11.7	11.7	11.8	25.0	25.0	24.2
Liberia Libéria	...	7.8	7.8	7.8	5.3	12.5	12.5	12.5	12.5	12.5
Libyan Arab Jamah. Jamah. arabe libyenne	...	...	...	...	...	4.7	7.7	7.7	7.7	7.7
Liechtenstein Liechtenstein	4.0	12.0	12.0	12.0	12.0	24.0	24.0	24.0	24.0	24.0
Lithuania Lituanie	...	10.6	10.6	10.6	22.0	22.0	24.8	22.7	17.7	19.1
Luxembourg Luxembourg	13.3	16.7	16.7	16.7	23.3	23.3	23.3	23.3	23.3	20.0
Madagascar Madagascar	6.5	8.0	3.8	3.8	6.9	6.9	6.9	7.9	7.9[4]	...
Malawi Malawi	9.8	9.3	9.3	9.3	14.0	13.6	13.6	13.0	13.0	20.8
Malaysia Malaisie	5.1	10.4	10.4	10.5	9.1	9.1	9.1	10.0	10.8	9.9
Maldives Maldives	6.3	6.0	6.0	6.0	12.0	12.0	12.0	12.0	12.0	6.5
Mali Mali	...	12.2	10.2	10.2	10.2	10.2	10.2	10.2	10.2	10.2
Malta Malte	2.9	9.2	9.2	9.2	9.2	9.2	9.2	9.2	8.7	8.7
Marshall Islands Iles Marshall	...	3.0	3.0	3.0	3.0	3.0	3.0	3.0	3.0	3.0
Mauritania Mauritanie	...	...	...	3.7	3.7	...	17.9	22.1	22.1	22.1
Mauritius Maurice	7.1	5.7	5.7	5.7	5.7	17.1	17.1	17.1	17.1	17.1
Mexico Mexique	12.0	16.0	16.0	22.6	22.6	24.2	22.6	23.2	23.2	27.6
Micronesia (Fed. States of) Micronésie (Etats féd. de)	...	0.0	0.0	0.0	0.0	0.0	0.0	0.0	0.0	0.0

Proportion of seats held by women in national parliament *(continued)*

Percentage, as of 31 January 2010

Proportion de sièges occupés par des femmes au parlement national *(suite)*

Pourcentage, données disponibles en 31 janvier 2010

Country or area Pays ou zone	1990	2002	2003	2004	2005	2006	2007	2008	2009	2010
Monaco Monaco	11.1	22.2	22.2	20.8	20.8	20.8	20.8	20.8	25.0	26.1
Mongolia Mongolie	24.9	10.5	10.5	10.5	6.8	6.7	6.6	6.6	4.1	3.9
Montenegro Monténégro	...	...	...	...	...	...	8.6	11.1	11.1	11.1
Morocco Maroc	0.0	0.6	10.8	10.8	10.8	10.8	10.8	10.5	10.5	10.5
Mozambique Mozambique	15.7	30.0	30.0	30.0	34.8	34.8	34.8	34.8	34.8	39.2
Namibia Namibie	6.9	25.0	26.4	26.4	25.0	26.9	26.9	26.9	26.9	26.9[11]
Nauru Nauru	5.6	0.0	0.0	0.0	0.0	0.0	0.0	0.0	0.0	0.0
Nepal Népal	6.1	5.9[12]	...	...	...	...	17.3[13]	17.3[13]	33.2	33.2
Netherlands Pays-Bas	21.3	36.0	36.7	36.7	36.7	36.7	36.7	39.3	41.3	42.0
New Zealand Nouvelle-Zélande	14.4	30.8	29.2	28.3	28.3	32.2	32.2	33.1	33.6	33.6
Nicaragua Nicaragua	14.8	20.7	20.7	20.7	20.7	20.7	18.5	18.5	18.5	20.7
Niger Niger	5.4	1.2	1.2	1.2	12.4	12.4	12.4	12.4	12.4	9.7
Nigeria Nigéria	...	3.4	3.4	6.7	4.7	6.4	6.1	7.0	7.0	7.0
Norway Norvège	35.8	35.8	36.4	36.4	38.2	37.9	37.9	36.1	36.1	39.6
Oman Oman	...	...	...	...	2.4	2.4	2.4	0.0	0.0	0.0
Pakistan Pakistan	10.1	...	21.6	21.6	21.3	21.3	21.3	21.1	22.5	22.2
Palau Palaos	...	0.0	0.0	0.0	0.0	0.0	0.0	0.0	0.0	0.0
Panama Panama	7.5	9.9	9.9	9.9	16.7	16.7	16.7	16.7	16.7	8.5
Papua New Guinea Papouasie-Nvl-Guinée	0.0	1.8	0.9	0.9	0.9	0.9	0.9	0.9	0.9	0.9
Paraguay Paraguay	5.6	2.5	2.5	10.0	10.0	10.0	10.0	10.0	12.5	12.5
Peru Pérou	5.6	18.3	18.3	18.3	18.3	18.3	29.2	29.2	29.2	27.5
Philippines Philippines	9.1	17.8	17.8	17.8	15.3	15.7	15.3	20.5	20.5	21.0
Poland Pologne	13.5	20.2	20.2	20.2	20.2	20.4	20.4	20.4	20.2	20.0
Portugal Portugal	7.6	18.7	19.1	19.1	19.1	21.3	21.3	28.3	28.3	27.4
Qatar Qatar	...	...	...	...	...	0.0	0.0	0.0	0.0	0.0
Republic of Moldova République de Moldova	...	12.9	12.9	12.9	15.8	21.8	21.8	21.8	21.8	23.8
Romania Roumanie	34.4	10.7	10.7	10.7	11.4	11.2	11.2	9.4	11.4	11.4
Russian Federation Fédération de Russie	...	7.6	7.6	9.8	9.8	9.8	9.8	14.0	14.0	14.0

Proportion of seats held by women in national parliament *(continued)*

Percentage, as of 31 January 2010

Proportion de sièges occupés par des femmes au parlement national *(suite)*

Pourcentage, données disponibles en 31 janvier 2010

Country or area Pays ou zone	1990	2002	2003	2004	2005	2006	2007	2008	2009	2010
Rwanda Rwanda	17.1	25.7	25.7	48.8	48.8	48.8	48.8	48.8	56.3	56.3
Saint Kitts and Nevis Saint-Kitts-et-Nevis	6.7	13.3	13.3	13.3	0.0	0.0	0.0	6.7	6.7	6.7
Saint Lucia Sainte-Lucie	0.0	...	11.1	11.1	11.1	11.1	5.6[14]	11.1	11.1	11.1
Saint Vincent-Grenadines Saint Vincent-Grenadines	9.5	22.7	22.7	22.7	22.7	18.2	18.2	18.2	18.2	21.7
Samoa Samoa	0.0	6.1	6.1	6.1	6.1	6.1	6.1	8.2	8.2	8.2
San Marino Saint-Marin	11.7	16.7	16.7	16.7	16.7	16.7	11.7	11.7	15.0	16.7
Sao Tome and Principe Sao Tomé-et-Principe	11.8	9.1	9.1	9.1	9.1	9.1	7.3	1.8	7.3	7.3
Saudi Arabia Arabie saoudite	...	...	...	0.0	0.0	0.0	0.0	0.0	0.0	0.0
Senegal Sénégal	12.5	16.7	19.2	19.2	19.2	19.2	19.2	22.0	22.0	22.7
Serbia Serbie	...	...	...	...	...	...	20.4	20.4	21.6	21.6
Serbia and Montenegro Serbie-et-Monténégro	...	7.2	7.2	7.9	7.9	7.9	...	...	...	...
Seychelles Seychelles	16.0	23.5	29.4	29.4	29.4	29.4	29.4	23.5	23.5	23.5
Sierra Leone Sierra Leone	...	8.8	14.5	14.5	14.5	14.5	14.5	13.2	13.2	13.2
Singapore Singapour	4.9	11.8	11.8	16.0	16.0	16.0	24.5	24.5	24.5	23.4
Slovakia Slovaquie	...	14.0	19.3	19.3	16.7	16.7	20.0	19.3	19.3	18.0
Slovenia Slovénie	...	12.2	12.2	12.2	12.2	12.2	12.2	12.2	13.3	14.4
Solomon Islands Iles Salomon	0.0	0.0	0.0	0.0	0.0	0.0	0.0	0.0	0.0	0.0
Somalia Somalie	4.0	...	...	...	...	8.0	7.8	8.2[15]	...	6.9
South Africa Afrique du Sud	2.8	29.8	29.8	29.8	32.8	32.8	32.8	33.0	33.0	44.5
Spain Espagne	14.6	28.3	28.3	28.3	36.0	36.0	36.0	36.6	36.3	36.6
Sri Lanka Sri Lanka	4.9	...	4.4	4.4	4.9	4.9	4.9	5.8	5.8	5.8
Sudan Soudan	...	9.7	9.7	9.7	9.7	14.7	17.8	18.1	18.1	18.9
Suriname Suriname	7.8	17.6	17.6	17.6	19.6	25.5	25.5	25.5	25.5	25.5
Swaziland Swaziland	3.6	3.1	3.1	10.8	10.8	10.8	10.8	10.8	13.8	13.6
Sweden Suède	38.4	42.7	45.3	45.3	45.3	45.3	47.3	47.0	47.0	46.4
Switzerland Suisse	14.0	23.0	23.0	25.0	25.0	25.0	25.0	28.5	28.5	29.0
Syrian Arab Republic Rép. arabe syrienne	9.2	10.4	10.4	12.0	12.0	12.0	12.0	12.0	12.4	12.4
Tajikistan Tadjikistan	...	12.7	12.7	12.7	12.7	17.5	17.5	17.5	17.5	17.5

Proportion of seats held by women in national parliament *(continued)*

Percentage, as of 31 January 2010

Proportion de sièges occupés par des femmes au parlement national *(suite)*

Pourcentage, données disponibles en 31 janvier 2010

Country or area Pays ou zone	1990	2002	2003	2004	2005	2006	2007	2008	2009	2010
Thailand Thaïlande	2.8	9.2	9.2	9.2	8.8	10.8	8.7	11.7	11.7	13.3
TFYR of Macedonia L'ex-R.Y. Macédoine	...	6.7	18.3	18.3	19.2	19.2	28.3	29.2	31.7	32.5
Timor-Leste Timor-Leste	...	...	26.1	26.1	25.3	25.3	25.3	29.2	29.2	29.2
Togo Togo	5.2	4.9	7.4	7.4	6.2	7.4	8.6	11.1	11.1	11.1
Tonga Tonga	0.0	0.0	...	0.0	0.0	3.4	3.3	3.3	3.1[16]	3.1
Trinidad and Tobago Trinité-et-Tobago	16.7	16.7	19.4	19.4	19.4	19.4	19.4	26.8	26.8	26.8
Tunisia Tunisie	4.3	11.5	11.5	11.5	22.8	22.8	22.8	22.8	22.8	27.6
Turkey Turquie	1.3	4.2	4.4	4.4	4.4	4.4	4.4	9.1	9.1	9.1
Turkmenistan Turkménistan	26.0	26.0	26.0	26.0	...	16.0	16.0	16.0	16.8	16.8
Tuvalu Tuvalu	7.7	0.0	0.0	0.0	0.0	0.0	0.0	0.0	0.0	0.0
Uganda Ouganda	12.2	24.7	24.7	24.7	23.9	23.9	29.8	30.7	30.7	31.5
Ukraine Ukraine	...	7.8	5.3	5.3	5.3	5.3	8.7	8.2	8.2	8.0
United Arab Emirates Emirats arabes unis	0.0	0.0	0.0	0.0	0.0	0.0	22.5	22.5	22.5	22.5
United Kingdom Royaume-Uni	6.3	17.9	17.9	17.9	18.1	19.7	19.7	19.5	19.5	19.5
United Rep. of Tanzania Rép.-Unie de Tanzanie	...	22.3	22.3	21.4	21.4	30.4	30.4	30.4	30.4	30.7
United States Etats-Unis	6.6	14.0	14.3	14.3	14.9	15.2	16.3	16.8	17.0	16.8
Uruguay Uruguay	6.1	12.1	12.1	12.1	12.1	11.1	11.1	12.1	12.1	14.1
Uzbekistan Ouzbékistan	...	7.2	7.2	7.2	17.5	17.5	17.5	17.5	17.5	22.0
Vanuatu Vanuatu	4.3	0.0	1.9	1.9	3.8	3.8	3.8	3.8	3.8	3.8
Venezuela (Boliv. Rep. of) Venezuela (Rép. boliv. du)	10.0	9.7	9.7	9.7	9.7	17.4	18.0	18.6	18.6	17.5
Viet Nam Viet Nam	17.7	26.0	27.3	27.3	27.3	27.3	27.3	25.8	25.8	25.8
Yemen Yémen	4.1	0.7	0.7	0.3	0.3	0.3	0.3	0.3	0.3	0.3
Zambia Zambie	6.6	12.0	12.0	12.0	12.0	12.7	14.6	15.2	15.2	14.0
Zimbabwe Zimbabwe	11.0	10.0	10.0	10.0	10.0	16.0	16.7	16.0	15.2	15.0

Source:
International Parliamentary Union (IPU), Geneva, *Women in National Parliaments*, PARLINE database, last accessed June 2010.

Source:
Union interparlementaire, Genève, *Les femmes dans les parlements*, la base de données PARLINE, dernier accès juin 2010.

9 Proportion of seats held by women in national parliament *(continued)*

Percentage, as of 31 January 2010

Proportion de sièges occupés par des femmes au parlement national *(suite)*

Pourcentage, données disponibles en 31 janvier 2010

1 In 2004, the number of seats in parliament was raised from 300 to 345, with the addition of 45 reserved seats for women. These reserved seats were filled in September and October 2005, being allocated to political parties in proportion to their share of the national vote received in the 2001 election.

2 This figure excludes the 45 reserved seats for women which were not yet filled in January 2009.

3 Data refers to the composition of the Legislative and Oversight Commission which assumed legislative and oversight functions in October 2008. The Commission is to be replaced by a new 124-member National Assembly, as provided for in the new Constitution of 2008, when elections are held in 2009.

4 Parliament has been dissolved or suspended for an indefinite period.

5 The parliament was dissolved following the December 2008 coup.

6 Situation for 1 January 2008 for directly elected members endorsed by the electoral commission. The additional twelve appointed seats and two ex-officio seats had yet to be filled.

7 In June 2005, a woman was appointed Minister for the first time in the country's history. As Cabinet Ministers also sit in Parliament, there was therefore one woman in Parliament.

8 No woman candidate was elected in the 2006 elections. One woman was appointed to the 16-member cabinet. As cabinet ministers also sit in parliament, there is therefore one woman out of a total of 65 members.

9 No woman candidate was elected in the 2006 elections. One woman was appointed to the 16-member cabinet sworn in July 2006. A new cabinet sworn in March 2007 included two women. As cabinet ministers also sit in parliament, there are two women out of a total of 65.

10 No woman candidate was elected in the 2008 elections. Two women were appointed to the 16-member cabinet sworn in June 2008. As cabinet ministers also sit in parliament, there are two women out of a total of 65 members. Four women were elected to the parliament in 2009.

11 Figure excludes 11 members yet to be sworn in.

12 The parliament (elected in the parliamentary elections in 1999) was dissolved on 22 May 2002. Women held 12 of the 205 (5.9%) seats in the outgoing parliament.

13 After the promulgation of the interim constitution in January 2007, the House of Representatives dissolved itself in favour of a 330-member interim legislature, called the Legislative Parliament. This interim legislature comprises all members of the previous parliament and other appointed members. It was replaced by an elected unicameral Constituent Assembly in April 2008.

14 No woman was elected in the 2006 elections. However one woman was appointed Speaker of the House and therefore became a member of the House.

15 Based on a peace agreement signed in Djibouti in November 2008, the statutory number of the Transitional Federal Parliament (TFP) increased from 275 to 550 members. On 28 January 2009, 200 of the 275 new TFP members were sworn in, bringing the total number of members to 475. However, the final composition, including the number of women members, is not yet available.

16 No women were elected in 2008, however one woman was appointed to the Cabinet. As cabinet ministers also sit in parliament, there is one woman out of a total of 32 members.

1 En 2004, le nombre de sièges parlementaires est passé de 300 à 345, les nouveaux sièges étant réservés aux femmes. Les sièges réservés ont été pourvus en septembre et en octobre 2005, au prorata des voix obtenues par les partis politiques lors des élections nationales de 2001.

2 Ce chiffre exclut les 45 sièges réservés aux femmes toujours vacants en janvier 2009.

3 Les données se réfèrent à la composition de la Commission législative et de contrôle en charge d'assurer les principales fonctions de la branche législative depuis octobre 2008. Après les élections qui seront tenues en 2009, la Commission législative et de contrôle sera remplacée par une nouvelle Assemblée nationale composée de 124 membres comme le prévoyait la nouvelle Constitution de 2008.

4 Le Parlement a été dissous ou suspendu pour une durée indéterminée.

5 L'Assemblée nationale a été dissoute après le coup d'État de décembre 2008.

6 Au 1er janvier 2008, la situation des membres directement élus et approuvés par la commission électorale est la suivante: les sièges des 12 membres nommés et 2 des membres de droits restent vacants.

7 En juin 2005, pour la première fois de son histoire, une femme fut nommée ministre. Comme les ministres du gouvernement siègent de droit au Parlement, il y avait donc une femme au Parlement.

8 Aucune femme n'a été élue en 2006. Une femme a été nommée parmi les 16 membres du gouvernement. Les ministres siégeant également au Parlement, le Parlement compte donc une femme sur un total de 65 membres.

9 Aucune femme n'a été élue en 2006. Une femme a été nommée parmi les 6 membres du gouvernement qui ont prêté serment en juillet 2006. Un nouveau gouvernement dont les membres ont prêté serment en mars 2007 inclut deux femmes. Les ministres siégeant également au Parlement, le Parlement compte donc deux femmes sur un total de 65 membres.

10 Aucune femme n'a été élue en 2008. Deux femmes ont été nommées parmi les 16 membres du gouvernement qui ont prêté serment en juin 2008. Les ministres siégeant également au Parlement, le Parlement compte donc deux femmes sur un total de 65 membres. Quatre femmes ont été élues au Parlement en 2009.

11 Ce chiffre ne tient pas compte de 11 membres qui n'avaient pas encore été assermentés.

12 Le parlement élu aux élections de 1999 a été dissous le 22 mai 2002. Les femmes y occupaient 12 des 205 sièges, soit 5.9%.

13 Après la promulgation de la constitution provisoire en janvier 2007, la Chambre des représentants a prononcé sa dissolution au profit d'une législature provisoire de 330 membres, baptisée Parlement législatif. Cet organe provisoire se compose de tous les membres du parlement précédent, ainsi que de membres nommés. Il a été remplacé en avril 2008 par une Assemblée constituante monocamérale.

14 Aucune femme n'a été élue en 2006. Une femme a cependant été nommée à la présidence de la chambre des députés et est donc devenue membre de cette dernière.

15 Suite à un accord de paix signé à Djibouti en novembre 2008, le nombre réglementaire de membres du Parlement transitoire fédéral (PTF) a été porté de 275 à 550. Le 28 janvier 2009, 200 des 275 nouveaux membres du PTF ont prêté serment, ce qui ramène le nombre total de membres à 475. Cependant, la composition finale ainsi que le nombre de femmes y siégeant n'est pas encore disponible.

16 Aucune femme n'a été élue en 2008. Cependant, une femme a été nommée au Gouvernement. Les ministres siégeant également au Parlement, le Parlement compte donc une femme sur un total de 32 membres.

10 Share of women in wage employment in the non-agricultural sector

Percentage of total employment

Proportion de femmes salariées dans le secteur non agricole

Pourcentage d'emploi total

Country or area Pays ou zone	1990	2000	2001	2002	2003	2004	2005	2006	2007	2008
Afghanistan *[1] Afghanistan *[1]	17.8	...	...	...	...	...	...	...	...	...
Albania[2] Albanie[2]	...	28.9	26.9	31.6	33.0	...	...	...	...	...
Algeria Algérie	...	...	13.4[2]	...	14.2[2]	14.5[2]	*12.2[3]	*14.1[3]	*13.1[3]	...
American Samoa[2] Samoa américaines[2]	41.7	...	...	...	...	...	...	...	...	...
Andorra Andorre	...	...	...	...	45.6	45.7	45.8	46.1	46.6	...
Anguilla Anguilla	...	...	47.7[2]	*48.8[3]	...	...	...	...	...	...
Antigua and Barbuda[4] Antigua-et-Barbuda[4]	...	...	50.6	50.6	50.6	50.6	50.6	50.6	50.6	50.6
Argentina Argentine	37.1	42.6	43.3	45.9	45.5	44.8	45.1	45.0	...	...
Armenia Arménie	...	52.1	51.1	49.5	47.4	50.1	44.1	45.7	44.8	...
Aruba Aruba	...	48.3	...	...	...	...	...	...	48.6	...
Australia Australie	*43.7	46.3	46.9	46.7	47.0	46.7	47.0	47.1	47.0	47.1
Austria Autriche	*41.5[2]	*43.7[2]	44.2	44.9	45.5	46.2	46.6	46.6	46.3	47.0
Azerbaijan Azerbaïdjan	...	47.6	47.0	46.6	46.2	44.9	46.5	46.1	44.6	43.6
Bahamas[4] Bahamas[4]	...	...	49.8	49.7	50.1	50.4	50.0	49.7	48.8	...
Bahrain Bahreïn	7.6	12.4	13.2	12.7	12.8	11.5	11.0	10.3	9.8	9.6
Bangladesh[2] Bangladesh[2]	...	24.7	...	...	21.6	...	20.1	...	...	...
Barbados Barbade	*46.8[4]	49.9[2]	50.1[2]	50.0[2]	51.1[2]	51.3[2]	...	...	...	...
Belarus Bélarus	*55.4[3]	55.9	56.0	*56.2[3]	*56.3[3]	*56.2[3]	*56.1[3]	*56.0[3]	*56.0[3]	*56.0[3]
Belgium Belgique	*38.7[3]	*43.4[3]	43.4	43.9	44.4	44.7	45.3	45.7	46.0	46.6
Belize Belize	...	...	*35.0[3]	*34.0[3]	...	...	36.5[2]	*35.9[3]	*37.7[3]	...
Benin[2] Bénin[2]	...	...	...	24.3	...	...	...	...	...	...
Bermuda Bermudes	48.7	49.8	49.3	49.4	48.9	48.7	48.6	48.5	48.7	...
Bhutan Bhoutan	...	...	...	...	...	...	16.6	...	...	...
Bolivia (Plurinational State of) *[2] Bolivie (État plurinational de) *[2]	35.2	38.6	38.1	38.2	...	36.1	37.7	42.4	38.1	...
Bosnia and Herzegovina[2] Bosnie-Herzégovine[2]	...	...	...	...	...	...	...	35.2	34.7	35.7
Botswana Botswana	33.5	*42.9	41.1	42.4	40.8	39.5	42.6	43.6	43.4	...
Brazil Brésil	*35.1	40.3	40.7	41.0	*41.4	*41.6	*41.5	*41.8	*41.6	...

10 Share of women in wage employment in the non-agricultural sector *(continued)*
Percentage of total employment

Proportion de femmes salariées dans le secteur non agricole *(suite)*
Pourcentage d'emploi total

Country or area Pays ou zone	1990	2000	2001	2002	2003	2004	2005	2006	2007	2008
British Virgin Islands [3] Iles Vierges britanniques [3]	...	49.8	49.9	50.2	50.4	49.3	49.1	...	...	...
Brunei Darussalam Brunéi Darussalam	...	30.3	28.9	29.0	30.3	...	...	...	...	...
Bulgaria Bulgarie	...	52.8	53.1	53.1	53.1	52.7	52.2	51.4	*51.3[3]	...
Burkina Faso [2] Burkina Faso [2]	12.5	...	...	...	...	...	...	...	...	...
Burundi [2] Burundi [2]	14.3	...	...	...	...	...	...	...	...	...
Cambodia Cambodge	...	41.1[2]	43.3[2]	...	...	*43.5[3]	...	...	...	...
Cameroon [2] Cameroun [2]	...	...	22.2	...	...	...	...	...	...	...
Canada Canada	46.9	48.3	48.8	48.8	49.2	49.4	49.4	49.5	49.8	49.9
Cape Verde [2] Cap-Vert [2]	...	38.9	...	...	...	...	...	...	...	...
Cayman Islands Iles Caïmanes	...	*51.2[3]	...	*51.8[3]	*54.2[3]	*52.2[3]	*49.5[3]	49.4[2]	49.3[2]	50.5[2]
Central African Rep. [3] Rép. centrafricaine [3]	...	...	...	...	46.8	...	...	...	...	...
Chad Tchad	3.8	...	...	...	...	...	...	...	...	...
Chile Chili	*37.3[4]	32.8	32.9	33.2	33.5	*34.2[4]	*34.4[4]	34.9	35.5	36.2
China Chine	37.8	...	...	...	...	...	...	...	...	...
China, Hong Kong SAR Chine, Hong Kong RAS	41.2	44.8	45.5	45.9	46.8	47.3	47.8	47.9	48.3	48.7
China, Macao SAR Chine, Macao RAS	42.7	48.9	48.8	50.2	49.0	49.4	49.5	48.1	48.1	...
Colombia Colombie	*41.8[4]	48.8	49.1	50.1	48.8	48.3	47.4	46.6	47.5	47.5
Congo *[1] Congo *[1]	26.1	...	...	...	...	...	...	...	...	...
Cook Islands Iles Cook	38.4	...	...	...	...	...	...	...	...	...
Costa Rica Costa Rica	37.2	39.3	40.1	*39.9[3]	39.5	38.5	39.6	40.7	41.1	41.5
Croatia Croatie	*43.2	47.0	46.7	46.9	46.1	45.7	45.9	46.9	45.5	45.8
Cuba Cuba	...	43.3	42.8	42.3	42.8	42.6	42.6	42.7	43.7	43.4
Cyprus Chypre	...	44.4	47.4	48.2	49.3	48.2	47.7	48.1	49.1	48.6
Czech Republic République tchèque	*51.0	46.5	46.6	46.7	46.8	47.1	46.6	46.4	46.3	46.0
Dem. Rep. of the Congo *[1] Rép. dém. du Congo *[1]	25.9	...	...	...	...	...	...	...	...	...
Denmark Danemark	*48.0[3]	48.5	48.9	49.0	48.3	48.8	48.7	48.8	49.0	49.3
Djibouti Djibouti	...	...	...	26.7	...	...	...	...	...	...
Dominica [2] Dominique [2]	...	...	43.8	...	...	...	...	...	...	...

10 Share of women in wage employment in the non-agricultural sector *(continued)*

Percentage of total employment

Proportion de femmes salariées dans le secteur non agricole *(suite)*

Pourcentage d'emploi total

Country or area Pays ou zone	1990	2000	2001	2002	2003	2004	2005	2006	2007	2008
Dominican Republic Rép. dominicaine	...	*37.3[2]	*36.9[2]	*38.2[2]	*39.0[2]	38.0	37.7	39.3	38.8	...
Ecuador Equateur	*30.9[2]	*39.3[2]	*38.7[2]	38.1	...	39.2	40.2	38.7	...	...
Egypt Egypte	20.5	19.0	20.7	22.4	19.9	18.8	17.7	18.1	19.0	...
El Salvador El Salvador	*45.5[4]	49.1	48.3	49.5	47.9	47.8	48.5	48.6	48.0	...
Equatorial Guinea *[1] Guinée équatoriale *[1]	10.5	...	...	...	...	...	...	...	...	...
Estonia Estonie	52.3	51.7	51.7	51.5	51.5	52.2	52.6	52.5	52.3	51.7
Ethiopia Ethiopie	...	...	...	...	...	40.6	*43.8[3]	*47.3[3]	...	...
Faeroe Islands[4] Iles Féroé[4]	...	...	...	...	...	...	45.8	...	...	...
Fiji Fidji	29.9	33.2	...	...	...	...	*29.6[2]	...	...	...
Finland Finlande	50.6	50.3	50.2	50.7	50.6	50.7	50.9	51.0	51.0	50.7
France France	*44.7	*47.4	*47.5	*47.9	48.2	48.3	48.6	48.9	49.3	49.2
French Guiana[2] Guyane française[2]	36.1	...	...	...	...	...	...	...	...	...
French Polynesia[2] Polynésie française[2]	...	42.4	41.8	42.5	42.2	42.7	42.5	42.8	42.7	...
Gambia *[1] Gambie *[1]	20.9	...	...	...	...	...	...	...	...	...
Georgia Géorgie	...	...	...	49.6	48.9	50.3	48.5	...	...	*46.1[2]
Germany Allemagne	...	45.1	45.5	45.9	46.4	46.6	46.6	46.9	46.9	46.8
Ghana[2] Ghana[2]	...	31.7	...	...	...	...	...	...	...	...
Gibraltar Gibraltar	34.5	39.7	39.9	40.2	41.6	41.5	41.9	41.5	41.0	...
Greece Grèce	35.0	39.1	39.6	39.8	40.1	40.9	41.0	41.6	42.0	41.9
Greenland[3] Groenland[3]	...	48.8	49.6	49.1	49.4	49.5	49.3	...	...	...
Guadeloupe[3] Guadeloupe[3]	...	...	...	45.7	...	...	...	...	...	...
Guam Guam	...	45.6	45.7	45.8	42.4	43.3	44.5	44.6	44.1	43.3
Guatemala Guatemala	36.8[4]	*40.0[3]	...	*40.3[3]	*42.0[3]	*39.4[3]	...	*43.0[3]	...	...
Guinea-Bissau *[1] Guinée-Bissau *[1]	10.8	...	...	...	...	...	...	...	...	...
Guyana[4] Guyana[4]	...	...	...	34.7	...	...	...	...	...	...
Haiti[2] Haïti[2]	44.2	...	...	...	...	...	...	...	...	...
Honduras Honduras	*33.3[4]	...	33.8[2]	32.9[2]	32.7[2]	34.2[2]	33.4[2]	34.0[2]	33.7[2]	...
Hungary Hongrie	...	48.6	48.5	48.4	49.1	48.9	48.7	48.3	48.0	48.3

10 Share of women in wage employment in the non-agricultural sector *(continued)*

Percentage of total employment

Proportion de femmes salariées dans le secteur non agricole *(suite)*

Pourcentage d'emploi total

Country or area Pays ou zone	1990	2000	2001	2002	2003	2004	2005	2006	2007	2008
Iceland Islande	...	52.2	52.3	53.0	52.5	51.8	52.2	50.9	50.0	49.4
India Inde	12.7	16.6	16.8	17.3	17.6	17.9	18.1	...	...	...
Indonesia Indonésie	29.2	31.7	30.7	29.7	29.5	29.0	30.3	31.3	30.9	32.4
Iran (Islamic Rep. of) Iran (Rép. islamique d')	10.5	13.6	11.6	12.0	12.1	13.0	16.1	...	...	...
Iraq Iraq	...	...	...	...	...	16.0	...	15.3	...	12.1
Ireland Irlande	41.7	46.3	46.5	47.5	47.4	47.5	47.7	47.5	48.2	49.2
Israel Israël	43.0	48.3	48.4	48.7	48.9	48.7	49.3	49.0	49.0	*49.3[2]
Italy Italie	*35.9[4]	39.8	40.6	40.9	41.2	42.7	42.6	42.8	43.0	43.5
Jamaica Jamaïque	*47.3[3]	45.0[2]	44.9[2]	46.2[2]	46.3[2]	45.2[2]	45.6[2]	45.8[2]	46.3[2]	48.2[2]
Japan Japon	38.0	40.0	40.4	40.6	40.8	41.2	41.3	41.6	41.6	41.8
Jordan Jordanie	...	14.4	14.1	14.9	13.9	...	13.7	15.5	15.8	15.7
Kazakhstan Kazakhstan	...	...	48.5	48.1	48.7	49.4	49.1	49.9	50.1	50.0
Kenya Kenya	21.4	...	...	...	...	...	...	...	...	...
Kiribati [2] Kiribati [2]	...	36.8	...	...	...	...	38.5	...	...	...
Korea, Dem. P. R. * [1] Corée, R. p. dém. de * [1]	40.7	...	...	...	...	...	...	...	...	...
Korea, Republic of Corée, République de	38.1	40.1	40.8	41.1	41.2	41.6	41.8	42.0	42.1	42.1
Kyrgyzstan Kirghizistan	...	45.8	45.6	44.9	47.3	49.4	51.9	52.2	50.8	...
Lao People's Dem. Rep. [3] Rép. dém. pop. lao [3]	...	...	...	...	...	...	50.2	...	...	...
Latvia Lettonie	...	53.1	52.5	53.1	53.3	53.2	53.4	52.8	52.0	52.7
Liberia Libéria	...	...	...	11.4	...	...	...	...	...	...
Libyan Arab Jamah. Jamah. arabe libyenne	...	...	15.8	...	...	...	...	...	...	...
Liechtenstein [4] Liechtenstein [4]	...	38.7	38.7	39.1	38.9	39.1	39.4	...	...	...
Lithuania Lituanie	*55.4	53.2	52.7	52.6	53.2	53.3	53.0	52.9	53.0	...
Luxembourg Luxembourg	...	...	...	...	40.6	41.9	42.4	43.2	43.8	43.3
Madagascar Madagascar	...	...	...	...	*37.2[2]	...	37.7	...	...	...
Malawi Malawi	10.5	...	...	...	...	...	...	...	...	...
Malaysia Malaisie	...	*37.9[2]	37.2	37.3	37.9	38.3	38.5	38.7	39.0	39.2
Maldives [2] Maldives [2]	15.8	40.6	...	...	...	...	...	30.0	...	...

10 Share of women in wage employment in the non-agricultural sector *(continued)*

Percentage of total employment

Proportion de femmes salariées dans le secteur non agricole *(suite)*

Pourcentage d'emploi total

Country or area Pays ou zone	1990	2000	2001	2002	2003	2004	2005	2006	2007	2008
Mali[2] Mali[2]	...	...	...	...	...	34.6	...	...	...	...
Malta Malte	...	32.7	31.2	33.8	33.0	32.9	33.6	34.4	35.5	35.1
Martinique[3] Martinique[3]	45.4	...	...	...	...	...	...	...	...	...
Mauritania Mauritanie	...	35.8	...	...	...	...	...	...	...	...
Mauritius Maurice	37.4	38.6	39.0	38.1	38.4	37.5	36.9	37.2	37.2	37.1
Mexico Mexique	...	37.3	37.3	37.5	36.9	37.5	39.1	39.3	39.4	39.4
Monaco[3] Monaco[3]	...	39.2	...	...	...	...	...	...	...	...
Mongolia Mongolie	...	48.6[2]	*48.9[4]	*49.9[4]	*49.3[4]	*51.2[4]	*51.2[4]	*52.0[4]	*51.2[4]	*51.1[4]
Montenegro Monténégro	...	44.0	44.3	...	...	...	43.4	...	...	...
Morocco[2] Maroc[2]	...	...	...	22.1	23.2	22.9	22.8	21.0	20.7	20.8
Mozambique *[1] Mozambique *[1]	11.4	...	...	...	...	...	...	...	...	...
Myanmar[4] Myanmar[4]	40.6	...	...	...	...	...	...	...	...	...
Namibia Namibie	...	42.8[2]	*40.7[3]	...	...	41.4[2]	...	...	...	...
Nepal *[2] Népal *[2]	...	...	14.0	...	...	...	...	...	...	...
Netherlands Pays-Bas	37.7	43.9	44.3	45.0	45.7	45.7	46.2	46.7	47.3	47.7
Netherlands Antilles Antilles néerlandaises	...	49.9[2]	*49.7[3]	*49.8[3]	*50.2[3]	*52.2[3]	*51.9[3]	*51.2[3]	*51.8[3]	*51.0[3]
New Zealand Nouvelle-Zélande	43.9	47.3	47.3	47.1	47.4	47.5	47.4	47.4	47.3	47.6
Nicaragua Nicaragua	...	...	...	...	39.5[2]	38.6[2]	38.3[2]	38.6[2]	*38.1[3]	...
Niger Niger	...	...	...	...	...	...	25.4	27.2	30.4	36.1
Nigeria[2] Nigéria[2]	...	18.6	19.3	20.1	20.8	21.0	21.1	...	...	...
Niue[4] Nioué[4]	...	...	43.1	...	...	...	...	...	...	...
Northern Mariana Islands[4] Iles Mariannes du Nord[4]	44.0	...	...	...	...	...	...	...	...	...
Norway Norvège	*47.0[4]	48.2	48.3	48.9	49.1	49.2	49.0	49.3	49.2	49.1
Occupied Palestinian Terr. Terr. palestinien occupé	...	13.5	15.9	17.0	16.8	17.9	16.1	17.1	17.0	17.9
Oman Oman	18.7	24.5	25.3	...	...	...	...	...	...	*21.9
Pakistan Pakistan	*7.7[4]	13.0[2]	13.0[2]	13.6[2]	13.6[2]	13.9[2]	13.9[2]	13.4[2]	13.2[2]	...
Palau Palaos	*39.5[3]	39.6[4]	...	...	...	...	...	...	...	...
Panama Panama	...	43.0	43.0	43.5	44.0	43.6	43.4	42.5	43.1	42.2

10 Share of women in wage employment in the non-agricultural sector *(continued)*
Percentage of total employment

Proportion de femmes salariées dans le secteur non agricole *(suite)*
Pourcentage d'emploi total

Country or area Pays ou zone	1990	2000	2001	2002	2003	2004	2005	2006	2007	2008
Papua New Guinea Papouasie-Nvl-Guinée	20.3	32.1	...	...	...	...	...	...	...	...
Paraguay Paraguay	41.0	*39.3[3]	...	*37.7[3]	*38.9[3]	*40.0[3]	*40.1[3]	*38.7[3]	40.2	39.5
Peru Pérou	...	33.3	34.6	35.0	36.0	34.8	35.1	34.9	36.8	37.5
Philippines Philippines	...	40.9	41.2	41.9	41.3	40.7	41.4	41.9	41.9	41.7
Poland Pologne	...	46.5	47.0	47.3	47.3	46.7	46.7	46.4	47.0	46.8
Portugal Portugal	42.5	45.7	46.2	46.4	46.9	47.4	47.3	47.3	47.6	47.6
Puerto Rico Porto Rico	46.5	39.6	41.3	40.7	40.1	*39.9[2]	*40.5[2]	*40.8[2]	*41.5[2]	*41.7[2]
Qatar Qatar	...	...	14.5	...	...	*15.5[4]	...	...	*12.5[4]	...
Republic of Moldova République de Moldova	...	52.8	52.6	53.6	54.6	54.6	54.9	53.5	54.6	54.1
Réunion Réunion	30.7	...	...	...	...	...	...	...	...	...
Romania Roumanie	*41.9[2]	45.5	45.7	45.2	45.3	46.5	46.2	46.6	46.1	45.8
Russian Federation Fédération de Russie	...	50.4	50.4	50.6	51.0	50.9	50.9	51.2	51.0	50.6
Rwanda Rwanda	...	33.0	...	...	...	...	...	...	...	...
Saint Helena[4] Sainte-Hélène[4]	...	...	...	...	...	...	...	...	...	47.6
Saint Lucia Sainte-Lucie	...	49.4[2]	...	*47.8[4]	*45.9[4]	*47.5[4]	...	...	...	...
Samoa[2] Samoa[2]	...	...	36.7	...	...	...	...	...	...	...
San Marino Saint-Marin	40.4	...	41.5	41.7	41.9	42.2	42.1	42.1	42.2	42.2
Saudi Arabia Arabie saoudite	...	14.0	14.2	14.0	...	...	...	*14.6[3]	*14.7[3]	*14.6[3]
Senegal Sénégal	...	...	10.6	...	...	...	...	...	...	...
Serbia Serbie	...	44.0	44.3	...	...	43.9	41.6	43.5	43.9	44.0
Sierra Leone Sierra Leone	...	...	...	...	...	23.2	...	...	...	...
Singapore *[2] Singapour *[2]	...	...	43.7	43.3	43.6	44.1	...	44.9	45.2	45.8
Slovakia Slovaquie	*46.8	48.9	49.0	48.6	48.7	48.5	48.1	47.2	47.4	47.7
Slovenia Slovénie	*47.8	48.0	47.7	47.9	47.4	47.6	47.4	47.9	46.8	...
Somalia *[1] Somalie *[1]	21.7	...	...	...	...	...	...	...	...	...
South Africa Afrique du Sud	...	*41.1[4]	*42.0[4]	*40.7[4]	*41.6[4]	*40.8[4]	*41.4[4]	*41.3[4]	42.0[2]	44.0[2]
Spain Espagne	32.3	38.9	39.4	40.0	40.7	41.5	42.3	43.0	43.7	44.9
Sri Lanka Sri Lanka	...	*30.2[2]	*30.4[2]	30.9	30.0	31.0	31.9	32.2	31.0	...

10 Share of women in wage employment in the non-agricultural sector *(continued)*

Percentage of total employment

Proportion de femmes salariées dans le secteur non agricole *(suite)*

Pourcentage d'emploi total

Country or area Pays ou zone	1990	2000	2001	2002	2003	2004	2005	2006	2007	2008
Sudan Soudan	22.2	...	...	...	...	...	...	...	...	...
Suriname *[2] Suriname *[2]	41.0	...	...	...	...	38.1	...	...	...	...
Sweden Suède	50.5	50.6	50.7	50.9	50.9	50.9	50.5	50.3	50.1	49.9
Switzerland Suisse	*43.4[4]	45.7	46.3	47.1	46.9	47.1	47.1	46.9	46.8	47.9
Syrian Arab Republic Rép. arabe syrienne	...	...	16.1	*15.9[4]	*16.1[4]	...	...	...	16.3	...
Tajikistan Tadjikistan	...	40.0	40.9	41.6	41.1	39.8	39.4	37.1	...	...
Thailand[2] Thaïlande[2]	41.9	44.1	44.3	44.2	44.5	44.0	45.4	45.1	45.0	45.4
TFYR of Macedonia L'ex-R.Y. Macédoine	38.3	41.6	41.9	42.2	44.1	43.2	42.6	42.6	43.0	41.9
Timor-Leste Timor-Leste	...	...	35.0	...	...	...	...	...	...	...
Togo *[1] Togo *[1]	41.0	...	...	...	...	...	...	...	...	...
Tokelau Tokélaou	...	...	37.0	...	...	...	...	...	...	...
Trinidad and Tobago Trinité-et-Tobago	35.6	40.0	39.9	41.4	41.9	43.5	43.9	...	...	...
Tunisia *[3] Tunisie *[3]	...	24.3	24.6	24.9	25.0	...	...	...	...	...
Turkey Turquie	...	*19.1	*19.5	*19.6	*20.4	*19.9	20.3	20.9	21.9	22.4
Turkmenistan Turkménistan	...	...	...	42.1	...	...	...	...	...	...
Turks and Calcos Islands[2] Iles Turques et Caïques[2]	...	...	...	...	41.0	42.2	41.6	40.5	38.1	...
Tuvalu[2] Tuvalu[2]	...	...	...	34.3	39.1	33.9	...	...	...	...
Uganda[4] Ouganda[4]	...	...	...	...	39.0	...	...	...	...	...
Ukraine Ukraine	46.6	52.9	...	54.4	54.4	55.1	54.9	54.6	54.7	54.6
United Arab Emirates Emirats arabes unis	...	...	...	...	...	...	...	...	...	20.1
United Kingdom Royaume-Uni	47.8	*51.6[2]	*52.0[2]	*52.1[2]	*52.0[2]	*52.4[2]	*52.4[2]	*52.4[2]	*52.2[2]	*52.3[2]
United Rep. of Tanzania Rép.-Unie de Tanzanie	...	...	...	...	...	...	...	30.5	...	...
United States Etats-Unis	46.6	47.4	47.4	47.5	47.7	47.5	47.3	47.3	47.4	47.7
Uruguay Uruguay	42.3	46.4	46.5	45.8	*48.1[2]	...	*48.8[2]	*45.1[2]	*45.5[2]	...
Uzbekistan *[3] Ouzbékistan *[3]	...	37.1	41.6	37.1	37.0	40.6	40.3	40.3	39.4	...
Vanuatu[2] Vanuatu[2]	...	...	...	...	...	37.5	37.9	38.3	37.8	38.9
Venezuela (Boliv. Rep. of)[4] Venezuela (Rép. boliv. du)[4]	35.2	39.8	41.4	41.8	42.2	42.1	41.6	41.0	41.4	41.6
Viet Nam[2] Viet Nam[2]	...	40.7	40.7	40.8	40.1	40.4	...	...	...	...

10 Share of women in wage employment in the non-agricultural sector *(continued)*

Percentage of total employment

Proportion de femmes salariées dans le secteur non agricole *(suite)*

Pourcentage d'emploi total

Country or area Pays ou zone	1990	2000	2001	2002	2003	2004	2005	2006	2007	2008
Yemen Yémen	...	7.0	*6.5	...	*6.1	6.0	...	6.3	6.2	...
Zambia [2] Zambie [2]	16.6	22.0	...	...	...	...	...	...	...	...
Zimbabwe Zimbabwe	15.4	20.4	21.5	21.9	...	...	...	...	...	...

Source:
International Labour Organization (ILO), Geneva, the ILO labour statistics database, last accessed June 2010.

1 Economically Active Population in non-agriculture.
2 Total paid employment.
3 Total employment.
4 Total employment in non-agriculture.

Source:
Bureau international du Travail (BIT), Genève, la base de données du BIT, dernier accès juin 2010.

1 Population active dans le secteur non agricole.
2 Emplois rémunérés (total).
3 Emploi total.
4 Population active totale dans le secteur non agricole.

11 Ratio of girls to boys in primary, secondary and tertiary education

Rapport filles/garçons dans l'enseignement primaire, secondaire et supérieur

Country or area	1991	2002	2003	2004	2005	2006	2007	2008	Pays ou zone
Afghanistan									**Afghanistan**
Primary education	0.55	0.46	0.57	0.44	0.59	0.64	0.63	0.66	Enseignement primaire
Secondary education	0.51	...	*0.35	0.21	0.33	0.37	0.38	...	Enseignement secondaire
Tertiary education	...	...	*0.28	0.28	...	...	...	...	Enseignement supérieur
Albania									**Albanie**
Primary education	1.01	0.98	0.99	1.00	...	...	...	...	Enseignement primaire
Secondary education	0.93	...	0.97	0.97	...	...	...	...	Enseignement secondaire
Tertiary education	1.13	1.52	1.56	1.57	...	...	...	...	Enseignement supérieur
Algeria									**Algérie**
Primary education	0.85	0.93	0.93	0.93	0.93	0.93	0.94	0.94	Enseignement primaire
Secondary education	0.80	*1.05	1.07	1.07	*1.08	...	...	...	Enseignement secondaire
Tertiary education	...	...	...	1.08	1.28	1.26	1.40	...	Enseignement supérieur
Andorra									**Andorre**
Primary education	...	0.99	0.99	*0.98	0.95	1.00	0.98	0.96	Enseignement primaire
Secondary education	...	1.05	1.05	*1.03	1.12	1.04	1.08	1.11	Enseignement secondaire
Tertiary education	...	1.05	1.01	*1.00	1.06	1.25	...	1.45	Enseignement supérieur
Angola									**Angola**
Primary education	0.92	...	...	...	...	...	...	0.81	Enseignement primaire
Secondary education *	...	0.83	...	...	...	...	...	...	Enseignement secondaire *
Tertiary education	...	0.65	...	...	...	...	...	...	Enseignement supérieur
Anguilla									**Anguilla**
Primary education	...	0.98	*1.01	*1.03	*1.06	*0.99	*0.97	*1.00	Enseignement primaire
Secondary education *	...	1.01	0.99	1.00	0.97	1.02	1.02	0.95	Enseignement secondaire *
Tertiary education *	...	...	...	4.23	3.11	4.86	4.96	5.01	Enseignement supérieur *
Antigua and Barbuda									**Antigua-et-Barbuda**
Primary education	...	...	...	...	...	...	0.94	0.92	Enseignement primaire
Secondary education	...	...	...	...	...	...	0.96	0.93	Enseignement secondaire
Argentina									**Argentine**
Primary education	...	0.99	0.99	0.99	0.99	0.98	0.99	...	Enseignement primaire
Secondary education	...	1.03	1.07	1.10	1.11	1.12	1.13	...	Enseignement secondaire
Tertiary education	...	1.50	1.52	1.43	1.46	1.52	1.52	...	Enseignement supérieur
Armenia									**Arménie**
Primary education	...	1.02	1.02	1.03	1.04	1.04	1.03	1.02	Enseignement primaire
Secondary education	1.12	1.06	1.04	1.02	1.03	1.04	1.05	1.05	Enseignement secondaire
Tertiary education	1.05	1.11	1.12	1.21	1.22	1.18	1.20	...	Enseignement supérieur
Aruba									**Aruba**
Primary education	...	0.93	0.92	0.92	0.95	0.97	0.96	0.96	Enseignement primaire
Secondary education	...	1.07	1.07	1.02	1.03	1.01	1.04	1.06	Enseignement secondaire
Tertiary education	...	1.49	1.43	1.50	1.48	1.53	1.41	1.39	Enseignement supérieur
Australia									**Australie**
Primary education	1.00	1.00	1.00	1.00	1.00	1.00	1.00	1.00	Enseignement primaire
Secondary education	1.03	0.97	0.97	0.96	0.96	0.95	0.96	0.95	Enseignement secondaire
Tertiary education	1.19	1.22	1.23	1.23	1.25	1.27	1.28	1.30	Enseignement supérieur
Austria									**Autriche**
Primary education	1.00	0.99	0.99	1.00	1.00	0.99	0.99	0.99	Enseignement primaire
Secondary education	0.92	0.95	0.95	0.94	0.95	0.96	0.96	0.96	Enseignement secondaire
Tertiary education	0.87	1.15	1.17	1.18	1.20	1.21	1.20	1.19	Enseignement supérieur
Azerbaijan									**Azerbaïdjan**
Primary education	0.99	0.99	0.97	0.98	0.98	0.97	0.99	0.99	Enseignement primaire
Secondary education	1.01	0.97	0.96	0.96	0.96	0.96	0.96	0.98	Enseignement secondaire
Tertiary education	0.67	0.81	0.83	0.88	0.91	0.94	0.88	0.83	Enseignement supérieur
Bahamas									**Bahamas**
Primary education	...	1.02	*1.01	*1.00	1.00	1.00	1.00	1.00	Enseignement primaire
Secondary education	...	1.06	*1.03	*1.01	1.01	1.01	1.04	1.03	Enseignement secondaire
Bahrain									**Bahreïn**
Primary education	1.00	1.00	1.01	1.00	0.99	0.99	...	0.98	Enseignement primaire
Secondary education	1.04	1.09	1.08	1.07	1.07	1.06	...	1.04	Enseignement secondaire
Tertiary education	1.36	...	1.88	*1.99	2.47	2.53	...	...	Enseignement supérieur

11 Ratio of girls to boys in primary, secondary and tertiary education *(continued)*
Rapport filles/garçons dans l'enseignement primaire, secondaire et supérieur *(suite)*

Country or area	1991	2002	2003	2004	2005	2006	2007	2008	Pays ou zone
Bangladesh									**Bangladesh**
Primary education	...	...	...	...	1.04	1.05	1.07	1.06	Enseignement primaire
Secondary education	...	1.09	1.09	1.02	1.06	1.05	1.05	...	Enseignement secondaire
Tertiary education	...	0.48	0.48	0.47	0.52	0.55	0.55	...	Enseignement supérieur
Belarus									**Bélarus**
Primary education	...	0.99	0.99	0.97	0.97	0.98	0.99	1.02	Enseignement primaire
Secondary education	...	1.04	1.03	1.01	1.02	1.02	1.02	...	Enseignement secondaire
Tertiary education	...	1.36	1.37	1.38	1.36	1.37	1.41	1.43	Enseignement supérieur
Belgium									**Belgique**
Primary education	1.01	0.99	0.99	1.00	1.00	0.99	1.00	1.00	Enseignement primaire
Secondary education	1.01	1.12	1.10	0.97	0.97	0.97	0.96	0.97	Enseignement secondaire
Tertiary education	0.97	1.17	1.18	1.20	1.23	1.24	1.26	1.26	Enseignement supérieur
Belize									**Belize**
Primary education	0.97	*0.96	0.98	0.97	0.96	0.97	0.99	0.97	Enseignement primaire
Secondary education	1.05	*1.04	*1.06	1.04	*1.01	1.06	1.07	1.08	Enseignement secondaire
Tertiary education	...	...	1.91	2.43	...	...	...	...	Enseignement supérieur
Benin									**Bénin**
Primary education	0.51	0.73	0.74	0.77	0.80	0.83	...	0.87	Enseignement primaire
Secondary education	...	*0.48	0.47	0.48	*0.57	...	...	...	Enseignement secondaire
Tertiary education	0.15	...	...	...	...	...	...	...	Enseignement supérieur
Bermuda									**Bermudes**
Primary education	...	1.02	1.00	1.06	1.03	0.85	...	...	Enseignement primaire
Secondary education	...	1.06	1.10	1.11	1.09	1.06	...	...	Enseignement secondaire
Tertiary education	...	*1.18	...	...	1.80	...	*2.38	...	Enseignement supérieur
Bhutan									**Bhoutan**
Primary education	...	*0.92	...	...	0.97	0.98	...	1.00	Enseignement primaire
Secondary education	...	*0.83	...	...	0.88	0.91	...	0.93	Enseignement secondaire
Tertiary education	...	...	...	...	...	0.59	0.51	0.59	Enseignement supérieur
Bolivia (Plurinational State of)									**Bolivie (État plurinational de)**
Primary education	...	0.99	0.99	*1.00	...	1.00	1.00	...	Enseignement primaire
Secondary education	...	*0.97	0.97	...	...	0.96	0.97	...	Enseignement secondaire
Tertiary education	...	...	...	...	...	...	0.84	...	Enseignement supérieur
Bosnia and Herzegovina									**Bosnie-Herzégovine**
Primary education	...	...	...	...	...	...	0.94	1.01	Enseignement primaire
Secondary education	...	...	...	...	...	...	1.04	1.02	Enseignement secondaire
Botswana									**Botswana**
Primary education	1.07	0.99	0.99	0.98	0.99	0.98	...	...	Enseignement primaire
Secondary education	1.18	1.06	1.05	*1.05	1.05	1.06	...	...	Enseignement secondaire
Tertiary education	0.73	1.02	1.02	1.10	1.13	1.15	...	...	Enseignement supérieur
Brazil									**Brésil**
Primary education	...	0.94	0.94	0.93	0.94	...	0.93	0.93	Enseignement primaire
Secondary education	...	1.10	1.11	1.10	1.10	...	1.11	1.11	Enseignement secondaire
Tertiary education	...	1.32	1.32	1.32	1.30	...	1.29	1.29	Enseignement supérieur
British Virgin Islands									**Iles Vierges britanniques**
Primary education	...	0.98	0.94	0.96	0.96	0.97	*0.96	...	Enseignement primaire
Secondary education	...	1.02	1.16	1.06	1.18	1.13	*1.11	...	Enseignement secondaire
Tertiary education	...	2.34	*2.65	2.33	*2.28	...	...	*8.30	Enseignement supérieur
Brunei Darussalam									**Brunéi Darussalam**
Primary education	0.94	1.00	1.01	1.00	1.00	0.99	0.99	1.00	Enseignement primaire
Secondary education	1.09	1.05	1.06	1.05	1.04	1.04	1.04	1.02	Enseignement secondaire
Tertiary education	1.04	1.74	1.85	1.97	2.02	1.99	1.88	1.99	Enseignement supérieur
Bulgaria									**Bulgarie**
Primary education	0.98	0.98	0.98	0.98	0.99	0.99	0.99	1.00	Enseignement primaire
Secondary education	1.00	0.98	0.97	0.96	0.96	0.96	0.96	0.96	Enseignement secondaire
Tertiary education	1.10	1.24	1.18	1.17	1.15	1.21	1.22	1.30	Enseignement supérieur
Burkina Faso									**Burkina Faso**
Primary education	0.64	0.74	0.75	0.79	0.80	0.82	0.84	0.87	Enseignement primaire
Secondary education	*0.54	*0.66	0.69	*0.70	0.71	0.73	0.73	0.74	Enseignement secondaire
Tertiary education	0.30	0.35	0.30	*0.30	0.46	0.46	0.46	0.50	Enseignement supérieur

11 Ratio of girls to boys in primary, secondary and tertiary education *(continued)*
Rapport filles/garçons dans l'enseignement primaire, secondaire et supérieur *(suite)*

Country or area	1991	2002	2003	2004	2005	2006	2007	2008	Pays ou zone
Burundi									**Burundi**
Primary education	0.84	0.78	0.81	0.83	0.86	0.91	0.93	0.95	Enseignement primaire
Secondary education	0.58	...	0.77	0.75	*0.74	*0.74	0.72	*0.71	Enseignement secondaire
Tertiary education	0.36	0.42	*0.46	0.38	*0.38	*0.43	...	...	Enseignement supérieur
Cambodia									**Cambodge**
Primary education	...	0.90	0.91	0.92	0.93	0.93	0.93	0.94	Enseignement primaire
Secondary education	...	0.60	0.64	*0.69	...	0.79	0.82	...	Enseignement secondaire
Tertiary education	...	0.41	*0.41	0.46	0.47	0.50	0.56	0.54	Enseignement supérieur
Cameroon									**Cameroun**
Primary education	0.86	0.86	0.85	0.86	*0.84	0.84	0.86	0.86	Enseignement primaire
Secondary education	0.71	...	*0.84	0.79	0.79	0.79	...	0.80	Enseignement secondaire
Tertiary education	0.20	*0.64	*0.64	*0.64	0.66	0.72	0.79	0.79	Enseignement supérieur
Canada									**Canada**
Primary education	0.98	*1.00	...	*0.99	1.00	1.00	...	...	Enseignement primaire
Secondary education	1.00	*1.02	...	...	0.98	0.98	...	...	Enseignement secondaire
Tertiary education	1.23	1.36	...	*1.36	...	...	...	...	Enseignement supérieur
Cape Verde									**Cap-Vert**
Primary education	*0.94	0.96	0.95	0.95	0.95	0.95	0.94	0.94	Enseignement primaire
Secondary education	...	1.04	1.09	1.09	...	...	...	...	Enseignement secondaire
Tertiary education	...	1.00	1.08	1.08	1.02	1.08	1.20	1.24	Enseignement supérieur
Cayman Islands									**Iles Caïmanes**
Primary education	...	*0.98	...	*0.95	*0.89	*0.96	*1.05	0.84	Enseignement primaire
Secondary education	...	*1.09	...	*1.10	*0.92	*1.06	*1.25	1.01	Enseignement secondaire
Tertiary education	...	...	...	...	...	*2.66	*2.72	1.98	Enseignement supérieur
Central African Rep.									**Rép. centrafricaine**
Primary education	0.64	0.67	0.69	0.66	0.69	0.69	0.70	0.71	Enseignement primaire
Secondary education	0.41	...	...	...	...	...	...	0.57	Enseignement secondaire
Tertiary education	0.15	...	...	...	...	0.28	...	0.35	Enseignement supérieur
Chad									**Tchad**
Primary education	0.45	0.65	0.66	0.66	0.67	0.68	0.70	0.70	Enseignement primaire
Secondary education	...	0.33	*0.32	0.33	*0.34	0.36	0.45	...	Enseignement secondaire
Tertiary education	...	...	0.11	0.14	0.06	...	...	0.15	Enseignement supérieur
Chile									**Chili**
Primary education	0.98	0.98	0.97	0.95	0.96	0.95	0.95	...	Enseignement primaire
Secondary education	1.02	1.02	1.01	1.01	1.01	1.02	1.03	...	Enseignement secondaire
Tertiary education	...	0.93	0.94	0.95	0.96	1.00	1.01	...	Enseignement supérieur
China									**Chine**
Primary education	0.92	1.03	1.03	...	...	1.04	1.04	1.04	Enseignement primaire
Secondary education	0.75	...	0.97	...	...	1.03	1.04	1.05	Enseignement secondaire
Tertiary education	...	...	0.83	0.89	0.91	0.96	1.00	1.04	Enseignement supérieur
China, Hong Kong SAR									**Chine, Hong Kong RAS**
Primary education	1.01	0.96	0.96	0.97	0.98	...	...	...	Enseignement primaire
Secondary education	1.05	0.97	0.99	1.00	1.01	1.01	1.02	1.02	Enseignement secondaire
Tertiary education	...	...	0.96	1.02	1.03	1.02	1.02	...	Enseignement supérieur
China, Macao SAR									**Chine, Macao RAS**
Primary education	0.96	0.94	0.93	0.92	0.92	0.94	0.93	0.94	Enseignement primaire
Secondary education	*1.11	1.04	1.04	1.01	1.00	0.99	0.98	0.97	Enseignement secondaire
Tertiary education	0.48	0.52	0.52	0.62	0.69	0.78	0.88	0.91	Enseignement supérieur
Colombia									**Colombie**
Primary education	1.02	0.99	*0.99	0.99	0.98	0.99	0.99	0.99	Enseignement primaire
Secondary education	1.19	1.11	*1.10	1.11	1.11	1.11	1.11	1.10	Enseignement secondaire
Tertiary education	1.07	1.08	*1.09	1.08	1.08	1.09	1.09	0.99	Enseignement supérieur
Comoros									**Comores**
Primary education	0.73	0.82	0.82	0.88	*0.88	...	...	0.92	Enseignement primaire
Secondary education	...	0.84	0.83	0.76	*0.76	...	...	...	Enseignement secondaire
Tertiary education	...	...	0.77	*0.77	...	...	...	...	Enseignement supérieur
Congo									**Congo**
Primary education	0.92	0.95	0.94	0.94	0.93	0.91	0.94	0.94	Enseignement primaire
Secondary education	...	*0.74	0.69	*0.86	...	...	...	...	Enseignement secondaire
Tertiary education	0.22	0.19	*0.19	...	...	...	...	...	Enseignement supérieur

Ratio of girls to boys in primary, secondary and tertiary education *(continued)*
Rapport filles/garçons dans l'enseignement primaire, secondaire et supérieur *(suite)*

Country or area	1991	2002	2003	2004	2005	2006	2007	2008	Pays ou zone
Costa Rica									**Costa Rica**
Primary education	0.99	0.98	*0.98	0.99	0.99	0.99	0.99	0.99	Enseignement primaire
Secondary education	1.06	1.08	*1.08	1.06	1.06	1.06	1.05	1.06	Enseignement secondaire
Tertiary education	0.85	...	*1.16	1.25	*1.26	...	...	...	Enseignement supérieur
Côte d'Ivoire									**Côte d'Ivoire**
Primary education	0.71	0.74	0.80	...	...	0.79	0.79	0.79	Enseignement primaire
Secondary education *	0.48	0.56	...	...	...	...	...	...	Enseignement secondaire *
Tertiary education	0.20	...	...	...	...	*0.49	0.50	...	Enseignement supérieur
Croatia									**Croatie**
Primary education	...	0.99	0.99	...	1.00	1.00	1.00	...	Enseignement primaire
Secondary education	...	1.02	1.02	...	1.03	1.03	1.03	...	Enseignement secondaire
Tertiary education	...	1.15	1.19	...	1.21	1.23	1.22	...	Enseignement supérieur
Cuba									**Cuba**
Primary education	0.97	0.96	0.96	0.96	0.97	0.97	0.98	0.98	Enseignement primaire
Secondary education	1.15	0.99	0.99	1.02	1.02	1.02	1.00	0.99	Enseignement secondaire
Tertiary education	1.40	1.27	1.37	*1.76	1.74	1.65	1.85	1.69	Enseignement supérieur
Cyprus									**Chypre**
Primary education	1.00	1.00	1.00	1.00	1.00	1.00	0.99	0.99	Enseignement primaire
Secondary education	1.02	1.02	1.02	1.03	1.02	1.02	1.02	1.01	Enseignement secondaire
Tertiary education	1.11	1.26	1.03	0.98	1.13	1.05	0.99	0.96	Enseignement supérieur
Czech Republic									**République tchèque**
Primary education	1.00	0.99	0.98	0.99	0.99	0.99	0.99	0.99	Enseignement primaire
Secondary education	0.97	1.03	1.03	1.01	1.02	1.02	1.01	1.01	Enseignement secondaire
Tertiary education	0.81	1.10	1.07	1.10	1.16	1.22	1.27	1.32	Enseignement supérieur
Dem. Rep. of the Congo									**Rép. dém. du Congo**
Primary education	0.74	0.78	...	...	...	...	0.81	0.83	Enseignement primaire
Secondary education	0.48	0.58	...	...	...	...	0.53	0.55	Enseignement secondaire
Tertiary education	0.18	...	...	...	...	...	0.35	...	Enseignement supérieur
Denmark									**Danemark**
Primary education	1.00	1.00	*1.00	1.00	1.00	1.00	1.00	...	Enseignement primaire
Secondary education	1.01	1.05	1.05	1.04	1.03	1.03	1.03	...	Enseignement secondaire
Tertiary education	1.14	1.39	1.42	1.41	1.39	1.39	1.41	...	Enseignement supérieur
Djibouti									**Djibouti**
Primary education	0.72	0.76	*0.78	0.79	0.82	0.81	0.86	0.88	Enseignement primaire
Secondary education	...	0.62	*0.66	0.69	0.66	0.67	0.69	0.70	Enseignement secondaire
Tertiary education	...	0.81	0.70	0.82	0.73	0.68	0.69	...	Enseignement supérieur
Dominica									**Dominique**
Primary education	...	0.97	0.99	0.99	1.02	1.02	*1.01	1.06	Enseignement primaire
Secondary education	...	1.06	1.04	0.99	1.00	0.98	*1.00	0.93	Enseignement secondaire
Tertiary education	...	...	...	...	...	...	...	3.26	Enseignement supérieur
Dominican Republic									**Rép. dominicaine**
Primary education	...	1.01	*1.01	0.95	0.95	0.95	0.94	0.93	Enseignement primaire
Secondary education	...	1.21	*1.21	1.21	1.19	1.20	1.20	1.19	Enseignement secondaire
Tertiary education	...	...	1.59	*1.59	...	...	...	...	Enseignement supérieur
Ecuador									**Equateur**
Primary education	...	1.00	1.00	1.00	1.00	1.00	1.00	*1.00	Enseignement primaire
Secondary education	...	1.01	1.02	1.00	1.01	1.02	1.01	*1.01	Enseignement secondaire
Tertiary education	...	...	...	...	...	...	1.22	1.15	Enseignement supérieur
Egypt									**Egypte**
Primary education	0.83	*0.94	*0.95	*0.96	0.94	0.94	0.95	...	Enseignement primaire
Secondary education	0.79	*0.93	*0.94	*0.94	...	...	...	...	Enseignement secondaire
Tertiary education	0.57	...	...	*0.77	...	...	...	...	Enseignement supérieur
El Salvador									**El Salvador**
Primary education	0.99	0.96	0.97	0.98	0.98	0.98	1.01	0.97	Enseignement primaire
Secondary education	1.11	0.98	0.99	0.99	1.00	1.02	1.02	1.02	Enseignement secondaire
Tertiary education	...	1.08	1.06	1.13	1.09	1.08	1.09	1.09	Enseignement supérieur
Equatorial Guinea									**Guinée équatoriale**
Primary education	...	0.91	0.97	...	0.95	...	0.95	...	Enseignement primaire
Secondary education *	...	0.57	...	...	...	...	...	...	Enseignement secondaire *
Tertiary education	0.14	...	...	...	...	...	...	...	Enseignement supérieur

Ratio of girls to boys in primary, secondary and tertiary education *(continued)*
Rapport filles/garçons dans l'enseignement primaire, secondaire et supérieur *(suite)*

Country or area	1991	2002	2003	2004	2005	2006	2007	2008	Pays ou zone
Eritrea									**Erythrée**
Primary education	0.95	0.80	0.80	0.80	0.80	0.81	0.83	0.82	Enseignement primaire
Secondary education	...	0.64	0.64	0.56	0.59	0.60	0.70	*0.71	Enseignement secondaire
Tertiary education	...	0.15	*0.15	0.15	...	...	...	...	Enseignement supérieur
Estonia									**Estonie**
Primary education	0.97	0.97	0.97	0.97	0.98	0.98	0.99	0.99	Enseignement primaire
Secondary education	...	1.03	1.04	1.03	1.02	1.03	1.02	1.03	Enseignement secondaire
Tertiary education	...	1.65	1.66	1.68	1.66	1.67	1.64	1.69	Enseignement supérieur
Ethiopia									**Ethiopie**
Primary education	0.66	0.71	0.73	0.77	0.83	0.86	0.88	0.89	Enseignement primaire
Secondary education	0.75	0.62	0.57	0.57	0.60	0.63	0.67	0.72	Enseignement secondaire
Tertiary education	0.22	0.36	0.34	0.34	0.32	0.32	0.35	0.31	Enseignement supérieur
Fiji									**Fidji**
Primary education	1.00	1.01	0.99	0.98	*0.98	0.98	0.97	0.99	Enseignement primaire
Secondary education	0.97	1.08	1.08	1.07	*1.07	1.10	1.12	1.07	Enseignement secondaire
Tertiary education	...	...	*1.20	1.20	*1.20	...	...	...	Enseignement supérieur
Finland									**Finlande**
Primary education	0.99	0.99	0.99	0.99	0.99	1.00	1.00	0.99	Enseignement primaire
Secondary education	1.19	1.11	1.10	1.05	1.04	1.04	1.05	1.05	Enseignement secondaire
Tertiary education	1.13	1.23	1.20	1.20	1.21	1.22	1.23	1.24	Enseignement supérieur
France									**France**
Primary education	0.98	0.99	0.99	0.99	0.99	0.99	0.99	0.99	Enseignement primaire
Secondary education	1.05	1.00	1.01	1.00	1.00	1.00	1.00	1.00	Enseignement secondaire
Tertiary education	1.17	1.25	1.26	1.26	1.27	1.27	1.28	1.28	Enseignement supérieur
Gabon									**Gabon**
Primary education	...	0.99	0.99	*0.99	...	...	...	...	Enseignement primaire
Gambia									**Gambie**
Primary education	*0.68	0.90	0.97	1.00	1.02	1.04	1.04	1.06	Enseignement primaire
Secondary education	0.49	0.71	0.75	0.82	0.82	...	0.89	0.94	Enseignement secondaire
Tertiary education	...	...	...	0.23	...	...	...	...	Enseignement supérieur
Georgia									**Géorgie**
Primary education	1.00	1.02	1.00	0.97	0.98	1.02	0.96	0.98	Enseignement primaire
Secondary education	0.97	0.98	0.97	0.98	0.96	*0.99	*0.95	0.96	Enseignement secondaire
Tertiary education	0.91	0.99	0.95	1.03	1.03	1.12	1.10	1.19	Enseignement supérieur
Germany									**Allemagne**
Primary education	*1.01	0.99	1.00	1.00	1.00	1.00	1.00	1.00	Enseignement primaire
Secondary education	*0.97	0.98	0.98	0.98	0.98	0.97	0.98	0.98	Enseignement secondaire
Tertiary education	0.73	...	...	...	...	...	...	...	Enseignement supérieur
Ghana									**Ghana**
Primary education	0.86	0.95	0.98	0.95	0.97	0.99	0.99	0.99	Enseignement primaire
Secondary education	...	*0.85	*0.85	0.84	*0.86	0.85	0.88	0.89	Enseignement secondaire
Tertiary education	0.30	...	...	...	0.56	0.53	0.54	...	Enseignement supérieur
Greece									**Grèce**
Primary education	0.99	0.99	1.00	0.99	1.00	1.00	1.00	...	Enseignement primaire
Secondary education	0.98	...	1.02	1.01	0.98	0.97	0.95	...	Enseignement secondaire
Tertiary education	0.99	1.15	1.14	1.17	1.14	1.13	1.10	...	Enseignement supérieur
Grenada									**Grenade**
Primary education	...	0.95	1.00	0.97	*0.97	...	0.98	0.95	Enseignement primaire
Secondary education	1.16	1.15	0.98	1.08	1.02	...	0.98	0.92	Enseignement secondaire
Guatemala									**Guatemala**
Primary education	0.87	0.91	*0.91	0.92	0.92	0.93	0.94	0.94	Enseignement primaire
Secondary education	...	0.89	*0.89	0.90	0.91	0.92	0.92	0.93	Enseignement secondaire
Tertiary education	...	0.72	*0.72	...	...	0.82	1.00	...	Enseignement supérieur
Guinea									**Guinée**
Primary education	0.48	0.75	0.77	0.79	0.82	0.84	0.86	0.85	Enseignement primaire
Secondary education	0.34	*0.42	*0.46	0.46	*0.51	0.53	*0.57	0.59	Enseignement secondaire
Tertiary education	0.07	...	*0.19	0.19	0.24	0.28	*0.34	0.34	Enseignement supérieur
Guinea-Bissau									**Guinée-Bissau**
Primary education *	0.55	...	...	...	...	...	...	...	Enseignement primaire *
Secondary education	0.47	...	...	...	...	...	...	...	Enseignement secondaire
Tertiary education	0.05	...	...	...	...	...	...	...	Enseignement supérieur

11 Ratio of girls to boys in primary, secondary and tertiary education *(continued)*
Rapport filles/garçons dans l'enseignement primaire, secondaire et supérieur *(suite)*

Country or area	1991	2002	2003	2004	2005	2006	2007	2008	Pays ou zone
Guyana									**Guyana**
Primary education	0.98	*0.98	0.98	*0.97	0.99	0.99	0.98	0.99	Enseignement primaire
Secondary education	1.06	*1.03	...	*1.02	0.98	*0.98	0.94	1.01	Enseignement secondaire
Tertiary education	0.74	...	...	1.88	2.07	2.18	2.12	1.42	Enseignement supérieur
Haiti									**Haïti**
Primary education	0.95	...	...	...	...	...	...	...	Enseignement primaire
Honduras									**Honduras**
Primary education	1.04	...	...	0.99	0.99	0.99	1.00	1.00	Enseignement primaire
Secondary education	1.23	...	...	...	...	...	1.25	1.27	Enseignement secondaire
Tertiary education	0.79	*1.39	1.41	*1.41	...	...	...	1.51	Enseignement supérieur
Hungary									**Hongrie**
Primary education	0.99	0.98	0.99	0.99	0.98	0.98	0.98	0.99	Enseignement primaire
Secondary education	1.01	1.01	1.00	0.99	0.99	0.99	0.99	0.98	Enseignement secondaire
Tertiary education	1.06	1.29	1.37	1.40	1.46	1.46	1.45	1.43	Enseignement supérieur
Iceland									**Islande**
Primary education	...	0.99	0.98	0.98	0.97	0.99	1.00	1.00	Enseignement primaire
Secondary education	0.96	1.06	1.06	1.03	1.02	1.03	1.06	1.03	Enseignement secondaire
Tertiary education	1.39	1.76	1.79	1.87	1.91	1.87	1.87	1.91	Enseignement supérieur
India									**Inde**
Primary education	0.76	0.87	0.96	*0.96	0.96	0.95	0.97	...	Enseignement primaire
Secondary education	...	0.74	0.81	0.81	0.82	0.83	0.86	...	Enseignement secondaire
Tertiary education	0.54	0.70	0.68	0.67	0.71	0.72	0.70	...	Enseignement supérieur
Indonesia									**Indonésie**
Primary education	0.98	0.98	0.98	0.98	*0.97	0.96	0.96	0.97	Enseignement primaire
Secondary education	0.83	0.99	0.99	0.99	*0.99	1.00	1.01	0.99	Enseignement secondaire
Tertiary education	...	0.87	0.80	0.79	*0.79	...	0.99	0.92	Enseignement supérieur
Iran (Islamic Rep. of)									**Iran (Rép. islamique d')**
Primary education	0.90	0.96	0.97	1.10	1.22	1.28	1.30	1.40	Enseignement primaire
Secondary education	0.75	0.94	0.94	0.97	0.97	0.98	1.02	0.98	Enseignement secondaire
Tertiary education	0.40	0.98	1.04	1.06	1.04	1.06	1.10	1.14	Enseignement supérieur
Iraq									**Iraq**
Primary education	0.84	*0.85	0.85	0.84	*0.84	...	...	...	Enseignement primaire
Secondary education	...	*0.61	0.72	0.67	*0.67	...	...	...	Enseignement secondaire
Tertiary education	...	*0.54	...	0.59	*0.59	...	...	...	Enseignement supérieur
Ireland									**Irlande**
Primary education	1.00	1.00	0.99	0.99	1.00	1.00	1.00	1.01	Enseignement primaire
Secondary education	1.09	1.09	1.09	1.08	1.09	1.08	1.07	1.06	Enseignement secondaire
Tertiary education	0.90	1.28	1.31	1.28	1.26	1.27	1.27	1.22	Enseignement supérieur
Israel									**Israël**
Primary education	1.04	1.00	1.00	1.01	1.01	1.02	1.01	1.01	Enseignement primaire
Secondary education	1.06	0.99	0.98	1.00	0.99	0.99	1.00	1.01	Enseignement secondaire
Tertiary education	1.01	1.38	1.33	1.33	1.34	1.29	1.32	1.31	Enseignement supérieur
Italy									**Italie**
Primary education	1.00	0.98	0.99	0.99	0.99	0.99	0.99	...	Enseignement primaire
Secondary education	1.00	0.97	*0.99	0.99	0.99	0.99	0.99	...	Enseignement secondaire
Tertiary education	0.94	1.33	1.33	1.34	1.36	1.39	1.41	...	Enseignement supérieur
Jamaica									**Jamaïque**
Primary education	*0.99	0.99	0.98	0.98	0.97	...	0.97	0.97	Enseignement primaire
Secondary education	*1.05	1.02	1.02	1.01	1.03	...	1.04	1.04	Enseignement secondaire
Tertiary education	*0.75	2.17	*2.29	...	...	...	...	2.22	Enseignement supérieur
Japan									**Japon**
Primary education	1.00	1.00	1.00	1.00	1.00	1.00	1.00	1.00	Enseignement primaire
Secondary education	1.02	1.01	1.01	1.00	1.00	1.00	1.00	1.00	Enseignement secondaire
Tertiary education	0.65	0.86	0.88	0.89	0.89	0.88	0.88	0.88	Enseignement supérieur
Jordan									**Jordanie**
Primary education	0.99	1.00	1.00	1.00	1.01	1.02	1.02	1.01	Enseignement primaire
Secondary education	1.04	1.03	1.03	1.02	1.03	1.03	1.04	1.04	Enseignement secondaire
Tertiary education	1.12	1.04	1.12	1.13	1.08	1.13	1.11	1.11	Enseignement supérieur
Kazakhstan									**Kazakhstan**
Primary education	...	1.00	1.00	1.00	1.00	1.00	1.00	1.00	Enseignement primaire
Secondary education	...	0.99	1.01	0.99	0.98	0.98	0.99	0.98	Enseignement secondaire
Tertiary education	...	1.25	1.33	1.38	1.43	1.43	1.44	1.44	Enseignement supérieur

11 Ratio of girls to boys in primary, secondary and tertiary education *(continued)*
Rapport filles/garçons dans l'enseignement primaire, secondaire et supérieur *(suite)*

Country or area	1991	2002	2003	2004	2005	2006	2007	2008	Pays ou zone
Kenya									**Kenya**
Primary education	0.97	0.95	0.95	0.94	0.96	0.97	0.99	0.98	Enseignement primaire
Secondary education	...	0.96	1.02	*0.94	0.96	0.93	0.88	0.92	Enseignement secondaire
Tertiary education	...	*0.54	...	0.60	*0.60	...	...	...	Enseignement supérieur
Kiribati									**Kiribati**
Primary education	...	*0.99	*0.98	*1.03	1.01	...	*1.02	...	Enseignement primaire
Secondary education	...	*1.17	*1.19	*1.18	1.14	...	*1.20	...	Enseignement secondaire
Korea, Republic of									**Corée, République de**
Primary education	1.01	0.97	0.97	0.97	0.97	0.97	0.98	0.98	Enseignement primaire
Secondary education	0.96	0.98	0.98	0.98	0.98	0.97	0.96	0.96	Enseignement secondaire
Tertiary education	0.49	0.62	0.63	0.64	0.65	0.66	0.67	0.69	Enseignement supérieur
Kuwait									**Koweït**
Primary education	0.95	1.00	1.01	1.00	0.98	0.99	0.98	0.98	Enseignement primaire
Secondary education	...	*1.05	1.04	1.06	1.05	1.05	1.02	1.04	Enseignement secondaire
Tertiary education	...	1.93	2.09	*2.14	...	...	...	...	Enseignement supérieur
Kyrgyzstan									**Kirghizistan**
Primary education	...	0.98	0.99	1.00	0.99	0.99	0.99	0.99	Enseignement primaire
Secondary education	1.02	1.00	1.01	1.01	1.01	1.01	1.01	1.01	Enseignement secondaire
Tertiary education	...	1.14	1.19	1.19	1.25	1.27	1.30	1.36	Enseignement supérieur
Lao People's Dem. Rep.									**Rép. dém. pop. lao**
Primary education	0.79	0.86	0.87	0.88	0.88	0.89	0.90	0.91	Enseignement primaire
Secondary education	...	0.73	0.74	0.75	0.76	0.78	0.79	0.81	Enseignement secondaire
Tertiary education	...	0.57	0.57	0.62	0.71	0.68	0.72	0.78	Enseignement supérieur
Latvia									**Lettonie**
Primary education	1.00	0.98	0.98	0.97	0.96	0.97	0.96	0.96	Enseignement primaire
Secondary education	1.02	1.01	1.00	1.00	1.00	1.01	1.03	1.03	Enseignement secondaire
Tertiary education	1.28	1.64	1.66	1.71	1.79	1.80	1.85	1.89	Enseignement supérieur
Lebanon									**Liban**
Primary education	...	...	...	...	...	0.97	0.97	0.97	Enseignement primaire
Secondary education	...	...	...	...	...	1.10	1.12	1.11	Enseignement secondaire
Tertiary education	...	1.10	1.16	1.09	1.13	1.15	1.20	1.24	Enseignement supérieur
Lesotho									**Lesotho**
Primary education	1.22	1.02	1.01	1.00	1.00	1.00	0.99	...	Enseignement primaire
Secondary education	1.42	1.28	1.27	*1.26	1.27	1.27	*1.32	...	Enseignement secondaire
Tertiary education	1.30	1.32	1.52	...	1.27	1.19	...	...	Enseignement supérieur
Liberia									**Libéria**
Primary education	0.66	...	...	...	...	0.90	...	0.90	Enseignement primaire
Secondary education	0.38	...	...	...	...	0.72	...	0.75	Enseignement secondaire
Tertiary education	0.29	...	...	...	...	...	...	...	Enseignement supérieur
Libyan Arab Jamah.									**Jamah. arabe libyenne**
Primary education	...	1.00	0.96	0.96	0.98	0.95	...	...	Enseignement primaire
Secondary education	...	1.06	*1.06	...	*1.19	1.17	...	...	Enseignement secondaire
Tertiary education	...	1.10	*1.10	...	...	...	...	...	Enseignement supérieur
Liechtenstein									**Liechtenstein**
Primary education	...	...	0.98	1.01	...	0.98	0.99	1.00	Enseignement primaire
Secondary education	...	...	0.88	0.87	...	0.88	0.87	0.86	Enseignement secondaire
Tertiary education	...	...	0.38	0.37	...	0.44	0.49	0.52	Enseignement supérieur
Lithuania									**Lituanie**
Primary education	*0.95	0.99	0.99	0.99	1.00	0.99	0.99	0.98	Enseignement primaire
Secondary education	...	0.98	0.98	0.99	1.00	1.00	1.00	1.00	Enseignement secondaire
Tertiary education	...	1.57	1.54	1.55	1.56	1.55	1.57	1.56	Enseignement supérieur
Luxembourg									**Luxembourg**
Primary education	1.08	1.00	1.01	1.01	1.01	1.01	1.01	1.01	Enseignement primaire
Secondary education	...	1.06	1.05	1.05	1.06	1.05	1.04	1.03	Enseignement secondaire
Tertiary education	...	*1.15	1.18	*1.17	...	1.12	...	...	Enseignement supérieur
Madagascar									**Madagascar**
Primary education	0.98	0.96	0.96	0.96	0.96	0.96	0.97	0.97	Enseignement primaire
Secondary education	*0.97	...	...	...	*0.96	0.95	0.95	0.94	Enseignement secondaire
Tertiary education	0.82	*0.83	*0.83	0.90	0.89	0.87	0.88	0.89	Enseignement supérieur

11 Ratio of girls to boys in primary, secondary and tertiary education *(continued)*
Rapport filles/garçons dans l'enseignement primaire, secondaire et supérieur *(suite)*

Country or area	1991	2002	2003	2004	2005	2006	2007	2008	Pays ou zone
Malawi									**Malawi**
Primary education	0.88	0.97	*1.00	1.03	1.03	1.04	1.04	1.03	Enseignement primaire
Secondary education	0.60	*0.78	*0.80	0.81	0.81	0.84	0.83	0.85	Enseignement secondaire
Tertiary education	0.34	*0.42	*0.41	*0.55	*0.55	*0.51	0.51	...	Enseignement supérieur
Malaysia									**Malaisie**
Primary education	0.99	1.00	1.00	1.00	1.00	0.99	1.00	...	Enseignement primaire
Secondary education	1.05	1.09	1.12	1.12	1.10	1.08	1.07	...	Enseignement secondaire
Tertiary education	...	1.25	1.36	1.26	1.29	1.24	1.29	...	Enseignement supérieur
Maldives									**Maldives**
Primary education	...	0.96	0.95	0.94	0.95	0.94	0.95	0.94	Enseignement primaire
Secondary education	...	1.15	1.11	*1.13	...	*1.05	...	...	Enseignement secondaire
Tertiary education	...	...	2.41	*2.40	...	...	...	...	Enseignement supérieur
Mali									**Mali**
Primary education	0.59	0.75	0.76	0.77	0.78	0.80	0.81	0.83	Enseignement primaire
Secondary education	0.51	...	0.54	0.59	*0.61	0.61	0.65	0.64	Enseignement secondaire
Tertiary education	0.16	0.49	*0.51	0.53	*0.53	...	0.45	0.45	Enseignement supérieur
Malta									**Malte**
Primary education	0.96	0.99	0.99	0.99	0.98	...	1.00	...	Enseignement primaire
Secondary education	0.94	0.99	0.99	0.93	0.97	...	1.02	...	Enseignement secondaire
Tertiary education	0.83	1.40	1.40	1.33	1.36	...	1.42	...	Enseignement supérieur
Marshall Islands									**Iles Marshall**
Primary education	...	*0.94	*0.94	*0.96	*0.96	...	0.97	...	Enseignement primaire
Secondary education	...	*1.04	*1.04	*1.05	*1.05	...	1.02	...	Enseignement secondaire
Tertiary education *	...	1.30	1.30	...	...	...	...	...	Enseignement supérieur *
Mauritania									**Mauritanie**
Primary education	0.78	1.01	1.03	1.04	1.06	1.05	1.06	1.07	Enseignement primaire
Secondary education	0.49	0.80	0.85	0.88	0.90	0.86	*0.89	...	Enseignement secondaire
Tertiary education	0.17	0.28	0.29	0.33	0.34	0.36	...	...	Enseignement supérieur
Mauritius									**Maurice**
Primary education	1.01	1.01	1.01	1.00	1.00	1.00	1.00	0.99	Enseignement primaire
Secondary education	*1.04	1.00	1.00	0.99	*0.99	*1.01	*1.01	*1.01	Enseignement secondaire
Tertiary education	0.73	*1.30	*1.42	*1.40	*1.27	*1.16	*1.16	*1.17	Enseignement supérieur
Mexico									**Mexique**
Primary education	0.97	0.99	0.99	0.99	0.98	0.98	0.98	0.98	Enseignement primaire
Secondary education	0.99	1.05	1.07	1.06	1.05	1.06	1.06	1.06	Enseignement secondaire
Tertiary education	...	0.96	0.97	0.98	0.99	0.98	0.98	0.98	Enseignement supérieur
Micronesia (Fed. States of)									**Micronésie (Etats féd. de)**
Primary education	...	...	...	0.99	0.98	...	1.01	...	Enseignement primaire
Secondary education	...	...	...	1.05	1.07	...	...	...	Enseignement secondaire
Mongolia									**Mongolie**
Primary education	1.02	1.01	1.00	0.99	1.00	1.00	1.00	0.99	Enseignement primaire
Secondary education	1.14	1.18	1.14	1.12	1.11	1.10	1.09	1.08	Enseignement secondaire
Tertiary education	1.89	1.71	1.66	1.62	1.60	1.56	1.55	1.57	Enseignement supérieur
Montserrat									**Montserrat**
Primary education	...	0.96	*0.96	0.97	1.04	*1.00	1.12	...	Enseignement primaire
Secondary education	...	1.13	*1.13	1.10	1.10	*0.98	1.02	...	Enseignement secondaire
Tertiary education *	...	...	...	...	...	...	...	4.99	Enseignement supérieur *
Morocco									**Maroc**
Primary education	0.69	0.89	0.90	0.90	0.89	0.89	0.90	0.91	Enseignement primaire
Secondary education	0.72	*0.81	0.82	0.83	*0.84	...	*0.86	...	Enseignement secondaire
Tertiary education	0.58	*0.76	0.80	0.83	0.81	0.81	0.89	0.89	Enseignement supérieur
Mozambique									**Mozambique**
Primary education	0.74	0.79	...	0.83	0.84	0.86	0.87	0.88	Enseignement primaire
Secondary education	0.57	0.66	...	0.70	0.69	0.72	0.73	0.75	Enseignement secondaire
Tertiary education	...	...	0.47	0.46	0.49	...	...	...	Enseignement supérieur
Myanmar									**Myanmar**
Primary education	0.95	1.00	1.00	1.00	1.00	0.99	...	0.99	Enseignement primaire
Secondary education	0.97	0.93	0.94	0.93	0.97	0.98	1.01	...	Enseignement secondaire
Tertiary education	...	...	...	...	...	...	1.37	...	Enseignement supérieur

11 Ratio of girls to boys in primary, secondary and tertiary education *(continued)*
Rapport filles/garçons dans l'enseignement primaire, secondaire et supérieur *(suite)*

Country or area	1991	2002	2003	2004	2005	2006	2007	2008	Pays ou zone
Namibia									**Namibie**
Primary education	1.03	1.01	1.00	1.00	1.00	1.00	0.99	0.99	Enseignement primaire
Secondary education	1.22	1.12	1.12	1.13	1.14	1.15	1.17	1.17	Enseignement secondaire
Tertiary education	1.75	1.37	1.13	1.13	0.88	0.88	...	1.32	Enseignement supérieur
Nauru									**Nauru**
Primary education	...	1.12	*0.99	1.02	1.04	0.97	*1.03	*1.06	Enseignement primaire
Secondary education	...	1.21	*1.07	1.16	1.14	1.21	*1.19	*1.23	Enseignement secondaire
Nepal									**Népal**
Primary education	0.63	0.86	...	...	...	...	...	...	Enseignement primaire
Secondary education	0.46	0.74	0.77	...	*0.86	*0.89	...	...	Enseignement secondaire
Tertiary education	0.33	0.27	0.34	0.40	...	...	...	...	Enseignement supérieur
Netherlands									**Pays-Bas**
Primary education	1.03	0.98	0.98	0.97	0.97	0.98	0.98	0.98	Enseignement primaire
Secondary education	0.92	0.97	0.98	0.98	0.98	0.98	0.98	0.98	Enseignement secondaire
Tertiary education	0.83	1.06	1.07	1.07	1.07	1.08	1.10	1.11	Enseignement supérieur
Netherlands Antilles									**Antilles néerlandaises**
Primary education	...	0.99	*0.99	...	...	...	...	...	Enseignement primaire
Secondary education	1.19	1.10	*1.09	...	...	...	...	...	Enseignement secondaire
Tertiary education	...	1.43	...	...	...	...	...	...	Enseignement supérieur
New Zealand									**Nouvelle-Zélande**
Primary education	0.99	*1.00	1.00	1.00	1.00	1.00	1.00	1.00	Enseignement primaire
Secondary education	1.01	1.12	1.11	1.07	1.07	1.05	1.03	1.05	Enseignement secondaire
Tertiary education	1.13	1.47	1.46	1.46	1.48	1.51	1.49	1.48	Enseignement supérieur
Nicaragua									**Nicaragua**
Primary education	1.06	0.99	0.99	0.98	0.97	0.98	0.98	0.98	Enseignement primaire
Secondary education	*1.20	1.17	*1.13	1.13	1.13	1.13	1.13	1.13	Enseignement secondaire
Tertiary education	0.96	1.08	*1.09	...	...	...	...	...	Enseignement supérieur
Niger									**Niger**
Primary education	0.60	0.70	0.71	0.71	0.72	0.73	0.74	0.78	Enseignement primaire
Secondary education	0.37	0.59	0.61	0.61	0.63	0.63	0.61	0.60	Enseignement secondaire
Tertiary education	0.13	...	*0.30	0.30	0.33	0.29	0.32	0.34	Enseignement supérieur
Nigeria									**Nigéria**
Primary education	0.79	0.82	*0.82	0.83	0.84	0.85	0.88	...	Enseignement primaire
Secondary education	...	*0.74	*0.76	*0.78	*0.81	*0.81	0.77	...	Enseignement secondaire
Tertiary education	...	...	*0.53	0.53	0.70	...	...	...	Enseignement supérieur
Niue									**Nioué**
Primary education	...	...	...	1.19	0.95	...	...	...	Enseignement primaire
Secondary education	...	...	...	0.95	1.07	...	...	...	Enseignement secondaire
Norway									**Norvège**
Primary education	1.00	1.00	1.00	1.00	1.00	1.01	1.00	1.00	Enseignement primaire
Secondary education	1.03	1.02	1.02	1.03	1.01	0.99	0.99	0.98	Enseignement secondaire
Tertiary education	1.19	1.54	1.54	1.53	1.53	1.54	1.58	1.62	Enseignement supérieur
Occupied Palestinian Terr.									**Terr. palestinien occupé**
Primary education	...	1.00	1.00	1.00	0.99	1.00	1.00	1.00	Enseignement primaire
Secondary education	...	1.06	1.06	1.05	1.05	1.06	1.06	1.07	Enseignement secondaire
Tertiary education	...	0.98	1.04	1.04	1.03	1.17	1.22	1.23	Enseignement supérieur
Oman									**Oman**
Primary education	0.92	0.98	0.99	0.99	1.00	1.00	1.01	1.01	Enseignement primaire
Secondary education	0.81	0.98	0.97	0.96	0.96	0.96	0.96	0.97	Enseignement secondaire
Tertiary education	0.97	*0.78	0.78	1.14	1.07	1.05	1.08	1.15	Enseignement supérieur
Pakistan									**Pakistan**
Primary education	...	0.68	0.72	0.73	0.76	0.78	0.82	0.83	Enseignement primaire
Secondary education	0.48	...	*0.79	*0.78	*0.78	0.78	0.76	0.76	Enseignement secondaire
Tertiary education	...	*0.81	0.81	0.79	0.88	0.85	0.85	0.85	Enseignement supérieur
Palau *									**Palaos** *
Primary education	...	...	0.78	0.93	0.94	...	1.02	...	Enseignement primaire
Secondary education	...	...	1.18	1.10	...	...	0.97	...	Enseignement secondaire
Tertiary education	...	2.15	...	...	...	...	...	...	Enseignement supérieur
Panama									**Panama**
Primary education	...	0.97	*0.97	0.97	0.97	0.97	0.97	0.97	Enseignement primaire
Secondary education	...	1.07	*1.07	1.07	1.07	1.09	1.08	1.08	Enseignement secondaire
Tertiary education	...	1.70	1.59	1.66	1.63	1.61	1.59	...	Enseignement supérieur

11 Ratio of girls to boys in primary, secondary and tertiary education *(continued)*
Rapport filles/garçons dans l'enseignement primaire, secondaire et supérieur *(suite)*

Country or area	1991	2002	2003	2004	2005	2006	2007	2008	Pays ou zone
Papua New Guinea									**Papouasie-Nvl-Guinée**
Primary education	0.85	0.84	0.85	0.86	0.84	0.84	...	...	Enseignement primaire
Secondary education	0.62	...	...	...	...	...	...	...	Enseignement secondaire
Paraguay									**Paraguay**
Primary education	0.97	0.96	0.97	0.97	0.97	0.97	0.97	...	Enseignement primaire
Secondary education	1.05	*1.02	1.01	1.02	1.03	1.04	1.04	...	Enseignement secondaire
Tertiary education	0.91	*1.40	*1.38	*1.34	*1.13	...	1.35	...	Enseignement supérieur
Peru									**Pérou**
Primary education	0.97	0.99	0.99	0.99	1.00	0.99	0.99	1.00	Enseignement primaire
Secondary education	0.94	0.93	0.96	0.98	0.97	1.00	1.00	0.99	Enseignement secondaire
Tertiary education *	...	1.07	1.07	1.02	1.03	1.06	...	...	Enseignement supérieur *
Philippines									**Philippines**
Primary education	0.99	0.99	0.99	0.99	0.99	0.99	0.98	0.98	Enseignement primaire
Secondary education	...	1.10	1.10	1.11	1.12	1.11	1.10	1.09	Enseignement secondaire
Tertiary education	...	1.30	1.28	1.28	1.23	1.24	...	1.24	Enseignement supérieur
Poland									**Pologne**
Primary education	0.98	0.99	1.00	1.00	1.00	1.00	1.00	...	Enseignement primaire
Secondary education	1.04	0.97	0.96	1.01	0.99	0.99	0.99	...	Enseignement secondaire
Tertiary education	1.34	1.42	1.42	1.40	1.40	1.40	1.40	...	Enseignement supérieur
Portugal									**Portugal**
Primary education	0.95	0.96	0.95	0.95	0.95	0.95	0.95	...	Enseignement primaire
Secondary education	1.16	...	1.09	1.10	1.10	1.09	1.07	...	Enseignement secondaire
Tertiary education	1.29	1.37	1.35	1.32	1.30	1.28	1.22	...	Enseignement supérieur
Qatar									**Qatar**
Primary education	0.93	0.96	0.97	0.97	0.98	0.98	0.98	0.99	Enseignement primaire
Secondary education	1.06	1.14	1.19	1.23	1.32	1.38	1.45	1.46	Enseignement secondaire
Tertiary education	3.34	4.09	5.01	5.68	*5.74	*6.26	6.12	6.05	Enseignement supérieur
Republic of Moldova									**République de Moldova**
Primary education	1.00	0.99	0.99	0.99	0.99	0.99	0.98	0.98	Enseignement primaire
Secondary education	1.09	1.03	1.04	1.05	1.04	1.04	1.03	1.03	Enseignement secondaire
Tertiary education	...	1.34	1.32	1.35	1.46	1.38	1.39	1.45	Enseignement supérieur
Romania									**Roumanie**
Primary education	1.00	0.98	0.98	0.98	0.99	0.99	0.99	0.99	Enseignement primaire
Secondary education	0.99	1.02	1.02	1.01	1.01	1.00	0.99	0.99	Enseignement secondaire
Tertiary education	0.93	1.25	1.24	1.27	1.26	1.30	1.33	1.34	Enseignement supérieur
Russian Federation									**Fédération de Russie**
Primary education	1.00	0.99	0.99	...	1.00	1.00	1.00	1.00	Enseignement primaire
Secondary education	...	...	1.00	0.99	0.99	0.98	0.98	0.97	Enseignement secondaire
Tertiary education	1.27	...	1.35	1.36	1.36	1.36	1.36	1.36	Enseignement supérieur
Rwanda									**Rwanda**
Primary education	0.97	0.99	1.00	1.02	*1.04	1.03	1.02	1.01	Enseignement primaire
Secondary education	0.74	...	0.88	0.89	*0.90	...	0.89	0.90	Enseignement secondaire
Tertiary education	...	0.50	0.56	0.62	*0.62	...	...	...	Enseignement supérieur
Saint Kitts and Nevis									**Saint-Kitts-et-Nevis**
Primary education	...	1.03	1.03	1.07	1.06	...	...	...	Enseignement primaire
Secondary education	...	0.98	1.06	*1.03	*0.98	...	...	...	Enseignement secondaire
Saint Lucia									**Sainte-Lucie**
Primary education	*0.95	0.97	0.94	0.94	0.95	0.92	0.95	0.97	Enseignement primaire
Secondary education	1.44	1.28	*1.11	1.09	1.18	1.17	1.11	1.04	Enseignement secondaire
Tertiary education	*1.37	...	*2.03	3.38	2.72	5.31	2.34	2.25	Enseignement supérieur
Saint Vincent-Grenadines									**Saint Vincent-Grenadines**
Primary education	0.99	0.95	0.97	0.95	0.90	...	0.95	0.92	Enseignement primaire
Secondary education	1.24	1.12	1.10	*1.08	1.25	...	...	1.11	Enseignement secondaire
Samoa									**Samoa**
Primary education	...	0.99	0.99	0.99	*0.99	...	0.99	...	Enseignement primaire
Secondary education	...	1.12	1.13	1.12	*1.12	...	...	...	Enseignement secondaire
Sao Tome and Principe									**Sao Tomé-et-Principe**
Primary education	...	*0.96	0.96	0.97	0.97	*0.97	1.00	0.98	Enseignement primaire
Secondary education	...	...	1.18	1.05	1.07	*1.07	1.08	1.07	Enseignement secondaire

11 Ratio of girls to boys in primary, secondary and tertiary education *(continued)*

Rapport filles/garçons dans l'enseignement primaire, secondaire et supérieur *(suite)*

Country or area	1991	2002	2003	2004	2005	2006	2007	2008	Pays ou zone
Saudi Arabia									**Arabie saoudite**
Primary education	0.85	...	...	...	0.97	...	0.96	0.96	Enseignement primaire
Secondary education	0.80	...	...	...	0.91	...	...	*0.85	Enseignement secondaire
Tertiary education	0.88	*1.62	1.56	1.57	1.50	1.46	...	1.65	Enseignement supérieur
Senegal									**Sénégal**
Primary education	0.73	0.90	0.92	0.95	0.96	0.98	1.00	1.02	Enseignement primaire
Secondary education	*0.53	0.67	0.69	0.72	0.75	*0.76	*0.76	0.81	Enseignement secondaire
Tertiary education	0.32	...	...	...	...	0.46	0.53	0.54	Enseignement supérieur
Serbia									**Serbie**
Primary education	...	*0.99	*1.00	*1.00	1.01	1.01	1.00	1.00	Enseignement primaire
Secondary education	...	*1.03	*1.03	*1.03	1.03	1.03	1.03	1.03	Enseignement secondaire
Tertiary education	...	...	...	...	...	...	1.29	1.29	Enseignement supérieur
Seychelles									**Seychelles**
Primary education	...	0.99	1.01	1.01	1.01	...	0.99	0.99	Enseignement primaire
Secondary education	...	1.00	1.04	1.08	1.06	...	1.13	1.19	Enseignement secondaire
Sierra Leone									**Sierra Leone**
Primary education	0.67	...	...	...	...	...	0.88	...	Enseignement primaire
Secondary education	0.54	...	...	...	...	...	0.66	...	Enseignement secondaire
Tertiary education *	...	0.38	...	...	...	...	...	...	Enseignement supérieur *
Slovakia									**Slovaquie**
Primary education	...	0.99	0.99	0.99	0.99	0.99	0.99	0.99	Enseignement primaire
Secondary education	...	1.01	1.01	1.01	1.01	1.01	1.01	1.01	Enseignement secondaire
Tertiary education	...	1.13	1.18	1.23	1.29	1.42	1.50	1.58	Enseignement supérieur
Slovenia									**Slovénie**
Primary education	...	0.99	0.99	1.00	0.99	0.99	0.99	0.99	Enseignement primaire
Secondary education	...	1.00	0.99	1.00	1.00	1.00	0.99	0.99	Enseignement secondaire
Tertiary education	1.32	1.45	1.37	1.40	1.45	1.48	1.47	1.46	Enseignement supérieur
Solomon Islands									**Iles Salomon**
Primary education	0.87	0.95	*0.95	*0.96	0.96	0.97	0.97	...	Enseignement primaire
Secondary education	0.61	0.82	*0.82	*0.84	0.84	0.84	0.84	...	Enseignement secondaire
Somalia									**Somalie**
Primary education	...	...	...	...	...	...	0.55	...	Enseignement primaire
Secondary education *	...	...	...	...	...	...	0.46	...	Enseignement secondaire *
South Africa									**Afrique du Sud**
Primary education	0.99	0.97	0.96	0.96	0.96	0.96	0.96	...	Enseignement primaire
Secondary education	1.18	1.07	1.07	1.07	1.06	*1.06	*1.05	...	Enseignement secondaire
Tertiary education	0.83	...	...	...	...	...	...	...	Enseignement supérieur
Spain									**Espagne**
Primary education	0.99	0.99	0.99	0.99	0.98	0.98	0.99	0.99	Enseignement primaire
Secondary education	1.07	1.06	1.05	1.06	1.06	1.06	1.06	1.06	Enseignement secondaire
Tertiary education	1.09	1.19	1.19	1.22	1.22	1.22	1.23	1.24	Enseignement supérieur
Sri Lanka									**Sri Lanka**
Primary education	0.96	*0.99	*1.00	...	*1.00	1.00	1.00	1.00	Enseignement primaire
Secondary education	1.09	*1.06	*1.06	*1.02	...	...	...	...	Enseignement secondaire
Tertiary education	0.48	...	...	...	...	...	...	...	Enseignement supérieur
Sudan									**Soudan**
Primary education	0.77	0.85	0.86	0.87	0.87	0.87	0.86	0.88	Enseignement primaire
Secondary education	0.79	0.94	0.92	0.92	0.94	0.96	0.93	0.91	Enseignement secondaire
Suriname									**Suriname**
Primary education	1.02	0.98	*0.98	...	0.96	0.96	0.94	0.95	Enseignement primaire
Secondary education	1.19	1.39	*1.34	...	1.29	1.32	1.33	1.28	Enseignement secondaire
Tertiary education	...	1.71	...	...	...	...	...	...	Enseignement supérieur
Swaziland									**Swaziland**
Primary education	0.99	0.93	0.95	0.94	0.93	0.93	0.93	...	Enseignement primaire
Secondary education	*0.96	1.02	1.01	0.97	1.01	1.02	0.90	...	Enseignement secondaire
Tertiary education	0.76	1.16	*1.16	1.07	1.06	0.97	...	...	Enseignement supérieur
Sweden									**Suède**
Primary education	1.00	1.03	1.03	1.00	1.00	1.00	1.00	0.99	Enseignement primaire
Secondary education	1.05	1.21	1.18	1.03	0.99	0.99	0.99	0.99	Enseignement secondaire
Tertiary education	1.22	1.54	1.55	1.54	1.55	1.55	1.57	1.59	Enseignement supérieur

11 Ratio of girls to boys in primary, secondary and tertiary education *(continued)*
Rapport filles/garçons dans l'enseignement primaire, secondaire et supérieur *(suite)*

Country or area	1991	2002	2003	2004	2005	2006	2007	2008	Pays ou zone
Switzerland									**Suisse**
Primary education	1.01	1.00	1.00	1.00	1.00	1.00	1.00	1.00	Enseignement primaire
Secondary education	0.94	0.94	0.94	0.94	0.94	0.94	0.95	0.95	Enseignement secondaire
Tertiary education	0.54	0.77	0.81	0.83	0.87	0.91	0.93	1.00	Enseignement supérieur
Syrian Arab Republic									**Rép. arabe syrienne**
Primary education	0.90	0.93	0.94	0.95	0.95	0.96	0.96	0.96	Enseignement primaire
Secondary education	0.73	0.91	0.93	0.93	0.94	0.95	0.97	0.98	Enseignement secondaire
Tertiary education	0.65	...	...	...	...	...	...	...	Enseignement supérieur
Tajikistan									**Tadjikistan**
Primary education	0.98	0.96	0.95	0.95	0.96	0.95	0.96	0.96	Enseignement primaire
Secondary education	...	0.82	0.83	0.84	0.83	0.83	0.84	0.87	Enseignement secondaire
Tertiary education	...	0.33	0.33	0.33	0.35	0.37	0.38	0.40	Enseignement supérieur
Thailand									**Thaïlande**
Primary education	0.98	0.98	*0.98	0.98	0.97	0.98	0.98	0.98	Enseignement primaire
Secondary education	0.99	*1.00	*1.01	1.08	*1.06	1.08	1.09	1.09	Enseignement secondaire
Tertiary education	0.94	1.09	*1.13	1.18	1.13	1.08	1.25	1.22	Enseignement supérieur
TFYR of Macedonia									**L'ex-R.Y. Macédoine**
Primary education	...	1.01	1.00	1.00	1.00	1.00	1.00	...	Enseignement primaire
Secondary education	...	0.98	0.98	0.98	0.98	...	0.98	0.97	Enseignement secondaire
Tertiary education	1.11	1.30	1.35	1.40	1.38	1.38	1.27	1.20	Enseignement supérieur
Timor-Leste									**Timor-Leste**
Primary education	...	...	...	0.93	0.92	...	0.94	0.94	Enseignement primaire
Secondary education	...	...	...	0.99	1.00	...	...	...	Enseignement secondaire
Tertiary education	...	1.27	...	...	...	...	...	...	Enseignement supérieur
Togo									**Togo**
Primary education	0.65	0.81	0.82	0.84	0.85	0.86	0.86	...	Enseignement primaire
Secondary education	0.34	0.48	0.49	0.51	0.53	0.54	*0.53	...	Enseignement secondaire
Tertiary education	0.16	...	...	...	...	...	...	...	Enseignement supérieur
Tokelau *									**Tokélaou ***
Primary education	...	1.08	1.29	1.35	...	...	...	...	Enseignement primaire
Secondary education	...	1.22	0.87	0.88	...	...	...	...	Enseignement secondaire
Tonga									**Tonga**
Primary education	0.98	0.98	0.96	0.96	0.98	0.97	...	...	Enseignement primaire
Secondary education	1.03	1.12	...	*1.08	...	1.03	...	...	Enseignement secondaire
Tertiary education	...	*1.65	1.66	*1.62	...	...	...	...	Enseignement supérieur
Trinidad and Tobago									**Trinité-et-Tobago**
Primary education	1.00	0.99	0.97	0.97	0.97	...	0.97	0.97	Enseignement primaire
Secondary education	1.04	*1.10	*1.09	1.07	1.04	...	*1.06	*1.07	Enseignement secondaire
Tertiary education	0.78	1.50	1.60	1.27	*1.28	...	...	...	Enseignement supérieur
Tunisia									**Tunisie**
Primary education	0.89	0.96	0.97	0.97	0.97	0.97	0.97	0.98	Enseignement primaire
Secondary education	0.79	1.04	1.08	...	1.10	*1.10	...	1.08	Enseignement secondaire
Tertiary education	0.66	1.22	1.27	1.35	1.39	1.41	1.50	1.49	Enseignement supérieur
Turkey									**Turquie**
Primary education	0.93	0.93	0.94	0.95	0.95	0.96	0.97	0.97	Enseignement primaire
Secondary education	0.62	0.73	0.73	0.78	0.84	0.84	0.85	0.89	Enseignement secondaire
Tertiary education	0.53	0.74	0.76	0.73	0.75	0.76	0.77	0.78	Enseignement supérieur
Turks and Caicos Islands									**Iles Turques et Caïques**
Primary education	...	0.96	0.95	*1.03	*1.04	...	...	...	Enseignement primaire
Secondary education *	...	1.02	1.00	0.98	0.94	...	...	...	Enseignement secondaire *
Tertiary education *	...	...	...	...	...	...	...	0.90	Enseignement supérieur *
Tuvalu									**Tuvalu**
Primary education	...	1.13	*1.11	1.07	0.99	0.99	...	...	Enseignement primaire
Uganda									**Ouganda**
Primary education	0.85	0.99	0.98	0.99	1.00	1.01	1.01	1.01	Enseignement primaire
Secondary education	...	*0.81	*0.81	0.81	*0.81	*0.83	*0.83	0.85	Enseignement secondaire
Tertiary education	0.38	*0.53	*0.53	0.63	...	0.77	...	0.80	Enseignement supérieur
Ukraine									**Ukraine**
Primary education	1.00	1.00	1.00	0.99	1.00	1.00	1.00	1.00	Enseignement primaire
Secondary education	1.04	1.00	1.00	0.99	0.92	0.98	0.99	0.98	Enseignement secondaire
Tertiary education	...	1.19	1.21	1.22	1.23	1.23	1.24	1.25	Enseignement supérieur

11 Ratio of girls to boys in primary, secondary and tertiary education *(continued)*
Rapport filles/garçons dans l'enseignement primaire, secondaire et supérieur *(suite)*

Country or area	1991	2002	2003	2004	2005	2006	2007	2008	Pays ou zone
United Arab Emirates									**Emirats arabes unis**
Primary education	0.97	0.97	0.98	0.98	0.99	0.99	1.00	...	Enseignement primaire
Secondary education	1.16	1.05	1.03	1.02	1.02	1.02	*1.02	...	Enseignement secondaire
Tertiary education	4.03	*2.85	*2.88	...	...	...	...	2.05	Enseignement supérieur
United Kingdom									**Royaume-Uni**
Primary education	1.01	1.00	1.00	1.00	1.00	1.01	1.01	1.00	Enseignement primaire
Secondary education	1.04	1.01	1.03	1.02	1.03	1.03	1.02	1.02	Enseignement secondaire
Tertiary education	0.96	1.26	1.30	1.37	1.39	1.40	1.40	1.40	Enseignement supérieur
United Rep. of Tanzania									**Rép.-Unie de Tanzanie**
Primary education	0.98	0.97	0.96	0.96	0.96	0.97	0.98	0.99	Enseignement primaire
Secondary education	0.77	...	...	...	...	...	...	...	Enseignement secondaire
Tertiary education	0.19	*0.31	0.44	0.41	*0.48	...	0.48	...	Enseignement supérieur
United States									**Etats-Unis**
Primary education	0.98	1.01	1.00	0.97	0.99	1.01	1.00	1.01	Enseignement primaire
Secondary education	1.01	0.99	1.00	1.02	1.02	0.99	1.01	1.00	Enseignement secondaire
Tertiary education	1.25	1.35	1.37	1.39	1.40	1.41	1.41	1.40	Enseignement supérieur
Uruguay									**Uruguay**
Primary education	0.99	0.98	0.98	0.97	0.98	0.97	0.97	...	Enseignement primaire
Secondary education	1.27	1.13	1.15	1.15	1.15	1.16	0.99	...	Enseignement secondaire
Tertiary education	1.31	...	...	...	...	1.68	1.75	...	Enseignement supérieur
Uzbekistan									**Ouzbékistan**
Primary education	0.98	0.98	0.99	0.98	0.98	0.98	0.98	0.98	Enseignement primaire
Secondary education	...	0.97	0.96	0.96	0.97	0.97	0.98	0.98	Enseignement secondaire
Tertiary education	...	0.80	0.77	0.79	0.70	0.71	0.71	0.68	Enseignement supérieur
Vanuatu									**Vanuatu**
Primary education	0.96	0.99	0.99	0.98	0.97	0.98	0.96	...	Enseignement primaire
Secondary education	0.80	0.94	0.84	0.86	...	...	...	...	Enseignement secondaire
Tertiary education	...	*0.57	0.59	*0.59	...	...	...	...	Enseignement supérieur
Venezuela (Boliv. Rep. of)									**Venezuela (Rép. boliv. du)**
Primary education	0.99	0.98	0.98	0.98	0.98	0.98	0.97	0.97	Enseignement primaire
Secondary education	1.24	1.16	1.15	1.14	1.13	1.12	1.12	1.10	Enseignement secondaire
Tertiary education	...	*1.09	*1.08	...	...	...	...	1.69	Enseignement supérieur
Yemen									**Yémen**
Primary education	...	0.66	0.69	0.71	0.74	...	...	0.80	Enseignement primaire
Secondary education	...	...	0.45	0.48	0.49	...	...	...	Enseignement secondaire
Tertiary education	...	...	...	0.38	0.37	0.39	0.42	...	Enseignement supérieur
Zambia									**Zambie**
Primary education	...	0.93	...	0.96	0.96	0.98	0.97	0.98	Enseignement primaire
Secondary education	...	0.83	...	0.79	0.81	...	0.89	0.83	Enseignement secondaire
Zimbabwe									**Zimbabwe**
Primary education	0.97	0.98	0.98	...	...	0.99	...	...	Enseignement primaire
Secondary education	0.79	0.88	0.90	...	...	0.92	...	...	Enseignement secondaire
Tertiary education *	...	0.68	0.62	...	...	...	...	...	Enseignement supérieur *

Source:
United Nations Educational, Scientific and Cultural Organization (UNESCO), Montreal, the UNESCO Institute for Statistics (UIS) database, last accessed September 2010.

Source:
L'Organisation des Nations Unies pour l'éducation, la science et la culture (UNESCO), Montréal, la base de données de l'institut de statistique de l'UNESCO (ISU), dernier accès septembre 2010.

Technical notes: tables 9-11

Tables 9-11: The three tables on gender presented in this chapter are all based on indicators for the Millennium Development Goals (MDGs). For more on MDGs, visit mdgs.un.org.

Table 9 shows the percentage of seats held by women members in single or lower chambers of national parliaments. National parliaments can be bicameral or unicameral. This table covers the single chamber in unicameral parliaments and the lower chamber in bicameral parliaments. It does not cover the upper chamber of bicameral parliaments. Seats are usually won by members in general parliamentary elections. Seats may also be filled by nomination, appointment, indirect election, rotation of members and by-election.

The proportion of seats held by women in national parliament is derived by dividing the total number of seats occupied by women by the total number of seats in parliament. There is no weighting or normalizing of statistics.

The source for this table is the Inter-Parliamentary Union (IPU). For more information visit www.ipu.org.

Table 10: The share of women in wage employment in the non-agricultural sector is the share of female workers in wage employment in the non-agricultural sector expressed as a percentage of total wage employment in that same sector.

The non-agricultural sector includes industry and services. "Industry" includes mining and quarrying (including oil production), manufacturing, construction, electricity, gas, and water, corresponding to divisions 2-5 in the International Standard Industrial Classification of All Economic Activities (ISIC-Rev.2) and to tabulation categories C-F in ISIC-Rev. 3. "Services" include wholesale and retail trade and restaurants and hotels; transport, storage, and communications; financing, insurance, real estate, and business services; and community, social, and personal services, corresponding to divisions 6-9 in ISIC-Rev. 2, and to tabulation categories G-Q in ISIC-Rev. 3.

Employment refers to people above a certain age who worked or held a job during a specified reference period (according to the ILO Resolution concerning statistics of the economically active population, employment, unemployment and underemployment, adopted by the Thirteenth International Conference of Labour Statisticians (ICLS), October 1982).

Wage employment refers only to wage earners and salaried employees, or "persons in paid employment jobs". Employees are typically remunerated by wages and salaries, but may be paid by commission from sales, piece-rates, bonuses or payments in kind such as food, housing, training, etc. These persons are in wage employment as opposed to self-employment – that is employers, own-account workers, members of producers'

Notes techniques : tableaux 9 à 11

Tableaux 9-11: ces trois tableaux sur la répartition des sexes figurant dans le présent chapitre reposent tous sur des indicateurs liés aux objectifs du Millénaire pour le développement. Pour plus d'informations sur les objectifs du Millénaire pour le développement, veuillez consulter le site Web suivant : mdgs.un.org.

Tableau 9 : ce tableau indique le pourcentage des sièges des chambres uniques ou basses des parlements nationaux occupés par des femmes. Les parlements nationaux peuvent être bicaméraux ou unicaméraux. Ce tableau porte sur la chambre unique des parlements unicaméraux et sur la chambre basse des parlements bicaméraux. Il ne porte pas sur la chambre haute des parlements bicaméraux. Les sièges sont habituellement attribués aux membres à l'issue d'élections parlementaires générales. Certains sièges peuvent aussi être pourvus à l'issue de nominations, d'élections indirectes, de roulement des membres et d'élections partielles.

La proportion d'élues est obtenue en divisant le nombre total de sièges occupés par des femmes par le nombre total de sièges que compte le parlement. Les statistiques ne sont ni pondérées ni normalisées.

La source de ce tableau est l'Union interparlementaire. Pour plus d'informations, veuillez consulter le site Web suivant : www.ipu.org.

Tableau 10 : la proportion des femmes rémunérées dans le secteur non agricole correspond au pourcentage du nombre total de salariés employés dans le secteur agricole qui sont des femmes.

Le secteur non agricole comprend l'industrie et les services. L'"industrie" comporte les industries extractives (y compris la production pétrolière), le secteur manufacturier, le bâtiment, l'électricité, le gaz et l'eau, correspondant aux divisions 2 à 5 de la Classification internationale type, par industrie, de toutes les branches d'activité économique (CITI) et aux catégories C à F de la CITI-Rev.3. Les "services" comportent le commerce de gros et de détail, la restauration et l'hôtellerie; les transports, l'entreposage et les communications; les finances, les assurances, l'immobilier et les services commerciaux; et les services communautaires, sociaux et personnels, correspondant aux divisions 6 à 9 de la CITI-Rev.2 et aux catégories G à Q de la CITI-Rev.3.

L'emploi se rapporte aux personnes d'un âge minimum donné qui ont travaillé ou occupé un emploi pendant une période donnée de référence (conformément à la résolution de l'OIT sur les statistiques de la population économiquement active, l'emploi, le chômage et le sous-emploi, adoptée par la treizième Conférence internationale des statisticiens du travail (CIST), octobre 1982).

L'emploi salarié se réfère uniquement aux travailleurs salariés ou recevant un traitement et aux personnes dans des emplois rémunérés. Les employés sont généra-

cooperatives and contributing family workers. The different statuses in employment are defined according to the ILO Resolution concerning the International Classification of Status in Employment (ICSE), adopted by the 15th ICLS (1993).

The source for this table is the International Labour Organization (ILO). For more information visit http://laborsta.ilo.org.

Table 11: Ratio of girls to boys (gender parity index) in primary, secondary and tertiary education is the ratio of the number of female students enrolled at primary, secondary and tertiary levels of education to the number of male students in each level. To standardize the effects of the population structure of the appropriate age groups, the Gender Parity Index (GPI) of the Gross Enrolment Ratio (GER) for each level of education is used.

The source for this table is the UNESCO Institute for Statistics (UIS). For more information visit www.uis.unesco.org.

lement rémunérés par des salaires et des traitements, mais leur rémunération peut aussi provenir de commissions, de travaux à la pièce, de primes ou d'avantages en nature tels que repas, logement, formation, etc. Il s'agit de salariés par opposition aux travailleurs indépendants – employeurs, travailleurs à leur compte, membres de coopératives de producteurs et travailleurs familiaux. Les différentes situations d'après la profession sont définies conformément à la résolution de l'OIT concernant la Classification internationale d'après la situation dans la profession (CISP), adoptée par la quinzième Conférence internationale des statisticiens du travail (CIST) (1993).

La source de ce tableau est l'Organisation internationale du Travail (OIT). Pour plus d'informations, veuillez consulter le site Web suivant : http://laborsta.ilo.org.

Tableau 11 : ce tableau indique la proportion de filles par rapport aux garçons (indice de parité des sexes) dans l'enseignement primaire, secondaire et supérieur, à savoir le rapport entre le nombre de filles inscrites dans l'enseignement primaire, secondaire et supérieur et le nombre de garçons à chaque niveau. Pour normaliser les effets de la pyramide des âges, l'indice de parité des sexes du taux brut de scolarisation pour chaque niveau d'enseignement est utilisé.

La source de ce tableau est l'Institut de statistique de l'UNESCO. Pour plus d'informations, veuillez consulter le site Web suivant : www.uis.unesco.org.

12 Education at the primary, secondary and tertiary levels

Number of students enrolled and percentage female

Enseignement primaire, secondaire et supérieur

Nombre d'élèves inscrits et pourcentage de sexe féminin

Country or area Pays ou zone	Year[t] Année[t]	Primary education Enseignement primaire		Secondary education Enseignement secondaire		Tertiary education Enseignement supérieur	
		Total	% F	Total	% F	Total	% F
Afghanistan Afghanistan	2004	4 430 142	29.1	594 306	16.3	27 648	20.4
	2005	4 318 819	35.7	651 453	23.4	...	...
	2006	4 669 110	37.2	1 006 841	25.4	...	...
	2007	4 718 077	36.9	1 035 782	26.1	...	...
	2008	4 887 523	38.2	...	...	...	...
Albania Albanie	2004	250 487	48.2	397 056	47.9	53 014	62.1
Algeria Algérie	2004	4 507 703	47.0	3 677 107	50.7	716 452	51.0
	2005	4 361 744	47.0	3 755 821[1]	50.7[1]	792 121	55.2
	2006	4 196 580	47.0	...	...	817 968	54.8
	2007	4 086 925	47.2	...	...	901 562	57.4
	2008	3 942 242	47.3	...	...	...	...
Andorra Andorre	2004	4 264	47.1	3 250	49.9	331	48.6
	2005	4 085	46.9	3 737	50.3	342	50.9
	2006	4 332	47.4	3 843	49.9	401	53.1
	2007	4 427	47.2	3 819	49.4	...	...
	2008	4 492	47.2	3 851	49.2	459	57.5
Angola Angola	2004	...	...	...	...	37 547	...
	2005	...	...	...	...	48 184	...
	2006	...	...	...	...	48 694	...
Anguilla Anguilla	2004	1 433	50.0	1 076	51.1	21	81.0
	2005	1 449	50.8	1 024	50.5	33	75.8
	2006	1 512	48.9	998	51.6	47	83.0
	2007	1 558	48.6	1 001	51.7	54	83.3
	2008	1 610	49.3	1 008	49.9	54	83.3
Antigua and Barbuda Antigua-et-Barbuda	2007	11 569	48.9	7 838	51.1	...	...
Argentina Argentine	2004	4 701 149	48.9	3 497 541	51.7	2 116 876	58.1
	2005	4 651 255	48.8	3 476 306	51.9	2 082 577	58.7
	2006	4 685 696	48.8	3 481 085	52.1	2 202 032	59.7
Armenia Arménie	2004	134 664	48.4	369 236	49.6	79 321	55.5
	2005	125 149	48.2	364 234	49.6	86 629	55.5
	2006	121 502	47.8	355 790	49.6	99 293	54.5
	2007	127 546	47.2	336 877	49.7	107 398	54.7
	2008	121 841	46.7	309 439	49.2	...	...
Aruba Aruba	2004	10 185	47.9	6 973	50.6	1 704	60.2
	2005	10 250	48.3	7 116	50.7	2 106	59.8
	2006	10 390	48.8	7 439	50.4	2 094	60.3
	2007	10 346	48.6	7 853	50.9	2 232	58.4
	2008	10 012	48.5	7 270	51.4	2 242	58.0
Australia Australie	2004	1 934 549	48.6	2 492 235	47.8	1 002 998	54.2
	2005	1 934 941	48.6	2 496 917	47.6	1 024 589	54.5
	2006	1 938 861	48.6	2 536 684	47.4	1 040 153	54.9
	2007	1 973 456	48.6	2 511 214	47.6	1 083 715	55.1
Austria Autriche	2004	372 963	48.7	770 391	47.4	238 522	53.3
	2005	362 822	48.7	781 292	47.5	244 410	53.7
	2006	355 293	48.5	782 981	47.7	253 139	53.8
	2007	347 249	48.4	777 792	47.8	260 975	53.7
Azerbaijan Azerbaïdjan	2004	607 007	47.8	1 085 632	48.0	122 770	46.0
	2005	568 097	47.7	1 069 980	47.9	128 634	46.8
	2006	538 339	47.1	1 051 591	47.6	131 507	47.5
	2007	512 976	47.2	1 029 853	47.6	135 164	45.7
	2008	496 697	46.9	1 151 357	47.8	141 896	44.3
Bahamas Bahamas	2004[1]	36 070	49.2	30 857	49.6	...	...
	2005	37 050	49.1	32 089	49.7	...	...
	2006	35 921	49.1	32 709	49.8	...	...
	2007	37 122	49.1	34 217	50.4	...	...

12 Education at the primary, secondary and tertiary levels *(continued)*

Number of students enrolled and percentage female

Enseignement primaire, secondaire et supérieur *(suite)*

Nombre d'élèves inscrits et pourcentage de sexe féminin

Country or area Pays ou zone	Year[t] Année[t]	Primary education Enseignement primaire		Secondary education Enseignement secondaire		Tertiary education Enseignement supérieur	
		Total	% F	Total	% F	Total	% F
Bahrain Bahreïn	2004	82 708	48.9	69 638	49.9	18 524[1]	63.1[1]
	2005	83 299	48.7	71 645	50.0	18 841	67.8
	2006	89 721	48.8	73 767	49.7	18 403	68.4
	2008	86 084	48.8	77 928	49.5	...	...
Bangladesh Bangladesh	2004	...	...	10 354 760	49.6	821 364	31.6
	2005	16 219 478	50.1	10 109 395	50.6	911 600	33.5
	2006	16 396 870	50.4	10 250 862	50.4	1 053 566	34.8
	2007	16 312 907	50.7	10 444 714	50.3	1 145 401	34.9
	2008[2]	16 001 605	50.5	...	...	...	...
Barbados Barbade	2004	22 327	48.9	21 300	49.7	...	...
	2005	22 249	49.2	21 418	49.4	...	...
	2006	22 461	48.7	20 855	50.2	...	...
	2007	22 584	49.3	20 651	50.0	11 405	68.0
	2008[2]	22 849	49.0	20 337	50.3	...	...
Belarus Bélarus	2004	403 841	47.8	969 768	49.1	507 360	57.1
	2005	379 577	47.8	928 488	49.1	528 508	56.8
	2006	367 736	48.1	878 943	49.1	544 328	56.8
	2007	361 493	48.2	823 253	49.2	556 526	57.5
	2008	362 377	49.2	...	...	576 679	57.8
Belgium Belgique	2004	747 111	48.8	805 778	48.0	386 110	53.8
	2005	738 580	48.8	814 539	48.0	389 547	54.4
	2006	732 808	48.8	821 996	48.1	394 427	54.7
	2007	732 411	48.9	825 293	48.0	393 687	55.0
Belize Belize	2004	48 996	48.7	31 224	50.3	722	70.2
	2005	50 389	48.4	31 377[1]	49.7[1]	...	...
	2006	51 497	48.6	30 084	50.7	...	...
	2007	51 898	49.0	30 475	51.0	...	...
	2008	51 994	48.6	31 120	51.4	...	...
	2009	...	...	...	...	3 581	64.2
Benin Bénin	2004	1 319 648	42.8	344 890	31.7	41 282	...
	2005	1 318 140	43.6	435 449[1]	35.4[1]	42 197	...
	2006	1 356 818	44.4	...	...	42 603	...
	2008	1 601 146	45.5	...	...	...	...
Bermuda Bermudes	2004	4 810	50.7	4 803	53.1	...	...
	2005	4 760	50.4	4 756	52.4	639	65.1
	2006	4 678	46.2	4 518	51.5	...	...
	2007	...	...	...	...	886	71.1
Bhutan Bhoutan	2005	99 458	48.7	42 144	47.2	...	...
	2006	102 225	48.9	45 035	47.8	4 141	32.7
	2007	...	...	...	...	3 998	30.6
	2008	106 100	49.5	52 098	48.2	5 051	34.8
	2009	108 842	49.7	56 543	49.5	...	...
Bolivia (Plurinational State of) Bolivie (État plurinational de)	2004[1]	1 541 559	49.0	...	...	346 056	...
	2006	1 508 194	49.0	1 043 127	48.1	...	...
	2007	1 512 002	49.0	1 052 014	48.4	352 554[2]	45.0[2]
Bosnia and Herzegovina Bosnie-Herzégovine	2007	191 588	46.9	344 567	49.6	99 414	...
Botswana Botswana	2004	328 692	49.3	169 727[1]	51.0[1]	10 197	46.4
	2005	326 500	49.3	168 720	50.9	10 950	49.8
	2006	330 417	49.1	174 843	51.1	...	...
Brazil Brésil	2004	18 979 209	47.2	25 155 104	51.5	4 275 027	56.3
	2005	18 661 105	47.6	24 863 112	51.6	4 572 297	55.9
	2007	17 996 083	47.2	23 423 870	51.7	5 272 877	55.7
British Virgin Islands Iles Vierges britanniques	2004	2 824	48.2	1 707	52.1	1 136	69.5
	2005	2 898	48.2	1 882	54.2	1 200[1]	68.8[1]
	2006	2 923	48.3	1 959	53.0	...	...
	2007	3 044	48.8	1 921	53.8	...	...

12 Education at the primary, secondary and tertiary levels *(continued)*
Number of students enrolled and percentage female

Enseignement primaire, secondaire et supérieur *(suite)*
Nombre d'élèves inscrits et pourcentage de sexe féminin

Country or area Pays ou zone	Year[t] Année[t]	Primary education Enseignement primaire		Secondary education Enseignement secondaire		Tertiary education Enseignement supérieur	
		Total	% F	Total	% F	Total	% F
Brunei Darussalam Brunéi Darussalam	2004	46 382	47.9	42 167	49.0	4 917	66.0
	2005	46 012	47.9	43 900	48.8	5 023	66.5
	2006	46 086	47.7	45 887	48.9	5 094	66.1
	2007	45 972	47.7	46 173	48.8	5 284	64.5
	2008	45 125	47.9	46 826	48.6	5 607	65.6
Bulgaria Bulgarie	2004	314 221	48.3	704 678	47.7	228 468	52.5
	2005	290 017	48.4	685 640	47.7	237 909	52.1
	2006	273 045	48.3	662 510	47.7	243 464	53.5
	2007	267 584	48.3	633 343	47.7	258 692	53.7
Burkina Faso Burkina Faso	2004	1 139 512	43.2	266 538[1]	40.3[1]	18 868[1]	22.4[1]
	2005	1 270 837	43.7	295 412	40.7	27 942	30.7
	2006	1 390 571	44.2	319 749	41.3	30 472	31.0
	2007	1 561 258	44.8	352 376	41.6	33 459	30.9
	2008	1 742 439	45.6	423 543	41.9	41 779	32.7
	2009	1 912 279	46.0	467 658	41.9	...	...
Burundi Burundi	2004	968 488	45.4	152 251	43.0	15 706	27.7
	2005	1 036 859	46.2	171 110[1]	42.5[1]	16 915	27.7[1]
	2006	1 324 937	47.7	192 296[1]	42.6[1]	17 953	30.5[1]
	2007	1 490 844	48.2	209 945	41.9	19 296	...
	2008	1 603 116	48.7	243 202[1]	41.4[1]	21 856	...
Cambodia Cambodge	2004	2 762 882	47.0	631 508[1]	40.2[1]	45 370	31.3
	2005	2 695 372	47.2	...	...	56 810	31.5
	2006	2 582 250	47.3	811 797	43.3	75 989	32.8
	2007	2 479 644	47.2	875 120	44.2	92 340	35.2
	2008	2 340 606	47.4	...	...	122 633	34.4
Cameroon Cameroun	2004	2 979 011	45.8	751 580	43.8	83 903[2]	38.8[1]
	2005	2 977 781	45.3[1]	784 203	43.8	99 864[2]	39.5[2]
	2006	2 998 135	45.3	698 444	44.0	120 298	41.8
	2007	3 120 357	45.9	...	...	132 134	43.9
	2008	3 201 477	45.9	1 127 691	44.2	147 631	44.1
Canada Canada	2004[1]	2 389 188	48.6	2 572 388	48.0	1 326 711	56.5
	2005	2 320 738	48.6	2 601 926	48.1	...	...
	2006	2 305 211	48.6	2 632 432	48.2	...	...
Cape Verde Cap-Vert	2004	85 138	48.6	49 790	52.2	3 036	52.6
	2005	82 952	48.5	...	...	3 910	51.0
	2006	81 434	48.6	...	...	4 567	52.1
	2007	78 801	48.3	...	...	5 289	54.6
	2008	76 299	48.2	...	...	6 658	55.5
Cayman Islands Iles Caïmanes	2004	3 361	48.5	2 701	50.8	...	...
	2005	3 240	48.4	2 824	47.8	...	...
	2006	3 461	48.1	2 899	49.0	567	71.6
	2007	3 706	48.2	3 010	49.5	626	70.0
	2008	3 736	47.9	3 198	51.9	907	68.8
Central African Rep. Rép. centrafricaine	2004	363 158	40.2	...	...	6 384	...
	2005	412 381	41.1	...	...	6 270[1]	...
	2006	418 825	41.1	...	...	4 462	22.5
	2007	494 985	41.4	...	...	...	...
	2008	522 187	41.9	...	...	9 641	25.0
Chad Tchad	2004	1 271 985	39.5	227 856	24.8	10 081	12.5
	2005	1 262 393	40.1	245 286[1]	25.5[1]	12 373	6.0
	2006	1 296 486	40.3	262 714	26.2	...	...
	2007	1 324 298	40.9	314 470	30.8	...	...
	2008	1 495 961	41.1	...	...	18 990	12.7
Chile Chili	2004	1 755 997	47.9	1 594 966	49.5	580 815	48.0
	2005	1 720 951	48.0	1 630 099	49.5	663 694	48.1
	2006	1 694 765	48.0	1 633 868	49.6	661 142	49.2
	2007	1 679 017	47.8	1 611 631	49.8	753 398	49.4

12 Education at the primary, secondary and tertiary levels *(continued)*

Number of students enrolled and percentage female

Enseignement primaire, secondaire et supérieur *(suite)*

Nombre d'élèves inscrits et pourcentage de sexe féminin

Country or area Pays ou zone	Year[t] Année[t]	Primary education Enseignement primaire		Secondary education Enseignement secondaire		Tertiary education Enseignement supérieur	
		Total	% F	Total	% F	Total	% F
China[3] Chine[3]	2004	...	...	...	...	18 090 814	45.5
	2005	...	...	...	...	20 601 219	46.0
	2006	108 925 227	46.8	101 195 119	47.7	23 360 535	47.1
	2007	107 394 752	46.6	101 830 969	47.7	25 346 279	47.9
China, Hong Kong SAR Chine, Hong Kong RAS	2004	472 863	48.1	492 779	48.9	147 724	51.2
	2005	451 171	48.0	498 354	48.9	152 294	51.1
	2006	429 892	48.0	500 708	48.8	155 324	50.5
	2007	414 501	47.9	510 284	48.8	157 858	50.1
	2008	389 937	47.8	513 787	48.7	...	...
China, Macao SAR Chine, Macao RAS	2004	39 872	46.7	46 509	49.6	24 815	40.5
	2005	37 401	46.8	46 539	49.4	23 420	42.8
	2006	34 739	47.2	46 393	49.3	23 291	45.9
	2007	32 932	46.9	45 410	49.2	23 868	48.8
	2008	30 487	47.1	41 271	49.2	25 407	49.8
Colombia Colombie	2004	5 259 033	48.7	4 050 525	51.7	1 112 574	51.3
	2005	5 298 257	48.5	4 297 228	51.6	1 223 594	51.3
	2006	5 296 190	48.6	4 509 406	51.8	1 314 972	51.5
	2007	5 292 476	48.8	4 684 033	51.7	1 372 674	51.5
	2008	5 285 523	48.8	4 772 189	51.4	1 487 186	49.1
Comoros Comores	2004	103 809	46.2	42 919	42.5	1 779[1]	43.2[1]
	2005[1]	106 700	46.2	43 349	42.5	...	...
Congo Congo	2004	584 370	48.1	232 026[1]	46.0[1]	...	...
	2005	597 304	47.9	...	...	...	...
	2006	617 010	47.2	...	...	...	...
	2007	621 702	48.0	...	...	...	...
	2008	628 081	48.0	...	...	...	...
Cook Islands Iles Cook	2004[1]	2 265	47.2	1 901	48.6	...	...
	2005	2 201	48.1	1 899	49.2	...	...
	2007	2 031	46.9	1 951	50.1	...	...
Costa Rica Costa Rica	2004	558 084	48.3	339 763	50.0	108 765	54.3
	2005	542 087	48.3	347 244	50.0	110 717[1]	54.3[1]
	2006	546 542	48.4	374 428	50.1	...	...
	2007	536 436	48.4	377 924	49.8	...	...
	2008	534 816	48.4	380 813	50.0	...	...
Côte d'Ivoire Côte d'Ivoire	2006	2 111 975	44.1	...	...	149 261[1]	32.7[1]
	2007	2 179 801	44.1	...	...	156 772	33.3
	2008	2 356 240	44.1	...	...	...	...
Croatia Croatie	2005	196 253	48.7	400 123	49.7	134 658	53.9
	2006	194 748	48.6	395 836	49.7	136 646	54.1
	2007	190 693	48.7	392 952	49.7	139 996	54.1
Cuba Cuba	2004	906 293	47.7	932 338	49.1	396 516	62.3[1]
	2005	895 045	47.8	937 493	49.1	471 858	62.1[2]
	2006	889 834	47.9	928 342	49.1	681 629	60.8
	2007	883 132	47.9	898 833	48.7	864 846	63.6
	2008	871 444	48.0	865 602	48.6	987 250	61.4
Cyprus Chypre	2004	61 731	48.8	64 534	49.2	20 849	47.9
	2005	61 247	48.7	64 293	49.2	20 078	52.0
	2006	59 710	48.8	64 714	49.2	20 587	50.9
	2007	57 785	48.6	64 853	49.3	22 227	50.1
Czech Republic République tchèque	2004	534 366	48.3	982 208	49.2	318 858	51.3
	2005	502 831	48.3	975 284	49.2	336 307	52.6
	2006	473 269	48.4	966 280	49.1	338 009	53.8
	2007	462 820	48.5	937 026	49.1	363 277	54.7
Dem. Rep. of the Congo Rép. dém. du Congo	2007	8 839 888	44.8	2 815 175	34.6	237 836	25.9[2]
	2008	9 973 365	45.5	3 129 488[2]	35.5[2]	306 400	...
Denmark Danemark	2004	419 806	48.7	449 750	49.8	217 130	57.9
	2005	414 103	48.7	464 952	49.5	232 255	57.4
	2006	415 793	48.7	463 617	49.4	228 893	57.4
	2007	415 793	48.7	475 140	49.4	232 194	57.6

12 Education at the primary, secondary and tertiary levels *(continued)*

Number of students enrolled and percentage female

Enseignement primaire, secondaire et supérieur *(suite)*

Nombre d'élèves inscrits et pourcentage de sexe féminin

Country or area Pays ou zone	Year[t] Année[t]	Primary education Enseignement primaire		Secondary education Enseignement secondaire		Tertiary education Enseignement supérieur	
		Total	% F	Total	% F	Total	% F
Djibouti Djibouti	2004	48 713	43.8	26 549	40.4	1 134	44.8
	2005	50 651	44.6	30 142	39.5	1 696	41.8
	2006	53 745	44.4	30 265	39.8	1 928	40.0
	2007	56 667	45.8	34 667	40.3	2 192	40.4
	2008	56 395	46.5	41 159	40.7	...	...
Dominica Dominique	2004	9 872	48.3	7 477	50.4	...	...
	2005	9 441	48.7	7 476	50.0	...	...
	2006	8 912	48.7	7 475	49.7	...	...
	2007	8 643	48.5	7 481	50.0	...	...
	2008	8 369	48.7	7 309	49.1	...	...
Dominican Republic Rép. dominicaine	2004	1 281 885	47.8	782 690	54.3	293 565[1]	61.3[1]
	2005	1 289 745	47.9	808 352	54.0	...	...
	2006	1 234 450	47.9	794 000	54.1	...	...
	2007	1 355 085	47.5	920 494	54.1	...	...
	2008	1 305 661	47.4	909 331	53.7	...	...
Ecuador Equateur	2004	1 989 665	49.0	996 535	49.3	...	...
	2005	1 997 624	49.0	1 053 175	49.4	...	...
	2006	2 006 430	48.9	1 103 258	49.6	...	...
	2007	2 039 168	49.0	1 141 866	49.5	443 509	54.4
	2008	...	...	...	...	534 522	52.9
Egypt Egypte	2004[1]	7 928 380	47.9	8 329 822	47.4	2 512 399	...
	2005	9 563 627	47.3	...	...	2 594 186[1]	...
	2006	9 794 591	47.4	...	...	...	...
	2007	9 988 181	47.6	...	...	...	...
El Salvador El Salvador	2004	1 045 485	48.2	520 332	49.9	120 264	55.7
	2005	1 045 484	48.2	524 202	50.0	122 431	54.7
	2006	1 035 100	48.2	529 057	50.3	124 956	54.7
	2007	1 075 041	49.1	536 017	50.3	132 246	54.8
	2008	993 795	48.2	539 277	50.1	138 615	54.6
Equatorial Guinea Guinée équatoriale	2005	75 809	48.7	...	...	...	...
	2007	81 099	48.6	...	...	...	...
Eritrea Erythrée	2004	374 997	44.2	194 124	36.2	4 612	13.1
	2005	377 512	44.4	216 944	37.2	...	...
	2006	364 263	44.4	227 786	37.6	...	...
	2007	331 855	45.1	218 369	41.4	...	...
	2008	314 034	44.8	229 079[1]	41.5[1]	...	...
	2009	...	...	...	...	9 949	24.5
Estonia Estonie	2004	92 098	47.9	124 382	49.4	65 659	61.8
	2005	85 539	47.9	124 493	49.1	67 760	61.5
	2006	79 589	48.0	120 286	49.3	68 286	61.6
	2007	76 026	48.3	114 141	49.3	68 767	61.1
Ethiopia Ethiopie	2004	8 269 663	43.5	2 140 751	36.3	172 111	25.2
	2005	10 019 729	45.1	2 488 465	37.3	191 212	24.4
	2006	10 971 581	46.1	2 992 589	38.5	180 286	24.2
	2007	12 174 719	46.5	3 430 129	40.0	255 454	25.7
	2008	12 741 814	47.0	3 696 385	41.9	264 822	23.8
Fiji Fidji	2004	113 449	48.0	102 023	50.1	12 783	53.1
	2005[1]	113 643	48.0	101 741	50.1	12 717	53.1
	2006	109 702	48.0	100 243	50.7	...	...
	2007	103 641	47.8	99 098	51.1	...	...
	2008	102 543	48.1	98 561	50.2	...	...
Finland Finlande	2004	387 934	48.8	425 966	50.0	299 888	53.4
	2005	381 785	48.9	430 596	50.0	305 996	53.6
	2006	372 128	48.9	432 565	50.0	308 966	53.9
	2007	364 902	48.9	432 607	50.1	309 163	54.0
France France	2004	3 783 197	48.6	5 826 848	49.0	2 160 300	55.0
	2005	4 015 490	48.5	6 036 192	49.0	2 187 383	55.2
	2006	4 051 861	48.5	5 993 897	48.9	2 201 201	55.3
	2007	4 105 628	48.5	5 940 366	48.9	2 179 505	55.3

12 Education at the primary, secondary and tertiary levels *(continued)*

Number of students enrolled and percentage female

Enseignement primaire, secondaire et supérieur *(suite)*

Nombre d'élèves inscrits et pourcentage de sexe féminin

Country or area Pays ou zone	Year[t] Année[t]	Primary education Enseignement primaire		Secondary education Enseignement secondaire		Tertiary education Enseignement supérieur	
		Total	% F	Total	% F	Total	% F
Gabon[1] Gabon[1]	2004	281 371	49.4	...	...	...	...
Gambia Gambie	2004	204 559	49.9	82 097	45.0	1 530	19.2
	2005	205 175	50.4	95 640	45.1	...	...
	2006	207 474	50.8	...	...	...	...
	2007	218 638	50.8	101 670	47.0	...	...
	2008	220 931	51.2	105 237	48.4	...	...
Georgia Géorgie	2004	363 951	48.2	312 333	49.1	155 058	50.5
	2005	338 222	48.3	316 430	48.8	174 255	50.4
	2006	326 597	48.8	314 427	49.8[1]	144 991	52.5
	2007	322 249	47.2	321 171	48.7[1]	141 303	52.0
	2008	311 265	47.0	305 388	48.7	129 926	54.1[2]
Germany Allemagne	2004	3 305 386	48.6	8 381 930	48.2	...	...
	2005	3 306 136	48.7	8 289 699	48.2	...	...
	2006	3 329 349	48.7	8 285 301	48.0	...	...
	2007	3 311 285	48.7	7 981 848	48.2	...	...
Ghana Ghana	2004	2 678 912	47.4	1 276 670	44.5	...	...
	2005	2 929 536	47.9	1 350 410[1]	45.0[1]	119 559	35.0
	2006	3 130 575	48.5	1 454 097	44.9	110 184	33.7
	2007	3 365 762	48.5	1 618 846	45.7	140 017	34.2
	2008	3 501 591	48.6	1 690 677	45.9	...	...
Gibraltar Gibraltar	2008	3 211	48.7	1 674	47.4	...	...
Greece Grèce	2004	657 492	48.2	695 838	48.3	597 007	51.7
	2005	650 242	48.5	715 537	47.7	646 587	51.1
	2006	645 324	48.6	704 515	47.7	653 003	50.9
	2007	639 083	48.6	682 012	47.1	602 858	50.4
Grenada Grenade	2004	15 819	48.6	13 660	51.4	...	...
	2005	16 072[1]	48.7[1]	13 675[2]	50.1[2]	...	...
	2007	13 733	48.7	13 060	49.0	...	...
	2008	13 873	47.7	12 469	47.3	...	...
Guatemala Guatemala	2004	2 280 706	47.5	698 561	47.4	...	...
	2005	2 345 301	47.6	754 496	47.6	...	...
	2006	2 405 041	47.8	809 131	47.8	112 215[2]	45.9[2]
	2007	2 448 976	47.9	864 154	48.0	233 885	50.8
	2008	2 500 575	48.0	902 796	48.3	...	...
Guinea Guinée	2004	1 147 388	43.3	344 630	30.7	17 218	15.6
	2005	1 206 743	44.1	420 057[1]	32.9[1]	23 788	18.6
	2006	1 258 038	44.8	482 825	34.0	42 711	21.4
	2007	1 317 791	45.2	530 590[1]	35.3[1]	68 261	24.4[1]
	2008	1 364 491	45.2	530 705	36.2	80 222	24.4
Guinea-Bissau Guinée-Bissau	2004	232 292	...	...	...	...	...
	2005	252 488	...	50 507	...	3 122	...
	2006	269 287	...	55 176	...	3 689	...
Guyana Guyana	2004	114 637[1]	48.7[1]	68 979[1]	50.8[1]	6 933	65.3
	2005	116 756	49.0	70 615	50.0	7 278	67.6
	2006	110 503	49.0	70 848[1]	50.2[1]	7 370	68.7
	2007	109 243	48.7	72 970	48.8	7 532	68.1
	2008	107 456	48.8	74 673	50.3	7 306	58.7
Honduras Honduras	2004	1 257 358	49.0	...	...	122 874[1]	58.6[1]
	2005	1 231 533	49.1	...	...	...	...
	2006	1 293 333	49.1	...	...	...	...
	2007	1 308 119	49.1	554 297	55.0	...	...
	2008	1 276 495	49.0	566 938	55.3	147 740[2]	60.0[2]
Hungary Hongrie	2004	446 610	48.4	963 242	48.7	422 177	57.3
	2005	430 561	48.3	960 215	48.7	436 012	58.4
	2006	415 858	48.3	948 856	48.7	438 702	58.5
	2007	399 250	48.2	937 323	48.7	431 572	58.3

12 Education at the primary, secondary and tertiary levels *(continued)*

Number of students enrolled and percentage female

Enseignement primaire, secondaire et supérieur *(suite)*

Nombre d'élèves inscrits et pourcentage de sexe féminin

Country or area Pays ou zone	Year[t] Année[t]	Primary education Enseignement primaire Total	% F	Secondary education Enseignement secondaire Total	% F	Tertiary education Enseignement supérieur Total	% F
Iceland Islande	2004	30 984	48.4	32 700	49.5	14 710	64.5
	2005	30 785	48.3	33 323	49.3	15 169	64.9
	2006	30 421	48.6	33 900	49.5	15 721	64.4
	2007	30 084	49.0	34 434	50.2	15 821	64.1
India Inde	2004	136 193 772[1]	46.8[1]	84 569 081	42.6	11 852 936	38.2
	2005	138 787 993	46.7	89 461 794	42.9	11 777 296	39.4
	2006	139 169 873	46.6	91 529 430	43.2	12 852 684	39.9
	2007	140 357 454	47.0	96 049 060	44.0	14 862 962	39.1
Indonesia Indonésie	2004	29 142 093	48.7	16 353 933	49.1	3 551 092	43.8
	2005	29 149 746	48.3[1]	15 993 187	49.0[1]	3 660 270[1]	43.7[1]
	2006	28 982 708	48.2	16 797 809	49.3	3 657 429	...
	2007	29 796 705	48.1	18 716 929	49.4	3 755 187	49.5
Iran (Islamic Rep. of) Iran (Rép. islamique d')	2004	7 306 634	51.1	9 440 807	48.0	1 954 920	51.4
	2005	7 307 056	53.7	9 066 410	48.1	2 126 274	51.0
	2006	7 273 911	54.7	8 805 028	48.2	2 398 811	51.6
	2007	7 152 492	55.1	8 323 213	49.1	2 828 528	52.4
	2008	7 027 775	57.1	8 187 132	48.2	3 391 852	53.0
Iraq Iraq	2004	4 334 609	44.3	1 706 234	38.9	412 545	36.2
	2005[1]	4 430 267	44.3	1 751 164	38.9	424 908	36.2
Ireland Irlande	2004	450 413	48.5	320 560	50.7	188 315	55.2
	2005	454 060	48.5	317 337	51.0	186 561	54.9
	2006	461 588	48.5	313 479	50.6	186 044	55.1
	2007	475 836	48.5	316 015	50.6	190 349	55.2
Israel Israël	2004	775 021	48.8	607 224	48.8	301 227	55.8
	2005	784 663	48.9	610 341	48.7	310 937	56.0
	2006	802 555	49.0	613 366	48.6	310 014	55.1
	2007	826 314	48.9	615 973	48.8	327 108	55.8
Italy Italie	2004	2 768 386	48.5	4 505 699	48.5	1 986 497	56.2
	2005	2 771 247	48.3	4 507 408	48.4	2 014 998	56.6
	2006	2 790 254	48.3	4 531 571	48.4	2 029 023	57.0
	2007	2 820 150	48.3	4 553 163	48.3	2 033 642	57.2
Jamaica Jamaïque	2004	331 286	48.9	245 533	49.9	...	...
	2005	326 411	48.8	246 332	50.1	...	...
	2007	310 021	49.0	257 186	50.4	...	...
Japan Japon	2004	7 257 223	48.8	7 894 456	48.9	4 031 604	45.9
	2005	7 231 854	48.8	7 710 439	48.8	4 038 302	45.9
	2006	7 229 135	48.8	7 561 241	48.8	4 084 861	45.7
	2007	7 220 111	48.8	7 427 059	48.8	4 032 625	45.6
Jordan Jordanie	2004	799 888	48.9	615 731	49.2	214 106	51.2
	2005	804 904	49.0	625 682	49.2	217 823	50.3
	2006	805 457	49.3	649 242	49.5	220 103	51.6
	2007	807 702	49.3	670 836	49.5	231 657	51.3
Kazakhstan Kazakhstan	2004	1 079 598	48.8	2 090 152	48.6	664 449	57.5
	2005	1 023 974	48.8	2 039 911	48.5	753 181	58.1
	2006	972 931	48.8	1 982 190	48.4	780 783	58.0
	2007	947 807	48.8	1 874 213	48.6	772 600	58.2
	2008	956 019	48.8	1 778 106	48.4	719 802	58.2
	2009	950 976	48.8	1 740 549	48.2	635 241	58.3
Kenya Kenya	2004	5 926 078	48.3	2 426 350[1]	48.2[1]	108 407	37.5
	2005	6 075 706	48.7	2 470 410	48.7	113 532[1]	37.3[1]
	2006	6 101 390	49.0	2 583 755	48.1	...	...
	2007	6 687 510	49.4	2 729 040	46.5	...	...
	2008	6 868 810	49.2	3 106 919	47.6	...	...
	2009	...	...	...	...	167 983	41.2
Kiribati Kiribati	2004	15 611	49.6	11 581	52.8	...	...
	2005	16 132	49.4	11 331	51.7	...	...
Korea, Republic of Corée, République de	2004	4 125 423	47.1	3 692 513	47.2	3 224 875	36.9
	2005	4 031 496	47.2	3 786 224	47.1	3 210 184	37.1
	2006	3 933 186	47.4	3 864 005	46.9	3 204 036	37.5
	2007	3 837 696	47.6	3 917 400	46.8	3 208 591	38.0

12 Education at the primary, secondary and tertiary levels *(continued)*
Number of students enrolled and percentage female

Enseignement primaire, secondaire et supérieur *(suite)*
Nombre d'élèves inscrits et pourcentage de sexe féminin

Country or area Pays ou zone	Year[t] Année[t]	Primary education Enseignement primaire Total	 % F	Secondary education Enseignement secondaire Total	 % F	Tertiary education Enseignement supérieur Total	 % F
Kuwait	2004	158 271	49.0	267 114	50.0	36 866[1]	64.3[1]
Koweït	2005	202 826	48.5	248 895	49.8	38 630	70.2
	2006	203 423	48.8	236 410	49.8	37 521	65.4
	2007	211 576	48.7	247 233	48.9	...	...
	2008	208 608	48.8	...	...	...	...
Kyrgyzstan	2004	444 417	49.0	732 618	49.6	205 224	54.0
Kirghizistan	2005	434 155	48.7	721 205	49.5	220 460	55.3
	2006	423 930	48.8	718 585	49.5	233 463	55.6
	2007	407 669	48.8	713 613	49.5	239 380	56.1
	2008	399 833	48.8	696 833[2]	49.4[2]	296 267	57.1
Lao People's Dem. Rep.	2004	884 629	45.9	379 579	42.2	33 760	38.0
Rép. dém. pop. lao	2005	890 821	46.0	393 856	42.5	47 424	41.2
	2006	891 881	46.1	395 382	43.1	56 716	40.0
	2007	891 807	46.4	403 833	43.4	75 003	41.5
	2008	900 817	46.6	412 375	43.9	89 457	43.2
Latvia	2004	92 453	48.1	275 586	48.8	127 656	62.3
Lettonie	2005	84 369	47.9	271 631	49.0	130 706	63.2
	2006	78 796	47.9	258 432	49.1	131 125	63.3
	2007	121 345[4]	47.8	195 745[4]	49.6	129 497	63.9
Lebanon	2004	...	...	...	...	154 635	52.3
Liban	2005	...	...	...	...	165 730	52.8
	2006	470 988	48.5	381 466	51.6	173 123	53.2
	2007	473 134	48.4	384 162	52.0	187 055	54.0
	2008	467 311	48.4	384 726	51.8	196 682	54.7
Lesotho	2004	427 009	49.7	89 864[1]	55.7[1]	...	...
Lesotho	2005	422 278	49.6	94 460	55.8	7 918	56.9
	2006	424 855	49.6	93 996	56.0	8 500	55.2
	2007	400 943	49.4	101 738[1]	56.8[1]	...	...
Liberia	2006	538 450	47.2	130 860	41.9	...	...
Libéria	2008	539 887	46.9	158 242	42.9	...	...
Libyan Arab Jamah.	2004	745 428	48.0	...	...	...	...
Jamah. arabe libyenne	2005	713 902	48.4	701 536	53.3[1]	...	...
	2006	755 338	47.7	732 614	52.9	...	...
Liechtenstein	2004	2 266	49.8	3 273	45.2	532	26.7
Liechtenstein	2005	2 242	50.0	3 142	45.6	527	28.8
	2006	2 247	50.7	3 190	45.6	636	30.4
	2007	2 244	50.9	3 169	45.9	673	31.8
Lithuania	2004	170 216	48.6	431 303	48.8	182 656	60.0
Lituanie	2005	158 105	48.6	423 706	48.8	195 405	60.1
	2006	150 422	48.4	410 507	48.9	198 868	59.9
	2007	143 814	48.3	393 889	48.9	199 855	60.1
Luxembourg	2004	34 603	48.7	35 208	50.2	3 042[1]	52.9[1]
Luxembourg	2005	35 016	48.8	35 946	50.4	...	...
	2006	35 431	48.9	37 009	50.0	2 692	51.6
	2007	35 668	48.7	38 209	49.9	...	...
Madagascar	2004	3 366 470	49.0	...	...	42 143	47.3
Madagascar	2005	3 597 731	48.9	621 173[1]	49.0[1]	44 948	47.0
	2006	3 698 906	49.0	726 998	48.7	49 680	46.5
	2007	3 837 343	49.2	833 568	48.8	58 313	47.0
	2008	4 020 322	49.2	945 245	48.6	62 069	47.2
Malawi	2004	2 841 640	50.3	505 303	44.6	5 782[2]	35.3[1]
Malawi	2005	2 868 038	50.2	516 462	44.7	5 810[2]	35.3[1]
	2006	2 933 557	50.5	565 467	45.5	6 298[1]	33.6[1]
	2007	2 943 248	50.4	574 003	45.2	6 458	33.6
	2008	3 197 928	50.2	636 416	45.6	...	...
Malaysia	2004	3 159 376	48.6	2 583 993	51.9	731 077	55.4
Malaisie	2005	3 202 008	48.6	2 489 117	51.3	696 760	56.0
	2006	3 133 399	48.6	...	...	737 267	54.8

12 Education at the primary, secondary and tertiary levels *(continued)*

Number of students enrolled and percentage female

Enseignement primaire, secondaire et supérieur *(suite)*

Nombre d'élèves inscrits et pourcentage de sexe féminin

Country or area Pays ou zone	Year ‡ Année ‡	Primary education Enseignement primaire		Secondary education Enseignement secondaire		Tertiary education Enseignement supérieur	
		Total	% F	Total	% F	Total	% F
Maldives Maldives	2004	63 300	47.7	28 878[1]	51.9[1]	73[1]	69.9[1]
	2005	57 873	47.8	...	...	...	...
	2006	54 770	47.7	32 645[1]	50.3[1]	...	...
	2007	50 270	47.8	...	...	...	...
	2008	47 082	47.8	...	...	...	...
Mali Mali	2004	1 396 791	43.1	388 418	36.7	28 578	34.6
	2005	1 505 903	43.4	429 716	37.5[1]	33 222	34.6[1]
	2006	1 609 979	44.0	474 976	37.5	...	...
	2007	1 716 956	44.4	533 849	39.1	66 094	31.1
	2008	1 823 037	44.8	612 012	38.6	67 839	31.1
Malta Malte	2004	31 064	48.2	41 723	46.8	7 867	55.9
	2005	29 596	48.0	38 479	48.6	9 441	56.3
	2007	27 782	48.5	36 977	49.0	9 811	57.4
Marshall Islands Iles Marshall	2004	8 250	47.5	5 846	49.8	...	...
	2005[1]	8 393	47.5	5 901	49.8	...	...
	2007	8 215	47.9	5 369	49.1	...	...
Mauritania Mauritanie	2004	434 181	49.4	88 926	45.3	9 292	23.7
	2005	443 615	50.0	92 796	45.9	8 758	24.6
	2006	465 970	49.8	98 946[2]	45.0[2]	10 157	25.7
	2007	483 776	50.0	102 130[1]	45.6[1]	11 794	...
	2008	473 688	50.3	99 258[1]	45.5[1]	...	...
Mauritius Maurice	2004	126 226	49.3	122 556	49.0	17 781	57.6
	2005	123 562	49.2	127 891[1]	49.1[1]	16 852	55.3
	2006	121 387	49.2	131 653[1]	49.5[1]	16 773	52.9
	2007	119 310	49.2	133 084[1]	49.5[1]	...	...
	2008	119 022	49.0	131 932[1]	49.6[1]	13 509	53.3
	2009	...	...	...	...	15 947	54.1
Mexico Mexique	2004	14 781 327	48.8	10 403 853	51.2	2 322 781	50.0
	2005	14 700 005	48.8	10 564 404	51.2	2 384 858	50.3
	2006	14 595 195	48.7	10 883 455	51.3	2 446 726	50.3
	2007	14 631 498	48.8	11 122 276	51.3	2 528 664	50.3
Micronesia (Fed. States of) Micronésie (Etats féd. de)	2004	19 105	48.3	13 506	48.8	...	...
	2005	18 793	48.1	13 634	49.3	...	...
	2007	18 512	49.0	14 742[1]	...	...	...
Monaco Monaco	2004	1 831	...	3 078	...	...	...
	2008	1 852	47.5	3 015	48.0	...	...
	2009	1 837	48.9	3 017	48.3	...	...
Mongolia Mongolie	2004	235 730	49.4	333 193	52.5	108 738	61.8
	2005	251 205	49.5	339 249	52.4	123 824	61.4
	2006	249 622	49.5	329 269	52.1	138 019	60.7
	2007	239 262	49.4	328 009	51.8	142 411	60.5
	2008	239 663	49.3	327 789	51.6	151 533	60.9
Montserrat Montserrat	2004	468	44.7	284	48.9	...	...
	2005	509	46.2	298	49.3	...	...
	2006	508	45.9	328	46.3	...	...
	2007	497	49.3	347	46.4	...	...
Morocco Maroc	2004	4 070 182	46.5	1 879 483	44.8	343 599	45.7
	2005	4 022 600	46.4	1 952 456[1]	45.1[1]	366 879	45.1
	2006	3 943 831	46.3	2 061 046	...	384 595	45.2
	2007	3 939 177	46.5	2 173 454	45.5[1]	369 142	47.6
	2008	3 878 640	46.7	...	...	401 093	47.3
Mozambique Mozambique	2004	3 569 473	45.3	243 428	41.1	22 256	31.6
	2005	3 942 829	45.7	305 877	40.9	28 298	33.1
	2006	4 172 749	46.2	367 395	41.8	...	...
	2007	4 563 633	46.4	444 926	42.2	...	...
	2008	4 904 434	46.7	512 266	42.8	...	...
Myanmar Myanmar	2004	4 932 646	49.7	2 544 437	48.0	...	...
	2005	4 948 198	49.9	2 589 312	49.1	...	...
	2006	4 969 445	49.6	2 696 307	49.3	...	...
	2007	5 013 582	...	2 686 198	49.9	507 660	57.9

Education at the primary, secondary and tertiary levels *(continued)*

Number of students enrolled and percentage female

Enseignement primaire, secondaire et supérieur *(suite)*

Nombre d'élèves inscrits et pourcentage de sexe féminin

Country or area Pays ou zone	Year[t] Année[t]	Primary education Enseignement primaire Total	% F	Secondary education Enseignement secondaire Total	% F	Tertiary education Enseignement supérieur Total	% F
Namibia Namibie	2004	403 412	50.0	144 289	53.0	12 197	53.2
	2005	404 198	49.8	148 104	53.1	13 566	46.7
	2006	402 529	49.8	152 637	53.4	13 185	46.7
	2007	409 508	49.6	158 162	53.9	...	...
	2008	407 402	49.5	163 873	53.8	19 707	56.8
Nauru Nauru	2004	1 529	47.4	508	52.4	...	...
	2005	1 812	48.2	600	50.7	...	...
	2006	1 393	47.1	815	51.7	...	...
	2007	1 235	48.6	689	51.4	...	...
Nepal Népal	2004	4 025 692	45.4	...	...	147 123	27.6
	2005	4 030 045	46.3	2 054 165	44.7[1]	...	...
	2006	4 502 697	47.4	1 983 561[1]	45.5[1]	...	...
	2007	4 515 059	48.3	1 998 990[1]	46.2[1]	255 354	...
	2008	4 418 713	48.9	2 305 166	46.7	...	...
Netherlands Pays-Bas	2004	1 283 014	48.2	1 396 696	48.5	543 396	50.9
	2005	1 277 990	48.2	1 410 547	48.4	564 983	51.0
	2006	1 277 478	48.2	1 423 262	48.4	579 622	51.1
	2007	1 280 571	48.3	1 444 057	48.4	590 121	51.5
New Zealand Nouvelle-Zélande	2004	353 062	48.5	503 241	50.3	243 425	58.4
	2005	352 845	48.5	526 152	50.2	239 983	58.7
	2006	350 810	48.6	522 325	49.8	237 784	59.0
	2007	349 080	48.8	526 974	49.3	242 650	58.7
Nicaragua Nicaragua	2004	941 957	48.6	416 405	52.7	...	...
	2005	945 089	48.4	437 853	52.7	...	...
	2006	966 206	48.4	448 258	52.6	...	...
	2007	952 964	48.5	470 520	52.5	...	...
	2008	944 341	48.4	462 198	52.6	...	...
Niger Niger	2004	980 033	40.3	158 343	38.5	8 774	27.4
	2005	1 064 056	40.8	181 641	39.1	10 799	29.6
	2006	1 126 073	41.1	216 961	38.8	11 208	26.6
	2007	1 235 065	41.5	213 991	37.9	10 869	28.5
	2008	1 389 194	42.7	232 498	37.6	12 823	29.6
	2009	1 554 102	43.1	...	...	15 293[1]	28.2[1]
Nigeria Nigéria	2004	21 395 510	44.7	6 580 011[1]	43.4[1]	1 289 656	34.6
	2005	22 115 432	44.9	6 703 139[1]	44.4[1]	1 391 527	40.7
	2006	22 861 884	45.4	6 436 449	44.2	...	...
	2007	21 632 070	46.0	6 068 160	43.0	...	...
Niue Nioué	2004	184	51.1	209	50.7	...	...
	2005	178	50.6	206	48.1	...	...
Norway Norvège	2004	432 345	48.7	400 159	49.5	213 845	59.6
	2005	429 652	48.7	403 026	48.9	213 940	59.6
	2006	429 680	48.8	412 311	48.5	214 711	59.8
	2007	430 747	48.7	419 698	48.3	215 237	60.3
Occupied Palestinian Terr. Terr. palestinien occupé	2004	388 948	49.0	628 495	50.1	121 928	49.5
	2005	387 138	48.8	656 797	50.1	138 139	49.5
	2006	381 904	49.0	685 585	50.4	150 128	52.7
	2007	383 559	49.0	701 715	50.5	169 373	53.7
	2008	...	...	...	...	180 905	53.9
Oman Oman	2004	306 210	48.6	286 413	47.9	41 578	51.8
	2005	297 120	48.8	292 783	47.7	48 483	50.8
	2006	287 938	48.9	299 484	47.8	68 154	49.9
	2007	278 461	49.1	306 377	47.8	69 018	53.1
	2008	271 407	49.2	307 094	48.0	72 632	54.3
Pakistan Pakistan	2004	16 207 286	40.8	8 249 163[1]	42.3[1]	520 666	42.7
	2005	17 257 947	41.8	7 994 299[1]	42.3[1]	782 621	45.1
	2006	16 687 658	42.5	8 421 015	42.4	820 347	44.5
	2007	17 979 190	43.6	9 145 084	41.8	954 698[2]	44.5[2]
	2008	18 175 801	43.8	9 339 991	41.8	973 792[2]	44.5[2]

12

Education at the primary, secondary and tertiary levels *(continued)*
Number of students enrolled and percentage female

Enseignement primaire, secondaire et supérieur *(suite)*
Nombre d'élèves inscrits et pourcentage de sexe féminin

Country or area Pays ou zone	Year ‡ Année ‡	Primary education Enseignement primaire		Secondary education Enseignement secondaire		Tertiary education Enseignement supérieur	
		Total	% F	Total	% F	Total	% F
Palau Palaos	2004	1 855	48.0	2 273	50.4	...	...
	2005[1]	1 913	48.1	2 282	...	...	...
	2007	1 544	47.8[1]	2 448	49.6[1]	...	...
Panama Panama	2004	429 837	48.3	253 900	50.8	128 558	61.6
	2005	430 152	48.2	256 224	50.8	126 242	61.2
	2006	436 945	48.3	257 378	51.0	130 838	60.9
	2007	446 176	48.3	260 694	50.8	132 660	60.6
	2008	445 107	48.2	266 760	51.0	...	...
Papua New Guinea Papouasie-Nvl-Guinée	2004	508 333	44.9	...	...	...	...
	2005	531 759	44.4	...	...	...	...
	2006	532 250	44.3	...	...	...	...
Paraguay Paraguay	2004	930 918	48.4	526 001	49.7	149 120[1]	56.6[1]
	2005	933 995	48.4	529 309	49.9	156 167[1]	52.3[1]
	2006	914 138	48.4	529 329	50.1	...	...
Peru Pérou	2004	4 133 386	49.0	2 661 880	49.6	896 501[1]	50.0[1]
	2005	4 077 361	49.1	2 691 311	49.6	909 315[1]	50.0[1]
	2006	4 026 316	49.0	2 760 349	49.9	952 437[1]	50.9[1]
	2007	3 993 965	49.0	2 861 313	50.0	...	...
Philippines Philippines	2004	13 017 973	48.5	6 308 792	51.6	2 420 997	55.2
	2005	13 083 744	48.6	6 352 482	51.7	2 402 649	54.2
	2006	13 006 648	48.5	6 301 582	51.7	2 483 988	54.5
	2007	13 145 210	48.5	6 365 985	51.4	...	...
Poland Pologne	2004	2 855 692	48.6	3 480 054	49.1	2 044 298	57.6
	2005	2 723 661	48.6	3 444 903	48.6	2 118 081	57.5
	2006	2 602 020	48.6	3 316 939	48.4	2 145 687	57.4
	2007	2 484 820	48.6	3 205 849	48.5	2 146 926	57.4
Portugal Portugal	2004	758 476	47.5	665 213	51.4	395 063	56.1
	2005	752 739	47.6	669 529	51.2	380 937	55.7
	2006	750 493	47.6	661 748	51.0	367 312	55.2
	2007	753 646	47.5	680 338	50.7	366 729	54.0
Qatar Qatar	2004	65 351	48.5	53 953	48.9	9 287	71.4
	2005	69 991	48.7	55 705	49.4	9 699[1]	68.2[1]
	2006	70 927	48.8	58 787	49.2	10 161[1]	67.6[1]
	2007	75 451	48.7	61 226	49.5	11 132	65.2
	2008	78 123	49.0	66 084	48.9	12 545	63.8
Republic of Moldova République de Moldova	2004	201 650	48.6	406 716	50.3	119 981	57.0
	2005	184 159	48.5	394 469	50.1	130 350	58.7
	2006	171 024	48.6	381 543	50.1	143 750	57.4
	2007	160 528	48.5	367 636	49.9	148 449[2]	57.3[2]
	2008	151 736	48.3	345 187	49.9	143 601	58.4
Romania Roumanie	2004	1 005 533	48.4	2 154 734	49.3	685 718	54.8
	2005	970 295	48.4	2 089 646	49.2	738 806	54.6
	2006	938 095	48.4	2 013 016	49.0	834 969	55.4
	2007	917 829	48.5	1 954 077	48.7	928 175	56.1
Russian Federation Fédération de Russie	2004	...	...	13 558 904	48.8	8 605 952	57.0
	2005	5 308 605	48.8	12 433 155	48.7	9 003 208	57.1
	2006	5 164 735	48.9	11 548 337	48.5	9 167 277	56.9
	2007	5 010 284	48.8	10 797 816	48.4	9 370 428	56.8
Rwanda Rwanda	2004	1 752 588	50.8	203 551	47.7	25 233	39.1
	2005[1]	1 851 879	51.3	218 227	47.8	26 378	39.0
	2006	2 019 991	51.3	...	...	...	...
	2007	2 150 430	50.9	266 518	47.6	...	...
	2008	2 190 270	50.9	288 036	47.9	45 128	...
Saint Kitts and Nevis Saint-Kitts-et-Nevis	2004	6 394	50.2	3 903[1]	52.0[1]	...	...
	2005	6 350	49.8	3 939[1]	50.7[1]	...	...
	2007	6 172	49.5	4 522	49.6	...	...
	2008	6 474	49.8	4 396	50.8	...	...

Country or area / Pays ou zone	Year [t] / Année [t]	Primary education / Enseignement primaire		Secondary education / Enseignement secondaire		Tertiary education / Enseignement supérieur	
		Total	% F	Total	% F	Total	% F
Saint Lucia / Sainte-Lucie	2004	23 821	48.3	14 209	52.6	2 285	77.8
	2005	23 573	48.6	13 786	54.3	2 197	73.8
	2006	24 046	47.8	14 377	53.9	1 628	84.6
	2007	22 028	48.7	15 146	52.5	1 438	70.7
	2008	20 938	49.1	16 014	50.9	2 577	69.7
Saint Vincent-Grenadines / Saint Vincent-Grenadines	2004	17 536	48.4	10 398	51.6[1]	...	...
	2005	17 858	47.0	9 780	55.2	...	...
	2007	15 928	48.3	...	...	...	...
	2008	15 532	47.4	11 641	52.3	...	...
Samoa / Samoa	2004	31 175	48.0	23 764	50.6	...	...
	2005[1]	31 596	48.0	24 242	50.7	...	...
	2007	30 199	48.0	...	...	...	...
San Marino / Saint-Marin	2004	1 445	...	...	...	...	...
	2008	1 573	47.6	2 223	48.7	929	57.4
Sao Tome and Principe / Sao Tomé-et-Principe	2004	29 784	48.7	7 423	50.5	...	...
	2005	30 468	48.6	8 091	51.1	...	...
	2006[1]	31 066	48.6	8 142	51.2	...	...
	2007	31 397	49.3	8 997	51.2	...	...
	2008	32 584	49.0	8 518	51.1	...	...
	2009	33 789	49.7	9 668	52.2	704	47.6
Saudi Arabia / Arabie saoudite	2004	...	...	...	...	573 732	58.7
	2005	3 097 604[2]	49.0[2]	2 609 567[2]	48.0[2]	603 671	58.1
	2006	...	...	...	...	636 445	57.9
	2007	3 173 807	48.8[2]	2 826 049	...	...	...
	2008	3 211 387	48.7	2 885 035	46.4	666 662	61.6
Senegal / Sénégal	2004	1 382 749	48.3	360 016	41.6	52 282	...
	2005	1 444 163	48.6	405 899	42.5	59 127[2]	...
	2006	1 473 464	49.2	447 425[1]	42.8[1]	62 539	31.7
	2007	1 572 178	49.6	505 097[1]	43.0[1]	71 211	34.6
	2008	1 618 303	50.2	592 831	44.3	91 359[2]	35.3[2]
Serbia / Serbie	2004[1]	328 439	48.8	641 743	49.5	...	...
	2005	324 490	48.8	632 761	49.5	...	...
	2006	312 469	48.8	622 854	49.6	...	...
	2007	297 816	48.7	615 135	49.4	238 710	55.3
	2008	289 785	48.8	608 456	49.4	237 598	55.4
Seychelles / Seychelles	2004	8 906	48.8	7 406	50.7	...	...
	2005	9 204	48.4	7 520	48.2	...	...
	2007	8 864	49.3	7 816	50.1	...	...
Sierra Leone / Sierra Leone	2007	1 322 205	47.5	239 579	41.0	...	...
Singapore / Singapour	2007	301 101	48.1	232 100	48.2	183 627	48.5
	2008	299 704	48.2	231 144	48.2	...	...
	2009	...	...	...	...	198 634	49.1
Slovakia / Slovaquie	2004	254 906	48.5	682 780	49.3	164 667	54.1
	2005	242 459	48.5	672 670	49.2	181 419	55.3
	2006	235 378	48.5	650 438	49.2	197 943	57.7
	2007	230 536	48.6	617 109	49.1	217 952	58.9
Slovenia / Slovénie	2004	93 371	48.6	187 817	48.8	104 396	56.9
	2005	93 156	48.4	181 299	48.7	112 228	57.8
	2006	93 274	48.4	174 330	48.7	114 794	58.4
	2007	95 173	48.4	165 467	48.5	115 944	58.3
Solomon Islands / Iles Salomon	2004[1]	70 906	46.8	22 157	43.5	...	...
	2005	75 082	46.8	22 487	43.5	...	...
	2006	80 649	47.1	26 345	43.5	...	...
	2007	83 232	47.1	27 332	43.5	...	...
South Africa / Afrique du Sud	2004	7 444 142	48.7	4 593 492	51.5	...	...
	2005	7 314 449	48.7	4 657 674	51.4	...	...
	2006	7 256 518	48.7	4 772 456[1]	51.3[1]	...	...
	2007	7 312 258	48.8	4 779 747[1]	51.0[1]	...	...

12 Education at the primary, secondary and tertiary levels *(continued)*

Number of students enrolled and percentage female

Enseignement primaire, secondaire et supérieur *(suite)*

Nombre d'élèves inscrits et pourcentage de sexe féminin

Country or area Pays ou zone	Year[t] Année[t]	Primary education Enseignement primaire		Secondary education Enseignement secondaire		Tertiary education Enseignement supérieur	
		Total	% F	Total	% F	Total	% F
Spain Espagne	2004	2 497 513	48.4	3 048 188	50.2	1 839 903	53.8
	2005	2 484 903	48.3	3 107 816	50.1	1 809 353	53.7
	2006	2 501 205	48.3	3 091 036	50.1	1 789 254	53.9
	2007	2 555 757	48.3	3 080 161	50.2	1 777 498	54.0
Sri Lanka Sri Lanka	2004[1]	1 612 318	...	2 332 326	49.5	...	...
	2005[1]	1 635 308	49.1	...	...	...	...
	2006	1 611 763	49.0	...	...	...	...
	2007	1 621 617	49.0	...	...	...	...
Sudan Soudan	2004	3 208 186	45.5	1 393 778	47.1	...	...
	2005	3 278 090	45.6	1 369 735	47.5	...	...
	2006	3 880 705	45.6	1 446 539	48.1	...	...
	2007	3 959 310	45.3	1 462 798	47.3	...	...
	2008	4 351 957	46.0	1 579 567	46.9	...	...
	2009	4 744 468	46.5	1 837 456	46.0	...	...
Suriname Suriname	2005	65 527	48.3	45 818	55.8	...	...
	2006	66 121	48.3	46 725	56.3	...	...
	2007	65 020	47.9	47 235	56.6	...	...
	2008	69 604	48.3	48 134	55.5	...	...
Swaziland Swaziland	2004	218 352	48.1	67 696	49.1	6 594	52.4
	2005	221 596	48.1	71 124	49.9	5 897	52.0
	2006	229 686	47.9	77 169	50.1	5 692	49.8
	2007	232 572	47.9	83 049	47.1	...	...
Sweden Suède	2004	690 758	48.6	711 798	49.5	429 623	59.6
	2005	658 461	48.7	735 494	48.6	426 723	59.6
	2006	626 847	48.7	750 567	48.6	422 614	59.6
	2007	601 120	48.6	760 491	48.5	413 710	59.9
Switzerland Suisse	2004	532 092	48.5	563 701	47.2	195 947	44.9
	2005	524 222	48.6	574 783	47.3	199 696	46.0
	2006	517 056	48.5	584 073	47.3	204 999	47.0
	2007	510 804	48.5	592 454	47.5	213 112	47.6
Syrian Arab Republic Rép. arabe syrienne	2004	2 192 764	47.6	2 249 116	47.2	...	...
	2005	2 252 145	47.8	2 389 383	47.4	...	...
	2006	2 279 545	47.8	2 464 688	47.7	...	...
	2007	2 310 168	47.8	2 549 444	48.2	...	...
	2008	2 356 403	47.9	2 626 228	48.5	...	...
Tajikistan Tadjikistan	2004	690 270	48.0	973 673	45.1	108 456	24.8
	2005	693 078	48.2	984 410	44.8	119 317	25.9
	2006	687 900	48.0	998 928	44.7	133 385	26.8
	2007	680 308	48.2	1 012 275	45.0	147 294	27.5
	2008	692 247	48.1	1 019 250	45.9	155 420	28.2
Thailand Thaïlande	2004	6 054 517	48.4	4 253 380	50.9	2 251 453	53.7
	2005	5 974 615	48.1	4 533 173	50.5[1]	2 359 127	52.4
	2006	5 843 512	48.4	4 530 029	50.8	2 338 572	51.0
	2007	5 703 756	48.4	4 789 339	51.1	2 503 572	54.5
	2008	5 564 622	48.4	4 728 761	51.0	2 430 047	54.0
TFYR of Macedonia L'ex-R.Y. Macédoine	2004	113 362	48.4	215 760	48.0	46 637	57.0
	2005	110 149	48.3	214 005	48.0	49 364	56.7
	2006	105 045	48.2	...	...	48 368	56.7
	2007	100 911	48.2	208 364	47.8	58 199	54.5
Timor-Leste Timor-Leste	2004	183 483	47.1	73 005	48.1	...	...
	2005	177 970	46.9	74 822	48.7	...	...
	2007	173 983	47.5	...	...	...	...
	2008	201 264	47.3	...	...	...	...
	2009	...	...	...	...	16 727	40.0
Togo Togo	2004	984 846	45.6	375 385	34.0	...	...
	2005	996 707	45.9	404 470	34.7	...	...
	2006	1 051 872	46.3	430 064	35.3	28 076[1]	...
	2007	1 021 617	46.4	408 964	34.6[1]	32 502	...
Tokelau[1] Tokélaou[1]	2004	243	57.2	175	45.1	...	...

Education at the primary, secondary and tertiary levels *(continued)*

Number of students enrolled and percentage female

Enseignement primaire, secondaire et supérieur *(suite)*

Nombre d'élèves inscrits et pourcentage de sexe féminin

Country or area Pays ou zone	Year[t] Année[t]	Primary education Enseignement primaire Total	% F	Secondary education Enseignement secondaire Total	% F	Tertiary education Enseignement supérieur Total	% F
Tonga Tonga	2004	17 113	46.9	14 032	49.2[1]	657[1]	59.8[1]
	2005	17 032	47.3	...	...	...	...
	2006	16 941	47.1	13 938	48.4	...	...
Trinidad and Tobago Trinité-et-Tobago	2004	137 313[2]	48.5[2]	105 381[2]	51.1[2]	16 751	55.4
	2005	129 703[2]	48.6[2]	97 080[2]	50.4[2]	16 920[1]	55.6[1]
	2007	130 242	48.5	98 490[1]	51.0[1]	...	...
	2008	130 880	48.5	95 275[1]	51.1[1]	...	...
Tunisia Tunisie	2004	1 228 347	47.7	1 210 012	...	291 842	56.5
	2005	1 184 301	47.7	1 239 468	51.1	311 569	57.2
	2006	1 134 414	47.7	1 247 046	51.0[1]	325 325	57.5
	2007	1 068 822	47.7	1 268 219	...	326 185	59.0
Turkey Turquie	2004	7 872 546[1]	47.6[1]	5 330 923[1]	42.0[1]	1 972 662	41.4
	2005	7 947 603[1]	47.7[1]	5 075 720[1]	44.2[1]	2 106 351	41.9
	2006	7 949 758[1]	47.9[1]	5 388 119[1]	44.5[1]	2 342 898	42.4
	2007	8 065 193[1]	47.7[1]	5 527 208[1]	44.4[1]	2 453 664	42.6
Turks and Caicos Islands Iles Turques et Caïques	2004	2 117	50.9	1 516	48.9	...	...
	2005	2 220	51.1	1 686[1]	47.8[1]	...	...
Tuvalu Tuvalu	2004	1 404	49.9	...	...	...	...
	2005	1 450	48.3	...	...	...	...
	2006	1 460	48.0	...	...	...	...
Uganda Ouganda	2004	7 377 292	49.4	732 792	44.4	88 360	38.4
	2005	7 223 879	49.6	760 337[1]	44.5[1]	...	...
	2006	7 363 721	49.9	849 129[1]	45.0[1]	92 605	43.3
	2007	7 537 971	49.9	1 001 987[1]	45.0[1]	...	...
	2008	7 963 979	49.9	1 145 459	45.8	107 728	44.3
Ukraine Ukraine	2004	1 850 734	48.6	4 445 974	48.5[2]	2 465 074	53.9[2]
	2005	1 945 715	48.7	4 042 827	46.8[2]	2 604 875	54.1
	2006	1 753 689	48.7	3 896 263	48.4[2]	2 740 342	54.2[2]
	2007	1 647 847	48.7[2]	3 708 736	48.7[2]	2 819 248	54.3
	2008	1 573 458	48.8[2]	3 498 524	48.3[2]	2 847 713	54.4[2]
United Arab Emirates Emirats arabes unis	2004	254 602	48.3	279 496	49.1	...	...
	2005	262 807	48.5	284 978	48.9	...	...
	2006	272 331	48.6	298 447	49.0	...	...
	2007	284 034	48.5	310 999[1]	48.8[1]	...	...
	2008	...	...	...	...	77 428	60.2
United Kingdom Royaume-Uni	2004	4 685 733	48.8	5 699 526	49.4	2 247 441	57.0
	2005	4 634 991	48.8	5 747 422	49.4	2 287 541	57.2
	2006	4 517 618	48.9	5 357 793	49.3	2 336 111	57.3
	2007	4 409 184	48.9	5 306 369	49.2	2 362 815	57.2
United Rep. of Tanzania Rép.-Unie de Tanzanie	2004	7 083 063	48.8	...	...	42 948	29.2
	2005	7 541 208	48.9	...	...	51 080[1]	32.4[1]
	2006	7 959 884	49.1	...	...	...	...
	2007	8 316 925	49.3	...	...	55 134	32.3
	2008	8 601 814	49.3	...	...	...	...
United States Etats-Unis	2004	24 559 494	48.1	24 185 786	49.2	16 900 471	57.1
	2005	24 454 602	48.6	24 431 934	49.2	17 272 044	57.2
	2006	24 319 033	49.0	24 552 317	48.6	17 487 475	57.4
	2007	24 492 041	48.8	24 731 027	48.9	17 758 870	57.4
Uruguay Uruguay	2004	366 205	48.3	339 057	52.6	...	...
	2005	365 536	48.4	323 087	52.6	...	...
	2006	365 388	48.3	323 027	52.8	113 368	61.9
	2007	359 439	48.3	294 852	48.8	158 841	62.9
Uzbekistan Ouzbékistan	2004	2 451 125	48.7	4 338 358	48.1	376 904	43.6
	2005	2 383 326	48.7	4 515 852	48.4	265 957	40.8
	2006	2 277 191	48.6	4 542 174	48.5	280 837	40.9
	2007	2 164 897	48.5	4 598 037	48.7	288 550	41.0
Vanuatu Vanuatu	2004	38 960	47.8	13 837	44.7	955[1]	36.1[1]
	2005	38 530	47.7	...	...	...	...
	2006	37 060	47.8	...	...	...	...
	2007	37 817	47.4	...	...	...	...

12 Education at the primary, secondary and tertiary levels *(continued)*

Number of students enrolled and percentage female

Enseignement primaire, secondaire et supérieur *(suite)*

Nombre d'élèves inscrits et pourcentage de sexe féminin

Country or area Pays ou zone	Year[ŧ] Année[ŧ]	Primary education Enseignement primaire		Secondary education Enseignement secondaire		Tertiary education Enseignement supérieur	
		Total	% F	Total	% F	Total	% F
Venezuela (Boliv. Rep. of) Venezuela (Rép. boliv. du)	2004	3 453 379	48.4	1 953 506	52.3	1 049 780[2]	...
	2005	3 449 290	48.5	2 028 388	52.1	...	...
	2006	3 452 062	48.4	2 104 857	51.9	...	...
	2007	3 521 139	48.3	2 174 619	51.8	...	...
	2008	3 439 199	48.3	2 224 214	51.4	2 109 331	62.1[2]
Viet Nam Viet Nam	2004	8 350 191	47.3	9 588 698	48.1	1 328 485[1]	40.9[1]
	2005	7 773 484	47.5	9 939 319	48.6	1 354 543	40.9
	2006	7 317 813	47.9	9 975 113	48.8	1 427 046	48.2
	2007	7 041 312	47.8	9 845 407	49.5	1 587 609	49.3
	2008	6 871 795	46.2	9 543 007	50.2	1 654 846	48.8
Yemen Yémen	2004	3 107 801	40.5	1 446 369	31.2	192 071	26.2
	2005	3 219 564	41.6	1 455 206	32.1	201 043	26.1
	2006	...	...	...	...	200 853	27.2
	2007	...	...	...	...	236 972	28.7
	2008	3 282 457	43.6	...	...	...	...
Zambia Zambie	2004	2 251 357	48.7	363 613	44.1	...	...
	2005	2 572 846	48.7	442 969	44.6	...	...
	2006	2 678 610	49.3	...	...	...	...
	2007	2 790 312	49.1	607 296	46.9	...	...
	2008	2 909 436	49.3	734 800	45.4	...	...
Zimbabwe Zimbabwe	2006	2 445 520	49.6	831 488	48.1	...	...

Source:
United Nations Educational, Scientific and Cultural Organization (UNESCO) Institute for Statistics, Montreal, the UNESCO Institute for Statistics (UIS) database, May 2010.

ŧ Data relate to the calendar year in which the academic year ends.

1 UIS estimation.
2 National estimation.
3 For statistical purposes, the data for China do not include those for the Hong Kong Special Administrative Region (Hong Kong SAR) and Macao Special Administrative Region (Macao SAR).
4 The first two grades of secondary education were reclassified to primary education.

Source :
L'Institut de statistique de l'Organisation des Nations Unies pour l'éducation, la science et la culture (UNESCO), Montréal, la base de données de l'institut de statistique de l'UNESCO (ISU), mai 2010.

ŧ Les données se réfèrent à l'année civile durant laquelle l'année scolaire se termine.

1 Estimation de l'ISU.
2 Estimation nationale.
3 Pour la présentation des statistiques, les données pour la Chine ne comprennent pas la Région Administrative Spéciale de Hong Kong (Hong Kong RAS) et la Région Administrative Spéciale de Macao (Macao RAS).
4 Les deux premières classes de l'enseignement secondaire sont desormais categoriseés dans l'enseignement primaire.

13 Public expenditure on education

Percentage of GNI and of government expenditure

Dépenses publiques afférentes à l'éducation

Pourcentage par rapport au RNB et aux dépenses du gouvernement

Country or area Pays ou zone	As % of Gross National Income (GNI) En % du Revenu National Brut (RNB)				As % of total government expenditure En % des dépenses totales du gouvernement			
	2005	2006	2007	2008	2005	2006	2007	2008
Andorra Andorre	1.7	2.3	2.6	...	...	...	...	...
Angola Angola	2.9	3.0	...	...	...	...	...	...
Anguilla Anguilla	4.0	...	...	...	14.0	...	...	10.7
Argentina Argentine	...	4.6	...	...	...	14.0	...	...
Armenia Arménie	2.6	2.6	2.9	...	14.6	15.0	15.0	...
Aruba Aruba	5.1	...	5.1	...	15.4	...	17.3	...
Australia Australie	5.0	5.4	...	...	14.0	14.0	...	...
Austria Autriche	5.5	...	...	...	10.9	...	...	...
Azerbaijan Azerbaïdjan	2.7	2.3	2.0	2.1	19.6	17.4	12.6	11.9
Bangladesh Bangladesh	...	2.3	2.4	2.2	...	14.2	15.8	14.0
Barbados Barbade	7.2	...	6.7	6.4	16.4	...	...	15.7
Belarus Bélarus	5.9	6.1	5.2	...	11.3	12.9	9.3	...
Belgium Belgique	5.9	6.0	...	...	12.1	12.4	...	...
Belize Belize	...	...	5.6	...	...	...	...	...
Benin Bénin	...	3.9	3.6	...	...	18.0	15.9	...
Bermuda Bermudes	2.0	1.2	...	...	...	...	...	...
Bhutan Bhoutan	7.5	...	...	5.2	17.2	...	...	...
Bolivia (Plurinational State of) Bolivie (État plurinational de)	...	5.8	...	...	...	...	...	...
Botswana Botswana	10.8	...	8.8	...	21.5	...	21.0	...
Brazil Brésil	4.6	5.1	...	...	14.5	16.2	...	...
British Virgin Islands Iles Vierges britanniques	3.3	4.0	3.4	...	12.5	...	14.6	...
Bulgaria Bulgarie	4.5	4.4	...	...	...	11.6	...	...
Burkina Faso Burkina Faso	4.5	4.5	4.6	...	16.4	15.4	...	...
Burundi Burundi	5.2	...	...	7.2	17.7	...	...	22.3
Cambodia Cambodge	...	...	1.7	...	...	...	12.4	...

13 Public expenditure on education *(continued)*
Percentage of GNI and of government expenditure

Dépenses publiques afférentes à l'éducation *(suite)*
Pourcentage par rapport au RNB et aux dépenses du gouvernement

Country or area Pays ou zone	As % of Gross National Income (GNI) En % du Revenu National Brut (RNB)				As % of total government expenditure En % des dépenses totales du gouvernement			
	2005	2006	2007	2008	2005	2006	2007	2008
Cameroon Cameroun	3.2	3.4	3.9	...	15.9	16.8	17.0	...
Canada Canada	5.0	...	...	...	...	...	...	...
Cape Verde Cap-Vert	...	6.3	5.8	5.8	...	15.6	16.4	16.7
Cayman Islands Iles Caïmanes	...	2.9	...	...	...	...	...	...
Central African Rep. Rép. centrafricaine	...	1.4	1.3	...	...	...	12.0	...
Chad Tchad	2.3	...	...	...	10.1	...	...	...
Chile Chili	3.7	3.6	3.8	...	16.0	16.0	18.2	...
China, Hong Kong SAR Chine, Hong Kong RAS	4.1	3.9	3.5	3.2	23.0	23.9	23.2	23.0
China, Macao SAR Chine, Macao RAS	2.6	2.6	2.0	...	14.1	14.9	16.2	...
Colombia Colombie	4.2	4.0	4.2	4.1	11.1	14.2	12.6	14.9
Congo Congo	2.5	...	...	...	8.1	...	...	...
Costa Rica Costa Rica	...	4.8	4.9	5.2	...	20.6	...	22.8
Côte d'Ivoire Côte d'Ivoire	...	...	...	4.8	...	...	...	24.6
Cuba Cuba	...	9.3	13.6	...	16.6	14.2	20.6	18.5
Cyprus Chypre	6.6	7.3	...	...	14.5	9.5	...	...
Czech Republic République tchèque	4.5	4.9	...	...	9.5	10.5	...	...
Denmark Danemark	8.2	7.8	...	...	15.5	15.5	...	...
Djibouti Djibouti	7.6	7.6	8.0	...	...	22.4	22.8	...
Dominica Dominique	...	...	4.6	5.0	...	...	10.7	11.3
Dominican Republic Rép. dominicaine	...	...	2.3	...	...	...	11.0	...
Egypt Egypte	4.8	4.0	3.7	3.6	16.0	12.0	12.6	12.1
El Salvador El Salvador	2.8	3.1	3.1[1]	3.7	...	...	13.1[1]	...
Eritrea Erythrée	...	2.0	...	...	...	...	...	...
Estonia Estonie	5.1	...	...	...	14.6	...	...	...
Ethiopia Ethiopie	...	5.5	5.5	...	...	17.5	23.3	...
Finland Finlande	6.3	6.1	...	...	12.5	12.6	...	...
France France	5.6	5.5	...	...	10.6	10.6	...	...

Country or area Pays ou zone	As % of Gross National Income (GNI) En % du Revenu National Brut (RNB)				As % of total government expenditure En % des dépenses totales du gouvernement			
	2005	2006	2007	2008	2005	2006	2007	2008
Georgia Géorgie	2.5	2.9	2.7	2.9	8.8	9.3	7.8	7.2
Germany Allemagne	4.5	4.4	...	...	9.7	9.7	...	...
Ghana Ghana	5.5	...	...	...	...	...	...	...
Greece Grèce	4.1	...	...	...	9.2	...	...	...
Guatemala Guatemala	...	3.0	3.1	...	...	...	...	...
Guinea Guinée	1.7	...	...	1.7	...	...	...	19.2
Guyana Guyana	9.0	8.4	6.3	...	14.5	15.5	12.5	...
Hungary Hongrie	5.8	5.7	...	...	10.9	10.4	...	...
Iceland Islande	7.9	8.1	...	...	18.0	18.1	...	...
India Inde	3.2	3.2	...	...	...	...	...	...
Indonesia [2] Indonésie [2]	3.0	3.8	3.6	...	14.9	17.2	17.5	...
Iran (Islamic Rep. of) Iran (Rép. islamique d')	4.8	5.2	5.6	4.8	22.8	18.6	19.5	20.0
Ireland Irlande	5.6	5.6	...	...	13.9	14.0	...	...
Israel Israël	6.2	6.2	...	...	...	...	...	...
Italy Italie	4.4	4.8	...	...	9.2	9.7	...	...
Jamaica Jamaïque	4.9	...	5.8	...	8.8	...	...	...
Japan Japon	3.5	3.4	...	...	9.5	9.5	...	...
Kazakhstan Kazakhstan	2.5	3.0	3.2	...	...	...	...	...
Kenya Kenya	7.4	7.0	...	...	17.9	...	...	...
Korea, Republic of Corée, République de	4.2	4.2	...	...	15.3	...	...	...
Kuwait Koweït	4.3	3.4 [2]	...	...	12.7	12.9 [2]	...	...
Kyrgyzstan Kirghizistan	5.1	5.6	6.7	...	24.4	25.0	25.6	...
Lao People's Dem. Rep. Rép. dém. pop. lao	2.5	3.1	3.2	2.4	11.7	14.0	15.8	12.2
Latvia Lettonie	...	5.2	...	...	...	13.4	...	...
Lebanon Liban	2.7	2.7	2.5	2.2	11.0	9.8	9.6	8.1
Lesotho Lesotho	11.4	11.3	...	9.9	29.8	28.1	...	23.7
Liberia Libéria	...	...	...	3.5	...	...	...	12.1

Public expenditure on education *(continued)*
Percentage of GNI and of government expenditure

Dépenses publiques afférentes à l'éducation *(suite)*
Pourcentage par rapport au RNB et aux dépenses du gouvernement

Country or area Pays ou zone	As % of Gross National Income (GNI) En % du Revenu National Brut (RNB)				As % of total government expenditure En % des dépenses totales du gouvernement			
	2005	2006	2007	2008	2005	2006	2007	2008
Lithuania Lituanie	5.0	5.0	...	...	14.7	14.4	...	...
Madagascar Madagascar	3.2	3.1	3.4	2.9	25.3	13.9	16.4	13.4
Malaysia Malaisie	7.8	4.8	...	...	...	...	...	...
Maldives Maldives	8.0	8.3	...	8.4	15.0	11.0	...	12.0
Mali Mali	4.3	...	...	3.9	14.8	...	...	19.5
Mauritania Mauritanie	2.3	2.8	...	...	8.3	10.1	...	15.6[2]
Mauritius Maurice	4.5	3.9	...	...	14.3	12.7	...	...
Mexico Mexique	5.1	4.9	...	...	...	...	...	...
Mongolia Mongolie	...	...	5.2	...	...	...	...	...
Morocco Maroc	5.9	5.6	...	...	27.2	26.1	...	...
Mozambique Mozambique	5.6	5.5	...	...	...	21.0	...	...
Namibia Namibie	...	6.1	...	6.6	...	...	...	22.4
Nepal Népal	...	...	...	3.7	...	...	...	...
Netherlands Pays-Bas	5.5	5.4	...	...	12.2	12.0	...	...
New Zealand Nouvelle-Zélande	6.9	6.7	6.6	...	15.5	19.7	...	...
Niger Niger	...	3.3	4.1	3.7	...	17.6	...	15.5
Norway Norvège	7.0	6.6	...	...	16.7	16.2	...	...
Oman Oman	3.6	4.1	...	...	24.2	31.1	...	...
Pakistan Pakistan	2.2	2.6	2.8	2.9	10.9	12.2	11.2	...
Panama Panama	...	...	...	4.1	...	...	...	18.0
Peru Pérou	2.9	2.8	2.7	...	...	15.4	16.4	...
Philippines Philippines	2.3	...	...	...	15.2	...	...	...
Poland Pologne	5.6	5.8	...	...	...	12.0	...	...
Portugal Portugal	5.5	5.5	...	...	11.3	11.3	...	...
Qatar Qatar	...	...	...	...	19.6	...	...	...
Republic of Moldova République de Moldova	6.4	6.7	7.6	7.5	19.4	20.2	19.8	19.8
Romania Roumanie	3.5	...	...	...	14.3	...	...	...

Public expenditure on education *(continued)*

Percentage of GNI and of government expenditure

Dépenses publiques afférentes à l'éducation *(suite)*

Pourcentage par rapport au RNB et aux dépenses du gouvernement

Country or area Pays ou zone	As % of Gross National Income (GNI) En % du Revenu National Brut (RNB)				As % of total government expenditure En % des dépenses totales du gouvernement			
	2005	2006	2007	2008	2005	2006	2007	2008
Russian Federation Fédération de Russie	3.9	4.0	...	...	...	...	...	...
Rwanda Rwanda	3.4	...	4.8	4.1	12.2	...	19.0	20.4
Saint Kitts and Nevis Saint-Kitts-et-Nevis	10.9	...	...	...	...	...	...	...
Saint Lucia Sainte-Lucie	6.0	7.1	...	6.8	16.9	19.1	...	12.9
Saint Vincent-Grenadines Saint Vincent-Grenadines	8.6	...	7.3	...	16.1	...	...	...
Senegal Sénégal	...	4.8	...	...	18.9	26.3	...	...
Seychelles Seychelles	...	5.2	...	...	...	12.6	...	...
Sierra Leone [2] Sierra Leone [2]	4.0	...	...	...	...	...	...	...
Singapore Singapour	...	...	...	3.0	...	...	...	15.3
Slovakia Slovaquie	4.0	3.9	...	...	...	10.2	...	...
Slovenia Slovénie	5.8	5.8	...	...	12.7	12.9	...	...
South Africa Afrique du Sud	5.5	5.5	5.4	5.3	17.9	17.6	17.4	16.2
Spain Espagne	4.3	4.4	...	...	11.0	11.1	...	...
Swaziland Swaziland	7.9	7.7	...	7.8	...	24.4	...	21.6
Sweden Suède	7.0	6.7	...	...	...	12.6	...	...
Switzerland Suisse	5.2	5.0	...	...	...	16.3	...	...
Syrian Arab Republic Rép. arabe syrienne	...	5.5	4.9	...	...	18.4	16.7	...
Tajikistan Tadjikistan	3.6	3.6	3.5	3.6	18.0	19.0	18.2	18.7
Thailand Thaïlande	4.4	5.0	4.8	...	25.0	25.0	20.9	...
Timor-Leste Timor-Leste	...	...	...	1.2	...	...	...	7.3
Togo Togo	3.5	3.7	3.8	...	18.7	16.6	17.2	...
Tunisia Tunisie	7.6	7.5	...	...	20.8	20.5	...	...
Turks and Caicos Islands Iles Turques et Caïques	...	...	...	...	11.8	...	...	...
Uganda Ouganda	...	...	...	3.8	...	...	...	18.9
Ukraine Ukraine	6.1	6.3	5.4	...	18.9	19.3	20.2	...
United Arab Emirates [2] Emirats arabes unis [2]	...	...	...	...	28.3	...	...	...
United Kingdom Royaume-Uni	5.4	5.5	...	...	12.5	11.9	...	...

13 Public expenditure on education *(continued)*

Percentage of GNI and of government expenditure

Dépenses publiques afférentes à l'éducation *(suite)*

Pourcentage par rapport au RNB et aux dépenses du gouvernement

Country or area Pays ou zone	As % of Gross National Income (GNI) En % du Revenu National Brut (RNB)				As % of total government expenditure En % des dépenses totales du gouvernement			
	2005	2006	2007	2008	2005	2006	2007	2008
United States Etats-Unis	5.3	5.7	...	...	13.7	14.8	...	...
Uruguay Uruguay	2.8	2.9	...	...	12.7	11.6	...	...
Vanuatu Vanuatu	...	...	...	6.2	...	...	...	28.1
Venezuela (Boliv. Rep. of) Venezuela (Rép. boliv. du)	...	3.7	3.6	...	...	...	...	...
Viet Nam Viet Nam	...	...	...	5.5	...	...	...	...
Yemen Yémen	...	...	...	5.7	...	...	...	16.0
Zambia Zambie	2.1	...	1.7	1.5	...	...	...	...

Source:
United Nations Educational, Scientific and Cultural Organization (UNESCO), Montreal, the UNESCO Institute for Statistics (UIS) database, last accessed April 2010.

1 National estimation.
2 UIS estimation.

Source:
L'Organisation des Nations Unies pour l'éducation, la science et la culture (UNESCO), Montréal, la base de données de l'Institut de statistique de l'UNESCO (ISU), dernier accès avril 2010.

1 Estimation nationale.
2 Estimation de l'ISU.

Technical notes: tables 12 and 13

Detailed data and explanatory notes on education can be found on the UNESCO Institute for Statistics web site www.uis.unesco.org. Brief notes which pertain to the statistical information shown in tables 12 and 13 are given below.

Table 12: The definitions and classifications applied by UNESCO are those set out in the *Revised Recommendation concerning the International Standardization of Education Statistics* (1978) and the 1976 and 1997 versions of the *International Standard Classification of Education* (ISCED). Data are presented in table 12 according to the terminology of the ISCED-97.

According to the ISCED, these educational levels are defined as follows:

Primary education (ISCED level 1): Programmes normally designed on a unit or project basis to give pupils a sound basic education in reading, writing and mathematics along with an elementary understanding of other subjects such as history, geography, natural science, social science, art and music. Religious instruction may also be featured. It is sometimes called elementary education.

Secondary education (ISCED levels 2 and 3): Lower secondary education (ISCED 2) is generally designed to continue the basic programmes of the primary level but the teaching is typically more subject-focused, requiring more specialized teachers for each subject area. The end of this level often coincides with the end of compulsory education. In upper secondary education (ISCED 3), the final stage of secondary education in most countries, education is often organized even more along subject lines and teachers typically need a higher or more subject-specific qualification than at ISCED level 2.

Tertiary education (ISCED levels 5 and 6): Programmes with an educational content more advanced than what is offered at ISCED levels 3 and 4. The first stage of tertiary education, ISCED level 5, covers level 5A, composed of largely theoretically based programmes intended to provide sufficient qualifications for gaining entry to advanced research programmes and professions with high skill requirements; and level 5B, where programmes are generally more practical, technical and/or occupationally specific. The second stage of tertiary education, ISCED level 6, comprises programmes devoted to advanced study and original research, and leading to the award of an advanced research qualification.

The ISCED-97 also introduced a new category or level between upper secondary and tertiary education called post-secondary non-tertiary education (ISCED level 4). This level includes programmes that lie between the upper-secondary and tertiary levels of education from an international point of view, even though

Notes techniques : tableaux 12 et 13

On trouvera des données détaillées et des notes explicatives sur l'éducation sur le site Web de l'Institut de statistique de l'UNESCO www.uis.unesco.org. Ci-après figurent des notes sommaires, relatives aux principaux éléments d'information statistique figurant dans les tableaux 12 et 13.

Tableau 12: Les définitions et classifications appliquées par l'UNESCO sont tirées de la *Recommandation révisée concernant la normalisation internationale des statistiques de l'éducation* (1978) et des versions de 1976 et de 1997 de la *Classification internationale type de l'éducation* (CITE). La terminologie utilisée dans le tableau 12 est celle de la CITE-1997.

Dans la CITE, les niveaux d'enseignement sont définis comme suit:

Enseignement primaire (niveau 1 de la CITE): Programmes s'articulant normalement autour d'une unité ou d'un projet visant à donner aux élèves un solide enseignement de base en lecture, en écriture et en mathématiques et des connaissances élémentaires dans d'autres matières telles que l'histoire, la géographie, les sciences naturelles, les sciences sociales, le dessin et la musique. Dans certains cas, une instruction religieuse est aussi considérée. Appelé parfois enseignement élémentaire.

Enseignement secondaire (niveaux 2 et 3 de la CITE): Le premier cycle de l'enseignement secondaire (CITE 2) est généralement destiné à compléter les programmes de base de l'enseignement primaire mais dont l'enseignement est généralement plus orienté vers les matières enseignées faisant appel à des enseignants plus spécialisés. La fin de ce niveau coïncide souvent avec celle de la scolarité obligatoire. Dans le deuxième cycle de l'enseignement secondaire (CITE 3), étape finale de l'enseignement secondaire dans plusieurs pays, l'enseignement est souvent organisé en une plus grande spécialisation et les enseignants doivent souvent être plus qualifiés ou spécialisés qu'au niveau 2 de la CITE.

Enseignement supérieur (niveaux 5 et 6 de la CITE): Programmes dont le contenu est plus avancé que celui offert aux niveaux 3 et 4 de la CITE. Le premier cycle de l'enseignement supérieur, niveau 5 de la CITE, couvre le niveau 5A, composé de programmes fondés dans une large mesure sur la théorie et destinés à offrir des qualifications suffisantes pour être admis à suivre des programmes de recherche de pointe ou à exercer une profession exigeant de hautes compétences; et le niveau 5B, dont les programmes sont dans une large mesure d'ordre pratique, technique et/ou spécifiquement professionnel. Le deuxième cycle de l'enseignement supérieur, niveau 6 de la CITE, comprend des programmes consacrés à des études approfondies et à des travaux de recherche originaux, et conduisant à l'obtention d'un titre

they might clearly be considered as upper-secondary or tertiary programmes in a national context. They are often not significantly more advanced than programmes at ISCED 3 (upper secondary) but they serve to broaden the knowledge of participants who have already completed a programme at level 3. The students are usually older than those at level 3. ISCED 4 programmes typically last between six months and two years.

Table 13: Public expenditure on education consists of current and capital expenditures on education by local, regional and national governments, including municipalities. Household contributions are excluded. Current expenditure on education includes expenditure for goods and services consumed within the current year and which would need to be renewed if needed the following year. It includes expenditure on: staff salaries and benefits; contracted or purchased services; other resources including books and teaching materials; welfare services; and other current expenditure such as subsidies to students and households, furniture and equipment, minor repairs, fuel, telecommunications, travel, insurance and rents. Capital expenditure on education includes expenditure for assets that last longer than one year. It includes expenditure for construction, renovation and major repairs of buildings and the purchase of heavy equipment or vehicles.

de chercheur hautement qualifié.

La CITE de 1997 a également introduit une nouvelle catégorie (ou nouveau niveau) entre l'enseignement secondaire et l'enseignement supérieur, appelée enseignement postsecondaire non supérieur (niveau 4 de la CITE). À ce niveau se trouvent des programmes qui, du point de vue des établissements, sont intermédiaires entre le deuxième cycle du secondaire et le premier cycle du supérieur, encore qu'il serait tout à fait possible de les considérer, dans le contexte national, comme appartenant au deuxième cycle du secondaire ou au supérieur. Ils ne sont souvent pas beaucoup plus avancés que des programmes du niveau 3 de la CITE (deuxième cycle du secondaire) mais servent à élargir les connaissances de ceux qui les suivent et qui ont déjà achevé un programme de niveau 3. Les étudiants y sont généralement plus âgés que ceux du niveau 3. Pour la plupart, ces programmes du niveau 4 de la CITE ont une durée comprise entre six mois et deux ans.

Tableau 13: Les données relatives aux dépenses publiques afférentes à l'éducation se rapportent aux dépenses courantes et en capital de l'éducation engagées par l'administration au niveau local, régional, national/central, y inclus les municipalités. Les contributions des ménages sont exclues. Les dépenses ordinaires (ou courantes) en éducation se réfèrent aux dépenses couvrant les biens et les services consommés dans l'année en cours et qui doivent être renouvelées périodiquement. Elles comprennent les dépenses en: salaires et avantages du personnel, services achetés ou assurés sous contrat, l'achat d'autres ressources y compris les manuels scolaires et du matériel pour l'enseignement, les services sociaux et d'autres dépenses de fonctionnement telles que les subventions aux étudiants et aux ménages, les fournitures et l'équipement, les réparations légères, les combustibles, les télécommunications, les voyages, les assurances et les loyers. Dépenses en capital pour l'éducation se réfèrent aux dépenses qui couvrent l'achat de biens d'une durée supérieure à une année. Elles peuvent comprendre les dépenses de construction, de rénovation et de grosses réparations de bâtiments, ainsi que l'achat d'équipements ou véhicules.

14

Telephones

Main telephone lines in operation (in thousands) and lines per 100 inhabitants

Téléphones

Nombre de lignes téléphoniques en service (en milliers) et lignes pour 100 habitants

Country or area	Fiscal year[&] Ex. budgét[&]	2003	2004	2005	2006	2007	2008	2009	Pays ou zone
Afghanistan									**Afghanistan**
Number (thousands)		37	50	100	90	81	101	129	Nombre (en milliers)
Per 100 inhabitants		0.2	0.2	0.4	0.4	0.3	0.4	0.5	Pour 100 habitants
Albania									**Albanie**
Number (thousands)		255	275	279	256	300	344	363	Nombre (en milliers)
Per 100 inhabitants		8.3	8.9	9.0	8.2	9.6	10.9	11.5	Pour 100 habitants
Algeria									**Algérie**
Number (thousands)		2 147	2 487	2 572	2 841	3 068	3 069	2 576	Nombre (en milliers)
Per 100 inhabitants		6.7	7.7	7.8	8.5	9.1	8.9	7.4	Pour 100 habitants
American Samoa									**Samoa américaines**
Number (thousands)		11	10	10	10	10	10	10	Nombre (en milliers)
Per 100 inhabitants		17.7	16.8	16.6	16.3	16.0	15.7	15.4	Pour 100 habitants
Andorra									**Andorre**
Number (thousands)		35[1]	35	35	37	37	37	38	Nombre (en milliers)
Per 100 inhabitants		47.4	45.4	44.4	44.7	44.6	44.3	44.3	Pour 100 habitants
Angola									**Angola**
Number (thousands)		85	94	97	98[2]	94	114	#303[3]	Nombre (en milliers)
Per 100 inhabitants		0.5	0.6	0.6	0.6	0.5	0.6	1.6	Pour 100 habitants
Antigua and Barbuda	(01/04)								**Antigua-et-Barbuda**
Number (thousands)		38	38	36	38	38	38	37	Nombre (en milliers)
Per 100 inhabitants		46.8	46.1	43.7	44.3	44.3	43.9	42.6	Pour 100 habitants
Argentina	(30/09)								**Argentine**
Number (thousands)[4]		8 604	8 761	9 442	9 460	9 500[5]	9 743[6]	9 764	Nombre (en milliers)[4]
Per 100 inhabitants		22.6	22.8	24.4	24.2	24.1	24.4	24.2	Pour 100 habitants
Armenia									**Arménie**
Number (thousands)		564	579	594	604	625	626	630	Nombre (en milliers)
Per 100 inhabitants		18.4	18.9	19.4	19.7	20.3	20.3	20.4	Pour 100 habitants
Aruba									**Aruba**
Number (thousands)		37	38	38	39	39	38	38	Nombre (en milliers)
Per 100 inhabitants		38.5	38.3	37.9	37.6	37.1	36.5	36.0	Pour 100 habitants
Australia	(30/06)								**Australie**
Number (thousands)		10 460[7]	10 370[7]	10 120[7]	9 940[7]	9 760[7]	9 370[7,8]	9 020[9]	Nombre (en milliers)
Per 100 inhabitants		52.6	51.5	49.6	48.2	46.8	44.5	42.4	Pour 100 habitants
Austria									**Autriche**
Number (thousands)[10,11]		3 877[12]	3 821[12]	3 739[12]	3 605[12]	3 407[12]	3 285	3 253	Nombre (en milliers)[10,11]
Per 100 inhabitants		47.7	46.7	45.4	43.6	41.0	39.4	38.9	Pour 100 habitants
Azerbaijan									**Azerbaïdjan**
Number (thousands)		941	1 013	1 094	1 177	1 253[13]	1 311[13]	1 397[13]	Nombre (en milliers)
Per 100 inhabitants		11.3	12.1	12.9	13.8	14.5	15.0	15.8	Pour 100 habitants
Bahamas									**Bahamas**
Number (thousands)		132	140	133	132	133	133	129	Nombre (en milliers)
Per 100 inhabitants		41.5	43.5	40.9	39.9	39.8	39.3	37.7	Pour 100 habitants
Bahrain									**Bahreïn**
Number (thousands)		186	192	194	194	204[14]	220[14]	238	Nombre (en milliers)
Per 100 inhabitants		26.7	26.9	26.6	26.1	26.8	28.4	30.1	Pour 100 habitants
Bangladesh	(30/06)								**Bangladesh**
Number (thousands)		742	831	1 070	1 134	1 187	1 344	1 523	Nombre (en milliers)
Per 100 inhabitants		0.5	0.6	0.7	0.7	0.8	0.8	0.9	Pour 100 habitants
Barbados	(01/04)								**Barbade**
Number (thousands)		134	136	135	134	134	150	136	Nombre (en milliers)
Per 100 inhabitants		53.2	53.7	53.3	52.9	52.7	58.8	53.0	Pour 100 habitants
Belarus									**Bélarus**
Number (thousands)		3 071	3 176	3 284	3 368	3 672	3 718	3 969	Nombre (en milliers)
Per 100 inhabitants		31.0	32.2	33.5	34.5	37.8	38.4	41.2	Pour 100 habitants
Belgium									**Belgique**
Number (thousands)		4 875[15]	4 801[15]	4 795[15]	4 728[15]	4 668[15]	4 457[15]	4 255	Nombre (en milliers)
Per 100 inhabitants		47.3	46.3	46.0	45.1	44.3	42.1	40.0	Pour 100 habitants
Belize	(01/04)								**Belize**
Number (thousands)		33	34	34	34	34	31	31	Nombre (en milliers)
Per 100 inhabitants		12.3	12.2	12.0	11.9	11.5	10.4	10.2	Pour 100 habitants
Benin									**Bénin**
Number (thousands)		67	73	76	77	111	103	127	Nombre (en milliers)
Per 100 inhabitants		0.9	1.0	1.0	1.0	1.3	1.2	1.4	Pour 100 habitants
Bermuda	(01/04)								**Bermudes**
Number (thousands)		54	54	52	58	58	58	58	Nombre (en milliers)
Per 100 inhabitants		84.8	84.2	81.8	89.6	89.2	89.0	89.0	Pour 100 habitants
Bhutan									**Bhoutan**
Number (thousands)		24	30	33	32	30	27	26	Nombre (en milliers)
Per 100 inhabitants		3.8	4.8	5.1	4.7	4.4	4.0	3.8	Pour 100 habitants

14 Telephones *(continued)*

Main telephone lines in operation (in thousands) and lines per 100 inhabitants

Téléphones *(suite)*

Nombre de lignes téléphoniques en service (en milliers) et lignes pour 100 habitants

Country or area	Fiscal year[&] Ex. budgét[&]	2003	2004	2005	2006	2007	2008	2009	Pays ou zone
Bolivia (Plur. State of)									**Bolivie (État plurin. de)**
Number (thousands)		610	625	646	667	678	690	810	Nombre (en milliers)
Per 100 inhabitants		6.9	6.9	7.0	7.1	7.1	7.1	8.2	Pour 100 habitants
Bosnia-Herzegovina									**Bosnie-Herzégovine**
Number (thousands)		938[16]	952[16]	969[16]	989[16]	1 064[16]	1 031[16]	999	Nombre (en milliers)
Per 100 inhabitants		24.8	25.2	25.6	26.2	28.2	27.3	26.5	Pour 100 habitants
Botswana	(01/04)								**Botswana**
Number (thousands)		131	132	136	132	137	142	144	Nombre (en milliers)
Per 100 inhabitants		7.3	7.3	7.4	7.1	7.2	7.4	7.4	Pour 100 habitants
Brazil									**Brésil**
Number (thousands)		39 205	39 579	39 853	38 800[17]	39 400	41 235	41 497	Nombre (en milliers)
Per 100 inhabitants		21.6	21.5	21.4	20.6	20.7	21.5	21.4	Pour 100 habitants
Brunei Darussalam									**Brunéi Darussalam**
Number (thousands)		82	83	84	80	80	81	81	Nombre (en milliers)
Per 100 inhabitants		23.0	22.9	22.7	21.2	20.7	20.6	20.2	Pour 100 habitants
Bulgaria									**Bulgarie**
Number (thousands)		2 818	2 727	2 490	2 399[11]	2 300[18]	2 190[18]	2 164[18,19]	Nombre (en milliers)
Per 100 inhabitants		35.9	35.0	32.2	31.2	30.1	28.8	28.7	Pour 100 habitants
Burkina Faso									**Burkina Faso**
Number (thousands)		67	85	91	99	122	144	167	Nombre (en milliers)
Per 100 inhabitants		0.5	0.6	0.7	0.7	0.8	0.9	1.1	Pour 100 habitants
Burundi									**Burundi**
Number (thousands)		24	28	31	28	29	30	32	Nombre (en milliers)
Per 100 inhabitants		0.3	0.4	0.4	0.4	0.4	0.4	0.4	Pour 100 habitants
Cambodia									**Cambodge**
Number (thousands)		31[20]	32[20]	33[20]	26[20]	38[20]	43[20]	54	Nombre (en milliers)
Per 100 inhabitants		0.2	0.2	0.2	0.2	0.3	0.3	0.4	Pour 100 habitants
Cameroon									**Cameroun**
Number (thousands)		97	99	100	131	189	255	324	Nombre (en milliers)
Per 100 inhabitants		0.6	0.6	0.6	0.7	1.0	1.3	1.7	Pour 100 habitants
Canada									**Canada**
Number (thousands)		20 612	20 563	18 148	18 236	18 282[21]	18 250	18 251	Nombre (en milliers)
Per 100 inhabitants		65.1	64.3	56.2	55.9	55.5	54.9	54.4	Pour 100 habitants
Cape Verde									**Cap-Vert**
Number (thousands)		72	72	72	72	72	72	72	Nombre (en milliers)
Per 100 inhabitants		15.5	15.3	15.0	14.8	14.6	14.4	14.3	Pour 100 habitants
Cayman Islands	(01/04)								**Iles Caïmanes**
Number (thousands)		38	38	38	38	38	38	38	Nombre (en milliers)
Per 100 inhabitants		79.0	75.1	72.3	70.3	69.1	68.3	67.7	Pour 100 habitants
Central African Rep.									**Rép. centrafricaine**
Number (thousands)		10	10	10	12	12	12	12	Nombre (en milliers)
Per 100 inhabitants		0.2	0.2	0.2	0.3	0.3	0.3	0.3	Pour 100 habitants
Chad									**Tchad**
Number (thousands)		12	13	13	13	13	13	13	Nombre (en milliers)
Per 100 inhabitants		0.1	0.1	0.1	0.1	0.1	0.1	0.1	Pour 100 habitants
Chile									**Chili**
Number (thousands)		3 252	3 318	3 436	3 384	3 460	3 526	3 575	Nombre (en milliers)
Per 100 inhabitants		20.4	20.6	21.1	20.5	20.8	21.0	21.1	Pour 100 habitants
China									**Chine**
Number (thousands)		262 747	311 756	350 445	367 786	365 637	340 810	313 680	Nombre (en milliers)
Per 100 inhabitants		20.3	23.9	26.7	27.8	27.5	25.5	23.3	Pour 100 habitants
China, Hong Kong SAR	(01/04)								**Chine, Hong Kong RAS**
Number (thousands)		3 806	3 763	3 793	3 836	4 125[22]	4 100	4 188	Nombre (en milliers)
Per 100 inhabitants		55.9	54.9	55.1	55.5	59.4	58.7	59.6	Pour 100 habitants
China, Macao SAR									**Chine, Macao RAS**
Number (thousands)		175	174	174	177	178[23]	176[23]	170[23]	Nombre (en milliers)
Per 100 inhabitants		37.5	36.5	35.8	35.3	34.7	33.4	31.7	Pour 100 habitants
Colombia									**Colombie**
Number (thousands)		7 848	7 589	7 679	7 860	7 936	8 054	7 500	Nombre (en milliers)
Per 100 inhabitants		18.8	17.9	17.8	18.0	17.9	17.9	16.4	Pour 100 habitants
Comoros									**Comores**
Number (thousands)		13	15	17	19	21	23[14]	25	Nombre (en milliers)
Per 100 inhabitants		2.2	2.5	2.7	3.0	3.3	3.5	3.8	Pour 100 habitants
Congo									**Congo**
Number (thousands)		7	14	16	18	20	22	24	Nombre (en milliers)
Per 100 inhabitants		0.2	0.4	0.5	0.5	0.6	0.6	0.7	Pour 100 habitants
Costa Rica									**Costa Rica**
Number (thousands)		1 159	1 343	1 389	1 330	1 437	1 438	1 493	Nombre (en milliers)
Per 100 inhabitants		27.7	31.6	32.1	30.2	32.2	31.8	32.6	Pour 100 habitants

14 Telephones *(continued)*

Main telephone lines in operation (in thousands) and lines per 100 inhabitants

Téléphones *(suite)*

Nombre de lignes téléphoniques en service (en milliers) et lignes pour 100 habitants

Country or area	Fiscal year[&] Ex. budgét[&]	2003	2004	2005	2006	2007	2008	2009	Pays ou zone
Côte d'Ivoire									**Côte d'Ivoire**
Number (thousands)		238	258	259	271	248	357	282	Nombre (en milliers)
Per 100 inhabitants		1.3	1.4	1.3	1.4	1.2	1.7	1.3	Pour 100 habitants
Croatia									**Croatie**
Number (thousands)		1 871	1 888	1 883	1 831	1 847	1 878	1 859	Nombre (en milliers)
Per 100 inhabitants		42.0	42.4	42.4	41.3	41.7	42.5	42.1	Pour 100 habitants
Cuba									**Cuba**
Number (thousands)		724	768	856	962	1 043	1 104	1 168	Nombre (en milliers)
Per 100 inhabitants		6.5	6.9	7.6	8.6	9.3	9.8	10.4	Pour 100 habitants
Cyprus									**Chypre**
Number (thousands)		424[11]	418	420	408	409	413	415	Nombre (en milliers)
Per 100 inhabitants		51.9	50.6	50.2	48.3	47.9	47.9	47.6	Pour 100 habitants
Czech Republic									**République tchèque**
Number (thousands)		3 626	3 428	3 217	2 888	2 403	2 264	2 092	Nombre (en milliers)
Per 100 inhabitants		35.6	33.7	31.6	28.2	23.4	21.9	20.2	Pour 100 habitants
Dem. Rep. of the Congo									**Rép. dém. du Congo**
Number (thousands)		10	11	11	10	4	37	40	Nombre (en milliers)
Per 100 inhabitants		^0.0	^0.0	^0.0	^0.0	^0.0	0.1	0.1	Pour 100 habitants
Denmark									**Danemark**
Number (thousands)[11]		3 614	3 491	3 348	3 099	2 825	2 491	2 062	Nombre (en milliers)[11]
Per 100 inhabitants		67.1	64.6	61.8	57.0	51.9	45.6	37.7	Pour 100 habitants
Djibouti									**Djibouti**
Number (thousands)		10	11	11	11	14	15	17	Nombre (en milliers)
Per 100 inhabitants		1.3	1.4	1.3	1.4	1.7	1.8	1.9	Pour 100 habitants
Dominica	(01/04)								**Dominique**
Number (thousands)		22	21	19	18	17	18	18	Nombre (en milliers)
Per 100 inhabitants		33.2	31.0	28.2	26.0	26.0	26.2	26.3	Pour 100 habitants
Dominican Republic									**Rép. dominicaine**
Number (thousands)		909	902	896	897	906	986	965	Nombre (en milliers)
Per 100 inhabitants		9.8	9.6	9.4	9.3	9.2	9.9	9.6	Pour 100 habitants
Ecuador									**Equateur**
Number (thousands)		1 531	1 591	1 680	1 775	1 823	1 904	2 004	Nombre (en milliers)
Per 100 inhabitants		12.0	12.3	12.9	13.4	13.7	14.1	14.7	Pour 100 habitants
Egypt	(30/06)								**Egypte**
Number (thousands)		8 736	9 535	10 474	10 890	11 229	11 853	10 313	Nombre (en milliers)
Per 100 inhabitants		11.8	12.6	13.6	13.9	14.0	14.5	12.4	Pour 100 habitants
El Salvador									**El Salvador**
Number (thousands)		753	888	971	1 037	1 080	1 077	1 099	Nombre (en milliers)
Per 100 inhabitants		12.5	14.7	16.0	17.0	17.7	17.6	17.8	Pour 100 habitants
Equatorial Guinea									**Guinée équatoriale**
Number (thousands)		10	11	10	10	10	10	10	Nombre (en milliers)
Per 100 inhabitants		1.7	1.8	1.6	1.6	1.6	1.5	1.5	Pour 100 habitants
Eritrea									**Erythrée**
Number (thousands)		38	39	38	38	37	40	48	Nombre (en milliers)
Per 100 inhabitants		0.9	0.9	0.8	0.8	0.8	0.8	1.0	Pour 100 habitants
Estonia									**Estonie**
Number (thousands)		461	444	442	452	495	498	493	Nombre (en milliers)
Per 100 inhabitants		34.1	32.9	32.8	33.6	36.9	37.1	36.8	Pour 100 habitants
Ethiopia	(30/06)								**Ethiopie**
Number (thousands)		405	484	610	725	880	897	915	Nombre (en milliers)
Per 100 inhabitants		0.6	0.7	0.8	0.9	1.1	1.1	1.1	Pour 100 habitants
Faeroe Islands									**Iles Féroé**
Number (thousands)		24	24	24	23	22	22	21	Nombre (en milliers)
Per 100 inhabitants		51.1	49.8	49.0	47.0	45.5	44.0	41.9	Pour 100 habitants
Fiji									**Fidji**
Number (thousands)		102	105	112	115	122	129	137	Nombre (en milliers)
Per 100 inhabitants		12.5	12.8	13.6	13.8	14.5	15.3	16.1	Pour 100 habitants
Finland									**Finlande**
Number (thousands)		2 568[24]	2 368[24]	2 120[24]	1 910[24]	1 740[24]	1 650[25]	1 430	Nombre (en milliers)
Per 100 inhabitants		49.3	45.3	40.4	36.3	32.9	31.1	26.9	Pour 100 habitants
France									**France**
Number (thousands)		33 913[15]	33 703[15]	33 707[15]	34 125[15]	34 800[15]	35 000[15]	35 500	Nombre (en milliers)
Per 100 inhabitants		56.3	55.6	55.2	55.6	56.4	56.4	56.9	Pour 100 habitants
French Guiana									**Guyane française**
Number (thousands)		51	51	51	51	51	51	48	Nombre (en milliers)
Per 100 inhabitants		27.2	26.2	25.2	24.5	23.8	23.2	21.3	Pour 100 habitants
French Polynesia									**Polynésie française**
Number (thousands)		54	53	53	54	54	55	54	Nombre (en milliers)
Per 100 inhabitants		21.6	21.2	20.9	20.7	20.6	20.5	20.2	Pour 100 habitants

14 Telephones *(continued)*

Main telephone lines in operation (in thousands) and lines per 100 inhabitants

Téléphones *(suite)*

Nombre de lignes téléphoniques en service (en milliers) et lignes pour 100 habitants

Country or area	Fiscal year[&] Ex. budgét[&]	2003	2004	2005	2006	2007	2008	2009	Pays ou zone
Gabon									**Gabon**
Number (thousands)		38	39	39	36	26[26]	27	27	Nombre (en milliers)
Per 100 inhabitants		2.9	2.9	2.9	2.6	1.9	1.8	1.8	Pour 100 habitants
Gambia	(01/04)								**Gambie**
Number (thousands)		42[27]	43[27]	44[27]	46[27]	49[27]	49[27]	49	Nombre (en milliers)
Per 100 inhabitants		2.9	2.9	2.9	2.9	3.0	2.9	2.9	Pour 100 habitants
Georgia	(01/04)								**Géorgie**
Number (thousands)		667	683	570	553	556	618	620	Nombre (en milliers)
Per 100 inhabitants		14.6	15.1	12.8	12.5	12.8	14.3	14.6	Pour 100 habitants
Germany									**Allemagne**
Number (thousands)[28]		54 233	54 526	54 791	54 400	53 100	51 100	48 700	Nombre (en milliers)[28]
Per 100 inhabitants		65.9	66.2	66.5	66.0	64.5	62.1	59.3	Pour 100 habitants
Ghana									**Ghana**
Number (thousands)		291	313	322	356	377	144	267	Nombre (en milliers)
Per 100 inhabitants		1.4	1.5	1.5	1.6	1.6	0.6	1.1	Pour 100 habitants
Gibraltar									**Gibraltar**
Number (thousands)		25	25	25	24	24	24	24	Nombre (en milliers)
Per 100 inhabitants		83.3	83.4	81.4	77.7	77.4	77.3	77.3	Pour 100 habitants
Greece									**Grèce**
Number (thousands)[11]		6 300	6 352	6 312	6 170	6 243	5 975	5 930	Nombre (en milliers)[11]
Per 100 inhabitants		57.2	57.5	57.0	55.7	56.2	53.7	53.1	Pour 100 habitants
Greenland									**Groenland**
Number (thousands)		25	25	32	36	23	23	22	Nombre (en milliers)
Per 100 inhabitants		44.4	44.1	56.2	62.8	40.4	39.8	38.5	Pour 100 habitants
Grenada									**Grenade**
Number (thousands)		33	33	27	28	29	29	29	Nombre (en milliers)
Per 100 inhabitants		32.0	32.0	26.8	26.9	27.7	27.6	27.5	Pour 100 habitants
Guam									**Guam**
Number (thousands)		66	66	66	66	66	66	66	Nombre (en milliers)
Per 100 inhabitants		40.2	39.5	38.9	38.3	37.8	37.3	36.9	Pour 100 habitants
Guatemala									**Guatemala**
Number (thousands)		944	1 132	1 248	1 355	1 414	1 449	1 413	Nombre (en milliers)
Per 100 inhabitants		7.8	9.1	9.8	10.4	10.6	10.6	10.1	Pour 100 habitants
Guernsey									**Guernesey**
Number (thousands)[11]		46	45	45	45	45	45	45	Nombre (en milliers)[11]
Per 100 inhabitants		81.9	80.9	85.1	89.8	...	...	...	Pour 100 habitants
Guinea									**Guinée**
Number (thousands)		26	26	25[29]	23	22	21	22	Nombre (en milliers)
Per 100 inhabitants		0.3	0.3	0.3	0.2	0.2	0.2	0.2	Pour 100 habitants
Guinea-Bissau									**Guinée-Bissau**
Number (thousands)		11	10	10	7	5	5	5	Nombre (en milliers)
Per 100 inhabitants		0.8	0.7	0.7	0.5	0.3	0.3	0.3	Pour 100 habitants
Guyana									**Guyana**
Number (thousands)		92	103	110	118	120	125	130	Nombre (en milliers)
Per 100 inhabitants		12.1	13.5	14.4	15.4	15.7	16.4	17.0	Pour 100 habitants
Haiti									**Haïti**
Number (thousands)		140	140	145	150	108	108	108	Nombre (en milliers)
Per 100 inhabitants		1.5	1.5	1.5	1.6	1.1	1.1	1.1	Pour 100 habitants
Honduras									**Honduras**
Number (thousands)		334	387	494	715	822	826	830	Nombre (en milliers)
Per 100 inhabitants		5.1	5.7	7.2	10.2	11.5	11.3	11.1	Pour 100 habitants
Hungary									**Hongrie**
Number (thousands)		3 603	3 564	3 416	3 360	3 251	3 094	3 069	Nombre (en milliers)
Per 100 inhabitants		35.6	35.3	33.9	33.4	32.4	30.9	30.7	Pour 100 habitants
Iceland									**Islande**
Number (thousands)		193[11]	190[11]	194[11]	189[11]	187	194	185	Nombre (en milliers)
Per 100 inhabitants		66.8	65.4	65.5	62.6	60.6	61.3	57.4	Pour 100 habitants
India	(01/04)								**Inde**
Number (thousands)		42 000	46 198	50 177	#40 770[30]	39 413	37 900	37 060	Nombre (en milliers)
Per 100 inhabitants		3.8	4.1	4.4	3.6	3.4	3.2	3.1	Pour 100 habitants
Indonesia									**Indonésie**
Number (thousands)		8 058	10 376	13 508	14 821	19 530	30 378	33 958	Nombre (en milliers)
Per 100 inhabitants		3.8	4.8	6.2	6.7	8.7	13.4	14.8	Pour 100 habitants
Iran (Islamic Rep. of)	(22/03)								**Iran (Rép. islamique d')**
Number (thousands)		15 341	16 342	20 339	22 627	23 835	24 800	25 804	Nombre (en milliers)
Per 100 inhabitants		22.2	23.4	28.7	31.6	32.9	33.8	34.8	Pour 100 habitants
Iraq	(30/06)								**Iraq**
Number (thousands)		1 183	1 034	1 115	1 248	1 365	1 082	1 108	Nombre (en milliers)
Per 100 inhabitants		4.4	3.8	3.9	4.3	4.6	3.6	3.6	Pour 100 habitants

Telephones *(continued)*

Main telephone lines in operation (in thousands) and lines per 100 inhabitants

Téléphones *(suite)*

Nombre de lignes téléphoniques en service (en milliers) et lignes pour 100 habitants

Country or area	Fiscal year[&] Ex. budgét[&]	2003	2004	2005	2006	2007	2008	2009	Pays ou zone
Ireland	(01/04)								**Irlande**
Number (thousands)		1 955[11]	2 015[11]	2 052[11]	2 177[31]	2 259[31]	2 202[31]	2 079[31,32]	Nombre (en milliers)
Per 100 inhabitants		48.6	49.1	49.0	51.0	51.9	49.6	46.1	Pour 100 habitants
Israel									**Israël**
Number (thousands)		2 913	2 896	2 936	3 005	3 075	3 224	3 250	Nombre (en milliers)
Per 100 inhabitants		45.1	44.1	43.9	44.1	44.4	45.7	45.3	Pour 100 habitants
Italy									**Italie**
Number (thousands)		26 596[11,33]	25 957[11,33]	25 049[11]	26 890[11]	22 417[11]	21 246[11]	21 300	Nombre (en milliers)
Per 100 inhabitants		45.9	44.5	42.7	45.6	37.8	35.6	35.6	Pour 100 habitants
Jamaica	(01/04)								**Jamaïque**
Number (thousands)		459	423	319	343	370	317	302	Nombre (en milliers)
Per 100 inhabitants		17.4	16.0	12.0	12.8	13.7	11.7	11.1	Pour 100 habitants
Japan	(01/04)								**Japon**
Number (thousands)		60 219	59 608	58 053[32]	56 029	52 346	48 427	44 364[32]	Nombre (en milliers)
Per 100 inhabitants		47.3	46.8	45.6	44.0	41.1	38.0	34.9	Pour 100 habitants
Jersey									**Jersey**
Number (thousands)		74	74	74	74	74	74	74	Nombre (en milliers)
Per 100 inhabitants		84.1	84.1	84.1	84.1	84.1	...	...	Pour 100 habitants
Jordan									**Jordanie**
Number (thousands)		623	638	628	614	559	519	501	Nombre (en milliers)
Per 100 inhabitants		11.9	11.8	11.3	10.7	9.4	8.5	7.9	Pour 100 habitants
Kazakhstan									**Kazakhstan**
Number (thousands)		2 228	2 550	2 708	2 928	3 237	3 458	3 763	Nombre (en milliers)
Per 100 inhabitants		14.9	16.9	17.8	19.1	21.0	22.3	24.1	Pour 100 habitants
Kenya	(30/06)								**Kenya**
Number (thousands)		328	299	287	293	464	646	664	Nombre (en milliers)
Per 100 inhabitants		1.0	0.9	0.8	0.8	1.2	1.7	1.7	Pour 100 habitants
Kiribati									**Kiribati**
Number (thousands)		4	4	4	4[34]	4	4	4	Nombre (en milliers)
Per 100 inhabitants		5.0	4.8	4.6	4.3	4.2	4.1	4.1	Pour 100 habitants
Korea, Dem. P. R.									**Corée, R. p. dém. de**
Number (thousands)		980	1 000	1 000	1 000	1 180	1 180	1 180	Nombre (en milliers)
Per 100 inhabitants		4.2	4.3	4.3	4.2	5.0	5.0	4.9	Pour 100 habitants
Korea, Republic of									**Corée, République de**
Number (thousands)		25 128[24]	23 568[24]	23 905[24]	22 431[24]	22 397[24]	21 325[24]	19 289	Nombre (en milliers)
Per 100 inhabitants		53.3	49.8	50.3	47.0	46.7	44.3	39.9	Pour 100 habitants
Kuwait									**Koweït**
Number (thousands)		487	497	505[35]	517	529	541	554	Nombre (en milliers)
Per 100 inhabitants		19.2	19.0	18.7	18.6	18.6	18.5	18.5	Pour 100 habitants
Kyrgyzstan									**Kirghizistan**
Number (thousands)		396	416	440	459	482	495	498	Nombre (en milliers)
Per 100 inhabitants		7.7	8.1	8.4	8.7	9.0	9.1	9.1	Pour 100 habitants
Lao People's Dem. Rep.									**Rép. dém. pop. lao**
Number (thousands)		70	75	91	92	95	128	132	Nombre (en milliers)
Per 100 inhabitants		1.2	1.3	1.5	1.5	1.6	2.1	2.1	Pour 100 habitants
Latvia									**Lettonie**
Number (thousands)		654	650	731	657	644	644	644	Nombre (en milliers)
Per 100 inhabitants		28.2	28.2	31.9	28.8	28.4	28.5	28.6	Pour 100 habitants
Lebanon									**Liban**
Number (thousands)		700	630	635	681	698[2]	750	750	Nombre (en milliers)
Per 100 inhabitants		17.7	15.6	15.6	16.5	16.8	17.9	17.8	Pour 100 habitants
Lesotho	(01/04)								**Lesotho**
Number (thousands)		35	37	48	53	48	41	40	Nombre (en milliers)
Per 100 inhabitants		1.8	1.9	2.4	2.6	2.3	2.0	1.9	Pour 100 habitants
Liberia									**Libéria**
Number (thousands)		...	...	...	...	2	2	2	Nombre (en milliers)
Per 100 inhabitants		...	...	...	...	0.1	0.1	0.1	Pour 100 habitants
Libyan Arab Jamah.									**Jamah. arabe libyenne**
Number (thousands)		750	800	852	909	969	1 033	1 101	Nombre (en milliers)
Per 100 inhabitants		13.2	13.8	14.4	15.0	15.7	16.4	17.1	Pour 100 habitants
Liechtenstein									**Liechtenstein**
Number (thousands)		20	20	20	20	20	20	20	Nombre (en milliers)
Per 100 inhabitants		58.5	58.1	57.6	56.4	55.4	55.0	54.6	Pour 100 habitants
Lithuania									**Lituanie**
Number (thousands)		824[27,36]	820	801	792	799	785	747	Nombre (en milliers)
Per 100 inhabitants		23.9	23.9	23.4	23.4	23.8	23.6	22.7	Pour 100 habitants
Luxembourg									**Luxembourg**
Number (thousands)[36,37]		245	245	245	248	248	261	274	Nombre (en milliers)[36,37]
Per 100 inhabitants		54.1	53.4	52.7	52.9	52.2	54.2	56.3	Pour 100 habitants

14 Telephones *(continued)*

Main telephone lines in operation (in thousands) and lines per 100 inhabitants

Téléphones *(suite)*

Nombre de lignes téléphoniques en service (en milliers) et lignes pour 100 habitants

Country or area	Fiscal year[&] Ex. budgét[&]	2003	2004	2005	2006	2007	2008	2009	Pays ou zone
Madagascar									**Madagascar**
Number (thousands)		60	59	92	130	134	165	181	Nombre (en milliers)
Per 100 inhabitants		0.4	0.3	0.5	0.7	0.7	0.9	0.9	Pour 100 habitants
Malawi									**Malawi**
Number (thousands)		85	93	103	130	175	175	175	Nombre (en milliers)
Per 100 inhabitants		0.7	0.7	0.8	0.9	1.2	1.2	1.1	Pour 100 habitants
Malaysia									**Malaisie**
Number (thousands)		4 572	4 446	4 366	4 342	4 350	4 292	4 312	Nombre (en milliers)
Per 100 inhabitants		18.5	17.7	17.0	16.6	16.4	15.9	15.7	Pour 100 habitants
Maldives									**Maldives**
Number (thousands)		30	32	32	32	33	47	49	Nombre (en milliers)
Per 100 inhabitants		10.6	10.9	11.0	10.9	11.0	15.4	15.8	Pour 100 habitants
Mali									**Mali**
Number (thousands)		61	66	76	83	80	81	81	Nombre (en milliers)
Per 100 inhabitants		0.5	0.6	0.6	0.7	0.6	0.6	0.6	Pour 100 habitants
Malta									**Malte**
Number (thousands)		208	207	202	208	230	241	253	Nombre (en milliers)
Per 100 inhabitants		52.4	51.6	50.2	51.5	56.7	59.2	61.8	Pour 100 habitants
Marshall Islands									**Iles Marshall**
Number (thousands)		4	4	4	4	4	4	4	Nombre (en milliers)
Per 100 inhabitants		8.2	7.9	7.8	7.6	7.4	7.3	7.1	Pour 100 habitants
Mauritania									**Mauritanie**
Number (thousands)		38	39	41	35	40	76	74	Nombre (en milliers)
Per 100 inhabitants		1.3	1.3	1.4	1.1	1.3	2.4	2.3	Pour 100 habitants
Mauritius									**Maurice**
Number (thousands)		348	354	357	357	361	365	379	Nombre (en milliers)
Per 100 inhabitants		28.3	28.5	28.5	28.3	28.4	28.5	29.4	Pour 100 habitants
Mexico									**Mexique**
Number (thousands)		16 330	18 073[2]	19 512	19 861	19 998	20 491	19 425	Nombre (en milliers)
Per 100 inhabitants		15.8	17.3	18.5	18.7	18.6	18.9	17.7	Pour 100 habitants
Micronesia (Fed. St. of)									**Micronésie (Et. féd. de)**
Number (thousands)		11	12	12	9	9	9	9	Nombre (en milliers)
Per 100 inhabitants		10.3	11.0	11.4	8.1	7.9	7.9	7.9	Pour 100 habitants
Mongolia									**Mongolie**
Number (thousands)		138	146	156	195	183	200	189[20]	Nombre (en milliers)
Per 100 inhabitants		5.6	5.8	6.1	7.6	7.0	7.6	7.1	Pour 100 habitants
Montenegro									**Monténégro**
Number (thousands)		...	290	349	353	358	362	367	Nombre (en milliers)
Per 100 inhabitants		...	45.9	55.9	56.9	57.7	58.2	58.7	Pour 100 habitants
Morocco									**Maroc**
Number (thousands)		1 219	1 309	1 341	1 266	2 394[14]	2 991[14]	3 516[14]	Nombre (en milliers)
Per 100 inhabitants		4.1	4.3	4.4	4.1	7.7	9.5	11.0	Pour 100 habitants
Mozambique									**Mozambique**
Number (thousands)		78	70	70	...	78	78	82	Nombre (en milliers)
Per 100 inhabitants		0.4	0.3	0.3	...	0.4	0.3	0.4	Pour 100 habitants
Myanmar									**Myanmar**
Number (thousands)		363	425	504	571	668	811	812	Nombre (en milliers)
Per 100 inhabitants		0.8	0.9	1.0	1.2	1.4	1.6	1.6	Pour 100 habitants
Namibia	(30/09)								**Namibie**
Number (thousands)		127	128	139	136	138	140	142	Nombre (en milliers)
Per 100 inhabitants		6.6	6.5	6.9	6.6	6.6	6.6	6.5	Pour 100 habitants
Nauru									**Nauru**
Number (thousands)		2	2	2	2	2	2	2	Nombre (en milliers)
Per 100 inhabitants		17.9	17.8	17.8	17.8	17.7	17.7	18.6	Pour 100 habitants
Nepal	(15/07)								**Népal**
Number (thousands)		372	418	485	612	701	805[38]	821[39]	Nombre (en milliers)
Per 100 inhabitants		1.4	1.6	1.8	2.2	2.5	2.8	2.8	Pour 100 habitants
Netherlands									**Pays-Bas**
Number (thousands)		7 846	7 861	7 600	7 450	7 404[40]	7 317[41]	7 320[42]	Nombre (en milliers)
Per 100 inhabitants		48.5	48.4	46.6	45.5	45.0	44.3	44.1	Pour 100 habitants
Netherlands Antilles									**Antilles néerlandaises**
Number (thousands)		83	84	85	86	87	88	89	Nombre (en milliers)
Per 100 inhabitants		45.5	45.6	45.6	45.5	45.3	45.1	44.9	Pour 100 habitants
New Caledonia									**Nouvelle-Calédonie**
Number (thousands)		52	53	55	58	60	63	66	Nombre (en milliers)
Per 100 inhabitants		22.9	23.1	23.5	24.2	24.8	25.6	26.4	Pour 100 habitants
New Zealand	(01/04)								**Nouvelle-Zélande**
Number (thousands)		1 798	1 801	1 729	1 762[43]	1 747[43]	1 750[32]	1 870	Nombre (en milliers)
Per 100 inhabitants		44.8	44.3	42.1	42.4	41.7	41.4	43.8	Pour 100 habitants

14 Telephones *(continued)*

Main telephone lines in operation (in thousands) and lines per 100 inhabitants

Téléphones *(suite)*

Nombre de lignes téléphoniques en service (en milliers) et lignes pour 100 habitants

Country or area	Fiscal year[&] Ex. budgét[&]	2003	2004	2005	2006	2007	2008	2009	Pays ou zone
Nicaragua									**Nicaragua**
Number (thousands)		205	214	221	248	249	252	255	Nombre (en milliers)
Per 100 inhabitants		3.9	4.0	4.0	4.5	4.5	4.4	4.4	Pour 100 habitants
Niger									**Niger**
Number (thousands)		23	24	24	24	24	65	65	Nombre (en milliers)
Per 100 inhabitants		0.2	0.2	0.2	0.2	0.2	0.4	0.4	Pour 100 habitants
Nigeria									**Nigéria**
Number (thousands)		889	1 028	1 223	1 688	#1 580[44]	1 308[44]	1 419[44]	Nombre (en milliers)
Per 100 inhabitants		0.7	0.7	0.9	1.2	1.1	0.9	0.9	Pour 100 habitants
Northern Mariana Islands									**Iles Mariannes du Nord**
Number (thousands)		22	23	23	24	24	25	25	Nombre (en milliers)
Per 100 inhabitants		29.5	29.2	29.1	29.0	28.9	28.9	28.9	Pour 100 habitants
Norway									**Norvège**
Number (thousands)		2 236	2 180	2 109	2 055	1 988	1 896	1 900	Nombre (en milliers)
Per 100 inhabitants		49.0	47.4	45.5	43.9	42.1	39.8	39.5	Pour 100 habitants
Occupied Palestinian Terr.									**Terr. palestinien occupé**
Number (thousands)		252	290	349	341	348	348	348	Nombre (en milliers)
Per 100 inhabitants		7.2	8.0	9.3	8.8	8.7	8.4	8.1	Pour 100 habitants
Oman									**Oman**
Number (thousands)		236	243	265	270	268	274	300	Nombre (en milliers)
Per 100 inhabitants		9.4	9.4	10.1	10.1	9.8	9.8	10.5	Pour 100 habitants
Pakistan	(30/06)								**Pakistan**
Number (thousands)		4 047	4 502	5 228	5 240	4 806	4 416	4 058	Nombre (en milliers)
Per 100 inhabitants		2.6	2.8	3.2	3.1	2.8	2.5	2.2	Pour 100 habitants
Palau									**Palaos**
Number (thousands)		7	8	8	7	7	7	7	Nombre (en milliers)
Per 100 inhabitants		37.0	38.7	39.6	36.2	36.8	36.1	34.5	Pour 100 habitants
Panama									**Panama**
Number (thousands)		381	425	470	488	495	524	537	Nombre (en milliers)
Per 100 inhabitants		12.2	13.4	14.6	14.9	14.8	15.4	15.6	Pour 100 habitants
Papua New Guinea									**Papouasie-Nvl-Guinée**
Number (thousands)		63	63	64	62	60	60	60	Nombre (en milliers)
Per 100 inhabitants		1.1	1.1	1.0	1.0	0.9	0.9	0.9	Pour 100 habitants
Paraguay									**Paraguay**
Number (thousands)		281	303	320	331	394	370	387	Nombre (en milliers)
Per 100 inhabitants		4.9	5.2	5.4	5.5	6.4	5.9	6.1	Pour 100 habitants
Peru									**Pérou**
Number (thousands)		1 839	2 050	2 251	2 401	2 673	2 878	2 965	Nombre (en milliers)
Per 100 inhabitants		6.8	7.5	8.1	8.5	9.4	10.0	10.2	Pour 100 habitants
Philippines									**Philippines**
Number (thousands)		3 340	3 437	3 367	3 633	3 940	4 076	4 100	Nombre (en milliers)
Per 100 inhabitants		4.1	4.1	3.9	4.2	4.4	4.5	4.5	Pour 100 habitants
Poland									**Pologne**
Number (thousands)		12 292	12 553	11 836	11 476	10 491	9 725	9 556	Nombre (en milliers)
Per 100 inhabitants		32.1	32.8	31.0	30.1	27.5	25.5	25.1	Pour 100 habitants
Portugal									**Portugal**
Number (thousands)		4 281	4 238	4 234	4 242	4 204	4 111	4 049	Nombre (en milliers)
Per 100 inhabitants		41.1	40.4	40.1	40.0	39.5	38.5	37.8	Pour 100 habitants
Puerto Rico									**Porto Rico**
Number (thousands)		1 213[2,45]	1 112[2,45]	1 038[45]	1 038[45]	1 013	949	870	Nombre (en milliers)
Per 100 inhabitants		31.3	28.5	26.5	26.4	25.7	23.9	21.9	Pour 100 habitants
Qatar									**Qatar**
Number (thousands)		185	191	205	228	237	263	285	Nombre (en milliers)
Per 100 inhabitants		25.2	23.9	23.2	22.8	20.9	20.6	20.2	Pour 100 habitants
Republic of Moldova									**Rép. de Moldova**
Number (thousands)		791	863	929	1 018	1 080	1 115	1 139	Nombre (en milliers)
Per 100 inhabitants		20.3	22.6	24.7	27.4	29.4	30.7	31.6	Pour 100 habitants
Romania									**Roumanie**
Number (thousands)		4 332	4 388	4 383	4 198	4 416	5 209	5 313	Nombre (en milliers)
Per 100 inhabitants		19.8	20.2	20.3	19.5	20.6	24.4	25.0	Pour 100 habitants
Russian Federation									**Fédération de Russie**
Number (thousands)		36 100	38 500[46]	40 100[46]	43 900	44 237	44 897	44 802	Nombre (en milliers)
Per 100 inhabitants		25.0	26.8	28.0	30.8	31.2	31.8	31.8	Pour 100 habitants
Rwanda									**Rwanda**
Number (thousands)		26	23	24	...	23	17	33	Nombre (en milliers)
Per 100 inhabitants		0.3	0.3	0.3	...	0.2	0.2	0.3	Pour 100 habitants
Saint Kitts and Nevis	(01/04)								**Saint-Kitts-et-Nevis**
Number (thousands)		24	20	20	21	20	20	21	Nombre (en milliers)
Per 100 inhabitants		49.1	42.0	41.3	41.5	40.6	39.9	39.6	Pour 100 habitants

14 Telephones *(continued)*

Main telephone lines in operation (in thousands) and lines per 100 inhabitants

Téléphones *(suite)*

Nombre de lignes téléphoniques en service (en milliers) et lignes pour 100 habitants

Country or area	Fiscal year[&] Ex. budget[&]	2003	2004	2005	2006	2007	2008	2009	Pays ou zone
Saint Lucia	(01/04)								**Sainte-Lucie**
Number (thousands)		49	42	39	41	41	41	41	Nombre (en milliers)
Per 100 inhabitants		30.2	25.7	23.6	24.5	24.3	24.0	23.8	Pour 100 habitants
Saint Vincent-Grenad.	(01/04)								**Saint Vincent-Grenad.**
Number (thousands)		21	19	23	23	23	23	23	Nombre (en milliers)
Per 100 inhabitants		19.6	17.5	20.7	20.8	21.0	20.9	21.1	Pour 100 habitants
Samoa									**Samoa**
Number (thousands)		13	16	20	23	26	29	32	Nombre (en milliers)
Per 100 inhabitants		7.4	9.2	10.9	12.6	14.4	16.1	17.8	Pour 100 habitants
San Marino									**Saint-Marin**
Number (thousands)		21	21	21	21	21	21	22	Nombre (en milliers)
Per 100 inhabitants		71.4	70.0	68.9	68.5	68.1	68.3	68.6	Pour 100 habitants
Sao Tome and Principe									**Sao Tomé-et-Principe**
Number (thousands)		7	7	7	8	8	8	8	Nombre (en milliers)
Per 100 inhabitants		4.7	4.7	4.7	4.9	4.9	4.8	4.8	Pour 100 habitants
Saudi Arabia									**Arabie saoudite**
Number (thousands)		3 503	3 695	3 844	3 951	3 996	4 100	4 171	Nombre (en milliers)
Per 100 inhabitants		15.6	16.0	16.3	16.4	16.2	16.3	16.2	Pour 100 habitants
Senegal									**Sénégal**
Number (thousands)		229	245	267	283	269	238	279	Nombre (en milliers)
Per 100 inhabitants		2.1	2.2	2.4	2.4	2.3	1.9	2.2	Pour 100 habitants
Serbia									**Serbie**
Number (thousands)		...	2 685	2 527	2 719	2 993	3 085	3 106	Nombre (en milliers)
Per 100 inhabitants		...	27.1	25.6	27.7	30.4	31.4	31.5	Pour 100 habitants
Seychelles	(01/04)								**Seychelles**
Number (thousands)		21	21	21	21	23[40,47]	22[47,48]	22[49]	Nombre (en milliers)
Per 100 inhabitants		25.8	25.8	25.9	24.9	27.3	26.6	26.2	Pour 100 habitants
Sierra Leone									**Sierra Leone**
Number (thousands)		25	27	28	29	30	32	33	Nombre (en milliers)
Per 100 inhabitants		0.5	0.5	0.5	0.6	0.6	0.6	0.6	Pour 100 habitants
Singapore	(01/04)								**Singapour**
Number (thousands)		1 890	1 857	1 844	1 854	1 862	1 857	1 852	Nombre (en milliers)
Per 100 inhabitants		45.5	44.2	43.2	42.5	41.5	40.2	39.1	Pour 100 habitants
Slovakia									**Slovaquie**
Number (thousands)		1 295	1 250	1 197	1 167	1 151	1 098	1 022	Nombre (en milliers)
Per 100 inhabitants		24.1	23.2	22.2	21.7	21.3	20.3	18.9	Pour 100 habitants
Slovenia									**Slovénie**
Number (thousands)		812[50]	811[50]	816[47,50]	837[47,50]	857[47,50]	1 010[51]	1 034	Nombre (en milliers)
Per 100 inhabitants		40.7	40.6	40.8	41.8	42.6	50.1	51.2	Pour 100 habitants
Solomon Islands	(01/04)								**Iles Salomon**
Number (thousands)		6[52]	7	7	8	8	8	8	Nombre (en milliers)
Per 100 inhabitants		1.4	1.5	1.6	1.6	1.6	1.6	1.6	Pour 100 habitants
Somalia									**Somalie**
Number (thousands)		100	100	100	100	100	100	100	Nombre (en milliers)
Per 100 inhabitants		1.3	1.2	1.2	1.2	1.1	1.1	1.1	Pour 100 habitants
South Africa	(01/04)								**Afrique du Sud**
Number (thousands)		4 821	4 850	4 729	4 642	4 532	4 425	4 320	Nombre (en milliers)
Per 100 inhabitants		10.3	10.2	9.8	9.5	9.2	8.9	8.6	Pour 100 habitants
Spain									**Espagne**
Number (thousands)		17 759	17 934	19 461	19 865	20 193	20 200	20 057	Nombre (en milliers)
Per 100 inhabitants		42.4	42.2	45.2	45.6	45.8	45.4	44.7	Pour 100 habitants
Sri Lanka									**Sri Lanka**
Number (thousands)		939	991	1 244	1 884	2 742	3 446	3 436	Nombre (en milliers)
Per 100 inhabitants		4.9	5.1	6.4	9.6	13.8	17.2	17.0	Pour 100 habitants
Sudan									**Soudan**
Number (thousands)		937	1 029	570	499	345	366	370	Nombre (en milliers)
Per 100 inhabitants		2.5	2.7	1.5	1.3	0.9	0.9	0.9	Pour 100 habitants
Suriname									**Suriname**
Number (thousands)		80	82	81	82	82	83	84	Nombre (en milliers)
Per 100 inhabitants		16.4	16.5	16.2	16.1	16.1	16.1	16.1	Pour 100 habitants
Swaziland	(01/04)								**Swaziland**
Number (thousands)		46	45	35	44	44	44	44	Nombre (en milliers)
Per 100 inhabitants		4.2	4.0	3.1	3.9	3.8	3.8	3.7	Pour 100 habitants
Sweden									**Suède**
Number (thousands)[11]		5 535	5 688	5 635	5 551	5 506	5 323	5 146	Nombre (en milliers)[11]
Per 100 inhabitants		61.7	63.1	62.2	60.9	60.1	57.8	55.6	Pour 100 habitants
Switzerland									**Suisse**
Number (thousands)[53]		5 323	5 253	5 150	5 022	4 927	*4 828	4 650	Nombre (en milliers)[53]
Per 100 inhabitants		72.5	71.1	69.2	67.1	65.6	64.0	61.4	Pour 100 habitants

14 Telephones *(continued)*

Main telephone lines in operation (in thousands) and lines per 100 inhabitants

Téléphones *(suite)*

Nombre de lignes téléphoniques en service (en milliers) et lignes pour 100 habitants

Country or area	Fiscal year& Ex. budgét&	2003	2004	2005	2006	2007	2008	2009	Pays ou zone
Syrian Arab Republic									**Rép. arabe syrienne**
Number (thousands)		2 411	2 658	2 903	3 243	3 452	3 633	3 871	Nombre (en milliers)
Per 100 inhabitants		13.4	14.4	15.2	16.4	16.8	17.1	17.7	Pour 100 habitants
Tajikistan									**Tadjikistan**
Number (thousands)		245	273	280	...	293	287	290	Nombre (en milliers)
Per 100 inhabitants		3.8	4.2	4.3	...	4.4	4.2	4.2	Pour 100 habitants
Thailand	(30/09)								**Thaïlande**
Number (thousands)		6 632	6 812	7 035	7 072	7 024	7 024	7 024	Nombre (en milliers)
Per 100 inhabitants		10.3	10.4	10.7	10.6	10.5	10.4	10.4	Pour 100 habitants
TFYR of Macedonia									**L'ex-R.Y. Macédoine**
Number (thousands)		525	537	534	491	464	457[54]	442[54]	Nombre (en milliers)
Per 100 inhabitants		25.9	26.4	26.2	24.1	22.7	22.4	21.7	Pour 100 habitants
Timor-Leste									**Timor-Leste**
Number (thousands) [11]		2	2	2	2	2	2	2	Nombre (en milliers) [11]
Per 100 inhabitants		0.2	0.2	0.2	0.2	0.2	0.2	0.2	Pour 100 habitants
Togo									**Togo**
Number (thousands)		61	66	63[55]	82	99	141	179	Nombre (en milliers)
Per 100 inhabitants		1.1	1.1	1.0	1.3	1.6	2.2	2.7	Pour 100 habitants
Tonga									**Tonga**
Number (thousands)		12	13	14	18	21	26	31	Nombre (en milliers)
Per 100 inhabitants		11.9	12.8	13.5	18.0	20.4	24.7	29.8	Pour 100 habitants
Trinidad and Tobago	(01/04)								**Trinité-et-Tobago**
Number (thousands)		319	322	322	326	307	315	315	Nombre (en milliers)
Per 100 inhabitants		24.4	24.5	24.4	24.6	23.1	23.6	23.5	Pour 100 habitants
Tunisia									**Tunisie**
Number (thousands)		1 164	1 204	1 257	1 268	1 273	1 239	1 279	Nombre (en milliers)
Per 100 inhabitants		12.0	12.3	12.7	12.7	12.6	12.2	12.4	Pour 100 habitants
Turkey									**Turquie**
Number (thousands)		18 917	19 125	18 978	18 832	18 201[22]	17 502	16 534	Nombre (en milliers)
Per 100 inhabitants		27.3	27.2	26.7	26.1	24.9	23.7	22.1	Pour 100 habitants
Turkmenistan									**Turkménistan**
Number (thousands)		376	388	398	424	458	478	478	Nombre (en milliers)
Per 100 inhabitants		8.0	8.1	8.2	8.6	9.2	9.5	9.4	Pour 100 habitants
Tuvalu									**Tuvalu**
Number (thousands)		1	1	1	1	1	2	2	Nombre (en milliers)
Per 100 inhabitants		7.2	7.7	9.1	11.2	13.2	15.2	17.1	Pour 100 habitants
Uganda	(30/06)								**Ouganda**
Number (thousands)		61	72	88	108	166	168	234	Nombre (en milliers)
Per 100 inhabitants		0.2	0.3	0.3	0.4	0.5	0.5	0.7	Pour 100 habitants
Ukraine									**Ukraine**
Number (thousands)		11 110	12 142	11 667	12 397	12 906	13 177	13 026	Nombre (en milliers)
Per 100 inhabitants		23.3	25.7	24.9	26.6	27.9	28.7	28.5	Pour 100 habitants
United Arab Emirates									**Emirats arabes unis**
Number (thousands)		1 136	1 188	1 237	1 310	1 386	1 508	1 561	Nombre (en milliers)
Per 100 inhabitants		30.2	30.2	30.2	30.9	31.7	33.6	33.9	Pour 100 habitants
United Kingdom	(01/04)								**Royaume-Uni**
Number (thousands) [11]		34 550	34 576	34 068	33 849	33 815[40]	33 209	33 615	Nombre (en milliers) [11]
Per 100 inhabitants		57.9	57.7	56.5	55.9	55.5	54.2	54.6	Pour 100 habitants
United Rep. of Tanzania									**Rép.-Unie de Tanzanie**
Number (thousands)		147	148	154	157	163	124[2]	173	Nombre (en milliers)
Per 100 inhabitants		0.4	0.4	0.4	0.4	0.4	0.3	0.4	Pour 100 habitants
United States									**Etats-Unis**
Number (thousands) [56]		182 933	177 691	175 161	167 460	158 418	154 655	155 000	Nombre (en milliers) [56]
Per 100 inhabitants		61.6	59.3	57.9	54.8	51.3	49.6	49.3	Pour 100 habitants
United States Virgin Is.									**Iles Vierges améric.**
Number (thousands)		70	71	72	73	73	74	75	Nombre (en milliers)
Per 100 inhabitants		63.7	64.7	65.4	66.1	66.9	67.7	68.5	Pour 100 habitants
Uruguay									**Uruguay**
Number (thousands)		938	997	1 006	987	965	959	953	Nombre (en milliers)
Per 100 inhabitants		28.2	30.0	30.3	29.6	28.9	28.6	28.4	Pour 100 habitants
Uzbekistan									**Ouzbékistan**
Number (thousands)		1 717	1 750	1 794	1 842	1 822	1 850	1 857	Nombre (en milliers)
Per 100 inhabitants		6.7	6.7	6.8	6.9	6.8	6.8	6.8	Pour 100 habitants
Vanuatu									**Vanuatu**
Number (thousands)		7	7	7	*8[34]	*9[34]	10	7	Nombre (en milliers)
Per 100 inhabitants		3.2	3.2	3.2	3.4	3.9	4.4	3.0	Pour 100 habitants
Venezuela (Bol. R. of)									**Venezuela (R. bol. du)**
Number (thousands)		2 956	3 346	3 651	4 217	5 195	6 418	6 867	Nombre (en milliers)
Per 100 inhabitants		11.5	12.7	13.7	15.5	18.8	22.8	24.0	Pour 100 habitants

14 Telephones *(continued)*

Main telephone lines in operation (in thousands) and lines per 100 inhabitants

Téléphones *(suite)*

Nombre de lignes téléphoniques en service (en milliers) et lignes pour 100 habitants

Country or area	Fiscal year& Ex. budgét&	2003	2004	2005	2006	2007	2008	2009	Pays ou zone
Viet Nam									**Viet Nam**
Number (thousands)		4 402	10 125	15 845	27 505	28 529	29 591	30 693	Nombre (en milliers)
Per 100 inhabitants		5.4	12.2	18.8	32.3	33.1	34.0	34.9	Pour 100 habitants
Yemen									**Yémen**
Number (thousands)		694	795	901	968	1 040	1 117	1 201	Nombre (en milliers)
Per 100 inhabitants		3.5	3.9	4.3	4.5	4.7	4.9	5.1	Pour 100 habitants
Zambia	(01/04)								**Zambie**
Number (thousands)		88	92	95	93	92	91	90	Nombre (en milliers)
Per 100 inhabitants		0.8	0.8	0.8	0.8	0.7	0.7	0.7	Pour 100 habitants
Zimbabwe	(30/06)								**Zimbabwe**
Number (thousands)		301	317	328	336	345	348	385	Nombre (en milliers)
Per 100 inhabitants		2.4	2.5	2.6	2.7	2.8	2.8	3.1	Pour 100 habitants

Source:
International Telecommunication Union (ITU), Geneva, the ITU database, last accessed October 2010.

& Fiscal year refers to the fiscal year used in each country or area. Countries or areas whose reference periods coincide with the calendar year ending 31 December are not footnoted. Those that have a fiscal year other than calendar year are denoted as follows:

22/03: Year beginning 22 March
01/04: Year beginning 1 April
30/06: Year ending 30 June
15/07: Year ending 15 July
30/09: Year ending 30 September

Source:
Union internationale des télécommunications (UIT), Genève, la base de données de l'UIT, dernier accès octobre 2010.

& Ex. budgét. fait référence à l'exercice budgétaire en vigueur dans chaque pays ou territoire. Les pays ou les territoires dont l'exercice budgétaire terminent le 31 décembre de l'année civile ne sont pas signalés. Dans le cas contraire, ils sont désignés de la manière suivante:

22/03 : Exercice commençant le 22 mars
01/04 : Exercice commençant le 1er avril
30/06 : Exercice se terminant le 30 juin
15/07 : Exercice se terminant le 15 juillet
30/09 : Exercice se terminant le 30 septembre

1 Analogic lines and XDSI lines.
2 June.
3 From this year, including copper line (171,562), DSL line (13,967), WiMax (43,146), CDMA (72,000) and VSAT (2,504) which are not included in previous years.
4 1994-2002 only refers to "Telefónica de Argentina S.A. y Telecom Argentina S.A." From 2002 all licensees are included (352 in 2003).
5 Only includes major telecommunication operators, representing about 85-90% of total.
6 Represents about 99% of total.
7 Excluding ISDN
8 Telstra
9 Communications Report 2008-09.
10 Measured in ISDN B channels equivalents.
11 Including ISDN channels.
12 VoB (Voice over Broadband) included.
13 Number of ISDN channels are not included.
14 Includes fixed wireless.
15 Including ISDN.
16 Including ISDN equivalents.
17 Conventional telephony terminals in service.
18 Number of subscribers of the incumbent operator and the alternative operators, including the ISDN lines.
19 Data as of 1 July 2009.
20 WLL lines included.
21 Retail lines.
22 November.
23 ISDN channels, fixed wireless subscribers and public payphones are not included in the figure.
24 Telephone subscribers.

1 Lignes analogiques et "XDSI".
2 Juin.
3 À partir de cette année, et contrairement aux années précédentes, les lignes en cuivre (171 562), DSL (13 967), WiMax (43 146), AMRC (72 000) et VSAT (2 504) sont comptabilisées.
4 Les chiffres de 1994-2002 ne concernent que "Telefónica de Argentina S.A. y Telecom Argentina S.A." À partir de 2002 tous les détenteurs de licence sont compris (352 en 2003).
5 Ne comprend que les principaux opérateurs de télécommunications, qui représentent de 85 à 90 % du total.
6 Représente environ 99% du total.
7 Non compris RNIS.
8 Telstra
9 Communications Report 2008-09.
10 Mesuré en équivalents canaux ISDN B.
11 RNIS inclus.
12 Comprend la VLB (Voix sur large bande).
13 Ne comprend pas le nombre de canaux ISDN.
14 Y compris les téléphones fixes sans fil.
15 RNIS inclus.
16 Y compris les équivalents du RNIS.
17 Terminaux de téléphonie conventionnelle en service.
18 Le nombre d'abonnés de l'opérateur historique et des opérateurs alternatifs, comprend les lignes ISDN.
19 Données du 1er Juillet 2009.
20 Y compris les lignes "WLL".
21 Lignes du commerce de détail.
22 Novembre.
23 Chiffre qui ne comprend pas les canaux ISDN, les abonnés au réseau fixe sans fil et les téléphones publics.
24 Abonnés au téléphone.

25 Including VoIP subscriptions.
26 Many cancellations of subscribers that had not paid, following privatization (February 2007).
27 Excluding public call offices.
28 Telephone channels including ISDN and own consumption, excluding public payphones.
29 ITU estimate.
30 Excluding WLL-F (Wireless in local loop-fixed) subscribers.
31 Including PSTN lines, ISDN paths, FWA subscription, public payphones and LLU.
32 December.
33 Data refer to Telecom Italia Wireline.
34 Based on Pacific Economic Survey 2008.
35 Indicates working lines.
36 Without ISDN channels.
37 Including digital lines.
38 April.
39 As of March 2010.
40 September.
41 Including telephone subscriptions over cable.
42 July.
43 Includes fibre and satellite fixed telephone connections.
44 Refers to active fixed/wireless lines.
45 Switched access lines.
46 October.
47 Including fixed VoIP (Voice over internet protocol) lines.
48 January 2009
49 Data collected at the end of June 2009.
50 Including ISDN subscribers.
51 Includes ISDN and VoIP connections (network termination points).
52 The number of fixed lines declined due to civil war.
53 Including ISDN access channels.
54 Internal and test lines of incumbent included.
55 Drop results from the termination of contract for clients that had not paid.
56 Data refer to "Local Loops".

25 Chiffre qui ne comprend pas les canaux ISDN, les abonnés au réseau fixe sans fil et les téléphones publics.
26 Nombreuses résiliations d'abonnements non payés après la privatisation (février 2007).
27 Cabines publiques exclues.
28 Voies téléphoniques, y compris RNIS et consommation personnelle, excluant les téléphones publics payants.
29 Estimation de l'UIT.
30 À l'exclusion des abonnés ayant un téléphone fixe en boucle locale sans fil.
31 Y compris les lignes du RTCP, du RNIS, les abonnements d'accès fixe sans fil, les cabines publiques et l'accès boucle locale dégroupée.
32 Décembre.
33 Les données se réfèrent au "Telecom Italia Wireline".
34 Basé sur l'Enquête économique sur le Pacifique de 2008.
35 Indique les lignes en service.
36 Sans RNIS.
37 Y compris les lignes digitales.
38 Avril.
39 En mars 2010.
40 Septembre.
41 Comprend les abonnements téléphoniques par câble.
42 Juillet.
43 Y compris les téléphones fixes sur réseau par fibre et par satellite.
44 Il s'agit des lignes en activité fixes/sans fil.
45 Lignes d'accès déviées.
46 Octobre.
47 Y compris les lignes de téléphonie par Internet (VoIP).
48 Janvier 2009
49 Données collectées à la fin juin 2009.
50 Y compris les abonnés au ISDN.
51 Y compris les connections ISDN et VoIP.
52 Le nombre de lignes fixes a diminué en raison de la guerre civile.
53 Comprend les canaux d'accès ISDN.
54 Intérieur et de lignes de test du titulaire du poste inclus.
55 La diminution est due à la résiliation des contrats de clients dont le compte était en souffrance.
56 Les données se réfèrent aux "Local Loops".

15 Cellular mobile telephone subscribers

Number (thousands) and per 100 inhabitants

Abonnés au téléphone mobile

Nombre (milliers) et pour 100 habitants

Country or area	Fiscal year & Ex. budgét. &	2003	2004	2005	2006	2007	2008	2009	Pays ou zone
Afghanistan									**Afghanistan**
Number (thousands)		200	600	1 200	2 520	4 668	7 899	12 000	Nombre (en milliers)
Per 100 inhabitants		1	3	5	10	18	29	43	Pour 100 habitants
Albania									**Albanie**
Number (thousands)		1 100	1 260	1 530	1 910	2 322	3 141	4 162	Nombre (en milliers)
Per 100 inhabitants		36	41	49	61	74	100	132	Pour 100 habitants
Algeria									**Algérie**
Number (thousands)		1 447	4 882	13 661	20 998	27 563	27 031	32 730	Nombre (en milliers)
Per 100 inhabitants		5	15	42	63	81	79	94	Pour 100 habitants
American Samoa									**Samoa américaines**
Number (thousands)		2	2	...	...	...	...	...	Nombre (en milliers)
Per 100 inhabitants		3	4	...	...	...	...	...	Pour 100 habitants
Andorra									**Andorre**
Number (thousands)		52	58	65	69	64	64	65	Nombre (en milliers)
Per 100 inhabitants		70	76	81	84	76	76	75	Pour 100 habitants
Angola									**Angola**
Number (thousands)		350	740	1 611	3 055[1]	4 962	6 773	8 109	Nombre (en milliers)
Per 100 inhabitants		2	5	10	18	28	38	44	Pour 100 habitants
Antigua and Barbuda	(01/04)								**Antigua-et-Barbuda**
Number (thousands)		46	54	86	110	112	137	135	Nombre (en milliers)
Per 100 inhabitants		57	66	103	130	131	158	154	Pour 100 habitants
Argentina	(30/09)								**Argentine**
Number (thousands)		7 842	13 512	22 156	31 510	40 402	46 509	51 891	Nombre (en milliers)
Per 100 inhabitants		21	35	57	81	102	117	129	Pour 100 habitants
Armenia									**Arménie**
Number (thousands)		114	203	318	1 260	1 876	2 336	2 620	Nombre (en milliers)
Per 100 inhabitants		4	7	10	41	61	76	85	Pour 100 habitants
Aruba									**Aruba**
Number (thousands)		70	98	103	109	114	121	128	Nombre (en milliers)
Per 100 inhabitants		72	99	102	106	109	115	120	Pour 100 habitants
Australia	(30/06)								**Australie**
Number (thousands)		14 347	16 480	18 420	19 760	21 260	22 120	24 220[2]	Nombre (en milliers)
Per 100 inhabitants		72	82	90	96	102	105	114	Pour 100 habitants
Austria									**Autriche**
Number (thousands)		7 274[3]	7 992	8 665	9 281[4]	9 912[4]	10 816	11 773	Nombre (en milliers)
Per 100 inhabitants		89	98	105	112	119	130	141	Pour 100 habitants
Azerbaijan									**Azerbaïdjan**
Number (thousands)		1 057	1 457	2 242	3 324	4 519	6 548	7 757	Nombre (en milliers)
Per 100 inhabitants		13	17	27	39	52	75	88	Pour 100 habitants
Bahamas									**Bahamas**
Number (thousands)		122	186	228	253	374	358[5]	359	Nombre (en milliers)
Per 100 inhabitants		39	58	70	77	112	106	105	Pour 100 habitants
Bahrain									**Bahreïn**
Number (thousands)		443	650	767	907	1 116	1 441	1 578	Nombre (en milliers)
Per 100 inhabitants		64	91	105	122	147	186	199	Pour 100 habitants
Bangladesh	(30/06)								**Bangladesh**
Number (thousands)		1 365	2 782	9 000	19 131	34 370[6]	44 640[7]	50 400[3]	Nombre (en milliers)
Per 100 inhabitants		1	2	6	12	22	28	31	Pour 100 habitants
Barbados	(01/04)								**Barbade**
Number (thousands)		140	200	206	237	258	289	337	Nombre (en milliers)
Per 100 inhabitants		56	79	81	93	101	113	132	Pour 100 habitants
Belarus									**Bélarus**
Number (thousands)		1 118	2 239	4 100	5 960	6 960	8 128	9 686	Nombre (en milliers)
Per 100 inhabitants		11	23	42	61	72	84	101	Pour 100 habitants
Belgium									**Belgique**
Number (thousands)		8 606	9 132	9 605	9 847	10 738	11 822	12 419	Nombre (en milliers)
Per 100 inhabitants		83	88	92	94	102	112	117	Pour 100 habitants

15 Cellular mobile telephone subscribers *(continued)*
Number (thousands) and per 100 inhabitants
Abonnés au téléphone mobile *(suite)*
Nombre (milliers) et pour 100 habitants

Country or area	Fiscal year & Ex. budgét. &	2003	2004	2005	2006	2007	2008	2009	Pays ou zone
Belize	(01/04)								**Belize**
Number (thousands)		60	75	85	100	118	160	162	Nombre (en milliers)
Per 100 inhabitants		22	27	30	35	40	53	53	Pour 100 habitants
Benin									**Bénin**
Number (thousands)		236	459	596	1 056	2 052	3 625	5 033	Nombre (en milliers)
Per 100 inhabitants		3	6	8	13	24	42	56	Pour 100 habitants
Bermuda	(01/04)								**Bermudes**
Number (thousands)		40	49	53	60	69	79	85	Nombre (en milliers)
Per 100 inhabitants		63	77	82	93	107	122	131	Pour 100 habitants
Bhutan									**Bhoutan**
Number (thousands)		2	19	36	82	149	251	327[8]	Nombre (en milliers)
Per 100 inhabitants		^0	3	6	12	22	37	47	Pour 100 habitants
Bolivia (Plurin. State of)									**Bolivie (État plurin. de)**
Number (thousands)		1 279	1 801	2 421	2 876	3 254	4 830	7 148	Nombre (en milliers)
Per 100 inhabitants		14	20	26	31	34	50	72	Pour 100 habitants
Bosnia and Herzegovina									**Bosnie-Herzégovine**
Number (thousands)		1 075	1 407	1 594	1 888	2 450	3 179	3 257	Nombre (en milliers)
Per 100 inhabitants		28	37	42	50	65	84	86	Pour 100 habitants
Botswana	(01/04)								**Botswana**
Number (thousands)		445	523	564	823	1 152	1 486	1 874	Nombre (en milliers)
Per 100 inhabitants		25	29	31	44	61	77	96	Pour 100 habitants
Brazil									**Brésil**
Number (thousands)		46 373	65 605	86 210	99 919	120 980	150 641	173 959	Nombre (en milliers)
Per 100 inhabitants		26	36	46	53	64	78	90	Pour 100 habitants
Brunei Darussalam									**Brunéi Darussalam**
Number (thousands)		177	202	233	301	366	399	*426	Nombre (en milliers)
Per 100 inhabitants		50	56	63	80	95	102	107	Pour 100 habitants
Bulgaria									**Bulgarie**
Number (thousands)		3 501	4 730	6 245	8 253	9 897	10 500	10 617	Nombre (en milliers)
Per 100 inhabitants		45	61	81	107	130	138	141	Pour 100 habitants
Burkina Faso									**Burkina Faso**
Number (thousands)		238[9]	396[9]	634[9]	1 017[9]	1 611	2 553	3 299	Nombre (en milliers)
Per 100 inhabitants		2	3	5	7	11	17	21	Pour 100 habitants
Burundi									**Burundi**
Number (thousands)		64	101	153	200	270	481	838	Nombre (en milliers)
Per 100 inhabitants		1	1	2	3	3	6	10	Pour 100 habitants
Cambodia									**Cambodge**
Number (thousands)		498	862	1 062	1 722	2 583	4 237	5 593	Nombre (en milliers)
Per 100 inhabitants		4	6	8	12	18	29	38	Pour 100 habitants
Cameroon									**Cameroun**
Number (thousands)		1 077	1 531	2 253	3 136	4 536	6 161	7 397	Nombre (en milliers)
Per 100 inhabitants		6	9	13	17	24	32	38	Pour 100 habitants
Canada									**Canada**
Number (thousands)		13 291	15 020	17 017	18 749	20 277	22 093	23 081	Nombre (en milliers)
Per 100 inhabitants		42	47	53	57	62	66	69	Pour 100 habitants
Cape Verde									**Cap-Vert**
Number (thousands)		53	66	82	109	152	278	392	Nombre (en milliers)
Per 100 inhabitants		12	14	17	22	31	56	78	Pour 100 habitants
Cayman Islands	(01/04)								**Iles Caïmanes**
Number (thousands)		21	34	...	...	...	...	...	Nombre (en milliers)
Per 100 inhabitants		44	67	...	...	...	...	...	Pour 100 habitants
Central African Rep.									**Rép. centrafricaine**
Number (thousands)		40	60	100	110	130	154	168	Nombre (en milliers)
Per 100 inhabitants		1	1	2	3	3	4	4	Pour 100 habitants
Chad									**Tchad**
Number (thousands)		65	123	210	466	918	1 809	2 686	Nombre (en milliers)
Per 100 inhabitants		1	1	2	5	9	17	24	Pour 100 habitants
Chile									**Chili**
Number (thousands)		7 268	9 261	10 570	12 451	13 955	14 797	16 450	Nombre (en milliers)
Per 100 inhabitants		46	57	65	76	84	88	97	Pour 100 habitants

15 Cellular mobile telephone subscribers *(continued)*

Number (thousands) and per 100 inhabitants

Abonnés au téléphone mobile *(suite)*

Nombre (milliers) et pour 100 habitants

Country or area	Fiscal year & Ex. budgét. &	2003	2004	2005	2006	2007	2008	2009	Pays ou zone
China [10]									**Chine** [10]
Number (thousands)		269 953	334 824	393 406	461 058	547 306	641 230	747 000	Nombre (en milliers)
Per 100 inhabitants		21	26	30	35	41	48	56	Pour 100 habitants
China, Hong Kong SAR	(01/04)								**Chine, Hong Kong RAS**
Number (thousands)		7 349	8 214	8 544	9 444	10 752[6]	11 580	12 207	Nombre (en milliers)
Per 100 inhabitants		108	120	124	137	155	166	174	Pour 100 habitants
China, Macao SAR									**Chine, Macao RAS**
Number (thousands)		364	432	533	636	794	933	1 037	Nombre (en milliers)
Per 100 inhabitants		78	91	109	127	155	177	193	Pour 100 habitants
Colombia									**Colombie**
Number (thousands)		6 186	10 401	21 850	29 763	33 941	41 365	42 160	Nombre (en milliers)
Per 100 inhabitants		15	25	51	68	77	92	92	Pour 100 habitants
Comoros									**Comores**
Number (thousands)		2	8	16	37	66	98	100	Nombre (en milliers)
Per 100 inhabitants		^0	1	3	6	10	15	15	Pour 100 habitants
Congo									**Congo**
Number (thousands)		330	384	558	918	1 288	1 807	2 171	Nombre (en milliers)
Per 100 inhabitants		10	11	16	26	36	50	59	Pour 100 habitants
Costa Rica									**Costa Rica**
Number (thousands)		778	923	1 101	1 444	1 508	1 887	1 950	Nombre (en milliers)
Per 100 inhabitants		19	22	25	33	34	42	43	Pour 100 habitants
Côte d'Ivoire									**Côte d'Ivoire**
Number (thousands)		1 281	1 674	2 349	4 065	7 468	10 449	13 346	Nombre (en milliers)
Per 100 inhabitants		7	9	12	21	37	51	63	Pour 100 habitants
Croatia									**Croatie**
Number (thousands)		2 537	2 836	3 650	4 395	5 035	5 880	6 035	Nombre (en milliers)
Per 100 inhabitants		57	64	82	99	114	133	137	Pour 100 habitants
Cuba									**Cuba**
Number (thousands)		35	76	136	153	198	332	443	Nombre (en milliers)
Per 100 inhabitants		^0	1	1	1	2	3	4	Pour 100 habitants
Cyprus									**Chypre**
Number (thousands)		552	658	783	868	988	1 017	978	Nombre (en milliers)
Per 100 inhabitants		68	80	94	103	116	118	112	Pour 100 habitants
Czech Republic									**République tchèque**
Number (thousands)		9 709	10 783	11 776	12 406	13 229	13 780	14 258	Nombre (en milliers)
Per 100 inhabitants		95	106	116	121	129	134	138	Pour 100 habitants
Dem. Rep. of the Congo									**Rép. dém. du Congo**
Number (thousands)		1 246	1 991	2 746	4 415	6 592	9 263	10 163	Nombre (en milliers)
Per 100 inhabitants		2	3	5	7	11	14	15	Pour 100 habitants
Denmark									**Danemark**
Number (thousands)		4 767	5 167	5 449	5 828	6 308[11]	6 862[11]	7 406[11]	Nombre (en milliers)
Per 100 inhabitants		88	96	101	107	116	126	135	Pour 100 habitants
Djibouti									**Djibouti**
Number (thousands)		23	34	44	45	70	113	129	Nombre (en milliers)
Per 100 inhabitants		3	4	5	5	8	13	15	Pour 100 habitants
Dominica	(01/04)								**Dominique**
Number (thousands)		24	42	52	72	89	100	106	Nombre (en milliers)
Per 100 inhabitants		35	62	77	106	133	150	159	Pour 100 habitants
Dominican Republic									**Rép. dominicaine**
Number (thousands)		2 092	2 534	3 623	4 606	5 513	7 210	8 630	Nombre (en milliers)
Per 100 inhabitants		23	27	38	48	56	72	86	Pour 100 habitants
Ecuador									**Equateur**
Number (thousands)		2 398	3 544	6 246	8 485	9 940	11 692	13 635	Nombre (en milliers)
Per 100 inhabitants		19	27	48	64	75	87	100	Pour 100 habitants
Egypt	(30/06)								**Egypte**
Number (thousands)		5 798	7 643	13 630	18 001	30 065	41 272	55 352	Nombre (en milliers)
Per 100 inhabitants		8	10	18	23	38	51	67	Pour 100 habitants
El Salvador									**El Salvador**
Number (thousands)		1 150	1 833	2 412	3 852	6 137	6 951	7 566	Nombre (en milliers)
Per 100 inhabitants		19	30	40	63	101	113	123	Pour 100 habitants

15 Cellular mobile telephone subscribers *(continued)*
Number (thousands) and per 100 inhabitants

Abonnés au téléphone mobile *(suite)*
Nombre (milliers) et pour 100 habitants

Country or area	Fiscal year & Ex. budgét. &	2003	2004	2005	2006	2007	2008	2009	Pays ou zone
Equatorial Guinea									**Guinée équatoriale**
Number (thousands)		42	62	97	140	220	346	445	Nombre (en milliers)
Per 100 inhabitants		7	10	16	22	34	52	66	Pour 100 habitants
Eritrea									**Erythrée**
Number (thousands)		0	20	40	62	84	109	141	Nombre (en milliers)
Per 100 inhabitants		0	^0	1	1	2	2	3	Pour 100 habitants
Estonia									**Estonie**
Number (thousands)		1 050	1 256	1 445	1 659	1 982[12]	2 524[13]	2 721[14]	Nombre (en milliers)
Per 100 inhabitants		78	93	107	123	148	188	203	Pour 100 habitants
Ethiopia	(30/06)								**Ethiopie**
Number (thousands)		51	156	411	867	1 209	1 955	4 052	Nombre (en milliers)
Per 100 inhabitants		^0	^0	1	1	2	2	5	Pour 100 habitants
Faeroe Islands									**Iles Féroé**
Number (thousands)		38	41	42	50	52	55	57	Nombre (en milliers)
Per 100 inhabitants		80	86	86	102	106	111	114	Pour 100 habitants
Fiji [15]									**Fidji** [15]
Number (thousands)		110	142	205	285	530	600	640	Nombre (en milliers)
Per 100 inhabitants		13	17	25	34	63	71	75	Pour 100 habitants
Finland									**Finlande**
Number (thousands)		4 747	4 988	5 270	5 670	6 080	6 830	7 700	Nombre (en milliers)
Per 100 inhabitants		91	95	100	108	115	129	145	Pour 100 habitants
France									**France**
Number (thousands)		41 702	44 544	48 088	51 662	55 358	57 972[7]	59 543[16]	Nombre (en milliers)
Per 100 inhabitants		69	73	79	84	90	93	96	Pour 100 habitants
French Guiana									**Guyane française**
Number (thousands)		92	98	...	...	...	...	218	Nombre (en milliers)
Per 100 inhabitants		49	50	...	...	...	...	96	Pour 100 habitants
French Polynesia									**Polynésie française**
Number (thousands)		60	96	120	152	175	187	208	Nombre (en milliers)
Per 100 inhabitants		24	38	47	59	67	70	77	Pour 100 habitants
Gabon [17]									**Gabon** [17]
Number (thousands)		300	489	737	898	1 169	1 300	1 373	Nombre (en milliers)
Per 100 inhabitants		23	36	54	64	82	90	93	Pour 100 habitants
Gambia	(01/04)								**Gambie**
Number (thousands)		149	175	247	404	800	1 166	1 433	Nombre (en milliers)
Per 100 inhabitants		10	12	16	26	50	70	84	Pour 100 habitants
Georgia	(01/04)								**Géorgie**
Number (thousands)		711	841	1 174	1 704	2 600	2 755	2 837	Nombre (en milliers)
Per 100 inhabitants		16	19	26	39	60	64	67	Pour 100 habitants
Germany									**Allemagne**
Number (thousands)		64 800	71 322	79 271	85 652[18]	96 233[18]	105 523[19]	105 000[19]	Nombre (en milliers)
Per 100 inhabitants		79	87	96	104	117	128	128	Pour 100 habitants
Ghana									**Ghana**
Number (thousands)		796	1 695	2 875	5 207	7 604	11 570	15 109	Nombre (en milliers)
Per 100 inhabitants		4	8	13	23	33	50	63	Pour 100 habitants
Gibraltar									**Gibraltar**
Number (thousands)		16[6]	18	20	22	24	26	29	Nombre (en milliers)
Per 100 inhabitants		53	60	65	71	77	84	92	Pour 100 habitants
Greece									**Grèce**
Number (thousands)		8 936	9 324	10 260	10 980[20]	12 295[20]	13 799[20]	13 295[20]	Nombre (en milliers)
Per 100 inhabitants		81	84	93	99	111	124	119	Pour 100 habitants
Greenland									**Groenland**
Number (thousands)		30	39	46	54	66	56	53	Nombre (en milliers)
Per 100 inhabitants		52	68	81	94	116	97	93	Pour 100 habitants
Grenada									**Grenade**
Number (thousands)		42	43	47	46	51	60	64	Nombre (en milliers)
Per 100 inhabitants		42	42	46	45	50	58	62	Pour 100 habitants
Guam									**Guam**
Number (thousands)		80	98	...	...	...	...	...	Nombre (en milliers)
Per 100 inhabitants		49	59	...	...	...	...	...	Pour 100 habitants

15 Cellular mobile telephone subscribers *(continued)*
Number (thousands) and per 100 inhabitants

Abonnés au téléphone mobile *(suite)*
Nombre (milliers) et pour 100 habitants

Country or area	Fiscal year & Ex. budgét. &	2003	2004	2005	2006	2007	2008	2009	Pays ou zone
Guatemala									**Guatemala**
Number (thousands)		2 035	3 168	4 510	7 179	11 898	14 949	17 307	Nombre (en milliers)
Per 100 inhabitants		17	26	35	55	89	109	123	Pour 100 habitants
Guernsey									**Guernesey**
Number (thousands)		42	44	...	...	...	...	...	Nombre (en milliers)
Per 100 inhabitants		74	79	...	...	...	...	...	Pour 100 habitants
Guinea									**Guinée**
Number (thousands)		112	155	189	...	2 000	3 840	5 607	Nombre (en milliers)
Per 100 inhabitants		1	2	2	...	21	39	56	Pour 100 habitants
Guinea-Bissau									**Guinée-Bissau**
Number (thousands)		1	39	99	157	296	500	560	Nombre (en milliers)
Per 100 inhabitants		^0	3	7	10	19	32	35	Pour 100 habitants
Guyana[21]									**Guyana**[21]
Number (thousands)		138	172	281	...	...	...	...	Nombre (en milliers)
Per 100 inhabitants		18	23	37	...	...	...	...	Pour 100 habitants
Haiti									**Haïti**
Number (thousands)		320	400	500	1 200	2 500	3 200	3 648	Nombre (en milliers)
Per 100 inhabitants		4	4	5	13	26	32	36	Pour 100 habitants
Honduras									**Honduras**
Number (thousands)		379	707	1 281	2 241	4 185	6 211	7 714	Nombre (en milliers)
Per 100 inhabitants		6	10	19	32	58	85	103	Pour 100 habitants
Hungary									**Hongrie**
Number (thousands)		7 945	8 727[22]	9 320	9 966	11 030	12 224	11 792	Nombre (en milliers)
Per 100 inhabitants		78	86	92	99	110	122	118	Pour 100 habitants
Iceland									**Islande**
Number (thousands)		280	290	283	302	328	337	349	Nombre (en milliers)
Per 100 inhabitants		97	100	96	100	106	107	108	Pour 100 habitants
India	(01/04)								**Inde**
Number (thousands)		33 690	52 220	90 140	166 050	233 620	346 890	525 090	Nombre (en milliers)
Per 100 inhabitants		3	5	8	14	20	29	44	Pour 100 habitants
Indonesia									**Indonésie**
Number (thousands)		18 495	30 337	46 910	63 803	93 387	140 578[3]	159 248	Nombre (en milliers)
Per 100 inhabitants		9	14	21	29	42	62	69	Pour 100 habitants
Iran (Islamic Rep. of)	(22/03)								**Iran (Rép. islamique d')**
Number (thousands)		3 450	5 076	8 511[23]	15 385	29 770	43 000	52 555	Nombre (en milliers)
Per 100 inhabitants		5	7	12	21	41	59	71	Pour 100 habitants
Iraq	(30/06)								**Iraq**
Number (thousands)		80	574	1 533	9 345	14 021	17 529	19 722	Nombre (en milliers)
Per 100 inhabitants		^0	2	5	32	48	58	64	Pour 100 habitants
Ireland	(01/04)								**Irlande**
Number (thousands)		3 500	3 860	4 270	4 690	4 971[24]	5 048	4 871[25]	Nombre (en milliers)
Per 100 inhabitants		87	94	102	110	114	114	108	Pour 100 habitants
Israel									**Israël**
Number (thousands)		6 618	7 222	7 757	8 404	8 902	8 982	9 022	Nombre (en milliers)
Per 100 inhabitants		103	110	116	123	128	127	126	Pour 100 habitants
Italy									**Italie**
Number (thousands)		56 770[26]	62 750	71 500	80 418	89 801	90 341	90 613	Nombre (en milliers)
Per 100 inhabitants		98	108	122	136	151	152	151	Pour 100 habitants
Jamaica	(01/04)								**Jamaïque**
Number (thousands)		1 576	1 838	1 981	2 275	2 684	2 723	2 971	Nombre (en milliers)
Per 100 inhabitants		60	69	74	85	100	101	109	Pour 100 habitants
Japan	(01/04)								**Japon**
Number (thousands)[27]		86 655	91 474	96 484	99 826	105 297	110 395[6]	114 917[6]	Nombre (en milliers)[27]
Per 100 inhabitants		68	72	76	78	83	87	90	Pour 100 habitants
Jersey									**Jersey**
Number (thousands)		81	84	...	...	...	...	...	Nombre (en milliers)
Per 100 inhabitants		92	95	...	...	...	...	...	Pour 100 habitants
Jordan									**Jordanie**
Number (thousands)		1 325	1 624	3 138	4 343	4 772	5 314	6 014	Nombre (en milliers)
Per 100 inhabitants		25	30	56	76	80	87	95	Pour 100 habitants

15 Cellular mobile telephone subscribers *(continued)*

Number (thousands) and per 100 inhabitants

Abonnés au téléphone mobile *(suite)*

Nombre (milliers) et pour 100 habitants

Country or area	Fiscal year & Ex. budgét. &	2003	2004	2005	2006	2007	2008	2009	Pays ou zone
Kazakhstan									**Kazakhstan**
Number (thousands)		1 331	2 447	5 398	7 776	12 323	14 911	14 995	Nombre (en milliers)
Per 100 inhabitants		9	16	36	51	80	96	96	Pour 100 habitants
Kenya	(30/06)								**Kenya**
Number (thousands)		1 591	2 546	4 612	7 340	11 349	16 304	19 365	Nombre (en milliers)
Per 100 inhabitants		5	7	13	20	30	42	49	Pour 100 habitants
Kiribati									**Kiribati**
Number (thousands)		1	1	1	1[28]	1	1	1	Nombre (en milliers)
Per 100 inhabitants		1	1	1	1	1	1	1	Pour 100 habitants
Korea, Dem. P. R.									**Corée, R. p. dém. de**
Number (thousands)		0[29]	0[29]	0[29]	0[29]	0[29]	0	69[3]	Nombre (en milliers)
Per 100 inhabitants		0	0	0	0	0	0	^0	Pour 100 habitants
Korea, Republic of									**Corée, République de**
Number (thousands)		33 592	36 586	38 342	40 197	43 498	45 607	47 944	Nombre (en milliers)
Per 100 inhabitants		71	77	81	84	91	95	99	Pour 100 habitants
Kuwait									**Koweït**
Number (thousands)		1 420	2 000	2 277	2 530	2 774	2 907	...	Nombre (en milliers)
Per 100 inhabitants		56	76	84	91	97	100	...	Pour 100 habitants
Kyrgyzstan									**Kirghizistan**
Number (thousands)		138	263	542	1 262	2 168	3 394	4 487	Nombre (en milliers)
Per 100 inhabitants		3	5	10	24	41	63	82	Pour 100 habitants
Lao People's Dem. Rep.									**Rép. dém. pop. lao**
Number (thousands)		112	204	658	1 010	1 478	2 022	3 235	Nombre (en milliers)
Per 100 inhabitants		2	4	11	17	24	33	51	Pour 100 habitants
Latvia									**Lettonie**
Number (thousands)		1 220	1 537	1 872	2 184	2 217	2 234	2 243	Nombre (en milliers)
Per 100 inhabitants		53	67	82	96	98	99	100	Pour 100 habitants
Lebanon									**Liban**
Number (thousands)		795	884	994	1 106	1 260	1 427[30]	1 526	Nombre (en milliers)
Per 100 inhabitants		20	22	24	27	30	34	36	Pour 100 habitants
Lesotho	(01/04)								**Lesotho**
Number (thousands)		126	196	250	358	456	593	661	Nombre (en milliers)
Per 100 inhabitants		6	10	13	18	22	29	32	Pour 100 habitants
Liberia									**Libéria**
Number (thousands)		47	94	160	280	563	732	842	Nombre (en milliers)
Per 100 inhabitants		2	3	5	8	16	19	21	Pour 100 habitants
Libyan Arab Jamah.									**Jamah. arabe libyenne**
Number (thousands)		127	500	2 000	3 928	4 500	4 828	5 004	Nombre (en milliers)
Per 100 inhabitants		2	9	34	65	73	77	78	Pour 100 habitants
Liechtenstein									**Liechtenstein**
Number (thousands)		*25	*26	*28	*29	*32	34	35	Nombre (en milliers)
Per 100 inhabitants		74	74	79	82	91	95	97	Pour 100 habitants
Lithuania									**Lituanie**
Number (thousands) [21]		2 102	3 051	4 353	4 718	4 912	5 023	4 962	Nombre (en milliers) [21]
Per 100 inhabitants		61	89	127	139	146	151	151	Pour 100 habitants
Luxembourg									**Luxembourg**
Number (thousands)		539	470[21]	510[21]	713[21]	685[21]	707[21]	719	Nombre (en milliers)
Per 100 inhabitants		119	102	110	152	144	147	148	Pour 100 habitants
Madagascar									**Madagascar**
Number (thousands)		284	334	510	1 046	2 157	4 835	5 997	Nombre (en milliers)
Per 100 inhabitants		2	2	3	6	12	25	31	Pour 100 habitants
Malawi									**Malawi**
Number (thousands)		135	222	421	620	1 051	1 781	2 400	Nombre (en milliers)
Per 100 inhabitants		1	2	3	4	7	12	16	Pour 100 habitants
Malaysia									**Malaisie**
Number (thousands)		11 124	14 611	19 545	19 464	23 347	27 713	30 379	Nombre (en milliers)
Per 100 inhabitants		45	58	76	75	88	103	111	Pour 100 habitants
Maldives									**Maldives**
Number (thousands)		66	113	204	271	314	436	458	Nombre (en milliers)
Per 100 inhabitants		23	39	70	91	104	143	148	Pour 100 habitants

15 Cellular mobile telephone subscribers *(continued)*

Number (thousands) and per 100 inhabitants

Abonnés au téléphone mobile *(suite)*

Nombre (milliers) et pour 100 habitants

Country or area	Fiscal year & Ex. budgét. &	2003	2004	2005	2006	2007	2008	2009	Pays ou zone
Mali									**Mali**
Number (thousands)		247	407	762	1 513	2 531	3 439	3 742	Nombre (en milliers)
Per 100 inhabitants		2	4	6	12	20	27	29	Pour 100 habitants
Malta									**Malte**
Number (thousands)		290	306	324	347	369	386	422	Nombre (en milliers)
Per 100 inhabitants		73	76	80	86	91	95	103	Pour 100 habitants
Marshall Islands									**Iles Marshall**
Number (thousands)		1	1	1	1	1	1	1	Nombre (en milliers)
Per 100 inhabitants		1	1	1	1	1	2	2	Pour 100 habitants
Mauritania									**Mauritanie**
Number (thousands)		351	522	746	1 060	1 414	2 092	2 182	Nombre (en milliers)
Per 100 inhabitants		12	18	25	35	45	65	66	Pour 100 habitants
Mauritius									**Maurice**
Number (thousands)		462	548	657	772	929	1 033	1 087	Nombre (en milliers)
Per 100 inhabitants		38	44	52	61	73	81	84	Pour 100 habitants
Mexico									**Mexique**
Number (thousands)		30 098	38 451	47 129	55 395	66 559	75 303	83 528	Nombre (en milliers)
Per 100 inhabitants		29	37	45	52	62	69	76	Pour 100 habitants
Micronesia (Fed. States of)									**Micronésie (Et. féd. de)**
Number (thousands)		6	13	14	19	27	34	38	Nombre (en milliers)
Per 100 inhabitants		5	12	13	17	25	31	34	Pour 100 habitants
Mongolia									**Mongolie**
Number (thousands)		319	429	557	775	1 195	1 763	2 249	Nombre (en milliers)
Per 100 inhabitants		13	17	22	30	46	67	84	Pour 100 habitants
Montenegro									**Monténégro**
Number (thousands)		...	484	543	644	703	735	752	Nombre (en milliers)
Per 100 inhabitants		...	77	87	104	113	118	120	Pour 100 habitants
Morocco									**Maroc**
Number (thousands)		7 360	9 337	12 393	16 005	20 029	22 816	25 311	Nombre (en milliers)
Per 100 inhabitants		25	31	41	52	64	72	79	Pour 100 habitants
Mozambique									**Mozambique**
Number (thousands)		436	708	1 504	2 339	3 080	4 405	5 971	Nombre (en milliers)
Per 100 inhabitants		2	3	7	11	14	20	26	Pour 100 habitants
Myanmar									**Myanmar**
Number (thousands)		67	92	129	214	248	367	448	Nombre (en milliers)
Per 100 inhabitants		^0	^0	^0	^0	1	1	1	Pour 100 habitants
Namibia	(30/09)								**Namibie**
Number (thousands)		224	286	449	609	800	1 052	1 217	Nombre (en milliers)
Per 100 inhabitants		12	15	22	30	38	49	56	Pour 100 habitants
Nepal	(15/07)								**Népal**
Number (thousands)		82	117	227	1 157	3 269[31]	4 200	7 618[32]	Nombre (en milliers)
Per 100 inhabitants		^0	^0	1	4	12	15	26	Pour 100 habitants
Netherlands									**Pays-Bas**
Number (thousands)		13 200	14 800	15 834	17 296	19 285	20 627	21 182[33]	Nombre (en milliers)
Per 100 inhabitants		82	91	97	106	117	125	128	Pour 100 habitants
Netherlands Antilles									**Antilles néerlandaises**
Number (thousands)		200	200	...	...	...	...	...	Nombre (en milliers)
Per 100 inhabitants		110	109	...	...	...	...	...	Pour 100 habitants
New Caledonia									**Nouvelle-Calédonie**
Number (thousands)		97	116	134	155	176	196	208	Nombre (en milliers)
Per 100 inhabitants		43	50	57	65	73	80	83	Pour 100 habitants
New Zealand	(01/04)								**Nouvelle-Zélande**
Number (thousands)		2 599	3 027	3 530	3 802	4 251[34]	4 620[3]	4 700	Nombre (en milliers)
Per 100 inhabitants		65	74	86	92	101	109	110	Pour 100 habitants
Nicaragua									**Nicaragua**
Number (thousands)		467	739	1 119	1 830	2 502	3 108	3 204	Nombre (en milliers)
Per 100 inhabitants		9	14	21	33	45	55	56	Pour 100 habitants
Niger									**Niger**
Number (thousands)		82	172	324	483	900[35]	1 898	2 599[36]	Nombre (en milliers)
Per 100 inhabitants		1	1	2	4	6	13	17	Pour 100 habitants

15 Cellular mobile telephone subscribers *(continued)*

Number (thousands) and per 100 inhabitants

Abonnés au téléphone mobile *(suite)*

Nombre (milliers) et pour 100 habitants

Country or area	Fiscal year & Ex. budgét. &	2003	2004	2005	2006	2007	2008	2009	Pays ou zone
Nigeria									**Nigéria**
Number (thousands)		3 149	9 147	18 587	32 322	#40 396[37]	62 988	73 099	Nombre (en milliers)
Per 100 inhabitants		2	7	13	22	27	42	47	Pour 100 habitants
Northern Mariana Islands									**Iles Mariannes du Nord**
Number (thousands)		19	20	...	...	...	...	...	Nombre (en milliers)
Per 100 inhabitants		25	26	...	...	...	...	...	Pour 100 habitants
Norway									**Norvège**
Number (thousands)		4 061	4 525	4 754	4 869	5 038	5 251	5 336	Nombre (en milliers)
Per 100 inhabitants		89	98	103	104	107	110	111	Pour 100 habitants
Occupied Palestinian Terr.									**Terr. palestinien occ.**
Number (thousands)		480	974	1 095	822	1 026	1 153	1 224	Nombre (en milliers)
Per 100 inhabitants		14	27	29	21	26	28	29	Pour 100 habitants
Oman									**Oman**
Number (thousands)		594	806	1 333	1 818	2 500	3 219	3 971	Nombre (en milliers)
Per 100 inhabitants		24	31	51	68	92	116	140	Pour 100 habitants
Pakistan	(30/06)								**Pakistan**
Number (thousands)		2 404	5 023	12 771	34 507	62 961[6]	88 020	102 980	Nombre (en milliers)
Per 100 inhabitants		2	3	8	20	36	50	57	Pour 100 habitants
Palau									**Palaos**
Number (thousands)		4	4	6	8	11	12	13	Nombre (en milliers)
Per 100 inhabitants		20	20	30	41	53	60	64	Pour 100 habitants
Panama									**Panama**
Number (thousands)		692	1 260	1 749	2 174	3 011	3 915	5 677	Nombre (en milliers)
Per 100 inhabitants		22	40	54	66	90	115	164	Pour 100 habitants
Papua New Guinea									**Papouasie-Nvl-Guinée**
Number (thousands)		18	48	75	100	300[28,38]	600	900	Nombre (en milliers)
Per 100 inhabitants		^0	1	1	2	5	9	13	Pour 100 habitants
Paraguay									**Paraguay**
Number (thousands)		1 770	1 749	1 887	3 233	4 694	5 954	5 619[39]	Nombre (en milliers)
Per 100 inhabitants		31	30	32	54	77	95	88	Pour 100 habitants
Peru									**Pérou**
Number (thousands)		2 930	4 093	5 583	8 772	15 417	20 952	24 700	Nombre (en milliers)
Per 100 inhabitants		11	15	20	31	54	73	85	Pour 100 habitants
Philippines									**Philippines**
Number (thousands)		22 510	32 936	34 779	42 869	57 345	68 117	74 489	Nombre (en milliers)
Per 100 inhabitants		27	39	41	49	65	75	81	Pour 100 habitants
Poland									**Pologne**
Number (thousands)		17 401	23 096	29 166	36 745	41 389	43 926	44 553	Nombre (en milliers)
Per 100 inhabitants		45	60	76	96	109	115	117	Pour 100 habitants
Portugal									**Portugal**
Number (thousands)		10 003	10 571	11 447	12 226	13 451	14 910	15 178	Nombre (en milliers)
Per 100 inhabitants		96	101	109	115	126	140	142	Pour 100 habitants
Puerto Rico									**Porto Rico**
Number (thousands)		1 709	1 848	1 993	2 199	2 432	2 544	2 716	Nombre (en milliers)
Per 100 inhabitants		44	47	51	56	62	64	68	Pour 100 habitants
Qatar									**Qatar**
Number (thousands)		377	490	717	920	1 264	1 683	2 472	Nombre (en milliers)
Per 100 inhabitants		51	62	81	92	111	131	175	Pour 100 habitants
Republic of Moldova									**Rép. de Moldova**
Number (thousands)		476	787	1 090	1 358	1 883	2 423	2 785	Nombre (en milliers)
Per 100 inhabitants		12	21	29	37	51	67	77	Pour 100 habitants
Romania									**Roumanie**
Number (thousands)		7 040	10 215	13 354	15 991[40]	20 417[40]	24 467[40]	25 377[40]	Nombre (en milliers)
Per 100 inhabitants		32	47	62	74	95	115	119	Pour 100 habitants
Russian Federation									**Fédération de Russie**
Number (thousands)		36 135	73 722	120 000	150 674[41]	171 200	199 522	230 500	Nombre (en milliers)
Per 100 inhabitants		25	51	84	106	121	141	164	Pour 100 habitants
Rwanda									**Rwanda**
Number (thousands)		131	137	223	314	635	1 323	2 429	Nombre (en milliers)
Per 100 inhabitants		2	2	2	3	7	14	24	Pour 100 habitants

15 Cellular mobile telephone subscribers *(continued)*

Number (thousands) and per 100 inhabitants

Abonnés au téléphone mobile *(suite)*

Nombre (milliers) et pour 100 habitants

Country or area	Fiscal year & Ex. budgét. &	2003	2004	2005	2006	2007	2008	2009	Pays ou zone
Saint Kitts and Nevis	(01/04)								**Saint-Kitts-et-Nevis**
Number (thousands)		22	29	51[6]	64	74	80	83	Nombre (en milliers)
Per 100 inhabitants		46	60	104	129	147	157	160	Pour 100 habitants
Saint Lucia	(01/04)								**Sainte-Lucie**
Number (thousands)		99	101	106	145	155	170	176	Nombre (en milliers)
Per 100 inhabitants		61	62	64	87	92	100	102	Pour 100 habitants
Saint Vincent-Grenadines	(01/04)								**Saint Vincent-Grenad.**
Number (thousands)		63	72	71	88	110	130	121[42]	Nombre (en milliers)
Per 100 inhabitants		58	66	65	80	101	119	111	Pour 100 habitants
Samoa									**Samoa**
Number (thousands)		11	16	24	46	86[38]	124	151	Nombre (en milliers)
Per 100 inhabitants		6	9	13	25	48	69	84	Pour 100 habitants
San Marino									**Saint-Marin**
Number (thousands)		17	17	17	17	18	24	24	Nombre (en milliers)
Per 100 inhabitants		58	58	57	57	56	77	77	Pour 100 habitants
Sao Tome and Principe									**Sao Tomé-et-Principe**
Number (thousands)		5	8	12	18	30	49	64	Nombre (en milliers)
Per 100 inhabitants		3	5	8	12	19	31	39	Pour 100 habitants
Saudi Arabia									**Arabie saoudite**
Number (thousands)		7 238	9 176	14 164	19 700	28 400	36 000	44 864	Nombre (en milliers)
Per 100 inhabitants		32	40	60	82	115	143	174	Pour 100 habitants
Senegal									**Sénégal**
Number (thousands)		782	1 121	1 730	2 983	3 631	5 389	6 901	Nombre (en milliers)
Per 100 inhabitants		7	10	15	26	31	44	55	Pour 100 habitants
Serbia									**Serbie**
Number (thousands)		...	4 730	5 511	6 644	8 453	9 619	9 912	Nombre (en milliers)
Per 100 inhabitants		...	48	56	68	86	98	101	Pour 100 habitants
Seychelles	(01/04)								**Seychelles**
Number (thousands)		49	54	59	70	77	93	92[43]	Nombre (en milliers)
Per 100 inhabitants		60	66	71	85	93	112	110	Pour 100 habitants
Sierra Leone									**Sierra Leone**
Number (thousands)		113	...	...	...	776	1 009	1 160	Nombre (en milliers)
Per 100 inhabitants		2	...	...	...	14	18	20	Pour 100 habitants
Singapore	(01/04)								**Singapour**
Number (thousands)		3 577	3 991[6]	4 385	4 789	5 924	6 376	6 652	Nombre (en milliers)
Per 100 inhabitants		86	95	103	110	132	138	140	Pour 100 habitants
Slovakia									**Slovaquie**
Number (thousands)		3 679[44]	4 275[44]	4 540[44]	4 893[44]	6 068[44]	#5 520[45]	5 498	Nombre (en milliers)
Per 100 inhabitants		68	79	84	91	112	102	102	Pour 100 habitants
Slovenia									**Slovénie**
Number (thousands)		1 739	1 849	1 759[46]	1 820	1 928	2 055	2 100	Nombre (en milliers)
Per 100 inhabitants		87	93	88	91	96	102	104	Pour 100 habitants
Solomon Islands	(01/04)								**Iles Salomon**
Number (thousands)		1	3	6	7	11[28]	30	30	Nombre (en milliers)
Per 100 inhabitants		^0	1	1	1	2	6	6	Pour 100 habitants
Somalia									**Somalie**
Number (thousands)		200	500	500	550	600	627	641	Nombre (en milliers)
Per 100 inhabitants		3	6	6	6	7	7	7	Pour 100 habitants
South Africa	(01/04)								**Afrique du Sud**
Number (thousands)		16 860	20 839	33 960	39 662	42 300[47]	45 000	46 436	Nombre (en milliers)
Per 100 inhabitants		36	44	71	82	86	91	93	Pour 100 habitants
Spain									**Espagne**
Number (thousands)		37 220	38 623	42 694	45 695	48 422	49 678	50 991	Nombre (en milliers)
Per 100 inhabitants		89	91	99	105	110	112	114	Pour 100 habitants
Sri Lanka									**Sri Lanka**
Number (thousands)		1 393	2 211	3 362	5 413	7 983	11 082	14 095	Nombre (en milliers)
Per 100 inhabitants		7	11	17	27	40	55	70	Pour 100 habitants
Sudan									**Soudan**
Number (thousands)		527[48]	1 049[48]	1 828[48]	4 683[48]	8 218[48]	11 991[48]	15 340	Nombre (en milliers)
Per 100 inhabitants		1	3	5	12	20	29	36	Pour 100 habitants

15 Cellular mobile telephone subscribers *(continued)*
Number (thousands) and per 100 inhabitants
Abonnés au téléphone mobile *(suite)*
Nombre (milliers) et pour 100 habitants

Country or area	Fiscal year & Ex. budgét. &	2003	2004	2005	2006	2007	2008	2009	Pays ou zone
Suriname									**Suriname**
Number (thousands)		169	213	233	320	380	416	764	Nombre (en milliers)
Per 100 inhabitants		35	43	47	63	74	81	147	Pour 100 habitants
Swaziland	(01/04)								**Swaziland**
Number (thousands)		85	145	200	250	380	532	656	Nombre (en milliers)
Per 100 inhabitants		8	13	18	22	33	46	55	Pour 100 habitants
Sweden									**Suède**
Number (thousands)		8 801	8 785[1]	9 104	9 607	10 177	10 892	11 426	Nombre (en milliers)
Per 100 inhabitants		98	97	100	105	111	118	124	Pour 100 habitants
Switzerland									**Suisse**
Number (thousands)		6 189	6 275	6 834	7 436	8 209	*8 897	9 255	Nombre (en milliers)
Per 100 inhabitants		84	85	92	99	109	118	122	Pour 100 habitants
Syrian Arab Republic									**Rép. arabe syrienne**
Number (thousands)		1 185	2 346	2 950	4 675	6 235	7 056	9 697[49]	Nombre (en milliers)
Per 100 inhabitants		7	13	15	24	30	33	44	Pour 100 habitants
Tajikistan									**Tadjikistan**
Number (thousands)		48	135	265	2 150	2 133	3 674	4 900	Nombre (en milliers)
Per 100 inhabitants		1	2	4	32	32	54	70	Pour 100 habitants
Thailand	(30/09)								**Thaïlande**
Number (thousands)		21 828	27 379	31 137	40 723	53 000	62 000	83 057	Nombre (en milliers)
Per 100 inhabitants		34	42	47	61	79	92	123	Pour 100 habitants
TFYR of Macedonia									**L'ex-R.Y. Macédoine**
Number (thousands)		776	986	1 261	1 417	1 947[1]	2 502	1 943[50]	Nombre (en milliers)
Per 100 inhabitants		38	48	62	70	95	123	95	Pour 100 habitants
Timor-Leste									**Timor-Leste**
Number (thousands)		20	26	33	49	78[38]	101	116	Nombre (en milliers)
Per 100 inhabitants		2	3	3	5	7	9	10	Pour 100 habitants
Togo									**Togo**
Number (thousands)		244	333	434	708	1 190	1 550	2 187	Nombre (en milliers)
Per 100 inhabitants		4	6	7	12	19	24	33	Pour 100 habitants
Tonga									**Tonga**
Number (thousands)		11	16	30	30	47	50	53	Nombre (en milliers)
Per 100 inhabitants		11	16	29	29	45	49	51	Pour 100 habitants
Trinidad and Tobago	(01/04)								**Trinité-et-Tobago**
Number (thousands)		336	651	924	1 519	1 510[51]	1 806	1 970	Nombre (en milliers)
Per 100 inhabitants		26	50	70	115	114	135	147	Pour 100 habitants
Tunisia									**Tunisie**
Number (thousands)		1 918	3 736	5 681	7 339	7 843	8 602	9 754	Nombre (en milliers)
Per 100 inhabitants		20	38	58	74	78	85	95	Pour 100 habitants
Turkey									**Turquie**
Number (thousands)		27 888	34 708	43 609	52 663	61 976	65 824	62 780[52]	Nombre (en milliers)
Per 100 inhabitants		40	49	61	73	85	89	84	Pour 100 habitants
Turkmenistan									**Turkménistan**
Number (thousands)		9	50	105	217[41]	382	1 135	1 500	Nombre (en milliers)
Per 100 inhabitants		^0	1	2	4	8	23	29	Pour 100 habitants
Tuvalu									**Tuvalu**
Number (thousands)		0	1	1	2	2	2	2	Nombre (en milliers)
Per 100 inhabitants		0	5	13	16	18	20	20	Pour 100 habitants
Uganda	(30/06)								**Ouganda**
Number (thousands)		776	1 165	1 315	2 009	4 195	8 555	9 384	Nombre (en milliers)
Per 100 inhabitants		3	4	5	7	14	27	29	Pour 100 habitants
Ukraine									**Ukraine**
Number (thousands)		6 498	13 735	30 014	49 076	55 240	55 694	55 333	Nombre (en milliers)
Per 100 inhabitants		14	29	64	105	119	121	121	Pour 100 habitants
United Arab Emirates									**Emirats arabes unis**
Number (thousands)		2 972	3 683	4 534	5 519	7 732	9 358[7]	10 672	Nombre (en milliers)
Per 100 inhabitants		79	94	111	130	177	209	232	Pour 100 habitants
United Kingdom	(01/04)								**Royaume-Uni**
Number (thousands)		54 256	59 688	65 472	70 078	73 836[3]	77 361	80 375	Nombre (en milliers)
Per 100 inhabitants		91	100	109	116	121	126	131	Pour 100 habitants

Cellular mobile telephone subscribers *(continued)*
Number (thousands) and per 100 inhabitants
Abonnés au téléphone mobile *(suite)*
Nombre (milliers) et pour 100 habitants

Country or area	Fiscal year [&] Ex. budgét. [&]	2003	2004	2005	2006	2007	2008	2009	Pays ou zone
United Rep. of Tanzania									**Rép.-Unie de Tanzanie**
Number (thousands)		1 942	1 942	3 390	5 767	8 323	13 007[1]	17 469	Nombre (en milliers)
Per 100 inhabitants		5	5	9	14	20	31	40	Pour 100 habitants
United States									**Etats-Unis**
Number (thousands)		160 637	184 819	213 000	241 800	263 000	270 500	298 404	Nombre (en milliers)
Per 100 inhabitants		54	62	70	79	85	87	95	Pour 100 habitants
United States Virgin Is.									**Iles Vierges améric.**
Number (thousands)		49	64	80	...	...	...	...	Nombre (en milliers)
Per 100 inhabitants		45	59	73	...	...	...	...	Pour 100 habitants
Uruguay									**Uruguay**
Number (thousands)		498	600	1 155	2 330	3 004	3 508	3 802	Nombre (en milliers)
Per 100 inhabitants		15	18	35	70	90	105	113	Pour 100 habitants
Uzbekistan									**Ouzbékistan**
Number (thousands)		321	544	720	2 530	5 691	12 375	16 418	Nombre (en milliers)
Per 100 inhabitants		1	2	3	10	21	46	60	Pour 100 habitants
Vanuatu									**Vanuatu**
Number (thousands)		8	11	13	15	26[38]	36	126	Nombre (en milliers)
Per 100 inhabitants		4	5	6	7	11	15	53	Pour 100 habitants
Venezuela (Boliv. Rep. of)									**Venezuela (R. bol. du)**
Number (thousands)		7 015	8 421	12 496	18 789	23 820	27 414	28 124[53]	Nombre (en milliers)
Per 100 inhabitants		27	32	47	69	86	97	98	Pour 100 habitants
Viet Nam									**Viet Nam**
Number (thousands)		2 742	4 960	9 593	15 505	23 730	70 000	88 566	Nombre (en milliers)
Per 100 inhabitants		3	6	11	18	28	80	101	Pour 100 habitants
Yemen									**Yémen**
Number (thousands)		675	1 483	2 278	2 978	3 436	3 700	3 842	Nombre (en milliers)
Per 100 inhabitants		3	7	11	14	15	16	16	Pour 100 habitants
Zambia	(01/04)								**Zambie**
Number (thousands)		241	464	950	1 663	2 639	3 539	4 407	Nombre (en milliers)
Per 100 inhabitants		2	4	8	14	21	28	34	Pour 100 habitants
Zimbabwe	(30/06)								**Zimbabwe**
Number (thousands)		364	426	647	849	1 226	1 655	2 991	Nombre (en milliers)
Per 100 inhabitants		3	3	5	7	10	13	24	Pour 100 habitants

Source:
International Telecommunication Union (ITU), Geneva, the ITU database, last accessed June 2010.

[&] Fiscal year refers to the fiscal year used in each country or area. Countries or areas whose reference periods coincide with the calendar year ending 31 December are not footnoted. Those that have a fiscal year other than calendar year are denoted as follows:

22/03: Year beginning 22 March
01/04: Year beginning 1 April
30/06: Year ending 30 June
15/07: Year ending 15 July
30/09: Year ending 30 September

1 June.
2 Communications Report 2008-09.
3 September.
4 Includes subscribers to public mobile data services.
5 Change from TDMA to GSM platform caused decrease in the number of subscriptions.
6 December.
7 Active subscriptions.
8 3G subscribers not included in the total number of mobile subscribers.
9 Including Celtel subscribers.

Source:
Union internationale des télécommunications (UIT), Genève, la base de données de l'UIT, dernier accès juin 2010.

[&] Ex. budgét. fait référence à l'exercice budgétaire en vigueur dans chaque pays ou territoire. Les pays ou les territoires dont l'exercice budgétaire terminent le 31 décembre de l'année civile ne sont pas signalés. Dans le cas contraire, ils sont désignés de la manière suivante:

22/03 : Exercice commençant le 22 mars
01/04 : Exercice commençant le 1er avril
30/06 : Exercice se terminant le 30 juin
15/07 : Exercice se terminant le 15 juillet
30/09 : Exercice se terminant le 30 septembre

1 Juin.
2 Communications Report 2008-09.
3 Septembre.
4 Y compris les abonnés aux services mobiles de données sur réseau public.
5 Le changement de la plateforme TDMA à celle du GSM a causé une baisse du nombre d'abonnements.
6 Décembre.
7 Abonnements actifs.
8 Les abonnes 3G ne sont pas inclus dans le nombre total d'abonnés à la téléphonie mobile.
9 Y compris les abonnés à Celtel.

15 Cellular mobile telephone subscribers *(continued)*

Number (thousands) and per 100 inhabitants

Abonnés au téléphone mobile *(suite)*

Nombre (milliers) et pour 100 habitants

10 For statistical purposes, the data for China do not include those for the Hong Kong Special Administrative Region (Hong Kong SAR), Macao Special Administrative Region (Macao SAR) and Taiwan Province of China.
11 Includes subscriptions for mobile broadband.
12 Including 300,000 inactive SIM cards.
13 Including 900,000 inactive SIM cards.
14 Includes an estimated 1.15 million inactive SIM cards of one operator.
15 Data refer to March of following year.
16 Total active prepaid customers + Total postpaid customers.
17 Includes inactive subscribers.
18 Including data services.
19 Excluding Data-only SIM cards.
20 Only active subscribers.
21 Active mobile subscribers
22 November.
23 October.
24 Excluding mobile broadband (HSDPA) subscriptions.
25 Decrease in the number of subscriptions was due to change in the definition of prepaid subscriptions (now includes only those that have done an event (outgoing call, SMS, MMS, Internet usage, etc)) that decrements their balance in the previous 90 days. Data refers to December.
26 30 June.
27 Including Personal Handy System (PHS).
28 Based on Pacific Economic Survey 2008.
29 Commercially not available.
30 Based on MTC Touch.
31 Refer to SNLP subscribers only.
32 As of March 2010.
33 July.
34 Telecom NZ and Vodafone NZ subscribers.
35 Estimate based on Celtel's Annual Report.
36 Based on Zain market share.
37 Includes active GSM & CDMA mobile lines.
38 Refers to mid-year.
39 Decrease due to database updating, excluding inactive accounts.
40 Active (last 6 months) SIM cards.
41 On basis of MTS (Moscow TeleSystems) Annual Report.
42 Decrease due to a change in policy. Inactive accounts for 3 months are being deactivated.
43 June 2009.
44 No distinction made between active or non-active subscribers.
45 From 1.01. 2008, only active mobile cellular subscribers are counted. Active subscribers are those that have used at least one payable service in the last 90 days.
46 New methodology of active subscribers.
47 Estimation based on Annual Reports of Vodacom, MTN and Cell C.
48 Canar counted as fixed line.
49 Data for 2009 is until 30/11/2009.
50 Refers to active subscribers that made electronic communication action in a period of 3 months (initiate and receive call, send and receive MMS and SMS, send and receive data, pay monthly fee…)
51 Only one telecom provider.
52 With the authorization of 3G services, the number of 3G exceeded 7 millions.
53 Data for the year 2009 is preliminary. Starting in 2009, figures reflect subscribers using mobile telephony during the reference period, that is subscribers who at least receive messages and/or calls.

10 Pour la présentation des statistiques, les données pour la Chine ne comprennent pas la Région Administrative Spéciale de Hong Kong (Hong Kong RAS), la Région Administrative Spéciale de Macao (Macao RAS) et la province de Taiwan.
11 Inclus les abonnements aux réseaux mobiles haut débit.
12 Y compris approximativement 300 000 cartes SIM inactives.
13 Y compris approximativement 900 000 cartes SIM inactives.
14 Y compris approximativement 1,15 million de cartes SIM inactives d'un opérateur.
15 Les données se réfèrent à mars de l'année suivante.
16 Nombre total de clients prépayés actifs + nombre total de clients post payés.
17 Y compris les abonnés inactifs.
18 Inclus les services mobiles de données
19 Non compris les cartes SIM "data-only".
20 Abonnés actifs uniquement.
21 Abonnés actifs.
22 Novembre.
23 Octobre.
24 À l'exclusion des abonnements au très haut débit mobile (HSDPA).
25 La baisse du nombre d'abonnements est due à une modification de la définition des abonnements prépayés. Ceux-ci incluent maintenant seulement ceux qui ont fait une action (appel sortant, SMS, MMS, utilisation de l'Internet, etc.) entraînant une diminution du solde au cours des derniers 90 jours. Les données concernent le mois de décembre.
26 30 juin.
27 Y compris le système PHS (Personal Handy System).
28 Basé sur l'Enquête économique sur le Pacifique de 2008.
29 Indisponible commercialement.
30 Basé sur MTC Touch.
31 Abonnés à SNPL seulement.
32 En mars 2010.
33 Juillet.
34 Abonnés à Telecom NZ et Vodafone NZ.
35 Estimations basées sur le rapport annuel de Celtel.
36 Basé sur la part de marché de Zain.
37 Y compris les lignes mobiles GSM et AMRC actives.
38 Données au milieu de l'année.
39 Baisse due à la mise à jour de la base de données qui exclue les comptes inactifs.
40 Cartes SIM actives (6 derniers mois).
41 Basé sur le rapport annuel de MTS (Moscow TeleSystems).
42 Baisse due à une modification des contrats: les comptes inactifs pendant 3 mois sont désactivés.
43 Juin 2009.
44 Aucune distinction entre abonnés actifs et abonnés non-actifs.
45 A compte du 1er janvier 2008, seuls les abonnés actifs sont comptés. Les abonnés actifs sont ceux qui ont au moins utilisé un service payant au cours des derniers 90 jours.
46 Nouvelle méthode de décompte des abonnés actifs.
47 Estimations basées sur les rapports annuels de Vodacom, MTN and Cell C.
48 Canar comptabilisé comme ligne fixe.
49 Les données de 2009 vont jusqu'au 30/11/2009.
50 Concerne les abonnés actifs ayant effectué une communication électronique durant une période de 3 mois (réception et émission d'appels, messages multimédias, SMS, ou de données, payer les frais mensuels, etc.).
51 Un seul fournisseur d'accès télécom.
52 Avec l'autorisation du service 3G, le nombre d'abonnés 3G a dépassé 7 millions.
53 Les données de l'année 2008 sont préliminaires. A partir de 2009, les données reflètent les abonnés qui utilisent le système de téléphonie mobile pendant la période de référence, c'est-à-dire qui reçoivent au moins des messages et/ou des appels.

16 Internet users

Estimated number (thousands) and number per 100 inhabitants

Usagers d'Internet

Nombre estimatif (en milliers) et nombre pour 100 habitants

Country or area	Fiscal year[&] Ex. budgét.[&]	2003	2004	2005	2006	2007	2008	2009	Pays ou zone
Afghanistan									**Afghanistan**
Number (thousands)		20	25	300	535	500	500	1 000	Nombre (milliers)
Per 100 inhabitants		^0	^0	1	2	2	2	4	Pour 100 habitants
Albania									**Albanie**
Number (thousands)		30	75	188	300	471	750	1 300[1]	Nombre (milliers)
Per 100 inhabitants		1	2	6	10	15	24	41	Pour 100 habitants
Algeria									**Algérie**
Number (thousands)		700	1 500	1 920	2 460	3 200	3 500	4 700	Nombre (milliers)
Per 100 inhabitants		2	5	6	7	9	10	13	Pour 100 habitants
Andorra									**Andorre**
Number (thousands)		10	21	30	40	59	59	67	Nombre (milliers)
Per 100 inhabitants		14	27	38	49	71	70	79	Pour 100 habitants
Angola									**Angola**
Number (thousands)		58	75	190	326	498	550	607	Nombre (milliers)
Per 100 inhabitants		^0	^0	1	2	3	3	3	Pour 100 habitants
Antigua and Barbuda	(01/04)								**Antigua-et-Barbuda**
Number (thousands)		14	20	29	53	60	65	65	Nombre (milliers)
Per 100 inhabitants		17	24	35	63	70	75	74	Pour 100 habitants
Argentina	(30/09)								**Argentine**
Number (thousands)		4 530	6 154	6 863	8 184	10 246	11 212	12 244	Nombre (milliers)
Per 100 inhabitants		12	16	18	21	26	28	30	Pour 100 habitants
Armenia									**Arménie**
Number (thousands)		140	150	161	173	185	191	208	Nombre (milliers)
Per 100 inhabitants		5	5	5	6	6	6	7	Pour 100 habitants
Aruba									**Aruba**
Number (thousands)		24	24	24	24	24	24	24	Nombre (milliers)
Per 100 inhabitants		25	24	24	23	23	23	23	Pour 100 habitants
Australia	(30/06)								**Australie**
Number (thousands)		11 837	12 364	12 899	13 440	14 300	15 170	15 757	Nombre (milliers)
Per 100 inhabitants		...	...	63	65	69	72	74	Pour 100 habitants
Austria									**Autriche**
Number (thousands)		3 337[3]	4 247[3]	4 771[3]	5 261[3]	5 763[3]	6 075[4]	*6 144	Nombre (milliers)
Per 100 inhabitants [2]		43	54	58	64	69	73	73	Pour 100 habitants [2]
Azerbaijan									**Azerbaïdjan**
Number (thousands)		...	...	679	1 024	1 554	2 445[5]	3 689	Nombre (milliers)
Per 100 inhabitants		...	...	8	12	18	28	42	Pour 100 habitants
Bahamas									**Bahamas**
Number (thousands)		84[6]	93[6]	103	110	90[6]	107[6]	116	Nombre (milliers)
Per 100 inhabitants		26[6]	29[6]	32	33	27[6]	32[6]	34	Pour 100 habitants
Bahrain									**Bahreïn**
Number (thousands)		150	153	155	210	250	403	649	Nombre (milliers)
Per 100 inhabitants		22	21	21	28	33	52	82	Pour 100 habitants
Bangladesh	(30/06)								**Bangladesh**
Number (thousands)		243	300	370	450	500	556	617	Nombre (milliers)
Per 100 inhabitants ^		0	0	0	0	0	0	0	Pour 100 habitants ^
Barbados	(01/04)								**Barbade**
Number (thousands)		100	126	142	...	...	...	...	Nombre (milliers)
Per 100 inhabitants		40	50	56	...	...	...	...	Pour 100 habitants
Belarus									**Bélarus**
Number (thousands)		1 607	2 461	2 600	2 700	2 810	3 107	4 437	Nombre (milliers)
Per 100 inhabitants		16	25	26	28	29	32	46	Pour 100 habitants
Belgium									**Belgique**
Number (thousands)		5 153[3]	5 581[3]	6 229[3]	6 721[3]	7 295[3]	7 546[3]	8 113	Nombre (milliers)
Per 100 inhabitants		50	54	60[2]	64[2]	69[2]	71[2]	76[2]	Pour 100 habitants
Belize	(01/04)								**Belize**
Number (thousands)		...	16	26	30	32	34	36	Nombre (milliers)
Per 100 inhabitants		...	6	9	10	11	11	12	Pour 100 habitants
Benin									**Bénin**
Number (thousands)		70	90	100	125	150	160	200	Nombre (milliers)
Per 100 inhabitants		1	1	1	2	2	2	2	Pour 100 habitants
Bermuda	(01/04)								**Bermudes**
Number (thousands)		36	39	42	45	48	51	54	Nombre (milliers)
Per 100 inhabitants		57	61	65	70	74	79	83	Pour 100 habitants
Bhutan									**Bhoutan**
Number (thousands)		15	20	25	30	40	45	50	Nombre (milliers)
Per 100 inhabitants		2	3	4	5	6	7	7	Pour 100 habitants
Bolivia (Plurinational State of)									**Bolivie (État plurinational de)**
Number (thousands)		310	400	480	580	1 000	1 050	1 103	Nombre (milliers)
Per 100 inhabitants		4	4	5	6	10	11	11	Pour 100 habitants

16 Internet users *(continued)*

Estimated number (thousands) and number per 100 inhabitants

Usagers d'Internet *(suite)*

Nombre estimatif (en milliers) et nombre pour 100 habitants

Country or area	Fiscal year & Ex. budgét.&	2003	2004	2005	2006	2007	2008	2009	Pays ou zone
Bosnia and Herzegovina									**Bosnie-Herzégovine**
Number (thousands)		150	585	806	950	1 055	1 308	1 422	Nombre (milliers)
Per 100 inhabitants		4	15	21	25	28	35	38	Pour 100 habitants
Botswana	(01/04)								**Botswana**
Number (thousands)		60	60	60	80	100	120	120	Nombre (milliers)
Per 100 inhabitants		3	3	3	4	5	6	6	Pour 100 habitants
Brazil									**Brésil**
Number (thousands)		23 977	35 070	39 118	53 020[7]	58 717[7]	72 028[3]	75 944[3]	Nombre (milliers)
Per 100 inhabitants		13	19	21	28[8]	31[8]	38[9]	39[9]	Pour 100 habitants
Brunei Darussalam									**Brunéi Darussalam**
Number (thousands)		70	108	135	159	174	267	319	Nombre (milliers)
Per 100 inhabitants		20	30	36	42	45	68	80	Pour 100 habitants
Bulgaria									**Bulgarie**
Number (thousands)		944	1 236[3]	1 545	2 083[3]	2 570	3 012	3 395[7]	Nombre (milliers)
Per 100 inhabitants		12	18[2]	20	27[2]	34[2]	40[2]	45[2]	Pour 100 habitants
Burkina Faso									**Burkina Faso**
Number (thousands)		48	53	65	90	110	140	178	Nombre (milliers)
Per 100 inhabitants		^0	^0	^0	1	1	1	1	Pour 100 habitants
Burundi									**Burundi**
Number (thousands)		14	25	40	50	55	65	65	Nombre (milliers)
Per 100 inhabitants		^0	^0	1	1	1	1	1	Pour 100 habitants
Cambodia									**Cambodge**
Number (thousands)		35	41	44	66	70	74	78	Nombre (milliers)
Per 100 inhabitants		^0	^0	^0	^0	^0	1	1	Pour 100 habitants
Cameroon									**Cameroun**
Number (thousands)		100	170	250	370	548	725	750	Nombre (milliers)
Per 100 inhabitants		1	1	1	2	3	4	4	Pour 100 habitants
Canada									**Canada**
Number (thousands)		20 247[3]	21 092[3]	21 942[3]	22 959[3]	24 000[3]	25 086	26 225	Nombre (milliers)
Per 100 inhabitants		64	66	68	70	73	75	78	Pour 100 habitants
Cape Verde									**Cap-Vert**
Number (thousands)		20	25	29	33	41	103	150	Nombre (milliers)
Per 100 inhabitants		4	5	6	7	8	21	30	Pour 100 habitants
Cayman Islands	(01/04)								**Iles Caïmanes**
Number (thousands)		...	...	20[10]	21	22	23	24	Nombre (milliers)
Per 100 inhabitants		...	...	38[10]	39	40	41	43	Pour 100 habitants
Central African Rep.									**Rép. centrafricaine**
Number (thousands)		6	9	11	13	16	19	23	Nombre (milliers)
Per 100 inhabitants		^0	^0	^0	^0	^0	^0	1	Pour 100 habitants
Chad									**Tchad**
Number (thousands)		30	35	40	60	90	130	188	Nombre (milliers)
Per 100 inhabitants		^0	^0	^0	1	1	1	2	Pour 100 habitants
Chile									**Chili**
Number (thousands)		4 064[3]	4 544[11]	5 081[11]	5 681[3]	5 162[11]	5 456[11]	5 767	Nombre (milliers)
Per 100 inhabitants		25	28	31	34	31	32	34	Pour 100 habitants
China[12]									**Chine**[12]
Number (thousands)		79 500	94 000	111 847	138 982[13]	212 581	298 000	384 000	Nombre (milliers)
Per 100 inhabitants		6	7	9	11[13]	16	22	29	Pour 100 habitants
China, Hong Kong SAR[14]	(01/04)								**Chine, Hong Kong RAS**[14]
Number (thousands)[3]		3 557	3 863	4 185	4 481	3 961	4 124	4 300	Nombre (milliers)[3]
Per 100 inhabitants		52	56	61	65	57	59	61	Pour 100 habitants
China, Macao SAR									**Chine, Macao RAS**
Number (thousands)		120	150	170	217	238	259	281	Nombre (milliers)
Per 100 inhabitants		26	31	35	43	46	49	52	Pour 100 habitants
Colombia									**Colombie**
Number (thousands)		3 084[15]	3 866	4 739	6 705	12 332	17 330	20 789[16]	Nombre (milliers)
Per 100 inhabitants		7[15]	9	11	15	28	39	46[16]	Pour 100 habitants
Comoros									**Comores**
Number (thousands)		5	8	20	21	22	23	24	Nombre (milliers)
Per 100 inhabitants		1	1	3	3	3	3	4	Pour 100 habitants
Congo									**Congo**
Number (thousands)		15	36	50	70	98	155	245	Nombre (milliers)
Per 100 inhabitants		^0	1	1	2	3	4	7	Pour 100 habitants
Costa Rica									**Costa Rica**
Number (thousands)		850	885	923	1 214	1 350	1 460	1 579	Nombre (milliers)
Per 100 inhabitants		20	21	21	28	30	32	34	Pour 100 habitants
Côte d'Ivoire									**Côte d'Ivoire**
Number (thousands)		140	160	200	300	450	660	968	Nombre (milliers)
Per 100 inhabitants		1	1	1	2	2	3	5	Pour 100 habitants

16 Internet users *(continued)*

Estimated number (thousands) and number per 100 inhabitants

Usagers d'Internet *(suite)*

Nombre estimatif (en milliers) et nombre pour 100 habitants

Country or area	Fiscal year [&] Ex. budgét. [&]	2003	2004	2005	2006	2007	2008	2009	Pays ou zone
Croatia									**Croatie**
Number (thousands)		1 014	1 375	1 472	1 685	1 835[3]	1 957[3]	2 234[3]	Nombre (milliers)
Per 100 inhabitants		23	31	33	38	41[2]	44[2]	51[2]	Pour 100 habitants
Cuba									**Cuba**
Number (thousands)		585[17]	940[17]	1 090[17]	1 250[17]	1 310[17]	1 450[17]	1 605	Nombre (milliers)
Per 100 inhabitants		5[17]	8[17]	10[17]	11[17]	12[17]	13[17]	14	Pour 100 habitants
Cyprus									**Chypre**
Number (thousands)		246[3]	264[3]	274[3]	303[3]	348[3]	365[3]	434[18]	Nombre (milliers)
Per 100 inhabitants		30	34[2]	33[2]	36	41[2]	42[2]	50[2]	Pour 100 habitants
Czech Republic									**République tchèque**
Number (thousands)		2 849[3]	3 212[3]	3 596[3]	4 901[3]	5 332[19]	6 498[20]	6 681[21]	Nombre (milliers)
Per 100 inhabitants [2]		34	36	35	48	52	63	64	Pour 100 habitants [2]
Dem. Rep. of the Congo									**Rép. dém. du Congo**
Number (thousands)		75	113	141	180	230	290	365	Nombre (milliers)
Per 100 inhabitants		^0	^0	^0	^0	^0	^0	1	Pour 100 habitants
Denmark									**Danemark**
Number (thousands)		3 822[3]	4 098[3]	4 482[3]	4 706[3]	4 630	4 641	4 751[22]	Nombre (milliers)
Per 100 inhabitants [2]		76	81	83	87	85	85	87	Pour 100 habitants [2]
Djibouti									**Djibouti**
Number (thousands)		5	6	8	10	14	19	26	Nombre (milliers)
Per 100 inhabitants		1	1	1	1	2	2	3	Pour 100 habitants
Dominica	(01/04)								**Dominique**
Number (thousands)		16	21	26	27	27	28	28	Nombre (milliers)
Per 100 inhabitants		24	30	39	39	40	41	42	Pour 100 habitants
Dominican Republic									**Rép. dominicaine**
Number (thousands)		731	833	1 095	1 436	1 733	2 072	2 701[23]	Nombre (milliers)
Per 100 inhabitants		8	9	11	15	18	21	27[23]	Pour 100 habitants
Ecuador									**Equateur**
Number (thousands)		570	625	783	977[24]	1 152	1 310	2 052	Nombre (milliers)
Per 100 inhabitants		4	5	6	7[2]	9	10	15	Pour 100 habitants
Egypt	(30/06)								**Egypte**
Number (thousands)		3 000	3 900	9 026	9 867	11 819	13 573	16 636	Nombre (milliers)
Per 100 inhabitants		4	5	12	13	15	17	20	Pour 100 habitants
El Salvador									**El Salvador**
Number (thousands)		215[24]	256[24]	382[24]	400[24]	421[24]	650[24]	889	Nombre (milliers)
Per 100 inhabitants		4[2]	4[2]	6[2]	7[2]	7[2]	11[2]	14	Pour 100 habitants
Equatorial Guinea									**Guinée équatoriale**
Number (thousands)		3	5	7	8	10	12	14	Nombre (milliers)
Per 100 inhabitants		1	1	1	1	2	2	2	Pour 100 habitants
Eritrea									**Erythrée**
Number (thousands)		30	50	80	100	120	200	250	Nombre (milliers)
Per 100 inhabitants		1	1	2	2	3	4	5	Pour 100 habitants
Estonia									**Estonie**
Number (thousands) [3]		613	681	828	854	889	947	970	Nombre (milliers) [3]
Per 100 inhabitants		45	53[2]	61[2]	64[2]	66[2]	71[2]	72[2]	Pour 100 habitants
Ethiopia	(30/06)								**Ethiopie**
Number (thousands)		75	113	164	238	291	360	445	Nombre (milliers)
Per 100 inhabitants		^0	^0	^0	^0	^0	^0	1	Pour 100 habitants
Faeroe Islands									**Iles Féroé**
Number (thousands)		28	32	33	34	38	38	38	Nombre (milliers)
Per 100 inhabitants		59	67	68	69	76	76	75	Pour 100 habitants
Fiji									**Fidji**
Number (thousands)		55	61	70	80	91	103	114	Nombre (milliers)
Per 100 inhabitants		7	7	8	10	11	12	13	Pour 100 habitants
Finland									**Finlande**
Number (thousands)		3 436[3]	3 677[3]	3 906[3]	4 192[3]	4 268[3]	4 438[3]	4 481	Nombre (milliers)
Per 100 inhabitants [2]		69	72	74	80	81	84	84	Pour 100 habitants [2]
France									**France**
Number (thousands)		21 765[25]	23 732[25]	26 156[25]	28 766[3]	40 787[3]	43 847[3]	44 625[3]	Nombre (milliers)
Per 100 inhabitants		36[25]	39[25]	43[25]	47[2]	66	71[2]	72[2]	Pour 100 habitants
French Guiana									**Guyane française**
Number (thousands)		31	38	42	46	50	54	58	Nombre (milliers)
Per 100 inhabitants		17	19	21	22	23	25	26	Pour 100 habitants
French Polynesia									**Polynésie française**
Number (thousands)		35	45	55	65	75	90	120	Nombre (milliers)
Per 100 inhabitants		14	18	22	25	29	34	45	Pour 100 habitants
Gabon									**Gabon**
Number (thousands)		35	40	67	77	82	90	99	Nombre (milliers)
Per 100 inhabitants		3	3	5	5	6	6	7	Pour 100 habitants

16 Internet users *(continued)*

Estimated number (thousands) and number per 100 inhabitants

Usagers d'Internet *(suite)*

Nombre estimatif (en milliers) et nombre pour 100 habitants

Country or area	Fiscal year[&] Ex. budgét.[&]	2003	2004	2005	2006	2007	2008	2009	Pays ou zone
Gambia	(01/04)								**Gambie**
Number (thousands)		35	49	58	82	100	114	130	Nombre (milliers)
Per 100 inhabitants		2	3	4	5	6	7	8	Pour 100 habitants
Georgia	(01/04)								**Géorgie**
Number (thousands)		117	176	271	332	360	1 024	1 300	Nombre (milliers)
Per 100 inhabitants		3	4	6	8	8	24	31	Pour 100 habitants
Germany									**Allemagne**
Number (thousands)[3]		44 191	50 315	56 623	59 455	61 889	64 092	65 124	Nombre (milliers)[3]
Per 100 inhabitants[2]		56	65	69	72	75	78	79	Pour 100 habitants[2]
Ghana									**Ghana**
Number (thousands)		250	368	401	610	880	997	1 297	Nombre (milliers)
Per 100 inhabitants		1	2	2	3	4	4	5	Pour 100 habitants
Gibraltar									**Gibraltar**
Number (thousands)		9	10	12	14	16	18	20	Nombre (milliers)
Per 100 inhabitants		28	33	39	45	52	58	65	Pour 100 habitants
Greece									**Grèce**
Number (thousands)[3]		1 791	2 179	2 709	3 576	3 987	4 587	4 971	Nombre (milliers)[3]
Per 100 inhabitants[2]		18	21	24	32	36	41	45	Pour 100 habitants[2]
Greenland									**Groenland**
Number (thousands)		31	32	33	34	35	36	36	Nombre (milliers)
Per 100 inhabitants		55	56	58	59	61	63	63	Pour 100 habitants
Grenada									**Grenade**
Number (thousands)		19	20	21	22	23	24	25	Nombre (milliers)
Per 100 inhabitants		19	20	20	21	22	23	24	Pour 100 habitants
Guam									**Guam**
Number (thousands)		55	60	65	75	80	85	90	Nombre (milliers)
Per 100 inhabitants		34	36	39	44	46	48	51	Pour 100 habitants
Guatemala									**Guatemala**
Number (thousands)		550	760	1 000	1 320	1 640	1 960	2 280	Nombre (milliers)
Per 100 inhabitants		5	6	8	10	12	14	16	Pour 100 habitants
Guernsey									**Guernesey**
Number (thousands)		33	36	39	42	44	46	48	Nombre (milliers)
Per 100 inhabitants		59	65	74	84	…	…	…	Pour 100 habitants
Guinea									**Guinée**
Number (thousands)		40	46	50	60	75	90	95	Nombre (milliers)
Per 100 inhabitants		^0	1	1	1	1	1	1	Pour 100 habitants
Guinea-Bissau									**Guinée-Bissau**
Number (thousands)		19	26	28	31	34	37	37	Nombre (milliers)
Per 100 inhabitants		1	2	2	2	2	2	2	Pour 100 habitants
Guyana									**Guyana**
Number (thousands)		140	145	160	175	190	205	220	Nombre (milliers)
Per 100 inhabitants		18	19	21	23	25	27	29	Pour 100 habitants
Haiti									**Haïti**
Number (thousands)		150	500	600	650	900	1 000	1 000	Nombre (milliers)
Per 100 inhabitants		2	5	6	7	9	10	10	Pour 100 habitants
Honduras									**Honduras**
Number (thousands)		318	378[27]	448[27]	549[27]	674[27]	703[27]	732[27]	Nombre (milliers)
Per 100 inhabitants[26]		5	6	7	8	9	10	10	Pour 100 habitants[26]
Hungary									**Hongrie**
Number (thousands)		2 191	2 803[3]	3 927[3]	4 731[3]	5 347[3]	6 111[3]	6 176[3]	Nombre (milliers)
Per 100 inhabitants		22	28	39[2]	47[2]	53[2]	61[2]	62[2]	Pour 100 habitants
Iceland									**Islande**
Number (thousands)[3]		234	240	258	270	279	287	302	Nombre (milliers)[3]
Per 100 inhabitants[2]		83	84	87	90	91	91	93	Pour 100 habitants[2]
India	(01/04)								**Inde**
Number (thousands)		18 480[28]	22 000[29]	27 000[29]	32 200[30]	46 000[30]	51 750	61 300	Nombre (milliers)
Per 100 inhabitants		2[28]	2	2	3[30]	4[30]	4	5	Pour 100 habitants
Indonesia									**Indonésie**
Number (thousands)		5 100	5 628	7 896	10 576	13 000	18 000	20 000	Nombre (milliers)
Per 100 inhabitants		2	3	4	5	6	8	9	Pour 100 habitants
Iran (Islamic Rep. of)	(22/03)								**Iran (Rép. islamique d')**
Number (thousands)		4 800	10 600	12 300	11 000	13 000	23 000	27 915	Nombre (milliers)
Per 100 inhabitants		7	15	17	15	18	31	38	Pour 100 habitants
Iraq	(30/06)								**Iraq**
Number (thousands)		30	36	200	275	275	300	325	Nombre (milliers)
Per 100 inhabitants		^0	^0	1	1	1	1	1	Pour 100 habitants
Ireland	(01/04)								**Irlande**
Number (thousands)[3]		1 229	1 375	1 742	2 341	2 637	2 899	3 043	Nombre (milliers)[3]
Per 100 inhabitants[2]		34	37	42	55	61	65	67	Pour 100 habitants[2]

Internet users *(continued)*

Estimated number (thousands) and number per 100 inhabitants

Usagers d'Internet *(suite)*

Nombre estimatif (en milliers) et nombre pour 100 habitants

Country or area	Fiscal year & Ex. budgét.&	2003	2004	2005	2006	2007	2008	2009	Pays ou zone
Israel									**Israël**
Number (thousands)		1 265	1 497	1 686	1 899	3 336[3]	3 500[31]	3 700	Nombre (milliers)
Per 100 inhabitants		20	23	25	28	48	50	52	Pour 100 habitants
Italy									**Italie**
Number (thousands)[3]		16 525	18 283	20 737	22 407	24 190	26 542	29 236	Nombre (milliers)[3]
Per 100 inhabitants[2]		29	33	35	38	41	45	49	Pour 100 habitants[2]
Jamaica	(01/04)								**Jamaïque**
Number (thousands)		800	1 067	1 232	1 300	1 500	1 540	1 581	Nombre (milliers)
Per 100 inhabitants		30	40	46	48	56	57	58	Pour 100 habitants
Japan	(01/04)								**Japon**
Number (thousands)		61 640[32]	79 480[33]	85 290[33]	87 540[33]	94 655[34]	95 979[34]	99 144[34]	Nombre (milliers)
Per 100 inhabitants		48[32]	62[33]	67[33]	69[33]	74	75	77	Pour 100 habitants
Jersey									**Jersey**
Number (thousands)		20	27	28	28	29	29	30	Nombre (milliers)
Per 100 inhabitants		23	31	31	32	32	...	...	Pour 100 habitants
Jordan									**Jordanie**
Number (thousands)		444	630	720	797	1 188	1 595	1 742	Nombre (milliers)
Per 100 inhabitants		8	12	13	14	20	26	28	Pour 100 habitants
Kazakhstan									**Kazakhstan**
Number (thousands)		300	400	450	500	620	1 707	5 300	Nombre (milliers)
Per 100 inhabitants		2	3	3	3	4	11	34	Pour 100 habitants
Kenya	(30/06)								**Kenya**
Number (thousands)		1 000	1 055	1 111	2 770	3 000	3 360	3 995	Nombre (milliers)
Per 100 inhabitants		3	3	3	8	8	9	10	Pour 100 habitants
Kiribati									**Kiribati**
Number (thousands)		2	2	2	2	2	2	2	Nombre (milliers)
Per 100 inhabitants		2	2	2	2	2	2	2	Pour 100 habitants
Korea, Republic of									**Corée, République de**
Number (thousands)		31 089[3]	33 446[3]	34 200[3]	35 395[3]	37 794[3]	39 003[3]	39 440	Nombre (milliers)
Per 100 inhabitants		66	71	72	74	79	81	82	Pour 100 habitants
Kuwait									**Koweït**
Number (thousands)		567	600	700	800	900	1 000	1 100	Nombre (milliers)
Per 100 inhabitants		22	23	26	29	32	34	37	Pour 100 habitants
Kyrgyzstan									**Kirghizistan**
Number (thousands)		200	263	550	650	750	850	2 194	Nombre (milliers)
Per 100 inhabitants		4	5	11	12	14	16	40	Pour 100 habitants
Lao People's Dem. Rep.									**Rép. dém. pop. lao**
Number (thousands)		19	21	50	70	100	220	300	Nombre (milliers)
Per 100 inhabitants		^0	^0	1	1	2	4	5	Pour 100 habitants
Latvia									**Lettonie**
Number (thousands)[3]		626	763	1 060	1 223	1 342	1 432	1 503	Nombre (milliers)[3]
Per 100 inhabitants		27	39[2]	46[2]	54[2]	59[2]	63[2]	67[2]	Pour 100 habitants
Lebanon									**Liban**
Number (thousands)		500	600	700	800	780	945[35]	1 000	Nombre (milliers)
Per 100 inhabitants		13	15	17	19	19	23[35]	24	Pour 100 habitants
Lesotho	(01/04)								**Lesotho**
Number (thousands)		30	43	51	60	70	73	77	Nombre (milliers)
Per 100 inhabitants		2	2	3	3	3	4	4	Pour 100 habitants
Liberia									**Libéria**
Number (thousands)		1	1	...	...	20	20	20	Nombre (milliers)
Per 100 inhabitants		^0	^0	...	...	1	1	1	Pour 100 habitants
Libyan Arab Jamah.									**Jamah. arabe libyenne**
Number (thousands)		160	205	232	260	291	323	354	Nombre (milliers)
Per 100 inhabitants		3	4	4	4	5	5	6	Pour 100 habitants
Liechtenstein									**Liechtenstein**
Number (thousands)		20	22	22	23	23	24	23	Nombre (milliers)
Per 100 inhabitants		59	64	63	64	65	66	64	Pour 100 habitants
Lithuania									**Lituanie**
Number (thousands)[3]		844	1 004	1 237	1 488	1 675	1 834	1 964	Nombre (milliers)[3]
Per 100 inhabitants[2]		26	31	36	44	50	55	60	Pour 100 habitants[2]
Luxembourg									**Luxembourg**
Number (thousands)[3]		239	300	327	340	375	395	424	Nombre (milliers)[3]
Per 100 inhabitants[2]		55	66	70	73	79	82	87	Pour 100 habitants[2]
Madagascar									**Madagascar**
Number (thousands)		71	90	100	110	121	316	320	Nombre (milliers)
Per 100 inhabitants		^0	1	1	1	1	2	2	Pour 100 habitants
Malawi									**Malawi**
Number (thousands)		36	46	53	60	139	316	716	Nombre (milliers)
Per 100 inhabitants		^0	^0	^0	^0	1	2	5	Pour 100 habitants

16

Internet users *(continued)*
Estimated number (thousands) and number per 100 inhabitants

Usagers d'Internet *(suite)*
Nombre estimatif (en milliers) et nombre pour 100 habitants

Country or area	Fiscal year[&] Ex. budgét.[&]	2003	2004	2005	2006	2007	2008	2009	Pays ou zone
Malaysia									**Malaisie**
Number (thousands)		8 643	10 637	12 465	13 475	14 793	15 074	15 824	Nombre (milliers)
Per 100 inhabitants		35	42	49	52	56	56	58	Pour 100 habitants
Maldives[36]									**Maldives**[36]
Number (thousands)		17	19	20	33	50	72	88	Nombre (milliers)
Per 100 inhabitants		6	7	7	11	17	24	28	Pour 100 habitants
Mali									**Mali**
Number (thousands)		35	50	60	88	100	200	250	Nombre (milliers)
Per 100 inhabitants		^0	^0	1	1	1	2	2	Pour 100 habitants
Malta									**Malte**
Number (thousands)[3]		126	139	166	163	190	204	241	Nombre (milliers)[3]
Per 100 inhabitants		32	35	41[2]	40[2]	47[2]	50[2]	59[2]	Pour 100 habitants
Marshall Islands									**Iles Marshall**
Number (thousands)		1	2	2	2	2	2	2	Nombre (milliers)
Per 100 inhabitants		3	4	4	4	4	4	4	Pour 100 habitants
Mauritania									**Mauritanie**
Number (thousands)		12	14	20	30	45	60	75	Nombre (milliers)
Per 100 inhabitants		^0	^0	1	1	1	2	2	Pour 100 habitants
Mauritius									**Maurice**
Number (thousands)		150	170	190	232[3]	257	282[3]	290	Nombre (milliers)
Per 100 inhabitants		12	14	15	18	20	22	23	Pour 100 habitants
Mexico									**Mexique**
Number (thousands)		15 375[3]	17 297[3]	19 450[3]	20 564[3]	22 104[3]	23 260	28 439	Nombre (milliers)
Per 100 inhabitants		15	17	18	19	21	21	26	Pour 100 habitants
Micronesia (Fed. States of)									**Micronésie (Etats féd. de)**
Number (thousands)		10	12	13	14	15	16	17	Nombre (milliers)
Per 100 inhabitants		9	11	12	13	14	14	15	Pour 100 habitants
Mongolia									**Mongolie**
Number (thousands)		143	200	268	310	320	330	350	Nombre (milliers)
Per 100 inhabitants		6	8	11	12	12	12	13	Pour 100 habitants
Montenegro									**Monténégro**
Number (thousands)		...	160	180	200	230	255	280	Nombre (milliers)
Per 100 inhabitants		...	25	29	32	37	41	45	Pour 100 habitants
Morocco									**Maroc**
Number (thousands)		1 000	3 500[37]	4 600[37]	6 100[37]	6 600[37]	10 300[37]	10 300	Nombre (milliers)
Per 100 inhabitants		3	12[37]	15[37]	20[37]	21[37]	33[37]	32	Pour 100 habitants
Mozambique									**Mozambique**
Number (thousands)		83	138	178	180	200	350	613	Nombre (milliers)
Per 100 inhabitants		0	1	1	1	1	2	3	Pour 100 habitants
Myanmar									**Myanmar**
Number (thousands)		11	12	32	89	107	109	110	Nombre (milliers)
Per 100 inhabitants ^		0	0	0	0	0	0	0	Pour 100 habitants ^
Namibia	(30/09)								**Namibie**
Number (thousands)		65	75	81	90	101	114	128	Nombre (milliers)
Per 100 inhabitants		3	4	4	4	5	5	6	Pour 100 habitants
Nepal	(15/07)								**Nepal**
Number (thousands)		100	120	225	317	398	499	626	Nombre (milliers)
Per 100 inhabitants		^0	^0	1	1	1	2	2	Pour 100 habitants
Netherlands									**Pays-Bas**
Number (thousands)[3]		10 401	11 129	13 182	13 539	14 126	14 448	14 872	Nombre (milliers)[3]
Per 100 inhabitants[2]		66	70	81	83	86	87	90	Pour 100 habitants[2]
New Caledonia									**Nouvelle-Calédonie**
Number (thousands)		60	70	76	80	85	85	85	Nombre (milliers)
Per 100 inhabitants		26	30	32	34	35	35	34	Pour 100 habitants
New Zealand	(01/04)								**Nouvelle-Zélande**
Number (thousands)		2 446	2 513	2 578	2 786	2 925	3 047	3 600	Nombre (milliers)
Per 100 inhabitants		61	62	63	67	70	72	84	Pour 100 habitants
Nicaragua									**Nicaragua**
Number (thousands)		100	125	140	155	170	185	200	Nombre (milliers)
Per 100 inhabitants		2	2	3	3	3	3	3	Pour 100 habitants
Niger									**Niger**
Number (thousands)		19	24	29	40	55	80	116	Nombre (milliers)
Per 100 inhabitants		^0	^0	^0	^0	^0	1	1	Pour 100 habitants
Nigeria									**Nigéria**
Number (thousands)		750	1 769	5 000	8 000	10 000	23 982	43 982	Nombre (milliers)
Per 100 inhabitants		1	1	4	6	7	16	28	Pour 100 habitants
Norway									**Norvège**
Number (thousands)[3]		3 412	3 441	3 801	3 860	4 103	4 317	4 431	Nombre (milliers)[3]
Per 100 inhabitants[2]		78	78	82	83	87	91	92	Pour 100 habitants[2]

16 Internet users *(continued)*

Estimated number (thousands) and number per 100 inhabitants

Usagers d'Internet *(suite)*

Nombre estimatif (en milliers) et nombre pour 100 habitants

Country or area	Fiscal year & Ex. budgét.&	2003	2004	2005	2006	2007	2008	2009	Pays ou zone
Occupied Palestinian Terr.									**Terr. palestinien occupé**
Number (thousands)		145	160	243	266	355	356	356	Nombre (milliers)
Per 100 inhabitants		4	4	6	7	9	9	8	Pour 100 habitants
Oman									**Oman**
Number (thousands)		183[38]	174[38]	175[38]	222[38]	455[3]	557	1 237[39]	Nombre (milliers)
Per 100 inhabitants		7[38]	7[38]	7[38]	8[38]	17	20	43[40]	Pour 100 habitants
Pakistan	(30/06)								**Pakistan**
Number (thousands)		8 000	10 000	10 500	12 000	17 500	18 500	20 350	Nombre (milliers)
Per 100 inhabitants		5	6	6	7	10	10	11	Pour 100 habitants
Palau									**Palaos**
Number (thousands)		4	5	...	...	...	...	...	Nombre (milliers)
Per 100 inhabitants		22	27	...	...	...	...	...	Pour 100 habitants
Panama									**Panama**
Number (thousands)		312	354	371	570	745	937	960	Nombre (milliers)
Per 100 inhabitants		10	11	11	17	22	28	28	Pour 100 habitants
Papua New Guinea									**Papouasie-Nvl-Guinée**
Number (thousands)		80	90	105	110	115	120	125	Nombre (milliers)
Per 100 inhabitants		1	2	2	2	2	2	2	Pour 100 habitants
Paraguay									**Paraguay**
Number (thousands)		120	200	467[41]	479[41]	687[41]	890[41]	1 000	Nombre (milliers)
Per 100 inhabitants		2	3	8[42]	8[42]	11[42]	14[42]	16	Pour 100 habitants
Peru									**Pérou**
Number (thousands)		2 850	3 220	4 600	6 498	7 000	7 128[43]	8 085[43]	Nombre (milliers)
Per 100 inhabitants		11	12	17	23	25	25[44]	28[44]	Pour 100 habitants
Philippines									**Philippines**
Number (thousands)		4 000	4 400	4 615	5 000	5 300	5 618	5 955	Nombre (milliers)
Per 100 inhabitants		5	5	5	6	6	6	6	Pour 100 habitants
Poland									**Pologne**
Number (thousands)[3]		9 522	11 065	14 825	17 013	18 532	20 245	22 451	Nombre (milliers)[3]
Per 100 inhabitants		25	33[2]	39[2]	45[2]	49[2]	53[2]	59[2]	Pour 100 habitants
Portugal									**Portugal**
Number (thousands)[3]		2 673	3 077	3 690	4 028	4 479	4 712	5 169	Nombre (milliers)[3]
Per 100 inhabitants[2]		30	32	35	38	42	44	48	Pour 100 habitants[2]
Puerto Rico									**Porto Rico**
Number (thousands)		764	862	916	1 000	1 100	1 000	1 000	Nombre (milliers)
Per 100 inhabitants		20	22	23	25	28	25	25	Pour 100 habitants
Qatar									**Qatar**
Number (thousands)		141	165	219	290	261	327	399	Nombre (milliers)
Per 100 inhabitants		19	21	25	29	23	26	28	Pour 100 habitants
Republic of Moldova									**République de Moldova**
Number (thousands)		288	406	550	728	750	850[45]	1 295	Nombre (milliers)
Per 100 inhabitants		7	11	15	20	20	23[45]	36	Pour 100 habitants
Romania									**Roumanie**
Number (thousands)[3]		1 942	2 704	3 583	5 312	6 070	6 925	7 787	Nombre (milliers)[3]
Per 100 inhabitants		9	12	17	25[2]	28[2]	32[2]	37[2]	Pour 100 habitants
Russian Federation									**Fédération de Russie**
Number (thousands)		12 000	18 500	21 800	25 689	35 000	45 400	59 700	Nombre (milliers)
Per 100 inhabitants		8	13	15	18	25	32	42	Pour 100 habitants
Rwanda									**Rwanda**
Number (thousands)		31	38	50[46]	...	200	300	450	Nombre (milliers)
Per 100 inhabitants		^0	^0	1	...	2	3	5	Pour 100 habitants
Saint Kitts and Nevis	(01/04)								**Saint-Kitts-et-Nevis**
Number (thousands)		11	12	13	14	15	16	17	Nombre (milliers)
Per 100 inhabitants		23	25	26	28	30	31	33	Pour 100 habitants
Saint Lucia	(01/04)								**Sainte-Lucie**
Number (thousands)		34	35	36	55	70	100	143	Nombre (milliers)
Per 100 inhabitants		21	21	22	33	42	59	83	Pour 100 habitants
Saint Vincent-Grenadines	(01/04)								**Saint Vincent-Grenadines**
Number (thousands)		7[47]	8[47]	10[47]	35[47]	57[47]	66[47]	76	Nombre (milliers)
Per 100 inhabitants		6[47]	7[47]	9[47]	32[47]	52[47]	60[47]	70	Pour 100 habitants
Samoa									**Samoa**
Number (thousands)		5	6	6	8	9	9	9	Nombre (milliers)
Per 100 inhabitants		3	3	3	4	5	5	5	Pour 100 habitants
San Marino									**Saint-Marin**
Number (thousands)		14	15	15	15	16	17	17	Nombre (milliers)
Per 100 inhabitants		50	51	50	50	50	55	54	Pour 100 habitants
Sao Tome and Principe									**Sao Tomé-et-Principe**
Number (thousands)		15	20	21	22	23	25	27	Nombre (milliers)
Per 100 inhabitants		10	13	14	14	15	15	16	Pour 100 habitants

16 Internet users *(continued)*

Estimated number (thousands) and number per 100 inhabitants

Usagers d'Internet *(suite)*

Nombre estimatif (en milliers) et nombre pour 100 habitants

Country or area	Fiscal year & Ex. budgét.&	2003	2004	2005	2006	2007	2008	2009	Pays ou zone
Saudi Arabia									**Arabie saoudite**
Number (thousands)		1 800	2 360	3 000	4 700	6 368	7 762	9 800	Nombre (milliers)
Per 100 inhabitants		8	10	13	19	26	31	38	Pour 100 habitants
Senegal									**Sénégal**
Number (thousands)		225	482	540	650	820	870[48]	923	Nombre (milliers)
Per 100 inhabitants		2	4	5	6	7	7[48]	7	Pour 100 habitants
Serbia									**Serbie**
Number (thousands)		...	600	2 592[3]	2 911[3]	3 259[3]	3 660[3]	4 107[3]	Nombre (milliers)
Per 100 inhabitants [2]		...	24	26	30	33	37	42	Pour 100 habitants [2]
Seychelles	(01/04)								**Seychelles**
Number (thousands)		12	20	21	29	32	34	34	Nombre (milliers)
Per 100 inhabitants		15	24	25	35	38	40	40	Pour 100 habitants
Sierra Leone									**Sierra Leone**
Number (thousands)		9	10	11	12	13	14	15	Nombre (milliers)
Per 100 inhabitants ^		0	0	0	0	0	0	0	Pour 100 habitants ^
Singapore	(01/04)								**Singapour**
Number (thousands)		2 236[3]	2 649[3]	2 639[3]	2 611[3]	3 105[3]	3 370[3]	3 658	Nombre (milliers)
Per 100 inhabitants		54	63	62	60	69	73	77	Pour 100 habitants
Slovakia									**Slovaquie**
Number (thousands)		2 317	2 500	2 972[3]	3 022[3]	3 334[3]	3 851[3]	4 064[3]	Nombre (milliers)
Per 100 inhabitants		43	53[2]	55[2]	56[2]	62[2]	71[2]	75[2]	Pour 100 habitants
Slovenia									**Slovénie**
Number (thousands) [3]		635	738	1 002	1 083	1 141	1 162	1 299	Nombre (milliers) [3]
Per 100 inhabitants		32	41[2]	50[2]	54[2]	57[2]	58[2]	64[2]	Pour 100 habitants
Solomon Islands	(01/04)								**Iles Salomon**
Number (thousands)		3	3	4	8	9	10	10	Nombre (milliers)
Per 100 inhabitants		1	1	1	2	2	2	2	Pour 100 habitants
Somalia									**Somalie**
Number (thousands)		30	86	90	94	98	102	106	Nombre (milliers)
Per 100 inhabitants		^0	1	1	1	1	1	1	Pour 100 habitants
South Africa	(01/04)								**Afrique du Sud**
Number (thousands)		3 283	4 000	3 600	3 700	3 966	4 187	4 420	Nombre (milliers)
Per 100 inhabitants		7	8	7	8	8	8	9	Pour 100 habitants
Spain									**Espagne**
Number (thousands)		15 338	17 149	20 617[3]	21 951[3]	24 277[3]	26 509[3]	28 118[3]	Nombre (milliers)
Per 100 inhabitants		40[2]	44[2]	48[2]	50	55	60[2]	63[2]	Pour 100 habitants
Sri Lanka									**Sri Lanka**
Number (thousands)		280	280	350	500	772	1 163	1 776	Nombre (milliers)
Per 100 inhabitants		1	1	2	3	4	6	9	Pour 100 habitants
Sudan									**Soudan**
Number (thousands)		200	300	500	3 200	3 500	4 200	4 200	Nombre (milliers)
Per 100 inhabitants		1	1	1	8	9	10	10	Pour 100 habitants
Suriname									**Suriname**
Number (thousands)		23	30	32	48	72	109	163	Nombre (milliers)
Per 100 inhabitants		5	6	6	9	14	21	31	Pour 100 habitants
Swaziland	(01/04)								**Swaziland**
Number (thousands)		27	36	42	42	47	80	90	Nombre (milliers)
Per 100 inhabitants		2	3	4	4	4	7	8	Pour 100 habitants
Sweden									**Suède**
Number (thousands) [3]		6 891	7 353	7 691	7 998	7 511	8 203	8 398	Nombre (milliers) [3]
Per 100 inhabitants [2]		79	84	85	88	82	89	91	Pour 100 habitants [2]
Switzerland									**Suisse**
Number (thousands)		4 697	4 923	5 077	5 301	5 021[49]	5 267[50]	5 480[51]	Nombre (milliers)
Per 100 inhabitants		64	67	68	71	67[49]	70[50]	72[51]	Pour 100 habitants
Syrian Arab Republic									**Rép. arabe syrienne**
Number (thousands)		610	800	1 080	1 550	3 470	3 565	3 935	Nombre (milliers)
Per 100 inhabitants		3	4	6	8	17	17	18	Pour 100 habitants
Tajikistan									**Tadjikistan**
Number (thousands)		4	5	20	250	484	600	700	Nombre (milliers)
Per 100 inhabitants		^0	^0	^0	4	7	9	10	Pour 100 habitants
Thailand	(30/09)								**Thaïlande**
Number (thousands)		6 000	6 970	9 909	11 413	13 416	16 100	17 486	Nombre (milliers)
Per 100 inhabitants		9	11	15	17	20	24	26	Pour 100 habitants
TFYR of Macedonia									**L'ex-R.Y. Macédoine**
Number (thousands) [3]		387	429	538	583	740	940	1 057	Nombre (milliers) [3]
Per 100 inhabitants		19	24[2]	26[2]	29[2]	36[2]	46[2]	52[2]	Pour 100 habitants
Timor-Leste									**Timor-Leste**
Number (thousands)		...	...	1	1	2	2	2	Nombre (milliers)
Per 100 inhabitants ^		...	...	0	0	0	0	0	Pour 100 habitants ^

16 Internet users *(continued)*

Estimated number (thousands) and number per 100 inhabitants

Usagers d'Internet *(suite)*

Nombre estimatif (en milliers) et nombre pour 100 habitants

Country or area	Fiscal year & Ex. budgét.&	2003	2004	2005	2006	2007	2008	2009	Pays ou zone
Togo									**Togo**
Number (thousands)		210	221	300	320	341	350	356	Nombre (milliers)
Per 100 inhabitants		4	4	5	5	5	5	5	Pour 100 habitants
Tonga									**Tonga**
Number (thousands)		3	4	5	6	7	8	8	Nombre (milliers)
Per 100 inhabitants		3	4	5	6	7	8	8	Pour 100 habitants
Trinidad and Tobago	(01/04)								**Trinité-et-Tobago**
Number (thousands)		340	355	382	397	429	456	485	Nombre (milliers)
Per 100 inhabitants		26	27	29	30	32	34	36	Pour 100 habitants
Tunisia									**Tunisie**
Number (thousands)		630	835	954	1 295	1 722	2 800	3 500	Nombre (milliers)
Per 100 inhabitants		6	9	10	13	17	28	34	Pour 100 habitants
Turkey									**Turquie**
Number (thousands)		8 550[52]	9 311[3]	11 003[3]	13 149[3]	20 901[3]	25 404[3]	26 410[3]	Nombre (milliers)
Per 100 inhabitants		12[2]	15[2]	15[2]	18[53]	29[2]	34	35	Pour 100 habitants
Turkmenistan									**Turkménistan**
Number (thousands)		20	36	48	65	70	75	80	Nombre (milliers)
Per 100 inhabitants		^0	1	1	1	1	1	2	Pour 100 habitants
Tuvalu									**Tuvalu**
Number (thousands)		2	2	3	3	4	4	4	Nombre (milliers)
Per 100 inhabitants		15	21	26	31	41	43	43	Pour 100 habitants
Uganda	(30/06)								**Ouganda**
Number (thousands)		125	200	500	750	1 125	2 500	3 200	Nombre (milliers)
Per 100 inhabitants		^0	1	2	3	4	8	10	Pour 100 habitants
Ukraine									**Ukraine**
Number (thousands)		1 500	1 650	1 760[54]	2 100	6 400[3]	10 400[3]	15 300	Nombre (milliers)
Per 100 inhabitants		3	3	4[54]	5	14	23	33	Pour 100 habitants
United Arab Emirates									**Emirats arabes unis**
Number (thousands)		1 110	1 185	1 321	1 708	2 260	3 229[55]	3 778	Nombre (milliers)
Per 100 inhabitants		29	30	32	40	52	72[55]	82	Pour 100 habitants
United Kingdom	(01/04)								**Royaume-Uni**
Number (thousands)[3]		36 292	37 590	41 929	41 687	45 729	47 999	51 442	Nombre (milliers)[3]
Per 100 inhabitants[2]		65	66	70	69	75	78	84	Pour 100 habitants[2]
United Rep. of Tanzania									**Rép.-Unie de Tanzanie**
Number (thousands)		250	333	384	390	400	520	676	Nombre (milliers)
Per 100 inhabitants		1	1	1	1	1	1	2	Pour 100 habitants
United States									**Etats-Unis**
Number (thousands)		183 196[3]	194 159[3]	205 767[3]	210 720[3]	221 724[3]	230 630[56]	239 894	Nombre (milliers)
Per 100 inhabitants		62	65	68	69	72	74[56]	76	Pour 100 habitants
United States Virgin Is.									**Iles Vierges américaines**
Number (thousands)		30	30	30	30	30	30	30	Nombre (milliers)
Per 100 inhabitants		27	27	27	27	27	27	27	Pour 100 habitants
Uruguay									**Uruguay**
Number (thousands)		530	567	668	850	968	1 340[57]	1 855	Nombre (milliers)
Per 100 inhabitants		16	17	20	26	29	40[57]	55	Pour 100 habitants
Uzbekistan									**Ouzbékistan**
Number (thousands)		492	675	880	1 700	2 015	2 469	4 689	Nombre (milliers)
Per 100 inhabitants		2	3	3	6	7	9	17	Pour 100 habitants
Vanuatu									**Vanuatu**
Number (thousands)		8	10	11	13	17	17	17	Nombre (milliers)
Per 100 inhabitants		4	5	5	6	7	7	7	Pour 100 habitants
Venezuela (Boliv. Rep. of)									**Venezuela (Rép. boliv. du)**
Number (thousands)		1 935	2 207	3 355	4 140	5 720	*7 222	8 847[58]	Nombre (milliers)
Per 100 inhabitants		8	8	13	15	21	*26	31	Pour 100 habitants
Viet Nam									**Viet Nam**
Number (thousands)		3 098	6 345	10 711	14 684	17 872	20 834	24 000	Nombre (milliers)
Per 100 inhabitants		4	8	13	17	21	24	27	Pour 100 habitants
Yemen									**Yémen**
Number (thousands)		120	180	220	270	320	370	420	Nombre (milliers)
Per 100 inhabitants		1	1	1	1	1	2	2	Pour 100 habitants
Zambia	(01/04)								**Zambie**
Number (thousands)		110	231	335	500	600	700	817	Nombre (milliers)
Per 100 inhabitants		1	2	3	4	5	6	6	Pour 100 habitants
Zimbabwe	(30/06)								**Zimbabwe**
Number (thousands)		800	820	1 000	1 220	1 351	1 421	1 422	Nombre (milliers)
Per 100 inhabitants		6	7	8	10	11	11	11	Pour 100 habitants

Source:
International Telecommunication Union (ITU), Geneva, the ITU database, last accessed July 2010.

& Fiscal year refers to the fiscal year used in each country or area. Countries or areas whose reference periods coincide with the calendar year ending 31 December are not footnoted. Those that have a fiscal year other than calendar year are denoted as follows:

22/03: Year beginning 22 March
01/04: Year beginning 1 April
30/06: Year ending 30 June
15/07: Year ending 15 July
30/09: Year ending 30 September

1 October.
2 Persons aged 16 to 74 years.
3 Estimated based on the percentage of Internet users as reported in surveys.
4 From RTR data request (NASE BB 2009).
5 Estimated based on % as reported in 2008 HH survey.
6 ITU estimate based on 3 times the number of subscribers.
7 Estimated based on % of Internet users as reported in surveys and taking into account urban/rural distribution and internet penetration as reported in Survey 2008.
8 Population age 10+. Estimated based on urban/rural distribution of Internet users in 2008 (as 2006 Survey collected only urban data).
9 Population age 10+ using internet in the last 3 months.
10 Tower Omnibus Survey
11 Estimated based on % of Internet users as reported in surveys in 2003 and 2006.
12 For statistical purposes, the data for China do not include those for the Hong Kong Special Administrative Region (Hong Kong SAR), Macao Special Administrative Region (Macao SAR) and Taiwan Province of China.
13 Population age 6+. Online at least one hour per week.
14 Population age 10+ who accessed Internet in previous year.
15 June.
16 September 2009. Based on the number of subscriptions. Multiplying factor consideres commercial, residential and community subscriptions and subscription bandwidth. The final result is also multiplied by a factor of repetition to avoid the duplicity of users. These factors are obtained through national surveys and are updated every 2 years.
17 Including users of the international network and also those having access only to the Cuban network.
18 Percent of users in the age range 16-74 according to statistical service.
19 Internet users 16+ (in the last 3 months), 45% of total number of individuals in 16+ socio-demographic group.
20 Internet users 16+ (in the last 3 months), 54% of total number of individuals in 16+ socio-demographic group.
21 Internet users 16+ (in the last 3 months), 55.9% of total number of individuals in 16+ socio-demographic group.

Source:
Union internationale des télécommunications (UIT), Genève, la base de données de l'UIT, dernier accès juillet 2010.

& Ex. budgét. fait référence à l'exercice budgétaire en vigueur dans chaque pays ou territoire. Les pays ou les territoires dont l'exercice budgétaire terminent le 31 décembre de l'année civile ne sont pas signalés. Dans le cas contraire, ils sont désignés de la manière suivante:

22/03 : Exercice commençant le 22 mars
01/04 : Exercice commençant le 1er avril
30/06 : Exercice se terminant le 30 juin
15/07 : Exercice se terminant le 15 juillet
30/09 : Exercice se terminant le 30 septembre

1 Octobre.
2 Personnes âgées de 16 à 74 ans.
3 Estimations basées sur le pourcentage d'utilisateurs d'Internet d'après les enquêtes.
4 D'après la demande de données RTR (NASE BB 2009).
5 Estimation fondée sur un pourcentage indiqué dans l'enquête HH 2008.
6 Estimation de l'UIT basée sur le nombre d'abonnés multiplié par 3.
7 Estimation fondée sur un pourcentage d'utilisateurs d'Internet tel qu'il figure dans les enquêtes, tenant compte de la répartition entre utilisateurs urbains et ruraux et du taux de pénétration de l'Internet indiqué dans l'enquête 2008.
8 Population âgée de plus de 10 ans. Estimation fondée sur la répartition entre usagers urbains et ruraux en 2008 (l'enquête 2006 n'a porté que sur les villes).
9 Population âgée de plus de 10 ans ayant employé Internet dans les trois derniers mois.
10 Tower Omnibus Survey
11 Estimation fondée sur le pourcentage d'utilisateurs d'Internet d'après les enquêtes 2003 et 2006.
12 Pour la présentation des statistiques, les données pour la Chine ne comprennent pas la Région Administrative Spéciale de Hong Kong (Hong Kong RAS), la Région Administrative Spéciale de Macao (Macao RAS) et la province de Taiwan.
13 Population âgée de plus de 6 ans. En ligne au moins une heure par semaine.
14 Population âgée de plus de 10 ans s'étant branchée sur l'Internet au cours de l'année écoulée.
15 Juin.
16 Septembre 2009. D'après le nombre d'abonnements. Les coefficients multiplicateurs tiennent compte du fait qu'un abonnement est commercial, résidentiel ou communautaire et de la bande passante. Le résultat final est multiplié par un coefficient de répétition pour éviter le double comptage des utilisateurs. Les coefficients proviennent d'enquêtes nationales et sont actualisés tous les deux ans.
17 Y compris les utilisateurs du réseau international et ceux qui n'ont accès qu'au réseau cubain.
18 Pourcentage d'utilisateurs dans la classe d'âge 16-74 ans d'après le service statistique.
19 Utilisateurs âgés de plus de 16 ans (au cours des trois derniers mois), 45 % de la population totale du groupe sociodémographique des plus de 16 ans.
20 Utilisateurs âgés de plus de 16 ans (au cours des trois derniers mois), 54 % de la population totale du groupe sociodémographique des plus de 16 ans.
21 Utilisateurs âgés de plus de 16 ans (au cours des trois derniers mois), 55,9 % de la population totale du groupe sociodémographique des plus de 16 ans.

16 Internet users *(continued)*

Estimated number (thousands) and number per 100 inhabitants

Usagers d'Internet *(suite)*

Nombre estimatif (en milliers) et nombre pour 100 habitants

22 A 2009 survey found that 86 % of people aged 16-74 are Internet users. This share has been expanded to the entire population. Population data from Statistics Denmark as of 31 December 2009.

23 Calculated based on Internet subscriptions. A factor of 3.9 is applied to residential subscriptions and a factor of 16 to business subscriptions. It can be overestimated as users can be double counted (estimated users at home and at work).

24 Estimated based on % of internet users between 16-74.

25 Population age 11+ using in the last month.

26 Population aged 5+.

27 Estimated based on % of internet users aged 5+.

28 December.

29 ITU estimate.

30 September.

31 Estimated based on % of Internet users as reported in 2007 survey.

32 PC-based only.

33 Including users accessing internet through cell phones, PHS and game console.

34 Estimated based on % of internet users aged 6+.

35 TRA estimates the number of Internet users based on the number of Internet subscribers (3 users for every subscriber).

36 Not from official survey data. Country estimated based on the assumption that every connection (except leased lines) serves 4 users (average household size) and a leased line serves 10 users. Mobile internet users are not included.

37 Using Internet at least once during the last month.

38 Based on the number of Internet subscribers, a multiplier of 3.54 was used to estimate the proportion of Internet users.

39 Fixed internet users are calculated based on actual fixed internet subscribers multiplied by a factor of 5.8 (453183). It also includes estimated (783475) mobile internet users.

40 Estimate based on actual fixed internet subscribers multiplied by a factor of 5.8 (453183). It also includes estimated (783475) mobile internet users.

41 Estimated based on % of internet users 10+.

42 Refer to users aged 10+

43 Estimation based on percentage of users aged 6+. Household Survey, INEI.

44 Population age 6+. INEI.

45 Based on RCC data.

46 No survey conducted yet. The figures provided are not from our databank.

47 Estimation based on GPRS subscribers, fixed and mobile.

48 Sonatel and Sentel.

49 Covers a limited number of users and a larger group of users: Age 14+. Period: October 07 to March 08.

50 Covers a limited number of users and a larger group of users: Age 14+. Period: October 08 to March 09.

51 Covers a limited number of users and a larger group of users: Age 14+. Estimation.

52 Refer to 16-74 years.

53 Estimated based on % of Internet users as reported in surveys in 2005 and 2007.

22 Selon une enquête de 2009, 86 % des habitants de 16 à 74 ans utilisent l'Internet. Cette proportion a été étendue à l'ensemble de la population. Données démographiques de Statistics Denmark en date du 31 décembre 2009.

23 D'après le nombre d'abonnements Internet. Un coefficient de 3,9 est appliqué pour les abonnements de particuliers et un coefficient de 16 pour les abonnements d'entreprises. Il peut y avoir surestimation en raison d'un double comptage (personnes qui utilisent Internet à la fois chez eux et au travail).

24 Estimation fondée sur le pourcentage d'utilisateurs d'Internet âgés de 16 à 74 ans.

25 Population âgée de plus de 11 ans utilisant au cours de dernier mois.

26 Population âgée de plus de 5 ans.

27 Estimation fondée sur un pourcentage d'utilisateurs d'Internet âgés de plus de 5 ans.

28 Décembre.

29 Estimation de l'UIT.

30 Septembre.

31 Estimation sur la base du pourcentage d'utilisateurs d'Internet tel qu'il figure dans l'enquête 2007.

32 Pour ordinateurs personnels seulement.

33 Comprend les utilisateurs qui naviguent sur Internet au moyen de téléphones mobiles, de téléphones PHS et de consoles de jeux.

34 Estimation fondée sur la base d'un pourcentage d'utilisateurs d'Internet âgés de plus de 6 ans.

35 L'Agence de régulation des télécommunications estime le nombre d'usagers de l'Internet sur la base du nombre d'abonnés (trois utilisateurs par abonné).

36 Chiffres ne provenant pas de données d'enquêtes officielles. Estimation par pays fondée sur le postulat que chaque abonnement (sauf lignes louées) dessert quatre usagers (taille moyenne du ménage) et que chaque ligne louée dessert 10 usagers. Les utilisateurs de l'Internet mobile ne sont pas inclus.

37 Ayant employé Internet au moins une fois durant le dernier mois.

38 D'après le nombre d'abonnés à l'Internet, la proportion d'utilisateurs de l'Internet étant estimée par un coefficient de multiplication de 3,54.

39 Le nombre d'utilisateurs de l'Internet fixes est calculé sur la base du nombre effectif d'abonnés à un raccordement fixe multiplié par un coefficient de 5,8 (453183). Il inclut le nombre estimatif d'utilisateurs de l'Internet mobile (783475).

40 Estimation fondée sur le nombre effectif d'abonnés à l'Internet – ligne fixe – multiplié par un facteur de 5,8 (453 183). Comprend le nombre estimatif d'usagers de l'Internet mobile (783 475).

41 Estimation fondée sur un pourcentage d'utilisateurs d'Internet âgés de plus de 10 ans.

42 Usagers âgés de plus de 10 ans.

43 Estimation fondée sur la base d'un pourcentage d'utilisateurs d'Internet âgés de plus de 6 ans. Household Survey, INEI.

44 Population âgée de plus de 6 ans. INEI.

45 D'après les données RCC.

46 Aucune enquête n'a encore été faite. Les chiffres fournis ne proviennent pas de notre base de données.

47 Estimation basée sur le nombre d'abonnés aux services GPRS (fixe et mobile).

48 Sonatel et Sentel.

49 Nombre limité d'usagers et un nombre d'usagers plus élevé: personnes âgées de plus de 14 ans. Période: octobre 07 à mars 08.

50 Nombre limité d'usagers et un nombre d'usagers plus élevé: personnes âgées de plus de 14 ans. Période: octobre 08 à mars 09.

51 Nombre limité d'usagers et un nombre d'usagers plus élevé: personnes âgées de plus de 14 ans. Estimation.

52 Population âgée de 16 à 74 ans.

53 Estimation fondée sur le pourcentage d'utilisateurs d'Internet d'après les enquêtes 2005 et 2007.

54 Estimated based on results of user survey applied to resident population aged 15-59 who used internet in the last 4 weeks.
55 Population age 15-74.
56 Pew Internet Project, "Usage over Time" http://www.pewinternet.org/Trend-Data/Usage-Over-Time.aspx
57 ANTEL from source: Radar.
58 Final year 2009.

54 Estimation basée sur les résultats d'enquête auprès de la population résidente âgée de 15 à 59 ans qui a utilisé l'internet dans les quatre dernières semaines.
55 Population âgée de 15 à 74 ans.
56 Pew Internet Project, "Usage over Time" http://www.pewinternet.org/Trend-Data/Usage-Over-Time.aspx
57 ANTEL de source: Radar.
58 Dernière année 2009.

Technical notes: tables 14-16

The statistics included in *Tables 14-16* were obtained from the statistics database (see www.itu.int) and the *Yearbook of Statistics, Telecommunication Services* of the International Telecommunication Union.

Table 14: This table shows the number of main (fixed) lines in operation and the main lines in operation per 100 inhabitants for the years indicated. Main telephone lines refer to the telephone lines connecting a customer's equipment to the Public Switched Telephone Network (PSTN) and which have a dedicated port on a telephone exchange. Note that in most countries, main lines also include public telephones. The number of main telephone lines per 100 inhabitants is calculated by dividing the number of main lines by the population and multiplying by 100.

Table 15: The number of mobile cellular telephone subscribers (as well as the number of subscribers per 100 inhabitants) refers to users of portable telephones subscribing to an automatic public mobile telephone service using cellular technology, which provides access to the Public Switched Telephone Network (PSTN). Users of both post-paid subscriptions and pre-paid accounts are included. The number of subscribers per 100 inhabitants is calculated by dividing the number of subscribers by the population and multiplying by 100.

Table 16: Many Internet users obtain access without paying directly, either as the member of a household, or from work or school. Therefore the number of Internet users will always be much larger than the number of subscribers, typically by a factor of 2-3 in developed countries or more in developing ones. The estimated number of Internet users is measured in a growing number of countries through regular surveys. In situations where surveys are not available, an estimate can be derived based on the number of subscribers. The number of users per 100 inhabitants is calculated by dividing the number of users by the population and multiplying by 100.

Notes techniques : tableaux 14 à 16

Les données présentées dans les *Tableaux 14 à 16* proviennent de la base de données (voir www.itu.int) et *l'Annuaire statistique, Services de télécommunications* de l'Union internationale des télécommunications.

Tableau 14: Ce tableau indique le nombre de lignes principales (fixes) en service et les lignes principales en service pour 100 habitants pour les années indiquées. Les lignes principales sont des lignes téléphoniques qui relient l'équipement terminal de l'abonné au Réseau de téléphone public connecté (RTPC) et qui possèdent un accès individualisé aux équipements d'un central téléphonique. Pour la plupart des pays, le nombre de lignes principales en service indiqué comprend également les lignes publiques. Le nombre de lignes principales pour 100 habitants se calcule en divisant le nombre de lignes principales par la population et en multipliant par 100.

Tableau 15: Les abonnés mobiles (et les abonnés mobiles pour 100 habitants) désignent les utilisateurs de téléphones portatifs abonnés à un service automatique public de téléphones mobiles ayant accès au Réseau de téléphone public connecté (RTPC). Sont pris en compte aussi bien les abonnements post-payés que les cartes prépayées. Le nombre d'abonnés pour 100 habitants se calcule en divisant le nombre d'abonnés par la population et en multipliant par 100.

Tableau 16: Un certain nombre d'utilisateurs de l'Internet y accèdent sans payer directement, soit en tant que membres d'un ménage, soit parce qu'ils l'utilisent au travail ou à l'école. C'est pourquoi le nombre d'utilisateurs de l'Internet sera toujours bien supérieur au nombre d'abonnés, généralement de deux à trois fois dans les pays développés et plus encore dans les pays en développement. Le nombre d'utilisateurs d'internet est recensé à l'aide d'enquêtes standards dans un nombre croissant de pays. Quand les enquêtes ne sont pas disponibles, il est estimé grâce au nombre d'abonnés. Le nombre d'utilisateurs pour 100 habitants est calculé en divisant le nombre d'utilisateurs par le nombre d'habitants, multiplié par 100.

Part Three

Economic activity

Chapter VI	National accounts (tables 17-21)
Chapter VII	Financial statistics (tables 22 and 23)
Chapter VIII	Labour force (tables 24 and 25)
Chapter IX	Prices (tables 26 and 27)
Chapter X	Agriculture, forestry and fishing (tables 28-33)
Chapter XI	Manufacturing (tables 34-48)
Chapter XII	Energy (tables 49 and 50)
Chapter XIII	Environment (tables 51-55)
Chapter XIV	Science and technology (tables 56 and 57)

Part Three of the *Yearbook* presents statistical series on production and consumption for a wide range of economic activities, and other basic series on major economic topics, for all countries or areas of the world for which data are available. Included are basic tables on national accounts, finance, labour force, prices, a wide range of agricultural, mined and manufactured commodities, energy, environment, research and development personnel and expenditure.

International economic topics such as external trade are covered in Part Four.

Troisième partie

Activité économique

Chapitre VI	Comptabilités nationales (tableaux 17 à 21)
Chapitre VII	Statistiques financières (tableaux 22 et 23)
Chapitre VIII	Main-d'œuvre (tableaux 24 et 25)
Chapitre IX	Prix (tableaux 26 et 27)
Chapitre X	Agriculture, forêts et pêche (tableaux 28 à 33)
Chapitre XI	Industries manufacturières (tableaux 34 à 48)
Chapitre XII	Energie (tableaux 49 et 50)
Chapitre XIII	Environnement (tableaux 51 à 55)
Chapitre XIV	Environnement (tableaux 56 et 57)

La troisième partie de l'*Annuaire* présente, pour une large gamme d'activités économiques, des séries statistiques sur la production et la consommation, et, pour tous les pays ou zones du monde pour lesquels des données sont disponibles, d'autres séries fondamentales ayant trait à des questions économiques importantes. Y figurent des tableaux de base consacrés à la comptabilité nationale, aux finances, à la main-d'œuvre, aux prix, à un large éventail de produits agricoles, miniers et manufacturés, à l'énergie, à l'environnement, au personnel employé à des travaux de recherche et développement et dépenses de recherche et développement.

Les questions économiques internationales comme le commerce extérieur sont traitées dans la quatrième partie.

17 Gross domestic product and gross domestic product per capita

In millions of US dollars at current and constant 1990 prices; per capita US dollars; real rates of growth

Produit intérieur brut et produit intérieur brut par habitant

En millions de dollars É.-U. aux prix courants et constants de 1990 ; par habitant en dollars É.U. ; taux de croissance réels

Country or area	2002	2003	2004	2005	2006	2007	2008	Pays ou zone
World								**Monde**
GDP at current prices	**33 186 252**	**37 291 961**	**41 975 038**	**45 424 395**	**49 178 037**	**55 276 671**	**60 819 579**	**PIB aux prix courants**
GDP per capita	**5 290**	**5 871**	**6 526**	**6 977**	**7 462**	**8 288**	**9 012**	**PIB par habitant**
GDP at constant prices	**30 355 717**	**31 182 582**	**32 462 596**	**33 598 970**	**34 957 792**	**36 332 066**	**37 124 191**	**PIB aux prix constants**
Growth rates	**2.0**	**2.7**	**4.1**	**3.5**	**4.0**	**3.9**	**2.2**	**Taux de croissance**
Afghanistan								**Afghanistan**
GDP at current prices	4 741	4 786	5 700	6 840	8 166	10 120	12 679	PIB aux prix courants
GDP per capita	216	210	241	279	322	385	466	PIB par habitant
GDP at constant prices	4 741	5 420	5 932	6 793	7 553	8 775	9 069	PIB aux prix constants
Growth rates	81.1	14.3	9.4	14.5	11.2	16.2	3.4	Taux de croissance
Albania								**Albanie**
GDP at current prices	4 443	5 696	7 305	8 159	9 082	10 871	13 119	PIB aux prix courants
GDP per capita	1 444	1 845	2 357	2 623	2 909	3 470	4 174	PIB par habitant
GDP at constant prices	2 884	3 050	3 224	3 411	3 599	3 820	4 079	PIB aux prix constants
Growth rates	4.2	5.8	5.7	5.8	5.5	6.1	6.8	Taux de croissance
Algeria								**Algérie**
GDP at current prices	56 948	68 017	85 351	103 220	117 288	134 304	170 453	PIB aux prix courants
GDP per capita	1 813	2 133	2 637	3 142	3 517	3 967	4 959	PIB par habitant
GDP at constant prices	78 562	83 983	88 350	92 856	94 528	97 363	100 284	PIB aux prix constants
Growth rates	4.7	6.9	5.2	5.1	1.8	3.0	3.0	Taux de croissance
Andorra								**Andorre**
GDP at current prices	1 456	1 918	2 322	2 540	2 824	3 245	3 712	PIB aux prix courants
GDP per capita	20 497	25 855	30 072	31 837	34 543	38 991	43 975	PIB par habitant
GDP at constant prices	1 628	1 738	1 850	1 960	2 093	2 123	2 199	PIB aux prix constants
Growth rates	5.9	6.8	6.5	5.9	6.8	1.4	3.6	Taux de croissance
Angola								**Angola**
GDP at current prices	11 432	13 956	15 963[1]	19 881[1]	24 331[1]	30 051[1]	34 999[1]	PIB aux prix courants
GDP per capita	754	892	989[1]	1 196[1]	1 424[1]	1 712[1]	1 942[1]	PIB par habitant
GDP at constant prices	13 794	14 250	15 844[1]	19 110[1]	22 658[1]	27 252[1]	31 285[1]	PIB aux prix constants
Growth rates	14.5	3.3	11.2	20.6	18.6	20.3	14.8	Taux de croissance
Anguilla								**Anguilla**
GDP at current prices	113	118	149	170	214	267	286	PIB aux prix courants
GDP per capita	9 348	9 311	11 310	12 419	15 194	18 397	19 291	PIB par habitant
GDP at constant prices	86	89	108	117	142	171	198	PIB aux prix constants
Growth rates	-1.4	2.6	21.6	8.3	21.6	20.7	15.3	Taux de croissance
Antigua and Barbuda								**Antigua-et-Barbuda**
GDP at current prices	714	753	815	868	1 003	1 155	1 217	PIB aux prix courants
GDP per capita	8 916	9 268	9 884	10 397	11 859	13 484	14 048	PIB par habitant
GDP at constant prices	560	589	632	661	745	819	840	PIB aux prix constants
Growth rates	2.5	5.2	7.2	4.7	12.6	10.0	2.5	Taux de croissance
Argentina								**Argentine**
GDP at current prices	102 042	129 596	153 129	183 196	214 267	262 451	333 322	PIB aux prix courants
GDP per capita	2 708	3 408	3 991	4 730	5 479	6 646	8 358	PIB par habitant
GDP at constant prices	182 072	198 162	216 055	235 887	255 857	277 998	298 045	PIB aux prix constants
Growth rates	-10.9	8.8	9.0	9.2	8.5	8.7	7.2	Taux de croissance
Armenia								**Arménie**
GDP at current prices	2 376	2 807	3 577	4 900	6 384	9 205	11 929	PIB aux prix courants
GDP per capita	776	917	1 168	1 599	2 081	2 996	3 877	PIB par habitant
GDP at constant prices	1 816	2 070	2 288	2 608	2 957	3 366	3 596	PIB aux prix constants
Growth rates	13.2	14.0	10.5	14.0	13.4	13.8	6.8	Taux de croissance
Aruba								**Aruba**
GDP at current prices	1 941	2 021	2 225	2 323	2 421	2 563	2 724	PIB aux prix courants
GDP per capita	20 452	20 818	22 439	22 995	23 577	24 604	25 831	PIB par habitant
GDP at constant prices	1 352	1 358	1 458	1 473	1 481	1 479	1 456	PIB aux prix constants
Growth rates	-2.2	0.5	7.4	1.0	0.6	-0.1	-1.6	Taux de croissance
Australia								**Australie**
GDP at current prices	424 694	545 654	660 151	738 812	787 418	947 365	1 016 897	PIB aux prix courants
GDP per capita	21 610	27 415	32 757	36 226	38 172	45 429	48 253	PIB par habitant
GDP at constant prices	472 892	491 808	505 578	520 746	537 928	557 729	563 166	PIB aux prix constants
Growth rates	3.2	4.0	2.8	3.0	3.3	3.7	1.0	Taux de croissance

Gross domestic product and gross domestic product per capita *(continued)*

In millions of US dollars at current and constant 1990 prices; per capita US dollars; real rates of growth

Produit intérieur brut et produit intérieur brut par habitant *(suite)*

En millions de dollars É.-U. aux prix courants et constants de 1990 ; par habitant en dollars É.-U. ; taux de croissance réels

Country or area	2002	2003	2004	2005	2006	2007	2008	Pays ou zone
Austria								**Autriche**
GDP at current prices	205 965	252 024	289 039	304 001	322 771	370 686	413 500	PIB aux prix courants
GDP per capita	25 479	30 980	35 308	36 928	39 019	44 623	49 596	PIB par habitant
GDP at constant prices	216 141	217 873	223 416	229 839	237 594	244 877	249 201	PIB aux prix constants
Growth rates	1.7	0.8	2.5	2.9	3.4	3.1	1.8	Taux de croissance
Azerbaijan								**Azerbaïdjan**
GDP at current prices	6 236	7 276	8 680	13 245	20 982	33 049	46 257	PIB aux prix courants
GDP per capita	757	876	1 036	1 567	2 457	3 829	5 298	PIB par habitant
GDP at constant prices	4 660	5 179	5 705	7 214	9 700	12 130	13 443	PIB aux prix constants
Growth rates	10.6	11.2	10.2	26.5	34.5	25.1	10.8	Taux de croissance
Bahamas								**Bahamas**
GDP at current prices	5 912	5 942	6 032	6 509	6 876	7 234	7 463	PIB aux prix courants
GDP per capita	18 870	18 722	18 764	19 996	20 864	21 684	22 102	PIB par habitant
GDP at constant prices	4 115	4 016	4 010	4 144	4 336	4 456	4 400	PIB aux prix constants
Growth rates	2.1	-2.4	-0.2	3.3	4.6	2.8	-1.3	Taux de croissance
Bahrain								**Bahreïn**
GDP at current prices	8 491	9 747	11 235	13 459	15 852	18 472	21 902	PIB aux prix courants
GDP per capita	12 482	14 007	15 787	18 499	21 320	24 320	28 240	PIB par habitant
GDP at constant prices	7 369	7 868	8 312	8 965	9 561	10 362	11 015	PIB aux prix constants
Growth rates	5.7	6.8	5.6	7.9	6.7	8.4	6.3	Taux de croissance
Bangladesh								**Bangladesh**
GDP at current prices	47 195	51 690	55 950	57 628	60 309	68 599	78 999	PIB aux prix courants
GDP per capita	324	349	371	376	388	435	494	PIB par habitant
GDP at constant prices	49 070	51 649	54 888	58 157	62 012	65 999	70 097	PIB aux prix constants
Growth rates	4.4	5.3	6.3	6.0	6.6	6.4	6.2	Taux de croissance
Barbados								**Barbade**
GDP at current prices	2 476	2 695	2 832	2 986	3 191	3 409	3 681	PIB aux prix courants
GDP per capita	9 847	10 696	11 213	11 789	12 568	13 393	14 422	PIB par habitant
GDP at constant prices	1 908	1 946	2 018	2 105	2 176	2 246	2 260	PIB aux prix constants
Growth rates	0.5	2.0	3.7	4.3	3.3	3.2	0.6	Taux de croissance
Belarus								**Bélarus**
GDP at current prices	14 595	17 825	23 142	30 210	36 962	45 276	60 302	PIB aux prix courants
GDP per capita	1 466	1 799	2 346	3 078	3 783	4 656	6 230	PIB par habitant
GDP at constant prices	18 336	19 618	21 860	23 924	26 316	28 573	31 426	PIB aux prix constants
Growth rates	5.0	7.0	11.4	9.4	10.0	8.6	10.0	Taux de croissance
Belgium								**Belgique**
GDP at current prices	251 896	310 063	359 625	375 705	399 205	458 390	504 202	PIB aux prix courants
GDP per capita	24 533	30 066	34 705	36 073	38 123	43 529	47 609	PIB par habitant
GDP at constant prices	256 470	259 012	266 694	271 621	279 735	287 446	290 530	PIB aux prix constants
Growth rates	1.5	1.0	3.0	1.9	3.0	2.8	1.1	Taux de croissance
Belize								**Belize**
GDP at current prices	932	988	1 055	1 115	1 214	1 277	1 374	PIB aux prix courants
GDP per capita	3 532	3 657	3 821	3 949	4 208	4 335	4 569	PIB par habitant
GDP at constant prices	740	809	847	873	922	924	959	PIB aux prix constants
Growth rates	5.1	9.3	4.6	3.1	5.6	0.3	3.8	Taux de croissance
Benin								**Bénin**
GDP at current prices	2 808	3 557	4 051	4 358	4 705	5 512	6 643	PIB aux prix courants
GDP per capita	395	483	532	554	579	657	767	PIB par habitant
GDP at constant prices	3 186	3 309	3 413	3 510	3 642	3 811	4 002	PIB aux prix constants
Growth rates	4.4	3.9	3.1	2.9	3.8	4.6	5.0	Taux de croissance
Bermuda								**Bermudes**
GDP at current prices	3 361	3 730	2 980	3 265	3 483	5 855	6 432	PIB aux prix courants
GDP per capita	52 995	58 559	46 602	50 885	54 102	90 698	99 383	PIB par habitant
GDP at constant prices	2 788	2 870	2 973	3 132	3 305	3 458	3 610	PIB aux prix constants
Growth rates	4.9	2.9	3.6	5.4	5.5	4.6	4.4	Taux de croissance
Bhutan								**Bhoutan**
GDP at current prices	544	631	713	827	893	1 246	1 327	PIB aux prix courants
GDP per capita	911	1 025	1 126	1 272	1 345	1 843	1 933	PIB par habitant
GDP at constant prices	554	594	634	679	718	871	929	PIB aux prix constants
Growth rates	10.9	7.2	6.8	7.1	5.8	21.4	6.6	Taux de croissance

17 Gross domestic product and gross domestic product per capita *(continued)*

In millions of US dollars at current and constant 1990 prices; per capita US dollars; real rates of growth

Produit intérieur brut et produit intérieur brut par habitant *(suite)*

En millions de dollars É.-U. aux prix courants et constants de 1990 ; par habitant en dollars É.-U. ; taux de croissance réels

Country or area	2002	2003	2004	2005	2006	2007	2008	Pays ou zone
Bolivia (Plurinational State of)								**Bolivie (État plurinational de)**
GDP at current prices	7 905	8 082	8 773	9 549	11 452	13 120	16 701	PIB aux prix courants
GDP per capita	913	915	974	1 040	1 224	1 378	1 723	PIB par habitant
GDP at constant prices	7 343	7 542	7 857	8 205	8 598	8 991	9 543	PIB aux prix constants
Growth rates	2.5	2.7	4.2	4.4	4.8	4.6	6.2	Taux de croissance
Bosnia and Herzegovina								**Bosnie-Herzégovine**
GDP at current prices	5 606	7 100	10 022	10 763	12 264	15 148	18 389	PIB aux prix courants
GDP per capita	1 485	1 877	2 650	2 846	3 243	4 009	4 874	PIB par habitant
GDP at constant prices	19 923	18 201	19 345	20 102	21 487	22 769	24 021	PIB aux prix constants
Growth rates	-8.2	-8.7	6.3	3.9	6.9	6.0	5.5	Taux de croissance
Botswana								**Botswana**
GDP at current prices	5 637	7 915	9 065	9 748	9 913	11 598	11 734	PIB aux prix courants
GDP per capita	3 181	4 413	4 993	5 301	5 316	6 129	6 108	PIB par habitant
GDP at constant prices	6 993	7 655	7 922	8 664	8 713	9 170	9 475	PIB aux prix constants
Growth rates	1.1	9.5	3.5	9.4	0.6	5.3	3.3	Taux de croissance
Brazil								**Brésil**
GDP at current prices	506 041	552 384	663 733	882 044	1 089 398	1 334 121	1 595 498	PIB aux prix courants
GDP per capita	2 825	3 043	3 610	4 740	5 790	7 017	8 311	PIB par habitant
GDP at constant prices	636 464	643 762	680 535	702 037	729 915	771 282	811 625	PIB aux prix constants
Growth rates	2.7	1.2	5.7	3.2	4.0	5.7	5.2	Taux de croissance
British Virgin Islands								**Iles Vierges britanniques**
GDP at current prices	816	743	832	931	1 041	1 134	1 215	PIB aux prix courants
GDP per capita	38 527	34 610	38 265	42 293	46 726	50 313	53 302	PIB par habitant
GDP at constant prices	821	722	800	878	900	915	939	PIB aux prix constants
Growth rates	-2.2	-12.1	10.9	9.7	2.5	1.8	2.5	Taux de croissance
Brunei Darussalam								**Brunéi Darussalam**
GDP at current prices	5 843	6 557	7 872	9 531	11 470	12 283	14 533	PIB aux prix courants
GDP per capita	16 779	18 445	21 700	25 755	30 390	31 917	37 048	PIB par habitant
GDP at constant prices	4 688	4 824	4 849	4 867	5 081	5 113	5 036	PIB aux prix constants
Growth rates	3.9	2.9	0.5	0.4	4.4	0.6	-1.5	Taux de croissance
Bulgaria								**Bulgarie**
GDP at current prices	15 600	19 985	24 648	27 188	31 656	39 551	49 904	PIB aux prix courants
GDP per capita	1 977	2 549	3 164	3 513	4 117	5 176	6 573	PIB par habitant
GDP at constant prices	19 143	20 101	21 436	22 775	24 162	25 652	27 195	PIB aux prix constants
Growth rates	5.6	5.0	6.6	6.3	6.1	6.2	6.0	Taux de croissance
Burkina Faso								**Burkina Faso**
GDP at current prices	3 239	4 325	5 029	5 426	5 771	6 757	7 949	PIB aux prix courants
GDP per capita	260	336	378	395	406	459	522	PIB par habitant
GDP at constant prices	5 808	6 274	6 565	7 029	7 417	7 685	8 031	PIB aux prix constants
Growth rates	4.7	8.0	4.6	7.1	5.5	3.6	4.5	Taux de croissance
Burundi								**Burundi**
GDP at current prices	628	595	680	796	959	936	1 111	PIB aux prix courants
GDP per capita	93	86	95	108	126	119	138	PIB par habitant
GDP at constant prices	1 035	1 023	1 068	1 077	1 132	1 173	1 226	PIB aux prix constants
Growth rates	4.5	-1.2	4.4	0.9	5.1	3.6	4.5	Taux de croissance
Cambodia								**Cambodge**
GDP at current prices	4 289	4 665	5 338	6 293	7 275	8 639	11 193	PIB aux prix courants
GDP per capita	325	347	391	454	516	603	769	PIB par habitant
GDP at constant prices	3 125	3 391	3 741	4 237	4 693	5 172	5 485	PIB aux prix constants
Growth rates	6.6	8.5	10.3	13.3	10.8	10.2	6.0	Taux de croissance
Cameroon								**Cameroun**
GDP at current prices	10 880	13 622	15 775	16 588	17 953	20 619	23 247	PIB aux prix courants
GDP per capita	654	800	906	931	984	1 105	1 218	PIB par habitant
GDP at constant prices	15 210	15 823	16 408	16 785	17 326	17 919	18 551	PIB aux prix constants
Growth rates	4.0	4.0	3.7	2.3	3.2	3.4	3.5	Taux de croissance
Canada								**Canada**
GDP at current prices	734 657	865 907	992 230	1 132 754	1 278 682	1 429 710	1 502 198	PIB aux prix courants
GDP per capita	23 460	27 362	31 027	35 062	39 189	43 396	45 166	PIB par habitant
GDP at constant prices	814 039	829 347	855 225	879 810	907 178	931 791	935 653	PIB aux prix constants
Growth rates	2.9	1.9	3.1	2.9	3.1	2.7	0.4	Taux de croissance

17 Gross domestic product and gross domestic product per capita *(continued)*

In millions of US dollars at current and constant 1990 prices; per capita US dollars; real rates of growth

Produit intérieur brut et produit intérieur brut par habitant *(suite)*

En millions de dollars É.-U. aux prix courants et constants de 1990 ; par habitant en dollars É.-U. ; taux de croissance réels

Country or area	2002	2003	2004	2005	2006	2007	2008	Pays ou zone
Cape Verde								**Cap-Vert**
GDP at current prices	621	814	924	1 006	1 202	1 456	1 715	PIB aux prix courants
GDP per capita	1 366	1 760	1 967	2 108	2 479	2 962	3 439	PIB par habitant
GDP at constant prices	663	694	724	771	854	920	975	PIB aux prix constants
Growth rates	5.3	4.7	4.3	6.5	10.8	7.8	5.9	Taux de croissance
Cayman Islands								**Iles Caïmanes**
GDP at current prices	1 855	1 924	2 027	2 316	2 442	2 643	2 822	PIB aux prix courants
GDP per capita	40 886	40 003	40 073	44 042	45 183	48 035	50 717	PIB par habitant
GDP at constant prices	1 289	1 315	1 327	1 413	1 478	1 511	1 560	PIB aux prix constants
Growth rates	1.7	2.0	0.9	6.5	4.6	2.3	3.3	Taux de croissance
Central African Rep.								**Rép. centrafricaine**
GDP at current prices	1 042	1 195	1 307	1 371	1 494	1 721	2 016	PIB aux prix courants
GDP per capita	268	302	324	334	358	404	464	PIB par habitant
GDP at constant prices	1 684	1 556	1 577	1 611	1 677	1 740	1 778	PIB aux prix constants
Growth rates	-0.6	-7.6	1.3	2.2	4.1	3.7	2.2	Taux de croissance
Chad								**Tchad**
GDP at current prices	1 987	2 723	4 415	5 873	6 300	7 008	8 354	PIB aux prix courants
GDP per capita	220	291	455	586	610	660	765	PIB par habitant
GDP at constant prices	2 629	3 004	4 016	4 333	4 341	4 347	4 362	PIB aux prix constants
Growth rates	8.5	14.3	33.7	7.9	0.2	0.2	0.3	Taux de croissance
Chile								**Chili**
GDP at current prices	67 266	73 990	95 653	118 250	146 437	163 915	169 573	PIB aux prix courants
GDP per capita	4 263	4 638	5 931	7 256	8 893	9 853	10 091	PIB par habitant
GDP at constant prices	65 803	68 381	72 512	76 543	79 866	83 936	86 484	PIB aux prix constants
Growth rates	2.2	3.9	6.0	5.6	4.3	5.1	3.0	Taux de croissance
China [2]								**Chine** [2]
GDP at current prices	1 454 040	1 647 918	1 936 502	2 302 719	2 779 871	3 460 288	4 327 024	PIB aux prix courants
GDP per capita	1 151	1 295	1 512	1 786	2 142	2 649	3 292	PIB par habitant
GDP at constant prices	1 288 775	1 417 691	1 560 947	1 723 332	1 923 344	2 173 608	2 370 258	PIB aux prix constants
Growth rates	9.1	10.0	10.1	10.4	11.6	13.0	9.1	Taux de croissance
China, Hong Kong SAR								**Chine, Hong Kong RAS**
GDP at current prices	163 781	158 572	165 886	177 772	190 003	207 169	215 558	PIB aux prix courants
GDP per capita	24 175	23 270	24 220	25 829	27 475	29 818	30 872	PIB par habitant
GDP at constant prices	115 274	118 739	128 792	137 913	147 594	156 992	160 794	PIB aux prix constants
Growth rates	1.8	3.0	8.5	7.1	7.0	6.4	2.4	Taux de croissance
China, Macao SAR								**Chine, Macao RAS**
GDP at current prices	6 824	7 925	10 342	11 603	14 404	18 918	21 798	PIB aux prix courants
GDP per capita	14 936	17 000	21 708	23 795	28 813	36 872	41 427	PIB par habitant
GDP at constant prices	4 772	5 448	6 995	7 477	8 749	10 986	12 438	PIB aux prix constants
Growth rates	10.1	14.2	28.4	6.9	17.0	25.6	13.2	Taux de croissance
Colombia								**Colombie**
GDP at current prices	93 016	91 702	113 774	144 580	162 347	207 786	243 744	PIB aux prix courants
GDP per capita	2 264	2 197	2 684	3 358	3 715	4 684	5 415	PIB par habitant
GDP at constant prices	72 900	76 262	79 819	84 385	90 244	97 054	99 514	PIB aux prix constants
Growth rates	2.5	4.6	4.7	5.7	6.9	7.6	2.5	Taux de croissance
Comoros								**Comores**
GDP at current prices	251	324	362	387	403	465	530	PIB aux prix courants
GDP per capita	436	550	601	628	639	720	802	PIB par habitant
GDP at constant prices	300	308	307	320	324	321	324	PIB aux prix constants
Growth rates	4.2	2.5	-0.2	4.2	1.2	-1.0	1.0	Taux de croissance
Congo								**Congo**
GDP at current prices	3 020	3 565	4 342	5 972	7 422	7 810	10 605	PIB aux prix courants
GDP per capita	950	1 093	1 300	1 748	2 129	2 199	2 934	PIB par habitant
GDP at constant prices	3 507	3 567	3 695	3 980	4 228	4 161	4 393	PIB aux prix constants
Growth rates	4.8	1.7	3.6	7.7	6.2	-1.6	5.6	Taux de croissance
Cook Islands								**Iles Cook**
GDP at current prices	102	143	171	184	180	211	215	PIB aux prix courants
GDP per capita	5 672	7 780	9 133	9 642	9 311	10 789	10 907	PIB par habitant
GDP at constant prices	83	90	94	94	95	96	99	PIB aux prix constants
Growth rates	2.6	8.2	4.3	^0.0	0.7	1.3	2.9	Taux de croissance

Gross domestic product and gross domestic product per capita *(continued)*

In millions of US dollars at current and constant 1990 prices; per capita US dollars; real rates of growth

Produit intérieur brut et produit intérieur brut par habitant *(suite)*

En millions de dollars É.-U. aux prix courants et constants de 1990 ; par habitant en dollars É.-U. ; taux de croissance réels

Country or area	2002	2003	2004	2005	2006	2007	2008	Pays ou zone
Costa Rica								**Costa Rica**
GDP at current prices	16 844	17 518	18 595	19 965	22 526	26 267	29 822	PIB aux prix courants
GDP per capita	4 108	4 191	4 369	4 613	5 125	5 891	6 599	PIB par habitant
GDP at constant prices	12 524	13 326	13 893	14 711	16 003	17 250	17 912	PIB aux prix constants
Growth rates	2.9	6.4	4.3	5.9	8.8	7.8	3.8	Taux de croissance
Côte d'Ivoire								**Côte d'Ivoire**
GDP at current prices	11 494	13 738	15 701	16 354	17 369	19 789	23 406	PIB aux prix courants
GDP per capita	636	744	833	850	883	983	1 137	PIB par habitant
GDP at constant prices	14 928	14 674	14 909	15 178	15 360	15 590	15 953	PIB aux prix constants
Growth rates	-1.6	-1.7	1.6	1.8	1.2	1.5	2.3	Taux de croissance
Croatia								**Croatie**
GDP at current prices	26 452	33 857	40 692	44 437	49 050	58 574	69 333	PIB aux prix courants
GDP per capita	5 923	7 597	9 144	10 002	11 058	13 225	15 677	PIB par habitant
GDP at constant prices	27 014	28 353	29 558	30 802	32 262	34 027	34 830	PIB aux prix constants
Growth rates	5.4	5.0	4.3	4.2	4.7	5.5	2.4	Taux de croissance
Cuba								**Cuba**
GDP at current prices	33 591	35 901	38 203	42 644	52 743	58 604	62 705	PIB aux prix courants
GDP per capita	3 016	3 217	3 417	3 810	4 709	5 230	5 596	PIB par habitant
GDP at constant prices	25 962	26 947	28 502	31 694	35 519	38 098	39 740	PIB aux prix constants
Growth rates	1.4	3.8	5.8	11.2	12.1	7.3	4.3	Taux de croissance
Cyprus [3]								**Chypre** [3]
GDP at current prices	10 523	13 303	15 804	16 978	18 410	21 421	24 827	PIB aux prix courants
GDP per capita	14 830	18 461	21 441	22 399	23 878	27 498	31 551	PIB par habitant
GDP at constant prices	9 536	9 718	10 126	10 526	10 962	11 449	11 868	PIB aux prix constants
Growth rates	2.1	1.9	4.2	4.0	4.1	4.5	3.7	Taux de croissance
Czech Republic								**République tchèque**
GDP at current prices	75 276	91 358	109 525	124 549	142 313	173 958	217 077	PIB aux prix courants
GDP per capita	7 387	8 974	10 758	12 217	13 919	16 941	21 036	PIB par habitant
GDP at constant prices	39 660	41 089	42 932	45 644	48 741	51 642	53 302	PIB aux prix constants
Growth rates	1.9	3.6	4.5	6.3	6.8	6.0	3.2	Taux de croissance
Dem. Rep. of the Congo								**Rép. dém. du Congo**
GDP at current prices	5 554	5 641	6 591	7 104	8 545	9 648	11 613	PIB aux prix courants
GDP per capita	103	101	115	120	141	154	181	PIB par habitant
GDP at constant prices	5 234	5 537	5 905	6 370	6 726	7 147	7 590	PIB aux prix constants
Growth rates	3.5	5.8	6.6	7.9	5.6	6.3	6.2	Taux de croissance
Denmark								**Danemark**
GDP at current prices	173 881	212 623	244 728	257 676	273 868	310 063	341 247	PIB aux prix courants
GDP per capita	32 372	39 468	45 300	47 567	50 423	56 943	62 520	PIB par habitant
GDP at constant prices	177 590	178 271	182 365	186 824	193 072	196 250	194 011	PIB aux prix constants
Growth rates	0.5	0.4	2.3	2.5	3.3	1.7	-1.1	Taux de croissance
Djibouti								**Djibouti**
GDP at current prices	592	628	666	709	770	848	981	PIB aux prix courants
GDP per capita	776	808	842	881	939	1 016	1 155	PIB par habitant
GDP at constant prices	541	558	575	594	622	652	690	PIB aux prix constants
Growth rates	2.6	3.2	3.0	3.2	4.8	4.8	5.8	Taux de croissance
Dominica								**Dominique**
GDP at current prices	255	263	285	299	316	336	364	PIB aux prix courants
GDP per capita	3 756	3 880	4 218	4 439	4 702	5 008	5 447	PIB par habitant
GDP at constant prices	184	188	200	207	217	220	226	PIB aux prix constants
Growth rates	-4.0	2.2	6.3	3.5	4.9	1.5	2.6	Taux de croissance
Dominican Republic								**Rép. dominicaine**
GDP at current prices	24 913	20 045	21 582	33 542	35 660	41 013	45 523	PIB aux prix courants
GDP per capita	2 734	2 167	2 298	3 518	3 686	4 179	4 574	PIB par habitant
GDP at constant prices	18 184	18 138	18 376	20 078	22 220	24 103	25 370	PIB aux prix constants
Growth rates	5.8	-0.3	1.3	9.3	10.7	8.5	5.3	Taux de croissance
Ecuador								**Equateur**
GDP at current prices	24 899	28 636	32 642	37 187	41 763	45 789	52 572	PIB aux prix courants
GDP per capita	1 972	2 242	2 527	2 847	3 163	3 432	3 900	PIB par habitant
GDP at constant prices	15 304	15 852	17 120	18 148	18 853	19 322	20 350	PIB aux prix constants
Growth rates	4.3	3.6	8.0	6.0	3.9	2.5	5.3	Taux de croissance

17 Gross domestic product and gross domestic product per capita *(continued)*

In millions of US dollars at current and constant 1990 prices; per capita US dollars; real rates of growth

Produit intérieur brut et produit intérieur brut par habitant *(suite)*

En millions de dollars É.-U. aux prix courants et constants de 1990 ; par habitant en dollars É.-U. ; taux de croissance réels

Country or area	2002	2003	2004	2005	2006	2007	2008	Pays ou zone
Egypt								**Egypte**
GDP at current prices	90 064	77 109	82 429	98 323	112 152	137 520	165 546	PIB aux prix courants
GDP per capita	1 236	1 038	1 089	1 274	1 427	1 718	2 031	PIB par habitant
GDP at constant prices	67 478	70 258	73 436	78 462	84 023	90 035	93 241	PIB aux prix constants
Growth rates	4.1	4.1	4.5	6.8	7.1	7.2	3.6	Taux de croissance
El Salvador								**El Salvador**
GDP at current prices	14 307	15 047	15 798	17 070	18 654	20 373	22 115	PIB aux prix courants
GDP per capita	2 386	2 501	2 617	2 818	3 067	3 336	3 605	PIB par habitant
GDP at constant prices	7 839	8 019	8 168	8 420	8 772	9 180	9 414	PIB aux prix constants
Growth rates	2.3	2.3	1.9	3.1	4.2	4.7	2.6	Taux de croissance
Equatorial Guinea								**Guinée équatoriale**
GDP at current prices	2 087	2 754	4 775	7 206	8 526	10 703	17 884	PIB aux prix courants
GDP per capita	3 723	4 778	8 059	11 836	13 632	16 666	27 130	PIB par habitant
GDP at constant prices	1 764	2 018	2 675	2 913	3 068	3 780	4 354	PIB aux prix constants
Growth rates	20.4	14.4	32.6	8.9	5.3	23.2	15.2	Taux de croissance
Eritrea								**Erythrée**
GDP at current prices	729	870	1 109	1 098	1 211	1 316	1 476	PIB aux prix courants
GDP per capita	184	210	258	246	262	275	300	PIB par habitant
GDP at constant prices	1 481	1 441	1 462	1 500	1 485	1 505	1 521	PIB aux prix constants
Growth rates	3.0	-2.7	1.5	2.6	-1.0	1.3	1.0	Taux de croissance
Estonia								**Estonie**
GDP at current prices	7 306	9 816	11 989	13 790	16 448	20 897	23 204	PIB aux prix courants
GDP per capita	5 384	7 256	8 884	10 239	12 232	15 561	17 298	PIB par habitant
GDP at constant prices	5 996	6 423	6 907	7 539	8 321	8 848	8 526	PIB aux prix constants
Growth rates	7.8	7.1	7.5	9.2	10.4	6.3	-3.6	Taux de croissance
Ethiopia								**Ethiopie**
GDP at current prices	7 768	8 539	10 035	12 286	15 134	19 200	25 727	PIB aux prix courants
GDP per capita	112	120	138	165	198	244	319	PIB par habitant
GDP at constant prices	16 423	16 068	18 249	20 406	22 617	25 136	27 978	PIB aux prix constants
Growth rates	1.5	-2.2	13.6	11.8	10.8	11.1	11.3	Taux de croissance
Fiji								**Fidji**
GDP at current prices	1 841	2 312	2 723	2 939	3 151	3 269	3 599	PIB aux prix courants
GDP per capita	2 265	2 827	3 309	3 549	3 782	3 897	4 264	PIB par habitant
GDP at constant prices	1 754	1 769	1 867	1 878	1 942	1 814	1 835	PIB aux prix constants
Growth rates	3.2	0.9	5.5	0.6	3.4	-6.6	1.2	Taux de croissance
Finland								**Finlande**
GDP at current prices	135 342	164 548	188 922	195 332	209 510	245 893	272 698	PIB aux prix courants
GDP per capita	26 034	31 568	36 139	37 246	39 808	46 542	51 409	PIB par habitant
GDP at constant prices	177 294	180 504	187 176	192 358	201 828	210 310	212 242	PIB aux prix constants
Growth rates	1.6	1.8	3.7	2.8	4.9	4.2	0.9	Taux de croissance
France [4]								**France** [4]
GDP at current prices	1 457 397	1 799 942	2 061 413	2 146 533	2 266 137	2 593 146	2 856 529	PIB aux prix courants
GDP per capita	23 663	29 023	33 012	34 152	35 836	40 774	44 675	PIB par habitant
GDP at constant prices	1 557 455	1 574 393	1 613 288	1 643 866	1 680 315	1 719 367	1 726 749	PIB aux prix constants
Growth rates	1.0	1.1	2.5	1.9	2.2	2.3	0.4	Taux de croissance
French Polynesia								**Polynésie française**
GDP at current prices	2 559	3 204	3 614	3 712	3 833	4 279	4 724	PIB aux prix courants
GDP per capita	10 491	12 929	14 364	14 538	14 807	16 311	17 781	PIB par habitant
GDP at constant prices	2 943	3 074	3 147	3 218	3 280	3 353	3 442	PIB aux prix constants
Growth rates	0.1	4.5	2.4	2.3	1.9	2.2	2.7	Taux de croissance
Gabon								**Gabon**
GDP at current prices	4 932	6 055	7 178	8 666	9 546	11 412	14 320	PIB aux prix courants
GDP per capita	3 826	4 601	5 346	6 329	6 840	8 026	9 888	PIB par habitant
GDP at constant prices	6 359	6 517	6 605	6 804	6 884	7 294	7 427	PIB aux prix constants
Growth rates	-0.3	2.5	1.4	3.0	1.2	5.9	1.8	Taux de croissance
Gambia								**Gambie**
GDP at current prices	578	509	527	629	691	823	1 057	PIB aux prix courants
GDP per capita	416	354	356	412	440	509	636	PIB par habitant
GDP at constant prices	1 044	1 068	1 061	1 084	1 156	1 228	1 288	PIB aux prix constants
Growth rates	0.5	2.3	-0.6	2.1	6.7	6.3	4.9	Taux de croissance

17

Gross domestic product and gross domestic product per capita *(continued)*

In millions of US dollars at current and constant 1990 prices; per capita US dollars; real rates of growth

Produit intérieur brut et produit intérieur brut par habitant *(suite)*

En millions de dollars É.-U. aux prix courants et constants de 1990 ; par habitant en dollars É.-U. ; taux de croissance réels

Country or area	2002	2003	2004	2005	2006	2007	2008	Pays ou zone
Georgia								**Géorgie**
GDP at current prices	3 396	3 991	5 126	6 411	7 745	10 173	12 792	PIB aux prix courants
GDP per capita	734	873	1 134	1 436	1 756	2 334	2 970	PIB par habitant
GDP at constant prices	3 515	3 904	4 133	4 529	4 954	5 565	5 679	PIB aux prix constants
Growth rates	5.5	11.1	5.9	9.6	9.4	12.3	2.0	Taux de croissance
Germany								**Allemagne**
GDP at current prices	2 017 013	2 442 118	2 745 215	2 789 633	2 912 283	3 316 145	3 649 469	PIB aux prix courants
GDP per capita	24 528	29 667	33 323	33 851	35 346	40 273	44 363	PIB par habitant
GDP at constant prices	2 137 262	2 132 615	2 158 367	2 175 041	2 239 433	2 294 531	2 323 661	PIB aux prix constants
Growth rates	0.0	-0.2	1.2	0.8	3.0	2.5	1.3	Taux de croissance
Ghana								**Ghana**
GDP at current prices	6 163	7 628	8 877	10 726	12 729	15 156	16 558	PIB aux prix courants
GDP per capita	301	364	414	489	568	663	709	PIB par habitant
GDP at constant prices	10 331	10 873	11 480	12 153	12 935	13 732	14 649	PIB aux prix constants
Growth rates	4.6	5.3	5.6	5.9	6.4	6.2	6.7	Taux de croissance
Greece								**Grèce**
GDP at current prices	147 395	193 458	230 766	245 790	267 465	312 303	355 874	PIB aux prix courants
GDP per capita	13 400	17 553	20 899	22 216	24 124	28 106	31 954	PIB par habitant
GDP at constant prices	127 981	135 125	141 768	145 877	152 437	158 589	163 239	PIB aux prix constants
Growth rates	3.4	5.6	4.9	2.9	4.5	4.0	2.9	Taux de croissance
Greenland								**Groenland**
GDP at current prices	1 169	1 426	1 645	1 703	1 738	2 122	1 740	PIB aux prix courants
GDP per capita	20 649	25 094	28 838	29 770	30 352	37 023	30 355	PIB par habitant
GDP at constant prices	1 218	1 214	1 246	1 271	1 327	1 401	1 405	PIB aux prix constants
Growth rates	-1.0	-0.4	2.7	2.0	4.5	5.5	0.4	Taux de croissance
Grenada								**Grenade**
GDP at current prices	437	480	469	554	561	608	644	PIB aux prix courants
GDP per capita	4 302	4 713	4 593	5 404	5 459	5 892	6 221	PIB par habitant
GDP at constant prices	326	354	331	371	364	377	385	PIB aux prix constants
Growth rates	2.1	8.4	-6.5	12.0	-1.9	3.7	2.1	Taux de croissance
Guatemala								**Guatemala**
GDP at current prices	20 777	21 918	23 965	27 211	30 193	34 031	38 977	PIB aux prix courants
GDP per capita	1 762	1 813	1 933	2 141	2 317	2 548	2 848	PIB par habitant
GDP at constant prices	10 850	11 125	11 475	11 850	12 476	13 270	13 804	PIB aux prix constants
Growth rates	3.9	2.5	3.2	3.3	5.3	6.4	4.0	Taux de croissance
Guinea								**Guinée**
GDP at current prices	3 209	3 621	4 014	3 257	3 285	4 039	4 970	PIB aux prix courants
GDP per capita	369	408	444	353	349	420	505	PIB par habitant
GDP at constant prices	4 540	4 593	4 701	4 841	4 962	5 049	5 249	PIB aux prix constants
Growth rates	4.2	1.2	2.3	3.0	2.5	1.8	4.0	Taux de croissance
Guinea-Bissau								**Guinée-Bissau**
GDP at current prices	204	239	270	301	308	357	404	PIB aux prix courants
GDP per capita	149	170	188	204	204	232	257	PIB par habitant
GDP at constant prices	246	245	250	259	264	274	282	PIB aux prix constants
Growth rates	-7.1	-0.6	2.2	3.5	1.8	3.7	3.1	Taux de croissance
Guyana								**Guyana**
GDP at current prices	726	743	788	825	915	1 075	1 178	PIB aux prix courants
GDP per capita	957	977	1 033	1 080	1 197	1 407	1 543	PIB par habitant
GDP at constant prices	660	653	675	660	644	703	726	PIB aux prix constants
Growth rates	1.1	-1.0	3.3	-2.2	-2.4	9.1	3.2	Taux de croissance
Haiti								**Haïti**
GDP at current prices	3 083	2 711	3 511	3 985	4 758	6 441	7 077	PIB aux prix courants
GDP per capita	344	298	379	423	497	663	717	PIB par habitant
GDP at constant prices	2 323	2 332	2 250	2 290	2 343	2 418	2 450	PIB aux prix constants
Growth rates	-0.3	0.4	-3.5	1.8	2.3	3.2	1.3	Taux de croissance
Honduras								**Honduras**
GDP at current prices	7 860	8 234	8 871	9 757	10 918	12 417	14 321	PIB aux prix courants
GDP per capita	1 211	1 243	1 313	1 416	1 553	1 731	1 957	PIB par habitant
GDP at constant prices	5 356	5 600	5 949	6 309	6 728	7 155	7 438	PIB aux prix constants
Growth rates	3.8	4.6	6.2	6.1	6.7	6.4	4.0	Taux de croissance

17 Gross domestic product and gross domestic product per capita *(continued)*

In millions of US dollars at current and constant 1990 prices; per capita US dollars; real rates of growth

Produit intérieur brut et produit intérieur brut par habitant *(suite)*

En millions de dollars É.-U. aux prix courants et constants de 1990 ; par habitant en dollars É.-U. ; taux de croissance réels

Country or area	2002	2003	2004	2005	2006	2007	2008	Pays ou zone
Hungary								**Hongrie**
GDP at current prices	66 496	84 326	102 076	110 196	113 006	138 757	154 668	PIB aux prix courants
GDP per capita	6 546	8 324	10 104	10 935	11 240	13 831	15 448	PIB par habitant
GDP at constant prices	43 093	44 927	47 022	48 843	50 781	51 400	51 713	PIB aux prix constants
Growth rates	4.4	4.3	4.7	3.9	4.0	1.2	0.6	Taux de croissance
Iceland								**Islande**
GDP at current prices	8 907	10 968	13 234	16 303	16 646	20 317	16 559	PIB aux prix courants
GDP per capita	31 182	38 066	45 419	55 127	55 232	65 935	52 490	PIB par habitant
GDP at constant prices	8 528	8 734	9 407	10 106	10 558	11 140	11 178	PIB aux prix constants
Growth rates	0.1	2.4	7.7	7.4	4.5	5.5	0.4	Taux de croissance
India								**Inde**
GDP at current prices	504 946	591 332	694 981	813 321	911 376	1 142 338	1 253 860	PIB aux prix courants
GDP per capita	468	540	624	719	794	981	1 061	PIB par habitant
GDP at constant prices	607 811	658 690	713 338	779 921	855 334	932 830	1 000 818	PIB aux prix constants
Growth rates	3.8	8.4	8.3	9.3	9.7	9.1	7.3	Taux de croissance
Indonesia								**Indonésie**
GDP at current prices	195 661	234 772	256 837	285 869	364 599	432 929	510 779	PIB aux prix courants
GDP per capita	928	1 099	1 187	1 304	1 643	1 927	2 247	PIB par habitant
GDP at constant prices	205 860	215 701	226 553	239 450	252 644	268 602	284 758	PIB aux prix constants
Growth rates	4.5	4.8	5.0	5.7	5.5	6.3	6.0	Taux de croissance
Iran (Islamic Rep. of)								**Iran (Rép. islamique d')**
GDP at current prices	135 525	136 646	162 747	194 175	226 531	290 021	346 611	PIB aux prix courants
GDP per capita	1 979	1 974	2 326	2 744	3 165	4 004	4 728	PIB par habitant
GDP at constant prices	147 556	157 827	164 765	172 847	183 481	197 242	204 141	PIB aux prix constants
Growth rates	7.2	7.0	4.4	4.9	6.2	7.5	3.5	Taux de croissance
Iraq								**Iraq**
GDP at current prices	17 437	10 621	16 844[1]	18 159[1]	20 647[1]	21 288[1]	23 709[1]	PIB aux prix courants
GDP per capita	667	395	611[1]	643[1]	715[1]	722[1]	788[1]	PIB par habitant
GDP at constant prices	19 398	12 977	20 005[1]	20 885[1]	23 007[1]	23 101[1]	25 359[1]	PIB aux prix constants
Growth rates	-6.9	-33.1	54.2	4.4	10.2	0.4	9.8	Taux de croissance
Ireland								**Irlande**
GDP at current prices	122 526	157 378	184 978	201 671	222 402	260 872	272 049	PIB aux prix courants
GDP per capita	31 091	39 144	45 080	48 165	52 072	59 904	61 314	PIB par habitant
GDP at constant prices	106 762	111 581	116 829	124 275	131 370	139 287	136 134	PIB aux prix constants
Growth rates	6.4	4.5	4.7	6.4	5.7	6.0	-2.3	Taux de croissance
Israel								**Israël**
GDP at current prices	111 797	117 845	125 773	133 203	143 807	163 958	199 497	PIB aux prix courants
GDP per capita	17 650	18 260	19 136	19 906	21 113	23 654	28 292	PIB par habitant
GDP at constant prices	100 555	102 351	107 496	113 013	118 871	125 253	130 340	PIB aux prix constants
Growth rates	-0.7	1.8	5.0	5.1	5.2	5.4	4.1	Taux de croissance
Italy								**Italie**
GDP at current prices	1 218 981	1 507 109	1 727 825	1 777 695	1 863 385	2 114 482	2 303 059	PIB aux prix courants
GDP per capita	21 168	26 017	29 642	30 313	31 592	35 655	38 640	PIB par habitant
GDP at constant prices	1 356 835	1 356 601	1 377 384	1 386 417	1 414 652	1 436 771	1 421 835	PIB aux prix constants
Growth rates	0.5	^0.0	1.5	0.7	2.0	1.6	-1.0	Taux de croissance
Jamaica								**Jamaïque**
GDP at current prices	9 677	9 399	10 135	11 152	11 989	12 894	15 084	PIB aux prix courants
GDP per capita	3 708	3 573	3 824	4 180	4 469	4 783	5 571	PIB par habitant
GDP at constant prices	5 639	5 836	5 917	5 978	6 140	6 228	6 155	PIB aux prix constants
Growth rates	1.0	3.5	1.4	1.0	2.7	1.4	-1.2	Taux de croissance
Japan								**Japon**
GDP at current prices	3 918 333	4 229 098	4 605 936	4 552 188	4 362 580	4 380 378	4 910 692	PIB aux prix courants
GDP per capita	30 829	33 231	36 158	35 718	34 229	34 384	38 578	PIB par habitant
GDP at constant prices	3 432 661	3 481 186	3 576 720	3 645 894	3 720 250	3 809 278	3 825 852	PIB aux prix constants
Growth rates	0.3	1.4	2.7	1.9	2.0	2.4	0.4	Taux de croissance
Jordan								**Jordanie**
GDP at current prices	9 582	10 196	11 411	12 629	14 839	17 005	21 268	PIB aux prix courants
GDP per capita	1 878	1 944	2 113	2 269	2 582	2 863	3 466	PIB par habitant
GDP at constant prices	7 095	7 391	8 024	8 676	9 368	10 202	11 008	PIB aux prix constants
Growth rates	5.8	4.2	8.6	8.1	8.0	8.9	7.9	Taux de croissance

Gross domestic product and gross domestic product per capita *(continued)*

In millions of US dollars at current and constant 1990 prices; per capita US dollars; real rates of growth

Produit intérieur brut et produit intérieur brut par habitant *(suite)*

En millions de dollars É.-U. aux prix courants et constants de 1990 ; par habitant en dollars É.-U. ; taux de croissance réels

Country or area	2002	2003	2004	2005	2006	2007	2008	Pays ou zone
Kazakhstan								**Kazakhstan**
GDP at current prices	24 637	30 834	43 152	57 124	81 004	104 850	132 474	PIB aux prix courants
GDP per capita	1 650	2 056	2 859	3 760	5 295	6 805	8 535	PIB par habitant
GDP at constant prices	25 664	28 058	30 748	33 730	37 298	40 541	41 879	PIB aux prix constants
Growth rates	9.8	9.3	9.6	9.7	10.6	8.7	3.3	Taux de croissance
Kenya								**Kenya**
GDP at current prices	13 151	14 905	16 091	18 769	22 479	26 950	30 552	PIB aux prix courants
GDP per capita	397	438	461	524	611	714	788	PIB par habitant
GDP at constant prices	13 896	14 300	15 028	15 900	16 917	18 094	18 458	PIB aux prix constants
Growth rates	0.6	2.9	5.1	5.8	6.4	7.0	2.0	Taux de croissance
Kiribati								**Kiribati**
GDP at current prices	44	57	65	65	63	70	78	PIB aux prix courants
GDP per capita	501	639	715	707	678	741	804	PIB par habitant
GDP at constant prices	36	39	40	41	39	38	41	PIB aux prix constants
Growth rates	4.9	7.4	1.6	1.8	-3.8	-1.8	6.3	Taux de croissance
Korea, Dem. P. R.								**Corée, R. p. dém. de**
GDP at current prices	10 910	11 051	11 168	13 031	13 764	14 375	13 337	PIB aux prix courants
GDP per capita	468	471	473	549	578	601	555	PIB par habitant
GDP at constant prices	12 105	12 321	12 597	13 077	12 933	12 642	13 115	PIB aux prix constants
Growth rates	1.2	1.8	2.2	3.8	-1.1	-2.3	3.7	Taux de croissance
Korea, Republic of								**Corée, République de**
GDP at current prices	575 930	643 760	721 976	844 866	951 773	1 049 239	929 124	PIB aux prix courants
GDP per capita	12 267	13 649	15 242	17 762	19 926	21 876	19 296	PIB par habitant
GDP at constant prices	552 767	568 260	594 508	618 034	650 040	683 230	698 424	PIB aux prix constants
Growth rates	7.2	2.8	4.6	4.0	5.2	5.1	2.2	Taux de croissance
Kosovo								**Kosovo**
GDP at current prices	2 438	2 827	3 070	3 138	3 293	3 865	4 649	PIB aux prix courants
GDP per capita	970	1 145	1 262	1 300	1 359	1 596	1 917	PIB par habitant
GDP at constant prices	2 830	2 664	2 639	2 742	2 851	2 968	2 999	PIB aux prix constants
Growth rates	1.2	-5.9	-1.0	3.9	4.0	4.1	1.0	Taux de croissance
Kuwait								**Koweït**
GDP at current prices	38 136	47 874	59 437	80 798	101 559	111 712	158 075	PIB aux prix courants
GDP per capita	15 634	18 916	22 712	29 925	36 550	39 182	54 152	PIB par habitant
GDP at constant prices	30 624	35 929	39 772	43 953	46 243	48 253	51 305	PIB aux prix constants
Growth rates	3.0	17.3	10.7	10.5	5.2	4.4	6.3	Taux de croissance
Kyrgyzstan								**Kirghizistan**
GDP at current prices	1 606	1 922	2 212	2 460	2 834	3 803	5 059	PIB aux prix courants
GDP per capita	317	376	428	471	537	711	934	PIB par habitant
GDP at constant prices	1 829	1 958	2 095	2 091	2 156	2 341	2 518	PIB aux prix constants
Growth rates	^0.0	7.0	7.0	-0.2	3.1	8.5	7.6	Taux de croissance
Lao People's Dem. Rep.								**Rép. dém. pop. lao**
GDP at current prices	1 746	2 031	2 397	2 740	3 325	4 112	5 326	PIB aux prix courants
GDP per capita	312	357	414	466	556	675	858	PIB par habitant
GDP at constant prices	1 784	1 887	2 017	2 164	2 344	2 529	2 719	PIB aux prix constants
Growth rates	5.9	5.8	6.9	7.3	8.3	7.9	7.5	Taux de croissance
Latvia								**Lettonie**
GDP at current prices	9 315	11 186	13 762	16 042	19 935	28 766	33 782	PIB aux prix courants
GDP per capita	3 986	4 820	5 969	6 999	8 744	12 679	14 956	PIB par habitant
GDP at constant prices	6 578	7 051	7 662	8 475	9 511	10 460	9 981	PIB aux prix constants
Growth rates	6.5	7.2	8.7	10.6	12.2	10.0	-4.6	Taux de croissance
Lebanon								**Liban**
GDP at current prices	18 712	19 802	21 465	21 558	22 100	24 668	28 504	PIB aux prix courants
GDP per capita	4 800	4 994	5 329	5 282	5 356	5 926	6 797	PIB par habitant
GDP at constant prices	5 754	5 927	6 223	6 287	6 287	6 758	7 333	PIB aux prix constants
Growth rates	-1.3	3.0	5.0	1.0	0.0	7.5	8.5	Taux de croissance
Lesotho								**Lesotho**
GDP at current prices	670	994	1 290	1 376	1 517	1 672	1 616	PIB aux prix courants
GDP per capita	346	508	653	690	753	823	788	PIB par habitant
GDP at constant prices	886	921	963	969	1 048	1 101	1 140	PIB aux prix constants
Growth rates	1.6	3.9	4.6	0.7	8.1	5.1	3.5	Taux de croissance

17 Gross domestic product and gross domestic product per capita *(continued)*

In millions of US dollars at current and constant 1990 prices; per capita US dollars; real rates of growth

Produit intérieur brut et produit intérieur brut par habitant *(suite)*

En millions de dollars É.-U. aux prix courants et constants de 1990 ; par habitant en dollars É.-U. ; taux de croissance réels

Country or area	2002	2003	2004	2005	2006	2007	2008	Pays ou zone
Liberia								**Libéria**
GDP at current prices	519	404	467	511	671	653	830	PIB aux prix courants
GDP per capita	170	129	145	153	193	180	219	PIB par habitant
GDP at constant prices	649	446	457	481	519	568	609	PIB aux prix constants
Growth rates	3.7	-31.3	2.6	5.3	7.8	9.5	7.1	Taux de croissance
Libyan Arab Jamah.								**Jamah. arabe libyenne**
GDP at current prices	21 913	26 236	33 293	45 451	55 077	62 668	90 822	PIB aux prix courants
GDP per capita	3 934	4 615	5 737	7 674	9 111	10 159	14 430	PIB par habitant
GDP at constant prices	40 106	45 320	47 315	52 184	55 688	58 521	62 453	PIB aux prix constants
Growth rates	-1.3	13.0	4.4	10.3	6.7	5.1	6.7	Taux de croissance
Liechtenstein								**Liechtenstein**
GDP at current prices	2 689	3 071	3 454	3 658	3 989	4 381	5 028	PIB aux prix courants
GDP per capita	79 947	90 297	100 503	105 380	113 838	123 970	141 114	PIB par habitant
GDP at constant prices	2 449	2 401	2 474	2 594	2 818	2 912	2 964	PIB aux prix constants
Growth rates	-1.0	-1.9	3.0	4.8	8.6	3.3	1.8	Taux de croissance
Lithuania								**Lituanie**
GDP at current prices	14 161	18 609	22 548	25 977	30 082	38 886	47 304	PIB aux prix courants
GDP per capita	4 084	5 388	6 559	7 604	8 877	11 587	14 244	PIB par habitant
GDP at constant prices	8 254	9 100	9 769	10 531	11 357	12 371	12 744	PIB aux prix constants
Growth rates	6.9	10.3	7.4	7.8	7.8	8.9	3.0	Taux de croissance
Luxembourg								**Luxembourg**
GDP at current prices	22 580	29 157	34 171	37 603	42 553	49 835	53 704	PIB aux prix courants
GDP per capita	50 417	64 332	74 510	81 035	90 633	104 907	111 743	PIB par habitant
GDP at constant prices	22 103	22 446	23 466	24 683	26 274	27 640	27 382	PIB aux prix constants
Growth rates	4.1	1.6	4.6	5.2	6.4	5.2	-0.9	Taux de croissance
Madagascar								**Madagascar**
GDP at current prices	4 397	5 474	4 364	5 039	5 515	7 417	9 330	PIB aux prix courants
GDP per capita	272	329	255	286	305	399	488	PIB par habitant
GDP at constant prices	3 386	3 717	3 912	4 092	4 298	4 569	4 800	PIB aux prix constants
Growth rates	-12.7	9.8	5.3	4.6	5.0	6.3	5.0	Taux de croissance
Malawi								**Malawi**
GDP at current prices	2 665	2 425	2 625	2 755	3 065	3 470	4 128	PIB aux prix courants
GDP per capita	212	188	198	202	218	240	278	PIB par habitant
GDP at constant prices	3 077	3 252	3 561	3 677	3 981	4 296	4 615	PIB aux prix constants
Growth rates	2.7	5.7	9.5	3.3	8.3	7.9	7.4	Taux de croissance
Malaysia								**Malaisie**
GDP at current prices	100 846	110 202	124 749	137 954	156 409	186 720	221 437	PIB aux prix courants
GDP per capita	4 159	4 459	4 956	5 382	5 994	7 031	8 197	PIB par habitant
GDP at constant prices	96 221	101 791	108 696	114 492	121 103	128 790	134 641	PIB aux prix constants
Growth rates	5.4	5.8	6.8	5.3	5.8	6.4	4.5	Taux de croissance
Maldives								**Maldives**
GDP at current prices	641	692	776	750	915	1 055	1 260	PIB aux prix courants
GDP per capita	2 284	2 434	2 692	2 564	3 087	3 509	4 131	PIB par habitant
GDP at constant prices	448	490	545	518	635	672	712	PIB aux prix constants
Growth rates	6.1	9.2	11.3	-5.0	22.5	6.0	5.8	Taux de croissance
Mali								**Mali**
GDP at current prices	3 189	4 222	4 982	5 486	6 123	7 145	8 599	PIB aux prix courants
GDP per capita	290	374	431	464	505	576	677	PIB par habitant
GDP at constant prices	4 367	4 699	4 805	5 100	5 368	5 598	5 863	PIB aux prix constants
Growth rates	4.3	7.6	2.3	6.1	5.3	4.3	4.7	Taux de croissance
Malta								**Malte**
GDP at current prices	4 233	4 994	5 616	5 959	6 417	7 459	8 253	PIB aux prix courants
GDP per capita	10 732	12 567	14 034	14 803	15 863	18 366	20 254	PIB par habitant
GDP at constant prices	4 242	4 229	4 276	4 426	4 565	4 734	4 808	PIB aux prix constants
Growth rates	2.6	-0.3	1.1	3.5	3.2	3.7	1.6	Taux de croissance
Marshall Islands								**Iles Marshall**
GDP at current prices	119	124	131	138	144	156	166	PIB aux prix courants
GDP per capita	2 229	2 272	2 353	2 426	2 483	2 633	2 737	PIB par habitant
GDP at constant prices	91	94	100	101	103	106	108	PIB aux prix constants
Growth rates	3.8	3.5	5.6	1.7	1.3	3.4	1.5	Taux de croissance

17

Gross domestic product and gross domestic product per capita *(continued)*

In millions of US dollars at current and constant 1990 prices; per capita US dollars; real rates of growth

Produit intérieur brut et produit intérieur brut par habitant *(suite)*

En millions de dollars É.-U. aux prix courants et constants de 1990 ; par habitant en dollars É.-U. ; taux de croissance réels

Country or area	2002	2003	2004	2005	2006	2007	2008	Pays ou zone
Mauritania								**Mauritanie**
GDP at current prices	1 145	1 281	1 486	1 743	2 579	2 839	3 271	PIB aux prix courants
GDP per capita	416	452	511	584	842	905	1 017	PIB par habitant
GDP at constant prices	1 456	1 537	1 641	1 730	2 240	2 262	2 313	PIB aux prix constants
Growth rates	1.8	5.6	6.7	5.4	29.4	1.0	2.2	Taux de croissance
Mauritius								**Maurice**
GDP at current prices	4 756	5 641	6 386	6 284	6 507	7 522	9 535	PIB aux prix courants
GDP per capita	3 901	4 583	5 142	5 018	5 156	5 917	7 450	PIB par habitant
GDP at constant prices	4 513	4 708	4 979	5 041	5 240	5 523	5 839	PIB aux prix constants
Growth rates	1.9	4.3	5.8	1.2	4.0	5.4	5.7	Taux de croissance
Mexico								**Mexique**
GDP at current prices	711 103	700 323	758 224	844 138	945 644	1 019 354	1 081 683	PIB aux prix courants
GDP per capita	6 969	6 788	7 273	8 014	8 887	9 484	9 964	PIB par habitant
GDP at constant prices	408 217	413 892	430 498	444 274	465 665	480 563	487 040	PIB aux prix constants
Growth rates	0.8	1.4	4.0	3.2	4.8	3.2	1.4	Taux de croissance
Micronesia (Fed. States of)								**Micronésie (Etats féd. de)**
GDP at current prices	222	228	224	232	238	238	238	PIB aux prix courants
GDP per capita	2 060	2 102	2 058	2 121	2 170	2 162	2 154	PIB par habitant
GDP at constant prices	167	172	166	165	163	157	151	PIB aux prix constants
Growth rates	0.9	2.9	-3.3	-0.5	-1.6	-3.6	-3.5	Taux de croissance
Monaco								**Monaco**
GDP at current prices	2 906	3 589	4 110	4 280	4 663	5 974	6 919	PIB aux prix courants
GDP per capita	90 080	111 015	126 914	131 885	143 346	183 151	211 501	PIB par habitant
GDP at constant prices	3 116	3 150	3 227	3 289	3 455	3 958	4 354	PIB aux prix constants
Growth rates	1.0	1.1	2.5	1.9	5.1	14.6	10.0	Taux de croissance
Mongolia								**Mongolie**
GDP at current prices	1 273	1 448	1 816	2 306	3 188	3 928	5 259	PIB aux prix courants
GDP per capita	519	583	721	905	1 235	1 504	1 991	PIB par habitant
GDP at constant prices	1 562	1 671	1 849	1 983	2 153	2 373	2 583	PIB aux prix constants
Growth rates	4.7	7.0	10.6	7.3	8.6	10.2	8.9	Taux de croissance
Montenegro								**Monténégro**
GDP at current prices	1 280	1 704	2 073	2 257	2 696	3 843	4 820	PIB aux prix courants
GDP per capita	1 969	2 662	3 285	3 614	4 338	6 189	7 744	PIB par habitant
GDP at constant prices	1 995	2 313	2 664	3 144	4 119	4 560	4 902	PIB aux prix constants
Growth rates	22.5	15.9	15.2	18.0	31.0	10.7	7.5	Taux de croissance
Montserrat								**Montserrat**
GDP at current prices	38	38	41	43	45	46	49	PIB aux prix courants
GDP per capita	8 109	7 590	7 656	7 656	7 754	7 858	8 272	PIB par habitant
GDP at constant prices	26	25	27	27	25	26	29	PIB aux prix constants
Growth rates	6.6	-3.1	6.8	0.4	-5.7	2.9	11.8	Taux de croissance
Morocco [5]								**Maroc** [5]
GDP at current prices	40 418	49 823	56 948	59 524	65 640	75 223	86 591	PIB aux prix courants
GDP per capita	1 370	1 671	1 889	1 952	2 128	2 409	2 740	PIB par habitant
GDP at constant prices	40 522	43 081	45 150	46 495	50 103	51 463	54 263	PIB aux prix constants
Growth rates	3.3	6.3	4.8	3.0	7.8	2.7	5.4	Taux de croissance
Mozambique								**Mozambique**
GDP at current prices	4 201	4 666	5 698	6 579	7 096	8 114	9 840	PIB aux prix courants
GDP per capita	218	236	281	316	332	371	440	PIB par habitant
GDP at constant prices	6 703	7 137	7 700	8 346	9 071	9 741	10 423	PIB aux prix constants
Growth rates	9.2	6.5	7.9	8.4	8.7	7.4	7.0	Taux de croissance
Myanmar								**Myanmar**
GDP at current prices	10 369	10 000	10 254	11 931	13 739	18 443[1]	28 663[1]	PIB aux prix courants
GDP per capita	219	210	214	247	282	375[1]	578[1]	PIB par habitant
GDP at constant prices	12 889	14 673	16 675	18 937	21 414	23 969[1]	25 057[1]	PIB aux prix constants
Growth rates	12.0	13.8	13.6	13.6	13.1	11.9	4.5	Taux de croissance
Namibia								**Namibie**
GDP at current prices	3 361	4 931	6 607	7 261	7 979	8 843	8 825	PIB aux prix courants
GDP per capita	1 770	2 549	3 352	3 614	3 895	4 234	4 143	PIB par habitant
GDP at constant prices	4 297	4 479	5 029	5 156	5 521	5 824	5 994	PIB aux prix constants
Growth rates	4.8	4.2	12.3	2.5	7.1	5.5	2.9	Taux de croissance

17 Gross domestic product and gross domestic product per capita *(continued)*

In millions of US dollars at current and constant 1990 prices; per capita US dollars; real rates of growth

Produit intérieur brut et produit intérieur brut par habitant *(suite)*

En millions de dollars É.-U. aux prix courants et constants de 1990 ; par habitant en dollars É.-U. ; taux de croissance réels

Country or area	2002	2003	2004	2005	2006	2007	2008	Pays ou zone
Nauru								**Nauru**
GDP at current prices	20	25	25	28	20	23	24	PIB aux prix courants
GDP per capita	2 025	2 470	2 478	2 786	1 999	2 283	2 396	PIB par habitant
GDP at constant prices	17	17	15	16	11	10	9	PIB aux prix constants
Growth rates	0.8	0.0	-14.5	6.3	-27.3	-9.8	-12.1	Taux de croissance
Nepal								**Népal**
GDP at current prices	6 321	7 049	8 000	9 165	9 994	12 359	13 406	PIB aux prix courants
GDP per capita	247	270	300	337	360	437	465	PIB par habitant
GDP at constant prices	6 948	7 273	7 500	7 779	8 027	8 405	8 875	PIB aux prix constants
Growth rates	4.0	4.7	3.1	3.7	3.2	4.7	5.6	Taux de croissance
Netherlands								**Pays-Bas**
GDP at current prices	437 827	538 292	609 890	638 471	677 332	776 125	870 998	PIB aux prix courants
GDP per capita	27 222	33 303	37 552	39 131	41 328	47 153	52 699	PIB par habitant
GDP at constant prices	410 779	412 158	421 376	430 000	444 517	459 900	469 641	PIB aux prix constants
Growth rates	0.1	0.3	2.2	2.1	3.4	3.5	2.1	Taux de croissance
Netherlands Antilles								**Antilles néerlandaises**
GDP at current prices	2 934	3 020	3 104	3 271	3 438	3 648	3 810	PIB aux prix courants
GDP per capita	16 215	16 564	16 850	17 543	18 181	18 987	19 512	PIB par habitant
GDP at constant prices	2 269	2 301	2 325	2 342	2 385	2 449	2 504	PIB aux prix constants
Growth rates	0.4	1.4	1.1	0.8	1.9	2.7	2.2	Taux de croissance
New Caledonia								**Nouvelle-Calédonie**
GDP at current prices	3 722	4 904	5 884	6 248	6 802	7 995	9 280	PIB aux prix courants
GDP per capita	16 669	21 586	25 470	26 601	28 495	32 965	37 678	PIB par habitant
GDP at constant prices	3 005	3 009	3 033	3 057	3 073	3 090	3 107	PIB aux prix constants
Growth rates	0.5	0.1	0.8	0.8	0.5	0.5	0.6	Taux de croissance
New Zealand								**Nouvelle-Zélande**
GDP at current prices	60 590	81 261	99 390	111 144	107 585	130 429	126 388	PIB aux prix courants
GDP per capita	15 294	20 249	24 459	27 038	25 903	31 108	29 879	PIB par habitant
GDP at constant prices	63 449	66 178	68 672	70 708	72 005	74 228	74 049	PIB aux prix constants
Growth rates	4.9	4.3	3.8	3.0	1.8	3.1	-0.2	Taux de croissance
Nicaragua								**Nicaragua**
GDP at current prices	4 187	4 406	4 790	5 215	5 634	6 239	6 961	PIB aux prix courants
GDP per capita	798	829	889	956	1 020	1 115	1 228	PIB par habitant
GDP at constant prices	4 308	4 477	4 692	4 883	5 055	5 215	5 371	PIB aux prix constants
Growth rates	1.6	3.9	4.8	4.1	3.5	3.2	3.0	Taux de croissance
Niger								**Niger**
GDP at current prices	2 065	2 640	2 897	3 369	3 647	4 247	5 210	PIB aux prix courants
GDP per capita	175	216	229	257	268	300	354	PIB par habitant
GDP at constant prices	3 699	3 982	3 950	4 282	4 531	4 680	4 956	PIB aux prix constants
Growth rates	5.4	7.7	-0.8	8.4	5.8	3.3	5.9	Taux de croissance
Nigeria								**Nigéria**
GDP at current prices	59 117	67 656	87 845	112 248	145 430	165 921	219 192	PIB aux prix courants
GDP per capita	451	504	639	797	1 008	1 123	1 450	PIB par habitant
GDP at constant prices	55 526	61 276	81 948	84 770	91 155	97 485	111 403	PIB aux prix constants
Growth rates	3.8	10.4	33.7	3.4	7.5	6.9	14.3	Taux de croissance
Norway								**Norvège**
GDP at current prices	191 928	225 110	258 579	302 013	336 732	388 475	451 830	PIB aux prix courants
GDP per capita	42 293	49 289	56 221	65 152	72 012	82 298	94 791	PIB par habitant
GDP at constant prices	175 193	176 969	183 807	188 842	193 149	199 203	203 450	PIB aux prix constants
Growth rates	1.5	1.0	3.9	2.7	2.3	3.1	2.1	Taux de croissance
Occupied Palestinian Terr.								**Terr. palestinien occupé**
GDP at current prices	3 433	3 841	4 198	4 480	4 383	4 942	6 159	PIB aux prix courants
GDP per capita	1 013	1 094	1 155	1 191	1 127	1 230	1 485	PIB par habitant
GDP at constant prices	3 193	3 668	4 106	4 382	4 174	4 123	4 206	PIB aux prix constants
Growth rates	-13.3	14.9	11.9	6.7	-4.8	-1.2	2.0	Taux de croissance
Oman								**Oman**
GDP at current prices	20 048	21 543	24 674	30 905	36 804	41 639	52 584	PIB aux prix courants
GDP per capita	8 071	8 529	9 601	11 806	13 784	15 273	18 879	PIB par habitant
GDP at constant prices	19 315	19 383	20 044	21 025	22 287	24 011	20 515	PIB aux prix constants
Growth rates	2.1	0.4	3.4	4.9	6.0	7.7	-14.6	Taux de croissance

17 Gross domestic product and gross domestic product per capita *(continued)*

In millions of US dollars at current and constant 1990 prices; per capita US dollars; real rates of growth

Produit intérieur brut et produit intérieur brut par habitant *(suite)*

En millions de dollars É.-U. aux prix courants et constants de 1990 ; par habitant en dollars É.-U. ; taux de croissance réels

Country or area	2002	2003	2004	2005	2006	2007	2008	Pays ou zone
Pakistan								**Pakistan**
GDP at current prices	81 637	97 669	111 569	128 090	144 732	172 513	178 762	PIB aux prix courants
GDP per capita	526	615	688	772	854	996	1 010	PIB par habitant
GDP at constant prices	88 046	94 533	101 782	108 069	114 569	121 387	128 610	PIB aux prix constants
Growth rates	4.9	7.4	7.7	6.2	6.0	6.0	6.0	Taux de croissance
Palau								**Palaos**
GDP at current prices	119	123	134	145	158	170	180	PIB aux prix courants
GDP per capita	6 046	6 165	6 671	7 188	7 799	8 380	8 812	PIB par habitant
GDP at constant prices	77	76	80	84	87	92	94	PIB aux prix constants
Growth rates	-3.5	-1.3	4.9	5.5	3.0	5.7	2.0	Taux de croissance
Panama								**Panama**
GDP at current prices	12 272	12 933	14 179	15 465	17 137	19 485	23 088	PIB aux prix courants
GDP per capita	4 006	4 146	4 465	4 785	5 213	5 828	6 793	PIB par habitant
GDP at constant prices	10 237	10 668	11 470	12 295	13 343	14 884	16 250	PIB aux prix constants
Growth rates	2.2	4.2	7.5	7.2	8.5	11.5	9.2	Taux de croissance
Papua New Guinea								**Papouasie-Nvl-Guinée**
GDP at current prices	3 048	3 716	4 177	4 866	5 528	6 199	8 007	PIB aux prix courants
GDP per capita	537	638	700	795	882	965	1 218	PIB par habitant
GDP at constant prices	5 252	5 483	5 514	5 730	5 862	6 226	6 699	PIB aux prix constants
Growth rates	2.0	4.4	0.6	3.9	2.3	6.2	7.6	Taux de croissance
Paraguay								**Paraguay**
GDP at current prices	5 092	5 552	6 950	7 473	9 275	12 222	16 101	PIB aux prix courants
GDP per capita	914	977	1 200	1 266	1 542	1 995	2 581	PIB par habitant
GDP at constant prices	5 551	5 765	6 002	6 175	6 442	6 878	7 277	PIB aux prix constants
Growth rates	-0.1	3.9	4.1	2.9	4.3	6.8	5.8	Taux de croissance
Peru								**Pérou**
GDP at current prices	56 775	61 356	69 701	79 389	92 319	107 329	128 933	PIB aux prix courants
GDP per capita	2 121	2 262	2 536	2 852	3 277	3 765	4 471	PIB par habitant
GDP at constant prices	45 775	47 621	49 991	53 403	57 537	62 633	68 750	PIB aux prix constants
Growth rates	5.0	4.0	5.0	6.8	7.7	8.9	9.8	Taux de croissance
Philippines								**Philippines**
GDP at current prices	76 814	79 634	86 930	98 829	117 566	144 062	168 580	PIB aux prix courants
GDP per capita	951	967	1 036	1 156	1 350	1 624	1 866	PIB par habitant
GDP at constant prices	63 581	66 716	70 972	74 486	78 508	84 151	88 052	PIB aux prix constants
Growth rates	4.5	4.9	6.4	5.0	5.4	7.2	4.6	Taux de croissance
Poland								**Pologne**
GDP at current prices	198 179	216 801	252 769	303 912	341 597	424 598	527 929	PIB aux prix courants
GDP per capita	5 170	5 663	6 610	7 956	8 951	11 135	13 855	PIB par habitant
GDP at constant prices	96 053	99 767	105 100	108 901	115 683	123 421	129 518	PIB aux prix constants
Growth rates	1.4	3.9	5.3	3.6	6.2	6.7	4.9	Taux de croissance
Portugal								**Portugal**
GDP at current prices	127 461	156 407	178 960	185 449	195 005	223 338	243 495	PIB aux prix courants
GDP per capita	12 313	15 009	17 065	17 584	18 401	20 988	22 805	PIB par habitant
GDP at constant prices	102 868	102 040	103 587	104 529	105 959	107 943	107 894	PIB aux prix constants
Growth rates	0.8	-0.8	1.5	0.9	1.4	1.9	^0.0	Taux de croissance
Puerto Rico								**Porto Rico**
GDP at current prices	74 827	79 209	82 809	86 157	88 902	93 263	97 466	PIB aux prix courants
GDP per capita	19 395	20 432	21 260	22 019	22 619	23 624	24 583	PIB par habitant
GDP at constant prices	50 910	52 456	52 890	52 809	52 079	51 364	51 462	PIB aux prix constants
Growth rates	0.1	3.0	0.8	-0.2	-1.4	-1.4	0.2	Taux de croissance
Qatar								**Qatar**
GDP at current prices	19 364	23 534	31 734	42 463	56 770	71 041	113 984	PIB aux prix courants
GDP per capita	28 288	32 171	39 815	47 957	56 736	62 451	88 990	PIB par habitant
GDP at constant prices	16 027	16 586	20 041	21 260	24 455	28 209	32 833	PIB aux prix constants
Growth rates	7.1	3.5	20.8	6.1	15.0	15.4	16.4	Taux de croissance
Republic of Moldova								**République de Moldova**
GDP at current prices	1 662	1 981	2 598	2 988	3 408	4 401	6 047	PIB aux prix courants
GDP per capita	420	509	680	795	919	1 200	1 664	PIB par habitant
GDP at constant prices	1 579	1 684	1 808	1 944	2 037	2 098	2 249	PIB aux prix constants
Growth rates	7.8	6.6	7.4	7.5	4.8	3.0	7.2	Taux de croissance

17 Gross domestic product and gross domestic product per capita *(continued)*

In millions of US dollars at current and constant 1990 prices; per capita US dollars; real rates of growth

Produit intérieur brut et produit intérieur brut par habitant *(suite)*

En millions de dollars É.-U. aux prix courants et constants de 1990 ; par habitant en dollars É.-U. ; taux de croissance réels

Country or area	2002	2003	2004	2005	2006	2007	2008	Pays ou zone
Romania								**Roumanie**
GDP at current prices	45 989	59 466	75 795	99 173	122 696	169 286	203 317	PIB aux prix courants
GDP per capita	2 097	2 724	3 488	4 584	5 696	7 892	9 518	PIB par habitant
GDP at constant prices	36 087	37 977	41 201	42 913	46 292	49 184	53 363	PIB aux prix constants
Growth rates	5.1	5.2	8.5	4.2	7.9	6.3	8.5	Taux de croissance
Russian Federation								**Fédération de Russie**
GDP at current prices	345 488	431 488	591 666	764 568	989 428	1 294 382	1 676 588	PIB aux prix courants
GDP per capita	2 377	2 984	4 113	5 340	6 942	9 119	11 858	PIB par habitant
GDP at constant prices	421 501	452 073	484 402	515 344	554 901	599 631	633 309	PIB aux prix constants
Growth rates	4.7	7.3	7.2	6.4	7.7	8.1	5.6	Taux de croissance
Rwanda								**Rwanda**
GDP at current prices	1 649	1 776	1 971	2 390	2 835	3 412	4 457	PIB aux prix courants
GDP per capita	193	205	223	266	308	361	458	PIB par habitant
GDP at constant prices	3 086	3 093	3 258	3 494	3 749	4 045	4 500	PIB aux prix constants
Growth rates	9.3	0.2	5.3	7.3	7.3	7.9	11.2	Taux de croissance
Saint Kitts and Nevis								**Saint-Kitts-et-Nevis**
GDP at current prices	351	362	400	439	488	527	555	PIB aux prix courants
GDP per capita	7 424	7 565	8 237	8 930	9 808	10 453	10 874	PIB par habitant
GDP at constant prices	246	247	266	279	297	305	314	PIB aux prix constants
Growth rates	1.1	0.5	7.6	4.8	6.4	2.7	3.0	Taux de croissance
Saint Lucia								**Sainte-Lucie**
GDP at current prices	705	748	801	879	933	960	1 025	PIB aux prix courants
GDP per capita	4 393	4 615	4 897	5 323	5 592	5 692	6 016	PIB par habitant
GDP at constant prices	518	542	567	602	623	636	647	PIB aux prix constants
Growth rates	2.7	4.7	4.6	6.2	3.5	1.9	1.7	Taux de croissance
Saint Vincent-Grenadines								**Saint Vincent-Grenadines**
GDP at current prices	365	382	414	438	490	544	602	PIB aux prix courants
GDP per capita	3 378	3 529	3 815	4 027	4 503	4 991	5 515	PIB par habitant
GDP at constant prices	282	291	309	315	346	369	387	PIB aux prix constants
Growth rates	3.7	3.3	6.1	1.9	9.9	6.7	5.0	Taux de croissance
Samoa								**Samoa**
GDP at current prices	264	322	385	435	449	544	534	PIB aux prix courants
GDP per capita	1 482	1 800	2 152	2 433	2 511	3 041	2 988	PIB par habitant
GDP at constant prices	161	169	177	186	188	200	193	PIB aux prix constants
Growth rates	3.2	4.8	4.8	5.4	1.0	6.4	-3.4	Taux de croissance
San Marino								**Saint-Marin**
GDP at current prices	880	1 123	1 317	1 375	1 469	1 688	1 900	PIB aux prix courants
GDP per capita	31 194	38 777	44 411	45 479	47 894	54 483	60 925	PIB par habitant
GDP at constant prices	1 001	1 040	1 088	1 113	1 156	1 196	1 219	PIB aux prix constants
Growth rates	0.3	3.9	4.6	2.3	3.9	3.5	1.9	Taux de croissance
Sao Tome and Principe								**Sao Tomé-et-Principe**
GDP at current prices	91	98	107	114	125	145	177	PIB aux prix courants
GDP per capita	625	664	711	746	803	919	1 108	PIB par habitant
GDP at constant prices	160	169	180	191	203	216	228	PIB aux prix constants
Growth rates	11.6	5.4	6.6	5.7	6.7	6.0	5.8	Taux de croissance
Saudi Arabia								**Arabie saoudite**
GDP at current prices	188 551	214 573	250 339	315 583	356 630	383 638	467 601	PIB aux prix courants
GDP per capita	8 599	9 538	10 856	13 365	14 766	15 544	18 555	PIB par habitant
GDP at constant prices	153 510	165 268	173 973	183 635	189 433	195 838	203 971	PIB aux prix constants
Growth rates	0.1	7.7	5.3	5.6	3.2	3.4	4.2	Taux de croissance
Senegal								**Sénégal**
GDP at current prices	5 334	6 860	8 031	8 708	9 358	11 283	13 288	PIB aux prix courants
GDP per capita	511	641	731	772	808	949	1 088	PIB par habitant
GDP at constant prices	8 834	9 423	9 977	10 538	10 796	11 308	11 589	PIB aux prix constants
Growth rates	0.7	6.7	5.9	5.6	2.4	4.8	2.5	Taux de croissance
Serbia [6]								**Serbie** [6]
GDP at current prices	15 108	19 676	23 711	25 300	29 492	40 423	50 946	PIB aux prix courants
GDP per capita	2 014	2 630	3 177	3 400	3 979	5 456	6 871	PIB par habitant
GDP at constant prices	17 998	18 438	19 968	21 089	22 188	23 720	25 008	PIB aux prix constants
Growth rates	3.9	2.5	8.3	5.6	5.2	6.9	5.4	Taux de croissance

17

Gross domestic product and gross domestic product per capita *(continued)*

In millions of US dollars at current and constant 1990 prices; per capita US dollars; real rates of growth

Produit intérieur brut et produit intérieur brut par habitant *(suite)*

En millions de dollars É.-U. aux prix courants et constants de 1990 ; par habitant en dollars É.-U. ; taux de croissance réels

Country or area	2002	2003	2004	2005	2006	2007	2008	Pays ou zone
Seychelles								**Seychelles**
GDP at current prices	849	854	854	917	1 020	1 026	926	PIB aux prix courants
GDP per capita	10 344	10 382	10 361	11 096	12 290	12 308	11 044	PIB par habitant
GDP at constant prices	678	635	623	663	725	795	788	PIB aux prix constants
Growth rates	1.3	-6.3	-2.0	6.6	9.3	9.7	-0.9	Taux de croissance
Sierra Leone								**Sierra Leone**
GDP at current prices	1 311	1 427	1 419	1 487	1 650	1 953	2 324	PIB aux prix courants
GDP per capita	289	301	288	291	313	360	418	PIB par habitant
GDP at constant prices	629	697	764	822	882	938	990	PIB aux prix constants
Growth rates	18.2	10.9	9.6	7.5	7.3	6.4	5.5	Taux de croissance
Singapore								**Singapour**
GDP at current prices	88 331	93 206	109 668	120 953	139 177	166 950	181 939	PIB aux prix courants
GDP per capita	21 437	22 437	26 119	28 346	31 890	37 228	39 423	PIB par habitant
GDP at constant prices	78 710	81 678	89 273	95 796	103 797	111 858	113 143	PIB aux prix constants
Growth rates	4.1	3.8	9.3	7.3	8.4	7.8	1.2	Taux de croissance
Slovakia								**Slovaquie**
GDP at current prices	24 471	33 267	42 225	47 897	55 877	75 029	94 957	PIB aux prix courants
GDP per capita	4 548	6 181	7 843	8 893	10 368	13 909	17 585	PIB par habitant
GDP at constant prices	19 473	20 395	21 446	22 850	24 792	27 376	29 125	PIB aux prix constants
Growth rates	4.8	4.7	5.2	6.6	8.5	10.4	6.4	Taux de croissance
Slovenia								**Slovénie**
GDP at current prices	23 070	29 058	33 724	35 695	38 899	47 179	54 383	PIB aux prix courants
GDP per capita	11 586	14 571	16 884	17 837	19 397	23 471	26 987	PIB par habitant
GDP at constant prices	23 240	23 899	24 924	26 008	27 543	29 406	30 447	PIB aux prix constants
Growth rates	4.0	2.8	4.3	4.4	5.9	6.8	3.5	Taux de croissance
Solomon Islands								**Iles Salomon**
GDP at current prices	274	333	375	414	457	584	656	PIB aux prix courants
GDP per capita	625	739	812	874	940	1 173	1 284	PIB par habitant
GDP at constant prices	226	241	253	266	285	313	332	PIB aux prix constants
Growth rates	-2.8	6.5	4.9	5.4	7.0	10.0	6.0	Taux de croissance
Somalia								**Somalie**
GDP at current prices	2 056	2 100	2 213	2 316	2 532	2 684	2 660	PIB aux prix courants
GDP per capita	264	263	271	277	296	307	298	PIB par habitant
GDP at constant prices	813	831	854	874	897	920	944	PIB aux prix constants
Growth rates	3.5	2.1	2.8	2.4	2.6	2.6	2.6	Taux de croissance
South Africa								**Afrique du Sud**
GDP at current prices	110 875	166 653	216 012	242 790	257 728	283 745	276 446	PIB aux prix courants
GDP per capita	2 400	3 557	4 550	5 050	5 299	5 770	5 566	PIB par habitant
GDP at constant prices	142 883	147 341	154 509	162 180	170 811	179 518	185 016	PIB aux prix constants
Growth rates	3.7	3.1	4.9	5.0	5.3	5.1	3.1	Taux de croissance
Spain								**Espagne**
GDP at current prices	686 278	883 633	1 044 299	1 130 170	1 232 283	1 437 916	1 604 224	PIB aux prix courants
GDP per capita	16 634	21 104	24 580	26 246	28 277	32 642	36 061	PIB par habitant
GDP at constant prices	730 775	753 402	778 015	806 135	837 484	868 159	878 219	PIB aux prix constants
Growth rates	2.7	3.1	3.3	3.6	3.9	3.7	1.2	Taux de croissance
Sri Lanka								**Sri Lanka**
GDP at current prices	17 102	18 882	20 662	24 406	28 280	32 348	40 713	PIB aux prix courants
GDP per capita	898	984	1 067	1 250	1 435	1 627	2 030	PIB par habitant
GDP at constant prices	14 035	14 869	15 678	16 657	17 934	19 151	20 293	PIB aux prix constants
Growth rates	4.0	5.9	5.5	6.2	7.7	6.8	6.0	Taux de croissance
Sudan								**Soudan**
GDP at current prices	18 134	22 197	26 637	33 153	43 888	56 101	70 276	PIB aux prix courants
GDP per capita	498	598	703	857	1 110	1 388	1 700	PIB par habitant
GDP at constant prices	36 478	38 706	45 608	49 564	54 227	59 931	64 458	PIB aux prix constants
Growth rates	6.7	6.1	17.8	8.7	9.4	10.5	7.6	Taux de croissance
Suriname [7]								**Suriname** [7]
GDP at current prices	1 095	1 274	1 477	1 785	2 136	2 425	2 869	PIB aux prix courants
GDP per capita	2 279	2 614	2 991	3 571	4 228	4 752	5 569	PIB par habitant
GDP at constant prices	721	766	827	860	899	947	1 018	PIB aux prix constants
Growth rates	2.8	6.3	8.0	3.9	4.5	5.4	7.5	Taux de croissance

17 Gross domestic product and gross domestic product per capita *(continued)*

In millions of US dollars at current and constant 1990 prices; per capita US dollars; real rates of growth

Produit intérieur brut et produit intérieur brut par habitant *(suite)*

En millions de dollars É.-U. aux prix courants et constants de 1990 ; par habitant en dollars É.-U. ; taux de croissance réels

Country or area	2002	2003	2004	2005	2006	2007	2008	Pays ou zone
Swaziland								**Swaziland**
GDP at current prices	1 224	1 854	2 421	2 588	2 951	3 062	2 767	PIB aux prix courants
GDP per capita	1 112	1 673	2 171	2 301	2 596	2 659	2 369	PIB par habitant
GDP at constant prices	1 436	1 495	1 541	1 576	1 628	1 692	1 736	PIB aux prix constants
Growth rates	1.7	4.1	3.1	2.3	3.2	4.0	2.6	Taux de croissance
Sweden								**Suède**
GDP at current prices	248 612	311 038	357 192	366 009	393 154	453 318	478 961	PIB aux prix courants
GDP per capita	27 860	34 677	39 607	40 370	43 142	49 494	52 035	PIB par habitant
GDP at constant prices	309 028	314 939	327 937	338 753	353 138	362 177	361 616	PIB aux prix constants
Growth rates	2.4	1.9	4.1	3.3	4.3	2.6	-0.2	Taux de croissance
Switzerland								**Suisse**
GDP at current prices	278 619	325 052	362 992	371 946	388 439	426 655	491 691	PIB aux prix courants
GDP per capita	38 265	44 294	49 098	49 986	51 927	56 787	65 200	PIB par habitant
GDP at constant prices	269 108	268 576	275 378	282 272	291 823	301 529	306 895	PIB aux prix constants
Growth rates	0.4	-0.2	2.5	2.5	3.4	3.3	1.8	Taux de croissance
Syrian Arab Republic								**Rép. arabe syrienne**
GDP at current prices	21 659	20 724	24 473	28 158	32 573	40 205	54 602	PIB aux prix courants
GDP per capita	1 242	1 154	1 322	1 473	1 646	1 961	2 572	PIB par habitant
GDP at constant prices	21 926	22 170	23 659	25 085	26 390	28 060	29 506	PIB aux prix constants
Growth rates	5.9	1.1	6.7	6.0	5.2	6.3	5.2	Taux de croissance
Tajikistan								**Tadjikistan**
GDP at current prices	1 221	1 555	2 076	2 312	2 142[1]	2 265[1]	2 480[1]	PIB aux prix courants
GDP per capita	194	244	322	354	323[1]	337[1]	363[1]	PIB par habitant
GDP at constant prices	1 325	1 472	1 624	1 733	1 555[1]	1 602[1]	1 728[1]	PIB aux prix constants
Growth rates	10.8	11.1	10.3	6.7	-10.2	3.0	7.9	Taux de croissance
Thailand								**Thaïlande**
GDP at current prices	126 877	142 640	161 340	176 352	206 993	246 053	282 158	PIB aux prix courants
GDP per capita	1 991	2 211	2 472	2 674	3 112	3 674	4 187	PIB par habitant
GDP at constant prices	142 065	152 209	161 865	169 318	178 167	186 944	195 876	PIB aux prix constants
Growth rates	5.3	7.1	6.3	4.6	5.2	4.9	4.8	Taux de croissance
TFYR of Macedonia								**L'ex-R.Y. Macédoine**
GDP at current prices	3 791	4 630	5 369	5 816	6 371	7 921	8 995	PIB aux prix courants
GDP per capita	1 873	2 282	2 642	2 857	3 126	3 883	4 407	PIB par habitant
GDP at constant prices	4 058	4 173	4 343	4 521	4 700	4 979	5 243	PIB aux prix constants
Growth rates	0.9	2.8	4.1	4.1	4.0	5.9	5.3	Taux de croissance
Timor-Leste								**Timor-Leste**
GDP at current prices	343	336	339	350	353	453	569	PIB aux prix courants
GDP per capita	396	370	356	353	343	426	518	PIB par habitant
GDP at constant prices	213	200	201	205	198	231	246	PIB aux prix constants
Growth rates	-6.7	-6.2	0.4	2.3	-3.4	16.2	6.8	Taux de croissance
Togo								**Togo**
GDP at current prices	1 472	1 674	1 935	2 082	2 197	2 541	2 877	PIB aux prix courants
GDP per capita	265	294	331	347	358	403	446	PIB par habitant
GDP at constant prices	1 898	2 007	2 054	2 079	2 121	2 195	2 220	PIB aux prix constants
Growth rates	-0.3	5.8	2.3	1.2	2.0	3.5	1.1	Taux de croissance
Tonga								**Tonga**
GDP at current prices	149	171	197	218	236	252	299	PIB aux prix courants
GDP per capita	1 490	1 700	1 951	2 136	2 303	2 445	2 891	PIB par habitant
GDP at constant prices	184	190	192	188	194	188	190	PIB aux prix constants
Growth rates	1.3	3.1	1.1	-2.2	3.2	-3.2	1.2	Taux de croissance
Trinidad and Tobago								**Trinité-et-Tobago**
GDP at current prices	9 008	11 305	13 280	15 935	19 345	21 717	24 205	PIB aux prix courants
GDP per capita	6 905	8 636	10 110	12 088	14 620	16 351	18 153	PIB par habitant
GDP at constant prices	8 787	10 056	10 856	11 440	12 961	13 674	14 153	PIB aux prix constants
Growth rates	7.9	14.4	8.0	5.4	13.3	5.5	3.5	Taux de croissance
Tunisia								**Tunisie**
GDP at current prices	21 048	24 968	28 276	29 097	31 092	35 617	39 415	PIB aux prix courants
GDP per capita	2 187	2 572	2 888	2 945	3 118	3 537	3 876	PIB par habitant
GDP at constant prices	20 900	22 060	23 393	24 332	25 670	27 300	28 964	PIB aux prix constants
Growth rates	1.9	5.6	6.0	4.0	5.5	6.4	6.1	Taux de croissance

17 Gross domestic product and gross domestic product per capita *(continued)*

In millions of US dollars at current and constant 1990 prices; per capita US dollars; real rates of growth

Produit intérieur brut et produit intérieur brut par habitant *(suite)*

En millions de dollars É.-U. aux prix courants et constants de 1990 ; par habitant en dollars É.-U. ; taux de croissance réels

Country or area	2002	2003	2004	2005	2006	2007	2008	Pays ou zone
Turkey								**Turquie**
GDP at current prices	232 530	303 008	392 156	482 986	530 917	657 277	741 448	PIB aux prix courants
GDP per capita	3 400	4 371	5 582	6 786	7 365	9 003	10 031	PIB par habitant
GDP at constant prices	290 678	305 983	334 632	362 746	387 752	405 016	409 310	PIB aux prix constants
Growth rates	6.2	5.3	9.4	8.4	6.9	4.5	1.1	Taux de croissance
Turkmenistan								**Turkménistan**
GDP at current prices [1]	4 531	4 779	5 162	6 026	6 929	7 940	8 845	PIB aux prix courants [1]
GDP per capita [1]	978	1 016	1 081	1 244	1 411	1 595	1 754	PIB par habitant [1]
GDP at constant prices [1]	2 524	2 606	2 737	3 094	3 446	3 846	4 223	PIB aux prix constants [1]
Growth rates	0.3	3.3	5.0	13.1	11.4	11.6	9.8	Taux de croissance
Turks and Caicos Islands								**Iles Turques et Caïques**
GDP at current prices	367	410	486	579	722	829	976	PIB aux prix courants
GDP per capita	15 671	15 681	16 972	18 955	22 730	25 564	29 880	PIB par habitant
GDP at constant prices	281	307	342	391	461	513	579	PIB aux prix constants
Growth rates	1.2	9.3	11.4	14.4	17.9	11.3	12.9	Taux de croissance
Tuvalu								**Tuvalu**
GDP at current prices	15 [8]	19	23	25	26	30	32	PIB aux prix courants
GDP per capita	1 519	1 939	2 341	2 548	2 623	3 050	3 213	PIB par habitant
GDP at constant prices	15 [9]	15	16	16	16	17	17	PIB aux prix constants
Growth rates	5.5	4.0	4.0	2.0	1.0	2.0	2.0	Taux de croissance
Uganda								**Ouganda**
GDP at current prices	6 670	7 050	8 436	10 040	11 011	13 572	15 829	PIB aux prix courants
GDP per capita	256	262	304	350	371	443	500	PIB par habitant
GDP at constant prices	8 793	9 335	9 876	10 865	11 630	12 636	13 841	PIB aux prix constants
Growth rates	4.7	6.2	5.8	10.0	7.1	8.6	9.5	Taux de croissance
Ukraine								**Ukraine**
GDP at current prices	42 393	50 133	64 881	86 142	107 753	142 719	180 335	PIB aux prix courants
GDP per capita	883	1 052	1 372	1 835	2 312	3 083	3 921	PIB par habitant
GDP at constant prices	44 799	49 097	55 062	56 562	60 719	65 541	66 884	PIB aux prix constants
Growth rates	5.3	9.6	12.2	2.7	7.4	7.9	2.1	Taux de croissance
United Arab Emirates								**Emirats arabes unis**
GDP at current prices	74 297	87 611	105 251	139 711	170 081	198 702	286 882	PIB aux prix courants
GDP per capita	20 691	23 267	26 762	34 167	40 184	45 533	63 966	PIB par habitant
GDP at constant prices	57 743	64 606	70 867	76 673	83 871	89 187	95 798	PIB aux prix constants
Growth rates	2.7	11.9	9.7	8.2	9.4	6.3	7.4	Taux de croissance
United Kingdom								**Royaume-Uni**
GDP at current prices	1 612 000	1 860 893	2 198 167	2 277 289	2 432 185	2 802 332	2 666 266	PIB aux prix courants
GDP per capita	27 142	31 188	36 662	37 791	40 152	46 016	43 544	PIB par habitant
GDP at constant prices	1 356 989	1 395 230	1 433 707	1 463 207	1 504 731	1 550 209	1 561 165	PIB aux prix constants
Growth rates	2.1	2.8	2.8	2.1	2.8	3.0	0.7	Taux de croissance
United Rep. of Tanzania [10]								**Rép.-Unie de Tanzanie [10]**
GDP at current prices	10 806	11 659	12 826	14 142	14 331	16 826	20 745	PIB aux prix courants
GDP per capita	309	325	348	373	368	419	502	PIB par habitant
GDP at constant prices	9 164	9 795	10 562	11 341	12 105	12 970	13 938	PIB aux prix constants
Growth rates	7.2	6.9	7.8	7.4	6.7	7.2	7.5	Taux de croissance
United States								**Etats-Unis**
GDP at current prices	10 417 600	10 908 000	11 630 900	12 364 100	13 116 500	13 741 600	14 096 717	PIB aux prix courants
GDP per capita	35 433	36 736	38 793	40 841	42 907	44 518	45 230	PIB par habitant
GDP at constant prices	8 158 495	8 364 302	8 669 584	8 924 843	9 172 839	9 358 408	9 463 005	PIB aux prix constants
Growth rates	1.6	2.5	3.7	2.9	2.8	2.0	1.1	Taux de croissance
Uruguay								**Uruguay**
GDP at current prices	13 607	12 046	13 686	17 363	20 023	24 254	32 186	PIB aux prix courants
GDP per capita	4 089	3 622	4 117	5 221	6 012	7 264	9 610	PIB par habitant
GDP at constant prices	11 146	11 236	11 798	12 678	13 268	14 273	15 544	PIB aux prix constants
Growth rates	-7.7	0.8	5.0	7.5	4.7	7.6	8.9	Taux de croissance
Uzbekistan								**Ouzbékistan**
GDP at current prices	9 877	10 155	12 016	13 751	17 077	22 355	25 712	PIB aux prix courants
GDP per capita	389	395	462	522	642	831	946	PIB par habitant
GDP at constant prices	15 755	16 448	17 714	18 955	20 338	22 270	24 052	PIB aux prix constants
Growth rates	4.2	4.4	7.7	7.0	7.3	9.5	8.0	Taux de croissance

Gross domestic product and gross domestic product per capita *(continued)*

In millions of US dollars at current and constant 1990 prices; per capita US dollars; real rates of growth

Produit intérieur brut et produit intérieur brut par habitant *(suite)*

En millions de dollars É.-U. aux prix courants et constants de 1990 ; par habitant en dollars É.-U. ; taux de croissance réels

Country or area	2002	2003	2004	2005	2006	2007	2008	Pays ou zone
Vanuatu								**Vanuatu**
GDP at current prices	230	280	330	370	415	507	558	PIB aux prix courants
GDP per capita	1 151	1 365	1 565	1 708	1 869	2 225	2 388	PIB par habitant
GDP at constant prices	189	195	206	219	236	252	266	PIB aux prix constants
Growth rates	-7.4	3.2	5.5	6.5	7.4	6.8	5.7	Taux de croissance
Venezuela (Boliv. Rep. of)								**Venezuela (Rép. boliv. du)**
GDP at current prices	92 889	83 529	112 451	145 514	183 477	228 071	319 889	PIB aux prix courants
GDP per capita	3 667	3 238	4 282	5 445	6 748	8 247	11 376	PIB par habitant
GDP at constant prices	54 498	50 272	59 465	65 600	72 076	78 469	82 294	PIB aux prix constants
Growth rates	8.9	-7.8	18.3	10.3	9.9	8.9	4.9	Taux de croissance
Viet Nam								**Viet Nam**
GDP at current prices	35 064	39 553	45 428	52 917	60 914	71 016	90 645	PIB aux prix courants
GDP per capita	434	483	547	629	716	825	1 041	PIB par habitant
GDP at constant prices	15 376	16 505	17 791	19 292	20 880	22 646	24 044	PIB aux prix constants
Growth rates	7.1	7.3	7.8	8.4	8.2	8.5	6.2	Taux de croissance
Yemen								**Yémen**
GDP at current prices	11 172	12 321	14 460	17 708	21 298	24 748	31 070	PIB aux prix courants
GDP per capita	580	621	708	842	984	1 111	1 356	PIB par habitant
GDP at constant prices	7 764	8 023	8 273	8 752	9 146	9 576	9 949	PIB aux prix constants
Growth rates	3.2	3.3	3.1	5.8	4.5	4.7	3.9	Taux de croissance
Zambia								**Zambie**
GDP at current prices	3 697	4 305	5 440	7 272	10 886	11 613	14 441	PIB aux prix courants
GDP per capita	337	384	474	619	906	943	1 144	PIB par habitant
GDP at constant prices	4 336	4 523	4 803	5 054	5 367	5 679	6 037	PIB aux prix constants
Growth rates	3.3	4.3	6.2	5.2	6.2	5.8	6.3	Taux de croissance
Zanzibar								**Zanzibar**
GDP at current prices	265	276	316	350	407	473	583	PIB aux prix courants
GDP per capita	270	273	304	326	356	415	496	PIB par habitant
GDP at constant prices	208	220	235	246	261	278	299	PIB aux prix constants
Growth rates	8.6	5.9	6.5	4.9	6.0	6.7	7.5	Taux de croissance
Zimbabwe								**Zimbabwe**
GDP at current prices	5 427[1,9]	5 004[1,9]	4 725	4 687[1]	4 575[1]	4 412[1]	3 912[1]	PIB aux prix courants
GDP per capita	434[1]	400[1]	378	376[1]	367[1]	354[1]	314[1]	PIB par habitant
GDP at constant prices	8 576[1,9]	7 743[1,9]	7 796	7 488[1]	7 082[1]	6 650[1]	5 813[1]	PIB aux prix constants
Growth rates	-4.9	-9.7	0.7	-4.0	-5.4	-6.1	-12.6	Taux de croissance

Source:
United Nations Statistics Division, New York, the national accounts database, last accessed January 2010.

Source:
Organisation des Nations Unies, Division de statistique, New York, la base de données sur les comptes nationaux, dernier accès janvier 2010.

1 Price-adjusted rates of exchange (PARE) are used for selected years for conversion to US dollars due to large distortions in the dollar levels of per capita GDP with the use of IMF market exchange rates.
2 For statistical purposes, the data for China do not include those for the Hong Kong Special Administrative Region (Hong Kong SAR) and Macao Special Administrative Region (Macao SAR).
3 Excludes northern Cyprus.
4 Includes Guadeloupe, Martinique, Réunion and French Guiana.
5 Including Western Sahara.
6 From 1990, excluding Kosovo and Metohia.
7 Excluding the informal sector.
8 GDP at market prices.
9 At factor cost.
10 Tanzania mainland only.

1 Pour certaines années, on utilise les Taux de change corrigés des prix (TCCP) pour effectuer la conversion en dollars des États-Unis, en raison des aberrations importantes relevées dans les niveaux du PNB exprimés en dollars après conversion à l'aide des taux de change du marché communiqués par le FMI.
2 Pour la présentation des statistiques, les données pour la Chine ne comprennent pas la Région Administrative Spéciale de Hong Kong (Hong Kong RAS) et la Région Administrative Spéciale de Macao (Macao RAS).
3 Exclu Chypre du nord.
4 Y compris Guadeloupe, Martinique, Réunion et Guyane française.
5 Y compris les données de Sahara occidental.
6 Après 1990, non compris Kosovo and Metohie.
7 Non compris le secteur informel.
8 PIB aux prix du marché.
9 Au coût des facteurs.
10 Tanzanie continentale seulement.

18 Implicit price deflators of gross domestic product

Index base: 1990 = 100

Déflateurs implicites des prix de produit intérieur brut

Indice base : 1990 = 100

Country or area Pays ou zone	Year Année	GDP at current prices PIB aux prix courants National currency Monnaie nationale	US dollars Dollars É.-U.	GDP at constant prices PIB aux prix constants National currency Monnaie nationale	GDP implicit price deflators PIB déflateurs implicites des prix National currency Monnaie nationale	US dollars Dollars É.-U.	Exchange rates Taux de change
Afghanistan Afghanistan	2000	91 232.7	74.9	74.9	121 797.2	100.0	121 797.2
	2006	222 448.0	225.5	208.5	106 672.1	108.1	98 667.4
	2007	275 898.5	279.4	242.3	113 880.3	115.3	98 740.2
	2008	342 450.0	350.1	250.4	136 768.3	139.8	97 826.9
Albania Albanie	2000	3 111.0	163.8	115.4	2 696.8	142.0	1 899.1
	2006	5 299.5	408.8	162.0	3 271.1	252.3	1 296.4
	2007	5 847.0	489.3	171.9	3 400.5	284.6	1 195.0
	2008	6 459.3	590.5	183.6	3 518.5	321.6	1 093.9
Algeria Algérie	2000	743.8	88.5	118.2	629.5	74.9	840.2
	2006	1 536.9	189.5	152.7	1 006.3	124.1	811.0
	2007	1 678.7	217.0	157.3	1 067.1	137.9	773.6
	2008	1 985.7	275.4	162.0	1 225.5	170.0	721.0
Andorra Andorre	2000	195.2	110.2	133.7	146.0	82.4	177.2
	2006	357.0	274.4	203.4	175.5	134.9	130.1
	2007	376.2	315.4	206.3	182.3	152.9	119.3
	2008	402.0	360.8	213.7	188.1	168.8	111.4
Angola Angola	2000	29 772.7[1]	88.7	113.4	26 248.6[1]	78.2	33 560.2[1]
	2006	1 295 551.9[1]	236.3[2]	220.1	588 654.9[1]	107.4[2]	548 178.4[1]
	2007	1 300 941.6[1]	291.9[2]	264.7	491 441.5[1]	110.3[2]	445 668.4[1]
	2008	1 335 811.7[1]	340.0[2]	303.9	439 566.9[1]	111.9[2]	392 926.6[1]
Anguilla Anguilla	2000	198.4	198.4	156.9	126.4	126.4	100.0
	2006	393.4	393.4	260.8	150.9	150.9	100.0
	2007	489.4	489.4	314.6	155.5	155.5	100.0
	2008	525.4	525.4	362.8	144.8	144.8	100.0
Antigua and Barbuda Antigua-et-Barbuda	2000	169.6	169.6	136.5	124.3	124.3	100.0
	2006	256.3	256.3	190.3	134.7	134.7	100.0
	2007	294.9	294.9	209.3	140.9	140.9	100.0
	2008	310.8	310.8	214.5	144.9	144.9	100.0
Argentina Argentine	2000	412.4	201.2	151.2	272.7	133.0	205.0
	2006	949.5	151.6	181.0	524.6	83.7	626.4
	2007	1 178.8	185.7	196.7	599.4	94.4	634.9
	2008	1 520.6	235.8	210.9	721.2	111.8	644.8
Armenia Arménie	2000	2 050 170.0	88.6	67.9	3 021 504.2	130.6	2 313 533.4
	2006	5 280 171.0	296.0	137.1	3 851 582.1	215.9	1 784 017.1
	2007	6 259 151.2	426.7	156.1	4 010 664.0	273.4	1 466 864.8
	2008	7 255 839.4	553.0	166.7	4 352 464.9	331.7	1 312 023.2
Aruba Aruba	2000	226.3	226.3	167.5	135.1	135.1	100.0
	2006	292.5	292.5	178.9	163.5	163.5	100.0
	2007	309.6	309.6	178.7	173.3	173.3	100.0
	2008	329.0	329.0	175.9	187.1	187.1	100.0
Australia Australie	2000	173.3	128.7	142.2	121.9	90.5	134.6
	2006	262.9	253.6	173.2	151.7	146.4	103.7
	2007	284.6	305.1	179.6	158.5	169.9	93.3
	2008	304.8	327.5	181.4	168.0	180.6	93.1
Austria Autriche	2000	152.4	116.0	128.3	118.7	90.4	131.4
	2006	188.9	195.8	144.1	131.1	135.9	96.5
	2007	198.8	224.9	148.5	133.9	151.4	88.4
	2008	207.2	250.8	151.2	137.1	165.9	82.6
Azerbaijan Azerbaïdjan	2000	1 609 174.6	80.9	58.9	2 733 946.1	137.5	1 988 264.7
	2006	6 393 656.2	322.1	148.9	4 294 268.3	216.3	1 985 185.7
	2007	9 672 749.0	507.3	186.2	5 195 184.6	272.5	1 906 703.9
	2008	12 962 380.6	710.0	206.3	6 281 967.2	344.1	1 825 595.4

18 Implicit price deflators of gross domestic product *(continued)*

Index base: 1990 = 100

Déflateurs implicites des prix de produit intérieur brut *(suite)*

Indice base : 1990 = 100

Country or area Pays ou zone	Year Année	GDP at current prices PIB aux prix courants National currency Monnaie nationale	US dollars Dollars É.-U.	GDP at constant prices PIB aux prix constants National currency Monnaie nationale	GDP implicit price deflators PIB déflateurs implicites des prix National currency Monnaie nationale	US dollars Dollars É.-U.	Exchange rates Taux de change
Bahamas Bahamas	2000	174.6	174.6	127.7	136.7	136.7	100.0
	2006	217.2	217.2	137.0	158.6	158.6	100.0
	2007	228.5	228.5	140.8	162.3	162.3	100.0
	2008	235.8	235.8	139.0	169.6	169.6	100.0
Bahrain Bahreïn	2000	187.0	187.0	155.9	119.9	119.9	100.0
	2006	369.2	369.2	222.7	165.8	165.8	100.0
	2007	430.3	430.3	241.4	178.3	178.3	100.0
	2008	510.2	510.2	256.6	198.9	198.9	100.0
Bangladesh Bangladesh	2000	243.8	161.6	158.7	153.6	101.9	150.8
	2006	427.4	214.3	220.4	193.9	97.3	199.4
	2007	485.8	243.8	234.6	207.1	103.9	199.2
	2008	557.2	280.8	249.1	223.6	112.7	198.4
Barbados Barbade	2000	148.8	148.8	113.4	131.2	131.2	100.0
	2006	185.5	185.5	126.5	146.7	146.7	100.0
	2007	198.2	198.2	130.6	151.8	151.8	100.0
	2008	214.0	214.0	131.4	162.9	162.9	100.0
Belarus Bélarus	2000	210.9[1]	55.3	88.5	238.3[1]	62.5	381.3[1]
	2006	1 830.6[1]	196.3	139.7	1 310.1[1]	140.5	932.8[1]
	2007	2 244.0[1]	240.4	151.7	1 479.1[1]	158.5	933.4[1]
	2008	2 975.3[1]	320.2	166.9	1 783.0[1]	191.9	929.2[1]
Belgium Belgique	2000	149.9	114.4	123.7	121.2	92.5	131.0
	2006	189.5	197.0	138.0	137.3	142.7	96.2
	2007	199.5	226.2	141.8	140.7	159.5	88.2
	2008	205.0	248.8	143.3	143.0	173.6	82.4
Belize Belize	2000	205.1	205.1	165.5	123.9	123.9	100.0
	2006	299.3	299.3	227.4	131.7	131.7	100.0
	2007	314.9	314.9	228.0	138.1	138.1	100.0
	2008	338.8	338.8	236.6	143.2	143.2	100.0
Benin Bénin	2000	334.4	127.9	155.6	214.9	82.2	261.5
	2006	489.8	255.0	197.4	248.1	129.2	192.1
	2007	525.9	298.8	206.6	254.6	144.7	176.0
	2008	592.2	360.1	216.9	273.0	166.0	164.5
Bermuda Bermudes	2000	169.1	169.1	130.7	129.4	129.4	100.0
	2006	174.4	174.4	165.5	105.4	105.4	100.0
	2007	293.2	293.2	173.2	169.3	169.3	100.0
	2008	322.1	322.1	180.8	178.2	178.2	100.0
Bhutan Bhoutan	2000	412.2	160.6	167.8	245.7	95.7	256.7
	2006	829.1	320.3	257.6	321.9	124.4	258.8
	2007	1 056.1	447.1	312.7	337.8	143.0	236.2
	2008	1 183.7	476.3	333.2	355.3	143.0	248.5
Bolivia (Plurinational State of) Bolivie (État plurinational de)	2000	336.3	172.5	144.8	232.3	119.2	194.9
	2006	594.1	235.3	176.6	336.3	133.2	252.5
	2007	667.0	269.5	184.7	361.1	145.9	247.5
	2008	781.5	343.1	196.1	398.6	175.0	227.8
Bosnia and Herzegovina Bosnie-Herzégovine	2000	1 077 911.7	58.4	303.3	355 368.4	19.3	1 846 269.8
	2006	2 144 451.3	158.2	277.1	773 944.5	57.1	1 355 938.8
	2007	2 427 746.3	195.3	293.6	826 847.1	66.5	1 242 816.4
	2008	2 753 612.1	237.1	309.8	888 939.5	76.6	1 161 231.6
Botswana Botswana	2000	435.3	158.7	181.6	239.6	87.4	274.2
	2006	891.4	284.2	249.7	356.9	113.8	313.7
	2007	1 096.9	332.4	262.9	417.3	126.5	330.0
	2008	1 234.2	336.3	271.6	454.4	123.8	366.9

18 Implicit price deflators of gross domestic product *(continued)*

Index base: 1990 = 100

Déflateurs implicites des prix de produit intérieur brut *(suite)*

Indice base : 1990 = 100

Country or area Pays ou zone	Year Année	GDP at current prices PIB aux prix courants National currency Monnaie nationale	GDP at current prices PIB aux prix courants US dollars Dollars É.-U.	GDP at constant prices PIB aux prix constants National currency Monnaie nationale	GDP implicit price deflators PIB déflateurs implicites des prix National currency Monnaie nationale	GDP implicit price deflators PIB déflateurs implicites des prix US dollars Dollars É.-U.	Exchange rates Taux de change
Brazil	2000	9 923 223.6	134.7	127.9	7 760 462.0	105.4	7 365 892.7
Brésil	2006	19 937 587.5	227.6	152.5	13 072 242.7	149.3	8 758 620.4
	2007	21 854 233.3	278.8	161.2	13 560 396.3	173.0	7 839 532.9
	2008	24 615 107.2	333.4	169.6	14 514 297.1	196.6	7 383 381.3
British Virgin Islands	2000	723.5	723.5	753.5	96.0	96.0	100.0
Iles Vierges britanniques	2006	992.3	992.3	857.4	115.7	115.7	100.0
	2007	1 081.0	1 081.0	872.4	123.9	123.9	100.0
	2008	1 158.1	1 158.1	894.6	129.5	129.5	100.0
Brunei Darussalam	2000	162.1	170.5	124.8	129.9	136.6	95.1
Brunéi Darussalam	2006	285.6	325.8	144.3	197.9	225.7	87.7
	2007	290.1	348.9	145.2	199.8	240.2	83.2
	2008	322.3	412.8	143.0	225.3	288.6	78.1
Bulgaria	2000	58 939.9	60.8	84.1	70 121.7	72.3	96 953.2
Bulgarie	2006	108 748.4	152.7	116.6	93 283.3	131.0	71 199.4
	2007	124 520.4	190.8	123.8	100 607.6	154.2	65 253.4
	2008	147 010.6	240.8	131.2	112 040.8	183.5	61 055.6
Burkina Faso	2000	219.3	83.9	166.0	132.1	50.5	261.5
Burkina Faso	2006	355.2	185.0	237.7	149.4	77.8	192.1
	2007	381.2	216.5	246.3	154.8	87.9	176.0
	2008	419.0	254.8	257.4	162.8	99.0	164.5
Burundi	2000	259.9	61.8	84.5	307.6	73.1	420.8
Burundi	2006	501.7	83.5	98.6	508.8	84.7	600.7
	2007	515.1	81.5	102.2	504.2	79.8	631.7
	2008	670.0	96.8	106.8	627.4	90.6	692.4
Cambodia	2000	2 352.5	261.1	193.0	1 218.6	135.2	901.1
Cambodge	2006	4 986.2	518.0	334.2	1 492.0	155.0	962.6
	2007	5 853.2	615.1	368.3	1 589.3	167.0	951.6
	2008	7 567.8	797.0	390.5	1 937.9	204.1	949.6
Cameroon	2000	205.0	78.4	118.1	173.6	66.4	261.5
Cameroun	2006	291.1	151.6	146.3	199.0	103.6	192.1
	2007	306.4	174.1	151.3	202.6	115.1	176.0
	2008	322.8	196.3	156.6	206.1	125.3	164.5
Canada	2000	158.3	124.4	133.3	118.7	93.3	127.3
Canada	2006	213.3	219.4	155.7	137.0	141.0	97.2
	2007	225.9	245.3	159.9	141.3	153.4	92.1
	2008	235.8	257.8	160.6	146.8	160.6	91.5
Cape Verde	2000	299.2	175.1	192.6	155.4	90.9	170.9
Cap-Vert	2006	489.6	390.1	277.2	176.6	140.7	125.5
	2007	543.9	472.8	298.8	182.1	158.2	115.0
	2008	598.4	556.7	316.4	189.2	176.0	107.5
Cayman Islands	2000	203.4	203.4	147.8	137.6	137.6	100.0
Iles Caïmanes	2006	286.4	286.4	173.4	165.2	165.2	100.0
	2007	301.4	310.0	177.3	170.0	174.9	97.2
	2008	321.8	331.1	183.0	175.8	180.9	97.2
Central African Rep.	2000	174.9	66.9	117.8	148.5	56.8	261.5
Rép. centrafricaine	2006	199.9	104.1	116.9	171.0	89.0	192.1
	2007	211.1	119.9	121.2	174.2	98.9	176.0
	2008	231.0	140.5	123.9	186.5	113.4	164.5
Chad	2000	235.0	89.9	140.9	166.8	63.8	261.5
Tchad	2006	784.8	408.6	281.6	278.7	145.1	192.1
	2007	800.2	454.6	282.0	283.8	161.2	176.0
	2008	891.2	541.8	282.9	315.0	191.5	164.5

Implicit price deflators of gross domestic product *(continued)*
Index base: 1990 = 100

Déflateurs implicites des prix de produit intérieur brut *(suite)*
Indice base : 1990 = 100

Country or area Pays ou zone	Year Année	GDP at current prices / PIB aux prix courants: National currency Monnaie nationale	GDP at current prices / PIB aux prix courants: US dollars Dollars É.-U.	GDP at constant prices / PIB aux prix constants: National currency Monnaie nationale	GDP implicit price deflators / PIB déflateurs implicites des prix: National currency Monnaie nationale	GDP implicit price deflators / PIB déflateurs implicites des prix: US dollars Dollars É.-U.	Exchange rates Taux de change
Chile	2000	397.2	224.4	185.9	213.6	120.7	177.0
Chili	2006	760.1	437.0	238.4	318.9	183.4	173.9
	2007	838.3	489.2	250.5	334.6	195.3	171.4
	2008	867.2	506.1	258.1	336.0	196.1	171.4
China [3]	2000	510.4	294.9	269.6	189.3	109.4	173.1
Chine [3]	2006	1 145.6	687.3	475.5	240.9	144.5	166.7
	2007	1 360.6	855.5	537.4	253.2	159.2	159.1
	2008	1 554.0	1 069.7	586.0	265.2	182.6	145.3
China, Hong Kong SAR	2000	220.0	220.0	146.5	150.2	150.2	100.0
Chine, Hong Kong RAS	2006	246.4	247.1	192.0	128.4	128.7	99.7
	2007	269.8	269.4	204.2	132.2	132.0	100.2
	2008	280.2	280.4	209.1	134.0	134.1	100.0
China, Macao SAR	2000	188.7	188.6	130.2	145.0	144.9	100.1
Chine, Macao RAS	2006	444.1	445.2	270.4	164.2	164.6	99.8
	2007	585.8	584.7	339.6	172.5	172.2	100.2
	2008	673.6	673.7	384.4	175.2	175.3	100.0
Colombia	2000	729.4	175.5	129.9	561.5	135.1	415.7
Colombie	2006	1 423.7	302.9	168.4	845.7	179.9	470.1
	2007	1 603.9	387.6	181.1	885.9	214.1	413.8
	2008	1 781.4	454.7	185.6	959.6	244.9	391.8
Comoros	2000	162.4	82.8	114.5	141.9	72.4	196.1
Comores	2006	238.2	165.4	132.9	179.3	124.5	144.0
	2007	251.8	190.7	131.6	191.4	145.0	132.0
	2008	268.3	217.5	132.8	202.0	163.7	123.4
Congo	2000	300.9	115.1	115.2	261.2	99.9	261.5
Congo	2006	509.3	265.2	151.1	337.1	175.5	192.1
	2007	491.2	279.1	148.7	330.4	187.7	176.0
	2008	623.2	378.9	157.0	397.1	241.4	164.5
Cook Islands	2000	181.3	138.1	132.4	136.9	104.3	131.3
Iles Cook	2006	283.1	307.7	162.0	174.8	190.0	92.0
	2007	292.3	360.1	164.0	178.2	219.5	81.2
	2008	308.2	366.8	168.8	182.6	217.3	84.0
Costa Rica	2000	739.8	219.8	166.0	445.7	132.4	336.5
Costa Rica	2006	1 733.8	310.5	220.6	785.9	140.8	558.3
	2007	2 042.7	362.1	237.8	859.0	152.3	564.1
	2008	2 362.3	411.1	246.9	956.7	166.5	574.6
Côte d'Ivoire	2000	234.9	89.8	127.4	184.3	70.5	261.5
Côte d'Ivoire	2006	280.5	146.1	129.2	217.2	113.1	192.1
	2007	292.9	166.4	131.1	223.4	126.9	176.0
	2008	323.7	196.8	134.1	241.3	146.7	164.5
Croatia	2000	53 640.2	73.4	84.8	63 258.1	86.5	73 121.8
Croatie	2006	86 928.7	168.6	110.9	78 402.0	152.0	51 568.9
	2007	95 393.2	201.3	116.9	81 573.3	172.1	47 388.3
	2008	103 874.1	238.3	119.7	86 778.3	199.1	43 594.3
Cuba	2000	141.9	106.7	86.6	163.9	123.2	133.0
Cuba	2006	244.9	184.1	124.0	197.5	148.5	133.0
	2007	272.1	204.6	133.0	204.6	153.8	133.0
	2008	291.1	218.9	138.7	209.8	157.8	133.0
Cyprus [4]	2000	218.6	160.9	155.5	140.6	103.5	135.9
Chypre [4]	2006	319.3	318.7	189.8	168.3	168.0	100.2
	2007	345.0	370.8	198.2	174.1	187.1	93.0
	2008	374.9	429.8	205.5	182.5	209.2	87.2

18 Implicit price deflators of gross domestic product *(continued)*

Index base: 1990 = 100

Déflateurs implicites des prix de produit intérieur brut *(suite)*

Indice base : 1990 = 100

Country or area Pays ou zone	Year Année	GDP at current prices PIB aux prix courants National currency Monnaie nationale	GDP at current prices PIB aux prix courants US dollars Dollars É.-U.	GDP at constant prices PIB aux prix constants National currency Monnaie nationale	GDP implicit price deflators PIB déflateurs implicites des prix National currency Monnaie nationale	GDP implicit price deflators PIB déflateurs implicites des prix US dollars Dollars É.-U.	Exchange rates Taux de change
Czech Republic République tchèque	2000	329.2	153.1	102.6	321.0	149.3	215.0
	2006	483.6	384.2	131.6	367.5	292.0	125.9
	2007	530.9	469.7	139.4	380.8	336.9	113.0
	2008	557.3	586.1	143.9	387.3	407.3	95.1
Dem. Rep. of the Congo Rép. dém. du Congo	2000	1 350 295.5[1]	57.3[2]	56.3	2 400 721.6[1]	101.8[2]	2 357 630.7[1]
	2006	18 187 364.8[1]	93.0	73.2	24 840 423.9[1]	127.0	19 554 408.7[1]
	2007	22 661 521.9[1]	105.0	77.8	29 128 780.7[1]	135.0	21 578 463.4[1]
	2008	28 751 727.2[1]	126.4	82.6	34 800 341.6[1]	153.0	22 744 213.2[1]
Denmark Danemark	2000	153.9	117.9	129.2	119.1	91.2	130.6
	2006	193.7	201.6	142.1	136.3	141.9	96.1
	2007	200.8	228.3	144.5	139.0	158.0	88.0
	2008	207.0	251.2	142.8	144.9	175.9	82.4
Djibouti Djibouti	2000	121.0	121.0	113.3	106.8	106.8	100.0
	2006	168.5	168.5	136.2	123.7	123.7	100.0
	2007	185.6	185.6	142.7	130.1	130.1	100.0
	2008	215.0	214.8	151.0	142.4	142.3	100.1
Dominica Dominique	2000	162.1	162.1	119.0	136.2	136.2	100.0
	2006	189.1	189.1	129.7	145.9	145.9	100.0
	2007	200.7	200.7	131.6	152.5	152.5	100.0
	2008	217.6	217.6	135.0	161.2	161.2	100.0
Dominican Republic Rép. dominicaine	2000	485.3	252.1	179.9	269.8	140.1	192.5
	2006	1 487.1	380.0	236.8	628.1	160.5	391.4
	2007	1 705.1	437.0	256.8	663.9	170.2	390.2
	2008	1 970.0	485.1	270.3	728.7	179.4	406.1
Ecuador Equateur	2000	141.7	141.7	123.9	114.3	114.3	100.0
	2006	371.3	371.3	167.6	221.5	221.5	100.0
	2007	407.1	407.1	171.8	237.0	237.0	100.0
	2008	467.4	467.4	180.9	258.4	258.4	100.0
Egypt Egypte	2000	319.7	252.7	159.3	200.7	158.6	126.5
	2006	594.5	284.6	213.2	278.9	133.5	208.9
	2007	716.6	348.9	228.5	313.7	152.7	205.4
	2008	831.3	420.0	236.6	351.4	177.6	197.9
El Salvador El Salvador	2000	273.6	273.6	156.9	174.4	174.4	100.0
	2006	388.5	388.5	182.7	212.7	212.7	100.0
	2007	424.4	424.4	191.2	221.9	221.9	100.0
	2008	460.6	460.6	196.1	234.9	234.9	100.0
Equatorial Guinea Guinée équatoriale	2000	2 311.2	883.8	655.3	352.7	134.9	261.5
	2006	12 290.5	6 399.6	2 302.9	533.7	277.9	192.1
	2007	14 142.7	8 034.3	2 837.1	498.5	283.2	176.0
	2008	22 079.9	13 424.5	3 268.4	675.6	410.7	164.5
Eritrea Erythrée	2000	446.7	96.2	179.9	248.3	53.4	464.5
	2006	1 223.5	164.9	202.2	605.1	81.5	742.1
	2007	1 329.6	179.2	204.9	648.9	87.5	742.1
	2008	1 490.9	200.9	207.0	720.2	97.1	742.1
Estonia Estonie	2000	11 970.8	99.9	91.7	13 058.6	109.0	11 985.9
	2006	25 703.7	291.9	147.7	17 405.0	197.7	8 805.1
	2007	29 952.2	370.9	157.0	19 073.9	236.2	8 076.4
	2008	31 108.1	411.8	151.3	20 557.4	272.1	7 554.1
Ethiopia Ethiopie	2000	284.4	71.7	132.0	215.5	54.3	397.0
	2006	561.8	133.7	199.8	281.2	66.9	420.2
	2007	733.3	169.6	222.1	330.3	76.4	432.4
	2008	1 048.0	227.3	247.2	424.1	92.0	461.2

18 Implicit price deflators of gross domestic product *(continued)*

Index base: 1990 = 100

Déflateurs implicites des prix de produit intérieur brut *(suite)*

Indice base : 1990 = 100

Country or area Pays ou zone	Year Année	GDP at current prices PIB aux prix courants		GDP at constant prices PIB aux prix constants	GDP implicit price deflators PIB déflateurs implicites des prix		Exchange rates Taux de change
		National currency Monnaie nationale	US dollars Dollars É.-U.	National currency Monnaie nationale	National currency Monnaie nationale	US dollars Dollars É.-U.	
Fiji Fidji	2000	183.3	127.6	126.3	145.2	101.0	143.7
	2006	279.0	238.7	147.0	189.8	162.3	116.9
	2007	269.2	247.5	137.3	196.0	180.2	108.8
	2008	293.4	272.6	139.0	211.1	196.1	107.6
Finland Finlande	2000	147.3	87.3	121.8	121.0	71.7	168.8
	2006	186.1	150.1	144.6	128.7	103.8	124.0
	2007	200.2	176.2	150.7	132.8	116.9	113.6
	2008	207.4	195.4	152.1	136.4	128.5	106.2
France [5] France [5]	2000	139.5	106.7	121.6	114.7	87.7	130.8
	2006	174.9	182.1	135.0	129.5	134.9	96.0
	2007	183.4	208.4	138.2	132.7	150.8	88.0
	2008	188.8	229.6	138.8	136.0	165.4	82.2
French Polynesia Polynésie française	2000	137.8	105.3	126.0	109.3	83.6	130.8
	2006	158.6	165.1	141.3	112.3	116.9	96.1
	2007	162.8	184.3	144.4	112.7	127.6	88.3
	2008	167.5	203.4	148.2	113.0	137.3	82.3
Gabon Gabon	2000	245.8	94.0	116.0	211.9	81.0	261.5
	2006	337.9	175.9	126.9	266.3	138.7	192.1
	2007	370.2	210.3	134.4	275.4	156.5	176.0
	2008	434.0	263.9	136.9	317.1	192.8	164.5
Gambia Gambie	2000	179.0	110.4	138.4	129.3	79.7	162.2
	2006	346.6	97.3	162.9	212.8	59.8	356.0
	2007	365.8	115.9	173.1	211.3	67.0	315.6
	2008	405.8	148.9	181.6	223.5	82.0	272.5
Georgia Géorgie	2000	40 287.1[6]	36.3	37.7	106 856.8[6]	96.2	111 124.0[6]
	2006	91 932.7[6]	91.8	58.7	156 522.9[6]	156.3	100 117.5[6]
	2007	113 291.9[6]	120.6	66.0	171 704.1[6]	182.8	93 935.3[6]
	2008	127 131.0[6]	151.7	67.3	188 828.2[6]	225.3	83 830.3[6]
Germany Allemagne	2000	145.6	110.8	123.1	118.3	90.0	131.4
	2006	163.9	169.9	130.6	125.5	130.1	96.5
	2007	171.1	193.4	133.8	127.8	144.5	88.4
	2008	175.9	212.9	135.5	129.8	157.1	82.6
Ghana Ghana	2000	1 336.5	80.0	152.3	877.7	52.5	1 671.6
	2006	5 744.9	204.4	207.7	2 766.7	98.4	2 811.4
	2007	6 978.7	243.3	220.5	3 165.7	110.4	2 868.3
	2008	8 418.6	265.8	235.2	3 579.8	113.0	3 167.1
Greece Grèce	2000	311.0	134.9	126.1	246.7	107.0	230.5
	2006	486.5	283.9	161.8	300.7	175.5	171.4
	2007	520.7	331.5	168.4	309.3	196.9	157.1
	2008	554.4	377.8	173.3	319.9	218.0	146.8
Greenland Groenland	2000	136.9	104.8	119.2	114.8	87.9	130.6
	2006	163.9	170.6	130.3	125.9	131.0	96.1
	2007	183.2	208.2	137.5	133.3	151.5	88.0
	2008	140.6	170.7	137.9	102.0	123.8	82.4
Grenada Grenade	2000	194.3	194.3	150.4	129.2	129.2	100.0
	2006	253.9	253.9	164.5	154.4	154.4	100.0
	2007	275.0	275.0	170.5	161.3	161.3	100.0
	2008	291.4	291.4	174.0	167.4	167.4	100.0
Guatemala Guatemala	2000	436.4	252.1	149.7	291.5	168.5	173.1
	2006	750.3	442.7	182.9	410.2	242.0	169.5
	2007	853.6	499.0	194.6	438.7	256.5	171.1
	2008	963.2	571.5	202.4	475.9	282.4	168.5

18

Implicit price deflators of gross domestic product *(continued)*

Index base: 1990 = 100

Déflateurs implicites des prix de produit intérieur brut *(suite)*

Indice base : 1990 = 100

Country or area Pays ou zone	Year Année	GDP at current prices PIB aux prix courants National currency Monnaie nationale	GDP at current prices PIB aux prix courants US dollars Dollars É.-U.	GDP at constant prices PIB aux prix constants National currency Monnaie nationale	GDP implicit price deflators PIB déflateurs implicites des prix National currency Monnaie nationale	GDP implicit price deflators PIB déflateurs implicites des prix US dollars Dollars É.-U.	Exchange rates Taux de change
Guinea Guinée	2000	292.2	110.4	149.0	196.1	74.1	264.6
	2006	877.8	116.6	176.1	498.5	66.2	753.1
	2007	1 009.2	143.3	179.2	563.2	80.0	704.2
	2008	1 215.0	176.3	186.3	652.3	94.7	689.0
Guinea-Bissau Guinée-Bissau	2000	1 954.9	92.3	113.4	1 723.3	81.4	2 117.6
	2006	2 049.1	131.8	113.0	1 813.0	116.6	1 555.2
	2007	2 181.6	153.0	117.2	1 861.3	130.6	1 425.4
	2008	2 307.7	173.3	120.8	1 909.7	143.4	1 331.9
Guyana Guyana	2000	830.0	179.9	161.2	514.9	111.6	461.5
	2006	1 168.8	230.8	162.6	719.0	142.0	506.4
	2007	1 388.8	271.3	177.4	782.8	152.9	511.8
	2008	1 512.5	297.2	183.1	825.8	162.3	508.9
Haiti Haïti	2000	569.4	134.5	90.1	632.3	149.3	423.4
	2006	1 471.3	182.1	89.7	1 641.1	203.1	808.2
	2007	1 816.8	246.4	92.5	1 963.6	266.3	737.2
	2008	2 105.2	270.8	93.7	2 246.0	288.9	777.5
Honduras Honduras	2000	713.1	197.6	138.2	516.1	143.0	360.9
	2006	1 379.3	300.2	185.0	745.6	162.3	459.5
	2007	1 568.7	341.4	196.7	797.4	173.5	459.5
	2008	1 809.2	393.7	204.5	884.7	192.5	459.5
Hungary Hongrie	2000	581.8	130.3	107.9	539.4	120.8	446.4
	2006	1 023.8	307.6	138.2	740.7	222.5	332.9
	2007	1 097.1	377.6	139.9	784.3	270.0	290.5
	2008	1 146.3	421.0	140.7	814.4	299.1	272.3
Iceland Islande	2000	184.1	136.5	128.6	143.2	106.1	134.9
	2006	314.5	261.2	165.7	189.9	157.7	120.4
	2007	350.4	318.8	174.8	200.4	182.4	109.9
	2008	394.4	259.8	175.4	224.9	148.1	151.8
India Inde	2000	367.5	143.1	170.4	215.8	84.0	256.8
	2006	721.9	278.9	261.7	275.8	106.6	258.9
	2007	825.8	349.6	285.5	289.3	122.5	236.2
	2008	953.7	383.7	306.3	311.4	125.3	248.6
Indonesia Indonésie	2000	599.9	131.3	151.2	396.8	86.8	457.0
	2006	1 441.4	290.0	201.0	717.3	144.3	497.0
	2007	1 708.1	344.4	213.7	799.5	161.2	496.0
	2008	2 138.3	406.3	226.5	944.1	179.4	526.3
Iran (Islamic Rep. of) Iran (Rép. islamique d')	2000	1 655.9	113.9	146.7	1 128.6	77.6	1 453.8
	2006	5 831.8	250.7	203.0	2 872.3	123.5	2 326.5
	2007	7 556.0	320.9	218.3	3 461.9	147.0	2 354.4
	2008	9 173.8	383.6	225.9	4 061.1	169.8	2 391.8
Iraq Iraq	2000	57 935.8	98.4[2]	119.4	48 505.6	82.4[2]	58 890.7
	2006	115 180.9	121.1[2]	134.9	85 363.4	89.7[2]	95 121.5
	2007	154 360.8	124.9[2]	135.5	113 935.1	92.2[2]	123 635.5
	2008	213 900.2	139.0[2]	148.7	143 821.8	93.5[2]	153 835.5
Ireland Irlande	2000	285.5	201.9	198.2	144.0	101.9	141.4
	2006	482.7	464.8	274.6	175.8	169.3	103.8
	2007	518.9	545.2	291.1	178.3	187.3	95.2
	2008	505.6	568.6	284.5	177.7	199.8	88.9
Israel Israël	2000	439.4	217.3	178.5	246.2	121.7	202.2
	2006	558.3	252.6	208.8	267.4	121.0	221.0
	2007	586.9	288.0	220.0	266.7	130.9	203.8
	2008	623.7	350.5	229.0	272.4	153.1	178.0

Implicit price deflators of gross domestic product *(continued)*
Index base: 1990 = 100

Déflateurs implicites des prix de produit intérieur brut *(suite)*
Indice base : 1990 = 100

Country or area Pays ou zone	Year Année	GDP at current prices PIB aux prix courants National currency Monnaie nationale	GDP at current prices PIB aux prix courants US dollars Dollars É.-U.	GDP at constant prices PIB aux prix constants National currency Monnaie nationale	GDP implicit price deflators PIB déflateurs implicites des prix National currency Monnaie nationale	GDP implicit price deflators PIB déflateurs implicites des prix US dollars Dollars É.-U.	Exchange rates Taux de change
Italy Italie	2000	169.8	96.8	117.0	145.1	82.7	175.4
	2006	211.8	164.4	124.8	169.7	131.7	128.8
	2007	220.3	186.6	126.8	173.8	147.2	118.1
	2008	224.2	203.2	125.4	178.7	162.0	110.3
Jamaica Jamaïque	2000	1 110.5	185.6	114.3	971.7	162.4	598.4
	2006	2 275.3	248.6	127.3	1 786.8	195.2	915.1
	2007	2 566.5	267.4	129.2	1 987.0	207.0	959.8
	2008	3 149.3	312.8	127.7	2 467.2	245.1	1 006.7
Japan Japon	2000	115.1	154.6	113.2	101.7	136.6	74.4
	2006	116.1	144.5	123.3	94.2	117.3	80.3
	2007	118.0	145.1	126.2	93.5	115.0	81.3
	2008	116.1	162.7	126.8	91.6	128.4	71.4
Jordan Jordanie	2000	224.8	210.5	158.5	141.9	132.8	106.8
	2006	394.3	369.1	233.0	169.2	158.4	106.8
	2007	451.9	423.0	253.8	178.1	166.7	106.8
	2008	564.3	529.0	273.8	206.1	193.2	106.7
Kazakhstan Kazakhstan	2000	2 715 557.2	61.7	69.4	3 910 934.5	88.8	4 403 103.7
	2006	10 668 084.9	273.1	125.8	8 483 156.4	217.2	3 906 084.7
	2007	13 421 411.9	353.5	136.7	9 818 871.7	258.6	3 796 566.9
	2008	16 645 458.1	446.7	141.2	11 788 507.1	316.3	3 726 710.0
Kenya Kenya	2000	379.6	114.2	119.8	316.8	95.3	332.4
	2006	640.8	203.7	153.3	418.1	132.9	314.7
	2007	717.3	244.2	163.9	437.6	148.9	293.8
	2008	835.7	276.8	167.2	499.7	165.5	301.9
Kiribati Kiribati	2000	264.5	196.5	159.2	166.2	123.4	134.6
	2006	281.7	271.8	166.9	168.8	162.8	103.7
	2007	281.4	301.7	164.0	171.6	184.0	93.3
	2008	309.3	332.4	174.3	177.5	190.7	93.1
Korea, Dem. P. R. Corée, R. p. dém. de	2000	71.5	72.2	78.5	91.1	91.9	99.1
	2006	6 097.0	93.6	88.0	6 930.9	106.4	6 512.5
	2007	6 266.2	97.8	86.0	7 287.4	113.7	6 409.0
	2008	5 810.6	90.7	89.2	6 514.0	101.7	6 405.5
Korea, Republic of Corée, République de	2000	310.0	194.0	180.4	171.8	107.5	159.8
	2006	466.9	346.1	236.4	197.5	146.4	134.9
	2007	501.0	381.6	248.5	201.6	153.6	131.3
	2008	526.1	337.9	254.0	207.1	133.0	155.7
Kosovo Kosovo	2000	40.8	31.1	47.3	86.3	65.7	131.4
	2006	67.6	70.0	60.6	111.4	115.5	96.5
	2007	72.7	82.2	63.1	115.2	130.2	88.4
	2008	81.7	98.8	63.8	128.1	155.0	82.6
Kuwait Koweït	2000	217.2	204.2	160.6	135.2	127.2	106.3
	2006	553.1	549.8	250.4	220.9	219.6	100.6
	2007	595.9	604.8	261.2	228.1	231.5	98.5
	2008	797.6	855.8	277.8	287.2	308.1	93.2
Kyrgyzstan Kirghizistan	2000	152 705.4	52.5	66.6	229 347.8	78.9	290 734.5
	2006	265 888.1	108.7	82.7	321 637.7	131.4	244 714.8
	2007	331 536.7	145.8	89.7	369 486.3	162.5	227 426.6
	2008	432 274.8	193.9	96.5	447 868.7	200.9	222 906.5
Lao People's Dem. Rep. Rép. dém. pop. lao	2000	2 128.7	191.0	184.0	1 156.9	103.8	1 114.5
	2006	5 513.8	384.1	270.8	2 036.4	141.9	1 435.5
	2007	6 445.8	475.1	292.2	2 206.3	162.6	1 356.9
	2008	7 629.1	615.3	314.1	2 429.1	195.9	1 239.9

18

Implicit price deflators of gross domestic product *(continued)*
Index base: 1990 = 100

Déflateurs implicites des prix de produit intérieur brut *(suite)*
Indice base : 1990 = 100

Country or area Pays ou zone	Year Année	GDP at current prices PIB aux prix courants National currency Monnaie nationale	US dollars Dollars É.-U.	GDP at constant prices PIB aux prix constants National currency Monnaie nationale	GDP implicit price deflators PIB déflateurs implicites des prix National currency Monnaie nationale	US dollars Dollars É.-U.	Exchange rates Taux de change
Latvia Lettonie	2000	7 608.5	88.5	64.6	11 785.0	137.0	8 602.0
	2006	17 891.9	225.1	107.4	16 659.1	209.6	7 948.3
	2007	23 670.4	324.8	118.1	20 040.0	275.0	7 287.1
	2008	26 014.0	381.5	112.7	23 081.7	338.5	6 819.5
Lebanon Liban	2000	1 286.6	593.2	200.1	642.9	296.4	216.9
	2006	1 704.8	786.0	223.6	762.4	351.5	216.9
	2007	1 902.8	877.4	240.4	791.6	365.0	216.9
	2008	2 198.8	1 013.8	260.8	843.0	388.7	216.9
Lesotho Lesotho	2000	380.9	142.0	153.4	248.3	92.6	268.2
	2006	719.6	275.0	190.0	378.7	144.7	261.7
	2007	825.4	303.1	199.6	413.4	151.8	272.3
	2008	935.5	293.0	206.7	452.7	141.8	319.3
Liberia Libéria	2000	108.4	108.4	124.9	86.7	86.7	100.0
	2006	137.8	137.8	106.5	129.3	129.3	100.0
	2007	134.0	134.0	116.7	114.9	114.9	100.0
	2008	170.3	170.3	125.0	136.3	136.3	100.0
Libyan Arab Jamah. Jamah. arabe libyenne	2000	214.4	118.6	121.3	176.8	97.7	180.9
	2006	787.3	169.7	171.6	458.8	98.9	463.9
	2007	861.1	193.1	180.3	477.5	107.1	445.9
	2008	1 196.9	279.9	192.5	622.0	145.4	427.7
Liechtenstein Liechtenstein	2000	212.4	174.7	175.3	121.2	99.7	121.6
	2006	253.3	280.6	198.2	127.8	141.6	90.3
	2007	266.3	308.2	204.8	130.0	150.5	86.4
	2008	275.8	353.7	208.5	132.3	169.6	78.0
Lithuania Lituanie	2000	33 595.9	115.3	73.0	46 034.1	158.0	29 134.3
	2006	60 815.4	303.4	114.5	53 097.0	264.9	20 046.1
	2007	72 087.8	392.2	124.8	57 781.8	314.3	18 381.8
	2008	81 901.3	477.1	128.5	63 725.5	371.2	17 167.9
Luxembourg Luxembourg	2000	209.6	160.0	163.5	128.2	97.9	131.0
	2006	323.2	335.9	207.4	155.9	162.0	96.2
	2007	346.9	393.3	218.2	159.0	180.3	88.2
	2008	349.3	423.9	216.1	161.6	196.1	82.4
Madagascar Madagascar	2000	570.3	125.9	118.7	480.3	106.0	452.9
	2006	1 283.8	179.1	139.6	919.9	128.3	716.9
	2007	1 510.2	240.8	148.4	1 017.9	162.3	627.1
	2008	1 731.9	302.9	155.9	1 111.3	194.4	571.7
Malawi Malawi	2000	2 171.0	99.5	130.4	1 664.7	76.3	2 182.0
	2006	6 327.3	127.0	164.9	3 837.0	77.0	4 984.2
	2007	7 371.7	143.7	178.0	4 142.4	80.8	5 128.7
	2008	8 810.2	171.0	191.2	4 608.6	89.5	5 152.1
Malaysia Malaisie	2000	288.2	205.2	198.7	145.1	103.3	140.5
	2006	464.0	342.1	264.9	175.2	129.2	135.6
	2007	519.1	408.4	281.7	184.3	145.0	127.1
	2008	597.4	484.4	294.5	202.8	164.5	123.3
Maldives Maldives	2000	389.1	315.7	207.0	188.0	152.6	123.2
	2006	620.3	462.9	321.0	193.3	144.2	134.0
	2007	715.2	533.7	340.1	210.3	156.9	134.0
	2008	854.0	637.3	359.9	237.3	177.1	134.0
Mali Mali	2000	276.7	105.8	149.1	185.6	71.0	261.5
	2006	468.5	244.0	213.9	219.1	114.1	192.1
	2007	501.2	284.7	223.1	224.7	127.6	176.0
	2008	563.6	342.7	233.6	241.3	146.7	164.5

18 Implicit price deflators of gross domestic product *(continued)*
Index base: 1990 = 100

Déflateurs implicites des prix de produit intérieur brut *(suite)*
Indice base : 1990 = 100

Country or area / Pays ou zone	Year / Année	GDP at current prices / PIB aux prix courants: National currency / Monnaie nationale	GDP at current prices / PIB aux prix courants: US dollars / Dollars É.-U.	GDP at constant prices / PIB aux prix constants: National currency / Monnaie nationale	GDP implicit price deflators / PIB déflateurs implicites des prix: National currency / Monnaie nationale	GDP implicit price deflators / PIB déflateurs implicites des prix: US dollars / Dollars É.-U.	Exchange rates / Taux de change
Malta / Malte	2000	210.7	152.8	164.9	127.8	92.7	137.9
	2006	270.2	251.9	179.2	150.8	140.6	107.3
	2007	287.2	292.8	185.8	154.5	157.6	98.1
	2008	298.8	324.0	188.7	158.3	171.7	92.2
Marshall Islands / Iles Marshall	2000	136.7	136.7	108.7	125.7	125.7	100.0
	2006	182.8	182.8	130.5	140.1	140.1	100.0
	2007	198.3	198.3	134.9	147.0	147.0	100.0
	2008	210.9	210.9	136.9	154.1	154.1	100.0
Mauritania / Mauritanie	2000	303.5	102.4	133.4	227.6	76.8	296.4
	2006	818.8	245.7	213.4	383.8	115.2	333.2
	2007	867.7	270.5	215.5	402.6	125.5	320.8
	2008	932.3	311.6	220.3	423.1	141.4	299.2
Mauritius / Maurice	2000	312.8	177.1	166.9	187.4	106.1	176.6
	2006	536.4	251.5	202.5	264.9	124.2	213.3
	2007	612.4	290.7	213.4	286.9	136.2	210.7
	2008	688.0	368.5	225.6	304.9	163.3	186.7
Mexico / Mexique	2000	743.2	221.1	140.7	528.3	157.1	336.2
	2006	1 272.3	328.3	161.7	786.9	203.1	387.5
	2007	1 375.2	353.9	166.9	824.2	212.1	388.5
	2008	1 486.2	375.6	169.1	878.8	222.1	395.7
Micronesia (Fed. States of) / Micronésie (Etats féd. de)	2000	149.8	149.8	114.2	131.2	131.2	100.0
	2006	164.4	164.4	112.3	146.5	146.5	100.0
	2007	164.3	164.3	108.2	151.8	151.8	100.0
	2008	164.1	164.1	104.4	157.1	157.1	100.0
Monaco / Monaco	2000	139.5	106.7	121.6	114.7	87.7	130.8
	2006	180.5	187.9	139.2	129.6	135.0	96.0
	2007	211.9	240.8	159.5	132.8	150.9	88.0
	2008	229.3	278.9	175.5	130.7	158.9	82.2
Mongolia / Mongolie	2000	7 539.6	74.9	99.6	7 570.1	75.2	10 066.8
	2006	23 884.5	219.2	148.0	16 136.7	148.1	10 896.2
	2007	29 571.7	270.1	163.1	18 126.1	165.6	10 948.5
	2008	39 413.5	361.6	177.6	22 192.6	203.6	10 899.6
Montenegro / Monténégro	2000	60.1	45.7	75.0	80.1	60.9	131.4
	2006	121.2	125.6	191.9	63.2	65.4	96.5
	2007	158.3	179.0	212.4	74.5	84.3	88.4
	2008	185.5	224.5	228.3	81.3	98.3	82.6
Montserrat / Montserrat	2000	51.8	51.8	38.5	134.7	134.7	100.0
	2006	66.9	66.9	37.4	178.7	178.7	100.0
	2007	68.8	68.8	38.5	178.6	178.6	100.0
	2008	72.8	72.8	43.0	169.1	169.1	100.0
Morocco[7] / Maroc[7]	2000	165.4	128.3	126.4	130.9	101.5	128.9
	2006	242.8	227.5	173.6	139.8	131.0	106.7
	2007	259.1	260.7	178.4	145.3	146.2	99.4
	2008	282.3	300.1	188.1	150.1	159.6	94.1
Mozambique / Mozambique	2000	2 379.2	145.2	184.1	1 292.3	78.9	1 638.9
	2006	6 534.1	239.0	305.5	2 138.8	78.2	2 734.0
	2007	7 600.6	273.3	328.1	2 316.6	83.3	2 781.3
	2008	8 557.0	331.4	351.1	2 437.5	94.4	2 581.8
Myanmar / Myanmar	2000	1 680.1	140.5	184.1	912.6	76.3	1 196.0
	2006	11 001.4	265.3	288.4	3 814.7	92.0	4 147.2
	2007	15 536.3	356.1[2]	304.2	5 108.0	117.1[2]	4 362.8
	2008	21 322.0	553.4[2]	310.2	6 872.8	178.4[2]	3 852.6

18 Implicit price deflators of gross domestic product *(continued)*

Index base: 1990 = 100

Déflateurs implicites des prix de produit intérieur brut *(suite)*

Indice base : 1990 = 100

Country or area Pays ou zone	Year Année	GDP at current prices / PIB aux prix courants: National currency Monnaie nationale	GDP at current prices / PIB aux prix courants: US dollars Dollars É.-U.	GDP at constant prices / PIB aux prix constants: National currency Monnaie nationale	GDP implicit price deflators / PIB déflateurs implicites des prix: National currency Monnaie nationale	GDP implicit price deflators / PIB déflateurs implicites des prix: US dollars Dollars É.-U.	Exchange rates Taux de change
Namibia	2000	391.3	145.9	151.3	258.7	96.4	268.2
Namibie	2006	779.4	297.8	206.1	378.2	144.5	261.7
	2007	898.8	330.1	217.4	413.5	151.9	272.3
	2008	1 051.7	329.4	223.7	470.1	147.2	319.3
Nauru	2000	86.8	64.5	58.7	147.9	109.9	134.6
Nauru	2006	71.9	69.4	39.3	182.9	176.5	103.7
	2007	74.0	79.4	35.5	208.9	223.9	93.3
	2008	77.7	83.5	31.1	249.6	268.2	93.1
Nepal	2000	367.0	151.6	163.0	225.2	93.0	242.1
Népal	2006	604.3	243.9	195.9	308.4	124.5	247.7
	2007	682.2	301.7	205.2	332.5	147.1	226.1
	2008	777.3	327.2	216.6	358.8	151.1	237.5
Netherlands	2000	171.5	130.6	136.6	125.6	95.6	131.4
Pays-Bas	2006	221.6	229.7	150.8	147.0	152.4	96.5
	2007	232.7	263.2	156.0	149.2	168.8	88.4
	2008	244.0	295.4	159.3	153.2	185.5	82.6
Netherlands Antilles	2000	144.2	144.2	112.6	128.1	128.1	100.0
Antilles néerlandaises	2006	173.6	173.6	120.5	144.1	144.1	100.0
	2007	184.2	184.2	123.7	148.9	148.9	100.0
	2008	192.4	192.4	126.5	152.1	152.1	100.0
New Caledonia	2000	176.5	134.9	117.7	149.9	114.6	130.8
Nouvelle-Calédonie	2006	258.4	268.9	121.5	212.6	221.3	96.1
	2007	279.2	316.1	122.2	228.5	258.7	88.3
	2008	302.0	366.9	122.9	245.8	298.7	82.3
New Zealand	2000	157.5	119.9	132.9	118.5	90.2	131.3
Nouvelle-Zélande	2006	225.4	245.0	164.0	137.5	149.4	92.0
	2007	241.1	297.0	169.0	142.6	175.7	81.2
	2008	244.3	287.8	168.6	144.9	170.7	84.9
Nicaragua	2000	12 327.0	137.0	137.6	8 960.9	99.6	9 001.0
Nicaragua	2006	23 219.1	186.2	167.1	13 895.3	111.5	12 467.9
	2007	27 000.0	206.2	172.4	15 664.3	119.7	13 091.3
	2008	31 628.6	230.1	177.5	17 815.2	129.6	13 746.5
Niger	2000	168.1	64.3	126.1	133.3	51.0	261.5
Niger	2006	270.1	140.7	174.8	154.6	80.5	192.1
	2007	288.3	163.8	180.5	159.7	90.7	176.0
	2008	330.5	201.0	191.1	172.9	105.1	164.5
Nigeria	2000	1 377.3	108.9	120.3	1 145.3	90.5	1 265.2
Nigéria	2006	5 462.8	341.3	213.9	2 553.4	159.5	1 600.5
	2007	6 094.7	389.4	228.8	2 663.8	170.2	1 565.1
	2008	7 448.4	514.4	261.5	2 848.8	196.8	1 447.9
Norway	2000	201.2	143.1	143.9	139.8	99.4	140.6
Norvège	2006	293.3	286.3	164.2	178.6	174.3	102.5
	2007	309.3	330.3	169.4	182.6	195.0	93.6
	2008	346.1	384.1	173.0	200.1	222.1	90.1
Occupied Palestinian Terr.	2000	216.7	216.7	208.1	104.1	104.1	100.0
Terr. palestinien occupé	2006	226.4	226.4	215.6	105.0	105.0	100.0
	2007	255.3	255.3	213.0	119.9	119.9	100.0
	2008	318.2	318.2	217.3	146.5	146.5	100.0
Oman	2000	168.3	168.3	155.1	108.5	108.5	100.0
Oman	2006	318.5	318.5	192.9	165.1	165.1	100.0
	2007	360.3	360.3	207.8	173.4	173.4	100.0
	2008	455.0	455.0	177.5	256.3	256.3	100.0

Implicit price deflators of gross domestic product *(continued)*

Index base: 1990 = 100

Déflateurs implicites des prix de produit intérieur brut *(suite)*

Indice base : 1990 = 100

Country or area Pays ou zone	Year Année	GDP at current prices PIB aux prix courants National currency Monnaie nationale	US dollars Dollars É.-U.	GDP at constant prices PIB aux prix constants National currency Monnaie nationale	GDP implicit price deflators PIB déflateurs implicites des prix National currency Monnaie nationale	US dollars Dollars É.-U.	Exchange rates Taux de change
Pakistan	2000	339.3	137.3	142.3	238.4	96.5	247.1
Pakistan	2006	703.1	253.2	200.4	350.8	126.3	277.7
	2007	844.5	301.8	212.4	397.7	142.1	279.8
	2008	1 014.4	312.7	225.0	450.8	139.0	324.4
Palau	2000	155.9	155.9	102.7	151.8	151.8	100.0
Palaos	2006	205.1	205.1	113.0	181.6	181.6	100.0
	2007	221.3	221.3	119.4	185.3	185.3	100.0
	2008	233.6	233.6	121.8	191.8	191.8	100.0
Panama	2000	191.2	191.2	163.9	116.7	116.7	100.0
Panama	2006	282.0	282.0	219.6	128.4	128.4	100.0
	2007	320.7	320.7	244.9	130.9	130.9	100.0
	2008	380.0	380.0	267.4	142.1	142.1	100.0
Papua New Guinea	2000	310.3	106.5	156.8	197.9	67.9	291.3
Papouasie-Nvl-Guinée	2006	538.5	168.2	178.4	301.8	94.3	320.1
	2007	585.9	188.7	189.5	309.2	99.6	310.5
	2008	689.0	243.7	203.9	337.9	119.5	282.7
Paraguay	2000	432.3	152.5	117.0	369.6	130.4	283.5
Paraguay	2006	913.5	199.4	138.5	659.8	144.0	458.2
	2007	1 075.1	262.7	147.8	727.2	177.7	409.2
	2008	1 218.3	346.1	156.4	778.9	221.3	352.1
Peru	2000	3 383.5	182.2	148.5	2 277.9	122.6	1 857.5
Pérou	2006	5 494.1	315.3	196.5	2 796.0	160.5	1 742.6
	2007	6 102.6	366.6	213.9	2 853.0	171.4	1 664.9
	2008	6 853.7	440.3	234.8	2 919.0	187.5	1 556.5
Philippines	2000	311.4	171.3	135.0	230.7	126.9	181.8
Philippines	2006	560.0	265.3	177.2	316.1	149.8	211.1
	2007	617.2	325.1	189.9	325.0	171.2	189.8
	2008	696.0	380.4	198.7	350.3	191.5	182.9
Poland	2000	1 213.9	265.3	144.9	837.5	183.1	457.5
Pologne	2006	1 728.6	529.2	179.2	964.6	295.3	326.7
	2007	1 916.6	657.8	191.2	1 002.4	344.0	291.4
	2008	2 073.8	817.9	200.7	1 033.6	407.6	253.6
Portugal	2000	228.4	149.6	132.9	171.8	112.6	152.7
Portugal	2006	290.4	259.0	140.8	206.3	184.0	112.1
	2007	304.9	296.7	143.4	212.6	206.9	102.8
	2008	310.6	323.5	143.3	216.7	225.7	96.0
Puerto Rico	2000	214.4	214.4	156.2	137.3	137.3	100.0
Porto Rico	2006	275.4	275.4	161.3	170.7	170.7	100.0
	2007	288.9	288.9	159.1	181.6	181.6	100.0
	2008	301.9	301.9	159.4	189.4	189.4	100.0
Qatar	2000	241.3	241.3	196.7	122.7	122.7	100.0
Qatar	2006	771.3	771.3	332.3	232.1	232.1	100.0
	2007	965.2	965.2	383.3	251.8	251.8	100.0
	2008	1 548.6	1 548.6	446.1	347.2	347.2	100.0
Republic of Moldova	2000	126 327.3	32.5	34.8	363 218.2	93.3	389 139.9
République de Moldova	2006	352 924.6	85.9	51.3	687 685.9	167.3	410 948.2
	2007	421 335.6	110.9	52.9	797 087.1	209.8	379 930.4
	2008	495 546.9	152.4	56.7	874 551.1	268.9	325 228.3
Romania	2000	93 043.1	96.1	84.3	110 371.4	114.1	96 775.3
Roumanie	2006	398 960.3	318.6	120.2	331 896.3	265.1	125 221.7
	2007	477 804.1	439.6	127.7	374 116.4	344.2	108 694.8
	2008	592 827.6	528.0	138.6	427 824.9	381.0	112 288.2

18 Implicit price deflators of gross domestic product *(continued)*

Index base: 1990 = 100

Déflateurs implicites des prix de produit intérieur brut *(suite)*

Indice base : 1990 = 100

Country or area Pays ou zone	Year Année	GDP at current prices PIB aux prix courants National currency Monnaie nationale	GDP at current prices PIB aux prix courants US dollars Dollars É.-U.	GDP at constant prices PIB aux prix constants National currency Monnaie nationale	GDP implicit price deflators PIB déflateurs implicites des prix National currency Monnaie nationale	GDP implicit price deflators PIB déflateurs implicites des prix US dollars Dollars É.-U.	Exchange rates Taux de change
Russian Federation Fédération de Russie	2000	1 222 955.4	45.6	67.2	1 819 530.1	67.8	2 682 636.8
	2006	4 503 608.9	173.7	97.4	4 623 793.8	178.3	2 593 161.3
	2007	5 542 801.1	227.2	105.3	5 266 214.0	215.9	2 439 607.2
	2008	6 975 173.2	294.3	111.2	6 274 693.0	264.7	2 370 182.1
Rwanda Rwanda	2000	320.5	68.8	104.1	307.7	66.1	465.6
	2006	735.5	111.6	147.6	498.4	75.6	659.1
	2007	877.5	134.3	159.2	551.1	84.3	653.4
	2008	1 146.1	175.4	177.1	647.1	99.1	653.3
Saint Kitts and Nevis Saint-Kitts-et-Nevis	2000	206.8	206.8	150.0	137.9	137.9	100.0
	2006	306.7	306.7	186.4	164.5	164.5	100.0
	2007	331.0	331.0	191.4	173.0	173.0	100.0
	2008	348.8	348.8	197.1	177.0	177.0	100.0
Saint Lucia Sainte-Lucie	2000	170.0	170.0	128.6	132.2	132.2	100.0
	2006	224.3	224.3	149.8	149.7	149.7	100.0
	2007	230.7	230.7	152.8	151.0	151.0	100.0
	2008	246.4	246.4	155.4	158.6	158.6	100.0
Saint Vincent-Grenadines Saint Vincent-Grenadines	2000	169.2	169.2	136.0	124.4	124.4	100.0
	2006	247.4	247.4	174.6	141.7	141.7	100.0
	2007	274.6	274.6	186.2	147.5	147.5	100.0
	2008	303.7	303.7	195.5	155.3	155.3	100.0
Samoa Samoa	2000	293.3	206.2	128.6	228.1	160.3	142.3
	2006	482.6	401.1	167.8	287.6	239.0	120.3
	2007	550.2	485.7	178.6	308.0	271.9	113.3
	2008	546.0	477.0	172.5	316.5	276.5	114.5
San Marino Saint-Marin	2000	240.5	137.1	167.4	143.6	81.9	175.4
	2006	335.2	260.2	204.8	163.7	127.1	128.8
	2007	353.0	298.9	211.9	166.6	141.1	118.1
	2008	371.3	336.5	215.9	172.0	155.9	110.3
Sao Tome and Principe Sao Tomé-et-Principe	2000	3 555.3	63.9	116.2	3 059.8	55.0	5 566.3
	2006	9 005.3	103.7	169.3	5 319.7	61.3	8 685.3
	2007	11 396.4	120.7	179.4	6 351.2	67.3	9 444.4
	2008	14 915.8	147.8	189.9	7 856.8	77.8	10 095.5
Saudi Arabia Arabie saoudite	2000	161.6	161.6	130.8	123.6	123.6	100.0
	2006	305.4	305.8	162.4	188.0	188.3	99.9
	2007	328.7	329.0	167.9	195.8	195.9	99.9
	2008	401.0	401.0	174.9	229.3	229.3	100.0
Senegal Sénégal	2000	197.2	75.4	135.3	145.8	55.8	261.5
	2006	289.7	150.8	174.0	166.5	86.7	192.1
	2007	320.1	181.9	182.3	175.6	99.8	176.0
	2008	352.2	214.2	186.8	188.6	114.7	164.5
Serbia [8] Serbie [8]	2000	284 845.3 [9]	27.0	50.7	562 119.9 [9]	53.2	1 056 812.1 [9]
	2006	1 468 049.1 [9]	91.1	68.5	2 142 601.1 [9]	132.9	1 612 005.8 [9]
	2007	1 751 699.3 [9]	124.8	73.3	2 391 457.9 [9]	170.4	1 403 325.1 [9]
	2008	2 069 034.5 [9]	157.3	77.2	2 679 302.3 [9]	203.7	1 315 178.9 [9]
Seychelles Seychelles	2000	179.5	167.7	153.1	117.3	109.6	107.1
	2006	235.6	227.8	162.0	145.4	140.6	103.4
	2007	287.9	229.3	177.7	162.0	129.0	125.6
	2008	366.6	206.9	176.1	208.1	117.5	177.2
Sierra Leone Sierra Leone	2000	1 289.5	93.4	45.4	2 840.1	205.6	1 381.4
	2006	3 254.6	166.4	88.9	3 659.8	187.1	1 955.8
	2007	3 881.5	196.9	94.6	4 103.3	208.2	1 971.1
	2008	4 554.3	234.4	99.8	4 562.9	234.8	1 943.3

18

Implicit price deflators of gross domestic product *(continued)*

Index base: 1990 = 100

Déflateurs implicites des prix de produit intérieur brut *(suite)*

Indice base : 1990 = 100

Country or area Pays ou zone	Year Année	GDP at current prices PIB aux prix courants National currency Monnaie nationale	GDP at current prices PIB aux prix courants US dollars Dollars É.-U.	GDP at constant prices PIB aux prix constants National currency Monnaie nationale	GDP implicit price deflators PIB déflateurs implicites des prix National currency Monnaie nationale	GDP implicit price deflators PIB déflateurs implicites des prix US dollars Dollars É.-U.	Exchange rates Taux de change
Singapore Singapour	2000	239.0	251.3	209.9	113.9	119.7	95.1
	2006	330.6	377.2	281.3	117.5	134.1	87.7
	2007	376.2	452.4	303.1	124.1	149.3	83.2
	2008	384.9	493.0	306.6	125.5	160.8	78.1
Slovakia Slovaquie	2000	318.3	124.1	109.4	290.9	113.4	256.4
	2006	562.6	340.1	150.9	372.8	225.4	165.4
	2007	628.2	456.7	166.6	377.0	274.1	137.6
	2008	687.8	578.0	177.3	387.9	326.0	119.0
Slovenia Slovénie	2000	2 162.4	109.9	120.1	1 800.2	91.5	1 966.9
	2006	3 628.3	215.0	152.2	2 383.3	141.2	1 687.5
	2007	4 033.5	260.8	162.5	2 481.6	160.4	1 546.7
	2008	4 344.1	300.6	168.3	2 581.3	178.6	1 445.2
Solomon Islands Iles Salomon	2000	327.0	162.5	121.5	269.2	133.8	201.2
	2006	660.3	219.4	136.9	482.3	160.3	300.9
	2007	849.8	280.8	150.6	564.3	186.5	302.6
	2008	963.8	315.1	159.6	603.8	197.4	305.9
Somalia Somalie	2000	1 139.7	208.3	76.4	1 491.9	272.6	547.2
	2006	2 052.2	254.7	90.2	2 274.1	282.3	805.6
	2007	2 224.0	270.0	92.6	2 402.1	291.7	823.6
	2008	2 204.1	267.6	95.0	2 320.2	281.7	823.6
South Africa Afrique du Sud	2000	318.2	118.6	119.8	265.7	99.1	268.2
	2006	602.2	230.1	152.5	394.9	150.9	261.7
	2007	689.8	253.3	160.3	430.4	158.1	272.3
	2008	788.0	246.8	165.2	477.1	149.4	319.3
Spain Espagne	2000	197.5	111.5	131.8	149.9	84.6	177.2
	2006	307.8	236.6	160.8	191.5	147.1	130.1
	2007	329.2	276.0	166.7	197.5	165.6	119.3
	2008	343.2	308.0	168.6	203.6	182.7	111.4
Sri Lanka Sri Lanka	2000	391.6	203.8	166.7	234.9	122.2	192.2
	2006	894.1	344.7	218.6	409.0	157.7	259.4
	2007	1 088.7	394.3	233.4	466.4	168.9	276.1
	2008	1 341.9	496.2	247.3	542.5	200.6	270.4
Sudan Soudan	2000	22 307.7	82.3	201.4	11 076.2	40.9	27 099.9
	2006	62 954.3	275.1	339.9	18 523.5	80.9	22 887.3
	2007	74 713.9	351.6	375.6	19 891.3	93.6	21 249.1
	2008	96 418.5	440.5	404.0	23 866.7	109.0	21 891.1
Suriname Suriname	2000	32 206.6	153.8	109.5	29 424.8	140.5	20 937.1
	2006	150 913.0	347.4	146.1	103 280.9	237.8	43 438.0
	2007	171 408.2	394.4	154.0	111 305.6	256.1	43 457.7
	2008	202 751.1	466.6	165.5	122 482.1	281.8	43 457.7
Swaziland Swaziland	2000	392.2	146.2	134.2	292.2	108.9	268.2
	2006	741.4	283.3	156.2	474.5	181.3	261.7
	2007	800.4	293.9	162.4	492.7	180.9	272.3
	2008	848.0	265.6	166.7	508.8	159.4	319.3
Sweden Suède	2000	155.3	100.4	122.0	127.3	82.2	154.8
	2006	200.3	160.7	144.3	138.8	111.3	124.7
	2007	211.5	185.2	148.0	142.9	125.2	114.2
	2008	218.0	195.7	147.8	147.5	132.5	111.4
Switzerland Suisse	2000	127.5	104.9	111.2	114.7	94.4	121.6
	2006	147.2	163.1	122.5	120.1	133.1	90.3
	2007	154.8	179.1	126.6	122.3	141.5	86.4
	2008	160.9	206.4	128.8	124.9	160.2	78.0

18 Implicit price deflators of gross domestic product *(continued)*
Index base: 1990 = 100

Déflateurs implicites des prix de produit intérieur brut *(suite)*
Indice base : 1990 = 100

Country or area Pays ou zone	Year Année	GDP at current prices / PIB aux prix courants: National currency Monnaie nationale	GDP at current prices / PIB aux prix courants: US dollars Dollars É.-U.	GDP at constant prices / PIB aux prix constants: National currency Monnaie nationale	GDP implicit price deflators / PIB déflateurs implicites des prix: National currency Monnaie nationale	GDP implicit price deflators / PIB déflateurs implicites des prix: US dollars Dollars É.-U.	Exchange rates Taux de change
Syrian Arab Republic Rép. arabe syrienne	2000	336.9	176.2	176.6	190.8	99.8	191.2
	2006	633.0	292.1	236.6	267.5	123.4	216.7
	2007	752.7	360.5	251.6	299.2	143.3	208.8
	2008	947.8	489.6	264.6	358.2	185.1	193.6
Tajikistan Tadjikistan	2000	2 447 671.2	30.0	38.0	6 433 714.3	78.9	8 159 761.9
	2006	12 787 945.2	74.7[2]	54.2	23 588 970.1	137.7[2]	17 125 187.3
	2007	17 540 274.0	79.0[2]	55.8	31 420 877.2	141.5[2]	22 213 833.2
	2008	24 122 328.8	86.4[2]	60.2	40 047 897.5	143.5[2]	27 908 168.1
Thailand Thaïlande	2000	225.4	143.8	154.7	145.7	93.0	156.8
	2006	359.0	242.5	208.7	172.0	116.2	148.1
	2007	388.9	288.3	219.0	177.6	131.6	134.9
	2008	430.4	330.6	229.5	187.6	144.1	130.2
TFYR of Macedonia L'ex-R.Y. Macédoine	2000	48 929.6	84.0	98.7	49 556.1	85.1	58 229.3
	2006	64 355.2	149.3	110.1	58 449.6	135.6	43 118.7
	2007	73 340.0	185.6	116.6	62 877.8	159.1	39 521.0
	2008	77 953.7	210.7	122.8	63 469.4	171.6	36 992.1
Timor-Leste Timor-Leste	2000	216.6	216.6	134.3	161.2	161.2	100.0
	2006	241.5	241.5	135.9	177.7	177.7	100.0
	2007	310.5	310.5	157.9	196.6	196.6	100.0
	2008	389.9	389.9	168.7	231.2	231.2	100.0
Togo Togo	2000	189.6	72.5	109.7	172.8	66.1	261.5
	2006	236.5	123.1	118.9	198.9	103.6	192.1
	2007	250.6	142.4	123.0	203.7	115.7	176.0
	2008	265.2	161.2	124.4	213.2	129.6	164.5
Tonga Tonga	2000	158.1	115.0	131.1	120.6	87.8	137.4
	2006	277.3	175.2	144.0	192.6	121.7	158.3
	2007	288.0	187.0	139.5	206.5	134.1	154.0
	2008	323.8	222.2	141.1	229.4	157.5	145.7
Trinidad and Tobago Trinité-et-Tobago	2000	238.5	160.9	154.2	154.7	104.3	148.2
	2006	566.9	381.7	255.8	221.7	149.3	148.5
	2007	638.0	428.5	269.8	236.5	158.8	148.9
	2008	706.2	477.6	279.3	252.9	171.0	147.9
Tunisia Tunisie	2000	246.4	157.9	158.9	155.1	99.4	156.1
	2006	382.6	252.5	208.5	183.6	121.1	151.5
	2007	422.0	289.2	221.7	190.3	130.5	145.9
	2008	449.0	320.1	235.2	190.9	136.1	140.3
Turkey Turquie	2000	31 542.0	131.6	143.4	22 003.9	91.8	23 967.2
	2006	143 534.2	262.1	191.4	74 976.4	136.9	54 758.5
	2007	162 081.1	324.5	200.0	81 055.6	162.3	49 946.7
	2008	182 642.7	366.1	202.1	90 380.2	181.2	49 893.6
Turkmenistan Turkménistan	2000	168.7[1]	135.4[2]	78.6	214.7[1]	172.3[2]	124.6[1]
	2006	747.4[1]	225.8[2]	112.3	665.5[1]	201.0[2]	331.0[1]
	2007	896.8[1]	258.7[2]	125.3	715.6[1]	206.5[2]	346.6[1]
	2008	1 075.3[1]	288.2[2]	137.6	781.5[1]	209.4[2]	373.1[1]
Turks and Caicos Islands Iles Turques et Caïques	2000	301.6	301.6	244.8	123.2	123.2	100.0
	2006	681.6	681.6	435.3	156.6	156.6	100.0
	2007	782.4	782.4	484.3	161.6	161.6	100.0
	2008	921.5	921.5	546.5	168.6	168.6	100.0
Tuvalu Tuvalu	2000	173.1[10]	128.6[10]	127.6[11]	135.7	100.8	134.6
	2006	279.5	269.7	169.9	164.6	158.8	103.7
	2007	293.7	314.8	173.3	169.5	181.7	93.3
	2008	310.0	333.1	176.7	175.4	188.5	93.1

18 Implicit price deflators of gross domestic product *(continued)*
Index base: 1990 = 100
Déflateurs implicites des prix de produit intérieur brut *(suite)*
Indice base : 1990 = 100

Country or area Pays ou zone	Year Année	GDP at current prices / PIB aux prix courants: National currency Monnaie nationale	GDP at current prices / PIB aux prix courants: US dollars Dollars É.-U.	GDP at constant prices / PIB aux prix constants: National currency Monnaie nationale	GDP implicit price deflators / PIB déflateurs implicites des prix: National currency Monnaie nationale	GDP implicit price deflators / PIB déflateurs implicites des prix: US dollars Dollars É.-U.	Exchange rates Taux de change
Uganda Ouganda	2000	602.0	157.0	195.5	308.0	80.3	383.5
	2006	1 164.2	272.6	288.0	404.3	94.7	427.1
	2007	1 350.4	336.0	312.8	431.7	107.4	401.9
	2008	1 572.4	391.9	342.7	458.9	114.4	401.2
Ukraine Ukraine	2000	10 175 971.9	34.7	43.2	23 557 544.3	80.2	29 363 925.4
	2006	32 558 861.7	119.5	67.3	48 372 089.5	177.5	27 257 621.9
	2007	43 124 233.4	158.2	72.7	59 355 062.6	217.8	27 257 621.9
	2008	56 834 182.0	199.9	74.1	76 653 674.1	269.6	28 430 085.1
United Arab Emirates Emirats arabes unis	2000	208.9	208.8	161.0	129.8	129.7	100.0
	2006	503.7	503.5	248.3	202.9	202.8	100.0
	2007	588.5	588.2	264.0	222.9	222.8	100.0
	2008	849.6	849.3	283.6	299.6	299.5	100.0
United Kingdom Royaume-Uni	2000	172.2	146.8	128.8	133.7	113.9	117.4
	2006	233.1	241.6	149.5	156.0	161.6	96.5
	2007	247.0	278.3	154.0	160.4	180.8	88.7
	2008	254.5	264.8	155.1	164.1	170.8	96.1
United Rep. of Tanzania [12] Rép.-Unie de Tanzanie [12]	2000	778.3	189.7	150.2	518.1	126.3	410.4
	2006	1 712.6	266.8	225.4	759.9	118.4	641.8
	2007	1 999.7	313.3	241.5	828.1	129.7	638.3
	2008	2 369.0	386.3	259.5	912.9	148.8	613.3
United States Etats-Unis	2000	169.6	169.6	138.4	122.5	122.5	100.0
	2006	227.8	227.8	159.3	143.0	143.0	100.0
	2007	238.7	238.7	162.6	146.8	146.8	100.0
	2008	244.9	244.9	164.4	149.0	149.0	100.0
Uruguay Uruguay	2000	2 555.7	247.0	136.0	1 879.6	181.7	1 034.6
	2006	4 460.9	216.7	143.6	3 106.5	150.9	2 058.5
	2007	5 268.3	262.5	154.5	3 410.3	169.9	2 007.0
	2008	6 240.2	348.4	168.2	3 709.3	207.1	1 791.3
Uzbekistan Ouzbékistan	2000	10 038 729.1	93.5	98.4	10 205 980.3	95.1	10 732 037.0
	2006	64 011 853.1	116.1	138.3	46 296 981.8	84.0	55 136 733.3
	2007	86 912 896.5	152.0	151.4	57 406 673.8	100.4	57 188 645.2
	2008	104 191 180.4	174.8	163.5	63 721 407.9	106.9	59 607 728.7
Vanuatu Vanuatu	2000	183.9	156.4	134.1	137.2	116.7	117.6
	2006	250.4	265.0	150.5	166.5	176.1	94.5
	2007	283.3	323.8	160.7	176.3	201.5	87.5
	2008	308.5	356.3	169.9	181.6	209.8	86.6
Venezuela (Boliv. Rep. of) Venezuela (Rép. boliv. du)	2000	3 611.5	249.1	123.0	2 936.9	202.6	1 449.8
	2006	17 860.2	390.2	153.3	11 653.2	254.6	4 577.8
	2007	22 201.0	485.0	166.9	13 305.4	290.7	4 577.8
	2008	31 138.8	680.2	175.0	17 794.5	388.7	4 577.8
Viet Nam Viet Nam	2000	1 052.7	481.7	207.6	507.1	232.1	218.5
	2006	2 322.2	941.2	322.6	719.8	291.7	246.7
	2007	2 726.1	1 097.3	349.9	779.1	313.6	248.4
	2008	3 522.2	1 400.6	371.5	948.0	377.0	251.5
Yemen Yémen	2000	1 187.4	270.0	195.2	608.2	138.3	439.8
	2006	3 065.6	572.1	245.7	1 247.8	232.9	535.8
	2007	3 596.6	664.8	257.2	1 398.2	258.4	541.0
	2008	4 527.5	834.6	267.2	1 694.1	312.3	542.5
Zambia Zambie	2000	8 888.8	86.6	106.9	8 311.8	80.9	10 270.5
	2006	34 606.6	290.9	143.4	24 127.7	202.8	11 895.6
	2007	41 012.1	310.4	151.8	27 025.2	204.5	13 214.4
	2008	47 724.9	385.9	161.3	29 583.4	239.2	12 366.4

18 Implicit price deflators of gross domestic product *(continued)*

Index base: 1990 = 100

Déflateurs implicites des prix de produit intérieur brut *(suite)*

Indice base : 1990 = 100

Country or area Pays ou zone	Year Année	GDP at current prices PIB aux prix courants: National currency Monnaie nationale	GDP at current prices PIB aux prix courants: US dollars Dollars É.-U.	GDP at constant prices PIB aux prix constants: National currency Monnaie nationale	GDP implicit price deflators PIB déflateurs implicites des prix: National currency Monnaie nationale	GDP implicit price deflators PIB déflateurs implicites des prix: US dollars Dollars É.-U.	Exchange rates Taux de change
Zanzibar Zanzibar	2000	894.7	218.0	160.7	556.8	135.7	410.4
	2006	2 394.9	373.1	239.1	1 001.8	156.1	641.8
	2007	2 766.8	433.5	255.0	1 085.2	170.0	638.3
	2008	3 277.8	534.4	274.0	1 196.4	195.1	613.3
Zimbabwe Zimbabwe	2000	1 681.3[11]	64.2[2,11]	105.7[11]	1 590.6	60.7[2]	2 619.0
	2006	3 818 384.6	52.2[2]	80.8	4 726 875.6	64.6[2]	7 316 989.0
	2007	378 390 054.0	50.3[2]	75.9	498 806 134.1	66.3[2]	751 915 212.1
	2008	49 619 073.1[9]	44.6[2]	66.3	74 839 222.6[9]	67.3[2]	111 202 041.9[9]

Source:
United Nations Statistics Division, New York, the national accounts database, last accessed January 2010.

1 Figures in millions.
2 Price-adjusted rates of exchange (PARE) are used for selected years for conversion to US dollars due to large distortions in the dollar levels of per capita GDP with the use of IMF market exchange rates.
3 For statistical purposes, the data for China do not include those for the Hong Kong Special Administrative Region (Hong Kong SAR), Macao Special Administrative Region (Macao SAR) and Taiwan Province of China.
4 Excludes northern Cyprus.
5 Includes Guadeloupe, Martinique, Réunion and French Guiana.
6 Figures in thousands.
7 Including Western Sahara.
8 Excluding Kosovo and Metohia.
9 Figures in billions.
10 GDP at market prices.
11 At factor cost.
12 Tanzania mainland only.

Source:
Organisation des Nations Unies, Division de statistique, New York, la base de données sur les comptes nationaux, dernier accès janvier 2010

1 Chiffres en millions.
2 Pour certaines années, on utilise les Taux de change corrigés des prix (TCCP) pour effectuer la conversion en dollars des États-Unis, en raison des aberrations importantes relevées dans les niveaux du PNB exprimés en dollars après conversion à l'aide des taux de change du marché communiqués par le FMI.
3 Pour la présentation des statistiques, les données pour la Chine ne comprennent pas la Région Administrative Spéciale de Hong Kong (Hong Kong RAS), la Région Administrative Spéciale de Macao (Macao RAS) et la province de Taiwan.
4 Exclu Chypre du nord.
5 Y compris Guadeloupe, Martinique, Réunion et Guyane française.
6 Données en milliers.
7 Y compris les données de Sahara occidental.
8 Non compris Kosovo et Metohia.
9 Chiffres en milliards.
10 PIB aux prix du marché.
11 Au coût des facteurs.
12 Tanzanie continentale seulement.

19 Gross domestic product by type of expenditure in current prices

Percentage distribution

Dépenses imputées au produit intérieur brut aux prix courants

Répartition en pourcentage

Country or area Pays ou zone	Year Année	GDP in current prices (mil. nat.cur.) PIB aux prix courants (millions monnaie nat.)	% of Gross domestic product – en % du Produit intérieur brut					
			Household final consumption expenditure Consom. finale des ménages	Govt. final consumption expenditure Consom. finale des admin. publiques	Gross fixed capital formation Formation brute de capital fixe	Changes in inventories Variation des stocks	Exports of goods and services Exportations de biens et services	Imports of goods and services Importations de biens et services
Afghanistan Afghanistan	2005	338 541	105.1	9.7	31.3	...	25.2	71.3
	2006	407 673	98.4	9.9	32.8	...	22.9	64.0
	2007	505 630	98.1	10.6	30.6	...	17.3	56.6
Albania Albanie	2004	750 785	78.0[1]	11.0	37.2	-3.8	22.0	44.4
	2005	814 797	78.0[1]	10.9	37.0	-1.3	22.8	47.5
	2006	891 000	78.3[1]	10.3	35.1	-0.5	24.7	48.0
Algeria[2] Algérie[2]	2001	4 260 811	43.4	14.7	22.7	4.8	36.4	21.8
	2002	4 537 691	43.8	15.4	24.5	6.4	35.4	25.5
	2003	5 264 187	40.4	14.8	24.0	6.3	38.2	23.8
Andorra[2] Andorre[2]	2005	2 042	...	...	...	...	...	...
	2006	2 251	...	...	...	...	...	...
	2007	2 371	...	...	...	...	...	...
Angola[2] Angola[2]	1988	239 640	45.5	32.9	14.6	0.0	32.8	25.8
	1989	278 866	48.2	28.9	11.2	0.9	33.8	23.1
	1990	308 062	44.7	28.5	11.1	0.6	38.9	23.8
Anguilla[2] Anguilla[2]	2004	402	86.2	16.4	33.1	...	56.1	91.8
	2005	458	80.7	18.6	34.0	...	67.2	100.6
	2006	579	84.9	20.3	38.4	...	58.9	102.4
Antigua and Barbuda[2] Antigua-et-Barbuda[2]	1984	468	69.8	18.5	23.6	0.0	73.7	85.6
	1985	541	71.5	18.3	28.0	0.0	75.7	93.5
	1986	642	69.7	18.9	36.1	0.0	75.2	99.9
Argentina Argentine	2005	531 939	61.3	11.9	21.5[3]	...	25.1	19.2
	2006	654 439	59.0	12.4	23.4[3]	...	24.8	19.2
	2007	812 456	58.6	12.9	24.2[3]	...	24.6	20.3
Armenia Arménie	2006	2 656 190	72.3[1]	10.1	35.5	0.4[4]	23.4	39.3
	2007	3 148 666	70.8[1]	10.6	36.4	0.9[4]	19.2	39.2
	2008	3 650 050	69.8[1]	12.3	39.0	0.9[4]	14.8	39.6
Aruba Aruba	2004	3 983	51.2	23.2	26.8	1.5	64.6	67.4
	2005	4 159	52.9	22.4	31.3	1.5	68.4	76.5
	2006	4 334	53.6	22.8	33.0	1.5	65.2	76.0
Australia Australie	2005	967 454	56.6[1]	17.9	27.0	0.1	20.3	21.8
	2006	1 045 674	55.9[1]	17.8	27.2	0.3	20.6	21.8
	2007	1 132 172	55.4[1]	17.7	28.3	0.4	20.7	22.5
Austria Autriche	2006	257 295	54.2[1]	18.4	21.7	0.8[4]	56.6	51.7
	2007	270 837	53.1[1]	18.2	22.2	0.6[4]	59.6	53.7
	2008	282 286	52.9[1]	18.3	22.4	0.9[4]	58.8	53.5
Azerbaijan Azerbaïdjan	2006	18 746	37.1[1]	8.5	29.7	0.2	66.5	38.8
	2007	28 361	33.4[1]	9.7	21.4	0.1	68.1	28.5
	2008	38 006[5]	34.9[1]	9.0	20.1	0.1	63.4	24.8
Bahamas Bahamas	2005	6 509	62.8	13.4	33.2	1.0	45.8	56.2
	2006	6 876	70.0	13.8	38.4	0.9	43.7	66.8
	2007	7 234	70.6	13.5	37.8	0.9	45.3	68.1
Bahrain[2] Bahreïn[2]	2006	5 960	35.5	14.2	25.8	-1.4[6]	98.8	72.9
	2007	6 946	33.5	14.1	26.4	0.6[6]	93.7	68.4
	2008	8 235[5]	30.8	13.5	31.9	1.4[6]	96.9	74.3
Bangladesh Bangladesh	2006	4 157 279	74.2	5.5	24.7	...	19.0[7]	25.2[7]
	2007	4 724 769	74.1	5.5	24.5	...	19.8	26.7
	2008	5 419 188	74.5	5.4	24.2	...	19.4	27.6
Barbados[2] Barbade[2]	2005	5 971	62.7	21.7	24.8	0.2	57.8	67.2
	2006	6 382	58.9	21.3	26.5	0.2	59.8	66.6
	2007	6 818	49.4	20.5	28.1	0.2	65.6	63.9
Belarus Bélarus	2006	79 266 985	51.5[1]	19.2	29.7	2.5	60.1	64.2
	2007	97 165 282	51.8[1]	18.5	31.4	2.7	60.9	67.2
	2008	128 828 759	52.1[1]	16.7	32.7	3.7	61.8	69.2

19 Gross domestic product by type of expenditure in current prices *(continued)*

Percentage distribution

Dépenses imputées au produit intérieur brut aux prix courants *(suite)*

Répartition en pourcentage

Country or area Pays ou zone	Year Année	GDP in current prices (mil. nat.cur.) PIB aux prix courants (millions monnaie nat.)	% of Gross domestic product – en % du Produit intérieur brut Household final consumption expenditure Consom. finale des ménages	Govt. final consumption expenditure Consom. finale des admin. publiques	Gross fixed capital formation Formation brute de capital fixe	Changes in inventories Variation des stocks	Exports of goods and services Exportations de biens et services	Imports of goods and services Importations de biens et services
Belgium Belgique	2006	318 223	52.4[1]	22.4	21.0	1.1	87.3	84.2
	2007	334 917	52.3[1]	22.2	21.7	0.9	88.8	85.8
	2008	344 206	53.5[1]	23.1	22.7	1.2	92.1	92.6
Belize Belize	2004	2 110	75.1	14.0	17.7	1.9	50.7	58.7
	2005	2 230	71.6	14.5	18.5	1.0	54.6	62.7
	2006	2 427	65.2	13.6	19.0	0.4	63.5	61.8
Benin[2] Bénin[2]	2006	2 460 244	76.6	12.1	19.6	1.0	18.5	27.7
	2007	2 641 661	75.8	12.3	19.9	0.8	19.5	28.3
	2008	2 974 771	75.2	11.8	20.3	0.3	19.8	27.5
Bermuda Bermudes	2004	2 980	76.4[1]	21.2	20.3	1.8	37.5	57.1
	2005	3 266	74.8[1]	20.4	19.4	0.7	37.1	52.5
	2006	3 483	74.3[1]	19.2	18.1	1.0	45.4	57.9
Bhutan Bhoutan	2005	36 462	40.0	21.7	50.9	0.3	38.7	62.2
	2006	40 448	38.5	21.6	46.5	0.3	52.4	60.7
	2007	51 522	39.1	18.8	38.7	0.1	53.9	55.6
Bolivia (Plurinat. State of)[2] Bolivie (État plurinat. de)[2]	2006	91 748	62.8[8]	14.4[9]	14.3	-0.4	41.8	32.8
	2007	103 009	63.2[8]	14.1[9]	16.1	-1.0	41.8	34.3
	2008	120 694	62.2[8]	13.3[9]	17.2	0.3	44.9	38.0
Bosnia and Herzegovina Bosnie-Herzégovine	2005	16 927	98.5[1]	21.6	28.9	0.1	33.0	74.7
	2006	19 121	95.4[1]	21.2	24.9	-1.0	36.6	66.4
	2007	21 647	92.5[1]	20.6	30.0	1.6	36.9	69.1
Botswana Botswana	2006	57 860	35.1[1]	20.4	23.1	1.7	49.7	32.0
	2007	71 199	33.2[1]	19.4	22.3	2.4	49.2	32.4
	2008	80 108	35.3[1]	20.1	25.0	5.2	47.9	38.1
Brazil Brésil	2004	1 941 498	59.8[1]	19.2	16.1	1.0	16.4	12.5
	2005	2 147 239	60.3[1]	19.9	15.9	0.3	15.1	11.5
	2006	2 369 797	60.3[1]	20.0	16.4	0.3	14.4	11.5
British Virgin Islands Iles Vierges britanniques	2005	931	37.2[1]	9.2	24.1	-1.6	108.9	77.7
	2006	1 041	36.7[1]	9.0	24.0	-1.6	109.5	77.5
	2007	1 134	36.2[1]	8.9	24.0	-1.7	110.0	77.4
Brunei Darussalam Brunéi Darussalam	2005	15 864	22.5	18.4	11.4	0.0	70.2	27.3
	2006	18 226	19.8	18.1	10.5	0.0	71.7	25.2
	2007	18 512	20.1	20.8	13.0	0.0	67.7	27.8
Bulgaria Bulgarie	2005	42 797	70.2[1]	18.0	24.2	3.8[4]	60.2	76.4
	2006	49 361	70.4[1]	16.6	25.9	5.8[4]	64.5	83.3
	2007	56 520	69.1[1]	16.2	29.8	7.0[4]	63.4	85.5
Burkina Faso Burkina Faso	2006	3 017 510	76.9	22.9	16.9	-2.8	11.5	25.5
	2007	3 238 186	76.2	22.9	20.9	-5.7	10.5	24.8
	2008	3 559 627	71.1	21.5	21.1	0.5	11.6	25.8
Burundi[2] Burundi[2]	1990	196 656	83.0	19.5	16.4	-0.6	8.0	26.2
	1991	211 898	83.9	17.0	18.1	-0.5	10.0	28.5
	1992	226 384	82.9	15.6	21.1	0.4	9.0	29.0
Cambodia Cambodge	2005	25 754 291	84.3[1]	5.8	18.9	-0.4	64.1	72.7
	2006	29 849 146	81.0[1]	5.3	19.3	1.2	68.6	76.0
	2007	35 039 310	78.2[1]	5.7	19.4	1.4	65.3	72.9
Cameroon Cameroun	2005	8 749 566	72.0[1]	10.0	17.7	1.4	20.5	21.5
	2006	9 387 481	71.5[1]	9.6	16.7	0.1	23.0	21.0
	2007	9 881 963	71.3[1]	...	16.9	-0.1	24.2	22.4
Canada Canada	2005	1 372 626	55.3[1]	19.0	21.3	0.7	37.8	34.1
	2006	1 450 490	55.4[1]	19.2	22.3	0.6	36.0	33.6
	2007	1 535 646	55.5[1]	19.3	22.6	0.6	34.7	32.7
Cape Verde[2] Cap-Vert[2]	2002	72 758	88.5	18.4	35.9	-0.1	20.9	63.7
	2003	79 527	86.5	20.1	31.1	-0.1	14.6	52.1
	2004	82 087	83.7	21.3	38.9	0.5	13.8	58.3
Cayman Islands[2] Iles Caïmanes[2]	1989	474	65.0	14.1	23.2	...	60.1	68.8
	1990	590	62.5	14.2	21.4	...	64.1	58.5
	1991	616	62.5	15.1	21.8	...	58.9	52.8

Gross domestic product by type of expenditure in current prices *(continued)*
Percentage distribution

Dépenses imputées au produit intérieur brut aux prix courants *(suite)*
Répartition en pourcentage

Country or area Pays ou zone	Year Année	GDP in current prices (mil. nat.cur.) PIB aux prix courants (millions monnaie nat.)	% of Gross domestic product – en % du Produit intérieur brut Household final consumption expenditure Consom. finale des ménages	Govt. final consumption expenditure Consom. finale des admin. publiques	Gross fixed capital formation Formation brute de capital fixe	Changes in inventories Variation des stocks	Exports of goods and services Exportations de biens et services	Imports of goods and services Importations de biens et services
Central African Rep. [2] Rép. centrafricaine [2]	1986	388 647	82.1	15.6	12.9	-0.1	18.2	28.6
	1987	360 942	80.6	17.5	12.9	-0.2	17.8	28.6
	1988	376 748	80.7	16.1	9.9	0.7	17.7	25.1
Chad Tchad	2006	3 294 117	26.2	23.3	16.0	-0.5	57.0	22.1
	2007	3 358 774	28.2	23.4	15.9	0.2	54.7	22.4
	2008	3 740 949[10]	26.8	23.2	15.1	0.8	55.1	21.1
Chile Chili	2006	77 830 577	54.4[1]	10.5	19.0	1.0	45.8	30.7
	2007	85 621 091	54.5[1]	11.0	19.9	0.7	47.2	33.3
	2008	88 535 187	71.2[11]	...	24.0	0.7	45.1	41.0
China [12] Chine [12]	2005	18 321 740	38.9	14.5	42.2	1.8	37.4	31.8
	2006	21 192 350	38.0	14.2	42.5	2.0	39.9	32.1
	2007	24 952 990	37.4	14.1	42.2	2.5	40.9	31.5
China, Hong Kong SAR Chine, Hong Kong RAS	2005	1 382 590	58.2[1]	8.8	20.9	-0.3	198.7	186.3
	2006	1 475 910	58.6[1]	8.3	21.8	-0.1	205.5	194.1
	2007	1 616 215	59.8[1]	8.0	20.3	0.9	207.3	196.4
China, Macao SAR Chine, Macao RAS	2005	92 951	27.1[1]	9.0	26.6	0.7	95.6	59.0
	2006	115 253	24.4[1]	7.8	34.1	0.9	90.9	58.2
	2007	152 025	21.7[1]	7.2	35.6	0.6	89.7	54.8
Colombia Colombie	2005	335 546 939	64.7[1]	17.5	19.5	2.1	17.3	21.0
	2006	383 322 872	62.9[1]	16.9	21.5	2.8	17.8	22.0
	2007	431 839 018	63.3[1]	16.6	22.0	2.3	16.9	21.0
Comoros [2] Comores [2]	1989	63 397	77.8	27.6	14.4	4.6	14.9	39.3
	1990	66 370	79.7	25.7	12.2	8.0	11.7	37.3
	1991	69 248	80.9	25.3	12.3	4.0	15.5	38.0
Congo [2] Congo [2]	1987	690 523	56.6[1]	20.6	20.9	-1.1	41.7	38.6
	1988	658 964	60.1[1]	21.1	19.6	-1.0	40.6	40.4
	1989	773 524	52.8	18.7	16.4	-0.5	47.6	35.0
Cook Islands [2] Iles Cook [2]	2005	261	...	...	...	...	73.3	61.8
	2006	278	...	...	...	...	80.9	70.5
	2007	287	...	...	...	...	93.8	87.5
Costa Rica Costa Rica	2005	9 538 977	67.3	13.8	18.7	5.6	48.5	54.0
	2006	11 517 822	66.2	13.5	19.9	6.5	49.1	55.3
	2007	13 570 071	66.9	13.3	21.8	2.8	48.8	53.6
Côte d'Ivoire [2] Côte d'Ivoire [2]	1998	7 457 508	65.1[1]	13.7	14.3	0.6	41.3	34.9
	1999	7 734 000	63.2[1]	14.6	14.5	-1.3	39.7	30.8
	2000	7 605 000	67.2[1]	15.5	12.3	-1.0	39.8	33.8
Croatia Croatie	2003	227 012	62.9[1]	18.5	25.0	1.5	42.9	50.8
	2004	245 550	61.8[1]	18.6	24.6	1.3	43.3	49.6
	2005	264 368	61.8[1]	18.4	24.6	1.7	42.6	49.1
Cuba Cuba	2005	42 644	52.9	33.6[13]	9.0	1.8	21.0	18.3
	2006	52 743	55.8	32.2[13]	10.4	1.3	18.7	18.5
	2007	58 604	51.7	35.4[13]	9.7	0.5	20.3	17.6
Cyprus Chypre	2005	13 462	64.6[1]	18.0	19.3	0.6	48.3	50.9
	2006	14 435	64.4[1]	18.6	20.6	0.1	48.0	51.8
	2007	15 596	66.3[1]	17.7	21.4	0.9	48.8	55.2
Czech Republic République tchèque	2006	3 215 642	48.8[1]	21.3	24.6	1.9[4]	76.6	73.1
	2007	3 530 249	48.1[1]	20.4	24.3	2.2[4]	80.2	75.1
	2008	3 705 868	49.7[1]	20.3	24.0	1.1[4]	76.8	71.8
Dem. Rep. of the Congo [2] Rép. dém. du Congo [2]	1987	326 946	77.1	22.4	20.3	5.3	63.2	88.2
	1988	622 822	...	37.2	19.0	3.7	81.0	...
	1989	2 146 811	...	14.4	13.4	3.2	46.5	...
Denmark Danemark	2006	1 628 630	48.7[1]	25.9	21.3	1.0[4]	52.0	48.9
	2007	1 687 892	49.0[1]	26.0	22.2	0.7[4]	52.3	50.2
	2008	1 739 716	48.9[1]	26.5	21.5	0.9[4]	54.7	52.5
Djibouti [2] Djibouti [2]	1996	88 233	64.6	33.6	19.3	-0.9	40.3	56.8
	1997	87 289	59.3	34.7	21.4	0.2	42.2	57.8
	1998	88 461	67.3	29.0	23.2	0.2	43.4	63.0

19 Gross domestic product by type of expenditure in current prices *(continued)*
Percentage distribution

Dépenses imputées au produit intérieur brut aux prix courants *(suite)*
Répartition en pourcentage

Country or area Pays ou zone	Year Année	GDP in current prices (mil. nat.cur.) PIB aux prix courants (millions monnaie nat.)	% of Gross domestic product – en % du Produit intérieur brut Household final consumption expenditure Consom. finale des ménages	Govt. final consumption expenditure Consom. finale des admin. publiques	Gross fixed capital formation Formation brute de capital fixe	Changes in inventories Variation des stocks	Exports of goods and services Exportations de biens et services	Imports of goods and services Importations de biens et services
Dominica[2] Dominique[2]	2004	770	70.0	18.1	27.3	...	45.2	67.2
	2005	809	75.0	18.8	28.6	...	42.4	72.1
	2006	854	70.3	18.9	28.9[3]	...	43.8	69.2
Dominican Republic Rép. dominicaine	2006	1 189 802	82.4	7.2	18.3	0.1	30.0	38.0
	2007	1 364 210	82.7	7.4	18.8	0.1	28.8	37.9
	2008	1 576 163	87.3	7.6	18.2	0.1	25.9	39.2
Ecuador Equateur	2005	37 187	66.0	11.1	22.0	1.8	30.9	31.8
	2006	41 763	64.4	11.0	22.3	1.1	34.0	32.9
	2007	45 789[5]	63.6	11.3	22.1	2.0	35.1	34.2
Egypt Egypte	2004	510 750	72.1[1]	11.1	15.5	0.7	28.8	28.3
	2005	568 192	72.9[1]	11.1	16.9	0.7	31.3	32.9
	2006	642 986	72.9[1]	10.7	18.7	0.6	32.2	35.1
El Salvador[2] El Salvador[2]	2005	17 070	92.4	9.6	15.3	0.4	26.6	44.3
	2006	18 654	93.8	9.6	16.1	0.0	27.8	47.2
	2007	20 373	95.9	9.2	16.1	0.0	27.1	48.3
Equatorial Guinea[2] Guinée équatoriale[2]	1989	42 256	54.3	22.2	19.6	0.0	40.4	36.6
	1990	44 349	53.2	15.3	34.6	-3.1	59.7	59.7
	1991	46 429	75.9	14.4	18.4	-2.3	28.4	34.7
Estonia Estonie	2005	173 530	55.6[1]	17.3	30.7	3.5[4]	80.0	86.3
	2006	205 038	55.2[1]	16.5	33.9	4.7[4]	80.9	92.4
	2007	238 929	55.2[1]	17.2	32.5	5.4[4]	74.4	85.3
Ethiopia Ethiopie	2006	131 642	84.1	12.1	24.2[3]	...	13.8	36.5
	2007	171 835	83.7	10.4	24.8[3]	...	12.7	32.1
	2008	245 585	87.0	9.8	21.2[3]	...	11.5	31.2
Fiji Fidji	2005	4 970	52.6	16.0	15.4	0.7	53.2	67.6
	2006	5 456	51.1	17.6	14.4	0.5	48.1	69.3
	2007	5 264	55.8	16.3	13.5	0.5	49.3	66.9
Finland Finlande	2006	167 009	51.4[1]	21.9	19.3	1.5[4]	45.2	40.2
	2007	179 659	50.5[1]	21.4	20.4	1.9[4]	45.7	40.7
	2008	186 164	51.4[1]	22.1	20.6	0.9[4]	44.2	40.3
France France	2006	1 806 430	56.8[1]	23.4	20.7	0.5[4]	26.7	28.0
	2007	1 894 646	56.6[1]	23.1	21.6	0.6[4]	26.5	28.4
	2008	1 950 085	57.1[1]	23.2	21.9	0.3[4]	26.4	28.9
French Guiana[2] Guyane française[2]	1990	6 526	64.4	35.0	47.8	-0.2	67.3	114.3
	1991	7 404	60.1	34.4	40.5	1.5	81.1	117.6
	1992	7 976	58.9	34.2	30.8	1.5	65.4	90.8
French Polynesia[2] Polynésie française[2]	2003	338 749	106.5	11.9	25.1	-0.1	17.3	60.6
	2004	347 345	98.2	11.1	25.6	0.4	17.4	52.7
	2005	356 156	105.7	9.1	25.0	0.3	17.6	57.8
Gabon[2] Gabon[2]	1999	2 855 800	39.2	16.9	25.1	-0.4	...	...
	2000	3 631 400	32.7	12.8	21.9	0.3	...	...
	2001	3 412 700	35.3	14.1	29.1	-2.3	...	...
Gambia Gambie	2005	17 987	81.9[1]	7.0	32.4	3.6	6.7	35.4
	2006	19 384	80.4[1]	6.0	35.4	3.3	1.2	32.2
	2007	20 460	88.6[1]	6.5	34.2	3.4	3.1	33.3
Georgia Géorgie	2006	13 790	78.7[1]	15.3	25.6	5.3	32.9	57.0
	2007	16 994	70.7[1]	21.9	25.7	6.3	31.2	58.0
	2008	19 070	73.3[1]	25.9	22.5	4.5	28.7	57.7
Germany Allemagne	2006	2 321 500	58.4[1]	18.3	18.2	-0.6[4]	45.3	39.7
	2007	2 422 900	56.7[1]	18.0	18.7	-0.5[4]	46.9	39.9
	2008	2 491 400	56.4[1]	18.1	19.2	0.1[4]	47.2	41.0
Ghana[2] Ghana[2]	2003	66 157 697	75.3[1]	17.7	22.9	^0.0	40.7	56.6
	2004	79 887 433	77.0[1]	16.5	28.4	^0.0	39.3	60.4
	2005	97 260 628	82.1[1]	15.3	29.0	^0.0	36.1	61.7
Greece Grèce	2006	213 207	71.7[1]	16.0	22.5	-0.9	23.3	32.6
	2007	228 180	71.2[1]	16.7	22.5	0.1	23.0	33.5
	2008	242 946	71.2[1]	16.8	19.3	1.5	23.1	31.9

19 Gross domestic product by type of expenditure in current prices *(continued)*

Percentage distribution

Dépenses imputées au produit intérieur brut aux prix courants *(suite)*

Répartition en pourcentage

Country or area Pays ou zone	Year Année	GDP in current prices (mil. nat.cur.) PIB aux prix courants (millions monnaie nat.)	% of Gross domestic product – en % du Produit intérieur brut: Household final consumption expenditure Consom. finale des ménages	Govt. final consumption expenditure Consom. finale des admin. publiques	Gross fixed capital formation Formation brute de capital fixe	Changes in inventories Variation des stocks	Exports of goods and services Exportations de biens et services	Imports of goods and services Importations de biens et services
Greenland [2] Groenland [2]	2003	9 397	...	55.7	...	...	24.3[14]	32.3[15]
	2004	9 855	...	54.0	...	...	23.2[14]	33.2[15]
	2005	10 210	...	51.1	...	...	23.9[14]	35.1[15]
Grenada [2] Grenade [2]	2004	1 267	69.1	17.3	40.5	...	40.5	67.4
	2005	1 495	76.7	16.4	50.7	...	27.8	71.6
	2006	1 516	80.1	16.0	38.0	...	28.8	62.9
Guadeloupe [2] Guadeloupe [2]	1990	15 201	92.8	30.8	33.9	1.1	4.9	63.5
	1991	16 415	87.3	31.0	33.0	1.0	6.1	58.4
	1992	17 972	84.1	29.3	27.8	1.3	4.5	47.0
Guatemala Guatemala	2004	190 440	85.5[1]	8.8	18.3	2.5[4]	27.0	42.1
	2005	207 729	87.7[1]	8.5	18.3	1.4[4]	25.1	41.0
	2006	229 548	87.8[1]	8.4	20.1	0.7[4]	25.0	41.9
Guinea Guinée	2004	8 147 563	66.6	11.8	24.7	1.6	23.0	27.5
	2005	10 703 666	65.4	8.1	27.6	2.0	32.1	35.2
	2006	15 094 203	64.7	8.2	29.8	2.4	38.0	43.1
Guinea-Bissau [2] Guinée-Bissau [2]	1990	510 094	100.9	11.4	13.8	0.9	12.0	39.0
	1991	854 985	100.6	12.6	10.4	0.9	13.4	38.0
	1992	1 530 010	111.1	10.7	...	...	8.2	56.5
Guyana [2] Guyana [2]	2005	164 873	73.4	26.9	32.3[3,16]	...	84.8	120.0[3]
	2006	183 084	65.3	24.2	45.2[3,16]	...	...	...
	2007	217 552	77.9	24.5	39.9[3,16]	...	...	...
Haiti [2] Haïti [2]	1997	51 578	103.1[11]	...	12.5	...	11.5	27.1
	1998	59 055	102.5[11]	...	12.9	...	13.2	28.6
	1999	66 425	101.8[11]	...	13.1	...	13.3	28.2
Honduras Honduras	2006	206 289	77.7[13]	15.0	27.3	1.0	56.1	77.1
	2007	234 622[5]	78.9[13]	16.7	32.4	1.0	51.8	80.7
	2008	270 597[5]	82.3[13]	16.0	33.4	1.3	48.6	81.6
Hungary Hongrie	2006	23 775 269	53.6[1]	22.8	21.6	2.7	77.1	77.8
	2007	25 479 405	53.4[1]	21.1	21.0	2.8	80.4	78.8
	2008	26 620 504	53.7[1]	21.3	20.1	3.6	81.4	80.2
Iceland Islande	2006	1 168 254	58.4[1]	24.4	34.0	1.2	32.0	50.0
	2007	1 301 410	58.0[1]	24.3	28.0	0.5	34.6	45.4
	2008	1 464 993	54.2[1]	24.6	23.9	0.2	44.7	47.6
India Inde	2005	35 867 431	57.4	10.5	31.0	3.8[4]	19.9	22.7
	2006	41 291 736	55.9	10.2	32.5	3.8[4]	22.2	25.2
	2007	47 233 996	55.0	10.1	34.0	4.7[4]	21.2	24.7
Indonesia Indonésie	2005	2 774 281 100	64.4	8.1	23.6	1.4	34.1	29.9
	2006	3 339 479 600	62.7	8.6	24.1	1.3	31.0	25.6
	2007	3 957 403 900	63.5	8.3	24.9	0.0	29.4	25.3
Iran (Islamic Rep. of) Iran (Rép. islamique d')	2005	1 740 580 500	44.0[1]	13.6	26.7	2.2	32.7	24.4
	2006	2 077 499 700	44.5[1]	14.7	25.9	3.7	31.9	24.0
	2007	2 691 727 900	44.4[1]	11.6	25.4	4.0	31.7	21.2
Iraq [2] Iraq [2]	2004	38 058 543	51.3	35.8	7.5	16.2	78.7	89.5
	2005	53 386 429	51.7	27.5	19.1	11.4	74.9	84.6
	2006	80 459 422	44.2	18.6	20.2	2.2	60.6	45.9
Ireland Irlande	2005	162 168	45.5[1]	15.4	26.6	0.5[4]	81.6	69.6
	2006	177 286	45.5[1]	15.4	26.8	0.8[4]	79.9	69.2
	2007	190 603	46.2[1]	15.9	26.3	0.0[4]	79.4	68.7
Israel Israël	2005	597 773	55.8[1]	25.7	16.4	2.5	42.9	43.2
	2006	640 776	55.1[1]	25.5	17.1	1.9	43.4	43.0
	2007	673 552	56.4[1]	25.2	18.7	1.4	43.2	44.9
Italy Italie	2006	1 485 377	59.1[1]	20.1	21.1	0.5[4]	27.7	28.6
	2007	1 544 915	58.7[1]	19.7	21.2	0.6[4]	29.0	29.2
	2008	1 572 243	59.1[1]	20.2	20.9	0.3[4]	28.8	29.3
Jamaica Jamaïque	2005	694 537	77.4	13.8	26.8	^0.0	35.4	53.5
	2006	788 179	77.6	13.9	28.0	0.3	39.6	59.4
	2007	889 027	81.6	14.0	26.4	0.2	37.9	60.1

19 Gross domestic product by type of expenditure in current prices *(continued)*

Percentage distribution

Dépenses imputées au produit intérieur brut aux prix courants *(suite)*

Répartition en pourcentage

Country or area Pays ou zone	Year Année	GDP in current prices (mil. nat.cur.) PIB aux prix courants (millions monnaie nat.)	% of Gross domestic product – en % du Produit intérieur brut					
			Household final consumption expenditure Consom. finale des ménages	Govt. final consumption expenditure Consom. finale des admin. publiques	Gross fixed capital formation Formation brute de capital fixe	Changes in inventories Variation des stocks	Exports of goods and services Exportations de biens et services	Imports of goods and services Importations de biens et services
Japan Japon	2005	501 734 400	57.0[1]	18.1	23.3	0.3	14.3	12.9
	2006	507 364 800	57.1[1]	17.9	23.3	0.4	16.1	14.9
	2007	515 804 800	56.3[1]	17.9	23.4	0.7	17.6	15.9
Jordan[2] Jordanie[2]	2004	8 091	81.0[1]	21.3	24.8	2.6	52.2	81.9
	2005	8 954	87.2[1]	19.5	30.5	3.5	52.5	93.4
	2006	10 521	80.1[1]	22.3	28.3	2.9	54.7	88.4
Kazakhstan Kazakhstan	2005	7 590 594	49.9[1]	11.2	28.0	3.0	53.5	44.7
	2006	10 213 731	45.7[1]	10.2	30.2	3.7	51.1	40.4
	2007	12 849 794	45.1[1]	11.1	30.0	5.5	49.4	42.8
Kenya Kenya	2005	1 418 071	75.2	17.4	18.7	-1.8	28.0	36.9
	2006	1 620 732	75.1	16.6	19.1	-1.1	27.2	38.0
	2007	1 814 229	76.4	17.2	19.5	0.7	26.6	38.8
Kiribati[2] Kiribati[2]	1980	21	92.8	36.4	44.0[17]	...	22.5	95.7
Korea, Republic of Corée, République de	2006	908 743 800	54.5[1]	14.5	28.7	0.9[4]	39.7	38.3
	2007	975 013 000	54.4[1]	14.7	28.5	0.9[4]	41.9	40.4
	2008	1 023 937 700	54.5[1]	15.3	29.3	...	52.9	54.1
Kosovo Kosovo	2004	3 007	85.2[1]	24.5	19.4	3.9	7.1	40.1
	2005	3 068	89.0[1]	23.0	19.3	4.2	7.0	42.5
	2006	3 192	90.5[1]	21.0	20.6	4.4	8.9	45.5
Kuwait[2] Koweït[2]	2005	23 593	32.2[1]	15.7	14.6	1.8	64.0	28.3
	2006	29 470	28.6[1]	13.9	16.0	0.2	65.5	24.2
	2007	31 750	30.5[1]	14.6	19.2	0.2	65.6	30.2
Kyrgyzstan Kirghizistan	2006	113 800	95.1[1]	18.0	23.0	1.2[4]	41.7	79.0
	2007	141 898	87.5[1]	17.1	24.6	2.0[4]	52.9	84.1
	2008	185 014	94.4[1]	16.5	22.7	2.0[4]	56.5	93.6
Latvia Lettonie	2005	9 059	62.5[1]	17.4	30.6	3.8[4]	47.8	62.2
	2006	11 172	65.2[1]	16.6	32.6	7.1[4]	44.9	66.3
	2007	14 780	62.3[1]	17.4	33.7	6.7[4]	42.2	62.4
Lebanon Liban	2003	29 851 000	101.8[11]	...	19.6	-0.4	16.7	37.7
	2004	32 359 000	100.4[11]	...	20.6	1.2	19.9	42.1
	2005	32 499 000	100.1[11]	...	22.0	-0.2	21.1	43.1
Lesotho Lesotho	2005	8 750	106.5[1]	35.8	24.5	0.2	48.6	119.2
	2006	10 269	99.9[1]	33.7	23.2	1.1	50.1	109.0
	2007	11 778	99.0[1]	33.8	24.4	-0.1	51.8	112.8
Liberia[2] Libéria[2]	2005	558	70.3[13]	28.5	1.6	-2.6	1.7	4.2
	2006	614	76.6[13]	26.4	3.7	-2.7	2.6	5.3
	2007	666	108.9[13]	38.9	3.3[3]	...	41.7	85.6
Libyan Arab Jamah.[2] Jamah. arabe libyenne[2]	1983	8 805	39.2	32.7	25.1	-1.1	42.1	38.0
	1984	8 013	38.6	33.6	25.3	0.5	41.4	39.4
	1985	8 277	37.6	31.7	19.7	0.4	37.4	26.7
Liechtenstein Liechtenstein	2004	4 296	...	...	...	...	...	...
	2005	4 555	...	...	...	...	...	...
	2006[5]	5 001	...	...	...	...	...	...
Lithuania Lituanie	2005	72 060	64.5[1]	18.7	22.8	1.1[4]	57.5	64.6
	2006	82 793	64.6[1]	19.3	25.2	1.2[4]	59.1	69.3
	2007	98 139	64.7[1]	18.2	28.0	2.5[4]	54.4	67.8
Luxembourg Luxembourg	2006	33 921	33.2[1]	15.4	18.5	1.3[4]	175.5	143.9
	2007	36 411	32.2[1]	15.3	19.5	0.5[4]	179.9	147.5
	2008	36 662	34.2[1]	16.0	20.1	1.2[4]	179.3	150.7
Madagascar[2] Madagascar[2]	2005	10 092 401	86.2	9.0	22.2	...	28.2	45.6
	2006	11 815 261	81.9	8.7	25.3	...	29.5	45.5
	2007	13 899 031	79.0	10.1	27.4	...	27.1	43.6
Malawi Malawi	2003	236 240	88.1[1]	8.7	14.1	3.0	26.7	40.6
	2004	285 870	89.6[1]	10.4	16.2	2.0	25.0	43.2
	2005	326 246	94.6[1]	10.8	20.2	2.5	24.0	52.2

19 Gross domestic product by type of expenditure in current prices *(continued)*
Percentage distribution

Dépenses imputées au produit intérieur brut aux prix courants *(suite)*
Répartition en pourcentage

Country or area Pays ou zone	Year Année	GDP in current prices (mil. nat.cur.) PIB aux prix courants (millions monnaie nat.)	% of Gross domestic product – en % du Produit intérieur brut Household final consumption expenditure Consom. finale des ménages	Govt. final consumption expenditure Consom. finale des admin. publiques	Gross fixed capital formation Formation brute de capital fixe	Changes in inventories Variation des stocks	Exports of goods and services Exportations de biens et services	Imports of goods and services Importations de biens et services
Malaysia	2005	522 445	44.8[1]	12.3	20.5	-0.5	117.5	94.6
Malaisie	2006	573 736	44.9[1]	11.9	20.8	0.1	116.7	94.5
	2007	641 864	45.6[1]	12.2	21.7	0.3	110.2	89.9
Maldives	2004	9 939	33.4	23.9	42.1	...	85.9	85.4
Maldives	2005	9 597	30.4	41.6	61.1	0.0	67.0	100.1
	2006	11 717	19.9	43.3	59.7	0.0	79.6	102.5
Mali[2]	2006	3 201 472	65.3	17.3	16.5	3.3	30.4	32.9
Mali[2]	2007	3 424 535	64.7	17.4	19.4	4.8	26.5	32.8
	2008	3 850 838	65.5	17.4	18.4	6.8	24.3	32.5
Malta	2005	2 061	64.7[1]	19.7	19.4	1.5[4]	77.1	82.4
Malte	2006	2 187	62.9[1]	20.0	19.7	1.1[4]	93.7	97.5
	2007	2 325	61.1[1]	19.3	19.6	2.8[4]	89.6	92.4
Martinique[2]	1990	19 320	83.6	29.7	26.7	1.9	8.4	50.3
Martinique[2]	1991	20 787	84.0	28.8	25.6	1.4	7.4	47.1
	1992	22 093	84.3	28.7	23.6	-0.9	6.8	42.5
Mauritania	2004	382 285	76.2	19.8	52.0	-6.2	39.9	81.7
Mauritanie	2005	462 779	61.1	31.6	69.2	2.0	40.0	103.8
	2006	692 823	54.6	24.7	25.3	3.6	59.0	67.1
Mauritius	2006	206 328	70.5	14.2	24.3	2.3	61.6	72.9
Maurice	2007	235 530	70.4	13.1	25.1	1.6	58.8	69.0
	2008	264 636[18]	72.4	13.2	25.4	2.1	54.0	67.1
Mexico	2005	9 199 316	66.8[13]	10.8	20.1	3.8	27.3	28.7
Mexique	2006	10 306 839	65.1[13]	10.5	20.8	4.9	28.2	29.5
	2007	11 139 674	65.6[13]	10.3	20.8	...	28.4	30.0
Micronesia (Fed. States of)	2005	232	...	...	...	...	15.9	...
Micronésie (Etats féd. de)	2006	238	...	...	...	...	15.6	...
	2007	238[5]	...	...	...	...	16.0	...
Mongolia	2005	2 779 578	55.6[1]	12.4	30.4	6.6[4]	64.3	68.2
Mongolie	2006	3 714 953	48.7[1]	11.4	32.3	2.8[4]	65.3	59.7
	2007	4 599 542	49.8[1]	13.0	37.0	3.2[4]	64.3	65.7
Montenegro	2005	1 815	69.9	29.9	18.0	-0.3	43.5	61.1
Monténégro	2006	2 149	77.3	27.0	21.9	3.6	49.4	79.1
	2007	2 808	76.8	27.6	24.3	3.7	46.5	79.0
Montserrat[2]	1984	94	96.4	20.6	23.7	2.7	13.6	56.9
Montserrat[2]	1985	100	96.3	20.3	24.7	1.5	11.7	54.4
	1986	114	89.5	18.7	33.0	2.8	10.1	53.9
Morocco	2005	527 679	57.5	19.4	27.5	1.3	32.3	37.9
Maroc	2006	577 344	57.5	18.5	28.1	1.3	34.2	39.7
	2007	616 254	58.4	18.2	31.2	1.2	35.7	44.9
Mozambique	2005	151 707	83.3[13]	13.0	18.7	-1.0	30.5	44.4
Mozambique	2006	180 242	79.5[13]	12.3	17.7	-0.7	30.4	39.3
	2007	209 661	79.5[13]	11.8	17.2	-0.8	29.4	37.0
Myanmar[2]	2003	7 716 616	89.0[11]	...	11.0	0.0	0.2	0.2
Myanmar[2]	2004	9 078 929	87.7[11]	...	11.8	0.4	0.2	0.1
	2005	12 286 765	86.7[11]	...	12.7	0.5	0.2	0.1
Namibia	2004	36 496	57.6[13]	24.7	25.2	0.5	45.9	52.0
Namibie	2005	39 711	52.6[13]	24.5	24.5	1.3	47.6	51.0
	2006	46 971	49.4[13]	22.5	26.1	0.7	52.2	52.5
Nepal	2005	654 055	82.3[1]	8.7	20.7	6.1	13.4	31.3
Népal	2006	727 089	81.1[1]	9.2	20.4	7.6	13.1	31.3
	2007	820 814	78.6[1]	9.9	21.0	10.9	12.0	32.6
Netherlands	2006	539 929	47.2[1]	25.1	19.7	-0.1[4]	73.0	65.0
Pays-Bas	2007	567 066	46.6[1]	25.1	20.0	-0.3[4]	74.9	66.3
	2008	594 608	46.2[1]	25.1	20.5	0.2[4]	76.9	68.8
Netherlands Antilles	2004	5 555	58.3[1]	18.8	29.4	-2.5	74.8	78.9
Antilles néerlandaises	2005	5 855	58.6[1]	19.1	28.9	-0.4	75.9	82.1
	2006	6 154	59.7[1]	18.7	29.6	0.2	78.1	86.3

19 Gross domestic product by type of expenditure in current prices *(continued)*

Percentage distribution

Dépenses imputées au produit intérieur brut aux prix courants *(suite)*

Répartition en pourcentage

Country or area Pays ou zone	Year Année	GDP in current prices (mil. nat.cur.) PIB aux prix courants (millions monnaie nat.)	% of Gross domestic product – en % du Produit intérieur brut Household final consumption expenditure Consom. finale des ménages	Govt. final consumption expenditure Consom. finale des admin. publiques	Gross fixed capital formation Formation brute de capital fixe	Changes in inventories Variation des stocks	Exports of goods and services Exportations de biens et services	Imports of goods and services Importations de biens et services
New Caledonia	2002	471 996	67.1	28.4	24.7	-0.2	18.1	38.1
Nouvelle-Calédonie	2003	518 545	64.0	27.2	28.9	0.6	20.6	41.3
	2004	565 528	62.4	25.6	25.1	1.5	22.0	36.6
New Zealand	2005	157 855	59.1[1]	18.1	24.1	0.7	27.8	30.1
Nouvelle-Zélande	2006	165 903	59.4[1]	18.6	23.5	-0.1	29.1	30.5
	2007	177 472	58.3[1]	18.8	23.3	0.8	29.0	29.8
Nicaragua	2006	93 007	81.4[1]	19.7	29.2	0.5	31.7	61.1
Nicaragua	2007	104 973	101.2[11]	19.6	30.5	3.2	33.4	68.3
	2008	125 246	104.0[11]	20.5	31.8	1.2	35.9	73.0
Niger	2006	1 906 837	72.9	15.0	22.6	1.0	18.1	29.5
Niger	2007	2 035 386	73.3	15.8	23.3	0.3	18.1	30.8
	2008	2 333 098	72.8	15.8	25.4	0.9	18.5	33.5
Nigeria	2006	18 709 787	60.3	6.9	8.3	^0.0	46.0	21.4
Nigéria	2007	20 874 172	74.5	7.9	9.2	^0.0	36.7	28.3
	2008	25 510 284[10]	69.7	8.2	8.9	^0.0	44.6	31.5
Norway	2006	2 159 573	40.8[1]	19.1	19.6	2.4	46.4	28.4
Norvège	2007	2 277 111	41.4[1]	19.6	21.3	1.8	45.8	29.8
	2008	2 548 322	38.9[1]	19.2	20.8	1.7	48.1	28.8
Occupied Palestinian Terr.	2004	4 198	108.4[1]	25.0	23.4	1.0	11.5	69.3
Terr. palestinien occupé	2005	4 480	103.8[1]	18.6	23.7	0.4	12.5	59.1
	2006	4 383	108.4[1]	19.8	29.9	0.6	12.7	71.4
Oman	2005	11 883	31.5[1]	19.9	23.1	-1.0	58.0	31.6
Oman	2006	14 151	31.1[1]	18.5	24.2	2.3	55.8	31.9
	2007	16 010[5]	35.2[1]	18.2	30.5	0.4	55.9	40.2
Pakistan	2006	7 623 205	75.0	10.8	20.5	1.6	15.2	23.2
Pakistan	2007	8 723 215	75.1	9.1	21.3	1.6	14.1	21.2
	2008	10 478 194	79.7	8.8	20.0	1.6	12.1	22.1
Panama	2005	15 465	62.1	13.2	16.8	1.5	75.5	69.1
Panama	2006	17 137	61.0	12.3	18.3	1.2	76.7	69.5
	2007	19 485	60.1	11.5	22.4	1.1	80.0	75.0
Papua New Guinea	2004	13 459	52.4	16.6	17.0	4.3	67.9	58.3
Papouasie-Nvl-Guinée	2005	15 095	48.0	16.1	16.5	1.0	74.5	56.1
	2006	16 897	47.1	16.8	13.6	2.1	82.8	62.4
Paraguay	2005	46 170 000	73.8	10.9	19.3	0.5	51.2	55.6
Paraguay	2006	52 270 000	73.7	11.2	19.1	0.6	53.7	58.2
	2007	61 511 651	74.1	10.8	17.4	0.7	50.9	53.9
Peru	2006	302 255	61.8	9.5	19.3	0.7	28.5	19.9
Pérou	2007	335 730	61.5	9.1	21.6	...	28.9	22.4
	2008	377 053	63.0	8.8	25.9	...	27.4	26.4
Philippines[2]	2005	5 444 039	69.3[13]	9.7	14.4	0.2	47.6	51.7
Philippines[2]	2006	6 032 835	70.1[13]	9.8	14.0	0.5	47.3	48.0
	2007	6 648 245	69.4[13]	9.7	14.8	0.4	42.6	42.2
Poland	2006	1 060 031	62.5[1]	18.3	19.7	1.4[4]	40.4	42.2
Pologne	2007	1 175 266	60.6[1]	18.0	21.6	2.7[4]	40.8	43.6
	2008	1 271 715	61.3[1]	18.5	22.0	1.9[4]	39.8	43.5
Portugal	2006	155 446	65.4[1]	20.7	21.7	0.5[4]	31.0	39.2
Portugal	2007	163 179	65.0[1]	20.3	21.8	0.4[4]	32.7	40.2
	2008	166 228	66.6[1]	20.7	21.7	0.6[4]	32.9	42.5
Puerto Rico[2]	2005	86 157	57.6[1]	12.0	13.7	0.4	80.2	64.0
Porto Rico[2]	2006	88 902	57.4[1]	11.8	13.1	0.3	79.5	63.3
	2007	93 263	58.3[1]	11.1	11.8	0.4	80.3	61.8
Qatar	2003	85 663	16.5	15.4	30.2	4.6	61.7	28.5
Qatar	2004	115 512	17.5	13.1	30.1	3.3	64.2	28.1
	2005	154 564	18.2	11.5	33.6	1.9	68.3	33.5
Republic of Moldova	2006	44 754	93.9[1]	20.0	28.4	4.4	45.3	91.9
République de Moldova	2007	53 430	93.5[1]	19.9	34.1	4.0	45.6	97.1
	2008[5]	62 840	93.5	20.3	34.1	2.9	40.7	91.5

19 Gross domestic product by type of expenditure in current prices *(continued)*
Percentage distribution

Dépenses imputées au produit intérieur brut aux prix courants *(suite)*
Répartition en pourcentage

Country or area Pays ou zone	Year Année	GDP in current prices (mil. nat.cur.) PIB aux prix courants (millions monnaie nat.)	% of Gross domestic product – en % du Produit intérieur brut Household final consumption expenditure Consom. finale des ménages	Govt. final consumption expenditure Consom. finale des admin. publiques	Gross fixed capital formation Formation brute de capital fixe	Changes in inventories Variation des stocks	Exports of goods and services Exportations de biens et services	Imports of goods and services Importations de biens et services
Réunion [2]	1992	33 787	76.1	28.4	28.6	2.1	3.4	38.6
Réunion [2]	1993	33 711	76.4	28.6	25.7	-0.4	3.1	36.2
	1994	35 266	78.0	28.9	28.1	0.1	2.9	38.0
Romania	2005	288 955	69.5[1]	17.4	23.7	-0.4[4]	33.1	43.2
Roumanie	2006	344 651	68.9[1]	16.7	25.6	0.8[4]	32.3	44.3
	2007[19]	412 762	67.3	15.6	30.4	0.7[4]	29.5	43.5
Russian Federation	2006	26 903 494	48.5[1]	17.1	18.2	3.2[4]	33.7	21.0
Fédération de Russie	2007	33 111 382	48.6[1]	17.2	20.7	3.5[4]	30.3	21.7
	2008	41 668 034	48.6[1]	16.7	21.5	4.0[4]	31.0	21.9
Rwanda [2]	2000	681 455	90.2	8.9	18.0	...	6.3	23.4
Rwanda [2]	2001	732 276	90.4	9.5	17.4	...	8.7	26.1
	2002	784 000	91.5	9.5	17.9	...	7.1	24.6
Saint Kitts and Nevis [2]	2006	1 319	62.4	18.2	37.8	...	47.4	65.8
Saint-Kitts-et-Nevis [2]	2007	1 382	67.1	18.7	40.9	...	42.5	69.3
	2008	1 490	70.3	18.8	40.9	...	40.3	70.3
Saint Lucia [2]	2005	2 374	68.7	18.4	23.3	...	56.8	67.1
Sainte-Lucie [2]	2006	2 520	81.5	16.4	29.2	...	46.7	73.9
	2007	2 592	84.4	15.5	27.2	...	45.8	72.9
Saint Vincent-Grenadines [2]	2005	1 182	68.7	19.8	32.2	...	45.8	66.5
Saint Vincent-Grenadines [2]	2006	1 324	69.4	18.7	35.6	...	43.2	66.9
	2007	1 469	...	19.8	...	...	38.8	73.8
San Marino [2]	2004	1 061	48.4[11]	...	53.6	2.2	186.1	190.3
Saint-Marin [2]	2005	1 106	48.2[11]	...	53.0	2.5	184.0	187.7
	2006	1 171	47.2[11]	...	51.1	2.0	197.0	197.3
Sao Tome and Principe [2]	1986	2 478	76.1	30.3	13.6	0.9	...	50.8
Sao Tomé-et-Principe [2]	1987	3 003	63.1	24.8	15.4	1.1	...	43.1
	1988	4 221	71.8	21.2	15.7	...	...	66.8
Saudi Arabia [2]	2006	1 335 581	26.6	23.3	17.5	1.3	63.2	31.8
Arabie saoudite [2]	2007	1 437 683	28.8	22.4	19.9	1.8	65.0	37.9
	2008	1 753 503	26.0	20.3	17.7	0.8	69.9	34.8
Senegal	2005	4 593 095	77.9[1]	13.0	23.3	1.2	27.0	42.4
Sénégal	2006	4 893 381	78.7[1]	13.9	26.5	-1.6	25.6	43.1
	2007	5 407 749	78.7[1]	14.8	26.9	-0.5	23.2	43.2
Serbia	2005	1 687 832[20]	76.9[1]	18.7	19.0	4.7[4]	28.7[21]	49.4[22]
Serbie	2006	1 980 237[20]	76.4[1]	18.7	20.8	2.9[4]	31.7[21]	52.4[22]
	2007	2 362 850[20]	73.6[1]	19.8	23.4	5.2[4]	30.6[21]	54.4[22]
Serbia and Montenegro	1998[2]	148 370	70.7[1]	28.2	11.6	-1.1[4]	23.4	32.8
Serbie-et-Monténégro	1999	191 099	68.0[1]	28.9	12.6	-0.5[4]	11.2	20.3
	2000	381 661	70.5[1]	28.3	15.4	-6.6[4]	9.2	16.8
Seychelles [2]	1998	3 201	50.0	31.2	34.0	0.6	-15.8[23]	...
Seychelles [2]	1999	3 330	45.3	27.8	41.5	1.8	-16.4[23]	...
	2000	3 424	39.4	27.1	35.7	0.5	-2.6[23]	...
Sierra Leone	2005	4 296 269	96.8[1]	15.2	8.3	2.4	18.9	41.6
Sierra Leone	2006	4 887 545	76.3[1]	15.6	7.4	22.1	19.2	40.6
	2007	5 829 011	74.4[1]	13.0	6.7	22.3	18.9	35.3
Singapore	2006	221 143	39.5	10.6	22.1	-2.0	243.4	213.2
Singapour	2007	251 610	38.6	9.7	24.0	-3.3	230.2	198.5
	2008	257 419	41.0	10.7	28.5	2.4	234.3	215.3
Slovakia	2006	55 082	56.8[1]	19.2	26.5	1.4[4]	84.4	88.3
Slovaquie	2007	61 501	55.9[1]	17.3	26.1	1.7[4]	86.5	87.5
	2008	67 331	56.5[1]	17.2	25.9	2.9[4]	82.6	85.0
Slovenia	2005	28 704	54.4[1]	19.0	25.3	1.8[4]	62.2	62.6
Slovénie	2006	31 008	53.0[1]	18.8	26.3	2.4[4]	66.6	67.1
	2007	34 471	52.2[1]	17.7	27.5	4.0[4]	70.2	71.5
Solomon Islands	2004	2 808	71.9[1]	28.5	10.0	1.4	30.9	42.4
Iles Salomon	2005	3 117	74.0[1]	36.0	12.5	1.3	34.1	54.6
	2006	3 475	74.4[1]	39.2	13.4	1.2	36.1	57.2

19 Gross domestic product by type of expenditure in current prices *(continued)*

Percentage distribution

Dépenses imputées au produit intérieur brut aux prix courants *(suite)*

Répartition en pourcentage

Country or area Pays ou zone	Year Année	GDP in current prices (mil. nat.cur.) PIB aux prix courants (millions monnaie nat.)	% of Gross domestic product – en % du Produit intérieur brut Household final consumption expenditure Consom. finale des ménages	Govt. final consumption expenditure Consom. finale des admin. publiques	Gross fixed capital formation Formation brute de capital fixe	Changes in inventories Variation des stocks	Exports of goods and services Exportations de biens et services	Imports of goods and services Importations de biens et services
Somalia [2] Somalie [2]	1985	87 290	90.5[24]	10.6[25]	8.9[25]	2.9[26]	4.2[14]	17.0[27]
	1986	118 781	89.1[24]	9.7[25]	16.8[25]	1.0[26]	5.8[14]	22.4[27]
	1987	169 608	88.8[24]	11.1[25]	16.8[25]	4.8[26]	5.9[14]	27.2[27]
South Africa Afrique du Sud	2006	1 745 217	62.3	19.8	18.8	1.8	29.7	32.9
	2007	1 999 086	61.4	19.7	21.1	0.8	31.5	34.6
	2008	2 283 777	60.6	20.4	23.2	-0.4	35.4	38.5
Spain Espagne	2006	982 303	57.4[1]	18.1	30.7	0.2	26.4	32.8
	2007	1 050 595	57.3[1]	18.3	31.0	0.2	26.5	33.3
	2008	1 095 163	57.2[1]	19.1	29.4	0.2	26.4	32.2
Sri Lanka Sri Lanka	2005	2 452 782	69.0	13.1	23.4	2.8	32.3	41.3
	2006	2 938 656	67.7	15.4	24.9	2.5	30.1	41.1
	2007	3 578 386	67.2	15.3	24.7	2.5	29.2	39.5
Sudan [2] Soudan [2]	1994	5 522 838	84.1	4.6	9.4	6.8	4.6	9.5
	#1996	10 330 678	81.9	7.5	12.3	9.6	8.0	19.2
	1997	16 769 372	85.6	5.4	12.2	5.7	10.2	19.2
Suriname [2] Suriname [2]	2004	3 453 039[28]	14.9[11]	14.9	93.9[3]	...	68.8	69.8
	2005	4 201 403[28]	...	...	...	...	66.6	82.3
	2006	5 039 810[28]	...	...	...	...	76.0	65.2
Swaziland Swaziland	2005	16 457	73.9	15.2	15.0	...	86.9	91.1
	2006	19 983	75.7	13.9	12.8	...	76.5	78.9
	2007	21 572	74.9	14.1	12.3	...	75.5	76.8
Sweden Suède	2006	2 900 790	47.3[1]	26.3	18.2	0.0[4]	51.5	43.3
	2007	3 063 873	46.7[1]	25.9	19.0	0.7[4]	52.6	44.9
	2008	3 156 881	46.5[1]	26.4	19.5	0.2[4]	54.2	46.8
Switzerland Suisse	2005	463 139	60.2[1]	11.7	21.2	0.4[4]	48.9	42.3
	2006	487 041	58.9[1]	11.2	21.4	0.8[4]	52.4	44.7
	2007	512 142	57.8[1]	10.8	22.0	0.3[4]	55.9	46.7
Syrian Arab Republic [2] Rép. arabe syrienne [2]	2005	1 493 766	66.5	13.8	24.1	-6.4	41.4	39.4
	2006	1 698 483	66.1	11.5	21.4	-5.7[4]	39.7	35.8
	2007	2 019 810	59.7	12.3	20.9	12.7[4]	38.6	37.8
Tajikistan Tadjikistan	2005	7 207	81.1[1]	14.6	11.1	0.5	54.3	72.8
	2006	9 335	80.4[1]	11.1	15.5	0.5	58.2	83.0
	2007	12 804	84.2[1]	8.9	23.2	1.4	51.0	86.3
Thailand [2] Thaïlande [2]	2005	7 092 893	57.2	11.9	28.9	2.5	73.6	74.7
	2006	7 841 297	55.8	11.8	28.0	0.4	73.7	70.2
	2007	8 493 311	53.7	12.2	26.5	0.1	73.2	65.3
TFYR of Macedonia L'ex-R.Y. Macédoine	2005	286 619	77.7[1,29]	18.8	17.0	3.8	45.5	62.8
	2006	310 915	78.2[1,29]	18.5	18.2	3.7	48.1	66.8
	2007	354 322	77.1[1,29]	17.5	20.2	4.0	53.4	72.3
Timor-Leste Timor-Leste	2001	412	51.7	54.6	35.3	3.5	12.3	57.4
	2002	385	53.0	51.8	30.9	3.1	11.3	50.1
	2003	388	51.5	49.7	27.0	2.7	13.9	44.8
Togo [2] Togo [2]	1984	304 800	66.0	14.0	21.2	-1.5	51.9	51.6
	1985	332 500	66.0	14.2	22.9	5.2	48.3	56.7
	1986	363 600	69.0	14.4	23.8	5.3	35.6	48.2
Tonga [2] Tonga [2]	2004	389	102.5	18.5	17.2	0.8	20.8	59.9
	2005	423	108.3	17.9	17.7	0.7	19.9	64.6
	2006	478	103.9	22.8	16.9	0.6	16.3	60.6
Trinidad and Tobago Trinité-et-Tobago	2005	100 386	53.7	11.7	14.3	0.4	61.1	41.2
	2006	122 108	37.1	10.7	12.3	0.5	75.9	36.5
	2007	137 427	47.2	11.1	11.8	1.0	65.5	36.6
Tunisia [2] Tunisie [2]	2005	37 751	62.9	15.3	22.5	-0.2	49.7	50.2
	2006	41 385	62.8	15.0	23.4	1.0	50.8	53.0
	2007	45 638	62.1	14.5	24.0	1.6	55.7	57.9
Turkey [2] Turquie [2]	2005	648 932	71.7	11.8	21.0	-1.0	21.9	25.4
	2006	758 391	70.5	12.3	22.3	-0.2	22.7	27.6
	2007	856 387	70.7	12.2	21.5	0.7	21.9	27.0

19 Gross domestic product by type of expenditure in current prices *(continued)*
Percentage distribution

Dépenses imputées au produit intérieur brut aux prix courants *(suite)*
Répartition en pourcentage

Country or area Pays ou zone	Year Année	GDP in current prices (mil. nat.cur.) PIB aux prix courants (millions monnaie nat.)	% of Gross domestic product – en % du Produit intérieur brut Household final consumption expenditure Consom. finale des ménages	Govt. final consumption expenditure Consom. finale des admin. publiques	Gross fixed capital formation Formation brute de capital fixe	Changes in inventories Variation des stocks	Exports of goods and services Exportations de biens et services	Imports of goods and services Importations de biens et services
Turkmenistan Turkménistan	2000	25 648 000	70.8[1]	...	...	...	...	...
	2001	35 118 973	70.8[1]	...	...	...	...	...
	2002	45 239 913	70.8[1]	...	...	...	...	...
Turks and Caicos Islands Iles Turques et Caïques	2005	579	50.3	17.2	38.7[3]	...	56.6	62.7
	2006	722	53.1	19.2	46.7[3]	...	62.8	81.9
	2007	829	55.3	17.3	47.4[3]	...	63.1	83.0
Tuvalu[2] Tuvalu[2]	1996	16[30]	...	...	67.6[3]	...	...	...
	1997	18[30]	...	...	51.2[3]	...	...	...
	1998	21[30]	...	...	54.9[3]	...	...	...
Uganda[2] Ouganda[2]	2005	17 877 944	74.9	13.7	21.3	0.2	15.2	25.3
	2006	20 166 191	80.0	13.4	20.5	0.3	14.9	29.0
	2007	23 391 981	80.4	11.9	22.4	0.3	16.1	31.1
Ukraine Ukraine	2006	544 153	59.6[1]	18.4	24.6	0.2[4]	46.6	49.5
	2007	720 731	59.6[1]	17.9	27.5	0.7[4]	44.8	50.6
	2008[5]	949 864	61.5	17.7	27.2	1.7[4]	46.8	54.9
United Arab Emirates[2] Emirats arabes unis[2]	2005	513 089	47.2	10.0	18.3	1.1	83.9	60.6
	2006	624 623[5]	43.5	9.3	19.4	1.1	85.6	58.8
	2007	729 732[5]	43.8	10.4	20.3	1.0	91.0	66.7
United Kingdom Royaume-Uni	2006	1 321 860	64.1[1]	21.6	17.2	0.3[4]	28.5	31.7
	2007	1 400 526	63.9[1]	21.1	17.7	0.6[4]	26.4	29.8
	2008	1 442 921	64.4[1]	21.9	16.7	0.1[4]	28.9	32.0
United Rep. of Tanzania[31] Rép.-Unie de Tanzanie[31]	2005	15 965 296	66.3	17.6	24.7	0.4	20.8	29.7
	2006	17 941 268	68.0	17.5	27.2	0.4	22.6	35.7
	2007	20 948 403	67.9	19.3	29.2	0.4	24.2	41.1
United States Etats-Unis	2005	12 364 100	70.3[1]	15.9	19.2	0.3	10.6	16.4
	2006	13 116 500	70.2[1]	15.9	19.3	0.4	11.3	17.1
	2007	13 741 600	70.7[1]	16.1	18.4	^0.0	12.1	17.2
Uruguay Uruguay	2006	482 016	70.3[13]	11.2	18.0	2.3	29.1	30.9
	2007	569 261[5]	68.8[13]	11.2	17.3	3.6	28.0	28.9
	2008	674 278[5]	69.4[13]	11.7	18.7	4.2	28.3	32.3
Uzbekistan Ouzbékistan	1999	2 128 660	62.1[1]	20.6	27.2	-10.1	0.1[23]	...
	2000	3 255 600	61.9[1]	18.7	24.0	-4.4	-0.2[23]	...
	2001	4 868 400	61.6[1]	18.4	25.7	-5.5	-0.3[23]	...
Vanuatu[2] Vanuatu[2]	2005	40 387	61.2	18.6	20.8	0.6	45.3	60.4
	2006	45 944	57.5	18.6	24.0	1.3	44.1	58.0
	2007	51 980	56.7	18.0	24.2	1.6	42.3	54.7
Venezuela (Boliv. Rep. of) Venezuela (Rép. boliv. du)	2004	212 683 082	49.2[1]	12.0	18.3	3.5[4]	36.2	19.2
	2005	304 086 815	46.8[1]	11.1	20.3	2.7[4]	39.7	20.5
	2006	393 926 240	47.0[1]	11.7	22.3	4.6[4]	36.5	22.1
Viet Nam Viet Nam	2006	974 266 206	63.3	6.0	33.4	3.5	-4.6[23]	...
	2007	1 143 715 362	64.8	6.1	38.3	4.9	-15.9[23]	...
	2008	1 477 716 636	67.3	6.2	36.0	5.1	-16.5[23]	...
Yemen Yémen	2005	3 391 262	60.8[1]	11.6	17.9	5.0	38.7	33.9
	2006	4 196 790	56.5[1]	13.0	17.2	12.9	36.9	36.6
	2007	4 923 687	53.7[1]	12.7	18.2	21.7	31.4	37.7
Zambia[2] Zambie[2]	2006	39 223 128	58.9	20.0	24.1	1.3	37.7	42.0
	2007	46 357 340	56.8	19.6	20.6	1.3	40.8	39.1
	2008	55 428 263	59.3	21.9	19.4	1.4	35.0	37.0
Zimbabwe Zimbabwe	2005	205 078 208	93.2[1]	4.5	7.1	0.2	23.3	28.2
	2006	1 030 061 188	97.0[1]	1.8	9.5	-1.7	35.3	42.0
	2007	15 767 745 314	89.7[1]	4.6	2.9	4.5	1.2	2.9

Source:
United Nations Statistics Division, New York, national accounts database, last accessed September 2010.

Source:
Organisation des Nations Unies, Division de statistique, New York, la base de données sur les comptes nationaux, dernier accès septembre 2010.

19 Gross domestic product by type of expenditure in current prices *(continued)*

Percentage distribution

Dépenses imputées au produit intérieur brut aux prix courants *(suite)*

Répartition en pourcentage

Data for most countries have been compiled in accordance with the concepts and definitions of the System of National Accounts 1993 (1993 SNA). Countries that follow the 1968 SNA are footnoted accordingly.

[+] Note: The national accounts data relate to the fiscal year used in each country, unless indicated otherwise. Countries whose reference periods coincide with the calendar year ending 31 December are not listed below.

Year beginning 21 March: Afghanistan, Iran (Islamic Republic).
Year beginning 1 April: Bermuda, India, Myanmar, New Zealand, Nigeria.
Year beginning 1 July: Australia, Bhutan, Cameroon, Gambia, Nicaragua, Pakistan, Puerto Rico, Saudi Arabia, Sierra Leone, Sudan, United Republic of Tanzania.
Year ending 30 June: Bangladesh, Botswana, Egypt, Swaziland, Tonga.
Year ending 7 July: Nepal.
Year ending 30 July: Ethiopia.
Year ending 30 September: Haiti.

Les données pour la majorité des pays sont compilées selon les concepts et définitions du Système de comptabilité nationale, 1993 (SCN93). Seuls les pays qui suivent toujours le SCN68 seront donc signalés par une note.

[+] Note : Sauf indication contraire, les données sur les comptes nationaux concernent l'exercice budgétaire utilisé dans chaque pays. Les pays ou territoires dont la période de référence coïncide avec l'année civile se terminant le 31 décembre ne sont pas répertoriés ci-dessous.

Exercice commençant le 21 mars: Afghanistan, Iran (République islamique d').
Exercice commençant le 1er avril: Bermudes, Inde, Myanmar, Nigéria, Nouvelle-Zélande.
Exercice commençant le 1er juillet: Arabie saoudite, Australie, Bhoutan, Cameroun, Gambie, Nicaragua, Pakistan, Porto Rico, Sierra Leone, Soudan, Rép.-Unie de Tanzanie.
Exercice se terminant le 30 juin: Bangladesh, Botswana, Égypte, Swaziland, Tonga.
Exercice se terminant le 7 juillet: Népal.
Exercice se terminant le 30 juillet: Éthiopie.
Exercice se terminant le 30 septembre: Haïti.

1 Including Final consumption expenditure of NPISH.
2 Data compiled in accordance with the System of National Accounts 1968 (1968 SNA).
3 Gross capital formation.
4 Including acquisitions less disposals of valuables.
5 Preliminary data.
6 Including net errors and omissions.
7 Discrepancy between components and total as one or more components has not been revised.
8 Refers to Total Individual Consumption.
9 Excludes individual consumption of general government.
10 Provisional data.
11 Final consumption expenditure.
12 For statistical purposes, the data for China do not include those for the Hong Kong Special Administrative Region (Hong Kong SAR), Macao Special Administrative Region (Macao SAR) and Taiwan Province of China.
13 Including "Non-profit institutions serving households" (NPISHs) final consumption expenditure.
14 Exports of goods only.
15 Imports of goods only.
16 Includes investment of public enterprises
17 Data have not been revised.
18 Forecast.
19 Semi-final data.
20 As from 1999: excluding Kosovo and Metohia.
21 Includes exports of goods and services to Montenegro.
22 Includes imports of goods and services from Montenegro.
23 Exports less imports.
24 Obtained as a residual.
25 Including the value of technical assistance from abroad.
26 Including livestock only.
27 Refers to imports of goods and non-factor services.
28 Excluding the informal sector.
29 Includes direct purchases in domestic market by non-residents.
30 GDP at market prices.
31 Tanganyika only.

1 Y compris les dépenses de consommation finale des NPISH.
2 Données compilées selon le Système de comptabilité nationale de 1968 (SCN 1968).
3 Formation brute de capital.
4 Y compris les acquisitions moins cessions d'objets de valeur.
5 Données préliminaires.
6 Y compris le montant net des erreurs et omissions.
7 Écart entre rubriques et total car une ou plusieurs rubriques n'ont pas été révisées.
8 Consommation individuelle totale.
9 Non compris la consommation individuelle de l'administrations publique.
10 Données provisoires.
11 Dépenses de consommation finale.
12 Pour la présentation des statistiques, les données pour la Chine ne comprennent pas la Région Administrative Spéciale de Hong Kong (Hong Kong RAS), la Région Administrative Spéciale de Macao (Macao RAS) et la province de Taiwan.
13 Y compris la consommation finale des institutions sans but lucratif au service des ménages.
14 Exportations de biens uniquement.
15 Importations de biens uniquement.
16 Y compris les investissements des entreprises publiques.
17 Les données n'ont pas été révisées.
18 Prévision.
19 Données demi-finales.
20 A partir de 1999: non compris Kosovo et Metohia.
21 Y compris exportations de biens et services à Monténégro.
22 Y compris importations de biens et services de Monténégro.
23 Exportations moins importations.
24 Obtenu comme valeur résiduelle.
25 Y compris la valeur de l'assistance technique étrangère.
26 Ne comprend que le bétail.
27 Concerne les importations de biens et de services autres que les services des facteurs.
28 Non compris le secteur informel.
29 Y compris les achats directs effectués sur le marché intérieur par les ménages non résidents.
30 PIB aux prix du marché.
31 Tanganyika seulement.

20 Value added by industries at current prices

Percentage distribution

Valeur ajoutée par branche d'activité aux prix courants

Répartition en pourcentage

Country or area Pays ou zone	Year Année	Value added, gross (mil. nat.cur) Valeur ajoutée, brute (mil. mon. nat.)	% of Value added – % de la valeur ajoutée Agriculture, hunting, forestry and fishing Agriculture, chasse, sylviculture et pêche	Mining and quarrying Activités extractives	Manu-facturing Activités de fabri-cation	Electricity, gas and water supply Electricité, gaz et eau	Construc-tion Construc-tion	Wholesale, retail trade, restaurants and hotels Commerce, restaurants, hôtels	Transport, storage & commu-nication Transports, entrepôts, communi-cations	Other activities Autres activités
Afghanistan Afghanistan	2006	396 094	38.8	0.3	17.2	0.1	9.0	10.3	7.7	13.2[1]
	2007	491 363	37.5	0.4	15.8	0.1	8.7	10.6	9.1	14.5[1]
	2008	524 331	31.6	0.5	16.2	0.1	9.5	11.4	9.9	17.1[1]
Albania Albanie	2005	737 636[2]	20.6	0.8	6.6	3.3	13.8	21.6	9.4	24.1
	2006	803 976[2]	19.5	0.7	7.5	2.8	14.2	20.8	9.2	25.4
	2007	883 469[2]	18.5	1.4	7.5	0.2	14.0	22.0	9.9	26.6
Algeria[3] Algérie[3]	2001	4 075 738	10.1	36.5	6.3	1.3	7.9	12.9	8.3	16.8
	2002	4 284 371	9.7	35.5	6.2	1.3	8.6	13.2	8.5	16.9
	2003	4 991 489	10.2	38.5	5.6	1.2	8.0	12.3	8.3	15.9
Andorra[3] Andorre[3]	2005	1 819	0.6	...	3.0	0.8	12.2	31.0	3.7	48.6
	2006	1 983	0.6	...	3.0	0.8	12.3	29.7	3.6	50.1
	2007	2 094	0.6	...	3.0	0.7	11.6	29.0	3.6	51.5
Angola[3] Angola[3]	1988	236 682	16.0	27.1	8.3	0.2	4.1	11.7	3.5	29.1[4,5]
	1989	276 075	19.3	29.7	6.2	0.2	3.3	11.4	3.0	27.1[4,5]
	1990	305 831	18.0	32.9	5.0	0.1	2.9	10.7	3.2	27.0[4,5]
Anguilla[3] Anguilla[3]	2004	340[6]	2.3	1.4	0.9	4.5	12.7	31.3	14.4	32.5[7]
	2005	393[6]	2.0	1.4	2.0	4.9	13.0	31.9	14.7	30.0[7]
	2006	465[6]	1.8	1.8	1.9	4.5	16.7	31.7	12.9	28.7[7]
Antigua and Barbuda[3] Antigua-et-Barbuda[3]	1986	567[6]	4.3	1.7	3.8	3.5	8.9	23.6	15.6	38.5
	1987	649[6]	4.5	2.2	3.5	3.5	11.3	24.1	15.6	35.3
	1988	776[6]	4.1	2.2	3.1	4.0	12.7	23.7	14.3	35.9
Argentina Argentine	2005	492 825[2,8]	9.4	5.8	23.2	1.7	4.9	14.3	9.0	31.7
	2006	604 792[2,8]	8.4	6.0	22.3	1.6	5.8	14.1	8.9	33.0
	2007	746 168[2,8]	9.4	4.8	21.3	1.5	6.2	14.2	8.6	34.0
Armenia Arménie	2006	2 458 817[9]	20.2	2.8	11.7	4.1	25.6	12.6	6.8	16.2
	2007	2 865 145[9]	19.8	2.4	10.3	3.8	27.1	12.3	7.0	17.3
	2008	3 289 779[9]	17.4	1.9	9.2	3.4	30.0	12.6	6.8	18.7
Aruba Aruba	2004	3 850	0.4[10]	...	3.9[11]	8.2[12]	6.5	21.7	8.5	50.8[7,13]
	2005	4 019	0.4[10]	...	3.9[11]	9.1[12]	6.7	21.5	8.5	49.9[7,13]
	2006	4 170	0.4[10]	...	3.9[11]	9.5[12]	7.5	19.8	8.3	50.6[7,13]
Australia Australie	2005	887 959	3.1	7.3	11.2	2.5	7.0	13.5	7.6	47.8[7]
	2006	962 501	2.4	8.5	10.7	2.3	7.5	12.9	7.6	48.1[7]
	2007	1 039 829	2.5	8.3	10.5	2.4	7.9	12.7	7.4	48.2[7]
Austria Autriche	2005	220 284	1.6	0.5	19.5	2.4	7.1	17.4	6.4	45.2
	2006	232 904	1.7	0.5	20.1	2.7	6.9	17.0	6.3	44.8
	2007	245 200	1.8	0.5	20.1	2.9	7.1	16.8	6.3	44.5
Azerbaijan Azerbaïdjan	2006	17 722[14]	7.5	53.8	6.1	0.7	8.2	6.2	7.0	11.6
	2007	26 490[14]	7.0	57.5	5.3	0.9	7.1	6.0	7.9	9.4
	2008	35 326[14]	6.3	56.5	4.5	0.8	8.2	6.5	7.5	10.5
Bahamas Bahamas	2004	5 876[9]	1.7	1.0	4.7	3.1	7.8	22.3	9.1	50.2
	2005	6 410[9]	1.5	0.9	4.5	3.2	9.3	22.4	9.4	48.8
	2006	6 714[9]	1.6	0.8	4.5	3.5	11.0	22.3	8.9	47.5
Bahrain[3] Bahreïn[3]	2006	5 892[14,15]	0.3	26.7	14.0	0.9	4.8	11.8	6.3	46.8[16]
	2007	6 866[14,15]	0.4	25.5	15.5	1.1	5.2	11.3	6.0	46.2[16]
	2008	8 147[14,15]	0.3	29.5	15.5	1.0	5.3	10.0	6.0	42.5[16]
Bangladesh Bangladesh	2006	4 004 536	19.6	1.2	17.2	1.3	8.2	14.9	10.8	26.7
	2007	4 568 143	19.2	1.2	17.8	1.2	8.2	15.2	10.7	26.5
	2008	5 237 639	19.1	1.2	18.0	1.1	8.3	15.7	10.5	26.2
Barbados[3] Barbade[3]	2005	4 940[6]	3.6	0.9	6.5	3.5	6.7	29.6	6.6	43.5
	2006	5 264[6,17]	3.4	1.0	6.8	3.7	6.8	28.6	6.3	52.1
	2007	5 574[6]	2.8	0.8	6.2	3.6	6.3	30.0	6.2	44.1
Belarus Bélarus	2006	69 637 780[9]	9.6	...	32.8	...	9.1	11.9	10.7	25.9
	2007	84 902 584[9]	9.2	...	31.8	...	9.8	12.3	10.7	26.3
	2008	112 327 320[9]	10.2	...	32.9	...	10.8	12.6	9.3	24.2
Belgium Belgique	2005	268 862	0.8	0.1	17.1	2.0	4.8	14.6	8.4	52.0
	2006	283 060	0.8	0.1	16.9	2.2	5.1	14.4	8.4	52.1
	2007	297 900	0.8	0.1	16.4	2.1	5.3	14.7	8.2	52.3

20 Value added by industries at current prices *(continued)*
Percentage distribution

Valeur ajoutée par branche d'activité aux prix courants *(suite)*
Répartition en pourcentage

Country or area Pays ou zone	Year Année	Value added, gross (mil. nat.cur) Valeur ajoutée, brute (mil. mon. nat.)	% of Value added – % de la valeur ajoutée Agriculture, hunting, forestry and fishing Agriculture, chasse, sylviculture et pêche	Mining and quarrying Activités extractives	Manufacturing Activités de fabrication	Electricity, gas and water supply Electricité, gaz et eau	Construction Construction	Wholesale, retail trade, restaurants and hotels Commerce, restaurants, hôtels	Transport, storage & communication Transports, entrepôts, communications	Other activities Autres activités
Belize	2004	1 822[14]	16.5	0.5	9.1	3.6	4.5	22.1	12.4	36.6
Belize	2005	1 928[14]	15.3	0.5	9.1	3.6	4.3	22.4	12.8	37.5
	2006	2 103[14]	14.0	0.5	12.3	4.2	4.1	21.8	12.0	36.4
Benin[3]	2006	2 256 825[2]	35.4	0.3	8.2	1.3	4.5	18.3	8.6	23.5
Bénin[3]	2007	2 419 751[2]	34.3	0.3	8.2	1.2	4.5	18.5	9.2	23.8
	2008	2 729 626[2]	35.4	0.3	7.8	1.1	4.6	19.0	9.1	22.8
Bermuda	2005	4 979[2]	0.8	...	1.6	1.6	6.5[10]	13.1	5.8	70.7
Bermudes	2006	5 593[2]	0.8	...	1.6	1.6	5.5[10]	12.5	5.2	72.8
	2007	6 149[2]	0.7	...	1.4	1.5	5.2[10]	12.0	5.2	73.9
Bhutan	2005	34 931[14]	23.6	1.6	7.3	10.4	17.8	6.6	11.1	21.5
Bhoutan	2006	38 884[14]	22.8	2.3	7.2	13.0	15.5	6.9	10.5	21.8
	2007	49 869[14]	19.2	1.8	6.6	24.2	13.9	6.0	9.3	18.9
Bolivia (Plur. State of)[3]	2006	72 318[14]	13.9	14.7	14.4	2.9	3.0	11.4	12.9	30.4
Bolivie (État plur. de)[3]	2007	80 081[14]	12.9	15.8	14.7	2.8	3.1	11.8	12.1	30.8
	2008	93 570[14]	13.5	18.4	14.4	2.6	3.0	12.0	10.8	29.4
Bosnia and Herzegovina	2005	14 344	10.3	2.3	10.9	6.1	5.0	18.3	9.2	37.9[18]
Bosnie-Herzégovine	2006	15 904	10.2	2.3	11.6	5.3	5.1	19.5	8.8	37.3[18]
	2007	18 038	9.5	2.4	12.9	4.4	5.6	19.4	8.7	37.1
Botswana	2006	55 521[6,9]	1.9	41.0	3.4	2.5	4.4	11.0	3.9	31.9[19,20]
Botswana	2007	68 541[6,9]	1.9	43.9	3.6	2.9	4.2	10.8	3.8	29.1[19,20]
	2008	76 817[6,9]	1.9	40.7	3.8	2.8	4.4	11.8	4.0	30.6[19,20]
Brazil	2004	1 666 258	6.9	1.9	19.2	3.9	5.1	18.1	8.6	36.3
Brésil	2005	1 842 253	5.7	2.5	18.1	3.8	4.9	18.4	8.9	37.7
	2006	2 034 734	5.5	2.9	17.4	3.8	4.7	19.1	8.6	38.0
British Virgin Islands	2005	940[2]	1.0	0.0	2.9	2.1	6.4	30.0	12.3	45.3
Iles Vierges britanniques	2006	1 057[2]	0.9	0.0	2.6	2.2	4.8	30.2	12.5	47.0
	2007	1 150[2]	0.8	0.0	2.3	2.2	6.9	29.6	12.2	46.1
Brunei Darussalam[21]	2005	15 864	0.9	55.9	12.3	0.7	2.6	3.3	2.9	21.4
Brunéi Darussalam[21]	2006	18 226	0.7	59.1	10.6	0.6	3.0	3.0	2.8	20.3
	2007	18 513	0.7	57.2	10.4	0.6	2.9	3.3	2.8	22.2
Bulgaria	2005	35 220	9.4	1.7	17.8	4.5	5.4	11.1	13.2	36.9
Bulgarie	2006	40 350	8.5	2.9	17.2	4.1	6.8	12.1	11.7	36.7
	2007	46 401	6.2	2.6	16.6	4.9	8.2	12.7	11.7	37.1
Burkina Faso	2006	2 783 982[9]	34.7	0.5	13.0	1.3	5.7	11.8	4.7	28.2
Burkina Faso	2007	2 973 044[9]	31.7	0.8	13.7	1.4	7.6	12.1	5.0	27.7
	2008	3 280 583[9]	31.4	1.3	13.6	1.4	7.6	9.6	8.2	27.0
Burundi[3]	1988	149 067	48.9	1.0[22]	16.5	...	2.9	12.9	2.6	15.2[7]
Burundi[3]	1989	175 627	47.0	1.2[22]	18.5	...	3.3	10.8	3.3	16.0[7]
	1990	192 050	52.4	0.8[22]	16.8	...	3.4	4.9	3.1	18.5[7]
Cambodia	2005	24 409 686[2]	32.4	0.4	18.8	0.5	6.7	14.3	7.8	19.2[23]
Cambodge	2006	28 344 453[2]	31.7	0.4	19.6	0.6	7.0	14.0	7.5	19.3[23]
	2007	32 637 867[2]	31.9	0.4	18.6	0.6	7.2	14.2	7.4	19.7[23]
Cameroon	2005	8 145 956[9]	20.4	9.0	18.7	1.0	3.1	22.9	5.9	19.0
Cameroun	2006	8 700 817[9]	20.9	11.0	17.8	1.1	3.1	22.1	6.2	17.8
	2007	9 157 142[9]	22.6	10.3	15.5	1.1	3.2	22.9	6.5	18.1
Canada	2002	1 068 767	2.2	5.0	17.6	2.9	5.4	13.8	7.2	45.9
Canada	2003	1 128 801	2.1	6.3	16.5	3.0	5.4	13.8	7.1	45.7
	2004	1 200 991	2.2	7.1	16.2	2.8	5.6	13.8	7.1	45.2
Cape Verde[3]	2004	73 094[14]	11.1	2.5	4.2	1.6	8.6	25.0	23.4	27.7[7,25]
Cap-Vert[3]	2005	79 118[14]	10.2	...	...	...	10.0	2.7[24]	22.0	25.5[25]
	2006	93 656[14]	9.4	...	...	...	10.0	3.3[24]	23.4	25.7[25]
Cayman Islands[3]	1989	473	0.4	0.6	1.9	3.2	11.0	24.5	11.0	47.6[26]
Iles Caïmanes[3]	1990	580	0.3	0.3	1.6	3.1	9.7	24.5	10.9	49.8[26]
	1991	605	0.3	0.3	1.5	3.1	9.1	22.8	10.7	52.1[26]
Central African Rep.[3]	1983	243 350	40.8	2.5	7.8[27]	0.5	2.1	21.2	4.2	20.8[28]
Rép. centrafricaine[3]	1984	268 725	40.7	2.8	8.1[27]	0.9	2.7	21.7	4.3	18.8[28]
	1985	308 549	42.4	2.5	7.5[27]	0.8	2.6	22.0	4.2	17.9[28]
Chad	2006	3 224 787	21.1	47.0	5.9	0.3	1.0	11.0	1.7	12.0
Tchad	2007	3 283 685	20.4	45.6	5.8	0.4	1.1	11.6	1.7	13.5
	2008	3 658 798	20.2	46.6	5.6	0.3	1.2	11.0	1.6	13.3

20 Value added by industries at current prices *(continued)*

Percentage distribution

Valeur ajoutée par branche d'activité aux prix courants *(suite)*

Répartition en pourcentage

Country or area Pays ou zone	Year Année	Value added, gross (mil. nat.cur) Valeur ajoutée, brute (mil. mon. nat.)	% of Value added – % de la valeur ajoutée							
			Agriculture, hunting, forestry and fishing Agriculture, chasse, sylviculture et pêche	Mining and quarrying Activités extractives	Manu-facturing Activités de fabri-cation	Electricity, gas and water supply Electricité, gaz et eau	Construc-tion Construc-tion	Wholesale, retail trade, restaurants and hotels Commerce, restaurants, hôtels	Transport, storage & commu-nication Transports, entrepôts, communi-cations	Other activities Autres activités
Chile Chili	2006	73 864 077[2,29]	4.0	23.5	14.2	3.0	6.5	8.7	7.8	32.4
	2007	81 [illegible]42 306[2,29]	3.7	23.9	13.9	2.7	6.9	8.6	7.3	33.1
	2008	83 849 975[2,29]	3.9	18.6	13.5	3.6	8.1	9.3	7.6	35.4
China[30] Chine[30]	2005	18 321 740[21]	12.2	5.6	32.8	3.7	5.5	7.4	5.9	9.5
	2006	21 192 350[21]	11.3	5.7	...	...	5.6	...	5.9	...
	2007	24 952 990[21]	11.3	43.0[31]	...	...	5.6	...	5.9	...
China, Hong Kong SAR Chine, Hong Kong RAS	2005	1 332 830[6]	0.1[32]	^0.0	3.4	3.0	2.9	29.0[33]	10.1	51.5[34,35]
	2006	1 423 299[6]	0.1[32]	^0.0	3.2	2.8	2.7	27.9[33]	9.6	53.6[34,35]
	2007	1 549 153[6]	0.1[32]	^0.0	2.5	2.5	2.6	27.0[33]	8.9	56.3[34]
China, Macao SAR Chine, Macao RAS	2005	75 145[2]	...	^0.0	4.1	1.8	8.4	11.5	4.5	69.7
	2006	94 618[2]	...	^0.0	3.7	1.6	12.7	10.9	4.0	67.0
	2007	121 350[2]	...	^0.0	2.7	1.0	13.3	11.3	3.6	68.1
Colombia Colombie	2005	309 644 778	9.6	7.2	17.0	3.6	6.3	13.5	7.3	35.6
	2006	355 062 370	9.3	7.6	17.2	3.4	7.2	13.5	7.3	34.6
	2007	395 628 923	8.9	7.0	17.6	3.3	7.5	13.4	7.4	34.9
Comoros[3] Comores[3]	1989	64 731	40.0	...	3.9	0.8	3.4	25.1	3.9	22.8
	1990	67 992	40.4	...	4.1	0.9	3.1	25.1	4.1	22.3
	1991	71 113	40.8	...	4.2	0.9	2.7	25.1	4.2	22.1
Congo[3] Congo[3]	1987	678 106	12.2	22.9	8.8	1.6	3.2	15.1	10.5	25.8
	1988	643 830	14.2	17.1	8.8	2.0	2.7	16.7	11.3	27.2
	1989	757 088	13.3	28.6	7.2	1.9	1.8	14.7	9.3	23.3
Cook Islands[3] Iles Cook[3]	2005	267[2,15]	12.5	...	3.6	1.8	2.9	39.5	13.4	26.6
	2006	284[2,15]	11.3	...	3.2	2.0	3.4	39.4	12.9	27.9
	2007	293[2,15]	11.9	...	3.6	2.1	3.7	37.9	12.5	28.3
Costa Rica Costa Rica	2005	9 027 072[9]	8.6	0.2	20.7	2.6	4.3	18.8	9.3	35.5[7]
	2006	10 855 048[9]	8.5	0.2	20.7	2.2	4.7	18.7	9.6	35.4[7]
	2007	12 709 110[9]	8.0	0.2	20.5	1.9	5.4	18.9	9.5	35.6[7]
Côte d'Ivoire[3] Côte d'Ivoire[3]	1998	6 984 000	25.6	0.6	21.9	1.6	2.3	20.4	6.0	21.3
	1999	7 449 000	23.2	0.3	22.2	2.0	3.5	21.9	5.7	21.1
	2000	7 323 000	24.8	0.3	22.4	1.6	2.9	19.0	5.5	23.2
Croatia Croatie	2003	191 455	6.8	0.6	18.2	2.5	6.6	18.3	8.8	38.1
	2004	209 382	7.2	0.7	18.2	2.8	7.1	16.9	9.3	37.7
	2005	226 184	6.5	0.8	17.5	2.7	7.4	17.2	9.1	38.9
Cuba Cuba	2005	34 906	5.6	1.6	9.5	1.5	6.8	14.1	10.4	50.5[20]
	2006	43 333	4.5	1.7	9.4	1.5	7.6	18.8	9.2	47.3[20]
	2007	48 072	5.0	2.3	10.1	1.5	6.6	16.9	9.2	48.5[20]
Cyprus Chypre	2005	12 107	2.8	0.4	8.8	2.1	8.2	19.8	8.1	49.8
	2006	12 934	2.4	0.4	7.9	2.1	8.6	19.9	7.7	51.1
	2007	13 818	2.2	0.4	7.5	2.0	9.1	19.9	7.4	51.6
Czech Republic République tchèque	2005	2 675 260	3.0	1.4	26.3	3.9	6.3	14.8	10.0	34.3
	2006	2 900 333	2.6	1.3	26.3	4.4	6.2	14.9	10.5	33.9
	2007	3 181 800	2.4	1.1	27.4	4.1	6.3	14.4	10.3	34.1
Denmark Danemark	2005	1 308 856	1.4	3.9	14.2	2.1	5.4	13.4	8.5	51.1
	2006	1 376 441	1.4	4.1	14.6	2.0	5.9	13.4	7.8	50.7
	2007	1 427 143	1.2	3.7	15.0	1.7	6.1	13.5	7.8	51.1
Djibouti[3] Djibouti[3]	1996	76 435	3.5[36]	0.2	2.8	6.8[37]	5.7	15.9	21.7	43.4
	1997	75 964	3.6[36]	0.2	2.8	6.6[37]	6.0	16.1	23.1	41.6
	1998	78 263	3.6[36]	0.2	2.7	5.3[37]	6.4	16.4	26.0	39.4
Dominica[3] Dominique[3]	2004	611[6,38]	18.7	0.8	8.3	6.4	8.3	15.5	13.4	37.0
	2005	641[6,38]	18.0	0.9	8.1	6.4	8.7	15.9	13.3	37.1
	2006	671[6,38]	17.6	0.9	7.9	5.7	9.2	16.4	13.8	37.0
Dominican Republic Rép. dominicaine	2006	1 135 019[2]	6.8	0.5	21.4	2.5	6.8	21.4	10.6	29.9
	2007	1 272 793[2]	6.4	0.7	20.6	2.4	7.0	21.5	11.0	30.5
	2008	1 509 374[2]	6.1	0.4	22.4	2.3	6.1	20.4	11.8	30.5
Ecuador Equateur	2005	35 067[2]	7.0	21.3[39]	3.5	1.5	8.8	14.3	11.8	31.7
	2006	39 724[2]	7.0	23.7[39]	2.1	1.4	9.6	13.8	11.0	31.5
	2007	43 638[2]	6.9	24.5[39]	2.0	1.4	9.5	13.8	10.4	31.4
Egypt Egypte	2004	534 427[2]	14.6	11.9	17.6	1.8	3.6	13.6	8.8	28.2
	2005	600 641[2]	14.9	12.5	16.8	1.5	3.8	13.4	10.2	26.9
	2006	675 373[2]	14.6	13.9	16.5	1.9	3.8	13.4	9.2	26.6

20 Value added by industries at current prices *(continued)*

Percentage distribution

Valeur ajoutée par branche d'activité aux prix courants *(suite)*

Répartition en pourcentage

Country or area Pays ou zone	Year Année	Value added, gross (mil. nat.cur) Valeur ajoutée, brute (mil. mon. nat.)	% of Value added – % de la valeur ajoutée Agriculture, hunting, forestry and fishing Agriculture, chasse, sylviculture et pêche	Mining and quarrying Activités extractives	Manu-facturing Activités de fabri-cation	Electricity, gas and water supply Electricité, gaz et eau	Construc-tion Construc-tion	Wholesale, retail trade, restaurants and hotels Commerce, restaurants, hôtels	Transport, storage & commu-nication Transports, entrepôts, communi-cations	Other activities Autres activités
El Salvador [3] El Salvador [3]	2005	16 432[2,15]	10.1	0.4	22.0	1.8	4.3	20.8	9.5	31.2[18]
	2006	17 853[2,15]	10.5	0.4	21.5	2.0	4.4	20.7	9.7	30.9[18]
	2007	19 545[2,15]	11.7	0.4	21.2	1.9	4.2	20.8	9.6	30.3[18]
Equatorial Guinea [3] Guinée équatoriale [3]	1989	40 948	56.1	...	1.3	3.1	3.7	8.8	2.0	25.0
	1990	42 765	53.6	...	1.3	3.4	3.8	7.6	2.2	28.0
	1991	43 932	53.1	...	1.4	3.1	3.0	7.6	1.9	30.0
Estonia Estonie	2005	152 718	3.6	1.0	17.2	3.4	7.5	16.2	11.7	39.5
	2006	179 749	3.1	1.0	17.2	3.1	8.5	16.8	11.5	38.8
	2007	207 723	2.8	1.0	17.6	2.7	9.1	16.1	10.9	39.9
Ethiopia Ethiopie	2006	122 950[2]	47.5	0.5	4.5	1.9	5.6	14.8	5.6	19.5
	2007	160 849[2]	47.2	0.5	4.4	1.9	5.8	15.8	4.9	19.4
	2008	230 429[2]	50.8	0.4	3.9	1.5	5.2	15.1	4.1	18.9
Fiji Fidji	2005	4 401[9]	13.9	0.8	12.8	2.6	5.2	19.2	16.9	28.7
	2006	4 919[9]	12.5	0.5	12.6	2.5	5.2	18.5	14.8	33.4
	2007	4 766[9]	13.1	^0.0	13.4	3.3	4.4	18.1	14.6	33.1
Finland Finlande	2005	136 423	3.0	0.3	23.1	2.1	5.9	12.2	10.4	43.1
	2006	145 023	2.7	0.4	23.7	2.3	6.0	12.0	10.1	42.8
	2007	156 912	3.2	0.3	23.6	2.2	6.4	11.7	9.8	42.6
France France	2006	1 614 341	2.1	0.2	12.6	1.7	6.0	12.6	6.4	58.5
	2007	1 697 408	2.2	0.2	12.3	1.6	6.3	12.4	6.4	58.6
	2008	1 752 430	2.0	0.2	11.9	1.7	6.7	12.2	6.4	58.9
French Guiana [3] Guyane française [3]	1990	6 454	10.1	7.6	...	0.7	12.8	13.5	7.7	47.5
	1991	7 385	7.4	7.6	...	0.5	12.1	13.1	12.3	47.0
	1992	8 052	7.2	9.0	...	0.6	10.8	11.9	11.4	49.1
French Polynesia [3] Polynésie française [3]	1991	305 211[21]	4.1	...	7.5	1.8[40]	5.7	...	...	29.3
	1992	314 265[21]	3.8	...	7.5	2.1[40]	5.9	...	...	29.5
	1993	329 266[21]	3.9	...	6.7	2.1[40]	5.7	...	...	29.0
Gabon [3] Gabon [3]	1987	986 000	10.9	28.4	7.1[41]	2.7	7.2	9.2	8.1	26.5
	1988	965 700	11.2	22.6	7.3[41]	3.0	5.2	14.4	9.1	27.3
	1989	1 128 400	10.4	32.3	5.7[41]	2.5	5.5	12.4	8.2	23.1
Gambia Gambie	2005	16 424[14]	29.7	1.8	6.2	0.9	6.8	30.9	12.4	15.7
	2006	17 419[14]	28.6	1.9	6.0	0.8	9.2	30.4	12.4	14.8
	2007	18 429[14]	28.9	2.0	6.0	0.8	8.3	30.7	12.5	15.0
Georgia Géorgie	2006	12 154[2]	12.7	1.1	12.6	3.1	7.8	18.1	13.1	31.5
	2007	14 774[2]	10.6	0.9	12.6	2.8	7.7	17.1	11.9	36.4
	2008	16 739[2]	10.2	0.8	12.1	2.5	6.0	18.2	11.4	38.7
Germany Allemagne	2005	2 024 890	0.9	0.2	22.7	2.3	4.0	12.0	5.7	52.3
	2006	2 093 300	0.9	0.2	23.2	2.3	3.8	12.2	5.7	51.7
	2007	2 171 210	0.9	0.2	23.9	2.2	4.0	11.8	5.8	51.1
Ghana [3] Ghana [3]	2006	107 038 630	38.8	5.6	9.2	3.4	10.1	7.7	5.0	20.2
	2007	129 666 740	36.9	6.3	8.2	2.6	10.7	7.7	5.0	22.5
	2008	155 842 260	36.5	8.3	7.9	2.5	10.9	7.6	4.9	21.4
Greece Grèce	2005	177 497	5.1	0.5	10.3	2.7	7.0	22.0	9.9	42.6
	2006	188 841	4.1	0.4	10.7	2.6	7.3	22.8	9.0	43.2
	2007	201 770	3.8	0.4	10.3	2.6	7.0	22.7	9.8	43.3
Grenada [3] Grenade [3]	2005	1 322[9]	4.4	0.5	4.9	4.7	17.1	12.7	19.3	36.5
	2006	1 346[9]	5.3	0.7	4.9	5.3	12.8	14.3	18.5	38.3
	2007	1 454[9]	5.0	0.6	4.7	5.3	10.9	14.6	17.8	41.1
Guadeloupe [3] Guadeloupe [3]	1990	15 036	6.7	5.4[42]	...	1.0	7.4	18.3	5.9	55.2
	1991	16 278	7.3	6.1[42]	...	1.4	7.0	16.5	6.0	55.5
	1992	17 968	6.7	6.9[42]	...	1.7	6.5	16.2	7.9	54.1
Guatemala Guatemala	2004	179 718[2]	13.6	1.1	20.0	3.0	5.0	19.2	6.1	32.0
	2005	197 129[2]	13.1	1.2	19.7	2.8	4.9	20.5	6.4	31.4
	2006	217 643[2]	11.9	1.5	19.7	2.7	5.5	20.5	7.0	31.3
Guinea Guinée	2004	7 445 143[38]	25.5	16.6	6.2	0.5	10.2	18.3	7.9	16.9[43,44]
	2005	9 578 049[38]	24.9	19.4	6.5	0.5	9.1	19.1	6.6	16.2[43,44]
	2006	13 491 019[38]	24.4	19.6	6.3	0.4	8.5	18.6	6.8	18.2[43,44]
Guinea-Bissau [3] Guinée-Bissau [3]	1989	358 875	44.6	7.9[31]	...	...	9.7	25.7	3.6	8.5[45]
	1990	510 094	44.6	8.2[31]	...	...	10.0	25.7	3.7	7.8[45]
	1991	854 985	44.7	8.5[31]	...	...	8.4	25.8	3.9	8.7[45]

20 Value added by industries at current prices *(continued)*
Percentage distribution

Valeur ajoutée par branche d'activité aux prix courants *(suite)*
Répartition en pourcentage

Country or area Pays ou zone	Year Année	Value added, gross (mil. nat.cur) Valeur ajoutée, brute (mil. mon. nat.)	% of Value added – % de la valeur ajoutée Agriculture, hunting, forestry and fishing Agriculture, chasse, sylviculture et pêche	Mining and quarrying Activités extractives	Manufacturing Activités de fabrication	Electricity, gas and water supply Electricité, gaz et eau	Construction Construction	Wholesale, retail trade, restaurants and hotels Commerce, restaurants, hôtels	Transport, storage & communication Transports, entrepôts, communications	Other activities Autres activités
Guyana[3]	2005	137 633[6]	34.6[46]	10.2	3.7	...	6.1[47]	5.1	11.1	29.3[48,49]
Guyana[3]	2006	154 000[6]	35.3[46]	9.7	3.6	...	6.4[47]	5.2	11.3	28.5[48,49]
	2007	171 190[6]	31.1[46]	11.2	3.7	...	6.8[47]	5.8	12.8	28.6[48,49]
Honduras	2006	188 387[14]	13.0[50]	1.3	21.4	1.2	6.0	18.0	7.4	36.3[7]
Honduras	2007	214 902[14]	12.9[50]	1.3	21.3	1.2	6.3	17.9	7.3	36.8[7]
	2008	250 076[14]	13.1	1.2	21.0	1.2	6.5	18.0	7.4	36.8[7]
Hungary	2005	18 833 973	4.2	0.2	22.2	2.9	4.9	12.6	7.8	45.2
Hongrie	2006	20 530 065	4.1	0.2	22.5	2.6	4.8	13.1	7.7	45.1
	2007	21 827 291	4.0	0.2	22.1	2.8	4.7	13.7	8.2	44.5
Iceland[6]	2003	716 948	7.5	0.1	13.3	3.5	7.6	11.4	8.0	49.2[51]
Islande[6]	2004	781 200	6.5	0.1	12.7	3.6	8.5	12.2	7.6	49.3[51]
	2005	852 669	5.8	0.1	10.1	4.0	9.5	12.3	6.2	52.7[51]
India	2005	33 399 759	18.9	2.8	16.1	2.1	7.9	16.1	8.4	27.6
Inde	2006	38 474 774	18.0	2.8	16.6	2.0	8.3	16.3	8.5	27.4
	2007	43 994 506	18.0	2.7	16.6	1.9	8.6	16.4	8.6	27.2
Indonesia	2005	2 774 281 100[21]	13.1	11.1	27.4	1.0	7.0	15.6	6.5	18.3[52,53]
Indonésie	2006	3 339 479 600[21]	13.0	11.0	27.5	0.9	7.5	15.0	6.9	18.1[52,53]
	2007	3 957 403 900[21]	13.8	11.1	27.0	0.9	7.7	14.9	6.7	17.8[52,53]
Iran (Islamic Rep. of)	2005	1 737 797 200	9.7	27.5[54]	10.5	1.2	3.5	10.7	6.6	30.3[7]
Iran (Rép. islamique d')	2006	2 079 653 069	9.8	26.3[54]	10.7	1.1	3.6	10.6	6.8	31.0[7]
	2007	2 679 463 956	9.5	27.0[54]	10.4	1.1	4.2	10.2	6.6	31.0[7]
Iraq[3]	2005	73 911 088[2,6]	6.9	57.5	1.3	0.8	3.6	5.7	8.0	16.2
Iraq[3]	2006	96 067 161[2,6]	5.8	55.2	1.5	0.8	3.6	6.6	7.0	19.4
	2007	108 402 971[2,6]	5.0	53.9	1.7	1.0	3.5	6.5	6.9	21.5
Ireland	2005	143 284[55]	1.9	0.4	23.5	1.2	9.9	12.7	5.3	45.2
Irlande	2006	156 485[55]	1.6	0.5	22.1	1.2	10.2	13.1	5.3	46.0
	2007	169 761[55]	1.7	0.4	21.9	1.4	9.9	12.8	5.2	46.8
Israel	2005	538 180[9]	2.0	...	15.1	2.1	4.7	10.3	7.6	58.2
Israël	2006	578 700[9]	1.9	...	15.9	1.9	4.9	10.4	7.6	57.3
	2007	617 315[9]	1.8	...	15.8	1.9	5.0	10.7	7.6	57.3
Italy	2005	1 284 444	2.2	0.4	18.4	2.0	6.0	15.4	7.7	47.8
Italie	2006	1 324 780	2.1	0.4	18.2	2.1	6.1	15.2	7.5	48.1
	2007	1 381 586	2.0	0.4	18.2	2.0	6.2	14.8	7.5	48.1
Jamaica	2005	637 816[2]	5.7	3.9	8.5	3.5	8.2	23.5	11.0	35.6
Jamaïque	2006	721 056[2]	5.5	3.8	8.3	3.6	7.9	23.8	11.2	36.0
	2007	812 991[2]	5.1	4.0	8.4	3.5	8.3	23.5	11.3	35.9
Japan	2005	522 494 500[9,56]	1.5	0.1	20.6	2.3	6.1	13.2[57,58]	6.4	49.7[28,59,]
Japon	2006	525 191 100[9,56]	1.4	0.1	20.5	2.2	6.1	13.0[57,58]	6.4	50.3[28,59,]
	2007	527 817 000[9,56]	1.4	0.1	20.6	1.9	5.9	13.0[57,58]	6.4	50.7[28,59,]
Jordan[3]	2004	7 415[2]	2.7	3.1	17.0	2.6	4.4	10.8	16.0	43.4
Jordanie[3]	2005	8 304[2]	3.0	3.4	16.9	2.3	4.6	10.7	15.1	44.1
	2006	9 528[2]	2.9	2.8	16.9	2.2	4.5	11.4	15.4	44.0
Kazakhstan	2005	7 288 444[2]	6.6	16.4	12.5	2.0	8.2	13.3	12.3	28.6
Kazakhstan	2006	9 853 931[2]	5.7	16.7	12.1	1.9	10.2	12.7	12.0	28.9
	2007	12 544 164[2]	5.8	15.4	11.8	1.8	9.7	13.6	11.8	30.2
Kenya	2005	1 261 183[38]	27.2	0.5	11.8	2.3	4.4	11.9	11.7	31.0
Kenya	2006	1 440 460[38]	26.8	0.5	11.6	2.0	4.4	12.2	12.7	30.8
	2007	1 603 161[38]	26.1	0.8	11.0	1.8	4.3	12.9	12.9	31.4
Kiribati	2006	142[2]	23.7	^0.0	4.6	0.3	2.3	6.5	11.7	51.0[1]
Kiribati	2007	151[2]	24.9	^0.0	5.2	0.2	2.0	6.1	11.7	49.9[1]
	2008	158[2]	26.0	^0.0	5.5	1.2	2.0	5.9	10.9	48.5[1]
Korea, Republic of	2005	775 889 600	3.3	0.3	27.8	2.3	7.6	11.0	7.0	40.7
Corée, République de	2006	814 686 100	3.2	0.2	27.5	2.3	7.5	11.1	6.8	41.5
	2007	874 782 000	2.9	0.2	27.6	2.2	7.4	11.0	6.8	41.9
Kosovo	2002	2 193	8.6	16.4[31]	...	...	9.5	12.1	4.1	49.4
Kosovo	2003	2 067	9.0	15.6[31]	...	...	10.7	12.6	4.2	47.9
	2004	2 076	8.6	15.1[31]	...	...	12.0	13.5	4.8	46.1
Kuwait[3]	2005	24 472[2,15]	0.3	50.1	7.0	1.3	1.8	4.8	5.0	29.6
Koweït[3]	2006	30 624[2,15]	0.2	53.9	5.3	1.1	1.7	4.1	6.3	27.3
	2007	33 178[2,15]	0.2	52.4	4.8	1.1	1.8	4.0	6.6	29.2

20 Value added by industries at current prices *(continued)*

Percentage distribution

Valeur ajoutée par branche d'activité aux prix courants *(suite)*

Répartition en pourcentage

Country or area Pays ou zone	Year Année	Value added, gross (mil. nat.cur) Valeur ajoutée, brute (mil. mon. nat.)	% of Value added – % de la valeur ajoutée Agriculture, hunting, forestry and fishing Agriculture, chasse, sylviculture et pêche	Mining and quarrying Activités extractives	Manu-facturing Activités de fabri-cation	Electricity, gas and water supply Electricité, gaz et eau	Construc-tion Construc-tion	Wholesale, retail trade, restaurants and hotels Commerce, restaurants, hôtels	Transport, storage & commu-nication Transports, entrepôts, communi-cations	Other activities Autres activités
Kyrgyzstan	2006	101 979[2]	32.0	0.5	12.3	3.9	3.0	22.0	6.8	19.7
Kirghizistan	2007	126 435[2]	30.2	0.5	11.1	3.1	4.0	21.5	8.4	21.3
	2008	165 754[2]	28.8	0.5	12.6	2.5	3.5	22.2	9.3	20.5
Lao People's Dem. Rep.	2005	30 324 846	44.8	3.1	20.7	2.7	3.0	12.8	6.3	6.7[20,61]
Rép. dém. pop. lao	2006	31 930 054	32.9	14.2	8.7	3.3	3.3	21.0	5.1	11.6[45]
	2007	37 579 039	32.4	11.7	9.1	2.7	3.8	23.2	5.1	12.1[45]
Latvia	2005	8 029	4.0	0.3	12.6	2.5	6.1	21.6	13.9	38.9
Lettonie	2006	9 836	3.5	0.3	11.8	2.4	7.4	22.7	11.4	40.4
	2007	13 060	3.6	0.4	11.4	2.4	9.0	21.6	10.2	41.4
Lebanon	2003	29 851 000[21]	5.5	...	11.8	0.6	7.4	22.4[62]	7.0	45.3[63,64]
Liban	2004	32 359 000[21]	5.3	...	11.7	0.2	7.4	24.0[62]	7.4	44.0[63,64]
	2005	32 499 000[21]	5.2	...	11.6	-0.6	8.2	23.2[62]	7.3	45.1[63,64]
Lesotho	2005	8 188[38]	7.7	2.9	18.1	4.8	5.0	14.7	6.2	41.6[7]
Lesotho	2006	9 659[38]	8.3	5.4	17.9	4.6	4.8	14.6	5.7	39.7[7]
	2007	11 099[38]	7.1	6.9	18.2	4.5	5.2	14.3	5.3	39.6[7]
Liberia[3]	2006	653	68.6	^0.0	6.7	0.8	3.1	11.8	6.3	2.8
Libéria[3]	2007	632	57.4	0.2	7.7	0.8	3.3	14.1	6.8	9.6
	2008	806	63.5	0.6	6.4	0.7	2.9	11.8	6.0	8.2
Libyan Arab Jamah	2005	66 921[9]	2.2	65.7	4.7	1.3	4.0	4.0	3.6	14.6
Jamah. arabe libyenne	2006	81 263[9]	2.0	68.5	4.4	1.2	3.9	3.5	3.4	13.1
	2007	89 362[9]	2.1	65.8	4.5	1.1	4.4	3.8	3.7	14.6
Lithuania	2005	65 164	4.8	0.5	20.8	4.0	7.5	18.7	12.7	30.9
Lituanie	2006	74 677	4.3	0.5	20.1	3.5	8.8	18.1	12.7	32.0
	2007	87 904	4.5	0.4	19.0	3.1	10.2	18.0	13.0	31.8
Luxembourg	2005	27 053	0.4	0.1	9.1	1.3	6.1	11.2	9.4	62.4
Luxembourg	2006	30 583	0.4	0.1	8.1	1.2	5.9	11.0	8.8	64.6
	2007	32 781	0.4	0.1	8.5	1.1	5.8	11.7	9.1	63.2
Madagascar[3]	2005	9 228 212	28.1	0.2	14.4	1.1	3.0	11.0	18.9	23.3
Madagascar[3]	2006	10 893 200	27.3	0.2	14.5	1.2	3.7	10.4	19.4	23.4
	2007	12 708 249	26.1	0.2	14.5	1.1	3.9	10.2	19.5	24.5
Malawi	2003	232 520[2]	33.9	1.2	11.1	1.6	4.3	14.3	6.1	27.4
Malawi	2004	273 761[2]	33.5	1.2	9.6	1.8	4.1	16.0	5.7	28.1
	2005	311 933[2]	31.4	1.3	8.7	1.7	4.5	17.4	6.0	29.0
Malaysia	2006	586 882[9]	8.6	14.6	28.8	2.6	2.7	12.4	6.6	23.8[65,66]
Malaisie	2007	652 660[9]	10.0	14.2	27.4	2.5	2.7	12.8	6.5	24.0[65,66]
	2008	751 190[9]	10.1	16.9	25.8	2.3	2.6	13.0	6.1	23.2[65,66]
Mali[3]	2007	3 092 048[2]	36.1	7.4	7.6	2.1	5.5	15.9	6.2	19.3
Mali[3]	2008	3 559 430[2]	39.7	6.8	5.8	2.1	5.4	15.7	6.2	18.3
	2009	3 805 563[2]	40.0	6.7	5.7	2.1	5.6	15.8	6.2	17.9
Malta	2005	1 768	2.7	0.3	17.3	0.9	3.9	19.1	9.9	45.9
Malte	2006	1 876	2.8	0.3	16.4	0.8	4.2	17.8	9.5	48.2
	2007	1 992	2.3	0.3	16.9	0.6	3.8	17.5	9.6	49.2
Marshall Islands[3]	1995	105	14.9	0.3	2.6	2.0	10.2	17.0	6.2	46.8
Iles Marshall[3]	1996	95	14.3	0.3	1.6	2.7	7.0	18.7	7.3	48.2
	1997[6]	90	14.3	0.4	1.7	3.1	7.0	17.9	7.9	47.7
Martinique[3]	1990	18 835	5.7	7.9[67]	...	2.5	4.9	18.9	6.2	53.9
Martinique[3]	1991	20 377	5.7	7.8[67]	...	2.4	5.3	18.9	6.3	53.6
	1992	21 869	5.1	8.1[67]	...	2.2	5.2	18.4	6.5	54.5
Mauritania	2004	350 893[9]	24.3	13.5	2.0	0.9	10.1	13.4	6.6	29.1
Mauritanie	2005	430 231[9]	18.0	18.7	6.6	0.9	8.2	12.9	7.4	27.4
	2006	649 007[9]	18.4	30.0	6.2	0.6	7.6	10.8	5.6	20.9
Mauritius	2007	218 499[2]	4.6	^0.0	18.8	1.7	6.0	20.6	11.2	37.0
Maurice	2008	248 151[2]	4.2	^0.0	18.9	2.0	6.5	19.7	10.4	38.2
	2009	262 979[2]	4.0	^0.0	18.4	2.2	6.4	18.2	10.6	40.2
Mexico	2004	8 241 720[2]	3.7	7.1[68]	19.1[68]	1.4	6.7	19.2	9.0	33.8
Mexique	2005	8 921 971[2]	3.4	7.3[68]	18.8[68]	1.4	6.7	18.9	9.2	34.2
	2006	10 059 082[2]	3.3	8.5[68]	18.9[68]	1.5	7.0	18.5	9.2	33.2
Mongolia	2005	2 467 840[6,14]	24.7	24.6	4.1	3.2	2.4	10.0	12.5	21.7
Mongolie	2006	3 309 699[6,14]	21.9	33.6	3.9	2.9	1.9	9.0	10.1	20.4
	2007	4 107 675[6,14]	23.0	32.6	4.5	2.5	1.9	8.5	10.7	20.5

Value added by industries at current prices *(continued)*
Percentage distribution

Valeur ajoutée par branche d'activité aux prix courants *(suite)*
Répartition en pourcentage

Country or area Pays ou zone	Year Année	Value added, gross (mil. nat.cur) Valeur ajoutée, brute (mil. mon. nat.)	% of Value added – % de la valeur ajoutée Agriculture, hunting, forestry and fishing Agriculture, chasse, sylviculture et pêche	Mining and quarrying Activités extractives	Manu-facturing Activités de fabri-cation	Electricity, gas and water supply Electricité, gaz et eau	Construc-tion Construc-tion	Wholesale, retail trade, restaurants and hotels Commerce, restaurants, hôtels	Transport, storage & commu-nication Transports, entrepôts, communi-cations	Other activities Autres activités
Montenegro	2005	1 522[9]	10.4	1.7	9.8	5.6	3.6	16.0	11.3	41.6
Monténégro	2006	1 757[9]	10.1	1.6	9.4	5.0	4.3	17.2	11.9	40.5
	2007	2 272[9]	8.5	1.4	8.5	3.7	4.2	18.9	12.4	42.4
Montserrat[3]	1985	90[6]	4.8	1.3	5.7	3.7	7.9	18.0	11.5	47.2
Montserrat[3]	1986	103[6]	4.3	1.4	5.6	3.7	11.3	18.7	11.6	43.4
	1987	118[6]	4.1	1.3	5.7	3.2	11.5	22.1	11.1	41.0
Morocco	2005	473 956[69]	14.7	1.9	16.6	3.1	6.7	14.6	7.3[50]	40.1[70]
Maroc	2006	517 948[69]	16.9	2.0	15.9	2.8	6.4	14.3	7.0[50]	39.6[70]
	2007	545 689[69]	13.7	2.4	15.2	2.9	6.8	14.9	7.9	41.8[70]
Mozambique	2005	140 829	26.4	1.0	15.1	5.4	3.2	14.5	10.3	24.1
Mozambique	2006	169 316[9]	27.1	1.4	15.6	5.7	3.1	15.1	9.7	22.4[7]
	2007	196 265[9]	28.4	1.6	14.5	5.7	2.9	15.7	9.4	21.8[7]
Myanmar[3,21]	2003	7 716 616	50.6	0.4[71]	9.8[72]	0.1[73]	3.9	22.6[74]	10.1	2.5
Myanmar[3,21]	2004	9 078 929	48.2	0.6[71]	11.6[72]	0.2[73]	3.9	22.3[74]	10.3	2.9
	2005	12 286 765	46.7	0.7[71]	12.8[72]	0.2[73]	3.8	21.7[74]	11.5	2.6[75]
Namibia	2005	42 313[38]	11.3	10.1	13.6	2.6	3.0	14.3	6.3	40.2
Namibie	2006	49 894[38]	10.5	13.3	15.6	2.0	3.8	13.7	5.1	37.2
	2007	57 625[38,50]	10.1	13.2	16.8	2.0	3.6	13.6	5.1	35.7
Nepal	2005	611 089[14]	34.6	0.5	7.8	2.2	6.7	16.3	10.0	25.0[7]
Népal	2006	675 484[14]	33.6	0.5	7.7	2.2	6.7	15.4	10.3	26.9[7]
	2007	768 832[14,76]	33.6	0.5	7.3	2.0	6.6	15.5	9.6	27.9[7]
Netherlands	2005	456 182	2.1	2.8	14.3	1.7	5.4	14.8	7.3	51.6
Pays-Bas	2006	478 734	2.2	3.3	13.7	1.8	5.5	14.9	7.1	51.4
	2007	503 088	2.0	3.0	13.7	2.0	5.6	14.9	7.0	51.7
Netherlands Antilles	2004	5 202[2]	0.7	...	6.3	4.2	5.1	16.7	9.5	57.5
Antilles néerlandaises	2005	5 474[2]	0.8	...	5.3	4.3	5.9	17.1	9.7	57.0
	2006	5 743[2]	0.6	...	6.4	3.9	5.4	18.1	9.8	55.7
New Caledonia	2002	435 713[2]	2.0	...	12.1[10]	1.9	9.3	13.4[77]	7.3	54.0[49]
Nouvelle-Calédonie	2003	477 656[2]	1.9	...	14.3[10]	1.7	9.3	13.0[77]	7.4	52.3[49]
	2004	520 059[2]	1.9	...	16.3[10]	1.8	8.9	12.7[77]	7.6	50.7[49]
New Zealand[78]	2000	111 279[9]	8.6	1.2	16.3	2.5	4.3	14.7	7.4	44.8
Nouvelle-Zélande[78]	2001	119 894[9]	8.9	1.2	15.8	2.4	4.4	15.5	7.2	44.5
	2002	126 137[9]	7.0	1.2	15.6	2.6	4.6	15.6	7.5	45.9
Nicaragua	2006	85 905[2]	18.0	1.3	17.5	3.2	6.2	14.7	5.8	33.3
Nicaragua	2007	97 873[2]	17.6	1.2	17.8	3.0	5.9	14.8	6.0	33.7
	2008	118 097[2]	18.2	1.0	17.9	3.1	6.1	14.4	5.9	33.3
Niger	2006	1 783 722[9]	45.8	2.2	5.8	1.4	2.7	15.4	7.0	19.8
Niger	2007	1 908 747[9]	43.5	5.1	5.6	1.4	2.7	15.2	7.1	19.4
	2008	2 199 222[9]	45.9	4.8	5.3	1.4	2.6	14.7	6.7	18.6
Nigeria	2006	18 564 805	32.0	37.8	2.6	0.2	1.3	15.1	3.3	7.7
Nigéria	2007	20 657 318	32.7	36.6	2.5	0.2	1.3	15.1	3.5	8.1
	2008	23 842 171	30.9	39.2	2.5	0.2	1.2	15.0	3.2	7.8
Norway	2006	1 921 295	1.5	27.8	10.0	2.6	4.5	9.5	7.5	36.7
Norvège	2007	2 018 450	1.4	25.0	10.4	2.2	5.0	10.0	7.5	38.4
	2008	2 296 798	1.2	29.2	9.5	2.6	4.8	9.2	6.5	36.9
Occupied Palestinian Terr.	2004	3 786[9]	7.8	0.8	14.6	3.6	6.3	11.7	6.8	44.3
Terr. palestinien occupé	2005	3 961[9]	6.4	0.5	13.4	3.2	7.0	12.1	6.9	45.7
	2006	3 869[9]	6.9	0.6	13.2	3.4	7.9	12.9	6.4	43.6
Oman	2005	11 939[14]	1.5	49.4	8.4	1.7	3.8	7.9	5.3	23.6
Oman	2006	14 156[14]	1.4	47.8	10.8	1.2	4.0	8.5	5.7	22.4
	2007	15 962[14,76]	1.3	45.5	10.5	1.2	4.8	9.8	6.2	22.6
Pakistan	2007	8 235 099[6]	20.5	3.1	19.0	2.1	2.7	17.5	12.3	22.8
Pakistan	2008	9 962 247[6]	20.2	3.0	19.6	1.5	2.7	18.4	11.8	22.8
	2009	12 459 544[6]	20.8	2.9	17.7	1.3	2.4	18.9	12.9	23.1
Palau	1999	111	4.1	0.2	1.5	3.1	7.4	31.7	8.9	43.3[79]
Palaos	2000	115	4.1	0.2	1.5	3.1	7.6	31.3	9.0	43.3[79]
	2001	118	4.0	0.2	1.5	3.2	7.8	31.1	9.2	43.1[79]
Panama	2005	14 845[2]	6.8	1.0	7.2	3.4	4.7	17.3	16.2	43.4
Panama	2006	16 554[2]	6.3	1.1	6.9	3.0	5.1	17.7	17.8	42.1
	2007	18 598[2]	5.7	1.3	6.7	2.8	5.7	17.8	18.0	42.0

20 Value added by industries at current prices *(continued)*
Percentage distribution

Valeur ajoutée par branche d'activité aux prix courants *(suite)*
Répartition en pourcentage

Country or area Pays ou zone	Year Année	Value added, gross (mil. nat.cur) Valeur ajoutée, brute (mil. mon. nat.)	% of Value added – % de la valeur ajoutée Agriculture, hunting, forestry and fishing Agriculture, chasse, sylviculture et pêche	Mining and quarrying Activités extractives	Manu-facturing Activités de fabri-cation	Electricity, gas and water supply Electricité, gaz et eau	Construc-tion Construc-tion	Wholesale, retail trade, restaurants and hotels Commerce, restaurants, hôtels	Transport, storage & commu-nication Transports, entrepôts, communi-cations	Other activities Autres activités
Papua New Guinea	2004	12 806[69]	35.5	25.0	6.6	2.1	9.2	7.0	2.4	14.1[80]
Papouasie-Nvl-Guinée	2005	14 437[69]	34.8	28.1	6.4	2.1	8.6	6.5	2.2	13.4[80]
	2006	16 200[69]	32.9	31.1	6.0	2.1	8.9	6.4	2.0	13.0[80]
Paraguay	2005	42 086 000	23.2	0.1	15.2	2.2	5.1	22.8	8.4	22.9
Paraguay	2006	47 584 000	22.2	0.1	15.0	2.2	5.2	24.0	8.3	23.0
	2007	55 843 241	24.2	0.1	14.1	1.9	5.9	22.6	8.7	22.4
Peru	2006	276 251	7.0	12.8	16.0	2.0	6.2	17.5	8.2	30.3
Pérou	2007	308 012	7.0	12.5	15.9	2.0	6.6	17.5	9.3	29.3
	2008	344 641	7.2	11.4	15.9	1.9	7.0	18.0	9.3	29.2
Philippines[3]	2005	5 444 038[21]	14.3	1.2	23.2	3.6	3.9	16.0	7.6	30.2
Philippines[3]	2006	6 032 833[21]	14.1	1.3	22.9	3.6	4.0	16.3	7.4	30.5
	2007	6 648 246[21]	14.1	1.6	22.0	3.5	4.6	16.5	7.2	30.5
Poland	2005	866 329	4.5	2.5	18.5	3.6	6.0	20.2	7.2	37.3
Pologne	2006	931 179	4.3	2.4	18.8	3.5	6.4	20.1	7.4	37.2
	2007	1 027 631	4.3	2.2	18.9	3.4	7.3	19.7	7.0	37.1
Portugal	2004	125 310	3.2	0.3	15.2	2.8	7.1	17.7	6.9	46.9
Portugal	2005	128 363	2.8	0.4	14.7	2.6	6.9	17.4	6.9	48.3
	2006	133 055	2.8	0.4	14.3	2.9	6.6	17.3	7.0	48.6
Puerto Rico[3]	2005	85 935[15]	0.5	0.1	41.5	2.3	2.0[81]	13.2	4.6	35.9
Porto Rico[3]	2006	88 966[15]	0.5	0.1	40.8	2.5	2.1[81]	13.2	4.4	36.5
	2007	92 687[15]	0.4	0.1	41.5	2.2	2.1[81]	13.4	4.3	36.0
Qatar	2003	87 622[2]	0.2	57.7	7.5	1.4	5.3	5.0	3.3	19.6
Qatar	2004	117 066[2]	0.2	53.7	10.2	1.3	5.5	5.3	3.4	20.4
	2005	157 810[2]	0.1	58.3	8.3	1.4	5.5	4.4	3.2	18.7
Republic of Moldova	2006	38 455[9]	16.9	0.6	14.6	2.0	4.6	14.6	13.8	33.0
République de Moldova	2007	45 629[9]	11.7	0.6	13.8	2.3	5.7	16.1	14.4	35.5
	2008[76]	53 213[9]	10.6	0.6	13.7	2.8	5.9	17.1	14.4	34.9
Réunion[3]	1990	27 417	4.0	9.1[42]	...	4.7	5.9	20.5	4.0	51.7[7]
Réunion[3]	1991	30 371	3.7	9.1[42]	...	4.1	7.1	19.9	4.6	51.5[7]
	1992	32 832	3.5	9.0[42]	...	4.1	6.8	20.0	4.5	50.1[7]
Romania	2005	255 233	9.5	1.5	24.0	2.6	7.4	13.0	11.5	30.5
Roumanie	2006	304 270	8.8	1.6	23.8	2.4	8.4	13.7	11.4	29.9
	2007[82]	365 967	6.4	27.0[31]	...	...	10.1	14.9	11.7	29.9
Russian Federation	2006	23 542 188[9]	5.0	10.7	18.1	3.2	5.2	21.0	9.7	27.0
Fédération de Russie	2007	29 259 010[9]	4.9	9.9	18.0	3.1	5.7	20.9	9.3	28.2
	2008	36 469 151[9]	4.9	9.2	17.5	3.0	6.5	21.7	9.4	28.0
Rwanda[3]	2000	680 822	40.7	0.3	10.0	0.6	8.9	10.4	7.3	22.0
Rwanda[3]	2001	731 919	41.4	0.5	9.9	0.5	8.5	10.2	7.5	21.5
	2002	794 978	43.1	0.5	9.5	0.4	8.1	10.0	7.5	20.9
Saint Kitts and Nevis[3]	2006	1 170[6,9]	2.5	0.3	8.2	2.4	12.9	19.9	14.5	39.3
Saint-Kitts-et-Nevis[3]	2007	1 258[6,9]	2.5	0.3	8.1	2.4	13.5	18.6	14.2	40.4
	2008	1 375[6,9]	2.2	0.3	7.9	2.3	13.5	18.3	14.6	40.9
Saint Lucia[3]	2004	1 928[9]	4.8	0.3	4.8	5.2	6.2	24.3	18.6	35.9
Sainte-Lucie[3]	2005	2 079[9]	3.6	0.3	5.5	4.7	7.3	24.9	18.5	35.3
	2006	2 206[9]	3.7	0.3	5.7	4.5	8.5	23.9	18.1	35.4
Saint Vincent-Grenadines[3]	2005	988[69]	8.2	0.2	6.0	5.6	12.1	21.8	19.1	34.9
Saint Vincent-Grenadines[3]	2006	1 085[69]	7.7	0.2	4.9	5.2	14.3	21.6	20.0	34.0
	2007	1 207[69]	7.9	0.2	4.4	5.0	15.4	21.5	20.0	33.6
Samoa	2006	1 264	11.2	...	13.1	4.6	12.0	20.3	13.8	24.8[1,83]
Samoa	2007	1 440	10.9	...	13.6	4.5	12.9	21.7	13.0	23.4[1,83]
	2008	1 430	10.6	...	11.5	4.7	12.6	22.6	13.4	24.4[1,83]
Sao Tome and Principe	2005	1 266 695[38]	18.6	0.6	6.9	2.3	9.2	25.1	14.6	24.7
Sao Tomé-et-Principe	2006	1 621 590[38]	16.9	0.7	6.5	2.3	12.1	24.6	15.2	23.7
	2007	1 950 717[38]	16.7	0.8	6.4	2.2	12.4	24.3	14.9	24.7
Saudi Arabia[3]	2006	1 342 131[2,15]	2.9	49.8	9.2	0.9	4.4	5.1	3.1	24.6[7]
Arabie saoudite[3]	2007	1 444 163[2,15]	2.8	50.7	9.2	0.9	4.5	5.1	3.1	23.6[7]
	2008	1 760 329[2,15]	2.3	57.1	8.3	0.7	4.0	4.6	2.8	20.1[7]
Senegal	2005	3 992 436	16.8	1.1	15.1	2.6	4.9	20.6	11.3	27.6
Sénégal	2006	4 231 818	15.0	0.9	14.2	2.7	5.5	20.5	12.5	28.7
	2007	4 664 876	13.7	0.9	14.2	2.9	5.5	20.7	12.9	29.2

Value added by industries at current prices *(continued)*

Percentage distribution

Valeur ajoutée par branche d'activité aux prix courants *(suite)*

Répartition en pourcentage

Country or area Pays ou zone	Year Année	Value added, gross (mil. nat.cur) Valeur ajoutée, brute (mil. mon. nat.)	% of Value added – % de la valeur ajoutée							
			Agriculture, hunting, forestry and fishing Agriculture, chasse, sylviculture et pêche	Mining and quarrying Activités extractives	Manu-facturing Activités de fabri-cation	Electricity, gas and water supply Electricité, gaz et eau	Construc-tion Construc-tion	Wholesale, retail trade, restaurants and hotels Commerce, restaurants, hôtels	Transport, storage & commu-nication Transports, entrepôts, communi-cations	Other activities Autres activités
Serbia Serbie	2005	1 428 626[2]	12.2	1.8	17.7	4.2	4.6	13.6	8.8	37.2
	2006	1 691 917[2]	11.3	1.7	18.4	4.4	4.8	14.2	8.2	37.0
	2007	2 019 768[2]	10.2	1.5	18.2	4.0	5.1	14.8	8.2	37.9
Serbia and Montenegro[84] Serbie-et-Monténégro[84]	2000	358 753	21.1	3.6	22.1	2.5	3.9	11.9	7.1	27.8
	2001	702 402	20.9	4.0	21.8	2.6	3.7	11.1	7.8	28.0
	2002	857 966	16.3	4.3	19.5	4.2	3.8	9.5	9.1	33.3
Seychelles Seychelles	2006	4 707[69]	3.5	...	10.9	2.2	6.5	19.4	17.2	44.6
	2007[85]	5 828[69]	3.0	...	11.3	1.5	6.2	25.5	15.5	41.8
	2008[86]	7 291[69]	2.9	...	10.3	1.3	6.8	29.6	14.4	39.2
Sierra Leone Sierra Leone	2005	4 147 635[2]	51.5	5.5	2.3	0.4	2.0	9.8	7.2	21.4
	2006	4 677 814[2]	53.0	4.3	2.3	0.3	1.9	10.0	7.4	20.7
	2007	5 604 440[2]	57.6	4.4	2.2	0.3	1.7	9.4	6.2	18.2
Singapore Singapour	2006	209 893[87]	0.1[88]	...	26.9	1.8	3.6	20.9	13.7	38.2[80]
	2007	235 099[87]	0.1[88]	...	24.9	1.7	3.9	20.6	13.6	40.8[80]
	2008	242 156[87]	0.1[88]	...	20.8	1.5	5.5	20.6	13.6	44.9[80]
Slovakia Slovaquie	2005	43 814	3.7	0.6	24.1	5.0	6.7	17.0	8.8	34.1
	2006	49 703	3.6	0.4	24.1	6.7	7.7	16.5	7.3	33.7
	2007	55 349	3.5	0.5	24.7	6.1	7.9	17.4	7.1	32.7
Slovenia Slovénie	2005	25 159	2.7	0.5	23.8	3.0	6.7	14.2	7.4	41.7
	2006	27 188	2.4	0.5	23.6	3.0	7.3	14.0	7.5	41.7
	2007	30 231	2.4	0.4	23.4	2.6	8.0	14.6	7.7	40.9
Solomon Islands Iles Salomon	2004	2 747	37.7	0.2	6.4	1.7	1.1	13.6	9.3	30.0
	2005	3 056	34.5	0.1	5.7	1.6	0.7	13.5	9.8	34.1
	2006	3 415	35.7	^0.0	4.8	1.3	0.6	14.0	9.4	34.2
Somalia[3] Somalie[3]	1985	84 050[6]	66.1	0.3	4.9	0.1	2.2	10.1	6.7	9.5
	1986	112 584[6]	62.5	0.4	5.5	0.2	2.7	10.3	7.3	11.1
	1987	163 175[6]	64.9	0.3	5.1	-0.5	2.9	10.7	6.8	9.8
South Africa Afrique du Sud	2006	1 548 808	2.9[50]	8.2	18.3	2.4	2.7	14.0	9.3	42.3
	2007	1 774 972	3.2	8.4	18.4	2.3	2.9	13.4	8.8	42.7
	2008	2 053 487	3.3	9.5	18.8	2.3	3.1	12.7	8.1	42.2
Spain Espagne	2005	813 776	3.2	0.3	15.8	2.0	11.5	18.2	6.9	42.0
	2006	874 845	2.9	0.3	15.5	2.0	12.2	18.0	6.8	42.4
	2007	942 002	2.9	0.3	15.2	2.0	12.3	17.6	6.8	43.0
Sri Lanka Sri Lanka	2005	2 194 796[6]	13.5	1.6	20.5	2.5	7.5	17.8	13.2	23.2
	2006	2 643 492[6]	13.0	1.7	20.2	2.6	8.1	17.5	13.2	23.6
	2007	3 262 023[6]	13.2	1.7	19.3	2.8	7.9	18.0	13.1	24.0
Sudan[3] Soudan[3]	1994	4 440 648	40.5	6.5[67]	...	0.7	3.8	46.6[89]	...	1.9
	#1996	9 015 824	37.1	9.6[67]	...	0.9	5.0	44.4[89]	...	3.0
	1997	15 865 432	40.5	9.1[67]	...	0.8	6.9	39.8[89]	...	2.8
Suriname[3] Suriname[3]	2005	4 588 065[9]	5.2	10.0	17.8	4.9	3.3	11.4	7.6	25.0
	2006	5 472 468[9]	5.0	10.3	18.9	4.5	3.7	10.9	6.7	25.1
	2007	6 243 595[9]	4.8	10.7	19.5	4.2	4.0	11.3	6.0	24.5
Swaziland Swaziland	2005	13 326[9]	8.5	0.3	37.8	1.4	4.3	11.3	6.5	29.9
	2006	15 105[9]	7.6	0.4	40.2	1.3	3.9	11.2	6.4	28.9
	2007	16 483[9]	7.7	0.3	40.6	1.2	3.4	11.4	7.1	28.2
Sweden Suède	2005	2 388 162	1.1	0.5	19.7	2.9	4.6	12.7	7.5	51.0
	2006	2 536 252	1.4	0.6	19.7	2.8	4.7	12.6	7.3	50.7
	2007	2 683 447	1.4	0.6	20.0	2.8	4.9	12.7	7.2	50.4
Switzerland Suisse	2004	424 751	1.4	0.2	18.9	2.0	5.6	15.9	6.6	49.4
	2005	435 870	1.3	0.2	19.3	2.0	5.7	15.8	6.6	49.2
	2006	458 153	1.2	0.2	19.9	2.0	5.6	15.6	6.5	49.1
Syrian Arab Republic[3,15] Rép. arabe syrienne[3,15]	2005	1 493 766[21]	20.5	24.8	2.5	0.3	2.6	20.4	10.8	18.2
	2006	1 698 480[21]	20.5	25.7	5.1	1.0	3.6	17.0	10.8	16.4
	2007	2 019 810[21]	20.4	23.9	6.0	1.1	3.4	17.4	9.9	17.9
Tajikistan Tadjikistan	2005	6 428[2]	23.8	...	25.6[90]	...	5.1	18.5	8.3	18.7
	2006	8 372[2]	23.9	...	23.7[90]	...	6.8	19.0	8.0	18.5
	2007	11 362[2]	21.9	...	20.7[90]	...	9.1	18.6	10.8	18.9
Thailand[3,21] Thaïlande[3,21]	2006	7 850 193	10.8	3.3	35.0	3.0	3.0	19.2	7.3	18.5
	2007	8 529 836	10.7	3.3	35.6	2.9	2.9	19.1	7.3	18.2
	2008	9 075 493	11.6	3.5	34.9	2.9	2.9	19.0	7.1	18.2

20 Value added by industries at current prices *(continued)*

Percentage distribution

Valeur ajoutée par branche d'activité aux prix courants *(suite)*

Répartition en pourcentage

Country or area Pays ou zone	Year Année	Value added, gross (mil. nat.cur) Valeur ajoutée, brute (mil. mon. nat.)	% of Value added – % de la valeur ajoutée Agriculture, hunting, forestry and fishing Agriculture, chasse, sylviculture et pêche	Mining and quarrying Activités extractives	Manu-facturing Activités de fabri-cation	Electricity, gas and water supply Electricité, gaz et eau	Construc-tion Construc-tion	Wholesale, retail trade, restaurants and hotels Commerce, restaurants, hôtels	Transport, storage & commu-nication Transports, entrepôts, communi-cations	Other activities Autres activités
TFYR of Macedonia	2005	248 952[9]	12.5	0.6	17.9	4.1	6.4	17.4	9.5	31.6
L'ex-R.Y. Macédoine	2006	274 484[9]	12.2	0.6	18.5	3.8	6.5	17.7	9.7	31.1
	2007	311 584[9]	10.6	0.8	21.0	3.1	6.8	17.1	9.4	31.1
Timor-Leste	2001	412	20.5	11.7	2.7	0.3	11.1	6.4	6.4	40.9[91]
Timor-Leste	2002	385	23.7	11.6	3.0	0.7	9.8	6.4	7.3	37.4[91]
	2003	388	25.1	14.3	3.1	0.9	8.0	6.5	8.0	34.2[91]
Togo[3]	1980	223 479	28.5	9.8	7.4	1.8	6.2	20.6	6.9	5.7
Togo[3]	1981	242 311	28.6	9.3	6.7	1.7	4.5	21.8	7.1	6.2
Tonga[3]	2004	338[2]	28.1	0.4	4.3	1.8	7.4	16.4	5.9	35.7[1,92]
Tonga[3]	2005	362[2]	27.4	0.5	3.8	2.2	7.5	16.4	5.6	36.7[1,92]
	2006	401[2]	25.1	0.4	3.1	2.4	7.6	14.9	5.4	41.1[1,92]
Trinidad and Tobago	2006	121 794[9]	0.4	30.2	21.5	0.8	7.0	15.6	4.1	20.3
Trinité-et-Tobago	2007	136 646[9]	0.4	27.0	22.5	1.1	8.4	15.0	5.1	20.4
	2008	150 824[9]	0.3	28.7	20.6	0.9	9.5	14.6	4.8	20.6
Tunisia[3,6]	2005	33 753[69]	12.4	5.6[93]	19.2	1.7[37]	6.4	17.1	11.5	28.6[94,95]
Tunisie[3,6]	2006	37 248[69]	12.3	6.8[93]	18.8	1.7[37]	6.3	16.9	11.8	28.4[94,95]
	2007	41 350[69]	11.4	8.8[93]	18.8	1.6[37]	6.0	16.3	12.2	28.0[94,95]
Turkey[3]	2005	571 714[2]	10.6	1.3	19.6	2.1	5.0	16.6	15.6	29.2
Turquie[3]	2006	668 418[2]	9.4	1.3	19.5	2.0	5.4	16.7	15.6	30.1
	2007	756 728[2]	8.7	1.4	18.7	2.1	5.6	16.2	15.5	31.8
Turkmenistan	1999	20 056 000	24.8	...	31.4[90]	...	12.2	4.1	6.7	20.8
Turkménistan	2000	25 648 000	22.9	...	35.0[90]	...	6.8	3.5	6.6	25.1
	2001	33 863 000	24.7	...	36.6[90]	...	5.7	4.2	5.4	23.5
Turks and Caicos Islands	2005	535[2]	1.2	1.0	2.2	4.4	12.1	33.4	10.2	35.5
Iles Turques et Caïques	2006	669[2]	1.0	1.2	1.9	3.8	15.0	33.1	8.6	35.4
	2007	767[2]	1.0	1.3	1.8	3.4	16.4	33.1	8.0	35.1
Tuvalu[3]	2000	25[96]	17.3	0.8	3.2	4.5	4.6	12.6	10.0	47.0
Tuvalu[3]	2001	27[96]	17.4	0.7	3.3	4.9	4.4	12.3	10.5	46.4
	2002	29[96]	15.9	0.8	3.5	5.0	4.8	12.9	11.9	45.3
Uganda[3]	2006	18 941 280[9]	24.0	0.3	7.4	4.1	11.9	18.8	6.4	27.1
Ouganda[3]	2007	21 847 741[9]	22.1	0.3	7.4	4.9	13.0	19.4	6.7	26.2
	2008	26 526 183[9]	22.9	0.3	7.7	4.4	13.0	19.7	7.3	24.6
Ukraine	2006	487 132[2]	8.4	4.5	22.5	3.8	4.3	15.2	11.5	29.7
Ukraine	2007	656 892[2]	7.2	4.8	21.8	3.5	4.6	15.5	10.7	31.7
	2008[76]	863 730[2]	7.4[97]	5.8	20.8	3.4	4.0	15.1[57]	10.6	32.9
United Arab Emirates[3]	2006	659 782[15]	1.3	33.6	12.8	1.5	6.6	16.7	5.5	21.9
Emirats arabes unis[3]	2007	777 167[15]	1.1	32.8	12.4	1.5	7.1	17.7	5.3	22.1
	2008	956 021[15]	0.9	36.2	11.8	1.4	7.2	17.0	4.9	20.4
United Kingdom	2003	1 030 928[9]	1.0	2.1	14.3	1.6	5.8	14.7	7.4	53.4
Royaume-Uni	2004	1 094 328[9]	0.9	2.0	13.7	1.6	5.9	14.7	7.2	54.2
	2005	1 148 553[9]	0.9	2.2	12.9	2.2	5.7	14.4	7.1	53.8
United Rep. of Tanzania[98]	2005	14 739 490	31.5	3.1	8.6	2.3	8.5	14.6	6.7	24.8
Rép.-Unie de Tanzanie[98]	2006	16 447 886	30.1	3.5	8.5	2.1	8.5	15.2	7.0	25.1
	2007	19 198 125	29.6	3.9	8.5	2.2	8.6	15.5	7.2	24.6
United States	2005	11 495 200[6,99,100]	1.2	1.9	14.1	2.1	5.3	16.4	6.4	60.2[101]
Etats-Unis	2006	12 190 100[6,99,100]	1.0	2.2	14.0	2.2	5.3	16.4	6.3	60.2[101]
	2007	12 778 400[6,99,100]	1.3	2.2	13.7	2.2	4.8	16.3	6.4	60.7[101]
Uruguay	2006	427 573[2]	10.0[10]	...	17.0	2.3	6.6	14.6	9.4	40.1[7]
Uruguay	2007	508 652[2]	9.7[10]	...	16.3	3.6	6.7	15.1	9.1	39.5[7]
	2008	608 779[2]	10.5[10]	...	17.2	1.7	7.0	15.7	9.7	38.2[7]
Uzbekistan	2000	2 788 137	34.9	...	15.8[90]	...	7.0	10.9	9.3	22.2
Ouzbékistan	2002	6 565 515	34.2	...	16.7[90]	...	5.6	11.3	...	22.9
	2003	8 369 111	33.3	...	17.6[90]	...	5.2	10.9	...	23.3
Vanuatu[3]	2005	42 625[2,15]	13.3	...	3.4	1.9	3.1	35.8	12.6	30.0[16,102]
Vanuatu[3]	2006	48 438[2,15]	13.7	...	3.0	1.9	3.2	35.9	12.2	30.0[16,102]
	2007	54 950[2,15]	13.6	...	2.9	1.9	3.5	35.6	12.2	30.3[16,102]
Venezuela (Boliv. Rep. of)	2004	200 008 986[9]	4.0	28.3	17.5	1.7	6.9	10.5	6.0	25.1
Venezuela (Rép. boliv. du)	2005	283 769 532[9]	4.0	32.4	16.2	1.4	6.9	11.1	5.8	22.2
	2006	369 059 760[9]	3.9	31.3	14.8	1.2	8.1	11.2	6.4	23.0
Viet Nam	2006	974 266 206[21]	20.4	10.2	21.2	3.4	6.6	17.3	4.5	16.2
Viet Nam	2007	1 143 715 434[21]	20.3	9.8	21.3	3.5	7.0	17.6	4.5	16.1
	2008	1 477 716 636[21]	22.1	8.9	21.1	3.2	6.5	18.2	4.5	15.4

20 Value added by industries at current prices *(continued)*

Percentage distribution

Valeur ajoutée par branche d'activité aux prix courants *(suite)*

Répartition en pourcentage

Country or area Pays ou zone	Year Année	Value added, gross (mil. nat.cur) Valeur ajoutée, brute (mil. mon. nat.)	Agriculture, hunting, forestry and fishing Agriculture, chasse, sylviculture et pêche	Mining and quarrying Activités extractives	Manu-facturing Activités de fabri-cation	Electricity, gas and water supply Electricité, gaz et eau	Construc-tion Construc-tion	Wholesale, retail trade, restaurants and hotels Commerce, restaurants, hôtels	Transport, storage & commu-nication Transports, entrepôts, communi-cations	Other activities Autres activités
			% of Value added – % de la valeur ajoutée							
Yemen Yémen	2005	3 422 599[9]	10.0	33.7	6.8	0.7	5.0	12.5	11.3	19.9
	2006	4 293 525[9]	9.1	30.8	7.7	0.7	4.9	14.2	12.0	20.6
	2007	5 063 149[9]	8.9	27.0	9.3	0.7	5.4	15.9	11.4	21.2
Zambia[3] Zambie[3]	2006	38 239 787[2]	20.4	4.2	10.5	3.0	14.3	20.0	4.3	23.3
	2007	45 247 919[2]	20.2	4.5	9.9	3.0	14.8	19.3	4.7	23.5
	2008	54 213 664[2]	19.8	4.2	9.6	2.8	16.4	18.6	4.5	24.0
Zanzibar Zanzibar	2005	345 283	26.8	0.9	5.6	1.9	7.1	20.0	9.1	28.5
	2006	447 968	33.6	0.9	5.2	2.2	8.5	18.8	7.7	23.1
	2007	510 461	31.3	0.9	4.8	2.2	10.1	19.9	8.0	22.8
Zimbabwe Zimbabwe	2005	195 467 764[14]	12.0	17.8	24.0	3.4	0.6	24.1	4.2	14.2
	2006	995 654 040[14]	15.6	24.0	28.4	2.7	1.5	17.0	2.1	8.7
	2007	15 644 561 426[14]	21.3	22.7	8.0	11.4	3.1	10.9	4.9	17.8

Source:
United Nations Statistics Division, New York, national accounts database, last accessed February 2010.

Data for most countries have been compiled in accordance with the concepts and definitions of the System of National Accounts 1993 (1993 SNA). Countries that follow the 1968 SNA are footnoted accordingly.

+ Note: The national accounts data generally relate to the fiscal year used in each country, unless indicated otherwise. Countries whose reference periods coincide with the calendar year ending 31 December are not listed below.

Year beginning 21 March: Afghanistan, Iran (Islamic Republic).
Year beginning 1 April: Bermuda, India, Myanmar, New Zealand, Nigeria.
Year beginning 1 July: Australia, Bhutan, Cameroon, Gambia, Nicaragua, Pakistan, Puerto Rico, Saudi Arabia, Sierra Leone, Sudan, United Republic of Tanzania.
Year ending 30 June: Bangladesh, Botswana, Egypt, Swaziland, Tonga.
Year ending 7 July: Nepal.
Year ending 30 July: Ethiopia.
Year ending 30 September: Haiti.

Source:
Organisation des Nations Unies, Division de statistique, New York, la base de données sur les comptes nationaux, dernier accès février 2010.

Les données pour la majorité des pays sont compilées selon les concepts et définitions du Système de comptabilité nationale, 1993 (SCN93). Seuls les pays qui suivent toujours le SCN68 seront donc signalés par une note.

+ Note : Sauf indication contraire, les données sur les comptes nationaux concernent généralement l'exercice budgétaire utilisé dans chaque pays. Les pays où territoires dont la période de référence coïncide avec l'année civile se terminant le 31 décembre ne sont pas répertoriés ci-dessous.

Exercice commençant le 21 mars: Afghanistan, Iran (République islamique d').
Exercice commençant le 1er avril: Bermudes, Inde, Myanmar, Nigéria, Nouvelle-Zélande.
Exercice commençant le 1er juillet: Arabie saoudite, Australie, Bhoutan, Cameroun, Gambie, Nicaragua, Pakistan, Porto Rico, Sierra Leone, Soudan, Rép.-Unie de Tanzanie.
Exercice se terminant le 30 juin: Bangladesh, Botswana, Égypte, Swaziland, Tonga.
Exercice se terminant le 7 juillet: Népal.
Exercice se terminant le 30 juillet: Éthiopie.
Exercice se terminant le 30 septembre: Haïti.

1 Includes ownership of dwellings.
2 Includes Financial intermediation services indirectly measured (FISIM) of total economy.
3 Data compiled in accordance with the System of National Accounts 1968 (1968 SNA).
4 Including finance and insurance.
5 Includes Hotels and restaurants; Real estate, renting and business activities and Private Households with employed persons.
6 At factor cost.
7 Including private households with employed persons.
8 Include some taxes on products (excise duties, taxes on gross revenue, export taxes).
9 Including Financial intermediation services indirectly measured (FISIM).
10 Including mining and quarrying.

1 Y compris la propriété des logements.
2 Y compris les services d'intermédiation financière mesurés indirectement par rapport à l'économie totale.
3 Données compilées selon le Système de comptabilité nationale de 1968 (SCN 1968).
4 Y compris les financés et les assurances.
5 Y compris l'hôtellerie et la restauration, les activités immobilières, de location et commerciales, et les ménages privés comptant des salariés.
6 Au coût des facteurs.
7 Y compris ménages privés avec les salariés.
8 Y compris les impôts sur les produits (droits d'accise, impôts sur le revenu brut, taxe à l'exportation).
9 Y compris les Services d'intermédiation financière mesurés indirectement (SIFMI).
10 Y compris les industries extractives.

20 Value added by industries at current prices *(continued)*

Percentage distribution

Valeur ajoutée par branche d'activité aux prix courants *(suite)*

Répartition en pourcentage

11 Excludes oil refining.
12 Includes oil refining.
13 Including education.
14 Excluding Financial intermediation services indirectly measured (FISIM).
15 At producers' prices.
16 Refers to other government services.
17 Discrepancy between Total Economy and breakdown by industry.
18 Includes imputed rentals of owner-occupied dwellings.
19 Including general government sector only.
20 Refers to Community, Social and Personal Services (Division 9 in ISIC Rev2.)
21 Value added refers to GDP.
22 Including electricity, gas and water.
23 Data refers to other services.
24 Restaurants and hotels only.
25 Refer to banking, insurance and house renting.
26 Excludes banks and insurance companies registered in Cayman Islands but with no physical presence in the Islands.
27 Including diamond cutting.
28 Includes hotels and restaurants.
29 At producers' prices (includes Other Taxes on Production, less Subsidies; and Taxes on fuel and tobacco).
30 For statistical purposes, the data for China do not include those for the Hong Kong Special Administrative Region (Hong Kong SAR) and Macao Special Administrative Region (Macao SAR).
31 Including manufacturing and electricity, gas and water supply.
32 Agriculture and fishing only.
33 Refers to Wholesale, retail and import/export trades, restaurants and hotels only. Repair of motor vehicles, motorcycles and personal and households goods are not included.
34 Refers to Community service provided by government unless otherwise specified.
35 Refers to Social service provided by non-profit making institutions and personal service provided by commercial establishments. Repair of motor vehicles, motorcycles and personal and households goods are included.
36 Excluding hunting.
37 Excluding gas.
38 Excludes Financial intermediation services indirectly measured (FISIM) but FISIM is included in tables by industry.
39 Including petroleum refining.
40 Including manufacturing of energy-generating products.
41 Including repair services.
42 Including "Manufacturing".
43 Refers to non market services
44 Includes public administration and defence.
45 Includes Education, Health, Social Work and other community services from the General Government.
46 Includes processing of sugar and rice.
47 Including engineering and sewage services.
48 Includes electricity and gas.
49 Includes Hotels and restaurants, Business activities and Private households with employed persons.
50 Discrepancy between components and total as one or more components has not been revised.
51 Includes Education and Social Work.
52 Refers to government administration, defense and other government services.
53 Refers to social and community services, recreational services, and personal and household services.
54 Including oil production.

11 Non compris le raffinage du pétrole.
12 Y compris le raffinage du pétrole.
13 Y compris l'enseignement.
14 Non compris les Services d'intermédiation financière mesurés indirectement (SIFMI).
15 Aux prix à la production.
16 Concerne d'autres services gouvernementaux.
17 Écart entre l'economie totale et la ventilation par industrie.
18 Y compris les loyers fictifs des logements occupés par leur propriétaire.
19 Comprend uniquement le secteur d'administation générale.
20 Correspond aux services fournis à la collectivité, aux services sociaux et aux services personnels (CITI Rév.2, branche 9).
21 La valeur ajoutée correspond au Produit Intérieur Brut.
22 Y compris l'électricité, le gaz, et l'eau.
23 Les données concernent les autres services.
24 Les restaurants et hôtels seulement.
25 Se rapporte aux banques, les assurances et la location.
26 Ne sont pas comprises les banques et les compagnies d'assurance qui sont domiciliées dans les îles Caïmanes, mais qui n'y sont pas présentes physiquement.
27 Y compris la taille de diamant.
28 Y compris les hôtels et restaurants.
29 Aux prix à la production (y compris les autres taxes à la production, déduction faite des subventions, et les taxes sur les carburants et le tabac).
30 Pour la présentation des statistiques, les données pour la Chine ne comprennent pas la Région Administrative Spéciale de Hong Kong (Hong Kong RAS) et la Région Administrative Spéciale de Macao (Macao RAS).
31 Y compris les activités de fabrication et la production et la distribution d'électricité, de gaz et d'eau.
32 Agriculture et la pêche seulement.
33 Se réfère à commerce de gros et de détail, commerce des importations/exportations, restaurants et hôtels seulement. Les réparations de véhicules à moteur, de motocycles et d'articles personnels et ménagers ne sont pas inclues.
34 Services communautaires fournis par les pouvoirs publics, sauf indication contraire.
35 Services sociaux fournis par des institutions sans but lucratif et services aux personnes fournis par des établissements commerciaux. Réparations de véhicules automobiles, de motocycles et de biens de consommation inclus.
36 Non compris la chasse.
37 Non compris le gaz.
38 Services d'intermédiation financière mesurés indirectement (SIFMI) non inclus, cependant les SIFMI sont inclus dans les tableaux par industries.
39 Y compris le raffinage du pétrole.
40 Y compris la fabrication de produits producteurs d'énergie.
41 Y compris les services de réparation.
42 Y compris "les industries manufacturières".
43 Services non marchands.
44 Y compris les administrations publiques et la défense nationale.
45 Y compris éducation, santé, action sociale et autres services sociaux de gouvernement général.
46 Traitement du sucre et du riz inclus.
47 Y compris génie civil et services d'égouts.
48 Y compris l'électricité et le gaz.
49 Y compris l'hôtellerie et la restauration, les activités immobilières, de location et commerciales, et les ménages privés comptant des salariés.
50 Écart entre rubriques et total car une ou plusieurs rubriques n'ont pas été révisées.
51 Education et travail social inclus.
52 Administrations publiques, défense nationale et autres services gouvernementaux.
53 Services sociaux et communautaires, services récréatifs et services aux personnes et aux ménages.
54 Y compris la production de pétrole.

20 Value added by industries at current prices *(continued)*

Percentage distribution

Valeur ajoutée par branche d'activité aux prix courants *(suite)*

Répartition en pourcentage

55 Financial intermediation services indirectly measured (FISIM) is distributed to uses.
56 Gross value added approximately at market prices.
57 Excludes hotels and restaurants, since those items are included in item "Community, social and personal services".
58 Excluding repair of motor vehicles, motorcycles and personal and household goods.
59 Includes renting and business activities.
60 Includes repair of motor vehicles, motorcycles and personal and household goods.
61 Includes non-profit institutions.
62 Wholesale and retail trade only.
63 Includes private education and private health services.
64 Includes Vehicles Repair, Hotels and Restaurant.
65 Includes insurance.
66 Includes owner occupied dwelling and private non profit services to households.
67 Including manufacturing.
68 Basic petroleum manufacturing is included in mining and quarrying.
69 Excludes Financial intermediation services indirectly measured (FISIM), but FISIM included in industry data.
70 Refers to industries, education and health and social work.
71 Includes energy.
72 Refers to processing and manufacturing.
73 Refers to electric power.
74 Refers to trade value.
75 Refers to Social and Administrative Services.
76 Preliminary data.
77 Excludes Hotels and restaurants.
78 Gross value added approximately at producers' prices.
79 Refers to all other services (Including Public administration and defence; compulsory social security; Education; health and social work; other community, social and personal services).
80 Including public administration and defense and compulsory social security.
81 Contract construction only.
82 Semi-final data.
83 Data refers to personal and other services.
84 Excluding Kosovo and Metohia.
85 Provisional data.
86 Data for this year refers to indicative data. Indicative estimates are at an early stage of development and are expected to be substantially improved with further work.
87 Excludes Financial intermediation services indirectly measured (FISIM).
88 Including quarrying.
89 Including Transport, storage and communications; Financial intermediation, real estate, renting and business activities; and Education, health and social work; other community, social and personal services, and Private households with employed persons.
90 Including mining and quarrying, electricity, gas and water.
91 Refers to other services, including government services, NGOs and UN peacekeeping operations.
92 Refer to entertainment, recreation and personal services.
93 Including crude petroleum and natural gas production.
94 Refers to market services.
95 Includes Hotels and restaurants and Real estate and business activities.
96 Derived from available data.
97 Excluding fishing.
98 Tanganyika only.

55 Services d'intermédiation financière mesurés indirectement (SIFMI) est distribué à ses utilisations.
56 Valeur brute ajoutée à environ aux prix du marché.
57 Non compris les hôtels et restaurants, car ils sont compris dans autres activités de services collectifs, sociaux et personnels.
58 Non compris les réparations de véhicules à moteur, de motocycles et d'articles personnels et ménagers.
59 Y compris activités économiques et locations et activités de services aux entreprises.
60 Y compris les réparations de véhicules à moteur, de motocycles et d'articles personnels et ménagers.
61 Y compris institutions sans but lucratif.
62 Commerce de gros et de détail seulement.
63 Y compris les services d'éducation et de santé privés.
64 Y compris la réparation de véhicules, l'hôtellerie et la restauration.
65 Y compris l'assurance.
66 Y compris logements occupés par leur propriétaire et services privées sans but lucratif aux ménages.
67 Y compris les industries manufacturières.
68 Les industries extractives y compris la fabrication de produits pétroliers de base.
69 Ne comprend pas les services d'intermédiation financière mesurés indirectement, mais ces services sont compris dans les données par secteurs intérieurs.
70 Industrie, éducation et santé et travail social.
71 Y compris l'énergie.
72 Se rapporte au Traitement et à la production.
73 Se rapporte à l'énergie électrique.
74 Correspond à la valeur des échanges.
75 Services sociaux et administratifs.
76 Données préliminaires.
77 Non compris les hôtels et restaurants.
78 Valeur brute ajoutée à environ aux prix à la production.
79 Ensemble des autres services (y compris les administrations publiques et la défense nationale, la sécurité sociale obligatoire, l'éducation, la santé et le travail social, les autres services communautaires et sociaux et les services aux personnes).
80 Y compris l'administration publique et la défense, et la sécurité sociale obligatoire.
81 Construction sous contrat seulement.
82 Données demi-finales.
83 Les données se réfèrent aux services personnelles et les autres services.
84 Non compris Kosovo et Metohia.
85 Données provisoires.
86 Les données concernant cette année sont indicatives. Il s'agit de premières estimations que de nouveaux travaux permettront d'affiner.
87 Ne comprend pas les services d'intermédiation financière mesurés indirectement
88 Y compris les carrières.
89 Comprend Transports, entreposage et communications ; Intermédiation financière, activités immobilières, de location et commerciales ; Éducation, santé et action sociale ; Autres services communautaires, sociaux et individuels, et Ménages privés comptant des salariés.
90 Y compris les industries extractives, l'électricité, gaz et l'eau.
91 Autres services, y compris les services gouvernementaux et ceux des ONG et les opérations de maintien de la paix des Nations Unies.
92 Services de loisirs et de récréation et services aux personnes.
93 Y compris la production de pétrole brut et de gaz naturel.
94 Services marchands.
95 Y compris l'hôtellerie et la restauration les activités commerciales
96 Calculés à partir des données disponibles.
97 Non compris la pêche.
98 Tanganyika seulement.

20 Value added by industries at current prices *(continued)*

Percentage distribution

Valeur ajoutée par branche d'activité aux prix courants *(suite)*

Répartition en pourcentage

99 Discrepancy between components and total as data for individual industries include all taxes less all subsidies.

100 Starting 1998 a new classification - NAICS98 - is used to compile data for Value Added.

101 From 1998 data, "Repairs and maintenance" is included in "Other community, social and personnel service activities".

102 Refers to personal services.

99 Les écarts entre le total et la somme de ses composantes tiennent au fait que les données de chaque industrie comprennent la totalité des taxes, moins la totalité des subventions.

100 A compter de 1998, une nouvelle classification – NAICS98 – est utilisée pour compiler les donnes sur la valeur ajoutée.

101 A compter de 1998, "réparations et entretien" sont inclus dans "Autres activités".

102 Services aux personnes.

21 Relationships among the principal national accounting aggregates

As a percentage of Gross Domestic Product (GDP)

Relations entre les principaux agrégats de la comptabilité nationale

En pourcentage du Produit Intérieur Brut (PIB)

Country or area Pays ou zone	Year Année	GDP at current prices (mil.nat.cur.) PIB aux prix courants (millions monnaie nat.)	As a percentage of GDP - En pourcentage du PIB Plus: Compensation of employees and property income from/to the rest of the world, net Plus : Rémunération des salariés et revenus de la propriété du/au reste du monde, net	Equals: Gross national income Égale : Revenu national brut	Plus: Net current transfers from/to the rest of the world Plus : Transferts courants du/au reste du monde, net	Equals: Gross national disposable income Égale : Revenu national disponible brut	Less: Final consumption expenditure Moins : Dépense de consommation finale	Equals: Gross savings Égale : Épargne brut
Algeria[1] Algérie[1]	2001	4 260 811	-2.9[2]	97.1	2.5	99.6	58.0	41.6
	2002	4 537 691	-3.9[2]	96.2	3.0	99.2	59.3	40.0
	2003	5 264 187	-3.6[2]	96.4	3.5	99.9	55.1	44.8
Angola[1] Angola[1]	1988	239 640	-11.1	88.9	-1.9	87.0	78.4	8.6
	1989	278 866	-10.5	89.5	-1.6	87.9	77.1	10.8
	1990	308 062	-12.4	87.6	-4.2	83.4	73.2	10.2
Anguilla[1] Anguilla[1]	2004	402	0.5	100.5	3.1	103.6	102.6	1.1
	2005	458	1.4	101.4	0.6	102.0	99.3	2.7
	2006	578	2.8	102.8	2.3	105.2	105.1	^0.0
Argentina Argentine	2005	531 939	-3.4	96.6	0.3	97.0	73.3	23.7
	2006	654 439	-2.4	97.6	0.3	97.9	71.4	26.4
	2007	812 456	-2.0	98.0	0.2	98.1	71.5	26.6
Armenia Arménie	2004	1 907 945	-4.0	96.0	11.6	107.6	92.7	15.0
	2005	2 242 881	-3.3	96.7	8.4	105.1	86.1	19.1
	2006	2 656 190	-3.6	96.5	9.0	105.5	82.3	23.1
Aruba Aruba	2000	3 327	-4.7	95.3	-1.7	93.5	72.0	21.5
	2001	3 399	-6.6	93.4	2.7	96.1	74.1	22.1
	2002	3 421	...	...	...	...	78.9	...
Australia[+] Australie[+]	2005	967 454	-3.9	96.1	-0.1	96.0	74.5	21.6
	2006	1 045 674	-4.4	95.6	0.0	95.6	73.7	21.8
	2007	1 132 172	-4.4	95.5	0.0	95.5	73.0	22.5
Austria Autriche	2006	257 295	-1.7	98.3	-0.7	97.6	72.6	25.0
	2007	270 837	-2.1	97.9	-0.5	97.4	71.3	26.1
	2008	282 286	-1.5	98.6	-0.6	98.0	71.2	26.8
Azerbaijan Azerbaïdjan	2005	12 523	-11.4	88.6	8.2	96.8	52.5	44.2
	2006	18 746	-12.0	88.0	5.6	93.6	45.6	47.9
	2007	28 361	-14.6	85.4	4.4	89.8	43.1	46.7
Bahamas Bahamas	2005	6 509	-2.0	98.0	1.3	99.3	76.2	23.1
	2006	6 876	-1.8	98.2	0.8	99.0	83.7	15.2
	2007	7 234	-2.7	97.4	0.4	97.8	84.1	13.7
Bahrain[1] Bahreïn[1]	2006	5 960	-2.4	97.6	-9.7	87.9	49.7	...
	2007	6 946	-1.6	98.4	-8.0	90.4	47.6	...
	2008	*8 235	-4.2	95.8	-8.1	87.7	44.2	...
Bangladesh[+] Bangladesh[+]	2006	4 157 279	6.5	106.5	0.9	107.4	79.8	27.7
	2007	4 724 769	...	107.5	0.8	108.3	79.7	28.7
	2008	5 419 188	...	108.0	1.1	109.2	79.9	29.2
Barbados[1] Barbade[1]	2002	4 952	-4.4	95.7	3.5	99.1	88.7	10.5
	2003	5 390	-4.0	96.0	3.4	99.5	88.9	10.6
	2004	5 632	-3.8	96.2	3.6	99.7	92.0	7.7
Belarus Bélarus	2006	79 266 985	-0.3	99.7	0.6	100.3	70.7	29.6
	2007	97 165 282	-0.9	99.1	0.4	99.5	70.3	29.2
	2008	128 828 759	-1.3	98.7	0.3	99.0	68.8	30.2
Belgium Belgique	2006	318 223	0.7	100.7	-1.2	99.5	74.8	24.6
	2007	334 917	0.6	100.6	-1.1	99.5	74.5	25.0
	2008	344 206	0.4	100.4	-1.3	99.1	76.7	22.4

21

Relationships among the principal national accounting aggregates *(continued)*
As a percentage of Gross Domestic Product (GDP)

Relations entre les principaux agrégats de comptabilité nationale *(suite)*
En pourcentage du Produit Intérieur Brut (PIB)

Country or area Pays ou zone	Year Année	GDP at current prices (mil.nat.cur.) PIB aux prix courants (millions monnaie nat.)	As a percentage of GDP - En pourcentage du PIB Plus: Compensation of employees and property income from/to the rest of the world, net Plus : Rémunération des salariés et revenus de la propriété du/au reste du monde, net	Equals: Gross national income Égale : Revenu national brut	Plus: Net current transfers from/to the rest of the world Plus : Transferts courants du/au reste du monde, net	Equals: Gross national disposable income Égale : Revenu national disponible brut	Less: Final consumption expenditure Moins : Dépense de consommation finale	Equals: Gross savings Égale : Épargne brut
Belize	2004	2 110	...	...	...	...	89.1	...
Belize	2005	2 230	...	...	...	...	86.1	...
	2006	2 427	...	...	...	...	78.8	...
Benin [1]	1989	479 200	...	99.2	11.1	110.2	94.4	12.6
Bénin [1]	1990	502 300	...	...	...	...	93.6	...
	1991	535 500	...	...	...	...	94.6	...
Bermuda [+]	2004	2 980	25.6	127.6	-5.3	122.3	97.6	24.8
Bermudes [+]	2005	3 265	26.9	128.8	-5.2	123.7	95.2	28.4
	2006	3 483	26.9	129.4	-2.7	126.7	93.4	33.2
Bhutan [+]	2005	36 462	-1.5	98.5	11.7	110.6	61.7	38.3
Bhoutan [+]	2006	40 448	-0.3	99.7	12.6	112.2	60.1	50.8
	2007	51 522	-2.3	97.8	9.4	107.2	57.9	44.3
Bolivia (Plurin. State of) [1]	2006	91 748	-4.3	95.7	6.8	102.5	77.1	25.3
Bolivie (État plurin.de) [1]	2007	103 009	-1.6	98.4	8.2	106.6	77.3	29.3
	2008	120 694	-3.3	96.8	7.7	104.4	75.5	28.9
Botswana [+]	2000	28 252	-5.3	83.0	^0.0	83.0	54.4	28.6
Botswana [+]	2001	34 774	-4.1	78.2	-0.1	78.1	49.4	28.7
	2002	35 671	-3.8	85.7	-0.1	85.6	55.7	29.9
Brazil	2004	1 941 498	-3.0	97.0	0.5	97.5	79.0	18.5
Brésil	2005	2 147 240	-2.9	97.1	0.4	97.5	80.2	17.4
	2006	2 369 797	-2.5	97.5	0.4	97.9	80.3	17.6
British Virgin Islands	2005	931	-7.1	92.9	5.3	98.2	46.4	51.9
Iles Vierges britanniques	2006	1 041	-6.6	93.5	5.2	98.7	45.7	52.9
	2007	1 134	-6.3	93.7	5.2	98.9	45.2	53.7
Bulgaria	2005	42 797	0.9	100.9	3.7	104.7	88.2	16.5
Bulgarie	2006	49 361	-2.5	97.5	2.7	100.2	87.0	13.1
	2007	56 520	-1.6	98.8	0.8	99.6	85.3	14.3
Burkina Faso	1999	1 836 037	-0.6	99.4	4.8	104.2	96.3	7.9
Burkina Faso	2000	1 863 300	-0.8	99.2	4.7	103.9	97.7	6.2
	2001	2 046 308	-0.9	99.1	4.4	103.5	99.8	3.7
Burundi [1]	1990	196 656	...	98.0	...	...	102.5	...
Burundi [1]	1991	211 898	...	99.0	...	...	100.9	...
	1992	226 384	...	98.7	...	...	98.5	...
Cambodia	2005	25 754 291	4.0	85.6	7.0	92.6[3]	90.1	4.3
Cambodge	2006	29 849 146	3.9	86.1	6.9	93.0[3]	86.2	9.1
	2007	35 039 310	...	...	...	...	83.9	...
Cameroon [+]	2000	6 612 385	-4.4	95.6	1.7	97.3	79.7	17.6
Cameroun [+]	2001	7 061 440	-3.4	96.6	0.5	97.1	81.0	16.1
	2002	7 583 077	-3.6	96.4	0.3	96.6	81.0	15.6
Canada	2005	1 372 626	-1.8	98.2	-0.1	98.1	74.3	23.9
Canada	2006	1 450 490	-0.9	99.1	-0.1	99.1	74.6	24.5
	2007	1 535 646	-1.4	98.6	-0.1	98.6	74.8	23.7
Cape Verde	1993	29 078	...	...	...	...	106.8	...
Cap-Vert	1994	33 497	...	...	...	...	104.5	...
	1995	37 705	...	...	...	...	109.1	...

21 Relationships among the principal national accounting aggregates *(continued)*

As a percentage of Gross Domestic Product (GDP)

Relations entre les principaux agrégats de comptabilité nationale *(suite)*

En pourcentage du Produit Intérieur Brut (PIB)

Country or area Pays ou zone	Year Année	GDP at current prices (mil.nat.cur.) PIB aux prix courants (millions monnaie nat.)	As a percentage of GDP - En pourcentage du PIB Plus: Compensation of employees and property income from/to the rest of the world, net Plus : Rémunération des salariés et revenus de la propriété du/au reste du monde, net	Equals: Gross national income Égale : Revenu national brut	Plus: Net current transfers from/to the rest of the world Plus : Transferts courants du/au reste du monde, net	Equals: Gross national disposable income Égale : Revenu national disponible brut	Less: Final consumption expenditure Moins : Dépense de consommation finale	Equals: Gross savings Égale : Épargne brut
Cayman Islands [1] Iles Caïmanes [1]	1989	474	-10.8	89.2	...	92.0	79.3	12.7
	1990	590	-10.3	89.7	...	92.2	76.8	15.4
	1991	616	-9.4	90.6	...	93.0	77.6	15.4
Chad Tchad	2004	2 332 311	...	62.9	...	...	...	...
	2005	3 098 019	...	56.3	...	...	...	...
	2006	3 294 117	...	55.7	...	...	...	...
Chile Chili	2005	66 192 596	-8.9	91.2	1.5	92.7	69.3	23.4
	2006	77 830 577	-12.6	87.5	2.4	89.8	64.9	24.9
	2007	85 621 091	-11.4	88.7	1.9	90.6	65.5	25.1
China Chine	2005	18 321 740	0.5	100.5	...	...	...	...
	2006	21 192 350	...	100.6	...	...	...	...
	2007	24 952 990	...	100.8	...	...	...	...
China, Hong Kong SAR Chine, Hong Kong RAS	2005	1 382 590	0.1	100.1	-1.2	98.9	67.0	31.9
	2006	1 475 910	1.9	101.9	-1.2	100.7	66.9	33.8
	2007	1 616 215	3.9	103.9	-1.2	102.6	67.8	34.8
Colombia Colombie	2005	335 546 939	-2.3	97.7	4.9	102.6	82.1	20.4
	2006	383 322 872	-2.7	97.3	4.8	102.2	79.9	22.3
	2007	431 839 018	-3.1	96.9	4.4	101.3	79.8	21.5
Comoros [1] Comores [1]	1989	63 397	...	100.7	...	...	...	...
	1990	66 370	...	99.8	12.3	112.1	105.5	6.7
	1991	69 248	...	99.6	...	...	...	...
Congo [1] Congo [1]	1986	640 407	-6.5	93.5	-1.3	92.2	84.4	7.8
	1987	690 523	-11.1	88.9	-1.6	87.3	77.2	10.2
	1988	658 964	-13.7	86.3	-1.8	84.5	81.2	3.3
Costa Rica Costa Rica	2005	9 538 977	-3.9	96.1	1.4	97.4	81.1	16.3
	2006	11 517 822	-3.2	96.8	1.6	98.3	79.7	18.6
	2007	13 570 071	-2.9	97.2	1.8	98.9	80.2	18.7
Côte d'Ivoire [1] Côte d'Ivoire [1]	1998	7 457 508	-5.7	94.3	-3.1	91.2	78.7	12.4
	1999	7 734 000	-6.9	92.1	-2.7	89.1	77.8	11.3
	2000	7 605 000	-5.7	94.3	-3.5	90.8	82.7	8.1
Cuba Cuba	2005	42 644	-1.5	98.5	-0.9	97.7	86.6	11.1
	2006	52 743	-1.2	98.8	0.5	99.4	88.0	11.3
	2007	58 604	-1.6	98.4	-0.3	98.0	87.1	10.9
Cyprus Chypre	2005	13 462	...	95.9	...	...	...	...
	2006	14 435	...	95.2	...	...	...	...
	2007	15 596	...	94.2	...	...	...	...
Czech Republic République tchèque	2006	3 215 642	-5.4	94.6	-0.3	94.3	70.0	24.3
	2007	3 530 249	-6.0	94.0	-0.5	93.5	68.4	25.0
	2008	3 705 868	-7.5	92.5	-0.7	91.8	70.0	21.8
Dem. Rep. of the Congo [1] Rép. dém. du Congo [1]	1983	59 134	...	95.7	...	...	76.9	...
	1984	99 723	...	88.5	...	...	49.5	...
	1985	147 263	...	97.2	...	...	59.4	...
Denmark Danemark	2006	1 628 630	1.9[4]	101.9	-2.0	99.9	74.6	25.2
	2007	1 687 892	0.5[4]	100.5	-1.9	98.6	75.0	23.6
	2008	1 739 716	1.9[4]	101.9	-2.0	99.9	75.5	24.4

21 Relationships among the principal national accounting aggregates *(continued)*

As a percentage of Gross Domestic Product (GDP)

Relations entre les principaux agrégats de comptabilité nationale *(suite)*

En pourcentage du Produit Intérieur Brut (PIB)

Country or area Pays ou zone	Year Année	GDP at current prices (mil.nat.cur.) PIB aux prix courants (millions monnaie nat.)	As a percentage of GDP - En pourcentage du PIB Plus: Compensation of employees and property income from/to the rest of the world, net Plus : Rémunération des salariés et revenus de la propriété du/au reste du monde, net	Equals: Gross national income Égale : Revenu national brut	Plus: Net current transfers from/to the rest of the world Plus : Transferts courants du/au reste du monde, net	Equals: Gross national disposable income Égale : Revenu national disponible brut	Less: Final consumption expenditure Moins : Dépense de consommation finale	Equals: Gross savings Égale : Épargne brut
Djibouti [1] Djibouti [1]	1996	88 233	1.0[2]	100.0	9.4	109.4	97.3	12.1
	1997	87 289	1.2[2]	99.9	8.3	108.2	94.2	14.0
	1998	88 461	1.2[2]	99.9	8.3	108.3	96.4	11.8
Dominica [1] Dominique [1]	1989	423	...	101.0	...	...	92.0	...
	1990	452	...	101.1	...	...	84.4	...
	1991	479	...	101.0	...	...	91.4	...
Dominican Republic Rép. dominicaine	1994	179 130	-2.2	97.8	6.7	104.5	81.4	23.1
	1995	209 646	-2.3	97.7	6.2	103.9	82.9	21.0
	1996	243 973	-5.4	94.6	6.1	100.7	82.2	18.5
Ecuador Equateur	2005	37 187	-5.2	94.8	7.2	101.9	77.1	24.8
	2006	41 763	-4.7	95.3	7.4	102.8	75.5	27.3
	2007	*45 789	-4.5	95.5	7.1	102.6	75.0	27.6
Egypt [+] Egypte [+]	2004	510 751	-0.8	99.2	4.6	103.8	83.3	20.6
	2005	568 192	-1.1	98.9	5.5	104.4	84.0	20.5
	2006	642 986	-0.5	99.6	4.7	104.3	83.6	20.7
El Salvador [1] El Salvador [1]	2005	17 070	-3.4	96.6	17.8	114.4	102.0	12.4
	2006	18 654	-2.8	97.2	18.6	115.8	103.3	12.4
	2007	20 373	-2.8	97.2	18.5	115.7	105.1	10.6
Estonia Estonie	2005	173 530	-4.2	96.1	0.1	96.2	72.9	23.3
	2006	205 038	-5.6	94.7	0.1	94.8	71.8	23.1
	2007	238 929	-8.0	92.2	0.4	92.6	72.4	20.2
Ethiopia [+] Ethiopie [+]	2006	131 641	0.2	100.2	13.8	114.0	96.2	17.8
	2007	171 834	0.2	100.2	14.8	115.1	94.1	21.0
	2008	245 585	0.2	100.2	14.0	114.1	96.8	17.3
Fiji Fidji	2005	4 970	-1.6	98.4	4.6	103.1	68.6	34.5
	2006	5 456	-3.9	96.2	3.4	99.6	68.7	30.8
	2007	5 264	-5.8	94.2	4.4	98.6	72.1	26.5
Finland Finlande	2006	167 009	1.0	101.0	-1.0	100.0	73.3	26.6
	2007	179 659	-0.1	100.0	-1.0	99.0	71.9	27.1
	2008	186 164	-0.7	99.3	-1.1	98.3	73.5	24.8
France France	2006	1 806 429	1.0[5]	101.0	-1.5	99.5	80.2	19.3
	2007	1 894 646	1.1[5]	101.1	-1.5	99.6	79.7	19.9
	2008	1 950 085	0.7[5]	100.7	-1.5	99.2	80.3	18.9
French Guiana [1] Guyane française [1]	1990	6 526	-1.9[2]	98.1	36.3	134.4	99.4	35.0
	1991	7 404	-5.8[2]	94.2	35.9	130.1	94.5	35.6
	1992	7 976	-6.9[2]	93.1	36.4	129.6	93.1	36.4
Gabon [1] Gabon [1]	1987	1 020 600	-6.2[2]	93.8	-4.2	89.7	72.4	17.3
	1988	1 013 600	-7.4[2]	92.6	-7.6	85.0	69.9	15.1
	1989	1 168 066	-8.6[2]	91.4	-6.1	85.3	66.8	18.5
Gambia [+1] Gambie [+1]	1991	2 920	...	98.3	...	115.7	96.7	19.0
	1992	3 078	...	98.7	...	114.1	94.4	19.7
	1993	3 243	...	98.5	...	114.4	93.3	21.1
Georgia Géorgie	2006	13 790	2.3	102.3	6.7	108.9	94.1	14.9
	2007	16 994	...	100.4	6.8	107.1	92.6	14.6
	2008	19 070	...	99.3	8.4	107.7	99.2	8.5

Relationships among the principal national accounting aggregates *(continued)*

As a percentage of Gross Domestic Product (GDP)

Relations entre les principaux agrégats de comptabilité nationale *(suite)*

En pourcentage du Produit Intérieur Brut (PIB)

Country or area Pays ou zone	Year Année	GDP at current prices (mil.nat.cur.) PIB aux prix courants (millions monnaie nat.)	As a percentage of GDP - En pourcentage du PIB					
			Plus: Compensation of employees and property income from/to the rest of the world, net Plus : Rémunération des salariés et revenus de la propriété du/au reste du monde, net	Equals: Gross national income Égale : Revenu national brut	Plus: Net current transfers from/to the rest of the world Plus : Transferts courants du/au reste du monde, net	Equals: Gross national disposable income Égale : Revenu national disponible brut	Less: Final consumption expenditure Moins : Dépense de consommation finale	Equals: Gross savings Égale : Épargne brut
Germany Allemagne	2006	2 321 500	1.8[5]	101.8	-1.2	100.6	76.7	23.9
	2007	2 422 900	1.7[5]	101.7	-1.2	100.5	74.7	25.9
	2008	2 491 400	1.6[5]	101.6	-1.2	100.5	74.5	26.0
Ghana [1] Ghana [1]	1994	5 205 200	...	98.0	...	...	...	...
	1995	7 752 600	...	98.0	...	...	...	...
	1996	11 339 200	...	98.1	...	...	...	...
Greece Grèce	2006	213 207	-2.1[5]	97.9	^0.0	97.9	87.7	10.2
	2007	228 180	-2.9[5]	97.2	-0.7	96.4	87.9	8.6
	2008	242 946	-3.6[5]	96.4	-0.2	96.2	88.0	8.1
Greenland [1] Groenland [1]	2003	9 397	-2.6	97.4	38.7	136.1	...	...
	2004	9 827	-2.5	97.5	36.7	134.2	...	...
	2005	10 210	-2.4	97.6	35.9	133.5	...	...
Grenada [1] Grenade [1]	1984	275	...	98.9	...	...	99.1	...
	1985	311	...	98.9	...	...	99.0	...
	1986	350	...	99.2	...	...	97.7	...
Guadeloupe [1] Guadeloupe [1]	1990	15 201	-2.5[2]	97.5	37.3	134.8	123.6	11.2
	1991	16 415	-3.4[2]	96.6	35.4	132.0	118.3	13.7
	1992	17 972	-3.0[2]	97.0	36.6	133.6	113.4	20.2
Guatemala Guatemala	2004	190 440	-1.4	98.6	11.3	109.9	94.3	15.6
	2005	207 729	-1.2	98.8	11.6	110.4	96.2	14.2
	2006	229 548	-1.1	99.0	13.0	112.0	96.1	15.9
Guinea-Bissau [1] Guinée-Bissau [1]	1986	46 973	-1.7	98.3	2.9	101.3	102.8	-1.5
	1987	92 375	-0.5	99.5	4.1	103.6	100.8	2.8
Guyana [1] Guyana [1]	2005	164 873	...	97.5	...	...	100.3	...
	2006	183 084	...	95.2	...	...	89.5	...
	2007	217 552	...	96.7	...	...	102.4	...
Haiti [+,1] Haïti [+,1]	1995	35 207	...	98.7	22.8	121.5	108.1	13.4
	1996	43 234	...	99.6	17.1	116.7	104.9	11.8
	1997	51 789	...	99.6	14.1	113.7	103.7	10.0
Honduras Honduras	2006	206 289	-5.0	95.0	22.4	116.7	92.7	25.8
	2007	*234 622	-3.3	*96.7	21.1	115.5	95.6	22.8
	2008	*270 597	-2.5	*97.5	...	...	98.3	...
Hungary Hongrie	2005	21 993 082	-5.5[6]	94.6	-0.8	93.7	77.7	16.0
	2006	23 775 269	-5.8[6]	94.2	-1.0	93.2	76.4	16.8
	2007	25 479 405	-6.9[6]	93.1	-1.0	92.1	74.6	17.6
Iceland Islande	2006	1 168 254	-7.2	92.8	-0.2	92.6	82.8	9.8
	2007	1 301 410	-5.0	95.0	-0.3	94.7	82.3	12.4
	2008	1 464 993	-31.4	68.6	-0.3	68.3	78.8	-10.5
India [+] Inde [+]	2005	35 867 431	-0.7	99.3	3.0	102.3	67.8	34.2
	2006	41 291 736	-0.7	99.3	3.1	102.3	66.1	35.7
	2007	47 233 996	-0.5	99.5	3.5	103.0	65.1	37.7
Indonesia [1] Indonésie [1]	2001	1 467 660 000	...	95.8	...	...	74.0	...
	2002	1 610 570 000	...	96.6	...	...	77.8	...
	2003	1 786 690 000	...	95.5	...	...	78.5	...

21

Relationships among the principal national accounting aggregates *(continued)*
As a percentage of Gross Domestic Product (GDP)

Relations entre les principaux agrégats de comptabilité nationale *(suite)*
En pourcentage du Produit Intérieur Brut (PIB)

Country or area Pays ou zone	Year Année	GDP at current prices (mil.nat.cur.) PIB aux prix courants (millions monnaie nat.)	As a percentage of GDP - En pourcentage du PIB Plus: Compensation of employees and property income from/to the rest of the world, net Plus : Rémunération des salariés et revenus de la propriété du/au reste du monde, net	Equals: Gross national income Égale : Revenu national brut	Plus: Net current transfers from/to the rest of the world Plus : Transferts courants du/au reste du monde, net	Equals: Gross national disposable income Égale : Revenu national disponible brut	Less: Final consumption expenditure Moins : Dépense de consommation finale	Equals: Gross savings Égale : Épargne brut
Iran (Islamic Rep. of) +	2005	1 740 580 500	-1.8	98.2	^0.0	98.2	57.6	40.6
Iran (Rép. islamique d') +	2006	2 077 499 700	-1.6	98.4	^0.0	98.4	59.2	39.2
	2007	2 691 728 400	-1.1	99.0	^0.0	98.9	56.0	42.9
Iraq [1]	2004	38 058 543	0.2	100.2	7.3	107.5	87.1	20.4
Iraq [1]	2005	53 386 429	2.0	102.0	9.1	111.1	79.2	31.9
	2006	80 459 422	1.6	101.6	-0.8	100.8	62.8	38.0
Ireland	2005	162 168	-14.2[5]	85.8	-1.0	84.8	60.9	24.0
Irlande	2006	177 286	-13.3[5]	86.7	-1.0	85.7	60.9	24.8
	2007	190 603	-14.9[5]	85.1	-1.2	83.9	62.1	21.8
Israel	2005	597 773	-1.2	98.8	4.5	103.3	81.5	21.8
Israël	2006	640 776	0.1	100.1	5.2	105.2	80.6	24.6
	2007	673 552	^0.0	100.0	4.4	104.4	81.6	22.8
Italy	2006	1 485 377	-0.2	99.8	-1.0	98.8	79.2	19.6
Italie	2007	1 544 915	-0.6	99.4	-0.9	98.4	78.5	20.0
	2008	1 572 243	-1.5	98.5	-1.0	97.5	79.3	18.2
Jamaica	2005	694 537	-6.1	93.9	14.2	108.1	91.3	16.8
Jamaïque	2006	788 179	-5.1	94.9	14.6	109.4	91.5	17.9
	2007	889 027	-6.7	93.4	15.3	108.7	95.6	13.1
Japan	2005	501 734 400	2.4	102.4	-0.1	102.3	75.1	26.8
Japon	2006	507 364 800	2.8	102.8	-0.2	102.7	75.0	26.9
	2007	515 804 800	3.3	103.3	-0.2	103.1	74.2	27.0
Jordan [1]	2004	8 091	1.7	101.7	28.5	130.2	102.3	27.9
Jordanie [1]	2005	8 954	2.4	102.3	21.1	123.3	106.7	16.7
	2006	10 521	3.4	103.4	20.4	123.7	102.5	21.3
Kazakhstan	2005	7 590 594	-9.4	90.6	-0.7	89.9	61.1	28.8
Kazakhstan	2006	10 213 731	-11.7	88.3	-1.5	86.8	55.9	30.9
	2007	12 849 794	-11.5	88.5	-2.0	86.5	56.2	30.3
Kenya	2005	1 418 071	-0.6	99.4	5.5	106.2	92.6	13.6
Kenya	2006	1 620 732	-0.3	99.7	8.0	107.7	91.7	16.0
	2007	1 814 229	-0.7	99.3	7.9	107.2	93.5	13.6
Kiribati [1]	2006	84	86.0[5]	186.0	...	...	...	...
Kiribati [1]	2007	84	86.7[5]	186.7	...	...	...	...
	2008	93	79.4[5]	179.4	...	...	...	...
Korea, Republic of	2006	908 743 800	0.2	100.2	-0.4	99.7	69.0	30.8
Corée, République de	2007	975 013 000	0.2	100.2	-0.3	99.9	69.1	30.8
	2008	1 023 937 700	0.7	100.7	0.0	100.6	69.7	30.9
Kuwait [1]	2005	23 593	11.0	111.0	-4.2	106.8	47.9	58.9
Koweït [1]	2006	29 470	13.0	113.0	-3.6	109.4	42.5	66.9
	2007	31 750	11.6	111.6	-4.5	107.0	45.1	61.9
Kyrgyzstan	2005	100 899	-3.3	96.7	13.5	110.2	102.1	8.2
Kirghizistan	2006	113 800	-1.2	98.8	25.2	123.9	113.1	10.8
	2007	141 898	-1.4	98.6	26.7	125.3	104.6	20.7
Latvia	2005	9 059	-1.8	98.7	3.2	101.9	80.0	21.9
Lettonie	2006	11 172	-3.4	97.1	1.9	99.0	81.8	17.2
	2007	14 780	-3.7	96.7	0.9	97.6	79.8	17.9

21

Relationships among the principal national accounting aggregates *(continued)*
As a percentage of Gross Domestic Product (GDP)

Relations entre les principaux agrégats de comptabilité nationale *(suite)*
En pourcentage du Produit Intérieur Brut (PIB)

Country or area Pays ou zone	Year Année	GDP at current prices (mil.nat.cur.) PIB aux prix courants (millions monnaie nat.)	As a percentage of GDP - En pourcentage du PIB Plus: Compensation of employees and property income from/to the rest of the world, net Plus : Rémunération des salariés et revenus de la propriété du/au reste du monde, net	Equals: Gross national income Égale : Revenu national brut	Plus: Net current transfers from/to the rest of the world Plus : Transferts courants du/au reste du monde, net	Equals: Gross national disposable income Égale : Revenu national disponible brut	Less: Final consumption expenditure Moins : Dépense de consommation finale	Equals: Gross savings Égale : Épargne brut
Lebanon Liban	2003	29 851 000	-1.2	98.8	17.0	115.8	101.8	14.0
	2004	32 359 000	-3.8	96.2	15.7	111.9	100.4	11.5
	2005	32 499 000	2.1	102.1	12.5	114.6	100.1	14.5
Lesotho Lesotho	2005	8 750	21.9	125.0	30.9	156.0	142.3	13.6
	2006	10 269	24.5	127.6	38.7	166.2	133.6	32.6
	2007	11 778	24.9	128.4	34.8	163.3	132.8	30.5
Liberia [1] Libéria [1]	1987	1 090	...	83.2	...	...	...	...
	1988	1 158	...	84.2	...	...	...	...
	1989	1 194	...	84.9	...	...	...	...
Libyan Arab Jamah. [1] Jamah. arabe libyenne [1]	1983	8 805	-7.0	91.0	-0.2	90.9	72.0	18.9
	1984	8 013	-4.7	92.7	-0.3	92.4	72.2	20.2
	1985	8 277	-3.0	96.7	-0.2	99.5	69.2	27.3
Liechtenstein Liechtenstein	2004	4 296	...	82.7	...	...	...	...
	2005	4 555	...	85.5	...	...	...	...
	2006	*5 001	...	88.0[7]	...	...	...	...
Lithuania Lituanie	2005	72 060	-2.5	98.3	1.7	100.0[8]	83.2	16.8[8]
	2006	82 793	-2.9	97.8	2.0	99.8[8]	83.8	16.0[8]
	2007	98 139	-4.2	96.1	2.2	98.3[8]	82.9	15.4[8]
Luxembourg Luxembourg	2005	30 237	-14.2[4]	85.9	...	...	52.0	...
	2006	33 921	-23.9[4]	76.1	...	...	48.6	...
	2007	36 411	-16.5[4]	83.5	...	...	47.5	...
Madagascar [1] Madagascar [1]	1980	689 800	...	99.9	...	...	...	...
Malawi [1] Malawi [1]	1994	11 209	-3.6	96.4	9.2	105.6	...	...
	1995	20 246	-3.1	96.9	9.6	105.0	...	...
	1996	23 993	-1.8	98.2	3.4	101.6	...	...
Malaysia Malaisie	2005	522 445	-4.6	95.4	-3.3	92.2	57.2	35.0
	2006	573 736	-3.0	97.0	-2.9	94.0	56.8	37.2
	2007	641 864	-2.1	97.9	-2.5	95.4	57.8	37.6
Maldives Maldives	2004	9 939	-5.5[2]	94.5	-7.0	87.5	56.5	31.0
	2005	9 607	-4.9[2]	95.1	4.9	100.0	71.9	28.1
	2006	11 608	-4.1[2]	95.9	5.7	101.6	67.7	33.9
Mali [1] Mali [1]	1990	683 300	-1.2[2]	98.8	11.5	110.3	94.3	16.1
	1991	691 400	-1.3[2]	98.7	13.0	111.9	100.4	11.5
	1992	737 400	-1.2[2]	98.8	11.4	110.2	96.4	13.8
Malta Malte	2005	2 061	-4.2	95.5	...	...	...	...
	2006	2 187	-4.2	95.6	...	...	...	...
	2007	2 325	-2.4	97.3	...	...	...	...
Martinique [1] Martinique [1]	1990	19 320	-4.2[2]	95.8	33.7	...	113.3	...
	1991	20 787	-4.4[2]	95.6	30.7	...	112.8	...
	1992	22 093	-3.9[2]	96.1	33.4	...	113.1	...
Mauritania Mauritanie	2002	311 087	10.8	110.8	8.8	119.6	96.4	23.2
	2003	336 818	4.6	104.6	10.8	115.4	102.7	12.6
	2004	395 268	4.4	104.4	7.3	111.7	92.9	18.8

21

Relationships among the principal national accounting aggregates *(continued)*

As a percentage of Gross Domestic Product (GDP)

Relations entre les principaux agrégats de comptabilité nationale *(suite)*

En pourcentage du Produit Intérieur Brut (PIB)

Country or area Pays ou zone	Year Année	GDP at current prices (mil.nat.cur.) PIB aux prix courants (millions monnaie nat.)	As a percentage of GDP - En pourcentage du PIB Plus: Compensation of employees and property income from/to the rest of the world, net Plus : Rémunération des salariés et revenus de la propriété du/au reste du monde, net	Equals: Gross national income Égale : Revenu national brut	Plus: Net current transfers from/to the rest of the world Plus : Transferts courants du/au reste du monde, net	Equals: Gross national disposable income Égale : Revenu national disponible brut	Less: Final consumption expenditure Moins : Dépense de consommation finale	Equals: Gross savings Égale : Épargne brut
Mauritius Maurice	2007	235 530	3.2	103.2	1.6	104.7	83.4	21.3
	2008	264 636	...	102.9	0.0	105.1	85.6	19.6
	2009	277 021	...	100.1	2.1	102.2	88.6	13.6
Mexico Mexique	2004	8 557 291	-1.4	98.7	2.3	100.9	77.1	23.8
	2005	9 199 316	-1.6	98.5	2.4	100.9	77.6	23.3
	2006	10 306 839	-1.4	98.6	2.5	101.1	75.6	25.5
Mongolia Mongolie	2005	2 779 578	3.6[5]	103.6	...	...	...	...
	2006	3 714 953	-0.3[5]	99.7	...	...	...	...
	2007	4 599 541	0.1[5]	100.1	...	...	...	...
Morocco Maroc	2005	527 679	-1.1	98.7	9.1	107.8	76.8	31.0
	2006	577 344	-1.4	98.6	9.6	108.2	76.1	32.2
	2007	616 254	...	98.6	...	...	76.6	32.2
Mozambique Mozambique	2005	151 707	-5.3	94.7	4.1	98.8	96.3	2.6
	2006	180 242	-8.0	92.0	5.9	97.9	91.9	6.0
	2007	209 661	-6.2	92.7	6.1	98.8	91.3	7.5
Myanmar + 1 Myanmar + 1	1996	791 980	...	100.0	...	100.0	88.5	11.4
	1997	1 109 554	...	100.0	...	100.0	88.1	11.9
	1998	1 559 996	...	100.0	...	100.0	89.4	10.6
Namibia Namibie	2006	54 028	-0.7	99.3	11.9	111.2	75.7	35.6
	2007	62 303	-2.0	98.0	11.3	109.3	82.1	27.2
	2008	72 904	-2.3	97.7	12.1	109.8	86.0	23.8
Nepal + Népal +	2005	654 055	0.8[4]	100.8	19.3	120.0	91.0	29.0
	2006	727 089	1.0[4]	101.0	17.7	118.8	90.3	28.5
	2007	*820 814	1.2[4]	101.2	19.3	120.5	88.5	32.0
Netherlands Pays-Bas	2006	539 929	3.2	103.2	-1.5	101.7	72.3	29.4
	2007	567 066	2.7	102.7	-1.5	101.2	71.7	29.5
	2008	594 608	-0.9	99.2	-1.4	97.7	71.3	26.5
Netherlands Antilles Antilles néerlandaises	2004	5 555	-0.5	99.5	1.9	101.4	77.1	24.3
	2005	5 855	-0.2	99.9	3.6	103.5	77.7	25.8
	2006	6 154	0.2	100.2	1.0	101.2	78.4	22.8
New Zealand + Nouvelle-Zélande +	2005	157 855	-7.0	93.0	0.1	93.1	77.2	15.9
	2006	165 903	-7.2	92.8	0.4	93.2	78.0	15.2
	2007	177 472	-7.5	92.5	0.4	92.9	77.1	15.8
Nicaragua + Nicaragua +	2006	93 007	-2.4[2]	97.6	19.0	116.5	99.7	16.8
	2007	104 973	-2.4[2]	97.6	18.9	116.5	101.2	15.3
	2008	125 246	-2.4[2]	97.6	16.4	113.9	104.0	9.9
Niger Niger	2006	1 906 837	^0.0	100.0	4.5	104.5	87.9	16.7
	2007	2 035 386	-0.1	99.9	4.3	104.2	89.1	15.1
	2008	2 333 098	-0.2	99.8	5.5	105.2	88.7	16.6
Nigeria + Nigéria +	2006	18 709 786	-1.7	98.3	7.1	105.5	67.2	38.3
	2007	20 874 172	-4.3	95.7	10.5	106.1	82.4	23.8
	2008	*25 510 284	-3.9	96.1	13.6	109.7	77.9	31.8
Norway Norvège	2006	2 159 573	0.1	100.1	-0.9	99.2	60.0	39.2
	2007	2 277 111	0.7	100.7	-0.8	100.0	61.0	39.0
	2008	2 548 322	0.9	100.9	-0.8	100.1	58.1	42.0

Relationships among the principal national accounting aggregates *(continued)*

As a percentage of Gross Domestic Product (GDP)

Relations entre les principaux agrégats de comptabilité nationale *(suite)*

En pourcentage du Produit Intérieur Brut (PIB)

Country or area Pays ou zone	Year Année	GDP at current prices (mil.nat.cur.) PIB aux prix courants (millions monnaie nat.)	Plus: Compensation of employees and property income from/to the rest of the world, net Plus : Rémunération des salariés et revenus de la propriété du/au reste du monde, net	Equals: Gross national income Égale : Revenu national brut	Plus: Net current transfers from/to the rest of the world Plus : Transferts courants du/au reste du monde, net	Equals: Gross national disposable income Égale : Revenu national disponible brut	Less: Final consumption expenditure Moins : Dépense de consommation finale	Equals: Gross savings Égale : Épargne brut
			As a percentage of GDP - En pourcentage du PIB					
Occupied Palestinian Terr. Terr. palestinien occupé	2004	4 198	5.5	105.5	18.0	123.5	133.4	-9.9
	2005	4 480	8.0	108.0	25.3	133.2	122.4	10.8
	2006	4 383	9.7	109.7	29.3	139.0	128.3	10.7
Oman Oman	2005	11 883	-3.1	...	-7.3	...	...	...
	2006	14 151	-2.5	...	-7.6	...	...	...
	2007	16 010	-2.3	...	-8.8	...	...	...
Pakistan [+] Pakistan [+]	2006	7 623 205	...	102.0	...	...	85.9	...
	2007	8 723 215	...	101.8	...	...	84.2	...
	2008	10 478 194	...	102.2	...	...	88.5	...
Panama Panama	2005	15 465	-9.3	90.7	1.1	91.8	75.2	16.6
	2006	17 137	-9.0	91.0	0.9	91.9	73.3	18.6
	2007	19 485	-9.0	91.0	0.8	91.8	71.5	20.3
Papua New Guinea Papouasie-Nvl-Guinée	2004	13 459	-10.5	89.5	5.9	95.5	69.0	26.5
	2005	15 095	-11.1	88.9	5.4	94.3	64.1	30.2
	2006	16 897	-14.6	85.4	4.3	89.7	63.9	25.8
Paraguay [1] Paraguay [1]	1993	11 991 719	...	100.4	...	100.4	88.0	12.4
	1994	14 960 131	...	100.5	...	100.5	95.2	5.3
	1995	19 699 000	...	100.9	...	100.9	92.5	8.4
Peru [1] Pérou [1]	1996	148 278	...	97.3	...	...	80.6	...
	1997	172 389	...	97.5	...	...	78.7	...
	1998	183 179	...	97.7	...	...	80.9	...
Philippines [1] Philippines [1]	2005	5 444 039	8.2	108.2	0.8	109.0	79.0	30.1
	2006	6 032 835	8.3	108.3	0.7	109.0	79.9	29.1
	2007	6 648 245	9.0	109.0	0.5	109.5	79.1	30.4
Poland Pologne	2005	983 302	-1.9	98.1	1.4	99.5	81.5	17.7
	2006	1 060 031	-2.5	97.5	1.4	98.8	80.8	18.0
	2007	1 175 266	-3.6	96.4	1.3	97.7	78.5	...
Portugal Portugal	2006	155 446	-3.6	96.4	1.3	97.8	86.0	11.7
	2007	163 179	-3.8	96.2	1.4	97.7	85.3	12.4
	2008	166 228	-4.0	96.0	1.5	97.5	87.3	10.3
Puerto Rico [+ 1] Porto Rico [+ 1]	2005	86 157	-34.5	65.5	11.8	77.2	69.6	7.0
	2006	88 902	-34.6	65.4	12.1	77.5	70.3	7.1
	2007	93 263	-35.4	64.6	13.4	78.0	69.4	7.1
Qatar Qatar	2003	85 663	-1.8[2]	98.2	-7.0	91.2	31.9	59.3
	2004	115 512	-7.1[2]	92.9	-7.1	85.8	30.5	55.3
	2005	154 564	-3.3[2]	96.7	-6.1	90.6	29.7	60.9
Republic of Moldova République de Moldova	2005	37 652	13.5	113.5	19.1	132.6	109.9	22.7
	2006	44 754	11.8	111.8	23.0	134.8	113.9	20.9
	2007	53 430	9.3	109.3	25.9	135.2	113.5	21.7
Réunion [1] Réunion [1]	1990	28 374	-2.5[2]	97.5	44.3	141.7	108.1	33.6
	1991	31 339	0.1[2]	100.7	42.7	143.4	103.5	39.9
	1992	33 787	-1.5[2]	98.4	43.6	142.1	104.5	37.6
Romania Roumanie	2005	288 955	-2.9	97.1	4.2	101.3	86.9	14.4
	2006	344 651	-3.4	96.7	4.8	101.4	85.6	15.9
	2007[9]	412 762	-3.3	96.7	...	...	...	...

21

Relationships among the principal national accounting aggregates *(continued)*

As a percentage of Gross Domestic Product (GDP)

Relations entre les principaux agrégats de comptabilité nationale *(suite)*

En pourcentage du Produit Intérieur Brut (PIB)

Country or area Pays ou zone	Year Année	GDP at current prices (mil.nat.cur.) PIB aux prix courants (millions monnaie nat.)	As a percentage of GDP - En pourcentage du PIB Plus: Compensation of employees and property income from/to the rest of the world, net Plus : Rémunération des salariés et revenus de la propriété du/au reste du monde, net	Equals: Gross national income Égale : Revenu national brut	Plus: Net current transfers from/to the rest of the world Plus : Transferts courants du/au reste du monde, net	Equals: Gross national disposable income Égale : Revenu national disponible brut	Less: Final consumption expenditure Moins : Dépense de consommation finale	Equals: Gross savings Égale : Épargne brut
Russian Federation	2004	17 048 122	-2.2	97.8	-0.1	97.7	66.9	30.9
Fédération de Russie	2005	21 625 372	-2.5	97.5	-0.2	97.3	66.4	30.9
	2006	26 903 494	-2.9	96.7	-0.1	96.6	66.0	30.6
Rwanda [1]	1987	171 430	-1.6	98.4	2.5	100.9	93.6	7.4
Rwanda [1]	1988	177 920	-2.0	98.0	2.9	100.9	93.6	7.3
	1989	192 220	-1.2	98.8	2.4	101.3	95.4	5.9
Saint Kitts and Nevis [1]	2006	1 319	-6.6	93.4	6.6	100.0	80.5	19.4
Saint-Kitts-et-Nevis [1]	2007	1 382	-6.1	94.0	6.5	100.5	85.8	14.7
	2008	1 519	-5.9	94.1	6.1	100.2	87.4	12.8
Saint Lucia [1]	2005	2 374	-8.3	91.8	1.6	93.3	87.1	6.2
Sainte-Lucie [1]	2006	2 520	-6.0	94.0	1.3	95.3	98.0	-2.7
	2007	2 592	-6.3	93.7	1.3	94.9	100.0	-5.0
Saint Vincent-Grenadines [1]	2005	1 182	-5.9	93.9	4.2	98.0	88.5	9.5
Saint Vincent-Grenadines [1]	2006	1 324	-4.3	95.1	4.1	99.1	88.1	11.0
	2007	1 469	-3.0	95.9	3.8	99.6	...	...
San Marino [1]	2003	995	...	89.6	-12.9	76.7	...	...
Saint-Marin [1]	2004	1 061	...	88.8	-12.8	76.1	...	...
	2005	1 106	...	87.7	-12.7	75.1	...	...
Saudi Arabia [1]	2005	1 182 514	0.1	100.1	-4.7	95.5	48.7	46.8
Arabie saoudite [1]	2006	1 335 581	1.1	101.1	-4.7	96.4	49.9	46.5
	2007	1 437 683	2.0	102.0	-4.4	97.5	51.2	46.3
Senegal	2005	4 593 095	-1.0	99.4 [10]	8.7	108.0	90.9	17.1
Sénégal	2006	4 893 381	-1.0	98.0 [10]	8.9	106.9	92.6	14.3
	2007	5 407 749	-0.5	99.4 [10]	10.7	110.1	93.6	16.5
Serbia	2005	1 747 459	...	...	...	...	...	...
Serbie	2006	2 042 048	...	...	...	...	...	...
	2007	2 349 241	...	...	...	...	...	...
Seychelles	2006	5 628	-4.3	95.7	...	...	...	...
Seychelles	*2007	6 877	-7.0	93.0	...	...	...	...
	2008	8 756	-11.9 [11]	88.1	...	...	...	...
Sierra Leone [+]	2005	4 296 269	-3.4 [5]	96.6	11.5	108.1	112.0	-3.9
Sierra Leone [+]	2006	4 887 545	-2.4 [5]	97.6	6.0	103.6	91.9	11.7
	2007	5 829 011	-5.3 [5]	94.7	5.1	99.7	87.4	12.3
Singapore	2006	221 143	-3.6	96.4	-1.2	95.2	50.1	45.5
Singapour	2007	251 610	-6.9	93.1	-1.3	91.8	48.3	44.2
	2008	257 419	-2.7	97.3	-1.5	95.8	51.7	45.7
Slovakia	2006	55 082	-2.4	97.6	-1.2	96.4	76.0	20.4
Slovaquie	2007	61 501	-2.8	97.2	-1.3	95.9	73.2	22.8
	2008	67 331	-2.5	97.5	-1.9	95.6	73.7	22.0
Slovenia	2005	28 704	-1.1	99.2	-0.5	98.7	73.4	25.3
Slovénie	2006	31 008	-1.4	98.8	-0.7	98.1	71.8	26.3
	2007	34 471	-2.2	98.0	-0.8	97.3	69.9	27.4
Solomon Islands [1]	1984	222	...	94.2	...	100.8	78.2	22.6
Iles Salomon [1]	1985	237	...	95.0	...	101.0	91.6	9.4
	1986	253	...	92.6	...	115.7	94.8	20.9

Relationships among the principal national accounting aggregates *(continued)*

As a percentage of Gross Domestic Product (GDP)

Relations entre les principaux agrégats de comptabilité nationale *(suite)*

En pourcentage du Produit Intérieur Brut (PIB)

Country or area Pays ou zone	Year Année	GDP at current prices (mil.nat.cur.) PIB aux prix courants (millions monnaie nat.)	As a percentage of GDP - En pourcentage du PIB Plus: Compensation of employees and property income from/to the rest of the world, net Plus : Rémunération des salariés et revenus de la propriété du/au reste du monde, net	Equals: Gross national income Égale : Revenu national brut	Plus: Net current transfers from/to the rest of the world Plus : Transferts courants du/au reste du monde, net	Equals: Gross national disposable income Égale : Revenu national disponible brut	Less: Final consumption expenditure Moins : Dépense de consommation finale	Equals: Gross savings Égale : Épargne brut
Somalia [1] Somalie [1]	1985	87 290	...	97.8	10.1	107.9	101.1	6.8
	1986	118 781	...	96.3	14.2	110.5	98.8	11.7
	1987	169 608	...	96.8	21.3	118.0	99.9	18.2
South Africa Afrique du Sud	2006	1 745 217	-2.0	98.0	-1.1	96.9	82.1	14.3
	2007	1 999 086	-3.2	96.8	-1.0	95.8	81.2	14.6
	2008	2 283 777	-3.2	96.8	-1.1	95.7	81.0	15.4
Spain Espagne	2006	982 303	-1.7	98.3	-1.0	97.4	75.5	21.9
	2007	1 050 595	-2.4	97.6	-0.9	96.7	75.6	21.1
	2008	1 095 163	-2.7	97.3	-1.0	96.3	76.3	20.0
Sri Lanka Sri Lanka	2005	2 452 782	-1.2	98.8	7.1	105.9	82.1	23.1
	2006	2 938 656	-1.4	98.6	6.7	105.4	83.0	21.7
	2007	3 578 386	-1.1	98.9	6.9	105.8	82.4	22.7
Sudan [+1] Soudan [+1]	1991	421 819	...	85.5	...	104.0	86.0	18.0
	1992	948 448	...	99.7	...	102.2	88.2	14.0
	1993	1 881 289	...	99.8	...	100.6	88.3	12.3
Suriname [1] Suriname [1]	2005	4 201 403 [12]	-2.7	97.3	1.5	98.8	...	...
	2006	5 039 810 [12]	-3.0	97.0	2.0	99.0	...	...
	2007	5 723 138 [12]	0.4	100.4	3.7	104.1	...	...
Swaziland [+] Swaziland [+]	2005	16 457	6.9	106.9	3.8	110.7	89.1	...
	2006	19 983	0.5	100.5	4.5	104.9	89.6	...
	2007	21 572	2.1	102.1	6.3	108.4	89.0	...
Sweden Suède	2006	2 900 790	1.7	101.7	-1.3	100.4	73.6	26.8
	2007	3 063 873	2.4	102.4	-1.2	101.2	72.6	28.7
	2008	3 156 881	2.2	102.2	-1.3	100.9	72.9	28.0
Switzerland Suisse	2005	463 139	9.4	109.4	-2.2	107.2	71.9	35.8
	2006	487 041	9.1	109.1	-3.0	106.1	70.1	36.6
	2007	512 142	6.6	106.6	...	...	68.6	...
Syrian Arab Republic [1] Rép. arabe syrienne [1]	2005	1 493 766	-4.5	95.5	0.8	96.3	80.3	16.0
	2006	1 698 480	-2.8	97.2	0.7	97.9	77.6	20.3
	2007	2 019 810	-1.7	98.3	0.5	98.8	72.0	26.9
Tajikistan Tadjikistan	2005	7 207	27.9	127.9	3.1	130.9	95.7	35.2
	2006	9 335	35.1	135.1	4.2	139.3	94.0	45.3
	2007	12 804	31.7	131.7	2.8	134.5	93.1	41.4
Thailand [1] Thaïlande [1]	2005	7 092 893	-4.9	95.2	1.7	96.9	69.1	27.7
	2006	7 841 297	-4.0	96.0	1.6	97.6	67.6	29.9
	2007	8 493 311	-3.8	96.2	1.6	97.8	65.9	31.8
TFYR of Macedonia L'ex-R.Y. Macédoine	2005	286 619	...	98.1	...	114.6	96.5	18.1
	2006	310 915	...	99.4	...	117.7	96.7	21.0
	2007	354 322	...	95.1	...	111.6	94.6	17.0
Togo [1] Togo [1]	1984	304 800	...	...	...	...	80.0	...
	1985	332 500	...	...	...	...	80.2	...
	1986	363 600	...	...	...	...	83.4	...
Tonga [+1] Tonga [+1]	2004	390	1.0	101.0	34.9	135.9	120.8	15.1
	2005	423	-2.1	97.9	35.7	133.6	126.2	7.3
	2006	479	2.7	102.7	34.2	137.0	126.5	10.4

21 Relationships among the principal national accounting aggregates *(continued)*

As a percentage of Gross Domestic Product (GDP)

Relations entre les principaux agrégats de comptabilité nationale *(suite)*

En pourcentage du Produit Intérieur Brut (PIB)

Country or area Pays ou zone	Year Année	GDP at current prices (mil.nat.cur.) PIB aux prix courants (millions monnaie nat.)	As a percentage of GDP - En pourcentage du PIB Plus: Compensation of employees and property income from/to the rest of the world, net Plus : Rémunération des salariés et revenus de la propriété du/au reste du monde, net	Equals: Gross national income Égale : Revenu national brut	Plus: Net current transfers from/to the rest of the world Plus : Transferts courants du/au reste du monde, net	Equals: Gross national disposable income Égale : Revenu national disponible brut	Less: Final consumption expenditure Moins : Dépense de consommation finale	Equals: Gross savings Égale : Épargne brut
Trinidad and Tobago	2005	100 386	-4.7[2]	95.3	0.3	95.6	65.4	30.2
Trinité-et-Tobago	2006	122 108	-4.8[2]	95.2	0.2	95.4	47.9	47.6
	2007	137 427	-4.4[2]	95.6	0.3	95.9	58.3	37.5
Tunisia [1]	2005	37 751	-5.6	94.4	5.1	99.5	78.2	21.3
Tunisie [1]	2006	41 385	-5.0	95.0	5.2	100.2	77.8	22.4
	2007	45 638	-5.6	94.4	5.3	99.6	76.6	23.1
Turkey [1]	2005	648 932	...	...	...	...	83.5	...
Turquie [1]	2006	758 391	...	...	...	...	82.9	...
	2007	856 387	...	...	...	...	82.9	...
Ukraine	2005	441 452	-1.1	98.9	3.4	102.2	76.5	25.7
Ukraine	2006	544 153	-1.6	98.4	3.0	101.4	78.1	23.3
	2007	720 731	-0.5	99.5	2.6	102.1	77.5	24.6
United Arab Emirates [1]	1988	87 106	0.3	100.3	-1.2	99.1	65.8	33.3
Emirats arabes unis [1]	1989	100 976	0.4	100.4	-0.7	99.7	61.7	38.0
	1990	124 008	-1.0	99.0	-8.9	90.1	54.9	35.1
United Kingdom	2006	1 321 860	0.7	100.7	-0.8	99.9	85.7	14.2
Royaume-Uni	2007	1 400 526	1.3	101.3	-0.9	100.5	85.0	15.5
	2008	1 442 921	2.2	102.2	-0.8	101.4	86.2	15.1
United Rep. of Tanzania [+ 13]	2005	15 965 296	-1.3	98.7	3.3	102.0	83.9	18.2
Rép.-Unie de Tanzanie [+ 13]	2006	17 941 268	-0.5	99.6	4.2	103.7	85.5	18.2
	2007	20 948 403	-0.4	99.7	4.1	103.7	87.2	16.5
United States	2005	12 364 100	0.8	101.3	-0.7	100.6	86.2	14.4
Etats-Unis	2006	13 116 500	0.6	101.8	-0.7	101.1	86.1	15.0
	2007	13 741 600	0.8	101.3	-0.8	100.5	86.8	13.7
Uruguay	2006	482 016	-2.2[2]	97.8	0.6	98.5	81.5	16.9
Uruguay	2007	*569 261	-1.6[2]	98.5	0.6	99.0	80.0	19.0
	2008	*674 278	-1.5[2]	98.5	0.5	98.9	81.0	17.9
Vanuatu [1]	2005	40 387	-7.0	93.0	5.4	98.3	79.8	4.8
Vanuatu [1]	2006	45 944	-4.9	95.1	6.1	101.2	76.1	11.3
	2007	51 980	-5.5	94.6	4.6	99.1	74.6	12.6
Venezuela (Boliv. Rep. of)	2004	212 683 082	-3.1	96.9	-0.1	96.8	61.2	35.7
Venezuela (Rép. boliv. du)	2005	304 086 815	-1.5	98.5	^0.0	98.4	57.8	40.6
	2006	393 926 240	-0.6	99.5	^0.0	99.4	58.7	40.7
Yemen [+]	2005	3 391 262	-8.7	91.3	7.5	98.8	72.4	26.5
Yémen [+]	2006	4 196 790	-5.5	94.5	6.1	100.6	69.5	31.1
	2007	4 923 687	-4.4	95.6	5.3	101.0	66.4	34.6
Zambia [1]	1986	12 963	-18.1[2]	81.9	-1.2	80.7	77.4	3.3
Zambie [1]	1987	19 778	-11.4[2]	88.6	0.5	89.1	82.0	7.1
	1988	27 275	-14.2[2]	85.8	1.0	86.9	79.8	7.1
Zimbabwe	2005	205 078 208	-1.6[5]	98.4	...	...	...	...
Zimbabwe	2006	1 030 061 188	-1.5[5]	98.5	...	...	...	...
	2007	15 767 745 314	-0.1[5]	99.9	...	...	...	...

21 Relationships among the principal national accounting aggregates *(continued)*

As a percentage of Gross Domestic Product (GDP)

Relations entre les principaux agrégats de comptabilité nationale *(suite)*

En pourcentage du Produit Intérieur Brut (PIB)

Source:
United Nations Statistics Division, New York, national accounts database, last accessed March 2010.

Data for most countries have been compiled in accordance with the concepts and definitions of the System of National Accounts 1993 (1993 SNA). Countries that follow the 1968 SNA are footnoted accordingly.

[+] Note: The national accounts data generally relate to the fiscal year used in each country, unless indicated otherwise. Countries whose reference periods coincide with the calendar year ending 31 December are not listed below.

Year beginning 21 March: Afghanistan, Iran (Islamic Republic).
Year beginning 1 April: Bermuda, India, Myanmar, New Zealand, Nigeria.
Year beginning 1 July: Australia, Bhutan, Cameroon, Gambia, Nicaragua, Pakistan, Puerto Rico, Saudi Arabia, Sierra Leone, Sudan, United Republic of Tanzania.
Year ending 30 June: Bangladesh, Botswana, Egypt, Swaziland, Tonga.
Year ending 7 July: Nepal.
Year ending 30 July: Ethiopia.
Year ending 30 September: Haiti.

Source:
Organisation des Nations Unies, Division de statistique, New York, la base de données sur les comptes nationaux, dernier accès mars 2010.

Les données pour la majorité des pays sont compilées selon les concepts et définitions du Système de comptabilité nationale, 1993 (SCN93). Seuls les pays qui suivent toujours le SCN68 seront donc signalés par une note.

[+] Note : Sauf indication contraire, les données sur les comptes nationaux concernent généralement l'exercice budgétaire utilisé dans chaque pays. Les pays où territoires dont la période de référence coïncide avec l'année civile se terminant le 31 décembre ne sont pas répertoriés ci-dessous.

Exercice commençant le 21 mars: Afghanistan, Iran (République islamique d').
Exercice commençant le 1er avril: Bermudes, Inde, Myanmar, Nigéria, Nouvelle-Zélande.
Exercice commençant le 1er juillet: Arabie saoudite, Australie, Bhoutan, Cameroun, Gambie, Nicaragua, Pakistan, Porto Rico, Sierra Leone, Soudan, Rép.-Unie de Tanzanie.
Exercice se terminant le 30 juin: Bangladesh, Botswana, Égypte, Swaziland, Tonga.
Exercice se terminant le 7 juillet: Népal.
Exercice se terminant le 30 juillet: Éthiopie.
Exercice se terminant le 30 septembre: Haïti.

1 Data compiled in accordance with the System of National Accounts 1968 (1968 SNA).
2 Property income - from and to the rest of the world, net.
3 Account does not balance.
4 Includes taxes less subsidies, net from-to-the Rest of the world.
5 Net Primary Income.
6 Includes net taxes less subsidies on production and imports -from/to the rest of the world
7 Preliminary data.
8 Including acquisitions less disposals of valuables.
9 Semi-final data.
10 Includes the adjustment for balance of payments.
11 Data for this year refers to indicative data. Indicative estimates are at an early stage of development and are expected to be substantially improved with further work.
12 Excluding the informal sector.
13 Tanzania mainland only.

1 Données compilées selon le Système de comptabilité nationale de 1968 (SCN 1968).
2 Revenus de la propriété - du et au reste du monde, net.
3 Le compte n'est pas équilibré.
4 Y compris les impôts moins les subventions, net du/au reste du monde.
5 Revenu primaire net.
6
7 Données préliminaires.
8 Y compris les acquisitions moins cessions d'objets de valeur.
9 Données demi-finales.
10 Y compris les données ajustées sur la balance des paiements.
11 Les données concernant cette année sont indicatives. Il s'agit de premières estimations que de nouveaux travaux permettront d'affiner.
12 Non compris le secteur informel.
13 Tanzanie continentale seulement.

Technical notes: tables 17-21

Detailed internationally comparable data on national accounts are compiled and published annually by the Statistics Division, Department of Economic and Social Affairs of the United Nations Secretariat. Data for national accounts aggregates for countries or areas are based on the concepts and definitions contained in *A System of National Accounts* (1968 SNA) and in *System of National Accounts 1993* (1993 SNA). A summary of the conceptual framework, classifications and definitions of transactions is found in the annual United Nations publication, *National Accounts Statistics: Main Aggregates and Detailed Tables*, which presents, in the form of analytical tables, a summary of selected principal national accounts aggregates based on official detailed national accounts data of over 200 countries and areas. Every effort has been made to present the estimates of the various countries or areas in a form designed to facilitate international comparability. The data for some countries or areas has been compiled according to the 1993 SNA. Data for those countries or areas which still follow the concepts and definitions of the 1968 SNA is indicated with a footnote. To the extent possible, any other differences in concept, scope, coverage and classification are footnoted as well. Detailed footnotes identifying these differences are also available in the annual national accounts publication mentioned above. Such differences should be taken into account in order to avoid misleading comparisons among countries or areas.

Table 17 shows gross domestic product (GDP) and GDP per capita in US dollars at current prices, GDP at constant 1990 prices and the corresponding real rates of growth. The table is designed to facilitate international comparisons of levels of income generated in production. In order to present comparable coverage for as many countries as possible, the official GDP national currency data are supplemented by estimates prepared by the Statistics Division, based on a variety of data derived from national and international sources. The conversion rates used to translate national currency data into US dollars are the period averages of market exchange rates (MERs) for members of the International Monetary Fund (IMF). These rates, which are published in the *International Financial Statistics*, are communicated to the IMF by national central banks and consist of three types: (a) market rates, determined largely by market forces; (b) official rates, determined by government authorities; and (c) principal rates for countries maintaining multiple exchange rate arrangements. Market rates always take priority and official rates are used only when a free market rate is not available.

For non-members of the IMF, averages of the United Nations operational rates, used for accounting pur-

Notes techniques: tableaux 17 à 21

La Division de statistique du Département des affaires économiques et sociales du Secrétariat de l'Organisation des Nations Unies établit et publie chaque année des données détaillées, comparables au plan international, sur les comptes nationaux. Les données relatives aux agrégats des différents pays et territoires sont établies en fonction des concepts et des définitions du *Système de comptabilité nationale* (SCN de 1968) et du *Système de comptabilité nationale 1993* (SCN de 1993). On trouvera un résumé de l'appareil conceptuel, des classifications et des définitions des opérations dans "*National Accounts Statistics: Main Aggregates and Detailed Tables*", publication annuelle des Nations Unies, qui présente, sous forme de tableaux analytiques, un choix d'agrégats essentiels de comptabilité nationale, issus des comptes nationaux détaillés de plus que 200 pays et territoires. On n'a rien négligé pour présenter les chiffres des différents pays et territoires sous une forme facilitant les comparaisons internationales. Pour plusieurs pays, les chiffres ont été établis selon le SCN de 1993. Les données des pays et territoires qui encore appliquent les concepts et les définitions du SCN de 1968 sont signalés par une note. Dans la mesure du possible, on signale également au moyen de notes les cas où les concepts, la portée, la couverture et la classification ne seraient pas les mêmes. Il y a en outre des notes détaillées explicitant ces différences dans la publication annuelle mentionnée plus haut. Il y a lieu de tenir compte de ces différences pour éviter de tenter des comparaisons qui donneraient matière à confusion.

Le *tableau 17* fait apparaître le produit intérieur brut (PIB) total et par habitant, exprimé en dollars des États-Unis aux prix courants et à prix constants (base 1990), ainsi que les taux de croissance correspondants. Le tableau est conçu pour faciliter les comparaisons internationales du revenu issu de la production. Afin que la couverture soit comparable pour le plus grand nombre possible de pays, la Division de statistique s'appuie non seulement sur les chiffres officiels du PIB exprimé dans la monnaie nationale, mais aussi sur diverses données provenant de sources nationales et internationales. Les taux de conversion utilisés pour exprimer les données nationales en dollars des États-Unis sont, pour les membres du Fonds monétaire international (FMI), les moyennes pour la période considérée des taux de change du marché. Ces derniers, publiés dans *Statistiques financières internationales*, sont communiqués au FMI par les banques centrales des pays et reposent sur trois types de taux : a) taux du marché, déterminés dans une large mesure par les facteurs du marché; b) taux officiels, déterminés par les pouvoirs publics; c) taux principaux, pour les pays pratiquant différents arrangements en matière

poses in United Nations transactions with member countries, are applied. These are based on official, commercial and/or tourist rates of exchange.

It should be noted that there are practical constraints in the use of MERs for conversion purposes. Their use may result in excessive fluctuations or distortions in the dollar income levels of a number of countries, particularly in those with multiple exchange rates, those coping with inordinate levels of inflation or countries experiencing misalignments caused by market fluctuations. Caution is therefore urged when making intercountry comparisons of incomes as expressed in US dollars.

Alternative methods of making international comparisons have been developed in recent years. One is the Purchasing Power Parities (PPPs) which have been developed as part of the International Comparison Programme; another is the World Bank Atlas method of conversion based on the average of the exchange rates of the current year and the two immediately preceding years that have been adjusted for differences in inflation rates between individual countries and the average of G-5 countries (Germany, France, Japan, the United Kingdom, and the United States). The Statistics Division of the United Nations has developed the Price-Adjusted Rates of Exchange method (PARE) which, like the Atlas method, is designed to adjust exchange rates that do not adequately reflect relative movements of domestic and international inflation. PARE is mainly applied to countries with fixed exchange rate regimes and countries going through a period of high inflation (e.g. transition countries from 1990-1995).

The GDP at constant price series, based primarily on data officially provided by countries or areas and partly on estimates made by the Statistics Division, is transformed into index numbers and rebased to 1990=100. The resulting data are then converted into US dollars at the rate prevailing in the base year 1990. The growth rates are based on the estimates of GDP at constant 1990 prices. The growth rate of the year in question is obtained by dividing the GDP of that year by the GDP of the preceding year.

Table 18 presents a desegregation of economic development by analyzing the movement of prices and exchange rates in relation to overall economic growth.

GDP indices based on current prices expressed in US dollars and national currencies are shown in columns 1 and 2. The annual changes of GDP in volume terms are reflected in column 3, where the indices are based on the movement of GDP at constant prices.

Column 4 presents indices of price changes of GDP expressed in national currency and column 5 includes indices of price changes of GDP in US dollars. The price indices in columns 4 and 5 are obtain by dividing,

de taux de change. On donne toujours la priorité aux taux du marché, n'utilisant les taux officiels que lorsqu'on n'a pas de taux du marché libre.

Pour les pays qui ne sont pas membres du FMI, on utilise les moyennes des taux de change opérationnels de l'ONU (qui servent à des fins comptables pour les opérations de l'ONU avec les pays qui en sont membres). Ces taux reposent sur les taux de change officiels, les taux du commerce et/ou les taux touristiques.

Il faut noter que l'utilisation des taux de change du marché pour la conversion des données se heurte à des obstacles pratiques. On risque, ce faisant, d'aboutir à des fluctuations excessives ou à des distorsions du revenu en dollars de certains pays, surtout dans le cas des pays qui pratiquent plusieurs taux de change et de ceux qui connaissent des taux d'inflation exceptionnels ou des décalages provenant des fluctuations du marché. Les comparaisons de revenu entre pays sont donc sujettes à caution lorsqu'on se fonde sur le revenu exprimé en dollars des États-Unis.

D'autres méthodes ont été élaborées ces dernières années pour les comparaisons internationales. L'une, celle de la parité de pouvoir d'achat (PPA), procède du Programme de comparaison internationale ; une autre méthode de conversion, celle de l'Atlas de la Banque mondiale, est basée sur la moyenne des taux de change de l'année en cours et des deux années immédiatement précédentes, ajustés en fonction des différences d'inflation entre les pays considérés et la moyenne des pays du G-5 (Allemagne, États-Unis, France, Japon, et Royaume-Uni). La Division de statistique de l'ONU a mis au point la méthode des Taux de Change Corrigés des Prix (TCCP) qui, comme celle de l'Atlas, est conçue pour corriger les taux de change qui ne rendent pas convenablement compte de l'évolution relative de l'inflation dans un pays par rapport à l'inflation à l'échelon international. Le TCCP sert surtout pour les pays à taux de change fixe et ceux qui connaissent une période de forte inflation (par ex. les pays en transition entre 1990 et 1995).

La série de statistiques du PIB à prix constants est fondée principalement sur des données officiellement communiquées par les pays, et en partie sur des estimations de la Division de statistique; les données permettent de calculer des indices, la base 100 correspondant à 1990. Les chiffres ainsi obtenus sont alors convertis en dollars des États-Unis au taux de change de l'année de base (1990). Les taux de croissance sont calculés à partir des estimations du PIB aux prix constants de 1990. Le taux de croissance de l'année considérée est obtenu en divisant le PIB de l'année par celui de l'année précédente.

Le *tableau 18* envisage le développement économique sous l'angle d'une analyse de l'évolution des prix et des taux de change par rapport à la croissance écono-

respectively, the indices of GDP at current prices in national currencies and in US dollars shown in columns 1 and 2, by the volume indices presented in column 3.

Column 6 provides an implied development in exchange rates derived either by dividing the GDP deflators in national currency (column 4) by the GDP deflators converted in US dollars (column 5), or by dividing the GDP indices expressed in national currencies by the US dollar indices listed in column 1 and 2, respectively.

Table 19 features the percentage distribution of GDP at current prices by expenditure breakdown. It shows the portions of GDP spent on consumption by the household sector (including the non-profit institutions serving households) and the government, the portions spent on gross fixed capital formation, on changes in inventories, and on exports of goods and services, deducting imports of goods and services. The percentages are derived from official data reported to the United Nations by the countries and published in the annual national accounts publication.

Table 20 shows the percentage distribution of value added originating from the various industry components of the *International Standard Industrial Classification of All Economic Activities, Revision 3* (ISIC Rev. 3). This table reflects the economic structure of production in the different countries or areas. The percentages are based on official gross value added at basic current prices broken down by the kind of economic activity: agriculture, hunting, forestry and fishing (categories A+B); mining and quarrying (C); manufacturing (D); electricity, gas and water supply (E); construction (F); wholesale and retail trade, repair of motor vehicles, motorcycles and personal and household goods, restaurants and hotels (G+H); transport, storage and communication (I) and "other activities", comprised of financial intermediation (J), real estate, renting and business activities (K), public administration and defence, compulsory social security (L), education (M), health and social work (N), other community, social and personal service activities (O) and private households with employed persons (P).

Table 21 presents the relationships among the principal national accounting aggregates, namely: gross domestic product (GDP), gross national income (GNI), gross national disposable income (GNDI) and gross savings. GNI is the term used in the 1993 SNA instead of the term Gross National Product (GNP) which was used in the 1968 SNA. The ratio of each aggregate to GDP is derived cumulatively by adding net primary income (or net factor income) from the rest of the world (GNI), adding net current transfers from the rest of the world (GNDI), and deducting final consumption to arrive at gross saving.

mique mondiale.

Les indices du PIB fondés sur les prix courants exprimés en monnaies nationales et en dollars des États-Unis sont indiqués dans les colonnes 1 et 2. L'évolution annuelle du PIB en volume apparaît dans la colonne 3, les indices étant fondés sur l'évolution du PIB à prix constants.

La colonne 4 présente l'évolution des indices des prix exprimés en monnaie nationale et la colonne 5 celle des indices des prix exprimés en dollars des États-Unis. Les indices de prix dans les colonnes 4 et 5 sont obtenus en divisant, respectivement, les indices du PIB fondés sur les prix courants exprimés en monnaies nationales et en dollars des États-Unis, qui sont indiqués dans les colonnes 1 et 2, par les indices de volume présentés dans la colonne 3.

La colonne 6 montre l'évolution implicite des taux de change obtenue soit en divisant les déflateurs du PIB en monnaie nationale (colonne 4) par les déflateurs du PIB convertis en dollars (colonne 5), soit en divisant les indices du PIB exprimés en monnaies nationales (colonne 1) par les indices exprimés en dollars des États-Unis (colonne 2).

Le *tableau 19* montre la répartition (en pourcentage) du PIB aux prix courants par catégorie de dépense. Il indique la part du PIB consacrée aux dépenses de consommation du secteur des ménages (y compris les institutions sans but lucratif au service des ménages) et des administrations publiques et celle qui est consacrée à l'investissement fixe brut, celle qui correspond aux variations de stocks et celle qui correspond aux exportations de biens et services, déduction faite des importations de biens et services. Ces pourcentages sont calculés à partir des chiffres officiels communiqués à l'ONU par les pays, publiés dans l'ouvrage annuel.

Le *tableau 20* montre la répartition (en pourcentage) de la valeur ajoutée par branche d'activité, selon le classement retenu dans la *Classification internationale type, par industrie, de toutes les branches d'activité économique, Révision 3* (CITI Révision 3). Il rend donc compte de la structure économique de la production dans chaque pays. Les pourcentages sont établis à partir des chiffres officiels de valeur ajoutée brute aux prix de base courants, répartis selon les différentes catégories d'activité économique: agriculture, chasse, sylviculture et pêche (catégories A + B); activités extractives (C); activités de fabrication (D); production et distribution d'électricité, de gaz et d'eau (E); construction (F); commerce de gros et de détail, réparation de véhicules automobiles, de motocycles et de biens personnels et domestiques, hôtels et restaurants (G + H); transports, entreposage et communications (I) et "autres activités", y compris intermédiation financière (J), immobilier, locations et activités de services aux entreprises (K), administra-

tion publique et défense, sécurité sociale obligatoire (L), éducation (M), santé et action sociale (N), autres activités de services collectifs, sociaux et personnels (O), et ménages privés employant du personnel domestique (P).

Le *tableau 21* montre les rapports entre les principaux agrégats de la comptabilité nationale, à savoir le produit intérieur brut (PIB), le revenu national brut (RNB), le revenu national brut disponible et l'épargne brute. Le revenu national brut est l'agrégat qui remplace dans le SCN de 1993 le produit national brut, utilisé dans le SCN de 1968. Chacun d'entre eux est obtenu par rapport au PIB, en ajoutant les revenus primaires nets (ou revenus nets de facteurs) engendrés dans le reste du monde, pour obtenir le revenu national brut; en ajoutant les transferts courants nets reçus de non-résidents, pour obtenir le revenu national disponible; en soustrayant la consommation finale pour obtenir l'épargne brute.

22 Rates of discount of central banks

Per cent per annum, end of period

Taux d'escompte des banques centrales

Pour cent par année, fin de la période

Country or area Pays ou zone	2000	2001	2002	2003	2004	2005	2006	2007	2008	2009
Albania [1] Albanie [1]	10.82	7.00	8.50	6.50	5.25	5.00	5.50	6.25	6.25	5.25
Algeria Algérie	6.00	6.00	5.50	4.50	4.00	4.00	4.00	4.00	4.00	4.00
Angola Angola	150.00	150.00	150.00	150.00	95.00	95.00	14.00	19.57	19.57	30.00
Anguilla Anguilla	8.00	7.00	7.00	6.50	6.50	6.50	6.50	6.50	6.50	6.50
Antigua and Barbuda Antigua-et-Barbuda	8.00	7.00	7.00	6.50	6.50	6.50	6.50	6.50	6.50	6.50
Aruba [1] Aruba [1]	6.50	6.50	6.50	5.00	5.00	5.00	5.00	5.00	5.00	3.00
Azerbaijan [2] Azerbaïdjan [2]	10.00	10.00	7.00	7.00	7.00	9.00	9.50	13.00	8.00	2.00
Bahamas Bahamas	5.75	5.75	5.75	5.75	5.75	5.25	5.25	5.25	5.25	5.25
Bangladesh Bangladesh	7.00	6.00	6.00	5.00	5.00	5.00	5.00	5.00	5.00	5.00
Barbados [1] Barbade [1]	10.00	7.50	7.50	7.50	7.50	10.00	12.00	12.00	10.00	7.00
Belarus [2] Bélarus [2]	80.00	48.00	38.00	28.00	17.00	11.00	10.00	10.00	12.00	13.50
Belize [3] Belize [3]	12.00	12.00	12.00	12.00	12.00	12.00	12.00	12.00	12.00	12.00
Benin Bénin	6.00	6.00	6.00	4.50	4.00	4.00	4.25	4.25	4.75	4.25
Bolivia (Plurinational State of) Bolivie (État plur. de)	10.00	8.50	12.50	7.50	6.00	5.25	5.25	6.50	13.00	3.00
Botswana [3] Botswana [3]	14.25	14.25	15.25	14.25	14.25	14.50	15.00	14.50	15.00	10.00
Brazil Brésil	18.52	21.43	30.42	23.92	24.55	25.34	19.98	17.85	20.48	15.17
Bulgaria [1] Bulgarie [1]	4.63	4.65	3.31	2.83	2.37	#2.05	3.26	4.58	5.77	0.55
Burkina Faso Burkina Faso	6.00	6.00	6.00	4.50	4.00	4.00	4.25	4.25	4.75	4.25
Burundi [4] Burundi [4]	14.00	14.00	15.50	14.50	14.50	14.50	11.07	10.12	10.08	10.00
Cameroon Cameroun	7.00	6.50	6.30	6.00	6.00	5.50	5.25	5.25	4.75	4.25
Canada [1] Canada [1]	6.00	2.50	3.00	3.00	2.75	3.50	4.50	4.50	1.75	0.50
Cape Verde Cap-Vert	...	11.50	10.00	8.50	8.50	8.50	8.50	8.50	7.50	7.50
Central African Rep. Rép. centrafricaine	7.00	6.50	6.30	6.00	6.00	5.50	5.25	5.25	4.75	4.25
Chad Tchad	7.00	6.50	6.30	6.00	6.00	5.50	5.25	5.25	4.75	4.25
Chile Chili	8.73	6.50	3.00	2.45	2.25	4.50	5.25	6.00	8.25	0.50
China [1] Chine [1]	3.24	3.24	2.70	2.70	3.33	3.33	3.33	3.33	2.79	2.79

Rates of discount of central banks *(continued)*

Per cent per annum, end of period

Taux d'escompte des banques centrales *(suite)*

Pour cent par année, fin de la période

Country or area Pays ou zone	2000	2001	2002	2003	2004	2005	2006	2007	2008	2009
China, Hong Kong SAR Chine, Hong Kong RAS	8.00	3.25	2.75	2.50	3.75	5.75	6.75	5.75	0.50	0.50
Colombia Colombie	18.28	13.25	10.00	12.00	11.25	10.75	9.50	11.50	11.50	5.50
Comoros Comores	5.63	5.89	4.79	3.83	3.55	3.59	4.34	5.36	5.36	2.22
Congo Congo	7.00	6.50	6.30	6.00	6.00	5.50	5.25	5.25	4.75	4.25
Costa Rica [5] Costa Rica [5]	31.50	28.75	31.25	26.00	26.00	27.00	24.75	17.00	25.00	23.00
Côte d'Ivoire Côte d'Ivoire	6.00	6.00	6.00	4.50	4.00	4.00	4.25	4.25	4.75	4.25
Croatia Croatie	5.90	5.90	4.50	4.50	4.50	4.50	4.50	9.00	9.00	9.00
Cyprus Chypre	7.00	5.50	5.00	4.50	5.50	4.25	4.50	5.00	...	...
Czech Republic [1] République tchèque [1]	5.25	4.50	2.75	2.00	2.50	2.00	2.50	3.50	2.25	1.00
Dem. Rep. of the Congo Rép. dém. du Congo	...	...	...	...	...	...	40.00	22.50	40.00	70.00
Denmark Danemark	4.75	3.25	2.86	2.00	2.00	2.25	3.50	4.00	3.50	1.00
Dominica Dominique	8.00	7.00	7.00	6.50	6.50	6.50	6.50	6.50	6.50	6.50
Ecuador Equateur	13.82	17.48	15.36	11.67	10.23	9.96	9.54	10.72	9.14	9.19
Egypt Egypte	12.00	11.00	10.00	10.00	10.00	10.00	9.00	9.00	11.50	8.50
Equatorial Guinea Guinée équatoriale	7.00	6.50	6.30	6.00	6.00	5.50	5.25	5.25	4.75	4.25
Euro Area [6,7] Zone euro [6,7]	5.75	4.25	3.75	3.00	3.00	3.25	4.50	5.00	3.00	1.75
Fiji [1] Fidji [1]	8.00	1.75	1.75	1.75	2.25	2.75	5.25	9.25	6.32	3.00
Gabon Gabon	7.00	6.50	6.30	6.00	6.00	5.50	5.25	5.25	4.75	4.25
Gambia Gambie	10.00	13.00	18.00	29.00	28.00	14.00	9.00	10.00	11.00	...
Ghana Ghana	27.00	27.00	24.50	21.50	18.50	15.50	12.50	13.50	17.00	18.00
Grenada Grenade	8.00	7.00	7.00	6.50	6.50	6.50	6.50	6.50	6.50	6.50
Guinea [2] Guinée [2]	11.50	16.25	16.25	16.25	16.25	22.25	...	...	...	...
Guinea-Bissau Guinée-Bissau	6.00	6.00	6.00	4.50	4.00	4.00	4.25	4.25	4.75	4.25
Guyana Guyana	11.75	8.75	6.25	5.50	6.00	6.00	6.75	6.50	6.75	6.75
Hungary Hongrie	11.00	9.75	8.50	12.50	9.50	6.00	8.00	7.50	10.00	6.25
Iceland Islande	12.40	12.00	8.20	7.70	10.25	12.00	15.25	15.25	22.00	14.55
India [1] Inde [1]	8.00	6.50	6.25	6.00	6.00	6.00	6.00	6.00	6.00	6.00
Indonesia Indonésie	14.53	17.62	12.93	8.31	7.43	12.75	9.75	8.00	10.83	6.46

22 Rates of discount of central banks *(continued)*

Per cent per annum, end of period

Taux d'escompte des banques centrales *(suite)*

Pour cent par année, fin de la période

Country or area Pays ou zone	2000	2001	2002	2003	2004	2005	2006	2007	2008	2009
Iraq Iraq	...	...	...	...	6.00	6.33	10.42	20.00	16.75	8.83
Israel Israël	8.21	5.67	9.18	5.20	3.90	4.44	5.00	4.00	2.50	1.00
Japan Japon	0.50	0.10	0.10	0.10	0.10	0.10	0.40	0.75	0.30	0.30
Jordan Jordanie	6.50	5.00	4.50	2.50	3.75	6.50	7.50	7.00	6.25	4.75
Kazakhstan [2] Kazakhstan [2]	14.00	9.00	7.50	7.00	7.00	8.00	9.00	11.00	10.50	7.00
Korea, Republic of Corée, République de	3.00	2.50	2.50	2.50	2.00	2.00	2.75	3.25	1.75	1.25
Kuwait Koweït	7.25	4.25	3.25	3.25	4.75	6.00	6.25	6.25	3.75	3.00
Lao People's Dem. Rep. [1] Rép. dém. pop. lao [1]	35.17	35.00	20.00	20.00	20.00	20.00	20.00	12.67	7.67	...
Latvia Lettonie	3.50	3.50	3.00	3.00	4.00	4.00	5.00	6.00	6.00	4.00
Lebanon Liban	20.00	20.00	20.00	20.00	20.00	12.00	12.00	12.00	12.00	10.00
Lesotho Lesotho	15.00	13.00	16.19	15.00	13.00	13.00	10.76	12.82	14.05	10.66
Libyan Arab Jamah. Jamah. arabe libyenne	5.00	5.00	5.00	5.00	4.00	4.00	4.00	4.00	5.00	4.00
Lithuania [1] Lituanie [1]	...	...	...	...	...	3.02	3.79	4.85	4.73	2.06
Malawi Malawi	50.23	46.80	40.00	35.00	25.00	25.00	20.00	15.00	15.00	15.00
Malaysia Malaisie	...	...	...	...	...	...	...	...	...	1.00
Maldives Maldives	...	18.00	18.54	19.00	18.25	18.00	...	#12.50	13.00	13.00
Mali [1] Mali [1]	6.00	6.00	6.00	4.50	4.00	4.00	4.25	4.25	4.75	4.25
Malta Malte	4.75	4.25	3.75	#3.00	3.00	3.25	3.75	...	...	...
Mauritania Mauritanie	13.00	11.00	11.00	11.00	11.00	14.00	14.00	12.00	...	...
Mongolia [1] Mongolie [1]	8.60	8.61	9.90	11.47	15.75	4.75	6.42	9.85	14.78	10.82
Montserrat Montserrat	8.00	7.00	7.00	6.50	6.50	6.50	6.50	6.50	6.50	6.50
Morocco Maroc	5.00	4.71	3.79	3.25	3.25	3.25	3.25	3.25	3.32	3.31
Mozambique Mozambique	9.95	9.95	9.95	9.95	9.95	9.95	9.95	9.95	9.95	9.95
Myanmar [1] Myanmar [1]	10.00	10.00	10.00	10.00	10.00	10.00	12.00	12.00	12.00	12.00
Namibia [8] Namibie [8]	11.25	9.25	12.75	7.75	7.50	7.00	9.00	10.50	10.00	7.00
Nepal [1] Népal [1]	7.50	6.50	5.50	5.50	5.50	6.00	6.25	6.25	6.50	6.50
Netherlands Antilles Antilles néerlandaises	6.00	6.00	6.00	...	...	...	...	...	...	...
New Zealand Nouvelle-Zélande	6.50	4.75	5.75	5.00	6.50	7.25	7.25	8.25	5.00	2.50

22 Rates of discount of central banks *(continued)*

Per cent per annum, end of period

Taux d'escompte des banques centrales *(suite)*

Pour cent par année, fin de la période

Country or area Pays ou zone	2000	2001	2002	2003	2004	2005	2006	2007	2008	2009
Niger Niger	6.00	6.00	6.00	4.50	4.00	4.00	4.25	4.25	4.75	4.25
Nigeria Nigéria	14.00	20.50	16.50	15.00	15.00	13.00	10.00	9.50	9.75	6.00
Norway Norvège	9.00	8.50	8.50	4.25	3.75	4.25	5.50	6.25	4.00	...
Oman Oman	7.30	7.50	7.50	7.50	#0.69	3.12	3.63	1.98	0.91	0.05
Pakistan Pakistan	13.00	10.00	7.50	7.50	7.50	9.00	9.50	10.00	15.00	12.50
Papua New Guinea Papouasie-Nvl-Guinée	9.79	11.73	11.71	#15.50	12.67	9.67	8.13	7.38	7.00	6.92
Paraguay Paraguay	20.00	20.00	20.00	20.00	20.00	20.00	20.00	20.00	20.00	...
Peru Pérou	14.00	5.00	4.50	3.25	3.75	4.00	5.25	5.75	7.25	2.05
Philippines Philippines	13.81	8.30	4.19	5.53	8.36	5.70	5.04	4.28	6.00	3.50
Poland Pologne	19.00	11.50	6.75	5.25	6.50	4.50	4.00	5.00	5.00	3.50
Qatar [3] Qatar [3]	...	...	1.70	1.33	2.60	4.50	5.50	5.50	5.50	5.50
Russian Federation [2] Fédération de Russie [2]	25.00	25.00	21.00	16.00	13.00	12.00	11.00	10.00	13.00	8.75
Rwanda Rwanda	11.69	13.00	13.00	14.50	14.50	12.50	12.50	12.50	11.25	...
Saint Kitts and Nevis Saint-Kitts-et-Nevis	8.00	7.00	7.00	6.50	6.50	6.50	6.50	6.50	6.50	6.50
Saint Lucia Sainte-Lucie	8.00	7.00	7.00	6.50	6.50	6.50	6.50	6.50	6.50	6.50
Saint Vincent-Grenadines Saint Vincent-Grenadines	8.00	7.00	7.00	6.50	6.50	6.50	6.50	6.50	6.50	6.50
Sao Tome and Principe Sao Tomé-et-Principe	17.00	15.50	15.50	14.50	14.50	18.20	28.00	28.00	28.00	16.00
Senegal Sénégal	6.00	6.00	6.00	4.50	4.00	4.00	4.25	4.25	4.75	4.25
Serbia [1] Serbie [1]	...	18.67	9.72	10.63	#17.21	19.16	15.35	9.57	17.75	9.92
Seychelles Seychelles	5.50	5.50	5.50	4.67	3.51	3.87	4.44	5.13	...	...
Slovakia Slovaquie	8.80	#7.75	6.50	6.00	4.00	3.00	4.75	4.25	...	...
Slovenia [1] Slovénie [1]	11.00	12.00	10.50	7.25	5.00	5.00	4.50	...	...	...
South Africa Afrique du Sud	12.00	9.50	13.50	8.00	7.50	7.00	9.00	11.00	11.50	7.00
Sri Lanka [4] Sri Lanka [4]	25.00	...	18.00	15.00	15.00	15.00	15.00	15.00	15.00	...
Swaziland Swaziland	11.00	9.50	13.50	8.00	7.50	7.00	9.00	11.00	11.00	6.50
Sweden [1] Suède [1]	2.00	2.00	#4.50	3.00	2.00	1.50	2.50	3.50	2.00	...
Switzerland Suisse	#3.20	1.59	0.50	0.11	0.54	0.73	1.90	2.05	0.05	0.05
Syrian Arab Republic Rép. arabe syrienne	5.00	5.00	5.00	5.00	5.00	5.00	5.00	5.00	5.00	5.00

22 Rates of discount of central banks *(continued)*

Per cent per annum, end of period

Taux d'escompte des banques centrales *(suite)*

Pour cent par année, fin de la période

Country or area Pays ou zone	2000	2001	2002	2003	2004	2005	2006	2007	2008	2009
Tajikistan [2] Tadjikistan [2]	20.60	20.00	#24.75	#15.00	10.00	9.00	12.00	15.00	13.50	8.00
Thailand Thaïlande	3.00	3.75	3.25	2.75	3.50	5.50	6.50	3.75	3.25	1.75
TFYR of Macedonia [1] L'ex-R.Y. Macédoine [1]	7.90	10.70	10.70	6.50	6.50	6.50	6.50	6.50	6.50	6.50
Togo Togo	6.00	6.00	6.00	4.50	4.00	4.00	4.25	4.25	4.75	4.25
Trinidad and Tobago [1] Trinité-et-Tobago [1]	13.00	13.00	7.25	7.00	7.00	8.00	10.00	10.00	10.75	7.25
Turkey Turquie	60.00	60.00	55.00	43.00	38.00	23.00	27.00	25.00	25.00	15.00
Uganda [1] Ouganda [1]	18.86	8.88	13.08	25.62	16.15	14.36	16.30	14.68	19.42	9.65
Ukraine [2] Ukraine [2]	27.00	12.50	7.00	7.00	9.00	9.50	8.50	8.00	12.00	10.25
United Rep. of Tanzania Rép.-Unie de Tanzanie	10.70	8.70	9.18	12.34	14.42	19.33	20.07	16.40	15.99	3.70
United States Etats-Unis	6.00	1.33	0.75	#2.00	3.15	5.16	6.25	4.83	0.86	0.50
Uruguay [9] Uruguay [9]	57.26	71.66	316.01	46.27	10.00	10.00	10.00	10.00	20.00	20.00
Vanuatu Vanuatu	7.00	6.50	6.50	6.50	6.50	6.25	6.00	6.00	6.00	6.00
Venezuela (Boliv. Rep. of) Venezuela (Rép. boliv. du)	38.00	37.00	40.00	28.50	28.50	28.50	28.50	28.50	33.50	29.50
Viet Nam [2] Viet Nam [2]	6.00	4.80	4.80	5.00	5.00	5.00	6.50	6.50	10.25	...
Zambia Zambie	25.67	40.10	27.87	14.35	16.68	14.81	8.79	11.73	14.49	8.39
Zimbabwe [1] Zimbabwe [1]	57.84	57.20	29.65	300.00	110.00	540.00	500.00	975.00	...	...

Source:
International Monetary Fund (IMF), Washington, D.C., the International Financial Statistics database, last accessed July 2010.

Source:
Fonds monétaire international (FMI), Washington, D.C., la base de données de Statistiques Financières Internationales, dernier accès juillet 2010.

1 Central Bank rate.
2 Refinance rate.
3 Lending rate.
4 Advance rate.
5 Discount rate: commercial.
6 "Euro Area" is an official descriptor for the European Economic and Monetary Union (EMU). The participating member states of the EMU are Austria, Belgium, Cyprus (beginning 2008), Finland, France, Germany, Greece (beginning 2001), Ireland, Italy, Luxembourg, Malta (beginning 2008), Netherlands, Portugal, Slovakia (beginning 2009), Slovenia (beginning 2007), and Spain.
7 Marginal lending facility rate.
8 Bank of Namibia overdraft rate.
9 Domestic currency.

1 Taux de la Banque centrale.
2 Taux de refinancement.
3 Taux prêteur.
4 Avances ordinaires à l'état.
5 Taux de l'escompte : effet de commerce.
6 L'expression "zone euro" est un intitulé officiel pour l'Union économique et monétaire (UEM) européenne. L'UEM est composée des pays membres suivants : Allemagne, Autriche, Belgique, Chypre (à partir de 2008), Espagne, Finlande, France, Grèce (à partir de 2001), Irlande, Italie, Luxembourg, Malte (à partir de 2008), Pays-Bas, Portugal, Slovaquie (à partir de 2009) et Slovénie (à partir de 2007).
7 Taux de facilité de prêt marginal.
8 Taux de découvert à la "Bank of Namibia".
9 Monnaie locale.

23 Short-term interest rates

Treasury bill and money market rates: per cent per annum

Taux d'intérêt à court terme

Taux des bons du trésor et du marché monétaire : pour cent par année

Country or area Pays ou zone	2000	2001	2002	2003	2004	2005	2006	2007	2008	2009
Afghanistan Afghanistan										
Money market Marché monétaire	...	...	...	...	...	...	2.50	5.65	...	...
Money market B [1] Marché monétaire B [1]	...	...	...	...	...	...	5.23	4.53	2.23	0.10
Albania Albanie										
Treasury bill Bons du trésor	10.80	7.72	9.49	8.81	6.79	5.52	5.49	5.93	6.24	6.27
Algeria Algérie										
Money market Marché monétaire	9.49	5.37	2.80	2.74	1.64	1.43	2.05	3.13	3.27	3.68
Treasury bill Bons du trésor	9.54	5.85	2.86	1.67	0.87	0.75	2.14	0.96	0.33	0.67
Anguilla Anguilla										
Money market Marché monétaire	5.25	#5.64	6.32	6.07	4.67	4.01	4.76	5.24	4.92	6.03
Antigua and Barbuda Antigua-et-Barbuda										
Money market Marché monétaire	5.25	#5.64	6.32	6.07	4.67	4.01	4.76	5.24	4.92	6.03
Treasury bill Bons du trésor	7.00	7.00	7.00	7.00	7.00	7.00	6.52	6.33	6.02	6.38
Argentina Argentine										
Money market Marché monétaire	8.15	24.90	41.35	3.74	1.96	4.11	7.20	8.67	10.07	10.23
Money market B [1] Marché monétaire B [1]	7.53	12.76	13.01	1.64	2.03	2.86	3.32	4.55	3.37	1.93
Armenia Arménie										
Money market Marché monétaire	18.63	19.40	12.29	7.51	4.18	3.17	4.34	4.47	6.75	6.25
Treasury bill Bons du trésor	24.40	#20.59	14.75	11.91	5.27	4.05	4.87	6.09	7.69	9.42
Aruba Aruba										
Money market Marché monétaire	3.37	2.19	0.45	0.18	0.11	0.51	2.27	2.53	0.45	0.05
Australia Australie										
Money market [2] Marché monétaire [2]	5.90	5.06	4.55	4.81	5.25	5.46	5.81	6.39	6.67	3.28
Treasury bill A Bons du trésor A	5.98	4.80	...	...	...	...	...	...	...	...
Azerbaijan Azerbaïdjan										
Treasury bill Bons du trésor	16.73	16.51	14.12	8.00	4.62	7.52	10.04	10.64	10.48	3.31
Bahamas Bahamas										
Treasury bill Bons du trésor	1.03	1.94	2.50	1.78	0.56	0.14	0.87	2.66	2.73	2.62
Bahrain Bahreïn										
Money market B Marché monétaire B	6.89	3.85	2.02	1.24	1.74	3.64	5.33	...	...	...
Treasury bill Bons du trésor	6.56	3.78	1.75	1.13	1.56	3.57	5.04	4.86	2.53	1.06
Barbados Barbade										
Treasury bill Bons du trésor	5.29	3.14	2.10	1.41	1.20	4.62	5.96	5.65	4.20	3.76
Belgium Belgique										
Treasury bill Bons du trésor	4.02	4.16	3.17	2.23	1.97	2.02	2.73	3.80	3.63	0.58
Belize [3] Belize [3]										
Treasury bill B Bons du trésor B	5.91	5.91	4.59	3.22	3.22	3.22	3.22	3.22	3.22	3.22

23 Short-term interest rates *(continued)*

Treasury bill and money market rates: per cent per annum

Taux d'intérêt à court terme *(suite)*

Taux des bons du trésor et du marché monétaire : pour cent par année

Country or area Pays ou zone	2000	2001	2002	2003	2004	2005	2006	2007	2008	2009
Benin[4] Bénin[4]										
Money market A Marché monétaire A	4.95	4.95	4.95	4.95	4.95	4.95	4.95	3.93	3.94	3.47
Bolivia (Plurinational State of) Bolivie (État plurinational de)										
Money market Marché monétaire	7.40	6.99	8.41	4.07	4.05	3.53	3.80	4.27	7.68	3.55
Money market B[1] Marché monétaire B[1]	5.68	3.57	2.96	2.12	3.02	3.37	4.62	4.59	6.36	1.63
Treasury bill Bons du trésor	10.99	11.48	12.41	9.93	7.41	4.96	4.56	6.04	8.31	2.86
Treasury bill B[1] Bons du trésor B[1]	7.02	4.19	3.56	2.53	3.34	2.85	3.68	4.31	4.87	0.65
Brazil Brésil										
Money market Marché monétaire	17.59	17.47	19.11	23.37	16.24	19.12	15.28	11.98	12.36	10.06
Treasury bill Bons du trésor	18.51	20.06	19.43	22.11	17.14	18.76	14.38	11.50	13.68	9.70
Treasury bill B[1] Bons du trésor B[1]	...	11.46	...	...	...	...	...	...	...	...
Bulgaria Bulgarie										
Money market B[5] Marché monétaire B[5]	3.02	3.74	2.47	1.95	1.95	#2.02	2.79	4.03	5.16	2.01
Treasury bill Bons du trésor	4.21	4.57	4.29	2.81	2.64	2.23	#2.58	3.79	...	...
Burkina Faso[4] Burkina Faso[4]										
Money market A Marché monétaire A	4.95	4.95	4.95	4.95	4.95	4.95	4.95	3.93	3.94	3.47
Burundi Burundi										
Treasury bill Bons du trésor	11.74	16.59	19.19	16.55	14.95	7.92	8.84	...	...	...
Canada Canada										
Money market A[6] Marché monétaire A[6]	5.52	4.11	2.45	2.93	2.25	2.66	4.02	4.35	2.96	0.39
Treasury bill Bons du trésor	5.49	3.77	2.59	2.87	2.22	2.73	4.03	4.15	2.39	0.35
Cape Verde Cap-Vert										
Treasury bill Bons du trésor	8.53	10.33	8.04	5.81	6.42	4.07	2.70	3.41	3.41	3.52
Chile Chili										
Money market Marché monétaire	10.09	6.81	4.08	2.72	1.88	3.48	5.02	5.36	7.11	1.95
China, Hong Kong SAR Chine, Hong Kong RAS										
Money market Marché monétaire	7.13	2.69	1.50	0.07	0.13	4.25	3.94	1.88	0.23	0.13
Treasury bill Bons du trésor	5.69	1.69	1.35	-0.08	0.07	3.65	3.29	1.96	0.05	0.07
China, Macao SAR[5] Chine, Macao RAS[5]										
Money market B Marché monétaire B	6.29	2.11	1.48	0.11	0.27	4.09	3.91	3.27	0.30	0.11
Colombia[5] Colombie[5]										
Money market B Marché monétaire B	10.87	10.43	6.06	6.95	7.01	6.19	6.49	8.66	9.73	5.65
Côte d'Ivoire[4] Côte d'Ivoire[4]										
Money market A Marché monétaire A	4.95	4.95	4.95	4.95	4.95	4.95	4.95	3.93	3.94	3.47
Croatia Croatie										
Money market Marché monétaire	6.88	3.42	1.61	3.19	5.08	3.25	2.46	5.11	6.08	7.53

Short-term interest rates *(continued)*
Treasury bill and money market rates: per cent per annum

Taux d'intérêt à court terme *(suite)*
Taux des bons du trésor et du marché monétaire : pour cent par année

Country or area Pays ou zone	2000	2001	2002	2003	2004	2005	2006	2007	2008	2009
Cyprus Chypre										
Money market Marché monétaire	5.96	4.93	3.42	3.35	4.01	3.27	2.90	4.01	...	...
Treasury bill Bons du trésor	6.02	5.80	4.04	3.51	4.44	4.34	2.56	3.59	...	...
Czech Republic République tchèque										
Money market Marché monétaire	5.42	4.69	2.63	2.08	2.56	2.17	2.55	4.11	3.63	1.54
Treasury bill Bons du trésor	5.37	5.06	2.72	2.04	2.57	1.96	2.51	3.55	3.62	1.29
Dem. Rep. of the Congo Rép. dém. du Congo										
Money market B Marché monétaire B	...	...	...	...	...	...	...	27.78	21.39	88.44
Denmark[7] Danemark[7]										
Money market B Marché monétaire B	4.98	...	3.56	2.38	2.16	2.20	3.18	#4.33	4.88	1.81
Dominica Dominique										
Money market Marché monétaire	5.25	#5.64	6.32	6.07	4.67	4.01	4.76	5.24	4.92	6.03
Treasury bill Bons du trésor	6.40	6.40	6.40	6.40	6.40	6.40	6.40	6.40	6.40	6.40
Dominican Republic Rép. dominicaine										
Money market Marché monétaire	18.28	13.47	14.50	24.24	36.76	12.57	10.60	8.24	12.24	8.08
Egypt Egypte										
Treasury bill Bons du trésor	9.10	7.20	5.50	6.90	9.90	8.57	9.53	6.85	11.37	9.84
El Salvador El Salvador										
Money market Marché monétaire	6.93	5.28	4.40	3.86	4.36	5.18	6.00	5.25	...	...
Estonia Estonie										
Money market Marché monétaire	5.68	5.31	3.88	2.92	2.50	2.38	3.16	4.87	6.66	5.93
Ethiopia Ethiopie										
Treasury bill Bons du trésor	2.74	3.06	1.30	#1.31	0.57	0.25	0.09	0.93	0.68	...
Euro Area Zone euro										
Money market A Marché monétaire A	4.39	4.26	3.26	2.26	2.05	2.12	3.01	3.98	3.78	1.00
Money market B[8] Marché monétaire B[8]	5.25	#5.64	6.32	6.07	4.67	4.01	4.76	5.24	4.92	6.03
Fiji Fidji										
Money market A[9] Marché monétaire A[9]	2.58	0.79	0.92	0.86	0.90	1.28	4.78	4.74	0.96	1.31
Treasury bill Bons du trésor	3.63	1.51	1.66	1.06	1.56	1.94	7.45	4.48	0.25	6.07
Finland[10] Finlande[10]										
Money market B Marché monétaire B	4.39	4.26	3.32	2.33	2.11	2.19	3.08	4.28	4.63	1.23
France France										
Treasury bill A Bons du trésor A	4.24	4.26	3.30	2.28	2.03	2.07	2.89	3.86	3.62	0.65
Georgia Géorgie										
Money market Marché monétaire	16.77	17.54	27.69	16.88	11.87	7.71	9.46	7.42	...	...
Treasury bill Bons du trésor	...	29.93	43.42	44.26	19.16	...	...	...	...	5.98

23 Short-term interest rates *(continued)*

Treasury bill and money market rates: per cent per annum

Taux d'intérêt à court terme *(suite)*

Taux des bons du trésor et du marché monétaire : pour cent par année

Country or area Pays ou zone	2000	2001	2002	2003	2004	2005	2006	2007	2008	2009
Germany Allemagne										
Money market B[7] Marché monétaire B[7]	4.11	4.37	3.28	2.32	2.05	2.09	2.84	3.86	3.82	0.63
Treasury bill Bons du trésor	4.32	3.66	2.97	1.98	2.00	2.03	3.08	...	...	...
Ghana Ghana										
Money market Marché monétaire	...	...	...	24.71	15.73	14.70	10.57	12.00	15.64	21.50
Treasury bill B[11] Bons du trésor B[11]	36.28	40.96	25.11	27.25	16.57	14.89	9.95	9.66	16.96	23.76
Greece[12] Grèce[12]										
Treasury bill A Bons du trésor A	6.22	4.08	3.50	2.34	2.27	2.33	3.44	4.45	4.81	1.62
Grenada Grenade										
Money market Marché monétaire	5.25	#5.64	6.32	6.07	4.67	4.01	4.76	5.24	4.94	6.03
Treasury bill Bons du trésor	6.50	#7.00	7.00	6.50	5.50	5.50	6.25	6.38	6.25	6.33
Guatemala Guatemala										
Money market Marché monétaire	9.33	10.58	9.11	6.65	6.16	6.54	6.56	...	...	...
Guinea-Bissau Guinée-Bissau										
Money market Marché monétaire	4.95	4.95	4.95	4.95	4.95	4.95	4.95	3.93	3.94	3.47
Guyana Guyana										
Treasury bill Bons du trésor	9.88	7.78	4.94	3.04	3.62	3.79	3.95	3.94	3.99	4.31
Hungary Hongrie										
Treasury bill Bons du trésor	11.03	10.79	8.91	8.22	11.33	6.95	6.87	7.67	8.90	8.48
Iceland Islande										
Money market Marché monétaire	11.61	14.51	11.21	5.14	6.22	9.05	12.41	13.96	16.05	11.15
Treasury bill B[13] Bons du trésor B[13]	11.12	11.03	8.01	4.93	6.04	8.80	13.41	15.13	17.88	11.38
India[7] Inde[7]										
Money market B Marché monétaire B	...	...	...	...	...	...	...	15.29	11.55	4.49
Indonesia[7] Indonésie[7]										
Money market B Marché monétaire B	10.32	15.03	13.54	7.76	5.38	6.78	9.18	6.02	8.48	7.16
Iraq[14] Iraq[14]										
Treasury bill A Bons du trésor A	...	...	...	...	...	8.90	9.49	21.00	17.68	...
Ireland[15] Irlande[15]										
Money market A Marché monétaire A	4.84	3.31	2.88	2.08	2.13	2.40	3.64	4.71	2.99	0.48
Israel Israël										
Treasury bill Bons du trésor	8.81	6.50	7.38	7.00	4.78	4.34	5.54	4.33	3.90	1.39
Italy Italie										
Money market Marché monétaire	4.39	4.26	3.32	2.33	2.10	2.18	3.09	4.29	4.67	1.28
Treasury bill Bons du trésor	4.53	4.05	3.26	2.19	2.08	2.17	3.18	4.04	3.76	0.96
Jamaica Jamaïque										
Money market Marché monétaire	19.90	19.10	15.09	25.53	12.79	10.96	9.37	9.04	10.78	8.79
Treasury bill Bons du trésor	18.24	16.71	15.54	25.94	15.47	13.39	12.79	12.56	15.89	19.95

Short-term interest rates *(continued)*

Treasury bill and money market rates: per cent per annum

Taux d'intérêt à court terme *(suite)*

Taux des bons du trésor et du marché monétaire : pour cent par année

Country or area Pays ou zone	2000	2001	2002	2003	2004	2005	2006	2007	2008	2009
Japan Japon										
Money market B[7] Marché monétaire B[7]	0.11	0.06	0.01	^0.00	^0.00	^0.00	0.13	0.47	0.46	0.11
Treasury bill B[16] Bons du trésor B[16]	0.23	0.03	0.01	^0.00	^0.00	^0.00	0.42	0.55	0.36	0.12
Jordan Jordanie										
Money market Marché monétaire	5.28	4.63	3.49	2.58	2.18	3.59	5.55	5.70	4.94	3.33
Kazakhstan Kazakhstan										
Treasury bill Bons du trésor	6.59	5.28	5.20	5.86	3.28	3.28	3.28	7.01	7.00	7.00
Kenya Kenya										
Treasury bill Bons du trésor	12.07	12.73	8.94	3.73	2.96	8.44	6.81	6.80	7.70	7.38
Korea, Republic of Corée, République de										
Money market[17] Marché monétaire[17]	5.16	4.69	4.21	4.00	3.65	3.33	4.19	4.77	4.78	1.98
Money market B Marché monétaire B	9.35	7.05	6.56	5.43	4.73	4.68	5.17	5.70	7.02	5.81
Kuwait Koweït										
Money market A[18] Marché monétaire A[18]	6.82	4.62	2.99	2.47	2.14	2.83	5.62	4.88	2.80	1.60
Treasury bill A[19,20] Bons du trésor A[19,20]	6.83	4.23	2.83	2.33	1.75	1.99	...	...	...	0.92
Kyrgyzstan Kirghizistan										
Money market Marché monétaire	24.26	11.92	6.30	4.65	4.78	3.24	2.83	3.18	7.62	7.81
Treasury bill Bons du trésor	32.26	19.08	10.15	7.21	4.94	4.40	4.75	4.90	13.16	10.57
Lao People's Dem. Rep. Rép. dém. pop. lao										
Treasury bill Bons du trésor	29.94	22.70	21.41	24.87	20.37	18.61	18.34	18.36	12.48	...
Latvia Lettonie										
Money market Marché monétaire	2.97	5.23	3.01	2.86	3.25	2.49	3.24	5.07	4.09	3.92
Treasury bill Bons du trésor	4.85	5.63	3.52	3.24	3.43	2.56	4.13	4.23	6.99	10.42
Lebanon Liban										
Treasury bill Bons du trésor	11.18	11.18	10.90	6.46	5.25	5.22	5.22	5.22	5.21	4.91
Lesotho Lesotho										
Treasury bill Bons du trésor	9.06	9.49	11.34	11.96	8.52	7.23	6.87	7.81	9.75	7.75
Libyan Arab Jamah.[21] Jamah. arabe libyenne[21]										
Money market B Marché monétaire B	4.00	4.00	4.00	4.00	4.00	...	...	...	...	...
Lithuania Lituanie										
Money market Marché monétaire	3.60	3.37	2.21	1.79	1.53	1.97	2.76	4.18	3.95	0.88
Money market B[1] Marché monétaire B[1]	6.10	4.03	1.92	1.72	1.73	2.59	3.06	4.25	2.92	0.44
Treasury bill Bons du trésor	9.27	5.68	3.72	2.61	2.25	2.36	2.95	4.23	5.35	8.54
Madagascar Madagascar										
Money market Marché monétaire	16.00	9.00	9.00	10.50	16.50	16.50	14.50	11.00	11.50	9.50
Treasury bill Bons du trésor	...	10.28	...	11.94	12.95	18.84	21.16	11.84	8.81	7.62
Malawi Malawi										
Treasury bill Bons du trésor	39.52	42.41	41.75	39.27	28.58	24.40	19.27	13.95	11.29	10.15

23 Short-term interest rates *(continued)*

Treasury bill and money market rates: per cent per annum

Taux d'intérêt à court terme *(suite)*

Taux des bons du trésor et du marché monétaire : pour cent par année

Country or area Pays ou zone	2000	2001	2002	2003	2004	2005	2006	2007	2008	2009
Malaysia Malaisie										
Money market A[9] Marché monétaire A[9]	2.66	2.79	2.73	2.74	2.70	2.72	3.38	3.50	3.47	2.12
Treasury bill A[19] Bons du trésor A[19]	2.86	2.79	2.73	2.79	2.40	2.48	3.23	3.43	3.39	2.05
Maldives Maldives										
Money market B[7] Marché monétaire B[7]	6.80	...	...	...	...	...	...	...	...	...
Treasury bill Bons du trésor	...	...	...	...	...	...	...	5.50	6.00	6.00
Mali[4] Mali[4]										
Money market A Marché monétaire A	4.95	4.95	4.95	4.95	4.95	4.95	4.95	3.93	3.94	3.47
Malta[19] Malte[19]										
Treasury bill A Bons du trésor A	4.89	4.93	4.03	3.29	2.94	3.18	3.49	4.25	4.54	1.23
Mauritania Mauritanie										
Treasury bill Bons du trésor	10.93	3.14	6.01	7.65	7.22	11.84	11.50	10.43	...	...
Mauritius Maurice										
Money market Marché monétaire	7.66	7.25	6.20	3.22	1.33	2.45	5.59	8.52	7.52	4.63
Mexico Mexique										
Money market B[22] Marché monétaire B[22]	16.96	12.89	8.17	6.83	7.15	9.59	7.51	7.66	8.28	5.93
Treasury bill Bons du trésor	15.24	11.31	7.09	6.23	6.82	9.20	7.19	7.19	7.68	5.43
Mongolia Mongolie										
Treasury bill Bons du trésor	...	...	...	...	10.39	13.73	6.73	6.82	...	...
Montenegro Monténégro										
Treasury bill Bons du trésor	...	...	...	...	10.39	6.03	1.15	0.56	...	4.43
Montserrat Montserrat										
Money market Marché monétaire	5.25	#5.64	6.32	6.07	4.67	4.01	4.76	5.24	4.92	6.03
Morocco Maroc										
Money market Marché monétaire	5.41	4.44	2.99	3.22	2.39	2.78	2.58	3.31	3.37	3.26
Mozambique Mozambique										
Money market Marché monétaire	16.12	#25.00	20.40	13.34	9.87	6.35	15.25	15.15	12.84	8.66
Treasury bill Bons du trésor	16.97	24.77	29.55	15.32	12.37	9.10	15.05	15.16	13.76	10.59
Namibia Namibie										
Money market Marché monétaire	9.19	9.53	10.46	10.03	6.93	6.93	7.12	8.61	9.37	7.75
Treasury bill Bons du trésor	10.26	9.29	11.00	10.51	7.78	7.09	7.26	8.59	9.64	8.19
Nepal Népal										
Treasury bill Bons du trésor	5.30	5.00	3.80	3.85	2.40	2.20	1.98	3.59	4.72	6.35
Netherlands Antilles[19] Antilles néerlandaises[19]										
Treasury bill A Bons du trésor A	6.15	6.15	5.15	2.80	3.86	3.52	5.39	6.04	4.40	1.35
New Zealand Nouvelle-Zélande										
Money market Marché monétaire	6.12	5.76	5.40	5.33	5.77	6.76	7.30	7.93	7.55	2.82
Treasury bill A[23] Bons du trésor A[23]	6.39	5.56	5.52	5.21	5.85	6.52	7.05	7.55	7.01	2.83

23 Short-term interest rates *(continued)*

Treasury bill and money market rates: per cent per annum

Taux d'intérêt à court terme *(suite)*

Taux des bons du trésor et du marché monétaire : pour cent par année

Country or area Pays ou zone	2000	2001	2002	2003	2004	2005	2006	2007	2008	2009
Niger[4] Niger[4]										
Money market A Marché monétaire A	4.95	4.95	4.95	4.95	4.95	4.95	4.95	3.93	3.94	3.47
Nigeria Nigéria										
Treasury bill Bons du trésor	15.50	17.50	19.03	14.79	14.34	7.63	9.99	6.85	8.20	3.79
Norway[7] Norvège[7]										
Money market B Marché monétaire B	6.72	7.38	7.05	4.45	2.17	2.26	3.12	...	6.06	...
Oman[9] Oman[9]										
Money market A Marché monétaire A	...	...	...	...	0.66	2.25	3.40	1.47	0.29	0.08
Pakistan Pakistan										
Money market B[7] Marché monétaire B[7]	8.57	8.49	5.53	2.14	2.70	6.83	8.89	9.30	12.33	11.96
Treasury bill A[24] Bons du trésor A[24]	8.38	10.71	6.08	1.87	2.49	7.18	8.54	8.99	11.37	12.52
Panama Panama										
Money market Marché monétaire	...	...	2.22	1.50	1.90	3.13	5.06	5.05	...	0.42
Papua New Guinea Papouasie-Nvl-Guinée										
Money market B[5] Marché monétaire B[5]	9.54	11.05	9.11	13.58	7.79	4.36	3.29	3.00	5.50	7.67
Treasury bill A[25] Bons du trésor A[25]	17.00	12.36	10.93	18.69	8.85	3.81	4.01	4.67	6.19	7.08
Paraguay Paraguay										
Money market Marché monétaire	10.70	13.45	13.19	13.02	1.33	2.29	8.33	3.93	4.50	8.94
Peru[5] Pérou[5]										
Money market Marché monétaire	11.41	3.15	3.80	2.51	3.00	3.34	4.51	4.99	6.54	1.24
Money market B[1] Marché monétaire B[1]	8.40	2.07	2.22	1.09	2.19	4.19	5.37	5.92	1.02	0.21
Philippines Philippines										
Money market Marché monétaire	10.84	9.75	7.15	6.97	7.05	7.31	7.84	7.02	5.48	4.54
Treasury bill A[14] Bons du trésor A[14]	9.91	9.73	5.49	5.87	7.32	6.13	5.29	3.38	...	...
Poland Pologne										
Money market Marché monétaire	17.55	17.14	9.49	5.69	5.67	5.34	4.10	4.42	5.75	3.18
Treasury bill Bons du trésor	17.42	14.73	8.22	5.38	6.60	4.90	4.19	4.70	6.27	4.56
Qatar Qatar										
Money market Marché monétaire	...	...	...	...	2.09	3.13	4.77	4.38	1.06	2.09
Republic of Moldova République de Moldova										
Money market Marché monétaire	20.77	11.04	5.13	11.51	13.19	5.87	9.50	12.19	15.58	...
Money market B[1] Marché monétaire B[1]	6.86	9.06	4.80	2.52	0.78	2.49	4.13	3.96	2.57	...
Treasury bill Bons du trésor	22.20	14.24	5.89	15.08	11.89	3.70	7.30	13.10	18.07	11.35
Romania Roumanie										
Money market Marché monétaire	44.78	40.97	29.05	18.95	20.01	8.99	8.34	7.55	11.37	10.92
Treasury bill A[14] Bons du trésor A[14]	51.86	42.18	27.03	15.07	...	...	...	7.11	10.42	10.90

23 Short-term interest rates *(continued)*

Treasury bill and money market rates: per cent per annum

Taux d'intérêt à court terme *(suite)*

Taux des bons du trésor et du marché monétaire : pour cent par année

Country or area Pays ou zone	2000	2001	2002	2003	2004	2005	2006	2007	2008	2009
Russian Federation Fédération de Russie										
Money market Marché monétaire	7.14	10.10	8.19	3.77	3.33	2.68	3.43	4.43	5.48	7.78
Treasury bill Bons du trésor	12.12	12.45	12.72	5.35	...	...	...	...	...	...
Rwanda Rwanda										
Money market B [5] Marché monétaire B [5]	...	10.29	10.09	10.13	11.02	8.28	8.26	7.21	7.13	...
Treasury bill Bons du trésor	...	8.89	9.32	11.18	12.52	8.35	9.86	#7.24	...	...
Saint Kitts and Nevis Saint-Kitts-et-Nevis										
Money market Marché monétaire	5.25	#5.64	6.32	6.07	4.67	4.01	4.76	5.24	4.92	6.03
Treasury bill Bons du trésor	6.50	7.50	7.50	7.17	7.00	7.00	7.00	7.00	7.00	6.85
Saint Lucia Sainte-Lucie										
Money market Marché monétaire	5.25	#5.64	6.32	6.07	4.67	4.01	4.76	5.24	4.92	6.03
Treasury bill Bons du trésor	6.02	5.84	5.84	5.44	5.50	4.64	5.17	#5.65	5.60	5.20
Saint Vincent-Grenadines Saint Vincent-Grenadines										
Money market Marché monétaire	5.25	#5.64	6.32	6.07	4.67	4.01	4.76	5.24	4.92	6.03
Treasury bill Bons du trésor	6.50	7.00	7.00	5.73	4.61	4.85	5.62	5.75	5.56	5.67
Senegal Sénégal										
Money market Marché monétaire	4.95	4.95	4.95	4.95	4.95	4.95	4.95	3.93	3.94	3.47
Serbia Serbie										
Money market Marché monétaire	...	31.91	15.48	12.69	12.86	20.51	16.51	10.31	18.52	11.01
Treasury bill Bons du trésor	...	...	...	20.02	21.17	14.58	10.24	4.42	9.61	10.34
Seychelles Seychelles										
Treasury bill Bons du trésor	5.00	5.00	5.00	4.61	3.17	3.34	3.70	3.92	7.07	12.97
Sierra Leone Sierra Leone										
Treasury bill Bons du trésor	26.22	13.74	15.15	15.68	26.14	22.98	17.71	18.41	15.48	...
Singapore Singapour										
Money market A [8] Marché monétaire A [8]	2.57	1.99	0.96	0.74	1.04	2.28	3.46	2.72	1.31	0.69
Treasury bill [19] Bons du trésor [19]	2.18	1.69	0.81	0.64	0.96	2.04	2.95	2.34	0.87	0.33
Slovakia Slovaquie										
Money market Marché monétaire	8.08	7.76	6.33	6.08	3.82	3.02	4.83	4.25	...	...
Slovenia Slovénie										
Money market Marché monétaire	6.95	6.90	4.93	5.59	4.40	3.73	3.38	4.08	4.27	0.90
Treasury bill Bons du trésor	10.94	10.88	8.73	6.53	4.17	3.66	3.30	3.90	3.88	1.26
Solomon Islands Iles Salomon										
Treasury bill A Bons du trésor A	7.05	8.23	6.87	5.85	6.00	4.53	#3.41	3.17	3.20	4.00
South Africa Afrique du Sud										
Money market Marché monétaire	9.54	#8.49	11.11	10.93	7.15	6.62	7.19	#9.22	11.32	8.15
Treasury bill Bons du trésor	10.11	9.68	11.16	10.67	7.53	6.91	7.34	9.12	10.81	7.85

23 Short-term interest rates *(continued)*

Treasury bill and money market rates: per cent per annum

Taux d'intérêt à court terme *(suite)*

Taux des bons du trésor et du marché monétaire : pour cent par année

Country or area Pays ou zone	2000	2001	2002	2003	2004	2005	2006	2007	2008	2009
Spain Espagne										
Money market B[7] Marché monétaire B[7]	4.11	4.36	3.28	2.31	2.04	2.09	2.83	3.85	3.85	0.68
Treasury bill Bons du trésor	4.61	3.92	3.34	2.21	2.17	2.19	3.26	4.07	3.71	1.00
Sri Lanka Sri Lanka										
Money market B[26] Marché monétaire B[26]	17.30	21.24	12.33	9.68	8.87	10.15	12.89	30.88	21.22	11.67
Treasury bill Bons du trésor	14.02	17.57	12.47	8.09	7.71	9.03	10.98	16.60	18.91	12.93
Swaziland Swaziland										
Money market Marché monétaire	5.54	5.06	7.31	6.98	4.12	3.47	4.40	6.67	8.17	5.40
Treasury bill Bons du trésor	8.30	7.16	8.59	10.61	7.94	7.08	7.54	9.03	10.77	7.93
Sweden Suède										
Money market B[7] Marché monétaire B[7]	3.81	4.09	4.19	3.29	...	...	...	...	...	...
Treasury bill A[27] Bons du trésor A[27]	3.96	4.00	4.07	3.03	2.11	1.72	2.33	3.55	3.91	0.40
Switzerland Suisse										
Money market Marché monétaire	3.50	1.65	0.44	0.09	0.55	0.63	1.94	2.00	0.01	0.05
Treasury bill Bons du trésor	2.93	2.68	0.94	0.16	0.37	0.71	1.36	2.16	1.33	0.00
Thailand Thaïlande										
Money market Marché monétaire	1.95	2.00	1.76	1.31	1.23	2.62	4.64	3.75	3.28	1.21
Treasury bill Bons du trésor	...	...	#1.92	1.35	1.30	2.67	4.66	3.48	3.19	1.24
Togo[4] Togo[4]										
Money market A Marché monétaire A	4.95	4.95	4.95	4.95	4.95	4.95	4.95	3.93	3.94	3.47
Trinidad and Tobago Trinité-et-Tobago										
Treasury bill Bons du trésor	10.56	8.55	4.83	4.71	4.77	4.86	6.07	6.91	7.01	2.69
Tunisia Tunisie										
Money market Marché monétaire	5.88	6.04	5.94	5.14	5.00	5.00	5.07	5.24	5.21	4.30
Turkey Turquie										
Money market B[5] Marché monétaire B[5]	56.72	91.95	49.51	36.16	21.42	14.73	15.59	17.24	16.00	9.24
Treasury bill Bons du trésor	37.77	93.24	59.50	34.90	22.08	15.49	18.37	17.65	...	...
Uganda[14] Ouganda[14]										
Treasury bill A Bons du trésor A	13.19	11.00	5.85	16.87	9.02	8.50	8.12	9.05	8.59	7.05
Ukraine Ukraine										
Money market Marché monétaire	18.34	16.57	5.50	7.90	6.34	4.16	3.59	2.27	13.71	12.64
Money market B[1] Marché monétaire B[1]	6.27	5.87	3.14	3.61	2.15	2.85	4.13	4.82	4.30	1.09
United Kingdom Royaume-Uni										
Money market A[28] Marché monétaire A[28]	5.77	5.08	3.89	3.59	4.29	4.70	4.77	5.67	4.68	0.53
Treasury bill Bons du trésor	5.80	4.77	3.86	3.55	4.43	4.55	4.65	5.52	4.30	0.53
Treasury bill B[29] Bons du trésor B[29]	5.83	4.79	3.96	3.55	4.44	4.59	4.67	5.60	4.35	0.54
United Rep. of Tanzania Rép.-Unie de Tanzanie										
Treasury bill Bons du trésor	9.78	4.21	3.53	6.26	8.35	10.67	11.64	13.38	8.11	7.14

23 Short-term interest rates *(continued)*
Treasury bill and money market rates: per cent per annum

Taux d'intérêt à court terme *(suite)*
Taux des bons du trésor et du marché monétaire : pour cent par année

Country or area Pays ou zone	2000	2001	2002	2003	2004	2005	2006	2007	2008	2009
United States Etats-Unis										
Money market A[30] Marché monétaire A[30]	6.31	3.61	1.69	1.11	1.49	3.38	5.03	4.99	2.12	0.26
Money market B[31] Marché monétaire B[31]	6.24	3.89	1.67	1.13	1.35	3.21	4.96	5.02	1.93	0.16
Treasury bill Bons du trésor	5.84	3.45	1.61	1.01	1.37	3.15	4.72	4.41	1.46	0.16
Treasury bill A[19] Bons du trésor A[19]	6.00	3.48	1.63	1.02	1.39	3.21	4.85	4.45	1.37	0.14
Uruguay Uruguay										
Money market Marché monétaire	14.82	22.11	86.10	20.76	3.57	1.25	1.60	4.11	9.80	8.60
Treasury bill Bons du trésor	...	...	...	32.53	14.75	4.14	4.54	7.11	...	11.87
Vanuatu[32] Vanuatu[32]										
Money market B Marché monétaire B	5.58	5.50	5.50	5.50	5.50	5.50	5.50	5.50	5.78	5.61
Venezuela (Boliv. Rep. of) Venezuela (Rép. boliv. du)										
Money market Marché monétaire	8.14	13.33	28.87	13.23	4.38	2.62	5.26	8.72	11.09	10.03
Viet Nam Viet Nam										
Treasury bill Bons du trésor	5.42	5.49	5.92	5.83	5.69	6.13	4.73	4.15	...	...
Yemen Yémen										
Treasury bill Bons du trésor	14.16	13.25	11.55	12.92	13.84	14.89	15.65	15.86	15.20	13.47
Zambia Zambie										
Treasury bill Bons du trésor	31.37	44.28	34.54	29.98	12.60	16.32	10.37	11.95	13.47	15.39
Zimbabwe[8] Zimbabwe[8]										
Money market A Marché monétaire A	64.98	21.52	32.35	110.05	129.58	...	...	...	...	...

Source:
International Monetary Fund (IMF), Washington, D.C., the database on International Financial Statistics, last accessed November 2010.

1 Foreign currency.
2 13 weeks.
3 Discount rate.
4 Overnight advances.
5 Interbank.
6 Overnight rate.
7 Call money rate.
8 3-month interbank rate.
9 Overnight interbank.
10 Average cost of Central Bank debt.
11 Discounted.
12 12 months.
13 Yield.
14 91 days.
15 1-month fixed rate.
16 Financing bill rate.
17 Corporate bond rate.
18 Interbank deposit rate (3 months).
19 3 months.
20 Central Bank bill rate.
21 Interbank call loans (maximum rate).
22 Bankers' acceptances.
23 New issue rate: 3-month treasury bills.
24 6 months.
25 182 days.

Source:
Fonds monétaire international (FMI), Washington, D.C., la base de données de Statistiques Financières Internationales, dernier accès novembre 2010.

1 Devises.
2 Treize semaines.
3 Taux de l'escompte.
4 Taux des avances à un jour.
5 Interbancaire.
6 Taux à un jour.
7 Taux de l'argent au jour le jour.
8 Taux interbancaire à trois mois.
9 Taux interbancaire à un jour.
10 Coût moyen de la dette à la Banque centrale.
11 Taux actualisé.
12 Douze mois.
13 Rendement.
14 Quatre-vingt-onze jours.
15 Taux forfaitaire à un mois.
16 Taux de facturation financière.
17 Taux des obligations de société.
18 Taux des dépôts interbancaires (à trois mois).
19 Trois mois.
20 Taux d'escompte de la Banque Centrale (a trois mois).
21 Prêts interbancaires remboursables sur demande (taux maximum).
22 Traite bancaire.
23 Taux des émissions nouvelles : bons du Trésor à trois mois.
24 Six mois.
25 182 jours.

26 Interbank call loans.
27 3-month discount notes.
28 Overnight interbank minimum.
29 Bond equivalent.
30 Commercial paper (3 months).
31 Federal funds rate.
32 Interbank borrowing rate.

26 Prêts interbancaires remboursables sur demande.
27 Billets à escompte à trois mois.
28 Taux minimum des prêts interbancaires à un jour.
29 Équivalant à obligation.
30 Effet de commerce (à trois mois).
31 Taux des fonds fédéraux.
32 Taux des prêts interbancaires.

Technical notes: tables 22 and 23

Detailed information and current figures relating to tables 22 and 23 are contained in *International Financial Statistics*, published by the International Monetary Fund (see also www.imf.org) and in the United Nations *Monthly Bulletin of Statistics*.

Table 22: The discount rates shown represent the rates at which the central bank lends or discounts eligible paper for deposit money banks, typically shown on an end-of-period basis.

Table 23: The rates shown represent short-term treasury bill rates and money market rates. The treasury bill rate is the rate at which short-term securities are issued or traded in the market. The money market rate is the rate on short-term lending between financial institutions. The naming conventions for money market rates and treasury bill yields sometimes vary among countries. In table 23, three money market and treasury bill descriptions are used: (i) "Money market"/"Treasury bill", (ii) "Money market A"/"Treasury bill A" and (iii) "Money market B"/"Treasury bill B". These distinctions are shown for those countries for which more than one type of money market rate or treasury bill yield is differentiated by the International Monetary Fund in *International Financial Statistics*. In this table, "Money market A" and "Treasury bill A" generally refer to those interest rates or yields whose durations have been specified (e.g. overnight, one month, 91 days, etc.) and "Money market B" and "Treasury bill B" refer to all others containing specific descriptors such as "call money rate", "foreign currency", "interbank", "discounted rate", etc.

Notes techniques : tableaux 22 et 23

Les informations détaillées et les chiffres courants concernant les tableaux 22 et 23 figurent dans les *Statistiques financières internationales* publiées par le Fonds monétaire international (voir aussi www.imf.org) et dans le *Bulletin mensuel de statistique* des Nations Unies.

Tableau 22: Les taux d'escomptes indiqués représentent les taux que la banque centrale applique à ses prêts ou auquel elle réescompte les effets escomptables des banques créatrices de monnaie (généralement, taux de fin de période).

Tableau 23: Les taux indiqués représentent le taux des bons du Trésor et le taux du marché monétaire à court terme. Le taux des bons du Trésor est le taux auquel les effets à court terme sont émis ou négociés sur le marché. Le taux du marché monétaire est le taux prêteur à court terme entre institutions financières. La manière dont par convention on dénomme les taux du marché monétaire et le rendement des bons du Trésor peut varier selon les pays. Dans le tableau 23, on utilise trois termes pour le marché monétaire et les bons du Trésor : i) "Marché monétaire"/ "Bons du Trésor", ii) "Marché monétaire A"/ "Bons du Trésor A", iii) "Marché monétaire B"/ "Bons du Trésor B". Ces distinctions apparaissent pour les pays où le Fonds monétaire international distingue dans *Statistiques financières internationales* plus d'un type de taux du marché monétaire ou de rendement de bons du Trésor. En général, dans ce tableau, "Marché monétaire A" et "Bons du Trésor A" désignent les taux d'intérêt ou les rendements dont la durée a été précisée (au jour le jour, à un mois, à 91 jours, etc.), "Marché monétaire B" et "Bons du Trésor B" désignant tous les autres assortis de descripteurs précis tels que taux de l'argent au jour le jour, en devises, interbancaire, taux escompté, etc.

24 Unemployment

Number (thousands) and percentage unemployed, by sex

Chômage

Nombre (milliers) et pourcentage des chômeurs, par sexe

Country or area, source § / Pays ou zone, source §	2002	2003	2004	2005	2006	2007	2008	2009
Austria [1,2] Autriche [1,2]								
MF [BA]	162.7	166.0	193.7	207.7	195.6	185.6	162.3	204.4
M [BA]	84.8	83.9	97.2	107.8	97.1	89.7	81.8	114.2
F [BA]	77.9	82.2	96.5	100.0	98.5	95.8	80.5	90.2
%MF [BA]	4.2	4.3	4.9	5.2	4.8	4.4	3.8	4.8
%M [BA]	4.0	4.0	4.5	4.9	4.3	3.9	3.6	5.0
%F [BA]	4.4	4.7	5.4	5.5	5.2	5.0	4.1	4.6
Belgium [2,3] Belgique [2,3]								
MF [BA]	330.6	362.3	379.1	390.4	383.2	353.0	333.4	379.6
M [BA]	167.1	191.9	190.9	196.2	191.0	174.4	170.2	203.9
F [BA]	163.5	170.4	188.2	194.2	192.2	178.6	163.2	175.6
%MF [BA]	7.5	8.2	8.4	8.5	8.3	7.5	7.0	7.9
%M [BA]	6.7	7.7	7.5	7.6	7.4	6.7	6.5	7.8
%F [BA]	8.6	8.9	9.5	9.5	9.3	8.5	7.6	8.1
Bulgaria [1,2] Bulgarie [1,2]								
MF [BA]	608.4	449.2	400.0	334.4	305.7	240.2	199.7	238.0
M [BA]	336.4	245.8	222.0	182.8	156.4	120.7	103.9	130.1
F [BA]	271.9	203.3	178.0	151.6	149.3	119.5	95.8	107.9
%MF [BA]	18.2	13.7	12.1	10.1	9.0	6.9	5.6	6.8
%M [BA]	18.9	14.1	12.6	10.3	8.7	6.5	5.5	7.0
%F [BA]	17.3	13.2	11.5	9.8	9.3	7.3	5.8	6.6
Croatia [1,2] Croatie [1,2]								
MF [BA]	263.4	252.3	246.9	226.7	198.7	170.8	149.2	159.7
M [BA]	128.1	125.2	118.3	113.4	94.5	81.4	67.9	75.6
F [BA]	135.2	127.1	128.6	113.4	104.2	89.4	81.3	84.2
%MF [BA]	14.8	14.2	13.7	12.7	11.2	9.6	8.4	9.1
%M [BA]	13.3	12.9	12.1	11.6	9.9	8.4	7.0	8.0
%F [BA]	16.6	15.8	15.7	13.9	12.8	11.2	10.1	10.3
Cyprus [1,2] Chypre [1,2]								
MF [BA]	11.8	14.1	16.4	19.2	17.3	15.5	14.3	21.3
M [BA]	5.3	6.8	7.1	8.8	8.3	7.4	6.8	11.3
F [BA]	6.5	7.3	9.3	10.4	9.0	8.1	7.5	10.0
%MF [BA]	3.6	4.1	4.7	5.3	4.6	4.0	3.6	5.3
%M [BA]	2.9	3.6	3.6	4.3	4.0	3.4	3.1	5.2
%F [BA]	4.5	4.8	6.0	6.5	5.4	4.6	4.2	5.5
Czech Republic [1,2] République tchèque [1,2]								
MF [BA]	373.3	398.4	425.7	410.2	371.7	276.6	229.8	352.2
M [BA]	168.5	174.1	201.2	186.7	169.2	123.7	102.6	175.4
F [BA]	204.8	224.3	224.5	223.5	202.4	152.9	127.2	176.8
%MF [BA]	7.3	7.8	8.3	7.9	7.2	5.3	4.4	6.7
%M [BA]	6.0	6.2	7.1	6.5	5.8	4.2	3.5	5.9
%F [BA]	9.0	9.9	9.9	9.8	8.9	6.7	5.6	7.7
Denmark [2,4] Danemark [2,4]								
MF [BA]	130.9	154.7	159.6	139.7	113.8	110.5	98.2	176.6
M [BA]	64.6	74.0	78.4	68.2	51.6	53.6	46.6	101.9
F [BA]	66.3	80.7	81.2	71.5	62.2	56.9	51.6	74.7
%MF [BA]	4.6	5.4	5.5	4.8	3.9	3.8	3.3	6.0
%M [BA]	4.3	4.8	5.1	4.4	3.3	3.5	3.0	6.5
%F [BA]	5.0	6.1	6.0	5.3	4.5	4.2	3.7	5.4
France [1,2] France [1,2]								
MF [BA]	2 334.4	2 475.6	2 577.8	2 596.9	2 603.8	2 380.1	2 232.6	2 754.6
M [BA]	1 120.7	1 196.6	1 237.2	1 243.5	1 259.8	1 167.6	1 093.0	1 401.1
F [BA]	1 213.6	1 279.0	1 340.6	1 353.4	1 344.0	1 212.5	1 139.6	1 353.4
%MF [BA]	8.6	9.0	9.3	9.3	9.2	8.4	7.8	9.5
%M [BA]	7.7	8.1	8.3	8.4	8.4	7.8	7.3	9.2
%F [BA]	9.7	9.9	10.3	10.3	10.1	9.0	8.4	9.8

Country or area, source § Pays ou zone, source §	2002	2003	2004	2005	2006	2007	2008	2009
Germany [1,2] Allemagne [1,2]								
MF [BA]	...	...	...	...	...	3 601.9	3 141.2	3 227.0
M [BA]	...	...	...	...	...	1 939.1	1 689.7	1 834.6
F [BA]	...	...	...	...	...	1 662.8	1 451.5	1 392.5
%MF [BA]	...	...	...	...	...	8.4	7.3	7.5
%M [BA]	...	...	...	...	...	8.5	7.4	8.0
%F [BA]	...	...	...	...	...	8.3	7.2	6.9
Hungary [1,2] Hongrie [1,2]								
MF [BA]	239.7	244.5	252.5	302.2	316.7	312.0	329.1	420.7
M [BA]	138.6	138.5	136.8	158.9	164.6	164.2	174.3	233.6
F [BA]	101.1	106.0	115.7	143.2	152.1	147.8	154.9	187.1
%MF [BA]	5.8	5.9	6.1	7.2	7.5	7.4	7.8	10.0
%M [BA]	6.2	6.1	6.1	7.0	7.2	7.1	7.6	10.3
%F [BA]	5.4	5.6	6.1	7.4	7.8	7.7	8.1	9.7
Ireland [1,2] Irlande [1,2]								
MF [BA]	82.6	86.5	87.7	89.7	95.2	101.4	141.3	258.7
M [BA]	51.3	54.0	54.8	54.4	57.0	62.1	94.3	181.6
F [BA]	31.3	32.5	32.8	35.3	38.2	39.3	47.0	77.1
%MF [BA]	4.5	4.6	4.5	4.4	4.5	4.6	6.3	11.9
%M [BA]	4.7	4.9	4.8	4.6	4.6	4.9	7.4	14.9
%F [BA]	4.1	4.1	4.0	4.1	4.2	4.1	4.9	8.0
Italy [1,2] Italie [1,2]								
MF [BA]	2 062.3	2 048.3	1 960.4	1 888.6	1 673.4	1 506.0	1 691.9	1 944.9
M [BA]	959.5	935.8	924.8	902.4	800.6	722.4	820.4	1 000.4
F [BA]	1 103.0	1 112.3	1 035.6	986.2	872.7	783.6	871.5	944.5
%MF [BA]	...	...	8.0	7.7	6.8	6.1	6.7	7.8
%M [BA]	...	...	6.4	6.2	5.4	4.9	5.5	6.8
%F [BA]	...	...	10.5	10.1	8.8	7.9	8.5	9.3
Luxembourg [1,2] Luxembourg [1,2]								
MF [BA]	4.9	7.4	9.8	9.3	9.5	8.8	10.5	11.7
M [BA]	2.2	3.4	4.2	4.2	4.1	4.0	5.0	5.9
F [BA]	2.7	3.9	5.6	5.2	5.4	4.8	5.5	5.8
%MF [BA]	2.6	3.8	5.0	4.6	4.6	4.2	4.9	5.1
%M [BA]	2.0	3.0	3.6	3.6	3.6	3.4	4.1	4.5
%F [BA]	3.5	4.9	6.8	6.0	6.0	5.1	5.9	5.9
Malta [1,2] Malte [1,2]								
MF [BA]	12.0	12.2	11.7	11.6	11.5	10.7	10.1	12.1
M [BA]	7.3	7.6	7.4	7.1	7.1	6.6	6.3	7.6
F [BA]	4.7	4.6	4.4	4.5	4.4	4.1	3.7	4.5
%MF [BA]	7.5	7.6	7.4	7.2	7.1	6.4	5.9	7.0
%M [BA]	6.6	6.9	6.6	6.4	6.3	5.9	5.6	6.6
%F [BA]	9.3	9.1	9.0	8.9	8.7	7.5	6.5	7.6
Netherlands [1,2] Pays-Bas [1,2]								
MF [BA]	253.8	340.9	419.4	441.2	365.6	305.7	267.5	326.6
M [BA]	127.5	187.1	227.3	227.0	178.6	146.7	133.6	175.0
F [BA]	126.3	153.8	192.1	214.2	187.0	159.0	133.8	151.6
%MF [BA]	3.1	4.2	5.1	5.3	4.4	3.6	3.1	3.7
%M [BA]	2.7	4.1	4.9	4.9	3.9	3.1	2.8	3.7
%F [BA]	3.5	4.3	5.3	5.8	5.0	4.1	3.4	3.8
Norway [2,5] Norvège [2,5]								
MF [BA]	87.2	100.2	102.0	108.6	83.5	63.5	65.0	81.3
M [BA]	48.3	56.9	58.3	59.7	45.4	34.0	36.6	49.2
F [BA]	38.9	43.3	43.6	48.9	38.2	29.4	28.5	32.1
%MF [BA]	3.7	4.2	4.3	4.5	3.4	2.5	2.5	3.1
%M [BA]	3.8	4.5	4.6	4.7	3.5	2.6	2.7	3.6
%F [BA]	3.5	3.9	3.9	4.3	3.3	2.5	2.3	2.6

24 Unemployment *(continued)*
Number (thousands) and percentage unemployed, by sex

Chômage *(suite)*
Nombre (milliers) et pourcentage des chômeurs, par sexe

Country or area, source § / Pays ou zone, source §	2002	2003	2004	2005	2006	2007	2008	2009
Poland [1,2] Pologne [1,2]								
MF [BA]	3 431.0	3 323.1	3 230.3	3 045.4	2 344.3	1 618.8	1 210.7	1 411.1
M [BA]	1 778.9	1 738.0	1 680.6	1 552.9	1 202.2	830.5	599.1	733.6
F [BA]	1 652.2	1 585.1	1 549.6	1 492.5	1 142.1	788.3	611.7	677.5
%MF [BA]	20.0	19.7	19.0	17.8	13.9	9.6	7.1	8.2
%M [BA]	19.2	19.0	18.2	16.6	13.0	9.0	6.4	7.8
%F [BA]	21.0	20.5	20.0	19.2	14.9	10.4	8.0	8.7
Portugal [1,2] Portugal [1,2]								
MF [BA]	270.5	342.3	365.0	422.3	427.8	448.6	427.1	528.6
M [BA]	121.4	160.9	172.9	198.1	194.8	196.8	194.3	261.3
F [BA]	149.1	181.4	192.2	224.1	233.1	251.8	232.7	267.4
%MF [BA]	5.1	6.4	6.7	7.7	7.8	8.1	7.7	9.6
%M [BA]	4.2	5.6	5.9	6.8	6.6	6.7	6.6	9.0
%F [BA]	6.1	7.3	7.7	8.8	9.1	9.7	9.0	10.3
Russian Federation [6] Fédération de Russie [6]								
MF [BA]	...	...	...	...	...	4 606.1	4 804.4	6 337.1
Slovakia [1,2] Slovaquie [1,2]								
MF [BA]	487.4	460.2	483.0	430.0	355.4	295.7	255.7	323.5
M [BA]	264.2	247.1	251.2	225.4	180.8	145.3	124.4	170.4
F [BA]	223.2	213.1	231.8	204.7	174.6	150.4	131.3	153.0
%MF [BA]	18.7	17.6	18.2	16.3	13.4	11.1	9.5	12.0
%M [BA]	18.6	17.4	17.4	15.5	12.3	9.9	8.4	11.4
%F [BA]	18.7	17.8	19.2	17.2	14.7	12.7	10.9	12.8
Slovenia [1,2] Slovénie [1,2]								
MF [BA]	61.3	64.2	63.3	66.0	60.8	49.9	45.5	61.0
M [BA]	31.0	33.1	31.9	33.2	26.9	22.3	22.6	33.3
F [BA]	30.3	31.1	31.4	32.8	33.9	27.6	23.0	27.7
%MF [BA]	6.3	6.7	6.3	6.5	6.0	4.9	4.4	5.9
%M [BA]	5.9	6.3	5.9	6.1	4.9	4.0	4.0	5.9
%F [BA]	6.8	7.1	6.9	7.1	7.2	5.9	4.8	5.8
Spain [2,5] Espagne [2,5]								
MF [BA]	2 095.1	2 173.6	2 143.8	1 912.5	1 837.1	1 833.9	2 590.6	4 149.5
M [BA]	914.3	958.7	951.7	862.9	791.5	815.2	1 311.0	2 292.1
F [BA]	1 180.8	1 214.9	1 192.1	1 049.6	1 045.6	1 018.7	1 279.6	1 857.4
%MF [BA]	11.1	11.1	10.6	9.2	8.5	8.3	11.3	18.0
%M [BA]	8.1	8.2	8.0	7.1	6.3	6.4	10.1	17.7
%F [BA]	15.7	15.3	14.3	12.2	11.6	10.9	13.0	18.4
Turkey [7,8] Turquie [7,8]								
MF [BA]	...	...	...	#2 375.3	2 328.6	2 360.8	2 605.0	3 459.9
M [BA]	...	...	...	#1 736.3	1 672.9	1 699.9	1 869.8	2 481.0
F [BA]	...	...	...	#638.8	655.8	660.9	735.0	978.9
United Kingdom [2,5] Royaume-Uni [2,5]								
MF [BA]	1 502.7	1 464.5	1 398.8	1 443.7	1 641.7	1 622.8	1 752.5	2 363.1
M [BA]	900.9	886.3	821.4	846.9	950.2	926.9	1 031.8	1 443.7
F [BA]	601.8	578.2	577.4	596.8	691.5	696.0	720.8	919.4
%MF [BA]	5.1	5.0	4.7	4.8	5.4	5.3	5.6	7.6
%M [BA]	5.7	5.5	5.1	5.2	5.8	5.6	6.1	8.6
%F [BA]	4.5	4.3	4.2	4.3	4.9	5.0	5.1	6.4
United States [9] Etats-Unis [9]								
MF [BA]	8 377.8	8 774.3	8 149.3	7 590.6	7 043.1	7 077.7	8 924.3	14 265.0
M [BA]	4 596.6	4 906.3	4 455.6	4 059.4	3 759.0	3 881.9	5 033.2	8 453.4
F [BA]	3 781.0	3 867.8	3 693.5	3 531.3	3 283.8	3 195.6	3 890.9	5 811.3
Venezuela (Boliv. Rep. of) [8] Venezuela (Rép. boliv. du) [8]								
MF [BA]	...	...	1 818.6	1 465.8	1 213.6	1 050.0	926.0	1 018.9
M [BA]	...	...	959.4	822.3	677.8	603.8	546.0	589.3
F [BA]	...	...	859.2	643.5	535.8	446.3	380.0	429.6

Source:
International Labour Office (ILO), Geneva, the ILO labour statistics database, last accessed December 2010.

Source:
Bureau international du Travail (BIT), Genève, la base de données du BIT, dernier accès décembre 2010.

§ Data source:
BA: Labour force sample surveys. Average of monthly data.

1 Persons aged 15 to 74 years.
2 Eurostat estimation based on labour force survey and registered unemployment figures.
3 Persons aged 15 to 64 years.
4 Persons aged 15 to 66 years.
5 Persons aged 16 to 74 years.
6 Persons aged 15 to 72 years.
7 Non-institutional civilian population.
8 Persons aged 15 years and over.
9 Persons aged 16 years and over.

§ Source de données :
BA: Enquêtes par sondage sur la main-d'œuvre. Moyenne des données mensuelles.

1 Personnes âgées de 15 à 74 ans.
2 Estimation d'Eurostat basée sur les enquêtes emploi et les données des chômeurs enregistrés.
3 Personnes âgées de 15 à 64 ans.
4 Personnes âgées de 15 à 66 ans.
5 Personnes âgées de 16 à 74 ans.
6 Personnes âgées de 15 à 72 ans.
7 Population civile non institutionnelle.
8 Personnes âgées de 15 ans et plus.
9 Personnes âgées de 16 ans et plus.

25 Employment by economic activity

Total employment and persons employed by ISIC rev. 3 categories (thousands)

Emploi par activité économique

Emploi total et personnes employées par branches de la CITI rév. 3 (milliers)

Country or area [&] Pays ou zone [&]	Year Année	Sex Sexe	Total employment Emploi total	ISIC Rev. 3 Tabulation categories [+] CITI Rév. 3 Catégories de classement [+] Categ. A Catég. A	Categ. B Catég. B	Categ. C Catég. C	Categ. D Catég. D	Categ. E Catég. E	Categ. F Catég. F	Categ. G Catég. G
Albania	2004	MF	931.0	545.0[1]	...	6.0	56.0	13.0	52.0	64.0
Albanie	2005	MF	932.1	545.0[1]	...	6.0	56.0	12.0	52.0	64.0
	2006	MF	935.0	542.0[1]	...	5.0	58.0	10.0	53.0	68.0
Algeria [3,4]	2001	M	5 345.2	1 132.4	69.4	111.0	406.8	99.1	643.8	761.6
Algérie [3,4]	2001	F	883.6	109.1	1.2	8.5	225.0	10.8	6.2	27.3
	2003	M	5 751.0	1 303.1	5.8	78.7	406.3	93.4	790.4	853.7
	2003	F	933.0	101.5	1.3	4.2	210.3	11.1	9.5	27.2
	2004	M	6 439.2	1 289.3	24.1	125.9	489.0	74.6	956.6	1 129.0
	2004	F	1 356.1	295.9	6.9	9.2	357.7	4.5	11.0	45.4
Anguilla [3,5,6]	2001	M	3.0	^0.0	0.1	^0.0	0.1	0.1	0.8	0.3
Anguilla [3,5,6]	2001	F	2.6	^0.0	^0.0	^0.0	0.1	^0.0	^0.0	0.3
Antigua and Barbuda [3]	2006	M	18.6	0.5	0.3	0.1	1.0	0.5	3.3	2.5
Antigua-et-Barbuda [3]	2006	F	18.5	0.2	^0.0	^0.0	0.7	0.1	0.1	2.8
	2007	M	19.0	0.6	0.3	0.1	1.0	0.5	3.4	2.5
	2007	F	18.8	0.2	^0.0	^0.0	0.7	0.1	0.1	2.9
	2008	M	19.3	0.6	0.3	0.1	1.1	0.5	3.4	2.6
	2008	F	19.1	0.2	^0.0	^0.0	0.7	0.1	0.1	2.9
Argentina [7,8]	2004[9]	M	5 446.9	65.7	8.4	30.6	925.4	33.8	717.8	1 230.0
Argentine [7,8]	2004[9]	F	3 968.0	32.0	2.9	2.6	435.0	10.2	14.0	715.7
	2005[9]	M	5 557.3	74.5	6.4	23.2	947.2	44.0	801.1	1 227.0
	2005[9]	F	4 081.4	25.3	1.0	7.7	412.5	5.0	21.9	724.8
	2006[10]	M	5 786.7	59.2	8.2	34.1	988.3	38.1	854.8	1 263.5
	2006[10]	F	4 253.8	13.6	0.8	5.7	422.3	6.0	29.9	755.2
Armenia [6]	2006	M	593.0	274.2	0.2	6.3	71.3	18.7	27.1	68.0
Arménie [6]	2006	F	499.4	230.1	...	1.3	39.2	4.1	2.6	37.9
	2007	M	571.4	248.6	0.2	7.2	67.8	18.6	28.5	66.5
	2007	F	530.1	258.1	0.0	1.4	35.9	4.2	2.6	39.6
	2008	M	570.9	224.5	0.4	6.9	61.1	19.7	57.2	68.2
	2008	F	546.7	268.5	0.1	1.4	33.8	4.8	3.2	45.0
Aruba [3,11]	1994	M	21.0	^0.0	0.0	^0.0	1.8	0.5	3.6	3.0
Aruba [3,11]	1994	F	14.9	^0.0	...	...	0.4	0.1	0.3	3.2
	1997	M	23.5	0.1	...	...	2.1	0.7	3.2	3.6
	1997	F	18.1	^0.0	...	...	0.5	0.1	0.2	3.7
	2007	M	27.2	0.3	...	^0.0	2.6	0.6	5.7	3.1
	2007	F	24.4	0.1	...	...	0.6	0.1	0.8	4.2
Australia [3,6]	2006	M	5 605.6	233.2	7.8	101.4	779.7	66.3	803.3	962.2
Australie [3,6]	2006	F	4 612.8	107.0	2.3	15.3	294.6	19.1	111.1	823.2
	2007	M	5 769.9	233.1	9.5	103.7	793.4	68.4	833.5	980.2
	2007	F	4 742.4	106.7	1.9	15.4	298.8	17.9	112.8	843.2
	2008	M	5 879.2	237.0	9.5	113.0	806.6	75.7	870.2	991.3
	2008	F	4 861.3	106.6	1.7	20.0	295.4	22.8	116.8	855.8
Austria [3,12]	2006	M	2 147.5	116.1	0.2	8.4	546.5	25.6	287.1	273.3
Autriche [3,12]	2006	F	1 780.7	100.5	0.0	1.4	195.0	5.7	36.6	337.5
	2007	M	2 208.5	123.5	0.3	7.5	543.1	24.2	288.8	305.1
	2007	F	1 819.4	107.2	0.3	1.3	187.4	6.0	40.2	340.5
	2008	M	2 222.1	123.2	0.6	8.4	515.8	20.9	286.6	309.2
	2008	F	1 867.9	104.1	0.3	2.3	179.1	4.7	45.5	354.6
Azerbaijan [3,13]	2006	M	2 105.7	752.9	8.8	54.7	98.4	46.8	217.4	312.9
Azerbaïdjan [3,13]	2006	F	1 880.2	811.9	2.6	6.0	49.2	5.6	14.4	433.1
	2007	M	2 020.5	708.7	1.7	38.9	141.7	34.0	216.8	186.8
	2007	F	1 993.5	834.3	2.7	5.2	52.3	6.1	11.9	472.7
	2008	M	2 048.3	785.0	3.6	35.2	114.6	32.5	187.4	206.7

25 Employment by economic activity *(continued)*

Total employment and persons employed by ISIC rev. 3 categories (thousands)

Emploi par activité économique *(suite)*

Emploi total et personnes employées par branches de la CITI rév. 3 (milliers)

ISIC Rev. 3 Tabulation categories[+]
CITI Rév. 3 Catégories de classement[+]

Categ. H Catég. H	Categ. I Catég. I	Categ. J Catég. J	Categ. K Catég. K	Categ. L Catég.L	Categ. M Catég. M	Categ. N Catég. N	Categ. O Catég. O	Categ. P Catég. P	Categ. Q Catég. Q	Country or area[&] Pays ou zone[&]
17.0	20.0	81.0[2]	...	...	48.0	27.0	...	...	...	Albania
15.0	19.0	90.0[2]	...	...	47.0	24.0	...	...	...	Albanie
16.0	19.0	90.0[2]	...	...	48.0	25.0	...	...	...	
78.4	322.5	55.0	50.5	926.3	403.4	128.6	126.7	23.4	6.3	Algeria[3,4]
4.2	17.4	13.1	9.5	81.9	206.9	88.5	60.0	12.2	1.9	Algérie[3,4]
97.6	384.5	49.5	53.6	958.6	400.3	143.2	124.0	4.6	2.4	
4.9	20.9	18.1	14.4	112.6	227.5	101.9	59.4	7.6	0.5	
154.6	419.8	46.1	56.0	990.1	372.4	135.2	141.8	19.2	2.8	
10.2	16.2	22.8	16.4	114.2	261.6	100.3	67.1	15.7	1.1	
0.6	0.3	0.1	0.2	0.3	0.1	^0.0	0.1	^0.0	...	Anguilla[3,5,6]
1.0	0.1	0.1	0.1	0.4	0.2	0.1	0.1	0.1	...	Anguilla[3,5,6]
2.2	2.0	0.4	0.9	2.3	0.4	0.3	1.3	0.3	0.3	Antigua and Barbuda[3]
3.3	1.1	0.8	0.7	2.5	1.5	1.6	1.7	1.2	0.2	Antigua-et-Barbuda[3]
2.3	2.0	0.4	0.9	2.4	0.4	0.3	1.3	0.3	0.3	
3.4	1.1	0.8	0.7	2.5	1.5	1.6	1.7	1.2	0.2	
2.3	2.1	0.4	0.9	2.4	0.5	0.3	1.3	0.3	0.3	
3.5	1.1	0.8	0.8	2.6	1.5	1.6	1.7	1.2	0.2	
167.6	561.5	92.0	436.2	466.2	154.9	196.6	287.6	53.1	...	Argentina[7,8]
153.5	86.4	51.8	240.2	306.7	557.4	455.9	242.3	649.3	...	Argentine[7,8]
171.2	548.3	93.0	459.4	429.7	174.6	173.8	311.2	56.4	2.1	
144.3	100.6	69.8	283.3	299.0	561.8	454.5	269.7	684.6	1.4	
213.9	557.4	95.9	528.3	444.4	185.9	163.5	317.1	18.2	2.0	
167.0	86.6	93.5	281.5	324.3	620.9	426.7	229.6	778.8	0.2	
3.8	33.4	3.1	13.8	19.5	23.9	11.4	18.3	...	...	Armenia[6]
3.9	15.2	3.5	9.5	15.4	76.9	37.4	22.5	...	...	Arménie[6]
3.9	33.0	4.0	16.1	20.8	25.0	11.9	19.4	...	...	
4.5	14.6	4.8	10.2	17.1	76.3	38.3	22.6	...	...	
5.8	36.4	4.5	15.6	21.5	23.7	8.5	17.0	...	...	
6.6	15.2	6.1	11.2	18.2	77.9	36.1	19.3	...	...	
3.2	2.3	0.4	1.1	2.6	0.5	0.4	1.6	0.1	^0.0	Aruba[3,11]
3.1	0.8	1.0	0.9	1.3	0.8	1.2	0.8	1.2	^0.0	Aruba[3,11]
3.7	2.3	0.5	1.9	2.7	0.5	0.4	1.7	0.0	...	
3.4	...	1.0	1.4	1.6	0.8	1.6	1.4	1.3	^0.0	
3.6	2.0	0.5	3.5	2.1	0.6	0.8	1.7	0.1	...	
5.1	0.9	1.4	3.4	1.9	1.0	2.3	1.5	1.1	^0.0	
282.6	468.7	181.2	693.3	342.2	233.3	234.8	215.7	0.1	...	Australia[3,6]
384.4	172.5	205.9	586.3	283.8	508.4	843.3	255.0	0.5	...	Australie[3,6]
308.9	496.5	197.3	703.2	345.0	252.2	227.0	217.6	0.4	...	
395.4	182.1	209.8	588.6	296.6	518.8	870.6	282.5	1.4	...	
312.7	512.6	188.0	717.7	337.7	249.8	234.6	222.3	0.3	...	
395.7	183.0	213.5	608.6	306.9	557.7	895.0	280.2	1.8	...	
85.8	182.4	67.5	178.9	144.4	66.8	80.2	80.6	0.4	3.4	Austria[3,12]
156.8	59.4	65.6	171.8	108.6	155.4	267.6	106.3	9.6	2.7	Autriche[3,12]
92.5	176.5	68.9	187.0	155.3	60.4	81.6	89.8	0.5	3.5	
166.2	66.7	66.1	176.3	120.1	151.3	265.7	113.1	8.2	2.9	
89.5	185.2	71.3	211.7	156.1	67.8	82.8	90.2	0.5	2.5	
161.6	59.7	71.2	186.7	122.2	161.7	282.0	116.4	11.2	4.6	
32.8	138.1	30.3	15.2	101.4	122.3	47.7	87.5	31.1	7.5	Azerbaijan[3,13]
15.7	16.4	23.6	4.7	38.9	229.8	118.4	71.2	36.9	1.8	Azerbaïdjan[3,13]
21.4	178.4	9.4	54.4	167.7	120.4	51.5	88.1	...	0.7	
5.7	25.1	8.4	75.3	107.9	213.9	129.2	43.0	...	...	
11.7	143.7	10.5	95.4	198.3	96.6	52.1	74.5	...	0.5	
11.7	23.3	24.6	99.4	51.2	214.7	128.4	64.1	...	...	

Employment by economic activity *(continued)*

Total employment and persons employed by ISIC rev. 3 categories (thousands)

Emploi par activité économique *(suite)*

Emploi total et personnes employées par branches de la CITI rév. 3 (milliers)

Country or area [&] Pays ou zone [&]	Year Année	Sex Sexe	Total employment Emploi total	ISIC Rev. 3 Tabulation categories [+] CITI Rév. 3 Catégories de classement [+] Categ. A Catég. A	Categ. B Catég. B	Categ. C Catég. C	Categ. D Catég. D	Categ. E Catég. E	Categ. F Catég. F	Categ. G Catég. G
Bahamas [3,6]	2006[5]	M	86.0	3.8[1]	...	2.0[15]	4.9	...	19.4	12.0
Bahamas [3,6]	2006[5]	F	80.5	0.4[1]	...	0.5[15]	2.5	...	1.2	12.5
	2007[14]	M	89.6	3.7[1]	...	2.3[15]	4.1	...	19.9	12.8
	2007[14]	F	81.9	0.2[1]	...	0.6[15]	2.4	...	1.4	12.1
	2008[14]	M	90.8	4.5[1]	...	2.3[15]	4.0	...	18.4	12.3
	2008[14]	F	84.1	0.6[1]	...	0.4[15]	2.2	...	1.0	12.1
Bahrain [3,14]	2001	M	231.5	2.2	2.2	2.6	42.7	2.4	26.0	31.1
Bahreïn [3,14]	2001	F	59.9	0.1	^0.0	0.2	7.2	0.1	0.4	3.4
Bangladesh [3,18]	2003	M	34 478.0	16 132.0	1 027.0	80.0	2 637.0	90.0	1 445.0	5 894.0
Bangladesh [3,18]	2003	F	9 844.0	5 754.0	17.0	2.0	1 706.0	8.0	97.0	214.0
	2005	M	36 080.0	14 168.0	916.0	44.0	3 926.0	73.0	1 421.0	6 705.0
	2005	F	11 277.0	7 504.0	179.0	7.0	1 298.0	3.0	104.0	403.0
Belgium [3,19]	2006	M	2 391.0	59.0	0.4	8.0	543.5	28.1	271.5	293.6
Belgique [3,19]	2006	F	1 871.5	24.0	...	1.4	171.7	7.0	21.4	265.9
	2007	M	2 443.7	55.3	0.6	7.0	545.8	25.2	278.2	308.7
	2007	F	1 936.6	24.9	0.4	2.1	178.8	9.1	23.8	280.3
	2008	M	2 460.7	59.1	0.9	5.1	554.9	31.5	295.0	294.8
	2008	F	1 985.2	20.4	0.1	1.1	172.6	8.9	26.8	276.2
Belize [14,20,21]	1998	M	50.1	17.1[1]	...	0.3	5.3	1.0	4.2	7.8
Belize [14,20,21]	1998	F	23.3	1.2[1]	...	...	2.3	0.2	0.1	5.1
	1999	M	53.7	19.8[1]	...	0.3	4.7	0.9	4.4	7.4
	1999	F	24.1	1.5[1]	...	^0.0	2.6	0.1	0.1	4.9
	2005	M	64.9	16.7	1.5	0.2	6.4	0.8	6.7	10.3
	2005	F	33.7	0.8	0.3	^0.0	3.2	0.2	0.2	6.6
Bermuda [3,5]	2000	M	19.0	0.4	0.1	0.1	0.8	0.3	3.6	2.4
Bermudes [3,5]	2000	F	17.9	^0.0	^0.0	^0.0	0.4	0.1	0.2	2.4
Bhutan [3,5]	2005	M	158.1	51.5	...	2.2	3.3	3.7	28.3	3.5
Bhoutan [3,5]	2005	F	90.7	57.1	...	0.6	1.6	0.4	2.6	3.3
Bolivia (Plurinational State of) [7,25]	2005	M	2 356.0	887.9	11.8	59.9	295.2	11.0	253.9	244.0
Bolivie (État plurinational de) [7,25]	2005	F	1 901.1	741.9	2.0	11.2	170.3	2.9	21.4	385.4
	2006	M	2 505.6	981.8	8.8	50.8	279.9	12.6	245.1	257.1
	2006	F	2 044.7	803.2	3.6	4.7	197.9	0.4	3.0	390.2
	2007	M	2 577.0	871.5	13.1	70.6	331.4	13.1	310.3	266.7
	2007	F	2 095.4	801.5	0.2	1.7	183.6	2.3	5.9	406.9
Botswana [21,25,26]	2000	M	269.4	58.9[1]	...	10.0	19.8	2.0	39.0	25.3
Botswana [21,25,26]	2000	F	214.0	36.4[1]	...	1.2	22.8	0.2	5.9	38.3
	2003	M	245.4	70.1[1]	...	11.3	18.3	3.5	35.7	20.9
	2003	F	217.0	28.0[1]	...	2.5	26.2	0.9	6.2	40.7
	2006	M	281.8	98.8[1]	...	12.5	16.0	2.6	23.1	27.9
	2006	F	257.4	62.6[1]	...	1.7	20.0	1.5	4.5	49.5
Brazil [4,7]	2005	M	50 493.7	11 581.9	373.0	292.9	7 687.4	299.1	5 494.4	9 566.3
Brésil [4,7]	2005	F	36 696.0	5 805.0	71.0	25.0	4 649.0	60.0	148.0	5 937.0
	2006	M	51 400.0	11 226.0	345.0	314.0	7 831.0	325.0	5 665.0	9 637.0
	2006	F	37 918.0	5 638.0	54.0	28.0	4 665.0	71.0	172.0	6 110.0
	2007	M	52 363.2	10 934.2	316.1	342.9	8 320.5	297.3	5 920.9	9 958.6
	2007	F	38 422.8	5 273.0	55.6	35.6	4 784.6	65.4	186.2	6 350.3
Brunei Darussalam [3,27]	2001	M	85.8	1.3	0.5	3.2	7.8	2.2	11.4	8.5
Brunéi Darussalam [3,27]	2001	F	60.4	0.2	^0.0	0.8	4.7	0.4	0.9	4.4
Bulgaria [3,21,25]	2005	M	1 591.4	170.6[1]	...	31.2	364.8	47.9	175.3	219.7
Bulgarie [3,21,25]	2005	F	1 388.7	94.8[1]	...	5.6	363.9	16.1	15.2	227.4
	2006	M	1 652.8	162.7[1]	...	31.2	375.6	44.2	212.2	239.3
	2006	F	1 457.2	89.4[1]	...	7.0	369.4	14.7	17.8	254.7
	2007	M	1 731.5	159.1[1]	...	28.7	377.0	47.2	267.9	246.4
	2007	F	1 521.1	86.3[1]	...	6.8	389.5	13.3	24.4	272.7

25 Employment by economic activity *(continued)*

Total employment and persons employed by ISIC rev. 3 categories (thousands)

Emploi par activité économique *(suite)*

Emploi total et personnes employées par branches de la CITI rév. 3 (milliers)

ISIC Rev. 3 Tabulation categories[+] CITI Rév. 3 Catégories de classement[+]										
Categ. H Catég. H	Categ. I Catég. I	Categ. J Catég. J	Categ. K Catég. K	Categ. L Catég.L	Categ. M Catég. M	Categ. N Catég. N	Categ. O Catég. O	Categ. P Catég. P	Categ. Q Catég. Q	Country or area[&] Pays ou zone[&]
10.8	7.3	7.9[16]	...	17.6[17]	...	...	...	...	...	Bahamas[3,6]
15.8	3.9	10.5[16]	...	33.2[17]	...	...	...	...	...	Bahamas[3,6]
11.5	9.3	8.0[16]	...	17.7[17]	...	...	...	...	...	
15.9	4.0	12.2[16]	...	33.0[17]	...	...	...	...	...	
11.0	9.3	8.3[16]	...	20.2[17]	...	...	...	...	...	
16.3	4.9	11.8[16]	...	34.6[17]	...	...	...	...	...	
11.2	11.6	4.6	14.7	48.1	5.7	3.2	8.8	7.7	1.6	Bahrain[3,14]
1.9	2.1	1.9	1.6	4.3	7.8	4.4	1.8	21.9	0.5	Bahreïn[3,14]
530.0	2 989.0	204.0	186.0	903.0	867.0	357.0	1 136.0	...	...	Bangladesh[3,18]
33.0	25.0	19.0	7.0	85.0	318.0	146.0	1 413.0	...	...	Bangladesh[3,18]
661.0	3 910.0	392.0	227.0	778.0	964.0	241.0	1 654.0	...	...	
51.0	66.0	115.0	11.0	104.0	343.0	122.0	968.0	...	...	
71.7	243.0	82.4	227.5	225.0	120.1	122.4	78.1	2.8	14.0	Belgium[3,19]
68.3	76.9	73.2	176.9	197.1	255.4	406.5	94.0	20.9	10.8	Belgique[3,19]
76.4	242.7	88.1	229.5	232.1	116.2	129.0	87.9	3.2	17.7	
74.4	73.4	74.5	184.5	199.5	262.3	405.7	97.2	30.7	15.0	
72.4	254.5	90.5	227.4	234.1	112.7	126.2	82.5	3.5	15.6	
69.6	77.3	85.2	190.5	202.8	262.9	437.9	99.4	38.5	15.2	
2.3	3.3	0.6	1.0	3.4	1.9[22]	...	1.3	0.4	0.2[23]	Belize[14,20,21]
3.0	0.5	0.6	0.4	1.5	4.6[22]	...	1.4	2.3	0.1[23]	Belize[14,20,21]
2.5	3.7	0.8	1.2	3.4	2.3[22]	...	1.7	0.5	0.1[23]	
3.3	0.5	0.7	0.3	1.6	4.7[22]	...	1.5	2.4	0.1[23]	
3.2	5.4	0.6	1.5	4.6	2.1	0.7	2.2	1.5	0.3	
5.5	0.9	1.0	0.6	2.2	4.1	2.0	1.7	4.3	0.3	
2.4	1.8	0.8	1.7	1.4	0.4	0.5	0.8	0.1	^0.0	Bermuda[3,5]
1.9	1.0	2.0	1.9	1.1	1.3	1.9	1.0	0.8	^0.0	Bermudes[3,5]
2.1	7.4	1.6	...	16.0	5.0	1.7	31.7[24]	...	...	Bhutan[3,5]
1.9	0.6	0.7	...	1.5	2.8	0.9	17.0[24]	...	...	Bhoutan[3,5]
38.5	231.2	4.1	65.6	62.5	91.4	21.7	70.6	3.1	3.8	Bolivia (Plurinat. State of)[7,25]
132.8	25.1	9.1	39.0	28.6	101.3	42.4	82.4	105.2	0.2	Bolivie (État plurinat. de)[7,25]
48.0	216.9	13.6	101.2	81.3	93.6	33.8	72.3	8.2	0.5	
1138.7	34.6	9.8	50.8	33.9	124.3	63.1	75.2	111.4	...	
33.8	242.2	17.3	94.1	107.7	92.0	39.9	66.5	5.9	0.3	
125.5	30.2	10.9	42.7	44.4	131.0	69.6	82.6	154.9	1.7	
2.4	10.8	2.0	11.7	47.6	18.3	4.4	11.0	2.8	0.2	Botswana[21,25,26]
7.4	3.0	2.3	6.1	25.7	24.3	7.8	11.0	18.4	0.1	Botswana[21,25,26]
3.8	9.4	1.5	9.2	36.2	14.2	4.5	4.0	2.4	0.2	
10.9	3.2	3.4	5.1	31.0	24.5	9.5	5.5	19.2	...	
3.8	10.5	3.0	15.6	34.5	15.2	5.4	5.2	7.2	0.5	
10.9	5.6	5.4	9.7	25.6	28.1	8.6	5.3	18.0	0.4	
1 587.1	3 441.6	501.4	3 286.6	2 634.2	1 037.4	702.0	1 369.8	453.0	3.0	Brazil[4,7]
1 600.0	525.0	506.0	1 650.0	1 633.0	3 647.0	2 275.0	1 932.0	6 214.0	4.0	Brésil[4,7]
1 644.0	3 535.0	539.0	3 541.0	2 766.0	1 054.0	760.0	1 556.0	460.0	1.0	
1 751.0	529.0	531.0	1 890.0	1 685.0	3 802.0	2 402.0	2 245.0	6 322.0	2.0	
1 615.1	3 779.7	603.1	3 520.3	2 777.9	1 127.3	764.2	1 490.9	418.3	2.4	
1 735.8	594.3	578.3	1 979.0	1 726.2	3 924.9	2 563.0	2 220.4	6 313.4	1.0	
3.8	3.4	5.1[16]	...	38.7[17]	...	...	...	...	...	Brunei Darussalam[3,27]
3.3	1.4	3.1[16]	...	41.1[17]	...	...	...	...	...	Brunéi Darussalam[3,27]
59.1	157.8	14.3	80.2	130.8	43.2	36.2	58.9[28]	...	...	Bulgaria[3,21,25]
91.1	56.1	23.5	61.4	83.3	164.0	123.4	61.9[28]	...	...	Bulgarie[3,21,25]
58.6	163.6	12.7	83.7	131.4	44.8	36.0	56.7[28]	...	...	
97.8	56.7	26.4	63.4	93.7	170.1	127.7	68.4[28]	...	...	
57.8	165.1	12.5	95.3	142.2	41.2	36.7	54.4[28]	...	...	
105.3	54.9	31.2	67.8	96.7	176.3	125.0	70.9[28]	...	...	

25

Employment by economic activity *(continued)*

Total employment and persons employed by ISIC rev. 3 categories (thousands)

Emploi par activité économique *(suite)*

Emploi total et personnes employées par branches de la CITI rév. 3 (milliers)

Country or area [&] Pays ou zone [&]	Year Année	Sex Sexe	Total employment Emploi total	ISIC Rev. 3 Tabulation categories [+] CITI Rév. 3 Catégories de classement [+] Categ. A Catég. A	Categ. B Catég. B	Categ. C Catég. C	Categ. D Catég. D	Categ. E Catég. E	Categ. F Catég. F	Categ. G Catég. G
Cambodia [7,29] Cambodge [7,29]	2004	MF	6 560.6	2 577.6	31.5	3.9	218.3	0.2	8.9	404.8
Canada [3,30,31]	2006	M	8 727.1	290.3	25.9	192.3	1 552.5	92.5	946.8	1 555.6
Canada [3,30,31]	2006	F	7 757.2	115.0	4.6	48.3	640.6	29.5	122.9	1 336.2
	2007	M	8 888.9	281.0	23.7	205.4	1 501.1	99.0	996.9	1 577.0
	2007	F	7 977.5	112.1	5.0	49.4	614.9	39.1	136.6	1 370.4
	2008	M	9 021.3	274.2	21.6	214.0	1 444.2	115.6	1 087.3	1 578.0
	2008	F	8 104.5	102.6	4.5	50.2	596.7	36.1	144.8	1 373.1
Cayman Islands [3,13]	2006[14]	M	18.4	0.6[1]	...	0.6[15]	0.2	...	6.0	2.3
Iles Caïmanes [3,13]	2006[14]	F	16.6	0.2[1]	...	0.1[15]	0.2	...	0.4	2.0
	2007[11]	M	18.3	0.6[1]	...	0.4[15]	0.5	...	5.2	1.8
	2007[11]	F	16.8	^0.0[1]	...	0.2[15]	0.1	...	0.4	1.8
	2008[11]	M	19.4	0.6[1]	...	...	...	0.4	5.3	2.1
	2008[11]	F	18.1	0.1[1]	...	...	...	0.2	0.5	2.6
Chile [3,14]	2002	M	3 303.9	425.6	55.8	66.5	471.4	28.5	385.0	665.1
Chili [3,14]	2002	F	1 782.0	50.7	13.6	4.1	147.0	4.4	14.7	326.6
China [33,34,35]	2005	M	70 794.0	2 806.0[1]	...	3 962.0	18 134.0	2 086.0	7 924.0	3 017.0
Chine [33,34,35]	2005	F	43 246.0	1 657.0[1]	...	1 130.0	13 975.0	913.0	1 342.0	2 423.0
	2006	M	72 675.0	2 717.0[1]	...	4 147.0	18 876.0	2 112.0	8 506.0	2 854.0
	2006	F	44 457.0	1 635.0[1]	...	1 150.0	14 640.0	913.0	1 381.0	2 303.0
	2007	M	74 841.0	2 690.0[1]	...	4 253.0	19 704.0	2 127.0	9 084.0	2 781.0
	2007	F	45 403.0	1 573.0[1]	...	1 097.0	14 950.0	907.0	1 424.0	2 288.0
China, Macao SAR [13,20]	2006	M	141.6	0.1	...	...	10.5	0.8	27.8	17.8
Chine, Macao RAS [13,20]	2006	F	123.5	0.1	...	...	19.1	0.1	3.2	18.6
	2007	M	160.5	...	...	...	8.7	1.0	33.9	19.3
	2007	F	139.8	...	...	...	15.4	0.2	4.7	19.1
	2008	M	172.3	0.3[36]	...	...	11.5	0.6	33.7	19.3
	2008	F	150.7	0.3[36]	...	...	13.1	0.2	4.7	20.3
Colombia [6,7]	2006	M	10 189.9	1 805.7	...	88.3	1 135.6	46.0	723.3	1 996.2
Colombie [6,7]	2006	F	6 490.9	253.5	...	13.7	862.4	16.9	32.0	1 650.3
	2007	M	10 399.9	2 645.3	...	95.4	1 347.9	70.9	872.8	2 346.9
	2007	F	6 676.5	389.7	...	7.8	1 013.5	12.7	32.3	1 997.5
	2008	M	10 611.0	2 654.4	...	142.0	1 355.6	63.3	852.1	2 438.5
	2008	F	6 814.7	400.1	...	7.1	980.0	15.4	26.4	2 166.8
Costa Rica [26,37]	2006	M	1 172.6	218.6	8.7	4.1	166.9	17.5	124.7	227.5
Costa Rica [26,37]	2006	F	657.3	28.4	0.5	0.6	77.0	4.6	2.0	124.7
	2007	M	1 222.6	209.8	9.0	2.3	170.6	16.7	146.5	237.3
	2007	F	703.1	34.9	0.9	0.3	81.0	4.4	5.3	129.2
	2008	M	1 229.5	205.1	6.2	1.8	155.3	21.9	148.3	242.8
	2008	F	728.2	30.0	0.4	0.4	84.3	6.1	4.1	134.8
Croatia [3,21,25]	2006	M	868.1	115.5	3.0	5.9	192.7	16.6	121.9	107.9
Croatie [3,21,25]	2006	F	718.3	106.7	0.6	1.4	109.3	6.1	11.2	126.0
	2007	M	897.3	104.0	3.4	*9.4	198.7	*21.7	131.4	106.0
	2007	F	717.1	102.0	...	...	113.6	*6.9	*11.0	124.0
	2008	M	905.1	108.1	*4.5	*8.1	199.9	*23.1	133.0	120.6
	2008	F	730.5	108.3	...	...	116.2	*5.5	*12.0	125.0
Cyprus [3,21,25,38]	2006	M	200.4	10.1	0.6	0.7	25.1	2.5	36.6	37.4
Chypre [3,21,25,38]	2006	F	156.9	4.6	^0.0	^0.0	12.2	0.4	3.4	25.8
	2007	M	209.5	12.0	0.6	0.5	25.4	2.4	40.7	37.9
	2007	F	168.5	3.9	0.2	^0.0	11.8	0.4	4.0	30.1
	2008	M	212.2	11.3	0.5	0.4	25.1	2.6	41.6	38.7
	2008	F	170.6	4.6	0.1	0.1	12.4	0.5	3.3	30.8

25

Employment by economic activity *(continued)*

Total employment and persons employed by ISIC rev. 3 categories (thousands)

Emploi par activité économique *(suite)*

Emploi total et personnes employées par branches de la CITI rév. 3 (milliers)

ISIC Rev. 3 Tabulation categories[+]
CITI Rév. 3 Catégories de classement[+]

Categ. H Catég. H	Categ. I Catég. I	Categ. J Catég. J	Categ. K Catég. K	Categ. L Catég.L	Categ. M Catég. M	Categ. N Catég. N	Categ. O Catég. O	Categ. P Catég. P	Categ. Q Catég. Q	Country or area[&] Pays ou zone[&]
25.1	5.2	3.0	4.8	17.5	33.1	11.9	42.7	14.5	3.0	Cambodia[7,29] Cambodge[7,29]
402.2	779.8	275.8	1 145.6	426.1	410.4	312.8	344.7	4.2	2.3	Canada[3,30,31]
612.8	317.3	469.1	925.5	408.0	748.0	1 472.7	472.5	55.0	1.0	Canada[3,30,31]
433.9	796.4	276.0	1 197.9	429.7	414.0	322.2	373.0	2.9	...	
635.5	328.6	484.2	944.8	432.4	769.1	1 523.9	495.3	56.7	...	
433.0	807.1	306.8	1 213.5	453.2	405.9	342.4	359.6	2.5	...	
640.4	341.1	479.4	962.5	470.5	787.0	1 561.0	507.0	70.3	...	
1.6	0.9	1.0	2.1	1.2	0.6[32]	...	1.1	0.3	...	Cayman Islands[3,13]
2.2	0.6	2.2	2.3	1.2	1.9[32]	...	0.7	2.7	...	Iles Caïmanes[3,13]
1.6	1.0	1.2	2.1	1.5	0.7[32]	...	1.2	0.2	...	
1.9	1.0	2.1	2.1	1.0	2.1[32]	...	0.9	2.6	^0.0	
2.1	0.9	1.4	2.5	1.1	0.7[32]	...	1.0	0.3	...	
2.2	0.8	2.4	2.5	1.0	2.3[32]	...	1.0	2.4	...	
66.6	318.3	51.0	313.1	165.1	115.9	67.9	77.7	28.7	1.3	Chile[3,14]
72.3	57.4	44.4	156.1	67.6	222.3	154.0	164.2	281.7	1.0	Chili[3,14]
823.0	4 429.0	1 873.0	3 988.0	9 039.0	7 700.0	2 080.0	724.0	...	...	China[33,34,35]
989.0	1 710.0	1 720.0	1 939.0	3 369.0	7 132.0	3 009.0	501.0	...	...	Chine[33,34,35]
844.0	4 480.0	1 888.0	4 224.0	9 170.0	7 706.0	2 125.0	717.0	...	...	
995.0	1 647.0	1 786.0	2 037.0	3 486.0	7 338.0	3 129.0	507.0	...	...	
850.0	4 538.0	1 968.0	4 434.0	9 352.0	7 732.0	2 187.0	729.0	...	...	
1 008.0	1 693.0	1 929.0	2 137.0	3 560.0	7 477.0	3 241.0	521.0	...	...	
14.6	12.0	2.9	9.9	14.0	3.7	1.4	25.6	0.3	...	China, Macao SAR[13,20]
15.4	4.8	4.0	6.4	6.4	7.7	4.1	26.9	6.6	0.1	Chine, Macao RAS[13,20]
16.7	11.8	3.1	11.7	14.2	3.8	1.7	33.9	0.5	...	
18.1	4.5	4.8	8.5	7.8	8.1	4.3	35.2	9.1	0.1	
20.5	11.8	2.8	14.5	13.0	3.5	2.0	38.3	0.3	...	
20.8	4.2	4.7	9.3	7.2	7.9	4.4	40.6	12.9	...	
...	907.7	113.1	505.5	...	...	1 028.8	...	...	...	Colombia[6,7]
...	190.2	91.7	305.7	...	...	2 154.2	...	...	...	Colombie[6,7]
...	1 180.3	106.4	560.1	...	...	1 167.2	...	...	...	
...	269.8	115.8	435.6	...	...	2 400.1	...	...	...	
...	1 178.9	111.5	650.5	...	...	1 146.7	...	...	...	
...	288.5	108.2	496.3	...	...	2 316.6	...	...	...	
41.8	104.0	23.3	73.4	55.8	30.6	23.8	34.1	14.2	0.9	Costa Rica[26,37]
56.0	14.5	14.9	34.8	30.7	77.8	38.7	31.7	116.9	1.7	Costa Rica[26,37]
44.3	108.8	25.8	84.3	54.6	34.3	23.3	35.9	14.1	0.8	
64.0	16.9	23.7	37.3	34.1	76.4	40.7	36.8	114.4	0.4	
41.7	119.6	26.3	88.7	58.6	31.0	23.1	43.5	8.4	1.2	
58.6	23.5	27.1	48.8	35.2	81.5	41.6	37.6	110.6	1.5	
39.7	81.9	11.1	44.7	53.8	21.4	18.7	31.6	0.5	...	Croatia[3,21,25]
50.1	22.3	27.7	36.4	44.9	70.7	66.1	33.9	3.7	...	Croatie[3,21,25]
46.2	89.8	*11.6	43.6	52.8	*23.2	*20.5	*34.0	...	...	
49.0	*25.0	*24.7	40.2	40.9	65.7	70.1	*37.1	*4.7	...	
42.0	87.3	*11.9	41.6	49.8	*22.2	*18.5	*33.0	...	...	
47.1	*21.5	*22.4	*41.1	44.3	69.3	73.8	*36.9	*4.4	...	
11.0	13.2	9.3	11.9	20.1	6.1	4.0	9.6	0.4	2.0	Cyprus[3,21,25,38]
12.9	7.0	9.6	14.8	9.8	18.7	10.2	12.0	14.4	1.0	Chypre[3,21,25,38]
10.6	13.4	8.7	14.4	19.6	7.5	4.9	8.8	0.2	2.1	
13.3	9.0	10.0	17.0	11.6	18.9	12.0	10.0	15.5	0.7	
12.5	13.4	8.5	14.6	18.4	7.4	5.5	9.2	0.3	2.1	
13.3	7.8	11.1	18.2	11.8	19.7	10.8	9.1	16.7	0.6	

25 Employment by economic activity *(continued)*

Total employment and persons employed by ISIC rev. 3 categories (thousands)

Emploi par activité économique *(suite)*

Emploi total et personnes employées par branches de la CITI rév. 3 (milliers)

Country or area [&] Pays ou zone [&]	Year Année	Sex Sexe	Total employment Emploi total	ISIC Rev. 3 Tabulation categories [+] CITI Rév. 3 Catégories de classement [+]						
				Categ. A Catég. A	Categ. B Catég. B	Categ. C Catég. C	Categ. D Catég. D	Categ. E Catég. E	Categ. F Catég. F	Categ. G Catég. G
Czech Republic [3] République tchèque [3]	2006	M	2 742.0	123.0[1]	...	48.0	856.0	60.0	403.0	286.0
	2006	F	2 086.0	58.0[1]	...	7.0	506.0	17.0	33.0	327.0
	2007	M	2 806.0	120.0	3.0	48.0	896.0	58.0	410.0	289.0
	2007	F	2 116.0	53.0	...	6.0	509.0	15.0	37.0	324.0
	2008	M	2 863.2	112.8	2.2	48.4	920.9	61.1	422.1	300.6
	2008	F	2 139.3	50.3	0.5	7.3	512.0	17.0	39.9	332.8
Denmark [39,40] Danemark [39,40]	2006	M	1 482.3	60.9	...	4.8	296.1	12.6	185.3	230.1
	2006	F	1 304.3	18.5	...	0.8	131.5	3.9	15.9	179.0
	2007	M	1 476.1	60.1	...	3.9	295.4	12.4	174.4	235.6
	2007	F	1 302.6	19.5	...	1.3	137.5	4.1	18.6	176.5
	2008	M	1 497.3	58.3	...	...	288.5	12.9	176.0	243.9
	2008	F	1 330.1	15.5	...	...	137.6	4.7	17.0	186.6
Dominican Republic [7] Rép. dominicaine [7]	2005	M	2 175.4	436.2	11.3	5.8	335.6	17.2	207.1	460.7
	2005	F	1 103.7	30.9	...	0.1	151.3	9.0	6.4	247.8
	2006	M	2 272.0	478.5	11.6	3.1	332.1	21.2	236.0	477.3
	2006	F	1 197.9	25.3	...	0.5	157.6	5.5	5.2	244.8
	2007	M	2 336.8	477.0	12.7	5.8	345.1	22.1	239.4	487.2
	2007	F	1 214.1	25.2	0.2	0.2	149.5	8.7	7.4	245.3
Ecuador [7,29,33] Equateur [7,29,33]	2004	M	2 288.5	247.5	34.2	14.6	335.6	17.3	239.9	589.5
	2004	F	1 570.1	73.3	3.3	1.5	203.4	5.6	8.8	506.7
	2005	M	2 327.8	218.7	38.4	10.6	361.4	15.4	249.4	597.3
	2005	F	1 564.0	54.8	12.7	0.1	175.7	3.4	9.4	501.6
	2006	M	2 416.5	222.8	42.2	14.2	368.3	15.7	278.2	623.0
	2006	F	1 615.1	62.2	6.8	1.6	187.2	3.6	11.9	528.8
Egypt [6,41,42] Egypte [6,41,42]	2006	M	16 559.4	4 529.7	160.5	49.5	2 188.3	229.2	1 806.9	1 964.6
	2006	F	3 884.2	1 679.2	1.3	3.8	192.5	21.2	16.0	207.3
	2007	M	17 089.5	4 587.7	144.2	34.8	2 190.4	245.9	2 051.5	2 048.8
	2007	F	4 634.3	2 153.5	0.6	0.7	221.8	36.4	26.6	258.2
	2008	M	18 041.0	4 932.0	150.0	35.0	2 365.0	277.0	2 243.0	2 124.0
	2008	F	4 466.0	2 034.0	1.0	2.0	202.0	20.0	25.0	263.0
El Salvador [7,34] El Salvador [7,34]	2005	M	1 330.6	399.3	11.3	2.2	181.1	5.5	127.0	277.1[43]
	2005	F	952.9	45.1	0.8	^0.0	188.1	0.9	2.3	397.0[43]
	2006	M	1 342.0	381.7	11.6	2.0	185.4	7.8	152.7	273.0[43]
	2006	F	995.1	46.1	1.4	...	183.1	1.2	5.0	425.8[43]
	2007	M	1 401.8	385.2	11.6	3.7	201.3	9.2	144.6	288.3[43]
	2007	F	1 017.3	37.1	2.0	...	202.3	1.0	3.8	432.3[43]
Estonia [21,25,45] Estonie [21,25,45]	2006	M	322.9	19.7	2.0	4.7	74.2	10.2	58.1	35.5
	2006	F	323.3	10.2	0.2	0.5	62.2	2.2	4.7	53.1
	2007	M	330.0	19.4	1.6	4.9	72.7	8.2	73.4	35.9
	2007	F	325.4	9.4	0.5	0.6	62.1	1.3	7.5	52.2
	2008	M	330.9	16.9	0.8	5.3	74.6	6.9	72.6	38.7
	2008	F	325.6	7.6	0.3	0.7	63.9	2.0	7.3	54.8
Ethiopia [6,7,33] Ethiopie [6,7,33]	2004[14]	M	1 625.6	168.3[1]	...	9.2	236.9	21.6	141.2	325.4
	2004[14]	F	1 228.8	56.8[1]	...	0.8	207.6	7.3	17.6	297.6
	2006[37]	M	1 913.2	224.8[1]	...	11.9	290.7	30.0	179.9	450.6
	2006[37]	F	1 923.6	106.2[1]	...	1.4	294.9	8.6	29.0	422.0
Finland [40,45] Finlande [40,45]	2006	M	1 288.0	80.0	1.0	5.0	317.0	13.0	152.0	155.0
	2006	F	1 178.0	33.0	...	...	125.0	4.0	10.0	149.0
	2007	M	1 310.0	80.0	1.0	4.0	323.0	12.0	162.0	156.0
	2007	F	1 202.0	31.0	1.0	1.0	122.0	4.0	11.0	154.0
	2008	M	1 336.6	80.9	0.8	4.3	321.4	13.0	171.3	163.4
	2008	F	1 216.8	32.2	0.6	...	116.3	4.3	12.8	150.5
France [3] France [3]	2006	M	13 381.5	655.5	15.1	25.4	2 825.2	193.1	1 545.5	1 809.6
	2006	F	11 752.0	258.0	3.0	3.6	1 159.6	52.8	159.9	1 543.3
	2007	M	13 521.9	605.0	13.0	19.2	2 768.8	156.2	1 599.6	1 920.2
	2007	F	12 043.3	256.5	1.4	5.2	1 181.0	44.3	155.4	1 618.7
	2008	M	13 670.2	539.6	17.4	21.6	2 746.2	154.7	1 683.0	1 784.7
	2008	F	12 243.0	230.4	1.7	3.9	1 131.0	46.5	177.0	1 636.6

25

Employment by economic activity *(continued)*

Total employment and persons employed by ISIC rev. 3 categories (thousands)

Emploi par activité économique *(suite)*

Emploi total et personnes employées par branches de la CITI rév. 3 (milliers)

ISIC Rev. 3 Tabulation categories [+] CITI Rév. 3 Catégories de classement [+]										
Categ. H Catég. H	Categ. I Catég. I	Categ. J Catég. J	Categ. K Catég. K	Categ. L Catég.L	Categ. M Catég. M	Categ. N Catég. N	Categ. O Catég. O	Categ. P Catég. P	Categ. Q Catég. Q	Country or area [&] Pays ou zone [&]
85.0	259.0	34.0	185.0	170.0	73.0	65.0	93.0	1.0	1.0	Czech Republic [3]
102.0	102.0	58.0	136.0	155.0	215.0	265.0	100.0	3.0	1.0	République tchèque [3]
79.0	263.0	38.0	200.0	165.0	72.0	67.0	96.0	1.0	1.0	
102.0	101.0	64.0	153.0	161.0	218.0	271.0	99.0	2.0	...	
80.7	268.7	44.4	204.7	169.5	68.5	62.8	94.8	0.7	...	
96.2	106.1	70.6	165.3	157.3	213.2	264.8	104.1	1.8	...	
33.4	124.1	44.9	159.3	86.4	87.7	75.1	77.1	...	...	Denmark [39,40]
43.3	52.0	48.1	116.6	81.8	123.3	411.9	73.6	...	...	Danemark [39,40]
37.7	123.2	43.0	158.6	83.4	88.2	88.2	71.5	0.3	...	
43.4	49.9	43.0	109.8	80.8	127.0	411.6	74.2	3.6	1.9	
38.6	114.9	43.5	178.4	88.5	88.4	87.8	70.6	...	...	
43.4	44.0	43.4	113.9	89.1	122.2	428.3	78.3	...	...	
88.6	215.5	34.5	66.3	44.2	29.2	100.3	18.9	0.5	...	Dominican Republic [7]
103.3	23.0	27.8	31.1	106.7	74.8	114.0	132.7	1.0	...	Rép. dominicaine [7]
100.4	230.1	31.8	60.6	95.0	42.1	27.1	110.0	15.0	...	
113.0	18.1	34.3	26.4	54.1	110.2	76.2	160.5	165.6	0.9	
104.5	234.4	33.1	62.6	105.8	55.4	28.2	103.9	19.5	0.2	
117.8	23.1	40.5	31.4	46.8	114.5	68.2	159.0	175.1	1.3	
62.2	233.9	26.3	138.0	124.9	100.6	47.4	68.5	7.0	1.2	Ecuador [7,29,33]
108.9	30.9	22.8	51.8	49.0	162.4	90.4	107.6	143.4	0.2	Equateur [7,29,33]
71.0	244.6	26.2	144.1	125.6	91.7	46.9	65.0	20.9	0.4	
119.8	35.5	25.7	55.6	42.6	167.2	85.1	93.7	180.8	0.3	
85.3	251.7	25.2	146.7	126.4	100.2	42.3	64.6	9.7	...	
140.1	40.7	22.7	54.0	43.9	180.7	73.7	98.2	158.0	0.9	
394.5	1 300.7	133.7	374.6	1 475.8	1 140.8	261.2	472.5	34.3	2.1	Egypt [6,41,42]
16.9	56.6	41.3	57.2	425.9	829.1	284.3	35.0	10.7	0.4	Egypte [6,41,42]
358.5	1 398.6	145.1	389.1	1 515.1	1 165.8	261.5	486.5	36.6	0.5	
12.3	53.8	49.8	62.6	459.4	914.0	311.6	52.0	15.0	0.5	
451.0	1 517.0	127.0	383.0	1 443.0	1 124.0	266.0	529.0	53.0	2.0	
11.0	58.0	39.0	65.0	447.0	918.0	317.0	46.0	13.0	1.0	
...	95.7	73.7 [16]	...	62.4	27.3	58.3 [44]	...	9.7	...	El Salvador [7,34]
...	10.8	34.5 [16]	...	26.0	58.4	100.3 [44]	...	88.6	...	El Salvador [7,34]
...	96.6	64.0 [16]	...	67.0	28.9	60.2 [44]	...	11.2	...	
...	8.2	36.0 [16]	...	25.2	52.8	104.6 [44]	...	105.8	...	
...	94.7	76.3 [16]	...	73.2	34.0	65.5 [44]	...	13.8	...	
...	8.6	38.0 [16]	...	25.5	56.0	112.9 [44]	...	97.9	...	
4.2	42.1	1.7	26.4	18.8	9.8	4.8	10.8	...	...	Estonia [21,25,45]
18.2	19.5	5.6	21.7	20.2	48.6	32.7	23.5	...	...	Estonie [21,25,45]
4.0	39.1	2.5	25.8	18.0	8.8	4.4	11.3	...	...	
18.8	19.3	6.9	23.7	21.2	45.6	32.0	24.3	...	...	
5.1	38.1	3.2	27.1	17.1	12.0	3.0	9.5	...	...	
19.1	17.7	7.2	24.8	21.3	47.6	28.7	22.8	...	...	
53.4	108.7	16.4	34.4	139.3	137.7 [22]	...	197.9	22.4	12.4	Ethiopia [6,7,33]
202.2	10.7	5.2	11.5	61.6	95.5 [22]	...	57.9	192.2	3.4	Ethiopie [6,7,33]
73.8	143.7	31.2	38.6	184.2	175.0 [22]	...	48.7	13.4	15.6	
296.2	10.9	13.2	17.8	84.4	139.4 [22]	...	300.8	188.2	9.5	
21.0	131.0	16.0	161.0	76.0	56.0	44.0	55.0	3.0	...	Finland [40,45]
57.0	50.0	31.0	127.0	61.0	114.0	328.0	82.0	4.0	1.0	Finlande [40,45]
23.0	126.0	17.0	172.0	73.0	56.0	42.0	55.0	3.0	...	
62.0	48.0	34.0	136.0	64.0	110.0	331.0	87.0	4.0	...	
23.0	124.9	17.3	180.4	73.0	53.6	40.9	56.6	4.0	...	
66.0	49.1	34.3	135.0	66.0	108.5	343.3	87.1	4.2	...	
463.2	1 070.0	333.4	1 468.7	1 193.2	562.9	622.2	488.7	85.4	7.8	France [3]
447.9	448.8	474.0	1 194.0	1 214.0	1 213.8	2 444.1	614.2	495.3	10.5	France [3]
434.0	1 134.9	337.7	1 446.6	1 236.0	555.1	665.1	502.0	98.9	8.4	
444.8	468.0	488.3	1 219.4	1 327.3	1 180.7	2 478.3	654.9	493.6	10.5	
456.7	1 151.0	324.8	1 530.5	1 274.8	583.5	670.7	514.3	108.5	7.4	
413.8	489.7	468.4	1 254.4	1 377.7	1 208.2	2 544.3	647.5	499.5	11.5	

25 Employment by economic activity *(continued)*

Total employment and persons employed by ISIC rev. 3 categories (thousands)

Emploi par activité économique *(suite)*

Emploi total et personnes employées par branches de la CITI rév. 3 (milliers)

Country or area [&] Pays ou zone [&]	Year Année	Sex Sexe	Total employment Emploi total	ISIC Rev. 3 Tabulation categories [+] CITI Rév. 3 Catégories de classement [+] Categ. A Catég. A	Categ. B Catég. B	Categ. C Catég. C	Categ. D Catég. D	Categ. E Catég. E	Categ. F Catég. F	Categ. G Catég. G
French Polynesia [3,29]	2002	M	53.4	3.4	3.1	0.3	4.8	0.5	7.4	6.8
Polynésie française [3,29]	2002	F	34.4	1.0	0.8	^0.0	2.4	0.1	0.4	4.7
Georgia [3,6]	2005	M	915.2	473.5	...	5.2	60.1	18.1	42.4	107.9
Géorgie [3,6]	2005	F	829.4	474.3	...	0.6	29.7	5.3	0.7	80.3
	2006	M	920.5	491.9	...	2.5	54.8	14.8	53.7	86.6
	2006	F	826.8	474.5	...	0.9	26.7	3.7	1.2	81.5
	2007	M	888.1	448.5	...	4.3	60.6	14.7	66.5	88.4
	2007	F	816.2	462.1	...	0.4	22.1	3.5	4.6	80.5
Germany [3,40]	2006	M	20 462.0	567.0	5.0	106.0	5 843.0	242.0	2 138.0	2 531.0
Allemagne [3,40]	2006	F	16 860.0	270.0	1.0	11.0	2 314.0	74.0	308.0	2 750.0
	2007	M	20 890.0	576.0	4.0	97.0	6 029.0	255.0	2 223.0	2 520.0
	2007	F	17 272.0	278.0	1.0	11.0	2 365.0	79.0	304.0	2 788.0
	2008	M	21 188.0	585.0	5.0	95.0	6 137.0	267.0	2 216.0	2 512.0
	2008	F	17 546.0	281.0	1.0	14.0	2 379.0	79.0	305.0	2 778.0
Greece [3,25,46]	2005	M	2 705.8	299.1	12.6	16.7	407.6	30.9	360.7	466.1
Grèce [3,25,46]	2005	F	1 676.2	231.3	1.6	1.1	152.7	6.8	6.6	316.0
	2006	M	2 725.7	295.6	11.6	16.9	411.1	33.8	350.7	460.4
	2006	F	1 727.1	227.4	1.4	1.3	152.1	7.0	7.9	328.8
	2007	M	2 762.0	289.0	13.0	16.9	404.5	31.6	386.7	463.4
	2007	F	1 758.0	218.3	2.1	1.3	154.4	8.5	7.7	337.3
Guatemala [6,7]	2006	M	3 338.7	1 462.6[1]	...	7.3	438.5	11.1	349.1	522.3[43]
Guatemala [6,7]	2006	F	2 051.8	328.8[1]	...	0.2	416.3	1.3	5.8	704.6[43]
Guyana [3]	2002	M	169.2	40.8	5.3	8.8	23.5	1.8	15.9	22.3
Guyana [3]	2002	F	70.4	4.8	0.3	0.7	7.1	0.5	0.3	15.6
Hungary [25,45]	2006	M	2 137.4	142.2[1]	...	13.0	530.7	48.7	300.0	269.6
Hongrie [25,45]	2006	F	1 792.7	48.6[1]	...	2.0	334.5	18.9	21.6	312.4
	2007	M	2 143.0	140.8[1]	...	12.7	533.3	48.0	307.3	277.0
	2007	F	1 783.2	42.1[1]	...	1.9	338.7	16.2	23.2	314.5
	2008	M	2 110.8	132.1[1]	...	8.2	537.7	44.0	284.7	279.7
	2008	F	1 768.6	42.0[1]	...	0.8	333.1	13.4	24.8	305.3
Iceland [13,47]	2006	M	92.0	4.5	4.0	0.1	14.0	1.1	13.9	13.6
Islande [13,47]	2006	F	77.5	1.8	0.3	...	6.1	0.3	0.8	10.0
	2007	M	96.6	4.2	4.3	0.1	13.4	1.3	15.2	14.4
	2007	F	80.7	1.8	0.2	...	5.7	0.4	0.6	11.1
	2008	M	97.1	2.9	3.9	0.1	14.4	1.4	16.4	13.2
	2008	F	81.5	1.5	0.4	...	5.9	0.4	1.1	10.0
Indonesia [3,27]	2006	M	61 977.3	24 972.1	1 397.2	817.7	7 005.5	202.7	4 574.5	9 416.4
Indonésie [3,27]	2006	F	33 479.6	13 631.7	135.2	105.9	4 884.4	25.3	122.9	7 966.8
	2007	M	63 148.0	24 290.0	1 693.0	874.0	7 119.0	154.0	5 120.0	8 508.0
	2007	F	36 782.0	15 081.0	142.0	120.0	5 249.0	21.0	133.0	8 024.0
	2008	M	63 899.0	24 294.0	1 620.0	938.0	7 129.0	184.0	5 311.0	8 716.0
	2008	F	38 653.0	15 262.0	156.0	132.0	5 421.0	17.0	128.0	8 437.0
Iran (Islamic Rep. of) [7]	2006	M	16 871.8	3 519.7	81.9	130.5	2 688.4	181.0	2 344.8	2 862.8
Iran (Rép. islamique d') [7]	2006	F	3 969.6	1 225.2	0.5	8.7	1 219.3	9.7	22.5	168.4
	2007	M	17 230.0	3 454.5	77.6	123.8	2 744.9	187.7	2 577.8	2 850.1
	2007	F	3 862.5	1 276.0	1.5	4.3	1 089.4	8.4	23.1	167.2
	2008	M	17 119.0	3 232.0	76.0	123.0	2 630.0	171.0	2 763.0	2 821.0
	2008	F	3 381.0	1 034.0	2.0	5.0	882.0	9.0	27.0	160.0
Iraq	2006	M	5 224.0	1 129.0	21.1	41.6	338.9	72.7	654.8	925.6
Iraq	2006	F	1 333.2	796.7	1.7	1.8	37.4	4.0	10.1	36.2
	2007	M	6 028.4	722.7	10.0	79.9	470.3	122.8	788.7	1 077.5
	2007	F	1 088.3	343.5	...	4.5	51.9	7.7	8.5	40.2
	2008	M	6 176.9	1 036.8	19.7	28.0	340.4	150.9	814.7	1 124.5
	2008	F	1 429.2	723.1	2.0	4.4	29.0	10.7	8.8	42.7

25 Employment by economic activity *(continued)*

Total employment and persons employed by ISIC rev. 3 categories (thousands)

Emploi par activité économique *(suite)*

Emploi total et personnes employées par branches de la CITI rév. 3 (milliers)

ISIC Rev. 3 Tabulation categories [+]
CITI Rév. 3 Catégories de classement [+]

Categ. H Catég. H	Categ. I Catég. I	Categ. J Catég. J	Categ. K Catég. K	Categ. L Catég.L	Categ. M Catég. M	Categ. N Catég. N	Categ. O Catég. O	Categ. P Catég. P	Categ. Q Catég. Q	Country or area [&] Pays ou zone [&]
3.3	3.7	0.6	2.2	11.8	2.2	1.3	1.8	0.4	...	French Polynesia [3,29]
4.4	2.0	0.9	1.5	6.2	3.9	2.9	1.6	1.7	...	Polynésie française [3,29]
7.6	57.9	7.2	15.8	56.1	29.6	12.0	18.1	0.6	2.9	Georgia [3,6]
8.7	11.3	6.1	10.1	25.7	101.2	46.0	20.1	8.6	0.4	Géorgie [3,6]
4.8	70.3	8.4	16.4	55.4	23.4	12.8	22.1	1.6	0.9	
12.1	7.5	5.9	10.5	23.1	108.8	39.4	19.8	10.1	1.4	
7.0	65.7	8.0	21.6	47.6	21.2	9.3	22.2	1.4	1.1	
11.0	6.0	9.3	13.1	16.7	103.0	50.6	21.7	9.8	1.8	
584.0	1 469.0	657.0	1 975.0	1 627.0	706.0	1 052.0	933.0	11.0	16.0	Germany [3,40]
796.0	591.0	650.0	1 760.0	1 274.0	1 468.0	3 213.0	1 192.0	176.0	13.0	Allemagne [3,40]
592.0	1 552.0	642.0	2 052.0	1 621.0	736.0	1 076.0	883.0	14.0	18.0	
836.0	596.0	661.0	1 857.0	1 295.0	1 501.0	3 322.0	1 175.0	192.0	12.0	
615.0	1 553.0	642.0	2 222.0	1 538.0	748.0	1 108.0	910.0	15.0	19.0	
844.0	593.0	659.0	1 949.0	1 298.0	1 542.0	3 407.0	1 202.0	201.0	14.0	
167.6	219.5	56.9	153.3	232.3	122.5	78.5	78.5	2.6	0.6	Greece [3,25,46]
136.6	48.3	56.1	136.1	111.4	189.8	141.7	75.1	65.0	...	Grèce [3,25,46]
168.8	227.2	61.2	147.3	251.6	126.7	79.8	79.6	3.3	0.1	
132.1	54.5	54.5	136.8	129.3	204.4	148.0	70.9	70.1	0.5	
173.7	215.3	57.1	162.7	249.1	123.1	86.5	83.5	4.5	1.3	
144.2	52.3	55.6	132.1	141.8	205.4	154.3	78.9	64.1	0.1	
...	146.6	129.3[16]	...	87.7	73.2	103.2[44]	...	...	8.0	Guatemala [6,7]
...	14.1	46.9[16]	...	27.8	146.6	354.2[44]	...	...	5.2	Guatemala [6,7]
2.0	15.0	1.4	4.6	8.7	3.1	1.3	6.5	1.3	0.2	Guyana [3]
3.6	1.9	1.7	2.9	6.4	10.0	4.3	3.2	4.9	0.3	Guyana [3]
69.3	218.9	27.8	157.7	151.0	72.2	60.0	75.5	0.2	0.6	Hungary [25,45]
87.9	82.4	52.5	125.1	148.2	250.7	209.5	96.9	1.5	...	Hongrie [25,45]
67.7	224.0	26.9	153.0	139.0	72.4	57.0	82.5	0.5	0.9	
88.4	77.7	56.9	129.9	146.3	243.9	203.4	97.8	2.0	0.3	
69.6	209.9	30.4	168.2	141.9	68.1	55.9	79.8	0.4	0.2	
87.6	77.5	64.3	138.4	146.7	242.6	193.2	97.1	1.5	0.3	
3.1	7.8	2.7	9.6	4.8	4.0	3.2	5.2	...	0.3	Iceland [13,47]
2.9	4.1	4.7	5.4	5.2	8.5	21.4	5.7	...	0.1	Islande [13,47]
2.5	7.4	3.6	11.4	4.5	4.6	3.9	5.5	...	0.3	
3.7	3.8	5.1	5.8	4.5	8.9	22.1	6.6	...	0.3	
2.8	7.8	3.8	10.5	4.7	4.8	4.2	6.1	...	0.0	
3.5	3.7	5.2	5.8	4.8	9.8	23.0	6.4	...	0.1	
914.3	5 372.3	447.2	505.9	2 275.3	1 512.2	289.8	1 511.4	723.4	8.8	Indonesia [3,27]
918.1	290.0	231.2	161.8	561.5	1 667.2	410.9	660.4	1 692.4	2.5	Indonésie [3,27]
1 865.0	5 587.0	472.0	523.0	2 138.0	1 620.0	273.0	2 406.0	460.0	2.0	
2 159.0	372.0	267.0	137.0	541.0	1 840.0	411.0	840.0	1 424.0	2.0	
1 798.0	5 466.0	454.0	574.0	2 000.0	1 490.0	303.0	3 021.0	525.0	7.0	
2 271.0	714.0	237.0	194.0	522.0	1 797.0	441.0	1 191.0	1 704.0	1.0	
177.4	1 867.4	235.5	358.1	1 212.3	668.5	239.5	281.0	11.5	0.7	Iran (Islamic Rep. of) [7]
9.6	42.8	42.3	65.4	110.8	656.6	213.1	153.7	17.6	0.7	Iran (Rép. islamique d') [7]
180.3	1 938.4	243.6	367.7	1 249.4	665.1	259.2	291.3	6.6	0.8	
12.8	37.6	37.9	70.0	104.1	656.0	201.5	150.3	21.3	^0.0	
194.0	2 021.0	243.0	444.0	1 216.0	618.0	243.0	303.0	5.0	1.0	
17.0	46.0	41.0	77.0	116.0	601.0	204.0	140.0	14.0	1.0	
52.9	606.7	19.8	35.2	656.5	275.7	106.2	282.9	0.6	3.8	Iraq
...	9.8	7.1	5.4	70.9	280.3	40.0	29.8	0.8	0.9	Iraq
102.7	683.7	18.2	239.1	630.9	260.8	155.0	477.8	...	...	
2.6	23.9	8.2	46.7	46.7	352.1	41.8	43.0	...	...	
60.3	595.2	11.9	32.2	904.5	339.5	162.6	543.2	6.2	6.3	
2.3	12.9	8.9	2.9	98.8	347.3	55.6	75.3	3.5	1.0	

25 Employment by economic activity *(continued)*

Total employment and persons employed by ISIC rev. 3 categories (thousands)

Emploi par activité économique *(suite)*

Emploi total et personnes employées par branches de la CITI rév. 3 (milliers)

Country or area [&] Pays ou zone [&]	Year Année	Sex Sexe	Total employment Emploi total	ISIC Rev. 3 Tabulation categories [+] CITI Rév. 3 Catégories de classement [+] Categ. A Catég. A	Categ. B Catég. B	Categ. C Catég. C	Categ. D Catég. D	Categ. E Catég. E	Categ. F Catég. F	Categ. G Catég. G
Lithuania [3,25]	2006	M	755.8	108.1	2.5	3.9	137.9	19.1	139.0	115.9
Lituanie [3,25]	2006	F	743.2	75.7	0.2	0.4	126.7	7.9	9.7	138.7
	2007	M	777.7	97.6	2.5	4.4	138.4	19.4	158.5	117.2
	2007	F	756.5	59.3	0.1	0.9	129.5	6.8	12.4	145.2
	2008	M	768.7	73.2	3.4	3.5	144.3	21.0	149.7	124.6
	2008	F	751.4	43.5	0.7	0.6	121.7	6.6	16.0	150.3
Luxembourg [21,51]	2006	MF	319.1	4.6[1]	...	0.3	33.7	1.6	33.6	43.1
Luxembourg [21,51]	2007	MF	333.2	5.0[1]	...	35.7[52]	...	...	35.3	85.2[53]
	2008	MF	348.7	5.0[1]	...	37.7[52]	...	...	38.4	89.6[53]
Madagascar [13,54]	2003	M	4 135.7	3 110.1	61.8	4.5	227.0	18.1	54.6	167.7
Madagascar [13,54]	2003	F	3 962.8	3 118.4	25.8	9.7	222.3	0.5	6.0	252.9
	2005	M	4 841.8	3 875.7	68.1	10.4	205.3	21.4	12.0	173.9
	2005	F	4 728.6	3 869.6	30.9	8.5	62.2	6.1	0.9	296.6
Malaysia [6,41]	2006	M	6 618.6	1 013.9	123.2	35.9	1 270.4	63.4	834.4	1 081.0
Malaisie [6,41]	2006	F	3 656.8	361.4	5.0	6.1	812.4	12.0	74.5	569.6
	2007	M	6 747.1	1 064.5	115.4	33.7	1 196.6	52.0	854.5	1 120.2
	2007	F	3 791.0	372.8	5.4	5.7	780.7	8.8	68.0	592.0
	2008	M	6 851.1	1 027.5	117.4	44.6	1 182.6	50.1	914.7	1 119.5
	2008	F	3 808.5	338.2	4.7	9.8	762.2	10.3	83.4	609.9
Maldives [25]	1995[26]	M	48.9	0.9	12.3	0.4	4.5	0.7	2.8	4.5
Maldives [25]	1995[26]	F	18.1	1.4	0.2	^0.0	7.6	0.1	^0.0	0.8
	2000[26]	M	57.4	1.1	9.2	0.4	4.3	1.0	3.6	4.8
	2000[26]	F	28.9	1.4	0.1	^0.0	6.8	0.1	0.1	1.0
	2006[3]	M	69.7	1.5	8.2	0.3	6.8	1.1	5.7	7.4
	2006[3]	F	40.5	2.7	0.2	^0.0	12.5	0.2	0.2	4.3
Mali [3]	2004	M	1 388.3	657.7	33.3	8.4	136.1	5.1	97.5	266.1
Mali [3]	2004	F	982.5	291.7	2.0	3.0	136.4	0.0	4.7	402.1
Malta [3]	2006	M	104.4	2.1	...	0.7	19.8	3.1	12.0	16.2
Malte [3]	2006	F	48.1	0.1	...	^0.0	6.7	0.2	0.2	7.7
	2007	M	104.4	2.3	...	...	19.4	2.8	11.1	16.5
	2007	F	51.1	0.2	...	...	6.2	0.2	0.4	8.1
	2008	M	107.5	2.6	0.4	0.6	19.2	3.5	12.0	16.9
	2008	F	53.5	0.2	^0.0	^0.0	5.1	0.2	0.5	8.1
Mauritius [6]	2006[3]	M	332.5	28.5	6.1	0.3	60.9	3.3	50.3	43.2
Maurice [6]	2006[3]	F	166.6	12.9	0.6	0.1	44.4	0.2	0.8	26.4
	#2007[56]	M	335.0	28.0	5.0	0.2	60.6	3.5	54.7	43.9
	#2007[56]	F	167.1	12.0	0.7	0.1	41.6	0.6	0.8	27.4
	2008[56]	M	341.0	28.1	4.7	0.3	59.6	3.2	56.1	44.8
	2008[56]	F	178.0	12.7	0.6	0.2	42.6	0.5	1.6	26.8
Mexico [20,46]	2006	M	26 597.9	5 141.3	157.2	147.9	4 357.5	150.2	3 352.0	5 380.2
Mexique [20,46]	2006	F	15 599.9	724.4	10.1	16.2	2 721.2	36.1	100.5	4 214.7
	2007	M	26 840.6	4 938.0	134.4	164.8	4 400.5	182.4	3 473.8	5 389.5
	2007	F	16 066.0	692.1	7.9	21.1	2 729.2	38.0	112.0	4 431.4
	2008	M	27 401.7	4 971.8	121.0	162.3	4 448.3	174.1	3 522.1	5 483.6
	2008	F	16 465.0	657.1	8.7	20.9	2 779.8	32.1	119.1	4 490.8
Mongolia [34,56]	2006	M	491.8	207.0[1]	...	26.8	21.4	16.3	31.4	64.5
Mongolie [34,56]	2006	F	518.1	184.4[1]	...	15.1	25.6	13.7	24.9	96.1
	2007	M	504.2	204.6[1]	...	29.5	21.9	18.2	34.2	65.7
	2007	F	519.9	181.0[1]	...	14.6	26.0	12.9	25.8	96.5
	2008	M	512.7	200.6[1]	...	29.9	22.7	18.2	38.2	66.9
	2008	F	529.0	177.0[1]	...	16.6	24.8	11.9	28.6	102.8
Montenegro [11,41]	2005	M	105.6	8.8	0.2	0.8	17.0	4.6	5.2	13.7
Monténégro [11,41]	2005	F	73.2	6.5	0.0	0.9	4.8	1.0	0.0	16.2

25 Employment by economic activity *(continued)*

Total employment and persons employed by ISIC rev. 3 categories (thousands)

Emploi par activité économique *(suite)*

Emploi total et personnes employées par branches de la CITI rév. 3 (milliers)

ISIC Rev. 3 Tabulation categories [+] CITI Rév. 3 Catégories de classement [+]									
Categ. I Catég. I	Categ. J Catég. J	Categ. K Catég. K	Categ. L Catég.L	Categ. M Catég. M	Categ. N Catég. N	Categ. O Catég. O	Categ. P Catég. P	Categ. Q Catég. Q	Country or area [&] Pays ou zone [&]
69.6	5.5	43.2	38.4	25.6	16.6	21.7	1.1	0.1	Lithuania [3,25]
29.3	11.1	35.1	37.2	106.0	89.1	42.1	2.4	...	Lituanie [3,25]
80.1	6.8	37.8	43.0	26.1	14.6	22.4	2.3	...	
31.3	15.5	37.5	40.5	118.2	86.1	44.7	1.5	...	
75.3	5.4	52.3	42.5	31.6	12.0	23.1	1.1	0.1	
29.2	14.8	49.0	40.8	116.9	83.7	41.7	2.7	0.1	
24.5	36.4	53.6	17.1	14.9	24.5	11.6	4.6	...	Luxembourg [21,51]
...	38.4	54.9	74.0[17]	...	...	...	...	...	Luxembourg [21,51]
...	41.3	59.5	77.1[17]	...	...	...	...	...	
108.1	4.4[16]	...	144.3	33.1	8.8	172.3	...	...	Madagascar [13,54]
9.1	1.3[16]	...	61.3	33.1	5.6	190.2	...	...	Madagascar [13,54]
80.8	2.7	...	133.6	18.5	5.1	203.8	...	...	
5.4	1.4	...	68.8	26.0	4.8	313.9	...	...	
449.9	120.5	317.8	486.5	209.7	70.6	135.2	19.6	1.0	Malaysia [6,41]
89.8	121.8	190.6	187.6	390.4	152.6	111.9	235.0	0.2	Malaisie [6,41]
450.2	142.2	343.5	514.6	221.7	74.9	144.9	19.5	1.0	
88.0	140.0	214.7	201.5	411.0	164.0	121.7	253.2	0.7	
487.0	134.2	342.7	536.4	226.1	76.2	158.4	29.4	0.9	
96.3	141.8	210.6	214.7	430.4	176.5	115.8	223.6	0.2	
5.8	1.4[16]	...	7.2[55]	...	...	...	...	...	Maldives [25]
0.6	0.7[16]	...	5.7[55]	...	...	...	...	...	Maldives [26]
7.2	1.1[16]	...	9.7[55]	...	...	...	...	...	
0.7	0.6[16]	...	8.4[55]	...	...	...	...	...	
6.2	0.3	0.9	11.7	2.7	1.3	2.1	...	0.1	
0.9	0.3	0.3	4.3	7.1	2.8	1.1	...	0.1	
51.8	4.4	3.5	33.3	35.6	11.4	23.8	18.8	...	Mali [3]
3.5	0.0	0.6	6.6	18.3	9.5	11.5	85.1	0.9	Mali [3]
8.9	3.5	6.2	10.1	4.4	5.3	3.5	...	...	Malta [3]
2.6	3.0	2.9	4.3	7.9	6.2	2.5	...	...	Malte [3]
9.4	3.0	7.1	10.0	4.7	5.1	3.7	...	...	
2.6	3.4	4.3	3.8	8.0	6.1	2.7	...	...	
9.8	2.8	7.5	9.6	4.7	5.4	4.4	0.0	0.2	
3.2	3.2	4.0	4.7	8.8	6.8	3.1	0.1	0.1	
30.0	5.5	15.2	29.7	13.0	7.6	11.7	2.6	0.2	Mauritius [6]
4.9	4.4	6.5	8.2	15.4	8.2	5.5	16.0	0.1	Maurice [6]
30.8	5.8	14.5	27.3	12.8	8.7	10.7	2.7	0.4	
5.1	4.5	7.0	7.4	16.1	9.4	5.8	16.1	0.1	
32.7	6.7	17.5	25.1	13.1	8.0	12.6	2.2	0.2	
5.6	6.7	8.9	8.9	17.0	8.6	7.2	16.9	0.1	
1 802.8	190.8	1 245.0	1 329.6	846.2	366.4	736.9	142.9	0.9	Mexico [20,46]
198.6	171.7	680.2	702.5	1 406.2	794.9	632.5	1 613.5	1.9	Mexique [20,46]
1 742.0	215.8	1 322.3	1 316.2	910.2	372.3	781.5	144.6	3.1	
201.0	187.8	727.3	725.1	1 409.2	840.3	592.4	1 713.7	4.1	
1 820.8	209.3	1 378.2	1 386.9	916.9	411.4	837.3	151.2	3.5	
213.5	196.6	811.0	785.1	1 409.1	841.5	632.1	1 700.6	0.3	
25.8	6.8	6.0	26.2	20.4	12.4	11.8	5.0	...	Mongolia [34,56]
15.4	10.0	6.0	20.7	41.6	26.9	11.1	5.6	...	Mongolie [34,56]
28.8	7.1	6.8	27.3	20.9	12.7	10.3	5.4	...	
15.3	10.3	7.7	21.2	43.9	27.5	9.4	6.2	...	
30.2	7.9	5.8	29.0	21.6	13.9	10.0	5.9	...	
16.1	11.9	6.2	21.9	44.6	28.4	9.7	5.9	...	
11.4	1.0	2.9	14.4	4.4	4.0	9.8	...	0.4	Montenegro [11,41]
3.2									
	1.2	1.6	8.4	9.1	8.3	8.0	...	0.0	Monténégro [11,41]

Employment by economic activity *(continued)*

Total employment and persons employed by ISIC rev. 3 categories (thousands)

Emploi par activité économique *(suite)*

Emploi total et personnes employées par branches de la CITI rév. 3 (milliers)

Country or area [&] Pays ou zone [&]	Year Année	Sex Sexe	Total employment Emploi total	ISIC Rev. 3 Tabulation categories [+] CITI Rév. 3 Catégories de classement [+]						
				Categ. A Catég. A	Categ. B Catég. B	Categ. C Catég. C	Categ. D Catég. D	Categ. E Catég. E	Categ. F Catég. F	Categ. G Catég. G
Morocco [3] Maroc [3]	2006	M	7 233.3	2 651.8[1]	...	39.3	760.8	39.2	783.1	1 461.6[43]
	2006	F	2 694.4	1 651.6[1]	...	0.6	381.2	3.6	6.5	140.8[43]
	2007	M	7 323.7	2 596.3[1]	...	873.1[52]	...	...	832.4	1 321.6[43]
	2007	F	2 732.6	1 638.8[1]	...	405.9[52]	...	...	6.4	113.7[43]
	2008	M	7 453.5	2 547.8[1]	...	891.1[52]	...	...	897.7	1 342.2[43]
	2008	F	2 735.8	1 620.5[1]	...	416.1[52]	...	...	6.0	114.8[43]
Namibia [58] Namibie [58]	2000	M	226.8	69.8	4.7	3.2	11.4	3.7	20.7	17.2
	2000	F	205.0	56.7	3.1	0.7	11.5	0.5	1.0	21.7
	2004	M	216.7	65.0	7.9	5.9	12.1	5.0	18.3	27.0
	2004	F	168.7	37.6	4.8	1.7	11.7	1.1	1.3	26.9
Nepal [7,59] Népal [7,59]	2001	M	5 606.8	3 370.6	7.2	10.3	456.9	33.2	235.3	521.6
	2001	F	4 293.4	3 125.6	1.2	5.7	415.3	115.0	51.1	342.1
Netherlands [3] Pays-Bas [3]	2006	M	4 475.0	191.0[1]	...	5.0	796.0	32.0	455.0	638.0
	2006	F	3 633.0	78.0[1]	...	2.0	227.0	11.0	45.0	562.0
	2007	M	4 548.0	179.0[1]	...	9.0	774.0	30.0	457.0	646.0
	2007	F	3 763.0	74.0[1]	...	2.0	229.0	11.0	43.0	565.0
	2008	M	4 594.0	160.0[1]	...	9.0	736.0	29.0	463.0	620.0
	2008	F	3 863.0	69.0[1]	...	...	237.0	11.0	46.0	566.0
Netherlands Antilles [3,11,60] Antilles néerlandaises [3,11,60]	2006	MF	52.1	0.5[1]	...	^0.0	3.5	0.8	3.9	9.5
	2007	MF	54.0	0.7[1]	...	0.1	3.8	0.8	4.0	9.2
	2008	MF	56.5	0.6[1]	...	0.1	3.9	0.8	5.1	9.8
New Caledonia [20] Nouvelle-Calédonie [20]	2006	MF	73.5	2.1[1]	...	1.1	6.9	0.8	6.9	8.7
	2007	MF	77.5	2.2[1]	...	1.2	7.4	0.8	7.6	9.0
	2008	MF	82.1	2.2[1]	...	1.2	8.2	0.8	8.1	9.4
New Zealand [3,6] Nouvelle-Zélande [3,6]	2006	M	1 146.3	100.4	1.3	4.1	203.4	6.0	162.5	196.0
	2006	F	988.4	50.3	...	...	77.2	2.3	22.6	172.4
	2007	M	1 165.0	103.7	1.9	4.4	201.6	7.0	164.4	197.8
	2007	F	1 009.5	49.7	...	...	77.6	1.8	20.9	179.9
	2008	M	1 164.9	100.1	2.1	3.6	194.7	9.7	158.9	201.6
	2008	F	1 023.2	49.3	0.5	0.4	83.3	2.3	20.2	185.6
Nicaragua [7] Nicaragua [7]	2004	M	1 239.3	509.2	11.0	4.8	135.5	6.1	94.3	199.1
	2004	F	733.8	77.2	0.6	0.8	119.3	0.7	1.0	193.5
	2005	M	1 296.6	523.6	12.2	4.2	157.5	7.4	90.9	201.0
	2005	F	784.3	64.5	0.9	1.2	144.8	1.8	1.7	218.3
	2006	M	1 303.5	528.7	14.5	5.9	153.1	5.3	99.1	195.6
	2006	F	786.3	64.9	1.0	0.8	136.1	1.2	1.7	213.5
Norway [45] Norvège [45]	2006	M	1 251.0	48.0	12.0	28.0	205.0	13.0	156.0	184.0
	2006	F	1 111.0	15.0	1.0	6.0	67.0	3.0	12.0	169.0
	2007	M	1 289.0	42.0	12.0	31.0	210.0	13.0	167.0	187.0
	2007	F	1 154.0	14.0	1.0	8.0	67.0	4.0	13.0	170.0
	2008	M	1 332.0	41.0	13.0	33.0	213.0	14.0	172.0	190.0
	2008	F	1 192.0	15.0	1.0	9.0	73.0	5.0	11.0	172.0
Occupied Palestinian Terr. [3] Terr. palestinien occupé [3]	2006	M	546.0	64.9	0.9	2.2	70.3	2.4	73.7	106.2
	2006	F	120.4	41.2	...	...	10.2	0.1	0.2	8.5
	2007	M	538.0	56.6	1.5	1.5	69.9	2.2	72.4	107.1
	2007	F	127.6	45.9	...	...	12.0	...	0.3	9.3
	2008	M	525.7	52.4	0.7	1.4	...	2.7	70.1	103.4
	2008	F	121.3	33.4	...	^0.0	...	0.1	0.6	8.1
Oman [6,26,61] Oman [6,26,61]	1996	M	226.8	9.3	7.8	7.4	3.5	0.3	6.3	13.5
	1996	F	25.4	1.2	0.1	0.2	1.3	^0.0	0.2	1.7
	2000	M	243.1	8.9	7.2	7.8	9.4	1.1	7.8	14.2
	2000	F	38.6	2.0	^0.0	0.7	4.5	^0.0	0.2	2.4
Palau [56] Palaos [56]	2007	MF	12.1	0.2	0.2	^0.0	0.4	...	1.2	1.9
	2008	MF	11.7	0.1	0.1	^0.0	0.4	...	1.0	1.8

25

Employment by economic activity *(continued)*

Total employment and persons employed by ISIC rev. 3 categories (thousands)

Emploi par activité économique *(suite)*

Emploi total et personnes employées par branches de la CITI rév. 3 (milliers)

ISIC Rev. 3 Tabulation categories + / CITI Rév. 3 Catégories de classement +										
Categ. H / Catég. H	Categ. I / Catég. I	Categ. J / Catég. J	Categ. K / Catég. K	Categ. L / Catég.L	Categ. M / Catég. M	Categ. N / Catég. N	Categ. O / Catég. O	Categ. P / Catég. P	Categ. Q / Catég. Q	Country or area & / Pays ou zone &
...	367.7	105.0[16]	...	1 016.2[55]	...	...	...	...	...	Morocco[3]
...	27.1	47.4[16]	...	433.3[55]	...	...	...	...	...	Maroc[3]
...	371.9	1 317.6[57]	...	...	...	...	...	...	...	
...	29.9	534.7[57]	...	...	...	...	...	...	...	
...	419.3	1 341.6[57]	...	...	...	...	...	...	...	
...	31.9	542.1[57]	...	...	...	...	...	...	...	
3.0	12.2	2.5	17.9	15.4	11.7	3.0	24.3	4.8	0.2	Namibia[58]
4.7	2.1	2.4	21.4	9.0	18.8	10.1	22.0	17.5	0.2	Namibie[58]
5.9	12.7	3.5	5.3	20.2	12.3	3.5	7.5	4.1	0.1	
7.2	3.1	4.1	4.1	10.5	18.9	10.5	5.2	20.0	0.0	
79.1	155.8	39.9	25.9	265.4	169.0	43.6	62.0	62.9	54.6	Nepal[7,59]
41.7	5.8	6.8	4.1	35.6	59.3	18.2	10.6	42.3	3.7	Népal[7,59]
158.0	369.0	141.0	591.0	327.0	205.0	226.0	148.0	...	...	Netherlands[3]
176.0	131.0	124.0	383.0	201.0	316.0	1 023.0	185.0	5.0	...	Pays-Bas[3]
167.0	372.0	137.0	632.0	328.0	210.0	230.0	171.0	...	...	
185.0	134.0	121.0	413.0	213.0	323.0	1 080.0	210.0	5.0	...	
159.0	376.0	133.0	669.0	326.0	215.0	238.0	168.0	...	...	
178.0	136.0	112.0	430.0	215.0	334.0	1 115.0	221.0	5.0	...	
4.2	3.1	3.9	5.2	4.8	2.6	4.4	3.6	2.0	0.1	Netherlands Antilles[3,11,60]
4.4	3.5	4.1	5.6	5.3	2.8	4.6	3.3	1.8	0.1	Antilles néerlandaises[3,11,60]
4.5	4.1	4.1	6.0	4.7	2.5	4.4	3.6	2.1	^0.0	
3.6	4.9	1.7	5.3	...	0.2	1.6	2.1	3.7	...	New Caledonia[20]
4.0	4.9	1.7	5.5	...	0.2	1.7	2.3	3.7	...	Nouvelle-Calédonie[20]
4.3	5.3	1.8	6.2	...	0.2	1.8	2.6	3.7	...	
33.1	80.8	32.6	133.6	63.8	49.4	33.8	40.6	...	...	New Zealand[3,6]
64.0	37.9	37.6	112.7	72.8	116.6	162.3	51.8	2.9	...	Nouvelle-Zélande[3,6]
39.9	84.6	32.7	129.9	67.2	50.3	32.1	40.9	...	...	
68.3	33.4	38.1	118.8	70.9	119.3	171.4	50.2	3.4	...	
40.3	86.7	29.7	134.0	63.4	48.1	36.6	48.0	...	...	
60.7	36.4	38.4	120.0	69.2	127.2	171.2	51.9	2.1	...	
20.9	74.6	8.1	33.9	44.5	26.8	19.5	32.3	16.7	2.1	Nicaragua[7]
53.0	5.4	8.7	10.0	23.8	59.7	36.4	52.6	89.6	1.5	Nicaragua[7]
16.3	80.6	8.8	40.4	47.4	28.6	18.7	34.4	18.4	5.9	
45.4	7.5	8.3	12.6	23.4	60.4	32.6	57.3	100.3	3.3	
18.1	82.3	7.5	42.1	44.6	28.5	19.6	33.0	22.6	3.1	
53.9	6.7	8.4	11.9	29.1	66.0	34.7	56.2	94.8	5.0	
25.0	117.0	28.0	157.0	79.0	67.0	86.0	44.0	1.0	...	Norway[45]
43.0	40.0	26.0	95.0	65.0	127.0	385.0	54.0	3.0	...	Norvège[45]
23.0	117.0	29.0	169.0	81.0	77.0	84.0	47.0	...	...	
45.0	40.0	26.0	101.0	73.0	138.0	392.0	58.0	3.0	...	
23.0	117.0	29.0	187.0	85.0	77.0	86.0	51.0	...	...	
45.0	39.0	26.0	103.0	78.0	143.0	416.0	56.0	1.0	...	
13.1	37.2	3.3	8.9	92.7	34.2	15.1	15.6	0.2	5.3	Occupied Palestinian Terr.[3]
0.4	1.1	1.2	2.3	6.2	33.5	9.3	3.8	0.2	2.0	Terr. palestinien occupé[3]
12.9	36.9	3.2	9.6	92.6	34.4	15.9	16.1	^0.0	5.1	
0.5	0.5	1.0	1.8	7.0	33.6	8.6	4.5	0.1	2.3	
18.7	31.3	3.8	...	94.4	32.6	16.7	14.3	0.3	4.6	
0.9	0.8	1.1	...	7.4	38.5	10.6	4.9	0.2	1.8	
0.6	14.6	4.9	2.7	141.3	9.6	3.3	0.9	^0.0	0.1	Oman[6,26,61]
0.2	0.3	1.9	0.7	6.6	8.3	2.4	0.1	...	^0.0	Oman[6,26,61]
2.3	19.5	4.7	1.9	133.6	17.8	5.2	1.2	^0.0	^0.0	
0.2	0.8	1.4	1.1	3.3	16.0	5.4	0.2	...	0.1	
1.7	0.9	0.2	0.7	3.0	0.6	0.1	0.3	0.9	^0.0	Palau[56]
1.7	0.9	0.1	0.7	3.0	0.6	0.1	0.3	0.8	^0.0	Palaos[56]

25 Employment by economic activity *(continued)*

Total employment and persons employed by ISIC rev. 3 categories (thousands)

Emploi par activité économique *(suite)*

Emploi total et personnes employées par branches de la CITI rév. 3 (milliers)

Country or area [&] / Pays ou zone [&]	Year / Année	Sex / Sexe	Total employment / Emploi total	Categ. A / Catég. A	Categ. B / Catég. B	Categ. C / Catég. C	Categ. D / Catég. D	Categ. E / Catég. E	Categ. F / Catég. F	Categ. G / Catég. G
				ISIC Rev. 3 Tabulation categories [+] / CITI Rév. 3 Catégories de classement [+]						
Panama [3,27]	2006	M	777.5	164.1	9.5	2.0	72.8	6.7	99.2	143.5
Panama [3,27]	2006	F	433.2	19.0	0.4	0.3	32.4	1.8	3.6	86.0
	2007	M	799.1	161.2	9.4	3.4	71.5	5.8	117.8	142.8
	2007	F	464.9	15.2	0.4	0.2	38.1	2.3	4.6	98.0
	2008	M	837.0	157.7	8.6	2.9	73.5	4.8	133.1	151.4
	2008	F	496.8	18.9	0.5	0.4	40.6	2.0	3.6	107.3
Papua New Guinea [7,37] / Papouasie-Nvl-Guinée [7,37]	2000	MF	2 344.7	1 666.2	30.0	9.3	25.6	2.2	48.3	353.2
Paraguay [7,62]	2007	M	1 653.6	551.2[1]	...	8.6	226.7	8.0	153.9	355.4[43]
Paraguay [7,62]	2007	F	1 062.8	249.4[1]	...	...	92.5	0.8	1.0	284.1[43]
	2008	M	1 726.4	537.2[1]	...	6.4	238.4	8.8	173.5	364.4[43]
	2008	F	1 084.1	208.0[1]	...	0.2	101.8	2.0	0.6	309.5[43]
Peru [20,33]	2006	M	4 821.9	567.1	41.3	89.0	730.5	21.4	420.0	795.2
Pérou [20,33]	2006	F	3 872.1	290.2	0.7	5.1	405.2	4.9	11.6	1 240.0
	2007	M	5 015.0	468.2	58.0	88.8	800.6	19.0	459.9	791.9
	2007	F	4 182.8	230.3	0.7	8.4	491.6	2.0	9.9	1 295.7
	2008	M	5 142.8	473.7	57.2	91.7	805.6	29.8	494.7	751.4
	2008	F	4 302.7	237.0	1.7	7.1	511.0	6.0	17.3	1 350.0
Philippines [3,63]	2006	M	20 013.0	7 382.0	1 327.0	124.0	1 653.0	107.0	1 648.0	2 464.0
Philippines [3,63]	2006	F	12 622.0	2 872.0	101.0	14.0	1 400.0	21.0	29.0	3 738.0
	2007	M	20 542.0	7 437.0	1 327.0	135.0	1 684.0	112.0	1 742.0	2 526.0
	2007	F	13 018.0	2 905.0	117.0	14.0	1 375.0	23.0	36.0	3 828.0
	2008	M	20 959.0	7 666.0	1 316.0	146.0	1 622.0	110.0	1 798.0	2 565.0
	2008	F	13 129.0	2 937.0	110.0	12.0	1 304.0	20.0	36.0	3 880.0
Poland [3,64]	2005	M	7 809.0	1 391.0	11.0	201.0	1 882.0	181.0	784.0	961.0
Pologne [3,64]	2005	F	6 307.0	1 048.0	2.0	25.0	949.0	47.0	59.0	1 059.0
	2006	M	8 081.0	1 316.0	9.0	212.0	1 989.0	172.0	864.0	963.0
	2006	F	6 513.0	977.0	1.0	26.0	1 000.0	51.0	61.0	1 097.0
	2007	M	8 403.0	1 270.0	6.0	215.0	2 084.0	170.0	991.0	1 038.0
	2007	F	6 838.0	969.0	1.0	33.0	1 078.0	48.0	63.0	1 226.0
Portugal [3]	2006	M	2 789.7	295.5	14.9[65]	16.2[65]	565.5	21.0	527.9	419.7
Portugal [3]	2006	F	2 369.8	292.2	1.3	1.4	414.9	5.1	25.1	331.6
	2007	M	2 789.3	294.7	15.8[65]	18.1[65]	551.4	26.3	545.5	416.2
	2007	F	2 380.4	289.7	1.3	1.2	402.6	7.4	25.3	334.0
	2008	M	2 797.1	290.5	17.0[65]	16.5[65]	540.5	26.2	529.8	432.3
	2008	F	2 400.7	287.2	0.9	1.5	376.4	6.3	23.8	345.1
Qatar [3,11]	2001	M	266.4	5.2	1.9	12.2	41.0	4.9	59.0	34.6
Qatar [3,11]	2001	F	43.9	...	...	1.0	0.1	0.1	0.3	1.1
	2006	M	452.6	12.5	3.2	25.9	62.0	4.4	124.7	67.6
	2006	F	76.7	...	...	1.3	0.7	0.2	0.8	2.3
	2007	M	726.8	15.9	3.6	41.3	71.0	5.1	306.2	98.3
	2007	F	100.8	...	...	2.4	0.9	0.4	1.1	3.3
Republic of Moldova [3]	2006	M	628.6	220.8	0.8	3.2	69.1	17.5	60.9	77.2
République de Moldova [3]	2006	F	628.7	200.8	0.0	0.2	65.3	6.0	6.4	96.9
	2007	M	621.5	219.7	0.8	3.2	65.4	19.2	68.6	75.5
	2007	F	625.7	188.1	0.0	0.5	63.1	6.7	7.1	100.8
	2008	M	628.8	210.7	1.2	3.3	67.9	17.4	73.3	81.7
	2008	F	622.3	176.7	0.0	0.5	68.4	6.0	9.5	105.9
Romania [3]	2006	M	5 074.0	1 508.7	...	101.2	1 028.8	148.6	501.6	483.1
Roumanie [3]	2006	F	4 239.3	1 331.7	...	18.5	949.4	49.0	56.0	566.3
	2007	M	5 116.3	1 443.9	...	95.1	1 052.5	134.9	610.1	530.9
	2007	F	4 237.0	1 312.8	...	14.2	921.3	41.0	68.4	620.5
	2008	M	5 157.4	1 408.8	...	93.1	1 045.4	127.4	676.1	542.0
	2008	F	4 211.7	1 281.1	...	14.1	884.4	34.0	70.3	636.2

25 Employment by economic activity *(continued)*

Total employment and persons employed by ISIC rev. 3 categories (thousands)

Emploi par activité économique *(suite)*

Emploi total et personnes employées par branches de la CITI rév. 3 (milliers)

ISIC Rev. 3 Tabulation categories [+] CITI Rév. 3 Catégories de classement [+]										
Categ. H Catég. H	Categ. I Catég. I	Categ. J Catég. J	Categ. K Catég. K	Categ. L Catég.L	Categ. M Catég. M	Categ. N Catég. N	Categ. O Catég. O	Categ. P Catég. P	Categ. Q Catég. Q	Country or area [&] Pays ou zone [&]
25.0	77.9	11.2	40.3	41.8	20.3	15.9	39.2	7.6	0.6	Panama [3,27]
39.5	12.9	15.2	22.4	28.5	42.4	32.4	28.9	67.3	0.2	Panama [3,27]
27.2	79.5	11.3	41.3	46.4	22.2	16.0	34.4	8.5	0.4	
42.3	12.4	17.5	25.7	33.2	43.1	34.6	29.4	67.7	0.3	
27.7	89.3	10.9	42.1	46.0	25.4	16.6	38.2	8.6	0.3	
43.1	11.6	17.5	29.6	32.7	49.2	38.5	31.9	68.8	0.6	
										Papua New Guinea [7,37]
4.4	24.5	3.7	27.5	32.0	27.1	12.3	31.4	15.5	0.2	Papouasie-Nvl-Guinée [7,37]
...	85.7	65.7[16]	...	198.1[55]	...	...	...	...	...	Paraguay [7,62]
...	15.8	38.6[16]	...	380.3[55]	...	...	...	...	...	Paraguay [7,62]
...	101.5	78.5[16]	...	217.7[55]	...	...	...	...	...	
...	16.9	42.3[16]	...	402.3[55]	...	...	...	...	...	
155.3	670.1	43.2	305.8	276.0	227.3	67.4	382.4	29.1	0.7	Peru [20,33]
475.7	80.6	31.3	121.0	120.4	318.4	133.7	186.4	446.9	...	Pérou [20,33]
174.1	738.0	41.1	316.6	316.1	258.7	86.4	370.5	26.4	0.4	
506.4	102.4	28.3	166.4	121.5	391.6	162.0	216.6	447.9	1.2	
172.7	797.4	51.6	331.2	311.7	248.8	101.0	402.3	21.9	...	
557.4	109.6	40.8	155.2	111.5	392.7	169.5	232.2	401.5	2.2	
402.0	2 329.0	148.0	508.0	927.0	249.0	99.0	405.0	239.0	1.0	Philippines [3,63]
484.0	154.0	196.0	275.0	558.0	750.0	260.0	396.0	1 374.0	...	Philippines [3,63]
409.0	2 428.0	156.0	578.0	950.0	259.0	101.0	434.0	262.0	2.0	
498.0	170.0	203.0	307.0	601.0	776.0	272.0	415.0	1 478.0	1.0	
436.0	2 425.0	156.0	624.0	1 023.0	269.0	114.0	426.0	262.0	1.0	
518.0	165.0	211.0	329.0	653.0	802.0	277.0	407.0	1 467.0	...	
87.0	658.0	94.0	485.0	451.0	251.0	158.0	213.0	1.0	...	Poland [3,64]
161.0	205.0	200.0	337.0	442.0	852.0	662.0	246.0	11.0	...	Pologne [3,64]
87.0	735.0	96.0	472.0	457.0	260.0	171.0	274.0	2.0	...	
185.0	207.0	232.0	365.0	460.0	880.0	700.0	260.0	9.0	...	
89.0	760.0	113.0	532.0	469.0	256.0	168.0	239.0	...	...	
202.0	213.0	250.0	422.0	469.0	872.0	703.0	272.0	16.0	...	
108.1	178.8	52.4	159.6	219.2	77.4	59.7	70.1	2.2	1.5[65]	Portugal [3]
171.9	60.8	37.7	134.9	135.1	241.3	270.1	94.8	150.2	1.4[65]	Portugal [3]
118.8	175.0	51.3	157.0	204.4	76.4	61.2	73.2	2.4	1.5[65]	
170.0	48.7	44.4	168.4	122.5	230.3	279.0	89.2	165.1	1.3[65]	
128.0	172.0	52.4	167.1	220.9	80.2	50.4	70.0	2.0	1.3[65]	
191.4	52.9	43.7	169.1	121.0	263.5	255.0	88.7	173.4	0.9[65]	
6.8	9.1	3.4	6.1	40.3	5.8	3.2	9.3	21.8	0.4	Qatar [3,11]
0.1	0.8	0.6	0.1	3.5	9.4	2.7	0.6	23.3	0.1	Qatar [3,11]
13.9	21.0	4.5	15.1	40.6	7.6	8.2	10.0	29.7	1.5	
1.1	2.8	1.6	0.8	6.4	15.1	8.5	2.0	32.8	0.2	
14.1	32.8	6.5	27.3	45.2	9.5	8.2	10.3	29.0	1.5	
2.1	3.1	2.6	1.1	7.4	16.7	12.9	2.5	43.8	0.2	
6.0	47.0	5.2	19.8	43.3	26.3	13.3	17.0	0.7	0.4	Republic of Moldova [3]
15.9	18.2	9.9	11.2	28.6	94.1	51.0	19.5	4.0	0.7	République de Moldova [3]
5.3	49.0	5.1	17.7	37.6	23.7	13.1	16.5	0.8	0.4	
16.2	19.7	10.4	11.2	28.6	93.2	54.3	20.6	4.5	0.5	
5.4	53.1	6.1	17.5	38.8	21.6	14.9	15.0	0.6	0.4	
15.8	17.7	10.9	12.9	29.4	90.4	53.2	20.7	3.9	0.5	
52.6	376.6	29.2	172.3	335.5	107.0	86.7	139.6[28]	...	...	Romania [3]
90.4	115.2	62.8	109.2	172.0	303.6	291.6	123.0[28]	...	...	Roumanie [3]
46.6	380.1	29.0	175.9	299.6	102.6	84.2	126.5[28]	...	...	
90.0	108.5	68.2	106.2	168.8	297.6	291.3	127.4[28]	...	...	
53.6	396.1	34.8	179.7	298.1	100.4	92.4	105.7[28]	...	...	
100.6	112.4	75.6	118.6	178.0	296.5	303.6	105.8[28]	...	...	

Employment by economic activity *(continued)*

Total employment and persons employed by ISIC rev. 3 categories (thousands)

Emploi par activité économique *(suite)*

Emploi total et personnes employées par branches de la CITI rév. 3 (milliers)

Country or area [&] Pays ou zone [&]	Year Année	Sex Sexe	Total employment Emploi total	ISIC Rev. 3 Tabulation categories [+] CITI Rév. 3 Catégories de classement [+] Categ. A Catég. A	Categ. B Catég. B	Categ. C Catég. C	Categ. D Catég. D	Categ. E Catég. E	Categ. F Catég. F	Categ. G Catég. G
Russian Federation [66] Fédération de Russie [66]	2006	M	34 695.0	4 069.0	144.0	926.0	7 163.0	1 441.0	3 606.0	4 090.0
	2006	F	34 160.0	2 622.0	31.0	272.0	5 309.0	622.0	856.0	6 509.0
	2007	M	35 650.0	3 764.0	157.0	1 044.0	7 073.0	1 390.0	4 047.0	4 313.0
	2007	F	34 920.0	2 391.0	34.0	280.0	5 252.0	627.0	886.0	6 783.0
	2008	M	36 139.0	3 671.0	119.0	1 053.0	6 844.0	1 497.0	4 500.0	4 141.0
	2008	F	34 826.0	2 324.0	22.0	296.0	4 819.0	619.0	913.0	6 633.0
Saint Helena [58] Sainte-Hélène [58]	1998[67]	M	1.1	0.2	^0.0	...	0.1	^0.0	0.3	0.1
	1998[67]	F	0.9	^0.0	...	...	^0.0	^0.0	^0.0	0.2
	2008[68]	M	1.2	0.1	^0.0	^0.0	0.1	0.1	0.2	0.1
	2008[68]	F	1.0	^0.0	^0.0	^0.0	^0.0	...	^0.0	0.2
Saint Lucia [3] Sainte-Lucie [3]	2002	M	32.1	4.4	0.4	...	2.0	0.5	4.6	3.4
	2002	F	26.4	2.3	^0.0	...	2.5	0.1	0.3	5.2
	2003	M	36.5	5.4	0.6	...	2.3	0.5	4.7	4.7
	2003	F	27.4	2.3	^0.0	...	2.3	0.1	0.2	5.7
	2004	M	34.8	5.9	0.7	...	2.3	0.4	4.8	4.4
	2004	F	27.4	2.6	0.1	...	2.4	0.1	0.2	5.4
Samoa [3]	2001	M	35.1	15.4	2.2	...	2.8[69]	0.8	1.6	1.5
Samoa [3]	2001	F	15.2	2.1	0.3	...	4.5[69]	0.1	0.1	1.3
San Marino [3,34] Saint-Marin [3,34]	2006	M	12.2	0.1	...	...	4.4	...	1.6	1.7
	2006	F	8.5	^0.0	...	...	1.8	...	0.1	1.5
	2007	M	12.7	0.1	...	...	4.6	...	1.6	1.8
	2007	F	8.8	^0.0	...	...	1.8	...	0.1	1.6
	2008	M	13.0	0.1	...	...	4.6	...	1.6	1.9
	2008	F	9.0	^0.0	...	...	1.8	...	0.1	1.7
Saudi Arabia [3] Arabie saoudite [3]	2006[14]	M	6 461.5	295.2[1]	...	102.1	495.7	79.5	835.4	1 200.3
	2006[14]	F	1 061.5	4.3[1]	...	0.1	9.4	...	1.5	9.8
	2007	M	6 664.0	359.8[1]	...	101.6	557.4	74.4	790.7	1 242.5
	2007	F	1 102.3	4.4[1]	...	1.2	8.3	...	2.9	7.8
	2008	M	6 837.2	381.9[1]	...	107.1	498.5	66.9	743.5	1 249.6
	2008	F	1 119.6	0.5[1]	...	0.6	10.4	0.0	2.3	8.3
Senegal [3]	2006	M	2 048.1	631.9	66.5	11.5	203.7	18.5	179.7	388.0
Sénégal [3]	2006	F	1 104.8	354.6	10.4	2.6	41.7	3.3	6.9	397.9
Serbia [3,11] Serbie [3,11]	2006	M	1 554.7	332.0	1.7	30.7	343.1	51.0	145.3	209.7
	2006	F	1 076.0	206.7	...	0.4	175.5	10.9	13.9	197.2
	2007	M	1 545.8	335.2	0.9	31.6	347.0	41.7	144.4	186.5
	2007	F	1 110.0	216.5	...	9.7	174.7	16.2	16.8	212.0
	2008	M	1 611.3	392.8	1.4	27.6	317.9	38.1	161.0	201.2
	2008	F	1 210.4	314.6	0.2	4.8	166.4	6.9	16.5	216.9
Sierra Leone [7,34]	2004	M	987.2	617.9	33.3	59.3	7.4	7.1	28.2	102.2
Sierra Leone [7,34]	2004	F	945.8	654.3	17.8	9.7	2.0	1.2	10.8	167.3
Singapore [59,71] Singapour [59,71]	2006	M	1 796.7	22.5[72]	...	...	301.7	...	95.0	301.1
	2007	M	1 803.2	20.7[72]	...	...	304.5	...	100.8	277.0
	2008	M	1 852.0	22.7[72]	...	...	311.9	...	105.5	269.5
Slovakia [3,74] Slovaquie [3,74]	2006	M	1 291.1	76.7[1]	...	15.3	380.5	33.9	213.1	129.4
	2006	F	1 010.3	24.2[1]	...	0.8	228.2	8.0	13.0	161.2
	2007	M	1 321.6	76.0[1]	...	15.5	403.3	33.4	224.2	129.3
	2007	F	1 035.6	23.3[1]	...	0.9	230.9	6.9	12.9	170.7
	2008	M	1 363.7	74.5[1]	...	12.8	412.3	35.2	242.6	124.8
	2008	F	1 070.0	23.5[1]	...	1.4	235.4	6.9	14.1	174.1
Slovenia [7,46] Slovénie [7,46]	2005	M	512.0	44.0	...	5.0	174.0	8.0	55.0	51.0
	2005	F	435.0	39.0	...	...	104.0	2.0	4.0	60.0
	2006	M	521.0	51.0	...	5.0	168.0	8.0	53.0	58.0
	2006	F	448.0	41.0	...	1.0	97.0	2.0	5.0	63.0
	2007	M	542.0	54.0	...	3.0	170.0	7.0	56.0	57.0
	2007	F	451.0	47.0	...	1.0	96.0	2.0	5.0	61.0

25 Employment by economic activity *(continued)*

Total employment and persons employed by ISIC rev. 3 categories (thousands)

Emploi par activité économique *(suite)*

Emploi total et personnes employées par branches de la CITI rév. 3 (milliers)

ISIC Rev. 3 Tabulation categories + CITI Rév. 3 Catégories de classement +										
Categ. H Catég. H	Categ. I Catég. I	Categ. J Catég. J	Categ. K Catég. K	Categ. L Catég.L	Categ. M Catég. M	Categ. N Catég. N	Categ. O Catég. O	Categ. P Catég. P	Categ. Q Catég. Q	Country or area & Pays ou zone &
292.0	4 343.0	359.0	2 327.0	3 005.0	1 198.0	943.0	779.0	4.0	2.0	Russian Federation[66]
1 100.0	1 868.0	701.0	1 820.0	1 871.0	5 000.0	3 953.0	1 609.0	17.0	1.0	Fédération de Russie[66]
281.0	4 593.0	417.0	2 496.0	3 076.0	1 268.0	964.0	762.0	5.0	...	
1 062.0	1 979.0	833.0	1 914.0	1 827.0	5 152.0	4 212.0	1 677.0	11.0	...	
308.0	4 722.0	410.0	2 511.0	3 275.0	1 225.0	1 041.0	808.0	9.0	4.0	
1 160.0	1 838.0	906.0	1 936.0	2 134.0	5 218.0	4 202.0	1 772.0	34.0	1.0	
^0.0	0.1	^0.0	^0.0	0.1	^0.0	^0.0	^0.0	^0.0	^0.0	Saint Helena[58]
^0.0	0.1	^0.0	^0.0	0.2	0.1	0.1	0.1	^0.0	^0.0	Sainte-Hélène[58]
^0.0	0.2	^0.0	0.1	0.1	^0.0	^0.0	0.1	^0.0	^0.0	
^0.0	^0.0	^0.0	0.1	0.1	0.1	0.2	0.1	^0.0	...	
2.9	2.4	0.3	0.9	3.2	0.5	0.1	0.9	0.5	...	Saint Lucia[3]
3.3	0.8	0.6	0.7	3.7	1.4	0.2	0.5	1.5	...	Sainte-Lucie[3]
3.3	3.1	0.6	1.1	3.6	0.6	0.1	0.8	0.5	...	
3.4	1.1	0.6	1.0	3.7	1.5	0.5	0.8	1.6	...	
3.0	2.5	0.4	1.5	3.7	0.2	0.1	1.1	0.2	...	
3.7	0.8	0.7	1.1	4.5	0.9	0.3	0.9	1.7	...	
0.8	1.6	0.5	0.2	2.1	0.9	0.3	1.6	2.0	0.2	Samoa[3]
0.8	0.3	0.6	0.1	1.2	1.5	0.5	0.5	0.9	0.3	Samoa[3]
0.1	0.3	0.5	1.5	1.3	0.1	0.4	0.3	...	...	San Marino[3,34]
0.1	0.2	0.4	1.2	1.1	0.5	0.8	0.7	...	...	Saint-Marin[3,34]
0.1	0.3	0.5	1.7	1.7	^0.0	^0.0	0.3	...	...	
0.1	0.2	0.4	1.2	2.3	^0.0	0.1	0.8	...	...	
0.1	0.4	0.5	1.7	1.7	^0.0	0.1	0.3	...	...	
0.1	0.2	0.5	1.3	2.3	^0.0	0.1	0.8	...	...	
239.8	289.5	81.5	245.3	1 394.8	490.2	235.2	162.3	307.0	7.9	Saudi Arabia[3]
1.5	1.8	5.1	7.3	31.2	417.0	90.3	6.9	474.6	0.7	Arabie saoudite[3]
246.0	331.8	79.3	245.8	1 367.6	513.0	248.9	168.2	327.1	9.9	
2.7	11.7	4.5	4.4	32.5	416.2	87.0	7.7	511.0	...	
274.1	359.7	81.4	305.9	1 469.8	534.1	282.0	157.3	319.8	5.6	
5.0	2.2	4.6	7.6	33.1	398.4	83.4	5.7	556.8	0.7	
12.2	135.9	11.8	...	118.7[70]	...	...	...	...	3.3	Senegal[3]
16.4	5.8	4.9	...	39.0[70]	...	...	...	...	3.7	Sénégal[3]
43.4	119.2	17.0	32.9	91.0	33.7	37.9	64.3	1.5	0.4	Serbia[3,11]
41.1	32.2	26.0	37.3	52.0	95.8	135.8	45.7	5.4	...	Serbie[3,11]
34.9	135.6	17.4	51.7	80.3	38.3	38.2	61.2	0.4	0.5	
37.4	34.2	25.7	37.2	61.6	79.7	128.2	52.9	6.0	1.0	
44.6	122.7	21.0	47.8	80.8	37.1	39.5	75.4	1.6	0.8	
39.2	34.4	35.6	44.0	54.9	85.4	136.8	48.5	5.0	0.3	
2.6	14.4	4.0	5.5	21.1	23.3	9.9	44.4	4.0	2.5	Sierra Leone[7,34]
2.3	1.3	2.9	5.3	4.9	11.3	10.0	39.1	4.3	1.3	Sierra Leone[7,34]
128.8	248.8	106.3	217.3	223.3[73]	...	70.8	81.0[28]	...	...	Singapore[59,71]
123.1	267.7	109.7	223.9	375.8[55]	...	...	...	...	...	Singapour[59,71]
120.0	269.4	123.6	237.5	391.9[55]	...	...	...	...	...	
35.5	116.9	19.4	75.7	82.5	40.7	29.9	41.0	0.2	0.1	Slovakia[3,74]
66.3	39.3	32.5	55.9	79.3	126.1	124.6	44.4	5.6	0.1	Slovaquie[3,74]
37.5	123.3	17.1	83.5	79.0	34.4	27.6	37.0	0.1	0.2	
64.5	42.0	30.5	62.3	80.9	129.0	127.2	45.1	8.1	0.6	
43.1	130.0	17.5	83.6	82.0	35.0	28.2	41.9	0.2	0.2	
64.6	47.7	37.7	74.3	85.2	128.8	125.9	44.5	5.6	0.5	
16.0	40.0	9.0	34.0	30.0	16.0	8.0	18.0	...	...	Slovenia[7,46]
25.0	13.0	14.0	28.0	29.0	53.0	43.0	19.0	...	...	Slovénie[7,46]
12.0	39.0	8.0	38.0	29.0	18.0	12.0	19.0	...	...	
26.0	15.0	13.0	28.0	30.0	57.0	48.0	20.0	1.0	...	
13.0	47.0	7.0	37.0	32.0	16.0	12.0	23.0	...	...	
24.0	13.0	15.0	28.0	26.0	62.0	45.0	20.0	1.0	...	

Employment by economic activity *(continued)*

Total employment and persons employed by ISIC rev. 3 categories (thousands)

Emploi par activité économique *(suite)*

Emploi total et personnes employées par branches de la CITI rév. 3 (milliers)

Country or area [&] Pays ou zone [&]	Year Année	Sex Sexe	Total employment Emploi total	ISIC Rev. 3 Tabulation categories [+] CITI Rév. 3 Catégories de classement [+] Categ. A Catég. A	Categ. B Catég. B	Categ. C Catég. C	Categ. D Catég. D	Categ. E Catég. E	Categ. F Catég. F	Categ. G Catég. G
South Africa [13,41] Afrique du Sud [13,41]	2006	M	7 320.0	662.0[1]	...	375.0	1 146.0	95.0	911.0	1 581.0[43]
	2006	F	5 480.0	426.0[1]	...	23.0	591.0	24.0	113.0	1 474.0[43]
	2007	M	7 554.0	798.0[1]	...	419.0	1 231.0	68.0	947.0	1 496.0[43]
	2007	F	5 668.0	366.0[1]	...	36.0	567.0	48.0	119.0	1 455.0[43]
	2008	M	7 672.0	520.0[1]	...	292.0	1 331.0	69.0	1 027.0	1 561.0[43]
	2008	F	6 041.0	257.0[1]	...	36.0	630.0	25.0	114.0	1 580.0[43]
Spain [12,47] Espagne [12,47]	2006	M	11 742.6	638.8	42.5	60.6	2 343.2	97.2	2 408.5	1 538.6
	2006	F	8 005.1	254.2	8.8	5.8	763.7	21.6	134.4	1 444.9
	2007	M	11 987.3	632.6	42.5	53.6	2 298.4	89.5	2 544.7	1 594.6
	2007	F	8 368.8	240.7	9.6	6.5	791.5	22.4	152.6	1 533.9
	2008	M	11 720.7	610.8	39.8	48.4	2 275.3	89.1	2 253.6	1 653.7
	2008	F	8 536.9	220.4	8.0	4.6	784.5	23.6	150.6	1 585.4
Sri Lanka [7,76] Sri Lanka [7,76]	2006	M	4 610.6	1 342.2[1]	...	507.2[15]	683.9	...	...	717.3
	2006	F	2 494.7	945.1[1]	...	19.7[15]	679.2	...	...	237.7
	2007	M	4 653.1	1 322.0[1]	...	523.5[15]	703.1	...	...	688.7
	2007	F	2 388.8	880.1[1]	...	19.0[15]	628.3	...	...	243.4
	2008	M	4 663.3	1 388.7[1]	...	510.5[15]	716.3	...	...	680.1
	2008	F	2 511.4	955.7[1]	...	22.6[15]	638.6	...	...	244.4
Suriname [3,27] Suriname [3,27]	2004	M	101.9	10.1[1]	...	8.4	8.1	1.4	13.5	15.7
	2004	F	54.8	2.5[1]	...	0.9	2.9	0.2	0.5	9.3
Sweden [77] Suède [77]	2006[78]	M	2 273.0	66.0	2.0	7.0	488.0	18.0	251.0	306.0
	2006[78]	F	2 067.0	18.0	...	1.0	165.0	7.0	19.0	230.0
	2007[45]	M	2 390.0	79.0	3.0	8.0	491.0	18.0	268.0	317.0
	2007[45]	F	2 150.0	20.0	...	1.0	166.0	7.0	22.0	240.0
	2008[45]	M	2 422.0	79.0	2.0	8.0	494.0	18.0	281.0	319.0
	2008[45]	F	2 171.0	20.0	...	1.0	161.0	6.0	24.0	244.0
Switzerland [3,46,81] Suisse [3,46,81]	2006	M	2 214.0	104.0[1]	...	473.0[52]	...	...	246.0	273.0
	2006	F	1 837.0	50.0[1]	...	180.0[52]	...	...	30.0	287.0
	2007	M	2 259.0	112.0[1]	...	495.0[52]	...	...	244.0	269.0
	2007	F	1 863.0	52.0[1]	...	173.0[52]	...	...	32.0	283.0
	2008	M	2 289.0	117.0[1]	...	494.0[52]	...	...	235.0	278.0
	2008	F	1 940.0	54.0[1]	...	185.0[52]	...	...	31.0	287.0
Syrian Arab Republic [3] Rép. arabe syrienne [3]	2007	M	4 316.4	780.8[1]	...	31.9	595.4	31.2	729.7	699.3
	2007	F	629.6	165.6[1]	...	2.8	37.6	2.3	6.2	27.9
Tajikistan [3] Tadjikistan [3]	2004	M	1 441.7	602.3	...	10.3	80.1	15.9	285.0	153.8
	2004	F	1 010.8	758.7	...	1.5	34.4	1.4	11.0	48.3
Thailand [3,6,82] Thaïlande [3,6,82]	2006	M	19 638.4	8 117.9	337.7	42.6	2 479.6	85.0	1 716.4	2 817.0
	2006	F	16 706.2	6 669.2	90.5	12.0	2 827.0	14.3	322.5	2 584.9
	2007	M	19 976.8	8 323.2	317.9	42.4	2 640.2	89.8	1 619.6	2 854.5
	2007	F	17 145.4	6 758.6	92.1	11.5	2 952.8	15.1	319.1	2 670.9
	2008	M	20 405.0	8 716.0	323.5	44.4	2 405.4	85.0	1 702.5	2 945.8
	2008	F	17 431.6	6 925.5	102.2	10.7	2 826.0	18.1	309.6	2 689.2
TFYR of Macedonia [3] L'ex-R.Y. Macédoine [3]	2006	M	352.0	70.1	0.3	3.6	64.7	13.7	40.3	45.0
	2006	F	218.4	44.4	^0.0	0.3	58.4	2.3	2.9	28.0
	2007	M	358.8	67.4	0.3	4.8	65.2	13.2	35.3	48.3
	2007	F	231.4	40.0	...	0.3	61.0	2.4	2.7	34.6
	2008	M	373.5	73.0	0.1	6.3	67.9	13.1	37.5	51.3
	2008	F	235.5	46.5	0.1	0.4	61.1	2.4	1.9	35.2
Tonga [3] Tonga [3]	2003	M	20.4	9.5	0.9	0.1	0.9	0.4	1.4	1.3
	2003	F	14.1	0.5	0.2	...	7.6	0.2	^0.0	1.6
Turkey [3,6] Turquie [3,6]	2006	M	16 520.0	3 272.0[1]	...	126.0	3 358.0	87.0	1 231.0	3 167.0
	2006	F	5 810.0	2 816.0[1]	...	2.0	828.0	6.0	36.0	563.0
	2007	M	15 382.0	2 578.0[1]	...	126.0	3 268.0	93.0	1 195.0	3 001.0
	2007	F	5 356.0	2 288.0[1]	...	2.0	821.0	4.0	35.0	568.0
	2008	M	15 598.0	2 663.0[1]	...	112.0	3 406.0	85.0	1 199.0	2 975.0
	2008	F	5 595.0	2 354.0[1]	...	3.0	828.0	7.0	42.0	600.0

25 Employment by economic activity *(continued)*

Total employment and persons employed by ISIC rev. 3 categories (thousands)

Emploi par activité économique *(suite)*

Emploi total et personnes employées par branches de la CITI rév. 3 (milliers)

ISIC Rev. 3 Tabulation categories +
CITI Rév. 3 Catégories de classement +

Categ. H Catég. H	Categ. I Catég. I	Categ. J Catég. J	Categ. K Catég. K	Categ. L Catég. L	Categ. M Catég. M	Categ. N Catég. N	Categ. O Catég. O	Categ. P Catég. P	Categ. Q Catég. Q	Country or area & Pays ou zone &
...	487.0	760.0[16]	...	1 055.0[75]	...	...	...	223.0	...	South Africa[13,41]
...	123.0	550.0[16]	...	1 264.0[75]	...	...	...	884.0	...	Afrique du Sud[13,41]
...	460.0	781.0[16]	...	1 027.0[75]	...	...	...	299.0	...	
...	135.0	558.0[16]	...	1 422.0[75]	...	...	...	945.0	...	
...	615.0	910.0[16]	...	1 086.0[75]	...	...	...	260.0	...	
...	152.0	736.0[16]	...	1 538.0[75]	...	...	...	972.0	...	
639.6	892.1	254.0	936.9	730.9	387.6	298.2	401.1	69.5	3.2	Spain[12,47]
763.1	266.0	218.5	920.5	490.7	721.2	882.6	414.3	691.1	3.8	Espagne[12,47]
652.4	907.2	266.9	1 007.9	744.2	388.0	288.7	411.5	63.3	1.1	
798.2	269.9	233.1	1 009.2	494.1	724.3	940.5	434.7	706.7	1.0	
640.5	906.4	276.9	1 021.0	755.7	404.7	295.6	394.8	53.0	1.4	
812.1	275.5	230.0	1 052.8	521.7	727.8	981.5	457.9	699.6	0.9	
93.7	407.6	156.0[16]	...	294.6	86.5	45.2	87.1[28]	16.0	...	Sri Lanka[7,76]
35.6	22.7	65.1[16]	...	105.9	190.3	64.4	36.8[28]	64.2	...	Sri Lanka[7,76]
85.2	435.2	151.8[16]	...	308.1	79.1	49.3	77.8[28]	27.0	...	
33.4	21.6	63.4[16]	...	124.9	180.4	66.7	26.8[28]	60.4	...	
...	...	162.6[16]	...	344.7	87.9	...	...	...	...	
...	...	73.4[16]	...	117.9	210.9	...	...	...	...	
1.9	7.6	1.4	4.5	16.3	1.8	1.6	5.0	...	...	Suriname[3,27]
2.9	1.1	1.3	1.9	11.7	6.6	5.2	4.9	...	...	Suriname[3,27]
58.0	203.0	37.0	370.0	113.0[79]	122.0	122.0	105.0[80]	...	...	Sweden[77]
69.0	71.0	47.0	233.0	136.0[79]	359.0	579.0	128.0[80]	...	...	Suède[77]
66.0	207.0	43.0	407.0	122.0[79]	125.0	123.0	108.0[80]	...	...	
77.0	74.0	45.0	258.0	138.0[79]	366.0	601.0	132.0[80]	...	...	
65.0	200.0	45.0	429.0	118.0[79]	123.0	120.0	117.0[80]	...	...	
83.0	75.0	48.0	268.0	143.0[79]	362.0	601.0	131.0[80]	...	...	
65.0	149.0	137.0	291.0	131.0[79]	121.0	108.0	112.0[80]	...	...	Switzerland[3,46,81]
95.0	68.0	94.0	175.0	93.0[79]	204.0	377.0	182.0[80]	...	...	Suisse[3,46,81]
65.0	155.0	139.0	313.0	120.0[79]	121.0	118.0	105.0[80]	...	...	
89.0	62.0	99.0	192.0	97.0[79]	205.0	397.0	178.0[80]	...	...	
64.0	159.0	142.0	315.0	122.0[79]	131.0	118.0	111.0[80]	...	...	
91.0	63.0	102.0	202.0	97.0[79]	212.0	423.0	189.0[80]	...	...	
54.5	342.8	6.5	110.6	566.1	181.1	64.8	121.0[28]	...	...	Syrian Arab Republic[3]
1.4	9.4	3.5	11.7	82.4	202.8	54.7	21.2[28]	...	...	Rép. arabe syrienne[3]
12.2	59.7	14.7	14.5	59.2	59.0	21.1	46.8	2.4	...	Tajikistan[3]
11.6	4.8	4.2	2.1	11.5	63.8	41.6	10.4	1.0	...	Tadjikistan[3]
777.2	887.4	147.8	371.7	784.0	454.4	143.7	307.9	34.0	...	Thailand[3,6,82]
1 437.7	165.5	201.9	287.6	386.1	625.5	459.1	402.4	187.9	0.4	Thaïlande[3,6,82]
761.3	873.2	152.4	417.1	890.6	473.6	154.9	305.5	31.9	0.9	
1 541.2	153.3	197.8	300.3	396.3	611.4	492.3	412.5	197.2	0.2	
822.8	916.3	179.2	396.4	853.5	435.5	174.3	364.7	21.3	0.4	
1 530.4	174.2	216.9	320.6	449.0	662.0	546.1	454.3	174.8	1.0	
12.9	25.6	3.3	7.5	27.6	14.7	9.8	12.7	0.1	0.3	TFYR of Macedonia[3]
6.1	4.4	3.8	7.9	11.7	18.7	22.8	5.6	0.3	0.7	L'ex-R.Y. Macédoine[3]
11.8	29.6	4.5	8.3	29.4	13.2	9.6	16.1	0.9	0.8	
5.7	5.9	4.5	7.6	12.0	21.1	23.4	8.6	0.6	1.1	
12.7	31.4	3.1	9.6	30.6	14.2	8.6	13.1	0.3	0.6	
6.4	6.3	4.6	6.7	11.6	19.5	24.3	7.9	0.5	0.2	
0.2	1.2	0.2	0.2	1.9	0.7	0.3	1.0	0.3	0.1	Tonga[3]
0.4	0.4	0.3	0.1	0.7	1.1	0.4	0.3	0.4	^0.0	Tonga[3]
885.0	1 086.0	154.0	581.0	1 077.0	537.0	287.0	673.0[28]	...	...	Turkey[3,6]
115.0	77.0	84.0	192.0	148.0	370.0	304.0	269.0[28]	...	...	Turquie[3,6]
851.0	1 055.0	152.0	607.0	1 083.0	488.0	261.0	623.0[28]	...	...	
138.0	81.0	96.0	200.0	177.0	380.0	299.0	266.0[28]	...	...	
850.0	1 002.0	153.0	691.0	1 089.0	503.0	256.0	615.0[28]	...	...	
148.0	87.0	107.0	219.0	176.0	418.0	338.0	269.0[28]	...	...	

25 Employment by economic activity *(continued)*

Total employment and persons employed by ISIC rev. 3 categories (thousands)

Emploi par activité économique *(suite)*

Emploi total et personnes employées par branches de la CITI rév. 3 (milliers)

Country or area [&] Pays ou zone [&]	Year Année	Sex Sexe	Total employment Emploi total	ISIC Rev. 3 Tabulation categories [+] CITI Rév. 3 Catégories de classement [+] Categ. A Catég. A	Categ. B Catég. B	Categ. C Catég. C	Categ. D Catég. D	Categ. E Catég. E	Categ. F Catég. F	Categ. G Catég. G
Turks and Caicos Islands [3] Iles Turques et Caïques [3]	2005	M	17.4	0.1	0.2	0.1	0.2	0.3	2.4	1.3
	2006	M	18.2	0.2	0.2	^0.0	0.2	0.2	3.2	1.5
	2007	M	19.6	0.1	0.1	^0.0	0.2	0.2	4.3	1.7
Uganda [7]	2003	M	4 618.0	2 771.2	78.7	18.5	337.4	4.6	115.8	637.9
Ouganda [7]	2003	F	4 642.0	3 507.1	4.6	9.3	227.5	4.7	4.9	436.3
Ukraine Ukraine	2006	MF	20 730.4	3 649.1[1]	...	4 036.9[52]	...	...	987.1	4 406.9[43]
	2007	MF	20 904.7	3 484.5[1]	...	3 973.0[52]	...	...	1 030.2	4 564.4[43]
	2008	MF	20 972.3	3 322.1[1]	...	3 871.4[52]	...	...	1 043.4	4 744.4[43]
United Arab Emirates [3,68]	2008	M	1 501.3	72.0	5.9	33.2	149.1	23.5	219.2	278.3
Emirats arabes unis [3,68]	2008	F	344.9	0.5	0.1	2.7	11.3	1.7	8.7	22.1
United Kingdom [46,56] Royaume-Uni [46,56]	2006	M	15 578.0	274.0	18.0	86.0	2 803.0	127.0	2 075.0	2 135.0
	2006	F	13 348.0	82.0	...	23.0	952.0	46.0	257.0	2 102.0
	2007	M	15 747.0	289.0	9.0	105.0	2 808.0	153.0	2 160.0	2 143.0
	2007	F	13 353.0	100.0	...	28.0	937.0	60.0	228.0	2 017.0
	2008	M	15 904.0	304.0	13.0	101.0	2 638.0	146.0	2 148.0	2 192.0
	2008	F	13 572.0	114.0	2.0	27.0	909.0	53.0	233.0	2 124.0
United Rep. of Tanzania [3]	2006	M	8 779.8	6 064.8	184.6	90.8	332.9	13.5	204.8	907.7
Rép.-Unie de Tanzanie [3]	2006	F	9 164.7	7 120.3	25.0	14.1	232.2	3.5	6.7	665.0
United States [6,56] Etats-Unis [6,56]	2006	M	77 502.0	1 663.0[1]	...	598.0	11 543.0	926.0	10 618.0	11 802.0
	2006	F	66 925.0	543.0[1]	...	89.0	4 834.0	259.0	1 131.0	9 526.0
	2007	M	78 254.0	1 604.0[1]	...	635.0	11 416.0	936.0	10 738.0	11 524.0
	2007	F	67 792.0	490.0[1]	...	101.0	4 885.0	257.0	1 119.0	9 414.0
	2008	M	77 486.0	1 650.0[1]	...	714.0	11 249.0	987.0	9 905.0	11 327.0
	2008	F	67 876.0	518.0[1]	...	105.0	4 655.0	239.0	1 069.0	9 258.0
Uruguay [20,25] Uruguay [20,25]	2005[33]	M	620.1	44.3[36]	...	...	107.2[83]	...	73.2	152.2[43]
	2005[33]	F	494.4	7.4[36]	...	...	62.0[83]	...	1.5	103.0[43]
	#2006	M	822.4	126.7[36]	...	...	138.0[83]	...	88.5	184.3[43]
	#2006	F	591.0	30.5[36]	...	...	71.6[83]	...	2.1	123.9[43]
	2007	M	852.9	132.9[36]	...	...	143.5[83]	...	99.3	183.5[43]
	2007	F	629.0	30.4[36]	...	...	76.4[83]	...	2.9	135.8[43]
Viet Nam [3,37] Viet Nam [3,37]	2002	M	20 355.6	11 460.7	948.6	156.5	1 972.1	97.8	1 357.3	1 521.5
	2002	F	19 806.7	12 184.7	323.3	87.8	2 078.8	20.3	133.6	2 785.0
	2003	M	20 959.2	11 072.5	1 023.1	194.7	2 203.6	103.9	1 631.8	1 673.1
	2003	F	20 216.5	12 164.2	311.3	127.4	2 308.0	24.3	164.7	2 834.2
	2004	M	21 649.3	11 041.3	1 059.3	182.7	2 429.1	117.6	1 774.1	1 778.0
	2004	F	20 666.3	12 027.3	369.9	112.2	2 520.8	24.1	182.5	2 918.0
Yemen [3]	1999	M	2 731.6	1 146.4	31.4	16.7	112.5	11.0	236.9	382.3
Yémen [3]	1999	F	890.1	781.3	...	1.0	23.0	0.8	1.3	11.9

25 Employment by economic activity *(continued)*

Total employment and persons employed by ISIC rev. 3 categories (thousands)

Emploi par activité économique *(suite)*

Emploi total et personnes employées par branches de la CITI rév. 3 (milliers)

ISIC Rev. 3 Tabulation categories [+]
CITI Rév. 3 Catégories de classement [+]

Categ. H Catég. H	Categ. I Catég. I	Categ. J Catég. J	Categ. K Catég. K	Categ. L Catég.L	Categ. M Catég. M	Categ. N Catég. N	Categ. O Catég. O	Categ. P Catég. P	Categ. Q Catég. Q	Country or area [&] Pays ou zone [&]
2.9	0.7	0.5	1.6	2.3	0.5[22]	...	1.0	1.6	...	Turks and Caicos Islands [3]
3.7	0.7	0.5	2.0	2.8	0.8[22]	...	1.0	0.9	...	Iles Turques et Caïques [3]
4.1	0.8	0.5	2.4	2.3	0.8[22]	...	1.2	0.4	...	
64.4	171.3	...	27.7	64.8	157.2	37.0	92.5	39.5	...	Uganda [7]
176.4	4.6	...	9.3	9.3	83.6	37.1	55.7	71.6	...	Ouganda [7]
...	1 428.8	286.0	1 041.9	1 033.7	1 690.5	1 356.7	812.8[28]	...	...	Ukraine
...	1 451.9	344.4	1 134.7	1 036.4	1 693.7	1 359.0	832.5[28]	...	...	Ukraine
...	1 465.8	394.9	1 150.4	1 067.5	1 702.4	1 369.9	840.1[28]	...	...	
63.9	119.0	41.3	132.8	154.2	38.2	24.3	50.2	90.5	2.9	United Arab Emirates [3,68]
8.6	13.6	17.4	15.1	16.1	45.7	24.3	9.1	146.1	0.9	Emirats arabes unis [3,68]
567.0	1 477.0	631.0	1 967.0	1 008.0	753.0	738.0	806.0	56.0	11.0	United Kingdom [46,56]
703.0	463.0	623.0	1 362.0	1 036.0	1 920.0	2 844.0	826.0	69.0	10.0	Royaume-Uni [46,56]
581.0	1 481.0	649.0	2 014.0	1 005.0	724.0	695.0	818.0	51.0	6.0	
717.0	475.0	614.0	1 470.0	1 033.0	1 921.0	2 767.0	863.0	69.0	4.0	
596.0	1 499.0	664.0	2 102.0	1 070.0	720.0	786.0	803.0	53.0	8.0	
688.0	464.0	615.0	1 500.0	1 022.0	1 966.0	2 855.0	871.0	84.0	5.0	
98.5	245.0	11.3	69.0	157.4	126.9	46.1	88.3	138.2	...	United Rep. of Tanzania [3]
279.0	13.1	6.2	13.0	27.3	98.7	59.1	38.2	563.3	...	Rép.-Unie de Tanzanie [3]
4 452.0	4 722.0	3 035.0	10 184.0	3 563.0	3 892.0	3 632.0	6 873.0[24]	...	...	United States [6,56]
5 023.0	1 547.0	4 219.0	7 920.0	2 961.0	8 630.0	13 784.0	6 459.0[24]	...	...	Etats-Unis [6,56]
4 525.0	4 836.0	3 030.0	10 613.0	3 720.0	3 962.0	3 794.0	6 922.0[24]	...	...	
5 057.0	1 621.0	4 276.0	8 190.0	3 026.0	8 866.0	14 040.0	6 449.0[24]	...	...	
4 592.0	4 954.0	3 056.0	10 524.0	3 707.0	3 994.0	3 805.0	7 022.0[24]	...	...	
5 203.0	1 547.0	4 223.0	7 965.0	3 056.0	9 174.0	14 429.0	6 436.0[24]	...	...	
...	49.1	64.0[16]	...	56.4	14.4	19.6	32.3[28]	7.4	...	Uruguay [20,25]
...	12.4	40.0[16]	...	29.7	53.3	61.5	32.0[28]	91.6	...	Uruguay [20,25]
...	61.5	61.1[16]	...	70.9	18.9	24.8	35.5[28]	11.2	...	
...	14.3	40.6[16]	...	33.6	59.5	68.9	33.7[28]	111.6	...	
...	68.5	67.4[16]	...	62.5	19.8	25.2	38.7[28]	11.6	...	
...	15.4	47.0[16]	...	31.8	64.4	72.0	36.0[28]	116.6	...	
145.3	1 117.4	59.0	113.8	432.4	318.7	115.6	468.7	69.2	0.9	Viet Nam [3,37]
375.7	149.9	71.0	70.6	157.6	739.9	163.3	343.3	121.0	1.1	Viet Nam [3,37]
195.3	1 150.5	74.0	144.4	457.5	335.1	135.1	480.2	84.1	0.4	
447.9	146.8	74.5	74.2	162.6	762.9	171.0	308.6	132.9	1.0	
176.1	1 128.2	80.8	142.6	516.0	359.6	140.1	624.6	97.4	1.8	
418.9	164.7	78.2	76.6	182.8	825.4	187.9	431.8	143.7	1.4	
42.0	121.0	9.3	18.0	347.7	171.0	31.8	49.1	3.4	0.3	Yemen [3]
0.9	1.5	1.7	0.9	10.3	38.2	10.6	4.0	2.2	0.3	Yémen [3]

Source:
International Labour Office (ILO), Geneva, the ILO labour statistics database, last accessed November 2010.

[+] Tabulation categories of ISIC Rev. 3 :

A. Agriculture, hunting and forestry.
B. Fishing.
C. Mining and quarrying.
D. Manufacturing.
E. Electricity, gas and water supply.
F. Construction.
G. Wholesale and retail trade, repair of motor vehicles, motor cycles and personal and household goods.
H. Hotels and restaurants.
I. Transport, storage and communications.

Source:
Bureau international du travail (BIT), Genève, la base de données du BIT, dernier accès novembre 2010.

[+] Catégories de classement de la CITI Rév. 3 :

A. Agriculture, chasse et sylviculture.
B. Pêche.
C. Activités extractives.
D. Activités de fabrication.
E. Production et distribution d'électricité, de gaz et d'eau.
F. Construction.
G. Commerce de gros et de détail; réparation de véhicules automobiles, de motocycles et de biens personnels et domestiques.
H. Hôtels et restaurants.

J. Financial intermediation.
K. Real estate, renting and business activities.
L. Public administration and defence; compulsory social security.
M. Education.
N. Health and social work.
O. Other community, social and personal service activities.
P. Private households with employed persons.
Q. Extra-territorial organizations and bodies.

& Data for most countries are collected from labour force surveys. The following countries are exceptions, with sources as follows:

Household surveys:
Madagascar
Senegal

Official estimates:
Mongolia
San Marino

Population census:
Anguilla
Aruba
Bahrain
Bermuda
Bhutan
Brunei Darussalam
Chile
French Polynesia
Guyana
Isle of Man
Kuwait
Maldives
Nepal
New Caledonia
Niue
Palau
Papua New Guinea
Saint Helena
Samoa
Sierra Leone
Suriname

1 Tabulation categories A-B.
2 Tabulation categories J-L and O-Q
3 Persons aged 15 years and over.
4 September.
5 May.
6 Excluding armed forces.
7 Persons aged 10 years and over.
8 Second semester.
9 28 urban agglomerations.
10 31 urban agglomerations.
11 October.
12 Excluding conscripts on compulsory military service.
13 Excluding armed forces and conscripts.
14 April.
15 Tabulation categories C and E.
16 Tabulation categories J-K.
17 Tabulation categories L-P.
18 Year ending in June of the year indicated.

I. Transports, entreposage et communications.
J. Intermédiation financière.
K. Immobilier, locations et activités de services aux entreprises.
L. Administration publique et défense; sécurité sociale obligatoire.
M. Education.
N. Santé et action sociale.
O. Autres activités de services collectifs, sociaux et personnels.
P. Ménages privés employant du personnel domestique.
Q. Organisations et organismes extraterritoriaux.

& Les données pour la plupart des pays sont extraites d'enquêtes par sondage sur la main-d'œuvre, sauf les pays ci-dessous dont les sources sont les suivantes :

Enquêtes auprès des ménages:
Madagascar
Sénégal

Evaluations officielles:
Mongolie
Saint-Marin

Recensement de la population:
Anguilla
Aruba
Bahreïn
Bermudes
Bhoutan
Brunéi Darussalam
Chili
Polynésie française
Guyana
Ile de Man
Koweït
Maldives
Népal
Nouvelle-Calédonie
Nioué
Palaos
Papouasie-Nouvelle-Guinée
Sainte Hélène
Samoa
Sierra-Leone
Suriname

1 Catégories de classement A à B.
2 Catégories de classement J à L et O à Q
3 Personnes âgées de 15 ans et plus.
4 Septembre.
5 Mai.
6 Non compris les militaires.
7 Personnes âgées de 10 ans et plus.
8 Second semestre.
9 28 agglomérations urbaines.
10 31 agglomérations urbaines.
11 Octobre.
12 Non compris les militaires du contingent.
13 Non compris les forces armées et les conscrits.
14 Avril.
15 Catégories de classement C et E.
16 Catégories de classement J à K.
17 Catégories de classement L à P.
18 Année se terminant en juin de l'année indiquée.

25 Employment by economic activity *(continued)*

Total employment and persons employed by ISIC rev. 3 categories (thousands)

Emploi par activité économique *(suite)*

Emploi total et personnes employées par branches de la CITI rév. 3 (milliers)

19 Including professional army.
20 Persons aged 14 years and over.
21 Including armed forces.
22 Tabulation categories M-N.
23 Tabulation categories Q and X. (Additional category X, not shown separately in the table, comprises activities which are not classifiable by economic activity).
24 Tabulation categories O-X. (Additional category X, not shown separately in the table, comprises activities which are not classifiable by economic activity).
25 Excluding conscripts.
26 Persons aged 12 years and over.
27 August.
28 Tabulation categories O-Q.
29 November.
30 Excluding full-time members of the armed forces.
31 Excluding residents of the Territories and indigenous persons living on reserves.
32 Tabulation categories M and N.
33 Urban areas.
34 December.
35 State-owned units, urban collective-owned units and other ownership units.
36 Tabulation categories A-C.
37 July.
38 Government-controlled area.
39 Persons aged 15 to 66 years.
40 Included armed forces and conscripts.
41 Persons aged 15 to 64 years.
42 May and November.
43 Tabulation categories G-H.
44 Tabulation categories N and O.
45 Persons aged 15 to 74 years.
46 Second quarter.
47 Persons aged 16 to 74 years.
48 Including self-defence forces.
49 Tabulation categories C and F.
50 Tabulation categories M and O.
51 Including border workers and employees of international organizations.
52 Tabulation categories C-E.
53 Tabulation categories G-I.
54 Persons aged 6 years and over.
55 Tabulation categories L-Q.
56 Persons aged 16 years and over.
57 Tabulation categories J-Q.
58 Persons aged 15 to 69 years.
59 June.
60 Curaçao.
61 Omanis.
62 Fourth quarter.
63 Excluding regular military living in barracks.
64 Excluding regular military living in barracks and conscripts.
65 Data not reliable; coefficient of variation greater than 20%.
66 Persons aged 15 to 72 years.
67 March.
68 February.
69 Including home-made handicrafts.
70 Tabulation categories L-N.
71 The data refer to the residents (Singapore citizens and permanent residents) aged 15 years and over.

19 Y compris les militaires de carrière.
20 Personnes âgées de 14 ans et plus.
21 Y compris les forces armées.
22 Catégories de classement M à N.
23 Catégories de classement Q et X. (la catégorie supplémentaire X, qui ne figure pas dans le tableau, comprend les activités qui ne peuvent être classées dans une activité économique).
24 Catégories de classement O à X. (la catégorie supplémentaire X, qui ne figure pas dans le tableau, comprend les activités qui ne peuvent être classées dans une activité économique).
25 Non compris les conscrits.
26 Personnes âgées de 12 ans et plus.
27 Août.
28 Catégories de classement O à Q.
29 Novembre.
30 Non compris les membres à temps complet des forces armées.
31 Non compris les habitants des Territoires et les populations indigènes vivant dans les réserves.
32 Catégories de classement M et N.
33 Régions urbaines.
34 Décembre.
35 Unités d'Etat, unités collectives urbaines et autres.
36 Catégories de classement A à C.
37 Juillet.
38 Région sous contrôle gouvernemental.
39 Personnes âgées de 15 à 66 ans.
40 Y compris les forces armées et les conscrits.
41 Personnes âgées de 15 à 64 ans.
42 Mai et novembre.
43 Catégories de classement G à H.
44 Catégories de classement N et O.
45 Personnes âgées de 15 à 74 ans.
46 Deuxième trimestre.
47 Personnes âgées de 16 à 74 ans.
48 Y compris les forces d'autodéfense.
49 Catégories de classement C et F.
50 Catégories de classement M et O.
51 Y compris les travailleurs frontaliers et les employés des organisations internationales.
52 Catégories de classement C à E.
53 Catégories de classement G à I.
54 Personnes âgées de 6 ans et plus.
55 Catégories de classement L à Q.
56 Personnes âgées de 16 ans et plus.
57 Catégories de classement J à Q.
58 Personnes âgées de 15 à 69 ans.
59 Juin.
60 Curaçao.
61 Omanais.
62 Quatrième trimestre.
63 Non compris les militaires de carrière vivant dans des casernes.
64 Non compris les militaires de carrière vivant dans des casernes et les conscrits.
65 Données non fiables; coefficient de variation supérieur à 20%.
66 Personnes âgées de 15 à 72 ans.
67 Mars.
68 Février.
69 Y compris l'artisanat fait main.
70 Catégories de classement L à N.
71 Les données font référence aux résidents (citoyens singapouriens et résidents permanents) âgés de 15 ans ou plus.

72 Tabulation categories A-C, E and X (additional category X, not shown separately in the table, comprises activities which are not classifiable by economic activity).
73 Tabulation categories L and M.
74 Excluding persons on child-care leave.
75 Tabulation categories L-O.
76 Excluding Northern and Eastern provinces.
77 Including professional army; excluding compulsory military service.
78 Persons aged 16 to 64 years.
79 Tabulation categories L and Q.
80 Tabulation categories O-P.
81 Excluding armed forces and seasonal border workers.
82 Third quarter.
83 Tabulation categories D-E.

72 Catégories de classement A à C, E et X. (la catégorie supplémentaire X, qui ne figure pas dans le tableau, comprend les activités qui ne peuvent être classées dans une activité économique).
73 Catégories de classement L et M.
74 Non compris les personnes en congé parental.
75 Catégories de classement L à O.
76 Non compris les provinces du Nord et de l'Est.
77 Y compris les militaires de carrière; non compris les militaires du contingent.
78 Personnes âgées de 16 à 64 ans.
79 Catégories de classement L et Q.
80 Catégories de classement O à P.
81 Non compris les forces armées et les travailleurs saisonniers et frontaliers.
82 Troisième trimestre.
83 Catégories de classement D à E.

Technical notes: tables 24 and 25

Detailed data on labour force and related topics are published in the ILO *Yearbook of Labour Statistics* and on the ILO web site http://laborsta.ilo.org. The series shown in the *Statistical Yearbook* give an overall picture of the availability and disposition of labour resources and, in conjunction with other macroeconomic indicators, can be useful for an overall assessment of economic performance. The ILO *Yearbook of Labour Statistics* provides a comprehensive description of the methodology underlying the labour series. Brief definitions of the major categories of labour statistics are given below.

"Unemployment" is defined to include persons above a certain age who, during a specified period of time were:

(a) "Without work", i.e. were not in paid employment or self-employment;

(b) "Currently available for work", i.e. were available for paid employment or self-employment during the reference period; and

(c) "Seeking work", i.e. had taken specific steps in a specified period to find paid employment or self-employment.

Persons not considered to be unemployed include:

(a) Persons intending to establish their own business or farm, but who had not yet arranged to do so and who were not seeking work for pay or profit;

(b) Former unpaid family workers not at work and not seeking work for pay or profit.

For various reasons, national definitions of employment and unemployment often differ from the recommended international standard definitions and thereby limit international comparability. Inter-country comparisons are also complicated by a variety of types of data collection systems used to obtain information on employed and unemployed persons.

"Employment" is defined to include persons above a specified age who, during a specified period of time, were in one of the following categories:

(a) "Paid employment", comprising persons who perform some work for pay or profit during the reference period or persons with a job but not at work due to temporary absence, such as vacation, strike, education leave;

(b) "Self-employment", comprising employers, own account workers, members of producers' cooperatives, persons engaged in production of goods and services for own consumption and unpaid family workers;

(c) Members of the armed forces, students, homemakers and others mainly engaged in non-economic activities during the reference period who, at the same time, were in paid employment or self-employment are considered as employed on the same basis as other categories.

Notes techniques : tableaux 24 et 25

Des données détaillées sur la main-d'œuvre et des sujets connexes sont publiées dans l'*Annuaire des Statistiques du Travail* du BIT et sur le site Web du BIT http://laborsta.ilo.org. Les séries indiquées dans l'*Annuaire des Statistiques* donnent un tableau d'ensemble des disponibilités de main-d'œuvre et de l'emploi de ces ressources et, combinées à d'autres indicateurs économiques, elles peuvent être utiles pour une évaluation générale de la performance économique. L'*Annuaire des statistiques du Travail* du BIT donne une description complète de la méthodologie employée pour établir les séries sur la main-d'œuvre. On trouvera ci-dessous quelques brèves définitions des grandes catégories de statistiques du travail.

Par "chômeurs", on entend les personnes dépassant un âge déterminé qui, pendant une période donnée, étaient:

(a) "sans emploi", c'est-à-dire sans emploi rémunéré ou indépendant;

(b) "disponibles", c'est-à-dire qui pouvaient être engagées pour un emploi rémunéré ou pouvaient s'adonner à un emploi indépendant au cours de la période de référence; et

(c) "à la recherche d'un emploi", c'est-à-dire qui avaient pris des mesures précises à un certain moment pour trouver un emploi rémunéré ou un emploi indépendant.

Ne sont pas considérés comme chômeurs:

(a) Les personnes qui, pendant la période de référence, avaient l'intention de créer leur propre entreprise ou exploitation agricole, mais n'avaient pas encore pris les dispositions nécessaires à cet effet et qui n'étaient pas à la recherche d'un emploi en vue d'une rémunération ou d'un profit;

(b) Les anciens travailleurs familiaux non rémunérés qui n'avaient pas d'emploi et n'étaient pas à la recherche d'un emploi en vue d'une rémunération ou d'un profit.

Pour diverses raisons, les définitions nationales de l'emploi et du chômage diffèrent souvent des définitions internationales types recommandées, limitant ainsi les possibilités de comparaison entre pays. Ces comparaisons se trouvent en outre compliquées par la diversité des systèmes de collecte de données utilisés pour recueillir des informations sur les personnes employées et les chômeurs.

Le terme "Emploi" désigne les personnes dépassant un âge déterminé qui, au cours d'une période donnée, se trouvaient dans l'une des catégories suivantes:

(a) La catégorie "emploi rémunéré", composée des per sonnes faisant un certain travail en échange d'une rémunération ou d'un profit pendant la période de référence, ou les personnes ayant un emploi, mais qui ne travaillaient pas en raison d'une absence temporaire

Table 24: Figures are presented in absolute numbers and in percentages. Data are normally annual averages of monthly, quarterly or semi-annual data.

The series generally represent the total number of persons wholly unemployed or temporarily laid-off. Percentage figures, where given, are calculated by comparing the number of unemployed to the total members of that group of the labour force on which the unemployment data are based.

Table 25 presents absolute figures on the distribution of employed persons by economic activity, according to ISIC rev. 3. The column for total employment includes economic activities not adequately defined and that are not accounted for in the other categories. Data are arranged as far as possible according to the major divisions of economic activity of the International Standard Industrial Classification of All Economic Activities.

(vacances, grève, congé d'études);

(b) La catégorie "emploi indépendant" regroupe les employeurs, les travailleurs indépendants, les membres de coopératives de producteurs et les personnes s'adonnant à la production de biens et de services pour leur propre consommation et la main -d'œuvre familiale non rémunérée;

(c) Les membres des forces armées, les étudiants, les aides familiales et autres personnes qui s'adonnaient essentiellement à des activités non économiques pendant la période de référence et qui, en même temps, avaient un emploi rémunéré ou indépendant, sont considérés comme employés au même titre que les personnes des autres catégories.

Tableau 24: Les chiffres sont présentés en valeur absolue et en pourcentage. Les données sont normalement des moyennes annuelles des données mensuelles, trimestrielles ou semestrielles.

Les séries représentent généralement le nombre total des chômeurs complets ou des personnes temporairement mises à pied. Les données en pourcentage, lorsqu'elles figurent dans le tableau, sont calculées en comparant le nombre de chômeurs au nombre total des personnes du groupe de main-d'œuvre sur lequel sont basées les données relatives au chômage.

Le tableau 25 présente les effectifs de personnes employées par activité économique, classés en fonction de la Révision 3. L'emploi total inclut les personnes employées à des activités économiques mal définies et qui ne sont pas classées ailleurs. Les données sont ventilées autant que possible selon les branches d'activité économique de la Classification internationale type, par industrie, de toutes les activités économiques.

26 Producer price indices

Index base: 2005 = 100

Indices des prix à la production

Indices base: 2005= 100

Country or area	2002	2003	2004	2006	2007	2008	2009	Pays ou zone
Argentina								**Argentine**
Domestic supply [1,2]	73.9	87.1	91.2	110.8	123.1	140.6	149.6	Offre intérieure [1,2]
Domestic production	72.2	86.3	93.1	111.0	123.5	140.9	150.5	Production intérieure
Agricultural products [2]	101.1	105.1	111.6	117.6	162.2	179.8	...	Produits agricoles [2]
Industrial products [2,3]	72.7	86.6	93.1	109.2	121.1	140.2	150.5	Produits industriels [2,3]
Imported goods [3]	94.6	96.5	99.2	108.1	118.5	138.1	139.2	Produits importés [3]
Armenia [4]								**Arménie** [4]
Industrial products	100.0	...	...	...	143.6	155.7	167.9	Produits industriels
Australia [5]								**Australie** [5]
Domestic supply	92.9	94.2	96.8	103.9	106.6	112.4	113.7	Offre intérieure
Domestic production	88.1	91.6	95.8	104.5	108.5	114.8	115.3	Production intérieure
Agricultural products	94.5	97.5	98.2	102.0	111.0	123.6	113.4	Produits agricoles
Industrial products [3,6,7]	90.3	90.8	94.4	107.9	110.5	119.6	113.1	Produits industriels [3,6,7]
Imported goods	113.8	104.8	98.9	104.1	100.0	109.1	109.0	Produits importés
Raw materials [6]	91.3	92.3	94.3	107.9	111.9	123.3	119.0	Matières premières [6]
Intermediate goods [6]	93.2[3]	94.1	95.5	106.8	111.0	120.0	117.3	Produits intermédiaires [6]
Consumer goods [6]	96.4	96.7	97.4	104.7	106.5	112.6	114.9	Biens de consommation [6]
Capital goods [6]	90.2	92.3	96.2	103.4	106.8	112.2	112.8	Biens d'équipement [6]
Austria								**Autriche**
Agricultural products	100.7	106.5	107.4	104.2	133.7	155.8	117.4	Produits agricoles
Industrial products	94.5	94.9	96.7	102.1	106.3	111.4	109.4	Produits industriels
Intermediate goods	95.7	94.9	97.8	102.3	107.2	111.6	108.6	Produits intermédiaires
Capital goods	99.5	99.4	99.4	101.4	104.0	104.8	109.3	Biens d'équipement
Bangladesh [8,9]								**Bangladesh** [8,9]
Domestic supply [2,10]	102.3	107.7	111.6	...	...	...	...	Offre intérieure [2,10]
Agricultural products [2,11]	101.7	108.0	112.3	...	...	...	...	Produits agricoles [2,11]
Industrial products [2,3,11]	104.6	106.7	109.8	...	...	...	...	Produits industriels [2,3,11]
Raw materials	103.4	112.7	107.2	...	...	...	...	Matières premières
Belarus								**Bélarus**
Domestic production	52.3	71.9	89.2	108.3	126.2	...	...	Production intérieure
Intermediate goods	47.0	70.6	88.8	109.1	132.9	...	...	Produits intermédiaires
Consumer goods	61.0	74.6	90.6	106.5	115.4	...	...	Biens de consommation
Capital goods	58.1	70.7	87.7	...	116.2	...	...	Biens d'équipement
Belgium								**Belgique**
Domestic production [12]	93.1	93.7	97.8	...	...	...	...	Production intérieure [12]
Industrial products	93.9	93.4	99.3	...	...	...	...	Produits industriels
Intermediate goods	90.6	90.9	96.4	...	...	...	...	Produits intermédiaires
Consumer goods	101.6	98.9	98.2	...	...	...	...	Biens de consommation
Capital goods	96.4	96.6	98.3	...	...	...	...	Biens d'équipement
Bolivia (Plur. State of) [9]								**Bolivie (État plur. de)** [9]
Industrial products [1]	103.9	107.3	...	...	...	158.1	154.7	Produits industriels [1]
Raw materials	107.7	116.9	...	...	...	...	...	Matières premières
Consumer goods [13]	103.3	105.9	...	...	...	150.9	151.3	Biens de consommation [13]
Capital goods [14]	108.8	110.5	...	...	...	156.2	191.0	Biens d'équipement [14]
Botswana [9]								**Botswana** [9]
Domestic supply	111.8	122.7	133.0	...	...	...	...	Offre intérieure
Brazil [9]								**Brésil** [9]
Domestic supply [15]	130.3	164.4	185.1	197.0	#310.8	...	...	Offre intérieure [15]
Agricultural products [15]	142.2	185.9	196.8	184.9	#363.4	...	...	Produits agricoles [15]
Industrial products [15]	127.3	160.7	180.3	200.2	#288.7	...	...	Produits industriels [15]
Raw materials [15]	132.6	169.0	190.9	187.0	...	...	...	Matières premières [15]
Consumer goods [15]	129.9	164.6	175.7	186.2	#294.7	...	...	Biens de consommation [15]
Capital goods	121.0	147.1	...	194.2	...	...	...	Biens d'équipement
Bulgaria								**Bulgarie**
Industrial products	86.1	88.5	93.3	108.7	117.4	133.0	127.3	Produits industriels
Intermediate goods	86.8	89.9	96.2	114.7	125.8	132.7	123.4	Produits intermédiaires
Capital goods	91.6	93.2	96.2	103.3	107.5	116.7	120.2	Biens d'équipement

26 Producer price indices *(continued)*

Index base: 2005= 100

Indices des prix à la production *(suite)*

Indices base: 2005= 100

Country or area	2002	2003	2004	2006	2007	2008	2009	Pays ou zone
Canada								**Canada**
Agricultural products [2]	109.5	104.9	102.4	99.5	108.2	118.3	...	Produits agricoles [2]
Industrial products [2,3]	96.8	95.5	98.5	102.3	104.0	108.5	104.8	Produits industriels [2,3]
Raw materials	77.5	79.0	88.3	111.3	119.8	135.1	104.8	Matières premières
Intermediate goods	92.4	92.0	97.4	104.2	106.8	112.3	105.9	Produits intermédiaires
Capital goods	109.9	104.5	102.0	97.8	95.9	96.8	101.0	Biens d'équipement
Chile								**Chili**
Domestic supply	86.8	92.6	94.9	107.0	114.1	133.1	133.5	Offre intérieure
Domestic production	83.4	89.2	93.6	108.2	115.8	135.8	135.1	Production intérieure
Agricultural products	87.4	87.5	92.6	108.4	123.3	140.4	139.8	Produits agricoles
Industrial products	84.2	90.8	94.4	106.1	112.3	131.8	129.8	Produits industriels
Imported goods	98.3	103.7	99.0	103.1	108.7	124.8	126.9	Produits importés
China, Hong Kong SAR [3]								**Chine, Hong Kong RAS [3]**
Industrial products	97.3	97.0	99.3	102.3	105.3	111.1	109.2	Produits industriels
Colombia								**Colombie**
Domestic supply [2]	84.5	92.2	97.0	104.2	105.2	112.8	115.0	Offre intérieure [2]
Domestic production	82.6	88.9	95.1	104.8	109.1	119.2	121.3	Production intérieure
Agricultural products [16]	84.0	89.1	93.4	103.9	107.4	115.5	121.9	Produits agricoles [16]
Industrial products [3]	85.6	93.7	98.3	103.9	104.1	109.4	112.3	Produits industriels [3]
Imported goods	90.8	103.5	103.2	102.0	92.4	92.1	94.5	Produits importés
Raw materials	80.7	89.5	98.4	103.0	103.8	108.4	112.0	Matières premières
Intermediate goods	82.1	90.7	96.1	105.1	106.2	115.0	114.6	Produits intermédiaires
Consumer goods	86.1	91.6	96.0	103.9	106.6	114.4	119.6	Biens de consommation
Capital goods	92.6	103.8	103.3	102.0	95.0	92.4	98.1	Biens d'équipement
Croatia								**Croatie**
Agricultural products [17,18]	82.4	81.5	85.2	83.9	87.8	100.0	85.8	Produits agricoles [17,18]
Industrial products	94.2	94.0	97.1	102.9	106.3	115.0	114.6	Produits industriels
Consumer goods	96.1	98.1	97.0	101.4	103.7	109.0	110.9	Biens de consommation
Capital goods	104.6	100.8	99.1	102.9	102.7	102.9	102.7	Biens d'équipement
Cyprus [3,19]								**Chypre [3,19]**
Industrial products	86.4	89.5	96.5	102.8	107.8	116.6	118.8	Produits industriels
Czech Republic								**République tchèque**
Agricultural products	105.1	102.1	110.4	101.1	118.1	128.5	96.6	Produits agricoles
Industrial products	92.4	91.9	97.0	101.6	105.8	110.5	107.0	Produits industriels
Denmark								**Danemark**
Domestic supply [2,15]	93.9	94.0	96.1	104.0	108.4	115.4	108.0	Offre intérieure [2,15]
Domestic production [2,15]	91.3	92.4	95.8	105.0	111.9	122.4	115.1	Production intérieure [2,15]
Imported goods [15]	96.4	95.3	96.2	103.3	105.8	110.1	103.6	Produits importés [15]
Raw materials	73.3	73.4	82.8	...	...	...	...	Matières premières
Consumer goods	95.8	96.6	98.6	...	...	...	...	Biens de consommation
Ecuador								**Equateur**
Domestic supply	...	...	87.3	112.1	...	139.0	113.2	Offre intérieure
Domestic production	78.8	...	...	104.2	...	125.6	125.4	Production intérieure
Agricultural products	...	...	...	101.6	...	141.4	...	Produits agricoles
Egypt [8,20]								**Egypte [8,20]**
Domestic production [10]	...	...	...	...	...	...	148.7	Production intérieure [10]
Agricultural products [21]	...	...	...	...	...	...	185.2	Produits agricoles [21]
Raw materials	...	...	...	...	...	...	144.5	Matières premières
Intermediate goods	...	...	...	...	...	...	135.7	Produits intermédiaires
Consumer goods	...	...	...	...	...	...	106.3	Biens de consommation
Capital goods	...	...	...	...	...	...	136.3	Biens d'équipement
Finland								**Finlande**
Domestic supply	95.0	96.9	96.3	105.7	109.9	116.1	108.7	Offre intérieure
Industrial products [3]	97.6	95.9	97.1	105.0	109.9	117.8	110.0	Produits industriels [3]
Intermediate goods	96.7	93.6	96.2	106.7	113.8	120.4	109.0	Produits intermédiaires
Consumer goods [22]	105.8	104.6	102.4	102.5	105.9	108.6	110.7	Biens de consommation [22]
Capital goods	105.3	101.4	99.7	101.9	105.2	109.1	109.6	Biens d'équipement
France								**France**
Domestic supply	...	...	...	103.8	106.7	112.4	...	Offre intérieure
Agricultural products	101.5	...	102.6	105.3	117.0	118.2	109.0	Produits agricoles
Intermediate goods	95.1	94.8	97.1	104.3	...	...	105.5	Produits intermédiaires
Consumer goods	...	99.9	99.8	99.5	...	...	100.3	Biens de consommation
Capital goods	...	99.2	99.0	101.1	...	...	104.0	Biens d'équipement

26 Producer price indices *(continued)*
Index base: 2005= 100

Indices des prix à la production *(suite)*
Indices base: 2005= 100

Country or area	2002	2003	2004	2006	2007	2008	2009	Pays ou zone
Georgia								**Géorgie**
Industrial products	86.1	89.0	93.1	111.0	123.7	135.8	128.4	Produits industriels
Germany								**Allemagne**
Domestic supply	96.5	95.6	96.8	104.2	106.0	111.0	...	Offre intérieure
Domestic production	...	...	...	105.4	106.8	112.6	108.0	Production intérieure
Agricultural products	96.3	96.0	96.6	107.4	117.7	121.2	101.5	Produits agricoles
Industrial products	96.2	94.1	95.6	105.5	107.8	106.3	103.4	Produits industriels
Imported goods	97.1	95.1	96.2	104.4	105.1	109.4	100.1	Produits importés
Intermediate goods	105.8	95.3	97.4	103.8	107.4	109.2	104.2	Produits intermédiaires
Consumer goods	100.5	98.2	98.9	101.6	104.0	106.7	105.7	Biens de consommation
Capital goods	90.4	99.2	99.3	100.6	101.6	100.6	101.5	Biens d'équipement
Greece								**Grèce**
Agricultural products	91.7	100.2	97.8	107.5	118.9	114.9	112.4	Produits agricoles
Industrial products [23,24]	89.1	91.2	94.4	107.3	111.7	123.0	115.8	Produits industriels [23,24]
Imported goods	88.5	89.1	91.9	104.2	106.9	114.5	112.5	Produits importés
Intermediate goods	91.3	93.4	96.3	107.3	113.8	123.4	122.0	Produits intermédiaires
Consumer goods	89.6	92.0	97.5	106.2	105.9	110.7	111.7	Biens de consommation
Capital goods	91.8	93.3	97.5	103.1	109.9	116.4	111.4	Biens d'équipement
Guatemala								**Guatemala**
Domestic supply	87.4	90.8	95.8	...	...	...	...	Offre intérieure
Domestic production	89.6	91.8	96.7	...	...	...	...	Production intérieure
Agricultural products	...	100.0	99.5	...	...	...	...	Produits agricoles
Industrial products	...	86.1	93.7	...	...	...	...	Produits industriels
Imported goods	...	89.8	94.9	...	...	...	...	Produits importés
India [25]								**Inde** [25]
Domestic supply	88.0	89.1	94.1	...	110.1	115.2	...	Offre intérieure
Agricultural products	92.8	94.1	98.7	...	109.7	117.7	...	Produits agricoles
Industrial products [3]	88.2	89.1	94.2	...	107.7	112.8	...	Produits industriels [3]
Raw materials [26]	81.3	84.3	94.4	...	106.4	119.6	...	Matières premières [26]
Indonesia								**Indonésie**
Domestic supply [24]	77.6	79.2	86.0	113.4	151.5	190.5	...	Offre intérieure [24]
Domestic production	83.7	86.1	89.5	123.4	180.3	226.9	...	Production intérieure
Agricultural products	90.3	90.2	93.2	115.8	193.2	248.4	...	Produits agricoles
Industrial products [3]	80.3	83.9	87.5	128.2	175.3	219.3	...	Produits industriels [3]
Imported goods [24]	81.2	79.8	87.4	118.3	151.3	190.8	...	Produits importés [24]
Raw materials	62.9	66.1	77.8	102.1	137.4	175.0	...	Matières premières
Intermediate goods	78.6	78.8	86.2	117.0	159.0	202.4	...	Produits intermédiaires
Consumer goods	89.9	90.0	92.0	115.5	167.7	206.6	...	Biens de consommation
Capital goods	88.3	88.5	92.8	105.5	120.9	139.9	...	Biens d'équipement
Iran (Islamic Rep. of)								**Iran (Rép. islamique d')**
Domestic supply [2]	71.5	77.1	93.4	109.6	125.5	151.6	165.8	Offre intérieure [2]
Agricultural products [11]	74.4	82.4	96.1	105.7	130.5	162.2	190.5	Produits agricoles [11]
Industrial products [11]	164.9	170.4	94.0	110.0	123.5	151.7	158.3	Produits industriels [11]
Raw materials [11]	64.9	...	...	113.1	132.1	...	...	Matières premières [11]
Ireland								**Irlande**
Domestic supply [2,9,27]	103.1	97.7	101.2	...	...	...	...	Offre intérieure [2,9,27]
Agricultural products [2,27]	97.3	96.5	...	104.1	112.8	120.3	102.2	Produits agricoles [2,27]
Industrial products [2,3,9,27]	100.5	92.4	...	...	...	...	...	Produits industriels [2,3,9,27]
Capital goods [9,11]	92.2	79.6	...	...	...	...	...	Biens d'équipement [9,11]
Israel [3,24]								**Israël** [3,24]
Industrial products	89.1	91.9	95.8	104.2	108.3	116.5	115.0	Produits industriels
Italy								**Italie**
Industrial products [24]	92.1	93.6	96.1	105.2	108.7	115.1	108.9	Produits industriels [24]
Intermediate goods	90.2	92.9	97.5	105.1	110.5	113.0	106.6	Produits intermédiaires
Consumer goods	96.1	98.4	99.4	101.7	104.3	107.9	106.9	Biens de consommation
Capital goods	95.7	96.7	98.3	101.7	103.9	109.0	109.0	Biens d'équipement

26 Producer price indices *(continued)*

Index base: 2005= 100

Indices des prix à la production *(suite)*

Indices base: 2005= 100

Country or area	2002	2003	2004	2006	2007	2008	2009	Pays ou zone
Japan								**Japon**
Domestic supply [2]	98.7	95.3	96.7	104.3	107.4	113.4	102.6	Offre intérieure [2]
Domestic production	97.9	97.1	98.4	102.2	104.0	108.8	103.1	Production intérieure
Agricultural products [11]	96.9	98.4	102.8	98.4	97.4	98.7	96.0	Produits agricoles [11]
Industrial products [11]	97.7	96.9	98.0	102.2	103.8	108.5	102.9	Produits industriels [11]
Imported goods	78.8	82.0	89.6	113.7	122.4	133.6	100.3	Produits importés
Raw materials	71.8	74.6	82.1	120.7	132.2	166.4	112.8	Matières premières
Intermediate goods	93.6	93.5	96.2	105.5	109.7	115.8	105.7	Produits intermédiaires
Consumer goods	102.3	100.6	100.0	99.8	100.0	101.0	96.8	Biens de consommation
Capital goods	108.5	104.2	101.8	99.4	98.9	98.0	96.0	Biens d'équipement
Jordan								**Jordanie**
Domestic supply [2]	85.2	86.2	93.5	106.5	115.5	138.0	139.3	Offre intérieure [2]
Agricultural products	79.2	79.9	90.4	107.4	120.9	149.6	150.6	Produits agricoles
Industrial products	84.0	86.2	91.4	115.8	126.3	196.8	164.4	Produits industriels
Intermediate goods	89.2	89.1	95.2	108.5	121.2	164.4	169.1	Produits intermédiaires
Consumer goods	96.9	98.2	98.2	101.6	104.7	117.1	117.7	Biens de consommation
Korea, Republic of								**Corée, République de**
Domestic supply	90.3	92.3	97.9	100.9	102.3	111.1	110.9	Offre intérieure
Agricultural products [11,28]	86.5	92.5	103.8	96.9	100.1	101.0	107.1	Produits agricoles [11,28]
Industrial products	88.6	90.2	96.9	102.9	99.8	103.9	102.2	Produits industriels
Raw materials	66.4	70.7	84.7	112.6	120.1	179.2	152.9	Matières premières
Intermediate goods	88.3	90.2	99.1	99.6	102.1	120.8	118.8	Produits intermédiaires
Consumer goods	94.3	95.8	98.7	99.5	99.6	105.4	108.3	Biens de consommation
Capital goods	101.2	99.8	102.1	97.4	96.6	105.9	115.0	Biens d'équipement
Kuwait [9]								**Koweït** [9]
Domestic supply	105.3	107.4	107.8	...	119.4	...	...	Offre intérieure
Domestic production	101.9	101.5	101.9	...	112.4	...	...	Production intérieure
Agricultural products	101.8	106.4	116.1	...	177.6	...	...	Produits agricoles
Industrial products	105.3	107.2	107.1	...	...	...	...	Produits industriels
Imported goods	106.3	109.0	109.3	...	121.3	...	...	Produits importés
Raw materials	108.2	...	...	...	152.0	...	...	Matières premières
Intermediate goods	103.6	...	...	...	132.1	...	...	Produits intermédiaires
Consumer goods	103.0	...	...	...	118.5	...	...	Biens de consommation
Capital goods	115.4	...	...	...	117.6	...	...	Biens d'équipement
Latvia								**Lettonie**
Domestic supply	82.8	85.6	92.7	110.4	128.2	...	...	Offre intérieure
Agricultural products	...	...	...	...	...	...	117.1	Produits agricoles
Intermediate goods	...	...	...	111.2	132.1	137.7	118.2	Produits intermédiaires
Capital goods	...	...	...	112.3	125.1	136.1	136.3	Biens d'équipement
Lithuania [24]								**Lituanie** [24]
Industrial products	82.5	82.2	88.5	107.4	113.9	133.8	111.6	Produits industriels
Luxembourg								**Luxembourg**
Industrial products	84.5	85.0	92.5	107.7	113.4	122.3	112.2	Produits industriels
Imported goods	86.2	88.2	96.2	...	120.8	...	...	Produits importés
Intermediate goods	79.4	80.7	91.0	109.0	117.5	126.5	108.2	Produits intermédiaires
Consumer goods [22]	104.7	99.4	99.4	99.6	99.2	101.0	103.6	Biens de consommation [22]
Capital goods	95.0	95.9	100.1	101.6	105.3	110.0	111.7	Biens d'équipement
Malaysia								**Malaisie**
Domestic supply	99.2	104.8	114.2	105.1	112.1	...	...	Offre intérieure
Domestic production	99.2	105.9	116.9	106.7	114.7	...	...	Production intérieure
Imported goods	117.0	117.9	120.2	102.2	107.0	108.9	...	Produits importés
Mexico								**Mexique**
Domestic supply [10,29]	85.6	92.9	98.7	109.3	...	...	125.8	Offre intérieure [10,29]
Agricultural products	81.8	90.8	96.5	111.3	...	...	133.2	Produits agricoles
Industrial products [3]	86.5	93.8	96.8	104.3	...	...	123.0	Produits industriels [3]
Raw materials [9]	103.3	115.8	...	...	...	...	...	Matières premières [9]
Consumer goods [11,29]	86.9	95.2	100.2	108.1	...	...	124.4	Biens de consommation [11,29]
Capital goods [10,11,29]	81.4	88.1	97.6	109.1	...	...	128.1	Biens d'équipement [10,11,29]
Montenegro								**Monténégro**
Industrial products	88.2	92.3	98.0	103.8	112.8	131.0	123.8	Produits industriels

26 Producer price indices *(continued)*

Index base: 2005= 100

Indices des prix à la production *(suite)*

Indices base: 2005= 100

Country or area	2002	2003	2004	2006	2007	2008	2009	Pays ou zone
Morocco								**Maroc**
Agricultural products	103.4	98.7	98.2	104.5	110.7	...	...	Produits agricoles
Industrial products [3]	86.1	87.3	91.7	105.9	107.8	127.4	108.0	Produits industriels [3]
Netherlands								**Pays-Bas**
Agricultural products [9]	103.3	105.4	...	...	...	...	...	Produits agricoles [9]
Imported goods	102.9	97.9	99.2	...	...	...	...	Produits importés
Raw materials	97.2	97.7	104.6	...	...	...	...	Matières premières
Intermediate goods	100.6	101.8	105.9	...	...	...	...	Produits intermédiaires
Consumer goods	103.5	104.8	107.6	...	...	...	...	Biens de consommation
Capital goods	104.6	106.2	107.9	...	...	...	...	Biens d'équipement
New Zealand								**Nouvelle-Zélande**
Agricultural products [2]	108.8	98.5	99.9	101.9	107.3	121.4	123.0	Produits agricoles [2]
Industrial products [2,30]	95.9	94.5	96.5	104.3	108.0	120.2	118.0	Produits industriels [2,30]
Intermediate goods [31]	94.2	93.7	95.0	106.8	109.0	119.8	118.0	Produits intermédiaires [31]
Norway								**Norvège**
Domestic supply	87.5	93.5	96.5	106.1	107.1	116.8	116.6	Offre intérieure
Domestic production	85.8	92.3	95.0	108.5	107.9	122.9	121.1	Production intérieure
Agricultural products	98.0	98.2	99.2	104.4	107.1	110.4	116.6	Produits agricoles
Industrial products [3]	92.5	93.8	96.7	103.0	107.6	116.0	116.3	Produits industriels [3]
Raw materials	97.1	96.5	97.9	101.6	112.5	114.7	110.3	Matières premières
Intermediate goods	95.9	96.1	98.0	103.0	109.8	117.3	119.3	Produits intermédiaires
Consumer goods	96.8	97.1	98.6	102.4	105.2	109.5	114.7	Biens de consommation
Capital goods	91.9	93.4	95.6	101.0	105.6	112.5	117.3	Biens d'équipement
Occupied Palestinian Terr.								**Terr. palestinien occupé**
Domestic supply	...	...	97.5	101.7	104.0	112.5	114.1	Offre intérieure
Domestic production	...	...	97.3	101.7	104.1	112.9	114.5	Production intérieure
Agricultural products	...	...	97.1	102.2	104.5	114.2	112.8	Produits agricoles
Industrial products [3]	...	...	97.4	101.1	103.6	111.6	115.4	Produits industriels [3]
Oman [9,32]								**Oman** [9,32]
Domestic supply	102.5	103.8	106.9	...	...	...	...	Offre intérieure
Pakistan [33]								**Pakistan** [33]
Domestic supply [2,10]	82.4	86.5	91.8	111.8	130.1	153.7	173.2	Offre intérieure [2,10]
Agricultural products	79.3	84.5	93.5	108.9	129.6	159.6	178.7	Produits agricoles
Industrial products [3]	91.0	96.2	97.2	103.1	110.3	120.9	133.2	Produits industriels [3]
Raw materials	95.2	108.9	90.6	113.4	128.4	151.3	195.3	Matières premières
Panama								**Panama**
Domestic supply	89.2	90.7	94.6	...	...	...	...	Offre intérieure
Peru								**Pérou**
Domestic supply	91.4	...	99.3	103.2	...	...	113.2	Offre intérieure
Domestic production	91.3	...	97.5	103.1	...	...	114.6	Production intérieure
Agricultural products [34]	88.9	...	98.4	104.7	...	...	136.1	Produits agricoles [34]
Industrial products [3,11]	91.0	...	97.4	103.0	...	...	110.5	Produits industriels [3,11]
Imported goods	91.6	...	98.5	103.5	...	...	108.0	Produits importés
Philippines [35]								**Philippines** [35]
Domestic supply	71.3	...	...	108.4	111.6	124.8	119.5	Offre intérieure
Poland								**Pologne**
Domestic production	...	...	...	103.5	107.6	113.4	116.1	Production intérieure
Industrial products	...	...	...	102.0	103.9	106.1	109.7	Produits industriels
Raw materials	...	...	...	106.1	110.7	125.9	134.2	Matières premières
Intermediate goods	...	...	...	104.6	112.1	115.7	112.8	Produits intermédiaires
Consumer goods	...	...	...	99.0	100.5	101.3	103.1	Biens de consommation
Capital goods	...	...	...	99.1	98.9	97.5	97.3	Biens d'équipement
Portugal								**Portugal**
Industrial products	92.8	93.6	96.1	104.7	108.0	112.9	108.6	Produits industriels
Intermediate goods	...	96.5	98.8	103.4	107.2	111.8	105.5	Produits intermédiaires
Consumer goods	97.4	98.1	98.9	102.7	104.3	106.1	105.0	Biens de consommation
Capital goods	96.3	96.9	98.4	102.3	104.9	107.4	107.6	Biens d'équipement
Romania								**Roumanie**
Industrial products	65.8	79.6	90.5	111.6	120.6	139.6	138.6	Produits industriels
Russian Federation								**Fédération de Russie**
Agricultural products	66.6	71.7	91.3	104.4	121.2	151.2	147.0	Produits agricoles
Industrial products	57.8	67.2	82.9	112.4	128.2	155.7	144.5	Produits industriels

Country or area	2002	2003	2004	2006	2007	2008	2009	Pays ou zone
Serbia [36]								**Serbie** [36]
Agricultural products [21]	...	...	...	100.0	113.4	145.8	142.9	Produits agricoles [21]
Industrial products	...	...	...	100.0	105.9	118.9	125.6	Produits industriels
Singapore								**Singapour**
Domestic supply [10]	86.6	88.6	91.2	105.0	105.5	113.1	97.5	Offre intérieure [10]
Domestic production [2,3]	100.1	96.1	94.6	102.4	101.2	104.2	90.7	Production intérieure [2,3]
Imported goods	95.9	96.7	95.1	102.9	101.3	103.9	95.7	Produits importés
Slovakia [37]								**Slovaquie** [37]
Agricultural products [21]	...	99.9	102.0	99.8	105.2	109.6	86.8	Produits agricoles [21]
Industrial products	85.0	90.8	93.3	102.8	104.7	111.1	...	Produits industriels
Slovenia								**Slovénie**
Agricultural products	98.8	101.6	99.6	105.4	113.7	131.0	112.4	Produits agricoles
Industrial products	91.0	93.3	97.3	102.4	108.0	114.0	113.6	Produits industriels
Intermediate goods	89.7	91.5	96.9	103.9	110.9	116.8	113.0	Produits intermédiaires
Consumer goods	91.6	95.3	98.1	101.6	104.8	110.7	110.2	Biens de consommation
Capital goods	95.1	94.7	96.2	100.2	101.1	104.7	103.0	Biens d'équipement
South Africa								**Afrique du Sud**
Domestic production [38]	92.2	94.3	96.5	107.7	119.5	136.6	136.5	Production intérieure [38]
Agricultural products	115.2	108.4	106.8	118.4	146.5	156.1	157.6	Produits agricoles
Imported goods	104.8	100.4	96.5	107.7	118.1	137.4	120.5	Produits importés
Spain								**Espagne**
Industrial products	91.0	92.3	95.5	105.4	109.2	116.3	112.4	Produits industriels
Intermediate goods	91.6	92.3	96.4	106.2	112.5	118.7	112.3	Produits intermédiaires
Consumer goods	92.7	94.8	97.3	103.2	105.7	110.3	109.6	Biens de consommation
Capital goods	95.6	96.7	98.1	103.0	106.5	109.2	110.0	Biens d'équipement
Sweden [24,39]								**Suède** [24,39]
Domestic supply [2]	93.8	93.0	94.9	105.4	109.5	115.3	114.2	Offre intérieure [2]
Domestic production [2]	94.5	95.0	97.4	104.9	110.6	115.7	114.6	Production intérieure [2]
Imported goods	92.8	90.6	93.2	105.8	108.4	113.2	113.8	Produits importés
Switzerland								**Suisse**
Domestic supply [2,10]	...	97.9	99.1	102.1	104.5	107.9	105.7	Offre intérieure [2,10]
Domestic production [2,10]	...	97.1	98.9	102.7	105.2	110.0	106.5	Production intérieure [2,10]
Agricultural products [2]	...	102.1	103.4	101.0	101.2	107.9	101.0	Produits agricoles [2]
Industrial products [10]	...	97.6	98.9	102.0	104.7	108.1	106.0	Produits industriels [10]
Imported goods [10]	...	97.6	98.3	103.1	106.4	109.9	101.8	Produits importés [10]
Intermediate goods	...	97.9	99.5	103.8	108.0	112.4	107.0	Produits intermédiaires
Consumer goods [22]	...	...	99.5	102.3	104.7	107.4	109.4	Biens de consommation [22]
Capital goods	...	97.4	98.3	101.7	104.4	106.3	106.6	Biens d'équipement
Syrian Arab Republic								**Rép. arabe syrienne**
Domestic supply [9]	101.0	...	...	...	...	...	...	Offre intérieure [9]
Raw materials	96.2	...	...	100.0	...	...	...	Matières premières
Intermediate goods	...	...	...	102.9	...	...	...	Produits intermédiaires
Consumer goods [40]	...	...	...	106.9	...	...	...	Biens de consommation [40]
Thailand								**Thaïlande**
Domestic supply [2,15]	...	85.9	91.6	107.1	...	...	119.5	Offre intérieure [2,15]
Agricultural products	...	73.0	83.9	120.1	...	...	174.3	Produits agricoles
Industrial products [3]	...	88.6	93.4	105.1	...	...	112.2	Produits industriels [3]
Raw materials	...	77.5	85.9	112.5	...	...	120.5	Matières premières
Intermediate goods	...	84.0	92.6	107.2	...	...	107.0	Produits intermédiaires
Consumer goods	76.8	80.8	87.2	110.4	...	...	165.4	Biens de consommation
Capital goods	...	90.4	92.5	100.3	...	...	101.6	Biens d'équipement
TFYR of Macedonia								**L'ex-R.Y. Macédoine**
Industrial products	...	...	...	107.3	110.0	121.3	113.4	Produits industriels
Intermediate goods	...	...	...	102.7	110.9	126.0	112.8	Produits intermédiaires
Capital goods	...	...	...	102.2	102.0	104.6	104.5	Biens d'équipement
Trinidad and Tobago [9]								**Trinité-et-Tobago** [9]
Domestic supply	102.2	103.1	106.7	...	...	...	...	Offre intérieure
Industrial products	101.5	102.9	...	...	...	...	...	Produits industriels
Tunisia								**Tunisie**
Domestic production	90.5	93.0	95.9	107.0	110.6	124.1	126.5	Production intérieure
Agricultural products	91.5	94.2	97.8	104.9	103.6	110.7	114.8	Produits agricoles
Industrial products [3]	92.2	95.3	97.2	104.7	107.2	115.4	117.4	Produits industriels [3]

26 Producer price indices *(continued)*

Index base: 2005= 100

Indices des prix à la production *(suite)*

Indices base: 2005= 100

Country or area	2002	2003	2004	2006	2007	2008	2009	Pays ou zone
Turkey								**Turquie**
Domestic supply [2,24,41]	65.6	82.4	94.5	109.1	116.2	131.0	132.6	Offre intérieure [2,24,41]
Agricultural products [42]	59.3	79.4	98.3	107.3	114.8	128.8	131.8	Produits agricoles [42]
Industrial products [3]	67.2	83.3	92.4	110.1	116.7	130.7	130.0	Produits industriels [3]
Ukraine								**Ukraine**
Agricultural products	...	...	...	102.4	141.3	151.9	...	Produits agricoles
Industrial products	...	...	...	109.6	131.0	177.8	189.5	Produits industriels
United Kingdom								**Royaume-Uni**
Domestic production [39]	95.8	96.8	98.2	102.2	104.8	112.5	113.9	Production intérieure [39]
Agricultural products	91.8	98.4	104.3	105.7	116.6	142.2	136.5	Produits agricoles
Industrial products [43]	98.0	98.6	99.1	101.8	103.7	108.6	110.7	Produits industriels [43]
Imported goods	102.2	102.4	99.9	103.0	104.2	117.8	121.2	Produits importés
Raw materials	88.0	88.5	90.5	109.5	112.8	137.2	132.4	Matières premières
Intermediate goods	93.2	94.8	97.5	103.9	109.1	118.9	119.0	Produits intermédiaires
Consumer goods	96.7	98.1	99.3	101.5	104.4	110.7	114.5	Biens de consommation
Capital goods	97.1	96.7	97.6	101.6	103.3	107.6	111.5	Biens d'équipement
United States								**Etats-Unis**
Domestic supply [2]	83.3	87.8	93.1	104.7	109.7	120.5	109.9	Offre intérieure [2]
Agricultural products [2,44]	83.5	94.1	104.9	98.8	120.9	136.2	113.6	Produits agricoles [2,44]
Industrial products [2]	82.7	86.9	92.1	105.4	109.4	120.0	109.2	Produits industriels [2]
Raw materials	59.5	74.4	87.1	101.9	113.9	138.3	96.1	Matières premières
Intermediate goods	83.0	86.8	92.6	106.5	110.8	122.3	112.0	Produits intermédiaires
Consumer goods	86.8	90.2	94.7	103.5	108.1	116.2	111.7	Biens de consommation
Capital goods	95.9	96.5	97.8	101.6	103.5	106.3	108.4	Biens d'équipement
Uruguay [45]								**Uruguay [45]**
Domestic production	64.4	89.5	102.6	105.9	118.4	138.5	141.4	Production intérieure
Agricultural products	69.0	104.2	118.6	101.3	126.5	155.4	181.0	Produits agricoles
Industrial products [3,10]	62.7	84.1	96.7	107.5	115.2	132.1	126.1	Produits industriels [3,10]
Venezuela (Boliv. R. of) [9,10]								**Venezuela (R. bol. du) [9,10]**
Domestic supply	...	253.2	...	435.2	506.7	...	819.2	Offre intérieure
Domestic production	...	236.6	...	421.1	497.2	...	817.8	Production intérieure
Agricultural products	...	184.2	...	380.1	492.6	...	1 131.2	Produits agricoles
Industrial products	...	191.4	...	321.6	373.2	...	572.6	Produits industriels
Imported goods	...	294.1	...	449.9	499.5	...	756.9	Produits importés
Viet Nam								**Viet Nam**
Agricultural products [42]	...	...	...	103.7	118.3	165.1	172.0	Produits agricoles [42]
Industrial products	...	...	...	104.2	111.4	135.6	144.2	Produits industriels
Imported goods	...	...	...	103.8	109.1	128.9	114.0	Produits importés

Source:
United Nations Statistics Division, New York, *Monthly Bulletin of Statistics*, August 2010, producer prices table.

Source:
Organisation des Nations Unies, Division de statistique, New York, *Bulletin mensuel de statistique*, août 2010, tableau des prix à la production.

1 Domestic agricultural products only.
2 Including exported products.
3 Manufacturing industry only.
4 Index base: 2002=100.
5 Including service industries.
6 The data refer to domestic production and imports.
7 Prices relate only to products for sale or transfer to other sectors or for use as capital equipment.
8 Annual figures: average of 12 months ending 30 June of the year stated.
9 Index base: 2000=100.
10 Excluding mining and quarrying.
11 Including imported products.
12 Excluding construction.
13 Non-durable goods only.
14 Including durable goods.
15 Agricultural products and products of manufacturing industry.

1 Produits agricoles intérieurs seulement.
2 Y compris les produits exportés.
3 Industries manufacturières seulement.
4 Base de l'indice: 2002=100.
5 Y compris industries de service.
6 Les données se réfèrent à la production intérieure et les importations.
7 Uniquement les prix des produits destinés à être vendus ou transférés à d'autres secteurs ou à être utilisés comme biens d'équipement.
8 Chiffres annuels : moyennes de douze mois finissant le 30 juin de l'année indiquée.
9 Indice base: 2000=100.
10 Non compris les industries extractives.
11 Y compris les produits importés.
12 Non compris construction.
13 Les biens non-durables seulement.
14 Y compris biens de consommation durables.
15 Produits agricoles et produits des industries manufacturières.

16 Including agriculture, forestry and livestock.
17 Forestry and fishing.
18 Index base: 2008=100
19 For government controlled areas.
20 Base: 1 July 2004 - 30 June 2005 = 100.
21 Including agriculture and fishing.
22 Durable goods only.
23 Finished products only.
24 Excluding electricity, gas and water.
25 Annual figures: average of 12 months ending 31 March of the year stated.
26 Primary articles include food, non-food articles and minerals.
27 Excluding Value Added Tax.
28 Including marine foods.
29 Mexico City.
30 Including all outputs of manufacturing.
31 Including all industrial inputs.
32 Muscat.
33 Annual figures: average of 12 months beginning 1 July of the year stated.
34 Excluding fishing.
35 Metro Manila.
36 Index base: 2006=100.
37 Prices of producers are surveyed without value added tax and without excise taxes.
38 Excluding gold mining.
39 Excluding agricultural products.
40 Index base: 1990=100.
41 Excluding industrial finished goods.
42 Including forestry and fishing.
43 Excluding food, beverages, petroleum and tobacco.
44 Excluding foods and feeds production.
45 Montevideo.

16 Y compris l'agriculture, la sylviculture et le bétail.
17 Exploitation forestière et pêche.
18 Base de l'indice: 2008=100
19 Pour les zones contrôlées par le gouvernement.
20 Base : le 1 juillet 2004 au 30 juin 2005=100.
21 Y compris l'agriculture et la pêche.
22 Biens durables seulement.
23 Produits finis uniquement.
24 Non compris l'électricité, le gaz et l'eau.
25 Chiffres annuels : moyennes de douze mois finissant le 31 mars de l'année indiquée.
26 Les articles primaires comprennent des articles des produits alimentaires, non- alimentaires et des minéraux.
27 Non compris taxe sur la valeur ajoutée.
28 Y compris l'alimentation marine.
29 Mexico.
30 Y compris toute la production du secteur manufacturière.
31 Tous les intrants industriels.
32 Muscat.
33 Chiffres annuels : moyennes de douze mois commençant le 1 juillet de l'année indiquée.
34 Non compris la pêche.
35 L'agglomération de Manille.
36 Base de l'indice: 2006=100.
37 Les enquêtes sur le prix à la production ne prennent pas en considération les taxes à la valeur ajoutée et excise.
38 Non compris l'extraction de l'or.
39 Non compris les produits agricoles.
40 Base de l'indice: 1990=100.
41 Non compris les produits finis industriels.
42 Y compris l'exploitation forestière et la pêche.
43 Non compris les produits alimentaires, les boissons, le pétrole et le tabac.
44 Non compris les produits alimentaires et d'affouragement.
45 Montevideo.

27 Consumer price indices

General and food (Index base: 2000 = 100)

Indices des prix à la consommation

Généraux et alimentation (Indices base : 2000 = 100)

Country or area	City - Ville	2002	2003	2004	2005	2006	2007	2008	2009	Pays ou zone
Albania										**Albanie**
General		108.4	110.8	114.0	116.7	119.5	123.0	127.1[2]	129.9	Généraux
Food		110.2[1]	115.0[1]	114.9[1]	114.3[1]	115.6[1]	119.0[1]	#124.3[3]	130.4	Alimentation
Algeria										**Algérie**
General		105.8	109.5	114.5	116.7	118.9	123.5	128.9	...	Généraux
Food		106.2	111.0	116.4	116.7	119.3	126.7	134.6	...	Alimentation
American Samoa										**Samoa américaines**
General [4]		103.4	108.5	116.1	122.1	125.7	...	...	...	Généraux [4]
Food		103.1	109.8	123.5	130.4	132.2	...	...	...	Alimentation
Andorra [5]										**Andorre** [5]
General (2001 = 100)		104.5	107.5	111.1	114.6	118.2	122.8	125.3	125.3	Généraux (2001 = 100)
Food (2001 = 100) [6]		106.2	109.9	111.9	113.1	116.2	119.8	123.2	122.7	Alimentation (2001 = 100) [6]
Angola	Luanda									**Angola**
General		527.6[2]	1 045.8	1 501.2	1 846.0	2 091.6	2 347.7[2]	2 640.5	3 003.0	Généraux
Food		508.6	1 062.4[2]	1 587.5	1 957.0	2 292.4	2 617.7	3 103.8	...	Alimentation
Anguilla										**Anguilla**
General		100.5	103.8	108.3	113.5	122.7	129.1	137.9	136.9	Généraux
Food		100.5	98.0	102.1	105.4	112.4	119.4	137.5	143.7	Alimentation
Argentina [7]	Buenos Aires									**Argentine** [7]
General		124.5	141.3	147.5	161.7	179.4	195.2[2]	211.9	225.5	Généraux
Food		132.0	157.3	165.1	183.3	205.5	228.5[2]	244.0	250.9	Alimentation
Armenia										**Arménie**
General		104.3[2]	109.2	116.3	117.0[2]	121.1	126.5	137.8	142.5	Généraux
Food		107.0[2]	114.4	125.8	126.8[2]	132.0	140.9	156.5	155.1	Alimentation
Aruba										**Aruba**
General		106.3	110.2	113.0	116.8	121.0	128.3	139.0[2]	136.0	Généraux
Food		106.7	110.1	114.4	118.7	124.1	137.6	156.8[2]	164.1	Alimentation
Australia										**Australie**
General		107.6	110.5	113.1	116.1	120.3	123.1	128.4	130.7	Généraux
Food		110.4	114.4	117.1	120.0	129.2	132.3	138.5	143.6	Alimentation
Austria										**Autriche**
General		104.5	105.9	108.1	110.6	112.3[2]	114.7	118.3	118.9	Généraux
Food		105.2[8]	107.3[8]	109.5[8]	111.0[8]	#112.5[3]	117.1	124.5	124.8	Alimentation
Azerbaijan										**Azerbaïdjan**
General		104.4	106.7	113.9	124.8	135.2	157.7	190.6	193.4	Généraux
Food [9]		106.5	109.9	120.9	134.1	150.2	174.6	224.4	221.0	Alimentation [9]
Bahamas	New Providence									**Bahamas**
General		104.2	107.4	108.6	110.8	112.8	115.6	120.8	...	Généraux
Food		104.1	104.7	107.8	111.2	116.4	120.6	128.6	...	Alimentation
Bahrain										**Bahreïn**
General		98.3	100.0	102.3	104.9	107.1[2]	110.6	114.4	117.6	Généraux
Food [9]		97.6	96.2	98.3	101.3	103.3[2]	108.0	119.8	130.6	Alimentation [9]
Bangladesh [10]										**Bangladesh** [10]
General		105.4	111.5[2]	118.4	126.7	135.3	147.6	160.7	169.4	Généraux
Food [6]		103.4	110.1[2]	118.3	127.8	137.5	151.9	168.7	177.9	Alimentation [6]
Barbados										**Barbade**
General		103.0	104.6	106.1	112.5	120.8	125.7	135.8	...	Généraux
Food		107.1	110.1	115.0	123.1	132.8	142.2	161.4	...	Alimentation
Belarus										**Bélarus**
General		229.8	295.0	348.3	384.3	411.2	445.9	512.0	578.3	Généraux
Food		217.9	267.6	320.1	358.2	380.1	417.4	491.1	559.8	Alimentation
Belgium										**Belgique**
General		104.2	105.8	108.0[2]	111.0	113.0	115.1	120.3	120.2	Généraux
Food		106.5	108.7	110.4[2]	112.5	115.0	119.2	126.1	127.4	Alimentation
Belize										**Belize**
General		103.4	106.1	109.3	113.1	118.2	120.9	128.6	127.2	Généraux
Food [9]		101.6	104.2	106.9	111.8	116.6	122.7	139.0	141.2	Alimentation [9]
Benin	Cotonou									**Bénin**
General		106.5	108.1	109.0	114.9	119.2	120.8	130.3	133.2	Généraux
Food [11]		108.0	105.5	104.7	114.4	113.8	112.6	132.9	140.3	Alimentation [11]

27

Consumer price indices *(continued)*
General and food (Index base: 2000 = 100)

Indices des prix à la consommation *(suite)*
Généraux et alimentation (Indices base : 2000 = 100)

Country or area	City - Ville	2002	2003	2004	2005	2006	2007	2008	2009	Pays ou zone
Bermuda										**Bermudes**
General		105.3	108.6	112.5	116.0	119.5[2]	124.1	130.0	132.4	Généraux
Food		103.5	105.6	108.2	111.4	113.6[2]	117.6	124.1	130.9	Alimentation
Bhutan										**Bhoutan**
General		106.0	107.6	110.9[2]	116.8	122.6	129.0	139.8	...	Généraux
Food		103.6	104.5	102.9[2]	108.8	114.2	123.5	138.2	...	Alimentation
Bolivia (Plurin. State of) [12]										**Bolivie (État plurin. de)** [12]
General		102.5	106.0	110.7	116.6	121.6	132.2	150.7[2]	155.8	Généraux
Food		99.7	103.2	109.3	115.7	122.2	138.9	174.5	176.8	Alimentation
Bosnia and Herzegovina										**Bosnie-Herzégovine**
General (2005 = 100)		...	...	...	100.0	106.1	107.7	115.7	115.3	Généraux (2005 = 100)
Food (2005 = 100)		...	...	...	100.0	108.3	111.4	124.8	123.7	Alimentation (2005 = 100)
Botswana										**Botswana**
General		115.1	125.8	134.4	146.1	163.0[2]	174.5	196.6	212.5	Généraux
Food		112.2	125.0	130.9	137.9	155.2[2]	172.7	207.7	237.4	Alimentation
Brazil										**Brésil**
General		115.9	132.9	141.7	151.4	157.8	163.5	172.8	181.2	Généraux
Food [8]		117.0	140.8	146.5	151.0	151.0	161.3	182.3	192.9	Alimentation [8]
British Virgin Islands										**Iles Vierges britanniques**
General		103.5	107.2	108.3	110.4	...	...	...	...	Généraux
Food		105.3	107.1	108.4	112.1	...	...	...	...	Alimentation
Brunei Darussalam										**Brunéi Darussalam**
General		98.3[2]	98.6	99.5	100.5	100.7	101.0	103.8	...	Généraux
Food		100.9[2]	100.0	101.7	102.2	102.5	104.7	109.9	...	Alimentation
Bulgaria										**Bulgarie**
General		113.6	116.3	123.4	129.6	139.1	150.7	169.3	174.0	Généraux
Food		106.5	105.4	112.5	117.0	123.4	140.0	163.4	162.3	Alimentation
Burkina Faso	Ouagadougou									**Burkina Faso**
General		107.3	109.5	109.0	116.0	118.8	118.5	131.1	134.6	Généraux
Food		112.2	110.3	104.9	120.2	120.0	117.9	145.4	...	Alimentation
Burundi	Bujumbura									**Burundi**
General		106.7	118.1	127.9	144.8	148.6	161.0	...	...	Généraux
Food		95.5	107.5	119.0	139.4	139.5	151.6	...	...	Alimentation
Cambodia	Phnom Penh									**Cambodge**
General		102.7	103.9	107.9	114.1	119.5	126.5	151.4	159.0[2]	Généraux
Food		99.7[9]	101.2[9]	107.6[9]	116.6[9]	124.2[9]	136.6[9]	#100.0[3]	64.1	Alimentation
Cameroon										**Cameroun**
General		107.4[13]	108.1[13]	108.4	110.5	116.2	117.2	123.5	...	Généraux
Food		112.1[13]	111.4[13]	109.2	110.4	117.9	119.1	130.0	...	Alimentation
Canada										**Canada**
General		104.9	107.8	109.8	112.2	114.5	116.9[2]	119.6	119.9	Généraux
Food		107.2	109.1	111.3	114.1	116.8	119.9[2]	124.1	130.2	Alimentation
Cape Verde										**Cap-Vert**
General		105.4	106.5	104.5	104.9	110.6	115.5[2]	123.4	124.6	Généraux
Food (2003 = 100)		...	#100.0[3]	96.6	96.4	102.7	107.9	117.7	120.0	Alimentation (2003 = 100)
Cayman Islands										**Iles Caïmanes**
General		103.6	104.2	108.8	116.8	117.7	121.1	126.1	124.4[2]	Généraux
Food		105.7	109.1	113.9	117.0	120.1	126.3	133.4	139.3[2]	Alimentation
Central African Rep.	Bangui									**Rép. centrafricaine**
General [4]		105.2	110.9	108.6	111.7	119.1	120.3	131.5	136.1	Généraux [4]
Food		106.8	112.4	107.2	110.9	118.9	121.1	134.9	...	Alimentation
Chad	N'Djamena									**Tchad**
General		117.5[2]	115.5	109.3	117.8	127.5	115.9	127.7[2]	140.6	Généraux
Food		125.8[2]	122.6	116.0	129.2	144.0	129.9	151.2[2]	164.6	Alimentation
Chile	Santiago									**Chili**
General		106.2	109.1	110.3	113.7	117.5	122.7	133.4	135.3[2]	Généraux
Food		102.9[8]	105.8[8]	104.4[8]	107.5[8]	110.6[8]	120.5[8]	139.8[8]	#147.4[3]	Alimentation
China										**Chine**
General		100.0	101.1	105.1	107.0	108.5	113.7	120.4	...	Généraux
Food		99.4	102.8	113.0	116.3	119.0	133.7	152.8	...	Alimentation

27

Consumer price indices *(continued)*
General and food (Index base: 2000 = 100)

Indices des prix à la consommation *(suite)*
Généraux et alimentation (Indices base : 2000 = 100)

Country or area	City - Ville	2002	2003	2004	2005	2006	2007	2008	2009	Pays ou zone
China, Hong Kong SAR										**Chine, Hong Kong RAS**
General		95.4	93.0	92.6	93.6[2]	95.5	97.4	101.6	95.1	Généraux
Food		97.1	95.7	96.7	98.4[2]	100.1	104.4	115.0	114.1	Alimentation
China, Macao SAR										**Chine, Macao RAS**
General		95.4	93.9	94.9	99.0[2]	104.1	109.9	119.4	120.8	Généraux
Food		96.5	95.3	97.4	101.3[2]	105.0	113.6	133.2	140.6	Alimentation
Colombia [14]										**Colombie** [14]
General		116.5	125.0	132.5	139.7	145.2	153.4	166.0	173.2[2]	Généraux
Food		118.4	127.2	134.6	143.1	150.5	162.5	182.6	189.6[2]	Alimentation
Congo [15]	Brazzaville									**Congo** [15]
General		104.4	103.8	106.4	109.6	116.8	119.9	128.7	135.1	Généraux
Food		102.9	96.9	90.8	95.7	105.3	112.9	122.1	131.3	Alimentation
Cook Islands	Rarotonga									**Iles Cook**
General		112.4	114.6	115.6	118.5	122.4	125.5[2]	135.4	144.4	Généraux
Food [16]		116.9	119.9	121.0	122.3	125.2	125.5[2]	132.9	147.2	Alimentation [16]
Costa Rica [17]										**Costa Rica** [17]
General		121.5	132.9	149.3	169.9	189.4[2]	207.1	234.9	253.3	Généraux
Food		121.8[11]	133.3[11]	151.6[11]	176.5[11]	...	#100.0[3,18]	123.9	134.0	Alimentation
Côte d'Ivoire [15]	Abidjan									**Côte d'Ivoire** [15]
General		107.6	111.1	112.7	117.1	119.9	122.2	130.0	131.3	Généraux
Food [11]		111.6	116.1	111.6	114.3	117.5	123.8	137.8	...	Alimentation [11]
Croatia										**Croatie**
General		106.3	108.2	110.4	114.0[2]	117.7	121.1	128.4	131.5	Généraux
Food		102.3	104.0	105.5	110.4[2]	113.1	116.9	128.6	130.6	Alimentation
Cuba										**Cuba**
General		106.1	108.2	105.9	108.9	114.5	122.6	124.5	...	Généraux
Food [8,19]		113.5	110.3	107.0	110.3	117.8	124.7	126.3	...	Alimentation [8,19]
Cyprus										**Chypre**
General		104.8	109.2	111.7	114.5	117.4[2]	120.2	125.8	126.2	Généraux
Food		108.9	114.4	119.0	120.9	126.7[2]	133.7	143.8	149.2	Alimentation
Czech Republic										**République tchèque**
General		106.6	106.6	109.7	111.7	114.6	117.9	125.4	...	Généraux
Food [20]		104.4	104.0	109.0	110.3	111.5	118.0	127.9	...	Alimentation [20]
Denmark										**Danemark**
General		104.8	107.0	108.3	110.2	112.3	114.2	118.1	119.7	Généraux
Food		106.1	107.7	106.6	107.3	110.2	115.1	123.8	123.7	Alimentation
Dominica										**Dominique**
General (2001 = 100)		100.2	101.6	104.1	105.8	108.6	112.1	119.2	119.6	Généraux (2001 = 100)
Food (2001 = 100)		101.5	101.9	104.8	107.4	111.8	117.7	131.5	138.7	Alimentation (2001 = 100)
Dominican Republic										**Rép. dominicaine**
General		114.6	146.1	221.2	230.5	247.9	263.1	291.1	295.3	Généraux
Food [11]		110.7	140.1	237.0	233.2	242.8	258.8	295.8	307.3	Alimentation [11]
Ecuador										**Equateur**
General		154.9	167.2	171.7	175.4[2]	181.2	185.4	200.9	211.3	Généraux
Food		142.5[11]	146.0[11]	147.7[11]	#100.0[3,21]	105.7	109.1	127.5	135.0	Alimentation
Egypt										**Egypte**
General		105.0	109.5	127.4[2]	133.7	143.9	157.6[2]	186.4	208.4	Généraux
Food		105.3[9]	112.3[9]	#100.0[3,22]	105.1	115.7	130.6[2]	162.0	188.1	Alimentation
El Salvador [12]										**El Salvador** [12]
General		105.7	107.9	112.7	118.0	122.8	128.4	137.7	138.5	Généraux
Food		106.6	108.6	115.5	122.6	126.3	134.2	150.5	144.0	Alimentation
Equatorial Guinea	Malabo									**Guinée équatoriale**
General		117.0	125.5	130.9	...	144.5	...	...	...	Généraux
Food		122.2	130.0	135.7	...	153.6	...	...	...	Alimentation
Estonia										**Estonie**
General		109.5	111.0	114.4	119.0	124.4	132.5	146.3	...	Généraux
Food		111.6	109.6	114.2	118.3	124.2	135.9	155.1	...	Alimentation
Ethiopia										**Ethiopie**
General (2001 = 100)		101.6	119.6	123.6	138.0	156.6	184.8[2]	266.8	289.4	Généraux (2001 = 100)
Food (2001 = 100)		102.6	130.9	134.8	153.3	175.2	214.3[2]	343.0	354.4	Alimentation (2001 = 100)

27

Consumer price indices *(continued)*
General and food (Index base: 2000 = 100)

Indices des prix à la consommation *(suite)*
Généraux et alimentation (Indices base : 2000 = 100)

Country or area	City - Ville	2002	2003	2004	2005	2006	2007	2008	2009	Pays ou zone
Faeroe Islands										**Iles Féroé**
General		105.2[2]	106.5	107.2	109.3	111.0	114.9	122.2	120.9	Généraux
Food		108.9[2]	109.5	109.9	111.1	114.1	118.9	127.1	128.0	Alimentation
Falkland Is. (Malvinas)	Stanley									**Iles Falkland (Malvinas)**
General		102.0	103.2	...	...	...	...	...	...	Généraux
Fiji										**Fidji**
General		105.0	109.5	112.5	115.1	118.1	123.7[2]	133.3	138.2	Généraux
Food		104.6	111.0	115.2	117.1	119.2	130.8[2]	145.8	155.6	Alimentation
Finland										**Finlande**
General		104.2	105.1	105.3	106.2	107.9[2]	110.6	115.0	115.0	Généraux
Food		107.4	108.1	108.9	109.2	110.7[2]	113.0	122.7	125.1	Alimentation
France										**France**
General		103.6	105.8	108.0	109.9	111.8	113.4	116.6	116.7	Généraux
Food		107.8	110.2	110.9	111.0	112.7	114.3	119.9	120.4	Alimentation
French Guiana										**Guyane française**
General		103.2	105.2	106.4	108.2	110.4	114.2	118.2	119.0	Généraux
Food		105.3	109.3	109.8	110.5	111.4	113.6	119.0	122.7	Alimentation
French Polynesia										**Polynésie française**
General		103.9	104.3[2]	104.8	105.8	108.7	110.9	114.4[2]	114.6	Généraux
Food		107.4	108.2[2]	110.6	113.2	117.5	121.0	126.6[2]	128.9	Alimentation
Gabon [15]	Libreville									**Gabon** [15]
General		102.3	104.4	104.9	104.9	109.1	112.7[2]	118.5	...	Généraux
Food		105.2[6]	107.1[6]	105.1[6]	105.5[6]	112.2[6]	#100.0[3,18]	107.8	...	Alimentation
Gambia	Banjul,Kombo St.Mary									**Gambie**
General		113.5	132.8	151.7	156.5	159.7[2]	168.3	175.8	183.8	Généraux
Food		117.2	141.2	164.0	169.2	172.2[2]	185.8	197.1	207.4	Alimentation
Georgia [23]										**Géorgie** [23]
General		110.5	115.8	122.4	132.5	144.6	158.0	173.8[2]	...	Généraux
Food [9]		114.6	122.7	132.2	149.6	167.1	183.4	204.0[2]	...	Alimentation [9]
Germany										**Allemagne**
General		103.4	104.5	106.2	108.3	110.1	112.5	115.5[2]	115.9	Généraux
Food		105.3	105.2	104.8	105.3	107.3	111.5	118.3[2]	116.8	Alimentation
Ghana										**Ghana**
General		151.8	193.3	217.7	250.7	278.0	331.9[2]	386.8	461.2	Généraux
Food		145.6	181.6	211.8	244.7	267.2	300.6[2]	346.2	400.6	Alimentation
Gibraltar										**Gibraltar**
General		102.5	105.2	107.6	110.9	113.8	116.9	121.2	124.6	Généraux
Food		107.2	111.3	115.1	117.4	120.5	124.4	132.1	143.4	Alimentation
Greece										**Grèce**
General		107.1	110.9	114.1	118.2[2]	122.0	125.5	130.7	132.3	Généraux
Food		110.7	116.2	116.8	117.5[2]	121.9	125.9	132.6	135.1	Alimentation
Greenland										**Groenland**
General		107.2	109.0	112.0	113.3	116.2	118.5	126.3	...	Généraux
Food		107.6	109.8	111.4	114.5	117.4	120.9	130.6	...	Alimentation
Grenada										**Grenade**
General		104.3	106.6	109.0	...	...	...	...	...	Généraux
Food		101.4	102.1	105.4	...	...	...	...	...	Alimentation
Guadeloupe										**Guadeloupe**
General		105.0	107.1	108.6	112.1	114.3	115.8	118.4	118.7	Généraux
Food		108.0	111.7	113.1	116.1	115.7	118.1	122.9	125.7	Alimentation
Guam										**Guam**
General		99.4	102.0	108.1	116.3	129.8	138.6	147.1[2]	149.7	Généraux
Food [8]		112.6	118.9	130.1	140.8	150.0	154.7	168.6[2]	179.4	Alimentation [8]
Guatemala	Guatemala									**Guatemala**
General		116.0	122.5	131.8	143.8	153.2	163.7	182.3	185.7	Généraux
Food		121.5	128.5	141.8	160.5	171.9	188.9	217.5	221.9	Alimentation
Guinea	Conakry									**Guinée**
General		108.4	122.4	141.1[2]	185.3	249.6	306.6	362.9	379.9	Généraux
Food		114.4[2,24]	138.8	168.3	230.6	328.6	422.2	509.2	545.4	Alimentation
Guinea-Bissau	Bissau									**Guinée-Bissau**
General (2003 = 100)		...	100.0	100.9	104.3	106.4	111.2	122.9	...	Généraux (2003 = 100)
Food (2003 = 100) [11]		...	#100.0[3]	101.1	104.8	105.2	111.3	129.1	...	Alimentation (2003 = 100) [11]

27 Consumer price indices *(continued)*
General and food (Index base: 2000 = 100)

Indices des prix à la consommation *(suite)*
Généraux et alimentation (Indices base : 2000 = 100)

Country or area	City - Ville	2002	2003	2004	2005	2006	2007	2008	2009	Pays ou zone
Guyana	Georgetown									**Guyana**
General		108.2	114.6	120.0	128.3	136.9	153.6	166.0	170.9	Généraux
Food [9]		104.5	108.5	113.3	121.7	130.0	150.3	172.3	171.6	Alimentation [9]
Haiti [7]										**Haïti [7]**
General		125.3	174.5	214.3	255.4[2]	286.9	311.3	359.7	359.7	Généraux
Food [11]		127.4	174.2	223.2	263.2[2]	300.2	324.5	388.6	378.5	Alimentation [11]
Honduras										**Honduras**
General		118.0	127.1	137.5	149.5	157.9	168.9	188.1	198.4	Généraux
Food		112.8	117.0	124.9	137.5	143.7	159.2	189.3	195.0	Alimentation
Hungary										**Hongrie**
General		115.0	120.3	128.5	133.1	138.3	149.3	158.4	165.0	Généraux
Food		119.9	123.2	131.2	134.5	144.8	161.5	177.9	185.7	Alimentation
Iceland [25]										**Islande [25]**
General		111.8	114.2	117.8	122.6	130.9	137.5	154.6	...	Généraux
Food		111.1	108.4	109.7	106.7	115.7	113.8	132.3	...	Alimentation
India [26]										**Inde [26]**
General		108.2	112.5	116.6	121.5	127.7[2]	136.1	147.5	163.2	Généraux
Food		104.9	108.4	111.5	115.0	124.7[2]	137.0	152.3	173.1	Alimentation
Indonesia										**Indonésie**
General		124.7	133.0	141.3[2]	156.0	176.5	187.8[2]	207.2	216.1	Généraux
Food		120.2	121.2	128.3[2]	140.3	161.9	180.4[2]	210.9	225.7	Alimentation
Iran (Islamic Rep. of)										**Iran (Rép. islamique d')**
General		127.3	148.2	170.1	192.9	216.0	246.1[2]	309.1	350.7	Généraux
Food		124.0[9]	145.9[9]	164.8[9]	186.3[9]	205.5[9]	#100.0[3,18]	131.0	146.5	Alimentation
Iraq										**Iraq**
General		130.9	185.5	235.6	322.6	494.3	646.8	664.0	645.4	Généraux
Food		118.0	137.5	149.5	182.9	237.5	270.4	300.0	323.0	Alimentation
Ireland										**Irlande**
General		109.7	113.5	116.0	118.8	123.5	129.5[2]	134.8	128.7	Généraux
Food		110.7	112.3	111.9	111.2	112.7	116.0[2]	123.5	119.2	Alimentation
Isle of Man										**Ile de Man**
General		104.1	107.3	112.8	117.5	121.0	125.9	132.4	133.1	Généraux
Food		113.0	119.6	126.3	131.0	135.1	141.2	152.3	166.5	Alimentation
Israel										**Israël**
General		106.9[2]	107.7	107.2	108.6	111.0[2]	111.5	116.6	114.7	Généraux
Food		105.4[2]	108.4	108.0	109.9	115.1[2]	119.5	133.2	116.8	Alimentation
Italy										**Italie**
General [19]		105.4	108.2	110.5	112.4	114.7	116.9	120.7	121.6	Généraux [19]
Food		107.9	111.3	113.7	113.7	115.6	119.0	125.4	127.7	Alimentation
Jamaica										**Jamaïque**
General		114.6	126.4	143.6	165.5	179.8	196.8[2]	240.1	263.2	Généraux
Food		109.7[8]	120.2[8]	136.5[8]	161.4[8]	172.0[8]	#194.8[3]	254.6	287.7	Alimentation
Japan										**Japon**
General		98.4	98.1	98.1	97.8	98.1	98.1	99.5	98.1	Généraux
Food		98.6	98.4	99.3	98.4	98.9	99.2	101.8	101.9	Alimentation
Jersey										**Jersey**
General		108.3	112.9	118.3	122.6	126.2	131.6	139.0	138.5	Généraux
Food		107.3	109.6	114.0	114.4	117.0	122.1	137.9	143.6	Alimentation
Jordan										**Jordanie**
General		103.6[2]	105.3	108.9	112.7	119.7	126.2	145.0	141.9	Généraux
Food [9]		100.5[2]	103.1	107.8	113.4	121.8	133.2	158.2	159.7	Alimentation [9]
Kazakhstan										**Kazakhstan**
General		114.7	122.1	130.5	140.3	152.4	168.8	197.5	...	Généraux
Food [11]		119.0	127.3	137.1	148.2	161.0	180.7	223.1	...	Alimentation [11]
Kenya										**Kenya**
General (2007 = 100)		...	...	...	...	...	100.0	116.2	126.9	Généraux (2007 = 100)
Food (2007=100)		...	...	...	...	...	100.0	123.1	138.6	Alimentation (2007 = 100)
Kiribati	Tarawa									**Kiribati**
General		109.4	111.4	110.3	110.0	108.3	112.9	125.3	...	Généraux
Food		109.7	112.8	112.8	112.7	108.3	114.4	133.4	...	Alimentation

27 Consumer price indices (continued)

General and food (Index base: 2000 = 100)

Indices des prix à la consommation (suite)

Généraux et alimentation (Indices base : 2000 = 100)

Country or area	City - Ville	2002	2003	2004	2005	2006	2007	2008	2009	Pays ou zone
Korea, Republic of										**Corée, République de**
General		106.9	110.7	114.7	117.8[2]	120.4	123.5	129.2	132.9	Généraux
Food		107.7[8]	112.4[8]	119.5[8]	#128.6[3]	129.2	132.4	139.1	149.5	Alimentation
Kosovo										**Kosovo**
General (2003 = 100)		98.8[27]	100.0	98.9	97.6	98.2	102.6	112.1	109.4	Généraux (2003 = 100)
Food (2003 = 100)		97.6[27]	100.0	98.9	96.5	99.7	100.7	116.9	111.7	Alimentation (2003 = 100)
Kuwait										**Koweït**
General		102.3	103.2	104.5	108.8	112.1	118.3	130.8	136.0	Généraux
Food		101.1	106.6	110.0	119.4	124.0	129.9	145.0	149.6	Alimentation
Kyrgyzstan										**Kirghizistan**
General		109.1	112.5	117.1	122.2	129.0	...	...	...	Généraux
Food		105.9	108.9	112.4	118.4	128.7	...	...	...	Alimentation
Lao People's Dem. Rep.										**Rép. dém. pop. lao**
General		119.3	137.7	152.1	163.0	174.1	182.0	195.9[2]	195.9	Généraux
Food		117.0	134.8	148.8	160.2	175.7[2]	190.0	210.7	214.7	Alimentation
Latvia										**Lettonie**
General		104.5	107.5	114.2	121.9	129.9	143.0	165.0	170.8	Généraux
Food		108.4[11]	111.2[11]	119.5[11]	#130.5[3]	141.1	160.1	189.4	189.3	Alimentation
Lebanon	Beirut									**Liban**
General		95.3	96.5	100.3	105.0	112.0	121.9	144.7	...	Généraux
Lesotho										**Lesotho**
General [4]		120.1	129.0	135.5	140.1	148.4	160.6	177.8	190.5	Généraux [4]
Food [1]		134.9	142.4	148.1	152.0	165.9	189.9	220.0	239.7	Alimentation [1]
Lithuania										**Lituanie**
General		101.6	100.4	101.6	104.3[2]	108.2	114.4	126.9	132.6	Généraux
Food		102.8	99.0	101.2	105.3[2]	111.7	124.3	144.1	146.5	Alimentation
Luxembourg										**Luxembourg**
General		104.8	106.9	109.3	112.0[2]	115.0	117.7	121.7	122.1	Généraux
Food		108.9	111.0	113.0	114.9[2]	117.6	121.5	128.1	129.9	Alimentation
Madagascar	Cinq régions									**Madagascar**
General		125.1	123.0	139.9	165.9	183.7	202.6	221.4	241.2	Généraux
Food [6]		117.2	112.9	134.7	170.2	180.8	202.1	223.2	241.6	Alimentation [6]
Malawi										**Malawi**
General		140.8	154.3	172.0	198.5	226.1	244.1	265.4	287.7	Généraux
Food		136.4	143.6	154.4	181.0	209.1	224.7	240.3	258.0	Alimentation
Malaysia										**Malaisie**
General		103.2	104.4	105.9	109.1[2]	113.0	115.3	121.5	122.3	Généraux
Food		101.4	102.7	105.0	108.8[2]	112.5	115.9	126.1	131.4	Alimentation
Maldives	Male									**Maldives**
General		101.6	98.7	105.0	108.5	110.0[2]	117.5	131.7	137.6	Généraux
Food		105.7[11]	99.3[11]	115.2[11]	117.6[11]	#104.0[3,21]	120.9	143.9	144.6	Alimentation
Mali	Bamako									**Mali**
General		110.4	109.1	105.6	112.4	114.1	115.7	126.3	...	Généraux
Food [6]		115.8	111.1	103.3	115.1	114.6	117.3	132.6	...	Alimentation [6]
Malta										**Malte**
General		105.2	105.8[2]	108.7	112.0	115.0	116.5	121.4	124.0	Généraux
Food		107.4	109.2[2]	109.5	111.4	113.6	118.5	128.1	136.2	Alimentation
Marshall Islands	Majuro									**Iles Marshall**
General		103.0	100.1	102.3	106.9	111.5	115.0	135.2	...	Généraux
Food		102.7	102.5	106.0	106.3	109.4	110.8	129.4	...	Alimentation
Martinique										**Martinique**
General		104.2	106.4	108.6	111.2	113.9	116.7	119.9	119.5	Généraux
Food		108.8	112.5	114.6	118.3	120.5	124.6	131.2	132.3	Alimentation
Mauritania										**Mauritanie**
General		108.9	114.4	124.2[2]	139.3	147.9	158.7	170.4	...	Généraux
Food		111.3	117.9[28]	131.2[2]	149.3	157.3	173.9	190.6	...	Alimentation
Mauritius										**Maurice**
General		112.2[2]	116.5	122.1	128.1	139.5	154.9[2,24]	166.5	170.8	Généraux
Food		112.2[2]	115.4	122.3	129.5	142.4	168.9[2,24]	190.7	198.5	Alimentation
Mexico										**Mexique**
General		111.7[2]	116.8	122.3	127.2	131.8	137.0	144.0	151.6	Généraux
Food [11]		109.6[2]	115.1	122.9	129.4	134.2	142.6	154.1	167.5	Alimentation [11]

27 Consumer price indices *(continued)*
General and food (Index base: 2000 = 100)

Indices des prix à la consommation *(suite)*
Généraux et alimentation (Indices base : 2000 = 100)

Country or area	City - Ville	2002	2003	2004	2005	2006	2007	2008	2009	Pays ou zone
Mongolia										**Mongolie**
General (2006 = 100)		...	...	...	...	100.0	109.6	140.3	151.0	Généraux (2006 = 100)
Food (2006 = 100)		...	...	...	...	100.0	112.9	158.2	160.9	Alimentation (2006 = 100)
Morocco										**Maroc**
General		103.4	104.6	106.2	107.3	110.8	113.0	117.4	...	Généraux
Food [9]		103.2	104.6	106.2	106.5	110.7	114.3	122.1	...	Alimentation [9]
Mozambique										**Mozambique**
General		130.4	145.4	162.0	173.3	196.9	214.9	246.5	255.1	Généraux
Food		132.3	148.8	165.0	173.9	203.6	224.6	266.9	285.6	Alimentation
Myanmar										**Myanmar**
General		190.2	259.8	271.6	297.1	356.5	481.3	610.3	...	Généraux
Food		201.2	274.3	277.5	303.2	365.7	493.9	638.3	...	Alimentation
Namibia										**Namibie**
General (2002 = 100)		100.0	107.2	111.6	114.1	119.9	127.9	141.1	153.6	Généraux (2002 = 100)
Food (2002 = 100)		100.0	109.5	110.4	112.0	119.3	133.8	156.6	173.4	Alimentation (2002 = 100)
Nepal										**Népal**
General		105.9	112.0	115.2	123.2	132.6	140.5	156.9	174.8	Généraux
Food		104.4	110.1	112.9	120.3	129.1	139.6	158.8	186.1	Alimentation
Netherlands										**Pays-Bas**
General		107.6	109.9	111.2	113.1	114.4	116.2[2]	119.1	120.6	Généraux
Food		110.5	111.7	107.8	106.5	108.3	109.4[2]	115.6	116.8	Alimentation
Netherlands Antilles	Curaçao									**Antilles néerlandaises**
General		102.1	103.8	105.3	109.4	113.0	116.4[2]	124.4	126.5	Généraux
Food		107.3	109.5	114.7	123.3	133.0	145.0[2]	171.6	188.6	Alimentation
New Caledonia	Nouméa									**Nouvelle-Calédonie**
General		104.1	105.4	106.3	107.6	110.7	111.8	115.1	116.2	Généraux
Food		105.0	107.0	108.3	109.7	113.0	114.5	119.1	122.3	Alimentation
New Zealand										**Nouvelle-Zélande**
General		105.4	107.3	109.7	113.0	116.8[2]	119.6	124.4	127.0	Généraux
Food		109.4[29]	109.4[29]	110.3[29]	113.1[29]	#114.4[3]	118.8	129.1	136.8	Alimentation
Nicaragua										**Nicaragua**
General (1999 = 100)		117.7	124.0	134.5	147.4	160.9	178.8	214.2	222.2[2]	Généraux (1999 = 100)
Food (1999 = 100)		115.7	120.7	133.6	149.0	162.5	188.9	242.8	252.4[2]	Alimentation (1999 = 100)
Niger [15]	Niamey									**Niger** [15]
General [4]		106.7	105.1	105.2	113.5	113.6	113.6	126.5	...	Généraux [4]
Food [9]		112.0	106.7	105.1	120.7	118.4	117.6	141.8	...	Alimentation [9]
Nigeria										**Nigéria**
General		134.2	153.1[2]	176.0	207.4	224.5	236.6	264.0	296.6	Généraux
Food		144.8	153.8[2]	175.8	216.3	228.4	232.6	270.0	309.6	Alimentation
Niue										**Nioué**
General		109.7	112.3[2]	116.6[30]	117.0	119.7	127.8	139.3	...	Généraux
Food		115.1	118.3[2]	121.2[30]	122.0	127.2	134.9	150.0	...	Alimentation
Norfolk Island										**Ile Norfolk**
General		105.9	109.1	118.6	125.2	134.5	140.8	148.0	152.3	Généraux
Food		112.4	118.4	123.4	129.9	137.3	148.4	160.9	169.8	Alimentation
Northern Mariana Islands	Saipan									**Iles Mariannes du Nord**
General		99.4	98.4[2]	99.3	99.8	104.7	111.9	117.2	119.9	Généraux
Food		93.0	90.7[2]	94.9	93.9	91.4	96.0	103.7	110.8	Alimentation
Norway										**Norvège**
General		104.4	106.9	107.4	109.1	111.6	112.4	116.7	119.2	Généraux
Food		96.5	99.7	101.5	103.1	104.6	107.4	111.9	116.6	Alimentation
Occupied Palestinian Terr.										**Terr. palestinien occupé**
General		107.0	111.7	115.1	119.1	123.6	126.9	139.3[2]	143.1	Généraux
Food		102.1	106.8	109.1	113.3	118.8	124.3	147.4[2]	152.7	Alimentation
Oman	Muscat									**Oman**
General		98.3	97.9	98.3	100.2[2]	103.3	108.5	122.6	128.4	Généraux
Food [9]		98.3	98.2	98.5	102.7[2]	108.3	118.9	145.2	150.2	Alimentation [9]
Pakistan										**Pakistan**
General		107.4[2]	110.5	118.7	129.5	139.7	150.3	180.8	205.5	Généraux
Food		105.9[2]	108.6	120.2	132.1	143.3	158.8	202.6	229.6	Alimentation

27 Consumer price indices *(continued)*

General and food (Index base: 2000 = 100)

Indices des prix à la consommation *(suite)*

Généraux et alimentation (Indices base : 2000 = 100)

Country or area	City - Ville	2002	2003	2004	2005	2006	2007	2008	2009	Pays ou zone
Panama [12]										**Panama** [12]
General (2003 = 100)		...	100.0	100.4	103.3	105.9	110.3	119.9	122.8	Généraux (2003 = 100)
Food (2003 = 100)		...	100.0	101.3	105.6	107.0	114.2	131.3	138.8	Alimentation (2003 = 100)
Papua New Guinea										**Papouasie-Nvl-Guinée**
General		122.2	140.2	143.2	145.7	149.2	150.6	166.8	178.3	Généraux
Food		128.3	145.3	146.1	151.2	159.3	160.3	187.0	200.4	Alimentation
Paraguay	Asunción									**Paraguay**
General		118.5	135.4	141.3	149.5	165.4	178.8	196.9[2]	202.1	Généraux
Food		114.4	139.3	149.8	156.2	182.5	213.2	246.1[2]	247.5	Alimentation
Peru [7]	Lima									**Pérou** [7]
General		102.2[2]	104.5	108.3	110.1	112.3	114.3	120.9	124.4	Généraux
Food		100.2[2]	101.0	106.6	107.6	110.2	113.0	123.3	128.5	Alimentation
Philippines										**Philippines**
General		110.1	113.9	120.6	129.8	137.9	141.8	155.0	160.0	Généraux
Food [11]		107.1	109.4	116.3	123.8	130.6	134.9	152.3	161.1	Alimentation [11]
Poland										**Pologne**
General		107.5	108.4	112.2	114.6	115.8	118.6	123.6	127.9	Généraux
Food [8]		104.6	103.0	108.6	110.6	111.2	115.9	122.5	127.8	Alimentation [8]
Portugal										**Portugal**
General [4]		108.1[2]	111.6	114.2	116.7	120.4	123.3	126.4[2]	125.2	Généraux [4]
Food		108.1[2]	110.9	112.1	111.3	114.2	117.0	121.1[2]	116.9	Alimentation
Puerto Rico										**Porto Rico**
General		113.6	122.5	137.1	156.1	179.0	191.1[2]	209.4	218.5	Généraux
Food		127.8	145.8	176.3	212.1	257.1	281.0[2]	331.5	377.5	Alimentation
Qatar										**Qatar**
General		101.6	104.0	111.0	120.9	135.2	153.6	176.9	...	Généraux
Food [9]		101.1	100.7	104.4	107.7	115.1	123.6	148.2	...	Alimentation [9]
Republic of Moldova										**République de Moldova**
General		115.6	129.2	145.3	162.7	183.5	206.2	232.6	232.4	Généraux
Food		115.5	131.2	147.9	168.0	183.4	203.4	234.8	221.6	Alimentation
Réunion										**Réunion**
General		105.1	106.3	108.1	110.4	113.2	114.8	118.2	118.8	Généraux
Food		108.3	107.5	107.5	108.8	111.2	114.0	121.5	124.3	Alimentation
Romania										**Roumanie**
General		164.8	189.9	212.5	231.7	246.9	258.8	279.1	294.7	Généraux
Food		160.5	184.1	201.5	213.8	222.0	230.7	251.9	260.1	Alimentation
Russian Federation										**Fédération de Russie**
General		140.6	159.9	177.3	199.7	219.1	238.8	272.5	...	Généraux
Food		136.5	151.8	167.4	190.3	208.4	227.2	274.6	...	Alimentation
Rwanda	Kigali									**Rwanda**
General		105.4	113.2[2]	126.7	138.3	150.6	164.2	189.5	210.8[2]	Généraux
Food		104.7	119.2[2]	141.7	156.1	171.5	185.0	215.2	248.3[2]	Alimentation
Saint Helena										**Sainte-Hélène**
General		104.2	108.1	112.5	115.8	120.8	126.4	136.5	147.3	Généraux
Food		99.0	102.7	108.8	112.7	117.1	117.2	131.2	150.6	Alimentation
Saint Lucia										**Sainte-Lucie**
General		105.0	106.0	107.6	111.8	114.4	...	...	...	Généraux
Food		101.9	104.1	104.9	112.4	116.1	...	...	...	Alimentation
Saint Pierre and Miquelon										**Saint-Pierre-et-Miquelon**
General		102.5	104.8	106.9	114.0	...	...	...	...	Généraux
Food		106.1	106.7	104.9	109.7	...	...	...	...	Alimentation
Saint Vincent-Grenadines	St. Vincent									**Saint Vincent-Grenadines**
General		101.5	101.8	104.8	108.7	112.0	119.8	131.8	...	Généraux
Food		101.6	100.9	105.6	111.3	115.3	123.9	142.1	...	Alimentation
Samoa										**Samoa**
General [4]		112.2	112.3	130.5[2]	133.0	138.1	145.7	162.4	...	Généraux [4]
Food		117.3	115.1	146.2[2]	146.7	152.5	164.3	187.5	...	Alimentation
San Marino										**Saint-Marin**
General (2003 = 100)		...	#100.0[3]	101.4	103.1	105.3	107.9	112.6	115.0	Généraux (2003 = 100)
Food (2003 = 100)		...	#100.0[3]	103.3	108.9	115.0	120.7	130.4	133.6	Alimentation (2003 = 100)

27

Consumer price indices *(continued)*
General and food (Index base: 2000 = 100)

Indices des prix à la consommation *(suite)*
Généraux et alimentation (Indices base : 2000 = 100)

Country or area	City - Ville	2002	2003	2004	2005	2006	2007	2008	2009	Pays ou zone
Sao Tome and Principe										**Sao Tomé-et-Principe**
General (1996 = 100)		385.0	422.7	478.9	561.0	690.4	818.5	1 080.4	1 263.6	Généraux (1996 = 100)
Food (1996 = 100)[6]		330.6	361.2	414.9	484.0	612.2	744.9	1 027.5	1 244.9	Alimentation (1996 = 100)[6]
Saudi Arabia[31]										**Arabie saoudite**[31]
General		98.6	97.3	99.5[2]	100.2	102.4	106.7	117.2	...	Généraux
Food[9]		100.0	96.9	104.4[2]	107.5	113.3	121.2	138.3	...	Alimentation[9]
Senegal	Dakar									**Sénégal**
General		105.4	105.3	105.9	107.7	110.0	116.4	123.1	121.8	Généraux
Food[9]		110.1	109.4	110.3	114.5	116.0	124.4	136.4	132.3	Alimentation[9]
Serbia										**Serbie**
General		233.0	256.1	284.2	330.0	368.7	392.4	442.8	477.3	Généraux
Food		209.8	211.5	235.1	280.9	310.1	328.7	397.4	414.7	Alimentation
Seychelles										**Seychelles**
General		106.3	109.8	114.0	115.1	114.6	122.1[2]	167.3	220.4	Généraux
Food		105.6	108.3	109.2	110.4	114.3	125.6[2]	173.8	244.6	Alimentation
Sierra Leone										**Sierra Leone**
General (2003 = 100)		...	100.0	114.9	131.8	142.5	160.8	182.6	199.0	Généraux (2003 = 100)
Food (2003 = 100)		...	100.0	120.1	137.6	141.0	159.3	186.4	203.2	Alimentation (2003 = 100)
Singapore										**Singapour**
General		100.6	101.1	102.8[2]	103.2	104.2	106.4	113.4	113.6[2]	Généraux
Food		100.5	101.1	103.2[2]	104.6	106.2	109.4	117.8	120.5[2]	Alimentation
Slovakia										**Slovaquie**
General		110.7	120.2	129.2	132.8	138.7	142.5	149.0	151.5	Généraux
Food		107.4	111.0	116.4	114.7	116.4	121.0	130.3	126.1	Alimentation
Slovenia[12]										**Slovénie**[12]
General		116.5	123.0	127.4	130.6[2]	133.8	138.6	146.5	147.7	Généraux
Food		117.5	123.1	124.2	124.3[2]	127.1	137.0	150.8	151.6	Alimentation
Solomon Islands	Honiara									**Iles Salomon**
General		119.5	129.4	138.7	149.3	161.2	178.1[2]	208.6	...	Généraux
Food		122.1	125.0	136.8	145.1	156.7	168.1[2]	208.7	...	Alimentation
South Africa										**Afrique du Sud**
General		115.4	122.1	123.8	128.0	134.0	143.5	160.0	171.4	Généraux
Food		122.0	131.9	134.9	137.9	147.8	163.1	190.0	#109.5[32]	Alimentation
Spain										**Espagne**
General		103.5	106.7	109.9	113.6	117.6[2]	120.9	125.8	125.5	Généraux
Food		104.7	109.0	113.2	116.3	121.5[2]	126.0	133.4	132.0	Alimentation
Sri Lanka	Colombo									**Sri Lanka**
General		125.1	133.0	143.0	159.7	181.5	#163.1[3,33]	199.9	206.8	Généraux
Food		127.5	134.9	145.5	163.0	184.6	#163.4[3,33]	213.3	219.2	Alimentation
Suriname	Paramaribo									**Suriname**
General (2001 = 100)		115.9	...	156.9[34]	171.4	190.7	203.0	232.8	...	Généraux (2001 = 100)
Food (2001 = 100)		118.1	...	157.8[34]	174.3	182.7	198.0	246.8	...	Alimentation (2001 = 100)
Swaziland										**Swaziland**
General		120.3	129.1	133.5	139.9	147.3	159.2[2]	179.8	193.2	Généraux
Food		129.8	145.7	155.7	169.2	194.1[2]	228.3	271.5	...	Alimentation
Sweden										**Suède**
General		104.6	106.6	107.0	107.5	109.0	111.4	115.2	114.9	Généraux
Food		106.2	106.6	106.1	105.4	106.2	108.3	115.8	119.2	Alimentation
Switzerland										**Suisse**
General		101.7	102.3	103.1	104.4	105.4[2]	106.1	108.8	108.2	Généraux
Food		104.4	105.7	106.3	105.5	105.4	106.0	109.3	109.1	Alimentation
Syrian Arab Republic										**Rép. arabe syrienne**
General		101.4	108.8[2]	113.5	121.9	134.1[2]	140.1	161.4	165.9	Généraux
Food		99.6	107.2[2]	112.8	122.5	138.1[2]	150.6	181.8	182.2	Alimentation
Thailand										**Thaïlande**
General		102.3	104.1	107.0[2]	111.8	117.0	119.6	126.1	125.0[2]	Généraux
Food		101.0	104.7	109.4[2]	114.9	120.1	125.0	139.4	145.6[2]	Alimentation
TFYR of Macedonia										**L'ex-R.Y. Macédoine**
General		107.4	108.7	108.3	108.8	112.3	114.9	124.4	123.4	Généraux
Food		108.8	107.3	104.0	102.7	105.0	109.1	125.8	123.8	Alimentation

Consumer price indices *(continued)*

General and food (Index base: 2000 = 100)

Indices des prix à la consommation *(suite)*

Généraux et alimentation (Indices base : 2000 = 100)

Country or area	City - Ville	2002	2003	2004	2005	2006	2007	2008	2009	Pays ou zone
Togo	Lomé									**Togo**
General		107.1	106.0	106.5	113.7	116.3	117.3	127.5	...	Généraux
Food [11]		109.3	103.1	101.9	113.0	111.7	114.9	138.3	...	Alimentation [11]
Tonga										**Tonga**
General [4]		119.6[2]	133.5	148.1	160.4	172.0	180.8	198.9	202.5	Généraux [4]
Food		130.6[2]	143.1	156.1	165.5	170.4	182.9	197.7	212.5	Alimentation
Trinidad and Tobago										**Trinité-et-Tobago**
General		110.0	114.2[2]	118.3	126.5	137.0	147.9	165.7	177.2	Généraux
Food		125.6	142.9[2]	161.1	198.1	244.1	286.7	360.9	406.7	Alimentation
Tunisia										**Tunisie**
General		104.8	107.6	111.5	113.8	118.9	122.6	128.8	133.6	Généraux
Food [8]		106.1	109.7	115.1	115.2	121.4	124.8	132.6	138.3	Alimentation [8]
Turkey										**Turquie**
General		223.8	280.4	310.1	329.5[2]	361.1	392.7	433.7	460.8	Généraux
Food		225.3[11]	290.0[11]	316.1[11]	#112.1[3,35]	123.0	138.2	155.9	168.4	Alimentation
Tuvalu	Funafuti									**Tuvalu**
General		106.7[2]	110.2	113.3	117.0	119.0	121.6[2]	...	...	Généraux
Food		109.4[2]	117.4	120.8	127.4	129.2	128.6[2]	...	...	Alimentation
Uganda										**Ouganda**
General		101.6	110.5	114.5	124.1	133.3	141.4[2]	158.5	179.2	Généraux
Food		92.5	106.7	111.4	126.1	139.1	142.8[2]	171.1	213.9	Alimentation
Ukraine										**Ukraine**
General		112.8	118.7	129.4	146.9	160.2	180.8	226.4	262.4	Généraux
Food [11]		114.4	121.5	135.1	157.5	166.6	182.4	247.0	273.9	Alimentation [11]
United Arab Emirates										**Emirats arabes unis**
General		105.8	109.1	114.6	121.7	133.0	147.8	166.0[2]	...	Généraux
Food		102.4[11]	104.7[11]	112.0[11]	117.0[11]	123.5[11]	130.4	#116.3[3,18]	...	Alimentation
United Kingdom										**Royaume-Uni**
General		103.5	106.5	109.6	112.7	116.3	121.3	126.1	125.5	Généraux
Food		104.0	105.4	106.0	107.3	109.6	114.6	125.2	131.8	Alimentation
United Rep. of Tanzania [36]										**Rép.-Unie de Tanzanie** [36]
General		109.9[2]	115.8	121.3	127.4	136.6	146.2	161.2	180.8	Généraux
Food		110.5[2]	117.8	127.5	133.5	142.9	152.9	172.3	202.4	Alimentation
United States [37]										**Etats-Unis** [37]
General		104.5	106.9	109.7	113.4	117.1	120.4	125.0	...	Généraux
Food		105.0	107.3	111.0	113.7	116.3	120.9	127.6	...	Alimentation
Uruguay	Montevideo									**Uruguay**
General		118.9	142.0	155.0	162.3	172.7	186.7	201.4	215.6	Généraux
Food		117.2	142.5	159.2	165.7	176.0	202.5	230.3	245.0	Alimentation
Vanuatu										**Vanuatu**
General		105.7	108.8	110.4	111.7	114.0	118.5	124.2	...	Généraux
Food		102.7	105.0	108.6	108.1	111.8	116.1	125.5	...	Alimentation
Venezuela (Boliv. Rep. of)	Caracas									**Venezuela (Rép. boliv. du)**
General		137.8	180.6	219.9	255.0	289.8	343.9	452.1[2]	581.4	Généraux
Food		149.0	205.2	274.6	332.5	399.3	506.3	738.0[2]	958.3	Alimentation
Viet Nam										**Viet Nam**
General		103.7	107.0	115.0	125.5	133.4[2]	143.8	177.0	...	Généraux
Food		106.1[11]	108.7[11]	119.8[11]	#136.2[3]	#144.8[2]	156.0	192.1	...	Alimentation
Yemen										**Yémen**
General		125.6	139.2	156.6	174.5	211.6	232.8	249.1[2]	...	Généraux
Food		121.2	141.4	168.3	199.9	269.5	317.9	323.2[2]	...	Alimentation
Zambia										**Zambie**
General		148.4	180.1	212.5	251.4	274.1	303.3	341.1	386.8	Généraux
Food [11]		151.1	184.5	214.7	254.5	267.1	281.1	319.9	365.5	Alimentation [11]
Zanzibar										**Zanzibar**
General (2001 = 100)		105.2	114.7	124.0	136.1	...	...	...	...	Généraux (2001 = 100)
Food (2001 = 100)		106.9	116.8	128.6	143.7	...	...	...	...	Alimentation (2001 = 100)
Zimbabwe [38]										**Zimbabwe** [38]
General		0.4	1.9	8.4	28.4	316.6	21 602.0	...	...	Généraux
Food		0.4	1.8	8.6	27.9	316.0	23 620.2	...	...	Alimentation

27

Consumer price indices *(continued)*
General and food (Index base: 2000 = 100)

Indices des prix à la consommation *(suite)*
Généraux et alimentation (Indices base : 2000 = 100)

Source:
International Labour Organization (ILO), Geneva, the ILO labour statistics database, last accessed October 2010.

1 Food only.
2 Series linked to former series.
3 Series replacing former series.
4 Excluding rent.
5 December.
6 Including beverages and tobacco.
7 Metropolitan area.
8 Including alcoholic beverages.
9 Including tobacco.
10 Government officials.
11 Including alcoholic beverages and tobacco.
12 Urban areas.
13 Douala and Yaoundé only.
14 Low-income group.
15 African population.
16 Excluding beverages.
17 Central area.
18 Index base: 2007=100
19 Excluding tobacco.
20 Including tobacco, beverages and public catering.
21 Index base: 2005=100.
22 Index base: 2004=100.
23 Five cities.
24 July-December.
25 Annual averages are based on the months February-December and the mean of January the following year.
26 Industrial workers.
27 May-December.
28 January-November.
29 Including restaurant meals and ready to eat food.
30 Average of the last three quarters.
31 All cities.
32 Index base: 2008=100
33 Index base: 2002=100.
34 March-December.
35 Index base: 2003=100.
36 Tanganyika only.
37 All urban consumers.
38 Due to lack of space, multiply each figure by 1000.

Source:
Bureau international du Travail (BIT), Genève, la base de données du BIT, dernier accès octobre 2010.

1 Alimentation seulement.
2 Série enchaînée à la précédente.
3 Série remplaçant la précédente.
4 Non compris le groupe "Loyer".
5 Décembre.
6 Y compris les boissons et le tabac.
7 Région métropolitaine.
8 Y compris les boissons alcoolisées.
9 Y compris le tabac.
10 Fonctionnaires.
11 Y compris les boissons alcoolisées et le tabac.
12 Régions urbaines.
13 Douala et Yaoundé seulement.
14 Familles à revenu modique.
15 Population Africaine.
16 Non compris les boissons.
17 Région centrale.
18 Base de l'indice: 2007=100.
19 Non compris le tabac.
20 Y compris le tabac, les boissons et la restauration.
21 Base de l'indice: 2005=100.
22 Indice base : 2004=100.
23 Cinq villes.
24 Juillet-décembre.
25 Les moyennes annuelles sont basées sur les mois de février-décembre et la moyenne de janvier de l'année suivante.
26 Ouvriers industriels.
27 Mai-décembre.
28 Janvier-novembre.
29 Y compris les repas au restaurant et plats à emporter.
30 Moyenne des trois derniers trimestres.
31 Ensemble des villes.
32 Base de l'indice: 2008=100
33 Indice base : 2002=100.
34 Mars-décembre.
35 Base de l'indice: 2003=100.
36 Tanganyika seulement.
37 Tous les consommateurs urbains.
38 En raison du manque de place, multiplier chaque chiffre par 1000.

Technical notes: tables 26 and 27

Table 26: The producer price index (PPI) can be generally described as an index for measuring the average change in the prices of goods and services either as they leave the place of production or as they enter the production process. As such, producer price indices can represent input prices (at purchasers' prices) and output prices (at basic or producer prices) with different levels of aggregation.

The industrial coverage of the PPI can vary across countries. Normally, the PPIs refer to indices related to the agricultural, mining, manufacturing, transport and telecommunications, and public utilities sectors. Many countries are progressively developing service industry PPIs for incorporation within their larger PPI frameworks. PPI prices should be actual transaction prices recorded at the time the transaction occurs (i.e. when ownership changes).

PPIs can be calculated in a number of different combinations. In this publication, the PPIs are classified according to the following scheme:

(a) Components of supply
- Domestic supply
- Domestic production for domestic market
- Agricultural products
- Industrial products
- Imported goods

(b) Stage of processing
- Raw materials
- Intermediate goods

(c) End-use
- Consumer goods
- Capital goods

Though a few countries are still compiling the wholesale price index (WPI), which is the precedent of the PPI, the WPI has been replaced in most countries by the PPI because of the broader coverage provided by the PPI in terms of products and industries and the conceptual concordance between the PPI and the System of National Accounts. The WPI would normally cover the price of products as they flow from the wholesaler to the retailer and is an index for measuring the price level changes in markets other than retail.

For a more detailed explanation about the PPI, please refer to the *Producer Price Index Manual: Theory and Practice* published by the International Monetary Fund in 2004.

Table 27: A consumer price index is usually estimated as a series of summary measures of the period-to-period proportional change in the prices of a fixed set of consumer goods and services of constant quantity and characteristics, acquired, used or paid for by the reference population. Each summary measure is constructed

Notes techniques : tableaux 26 et 27

Tableau 26: L'indice des prix à la production peut être caractérisé de manière générale comme un indice permettant de mesurer le changement moyen des prix des biens et des services soit au moment où ils quittent le lieu de production soit au moment où ils arrivent au processus de production. Les indices des prix à la production peuvent donc représenter les prix des intrants (aux prix d'acquisition) et les prix à la sortie de fabrique (aux prix de base, ou prix à la production), les agrégats étant de différents niveaux.

Les branches d'activité couvertes par l'indice des prix à la production peuvent n'être pas les mêmes d'un pays à l'autre. Normalement, l'indice concerne l'agriculture, les industries extractives, les industries manufacturières, les transports et télécommunications et les services publics de distribution. Nombre de pays mettent peu à peu au point des indices des prix à la production pour les services, de manière à pouvoir les intégrer à leurs indices des prix à la production plus généraux. Les prix servant pour ces indices doivent être des prix effectifs de transaction enregistrés au moment où s'effectue la transaction (au moment où le propriétaire change).

Les indices des prix à la production peuvent se calculer selon plusieurs combinaisons différentes. Dans la présente publication, on les classe de la manière ci-après:

(a) Eléments de l'offre
- Offre intérieure
- Production nationale pour le marché intérieur
- Produits agricoles
- Produits industriels
- Produits importés

(b) Stade de la transformation
- Matières premières
- Produits intermédiaires

(c) Utilisation finale
- Biens de consommation
- Biens d'équipement

Même s'il y a encore quelques pays qui compilent l'indice des prix de gros, qui est l'ancêtre de l'indice des prix à la production, la plupart l'ont remplacé par ce dernier, qui offre une couverture plus large de produits et de branches d'activité, et coïncide dans ses concepts avec le Système de comptabilité nationale. L'indice des prix de gros suivait normalement le prix des produits à mesure qu'ils passaient du grossiste au détaillant il permet de mesurer les changements du niveau des prix sur les marchés autres que le marché de détail.

Pour un complément de détails sur l'indice des prix à la production, on se reportera au "Producer Price Index

as a weighted average of a large number of elementary aggregate indices. Each of the elementary aggregate indices is estimated using a sample of prices for a defined set of goods and services obtained in, or by residents of, a specific region from a given set of outlets or other sources of consumption goods and services.

The table presents the general consumer price index for all groups of consumption items combined, and the food index including nonalcoholic beverages only. Where alcoholic beverages and/or tobacco are included, this is indicated in footnotes.

Manual, Theory and Practice" publié par le Fonds monétaire international en 2004.

Tableau 27: Un indice est généralement estimé à partir d'une suite de mesures synthétiques des variations relatives, d'une période à l'autre, des prix d'un ensemble fixe de biens et de services de consommation constants en quantité et par leurs caractéristiques, acquis, utilisés ou payés par la population de référence. Chaque mesure synthétique est obtenue comme une moyenne pondérée d'un grand nombre d'indices de prix d'agrégats élémentaires. L'indice de chaque agrégat élémentaire est estimé au moyen d'un échantillon de prix pour un ensemble fixe de biens et de services que se procurent les individus de la population de référence dans une région donnée, ou qui habitent cette région, auprès d'un ensemble spécifié de points de vente ou auprès d'autres fournisseurs de biens et de services de consommation.

Le tableau présente les indices généraux des prix à la consommation pour tous les groupes d'articles de consommation combinés, et un indice "Alimentation", y compris les boissons non alcoolisées seulement. Dans le cas où les boissons alcoolisées et/ou le tabac sont compris dans le groupe "alimentation", l'utilisateur sera informé par un appel de note.

28 Agricultural production

Index base: 1999-01 = 100

Production agricole

Indices base : 1999-01 = 100

Region, country or area Région, pays ou zone	Agriculture - Agriculture 2005	2006	2007	2008	2009	Food - Produits alimentaires 2005	2006	2007	2008	2009
World Monde	**112**	**114**	**116**	**120**	**121**	**112**	**113**	**116**	**121**	**121**
Africa Afrique	**117**	**122**	**121**	**127**	**129**	**118**	**124**	**122**	**128**	**131**
Algeria Algérie	137	143	131	131	161	137	143	131	131	161
Angola Angola	147	151	160	163	197	148	152	162	165	199
Benin Bénin	115	107	104	113	113	120	113	109	117	117
Botswana Botswana	111	113	113	113	113	111	113	113	113	113
Burkina Faso Burkina Faso	137	142	117	144	140	125	127	116	137	136
Burundi Burundi	110	110	111	109	109	112	109	113	110	110
Cameroon Cameroun	116	118	115	112	115	118	120	119	119	120
Cape Verde Cap-Vert	101	107	115	123	123	101	107	115	123	123
Central African Rep. Rép. centrafricaine	107	110	114	116	119	111	114	118	121	123
Chad Tchad	119	115	107	118	118	120	121	112	124	125
Comoros Comores	99	108	112	112	112	99	108	112	112	112
Congo Congo	117	122	120	124	124	117	122	120	124	124
Côte d'Ivoire Côte d'Ivoire	106	108	107	113	113	109	114	115	125	122
Dem. Rep. of the Congo Rép. dém. du Congo	97	97	97	97	97	97	97	98	98	98
Djibouti Djibouti	115	131	147	147	147	115	131	147	147	147
Egypt Egypte	115	121	128	130	135	116	122	130	132	137
Equatorial Guinea Guinée équatoriale	94	93	94	93	91	95	92	93	92	89
Eritrea Erythrée	104	114	123	124	124	104	115	124	125	125
Ethiopia Ethiopie	132	135	136	143	148	134	136	135	144	150
Gabon Gabon	100	101	103	103	103	100	101	103	103	103
Gambia Gambie	93	98	72	100	117	93	98	71	100	117
Ghana Ghana	127	129	130	144	154	127	130	131	145	155
Guinea Guinée	117	123	127	135	137	119	125	129	138	140
Guinea-Bissau Guinée-Bissau	113	119	121	121	122	113	119	121	121	122

28 Agricultural production (continued)
Index base: 1999-01=100

Production agricole (suite)
Indices base : 1999-01 = 100

Region, country or area Région, pays ou zone	Agriculture - Agriculture					Food - Produits alimentaires				
	2005	2006	2007	2008	2009	2005	2006	2007	2008	2009
Kenya Kenya	116	130	137	124	124	116	132	138	125	126
Lesotho Lesotho	94	92	94	75	75	92	89	92	72	72
Liberia Libéria	105	105	116	117	117	104	108	121	130	130
Libyan Arab Jamah. Jamah. arabe libyenne	104	102	108	108	108	103	102	108	108	108
Madagascar Madagascar	116	117	112	114	114	118	119	113	115	115
Malawi Malawi	89	121	138	142	142	86	119	139	137	137
Mali Mali	124	122	127	142	159	128	133	145	165	184
Mauritania Mauritanie	112	112	113	114	115	112	112	113	114	115
Mauritius Maurice	105	105	100	104	106	106	105	101	105	107
Morocco Maroc	123	147	122	137	137	123	148	123	138	137
Mozambique Mozambique	119	122	114	122	122	108	110	101	102	102
Namibia Namibie	96	97	102	100	100	96	96	102	100	100
Niger Niger	130	141	147	183	183	130	142	148	184	184
Nigeria Nigéria	123	132	124	132	133	123	132	124	133	133
Réunion Réunion	100	102	96	102	102	100	102	96	102	102
Rwanda Rwanda	124	129	129	133	134	125	129	130	134	134
Sao Tome and Principe Sao Tomé-et-Principe	102	107	112	109	111	102	107	113	109	111
Senegal Sénégal	101	88	78	121	129	101	87	78	121	130
Seychelles Seychelles	69	66	60	49	49	68	65	58	49	49
Sierra Leone Sierra Leone	170	204	201	200	200	173	208	205	204	204
Somalia Somalie	108	104	104	104	104	108	104	104	104	104
South Africa Afrique du Sud	111	108	108	121	119	112	109	110	123	120
Sudan Soudan	116	117	117	116	118	116	116	117	117	119
Swaziland Swaziland	113	113	109	109	109	117	117	114	114	114
Togo Togo	102	105	109	112	112	112	120	123	129	129
Tunisia Tunisie	118	122	123	126	116	118	122	123	126	116
Uganda Ouganda	105	104	106	109	111	106	105	107	109	111

28 Agricultural production *(continued)*
Index base: 1999-01=100

Production agricole *(suite)*
Indices base : 1999-01 = 100

Region, country or area Région, pays ou zone	Agriculture - Agriculture					Food - Produits alimentaires				
	2005	2006	2007	2008	2009	2005	2006	2007	2008	2009
United Rep. of Tanzania Rép.-Unie de Tanzanie	131	138	141	140	140	128	139	139	139	139
Western Sahara Sahara occidental	100	97	97	97	97	100	97	97	97	97
Zambia Zambie	127	130	128	130	144	113	120	117	119	135
Zimbabwe Zimbabwe	71	73	75	70	70	83	92	89	81	81
Americas Amériques	**112**	**113**	**118**	**120**	**119**	**111**	**113**	**119**	**121**	**120**
Antigua and Barbuda Antigua-et-Barbuda	103	105	108	112	112	103	105	108	112	112
Argentina Argentine	116	117	127	123	104	116	117	128	124	104
Bahamas Bahamas	104	109	115	115	115	104	109	115	115	115
Barbados Barbade	106	99	99	99	100	106	99	99	99	100
Belize Belize	113	121	111	108	105	113	121	111	108	105
Bermuda Bermudes	93	93	101	103	103	93	93	101	103	103
Bolivia (Plurinational State of) Bolivie (État plurinational de)	120	122	127	128	131	120	122	127	128	132
Brazil Brésil	127	131	141	149	146	126	131	140	148	146
British Virgin Islands Iles Vierges britanniques	100	100	100	100	100	100	100	100	100	100
Canada Canada	110	108	108	116	111	110	108	108	116	112
Cayman Islands Iles Caïmanes	97	97	97	97	97	97	97	97	97	97
Chile Chili	119	123	120	127	121	119	124	120	128	121
Colombia Colombie	114	117	121	127	129	114	117	122	128	129
Costa Rica Costa Rica	110	119	124	118	121	112	124	128	122	126
Cuba Cuba	90	77	84	85	88	90	77	84	85	89
Dominica Dominique	87	92	93	93	93	87	91	93	93	93
Dominican Republic Rép. dominicaine	117	129	132	129	129	119	130	134	131	131
Ecuador Equateur	126	131	134	140	144	128	135	138	144	149
El Salvador El Salvador	103	110	110	117	114	109	118	116	125	123
Falkland Is. (Malvinas) Iles Falkland (Malvinas)	99	99	103	103	103	96	96	103	103	103
French Guiana Guyane française	90	87	79	80	80	90	87	79	80	80
Greenland Groenland	99	99	99	99	99	99	99	99	99	99

28 Agricultural production *(continued)*

Index base: 1999-01=100

Production agricole *(suite)*

Indices base : 1999-01 = 100

Region, country or area Région, pays ou zone	Agriculture - Agriculture					Food - Produits alimentaires				
	2005	2006	2007	2008	2009	2005	2006	2007	2008	2009
Grenada Grenade	73	91	95	95	95	73	91	95	95	95
Guadeloupe Guadeloupe	88	80	79	80	80	88	80	79	80	80
Guatemala Guatemala	118	120	133	133	133	122	126	140	139	140
Guyana Guyana	92	96	96	97	97	92	96	96	97	97
Haiti Haïti	107	106	116	110	110	107	106	114	110	110
Honduras Honduras	139	145	146	146	145	145	151	153	154	152
Jamaica Jamaïque	99	105	103	102	102	99	105	103	101	102
Martinique Martinique	100	99	99	99	99	100	99	99	99	99
Mexico Mexique	109	115	117	119	117	109	115	117	120	118
Montserrat Montserrat	99	99	101	101	101	99	99	101	101	101
Netherlands Antilles Antilles néerlandaises	103	109	114	114	114	103	109	114	114	114
Nicaragua Nicaragua	130	128	136	131	131	131	132	136	135	135
Panama Panama	107	110	113	115	115	106	110	113	115	115
Paraguay Paraguay	122	132	148	145	126	123	135	154	153	134
Peru Pérou	121	132	136	145	149	122	132	137	147	151
Puerto Rico Porto Rico	91	93	94	94	94	91	93	93	94	94
Saint Kitts and Nevis Saint-Kitts-et-Nevis	63	57	60	65	65	63	57	60	65	65
Saint Lucia Sainte-Lucie	81	82	84	88	87	81	82	84	88	87
Saint Pierre and Miquelon Saint-Pierre-et-Miquelon	101	114	102	108	107	101	114	102	108	107
Saint Vincent-Grenadines Saint Vincent-Grenadines	110	111	116	117	117	110	112	117	118	118
Suriname Suriname	98	104	111	111	111	98	104	111	111	111
Trinidad and Tobago Trinité-et-Tobago	110	119	121	121	121	110	119	121	121	121
United States Etats-Unis	105	104	108	108	110	104	104	109	109	112
United States Virgin Is. Iles Vierges américaines	99	99	101	101	101	99	99	101	101	101
Uruguay Uruguay	124	130	126	137	143	126	132	128	140	146
Venezuela (Boliv. Rep. of) Venezuela (Rép. boliv. du)	104	110	117	123	123	105	111	118	124	124

28 Agricultural production *(continued)*
Index base: 1999-01=100

Production agricole *(suite)*
Indices base : 1999-01 = 100

Region, country or area Région, pays ou zone	Agriculture - Agriculture					Food - Produits alimentaires				
	2005	2006	2007	2008	2009	2005	2006	2007	2008	2009
Asia Asie	**116**	**119**	**123**	**126**	**128**	**115**	**118**	**122**	**126**	**128**
Afghanistan Afghanistan	121	109	120	105	126	123	110	122	106	128
Armenia Arménie	146	151	166	169	170	148	153	168	171	172
Azerbaijan Azerbaïdjan	141	140	141	147	154	139	142	145	153	162
Bahrain Bahreïn	112	127	127	118	118	112	127	127	118	118
Bangladesh Bangladesh	116	119	125	135	131	117	119	126	136	131
Bhutan Bhoutan	152	157	154	153	152	152	158	154	153	152
Brunei Darussalam Brunéi Darussalam	101	122	150	150	150	101	122	150	150	150
Cambodia Cambodge	140	152	160	174	182	141	153	161	175	183
China [1] Chine [1]	118	120	123	128	131	118	120	122	127	130
Cyprus Chypre	91	86	85	82	80	91	86	85	82	80
Georgia Géorgie	112	67	80	71	63	115	70	83	74	66
India Inde	108	114	122	124	121	107	112	121	123	119
Indonesia Indonésie	126	131	136	141	147	126	131	136	141	147
Iran (Islamic Rep. of) Iran (Rép. islamique d')	126	128	131	115	125	127	129	132	116	126
Iraq Iraq	109	115	112	92	94	110	117	113	94	95
Israel Israël	117	116	122	120	120	117	116	122	121	121
Japan Japon	97	96	96	97	95	97	96	97	97	95
Jordan Jordanie	132	138	138	146	148	132	138	138	146	148
Kazakhstan Kazakhstan	118	127	138	127	147	117	126	139	127	148
Korea, Dem. P. R. Corée, R. p. dém. de	115	113	106	111	111	115	114	107	112	112
Korea, Republic of Corée, République de	95	96	96	100	100	95	96	96	100	100
Kuwait Koweït	113	107	109	109	109	113	107	109	109	109
Kyrgyzstan Kirghizistan	100	101	103	103	108	101	103	105	106	112
Lao People's Dem. Rep. Rép. dém. pop. lao	122	124	135	150	152	125	128	136	149	152
Lebanon Liban	101	100	103	110	111	101	101	104	111	111
Malaysia Malaisie	126	132	132	141	139	125	131	132	143	143

Agricultural production *(continued)*

Index base: 1999-01=100

Production agricole *(suite)*

Indices base : 1999-01 = 100

Region, country or area Région, pays ou zone	Agriculture - Agriculture					Food - Produits alimentaires				
	2005	2006	2007	2008	2009	2005	2006	2007	2008	2009
Maldives Maldives	78	105	102	100	96	78	105	102	100	96
Mongolia Mongolie	71	72	78	89	109	71	72	78	88	109
Myanmar Myanmar	143	157	163	162	161	145	159	165	164	163
Nepal Népal	117	119	119	127	130	117	119	119	127	130
Occupied Palestinian Terr. Terr. palestinien occupé	111	99	100	101	100	111	99	100	101	100
Oman Oman	123	105	106	104	104	123	105	106	104	104
Pakistan Pakistan	115	117	122	126	130	115	117	124	128	132
Philippines Philippines	117	122	125	131	131	117	121	125	131	131
Qatar Qatar	63	67	81	81	81	63	67	81	81	81
Saudi Arabia Arabie saoudite	120	125	130	129	129	120	126	130	129	129
Singapore Singapour	97	111	115	104	120	97	111	115	104	120
Sri Lanka Sri Lanka	107	108	107	119	116	108	109	108	121	120
Syrian Arab Republic Rép. arabe syrienne	124	132	121	112	123	128	140	127	117	130
Tajikistan Tadjikistan	153	157	163	167	164	162	171	179	193	195
Thailand Thaïlande	111	114	125	125	125	110	114	125	125	125
Timor-Leste Timor-Leste	108	112	106	107	107	112	116	109	110	110
Turkey Turquie	110	112	107	111	114	111	113	109	114	117
Turkmenistan Turkménistan	143	126	131	130	130	152	142	138	141	141
United Arab Emirates Emirats arabes unis	63	62	61	63	63	63	62	61	63	63
Uzbekistan Ouzbékistan	129	137	139	149	149	132	145	150	159	169
Viet Nam Viet Nam	125	129	134	139	140	124	128	132	137	138
Yemen Yémen	113	123	135	140	144	112	122	135	139	144
Europe Europe	**101**	**100**	**99**	**105**	**104**	**101**	**100**	**99**	**105**	**104**
Albania Albanie	111	109	112	112	113	112	110	114	113	115
Austria Autriche	99	96	99	103	100	98	96	99	103	100
Belarus Bélarus	119	125	129	141	141	119	125	129	141	141
Belgium Belgique	95	94	96	94	97	95	94	96	94	97

28 Agricultural production *(continued)*
Index base: 1999-01=100
Production agricole *(suite)*
Indices base : 1999-01 = 100

Region, country or area Région, pays ou zone	Agriculture - Agriculture					Food - Produits alimentaires				
	2005	2006	2007	2008	2009	2005	2006	2007	2008	2009
Bosnia and Herzegovina Bosnie-Herzégovine	124	129	125	136	137	124	129	125	136	137
Bulgaria Bulgarie	82	86	67	92	86	80	86	66	92	85
Croatia Croatie	93	96	95	105	104	93	96	94	104	104
Czech Republic République tchèque	95	87	90	96	94	95	87	91	96	94
Denmark Danemark	102	100	102	106	107	102	100	102	106	107
Estonia Estonie	105	102	115	112	114	105	102	115	112	114
Faeroe Islands Iles Féroé	100	100	99	99	99	100	100	99	99	99
Finland Finlande	106	103	105	103	105	106	103	105	103	105
France France	97	93	92	95	97	97	93	92	95	97
Germany Allemagne	99	95	97	102	103	99	95	97	102	103
Greece Grèce	97	89	84	82	80	98	93	88	87	86
Hungary Hongrie	102	97	84	105	95	102	97	84	105	95
Iceland Islande	104	108	115	116	116	105	110	116	118	117
Ireland Irlande	95	96	96	95	92	95	96	96	95	92
Italy Italie	99	94	92	95	94	99	94	92	95	94
Latvia Lettonie	120	114	127	130	127	120	114	127	130	127
Liechtenstein Liechtenstein	100	100	96	96	96	100	100	96	96	96
Lithuania Lituanie	110	93	111	114	117	110	93	111	114	117
Luxembourg Luxembourg	97	98	95	101	101	97	98	95	101	102
Malta Malte	90	95	91	96	89	89	95	91	96	89
Netherlands Pays-Bas	94	94	95	98	100	94	94	95	98	100
Norway Norvège	97	97	98	101	94	97	97	98	101	94
Poland Pologne	95	93	99	99	102	95	93	99	99	102
Portugal Portugal	94	97	93	97	94	94	97	94	97	94
Republic of Moldova République de Moldova	110	104	80	113	99	112	107	82	116	102
Romania Roumanie	109	110	88	109	106	109	110	88	109	106
Russian Federation Fédération de Russie	113	115	116	124	122	113	115	116	124	122

28 Agricultural production *(continued)*

Index base: 1999-01=100

Production agricole *(suite)*

Indices base : 1999-01 = 100

Region, country or area Région, pays ou zone	Agriculture - Agriculture					Food - Produits alimentaires				
	2005	2006	2007	2008	2009	2005	2006	2007	2008	2009
Serbia and Montenegro Serbie-et-Monténégro	108	...	...	...	...	108	...	...	...	...
Slovakia Slovaquie	104	96	91	103	92	104	96	91	103	92
Slovenia Slovénie	102	97	95	97	95	102	97	95	97	95
Spain Espagne	96	103	102	103	99	96	103	103	103	100
Sweden Suède	97	91	93	94	97	97	92	93	94	97
Switzerland Suisse	99	99	101	103	105	99	99	101	103	105
TFYR of Macedonia L'ex-R.Y. Macédoine	105	106	108	113	114	105	107	110	117	116
Ukraine Ukraine	118	118	110	137	129	118	118	110	137	129
United Kingdom Royaume-Uni	98	98	95	100	98	98	98	95	100	98
Oceania Océanie	**103**	**92**	**94**	**99**	**98**	**105**	**94**	**98**	**104**	**102**
American Samoa Samoa américaines	124	126	126	126	126	124	126	126	126	126
Australia Australie	99	83	85	92	92	102	84	89	98	97
Cook Islands Iles Cook	51	51	63	63	63	51	51	63	63	63
Fiji Fidji	100	103	94	93	89	100	103	94	93	89
French Polynesia Polynésie française	117	109	112	111	111	117	109	112	111	111
Guam Guam	106	108	108	109	109	106	108	108	109	109
Kiribati Kiribati	125	125	128	125	125	125	125	128	125	125
Marshall Islands Iles Marshall	224	230	303	303	303	224	230	303	303	303
Micronesia (Fed. States of) Micronésie (Etats féd. de)	100	99	103	103	103	100	99	103	103	103
Nauru Nauru	100	100	106	106	106	100	100	106	106	106
New Caledonia Nouvelle-Calédonie	101	98	104	104	103	101	99	104	104	103
New Zealand Nouvelle-Zélande	113	115	117	116	113	115	116	119	118	114
Niue Nioué	101	101	105	105	105	101	101	105	105	105
Papua New Guinea Papouasie-Nvl-Guinée	109	114	118	118	118	109	115	119	119	119
Samoa Samoa	110	109	113	112	113	110	109	113	112	113
Solomon Islands Iles Salomon	117	114	117	118	119	117	114	117	118	119
Tokelau Tokélaou	100	100	100	100	100	100	100	100	100	100

28 Agricultural production *(continued)*

Index base: 1999-01=100

Production agricole *(suite)*

Indices base : 1999-01 = 100

Region, country or area Région, pays ou zone	Agriculture - Agriculture					Food - Produits alimentaires				
	2005	2006	2007	2008	2009	2005	2006	2007	2008	2009
Tonga Tonga	102	107	107	107	107	102	107	107	107	107
Tuvalu Tuvalu	111	111	114	114	114	111	111	114	114	114
Vanuatu Vanuatu	107	108	110	109	108	107	108	110	109	108
Wallis and Futuna Islands Iles Wallis et Futuna	99	101	104	104	104	99	101	104	104	104

Source:
Food and Agriculture Organization of the United Nations (FAO), Rome, FAOSTAT database, last accessed September 2010.

Source:
Organisation des Nations Unies pour l'alimentation et l'agriculture (FAO), Rome, la base de données FAOSTAT, dernier accès septembre 2010.

1 For statistical purposes, the data for China do not include those for the Hong Kong Special Administrative Region (Hong Kong SAR) and Macao Special Administrative Region (Macao SAR).

1 Pour la présentation des statistiques, les données pour la Chine ne comprennent pas la Région Administrative Spéciale de Hong Kong (Hong Kong RAS) et la Région Administrative Spéciale de Macao (Macao RAS).

29 Cereals

Production: thousand metric tons

Céréales

Production: milliers de tonnes

Region, country or area Région, pays ou zone	1999	2000	2001	2002	2003	2004	2005	2006	2007	2008
World Monde	**2 085 346**	**2 060 394**	**2 108 564**	**2 030 653**	**2 089 516**	**2 280 747**	**2 268 603**	**2 237 269**	**2 348 996**	**2 525 107**
Africa Afrique	**113 636**	**111 657**	**116 444**	**119 318**	**133 049**	**134 011**	**142 228**	**148 748**	**137 269**	**151 372**
Algeria Algérie	2 021	935	2 659	1 953	4 266	4 033	3 528	4 018	3 590	3 584
Angola Angola	541	510	586	717	717	668	871	724	731	731
Benin Bénin	974	993	943	926	1 043	1 109	1 152	934	1 159	1 298
Botswana Botswana	21	25	23	35	36	21	22	39	40	40
Burkina Faso Burkina Faso	2 700	2 286	3 109	3 119	3 564	2 902	3 650	3 681	3 109	4 326
Burundi Burundi	265	245	273	282	279	280	288	286	291	291
Cameroon Cameroun	1 185	1 275	1 356	1 499	1 584	1 684	1 660	1 412	1 512	1 512
Cape Verde Cap-Vert	36	24	20	5	12	10	4	4	3	12
Central African Rep. Rép. centrafricaine	161	166	183	193	202	210	230	236	246	246
Chad Tchad	1 231	930	1 321	1 212	1 618	1 213	1 853	1 913	1 972	2 019
Comoros Comores	21	21	21	21	21	21	21	21	21	21
Congo Congo	9	10	18	18	20	21	21	21	21	21
Côte d'Ivoire Côte d'Ivoire	1 264	1 286	1 308	1 330	1 334	1 378	1 425	1 442	1 244	1 472
Dem. Rep. of the Congo Rép. dém. du Congo	1 593	1 572	1 546	1 520	1 521	1 522	1 523	1 524	1 525	1 526
Egypt Egypte	19 401	20 106	18 561	20 194	20 682	20 823	22 411	22 503	21 565	22 811
Eritrea Erythrée	319	121	183	52	99	80	152	199	197	197
Ethiopia Ethiopie	8 393	8 020	9 586	9 002	9 533	10 697	13 365	13 390	11 846	13 012
Gabon Gabon	28	27	26	25	32	32	32	33	34	34
Gambia Gambie	151	176	200	139	205	224	206	215	151	235
Ghana Ghana	1 686	1 711	1 627	2 155	2 041	1 830	1 948	1 919	1 852	1 852
Guinea Guinée	1 656	1 801	1 721	1 846	1 984	2 136	2 290	2 445	2 601	3 188
Guinea-Bissau Guinée-Bissau	145	178	162	151	143	171	213	225	184	217
Kenya Kenya	2 802	2 591	3 369	3 046	3 352	3 199	3 585	3 937	3 614	2 861
Lesotho Lesotho	174	150	255	150	116	109	112	119	84	139
Liberia Libéria	196	183	145	110	100	110	155	164	232	295

29

Cereals *(continued)*
Production: thousand metric tons

Céréales *(suite)*
Production: milliers de tonnes

Region, country or area Région, pays ou zone	1999	2000	2001	2002	2003	2004	2005	2006	2007	2008
Libyan Arab Jamah. Jamah. arabe libyenne	213	222	218	217	217	218	234	213	213	209
Madagascar Madagascar	2 756	2 660	2 853	2 787	3 129	3 391	3 795	3 991	3 382	3 382
Malawi Malawi	2 636	2 631	1 866	1 711	2 143	1 718	1 302	2 786	3 440	2 846
Mali Mali	2 894	2 310	2 584	2 532	3 402	2 845	3 399	3 693	3 886	4 057
Mauritania Mauritanie	194	180	124	113	117	120	175	175	177	183
Mauritius Maurice	^0	1	^0	^0	^0	^0	^0	^0	1	1
Morocco Maroc	3 843	1 997	4 603	5 288	7 970	8 600	4 280	9 236	2 505	5 331
Mozambique Mozambique	1 912	1 587	1 585	1 662	1 813	2 007	1 922	1 747	1 454	1 601
Namibia Namibie	74	121	107	100	97	117	106	139	119	119
Niger Niger	2 853	2 127	3 162	3 243	3 568	2 730	3 669	4 034	3 844	5 010
Nigeria Nigéria	22 405	21 370	20 090	21 373	22 736	24 321	26 031	28 864	27 171	30 209
Réunion Réunion	12	12	12	12	12	12	3	12	12	12
Rwanda Rwanda	179	240	285	308	298	319	413	366	366	366
Sao Tome and Principe Sao Tomé-et-Principe	1	2	3	3	3	3	3	3	3	3
Senegal Sénégal	1 131	1 026	1 023	785	1 452	1 054	1 433	988	772	1 612
Sierra Leone Sierra Leone	280	222	334	466	496	614	824	1 163	1 100	1 100
Somalia Somalie	299	392	429	442	403	366	359	261	196	196
South Africa Afrique du Sud	10 065	14 528	10 706	13 046	11 821	12 028	14 177	9 454	9 514	14 467
Sudan Soudan	3 066	3 259	5 339	3 714	6 373	3 516	6 193	5 806	6 691	5 269
Swaziland Swaziland	125	114	84	69	70	69	76	68	27	27
Togo Togo	759	741	815	801	807	799	833	886	878	940
Tunisia Tunisie	1 837	1 118	1 391	550	2 318	2 164	2 136	1 649	2 027	1 227
Uganda Ouganda	2 178	2 112	2 309	2 368	2 508	2 274	2 459	2 557	2 631	2 716
United Rep. of Tanzania Rép.-Unie de Tanzanie	4 008	3 617	4 526	6 359	4 095	6 691	5 367	5 698	6 223	6 227
Western Sahara Sahara occidental	3	2	2	2	2	2	2	2	2	2
Zambia Zambie	1 003	1 208	950	755	1 366	1 381	1 067	1 604	1 537	1 630
Zimbabwe Zimbabwe	1 938	2 519	1 846	909	1 329	2 169	1 257	1 947	1 272	690

29 Cereals *(continued)*

Production: thousand metric tons

Céréales *(suite)*

Production: milliers de tonnes

Region, country or area Région, pays ou zone	1999	2000	2001	2002	2003	2004	2005	2006	2007	2008
Northern America Amérique septentrionale	**389 630**	**393 899**	**368 473**	**333 168**	**397 493**	**439 879**	**417 507**	**387 186**	**463 274**	**459 803**
Canada Canada	54 078	51 090	43 391	36 047	49 189	50 778	50 962	48 577	48 109	56 031
United States Etats-Unis	335 553	342 809	325 082	297 121	348 304	389 101	366 544	338 609	415 166	403 772
Latin America and the Caribbean Amérique latine et Caraïbes	**133 835**	**138 310**	**151 016**	**138 646**	**163 066**	**163 007**	**153 197**	**157 670**	**180 492**	**186 908**
Argentina Argentine	35 036	38 755	35 914	31 844	34 586	35 881	38 162	34 204	44 187	36 681
Belize Belize	62	48	57	57	56	49	59	45	63	60
Bolivia Bolivie	1 137	1 244	1 325	1 316	1 463	1 256	1 660	1 866	1 749	1 749
Brazil Brésil	47 431	45 897	57 117	50 879	67 453	63 951	55 669	59 149	69 442	79 682
Chile Chili	2 168	2 590	3 116	3 380	3 693	3 999	3 989	3 566	2 823	3 302
Colombia Colombie	3 411	4 080	3 934	3 956	4 625	4 853	4 268	3 972	4 214	4 707
Costa Rica Costa Rica	292	285	229	201	198	210	196	189	199	260
Cuba Cuba	797	826	900	1 001	1 076	889	732	744	809	762
Dominican Republic Rép. dominicaine	605	610	771	766	656	620	634	658	687	672
Ecuador Equateur	1 847	1 909	1 644	2 065	2 055	2 607	2 304	2 278	2 726	2 285
El Salvador El Salvador	857	779	760	814	791	822	895	937	1 050	1 234
French Guiana Guyane française	20	20	32	22	23	26	18	15	9	9
Guatemala Guatemala	1 134	1 161	1 199	1 155	1 147	1 170	1 158	1 276	1 390	1 390
Guyana Guyana	565	453	498	446	550	505	424	472	463	511
Haiti Haïti	475	431	363	376	382	398	406	415	520	420
Honduras Honduras	562	607	603	579	594	502	531	619	711	711
Jamaica Jamaïque	2	2	2	2	2	2	2	2	2	2
Mexico Mexique	27 430	27 991	31 056	28 770	31 334	32 312	29 060	32 155	34 311	36 141
Nicaragua Nicaragua	572	783	755	911	1 002	799	964	895	864	820
Panama Panama	265	303	342	371	409	341	334	325	332	324
Paraguay Paraguay	1 156	1 003	1 628	1 549	1 908	2 064	1 569	2 951	2 865	2 867
Peru Pérou	3 395	3 554	3 737	3 844	3 920	3 438	4 132	4 057	4 205	4 589
Puerto Rico Porto Rico	1	^0	^0	^0	^0	^0	^0	1	1	1

29 Cereals *(continued)*
Production: thousand metric tons

Céréales *(suite)*
Production: milliers de tonnes

Region, country or area Région, pays ou zone	1999	2000	2001	2002	2003	2004	2005	2006	2007	2008
Saint Vincent-Grenadines Saint Vincent-Grenadines	1	1	1	1	1	1	1	1	1	1
Suriname Suriname	180	164	191	157	194	175	164	183	179	183
Trinidad and Tobago Trinité-et-Tobago	4	7	5	7	5	5	5	5	5	5
Uruguay Uruguay	2 194	1 860	1 718	1 606	1 827	2 523	2 276	2 648	2 677	3 531
Venezuela (Boliv. Rep. of) Venezuela (Rép. boliv. du)	2 234	2 948	3 117	2 569	3 116	3 606	3 584	4 044	4 008	4 008
Asia Asie	**1 035 989**	**996 337**	**1 001 382**	**982 926**	**997 598**	**1 038 032**	**1 086 893**	**1 120 050**	**1 153 714**	**1 188 096**
Afghanistan Afghanistan	3 257	1 940	2 108	3 737	4 381	3 560	5 425	4 638	5 778	3 668
Armenia Arménie	297	221	364	412	310	460	399	215	457	409
Azerbaijan Azerbaïdjan	1 069	1 496	1 956	2 133	1 993	2 087	2 056	2 012	1 944	2 420
Bangladesh Bangladesh	36 403	39 503	38 029	39 341	40 015	37 759	41 147	42 048	44 711	49 103
Bhutan Bhoutan	157	107	115	93	108	158	193	179	169	169
Brunei Darussalam Brunéi Darussalam	^0	^0	^0	^0	1	1	1	1	1	1
Cambodia Cambodge	4 136	4 183	4 285	3 971	5 026	4 427	6 234	6 641	7 250	7 787
China Chine	455 192	407 337	398 395	399 998	376 123	413 164	429 370	452 785	457 670	481 009
Cyprus Chypre	127	48	127	142	165	111	70	67	64	57
Georgia Géorgie	771	418	704	662	742	663	680	320	419	408
India Inde	236 206	234 931	242 964	206 637	236 593	229 846	239 998	242 786	260 486	266 582
Indonesia Indonésie	60 070	61 575	59 808	61 075	63 024	65 314	66 675	66 064	70 445	76 575
Iran (Islamic Rep. of) Iran (Rép. islamique d')	14 186	12 874	14 945	19 861	20 942	21 986	21 906	22 407	22 397	18 109
Iraq Iraq	1 605	904	1 819	4 125	3 516	3 308	3 697	5 772	3 758	3 758
Israel Israël	123	183	242	271	306	273	308	245	284	204
Japan Japon	12 283	12 796	12 255	12 184	10 824	11 994	12 434	11 742	12 026	12 134
Jordan Jordanie	27	57	48	115	80	53	102	62	50	38
Kazakhstan Kazakhstan	14 248	11 539	15 866	15 929	14 741	12 339	13 740	16 461	20 090	15 542
Korea, Dem. P. R. Corée, R. p. dém. de	3 837	2 945	3 880	4 211	4 393	4 485	4 644	4 676	4 373	4 679
Korea, Republic of Corée, République de	7 458	7 501	7 860	7 083	6 355	7 115	6 816	6 647	6 312	7 205
Kuwait Koweït	3	3	3	5	3	3	3	3	4	4
Kyrgyzstan Kirghizistan	1 618	1 550	1 795	1 712	1 634	1 709	1 622	1 504	1 418	1 440

29 Cereals *(continued)*

Production: thousand metric tons

Céréales *(suite)*

Production: milliers de tonnes

Region, country or area Région, pays ou zone	1999	2000	2001	2002	2003	2004	2005	2006	2007	2008
Lao People's Dem. Rep. Rép. dém. pop. lao	2 199	2 319	2 447	2 541	2 518	2 733	2 941	3 114	3 401	3 818
Lebanon Liban	93	123	153	140	146	165	177	190	154	154
Malaysia Malaisie	2 094	2 206	2 162	2 267	2 329	2 336	2 389	2 267	2 458	2 467
Mongolia Mongolie	170	142	142	126	165	139	77	139	115	213
Myanmar Myanmar	20 776	21 966	22 717	22 695	24 165	25 875	28 978	32 274	32 900	31 950
Nepal Népal	6 930	7 116	7 120	7 215	7 360	7 747	7 767	7 657	7 329	8 069
Occupied Palestinian Terr. Terr. palestinien occupé	14	68	40	77	68	62	68	66	56	56
Oman Oman	11	12	13	14	14	19	15	14	16	16
Pakistan Pakistan	27 756	30 461	27 048	27 173	28 964	30 311	33 508	33 028	35 813	35 971
Philippines Philippines	16 371	16 901	17 480	17 590	18 116	19 910	19 856	21 409	22 977	23 744
Qatar Qatar	7	7	7	7	7	5	7	7	7	7
Saudi Arabia Arabie saoudite	2 454	2 167	2 592	2 853	2 949	3 189	3 007	3 043	3 042	3 042
Sri Lanka Sri Lanka	2 894	2 896	2 728	2 890	3 106	2 668	3 295	3 396	3 193	3 994
Syrian Arab Republic Rép. arabe syrienne	3 301	3 513	6 921	5 932	6 227	5 281	5 631	6 301	5 011	5 011
Tajikistan Tadjikistan	474	545	478	688	866	860	903	893	907	909
Thailand Thaïlande	28 661	30 523	31 215	30 526	31 485	33 021	34 508	33 550	35 964	34 423
Timor-Leste Timor-Leste	104	139	123	147	136	133	143	155	105	105
Turkey Turquie	28 886	32 249	29 571	30 831	30 807	34 045	36 354	34 637	29 250	29 280
Turkmenistan Turkménistan	1 567	1 751	1 832	2 461	2 667	2 785	3 035	3 489	2 886	2 886
Uzbekistan Ouzbékistan	4 311	3 914	4 056	5 535	6 106	5 860	6 531	6 632	6 749	6 706
Viet Nam Viet Nam	33 149	34 537	34 272	36 960	37 707	39 581	39 622	39 706	40 248	43 258
Yemen Yémen	694	672	700	560	418	490	562	809	1 029	714
Europe Europe	**375 978**	**384 854**	**431 397**	**436 595**	**355 704**	**470 388**	**428 031**	**403 406**	**391 282**	**504 365**
Albania Albanie	498	566	503	519	489	499	511	508	494	519
Austria Autriche	4 809	4 494	4 830	4 461	4 519	5 606	5 195	4 469	4 767	5 757
Belarus Bélarus	3 413	4 565	4 871	5 710	5 117	6 590	6 089	5 685	7 014	8 715
Belgium Belgique	...	2 513	2 359	2 639	2 561	2 932	2 787	2 606	2 622	3 112
Belgium-Luxembourg Belgique-Luxembourg	2 449	...	...	...	...	...	...	...	...	...

29 Cereals *(continued)*
Production: thousand metric tons

Céréales *(suite)*
Production: milliers de tonnes

Region, country or area Région, pays ou zone	1999	2000	2001	2002	2003	2004	2005	2006	2007	2008
Bosnia and Herzegovina Bosnie-Herzégovine	1 369	930	1 138	1 308	793	1 439	1 350	1 341	1 001	1 329
Bulgaria Bulgarie	5 221	4 389	6 076	6 770	3 814	7 463	5 839	5 532	3 203	7 016
Croatia Croatie	2 883	2 770	3 396	3 722	2 355	3 258	3 041	3 037	2 536	3 728
Czech Republic République tchèque	6 935	6 460	7 347	6 784	5 773	8 792	7 668	6 394	7 161	8 383
Denmark Danemark	8 774	9 413	9 423	8 804	9 051	8 963	9 283	8 632	8 220	9 095
Estonia Estonie	402	697	558	525	506	608	760	619	879	864
Finland Finlande	2 882	4 103	3 671	3 938	3 791	3 619	4 059	3 790	4 135	4 229
France France	64 342	65 698	60 237	69 657	54 940	70 517	64 104	61 584	59 330	70 094
Germany Allemagne	44 461	45 271	49 686	43 391	39 320	51 110	45 980	43 475	40 632	50 105
Greece Grèce	4 576	4 968	4 939	4 827	4 710	5 088	5 084	4 693	4 654	5 252
Hungary Hongrie	11 392	10 036	15 046	11 703	8 770	16 779	16 212	14 467	9 670	16 948
Ireland Irlande	2 011	2 174	2 166	1 964	2 147	2 501	1 940	2 090	2 006	2 385
Italy Italie	21 068	20 661	19 933	21 248	17 864	23 283	21 423	20 207	20 351	21 624
Latvia Lettonie	784	924	928	1 029	932	1 060	1 314	1 159	1 535	1 689
Lithuania Lituanie	2 048	2 657	2 344	2 539	2 626	2 859	2 811	1 858	3 017	3 422
Luxembourg Luxembourg	...	153	144	169	164	179	161	161	148	191
Malta Malte	11	12	12	12	12	12	12	12	14	11
Montenegro Monténégro	...	...	...	...	...	...	...	14	10	11
Netherlands Pays-Bas	1 368	1 732	1 672	1 740	1 820	1 823	1 775	1 675	1 520	1 964
Norway Norvège	1 218	1 300	1 220	1 143	1 287	1 445	1 298	1 169	1 202	1 347
Poland Pologne	25 750	22 341	26 960	26 877	23 391	29 635	26 928	21 776	27 143	27 664
Portugal Portugal	1 678	1 608	1 298	1 497	1 186	1 363	790	1 167	1 103	1 292
Republic of Moldova République de Moldova	2 142	1 905	2 550	2 539	1 583	2 943	2 772	2 222	887	3 132
Romania Roumanie	17 037	10 499	18 900	14 357	12 966	24 402	19 350	15 760	7 816	16 827
Russian Federation Fédération de Russie	53 845	64 326	83 398	84 859	65 562	76 231	76 564	76 479	80 190	106 392
Serbia Serbie	...	...	...	...	...	...	...	8 277	6 124	8 715
Serbia and Montenegro Serbie-et-Monténégro	8 615	5 263	9 040	8 327	5 568	9 893	9 534	...	...	...
Slovakia Slovaquie	2 830	2 204	3 414	3 196	2 491	3 798	3 585	2 929	2 793	4 137

Cereals *(continued)*
Production: thousand metric tons

Céréales *(suite)*
Production: milliers de tonnes

Region, country or area Région, pays ou zone	1999	2000	2001	2002	2003	2004	2005	2006	2007	2008
Slovenia Slovénie	480	497	500	614	402	586	580	497	535	583
Spain Espagne	17 988	24 556	18 050	21 710	21 412	24 809	14 226	19 036	23 963	23 889
Sweden Suède	4 931	5 604	5 382	5 398	5 290	5 508	5 051	4 128	5 058	5 314
Switzerland Suisse	1 055	1 206	1 094	1 101	847	1 089	1 057	1 013	1 014	1 021
TFYR of Macedonia L'ex-R.Y. Macédoine	638	564	475	556	472	682	645	602	469	613
Ukraine Ukraine	23 950	23 807	38 879	37 995	19 662	40 997	37 258	33 511	28 938	52 714
United Kingdom Royaume-Uni	22 125	23 989	18 959	22 966	21 511	22 028	20 998	20 832	19 130	24 281
Oceania Océanie	**36 278**	**35 337**	**39 853**	**20 001**	**42 606**	**35 430**	**40 746**	**20 209**	**22 965**	**34 563**
Australia Australie	35 369	34 447	38 877	19 029	41 631	34 564	39 840	19 369	21 998	33 527
Fiji Fidji	18	14	15	14	17	15	16	14	15	12
New Caledonia Nouvelle-Calédonie	2	5	5	4	6	5	6	4	6	6
New Zealand Nouvelle-Zélande	873	854	938	936	936	829	866	805	927	999
Papua New Guinea Papouasie-Nvl-Guinée	11	11	13	13	10	10	11	11	12	12
Solomon Islands Iles Salomon	5	5	5	5	5	6	6	6	6	6
Vanuatu Vanuatu	1	1	1	1	1	1	1	1	1	1

Source:
Food and Agriculture Organization of the United Nations (FAO), Rome, FAOSTAT data, last accessed May 2010.

Source:
Organisation des Nations Unies pour l'alimentation et l'agriculture (FAO), Rome, données FAOSTAT, dernier accès mai 2010.

30 Roundwood production

Solid volume of roundwood without bark: million cubic metres

Production de bois rond

Volume solide de bois rond sans écorce : millions de mètres cubes

Region, country or area Région, pays ou zone	2000	2001	2002	2003	2004	2005	2006	2007	2008	2009
World Monde	**3 430.1**	**3 332.1**	**3 359.6**	**3 413.0**	**3 478.2**	**3 559.5**	**3 532.5**	**3 551.0**	**3 410.5**	**3 290.9**
Africa Afrique	**594.9**	**591.2**	**599.8**	**611.3**	**619.8**	**636.3**	**664.1**	**678.7**	**687.8**	**684.8**
Algeria Algérie	7.2	7.4	7.5	7.5	7.7	7.7	7.8	8.0	8.1	8.1
Angola Angola	4.3	4.3	4.4	4.5	4.6	4.7	4.8	4.8	4.9	4.9
Benin Bénin	6.2	0.5	0.5	0.5	0.5	6.4	6.6	6.6	6.6	6.6
Botswana Botswana	0.7	0.7	0.7	0.8	0.8	0.8	0.8	0.8	0.8	0.8
Burkina Faso Burkina Faso	8.0	8.0	7.2	7.3	9.2	11.7	12.2	12.7	13.6	13.6
Burundi Burundi	5.8	8.3	8.4	8.6	8.7	8.9	9.0	9.2	9.3	9.3
Cameroon Cameroun	11.0	10.5	10.6	11.0	11.2	11.3	11.4	12.3	12.3	12.3
Central African Rep. Rép. centrafricaine	3.0	3.0	2.9	2.8	2.8	2.8	2.8	2.8	6.9	6.9
Chad Tchad	6.6	6.8	6.9	7.0	7.1	7.2	7.4	7.5	7.6	7.6
Congo Congo	2.5	2.8	3.1	3.3	3.5	3.6	3.6	3.7	3.7	3.7
Côte d'Ivoire Côte d'Ivoire	11.9	11.2	10.7	10.2	10.3	10.0	10.1	10.3	10.3	10.3
Dem. Rep. of the Congo Rép. dém. du Congo	68.6	69.8	71.1	72.5	73.9	75.3	76.4	77.7	78.8	78.8
Egypt Egypte	16.4	16.6	16.8	16.9	17.1	17.2	17.3	17.4	17.6	17.6
Equatorial Guinea Guinée équatoriale	1.1	1.1	1.0	0.9	0.9	0.9	0.9	0.6	0.6	0.6
Eritrea Erythrée	2.2	2.3	1.3	1.3	2.4	2.4	2.5	2.5	2.6	2.6
Ethiopia Ethiopie	89.9	91.3	92.7	94.5	96.0	97.4	98.6	100.1	101.4	101.4
Gabon Gabon	3.1	3.1	2.2	4.6	4.6	3.7	4.0	3.9	3.9	3.9
Gambia Gambie	0.7	0.7	0.7	0.7	0.8	0.8	0.8	0.8	0.8	0.8
Ghana Ghana	21.7	21.9	21.8	22.1	22.0	21.9	34.3	35.5	36.8	36.8
Guinea Guinée	12.1	12.1	12.2	12.2	12.3	12.3	12.4	12.4	12.5	12.5
Guinea-Bissau Guinée-Bissau	0.6	0.6	0.6	0.6	0.6	0.6	0.6	0.6	0.6	0.6
Kenya Kenya	21.6	21.7	21.8	21.9	22.2	26.7	27.6	27.6	22.4	22.4
Lesotho Lesotho	2.0	2.0	2.0	2.0	2.0	2.1	2.1	2.1	2.1	2.1
Liberia Libéria	5.8	6.1	6.7	6.3	5.9	6.1	6.4	6.6	6.9	6.9
Libyan Arab Jamah. Jamah. arabe libyenne	0.7	0.7	0.7	0.7	0.7	0.7	1.0	1.0	1.0	1.0

30 Roundwood production *(continued)*

Solid volume of roundwood without bark: million cubic metres

Production de bois rond *(suite)*

Volume solide de bois rond sans écorce : millions de mètres cubes

Region, country or area Région, pays ou zone	2000	2001	2002	2003	2004	2005	2006	2007	2008	2009
Madagascar Madagascar	9.8	10.0	10.3	10.7	11.0	11.2	13.3	19.5	12.2	12.2
Malawi Malawi	5.5	5.5	5.5	5.6	5.6	5.7	5.7	5.8	5.8	5.8
Mali Mali	5.1	5.2	5.3	5.3	5.4	5.4	5.5	5.6	5.6	5.6
Mauritania Mauritanie	1.4	1.5	1.5	1.5	1.6	1.6	1.7	1.7	1.8	1.8
Morocco Maroc	1.1	1.0	0.9	0.9	0.9	1.0	0.9	1.0	1.0	1.0
Mozambique Mozambique	18.0	18.0	18.0	18.0	18.0	18.0	18.0	18.0	18.0	18.0
Niger Niger	8.2	3.3	8.6	8.8	9.0	9.2	9.4	9.6	9.8	9.8
Nigeria Nigéria	68.8	69.1	69.5	69.9	70.3	70.7	71.0	71.4	71.8	71.8
Rwanda Rwanda	5.4	5.5	5.5	5.5	5.5	5.5	9.9	10.0	10.1	10.1
Senegal Sénégal	5.9	5.9	6.0	6.0	6.0	6.1	6.1	6.1	6.2	6.2
Sierra Leone Sierra Leone	5.5	5.5	5.5	5.5	5.5	5.5	5.6	5.6	5.6	5.6
Somalia Somalie	9.3	9.6	9.9	10.3	10.6	10.9	11.2	11.6	11.9	11.9
South Africa Afrique du Sud	30.6	30.6	30.6	33.2	33.3	30.2	30.1	30.1	39.4	36.5
Sudan Soudan	18.9	19.0	19.2	19.4	19.7	19.9	20.1	20.3	20.5	20.5
Swaziland Swaziland	0.9	0.9	0.9	0.9	0.9	0.9	1.3	1.3	1.4	1.4
Togo Togo	5.8	5.8	5.8	5.9	4.7	5.9	6.0	6.0	6.1	6.1
Tunisia Tunisie	2.3	2.3	2.3	2.3	2.3	2.4	2.4	2.4	2.4	2.4
Uganda Ouganda	37.3	37.8	38.3	38.9	39.5	40.1	40.7	41.4	42.0	42.0
United Rep. of Tanzania Rép.-Unie de Tanzanie	23.1	23.3	23.4	23.6	23.8	24.0	24.2	24.4	24.7	24.7
Zambia Zambie	8.9	8.7	8.9	9.2	9.5	9.8	10.1	10.0	10.2	10.2
Zimbabwe Zimbabwe	9.1	9.1	9.1	9.1	9.1	8.9	9.2	9.2	9.3	9.3
Northern America Amérique septentrionale	**668.4**	**635.0**	**646.1**	**628.2**	**669.8**	**670.5**	**641.0**	**585.9**	**515.5**	**452.1**
Canada Canada	201.8	185.9	198.1	179.6	208.1	203.1	183.9	160.8	134.9	107.3
United States Etats-Unis	466.5	449.1	448.0	448.5	461.7	467.3	457.0	425.1	380.5	344.8
Latin America and the Caribbean Amérique latine et Caraïbes	**425.0**	**412.4**	**421.0**	**449.8**	**446.1**	**463.7**	**465.7**	**477.8**	**482.7**	**482.7**
Argentina Argentine	10.0	9.3	9.3	13.7	14.9	14.2	13.9	13.6	13.6	13.6
Belize Belize	0.2	0.2	0.2	0.2	0.2	0.2	0.2	0.7	0.7	0.7
Bolivia (Plurinational State of) Bolivie (État plurinational de)	2.6	2.7	2.7	2.9	3.0	3.1	3.2	3.2	3.2	3.2

30 Roundwood production *(continued)*

Solid volume of roundwood without bark: million cubic metres

Production de bois rond *(suite)*

Volume solide de bois rond sans écorce : millions de mètres cubes

Region, country or area Région, pays ou zone	2000	2001	2002	2003	2004	2005	2006	2007	2008	2009
Brazil Brésil	235.4	223.3	230.9	255.9	243.3	255.7	257.5	261.4	256.3	256.3
Chile Chili	36.6	37.8	37.8	37.0	42.6	45.6	46.7	52.6	54.8	54.8
Colombia Colombie	13.1	12.5	11.6	12.0	10.5	11.9	10.5	10.4	12.2	12.2
Costa Rica Costa Rica	5.2	5.2	5.2	5.1	4.5	4.6	4.6	4.6	4.6	4.6
Cuba Cuba	1.8	1.7	2.8	2.6	2.5	2.6	2.3	2.2	2.0	2.0
Dominican Republic Rép. dominicaine	0.6	0.6	0.6	0.6	0.6	0.6	0.9	0.9	0.9	0.9
Ecuador Equateur	5.7	6.1	6.2	6.3	6.6	6.7	5.8	6.1	6.0	6.0
El Salvador El Salvador	5.2	5.2	5.2	4.8	4.9	4.9	4.9	4.9	4.9	4.9
French Guiana Guyane française	0.1	0.1	0.2	0.2	0.2	0.2	0.2	0.2	0.2	0.2
Guatemala Guatemala	15.0	15.3	15.7	15.9	16.3	16.7	17.1	17.4	17.8	17.8
Guyana Guyana	1.2	1.2	1.2	1.2	1.3	1.4	1.4	1.4	1.4	1.4
Haiti Haïti	2.2	2.2	2.2	2.2	2.2	2.2	2.2	2.3	2.3	2.3
Honduras Honduras	9.5	9.6	9.7	9.5	9.6	9.6	9.5	9.5	9.3	9.3
Jamaica Jamaïque	0.9	0.9	0.9	0.9	0.9	0.8	0.8	0.8	0.8	0.8
Mexico Mexique	45.7	45.2	44.0	44.4	45.2	44.6	44.7	44.9	45.1	45.1
Nicaragua Nicaragua	6.0	5.9	6.0	6.0	6.0	6.0	6.1	6.1	6.1	6.1
Panama Panama	1.3	1.3	1.3	1.3	1.3	1.4	1.3	1.3	1.3	1.3
Paraguay Paraguay	9.6	9.7	9.8	9.9	10.0	10.1	10.2	10.3	10.4	10.4
Peru Pérou	9.3	8.6	8.8	8.4	8.9	9.1	9.3	9.4	12.5	12.5
Suriname Suriname	0.2	0.2	0.2	0.2	0.2	0.2	0.2	0.2	0.2	0.2
Trinidad and Tobago Trinité-et-Tobago	0.1	0.1	0.1	0.1	0.1	0.1	0.1	0.1	0.1	0.1
Uruguay Uruguay	2.9	3.0	3.4	3.7	5.1	5.7	6.4	7.2	9.5	9.5
Venezuela (Boliv. Rep. of) Venezuela (Rép. boliv. du)	4.7	4.6	5.1	4.8	5.3	5.3	5.6	6.1	6.3	6.3
Asia Asie	**1 065.1**	**1 044.0**	**1 029.2**	**1 028.9**	**1 035.3**	**1 038.2**	**1 029.8**	**1 021.5**	**999.1**	**999.1**
Afghanistan Afghanistan	3.0	3.1	3.1	3.1	3.2	3.2	3.3	3.3	3.3	3.3
Armenia Arménie	0.1	^0.0	0.1	0.1	0.1	^0.0	0.1	^0.0	^0.0	^0.0
Azerbaijan Azerbaïdjan	^0.0	^0.0	0.1	^0.0	^0.0	^0.0	^0.0	^0.0	^0.0	^0.0
Bahrain Bahreïn	0.0	0.0	0.0	0.0	0.0	0.0	0.0	^0.0	^0.0	^0.0

30 Roundwood production *(continued)*

Solid volume of roundwood without bark: million cubic metres

Production de bois rond *(suite)*

Volume solide de bois rond sans écorce : millions de mètres cubes

Region, country or area Région, pays ou zone	2000	2001	2002	2003	2004	2005	2006	2007	2008	2009
Bangladesh Bangladesh	28.5	28.4	28.0	28.0	28.0	27.9	27.9	27.8	27.7	27.7
Bhutan Bhoutan	4.4	4.4	4.5	4.5	4.6	4.7	4.7	5.0	5.0	5.0
Brunei Darussalam Brunéi Darussalam	0.1	0.1	0.1	0.1	0.1	0.1	0.1	0.1	0.1	0.1
Cambodia Cambodge	10.3	10.0	9.9	9.7	9.5	9.3	9.3	9.0	8.9	8.9
China Chine	323.6	316.9	312.0	309.9	305.9	302.0	298.2	290.7	291.9	291.9
Georgia Géorgie	0.0	0.3	0.4	0.4	0.5	0.6	0.6	0.8	0.8	0.8
India Inde	296.1	296.7	319.4	321.0	326.6	328.7	329.4	330.2	331.0	331.0
Indonesia Indonésie	122.5	112.2	115.6	112.0	112.7	111.3	106.8	102.2	100.6	100.6
Iran (Islamic Rep. of) Iran (Rép. islamique d')	1.1	1.3	0.7	0.9	0.8	0.8	0.8	0.9	0.9	0.9
Iraq Iraq	0.1	0.1	0.1	0.1	0.1	0.1	0.1	0.1	0.1	0.1
Israel Israël	0.1	^0.0	^0.0	^0.0	^0.0	^0.0	^0.0	^0.0	^0.0	^0.0
Japan Japon	18.1	15.9	15.2	15.3	15.7	16.3	16.7	17.8	17.8	17.8
Jordan Jordanie	0.2	0.2	0.2	0.2	0.3	0.3	0.3	0.3	0.3	0.3
Kazakhstan Kazakhstan	0.6	0.7	0.5	0.3	0.5	0.9	0.1	0.2	0.2	0.2
Korea, Dem. P. R. Corée, R. p. dém. de	7.0	7.1	7.1	7.2	7.2	7.3	7.3	7.4	7.4	7.4
Korea, Republic of Corée, République de	4.0	4.0	4.1	4.1	4.7	4.8	4.9	5.2	5.2	5.2
Lao People's Dem. Rep. Rép. dém. pop. lao	6.4	6.5	6.3	6.3	6.2	6.1	6.1	6.1	6.1	6.1
Lebanon Liban	^0.0	0.1	0.1	0.1	0.1	0.1	0.1	0.1	0.1	0.1
Malaysia Malaisie	27.7	23.5	22.7	26.5	28.5	28.3	26.2	28.0	25.7	25.7
Mongolia Mongolie	0.6	0.7	0.7	0.7	0.7	0.7	0.7	0.8	0.7	0.7
Myanmar Myanmar	38.1	39.4	38.9	42.2	41.8	42.5	42.5	42.5	21.1	21.1
Nepal Népal	14.0	14.0	14.0	14.0	14.0	14.0	13.9	13.9	13.8	13.8
Pakistan Pakistan	33.6	33.2	27.7	28.0	28.7	29.3	29.0	32.5	32.7	32.7
Philippines Philippines	44.0	44.4	16.0	16.0	16.1	16.1	16.1	15.9	15.6	15.6
Sri Lanka Sri Lanka	6.6	6.5	6.5	6.4	6.3	6.3	6.3	6.1	6.1	6.1
Syrian Arab Republic Rép. arabe syrienne	0.1	0.1	0.1	0.1	0.1	0.1	0.1	0.1	0.1	0.1
Tajikistan Tadjikistan	0.0	0.0	0.0	0.0	0.1	0.1	0.1	0.1	0.1	0.1
Thailand Thaïlande	26.8	27.5	28.1	28.8	28.7	28.6	28.4	28.3	28.2	28.2

30 Roundwood production *(continued)*

Solid volume of roundwood without bark: million cubic metres

Production de bois rond *(suite)*

Volume solide de bois rond sans écorce : millions de mètres cubes

Region, country or area Région, pays ou zone	2000	2001	2002	2003	2004	2005	2006	2007	2008	2009
Timor-Leste Timor-Leste	0.0	0.0	0.0	0.0	0.0	0.0	0.0	0.0	0.0	0.0
Turkey Turquie	15.9	15.3	16.1	15.8	16.5	16.2	18.1	18.3	19.4	19.4
Viet Nam Viet Nam	30.9	30.8	30.7	26.4	26.5	31.1	31.0	27.5	27.9	27.9
Yemen Yémen	0.3	0.3	0.3	0.3	0.4	0.4	0.4	0.4	0.4	0.4
Europe Europe	**616.8**	**589.1**	**602.6**	**632.5**	**645.8**	**689.7**	**670.4**	**724.0**	**657.1**	**603.9**
Albania Albanie	0.4	0.3	0.3	0.3	0.3	0.3	0.3	0.4	0.4	0.4
Austria Autriche	13.3	13.5	14.8	17.1	16.5	16.5	19.1	21.3	21.8	16.7
Belarus Bélarus	6.1	6.5	6.9	7.5	8.6	8.7	8.8	8.8	8.8	8.8
Belgium Belgique	4.5	4.2	4.5	4.8	4.9	5.0	5.1	5.0	4.7	4.4
Bosnia and Herzegovina Bosnie-Herzégovine	4.3	3.8	4.2	4.1	4.0	3.8	4.1	3.8	4.0	3.4
Bulgaria Bulgarie	4.8	4.0	4.8	4.8	6.0	5.9	6.0	5.7	6.1	6.1
Croatia Croatie	3.7	3.5	3.6	3.8	3.8	4.0	4.5	4.2	4.5	4.2
Czech Republic République tchèque	14.4	14.4	14.5	15.1	15.6	15.5	17.7	18.5	16.2	16.2
Denmark Danemark	3.0	1.6	1.4	1.6	1.5	3.0	2.4	2.6	2.8	2.8
Estonia Estonie	8.9	10.2	10.5	10.5	6.8	5.5	5.4	4.5	4.9	4.9
Finland Finlande	54.3	52.2	53.4	54.2	54.4	52.3	50.8	56.6	50.7	41.7
France France	70.5	64.3	59.3	57.0	57.3	63.2	61.8	58.8	57.5	58.2
Germany Allemagne	53.7	39.5	42.4	51.2	54.5	56.9	62.3	76.7	55.4	56.6
Greece Grèce	2.2	1.9	1.6	1.7	1.7	1.5	1.6	1.7	1.7	1.7
Hungary Hongrie	5.9	5.8	5.8	5.8	5.7	5.9	5.9	5.6	5.4	5.2
Ireland Irlande	2.7	2.5	2.6	2.7	2.6	2.6	2.7	2.7	2.2	2.3
Italy Italie	9.3	8.1	7.5	8.2	8.7	8.7	8.6	8.1	8.7	7.6
Latvia Lettonie	14.3	12.8	13.5	12.9	12.8	12.8	12.8	12.2	8.8	10.4
Lithuania Lituanie	5.5	5.7	6.1	6.3	6.1	6.0	5.9	6.2	5.6	5.5
Luxembourg Luxembourg	0.3	0.3	0.3	0.3	0.3	0.2	0.3	0.3	0.4	0.4
Montenegro Monténégro	...	...	...	...	...	...	0.5	0.5	0.5	0.5
Netherlands Pays-Bas	1.0	0.9	0.8	1.0	1.0	1.1	1.1	1.0	1.1	1.0
Norway Norvège	8.2	9.0	8.7	8.3	8.8	9.7	9.8	10.5	10.3	8.9

30 Roundwood production *(continued)*

Solid volume of roundwood without bark: million cubic metres

Production de bois rond *(suite)*

Volume solide de bois rond sans écorce : millions de mètres cubes

Region, country or area Région, pays ou zone	2000	2001	2002	2003	2004	2005	2006	2007	2008	2009
Poland Pologne	26.0	25.0	27.1	30.8	32.7	31.9	32.4	35.9	34.3	34.9
Portugal Portugal	10.8	8.9	8.7	9.7	10.9	10.7	10.8	10.8	10.9	10.9
Republic of Moldova République de Moldova	0.1	0.1	0.1	0.2	0.2	0.2	0.4	0.4	0.4	0.4
Romania Roumanie	13.1	12.4	15.2	15.4	15.8	14.5	14.0	15.3	13.7	13.1
Russian Federation Fédération de Russie	158.1	164.7	165.0	174.0	178.4	185.0	190.6	207.0	181.4	151.4
Serbia Serbie	...	...	...	...	...	...	2.9	3.0	3.2	3.1
Serbia and Montenegro Serbie-et-Monténégro	3.4	2.5	2.9	3.2	3.5	3.2	...	...	...	...
Slovakia Slovaquie	6.2	5.8	5.8	6.4	7.2	9.3	7.9	8.1	9.3	9.1
Slovenia Slovénie	2.3	2.3	2.3	2.6	2.6	2.7	3.2	2.9	3.0	2.9
Spain Espagne	14.3	15.1	15.8	16.1	16.3	15.5	15.7	14.5	17.0	14.5
Sweden Suède	63.3	63.2	66.6	67.1	67.3	98.2	64.6	78.2	70.8	65.1
Switzerland Suisse	9.2	5.7	4.6	5.1	5.1	5.3	5.7	5.5	5.0	4.6
TFYR of Macedonia L'ex-R.Y. Macédoine	1.1	0.7	0.7	0.8	0.8	0.8	0.8	0.6	0.7	0.7
Ukraine Ukraine	9.9	9.9	12.3	13.8	14.9	14.6	15.8	16.9	16.9	16.9
United Kingdom Royaume-Uni	7.8	7.9	7.8	8.0	8.3	8.5	8.4	9.0	8.4	8.4
Oceania Océanie	**59.9**	**60.5**	**60.9**	**62.3**	**61.4**	**61.1**	**61.5**	**63.0**	**68.3**	**68.3**
Australia Australie	31.2	31.1	29.7	31.6	31.9	31.9	31.8	32.3	34.9	34.9
Fiji Fidji	0.5	0.5	0.4	0.4	0.5	0.5	0.5	0.5	0.6	0.6
New Zealand Nouvelle-Zélande	19.3	20.7	22.1	21.2	19.8	19.0	19.3	19.9	20.2	20.2
Papua New Guinea Papouasie-Nvl-Guinée	7.8	7.3	7.8	8.0	7.9	8.1	8.5	8.6	10.8	10.8
Samoa Samoa	0.1	0.1	0.1	0.1	0.1	0.1	0.1	0.1	0.1	0.1
Solomon Islands Iles Salomon	0.9	0.7	0.7	0.9	1.2	1.3	1.2	1.6	1.6	1.6
Vanuatu Vanuatu	0.1	0.1	0.1	0.1	0.1	0.1	0.1	0.1	0.1	0.1

Source:
Food and Agriculture Organization of the United Nations (FAO), Rome, FAOSTAT database, last accessed August 2010.

Source:
Organisation des Nations Unies pour l'alimentation et l'agriculture (FAO), Rome, la base de données de la FAOSTAT, dernier accès août 2010.

31 Fish production

Capture and aquaculture: metric tons

Production halieutique

Pêche de capture et aquaculture: tonnes

Country or area Pays ou zone	Capture production Captures					Aquaculture production Production de l'aquaculture				
	2004	2005	2006	2007	2008	2004	2005	2006	2007	2008
Afghanistan [1] Afghanistan [1]	1 000	1 000	1 000	1 000	1 000	...	...	...	...	...
Albania Albanie	6 083	6 455	7 676	7 505	7 368	1 569	1 473	1 970	2 008	1 858
Algeria Algérie	114 048	126 627	146 050	147 788	141 614	586[1]	368[1]	288	405	2 781[1]
American Samoa Samoa américaines	4 041	3 991	5 307	6 470	4 451	...	...	...	...	...
Angola Angola	240 094	202 742[1]	225 605	312 626	317 452	92[1]	126[1]	156[1]	190[1]	190[1]
Anguilla Anguilla	250[1]	250[1]	250[1]	250[1]	701	...	...	...	...	...
Antigua and Barbuda Antigua-et-Barbuda	2 527	2 999	3 092	3 092	3 521	...	...	...	...	...
Argentina Argentine	946 690	932 354	1 174 494	988 355	997 770	1 844	2 417	2 514	2 946	2 687
Armenia Arménie	1 031	989[1]	1 406[1]	4 715[1]	5 701[1]	813	739[1]	1 056[1]	1 615[1]	2 001[1]
Aruba Aruba	162	162[1]	145	159	151	...	...	...	...	...
Australia Australie	274 713	279 153	246 397	242 665	235 680	44 142	42 787	49 376	54 683	57 152
Austria Autriche	2 667	2 790	2 863	2 889	2 437	2 267	2 420	2 503	2 539	2 087
Azerbaijan Azerbaïdjan	9 442	9 115	4 093	3 056	1 606	184	114	110	113	89
Bahamas Bahamas	11 353	11 072	10 616	8 381	9 116	10	10	22	...	...
Bahrain Bahreïn	14 185	11 497	15 549	13 256	13 854	8	3	2	1	2
Bangladesh Bangladesh	2 102 026	2 215 957	2 328 545	2 440 011	2 563 296	914 752	882 091	892 049	945 812	1 005 542
Barbados Barbade	2 148	2 182	1 975	2 224	3 551	...	...	...	...	...
Belarus Bélarus	5 040	5 050[1]	5 050[1]	5 050[1]	5 050[1]	4 150	4 150[1]	4 150[1]	4 150[1]	4 150[1]
Belgium Belgique	27 474	24 981	23 147	24 669	22 735	739	414[1]	128	128	126
Belize Belize	15 576	15 023	11 841	15 861	14 170	11 428	10 858	7 624	7 700[1]	9 549[1]
Benin Bénin	39 994[1]	31 846[1]	41 921[1]	36 563[1]	37 675[1]	7	350	415	178	180[1]
Bermuda Bermudes	379	406	380	420	400	...	...	...	...	...
Bhutan [1] Bhoutan [1]	220	220	200	200	180	...	...	...	...	...
Bolivia (Plurin. State of) Bolivie (État plurin. de)	7 196	7 090	6 805[1]	6 585	7 428	450	430	455[1]	585	631
Bosnia and Herzegovina Bosnie-Herzégovine	8 399	9 075	9 626	9 625	9 625	6 394	7 070	7 621	7 620[1]	7 620[1]
Botswana Botswana	161	132	81	122	86	...	...	...	...	...

31 Fish production *(continued)*
Capture and aquaculture: metric tons

Production halieutique *(suite)*
Pêche de capture et aquaculture: tonnes

Country or area Pays ou zone	Capture production Captures 2004	2005	2006	2007	2008	Aquaculture production Production de l'aquaculture 2004	2005	2006	2007	2008
Brazil Brésil	1 015 285	1 007 414	1 050 160	1 071 624	1 064 576[1]	269 068	257 153	271 047	288 447	289 576[1]
British Indian Ocean Terr Terr. brit. de l'océan Indien	28	28	21	24	34	...	...	...	...	...
British Virgin Islands Iles Vierges britanniques	1 262	1 300[1]	1 308[1]	1 250[1]	1 200[1]	...	...	...	...	...
Brunei Darussalam Brunéi Darussalam	3 137	2 861	2 467	2 863	2 831	709	454	475	622	473
Bulgaria Bulgarie	10 741	8 579	10 789	12 929	14 018	2 489	3 145	3 257	4 032	5 157
Burkina Faso Burkina Faso	9 005[1]	9 055	9 700	10 498	11 005	5[1]	55[1]	200	298	405
Burundi Burundi	14 055	15 000[1]	15 950[1]	16 900[1]	17 966	200	200[1]	200[1]	200[1]	200[1]
Cambodia Cambodge	326 492	410 000	516 700	491 200[1]	470 950	20 675[1]	26 000[1]	34 200[1]	34 200[1]	39 950[1]
Cameroon Cameroun	129 330[1]	142 682	137 572	138 952	138 340[1]	330[1]	337	340[1]	340[1]	340[1]
Canada Canada	1 310 726	1 252 114	1 236 340	1 154 926	1 078 114	145 018	154 587	171 451	152 516	144 099
Cape Verde Cap-Vert	10 396	21 617	24 590	18 328	21 910	...	...	...	...	...
Cayman Islands Iles Caïmanes	125	125	125	125	125	...	...	...	...	...
Central African Rep. [1] Rép. centrafricaine [1]	15 000	15 000	15 000	15 000	15 000	...	...	...	...	...
Chad [1] Tchad [1]	60 000	55 000	50 000	45 000	40 000	...	...	...	...	...
Channel Islands Iles Anglo-Normandes	3 976	4 155	4 128	4 357	4 200	775	650	660[1]	791	972
Chile Chili	5 552 149	5 013 288	4 918 774	4 559 097	4 357 878	675 884[1]	723 875[1]	794 110[1]	779 779[1]	843 142[1]
China [2] Chine [2]	40 477 271	42 035 912	43 859 595	45 335 111	46 662 516	26 225 324[1]	27 728 349[1]	29 461 925[1]	30 936 873	32 143 572
China, Hong Kong SAR Chine, Hong Kong RAS	172 159[1]	166 094[1]	158 661[1]	158 661[1]	162 880[1]	4 615	4 130	4 125	4 514	4 754
China, Macao SAR [1] Chine, Macao RAS [1]	1 500	1 500	1 500	1 500	1 500	...	...	...	...	...
Colombia Colombie	171 932	182 000	179 777	196 400	201 400	60 072	61 000[1]	70 132	66 565[1]	66 400[1]
Comoros Comores	14 935	15 070	15 070[1]	16 000[1]	16 000[1]	...	...	...	...	...
Congo Congo	57 096	54 696	59 103	59 241	54 169	72	80	21	25	65
Cook Islands Iles Cook	4 044	3 948	3 574	3 259	2 999	...	...	...	...	...
Costa Rica Costa Rica	45 558	46 378	41 962[1]	47 500	48 785	24 708	24 038	19 962	25 765	27 035
Côte d'Ivoire Côte d'Ivoire	55 267	43 531	55 696	48 579	59 290[1]	866	866[1]	866[1]	1 290[1]	1 290[1]
Croatia Croatie	40 473	45 769	51 409	53 080	61 041	10 367	11 104	13 556	12 884	12 017
Cuba Cuba	63 637	51 279	54 739	60 417	60 895	27 562	22 635	27 186	31 648	33 039

31 Fish production *(continued)*

Capture and aquaculture: metric tons

Production halieutique *(suite)*

Pêche de capture et aquaculture: tonnes

Country or area Pays ou zone	Capture production Captures					Aquaculture production Production de l'aquaculture				
	2004	2005	2006	2007	2008	2004	2005	2006	2007	2008
Cyprus Chypre	3 743	4 303	4 788	4 950	5 414	2 175	2 387	2 633	2 504	3 403
Czech Republic République tchèque	23 912	24 697	25 077	24 723	24 559	19 384	20 455	20 431	20 447	20 395
Dem. Rep. of the Congo [1] Rép. dém. du Congo [1]	240 337	239 605	239 558	238 970	238 970	2 965	2 965	2 970	2 970	2 970
Denmark Danemark	1 133 410	949 610	904 896	684 087	725 539	42 814	39 012	37 188	31 168	35 337
Djibouti Djibouti	260[1]	260[1]	260[1]	265	450[1]	...	...	...	...	...
Dominica Dominique	703[1]	579	694	776	694	3[1]	...	...	...	...
Dominican Republic Rép. dominicaine	16 223	12 173	13 936	14 689	16 404	2 000	980	980[1]	980[1]	980[1]
Ecuador Equateur	447 772	545 937	619 015	555 267	606 339	108 673	138 562	169 588	171 020[1]	172 120[1]
Egypt Egypte	865 014	889 296	970 918	1 008 000	1 067 630	471 535	539 748	595 030	635 516	693 815
El Salvador El Salvador	44 634	43 317	46 296	52 368	51 766[1]	2 219	2 203	3 078	3 729	3 766[1]
Equatorial Guinea Guinée équatoriale	3 498[1]	3 748[1]	3 998[1]	4 530[1]	5 395	...	...	...	...	...
Eritrea Erythrée	7 404	4 027	8 813	1 932	1 665	...	...	...	...	...
Estonia Estonie	88 158	99 327	87 193	98 608	101 850	252	555	703	772	813
Ethiopia Ethiopie	10 005	9 450	9 890	13 253	16 770	...	...	...	...	...
Faeroe Islands Iles Féroé	645 463	588 715	641 696	612 088	541 277	46 077	23 455	18 574	29 954[1]	45 929[1]
Falkland Is. (Malvinas) Iles Falkland (Malvinas)	55 390	84 548	75 290	72 149	81 708	21	2	2	2	0
Fiji Fidji	47 663	42 564[1]	47 261	45 414	48 301[1]	99	99[1]	428	180	228
Finland Finlande	148 248	146 096	162 336	177 713	171 838	12 821	14 355	12 891	13 031	13 439
France France	842 359	819 215	812 986	751 002	694 953	242 634	245 115	238 119	237 618	237 833[1]
French Guiana Guyane française	5 551	5 322	4 479	4 857	3 957	37	37	37	...	...
French Polynesia Polynésie française	12 248	12 212	13 458	13 111	11 938	65	75	64	46	44
Gabon Gabon	46 127	43 907	41 611	38 619	30 120	80	78	126	124	124
Gambia Gambie	32 423	34 586	36 912	43 574	42 645	...	...	...	...	...
Georgia Géorgie	12 060	10 046	9 784	18 377	26 692	72	72[1]	75[1]	180	180[1]
Germany Allemagne	319 336	330 353	333 216	293 758	273 476	57 233	44 685	35 379	44 994	43 977
Ghana Ghana	400 338	393 020	369 189	324 550	355 425	950	1 154	2 270[1]	3 820[1]	5 594[1]
Greece Grèce	191 029	198 691	211 545	209 352	203 859	97 143	106 268	113 307	113 258	114 888

Country or area Pays ou zone	Capture production Captures					Aquaculture production Production de l'aquaculture				
	2004	2005	2006	2007	2008	2004	2005	2006	2007	2008
Greenland Groenland	225 088	234 864	252 959	233 754	233 754[1]	...	...	...	...	...
Grenada Grenade	2 033	2 047	2 166	2 404	2 383	...	...	...	...	...
Guadeloupe Guadeloupe	10 131[1]	10 131[1]	10 131[1]	10 137[1]	10 133[1]	31	31	31	37[1]	33[1]
Guam Guam	682	370	766	802	464	...	...	162	162	162[1]
Guatemala Guatemala	14 920	27 374	34 962	33 987	41 553	4 908	9 008[1]	16 293	16 400[1]	18 727
Guinea Guinée	93 947	105 137	98 489	74 823	74 000[1]	...	...	...	...	...
Guinea-Bissau [1] Guinée-Bissau [1]	6 650	7 155	7 310	6 750	6 750	...	...	...	...	...
Guyana Guyana	57 327	53 978	54 423[1]	48 108	42 460	608[1]	608	660[1]	660	292
Haiti Haïti	8 300	9 000[1]	10 000[1]	10 000[1]	10 000[1]	...	...	...	...	...
Honduras Honduras	41 043	68 021	74 287	69 467	59 984	27 036	49 249	55 356[1]	54 689	47 080
Hungary Hongrie	19 986	21 270	22 229	22 888	23 081	12 744	13 661	14 686	15 864	15 687
Iceland Islande	1 742 520	1 672 676	1 335 287	1 403 856	1 287 955	8 868	8 256	8 241	4 823	5 098
India Inde	6 189 695	6 658 740	7 020 108	6 971 533	7 583 563	2 798 686	2 967 378	3 180 863	3 112 240	3 478 690
Indonesia Indonésie	5 681 205	5 888 917	6 094 283	6 431 464	6 633 670	1 045 009	1 197 013	1 292 803	1 392 810	1 689 842
Iran (Islamic Rep. of) Iran (Rép. islamique d')	474 341	522 570	575 586	562 424	562 821	104 330	112 001	129 708	158 789	154 979
Iraq Iraq	26 883	47 870	74 126	73 589	53 718	13 947	17 941	14 867	15 810[1]	19 246
Ireland Irlande	338 584	327 689	264 886	271 972	262 552	58 355	60 050	53 122	57 101	57 210[1]
Isle of Man Ile de Man	2 627	2 764	1 209	3 760	2 770	...	...	...	...	...
Israel Israël	25 643	26 555	25 927	24 854	25 047	22 303	22 404	22 107	21 419	21 612[1]
Italy Italie	405 300	477 988	488 268	465 637	417 254	118 217	181 101	172 833	178 992	181 469[1]
Jamaica Jamaïque	17 966	18 766	25 924	22 164	19 123	4 495	5 670	8 019	5 616	5 948
Japan Japon	5 048 089	5 001 068	5 002 767	5 006 729	4 905 904[1]	761 174	737 429	723 916	761 704	721 474[1]
Jordan Jordanie	981	1 071	1 057	1 015	1 040	487	561	560	509	540
Kazakhstan Kazakhstan	34 445	37 887	35 148	41 628	55 902	589	1 102	528	386	321
Kenya Kenya	127 874	148 332	159 678	135 998	137 715	1 035	1 047	1 012	4 240	4 452
Kiribati Kiribati	30 750[1]	30 094[1]	25 073[1]	33 299	33 505	9[1]	12	12	5	5[1]
Korea, Dem. P. R. [1] Corée, R. p. dém. de [1]	268 600	268 600	268 600	268 600	268 600	63 700	63 700	63 700	63 700	63 700

31 Fish production *(continued)*

Capture and aquaculture: metric tons

Production halieutique *(suite)*

Pêche de capture et aquaculture: tonnes

Country or area Pays ou zone	Capture production Captures					Aquaculture production Production de l'aquaculture				
	2004	2005	2006	2007	2008	2004	2005	2006	2007	2008
Korea, Republic of Corée, République de	1 971 692	2 061 514	2 253 431	2 458 994	2 401 880	396 673	420 635	501 995	596 672	465 850
Kuwait Koweït	5 208	5 222	6 203	4 721	4 733[1]	375[1]	327	568	348	360[1]
Kyrgyzstan Kirghizistan	27	34	28	141	100	20	20[1]	20[1]	107	92
Lao People's Dem. Rep. Rép. dém. pop. lao	94 700	104 560	104 925	104 925	104 925	64 900[1]	78 000	78 000[1]	78 000[1]	78 000[1]
Latvia Lettonie	125 936	151 160	140 954	156 005	158 518	545	542	565	729	584
Lebanon Liban	4 656	4 601	4 614	4 614[1]	4 614[1]	790	803	803	803	803
Lesotho Lesotho	47	46	47	179	141	2	1	2	131	91
Liberia Libéria	13 725	12 147	8 894	14 488	7 890	...	...	...	...	...
Libyan Arab Jamah. Jamah. arabe libyenne	40 185[1]	37 778[1]	35 035[1]	32 161	47 885	288	388[1]	388[1]	240[1]	240[1]
Lithuania Lituanie	164 685	141 798	156 772	190 890	185 771	2 697	2 013	2 224	3 377	3 008
Madagascar Madagascar	143 119	141 344	144 106	158 245	129 344	8 803	9 396	11 233	11 287	9 580[1]
Malawi Malawi	57 196	60 407	74 287	68 000	71 719	733	812	1 500	1 500	1 700
Malaysia Malaisie	1 502 993	1 384 732	1 449 886	1 559 874	1 633 178	171 270	175 834	168 317	178 239	243 081
Maldives Maldives	157 982	185 806	184 070	144 056	133 002	...	...	...	...	...
Mali Mali	101 008[1]	101 008[1]	101 000[1]	100 640	100 821	1 008[1]	1 008[1]	1 000[1]	640	821
Malta Malte	2 006	2 142	2 445	3 783	2 971	868	736	1 115	2 548	1 692
Marshall Islands Iles Marshall	47 887	57 574	43 958	61 215	35 436	...	...	...	...	...
Martinique Martinique	6 282	5 582[1]	6 382	6 190	6 190	92	92	92	...	...
Mauritania Mauritanie	270 733	304 877	165 312	223 207	195 328	...	...	...	...	...
Mauritius Maurice	10 321	10 255	8 784	7 642	6 303	350	400	443	175	246
Mayotte Mayotte	2 476	2 358	5 912	11 789	12 765	170	164	140[1]	128	88
Mexico Mexique	1 360 753	1 450 051	1 508 978	1 609 182[1]	1 736 797[1]	104 263	132 981	154 295	128 236[1]	150 905[1]
Micronesia (Fed. States of) Micronésie (Etats féd. de)	30 122	30 000	12 683	17 621	21 699	...	...	...	...	...
Monaco[1] Monaco[1]	3	2	1	1	1	...	...	...	...	...
Mongolia Mongolie	305	366	326	185	88	...	...	...	...	...
Montenegro[1] Monténégro[1]	...	...	911	911	911	...	...	11	11	11
Montserrat[1] Montserrat[1]	50	50	50	50	50	...	...	...	...	...

31 Fish production *(continued)*

Capture and aquaculture: metric tons

Production halieutique *(suite)*

Pêche de capture et aquaculture: tonnes

Country or area Pays ou zone	Capture production Captures					Aquaculture production Production de l'aquaculture				
	2004	2005	2006	2007	2008	2004	2005	2006	2007	2008
Morocco Maroc	919 924	1 028 804	877 972	880 909	997 172	1 718	2 257	1 161	1 636	1 399[1]
Mozambique Mozambique	100 035	95 217	102 947	93 108	120 337	446	1 222	1 048	838	692[1]
Myanmar Myanmar	1 985 260	2 215 494	2 579 780	2 838 040	3 166 005	400 360[1]	485 220[1]	574 990[1]	604 660[1]	674 665
Namibia Namibie	571 760	554 026	509 622	413 341	372 850	50[1]	50[1]	52[1]	28	28[1]
Nauru Nauru	18	39	39[1]	39[1]	39[1]	...	...	...	...	...
Nepal Népal	39 947	42 463	45 425	46 779	48 750	20 000	22 480	25 409	26 679	27 250
Netherlands Pays-Bas	600 234	620 578	480 888	470 363	463 370	78 598	71 370	45 553	56 761	46 622
Netherlands Antilles Antilles néerlandaises	17 286	650[1]	6 247	4 018	16 698	...	...	...	...	...
New Caledonia Nouvelle-Calédonie	5 248	5 348	4 950	4 522	5 061	2 290	2 533	2 365	1 931	2 108
New Zealand Nouvelle-Zélande	637 646	649 723	583 273	605 574	562 616	92 220	105 302	107 524	111 908	112 358
Nicaragua Nicaragua	27 177	37 424	40 713	38 350	45 389	7 880	9 983	11 220	11 533	16 078
Niger Niger	51 506	50 058	29 875	29 768	30 000	40	40	40	40	40
Nigeria Nigéria	509 201	579 537	636 901	615 507	684 575	43 950	56 355	84 578	85 087	143 207
Niue Nioué	200[1]	203	160[1]	160[1]	160[1]	...	...	...	...	...
Northern Mariana Islands Iles Mariannes du Nord	169	214	221	231	292	...	...	...	...	...
Norway Norvège	3 161 266	3 054 847	2 968 782	3 220 395	3 274 571	636 802	661 877	712 373	841 560	843 730
Occupied Palestinian Terr. Terr. palestinien occupé	2 951	1 814	2 323	2 702	2 843	...	...	...	...	...
Oman Oman	165 531	157 544	147 815	151 919	145 751	515	218	146	175[1]	120
Pakistan Pakistan	556 993	515 472	611 246	570 280	586 512	76 653	80 622	121 825	130 092	135 098
Palau Palaos	1 084	937	972	1 003	1 027	5	5	5[1]	18[1]	20
Panama Panama	215 862	228 088	235 670	217 321	230 716	7 048	7 778	8 744	8 813	8 224
Papua New Guinea Papouasie-Nvl-Guinée	275 412	296 856	297 662	268 393	223 312	50[1]	55[1]	70[1]	70[1]	92[1]
Paraguay[1] Paraguay[1]	24 100	23 100	22 100	22 100	22 100	2 100	2 100	2 100	2 100	2 100
Peru Pérou	9 625 252	9 411 417	7 045 602	7 248 142	7 403 572	22 114	25 964	28 393	39 531	43 103
Philippines Philippines	2 722 394	2 826 104	2 941 419	3 208 410	3 301 418	512 220	557 251	623 369	709 715	741 142
Pitcairn[1] Pitcairn[1]	3	3	3	3	3	...	...	...	...	...
Poland Pologne	227 239	193 167	181 346	187 448	179 309	35 131	37 920	35 867	35 628	36 813

31 Fish production *(continued)*

Capture and aquaculture: metric tons

Production halieutique *(suite)*

Pêche de capture et aquaculture: tonnes

Country or area Pays ou zone	Capture production Captures					Aquaculture production Production de l'aquaculture				
	2004	2005	2006	2007	2008	2004	2005	2006	2007	2008
Portugal Portugal	228 001	218 453	236 978	245 782	246 647	6 700	6 696	7 894	7 416	6 458
Puerto Rico Porto Rico	2 845	2 862	2 308	1 719	1 837	417	311	266	44	44[1]
Qatar Qatar	11 134	13 946	16 412	15 226	17 724	0	11	36	36	36
Republic of Moldova République de Moldova	4 957	5 001	5 612	5 860	6 107	4 470	4 470[1]	5 000[1]	4 700[1]	4 700[1]
Réunion Réunion	3 480	4 443	3 709	3 925	2 905	107	161	161	...	...
Romania Roumanie	13 232	13 337	14 748	16 495	17 942	8 137	7 284	8 088	10 312	12 532
Russian Federation Fédération de Russie	3 048 874	3 308 928	3 385 399	3 553 647	3 490 424	109 802	114 752	105 525	105 503	115 420
Rwanda Rwanda	8 212	8 186[1]	8 800[1]	9 438	9 438[1]	386	386[1]	400[1]	388[1]	388[1]
Saint Helena Sainte-Hélène	1 061	1 130	1 120	837	794	...	...	...	...	...
Saint Kitts and Nevis Saint-Kitts-et-Nevis	484	450[1]	450[1]	450[1]	450[1]	...	...	...	...	...
Saint Lucia Sainte-Lucie	1 509	1 410	1 496	1 555	1 713	1	1	...	...	...
Saint Pierre and Miquelon Saint-Pierre-et-Miquelon	4 399	4 694	2 855	5 205	4 621	...	...	...	...	...
Saint Vincent-Grenadines Saint Vincent-Grenadines	8 647	1 740	4 738	5 250	3 828	...	...	...	...	...
Samoa Samoa	4 151	2 760	3 546	4 387	3 583	...	...	...	3	3[1]
Sao Tome and Principe Sao Tomé-et-Principe	4 141	4 196[1]	4 150[1]	4 250[1]	4 250[1]	...	...	...	...	...
Saudi Arabia Arabie saoudite	66 590	74 782	81 062	84 589	90 253[1]	11 172	14 375	15 586	18 497	22 253
Senegal Sénégal	457 057	421 513	392 101	435 702	447 954	204	193[1]	200[1]	200[1]	200[1]
Serbia Serbie	...	...	7 496	9 146	10 729	...	...	4 835	6 609	7 532
Serbia and Montenegro Serbie-et-Monténégro	7 004	7 022	...	...	...	4 616	4 554[1]	...	...	...
Seychelles Seychelles	101 610	109 076	93 022	65 358	69 020	1 175	772	704	368	289
Sierra Leone Sierra Leone	134 440	145 993	148 146	144 535	203 582	...	...	...	...	...
Singapore Singapour	7 579	7 837	11 676	8 025	5 141	5 406	5 917	8 573	4 503	3 518
Slovakia Slovaquie	2 783	2 648	2 981	3 193	2 726	1 180	955	1 263	1 199	1 071
Slovenia Slovénie	2 593	2 569	2 500	2 463	2 184	1 571	1 346	1 369	1 352	1 315
Solomon Islands Iles Salomon	34 977	30 066	39 499	31 278	26 216	...	...	...	1[1]	1[1]
Somalia [1] Somalie [1]	30 000	30 000	30 000	30 000	30 000	...	...	...	...	...
South Africa Afrique du Sud	891 213	820 561	621 653	681 426	646 901	3 109	2 895	3 037	2 669	3 215

31 Fish production *(continued)*

Capture and aquaculture: metric tons

Production halieutique *(suite)*

Pêche de capture et aquaculture: tonnes

Country or area Pays ou zone	Capture production Captures					Aquaculture production Production de l'aquaculture				
	2004	2005	2006	2007	2008	2004	2005	2006	2007	2008
Spain Espagne	1 102 922	1 072 023	1 253 688	1 100 817	1 165 629	293 319	219 367	292 918	281 240	249 062
Sri Lanka Sri Lanka	337 083	192 820	278 327	312 632	330 819	4 003	4 304	5 652	8 233	7 474
Sudan Soudan	64 600[1]	60 600[1]	58 600[1]	67 459	67 500[1]	1 600[1]	1 600[1]	1 600[1]	1 950	2 000[1]
Suriname Suriname	30 690	27 652	30 801	29 679	23 849	288	242	180	52	38
Swaziland [1] Swaziland [1]	70	70	70	70	70	...	...	...	...	...
Sweden Suède	275 911	262 239	276 800	243 618	238 931	5 989	5 880	7 549	5 365	7 595
Switzerland Suisse	2 807	2 689	2 636	2 591	2 796	1 205	1 214	1 214	1 214	1 214
Syrian Arab Republic Rép. arabe syrienne	17 210	16 980	17 166	17 881	15 591	8 682	8 533	8 902	8 425	8 595
Tajikistan Tadjikistan	210	172[1]	172[1]	172[1]	172[1]	26	26[1]	26[1]	26[1]	26
Thailand Thaïlande	4 093 048	4 077 443	3 962 261	3 643 817	3 820 430	1 255 238	1 299 815	1 403 318	1 347 214	1 370 029
TFYR of Macedonia L'ex-R.Y. Macédoine	1 172	1 114	735	1 218	1 453	959	868	646	1 096	1 331
Timor-Leste [1] Timor-Leste [1]	1 714	2 171	2 572	2 942	3 175	15	22	23	31	51
Togo Togo	28 138	27 869	25 005	20 031	20 126[1]	125[1]	125[1]	126[1]	126[1]	126[1]
Tokelau [1] Tokélaou [1]	200	200	200	200	200	...	...	...	...	...
Tonga Tonga	1 648	2 001[1]	2 505	2 549	2 142[1]	3	1	5	4	1
Trinidad and Tobago Trinité-et-Tobago	14 713	18 093	13 123	13 086	13 833	...	...	...	...	...
Tunisia Tunisie	113 839	111 720	113 922	107 162	103 569	2 308	2 603	2 634	3 367	3 328
Turkey Turquie	643 129	544 716	660 223	771 576	645 716	94 450	119 567	129 025	140 021	152 260
Turkmenistan Turkménistan	15 008	15 016[1]	15 016[1]	15 016[1]	15 016[1]	16	16[1]	16[1]	16[1]	16[1]
Turks and Caicos Islands Iles Turques et Caïques	5 681	5 495	6 022	4 830	6 133	4	4	4	0	0
Tuvalu Tuvalu	2 401	2 561	2 201[1]	2 201[1]	2 200[1]	1	1	1[1]	1[1]	...
Uganda Ouganda	377 328	427 575	399 491	551 110	502 250[1]	5 539	10 817	32 392	51 110	52 250[1]
Ukraine Ukraine	228 835	273 476	257 609	241 107	210 148	26 223	28 745	19 181	27 841	15 400
United Arab Emirates Emirats arabes unis	90 570[1]	87 305	83 070[1]	78 870[1]	75 281	570[1]	570[1]	570[1]	570[1]	1 206
United Kingdom Royaume-Uni	860 611	842 718	796 228	793 893	775 190	207 203	172 813	171 848	174 203	179 187
United Rep. of Tanzania [3] Rép.-Unie de Tanzanie [3]	362 513	376 042	334 304	328 540	325 491	13	12	13[1]	13[1]	15
United States Etats-Unis	5 549 156	5 393 145	5 359 023	5 281 964	4 840 986	606 549	513 107	519 258	525 292	500 114

31 Fish production *(continued)*

Capture and aquaculture: metric tons

Production halieutique *(suite)*

Pêche de capture et aquaculture: tonnes

Country or area Pays ou zone	Capture production Captures					Aquaculture production Production de l'aquaculture				
	2004	2005	2006	2007	2008	2004	2005	2006	2007	2008
United States Virgin Is. Iles Vierges américaines	1 522	1 269	1 625	1 137	1 075	...	...	10	10[1]	10[1]
Uruguay Uruguay	123 009	125 863	133 990	108 751	110 727	20	47	36	31	36
Uzbekistan Ouzbékistan	4 323	5 800[1]	7 200	6 226[1]	6 218[1]	3 093	3 800[1]	3 800	3 424[1]	3 418[1]
Vanuatu Vanuatu	112 132	148 082	87 775	92 132	60 906	1	1	114	31	40[1]
Venezuela (Boliv. Rep. of) Venezuela (Rép. boliv. du)	597 148[1]	417 206[1]	338 700[1]	276 303[1]	313 991[1]	24 006	14 622	23 355	19 950	18 627
Viet Nam Viet Nam	3 078 105	3 367 200	3 628 327	4 105 800	4 549 200	1 198 617	1 437 300[1]	1 657 727[1]	2 085 400[1]	2 461 700[1]
Wallis and Futuna Islands Iles Wallis et Futuna	299[1]	299[1]	599	599[1]	599[1]	...	...	...	...	...
Yemen Yémen	256 070[1]	238 270[1]	229 628[1]	179 905[1]	127 121	...	...	...	...	...
Zambia Zambie	72 850	71 052	65 446	79 418	85 043	5 125	5 125[1]	5 210	5 876	5 640
Zanzibar Zanzibar	23 488	23 210	24 418	23 580	24 514	...	...	...	...	...
Zimbabwe Zimbabwe	13 455[1]	12 872	12 950[1]	12 950[1]	12 950[1]	2 955	2 452	2 450[1]	2 450[1]	2 450[1]

Source:
Food and Agriculture Organization of the United Nations (FAO), Rome, FISHSTAT database, last accessed October 2010.

1 FAO estimate.
2 For statistical purposes, the data for China do not include those for the Hong Kong Special Administrative Region (Hong Kong SAR), Macao Special Administrative Region (Macao SAR) and Taiwan Province of China.
3 Tanganyika.

Source:
Organisation des Nations Unies pour l'alimentation et l'agriculture (FAO), Rome, les données des pêches de FISHSTAT, dernier accès octobre 2010.

1 Estimation de la FAO.
2 Pour la présentation des statistiques, les données pour la Chine ne comprennent pas la Région Administrative Spéciale de Hong Kong (Hong Kong RAS), la Région Administrative Spéciale de Macao (Macao RAS) et la province de Taiwan.
3 Tanganyika.

32 Livestock

Stocks: thousand head

Cheptel

Réserves: milliers de têtes

Region, country or area	2001	2002	2003	2004	2005	2006	2007	2008	Region, pays ou zone
World									**Monde**
Asses or mules	**54 626**	**54 484**	**54 013**	**53 860**	**54 032**	**54 305**	**54 418**	**54 703**	**Ânes ou mules**
Buffaloes	**166 362**	**168 789**	**171 682**	**172 651**	**174 526**	**176 189**	**177 377**	**180 703**	**Buffles**
Camels	**21 983**	**22 258**	**22 672**	**23 398**	**23 517**	**24 110**	**24 266**	**24 732**	**Chameaux**
Cattle	**1 317 527**	**1 325 877**	**1 336 639**	**1 344 221**	**1 350 572**	**1 362 050**	**1 360 614**	**1 347 473**	**Bovins**
Goats	**754 665**	**765 230**	**781 651**	**801 827**	**821 897**	**824 828**	**832 835**	**861 902**	**Caprins**
Horses	**57 114**	**56 199**	**56 986**	**57 747**	**58 735**	**58 852**	**58 932**	**58 770**	**Chevaux**
Pigs	**882 574**	**891 586**	**897 399**	**893 157**	**906 623**	**926 618**	**920 642**	**941 282**	**Porcins**
Sheep	**1 037 113**	**1 025 846**	**1 034 875**	**1 062 437**	**1 090 411**	**1 094 364**	**1 094 825**	**1 078 179**	**Ovins**
Africa									**Afrique**
Asses or mules	**15 983**	**16 654**	**16 687**	**17 062**	**17 702**	**18 170**	**18 948**	**19 620**	**Ânes ou mules**
Buffaloes	**3 532**	**3 550**	**3 777**	**3 845**	**3 898**	**3 937**	**4 105**	**5 023**	**Buffles**
Camels	**18 369**	**18 812**	**19 205**	**19 916**	**20 032**	**20 323**	**20 558**	**21 025**	**Chameaux**
Cattle	**231 903**	**237 597**	**241 012**	**243 147**	**251 513**	**255 417**	**261 476**	**269 961**	**Bovins**
Goats	**243 565**	**250 039**	**256 283**	**266 122**	**273 479**	**277 624**	**285 812**	**291 102**	**Caprins**
Horses	**3 852**	**4 085**	**4 130**	**4 190**	**4 241**	**4 336**	**4 480**	**4 519**	**Chevaux**
Pigs	**20 114**	**21 409**	**21 448**	**22 369**	**23 593**	**24 404**	**25 384**	**26 466**	**Porcins**
Sheep	**251 871**	**255 515**	**260 114**	**268 366**	**274 926**	**280 449**	**285 545**	**287 618**	**Ovins**
Algeria									**Algérie**
Asses or mules	224	215	215	201	201	195	190	190[1]	Ânes ou mules
Camels	245	245[1]	250	273	269	287	291	290[1]	Chameaux
Cattle	1 613	1 572	1 561	1 614	1 586	1 608	1 634	1 650[1]	Bovins
Goats	3 129	3 281	3 325	3 451	3 590	3 755	3 838	3 800[1]	Caprins
Horses	44	46	48	45	43	44	45[1]	45[1]	Chevaux
Pigs [1]	6	6	6	6	6	6	6	6	Porcins [1]
Sheep	17 299	17 588	17 503	18 293	18 909	19 616	20 155	20 000[1]	Ovins
Angola									**Angola**
Asses or mules [1]	5	5	5	5	5	5	5	5	Ânes ou mules [1]
Cattle	4 100[1]	4 150[1]	4 150[1]	3 681	4 150[1]	4 150[1]	4 160[1]	4 180[1]	Bovins
Goats [1]	2 150	2 050	2 050	2 050	2 050	2 050	2 060	2 100	Caprins [1]
Horses [1]	1	1	1	1	1	1	1	1	Chevaux [1]
Pigs [1]	800	780	780	780	780	780	782	785	Porcins [1]
Sheep	350[1]	340[1]	340[1]	297	340[1]	340[1]	340[1]	345[1]	Ovins
Benin									**Bénin**
Asses or mules [1]	1	1	1	1	1	1	1	1	Ânes ou mules [1]
Cattle	1 584	1 635	1 689	1 745	1 764	1 810	1 857	1 905	Bovins
Goats	1 250[1]	1 270[1]	1 300[1]	1 350[1]	1 372	1 410	1 440	1 472	Caprins
Horses [1]	1	1	1	1	1	1	1	1	Chevaux [1]
Pigs	277	286	297	309	303	315	327	341	Porcins
Sheep	655[1]	670[1]	670[1]	700[1]	739	759	776	793	Ovins
Botswana									**Botswana**
Asses or mules [1]	333	333	333	333	333	333	333	333	Ânes ou mules [1]
Cattle	2 468	2 000[1]	2 028	2 100[1]	2 300[1]	2 350[1]	2 400[1]	2 450[1]	Bovins
Goats	1 887	1 683	1 355	1 600[1]	1 950[1]	1 950[1]	1 960[1]	1 980[1]	Caprins
Horses [1]	33	33	33	33	33	33	33	33	Chevaux [1]
Pigs	5	8[1]	4	5[1]	5[1]	5[1]	5[1]	6[1]	Porcins
Sheep	306	273	220	250[1]	270[1]	300[1]	300[1]	305[1]	Ovins
Burkina Faso									**Burkina Faso**
Asses or mules	814[1]	863[1]	915	970[1]	1 028[1]	1 090[1]	1 156[1]	1 225[1]	Ânes ou mules
Camels	14[1]	15[1]	15	15[1]	15[1]	16[1]	16[1]	16[1]	Chameaux
Cattle	6 674[1]	6 985[1]	7 312	7 653[1]	8 010[1]	8 379[1]	8 764[1]	9 167[1]	Bovins
Goats	9 405[1]	9 715[1]	10 036	10 367[1]	10 709[1]	11 062[1]	11 428[1]	11 805[1]	Caprins
Horses	34[1]	35[1]	36	37[1]	39[1]	40[1]	41[1]	43[1]	Chevaux
Pigs	1 559[1]	1 715[1]	1 887	2 076[1]	2 284[1]	2 512[1]	2 763[1]	3 040[1]	Porcins
Sheep	6 409[1]	6 554[1]	6 703	6 854[1]	7 009[1]	7 164[1]	7 321[1]	7 482[1]	Ovins
Burundi									**Burundi**
Cattle	315[1]	324	355	374	396	434	479	480[1]	Bovins
Goats	780[1]	820[1]	850[1]	880[1]	900[1]	1 439	1 607	1 650[1]	Caprins
Pigs	80[1]	85[1]	90[1]	95[1]	95[1]	179	190	190[1]	Porcins
Sheep	230[1]	230	240	236	243	267	293	295[1]	Ovins

32 Livestock

Stocks: thousand head

Cheptel

Réserves: milliers de têtes

Region, country or area	2001	2002	2003	2004	2005	2006	2007	2008	Region, pays ou zone
Cameroon									**Cameroun**
Asses or mules [1]	38	39	39	40	40	40	40	40	Ânes ou mules [1]
Cattle	5 800[1]	5 600[2]	5 800[1]	5 900[1]	6 000[2]	6 000[1]	6 000[1]	6 000[1]	Bovins
Goats [1]	4 400	4 400	4 400	4 400	4 400	4 400	4 400	4 400	Caprins [1]
Horses [1]	17	17	17	17	17	17	17	17	Chevaux [1]
Pigs [1]	1 350	1 350	1 350	1 350	1 350	1 350	1 350	1 350	Porcins [1]
Sheep [1]	3 800	3 800	3 800	3 800	3 800	3 800	3 800	3 800	Ovins [1]
Cape Verde									**Cap-Vert**
Asses or mules [1]	16	16	16	16	16	16	16	16	Ânes ou mules [1]
Cattle	22[1]	22[1]	22	22	28[1]	33[1]	38	44[1]	Bovins
Goats	110[1]	112[1]	112	148	161[1]	175[1]	188	202[1]	Caprins
Horses [1]	^0	^0	^0	1	1	1	1	1	Chevaux [1]
Pigs [1]	200	200	200	205	205	210	217	224	Porcins [1]
Sheep	8[1]	9[1]	9	10	12[1]	13[1]	15	16[1]	Ovins
Central African Rep.									**Rép. centrafricaine**
Cattle	3 200	3 273	3 347	3 423[2]	3 430[1]	3 450[1]	3 450[1]	3 500[1]	Bovins
Goats	2 763	2 921	3 087	3 100[1]	3 100[1]	3 100[1]	3 100[1]	3 100[1]	Caprins
Pigs	707	738	771	805[2]	800[1]	800[1]	800[1]	800[1]	Porcins
Sheep	234	246	259	260[1]	260[1]	260[1]	260[1]	260[1]	Ovins
Chad									**Tchad**
Asses or mules	364	372[1]	380[1]	388[1]	388[1]	388[1]	389[1]	389[1]	Ânes ou mules
Camels [1]	877	927	977	1 027	1 077	1 127	1 327	1 358	Chameaux [1]
Cattle	5 992	6 128[2]	6 268[2]	6 400[1]	6 540[1]	6 680[1]	6 820[1]	6 964[1]	Bovins
Goats	5 304	5 463[2]	5 588[2]	5 717[1]	5 843[1]	5 971[1]	6 096[1]	6 224[1]	Caprins
Horses	255[2]	261[2]	267[2]	273[1]	275[1]	277[1]	279[1]	282[1]	Chevaux
Pigs [1]	22	24	24	25	25	26	27	28	Porcins [1]
Sheep	2 431	2 454[2]	2 511[2]	2 569[1]	2 628[1]	2 691[1]	2 982[1]	3 304[1]	Ovins
Comoros									**Comores**
Asses or mules [1]	5	5	5	5	5	5	5	5	Ânes ou mules [1]
Cattle	53[1]	55	45[2]	46[1]	47[1]	47[1]	47[1]	45[1]	Bovins
Goats	113	115[1]	115[1]	115[1]	115[1]	115[1]	115[1]	115[1]	Caprins
Sheep [1]	21	21	22	22	22	22	22	22	Ovins [1]
Congo									**Congo**
Cattle	90	93[1]	100[1]	110[1]	115[1]	115[1]	115[1]	115[1]	Bovins
Goats [1]	280	294	294	294	295	295	295	295	Caprins [1]
Pigs	46[1]	46	46[1]	46[1]	47[1]	47[1]	47[1]	47[1]	Porcins
Sheep [1]	96	98	98	98	99	99	99	100	Ovins [1]
Côte d'Ivoire									**Côte d'Ivoire**
Cattle	1 365	1 393	1 421	1 449	1 478	1 508	1 337	1 538	Bovins
Goats	1 138	1 161	1 184	1 208	1 232	1 257	945	1 282	Caprins
Pigs	302	308	313	319	325	330	324	320[1]	Porcins
Sheep	1 448	1 477	1 507	1 537	1 568	1 599	1 162	1 631	Ovins
Dem. Rep. of the Congo									**Rép. dém. du Congo**
Cattle	793	761	760	758	757	756	754	753	Bovins
Goats	4 067	4 004	4 010	4 016	4 022	4 028	4 034	4 046	Caprins
Pigs	1 000	953	955	957	959	961	963	965	Porcins
Sheep	911	897	898	899	900	900	901	902	Ovins
Djibouti									**Djibouti**
Asses or mules [1]	9	9	9	9	9	9	9	9	Ânes ou mules [1]
Camels	69	69	70[1]	72[1]	72[1]	69[1]	69[1]	69[1]	Chameaux
Cattle	297	297	297[1]	300[1]	300[1]	297[1]	297[1]	297[1]	Bovins
Goats	512	512	512[1]	512[1]	513[1]	512[1]	512[1]	512[1]	Caprins
Sheep	466	466	466[1]	468[1]	468[1]	466[1]	466[1]	466[1]	Ovins
Egypt									**Egypte**
Asses or mules [1]	3 051	3 071	3 071	3 071	3 071	3 071	3 071	3 071	Ânes ou mules [1]
Buffaloes	3 532	3 550[1]	3 777	3 845	3 898[2]	3 937	4 105	5 023	Buffles
Camels	134	127[2]	135[1]	135[1]	120[1]	148	84	107	Chameaux
Cattle	3 801	4 000[1]	4 227	4 369	4 500[1]	4 610	4 933	5 023	Bovins
Goats	3 497[2]	3 582[2]	3 811	3 889	3 915[2]	3 960	4 211	4 237	Caprins
Horses	53	62[2]	62[1]	62[1]	62[1]	54	66	66	Chevaux
Pigs	30	30[1]	31[1]	31[1]	30[1]	31[1]	31[1]	31[1]	Porcins
Sheep	4 671	5 105[2]	4 939	5 043	5 097[2]	5 385	5 467	5 023	Ovins

32 Livestock

Stocks: thousand head

Cheptel

Réserves: milliers de têtes

Region, country or area	2001	2002	2003	2004	2005	2006	2007	2008	Region, pays ou zone
Equatorial Guinea [1]									**Guinée équatoriale [1]**
Cattle	5	5	5	5	5	5	5	5	Bovins
Goats	9	9	9	9	9	9	9	9	Caprins
Pigs	6	6	6	6	6	6	6	6	Porcins
Sheep	38	38	38	38	38	38	38	38	Ovins
Eritrea [1]									**Erythrée [1]**
Camels	75	75	75	77	77	75	76	76	Chameaux
Cattle	1 950	1 900	1 927	1 930	1 950	1 950	1 960	1 960	Bovins
Goats	1 700	1 700	1 800	1 850	1 850	1 700	1 720	1 720	Caprins
Sheep	2 150	2 000	2 100	2 100	2 100	2 100	2 120	2 120	Ovins
Ethiopia									**Ethiopie**
Asses or mules	3 670	4 251	4 050[1]	4 194	4 565	4 826[1]	5 377[1]	5 795[2]	Ânes ou mules
Camels	2 222[1]	2 254[1]	2 286[1]	2 291[1]	2 324[1]	2 358[2]	2 400[1]	2 400[1]	Chameaux
Cattle	35 383	40 639	39 000[1]	38 749	40 390	43 125	45 000[1]	49 298[2]	Bovins
Goats	9 621	11 000[1]	12 000[1]	14 851	16 364	18 560	21 709	21 884[2]	Caprins
Horses	1 254	1 483	1 500[1]	1 518	1 569	1 655	1 776	1 787[2]	Chevaux
Pigs [1]	26	26	28	28	29	29	29	29	Porcins [1]
Sheep	11 438	14 322	16 000[1]	18 075	20 734	23 633	26 117	25 017[2]	Ovins
Gabon [1]									**Gabon [1]**
Cattle	36	36	35	35	35	35	36	37	Bovins
Goats	90	90	90	90	90	90	91	92	Caprins
Pigs	213	212	212	212	212	212	213	215	Porcins
Sheep	198	195	195	195	195	195	196	196	Ovins
Gambia									**Gambie**
Asses or mules [1]	35	35	35	35	35	35	35	35	Ânes ou mules [1]
Cattle	323	327	396	408	410	413	415	420	Bovins
Goats	228	262	297	287	296	305	371	374	Caprins
Horses [1]	17	17	17	17	17	17	17	17	Chevaux [1]
Pigs	14	16	16	16	16	16	24	25	Porcins
Sheep	129	146	203	209	215	221	183	200	Ovins
Ghana									**Ghana**
Asses or mules	14[1]	13	14[1]	14[1]	14[1]	14[1]	14[1]	14[1]	Ânes ou mules
Cattle	1 315	1 330	1 344	1 365[1]	1 385[1]	1 406[1]	1 427[1]	1 427[1]	Bovins
Goats	3 199	3 230	3 560	3 596[1]	3 632[1]	3 668[1]	3 705[1]	3 705[1]	Caprins
Horses	3[1]	3	3[1]	3[1]	3[1]	3[1]	3[1]	3[1]	Chevaux
Pigs	312	310	303	300	305[1]	229[1]	239[1]	239[1]	Porcins
Sheep	2 771	2 922	3 015	3 112[1]	3 211[1]	3 314[1]	3 420[1]	3 420[1]	Ovins
Guinea									**Guinée**
Asses or mules [1]	2	2	2	2	2	2	2	2	Ânes ou mules [1]
Cattle	3 034	3 200	3 376	3 561	3 756	3 962	4 180	4 409	Bovins
Goats	1 076	1 148	1 226	1 308	1 396	1 489	1 589	1 696	Caprins
Horses [1]	3	3	3	3	3	3	3	3	Chevaux [1]
Pigs	62	65	68	71	75	78	82	86	Porcins
Sheep	902	963	1 027	1 096	1 169	1 247	1 330	1 419	Ovins
Guinea-Bissau									**Guinée-Bissau**
Asses or mules [1]	5	5	5	5	5	5	5	5	Ânes ou mules [1]
Cattle	515[1]	515[1]	520[1]	520[1]	530[1]	550[1]	574	599[1]	Bovins
Goats	325[1]	325[1]	330[1]	330[1]	335[1]	350[1]	371	393[1]	Caprins
Horses [1]	2	2	2	2	2	2	2	2	Chevaux [1]
Pigs [1]	350	350	360	360	370	380	391	401	Porcins [1]
Sheep	285[1]	285[1]	290[1]	290[1]	300[1]	330[1]	358	389[1]	Ovins
Kenya									**Kenya**
Camels	819	889	895	1 194	931	1 058	1 006	1 133	Chameaux
Cattle	11 745	11 993	12 531	13 022	13 019	12 430	12 900	13 523	Bovins
Goats	10 980	11 226	11 946	13 391	13 883	12 856	13 966	14 478	Caprins
Horses [1]	2	2	2	2	2	2	2	2	Chevaux [1]
Pigs	333	336	415	380	320	321	304	330	Porcins
Sheep	8 238	8 208	8 195	10 299	10 034	9 871	9 429	9 907	Ovins
Lesotho									**Lesotho**
Asses or mules [1]	158	143	144	85	169	173	171	191	Ânes ou mules [1]
Cattle	732	645	682	677	729	688	695[1]	735[1]	Bovins
Goats	827	790	776	613	821	879	715[1]	750[1]	Caprins

32 Livestock

Stocks: thousand head

Cheptel

Réserves: milliers de têtes

Region, country or area	2001	2002	2003	2004	2005	2006	2007	2008	Region, pays ou zone
Horses	90	77	76	80	71	69	68[1]	65[1]	Chevaux
Pigs	116	103	70	112	135	216	220[1]	230[1]	Porcins
Sheep	1 083	1 031	936	1 045	1 041	905	1 025[1]	1 050[1]	Ovins
Liberia [1]									**Libéria** [1]
Cattle	36	36	36	36	36	37	38	39	Bovins
Goats	220	220	220	220	220	240	262	285	Caprins
Pigs	130	130	130	130	130	150	173	200	Porcins
Sheep	210	210	210	210	210	220	230	241	Ovins
Libyan Arab Jamah.									**Jamah. arabe libyenne**
Asses or mules [1]	30	30	30	30	30	30	30	30	Ânes ou mules [1]
Camels	45	46[1]	47[1]	47[1]	47[1]	47[1]	47[1]	47[1]	Chameaux
Cattle	130	130[1]	130[1]	130[1]	130[1]	130[1]	130[1]	130[1]	Bovins
Goats	1 263[2]	1 265[1]	1 265[1]	1 265[1]	1 265[1]	1 265[1]	1 265[1]	1 265[1]	Caprins
Horses	45[2]	45[2]	45[1]	45[1]	45[1]	45[1]	45[1]	45[1]	Chevaux
Sheep	4 500	4 500	4 500[1]	4 500[1]	4 500[1]	4 500[1]	4 500[1]	4 500[1]	Ovins
Madagascar									**Madagascar**
Cattle	8 800[1]	7 877	8 020	8 105	9 500	9 573	9 600[1]	9 700[1]	Bovins
Goats	1 180	1 220	1 252	1 397	1 219	1 249	1 250[1]	1 260[1]	Caprins
Horses [1]	0	0	0	0	0	0	0	0	Chevaux [1]
Pigs	462	531	605	676	1 247	1 300[1]	1 350[1]	1 360[1]	Porcins
Sheep	633	655	843	800[1]	695	712	715[1]	720[1]	Ovins
Malawi									**Malawi**
Asses or mules [1]	2	2	2	2	2	2	2	2	Ânes ou mules [1]
Cattle	749	753	782	765	778	799	871	947	Bovins
Goats	1 670	1 660	1 717	1 922	1 961	2 301	2 720	3 106	Caprins
Pigs	436	456	435	478	583	637	929	1 229	Porcins
Sheep	115	110	108	125[1]	157	175	186	189	Ovins
Mali									**Mali**
Asses or mules	971	1 047	1 133	1 232	1 347	1 480	1 617[1]	1 767[1]	Ânes ou mules
Camels	443	498	563	641	729	837	960[1]	1 100[1]	Chameaux
Cattle	6 116	6 321	6 552	6 811	7 103	7 431	7 843	8 278[1]	Bovins
Goats	7 315	7 585	7 903	8 274	8 706	9 207	9 667[1]	10 150[1]	Caprins
Horses	69	71	74	79	85	93	101[1]	111[1]	Chevaux
Pigs	61	65	71	85	90	105	71	75[1]	Porcins
Sheep	6 157	6 475	6 836	7 245	7 710	8 240	8 871	9 500[1]	Ovins
Mauritania									**Mauritanie**
Asses or mules [1]	158	158	158	158	158	158	158	158	Ânes ou mules [1]
Camels	1 411	1 467	1 511	1 556	1 603	1 600[1]	1 600[1]	1 600[1]	Chameaux
Cattle	1 565	1 564	1 600[1]	1 650[1]	1 692[2]	1 690[1]	1 690[1]	1 690[1]	Bovins
Goats	5 316	5 555	5 600[1]	5 600[1]	5 600[1]	5 600[1]	5 600[1]	5 600[1]	Caprins
Horses	20[2]	20[1]	20[1]	20[1]	20[1]	20[1]	20[1]	20[1]	Chevaux
Sheep	8 396	8 774	8 800[1]	8 850[1]	8 850[2]	8 850[2]	8 850[2]	8 850[1]	Ovins
Mauritius									**Maurice**
Cattle [1]	28	28	28	28	27	26	26	27	Bovins [1]
Goats	70[1]	55[1]	57[1]	40[1]	30[1]	24	25	25[1]	Caprins
Pigs	13[1]	11[1]	12[1]	12[1]	11[1]	16	17	12[1]	Porcins
Sheep [1]	12	12	11	11	11	13	11	1	Ovins [1]
Morocco									**Maroc**
Asses or mules	1 516	1 493	1 529	1 569	1 542	1 525	1 504	1 483	Ânes ou mules
Camels [1]	37	38	39	39	40	50	40	45	Chameaux [1]
Cattle	2 647	2 670	2 689	2 729	2 722	2 755	2 781	2 814	Bovins
Goats	5 133	5 090	5 208	5 359	5 332	5 355	5 284	5 118	Caprins
Horses	154	148	156	157	159	161	152	162	Chevaux
Pigs [1]	8	8	8	8	8	8	8	8	Porcins [1]
Sheep	17 172	16 336	16 743	17 026	16 872	17 260	16 894	17 078	Ovins
Mozambique									**Mozambique**
Asses or mules	21	33	41	42[1]	45[1]	45[1]	45[1]	45[1]	Ânes ou mules
Cattle	722	791	965	1 000[1]	1 100[1]	1 055	1 426	1 240	Bovins
Goats	5 047	4 912	4 753	4 800[1]	5 000[1]	4 950[1]	5 000[1]	5 000[1]	Caprins
Pigs [1]	185	190	190	195	200	180	182	182	Porcins [1]
Sheep	174	183	135	150[1]	165[1]	145	219	182	Ovins

32 Livestock

Stocks: thousand head

Cheptel

Réserves: milliers de têtes

Region, country or area	2001	2002	2003	2004	2005	2006	2007	2008	Region, pays ou zone
Namibia									**Namibie**
Asses or mules [1]	176	126	137	142	147	147	147	147	Ânes ou mules [1]
Cattle	2 509	2 330	2 336	2 309	3 134	2 384	2 500[1]	2 500[1]	Bovins
Goats	1 769	2 110	2 087	1 997	2 043	2 061	2 000[1]	2 000[1]	Caprins
Horses	53	48	50[1]	63	47	46	50[1]	50[1]	Chevaux
Pigs	22	24[1]	25[1]	29[1]	31[1]	25[1]	25[1]	25[1]	Porcins
Sheep	2 234	2 764	2 955	2 619	2 664	2 660	2 700[1]	2 700[1]	Ovins
Niger									**Niger**
Asses or mules	1 365	1 392	1 420	1 448	1 477	1 507	1 537	1 567	Ânes ou mules
Camels	1 487	1 506	1 526	1 545	1 565	1 586	1 606	1 627	Chameaux
Cattle	5 811	6 160	6 529	6 930	7 336	7 776	8 243	8 737	Bovins
Goats	9 697	9 991	10 390	10 806	11 238	11 688	12 155	12 641	Caprins
Horses	221	223	226	228	230	233	235	237	Chevaux
Pigs [1]	39	40	40	40	40	40	40	40	Porcins [1]
Sheep	8 010	8 291	8 581	8 881	9 192	9 514	9 847	10 191	Ovins
Nigeria									**Nigéria**
Asses or mules [1]	1 000	1 000	1 000	1 050	1 050	1 050	1 050	1 050	Ânes ou mules [1]
Camels [1]	18	18	18	18	18	19	19	19	Chameaux [1]
Cattle	15 133	15 149	15 164	15 700	15 875	16 066[1]	16 153	16 293	Bovins
Goats	45 260	46 400	47 552	48 700	49 959	51 224[1]	52 488	53 800	Caprins
Horses [1]	205	205	205	206	206	207	208	208	Chevaux [1]
Pigs	5 250	6 112	5 678	5 910[1]	6 141	6 390[1]	6 642	6 908	Porcins
Sheep	28 693	29 400	30 086	30 800	31 548	32 314[1]	33 080	33 874	Ovins
Réunion									**Réunion**
Cattle	30	31	32	34	36	36	35[2]	36[1]	Bovins
Goats	37	37	37	36	36	36	40	40[1]	Caprins
Pigs	78	79	83	88	77	73	79[2]	79[1]	Porcins
Sheep	2	2	1	1	1	1	1[1]	1[1]	Ovins
Rwanda									**Rwanda**
Cattle	816	815	992	1 004	1 004	1 000[1]	1 000[1]	1 000[1]	Bovins
Goats	757	920	941	1 264	1 340	1 400[1]	1 400[1]	1 400[1]	Caprins
Pigs	186	208	212	327	347	350[1]	350[1]	350[1]	Porcins
Sheep	278	301	372	470	464	470[1]	470[1]	470[1]	Ovins
Saint Helena [1]									**Sainte-Hélène** [1]
Cattle	1	1	1	1	1	1	1	1	Bovins
Goats	1	1	1	1	1	1	1	1	Caprins
Pigs	1	1	1	1	1	1	1	1	Porcins
Sheep	1	1	1	1	1	1	1	1	Ovins
Sao Tome and Principe [1]									**Sao Tomé-et-Principe** [1]
Cattle	4	4	5	5	5	5	5	5	Bovins
Goats	5	5	5	5	5	5	5	5	Caprins
Pigs	2	2	3	3	3	3	3	3	Porcins
Sheep	3	3	3	3	3	3	3	3	Ovins
Senegal									**Sénégal**
Asses or mules	407	400	400	412	413	415	438	441	Ânes ou mules
Camels	4	4	4	4	4	4	5	5	Chameaux
Cattle	3 061	2 997	3 018	3 039	3 091	3 137	3 163	3 208	Bovins
Goats	3 995	3 900	3 969	4 025	4 144	4 263	4 353	4 471	Caprins
Horses	492	496	500	504	514	518	518	522	Chevaux
Pigs	280	291	303	300	309	318	319	326	Porcins
Sheep	4 678	4 540	4 614	4 739	4 863	4 996	5 109	5 241	Ovins
Seychelles [1]									**Seychelles** [1]
Cattle	1	1	1	1	1	1	1	1	Bovins
Goats	5	5	5	5	5	5	5	5	Caprins
Pigs	18	15	13	10	8	8	8	8	Porcins
Sierra Leone									**Sierra Leone**
Cattle	150[1]	150	170	200	250	350	350[1]	350[1]	Bovins
Goats	200[1]	200	258	350	438	540	540[1]	540[1]	Caprins
Horses [1]	400	400	400	410	410	410	410	410	Chevaux [1]
Pigs	55[1]	52	52[1]	52[1]	52[1]	54[1]	55[1]	52[1]	Porcins
Sheep	150[1]	150	200	300	375	470	470[1]	470[1]	Ovins

32 Livestock

Stocks: thousand head

Cheptel

Réserves: milliers de têtes

Region, country or area	2001	2002	2003	2004	2005	2006	2007	2008	Region, pays ou zone
Somalia									**Somalie**
Asses or mules [1]	40	41	42	44	44	44	44	44	Ânes ou mules [1]
Camels	7 079	7 156[2]	7 200[1]	7 210[1]	7 230[1]	7 000[1]	7 000[1]	7 000[1]	Chameaux
Cattle	5 256	5 319[2]	5 350[1]	5 400[1]	5 500[1]	5 350[1]	5 350[1]	5 350[1]	Bovins
Goats [1]	12 700	12 750	13 000	13 800	14 600	12 700	12 700	12 700	Caprins [1]
Horses [1]	1	1	1	1	1	1	1	1	Chevaux [1]
Pigs [1]	4	4	5	5	5	4	4	4	Porcins [1]
Sheep	14 084	14 324[2]	14 350[1]	14 500[1]	14 700[1]	13 100[1]	13 100[1]	13 100[1]	Ovins
South Africa									**Afrique du Sud**
Asses or mules [1]	164	164	164	164	164	164	165	165	Ânes ou mules [1]
Cattle	13 500	13 635	13 538	13 512	13 790	13 532	13 911	14 398	Bovins
Goats	6 550[1]	6 452	6 358	6 372	6 356	6 400	6 265	6 741	Caprins
Horses [1]	270	270	270	270	270	270	270	270	Chevaux [1]
Pigs	1 592	1 663	1 662	1 651	1 656	1 662	1 651	1 683	Porcins
Sheep	28 800[1]	26 000[1]	25 820	25 360	25 334	24 983	25 082	25 233	Ovins
Sudan									**Soudan**
Asses or mules [1]	751	751	751	751	751	751	751	751	Ânes ou mules [1]
Camels	3 203	3 342	3 503	3 724	3 908	4 087	4 250	4 400	Chameaux
Cattle	38 325	38 183	39 760	39 760	40 468	40 994	41 000	41 400	Bovins
Goats	39 952	41 485	42 030	42 179	42 526	42 756	42 987	43 100	Caprins
Horses [1]	26	26	26	26	26	26	26	26	Chevaux [1]
Sheep	47 043	48 136	48 440	48 910	49 797	50 390	50 944	51 100	Ovins
Swaziland									**Swaziland**
Asses or mules [1]	15	15	15	15	15	15	15	15	Ânes ou mules [1]
Cattle	506	522[2]	600	610[1]	615[1]	580[1]	585[1]	585[1]	Bovins
Goats	422[1]	350[1]	274[2]	274[1]	274[1]	275[1]	276[1]	276[1]	Caprins
Horses [1]	1	1	1	1	1	1	2	2	Chevaux [1]
Pigs [1]	30	32	35	35	37	30	30	30	Porcins [1]
Sheep [1]	27	27	35	27	27	27	28	28	Ovins [1]
Togo									**Togo**
Asses or mules [1]	3	3	3	3	3	3	3	3	Ânes ou mules [1]
Cattle	297	306	315	325	334	344	355	366[1]	Bovins
Goats [1]	1 450	1 460	1 470	1 480	1 480	1 490	1 499	1 508	Caprins [1]
Horses [1]	2	2	2	2	2	2	2	2	Chevaux [1]
Pigs	413	434	456	478	502	527	554	582[1]	Porcins
Sheep [1]	1 600	1 700	1 800	1 850	1 850	1 900	1 950	2 002	Ovins [1]
Tunisia									**Tunisie**
Asses or mules [1]	311	311	311	311	311	311	311	311	Ânes ou mules [1]
Camels [1]	232	232	232	232	232	232	232	232	Chameaux [1]
Cattle	763	753	679	657	686	703	710	695	Bovins
Goats	1 450	1 449	1 379	1 412	1 427	1 497	1 551	1 496	Caprins
Horses	57	57[1]	57[1]	57[1]	57[1]	57[1]	57[1]	57[1]	Chevaux
Pigs [1]	6	6	6	6	6	6	6	6	Porcins [1]
Sheep	6 861	6 833	6 613	6 949	7 213	7 484	7 618	7 301	Ovins
Uganda									**Ouganda**
Asses or mules [1]	18	18	18	18	18	18	18	18	Ânes ou mules [1]
Cattle	6 144	6 328	6 519	6 567	6 770	6 973	7 182	7 398	Bovins
Goats	6 620	6 852	7 092	7 566	7 800	8 034	8 275	8 523	Caprins
Pigs	1 644	1 710	1 778	1 940	2 000	2 060	2 122	2 186	Porcins
Sheep	1 180	1 141	1 175	1 552	1 600	1 648	1 697	1 748	Ovins
United Rep. of Tanzania									**Rép.-Unie de Tanzanie**
Asses or mules [1]	182	182	182	182	182	182	182	182	Ânes ou mules [1]
Cattle	17 037	17 367	17 704	17 472	17 719	17 700[1]	18 000[1]	18 000[1]	Bovins
Goats	12 102	12 324	12 556	12 550[1]	12 550[1]	12 550[1]	12 550[1]	12 550[1]	Caprins
Pigs	455[1]	458	455	455[1]	455[1]	455[1]	455[1]	455[1]	Porcins
Sheep	3 508	3 514	3 945	3 950[1]	4 000[1]	4 000[1]	3 550[1]	3 550[1]	Ovins
Western Sahara [1]									**Sahara occidental [1]**
Asses or mules	1	1	1	1	1	1	1	1	Ânes ou mules
Camels	106	106	107	107	107	107	107	107	Chameaux
Cattle	107	...	...	...	...	...	...	...	Bovins
Goats	172	172	173	173	173	173	173	173	Caprins
Sheep	33	33	34	34	34	34	34	34	Ovins

32 Livestock

Stocks: thousand head

Cheptel

Réserves: milliers de têtes

Region, country or area	2001	2002	2003	2004	2005	2006	2007	2008	Région, pays ou zone
Zambia [1]									**Zambie** [1]
Asses or mules	2	2	2	2	2	2	2	2	Ânes ou mules
Cattle	2 700	2 900	2 900	2 800	2 900	2 800	2 850	2 850	Bovins
Goats	1 400	1 500	1 700	1 850	1 950	1 950	2 000	2 000	Caprins
Pigs	325	330	340	345	345	340	340	340	Porcins
Sheep	150	165	170	180	190	195	200	200	Ovins
Zimbabwe									**Zimbabwe**
Asses or mules [1]	109	111	113	113	113	113	113	113	Ânes ou mules [1]
Cattle	5 752	5 600[1]	5 400[1]	5 350[1]	5 300[1]	5 400[1]	5 400[1]	5 400[1]	Bovins
Goats	2 968	2 950[1]	2 970[1]	2 980[1]	2 960[1]	3 000[1]	3 000[1]	3 000[1]	Caprins
Horses [1]	27	27	28	28	28	28	28	28	Chevaux [1]
Pigs	604	605[1]	620[1]	620[1]	630[1]	625[1]	630[1]	630[1]	Porcins
Sheep	600	600[1]	550[1]	530[1]	500[1]	610[1]	610[1]	610[1]	Ovins
Americas									**Amériques**
Asses or mules	**13 772**	**13 588**	**13 595**	**13 538**	**13 499**	**13 670**	**13 588**	**13 480**	**Ânes ou mules**
Buffaloes	**1 125**	**1 121**	**1 155**	**1 140**	**1 180**	**1 164**	**1 139**	**1 139**	**Buffles**
Cattle	**468 171**	**478 171**	**492 650**	**501 669**	**503 133**	**507 896**	**504 478**	**480 940**	**Bovins**
Goats	**35 128**	**36 184**	**36 583**	**37 051**	**37 644**	**38 045**	**37 321**	**37 409**	**Caprins**
Horses	**29 968**	**30 072**	**31 201**	**32 182**	**33 374**	**33 561**	**33 489**	**33 594**	**Chevaux**
Pigs	**147 209**	**145 911**	**146 493**	**148 883**	**152 120**	**155 311**	**156 318**	**163 198**	**Porcins**
Sheep	**90 149**	**86 100**	**86 635**	**87 400**	**90 024**	**90 669**	**90 840**	**91 215**	**Ovins**
Antigua and Barbuda [1]									**Antigua-et-Barbuda** [1]
Asses or mules	1	2	2	2	2	2	2	2	Ânes ou mules
Cattle	14	14	14	14	14	14	15	15	Bovins
Goats	35	35	36	36	36	36	36	37	Caprins
Pigs	3	3	3	3	3	3	3	3	Porcins
Sheep	18	19	19	19	19	20	20	20	Ovins
Argentina									**Argentine**
Asses or mules [1]	275	275	283	283	283	283	283	283	Ânes ou mules [1]
Cattle	48 851	48 100	50 869[2]	50 768[2]	50 167[2]	50 700[1]	50 750[1]	50 750[1]	Bovins
Goats	3 387	4 000	4 200[1]	4 200[1]	4 200[1]	4 200[1]	4 250[1]	4 250[1]	Caprins
Horses [1]	3 600	3 650	3 655	3 655	3 655	3 650	3 680	3 680	Chevaux [1]
Pigs [1]	1 700	1 600	1 500	1 490	1 830	2 260	2 270	2 270	Porcins [1]
Sheep	13 500[1]	12 400	12 450[1]	12 450[1]	12 450[1]	12 400[1]	12 450[1]	12 450[1]	Ovins
Bahamas									**Bahamas**
Cattle	1	1[1]	1[1]	1[1]	1[1]	1[1]	1[1]	1[1]	Bovins
Goats	14	14[1]	14[1]	15[1]	15[1]	15[1]	15[1]	15[1]	Caprins
Pigs	5	5[1]	5[1]	5[1]	5[1]	5[1]	5[1]	5[1]	Porcins
Sheep	6	6[1]	6[1]	7[1]	7[1]	7[1]	7[1]	7[1]	Ovins
Barbados [1]									**Barbade** [1]
Asses or mules	4	4	4	4	4	4	4	4	Ânes ou mules
Cattle	21	19	17	15	13	11	11	11	Bovins
Goats	5	5	5	5	5	5	5	5	Caprins
Horses	1	1	1	1	1	1	1	1	Chevaux
Pigs	16	13	16	19	19	20	20	20	Porcins
Sheep	6	8	10	11	11	11	11	12	Ovins
Belize									**Belize**
Asses or mules [1]	4	5	5	5	5	5	5	5	Ânes ou mules [1]
Cattle	58	57	58	58	58[1]	68	73	81	Bovins
Horses [1]	5	5	5	5	5	5	5	5	Chevaux [1]
Pigs	28	23	21	21	21[1]	15	12	13	Porcins
Sheep	4	6	6	6	6[1]	8	10	10	Ovins
Bermuda [1]									**Bermudes** [1]
Cattle	1	1	1	1	1	1	1	1	Bovins
Horses	1	1	1	1	1	1	1	1	Chevaux
Pigs	1	1	1	1	1	1	1	1	Porcins
Bolivia (Plur. State of)									**Bolivie (État plur. de)**
Asses or mules [1]	712	714	717	717	717	717	717	717	Ânes ou mules [1]
Cattle	6 746	6 928	7 113	7 303	7 509	7 718	7 894	7 894[1]	Bovins
Goats	1 748	1 784	1 822	1 861	1 896	1 926	1 960	1 960[1]	Caprins
Horses	380[1]	400[1]	429	437	447	456	465	465[1]	Chevaux

32 Livestock

Stocks: thousand head

Cheptel

Réserves: milliers de têtes

Region, country or area	2001	2002	2003	2004	2005	2006	2007	2008	Region, pays ou zone
Pigs	1 956	2 059	2 166	2 282	2 390	2 488	2 592	2 592[1]	Porcins
Sheep	8 046	8 248	8 416	8 623	8 816	8 987	9 177	9 177[1]	Ovins
Brazil									**Brésil**
Asses or mules	2 585	2 556	2 554	2 552[2]	2 578[2]	2 573	2 507	2 507[1]	Ânes ou mules
Buffaloes	1 119	1 115	1 149	1 134	1 174	1 157	1 132	1 132[1]	Buffles
Cattle	176 389	185 347	195 552	204 513	207 157	205 886	199 752	175 437[2]	Bovins
Goats	9 537	9 429	9 582	10 047	10 307	10 401	9 450	9 500[1]	Caprins
Horses	5 801	5 774	5 828	5 787	5 787	5 749	5 602	5 650[1]	Chevaux
Pigs	32 605	32 013	32 305	33 085	34 064	35 174	35 945	40 000[1]	Porcins
Sheep	14 639	14 287	14 556	15 058	15 588	16 019	16 239	16 500[1]	Ovins
British Virgin Islands[1]									**Iles Vierges britanniques**[1]
Cattle	2	2	2	2	2	2	2	2	Bovins
Goats	10	10	10	10	10	10	10	10	Caprins
Pigs	2	2	2	2	2	2	2	2	Porcins
Sheep	6	6	6	6	6	6	6	6	Ovins
Canada									**Canada**
Asses or mules[1]	4	4	4	4	4	4	4	4	Ânes ou mules[1]
Cattle	13 608	13 752	13 466	14 555	14 925	14 655	14 155	13 895	Bovins
Goats[1]	30	30	30	30	30	30	30	30	Caprins[1]
Horses[1]	470	385	385	385	385	385	385	385	Chevaux[1]
Pigs	13 576	14 375	14 745	14 725	14 810	15 110	14 907	13 810	Porcins
Sheep	948	994	975	994	978	894	879	825	Ovins
Cayman Islands[1]									**Iles Caïmanes**[1]
Cattle	1	1	1	1	1	1	1	1	Bovins
Chile									**Chili**
Asses or mules	38[1]	39[1]	40[1]	40[1]	41[1]	40[1]	22	23[1]	Ânes ou mules
Cattle	3 980[2]	3 927[2]	3 932[2]	3 989[2]	3 985[1]	3 900[1]	3 789	3 800[1]	Bovins
Goats	705[1]	735[1]	715[1]	725[1]	735[1]	735[1]	739	740[1]	Caprins
Horses	445[1]	400[1]	365[1]	350[1]	335[1]	350[1]	320	320[1]	Chevaux
Pigs	2 170	2 305	2 166	2 314	2 572	2 855	2 957	2 960[1]	Porcins
Sheep	4 090[1]	4 050[1]	3 750[1]	3 680[1]	3 400[1]	3 400[1]	3 938	3 950[1]	Ovins
Colombia									**Colombie**
Asses or mules	800[1]	750[1]	700[1]	658[1]	571[1]	739	748	654	Ânes ou mules
Cattle	24 510	24 765	24 799	24 922	25 699	26 129	26 703	26 878	Bovins
Goats	1 136	1 105	1 120[1]	1 140[1]	1 160[1]	1 180[1]	1 200[1]	1 200[1]	Caprins
Horses	2 600[1]	2 600[1]	2 592	2 591	2 554	2 317	2 394	2 421	Chevaux
Pigs	2 500[1]	2 350[1]	2 100[1]	1 892	1 724	1 745[1]	1 914	1 830[1]	Porcins
Sheep	2 256	2 045	2 500[1]	2 831	3 333	3 300[1]	3 400[1]	3 400[1]	Ovins
Costa Rica									**Costa Rica**
Asses or mules[1]	13	13	13	13	13	13	13	13	Ânes ou mules[1]
Cattle	1 289	1 220	1 150	1 081	1 000[1]	1 100[1]	1 200[1]	1 287[1]	Bovins
Goats[1]	3	4	5	5	5	5	5	5	Caprins[1]
Horses[1]	115	115	115	115	115	115	120	120	Chevaux[1]
Pigs[1]	300	310	315	550	550	573	676	729	Porcins[1]
Sheep[1]	3	3	3	3	3	3	3	3	Ovins[1]
Cuba									**Cuba**
Asses or mules	31	31	31	31	30	30	30	31	Ânes ou mules
Cattle	4 038	3 972	4 025	3 943	3 704	3 737	3 787	3 821	Bovins
Goats	759	866	951	1 047	1 040	1 171	1 126	1 134	Caprins
Horses	431	438	452	464	470	483	506	534	Chevaux
Pigs	1 313	1 554	1 684	1 593	1 626	1 761	1 869	1 879	Porcins
Sheep	2 524	2 614	2 580	2 410	2 361	2 761	2 653	2 675	Ovins
Dominica[1]									**Dominique**[1]
Cattle	13	13	13	13	13	14	14	14	Bovins
Goats	10	10	10	10	10	10	10	10	Caprins
Pigs	5	5	5	5	5	5	5	5	Porcins
Sheep	8	8	8	8	8	8	8	8	Ovins
Dominican Republic									**Rép. dominicaine**
Asses or mules[1]	290	290	291	291	291	291	291	291	Ânes ou mules[1]
Cattle	2 107	2 160	2 207	2 509	2 200[1]	2 228	2 653[1]	2 653[1]	Bovins
Goats	187	188	189[1]	189[1]	190[1]	190[1]	190[1]	190[1]	Caprins
Horses[1]	340	342	343	343	345	348	350	350	Chevaux[1]

32 Livestock

Stocks: thousand head

Cheptel

Réserves: milliers de têtes

Region, country or area	2001	2002	2003	2004	2005	2006	2007	2008	Region, pays ou zone
Pigs	566	577[1]	578[1]	471[1]	580[1]	580[1]	580[1]	580[1]	Porcins
Sheep	106	121	122[1]	123[1]	123[1]	123[1]	123[1]	123[1]	Ovins
Ecuador									**Equateur**
Asses or mules	428[1]	298	306	298	295	304	281	265	Ânes ou mules
Cattle	4 657	5 016	4 985	5 082	4 971	5 035	4 727	4 892	Bovins
Goats	273	155	141	135	144	156	171	150	Caprins
Horses	525[1]	391	400	411	411	403	383	364	Chevaux
Pigs	1 402[1]	1 428	1 410	1 282	1 281	1 912	1 323	1 097	Porcins
Sheep	2 249	1 110	1 014	1 047	1 053	973	846	743	Ovins
El Salvador									**El Salvador**
Asses or mules [1]	27	27	27	27	27	27	27	27	Ânes ou mules [1]
Cattle	1 216	1 301	1 249	1 259	1 257	1 319	1 370	1 397	Bovins
Goats	12[1]	11	11[1]	11[1]	11[1]	11[1]	11[1]	11[1]	Caprins
Horses [1]	96	96	96	96	96	96	96	96	Chevaux [1]
Pigs	150	153	337	355	356	436	441	467	Porcins
Sheep [1]	5	5	5	5	5	5	5	5	Ovins [1]
Falkland Is. (Malvinas) [1]									**Iles Falkland (Malvinas)** [1]
Cattle	4	4	4	4	4	4	4	4	Bovins
Horses	1	1	1	1	1	1	1	1	Chevaux
Sheep	690	690	690	690	690	690	700	700	Ovins
French Guiana [1]									**Guyane française** [1]
Cattle	9	9	9	9	9	9	9	9	Bovins
Goats	1	1	1	1	1	1	1	1	Caprins
Pigs	11	11	11	11	11	11	11	11	Porcins
Sheep	3	3	3	3	3	3	3	3	Ovins
Greenland									**Groenland**
Sheep	20	19	19	19[1]	19[1]	19[1]	20[1]	20[1]	Ovins
Grenada [1]									**Grenade** [1]
Asses or mules	1	1	1	1	1	1	1	1	Ânes ou mules
Cattle	4	4	4	4	4	4	4	4	Bovins
Goats	7	7	7	7	7	7	7	7	Caprins
Pigs	3	3	3	3	3	3	3	3	Porcins
Sheep	13	13	13	13	13	13	13	13	Ovins
Guadeloupe									**Guadeloupe**
Cattle	63	89[2]	77[2]	73[2]	74[1]	73[1]	75[1]	75[1]	Bovins
Goats	47	48	48[2]	48[2]	48[1]	48[1]	48[1]	48[1]	Caprins
Horses [1]	1	1	1	1	1	1	1	1	Chevaux [1]
Pigs	29	33[2]	31[2]	24[2]	30[1]	30[1]	30[1]	30[1]	Porcins
Sheep	4	3[2]	3[2]	3[2]	3[1]	3[1]	3[1]	3[1]	Ovins
Guatemala									**Guatemala**
Asses or mules [1]	48	49	49	49	49	49	49	49	Ânes ou mules [1]
Cattle	2 500[1]	2 540[1]	2 540[1]	2 540[1]	2 453	2 796	3 261	3 261[1]	Bovins
Goats	112[1]	112[1]	112[1]	112[1]	112[1]	112[1]	101	101[1]	Caprins
Horses [1]	120	122	124	124	124	124	125	125	Chevaux [1]
Pigs	1 794	2 264	2 682	2 718	3 108	2 701	2 708	2 736	Porcins
Sheep	245	250[1]	260[1]	260[1]	260[1]	265[1]	265[1]	265[1]	Ovins
Guyana [1]									**Guyana** [1]
Asses or mules	1	1	1	1	1	1	1	1	Ânes ou mules
Cattle	120	110	110	110	110	110	110	110	Bovins
Goats	79	79	79	79	79	79	79	79	Caprins
Horses	2	2	2	2	2	2	2	2	Chevaux
Pigs	9	9	12	12	13	13	14	14	Porcins
Sheep	130	130	130	130	130	130	130	130	Ovins
Haiti [1]									**Haïti** [1]
Asses or mules	297	297	303	280	290	290	290	290	Ânes ou mules
Cattle	1 440	1 450	1 455	1 456	1 460	1 450	1 450	1 455	Bovins
Goats	1 942	1 943	1 944	1 900	1 910	1 900	1 900	1 910	Caprins
Horses	501	501	501	500	502	500	500	500	Chevaux
Pigs	1 001	1 001	1 002	1 000	1 001	1 000	1 000	1 001	Porcins
Sheep	152	153	154	154	154	153	153	154	Ovins
Honduras									**Honduras**
Asses or mules [1]	93	93	93	93	93	93	93	93	Ânes ou mules [1]

32 Livestock

Stocks: thousand head

Cheptel

Réserves: milliers de têtes

Region, country or area	2001	2002	2003	2004	2005	2006	2007	2008	Region, pays ou zone
Cattle	1 860	2 050	2 403	2 451	2 500	2 550[1]	2 600[1]	2 545	Bovins
Goats	32[1]	25	25	24	24	25[1]	25[1]	25[1]	Caprins
Horses [1]	180	180	181	181	181	181	181	181	Chevaux [1]
Pigs	538[2]	538	478	483	490	490[1]	490[1]	490[1]	Porcins
Sheep	14[1]	14	15	15	15	15[1]	15[1]	15[1]	Ovins
Jamaica [1]									**Jamaïque [1]**
Asses or mules	33	33	33	33	33	33	33	33	Ânes ou mules
Cattle	400	400	430	390	360	430	430	430	Bovins
Goats	440	440	440	440	440	440	440	440	Caprins
Horses	4	4	4	4	4	4	4	4	Chevaux
Pigs	180	150	170	197	262	221	186	186	Porcins
Sheep	1	1	1	1	2	1	1	1	Ovins
Martinique									**Martinique**
Cattle	28	24	25[1]	25[1]	25[1]	25[1]	25[1]	25[1]	Bovins
Goats	14	13	13	14[1]	14[1]	14[1]	14[1]	14[1]	Caprins
Horses	1	1	1[1]	1[1]	1[1]	1[1]	1[1]	1[1]	Chevaux
Pigs	26	20	19	20[1]	20[1]	20[1]	20[1]	20[1]	Porcins
Sheep	20	18	13	15[1]	15[1]	15[1]	15[1]	15[1]	Ovins
Mexico									**Mexique**
Asses or mules [1]	6 540	6 540	6 540	6 540	6 540	6 540	6 540	6 540	Ânes ou mules [1]
Cattle	30 621	31 390	31 477	31 248	28 763	31 163	31 950[1]	32 565[1]	Bovins
Goats	8 702	9 130	8 992	8 853	8 887	8 890	8 900[1]	8 831[1]	Caprins
Horses [1]	6 255	6 255	6 260	6 260	6 260	6 300	6 350	6 350	Chevaux [1]
Pigs	17 584	15 123	14 625	15 177	15 342	15 257	15 500[1]	15 528[1]	Porcins
Sheep	6 165	6 417	6 820	7 083	7 624	7 287	7 500[1]	7 825[1]	Ovins
Montserrat [1]									**Montserrat [1]**
Cattle	10	10	10	10	10	10	10	10	Bovins
Goats	7	7	7	7	7	7	7	7	Caprins
Pigs	1	1	1	1	1	1	1	1	Porcins
Sheep	5	5	5	5	5	5	5	5	Ovins
Netherlands Antilles [1]									**Antilles néerlandaises [1]**
Asses or mules	3	3	3	3	3	3	3	3	Ânes ou mules
Cattle	^0	1	^0	1	1	1	1	1	Bovins
Goats	13	13	14	14	14	14	14	14	Caprins
Pigs	2	2	2	3	3	3	3	3	Porcins
Sheep	9	9	9	9	9	9	9	9	Ovins
Nicaragua									**Nicaragua**
Asses or mules [1]	55	55	56	57	57	57	57	57	Ânes ou mules [1]
Cattle	3 300	3 350	3 500	3 400[2]	3 500[1]	3 600[1]	3 600[1]	3 600[1]	Bovins
Goats [1]	7	7	7	7	7	7	7	7	Caprins [1]
Horses [1]	248	250	260	265	268	268	268	268	Chevaux [1]
Pigs [1]	432	448	462	461	463	472	473	473	Porcins [1]
Sheep [1]	5	5	6	6	6	6	6	6	Ovins [1]
Panama									**Panama**
Asses or mules [1]	4	4	4	4	4	4	4	4	Ânes ou mules [1]
Cattle	1 533	1 533	1 498	1 480	1 565	1 562	1 526	1 603	Bovins
Goats	5	6	6[1]	6[1]	6[1]	6[1]	6[1]	6[1]	Caprins
Horses [1]	168	170	175	178	180	185	190	190	Chevaux [1]
Pigs	312	303	312	291	286	278	325	318	Porcins
Paraguay									**Paraguay**
Asses or mules [1]	47	48	50	50	50	50	50	50	Ânes ou mules [1]
Cattle	9 889	9 260	10 128	9 622	9 838	9 983	10 464	10 562	Bovins
Goats	124	125	136	159	160[1]	165[1]	167[1]	168[1]	Caprins
Horses	358	358[1]	360[1]	360[1]	370[1]	370[1]	380[1]	400[1]	Chevaux
Pigs	1 804	1 365	1 474	1 507	1 600[1]	1 650[1]	1 680[1]	1 700[1]	Porcins
Sheep	406	410	443	525	525[1]	550[1]	550[1]	560[1]	Ovins
Peru									**Pérou**
Asses or mules [1]	830	850	880	895	910	910	925	925	Ânes ou mules [1]
Cattle	4 962	4 990	5 133	5 181	5 241	5 241	5 421	5 421[1]	Bovins
Goats	1 998	1 942	1 984	1 959	1 957	1 937	1 926	1 926[1]	Caprins
Horses [1]	700	710	720	725	730	730	730	730	Chevaux [1]

32 Livestock

Stocks: thousand head

Cheptel

Réserves: milliers de têtes

Region, country or area	2001	2002	2003	2004	2005	2006	2007	2008	Region, pays ou zone
Pigs	2 781	2 849	2 992	3 004	3 005	3 074	3 116	3 116[1]	Porcins
Sheep	14 253	14 025	14 752	14 735	14 822	14 675	14 580	14 580[1]	Ovins
Puerto Rico									**Porto Rico**
Asses or mules [1]	5	5	5	5	5	5	5	5	Ânes ou mules [1]
Cattle	396	400	421	388	377	378[1]	380[1]	380[1]	Bovins
Goats	9[1]	9[1]	5	3	3	3[1]	3[1]	3[1]	Caprins
Horses	26[1]	26[1]	4	5	6	6[1]	7[1]	7[1]	Chevaux
Pigs	112	102	50[1]	50[1]	49	49[1]	50[1]	50[1]	Porcins
Sheep	16[1]	16[1]	6	5	6	6[1]	6[1]	6[1]	Ovins
Saint Kitts and Nevis									**Saint-Kitts-et-Nevis**
Cattle	4[1]	4[1]	4[1]	4[1]	5	6	7	7	Bovins
Goats	14[1]	14[1]	14[1]	14[1]	16	8	8	9	Caprins
Pigs	4[1]	4[1]	4[1]	4[1]	4[1]	6	7	6	Porcins
Sheep	14[1]	14[1]	14[1]	14[1]	13	6	6	7	Ovins
Saint Lucia									**Sainte-Lucie**
Asses or mules [1]	2	2	2	2	2	2	2	2	Ânes ou mules [1]
Cattle [1]	12	12	12	12	12	12	13	13	Bovins [1]
Goats	10[1]	10	10[1]	10[1]	10[1]	10[1]	9	9[1]	Caprins
Horses [1]	1	1	1	1	1	1	1	1	Chevaux [1]
Pigs	15[1]	15	15[1]	15[1]	15[1]	15[1]	20	16[1]	Porcins
Sheep	13[1]	13	13[1]	13[1]	13[1]	13[1]	8	13[1]	Ovins
Saint Vincent-Grenadines									**Saint Vincent-Grenadines**
Asses or mules [1]	1	1	1	1	1	1	1	1	Ânes ou mules [1]
Cattle	6[1]	6[1]	5	5[1]	5[1]	5[1]	5[1]	5[1]	Bovins
Goats	6[1]	6[1]	7	7[1]	7[1]	7[1]	7[1]	7[1]	Caprins
Pigs	10[1]	10[1]	9	9[1]	9[1]	9[1]	9[1]	9[1]	Porcins
Sheep	13[1]	13[1]	12	12[1]	12[1]	12[1]	12[1]	13[1]	Ovins
Suriname									**Suriname**
Cattle	120[1]	118[1]	115[1]	110[1]	95[1]	50	50	50	Bovins
Goats	7	7	6	7[1]	7[1]	6	4	4	Caprins
Pigs	23	25	23	28[1]	28[1]	28	28	27	Porcins
Sheep	8	7	7	7[1]	7[1]	7	7	6	Ovins
Trinidad and Tobago									**Trinité-et-Tobago**
Asses or mules [1]	4	4	4	4	4	4	4	4	Ânes ou mules [1]
Buffaloes [1]	6	6	6	6	6	6	6	6	Buffles [1]
Cattle	30[1]	32[1]	29	29	29[1]	29[1]	30[1]	30[1]	Bovins
Goats [1]	58	59	59	59	59	59	60	60	Caprins [1]
Horses [1]	1	1	1	1	1	1	1	1	Chevaux [1]
Pigs	41[1]	42[1]	41	43[1]	43[1]	43[1]	45[1]	45[1]	Porcins
Sheep [1]	3	4	3	3	3	3	4	4	Ovins [1]
United States									**Etats-Unis**
Asses or mules [1]	80	80	80	80	80	80	80	80	Ânes ou mules [1]
Cattle	97 277	96 723	96 100	94 888	95 438	96 702	97 003	96 669	Bovins
Goats	2 400[1]	2 530	2 530[1]	2 525[1]	2 715	2 837	2 934	3 015	Caprins
Horses	5 500[1]	6 000[1]	7 000[1]	8 000[1]	9 200	9 500[1]	9 500[1]	9 500[1]	Chevaux
Pigs	59 138	59 722	59 554	60 444	60 975	61 449	61 860	65 909	Porcins
Sheep	6 965	6 623	6 321	6 105	6 135	6 230	6 165	6 055	Ovins
United States Virgin Is. [1]									**Iles Vierges américaines** [1]
Cattle	8	8	8	8	8	8	8	8	Bovins
Goats	4	4	4	4	4	4	4	4	Caprins
Pigs	3	3	3	3	3	3	3	3	Porcins
Sheep	3	3	3	3	3	3	3	3	Ovins
Uruguay									**Uruguay**
Asses or mules [1]	5	5	5	5	5	5	5	6	Ânes ou mules [1]
Cattle	10 595	11 268	11 708	11 958	11 956	12 437	12 368	12 368[1]	Bovins
Goats [1]	15	15	16	16	16	17	17	17	Caprins [1]
Horses	590[1]	390[1]	437	429	432	525	427	427[1]	Chevaux
Pigs	282[1]	270	240	235	255	240	245	243[1]	Porcins
Sheep	12 083	10 801	9 975	9 766	10 847	11 087	10 323	10 323[1]	Ovins
Venezuela (Boliv. Rep. of)									**Venezuela (Rép. boliv. du)**
Asses or mules [1]	512	512	512	512	512	512	512	512	Ânes ou mules [1]
Cattle	15 474	15 791	15 989	16 232	16 615	16 739	16 778	16 900[1]	Bovins

32 Livestock

Stocks: thousand head

Cheptel

Réserves: milliers de têtes

Region, country or area	2001	2002	2003	2004	2005	2006	2007	2008	Region, pays ou zone
Goats	1 225	1 251	1 280	1 311	1 342	1 362	1 426	1 450[1]	Caprins
Horses [1]	500	500	500	500	500	500	510	510	Chevaux [1]
Pigs	2 780	2 825	2 922	3 047	3 264	3 303	2 971	3 000[1]	Porcins
Sheep	485	512	520	528	525	538	564	570[1]	Ovins
Asia									**Asie**
Asses or mules	**23 845**	**23 272**	**22 798**	**22 367**	**21 937**	**21 583**	**21 010**	**20 734**	**Ânes ou mules**
Buffaloes	**161 470**	**163 874**	**166 511**	**167 386**	**169 182**	**170 845**	**171 863**	**174 208**	**Buffles**
Camels	**3 603**	**3 434**	**3 454**	**3 474**	**3 478**	**3 780**	**3 701**	**3 700**	**Chameaux**
Cattle	**437 148**	**430 981**	**427 370**	**427 103**	**426 904**	**431 606**	**428 444**	**430 952**	**Bovins**
Goats	**456 464**	**459 924**	**468 745**	**478 942**	**491 454**	**490 163**	**490 866**	**514 449**	**Caprins**
Horses	**15 987**	**15 002**	**14 636**	**14 424**	**14 257**	**14 170**	**14 191**	**13 870**	**Chevaux**
Pigs	**517 275**	**523 718**	**525 985**	**524 069**	**534 536**	**547 750**	**535 720**	**555 015**	**Porcins**
Sheep	**407 998**	**403 461**	**413 825**	**428 105**	**446 537**	**454 958**	**457 782**	**452 317**	**Ovins**
Afghanistan									**Afghanistan**
Asses or mules [1]	945	945	945	947	949	943	944	1 233	Ânes ou mules [1]
Camels	224	175	181	190	188	174	186	183	Chameaux
Cattle	2 249	3 715	3 829	3 494	3 723	4 110	4 357	4 745	Bovins
Goats	5 003	7 281	7 425	7 648	6 977	6 746	5 387	6 386	Caprins
Horses	162	141	144	155	149	146	145	162	Chevaux
Sheep	13 955	8 773	9 074	10 136	10 773	9 259	8 105	10 710	Ovins
Armenia									**Arménie**
Asses or mules [1]	7	7	7	7	7	7	7	7	Ânes ou mules [1]
Cattle	497	514	536	566	573	592	620	629	Bovins
Goats	43	46	50	48	47	43	43	39	Caprins
Horses	11	12	12	13	12	12	13	12	Chevaux
Pigs	69	98	111	85	89	138	153	87	Porcins
Sheep	497	546	553	580	557	549	590	598	Ovins
Azerbaijan									**Azerbaïdjan**
Asses or mules	38	39	40	42	45	46	46	47	Ânes ou mules
Buffaloes	299	304	306	307	309	303	299	299	Buffles
Cattle	1 723	1 794	1 872	1 934	2 007	2 077	2 146	2 213	Bovins
Goats	533	556	594	604	601	594	578	587	Caprins
Horses	64	66	68	71	69	70	72	73	Chevaux
Pigs	19	17	20	20	23	23	21	19	Porcins
Sheep	5 553	6 003	6 392	6 676	6 887	7 105	7 291	7 523	Ovins
Bahrain									**Bahreïn**
Camels [1]	1	1	1	1	1	1	1	1	Chameaux [1]
Cattle	10	15	11[1]	9	9[1]	9[1]	9[1]	9[1]	Bovins
Goats	18[1]	23[1]	24[1]	25	25[2]	24	23	23[1]	Caprins
Sheep	27[1]	30[1]	35[1]	39	40[1]	42	41	41[1]	Ovins
Bangladesh									**Bangladesh**
Buffaloes	920	970	1 010	1 060	1 110	1 160	1 210	1 262[1]	Buffles
Cattle [1]	24 100	24 300	24 500	24 700	24 900	25 100	25 300	25 500	Bovins [1]
Goats [1]	34 400	36 900	39 600	42 500	45 600	48 900	52 500	56 400	Caprins [1]
Sheep [1]	1 143	1 194	1 260	1 330	1 400	1 480	1 560	1 644	Ovins [1]
Bhutan									**Bhoutan**
Asses or mules [1]	28	28	28	28	27	27	27	27	Ânes ou mules [1]
Buffaloes	2[1]	2	2[1]	2[1]	2[1]	2[1]	2[1]	2[1]	Buffles
Cattle	355[1]	355	372	372[1]	381	385[1]	385[1]	385[1]	Bovins
Goats	38[1]	31	30[1]	30[1]	30[1]	30[1]	30[1]	30[1]	Caprins
Horses	28[1]	29[1]	28	28[1]	25	26[1]	26[1]	26[1]	Chevaux
Pigs	41[1]	41	41	35[1]	28	35[1]	35[1]	35[1]	Porcins
Sheep	26[1]	23	21[1]	20[1]	18	18[1]	18[1]	18[1]	Ovins
Brunei Darussalam									**Brunéi Darussalam**
Buffaloes	6	6	6	5	5	5	5[1]	5[1]	Buffles
Cattle	2	1	1	1	1	1	1[1]	1[1]	Bovins
Goats	2	3	3	2	3	3	3[1]	3[1]	Caprins
Pigs [1]	1	1	1	2	2	2	2	2	Porcins [1]
Sheep [1]	3	3	4	4	4	3	3	3	Ovins [1]
Cambodia									**Cambodge**
Buffaloes	626	626	660	651	677	724	773	746	Buffles
Cattle	2 869	2 924	2 985	3 040	3 184	3 345	3 368	3 458	Bovins

32 Livestock

Stocks: thousand head

Cheptel

Réserves: milliers de têtes

Region, country or area	2001	2002	2003	2004	2005	2006	2007	2008	Region, pays ou zone
Horses [1]	27	27	28	28	28	28	28	28	Chevaux [1]
Pigs	2 115	2 105	2 304	2 429	2 689	2 741	2 389	2 216	Porcins
China [3]									**Chine [3]**
Asses or mules	13 757	13 177	12 693	12 164	11 659	11 376	10 757	10 105[1]	Ânes ou mules
Buffaloes	22 765	22 690	22 729	22 287	22 365	22 499	22 721	23 272[2]	Buffles
Camels	326	279	264	265	262	266	269	240	Chameaux
Cattle	100 929	95 555	93 100	92 207	90 134	87 548	82 073	82 624[2]	Bovins
Goats	149 641	145 785	148 568	149 844	152 134	146 782	137 862	149 377	Caprins
Horses	8 768	8 262	8 090	7 902	7 641	7 402	7 197	6 823	Chevaux
Pigs	423 601	426 399	424 641	420 739	428 506	440 365	425 225	446 423	Porcins
Sheep	130 026	130 628	133 997	143 395	152 035	151 337	146 018	136 436	Ovins
Cyprus									**Chypre**
Asses or mules [1]	7	7	7	7	7	7	7	7	Ânes ou mules [1]
Cattle	54	54	58	59	61	56	55	55[1]	Bovins
Goats	379	427	460	408	378	345	368	318	Caprins
Horses [1]	1	1	1	1	1	1	1	1	Chevaux [1]
Pigs	408	451	491	488	471	453	467	465	Porcins
Sheep	246	297	294	265	279	272	292	267	Ovins
Georgia									**Géorgie**
Asses or mules	11	10[1]	10[1]	10[1]	10[1]	10[1]	10[1]	10[1]	Ânes ou mules
Buffaloes	33	36	37	33	33	20	18	17	Buffles
Cattle	1 177	1 180	1 216	1 243	1 251	1 170	1 062	1 031	Bovins
Goats	81	92	88	93	116	96	92	83	Caprins
Horses	39	39	43	43	44	43	42[1]	42[1]	Chevaux
Pigs	443	445	446	474	484	455	344	110	Porcins
Sheep	547	568	611	629	689	720	697	624	Ovins
India									**Inde**
Asses or mules	910[1]	867[1]	826	826[1]	826[1]	826[1]	826[1]	826[1]	Ânes ou mules
Buffaloes	95 254[1]	96 588[1]	97 922	98 175[2]	98 875[2]	98 805[2]	98 700[2]	98 595[2]	Buffles
Camels	714	672	632	632[1]	632[1]	632[1]	632[1]	632[1]	Chameaux
Cattle	189 660	187 422	185 180	182 996[1]	180 837[1]	178 703[1]	176 594[1]	174 510[1]	Bovins
Goats	123 805[1]	124 077[1]	124 358	124 632[1]	124 906[1]	125 181[1]	125 456[1]	125 732[1]	Caprins
Horses	776[1]	763[1]	751	751[1]	751[1]	751[1]	751[1]	751[1]	Chevaux
Pigs	13 440[1]	13 480[1]	13 519	13 560[2]	13 600[2]	13 630[2]	13 700[2]	14 000[1]	Porcins
Sheep	60 113	60 787	61 469	62 157[1]	62 854[1]	63 558[1]	64 269[1]	64 989[1]	Ovins
Indonesia									**Indonésie**
Buffaloes	2 333	2 403	2 459	2 403	2 128	2 167	2 086	2 192	Buffles
Cattle	11 138	11 298	10 504	10 533	10 680	10 875	11 515	11 869	Bovins
Goats	12 464	12 549	12 722	12 781	13 409	13 790	14 470	15 806	Caprins
Horses	422	419	413	397	387	398	401	411	Chevaux
Pigs	5 369	5 927	6 151	5 980	6 801	6 218	6 711	7 376	Porcins
Sheep	7 401	7 641	7 811	8 075	8 327	8 980	9 860	8 356	Ovins
Iran (Islamic Rep. of)									**Iran (Rép. islamique d')**
Asses or mules [1]	1 775	1 775	1 775	1 775	1 775	1 775	1 775	1 775	Ânes ou mules [1]
Buffaloes	507	524	540[1]	560[1]	580[1]	600[1]	620[1]	630[1]	Buffles
Camels	146	146[1]	146[1]	146[1]	146[1]	146[1]	152[2]	152[1]	Chameaux
Cattle	8 500	7 445	7 335	7 631	7 819	7 892	7 609[2]	7 610[1]	Bovins
Goats	25 757	25 757	25 679	25 756	25 807	25 833	25 531[2]	25 300[1]	Caprins
Horses [1]	150	150	150	140	140	140	140	140	Chevaux [1]
Sheep	53 900	51 701	51 959	52 215	52 219	52 219[1]	53 800[2]	53 800[1]	Ovins
Iraq									**Iraq**
Asses or mules	396[1]	391[1]	391[2]	391[1]	391[1]	391[1]	391[1]	391[1]	Ânes ou mules
Buffaloes	109	120	115	111	213	410	120[1]	120[1]	Buffles
Camels	8	10	7	7	30	51	10[1]	10[1]	Chameaux
Cattle	1 458	1 500	1 425	1 516	1 648	1 130	1 500[1]	1 500[1]	Bovins
Goats	743	740[1]	715	549	523	1 650[1]	1 650[1]	1 650[1]	Caprins
Horses	48	48[1]	47	47[1]	47[1]	48[1]	48[1]	48[1]	Chevaux
Sheep	6 045	6 100[1]	6 255	4 473	4 449	6 200[1]	6 200[1]	6 200[1]	Ovins
Israel									**Israël**
Asses or mules [1]	7	7	7	7	7	7	7	7	Ânes ou mules [1]
Camels [1]	5	5	5	5	5	5	5	5	Chameaux [1]
Cattle	390	355	360	350	357	406	394	416	Bovins

32 Livestock

Stocks: thousand head

Cheptel

Réserves: milliers de têtes

Region, country or area	2001	2002	2003	2004	2005	2006	2007	2008	Region, pays ou zone
Goats	68	70	75	75	83	87	87	90	Caprins
Horses [1]	4	4	4	4	4	4	4	4	Chevaux [1]
Pigs	155[1]	195[1]	180	190	205	195	206	206	Porcins
Sheep	389	390	400	420	435	445	433	430	Ovins
Japan									**Japon**
Cattle	4 531	4 564	4 524	4 478	4 402	4 391	4 398	4 423	Bovins
Goats [1]	35	35	34	34	34	32	32	32	Caprins [1]
Horses	21[1]	25	25[1]	25[1]	25[1]	25[1]	25[1]	25[1]	Chevaux
Pigs	9 788	9 612	9 725	9 724	9 600[2]	9 620	9 759	9 745	Porcins
Sheep [1]	10	11	11	11	11	10	10	10	Ovins [1]
Jordan									**Jordanie**
Asses or mules [1]	15	21	15	16	14	12	12	12	Ânes ou mules [1]
Buffaloes	0[2]	0[2]	0[1]	0[1]	0[1]	0[1]	0[1]	0[1]	Buffles
Camels	6	6[1]	6	6	5	5[1]	5[1]	5[1]	Chameaux
Cattle	65	68	66	69	68	69	81	79	Bovins
Goats	426	557	547	501	516	474	569	1 083	Caprins
Horses	3	3[1]	3	3	3	4[1]	4[1]	4[1]	Chevaux
Sheep	1 484	1 458	1 476	1 529	1 890	1 972	2 251	2 300[1]	Ovins
Kazakhstan									**Kazakhstan**
Asses or mules [1]	30	30	30	30	31	30	30	30	Ânes ou mules [1]
Buffaloes [1]	9	9	9	9	9	10	10	10	Buffles [1]
Camels	98	104	108	115	126	131	139	143	Chameaux
Cattle	4 107	4 294	4 560	4 871	5 204	5 457	5 660	5 841	Bovins
Goats	1 042	1 271	1 486	1 827	1 891[2]	2 329	2 537	2 610	Caprins
Horses	976	990	1 019	1 064	1 120	1 164	1 236	1 291	Chevaux
Pigs	1 076	1 124	1 230	1 369	1 292	1 282	1 305	1 353	Porcins
Sheep	8 939	9 208	9 788	10 420	11 519[2]	12 006	12 814	13 470	Ovins
Korea, Dem. P. R.									**Corée, R. p. dém. de**
Cattle	570	575	576	566	570[1]	575[1]	576[1]	576	Bovins
Goats	2 566	2 693	2 717	2 736	2 900[1]	3 090[1]	3 260[1]	3 441	Caprins
Horses [1]	47	48	48	48	48	48	48	48	Chevaux [1]
Pigs	3 137	3 152	3 178	3 194	3 260[1]	3 300[1]	3 400[1]	2 178	Porcins
Sheep	189	170	171	171	170[1]	169[1]	168[1]	167	Ovins
Korea, Republic of									**Corée, République de**
Cattle	1 954	1 954	1 999	2 163	2 298	2 484	2 654	2 894	Bovins
Goats	440	444	483	527	523	467	372	300[1]	Caprins
Horses	13	14	16	19	20	23	25	27[1]	Chevaux
Pigs	8 720	8 974	9 231	8 908	8 962	9 382	9 606	9 153	Porcins
Sheep	1	1	1	1	1	1	2	2[1]	Ovins
Kuwait									**Koweït**
Camels	5	5	9[1]	6[1]	5[1]	5[1]	5[1]	5[1]	Chameaux
Cattle	20	25	27	28[1]	28	28[1]	28[1]	28[1]	Bovins
Goats	130	147	152	150[1]	150	160[1]	160[1]	160[1]	Caprins
Horses [1]	1	1	1	1	1	1	1	1	Chevaux [1]
Sheep	630	800	850[1]	900[1]	800	900[1]	900[1]	900[1]	Ovins
Kyrgyzstan									**Kirghizistan**
Asses or mules	41[1]	38[1]	38[2]	49[2]	44[2]	45[1]	45[1]	45[1]	Ânes ou mules
Cattle	947	970	988	1 004	1 035	1 075	1 117	1 168	Bovins
Goats	601	640	661	770	808	817	850	873	Caprins
Horses	354	354	361	341	347	345	348	356	Chevaux
Pigs	101	87	87	83	83	78	80	75	Porcins
Sheep	3 198	3 104	3 104	2 884	2 965	3 059	3 197	3 379	Ovins
Lao People's Dem. Rep.									**Rép. dém. pop. lao**
Buffaloes	1 051	1 089	1 111	1 125	1 096	1 108	1 123	1 155	Buffles
Cattle	1 217	1 221	1 244	1 281	1 272	1 321	1 353	1 499	Bovins
Goats	124	128	137	171	190	210	268	289	Caprins
Horses [1]	29	30	31	31	31	31	31	31	Chevaux [1]
Pigs	1 426	1 608	1 655	1 727	1 826	2 033	2 186	2 548	Porcins
Lebanon									**Liban**
Asses or mules	20[2]	20[2]	20[2]	20[2]	20[2]	20[2]	20[2]	20[1]	Ânes ou mules
Cattle	78	88	86	80	77	77	77	77[1]	Bovins
Goats	399	409	428	432	495	484	435	450[1]	Caprins

32 Livestock

Stocks: thousand head

Cheptel

Réserves: milliers de têtes

Region, country or area	2001	2002	2003	2004	2005	2006	2007	2008	Region, pays ou zone
Horses	4[2]	4[2]	4[2]	4[2]	4[2]	4[2]	4[2]	4[1]	Chevaux
Pigs	23	21	14	13	11	10	9	9[1]	Porcins
Sheep	329	298	303	305	337	370	324	330[1]	Ovins
Malaysia									**Malaisie**
Buffaloes	140[1]	131	133	138	133	131	130[1]	131[1]	Buffles
Cattle	742	748	753	787	781	774	785	790[1]	Bovins
Goats	247	233	247	264	288	286	285[1]	285[1]	Caprins
Horses [1]	4	5	7	7	7	7	7	7	Chevaux [1]
Pigs	1 973	2 047	2 071	2 111	2 036	2 092	2 866	1 861	Porcins
Sheep	129	126	115	115	116	112	120[1]	120[1]	Ovins
Mongolia									**Mongolie**
Asses or mules	1[1]	1[1]	1[1]	1[1]	0[1]	0	0	0	Ânes ou mules
Camels	323	285	253	257	254	254	261	266	Chameaux
Cattle	3 098	2 070	2 054	1 793	1 964	2 168	2 426	2 503	Bovins
Goats	10 270	9 591	8 858	10 653	13 267	15 452	18 348	19 969	Caprins
Horses	2 661	2 192	1 989	1 969	2 029	2 115	2 240	2 187	Chevaux
Pigs	15	18[1]	22[1]	27[1]	30[1]	33	36	29	Porcins
Sheep	13 876	11 937	11 797	10 756	12 885	14 815	16 990	18 362	Ovins
Myanmar									**Myanmar**
Asses or mules [1]	8	9	9	9	9	9	9	9	Ânes ou mules [1]
Buffaloes	2 502	2 552	2 598	2 649	2 705	2 770	2 842	2 924	Buffles
Cattle	11 243	11 551	11 728	11 939	12 123	12 364	12 634	12 929	Bovins
Goats	1 439	1 542	1 622	1 711	1 846	2 024	2 376	2 624	Caprins
Horses [1]	120	130	130	130	130	135	140	140	Chevaux [1]
Pigs	4 261	4 499	4 840	5 217	5 677	6 293	7 007	7 677	Porcins
Sheep	403	432	454	479	517	567	497	525	Ovins
Nepal									**Népal**
Buffaloes	3 624	3 701	3 840	3 953	4 081	4 203	4 367	4 497	Buffles
Cattle	6 983	6 979	6 954	6 966	6 994	7 003	7 044	7 091	Bovins
Goats	6 478	6 607	6 792	6 980	7 154	7 422	7 848	8 136	Caprins
Pigs	913	934	932	935	948	961	989	1 013	Porcins
Sheep	850	840	828	824	817	812	814	809	Ovins
Occ. Palestinian Terr.									**Terr. palestinien occupé**
Cattle	27	30	33	32	34	36	34	34[1]	Bovins
Goats	314	355	392	399	371	387	344	344[1]	Caprins
Sheep	616	758	829	812	803	794	745	745[1]	Ovins
Oman									**Oman**
Asses or mules [1]	29	29	29	29	29	29	29	29	Ânes ou mules [1]
Camels	121	118	120	116	117	120	122	122[1]	Chameaux
Cattle	314	320	326	333	302	308	314	314[1]	Bovins
Goats	998	1 018	1 039	1 059	1 557	1 598	1 620	1 620[1]	Caprins
Sheep	354	361	368	377	351	358	366	366[1]	Ovins
Pakistan									**Pakistan**
Asses or mules	4 083	4 168	4 258	4 353	4 450	4 425	4 505	4 589	Ânes ou mules
Buffaloes	23 335	24 030	24 800	25 500	26 300	27 335	28 165	29 883	Buffles
Camels	767	758	751	743	736	921	933	945	Chameaux
Cattle	22 424	22 858	23 303	23 757	24 218	29 559	30 673	31 830	Bovins
Goats	49 140	50 917	52 763	54 679	56 665	53 789	55 244	56 742	Caprins
Horses	321	318	317	315	313	344	346	348	Chevaux
Sheep	24 236	24 398	24 566	24 744	24 923	26 488	26 794	27 111	Ovins
Philippines									**Philippines**
Buffaloes	3 066	3 122	3 180	3 270	3 327	3 361	3 384	3 339	Buffles
Cattle	2 496	2 548	2 585	2 593	2 489	2 520	2 566	2 566	Bovins
Goats [1]	6 197	6 250	6 200	6 365	6 700	4 830	5 340	7 300	Caprins [1]
Horses [1]	230	230	230	230	230	230	232	232	Chevaux [1]
Pigs	11 063	11 653	12 364	12 562	12 140	13 047	13 459	13 070	Porcins
Sheep [1]	30	30	30	30	30	30	30	30	Ovins [1]
Qatar									**Qatar**
Camels	33	33	34	34	14	23	14[1]	14[1]	Chameaux
Cattle	10	10	10	10	7	7	8[1]	8[1]	Bovins
Goats	140	141	144	146	153	132	160[1]	160[1]	Caprins

32 Livestock

Stocks: thousand head

Cheptel

Réserves: milliers de têtes

Region, country or area	2001	2002	2003	2004	2005	2006	2007	2008	Region, pays ou zone
Horses	1	2	2	2	2	5	2[1]	2[1]	Chevaux
Sheep	150	153	156	159	112	115[1]	120[1]	120[1]	Ovins
Saudi Arabia									**Arabie saoudite**
Asses or mules	98	100[1]	100[1]	100[1]	100[1]	100[1]	100[1]	100[1]	Ânes ou mules
Camels	255	253	256[2]	269[2]	268[2]	260[1]	260[1]	260[1]	Chameaux
Cattle	306	322	332	342	352	369	372[1]	372[1]	Bovins
Goats	2 194	2 214	2 170[2]	2 240[2]	2 230[2]	2 200[1]	2 200[1]	2 200[1]	Caprins
Horses	3	3	3[1]	3[1]	3[1]	3[1]	3[1]	3[1]	Chevaux
Sheep	7 006	7 010	7 230[2]	7 897[2]	8 230[2]	7 000[1]	7 000[1]	7 000[1]	Ovins
Singapore [1]									**Singapour** [1]
Goats	1	1	1	1	1	1	1	1	Caprins
Pigs	100	250	250	250	250	260	260	260	Porcins
Sri Lanka									**Sri Lanka**
Buffaloes	290	282	280	302	308	314	318	319	Buffles
Cattle	1 153	1 113	1 139	1 161	1 185	1 185	1 206	1 196	Bovins
Goats	493	351[2]	415	405	395	382	389	377	Caprins
Horses [1]	2	2	2	2	2	2	2	2	Chevaux [1]
Pigs	68	82	68	79	85	92	94	89	Porcins
Sheep	12	9[2]	9	11	10	14	16	10	Ovins
Syrian Arab Republic									**Rép. arabe syrienne**
Asses or mules	177	137	133	128	117[2]	117[1]	117[1]	117[1]	Ânes ou mules
Buffaloes	2	3	4[1]	4	4	5	5[1]	5[1]	Buffles
Camels	12	13	15	20	23	27	25[1]	25[1]	Chameaux
Cattle	837	867	937	1 024	1 083	1 121	1 168	1 168[1]	Bovins
Goats	979	932	1 017	1 130	1 296	1 420	1 561	1 561[1]	Caprins
Horses	18	17	15	15	15	14	16[1]	16[1]	Chevaux
Sheep	12 362	13 497	15 293	17 565	19 651	21 380	22 865	22 865[1]	Ovins
Tajikistan									**Tadjikistan**
Asses or mules	117	138	138	147	156	164	169	171	Ânes ou mules
Buffaloes	15	16	16	14	15	15[1]	15[1]	15[1]	Buffles
Cattle	1 062	1 091	1 136	1 219	1 303	1 372	1 423	1 703	Bovins
Goats	744	779	842	920	1 040	1 160	1 210	1 424	Caprins
Horses	72	71	73	74	75	75	76	79	Chevaux
Pigs	1	1	0	1	1	1	1	1	Porcins
Sheep	1 478	1 490	1 591	1 672	1 782	1 894	1 955	2 374	Ovins
Thailand									**Thaïlande**
Buffaloes	1 524	1 613	1 690	1 738	1 771	1 763	1 744	1 699	Buffles
Cattle	4 640	4 820	5 048	5 297	5 610	6 042	6 481	6 700	Bovins
Goats	188	178	214	250	338	324	310[1]	310[1]	Caprins
Horses	8	8	7	3	6	2	2[1]	2[1]	Chevaux
Pigs	6 689	6 879	7 064	7 254	7 534	7 688	8 381	7 845	Porcins
Sheep	43	39	43	42	42	51	52[1]	52[1]	Ovins
Timor-Leste									**Timor-Leste**
Buffaloes	104	105[1]	107[1]	108[1]	110[1]	110[1]	110[1]	110[1]	Buffles
Cattle	166	168[1]	170[1]	171[1]	172[1]	171[1]	171[1]	171[1]	Bovins
Goats	79	80[1]	80[1]	81[1]	82[1]	80[1]	80[1]	80[1]	Caprins
Horses	45	48[1]	48[1]	48[1]	48[1]	48[1]	48[1]	48[1]	Chevaux
Pigs	339	340[1]	340[1]	346[1]	350[1]	346[1]	346[1]	346[1]	Porcins
Sheep	24	24[1]	25[1]	25[1]	26[1]	25[1]	25[1]	25[1]	Ovins
Turkey									**Turquie**
Asses or mules	588	559	512	490	452	404	364	364[1]	Ânes ou mules
Buffaloes	146	138	121	113	104	105	101	85	Buffles
Camels	1	1	1	1	1	1	1	1	Chameaux
Cattle	10 761	10 548	9 804	9 788	10 069	10 526	10 871	11 037	Bovins
Goats	7 201	7 022	6 780	6 772	6 610	6 517	6 286	5 594	Caprins
Horses	271	271	249	227	212	208	204	189	Chevaux
Pigs	3	3	4	7	4	2	1	2	Porcins
Sheep	28 492	26 972	25 174	25 432	25 201	25 304	25 462	23 975	Ovins
Turkmenistan									**Turkménistan**
Asses or mules [1]	25	25	25	25	25	25	25	25	Ânes ou mules [1]
Camels [1]	42	40	40	40	40	41	40	40	Chameaux [1]
Cattle	1 600	1 750[1]	1 900	2 000	2 025	2 065[2]	1 948[2]	1 948[1]	Bovins

32 Livestock

Stocks: thousand head

Cheptel

Réserves: milliers de têtes

Region, country or area	2001	2002	2003	2004	2005	2006	2007	2008	Region, pays ou zone
Goats	570[2]	650[1]	730[2]	750[2]	822[2]	904[2]	900[2]	900[1]	Caprins
Horses [1]	17	17	16	16	16	17	16	16	Chevaux [1]
Pigs	30	30[1]	30	30	30[1]	29[1]	30[1]	30[1]	Porcins
Sheep	8 230[2]	10 350[1]	12 570[2]	13 150[2]	14 267[2]	15 694[2]	15 500[2]	15 500[1]	Ovins
United Arab Emirates									**Emirats arabes unis**
Camels	233	246	259	250[1]	250[1]	342[1]	260[1]	260[1]	Chameaux
Cattle	102	107	113	115[1]	117[1]	120[1]	125[1]	125[1]	Bovins
Goats	1 355	1 430	1 495	1 500[1]	1 520[1]	1 550[1]	1 570[1]	1 570[1]	Caprins
Sheep	525	554	583	590[1]	580[1]	600[1]	615[1]	615[1]	Ovins
Uzbekistan									**Ouzbékistan**
Asses or mules	235[1]	245[1]	262	269	289	290[1]	290[1]	290[1]	Ânes ou mules
Camels	18[1]	17[1]	16	17	17	17	17[1]	17[1]	Chameaux
Cattle	5 344	5 478	5 879	6 243	6 571	7 045	7 043	7 458	Bovins
Goats	880[2]	1 033[2]	1 421	1 690	1 797	1 973	2 040[2]	2 000[2]	Caprins
Horses	150[1]	145[1]	148	152	158	162	162[1]	168	Chevaux
Pigs	89	75	90	87	87	93	92	92[1]	Porcins
Sheep	8 050[2]	8 200[2]	8 507	8 890	9 555	10 034	10 383[2]	10 625[2]	Ovins
Viet Nam									**Viet Nam**
Buffaloes	2 808	2 814	2 835	2 870	2 922	2 921	2 996	2 898	Buffles
Cattle	3 900	4 063	4 394	4 908	5 541[2]	6 511	6 725	6 338	Bovins
Goats	572	622	780	1 020	1 314	1 525	1 778	1 484	Caprins
Horses	113	111	112	113	111	87	104	121	Chevaux
Pigs	21 800	23 170	24 885	26 144	27 435	26 855	26 561	26 702	Porcins
Yemen									**Yémen**
Asses or mules [1]	500	500	500	500	500	500	500	500	Ânes ou mules [1]
Camels	264	267	350	353	357	359	365	373	Chameaux
Cattle	1 342	1 355	1 418	1 433	1 447	1 464	1 495	1 531	Bovins
Goats	7 246	7 318	7 707	7 785	7 864	8 042	8 414	8 708	Caprins
Horses	3	3	3[1]	3[1]	3[1]	3[1]	3[1]	3[1]	Chevaux
Sheep	6 483	6 548	7 819	7 899	7 980	8 197	8 589	8 889	Ovins
Europe									**Europe**
Asses or mules	**1 017**	**961**	**923**	**884**	**886**	**873**	**851**	**850**	**Ânes ou mules**
Buffaloes	**235**	**245**	**239**	**280**	**266**	**243**	**270**	**332**	**Buffles**
Camels	**12**	**12**	**13**	**7**	**7**	**7**	**7**	**7**	**Chameaux**
Cattle	**142 559**	**140 898**	**138 492**	**134 508**	**131 011**	**128 398**	**127 768**	**127 149**	**Bovins**
Goats	**18 738**	**18 214**	**19 148**	**18 635**	**18 392**	**17 992**	**17 871**	**17 993**	**Caprins**
Horses	**6 934**	**6 667**	**6 642**	**6 578**	**6 489**	**6 371**	**6 348**	**6 375**	**Chevaux**
Pigs	**192 435**	**194 724**	**197 907**	**192 354**	**190 773**	**193 516**	**197 705**	**191 130**	**Porcins**
Sheep	**136 169**	**135 017**	**135 480**	**137 993**	**137 906**	**137 146**	**136 470**	**133 925**	**Ovins**
Albania									**Albanie**
Asses or mules	127[2]	116[2]	107[2]	98[2]	96[2]	81[2]	76[2]	76[1]	Ânes ou mules
Cattle	708	690	684	654	655	634	577	577[1]	Bovins
Goats	1 027	929	1 015	944	941	940	876	876[1]	Caprins
Horses	67	65	63	58	53	51	46	46[1]	Chevaux
Pigs	106	114	132	143	147	152	147	147[1]	Porcins
Sheep	1 906	1 844	1 903	1 794	1 760	1 830	1 853	1 853[1]	Ovins
Austria									**Autriche**
Cattle	2 155	2 118	2 067	2 052	2 008	2 002	2 003	2 000	Bovins
Goats	70	59	58	55	56	55	53	60	Caprins
Horses	63[1]	60[1]	85[1]	80	85[1]	86[1]	87[1]	85[1]	Chevaux
Pigs	3 427	3 440	3 306	3 154	3 209	3 160	3 139	3 286	Porcins
Sheep	358	320	304	325	327	326	312	351	Ovins
Belarus									**Bélarus**
Asses or mules [1]	9	9	9	9	9	9	9	9	Ânes ou mules [1]
Cattle	4 221	4 085	4 005	3 924	3 963	3 980	3 989	4 007	Bovins
Goats	65	66	64	63	66	68	70	72	Caprins
Horses	217	209	202	192	181	168	156	147	Chevaux
Pigs	3 431	3 373	3 329	3 287	3 407	3 545	3 642	3 598	Porcins
Sheep	89	83	73	63	59	53	52	53	Ovins
Belgium									**Belgique**
Cattle	3 038	2 891	2 778	2 739	2 699	2 669	2 649	2 613	Bovins
Goats	21	25	26	25	26	26[1]	27[1]	27[1]	Caprins

32 Livestock

Stocks: thousand head

Cheptel

Réserves: milliers de têtes

Region, country or area	2001	2002	2003	2004	2005	2006	2007	2008	Region, pays ou zone
Horses	31	31	32	32	28	35	35	36	Chevaux
Pigs	6 834	6 735	6 539	6 355	6 318	6 295	6 255	6 269	Porcins
Sheep	156	146	146	151	152	154	151	132	Ovins
Bosnia and Herzegovina									**Bosnie-Herzégovine**
Buffaloes [1]	...	...	...	...	...	...	...	13	Buffles [1]
Cattle	440[1]	410[1]	440[1]	453	460	515	468	459	Bovins
Goats	101[1]	86[1]	81[1]	72	73	76	70	70	Caprins
Horses	38[1]	35[1]	30[1]	28	27	26	25	23	Chevaux
Pigs	483[1]	500[1]	540[1]	595	653	710	535	502	Porcins
Sheep	608[2]	633[2]	733[2]	893	903	1 005	1 033	1 031	Ovins
Bulgaria									**Bulgarie**
Asses or mules	210	180[1]	165[1]	144[1]	140[1]	140[1]	140[1]	140[1]	Ânes ou mules
Buffaloes	8	7	7	8	8	8	8	9	Buffles
Cattle	640	634	691	728	672	622	628	602	Bovins
Goats	970	675	754	725	718	608	549	495	Caprins
Horses	140	151	135[1]	126	125[1]	123[1]	120[1]	120[1]	Chevaux
Pigs	1 144	785	996	1 032	931	943	1 013	889	Porcins
Sheep	2 286	1 571	1 728	1 599	1 693	1 602	1 635	1 526	Ovins
Croatia									**Croatie**
Asses or mules [1]	4	4	4	4	4	4	4	4	Ânes ou mules [1]
Cattle	438	417	444	466	471	485	483	467	Bovins
Goats	93	97	86	126	134	103	103	92	Caprins
Horses	10	8	9	10	9	9	10	14	Chevaux
Pigs	1 234	1 286	1 347	1 489	1 205	1 488	1 488	1 348	Porcins
Sheep	539	580	587	722	796	769	680	646	Ovins
Czech Republic									**République tchèque**
Cattle	1 582	1 520	1 474	1 428	1 397	1 391	1 402	1 363	Bovins
Goats	28	14	13	12	13	16	17	17	Caprins
Horses	26	21	20	20	21	24	27	28	Chevaux
Pigs	3 594	3 441	3 363	3 127	2 877	2 830	2 433	1 917	Porcins
Sheep	90	96	103	116	140	169	184	183	Ovins
Denmark									**Danemark**
Cattle	1 907	1 796	1 724	1 646	1 570	1 535	1 566	1 564	Bovins
Horses	43	38	43	39	54	53	53	60	Chevaux
Pigs	12 608	12 732	12 949	13 233	13 534	13 361	13 723	12 738	Porcins
Sheep	152	131	144	141	173	170	157	136	Ovins
Estonia									**Estonie**
Cattle	253	261	254	257	250	250	245	242	Bovins
Goats	3	4	4	4	3	3	3	4	Caprins
Horses	4	6	5	6	5	5	5	5	Chevaux
Pigs	300	345	341	345	340	347	346	379	Porcins
Sheep	29	29	30	31	38	50	63	72	Ovins
Faeroe Islands [1]									**Iles Féroé** [1]
Cattle	2	2	2	2	2	2	2	2	Bovins
Sheep	68	68	68	68	68	68	68	68	Ovins
Finland									**Finlande**
Cattle	1 037	1 025	1 000	969	959	949	927	915	Bovins
Goats	7	7	5	7	7	7	6	6	Caprins
Horses	59	59	60	61	64	66	68	69	Chevaux
Pigs	1 261	1 315	1 375	1 365	1 401	1 436	1 448	1 483	Porcins
Sheep	96	96	98	109	90	117	119	122	Ovins
France									**France**
Asses or mules	31[1]	32[1]	32[1]	32[2]	32[1]	33[1]	31[1]	30[1]	Ânes ou mules
Cattle	20 462	20 116	19 597	19 320	19 310	19 418	19 359	19 887	Bovins
Goats	1 231	1 232	1 229	1 240	1 225	1 228	1 254	1 224	Caprins
Horses	343	345	350	344	426	423	422	420	Chevaux
Pigs	15 382	15 327	15 139	15 004	14 951	14 840	14 736	14 806	Porcins
Sheep	9 443	9 336	9 256	9 151	9 097	8 908	8 499	8 187	Ovins
Germany									**Allemagne**
Cattle	14 568	14 227	13 644	13 196	13 035	12 748	12 687	12 970	Bovins
Goats	140	160	160	165	170	170	180	190	Caprins
Horses	491	506	525	525[1]	500	510[1]	542	542[1]	Chevaux

32 Livestock

Stocks: thousand head

Cheptel

Réserves: milliers de têtes

Region, country or area	2001	2002	2003	2004	2005	2006	2007	2008	Region, pays ou zone
Pigs	25 784	26 103	26 334	25 659	26 858	26 521	27 125	26 687	Porcins
Sheep	2 700[1]	2 771	2 722	2 697	2 642	2 560	2 538	2 437	Ovins
Greece									**Grèce**
Asses or mules	96	89	84	79	73	75[1]	75[1]	75[1]	Ânes ou mules
Buffaloes	1	1[1]	1	1	1	1	1	1[1]	Buffles
Cattle	613	559	573	603	605	618	629	628[2]	Bovins
Goats	5 641	5 180	5 669	5 619	5 509	5 421	5 402	5 455[2]	Caprins
Horses	29	29[1]	28	27	27	27	27[1]	27[1]	Chevaux
Pigs	964	940	934	940	949	926	902	922	Porcins
Sheep	8 993	9 124	9 058	9 002	8 827	8 791	8 830	8 904[2]	Ovins
Hungary									**Hongrie**
Asses or mules [1]	4	4	4	4	4	4	4	4	Ânes ou mules [1]
Cattle	805	783	770	739	723	708	702	705	Bovins
Goats	103	90	87	85	74	79	70	67	Caprins
Horses	74	65	63	62	67	71	60	60	Chevaux
Pigs	4 834	4 822	5 082	4 913	4 059	3 853	3 987	3 860	Porcins
Sheep	1 129	1 136	1 103	1 296	1 397	1 405	1 298	1 231	Ovins
Iceland									**Islande**
Cattle	70	67	66	65	66	69	71	71	Bovins
Horses	74	71	71	72	75	76	77	77	Chevaux
Pigs	44[1]	37	44	36	41	42	41	42[1]	Porcins
Sheep	474	470	463	455	455	456	455	455	Ovins
Ireland									**Irlande**
Asses or mules	5[2]	5[2]	6[2]	6	6	6[1]	6[1]	6[1]	Ânes ou mules
Cattle	7 050	6 992	7 000	7 016	6 983	6 916	6 704	6 720	Bovins
Goats	8	8	8	8	7	7	7	9	Caprins
Horses	71	73	70	73	80	87	89	96	Chevaux
Pigs	1 743	1 785	1 726	1 653	1 688	1 643	1 588	1 467	Porcins
Sheep	5 056	4 807	4 829	6 777	6 392	5 973	5 522	5 061	Ovins
Italy									**Italie**
Asses or mules	33[1]	33[1]	33[1]	29[2]	33[1]	33[1]	33[1]	33[1]	Ânes ou mules
Buffaloes	182	194	185	223	210	205	231	294	Buffles
Cattle	6 050	6 739	6 505	6 504	6 304	6 255	6 117	6 283	Bovins
Goats	923	1 025	988	961	978	945	955	920	Caprins
Horses	285[1]	285[1]	290[1]	278	300[1]	290[1]	300[1]	300[1]	Chevaux
Pigs	8 646	8 766	9 166	9 157	8 972	9 200	9 281	9 273	Porcins
Sheep	6 809	8 311	8 138	7 952	8 106	7 954	8 227	8 237	Ovins
Latvia									**Lettonie**
Cattle	367	385	388	379	371	385	377	399	Bovins
Goats	10	12	13	15	15	15	14	13	Caprins
Horses	20	20	19	15	16	14	14	13	Chevaux
Pigs	394	429	453	444	436	428	417	414	Porcins
Sheep	29	29	32	39	39	42	41	54	Ovins
Liechtenstein [1]									**Liechtenstein** [1]
Cattle	6	6	6	6	6	6	6	6	Bovins
Pigs	3	3	3	3	3	3	3	3	Porcins
Sheep	3	3	3	3	3	3	3	3	Ovins
Lithuania									**Lituanie**
Cattle	748	752	779	812	792	800	839	788	Bovins
Goats	23	24	22	27	27	22	21	20	Caprins
Horses	68	65	61	64	64	63	61	56	Chevaux
Pigs	868	1 011	1 061	1 057	1 073	1 115	1 127	923	Porcins
Sheep	12	12	14	17	22	29	37	43	Ovins
Luxembourg									**Luxembourg**
Cattle	205	197	190	187	185	184	192	196	Bovins
Goats	1	1	2	2	2	2	3	3	Caprins
Horses	3	3	3	4	4	4	4	5	Chevaux
Pigs	79	80	84	85	90	84	83	81	Porcins
Sheep	8	9	9	10	10	10	9	9	Ovins
Malta									**Malte**
Asses or mules [1]	1	1	1	1	1	1	1	1	Ânes ou mules [1]
Cattle	19	19	19	18	19	20	19	19	Bovins

32 Livestock

Stocks: thousand head

Cheptel

Réserves: milliers de têtes

Region, country or area	2001	2002	2003	2004	2005	2006	2007	2008	Region, pays ou zone
Goats	5[1]	5	5	5	6	6	6	6	Caprins
Horses [1]	1	1	1	1	1	1	1	1	Chevaux [1]
Pigs	80	81	78	73	77	73	74	77	Porcins
Sheep	10	9	12	15	14	15	12	12	Ovins
Montenegro									**Monténégro**
Cattle	...	...	...	...	...	118	115	109	Bovins
Horses	...	...	...	...	...	7	6	6	Chevaux
Pigs	...	...	...	...	...	11	13	10	Porcins
Sheep	...	...	...	...	...	255	249	222	Ovins
Netherlands									**Pays-Bas**
Cattle	4 047	3 858	3 759	3 767	3 799	3 749	3 763	3 890	Bovins
Goats	221	232	268	290	310	340	355	390	Caprins
Horses	120	121	126	129	129[1]	129[1]	130[1]	130[1]	Chevaux
Pigs	13 073	11 648	11 169	11 153	11 312	11 356	11 663	12 026	Porcins
Sheep	1 296	1 186	1 185	1 236	1 363	1 376	1 369	1 213	Ovins
Norway									**Norvège**
Cattle	979	959	957	943	934	923	906	891	Bovins
Goats	75	74	72	72	73	72	72	70	Caprins
Horses	29	30	29	29	30	33	34	34[1]	Chevaux
Pigs	711	751	791	826	824	836	838	826	Porcins
Sheep	2 453	2 459	2 481	2 467	2 423	2 360	2 267	2 250	Ovins
Poland									**Pologne**
Cattle	5 734	5 533	5 489	5 353	5 483	5 606	5 696	5 757	Bovins
Goats	190[1]	190[1]	192	176	141	130	144	136	Caprins
Horses	546	330	333	321	312	307	329	325	Chevaux
Pigs	17 106	18 707	18 605	16 988	18 112	18 881	18 129	15 425	Porcins
Sheep	343	345	338	318	316	301	332	324	Ovins
Portugal									**Portugal**
Asses or mules [1]	175	175	165	165	165	165	165	165	Ânes ou mules [1]
Cattle	1 414	1 404	1 395	1 389	1 443	1 441	1 407	1 443	Bovins
Goats	623	561	538	502	547	551	509	496	Caprins
Horses [1]	17	17	17	17	17	18	19	19	Chevaux [1]
Pigs	2 338	2 389	2 334	2 249	2 348	2 344	2 295	2 374	Porcins
Sheep	3 578	3 459	3 457	3 356	3 541	3 583	3 549	3 145	Ovins
Republic of Moldova									**République de Moldova**
Asses or mules [1]	2	2	2	2	2	2	2	2	Ânes ou mules [1]
Cattle	394	405	410	373	331	310	299	232	Bovins
Goats	109	112	126	121	119	119	112	99	Caprins
Horses	71	77	78	77	72	69	67	58	Chevaux
Pigs	447	449	508	446	398	461	532	299	Porcins
Sheep	830	835	830	817	823	818	835	754	Ovins
Romania									**Roumanie**
Asses or mules [1]	31	28	28	28	29	29	29	29	Ânes ou mules [1]
Cattle	2 870	2 800	2 878	2 897	2 808	2 862	2 934	2 819	Bovins
Goats	538	525	633	678	661	687	727	865	Caprins
Horses	865	860	879	897	840	834	805	862	Chevaux
Pigs	4 797	4 447	5 058	5 145	6 495	6 622	6 815	6 565	Porcins
Sheep	7 657	7 251	7 312	7 447	7 425	7 611	7 678	8 469	Ovins
Russian Federation									**Fédération de Russie**
Asses or mules	20[1]	19[1]	18[1]	17[1]	22[1]	22	21	20	Ânes ou mules
Buffaloes	17	14	16	18	17	14	16	14	Buffles
Camels	12[1]	12[1]	12[1]	7	7	6	6	6	Chameaux
Cattle	27 294	27 107	26 524	24 935	22 988	21 474	21 515	21 473	Bovins
Goats	2 212	2 292	2 322	2 361	2 277	2 138	2 167	2 182	Caprins
Horses	1 619	1 578	1 499	1 499	1 409	1 319	1 304	1 323	Chevaux
Pigs	15 708	16 047	17 337	15 980	13 413	13 455	15 919	16 128	Porcins
Sheep	12 561	13 035	13 728	14 669	15 494	16 074	17 508	18 740	Ovins
Serbia									**Serbie**
Cattle	...	...	...	...	...	1 096	1 087	1 057	Bovins
Goats	...	...	...	...	...	139	149	155	Caprins
Horses	...	...	...	...	...	20	18	17	Chevaux

32 Livestock

Stocks: thousand head

Cheptel

Réserves: milliers de têtes

Region, country or area	2001	2002	2003	2004	2005	2006	2007	2008	Region, pays ou zone
Pigs	...	...	...	...	...	3 212	3 832	3 594	Porcins
Sheep	...	...	...	...	...	1 609	1 606	1 605	Ovins
Serbia and Montenegro									**Serbie-et-Monténégro**
Buffaloes	26	29	29[1]	29[1]	29[1]	...	...	...	Buffles
Cattle	1 341	1 306	1 294	1 276	1 196	...	...	...	Bovins
Goats	237	226	224	195	139	...	...	...	Caprins
Horses	41	39	34	35	33	...	...	...	Chevaux
Pigs	3 634	3 608	3 656	3 463	3 177	...	...	...	Porcins
Sheep	1 783	1 691	1 756	1 838	1 837	...	...	...	Ovins
Slovakia									**Slovaquie**
Cattle	645	625	608	593	540	528	508	488	Bovins
Goats	51	40	40	39	39	40	38	37	Caprins
Horses	10	8	8	8	8	8	8	8	Chevaux
Pigs	1 488	1 517	1 554	1 443	1 149	1 108	1 105	749	Porcins
Sheep	348	316	316	325	321	320	333	362	Ovins
Slovenia									**Slovénie**
Cattle	494	477	473	450	451	453	454	480	Bovins
Goats	22	20	22	23	23	25	28	28	Caprins
Horses	15	17	17	18[2]	19	19	19[1]	20	Chevaux
Pigs	604	600	656	621	534	547	575	543	Porcins
Sheep	96	94	107	106	119	129	132	131	Ovins
Spain									**Espagne**
Asses or mules [1]	255	250	250	250	252	252	252	252	Ânes ou mules [1]
Cattle	6 411	6 478	6 548	6 653	6 463	6 184	6 585	6 020	Bovins
Goats	2 876	3 047	3 164	2 833	2 905	2 957	2 892	2 959	Caprins
Horses	238	238[1]	238[1]	238[1]	240[1]	245[1]	250[1]	250[1]	Chevaux
Pigs	22 149	23 518	24 056	24 895	24 884	26 219	26 061	26 290	Porcins
Sheep	24 400	23 813	23 486	22 910	22 749	22 452	22 194	19 952	Ovins
Sweden									**Suède**
Cattle	1 652	1 637	1 607	1 628	1 605	1 590	1 560	1 547[2]	Bovins
Horses	86[1]	85[1]	95	96	96[1]	96[1]	95[1]	95[1]	Chevaux
Pigs	1 891	1 882	1 903	1 818	1 811	1 681	1 676	1 651[2]	Porcins
Sheep	432	452	448	466	471	505	509	521	Ovins
Switzerland									**Suisse**
Asses or mules	4	4	5	5	6	6[1]	3	3[1]	Ânes ou mules
Cattle	1 611	1 594	1 565	1 570	1 545	1 555	1 567	1 608	Bovins
Goats	63[1]	63	66	67	74	76	79	82	Caprins
Horses	50	51	53	54	55	56	58	59	Chevaux
Pigs	1 548	1 557	1 529	1 538	1 609	1 635	1 573	1 552	Porcins
Sheep	420	430	445	441	446	451	444	447	Ovins
TFYR of Macedonia									**L'ex-R.Y. Macédoine**
Buffaloes	1[1]	1	1	1	1[1]	1[1]	1[1]	1[1]	Buffles
Cattle	265[2]	259	260	255	248	255	254	254[1]	Bovins
Goats	63[1]	62[1]	62[1]	62[1]	62	64	126	126[1]	Caprins
Horses [1]	57	57	57	57	57	58	57	57	Chevaux [1]
Pigs	204	196	179	158	156	167	255	255[1]	Porcins
Sheep	1 251	1 234	1 239	1 432	1 244	1 249	818	818[1]	Ovins
Ukraine									**Ukraine**
Asses or mules [1]	12	11	12	12	12	12	12	12	Ânes ou mules [1]
Camels [1]	...	...	1	1	1	1	1	1	Chameaux [1]
Cattle	9 424	9 421	9 108	7 712	6 903	6 514	6 175	5 491	Bovins
Goats	912	998	1 034	965	879	757	693	645	Caprins
Horses	701	693	684	637	591	555	534	498	Chevaux
Pigs	7 652	8 370	9 204	7 322	6 466	7 053	8 055	7 020	Porcins
Sheep	963	967	950	893	875	872	925	1 034	Ovins
United Kingdom									**Royaume-Uni**
Cattle	10 600	10 343	10 517	10 551	10 770	10 579	10 304	10 107	Bovins
Goats	76	75	93	89	92	98	95	95[1]	Caprins
Horses	310[1]	320[1]	330[1]	350[1]	370[1]	388	384	384[1]	Chevaux
Pigs	5 845	5 588	5 047	5 161	4 864	4 933	4 834	4 714	Porcins
Sheep	36 716	35 834	35 846	35 848	35 253	34 722	33 946	33 131	Ovins

32 Livestock

Stocks: thousand head

Cheptel

Réserves: milliers de têtes

Region, country or area	2001	2002	2003	2004	2005	2006	2007	2008	Region, pays ou zone
Oceania									**Océanie**
Asses or mules	**9**	**9**	**9**	**9**	**9**	**9**	**9**	**9**	**Ânes ou mules**
Cattle	**37 745**	**38 230**	**37 114**	**37 793**	**38 011**	**38 733**	**38 447**	**38 471**	**Bovins**
Goats	**770**	**869**	**892**	**1 076**	**926**	**1 004**	**965**	**949**	**Caprins**
Horses	**373**	**372**	**377**	**373**	**375**	**413**	**424**	**412**	**Chevaux**
Pigs	**5 541**	**5 824**	**5 567**	**5 483**	**5 601**	**5 637**	**5 515**	**5 473**	**Porcins**
Sheep	**150 926**	**145 754**	**138 820**	**140 574**	**141 019**	**131 142**	**124 187**	**113 104**	**Ovins**
American Samoa [1]									**Samoa américaines** [1]
Pigs	11	11	11	11	11	11	11	11	Porcins
Australia									**Australie**
Asses or mules [1]	2	2	2	2	2	2	2	2	Ânes ou mules [1]
Cattle	27 721	27 870	26 664	27 465	27 782	28 393	28 037	28 000[1]	Bovins
Goats	295[1]	400[1]	420[1]	595	461	518	518	518[1]	Caprins
Horses	220[1]	220[1]	220[1]	219	221	257	265	270[1]	Chevaux
Pigs	2 748	2 940	2 658	2 548	2 708	2 733	2 605	2 605	Porcins
Sheep	110 900	106 166	99 252	101 287	101 125	91 028	85 711	79 000	Ovins
Cook Islands									**Iles Cook**
Goats	2[1]	2[1]	1	1[1]	1[1]	1[1]	1[1]	1[1]	Caprins
Pigs	40[1]	40[1]	30	32[1]	32[1]	32[1]	32[1]	32[1]	Porcins
Fiji									**Fidji**
Cattle [1]	340	320	310	310	310	310	315	315	Bovins [1]
Goats	246	250[1]	250[1]	260[1]	240[1]	260[1]	270[1]	270[1]	Caprins
Horses [1]	44	44	44	44	44	45	46	46	Chevaux [1]
Pigs	137	138[1]	139[1]	139[1]	140[1]	140[1]	145[1]	145[1]	Porcins
Sheep [1]	7	6	6	5	5	6	6	6	Ovins [1]
French Polynesia [1]									**Polynésie française** [1]
Cattle	9	6	8	9	7	7	7	7	Bovins
Goats	17	17	17	17	17	17	17	17	Caprins
Horses	2	2	2	2	2	2	2	2	Chevaux
Pigs	33	30	25	29	30	26	31	31	Porcins
Guam [1]									**Guam** [1]
Goats	1	1	1	1	1	1	1	1	Caprins
Pigs	5	5	5	5	5	5	5	5	Porcins
Kiribati [1]									**Kiribati** [1]
Pigs	11	12	12	12	12	13	13	13	Porcins
Micronesia (Fed. St. of) [1]									**Micronésie (Et. féd. de)** [1]
Cattle	14	14	14	14	14	14	14	14	Bovins
Goats	4	4	4	4	4	4	4	4	Caprins
Pigs	32	32	32	32	32	32	33	33	Porcins
Nauru [1]									**Nauru** [1]
Pigs	3	3	3	3	3	3	3	3	Porcins
New Caledonia									**Nouvelle-Calédonie**
Cattle	110[1]	111	111[1]	111[1]	100[1]	110[1]	115[1]	115[1]	Bovins
Goats	9[1]	8	8[1]	8[1]	8[1]	8[1]	8[1]	8[1]	Caprins
Horses [1]	12	12	12	12	12	12	12	12	Chevaux [1]
Pigs	26[1]	25	26[1]	31[1]	31[1]	29[1]	29[1]	29[1]	Porcins
Sheep	3[1]	2	2[1]	2[1]	2[1]	2[1]	2[1]	2[1]	Ovins
New Zealand									**Nouvelle-Zélande**
Cattle	9 281	9 637	9 728	9 600	9 511	9 609	9 654	9 715	Bovins
Goats	163	153	155	153	155[1]	155[1]	112	96	Caprins
Horses	77	76	80	77	77[1]	78[1]	80[1]	63	Chevaux
Pigs	354	342	377	389	341	356	367	325	Porcins
Sheep	40 010	39 572	39 552	39 271	39 880	40 098	38 460	34 088	Ovins
Niue [1]									**Nioué** [1]
Pigs	2	2	2	2	2	2	2	2	Porcins
Papua New Guinea									**Papouasie-Nvl-Guinée**
Cattle	88[2]	89[2]	90[2]	91[1]	92[1]	93[1]	94[1]	94[1]	Bovins
Goats	2[2]	2[2]	3[2]	3[1]	3[1]	3[1]	3[1]	3[1]	Caprins
Horses	2[2]	2[2]	2[2]	2[1]	2[1]	2[1]	2[1]	2[1]	Chevaux
Pigs	1 700[2]	1 800[2]	1 800[2]	1 800[1]	1 800[1]	1 800[1]	1 800[1]	1 800[1]	Porcins
Sheep	6[2]	7[2]	7[2]	7[1]	7[1]	7[1]	7[1]	7[1]	Ovins

32 Livestock

Stocks: thousand head

Cheptel

Réserves: milliers de têtes

Region, country or area	2001	2002	2003	2004	2005	2006	2007	2008	Region, pays ou zone
Samoa									**Samoa**
Asses or mules [1]	7	7	7	7	7	7	7	7	Ânes ou mules [1]
Cattle [1]	28	28	29	30	30	29	29	29	Bovins [1]
Horses [1]	2	2	2	2	2	2	2	2	Chevaux [1]
Pigs	201	201[1]	201[1]	201[1]	201[1]	201[1]	202[1]	202[1]	Porcins
Solomon Islands [1]									**Iles Salomon** [1]
Cattle	13	13	13	14	14	14	14	14	Bovins
Pigs	51	51	51	52	53	53	54	54	Porcins
Tokelau [1]									**Tokélaou** [1]
Pigs	1	1	1	1	1	1	1	1	Porcins
Tonga [1]									**Tonga** [1]
Cattle	11	11	11	11	11	11	11	11	Bovins
Goats	13	13	13	13	13	13	13	13	Caprins
Horses	11	11	11	11	11	11	12	12	Chevaux
Pigs	81	81	81	81	81	81	81	81	Porcins
Tuvalu [1]									**Tuvalu** [1]
Pigs	13	14	14	14	14	14	14	14	Porcins
Vanuatu									**Vanuatu**
Cattle	130[1]	130[1]	135[1]	138[1]	140[1]	143	156[1]	156[1]	Bovins
Goats	12[1]	13[1]	15[1]	16[1]	17[1]	18	12[1]	12[1]	Caprins
Horses [1]	3	3	3	3	3	3	3	3	Chevaux [1]
Pigs	68[1]	72[1]	75[1]	78[1]	80[1]	82	63[1]	63[1]	Porcins
Wallis and Futuna Is. [1]									**Iles Wallis et Futuna** [1]
Goats	7	7	7	7	7	7	7	7	Caprins
Pigs	25	25	25	25	25	25	25	25	Porcins

Source:
Food and Agriculture Organization of the United Nations (FAO), Rome, FAOSTAT data, last accessed August 2010.

Source:
Organisation des Nations Unies pour l'alimentation et l'agriculture (FAO), Rome, données FAOSTAT, dernier accès août 2010.

1 FAO estimate.
2 Unofficial figure.
3 For statistical purposes, the data for China do not include those for the Hong Kong Special Administrative Region (Hong Kong SAR) and Macao Special Administrative Region (Macao SAR).

1 Estimation de la FAO.
2 Chiffre non officiel.
3 Pour la présentation des statistiques, les données pour la Chine ne comprennent pas la Région Administrative Spéciale de Hong Kong (Hong Kong RAS) et la Région Administrative Spéciale de Macao (Macao RAS).

33 Fertilizers

Nitrogen, phosphate and potash: thousand metric tons of plant nutrients

Engrais

Azote, phosphates et potasse : milliers de tonnes d'éléments fertilisants

Country/area and type of fertilizer	Production 2005	Production 2006	Production 2007	Production 2008	Consumption - Consommation 2005	2006	2007	2008	Pays/zone et type d'engrais
Afghanistan									**Afghanistan**
Nitrogen	15.6	17.6	17.0	*17.0	25.1[1]	49.0[1]	27.3[1]	25.0[1]	Azote
Albania[1]									**Albanie**[1]
Nitrogen	...	...	...	...	16.9	24.0	25.3	18.0	Azote
Phosphate	...	...	...	...	10.0	7.6	6.9	5.4	Phosphates
Algeria									**Algérie**
Nitrogen	83.1	27.4	137.8	11.0	4.1[1]	43.8[1]	36.6[1]	23.1[1]	Azote
Phosphate	20.4	24.3	42.6	11.6	32.5[1]	31.8[1]	52.4[1]	20.8[1]	Phosphates
Potash[1]	...	...	...	...	19.2	23.4	22.7	7.3	Potasse[1]
Angola[1]									**Angola**[1]
Nitrogen	...	...	...	...	3.7	6.6	5.6	8.2	Azote
Phosphate	...	...	...	...	1.5	1.4	2.4	3.9	Phosphates
Potash	...	...	...	...	2.3	4.1	3.2	16.0	Potasse
Argentina									**Argentine**
Nitrogen	574.7	659.1	468.9	405.9	640.4[1]	787.7[1]	981.4[1]	762.0[1]	Azote
Phosphate[1]	...	...	...	...	513.2	618.3	766.2	436.4	Phosphates[1]
Potash[1]	...	...	...	...	43.9	37.3	47.1	43.4	Potasse[1]
Armenia[1]									**Arménie**[1]
Nitrogen	...	...	...	...	10.3	12.4	6.8	8.0	Azote
Phosphate	...	...	...	...	0.0	0.2	0.1	0.0	Phosphates
Australia									**Australie**
Nitrogen	*338.6	*337.2	*338.0	*338.0	954.4	841.9	793.9[1]	696.7	Azote
Phosphate	*596.8	*585.8	*586.0	*586.0	1 139.2	840.8	820.3[1]	693.8	Phosphates
Potash	...	...	...	...	273.3	220.8	209.1[1]	99.8	Potasse
Austria									**Autriche**
Nitrogen	...	...	...	...	101.8	97.2	82.6	84.1	Azote
Phosphate	...	...	...	...	38.6	36.6	28.3	29.7	Phosphates
Potash	...	...	...	...	47.0	46.1	40.8	36.9	Potasse
Azerbaijan[1]									**Azerbaïdjan**[1]
Nitrogen	...	...	...	...	17.6	20.4	16.8	29.7	Azote
Phosphate	...	...	...	...	3.2	2.1	1.3	6.0	Phosphates
Potash	...	...	...	...	3.8	2.1	1.6	3.2	Potasse
Bahrain									**Bahreïn**
Nitrogen	258.1	287.4	269.0	304.1	4.2[1]	13.6[1]	0.0[2]	17.9[1]	Azote
Potash[1]	...	...	...	...	0.2	^0.0	^0.0	...	Potasse[1]
Bangladesh									**Bangladesh**
Nitrogen	880.6	815.7	855.6	856.0[1]	993.3	1 098.9	1 048.5	*1 168.4	Azote
Phosphate	69.0	69.0	65.2	*65.0	326.7	298.6	256.1	*82.3	Phosphates
Potash	...	...	...	*0.0	244.4	124.8	136.8	*49.0	Potasse
Barbados[1]									**Barbade**[1]
Nitrogen	...	...	...	...	1.2	1.2	1.1	1.5	Azote
Phosphate	...	...	...	...	0.1	0.6	0.6	0.2	Phosphates
Potash	...	...	...	...	0.1	^0.0	^0.0	0.1	Potasse
Belarus									**Bélarus**
Nitrogen	682.1	711.5	749.5	728.0	406.0	479.3	447.3	523.5[1]	Azote
Phosphate	135.8	148.8	152.4	173.5	129.5	204.7	191.0	181.0[1]	Phosphates
Potash	4 887.0	4 565.1	5 097.4	5 066.1	393.9	601.1	566.8	605.1[1]	Potasse
Belize[1]									**Belize**[1]
Nitrogen	...	...	...	...	4.1	2.9	...	1.7	Azote
Phosphate	...	...	...	...	1.5	3.4	...	1.6	Phosphates
Potash ^	...	...	...	...	0.0	0.0	...	0.2	Potasse ^
Bhutan									**Bhoutan**
Nitrogen	0.0	0.0	0.0	0.0	0.9	0.8	0.8	0.8[1]	Azote
Phosphate	0.0	0.0	0.0	0.0	0.2	0.3	0.3	0.2[1]	Phosphates
Potash	0.0	0.0	0.0	0.0	0.2	0.1	0.2	0.2[1]	Potasse
Bolivia (Plurinational State of)									**Bolivie (Ét. pl. de)**
Nitrogen	...	...	...	...	12.2	8.7	11.7	13.5	Azote
Phosphate	...	...	...	...	7.8	4.1	8.5	4.6	Phosphates
Potash	...	...	...	...	4.7	2.7	2.4	1.6	Potasse

Country/area and type of fertilizer	Production 2005	Production 2006	Production 2007	Production 2008	Consumption - Consommation 2005	Consumption - Consommation 2006	Consumption - Consommation 2007	Consumption - Consommation 2008	Pays/zone et type d'engrais
Bosnia and Herzegovina [1]									**Bosnie-Herzégovine** [1]
Nitrogen	...	...	...	...	24.6	15.5	21.4	11.7	Azote
Phosphate	...	...	...	...	0.2	0.1	0.1	0.1	Phosphates
Potash	...	...	...	...	0.4	0.3	0.3	0.2	Potasse
Brazil									**Brésil**
Nitrogen	985.3	1 051.4	983.8	921.6	2 072.2[1]	2 197.5[1]	2 952.1[1]	2 479.2[1]	Azote
Phosphate	1 719.9	1 819.7	2 085.8	1 951.1	2 871.9[1]	3 002.6[1]	4 049.2[1]	3 450.1[1]	Phosphates
Potash	371.7	424.2	389.2	351.9	3 361.7[1]	3 434.0[1]	4 300.7[1]	4 179.3[1]	Potasse
Brunei Darussalam									**Brunéi Darussalam**
Nitrogen	0.0	0.0	0.0	0.0	0.3	0.1	0.4	0.1	Azote
Phosphate	0.0	0.0	0.0	0.0	0.1	0.1	0.3	0.1	Phosphates
Potash	0.0	0.0	0.0	0.0	0.2	0.0	0.4	0.1	Potasse
Bulgaria									**Bulgarie**
Nitrogen	*348.7	*294.3	*262.1	*250.0	189.9[1]	203.6[1]	200.1[1]	179.0[1]	Azote
Phosphate	*173.1	*173.3	*100.1	*115.8	39.3[1]	88.6[1]	7.3[1]	63.7[1]	Phosphates
Potash	*0.0	*0.0	*0.0	...	6.3[1]	8.3[1]	5.2[1]	7.6[1]	Potasse
Burkina Faso									**Burkina Faso**
Nitrogen	...	...	...	...	35.4	9.5[1]	6.0[1]	9.1[1]	Azote
Phosphate	...	...	...	...	22.1	8.9[1]	6.2[1]	7.7[1]	Phosphates
Potash	...	...	...	...	17.1	18.5[1]	14.0[1]	7.7[1]	Potasse
Burundi									**Burundi**
Nitrogen	...	...	...	...	1.1	1.5[1]	0.8[1]	1.0[1]	Azote
Phosphate	...	...	...	...	2.3	0.6[1]	0.7[1]	0.4[1]	Phosphates
Potash	...	...	...	...	^0.0	0.9[1]	0.2[1]	0.6[1]	Potasse
Cambodia [1]									**Cambodge** [1]
Nitrogen	...	...	...	...	42.9	51.3	50.1	59.5	Azote
Phosphate	...	...	...	...	26.6	27.6	23.4	18.8	Phosphates
Potash	...	...	...	...	5.2	3.9	7.3	10.1	Potasse
Cameroon									**Cameroun**
Nitrogen	0.0	...	...	...	22.8	26.6[1]	22.5[1]	31.6[1]	Azote
Phosphate	0.0	...	...	...	5.9	11.1[1]	6.2[1]	7.4[1]	Phosphates
Potash	0.0	...	...	...	18.2	16.5[1]	21.9[1]	12.2[1]	Potasse
Canada									**Canada**
Nitrogen	*3 109.0	3 283.0	3 297.0	3 245.4	1 776.7[1]	1 527.1[1]	2 128.4[1]	1 977.5[1]	Azote
Phosphate	*278.0	247.4	*200.0	*190.0	693.1[1]	604.3[1]	678.3[1]	590.5[1]	Phosphates
Potash	8 073.1[1]	10 047.0	10 807.2	6 795.0	*328.6	1 884.1[1]	431.8[1]	0.0[2]	Potasse
Chile									**Chili**
Nitrogen	130.8	116.5	164.9	*165.0	240.7[1]	254.9[1]	320.6[1]	337.0[1]	Azote
Phosphate	0.2	0.3	0.5	*0.5	124.6[1]	144.8[1]	143.0[1]	123.9[1]	Phosphates
Potash	528.3	476.5	508.8	559.0	265.1[1]	226.9[1]	214.1[1]	284.0[1]	Potasse
China									**Chine**
Nitrogen	28 014.6	31 181.6	*35 359.3	*35 584.8	28 016.0[1]	31 184.4[1]	32 541.6[1]	33 211.9[1]	Azote
Phosphate	12 238.1	12 961.0	*13 914.6	*13 518.7	12 754.0[1]	13 223.1[1]	12 493.7[1]	12 145.9[1]	Phosphates
Potash	1 236.0	1 755.0	2 016.0	2 133.0	7 084.7[1]	6 759.7[1]	7 904.5[1]	5 484.9[1]	Potasse
Colombia									**Colombie**
Nitrogen	205.9	272.7	299.3	208.4	481.6[1]	544.0[1]	574.1[1]	463.4[1]	Azote
Phosphate	79.5	159.0	156.6	114.9	198.4[1]	299.5[1]	285.5[1]	203.9[1]	Phosphates
Potash [1]	...	...	...	...	221.8	244.5	232.0	233.8	Potasse [1]
Congo [1]									**Congo** [1]
Nitrogen	...	...	...	...	^0.0	^0.0	0.3	0.4	Azote
Phosphate	...	...	...	...	^0.0	^0.0	0.7	^0.0	Phosphates
Potash	...	...	...	...	...	...	3.1	0.2	Potasse
Costa Rica [1]									**Costa Rica** [1]
Nitrogen	...	...	...	...	88.8	71.2	66.2	67.8	Azote
Phosphate	...	...	...	...	35.5	24.1	23.8	4.8	Phosphates
Potash	...	...	...	...	81.6	78.4	68.0	68.9	Potasse
Côte d'Ivoire [1]									**Côte d'Ivoire** [1]
Nitrogen	...	...	...	...	16.2	11.0	25.9	17.6	Azote
Phosphate	...	...	...	...	10.7	22.3	15.8	4.7	Phosphates
Potash	...	...	...	...	22.9	30.5	27.9	30.5	Potasse

33 Fertilizers *(continued)*

Nitrogen, phosphate and potash: thousand metric tons of plant nutrients

Engrais *(suite)*

Azote, phosphates et potasse : milliers de tonnes d'éléments fertilisants

Country/area and type of fertilizer	Production 2005	Production 2006	Production 2007	Production 2008	Consumption - Consommation 2005	2006	2007	2008	Pays/zone et type d'engrais
Croatia									**Croatie**
Nitrogen	323.2	329.9	348.4	352.8	124.9[1]	113.9[1]	130.6[1]	170.5[1]	Azote
Phosphate	111.7	120.5	125.8	118.6	76.4[1]	82.0[1]	77.7[1]	90.6[1]	Phosphates
Potash[1]	...	...	...	...	55.8	62.3	59.3	72.2	Potasse[1]
Cuba									**Cuba**
Nitrogen	12.7	17.4	17.5	16.9	30.7	41.5	47.4	50.8	Azote
Phosphate	4.1	3.7	1.7	3.5	13.8	17.8	16.4	31.7	Phosphates
Potash	6.1	5.6	2.6	5.2	37.7	44.0	52.8	59.3	Potasse
Cyprus									**Chypre**
Nitrogen	0.0	0.0	0.0	0.0	8.0[1]	10.1[1]	8.3[1]	4.8[1]	Azote
Phosphate	0.0	0.0	0.0	0.0	4.5[1]	6.6[1]	7.1[1]	2.1[1]	Phosphates
Potash	0.0	0.0	0.0	0.0	4.3[1]	5.6[1]	4.2[1]	2.6[1]	Potasse
Czech Republic									**République tchèque**
Nitrogen	*305.2	*332.6	*333.0	*333.0	342.1[1]	299.2	355.1[1]	321.2[1]	Azote
Phosphate	*23.2	*16.0	*16.0	*16.0	62.0[1]	25.5	68.9[1]	38.5[1]	Phosphates
Potash	*0.0	*0.0	*0.0	...	60.6[1]	28.2	70.3[1]	49.0[1]	Potasse
Dem. Rep. of the Congo									**Rép. dém. du Congo**
Nitrogen	0.0	0.0	0.0	0.0	0.4[1]	1.6[1]	2.9[1]	4.3[1]	Azote
Phosphate	0.0	0.0	0.0	0.0	^0.0[1]	0.2[1]	0.5[1]	0.9[1]	Phosphates
Potash	0.0	0.0	0.0	0.0	^0.0[1]	1.2[1]	0.8[1]	1.1[1]	Potasse
Denmark									**Danemark**
Nitrogen	*0.0	*0.0	*0.0	0.0	179.0	170.0	172.5	172.5	Azote
Phosphate	*0.0	*0.0	*0.0	0.0	41.7	39.8	40.7	40.7	Phosphates
Potash	*0.0	*0.0	*0.0	0.0	99.0	95.1	94.8	94.8	Potasse
Dominica									**Dominique**
Nitrogen	0.0	0.0	0.0	0.0	0.4[1]	0.2[1]	0.6[1]	0.2[1]	Azote
Phosphate	0.0	0.0	0.0	0.0	0.5[1]	0.2[1]	0.7[1]	^0.0[1]	Phosphates
Potash	0.0	0.0	0.0	0.0	0.2[1]	0.3[1]	^0.0[1]	^0.0[1]	Potasse
Ecuador[1]									**Equateur**[1]
Nitrogen	...	...	...	...	116.3	126.3	118.2	156.4	Azote
Phosphate	...	...	...	...	38.6	35.8	37.0	26.2	Phosphates
Potash	...	...	...	...	40.6	94.2	82.7	82.1	Potasse
Egypt									**Egypte**
Nitrogen	1 552.0	1 751.0	2 286.5	2 618.6	1 468.1[1]	1 039.7[1]	1 106.9[1]	1 721.1[1]	Azote
Phosphate	253.2	231.9	250.7	312.1	208.0[1]	193.8[1]	176.1[1]	229.9[1]	Phosphates
Potash[1]	...	...	...	...	48.5	50.5	72.3	55.6	Potasse[1]
El Salvador									**El Salvador**
Nitrogen	0.0	0.0	0.0	0.0	68.3[1]	52.4[1]	64.9[1]	59.3[1]	Azote
Phosphate	0.0	0.0	0.0	0.0	22.1[1]	12.9[1]	16.1[1]	7.5[1]	Phosphates
Potash	0.0	0.0	0.0	0.0	1.4[1]	0.5[1]	15.1[1]	14.2[1]	Potasse
Eritrea[1]									**Erythrée**[1]
Nitrogen	...	...	...	...	1.4	^0.0	0.7	...	Azote
Phosphate	...	...	...	...	...	^0.0	1.7	...	Phosphates
Potash ^	...	...	...	...	...	0.0	...	...	Potasse ^
Estonia									**Estonie**
Nitrogen	101.0	99.4	96.4	91.8	20.1[1]	22.6[1]	25.0[1]	35.5[1]	Azote
Phosphate	0.0	0.0	0.0	0.0	6.3[1]	8.1[1]	8.1[1]	9.6[1]	Phosphates
Potash	0.0	0.0	0.0	0.0	9.7[1]	11.6[1]	12.4[1]	15.0[1]	Potasse
Ethiopia									**Ethiopie**
Nitrogen	...	...	...	...	30.5	33.1	37.4	*37.5	Azote
Phosphate	...	...	...	...	59.3	64.5	67.2	*67.2	Phosphates
Potash	...	...	...	...	0.0	0.0	0.0	...	Potasse
Fiji[1]									**Fidji**[1]
Nitrogen	...	...	...	...	6.6	4.2	4.0	7.9	Azote
Phosphate ^	...	...	...	...	0.0	0.0	0.0	0.0	Phosphates ^
Potash ^	...	...	...	...	0.0	0.0	0.0	0.0	Potasse ^
Finland									**Finlande**
Nitrogen	*291.8	221.1	272.8	227.4	192.5[1]	158.3[1]	184.2[1]	171.6[1]	Azote
Phosphate	*73.0	103.4	69.5	163.8	29.8[1]	78.4[1]	42.3[1]	102.3[1]	Phosphates
Potash	*0.0	*0.0	*0.0	*0.0	77.9[1]	67.4[1]	52.2[1]	28.8[1]	Potasse

33 Fertilizers *(continued)*

Nitrogen, phosphate and potash: thousand metric tons of plant nutrients

Engrais *(suite)*

Azote, phosphates et potasse : milliers de tonnes d'éléments fertilisants

Country/area and type of fertilizer	Production 2005	Production 2006	Production 2007	Production 2008	Consumption - Consommation 2005	Consumption - Consommation 2006	Consumption - Consommation 2007	Consumption - Consommation 2008	Pays/zone et type d'engrais
France									**France**
Nitrogen	3 044.4	2 181.8	1 456.1	1 268.3	2 205.0	2 204.7	2 402.0	2 009.2	Azote
Phosphate	575.4	699.6	418.7	466.8	597.0	555.6	632.0	290.0	Phosphates
Potash	...	...	...	...	735.0	731.2	794.0	369.0	Potasse
French Polynesia [1]									**Polynésie française** [1]
Nitrogen	...	...	...	...	0.3	0.3	0.3	0.5	Azote
Phosphate	...	...	...	...	0.2	0.2	0.3	0.2	Phosphates
Potash	...	...	...	...	0.2	0.2	0.3	0.2	Potasse
Gabon [1]									**Gabon** [1]
Nitrogen	...	...	...	...	0.6	0.8	0.8	0.2	Azote
Phosphate	...	...	...	...	0.3	0.3	0.3	0.1	Phosphates
Potash	...	...	...	...	1.9	1.7	0.4	4.3	Potasse
Gambia									**Gambie**
Nitrogen	0.0	0.0	0.0	0.0	1.7[1]	1.5[1]	1.3[1]	0.3[1]	Azote
Phosphate	0.0	0.0	0.0	0.0	0.8[1]	0.6[1]	0.4[1]	0.3[1]	Phosphates
Potash	0.0	0.0	0.0	0.0	0.8[1]	0.6[1]	0.4[1]	0.3[1]	Potasse
Georgia									**Géorgie**
Nitrogen	110.4	127.5	131.8	133.9	24.1[1]	21.6[1]	18.5[1]	16.9[1]	Azote
Phosphate [1]	...	...	...	...	0.7	0.9	0.6	0.4	Phosphates [1]
Potash [1]	...	...	...	...	0.2	0.5	0.3	0.1	Potasse [1]
Germany									**Allemagne**
Nitrogen	1 253.8[1]	1 185.7[1]	1 504.5[1]	1 015.0[1]	1 785.0	1 599.8	1 807.2	1 560.6	Azote
Phosphate	51.0	48.3	61.5	101.4	273.9	264.6	316.7	174.3	Phosphates
Potash	3 395.3[1]	3 362.2[1]	2 889.2[1]	2 318.9[1]	426.1	442.6	511.3	179.2	Potasse
Ghana [1]									**Ghana** [1]
Nitrogen	...	...	...	...	11.1	30.2	19.1	10.0	Azote
Phosphate	...	...	...	...	6.3	15.2	13.2	9.9	Phosphates
Potash	...	...	...	...	6.6	38.9	13.4	8.4	Potasse
Greece									**Grèce**
Nitrogen	93.1	45.2	35.1	32.0	203.8[1]	172.6[1]	134.2[1]	173.2[1]	Azote
Phosphate	101.5	45.2	35.1	32.0	124.5[1]	86.1[1]	56.5[1]	68.5[1]	Phosphates
Potash	0.0	0.0	0.0	...	49.1[1]	63.3[1]	54.3[1]	60.3[1]	Potasse
Guatemala [1]									**Guatemala** [1]
Nitrogen	...	...	...	...	131.4	145.7	133.1	88.3	Azote
Phosphate	...	...	...	...	60.4	50.7	55.2	25.1	Phosphates
Potash	...	...	...	...	6.6	8.4	6.8	8.5	Potasse
Guinea [1]									**Guinée** [1]
Nitrogen	...	...	...	...	2.0	2.0	3.2	2.8	Azote
Phosphate	...	...	...	...	0.1	^0.0	0.1	0.4	Phosphates
Potash	...	...	...	...	0.5	0.4	0.1	0.5	Potasse
Guyana [1]									**Guyana** [1]
Nitrogen	...	...	...	...	6.2	8.3	6.4	18.3	Azote
Phosphate	...	...	...	...	1.6	1.5	7.3	5.6	Phosphates
Potash	...	...	...	...	1.5	3.9	^0.0	...	Potasse
Honduras [1]									**Honduras** [1]
Nitrogen	...	...	...	...	75.4	89.5	83.4	44.7	Azote
Phosphate	...	...	...	...	14.7	16.5	15.8	33.1	Phosphates
Potash	...	...	...	...	78.8	92.3	87.7	32.0	Potasse
Hungary									**Hongrie**
Nitrogen	*311.3	*302.0	223.0[1]	189.7[1]	348.5[1]	374.6[1]	320.0	294.0	Azote
Phosphate	...	...	...	...	89.8[1]	87.4[1]	97.7	74.0	Phosphates
Potash	...	...	...	...	106.2[1]	97.6[1]	126.0	63.0	Potasse
Iceland									**Islande**
Nitrogen	...	...	...	...	9.8	12.3	13.8	15.3	Azote
Phosphate	...	...	...	...	4.4	5.4	6.0	5.5	Phosphates
Potash	...	...	...	...	3.0	3.9	4.5	4.2	Potasse
India									**Inde**
Nitrogen	11 218.2	10 416.7	10 897.3	10 387.0	12 723.9	13 774.9	14 418.9	*14 909.8	Azote
Phosphate	4 092.6	2 715.1	4 645.4	2 347.0	5 210.0	5 550.2	5 518.1	*6 051.9	Phosphates
Potash	0.0	0.0	0.0	0.0	2 413.5	2 331.1	2 635.4	*3 312.8	Potasse

33 Fertilizers *(continued)*

Nitrogen, phosphate and potash: thousand metric tons of plant nutrients

Engrais *(suite)*

Azote, phosphates et potasse : milliers de tonnes d'éléments fertilisants

Country/area and type of fertilizer	Production 2005	2006	2007	2008	Consumption - Consommation 2005	2006	2007	2008	Pays/zone et type d'engrais
Indonesia									**Indonésie**
Nitrogen	2 875.7	2 808.3	2 947.3	3 189.1	2 411.9	2 435.5	2 503.3	2 675.6	Azote
Phosphate	345.1	307.7	349.8	349.1	327.8	354.1	385.0	353.2	Phosphates
Potash	*0.0	*0.0	*0.0	*0.0	564.2	607.7	810.7	1 130.8	Potasse
Iran (Islamic Rep. of)									**Iran (Rép. islam. d')**
Nitrogen	703.9	652.4	777.8	1 041.5	937.3[1]	1 203.3[1]	966.7[1]	1 061.8[1]	Azote
Phosphate	168.9	149.1	51.8	4.5	492.1[1]	558.0[1]	435.1[1]	362.0[1]	Phosphates
Potash	*0.0	*0.0	...	...	132.5[1]	141.2[1]	115.8[1]	124.9[1]	Potasse
Iraq									**Iraq**
Nitrogen	138.9	151.7	110.2	149.3	153.9[1]	167.0[1]	126.4[1]	164.1[1]	Azote
Phosphate	24.5	15.9	18.1	22.2	62.5[1]	55.0[1]	59.5[1]	63.6[1]	Phosphates
Ireland									**Irlande**
Nitrogen	0.0	0.0	0.0	0.0	359.9[1]	326.0[1]	303.4[1]	334.5[1]	Azote
Phosphate	0.0	0.0	0.0	0.0	124.1[1]	129.1[1]	118.7[1]	83.4[1]	Phosphates
Potash	0.0	0.0	0.0	0.0	150.6[1]	160.4[1]	139.2[1]	110.9[1]	Potasse
Israel									**Israël**
Nitrogen	*86.7	*89.0	111.7[1]	83.1[1]	48.8	47.5	59.4	45.9	Azote
Phosphate	*424.3	*450.0	411.3[1]	455.5[1]	11.8	12.2	11.3	10.1	Phosphates
Potash	*2 260.4	2 200.0	2 200.0	2 400.0	30.4	32.7	22.5	20.2	Potasse
Italy									**Italie**
Nitrogen	*444.6	*403.4	*400.0	*400.0	800.7	798.8	812.5	702.5	Azote
Phosphate	*23.0	*23.0	*20.0	*20.0	285.3	271.0	280.4	203.8	Phosphates
Potash	*0.0	*0.0	...	...	250.3	236.0	271.3	206.3	Potasse
Jamaica[1]									**Jamaïque**[1]
Nitrogen	...	...	...	...	6.4	4.8	3.8	4.9	Azote
Phosphate	...	...	...	...	4.6	1.8	^0.0	1.5	Phosphates
Potash	...	...	...	...	3.7	1.5	^0.0	0.0	Potasse
Japan									**Japon**
Nitrogen	767.3	770.5	769.9	647.2	553.5[1]	528.3[1]	514.5[1]	468.5[1]	Azote
Phosphate	306.1	290.0	296.8	236.2	611.1[1]	569.4[1]	593.0[1]	448.5[1]	Phosphates
Potash	*0.0	...	...	...	352.5[1]	347.8[1]	408.6[1]	281.6[1]	Potasse
Jordan									**Jordanie**
Nitrogen	118.3	162.3	158.8	150.0	21.9[1]	11.7[1]	36.9[1]	22.2[1]	Azote
Phosphate	302.2	331.4	342.7	315.4	43.0[1]	5.7[1]	16.5[1]	0.0[2]	Phosphates
Potash	1 097.4	1 036.0	1 142.1	*1 140.0	80.2[1]	114.5[1]	88.0[1]	28.2[1]	Potasse
Kazakhstan									**Kazakhstan**
Nitrogen	4.6	15.8	71.2	65.7	56.2[1]	80.7[1]	69.5[1]	60.8[1]	Azote
Phosphate	117.5	93.4	76.6	117.8	28.5[1]	51.6[1]	36.4[1]	0.0[2]	Phosphates
Potash	...	...	...	...	2.8[1]	0.0[2]	8.3[1]	9.1[1]	Potasse
Kenya									**Kenya**
Nitrogen	...	...	...	...	72.5	77.7	79.4	73.1	Azote
Phosphate	...	...	...	...	93.1	85.2	99.1	97.7	Phosphates
Potash	...	...	...	...	15.0	13.1	14.3	5.7	Potasse
Korea, Republic of									**Corée, République de**
Nitrogen	416.4	337.8	372.5	348.4	417.3	304.4	347.4	311.8	Azote
Phosphate	175.6	228.9	229.3	207.5	317.3	225.0	230.2	212.6	Phosphates
Potash	...	...	...	...	322.4	231.3	238.5	220.3	Potasse
Kuwait									**Koweït**
Nitrogen	374.4	455.4	424.1	442.5	47.8[1]	23.0[1]	0.0[2]	14.3[1]	Azote
Kyrgyzstan									**Kirghizistan**
Nitrogen	...	...	...	...	29.6	26.8	26.1	22.5	Azote
Phosphate	...	...	...	...	2.0	1.7	2.6	1.7	Phosphates
Potash	...	...	...	...	0.0	0.0	0.0	0.0	Potasse
Latvia									**Lettonie**
Nitrogen	0.0	0.0	0.0	0.0	40.9[1]	42.7[1]	47.7[1]	72.6[1]	Azote
Phosphate	0.0	0.0	0.0	0.0	14.7[1]	14.5[1]	16.0[1]	36.3[1]	Phosphates
Potash	0.0	0.0	0.0	0.0	18.7[1]	18.3[1]	16.7[1]	36.5[1]	Potasse
Lebanon									**Liban**
Nitrogen[1]	...	...	...	...	8.7	8.0	21.7	5.5	Azote[1]
Phosphate	*160.0	*150.0	*150.0	93.8	34.5[1]	32.0[1]	25.7[1]	1.2[1]	Phosphates
Potash[1]	...	...	...	...	1.3	0.5	12.7	1.4	Potasse[1]

33 Fertilizers *(continued)*

Nitrogen, phosphate and potash: thousand metric tons of plant nutrients

Engrais *(suite)*

Azote, phosphates et potasse : milliers de tonnes d'éléments fertilisants

Country/area and type of fertilizer	Production				Consumption - Consommation				Pays/zone et type d'engrais
	2005	2006	2007	2008	2005	2006	2007	2008	
Libyan Arab Jamah.									**Jam. arabe libyenne**
Nitrogen	384.1	380.4	359.3	276.9	75.6[1]	36.9[1]	68.7[1]	42.8[1]	Azote
Phosphate[1]	...	...	...	...	36.8	36.8	36.8	3.7	Phosphates[1]
Potash[1]	...	...	...	...	5.1	0.3	1.2	1.2	Potasse[1]
Lithuania									**Lituanie**
Nitrogen	670.2	628.3	746.8	688.1	...	28.4[1]	0.0[2]	17.2[1]	Azote
Phosphate	400.1	411.1	437.0	405.2	121.1[1]	81.8[1]	88.2[1]	73.1[1]	Phosphates
Potash	0.0	0.0	0.0	0.0	64.9[1]	78.9[1]	74.3[1]	57.1[1]	Potasse
Luxembourg									**Luxembourg**
Nitrogen	0.0	0.0	0.0	0.0	14.2	14.0	13.3	14.7[1]	Azote
Phosphate	0.0	0.0	0.0	0.0	2.2	1.7	1.7	1.7[1]	Phosphates
Potash	0.0	0.0	0.0	0.0	2.4	1.9	1.9	0.8[1]	Potasse
Madagascar[1]									**Madagascar**[1]
Nitrogen	...	...	...	...	7.3	3.7	4.4	7.5	Azote
Phosphate	...	...	...	...	4.6	2.0	2.5	2.4	Phosphates
Potash	...	...	...	...	4.5	1.7	2.6	2.9	Potasse
Malawi									**Malawi**
Nitrogen	...	0.1	0.1	0.2	66.2	83.0	84.3	2.6	Azote
Phosphate	...	...	...	...	19.7	24.0	25.4	3.2	Phosphates
Potash	...	...	...	...	11.7	14.5	15.5	...	Potasse
Malaysia									**Malaisie**
Nitrogen	*542.7	*616.2	*616.0	*616.0	586.0[1]	582.3[1]	667.3[1]	649.6[1]	Azote
Phosphate	*85.2	*74.0	*74.0	*74.0	163.9[1]	150.1[1]	158.9[1]	143.2[1]	Phosphates
Potash	*0.0	*0.0	*0.0	...	687.7[1]	879.5[1]	945.6[1]	880.9[1]	Potasse
Mali									**Mali**
Nitrogen	0.0	0.0	0.0	0.0	35.9	42.9	29.3	29.4	Azote
Phosphate	0.0	0.0	0.0	0.0	14.3	16.3	10.0	8.4	Phosphates
Potash	0.0	0.0	0.0	0.0	12.5	14.4	8.2	6.0	Potasse
Malta[1]									**Malte**[1]
Nitrogen	...	...	...	...	0.6	0.9	0.6	0.3	Azote
Phosphate	...	...	...	...	0.1	0.1	0.1	0.1	Phosphates
Potash	...	...	...	...	0.2	0.1	0.2	0.1	Potasse
Mauritius									**Maurice**
Nitrogen	0.0	0.0	0.0	0.0	9.9	8.6	*8.8	7.3[1]	Azote
Phosphate	0.0	0.0	0.0	0.0	5.8	3.4	*2.3	6.0[1]	Phosphates
Potash	0.0	0.0	0.0	0.0	14.2	9.4	*11.8	5.0[1]	Potasse
Mexico									**Mexique**
Nitrogen	368.2	260.9	262.1	262.0	1 219.5[1]	1 070.1[1]	1 095.1[1]	841.9[1]	Azote
Phosphate	79.6	84.8	84.7	85.0	438.2[1]	389.5[1]	362.5[1]	82.7[1]	Phosphates
Potash[1]	...	...	...	...	184.0	193.1	244.7	184.8	Potasse[1]
Mongolia[1]									**Mongolie**[1]
Nitrogen	...	...	...	...	3.7	6.5	6.0	6.9	Azote
Phosphate ^	...	...	...	...	...	0.0	...	0.0	Phosphates ^
Potash ^	...	...	...	...	...	0.0	0.0	0.0	Potasse ^
Morocco									**Maroc**
Nitrogen	264.1	298.9	275.5	293.6	337.4	321.4	304.8	275.1	Azote
Phosphate	1 042.1	1 154.6	1 168.4	791.3	114.4	101.7	112.9	97.0	Phosphates
Potash	*0.0	*0.0	*0.0	*0.0	66.3	62.2	56.8	61.4	Potasse
Mozambique[1]									**Mozambique**[1]
Nitrogen	...	...	...	...	6.4	17.2	11.5	...	Azote
Phosphate	...	...	...	...	0.4	2.8	1.1	...	Phosphates
Potash	...	...	...	...	0.3	2.7	1.3	...	Potasse
Myanmar									**Myanmar**
Nitrogen	2.1	3.6	3.1	2.3	9.8[1]	17.7[1]	33.5[1]	15.7[1]	Azote
Phosphate[1]	...	...	...	...	8.1	18.0	69.0	13.4	Phosphates[1]
Potash[1]	...	...	...	...	3.8	8.2	17.4	5.8	Potasse[1]
Namibia									**Namibie**
Nitrogen[1]	...	...	...	...	1.0	1.9	1.3	0.2	Azote[1]
Phosphate[1]	...	...	...	...	0.3	0.2	0.3	^0.0	Phosphates[1]
Potash	...	...	...	...	0.3[1]	0.2[1]	0.3[1]	0.0[2]	Potasse

33 Fertilizers *(continued)*

Nitrogen, phosphate and potash: thousand metric tons of plant nutrients

Engrais *(suite)*

Azote, phosphates et potasse : milliers de tonnes d'éléments fertilisants

Country/area and type of fertilizer	Production 2005	Production 2006	Production 2007	Production 2008	Consumption - Consommation 2005	Consumption - Consommation 2006	Consumption - Consommation 2007	Consumption - Consommation 2008	Pays/zone et type d'engrais
Nepal									**Népal**
Nitrogen	0.0	0.0	0.0	0.0	19.1[1]	25.6[1]	16.1[1]	5.5[1]	Azote
Phosphate	0.0	0.0	0.0	0.0	19.8[1]	12.6[1]	6.4[1]	0.3[1]	Phosphates
Potash	0.0	0.0	0.0	0.0	6.0[1]	11.0[1]	19.5[1]	12.4[1]	Potasse
Netherlands									**Pays-Bas**
Nitrogen	1 534.7	1 563.2	1 628.1	1 484.2	265.0	260.0	251.0	209.4[1]	Azote
Phosphate	204.7	171.8	168.5	120.5	44.0	42.0	39.0	37.6[1]	Phosphates
Potash	...	...	...	...	46.0	43.0	42.0	*40.0	Potasse
New Caledonia[1]									**Nouvelle-Calédonie**[1]
Nitrogen	...	...	...	...	0.8	0.6	0.8	0.5	Azote
Phosphate	...	...	...	...	0.5	0.4	0.5	0.4	Phosphates
Potash	...	...	...	...	0.6	0.6	0.5	0.4	Potasse
New Zealand									**Nouvelle-Zélande**
Nitrogen	174.0	129.8	*129.8	*129.8	309.8	268.8	277.5	262.7	Azote
Phosphate	132.2	113.6	*113.6	*113.6	821.1	708.0	701.5	505.7	Phosphates
Potash	0.0	0.0	*0.0	...	24.6	18.7	14.4	11.2	Potasse
Nicaragua[1]									**Nicaragua**[1]
Nitrogen	...	...	...	...	36.2	47.2	35.2	45.9	Azote
Phosphate	...	...	...	...	11.1	6.2	12.0	6.6	Phosphates
Potash	...	...	...	...	9.7	9.5	10.8	8.8	Potasse
Niger									**Niger**
Nitrogen	...	...	...	...	2.8	4.0	4.5[1]	5.0[1]	Azote
Phosphate	...	...	...	...	1.6	2.1	1.3[1]	0.8[1]	Phosphates
Potash	...	...	...	...	1.1	1.3	0.0[1]	0.5[1]	Potasse
Nigeria									**Nigéria**
Nitrogen	4.9	20.8	12.5	*12.5	215.9[1]	180.9[1]	56.0[1]	383.2[1]	Azote
Phosphate	2.8	12.5	6.6	*6.5	17.6[1]	25.8[1]	18.2[1]	67.3[1]	Phosphates
Potash	3.1	14.3	6.8	*6.8	9.1[1]	20.9[1]	14.1[1]	47.2[1]	Potasse
Norway									**Norvège**
Nitrogen	*453.4	*492.1	*497.7	*468.3	105.5	103.0	106.3	*104.3	Azote
Phosphate	*271.8	*300.4	*304.7	*289.7	28.6	28.3	27.7	*27.0	Phosphates
Potash	*0.0	*0.0	*0.0	*0.0	54.5	54.3	53.9	53.6[1]	Potasse
Oman									**Oman**
Nitrogen	478.9	778.8	875.4	897.9	30.1[1]	14.7[1]	0.9[1]	8.8[1]	Azote
Phosphate[1]	...	...	...	...	1.2	1.8	1.2	1.7	Phosphates[1]
Potash[1]	...	...	...	...	7.0	11.2	8.0	11.2	Potasse[1]
Pakistan									**Pakistan**
Nitrogen	2 424.8	2 464.7	2 442.4	2 544.9	2 818.8	2 865.4	2 712.0	2 818.7	Azote
Phosphate	343.9	323.5	292.6	330.5	871.4	919.3	824.8	482.1	Phosphates
Potash	...	...	...	...	35.3	34.1	40.3	22.5	Potasse
Panama									**Panama**
Nitrogen	0.0	0.0	0.0	0.0	15.6[1]	17.7[1]	14.5[1]	15.4[1]	Azote
Phosphate	0.0	0.0	0.0	0.0	1.6[1]	1.4[1]	1.8[1]	1.7[1]	Phosphates
Potash	0.0	0.0	0.0	0.0	1.6[1]	1.6[1]	2.1[1]	2.1[1]	Potasse
Papua New Guinea[1]									**Papouasie N. Guinée**[1]
Nitrogen	...	...	...	...	13.8	11.3	12.2	13.7	Azote
Phosphate	...	...	...	...	1.6	2.1	3.4	2.7	Phosphates
Potash	...	...	...	...	1.7	1.3	3.3	4.9	Potasse
Paraguay[1]									**Paraguay**[1]
Nitrogen	...	...	...	...	41.9	47.9	76.8	58.8	Azote
Phosphate	...	...	...	...	103.9	115.9	140.0	116.0	Phosphates
Potash	...	...	...	...	81.8	94.4	126.4	105.9	Potasse
Peru									**Pérou**
Nitrogen[1]	...	...	...	...	180.3	203.0	246.7	203.1	Azote[1]
Phosphate	0.4	0.3	0.4	0.3	65.4[1]	85.2[1]	65.8[1]	44.5[1]	Phosphates
Potash[1]	...	...	...	...	55.8	50.9	91.0	50.1	Potasse[1]
Philippines									**Philippines**
Nitrogen	138.5	116.1	97.3	*36.2	544.1[1]	468.5[1]	492.2[1]	473.6[1]	Azote
Phosphate	133.4	135.7	113.5	*35.2	137.3[1]	143.0[1]	149.8[1]	108.5[1]	Phosphates
Potash[1]	...	...	...	...	80.1	81.4	109.0	113.1	Potasse[1]

33 Fertilizers (continued)

Nitrogen, phosphate and potash: thousand metric tons of plant nutrients

Engrais (suite)

Azote, phosphates et potasse : milliers de tonnes d'éléments fertilisants

Country/area and type of fertilizer	Production 2005	Production 2006	Production 2007	Production 2008	Consumption - Consommation 2005	Consumption - Consommation 2006	Consumption - Consommation 2007	Consumption - Consommation 2008	Pays/zone et type d'engrais
Poland									**Pologne**
Nitrogen	1 735.5	1 714.3	1 832.9	1 856.8	996.5	1 056.2	1 142.3	1 473.0[1]	Azote
Phosphate	595.7	595.2	647.7	535.6	441.8	411.9	462.3	465.4[1]	Phosphates
Potash	*0.0	*0.0	...	...	527.8	502.6	537.4	455.0[1]	Potasse
Portugal									**Portugal**
Nitrogen	89.7[1]	55.4[1]	73.3[1]	66.7[1]	102.7	82.9	98.4	*98.5	Azote
Phosphate	67.3[1]	56.7[1]	66.7[1]	63.9[1]	77.3	64.3	67.5	*67.5	Phosphates
Potash	...	...	...	...	84.8	76.0	82.3	*82.3	Potasse
Qatar									**Qatar**
Nitrogen	1 370.2	1 338.1	1 363.4	1 378.6	7.3[1]	0.0[2]	70.4[1]	0.0[2]	Azote
Phosphate [2]	...	...	...	...	0.0	...	...	...	Phosphates [2]
Potash	...	...	...	...	0.0[2]	...	...	3.6[1]	Potasse
Republic of Moldova									**Rép. de Moldova**
Nitrogen	...	...	...	...	14.8	12.8	17.1	19.9	Azote
Phosphate	...	...	...	...	1.3	1.9	2.0	1.7	Phosphates
Potash	...	...	...	...	0.4	0.7	1.0	1.1	Potasse
Romania									**Roumanie**
Nitrogen	1 194.1	818.9	756.2	946.1	299.2	252.2	265.5	279.9	Azote
Phosphate	0.0	0.2	0.0	...	138.1	93.8	103.3	102.4	Phosphates
Potash	0.0	...	0.0	...	24.1	16.8	18.4	15.7	Potasse
Russian Federation									**Fédération de Russie**
Nitrogen	6 725.0	6 830.0	7 203.0	6 890.0	863.2	914.7	1 043.8	1 209.8	Azote
Phosphate	2 766.0	2 766.0	2 807.0	2 571.0	346.8	368.3	408.9	430.9	Phosphates
Potash	7 131.0	6 610.0	7 277.0	6 738.0	226.0	234.4	280.2	291.5	Potasse
Rwanda [1]									**Rwanda** [1]
Nitrogen	...	...	...	...	1.2	0.6	2.6	2.8	Azote
Phosphate	...	...	...	...	1.1	1.5	4.2	4.3	Phosphates
Potash	...	...	...	...	1.1	1.8	2.0	3.6	Potasse
Saudi Arabia									**Arabie saoudite**
Nitrogen	1 368.5	1 472.4	1 826.6	1 712.0	182.8[1]	228.7[1]	256.0[1]	180.4[1]	Azote
Phosphate	135.4	105.4	139.1	75.5	136.9[1]	106.4[1]	132.3[1]	65.1[1]	Phosphates
Potash	*0.0	*0.0	*0.0	*0.0	9.0[1]	5.7[1]	21.2[1]	13.7[1]	Potasse
Senegal									**Sénégal**
Nitrogen	15.9	2.6	5.9	3.5	12.2	1.6	1.4	1.8	Azote
Phosphate	32.5	7.1	22.5	12.0	11.6	3.3	3.4	4.1	Phosphates
Potash	*0.0	...	...	...	7.0	1.6	1.3	2.4	Potasse
Serbia									**Serbie**
Nitrogen	...	104.1	144.7	88.4	...	236.4[1]	292.0[1]	219.9[1]	Azote
Phosphate	...	22.1	25.2	33.4	...	69.5[1]	97.0[1]	66.8[1]	Phosphates
Potash	...	21.8	16.6	28.7	...	83.7[1]	95.0[1]	93.8[1]	Potasse
Serbia and Montenegro									**Serbie-et-Monténégro**
Nitrogen	184.5	...	...	...	277.0[1]	...	...	...	Azote
Phosphate	40.4	...	...	...	79.3[1]	...	...	...	Phosphates
Potash	39.1	...	...	...	91.8[1]	...	...	...	Potasse
Singapore									**Singapour**
Nitrogen [1]	...	...	...	...	9.1	10.7	9.7	6.8	Azote [1]
Phosphate	...	...	...	...	0.0[2]	0.1[1]	0.2[1]	0.1[1]	Phosphates
Potash	...	...	...	...	0.0[2]	0.0[2]	1.4[1]	2.9[1]	Potasse
Slovakia									**Slovaquie**
Nitrogen	*249.7	*221.5	*221.5	*221.5	81.5[1]	74.4[1]	113.0[1]	130.8[1]	Azote
Phosphate	*0.0	*0.0	...	...	18.6[1]	21.8[1]	28.6[1]	28.8[1]	Phosphates
Potash	*0.0	*0.0	...	...	17.4[1]	19.3[1]	23.0[1]	20.2[1]	Potasse
Slovenia									**Slovénie**
Nitrogen	^0.0	0.0	0.0	*0.0	28.9	29.9	29.2	24.9	Azote
Phosphate	^0.0	0.0	0.0	*0.0	13.2	13.0	12.7	11.9	Phosphates
Potash	^0.0	0.0	0.0	*0.0	16.0	14.4	14.9	14.6	Potasse
South Africa									**Afrique du Sud**
Nitrogen	*281.5	*166.9	154.1[1]	118.1[1]	347.3	428.7	439.5	424.1	Azote
Phosphate	*313.5	*130.5	162.8[1]	156.5[1]	159.5	203.8	192.5	185.0	Phosphates
Potash	*0.0	*0.0	...	...	116.8	152.9	136.9	111.4	Potasse

33 Fertilizers *(continued)*

Nitrogen, phosphate and potash: thousand metric tons of plant nutrients

Engrais *(suite)*

Azote, phosphates et potasse : milliers de tonnes d'éléments fertilisants

Country/area and type of fertilizer	Production 2005	Production 2006	Production 2007	Production 2008	Consumption - Consommation 2005	Consumption - Consommation 2006	Consumption - Consommation 2007	Consumption - Consommation 2008	Pays/zone et type d'engrais
Spain									**Espagne**
Nitrogen	794.7	715.6	710.3	674.9	937.1	974.3	1 017.2	739.8	Azote
Phosphate	331.2	310.2	362.4	298.0	455.0	406.3	495.5	271.6	Phosphates
Potash	643.5	580.5	621.3	596.4	422.6	412.2	471.1	319.2	Potasse
Sri Lanka									**Sri Lanka**
Nitrogen	...	...	...	...	181.6[1]	161.6[1]	161.6	204.8[1]	Azote
Phosphate	11.0	11.9	12.0	*12.0	36.9[1]	51.5[1]	51.1	77.7[1]	Phosphates
Potash	...	...	...	...	62.4[1]	77.5[1]	77.6	72.8[1]	Potasse
Sudan									**Soudan**
Nitrogen	0.0	0.0	0.0	...	39.7[1]	44.8[1]	55.8[1]	55.8[1]	Azote
Phosphate	0.0	0.0	0.0	...	10.3[1]	2.9[1]	2.9[1]	11.7[1]	Phosphates
Potash	0.0	0.0	0.0	...	0.2[1]	0.2[1]	10.4[1]	6.8[1]	Potasse
Suriname[1]									**Suriname**[1]
Nitrogen	...	...	...	...	4.2	7.5	5.2	14.5	Azote
Phosphate	...	...	...	...	0.3	0.6	0.7	5.7	Phosphates
Potash	...	...	...	...	0.7	0.9	1.0	5.7	Potasse
Sweden									**Suède**
Nitrogen	*53.2	*79.6	*80.0	*80.0	153.9[1]	210.5[1]	167.8[1]	228.3[1]	Azote
Phosphate	*24.0	*10.0	*10.0	*10.0	52.1[1]	37.7[1]	53.8[1]	87.4[1]	Phosphates
Potash	*0.0	*0.0	*0.0	...	34.2[1]	26.5[1]	14.5[1]	57.5[1]	Potasse
Switzerland[1]									**Suisse**[1]
Nitrogen	...	...	...	...	53.3	53.2	48.6	52.9	Azote
Phosphate	...	...	...	...	15.8	17.0	16.9	15.7	Phosphates
Potash	...	...	...	...	23.5	22.9	28.0	23.8	Potasse
Syrian Arab Republic									**Rép. arabe syrienne**
Nitrogen	129.2	164.0	141.0	148.7	266.4	275.6	263.1	270.2	Azote
Phosphate	127.8	113.2	100.3	75.4	121.9	109.6	109.0	131.2	Phosphates
Potash	...	...	...	...	8.8	9.6	9.8	12.1	Potasse
Tajikistan									**Tadjikistan**
Nitrogen	8.1	6.5	4.9	...	28.6	22.0	22.2	...	Azote
Phosphate	...	...	...	...	0.0	0.0	0.0	...	Phosphates
Potash	...	...	...	...	0.0	0.0	0.0	...	Potasse
Thailand									**Thaïlande**
Nitrogen	111.0	137.2	137.0	*130.0	1 042.7[1]	1 065.2[1]	1 230.2[1]	1 187.0[1]	Azote
Phosphate	57.2	6.4	6.4	*6.0	322.0[1]	419.9[1]	477.0[1]	376.5[1]	Phosphates
Potash[1]	...	...	...	...	348.7	312.3	380.7	425.9	Potasse[1]
TFYR of Macedonia[1]									**L'ex-R.Y. Macédoine**[1]
Nitrogen	...	...	...	...	18.1	17.1	18.6	15.8	Azote
Phosphate	...	...	...	...	5.4	4.5	5.3	4.6	Phosphates
Potash	...	...	...	...	4.3	3.7	4.6	3.8	Potasse
Togo									**Togo**
Nitrogen	0.0	0.0	0.0	...	6.9[1]	4.3[1]	5.5[1]	4.6[1]	Azote
Phosphate	0.0	0.0	0.0	...	6.7[1]	3.6[1]	4.5[1]	1.6[1]	Phosphates
Potash	0.0	0.0	0.0	...	6.7[1]	3.6[1]	4.5[1]	5.8[1]	Potasse
Tonga									**Tonga**
Nitrogen	0.0	0.0	0.0	0.0	0.5[1]	0.3[1]	0.0[1]	0.4[1]	Azote
Phosphate	0.0	0.0	0.0	0.0	0.8[1]	0.4[1]	0.1[1]	0.4[1]	Phosphates
Potash	0.0	0.0	0.0	0.0	0.1[1]	...	0.1[1]	0.2[1]	Potasse
Trinidad and Tobago									**Trinité-et-Tobago**
Nitrogen	344.1	316.5	328.0	*328.0	2.3[1]	7.0[1]	0.0[2]	56.5[1]	Azote
Phosphate[1]	...	...	...	...	0.7	6.3	0.4	0.3	Phosphates[1]
Potash[1]	...	...	...	...	1.0	15.6	1.3	1.6	Potasse[1]
Tunisia									**Tunisie**
Nitrogen	276.7	240.7	253.9	210.8	59.0[1]	66.5[1]	66.5[1]	47.8[1]	Azote
Phosphate	1 005.3	904.3	872.0	835.2	48.8[1]	97.1[1]	0.0[2]	42.4[1]	Phosphates
Potash[1]	...	...	...	...	8.2	1.1	1.1	0.9	Potasse[1]
Turkey									**Turquie**
Nitrogen	835.9	696.0	557.7	510.4	1 797.5[1]	1 805.7[1]	1 604.3[1]	1 399.9[1]	Azote
Phosphate	406.2	408.0	293.5	278.8	841.9[1]	716.7[1]	441.3[1]	415.6[1]	Phosphates
Potash	...	*0.0	*0.0	...	119.3[1]	109.1[1]	148.1[1]	96.8[1]	Potasse

33 Fertilizers *(continued)*

Nitrogen, phosphate and potash: thousand metric tons of plant nutrients

Engrais *(suite)*

Azote, phosphates et potasse : milliers de tonnes d'éléments fertilisants

Country/area and type of fertilizer	Production 2005	Production 2006	Production 2007	Production 2008	Consumption - Consommation 2005	Consumption - Consommation 2006	Consumption - Consommation 2007	Consumption - Consommation 2008	Pays/zone et type d'engrais
Uganda [1]									**Ouganda** [1]
Nitrogen	...	...	...	...	2.6	4.4	4.0	10.6	Azote
Phosphate	...	...	...	...	2.0	2.2	2.2	5.5	Phosphates
Potash	...	...	...	...	1.2	1.1	1.4	2.8	Potasse
Ukraine									**Ukraine**
Nitrogen	2 561.3	3 269.9	2 696.0	2 508.0	376.9	466.8	578.2	735.8	Azote
Phosphate	102.2	105.6	106.0	*106.0	101.6	128.9	168.8	173.5	Phosphates
Potash	...	...	...	...	79.4	103.7	149.5	155.5	Potasse
United Arab Emirates									**Emirats arabes unis**
Nitrogen	264.5	297.5	298.3	287.7	4.1[1]	41.7[1]	46.1[1]	19.9[1]	Azote
Phosphate	*0.0	*0.0	*0.0	*0.0	4.2[1]	2.5[1]	0.6[1]	0.6[1]	Phosphates
Potash	*0.0	*0.0	*0.0	*0.0	6.5[1]	2.0[1]	2.6[1]	1.4[1]	Potasse
United Kingdom									**Royaume-Uni**
Nitrogen	*660.4	*634.4	408.6[1]	*410.0	1 066.5	1 008.0	1 036.0	913.0	Azote
Phosphate	*164.5	*37.0	*35.0	46.4[1]	245.1	224.0	215.0	129.0	Phosphates
Potash	*655.8	*431.2	427.0	480.0	348.8	317.0	325.0	208.0	Potasse
United Rep. of Tanzania [1]									**Rép. U. de Tanzanie** [1]
Nitrogen	...	...	...	...	67.8	37.4	34.0	34.0	Azote
Phosphate	...	...	...	...	19.8	20.9	10.3	14.6	Phosphates
Potash	...	...	...	...	7.8	6.3	6.0	8.5	Potasse
United States									**Etats-Unis**
Nitrogen	8 317.5	8 168.6	8 516.3	7 848.3	11 013.7	11 625.4	11 585.1	10 963.2	Azote
Phosphate	11 439.2	10 701.8	10 959.9	9 215.1	4 120.8	4 113.6	3 970.6	3 342.8	Phosphates
Potash	1 200.0	1 100.0	1 100.0	1 200.0	4 448.1	4 508.0	4 399.1	3 269.4	Potasse
Uruguay									**Uruguay**
Nitrogen [1]	...	...	...	...	73.9	96.5	113.9	99.5	Azote [1]
Phosphate	*26.2	*22.4	12.8	*13.0	119.2[1]	109.1[1]	138.5[1]	90.8[1]	Phosphates
Potash	...	...	...	...	2.6[1]	2.0[1]	0.0[2]	3.8[1]	Potasse
Venezuela (Boliv. Rep. of)									**Venezuela (R. bol. du)**
Nitrogen	*705.0	*793.8	*794.0	*794.0	282.0[1]	191.2[1]	334.7[1]	375.7[1]	Azote
Phosphate	*40.0	*50.0	*50.0	*50.0	79.6[1]	84.5[1]	87.9[1]	94.9[1]	Phosphates
Potash [1]	...	...	...	...	77.1	97.0	89.4	158.2	Potasse [1]
Viet Nam									**Viet Nam**
Nitrogen	388.2	363.6	443.4	*419.0	1 047.2[1]	976.8[1]	1 124.6[1]	696.7[1]	Azote
Phosphate	249.0	171.7	*346.4	*406.8	552.9[1]	562.5[1]	764.5[1]	664.3[1]	Phosphates
Potash [1]	...	...	...	...	258.1	340.0	466.3	444.4	Potasse [1]
Yemen [1]									**Yémen** [1]
Nitrogen	...	...	...	...	3.9	8.9	26.2	17.0	Azote
Phosphate	...	...	...	...	0.9	0.1	...	...	Phosphates
Potash	...	...	...	...	0.1	2.5	3.0	1.2	Potasse
Zambia [1]									**Zambie** [1]
Nitrogen	...	...	...	...	51.6	49.2	55.8	53.2	Azote
Phosphate	...	...	...	...	4.8	8.6	11.6	8.9	Phosphates
Potash	...	...	...	...	19.9	19.6	28.0	55.9	Potasse
Zimbabwe									**Zimbabwe**
Nitrogen	*41.5	*37.1	*37.2	*37.2	48.4[1]	60.5[1]	57.4[1]	51.9[1]	Azote
Phosphate	*17.1	*25.9	*26.0	*26.0	20.8[1]	45.3[1]	30.3[1]	35.2[1]	Phosphates
Potash [1]	...	...	...	...	15.8	26.8	20.4	17.0	Potasse [1]

Source:
Food and Agriculture Organization of the United Nations (FAO), Rome, FAOSTAT data, last accessed September 2010.

1 Data obtained as a balance.
2 Apparent consumption has been set to zero due to utilization from stockpiles.

Source :
Organisation des Nations Unies pour l'alimentation et l'agriculture (FAO), Rome, données FAOSTAT, dernier accès septembre 2010.

1 Donnée obtenue par bilan.
2 La consommation apparente a été mise à zéro en raison de l'utilisation des réserves.

Technical notes: tables 28-33

The series shown on agriculture and fishing have been furnished by the Food and Agriculture Organization of the United Nations (FAO). They refer mainly to the long-term trends in the growth of agricultural output and the food supply, the output of principal agricultural commodities and fish production.

Agricultural production is defined to include all crops and livestock products except those used for seed and fodder and other intermediate uses in agriculture; for example deductions are made for eggs used for hatching. Intermediate input of seeds and fodder and similar items refer to both domestically produced and imported commodities. For further details, reference may be made to *FAO Statistical Yearbook*. FAO data are also available through the Internet at http://faostat.fao.org.

Table 28: "Agriculture" relates to the production of all crops and livestock products. The "Food Index" includes those commodities which are considered edible and contain nutrients.

The index numbers of agricultural output and food production are calculated by the Laspeyres formula with the base year period 1999-2001. The latter is provided in order to diminish the impact of annual fluctuations in agricultural output during base years on the indices for the period. Production quantities of each commodity are weighted by 1999-2001 average national producer prices and summed for each year. The index numbers are based on production data for a calendar year. These may differ in some instances from those actually produced and published by the individual countries themselves due to variations in concepts, coverage, weights and methods of calculation. Efforts have been made to estimate these methodological differences to achieve a better international comparability of data.

Detailed data on agricultural production are published by FAO in its *Statistical Yearbook*.

Table 29: The data on the production of cereals relate to crops harvested for dry grain only. Cereals harvested for hay, green feed or used for grazing are excluded.

Table 30: The data on roundwood refer to wood in the rough, wood in its natural state as felled or otherwise harvested, with or without bark, round, split, roughly squared or in other form (i.e. roots, stumps, burls, etc.). It may also be impregnated (e.g. telegraph poles) or roughly shaped or pointed. It comprises all wood obtained from removals, i.e. the quantities removed from forests and from trees outside the forest, including wood recovered from natural, felling and logging losses during the period—calendar year or forest year.

Table 31: The data cover (i) capture production from marine and inland fisheries and (ii) aquaculture,

Notes techniques : tableaux 28 à 33

Les séries présentées sur l'agriculture et la pêche ont été fournies par l'Organisation des Nations Unies pour l'alimentation et l'agriculture (FAO) et portent principalement sur les tendances à long terme de la croissance de la production agricole et des approvisionnements alimentaires, et sur la production des principales denrées agricoles et la production halieutique.

La production agricole se définit comme comprenant l'ensemble des produits agricoles et des produits de l'élevage à l'exception de ceux utilisés comme semences et comme aliments pour les animaux, et pour les autres utilisations intermédiaires en agriculture; par exemple, on déduit les œufs utilisés pour la reproduction. L'apport intermédiaire de semences et d'aliments pour les animaux et d'autres éléments similaires se rapportent à la fois à des produits locaux et importés. Pour tous détails complémentaires, on se reportera à *l'annuaire statistique de la FAO*. Des statistiques peuvent également être consultées sur le site Web de la FAO http://faostat.fao.org.

Tableau 28: "L'agriculture" se rapporte à la production de tous les produits de l'agriculture et de l'élevage. "L'indice des produits alimentaires" comprend les produits considérés comme comestibles et qui contiennent des éléments nutritifs.

Les indices de la production agricole et de la production alimentaire sont calculés selon la formule de Laspeyres avec les années 1999-2001 pour période de base. Le choix d'une période de plusieurs années permet de diminuer l'incidence des fluctuations annuelles de la production agricole pendant les années de base sur les indices pour cette période. Les quantités produites de chaque denrée sont pondérées par les prix nationaux moyens à la production de 1999-2001, et additionnées pour chaque année. Les indices sont fondés sur les données de production d'une année civile. Ils peuvent différer dans certains cas des indices effectivement établis et publiés par les pays eux-mêmes par suite de différences dans les concepts, la couverture, les pondérations et les méthodes de calcul. On s'est efforcé d'estimer ces différences méthodologiques afin de rendre les données plus facilement comparables à l'échelle internationale.

Des chiffres détaillés de production sont publiés dans l'*Annuaire statistique de la FAO*.

Tableau 29: Les données sur la production de céréales se rapportent uniquement aux céréales récoltées pour le grain sec; celles cultivées pour le foin, le fourrage vert ou le pâturage en sont exclues.

Tableau 30: Les données sur le bois rond se réfèrent au bois brut, bois à l'état naturel, tel qu'il a été abattu ou récolté autrement, avec ou sans écorce, fendu, grossièrement équarri ou sous une autre forme (par

and are expressed in terms of live weight. They include fish, crustaceans and molluscs but exclude sponges, corals, pearls, seaweed, crocodiles, and aquatic mammals (such as whales and dolphins).

The flag of the vessel is considered as the paramount indication of the nationality of the catch. Marine fisheries data include landings by domestic craft in foreign ports and exclude landings by foreign craft in domestic ports.

To separate aquaculture from capture fisheries production, at least two criteria must apply i.e., the human intervention in one or more of the phases of the growth cycle, and individual, corporate or state ownership of the organism reared and harvested.

Data on aquaculture production are published in the *FAO Yearbook of Fishery Statistics, Aquaculture Production*; capture production statistics are published in the *FAO Yearbook of Fishery Statistics, Capture Production.*

Table 32: The data refer to livestock numbers grouped into twelve-month periods ending 30 September of the year stated and cover all domestic animals irrespective of their age and place or purpose of their breeding.

Table 33: The data generally refer to the fertilizer year 1 July-30 June.

Nitrogenous fertilizers: data refer to the nitrogen content of commercial inorganic fertilizers.

Phosphate fertilizers: data refer to commercial phosphoric acid (P_2O_5) of super phosphates, ammonium phosphate and basic slag.

Potash fertilizers: data refer to K_2O content of commercial potash, muriate, nitrate and sulphate of potash, manure salts, kainit and nitrate of soda potash.

exemple, racines, souches, loupes, etc.). Il peut être également imprégné (par exemple, dans le cas des poteaux télégraphiques) et dégrossi ou taillé en pointe. Cette catégorie comprend tous les bois provenant des quantités enlevées en forêt ou provenant des arbres poussant hors forêt, y compris le volume récupéré sur les déchets naturels et les déchets d'abattage et de transport pendant la période envisagée (année civile ou forestière).

Tableau 31: Les données ont trait (i) à la pêche maritime et intérieure et (ii) à l'aquaculture, et sont exprimées en poids vif. Elles comprennent poissons, crustacés et mollusques, mais excluent éponges, coraux, perles, algues, crocodiles et les mammifères aquatiques (baleines, dauphins, etc.).

Le pavillon du navire est considéré comme la principale indication de la nationalité de la prise. Les données de pêche maritime comprennent les quantités débarquées par des bateaux nationaux dans des ports étrangers et excluent les quantités débarquées par des bateaux étrangers dans des ports nationaux.

Pour séparer la production d'aquaculture de la pêche de capture, au moins deux critères doivent se vérifier, c'est-à-dire l'intervention humaine dans une ou plusieurs des phases du cycle de croissance, et l'appartenance de l'organisme élevé et récolté à une personne physique, à une personne morale ou à l'état.

Les données sur la production de l'aquaculture sont publiées dans *l'Annuaire statistique des pêches, production de l'aquaculture*; celles sur les captures sont publiées dans *l'Annuaire statistique des pêches, captures*.

Tableau 32: Les statistiques sur les effectifs du cheptel sont groupées en périodes de 12 mois se terminant le 30 septembre de l'année indiquée et s'entendent de tous les animaux domestiques, quel que soit leur âge, leur emplacement ou le but de leur élevage.

Tableau 33: Les données sur les engrais se rapportent en général à une période d'un an comptée du 1er juillet au 30 juin.

Engrais azotés : les données se rapportent à la teneur en azote des engrais commerciaux inorganiques.

Engrais phosphatés : les données se rapportent à l'acide phosphorique (P_2O_5) et englobent la teneur en (P_2O_5) des superphosphates, du phosphate d'ammonium et des scories de déphosphoration.

Engrais potassiques : les données se rapportent à la teneur en K_2O des produits potassiques commerciaux, muriate, nitrate et sulfate de potasse, sels d'engrais, kaïnite et nitrate de soude potassique.

34 Sugar

Production and consumption: thousand metric tons; consumption per capita: kilograms

Sucre

Production et consommation : milliers de tonnes ; consommation per habitant : kilogrammes

Country or area	2002	2003	2004	2005	2006	2007	2008	Pays ou zone
World								**Monde**
Production	**142 091**	**148 125**	**147 285**	**141 377**	**152 211**	**166 338**	**162 463**	**Production**
Consumption	**137 513**	**141 248**	**146 598**	**147 163**	**153 149**	**157 265**	**163 244**	**Consommation**
Consumption per capita	**22**	**23**	**23**	**23**	**24**	**24**	**25**	**Consommation par habitant**
Afghanistan *								**Afghanistan** *
Consumption	70	90	120	145	160	185	210	Consommation
Consumption per capita	3	4	5	6	7	8	9	Consommation par habitant
Albania *								**Albanie** *
Production	3	3	3	3	5	4	4	Production
Consumption	75	75	78	80	80	85	85	Consommation
Consumption per capita	24	24	25	25	25	27	27	Consommation par habitant
Algeria *								**Algérie** *
Consumption	1 040	1 100	1 135	1 185	1 215	1 245	1 265	Consommation
Consumption per capita	33	35	35	36	36	37	37	Consommation par habitant
Angola								**Angola**
Production	0	0	0	0	0	0	0	Production
Consumption *	185	195	205	225	245	255	270	Consommation *
Consumption per capita *	13	13	13	14	15	15	16	Consommation par habitant *
Argentina								**Argentine**
Production	*1 680	1 952	1 857	2 165	2 470	2 198	2 448	Production
Consumption	*1 515	1 515	1 574	1 654	1 866	1 874	1 720	Consommation
Consumption per capita	*40	39	41	42	47	47	42	Consommation par habitant
Armenia								**Arménie**
Production	0	0	0	2	2	3	4	Production
Consumption	*74	87	*87	*87	*87	*88	*90	Consommation
Consumption per capita	*23	27	*27	*27	*27	*27	*28	Consommation par habitant
Australia								**Australie**
Production	5 614	5 315	5 530	5 393	4 729	4 627	4 619	Production
Consumption	1 100	1 089	1 043	1 034	*1 035	*1 040	1 221	Consommation
Consumption per capita	56	55	52	51	*50	*49	57	Consommation par habitant
Azerbaijan								**Azerbaïdjan**
Production	0	0	0	2	9	10	18	Production
Consumption *	160	160	165	165	170	170	175	Consommation *
Consumption per capita *	20	19	20	19	20	20	20	Consommation par habitant *
Bahamas								**Bahamas**
Consumption	9	11	12	13	14	14	13	Consommation
Consumption per capita	32	35	38	41	44	44	38	Consommation par habitant
Bangladesh								**Bangladesh**
Production	229	*166	*125	*120	*145	*170	*110	Production
Consumption *	635	695	790	880	995	1 055	1 120	Consommation *
Consumption per capita *	5	5	6	6	7	7	8	Consommation par habitant *
Barbados								**Barbade**
Production	*45	*36	*35	*40	32	34	*32	Production
Consumption *	14	14	15	15	15	15	15	Consommation *
Consumption per capita *	52	52	56	56	56	55	54	Consommation par habitant *
Belarus								**Bélarus**
Production	162	*255	*340	*435	*480	*495	541	Production
Consumption	410	*410	*415	*420	*425	*425	*430	Consommation
Consumption per capita	41	*42	*42	*43	*43	*44	*45	Consommation par habitant
Belize								**Belize**
Production	119	111	125	102	120	100	86	Production
Consumption	12	12	12	12	13	14	14	Consommation
Consumption per capita	44	44	42	42	44	45	44	Consommation par habitant
Benin *								**Bénin** *
Production	5	4	4	5	10	10	10	Production
Consumption	28	35	36	37	38	39	42	Consommation
Consumption per capita	4	5	5	5	5	4	5	Consommation par habitant
Bermuda								**Bermudes**
Consumption	2	2	2	2	2	2	2	Consommation
Consumption per capita	25	25	25	25	25	25	25	Consommation par habitant

34 Sugar *(continued)*

Production and consumption: thousand metric tons; consumption per capita: kilograms

Sucre *(suite)*

Production et consommation : milliers de tonnes ; consommation par habitant : kilogrammes

Country or area	2002	2003	2004	2005	2006	2007	2008	Pays ou zone
Bolivia (Plur. State of)								**Bolivie (État plur. de)**
Production	426	387	464	*400	*370	*375	*340	Production
Consumption *	300	305	310	320	325	335	340	Consommation *
Consumption per capita *	34	34	34	34	34	34	34	Consommation par habitant *
Bosnia and Herzegovina								**Bosnie-Herzégovine**
Consumption *	120	130	130	135	135	140	140	Consommation *
Consumption per capita *	31	34	34	35	35	36	36	Consommation par habitant *
Botswana								**Botswana**
Consumption	47	48	48	50	51	51	51	Consommation
Consumption per capita	28	28	28	29	29	29	29	Consommation par habitant
Brazil								**Brésil**
Production	23 567	25 730	27 290	28 135	31 622	33 199	32 290	Production
Consumption	10 520	10 217	10 857	10 950	12 513	12 474	11 856	Consommation
Consumption per capita	60	58	59	59	66	68	62	Consommation par habitant
Brunei Darussalam								**Brunéi Darussalam**
Consumption	10	11	11	11	11	11	12	Consommation
Consumption per capita	29	31	31	30	29	29	32	Consommation par habitant
Bulgaria * [1]								**Bulgarie** * [1]
Production	3	3	3	5	4	...	...	Production
Consumption	255	265	270	275	280	...	...	Consommation
Consumption per capita	33	34	35	36	37	...	...	Consommation par habitant
Burkina Faso *								**Burkina Faso** *
Production	40	40	40	40	40	40	40	Production
Consumption	60	65	65	75	80	85	85	Consommation
Consumption per capita	5	5	5	6	6	6	6	Consommation par habitant
Burundi								**Burundi**
Production	20	22	22	23	25	24	24	Production
Consumption	25	26	27	29	29	30	30	Consommation
Consumption per capita	3	3	4	4	4	4	4	Consommation par habitant
Cambodia *								**Cambodge** *
Consumption	115	120	130	170	185	195	210	Consommation
Consumption per capita	9	9	10	12	13	13	14	Consommation par habitant
Cameroon								**Cameroun**
Production	104	*120	*125	119	126	100	*100	Production
Consumption	145	*150	*145	92	112	129	*145	Consommation
Consumption per capita	10	*10	*8	5	6	7	*8	Consommation par habitant
Canada *								**Canada** *
Production	64	85	115	105	135	130	70	Production
Consumption	1 255	1 400	1 425	1 425	1 430	1 435	1 450	Consommation
Consumption per capita	40	44	45	44	43	43	43	Consommation par habitant
Cape Verde *								**Cap-Vert** *
Consumption	16	17	17	17	17	18	18	Consommation
Consumption per capita	36	37	36	35	35	37	37	Consommation par habitant
Central African Rep. *								**Rép. centrafricaine** *
Consumption	5	6	9	11	11	11	11	Consommation
Consumption per capita	1	2	3	4	4	4	4	Consommation par habitant
Chad								**Tchad**
Production	*32	*33	*30	*35	*35	35	36	Production
Consumption	*65	*75	*80	*85	*90	90	89	Consommation
Consumption per capita	*8	*9	*9	*10	*10	10	11	Consommation par habitant
Chile								**Chili**
Production	576	374	401	386	372	*370	*280	Production
Consumption	*685	*685	673	682	*695	*705	*725	Consommation
Consumption per capita	*46	*43	41	41	*42	*42	*44	Consommation par habitant
China [2]								**Chine** [2]
Production	9 805	11 433	10 912	*9 785	*10 682	*13 895	*15 405	Production
Consumption	*9 975	11 065	11 613	*11 785	*11 975	*13 825	*14 725	Consommation
Consumption per capita	*8	9	9	*9	*9	*10	*11	Consommation par habitant
China, Hong Kong SAR *								**Chine, Hong Kong RAS** *
Consumption	181	185	185	185	185	190	190	Consommation
Consumption per capita	27	28	27	27	27	27	27	Consommation par habitant

34 Sugar *(continued)*

Production and consumption: thousand metric tons; consumption per capita: kilograms

Sucre *(suite)*

Production et consommation : milliers de tonnes ; consommation par habitant : kilogrammes

Country or area	2002	2003	2004	2005	2006	2007	2008	Pays ou zone
China, Macao SAR								**Chine, Macao RAS**
Consumption	8	8	8	8	8	7	7	Consommation
Consumption per capita	17	18	21	17	15	12	12	Consommation par habitant
Colombia								**Colombie**
Production	2 523	2 646	2 740	2 683	2 415	2 277	2 036	Production
Consumption	1 356[3]	1 348	1 521	1 512	1 460	1 707[3]	1 720	Consommation
Consumption per capita	31	30	34	33	34	39	38	Consommation par habitant
Comoros								**Comores**
Consumption	9	9	9	9	9	10	10	Consommation
Consumption per capita	11	11	11	12	12	13	13	Consommation par habitant
Congo								**Congo**
Production	33	*45	*55	63	*65	56	67	Production
Consumption	32	*50	*55	76	*80	*80	*80	Consommation
Consumption per capita	10	*17	*18	24	*25	*27	*27	Consommation par habitant
Costa Rica								**Costa Rica**
Production	*360	*358	*405	398	348	373	351	Production
Consumption	*225	*230	*230	225	*230	235	229	Consommation
Consumption per capita	*56	*56	*54	53	*56	55	51	Consommation par habitant
Côte d'Ivoire *								**Côte d'Ivoire** *
Production	170	145	120	145	145	145	150	Production
Consumption	200	205	210	215	220	230	240	Consommation
Consumption per capita	11	11	11	11	11	11	12	Consommation par habitant
Croatia								**Croatie**
Production	160	116	192	221	*291	*216	*228	Production
Consumption *	180	185	190	200	200	200	205	Consommation *
Consumption per capita *	41	42	43	45	45	45	46	Consommation par habitant *
Cuba								**Cuba**
Production	3 522	2 278	*2 600	*1 300	1 239	1 193	1 446	Production
Consumption	698	682	*700	*700	741	690	692	Consommation
Consumption per capita	62	61	*62	*62	66	61	62	Consommation par habitant
Cyprus [1]								**Chypre** [1]
Consumption	33	36	...	...	...	...	...	Consommation
Consumption per capita	46	47	...	...	...	...	...	Consommation par habitant
Czech Republic [1]								**République tchèque** [1]
Production	523	522	...	...	...	...	...	Production
Consumption	475	399	...	...	...	...	...	Consommation
Consumption per capita	47	39	...	...	...	...	...	Consommation par habitant
Dem. Rep. of the Congo *								**Rép. dém. du Congo** *
Production	65	65	60	60	65	65	70	Production
Consumption	85	85	90	95	105	120	130	Consommation
Consumption per capita	2	2	2	2	2	2	2	Consommation par habitant
Djibouti								**Djibouti**
Consumption	13	14	15	16	16	16	16	Consommation
Consumption per capita	15	16	17	18	18	18	18	Consommation par habitant
Dominican Republic								**Rép. dominicaine**
Production	516	525	*530	*475	487	488	492	Production
Consumption	366	322	*360	*370	338	325	343	Consommation
Consumption per capita	44	36	*39	*38	36	34	36	Consommation par habitant
Ecuador								**Equateur**
Production	*475	*505	*490	*470	520	*495	*510	Production
Consumption *	480	485	485	488	490	495	505	Consommation *
Consumption per capita *	38	38	37	37	37	36	37	Consommation par habitant *
Egypt								**Egypte**
Production	*1 490	*1 425	1 489	*1 625	*1 725	1 851	1 699	Production
Consumption	*2 400	*2 500	*2 600	*2 675	*2 700	2 700	2 700	Consommation
Consumption per capita	*36	*35	*35	*37	*36	36	35	Consommation par habitant
El Salvador								**El Salvador**
Production	476	530	555	633	542	560	597	Production
Consumption	217	209	212	225	240	237	239	Consommation
Consumption per capita	33	33	33	35	35	37	42	Consommation par habitant

34 Sugar *(continued)*

Production and consumption: thousand metric tons; consumption per capita: kilograms

Sucre *(suite)*

Production et consommation : milliers de tonnes ; consommation par habitant : kilogrammes

Country or area	2002	2003	2004	2005	2006	2007	2008	Pays ou zone
Eritrea								**Erythrée**
Consumption	9	15	16	20	20	25	30	Consommation
Consumption per capita	2	3	4	4	4	5	6	Consommation par habitant
Estonia [1]								**Estonie** [1]
Consumption	73	80	...	...	...	...	...	Consommation
Consumption per capita	49	60	...	...	...	...	...	Consommation par habitant
Ethiopia								**Ethiopie**
Production	287	*295	*325	*345	*360	*340	*340	Production
Consumption	211	*260	*295	*320	*350	*370	*390	Consommation
Consumption per capita	3	*4	*4	*4	*5	*5	*5	Consommation par habitant
European Union (EU) [1]								**Union européenne (UE)** [1]
Production	18 268	16 578	21 843	21 698	18 098	18 445	16 376	Production
Consumption	14 370	14 137	17 691	16 765	17 527	19 315	20 471	Consommation
Consumption per capita	38	37	39	36	38	39	41	Consommation par habitant
Fiji								**Fidji**
Production	334	330	330	306	324	254	283	Production
Consumption [4]	53	55	58	55	61	70	52	Consommation [4]
Consumption per capita	64	66	69	66	71	85	65	Consommation par habitant
Gabon								**Gabon**
Production	*18	25	*19	*21	21	*21	*21	Production
Consumption	*20	*21	*21	*21	21	*22	*22	Consommation
Consumption per capita	*16	*16	*16	*15	15	*15	*15	Consommation par habitant
Gambia *								**Gambie** *
Consumption	65	70	70	70	75	75	75	Consommation
Consumption per capita	45	48	47	47	50	49	49	Consommation par habitant
Georgia *								**Géorgie** *
Production	0	0	0	0	0	0	0	Production
Consumption	120	125	135	135	135	137	138	Consommation
Consumption per capita	28	29	31	31	31	31	32	Consommation par habitant
Ghana *								**Ghana** *
Consumption	170	185	200	205	215	220	230	Consommation
Consumption per capita	9	9	10	10	10	10	10	Consommation par habitant
Gibraltar								**Gibraltar**
Consumption	2	2	2	2	1	1	1	Consommation
Consumption per capita	55	60	67	53	37	...	33	Consommation par habitant
Guatemala								**Guatemala**
Production	1 910	1 801	2 092	2 015	1 961	2 364	2 145	Production
Consumption	534	585	585	657	637	716	644	Consommation
Consumption per capita	45	48	47	52	49	54	47	Consommation par habitant
Guinea *								**Guinée** *
Production	25	26	26	25	25	25	20	Production
Consumption	100	110	110	120	125	130	140	Consommation
Consumption per capita	12	13	12	13	13	13	14	Consommation par habitant
Guinea-Bissau								**Guinée-Bissau**
Consumption	7	8	9	14	14	15	15	Consommation
Consumption per capita	6	6	7	11	10	11	11	Consommation par habitant
Guyana								**Guyana**
Production	331	*302	*320	246	*255	*265	*224	Production
Consumption	24	*25	*26	22	*25	*26	*26	Consommation
Consumption per capita	31	*33	*35	29	*33	*35	*35	Consommation par habitant
Haiti *								**Haïti** *
Production	5	0	0	0	0	0	0	Production
Consumption	170	175	175	185	185	190	195	Consommation
Consumption per capita	21	22	22	23	23	23	24	Consommation par habitant
Honduras								**Honduras**
Production	*320	300	357	*360	*385	*390	*380	Production
Consumption	*240	249	250	*250	*250	*260	*265	Consommation
Consumption per capita	*33	36	36	*36	*36	*37	*33	Consommation par habitant
Hungary [1]								**Hongrie** [1]
Production	347	257	...	...	...	...	...	Production
Consumption	313	282	...	...	...	...	...	Consommation
Consumption per capita	31	28	...	...	...	...	...	Consommation par habitant

34 Sugar *(continued)*

Production and consumption: thousand metric tons; consumption per capita: kilograms

Sucre *(suite)*

Production et consommation : milliers de tonnes ; consommation par habitant : kilogrammes

Country or area	2002	2003	2004	2005	2006	2007	2008	Pays ou zone
Iceland *								**Islande** *
Consumption	12	12	12	11	11	11	11	Consommation
Consumption per capita	41	41	41	37	36	35	35	Consommation par habitant
India								**Inde**
Production	19 525	21 702	14 432	15 216	22 347	29 090	25 936	Production
Consumption	17 857	18 625	19 858	20 110	20 110	20 878	22 550	Consommation
Consumption per capita	17	18	19	20	18	18	20	Consommation par habitant
Indonesia								**Indonésie**
Production	*2 150	*1 780	*2 225	*2 435	2 510	2 814	*2 895	Production
Consumption *	3 675	3 800	3 915	4 052	4 195	4 400	4 605	Consommation *
Consumption per capita *	17	18	18	18	19	20	20	Consommation par habitant *
Iran (Islamic Rep. of) *								**Iran (Rép. islamique d')** *
Production	995	1 270	1 310	1 300	1 425	1 250	805	Production
Consumption	1 975	2 025	2 060	2 110	2 160	2 225	2 290	Consommation
Consumption per capita	30	30	31	31	31	31	31	Consommation par habitant
Iraq *								**Iraq** *
Consumption	500	650	675	675	685	700	720	Consommation
Consumption per capita	20	25	25	24	24	24	24	Consommation par habitant
Israel *								**Israël** *
Consumption	410	425	440	455	460	470	480	Consommation
Consumption per capita	62	64	65	66	65	65	66	Consommation par habitant
Jamaica								**Jamaïque**
Production	175	154	181	126	144	163	140	Production
Consumption	126	129	111	123	98	109	128	Consommation
Consumption per capita	48	49	42	46	36	40	47	Consommation par habitant
Japan								**Japon**
Production	901	934	976	965	909	859	960	Production
Consumption	2 433	2 415	2 403	2 397	2 229	2 452	2 254	Consommation
Consumption per capita	19	19	19	19	17	19	18	Consommation par habitant
Jordan								**Jordanie**
Consumption	*200	216	*235	*255	*270	*280	*285	Consommation
Consumption per capita	*39	41	*44	*47	*48	*49	*49	Consommation par habitant
Kazakhstan								**Kazakhstan**
Production	46	62	40	*22	*26	*30	*15	Production
Consumption *	438	442	450	455	460	465	470	Consommation *
Consumption per capita *	29	30	30	30	30	30	30	Consommation par habitant *
Kenya								**Kenya**
Production	537	448	562	532	517	520	563	Production
Consumption	652	692	728	756	781	741	817	Consommation
Consumption per capita	21	21	22	23	23	20	22	Consommation par habitant
Korea, Dem. P. R.								**Corée, R. p. dém. de**
Consumption	*70	*75	*85	*90	*90	*90	95	Consommation
Consumption per capita	*3	*3	*4	*4	*4	*4	4	Consommation par habitant
Korea, Republic of [5]								**Corée, République de** [5]
Consumption	1 129	1 134	1 171	1 198	1 156	1 107	1 209	Consommation
Consumption per capita	24	24	24	25	24	23	25	Consommation par habitant
Kuwait *								**Koweït** *
Consumption	80	80	85	90	90	95	95	Consommation
Consumption per capita	35	34	36	37	36	36	35	Consommation par habitant
Kyrgyzstan								**Kirghizistan**
Production	41	75	88	45	*40	*15	*20	Production
Consumption *	115	120	120	120	125	130	130	Consommation *
Consumption per capita *	23	24	24	23	24	25	25	Consommation par habitant *
Lao People's Dem. Rep.								**Rép. dém. pop. lao**
Production	0	0	0	0	0	0	*10	Production
Consumption *	30	30	35	45	45	50	50	Consommation *
Consumption per capita *	5	5	6	8	8	9	8	Consommation par habitant *
Latvia [1]								**Lettonie** [1]
Production	77	75	...	...	...	...	...	Production
Consumption	78	73	...	...	...	...	...	Consommation
Consumption per capita	33	31	...	...	...	...	...	Consommation par habitant

Sugar *(continued)*

Production and consumption: thousand metric tons; consumption per capita: kilograms

Sucre *(suite)*

Production et consommation : milliers de tonnes ; consommation par habitant : kilogrammes

Country or area	2002	2003	2004	2005	2006	2007	2008	Pays ou zone
Lebanon								**Liban**
Production	0	0	0	4	*5	*5	*5	Production
Consumption	*140	*145	*150	151	*145	*150	*150	Consommation
Consumption per capita	*36	*39	*43	42	*40	*41	*40	Consommation par habitant
Liberia								**Libéria**
Production	0	0	0	0	0	0	0	Production
Consumption	10	10	10	15	15	16	16	Consommation
Consumption per capita	3	3	3	4	4	4	4	Consommation par habitant
Libyan Arab Jamah. *								**Jamah. arabe libyenne ***
Consumption	240	250	255	265	270	275	280	Consommation
Consumption per capita	45	46	46	47	47	47	47	Consommation par habitant
Lithuania [1]								**Lituanie** [1]
Production	150	143	...	...	...	...	...	Production
Consumption	89	89	...	...	...	...	...	Consommation
Consumption per capita	26	26	...	...	...	...	...	Consommation par habitant
Madagascar								**Madagascar**
Production	32	27	26	27	*20	*20	*16	Production
Consumption	104	117	129	132	*135	*140	*145	Consommation
Consumption per capita	7	7	8	7	*7	*7	*7	Consommation par habitant
Malawi								**Malawi**
Production	261	*257	*255	*265	*230	*280	*310	Production
Consumption *	145	150	155	160	165	170	175	Consommation *
Consumption per capita *	13	13	13	13	13	13	13	Consommation par habitant *
Malaysia *								**Malaisie ***
Production	110	80	80	80	55	60	35	Production
Consumption	1 090	1 175	1 215	1 225	1 250	1 275	1 295	Consommation
Consumption per capita	44	47	48	47	47	46	45	Consommation par habitant
Maldives								**Maldives**
Consumption	5	5	5	6	6	6	6	Consommation
Consumption per capita	18	17	17	19	21	20	19	Consommation par habitant
Mali *								**Mali ***
Production	32	34	35	35	34	34	35	Production
Consumption	90	95	95	100	105	110	115	Consommation
Consumption per capita	8	9	8	9	9	9	9	Consommation par habitant
Malta [1]								**Malte** [1]
Consumption	23	25	...	...	...	...	...	Consommation
Consumption per capita	59	63	...	...	...	...	...	Consommation par habitant
Mauritania *								**Mauritanie ***
Consumption	135	140	140	145	155	165	175	Consommation
Consumption per capita	48	48	45	44	45	45	45	Consommation par habitant
Mauritius								**Maurice**
Production	553	538	606	524	505	462	480	Production
Consumption	43	41	42	39	39	42	42	Consommation
Consumption per capita	35	34	34	32	31	33	33	Consommation par habitant
Mexico								**Mexique**
Production	5 073	5 442	5 672	5 619	5 412	5 420	5 940	Production
Consumption	5 069	5 328	5 300	4 877	4 979	4 944	5 031	Consommation
Consumption per capita	49	52	50	47	47	47	47	Consommation par habitant
Mongolia								**Mongolie**
Consumption	21	22	23	25	25	26	26	Consommation
Consumption per capita	9	9	9	10	10	10	10	Consommation par habitant
Morocco								**Maroc**
Production	*505	*505	*540	513	*450	*505	466	Production
Consumption	*1 100	1 057	*1 150	1 163	*1 170	*1 190	1 143	Consommation
Consumption per capita	*37	35	*38	39	*38	*39	36	Consommation par habitant
Mozambique								**Mozambique**
Production	*170	*225	205	265	243	244	250	Production
Consumption	*110	*120	134	135	144	169	172	Consommation
Consumption per capita	*5	*7	7	7	7	8	8	Consommation par habitant

34 Sugar *(continued)*

Production and consumption: thousand metric tons; consumption per capita: kilograms

Sucre *(suite)*

Production et consommation : milliers de tonnes ; consommation par habitant : kilogrammes

Country or area	2002	2003	2004	2005	2006	2007	2008	Pays ou zone
Myanmar *								**Myanmar** *
Production	125	135	150	150	155	160	180	Production
Consumption	120	135	150	155	165	175	185	Consommation
Consumption per capita	2	3	3	3	3	3	3	Consommation par habitant
Namibia *								**Namibie** *
Consumption	48	50	55	55	60	60	65	Consommation
Consumption per capita	26	27	30	30	33	33	35	Consommation par habitant
Nepal *								**Népal** *
Production	110	125	140	130	135	140	140	Production
Consumption	125	125	130	135	135	140	140	Consommation
Consumption per capita	5	5	5	5	5	5	5	Consommation par habitant
Netherlands Antilles *								**Antilles néerlandaises** *
Consumption	14	14	14	14	14	15	15	Consommation
Consumption per capita	82	78	76	76	76	83	82	Consommation par habitant
New Zealand *								**Nouvelle-Zélande** *
Consumption	220	225	230	225	225	225	225	Consommation
Consumption per capita	56	56	57	55	54	53	52	Consommation par habitant
Nicaragua								**Nicaragua**
Production	*370	333	*440	*470	*435	*505	*480	Production
Consumption *	175	190	200	205	210	215	220	Consommation *
Consumption per capita *	33	36	37	38	38	38	38	Consommation par habitant *
Niger *								**Niger** *
Production	10	15	10	10	10	10	10	Production
Consumption	65	70	70	75	75	80	80	Consommation
Consumption per capita	6	6	6	6	6	6	6	Consommation par habitant
Nigeria								**Nigéria**
Production	7	0	0	0	*30	55	21	Production
Consumption	1 317	1 046	1 222	1 236	*1 265	*1 295	1 570	Consommation
Consumption per capita	11	8	9	9	*8	*9	11	Consommation par habitant
Norway *								**Norvège** *
Consumption	175	175	170	170	165	165	160	Consommation
Consumption per capita	39	38	37	37	35	35	34	Consommation par habitant
Pakistan								**Pakistan**
Production	3 334	4 063	4 481	2 839	3 263	*4 355	4 997	Production
Consumption	*3 490	3 875	4 004	4 075	3 951	*4 250	4 538	Consommation
Consumption per capita	*24	26	29	27	25	*27	28	Consommation par habitant
Panama								**Panama**
Production	152	147	157	157	168	164	*175	Production
Consumption *	110	113	115	117	120	123	125	Consommation *
Consumption per capita *	36	38	36	37	36	36	36	Consommation par habitant *
Papua New Guinea								**Papouasie-Nvl-Guinée**
Production	53	50	46	44	*35	*35	*35	Production
Consumption	37	35	35	35	*35	*37	*38	Consommation
Consumption per capita	8	7	6	6	*6	*7	*7	Consommation par habitant
Paraguay *								**Paraguay** *
Production	115	116	115	117	120	120	120	Production
Consumption	110	115	115	120	120	125	125	Consommation
Consumption per capita	20	20	20	20	20	20	20	Consommation par habitant
Peru								**Pérou**
Production	*850	*970	813	695	805	*905	*1 005	Production
Consumption	*975	*995	967	896	*960	*1 025	*1 100	Consommation
Consumption per capita	*36	*37	35	32	*34	*36	*38	Consommation par habitant
Philippines								**Philippines**
Production	1 988	2 245	2 423	2 184	2 413	2 147	2 415	Production
Consumption	2 059	2 117	2 102	2 037	2 021	1 939	2 061	Consommation
Consumption per capita	26	26	25	24	23	22	23	Consommation par habitant
Poland [1]								**Pologne** [1]
Production	2 038	1 912	...	...	...	...	...	Production
Consumption	1 745	1 760	...	...	...	...	...	Consommation
Consumption per capita	45	46	...	...	...	...	...	Consommation par habitant

34 Sugar *(continued)*

Production and consumption: thousand metric tons; consumption per capita: kilograms

Sucre *(suite)*

Production et consommation : milliers de tonnes ; consommation par habitant : kilogrammes

Country or area	2002	2003	2004	2005	2006	2007	2008	Pays ou zone
Republic of Moldova								**République de Moldova**
Production	*125	107	111	133	161	75	134	Production
Consumption	*110	*115	106	*125	*130	*105	83	Consommation
Consumption per capita	*26	*32	29	*35	*36	*29	23	Consommation par habitant
Romania [1]								**Roumanie** [1]
Production	75	57	*55	67	*125	...	...	Production
Consumption	*570	*590	584	*595	*600	...	...	Consommation
Consumption per capita	*26	*27	27	*28	*28	...	...	Consommation par habitant
Russian Federation								**Fédération de Russie**
Production	1 757	1 892	2 496	2 719	3 459	*3 405	3 789	Production
Consumption	6 673	*6 850	*6 700	*6 600	*6 500	*6 500	6 180	Consommation
Consumption per capita	47	*47	*46	*46	*46	*46	44	Consommation par habitant
Rwanda *								**Rwanda** *
Production	3	3	5	5	10	10	10	Production
Consumption	14	14	16	19	20	20	21	Consommation
Consumption per capita	1	1	2	2	2	2	2	Consommation par habitant
Saint Kitts and Nevis								**Saint-Kitts-et-Nevis**
Production	*20	*15	*15	*10	0	0	0	Production
Consumption *	3	3	3	3	3	3	3	Consommation *
Consumption per capita *	42	42	42	42	42	36	31	Consommation par habitant *
Samoa								**Samoa**
Production	2	2	2	2	3	3	3	Production
Consumption	3	4	4	4	4	5	5	Consommation
Consumption per capita	12	15	15	15	15	19	18	Consommation par habitant
Saudi Arabia *								**Arabie saoudite** *
Consumption	650	690	720	790	820	850	880	Consommation
Consumption per capita	30	31	32	34	35	35	35	Consommation par habitant
Senegal *								**Sénégal** *
Production	95	90	90	90	95	95	100	Production
Consumption	175	175	180	185	190	200	205	Consommation
Consumption per capita	18	17	17	17	17	18	18	Consommation par habitant
Serbia *								**Serbie** *
Production	230	270	335	415	505	490	325	Production
Consumption	300	310	315	320	325	325	330	Consommation
Consumption per capita	40	41	42	43	44	44	45	Consommation par habitant
Sierra Leone *								**Sierra Leone** *
Production	7	5	6	6	6	6	6	Production
Consumption	21	22	25	26	27	28	30	Consommation
Consumption per capita	4	4	5	5	5	5	5	Consommation par habitant
Singapore *								**Singapour** *
Consumption	305	310	310	315	315	320	320	Consommation
Consumption per capita	73	74	73	72	70	70	68	Consommation par habitant
Slovakia [1]								**Slovaquie** [1]
Production	197	171	...	...	...	...	...	Production
Consumption	240	206	...	...	...	...	...	Consommation
Consumption per capita	45	38	...	...	...	...	...	Consommation par habitant
Slovenia [1]								**Slovénie** [1]
Production	44	55	...	...	...	...	...	Production
Consumption	90	100	...	...	...	...	...	Consommation
Consumption per capita	45	50	...	...	...	...	...	Consommation par habitant
Somalia *								**Somalie** *
Production	20	20	20	15	20	20	20	Production
Consumption	190	200	200	205	205	220	240	Consommation
Consumption per capita	19	25	23	22	21	21	21	Consommation par habitant
South Africa								**Afrique du Sud**
Production	2 767	2 418	2 234	2 507	2 338	2 433	2 415	Production
Consumption	1 478	1 436	1 484	1 565	1 699	1 771	1 831	Consommation
Consumption per capita	33	31	32	33	35	37	38	Consommation par habitant
Sri Lanka *								**Sri Lanka** *
Production	20	21	60	60	70	75	75	Production
Consumption	535	610	630	640	660	685	700	Consommation
Consumption per capita	28	32	32	32	33	34	34	Consommation par habitant

34 Sugar *(continued)*

Production and consumption: thousand metric tons; consumption per capita: kilograms

Sucre *(suite)*

Production et consommation : milliers de tonnes ; consommation par habitant : kilogrammes

Country or area	2002	2003	2004	2005	2006	2007	2008	Pays ou zone
Sudan								**Soudan**
Production	744	686	789	728	767	743	652	Production
Consumption	568	568	624	877	910	916	1 024	Consommation
Consumption per capita	17	16	18	25	26	26	25	Consommation par habitant
Suriname *								**Suriname ***
Production	10	5	5	5	7	7	7	Production
Consumption	20	20	20	21	21	22	22	Consommation
Consumption per capita	42	42	42	42	42	44	44	Consommation par habitant
Swaziland								**Swaziland**
Production	675	616	594	653	623	631	664	Production
Consumption *	45	50	45	45	50	50	55	Consommation *
Consumption per capita *	47	45	39	38	44	52	54	Consommation par habitant *
Switzerland								**Suisse**
Production	222	185	*225	221	198	*260	273	Production
Consumption	393	463	*475	526	558	*560	530	Consommation
Consumption per capita	54	63	*64	70	75	*74	70	Consommation par habitant
Syrian Arab Republic								**Rép. arabe syrienne**
Production	*120	*120	*105	*110	148	*160	*155	Production
Consumption *	760	775	790	800	825	835	840	Consommation *
Consumption per capita *	44	44	44	44	45	45	45	Consommation par habitant *
Tajikistan *								**Tadjikistan ***
Consumption	70	80	85	105	110	115	115	Consommation
Consumption per capita	11	12	13	15	16	16	16	Consommation par habitant
Thailand								**Thaïlande**
Production	6 438	7 737	7 462	4 589	5 646	7 147	7 774	Production
Consumption	1 978	2 073	2 303	2 352	2 464	2 476	2 310	Consommation
Consumption per capita	31	33	36	36	38	38	36	Consommation par habitant
TFYR of Macedonia								**L'ex-R.Y. Macédoine**
Production	*10	16	16	16	19	36	*35	Production
Consumption *	65	65	70	70	75	75	75	Consommation *
Consumption per capita *	32	32	34	34	37	37	37	Consommation par habitant *
Togo								**Togo**
Consumption *	45	48	50	60	62	65	66	Consommation *
Consumption per capita *	9	10	10	11	11	11	11	Consommation par habitant *
Trinidad and Tobago								**Trinité-et-Tobago**
Production	104	67	43	33	*25	*30	0	Production
Consumption	70	70	*75	*75	*75	*70	*70	Consommation
Consumption per capita	54	55	*59	*59	*59	*54	*53	Consommation par habitant
Tunisia								**Tunisie**
Consumption	319	*330	335	332	362	*375	347	Consommation
Consumption per capita	33	*33	34	33	36	*37	34	Consommation par habitant
Turkey								**Turquie**
Production	2 128	2 136	2 053	2 171	2 091	1 919	2 148	Production
Consumption	1 782	1 725	1 894	1 978	2 208	1 999	2 175	Consommation
Consumption per capita	26	24	27	27	30	28	30	Consommation par habitant
Turkmenistan								**Turkménistan**
Production	0	1	*2	*3	*3	*4	*4	Production
Consumption *	70	75	75	80	85	90	95	Consommation *
Consumption per capita *	15	15	14	14	13	13	13	Consommation par habitant *
Uganda								**Ouganda**
Production	180	192	213	211	208	197	259	Production
Consumption	*180	225	257	263	260	250	292	Consommation
Consumption per capita	*8	9	10	10	10	9	10	Consommation par habitant
Ukraine								**Ukraine**
Production	*1 545	1 690	*1 945	*2 060	*2 800	*2 025	*1 700	Production
Consumption *	2 100	2 300	2 300	2 350	2 350	2 350	2 300	Consommation *
Consumption per capita *	44	48	49	50	50	50	49	Consommation par habitant *
United Arab Emirates *								**Emirats arabes unis ***
Consumption	113	119	127	140	151	163	165	Consommation
Consumption per capita	30	30	31	34	36	39	39	Consommation par habitant

34 Sugar *(continued)*

Production and consumption: thousand metric tons; consumption per capita: kilograms

Sucre *(suite)*

Production et consommation : milliers de tonnes ; consommation par habitant : kilogrammes

Country or area	2002	2003	2004	2005	2006	2007	2008	Pays ou zone
United Rep. of Tanzania								**Rép.-Unie de Tanzanie**
Production	187	218	211	279	257	267	286	Production
Consumption	165	218	221	268	300	307	330	Consommation
Consumption per capita	5	6	6	7	8	8	8	Consommation par habitant
United States								**Etats-Unis**
Production	6 805	7 964	7 647	6 784	7 034	7 678	6 956	Production
Consumption	9 079	8 844	8 994	9 248	9 228	9 107	9 807	Consommation
Consumption per capita	32	30	31	31	31	30	32	Consommation par habitant
Uruguay *								**Uruguay ***
Production	7	6	7	6	6	6	7	Production
Consumption	110	115	120	120	120	120	125	Consommation
Consumption per capita	33	35	36	36	36	36	38	Consommation par habitant
Uzbekistan								**Ouzbékistan**
Production	*7	0	0	0	0	0	0	Production
Consumption *	490	495	495	505	510	510	515	Consommation *
Consumption per capita *	19	20	19	20	20	20	20	Consommation par habitant *
Venezuela (Boliv. Rep. of)								**Venezuela (Rép. boliv. du)**
Production	*550	*510	694	*690	*700	*700	*690	Production
Consumption	*925	*930	1 020	*1 050	*1 070	*1 080	*1 090	Consommation
Consumption per capita	*37	*36	39	*40	*40	*39	*39	Consommation par habitant
Viet Nam								**Viet Nam**
Production	*890	*975	*1 070	875	*995	1 251	*1 065	Production
Consumption	*950	*1 005	*1 035	906	*1 170	1 299	*1 350	Consommation
Consumption per capita	*12	*12	*13	11	*13	15	*16	Consommation par habitant
Yemen *								**Yémen ***
Consumption	445	470	480	495	510	525	540	Consommation
Consumption per capita	23	23	23	23	24	24	25	Consommation par habitant
Zambia								**Zambie**
Production	233	230	245	248	*250	237	207	Production
Consumption	116	104	115	95	*115	118	116	Consommation
Consumption per capita	11	9	10	8	*10	10	9	Consommation par habitant
Zimbabwe								**Zimbabwe**
Production	565	482	456	430	446	349	291	Production
Consumption	335	315	311	295	263	234	172	Consommation
Consumption per capita	27	25	27	25	23	22	17	Consommation par habitant

Source:
International Sugar Organization (ISO), London, the ISO database and the *Sugar Yearbook 2009.*

Source:
Organisation internationale du sucre (OIS), Londres, la base de données de l'OIS et l'*Annuaire du sucre 2009.*

1 Beginning 2004, data for Cyprus, Czech Republic, Estonia, Hungary, Latvia, Lithuania, Malta, Poland, Slovakia, and Slovenia are incorporated in the European Union data. From 2007 including figures of Bulgaria and Romania.

2 For statistical purposes, the data for China do not include those for the Hong Kong Special Administrative Region (Hong Kong SAR), Macao Special Administrative Region (Macao SAR) and Taiwan Province of China.

3 Including non-human consumption: 2002 - 16 750 tons; 2007 - 22 335 tons.

4 Including 7 546 tons sold to other Pacific Island nations in tons in 2002; 10 686 tons in 2004; 15 515 tons in 2006 and 13 398 tons in 2007.

5 Including sugar used for the production of mono-sodium glutamate and llysin: 2002 - 197 939 tons; 2003 - 226 191 tons; 2004 - 235 773 tons; 2005 - 241 101 tons; 2006 - 232 665 tons; 2007 - 223 344 tons; 2008 - 226 401.

1 À partir de 2004, les données pour Chypre, République tchèque, Estonie, Hongrie, Lettonie, Lituanie, Malta, Pologne, Slovaquie, Slovénie sont inclues dans les données de l'Union européenne. À partir de 2007, les données incluent également la Bulgarie et la Roumaine.

2 Pour la présentation des statistiques, les données pour la Chine ne comprennent pas la Région Administrative Spéciale de Hong Kong (Hong Kong RAS), la Région Administrative Spéciale de Macao (Macao RAS) et la province de Taiwan.

3 Dont consommation non humaine: 2002 - 16 750 tonnes; 2007 - 22 335 tonnes.

4 Y compris 7 546 tonnes vendues aux autres îles pacifiques en 2002; 10 686 tonnes en 2004, 15 515 tonnes en 2006 et 13 398 tonnes en 2007.

5 Y compris la sucre utilisée pour la production du glutamate monosodium et lysine: 2002 - 197 939 tonnes; 2003 - 226 191 tonnes; 2004 - 235 773 tonnes; 2005 - 241 101 tonnes; 2006 - 232 665 tonnes; 2007 - 223 344 tonnes; 2008 - 226 401.

35 Meat production

Thousand metric tons

Production de viande

Milliers de tonnes

Region, country or area	2001	2002	2003	2004	2005	2006	2007	2008	Région, pays ou zone
World									**Monde**
Buffalo	**2 792**	**2 858**	**2 832**	**2 949**	**3 013**	**3 116**	**3 226**	**3 248**	**Buffle**
Cattle	**55 274**	**56 816**	**57 210**	**58 085**	**59 132**	**60 687**	**61 865**	**61 670**	**Bovine**
Chicken	**60 477**	**63 124**	**64 588**	**67 211**	**69 188**	**71 257**	**75 076**	**78 155**	**Poulet**
Goat	**3 793**	**3 834**	**4 097**	**4 392**	**4 636**	**4 614**	**4 809**	**4 871**	**Chèvre**
Pig	**90 991**	**93 180**	**95 611**	**96 650**	**99 064**	**101 333**	**100 165**	**103 983**	**Porc**
Sheep	**7 637**	**7 623**	**7 675**	**7 708**	**7 881**	**8 155**	**8 330**	**8 248**	**Mouton**
Africa									**Afrique**
Buffalo	**189**	**203**	**229**	**269**	**270**	**270**	**270**	**270**	**Buffle**
Cattle	**3 993**	**4 197**	**4 325**	**4 397**	**4 610**	**4 830**	**4 876**	**4 915**	**Bovine**
Chicken	**2 975**	**3 078**	**3 117**	**3 172**	**3 259**	**3 352**	**3 538**	**3 552**	**Poulet**
Goat	**925**	**957**	**988**	**1 017**	**1 088**	**1 117**	**1 151**	**1 167**	**Chèvre**
Pig	**795**	**825**	**828**	**877**	**928**	**931**	**1 045**	**1 128**	**Porc**
Sheep	**1 141**	**1 133**	**1 158**	**1 178**	**1 208**	**1 256**	**1 253**	**1 249**	**Mouton**
Algeria									**Algérie**
Cattle	105	116[1]	121	125[2]	120[1]	122[1]	123[1]	125[1]	Bovine
Chicken [1]	236	243	253	253	253	253	254	254	Poulet [1]
Goat [1]	12	12	12	13	13	14	14	14	Chèvre [1]
Sheep [1]	165	165	165	172	178	185	187	187	Mouton [1]
Angola [1]									**Angola** [1]
Cattle	85	85	85	73	85	85	92	100	Bovine
Chicken	8	8	8	8	9	8	8	8	Poulet
Goat	10	9	9	9	9	10	11	11	Chèvre
Pig	29	28	28	28	28	28	28	28	Porc
Sheep	1	1	1	1	1	1	1	1	Mouton
Benin [1]									**Bénin** [1]
Cattle	19	20	20	21	22	23	23	24	Bovine
Chicken	12	12	12	15	15	16	17	22	Poulet
Goat	4	4	4	5	5	5	5	5	Chèvre
Pig	3	4	4	4	4	4	4	4	Porc
Sheep	2	2	2	2	3	3	3	3	Mouton
Botswana [1]									**Botswana** [1]
Cattle	34	29	27	35	35	35	35	35	Bovine
Chicken	9	9	6	6	5	5	6	6	Poulet
Goat	5	5	4	4	5	5	5	6	Chèvre
Sheep	2	2	1	1	2	2	2	2	Mouton
Burkina Faso [1]									**Burkina Faso** [1]
Cattle	88	92	96	101	106	111	116	116	Bovine
Chicken	27	28	29	30	31	32	33	34	Poulet
Goat	24	25	26	27	28	29	30	30	Chèvre
Pig	22	25	27	30	33	36	40	44	Porc
Sheep	15	15	16	16	16	17	17	17	Mouton
Burundi [1]									**Burundi** [1]
Cattle	9	9	10	10	11	12	13	7	Bovine
Chicken	6	6	6	7	7	7	7	7	Poulet
Goat	4	4	4	5	5	5	6	6	Chèvre
Pig	5	5	5	6	6	11	11	11	Porc
Sheep	1	1	1	1	1	1	1	^0	Mouton
Cameroon									**Cameroun**
Cattle	95[2]	90[1]	90[1]	93[1]	94[1]	94[1]	94[1]	94[1]	Bovine
Chicken [1]	30	30	30	30	30	30	31	30	Poulet [1]
Goat [1]	16	16	16	16	16	16	16	16	Chèvre [1]
Pig [1]	16	16	16	16	16	16	16	16	Porc [1]
Sheep [1]	16	16	16	16	16	16	16	16	Mouton [1]
Cape Verde									**Cap-Vert**
Cattle	1[1]	^0	^0	^0	1[1]	1[1]	1[1]	1[1]	Bovine
Chicken	^0	^0	^0	^0	^0	^0	1[1]	1[1]	Poulet
Goat [1]	^0	^0	^0	1	1	1	1	1	Chèvre [1]
Pig [1]	7	7	7	7	7	7	8	8	Porc [1]

35 Meat production *(continued)*

Thousand metric tons

Production de viande *(suite)*

Milliers de tonnes

Region, country or area	2001	2002	2003	2004	2005	2006	2007	2008	Région, pays ou zone
Central African Rep.									**Rép. centrafricaine**
Cattle	67	69	71[1]	74[2]	75[1]	76[1]	79[1]	82[1]	Bovine
Chicken	3[1]	4	4[1]	4[1]	4[1]	4[1]	5[1]	5[1]	Poulet
Goat	10[1]	11	12[1]	12[1]	12[1]	13[1]	14[1]	15[1]	Chèvre
Pig	13[1]	13	13	14[2]	14[1]	14[1]	14[1]	14[1]	Porc
Sheep[1]	1	1	2	2	2	2	2	2	Mouton[1]
Chad[1]									**Tchad[1]**
Cattle	77	76	78	80	82	84	86	89	Bovine
Chicken	5	5	5	5	5	5	5	5	Poulet
Goat	20	20	21	21	22	22	23	24	Chèvre
Pig	^0	^0	^0	^0	^0	1	1	1	Porc
Sheep	12	13	13	13	14	14	15	15	Mouton
Comoros[1]									**Comores[1]**
Cattle	1	1	1	1	1	1	1	1	Bovine
Chicken	1	1	1	1	1	1	1	1	Poulet
Congo[1]									**Congo[1]**
Cattle	2	2	2	2	2	2	2	2	Bovine
Chicken	6	5	5	6	6	6	6	6	Poulet
Goat	1	1	1	1	1	1	1	1	Chèvre
Pig	3	3	3	3	3	3	3	3	Porc
Côte d'Ivoire									**Côte d'Ivoire**
Cattle	32	28	26	28	30	31	29	33	Bovine
Chicken	21	22	21	24	23	22	23	23	Poulet
Goat	3	3	3	3	3	3	3	3	Chèvre
Pig	7	7	7	7	7	7	7	7	Porc
Sheep	8	7	7	8	8	9	7	8	Mouton
Dem. Rep. of the Congo									**Rép. dém. du Congo**
Cattle	13	12	12	12	12	12	12	12	Bovine
Chicken	11	11	11	11	11	11	11	11	Poulet
Goat	19	18	18	18	18	18	18	18	Chèvre
Pig	25	24	24	24	24	24	24	24	Porc
Sheep	3	3	3	3	3	3	3	3	Mouton
Djibouti[1]									**Djibouti[1]**
Cattle	6	6	6	4	5	2	6	6	Bovine
Goat	2	2	2	2	2	2	2	2	Chèvre
Sheep	2	2	2	2	2	2	2	2	Mouton
Egypt									**Egypte**
Buffalo	189	203	229	269	270[1]	270[1]	270[1]	270[1]	Buffle
Cattle	247[2]	252	287	325	320[1]	320[1]	332[1]	338[1]	Bovine
Chicken	539	548[1]	560[1]	560[1]	560[1]	616	705	629	Poulet
Goat	25[1]	26	21	17	18[1]	18[1]	18[1]	18[1]	Chèvre
Pig	3[2]	3[1]	2	2	2[1]	2[1]	3	2	Porc
Sheep	53	52	50	40	43[1]	43[1]	43[1]	43[1]	Mouton
Eritrea[1]									**Erythrée[1]**
Cattle	15	14	17	17	17	17	17	17	Bovine
Chicken	2	2	2	2	2	2	2	2	Poulet
Goat	6	6	6	6	6	6	6	6	Chèvre
Sheep	6	6	7	7	7	6	7	7	Mouton
Ethiopia[1]									**Ethiopie[1]**
Cattle	304	353	338	336	350	374	363	380	Bovine
Chicken	50	54	50	47	43	45	46	46	Poulet
Goat	29	33	36	44	49	55	65	65	Chèvre
Pig	1	1	2	2	2	2	2	2	Porc
Sheep	38	48	53	60	68	79	85	82	Mouton
Gabon[1]									**Gabon[1]**
Cattle	1	1	1	1	2	1	1	1	Bovine
Chicken	4	4	4	4	4	4	4	4	Poulet
Pig	3	3	3	3	3	3	3	3	Porc
Sheep	1	1	1	1	1	1	1	1	Mouton

35 Meat production *(continued)*
Thousand metric tons

Production de viande *(suite)*
Milliers de tonnes

Region, country or area	2001	2002	2003	2004	2005	2006	2007	2008	Région, pays ou zone
Gambia[1]									**Gambie**[1]
Cattle	3	3	4	4	4	4	4	4	Bovine
Chicken	1	1	1	1	1	1	1	1	Poulet
Goat	1	1	1	1	1	1	1	1	Chèvre
Pig	^0	^0	^0	^0	^0	^0	1	1	Porc
Sheep	^0	^0	1	1	1	1	1	1	Mouton
Ghana									**Ghana**
Cattle	24[1]	24[1]	24[1]	23	25	24	23[1]	25[1]	Bovine
Chicken[1]	21	23	26	28	29	31	42	44	Poulet[1]
Goat	11[1]	11[1]	12[1]	12	12	11	13[1]	14[1]	Chèvre
Pig[1]	11	10	10	10	10	12	17	17	Porc[1]
Sheep	10[1]	10[1]	10[1]	10	10	10	11[1]	11[1]	Mouton
Guinea									**Guinée**
Cattle	33[1]	34[1]	37[1]	39[1]	41[1]	44	47	49	Bovine
Chicken[1]	4	5	5	5	6	6	6	7	Poulet[1]
Goat	5[1]	5[1]	5[1]	6[1]	6[1]	7	8	8	Chèvre
Pig	2[1]	2[1]	2[1]	2[1]	2[1]	1	1[1]	2	Porc
Sheep	4[1]	4[1]	4[1]	4[1]	5[1]	5	5	6	Mouton
Guinea-Bissau[1]									**Guinée-Bissau**[1]
Cattle	5	5	5	5	5	5	5	6	Bovine
Chicken	1	1	1	1	1	2	2	2	Poulet
Goat	1	1	1	1	1	1	1	1	Chèvre
Pig	11	11	11	11	12	12	12	13	Porc
Sheep	1	1	1	1	1	1	1	1	Mouton
Kenya									**Kenya**
Cattle	282	319	343	350	396	430	445	368[1]	Bovine
Chicken	19	20	21	19	18	22	24	24[1]	Poulet
Goat[1]	34	35	36	41	42	43	45	46	Chèvre[1]
Pig	15[1]	11	15	15	13	17	16	17[1]	Porc
Sheep	34	39	36	36	37	35[1]	34[1]	34[1]	Mouton
Lesotho									**Lesotho**
Cattle	10[1]	10[1]	10[1]	10[1]	11[1]	3	11[1]	11[1]	Bovine
Chicken[1]	2	2	2	2	2	2	2	2	Poulet[1]
Goat	2[1]	2[1]	2[1]	2[1]	2[1]	2	2[1]	2[1]	Chèvre
Pig[1]	5	4	3	5	6	9	10	4	Porc[1]
Sheep	4[1]	4[1]	3[1]	4[1]	4[1]	5	4[1]	4[1]	Mouton
Liberia[1]									**Libéria**[1]
Cattle	1	1	1	1	1	1	1	1	Bovine
Chicken	7	7	8	8	8	9	9	10	Poulet
Goat	1	1	1	1	1	1	1	1	Chèvre
Pig	4	4	4	4	4	5	6	6	Porc
Sheep	1	1	1	1	1	1	1	1	Mouton
Libyan Arab Jamah.									**Jamah. arabe libyenne**
Cattle[1]	6	6	6	6	6	10	10	10	Bovine[1]
Chicken	99[1]	99[1]	99[1]	99[1]	99[1]	94	120	120[1]	Poulet
Goat[1]	6	7	9	10	11	12	12	12	Chèvre[1]
Sheep[1]	29	24	24	24	24	26	25	28	Mouton[1]
Madagascar[1]									**Madagascar**[1]
Cattle	119	112	115	115	134	134	135	150	Bovine
Chicken	36	36	36	36	36	36	37	37	Poulet
Goat	6	6	6	7	6	6	6	6	Chèvre
Pig	19	22	25	28	51	53	54	55	Porc
Sheep	2	2	3	3	3	3	3	3	Mouton
Malawi									**Malawi**
Cattle	19[1]	22	23	21[1]	21	24	27	29	Bovine
Chicken[1]	15	15	16	16	16	15	15	15	Poulet[1]
Goat	8[1]	10	10	10[1]	10	14	17	20	Chèvre
Pig	20[1]	21[1]	21[1]	22[1]	22[1]	21[1]	25	34	Porc
Sheep	^0[1]	^0	^0[1]	1	1	1	1	1	Mouton

35 Meat production *(continued)*
Thousand metric tons

Production de viande *(suite)*
Milliers de tonnes

Region, country or area	2001	2002	2003	2004	2005	2006	2007	2008	Région, pays ou zone
Mali									**Mali**
Cattle [1]	67	86	94	77	108	106	112	129	Bovine [1]
Chicken	27[1]	32[1]	34[1]	35[1]	36[1]	37	38	39[1]	Poulet
Goat [1]	28	31	33	34	36	38	40	43	Chèvre [1]
Pig [1]	2	2	2	3	3	3	2	2	Porc [1]
Sheep [1]	25	24	29	30	24	35	38	42	Mouton [1]
Mauritania [1]									**Mauritanie** [1]
Cattle	22	22	23	24	25	26	26	26	Bovine
Chicken	5	4	4	4	4	4	4	4	Poulet
Goat	13	14	14	15	15	15	15	15	Chèvre
Sheep	23	24	24	25	25	25	25	25	Mouton
Mauritius									**Maurice**
Cattle	2[1]	3[1]	3[1]	3[1]	3[1]	3[1]	2	2	Bovine
Chicken	27	29	30	33	33	36	40	42	Poulet
Pig	1	1	1	1	1	1	1	1	Porc
Morocco									**Maroc**
Cattle	145	170	150	140	157	160	160	170	Bovine
Chicken	255	280	320	325	370	370	380	440	Poulet
Goat	21	22	22	23	22	23	22	22	Chèvre
Pig [1]	1	1	1	1	1	1	1	1	Porc [1]
Sheep	125	110	105	105	115	120	120	120	Mouton
Mozambique [1]									**Mozambique** [1]
Cattle	11	12	15	17	19	16	22	19	Bovine
Chicken	31	33	23	20	19	22	22	22	Poulet
Goat	25	25	24	24	24	21	22	21	Chèvre
Pig	119	115	98	107	117	85	97	91	Porc
Sheep	1	1	1	1	1	1	1	1	Mouton
Namibia									**Namibie**
Cattle	57[1]	48[1]	49[1]	42[1]	39[1]	36	39[1]	39[1]	Bovine
Chicken [1]	8	8	8	9	10	10	10	10	Poulet [1]
Goat [1]	3	5	5	5	3	4	4	4	Chèvre [1]
Pig [1]	2	2	2	2	2	3	3	3	Porc [1]
Sheep	5[1]	8[1]	8[1]	7	10[1]	11[1]	12[1]	12[1]	Mouton
Niger [1]									**Niger** [1]
Cattle	130	142	149	161	170	177	192	220	Bovine
Chicken	11	11	11	12	12	11	11	11	Poulet
Goat	34	38	41	42	47	48	50	53	Chèvre
Pig	1	1	1	1	1	1	1	1	Porc
Sheep	29	30	31	35	36	37	39	35	Mouton
Nigeria [1]									**Nigéria** [1]
Cattle	279	280	280	280	261	284	287	294	Bovine
Chicken	184	190	201	211	219	232	243	243	Poulet
Goat	239	242	245	252	257	264	271	271	Chèvre
Pig	165	193	179	186	193	201	209	218	Porc
Sheep	128	130	131	134	137	141	145	145	Mouton
Réunion									**Réunion**
Cattle	2	2	2	2	2	2	2	2	Bovine
Chicken	13	14	14	14	14	14	14[2]	15[1]	Poulet
Pig	12	12	12	13	13	13	13[1]	13[1]	Porc
Rwanda [1]									**Rwanda** [1]
Cattle	19	20	24	23	24	29	31	37	Bovine
Chicken	2	2	2	2	2	2	2	2	Poulet
Goat	3	3	3	4	5	5	6	6	Chèvre
Pig	3	4	4	6	6	6	6	6	Porc
Sheep	1	1	1	1	1	1	1	1	Mouton
Sao Tome and Principe [1]									**Sao Tomé-et-Principe** [1]
Chicken	1	1	1	1	1	1	1	1	Poulet

35 Meat production *(continued)*

Thousand metric tons

Production de viande *(suite)*

Milliers de tonnes

Region, country or area	2001	2002	2003	2004	2005	2006	2007	2008	Région, pays ou zone
Senegal									**Sénégal**
Cattle	48	45	43	43	47	63	49	66	Bovine
Chicken	24	24	25	26	29	32	37	41	Poulet
Goat	9	9	9	10	11	13	13	14	Chèvre
Pig	9	11	10	9	10	10	11	11	Porc
Sheep	16	15	15	15	17	21	22	21	Mouton
Seychelles [1]									**Seychelles** [1]
Chicken	1	1	1	1	1	1	1	1	Poulet
Pig	1	1	1	1	^0	^0	^0	^0	Porc
Sierra Leone [1]									**Sierra Leone** [1]
Cattle	5	5	5	6	6	8	8	8	Bovine
Chicken	11	10	11	11	11	12	12	12	Poulet
Goat	^0	^0	1	1	1	1	1	1	Chèvre
Pig	2	2	2	2	2	2	2	2	Porc
Sheep	1	1	1	1	1	1	1	1	Mouton
Somalia [1]									**Somalie** [1]
Cattle	63	62	64	65	68	66	66	66	Bovine
Chicken	4	4	4	4	4	4	4	4	Poulet
Goat	36	39	40	40	39	42	42	42	Chèvre
Sheep	47	40	48	52	53	48	48	48	Mouton
South Africa									**Afrique du Sud**
Cattle	525	574	610	655	705	804	805[1]	777[1]	Bovine
Chicken	893	925	900	906	949	971	974[1]	974[1]	Poulet
Goat [1]	36	36	36	36	37	37	36	37	Chèvre [1]
Pig	111	111	134	145	147	151	225	296	Porc
Sheep	104	105	120	120	115	117	99[1]	94[1]	Mouton
Sudan									**Soudan**
Cattle [1]	320	325	340	340	350	350	340	340	Bovine [1]
Chicken	27[1]	27[1]	29[1]	37[1]	31[1]	25	26	27	Poulet
Goat	122[1]	126[1]	138	139	186	186[1]	186[1]	189[1]	Chèvre
Sheep [1]	150	144	144	145	148	148	148	152	Mouton [1]
Swaziland									**Swaziland**
Cattle	8	13	13[1]	15[1]	14[1]	18[1]	18[1]	18[1]	Bovine
Chicken [1]	6	5	10	7	7	5	5	5	Poulet [1]
Goat [1]	3	2	2	2	2	2	2	2	Chèvre [1]
Pig [1]	1	1	2	1	1	1	1	1	Porc [1]
Togo [1]									**Togo** [1]
Cattle	8	8	7	8	8	8	9	9	Bovine
Chicken	13	14	15	16	18	19	21	21	Poulet
Goat	4	4	4	4	4	4	4	4	Chèvre
Pig	6	7	7	7	8	8	9	9	Porc
Sheep	4	4	4	4	4	4	4	4	Mouton
Tunisia									**Tunisie**
Cattle	60	64	58	53	53	56	60	62	Bovine
Chicken	91	94	90	96	87	79	96	103	Poulet
Goat	9	10	9	9	11	11	11	11	Chèvre
Sheep	56	58	51	52	53	56	57	52	Mouton
Uganda									**Ouganda**
Cattle	101[1]	106	110[1]	106[1]	106[1]	106[1]	106[1]	106[1]	Bovine
Chicken [1]	49	54	38	38	38	38	38	38	Poulet [1]
Goat [1]	25	25	29	29	29	29	29	29	Chèvre [1]
Pig [1]	81	84	87	95	98	102	105	105	Porc [1]
Sheep [1]	6	6	8	8	6	6	6	6	Mouton [1]
United Rep. of Tanzania [1]									**Rép.-Unie de Tanzanie** [1]
Cattle	255	265	270	265	270	270	247	247	Bovine
Chicken	44	44	48	52	52	53	46	46	Poulet
Goat	30	31	31	31	31	31	31	31	Chèvre
Pig	13	13	13	13	13	13	13	13	Porc
Sheep	10	10	11	11	12	12	10	10	Mouton
Western Sahara [1]									**Sahara occidental** [1]
Goat	1	1	1	1	1	1	1	1	Chèvre

35 Meat production *(continued)*

Thousand metric tons

Production de viande *(suite)*

Milliers de tonnes

Region, country or area	2001	2002	2003	2004	2005	2006	2007	2008	Région, pays ou zone
Zambia [1]									**Zambie** [1]
Cattle	54	59	59	56	59	58	58	58	Bovine
Chicken	37	38	39	39	39	37	37	37	Poulet
Goat	5	6	7	7	8	8	8	8	Chèvre
Pig	11	11	11	11	11	11	11	11	Porc
Sheep	1	1	1	1	1	1	1	1	Mouton
Zimbabwe [1]									**Zimbabwe** [1]
Cattle	108	97	99	102	102	102	104	104	Bovine
Chicken	38	35	40	46	52	53	57	61	Poulet
Goat	13	15	15	14	14	14	15	14	Chèvre
Pig	29	29	29	29	29	30	30	30	Porc
Sheep	1	1	1	1	1	^0	^0	^0	Mouton
Northern America									**Amérique septentrionale**
Cattle	**13 244**	**13 722**	**13 242**	**12 638**	**12 661**	**13 190**	**13 257**	**13 127**	**Bovine**
Chicken	**15 220**	**15 650**	**15 650**	**16 421**	**17 041**	**17 214**	**17 658**	**18 036**	**Poulet**
Goat	**119**	**125**	**125**	**125**	**126**	**124**	**126**	**127**	**Chèvre**
Pig	**10 422**	**10 787**	**10 938**	**11 239**	**11 303**	**11 449**	**11 849**	**12 540**	**Porc**
Sheep	**115**	**116**	**108**	**106**	**103**	**101**	**99**	**98**	**Mouton**
Canada									**Canada**
Cattle	1 262	1 295	1 203	1 504	1 465	1 327	1 279	1 288	Bovine
Chicken	953	956	954	970	1 000	997	1 030	1 041	Poulet
Pig	1 731	1 858	1 882	1 936	1 920	1 898	1 898	1 941	Porc
Sheep	14	15	16	18	18	17	17	16	Mouton
United States									**Etats-Unis**
Cattle	11 982	12 427	12 039	11 135	11 196	11 863	11 979	11 839	Bovine
Chicken	14 267	14 467	14 696	15 451	16 041	16 217	16 628	16 994	Poulet
Pig	8 691	8 929	9 056	9 303	9 383	9 550	9 951	10 599	Porc
Sheep	101	101 [2]	92 [2]	88	85	84	83	82	Mouton
Latin America and the Caribbean									**Amérique latine et Caraïbes**
Cattle	**13 668**	**14 120**	**14 387**	**15 449**	**16 527**	**17 089**	**17 457**	**17 356**	**Bovine**
Chicken	**12 932**	**13 779**	**14 384**	**15 829**	**15 646**	**16 455**	**17 589**	**19 110**	**Poulet**
Goat	**119**	**125**	**125**	**125**	**126**	**127**	**128**	**129**	**Chèvre**
Pig	**5 226**	**5 463**	**5 733**	**5 820**	**5 695**	**5 869**	**6 269**	**6 407**	**Porc**
Sheep	**301**	**279**	**287**	**297**	**305**	**304**	**304**	**309**	**Mouton**
Antigua and Barbuda [1]									**Antigua-et-Barbuda** [1]
Cattle	1	1	1	1	1	1	1	1	Bovine
Argentina									**Argentine**
Cattle	2 461	2 493	2 658	3 024	2 980	2 800 [1]	2 830 [1]	2 830 [1]	Bovine
Chicken	951	699	738	866	1 010	1 159	1 160 [1]	1 160 [1]	Poulet
Goat [1]	9	9	10	10	10	10	10	10	Chèvre [1]
Pig	198	165	150	150 [1]	185 [1]	225 [1]	230 [1]	230 [1]	Porc
Sheep [1]	50	50	52	52	52	52	52	52	Mouton [1]
Bahamas									**Bahamas**
Chicken	7	7 [1]	8 [1]	8 [1]	6 [1]	6 [1]	7 [1]	7 [1]	Poulet
Barbados									**Barbade**
Chicken	12 [1]	11 [1]	12	14	15	14	14 [1]	14 [1]	Poulet
Pig	2	1	2	2	2	3	3 [1]	3 [1]	Porc
Belize									**Belize**
Cattle	1	2	2	3	2	2	2	2	Bovine
Chicken	10	14	14	14	14	14	13	13	Poulet
Pig	1	1	1	1	1	1	1	1	Porc
Bolivia (Plurinational State of)									**Bolivie (État plurinational de)**
Cattle	161	165	168	172	175 [1]	200 [1]	244	249	Bovine
Chicken	128	135	135	141 [1]	154 [1]	140 [1]	140 [1]	140 [1]	Poulet
Goat [1]	6	6	6	6	6	6	6	6	Chèvre [1]
Pig	97 [1]	101 [1]	104 [1]	108 [1]	108 [1]	110 [1]	112	114	Porc
Sheep	16	17	18	18	18 [1]	19 [1]	20 [1]	20 [1]	Mouton
Brazil									**Brésil**
Cattle	6 824	7 139	7 230	7 774	8 592 [2]	9 020 [2]	9 303 [2]	9 024 [2]	Bovine
Chicken	6 208	7 050	7 760	8 668	7 866	8 164	8 988	10 216	Poulet
Goat [1]	30	31	29	29	29	29	29	29	Chèvre [1]

35 Meat production *(continued)*

Thousand metric tons

Production de viande *(suite)*

Milliers de tonnes

Region, country or area	2001	2002	2003	2004	2005	2006	2007	2008	Région, pays ou zone
Pig	2 637	2 798	3 059	3 110	2 800[2]	2 830[2]	2 990[2]	3 015[2]	Porc
Sheep [1]	72	69	68	76	76	77	78	79	Mouton [1]
Chile									**Chili**
Cattle	218	200	192	208	216	238	242	240	Bovine
Chicken	408	379	389	446	457	523	486	510	Poulet
Goat [1]	5	5	5	5	5	5	6	6	Chèvre [1]
Pig	303	351	365	373	411	468	499	522	Porc
Sheep	11	10	10	10	9	11	10	11	Mouton
Colombia									**Colombie**
Cattle	700[1]	675[1]	642	717	792	827	856	917	Bovine
Chicken	596	649	678	709	763	850	925	1 011	Poulet
Goat [1]	6	6	7	7	7	7	7	7	Chèvre [1]
Pig	98	109	124	130	128	148	177	170	Porc
Sheep [1]	7	6	8	9	10	7	7	7	Mouton [1]
Costa Rica									**Costa Rica**
Cattle	74	68	74	70	81	75	81	88	Bovine
Chicken	77	77	72	84	91	98	107	103	Poulet
Pig	36	36	36	38	39	41	48	52	Porc
Cuba									**Cuba**
Cattle	75	66	56	55	60	56	54	62	Bovine
Chicken	70	35	34	36	29	31	34	33	Poulet
Goat	2	2	3	3	3	3	4	4	Chèvre
Pig	76	90	94	98	97	100	177	193	Porc
Sheep	6	7	7	7	7	7	8	9	Mouton
Dominica [1]									**Dominique** [1]
Cattle	1	1	1	1	1	1	1	1	Bovine
Dominican Republic									**Rép. dominicaine**
Cattle	71	72	69	71	73	84	101	101[1]	Bovine
Chicken	203	185	157	238	297	313	346	346[1]	Poulet
Goat [1]	1	1	1	1	1	1	1	1	Chèvre [1]
Pig	63	64	64	52	78	72[1]	72[1]	72[1]	Porc
Ecuador									**Equateur**
Cattle	188	203	206	207	209	211	233	248	Bovine
Chicken	208	209	211	208	210	300	336	330[1]	Poulet
Goat	1	1	1	1	1	1	1	1	Chèvre
Pig	140	145	154	161	162	163	189	213	Porc
Sheep	10	10	15	11	9	9	8	8	Mouton
El Salvador									**El Salvador**
Cattle	35	40	29	26	27	31	31	32	Bovine
Chicken	74	79	79	92	99	101	107	96	Poulet
Pig	9[1]	9[1]	8	8	11	14	9	9	Porc
Falkland Is. (Malvinas) [1]									**Iles Falkland (Malvinas)** [1]
Sheep	1	1	1	1	1	1	1	1	Mouton
French Guiana									**Guyane française**
Pig	1	1	1[1]	1[1]	1[1]	1[1]	1[1]	1[1]	Porc
Grenada [1]									**Grenade** [1]
Chicken	1	1	1	1	1	1	1	1	Poulet
Guadeloupe									**Guadeloupe**
Cattle	3[1]	3[2]	3[2]	3[2]	3[2]	3[2]	3[1]	3[1]	Bovine
Chicken [1]	1	1	1	1	1	1	1	1	Poulet [1]
Pig	1[1]	1	1[2]	1[2]	1[2]	1[2]	1[1]	1[1]	Porc
Guatemala									**Guatemala**
Cattle [1]	62	63	63	63	63	65	76	76	Bovine [1]
Chicken	144[2]	162	155[1]	147	151	168	151[1]	151[1]	Poulet
Pig [1]	39	49	58	58	67	58	58	58	Porc [1]
Sheep [1]	1	1	1	1	1	1	1	1	Mouton [1]
Guyana									**Guyana**
Cattle	2[2]	2[1]	2[1]	2[1]	2[1]	2[1]	2[1]	2[1]	Bovine
Chicken	12	17	24	24	23	21	25	23	Poulet
Pig [1]	1	1	1	1	1	1	1	1	Porc [1]
Sheep [1]	1	1	1	1	1	1	1	1	Mouton [1]

35 Meat production *(continued)*
Thousand metric tons

Production de viande *(suite)*
Milliers de tonnes

Region, country or area	2001	2002	2003	2004	2005	2006	2007	2008	Région, pays ou zone
Haiti [1]									**Haïti** [1]
Cattle	41	42	43	43	44	42	42	42	Bovine
Chicken	8	8	8	8	8	8	8	8	Poulet
Goat	7	7	7	6	6	6	6	6	Chèvre
Pig	31	33	33	33	33	33	33	33	Porc
Sheep	1	1	1	1	1	1	1	1	Mouton
Honduras									**Honduras**
Cattle	55	54	61	64	66	68	71	74	Bovine
Chicken	66	105	117	129	141	127	134	142	Poulet
Pig	10	9	8	9	9	11	11	12	Porc
Jamaica									**Jamaïque**
Cattle	13	14	14	11	10	6	6	6	Bovine
Chicken	83	84	94	96	102	105	107	107	Poulet
Goat	1	1	1	1	1	1	1	1	Chèvre
Pig	6	5	6	7	9	8	7	9	Porc
Martinique									**Martinique**
Cattle	2	2	2[1]	2[1]	2[1]	2[1]	2[1]	2[1]	Bovine
Chicken [1]	1	1	1	1	1	1	1	1	Poulet [1]
Pig	2	2	2[1]	2[1]	2[1]	2[1]	2[1]	2[1]	Porc
Mexico									**Mexique**
Cattle	1 445	1 468	1 504	1 544	1 558	1 613	1 635	1 667	Bovine
Chicken	1 928	2 076	2 116	2 280	2 437	2 464	2 542	2 581	Poulet
Goat	39	42	42	42	42	43	43	43	Chèvre
Pig	1 058	1 070	1 035	1 064	1 103	1 109	1 152	1 161	Porc
Sheep	36	38	42	44	46	48	49	51	Mouton
Montserrat [1]									**Montserrat** [1]
Cattle	1	1	1	1	1	1	1	1	Bovine
Nicaragua									**Nicaragua**
Cattle	54	60	66	75	76	85	93	96	Bovine
Chicken	55	56	62	67	71	84	90	91	Poulet
Pig	6	6	6	7	7	7	7	7	Porc
Panama									**Panama**
Cattle	67	65	61	64	66	67	65	68	Bovine
Chicken	88	89	87	87	95	96	113	115	Poulet
Pig	18	18	20	21	21	25	30	35	Porc
Paraguay									**Paraguay**
Cattle	231	234	229	215	249	300	265	276[1]	Bovine
Chicken [1]	36	36	37	42	42	45	28	35	Poulet [1]
Goat [1]	1	1	1	1	1	1	1	1	Chèvre [1]
Pig [1]	143	150	153	148	152	156	149	175	Porc [1]
Sheep [1]	2	3	3	3	3	3	3	3	Mouton [1]
Peru									**Pérou**
Cattle	132	134	138	146	153	163	163	163	Bovine
Chicken	518	556	578	579	656	710	770	877	Poulet
Goat	6	6	6	7	7	7	7	6	Chèvre
Pig	94	93	93	98	103	109	115	115	Porc
Sheep	32	31	32	34	34	34	34	33	Mouton
Puerto Rico									**Porto Rico**
Cattle	13	11	10	13	10	10[1]	10[1]	10[1]	Bovine
Chicken	52	54	47	50	50	50[1]	50[1]	50[1]	Poulet
Pig	10	9	9	12	11	11[1]	11[1]	12[1]	Porc
Saint Lucia [1]									**Sainte-Lucie** [1]
Chicken	1	1	1	1	2	1	2	2	Poulet
Pig	1	1	1	1	1	1	1	1	Porc
Saint Vincent-Grenadines [1]									**Saint Vincent-Grenadines** [1]
Pig	1	1	1	1	1	1	1	1	Porc
Suriname									**Suriname**
Cattle	2	2	2	1	1	2	2	2	Bovine
Chicken	5	6	6	6	7	6	10	8	Poulet
Pig	1	1	1	2	2	2	2	2	Porc
Trinidad and Tobago									**Trinité-et-Tobago**
Cattle	1	1	1	1[1]	1[1]	1[1]	1[1]	1[1]	Bovine

35 Meat production *(continued)*

Thousand metric tons

Production de viande *(suite)*

Milliers de tonnes

Region, country or area	2001	2002	2003	2004	2005	2006	2007	2008	Région, pays ou zone
Chicken	47	58	57	58	58[1]	58[1]	60[1]	60[1]	Poulet
Pig	2	3	3	3[1]	3[1]	3[1]	3[1]	3[1]	Porc
United States Virgin Is.[1]									**Iles Vierges américaines**[1]
Cattle	1	1	1	1	1	1	1	1	Bovine
Uruguay									**Uruguay**
Cattle	317[2]	412	424	497	590[1]	600[2]	560[2]	588[2]	Bovine
Chicken[1]	55	45	31	41	52	60	50	75	Poulet[1]
Pig	23	20	17	17	20	19	21	21	Porc
Sheep	51[1]	31	27	27	33[1]	31[1]	27[1]	27[1]	Mouton
Venezuela (Boliv. Rep. of)									**Venezuela (Rép. boliv. du)**
Cattle	418	429	435	376	425	516	481	483	Bovine
Chicken	877	893	676	686	739	735	780	802	Poulet
Goat	4	5	5	5	6	6	6	6	Chèvre
Pig	119	119	120	101	126	137	154	164	Porc
Sheep	2	2	2	2	3	3	3	3	Mouton
Asia									**Asie**
Buffalo	**2 602**	**2 653**	**2 601**	**2 677**	**2 737**	**2 845**	**2 951**	**2 975**	**Buffle**
Cattle	**10 180**	**10 507**	**10 838**	**11 294**	**11 335**	**11 748**	**12 253**	**12 435**	**Bovine**
Chicken	**18 677**	**19 691**	**20 472**	**20 507**	**21 582**	**22 506**	**23 576**	**24 480**	**Poulet**
Goat	**2 614**	**2 613**	**2 843**	**3 095**	**3 268**	**3 199**	**3 361**	**3 413**	**Chèvre**
Pig	**49 093**	**50 210**	**51 784**	**52 904**	**55 429**	**57 169**	**53 729**	**56 946**	**Porc**
Sheep	**3 530**	**3 636**	**3 717**	**3 759**	**3 841**	**4 074**	**4 171**	**4 117**	**Mouton**
Afghanistan									**Afghanistan**
Cattle	108[2]	150[2]	137	149	141	117	137	133	Bovine
Chicken[1]	13	24	28	31	32	24	18	21	Poulet[1]
Goat[1]	33	47	48	49	46	44	35	42	Chèvre[1]
Sheep[1]	114	72	74	82	88	75	66	87	Mouton[1]
Armenia									**Arménie**
Cattle	29	30	30	33	34	40	43	49	Bovine
Chicken	4	4	5	4	5	5	6	7	Poulet
Pig	9	10	12	9	9	14	13	8	Porc
Sheep	7	6	6	7	8	7	7	7	Mouton
Azerbaijan									**Azerbaïdjan**
Cattle	57	63	67	69	71	73	75	77	Bovine
Chicken	19	23	27	32	35	36	49	52	Poulet
Pig	1	1	1	2	2	1	1	1	Porc
Sheep	37	38	39	41	42	44	45	46	Mouton
Bahrain									**Bahreïn**
Cattle	1[1]	1[1]	1[1]	1	1[1]	1[1]	1[1]	1[1]	Bovine
Chicken	6	5	5	5	5[1]	6	5	6	Poulet
Goat[1]	5	6	5	6	6	6	6	6	Chèvre[1]
Sheep[1]	3	1	2	2	2	2	2	2	Mouton[1]
Bangladesh									**Bangladesh**
Buffalo[1]	4	4	5	5	5	5	5	6	Buffle[1]
Cattle	174[2]	178[2]	180[1]	181[1]	183[1]	184[1]	186[1]	187[1]	Bovine
Chicken[1]	101	108	116	123	130	138	147	151	Poulet[1]
Goat	129[2]	137[2]	147[1]	158[1]	169[1]	182[1]	195[1]	210[1]	Chèvre
Sheep	3[2]	3[2]	3[1]	3[1]	3[1]	3[1]	3[1]	4[1]	Mouton
Bhutan[1]									**Bhoutan**[1]
Cattle	5	5	5	5	5	5	5	5	Bovine
Pig	1	1	1	1	1	1	1	1	Porc
Brunei Darussalam									**Brunéi Darussalam**
Buffalo	^0	1[1]	^0	^0	^0	^0	^0	^0	Buffle
Cattle[1]	3	3	3	3	2	1	1	1	Bovine[1]
Chicken[1]	14	12	14	16	14	16	18	18	Poulet[1]
Cambodia[1]									**Cambodge**[1]
Buffalo	9	9	10	9	10	10	11	10	Buffle
Cattle	58	53	54	55	57	60	61	62	Bovine
Chicken	20	19	18	18	17	17	18	19	Poulet
Pig	108	107	117	123	135	139	120	110	Porc
China[3]									**Chine**[3]
Buffalo	379[2]	387[2]	305[2]	330[2]	345	288[2]	307[2]	306[2]	Buffle

35 Meat production *(continued)*
Thousand metric tons

Production de viande *(suite)*
Milliers de tonnes

Region, country or area	2001	2002	2003	2004	2005	2006	2007	2008	Région, pays ou zone
Cattle[2]	4 729	4 853	5 141	5 295	5 357	5 500	5 846	5 841	Bovine[2]
Chicken[2]	8 851	9 173	9 448	9 484	9 965	10 165	10 616	11 055	Poulet[2]
Goat[2]	1 198	1 163	1 360	1 568	1 704	1 704	1 830	1 828	Chèvre[2]
Pig	41 654	42 323	43 434	44 479	46 622	47 591	43 933	47 190	Porc
Sheep[2]	1 523	1 675	1 730	1 764	1 800	1 938	2 000	1 978	Mouton[2]
Cyprus									**Chypre**
Cattle	4	4	4	4	4	4	4	4	Bovine
Chicken	34	35	33	32	33	27	28	28	Poulet
Goat	7	8	5	4	4	4	4	4	Chèvre
Pig	51	52	54	55	55	53	55	59	Porc
Sheep	4	5	3	3	3	3	3	3	Mouton
Georgia									**Géorgie**
Cattle	47	49	50	50	49	33	31	25	Bovine
Chicken	13	13	13	15	17	11	12	13	Poulet
Pig	35	36	37	35	33	31	21	11	Porc
Sheep	8	8	8	9	10	3	4	4[2]	Mouton
India[1]									**Inde**[1]
Buffalo	1 274	1 292	1 311	1 330	1 349	1 368	1 388	1 407	Buffle
Cattle	970	958	947	936	925	914	903	896	Bovine
Chicken	439	464	491	520	550	582	617	649	Poulet
Goat	470	471	473	474	475	476	477	478	Chèvre
Pig	467	469	470	471	473	474	476	479	Porc
Sheep	223	226	229	232	233	236	238	237	Mouton
Indonesia									**Indonésie**
Buffalo	44	42	41	40	38	44	42	39	Buffle
Cattle	339	330	370	448	359	396	339	393	Bovine
Chicken	900	1 083	1 118	1 191	1 126	1 260	1 296	1 350	Poulet
Goat	49	58	64	57	51	65	64	66	Chèvre
Pig[1]	418	467	495	484	550	589	597	637	Porc[1]
Sheep	45	69	81	66	66	75	57	47	Mouton
Iran (Islamic Rep. of)									**Iran (Rép. islamique d')**
Buffalo[1]	12	13	13	13	14	14	15	15	Buffle[1]
Cattle	274	284	314	337	344[2]	356[2]	360[1]	360[1]	Bovine
Chicken	885	942	1 104	1 152	1 237	1 360	1 468	1 566	Poulet
Goat	111	105	105[1]	105[1]	111[1]	106[1]	106[1]	106[1]	Chèvre
Sheep	333	345	346[1]	347[1]	351[1]	389[1]	389[1]	390[1]	Mouton
Iraq									**Iraq**
Buffalo[1]	2	1	1	1	1	3	1	1	Buffle[1]
Cattle	49[1]	50[1]	34	43	47	41	31	43	Bovine
Chicken	83	95	25	46	85	60	81	49	Poulet
Goat[1]	4	4	4	4	5	6	11	14	Chèvre[1]
Sheep[1]	21	21	29	20	26	81	89	47	Mouton[1]
Israel									**Israël**
Cattle	62	80	91	83	90	108	105	117	Bovine
Chicken	318	324	334	350	370	402	420	440	Poulet
Goat	2	2	2	3	3	4	4	4	Chèvre
Pig	16	16	17	18	19	18	18	18	Porc
Sheep	5[2]	5[1]	5[1]	6[1]	6[1]	6[1]	6[1]	6[1]	Mouton
Japan									**Japon**
Cattle	459	537	496	514	499	497	504	520	Bovine
Chicken	1 216	1 229	1 240	1 242	1 273	1 367	1 366	1 369	Poulet
Pig	1 232	1 246	1 274	1 263	1 245	1 247	1 251	1 249	Porc
Jordan									**Jordanie**
Cattle	12[1]	12	10	16	8	15	14	19	Bovine
Chicken	117	110	123	127	133	116	134	140	Poulet
Goat	2	1	2	3	2	2	3	4	Chèvre
Sheep	12[2]	14	13	15	13	13	20	15	Mouton
Kazakhstan									**Kazakhstan**
Cattle	288	296	312	330	348	367	386	400	Bovine
Chicken	34	36	38	41	46	65	64	65	Poulet
Goat	5[2]	7	9[2]	11[2]	13[2]	17	19	21	Chèvre

35 Meat production *(continued)*

Thousand metric tons

Production de viande *(suite)*

Milliers de tonnes

Region, country or area	2001	2002	2003	2004	2005	2006	2007	2008	Région, pays ou zone
Pig	181	187	185	199	197	193	194	206	Porc
Sheep	92	94	87[2]	91[2]	94[2]	99	104	110	Mouton
Korea, Dem. P. R.[1]									**Corée, R. p. dém. de**[1]
Cattle	21	22	22	21	21	22	22	22	Bovine
Chicken	31	34	36	37	36	35	34	32	Poulet
Goat	11	11	11	11	12	13	13	14	Chèvre
Pig	145	163	163	165	168	170	175	180	Porc
Sheep	1	1	1	1	1	1	1	1	Mouton
Korea, Republic of									**Corée, République de**
Cattle	233	211	188	186	195	200	219	246	Bovine
Chicken	377	381	383[2]	386[2]	484[2]	510[2]	513[2]	488	Poulet
Goat[1]	3	3	3	3	3	3	2	2	Chèvre[1]
Pig	928	1 005	1 149[2]	960	899	1 000[2]	1 043[2]	1 056[2]	Porc
Kuwait									**Koweït**
Cattle[1]	2	3	3	3	2	2	2	2	Bovine[1]
Chicken	42	37	37	40[1]	32	42[1]	42[1]	42[1]	Poulet
Goat	^0[1]	1[1]	1[1]	1[1]	1	1[1]	1[1]	1[1]	Chèvre
Sheep	31[1]	37[1]	31[1]	30[1]	34	30[1]	30[1]	30[1]	Mouton
Kyrgyzstan									**Kirghizistan**
Cattle	100	105	94	95	91	91	91	93	Bovine
Chicken	5	6	6	5	5	5	5	6	Poulet
Goat	7	7	7	7	7	7[2]	7	7	Chèvre
Pig	26	23	22	25	19	20	20	19	Porc
Sheep	37	37	37	38	39	39[2]	40	40	Mouton
Lao People's Dem. Rep.									**Rép. dém. pop. lao**
Buffalo	17	17	18	19[1]	18[1]	18[1]	18[1]	19[1]	Buffle
Cattle	17	20	22	21[1]	23[1]	23[1]	24[1]	26[1]	Bovine
Chicken	11	11	14	15[1]	15[1]	16[1]	16[1]	17[1]	Poulet
Goat[1]	^0	^0	1	1	1	1	1	1	Chèvre[1]
Pig	32	32	36	37[1]	39[1]	43[1]	46[1]	54[1]	Porc
Lebanon									**Liban**
Cattle[1]	43	55	56	53	61	52	47	47	Bovine[1]
Chicken	109	116	119	129	122	132	135	135[1]	Poulet
Goat[1]	3	3	3	3	3	3	4	4	Chèvre[1]
Pig	2	2	1	1	1	1	1	1[1]	Porc
Sheep[1]	17	14	15	12	8	7	8	8	Mouton[1]
Malaysia									**Malaisie**
Buffalo[1]	3	4	4	5	5	5	5	5	Buffle[1]
Cattle[1]	16	18	20	21	22	22	22	22	Bovine[1]
Chicken	682	761	765	825	860[2]	922[2]	931[2]	931[1]	Poulet
Goat[1]	1	1	1	1	1	1	1	1	Chèvre[1]
Pig	185	193	198	204	200[1]	217	200	195	Porc
Mongolia									**Mongolie**
Cattle	67	61	44	52	45	44	47	54	Bovine
Goat	28	20[2]	19[2]	33[2]	37	33	39	48	Chèvre
Pig	1	^0	^0	^0	^0[1]	^0	^0	^0	Porc
Sheep	77	75[2]	62[2]	65[2]	57	55	68	72	Mouton
Myanmar									**Myanmar**
Buffalo	21[1]	22[1]	18	21	24	27	29	32	Buffle
Cattle	76	81	97	94	106	120	130	140	Bovine
Chicken	258	301	380	457	561	650	726	726[1]	Poulet
Goat	10	10	12	15	17	19	22	24	Chèvre
Pig	132	193	221	261	328	370	411	463	Porc
Sheep	3	3	3	4	5	5	5	5	Mouton
Nepal									**Népal**
Buffalo	125	128	131	134	139	142	147	152	Buffle
Cattle[1]	47	47	48	48	49	49	49	49	Bovine[1]
Chicken	13	14	15	16	15	16	16	17	Poulet
Goat	38	39	40	41	42	43	45	46	Chèvre
Pig	15	16	16	15	16	16	16	16	Porc
Sheep	3	3	3	3	3	3	3	3	Mouton

35 Meat production *(continued)*

Thousand metric tons

Production de viande *(suite)*

Milliers de tonnes

Region, country or area	2001	2002	2003	2004	2005	2006	2007	2008	Région, pays ou zone
Occupied Palestinian Terr.									**Terr. palestinien occupé**
Cattle	11[1]	8[1]	7[1]	5	5	5	5	5	Bovine
Chicken	75[1]	80[1]	63	57	69	54	45	47	Poulet
Goat[1]	3	4	5	5	5	5	5	5	Chèvre[1]
Sheep[1]	5	10	13	12	12	13	12	12	Mouton[1]
Oman									**Oman**
Cattle[1]	4	4	4	4	4	4	4	4	Bovine[1]
Chicken[1]	5	6	6	6	6	6	6	6	Poulet[1]
Goat	6[1]	8[1]	23	15	23	23[1]	24[1]	24[1]	Chèvre
Sheep	13[1]	13[1]	12[1]	11[1]	11[1]	12	13	11[1]	Mouton
Pakistan									**Pakistan**
Buffalo	480	494	508	524	540	668	688	708	Buffle
Cattle	428	437	445	455	464	632	656	680	Bovine
Chicken	339	355	372	378	384	512	554	601	Poulet
Goat	321	333	345	357	370	250	256	261	Chèvre
Sheep	159	159	161	161	162	149	151	154	Mouton
Philippines									**Philippines**
Buffalo	72	76	76	80	77	84	110	99	Buffle
Cattle	183	183	181	179	173	167	178	180	Bovine
Chicken	587	627	635	658	650	658	662	741	Poulet
Goat	33	34	33	34	36	45	50	53	Chèvre
Pig	1 266	1 332	1 385	1 366	1 415	1 565	1 617	1 606	Porc
Qatar									**Qatar**
Chicken	4	6	5	5[1]	5[1]	5[1]	5[1]	5[1]	Poulet
Goat[1]	1	1	1	1	1	1	1	1	Chèvre[1]
Sheep[1]	8	8	7	6	4	4	4	4	Mouton[1]
Saudi Arabia									**Arabie saoudite**
Cattle	22[2]	22[2]	22[2]	22	22	21[1]	29[1]	29[1]	Bovine
Chicken	505	467	468[2]	480[2]	537[2]	548[2]	559[2]	559[1]	Poulet
Goat	22[2]	22[2]	12[1]	14[1]	15[1]	15[1]	25[1]	25[1]	Chèvre
Sheep	76[2]	74[1]	76[1]	78[1]	81[1]	79[1]	78[1]	78[1]	Mouton
Singapore									**Singapour**
Chicken[1]	87	90	86	69	76	76	83	83	Poulet[1]
Pig	23	21	19	20	20	16	19	19	Porc
Sri Lanka									**Sri Lanka**
Buffalo[1]	3	3	3	4	4	4	4	4	Buffle[1]
Cattle	27	28	29	28	29	26	24	22	Bovine
Chicken	82	86	88	95	97	79	100	103	Poulet
Goat	2	2	1	1	1	1	1	1	Chèvre
Pig	2	2	2	2	2	2	2	2	Porc
Syrian Arab Republic									**Rép. arabe syrienne**
Cattle	42	47	47	48	55	60	66	64	Bovine
Chicken	114	123	159	170	162	174	173	179	Poulet
Goat	5	5	7	7	7	7	8	8	Chèvre
Sheep	169	121	153	161	180	187	205	185	Mouton
Tajikistan									**Tadjikistan**
Cattle	17	20	25	27	27	24	25	25	Bovine
Chicken	^0	^0	^0	^0	^0	1	1	1	Poulet
Pig	...	...	...	...	...	3	3	3	Porc
Sheep	13	16	20	21	27	29	30	36	Mouton
Thailand									**Thaïlande**
Cattle	176	183	190	204	248	232	197	236	Bovine
Chicken	1 230[2]	1 320[2]	1 227	878	950[2]	962	986	1 019	Poulet
Goat[1]	1	1	1	1	1	1	2	1	Chèvre[1]
Pig[1]	632	645	661	677	669	865	915	864	Porc[1]
Timor-Leste[1]									**Timor-Leste[1]**
Buffalo	1	1	1	1	1	1	1	1	Buffle
Cattle	1	1	1	1	1	1	1	1	Bovine
Chicken	1	1	1	1	1	1	1	1	Poulet
Pig	8	8	8	8	8	8	9	9	Porc
Turkey									**Turquie**
Buffalo	2	2	2	2	2	2	2	1	Buffle

35 Meat production *(continued)*
Thousand metric tons

Production de viande *(suite)*
Milliers de tonnes

Region, country or area	2001	2002	2003	2004	2005	2006	2007	2008	Région, pays ou zone
Cattle	332	328	290	365	322	341	432	371	Bovine
Chicken	615	696	872	877	937	918	1 068	1 088	Poulet
Goat [1]	48	47	45	45	43	43	43	42	Chèvre [1]
Sheep [1]	303	286	267	273	272	272	280	278	Mouton [1]
Turkmenistan									**Turkménistan**
Cattle	80[1]	92[2]	101[2]	100[1]	100[1]	102[1]	102[1]	102[1]	Bovine
Chicken	8[1]	11[2]	12[2]	13[1]	14[1]	14[1]	13[1]	13[1]	Poulet
Goat	5[1]	6[2]	6[2]	7[1]	7[1]	7[1]	6[1]	6[1]	Chèvre
Sheep	71[1]	83[2]	90[2]	95[1]	90[1]	93[1]	93[1]	93[1]	Mouton
United Arab Emirates [1]									**Emirats arabes unis [1]**
Cattle	8	9	25	26	10	11	10	10	Bovine
Chicken	28	29	41	35	34	29	26	36	Poulet
Goat	24	18	17	22	16	29	15	15	Chèvre
Sheep	15	17	14	8	13	11	7	7	Mouton
Uzbekistan									**Ouzbékistan**
Cattle	404[2]	425	456	494	518	552	551[2]	586[2]	Bovine
Chicken	15[2]	10	16	17	21	23	22[2]	24[2]	Poulet
Pig	11[2]	4	11	14	16	18	18[2]	19[2]	Porc
Sheep	75[2]	71	74	70	74	84	83[2]	88[2]	Mouton
Viet Nam									**Viet Nam**
Buffalo [1]	97	99	97	101	103	103	110	106	Buffle [1]
Cattle	98	102	108	120	142	159	206	194[1]	Bovine
Chicken	308	338	373	316	322	344	359	448	Poulet
Goat [1]	5	5	6	8	9	11	11	11	Chèvre [1]
Pig	1 515	1 654	1 795	2 012[2]	2 288	2 505	2 553	2 470[1]	Porc
Yemen									**Yémen**
Cattle	56	59	70	71	73	73	82	90	Bovine
Chicken	78	83	109	111	113	118	129	136	Poulet
Goat	24[1]	24[1]	22	22	23	23	26	30	Chèvre
Sheep	25[1]	26[1]	23	23	24	24	27	29	Mouton
Europe									**Europe**
Buffalo	**1**	**2**	**2**	**3**	**6**	**1**	**4**	**3**	**Buffle**
Cattle	**11 459**	**11 644**	**11 665**	**11 544**	**11 166**	**11 090**	**11 142**	**11 028**	**Bovine**
Chicken	**9 916**	**10 331**	**10 109**	**10 420**	**10 721**	**10 784**	**11 731**	**12 006**	**Poulet**
Goat	**121**	**122**	**126**	**136**	**131**	**126**	**128**	**121**	**Chèvre**
Pig	**24 959**	**25 353**	**25 774**	**25 275**	**25 180**	**25 390**	**26 750**	**26 443**	**Porc**
Sheep	**1 273**	**1 294**	**1 262**	**1 289**	**1 287**	**1 251**	**1 247**	**1 184**	**Mouton**
Albania									**Albanie**
Cattle	35[2]	38[2]	40	40[2]	41	49	50	40[2]	Bovine
Chicken	4	6	8	9	9	10	13	16	Poulet
Goat	7	7	7	8[2]	8[2]	7	9[2]	6[2]	Chèvre
Pig	8[2]	9[2]	9[2]	10[2]	11	11	13[2]	13[2]	Porc
Sheep	12[1]	12	12	14[2]	13	14	18[2]	15[2]	Mouton
Austria									**Autriche**
Cattle	215	212	208	206	204	216	218	224	Bovine
Chicken	88	88	88	89	89	85	95	97	Poulet
Goat	1	1	1	1	1	1	1	1	Chèvre
Pig	614[2]	653[2]	663[1]	657[1]	642[1]	586[1]	613[1]	533	Porc
Sheep	7	7	7	7	7	7	6	7	Mouton
Belarus									**Bélarus**
Cattle	231	227	211	224	256	272	274	269	Bovine
Chicken	85	85	87	101	115	145	165	193	Poulet
Pig	303	301	301	299	321	346	372	376	Porc
Sheep	3	2	2	2	1	1	1	1	Mouton
Belgium									**Belgique**
Cattle	285	305	275	281	267	287	288	267	Bovine
Chicken	406	459	424	468	450[1]	484[1]	448[1]	450[1]	Poulet
Pig	1 062	1 041	1 026	1 054	1 013	1 001	1 061	1 056	Porc
Sheep	5	3	3	4	3	3	3	3[1]	Mouton
Bosnia and Herzegovina									**Bosnie-Herzégovine**
Cattle	14[1]	16[1]	18[1]	19	24	22	24	26	Bovine
Chicken	6[1]	9[1]	12[1]	16	12	14	20	29	Poulet

Meat production *(continued)*

Thousand metric tons

Production de viande *(suite)*

Milliers de tonnes

Region, country or area	2001	2002	2003	2004	2005	2006	2007	2008	Région, pays ou zone
Pig	4[2]	6[2]	7[2]	8	9	10	9	9	Porc
Sheep	1[2]	1[2]	2[2]	1	2	2	2	2	Mouton
Bulgaria									**Bulgarie**
Cattle	69[2]	24	29	31	30	23	22	20	Bovine
Chicken	110	120	60	71	80	87	98	98	Poulet
Goat	7[2]	5	7	6	7	6	6	5	Chèvre
Pig	237	62	71	78	75	75	76	72	Porc
Sheep	44[2]	47[2]	13	14	18	18	15	16	Mouton
Croatia									**Croatie**
Cattle	26	27	28	32	33	36	33	36[2]	Bovine
Chicken	26[2]	35	41[2]	39[2]	31[2]	30[2]	31[2]	31[2]	Poulet
Pig	64[2]	65[2]	62[2]	80[1]	112[2]	112[2]	128[2]	121[2]	Porc
Sheep	2	2	3	2	3[2]	3[2]	3[2]	2[2]	Mouton
Czech Republic									**République tchèque**
Cattle	109	106	104	97	81	80	79	80	Bovine
Chicken	219	207	198	201	213	207	201	195	Poulet
Pig	415	416	411	426	380	359	360	336	Porc
Sheep	1	1	1	1	1	2	2	2	Mouton
Denmark									**Danemark**
Cattle	153	154	147	150	136	129	130	129	Bovine
Chicken	199	201	188	187	183	166	172	176	Poulet
Pig	1 716	1 759	1 762	1 810	1 793	1 749	1 802	1 707	Porc
Sheep	2	1	2	2	2	2	2	2	Mouton
Estonia									**Estonie**
Cattle	14	17	13	15	13	15	15	14	Bovine
Chicken	9	12	14	15	14	12	12	13	Poulet
Pig	34	40	40	41	40	42	43	46	Porc
Sheep	^0	^0	^0	^0	^0	1	1	^0	Mouton
Faeroe Islands[1]									**Iles Féroé**[1]
Sheep	1	1	1	1	1	1	1	1	Mouton
Finland									**Finlande**
Cattle	90	91	96	93	87	87	89	82	Bovine
Chicken	76	83	84	87	87	88	95	101	Poulet
Pig	174	184	193	198	204	208	213	217	Porc
Sheep	1	1	1	1	1	1	1	1	Mouton
France									**France**
Cattle	1 566	1 640	1 632	1 566	1 517	1 473	1 532	1 518	Bovine
Chicken	1 230	1 148	1 133	1 106	921	819	921	932	Poulet
Goat	7	7	7	7	7	7	8	7	Chèvre
Pig	2 315	2 346	2 339	2 293	2 274	2 011	2 031	2 029	Porc
Sheep	134	128	129	102	99	99	97	90	Mouton
Germany									**Allemagne**
Cattle	1 362	1 316	1 226	1 258	1 167	1 193	1 186	1 210	Bovine
Chicken	476	477	549	609	605	608	688	764	Poulet
Pig	4 074	4 110	4 239	4 323	4 500	4 663	4 985	5 111	Porc
Sheep	46	44	46	48	49	24	26	25	Mouton
Greece									**Grèce**
Cattle	60	62	62	77	72	73	76	68[2]	Bovine
Chicken	114	126	160	147	159	118	116	112[2]	Poulet
Goat	43	45	47	58	57	58	56	56[2]	Chèvre
Pig	137	110	111	108	109	108	102	105[2]	Porc
Sheep	79	82	80[1]	94	92	94	93	91[2]	Mouton
Hungary									**Hongrie**
Cattle	52	48	61	46	32	34	35	32	Bovine
Chicken	279	278	267	253	246	211	196	217	Poulet
Pig	556	580	510	540	454	489	499	461	Porc
Sheep	3	3[1]	1	2	1	1	1	1	Mouton
Iceland									**Islande**
Cattle	4	4	4	4	4	3	4	4	Bovine
Chicken	4	5	6	5	6	7	8	7	Poulet
Pig	5	6	6	6	5	6	6	7	Porc
Sheep	9	9	9	9	9	9	9	9	Mouton

35 Meat production *(continued)*

Thousand metric tons

Production de viande *(suite)*

Milliers de tonnes

Region, country or area	2001	2002	2003	2004	2005	2006	2007	2008	Région, pays ou zone
Ireland									**Irlande**
Cattle	579	540	568	564	546	572	581	537	Bovine
Chicken	90[2]	89[2]	90[2]	91[2]	92[2]	90[2]	85[2]	85[1]	Poulet
Pig	241	231	217	204	205	209	205	202	Porc
Sheep	78	67	63[2]	72	73	70	66	59	Mouton
Italy									**Italie**
Buffalo	1	2	1	3	6	1	4	2	Buffle
Cattle	1 133	1 134	1 127	1 145	1 102	1 109	1 119	1 057	Bovine
Chicken	794[2]	729	683	704	695	628	733	790	Poulet
Goat	4	4	3	3	3	3	2	2	Chèvre
Pig	1 510	1 536	1 590	1 590	1 515	1 559	1 603	1 606	Porc
Sheep	62	58	58	59	59	59	59	57	Mouton
Latvia									**Lettonie**
Cattle	19	16	21	22	20	21	23	21	Bovine
Chicken	9	11	12	14	17	21	21	23	Poulet
Pig	32	36	37	37	38	38	40	41	Porc
Sheep	^0	^0	^0	^0	^0	^0	^0	1	Mouton
Lithuania									**Lituanie**
Cattle	47	45	52	58	62	47	56	48	Bovine
Chicken	30	35	39	49	57	61	63	65	Poulet
Goat	1	1	1	^0	1	^0	^0	^0	Chèvre
Pig	72	95	105	113	119	106	99	76	Porc
Sheep	^0	^0	^0	^0	^0	^0	1	1	Mouton
Luxembourg									**Luxembourg**
Cattle	11	19	17	16	17	16	16[2]	16[2]	Bovine
Chicken [1]	15	16	16	10	10	12	12	12	Poulet [1]
Pig	11	11	12	11	11	10	10	10	Porc
Malta									**Malte**
Cattle	2	2	1	1	1	1	1	1	Bovine
Chicken	6	7	7	6	5	4	5	5	Poulet
Pig	10	10	10	8	9	8	8	9	Porc
Montenegro									**Monténégro**
Cattle	...	...	...	...	...	4	5	5[1]	Bovine
Chicken [1]	...	...	...	...	...	2	2	2	Poulet [1]
Pig	...	...	...	...	...	2[2]	2[2]	2[1]	Porc
Sheep	...	...	...	...	...	1[2]	1[2]	1[1]	Mouton
Netherlands									**Pays-Bas**
Cattle	372	384	365	386	396	384	386	378	Bovine
Chicken	701	683[2]	535	615	628	621	684	693	Poulet
Goat	^0	^0	^0	^0	^0	^0[1]	1[1]	1[1]	Chèvre
Pig	1 432	1 377	1 253	1 289	1 297	1 265	1 290	1 318	Porc
Sheep	18	17	15	15	13	16	16	14	Mouton
Norway									**Norvège**
Cattle	86	85	85	87	87	88	85	86	Bovine
Chicken	42	46	43	47	50	55	63	75	Poulet
Pig	105	105	105	114	113	116	118	123	Porc
Sheep	24	25	24	26	26	25	24	24	Mouton
Poland									**Pologne**
Cattle	316	281	317	311	310	363	380	393	Bovine
Chicken	668[1]	761[1]	637	704	796	824	896	730	Poulet
Pig	1 849	2 023	2 190	1 956	1 956	2 098	2 151	1 920	Porc
Sheep	1	1	1	2	1	1	2	1	Mouton
Portugal									**Portugal**
Cattle	95	106	105	118	118	105	91	109	Bovine
Chicken	239	206	182	196	198	193	223	237	Poulet
Goat	2	2	2	2	1	2	2	1	Chèvre
Pig	317	330	329	315	327	339	364	381	Porc
Sheep	22	24	22	22	22	23	24	22[2]	Mouton
Republic of Moldova									**République de Moldova**
Cattle	16	16	16	16	16	15	15	11	Bovine
Chicken	20	21	22	24	28	31	32	30	Poulet

35 Meat production *(continued)*

Thousand metric tons

Production de viande *(suite)*

Milliers de tonnes

Region, country or area	2001	2002	2003	2004	2005	2006	2007	2008	Région, pays ou zone
Pig	44	45	43	41	40	48	59	35	Porc
Sheep	3	3	3	3	2	2	2	2	Mouton
Romania									**Roumanie**
Cattle	145	156	185	162	190	159	165	150	Bovine
Chicken	284	340	344	303	309	273	312	316	Poulet
Goat	4	3	5	6	3	3	4	4	Chèvre
Pig	460	476	533	374	436	452	470	439	Porc
Sheep	48	51	62	67	49	42	50	47	Mouton
Russian Federation									**Fédération de Russie**
Cattle	1 873	1 957	1 990	1 951	1 794	1 705	1 690	1 769	Bovine
Chicken	862	938	1 030	1 152	1 346	1 580	1 869	2 001	Poulet
Goat	20	20	19	18	18	18	18	18	Chèvre
Pig	1 498	1 583	1 706	1 643	1 520	1 641	1 873	2 042	Porc
Sheep	114	115	114	125	134	139	150	156	Mouton
Serbia									**Serbie**
Cattle	...	...	...	...	...	83	95	99	Bovine
Chicken	...	...	...	...	...	75	70	76	Poulet
Pig [2]	...	...	...	...	...	566	643	558	Porc [2]
Sheep	...	...	...	...	...	20	20	23	Mouton
Serbia and Montenegro									**Serbie-et-Monténégro**
Cattle	165[2]	166[2]	164[2]	161[2]	156	...	...	...	Bovine
Chicken	64	67	59	65	67	...	...	...	Poulet
Goat [1]	1	1	1	1	1	...	...	...	Chèvre [1]
Pig	565[2]	617[2]	574[2]	539[2]	562	...	...	...	Porc
Sheep	22	19	21	24	21	...	...	...	Mouton
Slovakia									**Slovaquie**
Cattle	38	42	33	26	26	21	23	20	Bovine
Chicken	58[1]	85[1]	85	84	87	86	83	76	Poulet
Pig	153	154	183	165	140	122	114	102	Porc
Sheep	2	2	2	1	1	1	1	1	Mouton
Slovenia									**Slovénie**
Cattle	49	43	52	47	45	39	38	37	Bovine
Chicken	48[2]	44[2]	47[2]	43	46	44	43	52	Poulet
Pig	66	62	74	71	63	61	57	55	Porc
Sheep	1	1	1	1	2	2	2	2	Mouton
Spain									**Espagne**
Cattle	651	679	706	714	715	670	620	658	Bovine
Chicken	1 009[2]	1 191	1 185	1 083	1 084	1 065	1 131	1 082	Poulet
Goat	15	15	14	13	14	12	10	9	Chèvre
Pig	2 989	3 070	3 190	3 076	3 168	3 235	3 439	3 484	Porc
Sheep	236	237	236	231	224	214	203	157	Mouton
Sweden									**Suède**
Cattle	143	147	140	143	136	137	134	129	Bovine
Chicken	96	101	98	91	96	96	105	107	Poulet
Pig	276	284	288	295	275	264	265	271	Porc
Sheep	4	4	4	4	4	4	5	5	Mouton
Switzerland									**Suisse**
Cattle	138	140	137	134	132	135	133	135	Bovine
Chicken	47	51	53	60	58	48	58	62	Poulet
Goat	^0	^0	^0	^0	1	1	1	1	Chèvre
Pig	234	236	230	227	236	244	242	231	Porc
Sheep	6	6	6	7	6	6	5	5	Mouton
TFYR of Macedonia									**L'ex-R.Y. Macédoine**
Cattle	7[2]	7	9	9	8	7	7	7	Bovine
Chicken	5	4	4	3	4	4	4	3	Poulet
Pig	8	11	10	9	9	9	9	9	Porc
Sheep	6[1]	5	6	7	7	7	6	5	Mouton
Ukraine									**Ukraine**
Cattle	646	704	723	618	562	568	546	480	Bovine
Chicken	239	300	324	375	497	589	689	794	Poulet
Goat	7	9	9	8	8	7	8	9	Chèvre

35 Meat production *(continued)*

Thousand metric tons

Production de viande *(suite)*

Milliers de tonnes

Region, country or area	2001	2002	2003	2004	2005	2006	2007	2008	Région, pays ou zone
Pig	591	599	631	559	494	526	635	590	Porc
Sheep	8	8	8	8	8	8	8	8	Mouton
United Kingdom									**Royaume-Uni**
Cattle	645	694	699	719	762	847	882	862	Bovine
Chicken	1 263	1 272	1 295	1 295	1 334	1 289	1 270	1 259	Poulet
Pig	777	774	716	708	706	697	739	740	Porc
Sheep	267	307	303	312	331	330	325	326	Mouton
Oceania									**Océanie**
Cattle	**2 731**	**2 625**	**2 754**	**2 763**	**2 835**	**2 740**	**2 879**	**2 810**	**Bovine**
Chicken	**758**	**822**	**856**	**863**	**939**	**945**	**984**	**972**	**Poulet**
Goat	**14**	**17**	**16**	**19**	**23**	**24**	**19**	**19**	**Chèvre**
Pig	**496**	**542**	**554**	**535**	**530**	**526**	**522**	**519**	**Porc**
Sheep	**1 277**	**1 165**	**1 143**	**1 079**	**1 138**	**1 168**	**1 257**	**1 292**	**Mouton**
Australia									**Australie**
Cattle	2 119	2 028	2 073	2 033	2 162	2 077	2 226	2 155	Bovine
Chicken	619	667	690	694	760	773	812	802	Poulet
Goat [1]	11	14	14	17	20	22	16	16	Chèvre [1]
Pig	365	407	419	395	391	386	382	377	Porc
Sheep	715	644	597	561	595	626	684	694	Mouton
Cook Islands [1]									**Iles Cook** [1]
Pig	1	1	1	1	1	1	1	1	Porc
Fiji									**Fidji**
Cattle [1]	9	9	8	8	8	8	8	8	Bovine [1]
Chicken	8	11	12	13	12	14	14	14	Poulet
Goat	1	1	1	1	1	1	1	1	Chèvre
Pig [1]	4	4	4	4	4	4	4	4	Porc [1]
French Polynesia [1]									**Polynésie française** [1]
Chicken	1	1	1	1	1	1	1	1	Poulet
Pig	1	1	1	1	1	1	1	1	Porc
Kiribati [1]									**Kiribati** [1]
Chicken	^0	^0	^0	^0	^0	1	1	1	Poulet
Pig	1	1	1	1	1	1	1	1	Porc
Micronesia (Fed. States of) [1]									**Micronésie (Etats féd. de)** [1]
Pig	1	1	1	1	1	1	1	1	Porc
New Caledonia									**Nouvelle-Calédonie**
Cattle	4	4	4	4	4	3	3	3	Bovine
Chicken	1	1	1	1	1	1	1	1	Poulet
Pig	1[1]	1[1]	1[1]	2	2	2	2	2	Porc
New Zealand									**Nouvelle-Zélande**
Cattle	590	576	660	709	652	643	632	635	Bovine
Chicken	121	135	144	147	157	149	147	145	Poulet
Goat	2	1	1	2	1	1	2	1	Chèvre
Pig	47	47	47	52	50	51	51	51	Porc
Sheep	562	521	546	518	543	542	573	598	Mouton
Papua New Guinea [1]									**Papouasie-Nvl-Guinée** [1]
Cattle	3	3	3	3	3	3	3	3	Bovine
Chicken	5	6	6	6	6	6	6	6	Poulet
Pig	64	68	68	68	68	68	68	68	Porc
Samoa									**Samoa**
Cattle [1]	1	1	1	1	1	1	1	1	Bovine [1]
Chicken [1]	^0	^0	^0	^0	1	1	1	1	Poulet [1]
Pig	4	4[1]	4[1]	4[1]	4[1]	4[1]	4[1]	4[1]	Porc
Solomon Islands [1]									**Iles Salomon** [1]
Cattle	1	1	1	1	1	1	1	1	Bovine
Pig	2	2	2	2	2	2	2	2	Porc
Tonga [1]									**Tonga** [1]
Pig	1	1	1	1	1	2	2	2	Porc
Vanuatu									**Vanuatu**
Cattle	3	3	3	3	3	3	3	3	Bovine
Chicken [1]	1	1	1	1	1	1	^0	^0	Poulet [1]
Pig [1]	3	3	3	3	3	3	3	3	Porc [1]

35 Meat production *(continued)*

Thousand metric tons

Production de viande *(suite)*

Milliers de tonnes

Source:
Food and Agriculture Organization of the United Nations (FAO), Rome, FAOSTAT data, last accessed August 2010.

1 FAO estimate.
2 Unofficial figure.
3 For statistical purposes, the data for China do not include those for the Hong Kong Special Administrative Region (Hong Kong SAR), Macao Special Administrative Region (Macao SAR) and Taiwan Province of China.

Source:
Organisation des Nations Unies pour l'alimentation et l'agriculture (FAO), Rome, données FAOSTAT, dernier accès août 2010.

1 Estimation de la FAO.
2 Chiffre non officiel.
3 Pour la présentation des statistiques, les données pour la Chine ne comprennent pas la Région Administrative Spéciale de Hong Kong (Hong Kong RAS), la Région Administrative Spéciale de Macao (Macao RAS) et la province de Taiwan.

36 Beer production

Thousand hectolitres and millions of US dollars

Production de bière

Milliers d'hectolitres et millions de dollars É.-U.

A. Thousand hectoliters • Milliers d'hectolitres

Country or area Pays ou zone	1998	1999	2000	2001	2002	2003	2004	2005	2006	2007
Albania Albanie	93	87	86	117	150	144	296	285	348	366
Algeria Algérie	382	383	453	435	283	166	124	...	...	...
Angola [1] Angola [1]	1 288	1 609	...	...	...	...	...	...	...	...
Argentina Argentine	12 395	12 448	12 685	12 390	11 990	12 950	13 410	13 960	14 825	15 850
Armenia Arménie	133	84	79	100	71	73	88	108	126	116
Australia [2,3] Australie [2,3]	17 570	17 380	17 680	17 450	17 440	17 270	17 360	16 850	17 141	17 067
Austria Autriche	8 837	8 884	8 725	8 528	8 745	8 980	...	...	...	...
Azerbaijan Azerbaïdjan	12	69	71	117	125	133	184	249	309	328
Barbados Barbade	87	76	69	67	68	69	80	87	89	85
Belarus Bélarus	2 604	2 728	2 371	2 174	2 026	2 056	2 272	2 715	3 322	3 556
Belgium Belgique	14 763	15 094[4]	15 509[4]	15 068[4]	15 063[4]	15 924[4]	...	...	...	...
Belize Belize	42	66	92	...	...	...	...	...	...	...
Benin [5] Bénin [5]	329	347	...	...	...	...	...	...	...	...
Bolivia (Plur. State of) Bolivie (État plur. de)	186	166	...	...	...	...	...	...	...	...
Bosnia and Herzegovina Bosnie-Herzégovine	844	975	676[6]	480[6]	652[6]	#1 316	...	...	...	...
Botswana Botswana	1 019	1 591	1 976	1 692	1 396	1 198	...	...	...	...
Brazil Brésil	66 453	62 491	87 882	91 372	79 883	76 921	86 633	92 164	100 176	100 203
Bulgaria Bulgarie	3 765	3 890	3 977	4 097	3 888	4 355	3 997	4 287	4 778	5 284
Burkina Faso [5] Burkina Faso [5]	501	516	...	...	...	...	...	...	...	...
Burundi Burundi	1 036	1 084	892	702	752	876	973	1 013	1 220	...
Cameroon Cameroun	3 370	3 373	3 340	3 740	4 196	4 597	4 287	4 439	4 035	4 192
Canada Canada	24 352	24 605	24 515	25 551	25 368	19 299	...	...	...	...
Central African Rep. [5] Rép. centrafricaine [5]	219	243	...	...	...	...	...	...	...	...
Chile Chili	3 666	3 343	3 221	3 374	3 401	3 490	...	4 754	4 518	5 501
China [7,8] Chine [7,8]	162 693	...	...	...	...	...	...	...	...	...
Colombia Colombie	16 461	14 213	...	...	...	...	...	...	...	...

36 Beer production *(continued)*

Thousand hectolitres and millions of US dollars

Production de bière *(suite)*

Milliers d'hectolitres et millions de dollars É.-U.

A. Thousand hectoliters • Milliers d'hectolitres

Country or area Pays ou zone	1998	1999	2000	2001	2002	2003	2004	2005	2006	2007
Congo Congo	494	480	526	623	661	658	674	...	...	...
Croatia Croatie	3 759	3 663	3 847	3 799	3 624	3 679	3 606	3 496	3 689	3 810
Cuba Cuba	1 759	2 009	2 136	2 197	2 331	2 313	2 221	2 255	2 298	2 504
Cyprus Chypre	365	405	409	404	383	367	371	377	374	...
Czech Republic République tchèque	18 290	17 945	17 796	17 734	17 987	18 216	18 596	18 885	20 134	18 627
Denmark Danemark	8 044	8 205	7 455	7 233	8 202	8 352	8 550	8 493	7 915	8 016
Dominica Dominique	11	8	11	9	10	...	...	...	...	...
Dominican Republic Rép. dominicaine	2 993	3 484	3 666	3 176	3 554	3 553	3 547	4 408	2 134	...
Ecuador Equateur	633	555	353	...	...	...	...	...	...	...
Egypt Egypte	...	352	261	122	...	...	...	...	...	...
Estonia Estonie	744	957	950	1 015	1 044	1 040	1 189	1 346	1 411	1 388
Ethiopia Ethiopie	831[9]	921[9]	1 111[9]	1 605[9]	1 812	2 123	...	...	...	...
Fiji Fidji	170	185	179	180	200	150	200	220	220	190
Finland Finlande	4 341	4 733	4 574	4 650	4 777	4 606	4 948	4 527	4 557	4 499
France France	16 551	16 623	18 353	18 539	17 899	17 989	17 477	17 199	...	...
Gabon Gabon	847	778	812	867	792	754	...	...	...	...
Georgia Géorgie	97	126	234	257	273	284	476	...	...	...
Germany Allemagne	106 993	107 479	106 877	106 372	102 133	98 933	97 748	94 806	96 937	94 781
Greece Grèce	4 139	4 342	4 423	4 494	4 548	4 090	3 890	...	...	...
Guatemala Guatemala	1 363	1 443	1 406	...	...	...	...	...	...	...
Guyana Guyana	137	136	130	120	131	105	121	90	90	87
Hungary Hongrie	7 163	6 996	7 194	7 142	7 237	7 255	6 467	6 770	7 157	7 186
Iceland Islande	71	77	88	123	103	108	...	...	...	...
India Inde	4 332[10]	3 632[10]	3 025	2 352	2 696	3 609	2 704	2 955	3 722	...
Indonesia Indonésie	502	401	...	437	237	...	...	...	...	...
Iran (Islamic Rep. of) Iran (Rép. islamique d')	155[11]	127[11]	145[11]	...	...	...	352	518	663	1 017
Ireland Irlande	12 584	...	...	...	...	...	...	...	...	...
Italy Italie	11 073	11 123	11 173	11 375	11 208	13 994	13 692	...	...	...

36 Beer production *(continued)*

Thousand hectolitres and millions of US dollars

Production de bière *(suite)*

Milliers d'hectolitres et millions de dollars É.-U.

A. Thousand hectoliters • Milliers d'hectolitres

Country or area Pays ou zone	1998	1999	2000	2001	2002	2003	2004	2005	2006	2007
Jamaica Jamaïque	670	656	697	784	774	585	590	633	669	660
Japan [12] Japon [12]	63 297	58 573	55 081	51 855	46 215	41 323	37 833	36 169	34 079	33 048
Kazakhstan Kazakhstan	850	824	1 357	1 732	2 020	2 348	2 780	3 235	3 638	4 110
Kenya Kenya	2 630	1 885	2 029	1 843	1 919	2 223	2 447	2 663	3 116	3 934
Korea, Republic of Corée, République de	14 080	14 866	16 544	17 765	18 224	17 863	18 033	17 489	17 400	18 200
Kyrgyzstan Kirghizistan	129	122	124	87	71	77	116	123	110	140
Lao People's Dem. Rep. Rép. dém. pop. lao	...	...	480	576	652	702	827	927	1 059	...
Latvia Lettonie	721	946	931	989	1 199	1 364	1 313	1 285	1 383	1 414
Lesotho Lesotho	...	...	349	288	333	358	325	285	295	...
Lithuania Lituanie	1 557	1 852	2 065	2 174	2 683	2 520	2 782	2 916	2 958	2 878
Luxembourg Luxembourg	469	450	438	397	386	391	...	...	...	...
Madagascar Madagascar	297	446	467	502	439	...	92	93	103	...
Malawi Malawi	678	684	739	1 033	...	...	...	...	...	...
Mali Mali	66	62	74	71	75	78	78	149	101	108
Mauritius Maurice	376	358	375	328	348	378	364	389	360	338
Mexico Mexique	54 569	57 905	59 851	61 632	63 530	65 462	67 575	72 030	78 040	80 510
Montenegro Monténégro	...	...	...	...	301	553	491	52	517	534
Mozambique Mozambique	75	95	989	982	779	1 044	1 025	1 412	...	...
Namibia Namibie	...	...	1 111	1 168	1 226	1 208	1 256	1 188	1 316	1 369
Nepal [13] Népal [13]	139	188	217	233	228	242	250	260	...	...
Netherlands Pays-Bas	23 040 [14,15]	23 799 [14,15]	24 956 [14,15]	24 605 [15]	24 774 [15]	25 699	24 546 [14,15]	23 851 [14,15]	...	...
New Zealand Nouvelle-Zélande	3 206	3 146	2 980	3 070	3 093	3 127	3 060	3 036	2 909	2 862
Niger Niger	70	69	72	68	65	...	...	...	...	...
Nigeria Nigéria	...	...	...	4 049	4 142	4 011	4 067	4 073	...	...
Norway Norvège	1 833	2 651	...	2 462	2 377	...	2 352	2 442	2 410	...
Panama Panama	1 448	1 461	1 399	...	...	...	...	...	...	...
Peru Pérou	6 557	6 168	5 706	5 296	6 170	6 483	6 733	7 970	...	...
Poland Pologne	21 017	23 360	#24 739	15 069	26 715	28 412	29 794	31 343	33 531	36 351

36 Beer production *(continued)*
Thousand hectolitres and millions of US dollars

Production de bière *(suite)*
Milliers d'hectolitres et millions de dollars É.-U.

A. Thousand hectoliters • Milliers d'hectolitres

Country or area Pays ou zone	1998	1999	2000	2001	2002	2003	2004	2005	2006	2007
Portugal Portugal	6 617	6 641	6 718	6 509	6 689	7 110	7 712	7 702	8 337	...
Puerto Rico Porto Rico	263	259	...	...	...	...	...	...	...	...
Republic of Moldova [16] République de Moldova [16]	278	202	249	318	438	566	653	724	...	...
Romania Roumanie	9 989	11 133	12 664	12 087	11 513	13 087	14 159	14 713	17 554	18 865
Russian Federation Fédération de Russie	33 631	44 484	51 563	63 780	70 266	75 540	83 787	90 986	100 051	114 722
Saint Kitts and Nevis Saint-Kitts-et-Nevis	20	20	20	20	20	...	...	...	...	...
Serbia Serbie	...	...	...	...	...	...	...	6 569	6 451	6 547
Serbia and Montenegro Serbie-et-Monténégro	6 630	#6 786	6 734	6 063	5 764	6 049	...	...	...	...
Seychelles Seychelles	72	68	70	72	76	65	63	63	67	75
Sierra Leone Sierra Leone	489	...	382	983	1 116	924	942	1 012	1 101	...
Slovakia Slovaquie	4 478	4 473	4 491	4 216	4 747	4 684	3 877	3 810	3 987	3 557
Slovenia Slovénie	1 976	2 084	2 463	2 449	...	...	...	...	...	...
Spain Espagne	22 428	26 007	26 388	26 802	28 631	31 028	31 467	31 156	34 032	33 502
Sri Lanka Sri Lanka	...	...	...	...	...	...	...	...	0	...
Sweden Suède	4 763	4 718	4 686	4 522	4 527	4 255	3 870	3 952	4 381	4 447
Syrian Arab Republic Rép. arabe syrienne	97	121	91	100	104	100	109	111	107	...
Tajikistan Tadjikistan	9	7	4	8	9	9	11	13	16	16
Thailand Thaïlande	9 770	10 420	11 650	12 380	12 750	16 020	16 320	16 950	20 110	21 610
TFYR of Macedonia L'ex-R.Y. Macédoine	578	652	661	618	657	680	716	695	670	695
Togo Togo	...	...	...	...	...	...	313	325	345	...
Trinidad and Tobago Trinité-et-Tobago	517	522	625	...	...	...	...	...	...	...
Tunisia Tunisie	813	912	1 066	1 087	1 100	997	...	...	...	...
Turkey Turquie	7 130	7 188	7 649	7 441	7 845	8 363	8 812	8 936	9 059	...
Turkmenistan Turkménistan	29	37	52	79	84	...	...	...	...	...
Uganda Ouganda	1 105	1 178	1 261	1 079	989	826	1 149	1 359	1 616	...
Ukraine Ukraine	6 842	8 407	10 765	13 059	15 000	17 012	19 373	23 805	26 750	31 579
United Kingdom Royaume-Uni	60 915	62 510	54 206	57 032	60 646	64 253	73 622	...	...	...
United Rep. of Tanzania [17] Rép.-Unie de Tanzanie [17]	1 707	1 674	1 830	1 756	1 759	1 941	2 026	2 166	2 990	3 102

36

Beer production *(continued)*

Thousand hectolitres and millions of US dollars

Production de bière *(suite)*

Milliers d'hectolitres et millions de dollars É.-U.

A. Thousand hectoliters • Milliers d'hectolitres

Country or area Pays ou zone	1998	1999	2000	2001	2002	2003	2004	2005	2006	2007
Uruguay Uruguay	860	741	706	629	507	415	...	...	...	...
Uzbekistan [18] Ouzbékistan [18]	569	422	609	...	...	...	...	...	...	...
Viet Nam Viet Nam	6 700	6 898	7 791	8 712	9 398	11 189	13 428	14 606	15 472	16 553
Zimbabwe Zimbabwe	...	...	...	4 747	2 957	...	...	...	...	...

Source:
United Nations Statistics Division, New York, the *Industrial Commodity Statistics Yearbook 2007* and the industrial statistics database, last accessed February 2010.

1 Source: Economist Intelligence Unit (London).
2 Twelve months ending 30 June of the year stated.
3 Excluding light beer containing less than 1.15% by volume of alcohol.
4 Incomplete coverage.
5 Source: Afristat: Sub-Saharan African Observatory of Economics and Statistics (Bamako, Mali).
6 Excluding the Federation of Bosnia and Herzegovina.
7 For statistical purposes, the data for China do not include those for the Hong Kong Special Administrative Region (Hong Kong SAR), Macao Special Administrative Region (Macao SAR) and Taiwan Province of China.
8 Original data in metric tons.
9 Twelve months ending 7 July of the year stated.
10 Production by large- and medium-scale establishments only.
11 Production by establishments employing 10 or more persons.
12 Twelve months beginning 1 April of the year stated.
13 Twelve months beginning 16 July of the year stated.
14 Production by establishments employing 20 or more persons.
15 Sales.
16 Excluding the Transnistria region.
17 Tanganyika only.
18 Source: Statistical Yearbook for Asia and the Pacific, United Nations Economic and Social Commission for Asia and the Pacific (Bangkok).

Source:
Organisation des Nations Unies, Division de statistique, New York, *l'Annuaire de statistiques industrielles par produit 2007* et la base de données pour les statistiques industrielles, dernier accès février 2010.

1 Source: Economist Intelligence Unit (London).
2 Période de 12 mois finissant le 30 juin de l'année indiquée.
3 Non compris la bière légère contenant moins de 1.15 p. 100 en volume d'alcool.
4 Couverture incomplète.
5 Source : Afristat : Observatoire Economique et Statistique d'Afrique Subsaharienne (Bamako, Mali).
6 Non compris la Fédération de Bosnie et Herzégovine.
7 Pour la présentation des statistiques, les données pour la Chine ne comprennent pas la Région Administrative Spéciale de Hong Kong (Hong Kong RAS), la Région Administrative Spéciale de Macao (Macao RAS) et la province de Taiwan.
8 Données d'origine exprimées en tonnes.
9 Période de 12 mois finissant le 7 juillet de l'année indiquée.
10 Production des grandes et moyennes entreprises seulement.
11 Production des établissements employant 10 personnes ou plus.
12 Période de 12 mois commençant le 1er avril de l'année indiquée.
13 Période de 12 mois commençant le 16 juillet de l'année indiquée.
14 Production des établissements employant 20 personnes ou plus.
15 Ventes.
16 Non compris la région de Transnistrie.
17 Tanganyika seulement.
18 Source : Annuaire des Statistiques de l'Asie et Pacifique, Commission économique et sociale des Nations Unies pour l'Asie et le Pacifique (Bangkok).

36 Beer production

Thousand hectolitres and millions of US dollars

Production de bière

Milliers d'hectolitres et millions de dollars É.-U.

B. Millions of US dollars • Millions de dollars É.-U.

Country or area Pays ou zone	1998	1999	2000	2001	2002	2003	2004	2005	2006	2007
Albania Albanie	...	...	...	...	...	...	25.6	23.9	29.7	34.7
Azerbaijan Azerbaïdjan	...	...	3.1	6.3	6.1	6.7	10.4	16.4	21.2	29.4
Bolivia (Plur. State of) Bolivie (État plur. de)	143.0	123.2	...	...	...	...	...	...	...	...
Brazil Brésil	...	...	3 008.5	2 565.6	2 468.9	2 565.9	3 008.9	4 100.4	5 177.7	6 720.6
Bulgaria Bulgarie	83.5	99.9	90.9	92.9	96.3	116.0	133.3	148.7	178.3	241.7
Burkina Faso[1] Burkina Faso[1]	0.0	0.0	...	...	...	...	...	...	...	...
Canada Canada	2 355.2	...	...	...	2 499.6	2 739.2	...	...	...	...
Chile Chili	...	...	...	...	...	...	...	330.0	410.8	470.5
Congo Congo	46.9	43.8	41.4	46.7	59.2	67.2	74.6	...	...	...
Cyprus Chypre	...	...	...	...	40.9	46.4	51.2	49.6	52.3	...
Czech Republic République tchèque	...	...	...	496.2	603.9	771.8	905.4	1 018.0	1 136.4	1 328.4
Denmark Danemark	691.2	673.1	565.6	523.1	616.6	836.9	927.7	901.7	879.8	1 017.3
Dominican Republic Rép. dominicaine	389.8	432.5	465.7	439.1	453.7	326.1	...	...	...	...
Egypt Egypte	...	29.1	21.1	8.6	...	...	...	...	...	...
El Salvador El Salvador	59.2	...	...	...	...	...	...	...	...	...
Estonia Estonie	...	...	...	...	...	...	60.4	75.4	84.2	100.6
Finland Finlande	342.7	332.4	274.6	280.1	312.5	360.0	399.8	344.5	366.3	415.1
France France	...	...	1 544.1	1 560.6	1 647.9	2 074.4	2 170.4	2 183.8	...	...
Germany Allemagne	7 873.6	7 625.9	6 420.8	6 270.3	6 519.7	7 728.0	8 087.8	7 746.0	7 867.8	8 236.2
Greece Grèce	381.8	392.3	327.7	326.2	385.6	452.7	451.5	...	...	...
Hungary Hongrie	...	...	...	...	448.0	550.0	531.7	560.2	641.4	835.8
India Inde	...	...	...	...	...	241.0	270.1	324.0	...	...
Ireland Irlande	1 364.2	...	...	...	...	...	...	...	...	...
Italy Italie	...	...	...	...	...	1 582.5	1 753.6	...	...	...
Jordan Jordanie	...	...	...	...	...	...	17.3	19.0	19.4	20.2
Kenya Kenya	49.3	53.4	53.1	131.0	130.7	235.4	183.3	286.0	351.9	506.2

36

Beer production *(continued)*
Thousand hectolitres and millions of US dollars

Production de bière *(suite)*
Milliers d'hectolitres et millions de dollars É.-U.

B. Millions of US dollars • Millions de dollars É.-U.

Country or area Pays ou zone	1998	1999	2000	2001	2002	2003	2004	2005	2006	2007
Latvia Lettonie	...	52.5	49.2	47.0	56.7	...	...	68.6	77.4	97.4
Lithuania Lituanie	76.5	91.5	97.0	103.1	142.6	153.5	161.7	180.6	192.8	250.9
Madagascar Madagascar	...	...	...	...	...	...	5.2	...	...	...
Mexico Mexique	2 568.3	2 983.1	3 541.5	3 912.8	4 173.5	3 843.5	4 059.5	4 499.7	5 227.2	5 309.6
Mozambique Mozambique	...	...	...	...	...	534.9	693.0	934.4	...	...
Nepal Népal	...	...	...	31.5	...	...	...	...	...	34.9
Nigeria Nigéria	51.3	45.1	41.1	37.4	34.6	32.3	31.4	31.7	...	...
Norway Norvège	...	...	...	...	309.4	344.8	301.9	327.5	342.9	...
Peru Pérou	619.8	533.8	492.3	517.6	566.8	596.5	622.0	764.9	...	...
Poland Pologne	...	...	1 477.4	1 645.9	1 778.7	1 999.6	1 852.9	2 613.8	2 971.2	3 731.8
Portugal Portugal	467.3	425.0	399.1	404.9	319.7	404.2	475.6	522.3	536.9	...
Romania Roumanie	...	...	...	...	36.7	49.2	59.5	63.4	80.8	128.4
Slovakia Slovaquie	...	...	...	98.0	125.4	157.6	168.9	152.8	160.8	192.8
Slovenia Slovénie	153.5	136.7	127.8	126.4	...	...	...	...	...	...
Spain Espagne	...	...	...	...	...	...	3 188.6	3 428.6	3 531.4	4 396.2
Sri Lanka Sri Lanka	...	...	...	...	...	...	...	...	0.0	...
Sweden Suède	433.3	411.0	365.1	328.7	349.5	419.1	405.5	401.3	435.5	488.7
United Kingdom Royaume-Uni	7 770.0	7 485.9	5 242.6	5 194.1	5 513.4	6 117.5	7 677.5	...	...	...
United Rep. of Tanzania [2] Rép.-Unie de Tanzanie [2]	...	...	...	...	...	...	...	201.2	220.1	253.1
Uruguay Uruguay	74.6	64.4	63.8	54.4	...	30.6	...	...	...	...

Source:
United Nations Statistics Division, New York, the *Industrial Commodity Statistics Yearbook 2007* and the industrial statistics database, last accessed February 2010.

Source:
Organisation des Nations Unies, Division de statistique, New York, *l'Annuaire de statistiques industrielles par produit 2007* et la base de données pour les statistiques industrielles, dernier accès février 2010.

1 Source: Afristat: Sub-Saharan African Observatory of Economics and Statistics (Bamako, Mali).
2 Tanganyika only.

1 Source : Afristat : Observatoire Economique et Statistique d'Afrique Subsaharienne (Bamako, Mali).
2 Tanganyika seulement.

37 Cigarette production

Millions of cigarettes and millions of US dollars

Production de cigarettes

Millions de cigarettes et millions de dollars É.-U.

A. Millions of cigarettes • Millions de cigarettes

Country or area Pays ou zone	1998	1999	2000	2001	2002	2003	2004	2005	2006	2007
Albania Albanie	764[1]	647[1]	372[1]	126[1]	50	15	...	...	...	...
Andorra Andorre	1	1	1	1	1	2	2	3	1	...
Argentina Argentine	1 967	1 996	1 843	1 740	1 812	1 990	1 890	1 862	1 993	2 057
Armenia Arménie	2 489	3 132	2 109	1 623	2 815	3 222	2 720	3 020	2 825	2 911
Azerbaijan Azerbaïdjan	241	416	2 363	6 808	6 296	6 611	3 671	5 008	6 224	3 789
Bangladesh[2] Bangladesh[2]	19 889	19 558	19 732	20 120	20 384	22 499	...	...	...	...
Belarus Bélarus	7 296	9 259	10 356	11 182	10 524	10 442	12 627	12 008	15 650	18 699
Belgium Belgique	17 519	14 713[3]	...	...	...	...	...	...	...	...
Belize Belize	94	91	84	...	...	...	...	...	...	...
Bolivia Bolivie	1 538	1 404	...	...	...	...	...	...	...	...
Bosnia and Herzegovina Bosnie-Herzégovine	4 830	5 974	...	...	...	5 062	...	...	...	...
Brazil Brésil	...	...	17 860	15 820	100 193	21 099	96 828	120 167	120 574	88 214
Bulgaria Bulgarie	33 181	25 715	26 681	26 659	23 227	25 914	24 462	23 318	17 353	20 763
Burundi Burundi	317	353	286	293	312	354	376	419	410	...
Cameroon Cameroun	3 084	3 249	2 984	2 814	2 785	1 903	1 966	1 755	1 597	248
Canada Canada	48 854	47 224	46 068	44 403	37 127	...	...	...	...	...
Chile Chili	12 904	13 271	13 796	13 305	13 839	13 776	...	16 429	18 073	18 654
China[4] Chine[4]	34	33	34	34	35	36	...	...	...	...
China, Hong Kong SAR Chine, Hong Kong RAS	13 470	...	...	...	...	...	...	...	...	...
Colombia Colombie	12 472	15 182	...	...	...	...	...	...	...	...
Congo Congo	...	...	...	102	662	748	750	...	...	...
Croatia Croatie	11 987	12 785	13 692	14 738	15 047	15 613	14 256	14 578	14 457	14 415
Cuba Cuba	11 655	13 432	12 086	11 769	12 519	14 300	12 766	14 022	13 151	13 766
Cyprus Chypre	4 362	4 783	4 980	3 803	2 534	2 661	3 845	...	...	...
Denmark Danemark	12 392	11 749	11 413	11 089	12 039	12 898	13 458	14 867	14 553	15 274
Dominican Republic Rép. dominicaine	4 098	4 005	3 898	3 338	3 509	3 469	3 446	3 300	1 416	...

37 Cigarette production *(continued)*
Millions of cigarettes and millions of US dollars

Production de cigarettes *(suite)*
Millions de cigarettes et millions de dollars É.-U.

A. Millions of cigarettes • Millions de cigarettes

Country or area Pays ou zone	1998	1999	2000	2001	2002	2003	2004	2005	2006	2007
Ecuador Equateur	1 997	2 178	2 773	...	...	2 975	...	...	...	...
Egypt Egypte	52 000	52 336	56 614	61 000	62 018	63 396	63 395	55 468	55 123	...
Ethiopia Ethiopie	2 029[5]	1 829[5]	1 931[5]	1 904[5]	1 511	1 511	...	...	...	...
Fiji Fidji	410	446	396	389	422	416	454	420	457	456
Finland Finlande	4 062	4 877	3 981	3 999	4 130	3 946	868	...	...	...
France France	43 304	42 405	42 058	42 980	42 500	42 700	48 163	46 500	...	...
Gabon Gabon	463	670	859	880	860	...	...	...	...	...
Georgia Géorgie	601	132	296	1 615	1 894	2 972	2 808	...	...	...
Germany Allemagne	181 904	204 631	206 770	213 793	212 500	205 237	208 347	212 428	216 042	214 458
Ghana Ghana	1 399	1 158	1 166	1 481	1 800	...	...	...	...	...
Greece Grèce	31 705	31 535	34 256	25 516	28 091	26 249	28 048	...	...	...
Guatemala Guatemala	4 184	4 376	4 262	...	...	...	...	...	...	...
Honduras Honduras	3 814	4 586	5 655	5 984	6 010	...	...	...	...	...
Hungary Hongrie	26 849	22 985	21 608	20 787	21 748	20 181	12 119	...	...	...
India Inde	79 313[6]	82 504[6]	82 504[6]	60 577[7]	54 991[7]	49 769	54 748	75 711	85 747	...
Iran (Islamic Rep. of) Iran (Rép. islamique d')	14 335	20 081	13 800	13 363	12 700	12 200	13 930	14 270	14 200	17 387
Iraq Iraq	...	...	...	...	...	...	812	...	68	...
Ireland Irlande	6 452	6 176	6 461	6 807	6 599	...	...	...	...	...
Italy Italie	50 785	45 159	43 694[1]	45 368[1]	37 342	40 350	...	...	...	...
Jamaica Jamaïque	1 160	1 073	995	1 027	1 049	889	979	889	...	...
Japan[8] Japon[8]	336 600	332 200	324 500	313 900	...	...	...	...	...	...
Jordan[9] Jordanie[9]	1 144	*1 602	*1 300	...	...	...	...	...	...	...
Kazakhstan Kazakhstan	21 747	18 773	19 293	21 395	23 453	25 715	28 038	30 008	30 834	31 507
Kenya Kenya	7 599	7 231	6 009	5 850	4 631	4 753	5 351	7 324	10 262	12 204
Korea, Republic of Corée, République de	101 011	95 995	94 531	94 116	94 433	123 166	133 206	107 247	119 966	124 570
Kyrgyzstan Kirghizistan	862	2 103	3 169	3 013	2 927	3 102	3 170	3 179	3 086	3 053
Lao People's Dem. Rep. Rép. dém. pop. lao	1 104[8]	...	41	41	55	68	84	105	...	...
Latvia Lettonie	2 018	1 909	...	...	...	...	...	...	...	...

37 Cigarette production *(continued)*

Millions of cigarettes and millions of US dollars

Production de cigarettes *(suite)*

Millions de cigarettes et millions de dollars É.-U.

A. Millions of cigarettes • Millions de cigarettes

Country or area Pays ou zone	1998	1999	2000	2001	2002	2003	2004	2005	2006	2007
Lebanon [1] Liban [1]	672	945	1 009	...	...	...	...	...	...	...
Lithuania Lituanie	7 427	8 217	7 207	...	...	...	...	...	...	...
Madagascar Madagascar	3 303	...	...	...	...	...	8	8	8	...
Malawi Malawi	501	...	...	...	...	...	...	...	...	...
Malaysia Malaisie	15 504	27 271	25 618	23 079	23 971	24 669	23 340	22 798	23 723	23 004
Mali Mali	473	350	231	106	90	198	328	330	626	547
Mauritius Maurice	1 034	979	1 049	928	928	938	918	764	726	620
Mexico Mexique	44 917	45 373	44 400	44 904	43 834	41 856	40 752	41 439	44 295	39 763
Montenegro Monténégro	...	...	...	...	1 141	793	2 000	1 282	433	463
Mozambique Mozambique	950	1 084	1 417	1 359	1 255	1 390	...	...	...	...
Myanmar Myanmar	2 116	2 009	2 502	2 521	2 351	2 835	2 807	3 199	2 822	2 755
Nepal Népal	8 127[10]	7 315[10]	6 584[10]	6 979[10]	6 900[10]	6 812[10]	7 268[10]	...	...	6 081
New Zealand Nouvelle-Zélande	3 086	2 949	2 916	2 396	2 509	2 176	2 122	2 211	1 253	343
Nicaragua Nicaragua	1 789	780[11]	...	...	...	...	...	...	...	...
Nigeria Nigéria	...	...	...	1 798	1 854	1 776	1 809	1 813	...	...
Pakistan [2] Pakistan [2]	48	52	47	58	55	49	55	61	64	66
Panama Panama	284	...	...	...	...	...	...	...	...	...
Peru Pérou	3 115	3 581	3 605	3 310	3 766	2 707	2 168	1 460	...	...
Poland Pologne	96 741	95 056	#78 792	82 421	78 746	78 792	83 376	95 531	106 641	112 300
Portugal Portugal	15 889	18 189	20 561	23 376	25 581	24 950	26 415	27 013	26 608	...
Republic of Moldova [12] République de Moldova [12]	7 512	8 731	9 262	9 421	6 310	7 126	7 050	6 195	5 031	...
Romania Roumanie	...	...	...	...	38 033	37 808	28 677	34 541	31 881	37 831
Russian Federation Fédération de Russie	196 000	266 000	334 000	356 000	383 000	376 000	377 000	402 000	409 697	397 498
Serbia Serbie	...	...	...	...	...	...	...	18 127	18 267	21 304
Serbia and Montenegro Serbie-et-Monténégro	14 597	#13 126	14 451	13 968	15 388	...	...	...	...	...
Seychelles Seychelles	61	60	40	36	24	50	22	30	19	33
Spain Espagne	81 940	74 873	74 799	...	...	...	48 651	47 506	39 798	41 906
Sri Lanka Sri Lanka	5 797	5 333	4 889	*4 973	5 015[13]	4 765[13]	5 003[13]	...	...	...

37 Cigarette production *(continued)*

Millions of cigarettes and millions of US dollars

Production de cigarettes *(suite)*

Millions de cigarettes et millions de dollars É.-U.

A. Millions of cigarettes • Millions de cigarettes

Country or area Pays ou zone	1998	1999	2000	2001	2002	2003	2004	2005	2006	2007
Sweden Suède	5 692	6 060	5 958	5 959	...	...	...	...	...	...
Switzerland Suisse	34 453	32 139	34 299	33 565	37 160	38 140	39 059	42 190	48 937	54 348
Syrian Arab Republic [1] Rép. arabe syrienne [1]	10 398	10 991	11 097	12 007	12 863	13 412	...	...	...	...
Tajikistan Tadjikistan	191	209	667	1 155	585	468	508	714	497	616
Thailand Thaïlande	34 585	31 146	30 732	29 807	30 772	31 908	34 761	32 978	28 588	30 748
TFYR of Macedonia L'ex-R.Y. Macédoine	...	...	...	7 766	6 567	5 120	5 654	5 763	5 123	5 485
Trinidad and Tobago Trinité-et-Tobago	1 680	1 945	2 050	...	...	...	...	...	...	...
Tunisia Tunisie	9 813	11 066	12 231	12 354	13 230	13 227	...	...	...	...
Turkey Turquie	81 616[1]	75 135[1]	76 613[1]	77 160	131 561	111 881	103 371	104 170	128 278	...
Uganda Ouganda	1 866	1 602	1 344	1 220	1 092	...	...	...	...	...
Ukraine Ukraine	59 275	54 052	58 774	69 731	81 088	96 776	108 946	120 218	120 333	128 535
United Kingdom Royaume-Uni	152 998	143 794	139 125	109 025	124 896	89 639	85 691	...	...	...
United Rep. of Tanzania [14] Rép.-Unie de Tanzanie [14]	4 012	3 371	3 745	3 491	3 778	3 920	4 308	4 445	5 095	5 821
United States Etats-Unis	679 700	611 929	...	...	...	...	...	...	...	...
Uruguay Uruguay	10 187	11 161	10 894	9 616	8 449	5 718	...	...	...	...
Uzbekistan [8] Ouzbékistan [8]	7 582	10 668	7 766	...	...	...	...	...	...	...
Viet Nam Viet Nam	2 196	2 147	2 836	3 075	3 375	3 871	4 192	4 485	3 941	4 549
Yemen Yémen	5 980	5 760	4 780	6 020	5 780	5 960	...	...	...	...
Zimbabwe Zimbabwe	...	...	2 196	2 079	...	1 604	...	...	...	...

Source:
United Nations Statistics Division, New York, the industrial statistics database, last accessed April 2010.

Source:
Organisation des Nations Unies, Division de statistique, New York, et la base de données sur les statistiques industrielles, dernier accès avril 2010.

1 Original data in units of weight. Computed on the basis of one million cigarettes per ton.
2 Twelve months ending 30 June of the year stated.
3 Incomplete coverage.
4 For statistical purposes, the data for China do not include those for the Hong Kong Special Administrative Region (Hong Kong SAR), Macao Special Administrative Region (Macao SAR) and Taiwan Province of China.
5 Twelve months ending 7 July of the year stated.
6 Production by large- and medium-scale establishments only.
7 Production by establishments employing 50 or more persons.
8 Source: Statistical Yearbook for Asia and the Pacific, United Nations Economic and Social Commission for Asia and the Pacific (Bangkok).

1 Données d'origine exprimées en poids. Calcul sur la base d'un million de cigarettes par tonne.
2 Période de 12 mois finissant le 30 juin de l'année indiquée.
3 Couverture incomplète.
4 Pour la présentation des statistiques, les données pour la Chine ne comprennent pas la Région Administrative Spéciale de Hong Kong (Hong Kong RAS), la Région Administrative Spéciale de Macao (Macao RAS) et la province de Taiwan.
5 Période de 12 mois finissant le 7 juillet de l'année indiquée.
6 Production des grandes et moyennes entreprises seulement.
7 Production des établissements occupant 50 personnes ou plus.
8 Source : Annuaire des Statistiques de l'Asie et Pacifique, Commission économique et sociale des Nations Unies pour l'Asie et le Pacifique (Bangkok).

9 Source: "Bulletin of Industrial Statistics for the Arab Countries", United Nations Economic and Social Commission for Western Asia (Beirut).
10 Twelve months beginning 16 July of the year stated.
11 Beginning August 1999, national production discontinued.
12 Excluding the Transnistria region.
13 Source: "Country Economic Review", Asian Development Bank (Manila).
14 Tanganyika only.

9 Source: "Bulletin of Industrial Statistics for the Arab Countries", Commission économique et sociale pour l'Asie occidentale (Beyrouth).
10 Période de 12 mois commençant le 16 juillet de l'année indiquée.
11 A partir d'août 1999, la production nationale a été discontinuée.
12 Non compris la région de Transnistrie.
13 Source: "La Revue Economique du Pays", La Banque de Développement Asiatique (Manille).
14 Tanganyika seulement.

37 Cigarette production

Millions of cigarettes and millions of US dollars

Production de cigarettes

Millions de cigarettes et millions de dollars É.-U.

B. Millions of US dollars • Millions de dollars É.-U.

Country or area Pays ou zone	1998	1999	2000	2001	2002	2003	2004	2005	2006	2007
Azerbaijan Azerbaïdjan	...	...	2	48	28	28	25	30	37	26
Bolivia (Plurinational State of) Bolivie (État plurinational de)	15	15	...	...	...	...	...	...	...	...
Brazil Brésil	...	...	617	543	418	70	122	269	282	299
Bulgaria Bulgarie	208	171	162	164	157	208	230	247	175	228
Canada Canada	1 752	1 588	1 623	1 615	1 630	...	...	...	...	...
Chile Chili	...	...	...	...	...	...	...	199	245	273
China, Hong Kong SAR Chine, Hong Kong RAS	205	...	...	...	...	...	...	...	...	...
Congo Congo	0	0	0	2	14	18	22	...	...	...
Cyprus Chypre	...	...	104	108	106	132	171	159	41	...
Denmark Danemark	344	327	289	297	334	397	420	420	466	521
Dominican Republic Rép. dominicaine	206	212	220	204	205	143	...	...	...	...
Egypt Egypte	...	496	517	490	493	444	419	485	486	...
Finland Finlande	90	92	76	78	84	95	22	0	0	0
France France	...	...	757	771	843	991	1 033	1 045	...	...
Germany Allemagne	3 890	4 284	3 815	3 673	3 767	3 855	4 425	4 486	4 552	4 914
Greece Grèce	420	417	390	287	296	376	425	...	...	...
Hungary Hongrie	...	...	...	...	854	1 190	1 012	...	...	...
India Inde	...	...	...	...	...	971	1 072	1 101	...	...
Ireland Irlande	207	210	198	208	223	232	...	...	...	...
Jamaica Jamaïque	...	...	...	...	...	52	56	45	...	...
Jordan Jordanie	...	...	...	...	...	...	341	344	398	417
Kenya Kenya	70	59	19	47	34	42	20	33	46	70
Latvia Lettonie	...	14	...	...	...	...	...	...	...	...
Madagascar Madagascar	...	...	...	...	...	...	1	...	...	...
Mexico Mexique	1 057	1 255	1 385	1 610	1 742	1 645	1 665	1 993	2 210	2 340
Mozambique Mozambique	...	...	...	...	...	11	12	22	30	30

Cigarette production *(continued)*

Millions of cigarettes and millions of US dollars

Production de cigarettes *(suite)*

Millions de cigarettes et millions de dollars É.-U.

B. Millions of US dollars • Millions de dollars É.-U.

Country or area Pays ou zone	1998	1999	2000	2001	2002	2003	2004	2005	2006	2007
Nepal Népal	...	...	...	70	...	...	...	...	...	149
Nigeria Nigéria	...	...	...	2	1	1	1	1	...	...
Peru Pérou	49	63	74	69	80	68	53	37	...	...
Poland Pologne	...	...	2 108	2 476	2 695	689	1 969	4 041	4 325	5 462
Portugal Portugal	207	245	237	280	350	422	488	497	522	...
Romania Roumanie	...	...	...	...	50	67	80	55	105	132
Spain Espagne	...	...	...	...	...	...	1 132	1 038	640	799
Sweden Suède	117	123	97	87	...	...	...	0	0	0
United Kingdom Royaume-Uni	3 590	3 427	3 018	2 161	2 270	2 487	2 758	...	...	...
United Rep. of Tanzania [1] Rép.-Unie de Tanzanie [1]	1	1	^0	^0	...	...	...	...	...	...
Uruguay Uruguay	251	256	247	232	...	118	...	...	...	...

Source:
United Nations Statistics Division, New York, the industrial statistics database, last accessed April 2010.

1 Zanzibar.

Source:
Organisation des Nations Unies, Division de statistique, New York, et la base de données sur les statistiques industrielles, dernier accès avril 2010.

1 Zanzibar.

38 Production of footwear with uppers of leather

Thousand pairs and millions of US dollars

Production de chaussures à dessus en cuir naturel

Milliers de paires et millions de dollars É.-U.

A. Thousand pairs • Milliers de paires

Country or area Pays ou zone	1998	1999	2000	2001	2002	2003	2004	2005	2006	2007
Armenia Arménie	...	31	63	51	36	23	23	22	30	33
Azerbaijan Azerbaïdjan	...	...	114	218	339	456	288	261	311	302
Belarus Bélarus	12 533	12 449	12 455	11 275	9 346	8 635	9 020	8 821	9 487	9 811
Bolivia (Plur. State of) Bolivie (État plur. de)	175	251	...	...	...	...	...	...	...	...
Botswana Botswana	...	...	...	367 552	...	...	...	...	...	...
Brazil Brésil	...	...	205 040	212 569	197 153	190 027	210 046	216 116	208 863	206 604
Bulgaria Bulgarie	3 713	2 562	2 492	2 507	3 542	4 556	3 203	3 003	2 889	3 045
Chile Chili	...	...	...	...	...	...	...	5 178	3 791	3 628
China [1] Chine [1]	1 205 617	1 013 751	1 468 379	1 335 864	1 522 824	1 816 469	2 743 931	2 525 475	3 003 002	3 229 021
China, Hong Kong SAR Chine, Hong Kong RAS	178	200	381	542	523	572	504	...	...	...
China, Macao SAR Chine, Macao RAS	881	...	...	4 254	4 640	6 679	...	...	...	...
Croatia Croatie	...	...	...	...	...	...	4 312	3 914	3 805	4 026
Cuba Cuba	2 666	2 918	2 526	2 765	1 665	971	1 300	1 051	457	222
Cyprus Chypre	...	...	...	...	548	313	194	193	205	...
Czech Republic République tchèque	6 455	4 922	3 398	2 937	1 776	1 202	1 074	963	1 154	1 186
Denmark Danemark	9 784	9 673	9 590	1 584	1 811	1 738	1 781	1 897	1 887	1 824
El Salvador El Salvador	1 152	...	...	...	...	...	...	...	...	...
Estonia Estonie	...	...	...	...	...	...	1 124	778	879	908
Finland Finlande	2 569	2 294	1 895	1 866	1 877	1 698	1 651	1 584	1 171	969
Georgia Géorgie	...	...	17	7	^0	3	12	...	...	...
Germany Allemagne	22 203	20 675	17 501	16 129	21 183	17 418	19 294	18 648	14 733	15 725
Greece [2] Grèce [2]	4 836	...	...	...	...	...	...	...	...	...
Hungary Hongrie	...	...	...	...	3 347	3 739	2 999	2 098	1 555	4 955
Iran (Islamic Rep. of) Iran (Rép. islamique d')	...	...	...	...	...	...	5 004	7 076	9 217	6 497
Iraq Iraq	...	...	...	...	...	...	164	...	118	...

38 Production of footwear with uppers of leather *(continued)*

Thousand pairs and millions of US dollars

Production de chaussures à dessus en cuir naturel *(suite)*

Milliers de paires et millions de dollars É.-U.

A. Thousand pairs • Milliers de paires

Country or area Pays ou zone	1998	1999	2000	2001	2002	2003	2004	2005	2006	2007
Ireland Irlande	359	370	286	270	239	32	41	...	...	...
Italy Italie	...	...	...	...	...	205 316	218 417	...	...	...
Japan Japon	58 656	54 768	50 806	45 841	40 860	37 024	37 516	36 632	32 472	32 983
Kazakhstan Kazakhstan	116	59	127	264	218	206	210	367	314	508
Kenya Kenya	828	3 783	4 342	3 842	4 416	7 949	7 915	12 455	15 869	13 104
Kuwait Koweït	...	...	...	...	51	91	94	100	205	...
Kyrgyzstan Kirghizistan	59	63	56	30	24	6	8	6	7	...
Latvia Lettonie	...	382	305	285	...	...	...	...	...	...
Lesotho Lesotho	...	...	6 477	7 158	6 476	6 032	5 395	2 165	2 176	...
Lithuania Lituanie	785	1 056	609	848	781	566	680	402	300	309
Mexico Mexique	23 591	23 909	24 292	22 094	21 846	21 535	22 442	22 856	24 791	22 707
Montenegro Monténégro	...	...	...	...	327	241	12	...	...	...
Mozambique Mozambique	...	...	...	...	...	12	22	34	38	36
Nepal Népal	...	...	...	...	...	...	...	...	...	26
Nigeria Nigéria	...	...	...	1 779	1 798	1 770	1 782	1 783	...	...
Norway Norvège	...	...	...	...	...	33	...	...	...	...
Poland Pologne	...	...	...	...	12 933	12 439	10 898	10 877	11 993	12 919
Portugal Portugal	61 912	70 153	69 303	71 431	68 366	62 121	58 167	53 157	51 234	...
Republic of Moldova [3] République de Moldova [3]	...	...	...	...	...	...	1 557	1 814	1 802	2 243
Romania Roumanie	...	...	...	...	53 981	62 100	56 447	55 315	55 191	52 286
Russian Federation Fédération de Russie	16 986	18 918	21 048	22 095	21 443	22 512	21 330	21 162	22 984	23 791
Serbia Serbie	...	...	...	...	...	...	...	3 508	3 508	...
Slovakia Slovaquie	...	...	...	5 975	6 486	9 871	11 813	12 388	12 770	12 869
Slovenia Slovénie	4 279	3 480	3 359	3 258	2 942	2 462	2 485	2 083	1 862	2 138
Spain Espagne	...	...	...	...	...	...	87 210	72 668	70 844	71 002
Sweden Suède	582	691	540	498	544	351	379	360	334	379
Tajikistan Tadjikistan	123	72	110	100	84	46	49	33	30	38

38 Production of footwear with uppers of leather *(continued)*

Thousand pairs and millions of US dollars

Production de chaussures à dessus en cuir naturel *(suite)*

Milliers de paires et millions de dollars É.-U.

A. Thousand pairs • Milliers de paires

Country or area Pays ou zone	1998	1999	2000	2001	2002	2003	2004	2005	2006	2007
TFYR of Macedonia L'ex-R.Y. Macédoine	...	...	...	1 376	1 530	1 484	1 767	1 515	1 124	1 563
Ukraine Ukraine	...	...	...	...	...	10 476	9 742	8 899	9 465	8 611
United Kingdom Royaume-Uni	29 904	26 230[4]	22 369	20 331[5]	...	...	...	...	...	...
United Rep. of Tanzania[6] Rép.-Unie de Tanzanie[6]	...	71	...	0	0	0	0	0	0	0
Viet Nam Viet Nam	77 037	89 928	107 944	102 259	113 070	133 570	155 118	218 039	234 181	213 236

Source:
United Nations Statistics Division, New York, the *Industrial Commodity Statistics Yearbook 2007* and the industrial statistics database, last accessed February 2010.

Source:
Organisation des Nations Unies, Division de statistique, New York, *l'Annuaire de statistiques industrielles par produit 2007* et la base de données sur les statistiques industrielles, dernier accès février 2010.

1 For statistical purposes, the data for China do not include those for the Hong Kong Special Administrative Region (Hong Kong SAR), Macao Special Administrative Region (Macao SAR) and Taiwan Province of China.
2 Excluding children's sandals with leather uppers (incl. thong type sandals, flip flops).
3 Excluding the Transnistria region.
4 Excluding women's sandals with leather uppers (including thong type sandals and flip flops).
5 Excluding footwear with wood; cork or other outer soles and leather uppers (except outer soles of rubber, plastics or leather).
6 Tanganyika only.

1 Pour la présentation des statistiques, les données pour la Chine ne comprennent pas la Région Administrative Spéciale de Hong Kong (Hong Kong RAS), la Région Administrative Spéciale de Macao (Macao RAS) et la province de Taiwan.
2 Sandales pour enfants avec dessus en cuir naturel non comprises.
3 Non compris la région de Transnistrie.
4 Sandales pour femmes avec dessus en cuir naturel non comprises.
5 Chaussures à dessus en cuir avec des semelles en bois ou en liège non comprises.
6 Tanganyika seulement.

38 Production of footwear with uppers of leather

Thousand pairs and millions of US dollars

Production de chaussures à dessus en cuir naturel

Milliers de paires et millions de dollars É.-U.

B. Millions of US dollars • Millions de dollars É.-U.

Country or area Pays ou zone	1998	1999	2000	2001	2002	2003	2004	2005	2006	2007
Azerbaijan Azerbaïdjan	...	...	1.6	2.3	3.7	2.8	2.8	3.4	4.2	5.7
Bolivia Bolivie	5.4	13.9	...	...	...	...	...	...	...	...
Brazil Brésil	...	...	2 262.8	2 079.3	1 765.8	1 706.9	2 128.5	2 501.9	2 671.7	2 964.6
Bulgaria Bulgarie	34.1	19.6	15.5	22.0	29.4	42.7	21.6	31.8	31.4	50.4
Chile Chili	...	...	...	...	...	...	...	115.5	126.5	119.6
China, Hong Kong SAR Chine, Hong Kong RAS	2.5	3.5	4.1	6.8	6.6	6.1	6.7	...	...	...
China, Macao SAR Chine, Macao RAS	10.7	...	...	24.6	28.9	39.9	...	...	...	...
Cyprus Chypre	...	...	...	...	11.5	7.7	6.4	6.5	6.5	...
Czech Republic République tchèque	...	...	...	...	...	...	18.5	20.2	24.1	28.1
Denmark Danemark	241.7	231.9	213.5	29.6	36.2	40.7	45.8	50.2	50.8	51.1
El Salvador El Salvador	28.0	...	...	...	...	...	...	...	...	...
Estonia Estonie	...	...	...	...	...	...	11.3	11.8	13.3	15.5
Finland Finlande	106.8	89.5	74.6	72.5	76.2	85.8	83.2	83.3	64.0	63.1
France France	...	...	...	862.2	859.9	857.3	848.5	...	...	...
Germany Allemagne	586.2	553.3	431.2	408.2	598.4	549.5	615.4	588.4	485.4	561.9
Greece [1] Grèce [1]	129.5	...	...	...	...	...	...	...	...	...
Hungary Hongrie	...	...	...	...	68.6	81.9	71.3	63.2	44.4	123.0
Iraq Iraq	...	...	...	...	...	...	1.1	...	0.6	...
Ireland Irlande	12.2	12.9	8.2	7.1	6.5	1.2	7.4	...	...	...
Italy Italie	...	...	...	...	...	5 764.4	6 589.1	...	...	...
Japan Japon	2 159.2	2 283.3	2 225.4	1 828.4	1 578.7	1 493.2	1 610.7	1 501.3	1 340.8	1 374.1
Jordan Jordanie	...	...	...	...	...	...	15.2	18.2	27.6	25.3
Kenya Kenya	6.0	4.8	5.7	4.8	4.8	5.6	8.3	10.8	13.9	16.6
Latvia Lettonie	...	3.7	2.6	2.2	0.5	...	...	...	...	...
Lithuania Lituanie	10.8	9.8	6.5	9.4	10.3	10.2	10.9	8.3	7.3	8.1
Mexico Mexique	344.8	373.9	426.0	412.5	430.2	395.9	409.7	422.5	474.3	438.4

38 Production of footwear with uppers of leather *(continued)*

Thousand pairs and millions of US dollars

Production de chaussures à dessus en cuir naturel *(suite)*

Milliers de paires et millions de dollars É.-U.

B. Millions of US dollars • Millions de dollars É.-U.

Country or area Pays ou zone	1998	1999	2000	2001	2002	2003	2004	2005	2006	2007
Mozambique Mozambique	...	...	...	...	...	...	0.5	0.7	0.7	0.7
Nepal Népal	...	...	...	...	...	...	...	...	...	0.1
Nigeria Nigéria	...	...	...	5.7	5.2	4.9	4.8	4.8	...	...
Norway Norvège	...	...	...	...	4.6	1.9	1.5	...	...	...
Poland Pologne	...	...	...	...	202.1	213.7	221.0	248.9	312.6	393.1
Portugal Portugal	1 175.7	1 245.8	1 077.9	1 141.0	1 179.9	1 322.2	1 374.5	1 328.2	1 338.5	...
Romania Roumanie	...	...	...	...	65.4	89.5	96.0	153.6	121.6	123.9
Slovakia Slovaquie	...	...	...	77.4	89.4	187.1	246.6	271.5	298.3	354.4
Slovenia Slovénie	67.9	74.7	70.2	67.8	...	55.5	61.2	51.2	50.2	264.6
Spain Espagne	...	...	...	...	...	...	2 043.8	1 866.6	1 810.2	2 043.4
Sweden Suède	13.3	13.3	11.7	9.6	15.5	9.9	10.6	10.4	9.4	10.8
United Kingdom Royaume-Uni	925.4[2]	838.1[3]	648.0	590.1[2]	...	...	...	...	...	...
Uruguay Uruguay	26.8	22.5	14.7	14.0	...	3.9	...	...	...	...

Source:
United Nations Statistics Division, New York, the *Industrial Commodity Statistics Yearbook 2007* and the industrial statistics database, last accessed February 2010.

Source:
Organisation des Nations Unies, Division de statistique, New York, *l'Annuaire de statistiques industrielles par produit 2007* et la base de données sur les statistiques industrielles, dernier accès février 2010.

1 Excluding children's sandals with leather uppers (incl. thong type sandals, flip flops).
2 Excluding footwear with wood; cork or other outer soles and leather uppers (except outer soles of rubber, plastics or leather).
3 Excluding women's sandals with leather uppers (including thong type sandals and flip flops).

1 Sandales pour enfants avec dessus en cuir naturel non comprises.
2 Chaussures à dessus en cuir avec des semelles en bois ou en liège non comprises.
3 Sandales pour femmes avec dessus en cuir naturel non comprises.

39 Sawnwood production
Thousand cubic metres

Production de sciages
Milliers de mètres cubes

Region, country or area Région, pays ou zone	1999	2000	2001	2002	2003	2004	2005	2006	2007	2008
World Monde	**389 088**	**386 075**	**379 891**	**394 259**	**400 925**	**427 555**	**437 903**	**445 888**	**442 450**	**404 254**
Africa Afrique	**7 415**	**8 320**	**7 921**	**7 490**	**8 474**	**9 516**	**9 044**	**9 146**	**9 202**	**8 831**
Algeria Algérie	13	13	13	13	13	13	13	13	13	13
Angola Angola	5	5	5	5	5	5	5	5	5	5
Benin Bénin	13	13	32	46	31	31	31	146	84	84
Burkina Faso Burkina Faso	1	1	1	2	2	1	1	1	5	5
Burundi Burundi	80	83	83	83	83	83	83	83	83	83
Cameroon Cameroun	600	1 154	800	652	658	702	702	702	773	773
Central African Rep. Rép. centrafricaine	79	102	150	97	69	69	69	69	95	95
Chad Tchad	2	2	2	2	2	2	2	2	2	2
Congo Congo	74	93	126	170	168	200	209	268	268	268
Côte d'Ivoire Côte d'Ivoire	611	603	630	620	503	503	363	442	456	456
Dem. Rep. of the Congo Rép. dém. du Congo	70	40	10	35	15	15	15	15	15	15
Egypt Egypte	4	4	2	3	3	2	2	2	2	2
Equatorial Guinea Guinée équatoriale	4	4	4	4	4	4	4	4	4	4
Ethiopia Ethiopie	60	60	60	14	18	18	18	18	18	18
Gabon Gabon	98	88	112	176	231	133	230	235	230	230
Gambia Gambie	1	1	1	1	1	1	1	1	1	1
Ghana Ghana	454	475	480	461	496	480	520	527	520	513
Guinea Guinée	26	26	26	26	26	26	3	2	2	2
Guinea-Bissau Guinée-Bissau	16	16	16	16	16	16	16	16	16	16
Kenya Kenya	185	185	84	78	78	78	136	142	142	142
Liberia Libéria	4	10	20	30	25	50	50	60	60	80
Libyan Arab Jamah. Jamah. arabe libyenne	31	31	31	31	31	31	31	31	31	31
Madagascar Madagascar	102	485	400	95	493	893	893	887	888	503
Malawi Malawi	45	45	45	45	45	45	45	45	45	45

39 Sawnwood production *(continued)*
Thousand cubic metres
Production de sciages *(suite)*
Milliers de mètres cubes

Region, country or area Région, pays ou zone	1999	2000	2001	2002	2003	2004	2005	2006	2007	2008
Mali Mali	13	13	13	13	13	13	13	13	13	13
Mauritania Mauritanie	...	...	...	...	...	...	7	14	14	14
Mauritius Maurice	5	3	3	3	3	3	3	4	3	3
Morocco Maroc	83	83	83	83	83	83	83	83	83	83
Mozambique Mozambique	28	28	28	28	28	32	38	43	57	57
Niger Niger	4	4	4	4	4	4	4	4	4	4
Nigeria Nigéria	2 000	2 000	2 000	2 000	2 000	2 000	2 000	2 000	2 000	2 000
Réunion Réunion	2	2	2	2	2	2	2	2	2	2
Rwanda Rwanda	79	79	79	79	79	79	79	79	79	79
Sao Tome and Principe Sao Tomé-et-Principe	5	5	5	5	5	5	5	5	5	5
Senegal Sénégal	23	23	23	23	23	23	23	23	23	23
Sierra Leone Sierra Leone	5	5	5	5	5	5	5	5	5	5
Somalia Somalie	14	14	14	14	14	14	14	14	14	14
South Africa Afrique du Sud	1 498	1 498	1 498	1 498	2 171	2 824	2 217	2 091	2 091	2 091
Sudan Soudan	51	51	51	51	51	51	51	51	51	51
Swaziland Swaziland	102	102	102	102	102	102	102	102	102	102
Togo Togo	21	19	15	13	13	13	14	14	15	15
Tunisia Tunisie	20	20	20	20	20	20	20	20	20	20
Uganda Ouganda	264	264	264	264	264	264	125	117	117	117
United Rep. of Tanzania Rép.-Unie de Tanzanie	24	24	24	24	24	24	24	24	24	24
Zambia Zambie	157	157	157	157	157	157	157	157	157	157
Zimbabwe Zimbabwe	438	386	397	397	397	397	617	565	565	565
Northern America Amérique septentrionale	**143 026**	**141 541**	**139 723**	**147 124**	**143 051**	**154 019**	**157 206**	**151 613**	**137 661**	**114 417**
Canada Canada	50 412	50 465	53 708	58 481	56 892	60 952	60 187	58 709	52 284	41 548
United States Etats-Unis	92 615	91 076	86 015	88 643	86 159	93 067	97 020	92 903	85 377	72 869
Latin America and the Caribbean Amérique latine et Caraïbes	**36 621**	**36 653**	**38 169**	**39 249**	**39 961**	**41 624**	**41 915**	**44 726**	**44 533**	**44 567**
Argentina Argentine	1 408	821	2 130	2 130	1 388	1 562	1 739	2 103	1 516	1 516
Bahamas Bahamas	1	1	1	1	1	1	1	1	1	1

39 Sawnwood production *(continued)*
Thousand cubic metres
Production de sciages *(suite)*
Milliers de mètres cubes

Region, country or area Région, pays ou zone	1999	2000	2001	2002	2003	2004	2005	2006	2007	2008
Belize Belize	35	35	35	35	35	35	35	35	35	35
Bolivia (Plurinational State of) Bolivie (État plurinational de)	244	239	308	299	347	403	409	461	461	461
Brazil Brésil	20 530	21 600	21 950	22 488	23 090	23 480	23 557	23 797	24 414	24 987
Chile Chili	5 254	5 698	5 872	6 439	7 004	8 015	8 298	8 718	8 340	7 306
Colombia Colombie	730	587	539	527	599	622	407	389	382	641
Costa Rica Costa Rica	780	812	812	812	812	426	488	1 132	1 132	1 132
Cuba Cuba	146	179	190	147	181	189	220	243	195	182
Dominica Dominique	...	...	...	...	47	66	66	66	66	66
Dominican Republic Rép. dominicaine	0	0	0	0	0	0	15	58	56	39
Ecuador Equateur	1 455	715	794	750	750	755	755	1 382	1 480	1 407
El Salvador El Salvador	58	58	58	68	68	16	16	16	16	16
French Guiana Guyane française	15	15	15	15	15	15	15	15	15	15
Guadeloupe Guadeloupe	1	1	1	1	1	1	1	1	1	1
Guatemala Guatemala	235	340	340	340	366	366	366	366	366	366
Guyana Guyana	50	29	30	31	38	36	58	68	74	74
Haiti Haïti	14	14	14	14	14	14	14	14	14	14
Honduras Honduras	419	442	419	470	421	454	400	412	379	349
Jamaica Jamaïque	66	66	66	66	66	66	66	66	66	66
Martinique Martinique	1	1	1	1	1	1	1	1	1	1
Mexico Mexique	3 110	3 110	2 829	2 691	2 740	2 962	2 674	2 650	2 687	2 814
Nicaragua Nicaragua	148	148	65	45	45	67	54	54	54	54
Panama Panama	46	48	42	24	27	30	30	30	30	9
Paraguay Paraguay	550	550	550	550	550	550	550	550	550	550
Peru Pérou	835	646	506	626	528	671	743	856	948	1 140
Suriname Suriname	28	60	56	47	56	58	65	69	57	60
Trinidad and Tobago Trinité-et-Tobago	18	32	41	43	39	32	41	41	41	30
Uruguay Uruguay	269	203	203	224	230	252	268	293	308	284
Venezuela (Boliv. Rep. of) Venezuela (Rép. boliv. du)	174	202	301	364	501	479	562	838	848	950

39 Sawnwood production *(continued)*
Thousand cubic metres

Production de sciages *(suite)*
Milliers de mètres cubes

Region, country or area Région, pays ou zone	1999	2000	2001	2002	2003	2004	2005	2006	2007	2008
Asia Asie	**71 648**	**61 905**	**59 616**	**63 742**	**68 334**	**74 439**	**78 810**	**85 314**	**89 379**	**88 928**
Afghanistan Afghanistan	400	400	400	400	400	400	400	400	400	400
Armenia Arménie	...	4	4	4	3	2	2	2	1	^0
Azerbaijan Azerbaïdjan	...	1	^0	^0	^0	^0	^0	^0	1	2
Bangladesh Bangladesh	70	70	70	255	388	388	388	388	388	388
Bhutan Bhoutan	22	31	31	31	31	31	31	31	21	27
Brunei Darussalam Brunéi Darussalam	67	56	51	54	51	51	51	51	51	51
Cambodia Cambodge	26	20	5	10	4	6	4	2	4	4
China Chine	16 700	7 345	8 549	9 431	12 211	16 236	18 814	25 776	29 202	29 311
Cyprus Chypre	12	9	9	7	6	5	4	4	9	10
Georgia Géorgie	10	10	44	59	71	69	222	100	70	70
India Inde	8 400	7 900	7 900	10 990	11 880	13 661	14 789	14 789	14 789	14 789
Indonesia Indonésie	6 625	6 500	6 750	6 230	7 620	4 330	4 330	4 330	4 330	4 330
Iran (Islamic Rep. of) Iran (Rép. islamique d')	96	106	106	170	79	68	62	50	52	50
Iraq Iraq	12	12	12	12	12	12	12	12	12	12
Japan Japon	17 952	17 094	15 485	14 402	13 929	13 603	12 825	12 554	11 632	10 884
Kazakhstan Kazakhstan	183	244	224	232	265	134	139	149	111	111
Korea, Dem. P. R. Corée, R. p. dém. de	280	280	280	280	280	280	280	280	280	280
Korea, Republic of Corée, République de	4 300	4 544	4 420	4 410	4 380	4 366	4 366	4 366	4 366	4 366
Kyrgyzstan Kirghizistan	23	6	6	6	15	22	22	22	52	60
Lao People's Dem. Rep. Rép. dém. pop. lao	439	200	185	192	125	125	130	130	130	130
Lebanon Liban	9	9	9	9	9	9	9	9	9	9
Malaysia Malaisie	5 237	5 590	4 696	4 643	4 769	4 954	5 193	5 149	5 142	5 142
Mongolia Mongolie	300	300	300	300	300	300	300	300	300	300
Myanmar Myanmar	298	545	671	1 012	1 001	1 133	1 591	1 610	1 610	1 610
Nepal Népal	630	630	630	630	630	630	630	630	630	630
Pakistan Pakistan	1 075	1 087	1 180	1 180	1 180	1 260	1 288	1 313	1 363	1 381
Philippines Philippines	288	151	199	163	246	339	288	432	362	358

Region, country or area Région, pays ou zone	1999	2000	2001	2002	2003	2004	2005	2006	2007	2008
Singapore Singapour	25	25	25	25	25	25	25	25	25	25
Sri Lanka Sri Lanka	5	29	61	61	61	61	61	61	61	61
Syrian Arab Republic Rép. arabe syrienne	9	9	9	9	9	9	9	9	9	9
Thailand Thaïlande	178	220	233	288	288	2 814	2 868	2 868	2 868	2 868
Turkey Turquie	5 039	5 528	5 036	5 579	5 615	6 215	6 445	6 471	6 599	6 261
Viet Nam Viet Nam	2 937	2 950	2 036	2 667	2 450	2 900	3 232	3 000	4 500	5 000
Europe Europe	**122 822**	**129 501**	**126 558**	**127 933**	**132 212**	**138 649**	**141 757**	**145 840**	**152 111**	**137 909**
Albania Albanie	35	90	197	97	97	97	97	97	8	8
Austria Autriche	9 628	10 390	10 227	10 415	10 473	11 133	11 074	10 507	11 816	11 990
Belarus Bélarus	2 175	1 808	2 058	2 182	2 304	2 727	2 737	2 458	2 458	2 458
Belgium Belgique	...	1 150	1 275	1 175	1 215	1 235	1 285	1 520	1 555	1 400
Belgium-Luxembourg Belgique-Luxembourg	1 189	...	...	...	...	...	...	...	...	...
Bosnia and Herzegovina Bosnie-Herzégovine	330	320	310	738	888	1 319	1 319	1 319	987	987
Bulgaria Bulgarie	325	312	332	332	332	569	569	683	1 884	816
Croatia Croatie	685	642	574	640	585	582	624	669	702	721
Czech Republic République tchèque	3 584	4 106	3 889	3 800	3 805	3 940	4 003	5 080	5 454	4 636
Denmark Danemark	344	364	283	244	248	196	196	300	300	300
Estonia Estonie	1 200	1 436	1 623	1 825	1 954	2 029	2 063	1 958	1 584	1 300
Finland Finlande	12 768	13 420	12 770	13 390	13 745	13 544	12 269	12 227	12 477	9 881
France France	10 236	10 536	10 518	9 815	9 539	9 774	9 715	9 992	9 965	9 687
Germany Allemagne	16 096	16 340	16 131	17 119	17 596	19 538	21 931	24 420	25 063	23 060
Greece Grèce	140	123	123	196	191	191	191	108	108	108
Hungary Hongrie	308	291	264	293	299	205	215	186	235	207
Ireland Irlande	811	888	925	818	1 005	939	1 015	1 094	1 094	697
Italy Italie	1 630	1 630	1 600	1 605	1 590	1 580	1 590	1 748	1 700	1 384
Latvia Lettonie	3 640	3 900	3 840	3 947	3 951	3 988	4 227	4 320	3 459	2 545
Liechtenstein Liechtenstein	...	...	...	...	...	...	...	10	10	10
Lithuania Lituanie	1 150	1 300	1 200	1 300	1 400	1 450	1 445	1 466	1 380	1 109

39 Sawnwood production *(continued)*
Thousand cubic metres
Production de sciages *(suite)*
Milliers de mètres cubes

Region, country or area Région, pays ou zone	1999	2000	2001	2002	2003	2004	2005	2006	2007	2008
Luxembourg Luxembourg	...	133	133	133	133	133	133	133	...	202
Montenegro Monténégro	...	...	...	...	...	...	...	42	42	42
Netherlands Pays-Bas	362	390	268	258	269	273	279	265	273	243
Norway Norvège	2 336	2 280	2 253	2 225	2 186	2 230	2 326	2 389	2 402	2 228
Poland Pologne	4 137	4 262	3 083	3 180	3 360	3 743	3 360	3 607	4 417	3 786
Portugal Portugal	1 430	1 427	1 492	1 298	1 383	1 060	1 010	1 010	1 011	1 010
Republic of Moldova République de Moldova	6	5	5	5	31	31	31	31	34	34
Romania Roumanie	2 818	3 396	3 059	3 696	4 246	4 588	4 321	3 476	4 143	3 794
Russian Federation Fédération de Russie	19 100	20 000	19 600	19 240	20 155	21 355	22 033	22 127	24 258	21 613
Serbia Serbie	...	...	...	...	...	...	...	493	602	672
Serbia and Montenegro Serbie-et-Monténégro	364	504	391	432	514	575	497	...	...	...
Slovakia Slovaquie	1 265	1 265	1 265	1 265	1 651	1 837	2 621	2 440	2 781	2 842
Slovenia Slovénie	455	439	460	506	511	461	527	580	610	500
Spain Espagne	3 178	3 760	4 275	3 524	3 630	3 730	3 660	3 806	3 332	3 142
Sweden Suède	14 858	16 176	15 988	16 172	16 800	16 900	17 600	18 300	18 738	17 601
Switzerland Suisse	1 525	1 625	1 400	1 392	1 345	1 505	1 591	1 668	1 541	1 540
TFYR of Macedonia L'ex-R.Y. Macédoine	37	36	23	20	21	28	18	17	17	14
Ukraine Ukraine	2 141	2 127	1 995	1 950	2 019	2 392	2 416	2 385	2 525	2 525
United Kingdom Royaume-Uni	2 537	2 630	2 728	2 705	2 742	2 772	2 770	2 907	3 145	2 818
Oceania Océanie	**7 556**	**8 156**	**7 906**	**8 722**	**8 893**	**9 308**	**9 172**	**9 250**	**9 562**	**9 602**
Australia Australie	3 743	4 093	3 921	4 215	4 411	4 668	4 687	4 784	5 064	5 064
Fiji Fidji	64	72	72	84	84	112	125	125	90	90
New Caledonia Nouvelle-Calédonie	3	3	3	3	3	3	3	3	3	3
New Zealand Nouvelle-Zélande	3 653	3 910	3 821	4 301	4 289	4 419	4 249	4 234	4 301	4 341
Papua New Guinea Papouasie-Nvl-Guinée	40	40	40	70	60	60	61	61	61	61
Samoa Samoa	21	5	6	6	4	4	5	1	1	1
Solomon Islands Iles Salomon	12	12	12	12	12	12	12	12	12	12
Tonga Tonga	2	2	2	2	2	2	2	2	2	2

39 Sawnwood production *(continued)*

Thousand cubic metres

Production de sciages *(suite)*

Milliers de mètres cubes

Region, country or area Région, pays ou zone	1999	2000	2001	2002	2003	2004	2005	2006	2007	2008
Vanuatu Vanuatu	18	18	28	28	28	28	28	28	28	28

Source:
Food and Agriculture Organization of the United Nations (FAO), Rome, FAOSTAT database, last accessed May 2010.

Source:
Organisation des Nations Unies pour l'alimentation et l'agriculture (FAO), Rome, la base de données de la FAOSTAT, dernier accès mai 2010.

40 Paper and paperboard production

Thousand metric tons

Production de papiers et cartons

Milliers de tonnes

Region, country or area Région, pays ou zone	1999	2000	2001	2002	2003	2004	2005	2006	2007	2008
World **Monde**	**315 487**	**323 822**	**319 332**	**330 954**	**340 336**	**355 192**	**363 961**	**375 881**	**384 133**	**379 786**
Africa **Afrique**	**3 782**	**3 965**	**4 486**	**4 526**	**4 674**	**4 890**	**4 998**	**4 167**	**4 285**	**4 285**
Algeria Algérie	47	46	48	38	42	46	45	45	45	45
Dem. Rep. of the Congo Rép. dém. du Congo	3	3	3	3	3	3	3	3	3	3
Egypt Egypte	343	440	460	460	460	460	460	460	460	460
Ethiopia Ethiopie	10	12	12	11	14	16	16	16	16	16
Kenya Kenya	129	129	67	80	100	165	273	279	279	279
Libyan Arab Jamah. Jamah. arabe libyenne	6	6	6	6	6	6	6	6	6	6
Madagascar Madagascar	7	11	10	9	10	10	10	10	10	10
Mauritania Mauritanie	...	...	...	...	...	...	1	1	1	1
Morocco Maroc	109	109	129	129	129	129	129	129	129	129
Nigeria Nigéria	19	19	19	19	19	19	19	19	19	19
South Africa Afrique du Sud	2 900	2 982	3 523	3 579	3 645	3 774	3 774	2 915	3 033	3 033
Sudan Soudan	3	3	3	3	3	3	3	3	3	3
Tunisia Tunisie	94	94	94	77	95	106	106	106	106	106
Uganda Ouganda	3	3	3	3	3	3	3	3	3	3
United Rep. of Tanzania Rép.-Unie de Tanzanie	25	25	25	25	25	25	25	25	25	25
Zambia Zambie	4	4	4	4	4	4	4	4	4	4
Zimbabwe Zimbabwe	80	80	80	80	117	121	121	144	144	144
Northern America **Amérique septentrionale**	**108 950**	**107 211**	**101 083**	**101 952**	**100 676**	**102 546**	**103 195**	**102 506**	**101 283**	**95 951**
Canada Canada	20 280	20 959	19 834	20 073	19 964	20 462	19 498	18 189	17 367	15 773
United States Etats-Unis	88 670	86 252	81 249	81 879	80 712	82 084	83 697	84 317	83 916	80 178
Latin America and the Caribbean **Amérique latine et Caraïbes**	**13 837**	**14 498**	**15 507**	**15 772**	**16 601**	**17 949**	**18 812**	**16 514**	**16 290**	**16 333**
Argentina Argentine	1 012	1 270	1 141	1 417	1 444	1 586	2 080	1 545	1 516	1 516
Barbados Barbade	...	...	...	...	...	...	2	2	2	2
Brazil Brésil	6 255	6 473	7 354	7 354	7 811	8 221	8 411	5 834	5 835	5 947

40 Paper and paperboard production *(continued)*

Thousand metric tons

Production de papiers et cartons *(suite)*

Milliers de tonnes

Region, country or area Région, pays ou zone	1999	2000	2001	2002	2003	2004	2005	2006	2007	2008
Chile Chili	824	861	877	1 016	1 098	1 168	1 215	1 231	1 344	1 391
Colombia Colombie	733	771	771	847	864	899	919	990	1 013	1 025
Costa Rica Costa Rica	20	20	20	20	20	20	20	20	20	20
Cuba Cuba	57	57	57	25	33	27	30	27	31	34
Dominican Republic Rép. dominicaine	130	130	130	130	130	130	130	130	130	130
Ecuador Equateur	91	91	91	94	101	100	100	99	100	100
El Salvador El Salvador	56	56	56	56	56	56	56	56	56	56
Guatemala Guatemala	31	31	31	31	31	31	31	31	31	31
Honduras Honduras	95	95	95	95	95	95	95	95	95	95
Mexico Mexique	3 784	3 865	4 056	3 987	4 149	4 689	4 841	5 566	5 272	5 141
Paraguay Paraguay	13	13	13	13	13	13	13	13	13	13
Peru Pérou	63	83	86	88	91	91	91	124	132	132
Uruguay Uruguay	92	88	88	89	89	100	98	98	90	90
Venezuela (Boliv. Rep. of) Venezuela (Rép. boliv. du)	581	594	641	510	576	723	680	653	610	610
Asia Asie	**90 863**	**94 290**	**95 500**	**103 019**	**109 627**	**115 967**	**121 897**	**134 002**	**142 004**	**146 880**
Armenia Arménie	...	20	1	2	2	2	4	20	26	6
Azerbaijan Azerbaïdjan	...	28	146	144	8	8	5	3	^0	3
Bahrain Bahreïn	...	...	...	...	15	15	15	15	15	15
Bangladesh Bangladesh	46	46	46	46	83	58	58	58	58	58
Bhutan Bhoutan	...	...	...	...	...	...	...	...	8	10
China Chine	33 266	34 668	35 574	42 060	47 418	54 072	60 404	69 395	77 964	83 685
Georgia Géorgie	...	...	...	...	...	...	...	1	2	2
India Inde	3 845	3 794	4 094	4 105	4 075	4 434	4 183	4 183	4 183	4 183
Indonesia Indonésie	6 978	6 977	6 995	6 995	7 040	7 223	7 223	7 223	7 727	7 777
Iran (Islamic Rep. of) Iran (Rép. islamique d')	25	46	46	415	411	411	411	411	376	370
Iraq Iraq	20	30	33	33	27	33	33	33	33	33
Israel Israël	275	275	275	275	275	275	275	275	275	275
Japan Japon	30 631	31 828	30 717	30 686	30 457	29 253	29 295	29 459	28 930	28 360

40 Paper and paperboard production *(continued)*
Thousand metric tons

Production de papiers et cartons *(suite)*
Milliers de tonnes

Region, country or area Région, pays ou zone	1999	2000	2001	2002	2003	2004	2005	2006	2007	2008
Jordan Jordanie	32	19	27	25	54	54	54	54	54	54
Kazakhstan Kazakhstan	3	24	47	64	58	69	81	203	238	238
Korea, Dem. P. R. Corée, R. p. dém. de	80	80	80	80	80	80	80	80	80	80
Korea, Republic of Corée, République de	8 875	9 308	9 332	9 812	10 148	10 511	10 254	10 703	10 932	10 642
Kuwait Koweït	...	42	42	42	56	56	56	56	56	56
Kyrgyzstan Kirghizistan	...	2	7	16	3	2	2	2	^0	^0
Lebanon Liban	42	64	66	66	100	103	103	103	103	103
Malaysia Malaisie	859	791	851	851	983	946	954	1 069	1 062	1 062
Myanmar Myanmar	37	39	42	49	45	43	45	45	45	45
Nepal Népal	13	13	13	13	13	13	13	13	13	13
Pakistan Pakistan	574	592	1 027	1 027	1 027	848	872	872	891	1 079
Philippines Philippines	1 010	1 107	1 056	1 056	1 091	1 097	1 097	1 097	1 097	1 097
Saudi Arabia Arabie saoudite	...	50	70	70	214	279	279	279	279	279
Singapore Singapour	87	87	87	87	87	87	87	87	87	87
Sri Lanka Sri Lanka	25	24	25	25	25	25	25	25	25	25
Syrian Arab Republic Rép. arabe syrienne	1	11	15	15	62	75	75	75	75	75
Thailand Thaïlande	2 434	2 312	2 445	2 444	3 260	3 273	3 292	5 145	4 324	4 108
Turkey Turquie	1 349	1 567	1 513	1 643	1 643	1 643	1 643	1 643	1 643	1 643
United Arab Emirates Emirats arabes unis	...	55	58	58	78	81	81	81	81	81
Uzbekistan Ouzbékistan	...	8	8	9	11	11	11	11	11	11
Viet Nam Viet Nam	356	384	762	807	779	888	888	1 282	1 309	1 324
Yemen Yémen	...	...	...	...	...	...	...	...	1	1
Europe Europe	**94 675**	**100 144**	**99 245**	**102 166**	**104 857**	**109 825**	**110 863**	**114 530**	**116 207**	**112 924**
Albania Albanie	1	3	3	3	3	3	3	3	0	0
Austria Autriche	4 142	4 386	4 250	4 419	4 565	4 852	4 950	5 213	5 199	5 153
Belarus Bélarus	208	236	224	216	279	257	284	285	285	285
Belgium Belgique	...	1 727	1 662	1 704	1 919	1 957	1 897	1 897	1 931	2 006
Belgium-Luxembourg Belgique-Luxembourg	1 727	...	...	...	...	...	...	...	...	...

Paper and paperboard production *(continued)*

Thousand metric tons

Production de papiers et cartons *(suite)*

Milliers de tonnes

Region, country or area Région, pays ou zone	1999	2000	2001	2002	2003	2004	2005	2006	2007	2008
Bosnia and Herzegovina Bosnie-Herzégovine	...	...	...	...	60	81	81	118	115	115
Bulgaria Bulgarie	126	136	171	171	171	326	326	313	368	326
Croatia Croatie	417	406	451	467	463	464	592	564	545	535
Czech Republic République tchèque	770	804	864	870	950	934	969	1 042	1 023	932
Denmark Danemark	397	263	389	384	388	402	423	442	417	418
Estonia Estonie	48	54	70	75	64	66	64	78	78	69
Finland Finlande	12 947	13 509	12 502	12 789	13 058	14 036	12 391	14 189	14 709	13 549
France France	9 603	10 006	9 625	9 809	9 939	10 255	10 332	10 006	9 871	9 420
Germany Allemagne	16 742	18 182	17 879	18 526	19 310	20 391	21 679	22 656	23 317	22 842
Greece Grèce	545	496	495	493	493	510	510	412	409	409
Hungary Hongrie	473	506	495	517	546	579	571	553	552	424
Ireland Irlande	42	43	43	44	45	45	45	0	49	48
Italy Italie	8 568	9 129	8 926	9 317	9 491	9 667	9 999	10 008	10 112	9 467
Latvia Lettonie	19	16	24	33	38	38	39	57	60	52
Lithuania Lituanie	37	53	68	78	92	99	113	119	124	132
Luxembourg Luxembourg	...	...	...	...	...	...	...	...	19	31
Netherlands Pays-Bas	3 256	3 332	3 174	3 346	3 339	3 459	3 471	3 367	3 224	2 977
Norway Norvège	2 241	2 300	2 220	2 114	2 186	2 294	2 223	2 109	2 010	1 900
Poland Pologne	1 839	1 934	2 086	2 342	2 461	2 635	2 732	2 857	2 992	3 044
Portugal Portugal	1 163	1 290	1 419	1 537	1 530	1 664	1 570	1 644	1 644	1 669
Republic of Moldova République de Moldova	...	...	...	...	...	...	...	84	98	98
Romania Roumanie	289	340	395	370	443	454	371	432	558	421
Russian Federation Fédération de Russie	4 535	5 310	5 625	5 978	6 377	6 830	7 126	7 434	7 581	7 676
Serbia Serbie	...	...	...	...	...	...	...	231	245	268
Serbia and Montenegro Serbie-et-Monténégro	230	180	241	254	148	159	229	...	...	...
Slovakia Slovaquie	738	925	988	710	674	798	858	888	915	921
Slovenia Slovénie	417	411	633	704	417	497	763	760	794	672
Spain Espagne	4 435	4 765	5 131	5 365	5 437	5 526	5 697	6 898	6 713	7 048

40 Paper and paperboard production *(continued)*

Thousand metric tons

Production de papiers et cartons *(suite)*

Milliers de tonnes

Region, country or area Région, pays ou zone	1999	2000	2001	2002	2003	2004	2005	2006	2007	2008
Sweden Suède	10 071	10 782	10 534	10 724	11 062	11 589	11 775	12 066	12 361	12 374
Switzerland Suisse	1 748	1 589	1 729	1 805	1 818	1 777	1 751	1 526	1 705	1 698
TFYR of Macedonia L'ex-R.Y. Macédoine	14	17	15	19	18	16	20	20	20	23
Ukraine Ukraine	311	411	480	532	618	723	768	804	937	937
United Kingdom Royaume-Uni	6 576	6 605	6 434	6 452	6 455	6 442	6 241	5 454	5 228	4 983
Oceania Océanie	**3 381**	**3 713**	**3 511**	**3 519**	**3 900**	**4 014**	**4 195**	**4 162**	**4 064**	**3 412**
Australia Australie	2 564	2 836	2 672	2 645	3 090	3 097	3 244	3 221	3 192	2 541
New Zealand Nouvelle-Zélande	817	877	839	874	810	917	951	941	872	871

Source:
Food and Agriculture Organization of the United Nations (FAO), Rome, FAOSTAT database, last accessed May 2010.

Source:
Organisation des Nations Unies pour l'alimentation et l'agriculture (FAO), Rome, la base de données de la FAOSTAT, dernier accès mai 2010.

41 Cement production

Thousand metric tons and millions of US dollars

Production de ciment

Milliers de tonnes et millions de dollars É.-U.

A. Thousand metric tons • Milliers de tonnes

Country or area / Pays ou zone	1998	1999	2000	2001	2002	2003	2004	2005	2006	2007
Afghanistan / Afghanistan	116[1]	116[1]	25[1]	16[1]	27[1]	24	70[2]	30[3]	...	...
Albania / Albanie	84[1]	107[1]	180[1]	30[1]	50[1]	578	530	473	356	553
Algeria / Algérie	7 836[1]	7 685	8 703	8 710	8 941	8 192	9 543	...	...	...
Angola[2] / Angola[2]	*350	207	201	*200	*250	250	250	...	...	...
Argentina / Argentine	7 092	7 187	6 121	5 545	3 911	5 217	6 254	7 595	8 929	9 602
Armenia / Arménie	314	287	219	275	355	384	501	605	625	722
Australia[4] / Australie[4]	7 236	7 704	7 937	6 821	7 236	7 731	8 460	8 925	8 910	9 380
Austria[2] / Autriche[2]	...	...	3 776	3 863	3 800	3 800	3 800	...	...	...
Azerbaijan / Azerbaïdjan	201[1]	171[1]	251[1]	523[1]	848[1]	1 012[1]	1 428[1]	1 538	1 639	1 687
Bahrain / Bahreïn	230[1]	156[1]	89[1]	89[1]	67[1]	70[2]	75[2]	...	...	...
Bangladesh / Bangladesh	468[1]	1 514[1]	1 868[1]	2 340[4]	2 514[4]	2 565[4]	2 695[4]	2 943[4]	3 211[4]	3 439[3]
Barbados / Barbade	257	257	268	250	298	325	322	342	338	316
Belarus / Bélarus	2 035	1 998	1 847	1 803	2 171	2 472	2 731	3 131	3 495	3 821
Belgium / Belgique	6 852	7 463	7 150[2]	*7 500[2]	*8 000[2]	8 000[2]	8 000[2]	...	...	...
Benin / Bénin	520[1]	520[1]	250[1]	250[1]	250[1]	*250[2]	250[2]	...	...	...
Bhutan[2] / Bhoutan[2]	*150	*150	*150	*160	*160	*160	170	...	...	...
Bolivia (Plur. State of) / Bolivie (État plur. de)	938	1 234	1 072	983	1 011[5]	1 138[5]	1 276[5]	1 440	...	...
Bosnia and Herzegovina / Bosnie-Herzégovine	563	683	164[6]	145[6]	213[6]	#891	1 045[2]	...	...	...
Brazil / Brésil	39 942	40 248	37 562	38 302	37 462	34 653	34 159	38 864	41 555	64 973
Brunei Darussalam / Brunéi Darussalam	...	222	241[1]	234[1]	220[1]	235[2]	240[2]	234	184	...
Bulgaria / Bulgarie	1 723	2 047	2 207	2 061	2 141	2 398	2 943	3 600	4 064	4 383
Burkina Faso / Burkina Faso	50[2]	50[2]	50[1]	50[1]	50[1]	*30[2]	30[2]	...	...	...
Cambodia[2] / Cambodge[2]	150	...	...	...	...	...	...	...	...	...
Cameroon / Cameroun	740[1]	825	956	980	937	949	1 032	1 026	1 127	982
Canada / Canada	12 168	12 643	12 753	12 793	13 081	13 424[2]	14 017[2]	...	...	...
Chile / Chili	3 890	2 508	2 686	3 145	3 462[2]	3 622[2]	3 798[2]	4 014	4 000	4 368

41

Cement production *(continued)*
Thousand metric tons and millions of US dollars

Production de ciment *(suite)*
Milliers de tonnes et millions de dollars É.-U.

A. Thousand metric tons • Milliers de tonnes

Country or area Pays ou zone	1998	1999	2000	2001	2002	2003	2004	2005	2006	2007
China [7] Chine [7]	536 000	573 000	597 000	661 040	725 000	862 081	966 820	1 068 848	1 236 765	1 361 173
China, Hong Kong SAR Chine, Hong Kong RAS	1 539	1 387	1 284	1 279	1 206	1 189	1 039	1 005	1 255	1 300
Colombia Colombie	8 673	6 677	7 131	6 776	6 633	7 337[5]	7 822[5]	9 959[5]	...	...
Costa Rica [2] Costa Rica [2]	1 085	1 100	1 050	1 200	1 200	1 320	1 300	...	...	...
Côte d'Ivoire Côte d'Ivoire	650[1]	650[1]	650[1]	650[1]	650[1]	650[2]	650[2]	...	...	...
Croatia Croatie	3 873	2 712	2 852	3 246	3 378	3 571	3 514	3 481	3 622	3 587
Cuba Cuba	1 724	1 797	1 643	1 335	1 336	1 357	1 409	1 576	1 714	1 812
Cyprus Chypre	1 207	1 157	1 398	1 367	1 445	1 638	1 688	1 800	1 786	...
Czech Republic République tchèque	4 599	4 241	4 093	3 591	3 249	3 502	3 829	3 978	4 239	4 899
Dem. Rep. of the Congo [2] Rép. dém. du Congo [2]	134	159	161	192	*190	190	...	...	...	...
Denmark Danemark	2 548	2 422	2 536	2 576	2 545	2 580	2 892	2 881	2 937	2 871
Dominican Republic Rép. dominicaine	1 872	2 295	2 505	2 746	3 050	2 783	2 654	2 779	1 888	...
Ecuador Equateur	2 539	2 262	2 800[2]	2 947	3 113	3 100[2]	3 100[2]	...	...	...
Egypt Egypte	15 569[1]	11 933[1]	25 101[1]	26 811[1]	23 000[1]	16 281	...	...	...	...
El Salvador El Salvador	1 073	1 031[2]	1 064[2]	1 174[2]	1 318[2]	1 390[2]	1 400[2]	...	...	...
Eritrea [2] Erythrée [2]	50	*45	*45	*45	*45	*45	45	...	...	...
Estonia Estonie	321	358	329	405	466	506	614	733	856	...
Ethiopia Ethiopie	783[8]	767[8]	816[8]	819	919	890	1 300[2]	...	...	...
Fiji Fidji	89	99	87	98	102	100	111	143	143	144
Finland Finlande	1 232	1 310	1 422	1 325	1 198	1 493	1 691	1 321	1 513	1 743
France France	19 434	20 302	20 000[2]	20 652	20 244	20 544	...	...	...	...
French Guiana [2] Guyane française [2]	88	*88	*88	*58	*62	*62	62	...	...	...
Gabon Gabon	198[1]	162[1]	166[1]	240[1]	257[1]	261	350[2]	...	...	...
Georgia Géorgie	199	341	348	335	347	345	442	530[3]	777[3]	1 138[3]
Germany Allemagne	38 464	39 970	38 088	33 689	32 012	32 349[2]	31 954[2]	...	...	...
Ghana Ghana	1 573	1 851	1 673	1 490	1 414	1 900[2]	2 000[2]	...	...	...
Greece Grèce	14 207	13 624	14 147	15 563	15 500[2]	18 742[9]	15 000[2]	...	...	...
Guadeloupe * [2] Guadeloupe * [2]	230	230	230	230	230	230	230	...	...	...

41 Cement production (continued)

Thousand metric tons and millions of US dollars

Production de ciment (suite)

Milliers de tonnes et millions de dollars É.-U.

A. Thousand metric tons • Milliers de tonnes

Country or area Pays ou zone	1998	1999	2000	2001	2002	2003	2004	2005	2006	2007
Guatemala Guatemala	1 496	2 120	2 039	1 976	2 068	1 900[2]	1 900[2]	...	...	...
Guinea Guinée	277[1]	297[1]	300[1]	300[1]	300[1]	360[2]	360[2]	...	...	...
Haiti [2] Haïti [2]	...	...	...	204	290	200	300	...	...	...
Honduras Honduras	896[2]	980[2]	1 284[2]	*1 321[2]	*1 360[2]	1 400[2]	1 400[2]	1 384[5]	...	...
Hungary Hongrie	2 999	2 980	3 326	3 452	3 510	3 575	3 363	3 235	3 571	3 275
Iceland Islande	118	131	144	125	83	85	...	...	...	...
India Inde	87 646	100 230	99 227	106 491	111 778	117 035	125 338	140 512	154 746	...
Indonesia Indonésie	22 344[1]	22 806[1]	27 789[1]	18 629[1]	33 000[1]	40 476[1]	32 448[1]	33 916[3]	33 106[3]	35 033
Iran (Islamic Rep. of) Iran (Rép. islamique d')	20 049[1]	22 219[1]	23 276[1]	24 755[1]	30 000[1]	30 000[2]	30 000[2]	33 049	21 536	40 189
Iraq Iraq	2 000[1]	2 000[1]	2 000[1]	2 000[1]	2 000[1]	*1 000[2]	*3 000[2]	...	2 887	...
Ireland Irlande	2 395	2 616	2 784	2 779	2 693	3 065	3 348	...	...	...
Israel [2] Israël [2]	6 476	6 354	*5 703	*4 700	*4 584	*4 632	*4 494	...	...	...
Italy Italie	35 512	36 827	39 588	40 494	42 050	37 021[10]	37 843[10]	...	...	...
Jamaica Jamaïque	558	504[5]	521[5]	596	622	608	808	848[5]	763	774
Japan Japon	81 328	80 120	81 097	76 550	...	...	...	...	...	...
Jordan Jordanie	2 650[1]	2 688[1]	2 640[1]	3 149[1]	3 558	3 515	3 908	4 046	3 967	...
Kazakhstan Kazakhstan	622	838	1 175	2 029	2 128[1]	2 580[1]	3 660[1]	...	...	...
Kenya Kenya	1 453	1 389	1 348	1 319	1 537	1 659	1 886	2 182	2 406	2 615
Korea, Dem. P. R. [2] Corée, R. p. dém. de [2]	7 000	*4 000	*4 600	*5 160	*5 320	*5 540	5 500	...	...	...
Korea, Republic of Corée, République de	46 791	48 579	51 417	53 062	56 823	60 725	56 955	52 224	55 021	58 188
Kuwait Koweït	2 310[1]	947[1]	1 187[1]	921[1]	1 584[1]	1 863[1]	2 635	2 690	2 837	...
Kyrgyzstan Kirghizistan	709	386	453	469	533	757	870	973	1 051	1 230
Lao People's Dem. Rep. Rép. dém. pop. lao	80[2]	*80[2]	*92[2]	*92[2]	263	280	282	400	...	...
Latvia Lettonie	366	...	...	...	...	...	...	...	...	...
Lebanon Liban	3 316[1]	2 714[1]	2 808[1]	2 890[1]	2 852[1]	2 900[2]	2 900[2]	...	2 297	...
Liberia * [2] Libéria * [2]	10	15	71	63	54	30	30	...	...	...
Libyan Arab Jamah. [2] Jamah. arabe libyenne [2]	3 000	3 000	3 000	3 000	3 300	3 500	3 600	...	...	...
Lithuania Lituanie	781	668	559	541	601	599	753	840	1 054	1 088

41 Cement production *(continued)*

Thousand metric tons and millions of US dollars

Production de ciment *(suite)*

Milliers de tonnes et millions de dollars É.-U.

A. Thousand metric tons • Milliers de tonnes

Country or area Pays ou zone	1998	1999	2000	2001	2002	2003	2004	2005	2006	2007
Luxembourg Luxembourg	699	742	749	725	729	709	750[2]	...	...	...
Madagascar Madagascar	44	46[2]	48[2]	51	34	33[2]	23	29	33	...
Malawi Malawi	83	104	156[2]	111	174[2]	190[2]	190[2]	...	...	...
Malaysia Malaisie	10 379[1]	10 104[1]	11 445[1]	13 820[1]	14 336[1]	17 244[1]	17 328[1]	16 658	19 457	21 909
Mali Mali	10[1]	10[1]	10[1]	18[11]	...	...	...	...	...	...
Martinique *[2] Martinique *[2]	220	220	255	255	221	225	225	...	...	...
Mauritania Mauritanie	50[1]	50[1]	156[1]	181[1]	174[1]	*200[2]	*200[2]	...	...	...
Mexico Mexique	30 728	31 802	33 228	32 134	33 372	33 594	34 992	37 452	40 362	41 213
Mongolia Mongolie	109	104	92	68	148	162	62	112[3]	141	180
Morocco Maroc	7 155[1]	7 194[1]	7 497[1]	8 058[1]	8 486	9 277	9 796	10 289	11 357	12 787
Mozambique Mozambique	264[1]	266[1]	348[1]	421[1]	274[1]	582	552	564	774	771
Myanmar Myanmar	483	334	351	419	379	471	583	533	547	577
Nepal Népal	139[12]	191[12]	206[12]	215[12]	233[12]	255[12]	279[12]	278[12]	...	1 060
Netherlands Pays-Bas	3 200	3 200	3 200	*3 450[2]	*3 400[2]	*3 400[2]	*3 400[2]	...	...	...
New Caledonia Nouvelle-Calédonie	89	93	91	100	100	100[2]	115[2]	119	133	122
New Zealand[2] Nouvelle-Zélande[2]	950	*1 030	1 070	1 080	1 090	1 100	1 110	...	...	...
Nicaragua Nicaragua	412	536	568	588	507[5]	533[5]	521[5]	530[5]	...	...
Niger Niger	30[1]	30[1]	40[1]	40[1]	55[1]	40[2]	40[2]	...	...	...
Nigeria Nigéria	2 700[1]	2 500[1]	2 500[1]	1 756	1 760	1 747	1 754	1 754	...	...
Norway[2] Norvège[2]	1 676	1 827	1 851	*1 870	...	...	...	...	...	...
Occupied Palestinian Terr.[1] Terr. palestinien occupé[1]	...	...	...	40	29	...	...	...	...	...
Oman Oman	1 217[1]	1 990[1]	1 815[1]	1 370[1]	1 523[13]	1 593[13]	1 648[13]	...	...	...
Pakistan Pakistan	9 364	9 635	9 314	9 672	9 935	11 316[1]	12 862[4]	16 353[4]	18 564[4]	22 739[4]
Panama Panama	814	976	849[5]	698[5]	748[5]	889[5]	1 042[5]	...	...	...
Paraguay Paraguay	586	556	516	505	447	505	660[2]	...	...	...
Peru Pérou	4 069	3 327	3 658	3 589	4 115	4 203	4 602	5 108	...	...
Philippines Philippines	12 888	12 557	11 959	11 378	11 396	10 000[2]	13 057[3]	12 368[3]	12 033[3]	13 048[3]
Poland Pologne	14 970	15 555	#14 943	12 090	11 213	11 624	12 148	12 190	14 695	16 952

Cement production (continued)
Thousand metric tons and millions of US dollars

Production de ciment (suite)
Milliers de tonnes et millions de dollars É.-U.

A. Thousand metric tons • Milliers de tonnes

Country or area Pays ou zone	1998	1999	2000	2001	2002	2003	2004	2005	2006	2007
Portugal Portugal	9 845	10 057	10 293	10 168	9 728	8 598	8 839	8 427	8 327	...
Puerto Rico Porto Rico	1 646	1 757	...	...	...	...	...	...	...	...
Qatar Qatar	857[1]	959[1]	1 029[1]	1 209[1]	1 346[13]	1 340[13]	1 200[13]	...	...	...
Republic of Moldova [14] République de Moldova [14]	74	50	222	158	279	255	440	641	...	...
Réunion Réunion	342	263	258	*380[2]	*380[2]	*380[2]	*380[2]	...	...	...
Romania Roumanie	7 300	6 252	8 411	5 668	5 767	5 879	6 211	7 023	8 263	9 898
Russian Federation Fédération de Russie	25 974	28 529	32 389	35 271	37 705	40 998	45 615	48 534	54 731	59 933
Rwanda Rwanda	60	66	71[2]	91[2]	101[2]	105[2]	104[2]	...	...	...
Saudi Arabia Arabie saoudite	15 776[1]	16 381[1]	18 296[1]	20 976	23 452	24 200	25 470	26 064	...	...
Senegal Sénégal	847[1]	1 014	1 341	1 539	1 653	1 694	2 391	2 623	2 884	3 152
Serbia Serbie	...	...	...	...	...	...	...	2 276	2 565	2 676
Serbia and Montenegro Serbie-et-Monténégro	2 253	#1 575	2 117	2 418	2 396	2 075	2 240[2]	...	...	...
Sierra Leone Sierra Leone	41	45	73	113	144	170	181	172	163	...
Singapore [2] Singapour [2]	2 340	1 660	1 150	*600	*200	150	150	...	...	...
Slovakia Slovaquie	3 066	3 084	3 045	3 011	3 121	3 115	3 031	3 282	3 389	3 504
Slovenia Slovénie	...	...	...	1 186	...	...	...	...	...	...
South Africa Afrique du Sud	7 676	8 211	8 715	8 036[2]	8 525[2]	8 883[2]	12 348[2]	...	...	...
Spain [2] Espagne [2]	27 943	...	...	...	...	...	...	...	...	...
Sri Lanka Sri Lanka	2 151	2 354	2 432	2 123	973	1 163	1 400[2]	3 928[3]	4 579[3]	...
Sudan Soudan	198[15]	231[15]	146[15]	190[15]	220[15]	320[15]	244	244	227	327
Suriname Suriname	65[1]	65[1]	60[1]	65[1]	65[1]	*65[2]	*65[2]	...	...	...
Sweden Suède	2 373	2 293	2 613	2 644	2 765	2 841	2 731	2 791	3 074	3 033
Switzerland Suisse	*3 600[2]	3 548[2]	3 771[2]	3 950[2]	*4 000[2]	3 800[2]	3 955	...	...	...
Syrian Arab Republic Rép. arabe syrienne	5 016	5 134	4 631	5 428	5 399	5 224	5 098	5 218	4 965	...
Tajikistan Tadjikistan	18[1]	33[1]	55[1]	69[1]	89[1]	168[1]	192[1]	253	282	313
Thailand Thaïlande	22 722	25 354	25 499	27 913	31 679	32 530	35 626	37 872	39 408	35 668
TFYR of Macedonia L'ex-R.Y. Macédoine	461	563	801	630	778	832	812	887	924	902
Togo Togo	500[1]	600[1]	1 393	1 381	1 270	1 196	1 164	1 018	1 102	...

41

Cement production *(continued)*
Thousand metric tons and millions of US dollars

Production de ciment *(suite)*
Milliers de tonnes et millions de dollars É.-U.

A. Thousand metric tons • Milliers de tonnes

Country or area Pays ou zone	1998	1999	2000	2001	2002	2003	2004	2005	2006	2007
Trinidad and Tobago Trinité-et-Tobago	700	740	743	697	744	766	768	686	883	...
Tunisia [1] Tunisie [1]	4 588	4 860	5 647	5 721	6 020	6 480	6 192	...	...	...
Turkey Turquie	38 175	34 215	36 238	30 111	32 546	35 264	38 594	41 100	47 906	...
Turkmenistan Turkménistan	750[1]	780[1]	420[1]	448[1]	486[1]	200	450[2]	...	...	...
Uganda Ouganda	321	347	368	431	506	507	559	693	858	996
Ukraine Ukraine	5 591	5 828	5 311	5 786	7 157	8 923	10 648	12 165	13 739	15 019
United Arab Emirates Emirats arabes unis	7 066[1]	7 069[1]	6 100[1]	6 100[1]	6 500[1]	*8 000[2]	*8 000[2]	...	...	...
United Kingdom Royaume-Uni	14 764[10]	14 544[10]	12 452[2]	11 854[2]	*11 089[2]	11 215[2]	11 250[2]	...	...	...
United Rep. of Tanzania Rép.-Unie de Tanzanie	778[2]	833[16]	833[16]	901[16]	1 026[16]	1 187[16]	1 281[16]	1 367[16]	1 369[16]	1 629[16]
United States [17] Etats-Unis [17]	83 931	85 952	87 846	88 900	89 732	92 843	97 434	99 319	98 167	95 464
Uruguay Uruguay	940	839	688	1 015[2]	442[18]	489[18]	658[18]	691[18]	...	...
Uzbekistan Ouzbékistan	3 400[1]	3 300[1]	3 284[1]	3 722[3]	3 927[3]	4 062[3]	4 805[3]	5 068[3]	5 583[3]	6 043[3]
Venezuela (Bol. Rep. of) [5] Venezuela (Rép. bol. du) [5]	7 870	7 875	7 527	7 329	6 126	7 398	9 000	10 000	...	...
Viet Nam Viet Nam	9 738	10 489	13 298	16 073	21 121	24 127	26 153	30 808	32 690	37 102
Yemen Yémen	1 195[1]	1 454[1]	1 406[1]	1 449[1]	1 582[1]	1 541	1 546[2]	...	...	...
Zambia Zambie	351[2]	300[2]	335	309	343	424	480[2]	...	...	...
Zimbabwe Zimbabwe	1 066	1 105	1 000	549	*600[2]	*400[2]	*400[2]	...	...	...

Source:
United Nations Statistics Division, New York, the *Industrial Commodity Statistics Yearbook 2007* and the industrial statistics database, last accessed March 2010.

Source:
Organisation des Nations Unies, Division de statistique, New York, *l'Annuaire de statistiques industrielles par produit 2007* et la base de données sur les statistiques industrielles, dernier accès mars 2010.

1 Source: Organization of the Islamic Conference (Jeddah, Saudi Arabia).
2 Source: U. S. Geological Survey (Washington, D. C.).
3 Source: "Country Economic Review", Asian Development Bank (Manila).
4 Figures relate to 12 months ending 30 June of the year stated.
5 Source: United Nations Economic Commission for Latin America and the Caribbean (Santiago).
6 Excluding the Federation of Bosnia and Herzegovina.
7 For statistical purposes, the data for China do not include those for the Hong Kong Special Administrative Region (Hong Kong SAR), Macao Special Administrative Region (Macao SAR) and Taiwan Province of China.
8 Twelve months ending 7 July of the year stated.
9 Incomplete coverage.

1 Source: Organisation de la Conférence islamique (Djeddah, Arabie saoudite).
2 Source: U. S. Geological Survey (Washington, D. C.).
3 Source: "La Revue Economique du Pays", La Banque de Développement Asiatique (Manille).
4 Les chiffres font référence à une période de 12 mois se terminant le 30 juin de l'année indiquée.
5 Source: Commission économique des Nations Unies pour l'Amérique Latine et des Caraïbes (Santiago).
6 Non compris la Fédération de Bosnie et Herzégovine.
7 Pour la présentation des statistiques, les données pour la Chine ne comprennent pas la Région Administrative Spéciale de Hong Kong (Hong Kong RAS), la Région Administrative Spéciale de Macao (Macao RAS) et la province de Taiwan.
8 Période de 12 mois finissant le 7 juillet de l'année indiquée.
9 Couverture incomplète.

A. Thousand metric tons • Milliers de tonnes

10 Excluding Alumina cement.
11 Source: Afristat: Sub-Saharan African Observatory of Economics and Statistics (Bamako, Mali).
12 Twelve months beginning 16 July of the year stated.
13 Source: Arab Gulf Cooperation Council (Riyadh).
14 Excluding the Transnistria region.
15 Source: African Statistical Yearbook, Economic Commission for Africa (Addis Ababa).
16 Tanganyika only.
17 Excluding Puerto Rico.
18 Portland cement only.

10 Non compris Alumina ciment.
11 Source : Afristat : Observatoire Economique et Statistique d'Afrique Subsaharienne (Bamako, Mali).
12 Période de 12 mois commençant le 16 juillet de l'année indiquée.
13 Source: "Arab Gulf Cooperation Council (Riyad)".
14 Non compris la région de Transnistrie.
15 Source : Annuaire des Statistiques de l'Afrique, Conseil Economique pour l'Afrique (Addis-Abeba).
16 Tanganyika seulement.
17 Non compris Porto Rico.
18 Ciment Portland uniquement.

41 Cement production

Thousand metric tons and millions of US dollars

Production de ciment

Milliers de tonnes et millions de dollars É.-U.

B. Millions of US dollars • Millions de dollars É.-U.

Country or area Pays ou zone	1998	1999	2000	2001	2002	2003	2004	2005	2006	2007
Albania Albanie	...	...	...	...	...	...	36.7	32.0	27.8	49.7
Azerbaijan Azerbaïdjan	...	...	9.7	20.9	36.5	45.7	69.1	91.1	89.5	170.6
Bangladesh [1] Bangladesh [1]	...	...	...	175.9	174.6	168.8	175.5	186.2	217.1	...
Bolivia (Plur. State of) Bolivie (État plur. de)	117.6	104.3	...	...	...	...	...	...	...	...
Brazil Brésil	...	...	1 951.4	2 264.5	1 787.0	2 307.2	2 160.2	2 252.0	2 523.7	3 802.2
Bulgaria Bulgarie	74.4	82.2	74.4	81.5	94.8	128.1	187.3	245.2	312.3	416.4
Chile Chili	...	...	...	...	...	...	...	447.5	468.9	553.8
Cyprus Chypre	...	...	...	...	67.1	87.0	111.0	125.0	132.9	...
Czech Republic République tchèque	...	...	...	172.1	181.6	204.6	232.9	264.6	301.0	381.3
Denmark Danemark	219.6	210.7	198.9	194.0	188.6	215.3	246.4	253.8	311.6	317.5
Dominican Republic Rép. dominicaine	169.9	223.3	262.8	249.2	305.7	252.6	...	...	...	...
Egypt Egypte	...	621.4	704.4	672.2	795.1	457.3	...	...	...	...
El Salvador El Salvador	79.9	...	...	...	...	...	...	...	...	...
Estonia Estonie	...	...	...	...	...	...	31.9	40.0	53.2	...
Finland Finlande	81.2	85.2	77.4	76.1	78.1	92.5	118.0	116.9	139.2	182.7
France France	...	1 909.5	1 671.0	1 692.2	1 808.0	2 213.9	...	...	...	...
Germany Allemagne	2 423.0	2 403.5	2 044.4	1 783.4	1 633.8	1 532.7	1 774.4	1 917.6	2 126.9	2 503.1
Hungary Hongrie	...	...	...	...	197.4	242.0	261.9	257.1	271.3	320.9
Iraq Iraq	...	...	...	...	...	...	...	...	229.7	...
Ireland Irlande	201.2	209.0	179.2	173.1	183.6	248.1	310.7	...	...	...
Italy [2] Italie [2]	...	...	...	...	...	2 664.6	3 100.0	...	...	...
Jamaica Jamaïque	...	...	...	...	...	52.4	67.8	73.2	73.5	95.3
Japan Japon	163.0	214.2	248.7	177.3	193.9	258.5	283.3	260.8	208.3	138.6
Jordan Jordanie	...	...	...	...	...	...	225.3	290.7	408.8	453.6
Kenya Kenya	86.8	112.5	105.5	78.3	99.0	150.1	93.5	148.7	197.5	220.9
Lithuania Lituanie	30.6	26.2	20.5	21.0	24.6	27.3	36.6	42.0	65.7	92.6

41 Cement production *(continued)*

Thousand metric tons and millions of US dollars

Production de ciment *(suite)*

Milliers de tonnes et millions de dollars É.-U.

B. Millions of US dollars • Millions de dollars É.-U.

Country or area Pays ou zone	1998	1999	2000	2001	2002	2003	2004	2005	2006	2007
Madagascar Madagascar	...	...	...	...	...	...	0.8	...	...	...
Mexico Mexique	2 441.7	2 950.6	3 465.7	3 610.1	3 627.1	3 527.3	3 523.1	3 812.4	4 268.2	4 420.0
Mozambique Mozambique	...	...	...	...	...	32.0	51.9	73.1	80.6	87.9
Nepal Népal	...	...	...	27.6	...	...	...	...	...	111.3
Nigeria Nigéria	108.3	88.2	83.7	76.2	69.5	65.4	63.5	64.2	...	...
Philippines Philippines	551.5	558.6	529.1	569.9	618.9	535.2	433.7	469.8	520.3	768.0
Poland Pologne	...	...	597.8	593.2	604.1	635.8	690.0	779.6	1 030.8	1 544.8
Portugal Portugal	688.2	672.6	614.0	603.1	628.4	623.1	686.6	667.8	666.1	...
Romania Roumanie	...	...	...	...	26.5	29.9	43.4	56.0	69.1	106.8
Senegal Sénégal	...	...	...	0.1[3]	^0.0	...	...	...	...	...
Slovakia Slovaquie	...	...	...	118.9	142.4	165.9	186.4	216.5	239.0	307.9
Slovenia Slovénie	...	...	...	59.9	...	...	...	...	...	...
Sweden Suède	87.3	118.7	125.3	109.3	127.3	143.8	160.8	176.9	214.1	255.5
United Kingdom[2] Royaume-Uni[2]	1 176.2	1 192.9	...	...	...	...	...	...	...	...
United Rep. of Tanzania[4] Rép.-Unie de Tanzanie[4]	...	...	...	...	...	...	...	158.9	169.9	235.6
Uruguay Uruguay	83.0	69.1	60.5	56.7	...	31.7	...	...	...	...

Source:
United Nations Statistics Division, New York, the *Industrial Commodity Statistics Yearbook 2007* and the industrial statistics database, last accessed March 2010.

1 Figures relate to 12 months ending 30 June of the year stated.
2 Excluding Alumina cement.
3 Source: Afristat: Sub-Saharan African Observatory of Economics and Statistics (Bamako, Mali).
4 Tanganyika only.

Source:
Organisation des Nations Unies, Division de statistique, New York, *l'Annuaire de statistiques industrielles par produit 2007* et la base de données sur les statistiques industrielles, dernier accès mars 2010.

1 Les chiffres concernant aux 12 mois finissant le 30 Juin de l'année indiquée.
2 Non compris Alumina ciment.
3 Source : Afristat : Observatoire Economique et Statistique d'Afrique Subsaharienne (Bamako, Mali).
4 Tanganyika seulement.

42 Pesticide production

Metric tons and millions of US dollars

Production de pesticides

Tonnes et millions de dollars É.-U.

A. Metric tons • Milliers de tonnes

Country or area Pays ou zone	1998	1999	2000	2001	2002	2003	2004	2005	2006	2007
Austria Autriche	16 744	12 429	15 578	20 163	17 913	20 851	...	...	...	...
Bangladesh [1] Bangladesh [1]	7 701	9 086	9 063	8 880	8 577	3 773	...	...	...	...
Belgium [2] Belgique [2]	...	153 757	182 351	188 988	179 187	179 720	...	...	...	...
Bulgaria Bulgarie	...	...	...	...	...	...	2 882	3 576	3 282	3 537
Chile Chili	...	...	...	...	...	...	...	7 814	11 129	13 499
China [3] Chine [3]	382 100	386 500	397 200	411 800	481 400	420 000	485 300	434 300	505 300	577 700
Croatia Croatie	8 676	7 039	7 070	8 120	7 370	5 861	6 034	3 442	3 167	3 694
Cuba Cuba	5 965	6 944	6 896	9 099	3 840	3 469	2 304	2 757	1 616	1 998
Czech Republic République tchèque	21 432	19 128	19 064	18 037	18 687	18 759	16 727	17 264	18 457	19 481
Denmark Danemark	17 228	18 765	20 537	21 860	21 064	21 560	23 094	24 024	23 218	22 158
Ecuador Equateur	537	575	1 881	...	...	6 342	...	...	...	...
Estonia Estonie	...	...	...	...	...	...	...	82	...	...
Finland Finlande	2 039	1 835	1 842	...	...	...	...	...	...	...
Germany Allemagne	110 481[4]	97 261[4]	84 137[4]	85 849[4]	87 667[4]	93 616[4]	94 840[4]	129 313	122 699	151 424
Greece Grèce	11 368	11 249	11 366	8 960	...	8 797[2]	...	...	...	...
Hungary Hongrie	18 105	14 526	14 688	15 087	11 848	14 559	11 425	9 318	5 825	5 697
India Inde	...	...	...	...	...	1 569	462	138	...	...
Indonesia Indonésie	10 700	22 109	...	...	...	...	...	...	...	...
Iran (Islamic Rep. of) Iran (Rép. islamique d')	16 618[5]	28 634[5]	15 958[5]	26 340[5]	...	...	25 342	22 039	14 753	17 475
Ireland Irlande	5 362	6 614	3 198	4 771	1 459	7 664	10 356	...	...	...
Kazakhstan Kazakhstan	...	1 702	1 765	1 682	1 258	2 091	1 888	2 373	3 004	3 231
Kenya Kenya	1 180	1 188	679	370	530	1 331	2 234	1 616	1 639	923
Korea, Republic of Corée, République de	85 266	92 681	77 903	83 675	75 858	74 917	66 924	73 369	65 858	87 876
Latvia Lettonie	30	...	...	...	...	...	...	...	...	...
Lithuania Lituanie	354	295	372	613	...	469[4]	499[4]	461[4]	417[4]	537[6]
Mexico Mexique	58 637	61 206	62 062	54 938	58 340	58 359	51 449	62 297	65 197	64 299

42 Pesticide production *(continued)*
Metric tons and millions of US dollars

Production de pesticides *(suite)*
Tonnes et millions de dollars É.-U.

A. Metric tons • Milliers de tonnes

Country or area Pays ou zone	1998	1999	2000	2001	2002	2003	2004	2005	2006	2007
Mozambique Mozambique	...	...	...	...	...	...	62	54	...	...
Peru Pérou	1 975	1 405	1 185	1 191	1 139	1 192	1 216	1 446	...	...
Poland Pologne	29 930	30 219	...	22 547	22 251	27 013	28 403	35 102	34 973	39 981
Portugal [4] Portugal [4]	20 167	21 586	15 583	18 206	20 694	20 849	20 727	21 376	19 932	...
Romania Roumanie	5 197	4 154	3 611	3 669	2 921[4]	2 901[4]	2 786[4]	...	...	...
Russian Federation Fédération de Russie	5 830	9 756	10 641	12 864	10 916	8 275	8 369	10 115	12 815	15 506
Serbia Serbie	...	...	...	...	...	...	...	5 805	6 157	7 418
Serbia and Montenegro Serbie-et-Monténégro	8 630	#5 643	6 937	6 406	6 396	...	...	...	...	...
Slovakia Slovaquie	3 371	2 795	3 384	3 402[4]	4 115[4]	3 624[4]	3 684[4]	3 154[4]	2 764	2 630
South Africa Afrique du Sud	...	...	...	67 062	39 545	...	...	...	...	...
Spain Espagne	92 770	98 925	104 510	118 363	...	...	163 817	...	137 731	127 213
Sri Lanka Sri Lanka	...	...	...	...	...	...	...	...	0	23 686
Sweden Suède	2 262	2 004	2 021	2 126	5 822	4 958	3 828	3 680	5 472	3 293
TFYR of Macedonia L'ex-R.Y. Macédoine	172	127	177	39	46	55	59	75	170	64
Turkey Turquie	25 580	26 039	29 682	25 674	30 417	24 010	34 282	19 300	...	...
Ukraine Ukraine	1 852	1 840	1 070	2 669	1 894	1 742	1 502	2 143	2 175	3 602
United Kingdom Royaume-Uni	259 097	49 224	41 098	...	40 253	40 185	...	...	...	...
United Rep. of Tanzania [7] Rép.-Unie de Tanzanie [7]	40	30	16	24	65	31	688	523	880	1 132
Viet Nam Viet Nam	20 223[1]	*18 849	25 291	28 354	38 325	48 101	64 561	66 997	64 314	71 250

Source:
United Nations Statistics Division, New York, the *Industrial Commodity Statistics Yearbook 2007* and the industrial statistics database, last accessed March 2010.

Source:
Organisation des Nations Unies, Division de statistique, New York, l'*Annuaire de statistiques industrielles par produit 2007*, et la base de données sur les statistiques industrielles, dernier accès mars 2010.

1 Insecticides only.
2 Incomplete coverage.
3 For statistical purposes, the data for China do not include those for the Hong Kong Special Administrative Region (Hong Kong SAR), Macao Special Administrative Region (Macao SAR) and Taiwan Province of China.
4 On the basis of 100 per cent active substances.
5 Production by establishments employing 10 or more persons.
6 Including other carpets and rugs.
7 Tanganyika only.

1 Insecticides seulement.
2 Couverture incomplète.
3 Pour la présentation des statistiques, les données pour la Chine ne comprennent pas la Région Administrative Spéciale de Hong Kong (Hong Kong RAS), la Région Administrative Spéciale de Macao (Macao RAS) et la province de Taiwan.
4 Sur la base de 100 pour cent de substances actives.
5 Production des établissements employant 10 personnes ou plus.
6 Y compris les autres tapis et moquettes.
7 Tanganyika seulement.

42 Pesticide production

Metric tons and millions of US dollars

Production de pesticides

Tonnes et millions de dollars É.-U.

B. Millions of US dollars • Millions de dollars É.-U.

Country or area Pays ou zone	1998	1999	2000	2001	2002	2003	2004	2005	2006	2007
Brazil Brésil	...	...	1 794	1 901	1 731	2 263	2 809	3 014	3 299	4 721
Bulgaria Bulgarie	...	...	...	...	...	...	8	10	11	13
Canada Canada	295	224	...	...	280	397	...	...	...	...
Chile Chili	...	...	...	...	...	...	...	...	...	74
Cyprus Chypre	...	...	...	...	5	4	6	4	4	...
Czech Republic République tchèque	...	...	...	17	20	28	34	33	31	49
Denmark Danemark	89	79	76	73	81	135	194	192	167	196
Dominican Republic Rép. dominicaine	6	8	8	9	9	8	...	...	...	...
El Salvador El Salvador	15	...	...	...	...	...	...	...	...	...
Finland Finlande	10	9	8	7	7	8	7	9	8	8
France France	...	3 962	3 975	3 378	3 231	2 630	2 237	...	...	...
Germany Allemagne	2 368	1 824	1 396	1 608	1 790	2 150	2 421	2 471	2 454	3 318
Hungary Hongrie	...	...	...	...	50	52	56	45	29	28
India Inde	...	...	...	...	...	5	4	1	...	...
Ireland [1] Irlande [1]	18	20	20	22	21	27	35	...	...	...
Japan Japon	2 878	3 019	3 140	2 751	2 396	2 352	2 471	2 359	2 266	2 219
Jordan Jordanie	...	...	...	...	...	...	28	26	33	43
Kenya Kenya	3	3	3	4	3	6	11	9	9	5
Lithuania Lituanie	...	...	...	...	...	^0	^0	^0	1	1
Mexico Mexique	332	351	368	357	369	322	269	344	442	429
Mozambique Mozambique	...	...	...	...	...	...	181	155	...	...
Nepal Népal	...	...	...	0	...	...	...	...	...	220
Norway Norvège	...	...	...	...	...	...	...	...	16	...
Poland Pologne	...	...	...	64	64	80	88	122	130	158
Portugal Portugal	84 [2]	83 [2]	78 [2]	88 [2]	84 [2]	91 [2]	102	85	92	...
Romania Roumanie	...	...	...	...	2	2	2	2	2	1

42

Pesticide production *(continued)*
Metric tons and millions of US dollars

Production de pesticides *(suite)*
Tonnes et millions de dollars É.-U.

B. Millions of US dollars • Millions de dollars É.-U.

Country or area Pays ou zone	1998	1999	2000	2001	2002	2003	2004	2005	2006	2007
Slovakia Slovaquie	...	...	...	7[2]	8[2]	8[2]	9[2]	8	7	5
Slovenia Slovénie	26	21	19	18	21	24	23	35	42	...
Spain Espagne	...	...	...	...	...	...	1 166	...	832	965
Sri Lanka Sri Lanka	...	...	...	...	...	71	...	...	...	...
Sweden Suède	15	14	13	11	15	15	15	16	16	19
United Rep. of Tanzania[3] Rép.-Unie de Tanzanie[3]	...	...	...	...	...	...	...	6	8	...
Uruguay Uruguay	8	7	3	8	...	14	...	...	...	...

Source:
United Nations Statistics Division, New York, the *Industrial Commodity Statistics Yearbook 2007* and the industrial statistics database, last accessed March 2010.

1 Data converted from Prodcom. Exclusion of some Prodcom codes may result in understating actual production.
2 On the basis of 100 per cent active substances.
3 Tanganyika only.

Source:
Organisation des Nations Unies, Division de statistique, New York, *l'Annuaire de statistiques industrielles par produit 2007* et la base de données sur les statistiques industrielles, dernier accès mars 2010.

1 Les données sont converties à partir Prodcom. Exclusion de certains codes Prodcom peut entraîner une sous-estimer la production réelle.
2 Sur la base de 100 pour cent de substances actives.
3 Tanganyika seulement.

43 Pig iron and crude steel production

Thousand metric tons and millions of US dollars

Production de fonte et acier brut

Milliers de tonnes et millions de dollars É.-U.

A. Thousand metric tons • Milliers de tonnes

Country or area	2000	2001	2002	2003	2004	2005	2006	2007	Pays ou zone
Albania									**Albanie**
Crude steel and semi-finished prod.	5[1]	80[1]	140[1]	140[1]	143[1]	145[1]	123	136	Acier brut et demi-prod.
Algeria									**Algérie**
Pig iron and spiegeleisen [1,2]	762	895	959	1 026	977	952	1 093	1 193	Fontes brutes et fontes spiegel [1,2]
Crude steel and semi-finished prod.	689	861	991	964	978	1 007[1]	1 158[1]	1 278[1]	Acier brut et demi-prod.
Angola [1]									**Angola** [1]
Crude steel and semi-finished prod.	9	...	...	...	...	...	...	...	Acier brut et demi-prod.
Argentina									**Argentine**
Pig iron and spiegeleisen	3 602	3 193	3 650	4 140	4 148	4 467	4 428	4 393	Fontes brutes et fontes spiegel
Crude steel and semi-finished prod.	4 472	4 107	4 354	5 033	5 133	5 386	5 533	5 387	Acier brut et demi-prod.
Australia [1]									**Australie** [1]
Pig iron and spiegeleisen [2]	7 049	6 017	6 106	6 116	5 735	6 203	6 433	6 369	Fontes brutes et fontes spiegel [2]
Crude steel and semi-finished prod.	7 129	7 033	7 527	7 544	7 414	7 757	7 881	7 939	Acier brut et demi-prod.
Austria [1]									**Autriche** [1]
Pig iron and spiegeleisen [2]	4 318	4 375	4 669	4 677	4 847	5 444	5 547	5 908	Fontes brutes et fontes spiegel [2]
Crude steel and semi-finished prod.	5 707	5 869	6 189	6 261	6 530	7 031	7 129	7 578	Acier brut et demi-prod.
Azerbaijan									**Azerbaïdjan**
Pig iron and spiegeleisen	^0	1	1	1	1	2	1	^0	Fontes brutes et fontes spiegel
Crude steel and semi-finished prod.	...	5	33	55	88	284	55	76	Acier brut et demi-prod.
Belarus									**Bélarus**
Crude steel and semi-finished prod.	1 623	1 611	1 607	1 694	1 920[1]	2 076	2 297	2 387	Acier brut et demi-prod.
Belgium [1]									**Belgique** [1]
Pig iron and spiegeleisen [2]	8 471	7 732	7 988	7 813	8 224	7 254	7 516	6 577	Fontes brutes et fontes spiegel [2]
Crude steel and semi-finished prod.	11 636	10 762	11 343	11 114	11 698	10 422	11 631	10 692	Acier brut et demi-prod.
Bosnia and Herzegovina [1]									**Bosnie-Herzégovine** [1]
Crude steel and semi-finished prod.	77	84	74	75	75	269	490	533	Acier brut et demi-prod.
Brazil									**Brésil**
Pig iron and spiegeleisen	27 723[1,2]	27 391[1,2]	29 644[1,2]	32 038[1,2]	8 455[2]	10 326	10 110	10 504	Fontes brutes et fontes spiegel
Crude steel and semi-finished prod.	27 865[1]	26 717[1]	29 604[1]	31 147[1]	18 814	18 620	19 039	20 128	Acier brut et demi-prod.
Bulgaria									**Bulgarie**
Pig iron and spiegeleisen [1,2]	...	...	...	...	1 158	...	...	1 069	Fontes brutes et fontes spiegel [1,2]
Crude steel and semi-finished prod.	98	300	...	...	282	104	160	1 909[1]	Acier brut et demi-prod.
Canada [1]									**Canada** [1]
Pig iron and spiegeleisen [2]	8 904	8 302	8 670	8 554	8 828	8 274	8 305	8 579	Fontes brutes et fontes spiegel [2]
Crude steel and semi-finished prod.	16 595	15 276	16 002	15 929	16 305	15 327	15 493	15 572	Acier brut et demi-prod.
Chile									**Chili**
Pig iron and spiegeleisen [1,2]	1 024	897	964	988	1 137	1 074	1 115	1 147	Fontes brutes et fontes spiegel [1,2]
Crude steel and semi-finished prod.	1 352[1]	1 247[1]	1 279[1]	1 377[1]	1 579[1]	289[1]	224[1]	^0[3]	Acier brut et demi-prod.
China [1,4]									**Chine** [1,4]
Pig iron and spiegeleisen [2]	131 034	147 067	170 745	213 785	256 738	344 732	413 635	471 419	Fontes brutes et fontes spiegel [2]
Crude steel and semi-finished prod.	127 236	150 906	182 249	222 413	280 486	355 790	422 660	494 899	Acier brut et demi-prod.
Colombia [1]									**Colombie** [1]
Pig iron and spiegeleisen [2]	285	319	311	283	312	325	360	341	Fontes brutes et fontes spiegel [2]
Crude steel and semi-finished prod.	660	638	664	668	730	842	1 220	1 245	Acier brut et demi-prod.
Croatia									**Croatie**
Crude steel and semi-finished prod.	71[1]	58[1]	34[1]	41[1]	86[1]	73[1]	93	0	Acier brut et demi-prod.
Cuba									**Cuba**
Pig iron and spiegeleisen	327	270	264	210	193	245	257	262	Fontes brutes et fontes spiegel
Crude steel and semi-finished prod.	304	250	247	193	178	226	237	247	Acier brut et demi-prod.
Czech Republic									**République tchèque**
Pig iron and spiegeleisen	4 621[1,2]	4 671[1,2]	4 840[1,2]	5 207[1,2]	5 384[1,2]	...	5 184	5 288	Fontes brutes et fontes spiegel
Crude steel and semi-finished prod.	6 216[1]	6 316[1]	6 512[1]	6 783[1]	7 033[1]	5 363	5 955	6 159	Acier brut et demi-prod.
Dem. Rep. of the Congo [1]									**Rép. dém. du Congo** [1]
Crude steel and semi-finished prod.	30	30	30	30	30	30	30	...	Acier brut et demi-prod.
Denmark									**Danemark**
Crude steel and semi-finished prod.	801[1]	751[1]	392[1]	...	...	43	0	^0	Acier brut et demi-prod.
Dominican Republic [1]									**Rép. dominicaine** [1]
Crude steel and semi-finished prod.	39	...	...	...	...	...	...	...	Acier brut et demi-prod.
Ecuador [1]									**Equateur** [1]
Crude steel and semi-finished prod.	58	60	69	80	72	84	85	87	Acier brut et demi-prod.

43 Pig iron and crude steel production *(continued)*

Thousand metric tons and millions of US dollars

Production de fonte et acier brut *(suite)*

Milliers de tonnes et millions de dollars É.-U.

A. Thousand metric tons • Milliers de tonnes

Country or area	2000	2001	2002	2003	2004	2005	2006	2007	Pays ou zone
Egypt[1]									**Egypte**[1]
Pig iron and spiegeleisen[2]	990	1 160	1 100	1 080	1 000	1 100	1 100	1 000	Fontes brutes et fontes spiegel[2]
Crude steel and semi-finished prod.	...	...	4 316	4 398	4 810	5 603	6 054	6 224	Acier brut et demi-prod.
El Salvador[1]									**El Salvador**[1]
Crude steel and semi-finished prod.	41	39	49	57	59	48	72	73	Acier brut et demi-prod.
Estonia[1]									**Estonie**[1]
Crude steel and semi-finished prod.	1	1	1	1	1	1	...	...	Acier brut et demi-prod.
Finland									**Finlande**
Pig iron and spiegeleisen	2 983[1,2]	2 852[1,2]	2 828[1,2]	3 092[1,2]	3 037[1,2]	4 000	3 158[1,2]	4 985	Fontes brutes et fontes spiegel
Crude steel and semi-finished prod.	4 096[1]	3 938[1]	4 003[1]	4 766[1]	4 832[1]	4 738[1]	274	183	Acier brut et demi-prod.
France[1]									**France**[1]
Pig iron and spiegeleisen[2]	13 916	12 298	13 510	12 972	13 198	12 705	13 013	12 426	Fontes brutes et fontes spiegel[2]
Crude steel and semi-finished prod.	20 954	19 343	20 258	19 758	20 770	19 481	19 852	19 250	Acier brut et demi-prod.
Germany									**Allemagne**
Pig iron and spiegeleisen	1 304	1 393	1 661	1 694	1 595	1 523	1 702	1 750	Fontes brutes et fontes spiegel
Crude steel and semi-finished prod.	20 261	21 534	12 404	12 631	12 469	11 655	11 828	12 857	Acier brut et demi-prod.
Ghana[1]									**Ghana**[1]
Crude steel and semi-finished prod.	25	25	25	25	25	25	25	25	Acier brut et demi-prod.
Greece[1]									**Grèce**[1]
Crude steel and semi-finished prod.	1 088	1 281	1 835	1 701	1 967	2 266	2 416	2 554	Acier brut et demi-prod.
Guatemala[1]									**Guatemala**[1]
Crude steel and semi-finished prod.	167	202	216	226	232	207	292	349	Acier brut et demi-prod.
Hungary									**Hongrie**
Pig iron and spiegeleisen	1 340[1,2]	1 226[1,2]	1 335[1,2]	1 333[1,2]	1	...	...	...	Fontes brutes et fontes spiegel
Crude steel and semi-finished prod.	1 871[1]	1 956[1]	2 053[1]	1 989[1]	118	164	138	126	Acier brut et demi-prod.
India[1]									**Inde**[1]
Pig iron and spiegeleisen[2]	21 321	21 875	24 315	26 550	25 117	27 125	28 256	28 828	Fontes brutes et fontes spiegel[2]
Crude steel and semi-finished prod.	26 924	27 291	28 814	31 779	32 626	45 780	49 450	53 080	Acier brut et demi-prod.
Indonesia									**Indonésie**
Crude steel and semi-finished prod.	2 848[1]	2 781[1]	2 462[1]	2 042[1]	3 682[1]	3 675[1]	3 759[1]	1 237	Acier brut et demi-prod.
Iran (Islamic Rep. of)									**Iran (Rép. islamique d')**
Pig iron and spiegeleisen	2 202[1,2]	2 183[1,2]	2 182[1,2]	2 231[1,2]	2 096[1,2]	2 305[1,2]	229	305	Fontes brutes et fontes spiegel
Crude steel and semi-finished prod.	6 600[1]	6 916[1]	7 321[1]	7 869[1]	8 682[1]	2 310	2 487	2 266	Acier brut et demi-prod.
Ireland[1]									**Irlande**[1]
Crude steel and semi-finished prod.	360	150	...	...	...	...	...	...	Acier brut et demi-prod.
Israel[1]									**Israël**[1]
Crude steel and semi-finished prod.	280	280	280	280	280	300	300	300	Acier brut et demi-prod.
Italy[1]									**Italie**[1]
Pig iron and spiegeleisen[2]	11 220	11 220	9 775	10 148	10 604	11 423	11 497	11 110	Fontes brutes et fontes spiegel[2]
Crude steel and semi-finished prod.	26 759	26 545	26 066	27 058	28 604	29 350	31 624	31 553	Acier brut et demi-prod.
Japan									**Japon**
Pig iron and spiegeleisen	5 244	5 325	5 153	4 904	4 759	4 457	4 691	4 730	Fontes brutes et fontes spiegel
Crude steel and semi-finished prod.	11 884	11 350	11 965	12 476	14 340	13 452	14 044	14 602	Acier brut et demi-prod.
Jordan[1]									**Jordanie**[1]
Crude steel and semi-finished prod.	30	30	134	135	140	150	150	150	Acier brut et demi-prod.
Kazakhstan									**Kazakhstan**
Pig iron and spiegeleisen	4 010	3 906	4 009	4 138	4 283	3 582	3 369	3 795	Fontes brutes et fontes spiegel
Crude steel and semi-finished prod.	4 799	4 691	9 081	9 360	9 903	7 196	5 007	4 970	Acier brut et demi-prod.
Kenya[1]									**Kenya**[1]
Crude steel and semi-finished prod.	20	20	20	20	20	20	20	20	Acier brut et demi-prod.
Korea, Dem. P. R.[1]									**Corée, R. p. dém. de**[1]
Pig iron and spiegeleisen[2]	250	250	250	250	250	250	250	...	Fontes brutes et fontes spiegel[2]
Crude steel and semi-finished prod.	300	300	300	300	300	300	300	300	Acier brut et demi-prod.
Korea, Republic of									**Corée, République de**
Pig iron and spiegeleisen[1,2]	24 937	25 898	26 570	27 314	27 556	27 309	27 559	29 437	Fontes brutes et fontes spiegel[1,2]
Crude steel and semi-finished prod.	43 423	44 199	45 482	46 561	46 466	46 123	48 259	51 003	Acier brut et demi-prod.
Latvia[1]									**Lettonie**[1]
Crude steel and semi-finished prod.	498	515	520	520	520	550	...	696	Acier brut et demi-prod.
Libyan Arab Jamah.[1]									**Jamah. arabe libyenne**[1]
Crude steel and semi-finished prod.	1 055	846	886	1 007	1 026	1 255	1 151	1 250	Acier brut et demi-prod.
Luxembourg[1]									**Luxembourg**[1]
Crude steel and semi-finished prod.	2 571	2 725	2 719	2 675	2 684	2 194	2 802	2 858	Acier brut et demi-prod.

43

Pig iron and crude steel production *(continued)*
Thousand metric tons and millions of US dollars

Production de fonte et acier brut *(suite)*
Milliers de tonnes et millions de dollars É.-U.

A. Thousand metric tons • Milliers de tonnes

Country or area	2000	2001	2002	2003	2004	2005	2006	2007	Pays ou zone
Malaysia [1]									**Malaisie** [1]
Crude steel and semi-finished prod.	3 650	4 100	4 722	3 960	5 698	5 296	5 834	6 895	Acier brut et demi-prod.
Mauritania [1]									**Mauritanie** [1]
Crude steel and semi-finished prod.	5	5	5	5	5	5	5	5	Acier brut et demi-prod.
Mexico									**Mexique**
Pig iron and spiegeleisen [1,2]	4 856	4 373	3 996	4 183	4 278	4 047	3 790	4 078	Fontes brutes et fontes spiegel [1,2]
Crude steel and semi-finished prod.	13 881	12 706	12 831	14 080	15 238	14 619	14 738	15 239	Acier brut et demi-prod.
Mongolia [1]									**Mongolie** [1]
Crude steel and semi-finished prod.	35	35	35	35	35	35	35	35	Acier brut et demi-prod.
Montenegro									**Monténégro**
Crude steel and semi-finished prod.	...	...	17	6	30	28	20	38	Acier brut et demi-prod.
Morocco [1]									**Maroc** [1]
Pig iron and spiegeleisen [2]	15	15	15	15	15	15	15	15	Fontes brutes et fontes spiegel [2]
Crude steel and semi-finished prod.	5	5	5	5	5	205	314	512	Acier brut et demi-prod.
Myanmar [1]									**Myanmar** [1]
Crude steel and semi-finished prod.	25	25	25	25	25	25	25	25	Acier brut et demi-prod.
Netherlands [1]									**Pays-Bas** [1]
Pig iron and spiegeleisen [2]	4 970	5 305	5 367	5 846	6 011	6 031	5 417	6 412	Fontes brutes et fontes spiegel [2]
Crude steel and semi-finished prod.	5 666	6 037	6 117	6 571	6 848	6 919	6 372	7 368	Acier brut et demi-prod.
New Zealand [1]									**Nouvelle-Zélande** [1]
Pig iron and spiegeleisen [2]	603	646	617	700	719	652	664	679	Fontes brutes et fontes spiegel [2]
Crude steel and semi-finished prod.	702	826	765	853	885	889	810	845	Acier brut et demi-prod.
Nigeria [1]									**Nigéria** [1]
Crude steel and semi-finished prod.	...	...	...	...	40	100	100	100	Acier brut et demi-prod.
Norway [1]									**Norvège** [1]
Pig iron and spiegeleisen [2]	70	70	...	...	...	100	100	100	Fontes brutes et fontes spiegel [2]
Crude steel and semi-finished prod.	679	640	...	...	...	705	684	708	Acier brut et demi-prod.
Pakistan									**Pakistan**
Pig iron and spiegeleisen [2]	1 000[1]	1 067[1]	1 000[1]	1 000[1]	1 180[5]	1 137[5]	768[5]	900[1]	Fontes brutes et fontes spiegel [2]
Crude steel and semi-finished prod. [1]	950	953	970	1 000	1 145	825	1 040	1 090	Acier brut et demi-prod. [1]
Paraguay [1]									**Paraguay** [1]
Pig iron and spiegeleisen [2]	82	72	87	98	119	123	128	110	Fontes brutes et fontes spiegel [2]
Crude steel and semi-finished prod.	77	71	80	91	107	101	115	95	Acier brut et demi-prod.
Peru [1]									**Pérou** [1]
Pig iron and spiegeleisen [2]	327	316	240	226	272	263	306	351	Fontes brutes et fontes spiegel [2]
Crude steel and semi-finished prod.	751	690	611	609	726	790	896	881	Acier brut et demi-prod.
Philippines [1]									**Philippines** [1]
Crude steel and semi-finished prod.	426	500	550	500	400	470	558	718	Acier brut et demi-prod.
Poland									**Pologne**
Pig iron and spiegeleisen	6 492[1,2]	5 440[1,2]	5 294[1,2]	5 632[1,2]	6 400[1,2]	4 477[1,2]	5 333[1,2]	5 804	Fontes brutes et fontes spiegel
Crude steel and semi-finished prod.	10 498[1]	8 809[1]	8 368[1]	9 107[1]	10 593[1]	8 336[1]	10 008[1]	0	Acier brut et demi-prod.
Portugal									**Portugal**
Pig iron and spiegeleisen	379[1,2]	82[1,2]	0	0	0	0	0	...	Fontes brutes et fontes spiegel
Crude steel and semi-finished prod.	1 088[1]	728[1]	920	1 000	...	...	1 400[1]	1 400[1]	Acier brut et demi-prod.
Qatar [1]									**Qatar** [1]
Crude steel and semi-finished prod.	729	891	1 027	1 055	1 089	1 057	1 003	1 147	Acier brut et demi-prod.
Republic of Moldova [6]									**République de Moldova** [6]
Crude steel and semi-finished prod.	908[1]	967[1]	514[1]	850[1]	1 012	...	785[1]	965[1]	Acier brut et demi-prod.
Romania [1]									**Roumanie** [1]
Pig iron and spiegeleisen [2]	2 985	3 085	3 976	4 101	4 244	4 098	3 975	3 923	Fontes brutes et fontes spiegel [2]
Crude steel and semi-finished prod.	4 672	4 935	5 491	5 691	6 042	6 280	6 263	6 261	Acier brut et demi-prod.
Russian Federation									**Fédération de Russie**
Pig iron and spiegeleisen	44 584	45 016	46 691	48 812	50 427	49 175	52 362	51 516	Fontes brutes et fontes spiegel
Crude steel and semi-finished prod.	59 150	59 030	59 883	62 839	65 646	66 262	70 816	72 370	Acier brut et demi-prod.
Saudi Arabia [1]									**Arabie saoudite** [1]
Crude steel and semi-finished prod.	2 981	3 413	3 570	3 944	3 902	4 186	3 974	4 644	Acier brut et demi-prod.
Serbia									**Serbie**
Pig iron and spiegeleisen	...	...	...	...	...	1 115	1 529	1 377	Fontes brutes et fontes spiegel
Crude steel and semi-finished prod.	...	...	...	...	...	1	1	...	Acier brut et demi-prod.
Serbia and Montenegro [1]									**Serbie-et-Monténégro** [1]
Pig iron and spiegeleisen [2]	598	456	485	635	1 003	1 208	1 762	...	Fontes brutes et fontes spiegel [2]
Crude steel and semi-finished prod.	696	595	591	711	1 175	1 292	1 823	...	Acier brut et demi-prod.

43 Pig iron and crude steel production *(continued)*

Thousand metric tons and millions of US dollars

Production de fonte et acier brut *(suite)*

Milliers de tonnes et millions de dollars É.-U.

A. Thousand metric tons • Milliers de tonnes

Country or area	2000	2001	2002	2003	2004	2005	2006	2007	Pays ou zone
Singapore [1]									**Singapour** [1]
Crude steel and semi-finished prod.	603	456	460	561	610	572	607	640	Acier brut et demi-prod.
Slovakia									**Slovaquie**
Pig iron and spiegeleisen [1,2]	3 166	3 255	3 533	3 892	3 765	3 681	4 145	4 012	Fontes brutes et fontes spiegel [1,2]
Crude steel and semi-finished prod.	3 733	181	119	95	515	280	663	516	Acier brut et demi-prod.
Slovenia									**Slovénie**
Crude steel and semi-finished prod.	6	...	481[1]	...	...	583[1]	...	...	Acier brut et demi-prod.
South Africa [1]									**Afrique du Sud** [1]
Pig iron and spiegeleisen [2]	6 292	5 820	5 823	6 234	6 011	6 130	6 159	5 358	Fontes brutes et fontes spiegel [2]
Crude steel and semi-finished prod.	8 481	8 821	9 095	9 481	9 500	9 494	9 718	9 098	Acier brut et demi-prod.
Spain									**Espagne**
Pig iron and spiegeleisen [1,2]	4 059	4 219	4 021	3 645	4 036	4 160	...	3 976	Fontes brutes et fontes spiegel [1,2]
Crude steel and semi-finished prod.	15 874[1]	16 504[1]	16 408[1]	16 286[1]	17 621[1]	502	600	581	Acier brut et demi-prod.
Sri Lanka [1]									**Sri Lanka** [1]
Crude steel and semi-finished prod.	30	30	30	30	30	30	30	30	Acier brut et demi-prod.
Sweden									**Suède**
Pig iron and spiegeleisen	3 145[1,2]	3 614[1,2]	3 703[1,2]	3 710[1,2]	3 871[1,2]	0	0	0	Fontes brutes et fontes spiegel
Crude steel and semi-finished prod.	5 227[1]	5 518[1]	5 754[1]	5 707[1]	5 978[1]	3 154	3 192	3 344	Acier brut et demi-prod.
Switzerland [1]									**Suisse** [1]
Pig iron and spiegeleisen [2]	80	80	80	80	80	80	80	...	Fontes brutes et fontes spiegel [2]
Crude steel and semi-finished prod.	1 000	1 000	1 000	1 000	1 000	1 158	1 252	1 264	Acier brut et demi-prod.
Syrian Arab Republic [1]									**Rép. arabe syrienne** [1]
Crude steel and semi-finished prod.	70	70	70	70	70	70	70	70	Acier brut et demi-prod.
Thailand [1]									**Thaïlande** [1]
Crude steel and semi-finished prod.	2 100	2 127	2 538	3 551	4 533	5 161	5 210	5 565	Acier brut et demi-prod.
TFYR of Macedonia									**L'ex-R.Y. Macédoine**
Crude steel and semi-finished prod.	161[1]	260[1]	260[1]	291[1]	309[1]	313	354	366	Acier brut et demi-prod.
Trinidad and Tobago									**Trinité-et-Tobago**
Crude steel and semi-finished prod.	741[1]	668[1]	817	896	790	712	673	682[1]	Acier brut et demi-prod.
Tunisia [1]									**Tunisie** [1]
Pig iron and spiegeleisen [2]	195	191	152	45	...	...	...	...	Fontes brutes et fontes spiegel [2]
Crude steel and semi-finished prod.	229	239	200	86	66	115	160	160	Acier brut et demi-prod.
Turkey									**Turquie**
Pig iron and spiegeleisen [1,2]	5 333	5 289	5 003	5 706	5 836	5 970	5 952	6 235	Fontes brutes et fontes spiegel [1,2]
Crude steel and semi-finished prod.	14 325[1]	14 981[1]	16 467[1]	18 298[1]	20 478[1]	20 965[1]	23 308	25 754[1]	Acier brut et demi-prod.
Uganda [1]									**Ouganda** [1]
Crude steel and semi-finished prod.	30	30	30	30	30	30	30	30	Acier brut et demi-prod.
Ukraine									**Ukraine**
Pig iron and spiegeleisen	25 699	26 379	27 633	29 459	30 978	30 746	32 929	35 650	Fontes brutes et fontes spiegel
Crude steel and semi-finished prod.	31 767[1]	33 108[1]	34 050[1]	50 564	51 232	50 458	54 020	56 708	Acier brut et demi-prod.
United Arab Emirates [1]									**Emirats arabes unis** [1]
Crude steel and semi-finished prod.	90	90	90	90	90	90	90	90	Acier brut et demi-prod.
United Kingdom [1]									**Royaume-Uni** [1]
Pig iron and spiegeleisen [2]	10 890	9 870	8 561	10 228	10 180	10 189	10 696	10 960	Fontes brutes et fontes spiegel [2]
Crude steel and semi-finished prod.	15 155	13 543	11 667	13 268	13 766	13 239	13 871	14 317	Acier brut et demi-prod.
United States									**Etats-Unis**
Pig iron and spiegeleisen [2]	47 900	42 100	40 200	40 600	42 300	37 200	37 900	36 300	Fontes brutes et fontes spiegel [2]
Crude steel and semi-finished prod. [7]	102 000	90 100	91 600	93 700	99 700	94 900	98 200	98 100	Acier brut et demi-prod. [7]
Uruguay [1]									**Uruguay** [1]
Crude steel and semi-finished prod.	38	31	34	40	58	64	57	71	Acier brut et demi-prod.
Uzbekistan [1]									**Ouzbékistan** [1]
Crude steel and semi-finished prod.	407	433	450	499	602	595	730	645	Acier brut et demi-prod.
Venezuela (Boliv. Rep. of) [1]									**Venezuela (Rép. boliv. du)** [1]
Crude steel and semi-finished prod.	3 835	3 813	4 164	3 930	4 561	4 910	4 864	5 005	Acier brut et demi-prod.
Viet Nam									**Viet Nam**
Pig iron and spiegeleisen	41	31	172	380	294	91	80	109	Fontes brutes et fontes spiegel
Crude steel and semi-finished prod.	36	231	412	591	670	474	827	890	Acier brut et demi-prod.
Zimbabwe [1]									**Zimbabwe** [1]
Pig iron and spiegeleisen [2]	277	156	122	182	125	129	38	38	Fontes brutes et fontes spiegel [2]
Crude steel and semi-finished prod.	258	149	105	152	135	107	24	23	Acier brut et demi-prod.

43 Pig iron and crude steel production *(continued)*

Thousand metric tons and millions of US dollars

Production de fonte et acier brut *(suite)*

Milliers de tonnes et millions de dollars É.-U.

A. Thousand metric tons • Milliers de tonnes

Source:
United Nations Statistics Division, New York, the *Industrial Commodity Statistics Yearbook 2007* and the industrial statistics database, last accessed February 2010.

1 Source: International Iron and Steel Institute (Brussels).
2 Excluding spiegeleisen.
3 Incomplete coverage.
4 For statistical purposes, the data for China do not include those for the Hong Kong Special Administrative Region (Hong Kong SAR), Macao Special Administrative Region (Macao SAR) and Taiwan Province of China.
5 Twelve months ending 30 June of the year stated.
6 Excluding the Transnistria region.
7 Source: American Iron and Steel Institute (AISI).

Source:
Organisation des Nations Unies, Division de statistique, New York, l'*Annuaire de statistiques industrielles par produit 2007* et la base de données sur les statistiques industrielles, dernier accès février 2010.

1 Source: Institut international du fer et de l'acier (Bruxelles).
2 Non compris la fonte spiegel.
3 Couverture incomplète.
4 Pour la présentation des statistiques, les données pour la Chine ne comprennent pas la Région Administrative Spéciale de Hong Kong (Hong Kong RAS), la Région Administrative Spéciale de Macao (Macao RAS) et la province de Taiwan.
5 Période de 12 mois finissant le 30 juin de l'année indiquée.
6 Non compris la région de Transnistrie.
7 Source: Institut américain du fer et de l'acier.

43 Pig iron and crude steel production

Thousand metric tons and millions of US dollars

Production de fonte et acier brut

Milliers de tonnes et millions de dollars É.-U.

B. Millions of US dollars • Millions de dollars É.-U.

Country or area	2000	2001	2002	2003	2004	2005	2006	2007	Pays ou zone
Azerbaijan									**Azerbaïdjan**
Pig iron and spiegeleisen	0.1	0.2	0.2	0.3	0.4	0.7	0.9	0.3	Fontes brutes et fontes spiegel
Crude steel and semi-finished prod.	...	0.8	6.0	12.4	23.6	78.9	15.7	35.7	Acier brut et demi-prod.
Brazil									**Brésil**
Pig iron and spiegeleisen	507.6	460.5	593.0	767.3	1 670.1	2 248.6	2 418.8	2 975.1	Fontes brutes et fontes spiegel
Crude steel and semi-finished prod.	1 875.9	1 440.4	1 638.2	2 155.6	2 561.3	2 670.8	2 837.7	3 642.8	Acier brut et demi-prod.
Bulgaria									**Bulgarie**
Crude steel and semi-finished prod.	16.5	46.2	0.0	0.0	104.1	36.8	66.1	...	Acier brut et demi-prod.
Chile									**Chili**
Pig iron and spiegeleisen	...	...	...	...	...	0.7	0.3	0.2	Fontes brutes et fontes spiegel
Crude steel and semi-finished prod.	...	...	...	...	...	172.2	163.1	1.0[1]	Acier brut et demi-prod.
Czech Republic									**République tchèque**
Pig iron and spiegeleisen	...	...	...	...	...	...	1 593.7	1 638.9	Fontes brutes et fontes spiegel
Crude steel and semi-finished prod.	...	...	746.9	773.8	...	2 644.4	2 855.6	3 402.7	Acier brut et demi-prod.
Denmark									**Danemark**
Crude steel and semi-finished prod.	31.0	22.4	18.9	23.3	32.7	44.2	2.5	3.9	Acier brut et demi-prod.
Finland									**Finlande**
Pig iron and spiegeleisen	0.9	3.6	0.9	1.1	1.2	1.2	3.8	1.5	Fontes brutes et fontes spiegel
Crude steel and semi-finished prod.	30.4	22.4	44.2	310.4	540.1	485.0	286.0	118.5	Acier brut et demi-prod.
France									**France**
Crude steel and semi-finished prod.	32.1	36.0	37.5	...	...	...	...	...	Acier brut et demi-prod.
Germany									**Allemagne**
Pig iron and spiegeleisen	169.5	188.6	227.8	274.0	343.7	350.9	467.2	545.7	Fontes brutes et fontes spiegel
Crude steel and semi-finished prod.	2 586.6	2 729.3	2 698.3	3 408.0	4 161.7	5 174.3	5 534.3	7 047.2	Acier brut et demi-prod.
Hungary									**Hongrie**
Pig iron and spiegeleisen	...	...	...	...	0.2	...	...	...	Fontes brutes et fontes spiegel
Crude steel and semi-finished prod.	...	...	52.6	46.0	51.8	79.7	72.1	82.8	Acier brut et demi-prod.
Japan									**Japon**
Pig iron and spiegeleisen	806.8	578.1	663.0	677.4	940.3	1 169.6	1 204.9	1 261.9	Fontes brutes et fontes spiegel
Crude steel and semi-finished prod.	3 111.1	2 717.4	2 663.8	3 337.0	4 641.6	5 861.8	6 555.6	8 143.1	Acier brut et demi-prod.
Jordan									**Jordanie**
Crude steel and semi-finished prod.	...	...	...	...	18.5	22.3	22.2	21.5	Acier brut et demi-prod.
Mexico									**Mexique**
Crude steel and semi-finished prod.	3 563.8	3 359.1	3 286.5	3 664.5	5 225.0	5 249.5	5 881.9	6 798.1	Acier brut et demi-prod.
Poland									**Pologne**
Pig iron and spiegeleisen	51.4	29.6	20.8	29.4	58.1	...	...	32.1	Fontes brutes et fontes spiegel
Crude steel and semi-finished prod.	596.7	562.1	530.0	495.0	1 163.1	818.1	...	0.0	Acier brut et demi-prod.
Romania									**Roumanie**
Pig iron and spiegeleisen	...	...	0.1	0.3	0.2	0.3	0.4	0.6	Fontes brutes et fontes spiegel
Crude steel and semi-finished prod.	...	...	11.9	12.7	32.9	37.4	37.8	64.0	Acier brut et demi-prod.
Slovakia									**Slovaquie**
Pig iron and spiegeleisen	...	...	...	40.7	102.1	...	...	...	Fontes brutes et fontes spiegel
Crude steel and semi-finished prod.	...	43.0	35.7	31.2	180.6	118.8	287.0	257.5	Acier brut et demi-prod.
Slovenia									**Slovénie**
Crude steel and semi-finished prod.	4.9	...	...	...	...	...	...	...	Acier brut et demi-prod.
Spain									**Espagne**
Crude steel and semi-finished prod.	...	...	...	...	118.0	248.7	306.1	355.9	Acier brut et demi-prod.
Sweden									**Suède**
Crude steel and semi-finished prod.	1 623.4	1 278.0	1 465.1	1 008.7	1 398.0	1 631.7	2 070.2	2 474.5	Acier brut et demi-prod.
Uruguay									**Uruguay**
Crude steel and semi-finished prod.	0.2	0.2	...	0.7	...	...	...	...	Acier brut et demi-prod.

Source:
United Nations Statistics Division, New York, the *Industrial Commodity Statistics Yearbook 2007* and the industrial statistics database, last accessed February 2010.

Source:
Organisation des Nations Unies, Division de statistique, New York, l'*Annuaire de statistiques industrielles par produit 2007* et la base de données sur les statistiques industrielles, dernier accès février 2010.

1 Incomplete coverage.

1 Couverture incomplète.

44 Production of aluminium, unwrought

Thousand metric tons and millions of US dollars

Production d'aluminium non travaillé

Milliers de tonnes et millions de dollars É.-U.

A. Thousand metric tons • Milliers de tonnes

Country or area Pays ou zone	1998	1999	2000	2001	2002	2003	2004	2005	2006	2007
Argentina Argentine	187	206	261	248	269	272	272	271	273	286
Australia [1] Australie [1]	1 589	1 686	...	...	...	...	...	...	...	...
Austria Autriche	126	143[2]	158[2]	158[2]	...	...	...	...	...	...
Azerbaijan Azerbaïdjan	...	...	...	...	...	19[3]	30[3]	0	0	0
Bahrain Bahreïn	501[3]	502	512	523[3]	519[3]	532[3]	530[3]	...	...	...
Bosnia and Herzegovina Bosnie-Herzégovine	32	57	95[3]	96[3]	103[3]	113	115[3]	...	...	...
Brazil Brésil	1 388[2]	1 440[3]	1 035	951	1 449	1 195	1 275	1 307	1 267	1 557
Bulgaria Bulgarie	...	...	1	...	...	0	0	0	0	0
Cameroon Cameroun	89	94	100	85	72	79	86	86	91	90
Canada Canada	2 485[2]	2 502	2 373[3]	2 583[3]	2 709[3]	808	2 592[3]	...	...	...
China [4] Chine [4]	2 362	2 809	2 989	3 576	4 511	5 866	6 690	7 787	9 266	12 340
Croatia Croatie	4	14	5	0	1	^0	^0	^0	^0	0
Czech Republic République tchèque	45[3]	40[3]	40[3]	...	...	...	...	0	0	0
Denmark Danemark	0	0	0	0	0	0	0	3	1	0
Egypt Egypte	187[5]	193[3]	189[3]	191[3]	195[3]	195[3]	215[3]	...	...	...
Finland Finlande	2	...	...	...	...	...	...	0	0	0
France * France *	663	694	701	713	713	685	...	...	...	...
Germany Allemagne	375	395	404	404	410	438	...	329	225	280
Ghana Ghana	56	114	156	162	133	...	...	...	...	...
Greece Grèce	161	161	168[3]	166[3]	165[3]	166[6]	165[3]	...	...	...
Hungary Hongrie	92	89	89[3]	110[3]	...	...	2	...	...	...
Iceland Islande	160	161	167	169	194	286	192	180	...	446
India Inde	542[3]	614[3]	644[3]	624[3]	671[3]	...	124	209	...	...
Indonesia Indonésie	133[2]	112[2,7]	160[3]	180[3]	*160[3]	200[3]	230[3]	...	...	...
Iran (Islamic Rep. of) Iran (Rép. islamique d')	137[2]	164[2]	146[3]	160[3]	169[3]	170[3]	170[3]	336	218	216
Italy Italie	690	689	757	766	782	#74	76	...	...	...

44 Production of aluminium, unwrought *(continued)*

Thousand metric tons and millions of US dollars

Production d'aluminium non travaillé *(suite)*

Milliers de tonnes et millions de dollars É.-U.

A. Thousand metric tons • Milliers de tonnes

Country or area Pays ou zone	1998	1999	2000	2001	2002	2003	2004	2005	2006	2007
Korea, Republic of Corée, République de	...	...	312	325	357	356	454	463	...	...
Kuwait Koweït	4	7	7	7	6	6	6	7	10	...
Mozambique Mozambique	...	...	54[3]	266[3]	273[3]	409	548	549	567	573
Netherlands Pays-Bas	366	391	405	294[3]	284[3]	278[3]	326[3]	...	...	...
New Zealand Nouvelle-Zélande	389[2]	348[3]	328[3]	322[3]	335[3]	340[3]	350[3]	...	...	...
Norway Norvège	1 058[2]	1 199[3]	1 280[3]	1 291[3]	...	...	...	...	...	...
Poland Pologne	54	51	#12	12	14	15	14	11	18	20
Romania [8,9] Roumanie [8,9]	175	174	181	183	190	205	...	...	...	...
Russian Federation [3] Fédération de Russie [3]	3 005	3 146	3 245	3 300	3 347	3 478	3 593	...	...	...
Serbia Serbie	...	...	...	...	...	...	...	^0	1	2
Serbia and Montenegro Serbie-et-Monténégro	61	#73	88	100	112	117	115[3]	...	...	...
Slovakia Slovaquie	121	109	110	...	...	...	...	...	...	...
South Africa [3] Afrique du Sud [3]	677	689	673	662	707	738	863	...	...	...
Spain Espagne	570[2]	588[2]	366[3]	376[3]	380[3]	389[3]	...	...	...	82
Suriname Suriname	28	7	...	...	2	...	...	...	...	...
Sweden Suède	31	36	35	35	29	28	...	...	^0	0
Switzerland Suisse	47[2]	41[2]	36[3]	36[3]	40[3]	44[3]	45[3]	...	...	...
Tajikistan Tadjikistan	196	229	269[3]	289[3]	306[3]	319[3]	358[3]	...	...	...
TFYR of Macedonia L'ex-R.Y. Macédoine	7	6	4	3	5	5	...	...	...	...
Turkey Turquie	62	62	62	62	63	63	60[3]	27	...	...
Ukraine [3] Ukraine [3]	178	226	104	106	112	...	...	...	...	...
United Arab Emirates [3] Emirats arabes unis [3]	...	...	0	1	1	1	1	...	...	...
United Kingdom [3] Royaume-Uni [3]	494	547	305	341	344	343	360	...	...	...
United States Etats-Unis	3 713	3 779	3 668	2 637	2 707	2 703	2 516	2 481	2 284	2 554
Venezuela (Boliv. Rep. of) Venezuela (Rép. boliv. du)	617[2]	595[2]	571[3]	571[3]	605[3]	601[3]	624[3]	...	...	...

Source:
United Nations Statistics Division, New York, the *Industrial Commodity Statistics Yearbook 2007* and the industrial statistics database, last accessed April 2010.

Source:
Organisation des Nations Unies, Division de statistique, *l'Annuaire de statistiques industrielles par produit 2007* et la base de données sur les statistiques industrielles, dernier accès avril 2010.

44

Production of aluminium, unwrought *(continued)*

Thousand metric tons and millions of US dollars

Production d'aluminium non travaillé *(suite)*

Milliers de tonnes et millions de dollars É.-U.

A. Thousand metric tons • Milliers de tonnes

1 Twelve months ending 30 June of the year stated.
2 Source: World Metal Statistics (London).
3 Source: U. S. Geological Survey (Washington, D. C.).
4 For statistical purposes, the data for China do not include those for the Hong Kong Special Administrative Region (Hong Kong SAR), Macao Special Administrative Region (Macao SAR) and Taiwan Province of China.
5 Including aluminium plates, shapes and bars.
6 Incomplete coverage.
7 Primary metal production only.
8 Including alloys.
9 Including pure content of virgin alloys.

1 Période de 12 mois finissant le 30 juin de l'année indiquée.
2 Source: World Metal Statistics (Londres).
3 Source: U. S. Geological Survey (Washington, D. C.).
4 Pour la présentation des statistiques, les données pour la Chine ne comprennent pas la Région Administrative Spéciale de Hong Kong (Hong Kong RAS), la Région Administrative Spéciale de Macao (Macao RAS) et la province de Taiwan.
5 Y compris les tôles, les profilés et les barres d'aluminium.
6 Couverture incomplète.
7 Production du métal de première fusion seulement.
8 Y compris les alliages.
9 Y compris la teneur pure des alliages de première fusion.

44 Production of aluminium, unwrought

Thousand metric tons and millions of US dollars

Production d'aluminium non travaillé

Milliers de tonnes et millions de dollars É.-U.

B. Millions of US dollars • Millions de dollars É.-U.

Country or area Pays ou zone	1998	1999	2000	2001	2002	2003	2004	2005	2006	2007
Brazil Brésil	...	...	1 442	1 305	1 345	1 499	1 991	2 179	2 935	3 323
Bulgaria Bulgarie	...	...	1	...	...	0	0	0	0	0
Canada Canada	741	789	985	1 086	1 090	1 195	...	...	...	...
Denmark Danemark	0	0	0	0	0	2	3	7	4	...
Finland Finlande	8	0	0	0	...	...	...	0	0	0
Germany Allemagne	441	512	423	441	469	642	653	542	534	725
Hungary Hongrie	...	...	...	...	...	...	4	...	...	...
Iceland Islande	...	...	...	...	...	...	370	375	...	1 246
India Inde	...	...	...	...	...	10	28	99	...	...
Italy Italie	...	...	...	...	...	111	139	...	...	...
Mozambique Mozambique	...	...	...	...	...	563	882	1 083	1 451	1 505
Poland Pologne	...	...	16	17	20	22	23	18	41	47
Spain Espagne	...	...	...	...	...	...	...	...	...	226
Sweden Suède	37	38	38	36	29	35	1	...	1	0
United Kingdom Royaume-Uni	154	156	152	180	174	153	176	...	...	...

Source:
United Nations Statistics Division, New York, the *Industrial Commodity Statistics Yearbook 2007* and the industrial statistics database, last accessed March 2010.

Source:
Organisation des Nations Unies, Division de statistique, *l'Annuaire de statistiques industrielles par produit 2007* et la base de données sur les statistiques industrielles, dernier accès mars 2010.

45 Radio and television receivers production

Physical quantities in thousands and monetary value in millions of US dollars

Production de récepteurs de radio et de télévision

Quantités physiques en milliers et valeurs monétaires en millions de dollars E.–U.

A. Quantities: thousands • Quantités : milliers

Country or area Pays ou zone	Radio receivers Récepteurs de radio					Television receivers Récepteurs de télévision				
	2003	2004	2005	2006	2007	2003	2004	2005	2006	2007
Algeria Algérie	...	...	...	...	...	292	206	...	...	...
Argentina Argentine	203	340	301	517	679	332	941	1 627	2 042	2 219
Azerbaijan Azerbaïdjan	...	...	...	...	...	...	...	7	5	...
Bangladesh [1] Bangladesh [1]	13	15	20	24	...	131	141	172	192	...
Belarus Bélarus	31	22	13	8	5	690	1 262	1 308	1 067	702
Brazil Brésil	3 905	6 335	5 813	5 913	...	6 952	10 872	13 236	15 346	17 555
Bulgaria Bulgarie	...	...	...	...	...	...	...	159	249	...
Cuba Cuba	6	66	214	522	26	325	100	128	150	118
Czech Republic République tchèque	...	...	...	...	8 795	...	...	...	...	...
Denmark Danemark	68	64	49	125	107	...	...	273	84	...
France France	3 498	...	...	...	...	...	...	...	...	...
Germany Allemagne	...	...	...	...	...	1 565	2 564	2 209	2 207	2 009
Hungary Hongrie	2 991	2 840	2 248	2 258	2 341	...	4 892	5 832	8 350	9 891
India Inde	0	...	...	...	...	3 572	5 044	6 060	5 853	...
Iran (Islamic Rep. of) Iran (Rép. islamique d')	^0	^0	1	1	^0	...	...	...	...	...
Iraq Iraq	...	...	...	29	...	...	...	...	4	...
Ireland Irlande	174	1 490	...	...	...	...	...	...	...	...
Japan Japon	2 892	1 605	1 769	1 456	1 941	10 404	10 521	11 072	15 740	13 798
Kazakhstan Kazakhstan	...	...	^0	0	0	...	...	346	410	323
Korea, Republic of Corée, République de	318	31	1	...	...	7 336	6 425	5 843	...	...
Kyrgyzstan Kirghizistan	...	...	...	...	...	8	3	2	...	22
Malaysia Malaisie	27 634	28 587	19 245	28 433	46 253	9 915	9 895	10 409	7 594	6 028
Mexico Mexique	1 580	1 310	903	781	1 068	...	...	...	...	...
Nigeria Nigéria	26	26	26	...	...	3	3	3	...	...
Poland Pologne	...	...	15	18	...	...	...	6 525	8 920	13 147

45 Radio and television receivers production *(continued)*

Physical quantities in thousands and monetary value in millions of US dollars

Production de récepteurs de radio et de télévision *(suite)*

Quantités physiques en milliers et valeurs monétaires en millions de dollars E.–U.

A. Quantities: thousands • Quantités : milliers

Country or area Pays ou zone	Radio receivers Récepteurs de radio					Television receivers Récepteurs de télévision				
	2003	2004	2005	2006	2007	2003	2004	2005	2006	2007
Portugal Portugal	7 310	7 805	9 487	10 592	...	0	0	0	0	...
Republic of Moldova République de Moldova	3	6	3	^0	...	...	...	...	...	...
Russian Federation Fédération de Russie	278	194	313	184	152	2 383	4 691	6 278	4 601	6 823
South Africa [2] Afrique du Sud [2]	...	...	...	...	...	359	...	...	...	...
Spain Espagne	47	71	110	151	150	...	...	3 084	2 991	3 010
Sweden Suède	...	...	275	145	367	...	...	344	0	0
Thailand Thaïlande	...	...	...	...	...	6 538	6 942	6 916	6 255	6 074
Ukraine Ukraine	21	106	18	2	1	415	443	651	434	514
Viet Nam Viet Nam	24	24	25	23	37	...	...	...	...	...

Source:
United Nations Statistics Division, New York, the *Industrial Commodity Statistics Yearbook 2007* and the industrial statistics database, last accessed April 2010.

Source:
Organisation des Nations Unies, Division de statistique, New York, *l'Annuaire de statistiques industrielles par produit 2007* et la base de données sur les statistiques industrielles, dernier accès avril 2010.

1 Twelve months ending 30 June of the year stated.
2 Source: African Statistical Yearbook, Economic Commission for Africa (Addis Ababa).

1 Période de 12 mois finissant le 30 juin de l'année indiquée.
2 Source : Annuaire des Statistiques de l'Afrique, Conseil Economique pour l'Afrique (Addis-Abeba).

45 Radio and television receivers production

Physical quantities in thousands and monetary value in millions of US dollars

Production de récepteurs de radio et de télévision

Quantités physiques en milliers et valeurs monétaires en millions de dollars E.–U.

B. Value: millions of US dollars • Valeur : millions de dollars E.–U.

Country or area Pays ou zone	Radio receivers Récepteurs de radio					Television receivers Récepteurs de télévision				
	2003	2004	2005	2006	2007	2003	2004	2005	2006	2007
Azerbaijan Azerbaïdjan	...	...	...	...	...	...	...	1	1	0
Bangladesh [1] Bangladesh [1]	^0	^0	^0	^0	...	18	19	22	24	...
Brazil Brésil	504	702	621	587	691	826	1 313	2 015	2 659	3 151
Bulgaria Bulgarie	0	0	0	...	...	...	...	12	17	7
Czech Republic République tchèque	...	...	...	...	701	...	...	...	...	...
Denmark Danemark	66	65	64	90	7	...	...	267	188	0
Finland Finlande	...	...	0	0	0	...	...	2	0	0
France France	543	531	...	...	...	...	...	...	...	...
Germany Allemagne	...		...	...	...	483	642	603	694	773
Hungary Hongrie	274	317	342	311	378	...	1 164	1 601	2 862	4 532
Ireland Irlande	88	130	...	...	...	...	...	...	...	...
Japan Japon	198	107	116	91	131	5 942	8 353	8 831	11 120	10 517
Mexico Mexique	224	204	155	121	135	...	...	...	...	...
Nepal Népal	...	...	...	...	8		...	...	...	...
Poland Pologne	...	...	0	...	...	...	...	1 715	2 920	4 707
Portugal Portugal	906	1 007	1 093	1 128	...	0	0	0	0	...
Spain Espagne	...	15	12	16	18	...	...	1 786	2 532	2 925
Sweden Suède	...	...	13	8	37	...	...	32	0	0

Source:
United Nations Statistics Division, New York, the *Industrial Commodity Statistics Yearbook 2007* and the industrial statistics database, last accessed April 2010.

Source:
Organisation des Nations Unies, Division de statistique, New York, *l'Annuaire de statistiques industrielles par produit 2007* et la base de données sur les statistiques industrielles, dernier accès avril 2010.

1 Twelve months ending 30 June of the year stated.

1 Période de 12 mois finissant le 30 juin de l'année indiquée.

46 Passenger cars production

Thousands of cars and millions of US dollars

Production de voitures de tourisme

Milliers de voitures et millions de dollars É.-U.

A. Thousands of cars • Milliers de voitures

Country or area Pays ou zone	1998	1999	2000	2001	2002	2003	2004	2005	2006	2007
Argentina Argentine	435	291	325	227	153	161	244	299	409	513
Australia [1] Australie [1]	313	340	314	340	319	358	414	399	352	335
Azerbaijan Azerbaïdjan	...	...	...	...	...	...	^0	^0	1	^0
Bangladesh [1] Bangladesh [1]	...	...	...	1	1	1	1	^0	^0	...
Belarus Bélarus	1	^0	^0	^0	^0	^0	^0	^0	^0	^0
Brazil Brésil	...	...	1 320	1 467	1 444	1 472	1 876	2 182	3 706	2 557
Chile Chili	...	...	...	...	...	...	...	...	...	12
Colombia [2] Colombie [2]	...	...	...	...	...	...	40	52	45	68
Denmark Danemark	1	1	1	1	1	1	1	1	^0	^0
Finland Finlande	31	34	38	42	41	19	10	22	33	24
Germany Allemagne	5 459	...	...	...	5 561	5 624	...	5 945	5 965	6 399
Hungary Hongrie	...	...	...	...	...	...	116	...	182	289
India Inde	...	...	506	573	575	538	732	1 031	...	...
Iran (Islamic Rep. of) Iran (Rép. islamique d')	...	...	...	...	...	...	...	844	923	953
Japan Japon	...	...	...	...	9 244	9 409	9 605	9 588	10 684	9 522
Kazakhstan Kazakhstan	...	...	...	...	...	3	3	2	3	6
Kenya Kenya	...	...	...	...	^0	1	^0	^0	^0	^0
Korea, Republic of Corée, République de	1 437	1 924	2 626	2 477	2 653	2 767	3 133	3 356	3 489	...
Malaysia Malaisie	149	258	301	384	419	348	385	423	366	334
Mexico Mexique	947	988	1 294	1 273	1 247	1 028	993	1 128	1 430	1 501
Nigeria Nigéria	...	...	...	2	2	2	2	2	...	...
Poland Pologne	...	...	534	365	292	333	522	540	631	...
Portugal Portugal	189	184	187	195	190	168	157	142	148	...
Romania Roumanie	...	...	...	...	66	74	104	173	200	231
Russian Federation Fédération de Russie	840	954	969	1 022	981	1 012	1 110	1 069	1 178	1 294
Serbia Serbie	...	...	...	...	...	...	...	16	11	9

46 Passenger cars production *(continued)*

Thousands of cars and millions of US dollars

Production de voitures de tourisme *(suite)*

Milliers de voitures et millions de dollars É.-U.

A. Thousands of cars • Milliers de voitures

Country or area Pays ou zone	1998	1999	2000	2001	2002	2003	2004	2005	2006	2007
Slovakia Slovaquie	...	...	...	182	226	242	186	177	263	525
Slovenia Slovénie	126	...	...	...	...	...	...	...	...	...
Spain Espagne	...	...	...	...	...	...	2 482	2 375	2 220	2 385
Sudan Soudan	...	...	...	...	...	...	1	2	2	2
Sweden Suède	214	235	278	272	260	297	318	309	310	315
Thailand Thaïlande	32	73	97	156	169	252	299	278	299	315
Ukraine Ukraine	26	10	17	26	44	98	174	192	267	380
United Kingdom [3] Royaume-Uni [3]	...	2 208	...	...	...	...	...	...	...	...
Venezuela (Boliv. Rep. of) [2] Venezuela (Rép. boliv. du) [2]	...	...	...	...	...	...	24	139	120	129
Viet Nam Viet Nam	5	6	14	21	30	48	51	59	48	72

Source:
United Nations Statistics Division, New York, the *Industrial Commodity Statistics Yearbook 2007* and the industrial statistics database, last accessed April 2010

Source:
Organisation des Nations Unies, Division de statistique, New York, *l'Annuaire de statistiques industrielles par produit 2007* et la base de données sur les statistiques industrielles, dernier accès avril 2010

1 Twelve months ending 30 June of the year stated.
2 Source: United Nations Economic Commission for Latin America and the Caribbean (Santiago).
3 Excluding motor cars and other motor vehicles principally designed for the transport of persons (except public-transport type vehicles, vehicles specially designed for travelling on snow, and golf cars and similar vehicles).

1 Période de 12 mois finissant le 30 juin de l'année indiquée.
2 Source: Commission économique des Nations Unies pour l'Amérique Latine et des Caraïbes (Santiago).
3 Voitures de tourisme et autres véhicules automobiles principalement conçus pour le transport des personnes (autres que les véhicules automobiles pour le transport en commun des personnes, les véhicules spécialement conçus pour se déplacer sur la neige et les véhicules spéciaux pour le transport des personnes sur les terrains de golf et véhicules similaires).

46 Passenger cars production

Thousands of cars and millions of US dollars

Production de voitures de tourisme

Milliers de voitures et millions de dollars É.-U.

B. Millions of US dollars • Millions de dollars É.-U.

Country or area Pays ou zone	1998	1999	2000	2001	2002	2003	2004	2005	2006	2007
Azerbaijan Azerbaïdjan	...	...	0	0	0	0	^0	1	4	3
Bangladesh [1] Bangladesh [1]	...	...	...	14	14	11	9	5	7	...
Brazil Brésil	...	...	9 213	9 617	9 058	10 059	13 207	18 943	22 449	29 878
Chile Chili	...	...	...	...	...	...	...	...	...	223
Denmark Danemark	6	5	6	8	6	1	2	2	1	1
Finland Finlande	101	107	105	121	120	71	50	679	956	773
France France	...	...	40 465	43 422	...	...	...	...	...	...
Germany Allemagne	100 083	...	...	...	112 014	134 199	...	159 711	166 926	195 846
Hungary Hongrie	...	...	...	...	...	...	1 662	...	2 380	4 650
India Inde	...	...	...	...	...	2 434	3 517	5 163	...	...
Ireland Irlande	5	7	7	6	5	10	14	...	...	...
Japan Japon	99 221	112 839	115 772	106 946	111 009	124 695	132 071	137 959	150 359	124 456
Kenya Kenya	...	...	...	...	^0	1	^0	^0	^0	^0
Mexico Mexique	10 392	11 942	16 369	17 198	16 247	13 100	12 128	15 144	19 810	20 374
Nigeria Nigéria	19	16	15	14	13	12	12	12	...	...
Poland Pologne	...	...	2 608	1 806	1 510	2 147	4 219	5 298	6 403	...
Portugal Portugal	2 683	2 604	2 368	2 466	2 312	2 371	2 419	2 159	2 515	...
Romania Roumanie	...	...	...	...	28	37	63	120	155	213
Slovakia Slovaquie	...	...	...	1 663	2 194	3 954	4 199	3 831	6 107	10 448
Slovenia Slovénie	1 022	...	...	...	...	...	...	...	...	...
Spain Espagne	...	...	...	...	...	...	28 665	27 108	28 211	34 671
Sweden Suède	4 816	5 268	5 779	5 426	5 389	7 553	9 036	8 914	9 416	10 517
United Kingdom [2] Royaume-Uni [2]	...	31 321	...	...	...	...	...	...	...	...
Uruguay Uruguay	164	106	128	92	...	1	...	...	...	...

46

Passenger cars production *(continued)*

Thousands of cars and millions of US dollars

Production de voitures de tourisme *(suite)*

Milliers de voitures et millions de dollars É.-U.

B. Millions of US dollars • Millions de dollars É.-U.

Source:
United Nations Statistics Division, New York, the *Industrial Commodity Statistics Yearbook 2007* and the industrial statistics database, last accessed March 2010.

1 Twelve months ending 30 June of the year stated.
2 Excluding motor cars and other motor vehicles principally designed for the transport of persons (except public-transport type vehicles, vehicles specially designed for travelling on snow, and golf cars and similar vehicles).

Source:
Organisation des Nations Unies, Division de statistique, New York, *l'Annuaire de statistiques industrielles par produit 2007* et la base de données sur les statistiques industrielles, dernier accès mars 2010.

1 Période de 12 mois finissant le 30 juin de l'année indiquée.
2 Voitures de tourisme et autres véhicules automobiles principalement conçus pour le transport des personnes (autres que les véhicules automobiles pour le transport en commun des personnes, les véhicules spécialement conçus pour se déplacer sur la neige et les véhicules spéciaux pour le transport des personnes sur les terrains de golf et véhicules similaires).

47 Production of refrigerators for household use

Thousands of refrigerators and millions of US dollars

Production de réfrigérateurs à usage domestique

Milliers de réfrigérateurs et millions de dollars É.-U.

A. Thousands of refrigerators • Milliers de réfrigérateurs

Country or area Pays ou zone	1998	1999	2000	2001	2002	2003	2004	2005	2006	2007
Algeria Algérie	215	181	117	64	153	150	215	...	...	...
Argentina [1] Argentine [1]	512	456	405	311	197	200	321	458	532	777
Australia Australie	441	427	...	...	...	...	...	...	...	...
Azerbaijan Azerbaïdjan	3	1	1	2	4	5	10	13	14	11
Belarus Bélarus	802	802	812	830	856	886	953	995	1 050	1 072
Brazil Brésil	3 034	2 796	...	...	...	...	...	...	...	...
Chile Chili	229	242	271	280	230	232	...	...	...	...
China [2] Chine [2]	10 600	12 100	12 790	13 513	15 989	22 426	30 076	29 871	35 309	43 971
Cuba Cuba	6	10	9	9	10	8	7	0	0	...
Denmark Danemark	1 046	1 061	1 008	863	805	798	667	511	515	364
Ecuador Equateur	88	38	55	...	...	142	...	...	...	...
Egypt Egypte	...	527	191	451	640	808	663	685	698	...
Finland Finlande	107	...	...	...	0	...	...	...	...	...
France France	640	509	555	542	528	544	...	...	...	...
Germany Allemagne	...	...	...	...	2 354	2 107	2 061	2 152	2 460	2 388
Greece Grèce	...	...	...	...	...	381	...	...	...	...
Hungary Hongrie	708	849	995	1 058	1 866	1 883	1 625	1 535	1 683	1 520
India Inde	1 902	2 012	2 009	2 469	2 735	3 715	4 360	5 159	6 490	...
Indonesia Indonésie	417	240	774	...	...	...	...	...	...	...
Iran (Islamic Rep. of) Iran (Rép. islamique d')	1 200	1 236	973	917	978	946	799	775	854	1 065
Ireland Irlande	...	15	...	10	10	11	12	...	...	...
Italy Italie	6 280	6 582	6 987	6 936	7 088	7 197	7 201	...	...	...
Japan Japon	4 851	4 543	4 224	3 875	3 317	2 859	...	...	...	...
Kazakhstan Kazakhstan	...	...	2	...	...	...	...	0	0	0
Korea, Republic of Corée, République de	3 790	4 735	6 304	6 448	8 254	7 267	7 122	6 960	6 579	...
Lithuania Lituanie	116	118	101	94	111	98	107	89	84	100

47

Production of refrigerators for household use *(continued)*
Thousands of refrigerators and millions of US dollars

Production de réfrigérateurs à usage domestique *(suite)*
Milliers de réfrigérateurs et millions de dollars É.-U.

A. Thousands of refrigerators • Milliers de réfrigérateurs

Country or area Pays ou zone	1998	1999	2000	2001	2002	2003	2004	2005	2006	2007
Malaysia Malaisie	206	194	215	186	172	187	...	...	...	...
Mexico Mexique	1 986	2 083	2 049	2 071	2 222	2 162	2 291	2 844	3 043	2 650
Peru Pérou	118	42	51	*68	64	*46	69	76	...	...
Poland Pologne	714	726	#172	152	101	215	273	329	251	...
Portugal Portugal	403	430	424	417	440	452	399	166	208	...
Romania Roumanie	366[3]	323[3]	341[3]	313[3]	212	319	260	251	424	442
Russian Federation Fédération de Russie	1 043	1 173	1 327	1 719	1 938	2 218	2 589	2 778	2 995	3 539
Serbia and Montenegro Serbie-et-Monténégro	48	#5	20	...	10	...	...	...	...	...
Slovakia Slovaquie	228	206	177	53	...	...	...	...	...	...
South Africa Afrique du Sud	399	440	508	662	702	711	...	...	...	...
Spain Espagne	2 415	2 107	2 153	...	...	...	...	...	...	...
Sudan Soudan	...	...	...	...	...	...	47	47	48	96
Sweden Suède	368	549	575	593	627	655	639	625	632	565
Syrian Arab Republic Rép. arabe syrienne	149	139	120	133	135	119	143	182	192	...
Tajikistan Tadjikistan	1	2	2	2	1	1	2	1	1	...
Thailand[4] Thaïlande[4]	1 631	...	...	...	...	...	...	...	...	...
TFYR of Macedonia L'ex-R.Y. Macédoine	4	...	...	9	1	...	...	...	...	0
Turkey Turquie	1 993	2 083	2 405	2 245	3 017	4 011	4 867	5 099	6 223	...
Ukraine Ukraine	407	427	474	548	635	340	313	313	437	439
United Kingdom[5] Royaume-Uni[5]	662	620	581	565	476	745	317	...	...	...
United States[6,7] Etats-Unis[6,7]	11 279	11 716	12 355	11 776	11 145	11 639	...	...	...	...
Uzbekistan[8] Ouzbékistan[8]	16	2	1	...	...	...	...	...	...	...
Viet Nam Viet Nam	...	...	174	223	342	479	621	693	793	946

Source:
United Nations Statistics Division, New York, the *Industrial Commodity Statistics Yearbook 2007* and the industrial statistics database, last accessed March 2010.

Source:
Organisation des Nations Unies, Division de statistique, New York, *l'Annuaire de statistiques industrielles par produit 2007* et la base de données sur les statistiques industrielles, dernier accès mars 2010.

1 All refrigerators, freezers and combined refrigerator-freezers.

2 For statistical purposes, the data for China do not include those for the Hong Kong Special Administrative Region (Hong Kong SAR),

1 Tous réfrigérateurs, congélateurs et combinaisons réfrigérateurs-congélateurs.

2 Pour la présentation des statistiques, les données pour la Chine ne comprennent pas la Région Administrative Spéciale de Hong Kong

A. Thousands of refrigerators • Milliers de réfrigérateurs

Macao Special Administrative Region (Macao SAR) and Taiwan Province of China.

3 Including freezers.

4 Beginning 1999, series discontinued.

5 Excluding refrigerators of household type such as compression-type, absorption-type, electrical, and other household type refrigerators; freezers of the chest type, not exceeding 800 litres capacity; freezers of the upright type, not exceeding 900 litres capacity.

6 Shipments.

7 Electric domestic refrigerators only.

8 Source: Statistical Yearbook for Asia and the Pacific, United Nations Economic and Social Commission for Asia and the Pacific (Bangkok).

(Hong Kong RAS), la Région Administrative Spéciale de Macao (Macao RAS) et la province de Taiwan.

3 Y compris les congélateurs.

4 A partir de 1999, les séries ont été discontinuées.

5 Réfrigérateurs de type ménager comme les réfrigérateurs à compression, à absorption, électriques, et autres réfrigérateurs de type ménager; meubles congélateurs conservateurs du type coffre, d'une capacité n'excédant pas 800 litres; meubles congélateurs conservateurs du type armoire, d'une capacité n'excédant pas 900 litres.

6 Expéditions.

7 Réfrigérateurs électriques de ménage seulement.

8 Source : Annuaire des Statistiques de l'Asie et Pacifique, Commission économique et sociale des Nations Unies pour l'Asie et le Pacifique (Bangkok).

47 Production of refrigerators for household use

Thousands of refrigerators and millions of US dollars

Production de réfrigérateurs à usage domestique

Milliers de réfrigérateurs et millions de dollars É.-U.

B. Millions of US dollars • Millions de dollars É.-U.

Country or area Pays ou zone	1998	1999	2000	2001	2002	2003	2004	2005	2006	2007
Azerbaijan Azerbaïdjan	...	...	^0	^0	1	1	2	2	2	2
Denmark Danemark	258	262	210	184	183	209	190	146	152	131
Egypt Egypte	...	118	77	152	116	120	111	121	159	...
Finland Finlande	21	9	8	5	8	6	6	5	...	9
France France	...	81	50	0	0	42	...	...	...	...
Germany Allemagne	...	...	...	...	590	647	725	824	932	1 005
Hungary Hongrie	...	...	...	...	190	238	216	212	235	249
Ireland Irlande	10	12	10	6	8	10	12	...	...	...
Italy Italie	...	...	...	...	...	1 353	1 499	...	...	...
Lithuania Lituanie	18	16	12	11	17	16	19	16	15	20
Mexico Mexique	456	499	522	542	556	474	462	799	903	835
Nigeria [1] Nigéria [1]	9	8	7	7	6	6	5	6	...	...
Norway Norvège	...	...	...	...	...	...	8	10	6	...
Poland Pologne	...	...	...	...	...	...	...	34	...	...
Portugal Portugal	76	73	57	50	72	89	91	40	50	...
Romania Roumanie	...	...	...	...	3	5	4	3	7	8
Slovakia Slovaquie	...	...	...	7	...	...	...	...	...	...
Sweden Suède	256	184	161	123	204	253	271	265	287	294
United Kingdom [2] Royaume-Uni [2]	118	114	103	109	99	97	113	...	...	...

Source:
United Nations Statistics Division, New York, the *Industrial Commodity Statistics Yearbook 2007* and the industrial statistics database, last accessed April 2010.

Source:
Organisation des Nations Unies, Division de statistique, New York, *l'Annuaire de statistiques industrielles par produit 2007* et la base de données sur les statistiques industrielles, dernier accès avril 2010.

1 All refrigerators, freezers and combined refrigerator-freezers.

2 Excluding refrigerators of household type such as compression-type, absorption-type, electrical, and other household type refrigerators; freezers of the chest type, not exceeding 800 litres capacity; freezers of the upright type, not exceeding 900 litres capacity.

1 Tous réfrigérateurs, congélateurs et combinaisons réfrigérateurs-congélateurs.

2 Réfrigérateurs de type ménager comme les réfrigérateurs à compression, à absorption, électriques, et autres réfrigérateurs de type ménager; meubles congélateurs conservateurs du type coffre, d'une capacité n'excédant pas 800 litres; meubles congélateurs conservateurs du type armoire, d'une capacité n'excédant pas 900 litres.

48 Production of household washing and drying machines

Thousands of machines and millions of US dollars

Production de machines à laver et à sécher le linge, de type ménager

Milliers de machines et millions de dollars É.-U.

A. Thousands of machines • Milliers de machines

Country or area Pays ou zone	1998	1999	2000	2001	2002	2003	2004	2005	2006	2007
Argentina Argentine	624	635	694	558	263	608	919	1 102	1 243	1 546
Australia Australie	321	354	...	...	...	...	...	...	...	...
Azerbaijan Azerbaïdjan	...	...	...	...	...	...	...	...	36	...
Belarus Bélarus	91	92	88	81	66	63	50	37	13	163
Brazil Brésil	1 851	1 940	3 216	2 495	2 875	4 428	3 708	3 794	4 402	5 856
Chile Chili	...	...	...	...	...	...	...	117	440	449
China [1] Chine [1]	12 073	13 422	14 430	13 416	15 958	19 645	25 334	30 355	35 605	40 051
Cuba Cuba	...	...	35	49	45	15	5	...	...	...
Egypt Egypte	201	159	7	7	27	86	...	...	...	...
Finland Finlande	...	...	...	...	...	...	...	...	6	4
France France	1 941 [2]	2 229 [2]	2 751	3 259	3 404	3 618	...	...	...	...
Germany Allemagne	...	5 857	5 770	5 789	5 988	5 836	5 319	4 233	3 299	...
Greece [3] Grèce [3]	...	...	...	...	...	5	...	...	...	...
Hungary Hongrie	...	...	...	...	...	...	26	...	...	...
India Inde	...	...	715	779	1 165	1 438	1 589	1 757	1 945	...
Indonesia Indonésie	33	48	110	92	96	...	...	...	...	...
Iran (Islamic Rep. of) Iran (Rép. islamique d')	175	193	288	296	411	363	335	430	418	780
Italy Italie	8 119	7 367	8 186	8 507	8 884	9 905	9 829	...	...	...
Japan Japon	5 076	4 833	4 662	4 546	3 982	3 882	3 930	3 839	3 848	3 159
Kazakhstan Kazakhstan	3	2	5	11	17	20	50	73	102	127
Korea, Republic of Corée, République de	2 643	2 822	3 271	3 529	4 183	4 977	5 226	5 665	...	...
Latvia Lettonie	2	...	...	...	...	...	...	...	...	...
Mexico Mexique	1 037	1 250	1 337	1 240	1 220	1 091	1 074	988	1 042	962
Poland Pologne	416	448	...	...	...	...	...	2 338	3 287	3 742
Republic of Moldova République de Moldova	43	18	25	25	40	48	55	36	22	...
Romania Roumanie	36	28	25	24	28	37	43	25	23	23

48 Production of household washing and drying machines *(continued)*

Thousands of machines and millions of US dollars

Production de machines à laver et à sécher le linge, de type ménager *(suite)*

Milliers de machines et millions de dollars É.-U.

A. Thousands of machines • Milliers de machines

Country or area Pays ou zone	1998	1999	2000	2001	2002	2003	2004	2005	2006	2007
Russian Federation Fédération de Russie	862	999	954	1 039	1 369	1 330	1 452	1 582	2 016	2 713
Serbia and Montenegro Serbie-et-Monténégro	30	#12	10	5	4	...	...	...	...	...
South Africa Afrique du Sud	44	45	35	...	...	...	...	...	...	...
Spain Espagne	2 281	...	...	...	2 702	...	2 809	...	2 716	2 478
Sweden Suède	170	182	176	206	189	182	182	187	179	151
Syrian Arab Republic Rép. arabe syrienne	68	65	66	62	85	85	87	77	85	...
Thailand [4] Thaïlande [4]	800	...	...	...	...	...	...	...	...	...
Turkey Turquie	1 408	1 249	1 346	1 034	1 687	2 471	4 058	4 433	5 410	...
Ukraine Ukraine	138 [5]	127 [5]	125 [5]	166 [5]	232 [5]	255	345	322	208	173
United Kingdom Royaume-Uni	1 111	1 321 [6]	1 350 [6]	1 549 [6]	1 592 [6]	1 450 [6]	1 670 [6]	...	...	...
United States Etats-Unis	7 504 [2]	7 991 [2]	8 043	7 992 [2]	8 959 [2]	9 531 [2]	...	...	...	...
Uzbekistan [7] Ouzbékistan [7]	5	0	0	...	...	...	...	...	...	...
Viet Nam Viet Nam	...	...	159	168	211	283	514	337	340	415

Source:
United Nations Statistics Division, New York, the *Industrial Commodity Statistics Yearbook 2007* and the industrial statistics database, last accessed April 2010.

1 For statistical purposes, the data for China do not include those for the Hong Kong Special Administrative Region (Hong Kong SAR) and Macao Special Administrative Region (Macao SAR).
2 Shipments.
3 Incomplete coverage.
4 Beginning 1999, series discontinued.
5 Excluding household drying machines.
6 Excluding household washing machines and drying machines, including machines that both wash and dry.
7 Source: Statistical Yearbook, Commonwealth of Independent States (Moscow).

Source:
Organisation des Nations Unies, Division de statistique, New York, *l'Annuaire de statistiques industrielles par produit 2007* et la base de données pour les statistiques industrielles, dernier accès avril 2010.

1 Pour la présentation des statistiques, les données pour la Chine ne comprennent pas la Région Administrative Spéciale de Hong Kong (Hong Kong RAS) et la Région Administrative Spéciale de Macao (Macao RAS).
2 Expéditions.
3 Couverture incomplète.
4 A partir de 1999, les séries ont été discontinuées.
5 Non compris les machines à sécher le linge, de type ménager.
6 Code machines à laver le linge, même avec dispositif de séchage, et machines à sécher le linge.
7 Source: Annuaire des Statistiques, Communauté des États indépendants (Moscou).

48 Production of household washing and drying machines

Thousands of machines and millions of US dollars

Prdocution de machines à laver et à sécher le linge, de type ménager

Milliers de machines et millions de dollars É.-U.

B. Millions of US dollars • Millions de dollars É.-U.

Country or area Pays ou zone	1998	1999	2000	2001	2002	2003	2004	2005	2006	2007
Brazil Brésil	...	...	265	216	216	277	378	501	637	946
Chile Chili	...	...	...	...	...	...	...	9	54	57
Egypt Egypte	...	73	1	3	9	22	...	...	...	...
Finland Finlande	14	12	13	10	9	2	2	2	3	2
France France	...	655	84	...	...	448	466	...	...	...
Germany Allemagne	...	2 151	1 938	1 889	2 030	2 202	2 204	2 202	1 936	...
Hungary Hongrie	...	...	...	...	...	...	2	...	...	...
India Inde	...	...	...	...	...	191	213	206	...	...
Italy Italie	...	...	...	...	...	2 321	2 420	...	...	...
Japan Japon	1 379	1 557	1 623	1 388	1 115	1 199	1 305	1 321	1 293	1 109
Jordan Jordanie	...	...	...	...	...	...	0	0	1	0
Mexico Mexique	115	153	166	160	145	110	116	95	99	102
Poland Pologne	...	...	...	...	...	...	...	563	846	1 085
Spain Espagne	...	...	...	...	...	...	667	...	665	653
Sweden Suède	94	99	88	97	91	98	111	142	103	106
United Kingdom [1] Royaume-Uni [1]	...	188	178	200	214	232	295	...	...	...
United States [2] Etats-Unis [2]	3 327	4 030[3]	4 047[3]	4 162[3]	4 447[3]	4 770[3]	5 130[3]	5 236[3]	5 184[3]	6 513[3]

Source:
United Nations Statistics Division, New York, the *Industrial Commodity Statistics Yearbook 2007* and the industrial statistics database, last accessed April 2010.

1 Excluding household washing machines and drying machines, including machines that both wash and dry.
2 Including parts thereof.
3 Shipments.

Source:
Organisation des Nations Unies, Division de statistique, New York, *l'Annuaire de statistiques industrielles par produit 2007* et la base de données pour les statistiques industrielles, dernier accès avril 2010.

1 Code machines à laver le linge, même avec dispositif de séchage, et machines à sécher le linge.
2 Y compris leurs pièces.
3 Expéditions.

Technical notes: tables 34-48

Industrial activity includes mining and quarrying, manufacturing and the production of electricity, gas and water. These activities correspond to the major divisions 2, 3 and 4 respectively of the *International Standard Industrial Classification of All Economic Activities*.

Many of the tables are based primarily on data compiled for the United Nations *Industrial Commodity Statistics Yearbook*. Data taken from alternate sources are footnoted.

The methods used by countries for the computation of industrial output are, as a rule, consistent with those described in the United Nations *International Recommendations for Industrial Statistics* and provide a satisfactory basis for comparative analysis. In some cases, however, the definitions and procedures underlying computations of output differ from approved guidelines. The differences, where known, are indicated in the footnotes to each table.

Table 34: The statistics on sugar were obtained from the database and the *Sugar Yearbook* of the International Sugar Organization. The data shown cover the production and consumption of centrifugal sugar from both beet and cane, and refer to calendar years.

The consumption data relate to the apparent consumption of centrifugal sugar in the country concerned, including sugar used for the manufacture of sugar-containing products whether exported or not and sugar used for purposes other than human consumption as food. Unless otherwise specified, the statistics are expressed in terms of raw value (i.e. sugar polarizing at 96 degrees). The world total also includes data for countries not shown separately whose sugar consumption was less than 10,000 metric tons.

Table 35: The data refer to meat from animals slaughtered within the national boundaries irrespective of the origin of the animals. Production figures of cattle, chicken, buffalo, pig (including bacon and ham), sheep and goat meat are in terms of carcass weight, excluding edible offal, tallow and lard. All data refer to total meat production, i.e. from both commercial and farm slaughter.

Table 36: The data refer to beer made from malt, including ale, stout, and porter.

Table 37 presents data on cigarettes only, unless otherwise indicated.

Table 38 presents data on footwear with uppers of leather, other than sports footwear, footwear incorporating a protective metal toe-cap and miscellaneous special footwear.

Table 39: The data refer to the aggregate of sawnwood and sleepers, coniferous or non-coniferous. The data cover wood planed, unplaned, grooved, tongued and

Notes techniques : tableaux 34 à 48

L'activité industrielle comprend les industries extractives (mines et carrières), les industries manufacturières et la production d'électricité, de gaz et d'eau. Ces activités correspondent aux grandes divisions 2, 3 et 4, respectivement, de la *Classification internationale type par industrie de toutes les branches d'activité économique*.

Un grand nombre de ces tableaux sont établis principalement sur la base de données compilée pour l'*Annuaire de statistiques industrielles par produit* des Nations Unies. Les données tirées d'autres sources sont signalées par une note.

En règle générale, les méthodes employées par les pays pour le calcul de leur production industrielle sont conformes à celles dans *Recommandations internationales concernant les statistiques industrielles* des Nations Unies et offrent une base satisfaisante pour une analyse comparative. Toutefois, dans certains cas, les définitions des méthodes sur lesquelles reposent les calculs de la production diffèrent des directives approuvées. Lorsqu'elles sont connues, les différences sont indiquées par une note.

Tableau 34: Les données sur le sucre proviennent de la base de données et de l'*Annuaire du sucre* de l'Organisation internationale du sucre. Les données présentées portent sur la production et la consommation de sucre centrifugé à partir de la betterave et de la canne à sucre, et se rapportent à des années civiles.

Les données de la consommation se rapportent à la consommation apparente de sucre centrifugé dans le pays en question, y compris le sucre utilisé pour la fabrication de produits à base de sucre, exportés ou non, et le sucre utilisé à d'autres fins que pour la consommation alimentaire humaine. Sauf indication contraire, les statistiques sont exprimées en valeur brute (sucre polarisant à 96 degrés). Le total mondial compris également les données relatives aux pays où la consommation de sucre est inférieure à 10.000 tonnes.

Le tableau 35 indique la production de viande provenant des animaux abattus à l'intérieur des frontières nationales, quelle que soient leurs origines. Les chiffres de production de viande bovine, de buffle, de poulet, de porc (y compris le bacon et le jambon), de mouton et de chèvre se rapportent à la production en poids de carcasses et ne comprennent pas le saindoux, le suif et les abats comestibles. Toutes les données se rapportent à la production totale de viande, c'est-à-dire à la fois aux animaux abattus à des fins commerciales et des animaux sacrifiés à la ferme.

Tableau 36: Les données se rapportent à la bière produite à partir du malte, y compris ale, stout et porter (bière anglaise, blonde et brune).

Le *tableau 37* se rapporte seulement aux cigarettes,

the like, sawn lengthwise or produced by a profile-chipping process, and planed wood which may also be finger-jointed, tongued or grooved, chamfered, rabbeted, V-jointed, beaded and so on. Wood flooring is excluded. Sleepers may be sawn or hewn.

Table 40 presents statistics on the production of all paper and paper board. The data cover newsprint, printing and writing paper, construction paper and paperboard, household and sanitary paper, special thin paper, wrapping and packaging paper and paperboard.

Table 41: Statistics on all hydraulic cements used for construction (Portland, aluminous, slag, and so on) are shown, except in the form of clinkers.

Table 42 presents statistics on pesticides, including insecticides, rodenticides, fungicides, herbicides, anti-sprouting products and plant-growth regulators, disinfectants and similar products, put up in forms or packings for retail sale or as preparations or articles (for example, sulphur-treated bands, wicks and candles, and fly-papers).

Table 43: The data on crude steel and steel semi-finished products refer to ingots, other primary forms, and semi-finished products of iron, non-alloy steel, stainless steel or other alloy steel.

The data on pig iron and spiegeleisen refer to non-alloy pig iron, alloy pig iron and spiegeleisen, in pigs, blocks or other primary forms.

Table 44: The data refer to unwrought aluminium obtained by electrolytic reduction of alumina (primary) and re-melting metal waste or scrap (secondary).

Table 45: The data on radio receivers include radio-broadcast receivers capable of operating without an external source of power, including apparatus capable of receiving also radio-telephony or radio-telegraphy, whether combined with sound recording or reproducing apparatus or not; radio-broadcast receivers not capable of operating without an external source of power, of a kind used in motor vehicles, including apparatus capable of receiving also radio-telephony or radio-telegraphy, whether combined with sound recording or reproducing apparatus or not; other radio-broadcast receivers, including apparatus capable of receiving also radio-telephony or radio-telegraphy, whether combined with sound recording or reproducing apparatus or not.

The data on television receivers include colour, black and white and other monochrome. Also includes television receivers with a video recorder or player, flat panel colour TV receivers, tuner blocks for CTV/VCR and cable TV receiver units and satellite TV receivers/decoders.

Table 46 presents statistics on passenger cars, including motor cars and other motor vehicles principally designed for the transport of persons (except public-transport type vehicles, vehicles specially designed for

sauf indication contraire.

Le *tableau 38* se rapporte aux chaussures à dessus en cuir naturel, autres que les chaussures de sport, les chaussures comportant à l'avant une coquille de protection en métal et les chaussures spéciales diverses.

Tableau 39: Les données font référence à un agrégat des sciages de bois de conifères et de non-conifères et des traverses de chemins de fer. Elles comprennent les bois rabotés, non rabotés, rainés, languetés, etc. sciés en long ou obtenus à l'aide d'un procédé de profilage par enlèvement de copeaux et les bois rabotés qui peuvent être également à joints digitiformes languetés ou rainés, chanfreinés, à feuillures, à joints en V, à rebords, etc. Cette rubrique ne comprend pas les éléments de parquet en bois. Les traverses de chemin de fer comprennent les traverses sciées ou équarries à la hache.

Le *tableau 40* présente les statistiques sur la production de tout papier et carton. Les données comprennent le papier journal, les papiers d'impression et d'écriture, les papiers et cartons de construction, les papiers de ménage et les papiers hygiéniques, les papiers minces spéciaux, les papiers d'empaquetage et d'emballage et carton.

Tableau 41: Les données sur tous les ciments hydrauliques utilisés dans la construction (portland, alumineux, de laitier, etc.) sont présentées, autres que sous forme de "clinkers".

Le *tableau 42* présente les statistiques sur la production des pesticides, y compris des insecticides, anti-rongeurs, fongicides, herbicides, inhibiteurs de germination et régulateurs de croissance pour plantes, désinfectants et produits similaires, présentés dans des formes ou emballages de vente au détail ou à l'état de préparations ou sous forme d'articles (rubans, mèches et bougies soufrés et papier tue mouches, par exemple).

Tableau 43: Les données sur l'acier brut et demi-produits se rapportent aux lingots, autres formes primaires, et demi produits en fer, en aciers non alliés, aciers inoxydables ou autres aciers alliés.

Les données sur les fontes brutes et fontes spiegel se rapportent aux fontes brutes non alliées, fontes brutes alliées et fontes spiegel, en gueuses, saumons ou autres formes primaires.

Tableau 44: Les données se rapportent à la production d'aluminium non travaillé obtenue par réduction électrolytique de l'alumine (formes primaires) et par refonte de déchets et débris de métal (formes secondaires).

Tableau 45: Les données sur les récepteurs de radio comprennent les appareils récepteurs de radiodiffusion pouvant fonctionner sans source d'énergie extérieure, y compris les appareils pouvant recevoir également la radiotéléphonie ou la radiotélégraphie, même combinés à un appareil d'enregistrement ou de reproduction du

travelling on snow, and golf cars and similar vehicles).

Table 47: The data refer to refrigerators of household type such as compression-type, absorption-type, electrical, and other household type refrigerators; freezers of the chest type, not exceeding 800 litre capacity; freezers of the upright type, not exceeding 900 litre capacity.

Table 48 presents statistics on household washing machines and drying machines, including machines that both wash and dry.

son; appareils récepteurs de radiodiffusion ne pouvant fonctionner qu'avec une source d'énergie extérieure, du type utilisé dans les véhicules automobiles, y compris les appareils pouvant recevoir également la radiotéléphonie ou la radiotélégraphie, même combinés à un appareil d'enregistrement ou de reproduction du son; autres appareils récepteurs de radiodiffusion, y compris les appareils pouvant recevoir également la radiotéléphonie ou la radiotélégraphie, même combinés à un appareil d'enregistrement ou de reproduction du son.

Les données sur les appareils récepteurs de télévision y compris couleur, en noir et blanc ou en autres monochromes. Y compris les appareils incorporant un appareil d'enregistrement ou de reproduction vidéo phonique, les récepteurs de télévision avec écran plat (écran à cristaux liquides ou écran à plasma), récepteurs de signaux vidéo phoniques (tuner) et autres appareils récepteurs téléviseur sans écran.

Le *tableau 46* présente les statistiques sur les voitures de tourisme et autres véhicules automobiles principalement conçus pour le transport des personnes (autres que les véhicules automobiles pour le transport en commun des personnes, les véhicules spécialement conçus pour se déplacer sur la neige et les véhicules spéciaux pour le transport des personnes sur les terrains de golf et véhicules similaires).

Tableau 47: Les données se rapportent à la production des réfrigérateurs de type ménager comme les réfrigérateurs à compression, à absorption, électriques, et autres réfrigérateurs de type ménager; meubles congélateurs conservateurs du type coffre, d'une capacité n'excédant pas 800 litres; meubles congélateurs conservateurs du type armoire, d'une capacité n'excédant pas 900 litres.

Le *tableau 48* présente les statistiques sur les machines à laver le linge, même avec dispositif de séchage, et machines à sécher le linge.

49 Production, trade and consumption of commercial energy

Thousand metric tons of oil equivalent and kilograms per capita

Production, commerce et consommation d'énergie commerciale

Milliers de tonnes d'équivalent pétrole et kilogrammes par habitant

Region, country or area	Year Année	Primary energy production – Production d'énergie primaire Total Totale	Solids Solides	Liquids Liquides	Gas Gaz	Electricity Electricité	Changes in stocks Variations des stocks	Imports Importations	Exports Exportations
World	**2004**	**9 870 894**	**2 891 230**	**3 928 973**	**2 555 309**	**495 381**	**8 680**	**4 283 776**	**4 223 457**
	2005	**10 219 370**	**3 083 173**	**3 994 035**	**2 631 735**	**510 428**	**5 394**	**4 385 395**	**4 392 055**
	2006	**10 510 653**	**3 250 954**	**4 016 730**	**2 717 996**	**524 973**	**62 023**	**4 501 744**	**4 492 936**
	2007	**10 667 728**	**3 361 440**	**4 019 974**	**2 760 599**	**525 714**	**-603**	**4 616 603**	**4 508 391**
Africa	**2004**	**767 719**	**131 589**	**482 572**	**144 550**	**9 008**	**-1 445**	**88 051**	**523 344**
	2005	**826 081**	**132 909**	**510 843**	**173 341**	**8 988**	**-547**	**98 018**	**565 541**
	2006	**853 027**	**132 754**	**518 810**	**191 989**	**9 474**	**1 077**	**97 507**	**593 654**
	2007	**857 608**	**134 185**	**524 729**	**189 090**	**9 603**	**-360**	**104 027**	**591 372**
Algeria	2004	188 091	...	111 250	76 819	22	*153	1 235	141 742
	2005	200 102	...	114 397	85 657	48	65	1 118	144 487
	2006	204 239	...	112 387	91 833	19	717	1 355	151 790
	2007	194 718	...	112 902	81 796	19	-725	1 404	142 758
Angola	2004	50 421	...	49 571	699	150	780	777	47 710
	2005	63 253	...	62 456	606	191	129	883	61 064
	2006	72 030	...	71 168	634	229	612	1 152	69 149
	2007	86 641	...	85 645	774	222	77	1 857	84 114
Benin	2004	0	...	...	...	0	21	1 296	436
	2005	0	...	...	...	0	-15	1 195	311
	2006	0	...	...	...	0	-14	1 595	531
	2007	0	...	...	...	0	0	1 640	519
Botswana	2004	638	638	...	...	...	...	807	...
	2005	677	677	...	...	...	...	821	...
	2006	700	700	...	...	...	...	861	...
	2007	727	727	...	...	...	...	907	...
Burkina Faso	2004	9	...	...	...	9	-20	370	...
	2005	9	...	...	...	9	-6	396	...
	2006	7	...	...	...	7	-86	394	...
	2007	10	...	...	...	10	-10	559	...
Burundi	2004	10	2	...	...	8	*13	72	...
	2005	10	2	...	...	9	-2	62	...
	2006	10	*2	...	...	8	4	73	...
	2007	12	2	...	...	10	2	68	...
Cameroon	2004	4 693	...	4 356	0	337	1	2 336	5 468
	2005	4 405	...	4 081	0	324	-110	1 963	5 020
	2006	4 661	...	4 326	0	335	35	2 468	5 308
	2007	5 180	...	4 465	384	331	48	2 305	4 846
Cape Verde	2004	1	...	...	...	1	...	*96	...
	2005	1	...	...	...	1	...	*109	...
	2006	1	...	...	...	1	...	*111	...
	2007	*1	...	...	...	1	...	*112	...
Central African Rep.	*2004	7	...	...	...	7	...	105	...
	*2005	9	...	...	...	9	...	105	...
	*2006	9	...	...	...	9	...	112	...
	2007	11	...	...	...	11	...	*115	...
Chad	2004	8 505	...	8 505	...	...	...	*78	8 440
	2005	8 808	...	8 808	...	...	...	*84	8 741
	2006	7 874	...	7 874	...	...	...	*86	7 806
	2007	*7 190	...	7 190	...	...	...	*87	7 105
Comoros	*2004	0	...	...	...	0	...	34	...
	*2005	0	...	...	...	0	...	37	...
	*2006	0	...	...	...	0	...	41	...
	2007	0	...	...	...	0	...	*41	...
Congo	2004	11 679	...	11 626	18	34	...	81	11 124
	2005	12 717	...	12 665	21	31	...	116	12 314
	2006	14 382	...	14 328	22	32	...	133	14 035
	2007	11 548	...	11 499	20	29	...	170	11 175

49 Production, trade and consumption of commercial energy *(continued)*

Thousand metric tons of oil equivalent and kilograms per capita

Production, commerce et consommation d'énergie commerciale *(suite)*

Milliers de tonnes d'équivalent pétrole et kilogrammes par habitant

Bunkers - Soutes			Consumption - Consommation							
Air Avion	Sea Maritime	Unallocated Non distribué	Per capita Par habitant	Total Totale	Solids Solides	Liquids Liquides	Gas Gaz	Electricity Electricité	Year Année	Région, pays ou zone
114 253	**159 021**	**473 603**	**1 446**	**9 175 656**	**2 938 180**	**3 194 053**	**2 547 745**	**495 678**	**2004**	**Monde**
121 272	**169 113**	**464 188**	**1 470**	**9 452 743**	**3 088 008**	**3 225 100**	**2 628 947**	**510 688**	**2005**	
124 118	**178 886**	**472 707**	**1 487**	**9 681 727**	**3 244 120**	**3 241 633**	**2 670 996**	**524 978**	**2006**	
128 558	**186 367**	**478 419**	**1 511**	**9 983 198**	**3 396 945**	**3 286 285**	**2 773 737**	**526 232**	**2007**	
4 510	**6 072**	**24 601**	**345**	**298 688**	**103 438**	**113 533**	**72 541**	**9 176**	**2004**	**Afrique**
5 067	**6 405**	**29 909**	**358**	**317 724**	**102 078**	**117 824**	**88 675**	**9 147**	**2005**	
5 072	**5 660**	**21 427**	**355**	**323 644**	**103 176**	**122 058**	**88 769**	**9 642**	**2006**	
5 428	**5 569**	**26 188**	**354**	**333 439**	**107 068**	**126 769**	**89 614**	**9 988**	**2007**	
219	332	16 217	947	30 664	524	10 110	20 008	23	2004	Algérie
318	331	15 763	1 223	40 257	644	9 847	29 720	45	2005	
371	317	15 457	1 103	36 943	734	9 579	26 604	26	2006	
365	349	16 838	1 072	36 537	830	10 884	24 803	20	2007	
343	0	-280	232	2 645	...	1 796	699	150	2004	Angola
286	1	20	225	2 637	...	1 840	606	191	2005	
340	1	137	245	2 943	...	2 080	634	229	2006	
328	0	239	305	3 739	...	2 744	774	222	2007	
25	...	...	99	814	...	764	...	50	2004	Bénin
24	...	...	103	875	...	824	...	51	2005	
25	...	...	120	1 055	...	1 004	...	51	2006	
26	...	...	121	1 095	...	1 044	...	51	2007	
8	...	...	849	1 437	650	648	...	139	2004	Botswana
10	...	...	871	1 488	678	659	...	151	2005	
10	...	...	902	1 551	722	678	...	151	2006	
10	...	...	935	1 623	769	702	...	152	2007	
17	...	...	29	382	...	365	...	17	2004	Burkina Faso
21	...	...	28	390	...	370	...	19	2005	
16	...	...	33	470	...	451	...	19	2006	
14	...	...	38	565	...	545	...	20	2007	
7	...	...	8	62	2	47	...	13	2004	Burundi
7	...	...	9	67	2	51	...	15	2005	
7	...	...	9	73	*2	58	...	13	2006	
6	...	...	9	72	2	53	...	17	2007	
71	15	153	76	1 321	...	984	0	337	2004	Cameroun
64	12	107	72	1 275	...	951	0	324	2005	
42	42	216	82	1 486	...	1 151	0	335	2006	
64	52	80	128	2 396	...	1 681	384	331	2007	
...	*7	...	*190	*89	...	*89	...	1	2004	Cap-Vert
...	*10	...	*209	*99	...	*99	...	1	2005	
...	*10	...	*210	*102	...	*101	...	1	2006	
...	*10	...	*209	*103	...	*102	...	1	2007	
27	...	...	21	85	...	78	...	7	*2004	Rép. centrafricaine
27	...	...	21	87	...	78	...	9	*2005	
29	...	...	22	93	...	83	...	9	*2006	
*30	...	...	*22	*96	...	*85	...	11	2007	
*19	...	66	*6	*60	...	*60	...	...	2004	Tchad
*20	...	67	*6	*65	...	*65	...	...	2005	
*20	...	67	*6	*66	...	*66	...	...	2006	
*20	...	85	*6	*67	...	*67	...	...	2007	
...	...	...	53	34	...	34	...	0	*2004	Comores
...	...	...	56	37	...	37	...	0	*2005	
...	...	...	60	42	...	41	...	0	*2006	
...	...	...	*58	*41	...	*41	...	0	2007	
...	0	253	108	383	...	295	18	69	2004	Congo
...	0	118	111	401	...	314	21	66	2005	
...	0	25	123	454	...	365	22	67	2006	
...	28	27	129	487	...	400	20	67	2007	

49 Production, trade and consumption of commercial energy *(continued)*

Thousand metric tons of oil equivalent and kilograms per capita

Production, commerce et consommation d'énergie commerciale *(suite)*

Milliers de tonnes d'équivalent pétrole et kilogrammes par habitant

Region, country or area	Year Année	Primary energy production – Production d'énergie primaire: Total Totale	Solids Solides	Liquids Liquides	Gas Gaz	Electricity Electricité	Changes in stocks: Variations des stocks	Imports Importations	Exports Exportations
Côte d'Ivoire	2004	2 726	...	1 126	1 450	150	-238	3 617	3 340
	2005	3 737	...	1 994	1 619	123	*-31	4 265	4 516
	2006	4 786	...	3 135	1 521	130	-204	3 724	5 711
	2007	3 691	...	2 418	1 118	155	-145	3 720	4 853
Dem. Rep. of the Congo	2004	1 696	76	1 033	...	587	...	724	1 163
	2005	1 704	84	984	...	636	...	735	1 144
	2006	1 649	87	886	...	676	...	754	1 005
	2007	1 637	90	836	...	712	...	799	928
Djibouti	2004	...	...	...	...	...	...	307	...
	2005	...	...	...	...	...	...	318	...
	2006	...	...	...	...	...	...	331	...
	2007	...	...	...	...	...	...	331	...
Egypt	2004	66 181	20	33 706	31 323	1 132	*-398	3 901	9 651
	2005	79 955	20	32 628	46 172	1 135	0	6 959	18 484
	2006	84 781	15	34 056	49 545	1 164	-89	7 075	19 963
	2007	85 876	15	33 434	51 022	1 405	-159	7 611	19 282
Equatorial Guinea	2004	23 389	...	22 790	*598	*1	...	*188	21 731
	2005	24 482	...	23 406	*1 076	*1	...	*195	22 286
	2006	24 165	...	22 850	*1 314	*1	...	*209	21 669
	2007	25 161	...	23 603	*1 558	0	...	*214	22 355
Eritrea	2004	0	...	...	...	0	-28	229	3
	2005	0	...	...	...	0	-47	197	0
	2006	0	...	...	...	0	-32	153	0
	2007	0	...	...	...	0	-33	156	0
Ethiopia	2004	217	...	...	...	217	-397	1 349	...
	2005	245	...	...	...	245	-209	1 504	...
	2006	280	...	...	...	280	-218	1 676	...
	2007	290	...	...	...	290	-186	1 918	...
Gabon	2004	10 930	...	10 736	117	77	-190	88	10 351
	2005	10 876	...	10 690	116	70	-190	149	10 270
	2006	10 944	...	10 736	127	81	-265	183	10 363
	2007	10 767	...	10 553	145	69	-123	216	10 098
Gambia	2004	...	...	...	...	...	...	*110	*2
	2005	...	...	...	...	...	...	*110	*2
	2006	...	...	...	...	...	...	*116	*2
	2007	...	...	...	...	...	...	135	2
Ghana	2004	454	...	...	...	454	-6	2 467	432
	2005	484	...	...	...	484	-6	2 726	458
	2006	483	...	...	...	483	-6	3 170	293
	2007	320	...	...	...	320	-6	3 325	286
Guinea	2004	48	...	...	0	48	...	*405	...
	2005	43	...	...	0	42	...	*412	...
	2006	40	...	...	0	40	...	*413	...
	2007	46	...	...	0	46	...	*425	...
Guinea-Bissau *	2004	...	...	...	...	...	...	96	...
	2005	...	...	...	...	...	...	97	...
	2006	...	...	...	...	...	...	101	...
	2007	...	...	...	...	...	...	106	...
Kenya	2004	357	...	...	...	357	0	3 673	424
	2005	347	...	...	...	347	48	3 600	241
	2006	350	...	...	...	350	-201	3 823	221
	2007	394	...	...	...	394	0	3 539	181
Lesotho	2004	26	...	...	...	26	...	3	...
	2005	30	...	...	...	30	...	3	...
	2006	17	...	...	...	17	...	2	...
	2007	17	...	...	...	17	...	2	...

49

Production, trade and consumption of commercial energy *(continued)*

Thousand metric tons of oil equivalent and kilograms per capita

Production, commerce et consommation d'énergie commerciale *(suite)*

Milliers de tonnes d'équivalent pétrole et kilogrammes par habitant

Bunkers - Soutes			Consumption - Consommation							
Air Avion	Sea Maritime	Unallocated Non distribué	Per capita Par habitant	Total Totale	Solids Solides	Liquids Liquides	Gas Gaz	Electricity Electricité	Year Année	Région, pays ou zone
92	91	435	141	2 623	...	1 143	1 450	29	2004	Côte d'Ivoire
92	75	658	141	2 692	...	1 069	1 619	3	2005	
92	65	168	136	2 679	...	1 120	1 521	38	2006	
50	109	377	107	2 166	...	959	1 118	88	2007	
121	2	0	20	1 133	251	420	...	463	2004	Rép. dém. du Congo
120	2	0	20	1 173	264	428	...	482	2005	
120	2	0	21	1 276	278	435	...	563	2006	
138	2	0	21	1 368	293	444	...	631	2007	
99	*75	...	169	133	...	133	...	...	2004	Djibouti
104	*74	...	173	139	...	139	...	...	2005	
104	*84	...	174	143	...	143	...	...	2006	
104	*84	...	171	143	...	143	...	...	2007	
712	1 843	3 242	773	55 032	893	25 089	27 978	1 072	2004	Egypte
761	1 973	4 544	855	61 151	893	27 068	32 123	1 068	2005	
801	1 082	5 999	890	64 100	780	28 010	34 176	1 134	2006	
998	991	4 211	926	68 164	934	29 918	35 955	1 357	2007	
*33	...	1 050	*1 610	*762	...	*163	*598	*1	2004	Guinée équatoriale
*34	...	1 109	*2 581	*1 249	...	*173	*1 076	*1	2005	
*35	...	1 167	*3 030	*1 503	...	*188	*1 314	*1	2006	
*35	...	1 227	*3 469	*1 759	...	*200	*1 558	0	2007	
11	...	...	56	243	...	243	...	0	2004	Erythrée
9	...	...	52	235	...	235	...	0	2005	
7	...	...	38	177	...	177	...	0	2006	
5	...	...	38	184	...	183	...	0	2007	
99	...	...	26	1 864	...	1 647	...	217	2004	Ethiopie
151	...	...	25	1 808	...	1 563	...	245	2005	
183	...	...	27	1 992	...	1 711	...	280	2006	
226	...	...	29	2 168	...	1 878	...	290	2007	
67	149	35	444	606	...	412	117	77	2004	Gabon
69	153	25	500	697	...	511	116	70	2005	
65	155	97	499	712	...	504	127	81	2006	
54	155	23	545	775	...	562	145	69	2007	
...	...	...	*76	*108	...	*107	2	...	2004	Gambie
...	...	...	*75	*108	...	*107	2	...	2005	
...	...	...	*75	*114	...	*112	2	...	2006	
...	...	...	81	133	...	131	2	...	2007	
116	19	7	113	2 353	...	1 880	...	472	2004	Ghana
128	0	-70	127	2 700	...	2 201	...	499	2005	
162	40	18	141	3 146	...	2 674	...	472	2006	
77	45	-31	143	3 274	...	2 938	...	336	2007	
*22	...	...	*49	*431	...	*383	0	48	2004	Guinée
*23	...	...	*48	*432	...	*389	0	42	2005	
*23	...	...	*47	*430	...	*390	0	40	2006	
*26	...	...	*48	*446	...	*399	0	46	2007	
10	...	...	66	86	...	86	...	...	2004	Guinée-Bissau *
10	...	...	66	87	...	87	...	...	2005	
10	...	...	67	90	...	90	...	...	2006	
11	...	...	68	95	...	95	...	...	2007	
...	37	331	95	3 239	76	2 792	...	371	2004	Kenya
...	42	114	99	3 502	76	3 079	...	348	2005	
...	47	235	106	3 870	84	3 440	...	347	2006	
...	26	-6	100	3 732	77	3 264	...	391	2007	
...	...	...	14	28	...	...	...	28	2004	Lesotho
...	...	...	17	33	...	...	...	33	2005	
...	...	...	10	19	...	...	...	19	2006	
...	...	...	10	19	...	...	...	19	2007	

49 Production, trade and consumption of commercial energy *(continued)*

Thousand metric tons of oil equivalent and kilograms per capita

Production, commerce et consommation d'énergie commerciale *(suite)*

Milliers de tonnes d'équivalent pétrole et kilogrammes par habitant

Region, country or area	Year Année	Primary energy production – Production d'énergie primaire: Total Totale	Solids Solides	Liquids Liquides	Gas Gaz	Electricity Electricité	Changes in stocks Variations des stocks	Imports Importations	Exports Exportations
Liberia	2004	...	...	...	...	...	...	205	*1
	2005	...	...	...	...	...	...	236	*1
	2006	...	...	...	...	...	...	242	*1
	2007	...	...	...	...	...	...	216	*1
Libyan Arab Jamah.	2004	86 327	...	79 012	7 315	...	...	0	64 978
	2005	94 886	...	84 630	10 256	...	...	13	74 316
	2006	102 485	...	89 052	13 433	...	...	11	81 924
	2007	102 344	...	87 405	14 939	...	...	7	81 544
Madagascar	2004	55	...	...	...	55	2	749	116
	2005	*57	...	...	...	*57	*-34	681	0
	2006	*52	...	...	...	*52	8	672	0
	2007	46	...	...	...	46	-17	709	0
Malawi	2004	142	35	...	...	107	...	*298	*11
	2005	145	31	...	...	113	...	280	*8
	2006	155	*38	...	...	116	...	281	*8
	2007	*163	*42	...	...	121	...	*272	*8
Mali	2004	*21	...	...	...	*21	...	*210	...
	2005	*22	...	...	...	*22	...	*211	...
	*2006	23	...	...	...	23	...	211	...
	2007	23	...	...	...	*23	...	*216	...
Mauritania	2004	0	...	0	...	...	1	516	0
	2005	0	...	0	...	...	1	538	0
	2006	1 526	...	1 526	...	...	92	521	1 433
	2007	749	...	749	...	...	99	601	648
Mauritius	2004	10	...	...	...	10	14	1 260	...
	2005	10	...	...	...	10	-15	1 343	...
	2006	7	...	...	...	7	-58	1 384	...
	2007	7	...	...	...	7	39	1 542	...
Morocco	2004	214	...	11	47	156	-269	12 488	778
	2005	190	...	7	43	140	57	13 940	576
	2006	226	...	11	62	153	-54	13 965	344
	2007	212	...	14	60	138	-155	14 888	625
Mozambique	2004	2 265	12	...	1 249	1 003	-8	1 422	2 162
	2005	3 245	2	...	2 103	1 140	-15	1 337	3 073
	2006	3 811	29	...	2 516	1 265	19	1 412	3 555
	2007	3 943	17	...	2 545	1 381	25	1 420	3 432
Namibia	2004	136	...	...	...	136	...	965	2
	2005	133	...	...	...	133	...	1 028	3
	2006	119	...	...	...	119	...	1 106	3
	2007	134	...	...	...	134	...	1 173	3
Niger	2004	110	110	...	...	...	...	185	...
	2005	100	100	...	...	...	...	184	...
	2006	*101	*101	...	...	...	...	184	...
	2007	*102	*102	...	...	...	...	212	...
Nigeria	2004	150 196	2	128 734	20 866	594	224	7 680	136 250
	2005	155 588	6	133 807	21 250	526	-1	7 959	136 660
	2006	152 288	6	125 057	26 562	663	-42	7 749	137 297
	2007	*145 640	6	114 794	30 290	551	-86	8 579	133 097
Réunion *	2004	50	...	...	...	50	...	811	...
	2005	50	...	...	...	50	...	813	...
	2006	50	...	...	...	50	...	815	...
	2007	57	...	...	...	57	...	827	...
Rwanda	2004	8	...	...	*0	7	0	*181	0
	2005	6	...	...	*1	5	0	*179	0
	2006	4	...	...	*1	4	4	181	0
	2007	3	...	...	*1	3	-1	188	0
Saint Helena	2004	...	...	...	...	...	...	3	...
	*2005	...	...	...	...	...	...	3	...
	*2006	...	...	...	...	...	...	3	...
	2007	...	...	...	...	...	...	4	...

Production, trade and consumption of commercial energy *(continued)*
Thousand metric tons of oil equivalent and kilograms per capita

Production, commerce et consommation d'énergie commerciale *(suite)*
Milliers de tonnes d'équivalent pétrole et kilogrammes par habitant

Bunkers - Soutes			Consumption - Consommation							
Air Avion	Sea Maritime	Unallocated Non distribué	Per capita Par habitant	Total Totale	Solids Solides	Liquids Liquides	Gas Gaz	Electricity Electricité	Year Année	Région, pays ou zone
*3	*13	...	58	188	...	188	...	...	2004	Libéria
*3	*13	...	66	219	...	219	...	...	2005	
*3	*13	...	65	225	...	225	...	...	2006	
*3	*13	...	55	199	...	199	...	...	2007	
215	89	4 714	2 814	16 332	...	10 105	6 226	0	2004	Jamah. arabe libyenne
191	89	4 719	2 631	15 584	...	10 225	5 355	4	2005	
179	89	4 549	2 606	15 755	...	9 952	5 800	3	2006	
188	89	4 518	2 596	16 012	...	10 136	5 879	-2	2007	
2	*17	-56	42	721	*7	659	...	55	2004	Madagascar
1	*14	0	43	757	*7	693	...	*57	2005	
1	*17	0	38	698	*7	639	...	*52	2006	
1	*20	0	40	751	*7	698	...	46	2007	
...	...	...	*36	*429	*40	*283	...	106	2004	Malawi
...	...	...	34	417	41	263	...	112	2005	
...	...	...	34	428	*41	272	...	116	2006	
...	...	...	*32	*426	*42	*264	...	119	2007	
21	...	...	*18	*211	...	*189	...	*21	2004	Mali
21	...	...	*18	*212	...	*190	...	*22	2005	
21	...	...	17	213	...	190	...	23	*2006	
*22	...	...	*18	*218	...	*194	...	*23	2007	
25	*5	0	167	485	0	479	...	6	2004	Mauritanie
26	*5	0	174	506	0	495	...	11	2005	
18	*5	0	166	498	0	487	...	11	2006	
17	*5	0	189	581	0	571	...	*9	2007	
91	146	...	835	1 019	202	806	...	10	2004	Maurice
100	192	...	866	1 077	255	812	...	10	2005	
103	172	...	936	1 173	339	828	...	7	2006	
121	195	...	947	1 194	401	786	...	7	2007	
331	13	987	364	10 862	3 612	6 917	47	286	2004	Maroc
380	13	1 045	400	12 059	3 716	7 713	421	209	2005	
430	13	1 138	404	12 320	3 878	7 584	532	325	2006	
499	13	1 121	416	12 997	3 978	7 980	604	436	2007	
41	43	...	76	1 449	0	541	3	906	2004	Mozambique
45	3	...	76	1 476	0	475	68	933	2005	
56	3	...	80	1 589	0	501	79	1 009	2006	
65	0	...	90	1 841	6	613	145	1 076	2007	
...	...	...	572	1 100	1	830	...	269	2004	Namibie
...	...	...	592	1 159	14	868	...	277	2005	
...	...	...	613	1 222	45	894	...	283	2006	
...	...	...	643	1 304	54	943	...	307	2007	
12	...	...	23	284	110	148	...	25	2004	Niger
13	...	...	21	271	100	142	...	29	2005	
11	...	...	21	273	*101	142	...	31	2006	
12	...	...	21	301	*102	165	...	34	2007	
197	523	719	155	19 963	4	10 354	9 011	594	2004	Nigéria
497	476	5 100	156	20 815	7	10 369	9 912	526	2005	
235	609	524	153	21 415	7	10 736	10 008	663	2006	
241	609	253	136	20 104	7	9 595	9 951	551	2007	
...	33	...	1 081	828	...	778	...	50	2004	Réunion *
...	33	...	1 068	829	...	780	...	50	2005	
...	34	...	1 062	831	...	781	...	50	2006	
...	36	...	1 051	847	...	791	...	57	2007	
*12	...	...	*19	*177	...	*159	*0	17	2004	Rwanda
*12	...	...	*19	*172	...	*159	*1	13	2005	
*12	...	...	18	168	...	159	*1	9	2006	
*12	...	...	19	179	...	169	*1	10	2007	
...	...	...	345	3	...	3	...	...	2004	Sainte-Hélène
...	...	...	411	3	...	3	...	...	*2005	
...	...	...	430	3	...	3	...	...	*2006	
...	...	...	543	4	...	4	...	...	2007	

49 Production, trade and consumption of commercial energy *(continued)*

Thousand metric tons of oil equivalent and kilograms per capita

Production, commerce et consommation d'énergie commerciale *(suite)*

Milliers de tonnes d'équivalent pétrole et kilogrammes par habitant

Region, country or area	Year Année	Primary energy production – Production d'énergie primaire: Total Totale	Solids Solides	Liquids Liquides	Gas Gaz	Electricity Electricité	Changes in stocks: Variations des stocks	Imports Importations	Exports Exportations
Sao Tome and Principe	2004	1	...	...	...	1	...	*38	...
	2005	0	...	...	...	0	...	*43	...
	*2006	1	...	...	...	1	...	43	...
	2007	1	...	...	...	1	...	*43	...
Senegal	2004	12	...	...	12	0	-42	1 708	187
	2005	13	...	...	13	0	83	1 967	273
	2006	12	...	...	12	0	-132	1 189	145
	2007	10	...	...	10	0	-48	1 787	343
Seychelles	2004	...	...	...	...	...	...	392	2
	2005	...	...	...	...	...	...	357	2
	2006	...	...	...	...	...	...	381	2
	2007	...	...	...	...	...	...	314	1
Sierra Leone	2004	1	...	...	...	1	...	*454	20
	2005	2	...	...	...	2	...	*544	*22
	*2006	0	...	...	...	0	...	526	23
	2007	2	...	...	...	2	...	*550	*23
Somalia	2004	*1	...	...	...	*1	...	*281	*21
	2005	*1	...	...	...	*1	...	*284	*21
	2006	*1	...	...	...	*1	...	*308	*49
	2007	1	...	...	...	1	...	*317	*42
South Africa [1]	2004	133 073	127 999	1 680	1 843	1 551	-1 286	23 586	40 592
	2005	134 013	129 140	1 555	1 982	1 337	0	27 415	44 797
	2006	133 841	129 034	1 506	1 804	1 497	0	25 302	44 334
	2007	134 838	130 553	1 185	1 787	1 314	0	26 782	38 608
Sudan	2004	15 091	...	15 000	...	91	116	385	11 820
	2005	15 357	...	15 250	...	107	-171	314	12 013
	2006	16 668	...	16 550	...	118	907	538	12 482
	2007	23 525	...	23 400	...	125	942	486	19 025
Swaziland	2004	319	310	...	...	9	*4	*402	310
	2005	329	316	...	...	14	*-13	*373	316
	2006	*324	*310	...	...	13	*3	*396	*310
	2007	*338	*323	...	...	15	*3	*413	*323
Togo	2004	7	...	...	...	7	-1	420	...
	2005	6	...	...	...	6	-18	394	...
	2006	8	...	...	...	8	-46	311	...
	2007	8	...	...	...	8	-39	344	...
Tunisia	2004	5 526	...	3 436	2 074	17	39	5 677	3 884
	2005	5 598	...	3 484	2 098	16	-113	5 720	3 953
	2006	5 628	...	3 363	2 254	11	60	5 776	3 719
	2007	6 793	...	4 639	2 147	8	80	6 228	4 960
Uganda	2004	167	...	...	...	167	...	518	17
	2005	156	...	...	...	156	...	663	5
	2006	107	...	...	...	107	...	785	4
	2007	121	...	...	...	121	...	943	6
United Rep. of Tanzania	2004	367	45	...	119	203	...	1 209	...
	2005	534	52	...	329	153	...	1 293	...
	2006	528	56	...	349	123	...	1 366	...
	2007	771	59	...	495	216	...	1 468	...
Western Sahara *	2004	...	...	...	...	...	...	85	...
	2005	...	...	...	...	...	...	85	...
	2006	...	...	...	...	...	...	85	...
	2007	...	...	...	...	...	...	85	...
Zambia	2004	865	137	...	...	727	56	657	35
	2005	908	144	...	...	764	60	691	37
	2006	956	153	...	...	802	65	725	45
	2007	1 005	163	...	...	842	68	767	49

49 Production, trade and consumption of commercial energy *(continued)*

Thousand metric tons of oil equivalent and kilograms per capita

Production, commerce et consommation d'énergie commerciale *(suite)*

Milliers de tonnes d'équivalent pétrole et kilogrammes par habitant

Bunkers - Soutes			Consumption - Consommation							
Air Avion	Sea Maritime	Unallocated Non distribué	Per capita Par habitant	Total Totale	Solids Solides	Liquids Liquides	Gas Gaz	Electricity Electricité	Year Année	Région, pays ou zone
...	...	...	*256	*38	...	*38	...	1	2004	Sao Tomé-et-Principe
...	...	...	*283	*43	...	*43	...	0	2005	
...	...	...	282	44	...	43	...	1	*2006	
...	...	...	*278	*44	...	*43	...	1	2007	
233	0	39	123	1 303	111	1 155	12	25	2004	Sénégal
234	0	22	126	1 368	110	1 222	13	23	2005	
224	0	10	87	954	133	789	12	20	2006	
*248	*12	24	102	1 218	211	982	10	16	2007	
*31	*103	...	3 100	256	...	258	...	-2	2004	Seychelles
*27	*100	...	2 753	228	...	230	...	-2	2005	
*30	*106	...	2 877	243	...	246	...	-2	2006	
*29	*79	...	2 416	205	...	206	...	-1	2007	
*27	*71	*63	*56	*274	...	*273	...	1	2004	Sierra Leone
*27	*92	*107	*58	*298	...	*297	...	2	2005	
29	87	101	54	286	...	286	...	0	*2006	
*30	*87	*103	*57	*309	...	*307	...	2	2007	
*52	*20	*1	24	188	...	187	...	*1	2004	Somalie
*52	*21	*1	23	190	...	189	...	*1	2005	
*52	*21	*-3	22	190	...	189	...	*1	2006	
*59	*22	*-3	23	199	...	198	...	1	2007	
772	2 390	-3 725	2 531	117 915	94 645	18 925	3 090	1 256	2004	Afrique du Sud [1]
755	2 647	-3 932	2 499	117 161	92 782	19 207	4 037	1 135	2005	
783	2 604	-8 381	2 528	119 802	93 633	20 772	4 242	1 155	2006	
886	2 504	-3 153	2 538	122 775	97 079	20 446	4 186	1 064	2007	
142	8	212	92	3 178	...	3 087	...	91	2004	Soudan
201	8	188	97	3 431	...	3 324	...	107	2005	
226	8	-337	108	3 921	...	3 803	...	118	2006	
205	8	47	98	3 782	...	3 657	...	125	2007	
*1	...	...	*368	*406	104	*215	...	88	2004	Swaziland
1	...	...	*355	*399	101	*214	...	84	2005	
*1	...	...	*354	*406	*102	*213	...	90	2006	
1	...	...	*444	*423	*106	*222	...	95	2007	
40	5	...	75	383	...	333	...	49	2004	Togo
50	3	...	68	365	...	315	...	50	2005	
35	2	...	61	327	...	276	...	51	2006	
31	2	...	66	359	...	307	...	52	2007	
...	0	94	724	7 186	...	4 009	3 162	15	2004	Tunisie
...	0	159	730	7 319	...	4 049	3 257	13	2005	
...	9	191	733	7 424	...	4 065	3 348	12	2006	
...	0	156	765	7 825	...	4 233	3 583	8	2007	
...	...	...	26	668	...	518	...	150	2004	Ouganda
...	...	...	31	814	...	663	...	151	2005	
...	...	...	32	887	...	785	...	102	2006	
...	...	...	37	1 059	...	943	...	116	2007	
79	23	...	41	1 473	45	1 097	119	212	2004	Rép.-Unie de Tanzanie
86	23	...	46	1 719	52	1 173	329	165	2005	
91	23	...	47	1 781	56	1 242	349	134	2006	
97	23	...	54	2 119	59	1 344	495	221	2007	
6	...	...	190	79	...	79	...	...	2004	Sahara occidental *
6	...	...	179	79	...	79	...	...	2005	
6	...	...	171	79	...	79	...	...	2006	
6	...	...	164	79	...	79	...	...	2007	
51	...	43	121	1 338	90	540	...	708	2004	Zambie
53	...	46	122	1 404	95	566	...	743	2005	
56	...	48	124	1 467	101	586	...	780	2006	
59	...	51	127	1 545	107	618	...	819	2007	

49 Production, trade and consumption of commercial energy *(continued)*

Thousand metric tons of oil equivalent and kilograms per capita

Production, commerce et consommation d'énergie commerciale *(suite)*

Milliers de tonnes d'équivalent pétrole et kilogrammes par habitant

Region, country or area	Year Année	Primary energy production – Production d'énergie primaire: Total Totale	Solids Solides	Liquids Liquides	Gas Gaz	Electricity Electricité	Changes in stocks: Variations des stocks	Imports Importations	Exports Exportations
Zimbabwe	2004	2 677	2 202	...	...	475	13	822	143
	2005	2 837	2 335	...	...	502	5	967	128
	2006	2 700	2 223	...	...	477	-2	929	129
	2007	2 536	2 087	...	...	448	-12	886	131
America, North	**2004**	**2 132 755**	**590 011**	**684 653**	**717 308**	**140 783**	**381**	**961 933**	**476 523**
	2005	**2 119 134**	**601 043**	**665 043**	**709 479**	**143 568**	**-5 036**	**992 180**	**476 522**
	2006	**2 158 513**	**614 723**	**667 045**	**730 105**	**146 640**	**34 567**	**992 574**	**488 753**
	2007	**2 168 216**	**607 401**	**668 381**	**746 382**	**146 051**	**-15 814**	**1 010 013**	**509 951**
Anguilla	2004	...	...	...	...	...	...	14	...
	2005	...	...	...	...	...	...	17	...
	2006	...	...	...	...	...	...	18	...
	2007	...	...	...	...	...	...	17	...
Antigua and Barbuda *	2004	...	...	...	...	...	...	196	8
	2005	...	...	...	...	...	...	199	9
	2006	...	...	...	...	...	...	205	10
	2007	...	...	...	...	...	...	211	11
Aruba	2004	*120	...	*120	...	...	...	*10 706	10 495
	2005	*120	...	*120	...	...	...	10 713	10 495
	*2006	120	...	120	...	...	...	10 713	10 495
	*2007	125	...	125	...	...	...	10 839	10 600
Bahamas *	2004	...	...	...	...	...	...	3 209	2 247
	2005	...	...	...	...	...	...	3 265	2 257
	2006	...	...	...	...	...	...	3 273	2 256
	2007	...	...	...	...	...	...	3 281	2 258
Barbados	2004	89	...	65	23	...	...	351	64
	2005	90	...	66	25	...	...	364	64
	2006	77	...	52	25	...	...	372	51
	2007	*84	...	*56	28	...	...	*372	*55
Belize	2004	6	...	...	...	6	...	*170	...
	2005	7	...	...	...	7	...	*178	...
	2006	16	...	...	...	16	...	*178	...
	2007	14	...	...	...	14	...	181	...
Bermuda	*2004	...	...	...	...	...	...	243	...
	2005	...	...	...	...	...	...	181	...
	2006	...	...	...	...	...	...	211	...
	2007	...	...	...	...	...	...	225	...
British Virgin Islands *	2004	...	...	...	...	...	...	29	...
	2005	...	...	...	...	...	...	30	...
	2006	...	...	...	...	...	...	33	...
	2007	...	...	...	...	...	...	33	...
Canada	2004	384 673	32 180	147 681	167 591	37 221	-7 011	79 055	220 971
	2005	388 173	31 801	145 830	171 231	39 311	-5 780	78 982	220 831
	2006	396 969	32 536	153 101	172 121	39 211	-1 153	76 071	224 967
	2007	400 185	33 900	158 928	167 366	39 991	-8 620	80 306	237 670
Cayman Islands *	2004	...	...	...	...	...	...	186	...
	2005	...	...	...	...	...	...	194	...
	2006	...	...	...	...	...	...	201	...
	2007	...	...	...	...	...	...	203	...
Costa Rica	2004	676	...	...	...	676	15	2 169	88
	2005	681	...	...	...	681	3	2 105	6
	2006	696	...	...	...	696	17	2 328	34
	2007	709	...	...	...	709	-23	2 467	3
Cuba	2004	4 311	...	3 648	656	8	461	4 863	...
	2005	3 923	...	3 225	692	6	583	5 916	...
	2006	4 121	...	3 101	1 011	8	203	4 981	...
	2007	4 169	...	3 053	1 105	10	95	5 350	...

49

Production, trade and consumption of commercial energy *(continued)*

Thousand metric tons of oil equivalent and kilograms per capita

Production, commerce et consommation d'énergie commerciale *(suite)*

Milliers de tonnes d'équivalent pétrole et kilogrammes par habitant

Bunkers - Soutes			Consumption - Consommation							
Air Avion	Sea Maritime	Unallocated Non distribué	Per capita Par habitant	Total Totale	Solids Solides	Liquids Liquides	Gas Gaz	Electricity Electricité	Year Année	Région, pays ou zone
8	...	...	256	3 334	2 073	611	...	650	2004	Zimbabwe
8	...	...	279	3 662	2 241	664	...	758	2005	
8	...	...	264	3 494	2 133	640	...	721	2006	
8	...	...	247	3 295	2 003	614	...	677	2007	
20 935	**29 377**	**65 192**	**4 938**	**2 502 280**	**588 343**	**1 054 862**	**718 280**	**140 796**	**2004**	**Amérique du Nord**
21 596	**30 487**	**54 138**	**4 952**	**2 533 609**	**596 472**	**1 074 851**	**718 719**	**143 567**	**2005**	
20 509	**32 522**	**55 685**	**4 874**	**2 519 050**	**590 117**	**1 063 026**	**719 369**	**146 538**	**2006**	
21 343	**35 158**	**46 144**	**4 927**	**2 581 447**	**596 552**	**1 075 976**	**762 435**	**146 485**	**2007**	
...	...	...	1 092	14	...	14	...	...	2004	Anguilla
...	...	...	1 250	17	...	17	...	...	2005	
...	...	...	1 242	18	...	18	...	...	2006	
...	...	...	1 163	17	...	17	...	...	2007	
50	3	...	1 671	135	...	135	...	...	2004	Antigua-et-Barbuda *
50	3	...	1 659	137	...	137	...	...	2005	
50	3	...	1 695	143	...	143	...	...	2006	
52	3	...	1 716	146	...	146	...	...	2007	
*75	...	*5	2 566	251	...	251	...	...	2004	Aruba
*77	...	5	2 541	256	...	256	...	...	2005	
77	...	5	2 487	256	...	256	...	...	*2006	
79	...	25	2 501	260	...	260	...	...	*2007	
44	254	...	2 071	664	2	662	...	...	2004	Bahamas *
46	266	...	2 141	696	2	694	...	...	2005	
47	264	...	2 144	706	3	703	...	...	2006	
49	266	...	2 124	709	3	707	...	...	2007	
...	...	0	1 376	375	...	352	23	...	2004	Barbade
...	...	0	1 429	390	...	366	25	...	2005	
...	...	0	1 451	398	...	373	25	...	2006	
...	...	*0	*1 461	*401	...	*373	28	...	2007	
*22	...	...	*561	*155	...	*128	...	26	2004	Belize
*23	...	...	*572	*161	...	*133	...	28	2005	
*23	...	...	*596	*172	...	*138	...	34	2006	
17	...	...	605	178	...	143	...	35	2007	
18	3	...	3 509	222	...	222	...	...	*2004	Bermudes
*18	*15	...	2 331	148	...	148	...	...	2005	
*20	18	...	2 717	173	...	173	...	...	2006	
*37	18	...	2 662	170	...	170	...	...	2007	
...	...	...	1 330	29	...	29	...	...	2004	Iles Vierges britanniques *
...	...	...	1 357	30	...	30	...	...	2005	
...	...	...	1 464	33	...	33	...	...	2006	
...	...	...	1 442	33	...	33	...	...	2007	
885	617	17 030	7 227	231 237	27 991	80 229	86 695	36 321	2004	Canada
835	604	16 502	7 247	234 162	27 935	79 350	89 617	37 260	2005	
825	549	15 928	7 103	231 923	28 171	77 863	88 322	37 568	2006	
508	652	12 969	7 196	237 311	30 276	81 420	87 802	37 814	2007	
23	...	...	3 699	164	...	164	...	...	2004	Iles Caïmanes *
24	...	...	3 513	170	...	170	...	...	2005	
25	...	...	3 387	176	...	176	...	...	2006	
25	...	...	3 293	178	...	178	...	...	2007	
...	...	99	632	2 643	81	1 906	...	655	2004	Costa Rica
...	...	34	643	2 742	77	1 984	...	682	2005	
...	...	38	674	2 934	41	2 189	...	703	2006	
...	...	23	714	3 173	81	2 368	...	723	2007	
...	72	49	758	8 592	18	7 910	656	8	2004	Cuba
...	73	727	752	8 457	23	7 735	692	6	2005	
...	*55	569	736	8 275	*20	7 236	1 011	8	2006	
...	56	191	814	9 177	15	8 046	1 105	10	2007	

Production, trade and consumption of commercial energy *(continued)*

Thousand metric tons of oil equivalent and kilograms per capita

Production, commerce et consommation d'énergie commerciale *(suite)*

Milliers de tonnes d'équivalent pétrole et kilogrammes par habitant

Region, country or area	Year Année	Primary energy production – Production d'énergie primaire: Total Totale	Solids Solides	Liquids Liquides	Gas Gaz	Electricity Electricité	Changes in stocks Variations des stocks	Imports Importations	Exports Exportations
Dominica	2004	3	...	...	...	3	...	36	...
	2005	2	...	...	...	2	...	*38	...
	*2006	3	...	...	...	3	...	39	...
	*2007	3	...	...	...	3	...	40	...
Dominican Republic	2004	136	...	...	...	136	36	6 217	...
	2005	163	...	...	...	163	-5	6 224	...
	2006	121	...	...	...	121	-19	6 325	...
	2007	120	...	...	...	120	-27	6 479	...
El Salvador	2004	206	...	...	...	206	38	2 284	274
	2005	234	...	...	...	234	65	2 215	122
	2006	267	...	...	...	267	53	2 157	78
	2007	268	...	...	...	268	85	2 385	180
Greenland	2004	...	...	...	...	...	...	207	53
	2005	...	...	...	...	...	...	244	51
	2006	...	...	...	...	...	...	223	48
	2007	...	...	...	...	...	...	243	52
Grenada	2004	...	...	...	...	...	...	82	...
	2005	...	...	...	...	...	...	86	...
	2006	...	...	...	...	...	...	88	...
	2007	...	...	...	...	...	...	90	...
Guadeloupe *	2004	...	...	...	...	...	...	748	...
	2005	...	...	...	...	...	...	772	...
	2006	...	...	...	...	...	...	781	...
	2007	...	...	...	...	...	...	790	...
Guatemala	2004	1 311	...	1 102	...	209	25	3 815	1 414
	2005	1 282	...	1 004	...	278	162	3 828	966
	2006	1 209	...	880	...	329	-211	3 642	979
	2007	1 145	...	833	...	312	207	4 176	841
Haiti	2004	22	...	...	...	22	...	639	...
	2005	23	...	...	...	23	...	670	...
	2006	23	...	...	...	23	...	685	...
	2007	13	...	...	...	13	...	773	...
Honduras	2004	202	...	...	...	202	-2	2 255	27
	2005	148	...	...	...	148	-109	2 205	25
	2006	178	...	...	...	178	269	2 425	40
	2007	190	...	...	...	190	-118	2 739	182
Jamaica	2004	17	...	...	...	17	12	3 674	124
	2005	17	...	...	...	17	26	3 431	0
	2006	19	...	...	...	19	-11	4 121	0
	2007	18	...	...	...	18	42	4 802	0
Martinique	2004	...	...	...	...	...	...	793	*225
	2005	...	...	...	...	...	...	814	*225
	2006	...	...	...	...	...	...	840	*225
	2007	...	...	...	...	...	...	866	*224
Mexico	2004	239 616	4 749	191 899	39 440	3 528	1 243	24 867	109 241
	2005	238 277	5 159	188 168	41 004	3 945	251	27 750	104 306
	2006	238 456	5 510	183 780	45 037	4 128	558	31 431	104 115
	2007	233 700	6 000	176 050	47 748	3 901	622	37 769	96 622
Montserrat *	2004	...	...	...	...	...	...	24	...
	2005	...	...	...	...	...	...	24	...
	2006	...	...	...	...	...	...	26	...
	2007	...	...	...	...	...	...	27	...
Netherlands Antilles	2004	...	...	...	...	...	...	14 091	8 637
	2005	...	...	...	...	...	...	14 564	9 311
	2006	...	...	...	...	...	...	13 799	8 647
	2007	...	...	...	...	...	...	14 473	9 243

49

Production, trade and consumption of commercial energy *(continued)*

Thousand metric tons of oil equivalent and kilograms per capita

Production, commerce et consommation d'énergie commerciale *(suite)*

Milliers de tonnes d'équivalent pétrole et kilogrammes par habitant

Bunkers - Soutes			Consumption - Consommation							
Air Avion	Sea Maritime	Unallocated Non distribué	Per capita Par habitant	Total Totale	Solids Solides	Liquids Liquides	Gas Gaz	Electricity Electricité	Year Année	Région, pays ou zone
...	...	...	543	39	...	36	...	3	2004	Dominique
...	...	...	*563	*41	...	*38	...	2	2005	
...	...	...	578	42	...	39	...	3	*2006	
...	...	...	591	43	...	40	...	3	*2007	
101	...	192	662	6 023	544	5 218	125	136	2004	Rép. dominicaine
100	...	156	665	6 135	333	5 386	253	163	2005	
99	...	54	674	6 311	560	5 322	309	121	2006	
96	...	-24	690	6 553	576	5 449	407	120	2007	
75	...	-28	315	2 131	1	1 891	...	239	2004	El Salvador
78	...	149	296	2 035	1	1 775	...	258	2005	
75	...	48	310	2 170	1	1 903	...	267	2006	
97	...	23	319	2 269	1	1 997	...	271	2007	
*11	...	...	2 526	142	...	142	...	...	2004	Groenland
*17	...	...	3 139	177	...	177	...	...	2005	
*19	...	...	2 760	157	...	157	...	...	2006	
*19	...	...	3 055	173	...	173	...	...	2007	
*8	...	...	707	74	...	74	...	...	2004	Grenade
*7	...	...	749	79	...	79	...	...	2005	
*7	...	...	765	81	...	81	...	...	2006	
*9	...	...	755	81	...	81	...	...	2007	
103	...	...	1 449	644	...	644	...	...	2004	Guadeloupe *
108	...	...	1 491	664	...	664	...	...	2005	
110	...	...	1 503	672	...	672	...	...	2006	
111	...	...	1 513	679	...	679	...	...	2007	
44	122	0	284	3 521	323	3 025	...	173	2004	Guatemala
38	122	46	297	3 776	412	3 113	...	251	2005	
38	122	116	292	3 808	431	3 054	...	322	2006	
28	122	60	304	4 063	462	3 300	...	301	2007	
24	...	...	76	638	...	616	...	22	2004	Haïti
24	...	...	79	669	...	646	...	23	2005	
25	...	...	80	684	...	660	...	23	2006	
21	...	...	88	765	...	752	...	13	2007	
29	...	...	342	2 403	122	2 049	...	233	2004	Honduras
28	...	...	335	2 409	128	2 128	...	153	2005	
30	...	...	307	2 264	133	1 951	...	180	2006	
26	...	...	377	2 840	141	2 508	...	191	2007	
*186	25	59	1 228	3 286	46	3 223	...	17	2004	Jamaïque
183	30	7	1 208	3 203	42	3 144	...	17	2005	
236	30	12	1 454	3 872	22	3 831	...	19	2006	
248	30	10	1 665	4 490	25	4 447	...	18	2007	
*4	*45	*-97	*1 564	*616	...	*616	...	...	2004	Martinique
*4	*45	*-80	*1 560	*620	...	*620	...	...	2005	
*4	*45	*-62	*1 577	*627	...	*627	...	...	2006	
*5	*47	*-47	*1 600	*637	...	*637	...	...	2007	
2 491	774	8 435	1 382	142 299	7 498	82 786	48 570	3 445	2004	Mexique
2 581	877	10 141	1 423	147 870	8 975	85 936	49 117	3 842	2005	
2 763	880	8 518	1 459	153 053	9 069	85 954	53 968	4 062	2006	
3 064	873	9 438	1 496	160 848	9 097	91 778	56 173	3 800	2007	
...	1	...	4 676	23	...	23	...	...	2004	Montserrat *
...	1	...	5 126	23	...	23	...	...	2005	
...	1	...	5 489	25	...	25	...	...	2006	
...	1	...	5 808	26	...	26	...	...	2007	
72	1 767	1 162	13 725	2 453	...	2 453	...	...	2004	Antilles néerlandaises
73	1 792	1 899	8 109	1 488	...	1 488	...	...	2005	
74	1 824	1 911	7 105	1 342	...	1 342	...	...	2006	
75	1 857	1 289	10 379	2 009	...	2 009	...	...	2007	

Production, trade and consumption of commercial energy *(continued)*

Thousand metric tons of oil equivalent and kilograms per capita

Production, commerce et consommation d'énergie commerciale *(suite)*

Milliers de tonnes d'équivalent pétrole et kilogrammes par habitant

Region, country or area	Year Année	Primary energy production – Production d'énergie primaire Total Totale	Solids Solides	Liquids Liquides	Gas Gaz	Electricity Electricité	Changes in stocks Variations des stocks	Imports Importations	Exports Exportations
Nicaragua	2004	50	...	...	...	50	-40	1 286	7
	2005	61	...	...	...	61	37	1 317	8
	2006	53	...	...	...	53	23	1 421	20
	2007	47	...	...	...	47	52	1 531	*3
Panama	2004	325	...	...	...	325	-191	1 758	11
	2005	320	...	...	...	320	0	2 026	4
	2006	308	...	...	...	308	0	2 316	4
	2007	315	...	...	...	315	-405	2 051	11
Puerto Rico	2004	12	...	...	...	12	...	633	...
	2005	12	...	...	...	12	...	633	...
	2006	*13	...	...	...	*13	...	660	...
	2007	26	...	...	...	26	...	686	...
Saint Kitts and Nevis *	2004	...	...	...	...	...	...	76	...
	2005	...	...	...	...	...	...	79	...
	2006	...	...	...	...	...	...	79	...
	2007	...	...	...	...	...	...	83	...
Saint Lucia *	2004	...	...	...	...	...	...	125	...
	2005	...	...	...	...	...	...	129	...
	2006	...	...	...	...	...	...	125	...
	2007	...	...	...	...	...	...	134	...
Saint Pierre and Miquelon *	2004	...	...	...	...	...	...	27	...
	2005	...	...	...	...	...	...	28	...
	2006	...	...	...	...	...	...	28	...
	2007	...	...	...	...	...	...	29	...
Saint Vincent-Grenadines	2004	2	...	...	...	2	...	*64	...
	*2005	2	...	...	...	2	...	65	...
	*2006	3	...	...	...	3	...	67	...
	2007	3	...	...	...	3	...	*67	...
Trinidad and Tobago	2004	31 847	...	7 385	24 462	...	313	4 659	21 483
	2005	33 934	...	8 444	25 490	...	78	4 577	24 016
	2006	37 516	...	8 463	29 052	...	-471	4 892	26 746
	2007	40 208	...	8 208	32 000	...	-291	5 411	28 595
Turks and Caicos Islands *	2004	...	...	...	...	...	...	35	...
	2005	...	...	...	...	...	...	41	...
	2006	...	...	...	...	...	...	48	...
	2007	...	...	...	...	...	...	52	...
United States	2004	1 469 130	553 082	332 753	485 136	98 160	5 482	792 347	101 155
	2005	1 451 666	564 083	318 187	471 037	98 358	-347	818 276	103 826
	2006	1 478 346	576 677	317 547	482 858	101 264	35 311	817 773	110 039
	2007	1 486 872	567 500	321 128	498 134	100 109	-7 434	820 830	123 400
America, South	**2004**	**536 330**	**42 229**	**346 886**	**96 691**	**50 525**	**-735**	**103 167**	**261 443**
	2005	**561 211**	**46 620**	**362 478**	**98 645**	**53 468**	**732**	**93 729**	**270 510**
	2006	**571 244**	**51 170**	**360 025**	**103 914**	**56 136**	**-2 677**	**97 895**	**272 644**
	2007	**564 609**	**53 747**	**350 805**	**102 479**	**57 578**	**6 114**	**108 565**	**252 074**
Argentina	2004	88 171	30	43 912	40 921	3 307	-115	3 093	22 233
	2005	86 000	15	42 189	40 253	3 544	147	4 587	20 082
	2006	88 717	252	42 362	42 155	3 948	5	3 543	16 478
	2007	86 587	65	40 892	42 363	3 268	-275	4 310	9 879
Bolivia (Plurinational State of)	2004	12 514	...	2 588	9 742	185	0	193	8 342
	2005	14 087	...	2 784	11 093	211	38	255	10 172
	2006	14 655	...	2 654	11 815	186	60	376	10 762
	2007	15 557	...	2 448	12 909	199	-13	437	11 185
Brazil	2004	127 868	2 402	86 852	10 032	28 582	-775	51 604	22 419
	2005	139 024	2 779	96 133	10 249	29 863	-226	46 181	23 303
	2006	146 068	2 613	101 894	10 386	31 174	-424	47 919	29 438
	2007	152 568	2 650	106 569	10 127	33 221	1 286	55 662	33 742

49

Production, trade and consumption of commercial energy *(continued)*
Thousand metric tons of oil equivalent and kilograms per capita

Production, commerce et consommation d'énergie commerciale *(suite)*
Milliers de tonnes d'équivalent pétrole et kilogrammes par habitant

Bunkers - Soutes			Consumption - Consommation							
Air Avion	Sea Maritime	Unallocated Non distribué	Per capita Par habitant	Total Totale	Solids Solides	Liquids Liquides	Gas Gaz	Electricity Electricité	Year Année	Région, pays ou zone
20	...	11	249	1 338	...	1 288	...	50	2004	Nicaragua
18	...	9	240	1 306	...	1 244	...	62	2005	
18	...	20	253	1 395	...	1 337	...	58	2006	
27	...	24	263	1 473	...	1 420	...	53	2007	
174	...	...	658	2 088	1	1 767	...	321	2004	Panama
186	...	...	668	2 156	1	1 834	...	321	2005	
218	...	...	731	2 402	1	2 094	...	307	2006	
265	...	...	747	2 496	150	2 041	...	305	2007	
...	...	...	166	645	...	...	633	12	2004	Porto Rico
...	...	...	165	646	...	...	633	12	2005	
...	...	...	171	673	...	...	660	*13	2006	
...	...	...	181	712	...	...	686	26	2007	
...	...	...	1 679	76	...	76	...	...	2004	Saint-Kitts-et-Nevis *
...	...	...	1 742	79	...	79	...	...	2005	
...	...	...	1 735	79	...	79	...	...	2006	
...	...	...	1 816	83	...	83	...	...	2007	
...	5	...	741	120	...	120	...	...	2004	Sainte-Lucie *
...	6	...	747	123	...	123	...	...	2005	
...	6	...	713	119	...	119	...	...	2006	
...	6	...	756	128	...	128	...	...	2007	
...	6	...	2 920	20	...	20	...	...	2004	Saint-Pierre-et-Miquelon *
...	6	...	3 060	21	...	21	...	...	2005	
...	6	...	3 054	21	...	21	...	...	2006	
...	6	...	3 193	22	...	22	...	...	2007	
...	...	...	*634	*66	...	*64	...	2	2004	Saint Vincent-Grenadines
...	...	...	649	67	...	65	...	2	*2005	
...	...	...	675	70	...	67	...	3	*2006	
...	...	...	*679	*70	...	*67	...	3	2007	
6	898	1 524	9 313	12 283	...	632	11 651	...	2004	Trinité-et-Tobago
60	264	1 016	9 877	13 078	...	908	12 170	...	2005	
73	273	957	11 167	14 830	...	890	13 940	...	2006	
83	265	939	12 024	16 028	...	1 047	14 981	...	2007	
...	...	...	1 255	35	...	35	...	...	2004	Iles Turques et Caïques *
...	...	...	1 327	41	...	41	...	...	2005	
...	...	...	1 437	48	...	48	...	...	2006	
...	...	...	1 485	52	...	52	...	...	2007	
16 469	24 786	36 752	7 084	2 076 835	551 716	856 060	569 926	99 132	2004	Etats-Unis
17 020	26 383	23 526	7 096	2 099 536	558 542	874 298	566 211	100 484	2005	
15 653	28 445	27 571	6 959	2 079 100	551 665	863 453	561 134	102 848	2006	
16 405	30 956	21 223	7 039	2 123 152	555 725	863 379	601 252	102 796	2007	
4 443	**5 512**	**24 724**	**937**	**344 111**	**20 888**	**175 894**	**96 762**	**50 566**	**2004**	**Amérique du Sud**
4 532	**6 124**	**24 752**	**936**	**348 290**	**21 597**	**174 353**	**98 681**	**53 659**	**2005**	
4 895	**5 966**	**27 708**	**956**	**360 603**	**21 696**	**178 460**	**104 007**	**56 440**	**2006**	
4 193	**5 205**	**30 987**	**974**	**374 600**	**22 903**	**191 019**	**102 768**	**57 911**	**2007**	
748	514	9 516	1 527	58 368	580	19 301	34 882	3 606	2004	Argentine
724	695	8 284	1 572	60 655	897	20 198	35 683	3 877	2005	
697	741	9 328	1 668	65 009	753	22 224	37 882	4 151	2006	
760	895	9 546	1 781	70 092	1 081	23 642	41 443	3 926	2007	
...	...	182	453	4 183	...	1 982	2 016	185	2004	Bolivie (État plurinational de)
...	...	499	385	3 633	...	1 902	1 520	211	2005	
...	...	163	420	4 045	...	2 069	1 791	186	2006	
...	...	421	448	4 402	...	2 339	1 864	199	2007	
1 090	3 348	9 291	794	144 100	14 363	80 429	17 512	31 796	2004	Brésil
1 100	3 497	9 824	802	147 706	13 923	81 990	18 572	33 220	2005	
1 271	3 393	9 991	805	150 318	13 779	82 383	19 441	34 714	2006	
1 386	2 339	10 399	829	159 078	14 591	88 241	19 686	36 560	2007	

Production, trade and consumption of commercial energy *(continued)*

Thousand metric tons of oil equivalent and kilograms per capita

Production, commerce et consommation d'énergie commerciale *(suite)*

Milliers de tonnes d'équivalent pétrole et kilogrammes par habitant

		Primary energy production – Production d'énergie primaire					Changes in stocks		
Region, country or area	Year Année	Total Totale	Solids Solides	Liquids Liquides	Gas Gaz	Electricity Electricité	Variations des stocks	Imports Importations	Exports Exportations
Chile	2004	3 997	158	423	1 526	1 890	451	22 919	1 475
	2005	4 820	369	389	1 784	2 278	267	22 817	1 619
	2006	5 016	458	330	1 723	2 505	790	24 100	1 941
	2007	3 916	165	559	1 202	1 990	1 812	25 152	1 141
Colombia	2004	71 600	34 900	26 770	6 481	3 449	8	319	48 347
	2005	74 924	38 391	26 301	6 800	3 430	357	947	50 662
	2006	80 037	42 637	26 901	6 813	3 685	-1 324	688	55 668
	2007	83 615	45 436	27 539	6 814	3 826	1 223	705	56 515
Ecuador	2004	28 077	...	26 888	552	637	-122	2 078	20 442
	2005	28 195	...	27 022	434	740	297	2 752	20 670
	2006	29 540	...	28 066	707	766	74	3 230	21 626
	2007	*28 352	...	26 760	728	863	364	3 557	19 833
Falkland Is. (Malvinas)	2004	3	3	...	...	...	...	*13	...
	*2005	3	3	...	...	...	...	13	...
	2006	3	3	...	...	...	...	*15	...
	*2007	3	3	...	...	...	...	15	...
French Guiana *	2004	...	...	...	...	...	...	287	...
	2005	...	...	...	...	...	...	287	...
	2006	...	...	...	...	...	...	298	...
	2007	...	...	...	...	...	...	304	...
Guyana	2004	...	...	...	...	...	...	492	...
	2005	...	...	...	...	...	...	508	...
	2006	...	...	...	...	...	...	513	...
	2007	...	...	...	...	...	...	513	...
Paraguay	2004	4 464	...	0	...	4 464	-12	1 292	3 869
	2005	4 403	...	5	...	4 399	-26	1 179	3 765
	2006	4 628	...	5	...	4 624	-13	1 241	3 929
	2007	4 623	...	4	...	4 619	5	1 311	3 880
Peru	2004	7 180	15	4 695	963	1 507	36	6 542	2 924
	2005	8 762	29	5 391	1 624	1 717	-94	6 550	3 452
	2006	9 400	73	5 620	1 859	1 847	1 180	6 631	3 339
	2007	10 435	77	6 081	2 596	1 681	1 406	8 379	4 158
Suriname	2004	678	...	612	...	66	...	272	142
	2005	708	...	637	...	71	...	284	148
	2006	731	...	656	...	75	...	290	152
	2007	731	...	656	...	75	...	290	152
Uruguay	2004	411	...	...	...	411	78	2 763	353
	2005	575	...	...	...	575	-129	2 586	444
	2006	309	...	...	...	309	39	2 942	239
	2007	694	...	...	...	694	-163	2 442	291
Venezuela (Boliv. Rep. of)	2004	191 366	4 721	154 146	26 473	6 025	-283	11 300	130 896
	2005	199 710	5 034	161 628	26 408	6 640	100	4 783	136 193
	2006	192 142	5 134	151 537	28 455	7 016	-3 064	6 109	129 072
	2007	177 530	5 352	139 297	25 740	7 142	468	5 486	111 297
Asia	**2004**	**3 983 408**	**1 572 786**	**1 632 765**	**664 544**	**113 312**	**-523**	**1 518 623**	**1 562 465**
	2005	**4 261 712**	**1 735 153**	**1 687 563**	**717 210**	**121 787**	**-2 989**	**1 545 645**	**1 651 099**
	2006	**4 480 559**	**1 886 983**	**1 709 436**	**754 597**	**129 544**	**1 993**	**1 622 458**	**1 712 135**
	2007	***4 625 554**	**1 989 634**	**1 704 189**	**801 463**	**130 268**	**6 236**	**1 727 459**	**1 708 710**
Afghanistan	2004	76	24	...	3	50	...	197	...
	*2005	77	23	...	2	51	...	210	...
	*2006	77	23	...	2	52	...	211	...
	*2007	78	23	...	3	52	...	217	...
Armenia	2004	380	...	...	...	380	...	1 586	99
	2005	386	...	...	...	386	...	1 924	129
	2006	384	...	...	...	384	...	1 928	85
	2007	379	...	...	...	379	...	2 261	62

49

Production, trade and consumption of commercial energy *(continued)*
Thousand metric tons of oil equivalent and kilograms per capita

Production, commerce et consommation d'énergie commerciale *(suite)*
Milliers de tonnes d'équivalent pétrole et kilogrammes par habitant

Bunkers - Soutes			Consumption - Consommation							
Air Avion	Sea Maritime	Unallocated Non distribué	Per capita Par habitant	Total Totale	Solids Solides	Liquids Liquides	Gas Gaz	Electricity Electricité	Year Année	Région, pays ou zone
597	...	513	1 483	23 880	3 144	10 893	7 789	2 054	2004	Chili
641	...	294	1 526	24 816	3 133	11 670	7 550	2 463	2005	
682	...	194	1 552	25 508	3 910	11 940	6 957	2 702	2006	
766	...	208	1 515	25 142	3 855	15 438	3 720	2 130	2007	
587	395	989	477	21 593	1 941	9 863	6 481	3 308	2004	Colombie
616	415	1 355	488	22 466	2 700	9 685	6 800	3 281	2005	
663	468	2 557	485	22 693	2 467	9 882	6 813	3 531	2006	
507	391	3 437	468	22 246	2 391	9 288	6 813	3 754	2007	
278	226	1 575	595	7 757	...	6 426	552	779	2004	Equateur
314	222	742	659	8 703	...	7 383	434	887	2005	
328	248	987	709	9 506	...	7 897	707	901	2006	
340	274	1 036	740	10 062	...	8 400	728	934	2007	
...	...	...	*5 523	*16	*3	*13	...	...	2004	Iles Falkland (Malvinas)
...	...	...	5 504	16	3	13	...	...	*2005	
...	...	...	*6 188	*18	*3	*15	...	...	2006	
...	...	...	6 095	18	3	15	...	...	*2007	
18	...	...	1 408	269	...	269	...	...	2004	Guyane française *
18	...	...	1 378	269	...	269	...	...	2005	
20	...	...	1 413	278	...	278	...	...	2006	
20	...	...	1 408	284	...	284	...	...	2007	
12	...	...	635	479	...	479	...	...	2004	Guyana
13	...	...	653	495	...	495	...	...	2005	
13	...	...	658	500	...	500	...	...	2006	
13	...	...	666	500	...	500	...	...	2007	
19	...	2	324	1 878	...	1 282	...	595	2004	Paraguay
19	...	1	309	1 823	...	1 189	...	634	2005	
24	...	0	321	1 929	...	1 235	...	694	2006	
24	...	0	330	2 024	...	1 285	...	738	2007	
443	57	-545	399	10 807	857	7 480	963	1 507	2004	Pérou
313	228	313	408	11 100	902	6 856	1 624	1 717	2005	
466	100	-208	407	11 152	745	6 701	1 859	1 847	2006	
169	152	987	436	11 941	937	6 727	2 596	1 681	2007	
...	...	144	1 364	664	0	598	...	66	2004	Suriname
...	...	149	1 395	696	0	624	...	71	2005	
...	...	155	1 416	714	0	639	...	75	2006	
...	...	155	1 401	714	0	639	...	75	2007	
45	340	25	706	2 332	1	1 626	94	611	2004	Uruguay
43	356	91	712	2 355	1	1 626	89	639	2005	
57	248	104	774	2 565	2	1 909	102	552	2006	
68	325	53	767	2 562	3	1 789	95	676	2007	
606	633	3 031	2 594	67 783	0	35 252	26 473	6 058	2004	Venezuela (Rép. boliv. du)
732	711	3 200	2 391	63 558	36	30 453	26 408	6 660	2005	
674	767	4 436	2 455	66 366	36	30 787	28 455	7 088	2006	
140	829	4 747	2 385	65 535	43	32 431	25 823	7 237	2007	
34 979	**64 305**	**289 336**	**924**	**3 551 468**	**1 706 367**	**1 077 891**	**653 912**	**113 298**	**2004**	**Asie**
37 883	**70 308**	**284 548**	**968**	**3 766 507**	**1 855 704**	**1 088 211**	**700 791**	**121 800**	**2005**	
39 753	**75 873**	**301 099**	**1 008**	**3 972 163**	**2 002 096**	**1 095 916**	**744 667**	**129 485**	**2006**	
41 826	**80 997**	**308 358**	**1 055**	**4 206 884**	**2 144 928**	**1 128 323**	**803 874**	**129 759**	**2007**	
0	...	...	12	273	24	188	3	58	2004	Afghanistan
10	...	...	11	277	23	191	2	60	*2005	
10	...	...	11	278	23	191	2	62	*2006	
10	...	...	11	284	23	196	3	63	*2007	
39	...	0	569	1 828	0	311	1 201	315	2004	Arménie
45	...	0	664	2 136	0	333	1 488	316	2005	
40	...	0	679	2 187	1	312	1 525	350	2006	
61	...	0	781	2 517	2	313	1 826	376	2007	

49 Production, trade and consumption of commercial energy *(continued)*

Thousand metric tons of oil equivalent and kilograms per capita

Production, commerce et consommation d'énergie commerciale *(suite)*

Milliers de tonnes d'équivalent pétrole et kilogrammes par habitant

Region, country or area	Year	Primary energy production – Production d'énergie primaire					Changes in stocks	Imports	Exports
	Année	Total Totale	Solids Solides	Liquids Liquides	Gas Gaz	Electricity Electricité	Variations des stocks	Importations	Exportations
Azerbaijan	2004	20 457	...	15 565	4 655	237	42	4 861	11 405
	2005	27 652	...	22 231	5 161	259	904	4 686	16 770
	2006	38 599	...	32 290	6 092	217	-126	4 412	27 985
	2007	52 975	...	42 698	10 074	203	24	98	39 636
Bahrain	2004	16 720	...	10 168	6 552	...	-315	3 326	9 927
	2005	17 083	...	10 143	6 941	...	-250	3 980	10 082
	2006	17 324	...	9 970	7 354	...	-513	3 760	9 746
	2007	18 049	...	9 954	8 095	...	-307	3 812	9 665
Bangladesh	2004	11 374	...	97	11 171	105	-56	4 269	...
	2005	12 225	...	104	12 010	111	-326	4 495	...
	2006	13 191	...	100	12 972	119	-117	4 537	...
	2007	*14 070	...	91	13 859	120	-109	4 572	...
Bhutan	2004	223	21	...	...	202	0	114	156
	2005	287	60	...	...	228	*31	152	202
	2006	457	69	...	...	389	*-32	82	359
	2007	638	74	...	...	564	0	94	488
Brunei Darussalam	2004	21 739	...	10 338	11 401	...	55	0	19 392
	2005	21 309	...	10 116	11 193	...	-11	26	19 153
	2006	22 598	...	10 833	11 765	...	-68	0	20 549
	2007	*21 149	...	9 729	11 420	...	-40	0	18 148
Cambodia	2004	2	...	...	...	2	...	1 202	...
	2005	4	...	...	...	4	...	1 278	...
	2006	5	...	...	...	5	...	1 404	...
	2007	4	...	...	...	4	...	1 519	...
China [2]	2004	1 400 556	1 150 567	175 873	39 628	34 488	-4	176 761	79 353
	2005	1 540 362	1 273 231	181 353	47 076	38 702	-3 043	178 910	74 404
	2006	1 653 788	1 370 407	184 766	55 956	42 659	-4 061	199 275	68 516
	2007	1 759 178	1 458 750	186 318	66 078	48 033	15 286	232 675	63 597
China, Hong Kong SAR	2004	...	...	...	...	...	-22	24 365	1 618
	2005	...	...	...	...	...	37	23 619	1 769
	2006	...	...	...	...	...	632	25 222	1 582
	2007	...	...	...	...	...	1 142	27 051	1 311
China, Macao SAR	2004	...	...	...	...	...	19	595	...
	2005	...	...	...	...	...	-4	627	...
	2006	...	...	...	...	...	8	625	...
	2007	...	...	...	...	...	9	664	...
Cyprus	2004	0	...	...	...	0	-62	2 398	...
	2005	0	...	...	...	0	71	2 799	...
	2006	0	...	...	...	0	120	2 959	...
	2007	0	...	...	...	0	-56	2 868	...
Georgia	2004	634	5	98	11	520	0	1 699	106
	2005	618	3	67	12	536	0	2 059	90
	2006	551	6	64	17	463	0	2 338	77
	2007	666	8	57	15	586	-2	2 493	100
India	2004	299 700	228 921	37 958	24 075	8 748	1 532	120 102	15 877
	2005	314 407	243 028	36 651	24 490	10 238	5 996	130 539	16 996
	2006	330 977	257 109	38 468	24 006	11 395	5 918	148 024	24 074
	2007	348 940	272 957	38 571	25 585	11 827	1 254	165 245	29 895
Indonesia	2004	208 561	86 398	52 909	67 850	1 404	*543	40 530	134 141
	2005	219 741	104 097	50 122	64 028	1 493	506	37 724	141 307
	2006	249 725	135 997	47 741	64 588	1 400	467	32 932	165 938
	2007	244 802	128 669	50 940	63 619	1 574	590	36 324	149 109
Iran (Islamic Rep. of)	2004	284 719	872	199 365	83 567	914	13	12 821	136 432
	2005	314 629	931	215 845	96 462	1 390	0	12 807	158 928
	2006	317 881	1 070	214 023	101 215	1 573	48	16 039	147 367
	2007	325 234	1 144	218 241	104 291	1 559	-1 544	19 279	153 843

Production, trade and consumption of commercial energy *(continued)*

Thousand metric tons of oil equivalent and kilograms per capita

Production, commerce et consommation d'énergie commerciale *(suite)*

Milliers de tonnes d'équivalent pétrole et kilogrammes par habitant

Bunkers - Soutes			Consumption - Consommation							
Air Avion	Sea Maritime	Unallocated Non distribué	Per capita Par habitant	Total Totale	Solids Solides	Liquids Liquides	Gas Gaz	Electricity Electricité	Year Année	Région, pays ou zone
195	...	255	1 616	13 421	...	4 025	9 042	354	2004	Azerbaïdjan
28	...	438	1 692	14 199	...	4 839	8 997	362	2005	
104	...	449	1 721	14 599	...	4 369	9 938	293	2006	
110	...	935	1 441	12 367	...	3 634	8 550	183	2007	
521	...	2 313	10 749	7 601	...	1 049	6 552	...	2004	Bahreïn
563	...	2 499	11 273	8 169	...	1 228	6 941	...	2005	
577	...	2 438	11 899	8 835	...	1 482	7 354	...	2006	
606	...	2 408	12 483	9 489	...	1 394	8 095	...	2007	
242	36	527	109	14 894	350	3 267	11 171	105	2004	Bangladesh
279	36	582	117	16 149	350	3 678	12 010	111	2005	
274	36	569	120	16 966	350	3 525	12 972	119	2006	
245	36	485	125	17 986	350	3 657	13 859	120	2007	
1	...	...	288	180	50	65	...	64	2004	Bhoutan
1	...	...	322	204	71	70	...	63	2005	
1	...	...	327	211	62	73	...	76	2006	
1	...	...	370	244	70	75	...	98	2007	
...	...	95	6 108	2 197	...	623	1 574	...	2004	Brunéi Darussalam
...	...	-51	6 061	2 243	...	649	1 594	...	2005	
...	...	-120	5 842	2 237	...	664	1 573	...	2006	
...	...	102	7 536	2 939	...	684	2 255	...	2007	
21	...	...	87	1 184	...	1 176	...	7	2004	Cambodge
21	...	...	91	1 261	...	1 250	...	11	2005	
26	...	...	98	1 383	...	1 369	...	14	2006	
29	...	...	104	1 494	...	1 476	...	19	2007	
129	289	80 617	1 093	1 416 932	1 104 029	241 481	37 456	33 966	2004	Chine[2]
321	927	78 315	1 203	1 568 347	1 240 395	245 348	44 433	38 170	2005	
439	1 440	86 892	1 297	1 699 838	1 349 546	253 880	54 345	42 067	2006	
121	1 536	89 719	1 379	1 821 595	1 436 637	270 471	67 342	47 146	2007	
3 244	7 722	...	1 740	11 803	5 244	3 929	2 049	580	2004	Chine, Hong Kong RAS
3 764	5 718	...	1 810	12 331	5 839	3 884	2 048	559	2005	
3 836	7 329	...	1 725	11 843	5 733	3 399	2 164	548	2006	
3 904	8 355	...	1 702	12 339	6 287	3 586	1 870	595	2007	
...	...	...	1 239	576	...	563	...	13	2004	Chine, Macao RAS
...	...	...	1 291	630	...	601	...	29	2005	
...	...	...	1 229	617	...	534	...	83	2006	
...	...	...	1 246	655	...	510	...	145	2007	
304	54	6	2 844	2 096	40	2 056	...	0	2004	Chypre
300	291	0	2 819	2 137	37	2 100	...	0	2005	
310	296	0	2 898	2 234	38	2 196	...	0	2006	
296	275	0	3 001	2 353	35	2 318	...	0	2007	
38	...	21	502	2 168	7	527	1 004	630	2004	Géorgie
38	...	15	581	2 534	11	676	1 195	652	2005	
38	...	15	627	2 759	13	682	1 534	530	2006	
48	...	29	680	2 983	28	838	1 548	569	2007	
2 900	7	34 005	337	365 482	246 275	86 238	24 075	8 893	2004	Inde
3 400	5	37 175	346	381 375	259 810	86 704	24 490	10 371	2005	
4 101	4	38 018	364	406 886	278 181	93 069	24 006	11 631	2006	
4 771	15	41 513	385	436 736	302 255	96 645	25 585	12 252	2007	
794	358	1 590	514	111 664	20 000	59 288	30 972	1 404	2004	Indonésie
729	374	2 733	509	111 816	22 813	59 148	28 362	1 493	2005	
717	394	1 875	509	113 267	27 230	54 129	30 508	1 400	2006	
763	419	5 043	555	125 203	38 946	54 868	29 815	1 574	2007	
812	619	8 003	2 248	151 661	1 117	63 828	85 773	943	2004	Iran (Rép. islamique d')
880	556	2 043	2 410	165 028	1 267	65 553	96 877	1 331	2005	
1 032	459	9 878	2 484	175 135	1 357	70 505	101 720	1 553	2006	
1 047	842	11 036	2 491	179 289	1 381	71 602	104 806	1 501	2007	

49 Production, trade and consumption of commercial energy *(continued)*

Thousand metric tons of oil equivalent and kilograms per capita

Production, commerce et consommation d'énergie commerciale *(suite)*

Milliers de tonnes d'équivalent pétrole et kilogrammes par habitant

Region, country or area	Year Année	Primary energy production – Production d'énergie primaire Total Totale	Solids Solides	Liquids Liquides	Gas Gaz	Electricity Electricité	Changes in stocks Variations des stocks	Imports Importations	Exports Exportations
Iraq	2004	99 966	...	99 016	908	42	459	6 651	74 766
	2005	93 126	...	91 766	1 316	45	448	7 962	67 783
	2006	97 416	...	96 058	1 316	42	-1 749	8 992	73 128
	2007	102 688	...	101 319	1 325	44	0	11 526	80 565
Israel	2004	1 143	97	2	1 041	3	-201	22 131	3 590
	2005	1 529	91	2	1 433	3	548	21 713	3 926
	2006	2 105	99	2	2 002	1	-186	22 087	3 290
	2007	1 962	94	...	1 866	1	137	8 076	179
Japan	2004	37 244	...	692	2 994	33 558	-1 138	428 408	5 268
	2005	38 006	...	734	3 215	34 057	2 486	430 051	9 121
	2006	39 187	...	726	3 547	34 915	-1 231	425 573	10 507
	2007	35 174	...	784	3 974	30 416	-270	438 157	14 603
Jordan	2004	247	...	1	241	5	112	6 393	0
	2005	205	...	1	199	5	163	7 118	0
	2006	191	...	1	185	5	-6	6 943	3
	2007	171	...	1	165	6	56	7 388	15
Kazakhstan	2004	119 676	38 198	60 185	20 601	693	400	17 216	81 703
	2005	124 352	38 071	62 329	23 277	675	359	16 889	83 103
	2006	133 379	42 271	65 850	24 591	668	269	19 103	89 742
	2007	141 513	45 192	68 067	27 552	703	465	15 595	81 788
Korea, Dem. P. R.	2004	21 217	20 142	...	...	1 075	...	1 368	1 100
	2005	23 187	22 058	...	...	1 129	...	1 202	1 963
	2006	23 435	22 350	...	...	1 085	...	989	1 737
	2007	20 565	19 423	...	...	1 142	...	1 077	2 619
Korea, Republic of	2004	13 122	1 368	4	0	11 750	913	199 949	25 402
	2005	14 847	1 214	65	490	13 079	-4 447	196 501	29 636
	2006	14 996	1 210	87	436	13 262	2 989	210 174	32 370
	2007	14 463	1 237	111	353	12 762	-2 109	214 282	31 945
Kuwait	2004	135 274	...	124 221	11 053	...	...	113	93 408
	2005	150 065	...	137 670	12 394	...	...	0	105 226
	2006	154 727	...	141 990	12 737	...	...	0	111 831
	2007	150 534	...	138 134	12 400	...	...	0	107 064
Kyrgyzstan	2004	1 448	135	74	27	1 212	-10	1 791	464
	2005	1 422	99	74	23	1 226	0	1 715	357
	2006	1 463	95	71	18	1 280	0	1 668	320
	2007	1 395	113	68	14	1 199	0	1 830	315
Lao People's Dem. Rep. *	2004	561	284	...	...	277	...	154	313
	2005	585	296	...	...	289	...	161	319
	2006	598	299	...	...	298	...	157	318
	2007	687	397	...	...	290	...	159	412
Lebanon	2004	97	...	...	...	97	1	5 002	...
	2005	90	...	...	...	90	-417	4 812	...
	2006	60	...	...	...	60	0	4 443	...
	2007	*50	...	...	...	50	-19	3 805	...
Malaysia	2004	90 490	268	37 632	52 089	501	397	29 557	49 128
	2005	95 925	477	37 627	57 375	446	500	27 722	52 132
	2006	98 907	631	37 018	60 650	608	114	28 702	52 605
	2007	96 647	576	35 179	60 334	558	99	34 193	48 405
Maldives	2004	...	...	...	...	...	...	250	...
	2005	...	...	...	...	...	...	225	...
	2006	...	...	...	...	...	...	288	...
	2007	...	...	...	...	...	...	299	...
Mongolia	2004	2 111	2 111	...	...	...	...	595	361
	2005	2 311	2 311	...	...	...	...	582	490
	2006	2 482	2 482	...	...	...	...	669	569
	2007	2 840	2 840	...	...	...	...	822	756

49

Production, trade and consumption of commercial energy *(continued)*
Thousand metric tons of oil equivalent and kilograms per capita

Production, commerce et consommation d'énergie commerciale *(suite)*
Milliers de tonnes d'équivalent pétrole et kilogrammes par habitant

Bunkers - Soutes			Consumption - Consommation							
Air Avion	Sea Maritime	Unallocated Non distribué	Per capita Par habitant	Total Totale	Solids Solides	Liquids Liquides	Gas Gaz	Electricity Electricité	Year Année	Région, pays ou zone
1 200	...	2 678	1 014	27 514	...	26 450	908	156	2004	Iraq
774	...	3 160	1 052	28 924	...	27 444	1 316	164	2005	
812	...	4 415	1 034	29 801	...	28 331	1 316	154	2006	
837	...	2 185	1 032	30 627	...	29 142	1 325	160	2007	
*4	229	-240	2 922	19 893	7 993	10 980	1 041	-122	2004	Israël
*4	259	-1 272	2 854	19 776	7 403	11 080	1 433	-140	2005	
4	261	-412	3 010	21 234	7 963	11 427	2 002	-157	2006	
...	...	...	1 354	9 722	8 034	...	1 866	-178	2007	
6 952	5 360	24 882	3 361	424 328	116 469	195 864	78 438	33 558	2004	Japon
7 000	6 024	24 330	3 320	419 096	110 997	195 614	78 428	34 057	2005	
6 498	5 666	26 969	3 300	416 351	112 387	182 964	86 085	34 915	2006	
6 032	5 650	23 929	3 357	423 387	117 095	183 576	92 299	30 416	2007	
79	48	192	1 217	6 209	...	4 804	1 329	76	2004	Jordanie
162	79	303	1 209	6 616	...	5 009	1 538	69	2005	
74	41	163	1 225	6 860	...	4 811	2 004	46	2006	
97	38	128	1 262	7 225	...	4 811	2 406	8	2007	
223	...	2 846	3 445	51 720	27 583	8 281	15 351	506	2004	Kazakhstan
241	...	1 135	3 724	56 403	28 217	8 097	19 364	725	2005	
254	...	10	4 064	62 207	30 318	10 291	20 858	740	2006	
309	...	3 456	4 591	71 090	33 707	10 456	26 254	673	2007	
...	...	13	909	21 473	19 296	1 102	...	1 075	2004	Corée, R. p. dém. de
...	...	10	949	22 417	20 362	925	...	1 129	2005	
...	...	7	957	22 681	20 887	708	...	1 085	2006	
...	...	7	799	19 016	17 028	847	...	1 142	2007	
1 286	7 135	23 234	3 226	155 102	50 672	64 582	28 097	11 750	2004	Corée, République de
2 374	10 169	19 528	3 191	154 088	49 265	61 326	30 417	13 079	2005	
2 891	10 182	22 019	3 203	154 719	52 521	57 039	31 898	13 262	2006	
3 076	9 455	25 246	3 309	161 131	57 603	56 142	34 623	12 762	2007	
552	567	16 062	11 441	24 797	...	13 744	11 053	...	2004	Koweït
594	528	15 696	12 481	28 020	...	15 626	12 394	...	2005	
572	634	15 101	11 421	26 588	...	13 852	12 737	...	2006	
626	500	15 808	11 007	26 536	...	14 136	12 400	...	2007	
...	...	2	546	2 783	555	559	744	926	2004	Kirghizistan
...	...	-8	542	2 788	516	591	686	995	2005	
...	...	-13	544	2 824	480	564	717	1 063	2006	
...	...	5	550	2 905	499	643	769	995	2007	
...	...	...	69	402	229	136	...	38	2004	Rép. dém. pop. lao *
...	...	...	76	427	236	137	...	55	2005	
...	...	...	76	436	239	138	...	59	2006	
...	...	...	74	434	241	142	...	51	2007	
131	17	...	1 248	4 950	140	4 695	...	115	2004	Liban
152	17	...	1 284	5 151	140	4 882	...	129	2005	
106	17	...	1 080	4 379	140	4 100	...	140	2006	
134	19	...	990	3 722	140	3 448	...	134	2007	
2 074	85	8 469	2 341	59 893	9 293	21 392	28 753	456	2004	Malaisie
1 954	59	8 361	2 321	60 640	7 575	21 699	31 113	254	2005	
2 010	50	7 390	2 456	65 441	7 800	21 468	35 781	391	2006	
2 160	65	7 121	2 686	72 989	8 602	23 314	40 711	363	2007	
...	...	...	863	250	...	250	...	...	2004	Maldives
...	...	...	767	225	...	225	...	...	2005	
...	...	...	965	288	...	288	...	...	2006	
...	...	...	979	299	...	299	...	...	2007	
...	...	...	931	2 345	1 751	580	...	14	2004	Mongolie
...	...	...	943	2 403	1 822	567	...	13	2005	
...	...	...	1 001	2 582	1 915	655	...	13	2006	
...	...	...	1 112	2 907	2 085	805	...	16	2007	

Production, trade and consumption of commercial energy *(continued)*
Thousand metric tons of oil equivalent and kilograms per capita

Production, commerce et consommation d'énergie commerciale *(suite)*
Milliers de tonnes d'équivalent pétrole et kilogrammes par habitant

Region, country or area	Year Année	Primary energy production – Production d'énergie primaire Total Totale	Solids Solides	Liquids Liquides	Gas Gaz	Electricity Electricité	Changes in stocks Variations des stocks	Imports Importations	Exports Exportations
Myanmar	2004	11 444	645	1 025	9 567	207	0	1 154	47 510
	2005	14 361	794	1 116	12 193	258	0	1 268	46 370
	2006	13 982	819	1 059	11 818	286	57	907	46 644
	2007	14 903	864	1 057	12 681	301	68	979	44 346
Nepal	2004	213	6	...	...	207	...	883	10
	2005	231	6	...	...	225	...	1 011	11
	2006	239	6	...	...	233	...	1 041	12
	2007	247	6	...	...	240	...	1 070	12
Occupied Palestinian Terr.	2004	...	...	...	...	...	0	862	15
	2005	...	...	...	...	...	0	1 185	18
	2006	...	...	...	...	...	0	1 032	0
	2007	...	...	...	...	...	0	1 058	0
Oman	2004	55 938	...	39 084	16 854	...	-1 021	422	46 249
	2005	57 721	...	38 763	18 958	...	-1 567	378	46 616
	2006	59 321	...	36 912	22 409	...	677	735	44 261
	2007	58 395	...	35 564	22 831	...	1 683	768	43 025
Pakistan	2004	37 578	2 169	3 444	29 518	2 448	558	16 347	302
	2005	39 586	2 304	3 583	30 831	2 867	206	16 664	411
	2006	39 329	1 723	3 702	30 959	2 944	475	19 610	440
	2007	40 046	1 950	3 827	31 537	2 733	393	21 678	405
Philippines	2004	5 243	1 289	19	2 311	1 624	-253	20 884	613
	2005	5 985	1 337	29	3 047	1 573	-259	20 914	1 164
	2006	5 669	819	25	3 064	1 761	57	19 221	2 060
	2007	6 517	1 209	53	3 633	1 621	-474	19 501	2 495
Qatar	2004	78 681	...	42 174	36 506	...	-768	0	61 050
	2005	85 741	...	43 055	42 686	...	-1 307	0	64 030
	2006	94 614	...	47 361	47 252	...	-42	55	75 265
	2007	107 949	...	49 046	58 902	...	*59	204	82 867
Saudi Arabia	2004	547 073	...	495 418	51 655	...	-46	1 524	396 053
	2005	575 237	...	518 469	56 768	...	25	1 875	415 194
	2006	569 645	...	510 048	59 598	...	-119	3 711	404 994
	2007	550 703	...	489 468	61 236	...	300	3 774	382 137
Singapore	2004	...	...	...	...	...	-2 310	97 980	47 157
	2005	...	...	...	...	...	-4 405	105 496	50 712
	2006	...	...	...	...	...	-4 509	112 321	55 656
	2007	...	...	...	...	...	-6 967	117 310	60 312
Sri Lanka	2004	255	...	...	...	255	-2	4 086	38
	2005	297	...	...	...	297	41	4 013	0
	2006	399	...	...	...	399	120	4 174	0
	2007	340	...	...	...	340	25	4 229	0
Syrian Arab Republic	2004	30 167	...	23 409	6 393	365	-20	*2 877	12 645
	2005	28 138	...	22 349	5 493	296	18	*4 092	10 931
	2006	25 255	...	20 175	4 736	343	440	5 778	8 822
	2007	24 220	...	19 308	4 609	303	70	7 897	8 332
Tajikistan	2004	1 498	41	19	33	1 405	...	2 236	387
	2005	1 565	57	22	27	1 459	...	2 316	372
	2006	1 541	65	22	18	1 436	...	2 539	371
	2007	1 620	109	26	13	1 472	...	2 745	371
Thailand	2004	36 442	8 824	10 351	16 747	520	-981	58 673	8 564
	2005	39 592	9 184	11 907	18 002	499	-1 285	58 271	8 938
	2006	40 196	8 359	12 948	18 191	699	-1 969	61 115	10 311
	2007	41 701	8 023	13 809	19 171	698	-1 869	59 116	9 218
Timor-Leste *	2004	7 367	...	7 367	...	...	...	58	7 291
	2005	7 394	...	7 394	...	...	...	58	7 318
	2006	7 407	...	7 407	...	...	...	59	7 330
	2007	7 420	...	7 420	...	...	...	61	7 343

49

Production, trade and consumption of commercial energy *(continued)*

Thousand metric tons of oil equivalent and kilograms per capita

Production, commerce et consommation d'énergie commerciale *(suite)*

Milliers de tonnes d'équivalent pétrole et kilogrammes par habitant

Bunkers - Soutes			Consumption - Consommation							
Air Avion	Sea Maritime	Unallocated Non distribué	Per capita Par habitant	Total Totale	Solids Solides	Liquids Liquides	Gas Gaz	Electricity Electricité	Year Année	Région, pays ou zone
66	3	60	85	4 617	110	1 795	2 504	207	2004	Myanmar
51	3	57	110	6 107	124	1 879	3 845	258	2005	
77	3	50	97	5 486	138	1 667	3 395	286	2006	
65	3	46	97	5 556	145	1 705	3 405	301	2007	
54	...	...	42	1 032	180	635	...	218	2004	Népal
60	...	...	46	1 170	287	653	...	231	2005	
62	...	...	47	1 207	297	670	...	239	2006	
64	...	...	47	1 241	307	687	...	247	2007	
...	...	...	248	847	...	623	...	223	2004	Terr. palestinien occupé
...	...	...	333	1 166	...	920	...	246	2005	
...	...	...	286	1 032	...	765	...	266	2006	
...	...	...	281	1 058	...	784	...	274	2007	
205	1	150	4 461	10 776	...	3 314	7 463	...	2004	Oman
230	1	325	4 980	12 494	...	3 415	9 079	...	2005	
322	0	95	5 705	14 702	...	4 315	10 387	...	2006	
268	0	-99	5 207	14 286	...	3 665	10 622	...	2007	
168	63	1 410	346	51 425	4 460	14 998	29 510	2 457	2004	Pakistan
214	80	1 605	350	53 733	4 272	15 752	30 829	2 880	2005	
176	102	1 589	358	56 156	4 667	17 574	30 956	2 959	2006	
170	132	1 822	369	58 803	6 097	18 420	31 536	2 750	2007	
*619	139	867	292	24 143	5 478	14 730	2 311	1 624	2004	Philippines
*722	120	785	286	24 367	6 472	13 276	3 047	1 573	2005	
800	126	433	246	21 414	4 674	12 450	2 529	1 761	2006	
1 070	232	604	249	22 090	5 060	12 376	3 033	1 621	2007	
366	...	1 126	22 349	16 907	...	3 032	13 875	...	2004	Qatar
468	...	1 147	24 090	21 403	...	3 420	17 983	...	2005	
604	...	1 107	17 025	17 736	...	3 941	13 794	...	2006	
766	...	2 404	17 989	22 058	...	4 208	17 850	...	2007	
1 695	2 249	26 945	5 394	121 701	...	70 046	51 655	...	2004	Arabie saoudite
1 707	2 282	27 974	5 620	129 931	...	73 163	56 768	...	2005	
1 774	2 661	26 916	5 791	137 129	...	77 532	59 598	...	2006	
1 842	2 786	24 621	5 786	142 790	...	81 554	61 236	...	2007	
2 980	23 395	13 136	3 269	13 622	6	7 742	5 875	...	2004	Singapour
3 184	25 292	15 907	3 471	14 806	2	8 208	6 595	...	2005	
3 440	27 788	15 382	3 309	14 564	4	7 867	6 692	...	2006	
3 604	31 305	14 089	3 262	14 967	8	8 175	6 785	...	2007	
132	119	118	203	3 937	67	3 615	...	255	2004	Sri Lanka
134	169	139	196	3 828	67	3 464	...	297	2005	
123	137	161	205	4 032	67	3 566	...	399	2006	
105	170	143	208	4 126	48	3 738	...	340	2007	
120	...	815	1 093	19 483	3	12 723	6 393	365	2004	Rép. arabe syrienne
108	...	1 536	1 083	19 637	3	13 846	5 493	296	2005	
145	...	513	1 128	21 112	3	16 099	4 736	274	2006	
*103	...	1 062	1 176	22 549	*3	17 601	4 609	337	2007	
4	...	15	496	3 327	45	1 319	528	1 436	2004	Tadjikistan
4	...	17	509	3 488	60	1 411	537	1 480	2005	
4	...	16	517	3 690	68	1 590	543	1 488	2006	
4	...	21	589	3 968	113	1 774	601	1 480	2007	
2	1 389	11 070	1 170	75 072	14 818	35 185	24 289	779	2004	Thaïlande
2	1 588	11 599	1 188	77 021	15 486	34 473	26 238	823	2005	
3	1 610	12 398	1 209	78 957	17 595	33 609	26 675	1 078	2006	
3	1 550	9 530	1 265	82 385	18 590	34 739	28 052	1 004	2007	
...	...	76	57	58	...	58	...	...	2004	Timor-Leste *
...	...	76	56	58	...	58	...	...	2005	
...	...	76	56	59	...	59	...	...	2006	
...	...	76	56	61	...	61	...	...	2007	

49

Production, trade and consumption of commercial energy *(continued)*

Thousand metric tons of oil equivalent and kilograms per capita

Production, commerce et consommation d'énergie commerciale *(suite)*

Milliers de tonnes d'équivalent pétrole et kilogrammes par habitant

		Primary energy production – Production d'énergie primaire					Changes in stocks		
Region, country or area	Year Année	Total Totale	Solids Solides	Liquids Liquides	Gas Gaz	Electricity Electricité	Variations des stocks	Imports Importations	Exports Exportations
Turkey	2004	17 386	10 530	2 251	629	3 975	-454	64 609	4 515
	2005	17 300	10 806	2 258	821	3 415	-611	69 324	4 939
	2006	19 898	13 085	2 162	828	3 823	185	76 886	5 998
	2007	21 390	15 300	2 146	817	3 127	970	84 293	6 015
Turkmenistan	2004	63 541	...	10 148	53 393	0	...	87	46 693
	2005	66 862	...	9 849	57 013	0	...	87	49 066
	2006	67 359	...	10 120	57 239	0	...	87	48 820
	2007	72 346	...	10 012	62 334	0	...	87	52 876
United Arab Emirates	2004	168 561	...	125 442	43 119	...	...	14 690	113 577
	2005	170 024	...	126 663	43 361	...	...	16 349	114 860
	2006	181 568	...	136 096	45 472	...	...	17 063	123 385
	2007	180 829	...	133 959	46 870	...	...	23 660	123 025
Uzbekistan	2004	62 239	727	7 533	53 415	564	17	2 174	10 300
	2005	61 910	809	6 149	54 425	527	19	1 952	12 404
	2006	63 753	842	5 738	56 628	545	20	1 984	12 645
	2007	65 844	884	5 571	58 839	550	21	1 978	14 482
Viet Nam	2004	47 103	19 144	20 597	5 843	1 519	550	11 526	27 646
	2005	50 690	23 865	19 011	6 002	1 811	552	12 346	32 272
	2006	52 948	27 145	17 223	6 524	2 057	1 449	12 247	33 063
	2007	55 216	29 738	16 310	6 599	2 569	-2 847	14 165	39 008
Yemen	2004	20 067	...	20 067	...	...	912	2 639	15 347
	2005	19 882	...	19 882	...	...	955	2 795	14 898
	2006	18 210	...	18 210	...	...	1 509	3 424	12 997
	2007	16 055	...	16 055	...	...	234	3 283	11 608
Europe	**2004**	**2 182 141**	**359 496**	**752 392**	**892 715**	**177 538**	**10 552**	**1 573 230**	**1 224 058**
	2005	**2 172 467**	**362 394**	**741 517**	**889 897**	**178 658**	**14 501**	**1 614 329**	**1 244 586**
	2006	**2 167 574**	**360 499**	**735 404**	**892 561**	**179 110**	**28 357**	**1 647 397**	**1 241 011**
	2007	**2 152 622**	**356 795**	**743 625**	**874 074**	**178 129**	**-2 571**	**1 619 620**	**1 248 322**
Albania	2004	933	26	420	17	470	...	1 048	28
	2005	949	22	447	18	462	...	955	0
	2006	975	22	505	18	430	...	920	0
	2007	*849	22	570	18	240	...	1 141	0
Andorra	2004	8	...	...	...	8	*0	225	...
	2005	7	...	...	...	7	0	231	...
	2006	6	...	...	...	6	0	224	...
	2007	5	...	...	...	5	0	222	...
Austria	2004	6 449	55	1 099	1 865	3 431	227	27 692	3 766
	2005	5 951	0	1 018	1 498	3 436	222	29 702	4 328
	2006	6 206	0	1 067	1 751	3 388	763	30 387	5 106
	2007	6 450	0	1 188	1 777	3 484	489	29 718	5 959
Belarus	2004	2 498	453	1 804	237	3	203	37 874	12 693
	2005	2 524	525	1 785	210	3	-102	39 380	14 746
	2006	2 469	483	1 780	202	3	16	42 362	15 894
	2007	2 519	570	1 760	185	3	-295	41 122	14 275
Belgium	2004	4 268	49	0	1	4 219	110	78 786	24 994
	2005	4 293	29	13	1	4 250	387	77 672	25 683
	2006	4 214	8	22	2	4 182	110	76 983	24 176
	2007	4 489	0	153	1	4 334	-983	76 469	25 039
Bosnia and Herzegovina	2004	5 657	5 143	...	...	514	3	1 776	578
	2005	5 938	5 423	...	...	516	-15	2 012	681
	2006	6 303	5 800	...	...	504	-15	2 204	831
	2007	6 468	6 124	...	...	344	-15	2 380	787
Bulgaria	2004	6 421	4 345	30	311	1 735	461	12 340	2 899
	2005	6 523	4 040	30	442	2 011	-7	13 092	3 306
	2006	6 745	4 210	34	429	2 072	-178	14 276	4 394
	2007	6 646	4 794	29	282	1 541	99	15 231	4 397

Production, trade and consumption of commercial energy *(continued)*

Thousand metric tons of oil equivalent and kilograms per capita

Production, commerce et consommation d'énergie commerciale *(suite)*

Milliers de tonnes d'équivalent pétrole et kilogrammes par habitant

Bunkers - Soutes			Consumption - Consommation							
Air Avion	Sea Maritime	Unallocated Non distribué	Per capita Par habitant	Total Totale	Solids Solides	Liquids Liquides	Gas Gaz	Electricity Electricité	Year Année	Région, pays ou zone
974	1 008	3 462	1 019	72 490	22 229	25 556	20 788	3 917	2004	Turquie
1 090	1 072	3 720	1 060	76 414	22 678	25 097	25 324	3 315	2005	
986	991	4 559	1 152	84 064	26 541	24 985	28 859	3 680	2006	
1 159	853	4 033	1 254	92 654	30 473	25 384	33 804	2 993	2007	
...	...	797	3 386	16 137	...	3 478	12 760	-101	2004	Turkménistan
...	...	774	3 540	17 108	...	3 591	13 625	-108	2005	
...	...	800	3 639	17 826	...	4 262	13 679	-115	2006	
...	...	790	3 780	18 767	...	3 996	14 897	-125	2007	
3 276	10 832	8 620	12 482	46 946	...	9 524	37 422	...	2004	Emirats arabes unis
3 609	12 050	7 927	11 671	47 926	...	9 945	37 981	...	2005	
3 704	13 143	7 873	11 947	50 526	...	10 378	40 148	...	2006	
3 861	14 233	6 865	12 901	56 505	...	10 878	45 626	...	2007	
...	...	1 278	2 015	52 818	710	5 956	45 597	556	2004	Ouzbékistan
...	...	1 040	1 895	50 400	790	4 864	44 226	520	2005	
...	...	970	1 931	52 102	822	4 540	46 203	537	2006	
...	...	941	1 914	52 378	863	4 408	46 564	543	2007	
266	...	182	366	29 986	10 999	11 625	5 843	1 519	2004	Viet Nam
265	...	119	359	29 827	11 344	12 099	4 573	1 811	2005	
287	...	95	360	30 303	11 341	12 081	4 824	2 057	2006	
274	...	84	386	32 862	11 375	12 846	6 071	2 569	2007	
106	126	1 426	243	4 789	...	4 789	...	...	2004	Yémen
118	126	1 503	250	5 077	...	5 077	...	...	2005	
115	126	1 573	254	5 314	...	5 314	...	...	2006	
130	126	1 576	263	5 663	...	5 663	...	...	2007	
45 958	**52 523**	**72 856**	**3 226**	**2 349 424**	**466 984**	**727 780**	**977 033**	**177 627**	**2004**	**Europe**
48 363	**54 524**	**73 099**	**3 221**	**2 351 723**	**456 266**	**724 224**	**992 678**	**178 556**	**2005**	
50 255	**57 436**	**67 072**	**3 242**	**2 370 840**	**470 615**	**737 174**	**984 246**	**178 805**	**2006**	
51 546	**58 171**	**67 007**	**3 207**	**2 349 768**	**469 994**	**719 194**	**982 577**	**178 003**	**2007**	
59	...	164	555	1 730	28	1 198	17	487	2004	Albanie
71	...	236	508	1 597	25	1 059	18	494	2005	
86	...	276	486	1 533	25	1 008	18	483	2006	
103	...	350	486	1 537	25	1 012	18	483	2007	
*0	...	...	3 037	233	0	188	...	45	2004	Andorre
*0	...	...	3 034	238	0	192	...	46	2005	
*0	...	...	2 825	229	0	182	...	47	2006	
0	...	...	2 756	227	0	179	...	48	2007	
502	...	1 195	3 495	28 451	3 961	12 316	8 479	3 696	2004	Autriche
566	...	961	3 604	29 577	4 089	12 703	9 120	3 665	2005	
593	...	1 238	3 489	28 893	4 040	12 576	8 300	3 977	2006	
570	...	1 421	3 335	27 729	3 916	11 993	7 767	4 053	2007	
...	...	3 040	2 487	24 436	553	5 130	18 469	283	2004	Bélarus
...	...	2 442	2 539	24 817	547	5 095	18 825	350	2005	
...	...	3 131	2 650	25 790	522	5 722	19 168	378	2006	
...	...	3 706	2 679	25 955	493	5 805	19 281	377	2007	
1 360	7 978	3 846	4 306	44 767	5 726	17 963	16 190	4 887	2004	Belgique
1 287	7 895	3 759	4 112	42 954	5 050	17 430	15 682	4 792	2005	
1 182	8 545	2 887	4 214	44 297	4 768	17 811	16 663	5 056	2006	
1 017	9 560	4 359	3 951	41 966	4 254	16 207	16 589	4 917	2007	
...	...	21	1 778	6 830	5 070	1 131	283	347	2004	Bosnie-Herzégovine
...	...	9	1 893	7 275	5 482	1 060	336	397	2005	
...	...	9	1 999	7 681	5 867	1 133	359	322	2006	
...	...	7	2 099	8 068	6 198	1 194	384	292	2007	
154	117	503	1 880	14 627	6 976	3 638	2 784	1 230	2004	Bulgarie
189	112	796	1 966	15 220	6 840	3 891	3 130	1 359	2005	
181	108	902	2 028	15 615	6 979	3 993	3 237	1 406	2006	
183	53	1 049	2 107	16 097	7 913	3 663	3 365	1 156	2007	

49 Production, trade and consumption of commercial energy *(continued)*

Thousand metric tons of oil equivalent and kilograms per capita

Production, commerce et consommation d'énergie commerciale *(suite)*

Milliers de tonnes d'équivalent pétrole et kilogrammes par habitant

Region, country or area	Year Année	Primary energy production – Production d'énergie primaire: Total Totale	Solids Solides	Liquids Liquides	Gas Gaz	Electricity Electricité	Changes in stocks: Variations des stocks	Imports Importations	Exports Exportations
Croatia	2004	3 876	...	1 274	1 995	606	-6	7 678	2 216
	2005	3 833	...	1 206	2 072	554	4	7 864	2 326
	2006	4 156	...	1 165	2 463	528	69	7 840	2 605
	2007	4 079	...	1 072	2 625	381	-32	8 211	2 548
Czech Republic	2004	27 668	24 337	640	206	2 485	29	19 811	7 210
	2005	26 837	23 570	681	197	2 388	400	21 167	7 344
	2006	27 036	23 880	443	189	2 524	372	22 064	8 195
	2007	26 730	23 652	420	180	2 478	-730	21 034	8 461
Denmark	2004	29 326	...	19 319	9 438	569	129	13 736	24 395
	2005	29 580	...	18 580	10 429	571	323	13 144	24 561
	2006	27 820	...	16 926	10 367	527	-521	13 731	22 768
	2007	25 069	...	15 256	9 194	619	-89	13 382	19 757
Estonia	2004	3 220	3 217	...	...	3	-112	2 238	250
	2005	3 381	3 375	...	...	7	1	2 030	210
	2006	3 300	3 292	...	...	8	130	2 161	153
	2007	3 847	3 837	...	...	10	23	2 356	322
Faeroe Islands	2004	9	...	...	...	9	...	*219	...
	2005	9	...	...	...	9	...	*222	...
	2006	10	...	...	...	10	...	*224	...
	2007	10	...	...	...	10	...	*226	...
Finland	2004	4 145	885	...	...	3 260	-1 354	26 559	5 745
	2005	5 376	2 175	...	...	3 201	679	23 691	4 685
	2006	6 196	3 224	...	...	2 972	523	26 015	5 262
	2007	4 338	1 088	...	...	3 250	-1 582	26 259	5 979
France [3]	2004	47 758	542	1 944	1 040	44 233	-1 026	171 379	27 864
	2005	46 877	383	1 795	890	43 808	1 203	177 781	30 462
	2006	47 318	281	1 780	1 033	44 225	1 800	174 123	30 428
	2007	46 985	236	2 149	922	43 678	-1 220	166 752	28 513
Germany	2004	98 169	58 338	4 448	16 379	19 003	1 325	249 348	34 710
	2005	96 685	56 488	5 613	15 816	18 769	1 594	251 620	38 740
	2006	95 697	53 371	7 137	15 627	19 562	1 280	256 176	41 625
	2007	95 317	54 551	8 241	14 314	18 210	-3 182	243 359	42 771
Gibraltar	2004	...	...	...	...	...	...	1 279	...
	2005	...	...	...	...	...	...	1 304	...
	2006	...	...	...	...	...	...	1 341	...
	2007	...	...	...	...	...	...	1 382	...
Greece	2004	9 257	8 547	134	32	544	1 016	30 674	5 041
	2005	9 251	8 538	101	20	591	-498	29 657	5 663
	2006	9 039	8 170	137	29	703	383	32 289	6 814
	2007	8 996	8 362	163	25	447	217	32 688	7 107
Guernsey	2004	...	...	...	...	...	...	23	...
	2005	...	...	...	...	...	...	25	...
	2006	...	...	...	...	...	...	24	...
	2007	...	...	...	...	...	...	17	...
Hungary	2004	7 768	2 182	1 914	2 630	1 043	-31	19 959	2 619
	2005	7 336	1 748	1 788	2 592	1 208	136	22 495	3 360
	2006	7 303	1 757	1 708	2 661	1 177	154	22 557	3 762
	2007	6 838	1 733	1 571	2 245	1 290	-194	21 766	3 855
Iceland	2004	963	...	...	222	741	31	1 047	...
	2005	953	...	...	207	746	20	1 032	...
	2006	1 083	...	...	230	853	-28	1 050	...
	2007	1 233	...	...	203	1 030	-8	1 170	...
Ireland	2004	1 795	889	0	765	141	411	15 086	1 241
	2005	1 502	810	1	512	179	48	15 106	1 393
	2006	1 459	766	3	456	233	143	15 533	1 283
	2007	1 256	575	15	410	256	-481	15 668	1 237

49 Production, trade and consumption of commercial energy *(continued)*

Thousand metric tons of oil equivalent and kilograms per capita

Production, commerce et consommation d'énergie commerciale *(suite)*

Milliers de tonnes d'équivalent pétrole et kilogrammes par habitant

Bunkers - Soutes			Consumption - Consommation							
Air Avion	Sea Maritime	Unallocated Non distribué	Per capita Par habitant	Total Totale	Solids Solides	Liquids Liquides	Gas Gaz	Electricity Electricité	Year Année	Région, pays ou zone
29	24	468	1 988	8 823	818	4 352	2 731	922	2004	Croatie
40	25	344	2 016	8 957	788	4 534	2 641	994	2005	
40	20	361	2 005	8 902	738	4 540	2 612	1 012	2006	
44	24	240	2 107	9 465	803	4 733	3 001	928	2007	
291	...	2 035	3 715	37 915	21 322	6 784	8 675	1 133	2004	République tchèque
318	...	2 292	3 679	37 650	20 779	6 986	8 582	1 302	2005	
335	...	2 217	3 692	37 980	21 156	6 954	8 433	1 438	2006	
345	...	1 991	3 631	37 698	21 459	7 172	7 978	1 089	2007	
821	806	-96	3 174	17 008	4 361	7 171	5 155	322	2004	Danemark
864	833	64	2 977	16 079	3 716	6 780	4 895	689	2005	
869	1 081	-22	3 208	17 376	5 478	6 915	5 052	-69	2006	
890	1 119	12	3 084	16 761	4 705	6 994	4 525	538	2007	
28	153	...	3 809	5 139	3 545	885	861	-152	2004	Estonie
42	122	...	3 741	5 035	3 388	891	889	-132	2005	
29	216	...	3 672	4 933	3 209	883	898	-57	2006	
51	252	...	4 141	5 556	3 860	1 001	893	-198	2007	
*2	...	...	*4 672	*225	...	*217	...	9	2004	Iles Féroé
*3	...	...	*4 727	*228	...	*219	...	9	2005	
*3	...	...	*4 781	*231	...	*221	...	10	2006	
*3	...	...	*4 829	*233	...	*223	...	10	2007	
418	524	-645	4 976	26 017	7 499	10 450	4 389	3 678	2004	Finlande
420	515	-1 238	4 576	24 006	4 924	10 420	3 998	4 664	2005	
467	566	-1 055	5 022	26 447	7 444	10 744	4 307	3 952	2006	
539	465	-1 437	5 047	26 633	7 299	10 868	4 136	4 329	2007	
5 394	3 051	9 937	2 868	173 918	13 907	76 682	44 418	38 910	2004	France [3]
5 459	2 781	11 016	2 848	173 736	14 307	75 287	45 521	38 621	2005	
5 714	2 889	6 905	2 831	173 705	13 200	77 844	43 883	38 778	2006	
5 924	2 961	7 096	2 762	170 464	13 343	75 665	42 663	38 793	2007	
6 201	2 704	6 286	3 591	296 290	85 817	104 211	87 485	18 778	2004	Allemagne
6 674	2 532	6 403	3 545	292 363	81 687	102 453	89 847	18 376	2005	
7 014	2 624	4 941	3 574	294 389	82 300	105 649	88 338	18 102	2006	
7 270	3 129	4 954	3 449	283 734	86 943	94 835	85 170	16 786	2007	
4	1 153	...	4 234	122	...	122	...	...	2004	Gibraltar
4	1 175	...	4 335	125	...	125	...	...	2005	
4	1 207	...	4 496	130	...	130	...	...	2006	
4	1 244	...	4 576	134	...	134	...	...	2007	
809	3 263	-683	2 756	30 484	9 100	18 122	2 476	787	2004	Grèce
781	2 909	-1 353	2 828	31 406	8 949	18 926	2 615	916	2005	
937	3 141	-1 970	2 873	32 025	8 430	19 478	3 052	1 064	2006	
958	3 205	-2 369	2 910	32 566	8 820	19 203	3 722	821	2007	
...	...	...	379	23	...	...	...	23	2004	Guernesey
...	...	...	409	25	...	...	...	25	2005	
...	...	...	390	24	...	...	...	24	2006	
...	...	...	274	17	...	...	...	17	2007	
233	...	1 363	2 329	23 543	3 404	5 440	13 014	1 685	2004	Hongrie
270	...	1 681	2 417	24 383	3 088	6 111	13 440	1 743	2005	
273	...	1 512	2 399	24 159	3 058	6 560	12 744	1 797	2006	
250	...	1 388	2 318	23 305	3 110	6 651	11 912	1 632	2007	
119	71	126	5 683	1 663	103	597	222	741	2004	Islande
134	65	128	5 538	1 639	99	586	207	746	2005	
179	35	163	5 863	1 784	78	624	230	853	2006	
167	67	210	6 536	1 967	114	620	203	1 030	2007	
691	151	6	3 556	14 381	2 313	7 741	4 050	276	2004	Irlande
798	105	136	3 420	14 128	2 705	7 213	3 855	355	2005	
814	125	-141	3 487	14 768	2 426	7 497	4 459	386	2006	
973	111	103	3 483	14 981	2 286	7 566	4 760	370	2007	

Production, trade and consumption of commercial energy *(continued)*
Thousand metric tons of oil equivalent and kilograms per capita

Production, commerce et consommation d'énergie commerciale *(suite)*
Milliers de tonnes d'équivalent pétrole et kilogrammes par habitant

Region, country or area	Year Année	Primary energy production – Production d'énergie primaire: Total Totale	Solids Solides	Liquids Liquides	Gas Gaz	Electricity Electricité	Changes in stocks Variations des stocks	Imports Importations	Exports Exportations
Isle of Man	2004	0	...	...	...	0	...	21	1
	2005	0	...	...	...	0	...	4	4
	2006	0	...	...	...	0	...	4	2
	2007	0	...	...	...	0	...	4	6
Italy[4]	2004	22 475	62	5 698	11 795	4 920	-187	188 232	22 765
	2005	21 686	60	6 288	10 985	4 353	-1 621	193 961	26 804
	2006	20 438	13	5 966	9 991	4 468	3 157	196 028	25 398
	2007	19 109	100	6 039	8 832	4 138	-1 033	193 435	28 791
Jersey	2004	...	...	...	...	...	...	54	...
	2005	...	...	...	...	...	...	56	...
	2006	...	...	...	...	...	...	57	...
	2007	...	...	...	...	...	...	51	...
Latvia	2004	274	3	0	...	272	455	3 862	392
	2005	294	3	2	...	290	125	3 756	557
	2006	249	3	9	...	236	203	3 855	290
	2007	258	3	16	...	240	-85	3 727	317
Lithuania	2004	1 820	11	381	49	1 380	156	12 277	7 749
	2005	1 360	16	337	48	960	85	12 828	7 598
	2006	1 146	13	271	48	814	138	12 472	6 892
	2007	1 230	12	235	47	937	129	10 446	4 467
Luxembourg	2004	79	...	1	...	78	-13	4 936	284
	2005	83	...	1	...	82	-19	5 013	284
	2006	87	...	1	...	86	29	5 064	289
	2007	121	...	34	...	86	-36	4 874	255
Malta	2004	...	...	...	...	...	...	1 940	...
	2005	...	...	...	...	...	...	1 646	...
	2006	...	...	...	...	...	...	1 690	...
	2007	...	...	...	...	...	...	1 844	...
Montenegro	2005	510	350	...	...	160	...	446	92
	2006	558	408	...	...	150	...	*508	91
	2007	435	324	...	...	110	...	499	65
Netherlands	2004	71 903	...	2 975	68 428	500	432	130 345	107 467
	2005	65 701	...	2 652	62 517	532	1 179	143 676	112 600
	2006	64 302	...	2 161	61 595	545	95	151 561	121 404
	2007	64 263	...	2 750	60 844	669	70	150 811	119 990
Norway[5]	2004	235 004	1 949	144 453	79 176	9 426	-403	6 059	211 735
	2005	231 554	987	133 506	85 285	11 775	346	5 443	205 904
	2006	223 873	1 607	124 284	87 632	10 349	516	5 578	197 689
	2007	221 205	2 681	120 078	86 756	11 690	-769	5 805	198 314
Poland	2004	74 794	69 201	900	4 364	330	341	34 033	17 996
	2005	74 484	68 875	956	4 316	336	1 959	36 256	18 370
	2006	73 118	67 577	948	4 312	282	-304	40 070	18 147
	2007	68 329	62 878	824	4 330	298	-34	42 295	15 147
Portugal	2004	950	...	0	...	950	-413	23 847	1 703
	2005	599	...	0	...	599	415	25 892	2 148
	2006	1 315	...	70	...	1 245	55	24 487	3 186
	2007	1 427	...	162	...	1 265	-305	23 151	2 397
Republic of Moldova	2004	13	...	8	0	5	-5	2 037	43
	2005	12	...	5	0	7	3	2 137	3
	2006	11	...	4	0	7	-28	2 098	2
	2007	11	...	8	0	3	37	2 055	1
Romania	2004	24 654	5 502	5 724	11 531	1 897	1 010	16 383	4 633
	2005	24 129	5 383	5 751	10 780	2 215	-340	16 852	6 259
	2006	24 408	6 044	5 676	10 625	2 063	-648	17 360	5 737
	2007	23 430	6 190	4 941	10 263	2 036	611	16 578	4 628

49

Production, trade and consumption of commercial energy *(continued)*
Thousand metric tons of oil equivalent and kilograms per capita

Production, commerce et consommation d'énergie commerciale *(suite)*
Milliers de tonnes d'équivalent pétrole et kilogrammes par habitant

Bunkers - Soutes			Consumption - Consommation							
Air Avion	Sea Maritime	Unallocated Non distribué	Per capita Par habitant	Total Totale	Solids Solides	Liquids Liquides	Gas Gaz	Electricity Electricité	Year Année	Région, pays ou zone
...	...	...	269	21	...	...	...	21	2004	Ile de Man
...	...	...	-4	0	...	...	...	0	2005	
...	...	...	33	3	...	...	...	3	2006	
...	...	...	-29	-2	...	...	...	-2	2007	
2 704	3 381	1 611	3 102	180 432	16 595	81 638	73 354	8 844	2004	Italie[4]
2 864	3 411	1 110	3 124	183 078	16 485	79 512	78 501	8 580	2005	
3 052	3 515	556	3 067	180 787	16 663	78 909	76 880	8 336	2006	
3 258	3 557	-626	3 008	178 597	16 786	76 437	77 257	8 117	2007	
...	...	...	613	54	...	...	...	54	2004	Jersey
...	...	...	632	56	...	...	...	56	2005	
...	...	...	643	57	...	...	...	57	2006	
...	...	...	563	51	...	...	...	51	2007	
48	205	3	1 311	3 033	51	1 050	1 480	452	2004	Lettonie
59	264	4	1 323	3 043	61	999	1 509	475	2005	
66	200	20	1 453	3 325	55	1 255	1 563	452	2006	
80	181	31	1 520	3 461	80	1 373	1 511	498	2007	
11	115	147	1 723	5 918	206	2 294	2 657	761	2004	Lituanie
46	146	122	1 813	6 192	226	2 462	2 799	704	2005	
53	141	-100	1 913	6 494	311	2 631	2 775	777	2006	
72	121	-945	2 320	7 832	299	3 454	3 260	819	2007	
427	...	...	9 424	4 317	94	2 522	1 333	368	2004	Luxembourg
433	...	...	9 453	4 397	82	2 644	1 310	362	2005	
407	...	...	9 364	4 426	110	2 553	1 371	391	2006	
436	...	...	9 041	4 340	80	2 497	1 336	427	2007	
102	1 000	...	2 079	837	...	837	...	...	2004	Malte
89	676	...	2 180	881	...	881	...	...	2005	
77	772	...	2 068	841	...	841	...	...	2006	
91	865	...	2 180	889	...	889	...	...	2007	
...	...	...	1 388	864	423	*127	...	314	2005	Monténégro
...	...	...	1 562	975	496	*167	...	311	2006	
...	...	...	1 390	869	369	*167	...	333	2007	
3 518	14 965	-4 630	4 951	80 495	7 931	29 842	40 828	1 895	2004	Pays-Bas
3 616	17 178	-2 472	4 735	77 276	7 465	28 458	39 249	2 105	2005	
3 666	17 830	-825	4 511	73 694	6 730	26 463	38 111	2 391	2006	
3 684	16 433	4 094	4 322	70 804	7 115	24 485	37 024	2 180	2007	
242	520	1 367	5 989	27 603	927	9 920	6 345	10 411	2004	Norvège[5]
272	701	1 536	6 082	28 238	776	10 319	6 403	10 740	2005	
378	507	467	6 415	29 894	713	11 905	6 853	10 423	2006	
369	665	517	5 928	27 914	753	11 419	4 915	10 827	2007	
286	258	1 921	2 306	88 025	56 081	19 213	13 201	-469	2004	Pologne
324	328	2 123	2 296	87 635	55 396	19 271	13 594	-625	2005	
431	300	2 371	2 419	92 242	58 517	20 640	13 748	-663	2006	
450	253	2 175	2 430	92 633	57 063	21 981	13 752	-162	2007	
695	670	1 102	2 003	21 040	3 319	12 542	3 670	1 507	2004	Portugal
721	589	1 227	2 028	21 390	3 308	12 729	4 167	1 186	2005	
772	647	961	1 907	20 182	3 370	11 055	4 044	1 713	2006	
885	679	1 170	1 862	19 752	2 867	10 744	4 232	1 909	2007	
0	...	0	558	2 013	84	650	1 022	258	2004	Rép. de Moldova
0	...	0	596	2 144	76	659	1 148	261	2005	
0	...	0	595	2 134	91	643	1 147	254	2006	
0	...	-3	568	2 031	45	675	1 056	255	2007	
137	0	1 799	1 544	33 459	8 125	8 051	15 487	1 795	2004	Roumanie
111	0	1 326	1 555	33 624	7 915	8 252	15 492	1 966	2005	
137	0	1 827	1 608	34 715	8 554	8 420	16 046	1 695	2006	
109	34	1 232	1 550	33 393	8 625	8 483	14 429	1 856	2007	

49 Production, trade and consumption of commercial energy *(continued)*
Thousand metric tons of oil equivalent and kilograms per capita

Production, commerce et consommation d'énergie commerciale *(suite)*
Milliers de tonnes d'équivalent pétrole et kilogrammes par habitant

Region, country or area	Year	Primary energy production – Production d'énergie primaire					Changes in stocks		
Region, country or area	Year Année	Total Totale	Solids Solides	Liquids Liquides	Gas Gaz	Electricity Electricité	Variations des stocks	Imports Importations	Exports Exportations
Russian Federation	2004	1 160 339	108 768	457 537	566 269	27 764	6 775	22 063	17 094
	2005	1 188 192	119 007	467 819	573 466	27 899	6 859	20 337	18 159
	2006	1 210 122	119 645	477 262	584 652	28 563	13 924	20 843	12 797
	2007	1 220 659	121 887	489 230	580 349	29 193	9 286	20 476	7 832
Serbia and Montenegro	2004	10 661	8 767	652	285	956	0	6 730	111 137
	2005	9 457	7 519	649	254	1 035	0	6 418	101 443
	2006	9 663	7 812	646	262	943	-21	6 778	88 720
	2007	9 614	7 890	641	220	863	-43	6 941	86 241
Slovakia	2004	2 906	817	53	210	1 826	582	17 883	170 879
	2005	2 831	637	65	196	1 932	95	17 867	175 669
	2006	2 823	562	69	250	1 942	-174	17 650	183 369
	2007	2 506	539	81	171	1 716	463	18 118	184 831
Slovenia	2004	1 872	1 045	0	5	821	40	4 402	171 451
	2005	1 794	987	0	4	804	9	4 660	178 585
	2006	1 778	983	5	4	786	-93	4 791	179 566
	2007	1 764	986	4	3	771	-49	4 783	...
Spain	2004	17 056	6 453	474	344	9 785	-761	124 661	...
	2005	15 602	6 265	426	160	8 752	1 756	133 678	...
	2006	16 180	6 049	313	70	9 748	2 625	135 944	...
	2007	16 084	5 672	527	89	9 796	-1 469	135 435	*118
Sweden	2004	12 318	267	141	...	11 910	-385	32 030	*134
	2005	12 974	211	193	...	12 570	722	31 767	*124
	2006	11 615	185	277	...	11 152	-182	31 369	*119
	2007	12 112	155	384	...	11 572	-534	30 381	...
Switzerland[6]	2004	5 400	...	3	28	5 370	5	17 977	...
	2005	4 887	...	7	26	4 854	128	19 249	...
	2006	5 261	...	8	31	5 223	64	19 031	...
	2007	5 606	...	12	30	5 564	-261	17 506	...
TFYR of Macedonia	2004	2 080	1 953	0	...	127	4	1 314	...
	2005	1 983	1 854	0	...	128	-60	1 516	...
	2006	1 931	1 789	0	...	142	16	1 627	...
	2007	1 844	1 754	3	...	87	-90	1 648	...
Ukraine	2004	62 735	30 771	4 370	19 087	8 508	289	87 354	...
	2005	63 764	31 209	4 471	19 374	8 710	-2 214	77 322	...
	2006	62 969	31 864	4 600	17 623	8 882	1 587	68 533	...
	2007	61 401	30 375	4 550	17 632	8 843	3 475	70 930	...
United Kingdom	2004	214 619	14 917	95 998	96 006	7 697	1 213	116 012	...
	2005	192 765	11 905	85 332	87 581	7 947	677	123 369	...
	2006	178 394	10 680	80 127	80 009	7 579	2 398	137 514	...
	2007	169 090	9 803	80 520	72 125	6 643	-3 955	137 271	30
Oceania	**2004**	**268 541**	**195 119**	**29 706**	**39 501**	**4 215**	**450**	**38 773**	**30**
	2005	**278 764**	**205 052**	**26 591**	**43 163**	**3 958**	**-1 266**	**41 495**	***31**
	2006	**279 736**	**204 826**	**26 011**	**44 831**	**4 068**	**-1 295**	**43 914**	***32**
	2007	**299 120**	**219 678**	**28 245**	**47 111**	**4 085**	**5 793**	**46 919**	**2 267**
Australia	2004	255 546	192 112	26 451	35 557	1 426	309	27 428	1 908
	2005	265 895	201 995	23 085	39 372	1 443	-1 186	29 931	2 142
	2006	265 953	201 355	22 143	40 928	1 526	-1 570	32 169	2 389
	2007	285 470	216 859	24 304	42 816	1 491	4 871	35 681	...
Cook Islands	2004	...	...	...	...	...	...	18	...
	2005	...	...	...	...	...	...	20	...
	*2006	...	...	...	...	...	...	21	...
	*2007	...	...	...	...	...	...	23	...
Fiji	2004	*58	...	...	...	*58	*-1	1 056	...
	2005	*58	...	...	...	*58	*-1	941	...
	2006	59	...	...	...	59	*-1	975	...
	2007	62	...	...	...	62	*-1	899	

49

Production, trade and consumption of commercial energy *(continued)*

Thousand metric tons of oil equivalent and kilograms per capita

Production, commerce et consommation d'énergie commerciale *(suite)*

Milliers de tonnes d'équivalent pétrole et kilogrammes par habitant

Bunkers - Soutes			Consumption - Consommation							
Air Avion	Sea Maritime	Unallocated Non distribué	Per capita Par habitant	Total Totale	Solids Solides	Liquids Liquides	Gas Gaz	Electricity Electricité	Year Année	Région, pays ou zone
4 789	...	24 773	4 181	601 348	87 514	101 183	385 543	27 109	2004	Fédération de Russie
5 178	...	27 938	4 212	602 835	86 988	100 183	388 830	26 835	2005	
5 470	...	28 390	4 352	620 159	89 809	104 235	398 911	27 203	2006	
5 519	...	25 313	4 411	626 854	85 862	105 808	407 091	28 092	2007	
47	...	910	1 491	15 678	9 265	2 911	2 569	933	2004	Serbie-et-Monténégro
50	...	853	1 340	14 028	8 031	2 979	2 151	867	2005	
54	...	718	1 413	14 773	8 623	3 064	2 213	873	2006	
48	...	406	1 449	15 149	8 582	3 534	2 177	856	2007	
27	...	76	2 862	15 406	4 520	3 059	6 161	1 666	2004	Slovaquie
39	...	109	2 893	15 588	4 221	3 122	6 593	1 652	2005	
40	...	257	2 829	15 252	4 503	2 978	6 030	1 741	2006	
50	...	179	2 747	14 826	4 096	3 161	5 705	1 864	2007	
20	0	52	2 716	5 425	1 340	2 331	999	754	2004	Slovénie
23	22	56	2 740	5 483	1 293	2 382	1 032	776	2005	
25	30	51	2 757	5 538	1 300	2 449	999	790	2006	
32	49	44	2 751	5 532	1 317	2 408	1 016	790	2007	
3 103	7 376	7 884	2 743	117 090	20 923	58 674	27 969	9 525	2004	Espagne
3 113	8 094	5 893	2 839	123 195	20 495	60 904	33 160	8 636	2005	
3 245	8 451	5 257	2 798	123 308	18 368	60 770	34 704	9 466	2006	
3 413	8 649	3 876	2 815	126 341	20 075	61 571	35 394	9 301	2007	
628	1 937	2 027	3 118	28 041	2 900	12 429	983	11 729	2004	Suède
634	1 978	2 099	3 048	27 525	2 671	11 983	936	11 934	2005	
663	2 126	1 914	2 953	26 812	2 618	11 542	980	11 672	2006	
654	2 115	2 363	2 916	26 578	2 648	11 232	1 012	11 686	2007	
1 155	9	-21	2 586	19 266	144	10 772	3 040	5 309	2004	Suisse [6]
1 180	12	-20	2 628	19 606	167	10 920	3 118	5 400	2005	
1 247	9	-47	2 646	19 804	167	11 144	3 037	5 455	2006	
1 312	9	-74	2 439	18 420	171	9 905	2 958	5 386	2007	
6	...	11	1 556	3 163	2 046	824	65	229	2004	L'ex-R.Y. Macédoine
6	...	11	1 577	3 211	2 026	849	70	266	2005	
4	...	24	1 545	3 153	1 888	894	75	296	2006	
7	...	-15	1 627	3 326	1 920	1 010	95	301	2007	
378	...	4 711	2 677	126 553	33 005	11 966	73 532	8 050	2004	Ukraine
376	...	1 219	2 738	128 907	33 796	12 436	74 683	7 992	2005	
335	...	1 005	2 582	120 742	36 634	13 187	62 937	7 984	2006	
359	...	668	2 606	120 416	37 328	14 112	60 922	8 055	2007	
10 517	2 092	1 547	3 578	213 581	37 410	70 732	97 097	8 341	2004	Royaume-Uni
11 308	2 056	2 289	3 506	211 091	37 902	70 195	94 332	8 663	2005	
11 412	2 352	2 874	3 477	210 638	41 376	70 967	90 069	8 225	2006	
11 425	2 373	3 521	3 357	204 668	38 373	68 132	91 071	7 092	2007	
3 429	**1 232**	**-3 106**	**3 942**	**129 685**	**52 160**	**44 092**	**29 218**	**4 215**	**2004**	**Océanie**
3 831	**1 265**	**-2 258**	**4 040**	**134 890**	**55 892**	**45 637**	**29 403**	**3 958**	**2005**	
3 634	**1 430**	**-284**	**3 991**	**135 427**	**56 419**	**45 000**	**29 939**	**4 068**	**2006**	
4 222	**1 267**	**-265**	**3 966**	**137 059**	**55 499**	**45 004**	**32 471**	**4 085**	**2007**	
2 266	842	-3 004	5 532	111 352	50 068	34 583	25 274	1 426	2004	Australie
2 654	857	-2 240	5 735	116 958	53 602	36 301	25 612	1 443	2005	
2 387	988	-418	5 683	117 632	54 115	35 954	26 037	1 526	2006	
2 990	815	-282	5 677	119 628	53 779	36 182	28 176	1 491	2007	
...	...	...	909	18	...	18	...	...	2004	Iles Cook
...	...	...	1 014	20	...	20	...	...	2005	
...	...	...	1 033	21	...	21	...	...	*2006	
...	...	...	1 067	23	...	23	...	...	*2007	
*232	*82	...	798	666	*2	607	...	*58	2004	Fidji
*227	*72	...	686	578	*1	518	...	*58	2005	
*290	*67	...	655	559	*1	499	...	59	2006	
281	*66	...	626	524	*1	462	...	62	2007	

49 Production, trade and consumption of commercial energy *(continued)*

Thousand metric tons of oil equivalent and kilograms per capita

Production, commerce et consommation d'énergie commerciale *(suite)*

Milliers de tonnes d'équivalent pétrole et kilogrammes par habitant

		Primary energy production – Production d'énergie primaire					Changes in stocks		
Region, country or area	Year Année	Total Totale	Solids Solides	Liquids Liquides	Gas Gaz	Electricity Electricité	Variations des stocks	Imports Importations	Exports Exportations
French Polynesia	2004	13	...	...	...	13	...	311	...
	2005	11	...	...	...	11	...	333	...
	2006	13	...	...	...	13	...	326	...
	2007	14	...	...	...	14	...	*321	...
Kiribati *	2004	...	...	...	...	...	...	10	...
	2005	...	...	...	...	...	...	10	...
	2006	...	...	...	...	...	...	12	...
	2007	...	...	...	...	...	...	13	...
Marshall Islands *	2004	...	...	...	...	...	...	29	...
	2005	...	...	...	...	...	...	29	...
	2006	...	...	...	...	...	...	30	...
	2007	...	...	...	...	...	...	32	...
Nauru *	2004	...	...	...	...	...	...	53	...
	2005	...	...	...	...	...	...	53	...
	2006	...	...	...	...	...	...	53	...
	2007	...	...	...	...	...	...	54	...
New Caledonia	2004	29	...	...	...	29	...	808	30
	2005	31	...	...	...	31	...	892	*31
	2006	27	...	...	...	27	...	881	*30
	2007	37	...	...	...	37	...	913	*32
New Zealand	2004	10 572	3 007	1 121	3 837	2 606	347	7 360	2 102
	2005	9 984	3 057	1 044	3 549	2 333	-79	7 327	2 372
	2006	10 478	3 471	1 000	3 643	2 363	-18	7 435	2 761
	2007	11 276	2 819	2 001	4 056	2 400	358	7 507	3 173
Niue *	2004	...	...	...	...	...	...	1	...
	2005	...	...	...	...	...	...	1	...
	2006	...	...	...	...	...	...	1	...
	2007	...	...	...	...	...	...	1	...
Palau *	2004	2	...	...	...	2	...	77	...
	2005	2	...	...	...	2	...	79	...
	2006	2	...	...	...	2	...	83	...
	2007	2	...	...	...	2	...	86	...
Papua New Guinea	2004	2 318	...	2 134	107	77	*-204	1 410	2 147
	2005	2 780	...	2 462	241	77	0	1 666	2 487
	2006	3 200	...	2 867	259	74	294	1 713	2 726
	2007	2 255	...	1 940	*239	*75	565	1 163	1 538
Samoa	2004	4	...	...	...	4	...	*52	...
	2005	4	...	...	...	4	...	*53	...
	2006	5	...	...	...	5	...	*53	...
	*2007	5	...	...	...	5	...	54	...
Solomon Islands *	2004	...	...	...	...	...	...	61	...
	2005	...	...	...	...	...	...	61	...
	2006	...	...	...	...	...	...	63	...
	2007	...	...	...	...	...	...	69	...
Tonga	2004	...	...	...	...	...	...	58	...
	*2005	...	...	...	...	...	...	58	...
	*2006	...	...	...	...	...	...	58	...
	*2007	...	...	...	...	...	...	59	...
Vanuatu *	2004	...	...	...	...	...	...	30	...
	2005	...	...	...	...	...	...	30	...
	2006	...	...	...	...	...	...	31	...
	2007	...	...	...	...	...	...	35	...
Wallis and Futuna Islands	2004	...	...	...	...	...	...	9	...
	2005	...	...	...	...	...	...	9	...
	2006	...	...	...	...	...	...	9	...
	2007	...	...	...	...	...	...	10	...

49 Production, trade and consumption of commercial energy *(continued)*

Thousand metric tons of oil equivalent and kilograms per capita

Production, commerce et consommation d'énergie commerciale *(suite)*

Milliers de tonnes d'équivalent pétrole et kilogrammes par habitant

Bunkers - Soutes			Consumption - Consommation							
Air Avion	Sea Maritime	Unallocated Non distribué	Per capita Par habitant	Total Totale	Solids Solides	Liquids Liquides	Gas Gaz	Electricity Electricité	Year Année	Région, pays ou zone
*6	*46	...	1 085	272	...	259	...	13	2004	Polynésie française
*6	*47	...	1 145	291	...	280	...	11	2005	
*6	*50	...	1 105	283	...	270	...	13	2006	
*6	*50	...	*1 077	*280	...	*265	...	14	2007	
2	...	...	82	8	...	8	...	...	2004	Kiribati *
2	...	...	80	8	...	8	...	...	2005	
2	...	...	98	10	...	10	...	...	2006	
2	...	...	105	11	...	11	...	...	2007	
...	...	...	503	29	...	29	...	...	2004	Iles Marshall *
...	...	...	505	29	...	29	...	...	2005	
...	...	...	584	30	...	30	...	...	2006	
...	...	...	616	32	...	32	...	...	2007	
7	...	...	3 590	46	...	46	...	...	2004	Nauru *
7	...	...	3 524	46	...	46	...	...	2005	
7	...	...	3 457	46	...	46	...	...	2006	
7	...	...	3 506	47	...	47	...	...	2007	
11	...	...	3 451	796	197	571	...	29	2004	Nouvelle-Calédonie
10	...	...	3 768	882	182	669	...	31	2005	
14	...	...	3 631	864	198	639	...	27	2006	
12	...	...	3 769	906	171	698	...	37	2007	
846	231	-238	3 605	14 643	1 894	6 306	3 836	2 606	2004	Nouvelle-Zélande
867	258	-331	3 470	14 224	2 107	6 235	3 549	2 333	2005	
868	292	-93	3 404	14 102	2 105	5 991	3 643	2 363	2006	
858	304	-66	3 348	14 155	1 549	6 150	4 055	2 400	2007	
...	...	...	576	1	...	1	...	...	2004	Nioué *
...	...	...	581	1	...	1	...	...	2005	
...	...	...	605	1	...	1	...	...	2006	
...	...	...	680	1	...	1	...	...	2007	
15	...	...	3 075	63	...	62	...	2	2004	Palaos *
15	...	...	3 112	65	...	64	...	2	2005	
15	...	...	3 168	69	...	67	...	2	2006	
-17	...	...	3 218	71	...	69	...	2	2007	
*38	*32	136	265	1 579	...	1 395	107	77	2004	Papouasie-Nvl-Guinée
*38	*32	312	258	1 577	...	1 259	241	77	2005	
*39	*32	226	255	1 596	...	1 263	259	74	2006	
*40	*32	84	180	1 158	...	844	*239	*75	2007	
...	...	...	*308	*56	...	*52	...	4	2004	Samoa
...	...	...	*311	*57	...	*53	...	4	2005	
...	...	...	*309	*57	...	*53	...	5	2006	
...	...	...	312	58	...	54	...	5	*2007	
3	...	...	127	58	...	58	...	...	2004	Iles Salomon *
3	...	...	124	58	...	58	...	...	2005	
3	...	...	123	59	...	59	...	...	2006	
5	...	...	129	64	...	64	...	...	2007	
*1	...	...	565	57	...	57	...	...	2004	Tonga
1	...	...	555	57	...	57	...	...	*2005	
1	...	...	555	57	...	57	...	...	*2006	
1	...	...	564	58	...	58	...	...	*2007	
...	...	...	139	30	...	30	...	...	2004	Vanuatu *
...	...	...	138	30	...	30	...	...	2005	
...	...	...	139	31	...	31	...	...	2006	
...	...	...	154	35	...	35	...	...	2007	
1	...	...	564	9	...	9	...	...	2004	Iles Wallis et Futuna
1	...	...	555	9	...	9	...	...	2005	
1	...	...	537	9	...	9	...	...	2006	
1	...	...	538	9	...	9	...	...	2007	

Source:
United Nations Statistics Division, New York, the energy statistics database, last accessed June 2010.

1 Refers to the Southern African Customs Union.
2 For statistical purposes, the data for China do not include those for the Hong Kong Special Administrative Region (Hong Kong SAR), Macao Special Administrative Region (Macao SAR) and Taiwan Province of China.
3 Including Monaco.
4 Including San Marino.
5 Including Svalbard and Jan Mayen Islands.
6 Including Liechtenstein.

49 Production, trade and consumption of commercial energy *(continued)*

Thousand metric tons of oil equivalent and kilograms per capita

Production, commerce et consommation d'énergie commerciale *(suite)*

Milliers de tonnes d'équivalent pétrole et kilogrammes par habitant

Source:
Organisation des Nations Unies, Division de statistique, New York, la base de données pour les statistiques de l'énergie, dernier accès juin 2010.

1 Se réfèrent à l'Union douanière d'Afrique australe.
2 Pour la présentation des statistiques, les données pour la Chine ne comprennent pas la Région Administrative Spéciale de Hong Kong (Hong Kong RAS), la Région Administrative Spéciale de Macao (Macao RAS) et la province de Taiwan.
3 Y compris Monaco.
4 Y compris Saint-Marin.
5 Y compris îles Svalbard et Jan Mayen.
6 Y compris Liechtenstein.

50 Energy production

Production de l'énergie

Region, country or area Région, pays ou zone	Year Année	Hard coal, lignite and peat Houille, lignite et tourbe	Crude petroleum and NGL Pétrole brut et LGN	Motor gasoline Essence auto	Jet fuel Carbu-réacteurs	Gas-diesel oil Gazole/ carburant diesel	Residual fuel oil Mazout résiduel	Liquefied petroleum gas Gaz de pétrole liquéfiés	Natural gas Gaz naturel	Electricity Electricité
		Thousand metric tons – Milliers de tonnes							Terajoules Térajoules	Million kWh Millions kWh
World	**2004**	**5 593 876**	**3 885 483**	**891 085**	**217 988**	**1 123 331**	**599 610**	**243 602**	**106 951 798**	**17 548 456**
Monde	**2005**	**5 930 382**	**3 946 007**	**890 776**	**225 584**	**1 162 928**	**598 009**	**245 048**	**110 154 472**	**18 345 083**
	2006	**6 229 338**	**3 962 468**	**891 788**	**229 368**	**1 180 344**	**592 097**	**248 643**	**113 762 209**	**19 062 472**
	2007	**6 428 321**	**3 955 731**	**894 129**	**231 754**	**1 197 261**	**588 093**	**248 834**	**115 547 689**	**19 907 388**
Africa	**2004**	**248 305**[1]	**477 272**	**21 292**	**8 019**	**36 082**	**34 173**	**13 102**	**6 052 025**	**540 706**
Afrique	**2005**	**250 740**[1]	**505 229**	**18 497**	**8 419**	**37 739**	**35 956**	**13 311**	**7 257 439**	**564 670**
	2006	**250 456**[1]	**513 209**	**20 221**	**7 809**	**38 907**	**34 028**	**13 411**	**8 038 203**	**594 638**
	2007	**253 198**[1]	**519 143**	**19 977**	**8 336**	**35 170**	**32 740**	**13 972**	**7 916 816**	**621 148**
Algeria	2004	...	107 432	1 925	986	6 340	5 560	9 223	3 216 262	31 250
Algérie	2005	...	110 583	2 059	1 069	5 946	5 055	9 337	3 586 296	32 875
	2006	...	108 818	2 320	855	6 385	5 337	8 750	3 844 884	35 226
	2007	...	109 311	2 100	1 034	6 388	5 518	9 186	3 424 650	37 196
Angola	2004	...	49 562	96	302	669	604	147	29 266	2 240
Angola	2005	...	62 446	134	290	675	609	156	25 364	2 632
	2006	...	71 118	98	313	681	587	651	26 534	2 959
	2007	...	85 591	56	351	513	601	711	32 387	3 171
Benin	2004	...	...	...	...	...	...	...	...	81
Bénin	2005	...	...	...	...	...	...	...	...	107
	2006	...	...	...	...	...	...	...	...	128
	2007	...	...	...	...	...	...	...	...	132
Botswana	2004	911[2]	...	...	...	...	...	...	...	991
Botswana	2005	967[2]	...	...	...	...	...	...	...	971
	2006	1 000[2]	...	...	...	...	...	...	...	1 042
	2007	1 038[2]	...	...	...	...	...	...	...	1 119
Burkina Faso	2004	...	...	...	...	...	...	...	...	473
Burkina Faso	2005	...	...	...	...	...	...	...	...	516
	2006	...	...	...	...	...	...	...	...	548
	2007	...	...	...	...	...	...	...	...	612
Burundi	2004	5[3]	...	...	...	...	...	...	...	94
Burundi	2005	5[3]	...	...	...	...	...	...	...	102
	2006	*5[3]	...	...	...	...	...	...	...	95
	2007	5[3]	...	...	...	...	...	...	...	119
Cameroon	2004	...	4 356[4]	402	69	607	388	28	0	4 110
Cameroun	2005	...	4 081[4]	393	62	610	341	26	0	4 004
	2006	...	4 326[4]	320	71	569	354	22	0	5 106
	2007	...	4 465[4]	390	73	694	387	19	16 090	5 753
Cape Verde	2004	...	...	...	...	...	...	...	...	220
Cap-Vert	2005	...	...	...	...	...	...	...	...	237
	2006	...	...	...	...	...	...	...	...	252
	2007	...	...	...	...	...	...	...	...	269
Central African Rep.	*2004	...	...	...	...	...	...	...	...	111
Rép. centrafricaine	*2005	...	...	...	...	...	...	...	...	128
	*2006	...	...	...	...	...	...	...	...	139
	2007	...	...	...	...	...	...	...	...	160
Chad	2004	...	8 505[4]	...	...	...	...	...	...	*97
Tchad	2005	...	8 808[4]	...	...	...	...	...	...	*100
	2006	...	7 874[4]	...	...	...	...	...	...	*102
	2007	...	7 190[4]	...	...	...	...	...	...	*105
Comoros *	2004	...	...	...	...	...	...	...	...	44
Comores *	2005	...	...	...	...	...	...	...	...	48
	2006	...	...	...	...	...	...	...	...	51
	2007	...	...	...	...	...	...	...	...	50
Congo	2004	...	11 595	49	47	120	295	5	769	465
Congo	2005	...	12 636	47	45	110	210	5	890	434
	2006	...	14 296	53	53	123	377	7	923	453
	2007	...	11 490	63	55	141	437	7	824	407
Côte d'Ivoire	2004	...	1 126[4]	436	88	1 180	431	96	60 709	5 403
Côte d'Ivoire	2005	...	1 994[4]	494	88	1 205	687	87	67 803	5 566
	2006	...	3 135[4]	605	88	1 269	521	101	63 681	5 535
	2007	...	2 418[4]	564	47	1 089	500	38	46 824	5 631

Region, country or area Région, pays ou zone	Year Année	Hard coal, lignite and peat Houille, lignite et tourbe	Crude petroleum and NGL Pétrole brut et LGN	Motor gasoline Essence auto	Jet fuel Carbu-réacteurs	Gas-diesel oil Gazole/ carburant diesel	Residual fuel oil Mazout résiduel	Liquefied petroleum gas Gaz de pétrole liquéfiés	Natural gas Gaz naturel	Electricity Electricité
		Thousand metric tons – Milliers de tonnes							Terajoules Térajoules	Million kWh Millions kWh
Dem. Rep. of the Congo	2004	108[2]	1 033[4]	...	...	...	...	...	...	6 852
Rép. dém. du Congo	2005	120[2]	984[4]	...	...	...	...	...	...	7 419
	2006	124[2]	886[4]	...	...	...	...	...	...	7 886
	2007	128[2]	836[4]	...	...	...	...	...	...	8 302
Djibouti	2004	...	...	...	...	...	...	...	...	215
Djibouti	2005	...	...	...	...	...	...	...	...	255
	2006	...	...	...	...	...	...	...	...	280
	2007	...	...	...	...	...	...	...	...	292
Egypt	2004	33[2]	33 363	*5 000	2 080	7 922	11 273	1 724	1 311 413	101 299
Egypte	2005	33[2]	32 217	2 972	2 146	8 179	11 643	1 713	1 933 144	111 690
	2006	25[2]	33 459	3 659	2 033	8 440	10 653	1 711	2 074 343	118 407
	2007	25[2]	32 913	4 195	2 422	8 803	10 989	1 898	2 136 170	128 129
Equatorial Guinea *	2004	...	22 413	...	...	...	...	81	25 030	85
Guinée équatoriale *	2005	...	23 007	...	...	...	...	84	45 030	90
	2006	...	22 430	...	...	...	...	86	55 030	95
	2007	...	23 155	...	...	...	...	92	65 250	95
Eritrea	2004	...	...	...	...	...	...	...	...	283
Erythrée	2005	...	...	...	...	...	...	...	...	289
	2006	...	...	...	...	...	...	...	...	269
	2007	...	...	...	...	...	...	...	...	288
Ethiopia	2004	...	...	...	...	...	...	...	...	2 540
Ethiopie	2005	...	...	...	...	...	...	...	...	2 872
	2006	...	...	...	...	...	...	...	...	3 270
	2007	...	...	...	...	...	...	...	...	3 503
Gabon	2004	...	10 736[4]	68	45	228	324	9	4 912	1 537
Gabon	2005	...	10 690[4]	79	60	225	305	10	4 856	1 610
	2006	...	10 736[4]	44	52	213	324	7	5 320	1 732
	2007	...	10 553[4]	56	59	260	356	14	6 071	1 844
Gambia	*2004	...	...	...	...	...	...	...	...	185
Gambie	*2005	...	...	...	...	...	...	...	...	203
	*2006	...	...	...	...	...	...	...	...	216
	2007	...	...	...	...	...	...	...	...	229
Ghana	2004	...	...	580	107	568	199	66	...	6 044
Ghana	2005	...	...	567	113	520	242	78	...	6 793
	2006	...	...	291	46	204	156	30	...	8 435
	2007	...	...	493	66	398	49	67	...	6 984
Guinea	2004	...	...	...	...	...	...	...	4	973
Guinée	2005	...	...	...	...	...	...	...	4	911
	2006	...	...	...	...	...	...	...	4	872
	2007	...	...	...	...	...	...	...	4	973
Guinea-Bissau *	2004	...	...	...	...	...	...	...	...	63
Guinée-Bissau *	2005	...	...	...	...	...	...	...	...	64
	2006	...	...	...	...	...	...	...	...	66
	2007	...	...	...	...	...	...	...	...	70
Kenya	2004	...	...	275	212	387	620	27	...	6 442
Kenya	2005	...	...	266	205	374	549	26	...	6 737
	2006	...	...	179	226	368	596	30	...	7 323
	2007	...	...	207	223	397	534	33	...	6 773
Lesotho	2004	...	...	...	...	...	...	...	...	300
Lesotho	2005	...	...	...	...	...	...	...	...	350
	2006	...	...	...	...	...	...	...	...	200
	2007	...	...	...	...	...	...	...	...	200
Liberia	2004	...	...	...	...	...	...	...	...	330
Libéria	*2005	...	...	...	...	...	...	...	...	338
	*2006	...	...	...	...	...	...	...	...	351
	*2007	...	...	...	...	...	...	...	...	353
Libyan Arab Jamah.	2004	...	78 738	1 507	1 504	4 782	4 597	846	306 280	20 202
Jamah. arabe libyenne	2005	...	84 308	1 237	1 339	4 849	4 443	851	429 400	22 317
	2006	...	88 630	1 237	1 255	4 503	4 419	907	562 400	23 992
	2007	...	86 942	1 295	1 323	4 542	4 310	876	625 480	25 694
Madagascar	2004	...	...	62	*1	79	128	3	...	990
Madagascar	2005	...	...	0	0	0	0	0	...	*1 035
	2006	...	...	0	0	0	0	0	...	*990
	2007	...	...	0	0	0	0	0	...	935

Region, country or area Région, pays ou zone	Year Année	Hard coal, lignite and peat Houille, lignite et tourbe	Crude petroleum and NGL Pétrole brut et LGN	Motor gasoline Essence auto	Jet fuel Carbu-réacteurs	Gas-diesel oil Gazole/ carburant diesel	Residual fuel oil Mazout résiduel	Liquefied petroleum gas Gaz de pétrole liquéfiés	Natural gas Gaz naturel	Electricity Electricité
		Thousand metric tons – Milliers de tonnes							Terajoules Térajoules	Million kWh Millions kWh
Malawi Malawi	2004	50[2]	...	...	...	...	...	...	...	1 452
	2005	45[2]	...	...	...	...	...	...	...	1 537
	2006	*55[2]	...	...	...	...	...	...	...	1 580
	2007	*60[2]	...	...	...	...	...	...	...	1 637
Mali * Mali *	2004	...	...	...	...	...	...	...	...	465
	2005	...	...	...	...	...	...	...	...	475
	2006	...	...	...	...	...	...	...	...	489
	2007	...	...	...	...	...	...	...	...	495
Mauritania Mauritanie	2004	...	...	...	...	...	...	...	...	505
	2005	...	...	...	...	...	...	...	...	479
	2006	...	1 526[4]	...	...	...	...	...	...	569
	2007	...	749[4]	...	...	...	...	...	...	587
Mauritius Maurice	2004	...	...	...	...	...	...	...	...	2 165
	2005	...	...	...	...	...	...	...	...	2 271
	2006	...	...	...	...	...	...	...	...	2 350
	2007	...	...	...	...	...	...	...	...	2 465
Morocco Maroc	2004	...	11[4]	257	174	2 254	2 264	104	1 977	19 336
	2005	...	7[4]	372	264	2 295	2 545	204	1 782	22 456
	2006	...	10[4]	373	236	2 033	2 265	192	2 600	23 192
	2007	...	14[4]	365	292	1 996	2 269	170	2 494	22 858
Mozambique Mozambique	2004	17[2]	...	...	...	...	...	...	52 312	11 714
	2005	3[2]	...	...	...	...	...	...	88 029	13 285
	2006	41[2]	...	...	...	...	...	...	105 358	14 737
	2007	24[2]	...	...	...	...	...	...	106 540	16 076
Namibia Namibie	2004	...	...	...	...	...	...	...	...	1 588
	2005	...	...	...	...	...	...	...	...	1 585
	2006	...	...	...	...	...	...	...	...	1 491
	2007	...	...	...	...	...	...	...	...	1 694
Niger Niger	2004	200[2]	...	...	...	...	...	...	...	*212
	2005	182[2]	...	...	...	...	...	...	...	*195
	2006	183[2]	...	...	...	...	...	...	...	*179
	*2007	185[2]	...	...	...	...	...	...	...	197
Nigeria Nigéria	2004	3[2]	128 308	534	189	1 179	1 866	17	873 602	20 224
	2005	8[2]	133 199	275	480	980	2 877	17	889 679	20 468
	2006	8[2]	124 569	993	226	1 260	2 159	20	1 112 098	23 110
	2007	8[2]	114 310	287	232	623	1 002	1	1 268 182	22 978
Réunion * Réunion *	2004	...	...	...	...	...	...	...	...	1 652
	2005	...	...	...	...	...	...	...	...	1 680
	2006	...	...	...	...	...	...	...	...	1 710
	2007	...	...	...	...	...	...	...	...	1 792
Rwanda Rwanda	2004	...	...	...	...	...	...	...	*20	93
	2005	...	...	...	...	...	...	...	*23	113
	2006	...	...	...	...	...	...	...	*24	171
	2007	...	...	...	...	...	...	...	*24	169
Saint Helena Sainte-Hélène	2004	...	...	...	...	...	...	...	...	8
	*2005	...	...	...	...	...	...	...	...	8
	2006	...	...	...	...	...	...	...	...	8
	2007	...	...	...	...	...	...	...	...	8
Sao Tome and Principe Sao Tomé-et-Principe	2004	...	...	...	...	...	...	...	...	37
	2005	...	...	...	...	...	...	...	...	41
	*2006	...	...	...	...	...	...	...	...	42
	*2007	...	...	...	...	...	...	...	...	43
Senegal Sénégal	2004	...	...	148	132	471	327	10	506	2 061
	2005	...	...	118	89	356	279	3	533	1 908
	2006	...	...	46	31	115	111	0	483	1 962
	2007	...	...	77	48	339	187	0	407	2 124
Seychelles Seychelles	2004	...	...	...	...	...	...	...	...	226
	2005	...	...	...	...	...	...	...	...	231
	2006	...	...	...	...	...	...	...	...	252
	2007	...	...	...	...	...	...	...	...	271
Sierra Leone Sierra Leone	2004	...	...	*32	*21	*90	*45	...	...	120
	2005	...	...	*32	*21	*60	*35	...	...	84
	*2006	...	...	33	22	60	40	...	...	41
	*2007	...	...	33	22	60	40	...	...	60

50 Energy production *(continued)*
Production de l'énergie *(suite)*

Region, country or area Région, pays ou zone	Year Année	Hard coal, lignite and peat Houille, lignite et tourbe	Crude petroleum and NGL Pétrole brut et LGN	Motor gasoline Essence auto	Jet fuel Carbu-réacteurs	Gas-diesel oil Gazole/carburant diesel	Residual fuel oil Mazout résiduel	Liquefied petroleum gas Gaz de pétrole liquéfiés	Natural gas Gaz naturel	Electricity Electricité
		Thousand metric tons – Milliers de tonnes							Terajoules Térajoules	Million kWh Millions kWh
Somalia	2004	...	...	5	65	10	25	0	...	291
Somalie	2005	...	...	5	65	10	25	0	...	301
	2006	...	...	5	65	10	25	31	...	307
	2007	...	...	5	65	11	25	31	...	326
South Africa[5]	2004	242 821[2]	1 665	8 343	1 778	7 141	4 192	305	77 172	244 607
Afrique du Sud[5]	2005	244 986[2]	1 541	7 858	1 840	9 201	5 040	297	82 976	244 920
	2006	244 784[2]	1 492	7 938	1 908	9 873	4 906	327	75 529	253 798
	2007	247 666[2]	1 173	7 876	1 688	6 219	4 118	293	74 808	263 479
Sudan	2004	...	15 000[4]	1 228	192	1 400	361	300	...	3 883
Soudan	2005	...	15 250[4]	1 247	214	1 423	377	305	...	4 124
	2006	...	16 550[4]	1 712	294	1 952	504	419	...	4 209
	2007	...	23 400[4]	1 639	303	1 873	677	430	...	4 541
Swaziland	2004	443[2]	...	...	...	...	...	...	...	*354
Swaziland	2005	451[2]	...	...	...	...	...	...	...	408
	*2006	444[2]	...	...	...	...	...	...	...	436
	*2007	462[2]	...	...	...	...	...	...	...	454
Togo	2004	...	...	...	...	...	...	...	...	186
Togo	2005	...	...	...	...	...	...	...	...	189
	2006	...	...	...	...	...	...	...	...	221
	2007	...	...	...	...	...	...	...	...	196
Tunisia	2004	...	3 429	226	0	432	595	108	86 816	12 455
Tunisie	2005	...	3 478	216	0	482	609	109	87 857	13 007
	2006	...	3 355	178	4	506	604	110	94 391	14 122
	2007	...	4 633	134	0	556	646	103	89 876	14 060
Uganda	2004	...	...	...	...	...	...	...	...	1 942
Ouganda	2005	...	...	...	...	...	...	...	...	1 880
	2006	...	...	...	...	...	...	...	...	1 615
	2007	...	...	...	...	...	...	...	...	1 952
United Rep. of Tanzania	2004	65[2]	...	...	...	...	...	...	4 975	2 893
Rép.-Unie de Tanzanie	2005	75[2]	...	...	...	...	...	...	13 774	3 035
	2006	80[2]	...	...	...	...	...	...	14 600	2 776
	2007	84[2]	...	...	...	...	...	...	20 735	4 175
Western Sahara	2004	...	...	...	...	...	...	...	...	90
Sahara occidental	2005	...	...	...	...	...	...	...	...	90
	*2006	...	...	...	...	...	...	...	...	90
	*2007	...	...	...	...	...	...	...	...	90
Zambia	2004	233[2]	...	118	27	223	79	3	...	8 512
Zambie	2005	244[2]	...	126	29	239	85	3	...	8 938
	2006	260[2]	...	134	31	253	90	3	...	9 385
	2007	276[2]	...	142	33	268	95	3	...	9 853
Zimbabwe	2004	3 415[2]	...	...	...	...	...	...	...	9 718
Zimbabwe	2005	3 621[2]	...	...	...	...	...	...	...	10 269
	2006	3 447[2]	...	...	...	...	...	...	...	9 776
	2007	3 237[2]	...	...	...	...	...	...	...	9 180
America, North	**2004**	**1 095 008[6]**	**670 180**	**409 252**	**82 416**	**247 424**	**78 484**	**77 046**	**30 032 263**	**5 109 229**
Amérique du Nord	**2005**	**1 114 691[6]**	**649 690**	**408 097**	**82 984**	**253 940**	**75 570**	**73 518**	**29 704 467**	**5 271 637**
	2006	**1 145 829[6]**	**649 327**	**404 150**	**79 681**	**258 824**	**72 427**	**71 387**	**30 568 028**	**5 280 363**
	2007	**1 133 717[6]**	**646 454**	**403 768**	**78 441**	**263 735**	**75 914**	**70 925**	**31 249 512**	**5 369 816**
Anguilla	2004	...	...	...	...	...	...	...	...	62
Anguilla	2005	...	...	...	...	...	...	...	...	72
	2006	...	...	...	...	...	...	...	...	80
	2007	...	...	...	...	...	...	...	...	80
Antigua and Barbuda *	2004	...	...	...	...	...	...	...	...	111
Antigua-et-Barbuda *	2005	...	...	...	...	...	...	...	...	114
	2006	...	...	...	...	...	...	...	...	116
	2007	...	...	...	...	...	...	...	...	118
Aruba	2004	...	*120[4]	...	...	...	...	...	...	866
Aruba	2005	...	*120[4]	...	...	...	...	...	...	911
	2006	...	*120[4]	...	...	...	...	...	...	910
	2007	...	*125[4]	...	...	...	...	...	...	936
Bahamas *	2004	...	...	...	...	...	...	...	...	2 087
Bahamas *	2005	...	...	...	...	...	...	...	...	2 090
	2006	...	...	...	...	...	...	...	...	2 100
	2007	...	...	...	...	...	...	...	...	2 110

Region, country or area Région, pays ou zone	Year Année	Hard coal, lignite and peat Houille, lignite et tourbe	Crude petroleum and NGL Pétrole brut et LGN	Motor gasoline Essence auto	Jet fuel Carbu-réacteurs	Gas-diesel oil Gazole/ carburant diesel	Residual fuel oil Mazout résiduel	Liquefied petroleum gas Gaz de pétrole liquéfiés	Natural gas Gaz naturel	Electricity Electricité
		Thousand metric tons – Milliers de tonnes							Terajoules Térajoules	Million kWh Millions kWh
Barbados Barbade	2004	...	*65	...	...	...	...	1	973	895
	2005	...	*65	...	...	...	...	1	1 028	930
	2006	...	*52	...	...	...	...	1	1 048	948
	2007	...	*56	...	...	...	...	1	1 177	948
Belize Belize	2004	...	...	...	...	...	...	...	...	150
	2005	...	...	...	...	...	...	...	...	158
	2006	...	...	...	...	...	...	...	...	214
	2007	...	...	...	...	...	...	...	...	197
Bermuda Bermudes	2004	...	...	...	...	...	...	...	...	667
	2005	...	...	...	...	...	...	...	...	617
	2006	...	...	...	...	...	...	...	...	631
	2007	...	...	...	...	...	...	...	...	643
British Virgin Islands * Iles Vierges brit. *	2004	...	...	...	...	...	...	...	...	45
	2005	...	...	...	...	...	...	...	...	45
	2006	...	...	...	...	...	...	...	...	48
	2007	...	...	...	...	...	...	...	...	48
Canada Canada	2004	65 997[6]	145 983	33 024	4 597	31 590	8 724	1 955	7 016 682	598 514
	2005	65 345[6]	144 080	32 270	4 363	30 745	8 263	1 779	7 169 112	628 194
	2006	66 440[6]	151 265	30 889	3 869	30 704	7 763	1 730	7 206 362	612 594
	2007	68 446[6]	156 827	32 630	4 038	31 223	8 407	1 878	7 007 286	639 841
Cayman Islands Iles Caïmanes	2004	...	...	...	...	...	...	...	...	451
	2005	...	...	...	...	...	...	...	...	482
	2006	...	...	...	...	...	...	...	...	555
	2007	...	...	...	...	...	...	...	...	604
Costa Rica Costa Rica	2004	...	...	14	...	163	247	2	...	8 209
	2005	...	...	64	...	148	235	2	...	8 252
	2006	...	...	105	...	230	295	4	...	8 697
	2007	...	...	132	...	248	328	4	...	9 050
Cuba Cuba	2004	...	3 253[4]	331	0	385	858	63	27 470	15 633
	2005	...	2 935[4]	407	0	365	859	82	28 992	15 341
	2006	...	2 900[4]	317	9	420	892	62	42 337	16 469
	2007	...	2 905[4]	392	56	464	940	59	46 280	17 621
Dominica Dominique	2004	...	...	...	...	...	...	...	...	79
	2005	...	...	...	...	...	...	...	...	84
	*2006	...	...	...	...	...	...	...	...	85
	*2007	...	...	...	...	...	...	...	...	85
Dominican Republic Rép. dominicaine	2004	...	...	445	54	417	839	33	...	13 759
	2005	...	...	447	56	423	812	35	...	12 899
	2006	...	...	440	59	424	762	33	...	14 150
	2007	...	...	404	45	359	753	25	...	14 839
El Salvador El Salvador	2004	...	...	143	49	199	543	14	...	4 468
	2005	...	...	112	51	198	419	16	...	4 788
	2006	...	...	112	39	176	437	17	...	5 597
	2007	...	...	117	49	229	477	20	...	5 806
Greenland * Groenland *	2004	...	...	...	...	...	...	...	...	305
	2005	...	...	...	...	...	...	...	...	305
	2006	...	...	...	...	...	...	...	...	305
	2007	...	...	...	...	...	...	...	...	325
Grenada Grenade	2004	...	...	...	...	...	...	...	...	157
	2005	...	...	...	...	...	...	...	...	166
	2006	...	...	...	...	...	...	...	...	171
	2007	...	...	...	...	...	...	...	...	171
Guadeloupe * Guadeloupe *	2004	...	...	...	...	...	...	...	...	1 180
	2005	...	...	...	...	...	...	...	...	1 190
	2006	...	...	...	...	...	...	...	...	1 225
	2007	...	...	...	...	...	...	...	...	1 227
Guatemala Guatemala	2004	...	1 102[4]	0	0	0	...	...	...	7 009
	2005	...	1 004[4]	1	0	25	...	...	...	7 555
	2006	...	880[4]	1	0	22	...	...	...	7 916
	2007	...	833[4]	0	1	25	...	...	...	8 755
Haiti Haïti	2004	...	...	...	...	...	...	...	...	547
	2005	...	...	...	...	...	...	...	...	556
	2006	...	...	...	...	...	...	...	...	570
	2007	...	...	...	...	...	...	...	...	469

50 Energy production *(continued)*
Production de l'énergie *(suite)*

Region, country or area Région, pays ou zone	Year Année	Hard coal, lignite and peat Houille, lignite et tourbe	Crude petroleum and NGL Pétrole brut et LGN	Motor gasoline Essence auto	Jet fuel Carbu-réacteurs	Gas-diesel oil Gazole/carburant diesel	Residual fuel oil Mazout résiduel	Liquefied petroleum gas Gaz de pétrole liquéfiés	Natural gas Gaz naturel	Electricity Electricité
		Thousand metric tons – Milliers de tonnes							Terajoules Térajoules	Million kWh Millions kWh
Honduras Honduras	2004	...	...	...	...	...	...	...	...	4 877
	2005	...	...	...	...	...	...	...	...	5 545
	2006	...	...	...	...	...	...	...	...	5 487
	2007	...	...	...	...	...	...	...	...	6 316
Jamaica Jamaïque	2004	...	...	95	63	129	370	7	...	7 249
	2005	...	...	52	41	87	268	0	...	7 576
	2006	...	...	124	63	226	561	9	...	7 528
	2007	...	...	104	53	190	473	8	...	7 782
Martinique * Martinique *	2004	...	...	163	...	178	310	27	...	1 195
	2005	...	...	164	...	179	310	27	...	1 205
	2006	...	...	164	...	179	312	27	...	1 215
	2007	...	...	165	...	180	313	28	...	1 225
Mexico Mexique	2004	9 882[6]	190 897	19 855	2 770	16 057	21 089	10 707	1 651 290	224 077
	2005	10 755[6]	187 205	20 399	3 125	17 157	20 019	10 211	1 716 773	234 895
	2006	11 487[6]	182 811	20 658	3 172	17 692	16 914	10 255	1 885 615	249 648
	2007	12 514[6]	174 954	21 563	3 232	18 011	17 252	9 662	1 999 118	257 455
Montserrat Montserrat	2004	...	...	...	...	...	...	...	...	21
	*2005	...	...	...	...	...	...	...	...	22
	*2006	...	...	...	...	...	...	...	...	22
	*2007	...	...	...	...	...	...	...	...	23
Netherlands Antilles Antilles néerlandaises	2004	...	...	2 032	776	2 532	3 190	42	...	1 210
	2005	...	...	2 171	862	2 463	3 647	83	...	1 248
	2006	...	...	1 781	815	2 481	3 487	77	...	1 271
	2007	...	...	1 987	783	2 350	4 056	83	...	1 294
Nicaragua Nicaragua	2004	...	...	99	19	210	427	17	...	2 822
	2005	...	...	87	25	183	378	15	...	2 866
	2006	...	...	91	27	199	404	15	...	2 958
	2007	...	...	87	35	198	395	16	...	3 209
Panama Panama	2004	...	...	...	...	...	...	...	...	5 761
	2005	...	...	...	...	...	...	...	...	5 827
	2006	...	...	...	...	...	...	...	...	5 989
	2007	...	...	...	...	...	...	...	...	6 476
Puerto Rico Porto Rico	2004	...	...	...	...	...	...	...	...	24 130
	2005	...	...	...	...	...	...	...	...	24 960
	2006	...	...	...	...	...	...	...	...	23 838
	2007	...	...	...	...	...	...	...	...	23 720
Saint Kitts and Nevis * Saint-Kitts-et-Nevis *	2004	...	...	...	...	...	...	...	...	130
	2005	...	...	...	...	...	...	...	...	133
	2006	...	...	...	...	...	...	...	...	135
	2007	...	...	...	...	...	...	...	...	137
Saint Lucia Sainte-Lucie	2004	...	...	...	...	...	...	...	...	309
	2005	...	...	...	...	...	...	...	...	324
	2006	...	...	...	...	...	...	...	...	331
	2007	...	...	...	...	...	...	...	...	346
Saint Pierre-Miquelon * Saint-Pierre-et-Miq. *	2004	...	...	...	...	...	...	...	...	52
	2005	...	...	...	...	...	...	...	...	54
	2006	...	...	...	...	...	...	...	...	54
	2007	...	...	...	...	...	...	...	...	55
Saint Vincent-Grenadines Saint Vincent-Gren.	2004	...	...	...	...	...	...	...	...	121
	*2005	...	...	...	...	...	...	...	...	124
	*2006	...	...	...	...	...	...	...	...	130
	*2007	...	...	...	...	...	...	...	...	135
Trinidad and Tobago Trinité-et-Tobago	2004	...	7 308	1 096	615	1 421	2 971	710	1 024 185	6 430
	2005	...	8 373	1 350	827	1 764	3 180	686	1 067 201	7 058
	2006	...	8 382	1 240	755	1 804	2 934	771	1 216 368	7 045
	2007	...	8 118	1 273	746	1 736	3 027	848	1 339 773	7 662
Turks and Caicos Islands Iles Turq. et Caïques	2004	...	...	...	...	...	...	...	...	117
	2005	...	...	...	...	...	...	...	...	132
	2006	...	...	...	...	...	...	...	...	158
	2007	...	...	...	...	...	...	...	...	182
United States Etats-Unis	2004	1 019 129[6]	321 452	351 954	73 473	194 143	38 916	63 468	20 311 663	4 174 484
	2005	1 038 591[6]	305 908	350 574	73 634	200 203	37 180	60 581	19 721 361	4 293 860
	2006	1 067 902[6]	302 917	348 229	70 873	204 267	37 666	58 386	20 216 298	4 300 109
	2007	1 052 757[6]	302 636	344 914	69 403	208 522	39 493	58 293	20 855 878	4 348 856

Region, country or area Région, pays ou zone	Year Année	Hard coal, lignite and peat Houille, lignite et tourbe	Crude petroleum and NGL Pétrole brut et LGN	Motor gasoline Essence auto	Jet fuel Carbu-réacteurs	Gas-diesel oil Gazole/carburant diesel	Residual fuel oil Mazout résiduel	Liquefied petroleum gas Gaz de pétrole liquéfiés	Natural gas Gaz naturel	Electricity Electricité
		Thousand metric tons – Milliers de tonnes							Terajoules Térajoules	Million kWh Millions kWh
United States Virgin Is. * Iles Vierges améric. *	2004	...	...	...	...	...	...	...	...	1 050
	2005	...	...	...	...	...	...	...	...	1 060
	2006	...	...	...	...	...	...	...	...	1 065
	2007	...	...	...	...	...	...	...	...	1 070
America, South Amérique du Sud	**2004**	**66 166[1]**	**337 767**	**46 530**	**10 659**	**71 705**	**45 944**	**16 423**	**4 048 251**	**789 852**
	2005	**73 139[1]**	**352 400**	**48 540**	**10 544**	**71 688**	**44 528**	**18 130**	**4 130 087**	**825 143**
	2006	**80 036[1]**	**348 851**	**47 478**	**10 437**	**71 980**	**46 038**	**18 282**	**4 350 658**	**866 663**
	2007	**83 992[1]**	**336 993**	**47 718**	**10 034**	**73 370**	**47 130**	**18 302**	**4 290 591**	**907 766**
Argentina Argentine	2004	51[2]	43 297	4 550	1 209	10 294	2 368	4 431	1 713 297	100 260
	2005	25[2]	41 582	4 883	1 264	9 946	2 795	4 290	1 685 308	107 053
	2006	427[2]	41 736	4 563	1 191	10 685	3 422	4 643	1 764 945	115 197
	2007	110[2]	40 307	4 846	1 283	10 970	4 267	4 215	1 773 634	115 428
Bolivia (Plur. State of) Bolivie (État plur. de)	2004	...	2 564	552	122	622	0	322	407 861	4 542
	2005	...	2 759	420	125	601	0	333	464 428	5 230
	2006	...	2 628	500	131	620	1	353	494 677	5 293
	2007	...	2 423	531	114	661	0	356	540 493	5 734
Brazil Brésil	2004	5 406[2]	78 846	13 738	3 357	34 079	16 074	5 144	420 030	387 451
	2005	6 255[2]	87 325	14 337	3 337	33 368	15 461	5 780	429 095	402 938
	2006	5 881[2]	92 144	14 981	3 037	33 597	15 661	5 405	434 855	419 336
	2007	5 965[2]	94 206	15 733	3 263	34 035	15 707	5 731	423 995	444 583
Chile Chili	2004	233[2]	404	2 384	650	3 693	2 294	542	63 901	51 208
	2005	544[2]	372	2 257	574	3 534	2 306	499	74 703	52 484
	2006	674[2]	316	2 482	660	3 717	2 646	530	72 145	55 320
	2007	243[2]	527	2 349	537	3 623	2 445	781	50 334	58 509
Colombia Colombie	2004	53 693[2]	26 766	4 963	861	3 689	3 330	688	271 346	50 228
	2005	59 064[2]	26 283	4 252	858	3 660	3 056	689	284 720	50 665
	2006	65 596[2]	26 768	3 618	718	4 457	2 792	694	285 242	54 755
	2007	69 902[2]	27 390	3 164	537	4 395	3 318	727	285 275	55 314
Ecuador Equateur	2004	...	26 880	1 533	279	1 698	3 195	259	23 103	12 585
	2005	...	27 013	1 610	310	1 685	3 352	246	18 165	13 404
	2006	...	28 058	1 744	337	1 662	3 406	237	29 618	14 814
	2007	...	26 754	1 940	357	1 603	3 323	165	30 478	17 339
Falkland Is. (Malvinas) Iles Falkland (Malvin.)	2004	13[3]	...	...	...	...	...	...	...	*16
	*2005	13[3]	...	...	...	...	...	...	...	17
	2006	13[3]	...	...	...	...	...	...	...	*17
	*2007	13[3]	...	...	...	...	...	...	...	17
French Guiana Guyane française	2004	...	...	...	...	...	...	...	...	430
	2005	...	...	...	...	...	...	...	...	430
	2006	...	...	...	...	...	...	...	...	430
	2007	...	...	...	...	...	...	...	...	435
Guyana Guyana	2004	...	...	...	...	...	...	...	...	835
	2005	...	...	...	...	...	...	...	...	862
	2006	...	...	...	...	...	...	...	...	867
	2007	...	...	...	...	...	...	...	...	867
Paraguay Paraguay	2004	...	...	8	...	33	20	...	...	51 921
	2005	...	...	4	...	16	11	...	...	51 156
	2006	...	...	0	...	0	0	...	...	53 774
	2007	...	...	0	...	0	0	...	...	53 715
Peru Pérou	2004	22[2]	4 653	1 744	418	2 036	3 324	396	40 321	24 415
	2005	43[2]	5 281	2 220	270	2 532	2 958	738	68 008	25 660
	2006	107[2]	5 501	2 208	504	2 780	2 878	777	77 826	27 358
	2007	112[2]	5 963	2 356	565	3 063	2 693	788	108 691	29 931
Suriname Suriname	2004	...	612[4]	...	...	39	335	...	...	1 509
	2005	...	637[4]	...	...	41	349	...	...	1 571
	2006	...	656[4]	...	...	41	360	...	...	1 618
	2007	...	656[4]	...	...	41	360	...	...	1 618
Uruguay Uruguay	2004	...	...	503	44	807	518	86	...	5 899
	2005	...	...	447	41	810	505	91	...	7 683
	2006	...	...	396	53	760	381	77	...	5 618
	2007	...	...	352	61	637	368	65	...	9 424
Venezuela (Bol. Rep. of) Venezuela (R. bol. du)	2004	6 748[2]	153 745	16 555	3 719	14 715	14 486	4 555	1 108 392	98 552
	2005	7 195[2]	161 148	18 110	3 765	15 495	13 735	5 464	1 105 660	105 990
	2006	7 338[2]	151 044	16 986	3 806	13 661	14 491	5 566	1 191 350	112 266
	2007	7 647[2]	138 767	16 447	3 317	14 342	14 649	5 474	1 077 691	114 852

Region, country or area Région, pays ou zone	Year Année	Hard coal, lignite and peat Houille, lignite et tourbe	Crude petroleum and NGL Pétrole brut et LGN	Motor gasoline Essence auto	Jet fuel Carbu-réacteurs	Gas-diesel oil Gazole/carburant diesel	Residual fuel oil Mazout résiduel	Liquefied petroleum gas Gaz de pétrole liquéfiés	Natural gas Gaz naturel	Electricity Electricité
		Thousand metric tons – Milliers de tonnes							Terajoules Térajoules	Million kWh Millions kWh
Asia	**2004**	**2 785 528[6]**	**1 623 401**	**199 198**	**63 325**	**414 001**	**247 286**	**94 234**	**27 823 147**	**6 130 260**
Asie	**2005**	**3 074 823[6]**	**1 677 418**	**201 202**	**70 135**	**434 329**	**246 838**	**96 511**	**30 028 144**	**6 622 954**
	2006	**3 337 507[6]**	**1 699 131**	**205 413**	**75 863**	**444 732**	**245 192**	**99 911**	**31 593 452**	**7 171 863**
	2007	**3 528 022[6]**	**1 693 346**	**214 091**	**79 747**	**458 693**	**238 393**	**102 485**	**33 555 664**	**7 808 586**
Afghanistan	2004	34[2]	...	...	...	...	...	...	119	929
Afghanistan	2005	33[2]	...	...	...	...	...	...	*100	*962
	2006	33[2]	...	...	...	...	...	...	*100	*976
	*2007	33[2]	...	...	...	...	...	...	105	999
Armenia	2004	...	...	...	...	...	...	...	...	6 030
Arménie	2005	...	...	...	...	...	...	...	...	6 317
	2006	...	...	...	...	...	...	...	...	5 941
	2007	...	...	...	...	...	...	...	...	5 898
Azerbaijan	2004	...	15 549	852	504	1 789	2 521	182	194 905	21 743
Azerbaïdjan	2005	...	22 214	906	629	2 101	3 061	185	216 096	22 872
	2006	...	32 268	1 043	693	2 095	2 899	205	255 073	24 542
	2007	...	42 598	1 129	761	2 109	2 340	187	421 780	21 847
Bahrain	2004	...	10 111	755	2 178	4 500	2 734	204	274 330	8 448
Bahreïn	2005	...	10 081	789	2 276	4 702	2 857	218	290 590	8 698
	2006	...	9 909	766	2 210	4 566	2 775	215	307 881	9 822
	2007	...	9 898	772	2 227	4 601	2 797	197	338 924	10 908
Bangladesh	2004	...	90[7]	136	2	274	53	16	467 723	20 820
Bangladesh	2005	...	96[7]	145	1	293	57	12	502 829	22 006
	2006	...	93[7]	140	1	284	55	8	543 096	23 703
	2007	...	84[7]	127	4	258	49	12	580 266	24 378
Bhutan	2004	30[2]	...	...	...	...	...	...	...	2 355
Bhoutan	2005	85[2]	...	...	...	...	...	...	...	2 648
	2006	98[2]	...	...	...	...	...	...	...	4 521
	2007	105[2]	...	...	...	...	...	...	...	6 562
Brunei Darussalam	2004	...	10 291	201	80	173	89	15	477 318	3 236
Brunéi Darussalam	2005	...	10 075	196	78	178	92	15	468 618	3 264
	2006	...	10 788	209	79	190	103	15	492 586	3 298
	2007	...	9 682	217	80	189	97	15	478 121	3 395
Cambodia	2004	...	...	...	...	...	...	...	...	765
Cambodge	2005	...	...	...	...	...	...	...	...	880
	2006	...	...	...	...	...	...	...	...	1 000
	2007	...	...	...	...	...	...	...	...	1 349
China [8]	2004	1 992 324[2]	175 873[4]	52 236	...	98 436	20 293	14 170	1 659 129	2 193 736
Chine [8]	2005	2 204 729[2]	181 353[4]	53 884	...	110 902	17 674	14 327	1 970 965	2 497 441
	2006	2 373 000[2]	184 766[4]	55 473	...	117 624	17 847	17 453	2 342 769	2 865 726
	2007	2 525 974[2]	186 318[4]	58 695	...	123 591	19 673	19 447	2 766 547	3 281 553
China, Hong Kong SAR	2004	...	...	...	...	...	...	...	...	37 129
Chine, Hong Kong RAS	2005	...	...	...	...	...	...	...	...	38 448
	2006	...	...	...	...	...	...	...	...	38 613
	2007	...	...	...	...	...	...	...	...	38 948
China, Macao SAR	2004	...	...	...	...	...	...	...	...	1 973
Chine, Macao RAS	2005	...	...	...	...	...	...	...	...	2 027
	2006	...	...	...	...	...	...	...	...	1 669
	2007	...	...	...	...	...	...	...	...	1 520
Cyprus	2004	...	...	40	...	88	112	9	...	4 200
Chypre	2005	...	...	0	...	0	0	0	...	4 377
	2006	...	...	0	...	0	0	0	...	4 652
	2007	...	...	0	...	0	0	0	...	4 871
Georgia	2004	8[2]	98[4]	...	...	2	14	...	461	6 924
Géorgie	2005	5[2]	67[4]	...	...	1	4	...	516	7 267
	2006	11[2]	64[4]	...	...	0	4	...	712	7 599
	2007	14[2]	57[4]	...	...	0	13	...	628	8 329
India	2004	412 952[6]	37 665	11 057	5 201	47 426	14 970	7 825	1 007 951	665 986
Inde	2005	437 105[6]	36 323	10 502	6 196	48 495	14 305	7 710	1 025 355	697 470
	2006	462 117[6]	38 138	12 539	7 805	54 268	15 697	8 408	1 005 064	752 454
	2007	491 062[6]	38 243	14 167	9 107	59 032	15 804	8 792	1 071 204	813 102
Indonesia	2004	143 489[6]	52 658	8 825	1 414	14 661	10 995	2 514	2 840 728	120 160
Indonésie	2005	172 465[6]	49 835	8 325	1 418	13 889	10 105	1 819	2 680 743	127 369
	2006	224 123[6]	47 469	8 411	1 256	13 216	9 686	1 428	2 704 155	133 108
	2007	213 446[6]	50 703	8 363	1 087	11 828	9 538	1 410	2 663 613	142 236

Region, country or area Région, pays ou zone	Year Année	Hard coal, lignite and peat Houille, lignite et tourbe	Crude petroleum and NGL Pétrole brut et LGN	Motor gasoline Essence auto	Jet fuel Carbu-réacteurs	Gas-diesel oil Gazole/ carburant diesel	Residual fuel oil Mazout résiduel	Liquefied petroleum gas Gaz de pétrole liquéfiés	Natural gas Gaz naturel	Electricity Electricité
		Thousand metric tons – Milliers de tonnes							Terajoules Térajoules	Million kWh Millions kWh
Iran (Islamic Rep. of) Iran (Rép. islamique d')	2004	1 246[2]	198 783	10 836	795	23 771	25 840	4 146	3 498 799	166 023
	2005	1 330[2]	214 914	11 394	848	24 375	26 241	3 689	4 038 674	180 461
	2006	1 529[2]	213 079	12 047	1 042	24 762	26 351	4 086	4 237 681	200 227
	2007	1 634[2]	217 177	12 131	992	25 093	25 168	4 538	4 366 450	211 779
Iraq Iraq	2004	...	98 951	3 278	607	4 906	6 942	938	38 000	32 295
	2005	...	91 699	3 185	590	4 766	6 479	951	55 100	34 000
	2006	...	95 985	3 233	599	4 838	5 988	1 032	55 100	31 869
	2007	...	101 244	2 212	409	4 995	5 595	1 065	55 480	33 183
Israel Israël	2004	439[9]	2[4]	2 467	...	2 750	3 168	532	43 585	48 481
	2005	413[9]	2[4]	2 729	...	3 042	3 504	566	59 988	49 843
	2006	452[9]	2[4]	2 592	...	3 231	3 223	471	83 815	51 811
	2007	429[9]	...	...	...	...	...	...	78 117	55 091
Japan Japon	2004	...	663	42 716	7 902	57 059	30 985	4 448	125 356	1 076 244
	2005	...	703	43 259	8 896	57 700	31 649	4 895	134 612	1 098 298
	2006	...	693	42 437	10 433	54 711	28 536	4 644	148 485	1 102 802
	2007	...	747	42 801	11 663	55 300	29 545	4 409	166 369	1 133 711
Jordan Jordanie	2004	...	1[4]	579	291	1 223	1 516	112	10 098	8 970
	2005	...	1[4]	613	338	1 395	1 466	118	8 315	9 651
	2006	...	1[4]	675	312	1 412	1 345	139	7 754	11 120
	2007	...	1[4]	706	301	1 292	1 215	119	6 908	12 838
Kazakhstan Kazakhstan	2004	86 875[6]	59 485	1 928	244	2 888	2 708	1 507	862 531	66 942
	2005	86 586[6]	61 486	2 359	207	3 705	3 874	1 478	974 571	67 916
	2006	96 231[6]	65 003	2 345	254	3 888	3 333	1 106	1 029 558	71 653
	2007	102 754[6]	67 125	2 633	269	4 295	2 584	1 262	1 153 539	76 621
Korea, Dem. P. R. Corée, R. p. dém. de	2004	31 711[6]	...	188	...	203	117	...	...	21 974
	2005	34 610[6]	...	159	...	171	98	...	...	22 913
	2006	35 107[6]	...	122	...	131	75	...	...	22 436
	2007	30 339[6]	...	146	...	157	90	...	...	21 523
Korea, Republic of Corée, République de	2004	3 191[2]	0[4]	8 850	9 665	29 048	29 912	3 326	0	368 162
	2005	2 832[2]	54[4]	8 654	10 755	31 508	31 305	3 213	20 495	389 390
	2006	2 824[2]	45[4]	8 707	12 021	32 392	30 793	3 098	18 275	404 021
	2007	2 886[2]	31[4]	8 505	13 379	34 314	27 363	2 927	14 770	427 317
Kuwait Koweït	2004	...	123 501	1 931	2 258	12 204	9 760	3 515	462 773	41 256
	2005	...	136 982	2 812	1 586	12 397	9 166	3 368	518 914	43 734
	2006	...	141 245	3 023	2 619	11 079	11 951	3 671	533 264	47 607
	2007	...	137 416	2 852	2 827	11 475	11 559	3 447	519 174	48 753
Kyrgyzstan Kirghizistan	2004	461[6]	74[4]	19	...	27	42	...	1 132	16 312
	2005	335[6]	74[4]	13	...	31	42	...	975	16 415
	2006	322[6]	71[4]	10	...	31	42	...	741	17 082
	2007	395[6]	69[4]	14	...	52	56	...	581	16 237
Lao People's Dem. Rep. * Rép. dém. pop. lao *	2004	590[2]	...	...	...	...	...	...	...	3 541
	2005	620[2]	...	...	...	...	...	...	...	3 685
	2006	624[2]	...	...	...	...	...	...	...	3 799
	2007	987[2]	...	...	...	...	...	...	...	3 667
Lebanon Liban	2004	...	...	...	...	...	...	...	...	11 054
	2005	...	...	...	...	...	...	...	...	11 125
	2006	...	...	...	...	...	...	...	...	10 654
	2007	...	...	...	...	...	...	...	...	11 348
Malaysia Malaisie	2004	382[2]	37 568	4 496	2 608	9 463	1 828	1 303	2 180 862	82 282
	2005	682[2]	37 468	4 040	2 472	9 020	1 792	2 470	2 402 160	87 300
	2006	902[2]	36 858	4 270	2 523	8 734	1 992	2 503	2 539 294	91 563
	2007	823[2]	35 005	5 029	3 040	8 891	2 006	3 021	2 526 083	101 325
Maldives Maldives	2004	...	...	...	...	...	...	...	...	160
	*2005	...	...	...	...	...	...	...	...	185
	2006	...	...	...	...	...	...	...	...	212
	2007	...	...	...	...	...	...	...	...	245
Mongolia Mongolie	2004	6 865[6]	...	...	...	...	...	...	...	3 303
	2005	7 517[6]	...	...	...	...	...	...	...	3 419
	2006	8 074[6]	...	...	...	...	...	...	...	3 544
	2007	9 238[6]	...	...	...	...	...	...	...	3 701
Myanmar Myanmar	2004	1 052	1 024	309	61	196	49	19	400 544	5 608
	2005	1 360	1 115	303	46	173	48	20	510 497	6 015
	2006	1 412	1 058	357	52	274	41	10	494 789	6 164
	2007	1 489	1 056	371	52	254	56	18	530 917	6 501

Region, country or area Région, pays ou zone	Year Année	Hard coal, lignite and peat Houille, lignite et tourbe	Crude petroleum and NGL Pétrole brut et LGN	Motor gasoline Essence auto	Jet fuel Carbu-réacteurs	Gas-diesel oil Gazole/ carburant diesel	Residual fuel oil Mazout résiduel	Liquefied petroleum gas Gaz de pétrole liquéfiés	Natural gas Gaz naturel	Electricity Electricité
		Thousand metric tons – Milliers de tonnes							Terajoules Térajoules	Million kWh Millions kWh
Nepal Népal	2004	9[2]	...	...	...	...	...	...	...	2 416
	2005	9[2]	...	...	...	...	...	...	...	2 622
	2006	9[2]	...	...	...	...	...	...	...	2 719
	2007	9[2]	...	...	...	...	...	...	...	2 806
Occ. Palestinian Terr. Terr. palestinien occ.	2004	...	...	...	...	...	...	...	...	396
	2005	...	...	...	...	...	...	...	...	501
	2006	...	...	...	...	...	...	...	...	345
	2007	...	...	...	...	...	...	...	...	417
Oman Oman	2004	...	39 073	593	178	864	2 121	78	705 655	11 499
	2005	...	38 750	494	224	951	2 299	95	793 713	12 648
	2006	...	36 899	597	292	905	2 244	104	938 220	13 585
	2007	...	35 550	469	272	650	1 937	150	955 879	14 443
Pakistan Pakistan	2004	4 587[2]	3 429	1 326	1 185	3 603	3 132	412	1 235 848	85 628
	2005	4 871[2]	3 556	1 186	1 258	3 419	3 358	558	1 290 846	93 629
	2006	3 643[2]	3 673	1 218	1 165	3 383	3 193	583	1 296 194	98 213
	2007	4 124[2]	3 798	1 337	1 009	3 697	3 324	578	1 320 373	95 661
Philippines Philippines	2004	2 730[6]	19[4]	1 501	590	3 004	3 537	263	96 743	55 957
	2005	2 831[6]	29[4]	1 629	665	3 399	3 463	322	127 566	56 549
	2006	1 735[6]	24[4]	1 590	714	3 575	3 057	327	128 296	56 819
	2007	2 561[6]	24[4]	1 409	729	3 511	3 093	250	152 115	59 647
Qatar Qatar	2004	...	41 713	1 709	956	979	618	1 622	1 528 453	13 233
	2005	...	42 553	1 722	916	924	356	1 606	1 787 162	14 396
	2006	...	46 797	1 693	1 045	1 020	734	1 748	1 978 365	15 325
	2007	...	48 274	1 957	1 106	1 030	410	1 775	2 466 127	16 079
Saudi Arabia Arabie saoudite	2004	...	491 685	13 605	4 923	31 486	25 944	29 719	2 162 680	159 875
	2005	...	514 624	13 400	6 627	31 685	26 722	30 979	2 376 770	176 124
	2006	...	506 289	12 025	6 193	32 412	27 177	30 641	2 495 244	179 782
	2007	...	485 786	15 050	5 388	31 971	26 185	29 777	2 563 812	189 076
Singapore Singapour	2004	...	...	3 948	6 481	11 711	7 170	981	...	36 810
	2005	...	...	4 879	7 610	14 474	8 862	882	...	38 213
	2006	...	...	4 699	7 458	13 939	8 534	669	...	39 442
	2007	...	...	4 574	8 102	13 567	8 306	663	...	41 134
Sri Lanka Sri Lanka	2004	...	...	203	126	693	855	15	...	8 158
	2005	...	...	161	114	591	762	13	...	8 769
	2006	...	...	194	131	628	809	15	...	9 389
	2007	...	...	163	171	445	810	16	...	9 814
Syrian Arab Republic Rép. arabe syrienne	2004	...	23 405	1 338	245	4 123	5 015	336	267 670	32 077
	2005	...	22 341	1 257	221	3 934	4 938	428	229 970	34 935
	2006	...	20 160	1 399	208	4 151	5 036	510	198 305	37 504
	2007	...	19 282	1 278	183	3 824	4 862	463	192 959	38 644
Tajikistan Tadjikistan	2004	68[6]	19[4]	...	...	...	...	...	1 368	16 491
	2005	91[6]	22[4]	...	...	...	...	...	1 113	17 090
	2006	102[6]	22[4]	...	...	...	...	...	760	16 935
	2007	165[6]	26[4]	...	...	...	...	...	551	17 494
Thailand Thaïlande	2004	20 060[9]	9 903	6 674	3 774	17 511	6 335	3 917	701 157	125 727
	2005	20 878[9]	11 418	6 428	3 711	16 378	6 409	4 011	753 708	132 197
	2006	19 001[9]	12 406	6 331	4 299	16 737	6 578	4 032	761 621	138 742
	2007	18 239[9]	13 179	6 311	3 992	18 381	7 333	4 291	802 644	143 378
Timor-Leste * Timor-Leste *	2004	...	6 835	...	...	...	...	2 200	...	97
	2005	...	6 860	...	...	...	...	2 210	...	112
	2006	...	6 872	...	...	...	...	2 215	...	123
	2007	...	6 884	...	...	...	...	2 220	...	135
Turkey Turquie	2004	46 377[6]	2 251[4]	3 479	1 767	7 665	7 845	762	26 350	150 698
	2005	58 340[6]	2 258[4]	3 609	1 997	7 601	7 208	766	34 355	161 956
	2006	64 255[6]	2 160[4]	3 659	1 644	7 549	7 271	808	34 662	176 299
	2007	75 364[6]	2 134[4]	4 098	2 336	7 016	6 369	762	34 202	191 558
Turkmenistan Turkménistan	2004	...	10 091	1 270	297	2 522	1 752	...	2 235 451	11 920
	2005	...	9 794	1 313	307	2 607	1 811	...	2 387 007	12 820
	2006	...	10 063	1 564	366	3 105	2 157	...	2 396 479	13 650
	2007	...	9 956	1 464	342	2 908	2 020	...	2 609 794	14 880
United Arab Emirates Emirats arabes unis	2004	...	124 521	1 746	5 400	4 754	1 291	7 252	1 805 310	52 417
	2005	...	125 751	1 866	5 404	4 262	1 299	7 526	1 815 450	60 698
	2006	...	135 162	2 626	5 385	4 428	1 173	7 807	1 903 835	66 768
	2007	...	133 044	2 336	4 948	4 242	1 102	8 140	1 962 366	76 106

Region, country or area Région, pays ou zone	Year Année	Hard coal, lignite and peat Houille, lignite et tourbe	Crude petroleum and NGL Pétrole brut et LGN	Motor gasoline Essence auto	Jet fuel Carbu-réacteurs	Gas-diesel oil Gazole/carburant diesel	Residual fuel oil Mazout résiduel	Liquefied petroleum gas Gaz de pétrole liquéfiés	Natural gas Gaz naturel	Electricity Electricité
		Thousand metric tons – Milliers de tonnes							Terajoules Térajoules	Million kWh Millions kWh
Uzbekistan Ouzbékistan	2004	2 699[9]	7 295	1 736	296	1 879	1 814	40	2 236 391	51 030
	2005	3 003[9]	5 962	1 418	242	1 535	1 482	32	2 278 677	47 706
	2006	3 126[9]	5 560	1 323	226	1 433	1 383	30	2 370 882	49 299
	2007	3 282[9]	5 396	1 284	220	1 391	1 342	29	2 463 465	48 950
Viet Nam Viet Nam	2004	27 349[2]	20 557	...	...	...	...	335	244 623	46 029
	2005	34 093[2]	18 975	...	...	...	...	343	251 295	53 462
	2006	38 778[2]	17 192	...	...	...	...	302	273 147	61 794
	2007	42 483[2]	16 281	...	...	...	...	281	276 269	69 487
Yemen Yémen	2004	...	20 015	1 219	321	809	409	89	...	4 365
	2005	...	19 830	1 179	403	902	512	84	...	4 768
	2006	...	18 158	1 022	396	777	519	69	...	5 387
	2007	...	16 000	1 127	486	991	676	72	...	6 027
Europe Europe	**2004**	**1 041 517**	**747 405**	**199 706**	**48 702**	**340 617**	**192 201**	**41 318**	**37 342 293**	**4 691 697**
	2005	**1 044 380**	**734 883**	**199 523**	**48 304**	**352 247**	**193 453**	**42 133**	**37 227 205**	**4 762 999**
	2006	**1 042 291**	**726 210**	**200 812**	**50 436**	**354 086**	**192 875**	**43 816**	**37 334 898**	**4 844 649**
	2007	**1 035 176**	**731 859**	**194 116**	**50 044**	**354 898**	**192 502**	**41 408**	**36 562 645**	**4 892 015**
Albania Albanie	2004	109[9]	420[4]	35	16	73	67	1	636	5 559
	2005	92[9]	447[4]	14	0	72	68	0	670	5 443
	2006	92[9]	505[4]	0	0	99	48	0	670	5 094
	2007	92[9]	570[4]	0	0	82	32	0	670	2 860
Andorra Andorre	2004	...	...	...	...	...	...	...	...	94
	2005	...	...	...	...	...	...	...	...	85
	2006	...	...	...	...	...	...	...	...	74
	2007	...	...	...	...	...	...	...	...	76
Austria Autriche	2004	236[10]	1 061	1 738	455	3 529	1 032	57	77 550	64 125
	2005	1[10]	965	1 798	592	3 894	1 009	107	62 081	65 681
	2006	1[10]	983	1 615	526	3 685	915	50	72 756	63 445
	2007	1[10]	982	1 702	604	3 461	880	70	73 899	63 357
Belarus Bélarus	2004	1 993[3]	1 804[4]	2 842	...	5 845	5 501	418	9 942	31 210
	2005	2 308[3]	1 785[4]	3 330	...	6 426	6 313	459	8 806	30 961
	2006	2 125[3]	1 780[4]	3 498	...	6 616	6 329	483	8 458	31 811
	2007	2 507[3]	1 760[4]	3 181	...	6 679	6 195	439	7 763	31 829
Belgium Belgique	2004	181[9]	...	5 789	2 143	12 327	8 380	511	...	85 643
	2005	109[9]	...	5 056	1 678	11 938	8 042	462	...	86 944
	2006	29[9]	...	5 357	1 744	12 660	7 128	403	...	85 391
	2007	0	...	5 041	1 751	12 737	7 391	464	...	88 624
Bosnia and Herzegovina Bosnie-Herzégovine	2004	12 275[6]	...	26	...	42	78	3	...	12 734
	2005	12 665[6]	...	18	...	31	74	2	...	12 637
	2006	13 753[6]	...	18	...	31	74	2	...	13 346
	2007	14 455[6]	...	14	...	24	58	2	...	11 824
Bulgaria Bulgarie	2004	26 485	30[4]	1 401	142	1 915	965	103	12 432	41 621
	2005	24 695	30[4]	1 381	144	2 270	1 230	105	17 884	44 365
	2006	25 678	28[4]	1 560	151	2 521	1 512	127	17 391	45 843
	2007	28 633	26[4]	1 466	183	2 376	1 550	136	10 966	43 297
Croatia Croatie	2004	...	*1 246	1 226	91	1 741	1 012	443	83 528	13 295
	2005	...	*1 178	1 168	99	1 603	1 160	431	86 769	12 462
	2006	...	*1 139	1 083	67	1 565	1 097	399	103 113	12 430
	2007	...	*1 050	1 202	97	1 676	1 180	433	109 900	12 245
Czech Republic République tchèque	2004	64 076[6]	565[4]	1 289	147	2 673	394	181	7 555	84 333
	2005	62 026[6]	569[4]	1 467	132	3 067	581	184	7 170	82 578
	2006	62 912[6]	344[4]	1 594	121	3 128	381	204	6 853	84 361
	2007	62 626[6]	330[4]	1 555	145	2 902	417	192	6 524	88 198
Denmark Danemark	2004	...	19 262[4]	1 986	606	3 329	1 557	164	395 033	40 433
	2005	...	18 517[4]	1 919	507	3 224	1 405	145	436 520	36 243
	2006	...	16 839[4]	1 987	608	3 298	1 471	166	433 718	45 613
	2007	...	15 169[4]	1 962	542	3 198	1 415	159	384 607	39 154
Estonia Estonie	2004	14 272[10]	...	...	...	...	...	...	...	10 304
	2005	14 969[10]	...	...	...	...	...	...	...	10 205
	2006	14 602[10]	...	...	...	...	...	...	...	9 731
	2007	17 019[10]	...	...	...	...	...	...	...	12 190
Faeroe Islands Iles Féroé	2004	...	...	...	...	...	...	...	...	249
	2005	...	...	...	...	...	...	...	...	245
	2006	...	...	...	...	...	...	...	...	260
	2007	...	...	...	...	...	...	...	...	269

Region, country or area Région, pays ou zone	Year Année	Hard coal, lignite and peat Houille, lignite et tourbe	Crude petroleum and NGL Pétrole brut et LGN	Motor gasoline Essence auto	Jet fuel Carbu-réacteurs	Gas-diesel oil Gazole/ carburant diesel	Residual fuel oil Mazout résiduel	Liquefied petroleum gas Gaz de pétrole liquéfiés	Natural gas Gaz naturel	Electricity Electricité
		Thousand metric tons – Milliers de tonnes							Terajoules Térajoules	Million kWh Millions kWh
Finland Finlande	2004	3 633[3]	...	4 321	714	5 078	1 445	267	...	85 847
	2005	8 928[3]	...	4 061	592	4 964	1 318	315	...	70 550
	2006	13 235[3]	...	4 298	715	5 502	1 272	402	...	82 304
	2007	4 466[3]	...	4 348	717	5 863	1 402	350	...	81 249
France [11] France [11]	2004	872[2]	1 513	16 878	5 616	34 421	11 887	2 979	43 530	574 275
	2005	617[2]	1 320	16 271	5 478	33 590	11 823	2 868	37 275	576 164
	2006	452[2]	1 100	17 195	5 633	33 733	11 955	2 774	43 252	574 558
	2007	380[2]	1 013	16 479	5 536	34 392	11 411	...	38 585	569 840
Germany Allemagne	2004	211 210	3 463[4]	26 467	4 424	49 551	14 013	2 918	685 342	615 287
	2005	206 054	3 471[4]	27 240	4 252	52 137	13 340	2 951	661 721	620 574
	2006	200 184	3 383[4]	26 576	4 412	50 854	13 684	2 925	653 696	636 761
	2007	204 594	3 361[4]	25 891	4 592	49 314	13 669	3 065	598 741	637 100
Gibraltar Gibraltar	2004	...	...	...	...	...	...	...	...	136
	2005	...	...	...	...	...	...	...	...	145
	2006	...	...	...	...	...	...	...	...	151
	2007	...	...	...	...	...	...	...	...	155
Greece Grèce	2004	70 041[9]	*133	3 629	1 720	5 369	7 095	598	1 337	59 346
	2005	69 398[9]	*100	4 058	1 737	5 653	6 956	655	851	60 020
	2006	64 787[9]	*94	4 327	1 423	6 452	6 953	653	1 209	60 789
	2007	66 308[9]	81	4 318	1 719	6 562	7 116	645	1 026	63 496
Guernsey Guernesey	2004	...	...	...	...	...	...	...	...	63
	2005	...	...	...	...	...	...	...	...	53
	2006	...	...	...	...	...	...	...	...	80
	2007	...	...	...	...	...	...	...	...	158
Hungary Hongrie	2004	11 242[9]	1 852	1 439	239	2 989	313	408	109 251	33 708
	2005	9 570[9]	1 724	1 321	266	3 515	218	394	107 626	35 756
	2006	9 952[9]	1 637	1 302	280	3 498	232	373	110 660	35 859
	2007	9 818[9]	1 502	1 322	273	3 722	200	379	93 251	39 960
Iceland Islande	2004	...	...	...	...	...	...	...	...	8 623
	2005	...	...	...	...	...	...	...	...	8 683
	2006	...	...	...	...	...	...	...	...	9 930
	2007	...	...	...	...	...	...	...	...	11 982
Ireland Irlande	2004	4 395[3]	...	552	...	964	966	53	32 025	25 569
	2005	3 956[3]	...	683	...	1 097	948	57	21 437	25 970
	2006	3 694[3]	...	634	...	1 121	1 101	51	19 107	28 046
	2007	2 772[3]	...	487	...	1 186	1 250	36	17 181	28 226
Isle of Man Ile de Man	2004	...	...	...	...	...	...	...	...	189
	2005	...	...	...	...	...	...	...	...	435
	2006	...	...	...	...	...	...	...	...	396
	2007	...	...	...	...	...	...	...	...	462
Italy [12] Italie [12]	2004	98[2]	5 445[4]	20 662	3 787	39 536	17 543	2 613	493 813	303 347
	2005	95[2]	6 111[4]	21 189	3 910	39 844	19 032	2 517	459 905	303 699
	2006	21[2]	5 769[4]	20 967	4 081	39 805	17 621	2 275	418 301	314 121
	2007	158[2]	5 860[4]	21 417	4 034	41 079	17 357	2 349	369 799	313 888
Jersey Jersey	2004	...	...	...	...	...	...	...	...	46
	2005	...	...	...	...	...	...	...	...	29
	2006	...	...	...	...	...	...	...	...	37
	2007	...	...	...	...	...	...	...	...	101
Latvia Lettonie	2004	13[3]	...	...	...	...	...	...	...	4 689
	2005	12[3]	...	...	...	...	...	...	...	4 905
	2006	14[3]	...	...	...	...	...	...	...	4 891
	2007	11[3]	...	...	...	...	...	...	...	4 771
Lithuania Lituanie	2004	50[3]	372	2 401	850	2 523	1 673	526	...	19 274
	2005	70[3]	318	2 564	832	2 781	1 799	555	...	14 784
	2006	55[3]	250	2 232	764	2 246	1 938	474	...	12 482
	2007	53[3]	199	1 614	503	1 493	1 381	330	...	14 007
Luxembourg Luxembourg	2004	...	...	...	...	...	...	...	...	4 121
	2005	...	...	...	...	...	...	...	...	4 135
	2006	...	...	...	...	...	...	...	...	4 333
	2007	...	...	...	...	...	...	...	...	4 002
Malta Malte	2004	...	...	...	...	...	...	...	...	2 216
	2005	...	...	...	...	...	...	...	...	2 240
	2006	...	...	...	...	...	...	...	...	2 261
	2007	...	...	...	...	...	...	...	...	2 296

Region, country or area Région, pays ou zone	Year Année	Hard coal, lignite and peat Houille, lignite et tourbe	Crude petroleum and NGL Pétrole brut et LGN	Motor gasoline Essence auto	Jet fuel Carbu-réacteurs	Gas-diesel oil Gazole/carburant diesel	Residual fuel oil Mazout résiduel	Liquefied petroleum gas Gaz de pétrole liquéfiés	Natural gas Gaz naturel	Electricity Electricité
		Thousand metric tons – Milliers de tonnes							Terajoules Térajoules	Million kWh Millions kWh
Montenegro Monténégro	2005	1 297[9]	...	...	...	...	...	...	...	2 864
	2006	1 512[9]	...	...	...	...	...	...	...	2 952
	2007	1 203[9]	...	...	...	...	...	...	...	2 144
Netherlands Pays-Bas	2004	...	2 910	15 539	6 935	20 234	13 073	5 070	2 864 924	100 770
	2005	...	2 530	14 234	6 990	21 346	12 394	4 579	2 617 469	100 219
	2006	...	2 022	13 794	6 914	19 685	12 151	4 069	2 578 865	96 733
	2007	...	2 576	10 756	6 597	19 332	11 974	1 518	2 547 408	103 241
Norway [13] Norvège [13]	2004	2 904[2]	143 855	3 261	423	6 241	1 845	6 423	3 314 956	110 699
	2005	1 471[2]	132 839	3 829	644	6 835	1 610	6 628	3 570 726	138 005
	2006	2 395[2]	123 581	4 134	644	7 102	1 957	8 255	3 668 327	121 580
	2007	3 995[2]	119 385	3 942	575	6 817	2 066	8 136	3 632 319	137 471
Poland Pologne	2004	162 428[6]	886[4]	3 978	679	7 371	2 754	259	182 698	154 159
	2005	159 540[6]	848[4]	4 117	644	7 459	2 537	284	180 700	156 936
	2006	156 067[6]	796[4]	4 155	853	8 336	2 824	282	180 514	161 742
	2007	145 850[6]	721[4]	3 867	801	8 787	2 831	243	181 274	159 348
Portugal Portugal	2004	...	...	2 551	779	4 703	2 969	365	...	45 105
	2005	...	...	2 466	854	4 906	3 062	391	...	46 575
	2006	...	...	2 750	856	5 102	2 920	406	...	49 041
	2007	...	...	2 591	745	4 634	2 622	366	...	47 253
Republic of Moldova République de Moldova	2004	...	8[4]	...	...	...	...	...	8	1 022
	2005	...	5[4]	...	...	...	...	...	8	1 229
	2006	...	4[4]	...	...	...	...	...	5	1 192
	2007	...	8[4]	...	...	3	...	...	4	1 100
Romania Roumanie	2004	31 800[10]	*5 705	3 419	177	4 170	1 559	366	482 759	56 499
	2005	*31 114[10]	*5 733	4 237	191	4 709	1 707	658	451 305	59 413
	2006	34 932[10]	*5 659	4 145	238	4 593	1 303	677	444 656	62 697
	2007	35 781[10]	*4 905	3 799	278	4 660	1 186	754	429 507	61 673
Russian Federation Fédération de Russie	2004	260 431	456 253	30 505	9 283	55 389	58 330	8 760	23 693 333	931 865
	2005	284 530	466 448	32 011	10 036	60 003	62 365	9 428	23 996 973	953 074
	2006	285 928	475 827	34 368	10 602	64 166	65 189	10 368	24 463 654	995 794
	2007	290 308	487 681	35 097	10 699	66 301	67 690	10 856	24 283 317	1 015 333
Serbia Serbie	2004	41 157[6]	652[4]	671	56	1 315	853	95	11 951	37 686
	2005	35 244[6]	649[4]	630	53	1 234	801	89	10 631	36 474
	2006	36 780[6]	646[4]	1 038	45	1 038	674	75	10 970	36 481
	2007	37 148[6]	641[4]	624	57	1 091	796	98	9 197	36 523
Slovakia Slovaquie	2004	2 952[9]	*42	1 670	61	2 598	585	206	6 367	30 567
	2005	2 511[9]	*34	1 584	36	2 455	543	181	5 831	31 455
	2006	2 201[9]	*31	1 449	46	2 587	654	137	7 976	31 418
	2007	2 111[9]	*24	1 596	78	2 819	544	143	4 926	28 056
Slovenia Slovénie	2004	4 809[9]	...	...	...	...	...	...	201	15 271
	2005	4 540[9]	...	...	...	...	...	...	160	15 117
	2006	4 522[9]	...	...	...	...	...	...	160	15 115
	2007	4 535[9]	...	...	...	...	...	...	120	15 043
Spain Espagne	2004	20 487[6]	255[4]	10 434	2 713	21 563	9 125	1 058	14 398	280 007
	2005	19 481[6]	166[4]	10 152	2 653	23 457	9 019	1 050	6 694	294 077
	2006	18 447[6]	139[4]	10 038	2 612	23 844	9 245	1 522	2 930	299 454
	2007	17 182[6]	142[4]	9 232	2 562	23 933	9 340	1 436	3 744	303 292
Sweden Suède	2004	893[3]	...	4 506	208	7 238	5 450	423	...	151 726
	2005	708[3]	...	4 045	70	6 951	5 576	433	...	158 434
	2006	621[3]	...	4 182	179	7 204	5 226	302	...	143 299
	2007	520[3]	...	3 679	196	6 414	4 246	261	...	148 849
Switzerland [14] Suisse [14]	2004	...	...	1 362	350	2 148	701	196	...	65 299
	2005	...	...	1 268	212	2 170	611	197	...	59 612
	2006	...	...	1 465	228	2 573	583	223	...	64 038
	2007	...	...	1 280	183	2 172	587	202	...	67 950
TFYR of Macedonia L'ex-R.Y. Macédoine	2004	7 245[9]	...	146	0	359	282	20	...	6 667
	2005	6 881[9]	...	183	23	394	295	24	...	6 945
	2006	6 639[9]	...	190	33	443	327	29	...	7 009
	2007	6 509[9]	...	180	17	424	402	25	...	6 729
Ukraine Ukraine	2004	60 133	*4 269	4 394	473	6 544	7 766	754	799 130	182 165
	2005	61 000	*4 374	4 609	512	5 531	5 889	766	811 148	186 055
	2006	62 133	*4 506	3 926	400	4 519	3 834	758	737 856	193 381
	2007	59 134	*4 459	4 161	384	4 368	3 475	824	738 205	196 251

Region, country or area Région, pays ou zone	Year Année	Hard coal, lignite and peat Houille, lignite et tourbe	Crude petroleum and NGL Pétrole brut et LGN	Motor gasoline Essence auto	Jet fuel Carbu-réacteurs	Gas-diesel oil Gazole/carburant diesel	Residual fuel oil Mazout résiduel	Liquefied petroleum gas Gaz de pétrole liquéfiés	Natural gas Gaz naturel	Electricity Electricité
		Thousand metric tons – Milliers de tonnes							Terajoules Térajoules	Million kWh Millions kWh
United Kingdom Royaume-Uni	2004	25 097[2]	95 374	24 589	5 615	28 839	12 988	5 080	4 019 594	395 853
	2005	20 498[2]	84 722	22 620	5 167	28 691	11 728	5 218	3 666 845	400 524
	2006	18 528[2]	79 148	21 443	6 261	26 080	12 277	4 952	3 349 811	398 327
	2007	17 007[2]	79 414	21 313	6 176	26 397	11 809	4 880	3 019 712	396 143
Oceania Océanie	**2004**	**357 352[6]**	**29 458**	**15 107**	**4 867**	**13 503**	**1 521**	**1 479**	**1 653 819**	**286 712**
	2005	**372 609[6]**	**26 387**	**14 917**	**5 198**	**12 985**	**1 664**	**1 445**	**1 807 130**	**297 680**
	2006	**373 219[6]**	**25 740**	**13 714**	**5 143**	**11 815**	**1 537**	**1 836**	**1 876 971**	**304 295**
	2007	**394 217[6]**	**27 936**	**14 460**	**5 153**	**11 396**	**1 414**	**1 742**	**1 972 460**	**308 057**
American Samoa Samoa américaines	2004	...	...	...	...	...	...	...	...	188
	2005	...	...	...	...	...	...	...	...	189
	*2006	...	...	...	...	...	...	...	...	193
	*2007	...	...	...	...	...	...	...	...	196
Australia Australie	2004	352 197[6]	26 218	13 453	3 937	11 590	1 071	1 312	1 488 699	234 543
	2005	367 342[6]	22 895	13 218	4 221	10 790	1 085	1 271	1 648 435	245 495
	2006	367 452[6]	21 886	12 153	4 128	9 466	1 051	1 679	1 713 590	251 659
	2007	389 383[6]	24 004	12 992	4 238	9 270	952	1 639	1 792 629	254 965
Cook Islands Iles Cook	2004	...	...	...	...	...	...	...	...	30
	2005	...	...	...	...	...	...	...	...	30
	2006	...	...	...	...	...	...	...	...	32
	2007	...	...	...	...	...	...	...	...	34
Fiji Fidji	*2004	...	...	...	...	...	...	...	...	816
	*2005	...	...	...	...	...	...	...	...	823
	2006	...	...	...	...	...	...	...	...	840
	2007	...	...	...	...	...	...	...	...	836
French Polynesia Polynésie française	2004	...	...	...	...	...	...	...	...	643
	2005	...	...	...	...	...	...	...	...	631
	2006	...	...	...	...	...	...	...	...	657
	2007	...	...	...	...	...	...	...	...	687
Guam Guam	2004	...	...	...	...	...	...	...	...	1 878
	2005	...	...	...	...	...	...	...	...	1 897
	2006	...	...	...	...	...	...	...	...	1 891
	2007	...	...	...	...	...	...	...	...	1 879
Kiribati Kiribati	2004	...	...	...	...	...	...	...	...	21
	2005	...	...	...	...	...	...	...	...	22
	2006	...	...	...	...	...	...	...	...	24
	2007	...	...	...	...	...	...	...	...	24
Marshall Islands Iles Marshall	2004	...	...	...	...	...	...	...	...	101
	2005	...	...	...	...	...	...	...	...	101
	*2006	...	...	...	...	...	...	...	...	104
	*2007	...	...	...	...	...	...	...	...	108
Nauru * Nauru *	2004	...	...	...	...	...	...	...	...	32
	2005	...	...	...	...	...	...	...	...	33
	2006	...	...	...	...	...	...	...	...	33
	2007	...	...	...	...	...	...	...	...	35
New Caledonia Nouvelle-Calédonie	2004	...	...	...	...	...	...	...	...	1 678
	2005	...	...	...	...	...	...	...	...	1 883
	2006	...	...	...	...	...	...	...	...	1 872
	2007	...	...	...	...	...	...	...	...	1 926
New Zealand Nouvelle-Zélande	2004	5 155[6]	1 106	1 627	930	1 763	350	167	160 640	42 901
	2005	5 267[6]	1 030	1 645	887	1 785	439	156	148 597	43 136
	2006	5 767[6]	987	1 482	909	1 819	381	135	152 529	43 519
	2007	4 834[6]	1 992	1 423	837	1 731	400	100	169 811	43 845
Niue * Nioué *	2004	...	...	...	...	...	...	...	...	3
	2005	...	...	...	...	...	...	...	...	3
	2006	...	...	...	...	...	...	...	...	3
	2007	...	...	...	...	...	...	...	...	3
Palau * Palaos *	2004	...	...	...	...	...	...	...	...	128
	2005	...	...	...	...	...	...	...	...	134
	2006	...	...	...	...	...	...	...	...	151
	2007	...	...	...	...	...	...	...	...	154
Papua New Guinea Papouasie-Nvl-Guinée	2004	...	2 134[4]	27	0	150	100	0	4 480	3 468
	2005	...	2 462[4]	54	90	410	140	18	10 098	3 002
	2006	...	2 867[4]	79	106	530	105	22	10 852	3 012
	2007	...	1 940[4]	45	78	395	62	3	*10 020	*3 049

Region, country or area Région, pays ou zone	Year Année	Hard coal, lignite and peat Houille, lignite et tourbe	Crude petroleum and NGL Pétrole brut et LGN	Motor gasoline Essence auto	Jet fuel Carbu-réacteurs	Gas-diesel oil Gazole/ carburant diesel	Residual fuel oil Mazout résiduel	Liquefied petroleum gas Gaz de pétrole liquéfiés	Natural gas Gaz naturel	Electricity Electricité
		Thousand metric tons – Milliers de tonnes							Terajoules Térajoules	Million kWh Millions kWh
Samoa Samoa	2004	...	...	...	...	...	...	...	...	106
	2005	...	...	...	...	...	...	...	...	111
	2006	...	...	...	...	...	...	...	...	116
	*2007	...	...	...	...	...	...	...	...	118
Solomon Islands Iles Salomon	2004	...	...	...	...	...	...	...	...	63
	2005	...	...	...	...	...	...	...	...	74
	2006	...	...	...	...	...	...	...	...	75
	2007	...	...	...	...	...	...	...	...	85
Tonga Tonga	2004	...	...	...	...	...	...	...	...	47
	*2005	...	...	...	...	...	...	...	...	48
	*2006	...	...	...	...	...	...	...	...	45
	*2007	...	...	...	...	...	...	...	...	43
Tuvalu Tuvalu	2004	...	...	...	...	...	...	...	...	4
	2005	...	...	...	...	...	...	...	...	4
	2006	...	...	...	...	...	...	...	...	4
	2007	...	...	...	...	...	...	...	...	4
Vanuatu * Vanuatu *	2004	...	...	...	...	...	...	...	...	44
	2005	...	...	...	...	...	...	...	...	45
	2006	...	...	...	...	...	...	...	...	45
	2007	...	...	...	...	...	...	...	...	46
Wallis and Futuna Islands Iles Wallis et Futuna	2004	...	...	...	...	...	...	...	...	19
	2005	...	...	...	...	...	...	...	...	20
	2006	...	...	...	...	...	...	...	...	20
	2007	...	...	...	...	...	...	...	...	20

Source:
United Nations Statistics Division, New York, the energy statistics database, last accessed June 2010.

1 Hardcoal and peat only.
2 Hard coal only.
3 Peat only.
4 Crude petroleum only.
5 Refers to the Southern African Customs Union.
6 Hardcoal and lignite only.
7 Natural gas liquids only.
8 For statistical purposes, the data for China do not include those for the Hong Kong Special Administrative Region (Hong Kong SAR), Macao Special Administrative Region (Macao SAR) and Taiwan Province of China.
9 Lignite only.
10 Lignite and peat only.
11 Including Monaco.
12 Including San Marino.
13 Including Svalbard and Jan Mayen Islands.
14 Including Liechtenstein.

Source:
Organisation des Nations Unies, Division de statistique, New York, la base de données pour les statistiques de l'énergie, dernier accès juin 2010.

1 Houille et tourbe seulement.
2 Houille seulement.
3 Tourbe seulement.
4 Pétrole brut seulement.
5 Se réfèrent à l'Union douanière d'afrique australe.
6 Houille et lignite seulement.
7 Liquides de gaz naturel seulement.
8 Pour la présentation des statistiques, les données pour la Chine ne comprennent pas la Région Administrative Spéciale de Hong Kong (Hong Kong RAS), la Région Administrative Spéciale de Macao (Macao RAS) et la province de Taiwan.
9 Lignite seulement.
10 Lignite et tourbe seulement.
11 Y compris Monaco.
12 Y compris Saint-Marin.
13 Y compris îles Svalbard et Jan Mayen.
14 Y compris Liechtenstein.

Technical notes: tables 49 and 50

Table 49: Data are presented in metric tons of oil equivalent (TOE), to which the individual energy commodities are converted in the interests of international uniformity and comparability.

To convert from original units to TOE, the data in original units (metric tons, terajoules, kilowatt hours, cubic metres) are multiplied by conversion factors. For a list of the relevant conversion factors and a detailed description of methods, see the *United Nations Energy Statistics Yearbook* and related methodological publications.

Included in the production of commercial primary energy for solids are hard coal, lignite, peat and oil shale; liquids are comprised of crude petroleum and natural gas liquids; gas comprises natural gas; and electricity is comprised of primary electricity generation from hydro, nuclear, geothermal, wind, tide, wave and solar sources.

In general, data on stocks refer to changes in stocks of producers, importers and/or industrial consumers at the beginning and end of each year.

International trade of energy commodities is based on the "general trade" system, that is, all goods entering and leaving the national boundary of a country are recorded as imports and exports.

Sea/air bunkers refer to the amounts of fuels delivered to ocean-going ships or aircraft of all flags engaged in international traffic. Consumption by ships engaged in transport in inland and coastal waters, or by aircraft engaged in domestic flights, is not included.

Data on consumption refer to "apparent consumption" and are derived from the formula "production + imports – exports – bunkers +/- stock changes". Accordingly, the series on apparent consumption may in some cases represent only an indication of the magnitude of actual gross inland availability.

Included in the consumption of commercial energy for solids are consumption of primary forms of solid fuels, net imports and changes in stocks of secondary fuels; liquids are comprised of consumption of energy petroleum products including feedstocks, natural gasoline, condensate, refinery gas and input of crude petroleum to thermal power plants; gases include the consumption of natural gas, net imports and changes in stocks of gasworks and coke oven gas; and electricity is comprised of production of primary electricity and net imports of electricity.

Table 50: The definitions of the energy commodities are as follows:

– Hard coal: Coal that has a high degree of coalification with a gross calorific value above 23,865 KJ/kg (5,700 kcal/kg) on an ash free but moist basis, and a mean random reflectance of vitrinite of at least 0.6. Slurries, middlings and other low-grade coal products, which cannot be classified according to the type of coal from which they are ob-

Notes techniques : tableaux 49 et 50

Tableau 49 : Les données relatives aux divers produits énergétiques ont été converties en tonnes d'équivalent pétrole (TEP), dans un souci d'uniformité et pour permettre les comparaisons entre la production de différents pays.

Pour passer des unités de mesure d'origine à l'unité commune, les données en unités d'origine (tonnes, terajoules, kilowattheures, mètres cubes) sont multipliées par des facteurs de conversion. Pour une liste des facteurs de conversion appropriée et pour des descriptions détaillées des méthodes appliquées, se reporter à *l'Annuaire des statistiques de l'énergie des Nations Unies* et aux publications méthodologiques apparentées.

Sont compris dans la production d'énergie primaire commerciale: pour les solides, la houille, le lignite, la tourbe et le schiste bitumineux; pour les liquides, le pétrole brut et les liquides de gaz naturel; pour les gaz, le gaz naturel; pour l'électricité, l'électricité primaire de source hydraulique, nucléaire, géothermique, éolienne, marémotrice, des vagues et solaire.

En général, les variations des stocks se rapportent aux différences entre les stocks des producteurs, des importateurs ou des consommateurs industriels au début et à la fin de chaque année.

Le commerce international des produits énergétiques est fondé sur le système du "commerce général", c'est-à-dire que tous les biens entrant sur le territoire national d'un pays ou en sortant sont respectivement enregistrés comme importations et exportations.

Les soutes maritimes/aériens se rapportent aux quantités de combustibles livrées aux navires de mer et aéronefs assurant des liaisons commerciales internationales, quel que soit leur pavillon. La consommation des navires effectuant des opérations de transport sur les voies navigables intérieures ou dans les eaux côtières n'est pas incluse, tout comme celle des aéronefs effectuant des vols intérieurs.

Les données sur la consommation se rapportent à la "consommation apparente" et sont obtenues par la formule "production + importations – exportations – soutes +/- variations des stocks". En conséquence, les séries relatives à la consommation apparente peuvent occasionnellement ne donner qu'une indication de l'ordre de grandeur des disponibilités intérieures brutes réelles.

Sont compris dans la consommation d'énergie commerciale: pour les solides, la consommation de combustibles solides primaires, les importations nettes et les variations de stocks de combustibles solides secondaires; pour les liquides, la consommation de produits pétroliers énergétiques y compris les charges d'alimentation des usines de traitement, l'essence naturelle, le condensat et le gaz de raffinerie ainsi que le pétrole brut consommé dans les centrales thermiques pour la production d'électricité; pour les gaz, la consommation de gaz naturel, les importations nettes et les variations

tained, are included under hard coal.

– Lignite: Non-agglomerating coal with a low degree of coalification which retained the anatomical structure of the vegetable matter from which it was formed. Its gross calorific value is less than 17,435 KJ/kg (4,165 kcal/kg), and it contains greater than 31 per cent volatile matter on a dry mineral matter free basis.

– Peat: a solid fuel formed from the partial decomposition of dead vegetation under conditions of high humidity and limited air access (initial stage of coalification). Only peat used as fuel is included. Its principal use is as a household fuel.

– Crude petroleum: A mineral oil consisting of a mixture of hydrocarbons of natural origin, yellow to black in colour, of variable density and viscosity. Data in this category also includes lease or field condensate (separator liquids) which is recovered from gaseous hydrocarbons in lease separation facilities, as well as synthetic crude oil, mineral oils extracted from bituminous minerals such as shales and bituminous sand, and oils from coal liquefaction.

– Natural gas liquids (NGL): Liquid or liquefied hydrocarbons produced in the manufacture, purification and stabilization of natural gas. NGLs include, but are not limited to, ethane, propane, butane, pentane, natural gasoline, and plant condensate.

– Motor gasoline: Light hydrocarbon oil for use in internal combustion engines such as motor vehicles, excluding aircraft. It distills between 35°C and 200°C, and is treated to reach a sufficiently high octane number of generally between 80 and 100 RON. Treatment may be by re-forming, blending with an aromatic fraction, or the addition of benzole or other additives (such as tetraethyl lead).

– Jet fuel: Consists of gasoline-type jet fuel and kerosene-type jet fuel. Gasoline-type jet fuel: All light hydrocarbon oils for use in aviation gas-turbine engines. It distills between 100°C and 250°C with at least 20% of volume distilling at 143°C. It is obtained by blending kerosene and gasoline or naphtha in such a way that the aromatic content does not exceed 25% in volume. Additives are included to reduce the freezing point to -58°C or lower, and to keep the Reid vapour pressure between 0.14 and 0.21 kg/cm2. Kerosene-type jet fuel: Medium oil for use in aviation gas-turbine engines with the same distillation characteristics and flash point as kerosene, with a maxi-mum aromatic content of 20% in volume. It is treated to give a kinematic viscosity of less than 15 cSt at -34°C and a freezing point below -50°C.

– Gas-diesel oil (distillate fuel oil): Heavy oils distilling between 200°C and 380°C, but distilling less than 65% in volume at 250°C, including losses, and 85% or more at 350°C. Its flash point is always above 50°C and its specific gravity is higher than 0.82. Heavy oils obtained by blending are grouped together with gas oils on the condition that their kinematic viscosity does not exceed 27.5 cSt at 38°C.

de stocks de gaz d'usines à gaz et de gaz de cokerie; pour l'électricité, la production d'électricité primaire et les importations nettes d'électricité.

Tableau 50: Les définitions des produits énergétiques sont données ci-après :

– Houille: Charbon à haut degré de houillification et à pouvoir calorifique brut supérieur à 23 865 kJ/kg (5 700 kcal/kg), valeur mesurée pour un combustible exempt de cendres, mais humide et ayant un indice moyen de réflectance de la vitrinite au moins égal à 0,6. Les schlamms, les mixtes et autres produits du charbon de faible qualité qui ne peuvent être classés en fonction du type de charbon dont ils sont dérivés, sont inclus dans cette rubrique.

– Lignite: Le charbon non agglutinant d'un faible degré de houillification qui a gardé la structure anatomique des végétaux dont il est issu. Son pouvoir calorifique supérieur est inférieur à 17 435 kJ/kg (4 165 kcal/kg) et il contient plus de 31% de matières volatiles sur produit sec exempt de matières minérales.

–Tourbe : Combustible solide issu de la décomposition partielle de végétaux morts dans des conditions de forte humidité et de faible circulation d'air (phase initiale de la houillification). N'est prise en considération ici que la tourbe utilisée comme combustible. La tourbe est utilisée principalement comme combustible domestique.

– Pétrole brut: Huile minérale constituée d'un mélange d'hydrocarbures d'origine naturelle, de couleur variant du jaune au noir, d'une densité et d'une viscosité variable. Figurent également dans cette rubrique les condensats directement récupérés sur les sites d'exploitation des hydrocarbures gazeux (dans les installations prévues pour la séparation des phases liquide et gazeuse), le pétrole brut synthétique, les huiles minérales brutes extraites des roches bitumineuses telles que schistes, sables asphaltiques et les huiles issues de la liquéfaction du charbon.

– Liquides de gaz naturel (LGN): Hydrocarbures liquides ou liquéfiés produits lors de la fabrication, de la purification et de la stabilisation du gaz naturel. Les liquides de gaz naturel comprennent l'éthane, le propane, le butane, le pentane, l'essence naturelle et les condensats d'usine, sans que la liste soit limitative.

– Essence auto : Hydrocarbure léger utilisé dans les moteurs à combustion interne, tels que ceux des véhicules à moteur, à l'exception des aéronefs. Sa température de distillation se situe entre 35°C et 200°C et il est traité de façon à atteindre un indice d'octane suffisamment élevé, généralement entre 80 et 100 IOR. Le traitement peut consister en reformage, mélange avec une fraction aromatique, ou adjonction de benzol ou d'autres additifs (tels que du plomb tétraéthyle).

– Carburéacteurs: Comprennent les carburéacteurs du type essence et les carburéacteurs du type kérosène. Carburéacteurs du type essence: Comprennent tous les hydrocarbures légers utilisés dans les turboréacteurs d'aviation. Leur

Also included are middle distillates intended for the petrochemical industry. Gas-diesel oils are used as a fuel for internal combustion in diesel engines, as a burner fuel in heating installations, such as furnaces, and for enriching water gas to increase its luminosity. Other names for this product are diesel fuel, diesel oil and gas oil.

– Residual fuel oil: Heavy oil that makes up the distillation residue. It comprises all fuels (including those obtained by blending) with a kinematic viscosity above 27.5 cSt at 38°C. Its flash point is always above 50°C and its specific gravity is higher than 0.90. It is commonly used by ships and industrial large-scale heating installations as a fuel in furnaces or boilers.

– Liquefied petroleum gas (LPG): Hydrocarbons which are gaseous under conditions of normal temperature and pressure but are liquefied by compression or cooling to facilitate storage, handling and transportation. It comprises propane, butane, or a combination of the two. Also included is ethane from petroleum refineries or natural gas producers' separation and stabilization plants.

– Natural gas: Gases consisting mainly of methane occurring naturally in underground deposits. It includes both non associated gas (originating from fields producing only hydrocarbons in gaseous form) and associated gas (originating from fields producing both liquid and gaseous hydrocarbons), as well as methane recovered from coal mines and sewage gas. Production of natural gas refers to dry marketable production, measured after purification and extraction of natural gas liquids and sulphur. Extraction losses and the amounts that have been re-injected, flared, and vented are excluded from the data on production.

– Electricity production refers to gross production, which includes the consumption by station auxiliaries and any losses in the transformers that are considered integral parts of the station. Included also is total electric energy produced by pumping installations without deduction of electric energy absorbed by pumping.

température de distillation se situe entre 100°C et 250°C et donne au moins 20% en volume de distillat à 143°C. Ils sont obtenus par mélange de pétrole lampant et d'essence ou de naphta de façon que la teneur en composés aromatiques ne dépasse pas 25% en volume. Des additifs y sont ajoutés afin d'abaisser le point de congélation à -58°C ou au-dessous, et de maintenir la tension de vapeur Reid entre 0,14 et 0,21 kg/cm2. Carburéacteurs du type kerosene: Huiles moyennement visqueuses utilisées dans les turboréacteurs d'aviation, ayant les mêmes caractéristiques de distillation et le même point d'éclair que le pétrole lampant et une teneur en composés aromatiques ne dépassant pas 20% en volume. Elles sont traitées de façon à atteindre une viscosité cinématique de moins de 15 cSt à -34°C et un point de congélation inférieur à -50°C.

– Gazole/carburant diesel (mazout distillé):Huiles lourdes dont la température de distillation se situe entre 200°C et 380°C, mais qui donnent moins de 65% en volume de distillat à 250°C (y compris les pertes) et 85% ou davantage à 350°C. Leur point d'éclair est toujours supérieur à 50°C et leur densité supérieure à 0,82. Les huiles lourdes obtenues par mélange sont classées dans la même catégorie que les gazoles à condition que leur viscosité cinématique ne dépasse pas 27,5 cSt à 38°C. Sont compris dans cette rubrique les distillats moyens destinés à l'industrie pétrochimique. Les gazoles servent de carburant pour la combustion interne dans les moteurs diesel, de combustible dans les installations de chauffage telles que les chaudières, et d'additifs destinés à augmenter la luminosité de la flamme du gaz à l'eau. Ce produit est aussi connu sous les appellations de gazole ou gasoil et carburant ou combustible diesel.

– Gaz de pétrole liquéfiés (GPL): Hydrocarbures qui sont à l'état gazeux dans des conditions de température et de pression normales mais sont liquéfiés par compression ou refroidissement pour en faciliter l'entreposage, la manipulation et le transport. Dans cette rubrique figurent le propane et le butane ou un mélange de ces deux hydrocarbures. Est également inclus l'éthane produit dans les raffineries ou dans les installations de séparation et de stabilisation des producteurs de gaz naturel.

– Gaz naturel: gaz constitué essentiellement de méthane, extraits de gisements naturels souterrains. Il peut s'agir aussi bien de gaz non associé (provenant de gisements qui produisent uniquement des hydrocarbures gazeux) que de gaz associé (provenant de gisements qui produisent à la fois des hydrocarbures liquides et gazeux) ou de méthane récupéré dans les mines de charbon et le gaz de gadoues. La production de gaz naturel se rapporte à la production de gaz commercialisable sec, mesurée après purification et extraction des condensats de gaz naturel et du soufre. Les quantités réinjectées, brûlées à la torchère ou éventées et les pertes d'extraction sont exclues des données sur la production.

– La production d'électricité se rapporte à la production brute, qui comprend la consommation des équipements

auxiliaires des centrales et les pertes au niveau des transformateurs considérés comme faisant partie intégrante de ces centrales, ainsi que la quantité totale d'énergie électrique produite par les installations de pompage sans déductions de l'énergie électrique absorbée par ces dernières.

51 Land

As of 2008, thousand hectares

Terres

En 2008, milliers d'hectares

Country or area Pays ou zone	Area – Superficie: Total land Superficie totale	Area – Superficie: Arable land Terres arables	Area – Superficie: Permanent crops Cultures permanentes	Area – Superficie: Forest cover Superficie forestière	Net change from 2000 to 2008 / Variation nette de 2000 à 2008: Arable land Terres arables	Net change from 2000 to 2008 / Variation nette de 2000 à 2008: Permanent crops Cultures permanentes	Net change from 2000 to 2008 / Variation nette de 2000 à 2008: Forest cover Superficie forestière
World [1] Monde [1]	**13 003 469**	**1 380 515**	**146 242**	**4 044 221**	**-1 824**	**14 170**	**-40 351**
Africa [1] Afrique [1]	**2 964 388**	**222 802**	**28 063**	**681 239**	**26 067**	**3 097**	-27 326
Americas [1] Amériques [1]	**3 889 231**	**365 430**	**29 844**	**1 576 868**	**1 751**	**1 313**	-32 355
Asia [1] Asie [1]	**3 093 791**	**470 277**	**70 977**	**589 126**	**-14 929**	**10 504**	18 962
Europe [1] Europe [1]	**2 207 405**	**276 987**	**15 859**	**1 003 460**	**-10 454**	**-869**	5 221
Oceania [1] Océanie [1]	**848 655**	**45 020**	**1 499**	**193 528**	**-4 259**	**125**	-4 853
Afghanistan Afghanistan	65 223[2]	7 794	116	1 350[2]	111	46	0[2]
Albania Albanie	2 740	610	87	779[2]	32	-34	10[2]
Algeria Algérie	238 174	7 489	935	1 510[2]	-173	405	-69[2]
American Samoa Samoa américaines	20	2[2]	3[2]	18[2]	0[2]	0[2]	0[2]
Andorra Andorre	47	1[2]	...	16[2]	0[2]	...	0[2]
Angola Angola	124 670	3 400[2]	290[2]	58 730[2]	400[2]	-10[2]	-998[2]
Anguilla Anguilla	9	...	...	6[2]	...	...	0[2]
Antigua and Barbuda Antigua-et-Barbuda	44	8[2]	1[2]	10[2]	0[2]	0[2]	0[2]
Argentina [2] Argentine [2]	273 669	32 000	1 000	29 880	4 100	0	-1 981
Armenia Arménie	2 848	449	54	270[2]	-1	16	-34[2]
Aruba Aruba	18	2[2]	...	0[2]	0[2]	...	0[2]
Australia Australie	768 230	44 024[2]	350[2]	151 148[2]	-3 280[2]	54[2]	-3 772[2]
Austria Autriche	8 245	1 374	66	3 877	-25	-5	39
Azerbaijan Azerbaïdjan	8 263	1 860	228	936[2]	35	-9	0[2]
Bahamas [2] Bahamas [2]	1 001	7	4	515	0	0	0
Bahrain Bahreïn	76	1[2]	3[2]	0[2]	-1[2]	0[2]	0[2]
Bangladesh [2] Bangladesh [2]	13 017	7 900	800	1 447	-164	380	-21
Barbados Barbade	43	16[2]	1[2]	8[2]	0[2]	0[2]	0[2]
Belarus Bélarus	20 290[2]	5 516	121	8 552[2]	-617	-3	279[2]

51 Land (continued)

As of 2008, thousand hectares

Terres (suite)

En 2008, milliers d'hectares

Country or area Pays ou zone	Area – Superficie: Total land Superficie totale	Arable land Terres arables	Permanent crops Cultures permanentes	Forest cover Superficie forestière	Net change from 2000 to 2008 / Variation nette de 2000 à 2008: Arable land Terres arables	Permanent crops Cultures permanentes	Forest cover Superficie forestière
Belgium Belgique	3 028	845	23	676[2]	-17	2	8[2]
Belize[2] Belize[2]	2 281	70	32	1 412	6	-3	-77
Benin[2] Bénin[2]	11 062	2 550	295	4 661	170	30	-400
Bermuda Bermudes	5	1	...	1[2]	0	...	0[2]
Bhutan Bhoutan	3 839	128[2]	28[2]	3 227[2]	-2[2]	4[2]	86[2]
Bolivia (Plurinational State of) Bolivie (État plurinational de)	108 330	3 600[2]	219[2]	57 811[2]	600[2]	51[2]	-2 280[2]
Bosnia and Herzegovina Bosnie-Herzégovine	5 120	1 008	90	2 185[2]	8	-10	0[2]
Botswana[2] Botswana[2]	56 673	250	2	11 588	-100	1	-947
Brazil[2] Brésil[2]	845 942	61 000	7 500	523 911	3 300	0	-22 032
British Virgin Islands Iles Vierges britanniques	15	1[2]	1[2]	4[2]	0[2]	0[2]	0[2]
Brunei Darussalam[2] Brunéi Darussalam[2]	527	3	5	384	1	1	-13
Bulgaria Bulgarie	10 861[2]	3 061	184	3 817[2]	-465	-68	442[2]
Burkina Faso[2] Burkina Faso[2]	27 360	6 300	60	5 769	2 260	0	-479
Burundi[2] Burundi[2]	2 568	900	390	176	-60	30	-22
Cambodia[2] Cambodge[2]	17 652	3 900	155	10 349	200	15	-1 197
Cameroon Cameroun	47 271	5 963	1 200[2]	20 356[2]	3	0[2]	-1 760[2]
Canada[3] Canada[3]	909 351	45 100[2]	7 050[2]	310 134[2]	-710[2]	682[2]	0[2]
Cape Verde Cap-Vert	403	65[2]	3[2]	84[2]	21[2]	1[2]	2[2]
Cayman Islands Iles Caïmanes	24	0[2]	1[2]	13[2]	0[2]	0[2]	0[2]
Central African Rep. Rép. centrafricaine	62 298	1 930[2]	80[2]	22 665[2]	0[2]	-14[2]	-238[2]
Chad[2] Tchad[2]	125 920	4 300	30	11 683	780	0	-634
Channel Islands Iles Anglo-Normandes	19	4[2]	...	1[2]	0[2]	...	0[2]
Chile Chili	74 353	1 265[2]	457[2]	16 156[2]	-485[2]	97[2]	322[2]
China[2] Chine[2]	932 749[4]	108 642[4]	13 901[4]	201 334[4]	-12 374[4]	2 715[4]	24 333
Colombia Colombie	110 950	1 830[2]	1 631[2]	60 701[2]	-988[2]	-96[2]	-808[2]
Comoros Comores	186	80[2]	55[2]	4[2]	0[2]	5[2]	-4[2]

51 Land *(continued)*

As of 2008, thousand hectares

Terres *(suite)*

En 2008, milliers d'hectares

Country or area Pays ou zone	Area – Superficie Total land Superficie totale	Arable land Terres arables	Permanent crops Cultures permanentes	Forest cover Superficie forestière	Net change from 2000 to 2008 Variation nette de 2000 à 2008 Arable land Terres arables	Permanent crops Cultures permanentes	Forest cover Superficie forestière
Congo [2] Congo [2]	34 150	490	52	22 435	0	2	-121
Cook Islands Iles Cook	24	2[2]	1[2]	16[2]	-1[2]	-2[2]	0[2]
Costa Rica [2] Costa Rica [2]	5 106	200	300	2 559	-10	20	183
Côte d'Ivoire [2] Côte d'Ivoire [2]	31 800	2 800	4 250	10 404	0	450	76
Croatia [5] Croatie [5]	5 596	860	86	1 913[2]	18	17	28[2]
Cuba [2] Cuba [2]	10 644	3 570	400	2 801	66	-150	366
Cyprus [6] Chypre [6]	924	82	32	173[2]	-16	-10	1[2]
Czech Republic République tchèque	7 725	3 026	239	2 653	-56	3	16
Dem. Rep. of the Congo [2] Rép. dém. du Congo [2]	226 705	6 700	750	154 758	0	-50	-2 491
Denmark Danemark	4 243	2 400	7	540[2]	119	-1	54[2]
Djibouti [2] Djibouti [2]	2 318	1	...	6	0	...	0
Dominica Dominique	75	5[2]	16[2]	45[2]	0[2]	2[2]	-2[2]
Dominican Republic [2] Rép. dominicaine [2]	4 832	800	500	1 972	-18	0	596
Ecuador Equateur	24 836[2]	1 236	1 264	10 260[2]	-380	-99	-1 581[2]
Egypt Egypte	99 545[2]	2 773	769	69[2]	-28	279	10[2]
El Salvador [2] El Salvador [2]	2 072	685	230	296	35	-20	-36
Equatorial Guinea Guinée équatoriale	2 805	131[2]	75[2]	1 650[2]	1[2]	-25[2]	-93[2]
Eritrea [2] Erythrée [2]	10 100	670	2	1 541	110	-1	-35
Estonia Estonie	4 239	598	8	2 231[2]	-245	-4	-12[2]
Ethiopia Ethiopie	100 000[2]	13 606	907	12 578[2]	3 606	245	-1 127[2]
Faeroe Islands Iles Féroé	140	3[2]	...	0[2]	0[2]	...	0[2]
Falkland Is. (Malvinas) Iles Falkland (Malvinas)	1 217	...	...	0[2]	...	...	0[2]
Fiji [2] Fidji [2]	1 827	170	83	1 007	0	0	27
Finland Finlande	30 390	2 256	8	22 157[2]	73	-2	-302[2]
France [2,7] France [2,7]	54 766	18 260	1 071	15 858	-180	-71	505
French Guiana [2] Guyane française [2]	8 220	13	4	8 089	1	0	-29

51 Land *(continued)*

As of 2008, thousand hectares

Terres *(suite)*

En 2008, milliers d'hectares

Country or area Pays ou zone	Area – Superficie				Net change from 2000 to 2008 Variation nette de 2000 à 2008		
	Total land Superficie totale	Arable land Terres arables	Permanent crops Cultures permanentes	Forest cover Superficie forestière	Arable land Terres arables	Permanent crops Cultures permanentes	Forest cover Superficie forestière
French Polynesia [2] Polynésie française [2]	366	3	22	145	0	2	40
Gabon Gabon	25 767	325[2]	150[2]	22 000[2]	0[2]	-20[2]	0[2]
Gambia [2] Gambie [2]	1 000	390	5	476	110	0	15
Georgia Géorgie	6 949	468	115	2 747[2]	-325	-154	-21[2]
Germany Allemagne	34 863	11 933	200	11 076[2]	129	-16	0[2]
Ghana [2] Ghana [2]	22 754	4 400	2 850	5 171	450	700	-923
Gibraltar Gibraltar	1	...	...	0[2]	...	...	0[2]
Greece [2] Grèce [2]	12 890	2 100	1 125	3 843	-641	12	242
Greenland Groenland	41 045	...	...	0[2]	...	...	0[2]
Grenada Grenade	34	2[2]	9[2]	17[2]	1[2]	-1[2]	0[2]
Guadeloupe Guadeloupe	169	21	3	65[2]	2	-3	-2[2]
Guam Guam	54	1[2]	10[2]	26[2]	-1[2]	0[2]	0[2]
Guatemala Guatemala	10 716	1 325	943	3 769[2]	-70	373	-439[2]
Guinea [2] Guinée [2]	24 572	2 400	690	6 616	1 030	65	-288
Guinea-Bissau [2] Guinée-Bissau [2]	2 812	300	250	2 042	0	2	-78
Guyana [2] Guyana [2]	19 685	420	25	15 205	-30	-3	0
Haiti [2] Haïti [2]	2 756	1 000	300	103	100	-20	-6
Honduras [2] Honduras [2]	11 189	1 018	410	5 432	-50	51	-960
Hungary Hongrie	8 961	4 573	195	2 011[2]	-29	-6	104[2]
Iceland Islande	10 025	7	...	28[2]	0	...	10[2]
India [2] Inde [2]	297 319	158 145	11 175	68 144	-4 572	1 975	2 754
Indonesia Indonésie	181 157	22 000[2]	15 100[2]	95 802[2]	1 500[2]	2 000[2]	-3 607[2]
Iran (Islamic Rep. of) Iran (Rép. islamique d')	162 855	17 037	1 733	11 075	2 113	373	0
Iraq [2] Iraq [2]	43 737	5 200	250	825	200	-50	7
Ireland Irlande	6 889	1 101	3	721[2]	24	1	86[2]
Isle of Man Ile de Man	57	5[2]	...	3[2]	-4[2]	...	0[2]

Land *(continued)*

As of 2008, thousand hectares

Terres *(suite)*

En 2008, milliers d'hectares

Country or area Pays ou zone	Area – Superficie: Total land Superficie totale	Area – Superficie: Arable land Terres arables	Area – Superficie: Permanent crops Cultures permanentes	Area – Superficie: Forest cover Superficie forestière	Net change from 2000 to 2008 / Variation nette de 2000 à 2008: Arable land Terres arables	Net change from 2000 to 2008 / Variation nette de 2000 à 2008: Permanent crops Cultures permanentes	Net change from 2000 to 2008 / Variation nette de 2000 à 2008: Forest cover Superficie forestière
Israel[8] Israël[8]	2 164[2]	302[2]	77	154[2]	-36[2]	-9	1[2]
Italy Italie	29 414[2]	7 132[2]	2 636	8 993[2]	-1 347[2]	-169	624[2]
Jamaica[2] Jamaïque[2]	1 083	125	110	338	-15	0	-3
Japan Japon	36 450[2]	4 308	320	24 961[2]	-166	-36	85[2]
Jordan Jordanie	8 824	150	81	98[2]	-41	-7	0[2]
Kazakhstan[2] Kazakhstan[2]	269 970	22 700	100	3 320	1 165	-36	-45
Kenya[2] Kenya[2]	56 914	5 300	500	3 489	409	20	-93
Kiribati[2] Kiribati[2]	81	2	32	12	0	0	0
Korea, Dem. P. R.[2] Corée, R. p. dém. de[2]	12 041	2 700	200	5 919	100	0	-1 014
Korea, Republic of Corée, République de	9 692[2]	1 553[2]	194	6 235[2]	-165[2]	-6	-53[2]
Kuwait Koweït	1 782	11[2]	4[2]	6[2]	1[2]	2[2]	1[2]
Kyrgyzstan Kirghizistan	19 180[2]	1 280	73	920[2]	-77	6	62[2]
Lao People's Dem. Rep. Rép. dém. pop. lao	23 080	1 250[2]	95[2]	15 907[2]	373[2]	14[2]	-625[2]
Latvia Lettonie	6 220[9]	1 170[9]	7[9]	3 331[2,9]	200[9]	-5[9]	90[2]
Lebanon[2] Liban[2]	1 023	144	142	137	15	1	6
Lesotho Lesotho	3 036	355[2]	4[2]	44[2]	25[2]	0[2]	2[2]
Liberia[2] Libéria[2]	9 632	400	218	4 389	20	8	-240
Libyan Arab Jamah. Jamah. arabe libyenne	175 954	1 750[2]	300[2]	217[2]	-65[2]	-35[2]	0[2]
Liechtenstein Liechtenstein	16	4[2]	...	7[2]	0[2]	...	0[2]
Lithuania Lituanie	6 268	1 862	27	2 144[2]	-1 017	-16	124[2]
Luxembourg Luxembourg	259	62	1	87[2]	0	0	0[2]
Madagascar[2] Madagascar[2]	58 154	2 950	600	12 667	50	0	-455
Malawi[2] Malawi[2]	9 408	3 500	122	3 303	750	2	-264
Malaysia[2] Malaisie[2]	32 855	1 800	5 785	20 630	-20	0	-961
Maldives Maldives	30	4[2]	4[2]	1[2]	0[2]	-1[2]	0[2]
Mali[2] Mali[2]	122 019	4 850	130	12 648	261	45	-633

51 Land (continued)

As of 2008, thousand hectares

Terres (suite)

En 2008, milliers d'hectares

Country or area Pays ou zone	Area – Superficie Total land Superficie totale	Arable land Terres arables	Permanent crops Cultures permanentes	Forest cover Superficie forestière	Net change from 2000 to 2008 / Variation nette de 2000 à 2008 Arable land Terres arables	Permanent crops Cultures permanentes	Forest cover Superficie forestière
Malta Malte	32	9[2]	2[2]	0[2]	1[2]	1[2]	0[2]
Marshall Islands Iles Marshall	18	2[2]	8[2]	13[2]	1[2]	0[2]	0[2]
Martinique Martinique	106[2]	11	6	49[2]	0	-4	0[2]
Mauritania Mauritanie	103 070	400[2]	11[2]	252[2]	-88[2]	-1[2]	-65[2]
Mauritius Maurice	203	87[2]	4[2]	35[2]	-13[2]	0[2]	-4[2]
Mayotte Mayotte	38	7[2]	13[2]	14[2]	0[2]	0[2]	-2[2]
Mexico[2] Mexique[2]	194 395	24 800	2 700	65 112	-300	400	-1 639
Micronesia (Fed. States of) Micronésie (Etats féd. de)	70	3[2]	17[2]	64[2]	0[2]	0[2]	0[2]
Mongolia[2] Mongolie[2]	155 356	850	2	11 062	-324	0	-655
Montenegro Monténégro	1 345[2]	173	16	543[2]	-1[10]	0[10]	0[2,10]
Montserrat Montserrat	10	2[2]	...	3[2]	0[2]	...	0[2]
Morocco Maroc	44 630[2]	8 055	926	5 111[2]	-712	41	94[2]
Mozambique Mozambique	78 638	4 500[2]	250[2]	39 445[2]	600[2]	0[2]	-1 743[2]
Myanmar[2] Myanmar[2]	65 352	10 600	1 100	32 392	691	511	-2 476
Namibia[2] Namibie[2]	82 329	800	8	7 438	-16	4	-594
Nauru Nauru	2	...	^0[2]	0[2]	...	0[2]	0[2]
Nepal[11] Népal[11]	14 335	2 357	118	3 636[2]	3	13	-264[2]
Netherlands Pays-Bas	3 376	1 067	35	365[2]	157	1	5[2]
Netherlands Antilles Antilles néerlandaises	80	8[2]	...	1[2]	0[2]	...	0[2]
New Caledonia[2] Nouvelle-Calédonie[2]	1 828	8	5	839	2	1	0
New Zealand Nouvelle-Zélande	26 331	453	69	8 286[2]	-1 047	19	20
Nicaragua Nicaragua	12 034	1 900[2]	230[2]	3 254[2]	-17[2]	-4[2]	-560[2]
Niger[2] Niger[2]	126 670	14 493	43	1 229	513	23	-99
Nigeria[2] Nigéria[2]	91 077	37 500	3 000	9 860	7 500	350	-3 277
Niue Nioué	26	1[2]	3[2]	19[2]	0[2]	0[2]	-1[2]
Norfolk Island Ile Norfolk	4	...	...	0[2]	...	...	0[2]

51 Land *(continued)*

As of 2008, thousand hectares

Terres *(suite)*

En 2008, milliers d'hectares

Country or area Pays ou zone	Area – Superficie Total land Superficie totale	Arable land Terres arables	Permanent crops Cultures permanentes	Forest cover Superficie forestière	Net change from 2000 to 2008 Variation nette de 2000 à 2008 Arable land Terres arables	Permanent crops Cultures permanentes	Forest cover Superficie forestière
Northern Mariana Islands Iles Mariannes du Nord	46	1[2]	1[2]	31[2]	0[2]	0[2]	-1[2]
Norway Norvège	30 547	845	5	9 912[2]	-34	0	611[2]
Occupied Palestinian Terr. Terr. palestinien occupé	602	101[2]	117	9[2]	-1[2]	-3	0[2]
Oman Oman	30 950	55[2]	39[2]	2[2]	17[2]	-3[2]	0
Pakistan Pakistan	77 088	20 347[2]	853	1 773[2]	-945[2]	195	-343[2]
Palau[2] Palaos[2]	46	1	2	40	0	0	1
Panama[2] Panama[2]	7 434	548	147	3 275	0	0	-94
Papua New Guinea[2] Papouasie-Nvl-Guinée[2]	45 286	270	650	29 010	65	30	-1 123
Paraguay[2] Paraguay[2]	39 730	4 200	100	17 939	1 180	10	-1 429
Peru[2] Pérou[2]	128 000	3 650	790	68 292	-50	205	-921
Philippines[2] Philippines[2]	29 817	5 300	5 000	7 555	266	350	438
Pitcairn Pitcairn	5	...	...	4[2]	...	...	0[2]
Poland Pologne	30 422	12 571	399	9 282[2]	-1 422	62	223[2]
Portugal[2] Portugal[2]	9 147	1 050	585	3 448	-590	-115	28
Puerto Rico[2] Porto Rico[2]	887	60	37	534	0	-5	70
Qatar Qatar	1 159	13[2]	3[2]	0[2]	0[2]	0[2]	0[2]
Republic of Moldova République de Moldova	3 289	1 822	303	377[2]	-5	-32	53[2]
Réunion Réunion	250	33	3	87[2]	-4	-1	0[2]
Romania Roumanie	22 990	8 721	375	6 500[2]	-660	-152	134[2]
Russian Federation Fédération de Russie	1 637 687	121 649	1 793	808 970[2]	-2 725	-71	-299[2]
Rwanda[2] Rwanda[2]	2 467	1 290	280	415	390	30	71
Saint Helena[2,12] Sainte-Hélène[2,12]	39	4	...	2	0	...	0
Saint Kitts and Nevis Saint-Kitts-et-Nevis	26	4	0[2]	11[2]	-3	0[2]	0[2]
Saint Lucia[2] Sainte-Lucie[2]	61	3	7	47	1	-5	0
Saint Pierre and Miquelon[2] Saint-Pierre-et-Miquelon[2]	23	3	...	3	0	...	0
Saint Vincent-Grenadines Saint Vincent-Grenadines	39	5[2]	3[2]	27[2]	0[2]	0[2]	1[2]

Country or area Pays ou zone	Area – Superficie				Net change from 2000 to 2008 Variation nette de 2000 à 2008		
	Total land Superficie totale	Arable land Terres arables	Permanent crops Cultures permanentes	Forest cover Superficie forestière	Arable land Terres arables	Permanent crops Cultures permanentes	Forest cover Superficie forestière
Samoa[2] Samoa[2]	283	25	38	171	0	3	0
San Marino Saint-Marin	6	1[2]	...	0[2]	0[2]	...	0[2]
Sao Tome and Principe[2] Sao Tomé-et-Principe[2]	96	9	45	27	3	0	0
Saudi Arabia[2] Arabie saoudite[2]	214 969	3 446	230	977	-146	37	0
Senegal[2] Sénégal[2]	19 253	3 500	54	8 553	450	-1	-345
Serbia Serbie	8 836[2]	3 302	300	2 618[2]	-16[10]	0[10]	95[2,10]
Seychelles[2] Seychelles[2]	46	1	3	41	0	-1	0
Sierra Leone[2] Sierra Leone[2]	7 162	1 795	135	2 765	1 305	0	-157
Singapore[2] Singapour[2]	70	1	^0	2	-1	0	0
Slovakia Slovaquie	4 810	1 382	23	1 933[2]	-146	-24	12[2]
Slovenia Slovénie	2 014	181	26	1 249[2]	8	-5	16[2]
Solomon Islands[2] Iles Salomon[2]	2 799	16	60	2 224	2	5	-44
Somalia[2] Somalie[2]	62 734	1 000	27	6 901	-43	3	-614
South Africa[2] Afrique du Sud[2]	121 447	14 500	950	9 241	-253	-9	0
Spain[2] Espagne[2]	49 911	12 500	4 800	17 821	-900	-104	833
Sri Lanka Sri Lanka	6 271	1 250[2]	950[2]	1 889[2]	335[2]	-45[2]	-193[2]
Sudan Soudan	237 600[2]	20 698	208	70 057[2]	4 465	91	-434[2]
Suriname Suriname	15 600	49	7[2]	14 765[2]	-8	-3[2]	-11[2]
Swaziland[2] Swaziland[2]	1 720	178	14	554	0	1	36
Sweden Suède	41 034	2 626	9[2]	28 203[2]	-77	6[2]	814[2]
Switzerland Suisse	4 000[2]	408	23	1 231[2]	-5	-1	37[2]
Syrian Arab Republic Rép. arabe syrienne	18 364	4 699	967	479[2]	157	157	47[2]
Tajikistan[2] Tadjikistan[2]	13 996	738	133	410	-46	31	0
Thailand[2] Thaïlande[2]	51 089	15 200	3 650	18 942	-454	270	-62
TFYR of Macedonia L'ex-R.Y. Macédoine	2 523	432	36	989[2]	-123	-8	31[2]
Timor-Leste[2] Timor-Leste[2]	1 487	160	65	764	40	-2	-90

51 Land *(continued)*

As of 2008, thousand hectares

Terres *(suite)*

En 2008, milliers d'hectares

Country or area Pays ou zone	Area – Superficie Total land Superficie totale	Arable land Terres arables	Permanent crops Cultures permanentes	Forest cover Superficie forestière	Net change from 2000 to 2008 Variation nette de 2000 à 2008 Arable land Terres arables	Permanent crops Cultures permanentes	Forest cover Superficie forestière
Togo[2] Togo[2]	5 439	2 460	170	327	-50	50	-159
Tokelau Tokélaou	1	...	1[2]	0[2]	...	0[2]	0[2]
Tonga Tonga	72	15[2]	12[2]	9[2]	0[2]	1[2]	0[2]
Trinidad and Tobago Trinité-et-Tobago	513	25[2]	22[2]	228[2]	-10[2]	-3[2]	-6[2]
Tunisia Tunisie	15 536	2 835	2 206	973[2]	-29	80	136[2]
Turkey Turquie	76 963	21 555	2 950	11 096[2]	-2 271	397	950[2]
Turkmenistan[2] Turkménistan[2]	46 993	1 850	68	4 127	230	3	0
Turks and Caicos Islands Iles Turques et Caïques	95	1[2]	...	34[2]	0[2]	...	0[2]
Tuvalu Tuvalu	3	...	2[2]	1[2]	...	0[2]	0[2]
Uganda[2] Ouganda[2]	19 710	5 650	2 250	3 164	590	150	-705
Ukraine Ukraine	57 932	32 474	900	9 653[2]	-90	-32	143[2]
United Arab Emirates[2] Emirats arabes unis[2]	8 360	65	200	315	5	13	5
United Kingdom Royaume-Uni	24 193	6 005	46	2 867[2]	129	-6	74[2]
United Rep. of Tanzania Rép.-Unie de Tanzanie	88 580	9 600[2]	1 350[2]	34 235[2]	800[2]	150[2]	-3 227[2]
United States Etats-Unis	914 742	170 500[2]	2 700[2]	303 256[2]	-4 868[2]	0[2]	3 061[2]
United States Virgin Is. Iles Vierges américaines	35	1[2]	1[2]	21[2]	-1[2]	0[2]	-1[2]
Uruguay Uruguay	17 502	1 640[2]	33	1 654[2]	267[2]	-9	242[2]
Uzbekistan[2] Ouzbékistan[2]	42 540	4 300	320	3 283	-175	-30	71
Vanuatu[2] Vanuatu[2]	1 219	20	125	440	0	12	0
Venezuela (Boliv. Rep. of)[2] Venezuela (Rép. boliv. du)[2]	88 205	2 700	650	46 850	105	-150	-2 301
Viet Nam[2] Viet Nam[2]	31 007	6 300	3 115	13 509	100	1 177	1 784
Wallis and Futuna Islands Iles Wallis et Futuna	14	1[2]	5[2]	6[2]	0[2]	0[2]	0[2]
Western Sahara Sahara occidental	26 600	4[2]	...	707[2]	-1[2]	...	0[2]
Yemen Yémen	52 797[2]	1 279[2]	327	549[2]	-266[2]	203	0[2]
Zambia[2] Zambie[2]	74 339	2 355	29	49 801	130	2	-1 333
Zimbabwe[2] Zimbabwe[2]	38 685	3 730	120	16 278	500	0	-2 616

Source:
Food and Agriculture Organization of the United Nations (FAO), Rome, FAOSTAT data, last accessed September 2010.

1 May include official, semi-official or estimated data.
2 FAO estimate.
3 Data relating to "Permanent Crops" is largely the area on farms that is covered by "Forest and Woodland": whereas, the area used to cultivate fruit and fibre crops, which is less than one percent of the land in crops is included in the "Arable Land" category.
4 For statistical purposes, the data for China do not include those for the Hong Kong Special Administrative Region (Hong Kong SAR), Macao Special Administrative Region (Macao SAR) and Taiwan Province of China.
5 Starting in 1996 the "Arable land" figures exclude non-cultivated arable land; the "Permanent meadows and pastures" figures exclude state-owned land not currently used for agricultural production. Source: "Statistical yearbook of the Republic of Croatia, 2006": Central Bureau of Statistics, Croatia.
6 As a result of the present situation in Cyprus, data refer to the government controlled area only, except for total country area where data refer to all Cyprus.
7 Data exclude the overseas departments (French Guiana, Guadeloupe, Martinique and Réunion).
8 Data relating to "Country area" and "Land area" include the Golan Heights.
9 Starting in 1995, land use statistics have been re-calculated by excluding the unutilized agricultural area.
10 Net change from 2006 to 2008.
11 Data on Agricultural area irrigated and data on Arable land and Permanent crops refer to agricultural holdings operated by the households. The agricultural activities undertaken by governmental organizations, business, etc. are excluded.
12 Data for Saint Helena include those for Ascension and Tristan da Cunha.

Source :
Organisation des Nations Unies pour l'alimentation et l'agriculture (FAO), Rome, données FAOSTAT, dernier accès septembre 2010.

1 Les données peuvent être officielles, semi-officielles ou estimatives.
2 Estimation de la FAO.
3 Les données relatives aux « Cultures permanentes » représentent la superficie des terres des exploitations agricoles couvertes par « Superficie forestière », tandis que la superficie des terres utilisées pour la culture des fruits et des plantes textiles, qui représente moins de un pour cent des terres cultivées est comprise dans « Terres arables ».
4 Pour la présentation des statistiques, les données pour la Chine ne comprennent pas la Région Administrative Spéciale de Hong Kong (Hong Kong RAS), la Région Administrative Spéciale de Macao (Macao RAS) et la province de Taiwan.
5 Depuis 1996, les chiffres relatifs aux « Terres arables » ne concernent pas les terres arables non cultivées; les « Prairies et pâturages permanents » ne comprennent pas les terres appartenant à l'État qui ne sont pas utilisées pour la production agricole. Source : Annuaire statistique de la République de Croatie pour 2006, Bureau central de la statistique de la Croatie.
6 Étant donné la situation actuelle à Chypre, les données portent uniquement sur les terres contrôlées par le Gouvernement, sauf la superficie totale du pays qui correspond à la totalité de Chypre.
7 Les données ne concernent pas les départements d'outre-mer (Guyane française, Guadeloupe, Martinique et Réunion).
8 Données par pays et par territoire, comprennent les hauteurs du Golan.
9 Depuis 1995, les statistiques de l'utilisation des sols sont recalculées en excluant la superficie agricole non exploitée.
10 Variation nette de 2006 à 2008.
11 Les données concernant la « Superficie agricole irriguée » et celles concernant les « Terres arables » et les « Cultures permanentes » concernent les exploitations agricoles gérées par les ménages. Les activités agricoles des organisations gouvernementales, des entreprises privées, etc. sont exclues.
12 Les données concernant Sainte-Hélène comprennent celles relatives à Ascension et à Tristan da Cunha.

52

CO_2 emission estimates

From fossil fuel combustion, cement production and gas flared (thousand metric tons of carbon dioxide)

Estimation des émissions de CO_2

Dues à la combustion de combustibles fossiles, à la production de ciment et au gaz brûlés à la torchère (milliers de tonnes de dioxyde de carbone)

Country or area Pays ou zone	1998	1999	2000	2001	2002	2003	2004	2005	2006	2007
Afghanistan Afghanistan	1 056	832	781	645	359	583	704	700	697	715
Albania Albanie	1 753	2 992	3 029	3 231	3 751	4 169	5 057	4 492	4 184	4 243
Algeria Algérie	107 080	117 252	116 864	113 761	121 004	122 052	121 953	138 855	133 530	140 120
Andorra Andorre	484	513	524	524	532	535	565	576	546	539
Angola Angola	7 308	9 156	9 542	9 732	12 666	8 628	18 023	19 772	20 689	24 763
Anguilla Anguilla	26	26	33	37	37	40	44	51	51	51
Antigua and Barbuda Antigua-et-Barbuda	334	348	345	345	363	389	407	411	425	436
Argentina Argentine	137 674	145 488	141 077	140 472	131 407	143 211	155 451	158 440	171 597	183 728
Armenia Arménie	3 407	3 058	3 465	3 542	3 003	3 429	3 645	4 349	4 378	5 057
Aruba Aruba	1 694	1 709	2 259	2 266	2 288	2 292	2 292	2 310	2 310	2 398
Australia Australie	349 986	328 020	329 077	322 428	336 176	339 777	340 609	364 265	371 775	374 045
Austria Autriche	62 940	61 741	61 752	63 611	65 141	70 164	69 475	72 753	71 774	68 731
Azerbaijan Azerbaïdjan	31 595	29 299	30 546	29 439	30 007	31 694	33 480	35 192	35 068	31 775
Bahamas Bahamas	1 793	1 797	1 797	1 797	2 083	1 870	2 010	2 109	2 138	2 149
Bahrain Bahreïn	18 405	18 020	19 758	15 082	16 821	17 580	18 056	19 684	21 294	22 464
Bangladesh Bangladesh	24 041	25 233	27 862	32 449	33 700	35 489	37 092	40 113	41 613	43 751
Barbados Barbade	1 140	1 210	1 188	1 221	1 228	1 192	1 272	1 316	1 338	1 346
Belarus Bélarus	59 713	58 459	59 200	58 617	59 893	62 607	65 148	64 341	68 855	66 802
Belgium Belgique	119 412	116 013	115 588	115 756	107 832	115 085	111 810	107 678	107 179	103 035
Belize Belize	370	601	689	711	359	374	381	396	407	425
Benin Bénin	1 214	1 562	1 617	1 738	2 054	2 281	2 387	2 567	3 729	3 876
Bermuda Bermudes	462	495	495	495	524	510	671	444	521	513
Bhutan Bhoutan	385	385	400	414	513	466	469	565	546	579
Bolivia (Plurinational State of) Bolivie (État plurinational de)	10 326	9 769	9 520	8 830	8 346	12 530	11 712	11 463	11 408	13 190
Bosnia and Herzegovina Bosnie-Herzégovine	16 692	19 395	22 702	20 286	22 134	22 809	24 180	25 610	27 484	29 024
Botswana Botswana	3 825	3 535	4 272	4 334	4 485	4 265	4 386	4 525	4 749	4 998

52 CO_2 emission estimates *(continued)*

From fossil fuel combustion, cement production and gas flared (thousand metric tons of carbon dioxide)

Estimation des émissions de CO_2 *(suite)*

Dues à la combustion de combustibles fossiles, à la production de ciment et au gaz brûlés à la torchère (milliers de tonnes de dioxyde de carbone)

Country or area Pays ou zone	1998	1999	2000	2001	2002	2003	2004	2005	2006	2007
Brazil Brésil	314 013	322 069	330 125	339 894	335 186	324 753	341 167	349 967	352 542	368 317
British Virgin Islands Iles Vierges britanniques	59	59	59	59	66	77	84	88	99	99
Brunei Darussalam Brunéi Darussalam	5 985	4 598	6 527	6 197	5 966	5 823	6 076	5 688	5 471	7 605
Bulgaria Bulgarie	50 271	43 120	43 054	45 518	43 494	46 879	45 291	46 996	48 085	51 782
Burkina Faso Burkina Faso	895	968	1 078	1 038	1 041	1 118	1 148	1 173	1 404	1 694
Burundi Burundi	301	293	301	216	220	165	161	165	191	180
Cambodia Cambodge	2 233	2 197	2 255	2 644	2 860	3 128	3 498	3 722	4 074	4 441
Cameroon Cameroun	3 209	3 080	3 432	3 421	3 418	4 301	3 942	3 696	4 268	6 168
Canada Canada	478 881	477 869	537 403	527 131	521 832	554 663	553 926	559 837	547 241	557 340
Cape Verde Cap-Vert	154	172	187	209	246	253	268	297	308	308
Cayman Islands Iles Caïmanes	286	282	455	455	469	480	495	517	535	539
Central African Rep. Rép. centrafricaine	249	264	268	246	246	235	235	235	249	253
Chad Tchad	114	121	176	172	169	381	378	400	407	385
Chile Chili	58 987	62 225	60 095	54 019	56 072	56 409	64 066	65 430	67 983	71 705
China Chine	3 324 345	3 318 045	3 405 096	3 487 365	3 694 040	4 346 796	5 094 739	5 614 071	6 113 278	6 538 367
China, Hong Kong SAR Chine, Hong Kong RAS	39 233	42 754	40 583	37 972	36 952	40 066	38 412	40 550	38 555	39 963
China, Macao SAR Chine, Macao RAS	1 566	1 533	1 635	1 687	1 525	1 536	1 727	1 837	1 632	1 555
Colombia Colombie	65 977	56 512	57 924	56 274	55 661	57 422	53 773	59 178	61 562	63 439
Comoros Comores	73	81	84	88	92	99	103	110	121	121
Congo Congo	777	821	1 049	862	708	1 085	1 903	1 606	1 463	1 588
Cook Islands Iles Cook	22	29	29	33	29	33	55	62	66	66
Costa Rica Costa Rica	5 317	5 523	5 475	5 761	6 326	6 626	6 931	6 942	7 437	8 119
Côte d'Ivoire Côte d'Ivoire	6 912	6 267	6 791	7 726	7 286	5 460	7 664	8 166	6 883	6 384
Croatia Croatie	21 111	21 126	20 249	21 243	22 391	24 045	23 586	23 619	23 685	24 840
Cuba Cuba	24 444	25 277	26 039	25 453	26 091	25 453	24 936	25 020	26 032	27 055
Cyprus Chypre	6 641	6 755	6 850	6 846	7 022	7 748	7 334	7 503	7 789	8 199
Czech Republic République tchèque	127 857	113 200	125 950	125 147	122 316	124 425	124 623	122 808	123 648	124 964
Dem. Rep. of the Congo Rép. dém. du Congo	2 534	2 248	1 646	1 566	1 650	1 698	2 208	2 277	2 351	2 435

52 CO_2 emission estimates *(continued)*

From fossil fuel combustion, cement production and gas flared (thousand metric tons of carbon dioxide)

Estimation des émissions de CO_2 *(suite)*

Dues à la combustion de combustibles fossiles, à la production de ciment et au gaz brûlés à la torchère (milliers de tonnes de dioxyde de carbone)

Country or area Pays ou zone	1998	1999	2000	2001	2002	2003	2004	2005	2006	2007
Denmark Danemark	55 500	50 696	47 154	49 013	51 624	55 933	50 579	46 762	53 898	49 996
Djibouti Djibouti	411	444	403	385	400	407	458	473	488	488
Dominica Dominique	77	81	103	114	103	114	106	114	117	121
Dominican Republic Rép. dominicaine	18 683	18 870	20 117	20 235	21 500	21 533	19 970	19 893	20 359	20 759
Ecuador Equateur	22 229	21 272	20 942	23 447	24 690	25 948	26 234	26 344	29 288	29 989
Egypt Egypte	122 265	125 195	141 330	125 826	126 688	131 961	144 054	163 354	178 400	184 659
El Salvador El Salvador	5 812	5 699	5 743	5 948	6 040	6 381	6 179	6 293	6 461	6 700
Equatorial Guinea Guinée équatoriale	169	473	455	3 095	4 980	6 018	4 679	4 712	4 752	4 796
Eritrea Erythrée	590	620	609	634	642	722	759	733	561	579
Estonia Estonie	17 679	15 992	15 988	16 395	15 970	18 368	18 738	18 251	17 550	20 473
Ethiopia Ethiopie	5 027	5 075	5 831	4 309	4 481	4 947	5 607	5 489	6 007	6 509
Faeroe Islands Iles Féroé	664	671	656	660	667	675	675	682	689	697
Falkland Is. (Malvinas) Iles Falkland (Malvinas)	37	37	37	44	44	48	51	51	59	59
Fiji Fidji	730	832	862	1 122	858	1 657	1 889	1 635	1 566	1 459
Finland Finlande	56 989	55 423	52 141	56 424	61 078	68 888	66 970	54 605	66 076	64 176
France [1] France [1]	409 094	371 309	365 560	385 809	380 448	387 620	390 165	392 230	380 891	371 757
French Guiana Guyane française	968	939	843	836	851	851	851	851	876	895
French Polynesia Polynésie française	572	576	649	737	748	821	788	854	821	807
Gabon Gabon	1 753	1 562	1 214	1 371	1 492	1 514	1 591	1 863	2 072	2 035
Gambia Gambie	235	257	275	282	315	315	323	323	337	396
Georgia Géorgie	4 961	4 345	4 536	3 770	3 388	3 773	3 927	4 771	5 504	6 032
Germany Allemagne	894 381	824 466	832 101	855 757	830 909	835 658	828 522	809 597	811 881	787 936
Ghana Ghana	6 410	6 560	6 300	6 920	7 415	7 594	6 725	7 473	9 123	9 809
Gibraltar Gibraltar	312	323	334	345	345	356	367	378	392	407
Greece Grèce	87 810	86 637	91 616	93 806	93 670	95 720	97 157	98 690	97 271	98 118
Greenland Groenland	532	543	532	539	539	535	429	535	473	521
Grenada Grenade	191	205	205	220	216	220	216	235	242	242
Guadeloupe Guadeloupe	1 525	1 588	2 076	2 090	2 028	2 043	2 061	2 127	2 142	2 164

52

CO_2 emission estimates *(continued)*

From fossil fuel combustion, cement production and gas flared (thousand metric tons of carbon dioxide)

Estimation des émissions de CO_2 *(suite)*

Dues à la combustion de combustibles fossiles, à la production de ciment et au gaz brûlés à la torchère (milliers de tonnes de dioxyde de carbone)

Country or area Pays ou zone	1998	1999	2000	2001	2002	2003	2004	2005	2006	2007
Guatemala Guatemala	8 753	8 929	9 916	10 627	11 173	10 671	11 287	12 160	12 295	12 930
Guinea Guinée	1 243	1 272	1 280	1 298	1 324	1 342	1 342	1 360	1 360	1 390
Guinea-Bissau Guinée-Bissau	216	246	198	198	209	249	257	264	275	286
Guyana Guyana	1 654	1 650	1 580	1 518	1 547	1 500	1 445	1 492	1 507	1 507
Haiti Haïti	1 232	1 331	1 368	1 569	1 826	1 734	1 988	2 076	2 120	2 398
Honduras Honduras	4 650	4 741	5 031	5 713	6 091	6 769	7 367	7 620	7 107	8 834
Hungary Hongrie	61 015	60 271	57 194	57 073	56 934	59 860	58 144	58 980	57 807	56 472
Iceland Islande	2 101	2 068	2 164	2 101	2 171	2 167	2 233	2 204	2 237	2 340
India Inde	1 071 912	1 144 390	1 186 663	1 203 843	1 226 791	1 281 914	1 346 596	1 411 128	1 504 346	1 612 362
Indonesia Indonésie	210 211	237 596	258 120	289 066	303 507	306 066	333 778	341 093	342 828	397 143
Iran (Islamic Rep. of) Iran (Rép. islamique d')	316 176	316 671	339 242	357 085	375 211	399 659	423 483	426 956	481 976	495 987
Iraq Iraq	72 372	72 328	74 539	86 769	88 312	82 504	91 360	96 904	103 695	100 127
Ireland Irlande	38 133	40 077	40 887	43 784	43 480	42 849	43 223	43 223	43 109	44 319
Israel Israël	62 779	62 156	62 691	65 749	63 146	65 122	63 201	59 211	65 779	66 739
Italy [2] Italie [2]	441 642	437 081	447 385	447 726	450 055	465 551	467 443	468 294	465 225	456 428
Jamaica Jamaïque	9 729	9 773	10 319	10 627	10 301	10 722	10 561	10 165	12 152	13 964
Japan Japon	1 228 804	1 196 102	1 229 794	1 222 438	1 237 708	1 259 266	1 264 532	1 242 427	1 235 977	1 254 543
Jordan Jordanie	14 543	14 569	15 508	16 003	16 887	17 492	19 237	21 335	20 726	21 452
Kazakhstan Kazakhstan	125 063	116 493	127 769	147 912	151 946	153 816	172 158	177 233	192 129	227 394
Kenya Kenya	10 037	10 172	10 418	9 369	7 968	8 841	10 587	10 953	12 446	11 236
Kiribati Kiribati	33	29	33	26	26	26	26	26	29	33
Korea, Dem. P. R. Corée, R. p. dém. de	64 928	71 396	76 967	79 922	76 530	78 210	79 926	83 476	85 034	70 711
Korea, Republic of Corée, République de	365 409	404 144	442 046	449 189	474 546	474 814	490 582	463 058	470 619	503 321
Kuwait Koweït	63 421	66 002	71 107	67 465	63 982	73 263	81 338	89 878	86 343	86 145
Kyrgyzstan Kirghizistan	5 988	4 679	4 646	3 850	4 950	5 379	5 761	5 570	5 567	6 080
Lao People's Dem. Rep. Rép. dém. pop. lao	895	902	1 060	1 199	1 324	1 357	1 397	1 426	1 518	1 536
Latvia Lettonie	7 880	6 634	6 098	6 777	6 560	7 004	7 066	7 063	7 466	7 825
Lebanon Liban	15 999	16 601	15 354	16 208	16 039	18 929	16 839	17 547	15 031	13 355

52

CO$_2$ emission estimates *(continued)*

From fossil fuel combustion, cement production and gas flared (thousand metric tons of carbon dioxide)

Estimation des émissions de CO$_2$ *(suite)*

Dues à la combustion de combustibles fossiles, à la production de ciment et au gaz brûlés à la torchère (milliers de tonnes de dioxyde de carbone)

Country or area Pays ou zone	1998	1999	2000	2001	2002	2003	2004	2005	2006	2007
Liberia Libéria	389	407	436	502	502	532	627	737	755	675
Libyan Arab Jamah. Jamah. arabe libyenne	48 133	47 231	49 754	51 074	51 547	53 113	54 345	56 043	56 695	57 334
Lithuania Lituanie	16 197	13 693	12 193	12 699	12 915	13 080	13 539	14 316	14 507	15 280
Luxembourg Luxembourg	7 356	7 686	8 236	8 581	9 424	9 919	11 067	11 327	11 313	10 843
Madagascar Madagascar	1 738	1 925	2 450	2 127	1 698	1 918	1 900	2 175	2 021	2 252
Malawi Malawi	792	1 100	1 030	1 030	1 008	1 038	1 067	1 038	1 071	1 056
Malaysia Malaisie	114 187	107 934	126 603	136 717	135 129	160 266	168 040	183 445	185 418	194 476
Maldives Maldives	334	466	499	576	689	598	752	678	869	898
Mali Mali	517	539	543	546	554	539	565	568	568	579
Malta Malte	2 145	2 347	2 065	2 486	2 299	2 582	2 574	2 699	2 574	2 725
Marshall Islands Iles Marshall	70	66	77	81	84	84	88	84	92	99
Martinique Martinique	2 057	2 006	2 043	1 602	1 555	1 646	1 727	1 793	1 870	1 947
Mauritania Mauritanie	1 111	1 199	1 195	1 283	1 412	1 452	1 613	1 657	1 665	1 951
Mauritius Maurice	2 197	2 468	2 769	2 967	2 981	3 146	3 198	3 410	3 777	3 887
Mexico Mexique	388 244	390 290	390 092	404 565	399 355	415 185	417 708	440 916	447 741	471 459
Micronesia (Fed. States of) Micronésie (Etats féd. de)	...	55	55	55	55	55	55	55	55	62
Mongolia Mongolie	7 708	7 554	7 506	7 884	8 287	8 034	8 551	8 808	9 443	10 583
Montserrat Montserrat	51	48	55	59	66	70	70	70	77	77
Morocco Maroc	32 039	33 153	33 905	37 715	38 254	37 561	40 590	43 861	45 034	46 406
Mozambique Mozambique	1 133	1 188	1 349	1 580	1 588	1 918	1 933	1 856	2 039	2 600
Myanmar Myanmar	8 078	8 830	8 889	7 349	8 174	9 611	11 470	14 536	13 025	13 190
Namibia Namibie	1 995	1 771	1 764	2 087	2 215	2 362	2 497	2 659	2 853	3 036
Nauru Nauru	139	136	136	139	139	143	143	143	143	143
Nepal Népal	2 252	3 220	3 234	3 454	2 710	2 952	2 769	3 234	3 333	3 425
Netherlands Pays-Bas	175 488	163 013	166 306	168 326	172 785	176 214	177 824	173 031	165 576	173 244
Netherlands Antilles Antilles néerlandaises	282	2 116	5 706	5 809	5 603	5 489	5 765	5 717	5 556	6 238
New Caledonia Nouvelle-Calédonie	1 804	2 035	2 299	2 120	2 428	2 750	2 552	2 802	2 776	2 849
New Zealand Nouvelle-Zélande	30 058	31 668	32 691	34 143	33 641	33 810	33 604	33 359	33 388	32 662

52

CO_2 emission estimates *(continued)*

From fossil fuel combustion, cement production and gas flared (thousand metric tons of carbon dioxide)

Estimation des émissions de CO_2 *(suite)*

Dues à la combustion de combustibles fossiles, à la production de ciment et au gaz brûlés à la torchère (milliers de tonnes de dioxyde de carbone)

Country or area Pays ou zone	1998	1999	2000	2001	2002	2003	2004	2005	2006	2007
Nicaragua Nicaragua	3 421	3 627	3 843	4 015	3 803	4 107	4 125	3 979	4 312	4 591
Niger Niger	1 038	1 041	766	763	829	880	880	825	832	909
Nigeria Nigéria	40 183	44 789	79 182	83 351	98 125	93 138	97 594	110 461	97 865	95 272
Niue Nioué	4	4	4	4	4	4	4	4	4	4
Norway Norvège	34 591	41 023	38 812	41 133	37 433	42 563	46 355	46 380	49 343	42 757
Occupied Palestinian Terr. Terr. palestinien occupé	609	660	799	1 353	1 166	1 280	1 870	2 743	2 266	2 325
Oman Oman	16 667	20 818	22 057	20 444	25 544	31 943	30 971	34 176	39 717	37 319
Pakistan Pakistan	97 663	100 384	106 449	108 283	114 084	118 895	131 620	136 636	145 855	156 394
Palau Palaos	117	117	117	183	183	191	191	194	205	213
Panama Panama	5 948	5 669	5 790	7 008	5 834	6 153	5 842	6 054	6 839	7 250
Papua New Guinea Papouasie-Nvl-Guinée	2 838	2 464	2 688	3 231	3 513	3 968	4 481	4 613	4 620	3 366
Paraguay Paraguay	4 503	4 503	3 689	3 821	3 898	4 070	4 089	3 832	3 986	4 133
Peru Pérou	27 833	29 373	30 319	27 191	27 216	26 417	31 932	37 209	35 005	42 988
Philippines Philippines	75 650	73 021	78 888	76 952	75 790	75 775	78 650	80 612	67 579	70 916
Poland Pologne	326 994	317 254	301 691	302 806	296 932	304 790	305 039	303 635	319 227	317 379
Portugal Portugal	58 071	64 642	63 201	62 489	66 820	61 254	62 878	65 082	59 453	58 111
Qatar Qatar	32 402	31 408	34 730	28 001	28 012	30 564	40 286	56 820	49 541	63 054
Republic of Moldova République de Moldova	6 271	4 503	3 513	3 715	3 986	4 309	4 569	4 928	5 020	4 705
Réunion Réunion	2 512	2 369	2 475	2 699	2 695	2 728	2 754	2 758	2 772	2 802
Romania Roumanie	103 681	86 244	87 707	93 292	89 834	93 428	92 665	91 866	98 558	94 183
Russian Federation Fédération de Russie	1 422 356	1 424 068	1 443 716	1 442 561	1 433 089	1 481 915	1 500 071	1 515 567	1 564 727	1 537 357
Rwanda Rwanda	642	671	686	689	689	682	689	689	689	715
Saint Helena Sainte-Hélène	18	22	11	11	11	11	11	11	11	11
Saint Kitts and Nevis Saint-Kitts-et-Nevis	103	103	103	183	198	220	227	235	235	249
Saint Lucia Sainte-Lucie	308	319	330	363	326	359	356	367	352	381
Saint Pierre and Miquelon Saint-Pierre-et-Miquelon	55	55	55	55	59	66	62	66	66	66
Saint Vincent-Grenadines Saint Vincent-Grenadines	165	169	158	180	187	194	194	198	202	202
Samoa Samoa	132	139	139	143	143	150	154	158	158	161

52

CO_2 emission estimates *(continued)*

From fossil fuel combustion, cement production and gas flared (thousand metric tons of carbon dioxide)

Estimation des émissions de CO_2 *(suite)*

Dues à la combustion de combustibles fossiles, à la production de ciment et au gaz brûlés à la torchère (milliers de tonnes de dioxyde de carbone)

Country or area Pays ou zone	1998	1999	2000	2001	2002	2003	2004	2005	2006	2007
Sao Tome and Principe Sao Tomé-et-Principe	81	88	88	92	106	110	114	128	128	128
Saudi Arabia Arabie saoudite	207 288	227 229	297 749	295 843	323 459	323 697	346 047	367 067	384 386	402 450
Senegal Sénégal	3 429	3 700	3 938	4 331	4 547	5 013	5 280	5 534	4 386	5 478
Serbia and Montenegro Serbie-et-Monténégro	53 663	36 996	41 096	44 132	47 202	50 476	54 737	51 221	54 330	53 593
Seychelles Seychelles	440	513	565	642	543	557	774	697	744	623
Sierra Leone Sierra Leone	594	583	631	858	1 192	1 225	1 067	1 261	1 239	1 313
Singapore Singapour	61 895	52 346	52 346	52 548	51 147	49 138	50 924	59 563	56 222	54 191
Slovakia Slovaquie	43 230	39 864	36 531	39 358	39 237	39 479	38 738	39 175	38 918	36 985
Slovenia Slovénie	15 174	15 027	14 444	14 503	14 642	14 873	14 921	14 925	15 170	15 108
Solomon Islands Iles Salomon	161	165	165	172	172	180	180	180	180	198
Somalia Somalie	...	...	517	502	572	576	576	579	576	601
South Africa Afrique du Sud	372 219	371 034	368 611	362 743	347 687	380 862	414 213	408 229	403 733	433 527
Spain Espagne	274 684	282 385	294 442	297 834	314 526	321 097	339 429	353 462	350 796	359 260
Sri Lanka Sri Lanka	7 763	8 537	10 161	10 246	11 008	10 660	11 965	11 643	11 742	12 314
Sudan Soudan	4 697	5 093	5 534	6 370	8 119	8 999	10 374	11 001	10 814	11 522
Suriname Suriname	2 164	2 153	2 127	2 266	2 252	2 241	2 285	2 380	2 439	2 439
Swaziland Swaziland	1 214	1 239	1 188	1 144	1 126	1 041	1 030	1 019	1 016	1 063
Sweden Suède	55 064	51 202	50 106	50 850	57 073	55 148	54 312	51 840	49 383	49 248
Switzerland Suisse	42 005	40 700	39 090	42 999	40 770	40 256	40 480	41 426	41 943	37 994
Syrian Arab Republic Rép. arabe syrienne	62 709	64 913	63 344	60 660	71 341	69 772	71 617	72 541	64 349	69 893
Tajikistan Tadjikistan	5 445	5 523	4 268	4 976	4 646	5 049	5 427	5 805	6 392	7 228
Thailand Thaïlande	186 504	196 947	201 549	217 086	230 636	245 674	263 694	270 430	279 143	277 511
TFYR of Macedonia L'ex-R.Y. Macédoine	12 625	11 723	12 064	11 998	10 935	11 309	11 228	11 236	10 876	11 276
Timor-Leste Timor-Leste	...	...	...	...	161	161	176	176	180	183
Togo Togo	1 166	1 536	1 357	1 162	1 232	1 463	1 397	1 338	1 221	1 316
Tonga Tonga	110	128	121	139	143	176	172	172	172	176
Trinidad and Tobago Trinité-et-Tobago	19 318	22 816	24 514	25 024	26 890	27 697	31 555	30 949	34 481	37 037
Tunisia Tunisie	18 001	18 331	19 923	20 818	21 016	21 397	22 446	22 801	23 128	23 869

52 CO_2 emission estimates *(continued)*

From fossil fuel combustion, cement production and gas flared (thousand metric tons of carbon dioxide)

Estimation des émissions de CO_2 *(suite)*

Dues à la combustion de combustibles fossiles, à la production de ciment et au gaz brûlés à la torchère (milliers de tonnes de dioxyde de carbone)

Country or area Pays ou zone	1998	1999	2000	2001	2002	2003	2004	2005	2006	2007
Turkey Turquie	205 422	196 768	216 148	194 538	205 678	218 509	225 407	237 369	261 571	288 681
Turkmenistan Turkménistan	26 047	35 115	35 647	39 681	41 074	43 161	39 640	41 760	44 107	45 808
Turks and Caicos Islands Iles Turques et Caïques	15	15	15	15	99	103	103	121	143	158
Uganda Ouganda	1 338	1 393	1 533	1 632	1 705	1 720	1 834	2 340	2 706	3 205
Ukraine Ukraine	314 695	317 779	304 988	305 850	303 298	337 654	328 809	326 554	315 171	317 537
United Arab Emirates Emirats arabes unis	98 892	89 038	126 754	113 783	83 659	106 365	112 878	115 628	121 462	135 540
United Kingdom Royaume-Uni	554 139	535 551	544 428	552 353	531 972	542 782	545 338	543 713	554 021	539 617
United Rep. of Tanzania Rép.-Unie de Tanzanie	2 556	2 538	2 651	3 128	3 590	3 806	4 353	5 086	5 379	6 043
United States [3] Etats-Unis [3]	5 483 668	5 556 587	5 742 526	5 630 110	5 695 562	5 689 629	5 799 254	5 842 558	5 759 214	5 838 381
Uruguay Uruguay	5 688	6 725	5 306	5 093	4 620	4 595	5 827	5 992	6 865	6 219
Uzbekistan Ouzbékistan	118 052	117 421	118 851	120 963	125 873	121 686	118 514	112 504	115 613	116 090
Vanuatu Vanuatu	84	84	81	84	84	88	88	88	92	103
Venezuela (Boliv. Rep. of) Venezuela (Rép. boliv. du)	167 322	172 617	152 415	172 525	193 262	192 103	173 698	164 032	160 549	165 550
Viet Nam Viet Nam	47 807	48 063	53 597	59 977	71 360	79 431	101 682	103 464	104 832	111 378
Wallis and Futuna Islands Iles Wallis et Futuna	...	...	...	15	18	26	26	29	29	29
Western Sahara Sahara occidental	224	235	238	238	238	238	238	238	238	238
Yemen Yémen	12 200	13 902	14 628	16 259	15 764	17 305	18 881	20 044	20 792	21 976
Zambia Zambie	2 314	1 808	1 819	1 907	1 969	2 127	2 244	2 365	2 563	2 692
Zimbabwe Zimbabwe	14 254	15 841	13 898	12 574	11 940	10 638	9 934	10 788	10 356	9 637

Source:
Carbon Dioxide Information Analysis Center (CDIAC) of the Oak Ridge National Laboratory, Oak Ridge, Tennessee, U.S.A., database on national CO_2 emission estimates, last accessed July 2010.

1 Including Monaco.
2 Including San Marino.
3 Include emissions from American Samoa, Guam, Puerto Rico, the U.S. Virgin Islands, and Wake Island.

Source:
"Carbon Dioxide Information Analysis Center (CDIAC) of the Oak Ridge National Laboratory, Oak Ridge, Tennessee, U.S.A.", la base de données des estimations nationales des émissions de CO_2, dernier accès juillet 2010.

1 Y compris Monaco.
2 Y compris Saint-Marin.
3 Y compris Samoa américaines, Guam, Porto Rico, les Iles Vierges des Etats-Unis et l'Ile de Wake.

53 Ozone-depleting chlorofluorocarbons (CFCs)

Consumption: ozone-depleting potential (ODP) metric tons

Chlorofluorocarbones (CFC) qui appauvrissent la couche d'ozone

Consommation : tonnes de potentiel de destruction de l'ozone (PDO)

Country or area Pays ou zone	1990	2000	2001	2002	2003	2004	2005	2006	2007	2008
Afghanistan Afghanistan	...	...	...	...	...	177.9	141.2	94.5	55.2	40.0
Albania Albanie	...	61.9	68.8	49.9	35.0	36.6	14.3	15.2	4.1	0.0
Algeria Algérie	...	1 474.6	1 021.8	1 761.8	1 761.8	1 045.0	859.0	302.6	200.0	149.6
Angola Angola	...	107.0	114.8	105.0	104.2	75.6	52.0	42.1	17.0	9.7
Antigua and Barbuda Antigua-et-Barbuda	421.3	5.0	3.1	3.7	1.5	1.9	1.1	1.1	0.0	0.1
Argentina Argentine	2 138.2	2 396.7	3 293.1	2 139.2	2 255.2	2 211.6	1 675.5	1 654.2	529.0	50.9
Armenia Arménie	...	25.0	162.7	172.7	172.7	110.7	84.0	59.0	25.0	13.6
Australia Australie	7 416.4	6.5	6.0	9.8	1.1	-61.8[1]	-51.4[1]	-80.0[1]	-55.0[1]	-42.0[1]
Azerbaijan Azerbaïdjan	...	87.8	52.0	12.0	10.2	15.1	21.9	0.0	0.0	0.0
Bahamas Bahamas	...	65.9	63.0	55.4	29.6	18.8	13.0	4.0	0.0	0.0
Bahrain Bahreïn	107.0	113.1	106.0	94.6	85.8	64.8	58.7	32.4	14.7	11.7
Bangladesh Bangladesh	195.1	805.0	807.9	328.0	333.0	294.9	263.0	196.2	154.9	158.3
Barbados Barbade	20.9	8.1	12.5	9.5	8.6	14.1	6.7	7.9	1.9	1.1
Belarus Bélarus	1 230.0	0.0	0.0	0.0	0.0	0.0	0.0	0.0	0.0	0.0
Belize Belize	...	15.5	28.0	21.7	15.1	12.2	9.6	3.9	2.2	0.0
Benin Bénin	57.7	54.6	54.0	35.5	17.3	11.5	10.0	14.2	7.9	5.2
Bhutan Bhoutan	...	0.0	...	...	...	0.1	0.1	0.1	0.0	0.0
Bolivia (Plurin. State of) Bolivie (État plurin. de)	...	78.8	76.7	65.5	32.1	42.4	26.7	33.1	2.4	2.6
Bosnia and Herzegovina Bosnie-Herzégovine	0.0	175.9	199.7	243.6	230.0	187.9	50.8	32.6	22.1	8.8
Botswana Botswana	...	2.5	4.0	3.6	5.1	2.7	1.9	0.7	0.6	0.3
Brazil Brésil	8 538.8	9 275.1	6 230.9	3 000.6	3 224.3	1 870.5	967.2	477.8	318.1	290.4
Brunei Darussalam Brunéi Darussalam	...	46.6	31.4	43.4	32.3	60.2	39.0	27.8	9.9	2.4
Bulgaria Bulgarie	2 034.0	0.0	0.0	0.0	0.0	0.0	0.0	0.0	...	...
Burkina Faso Burkina Faso	27.8	25.4	19.6	16.3	13.2	10.5	7.4	5.2	4.2	0.0
Burundi Burundi	43.0	53.8	46.5	19.1	9.2	3.9	3.5	3.5	3.1	1.0
Cambodia Cambodge	...	94.2	94.2	94.2	86.7	70.4	44.5	28.3	11.6	1.4

53 Ozone-depleting chlorofluorocarbons (CFCs) *(continued)*

Consumption: ozone-depleting potential (ODP) metric tons

Chlorofluorocarbones (CFC) qui appauvrissent la couche d'ozone *(suite)*

Consommation : tonnes de potentiel de destruction de l'ozone (PDO)

Country or area Pays ou zone	1990	2000	2001	2002	2003	2004	2005	2006	2007	2008
Cameroon Cameroun	77.7	368.7	364.1	226.0	220.5	148.5	120.0	103.0	25.0	17.0
Canada Canada	13 173.6	10.1	0.1	-12.6[1]	-0.2[1]	0.0	0.0	0.0	0.0	0.0
Cape Verde Cap-Vert	2.2	1.9	1.9	1.8	1.8	1.5	0.9	0.0	0.0	0.0
Central African Rep. Rép. centrafricaine	...	4.3	4.0	4.4	4.1	3.9	2.6	2.0	1.3	0.0
Chad Tchad	26.1	36.5	31.6	27.1	22.8	14.2	11.3	9.2	5.1	2.2
Chile Chili	662.3	576.0	470.2	370.2	424.5	230.8	221.5	181.8	19.2	47.9
China Chine	41 829.0[2]	39 123.6[3]	33 922.6[3]	30 621.2[3]	22 808.8[3]	17 902.5[3]	13 123.8[3]	12 414.9[3]	5 832.1[3]	263.0[3]
Colombia Colombie	2 025.8	1 149.3	1 164.8	907.0	1 058.1	898.5	556.9	660.4	263.1	208.0
Comoros Comores	...	2.7	1.9	1.8	1.2	1.1	0.9	0.8	0.3	0.0
Congo Congo	...	11.4	2.5	5.5	7.0	4.7	3.7	3.3	1.5	1.4
Cook Islands Iles Cook	...	0.0	...	...	0.0	0.0	0.0	0.0	0.0	0.0
Costa Rica Costa Rica	...	105.9	144.6	137.4	142.5	111.5	96.1	55.7	27.9	13.9
Côte d'Ivoire Côte d'Ivoire	...	206.4	148.0	106.5	93.4	79.4	70.1	85.5	35.5	12.0
Croatia Croatie	464.0	171.2	113.8	140.1	88.7	78.2	43.5	-31.4[1]	-5.0[1]	0.0
Cuba Cuba	778.4	533.7	504.0	488.8	481.0	445.1	208.6	239.5	83.5	74.4
Cyprus Chypre	240.1	165.0	137.6	131.8	62.5	...	...	...	...	...
Czech Republic République tchèque	...	5.1	2.9	3.7	-4.4[1]	...	...	...	...	...
Dem. Rep. of the Congo Rép. dém. du Congo	...	386.6	639.4	569.4	566.9	329.1	268.7	170.7	48.9	8.6
Djibouti Djibouti	...	20.7	18.0	15.8	12.1	8.8	7.1	3.1	2.2	0.9
Dominica Dominique	...	2.1	1.6	3.0	1.4	1.0	1.4	0.5	0.0	0.0
Dominican Republic Rép. dominicaine	...	401.9	485.8	329.8	266.5	310.4	204.3	156.2	24.4	4.5
Ecuador Equateur	603.6	230.5	207.0	229.6	256.3	147.4	132.5	63.0	28.3	8.2
Egypt Egypte	2 144.0	1 267.0	1 334.8	1 294.0	1 102.2	1 047.6	821.2	593.6	241.6	187.8
El Salvador El Salvador	...	99.1	116.9	101.6	97.5	75.6	119.2	64.4	34.7	0.0
Equatorial Guinea Guinée équatoriale	20.0	23.2	23.8	17.5	13.6	10.0	8.1	4.6	4.6	2.3
Eritrea Erythrée	...	48.8	...	...	...	...	30.2	4.2	3.1	2.8
Estonia Estonie	...	15.7	-0.4[1]	0.0	0.0	...	...	...	...	...

53 Ozone-depleting chlorofluorocarbons (CFCs) *(continued)*

Consumption: ozone-depleting potential (ODP) metric tons

Chlorofluorocarbones (CFC) qui appauvrissent la couche d'ozone *(suite)*

Consommation : tonnes de potentiel de destruction de l'ozone (PDO)

Country or area Pays ou zone	1990	2000	2001	2002	2003	2004	2005	2006	2007	2008
Ethiopia Ethiopie	...	39.2	34.6	30.0	28.0	16.0	15.0	12.9	4.9	4.3
European Union (EU) Union européenne (UE)	170 331.4[4]	2 168.8[5]	2 136.4[5]	-265.8[1,5]	294.6[5]	195.8[6]	-1 151.6[1,6]	-2.5[1,6]	-106.7[1,7]	-552.0[1,7]
Fiji Fidji	37.8	0.0	0.0	0.0	0.0	0.0	0.0	0.0	0.0	0.0
Gabon Gabon	...	13.7	6.4	5.0	5.0	4.5	2.1	1.2	0.0	0.0
Gambia Gambie	15.0	6.1	5.8	4.7	5.1	0.2	0.7	1.0	0.6	0.4
Georgia Géorgie	...	21.5	18.8	15.5	12.6	8.6	8.2	5.8	2.7	0.0
Ghana Ghana	106.6	47.0	35.6	21.2	32.0	35.6	17.5	13.1	4.2	0.0
Grenada Grenade	...	2.9	1.3	2.1	2.1	1.9	0.6	0.0	0.0	0.0
Guatemala Guatemala	357.3	187.9	265.0	239.6	147.1	65.4	57.5	12.7	5.9	1.4
Guinea Guinée	28.0	37.5	35.4	31.3	25.9	16.7	9.3	4.9	2.9	1.6
Guinea-Bissau Guinée-Bissau	22.2	26.0	26.9	27.2	29.4	25.2	12.5	13.1	2.9	1.4
Guyana Guyana	18.9	24.4	19.8	14.3	10.4	11.9	23.5	8.8	0.1	0.0
Haiti Haïti	...	169.0	169.0	181.2	115.9	132.5	81.4	50.4	9.0	2.3
Honduras Honduras	...	172.3	121.6	131.2	219.1	167.8	122.6	94.7	39.7	23.4
Hungary Hongrie	4 390.0	0.5	0.0	0.3	-1.3[1]	...	...	...	...	...
Iceland Islande	132.7	0.0	0.0	0.0	0.0	0.0	0.0	0.0	0.0	0.0
India Inde	0.0	5 614.3	4 514.3	3 917.7	2 631.5	2 241.6	1 957.8	3 560.3	998.2	216.5
Indonesia Indonésie	...	5 411.1	5 003.3	5 506.3	4 829.3	3 925.5	2 385.3	231.0	202.6	0.0
Iran (Islamic Rep. of) Iran (Rép. islamique d')	1 365.8	4 156.5	4 204.8	4 437.8	4 088.8	3 471.9	2 221.0	953.3	549.5	240.6
Iraq Iraq	...	...	...	...	...	...	...	1 414.1	1 686.1	1 597.1
Israel Israël	...	0.0	0.0	0.0	0.0	0.0	0.0	0.0	0.0	0.0
Jamaica Jamaïque	423.9	59.8	48.6	31.7	16.2	16.0	5.0	0.0	0.0	0.0
Japan Japon	97 723.2	-24.2[1]	-5.5[1]	19.5	4.0	0.0	0.0	0.0	-5.0[1]	-0.7[1]
Jordan Jordanie	540.0	354.0	321.0	90.0	74.4	58.4	59.6	21.8	24.0	6.0
Kazakhstan Kazakhstan	1 214.3	523.9	290.0	112.0	30.4	11.2	0.0	0.0	0.0	0.0
Kenya Kenya	230.0	203.3	168.6	152.3	168.6	131.7	160.6	57.7	22.7	7.5
Kiribati Kiribati	...	0.0	0.0	0.0	0.0	0.0	0.0	0.0	0.0	0.0

53 Ozone-depleting chlorofluorocarbons (CFCs) *(continued)*

Consumption: ozone-depleting potential (ODP) metric tons

Chlorofluorocarbones (CFC) qui appauvrissent la couche d'ozone *(suite)*

Consommation : tonnes de potentiel de destruction de l'ozone (PDO)

Country or area Pays ou zone	1990	2000	2001	2002	2003	2004	2005	2006	2007	2008
Korea, Dem. P. R. Corée, R. p. dém. de	...	77.0	320.8	299.0	587.4	7.3	91.8	24.5	40.7	33.5
Korea, Republic of Corée, République de	...	7 395.4	6 802.2	6 646.6	5 171.6	5 012.2	2 730.0	3 026.2	1 209.6	1 114.8
Kuwait Koweït	...	419.9	354.2	349.0	247.4	233.0	152.7	106.8	68.0	33.0
Kyrgyzstan Kirghizistan	...	53.5	53.0	38.0	33.0	22.9	8.1	5.3	4.2	5.0
Lao People's Dem. Rep. Rép. dém. pop. lao	...	44.6	41.2	42.3	35.3	23.1	19.5	17.8	6.4	2.0
Latvia Lettonie	...	35.2	0.0	0.0	0.0	...	...	...	...	...
Lebanon Liban	...	527.9	533.4	491.7	480.2	347.0	287.3	224.4	74.5	33.8
Lesotho Lesotho	...	2.4	1.8	1.6	1.4	1.2	0.0	0.0	0.0	0.0
Liberia Libéria	26.1	41.4	25.1	32.8	26.3	14.2	5.0	5.0	1.8	0.6
Libyan Arab Jamah. Jamah. arabe libyenne	66.6	985.4	985.4	985.4	704.1	459.0	252.0	115.7	57.5	21.9
Liechtenstein Liechtenstein	3.4	0.0	0.0	0.0	0.0	-0.1[1]	0.0	0.0	0.0	0.0
Lithuania Lituanie	4 178.9	36.5	0.0	0.0	0.0	...	...	...	...	...
Madagascar Madagascar	...	12.4	9.9	7.8	7.2	7.1	7.0	2.3	2.1	0.8
Malawi Malawi	...	21.5	19.0	19.0	18.7	11.4	5.6	3.6	2.3	0.0
Malaysia Malaisie	3 384.2	1 979.8	1 946.9	1 605.5	1 174.4	1 128.5	668.3	564.2	234.2	173.7
Maldives Maldives	3.5	4.6	14.0	2.8	0.0	0.0	0.0	2.1	0.0	0.0
Mali Mali	0.0	29.2	27.0	26.0	26.0	25.0	25.0	16.2	11.0	3.0
Malta Malte	179.4	67.6	63.1	10.3	14.0	...	...	...	...	...
Marshall Islands Iles Marshall	1.2	0.5	0.2	0.2	0.2	0.0	0.0	0.0	0.0	0.0
Mauritania Mauritanie	...	14.2	15.0	14.7	14.3	7.1	6.1	3.0	1.3	1.0
Mauritius Maurice	...	19.1	14.5	7.3	4.0	3.4	-0.1[1]	1.0	0.0	0.0
Mexico Mexique	12 037.2	3 059.5	2 223.9	1 946.7	1 983.2	3 208.4	1 604.0	-441.3[1]	-480.6[1]	-130.4[1]
Micronesia (Fed. States of) Micronésie (Etats féd. de)	...	1.0	1.1	1.9	1.7	1.5	0.4	0.0	0.5	0.0
Monaco Monaco	...	0.0	0.0	0.0	0.0	0.0	0.0	0.0	0.0	0.0
Mongolia Mongolie	...	11.2	9.3	6.9	5.7	4.1	3.7	2.2	1.0	0.4
Montenegro Monténégro	...	...	...	...	...	...	...	14.0	3.5	0.1
Morocco Maroc	604.2	564.0	435.2	668.6	474.8	329.0	38.7	40.0	24.1	0.0

53 Ozone-depleting chlorofluorocarbons (CFCs) *(continued)*

Consumption: ozone-depleting potential (ODP) metric tons

Chlorofluorocarbones (CFC) qui appauvrissent la couche d'ozone *(suite)*

Consommation : tonnes de potentiel de destruction de l'ozone (PDO)

Country or area Pays ou zone	1990	2000	2001	2002	2003	2004	2005	2006	2007	2008
Mozambique Mozambique	...	9.9	8.4	9.9	1.7	1.6	1.2	2.7	2.3	2.3
Myanmar Myanmar	...	26.3	39.4	43.5	51.6	29.6	14.8	0.0	0.0	0.0
Namibia Namibie	...	22.1	24.0	20.0	17.2	7.7	0.0	0.0	0.0	0.0
Nauru Nauru	...	0.4	0.4	0.0	0.0	0.0	0.0	0.0	0.0	...
Nepal Népal	...	94.0	0.0	0.0	0.0	0.0	0.0	0.0	0.0	0.0
New Zealand Nouvelle-Zélande	558.4	-2.6[1]	0.0	-4.7[1]	0.0	-1.1[1]	0.0	0.0	0.0	0.0
Nicaragua Nicaragua	86.5	44.4	35.2	54.9	29.9	48.4	36.0	27.6	3.7	0.0
Niger Niger	16.0	39.9	29.1	26.6	24.5	23.0	15.1	15.9	4.3	2.9
Nigeria Nigéria	934.0	4 094.8	3 665.5	3 286.7	2 662.4	2 116.1	466.1	454.0	17.5	16.5
Niue Nioué	...	0.0	...	...	0.0	0.0	0.0	0.0	0.0	0.0
Norway Norvège	722.4	-39.8[1]	-48.1[1]	-73.5[1]	-65.5[1]	-54.6[1]	-21.8[1]	-26.7[1]	-64.2[1]	-3.8[1]
Oman Oman	...	282.1	207.3	179.5	134.5	98.7	54.3	25.8	10.1	8.5
Pakistan Pakistan	751.0	1 945.3	1 666.3	1 647.0	1 124.0	805.0	453.0	626.0	170.3	167.4
Palau Palaos	...	0.6	0.6	0.1	1.0	0.9	0.2	0.1	0.1	0.1
Panama Panama	252.1	249.9	180.4	195.3	168.5	134.7	92.8	43.7	28.4	11.5
Papua New Guinea Papouasie-Nvl-Guinée	...	47.9	15.0	34.6	22.7	17.2	15.1	3.1	4.5	-1.6[1]
Paraguay Paraguay	...	153.5	116.0	96.9	91.8	141.0	250.7	102.9	12.3	27.3
Peru Pérou	800.7	347.0	189.0	196.5	178.4	145.7	127.7	87.2	0.0	0.0
Philippines Philippines	2 981.2	2 905.2	2 049.4	1 644.5	1 422.4	1 389.8	1 014.2	603.4	143.1	169.4
Poland Pologne	4 939.0	174.8	179.0	201.5	126.3	...	...	...	...	...
Qatar Qatar	...	85.8	85.4	86.7	95.1	63.7	37.0	31.4	13.0	5.1
Republic of Moldova République de Moldova	...	31.7	23.5	29.6	18.9	20.0	14.4	12.0	9.2	0.0
Romania Roumanie	...	360.6	185.7	359.4	362.1	116.7	180.2	0.0	...	...
Russian Federation Fédération de Russie	98 752.0	23 820.8	0.0	0.0	258.0	373.6	349.0	394.7	363.0	324.0
Rwanda Rwanda	30.2	30.1	30.1	30.1	30.1	27.1	12.3	12.0	4.1	1.2
Saint Kitts and Nevis Saint-Kitts-et-Nevis	...	7.0	6.6	5.3	2.8	3.3	1.5	0.6	0.1	0.0
Saint Lucia Sainte-Lucie	...	4.2	4.1	7.6	2.5	0.8	1.5	0.8	0.0	0.0

53 Ozone-depleting chlorofluorocarbons (CFCs) *(continued)*

Consumption: ozone-depleting potential (ODP) metric tons

Chlorofluorocarbones (CFC) qui appauvrissent la couche d'ozone *(suite)*

Consommation : tonnes de potentiel de destruction de l'ozone (PDO)

Country or area Pays ou zone	1990	2000	2001	2002	2003	2004	2005	2006	2007	2008
Saint Vincent-Grenadines Saint Vincent-Grenadines	...	6.0	6.9	6.0	3.1	2.1	1.0	0.5	0.2	0.0
Samoa Samoa	...	0.6	2.0	2.2	0.0	0.0	0.0	0.0	0.0	0.0
Sao Tome and Principe Sao Tomé-et-Principe	2.5	3.9	4.1	4.3	4.6	4.0	2.3	1.7	0.4	0.2
Saudi Arabia Arabie saoudite	...	1 593.6	1 593.0	1 531.0	1 300.0	1 150.0	878.5	850.0	657.8	365.0
Senegal Sénégal	96.8	116.5	98.0	71.9	51.0	40.0	30.0	25.0	15.0	10.0
Serbia Serbie	1 448.8	309.7	263.3	371.7	412.0	282.8	52.1	233.8	53.5	76.7
Seychelles Seychelles	2.7	0.8	0.7	1.5	0.6	0.0	0.0	0.0	0.0	0.0
Sierra Leone Sierra Leone	79.1	75.9	92.9	80.8	66.3	64.5	26.2	18.2	10.4	4.2
Singapore Singapour	3 166.6	21.7	21.6	0.9	11.1	6.6	-0.7[1]	0.0	0.0	0.0
Slovakia Slovaquie	...	1.7	3.3	0.8	0.6	...	...	...	...	...
Slovenia Slovénie	343.4	0.3	2.6	0.4	0.6	...	...	...	...	...
Solomon Islands Iles Salomon	1.6	0.3	0.6	0.5	0.8	1.1	0.9	1.4	0.0	0.0
Somalia Somalie	205.8	65.6	86.9	98.5	108.2	97.2	88.2	84.6	79.5	20.0
South Africa Afrique du Sud	6 804.5	80.5	16.0	86.6	60.8	61.8	30.0	0.0	0.0	0.0
Sri Lanka Sri Lanka	209.5	220.3	190.4	185.0	179.9	155.7	149.2	105.3	62.2	0.0
Sudan Soudan	...	291.5	266.0	253.0	216.0	203.0	185.0	120.0	61.0	44.8
Suriname Suriname	...	44.0	46.0	46.0	12.3	9.2	7.5	0.1	0.1	0.0
Swaziland Swaziland	...	0.1	1.3	1.2	1.9	3.1	1.5	0.2	0.0	0.0
Switzerland Suisse	2 920.2	-5.8[1]	-1.6[1]	-3.4[1]	-9.1[1]	-19.0[1]	-30.0[1]	0.0	0.0	0.0
Syrian Arab Republic Rép. arabe syrienne	1 272.2	1 174.7	1 392.2	1 201.6	1 124.6	928.3	869.7	541.2	282.0	166.0
Tajikistan Tadjikistan	...	28.0	28.3	11.8	4.7	0.0	0.0	0.0	0.0	0.0
Thailand Thaïlande	6 660.2	3 568.3	3 375.1	2 177.3	1 857.0	1 358.3	1 259.9	453.7	321.6	190.3
TFYR of Macedonia L'ex-R.Y. Macédoine	...	49.5	46.7	34.1	49.3	8.8	11.8	7.0	0.0	0.0
Timor-Leste Timor-Leste	...	21.4	...	...	...	...	...	...	2.3	...
Togo Togo	41.0	37.5	34.7	35.3	33.7	26.4	18.6	10.1	5.0	3.2
Tonga Tonga	...	0.5	0.7	0.8	0.3	0.0	0.0	0.0	0.0	0.0
Trinidad and Tobago Trinité-et-Tobago	137.9	101.3	79.2	63.6	62.5	35.0	18.3	2.9	0.0	0.0

53 Ozone-depleting chlorofluorocarbons (CFCs) *(continued)*

Consumption: ozone-depleting potential (ODP) metric tons

Chlorofluorocarbones (CFC) qui appauvrissent la couche d'ozone *(suite)*

Consommation : tonnes de potentiel de destruction de l'ozone (PDO)

Country or area Pays ou zone	1990	2000	2001	2002	2003	2004	2005	2006	2007	2008
Tunisia Tunisie	730.0	555.0	570.0	465.8	362.5	271.0	205.0	59.0	17.7	12.2
Turkey Turquie	3 518.6	820.2	731.2	698.9	440.9	257.6	132.8	0.2	0.0	-0.1[1]
Turkmenistan Turkménistan	140.8	21.0	57.7	10.5	43.4	58.4	17.9	16.8	5.6	1.2
Tuvalu Tuvalu	...	0.0	0.0	0.0	0.0	0.0	0.0	0.0	0.0	0.0
Uganda Ouganda	14.3	12.7	13.4	12.7	4.1	0.2	0.2	0.0	0.0	0.0
Ukraine Ukraine	4 518.0	838.7	1 076.5	119.7	77.8	80.0	53.1	0.0	0.0	0.0
United Arab Emirates Emirats arabes unis	447.6	476.2	423.4	370.4	317.5	291.0	264.6	132.3	79.4	52.9
United Rep. of Tanzania Rép.-Unie de Tanzanie	...	215.5	131.2	71.5	148.2	98.8	98.9	54.0	26.5	13.9
United States Etats-Unis	198 308.2	2 613.0	2 805.2	1 357.2	1 605.2	1 153.6	1 496.6	752.7	-68.6[1]	-569.2[1]
Uruguay Uruguay	...	106.8	102.3	75.2	111.4	90.9	97.6	81.9	29.3	26.4
Uzbekistan Ouzbékistan	...	41.7	15.3	0.0	0.0	0.0	0.0	0.0	0.0	0.0
Vanuatu Vanuatu	...	0.0	0.0	0.0	0.0	0.0	0.0	0.0	0.3	0.7
Venezuela (Boliv. Rep. of) Venezuela (Rép. boliv. du)	3 343.1	2 705.9	2 546.2	1 552.8	1 313.5	2 944.6	1 841.8	2 641.8	-114.4[1]	-15.0[1]
Viet Nam Viet Nam	...	220.0	243.0	235.5	243.7	241.0	234.8	148.7	37.8	20.4
Yemen Yémen	...	1 045.0	1 023.4	959.9	758.6	746.4	710.5	394.7	268.7	247.7
Zambia Zambie	34.6	23.3	11.8	10.6	10.4	10.0	9.5	6.6	4.1	2.0
Zimbabwe Zimbabwe	...	145.0	259.4	129.1	117.5	112.9	49.0	63.0	54.3	7.0

Source:
United Nations Environment Programme (UNEP), Ozone Secretariat (Nairobi), data access centre, last accessed June 2010.

Source:
Secrétariat de l'ozone du programme des Nations Unies pour l'environnement (PNUE) (Nairobi), centre de communication de données, dernier accès juin 2010.

1 Negative numbers can occur when destruction and/or exports exceed production plus imports, implying that the destruction and/or exports are from stockpiles.

2 Data include those for Taiwan Province of China.

3 Data include those for Hong Kong Special Administrative Region (Hong Kong SAR) and Taiwan Province of China.

4 European Community (EC) consumption figures for the years before 1995 contain data reported for the 12 members of the community at the time, namely Belgium, Denmark, France, Germany, Greece, Ireland, Italy, Luxembourg, Netherlands, Portugal, Spain and United Kingdom of Great Britain and Northern Ireland.

1 Il peut y avoir des chiffres négatifs, lorsque les quantités exportées, ajoutées aux quantités détruites, sont supérieures aux quantités effectivement produites ajoutées aux quantités importées, ce qui est le cas par exemple lorsque les exportations proviennent des stocks reportés d'un exercice précédent.

2 Les données comprennent les chiffres pour la province de Taiwan.

3 Les données comprennent les chiffres pour la Région Administrative Spéciale de Hong Kong (Hong Kong RAS), et la province de Taiwan.

4 Les chiffres sur la consommation dans la Communauté européenne pour les années avant 1995 englobent des données communiquées par les 12 pays qui étaient alors membres de la Communauté, à savoir l'Allemagne, la Belgique, le Danemark, l'Espagne, la France, la Grèce, l'Irlande, l'Italie, le Luxembourg, les Pays-Bas, le Portugal, et le Royaume-Uni de Grande-Bretagne et d'Irlande du Nord.

5 European Community (EC) consumption figures for the years between 1995 and 2003 cover 15 members of the community at the time, namely Austria, Belgium, Denmark, Finland, France, Germany, Greece, Ireland, Italy, Luxembourg, Netherlands, Portugal, Spain, Sweden and United Kingdom of Great Britain and Northern Ireland.

6 European Community (EC) consumption figures for the years between 2004 and 2006 cover 25 members of the community at the time, namely Austria, Belgium, Cyprus, Czech Republic, Denmark, Estonia, Finland, France, Germany, Greece, Hungary, Ireland, Italy, Latvia, Lithuania, Luxembourg, Malta, Netherlands, Poland, Portugal, Slovakia, Slovenia, Spain, Sweden and United Kingdom of Great Britain and Northern Ireland.

7 European Community (EC) consumption figures for the years starting 2007 onwards covers 27 members of the community at the time, namely Austria, Belgium, Bulgaria, Cyprus, Czech Republic, Denmark, Estonia, Finland, France, Germany, Greece, Hungary, Ireland, Italy, Latvia, Lithuania, Luxembourg, Malta, Netherlands, Poland, Portugal, Romania, Slovakia, Slovenia, Spain, Sweden and United Kingdom of Great Britain and Northern Ireland.

5 Les chiffres sur la consommation dans la Communauté européenne pour les années comprises entre 1995 et 2003 englobent des données communiquées par les 15 pays qui étaient alors membres de la Communauté, à savoir l'Allemagne, l'Autriche, la Belgique, le Danemark, l'Espagne, la Finlande, la France, la Grèce, l'Irlande, l'Italie, le Luxembourg, les Pays-Bas, le Portugal, le Royaume-Uni de Grande-Bretagne et d'Irlande du Nord et la Suède.

6 Les chiffres sur la consommation dans la Communauté européenne pour les années comprises entre 2004 et 2006 englobent des données communiquées par les 25 pays qui étaient alors membres de la Communauté, à savoir l'Allemagne, l'Autriche, la Belgique, Chypre, le Danemark, l'Espagne, l'Estonie, la Finlande, la France, la Grèce, la Hongrie, l'Irlande, l'Italie, la Lettonie, la Lituanie, le Luxembourg, Malte, les Pays-Bas, la Pologne, le Portugal, la République tchèque, le Royaume-Uni de Grande-Bretagne et d'Irlande du Nord, la Slovaquie, la Slovénie et la Suède.

7 Les chiffres sur la consommation dans la Communauté européenne depuis 2007 englobent des données communiquées par les 27 pays qui étaient alors membres de la Communauté, à savoir l'Allemagne, l'Autriche, la Belgique, la Bulgarie, Chypre, le Danemark, l'Espagne, l'Estonie, la Finlande, la France, la Grèce, la Hongrie, l'Irlande, l'Italie, la Lettonie, la Lituanie, le Luxembourg, Malte, les Pays-Bas, la Pologne, le Portugal, la République tchèque, la Roumanie, le Royaume-Uni de Grande-Bretagne et d'Irlande du Nord, la Slovaquie, la Slovénie et la Suède.

54 Threatened species

Number by taxonomic group

Espèces menacées

Nombre par groupe taxonomique

Country or area Pays ou zone	Year Année	Mammals Mammifères	Birds Oiseaux	Reptiles Reptiles	Amphibians Amphibiens	Fishes Poissons	Molluscs Mollusques	Invertebrates Invertébrés	Plants Plantes	Total
Afghanistan	2006	16	18	1	1	0	0	1	1	38
Afghanistan	2008	11	13	1	1	3	0	1	2	32
	2010	11	13	1	1	5	0	1	2	34
Albania	2006	2	9	4	2	22	0	4	0	43
Albanie	2008	3	6	4	2	33	0	4	0	52
	2010	3	6	4	2	38	42	5	0	100
Algeria	2006	15	13	7	3	18	0	14	3	73
Algérie	2008	14	11	7	3	23	0	14	3	75
	2010	14	11	8	3	33	8	13	15	105
American Samoa	2006	3	11	2	0	5	5	0	1	27
Samoa américaines	2008	1	8	2	0	8	5	52	1	77
	2010	1	8	4	0	8	5	52	1	79
Andorra	2006	2	0	1	0	1	1	3	0	8
Andorre	2008	2	0	1	0	2	1	3	0	9
	2010	2	0	1	0	1	1	3	0	8
Angola	2006	14	21	5	0	16	5	1	26	88
Angola	2008	14	18	4	0	22	4	1	26	89
	2010	15	21	4	0	37	6	1	33	117
Anguilla	2006	1	0	4	0	12	0	0	3	20
Anguilla	2008	1	0	3	0	14	0	10	3	31
	2010	1	0	5	0	14	0	10	3	33
Antigua and Barbuda	2006	1	1	5	0	12	0	0	4	23
Antigua-et-Barbuda	2008	2	1	6	0	14	0	11	4	38
	2010	2	1	6	0	14	0	11	4	38
Argentina	2006	32	57	5	33	22	0	10	44	203
Argentine	2008	35	49	5	29	31	0	10	44	203
	2010	37	50	5	29	36	0	12	44	213
Armenia	2006	11	12	5	0	1	0	6	1	36
Arménie	2008	9	12	5	0	4	0	6	1	37
	2010	9	10	7	0	3	0	6	1	36
Aruba	2006	2	2	3	0	13	0	1	0	21
Aruba	2008	3	1	2	0	15	0	1	0	22
	2010	2	1	2	0	15	0	1	1	22
Australia	2006	64	65	39	47	85	176	107	56	639
Australie	2008	57	49	38	48	84	175	282	55	788
	2010	55	52	43	47	100	175	314	67	853
Austria	2006	6	12	1	0	7	22	21	4	73
Autriche	2008	4	9	1	0	9	22	21	4	70
	2010	3	8	1	0	11	33	22	4	82
Azerbaijan	2006	11	13	5	0	5	0	5	0	39
Azerbaïdjan	2008	7	15	5	0	9	0	4	0	40
	2010	7	15	9	0	10	0	4	0	45
Bahamas	2006	5	10	7	0	17	0	1	5	45
Bahamas	2008	7	5	6	0	20	0	11	5	54
	2010	7	5	7	0	25	0	11	7	62
Bahrain	2006	2	7	4	0	6	0	0	0	19
Bahreïn	2008	3	4	4	0	6	0	13	0	30
	2010	3	4	4	0	8	0	13	0	32
Bangladesh	2006	31	32	21	2	13	0	0	12	111
Bangladesh	2008	34	28	20	1	12	0	2	12	109
	2010	34	29	21	1	19	0	2	16	122
Barbados	2006	1	3	4	0	12	0	0	2	22
Barbade	2008	3	1	4	0	15	0	10	2	35
	2010	3	1	4	0	16	0	10	2	36
Belarus	2006	6	5	0	0	0	0	8	0	19
Bélarus	2008	4	4	0	0	1	0	8	0	17
	2010	4	4	0	0	2	0	6	0	16

54 Threatened species *(continued)*
Number by taxonomic group
Espèces menacées *(suite)*
Nombre par groupe taxonomique

Country or area Pays ou zone	Year Année	Mammals Mammifères	Birds Oiseaux	Reptiles Reptiles	Amphibians Amphibiens	Fishes Poissons	Molluscs Mollusques	Invertebrates Invertébrés	Plants Plantes	Total
Belgium	2006	9	12	0	0	8	4	8	0	41
Belgique	2008	3	2	0	0	9	4	8	1	27
	2010	3	2	0	0	10	4	7	1	27
Belize	2006	5	3	5	6	19	0	1	30	69
Belize	2008	7	3	5	6	22	0	12	30	85
	2010	8	4	5	6	25	0	12	32	92
Benin	2006	12	2	5	0	12	0	0	14	45
Bénin	2008	10	4	4	0	15	0	0	14	47
	2010	11	5	4	0	27	0	1	14	62
Bermuda	2006	2	3	2	0	13	0	25	4	49
Bermudes	2008	4	1	2	0	12	0	28	4	51
	2010	4	1	2	0	11	0	28	4	50
Bhutan	2006	25	18	1	2	0	0	1	7	54
Bhoutan	2008	28	17	1	1	0	0	1	7	55
	2010	27	17	2	1	3	0	1	8	59
Bolivia (Plurinational State of)	2006	24	32	3	23	0	0	1	71	154
Bolivie (État plurinational de)	2008	19	29	2	39	0	0	1	71	161
	2010	20	33	3	34	0	0	1	72	163
Bosnia and Herzegovina	2006	8	9	2	1	25	0	10	1	56
Bosnie-Herzégovine	2008	4	6	2	1	27	0	10	1	51
	2010	4	6	2	1	31	8	14	1	67
Botswana	2006	8	9	0	0	0	0	0	0	17
Botswana	2008	6	7	0	0	2	0	0	0	15
	2010	7	9	0	0	2	0	0	0	18
Bouvet Island Ile Bouvet	2010	0	1	0	0	1	0	0	0	2
Brazil	2006	73	124	22	28	58	21	13	382	721
Brésil	2008	82	122	22	30	64	21	15	382	738
	2010[1]	80	123	28	30	80	21	24	387	773
British Indian Ocean Terr.	2006	0	0	2	0	5	0	0	1	8
Terr. brit. de l'océan Indien	2008	0	0	2	0	9	0	65	1	77
	2010	0	0	2	0	8	0	65	1	76
British Virgin Islands	2006	1	1	6	2	11	0	0	10	31
Iles Vierges britanniques	2008	1	1	6	2	12	0	10	10	42
	2010	1	1	6	2	13	0	10	10	43
Brunei Darussalam	2006	15	25	5	15	7	0	0	101	168
Brunéi Darussalam	2008	35	21	5	3	8	0	0	99	171
	2010	34	19	6	3	8	0	1	99	170
Bulgaria	2006	13	12	2	0	12	0	8	0	47
Bulgarie	2008	7	12	2	0	17	0	7	0	45
	2010	7	12	2	0	18	18	9	0	66
Burkina Faso	2006	9	3	1	0	0	0	0	2	15
Burkina Faso	2008	8	5	1	0	0	0	0	2	16
	2010	9	6	1	0	4	1	0	3	24
Burundi	2006	12	11	0	6	18	1	4	2	54
Burundi	2008	9	8	0	6	18	1	4	2	48
	2010	10	10	0	6	17	4	3	2	52
Cambodia	2006	29	25	15	6	15	0	0	32	122
Cambodge	2008	37	25	12	3	18	0	67	31	193
	2010	37	24	15	3	28	0	67	30	204
Cameroon	2006	43	18	4	53	39	1	1	355	514
Cameroun	2008	41	15	3	53	43	1	3	355	514
	2010	39	16	4	53	110	11	13	378	624
Canada	2006	18	21	3	1	26	2	10	1	82
Canada	2008	12	16	3	1	26	2	10	2	72
	2010	12	15	3	1	32	2	10	2	77
Cape Verde	2006	3	5	3	0	15	0	0	2	28
Cap-Vert	2008	3	4	1	0	18	0	0	2	28
	2010	3	4	1	0	20	0	0	3	31

Threatened species *(continued)*
Number by taxonomic group
Espèces menacées *(suite)*
Nombre par groupe taxonomique

Country or area Pays ou zone	Year Année	Mammals Mammifères	Birds Oiseaux	Reptiles Reptiles	Amphibians Amphibiens	Fishes Poissons	Molluscs Mollusques	Invertebrates Invertébrés	Plants Plantes	Total
Cayman Islands Iles Caïmanes	2006	0	3	6	0	11	1	0	2	23
	2008	1	1	4	0	14	1	10	2	33
	2010	1	1	4	0	15	1	10	2	34
Central African Rep. Rép. centrafricaine	2006	12	3	1	0	0	0	0	15	31
	2008	7	5	1	0	0	0	0	15	28
	2010	8	7	1	0	3	0	0	17	36
Chad Tchad	2006	14	5	1	0	0	1	0	2	23
	2008	12	7	1	0	0	1	0	2	23
	2010	13	9	1	0	1	4	0	2	30
Chile Chili	2006	22	35	1	21	12	0	2	39	132
	2008	21	32	1	21	18	0	8	40	141
	2010	20	34	1	21	19	0	9	41	145
China [2] Chine [2]	2006	84	88	34	91	59	1	5	442	804
	2008	74	85	30	90	70	1	20	446	816
	2010	74	85	31	87	97	8	24	453	859
China, Hong Kong SAR Chine, Hong Kong RAS	2006	1	20	1	3	9	1	2	6	43
	2008	2	16	1	5	13	1	4	6	48
	2010	2	17	2	5	11	1	5	6	49
China, Macao SAR Chine, Macao RAS	2008	0	4	0	0	6	0	0	0	10
	2010	0	4	0	0	5	0	0	0	9
Christmas Is. Ile Christmas	2006	0	5	3	0	5	0	0	1	14
	2008	1	5	3	0	5	0	16	1	31
	2010	3	5	4	0	4	0	16	1	33
Cocos (Keeling) Islands Iles des Cocos (Keeling)	2006	0	1	1	0	4	1	0	0	7
	2008	2	0	1	0	7	0	17	0	27
	2010	2	0	1	0	8	0	17	0	28
Colombia Colombie	2006	38	88	16	217	28	0	2	225	614
	2008	52	86	15	214	31	0	31	223	652
	2010	51	91	19	213	50	0	30	227	681
Comoros Comores	2006	3	10	2	0	5	0	4	5	29
	2008	5	8	2	0	7	0	62	5	89
	2010	5	8	2	0	6	0	63	5	89
Congo Congo	2006	14	4	2	0	12	1	4	36	73
	2008	11	3	2	0	15	1	3	35	70
	2010	11	3	2	0	45	5	0	37	103
Cook Islands Iles Cook	2006	1	15	2	0	6	0	0	1	25
	2008	1	15	1	0	7	0	25	1	50
	2010	1	15	2	0	9	0	25	1	53
Costa Rica Costa Rica	2006	11	19	8	64	15	0	12	111	240
	2008	8	17	8	59	19	0	28	111	250
	2010	9	19	8	60	46	0	27	116	285
Côte d'Ivoire Côte d'Ivoire	2006	25	11	5	15	15	1	0	109	181
	2008	24	14	4	13	19	1	0	105	180
	2010	24	14	6	13	43	3	1	106	210
Croatia Croatie	2006	7	11	2	2	40	0	13	0	75
	2008	7	11	2	2	46	0	15	1	84
	2010	7	10	2	2	56	6	15	3	101
Cuba Cuba	2006	11	18	7	47	26	0	5	163	277
	2008	14	17	8	49	28	0	15	163	294
	2010	14	17	13	49	30	0	15	166	304
Cyprus Chypre	2006	4	12	4	0	9	0	0	7	36
	2008	5	5	4	0	12	0	0	7	33
	2010	5	5	4	0	17	0	4	8	43
Czech Republic République tchèque	2006	7	11	0	0	10	2	16	4	50
	2008	2	6	0	0	5	2	16	4	35
	2010	2	6	0	0	2	2	17	4	33
Dem. Rep. of the Congo Rép. dém. du Congo	2006	29	30	4	13	24	14	13	66	193
	2008	29	31	3	13	25	13	11	65	190
	2010	30	34	3	14	81	43	8	83	296

Threatened species *(continued)*
Number by taxonomic group

Espèces menacées *(suite)*
Nombre par groupe taxonomique

Country or area Pays ou zone	Year Année	Mammals Mammifères	Birds Oiseaux	Reptiles Reptiles	Amphibians Amphibiens	Fishes Poissons	Molluscs Mollusques	Invertebrates Invertébrés	Plants Plantes	Total
Denmark	2006	4	12	0	0	10	1	10	3	40
Danemark	2008	2	2	0	0	13	1	10	3	31
	2010	2	2	0	0	14	2	10	3	33
Djibouti	2006	7	6	2	0	12	0	0	2	29
Djibouti	2008	8	7	0	0	14	0	50	2	81
	2010	8	6	0	0	15	0	50	2	81
Dominica	2006	2	5	4	2	13	0	0	11	37
Dominique	2008	3	3	3	2	15	0	11	11	48
	2010	3	3	4	2	15	0	11	10	48
Dominican Republic	2006	5	14	10	31	12	0	6	30	108
Rép. dominicaine	2008	6	14	11	30	15	0	18	30	124
	2010	6	14	13	30	17	0	16	30	126
Ecuador	2006	34	76	11	165	14	48	0	1 832	2 180
Equateur	2008	43	69	11	171	15	48	12	1 839	2 208
	2010	43	71	22	171	49	48	14	1 837	2 255
Egypt	2006	14	18	11	0	17	0	1	2	63
Egypte	2008	17	10	11	0	24	0	46	2	110
	2010	17	10	10	0	36	0	46	2	121
El Salvador	2006	4	4	7	11	7	0	0	26	59
El Salvador	2008	5	3	7	10	7	0	6	26	64
	2010	5	5	7	10	12	0	6	27	72
Equatorial Guinea	2006	18	5	3	5	10	0	0	63	104
Guinée équatoriale	2008	18	5	4	4	13	0	0	63	107
	2010	19	5	5	4	27	0	2	68	130
Eritrea	2006	13	8	6	0	12	0	0	3	42
Erythrée	2008	9	9	6	0	14	0	50	3	91
	2010	10	10	6	0	18	0	50	3	97
Estonia	2006	5	4	0	0	2	0	4	0	15
Estonie	2008	1	3	0	0	4	0	4	0	12
	2010	1	3	0	0	4	0	3	0	11
Ethiopia	2006	40	21	1	9	3	3	12	22	111
Ethiopie	2008	31	22	1	9	2	3	11	22	101
	2010	32	23	1	9	14	4	11	26	120
Faeroe Islands	2006	4	0	0	0	8	0	0	0	12
Iles Féroé	2008	5	0	0	0	9	0	0	0	14
	2010	5	0	0	0	8	0	0	0	13
Falkland Is. (Malvinas)	2006	4	18	0	0	2	0	0	5	29
Iles Falkland (Malvinas)	2008	4	10	0	0	5	0	0	5	24
	2010	4	10	0	0	4	0	0	5	23
Fiji	2006	5	12	6	1	9	3	0	66	102
Fidji	2008	6	10	6	1	11	3	87	66	190
	2010	6	13	6	1	11	3	87	65	192
Finland	2006	4	11	0	0	3	1	9	1	29
Finlande	2008	1	4	0	0	5	1	9	1	21
	2010	1	4	0	0	5	1	6	1	18
France	2006	16	17	5	2	23	34	29	7	133
France	2008	9	6	5	2	31	34	40	8	135
	2010	9	7	4	2	40	62	29	15	168
French Guiana	2006	9	0	7	3	18	0	0	16	53
Guyane française	2008	6	0	6	3	21	0	0	16	52
	2010	7	0	6	3	24	0	0	16	56
French Polynesia	2006	3	35	2	0	10	30	0	47	127
Polynésie française	2008	1	32	1	0	13	29	26	47	149
	2010	1	32	1	0	20	33	26	47	160
Gabon	2006	13	5	4	4	16	0	0	108	150
Gabon	2008	13	5	3	3	21	0	0	108	153
	2010	14	5	3	3	59	0	0	120	204
Gambia	2006	10	2	2	0	14	0	0	4	32
Gambie	2008	9	5	2	0	16	0	0	4	36
	2010	10	6	2	0	21	0	0	4	43

54 Threatened species *(continued)*

Number by taxonomic group

Espèces menacées *(suite)*

Nombre par groupe taxonomique

Country or area Pays ou zone	Year Année	Mammals Mammifères	Birds Oiseaux	Reptiles Reptiles	Amphibians Amphibiens	Fishes Poissons	Molluscs Mollusques	Invertebrates Invertébrés	Plants Plantes	Total
Georgia	2006	13	10	7	1	9	0	9	0	49
Géorgie	2008	10	10	7	1	12	0	9	0	49
	2010	10	10	7	1	9	0	9	0	46
Germany	2006	10	16	0	0	15	9	21	12	83
Allemagne	2008	6	6	0	0	20	9	21	12	74
	2010	6	6	0	0	21	10	24	12	79
Ghana	2006	18	9	5	10	13	0	0	117	172
Ghana	2008	17	8	4	10	17	0	1	117	174
	2010	16	9	5	11	42	0	1	118	202
Gibraltar	2006	1	5	0	0	10	2	0	0	18
Gibraltar	2008	5	3	0	0	10	2	0	0	20
	2010	5	3	0	0	12	2	0	0	22
Greece	2006	12	15	5	5	49	1	13	11	111
Grèce	2008	10	11	5	5	62	1	13	11	118
	2010	10	11	8	5	73	9	27	13	156
Greenland	2006	8	3	0	0	6	0	0	1	18
Groenland	2008	6	0	0	0	6	0	0	1	13
	2010	6	0	0	0	7	0	0	1	14
Grenada	2006	1	3	4	1	13	0	0	3	25
Grenade	2008	3	1	4	1	15	0	10	3	37
	2010	3	1	4	1	15	0	10	3	37
Guadeloupe	2006	6	4	6	3	12	1	0	7	39
Guadeloupe	2008	5	1	5	3	14	1	15	7	51
	2010	5	1	7	3	14	1	15	8	54
Guam	2006	2	11	2	0	7	6	0	4	32
Guam	2008	2	12	2	0	9	6	0	4	35
	2010	2	14	2	0	6	6	0	4	34
Guatemala	2006	9	11	11	79	16	2	5	86	219
Guatemala	2008	16	11	13	80	16	2	7	83	228
	2010	16	10	13	81	20	2	6	82	230
Guernsey Guernesey	2010	0	0	0	0	2	0	0	0	2
Guinea	2006	22	10	3	8	15	0	3	22	83
Guinée	2008	22	12	2	5	19	0	4	22	86
	2010	22	13	4	5	63	1	4	22	134
Guinea-Bissau	2006	9	1	3	0	15	0	0	4	32
Guinée-Bissau	2008	11	2	2	0	18	0	0	4	37
	2010	12	3	3	0	30	0	0	4	52
Guyana	2006	11	3	6	9	18	0	1	23	71
Guyana	2008	8	3	5	7	22	0	1	22	68
	2010	9	3	5	4	25	0	1	22	69
Haiti	2006	4	13	9	47	13	0	4	29	119
Haïti	2008	5	13	8	46	15	0	14	29	130
	2010	5	13	13	46	17	0	14	29	137
Holy See Saint-Siège	2010	1	0	0	0	0	0	0	0	1
Honduras	2006	9	6	11	59	16	0	1	110	212
Honduras	2008	6	7	11	59	19	0	18	110	230
	2010	7	9	12	60	22	0	17	113	240
Hungary	2006	9	12	1	0	10	1	26	1	60
Hongrie	2008	2	9	1	0	9	1	25	1	48
	2010	2	9	1	0	8	1	25	1	47
Iceland	2006	8	2	0	0	10	0	0	0	20
Islande	2008	5	0	0	0	12	0	0	0	17
	2010	5	0	0	0	12	0	0	0	17
India	2006	89	82	26	68	35	2	20	247	569
Inde	2008	96	76	25	65	40	2	109	246	659
	2010	94	78	30	66	122	2	111	255	758

54 Threatened species *(continued)*
Number by taxonomic group
Espèces menacées *(suite)*
Nombre par groupe taxonomique

Country or area Pays ou zone	Year Année	Mammals Mammifères	Birds Oiseaux	Reptiles Reptiles	Amphibians Amphibiens	Fishes Poissons	Molluscs Mollusques	Invertebrates Invertébrés	Plants Plantes	Total
Indonesia	2006	146	121	28	39	105	3	28	387	857
Indonésie	2008	183	115	27	33	111	3	229	386	1 087
	2010	183	119	31	32	138	3	243	393	1 142
Iran (Islamic Rep. of)	2006	25	19	9	4	15	0	5	1	78
Iran (Rép. islamique d')	2008	16	20	9	4	21	0	19	1	90
	2010	16	21	12	4	29	0	19	1	102
Iraq	2006	12	18	2	2	5	0	2	0	41
Iraq	2008	13	18	2	1	6	0	15	0	55
	2010	13	18	2	1	11	0	15	0	60
Ireland	2006	4	9	0	0	7	1	2	1	24
Irlande	2008	5	1	0	0	16	1	2	1	26
	2010	5	1	0	0	18	1	1	1	27
Isle of Man Ile de Man	2010	0	0	0	0	2	0	0	0	2
Israel	2006	16	21	10	0	24	5	6	0	82
Israël	2008	15	13	10	1	31	5	52	0	127
	2010	15	13	9	1	35	5	53	0	131
Italy	2006	12	16	5	6	30	16	42	20	147
Italie	2008	7	8	5	8	33	16	42	19	138
	2010	7	8	4	9	42	30	47	27	174
Jamaica	2006	5	12	9	17	13	0	5	208	269
Jamaïque	2008	5	10	9	17	15	0	15	209	280
	2010	5	10	9	17	17	0	15	209	282
Japan	2006	38	56	11	20	35	25	18	12	215
Japon	2008	27	40	12	20	40	25	133	12	309
	2010	28	40	12	19	59	25	132	15	330
Jersey Jersey	2010	0	0	0	0	2	0	0	0	2
Jordan	2006	12	15	5	0	12	0	3	0	47
Jordanie	2008	13	8	5	0	14	0	49	0	89
	2010	13	10	5	0	13	0	48	1	90
Kazakhstan	2008	16	21	2	1	13	0	4	16	73
Kazakhstan	2010	16	21	1	1	14	0	4	16	73
Kenya	2006	32	27	5	6	68	16	16	104	274
Kenya	2008	27	27	5	7	71	16	55	103	311
	2010	28	30	6	7	66	17	55	129	338
Kiribati	2006	0	6	2	0	4	1	0	0	13
Kiribati	2008	1	5	1	0	7	1	72	0	87
	2010	1	6	1	0	9	1	72	0	90
Korea, Dem. P. R.	2006	13	23	0	1	8	0	2	3	50
Corée, R. p. dém. de	2008	9	20	0	1	8	0	2	3	43
	2010	9	22	0	1	12	0	2	6	52
Korea, Republic of	2006	12	35	0	1	10	0	2	0	60
Corée, République de	2008	9	30	0	2	14	0	3	0	58
	2010	9	30	0	2	17	0	3	3	64
Kuwait	2006	5	12	2	0	9	0	0	0	28
Koweït	2008	6	8	2	0	10	0	13	0	39
	2010	6	9	2	0	11	0	13	0	41
Kyrgyzstan	2006	9	6	2	0	0	0	3	1	21
Kirghizistan	2008	6	12	2	0	3	0	3	14	40
	2010	6	12	2	0	3	0	3	14	40
Lao People's Dem. Rep.	2006	35	24	12	9	6	0	0	20	106
Rép. dém. pop. lao	2008	46	23	11	5	6	0	3	21	115
	2010	45	22	12	5	23	0	3	22	132
Latvia	2006	5	9	0	0	4	0	9	0	27
Lettonie	2008	1	4	0	0	6	1	9	0	21
	2010	1	3	0	0	5	1	8	0	18
Lebanon	2006	9	10	7	0	10	0	3	0	39
Liban	2008	10	6	6	0	15	0	3	0	40
	2010	10	7	6	0	21	0	5	1	50

54

Threatened species *(continued)*

Number by taxonomic group

Espèces menacées *(suite)*

Nombre par groupe taxonomique

Country or area Pays ou zone	Year Année	Mammals Mammifères	Birds Oiseaux	Reptiles Reptiles	Amphibians Amphibiens	Fishes Poissons	Molluscs Mollusques	Invertebrates Invertébrés	Plants Plantes	Total
Lesotho	2006	3	7	0	2	1	0	1	1	15
Lesotho	2008	2	5	0	0	1	0	2	1	11
	2010	2	7	0	0	1	0	2	4	16
Liberia	2006	21	11	4	11	14	1	1	46	109
Libéria	2008	20	11	4	4	19	1	6	46	111
	2010	19	11	5	4	52	1	8	47	147
Libyan Arab Jamah.	2006	9	8	5	0	8	0	0	1	31
Jamah. arabe libyenne	2008	12	0	5	0	14	0	0	1	36
	2010	12	4	5	0	21	0	0	2	44
Liechtenstein	2006	2	1	0	0	0	0	4	0	7
Liechtenstein	2008	0	0	0	0	0	0	4	0	4
	2010	0	0	0	0	0	0	2	0	2
Lithuania	2006	6	5	0	0	4	0	6	0	21
Lituanie	2008	3	4	0	0	6	0	6	0	19
	2010	3	4	0	0	5	0	5	0	17
Luxembourg	2006	3	3	0	0	0	2	2	0	10
Luxembourg	2008	0	0	0	0	1	2	2	0	5
	2010	0	0	0	0	1	2	2	0	5
Madagascar	2006	48	36	18	55	72	24	8	277	538
Madagascar	2008	62	35	19	64	75	24	76	281	636
	2010	63	35	35	67	83	24	76	280	663
Malawi	2006	7	13	0	5	102	9	7	14	157
Malawi	2008	6	12	0	5	101	9	7	14	154
	2010	7	14	0	5	101	8	9	14	158
Malaysia	2006	51	43	22	47	45	19	2	688	917
Malaisie	2008	70	42	21	47	49	19	207	686	1 141
	2010	70	45	24	47	60	31	211	692	1 180
Maldives	2006	1	2	2	0	10	0	0	0	15
Maldives	2008	2	0	3	0	12	0	38	0	55
	2010	2	0	3	0	15	0	39	0	59
Mali	2006	15	7	1	0	1	0	0	6	30
Mali	2008	11	6	1	0	1	0	0	6	25
	2010	12	7	1	0	3	0	0	6	29
Malta	2006	1	10	0	0	11	3	0	3	28
Malte	2008	3	3	0	0	13	3	0	3	25
	2010	3	3	0	0	14	3	0	3	26
Marshall Islands	2006	1	2	2	0	8	1	0	0	14
Iles Marshall	2008	2	5	1	0	10	1	66	0	85
	2010	2	4	2	0	9	1	66	0	84
Martinique	2006	1	4	5	2	12	1	0	8	33
Martinique	2008	2	2	6	2	10	1	0	8	31
	2010	2	2	7	2	9	1	0	8	31
Mauritania	2006	12	6	3	0	17	0	1	0	39
Mauritanie	2008	14	8	3	0	23	0	1	0	49
	2010	15	9	3	0	30	0	1	0	58
Mauritius	2006	4	17	7	0	9	27	5	88	157
Maurice	2008	6	11	7	0	11	27	69	88	219
	2010	6	11	7	0	12	27	71	88	222
Mayotte	2006	1	4	2	0	1	0	1	0	9
Mayotte	2008	1	3	2	0	3	0	59	0	68
	2010	1	3	2	0	3	0	60	0	69
Mexico	2006	74	62	21	204	109	5	35	261	771
Mexique	2008	100	54	95	211	114	5	57	261	897
	2010	99	55	94	211	150	5	74	255	943
Micronesia (Fed. States of)	2006	5	8	2	0	8	4	0	6	33
Micronésie (Etats féd. de)	2008	6	9	3	0	13	4	104	5	144
	2010	7	10	4	0	14	4	104	5	148
Monaco	2006	0	0	0	0	6	0	0	0	6
Monaco	2008	2	0	0	0	12	0	0	0	14
	2010	2	0	0	0	9	0	0	0	11

54 Threatened species (continued)

Number by taxonomic group

Espèces menacées (suite)

Nombre par groupe taxonomique

Country or area Pays ou zone	Year Année	Mammals Mammifères	Birds Oiseaux	Reptiles Reptiles	Amphibians Amphibiens	Fishes Poissons	Molluscs Mollusques	Invertebrates Invertébrés	Plants Plantes	Total
Mongolia	2006	14	22	0	0	1	0	3	0	40
Mongolie	2008	11	21	0	0	1	0	3	0	36
	2010	11	21	0	0	1	0	3	0	36
Montserrat	2006	2	2	5	1	12	0	0	3	25
Montserrat	2008	3	2	2	1	14	0	11	3	36
	2010	3	2	2	1	13	0	11	3	35
Morocco	2006	17	14	10	2	25	0	9	2	79
Maroc	2008	18	10	10	2	31	0	9	2	82
	2010	18	10	11	2	45	33	7	31	157
Mozambique	2006	15	24	5	7	39	4	2	47	143
Mozambique	2008	11	21	5	3	45	4	54	46	189
	2010	12	23	8	3	52	4	55	52	209
Myanmar	2006	40	49	26	7	15	1	1	38	177
Myanmar	2008	45	41	22	0	17	1	63	38	227
	2010	45	41	24	0	33	1	63	42	249
Namibia	2006	10	22	5	2	16	1	1	24	81
Namibie	2008	11	21	4	1	21	0	0	24	82
	2010	12	24	4	1	25	0	0	26	92
Nauru	2006	0	2	0	0	5	0	0	0	7
Nauru	2008	1	2	0	0	8	0	62	0	73
	2010	1	2	0	0	9	0	62	0	74
Nepal	2006	32	34	9	3	0	0	0	7	85
Népal	2008	32	32	7	3	0	0	0	7	81
	2010	31	33	8	3	8	1	2	7	93
Netherlands	2006	10	13	0	0	9	1	6	0	39
Pays-Bas	2008	4	2	0	0	11	1	5	0	23
	2010	4	2	0	0	12	1	5	0	24
Netherlands Antilles	2006	2	4	6	0	13	0	0	2	27
Antilles néerlandaises	2008	4	1	6	0	15	0	11	2	39
	2010	3	1	5	0	15	0	11	3	38
New Caledonia	2006	6	16	3	0	12	11	1	217	266
Nouvelle-Calédonie	2008	9	14	2	0	17	11	84	218	355
	2010	9	15	13	0	24	11	86	257	415
New Zealand	2006	8	80	12	4	16	5	9	21	155
Nouvelle-Zélande	2008	8	69	12	4	14	5	10	21	143
	2010	9	70	13	4	21	5	10	21	153
Nicaragua	2006	6	8	8	10	19	2	3	39	95
Nicaragua	2008	5	9	8	10	21	2	17	39	111
	2010	6	11	8	10	26	2	15	43	121
Niger	2006	13	2	1	0	2	0	1	2	21
Niger	2008	11	5	0	0	2	0	1	2	21
	2010	12	6	0	0	4	1	1	2	26
Nigeria	2006	30	10	5	19	16	0	1	172	253
Nigéria	2008	27	12	4	13	21	0	3	171	251
	2010	27	13	4	13	56	1	11	172	297
Niue	2006	0	8	1	0	4	0	0	0	13
Nioué	2008	2	8	1	0	7	0	23	0	41
	2010	2	8	3	0	7	0	23	0	43
Norfolk Island	2006	0	19	2	0	2	12	0	1	36
Ile Norfolk	2008	0	15	2	0	2	12	9	1	41
	2010	0	14	2	0	3	12	9	1	41
Northern Mariana Islands	2006	2	13	2	0	6	4	0	5	32
Iles Mariannes du Nord	2008	5	14	1	0	9	4	47	5	85
	2010	5	15	1	0	8	4	47	5	85
Norway	2006	10	7	0	0	9	1	8	2	37
Norvège	2008	7	2	0	0	14	1	8	2	34
	2010	7	2	0	0	18	1	6	2	36
Occupied Palestinian Terr.	2006	0	4	4	0	0	0	1	0	9
Terr. palestinien occupé	2008	3	7	4	1	1	0	1	0	17
	2010	3	8	4	1	0	0	2	0	18

54 Threatened species (continued)
Number by taxonomic group
Espèces menacées (suite)
Nombre par groupe taxonomique

Country or area Pays ou zone	Year Année	Mammals Mammifères	Birds Oiseaux	Reptiles Reptiles	Amphibians Amphibiens	Fishes Poissons	Molluscs Mollusques	Invertebrates Invertébrés	Plants Plantes	Total
Oman	2006	13	14	4	0	21	0	4	6	62
Oman	2008	9	9	4	0	20	0	26	6	74
	2010	9	10	4	0	24	0	26	6	79
Pakistan	2006	23	32	9	0	20	0	0	2	86
Pakistan	2008	23	27	10	0	22	0	15	2	99
	2010	23	26	10	0	33	0	15	2	109
Palau	2006	3	2	2	0	7	5	0	4	23
Palaos	2008	4	2	2	0	12	5	97	4	126
	2010	4	4	2	0	12	5	97	4	128
Panama	2006	18	20	7	60	19	0	2	196	322
Panama	2008	14	17	7	49	19	0	20	194	320
	2010	15	17	7	50	36	0	20	202	347
Papua New Guinea	2006	58	32	10	10	37	2	10	142	301
Papouasie-Nvl-Guinée	2008	41	36	9	11	38	2	167	142	446
	2010	39	37	11	11	41	2	169	143	453
Paraguay	2006	9	29	2	2	0	0	0	12	54
Paraguay	2008	8	27	2	0	0	0	0	10	47
	2010	8	27	3	0	0	0	0	10	48
Peru	2006	46	98	8	86	8	0	2	276	524
Pérou	2008	53	93	6	96	10	0	3	275	536
	2010	54	96	8	97	19	0	3	274	551
Philippines	2006	51	74	9	48	58	3	17	215	475
Philippines	2008	39	67	9	48	60	3	199	216	641
	2010	39	72	38	48	65	3	210	222	697
Pitcairn	2006	0	11	1	0	4	5	0	7	28
Pitcairn	2008	2	10	0	0	6	5	10	7	40
	2010	2	10	0	0	8	5	10	7	42
Poland	2006	13	14	0	0	4	1	15	4	51
Pologne	2008	5	6	0	0	6	1	15	4	37
	2010	5	6	0	0	6	1	15	4	37
Portugal	2006	15	16	3	0	36	67	15	15	167
Portugal	2008	11	8	2	1	38	67	16	16	159
	2010	11	9	3	1	47	66	13	21	171
Puerto Rico	2006	2	13	8	13	11	0	1	54	102
Porto Rico	2008	3	8	9	14	13	0	1	53	101
	2010	3	8	9	14	15	0	1	53	103
Qatar	2006	1	7	2	0	6	0	0	0	16
Qatar	2008	2	4	1	0	7	0	13	0	27
	2010	2	5	1	0	11	0	13	0	32
Republic of Moldova	2006	5	8	1	0	9	0	4	0	27
République de Moldova	2008	4	9	1	0	9	0	4	0	27
	2010	4	9	2	0	9	0	3	0	27
Réunion	2006	4	10	2	0	5	14	2	16	53
Réunion	2008	5	6	0	0	6	14	58	15	104
	2010	5	6	0	0	5	14	59	15	104
Romania	2006	15	14	2	0	13	0	22	1	67
Roumanie	2008	7	12	2	0	16	0	22	1	60
	2010	7	12	2	0	18	0	24	1	64
Russian Federation	2006	44	53	6	0	22	1	28	7	161
Fédération de Russie	2008	33	51	6	0	32	1	28	7	158
	2010	32	18	8	0	35	1	24	8	126
Rwanda	2006	17	12	0	8	9	0	5	3	54
Rwanda	2008	19	10	0	8	9	0	3	3	52
	2010	20	12	0	8	9	0	2	4	55
Saint Helena	2006	1	20	1	0	11	0	2	26	61
Sainte-Hélène	2008	2	18	1	0	11	0	2	26	60
	2010	2	19	1	0	9	0	2	27	60
Saint Kitts and Nevis	2006	1	1	5	1	12	0	0	2	22
Saint-Kitts-et-Nevis	2008	2	1	5	1	14	0	10	2	35
	2010	2	1	5	1	15	0	10	2	36

54 Threatened species *(continued)*
Number by taxonomic group
Espèces menacées *(suite)*
Nombre par groupe taxonomique

Country or area Pays ou zone	Year Année	Mammals Mammifères	Birds Oiseaux	Reptiles Reptiles	Amphibians Amphibiens	Fishes Poissons	Molluscs Mollusques	Invertebrates Invertébrés	Plants Plantes	Total
Saint Lucia	2006	2	5	6	0	11	0	0	6	30
Sainte-Lucie	2008	2	5	5	0	15	0	11	6	44
	2010	2	5	6	0	16	0	11	6	46
Saint Pierre and Miquelon	2006	0	0	0	0	1	0	0	0	1
Saint-Pierre-et-Miquelon	2008	3	1	0	0	1	0	0	0	5
	2010	3	1	0	0	0	0	0	0	4
Saint Vincent-Grenadines	2006	3	3	4	1	12	0	0	4	27
Saint Vincent-Grenadines	2008	2	2	3	1	16	0	10	4	38
	2010	2	2	3	1	16	0	10	4	38
Samoa	2006	3	8	2	0	5	1	0	2	21
Samoa	2008	2	7	1	0	8	1	52	2	73
	2010	2	7	3	0	11	1	52	2	78
San Marino	2008	0	0	0	0	1	0	0	0	1
Saint-Marin	2010	0	0	0	0	0	0	0	0	0
Sao Tome and Principe	2008	5	10	3	3	8	1	1	35	66
Sao Tomé-et-Principe	2010	5	10	4	3	11	1	1	35	70
Saudi Arabia	2006	12	18	2	0	13	0	2	3	50
Arabie saoudite	2008	9	14	2	0	16	0	53	3	97
	2010	9	14	2	0	22	0	53	3	103
Senegal	2006	15	6	7	0	23	0	0	7	58
Sénégal	2008	15	8	6	0	28	0	0	7	64
	2010	16	9	6	0	41	0	1	9	82
Seychelles	2006	4	13	10	6	12	2	3	45	95
Seychelles	2008	5	10	10	6	14	2	63	45	155
	2010	5	10	10	6	14	36	64	45	190
Sierra Leone	2006	15	10	3	2	12	0	2	47	91
Sierra Leone	2008	16	10	3	2	16	0	0	47	94
	2010	17	10	3	2	45	3	3	48	131
Singapore	2006	5	14	5	0	20	0	1	55	100
Singapour	2008	12	14	4	0	22	0	161	54	267
	2010	11	17	5	0	25	0	162	57	277
Slovakia	2006	8	13	1	0	9	6	13	2	52
Slovaquie	2008	3	7	1	0	7	6	13	2	39
	2010	3	7	0	0	5	2	15	2	34
Slovenia	2006	7	8	1	2	21	0	42	0	81
Slovénie	2008	4	4	1	2	24	0	42	0	77
	2010	4	4	0	2	26	18	41	0	95
Solomon Islands	2006	20	20	4	2	7	2	4	16	75
Iles Salomon	2008	17	20	4	2	12	2	138	16	211
	2010	20	20	6	2	15	2	139	16	220
Somalia	2006	15	13	3	0	21	1	1	17	71
Somalie	2008	14	12	3	0	26	1	50	17	123
	2010	15	11	4	0	26	1	50	21	128
South Africa	2006	28	38	20	21	58	18	123	73	379
Afrique du Sud	2008	23	35	19	21	65	24	137	74	398
	2010	24	39	21	20	81	21	138	97	441
Spain	2006	20	21	18	6	44	27	35	48	219
Espagne	2008	16	15	18	6	52	27	35	49	218
	2010	16	15	19	6	62	28	39	55	240
Sri Lanka	2006	21	17	8	52	29	0	52	280	459
Sri Lanka	2008	30	13	8	53	31	0	119	280	534
	2010	30	14	11	53	41	0	120	283	552
Sudan	2006	19	11	3	0	11	0	2	17	63
Soudan	2008	14	13	3	0	13	0	45	17	105
	2010	15	14	3	0	17	0	45	18	112
Suriname	2006	11	0	6	2	19	0	0	27	65
Suriname	2008	7	0	5	1	20	0	0	26	59
	2010	8	0	5	1	24	0	1	26	65

54

Threatened species *(continued)*

Number by taxonomic group

Espèces menacées *(suite)*

Nombre par groupe taxonomique

Country or area Pays ou zone	Year Année	Mammals Mammifères	Birds Oiseaux	Reptiles Reptiles	Amphibians Amphibiens	Fishes Poissons	Molluscs Mollusques	Invertebrates Invertébrés	Plants Plantes	Total
Svalbard and Jan Mayen Is.	2006	6	3	0	0	2	0	0	0	11
Svalbard et îles Jan Mayen	2008	1	0	0	0	2	0	0	0	3
	2010	1	0	0	0	2	0	0	0	3
Swaziland	2006	8	8	0	1	0	0	0	11	28
Swaziland	2008	4	7	0	0	3	0	0	11	25
	2010	5	9	0	0	4	0	0	11	29
Sweden	2006	5	11	0	0	9	1	12	3	41
Suède	2008	1	3	0	0	12	1	12	3	32
	2010	1	3	0	0	11	1	10	3	29
Switzerland	2006	4	9	0	1	8	0	29	3	54
Suisse	2008	2	2	0	1	11	0	29	3	48
	2010	2	2	0	1	9	0	28	3	45
Syrian Arab Republic	2006	10	14	7	0	22	0	5	0	58
Rép. arabe syrienne	2008	16	13	6	0	27	0	6	0	68
	2010	16	13	6	0	33	0	7	3	78
Tajikistan	2006	10	10	1	0	5	0	2	2	30
Tadjikistan	2008	8	9	1	0	8	0	2	14	42
	2010	8	9	2	0	5	0	2	14	40
Thailand	2006	38	49	22	3	49	1	0	88	250
Thaïlande	2008	57	44	22	4	50	1	179	86	443
	2010	57	45	23	4	72	1	184	91	477
TFYR of Macedonia	2006	9	11	2	0	8	0	5	0	35
L'ex-R.Y. Macédoine	2008	5	10	2	0	14	0	5	0	36
	2010	5	10	2	0	14	54	5	0	90
Timor-Leste	2008	4	5	1	0	5	0	0	0	15
Timor-Leste	2010	4	7	2	0	5	0	0	0	18
Togo	2006	12	2	4	3	12	0	0	10	43
Togo	2008	10	2	3	3	16	0	0	10	44
	2010	11	3	3	2	24	0	1	10	54
Tokelau	2006	0	1	2	0	4	0	0	0	7
Tokélaou	2008	0	1	1	0	7	0	31	0	40
	2010	0	1	2	0	7	0	31	0	41
Tonga	2006	2	4	3	0	5	2	0	3	19
Tonga	2008	2	4	2	0	9	2	33	4	56
	2010	2	4	3	0	10	2	33	4	58
Trinidad and Tobago	2006	1	4	5	9	18	0	0	1	38
Trinité-et-Tobago	2008	2	2	5	9	19	0	10	1	48
	2010	2	2	5	9	19	0	10	1	48
Tunisia	2006	15	9	4	2	14	0	7	0	51
Tunisie	2008	14	8	4	1	20	0	7	0	54
	2010	13	7	5	1	31	5	6	7	75
Turkey	2006	18	16	13	10	52	0	11	3	123
Turquie	2008	17	15	13	10	60	0	13	3	131
	2010	17	15	20	11	67	0	15	5	150
Turkmenistan	2006	16	14	1	0	9	0	5	0	45
Turkménistan	2008	9	15	1	0	12	0	5	3	45
	2010	9	15	2	0	11	0	5	3	45
Turks and Caicos Islands	2006	1	2	5	0	11	0	0	2	21
Iles Turques et Caïques	2008	2	2	4	0	14	0	10	2	34
	2010	2	2	4	0	14	0	10	2	34
Tuvalu	2006	0	1	2	0	6	2	0	0	11
Tuvalu	2008	2	1	1	0	8	1	70	0	83
	2010	2	1	2	0	9	1	70	0	85
Uganda	2006	28	15	1	10	49	10	17	40	170
Ouganda	2008	21	18	0	6	54	10	12	38	159
	2010	22	19	1	7	61	9	6	41	166
Ukraine	2006	17	13	2	0	14	0	14	1	61
Ukraine	2008	11	12	2	0	20	0	14	1	60
	2010	11	12	1	0	21	0	15	1	61

54 Threatened species *(continued)*

Number by taxonomic group

Espèces menacées *(suite)*

Nombre par groupe taxonomique

Country or area Pays ou zone	Year Année	Mammals Mammifères	Birds Oiseaux	Reptiles Reptiles	Amphibians Amphibiens	Fishes Poissons	Molluscs Mollusques	Invertebrates Invertébrés	Plants Plantes	Total
United Arab Emirates	2006	7	12	2	0	8	0	2	0	31
Emirats arabes unis	2008	7	8	2	0	9	0	16	0	42
	2010	7	10	2	0	13	0	16	0	48
United Kingdom	2006	10	13	0	0	14	2	8	13	60
Royaume-Uni	2008	5	2	0	0	34	2	8	14	65
	2010	5	2	0	0	41	2	9	14	73
United Rep. of Tanzania	2006	35	39	5	41	130	17	25	241	533
Rép.-Unie de Tanzanie	2008	34	40	5	49	138	17	66	240	589
	2010	35	42	14	50	172	15	65	298	691
United States	2006	41	79	27	53	159	273	303	243	1 178
Etats-Unis	2008	37	74	32	56	164	273	312	244	1 192
	2010	37	74	32	56	177	273	258	245	1 152
United States Virgin Is.	2006	2	5	5	2	10	0	0	11	35
Iles Vierges américaines	2008	1	1	6	2	12	0	10	10	42
	2010	2	1	4	2	12	0	0	12	33
Uruguay	2006	7	26	3	4	22	0	1	1	64
Uruguay	2008	10	24	4	4	28	0	1	1	72
	2010	11	23	4	5	35	0	1	1	80
Uzbekistan	2006	10	16	2	0	5	0	1	1	35
Ouzbékistan	2008	11	15	2	0	8	0	1	15	52
	2010	10	15	2	0	7	0	1	15	50
Vanuatu	2006	5	8	2	0	7	2	0	10	34
Vanuatu	2008	8	8	2	0	11	1	78	10	118
	2010	8	7	3	0	14	1	78	10	121
Venezuela (Boliv. Rep. of)	2006	26	25	13	71	26	0	3	69	233
Venezuela (Rép. boliv. du)	2008	32	26	13	71	29	0	19	69	259
	2010	32	27	14	72	34	0	21	70	270
Viet Nam	2006	45	42	27	18	30	0	0	148	310
Viet Nam	2008	54	39	27	17	33	0	91	147	408
	2010	54	40	30	16	46	0	92	146	424
Wallis and Futuna Islands	2006	0	9	1	0	3	0	0	1	14
Iles Wallis et Futuna	2008	0	9	0	0	6	0	57	1	73
	2010	0	9	1	0	6	0	57	1	74
Western Sahara	2006	9	4	2	0	14	0	1	0	30
Sahara occidental	2008	11	1	0	0	19	0	1	0	32
	2010	11	1	0	0	26	0	1	0	39
Yemen	2006	9	14	2	1	13	2	4	159	204
Yémen	2008	9	13	3	1	18	2	61	159	266
	2010	9	14	3	1	21	1	61	159	269
Zambia	2006	12	12	0	1	6	4	3	8	46
Zambie	2008	8	12	0	1	10	3	1	8	43
	2010	9	14	0	1	20	13	1	9	67
Zimbabwe	2006	10	11	0	6	0	0	5	18	50
Zimbabwe	2008	8	11	0	6	3	0	4	17	49
	2010	9	13	3	6	3	0	5	16	55

Source:
The World Conservation Union (IUCN) / Species Survival Commission (SSC), Gland, Switzerland and Cambridge, United Kingdom, IUCN Red List of Threatened Species, 2006, 2008 and 2010.

Source:
Union mondiale pour la nature (UICN) / Commission de la sauvegarde des espèces, Gland, Suisse, et Cambridge, Royaume-Uni, La liste rouge des espèces menacées de l'UICN, 2006, 2008 et 2010.

1 The figures for Amphibians displayed here are those that were agreed at the GAA Brazil workshop in April 2003; the "consistent Red List Categories" were not yet accepted by the Brazilian experts.

1 Les chiffres concernant les amphibiens sont ceux qui ont été convenus lors de l'atelier de l'Évaluation mondiale des amphibiens du Brésil en avril 2003 ; les "catégories conformes à la Liste rouge" n'ont pas encore été acceptées par les experts brésiliens.

2 For statistical purposes, the data for China do not include those for the Hong Kong Special Administrative Region (Hong Kong SAR), Macao Special Administrative Region (Macao SAR) and Taiwan Province of China.

2 Pour la présentation des statistiques, les données pour la Chine ne comprennent pas la Région Administrative Spéciale de Hong Kong (Hong Kong RAS), la Région Administrative Spéciale de Macao (Macao RAS) et la province de Taiwan.

55 Water supply and sanitation coverage

Accès à l'eau et à l'assainissement

Country or area Pays ou zone	Year Année	Improved drinking water sources – Un système amélioré de distribution d'eau potable: Urban (%) Urbaine (%)	Rural (%) Rurale (%)	Total (%) Totale (%)	Improved sanitation facilities – Un système amélioré d'assainissement: Urban (%) Urbaine (%)	Rural (%) Rurale (%)	Total (%) Totale (%)
		Proportion of population with access to: - Pourcentage de la population ayant accès à :					
Afghanistan Afghanistan	1995	12	1	3	36	27	29
	2000	36	17	21	46	28	32
	2008	78	39	48	60	30	37
Albania Albanie	1990	100	...	...	...	...	...
	1995	100	94	96	97	81	87
	2000	100	95	97	97	85	90
	2008	96	98	97	98	98	98
Algeria Algérie	1990	100	88	94	99	77	88
	1995	98	86	93	99	78	90
	2000	93	84	89	99	82	92
	2008	85	79	83	98	88	95
Andorra Andorre	1990	100	100	100	100	100	100
	1995	100	100	100	100	100	100
	2000	100	100	100	100	100	100
	2008	100	100	100	100	100	100
Angola Angola	1990	30	40	36	58	6	25
	1995	32	40	36	60	7	30
	2000	43	40	41	70	11	40
	2008	60	38	50	86	18	57
Anguilla Anguilla	1990	...	...	...	99	...	99
	1995	60	...	60	99	...	99
	2000	60	...	60	99	...	99
	2008	...	...	...	99	...	99
Antigua and Barbuda Antigua-et-Barbuda	1990	95	...	...	98	...	...
	1995	95	89	91	98	94	95
	2000	95	89	91	98	94	95
	2008	95	...	...	98	...	...
Argentina Argentine	1990	97	72	94	93	73	90
	1995	98	75	95	93	75	91
	2000	98	78	96	92	77	91
	2008	98	80	97	91	77	90
Armenia Arménie	1990	99	...	...	95	...	...
	1995	99	78	92	95	75	88
	2000	99	83	93	95	77	89
	2008	98	93	96	95	80	90
Aruba Aruba	1990	100	100	100	...	...	...
	1995	100	100	100	...	...	...
	2000	100	100	100	...	...	...
	2008	100	100	100	...	...	...
Australia Australie	1990	100	100	100	100	100	100
	1995	100	100	100	100	100	100
	2000	100	100	100	100	100	100
	2008	100	100	100	100	100	100
Austria Autriche	1990	100	100	100	100	100	100
	1995	100	100	100	100	100	100
	2000	100	100	100	100	100	100
	2008	100	100	100	100	100	100
Azerbaijan Azerbaïdjan	1990	88	49	70	...	...	...
	1995	88	52	71	70	43	57
	2000	88	59	74	73	50	62
	2008	88	71	80	85	39	45
Bahamas Bahamas	1990	98	...	...	100	100	100
	1995	98	86	96	100	100	100
	2000	98	86	96	100	100	100
	2008	98	...	...	100	100	100

55 Water supply and sanitation coverage *(continued)*

Accès à l'eau et à l'assainissement *(suite)*

Country or area Pays ou zone	Year Année	Improved drinking water sources / Un système amélioré de distribution d'eau potable: Urban (%) Urbaine (%)	Rural (%) Rurale (%)	Total (%) Totale (%)	Improved sanitation facilities / Un système amélioré d'assainissement: Urban (%) Urbaine (%)	Rural (%) Rurale (%)	Total (%) Totale (%)
Bahrain Bahreïn	1990	100	...	...	100	...	...
	1995	100	...	...	100	...	...
	2000	100	...	...	100	...	...
	2008	100	...	...	100	...	...
Bangladesh [1] Bangladesh [1]	1990	88	76	78	57	28	34
	1995	87	76	78	56	33	38
	2000	86	77	79	56	40	44
	2008	85	78	80	55	52	53
Barbados Barbade	1990	100	100	100	100	100	100
	1995	100	100	100	100	100	100
	2000	100	100	100	100	100	100
	2008	100	100	100	100	100	100
Belarus Bélarus	1990	100	99	100	...	...	...
	1995	100	99	100	91	96	93
	2000	100	99	100	91	96	93
	2008	100	99	100	91	97	93
Belgium Belgique	1990	100	100	100	100	100	100
	1995	100	100	100	100	100	100
	2000	100	100	100	100	100	100
	2008	100	100	100	100	100	100
Belize Belize	1990	89	63	75	73	75	74
	1995	92	73	82	79	78	78
	2000	95	83	89	84	81	82
	2008	99	100	99	93	86	90
Benin Bénin	1990	72	47	56	14	1	5
	1995	75	53	61	17	2	8
	2000	78	59	66	19	3	9
	2008	84	69	75	24	4	12
Bhutan Bhoutan	2000	99	88	91	87	54	62
	2008	99	88	92	87	54	65
Bolivia (Plurinational State of) Bolivie (État plur. de)	1990	92	42	70	29	6	19
	1995	93	49	75	30	7	21
	2000	94	56	79	32	8	23
	2008	96	67	86	34	9	25
Bosnia and Herzegovina Bosnie-Herzégovine	1995	99	96	97	98	93	95
	2000	99	96	97	98	93	95
	2008	100	98	99	99	92	95
Botswana Botswana	1990	100	88	93	58	20	36
	1995	100	89	94	63	25	44
	2000	99	89	94	67	31	50
	2008	99	90	95	74	39	60
Brazil Brésil	1990	96	65	88	81	35	69
	1995	97	70	91	82	35	72
	2000	97	75	93	84	36	75
	2008	99	84	97	87	37	80
British Virgin Islands Iles Vierges britanniques	1990	98	98	98	100	100	100
	1995	98	98	98	100	100	100
	2000	98	98	98	100	100	100
	2008	98	98	98	100	100	100
Bulgaria Bulgarie	1990	100	99	100	100	98	99
	1995	100	100	100	100	99	100
	2000	100	100	100	100	100	100
	2008	100	100	100	100	100	100
Burkina Faso Burkina Faso	1990	73	36	41	28	2	6
	1995	79	44	49	29	3	7
	2000	85	55	60	31	4	8
	2008	95	72	76	33	6	11

Proportion of population with access to: - Pourcentage de la population ayant accès à :

Country or area Pays ou zone	Year Année	Proportion of population with access to: - Pourcentage de la population ayant accès à : Improved drinking water sources Un système amélioré de distribution d'eau potable			Improved sanitation facilities Un système amélioré d'assainissement		
		Urban (%) Urbaine (%)	Rural (%) Rurale (%)	Total (%) Totale (%)	Urban (%) Urbaine (%)	Rural (%) Rurale (%)	Total (%) Totale (%)
Burundi Burundi	1990	97	68	70	41	44	44
	1995	93	69	71	44	45	45
	2000	89	70	72	46	45	45
	2008	83	71	72	49	46	46
Cambodia Cambodge	1990	52	33	35	38	5	9
	1995	54	34	37	40	6	11
	2000	64	42	46	50	10	17
	2008	81	56	61	67	18	29
Cameroon Cameroun	1990	77	31	50	65	35	47
	1995	82	37	57	63	35	48
	2000	86	43	64	60	35	47
	2008	92	51	74	56	35	47
Canada Canada	1990	100	99	100	100	99	100
	1995	100	99	100	100	99	100
	2000	100	99	100	100	99	100
	2008	100	99	100	100	99	100
Cape Verde Cap-Vert	1995	86	78	82	64	17	40
	2000	86	80	83	64	24	45
	2008	85	82	84	65	38	54
Cayman Islands Iles Caïmanes	1990	...	...	...	96	...	96
	1995	93	...	93	96	...	96
	2000	93	...	93	96	...	96
	2008	95	...	95	96	...	96
Central African Rep. Rép. centrafricaine	1990	78	47	58	21	5	11
	1995	81	48	60	25	9	15
	2000	85	49	63	32	16	22
	2008	92	51	67	43	28	34
Chad Tchad	1990	48	36	38	20	2	6
	1995	54	39	42	21	2	6
	2000	60	41	45	22	3	7
	2008	67	44	50	23	4	9
Chile Chili	1990	99	48	90	91	48	84
	1995	99	57	92	93	59	88
	2000	99	66	94	96	71	92
	2008	99	75	96	98	83	96
China Chine	1990	97	56	67	48	38	41
	1995	97	63	74	52	42	45
	2000	98	70	80	55	46	49
	2008	98	82	89	58	52	55
Colombia Colombie	1990	98	68	88	80	43	68
	1995	98	70	90	80	46	70
	2000	99	71	91	80	50	72
	2008	99	73	92	81	55	74
Comoros Comores	1990	98	83	87	34	11	17
	1995	96	87	90	36	17	22
	2000	93	92	92	42	23	28
	2008	91	97	95	50	30	36
Congo Congo	2000	95	34	70	31	29	30
	2008	95	34	71	31	29	30
Cook Islands Iles Cook	1990	99	87	94	100	91	96
	1995	99	87	94	100	92	97
	2000	99	87	95	100	99	100
	2008	98	...	...	100	100	100
Costa Rica Costa Rica	1990	99	86	93	94	91	93
	1995	99	88	94	95	92	94
	2000	99	89	95	95	94	95
	2008	100	91	97	95	96	95

55 Water supply and sanitation coverage *(continued)*

Accès à l'eau et à l'assainissement *(suite)*

Country or area Pays ou zone	Year Année	Improved drinking water sources / Un système amélioré de distribution d'eau potable: Urban (%) Urbaine (%)	Rural (%) Rurale (%)	Total (%) Totale (%)	Improved sanitation facilities / Un système amélioré d'assainissement: Urban (%) Urbaine (%)	Rural (%) Rurale (%)	Total (%) Totale (%)
Côte d'Ivoire Côte d'Ivoire	1990	90	67	76	38	8	20
	1995	91	67	77	38	9	21
	2000	92	67	78	37	10	22
	2008	93	68	80	36	11	23
Croatia Croatie	1995	100	97	99	99	98	99
	2000	100	97	99	99	98	99
	2008	100	97	99	99	98	99
Cuba Cuba	1990	93	53	82	86	64	80
	1995	94	63	86	88	69	83
	2000	95	73	90	90	73	86
	2008	96	89	94	94	81	91
Cyprus Chypre	1990	100	100	100	100	100	100
	1995	100	100	100	100	100	100
	2000	100	100	100	100	100	100
	2008	100	100	100	100	100	100
Czech Republic République tchèque	1990	100	100	100	100	98	100
	1995	100	100	100	100	98	99
	2000	100	100	100	99	97	98
	2008	100	100	100	99	97	98
Dem. Rep. of the Congo Rép. dém. du Congo	1990	90	27	45	23	4	9
	1995	88	27	44	23	7	12
	2000	85	27	44	23	13	16
	2008	80	28	46	23	23	23
Denmark Danemark	1990	100	100	100	100	100	100
	1995	100	100	100	100	100	100
	2000	100	100	100	100	100	100
	2008	100	100	100	100	100	100
Djibouti Djibouti	1990	80	69	77	73	45	66
	1995	81	67	78	72	42	66
	2000	88	61	84	69	30	63
	2008	98	52	92	63	10	56
Dominica Dominique	1995	96	92	95	80	84	81
	2000	96	92	95	80	84	81
Dominican Republic Rép. dominicaine	1990	98	76	88	83	61	73
	1995	95	78	88	84	65	76
	2000	92	80	87	85	69	79
	2008	87	84	86	87	74	83
Ecuador Equateur	1990	81	62	72	86	48	69
	1995	86	70	79	89	59	76
	2000	91	78	86	92	70	83
	2008	97	88	94	96	84	92
Egypt Egypte	1990	96	86	90	91	57	72
	1995	97	90	93	93	68	79
	2000	99	93	96	95	79	86
	2008	100	98	99	97	92	94
El Salvador El Salvador	1990	90	58	74	88	62	75
	1995	91	63	78	88	68	79
	2000	92	68	82	89	74	83
	2008	94	76	87	89	83	87
Equatorial Guinea Guinée équatoriale	1995	45	42	43	60	46	51
	2000	45	42	43	60	46	51
Eritrea Erythrée	1990	62	39	43	58	0	9
	1995	64	42	46	57	1	10
	2000	70	50	54	54	2	11
	2008	74	57	61	52	4	14
Estonia Estonie	1990	99	97	98	...	...	...
	1995	99	97	98	96	94	95
	2000	99	97	98	96	94	95
	2008	99	97	98	96	94	95

Country or area Pays ou zone	Year Année	Proportion of population with access to: - Pourcentage de la population ayant accès à : Improved drinking water sources Un système amélioré de distribution d'eau potable Urban (%) Urbaine (%)	Rural (%) Rurale (%)	Total (%) Totale (%)	Improved sanitation facilities Un système amélioré d'assainissement Urban (%) Urbaine (%)	Rural (%) Rurale (%)	Total (%) Totale (%)
Ethiopia Ethiopie	1990	77	8	17	21	1	4
	1995	82	12	22	23	2	5
	2000	88	18	28	26	5	8
	2008	98	26	38	29	8	12
Fiji Fidji	1990	92	...	...	92	...	...
	1995	93	...	...	94	...	...
	2000	93	...	...	96	...	...
Finland Finlande	1990	100	100	100	100	100	100
	1995	100	100	100	100	100	100
	2000	100	100	100	100	100	100
	2008	100	100	100	100	100	100
France France	1990	100	100	100	100	100	100
	1995	100	100	100	100	100	100
	2000	100	100	100	100	100	100
	2008	100	100	100	100	100	100
French Guiana Guyane française	1995	88	71	84	85	57	78
	2000	88	71	84	85	57	78
French Polynesia Polynésie française	1990	100	100	100	99	97	98
	1995	100	100	100	99	97	98
	2000	100	100	100	99	97	98
	2008	100	100	100	99	97	98
Gabon Gabon	1995	95	49	84	38	29	36
	2000	95	47	85	37	30	36
	2008	95	41	87	33	30	33
Gambia Gambie	1990	85	67	74	...	...	...
	1995	88	72	79	63	58	60
	2000	91	77	84	65	61	63
	2008	96	86	92	68	65	67
Georgia Géorgie	1990	94	66	81	97	95	96
	1995	94	69	82	97	95	96
	2000	97	80	89	96	94	95
	2008	100	96	98	96	93	95
Germany Allemagne	1990	100	100	100	100	100	100
	1995	100	100	100	100	100	100
	2000	100	100	100	100	100	100
	2008	100	100	100	100	100	100
Ghana Ghana	1990	84	37	54	11	4	7
	1995	86	47	63	13	5	8
	2000	88	58	71	15	5	9
	2008	90	74	82	18	7	13
Greece Grèce	1990	99	92	96	100	92	97
	1995	100	95	98	99	94	97
	2000	100	98	99	99	96	98
	2008	100	99	100	99	97	98
Grenada Grenade	1990	97	...	...	96	97	97
	1995	97	93	94	96	97	97
	2000	97	93	94	96	97	97
	2008	97	...	...	96	97	97
Guadeloupe Guadeloupe	1990	98	...	...	...	...	...
	1995	98	93	98	94	...	...
	2000	98	93	98	94	...	...
	2008	98	...	...	95	...	...
Guam Guam	1990	100	100	100	99	98	99
	1995	100	100	100	99	98	99
	2000	100	100	100	99	98	99
	2008	100	100	100	99	98	99

55 Water supply and sanitation coverage *(continued)*

Accès à l'eau et à l'assainissement *(suite)*

Country or area Pays ou zone	Year Année	Proportion of population with access to: - Pourcentage de la population ayant accès à : Improved drinking water sources / Un système amélioré de distribution d'eau potable — Urban (%) Urbaine (%)	Rural (%) Rurale (%)	Total (%) Totale (%)	Improved sanitation facilities / Un système amélioré d'assainissement — Urban (%) Urbaine (%)	Rural (%) Rurale (%)	Total (%) Totale (%)
Guatemala Guatemala	1990	91	75	82	84	51	65
	1995	93	80	86	85	57	69
	2000	95	84	89	87	63	74
	2008	98	90	94	89	73	81
Guinea Guinée	1990	87	38	52	18	6	9
	1995	88	45	58	23	8	12
	2000	88	51	62	27	9	15
	2008	89	61	71	34	11	19
Guinea-Bissau Guinée-Bissau	1990	...	37	...	...	...	...
	1995	78	41	52	41	6	16
	2000	79	45	55	43	7	18
	2008	83	51	61	49	9	21
Guyana Guyana	1995	92	85	87	85	76	79
	2000	93	87	89	85	77	79
	2008	98	93	94	85	80	81
Haiti Haïti	1990	62	41	47	44	19	26
	1995	65	45	52	40	18	25
	2000	67	49	55	34	15	22
	2008	71	55	63	24	10	17
Honduras Honduras	1990	91	59	72	68	28	44
	1995	92	64	76	71	37	51
	2000	93	69	80	75	47	59
	2008	95	77	86	80	62	71
Hungary Hongrie	1990	98	91	96	100	100	100
	1995	99	94	97	100	100	100
	2000	100	98	99	100	100	100
	2008	100	100	100	100	100	100
Iceland Islande	1990	100	100	100	100	100	100
	1995	100	100	100	100	100	100
	2000	100	100	100	100	100	100
	2008	100	100	100	100	100	100
India Inde	1990	90	66	72	49	7	18
	1995	91	71	76	50	10	21
	2000	93	76	81	52	14	25
	2008	96	84	88	54	21	31
Indonesia Indonésie	1990	92	62	71	58	22	33
	1995	91	65	74	60	26	38
	2000	90	67	77	63	30	44
	2008	89	71	80	67	36	52
Iran (Islamic Rep. of) Iran (Rép. islamique d')	1990	98	83	91	86	78	83
	1995	98	83	92	86	78	83
	2000	98	83	93	86	78	83
	2008	98	...	...	...	...	...
Iraq Iraq	1990	97	44	81	...	...	...
	1995	97	44	80	76	46	67
	2000	95	49	80	76	54	69
	2008	91	55	79	76	66	73
Ireland Irlande	1990	100	100	100	100	98	99
	1995	100	100	100	100	98	99
	2000	100	100	100	100	98	99
	2008	100	100	100	100	98	99
Israel Israël	1990	100	100	100	100	100	100
	1995	100	100	100	100	100	100
	2000	100	100	100	100	100	100
	2008	100	100	100	100	100	100
Italy Italie	1990	100	100	100	...	...	...
	1995	100	100	100	...	...	...
	2000	100	100	100	...	...	...
	2008	100	100	100	...	...	...

Country or area Pays ou zone	Year Année	Improved drinking water sources / Un système amélioré de distribution d'eau potable: Urban (%) Urbaine (%)	Rural (%) Rurale (%)	Total (%) Totale (%)	Improved sanitation facilities / Un système amélioré d'assainissement: Urban (%) Urbaine (%)	Rural (%) Rurale (%)	Total (%) Totale (%)
Jamaica Jamaïque	1990	98	88	93	82	83	83
	1995	98	88	93	82	83	82
	2000	98	88	93	82	83	82
	2008	98	89	94	82	84	83
Japan Japon	1990	100	100	100	100	100	100
	1995	100	100	100	100	100	100
	2000	100	100	100	100	100	100
	2008	100	100	100	100	100	100
Jordan Jordanie	1990	99	91	97	98	...	...
	1995	98	91	96	98	95	97
	2000	98	91	96	98	96	98
	2008	98	91	96	98	97	98
Kazakhstan Kazakhstan	1990	99	92	96	96	97	96
	1995	99	92	96	96	97	96
	2000	99	91	96	97	97	97
	2008	99	90	95	97	98	97
Kenya Kenya	1990	91	32	43	24	27	26
	1995	89	38	48	25	28	27
	2000	87	43	52	26	30	29
	2008	83	52	59	27	32	31
Kiribati Kiribati	1990	76	33	48	36	21	26
	1995	77	41	54	41	21	28
	2000	77	50	62	47	22	33
Korea, Dem. P. R. Corée, R. p. dém. de	1990	100	100	100	...	...	...
	1995	100	100	100	58	60	59
	2000	100	100	100	58	60	59
	2008	100	100	100	...	...	...
Korea, Republic of Corée, République de	1990	97	...	...	100	100	100
	1995	97	67	90	100	100	100
	2000	98	75	93	100	100	100
	2008	100	88	98	100	100	100
Kuwait Koweït	1990	99	99	99	100	100	100
	1995	99	99	99	100	100	100
	2000	99	99	99	100	100	100
	2008	99	99	99	100	100	100
Kyrgyzstan Kirghizistan	1990	98	...	...	94	...	...
	1995	98	66	78	94	93	93
	2000	98	73	82	94	93	93
	2008	99	85	90	94	93	93
Lao People's Dem. Rep. Rép. dém. pop. lao	1995	78	37	44	56	10	18
	2000	77	40	48	62	16	26
	2008	72	51	57	86	38	53
Latvia Lettonie	1990	100	96	99	...	...	...
	1995	100	96	99	...	...	...
	2000	100	96	99	82	71	78
	2008	100	96	99	82	71	78
Lebanon Liban	1990	100	100	100	100	...	...
	1995	100	100	100	100	87	98
	2000	100	100	100	100	87	98
	2008	100	100	100	100	...	...
Lesotho Lesotho	1990	88	57	61	29	32	32
	1995	89	59	64	30	31	31
	2000	92	69	74	35	28	29
	2008	97	81	85	40	25	29
Liberia Libéria	1990	86	34	58	21	3	11
	1995	84	39	61	22	4	13
	2000	82	44	65	23	4	14
	2008	79	51	68	25	4	17

Proportion of population with access to: - Pourcentage de la population ayant accès à :

55 Water supply and sanitation coverage *(continued)*

Accès à l'eau et à l'assainissement *(suite)*

Country or area Pays ou zone	Year Année	Proportion of population with access to: - Pourcentage de la population ayant accès à : Improved drinking water sources Un système amélioré de distribution d'eau potable			Improved sanitation facilities Un système amélioré d'assainissement		
		Urban (%) Urbaine (%)	Rural (%) Rurale (%)	Total (%) Totale (%)	Urban (%) Urbaine (%)	Rural (%) Rurale (%)	Total (%) Totale (%)
Libyan Arab Jamah. Jamah. arabe libyenne	1990	54	55	54	97	96	97
	1995	54	55	54	97	96	97
	2000	54	55	54	97	96	97
	2008	...	...	...	97	96	97
Luxembourg Luxembourg	1990	100	100	100	100	100	100
	1995	100	100	100	100	100	100
	2000	100	100	100	100	100	100
	2008	100	100	100	100	100	100
Madagascar Madagascar	1990	78	16	31	14	6	8
	1995	76	20	34	14	7	9
	2000	73	24	37	15	8	10
	2008	71	29	41	15	10	11
Malawi Malawi	1990	90	33	40	50	41	42
	1995	92	45	51	50	46	47
	2000	93	58	63	51	50	50
	2008	95	77	80	51	57	56
Malaysia Malaisie	1990	94	82	88	88	81	84
	1995	96	88	92	91	85	88
	2000	99	93	97	94	90	92
	2008	100	99	100	96	95	96
Maldives Maldives	1990	100	87	90	100	58	69
	1995	100	87	90	100	60	70
	2000	100	87	91	100	74	81
	2008	99	86	91	100	96	98
Mali Mali	1990	54	22	29	36	23	26
	1995	61	28	36	39	25	29
	2000	69	34	44	41	28	32
	2008	81	44	56	45	32	36
Malta Malte	1990	100	98	100	100	100	100
	1995	100	99	100	100	100	100
	2000	100	100	100	100	100	100
	2008	100	100	100	100	100	100
Marshall Islands Iles Marshall	1990	94	97	95	77	41	64
	1995	94	98	95	79	44	67
	2000	93	98	95	80	48	69
	2008	92	99	94	83	53	73
Martinique Martinique	1990	100	...	...	...	...	...
	1995	100	...	...	93	...	...
	2000	100	...	...	94	...	...
	2008	100	...	...	95	...	...
Mauritania Mauritanie	1990	36	26	30	29	8	16
	1995	41	32	36	31	9	18
	2000	45	37	40	38	9	21
	2008	52	47	49	50	9	26
Mauritius Maurice	1990	100	99	99	93	90	91
	1995	100	99	99	93	90	91
	2000	100	99	99	93	90	91
	2008	100	99	99	93	90	91
Mexico Mexique	1990	94	64	85	80	30	66
	1995	94	71	88	83	41	72
	2000	95	77	90	85	51	76
	2008	96	87	94	90	68	85
Micronesia (Fed. States of) Micronésie (Etats féd. de)	1990	93	87	89	55	20	29
	1995	94	89	90	56	18	28
	2000	94	92	92	59	16	26
	2008	95	...	...	...	...	...

Country or area Pays ou zone	Year Année	Proportion of population with access to: - Pourcentage de la population ayant accès à : Improved drinking water sources Un système amélioré de distribution d'eau potable Urban (%) Urbaine (%)	Rural (%) Rurale (%)	Total (%) Totale (%)	Improved sanitation facilities Un système amélioré d'assainissement Urban (%) Urbaine (%)	Rural (%) Rurale (%)	Total (%) Totale (%)
Monaco Monaco	1990	100	...	100	100	...	100
	1995	100	...	100	100	...	100
	2000	100	...	100	100	...	100
	2008	100	...	100	100	...	100
Mongolia Mongolie	1990	81	27	58	...	...	...
	1995	82	28	59	67	25	49
	2000	88	37	66	66	26	49
	2008	97	49	76	64	32	50
Montenegro Monténégro	2000	100	96	98	96	86	92
	2008	100	96	98	96	86	92
Montserrat Montserrat	1990	100	100	100	96	96	96
	1995	100	100	100	96	96	96
	2000	100	100	100	96	96	96
	2008	100	100	100	96	96	96
Morocco Maroc	1990	94	55	74	81	27	53
	1995	95	56	76	82	35	59
	2000	96	58	78	82	43	64
	2008	98	60	81	83	52	69
Mozambique Mozambique	1990	73	26	36	36	4	11
	1995	73	26	38	36	4	12
	2000	75	27	42	37	4	14
	2008	77	29	47	38	4	17
Myanmar Myanmar	1990	87	47	57	...	...	...
	1995	85	51	60	77	39	49
	2000	80	60	66	81	59	65
	2008	75	69	71	86	79	81
Namibia Namibie	1990	99	51	64	66	9	25
	1995	99	62	73	64	11	27
	2000	99	72	81	63	13	29
	2008	99	88	92	60	17	33
Nauru Nauru	2008	90	...	...	50	...	...
Nepal Népal	1990	96	74	76	41	8	11
	1995	95	78	80	44	13	16
	2000	94	81	83	47	19	23
	2008	93	87	88	51	27	31
Netherlands Pays-Bas	1990	100	100	100	100	100	100
	1995	100	100	100	100	100	100
	2000	100	100	100	100	100	100
	2008	100	100	100	100	100	100
New Zealand Nouvelle-Zélande	1990	100	100	100	...	88	...
	1995	100	100	100	...	88	...
	2000	100	100	100	...	...	...
	2008	100	100	100	...	...	...
Nicaragua Nicaragua	1990	92	54	74	59	26	43
	1995	94	58	77	60	29	46
	2000	95	62	80	61	32	48
	2008	98	68	85	63	37	52
Niger Niger	1990	57	31	35	19	2	5
	1995	68	33	39	23	2	5
	2000	78	35	42	27	3	7
	2008	96	39	48	34	4	9
Nigeria Nigéria	1990	79	30	47	39	36	37
	1995	78	33	50	38	34	36
	2000	77	36	53	37	32	34
	2008	75	42	58	36	28	32

55 Water supply and sanitation coverage *(continued)*

Accès à l'eau et à l'assainissement *(suite)*

Country or area Pays ou zone	Year Année	Proportion of population with access to: - Pourcentage de la population ayant accès à : Improved drinking water sources / Un système amélioré de distribution d'eau potable: Urban (%) Urbaine (%)	Rural (%) Rurale (%)	Total (%) Totale (%)	Improved sanitation facilities / Un système amélioré d'assainissement: Urban (%) Urbaine (%)	Rural (%) Rurale (%)	Total (%) Totale (%)
Niue Nioué	1990	100	100	100	100	100	100
	1995	100	100	100	100	100	100
	2000	100	100	100	100	100	100
	2008	100	100	100	100	100	100
Northern Mariana Islands Iles Mariannes du Nord	1990	98	100	98	85	78	84
	1995	98	99	98	89	86	89
	2000	98	97	98	92	93	92
	2008	98	97	98	...	96	...
Norway Norvège	1990	100	100	100	100	100	100
	1995	100	100	100	100	100	100
	2000	100	100	100	100	100	100
	2008	100	100	100	100	100	100
Occupied Palestinian Terr. Terr. palestinien occupé	1990	100	...	...	...	...	...
	1995	100	84	95	91	84	89
	2000	95	88	93	91	84	89
	2008	91	91	91	91	84	89
Oman Oman	1990	84	72	80	97	61	85
	1995	84	72	81	97	61	87
	2000	87	74	83	97	61	87
	2008	92	77	88	97	...	...
Pakistan Pakistan	1990	96	81	86	73	8	28
	1995	95	83	87	73	14	33
	2000	95	85	88	72	20	37
	2008	95	87	90	72	29	45
Palau Palaos	1990	73	98	81	76	54	69
	1995	74	97	81	81	53	73
	2000	78	95	83	92	52	80
	2008	...	...	...	96	...	...
Panama Panama	1990	99	66	84	73	40	58
	1995	98	71	87	74	43	62
	2000	97	77	90	74	47	65
	2008	97	83	93	75	51	69
Papua New Guinea Papouasie-Nvl-Guinée	1990	89	32	41	78	42	47
	1995	89	32	40	78	42	47
	2000	88	32	39	75	42	46
	2008	87	33	40	71	41	45
Paraguay Paraguay	1990	81	25	52	61	15	37
	1995	87	38	64	70	23	48
	2000	92	51	74	79	31	58
	2008	99	66	86	90	40	70
Peru Pérou	1990	88	45	75	71	16	54
	1995	89	50	77	74	22	59
	2000	90	54	79	77	27	62
	2008	90	61	82	81	36	68
Philippines Philippines	1990	93	76	84	70	46	58
	1995	93	79	87	73	52	63
	2000	93	82	88	76	59	69
	2008	93	87	91	80	69	76
Poland Pologne	1990	100	100	100	96	...	...
	1995	100	100	100	96	...	...
	2000	100	100	100	96	80	90
	2008	100	100	100	96	80	90
Portugal Portugal	1990	98	94	96	97	87	92
	1995	98	96	97	98	92	95
	2000	99	98	99	99	96	98
	2008	99	100	99	100	100	100

Country or area Pays ou zone	Year Année	Proportion of population with access to: - Pourcentage de la population ayant accès à : Improved drinking water sources Un système amélioré de distribution d'eau potable: Urban (%) Urbaine (%)	Rural (%) Rurale (%)	Total (%) Totale (%)	Improved sanitation facilities Un système amélioré d'assainissement: Urban (%) Urbaine (%)	Rural (%) Rurale (%)	Total (%) Totale (%)
Qatar Qatar	1990	100	100	100	100	100	100
	1995	100	100	100	100	100	100
	2000	100	100	100	100	100	100
	2008	100	100	100	100	100	100
Republic of Moldova République de Moldova	1995	98	89	93	...	...	...
	2000	97	88	92	85	74	79
	2008	96	85	90	85	74	79
Romania Roumanie	1990	...	...	...	88	52	71
	1995	...	...	...	88	53	72
	2000	...	...	...	88	54	72
	2008	...	...	...	88	54	72
Russian Federation Fédération de Russie	1990	98	81	93	93	70	87
	1995	98	83	94	93	70	87
	2000	98	86	95	93	70	87
	2008	98	89	96	93	70	87
Rwanda Rwanda	1990	96	66	68	35	22	23
	1995	91	65	67	39	31	32
	2000	85	64	67	43	40	40
	2008	77	62	65	50	55	54
Saint Kitts and Nevis Saint-Kitts-et-Nevis	1990	99	99	99	96	96	96
	1995	99	99	99	96	96	96
	2000	99	99	99	96	96	96
	2008	99	99	99	96	96	96
Saint Lucia Sainte-Lucie	1990	98	98	98	...	...	...
	1995	98	98	98	89	89	89
	2000	98	98	98	89	89	89
	2008	98	98	98	...	...	...
Saint Vincent-Grenadines Saint Vincent-Grenadines	1990	...	...	...	...	96	...
	1995	...	93	...	...	96	...
	2000	...	93	...	...	96	...
	2008	...	...	...	...	96	...
Samoa Samoa	1990	99	89	91	100	98	98
	1995	96	88	90	100	99	99
	2000	92	88	89	100	100	100
	2008	...	...	...	100	100	100
Sao Tome and Principe Sao Tomé-et-Principe	1995	85	65	75	27	14	20
	2000	86	70	79	27	15	21
	2008	89	88	89	30	19	26
Saudi Arabia Arabie saoudite	1990	97	63	89	100	...	...
	1995	97	63	90	100	...	...
	2000	97	...	...	100	...	...
	2008	97	...	...	100	...	...
Senegal Sénégal	1990	88	43	61	62	22	38
	1995	89	46	63	64	26	41
	2000	90	48	65	66	31	45
	2008	92	52	69	69	38	51
Serbia Serbie	2000	99	98	99	96	88	92
	2008	99	98	99	96	88	92
Seychelles Seychelles	2000	84	...	...	94	...	...
	2008	100	...	...	97	...	...
Sierra Leone Sierra Leone	1995	72	49	57	21	4	10
	2000	75	44	55	21	5	11
	2008	86	26	49	24	6	13
Singapore Singapour	1990	100	...	100	99	...	99
	1995	100	...	100	99	...	99
	2000	100	...	100	100	...	100
	2008	100	...	100	100	...	100

55 Water supply and sanitation coverage *(continued)*

Accès à l'eau et à l'assainissement *(suite)*

Country or area Pays ou zone	Year Année	Proportion of population with access to: - Pourcentage de la population ayant accès à : Improved drinking water sources / Un système amélioré de distribution d'eau potable — Urban (%) Urbaine (%)	Rural (%) Rurale (%)	Total (%) Totale (%)	Improved sanitation facilities / Un système amélioré d'assainissement — Urban (%) Urbaine (%)	Rural (%) Rurale (%)	Total (%) Totale (%)
Slovakia Slovaquie	1990	...	...	...	100	100	100
	1995	...	...	...	100	100	100
	2000	100	100	100	100	100	100
	2008	100	100	100	100	99	100
Slovenia Slovénie	1990	100	99	100	100	100	100
	1995	100	99	100	100	100	100
	2000	100	99	100	100	100	100
	2008	100	99	99	100	100	100
Solomon Islands Iles Salomon	1990	...	...	...	98	...	...
	1995	94	65	69	98	18	30
	2000	94	65	70	98	18	31
	2008	...	...	...	98	...	...
Somalia Somalie	1995	22	20	21	42	12	21
	2000	36	17	23	45	10	22
	2008	67	9	30	52	6	23
South Africa Afrique du Sud	1990	98	66	83	80	58	69
	1995	98	67	84	81	59	71
	2000	98	71	86	82	61	73
	2008	99	78	91	84	65	77
Spain Espagne	1990	100	100	100	100	100	100
	1995	100	100	100	100	100	100
	2000	100	100	100	100	100	100
	2008	100	100	100	100	100	100
Sri Lanka Sri Lanka	1990	91	62	67	85	67	70
	1995	93	69	73	86	74	76
	2000	95	77	80	87	81	82
	2008	98	88	90	88	92	91
Sudan Soudan	1990	85	58	65	63	23	34
	1995	79	56	63	60	21	33
	2000	73	55	61	58	20	34
	2008	64	52	57	55	18	34
Suriname Suriname	1990	99	...	...	90	...	...
	1995	99	71	91	90	64	82
	2000	98	73	91	90	65	83
	2008	97	81	93	90	66	84
Swaziland Swaziland	1995	85	43	53	60	45	48
	2000	86	46	55	60	46	49
	2008	92	61	69	61	53	55
Sweden Suède	1990	100	100	100	100	100	100
	1995	100	100	100	100	100	100
	2000	100	100	100	100	100	100
	2008	100	100	100	100	100	100
Switzerland Suisse	1990	100	100	100	100	100	100
	1995	100	100	100	100	100	100
	2000	100	100	100	100	100	100
	2008	100	100	100	100	100	100
Syrian Arab Republic Rép. arabe syrienne	1990	96	75	85	94	72	83
	1995	96	76	86	95	73	84
	2000	95	79	87	95	82	89
	2008	94	84	89	96	95	96
Tajikistan Tadjikistan	1990	...	...	...	93	...	...
	1995	91	45	58	93	87	89
	2000	92	49	60	94	89	90
	2008	94	61	70	95	94	94
Thailand Thaïlande	1990	97	89	91	93	74	80
	1995	98	92	94	94	83	86
	2000	98	95	96	94	92	93
	2008	99	98	98	95	96	96

Country or area / Pays ou zone	Year / Année	Proportion of population with access to: - Pourcentage de la population ayant accès à : Improved drinking water sources / Un système amélioré de distribution d'eau potable			Improved sanitation facilities / Un système amélioré d'assainissement		
		Urban (%) / Urbaine (%)	Rural (%) / Rurale (%)	Total (%) / Totale (%)	Urban (%) / Urbaine (%)	Rural (%) / Rurale (%)	Total (%) / Totale (%)
TFYR of Macedonia / L'ex-R.Y. Macédoine	2000	100	99	100	92	82	88
	2008	100	99	100	92	82	89
Timor-Leste / Timor-Leste	2000	69	47	52	55	25	32
	2008	86	63	69	76	40	50
Togo / Togo	1990	79	36	49	25	8	13
	1995	81	37	52	25	7	13
	2000	83	39	55	24	5	12
	2008	87	41	60	24	3	12
Tokelau / Tokélaou	1990	...	90	90	...	41	41
	1995	...	91	91	...	45	45
	2000	...	93	93	...	63	63
	2008	...	97	97	...	93	93
Tonga / Tonga	1990	...	...	...	98	96	96
	1995	100	100	100	98	96	96
	2000	100	100	100	98	96	96
	2008	100	100	100	98	96	96
Trinidad and Tobago / Trinité-et-Tobago	1990	92	88	88	93	93	93
	1995	94	90	90	92	92	92
	2000	95	91	91	92	92	92
	2008	98	93	94	92	92	92
Tunisia / Tunisie	1990	95	62	81	95	44	74
	1995	96	69	86	95	51	78
	2000	98	77	90	95	57	81
	2008	99	84	94	96	64	85
Turkey / Turquie	1990	94	73	85	96	66	84
	1995	95	79	89	96	68	85
	2000	97	85	93	96	71	87
	2008	100	96	99	97	75	90
Turkmenistan / Turkménistan	1990	97	...	...	99	97	98
	1995	97	72	83	99	97	98
	2000	97	72	83	99	97	98
	2008	97	...	...	99	97	98
Turks and Caicos Islands / Iles Turques et Caïques	1990	100	100	100	98	...	...
	1995	100	100	100	98	94	96
	2000	100	100	100	98	94	96
	2008	100	100	100	98	...	...
Tuvalu / Tuvalu	1990	92	89	90	86	76	80
	1995	93	91	92	86	78	82
	2000	95	93	94	87	79	83
	2008	98	97	97	88	81	84
Uganda / Ouganda	1990	78	39	43	35	40	39
	1995	81	46	50	36	43	42
	2000	85	53	57	37	45	44
	2008	91	64	67	38	49	48
Ukraine / Ukraine	1990	99	...	...	97	91	95
	1995	99	91	96	97	91	95
	2000	99	92	97	97	91	95
	2008	98	97	98	97	90	95
United Arab Emirates / Emirats arabes unis	1990	100	100	100	98	95	97
	1995	100	100	100	98	95	97
	2000	100	100	100	98	95	97
	2008	100	100	100	98	95	97
United Kingdom / Royaume-Uni	1990	100	100	100	100	100	100
	1995	100	100	100	100	100	100
	2000	100	100	100	100	100	100
	2008	100	100	100	100	100	100

Country or area Pays ou zone	Year Année	Proportion of population with access to: - Pourcentage de la population ayant accès à : Improved drinking water sources Un système amélioré de distribution d'eau potable			Improved sanitation facilities Un système amélioré d'assainissement		
		Urban (%) Urbaine (%)	Rural (%) Rurale (%)	Total (%) Totale (%)	Urban (%) Urbaine (%)	Rural (%) Rurale (%)	Total (%) Totale (%)
United Rep. of Tanzania Rép.-Unie de Tanzanie	1990	94	46	55	27	23	24
	1995	90	45	54	28	23	24
	2000	86	45	54	29	22	24
	2008	80	45	54	32	21	24
United States Etats-Unis	1990	100	94	99	100	99	100
	1995	100	94	99	100	99	100
	2000	100	94	99	100	99	100
	2008	100	94	99	100	99	100
Uruguay Uruguay	1990	98	79	96	95	83	94
	1995	98	81	96	95	84	94
	2000	99	88	98	97	90	96
	2008	100	100	100	100	99	100
Uzbekistan Ouzbékistan	1990	97	85	90	95	76	84
	1995	97	85	90	96	78	85
	2000	98	83	89	97	87	91
	2008	98	81	87	100	100	100
Vanuatu Vanuatu	1990	91	49	57	...	...	...
	1995	92	58	65	53	30	35
	2000	93	66	72	57	36	41
	2008	96	79	83	66	48	52
Venezuela (Boliv. Rep. of) Venezuela (Rép. boliv. du)	1990	93	71	90	89	45	82
	1995	94	73	91	91	50	86
	2000	94	74	92	93	54	89
Viet Nam Viet Nam	1990	88	51	58	61	29	35
	1995	91	62	68	70	40	47
	2000	94	74	79	79	50	57
	2008	99	92	94	94	67	75
Wallis and Futuna Islands Iles Wallis et Futuna	1990	...	100	100	...	96	96
	1995	...	100	100	...	96	96
	2000	...	100	100	...	96	96
	2008	...	100	100	...	96	96
Yemen Yémen	1990	...	...	...	64	6	18
	1995	88	60	67	73	14	28
	2000	82	59	65	81	21	37
	2008	72	57	62	94	33	52
Zambia Zambie	1990	89	23	49	62	36	46
	1995	88	29	51	61	38	47
	2000	88	36	54	60	40	47
	2008	87	46	60	59	43	49
Zimbabwe Zimbabwe	1990	99	70	78	58	37	43
	1995	99	70	79	57	37	43
	2000	99	71	80	57	37	44
	2008	99	72	82	56	37	44

Source:
World Health Organization (WHO) and United Nations Children's Fund (UNICEF), Geneva and New York, the WHO/UNICEF Joint Monitoring Programme for the Water and Sanitation database, last accessed July 2010.

Source :
Organisation mondial de la santé (OMS) et Fonds des Nations Unies pour l'enfance (UNICEF), Genève et New York, la base de données de la Programme commun OMS/UNICEF de surveillance de l'eau et de l'assainissement, dernier accès juillet 2010.

1 Bangladesh figures have been corrected since JMP 2010 report.

1 Les données du Bangladesh ont été corrigées depuis le rapport du JMP de 2010.

Technical notes: tables 51-55

Table 51: The data on land are compiled by the Food and Agriculture Organization of the United Nations (FAO). FAO's definitions of the land categories are as follows:

Land area: Total area excluding area under inland water bodies. The definition of inland water bodies generally includes major rivers and lakes.

Arable land: Land under temporary crops (double-cropped areas are counted only once); temporary meadows for mowing or pasture; land under market and kitchen gardens; and land temporarily fallow (less than five years). Abandoned land resulting from shifting cultivation is not included in this category. Data for "arable land" are not meant to indicate the amount of land that is potentially cultivable.

Permanent crops: Land cultivated with crops that occupy the land for long periods and need not be replanted after each harvest, such as cocoa, coffee and rubber. This category includes land under flowering shrubs, fruit trees, nut trees and vines, but excludes land under trees grown for wood or timber.

Forest: In the *Global Forest Resources Assessment 2010* the following definition is used for forest: Land spanning more than 0.5 hectares with trees higher than 5 metres and a canopy cover of more than 10 percent, or trees able to reach these thresholds *in situ*. It does not include land that is predominantly under agricultural or urban land use.

Table 52: The source of the data presented on the emissions of carbon dioxide (CO_2) is the Carbon Dioxide Information Analysis Centre (CDIAC) of the Oak Ridge National Laboratory in the USA.

The CDIAC estimates of CO_2 emissions are derived primarily from United Nations energy statistics on the consumption of liquid and solid fuels and gas consumption and flaring, and from cement production estimates from the Bureau of Mines of the U.S. Department of Interior. The emissions presented in the table are in units of 1,000 metric tons of CO_2; to convert CO_2 into carbon, divide the data by 3.66406. Full details of the procedures for calculating emissions are given in Global, Regional, and National Annual $C0_2$ Emissions Estimates from Fossil Fuel Burning, Hydraulic Cement Production, and Gas Flaring and on the CDIAC web site (see http://cdiac.esd.ornl.gov). Relative to other industrial sources for which CO_2 emissions are estimated, statistics on gas flaring activities are sparse and sporadic. In countries where gas flaring activities account for a considerable proportion of the total CO_2 emissions, the sporadic nature of gas flaring statistics may produce spurious or misleading trends in national CO_2 emissions over the period covered by the table.

Table 53: Chlorofluorocarbons (CFCs) are synthetic compounds formerly used as refrigerants and aerosol propel-

Notes techniques : tableaux 51 à 55

Tableau 51: Les données relatives aux terres sont compilées par l'Organisation des Nations Unies pour l'alimentation et l'agriculture (FAO). Les définitions de la FAO en ce qui concerne les terres sont les suivantes:

Superficie totale des terres: Superficie totale, à l'exception des eaux intérieures. Les eaux intérieures désignent généralement les principaux fleuves et lacs.

Terres arables: Terres affectées aux cultures temporaires (les terres sur lesquelles est pratiquée la double culture ne sont comptabilisées qu'une fois), prairies temporaires à faucher ou à pâturer, jardins maraîchers ou potagers et terres en jachère temporaire (moins de cinq ans). Cette définition ne comprend pas les terres abandonnées du fait de la culture itinérante. Les données relatives aux terres arables ne peuvent être utilisées pour calculer la superficie des terres aptes à l'agriculture.

Cultures permanentes: Superficie des terres avec des cultures qui occupent la terre pour de longues périodes et qui ne nécessitent pas d'être replantées après chaque récolte, comme le cacao, le café et le caoutchouc. Cette catégorie comprend les terres plantées d'arbustes à fleurs, d'arbres fruitiers, d'arbres à noix et de vignes, mais ne comprend pas les terres plantées d'arbres destinés à la coupe.

Superficie forestière: Dans *l'Évaluation des ressources forestières mondiales 2010*, la FAO a défini les forêts comme suit : Terres occupant une superficie de plus de 0,5 hectares avec des arbres atteignant une hauteur supérieure à cinq mètres et un couvert arboré de plus de dix pour cent, ou avec des arbres capables d'atteindre ces seuils en situ. Sont exclues les terres à vocation agricole ou urbaine prédominante.

Tableau 52: Les données sur les émissions de dioxyde de carbone (CO_2) proviennent du "Carbon Dioxide Information Analysis Center" (CDIAC) du "Oak Ridge National Laboratory" (États-Unis).

Les estimations du "Carbon Dioxide Information Analysis Center" sont obtenues essentiellement à partir des statistiques de l'énergie des Nations Unies relatives à la consommation de combustibles liquides et solides, à la production et à la consommation de gaz de torche, et des chiffres de production de ciment du "Bureau of Mines" du "Department of Interior" des États-Unis. Les émissions sont indiquées en milliers de tonnes de dioxyde de carbone (à diviser par 3.66406 pour avoir les chiffres de carbone). On peut voir dans le détail les méthodes utilisées pour calculer les émissions dans "Global, Regional, and National Annual $C0_2$ Emissions Estimates from Fossil Fuel Burning, Hydraulic Cement Production, and Gas Flaring" et sur le site Web du Carbon Dioxide Information Analysis Center (voir http://cdiac.esd.ornl.gov). Par rapport à d'autres sources industrielles pour lesquelles on calcule les émissions de CO_2, les statistiques sur la production de gaz de

lants and known to be harmful to the ozone layer of the atmosphere. In the Montreal Protocol on Substances that Deplete the Ozone Layer, CFCs to be measured are found in vehicle air conditioning units, domestic and commercial refrigeration and air conditioning/heat pump equipment, aerosol products, portable fire extinguishers, insulation boards, panels and pipe covers, and pre-polymers.

The Parties to the Montreal Protocol on Substances that Deplete the Ozone Layer report data on CFCs to the Ozone Secretariat of the United Nations Environment Programme. The data on CFCs are shown in ozone depleting potential (ODP) tons that are calculated by multiplying the quantities in metric tons reported by the Parties, by the ODP of that substance, and added together.

Consumption is defined as production plus imports, minus exports of controlled substances. Feedstocks are exempt and are therefore subtracted from the imports and/or production. Similarly, the destroyed amounts are also subtracted. Negative numbers can occur when destruction and/or exports exceed production plus imports, implying that the destruction and/or exports are from stockpiles.

Table 54: Data on the number of threatened species in each group of animals and plants are compiled by the World Conservation Union (IUCN)/Species Survival Commission (SSC) and published in the IUCN Red List of Threatened Species.

The list provides a catalogue of those species that are considered globally threatened. The categories used in the Red List are as follows: Extinct, Extinct in the Wild, Critically Endangered, Endangered, Vulnerable, Near Threatened and Data Deficient.

Table 55: The proportion of the population with sustainable access to an improved water source, urban and rural, is the percentage of the population who use any of the following types of water supply for drinking: piped water, public tap, borehole or pump, protected well, protected spring or rainwater. Improved water sources do not include vendor-provided water, bottled water, tanker trucks or unprotected wells and springs.

Proportion of the urban and rural population with access to improved sanitation refers to the percentage of the population with access to facilities that hygienically separate human excreta from human, animal and insect contact. Facilities such as sewers or septic tanks, poor-flush latrines and simple pit or ventilated improved pit latrines are assumed to be adequate, provided that they are not public, according to the World Health Organization and United Nations Children's Fund. To be effective, facilities must be correctly constructed and properly maintained.

torche sont rares et sporadiques. Dans les pays où cette production représente une proportion considérable de l'ensemble des émissions de dioxyde de carbone, on peut voir apparaître de ce fait des chiffres parasites ou trompeurs pour ce qui est des tendances des émissions nationales de dioxyde de carbone durant la période visée par le tableau.

Tableau 53: Les chlorofluorocarbones (CFC) sont des substances de synthèse utilisées comme réfrigérants et propulseurs d'aérosols, dont on sait qu'elles appauvrissent la couche d'ozone. Aux termes du Protocole de Montréal relatif à des substances qui appauvrissent la couche d'ozone, la production de certains CFC doit être mesurée : ils sont utilisés dans les climatiseurs de véhicules, le matériel domestique et commercial de réfrigération et de climatisation (pompes à chaleur), les produits sous forme d'aérosols, les extincteurs d'incendie portables, les planches, panneaux et gaines isolants, et les prépolymères.

Les Parties au Protocole de Montréal communiquent leurs données concernant les CFC au secrétariat de l'ozone du Programme des Nations Unies pour l'environnement. Les données sur les CFC, indiquées en tonnes de potentiel de destruction de l'ozone (PDO), sont calculées en multipliant le nombre de tonnes signalé par les Parties par le potentiel de destruction coefficient de la substance considérée, et en faisant la somme de ces PDO.

La consommation est définie comme production de substances contrôlées, plus les importations, moins les exportations. Les produits intermédiaires de l'industrie sont exemptés, et on les soustrait donc des importations et/ou de la production. De même, on soustrait aussi les quantités détruites. On peut obtenir des quantités négatives, lorsque les quantités détruites et/ou exportées sont supérieures à la somme production + importations, ce qui signifie que les quantités détruites ou exportées ont été prélevées sur les stocks accumulés.

Tableau 54: Les données relatives aux espèces menacées pour chaque groupe d'animaux et de plantes, réunies par la Commission de la sauvegarde des espèces de l'Union mondiale pour la nature (UICN), sont publiées dans la Liste rouge des espèces menacées de l'UICN.

Cette liste répertorie les espèces animales considérées comme menacées à l'échelle mondiale, réparties entre les catégories ci-après : éteintes, éteintes à l'état sauvage, gravement menacées d'extinction, menacées d'extinction, vulnérables, quasi menacées, et catégorie à données insuffisantes.

Tableau 55: La proportion de la population ayant accès de façon durable à une source d'eau améliorée (zones urbaines et rurales) est le pourcentage de la population qui utilise l'un quelconque des types suivants d'approvisionnement en eau de boisson : eau courante, fontaine publique, forage ou pompe, puits protégé, source protégée ou eau de pluie. Les sources d'eau améliorées ne comprennent pas l'eau fournie par un vendeur, l'eau en bouteille, l'eau fournie par un camion-citerne ou les puits et sources non protégés.

La proportion de la population ayant accès à un système d'assainissement amélioré (zones urbaines et rurales) se

réfère au pourcentage de la population ayant accès aux installations qui dans des conditions hygiéniques empêchent l'homme, l'animal ou l'insecte d'entrer en contact avec des excréta humains. Les dispositifs tels que les égouts ou les fosses septiques, les latrines à siphon hydraulique et les latrines simples ou les latrines améliorées à fosse ventilée sont considérés comme appropriés, à condition de ne pas être publics, aux termes du l'Organisation mondiale de la santé et du Fonds des Nations Unies pour l'enfance. Pour être efficaces, ces installations doivent être bien construites et correctement entretenues.

56 Personnel in research and development (R & D)

Full-time equivalent (FTE)

Personnel employé dans la recherche et le développement (R - D)

Equivalent temps plein (ETP)

Country or area Pays ou zone	Year Année	Total R & D personnel Total du personnel de R - D	Researchers Chercheurs		Technicians and equivalent staff Techniciens et personnel assimilé		Other supporting staff Autre personnel de soutien	
			Total M & W Total H & F	Women Femmes	Total M & W Total H & F	Women Femmes	Total M & W Total H & F	Women Femmes
Algeria [1] Algérie [1]	2005	7 331	5 593	2 043	1 134	...	604	...
Argentina Argentine	2002	37 413	26 083	12 593	6 072	...	5 258	...
	2003	39 393	27 367	13 271	6 428	...	5 598	...
	2004	42 454	29 471	14 370	6 967	...	6 016	...
	2005	45 361	31 868	15 416	7 788	...	5 705	...
	2006	49 359	35 040	17 081	8 151	...	6 168	...
	2007	53 187	38 681	20 418[2]	7 732	...	6 774	...
Armenia [1,3] Arménie [1,3]	2002	6 737[4]	4 927[4]	2 314	451[4]	...	1 359[4]	...
	2003	6 277[4]	4 667[4]	2 138	313[4]	...	1 297[4]	...
	2004	6 685[4]	4 788[4]	2 235	423[4]	...	1 474[4]	...
	2005	6 892[4]	5 056[4]	2 329	345[4]	...	1 491[4]	...
	2006	6 723[4]	4 838	2 217	296	...	#782	...
	2007	5 669[4]	4 114	1 840	331	...	811[4]	...
Australia Australie	2002	107 209	73 173	...	...	...	...	...
	2004	116 194	81 192	...	...	...	...	...
	2006	126 070	87 140	...	...	...	...	...
Austria Autriche	2002	38 893	24 124	3 811	10 194	2 683	4 575	2 068
	2004	42 891	25 955	4 740	12 067	2 901	4 869	2 471
	2005[5]	47 275	28 148	...	...	...	...	...
	2006	49 377	29 199	5 669	14 822	3 486	5 357	2 452
	2007	53 252	31 676	6 521	16 278	3 673	5 299	2 424
	2008	57 494	34 377	...	...	...	...	...
Azerbaijan [3] Azerbaïdjan [3]	2002	16 019[4]	10 195	5 236	1 609	...	4 215[4]	...
	2003	17 190[4]	10 830	5 541	1 825	...	#2 814	...
	2004	17 712[4]	11 531	6 110	1 749	...	2 849	...
	2005	18 164[4]	11 603	6 056	1 825	...	3 086	...
	2006	17 973[4]	11 698	6 029	2 013	...	2 905	...
	2007	18 079[4]	11 280	5 866	2 073	...	3 194	...
Belarus [3] Bélarus [3]	2002	26 871	18 557	8 361	2 050	...	6 264	...
	2003	#29 981[4]	17 702	7 785	2 337	...	5 999	...
	2004	28 750[4]	17 034	7 556	2 068	...	5 844	...
	2005	30 222[4]	18 267	7 897	2 112	...	5 763	...
	2006	30 544[4]	18 494	8 078	2 263	...	5 715	...
	2007	31 294[4]	18 995	8 228	2 312	...	5 880	...
Belgium Belgique	2002	52 054	30 668	8 316	15 358	4 498	6 028	2 640
	2003	52 257	30 917	8 585	15 293	4 572	6 046	2 669
	2004	52 253	32 400	9 287	14 722	4 425	5 130	2 606
	2005	53 517	33 146	9 769	15 047	4 585	5 324	2 702
	2006	55 714	34 879	10 586	14 325	3 920	6 510	3 301
	2007	57 963	36 318	11 150	14 815	4 010	6 830	3 397
	*2008	58 733	36 382	...	...	...	...	...
Benin [1,3,5] Bénin [1,3,5]	2007	...	1 000	...	...	...	...	...
Bosnia and Herzegovina [1] Bosnie-Herzégovine [1]	2003	614	232	...	170	...	213	...
	2004	688	239	...	197	...	250	...
	2005	731	253	...	198	...	280	...
	#2006	1 284	671	...	245	...	368	...
	2007	1 554	745	...	270	...	536	...
Botswana [1,3,6] Botswana [1,3,6]	2005	2 140	1 732	533	408	...	...	...

Personnel in research and development (R & D) *(continued)*
Full-time equivalent (FTE)

Personnel employé dans la recherche et le développement (R - D) *(suite)*
Equivalent temps plein (ETP)

Country or area Pays ou zone	Year Année	Total R & D personnel Total du personnel de R - D	Researchers Chercheurs		Technicians and equivalent staff Techniciens et personnel assimilé		Other supporting staff Autre personnel de soutien	
			Total M & W Total H & F	Women Femmes	Total M & W Total H & F	Women Femmes	Total M & W Total H & F	Women Femmes
Brazil [3]	2002	215 864	122 699	56 442[2]	...	...	93 165	...
Brésil [3]	2003	246 782	135 080	62 137	...	...	111 702	...
	2004	279 128	147 244	69 205[2]	...	...	131 884	...
	2005	328 932	177 941	83 632[2]	...	...	150 991	...
	2006	348 865	188 163	90 318[2]	...	...	160 702	...
	2007	373 221	199 427	95 725	...	...	173 794	...
	2008	397 720	210 716	...	...	...	187 004	...
Brunei Darussalam [1]	2002[7]	140	99	...	...	...	...	...
Brunéi Darussalam [1]	2003[7]	140	98	...	...	...	...	...
	#2004	...	102	...	...	...	...	...
Bulgaria	2002	15 029	9 223	4 353	3 713	2 374	2 093	1 379
Bulgarie	2003	15 453	9 589	4 535	3 735	2 294	2 129	1 396
	2004	15 647	9 827	4 642	3 721	2 236	2 099	1 371
	2005	15 853	10 053	4 673	3 778	2 256	2 022	1 349
	2006	16 321	10 336	4 690	3 843	2 263	2 142	1 362
	2007	16 940	11 203	5 350	3 638	2 101	2 099	1 309
	*2008	17 219	11 384	...	...	...	...	...
Burkina Faso [3]	2002	828[1,8]	236[1,8]	34	244[1,8]	...	348[1,8]	...
Burkina Faso [3]	2003	888[1,8]	251[1,8]	32	260[1,8]	...	377[1,8]	...
	2004	890[1,8]	293[1,8]	34	227[1,8]	...	370[1,8]	...
	2005	942[1,8]	301[1,8]	37	225[1,8]	...	416[1,8]	...
	#2007	1 054[1]	187[1,8]	25	391[1,8]	...	476[1,8]	...
Cambodia [1,5] Cambodge [1,5]	2002	494	223	50	170	...	102	...
Cameroon [1,3,8] Cameroun [1,3,8]	2005	...	462	88	...	...	...	...
Canada	2002	183 422	116 032	...	42 676	...	24 714	...
Canada	2003	196 505	123 301	...	46 057	...	27 147	...
	2004	210 557	130 383	...	51 612	...	28 562	...
	2005	218 612	136 759	...	52 771	...	29 082	...
	*2006[5]	224 106	139 011	...	55 146	...	29 949	...
Cape Verde [1] Cap-Vert [1]	2002	151	60	...	15	...	76	...
Central African Rep. [3]	2005[1]	...	11	...	...	...	...	...
Rép. centrafricaine [3]	2006[1]	...	20	...	...	...	...	...
	2007	...	41[1]	17	...	...	...	...
Chile [3]	2002	...	8 507	2 785	...	...	...	...
Chili [3]	#2003	28 220	17 212	5 168	7 273	...	3 735	...
	2004	30 583	18 365	5 503	7 912	...	4 306	...
China [9,10]	2002	1 035 200	810 525	...	...	...	...	...
Chine [9,10]	2003	1 094 830	862 108	...	...	...	...	...
	2004	1 152 620	926 252	...	...	...	...	...
	2005	1 364 800	1 118 700	...	...	...	...	...
	2006	1 502 470	1 223 760	...	...	...	...	...
	2007	1 736 160	1 423 380	...	...	...	...	...
China, Hong Kong SAR	2002	12 890	10 639	...	1 532	...	719	...
Chine, Hong Kong RAS	2003	16 864	13 497	...	2 138	...	1 228	...
	2004	18 846	14 594	...	2 904	...	1 348	...
	2005	22 053	18 024	...	2 346	...	1 683	...
	2006	22 977	18 326	...	3 176	...	1 475	...
China, Macao SAR [1,5]	2002	196	105	16	81	...	10	...
Chine, Macao RAS [1,5]	2003	249	147	27	94	...	8	...
	2004	349	244	48	97	...	8	...
	2005	409	298	62	102	...	9	...

56 Personnel in research and development (R & D) *(continued)*

Full-time equivalent (FTE)

Personnel employé dans la recherche et le développement (R - D) *(suite)*

Equivalent temps plein (ETP)

Country or area Pays ou zone	Year Année	Total R & D personnel Total du personnel de R - D	Researchers Chercheurs		Technicians and equivalent staff Techniciens et personnel assimilé		Other supporting staff Autre personnel de soutien	
			Total M & W Total H & F	Women Femmes	Total M & W Total H & F	Women Femmes	Total M & W Total H & F	Women Femmes
Colombia[3] Colombie[3]	2002	...	10 292	3 542	...	...	...	...
	2003	...	11 481	4 004	...	...	...	...
	2004	...	12 651	4 526	...	...	...	...
	2005	...	13 214	4 804	...	...	...	...
	2006	...	13 242	4 815	...	...	...	...
	2007	...	12 017	4 372	...	...	...	...
Costa Rica[3] Costa Rica[3]	2002	...	1 193	453	...	...	...	...
	2003	...	1 171	480	...	...	...	...
	2004	...	1 076	447	...	...	...	...
	2005	...	1 444	569	...	...	...	...
	#2006	4 298	3 164	1 200	...	...	1 134	443
	2007	4 660	3 521	1 306	...	...	1 139	366
Côte d'Ivoire[1] Côte d'Ivoire[1]	2005	...	1 269	210	...	...	...	...
Croatia Croatie	2002	12 960	8 572	3 651	1 981	1 086	2 407	1 744
	2003	9 148	5 861	2 799	2 056	1 046	1 231	934
	2004	11 162	7 140	3 256	2 573	1 226	1 449	1 051
	2005	9 270	5 727	2 710	2 633	1 196	910	584
	2006	9 516	5 778	2 680	2 843	1 359	895	597
	2007	10 124	6 129	2 893	2 846	1 433	1 149	795
	2008	10 583	6 697	...	2 675	...	1 212	...
Cuba[3] Cuba[3]	2002	34 326	6 057	...	...	...	28 269[11]	...
	2003	33 855	5 075	...	...	...	28 780[11]	...
	2004	34 094	5 115	...	...	...	28 979[11]	...
	2005	33 988	5 526	2 703	...	...	28 462[11]	...
	2006	29 810	5 491	2 724	...	...	24 319	...
	2007	#17 915	5 236	2 408	...	...	#12 679	...
	2008	18 625	5 525	2 680	...	...	13 100	...
Cyprus Chypre	2002	822	435	137	206	80	181	95
	2003	922	490	157	239	87	194	107
	2004	1 017	583	197	243	95	191	105
	2005	1 157	682	239	273	98	201	105
	2006	1 226	748	254	270	103	207	108
	2007	1 244	799	272	266	113	179	87
	*2008	1 315	885	...	...	...	...	...
Czech Republic République tchèque	2002	26 032	14 974	3 917	8 090	3 216	2 968	1 351
	2003	27 957	15 809	4 121	9 001	3 347	3 147	1 403
	2004	28 765	16 300	4 052	9 446	3 407	3 020	1 348
	#2005	43 370	24 169	6 349	13 773	5 153	5 429	2 633
	2006	47 729	26 267	6 652	15 840	5 672	5 622	2 731
	2007	49 192	27 878	7 093	15 431	5 641	5 883	2 916
	2008	50 808	29 785	7 559	15 133	5 259	5 890	2 888
Dem. Rep. of the Congo[3,4] Rép. dém. du Congo[3,4]	2004	31 923	9 072	...	1 444	...	21 407	...
	2005	33 478	10 411	...	1 510	...	21 557	...
Denmark Danemark	2002	42 406	#25 547	#6 802	...	...	...	...
	2003	41 607	24 882	6 926	...	...	...	...
	2004	42 687	26 167	...	...	...	...	...
	2005	43 499	28 179	8 113	10 782	5 364	4 538	2 534
	2006	44 878	28 846	...	10 894	...	5 138	...
	#2007	46 897	30 174	8 843	11 527	4 867	5 196	2 570
	2008[5]	48 096	30 945	...	11 821	...	5 329	...
Ecuador[3] Equateur[3]	2002	1 271	696	160	...	...	575	...
	2003	1 555	845	241	...	...	710	...
	#2006	2 301	1 555	645	414	171	332	...
	2007	2 853	1 615	725	471	211	767	...

56 Personnel in research and development (R & D) *(continued)*

Full-time equivalent (FTE)

Personnel employé dans la recherche et le développement (R - D) *(suite)*

Equivalent temps plein (ETP)

Country or area Pays ou zone	Year Année	Total R & D personnel Total du personnel de R - D	Researchers / Chercheurs: Total M & W Total H & F	Researchers / Chercheurs: Women Femmes	Technicians and equivalent staff / Techniciens et personnel assimilé: Total M & W Total H & F	Technicians and equivalent staff / Techniciens et personnel assimilé: Women Femmes	Other supporting staff / Autre personnel de soutien: Total M & W Total H & F	Other supporting staff / Autre personnel de soutien: Women Femmes
Egypt[3] Egypte[3]	2007	...	95 947[1]	34 725[2]	30 295[1]	...	...	...
El Salvador[3] El Salvador[3]	2003	...	252	78	...	...	...	...
	2004	...	258	80	...	...	...	...
	2005	...	260	81	...	...	...	...
	2006	...	263	82	...	...	...	...
	2007	...	274	85	...	...	...	...
	#2008	...	401	132	...	...	...	...
Estonia Estonie	2002	4 129	3 059	1 262	524	317	546	394
	2003	4 144	3 017	1 273	573	362	554	393
	2004	4 735	3 369	1 390	654	370	712	488
	2005	4 362	3 331	1 317	567	274	464	305
	2006	4 741	3 513	1 418	776	339	452	237
	2007	5 002	3 690	1 531	805	368	507	266
	*2008	5 086	3 979	...	828	...	279	...
Ethiopia Ethiopie	2005	5 112	1 608	111	779	...	2 725	...
	2007	6 051	1 615	125	978	...	3 458	...
Finland[3] Finlande[3]	2002	73 121	50 215[12]	15 025[12]	...	...	...	...
	2003	74 773	53 430[12]	15 931[12]	...	...	...	...
	2004	76 687	#51 219	#14 834	...	...	...	...
	2005	77 275	50 773	15 349	...	...	...	...
	2006	79 911	53 273	16 808	...	...	...	...
	2007	79 507	53 420	16 824	...	...	...	...
France France	2002	339 847	186 420	...	...	...	...	...
	2003	342 307	192 790	...	...	...	...	...
	2004	352 003	202 377	...	106 415	...	43 211	...
	2005	349 681	202 507	...	105 171	...	42 003	...
	2006	365 814	210 591	...	114 525	...	40 698	...
	2007	372 326	215 755	...	115 992	...	40 578	...
Gabon[1,3] Gabon[1,3]	2004	188	80	25	68	...	40	...
	2006	322	150	37	42	13	130	40
Gambia[3] Gambie[3]	2002	77[1]	40[1]	^0	25[1]	...	12[1]	...
	2003	81[1]	44[1]	^0	25[1]	...	12[1]	...
	2004[1]	82	44	3	28	...	10	...
	2005[1]	84	46	4	28	...	10	...
Georgia[3] Géorgie[3]	2002	16 031	11 997	6 165	1 246	...	2 788	...
	2003	17 819	11 572	5 809	1 895	...	4 352	...
	2004	16 698	10 910	5 664	2 262	...	3 526	...
	2005	13 415	8 112	4 275	1 810	...	3 493	...
Germany Allemagne	2002[5]	480 004	265 812	...	...	...	...	...
	2003	472 533	268 942	43 855	89 956	...	113 634	...
	2004	470 729	270 215	...	87 873	...	112 640	...
	2005	475 278	272 148	48 205	94 578	...	108 553	...
	2006	487 935	279 822	...	98 922	...	109 190	...
	2007	506 450	290 853	...	107 150	...	108 447	...
Greece Grèce	2003	31 849	15 631	5 198	9 207	2 661	7 011	3 223
	2005	33 603	19 593	6 213	8 450	3 070	5 559	3 007
	2006[5]	35 140	19 907	...	...	...	...	...
	2007[5]	35 629	20 817	...	...	...	...	...
Guatemala[1,3] Guatemala[1,3]	2005	851	615	262	192	52	370	90
	2006	858	547	135	189	50	386	69
	2007	1 223	634	201	695	251	371	110
Honduras[3] Honduras[3]	2002	2 321	516	149	...	...	1 805	830
	2003	2 280	539	143	...	...	1 741	731

56 Personnel in research and development (R & D) *(continued)*
Full-time equivalent (FTE)

Personnel employé dans la recherche et le développement (R - D) *(suite)*
Equivalent temps plein (ETP)

Country or area Pays ou zone	Year Année	Total R & D personnel Total du personnel de R - D	Researchers Chercheurs		Technicians and equivalent staff Techniciens et personnel assimilé		Other supporting staff Autre personnel de soutien	
			Total M & W Total H & F	Women Femmes	Total M & W Total H & F	Women Femmes	Total M & W Total H & F	Women Femmes
Hungary[3] Hongrie[3]	2002[13]	48 727	29 764	10 039	8 965	5 590	9 998	6 617
	2003[13]	48 681	30 292	10 647	8 659	5 552	9 730	6 350
	#2004	49 615	30 420	10 484	8 873	5 910	10 322	7 138
	2005	49 723	31 407	10 731	8 663	5 803	9 653	6 679
	2006	50 411	32 786	10 973	8 441	5 377	9 184	6 073
	2007	49 485	33 059	11 077	8 474	5 147	7 952	5 287
Iceland Islande	2002[5]	2 797	...	...	...	...	...	...
	2003	2 940	1 917	690	594	...	429	...
	2005	3 226	2 155	784	669	299	402	181
	2006	3 415	2 400	874	652	282	363	156
	2007	2 982	2 208	805	517	213	257	102
	2008	3 117	2 308	841	540	222	269	107
India[6] Inde[6]	2005	391 149	154 827[5]	19 707[14]	105 808	15 802	130 514	25 541
Indonesia[3] Indonésie[3]	2005	55 118[1]	35 564[1]	10 874	9 253[1]	...	10 301[1]	...
Iran (Islamic Rep. of)[3] Iran (Rép. islamique d')[3]	2004	91 584	51 899	10 300	22 186	...	17 499	...
	2006	101 457	67 795	15 587	18 429	...	15 233	...
Ireland Irlande	2002	13 582	9 376	2 602	2 369	586	1 837	672
	2003	14 450	10 039	2 883	2 511	633	1 900	702
	2004	15 713	11 010	3 069	2 717	729	1 986	834
	2005	16 690	11 587	3 241	3 043	797	2 060	881
	2006	17 507	12 184	3 561	2 968	783	2 355	1 023
	2007	18 212	12 669	*3 856	2 934	*797	2 610	*1 199
	*2008	19 348	13 709	...	3 033	...	2 605	...
Italy Italie	2002	164 023	71 242	...	...	...	...	...
	2003	161 828	70 332	20 105	...	...	...	...
	2004	164 026	72 012	20 938	...	...	...	...
	2005	175 248	82 489	26 797	...	...	...	...
	2006	192 002	88 430	29 107	...	...	...	...
	2007	208 376	93 000	...	...	...	...	...
	*2008	236 261	96 303	...	...	...	...	...
Japan[3] Japon[3]	2002	1 032 830	791 224	88 674	76 490	22 964	165 112	61 044
	2003	1 081 100	830 545	96 133	82 007	24 650	168 546	62 433
	2004	1 096 080	830 474	98 690	87 886	25 696	177 719	65 308
	2005	1 122 680	861 901	102 948	85 509	27 562	175 269	65 753
	2006	1 148 840	874 690	108 547	87 721	27 774	186 425	67 387
	2007	1 157 570	883 386	114 942	93 841	30 051	180 343	65 469
Jordan[3] Jordanie[3]	2003	42 153	15 891	3 385	19 322	2 073	6 940	2 101
Kazakhstan[3] Kazakhstan[3]	2002	15 998[4]	9 366	4 558	1 364	...	2 990	...
	2003	16 578[4]	9 899	4 809	1 300	...	3 018	...
	2004	16 715[4]	10 382	5 017	1 102	...	3 112	...
	2005	18 912[4]	11 910	6 013	1 270	...	3 133	...
	2006	19 563[4]	12 404	6 140	1 281	...	3 214	...
	2007	17 774[4]	11 524	5 987	1 290	...	2 824	...
	2008	16 304[4]	10 780	5 526	1 166	...	2 349	...
Korea, Republic of[3] Corée, République de[3]	2002[15]	279 806	189 888	22 057	69 021	17 460	20 897	7 792
	2003[15]	297 060	198 171	22 613	75 283	18 158	23 606	8 845
	2004[15]	312 314	209 979	25 198	76 730	18 908	25 605	9 401
	2005[15]	335 428	234 702	30 174	75 179	19 123	25 547	9 732
	2006[15]	365 794	256 598	33 682	80 079	21 223	29 117	10 478
	#2007	421 549	289 098	42 977	94 319	28 734	38 132	14 713

56 Personnel in research and development (R & D) *(continued)*

Full-time equivalent (FTE)

Personnel employé dans la recherche et le développement (R - D) *(suite)*

Equivalent temps plein (ETP)

Country or area Pays ou zone	Year Année	Total R & D personnel Total du personnel de R - D	Researchers Chercheurs		Technicians and equivalent staff Techniciens et personnel assimilé		Other supporting staff Autre personnel de soutien	
			Total M & W Total H & F	Women Femmes	Total M & W Total H & F	Women Femmes	Total M & W Total H & F	Women Femmes
Kuwait [1,8] Koweït [1,8]	2002	744	346	...	86	...	312	...
	2003	771	358	...	90	...	323	...
	2004	786	373	...	93	...	320	...
	2005	800	384	...	96	...	320	...
	2006	812	392	...	98	...	322	...
	2007	869	472	166	94	...	303	...
Kyrgyzstan [3] Kirghizistan [3]	2002	2 922	2 065	1 019	257	...	600	...
	2003	#3 207[4]	1 979	990	229	...	491	...
	2004	3 369[4]	2 019	971	307	...	518	...
	2005	3 419[4]	2 187	977	226	...	498	...
	2006	3 287[4]	2 154	967	205	...	457	...
	2007	3 140[4]	2 034	888	204	...	480	...
Lao People's Dem. Rep. [1,7] Rép. dém. pop. lao [1,7]	2002	268	87	...	...	...	...	...
Latvia Lettonie	2002	5 294	3 451	1 835	660	367	1 183	726
	2003	4 858	3 203	1 707	742	416	913	598
	2004	5 103	3 324	1 806	802	456	977	619
	2005	5 483	3 282	1 636	1 062	554	1 139	594
	2006	6 520	4 024	1 868	1 483	711	1 013	623
	2007	6 378	4 223	2 063	1 126	596	1 029	661
	2008	6 533	4 370	...	1 227	...	936	...
Lesotho Lesotho	2002	26[1]	12[1]	5[14]	5[1]	...	9[1]	...
	2003	26[1]	15[1]	8[14]	5[1]	...	6[1]	...
	2004	51[1]	20[1]	10[14]	21[1]	...	10[1]	...
Libyan Arab Jamah. [3] Jamah. arabe libyenne [3]	2004	772	215	...	164	...	...	...
	2006	1 253	339	...	185	...	...	...
	2007	1 283	373	...	258	...	...	...
Lithuania Lituanie	2002	9 531	6 326	2 989	1 490	1 058	1 715	1 054
	2003	9 648	6 606	3 196	1 476	1 029	1 566	970
	2004	10 557	7 356	3 481	1 531	992	1 670	1 054
	2005	11 002	7 637	3 706	1 436	939	1 929	1 280
	2006	11 443	8 036	3 907	1 402	899	2 005	1 323
	2007	12 656	8 489	4 116	1 778	1 017	2 389	1 612
	2008	12 632	8 458	...	1 836	...	2 338	...
Luxembourg Luxembourg	2003	4 010	1 949	...	1 685[5]	...	376[5]	...
	2004	4 318	2 031	...	...	...	...	...
	2005	4 392	2 227	392	1 558	258	607	250
	2006	4 377	2 054	...	1 284	...	1 038	...
	2007[5]	4 605	2 201	...	1 321	...	1 083	...
	*2008	4 744	2 282	...	1 356	...	1 106	...
Madagascar Madagascar	2002	1 712[1]	788[1]	241	245[1]	...	679[1]	...
	2003	1 696[1]	814[1]	259	188[1]	...	694[1]	...
	2004	1 706[1]	848[1]	279	175[1]	...	683[1]	...
	2005	1 686[1]	879[1]	298	195[1]	...	612[1]	...
	2006	1 715[1]	899[1]	303	278[1]	...	538[1]	...
	2007	1 778[1]	937[1]	320	280[1]	...	561[1]	...
Malaysia Malaisie	2002	10 731	7 157	2 451	1 379	...	2 195	...
	2004	17 887	12 670	4 701	1 598	...	3 619	...
	2006	13 416	9 694	3 757	1 142	...	2 579	...
Mali Mali	2006	672[1]	513[1]	68	159[1,16]	...	...	...

56

Personnel in research and development (R & D) *(continued)*
Full-time equivalent (FTE)

Personnel employé dans la recherche et le développement (R - D) *(suite)*
Equivalent temps plein (ETP)

Country or area Pays ou zone	Year Année	Total R & D personnel Total du personnel de R - D	Researchers Chercheurs		Technicians and equivalent staff Techniciens et personnel assimilé		Other supporting staff Autre personnel de soutien	
			Total M & W Total H & F	Women Femmes	Total M & W Total H & F	Women Femmes	Total M & W Total H & F	Women Femmes
Malta Malte	2002	475	272	...	45	...	158	...
	2003	413	276	...	...	...	...	...
	#2004	717	436	109	147	17	134	64
	2005	825	479	121	222	20	124	65
	2006	862	521	132	221	23	120	63
	2007	*862	*494	127	*267	28	*100	55
	*2008	905	524	...	268	...	113	...
Mexico Mexique	2002[17]	53 379	31 132	...	11 279	...	10 968	...
	2003	59 875	33 558	...	15 304	...	11 013	...
	#2004	75 112	39 724	...	22 289	...	13 099	...
	2005	83 685	43 922	...	25 796	...	13 967	...
	2006	66 967	36 264	...	19 328	...	11 375	...
	2007	70 293	37 930	...	20 037	...	12 326	...
Monaco[1] Monaco[1]	2004	18	9	4	6	...	3	...
	2005	18	10	5	5	...	3	...
Mongolia[3] Mongolie[3]	2002	2 879[1]	1 973[1]	923	177[1]	...	729[1]	...
	2003	2 638[1]	1 995[1]	909	154[1]	...	489[1]	...
	2004	2 642[1]	1 991[1]	907	146[1]	...	505[1]	...
	2005	2 283[1]	1 731[1]	819	81[1]	...	471[1]	...
	2006	2 316[1]	1 707[1]	822	114[1]	...	495[1]	...
	2007	2 379[1]	1 740[1]	837	120[1]	...	519[1]	...
Montenegro[3] Monténégro[3]	2003	1 227	602	235	312	...	313	...
	2004	1 200	597	236	259	...	344	...
	2005	1 246	633	252	290	...	323	...
	2006	1 233	602	231	282	...	349	...
	2007	1 344	671	277	276	...	397	...
Morocco[1,3] Maroc[1,3]	2002	...	25 790	5 133[14]	...	...	...	...
	2003	26 571	23 559	6 049[14]	1 420	...	1 592	...
	2004	27 495	24 483	6 872	1 420	...	1 592	...
	2005	27 549	24 835	6 580	1 042	...	1 672	...
	2006	31 326	28 089	7 322[14]	1 467	...	1 770	...
Mozambique[3] Mozambique[3]	2002[14]	2 467[6]	468[6]	...	1 999[16]	...	...	...
	2006	#1 532[1]	#337[1]	113	#753[1]	...	#442[1]	...
Myanmar[1] Myanmar[1]	2002	7 418	837	...	6 499	...	82	...
Nauru[1,3] Nauru[1,3]	2003	77	19	3	18	...	36	...
Nepal[3,5] Népal[3,5]	2002	13 500	3 000	450	6 000	...	4 500	...
Netherlands Pays-Bas	2002	87 423	38 159	...	28 026	...	21 238	...
	2003	85 986	37 282	...	28 508	...	20 196	...
	# *2004	90 624	47 225	...	...	...	...	...
	*2005	88 442	46 767	...	...	...	...	...
	*2006	92 824	52 039	...	...	...	...	...
	*2007	88 584	49 726	...	...	...	...	...
	*2008	88 723	51 052	...	...	...	...	...
New Zealand[3] Nouvelle-Zélande[3]	2003	36 875	25 486	...	5 554	...	5 835	...
	2005	37 310	27 570	...	5 303	...	4 437	...
	2007	43 600	29 700	...	7 700	...	6 250	...
Nicaragua[3] Nicaragua[3]	2002	456	256	96[14]	...	...	200	...
	2004	371	326	...	45	15	...	...
Niger[1] Niger[1]	2002	594	104	...	118	...	372	...
	2003	569	100	...	115	...	354	...
	2004	599	106	...	133	...	360	...
	2005	595	101	...	137	...	357	...

56 Personnel in research and development (R & D) *(continued)*

Full-time equivalent (FTE)

Personnel employé dans la recherche et le développement (R - D) *(suite)*

Equivalent temps plein (ETP)

Country or area Pays ou zone	Year Année	Total R & D personnel Total du personnel de R - D	Researchers Chercheurs		Technicians and equivalent staff Techniciens et personnel assimilé		Other supporting staff Autre personnel de soutien	
			Total M & W Total H & F	Women Femmes	Total M & W Total H & F	Women Femmes	Total M & W Total H & F	Women Femmes
Nigeria [1,3] Nigéria [1,3]	2002	50 271	18 973	3 475	8 986	...	22 312	...
	2003	55 556	22 690	4 246	9 107	...	23 759	...
	2004	...	24 727	4 286	9 847	...	...	...
	2005	66 574	28 533	4 839	10 854	...	27 187	...
Norway [3] Norvège [3]	2002	51 086	...	...	...	...	...	...
	2003	51 175	35 700	10 505	...	...	...	...
	2005	54 341	36 998	11 740	...	...	...	...
	2007	59 590	41 752	13 924	...	...	...	...
Occupied Palestinian Terr. [1,3] Terr. palestinien occupé [1,3]	2002	81	...	...	...	...	...	...
	2003	141	...	...	...	...	...	...
	2004	209	...	...	...	...	...	...
	2005	195	...	...	...	...	...	...
Pakistan Pakistan	2005	53 159	12 689	2 053	6 471	...	33 999	...
	2007	#69 619	#26 338	6 153	11 113	...	32 168	...
Panama [3] Panama [3]	2002	1 688	416	154	...	...	1 272	442
	2003	1 795	432	158	...	...	1 363	477
	2004	#1 446	484	199	332	130	#630	#245
	2005	#1 802	507	...	...	...	#1 295	...
	2007	1 828	572	187	402	...	854	...
Paraguay [3] Paraguay [3]	2002	1 721	794	398	...	...	927	515
	2003	1 734	800	406	...	...	934	504
	2004	1 873	864	444	...	...	1 009	525
	2005	#1 142	787	368	...	...	#355	#179
Peru [3] Pérou [3]	2004	8 434	4 965	...	1 757	...	1 712	...
Philippines Philippines	2003	9 390[4]	5 860	3 089[2]	938	...	2 502	...
	2005	9 407[4]	6 896	3 500	897	...	1 440	...
Poland Pologne	2002	76 214	56 725	...	11 435	...	8 054	...
	2003	77 040	58 595	21 947	10 881	...	7 564	...
	2004	78 362	60 944	22 684	10 044	...	7 374	...
	2005	76 761	62 162	24 521	8 947	...	5 652	...
	2006	73 554	59 573	22 903	8 662	...	5 320	...
	2007	75 309	61 395	24 186	8 631	...	5 283	...
	2008	74 596	61 831	...	7 264	...	5 501	...
Portugal Portugal	2002[5]	24 250	18 984	8 538	3 031	1 164	2 235	1 131
	2003	25 529	20 242	9 136	3 189	1 272	2 098	1 214
	2004[5]	25 629	20 684	9 333	3 054	1 224	1 891	1 084
	2005	25 728	21 126	9 530	2 918	1 177	1 683	954
	2006[5]	30 531	24 651	10 944	3 605	1 352	2 274	1 063
	2007	35 334	28 176	12 359	4 292	1 527	2 866	1 173
	# *2008	49 114	40 563	...	...	...	...	...
Republic of Moldova République de Moldova	2003	5 005[14]	2 737[14]	1 242	403[14]	...	1 865[14]	...
	2004	4 797[14]	2 725[14]	1 220	354[14]	...	1 718[14]	...
	2005	4 672[14]	2 583[14]	1 120	334[14]	...	1 755[14]	...
	2006	4 505[14]	2 507[14]	1 045	362[14]	...	1 636[14]	...
	2007	4 587[14]	2 592[14]	1 170	417[14]	...	1 578[14]	...
Romania Roumanie	2002	32 799	20 286	9 181	6 436	3 540	6 077	2 763
	2003	33 077	20 965	9 340	5 434	3 174	6 678	3 147
	2004	33 361	21 257	9 480	5 525	3 199	6 579	2 916
	2005	33 222	22 958	10 617	4 998	2 859	5 266	2 414
	2006	30 802	20 506	8 956	4 496	2 625	5 800	2 734
	2007	28 977	18 808	8 242	4 361	2 392	5 808	2 631
	2008	30 390	19 394	...	4 620	...	6 376	...

56 Personnel in research and development (R & D) *(continued)*

Full-time equivalent (FTE)

Personnel employé dans la recherche et le développement (R - D) *(suite)*

Equivalent temps plein (ETP)

Country or area Pays ou zone	Year Année	Total R & D personnel Total du personnel de R - D	Researchers Chercheurs		Technicians and equivalent staff Techniciens et personnel assimilé		Other supporting staff Autre personnel de soutien	
			Total M & W Total H & F	Women Femmes	Total M & W Total H & F	Women Femmes	Total M & W Total H & F	Women Femmes
Russian Federation[3,14] Fédération de Russie[3,14]	2002	870 878	414 676	179 120	74 599	...	381 603	...
	2003	858 470	409 775	177 538	71 729	...	376 966	...
	2004	839 338	401 425	172 177	69 963	...	367 950	...
	2005	813 207	391 121	165 993	65 982	...	356 104	...
	2006	807 066	388 939	163 972	66 031	...	352 096	...
	2007	801 135	392 849	164 385	64 569	...	343 717	...
	2008	761 252	375 804	157 149	60 218	...	325 230	...
Saint Vincent-Grenadines[3] Saint Vincent-Grenadines[3]	2002	131	21	...	110	...	...	...
Saudi Arabia[1,3] Arabie saoudite[1,3]	2002[18]	4 182	1 513	263	1 674	...	995	...
	#2007[8]	1 612	1 024	...	419	...	169	...
Senegal[5] Sénégal[5]	2006	3 299[1]	3 011[1]	301	...	...	288[1]	...
	2007[1]	3 565	3 277	327	...	...	288	...
Serbia[3] Serbie[3]	2002	21 291[4,19]	10 855[4,19]	4 663	4 631[4,19]	...	5 805[4,19]	...
	2003	22 054[4,19]	11 353[4,19]	4 968	4 732[4,19]	...	5 969[4,19]	...
	2004	22 485[4,19]	11 637[4,19]	5 071	4 844[4,19]	...	6 004[4,19]	...
	2005	22 641[4,19]	11 551[4,19]	5 050	4 894[4,19]	...	6 196[4,19]	...
	2006	22 707[4,19]	12 079[4,19]	5 405	4 756[4,19]	...	5 872[4,19]	...
	#2007	18 153[19]	10 580[19]	4 975	2 408[19]	...	5 165[19]	...
Seychelles Seychelles	2005	180[1]	13[1]	4	53[1]	...	114[1]	...
Singapore[3] Singapour[3]	2002	26 824	21 531	5 517	2 398	953	2 895	1 701
	2003	28 825	23 513	5 938	2 549	1 009	2 763	1 823
	2004	31 006	25 251	6 506	2 823	1 121	2 932	1 901
	2005	34 522	27 969	7 346	3 265	1 326	3 288	2 095
	2006	36 191	29 478	7 986	3 291	1 311	3 422	2 290
	2007	38 255	31 657	8 665	3 224	1 279	3 374	2 278
Slovakia Slovaquie	2002	13 631	9 181	3 749	3 032	1 586	1 418	828
	2003	13 354	9 627	3 946	2 483	1 433	1 244	735
	2004	14 329	10 718	4 427	2 403	1 331	1 209	664
	2005	14 404	10 921	4 484	2 245	1 218	1 238	670
	2006	15 028	11 776	4 959	2 284	1 220	969	603
	2007	15 421	12 354	5 116	2 238	1 238	829	533
	2008	15 576	12 587	5 330	2 117	1 139	872	551
Slovenia Slovénie	2002	8 615	4 642	1 606	3 140	1 199	833	450
	2003	6 805	3 775	1 202	2 281	838	749	415
	2004	7 132	4 030	1 288	2 323	882	779	427
	2005	8 994	5 253	1 777	2 820	1 067	921	501
	2006	9 793	5 857	1 941	2 954	1 148	982	535
	2007	10 369	6 250	2 106	3 089	1 176	1 030	542
	2008	11 594	7 032	...	3 418	...	1 144	...
South Africa Afrique du Sud	2003	25 189	14 131	5 059	5 142	1 992	5 916	2 300
	2004	29 697	17 915	6 623	5 176	1 631	6 606	2 913
	2005	28 798	17 303	6 272	5 248	1 749	6 247	2 928
	2006	30 984	18 573	7 114	6 332	2 201	6 080	2 700
	2007[6]	31 354	19 320	...	6 061	...	5 974	...
Spain Espagne	2002	134 258	83 318	29 767	30 376	9 561	20 564	9 068
	2003	151 487	92 523	33 985	36 278	11 381	22 687	9 891
	2004	161 933	100 994	37 580	37 871	12 578	23 068	10 353
	2005	174 773	109 720	41 371	39 904	13 259	25 149	11 390
	2006	188 978	115 798	43 431	44 842	15 809	28 337	12 932
	2007	201 108	122 624	46 458	50 341	18 263	28 143	13 448
	2008	215 676	130 986	...	...	...	...	...
Sri Lanka Sri Lanka	2004	5 475	2 679	861	1 474	...	1 322	...
	2006	4 513	1 833	754	1 272	...	1 408	...

56 Personnel in research and development (R & D) *(continued)*
Full-time equivalent (FTE)

Personnel employé dans la recherche et le développement (R - D) *(suite)*
Equivalent temps plein (ETP)

Country or area Pays ou zone	Year Année	Total R & D personnel Total du personnel de R - D	Researchers Chercheurs		Technicians and equivalent staff Techniciens et personnel assimilé		Other supporting staff Autre personnel de soutien	
			Total M & W Total H & F	Women Femmes	Total M & W Total H & F	Women Femmes	Total M & W Total H & F	Women Femmes
Sudan[3,5] Soudan[3,5]	2002	18 604	9 100	2 754	3 674	...	5 830	...
	2003	18 808	9 200	2 784	3 714	...	5 894	...
	2004	19 772	9 340	2 830	4 641	...	5 791	...
	2005	23 726	11 208	4 483	5 569	...	6 949	...
Sweden Suède	2003	72 978	48 186	...	...	...	...	...
	2004	72 459	48 784	...	...	...	...	...
	2005	#77 704	#55 090	16 002[12]	...	...	...	...
	2006	78 715	55 729	...	...	...	...	...
	2007	#76 827[14]	#47 775[14]	#13 743[14]	17 140	...	11 532	...
	2008[5]	77 549	48 220	...	...	...	...	...
Switzerland[3] Suisse[3]	2004	84 090	43 220	11 555	19 775	3 590	21 095	10 960
Tajikistan[3] Tadjikistan[3]	2002	2 628[4]	1 752	701	312	...	564[4]	...
	2003	2 425[4]	1 544	438	270	...	611[4]	...
	2004	2 487[4]	1 548	407	247	...	692[4]	...
	2005	3 220[4]	1 993	...	324	...	903[4]	...
	2006	3 110[4]	1 895	735	202	...	1 013[4]	...
	2007	2 075[4]	1 286	...	253	...	536[4]	...
Thailand Thaïlande	2003	42 379	18 114	...	13 139	...	11 126	...
	2005	36 967	20 506	10 241	10 520	...	5 941	...
TFYR of Macedonia L'ex-R.Y. Macédoine	2002	1 518	1 164	571	140	...	214	...
	2003	1 464	1 118	557	137	...	209	...
	2004	1 447	1 069	538	195	...	183	...
	2005	1 434	1 113	576	168	...	153	...
	2006	1 357	1 062	547	152	...	143	...
Togo Togo	2003	235	142	...	93	...	...	...
	2004	228	137	...	91[2]	...	...	...
	#2005	312	186	...	126	...	...	...
	2006	230	136	...	94	...	...	...
	#2007	320	216	21[14]	104	...	...	...
Trinidad and Tobago[3] Trinité-et-Tobago[3]	2003	...	518	208	...	...	...	...
	2004	#908	550	213	#358	#132	...	...
	2005	1 103	603	203	500	229	...	...
	2006	1 243	690	267	553	261	...	...
	2007	1 117	634	241	483	...	...	...
Tunisia Tunisie	2002	11 510	9 910[4]	...	329[1,8]	...	1 271[1,8]	...
	2003	12 857	11 265[4]	5 471	357[1,8]	...	1 235[1,8]	...
	2004	14 556	12 950[4]	6 145	379[1,8]	...	1 227[1,8]	...
	2005	16 289	14 650[4]	6 995	413[1,8]	...	1 226[1,8]	...
	2006	17 466	15 833[4]	...	428[1,8]	...	1 205[1,8]	...
Turkey Turquie	2002	28 964[14]	23 995	8 211	2 567[14]	415[14]	2 402[14]	511[14]
	2003	38 308[14]	32 660	11 229	3 092[14]	565[14]	2 556[14]	650[14]
	2004	39 960[14]	33 876	11 815	3 341[14]	637[14]	2 743[14]	677[14]
	2005	49 251[14]	39 139	13 381	4 753[14]	988[14]	5 360[14]	978[14]
	2006	54 444[14]	42 664	14 567	5 724[14]	1 074[14]	6 056[14]	1 131[14]
	2007	63 377[14]	49 668	16 942	7 420[14]	1 291[14]	6 289[14]	1 258[14]
Uganda[3] Ouganda[3]	2002	1 370	630	236	384	...	356	...
	2003	1 468	675	253	411	...	382	...
	2004	1 573	724	272	440	...	409	...
	2005	1 686	776	291	472	...	438	...
	2006	1 807	831	312	506	...	470	...
	2007	1 937	891	365	542	...	504	...

56 Personnel in research and development (R & D) *(continued)*

Full-time equivalent (FTE)

Personnel employé dans la recherche et le développement (R - D) *(suite)*

Equivalent temps plein (ETP)

Country or area Pays ou zone	Year Année	Total R & D personnel Total du personnel de R - D	Researchers Chercheurs		Technicians and equivalent staff Techniciens et personnel assimilé		Other supporting staff Autre personnel de soutien	
			Total M & W Total H & F	Women Femmes	Total M & W Total H & F	Women Femmes	Total M & W Total H & F	Women Femmes
Ukraine [3] Ukraine [3]	2002	142 763	85 211	36 557	22 236	...	35 316	...
	2003	139 470	83 890	36 174	20 951	...	34 629	...
	2004	140 284	85 742	37 634	20 861	...	33 681	...
	2005	#170 579[4]	85 246	37 586	20 266	...	32 052	...
	2006	160 788[4]	80 497	35 542	19 748	...	30 204	...
	2007	155 549[4]	78 832	34 596	17 988	...	28 896	...
United Kingdom Royaume-Uni	2002[20]	308 776	198 163	...	...	...	...	...
	2003[20]	315 846	216 690	...	...	...	...	...
	2004[20]	318 886	228 969	...	...	...	...	...
	2005[5]	#324 917[14]	#248 599	...	41 494	...	34 824[14]	...
	2006[5]	334 804[14]	254 009	...	44 138	...	36 657[14]	...
	2007[5]	349 360[14]	254 599	...	53 502	...	41 254[14]	...
	*2008	358 284[14]	261 406	...	54 698	...	42 180[14]	...
United States [20] Etats-Unis [20]	2002	...	1 342 450	...	...	...	...	...
	2003	...	1 430 550	...	...	...	...	...
	2004	...	1 393 520	...	...	...	...	...
	2005	...	1 387 880	...	...	...	...	...
	2006	...	1 425 550	...	...	...	...	...
Uruguay [3] Uruguay [3]	2002	4 323	3 839	1 813	...	...	484	114
	2006	3 436	3 182	1 349	172	84	82	#69
	2008	...	2 153	1 127	...	...	...	...
Venezuela (Boliv. Rep. of) [3] Venezuela (Rép. boliv. du) [3]	2002	...	2 077[1]	923	...	...	...	...
	2003	...	2 827[1]	1 345	...	...	...	...
	2004	...	3 148[1]	1 529	...	...	...	...
	2005	...	3 710[1]	1 843	...	...	...	...
	2006	...	4 626[1]	2 330	...	...	...	...
	2007	...	5 222[1]	2 710	...	...	...	...
	2008	...	6 038	3 209	...	...	...	...
Viet Nam Viet Nam	2002	11 356	9 328	...	...	...	...	...
Zambia [3] Zambie [3]	#2002	1 084[1]	268[1]	31[14]	276[1]	...	540[1]	...
	2003	1 141[1]	288[1]	36[14]	295[1]	...	558[1]	...
	2004	1 307[1]	356[1]	79[14]	376[1]	...	575[1]	...
	2005	3 285[1]	792[1]	116[14]	1 240[1]	...	1 253[1]	...

Source:
United Nations Educational, Scientific and Cultural Organization (UNESCO) Institute for Statistics, Montreal, the UNESCO Institute of Statistics database, last accessed October 2010.

Source:
L'Institut de statistique de l'Organisation des Nations Unies pour l'éducation, la science et la culture (UNESCO), Montréal, la base de données de l'Institut de statistique de l'UNESCO, dernier accès octobre 2010.

1 Partial data.
2 UIS estimation.
3 Head count instead of Full-time equivalent.
4 Overestimated or based on overestimated data.
5 National estimation.
6 Source: National publication.
7 Source: Regional publication.
8 Government only.
9 Do not correspond exactly to Frascati Manual recommendations.

1 Données partielles.
2 Estimation de l'ISU.
3 Personnes physiques au lieu d'Equivalents temps plein.
4 Surestimé ou fondé sur des données surestimées.
5 Estimation nationale.
6 Source : Publication statistique nationale.
7 Source: Publication régionale.
8 Etat seulement.
9 Ne corresponds pas exactement aux recommandations du Manuel de Frascati.

56

Personnel in research and development (R & D) *(continued)*

Full-time equivalent (FTE)

Personnel employé dans la recherche et le développement (R - D) *(suite)*

Equivalent temps plein (ETP)

10 For statistical purposes, the data for China do not include those for the Hong Kong Special Administrative Region (Hong Kong SAR), Macao Special Administrative Region (Macao SAR) and Taiwan Province of China.

11 Including technicians and equivalent staff.

12 University graduates instead of researchers.

13 Defence excluded (all or mostly).

14 Underestimated or based on underestimated data.

15 Excluding R&D in the Social sciences and Humanities.

16 Including other supporting staff.

17 Source : "Red Ibero Americana de Indicadores de Ciencia y Tecnologia (RICYT)".

18 Data refer to the higher education sector only.

19 Excluding data from some regions, provinces or states.

20 OECD estimation.

10 Pour la présentation des statistiques, les données pour la Chine ne comprennent pas la Région Administrative Spéciale de Hong Kong (Hong Kong RAS), la Région Administrative Spéciale de Macao (Macao RAS) et la province de Taiwan.

11 Y compris les techniciens y le personnel assimilé.

12 Diplômes universitaires au lieu de chercheurs.

13 A l'exclusion de la défense (en totalité ou en grande partie).

14 Sous-estimé ou basé sur des données sous-estimées.

15 À l'exclusion de la recherche-développement en sciences sociales et sciences humaines.

16 Y compris autre personnel de soutien.

17 Source : "Red IberoAmericana de Indicadores de Ciencia y Tecnologia (RICYT)".

18 Les données se réfèrent au secteur de l'enseignement supérieur seulement.

19 Non compris les données de certaines régions, provinces ou états.

20 Estimation de l'OCDE.

57 Gross domestic expenditure on R & D

As a percentage of GDP and by source of funds

Dépenses intérieures brutes de recherche et développement

En pourcentage du PIB et répartition par source de financement

Country or area Pays ou zone	Year Année	Expenditure on R&D as a % of GDP Dépenses en R&D en % du PIB	Source of funds (%) / Source de financement (%) Business enterprises Entreprises	Government Etat	Higher education Enseigne ment supérieur	Private non-profit Institut. privées sans but lucratif	Funds from abroad Fonds de l'étranger	Not distributed Non répartis
Algeria [1]	2003	0.2	...	...	...	...	...	...
Algérie [1]	2004	0.2	...	...	...	...	...	...
	2005	0.1	...	...	...	...	...	...
Argentina	2005	0.5	31.0	65.3	1.4	1.5	0.8	0.0
Argentine	2006	0.5	29.4	66.9	1.4	1.6	0.8	0.0
	2007	0.5	29.3	67.6	1.4	1.1	0.6	0.0
Armenia [1]	2005	0.2	...	53.8	...	...	5.7	40.5
Arménie [1]	2006	0.2	...	64.2	...	...	10.1	25.6
	2007	0.2	...	50.3	...	...	11.3	38.5
Australia	2002	1.7	50.7	41.2	0.2	#1.7	3.6	2.7[2]
Australie	2004	1.8	54.6	40.3	0.4	1.9	2.9	0.0
	2006	2.1	58.3	37.3	0.1	1.8	2.4	0.0
Austria	2007	2.5	48.7	32.3	0.6	0.5	17.9	0.0
Autriche	2008[3]	2.7	46.3	37.2	...	0.4	16.1	...
	2009[3]	...	45.0	39.9	...	0.4	14.8	...
Azerbaijan	2005	0.2	18.7	77.5	0.0	1.3	2.4	0.0
Azerbaïdjan	2006	0.2	18.3	79.7	...	2.0	^0.0	0.0
	2007	0.2	20.8	76.5	0.0	2.6	0.1	0.0
Belarus	2005	0.7	21.2	71.9	0.7	0.0	6.3	0.0
Bélarus	2006	0.7	20.7	71.8	0.7	0.0	6.8	0.0
	2007	1.0	#45.1	#49.2	0.3	0.1	5.3	0.0
Belgium	2005	1.8	59.7	24.7	2.6	0.6	12.4	0.0
Belgique	2006	1.9	61.0	22.4	2.5	0.7	13.3	0.0
	2007	1.9	61.4	22.2	2.8	0.7	13.0	0.0
Bermuda Bermudes	1997	0.1	...	...	...	...	...	...
Bolivia (Plurinational State of)	2000	0.3	22.0	22.0	32.0	15.0	9.0	0.0
Bolivie (État plurin. de)	2001	0.3	18.0	21.0	33.0	17.0	11.0	0.0
	2002	0.3	16.0	20.0	31.0	19.0	14.0	0.0
Botswana [4] Botswana [4]	2005	0.5	...	...	...	...	...	...
Brazil	2005	1.0	48.3	49.7	2.0	...	...	0.0
Brésil	2006	1.0	47.7	50.4	2.0	...	...	0.0
	2007	1.1	44.7	52.9	2.4	...	...	0.0
Brunei Darussalam	2002	^0.0[1,5]	8.8	91.2	0.0	0.0	...	0.0
Brunéi Darussalam	2003	^0.0[1,5]	6.7	86.8	0.0	0.0	6.6	0.0
	#2004	^0.0[1,5]	1.6	91.0	7.4	0.0	0.0	0.0
Bulgaria	2005	0.5	27.8	63.9	0.4	0.3	7.6	0.0
Bulgarie	2006	0.5	30.6	61.9	0.7	0.4	6.5	0.0
	2007	0.5	34.2	56.7	1.0	0.5	7.6	0.0
Burkina Faso	2004	0.2[1]	...	100.0	...	...	...	...
Burkina Faso	2005	0.2[1]	...	100.0	...	...	...	...
	#2007	0.1[1]	...	72.3	...	...	24.5	3.2
Cambodia [1,3] Cambodge [1,3]	2002	^0.0	...	17.9	...	43.0	28.4	10.6
Canada	2007	1.9	47.8	32.9[3]	6.6[3]	3.3	9.4	0.0
Canada	2008	*1.8	*47.6	*33.0[3]	*6.7[3]	*3.3	*9.3	0.0
	2009	...	*47.5	*33.1[3]	*6.8[3]	*3.3	*9.3	0.0
Chile	2002	0.7	33.2	54.6	0.4	0.3	11.3	0.0
Chili	2003	0.7	43.6	43.2	0.8	0.4	12.0	0.0
	2004	0.7	45.8	44.4	0.8	0.3	8.7	0.0
China	2005	1.3	67.0	26.3	...	...	0.9	5.7[2]
Chine	2006	1.4	69.1	24.7	...	...	1.6	4.6[2]
	2007	1.4	70.4	24.6	...	...	1.3	3.7[2]
China, Hong Kong SAR	2004	0.7	47.8[6]	47.0	0.1	0.0	5.1	0.0
Chine, Hong Kong RAS	2005	0.8	53.0[6]	44.1	0.4	0.0	2.5	0.0
	2006	0.8	52.8[6]	43.1	0.2	0.0	3.9	0.0

Gross domestic expenditure on R & D *(continued)*

As a percentage of GDP and by source of funds

Dépenses intérieures brutes de recherche et développement *(suite)*

En pourcentage du PIB et répartition par source de financement

Country or area Pays ou zone	Year Année	Expenditure on R&D as a % of GDP Dépenses en R&D en % du PIB	Source of funds (%) / Source de financement (%) Business enterprises Entreprises	Government Etat	Higher education Enseigne ment supérieur	Private non-profit Institut. privées sans but lucratif	Funds from abroad Fonds de l'étranger	Not distributed Non répartis
China, Macao SAR[1,3]	2003	0.1	...	...	...	...	...	...
Chine, Macao RAS[1,3]	2004	0.1	...	...	...	...	...	...
	2005	0.1	...	...	...	...	...	...
Colombia	2005	0.2	27.2	37.8	27.1	2.4	5.5	0.0
Colombie	2006	0.2	28.0	38.5	24.9	4.2	4.4	0.0
	2007	0.2	27.2	37.7	25.6	5.4	4.1	0.0
Costa Rica	2004	0.4	...	...	...	...	...	...
Costa Rica	2006	0.4	...	...	...	...	...	...
	2007	0.3	...	...	...	...	...	...
Croatia	2006	0.8	34.6	55.8	2.5	0.2	6.8	0.0
Croatie	2007	0.8	35.5	50.4	3.0	0.2	10.9	0.0
	2008	0.9	40.8	49.3	1.9	0.2	7.9	0.0
Cuba	2006	0.4	35.0	60.0	...	...	5.0	0.0
Cuba	2007	0.4	35.0	60.0	...	...	5.0	0.0
	2008	0.5	#18.0	#69.0	...	...	#13.0	0.0
Cyprus	2006	0.4	15.9	66.5	4.1	1.3	12.1	0.0
Chypre	2007	0.4	16.4	64.6	2.8	1.7	14.5	0.0
	*2008	0.5	...	...	...	...	...	...
Czech Republic	2006	1.5	56.9	39.0	1.0	0.0	3.1	0.0
République tchèque	2007	1.5	54.0	41.2	0.8	0.0	4.1	0.0
	2008	1.5	52.2	41.3	1.2	0.0	5.3	0.0
Dem. Rep. of the Congo	2004	0.4[7,8]	...	100.0	...	...	...	...
Rép. dém. du Congo	2005	0.5[7,8]	...	100.0	...	...	...	...
Denmark	2006	2.5	...	...	...	...	...	...
Danemark	2007	#2.6	#60.6	#26.0	#0.3	#3.6	#9.7	0.0
	2008	2.7[3]	61.1[3]	25.3[3]	0.3[3]	3.6[3]	9.7[3]	0.0
Ecuador	2003	0.1	...	...	...	...	...	...
Equateur	#2006	0.1	17.4	69.3	4.0	1.2	4.2	4.0
	2007	0.1	21.5	58.1	3.9	3.3	7.0	6.2
Egypt[1]	2005	0.2	...	...	...	...	...	...
Egypte[1]	2006	0.3	...	...	...	...	...	...
	2007	0.2	...	...	...	...	...	...
El Salvador	1998	0.1	1.2	51.9	13.2	10.4	23.4	0.0
El Salvador	2007	0.1	1.8	50.4	39.4	0.9	7.4	0.0
Estonia	2006	1.1	38.1	44.6	0.9	0.1	16.3	0.0
Estonie	2007	1.1	41.6	45.6	0.9	0.2	11.7	0.0
	2008	*1.3	33.6	50.0	0.5	0.3	15.5	...
Ethiopia	2005	0.2[1]	...	69.2	...	0.1	30.8	0.0
Ethiopie	2007	0.2[1]	...	71.7	0.0	0.7	27.0	0.5
Finland	2006	3.4	66.6	25.1	0.3	1.0	7.1	0.0
Finlande	2007	3.5	68.2	24.1	0.3	1.0	6.5	0.0
	2008[3]	3.5	...	...	...	...	...	...
France	2006	2.1	52.3	38.5	1.3	0.8	7.0	0.0
France	2007	*2.0	*52.0	*38.3	*1.3	*0.8	*7.5	0.0
	2008	*2.0	*50.5	*39.4	*1.3	*0.8	*8.0	0.0
Georgia	2003	0.2	...	...	...	...	...	...
Géorgie	2004	0.2	...	...	...	...	...	...
	2005	0.2	...	...	...	...	...	...
Germany	2005	2.5	67.6	28.4	...	0.3	3.7	...
Allemagne	2006	2.5	68.2	27.7	...	0.4	3.8	...
	2007	2.5	67.9	27.7	...	0.4	4.0	...
Greece	2005	0.6	31.1	46.8	1.7	1.5	19.0	0.0
Grèce	2006[3]	0.6	...	...	...	...	...	...
	2007[3]	0.6	...	...	...	...	...	...
Guatemala	2005	^0.0[1]	...	42.1[1]	57.9[1]	...	...	0.0
Guatemala	2006	^0.0[1]	...	#36.5[1]	#23.7[1]	...	#39.8[1]	0.0
	2007	0.1[1]	...	27.9[1]	21.7[1]	...	50.5[1]	0.0
Hungary	2005	0.9	39.4	49.4	...	0.3	10.7	0.1[2]
Hongrie	2006	1.0	43.3	44.8	...	0.6	11.3	...
	2007	1.0	43.9	44.4	...	0.6	11.1	...

57 Gross domestic expenditure on R & D *(continued)*

As a percentage of GDP and by source of funds

Dépenses intérieures brutes de recherche et développement *(suite)*

En pourcentage du PIB et répartition par source de financement

Country or area Pays ou zone	Year Année	Expenditure on R&D as a % of GDP Dépenses en R&D en % du PIB	Source of funds (%) / Source de financement (%) Business enterprises Entreprises	Government Etat	Higher education Enseignement supérieur	Private non-profit Institut. privées sans but lucratif	Funds from abroad Fonds de l'étranger	Not distributed Non répartis
Iceland Islande	2006	3.0	49.3	39.6	0.0	0.6	10.6	0.0
	2007	2.7	50.3	38.8	0.0	0.8	10.0	0.0
	2008	*2.7	*50.4	*38.8	0.0	*0.8	*10.0	0.0
India Inde	2005[4]	0.8	25.9	69.8	4.4	...	...	...
	2006	0.8[3,4]	27.7[3,4]	67.9[3,4]	4.4[3,4]	...	...	0.0
	2007	0.8[3,4]	29.6[3,4]	66.0[3,4]	4.4[3,4]	...	...	0.0
Indonesia Indonésie	2000	0.1[1,5]	25.7[1,6]	72.7	1.1	...	...	0.5
	2001	^0.0[1,5]	14.7[1,6]	84.5	0.2	0.0	...	0.7
	^#2005[1]	0.0	...	...	...	...	...	...
Iran (Islamic Rep. of) Iran (Rép. islamique d')	2004	0.6	19.6	69.0	11.4	...	...	0.0
	2005	0.7	12.2	76.2	11.6	...	...	0.0
	2006	0.7	14.2	74.6	11.2	...	...	0.0
Ireland Irlande	2006	1.3	53.4	31.9	0.3	1.5	12.9	0.0
	*2007	1.3	49.6	32.2	0.4	1.9	15.9	...
	*2008	1.4	...	...	...	...	...	...
Israel Israël	2006	*4.4[9]	*77.2[9]	*15.9[9]	2.2	1.7	*3.0[9]	...
	2007	4.8	...	...	...	...	...	...
	*2008[9]	4.9	...	...	...	...	...	...
Italy Italie	2005	1.1	39.7	50.7	0.1	1.6	8.0	0.0
	2006	1.1	40.4	47.0	1.4	2.9	8.3	0.0
	2007	1.2	42.0	44.3	1.3	2.9	9.5	0.0
Jamaica Jamaïque	2001	0.1	...	...	...	...	...	...
	2002	0.1	...	...	...	...	...	...
Japan Japon	2005	3.3	76.1	16.8[10]	6.1[10]	0.7	0.3	0.0
	2006	3.4	77.1	16.2[10]	5.7[10]	0.7	0.4	0.0
	2007	3.4	77.7	15.6[10]	5.6[10]	0.7	0.3	0.0
Jordan Jordanie	2002	0.3	...	...	...	...	...	...
Kazakhstan Kazakhstan	2007	0.2	44.5	37.4	15.3	1.1	1.7	0.0
	2008	0.2	50.7	31.4	14.7	2.2	1.0	0.0
	2009	...	13.5	38.5	15.2	32.7	^0.0	0.0
Korea, Republic of Corée, République de	2005	2.8[11]	75.0[11]	23.0[11]	0.9[11]	0.4[11]	0.7[11]	0.0
	2006	3.0[11]	75.4[11]	23.1[11]	0.8[11]	0.3[11]	0.3[11]	0.0
	2007	#3.2	#73.7	#24.8	#1.0	#0.3	#0.2	0.0
Kuwait Koweït	2005	0.1[1]	7.3	92.3	...	0.4	...	...
	2006	0.1[1]	6.6	93.4	...	...	...	...
	2007	0.1[1]	2.4	97.6	...	...	...	...
Kyrgyzstan Kirghizistan	2004	0.2	45.9	53.4	0.0	0.0	0.7	0.0
	2005	0.2	36.4	63.6	0.0	0.0	0.0	0.0
	2006	0.2	...	...	...	...	...	...
Lao People's Dem. Rep. Rép. dém. pop. lao	2002	^0.0[1,5]	36.0[1,5]	8.0[1,5]	2.0[1,5]	0.0	54.0[1,5]	0.0
Latvia Lettonie	2006	0.7	52.7	38.2	1.5	...	7.5	0.0
	2007	0.6	36.4	49.9	0.9	...	12.7	0.0
	2008	0.6	27.0	47.3	2.5	...	23.1	...
Lesotho[1] Lesotho[1]	^2002	0.0	...	...	...	...	...	...
	2003	0.1	...	...	...	...	...	...
	2004	0.1	...	...	...	...	...	...
Lithuania Lituanie	2006	0.8	26.2	53.6	5.3	0.6	14.3	0.0
	2007	0.8	24.5	47.9	7.5	0.5	19.6	0.0
	2008	0.8	21.4	55.6	7.2	0.3	15.5	0.0
Luxembourg Luxembourg	2003	1.6	80.4	11.2	0.0	0.1	8.3	0.0
	2005	1.6	79.7	16.6	0.0	0.1	3.6	0.0
	2007	1.6[3]	76.0	18.2	0.0[3]	0.1	5.7	0.0
Madagascar Madagascar	2005	0.2[1]	...	38.6	51.2	...	10.2	...
	2006	0.2[1]	...	28.4	52.4	...	19.2	...
	2007	0.1[1]	...	32.0	59.6	...	8.4	...
Malaysia Malaisie	2002	0.7	51.5	32.1	4.9	0.0	11.5	0.0
	2004	0.6	71.2	21.5	6.9	0.0	0.4	0.0
	2006	0.6	84.7	5.0	9.7	0.0	0.2	0.4

57 Gross domestic expenditure on R & D *(continued)*

As a percentage of GDP and by source of funds

Dépenses intérieures brutes de recherche et développement *(suite)*

En pourcentage du PIB et répartition par source de financement

Country or area Pays ou zone	Year Année	Expenditure on R&D as a % of GDP Dépenses en R&D en % du PIB	Source of funds (%) / Source de financement (%) Business enterprises Entreprises	Government Etat	Higher education Enseigne ment supérieur	Private non-profit Institut. privées sans but lucratif	Funds from abroad Fonds de l'étranger	Not distributed Non répartis
Malta Malte	2006	0.6	45.7	26.8	...	...	27.5	0.0
	2007	*0.6	51.5	26.3	...	...	22.2	0.0
	2008	...	50.8	28.1	...	0.1	21.0	0.0
Mauritius [7,8] Maurice [7,8]	2003	0.3	...	100.0	...	...	...	...
	2004	0.4	...	100.0	...	...	...	...
	2005	0.4	...	100.0	...	...	...	...
Mexico Mexique	2005	0.4	41.5	49.2	7.3	0.9	1.1	0.0
	2006	0.4	44.8	50.3	3.2	0.1	1.6	0.0
	2007	0.4	45.1	50.2	3.2	0.1	1.4	0.0
Monaco [1] Monaco [1]	2004	...	...	97.0	...	...	...	3.0
	2005	...	...	98.8	...	...	...	1.2
Mongolia Mongolie	2005	0.3[1]	10.4	77.8	0.8	0.0	4.4	6.5
	2006	0.2[1]	8.2	79.5	0.8	0.0	1.7	9.8
	2007	0.2[1]	3.1	82.4	0.5	0.0	1.6	12.4
Montenegro Monténégro	2005	0.9	...	...	...	...	...	...
	2006	1.2	...	...	...	...	...	...
	2007	1.1	...	...	...	...	...	...
Morocco Maroc	2002	0.5[1]	21.6[1]	37.1[1]	41.2[1]	...	...	0.0
	2003	0.7[1]	12.3[1]	40.3[1]	47.4[1]	...	...	0.0
	2006	0.6[1]	22.7[1]	74.7[1]	...	...	2.6[1]	0.0
Mozambique Mozambique	2002[4,7,12]	0.5	...	34.7	...	...	65.3	...
	2006	0.5	...	...	...	...	...	...
Myanmar [1] Myanmar [1]	2000	0.1	...	...	...	...	...	...
	2001	0.1	...	...	...	...	...	...
	2002	0.2	...	...	...	...	...	...
Netherlands Pays-Bas	2002	1.7	50.0	37.1	0.1	1.1	11.6	0.0
	2003	1.8	51.1	36.2	0.1	1.3	11.3	0.0
	*#2004	1.8	...	...	...	...	...	...
New Zealand Nouvelle-Zélande	2003	1.2	38.2	43.8	8.8	2.1	7.1	0.0
	2005	1.2	41.1	43.2	8.9	1.7	5.2	0.0
	2007	1.2	40.1	42.7	8.7	3.7	4.8	0.0
Nicaragua Nicaragua	1997	0.1	...	...	...	...	...	...
	^2002	0.0	...	...	...	...	...	...
Norway Norvège	2003	1.7	49.2	41.9	0.6	0.8	7.4	0.0
	2005	1.5	46.4	44.0	0.7	0.9	8.0	0.0
	2007	1.6	45.3	44.9	0.6	0.9	8.3	0.0
Pakistan Pakistan	2002[3]	0.2[1]	...	100.0	...	...	...	...
	2005	0.4	...	87.0	11.9	...	0.3	0.8
	2007	0.7	...	82.9	12.9	1.8	1.0	1.5
Panama Panama	2004	0.2	0.1	35.0	2.6	2.5	59.8	0.0
	2005	0.2	0.4	38.5	1.4	0.7	58.9	0.0
	2006	0.2	...	...	...	...	...	...
Paraguay Paraguay	2003	0.1	0.0	63.2	12.7	2.3	21.8	0.0
	2004	0.1	0.0	63.1	12.7	2.3	21.9	0.0
	2005	0.1	#0.3	#74.9	#8.6	#2.0	#14.2	0.0
Peru Pérou	2002	0.1	...	...	...	...	...	...
	2003	0.1	...	...	...	...	...	...
	2004	0.1	...	...	...	...	...	...
Philippines Philippines	2002	0.1	68.6	19.1	5.9	0.2	5.5	0.7
	2003	0.1	69.1	21.9	4.8	0.4	3.8	0.1
	2005	0.1	62.6	25.6	6.0	0.7	4.8	0.3
Poland Pologne	2006	0.6	33.1	57.5	2.2	0.3	7.0	0.0
	2007	0.6	34.3	58.6	0.2	0.2	6.7	0.0
	2008	0.6	30.5	59.8	4.1	0.2	5.4	0.0
Portugal Portugal	2006[3]	1.0	43.0	48.6	0.8	2.5	5.2	...
	2007	1.2	47.0	44.6	0.7	2.3	5.4	0.0
	#2008	1.5	...	...	...	...	...	...
Republic of Moldova République de Moldova	2005	0.4	...	...	...	...	3.8	96.2
	2006	0.4	...	...	...	...	2.6	97.4
	2007	0.5	...	...	...	...	2.7	97.3

57 Gross domestic expenditure on R & D *(continued)*

As a percentage of GDP and by source of funds

Dépenses intérieures brutes de recherche et développement *(suite)*

En pourcentage du PIB et répartition par source de financement

Country or area Pays ou zone	Year Année	Expenditure on R&D as a % of GDP Dépenses en R&D en % du PIB	Source of funds (%) / Source de financement (%)					
			Business enterprises Entreprises	Government Etat	Higher education Enseignement supérieur	Private non-profit Institut. privées sans but lucratif	Funds from abroad Fonds de l'étranger	Not distributed Non répartis
Romania	2006	0.5	30.4	64.1	1.2	0.2	4.1	0.0
Roumanie	2007	0.5	26.9	67.1	1.4	0.0	4.5	0.0
	2008	0.6	23.3	70.1	2.6	0.0	4.0	0.0
Russian Federation	2006	1.1	28.8	61.1	0.6	0.1	9.4	0.0
Fédération de Russie	2007	1.1	29.4	62.6	0.6	0.1	7.2	0.0
	2008	1.0	28.7	64.7	0.5	0.2	5.9	0.0
Saint Lucia[7]	1998	0.8	...	...	...	...	...	...
Sainte-Lucie[7]	1999	0.4	...	...	...	...	...	...
Saint Vincent-Grenadines	2001	0.1	...	...	...	...	...	...
Saint Vincent-Grenadines	2002	0.2	...	...	...	...	...	...
Senegal[3] Sénégal[3]	2005	0.1[1]	...	100.0	...	...	...	...
Serbia[13]	2005	0.4	...	...	...	...	...	...
Serbie[13]	2006	0.5	...	...	...	...	...	...
	2007	0.4	...	...	...	...	...	...
Seychelles	2003	0.4	...	...	...	...	...	...
Seychelles	2004	0.4	...	...	...	...	...	...
	2005	0.3	...	...	...	...	...	...
Singapore	2005	2.3	58.8	36.4	0.5	...	4.4	...
Singapour	2006	2.3	58.3	36.4	0.9	...	4.4	...
	2007	2.5	59.8	34.9	0.9	...	4.3	...
Slovakia	2006	0.5	35.0	55.6[14]	0.3	0.1	9.1	0.0
Slovaquie	2007	0.5	35.6	53.9[14]	0.2	0.1	10.2	0.0
	2008	0.5	34.7	52.3[14]	0.3	0.4	12.3	0.0
Slovenia	2006	1.6	59.3	34.4	0.3	0.2	5.8	0.0
Slovénie	2007	1.5	58.3	35.6	0.4	0.0	5.8	0.0
	2008	1.7	62.8	31.3	0.3	0.0	5.6	0.0
South Africa	2005	0.9	43.9	38.2	3.0	1.4	13.6	0.0
Afrique du Sud	2006	0.9	44.8	40.4	3.3	1.0	10.6	0.0
	2007[4]	0.9	...	...	...	...	...	...
Spain	2005	1.1	46.3	43.0	4.1	0.9	5.7	0.0
Espagne	2006	1.2	47.1	42.5	3.9	0.6	5.9	0.0
	2007	1.3	45.5	43.7	3.3	0.5	7.0	0.0
Sri Lanka	2000	0.1[1,3]	7.7[1,3]	51.7[1,3]	18.5[1,3]	0.0	4.5[1,3]	17.5[1,3]
Sri Lanka	#2004	0.2	0.6[6]	67.5[15]	...	...	22.6	9.3
	2006	0.2	19.0[6]	65.2[15]	...	...	4.8	10.9
Sudan[3]	2003	0.3	...	...	...	...	...	...
Soudan[3]	2004	0.3	...	...	...	...	...	...
	2005	0.3	...	...	...	...	...	...
Sweden	2003	3.8[14]	65.1[14]	24.3[14]	0.1[14]	3.1[14]	7.3[14]	0.0
Suède	2005	#3.6	#63.9	#24.4	#0.7	#2.9	#8.1	0.0
	2007	3.6	64.0	22.2	0.7	3.8	9.3	0.0
Switzerland	1996	2.7	67.5	26.9	1.3	1.2	3.1	0.0
Suisse	2000	2.5	69.1	23.2	2.1	1.4	4.3	0.0
	2004	2.9	69.7	22.7	1.5	0.8	5.2	0.0
Tajikistan	2004	0.1	4.8	64.7	0.1	...	...	30.4
Tadjikistan	2005	0.1	2.2	91.9	0.3	...	...	5.5
	2006	0.1	...	...	...	...	...	...
Thailand	2004[3]	0.3	35.5	...	...	...	...	64.5
Thaïlande	2005	0.2	48.7	31.5	14.9	0.7	1.8	2.4
	2006[3]	0.2	...	...	...	...	...	...
TFYR of Macedonia	2001	0.3	10.0[3]	70.3[3]	6.9[3]	3.3[3]	9.4[3]	0.0
L'ex-R.Y. Macédoine	2002	0.3	7.8[3]	76.3[3]	7.3[3]	0.0[3]	8.6[3]	0.0
	2003	0.2	...	...	...	...	...	...
Trinidad and Tobago	2005	0.1	...	...	...	...	...	...
Trinité-et-Tobago	2006	0.1	...	...	...	...	...	...
	2007	0.1	...	...	...	...	...	...
Tunisia	2003	0.7	9.6	47.0	34.2	0.0	7.5	1.7
Tunisie	2004	1.0	12.6	35.4	28.0	0.0	9.4	14.6
	2005	1.0[3]	14.1[3]	45.1[3]	30.5[3]	0.0	10.4[3]	0.0

57 Gross domestic expenditure on R & D *(continued)*

As a percentage of GDP and by source of funds

Dépenses intérieures brutes de recherche et développement *(suite)*

En pourcentage du PIB et répartition par source de financement

Country or area Pays ou zone	Year Année	Expenditure on R&D as a % of GDP Dépenses en R&D en % du PIB	Source of funds (%) / Source de financement (%)					
			Business enterprises Entreprises	Government Etat	Higher education Enseignement supérieur	Private non-profit Institut. Institut. privées sans but lucratif	Funds from abroad Fonds de l'étranger	Not distributed Non répartis
Turkey Turquie	2005	0.6	43.3	50.1	0.0	5.8[17]	0.8	0.0
	2006	0.6	46.0	48.6	0.0[16]	4.8[17]	0.5	0.0
	2007	0.7	48.4	47.1	0.0[16]	4.0[17]	0.5	0.0
Uganda Ouganda	2005	0.2	1.7	41.5	0.0	0.0	56.9	0.0
	2006	0.3	0.0	50.1	0.0	0.0	49.9	0.0
	2007	0.4	7.5	41.7	0.0	0.0	50.7	0.0
Ukraine Ukraine	2005	1.0	32.3[2]	40.1[2]	0.1[2]	0.4[2]	24.4[2]	2.8[2]
	2006	0.9	#32.5	#46.3	#0.1	#0.1	#19.4	#1.5
	2007	0.9	30.2	52.2	0.2	0.1	15.9	1.3
United Kingdom Royaume-Uni	2006	1.8	45.2	31.9	1.3	4.6	17.0	0.0
	2007	1.8	46.7	30.2	1.2	4.5	17.4	0.0
	2008	*1.9	*47.2	*29.5	*1.2	*4.5	*17.6	0.0
United States Etats-Unis	2006	2.7[18]	65.4[17,18]	29.3[18]	2.7[18]	2.7[18]	0.0	0.0
	2007	2.7[18]	66.2[17,18]	28.3[18]	2.7[18]	2.8[18]	0.0	0.0
	2008	*2.8[18]	*67.3[17,18]	*27.0[18]	*2.7[18]	*3.0[18]	0.0	0.0
Uruguay Uruguay	2006	0.3	32.8	40.0	26.9	...	0.3	0.0
	2007	0.4	38.3	43.2	18.5	...	...	0.0
	2008	0.6	#24.6	#60.2	#12.9	...	#2.3	0.0
Viet Nam Viet Nam	2002	0.2	18.1	74.1	0.7[6]	0.0	6.3	0.8

Source:
United Nations Educational, Scientific and Cultural Organization (UNESCO) Institute for Statistics, Montreal, the UNESCO Institute of Statistics database, last accessed October 2010.

1 Partial data.
2 UIS estimation.
3 National estimation.
4 Source: National publication.
5 Source: Regional publication.
6 Including private non-profit funds.
7 Overestimated or based on overestimated data.
8 Based on R&D budget instead of R&D expenditure.
9 Defence excluded (all or mostly).
10 OECD estimation.
11 Excluding R&D in the Social sciences and Humanities.
12 Science and technology budget instead of research and development expenditure.
13 Excluding data from some regions, provinces or states.
14 Underestimated or based on underestimated data.
15 Including higher education.
16 Included elsewhere.
17 Including other classes.
18 Excluding most or all capital expenditure.

Source:
L'Institut de statistique de l'Organisation des Nations Unies pour l'éducation, la science et la culture (UNESCO), Montréal, la base de données de l'Institut de statistique de l'UNESCO, dernier accès octobre 2010.

1 Données partielles.
2 Estimation de l'ISU.
3 Estimation nationale.
4 Source : Publication statistique nationale.
5 Source: Publication régionale.
6 Y compris les fonds privés à but non lucratif.
7 Surestimé ou fondé sur des données surestimées.
8 Basé sur le budget de la recherche-développement au lieu des dépenses.
9 A l'exclusion de la défense (en totalité ou en grande partie).
10 Estimation de l'OCDE.
11 À l'exclusion de la recherche-développement en sciences sociales et sciences humaines.
12 Budget science et technologie au lieu de dépenses de recherche et développement.
13 Non compris les données de certaines régions, provinces ou états.
14 Sous-estimé ou basé sur des données sous-estimées.
15 Y compris l'enseignement supérieur.
16 Inclus ailleurs.
17 Comprend d'autres catégories.
18 A l'exclusion des dépenses d'équipement (en totalité ou en grande partie).

Technical notes: tables 56-57

Research and experimental development (R&D) is defined as any creative work undertaken on a systematic basis in order to increase the stock of knowledge, including knowledge of man, culture and society, and the use of this stock of knowledge to devise new applications.

Table 56: The data presented on human resources in research and development (R&D) are compiled by the UNESCO Institute for Statistics. Data for certain countries are provided to UNESCO by OECD, EUROSTAT and the Network on Science and Technology Indicators (RICYT).

The definitions and classifications applied by UNESCO in the table are based on those set out in the *Recommendation concerning the International Standardization of Statistics on Science and Technology* (UNESCO, 1978) and in the *Frascati Manual* (OECD, 2002).

The three categories of personnel shown are defined as follows:

Researchers are professionals engaged in the conception or creation of new knowledge, products, processes, methods and systems, and in the planning and management of R&D projects. Postgraduate students engaged in R&D are considered as researchers.

Technicians and equivalent staff comprise persons whose main tasks require technical knowledge and experience in one or more fields of engineering, physical and life sciences, or social sciences and humanities. They participate in R&D by performing scientific and technical tasks involving the application of concepts and operational methods, normally under the supervision of researchers. As distinguished from technicians participating in the R&D under the supervision of researchers in engineering, physical and life sciences, equivalent staff perform the corresponding R&D tasks in the social sciences and humanities.

Other supporting staff includes skilled and unskilled craftsmen, secretarial and clerical staff participating in or directly associated with R&D projects. Included in this category are all managers and administrators dealing mainly with financial and personnel matters and general administration, insofar as their activities are a direct service to R&D.

Headcount data reflect the total number of persons employed in R&D, independently from their dedication. Full-time equivalent may be thought of as one person-year. Thus, a person who normally spends 30% of his/her time on R&D and the rest on other activities (such as teaching, university administration and student counselling) should be considered as 0.3 FTE. Similarly, if a full-time R&D worker is employed at an R&D unit for only six months, this results in an FTE of 0.5.

More information can be found on the UNESCO Institute for Statistics web site www.uis.unesco.org.

Table 57: The data presented on gross domestic ex-

Notes techniques : tableaux 56 et 57

La recherche et le développement expérimental (R-D) englobe tous les travaux de création entrepris de façon systématique en vue d'accroître la somme des connaissances, y compris la connaissance de l'homme, de la culture et de la société, ainsi que l'utilisation de cette somme de connaissances pour de nouvelles applications.

Tableau 56: Les données présentées sur le personnel employé dans la recherche et le développement (R-D) sont compilées par l'Institut de statistique de l'UNESCO. Les données de certains pays ont été fournies à l'UNESCO par l'OCDE, EUROSTAT et "la Red de Indicadores de Ciencia y Technología (RICYT)".

Les définitions et classifications appliquées par l'UNESCO sont basées sur la *Recommandation concernant la normalisation internationale des statistiques relatives à la science et à la technologie* (UNESCO, 1978) et sur le *Manuel de Frascati* (OCDE, 2002).

Les trois catégories du personnel présentées sont définies comme suivant:

Les chercheurs sont des spécialistes travaillant à la conception ou à la création de connaissances, de produits, de procédés, de méthodes et de systèmes, et dans la planification et la gestion de projets de R-D. Les étudiants diplômés ayant des activités de R-D sont considérés comme des chercheurs.

Techniciens et personnel assimilé comprend des personnes dont les tâches principales requièrent des connaissances et une expérience technique dans un ou plusieurs domaines de l'ingénierie, des sciences physiques et de la vie ou des sciences sociales et humaines. Ils participent à la R-D en exécutant des tâches scientifiques et techniques faisant intervenir l'application de principes et de méthodes opérationnelles, généralement sous le contrôle de chercheurs. Pour se distinguer des techniciens qui participent à la R-D sous le contrôle de chercheurs dans les domaines de l'ingénierie, des sciences physiques et de la vie, le personnel assimilé effectue des travaux correspondants dans les sciences sociales et humaines.

Autre personnel de soutien comprend les travailleurs, qualifiés ou non, et le personnel de secrétariat et de bureau qui participent à l'exécution des projets de R-D ou qui sont directement associés à l'exécution de tels projets. Sont inclus dans cette catégorie les gérants et administrateurs qui s'occupent principalement de problèmes financiers, le personnel et l'administration en général, dans la mesure où leurs activités ont une relation directe avec la R-D.

Personnes physiques est le nombre total de personnes qui sont principalement ou partiellement affectées à la R-D. Ce dénombrement inclut les employés à 'temps plein' et les employés à 'temps partiel'. Équivalent temps plein (ETP) peut être considéré comme une année-personne. Ainsi, une personne qui consacre 30% de son temps en R&D et le res-

penditure on research and development are compiled by the UNESCO Institute for Statistics. Data for certain countries are provided to UNESCO by OECD, EUROSTAT and the Network on Science and Technology Indicators (RICYT).

Gross domestic expenditure on R&D (GERD) is total intramural expenditure on R&D performed on the national territory during a given period. It includes R&D performed within a country and funded from abroad but excludes payments made abroad for R&D.

The sources of funds for GERD are classified according to the following five categories:

Business enterprise funds include funds allocated to R&D by all firms, organizations and institutions whose primary activity is the market production of goods and services (other than the higher education sector) for sale to the general public at an economically significant price, and those private non-profit institutes mainly serving these firms, organizations and institutions.

Government funds refer to funds allocated to R&D by the central (federal), state or local government authorities. These include all departments, offices and other bodies which furnish, but normally do not sell to the community, those common services, other than higher education, which cannot be conveniently and economically provided, as well as those that administer the state and the economic and social policy of the community. Public enterprises funds are included in the business enterprise funds sector. Government funds also include private non-profit institutes controlled and mainly financed by government.

Higher education funds include funds allocated to R&D by institutions of higher education comprising all universities, colleges of technology, other institutes of post-secondary education, and all research institutes, experimental stations and clinics operating under the direct control of or administered by or associated with higher educational establishments.

Private non-profit funds are funds allocated to R&D by non-market, private non-profit institutions serving the general public, as well as by private individuals and households.

Funds from abroad refer to funds allocated to R&D by institutions and individuals located outside the political frontiers of a country except for vehicles, ships, aircraft and space satellites operated by domestic organizations and testing grounds acquired by such organizations, and by all international organizations (except business enterprises) including their facilities and operations within the country's borders.

The absolute figures for R&D expenditure should not be compared country by country. Such comparisons would require the conversion of national currencies into a common currency by means of special R&D exchange rates. Official exchange rates do not always reflect the real costs of R&D activities and comparisons are based on such rates

te à d'autres activités (enseignement, administration universitaire ou direction d'étudiants) compte pour 0.3 ETP en R&D. De façon analogue, si un employé travaille à temps plein dans un centre de R&D pendant six mois seulement, il compte pour 0.5 ETP.

Pour tout renseignement complémentaire, voir le site Web de l'Institut de statistique de l'UNESCO www.uis.unesco.org.

Tableau 57: Les données présentées sur les dépenses intérieures brutes de recherche et développement sont compilées par l'Institut de statistique de l'UNESCO. Les données de certains pays ont été fournies à l'UNESCO par l'OCDE, EUROSTAT et "la Red de Indicadores de Ciencia y Technología (RICYT)".

La dépense intérieure brute de R-D (DIRD) est la dépense totale intra-muros afférente aux travaux de R-D exécutés sur le territoire national pendant une période donnée. Elle comprend la R-D exécutée sur le territoire national et financée par l'étranger mais ne tient pas compte des paiements effectués à l'étranger pour des travaux de R-D.

Les sources de financement pour la DIRD sont classées selon les cinq catégories suivantes:

Les fonds des entreprises incluent les fonds alloués à la R-D par toutes les firmes, organismes et institutions dont l'activité première est la production marchande de biens ou de services (autres que dans le secteur d'enseignement supérieur) en vue de leur vente au public, à un prix qui correspond à la réalité économique, et les institutions privées sans but lucratif principalement au service de ces entreprises, organismes et institutions.

Les fonds de l'Etat sont les fonds fournis à la R-D par le gouvernement central (fédéral), d'état ou par les autorités locales. Ceci inclut tous les ministères, bureaux et autres organismes qui fournissent, sans normalement les vendre, des services collectifs autres que d'enseignement supérieur, qu'il n'est pas possible d'assurer de façon pratique et économique par d'autres moyens et qui, de surcroît, administrent les affaires publiques et appliquent la politique économique et sociale de la collectivité. Les fonds des entreprises publiques sont compris dans ceux du secteur des entreprises. Les fonds de l'Etat incluent également les institutions privées sans but lucratif contrôlées et principalement financées par l'Etat.

Les fonds de l'enseignement supérieur inclut les fonds fournis à la R-D par les établissements d'enseignement supérieur tels que toutes les universités, grandes écoles, instituts de technologie et autres établissements postsecondaires, ainsi que tous les instituts de recherche, les stations d'essais et les cliniques qui travaillent sous le contrôle direct des établissements d'enseignement supérieur ou qui sont administrés par ces derniers ou leur sont associés.

Les fonds d'institutions privées sans but lucratif sont les fonds destinés à la R-D par les institutions privées sans

can result in misleading conclusions, although they can be used to indicate a gross order of magnitude.

More information can be found on the UNESCO Institute for Statistics web site www.uis.unesco.org.

but lucratif non marchandes au service du public, ainsi que par les simples particuliers ou les ménages.

Les fonds étrangers concernent les fonds destinés à la R-D par les institutions et les individus se trouvant en dehors des frontières politiques d'un pays, à l'exception des véhicules, navires, avions et satellites utilisés par des institutions nationales, ainsi que des terrains d'essai acquis par ces institutions, et par toutes les organisations internationales (à l'exception des entreprises), y compris leurs installations et leurs activités à l'intérieur des frontières d'un pays.

Il faut éviter de comparer les chiffres absolus concernant les dépenses de R-D d'un pays à l'autre. On ne pourrait procéder à des comparaisons détaillées qu'en convertissant en une même monnaie les sommes libellées en monnaie nationale au moyen de taux de change spécialement applicables aux activités de R-D. Les taux de change officiels ne reflètent pas toujours le coût réel des activités de R-D, et les comparaisons établies sur la base de ces taux peuvent conduire à des conclusions trompeuses; toutefois, elles peuvent être utilisées pour donner une idée de l'ordre de grandeur.

Pour tout renseignement complémentaire, voir le site Web de l'Institut de statistique de l'UNESCO www.uis.unesco.org.

Part Four

International economic relations

Part Four of the *Yearbook* presents statistics on international economic relations in areas of international merchandise trade, international tourism and transport and assistance to developing countries. The series cover all countries or areas of the world for which data have been made available.

Quatrième partie

Relations économiques internationales

La quatrième partie de l'*Annuaire* présente des statistiques sur les relations économiques internationales dans les domaines du commerce international des marchandises, du tourisme international et transport et l'assistance aux pays en développement. Les séries couvrent tous les pays ou les zones du monde pour lesquels de données sont disponibles.

Total imports and exports

Imports c.i.f., exports f.o.b. and balance, value in million US dollars

Importations et exportations totales

Importations c.a.f., exportations f.o.b. et balance, valeur en millions de dollars E.-U.

Region, country or area &	Sys.ᵗ	2002	2003	2004	2005	2006	2007	2008	Région, pays ou zone &
World									**Monde**
Imports		**6 535 814**	**7 615 974**	**9 296 007**	**10 577 018**	**12 148 540**	**13 993 954**	**16 157 456**	**Importations**
Exports		**6 409 332**	**7 458 824**	**9 075 250**	**10 348 347**	**11 969 551**	**13 800 097**	**15 926 318**	**Exportations**
Balance		**-126 482**	**-157 150**	**-220 758**	**-228 671**	**-178 989**	**-193 857**	**-231 138**	**Balance**
Developed economies [1,2]									**Economies développées [1,2]**
Imports		**4 460 332**	**5 178 028**	**6 173 359**	**6 870 129**	**7 783 166**	**8 788 017**	**9 812 260**	**Importations**
Exports		**4 155 593**	**4 785 854**	**5 642 630**	**6 146 099**	**6 939 981**	**7 951 202**	**8 878 956**	**Exportations**
Balance		**-304 739**	**-392 174**	**-530 728**	**-724 030**	**-843 185**	**-836 815**	**-933 304**	**Balance**
Asia and the Pacific - Developed economies									**Asie et Pacifique - Economies développées**
Imports		**424 949**	**490 733**	**587 170**	**666 504**	**745 317**	**816 094**	**997 513**	**Importations**
Exports		**496 148**	**560 076**	**672 507**	**722 547**	**795 698**	**877 736**	**1 004 265**	**Exportations**
Balance		**71 199**	**69 343**	**85 337**	**56 043**	**50 381**	**61 642**	**6 753**	**Balance**
Australia	G								**Australie**
Imports		72 693	89 089	109 383	125 283	139 279	165 364	200 564	Importations
Exports		65 036	71 551	86 420	105 833	123 316	141 122	187 249	Exportations
Balance		-7 657	-17 539	-22 962	-19 449	-15 963	-24 241	-13 314	Balance
Japan	G								**Japon**
Imports		337 209	383 085	454 592	514 988	579 609	619 845	762 575	Importations
Exports		416 730	471 999	565 743	594 986	649 948	709 668	786 434	Exportations
Balance		79 520	88 914	111 150	79 998	70 340	89 823	23 859	Balance
New Zealand	G								**Nouvelle-Zélande**
Imports		15 046	18 559	23 195	26 234	26 430	30 885	34 374	Importations
Exports		14 382	16 527	20 344	21 729	22 434	26 946	30 582	Exportations
Balance		-664	-2 033	-2 850	-4 505	-3 996	-3 939	-3 792	Balance
Europe - Developed economies									**Europe - Economies développées**
Imports		**2 611 966**	**3 143 741**	**3 786 038**	**4 143 406**	**4 768 808**	**5 569 512**	**6 235 571**	**Importations**
Exports		**2 713 561**	**3 227 891**	**3 846 503**	**4 156 500**	**4 716 035**	**5 493 539**	**6 120 812**	**Exportations**
Balance		**101 596**	**84 150**	**60 465**	**13 093**	**-52 773**	**-75 974**	**-114 759**	**Balance**
Andorra	S								**Andorre**
Imports		1 200	1 513	1 762	1 796	1 780	1 917	1 931	Importations
Exports		63	89	123	142	150	127	96	Exportations
Balance		-1 136	-1 424	-1 639	-1 654	-1 630	-1 790	-1 835	Balance
Austria	S								**Autriche**
Imports		72 796	91 595	113 344	119 950	130 945	156 760	176 087	Importations
Exports		73 113	89 257	111 720	117 722	130 376	157 317	173 090	Exportations
Balance		316	-2 339	-1 623	-2 228	-570	557	-2 997	Balance
Belgium	S								**Belgique**
Imports		198 125	234 947	285 596	318 768	351 908	413 565	470 439	Importations
Exports		215 867	255 598	306 816	335 868	366 938	432 287	476 826	Exportations
Balance		17 742	20 650	21 220	17 100	15 030	18 723	6 387	Balance
Croatia	G								**Croatie**
Imports		10 722	14 209	16 589	18 560	21 488	25 830	30 728	Importations
Exports		4 904	6 187	8 024	8 773	10 376	12 364	14 112	Exportations
Balance		-5 818	-8 022	-8 565	-9 788	-11 112	-13 465	-16 617	Balance
Czech Republic	S								**République tchèque**
Imports		42 773	53 807	71 635	76 343	93 453	118 467	141 825	Importations
Exports		38 488	48 715	67 198	77 988	95 165	122 760	146 071	Exportations
Balance		-4 285	-5 092	-4 438	1 645	1 712	4 293	4 246	Balance
Denmark	S								**Danemark**
Imports		48 890	56 227	66 845	74 265	85 103	98 859	111 326	Importations
Exports		56 308	65 280	75 568	83 569	91 703	102 865	115 775	Exportations
Balance		7 418	9 052	8 723	9 303	6 600	4 006	4 450	Balance
Estonia	S								**Estonie**
Imports		4 810	6 480	8 334	10 188	13 472	15 170	16 024	Importations
Exports		3 448	4 539	5 934	7 676	9 705	10 948	12 403	Exportations
Balance		-1 363	-1 942	-2 400	-2 513	-3 767	-4 222	-3 621	Balance
Faeroe Islands	G								**Iles Féroé**
Imports		524	630	628	743	790	976	977	Importations

58 Total imports and exports *(continued)*

Imports c.i.f., exports f.o.b., and balance, value in million US dollars

Importations et exportations totales *(suite)*

Importations c.a.f., exportations f.o.b. et balance, valeur en millions de dollars E.-U.

Region, country or area &	Sys.†	2002	2003	2004	2005	2006	2007	2008	Région, pays ou zone &
Exports		541	653	616	599	651	739	825	Exportations
Balance		17	22	-12	-144	-139	-237	-152	Balance
Finland	G								**Finlande**
Imports		33 642	41 601	50 677	58 474	69 447	81 756	92 125	Importations
Exports		44 671	52 514	60 916	65 240	77 287	90 091	96 879	Exportations
Balance		11 029	10 913	10 239	6 765	7 840	8 335	4 754	Balance
France [3]	S								**France** [3]
Imports		312 506	370 888	443 577	486 489	539 658	623 483	707 063	Importations
Exports		312 237	366 121	425 198	443 886	488 432	550 662	606 494	Exportations
Balance		-269	-4 767	-18 378	-42 603	-51 226	-72 822	-100 569	Balance
Germany	S								**Allemagne**
Imports		490 230	604 742	715 903	780 514	922 376	1 055 997	1 205 522	Importations
Exports		615 695	751 829	909 513	977 970	1 122 112	1 323 818	1 467 244	Exportations
Balance		125 465	147 087	193 610	197 456	199 736	267 822	261 722	Balance
Gibraltar									**Gibraltar**
Imports		385	468	535	550	676	853	824	Importations
Exports		148	147	199	199	242	304	281	Exportations
Balance		-236	-320	-336	-351	-434	-548	-543	Balance
Greece	S								**Grèce**
Imports		31 164	44 375	51 559	49 817	59 121	75 100	77 831	Importations
Exports		10 315	13 195	14 996	15 511	20 180	23 472	25 231	Exportations
Balance		-20 849	-31 180	-36 564	-34 306	-38 940	-51 628	-52 600	Balance
Greenland	G								**Groenland**
Imports		391	465	546	593	618	678	871	Importations
Exports		307	349	382	402	396	431	489	Exportations
Balance		-84	-117	-164	-190	-222	-247	-383	Balance
Hungary	S								**Hongrie**
Imports		37 787	47 602	59 636	65 783	77 206	94 375	106 380	Importations
Exports		34 512	42 532	54 893	62 179	74 217	93 377	107 466	Exportations
Balance		-3 276	-5 070	-4 744	-3 604	-2 989	-997	1 085	Balance
Iceland	G								**Islande**
Imports		2 274	2 788	3 551	4 554	5 077	6 354	5 614	Importations
Exports		2 227	2 385	2 896	2 944	3 241	4 509	5 191	Exportations
Balance		-47	-403	-654	-1 610	-1 836	-1 845	-423	Balance
Ireland	G								**Irlande**
Imports		51 508	53 315	61 413	69 177	83 889	85 624	82 658	Importations
Exports		87 497	92 431	104 204	109 605	104 639	122 622	126 144	Exportations
Balance		35 990	39 117	42 791	40 428	20 750	36 998	43 486	Balance
Italy	S								**Italie**
Imports		246 613	297 405	355 269	384 837	440 852	509 937	558 422	Importations
Exports		254 219	299 468	353 544	372 962	416 231	499 933	548 842	Exportations
Balance		7 606	2 063	-1 726	-11 875	-24 621	-10 004	-9 579	Balance
Latvia	S								**Lettonie**
Imports		4 053	5 242	7 048	8 592	11 430	15 185	15 778	Importations
Exports		2 284	2 893	3 983	5 108	5 896	7 892	9 281	Exportations
Balance		-1 769	-2 350	-3 066	-3 483	-5 535	-7 293	-6 497	Balance
Lithuania	G								**Lituanie**
Imports		7 524	9 668	12 386	15 510	19 413	24 445	31 118	Importations
Exports		5 231	6 970	9 307	11 782	14 153	17 162	23 756	Exportations
Balance		-2 294	-2 698	-3 079	-3 729	-5 259	-7 283	-7 362	Balance
Luxembourg	S								**Luxembourg**
Imports		11 602	13 694	16 829	17 565	19 434	22 168	25 045	Importations
Exports		8 499	9 980	12 181	12 699	14 172	16 021	17 856	Exportations
Balance		-3 103	-3 714	-4 648	-4 866	-5 262	-6 147	-7 189	Balance
Malta	G								**Malte**
Imports		2 840	3 399	3 824	3 807	4 073	4 508	4 887	Importations
Exports		2 223	2 468	2 628	2 376	2 705	2 985	2 916	Exportations
Balance		-616	-931	-1 196	-1 432	-1 368	-1 523	-1 971	Balance
Netherlands	S								**Pays-Bas**
Imports		194 130	234 014	284 020	310 600	358 510	421 084	495 043	Importations
Exports		219 857	264 849	318 066	349 844	399 635	476 806	541 445	Exportations
Balance		25 727	30 835	34 046	39 244	41 125	55 722	46 402	Balance

58 Total imports and exports *(continued)*

Imports c.i.f., exports f.o.b., and balance, value in million US dollars

Importations et exportations totales *(suite)*

Importations c.a.f., exportations f.o.b. et balance, valeur en millions de dollars E.-U.

Region, country or area &	Sys.‡	2002	2003	2004	2005	2006	2007	2008	Région, pays ou zone &
Norway	G								**Norvège**
Imports		34 889	39 284	48 062	54 786	63 349	79 777	87 878	Importations
Exports		59 576	67 103	81 709	101 917	120 550	137 975	165 239	Exportations
Balance		24 687	27 818	33 646	47 131	57 200	58 198	77 362	Balance
Poland	S								**Pologne**
Imports		55 141	68 153	89 094	100 759	127 260	162 437	204 873	Importations
Exports		41 032	53 699	74 831	89 214	110 941	138 756	168 674	Exportations
Balance		-14 108	-14 454	-14 264	-11 545	-16 319	-23 680	-36 200	Balance
Portugal	S								**Portugal**
Imports		38 326	40 843	49 225	53 399	65 605	76 369	89 736	Importations
Exports		25 536	30 714	33 023	32 129	42 890	50 241	57 057	Exportations
Balance		-12 791	-10 129	-16 201	-21 270	-22 715	-26 128	-32 679	Balance
Slovakia	S								**Slovaquie**
Imports		17 460	23 760	30 469	36 168	47 250	62 102	74 034	Importations
Exports		14 478	21 966	27 605	31 997	41 939	57 766	70 982	Exportations
Balance		-2 983	-1 794	-2 864	-4 171	-5 311	-4 336	-3 052	Balance
Slovenia	S								**Slovénie**
Imports		10 933	13 853	17 571	19 626	23 014	29 481	34 000	Importations
Exports		10 357	12 767	15 879	17 896	20 985	26 553	29 254	Exportations
Balance		-576	-1 086	-1 692	-1 730	-2 029	-2 928	-4 747	Balance
Spain	S								**Espagne**
Imports		163 575	208 553	257 672	287 610	326 046	382 651	417 049	Importations
Exports		123 563	156 024	182 156	191 021	213 350	246 752	277 695	Exportations
Balance		-40 012	-52 529	-75 516	-96 589	-112 697	-135 899	-139 353	Balance
Sweden	G								**Suède**
Imports		67 667	84 197	100 791	111 324	126 609	148 977	165 122	Importations
Exports		82 965	102 405	123 307	130 205	147 236	166 834	183 093	Exportations
Balance		15 298	18 208	22 516	18 881	20 627	17 856	17 971	Balance
Switzerland	S								**Suisse**
Imports		82 387	95 600	110 324	119 784	132 030	153 181	173 684	Importations
Exports		87 370	100 744	117 820	126 099	141 679	164 809	191 810	Exportations
Balance		4 983	5 144	7 496	6 314	9 649	11 627	18 126	Balance
United Kingdom	G								**Royaume-Uni**
Imports		335 490	380 889	451 870	483 066	547 543	622 125	631 551	Importations
Exports		276 340	304 372	341 652	371 381	428 261	434 790	458 785	Exportations
Balance		-59 150	-76 517	-110 219	-111 685	-119 282	-187 335	-172 766	Balance
North America - Developed economies									**Amerique du Nord - Economies développées**
Imports		**1 423 418**	**1 543 554**	**1 800 150**	**2 060 219**	**2 269 041**	**2 402 411**	**2 579 176**	**Importations**
Exports		**945 884**	**997 886**	**1 123 620**	**1 267 052**	**1 428 248**	**1 579 927**	**1 753 878**	**Exportations**
Balance		**-477 534**	**-545 668**	**-676 530**	**-793 167**	**-840 793**	**-822 484**	**-825 298**	**Balance**
Bermuda	G								**Bermudes**
Imports		747	833	988	985	1 094	1 150	1 145	Importations
Exports		56	52	73	49	25	23	25	Exportations
Balance		-691	-781	-915	-936	-1 069	-1 127	-1 120	Balance
Canada [4]	G								**Canada** [4]
Imports		221 962	239 085	273 084	323 365	348 958	379 792	407 167	Importations
Exports		252 407	272 699	304 623	359 411	389 513	416 431	452 170	Exportations
Balance		30 445	33 614	31 538	36 046	40 555	36 640	45 003	Balance
United States [5]	G								**Etats-Unis** [5]
Imports		1 200 230	1 303 050	1 525 370	1 735 060	1 918 080	2 020 400	2 169 490	Importations
Exports		693 103	724 771	818 520	907 158	1 038 270	1 162 980	1 301 110	Exportations
Balance		-507 127	-578 279	-706 850	-827 902	-879 810	-857 420	-868 380	Balance
South-eastern Europe									**Europe du Sud-est**
Imports		**39 735**	**51 780**	**69 656**	**82 988**	**103 591**	**140 431**	**170 945**	**Importations**
Exports		**24 375**	**30 993**	**41 293**	**49 008**	**61 184**	**76 807**	**94 026**	**Exportations**
Balance		**-15 360**	**-20 787**	**-28 363**	**-33 980**	**-42 407**	**-63 624**	**-76 919**	**Balance**
Albania	G								**Albanie**
Imports		1 503	1 864	2 309	2 618	3 058	4 188	5 251	Importations
Exports		340	448	605	658	798	1 078	1 355	Exportations
Balance		-1 164	-1 416	-1 703	-1 960	-2 261	-3 110	-3 896	Balance

58 Total imports and exports *(continued)*

Imports c.i.f., exports f.o.b., and balance, value in million US dollars

Importations et exportations totales *(suite)*

Importations c.a.f., exportations f.o.b. et balance, valeur en millions de dollars E.-U.

Region, country or area &	Sys.†	2002	2003	2004	2005	2006	2007	2008	Région, pays ou zone &
Bosnia and Herzegovina	S								**Bosnie-Herzégovine**
Imports		4 068	4 769	5 918	7 073	7 344	9 772	12 282	Importations
Exports		1 020	1 369	1 794	2 401	3 324	4 166	5 064	Exportations
Balance		-3 048	-3 399	-4 124	-4 673	-4 020	-5 606	-7 218	Balance
Bulgaria	S								**Bulgarie**
Imports		7 987	10 887	14 467	18 162	23 270	30 086	37 018	Importations
Exports		5 749	7 540	9 931	11 739	15 101	18 575	22 485	Exportations
Balance		-2 238	-3 346	-4 536	-6 423	-8 168	-11 511	-14 532	Balance
Montenegro	S								**Monténégro**
Imports		...	...	...	...	1 874	3 206	...	Importations
Exports		...	...	...	...	791	827	...	Exportations
Balance		...	...	...	...	-1 082	-2 378	...	Balance
Romania	S								**Roumanie**
Imports		17 862	24 003	32 664	40 463	51 106	69 602	82 965	Importations
Exports		13 876	17 619	23 485	27 730	32 336	40 042	49 539	Exportations
Balance		-3 986	-6 384	-9 179	-12 733	-18 770	-29 560	-33 426	Balance
Serbia	S								**Serbie**
Imports		...	...	...	...	13 188	18 400	22 946	Importations
Exports		...	...	...	...	6 437	8 817	11 004	Exportations
Balance		...	...	...	...	-6 752	-9 584	-11 942	Balance
Serbia and Montenegro	S								**Serbie-et-Monténégro**
Imports		6 320	7 952	11 366	...	...	...	...	Importations
Exports		2 275	2 650	3 801	...	...	...	...	Exportations
Balance		-4 045	-5 302	-7 565	...	...	...	...	Balance
TFYR of Macedonia	S								**L'ex-R.Y. Macédoine**
Imports		1 995	2 306	2 932	3 228	3 752	5 177	6 844	Importations
Exports		1 116	1 367	1 676	2 041	2 398	3 302	3 920	Exportations
Balance		-880	-939	-1 256	-1 187	-1 355	-1 875	-2 923	Balance
CIS§									**CEI§**
Imports		**89 168**	**113 555**	**150 032**	**188 007**	**254 079**	**351 907**	**469 584**	**Importations**
Exports		**152 614**	**191 322**	**263 182**	**339 428**	**426 786**	**510 893**	**712 799**	**Exportations**
Balance		**63 445**	**77 766**	**113 149**	**151 421**	**172 707**	**158 985**	**243 215**	**Balance**
Asia									**Asie**
Imports		**15 884**	**20 227**	**27 203**	**34 162**	**46 172**	**59 152**	**73 449**	**Importations**
Exports		**19 280**	**23 864**	**34 099**	**46 656**	**66 380**	**84 049**	**143 856**	**Exportations**
Balance		**3 396**	**3 637**	**6 897**	**12 494**	**20 208**	**24 897**	**70 407**	**Balance**
Armenia	S								**Arménie**
Imports		987	1 280	1 351	1 768	2 194	3 282	4 427	Importations
Exports		505	686	715	950	1 004	1 219	1 057	Exportations
Balance		-482	-594	-636	-818	-1 190	-2 063	-3 370	Balance
Azerbaijan	G								**Azerbaïdjan**
Imports		1 666	2 626	3 516	4 211	5 269	5 709	7 200	Importations
Exports		2 167	2 590	3 743	7 649	13 015	21 269	...	Exportations
Balance		502	-36	227	3 438	7 745	15 561	...	Balance
Georgia	G								**Géorgie**
Imports		796	1 141	1 846	2 490	3 678	5 217	6 066	Importations
Exports		346	461	647	865	993	1 240	1 507	Exportations
Balance		-450	-680	-1 199	-1 624	-2 685	-3 977	-4 559	Balance
Kazakhstan	G								**Kazakhstan**
Imports		6 584	8 409	12 781	17 353	24 956	32 940	39 011	Importations
Exports		9 670	12 927	20 093	27 849	40 470	46 540	77 192	Exportations
Balance		3 086	4 518	7 312	10 497	15 515	13 600	38 180	Balance
Kyrgyzstan	S								**Kirghizistan**
Imports		587	717	941	1 101	1 718	2 412	4 072	Importations
Exports		486	582	733	672	794	1 134	1 618	Exportations
Balance		-101	-135	-208	-429	-924	-1 278	-2 455	Balance
Tajikistan	G								**Tadjikistan**
Imports		721	881	1 191	1 354	1 723	2 455	3 270	Importations
Exports		737	797	915	891	1 399	1 468	1 406	Exportations
Balance		16	-84	-276	-464	-324	-987	-1 864	Balance
Turkmenistan	G								**Turkménistan**
Imports		2 119	2 512	...	...	...	...	...	Importations

58

Total imports and exports *(continued)*

Imports c.i.f., exports f.o.b., and balance, value in million US dollars

Importations et exportations totales *(suite)*

Importations c.a.f., exportations f.o.b. et balance, valeur en millions de dollars E.-U.

Region, country or area &	Sys.†	2002	2003	2004	2005	2006	2007	2008	Région, pays ou zone &
Exports		2 856	2 632	...	...	...	...	...	Exportations
Balance		736	120	...	...	...	...	...	Balance
Uzbekistan	G								**Ouzbékistan**
Imports		2 425	2 662	3 392	3 666	4 380	4 848	7 076	Importations
Exports		2 513	3 189	4 280	4 749	5 617	8 029	10 369	Exportations
Balance		88	527	888	1 083	1 237	3 181	3 293	Balance
Europe									**Europe**
Imports		**73 285**	**93 328**	**122 830**	**153 845**	**207 907**	**292 755**	**396 135**	**Importations**
Exports		**133 334**	**167 458**	**229 083**	**292 772**	**360 406**	**426 843**	**568 943**	**Exportations**
Balance		**60 049**	**74 130**	**106 253**	**138 927**	**152 499**	**134 088**	**172 808**	**Balance**
Belarus	G								**Bélarus**
Imports		9 092	11 558	16 491	16 708	22 351	28 693	39 483	Importations
Exports		8 021	9 946	13 774	15 979	19 734	24 275	32 902	Exportations
Balance		-1 071	-1 612	-2 717	-729	-2 618	-4 418	-6 581	Balance
Republic of Moldova	G								**République de Moldova**
Imports		1 039	1 403	1 773	2 293	2 710	3 690	4 081	Importations
Exports		644	789	980	1 091	1 060	1 342	1 335	Exportations
Balance		-395	-614	-793	-1 202	-1 650	-2 348	-2 746	Balance
Russian Federation	G								**Fédération de Russie**
Imports		46 177	57 347	75 569	98 708	137 807	199 754	267 037	Importations
Exports		106 712	133 656	181 663	241 473	301 244	351 930	467 704	Exportations
Balance		60 535	76 309	106 093	142 766	163 437	152 176	200 667	Balance
Ukraine	G								**Ukraine**
Imports		16 977	23 020	28 997	36 136	45 039	60 618	85 534	Importations
Exports		17 957	23 067	32 666	34 228	38 368	49 296	67 003	Exportations
Balance		980	47	3 669	-1 908	-6 671	-11 322	-18 532	Balance
Northern Africa									**Afrique du Nord**
Imports		**50 284**	**52 759**	**67 975**	**80 229**	**87 531**	**112 542**	**164 706**	**Importations**
Exports		**48 053**	**60 740**	**78 996**	**109 208**	**129 990**	**150 384**	**208 063**	**Exportations**
Balance		**-2 231**	**7 981**	**11 021**	**28 979**	**42 459**	**37 843**	**43 357**	**Balance**
Algeria	S								**Algérie**
Imports		11 969	12 392	18 166	20 356	20 985	...	...	Importations
Exports		18 801	23 206	31 300	46 000	52 760	...	...	Exportations
Balance		6 832	10 814	13 133	25 644	31 775	...	...	Balance
Egypt[6]	S								**Egypte**[6]
Imports		12 496	10 878	12 831	19 816	20 722	27 063	48 775	Importations
Exports		4 687	6 163	7 683	10 652	13 694	16 200	26 246	Exportations
Balance		-7 809	-4 715	-5 149	-9 163	-7 028	-10 863	-22 528	Balance
Libyan Arab Jamah.	G								**Jamah. arabe libyenne**
Imports		4 412	4 311	6 333	6 058	6 965	8 626	...	Importations
Exports		9 837	14 557	20 403	30 869	39 271	45 075	...	Exportations
Balance		5 425	10 246	14 069	24 811	32 306	36 449	...	Balance
Morocco	S								**Maroc**
Imports		11 864	14 250	17 807	20 805	23 977	30 149	40 566	Importations
Exports		7 849	8 778	9 917	11 185	12 744	13 864	18 525	Exportations
Balance		-4 014	-5 472	-7 890	-9 621	-11 233	-16 285	-22 041	Balance
Tunisia	G								**Tunisie**
Imports		9 526	10 910	12 818	13 177	14 865	18 980	24 612	Importations
Exports		6 871	8 027	9 685	10 494	11 513	15 029	19 319	Exportations
Balance		-2 655	-2 883	-3 133	-2 683	-3 352	-3 951	-5 293	Balance
Sub-Saharan Africa									**Afrique subsaharienne**
Imports		**85 245**	**111 549**	**141 670**	**173 968**	**211 018**	**248 466**	**292 902**	**Importations**
Exports		**92 410**	**112 391**	**150 126**	**203 161**	**232 864**	**275 814**	**357 760**	**Exportations**
Balance		**7 165**	**842**	**8 456**	**29 193**	**21 846**	**27 348**	**64 859**	**Balance**
Angola	S								**Angola**
Imports		3 760	5 480	5 832	8 353	11 600	...	14 544	Importations
Exports		7 516	9 237	12 975	23 670	31 084	44 396	72 179	Exportations
Balance		3 756	3 757	7 143	15 317	19 484	...	57 634	Balance
Benin	S								**Bénin**
Imports		729	898	896	894	960	1 110	1 983	Importations
Exports		451	541	564	574	572	593	1 046	Exportations
Balance		-278	-357	-332	-321	-388	-517	-937	Balance

58 Total imports and exports *(continued)*

Imports c.i.f., exports f.o.b., and balance, value in million US dollars

Importations et exportations totales *(suite)*

Importations c.a.f., exportations f.o.b. et balance, valeur en millions de dollars E.-U.

Region, country or area [&]	Sys.[t]	2002	2003	2004	2005	2006	2007	2008	Région, pays ou zone [&]
Botswana	G								**Botswana**
Imports		1 865	2 472	3 236	3 177	3 045	4 170	...	Importations
Exports		2 445	2 809	3 516	4 464	4 487	5 304	...	Exportations
Balance		580	337	280	1 287	1 442	1 134	...	Balance
Burkina Faso	G								**Burkina Faso**
Imports		746	932	1 273	1 374	1 504	1 707	1 794	Importations
Exports		248	320	480	467	588	660	618	Exportations
Balance		-498	-612	-793	-907	-916	-1 047	-1 175	Balance
Burundi	S								**Burundi**
Imports		129	157	176	267	431	319	402	Importations
Exports		30	38	47	56	58	62	54	Exportations
Balance		-99	-119	-129	-211	-372	-257	-348	Balance
Cameroon	S								**Cameroun**
Imports		1 876	2 176	2 411	2 725	3 161	3 776	4 326	Importations
Exports		1 814	2 297	2 481	2 785	3 590	3 769	4 312	Exportations
Balance		-62	122	70	60	430	-7	-14	Balance
Cape Verde	G								**Cap-Vert**
Imports		276	352	432	438	543	753	821	Importations
Exports		11	13	15	18	21	19	32	Exportations
Balance		-266	-339	-417	-420	-522	-734	-790	Balance
Central African Rep.	S								**Rép. centrafricaine**
Imports		122	119	152	175	203	231	307	Importations
Exports		150	128	126	127	159	196	181	Exportations
Balance		27	9	-26	-48	-44	-34	-125	Balance
Chad	S								**Tchad**
Imports		1 638	788	953	954	1 304	1 495	1 695	Importations
Exports		184	599	2 192	3 164	3 398	3 438	4 785	Exportations
Balance		-1 454	-189	1 239	2 210	2 093	1 943	3 090	Balance
Comoros	S								**Comores**
Imports		53	70	86	98	116	120	189	Importations
Exports		19	27	19	12	10	9	15	Exportations
Balance		-34	-43	-67	-86	-106	-112	-174	Balance
Congo	S								**Congo**
Imports		695	856	905	1 503	1 909	2 985	2 840	Importations
Exports		2 290	2 686	3 410	4 788	6 796	6 116	9 018	Exportations
Balance		1 596	1 830	2 505	3 285	4 887	3 130	6 177	Balance
Côte d'Ivoire	S								**Côte d'Ivoire**
Imports		2 462	3 237	4 299	5 246	5 222	6 110	7 150	Importations
Exports		5 279	5 803	6 955	7 693	8 368	8 423	10 100	Exportations
Balance		2 817	2 566	2 655	2 447	3 146	2 313	2 950	Balance
Dem. Rep. of the Congo	S								**Rép. dém. du Congo**
Imports		1 081	1 594	1 986	2 270	2 740	2 950	4 100	Importations
Exports		1 132	1 374	1 850	2 190	2 320	2 600	3 950	Exportations
Balance		51	-220	-137	-80	-420	-350	-150	Balance
Djibouti	G								**Djibouti**
Imports		197	238	261	277	336	410	580	Importations
Exports		36	37	38	40	55	60	69	Exportations
Balance		-161	-201	-223	-238	-281	-350	-512	Balance
Equatorial Guinea	G								**Guinée équatoriale**
Imports		508	1 237	1 563	2 108	2 624	3 098	3 230	Importations
Exports		2 121	2 803	4 588	6 989	8 227	10 095	...	Exportations
Balance		1 613	1 566	3 024	4 880	5 602	6 996	...	Balance
Ethiopia	G								**Ethiopie**
Imports		1 622	2 119	3 087	4 127	4 805	5 307	...	Importations
Exports		480	496	678	903	1 036	1 290	1 499	Exportations
Balance		-1 142	-1 623	-2 409	-3 224	-3 768	-4 018	...	Balance
Gabon	S								**Gabon**
Imports		943	1 043	1 213	1 473	1 726	2 198	2 542	Importations
Exports		2 413	2 827	3 612	4 863	5 254	5 943	8 324	Exportations
Balance		1 470	1 784	2 398	3 390	3 528	3 746	5 782	Balance
Gambia	G								**Gambie**
Imports		159	156	229	237	259	306	322	Importations

58 Total imports and exports (continued)

Imports c.i.f., exports f.o.b., and balance, value in million US dollars

Importations et exportations totales (suite)

Importations c.a.f., exportations f.o.b. et balance, valeur en millions de dollars E.-U.

Region, country or area &	Sys.†	2002	2003	2004	2005	2006	2007	2008	Région, pays ou zone &
Exports		12	8	10	8	11	13	14	Exportations
Balance		-147	-148	-219	-229	-248	-294	-309	Balance
Ghana	G								**Ghana**
Imports		2 712	3 210	4 074	5 754	6 498	7 978	10 351	Importations
Exports		...	...	...	2 802	3 735	4 322	5 625	Exportations
Balance		...	...	...	-2 952	-2 763	-3 656	-4 727	Balance
Guinea	S								**Guinée**
Imports		667	640	690	820	900	1 190	1 600	Importations
Exports		709	609	726	890	900	1 100	1 300	Exportations
Balance		42	-31	36	70	0	-90	-300	Balance
Guinea-Bissau	G								**Guinée-Bissau**
Imports		59	66	96	119	111	111	159	Importations
Exports		54	65	87	80	75	70	98	Exportations
Balance		-5	-1	-9	-39	-36	-42	-62	Balance
Kenya	G								**Kenya**
Imports		3 245	3 725	4 553	6 149	7 311	8 989	11 074	Importations
Exports		2 116	2 411	2 684	3 293	3 437	4 080	4 972	Exportations
Balance		-1 129	-1 314	-1 869	-2 856	-3 874	-4 910	-6 102	Balance
Lesotho	G								**Lesotho**
Imports		815	1 121	1 440	1 410	1 466	1 733	2 005	Importations
Exports		376	485	713	675	690	810	890	Exportations
Balance		-438	-636	-727	-735	-776	-922	-1 116	Balance
Liberia	S								**Libéria**
Imports		...	...	337	310	467	502	865	Importations
Exports		...	...	104	131	158	200	262	Exportations
Balance		...	...	-233	-179	-309	-301	-603	Balance
Madagascar	S								**Madagascar**
Imports		629	1 311	1 616	1 685	1 796	2 625	4 040	Importations
Exports		490	863	946	837	983	1 214	1 345	Exportations
Balance		-139	-449	-670	-848	-814	-1 411	-2 695	Balance
Malawi	G								**Malawi**
Imports		691	785	932	1 163	1 206	1 380	1 700	Importations
Exports		405	520	483	501	541	670	790	Exportations
Balance		-286	-265	-449	-662	-665	-710	-910	Balance
Mali	S								**Mali**
Imports		927	1 270	1 365	1 623	1 843	1 999	2 550	Importations
Exports		873	926	979	1 092	1 553	1 631	1 650	Exportations
Balance		-54	-345	-386	-531	-290	-367	-900	Balance
Mauritania	S								**Mauritanie**
Imports		357	387	1 346	1 344	1 089	1 417	1 644	Importations
Exports		320	321	435	556	1 268	1 410	1 627	Exportations
Balance		-37	-66	-911	-787	180	-8	-17	Balance
Mauritius	G								**Maurice**
Imports		2 159	2 364	2 771	3 157	3 627	3 894	4 670	Importations
Exports		1 801	1 899	1 993	2 138	2 329	2 238	2 402	Exportations
Balance		-358	-465	-778	-1 018	-1 298	-1 656	-2 268	Balance
Mozambique	S								**Mozambique**
Imports		1 543	1 753	2 035	2 408	2 869	3 210	4 100	Importations
Exports		810	1 045	1 504	1 783	2 381	2 650	2 600	Exportations
Balance		-733	-708	-531	-625	-488	-560	-1 500	Balance
Namibia	G								**Namibie**
Imports		1 484	1 999	2 432	2 659	2 904	3 348	4 520	Importations
Exports		1 077	1 269	1 833	2 067	2 638	2 992	2 960	Exportations
Balance		-407	-730	-600	-592	-266	-355	-1 560	Balance
Niger	S								**Niger**
Imports		474	630	757	797	956	982	1 444	Importations
Exports		278	353	439	479	520	651	817	Exportations
Balance		-196	-277	-318	-319	-436	-331	-627	Balance
Nigeria	G								**Nigéria**
Imports		7 547	10 853	14 164	21 314	26 760	37 576	42 378	Importations
Exports		15 107	19 887	31 148	55 145	57 444	65 133	80 615	Exportations
Balance		7 560	9 034	16 984	33 831	30 684	27 557	38 237	Balance

Total imports and exports *(continued)*
Imports c.i.f., exports f.o.b., and balance, value in million US dollars

Importations et exportations totales *(suite)*
Importations c.a.f., exportations f.o.b. et balance, valeur en millions de dollars E.-U.

Region, country or area &	Sys.ŧ	2002	2003	2004	2005	2006	2007	2008	Région, pays ou zone &
Rwanda	G								**Rwanda**
Imports		203	245	284	432	484	736	...	Importations
Exports		56	58	98	125	135	176	...	Exportations
Balance		-147	-187	-186	-306	-349	-559	...	Balance
Sao Tome and Principe	S								**Sao Tomé-et-Principe**
Imports		31	41	41	50	71	67	99	Importations
Exports		5	7	4	3	4	3	7	Exportations
Balance		-26	-34	-38	-46	-67	-64	-93	Balance
Senegal	G								**Sénégal**
Imports		2 038	2 395	2 844	3 193	3 442	4 261	...	Importations
Exports		1 070	1 259	1 506	1 576	1 559	1 663	...	Exportations
Balance		-968	-1 136	-1 337	-1 617	-1 884	-2 597	...	Balance
Seychelles	G								**Seychelles**
Imports		421	412	497	676	758	777	...	Importations
Exports		227	274	291	340	380	356	...	Exportations
Balance		-194	-138	-206	-336	-378	-421	...	Balance
Sierra Leone	S								**Sierra Leone**
Imports		264	303	286	345	389	445	560	Importations
Exports		49	92	139	159	216	244	220	Exportations
Balance		-216	-211	-148	-186	-173	-200	-340	Balance
South Africa [7,8]	G								**Afrique du Sud** [7,8]
Imports		29 281	41 120	53 483	62 325	78 746	88 450	...	Importations
Exports		29 733	36 503	46 148	51 640	58 197	69 787	84 488	Exportations
Balance		452	-4 617	-7 334	-10 685	-20 549	-18 662	...	Balance
Sudan [9]	G								**Soudan** [9]
Imports		2 446	2 882	4 075	6 757	8 074	8 450	9 200	Importations
Exports		1 949	2 542	3 778	4 824	5 657	...	12 450	Exportations
Balance		-497	-340	-297	-1 933	-2 417	...	3 250	Balance
Swaziland	G								**Swaziland**
Imports		1 037	1 654	1 961	2 138	2 379	2 460	2 199	Importations
Exports		964	1 536	1 938	2 226	2 479	2 657	1 790	Exportations
Balance		-73	-118	-23	88	100	197	-410	Balance
Togo	S								**Togo**
Imports		595	775	883	1 194	1 346	1 483	1 540	Importations
Exports		430	600	601	659	619	705	790	Exportations
Balance		-165	-176	-281	-535	-726	-778	-750	Balance
Uganda	G								**Ouganda**
Imports		1 112	1 251	2 020	1 895	2 503	3 466	4 802	Importations
Exports		442	563	885	821	970	1 557	2 170	Exportations
Balance		-670	-688	-1 136	-1 075	-1 533	-1 909	-2 632	Balance
United Rep. of Tanzania	G								**Rép.-Unie de Tanzanie**
Imports		1 661	2 125	2 515	2 661	4 254	5 337	7 081	Importations
Exports		902	1 129	1 336	1 479	1 655	2 022	2 674	Exportations
Balance		-758	-996	-1 179	-1 182	-2 598	-3 315	-4 407	Balance
Zambia	S								**Zambie**
Imports		1 284	1 576	2 018	2 567	2 931	4 014	5 023	Importations
Exports		961	981	1 576	1 780	3 828	4 915	5 039	Exportations
Balance		-323	-595	-442	-786	896	901	16	Balance
Zimbabwe	G								**Zimbabwe**
Imports		1 751	1 710	2 204	2 330	2 250	2 420	2 900	Importations
Exports		2 012	1 670	1 887	1 840	2 020	2 050	2 150	Exportations
Balance		261	-40	-317	-490	-230	-370	-750	Balance
Latin America and the Caribbean									**Amérique latine et Caraïbes**
Imports		**344 417**	**356 832**	**435 053**	**515 193**	**614 268**	**734 392**	**897 319**	**Importations**
Exports		**344 457**	**374 986**	**461 451**	**559 285**	**669 067**	**759 640**	**883 718**	**Exportations**
Balance		**41**	**18 154**	**26 397**	**44 092**	**54 798**	**25 248**	**-13 601**	**Balance**
Caribbean									**Caraïbes**
Imports		**26 866**	**27 762**	**30 141**	**37 904**	**44 346**	**50 481**	**61 325**	**Importations**
Exports		**10 318**	**11 673**	**13 514**	**17 512**	**24 049**	**26 532**	**30 410**	**Exportations**
Balance		**-16 548**	**-16 089**	**-16 626**	**-20 393**	**-20 297**	**-23 949**	**-30 915**	**Balance**
Anguilla	S								**Anguilla**
Imports		74	80	105	133	143	...	...	Importations

58

Total imports and exports *(continued)*

Imports c.i.f., exports f.o.b., and balance, value in million US dollars

Importations et exportations totales *(suite)*

Importations c.a.f., exportations f.o.b. et balance, valeur en millions de dollars E.-U.

Region, country or area [&]	Sys.[†]	2002	2003	2004	2005	2006	2007	2008	Région, pays ou zone [&]
Exports		4	4	6	7	13	...	...	Exportations
Balance		-69	-76	-100	-126	-130	...	...	Balance
Antigua and Barbuda	G								**Antigua-et-Barbuda**
Imports		400	422	454	497	615	750	840	Importations
Exports		39	45	57	82	72	77	90	Exportations
Balance		-360	-377	-397	-415	-543	-673	-750	Balance
Aruba	S								**Aruba**
Imports		841	848	875	1 028	1 041	1 114	1 111	Importations
Exports		128	83	80	102	109	98	99	Exportations
Balance		-713	-764	-796	-927	-932	-1 016	-1 013	Balance
Bahamas [10]	G								**Bahamas [10]**
Imports		1 728	1 762	1 905	2 230	2 401	2 449	2 354	Importations
Exports		446	425	477	562	674	485	560	Exportations
Balance		-1 282	-1 337	-1 428	-1 668	-1 726	-1 965	-1 794	Balance
Barbados	G								**Barbade**
Imports		1 071	1 195	1 413	1 604	1 586	1 709	1 879	Importations
Exports		242	250	278	359	385	419	445	Exportations
Balance		-829	-946	-1 135	-1 245	-1 201	-1 291	-1 433	Balance
Cayman Islands	G								**Iles Caïmanes**
Imports		605	666	877	1 191	1 042	1 032	1 052	Importations
Exports		3	24	25	60	26	27	17	Exportations
Balance		-602	-642	-852	-1 130	-1 017	-1 005	-1 035	Balance
Cuba	S								**Cuba**
Imports		4 151	4 613	5 562	8 130	10 174	10 889	14 249	Importations
Exports		1 504	1 672	2 188	2 159	2 980	3 998	...	Exportations
Balance		-2 647	-2 941	-3 374	-5 972	-7 194	-6 892	...	Balance
Dominica	S								**Dominique**
Imports		116	128	144	165	167	190	225	Importations
Exports		46	41	44	46	41	40	44	Exportations
Balance		-70	-87	-101	-119	-125	-150	-181	Balance
Dominican Republic [4,11]	G								**Rép. dominicaine [4,11]**
Imports		6 037	5 266	5 368	7 207	8 745	11 289	14 020	Importations
Exports		834	1 041	1 251	1 398	1 933	2 635	2 405	Exportations
Balance		-5 204	-4 225	-4 117	-5 809	-6 812	-8 654	-11 615	Balance
Grenada	S								**Grenade**
Imports		202	254	233	319	280	345	320	Importations
Exports		58	42	30	39	20	37	25	Exportations
Balance		-144	-213	-203	-279	-260	-308	-295	Balance
Haiti	G								**Haïti**
Imports		1 122	1 187	1 317	1 449	1 880	1 681	2 310	Importations
Exports		279	346	394	470	480	522	475	Exportations
Balance		-842	-841	-923	-979	-1 401	-1 159	-1 835	Balance
Jamaica	G								**Jamaïque**
Imports		3 533	3 633	3 772	4 458	5 314	6 394	7 734	Importations
Exports		1 114	1 177	1 390	1 499	1 874	2 070	2 542	Exportations
Balance		-2 419	-2 457	-2 382	-2 959	-3 440	-4 324	-5 192	Balance
Montserrat	S								**Montserrat**
Imports		25	28	29	30	30	30	33	Importations
Exports		1	2	4	1	1	2	4	Exportations
Balance		-24	-27	-24	-28	-29	-28	-29	Balance
Netherlands Antilles	S								**Antilles néerlandaises**
Imports		2 268	2 606	1 948	2 277	2 590	2 880	3 130	Importations
Exports		1 609	1 161	762	962	1 125	1 180	1 140	Exportations
Balance		-659	-1 445	-1 186	-1 315	-1 465	-1 700	-1 990	Balance
Saint Kitts and Nevis	S								**Saint-Kitts-et-Nevis**
Imports		201	205	182	210	250	275	285	Importations
Exports		27	48	42	34	40	40	39	Exportations
Balance		-174	-157	-140	-176	-210	-235	-246	Balance
Saint Lucia	S								**Sainte-Lucie**
Imports		309	403	437	479	592	635	690	Importations
Exports		49	85	63	64	65	77	120	Exportations
Balance		-260	-318	-374	-415	-527	-558	-570	Balance

Total imports and exports *(continued)*
Imports c.i.f., exports f.o.b., and balance, value in million US dollars

Importations et exportations totales *(suite)*
Importations c.a.f., exportations f.o.b. et balance, valeur en millions de dollars E.-U.

Region, country or area &	Sys.†	2002	2003	2004	2005	2006	2007	2008	Région, pays ou zone &
Saint Vincent-Grenadines	S								**Saint Vincent-Grenadines**
Imports		174	201	226	240	271	310	360	Importations
Exports		38	38	37	40	38	50	47	Exportations
Balance		-136	-163	-189	-201	-233	-260	-313	Balance
Trinidad and Tobago	S								**Trinité-et-Tobago**
Imports		3 644	3 892	4 858	5 725	6 484	7 481	9 596	Importations
Exports		3 883	5 178	6 374	9 611	14 154	14 744	18 644	Exportations
Balance		239	1 286	1 516	3 887	7 670	7 264	9 048	Balance
Turks and Caicos Islands	G								**Iles Turques et Caïques**
Imports		177	171	220	304	498	581	591	Importations
Exports		9	10	12	15	18	16	25	Exportations
Balance		-169	-161	-208	-289	-480	-564	-566	Balance
Latin America									**Amérique latine**
Imports		**317 550**	**329 070**	**404 913**	**477 289**	**569 922**	**683 912**	**835 993**	**Importations**
Exports		**334 139**	**363 313**	**447 936**	**541 774**	**645 018**	**733 108**	**853 308**	**Exportations**
Balance		**16 589**	**34 243**	**43 024**	**64 485**	**75 096**	**49 197**	**17 315**	**Balance**
Argentina	S								**Argentine**
Imports		8 990	13 833	22 445	28 693	34 158	44 707	57 413	Importations
Exports		25 650	29 566	34 576	40 351	46 568	55 779	70 588	Exportations
Balance		16 660	15 732	12 131	11 658	12 410	11 072	13 174	Balance
Belize	G								**Belize**
Imports		525	552	514	593	676	684	837	Importations
Exports		169	205	213	208	266	254	271	Exportations
Balance		-356	-347	-301	-385	-410	-430	-566	Balance
Bolivia (Plurinational State of)	G								**Bolivie (État plurinational de)**
Imports		1 770	1 616	1 844	2 341	2 814	3 457	4 987	Importations
Exports		1 299	1 598	2 146	2 791	3 875	4 458	6 448	Exportations
Balance		-471	-18	302	450	1 060	1 001	1 461	Balance
Brazil	G								**Brésil**
Imports		49 723	50 881	66 433	77 628	95 836	126 564	182 361	Importations
Exports		60 439	73 203	96 678	118 529	137 807	160 649	197 942	Exportations
Balance		10 716	22 322	30 244	40 901	41 971	34 085	15 581	Balance
Chile	S								**Chili**
Imports		17 092	19 322	24 794	32 735	38 406	47 164	61 903	Importations
Exports		18 180	21 664	32 520	41 267	58 680	67 666	66 456	Exportations
Balance		1 088	2 342	7 727	8 532	20 274	20 502	4 553	Balance
Colombia	G								**Colombie**
Imports		12 711	13 889	16 746	21 204	26 046	33 164	39 320	Importations
Exports		11 911	13 080	16 224	21 146	24 388	29 786	38 265	Exportations
Balance		-800	-809	-522	-59	-1 658	-3 378	-1 055	Balance
Costa Rica	S								**Costa Rica**
Imports		7 188	7 663	8 268	9 812	11 520	12 953	15 366	Importations
Exports		5 264	6 102	6 301	7 026	8 216	9 340	9 575	Exportations
Balance		-1 924	-1 561	-1 967	-2 786	-3 305	-3 613	-5 791	Balance
Ecuador	G								**Equateur**
Imports		6 431	6 703	8 226	10 287	12 114	13 565	18 692	Importations
Exports		5 042	6 223	7 753	10 100	12 728	13 852	18 490	Exportations
Balance		-1 390	-480	-473	-187	615	287	-202	Balance
El Salvador	S								**El Salvador**
Imports		5 184	5 754	6 329	6 834	7 628	8 677	9 754	Importations
Exports		2 995	3 128	3 305	3 387	3 513	3 977	4 579	Exportations
Balance		-2 189	-2 626	-3 024	-3 448	-4 115	-4 700	-5 175	Balance
Guatemala	S								**Guatemala**
Imports		6 304	6 722	7 812	8 810	10 157	11 861	12 835	Importations
Exports		2 473	2 632	2 939	3 477	3 665	4 468	5 412	Exportations
Balance		-3 831	-4 090	-4 873	-5 333	-6 492	-7 393	-7 423	Balance
Guyana	S								**Guyana**
Imports		576	576	652	788	889	1 060	1 289	Importations
Exports		496	513	593	553	588	677	782	Exportations
Balance		-81	-63	-59	-235	-301	-383	-507	Balance
Honduras	S								**Honduras**
Imports		3 082	3 448	4 212	4 853	5 695	6 762	8 807	Importations

58 Total imports and exports *(continued)*

Imports c.i.f., exports f.o.b., and balance, value in million US dollars

Importations et exportations totales *(suite)*

Importations c.a.f., exportations f.o.b. et balance, valeur en millions de dollars E.-U.

Region, country or area &	Sys.†	2002	2003	2004	2005	2006	2007	2008	Région, pays ou zone &
Exports		1 240	1 359	1 640	1 892	2 054	2 120	2 558	Exportations
Balance		-1 842	-2 089	-2 572	-2 960	-3 641	-4 642	-6 249	Balance
Mexico [4,12]	G								**Mexique** [4,12]
Imports		168 679	170 490	197 347	221 414	256 130	283 264	310 561	Importations
Exports		160 682	165 396	189 084	213 891	250 441	272 055	291 827	Exportations
Balance		-7 997	-5 094	-8 263	-7 523	-5 689	-11 209	-18 734	Balance
Nicaragua	G								**Nicaragua**
Imports		1 754	1 879	2 212	2 595	3 000	3 579	4 300	Importations
Exports		561	605	756	858	1 027	1 194	1 473	Exportations
Balance		-1 193	-1 275	-1 457	-1 737	-1 973	-2 385	-2 827	Balance
Panama [13]	S								**Panama** [13]
Imports		2 982	3 086	3 594	4 180	4 831	6 872	9 050	Importations
Exports		846	864	944	1 018	1 093	1 164	1 247	Exportations
Balance		-2 136	-2 222	-2 651	-3 162	-3 738	-5 709	-7 803	Balance
Paraguay	S								**Paraguay**
Imports		1 672	2 228	3 097	3 715	5 879	7 220	10 180	Importations
Exports		951	1 242	1 627	1 688	1 906	2 817	4 463	Exportations
Balance		-721	-986	-1 470	-2 027	-3 972	-4 403	-5 717	Balance
Peru	S								**Pérou**
Imports		7 440	8 244	9 812	12 084	14 897	19 580	28 373	Importations
Exports		7 714	9 091	12 809	17 368	23 830	27 882	31 529	Exportations
Balance		274	846	2 997	5 284	8 933	8 301	3 157	Balance
Suriname	G								**Suriname**
Imports		492	704	742	770	820	940	1 350	Importations
Exports		469	638	895	950	1 200	1 310	1 730	Exportations
Balance		-23	-66	152	180	380	370	380	Balance
Uruguay	G								**Uruguay**
Imports		1 964	2 190	3 114	3 879	4 757	5 667	8 943	Importations
Exports		1 861	2 206	2 931	3 405	3 953	4 485	6 421	Exportations
Balance		-103	16	-183	-474	-804	-1 182	-2 523	Balance
Venezuela (Boliv. Rep. of)	G								**Venezuela (Rép. boliv. du)**
Imports		12 963	9 256	16 679	24 027	33 615	46 097	49 602	Importations
Exports		25 890	23 990	33 994	51 859	59 208	69 165	93 242	Exportations
Balance		12 927	14 734	17 315	27 832	25 593	23 068	43 640	Balance
Eastern Asia									**Asie orientale**
Imports		**772 644**	**956 361**	**1 231 411**	**1 409 907**	**1 646 240**	**1 909 582**	**2 206 817**	**Importations**
Exports		**827 093**	**1 010 358**	**1 293 254**	**1 530 470**	**1 840 228**	**2 185 638**	**2 473 784**	**Exportations**
Balance		**54 448**	**53 997**	**61 843**	**128 564**	**193 987**	**276 056**	**266 968**	**Balance**
China [14]	S								**Chine** [14]
Imports		295 170	412 760	561 229	659 953	791 605	956 284	1 131 620	Importations
Exports		325 596	438 228	593 326	761 953	969 380	1 217 815	1 428 660	Exportations
Balance		30 426	25 468	32 097	102 000	177 775	261 531	297 040	Balance
China, Hong Kong SAR	G								**Chine, Hong Kong RAS**
Imports		207 644	231 896	271 074	299 533	334 681	367 864	388 505	Importations
Exports		200 092	223 762	259 260	289 337	316 816	344 629	362 675	Exportations
Balance		-7 552	-8 134	-11 814	-10 196	-17 865	-23 235	-25 830	Balance
China, Macao SAR	G								**Chine, Macao RAS**
Imports		2 530	2 755	3 478	3 913	4 565	5 366	5 365	Importations
Exports		2 356	2 581	2 812	2 476	2 557	2 543	1 997	Exportations
Balance		-174	-174	-666	-1 438	-2 008	-2 823	-3 368	Balance
Korea, Republic of	G								**Corée, République de**
Imports		152 126	178 827	224 463	261 238	309 383	356 648	435 275	Importations
Exports		162 471	193 817	253 845	284 419	325 465	371 554	422 007	Exportations
Balance		10 345	14 990	29 382	23 181	16 082	14 906	-13 268	Balance
Mongolia	G								**Mongolie**
Imports		691	801	1 021	1 184	1 486	2 117	3 616	Importations
Exports		524	616	870	1 065	1 543	1 889	2 539	Exportations
Balance		-167	-185	-151	-119	57	-228	-1 077	Balance
Southern Asia									**Asie australe**
Imports		**106 816**	**131 158**	**175 434**	**235 692**	**274 923**	**329 969**	**447 794**	**Importations**
Exports		**94 836**	**116 083**	**145 486**	**187 124**	**232 797**	**268 090**	**333 595**	**Exportations**
Balance		**-11 980**	**-15 075**	**-29 948**	**-48 568**	**-42 126**	**-61 879**	**-114 199**	**Balance**

58 Total imports and exports *(continued)*

Imports c.i.f., exports f.o.b., and balance, value in million US dollars

Importations et exportations totales *(suite)*

Importations c.a.f., exportations f.o.b. et balance, valeur en millions de dollars E.-U.

Region, country or area &	Sys.†	2002	2003	2004	2005	2006	2007	2008	Région, pays ou zone &
Afghanistan	G								**Afghanistan**
Imports		2 452	2 101	2 177	...	...	...	...	Importations
Exports		100	144	314	...	...	...	...	Exportations
Balance		-2 352	-1 957	-1 863	...	...	...	...	Balance
Bangladesh	G								**Bangladesh**
Imports		7 913	9 516	12 611	12 881	14 964	17 263	22 473	Importations
Exports		4 566	5 263	6 615	7 233	9 103	10 233	11 777	Exportations
Balance		-3 348	-4 253	-5 996	-5 648	-5 861	-7 030	-10 695	Balance
Bhutan	G								**Bhoutan**
Imports		196	249	411	387	419	480	560	Importations
Exports		113	133	183	258	414	601	580	Exportations
Balance		-84	-116	-228	-129	-5	120	20	Balance
India [15]	G								**Inde** [15]
Imports		56 496	72 559	99 757	142 865	172 835	216 760	303 525	Importations
Exports		50 353	58 964	76 647	99 618	120 968	147 032	182 019	Exportations
Balance		-6 143	-13 595	-23 110	-43 247	-51 867	-69 728	-121 505	Balance
Iran (Islamic Rep. of) [16,17]	S								**Iran (Rép. islamique d')** [16,17]
Imports		20 617	24 798	31 976	40 041	40 772	45 000	57 230	Importations
Exports		24 440	33 750	41 697	56 252	77 012	83 000	...	Exportations
Balance		3 823	8 952	9 721	16 211	36 240	38 000	...	Balance
Maldives	G								**Maldives**
Imports		392	471	642	745	927	1 096	1 388	Importations
Exports		90	113	122	103	135	108	126	Exportations
Balance		-301	-358	-519	-641	-791	-989	-1 262	Balance
Nepal	G								**Népal**
Imports		1 418	1 755	1 939	2 284	2 490	2 911	3 558	Importations
Exports		568	662	772	863	838	889	1 096	Exportations
Balance		-850	-1 093	-1 167	-1 421	-1 652	-2 022	-2 462	Balance
Pakistan	G								**Pakistan**
Imports		11 227	13 038	17 949	25 356	29 828	32 590	42 326	Importations
Exports		9 908	11 930	13 379	16 050	16 932	17 837	20 323	Exportations
Balance		-1 319	-1 107	-4 570	-9 306	-12 896	-14 753	-22 003	Balance
Sri Lanka	G								**Sri Lanka**
Imports		6 105	6 672	7 973	8 833	10 259	11 301	14 022	Importations
Exports		4 699	5 125	5 757	6 347	6 886	7 740	8 374	Exportations
Balance		-1 406	-1 547	-2 216	-2 487	-3 373	-3 560	-5 647	Balance
South-eastern Asia									**Asie du Sud-est**
Imports		**362 310**	**398 695**	**500 677**	**600 761**	**686 185**	**774 484**	**947 407**	**Importations**
Exports		**407 511**	**453 756**	**569 597**	**653 612**	**771 859**	**869 292**	**1 005 876**	**Exportations**
Balance		**45 202**	**55 061**	**68 920**	**52 851**	**85 674**	**94 808**	**58 469**	**Balance**
Brunei Darussalam	S								**Brunéi Darussalam**
Imports		1 556	1 327	1 427	...	...	...	...	Importations
Exports		3 701	4 424	5 069	...	...	...	...	Exportations
Balance		2 145	3 097	3 642	...	...	...	...	Balance
Cambodia	S								**Cambodge**
Imports		2 318	2 560	3 193	3 927	4 749	5 300	6 510	Importations
Exports		1 923	2 118	2 798	3 200	3 800	4 400	4 290	Exportations
Balance		-395	-442	-395	-727	-949	-900	-2 220	Balance
Indonesia	S								**Indonésie**
Imports		37 730	41 568	55 008	75 631	78 781	93 088	129 767	Importations
Exports		58 774	64 109	72 164	86 721	103 493	118 728	147 640	Exportations
Balance		21 043	22 542	17 156	11 090	24 712	25 640	17 873	Balance
Lao People's Dem. Rep.	S								**Rép. dém. pop. lao**
Imports		447	462	713	882	1 060	1 067	1 803	Importations
Exports		301	335	363	553	882	842	828	Exportations
Balance		-146	-127	-349	-329	-177	-225	-976	Balance
Malaysia	G								**Malaisie**
Imports		79 869	81 948	105 298	114 410	131 079	146 772	163 900	Importations
Exports		93 265	99 369	125 745	140 870	160 574	176 026	208 986	Exportations
Balance		13 396	17 421	20 446	26 460	29 495	29 254	45 086	Balance
Myanmar	G								**Myanmar**
Imports		2 348	2 092	2 196	1 927	2 564	3 277	4 299	Importations

58

Total imports and exports *(continued)*

Imports c.i.f., exports f.o.b., and balance, value in million US dollars

Importations et exportations totales *(suite)*

Importations c.a.f., exportations f.o.b. et balance, valeur en millions de dollars E.-U.

Region, country or area &	Sys.†	2002	2003	2004	2005	2006	2007	2008	Région, pays ou zone &
Exports		3 046	2 485	2 380	3 813	4 585	6 313	6 950	Exportations
Balance		698	392	184	1 887	2 021	3 036	2 651	Balance
Philippines	G								**Philippines**
Imports		37 202	39 502	42 345	46 963	54 077	57 708	60 492	Importations
Exports		36 510	36 231	39 680	39 879	47 413	50 270	49 205	Exportations
Balance		-692	-3 271	-2 664	-7 084	-6 665	-7 438	-11 287	Balance
Singapore	G								**Singapour**
Imports		116 448	127 935	163 851	200 050	238 711	263 155	319 781	Importations
Exports		125 177	144 183	198 633	229 652	271 809	299 270	338 201	Exportations
Balance		8 729	16 248	34 782	29 602	33 098	36 115	18 421	Balance
Thailand	S								**Thaïlande**
Imports		64 645	75 824	94 410	118 158	128 654	140 812	178 776	Importations
Exports		68 108	80 324	96 248	110 178	130 795	153 092	172 822	Exportations
Balance		3 463	4 499	1 838	-7 980	2 142	12 280	-5 954	Balance
Viet Nam	G								**Viet Nam**
Imports		19 746	25 256	31 969	36 978	44 410	60 869	79 293	Importations
Exports		16 706	20 149	26 485	32 442	39 605	48 302	60 938	Exportations
Balance		-3 040	-5 107	-5 484	-4 536	-4 805	-12 567	-18 355	Balance
Western Asia									**Asie occidentale**
Imports		**216 978**	**255 723**	**340 513**	**409 086**	**475 082**	**589 555**	**730 895**	**Importations**
Exports		**257 774**	**316 588**	**422 766**	**555 703**	**656 272**	**742 297**	**967 136**	**Exportations**
Balance		**40 796**	**60 865**	**82 253**	**146 618**	**181 189**	**152 742**	**236 241**	**Balance**
Bahrain	G								**Bahreïn**
Imports		4 988	5 657	7 385	8 790	9 022	11 293	12 530	Importations
Exports		5 786	6 624	7 556	10 160	11 625	13 394	18 865	Exportations
Balance		798	966	171	1 370	2 603	2 101	6 335	Balance
Cyprus	G								**Chypre**
Imports		3 863	4 288	5 659	6 282	6 951	8 687	10 848	Importations
Exports		770	834	1 081	1 303	1 153	1 254	1 721	Exportations
Balance		-3 094	-3 455	-4 577	-4 979	-5 798	-7 433	-9 128	Balance
Israel [18]	S								**Israël** [18]
Imports		35 517	36 303	42 864	47 142	50 334	59 039	67 656	Importations
Exports		29 347	31 784	38 618	42 770	46 789	54 065	60 825	Exportations
Balance		-6 170	-4 519	-4 245	-4 371	-3 544	-4 973	-6 831	Balance
Jordan	G								**Jordanie**
Imports		5 076	5 743	8 128	10 506	11 447	13 511	16 764	Importations
Exports		2 770	3 082	3 922	4 302	5 175	5 725	7 788	Exportations
Balance		-2 306	-2 662	-4 206	-6 204	-6 272	-7 786	-8 976	Balance
Kuwait	S								**Koweït**
Imports		9 007	10 992	12 630	15 534	17 243	21 353	24 875	Importations
Exports		15 363	20 677	28 599	45 189	56 016	62 702	87 467	Exportations
Balance		6 356	9 685	15 968	29 655	38 774	41 350	62 591	Balance
Lebanon	G								**Liban**
Imports		6 560	7 315	9 609	9 633	9 401	11 819	16 142	Importations
Exports		1 238	1 813	2 199	2 337	2 283	2 817	3 479	Exportations
Balance		-5 322	-5 502	-7 410	-7 296	-7 117	-9 002	-12 663	Balance
Occupied Palestinian Terr.	S								**Terr. palestinien occupé**
Imports		1 516	1 800	2 373	2 668	2 759	3 141	...	Importations
Exports		241	280	313	335	367	513	...	Exportations
Balance		-1 275	-1 521	-2 061	-2 332	-2 392	-2 628	...	Balance
Oman	G								**Oman**
Imports		6 005	6 572	8 865	8 827	10 915	15 978	22 925	Importations
Exports		11 172	11 669	13 341	18 692	21 585	24 136	37 719	Exportations
Balance		5 166	5 096	4 476	9 865	10 670	8 158	14 795	Balance
Qatar	S								**Qatar**
Imports		4 052	4 897	6 005	10 061	16 441	22 045	26 850	Importations
Exports		10 978	13 383	18 684	25 762	34 052	42 020	...	Exportations
Balance		6 926	8 485	12 680	15 702	17 610	19 975	...	Balance
Saudi Arabia	S								**Arabie saoudite**
Imports		32 293	36 915	44 744	59 458	69 800	90 215	115 133	Importations
Exports		72 453	93 245	125 997	180 736	211 306	234 145	...	Exportations
Balance		40 160	56 331	81 253	121 278	141 506	143 930	...	Balance

58 Total imports and exports *(continued)*

Imports c.i.f., exports f.o.b., and balance, value in million US dollars

Importations et exportations totales *(suite)*

Importations c.a.f., exportations f.o.b. et balance, valeur en millions de dollars E.-U.

Region, country or area &	Sys.†	2002	2003	2004	2005	2006	2007	2008	Région, pays ou zone &
Syrian Arab Republic	S								**Rép. arabe syrienne**
Imports		5 097	5 119	8 411	10 862	11 488	14 655	18 320	Importations
Exports		6 520	5 731	7 485	9 174	10 919	11 546	14 300	Exportations
Balance		1 423	611	-926	-1 688	-569	-3 109	-4 020	Balance
Turkey	S								**Turquie**
Imports		51 554	69 340	97 540	116 774	139 576	169 792	201 823	Importations
Exports		36 059	47 253	63 167	73 476	85 535	107 136	132 003	Exportations
Balance		-15 495	-22 087	-34 373	-43 298	-54 041	-62 656	-69 820	Balance
United Arab Emirates	G								**Emirats arabes unis**
Imports		42 652	52 074	72 082	84 654	97 864	121 100	158 900	Importations
Exports		52 163	67 135	90 997	117 287	142 505	154 000	...	Exportations
Balance		9 511	15 061	18 915	32 633	44 641	32 900	...	Balance
Yemen	S								**Yémen**
Imports		2 927	3 680	3 988	4 885	5 300	5 892	...	Importations
Exports		3 683	3 923	4 676	6 376	7 315	7 160	...	Exportations
Balance		755	243	688	1 491	2 015	1 268	...	Balance
Oceania									**Océanie**
Imports		**7 884**	**9 532**	**10 227**	**11 059**	**12 456**	**14 610**	**16 828**	**Importations**
Exports		**4 616**	**5 753**	**6 470**	**7 248**	**8 524**	**10 042**	**10 604**	**Exportations**
Balance		**-3 269**	**-3 779**	**-3 758**	**-3 811**	**-3 932**	**-4 568**	**-6 223**	**Balance**
American Samoa [19]	S								**Samoa américaines** [19]
Imports		499	624	604	520	579	650	680	Importations
Exports		388	460	446	374	439	450	460	Exportations
Balance		-111	-164	-158	-146	-141	-200	-220	Balance
Cook Islands	G								**Iles Cook**
Imports		47	71	76	81	100	99	140	Importations
Exports		5	9	7	5	3	5	4	Exportations
Balance		-42	-62	-69	-76	-96	-94	-136	Balance
Fiji	G								**Fidji**
Imports		906	1 208	1 444	1 607	1 802	1 801	2 245	Importations
Exports		519	674	693	701	679	755	907	Exportations
Balance		-386	-533	-751	-906	-1 123	-1 046	-1 338	Balance
French Polynesia	S								**Polynésie française**
Imports		1 336	1 688	1 500	1 723	1 656	1 863	2 237	Importations
Exports		168	151	199	217	235	197	207	Exportations
Balance		-1 169	-1 537	-1 301	-1 506	-1 420	-1 667	-2 030	Balance
Guam	G								**Guam**
Imports		...	...	...	...	501	688	649	Importations
Exports		...	...	53	52	53	91	105	Exportations
Balance		...	...	...	...	-448	-596	-544	Balance
Kiribati [4]	G								**Kiribati** [4]
Imports		50	52	59	74	63	70	55	Importations
Exports		3	3	2	4	6	10	15	Exportations
Balance		-46	-49	-57	-70	-57	-60	-40	Balance
New Caledonia	S								**Nouvelle-Calédonie**
Imports		1 013	1 532	1 641	1 774	2 117	2 836	3 213	Importations
Exports		495	788	1 036	1 090	1 349	2 165	1 344	Exportations
Balance		-518	-745	-606	-684	-768	-671	-1 869	Balance
Niue	G								**Nioué**
Imports		2	2	8	...	4	7	8	Importations
Exports		^0	^0	^0	^0	1	3	^0	Exportations
Balance		-2	-2	-8	...	-2	-4	-8	Balance
Papua New Guinea	G								**Papouasie-Nvl-Guinée**
Imports		1 235	1 368	1 681	1 728	2 287	2 945	3 550	Importations
Exports		1 641	2 206	2 552	3 273	4 166	4 683	5 805	Exportations
Balance		406	838	871	1 546	1 879	1 737	2 255	Balance
Samoa	S								**Samoa**
Imports		127	128	155	187	219	227	249	Importations
Exports		14	15	11	12	11	15	11	Exportations
Balance		-114	-113	-145	-175	-208	-212	-238	Balance
Solomon Islands	S								**Iles Salomon**
Imports		67	83	85	185	210	250	315	Importations

58 Total imports and exports *(continued)*

Imports c.i.f., exports f.o.b., and balance, value in million US dollars

Importations et exportations totales *(suite)*

Importations c.a.f., exportations f.o.b. et balance, valeur en millions de dollars E.-U.

Region, country or area &	Sys.ŧ	2002	2003	2004	2005	2006	2007	2008	Région, pays ou zone &
Exports		58	74	97	105	120	166	190	Exportations
Balance		-9	-9	12	-80	-90	-84	-125	Balance
Tonga	G								**Tonga**
Imports		89	94	105	120	130	143	149	Importations
Exports		14	18	15	10	11	9	9	Exportations
Balance		-75	-76	-90	-110	-119	-134	-140	Balance
Tuvalu	G								**Tuvalu**
Imports		11	8	11	13	13	16	...	Importations
Exports ^		0	0	0	0	0	0	...	Exportations
Balance		-11	-8	-11	-13	-13	-16	...	Balance
Vanuatu	G								**Vanuatu**
Imports		90	106	128	149	160	202	265	Importations
Exports		20	27	38	38	37	30	35	Exportations
Balance		-70	-79	-90	-111	-123	-172	-230	Balance
Non Petroleum Exports of Asia Middle East [20]									**Exp. non pétrolières de Moyen-Orient d'Asie [20]**
Exports		**92 853**	**86 061**	**79 766**	**73 931**	**68 523**	**63 510**	**58 864**	**Exportations**
	Additional country groupings · Groupements supplémentaires de pays								
ANCOM§									**ANCOM§**
Imports		41 315	39 708	53 308	69 944	89 486	115 863	140 974	Importations
Exports		51 855	53 981	72 926	103 264	124 029	145 143	187 974	Exportations
Balance		10 540	14 273	19 618	33 320	34 543	29 280	47 001	Balance
APEC§									**CEAP§**
Imports		3 213 144	3 634 493	4 414 659	5 088 639	5 777 939	6 433 815	7 375 913	Importations
Exports		2 962 304	3 344 756	4 067 103	4 686 541	5 459 718	6 219 441	7 083 035	Exportations
Balance		-250 841	-289 738	-347 556	-402 098	-318 221	-214 374	-292 877	Balance
ASEAN§									**ANASE§**
Imports		362 310	398 474	500 410	600 439	685 796	774 016	946 842	Importations
Exports		407 511	453 727	569 565	653 578	771 822	869 252	1 005 833	Exportations
Balance		45 202	55 253	69 155	53 139	86 026	95 236	58 991	Balance
CACM§									**MCAC§**
Imports		23 512	25 466	28 833	32 904	37 999	43 831	51 061	Importations
Exports		12 532	13 825	14 941	16 640	18 475	21 098	23 596	Exportations
Balance		-10 980	-11 641	-13 892	-16 264	-19 524	-22 732	-27 465	Balance
CARICOM§									**CARICOM§**
Imports		14 116	15 143	16 879	19 557	22 255	24 934	30 100	Importations
Exports		7 356	9 032	10 891	14 519	19 899	20 804	25 817	Exportations
Balance		-6 761	-6 111	-5 988	-5 038	-2 357	-4 130	-4 283	Balance
COMESA§									**COMESA§**
Imports		35 312	37 681	48 166	62 365	70 031	84 716	119 663	Importations
Exports		27 654	36 019	47 288	63 459	79 213	92 215	130 434	Exportations
Balance		-7 658	-1 661	-878	1 094	9 182	7 499	10 771	Balance
ECOWAS§									**CEDEAO§**
Imports		19 792	25 865	32 625	43 657	51 201	66 512	78 951	Importations
Exports		26 824	32 619	45 691	71 771	76 339	85 428	105 310	Exportations
Balance		7 032	6 754	13 066	28 114	25 138	18 916	26 360	Balance
EMCCA§									**CEMAC§**
Imports		5 782	6 218	7 198	8 939	10 927	13 783	14 940	Importations
Exports		8 972	11 340	16 409	22 716	27 423	29 556	40 157	Exportations
Balance		3 190	5 122	9 211	13 778	16 496	15 773	25 217	Balance
LAIA§									**ALAI§**
Imports		293 585	303 265	376 100	446 138	534 826	641 338	786 584	Importations
Exports		321 122	348 929	432 529	524 553	626 365	712 592	829 350	Exportations
Balance		27 537	45 664	56 429	78 415	91 539	71 253	42 766	Balance
LDC§									**PMA§**
Imports		49 630	59 369	73 339	85 914	102 530	116 073	148 247	Importations
Exports		37 684	44 090	59 079	80 520	99 944	124 552	172 092	Exportations
Balance		-11 946	-15 278	-14 259	-5 394	-2 586	8 479	23 845	Balance
MERCOSUR§									**MERCOSUR§**
Imports		62 348	69 132	95 089	113 915	140 630	184 158	258 898	Importations

58

Total imports and exports *(continued)*

Imports c.i.f., exports f.o.b., and balance, value in million US dollars

Importations et exportations totales *(suite)*

Importations c.a.f., exportations f.o.b. et balance, valeur en millions de dollars E.-U.

Region, country or area &	Sys.t	2002	2003	2004	2005	2006	2007	2008	Région, pays ou zone &
Exports		88 900	106 217	135 811	163 973	190 235	223 730	279 414	Exportations
Balance		26 552	37 084	40 722	50 058	49 604	39 572	20 516	Balance
NAFTA§									**ALENA§**
Imports		1 590 871	1 712 625	1 995 801	2 279 839	2 523 168	2 683 456	2 887 218	Importations
Exports		1 106 192	1 162 866	1 312 227	1 480 460	1 678 224	1 851 466	2 045 107	Exportations
Balance		-484 679	-549 759	-683 575	-799 379	-844 944	-831 989	-842 111	Balance
OECD§									**OCDE§**
Imports		4 788 475	5 539 803	6 622 336	7 388 388	8 390 116	9 477 139	10 621 133	Importations
Exports		4 485 233	5 155 191	6 101 558	6 662 853	7 536 094	8 622 357	9 631 272	Exportations
Balance		-303 242	-384 612	-520 778	-725 535	-854 022	-854 782	-989 861	Balance
OPEC§									**OPEP§**
Imports		199 303	225 266	302 077	388 783	449 481	558 309	714 023	Importations
Exports		325 595	398 556	531 841	747 391	896 525	1 014 108	1 345 132	Exportations
Balance		126 292	173 291	229 763	358 608	447 044	455 800	631 109	Balance
EU-25									**UE-25**
Imports		2 483 449	2 993 536	3 610 246	3 948 915	4 550 568	5 309 312	5 944 784	Importations
Exports		2 559 502	3 051 417	3 636 198	3 917 131	4 440 299	5 173 965	5 744 979	Exportations
Balance		76 054	57 881	25 952	-31 784	-110 269	-135 347	-199 805	Balance
Extra-EU-25 21									**Extra-UE-25 21**
Imports		889 542	1 063 891	1 283 846	1 456 866	1 702 321	1 967 370	...	Importations
Exports		854 112	999 614	1 205 511	1 330 464	1 489 696	1 742 459	...	Exportations
Balance		-35 430	-64 277	-78 335	-126 402	-212 625	-224 911	...	Balance
EU-27									**UE-27**
Imports		2 509 297	3 028 426	3 657 377	4 007 540	4 624 944	5 409 000	6 064 767	Importations
Exports		2 579 127	3 076 576	3 669 615	3 956 600	4 487 737	5 232 582	5 817 003	Exportations
Balance		69 830	48 150	12 238	-50 940	-137 207	-176 418	-247 763	Balance
Extra-EU-27 21									**Extra-UE-27 21**
Imports		884 628	1 057 654	1 277 865	1 465 103	1 698 154	1 967 044	2 306 747	Importations
Exports		843 095	984 114	1 185 169	1 307 303	1 457 176	1 703 272	1 925 568	Exportations
Balance		-41 534	-73 540	-92 697	-157 800	-240 978	-263 773	-381 179	Balance
World exc. intra-EU27									**Monde excl. intra-UE27**
Imports		4 911 145	5 645 202	6 916 496	8 034 581	9 221 750	10 551 999	12 399 436	Importations
Exports		4 673 300	5 366 362	6 590 804	7 699 051	8 938 991	10 270 787	12 034 882	Exportations
Balance		-237 845	-278 840	-325 692	-335 530	-282 759	-281 212	-364 553	Balance

Source:
United Nations Statistics Division, New York, trade statistics database, last accessed January 2010.

& The regional totals for imports and exports have been adjusted to exclude the re-exports of countries or areas comprising each region.

§ For member states of this grouping, see Annex I – Other groupings. The totals have been calculated for all periods shown according to the current composition.

t Systems of trade: Two systems of recording trade, the General trade system (G) and the Special trade system (S), are in common use. They differ mainly in the way warehoused and re-exported goods are recorded. See the Technical notes for an explanation of the trade systems.

1 This classification is intended for statistical convenience and does not, necessarily, express a judgement about the stage reached by a particular country in the development process.

2 Developed economies of the Asia-Pacific region, Europe, and North America.

Source:
Organisation des Nations Unies, Division de statistique, New York, la base de données pour les statistiques du commerce extérieur, dernier accès janvier 2010.

& Les totaux régionaux pour importations et exportations ont été ajustés pour exclure les réexportations des pays ou zones qui comprennent la région.

§ Pour les Etats membres de ce groupements, voir annexe I – Autres groupements. Les totales ont été calculés pour toutes les périodes données suivant la composition présente.

t Systèmes de commerce : Deux systèmes d'enregistrement du commerce sont couramment utilisés, le Commerce général (G) et le Commerce spécial (S). Ils ne diffèrent que par la façon dont sont enregistrées les marchandises entreposées et les marchandises réexportées. Voir les Notes techniques pour une explication des Systèmes de commerce.

1 Cette classification est utilisée pour plus de commodité dans la présentation des statistiques et n'implique pas nécessairement un jugement quant au stage de développement auquel est parvenu un pays donné.

2 Économies développées de la région Asie-Pacifique, de l'Europe, et de l'Amérique de Nord.

58

Total imports and exports *(continued)*

Imports c.i.f., exports f.o.b., and balance, value in million US dollars

Importations et exportations totales *(suite)*

Importations c.a.f., exportations f.o.b. et balance, valeur en millions de dollars E.-U.

3 Trade data for France include the import and export values of French Guiana, Guadeloupe, Martinique, and Réunion.

4 Imports FOB.

5 Including the trade of the U.S. Virgin Islands and Puerto Rico but excluding shipments of merchandise between the United States and its other possessions (Guam, American Samoa, etc.). Data include imports and exports of non-monetary gold.

6 Imports exclude petroleum imported without stated value. Exports cover domestic exports.

7 Exports include gold.

8 Beginning in January 1998, foreign trade data refer to South Africa only, excluding intra-trade of the Southern African Common Customs Area. Prior to January 1998, trade data refer to the Southern African Common Customs Area, which includes Botswana, Lesotho, Namibia, South Africa and Swaziland.

9 Year ending June 30 through 1994. Year ending December 31 thereafter.

10 Trade statistics exclude certain oil and chemical products.

11 Export and import values exclude trade in the processing zone.

12 Trade data include maquiladoras and exclude goods from customs-bonded warehouses. Total exports include revaluation and exports of silver.

13 Exports include re-exports and petroleum products.

14 For statistical purposes, the data for China do not include those for the Hong Kong Special Administrative Region (Hong Kong SAR), Macao Special Administrative Region (Macao SAR) and Taiwan Province of China.

15 Excluding military goods, fissionable materials, bunkers, ships, and aircraft.

16 Data include oil and gas. Data on the value and volume of oil exports and on the value of total exports are rough estimates based on information published in various petroleum industry journals.

17 Year ending 20 March of the years stated.

18 Imports and exports net of returned goods. The figures also exclude Judea and Samaria and the Gaza area.

19 Year ending 30 September.

20 Data refer to total exports less petroleum exports of Asia Middle East countries where petroleum, in this case, is the sum of SITC groups 333, 334 and 335.

21 Excluding intra-EU trade.

3 Les valeurs de commerce pour la France comprennent les valeurs des importations et des exportations de la Guyane française, la Guadeloupe, la Martinique, et la Réunion.

4 Importations FOB.

5 Y compris le commerce des Iles Vierges américaines et de Porto Rico mais non compris les échanges de marchandises, entre les Etats-Unis et leurs autres possessions (Guam, Samoa américaines, etc.). Les données comprennent les importations et exportations d'or non-monétaire.

6 Non compris le pétrole brute dont la valeur des importations ne sont pas stipulée. Les exportations sont les exportations d'intérieur.

7 Les exportations comprennent l'or.

8 A compter de janvier 1998, les données sur le commerce extérieur ne se rapportent qu'à l'Afrique du Sud. et ne tiennent pas compte des échanges commerciaux entre les pays de l'Union douanière de l'Afrique du Sud, qui incluait l'Afrique du Sud, Botswana, Lesotho, Namibie, et Swaziland.

9 Année finissant juin 30 à 1994. Année finissant décembre 31 ensuite.

10 Les statistiques commerciales font exclusion de certains produits pétroliers et chimiques.

11 Les valeurs à l'exportation et à l'importation excluent le commerce de la zone de transformation.

12 Les statistiques du commerce extérieur comprennent maquiladoras et ne comprennent pas les marchandises provenant des entrepôts en douane. Les exportations comprennent la réévaluation et les données sur les exportations d'argent.

13 Exportations comprennent réexportations et produits pétroliers.

14 Pour la présentation des statistiques, les données pour la Chine ne comprennent pas la Région Administrative Spéciale de Hong Kong (Hong Kong RAS), la Région Administrative Spéciale de Macao (Macao RAS) et la province de Taiwan.

15 A l'exclusion des marchandises militaires, des matières fissibles, des soutes, des bateaux, et de l'avion.

16 Les données comprennent le pétrole et le gaz. La valeur des exportations de pétrole et des exportations totales sont des évaluations grossières basées sur l'information publiée à divers journaux d'industrie de pétrole.

17 Année finissant le 20 mars de l'année indiquée.

18 Importations et exportations nets, ne comprenant pas les marchandises retournées. Sont également exclues les données de la Judée et de Samara et ainsi que la zone de Gaza.

19 Année finissant le 30 septembre.

20 Les données se rapportent aux exportations totales moins les exportations pétrolières de Moyen-Orient d'Asie. Dans ce cas, le pétrole est la somme des groupes CTCI 333, 334 et 335.

21 Non compris le commerce de l'intra-UE.

59 Total imports and exports: index numbers

Index base : 2000 = 100

Importations et exportations totales : indices

Indices base : 2000 = 100

Country or area	1999	2001	2002	2003	2004	2005	2006	2007	2008	Pays ou zone
Argentina										**Argentine**
Imports: volume	101	83	38	58	87	108	125	150	176	Importations : volume
Imports: unit value	100	97	94	94	102	105	108	115	128	Importations : valeur unitaire
Exports: volume	97	104	105	110	118	135	143	154	156	Exportations : volume
Exports: unit value	91	97	93	102	111	113	122	137	171	Exportations : valeur unitaire
Terms of trade	91	99	99	108	110	107	113	119	134	Termes de l'échange
Purchasing power of exports	89	104	104	120	129	145	163	183	209	Pouvoir d'achat des exportations
Australia										**Australie**
Imports: volume	92	96	108	120	137	129	145	155	186	Importations : volume
Imports: unit value [1]	102	94	95	104	111	117	120	128	141	Importations : valeur unitaire [1]
Exports: volume	91	103	104	102	106	119	141	144	191	Exportations : volume
Exports: unit value [1]	96	98	100	111	129	153	175	196	246	Exportations : valeur unitaire [1]
Terms of trade	94	104	106	106	116	131	146	153	174	Termes de l'échange
Purchasing power of exports	86	107	110	108	123	156	205	220	332	Pouvoir d'achat des exportations
Austria										**Autriche**
Imports: volume	87	103	107	111	118	125	132	137	145	Importations : volume
Imports: unit value	115	97	100	114	125	123	130	144	162	Importations : valeur unitaire
Exports: volume	94	106	112	117	127	132	144	149	157	Exportations : volume
Exports: unit value	105	95	101	114	126	126	132	146	164	Exportations : valeur unitaire
Terms of trade	91	98	101	100	101	102	102	101	102	Termes de l'échange
Purchasing power of exports	86	104	114	117	128	135	147	151	160	Pouvoir d'achat des exportations
Belgium										**Belgique**
Imports: volume	91	101	109	111	118	126	132	139	139	Importations : volume
Imports: unit value	102	100	103	120	136	143	151	168	193	Importations : valeur unitaire
Exports: volume	91	102	111	113	121	126	131	135	133	Exportations : volume
Exports: unit value	105	99	104	121	135	142	149	170	190	Exportations : valeur unitaire
Terms of trade	102	100	101	100	99	99	99	101	98	Termes de l'échange
Purchasing power of exports	93	102	112	113	120	125	129	137	131	Pouvoir d'achat des exportations
Bolivia (Plur. State of)										**Bolivie (État plurinational de)**
Exports: volume	88	107	129	145	173	126	142	153	...	Exportations : volume
Exports: unit value	78	91	81	91	122	169	252	292	402	Exportations : valeur unitaire
Brazil										**Brésil**
Imports: volume	92	101	99	136	111	101	110	128	134	Importations : volume
Imports: unit value	96	99	86	64	102	131	148	168	231	Importations : valeur unitaire
Exports: volume	93	111	121	131	154	162	173	189	192	Exportations : volume
Exports: unit value	94	95	91	101	114	133	144	154	187	Exportations : valeur unitaire
Terms of trade	98	96	106	158	112	101	97	92	81	Termes de l'échange
Purchasing power of exports	91	107	128	208	173	165	168	173	155	Pouvoir d'achat des exportations
Bulgaria										**Bulgarie**
Imports: unit value	...	96	98	112	130	140	156	182	208	Importations : valeur unitaire
Exports: unit value	...	95	95	114	133	142	162	194	227	Exportations : valeur unitaire
Terms of trade	...	99	98	102	102	102	104	107	109	Termes de l'échange
Canada										**Canada**
Imports: volume	96	94	96	100	108	116	123	130	130	Importations : volume
Imports: unit value	93	96	95	100	106	114	122	128	137	Importations : valeur unitaire
Exports: volume	91	96	97	95	100	102	103	105	97	Exportations : volume
Exports: unit value	98	101	96	106	117	130	140	151	166	Exportations : valeur unitaire
Terms of trade	105	105	101	106	110	114	114	118	121	Termes de l'échange
Purchasing power of exports	96	101	97	101	111	117	118	123	117	Pouvoir d'achat des exportations
China, Hong Kong SAR										**Chine, Hong Kong RAS**
Imports: volume	85	98	106	119	136	148	162	179	184	Importations : volume
Imports: unit value	100	97	93	93	96	98	101	102	107	Importations : valeur unitaire
Exports: volume	85	97	105	120	138	154	169	183	189	Exportations : volume
Exports: unit value	101	98	95	94	95	96	97	99	103	Exportations : valeur unitaire
Terms of trade	101	101	102	101	99	98	97	97	96	Termes de l'échange
Purchasing power of exports	86	97	107	121	137	151	164	177	182	Pouvoir d'achat des exportations
Colombia										**Colombie**
Imports: unit value	103	98	95	95	103	114	114	117	125	Importations : valeur unitaire
Exports: unit value	96	89	84	87	96	111	119	130	159	Exportations : valeur unitaire
Terms of trade	93	91	89	92	93	97	104	111	128	Termes de l'échange

59 Total imports and exports: index numbers *(continued)*

Index base : 2000 = 100

Importations et exportations totales : indices *(suite)*

Indices base : 2000 = 100

Country or area	1999	2001	2002	2003	2004	2005	2006	2007	2008	Pays ou zone
Czech Republic										**République tchèque**
Imports: unit value	99	101	107	123	137	148	158	175	201	Importations : valeur unitaire
Exports: unit value	105	102	111	130	147	155	164	185	210	Exportations : valeur unitaire
Terms of trade	105	101	104	105	107	105	104	106	105	Termes de l'échange
Denmark										**Danemark**
Imports: volume	93	102	108	106	113	122	135	140	137	Importations : volume
Imports: unit value	108	98	102	119	133	138	142	162	178	Importations : valeur unitaire
Exports: volume	92	103	109	107	110	116	122	126	128	Exportations : volume
Exports: unit value	108	99	103	122	136	143	150	163	178	Exportations : valeur unitaire
Terms of trade	100	101	101	102	102	104	105	100	100	Termes de l'échange
Purchasing power of exports	92	104	110	109	113	121	128	126	129	Pouvoir d'achat des exportations
Dominica										**Dominique**
Imports: volume	97	98	82	...	...	...	...	...	...	Importations : volume
Imports: unit value	95	95	91	...	...	...	...	...	...	Importations : valeur unitaire
Exports: volume	92	78	72	...	...	...	...	...	...	Exportations : volume
Exports: unit value	113	101	101	...	...	...	...	...	...	Exportations : valeur unitaire
Terms of trade	119	106	111	...	...	...	...	...	...	Termes de l'échange
Purchasing power of exports	110	82	80	...	...	...	...	...	...	Pouvoir d'achat des exportations
Ecuador										**Equateur**
Imports: volume	96	119	148	161	168	204	229	262	274	Importations : volume
Exports: volume	93	101	99	107	133	117	143	139	140	Exportations : volume
Exports: unit value	77	88	94	107	118	150	182	209	284	Exportations : valeur unitaire
Estonia										**Estonie**
Imports: unit value	109	98	103	121	135	140	148	167	189	Importations : valeur unitaire
Exports: unit value	107	129	136	173	194	199	210	247	276	Exportations : valeur unitaire
Terms of trade	98	132	132	143	144	143	142	148	146	Termes de l'échange
Finland										**Finlande**
Imports: volume	96	97	104	103	108	114	127	128	130	Importations : volume
Imports: unit value	101	98	97	115	131	146	152	170	189	Importations : valeur unitaire
Exports: volume	92	99	104	106	112	111	124	120	121	Exportations : volume
Exports: unit value	102	96	94	107	117	127	126	141	154	Exportations : valeur unitaire
Terms of trade	101	97	97	93	89	87	83	83	81	Termes de l'échange
Purchasing power of exports	93	97	101	98	99	96	103	100	99	Pouvoir d'achat des exportations
France										**France**
Imports: volume	87	116	112	112	125	136	147	154	162	Importations : volume
Imports: unit value	108	96	95	114	123	122	124	137	147	Importations : valeur unitaire
Exports: volume	89	119	112	110	118	125	137	140	145	Exportations : volume
Exports: unit value	114	97	97	118	127	127	127	139	147	Exportations : valeur unitaire
Terms of trade	105	102	103	104	104	104	102	101	100	Termes de l'échange
Purchasing power of exports	93	121	115	114	123	130	141	142	145	Pouvoir d'achat des exportations
Germany										**Allemagne**
Imports: volume	89	101	100	110	121	126	133	147	150	Importations : volume
Imports: unit value	104	97	98	111	121	123	129	144	160	Importations : valeur unitaire
Exports: volume	87	103	104	115	129	136	151	163	165	Exportations : volume
Exports: unit value	111	99	102	119	129	130	132	147	160	Exportations : valeur unitaire
Terms of trade	107	102	104	107	107	105	102	103	100	Termes de l'échange
Purchasing power of exports	93	105	109	123	139	143	154	167	166	Pouvoir d'achat des exportations
Greece										**Grèce**
Imports: volume	90	...	...	...	...	...	...	...	...	Importations : volume
Imports: unit value [1]	115	100	106	127	144	158	165	185	213	Importations : valeur unitaire [1]
Exports: volume	96	...	...	...	...	...	...	...	...	Exportations : volume
Exports: unit value [1]	107	98	104	124	143	149	158	177	202	Exportations : valeur unitaire [1]
Terms of trade	93	98	98	98	99	95	95	96	95	Termes de l'échange
Purchasing power of exports	90	...	...	...	...	...	...	...	...	Pouvoir d'achat des exportations
Honduras										**Honduras**
Exports: volume	70	102	100	93	112	96	103	114	118	Exportations : volume
Exports: unit value	101	101	96	83	102	125	128	135	161	Exportations : valeur unitaire

59 Total imports and exports: index numbers *(continued)*

Index base : 2000 = 100

Importations et exportations totales : indices *(suite)*

Indices base : 2000 = 100

Country or area	1999	2001	2002	2003	2004	2005	2006	2007	2008	Pays ou zone
Hungary										**Hongrie**
Imports: volume	83	104	109	120	139	147	168	189	197	Importations : volume
Imports: unit value	106	101	107	123	135	138	142	156	171	Importations : valeur unitaire
Exports: volume	82	108	114	125	147	164	194	225	234	Exportations : volume
Exports: unit value	108	101	107	122	134	134	136	149	160	Exportations : valeur unitaire
Terms of trade	103	100	100	100	99	97	95	95	94	Termes de l'échange
Purchasing power of exports	84	107	114	124	146	159	185	214	219	Pouvoir d'achat des exportations
Iceland										**Islande**
Imports: volume	96	90	...	...	...	...	...	...	...	Importations : volume
Imports: unit value	101	97	...	...	...	...	...	...	...	Importations : valeur unitaire
Exports: volume	100	107	...	...	...	...	...	...	...	Exportations : volume
Exports: unit value	106	99	...	...	...	...	...	...	...	Exportations : valeur unitaire
Terms of trade	104	102	...	...	...	...	...	...	...	Termes de l'échange
Purchasing power of exports	104	109	...	...	...	...	...	...	...	Pouvoir d'achat des exportations
India										**Inde**
Imports: volume	101	105	115	139	155	197	239	290	...	Importations : volume
Imports: unit value	96	96	104	113	134	143	135	178	...	Importations : valeur unitaire
Exports: volume	81	104	126	134	152	185	193	212	...	Exportations : volume
Exports: unit value	101	94	92	107	122	130	148	161	...	Exportations : valeur unitaire
Terms of trade	105	98	89	95	91	91	110	90	...	Termes de l'échange
Purchasing power of exports	85	102	112	127	138	169	212	191	...	Pouvoir d'achat des exportations
Indonesia										**Indonésie**
Exports: volume	84	121	100	97	101	64	...	...	...	Exportations : volume
Exports: unit value	65	90	96	103	120	81	...	...	...	Exportations : valeur unitaire
Ireland										**Irlande**
Imports: volume	86	99	97	90	98	112	117	119	110	Importations : volume
Imports: unit value	107	100	101	112	120	121	126	137	149	Importations : valeur unitaire
Exports: volume	84	105	104	99	110	113	117	120	120	Exportations : volume
Exports: unit value	110	99	104	115	116	119	118	125	131	Exportations : valeur unitaire
Terms of trade	103	98	102	103	97	99	94	91	88	Termes de l'échange
Purchasing power of exports	86	103	107	103	107	111	110	110	105	Pouvoir d'achat des exportations
Israel										**Israël**
Imports: volume	88	93	93	92	103	105	105	114	116	Importations : volume
Imports: unit value	97	99	99	104	112	120	127	138	157	Importations : valeur unitaire
Exports: volume	80	96	97	101	116	119	124	137	134	Exportations : volume
Exports: unit value	100	96	96	100	106	114	119	127	147	Exportations : valeur unitaire
Terms of trade	103	98	98	96	95	95	94	92	93	Termes de l'échange
Purchasing power of exports	82	94	95	97	110	113	116	126	124	Pouvoir d'achat des exportations
Italy										**Italie**
Imports: volume	93	101	101	102	108	108	113	116	108	Importations : volume
Imports: unit value	99	98	102	122	138	149	165	185	217	Importations : valeur unitaire
Exports: volume	92	103	101	99	104	104	110	115	109	Exportations : volume
Exports: unit value	107	99	106	126	142	149	158	181	206	Exportations : valeur unitaire
Terms of trade	108	101	103	104	103	100	96	98	95	Termes de l'échange
Purchasing power of exports	99	104	104	103	106	104	105	113	104	Pouvoir d'achat des exportations
Japan										**Japon**
Imports: volume	90	99	100	107	115	118	123	119	119	Importations : volume
Imports: unit value	91	87	86	91	101	112	120	133	164	Importations : valeur unitaire
Exports: volume	91	90	97	102	113	114	123	130	128	Exportations : volume
Exports: unit value	95	94	89	96	104	109	110	115	127	Exportations : valeur unitaire
Terms of trade	105	107	104	105	103	98	92	86	77	Termes de l'échange
Purchasing power of exports	96	97	101	108	116	111	113	112	99	Pouvoir d'achat des exportations
Jordan										**Jordanie**
Imports: volume	84	103	104	109	136	155	154	162	166	Importations : volume
Imports: unit value	97	102	105	115	130	148	162	184	221	Importations : valeur unitaire
Exports: volume	93	123	142	152	190	182	188	173	158	Exportations : volume
Exports: unit value	105	101	102	102	114	131	143	170	261	Exportations : valeur unitaire
Terms of trade	107	99	97	88	87	88	88	92	118	Termes de l'échange
Purchasing power of exports	100	122	137	135	166	161	166	160	186	Pouvoir d'achat des exportations

59 Total imports and exports: index numbers *(continued)*

Index base : 2000 = 100

Importations et exportations totales : indices *(suite)*

Indices base : 2000 = 100

Country or area	1999	2001	2002	2003	2004	2005	2006	2007	2008	Pays ou zone
Kenya										**Kenya**
Imports: volume	87	...	...	...	...	...	...	...	...	Importations : volume
Imports: unit value	98	...	...	...	...	...	...	...	...	Importations : valeur unitaire
Exports: unit value	101	...	...	...	...	...	...	...	...	Exportations : valeur unitaire
Terms of trade	103	...	...	...	...	...	...	...	...	Termes de l'échange
Korea, Republic of										**Corée, République de**
Imports: volume	84	98	110	118	132	140	155	169	172	Importations : volume
Imports: unit value	87	91	88	96	107	117	126	134	164	Importations : valeur unitaire
Exports: volume	83	101	114	134	163	178	202	223	238	Exportations : volume
Exports: unit value	100	87	83	85	92	93	93	96	102	Exportations : valeur unitaire
Terms of trade	114	96	95	89	85	79	74	72	62	Termes de l'échange
Purchasing power of exports	95	96	108	119	140	141	149	160	148	Pouvoir d'achat des exportations
Latvia										**Lettonie**
Imports: unit value	97	98	106	122	140	150	166	191	224	Importations : valeur unitaire
Exports: unit value	105	99	104	121	145	153	169	209	242	Exportations : valeur unitaire
Terms of trade	108	101	98	99	104	102	102	109	108	Termes de l'échange
Libyan Arab Jamah.										**Jamah. arabe libyenne**
Imports: volume	147	173	214	...	...	...	...	...	...	Importations : volume
Imports: unit value	115	83	48	...	...	...	...	...	...	Importations : valeur unitaire
Exports: volume	108	110	95	...	...	...	...	...	...	Exportations : volume
Exports: unit value	72	87	88	...	...	...	...	...	...	Exportations : valeur unitaire
Terms of trade	63	104	185	...	...	...	...	...	...	Termes de l'échange
Purchasing power of exports	68	115	175	...	...	...	...	...	...	Pouvoir d'achat des exportations
Lithuania										**Lituanie**
Imports: volume	...	120	143	155	182	209	233	229	224	Importations : volume
Imports: unit value	95	97	101	117	127	138	151	174	211	Importations : valeur unitaire
Exports: volume	...	125	145	161	185	214	234	227	240	Exportations : volume
Exports: unit value	94	97	101	120	137	151	160	185	216	Exportations : valeur unitaire
Terms of trade	99	101	100	102	108	109	106	106	102	Termes de l'échange
Purchasing power of exports	...	126	146	164	199	233	247	241	245	Pouvoir d'achat des exportations
Malaysia										**Malaisie**
Imports: volume	...	92	97	...	...	...	...	...	...	Importations : volume
Imports: unit value	...	98	99	...	...	...	...	...	...	Importations : valeur unitaire
Exports: volume	...	96	102	...	...	...	...	...	...	Exportations : volume
Exports: unit value	...	94	93	...	...	...	...	...	...	Exportations : valeur unitaire
Terms of trade	...	96	94	...	...	...	...	...	...	Termes de l'échange
Purchasing power of exports	...	92	96	...	...	...	...	...	...	Pouvoir d'achat des exportations
Mauritius										**Maurice**
Imports: volume	107	98	103	96	102	107	111	114	116	Importations : volume
Imports: unit value	100	97	99	80	90	98	102	111	134	Importations : valeur unitaire
Exports: volume	98	116	121	92	89	96	106	95	96	Exportations : volume
Exports: unit value	106	92	98	84	92	90	89	96	102	Exportations : valeur unitaire
Terms of trade	106	95	98	105	101	92	87	87	76	Termes de l'échange
Purchasing power of exports	103	110	119	96	90	89	93	82	73	Pouvoir d'achat des exportations
Mexico										**Mexique**
Imports: unit value	97	101	100	103	108	114	119	125	136	Importations : valeur unitaire
Exports: unit value	93	98	100	105	117	127	137	144	158	Exportations : valeur unitaire
Terms of trade	96	97	100	102	108	112	115	114	116	Termes de l'échange
Morocco										**Maroc**
Imports: volume	89	98	105	113	127	140	155	176	...	Importations : volume
Imports: unit value	107	97	98	110	121	129	134	152	...	Importations : valeur unitaire
Exports: volume	92	102	107	104	103	118	127	131	...	Exportations : volume
Exports: unit value	110	94	99	116	127	128	135	150	...	Exportations : valeur unitaire
Terms of trade	103	97	101	105	105	99	100	98	...	Termes de l'échange
Purchasing power of exports	95	99	107	110	108	117	128	129	...	Pouvoir d'achat des exportations
Netherlands										**Pays-Bas**
Imports: volume	96	97	95	98	106	121	133	141	146	Importations : volume
Imports: unit value	103	101	101	118	131	129	135	151	169	Importations : valeur unitaire
Exports: volume	92	102	103	106	116	122	134	144	147	Exportations : volume
Exports: unit value	101	100	100	116	127	134	140	155	174	Exportations : valeur unitaire
Terms of trade	98	99	98	99	96	104	104	103	103	Termes de l'échange
Purchasing power of exports	90	100	101	104	112	127	139	149	152	Pouvoir d'achat des exportations

59 Total imports and exports: index numbers *(continued)*

Index base : 2000 = 100

Importations et exportations totales : indices *(suite)*

Indices base : 2000 = 100

Country or area	1999	2001	2002	2003	2004	2005	2006	2007	2008	Pays ou zone
New Zealand										**Nouvelle-Zélande**
Imports: volume	103	102	111	124	142	151	150	164	171	Importations : volume
Imports: unit value	100	94	98	109	118	125	126	169	145	Importations : valeur unitaire
Exports: volume	95	103	109	112	119	118	120	127	126	Exportations : volume
Exports: unit value	99	101	99	111	129	138	138	179	184	Exportations : valeur unitaire
Terms of trade	99	107	102	102	109	111	110	106	127	Termes de l'échange
Purchasing power of exports	93	110	111	115	130	130	131	135	159	Pouvoir d'achat des exportations
Norway										**Norvège**
Imports: volume [2]	94	101	103	106	118	129	142	156	157	Importations : volume [2]
Imports: unit value [2]	109	98	104	116	127	133	139	159	173	Importations : valeur unitaire [2]
Exports: volume [2]	95	105	107	107	108	108	106	107	107	Exportations : volume [2]
Exports: unit value [2]	78	93	94	104	127	161	194	213	270	Exportations : valeur unitaire [2]
Terms of trade	71	95	91	90	100	122	139	134	156	Termes de l'échange
Purchasing power of exports	68	99	97	97	109	131	147	143	167	Pouvoir d'achat des exportations
Pakistan										**Pakistan**
Imports: volume	101	112	123	123	142	165	153	169	184	Importations : volume
Imports: unit value	93	94	95	109	122	138	151	167	216	Importations : valeur unitaire
Exports: volume	89	102	109	110	103	126	127	124	133	Exportations : volume
Exports: unit value	109	94	90	96	103	103	106	110	124	Exportations : valeur unitaire
Terms of trade	118	100	95	89	85	75	70	66	57	Termes de l'échange
Purchasing power of exports	105	102	104	98	87	95	89	81	76	Pouvoir d'achat des exportations
Panama										**Panama**
Exports: volume	105	...	81	84	83	98	100	105	82	Exportations : volume
Papua New Guinea										**Papouasie-Nvl-Guinée**
Exports: volume	...	94	88	105	99	106	92	94	100	Exportations : volume
Exports: unit value	79	90	85	101	126	156	247	271	329	Exportations : valeur unitaire
Peru										**Pérou**
Exports: volume	88	114	126	122	135	134	126	138	154	Exportations : volume
Exports: unit value	75	84	87	97	128	170	280	307	251	Exportations : valeur unitaire
Philippines										**Philippines**
Imports: volume	95	98	116	118	137	123	126	...	...	Importations : volume
Imports: unit value [1]	118	84	83	82	81	97	113	...	...	Importations : valeur unitaire [1]
Exports: volume	87	89	104	98	110	104	124	...	...	Exportations : volume
Exports: unit value [1]	121	84	77	79	75	84	88	...	...	Exportations : valeur unitaire [1]
Terms of trade	103	100	93	96	93	87	78	...	...	Termes de l'échange
Purchasing power of exports	89	88	97	94	102	90	97	...	...	Pouvoir d'achat des exportations
Poland										**Pologne**
Imports: volume	90	104	111	119	140	148	173	200	218	Importations : volume
Imports: unit value [1]	103	100	101	116	131	141	151	171	198	Importations : valeur unitaire [1]
Exports: volume	80	114	122	143	170	189	220	242	262	Exportations : volume
Exports: unit value [1]	108	102	107	118	139	150	160	186	213	Exportations : valeur unitaire [1]
Terms of trade	105	102	105	102	107	107	107	109	107	Termes de l'échange
Purchasing power of exports	83	116	129	146	182	201	235	263	280	Pouvoir d'achat des exportations
Portugal										**Portugal**
Imports: volume	...	97	94	94	...	...	...	...	...	Importations : volume
Imports: unit value [1]	106	89	91	110	...	...	...	...	...	Importations : valeur unitaire [1]
Exports: volume	...	95	95	97	...	...	...	...	...	Exportations : volume
Exports: unit value [1]	109	93	96	112	...	...	...	...	...	Exportations : valeur unitaire [1]
Terms of trade	103	105	106	102	...	...	...	...	...	Termes de l'échange
Purchasing power of exports	...	99	101	99	...	...	...	...	...	Pouvoir d'achat des exportations
Republic of Moldova										**République de Moldova**
Imports: volume	...	118	139	180	205	248	267	330	379	Importations : volume
Imports: unit value	...	97	92	95	119	124	130	156	213	Importations : valeur unitaire
Exports: volume	...	122	142	170	199	215	197	232	254	Exportations : volume
Exports: unit value	...	93	87	88	107	107	107	127	164	Exportations : valeur unitaire
Terms of trade	...	96	95	93	90	86	83	82	77	Termes de l'échange
Purchasing power of exports	...	117	134	158	178	186	163	190	196	Pouvoir d'achat des exportations

Total imports and exports: index numbers *(continued)*

Index base : 2000 = 100

Importations et exportations totales : indices *(suite)*

Indices base : 2000 = 100

Country or area	1999	2001	2002	2003	2004	2005	2006	2007	2008	Pays ou zone
Romania										**Roumanie**
Imports: volume	...	124	143	169	207	244	293	369	394	Importations : volume
Imports: unit value	105	96	96	106	106	112	116	100	103	Importations : valeur unitaire
Exports: volume	...	112	132	144	166	179	191	204	225	Exportations : volume
Exports: unit value	102	98	102	119	125	137	148	107	111	Exportations : valeur unitaire
Terms of trade	97	102	106	112	118	122	127	108	108	Termes de l'échange
Purchasing power of exports	...	114	139	161	195	218	244	221	243	Pouvoir d'achat des exportations
Russian Federation										**Fédération de Russie**
Imports: volume	...	123	136	168	222	288	398	...	470	Importations : volume
Exports: volume	...	99	105	133	180	240	303	...	261	Exportations : volume
Serbia										**Serbie**
Imports: volume	...	...	...	...	...	...	...	129	108	Importations : volume
Imports: unit value	...	...	...	...	...	...	...	106	116	Importations : valeur unitaire
Exports: volume	...	...	...	...	...	...	...	126	108	Exportations : volume
Exports: unit value	...	...	...	...	...	...	...	110	113	Exportations : valeur unitaire
Terms of trade	...	...	...	...	...	...	...	104	98	Termes de l'échange
Purchasing power of exports	...	...	...	...	...	...	...	131	106	Pouvoir d'achat des exportations
Seychelles										**Seychelles**
Imports: volume	105	...	...	...	...	...	...	...	...	Importations : volume
Imports: unit value	120	...	...	...	...	...	...	...	...	Importations : valeur unitaire
Exports: volume	78	...	...	...	...	...	...	...	...	Exportations : volume
Exports: unit value	114	...	...	...	...	...	...	...	...	Exportations : valeur unitaire
Terms of trade	94	...	...	...	...	...	...	...	...	Termes de l'échange
Purchasing power of exports	73	...	...	...	...	...	...	...	...	Pouvoir d'achat des exportations
Singapore										**Singapour**
Imports: volume	88	89	90	96	117	134	148	158	174	Importations : volume
Imports: unit value [1]	93	97	96	99	104	111	119	124	136	Importations : valeur unitaire [1]
Exports: volume	86	95	100	116	155	173	192	208	217	Exportations : volume
Exports: unit value [1]	96	93	91	90	93	96	103	104	113	Exportations : valeur unitaire [1]
Terms of trade	103	96	94	91	89	87	86	84	83	Termes de l'échange
Purchasing power of exports	89	91	95	106	139	151	165	176	180	Pouvoir d'achat des exportations
Slovakia										**Slovaquie**
Imports: unit value	...	...	106	129	147	157	177	196	235	Importations : valeur unitaire
Exports: unit value	...	...	105	139	174	191	204	221	248	Exportations : valeur unitaire
Terms of trade	...	...	99	108	118	121	116	112	106	Termes de l'échange
Slovenia										**Slovénie**
Imports: volume	96	101	105	111	...	...	...	...	...	Importations : volume
Imports: unit value	104	100	104	124	141	152	164	175	183	Importations : valeur unitaire
Exports: volume	89	105	110	115	...	...	...	...	...	Exportations : volume
Exports: unit value	109	100	106	126	142	149	159	168	171	Exportations : valeur unitaire
Terms of trade	105	100	102	102	101	98	97	96	94	Termes de l'échange
Purchasing power of exports	94	105	112	117	...	...	...	...	...	Pouvoir d'achat des exportations
South Africa										**Afrique du Sud**
Imports: volume	93	100	105	115	131	144	...	...	...	Importations : volume
Imports: unit value	98	94	93	116	136	144	...	...	...	Importations : valeur unitaire
Exports: volume	91	102	102	103	105	112	...	...	...	Exportations : volume
Exports: unit value	100	96	96	123	148	156	...	...	...	Exportations : valeur unitaire
Terms of trade	102	101	104	107	109	109	...	...	...	Termes de l'échange
Purchasing power of exports	92	103	106	109	114	122	...	...	...	Pouvoir d'achat des exportations
Spain										**Espagne**
Imports: volume	92	104	109	117	129	137	149	159	154	Importations : volume
Imports: unit value [1]	102	96	99	116	131	138	143	158	177	Importations : valeur unitaire [1]
Exports: volume	89	104	107	114	120	121	127	133	135	Exportations : volume
Exports: unit value [1]	109	98	102	121	134	140	148	166	182	Exportations : valeur unitaire [1]
Terms of trade	106	101	103	104	102	102	103	105	103	Termes de l'échange
Purchasing power of exports	94	106	111	118	123	123	132	139	139	Pouvoir d'achat des exportations

59 Total imports and exports: index numbers *(continued)*

Index base : 2000 = 100

Importations et exportations totales : indices *(suite)*

Indices base : 2000 = 100

Country or area	1999	2001	2002	2003	2004	2005	2006	2007	2008	Pays ou zone
Sri Lanka										**Sri Lanka**
Imports: volume	90	91	101	111	122	126	135	140	147	Importations : volume
Imports: unit value	...	98	90	...	...	...	...	...	...	Importations : valeur unitaire
Exports: volume	84	92	93	98	106	113	97	126	126	Exportations : volume
Exports: unit value	101	97	91	97	101	104	109	113	119	Exportations : valeur unitaire
Terms of trade	...	98	101	...	...	...	...	...	...	Termes de l'échange
Purchasing power of exports	...	90	94	...	...	...	...	...	...	Pouvoir d'achat des exportations
Sweden										**Suède**
Imports: volume	89	95	94	100	108	116	126	138	141	Importations : volume
Imports: unit value [1]	103	93	99	117	132	139	149	166	183	Importations : valeur unitaire [1]
Exports: volume	90	98	101	106	117	122	133	136	138	Exportations : volume
Exports: unit value [1]	106	90	94	111	121	124	131	149	158	Exportations : valeur unitaire [1]
Terms of trade	104	97	95	95	92	90	88	89	87	Termes de l'échange
Purchasing power of exports	93	96	96	101	108	109	117	121	119	Pouvoir d'achat des exportations
Switzerland										**Suisse**
Imports: volume	93	101	99	100	104	106	117	119	121	Importations : volume
Imports: unit value	107	100	105	121	135	143	149	162	181	Importations : valeur unitaire
Exports: volume	93	103	105	105	111	115	132	132	136	Exportations : volume
Exports: unit value	109	101	107	124	137	141	143	158	182	Exportations : valeur unitaire
Terms of trade	103	101	102	102	102	99	96	97	100	Termes de l'échange
Purchasing power of exports	95	104	106	107	113	114	127	128	137	Pouvoir d'achat des exportations
Thailand										**Thaïlande**
Imports: volume	82	89	100	112	137	162	164	171	192	Importations : volume
Imports: unit value	95	109	102	107	110	117	124	131	147	Importations : valeur unitaire
Exports: volume	82	92	101	109	119	143	159	178	185	Exportations : volume
Exports: unit value	102	102	97	105	118	113	119	126	139	Exportations : valeur unitaire
Terms of trade	107	93	95	99	108	97	96	96	94	Termes de l'échange
Purchasing power of exports	88	85	96	108	128	138	152	171	174	Pouvoir d'achat des exportations
Turkey										**Turquie**
Imports: volume	75	75	91	113	137	153	166	187	185	Importations : volume
Imports: unit value	96	100	98	111	129	138	150	164	197	Importations : valeur unitaire
Exports: volume	90	122	142	169	192	212	238	265	283	Exportations : volume
Exports: unit value	104	97	96	108	126	133	138	155	180	Exportations : valeur unitaire
Terms of trade	109	98	97	97	98	97	92	95	91	Termes de l'échange
Purchasing power of exports	98	119	137	164	188	205	220	251	258	Pouvoir d'achat des exportations
United Kingdom										**Royaume-Uni**
Imports: volume	91	105	110	112	120	128	141	137	134	Importations : volume
Imports: unit value [1]	104	94	96	104	116	120	125	138	145	Importations : valeur unitaire [1]
Exports: volume	89	102	101	101	102	111	124	112	112	Exportations : volume
Exports: unit value [1]	106	94	97	108	121	126	130	143	152	Exportations : valeur unitaire [1]
Terms of trade	102	99	102	104	105	105	104	104	105	Termes de l'échange
Purchasing power of exports	91	101	103	105	107	117	129	116	117	Pouvoir d'achat des exportations
United States										**Etats-Unis**
Imports: volume	90	97	101	107	118	125	132	133	128	Importations : volume
Imports: unit value [1]	94	96	94	97	102	110	115	120	134	Importations : valeur unitaire [1]
Exports: volume [3]	90	94	90	93	101	109	120	128	135	Exportations : volume [3]
Exports: unit value [1,3]	98	99	98	100	104	107	111	116	123	Exportations : valeur unitaire [1,3]
Terms of trade	105	103	104	103	101	97	96	97	92	Termes de l'échange
Purchasing power of exports	95	97	94	96	102	105	115	124	124	Pouvoir d'achat des exportations
Uruguay										**Uruguay**
Imports: unit value	96	94	87	...	...	...	...	...	...	Importations : valeur unitaire
Exports: unit value	101	98	93	...	...	...	...	...	...	Exportations : valeur unitaire
Terms of trade	106	104	106	...	...	...	...	...	...	Termes de l'échange
Venezuela (Boliv. Rep. of) [1]										**Venezuela (Rép. boliv. du) [1]**
Imports: unit value	102	105	105	112	123	126	132	151	179	Importations : valeur unitaire

59

Total imports and exports: index numbers *(continued)*

Index base : 2000 = 100

Importations et exportations totales : indices *(suite)*

Indices base : 2000 = 100

Source:
United Nations Statistics Division, New York, trade statistics database, last accessed January 2010.

1 Price indices.
2 Index numbers exclude ships.
3 Excluding military goods.

Source:
Organisation des Nations Unies, Division de statistique, New York, la base de données pour les statistiques du commerce extérieur, dernier accès janvier 2010.

1 Les indices des prix.
2 Les indices excluent les navires.
3 Non compris les biens militaires.

Manufactured goods exports

Unit value and volume indices: 2000 = 100; value: thousand million US dollars

Exportations des produits manufacturés

Indices de valeur unitaire et de volume: 2000 = 100; valeur: milliards de dollars des E.-U.

Region, country or area Région, pays ou zone	1999	2000	2001	2002	2003	2004	2005	2006	2007	2008
Total Total										
Unit value indices, US $[1]										
Indices de valeur unitaire, $ des E.-U.[1]	103	100	98	98	104	110	111	114	125	131
Unit value indices, SDRs										
Indices de valeur unitaire, DTS	99	100	102	99	99	97	99	102	107	109
Volume indices										
Indices de volume	88	100	100	103	111	128	139	153	145	146
Value, thousand million US $										
Valeur, milliards de $ des E.-U.	4 194.4	4 620.8	4 548.3	4 648.6	5 356.1	6 495.7	7 135.9	8 104.2	8 379.8	8 882.1
Developed economies Economies développées										
Unit value indices, US $										
Indices de valeur unitaire, $ des E.-U.	105	100	98	99	108	116	120	123	133	139
Unit value indices, SDRs										
Indices de valeur unitaire, DTS	101	100	102	100	102	103	107	110	114	116
Volume indices										
Indices de volume	89	100	102	101	105	115	120	130	136	136
Value, thousand million US $										
Valeur, milliards de $ des E.-U.	3 021.0	3 209.4	3 215.6	3 196.4	3 653.2	4 312.7	4 590.7	5 128.2	5 793.1	6 099.6
Americas Amériques										
Unit value indices, US $										
Indices de valeur unitaire, $ des E.-U.	99	100	99	100	103	106	108	111	115	118
Volume indices										
Indices de volume	91	100	101	88	88	97	104	113	119	120
Value, thousand million US $										
Valeur, milliards de $ des E.-U.	703.7	780.3	781.7	685.3	704.0	803.2	872.2	983.2	1 070.3	1 105.3
Canada Canada										
Unit value indices, US $										
Indices de valeur unitaire, $ des E.-U.	99	100	98	96	103	112	119	128	135	...
Unit value indices, national currency										
Indices de val. unitaire, monnaie nat.	99	100	102	102	98	98	97	98	97	...
Volume indices										
Indices de volume	90	100	94	94	92	97	100	99	100	...
Value, thousand million US $										
Valeur, milliards de $ des E.-U.	165.6	184.0	169.1	166.6	173.6	200.2	219.2	234.6	247.8	235.1
United States Etats-Unis										
Unit value indices, US $[2]										
Indices de valeur unitaire, $ des E.-U.[2]	99	100	100	102	103	104	104	107	110	116
Unit value indices, national currency[2]										
Indices de val. unitaire, monnaie nat.[2]	99	100	100	102	103	104	104	107	110	116
Volume indices										
Indices de volume	91	100	103	86	87	97	105	118	126	126
Value, thousand million US $										
Valeur, milliards de $ des E.-U.	538.1	596.3	612.6	518.8	530.4	603.0	653.1	748.6	822.5	870.2
Europe Europe										
Unit value indices, US $										
Indices de valeur unitaire, $ des E.-U.	110	100	99	100	112	122	125	130	142	149
Volume indices										
Indices de volume	89	100	106	108	113	124	128	139	145	145
Value, thousand million US $										
Valeur, milliards de $ des E.-U.	1 856.3	1 903.5	1 986.4	2 051.3	2 426.2	2 877.4	3 055.3	3 426.3	3 927.2	4 136.1
Austria Autriche										
Unit value indices, US $										
Indices de valeur unitaire, $ des E.-U.	118	100	94	100	...	...	...	...	...	...
Unit value indices, national currency										
Indices de val. unitaire, monnaie nat.	102	100	98	98	...	...	...	...	...	...
Volume indices										
Indices de volume	86	100	124	118	...	...	...	...	...	...
Value, thousand million US $										
Valeur, milliards de $ des E.-U.	50.4	49.8	58.3	59.0	76.8	96.7	100.2	114.0	133.6	150.0

60 Manufactured goods exports *(continued)*

Unit value and volume indices: 2000 = 100; value: thousand million US dollars

Exportations des produits manufacturés *(suite)*

Indices de valeur unitaire et de volume: 2000 = 100; valeur: milliards de dollars des E.-U.

Region, country or area Région, pays ou zone	1999	2000	2001	2002	2003	2004	2005	2006	2007	2008
Belgium Belgique										
Unit value indices, US $ Indices de valeur unitaire, $ des E.-U.	108	100	99	106	125	141	148	156	178	186
Unit value indices, national currency Indices de val. unitaire, monnaie nat.	94	100	102	103	103	105	110	115	120	116
Volume indices Indices de volume	92	100	100	100	100	106	107	107	109	112
Value, thousand million US $ Valeur, milliards de $ des E.-U.	131.8	132.5	131.6	139.5	166.3	198.7	209.9	222.3	258.2	274.5
Denmark Danemark										
Unit value indices, US $ Indices de valeur unitaire, $ des E.-U.	112	100	100	103	122	136	138	141	145	157
Unit value indices, national currency Indices de val. unitaire, monnaie nat.	97	100	102	100	101	101	102	103	97	98
Volume indices Indices de volume	95	100	105	114	119	119	129	137	149	154
Value, thousand million US $ Valeur, milliards de $ des E.-U.	33.8	31.8	33.5	37.2	46.4	51.4	56.6	61.1	68.8	76.7
Finland Finlande										
Unit value indices, US $ Indices de valeur unitaire, $ des E.-U.	104	100	95	100	117	120	131	141	166	177
Unit value indices, national currency Indices de val. unitaire, monnaie nat.	90	100	98	98	96	89	97	104	112	111
Volume indices Indices de volume	89	100	103	98	98	109	108	116	116	115
Value, thousand million US $ Valeur, milliards de $ des E.-U.	36.7	39.7	38.9	38.9	45.4	51.8	56.1	65.1	76.8	81.3
France France										
Unit value indices, US $ Indices de valeur unitaire, $ des E.-U.	113	100	98	84	101	111	111	109	118	124
Unit value indices, national currency Indices de val. unitaire, monnaie nat.	98	100	101	83	83	82	82	81	80	78
Volume indices Indices de volume	86	100	119	120	118	127	132	148	152	159
Value, thousand million US $ Valeur, milliards de $ des E.-U.	242.5	249.2	290.2	251.9	298.5	351.8	365.3	404.9	449.2	489.7
Germany Allemagne										
Unit value indices, US $ Indices de valeur unitaire, $ des E.-U.	111	100	99	104	118	128	128	132	143	155
Unit value indices, national currency Indices de val. unitaire, monnaie nat.	97	100	102	102	96	95	95	97	97	97
Volume indices Indices de volume	86	100	105	107	114	128	138	152	166	153
Value, thousand million US $ Valeur, milliards de $ des E.-U.	461.1	481.0	499.2	534.8	644.3	790.3	849.0	970.0	1 143.7	1 142.6
Greece Grèce										
Unit value indices, US $ Indices de valeur unitaire, $ des E.-U.	107	100	...	...	...	...	...	...	...	...
Unit value indices, national currency Indices de val. unitaire, monnaie nat.	90	100	...	...	...	...	...	...	...	...
Volume indices Indices de volume	86	100	...	...	...	...	...	...	...	...
Value, thousand million US $ Valeur, milliards de $ des E.-U.	5.6	6.1	6.0	5.7	8.7	8.5	10.7	12.0	14.0	15.4
Iceland Islande										
Value, thousand million US $ Valeur, milliards de $ des E.-U.	0.6	0.6	0.7	0.7	0.8	1.0	1.1	1.3	1.9	2.9
Ireland Irlande										
Value, thousand million US $ Valeur, milliards de $ des E.-U.	59.6	65.6	75.1	77.7	79.4	88.7	94.0	96.5	101.9	107.7

60 Manufactured goods exports *(continued)*

Unit value and volume indices: 2000 = 100; value: thousand million US dollars

Exportations des produits manufacturés *(suite)*

Indices de valeur unitaire et de volume: 2000 = 100; valeur: milliards de dollars des E.-U.

Region, country or area Région, pays ou zone	1999	2000	2001	2002	2003	2004	2005	2006	2007	2008
Italy Italie										
Unit value indices, US $ [3] Indices de valeur unitaire, $ des E.-U. [3]	113	100	100	...	104	...	118	125	136	139
Volume indices Indices de volume	86	100	105	...	119	...	128	135	148	156
Value, thousand million US $ Valeur, milliards de $ des E.-U.	206.7	212.6	223.2	226.1	262.5	309.7	320.2	357.9	426.3	460.0
Netherlands Pays-Bas										
Unit value indices, US $ [3] Indices de valeur unitaire, $ des E.-U. [3]	109	100	104	104	120	130	139	144	175	...
Unit value indices, national currency Indices de val. unitaire, monnaie nat.	95	100	107	102	98	97	103	106	118	...
Volume indices Indices de volume	88	100	115	117	122	135	136	147	148	...
Value, thousand million US $ Valeur, milliards de $ des E.-U.	122.2	127.5	152.8	154.6	186.1	224.7	240.4	271.0	331.4	350.9
Norway Norvège										
Unit value indices, US $ Indices de valeur unitaire, $ des E.-U.	106	100	97	100	110	126	131	145	169	177
Unit value indices, national currency Indices de val. unitaire, monnaie nat.	94	100	99	91	89	96	96	106	112	111
Volume indices Indices de volume	96	100	92	110	110	112	119	129	141	148
Value, thousand million US $ Valeur, milliards de $ des E.-U.	16.8	16.6	14.8	18.3	20.3	23.5	25.9	31.1	39.5	43.6
Portugal Portugal										
Unit value indices, US $ [3] Indices de valeur unitaire, $ des E.-U. [3]	110	100	99	...	...	...	...	...	...	...
Volume indices Indices de volume	93	100	103	...	...	...	...	...	...	...
Value, thousand million US $ Valeur, milliards de $ des E.-U.	21.3	21.0	21.4	22.4	27.5	30.5	28.8	32.1	32.9	39.7
Spain Espagne										
Value, thousand million US $ Valeur, milliards de $ des E.-U.	88.7	89.4	91.4	99.0	124.0	142.8	150.1	166.8	196.8	209.2
Sweden Suède										
Unit value indices, US $ Indices de valeur unitaire, $ des E.-U.	106	100	...	...	...	...	...	...	...	...
Unit value indices, national currency Indices de val. unitaire, monnaie nat.	96	100	...	...	...	...	...	...	...	...
Volume indices Indices de volume	100	100	...	...	...	...	...	...	...	...
Value, thousand million US $ Valeur, milliards de $ des E.-U.	71.1	67.2	58.7	66.9	82.4	101.0	111.0	124.1	143.1	150.9
Switzerland Suisse										
Unit value indices, US $ Indices de valeur unitaire, $ des E.-U.	109	100	104	109	...	...	...	...	...	...
Volume indices Indices de volume	94	100	97	99	...	...	...	...	...	...
Value, thousand million US $ Valeur, milliards de $ des E.-U.	80.0	78.2	78.8	84.5	96.8	113.7	123.3	138.2	157.8	182.0
United Kingdom Royaume-Uni										
Unit value indices, US $ Indices de valeur unitaire, $ des E.-U.	108	100	95	98	108	120	120	123	133	135
Unit value indices, national currency Indices de val. unitaire, monnaie nat.	101	100	99	99	100	99	100	101	101	111
Volume indices Indices de volume	90	100	96	102	103	104	111	124	113	114
Value, thousand million US $ Valeur, milliards de $ des E.-U.	225.6	232.5	210.2	232.6	258.1	290.2	310.5	355.4	348.4	356.3

60 Manufactured goods exports *(continued)*

Unit value and volume indices: 2000 = 100; value: thousand million US dollars

Exportations des produits manufacturés *(suite)*

Indices de valeur unitaire et de volume: 2000 = 100; valeur: milliards de dollars des E.-U.

Region, country or area Région, pays ou zone	1999	2000	2001	2002	2003	2004	2005	2006	2007	2008
Other developed economies Autres économies développées										
Unit value indices, US $ Indices de valeur unitaire, $ des E.-U.	98	100	93	91	97	107	113	114	119	128
Volume indices Indices de volume	90	100	91	96	103	112	112	120	127	128
Value, thousand million US $ Valeur, milliards de $ des E.-U.	461.0	525.6	447.5	459.8	523.1	632.1	663.2	718.6	795.7	858.1
Australia Australie										
Unit value indices, US $ Indices de valeur unitaire, $ des E.-U.	97	100	93	92	101	133	151	203	245	223
Unit value indices, national currency Indices de val. unitaire, monnaie nat.	87	100	104	97	89	104	114	156	169	153
Volume indices Indices de volume	91	100	99	104	103	88	88	73	73	85
Value, thousand million US $ Valeur, milliards de $ des E.-U.	18.7	21.2	19.5	20.2	22.0	25.0	28.2	31.6	38.1	40.3
Israel Israël										
Unit value indices, US $ Indices de valeur unitaire, $ des E.-U.	83	100	98	95	95	99	109	118	124	126
Volume indices Indices de volume	98	100	95	98	105	124	125	123	134	135
Value, thousand million US $ Valeur, milliards de $ des E.-U.	24.2	29.7	27.6	27.5	29.5	36.5	40.5	43.3	49.4	50.7
Japan Japon										
Unit value indices, US $ Indices de valeur unitaire, $ des E.-U.	98	100	94	92	97	107	112	112	117	129
Unit value indices, national currency Indices de val. unitaire, monnaie nat.	104	100	110	106	105	107	114	121	127	124
Volume indices Indices de volume	89	100	89	94	100	110	109	117	123	121
Value, thousand million US $ Valeur, milliards de $ des E.-U.	397.5	454.8	378.0	391.8	443.3	534.1	553.7	597.3	654.1	707.8
New Zealand Nouvelle-Zélande										
Unit value indices, US $ Indices de valeur unitaire, $ des E.-U.	96	100	98	99	112	125	136	140	155	163
Unit value indices, national currency Indices de val. unitaire, monnaie nat.	83	100	105	97	88	86	88	98	96	104
Volume indices Indices de volume	99	100	108	105	109	116	115	117	119	113
Value, thousand million US $ Valeur, milliards de $ des E.-U.	4.5	4.7	5.0	4.9	5.7	6.8	7.3	7.7	8.6	8.7
South Africa Afrique du Sud										
Value, thousand million US $ Valeur, milliards de $ des E.-U.	16.1	15.2	17.5	15.3	22.5	29.7	33.5	38.7	45.5	50.7
Developing Countries, Total Les pays en développement, total										
Unit value indices, US $ Indices de valeur unitaire, $ des E.-U.	97	100	98	96	97	99	98	102	110	117
Unit value indices, SDRs Indices de valeur unitaire, DTS	93	100	102	98	92	87	87	91	94	97
Volume indices Indices de volume	86	100	96	107	124	157	184	208	167	169
Value, thousand million US $ Valeur, milliards de $ des E.-U.	1 173.3	1 411.4	1 332.7	1 452.2	1 702.8	2 183.0	2 545.1	2 976.0	2 586.6	2 782.5
China, Hong Kong SAR Chine, Hong Kong RAS										
Unit value indices, US $ Indices de valeur unitaire, $ des E.-U.	102	100	95	93	93	94	96	93	94	99
Unit value indices, national currency Indices de val. unitaire, monnaie nat.	101	100	96	93	93	94	96	93	94	99
Volume indices Indices de volume	93	100	88	93	70	71	75	77	60	45
Value, thousand million US $ Valeur, milliards de $ des E.-U.	21.2	22.4	18.9	19.4	14.7	15.1	16.3	16.0	12.5	10.0

60 Manufactured goods exports *(continued)*

Unit value and volume indices: 2000 = 100; value: thousand million US dollars

Exportations des produits manufacturés *(suite)*

Indices de valeur unitaire et de volume: 2000 = 100; valeur: milliards de dollars des E.-U.

Region, country or area / Région, pays ou zone	1999	2000	2001	2002	2003	2004	2005	2006	2007	2008
India Inde										
Unit value indices, US $ / Indices de valeur unitaire, $ des E.-U.	121	100	92	99	...	...	...	...	...	...
Unit value indices, national currency / Indices de val. unitaire, monnaie nat.	116	100	95	107	...	...	...	...	...	...
Volume indices / Indices de volume	69	100	105	115	...	...	...	...	...	...
Value, thousand million US $ / Valeur, milliards de $ des E.-U.	29.3	35.0	33.5	39.9	48.8	59.1	74.1	86.1	96.9	116.7
Korea, Republic of Corée, République de										
Unit value indices, US $ / Indices de valeur unitaire, $ des E.-U.	96	100	92	82	83	92	96	101	106	99
Unit value indices, national currency / Indices de val. unitaire, monnaie nat.	101	100	105	91	87	93	87	85	87	94
Volume indices / Indices de volume	87	100	95	97	118	145	175	188	203	241
Value, thousand million US $ / Valeur, milliards de $ des E.-U.	130.6	156.9	137.3	125.4	153.0	207.9	262.8	297.5	338.6	373.2
Pakistan Pakistan										
Unit value indices, US $ / Indices de valeur unitaire, $ des E.-U.	106	100	100	96	101	108	106	108	108	108
Unit value indices, national currency / Indices de val. unitaire, monnaie nat.	100	100	117	108	111	119	119	123	124	143
Volume indices / Indices de volume	90	100	101	114	140	137	155	160	163	179
Value, thousand million US $ / Valeur, milliards de $ des E.-U.	7.4	7.7	7.8	8.4	10.9	11.4	12.7	13.4	13.6	14.9
Singapore Singapour										
Unit value indices, US $ / Indices de valeur unitaire, $ des E.-U.	101	100	98	100	99	98	78	81	109	109
Unit value indices, national currency / Indices de val. unitaire, monnaie nat.	...	100	...	...	...	...	76	75	95	89
Volume indices / Indices de volume	82	100	89	90	104	129	188	225	180	184
Value, thousand million US $ / Valeur, milliards de $ des E.-U.	99.7	119.3	103.7	106.7	122.8	151.7	175.7	217.4	233.8	240.3
Turkey Turquie										
Unit value indices, US $ [4] / Indices de valeur unitaire, $ des E.-U. [4]	105	100	99	96	108	124	130	127	137	171
Volume indices / Indices de volume	88	100	114	138	162	189	204	240	279	269
Value, thousand million US $ / Valeur, milliards de $ des E.-U.	21.2	23.1	26.1	30.8	40.3	54.2	61.1	70.9	88.7	106.3

Source:
United Nations Statistics Division, New York, trade statistics database, last accessed January 2010.

1 Excluding trade of the countries of Eastern Europe and the former USSR.
2 Derived from price indices; national unit value index is discontinued.
3 Calculated by the United Nations Statistics Division.
4 Industrial products.

Source:
Organisation des Nations Unies, Division de statistique, New York, la base de données pour les statistiques du commerce extérieur, dernier accès janvier 2010.

1 Non compris le commerce des pays de l'Europe de l'Est et l'ex-URSS.
2 Calculés à partir des indices des prix; l'indice de la valeur unitaire nationale est discontinué.
3 Calculés par la Division de statistique des Nations Unies.
4 Produits industriels.

Technical notes: tables 58-60

Current data (annual, monthly and/or quarterly) for most of the series are published regularly by the United Nations Statistics Division in the *Monthly Bulletin of Statistics*. More detailed descriptions of the tables and notes on methodology appear in the *International Trade Statistics Yearbook*.

Data are obtained from data supplied by the governments for dissemination in United Nations publications, from national published sources and from data published by other international organisations.

Statistical Territory
The statistics reported by each country refer to its statistical territory which may coincide with its economic territory or with some part of it.

Systems of trade
There are two trade systems in common use by which international merchandise trade statistics are compiled - the general trade system and the special trade system:

(a) The general trade system is in use when the statistical territory of a country coincides with its economic territory.

(b) The special trade system (strict definition) is in use when the statistical territory comprises only the free circulation area, that is, the part within which goods may be disposed of without customs restriction. A "relaxed" definition of the special trade system is in use when (i) goods that enter a country for or leave it after inward processing and (ii) goods that enter or leave an industrial free zone are also recorded and included in international merchandise trade statistics.

Valuation
Goods are, in general, valued based on the transaction value. It is recommended that the statistical value of imported goods be a CIF-type value and the statistical value of exported goods an FOB-type value. FOB-type values include the transaction value of the goods and the value of services performed to deliver goods to the border of the exporting country. CIF-type values include the transaction value of the goods, the value of services performed to deliver goods to the border of the exporting country and the value of the services performed to deliver the goods from the border of the exporting country to the border of the importing country.

Currency conversion
Conversion of values from national currencies into United States dollars is done by means of external trade conversion factors which are generally weighted averages of exchange rates, the weight being the corresponding monthly value of imports or exports.

Notes techniques : tableaux 58 à 60

La Division de statistique des Nations Unies publie régulièrement dans le *Bulletin mensuel de statistique* des données courantes (annuelles, mensuelles et/ou trimestrielles) pour la plupart des séries de ces tableaux. Des descriptions plus détaillées des tableaux et des notes méthodologiques figurent dans l'*Annuaire statistique du Commerce international.*

Les données proviennent de publications nationales, des informations fournies par les gouvernements pour les publications des Nations Unies ainsi que des publications d'autres organisations internationales.

Territoire statistique
Les statistiques fournies par chaque pays se rapportent au territoire statistique. Celui-ci peut coïncider avec le territoire économique en totalité ou en partie.

Systèmes de commerce
Il existe deux systèmes de commerce qui servent couramment pour les statistiques du commerce international de marchandises - le système de commerce général et le système de commerce spécial:

(a) Le système de commerce général est utilisé lorsque le territoire statistique d'un pays coïncide avec son territoire économique.

(b) Le système de commerce spécial (définition stricte) est appliqué lorsque le territoire statistique ne comprend que la zone de libre circulation, c'est-à-dire la zone à l'intérieur de laquelle les biens peuvent être écoulés librement sans restriction douanière. Une définition "assouplie" du système de commerce spécial est utilisée lorsque (i) les biens qui entrent dans un pays en vue de ou le quittent après un perfectionnement actif et (ii) les biens qui entrent ou quittent une zone franche industrielle sont également enregistrés et inclus dans les statistiques du commerce international de marchandises.

Evaluation
En général, les marchandises sont évaluées à la valeur de la transaction. Il est recommandé d'adopter une valeur de type CIF pour la valeur statistique des biens importés et une valeur de type FOB pour la valeur statistique des biens exportés. Les valeurs FOB comprennent la valeur transactionnelle des biens et la valeur des services fournis pour acheminer les biens jusqu'à la frontière du pays exportateur. Les valeurs CIF comprennent la valeur transactionnelle des biens, la valeur des services fournis pour acheminer les biens jusqu'à la frontière du pays exportateur et la valeur des services fournis pour acheminer les biens de la frontière du pays exportateur jusqu'à la frontière du pays importateur.

Coverage
The statistics relate to merchandise trade. It is recommended that international merchandise trade statistics record all goods which add to or subtract from the stock of material resources of a country by entering (imports) or leaving (exports) its economic territory. Goods simply being transported through a country (goods in transit) or temporarily admitted or withdrawn (except for goods for inward or outward processing) do not add to or subtract from the stock of material resources of a country and are not included in the international merchandise trade statistics. For details and a list of inclusions and exclusions see *International Merchandise Trade Statistics, Concepts and Definitions, Revision 2.*

Commodity classification
The commodity classification of trade is in accordance with the United Nations *Standard International Trade Classification* (SITC).

World and regional totals
The regional, economic and world totals have been adjusted: (a) to include estimates for countries or areas for which full data are not available; (b) to include countries or areas not listed separately; and (c) where possible, to eliminate incomparabilities owing to geographical changes, by adjusting the figures for periods before the change to be comparable to those for periods after the change.

Volume and unit value index numbers
These index numbers show the changes in the volume of imports or exports (volume index) and the average price of imports or exports (unit value or price index).

Description of tables
Table 58: The regional totals for imports and exports have been adjusted to exclude the re-exports of countries or areas comprising each region. Estimates for certain countries or areas not shown separately as well as for those shown separately but for which no data are yet available are included in the regional and world totals.

Export and import values in terms of U.S. dollars are obtained from data published by the International Monetary Fund (IMF) in the publication *International Financial Statistics*, from the replies to the *Monthly Bulletin of Statistics* questionnaires and from national sources.

Table 59: These index numbers show the changes in the volume (quantum index) and the average price (unit value or price index) of total imports and exports.

The indices are obtained from data published by the International Monetary Fund (IMF) in the publication *International Financial Statistics*, from the replies

Conversion des monnaies
La conversion en dollars des Etats-Unis de valeurs exprimées en monnaie nationale se fait par application de coefficients de conversion du commerce extérieur, qui sont généralement les moyennes pondérées des taux de change, le poids étant la valeur mensuelle correspondante des importations ou des exportations.

Couverture
Les statistiques se rapportent au commerce des marchandises. Il est recommandé d'enregistrer dans les statistiques du commerce international de marchandises tous les biens dont l'entrée (importations) ou la sortie (exportations) du territoire économique fait augmenter ou diminuer le stock des ressources matérielles du territoire économique du pays considéré. Les biens simplement transportés à travers le pays (biens en transit) ou admis ou expédiés temporairement (à l'exception des biens destinés au perfectionnement actif ou passif) ne font ni augmenter ni diminuer le stock de ressources matérielles d'un pays et ne sont donc pas à inclure dans les statistiques du commerce international de marchandises. Pour plus de détails et une liste des inclusions et exclusions, voir *Statistiques du commerce international des marchandises : concepts et définitions, révision 2.*

Classification par marchandise
La classification par marchandise du commerce extérieur est celle adoptée dans la *Classification Type pour le Commerce International* des Nations Unies (CTCI).

Totaux mondiaux et régionaux
Les totaux économiques, régionaux et mondiaux ont été ajustés de manière: (a) à inclure les estimations pour les pays ou régions pour lesquels on ne disposait pas de données complètes; (b) à inclure les pays ou régions non indiqués séparément ; et (c) à éliminer, dans la mesure du possible, les données non comparables par suite de changements géographiques, en ajustant les chiffres correspondant aux périodes avant le changement de manière à les rendre comparables à ceux des périodes après le changement.

Indices de volume et de valeur unitaire
Ces indices indiquent les variations du volume des importations ou des exportations (indice de volume) et du prix moyen des importations ou des exportations (indice de valeur unitaire ou de prix).

Description des tableaux
Tableau 58: Les totaux régionaux des importations et des exportations ont été ajustés afin d'exclure les réexportations des pays ou zones que comprend une région donnée. Les totaux régionaux et mondiaux comprennent des estimations pour certains pays ou zones ne figurant

to the *Monthly Bulletin of Statistics* questionnaires and from national sources.

Unit value indices obtained from national indices are rebased, where necessary, so that 2000=100. Indices in national currency are converted into US dollars using conversion factors obtained by dividing the weighted average exchange rate of a given currency in the current period by the weighted average exchange rate in the base period. The terms of trade figures are calculated by dividing export unit value indices by the corresponding import unit value indices. The product of the terms of trade and the volume index of exports is called the index of the purchasing power of exports. The footnotes to countries appearing in table 58 also apply to the index numbers in this table.

Table 60: Manufactured goods are defined here to comprise sections 5 through 8 of the Standard International Trade Classification (SITC). These sections are: chemicals and related products, manufactured goods classified chiefly by material, machinery and transport equipment and miscellaneous manufactured articles.

The unit value indices are obtained from national sources including replies to the *Monthly Bulletin of Statistics* questionnaires, except those of a few countries which the United Nations Statistics Division compiles using their quantity and value figures. For countries that do not compile indices for manufactured goods exports conforming to the above definition, sub-indices are aggregated to approximate an index of SITC sections 5-8.

Unit value indices obtained from national indices are rebased, where necessary, so that 2000=100. Indices in national currency are converted into US dollars using conversion factors obtained by dividing the weighted average exchange rate of a given currency in the current period by the weighted average exchange rate in the base period. All aggregate unit value indices are current period weighted.

The indices in Special Drawing Rights (SDRs) are calculated by multiplying the equivalent aggregate indices in United States dollars by conversion factors obtained by dividing the SDR/US$ exchange rate in the current period by the rate in the base period.

The volume indices are derived from the value data and the unit value indices. All aggregate volume indices are base period weighted.

pas séparément mais pour lesquels les données ne sont pas encore disponibles.

Les valeurs en dollars des E.-U. des exportations et des importations ont été obtenues à partir des données publiées par le Fonds Monétaire International dans *Statistiques Financières Internationales,* des réponses aux questionnaires du *Bulletin Mensuel de Statistique* et des sources nationales.

Tableau 59: Ces indices indiquent les variations du volume (indice de quantum) et du prix moyen (indice de valeur unitaire ou de prix) des importations et des exportations totales.

Les indices sont obtenus à partir des données publiées par le Fonds Monétaire International dans *Statistiques Financières Internationales,* des réponses aux questionnaires du *Bulletin Mensuel de Statistique* et des sources nationales.

Les indices de valeur unitaire obtenus à partir des indices nationaux sont ajustés sur la base 2000=100. On convertit les indices en monnaie nationale en indices en dollars des Etats-Unis en utilisant des facteurs de conversion obtenus en divisant la moyenne pondérée des taux de change d'une monnaie donnée pendant la période courante par la moyenne pondérée des taux de change de la période de base. Les chiffres relatifs aux termes de l'échange se calculent en divisant les indices de valeur unitaire des exportations par les indices correspondants de valeur unitaire des importations. Le produit de la valeur des termes de l'échange et de l'indice du volume des exportations est appelé indice du pouvoir d'achat des exportations. Les notes figurant au bas du tableau 58 concernant certains pays s'appliquent également aux indices du présent tableau.

Tableau 60: Les produits manufacturés se définissent comme correspondant aux sections 5 à 8 de la Classification Type pour le Commerce International (CTCI). Ces sections sont: produits chimiques et produits liés connexes, biens manufacturés classés principalement par matière première, machines et équipements de transport et articles divers manufacturés.

Les indices de valeur unitaire sont obtenus de sources nationales y compris les réponses aux questionnaires du *Bulletin Mensuel de Statistique*, à l'exception de ceux de certains pays que la Division de statistique des Nations Unies compile en utilisant les chiffres de ces pays relatifs aux quantités et aux valeurs. Pour les pays qui n'établissent pas d'indices conformes à la définition ci-dessus pour leurs exportations de produits manufacturés, on fait la synthèse de sous-indices de manière à établir un indice proche de celui des sections 5 à 8 de la CTCI.

Le cas échéant, les indices de valeur unitaire obtenus à partir des indices nationaux sont ajustés sur la base

2000=100. On convertit les indices en monnaie nationale en indices en dollars des Etats-Unis en utilisant des facteurs de conversion obtenus en divisant la moyenne pondérée des taux de change d'une monnaie donnée pendant la période courante par la moyenne pondérée des taux de change de la période de base. Tous les indices globaux de valeur unitaire sont pondérés pour la période courante.

On calcule les indices en Droits de Tirages Spéciaux (DTS) en multipliant les indices globaux équivalents en dollars des Etats-Unis par les facteurs de conversion obtenus en divisant le taux de change DTS/dollars E.-U. de la période courante par le taux correspondant de la période de base.

On détermine les indices de volume à partir des données de valeur et des indices de valeur unitaire. Tous les indices globaux de volume sont pondérés par rapport à la période de base.

61 Tourist/visitor arrivals by region of origin

Number

Arrivées de touristes/visiteurs par région de provenance

Nombre

Country or area of destination and region of origin+	Series& Série&	2004	2005	2006	2007	2008	Pays ou zone de destination et région de provenance+
Albania	VFN						**Albanie**
Total [1]		645 409	747 837	937 038	1 126 514	1 419 191	Total [1]
Africa		174	174	220	319	317	Afrique
Americas		25 519	34 816	42 241	51 881	60 978	Amériques
East Asia/Pacific		4 288	5 444	7 592	9 674	15 419	Asie de l'Est/Pacifique
Europe		609 821	703 205	857 358	1 060 975	1 335 227	Europe
Middle East		775	837	1 068	1 262	1 209	Moyen-Orient
South Asia		410	354	376	376	484	Asie du Sud
Region not specified		4 422	3 007	28 183	2 027	5 557	Région non spécifiée
Algeria	VFN						**Algérie**
Total [2]		1 233 719	1 443 090	1 637 582	1 743 084	1 771 749	Total [2]
Africa		131 066	161 182	159 869	157 554	194 403	Afrique
Americas		6 830	8 117	9 724	10 271	10 939	Amériques
East Asia/Pacific		9 401	15 157	19 207	27 590	39 227	Asie de l'Est/Pacifique
Europe		198 230	227 618	252 553	270 881	267 552	Europe
Middle East		23 035	29 132	37 005	44 892	44 576	Moyen-Orient
Region not specified		865 157	1 001 884	1 159 224	1 231 896	1 215 052	Région non spécifiée
American Samoa	TFN						**Samoa américaines**
Total		...	24 496	25 347	...	...	Total
Africa		...	11	7	...	...	Afrique
Americas		...	6 899	7 205	...	...	Amériques
East Asia/Pacific		...	16 933	17 640	...	...	Asie de l'Est/Pacifique
Europe		...	382	358	...	...	Europe
Middle East		...	8	5	...	...	Moyen-Orient
South Asia		...	37	49	...	...	Asie du Sud
Region not specified		...	226	83	...	...	Région non spécifiée
Andorra	TFR						**Andorre**
Total		2 791 116	2 418 409	2 226 922	2 189 421	2 059 451	Total
Europe		2 791 116	2 418 409	2 226 922	2 189 421	2 059 451	Europe
Angola	TFR						**Angola**
Total		194 329	209 956	121 426	194 730	294 258	Total
Africa		41 873	43 138	18 921	33 098	38 059	Afrique
Americas		34 045	36 140	20 847	38 067	59 358	Amériques
East Asia/Pacific		16 061	15 358	15 248	28 299	59 051	Asie de l'Est/Pacifique
Europe		101 180	110 025	63 459	89 344	129 838	Europe
Middle East		1 170	3 151	896	1 639	1 842	Moyen-Orient
South Asia		...	2 144	2 055	4 283	6 110	Asie du Sud
Anguilla	TFR						**Anguilla**
Total [1]		53 987	62 084	72 962	77 652	68 284	Total [1]
Americas		44 799	52 054	61 746	63 792	57 024	Amériques
Europe		7 667	8 113	9 218	10 795	8 943	Europe
Region not specified		1 521	1 917	1 998	3 065	2 317	Région non spécifiée
Antigua and Barbuda	TFR						**Antigua-et-Barbuda**
Total [1,3]		245 797	245 384	253 669	261 802	265 844	Total [1,3]
Americas		129 316	128 287	138 547	140 823	151 785	Amériques
Europe		113 033	108 268	106 538	115 454	110 266	Europe
Region not specified		3 448	8 829	8 584	5 525	3 793	Région non spécifiée
Argentina	TFN						**Argentine**
Total [1]		3 456 526	3 822 666	4 172 533	4 561 743	4 665 359	Total [1]
Americas		2 721 888	2 983 895	3 282 925	3 608 724	3 678 220	Amériques
Europe		546 184	630 888	661 694	737 634	769 848	Europe
Region not specified		188 454	207 883	227 914	215 385	217 291	Région non spécifiée
Armenia	TFR						**Arménie**
Total		262 959	318 563	382 136	510 622	558 443	Total
Africa		184	335	396	496	643	Afrique
Americas		75 496	85 994	97 525	127 155	135 550	Amériques
East Asia/Pacific		9 355	13 592	15 557	23 005	24 365	Asie de l'Est/Pacifique
Europe		127 242	160 479	203 539	278 209	308 266	Europe
Middle East		23 131	28 182	32 621	40 849	43 800	Moyen-Orient
South Asia		27 551	29 981	32 498	40 908	45 819	Asie du Sud

61 Tourist/visitor arrivals by region of origin *(continued)*

Number

Arrivées de touristes/visiteurs par région de provenance *(suite)*

Nombre

Country or area of destination and region of origin+	Series& Série&	2004	2005	2006	2007	2008	Pays ou zone de destination et région de provenance+
Aruba	TFR						**Aruba**
Total		728 157	732 514	694 372	771 822	826 677	Total
Americas		665 489	666 454	629 925	703 367	748 922	Amériques
East Asia/Pacific		211	191	199	148	157	Asie de l'Est/Pacifique
Europe		60 428	63 181	61 993	67 446	73 772	Europe
Region not specified		2 029	2 688	2 255	861	3 826	Région non spécifiée
Australia	VFR						**Australie**
Total[4]		5 214 981	5 499 050	5 532 435	5 644 077	5 585 826	Total[4]
Africa		67 711	70 877	77 615	85 570	93 239	Afrique
Americas		561 454	584 395	611 140	628 777	644 162	Amériques
East Asia/Pacific		3 205 477	3 374 765	3 314 747	3 386 832	3 244 424	Asie de l'Est/Pacifique
Europe		1 261 477	1 330 233	1 367 738	1 355 280	1 381 169	Europe
Middle East		43 484	49 195	52 401	62 743	74 696	Moyen-Orient
South Asia		75 233	89 356	108 324	124 690	148 089	Asie du Sud
Region not specified		145	229	470	185	47	Région non spécifiée
Austria	TCER						**Autriche**
Total[5]		19 373 971	19 952 350	20 268 533	20 773 316	21 935 409	Total[5]
Africa		32 114	42 259	42 553	40 472	39 957	Afrique
Americas		673 693	691 644	780 232	755 989	672 610	Amériques
East Asia/Pacific		755 406	792 197	797 159	747 319	705 701	Asie de l'Est/Pacifique
Europe		17 466 740	18 030 663	18 264 769	18 795 014	19 993 474	Europe
Middle East		43 203	67 833	75 217	91 354	102 099	Moyen-Orient
South Asia		39 882	39 204	49 684	46 210	46 990	Asie du Sud
Region not specified		362 933	288 550	258 919	296 958	374 578	Région non spécifiée
Azerbaijan	VFR						**Azerbaïdjan**
Total		1 348 655	1 177 277	1 193 742	1 332 701	1 898 936	Total
Africa		661	544	807	835	1 630	Afrique
Americas		12 358	11 272	10 133	11 021	17 329	Amériques
East Asia/Pacific		6 051	6 825	7 205	8 391	16 190	Asie de l'Est/Pacifique
Europe		1 050 943	945 662	1 007 670	1 104 267	1 541 306	Europe
Middle East		2 143	1 942	1 888	1 854	3 716	Moyen-Orient
South Asia		275 147	211 032	165 144	205 242	316 514	Asie du Sud
Region not specified		1 352	...	895	1 091	2 251	Région non spécifiée
Bahamas	TFR						**Bahamas**
Total		1 561 312	1 608 153	1 600 862	1 527 727	1 463 006	Total
Africa		1 443	1 556	1 685	1 812	1 785	Afrique
Americas		1 455 375	1 484 921	1 485 158	1 404 000	1 331 022	Amériques
East Asia/Pacific		6 913	7 215	6 996	6 861	6 902	Asie de l'Est/Pacifique
Europe		84 126	85 874	82 824	87 931	94 560	Europe
Middle East		618	539	604	644	670	Moyen-Orient
South Asia		352	345	524	580	696	Asie du Sud
Region not specified		12 485	27 703	23 071	25 899	27 371	Région non spécifiée
Bahrain	VFN						**Bahreïn**
Total[1]		5 667 331	6 313 232	7 288 716	7 833 609	...	Total[1]
Africa		76 325	82 121	98 749	109 114	...	Afrique
Americas		200 481	189 778	234 467	267 496	...	Amériques
East Asia/Pacific		267 978	287 257	374 335	390 262	...	Asie de l'Est/Pacifique
Europe		333 920	357 623	429 750	506 891	...	Europe
Middle East		4 140 624	4 676 446	5 209 825	5 451 041	...	Moyen-Orient
South Asia		648 003	720 007	941 590	1 108 805	...	Asie du Sud
Bangladesh	TFN						**Bangladesh**
Total		271 270	207 662	200 311	289 110	...	Total
Africa		2 147	1 730	1 953	2 001	...	Afrique
Americas		37 404	18 673	25 129	45 706	...	Amériques
East Asia/Pacific		51 230	35 887	37 032	57 135	...	Asie de l'Est/Pacifique
Europe		77 307	48 961	56 709	77 345	...	Europe
Middle East		3 243	2 861	4 021	4 530	...	Moyen-Orient
South Asia		99 939	99 458	75 467	102 393	...	Asie du Sud
Region not specified		...	92	...	...	...	Région non spécifiée

61 Tourist/visitor arrivals by region of origin *(continued)*
Number
Arrivées de touristes/visiteurs par région de provenance *(suite)*
Nombre

Country or area of destination and region of origin+	Series& Série&	2004	2005	2006	2007	2008	Pays ou zone de destination et région de provenance+
Barbados	TFR						**Barbade**
Total		551 502	547 534	562 558	574 533	567 667	Total
Africa		753	1 117	988	3 331	1 389	Afrique
Americas		301 268	311 222	312 317	303 404	309 043	Amériques
East Asia/Pacific		2 679	2 710	2 758	10 450	4 147	Asie de l'Est/Pacifique
Europe		245 919	230 167	241 141	250 924	250 022	Europe
Middle East		145	154	230	481	337	Moyen-Orient
South Asia		627	756	784	3 538	1 113	Asie du Sud
Region not specified		111	1 408	4 340	2 405	1 616	Région non spécifiée
Belarus	TFN						**Bélarus**
Total[6]		67 297	90 588	89 101	104 890	91 232	Total[6]
Africa		47	399	148	499	73	Afrique
Americas		5 892	4 663	4 292	5 587	1 401	Amériques
East Asia/Pacific		2 150	1 860	1 815	2 386	1 054	Asie de l'Est/Pacifique
Europe		58 524	82 247	80 956	95 003	87 752	Europe
Middle East		415	825	1 318	818	473	Moyen-Orient
South Asia		269	594	572	597	479	Asie du Sud
Belgium	TCER						**Belgique**
Total[7]		6 709 740	6 747 123	6 994 819	7 044 719	7 164 765	Total[7]
Africa		60 872	62 455	65 438	62 449	63 250	Afrique
Americas		382 249	390 160	407 403	420 845	399 047	Amériques
East Asia/Pacific		318 231	298 360	304 773	301 959	267 943	Asie de l'Est/Pacifique
Europe		5 800 440	5 835 628	6 035 866	6 061 187	6 187 002	Europe
Middle East		17 664	19 793	20 978	20 284	22 067	Moyen-Orient
South Asia		33 152	34 844	32 673	43 785	64 480	Asie du Sud
Region not specified		97 132	105 883	127 688	134 210	160 976	Région non spécifiée
Belize	TFN						**Belize**
Total[2]		230 835	236 573	247 309	251 422	245 026	Total[2]
Africa		349	348	359	491	512	Afrique
Americas		185 254	190 301	199 315	201 679	195 645	Amériques
East Asia/Pacific		4 285	4 384	4 516	5 482	5 234	Asie de l'Est/Pacifique
Europe		32 768	33 466	34 373	34 175	34 269	Europe
Middle East		481	369	381	435	588	Moyen-Orient
Region not specified		7 698	7 705	8 365	9 160	8 778	Région non spécifiée
Benin	TFR						**Bénin**
Total *		173 500	176 000	180 006	186 394	188 000	Total *
Africa		147 536	140 185	152 000	153 016	117 929	Afrique
Americas		360	500	972	2 299	3 926	Amériques
East Asia/Pacific		261	321	633	780	1 633	Asie de l'Est/Pacifique
Europe		25 157	31 500	22 257	26 283	50 706	Europe
Middle East		61	518	644	1 762	291	Moyen-Orient
South Asia		125	2 956	3 500	2 254	691	Asie du Sud
Region not specified		...	20	...	...	12 824	Région non spécifiée
Bermuda	TFR						**Bermudes**
Total[3]		271 620	269 591	298 973	305 548	263 613	Total[3]
Americas		235 546	232 661	255 400	257 342	216 595	Amériques
East Asia/Pacific		834	639	647	714	795	Asie de l'Est/Pacifique
Europe		25 873	26 678	32 347	35 938	35 003	Europe
Region not specified		9 367	9 613	10 579	11 554	11 220	Région non spécifiée
Bhutan	TFN						**Bhoutan**
Total		9 249	13 626	17 348	21 094	27 642	Total
Africa		14	45	88	65	77	Afrique
Americas		3 607	5 168	5 627	6 653	8 240	Amériques
East Asia/Pacific		1 680	2 759	4 317	5 393	7 412	Asie de l'Est/Pacifique
Europe		3 905	5 619	7 267	8 929	11 778	Europe
Middle East		...	7	12	15	29	Moyen-Orient
South Asia		19	17	30	39	106	Asie du Sud
Region not specified		24	11	7	...	...	Région non spécifiée

61 Tourist/visitor arrivals by region of origin *(continued)*
Number
Arrivées de touristes/visiteurs par région de provenance *(suite)*
Nombre

Country or area of destination and region of origin+	Series& Série&	2004	2005	2006	2007	2008	Pays ou zone de destination et région de provenance+
Bolivia (Plur. State of)	THSN						**Bolivie (État plur. de)**
Total[8]		390 888	413 267	496 489	...	...	Total[8]
Africa		1 278	1 661	1 484	...	...	Afrique
Americas		227 280	250 107	300 893	...	...	Amériques
East Asia/Pacific		18 917	19 878	26 999	...	...	Asie de l'Est/Pacifique
Europe		143 413	141 621	167 113	...	...	Europe
Bonaire	TFR						**Bonaire**
Total		63 156	62 550	63 552	74 309	74 342	Total
Americas		34 576	32 244	35 093	42 191	43 112	Amériques
Europe		27 973	30 066	28 202	31 427	30 768	Europe
Region not specified		607	240	257	691	462	Région non spécifiée
Bosnia and Herzegovina	TCER						**Bosnie-Herzégovine**
Total		190 300	217 273	255 764	306 452	321 511	Total
Americas		8 442	8 030	10 195	10 341	8 862	Amériques
East Asia/Pacific		2 177	2 355	2 869	4 399	5 348	Asie de l'Est/Pacifique
Europe		176 588	203 564	238 976	286 280	300 672	Europe
Middle East		132	46	175	252	330	Moyen-Orient
South Asia		116	265	51	233	151	Asie du Sud
Region not specified		2 845	3 013	3 498	4 947	6 148	Région non spécifiée
Botswana	TFR						**Botswana**
Total *		1 522 807	...	1 425 994	1 455 151	...	Total *
Africa		1 353 125	...	1 239 719	1 297 231	...	Afrique
Americas		21 023	...	24 866	29 089	...	Amériques
East Asia/Pacific		11 848	...	15 252	15 063	...	Asie de l'Est/Pacifique
Europe		58 432	...	67 205	67 559	...	Europe
Middle East		...	...	10	...	...	Moyen-Orient
South Asia		2 223	...	3 772	2 080	...	Asie du Sud
Region not specified		76 156	...	75 170	44 129	...	Région non spécifiée
Brazil	TFR						**Brésil**
Total		4 793 703	5 358 170	5 017 251	5 025 834	5 050 099	Total
Africa		64 678	75 676	83 721	75 435	75 824	Afrique
Americas		2 703 442	2 998 060	2 717 273	2 779 164	2 883 839	Amériques
East Asia/Pacific		155 605	177 381	216 976	205 730	256 271	Asie de l'Est/Pacifique
Europe		1 860 259	2 097 357	1 979 817	1 938 165	1 814 146	Europe
Middle East		6 064	7 002	18 172	25 967	...	Moyen-Orient
South Asia		...	...	...	...	19 456	Asie du Sud
Region not specified		3 655	2 694	1 292	1 373	563	Région non spécifiée
British Virgin Islands	VFR						**Iles Vierges britanniques**
Total		812 908	820 766	...	...	...	Total
Americas		598 633	600 732	...	...	...	Amériques
Europe		199 790	203 004	...	...	...	Europe
Region not specified		14 485	17 030	...	...	...	Région non spécifiée
Brunei Darussalam	TFN						**Brunéi Darussalam**
Total[3]		119 000	126 217	158 095	178 540	225 757	Total[3]
Americas		2 000	3 313	3 943	5 116	5 652	Amériques
East Asia/Pacific		11 000	75 781	100 160	144 488	186 475	Asie de l'Est/Pacifique
Europe		14 000	14 428	20 847	20 796	22 765	Europe
Middle East		...	210	654	574	...	Moyen-Orient
South Asia		...	...	...	5 195	5 317	Asie du Sud
Region not specified		92 000	32 485	32 491	2 371	5 548	Région non spécifiée
Bulgaria	VFR						**Bulgarie**
Total		6 981 597	7 282 455	7 499 117	7 725 747	8 532 972	Total
Africa		2 937	2 774	2 668	1 734	...	Afrique
Americas		67 605	76 514	85 158	89 790	85 723	Amériques
East Asia/Pacific		32 067	35 127	38 186	43 563	...	Asie de l'Est/Pacifique
Europe		6 806 650	7 087 954	7 286 509	7 371 761	8 144 199	Europe
Middle East		16 124	17 569	14 284	18 823	...	Moyen-Orient
South Asia		12 199	11 396	13 267	15 000	...	Asie du Sud
Region not specified		44 015	51 121	59 045	185 076	303 050	Région non spécifiée

61 Tourist/visitor arrivals by region of origin *(continued)*
Number
Arrivées de touristes/visiteurs par région de provenance *(suite)*
Nombre

Country or area of destination and region of origin+	Series& Série&	2004	2005	2006	2007	2008	Pays ou zone de destination et région de provenance+
Burkina Faso	THSN						**Burkina Faso**
Total [2]		222 201	244 728	263 978	288 965	225 651	Total [2]
Africa		96 385	100 674	108 019	121 174	93 169	Afrique
Americas		12 991	14 724	15 814	20 473	14 817	Amériques
East Asia/Pacific		4 550	6 582	6 387	11 563	5 038	Asie de l'Est/Pacifique
Europe		99 742	113 496	123 426	126 544	103 537	Europe
Middle East		1 982	2 220	2 022	2 066	1 682	Moyen-Orient
Region not specified		6 551	7 032	8 310	7 145	7 408	Région non spécifiée
Burundi	TFN						**Burundi**
Total [9]		133 228	148 418	201 241	...	...	Total [9]
Africa		1 333	49 473	140 868	...	...	Afrique
Americas		5 908	9 956	4 025	...	...	Amériques
East Asia/Pacific		4 528	4 023	10 062	...	...	Asie de l'Est/Pacifique
Europe		29 409	29 486	32 199	...	...	Europe
Region not specified		92 050	55 480	14 087	...	...	Région non spécifiée
Cambodia	TFR						**Cambodge**
Total		987 359	1 333 000	1 591 350	1 872 567	2 001 434	Total
Africa		...	...	...	3 270	4 040	Afrique
Americas		122 169	152 328	159 429	194 706	204 878	Amériques
East Asia/Pacific		589 230	786 506	1 022 181	1 241 882	1 312 218	Asie de l'Est/Pacifique
Europe		242 811	310 006	314 194	417 096	463 602	Europe
Middle East		...	...	...	1 059	947	Moyen-Orient
South Asia		7 132	7 516	9 245	14 554	15 749	Asie du Sud
Region not specified		26 017	76 644	86 301	...	...	Région non spécifiée
Cameroon	THSN						**Cameroun**
Total		189 856	176 372	184 549	...	...	Total
Africa		80 013	88 739	97 596	...	...	Afrique
Americas		11 593	10 002	8 999	...	...	Amériques
East Asia/Pacific		4 248	4 580	5 042	...	...	Asie de l'Est/Pacifique
Europe		83 272	68 058	62 668	...	...	Europe
Middle East		4 583	2 007	3 501	...	...	Moyen-Orient
Region not specified		6 147	2 986	6 743	...	...	Région non spécifiée
Canada	TFR						**Canada**
Total		19 144 810	18 770 552	18 265 406	17 934 881	17 142 102	Total
Africa		58 210	61 842	72 388	75 525	79 927	Afrique
Americas		15 518 243	14 867 460	14 372 551	13 946 446	13 111 691	Amériques
East Asia/Pacific		1 221 081	1 282 007	1 282 472	1 266 536	1 230 626	Asie de l'Est/Pacifique
Europe		2 202 397	2 397 419	2 359 997	2 443 093	2 497 509	Europe
Middle East		47 637	52 131	59 270	67 512	77 272	Moyen-Orient
South Asia		96 342	109 693	118 728	135 769	145 077	Asie du Sud
Cape Verde	THSR						**Cap-Vert**
Total		157 052	197 844	241 742	267 188	285 141	Total
Africa		10 034	9 432	4 659	307	193	Afrique
Americas		1 472	2 102	5 949	4 932	4 004	Amériques
Europe		136 304	173 318	207 964	228 165	234 309	Europe
Region not specified		9 242	12 992	23 170	33 784	46 635	Région non spécifiée
Cayman Islands	TFR						**Iles Caïmanes**
Total [3]		259 929	167 802	267 257	291 503	302 879	Total [3]
Africa		321	325	435	530	538	Afrique
Americas		242 012	152 735	247 420	268 141	278 584	Amériques
East Asia/Pacific		1 216	1 129	1 370	1 720	1 626	Asie de l'Est/Pacifique
Europe		15 938	13 221	17 516	20 432	21 419	Europe
Middle East		72	24	53	116	99	Moyen-Orient
South Asia		176	97	158	158	214	Asie du Sud
Region not specified		194	271	305	406	399	Région non spécifiée

Tourist/visitor arrivals by region of origin *(continued)*
Number

Arrivées de touristes/visiteurs par région de provenance *(suite)*
Nombre

Country or area of destination and region of origin+	Series& Série&	2004	2005	2006	2007	2008	Pays ou zone de destination et région de provenance+
Central African Rep.	TFN						**Rép. centrafricaine**
Total [3]		8 156	11 969	*13 764	17 117	30 611	Total [3]
Africa		3 501	6 156	7 079	8 306	16 038	Afrique
Americas		449	639	735	944	1 300	Amériques
East Asia/Pacific		317	373	429	529	2 174	Asie de l'Est/Pacifique
Europe		3 674	4 349	5 001	6 708	10 559	Europe
Middle East		192	397	457	560	448	Moyen-Orient
Region not specified		23	55	63	70	92	Région non spécifiée
Chad	THSN						**Tchad**
Total		25 899	29 356	15 863	24 794	...	Total
Africa		5 855	6 695	4 226	6 365	...	Afrique
Americas		5 609	5 976	2 316	5 002	...	Amériques
East Asia/Pacific		398	550	490	1 427	...	Asie de l'Est/Pacifique
Europe		12 690	14 805	8 723	11 250	...	Europe
Middle East		1 347	1 330	108	750	...	Moyen-Orient
Chile	TFN						**Chili**
Total		1 785 024	2 027 082	2 252 952	2 506 756	2 698 659	Total
Africa		3 653	3 544	4 150	4 286	5 080	Afrique
Americas		1 360 342	1 553 381	1 754 599	1 967 792	2 154 437	Amériques
East Asia/Pacific		69 883	74 927	83 683	90 673	87 960	Asie de l'Est/Pacifique
Europe		344 774	384 886	401 775	436 770	446 575	Europe
Middle East		812	682	2 015	1 297	504	Moyen-Orient
South Asia		3 605	4 257	4 100	4 410	3 957	Asie du Sud
Region not specified		1 955	5 405	2 630	1 528	146	Région non spécifiée
China [10]	VFN						**Chine** [10]
Total		109 038 218	120 292 255	124 942 096	131 873 287	130 027 393	Total
Africa		154 223	210 533	255 288	327 142	323 921	Afrique
Americas		1 789 500	2 145 758	2 405 829	2 721 034	2 581 855	Amériques
East Asia/Pacific		102 393 763	112 053 459	115 700 406	120 956 213	119 584 350	Asie de l'Est/Pacifique
Europe		4 096 999	5 165 588	5 769 346	6 936 600	6 688 442	Europe
Middle East		84 376	110 966	136 429	179 771	178 131	Moyen-Orient
South Asia		514 163	599 435	670 505	749 103	668 806	Asie du Sud
Region not specified		5 194	6 516	4 293	3 424	1 888	Région non spécifiée
China, Hong Kong SAR	TFR						**Chine, Hong Kong RAS**
Total		13 655 100	14 773 200	15 821 400	17 153 900	17 319 400	Total
Africa		91 100	116 600	123 400	126 500	119 000	Afrique
Americas		1 091 600	1 196 700	1 229 500	1 330 100	1 231 800	Amériques
East Asia/Pacific		11 368 600	12 124 500	12 989 900	14 022 400	14 311 900	Asie de l'Est/Pacifique
Europe		888 700	1 083 900	1 198 700	1 368 600	1 325 700	Europe
Middle East		55 600	71 000	88 100	101 600	99 500	Moyen-Orient
South Asia		159 500	180 500	191 800	204 700	231 500	Asie du Sud
China, Macao SAR	VFN						**Chine, Macao RAS**
Total [11,12]		16 672 556	18 711 187	21 998 580	26 992 995	22 907 724	Total [11,12]
Africa		6 042	8 082	13 693	30 049	21 820	Afrique
Americas		147 953	182 830	218 728	306 510	312 914	Amériques
East Asia/Pacific		16 361 807	18 321 056	21 525 911	26 325 474	22 197 796	Asie de l'Est/Pacifique
Europe		128 887	161 204	188 196	252 322	265 916	Europe
Middle East		1 905	2 679	3 747	7 276	7 009	Moyen-Orient
South Asia		23 771	32 335	42 604	64 532	94 723	Asie du Sud
Region not specified		2 191	3 001	5 701	6 832	7 546	Région non spécifiée
Colombia	VFN						**Colombie**
Total [13]		790 940	933 243	1 053 348	1 195 443	1 222 966	Total [13]
Africa		935	1 380	1 703	3 929	1 969	Afrique
Americas		617 896	730 495	826 746	943 562	969 075	Amériques
East Asia/Pacific		13 294	15 395	17 118	24 427	21 228	Asie de l'Est/Pacifique
Europe		155 657	182 822	204 533	219 810	226 803	Europe
Middle East		1 399	1 167	1 349	1 339	1 188	Moyen-Orient
South Asia		1 404	1 618	1 819	2 292	2 492	Asie du Sud
Region not specified		355	366	80	84	211	Région non spécifiée

61 Tourist/visitor arrivals by region of origin *(continued)*

Number

Arrivées de touristes/visiteurs par région de provenance *(suite)*

Nombre

Country or area of destination and region of origin+	Series& Série&	2004	2005	2006	2007	2008	Pays ou zone de destination et région de provenance+
Comoros	TFN						**Comores**
Total[3]		17 603	19 551	17 060	14 582	...	Total[3]
Africa		6 344	8 793	6 123	4 241	...	Afrique
Americas		162	83	358	420	...	Amériques
East Asia/Pacific		165	543	582	382	...	Asie de l'Est/Pacifique
Europe		10 562	9 625	9 470	9 450	...	Europe
Region not specified		370	507	527	89	...	Région non spécifiée
Congo	THSR						**Congo**
Total		31 286	34 690	43 317	...	...	Total
Africa		11 951	13 201	20 159	...	...	Afrique
Americas		1 177	1 537	1 394	...	...	Amériques
Europe		11 365	12 545	14 198	...	...	Europe
Region not specified		6 793	7 407	7 566	...	...	Région non spécifiée
Cook Islands	TFR						**Iles Cook**
Total[14]		83 333	88 405	92 328	97 316	94 720	Total[14]
Americas		8 445	6 463	7 681	6 958	5 676	Amériques
East Asia/Pacific		53 962	63 319	66 039	74 583	75 198	Asie de l'Est/Pacifique
Europe		20 410	18 162	18 109	15 350	13 454	Europe
Region not specified		516	461	499	425	392	Région non spécifiée
Costa Rica	TFN						**Costa Rica**
Total		1 452 926	1 679 051	1 725 261	1 979 789	2 089 174	Total
Africa		1 194	1 164	1 204	1 621	1 852	Afrique
Americas		1 213 784	1 411 640	1 456 947	1 670 551	1 754 547	Amériques
East Asia/Pacific		16 043	23 687	23 425	25 730	28 197	Asie de l'Est/Pacifique
Europe		215 072	241 751	243 100	281 515	299 798	Europe
Region not specified		6 833	809	585	372	4 780	Région non spécifiée
Croatia	TCER						**Croatie**
Total[15]		7 911 874	8 466 886	8 658 876	9 306 691	9 415 105	Total[15]
Africa		...	...	...	12 494	11 905	Afrique
Americas		119 485	140 031	182 916	242 026	223 467	Amériques
East Asia/Pacific		58 370	83 273	132 824	212 482	280 281	Asie de l'Est/Pacifique
Europe		7 692 506	8 192 055	8 281 634	8 839 689	8 899 452	Europe
Region not specified		41 513	51 527	61 502	...	...	Région non spécifiée
Cuba	VFR						**Cuba**
Total		2 048 572	2 319 324	2 220 558	2 152 221	2 348 340	Total
Africa		5 868	6 619	6 636	6 611	7 346	Afrique
Americas		1 025 756	1 215 857	1 149 135	1 172 933	1 380 232	Amériques
East Asia/Pacific		33 861	41 858	43 819	42 311	44 225	Asie de l'Est/Pacifique
Europe		976 727	1 047 659	1 013 264	924 025	909 086	Europe
Middle East		1 517	1 622	1 643	1 734	1 981	Moyen-Orient
South Asia		4 176	5 149	5 248	4 021	5 156	Asie du Sud
Region not specified		667	560	813	586	314	Région non spécifiée
Curaçao	TFR						**Curaçao**
Total[3]		223 439	222 061	234 400	299 730	408 942	Total[3]
Americas		128 873	123 353	126 522	174 261	264 986	Amériques
Europe		89 752	94 957	104 248	121 383	136 747	Europe
Region not specified		4 814	3 751	3 630	4 086	7 209	Région non spécifiée
Cyprus	TFR						**Chypre**
Total		2 349 012	2 470 063	2 400 924	2 416 081	2 403 750	Total
Africa		4 936	7 097	6 641	7 139	7 535	Afrique
Americas		22 924	28 984	26 353	30 352	27 777	Amériques
East Asia/Pacific		13 042	15 043	16 262	16 548	16 567	Asie de l'Est/Pacifique
Europe		2 263 145	2 375 402	2 307 885	2 304 366	2 299 530	Europe
Middle East		41 379	40 233	39 291	50 896	48 280	Moyen-Orient
South Asia		1 992	2 777	3 808	6 432	3 751	Asie du Sud
Region not specified		1 594	527	684	348	310	Région non spécifiée
Czech Republic	TCEN						**République tchèque**
Total		6 061 225	6 336 128	6 435 474	6 679 704	6 649 410	Total
Africa		15 394	18 539	19 411	19 520	22 934	Afrique
Americas		380 056	400 840	435 280	441 493	434 061	Amériques
East Asia/Pacific		351 652	420 989	492 842	503 899	501 793	Asie de l'Est/Pacifique
Europe		5 314 123	5 495 760	5 487 941	5 714 792	5 690 622	Europe

Country or area of destination and region of origin+	Series& Série&	2004	2005	2006	2007	2008	Pays ou zone de destination et région de provenance+
Dem. Rep. of the Congo	TFN						**Rép. dém. du Congo**
Total		36 238[3]	61 007	55 148	47 492[3]	49 971[3]	Total
Africa		14 531	36 489	33 089	27 767	27 969	Afrique
Americas		4 592	3 824	3 309	2 933	3 665	Amériques
East Asia/Pacific		3 998	5 943	5 515	5 478	5 233	Asie de l'Est/Pacifique
Europe		13 117	14 751	13 235	11 314	13 104	Europe
Denmark	TCER						**Danemark**
Total		4 421 442[16]	4 698 668	4 742 144[16]	4 770 311	4 502 912	Total
Americas		126 276	147 289	159 593	140 200	142 276	Amériques
East Asia/Pacific		82 957	110 098	109 878	102 544	93 637	Asie de l'Est/Pacifique
Europe		4 065 043	4 357 752	4 351 490	4 403 961	4 186 746	Europe
Region not specified		147 166	83 529	121 183	123 606	80 253	Région non spécifiée
Dominica	TFR						**Dominique**
Total		80 087	79 257	84 041	81 086	...	Total
Americas		69 115	68 164	71 832	69 429	...	Amériques
East Asia/Pacific		387	529	495	514	...	Asie de l'Est/Pacifique
Europe		10 208	10 258	11 303	10 784	...	Europe
Region not specified		377	306	411	359	...	Région non spécifiée
Dominican Republic	TFR						**Rép. dominicaine**
Total[2,3]		3 450 180	3 690 692	3 965 055	3 979 582	3 979 672	Total[2,3]
Americas		1 597 342	1 711 341	1 947 796	2 046 288	2 127 963	Amériques
East Asia/Pacific		3 511	4 280	4 631	7 672	7 624	Asie de l'Est/Pacifique
Europe		1 271 299	1 371 663	1 388 757	1 343 209	1 310 611	Europe
South Asia		249	337	279	663	754	Asie du Sud
Region not specified		577 779	603 071	623 592	581 750	532 720	Région non spécifiée
Ecuador	VFN						**Equateur**
Total[1]		818 927	859 888	840 555	937 487	1 005 297	Total[1]
Africa		2 191	1 919	1 240	1 360	1 560	Afrique
Americas		662 019	690 743	642 075	729 610	753 266	Amériques
East Asia/Pacific		18 075	17 891	18 212	23 828	34 134	Asie de l'Est/Pacifique
Europe		133 868	146 677	144 856	179 700	198 177	Europe
Middle East		551	444	279	302	443	Moyen-Orient
South Asia		2 223	1 747	823	1 093	1 666	Asie du Sud
Region not specified		...	467	33 070	1 594	16 051	Région non spécifiée
Egypt	VFN						**Egypte**
Total[1]		8 103 609	8 607 807	9 082 777	11 090 863	12 835 351	Total[1]
Africa		244 662	263 847	301 866	387 221	400 979	Afrique
Americas		257 418	297 675	340 530	429 863	486 099	Amériques
East Asia/Pacific		296 189	411 048	389 304	526 196	494 891	Asie de l'Est/Pacifique
Europe		5 919 575	6 047 194	6 259 732	7 936 508	9 621 738	Europe
Middle East		1 317 883	1 511 285	1 706 423	1 686 953	1 675 960	Moyen-Orient
South Asia		63 310	73 000	80 501	105 874	116 199	Asie du Sud
Region not specified		4 572	3 758	4 421	18 248	39 485	Région non spécifiée
El Salvador	TFN						**El Salvador**
Total		950 745	1 127 141	1 278 927	1 338 543	1 384 773	Total
Africa		580	624	753	569	172	Afrique
Americas		908 148	1 086 016	1 239 978	1 285 051	1 342 824	Amériques
East Asia/Pacific		9 408	9 716	9 677	11 699	8 556	Asie de l'Est/Pacifique
Europe		32 597	30 759	28 503	41 190	33 198	Europe
Middle East		12	26	16	34	23	Moyen-Orient
Eritrea	VFN						**Erythrée**
Total[2]		87 298	83 307	78 451	80 503	69 897	Total[2]
Africa		4 503	3 182	3 645	5 051	4 929	Afrique
Americas		2 559	2 263	1 474	983	858	Amériques
East Asia/Pacific		2 484	2 267	2 275	1 935	1 824	Asie de l'Est/Pacifique
Europe		10 142	8 364	5 983	5 408	5 182	Europe
Middle East		4 196	3 862	3 241	2 249	1 494	Moyen-Orient
South Asia		2 420	2 985	2 895	2 973	395	Asie du Sud
Region not specified		60 994	60 384	58 938	61 904	55 215	Région non spécifiée

61 Tourist/visitor arrivals by region of origin *(continued)*
Number

Arrivées de touristes/visiteurs par région de provenance *(suite)*
Nombre

Country or area of destination and region of origin+	Series& Série&	2004	2005	2006	2007	2008	Pays ou zone de destination et région de provenance+
Estonia	TCER						**Estonie**
Total		1 374 414	1 453 418	1 427 583	1 380 323	1 433 346	Total
Africa		641	1 033	723	1 013	1 152	Afrique
Americas		23 448	24 037	24 359	27 787	24 990	Amériques
East Asia/Pacific		13 456	15 130	17 663	17 101	18 164	Asie de l'Est/Pacifique
Europe		1 333 979	1 411 062	1 382 143	1 332 798	1 388 201	Europe
Region not specified		2 890	2 156	2 695	1 624	839	Région non spécifiée
Ethiopia	TFR						**Ethiopie**
Total[9,17]		184 079	227 398	290 458	311 947	330 157	Total[9,17]
Africa		64 304	82 436	89 923	91 674	115 999	Afrique
Americas		33 895	41 380	61 353	68 289	59 240	Amériques
East Asia/Pacific		10 319	13 243	20 058	26 341	23 141	Asie de l'Est/Pacifique
Europe		52 123	62 295	76 466	88 666	95 354	Europe
Middle East		18 184	19 936	30 556	27 537	25 228	Moyen-Orient
South Asia		5 216	8 108	7 975	9 440	11 195	Asie du Sud
Region not specified		38	...	4 127	...	...	Région non spécifiée
Fiji	TFR						**Fidji**
Total[1]		504 075	545 145	548 589	539 881	585 031	Total[1]
Americas		77 646	75 265	81 003	81 679	81 538	Amériques
East Asia/Pacific		352 743	388 910	393 994	387 941	430 808	Asie de l'Est/Pacifique
Europe		70 388	69 595	65 040	61 096	63 447	Europe
Region not specified		3 298	11 375	8 552	9 165	9 238	Région non spécifiée
Finland	TCER						**Finlande**
Total		2 083 487[18]	2 080 194	2 316 967	2 472 449	2 494 334	Total
Africa		3 301	4 235	5 236	5 340	4 988	Afrique
Americas		111 245	105 992	110 530	117 098	107 107	Amériques
East Asia/Pacific		167 808	158 128	188 447	193 835	177 552	Asie de l'Est/Pacifique
Europe		1 698 936	1 712 228	1 884 448	2 017 072	2 056 016	Europe
Middle East		3 168	3 613	3 824	3 316	3 866	Moyen-Orient
South Asia		5 965	7 445	10 707	15 651	18 910	Asie du Sud
Region not specified		93 064	88 553	113 775	120 137	125 895	Région non spécifiée
France	TFR						**France**
Total[19]		74 433 000	74 988 000	77 916 000	80 851 000	79 220 000	Total[19]
Africa		1 597 000	1 421 000	1 434 000	1 576 000	1 765 000	Afrique
Americas		4 785 000	4 950 000	5 406 000	6 023 000	5 963 000	Amériques
East Asia/Pacific		2 697 000	2 827 000	3 139 000	3 206 000	3 484 000	Asie de l'Est/Pacifique
Europe		64 789 000	65 217 000	67 393 000	69 271 000	67 305 000	Europe
Middle East		565 000	573 000	544 000	775 000	703 000	Moyen-Orient
French Guiana	TFR						**Guyane française**
Total		...	94 920	...	108 801	...	Total
Americas		...	25 439	...	37 101	...	Amériques
Europe		...	63 501	...	67 130	...	Europe
Region not specified		...	5 980	...	4 570	...	Région non spécifiée
French Polynesia	TFR						**Polynésie française**
Total[1,3]		211 828	208 045	221 549	218 241	196 496	Total[1,3]
Africa		257	235	255	764	338	Afrique
Americas		86 032	80 067	88 991	81 445	70 506	Amériques
East Asia/Pacific		45 083	45 655	48 344	50 260	42 386	Asie de l'Est/Pacifique
Europe		79 944	81 643	82 580	85 205	82 838	Europe
Middle East		172	165	226	343	182	Moyen-Orient
South Asia		75	69	116	224	246	Asie du Sud
Region not specified		265	211	1 037	...	...	Région non spécifiée
Gambia	TFN						**Gambie**
Total[2,20]		90 095	107 904	124 800	142 626	146 759	Total[2,20]
Africa		282	2 896	3 961	3 247	2 568	Afrique
Americas		3 248	1 387	2 189	1 639	1 786	Amériques
East Asia/Pacific		...	181	153	147	74	Asie de l'Est/Pacifique
Europe		84 267	92 763	101 493	121 038	123 313	Europe
Region not specified		2 298	10 677	17 004	16 555	19 018	Région non spécifiée

Country or area of destination and region of origin+	Series& Série&	2004	2005	2006	2007	2008	Pays ou zone de destination et région de provenance+
Georgia	VFR						**Géorgie**
Total		368 312	560 021	983 114	1 051 769	1 290 107	Total
Africa		788	429	755	874	635	Afrique
Americas		11 209	14 842	19 417	16 861	17 489	Amériques
East Asia/Pacific		4 952	3 246	13 754	9 424	9 464	Asie de l'Est/Pacifique
Europe		342 596	533 129	935 747	1 009 669	1 243 783	Europe
Middle East		1 563	973	2 105	2 490	3 245	Moyen-Orient
South Asia		6 635	6 641	9 977	10 873	13 457	Asie du Sud
Region not specified		569	761	1 359	1 578	2 034	Région non spécifiée
Germany	TCER						**Allemagne**
Total		20 136 979	21 500 067	23 569 145	24 420 672	24 884 017	Total
Africa		146 454	144 391	167 005	163 564	159 670	Afrique
Americas		2 337 209	2 397 527	2 782 911	2 705 989	2 572 554	Amériques
East Asia/Pacific		1 931 265	2 000 752	2 176 143	2 104 663	1 990 945	Asie de l'Est/Pacifique
Europe		14 918 028	16 099 891	17 504 005	18 423 468	19 095 571	Europe
Middle East		160 110	185 497	202 369	222 556	241 786	Moyen-Orient
Region not specified		643 913	672 009	736 712	800 432	823 491	Région non spécifiée
Ghana	TFN						**Ghana**
Total[2]		583 819	428 533	497 129	...	...	Total[2]
Africa		198 638	172 913	140 066	...	...	Afrique
Americas		49 031	62 572	73 858	...	...	Amériques
East Asia/Pacific		28 081	11 186	7 917	...	...	Asie de l'Est/Pacifique
Europe		144 724	100 509	95 728	...	...	Europe
Middle East		4 428	10 632	9 602	...	...	Moyen-Orient
South Asia		...	10 900	14 132	...	...	Asie du Sud
Region not specified		158 917	59 821	155 826	...	...	Région non spécifiée
Greece	TFN						**Grèce**
Total[21]		13 312 629	14 765 463	16 039 216	16 165 265	15 938 806	Total[21]
Africa		23 073	22 961	30 296	46 325	44 569	Afrique
Americas		236 274	416 746	513 402	842 815	849 014	Amériques
East Asia/Pacific		226 973	253 686	315 691	230 309	217 999	Asie de l'Est/Pacifique
Europe		12 766 224	13 996 356	15 104 338	14 987 571	14 766 811	Europe
Middle East		55 257	72 057	70 616	46 276	47 702	Moyen-Orient
South Asia		4 828	3 657	4 873	641	847	Asie du Sud
Region not specified		...	...	...	11 328	11 864	Région non spécifiée
Grenada	TFN						**Grenade**
Total[2]		133 865	98 548	118 654	130 096	130 363	Total[2]
Africa		562	325	461	965	644	Afrique
Americas		77 126	58 629	65 292	63 796	66 159	Amériques
East Asia/Pacific		722	1 054	1 515	3 382	1 129	Asie de l'Est/Pacifique
Europe		36 222	22 423	32 556	42 111	44 676	Europe
Middle East		132	121	110	87	97	Moyen-Orient
Region not specified		19 101	15 996	18 720	19 755	17 658	Région non spécifiée
Guadeloupe	THSR						**Guadeloupe**
Total		455 981[22]	371 985[23]	...	...	...	Total
Europe		406 204	369 800	...	...	...	Europe
Region not specified		49 777	2 185	...	...	...	Région non spécifiée
Guam	TFR						**Guam**
Total[14]		1 159 881	1 227 587	1 211 674	1 224 894	1 140 499	Total[14]
Americas		46 754	46 362	44 813	50 267	53 552	Amériques
East Asia/Pacific		1 068 997	1 133 807	1 134 264	1 124 725	1 032 999	Asie de l'Est/Pacifique
Europe		1 511	1 750	1 380	1 564	1 678	Europe
Region not specified		42 619	45 668	31 217	48 338	52 270	Région non spécifiée
Guatemala	VFN						**Guatemala**
Total		1 181 526	1 315 646	1 502 069	1 627 551	1 715 426	Total
Americas		1 006 614	1 148 318	1 325 209	1 443 662	1 517 540	Amériques
East Asia/Pacific		23 167	24 921	27 914	30 245	30 480	Asie de l'Est/Pacifique
Europe		149 871	139 996	147 227	151 807	165 025	Europe
Middle East		365	1 182	485	454	281	Moyen-Orient
Region not specified		1 509	1 229	1 234	1 383	2 100	Région non spécifiée

61

Tourist/visitor arrivals by region of origin *(continued)*
Number

Arrivées de touristes/visiteurs par région de provenance *(suite)*
Nombre

Country or area of destination and region of origin+	Series& Série&	2004	2005	2006	2007	2008	Pays ou zone de destination et région de provenance+
Guinea	TFR						**Guinée**
Total [24]		42 041	45 334	46 096	...	...	Total [24]
Africa		17 915	17 008	6 562	...	...	Afrique
Americas		4 377	5 336	2 260	...	...	Amériques
East Asia/Pacific		2 160	2 545	2 002	...	...	Asie de l'Est/Pacifique
Europe		15 564	18 007	13 717	...	...	Europe
Middle East		1 040	628	755	...	...	Moyen-Orient
South Asia		985	1 251	20 800	...	...	Asie du Sud
Region not specified		...	559	...	...	...	Région non spécifiée
Guinea-Bissau	TFN						**Guinée-Bissau**
Total [25]		...	4 978	11 617	30 092	...	Total [25]
Africa		...	1 224	2 705	13 354	...	Afrique
Americas		...	451	1 992	2 409	...	Amériques
East Asia/Pacific		...	102	1 601	2 884	...	Asie de l'Est/Pacifique
Europe		...	3 123	5 063	10 289	...	Europe
Middle East		...	12	94	356	...	Moyen-Orient
South Asia		...	66	162	800	...	Asie du Sud
Guyana	TFR						**Guyana**
Total [26]		121 989	116 596	113 474	131 487	132 776	Total [26]
Americas		111 078	105 468	102 627	115 812	90 221	Amériques
Europe		9 056	8 704	8 390	9 686	9 208	Europe
Region not specified		1 855	2 424	2 457	5 989	33 347	Région non spécifiée
Haiti	TFR						**Haïti**
Total [3]		96 439	112 267	107 783	386 060 [9]	304 021 [9]	Total [3]
Americas		90 615	103 595	98 898	331 986	261 438	Amériques
Europe		4 246	6 720	6 782	23 372	18 405	Europe
Region not specified		1 578	1 952	2 103	30 702	24 178	Région non spécifiée
Honduras	TFN						**Honduras**
Total		640 981	673 035	738 667	831 433	899 319	Total
Africa		251	231	330	209	232	Afrique
Americas		584 831	610 179	666 017	785 225	809 665	Amériques
East Asia/Pacific		7 542	8 437	11 069	7 001	8 013	Asie de l'Est/Pacifique
Europe		47 504	53 482	60 324	38 226	80 519	Europe
Middle East		109	90	135	100	115	Moyen-Orient
South Asia		278	321	396	250	290	Asie du Sud
Region not specified		466	295	396	422	485	Région non spécifiée
Hungary	VFN						**Hongrie**
Total [27]		36 104 954	38 554 561	40 962 830	42 466 159 [28]	...	Total [27]
Africa		14 050	13 502	16 675	18 382	...	Afrique
Americas		478 255	490 440	521 151	532 683	...	Amériques
East Asia/Pacific		236 915	272 207	290 992	312 426	...	Asie de l'Est/Pacifique
Europe		35 318 166	37 744 758	40 100 380	41 558 891	...	Europe
Middle East		9 593	9 538	9 477	13 527	...	Moyen-Orient
South Asia		14 630	15 179	15 500	17 533	...	Asie du Sud
Region not specified		33 345	8 937	8 655	12 717	...	Région non spécifiée
Hungary	TCEN						**Hongrie**
Total [29]		3 269 868	3 446 362	3 309 753	3 451 186	3 516 030	Total [29]
Africa		12 379	10 310	7 557	9 540	9 091	Afrique
Americas		202 180	218 304	244 890	252 473	238 414	Amériques
East Asia/Pacific		104 805	132 564	122 687	116 151	102 804	Asie de l'Est/Pacifique
Europe		2 860 588	2 985 842	2 827 586	3 073 022	3 040 128	Europe
Region not specified		89 916	99 342	107 033	...	125 593	Région non spécifiée
Iceland	TCEN						**Islande**
Total		836 230	871 401	970 821	1 054 016	1 106 017	Total
Africa		...	1 104	1 508	1 356	2 219	Afrique
Americas		74 857	84 839	86 650	85 847	86 773	Amériques
East Asia/Pacific		10 520	29 723	32 943	29 481	30 275	Asie de l'Est/Pacifique
Europe		706 580	714 982	785 148	850 326	918 025	Europe
Region not specified		44 273	40 753	64 572	87 006	68 725	Région non spécifiée

61 Tourist/visitor arrivals by region of origin *(continued)*

Number

Arrivées de touristes/visiteurs par région de provenance *(suite)*

Nombre

Country or area of destination and region of origin+	Series& Série&	2004	2005	2006	2007	2008	Pays ou zone de destination et région de provenance+
India	TFN						**Inde**
Total [1]		3 457 477	3 918 610	4 447 167	5 081 504	5 282 603	Total [1]
Africa		111 711	130 753	137 285	151 355	136 424	Afrique
Americas		690 169	804 394	912 051	1 049 595	1 070 802	Amériques
East Asia/Pacific		511 681	584 753	702 147	822 575	866 463	Asie de l'Est/Pacifique
Europe		1 257 239	1 434 983	1 662 362	1 900 413	1 955 824	Europe
Middle East		80 073	86 450	98 439	118 469	166 404	Moyen-Orient
South Asia		790 698	841 969	908 916	982 468	1 051 846	Asie du Sud
Region not specified		15 906	35 308	25 967	56 629	34 840	Région non spécifiée
Indonesia	TFR						**Indonésie**
Total		5 321 165	5 002 101	4 871 351	5 505 759	6 234 497	Total
Africa		35 507	27 450	22 655	27 777	29 753	Afrique
Americas		209 779	209 511	184 525	220 202	239 678	Amériques
East Asia/Pacific		4 265 551	3 837 107	3 795 481	4 315 873	4 848 796	Asie de l'Est/Pacifique
Europe		720 706	798 408	730 398	796 730	924 745	Europe
Middle East		35 783	60 601	55 033	55 348	67 271	Moyen-Orient
South Asia		53 839	69 024	83 259	89 829	124 254	Asie du Sud
Ireland	TFR						**Irlande**
Total		6 953 000	7 334 000	8 001 000	8 333 000	8 026 000	Total
Africa		42 000	39 000	48 000	39 000	54 000	Afrique
Americas		975 000	956 000	1 058 000	1 099 000	985 000	Amériques
East Asia/Pacific		259 000	226 000	237 000	249 000	256 000	Asie de l'Est/Pacifique
Europe		5 677 000	6 113 000	6 658 000	6 946 000	6 731 000	Europe
Israel	TFR						**Israël**
Total [1]		1 505 606	1 902 787	1 825 207	2 066 852	2 572 317	Total [1]
Africa		40 122	41 450	54 337	66 023	73 866	Afrique
Americas		486 508	602 578	606 771	672 870	783 253	Amériques
East Asia/Pacific		65 953	87 572	94 407	109 873	130 005	Asie de l'Est/Pacifique
Europe		860 916	1 113 772	1 018 364	1 171 006	1 521 264	Europe
Middle East		28 561	29 946	20 613	13 433	17 912	Moyen-Orient
South Asia		15 155	22 911	23 219	27 631	33 209	Asie du Sud
Region not specified		8 391	4 558	7 496	6 016	12 808	Région non spécifiée
Italy	TFN						**Italie**
Total [30]		37 070 774	36 512 502	41 057 835	43 654 121	42 733 683	Total [30]
Africa		205 617	250 705	253 863	264 662	300 031	Afrique
Americas		2 988 243	3 250 285	3 579 393	3 440 062	3 394 811	Amériques
East Asia/Pacific		1 088 281	1 111 603	1 188 782	1 326 583	1 253 482	Asie de l'Est/Pacifique
Europe		32 521 819	31 571 338	35 598 434	38 207 532	37 342 335	Europe
Middle East		129 760	212 716	246 956	242 048	235 613	Moyen-Orient
South Asia		135 290	115 193	189 745	173 234	207 411	Asie du Sud
Region not specified		1 764	662	662	...	...	Région non spécifiée
Jamaica	TFR						**Jamaïque**
Total [3,9]		1 414 786	1 478 663	1 678 905	1 700 785	1 767 271	Total [3,9]
Africa		1 139	889	1 032	1 449	1 213	Afrique
Americas		1 161 840	1 233 846	1 411 339	1 398 318	1 470 488	Amériques
East Asia/Pacific		7 971	8 129	8 240	8 620	7 863	Asie de l'Est/Pacifique
Europe		242 904	234 952	257 224	290 269	286 142	Europe
Middle East		350	347	394	477	577	Moyen-Orient
South Asia		554	464	600	1 604	923	Asie du Sud
Region not specified		28	36	76	48	65	Région non spécifiée
Japan	VFN						**Japon**
Total [1]		6 137 905	6 727 926	7 334 077	8 346 969	8 350 835	Total [1]
Africa		16 946	20 583	18 678	20 114	20 542	Afrique
Americas		951 074	1 032 140	1 035 300	1 054 019	1 005 692	Amériques
East Asia/Pacific		4 337 788	4 761 395	5 362 608	6 267 798	6 306 921	Asie de l'Est/Pacifique
Europe		744 142	817 092	817 670	897 944	909 626	Europe
Middle East		3 285	3 072	3 218	3 294	3 956	Moyen-Orient
South Asia		83 856	92 676	95 555	102 860	102 991	Asie du Sud
Region not specified		814	968	1 048	940	1 107	Région non spécifiée

61 Tourist/visitor arrivals by region of origin *(continued)*
Number
Arrivées de touristes/visiteurs par région de provenance *(suite)*
Nombre

Country or area of destination and region of origin+	Series& Série&	2004	2005	2006	2007	2008	Pays ou zone de destination et région de provenance+
Jordan	TFN						**Jordanie**
Total[2]		2 852 803	2 986 589	3 225 409	3 430 954	3 728 726	Total[2]
Africa		19 938	30 234	50 670	54 708	49 884	Afrique
Americas		93 477	111 975	163 918	177 782	200 371	Amériques
East Asia/Pacific		60 121	64 191	82 943	126 069	146 029	Asie de l'Est/Pacifique
Europe		374 428	391 846	424 583	570 859	657 628	Europe
Middle East		1 780 755	1 828 735	1 879 541	1 689 532	1 777 094	Moyen-Orient
South Asia		37 885	42 947	41 884	64 895	73 571	Asie du Sud
Region not specified		486 199	516 661	581 870	747 109	824 149	Région non spécifiée
Kazakhstan	VFR						**Kazakhstan**
Total		4 291 040	4 364 949	4 706 742	5 310 582	4 721 456	Total
Africa		1 506	1 703	5 023	2 272	1 805	Afrique
Americas		32 345	30 768	31 978	33 222	28 860	Amériques
East Asia/Pacific		96 660	113 842	152 929	219 908	212 003	Asie de l'Est/Pacifique
Europe		4 125 909	4 194 081	4 486 983	5 018 562	4 447 837	Europe
Middle East		1 984	2 276	3 212	4 551	3 832	Moyen-Orient
South Asia		20 849	19 036	21 811	26 372	23 064	Asie du Sud
Region not specified		11 787	3 243	4 806	5 695	4 055	Région non spécifiée
Kenya	VFR						**Kenya**
Total[1]		1 360 000	1 675 000	1 840 000	2 004 000	...	Total[1]
Africa		827 000	999 000	1 035 000	1 170 000	...	Afrique
Americas		70 000	94 000	111 000	133 000	...	Amériques
East Asia/Pacific		47 000	65 000	78 000	80 000	...	Asie de l'Est/Pacifique
Europe		381 000	474 000	568 000	580 000	...	Europe
Middle East		16 000	22 000	23 000	14 000	...	Moyen-Orient
South Asia		19 000	21 000	25 000	27 000	...	Asie du Sud
Kiribati	TFN						**Kiribati**
Total[3,31]		3 404	4 137	4 406	4 709	3 871	Total[3,31]
Americas		430	1 032	760	1 109	928	Amériques
East Asia/Pacific		2 147	2 399	2 744	3 069	2 481	Asie de l'Est/Pacifique
Europe		104	182	232	297	304	Europe
Region not specified		723	524	670	234	158	Région non spécifiée
Korea, Republic of	VFN						**Corée, République de**
Total[2,32]		5 818 138	6 022 752	6 155 046	6 448 240	6 890 841	Total[2,32]
Africa		14 649	14 464	16 071	19 210	20 720	Afrique
Americas		610 562	640 050	673 118	716 336	744 615	Amériques
East Asia/Pacific		4 252 976	4 441 757	4 554 010	4 696 553	5 035 206	Asie de l'Est/Pacifique
Europe		531 257	540 694	571 648	605 440	645 501	Europe
Middle East		11 155	13 050	14 964	15 859	18 208	Moyen-Orient
South Asia		95 398	92 189	95 430	100 662	118 036	Asie du Sud
Region not specified		302 141	280 548	229 805	294 180	308 555	Région non spécifiée
Kuwait	VFN						**Koweït**
Total		3 056 093	3 474 267	3 899 105	4 481 616	4 735 910	Total
Africa		29 144	35 339	43 420	54 708	64 768	Afrique
Americas		115 260	131 644	155 203	189 775	219 039	Amériques
East Asia/Pacific		158 006	184 548	226 747	235 562	244 241	Asie de l'Est/Pacifique
Europe		125 509	136 877	154 765	177 528	181 162	Europe
Middle East		1 769 220	2 004 725	2 222 558	2 618 506	2 778 066	Moyen-Orient
South Asia		855 730	977 946	1 092 846	1 191 690	1 224 937	Asie du Sud
Region not specified		3 224	3 188	3 566	13 847	23 697	Région non spécifiée
Kyrgyzstan	TFR						**Kirghizistan**
Total[33]		398 078	319 303	765 850	1 655 833	2 435 386	Total[33]
Americas		12 266	13 023	14 140	15 407	9 580	Amériques
East Asia/Pacific		16 766	21 993	26 288	30 813	30 152	Asie de l'Est/Pacifique
Europe		356 982	273 696	715 435	1 595 211	2 383 543	Europe
Middle East		...	108	134	168	194	Moyen-Orient
South Asia		5 864	6 364	5 142	7 262	6 838	Asie du Sud
Region not specified		6 200	4 119	4 711	6 972	5 079	Région non spécifiée

61 Tourist/visitor arrivals by region of origin *(continued)*
Number

Arrivées de touristes/visiteurs par région de provenance *(suite)*
Nombre

Country or area of destination and region of origin+	Series& Série&	2004	2005	2006	2007	2008	Pays ou zone de destination et région de provenance+
Lao People's Dem. Rep.	VFN						**Rép. dém. pop. lao**
Total		894 806	1 095 315	1 215 107	1 623 943	1 736 787	Total
Americas		47 153	60 061	60 883	61 463	75 266	Amériques
East Asia/Pacific		728 262	897 177	1 006 564	1 404 095	1 479 847	Asie de l'Est/Pacifique
Europe		116 180	134 472	143 716	152 023	172 846	Europe
South Asia		1 845	2 096	2 100	2 361	2 652	Asie du Sud
Region not specified		1 366	1 509	1 844	4 001	6 176	Région non spécifiée
Latvia	TCER						**Lettonie**
Total		545 366	730 146	816 297	844 828	944 690	Total
Africa		83	71	137	132	389	Afrique
Americas		21 091	20 423	22 517	20 849	24 690	Amériques
East Asia/Pacific		9 511	9 941	10 131	11 387	13 464	Asie de l'Est/Pacifique
Europe		500 979	680 362	757 385	794 241	897 356	Europe
Middle East		196	524	233	390	368	Moyen-Orient
South Asia		308	570	620	626	969	Asie du Sud
Region not specified		13 198	18 255	25 274	17 203	7 454	Région non spécifiée
Lebanon	TFN						**Liban**
Total[34]		1 278 469	1 139 524	1 062 625	1 017 072	1 332 533	Total[34]
Africa		45 095	31 073	39 021	59 861	50 732	Afrique
Americas		152 175	136 904	130 117	121 596	176 647	Amériques
East Asia/Pacific		92 285	87 813	74 461	63 579	89 452	Asie de l'Est/Pacifique
Europe		337 337	316 561	269 263	277 873	348 262	Europe
Middle East		520 230	436 549	433 323	388 292	532 871	Moyen-Orient
South Asia		128 120	129 315	115 243	104 729	133 067	Asie du Sud
Region not specified		3 227	1 309	1 197	1 142	1 502	Région non spécifiée
Lesotho	VFR						**Lesotho**
Total		303 530	303 578	356 913	300 350	293 073	Total
Africa		290 295	289 342	329 838	271 475	259 407	Afrique
Americas		1 375	1 490	3 412	3 385	4 556	Amériques
East Asia/Pacific		2 551	2 657	3 456	4 816	5 566	Asie de l'Est/Pacifique
Europe		7 568	7 930	19 641	19 772	22 717	Europe
Middle East		...	...	117	400	385	Moyen-Orient
South Asia		...	...	318	304	404	Asie du Sud
Region not specified		1 741	2 159	131	198	38	Région non spécifiée
Libyan Arab Jamah.	VFN						**Jamah. arabe libyenne**
Total		...	...	125 000	105 997	...	Total
Africa		...	...	...	163	...	Afrique
Americas		...	...	3 000	813	...	Amériques
East Asia/Pacific		...	...	5 000	3 683	...	Asie de l'Est/Pacifique
Europe		...	...	117 000	101 288	...	Europe
Middle East		...	...	...	23	...	Moyen-Orient
South Asia		...	...	...	27	...	Asie du Sud
Liechtenstein	THSR						**Liechtenstein**
Total		48 501	49 767	54 856	58 258	58 454	Total
Africa		198	170	189	216	177	Afrique
Americas		2 739	2 888	2 999	3 156	2 439	Amériques
East Asia/Pacific		1 728	1 635	1 740	1 724	1 679	Asie de l'Est/Pacifique
Europe		43 836	44 944	49 818	53 053	54 067	Europe
South Asia		...	47	59	62	73	Asie du Sud
Region not specified		...	83	51	47	19	Région non spécifiée
Lithuania	TCER						**Lituanie**
Total		590 043	681 487	759 041	849 006	909 983	Total
Africa		525	1 159	1 360	961	1 253	Afrique
Americas		22 385	23 626	25 955	27 188	26 322	Amériques
East Asia/Pacific		15 472	15 032	16 260	15 953	19 215	Asie de l'Est/Pacifique
Europe		538 078	623 045	694 241	791 281	849 313	Europe
Region not specified		13 583	18 625	21 225	13 623	13 880	Région non spécifiée
Luxembourg	TCER						**Luxembourg**
Total		877 712	912 798	908 171	917 334	878 900	Total
Americas		29 777	32 249	34 516	33 255	32 482	Amériques
Europe		806 575	840 259	831 114	841 388	807 742	Europe
Region not specified		41 360	40 290	42 541	42 691	38 676	Région non spécifiée

61 Tourist/visitor arrivals by region of origin *(continued)*
Number
Arrivées de touristes/visiteurs par région de provenance *(suite)*
Nombre

Country or area of destination and region of origin+	Series& Série&	2004	2005	2006	2007	2008	Pays ou zone de destination et région de provenance+
Madagascar	TFN						**Madagascar**
Total [3]		228 785	277 422	311 730	344 348	375 010	Total [3]
Africa		39 302	52 277	58 520	64 013	83 802	Afrique
Americas		9 180	13 853	15 587	13 671	11 250	Amériques
East Asia/Pacific		3 432	6 404	7 206	14 084	16 500	Asie de l'Est/Pacifique
Europe		175 727	202 530	228 452	246 837	261 936	Europe
Region not specified		1 144	2 358	1 965	5 743	1 522	Région non spécifiée
Malawi	TFR						**Malawi**
Total [27]		427 360	437 718	637 780	734 598	742 457	Total [27]
Africa		335 651	336 856	483 615	559 149	574 544	Afrique
Americas		20 828	18 725	36 162	47 225	44 561	Amériques
East Asia/Pacific		11 313	8 698	10 030	12 835	11 588	Asie de l'Est/Pacifique
Europe		48 929	60 437	94 266	99 226	98 330	Europe
Middle East		...	...	5 730	1 613	1 581	Moyen-Orient
South Asia		6 815	9 549	...	13 366	10 194	Asie du Sud
Region not specified		3 824	3 453	7 977	1 184	1 659	Région non spécifiée
Malaysia	TFR						**Malaisie**
Total [35]		15 703 406	16 431 055	17 546 863	20 972 822	22 052 488	Total [35]
Africa		136 587	128 208	157 342	307 797	127 361	Afrique
Americas		271 901	274 915	312 478	472 164	345 217	Amériques
East Asia/Pacific		13 983 381	14 685 975	15 478 386	17 656 571	18 972 997	Asie de l'Est/Pacifique
Europe		540 306	618 188	673 118	829 653	1 026 032	Europe
Middle East		124 331	145 448	173 750	225 153	216 351	Moyen-Orient
South Asia		248 673	321 246	390 189	686 614	826 028	Asie du Sud
Region not specified		398 227	257 075	361 600	794 870	538 502	Région non spécifiée
Maldives	TFN						**Maldives**
Total [3]		616 716	395 320	601 923	675 889	683 012	Total [3]
Africa		5 325	3 460	4 169	4 846	5 694	Afrique
Americas		9 385	7 238	10 813	14 198	14 485	Amériques
East Asia/Pacific		99 735	55 985	102 277	124 674	127 151	Asie de l'Est/Pacifique
Europe		475 707	306 856	457 535	495 371	497 560	Europe
Middle East		4 517	2 404	4 372	6 450	9 205	Moyen-Orient
South Asia		22 047	19 377	22 757	30 350	28 917	Asie du Sud
Mali	THSN						**Mali**
Total		112 654	142 814	152 660	164 124	189 511	Total
Africa		29 256	35 985	38 892	29 378	47 418	Afrique
Americas		12 494	13 287	18 507	17 564	19 519	Amériques
East Asia/Pacific		3 117	2 090	1 636	1 416	4 672	Asie de l'Est/Pacifique
Europe		64 252	80 968	86 443	104 308	100 819	Europe
Middle East		1 524	1 064	1 128	1 190	4 176	Moyen-Orient
Region not specified		2 011	9 420	6 054	10 268	12 907	Région non spécifiée
Malta	TFN						**Malte**
Total [36]		1 156 028	1 170 610	1 124 233	1 243 508	1 290 856	Total [36]
Americas		18 720	18 136	16 970	20 423	18 021	Amériques
Europe		982 623	1 006 530	955 176	1 043 222	1 078 531	Europe
Middle East		12 831	10 662	9 198	9 259	9 403	Moyen-Orient
Region not specified		141 854	135 282	142 889	170 604	184 901	Région non spécifiée
Marshall Islands	TFR						**Iles Marshall**
Total		9 007[14]	9 173[14]	5 780[3]	7 200[3]	6 022[3]	Total
Americas		2 099	1 721	1 472	1 703	1 480	Amériques
East Asia/Pacific		4 466	5 577	3 850	4 382	3 663	Asie de l'Est/Pacifique
Europe		160	160	180	278	177	Europe
Region not specified		2 282	1 715	278	837	702	Région non spécifiée
Martinique	TFR						**Martinique**
Total		470 890	484 127	503 475	501 491	...	Total
Americas		73 011	81 247	79 335	92 980	...	Amériques
Europe		396 138	399 083	422 453	405 231	...	Europe
Region not specified		1 741	3 797	1 687	3 280	...	Région non spécifiée

Tourist/visitor arrivals by region of origin *(continued)*

Number

Arrivées de touristes/visiteurs par région de provenance *(suite)*

Nombre

Country or area of destination and region of origin+	Series& Série&	2004	2005	2006	2007	2008	Pays ou zone de destination et région de provenance+
Mauritius	TFR						**Maurice**
Total		718 861	761 063	788 276	906 971	930 456	Total
Africa		175 295	184 821	189 026	210 553	213 383	Afrique
Americas		8 380	8 791	9 759	10 462	13 709	Amériques
East Asia/Pacific		27 026	28 924	34 103	39 681	39 843	Asie de l'Est/Pacifique
Europe		477 347	503 037	510 872	596 132	608 929	Europe
Middle East		3 883	3 737	4 715	4 591	7 158	Moyen-Orient
South Asia		26 558	31 087	39 070	44 762	45 848	Asie du Sud
Region not specified		372	666	731	790	1 586	Région non spécifiée
Mexico	TFN						**Mexique**
Total [9]		...	21 914 917	21 352 605	21 369 721	22 637 405	Total [9]
Americas		...	19 012 275	18 713 395	18 788 222	19 890 916	Amériques
East Asia/Pacific		...	92 007	99 723	109 488	105 797	Asie de l'Est/Pacifique
Europe		...	1 134 228	1 295 430	1 423 432	1 511 467	Europe
Region not specified		...	1 676 407	1 244 057	1 048 579	1 129 225	Région non spécifiée
Mexico	TFR						**Mexique**
Total [9]		20 617 746	21 914 917	21 352 605	21 369 721	22 637 405	Total [9]
Americas		19 705 636	20 691 415	20 094 345	20 016 280	18 853 129	Amériques
Region not specified		912 110	1 223 502	1 258 260	1 353 441	3 784 276	Région non spécifiée
Micronesia (Fed. States of)	TFR						**Micronésie (Etats féd. de)**
Total [37]		19 260	18 958	19 136	21 146	25 627	Total [37]
Americas		7 744	7 955	8 256	8 471	9 203	Amériques
East Asia/Pacific		9 982	8 895	8 361	10 082	13 442	Asie de l'Est/Pacifique
Europe		1 408	2 019	2 398	2 452	2 788	Europe
Region not specified		126	89	121	141	194	Région non spécifiée
Monaco	THSN						**Monaco**
Total		250 159	285 675	313 070	327 985	323 705	Total
Africa		2 230	2 601	2 826	3 293	2 832	Afrique
Americas		25 132	28 626	34 071	40 910	35 368	Amériques
East Asia/Pacific		12 653	11 746	10 632	12 382	12 535	Asie de l'Est/Pacifique
Europe		190 326	214 131	239 872	244 497	260 856	Europe
Middle East		3 367	3 190	3 694	4 318	7 045	Moyen-Orient
Region not specified		16 451	25 381	21 975	22 585	5 069	Région non spécifiée
Mongolia	TFN						**Mongolie**
Total		300 537	337 790	385 989	451 788	446 317	Total
Africa		263	297	502	691	592	Afrique
Americas		12 198	12 913	14 433	15 401	15 805	Amériques
East Asia/Pacific		188 250	223 411	245 760	283 267	266 582	Asie de l'Est/Pacifique
Europe		98 592	100 123	124 002	149 077	159 884	Europe
Middle East		249	232	159	480	610	Moyen-Orient
South Asia		966	792	1 129	1 202	1 407	Asie du Sud
Region not specified		19	22	4	1 670	1 437	Région non spécifiée
Montenegro	TCEN						**Monténégro**
Total		188 060	272 005	377 798	984 138	1 030 825	Total
Americas		3 354	4 302	7 324	8 894	9 084	Amériques
East Asia/Pacific		752	1 047	1 680	2 293	2 839	Asie de l'Est/Pacifique
Europe		181 943	263 973	366 028	968 475	1 013 406	Europe
Region not specified		2 011	2 683	2 766	4 476	5 496	Région non spécifiée
Montserrat	TFR						**Montserrat**
Total		10 138	9 690	7 991	7 746	7 360	Total
Americas		6 822	6 448	5 427	5 311	4 989	Amériques
East Asia/Pacific		1	3	5	5	...	Asie de l'Est/Pacifique
Europe		3 197	3 196	2 501	2 366	2 333	Europe
Region not specified		118	43	58	64	38	Région non spécifiée

61 Tourist/visitor arrivals by region of origin *(continued)*
Number

Arrivées de touristes/visiteurs par région de provenance *(suite)*
Nombre

Country or area of destination and region of origin+	Series& Série&	2004	2005	2006	2007	2008	Pays ou zone de destination et région de provenance+
Morocco	TFN						**Maroc**
Total[2]		5 476 713	5 843 377	6 558 333	7 407 617	7 878 639	Total[2]
Africa		123 070	143 855	165 307	192 668	213 611	Afrique
Americas		127 955	140 179	173 052	196 037	201 867	Amériques
East Asia/Pacific		48 874	51 745	65 234	73 910	76 127	Asie de l'Est/Pacifique
Europe		2 309 502	2 607 668	3 025 107	3 406 184	3 563 990	Europe
Middle East		84 298	91 029	105 632	115 832	127 486	Moyen-Orient
South Asia		6 486	7 723	8 795	11 592	11 901	Asie du Sud
Region not specified		2 776 528	2 801 178	3 015 206	3 411 394	3 683 657	Région non spécifiée
Mozambique	VFR						**Mozambique**
Total		711 060	954 433	1 095 000	1 259 000	2 617 424[38]	Total
Africa		623 240	851 999	977 468	1 043 310	2 143 268	Afrique
Americas		5 647	12 399	14 226	18 799	32 436	Amériques
East Asia/Pacific		...	8 036	9 220	12 680	...	Asie de l'Est/Pacifique
Europe		56 508	47 999	55 074	66 233	158 015	Europe
Region not specified		25 665	34 000	39 012	117 978	283 705	Région non spécifiée
Myanmar	TFN						**Myanmar**
Total[39]		241 938	232 218	263 514	248 076	193 319	Total[39]
Africa		395	488	502	432	539	Afrique
Americas		20 451	20 701	22 880	19 331	16 158	Amériques
East Asia/Pacific		141 683	129 922	148 282	142 904	124 242	Asie de l'Est/Pacifique
Europe		65 411	67 933	80 791	72 827	40 885	Europe
Middle East		1 831	1 920	2 177	2 281	1 379	Moyen-Orient
South Asia		12 167	11 254	8 882	10 301	10 116	Asie du Sud
Namibia	TFN						**Namibie**
Total		...	777 888	833 344	928 914	...	Total
Africa		...	601 737	628 588	690 148	...	Afrique
Americas		...	11 979	16 325	19 342	...	Amériques
East Asia/Pacific		...	4 274	4 645	5 783	...	Asie de l'Est/Pacifique
Europe		...	146 361	166 972	194 605	...	Europe
Region not specified		...	13 537	16 814	19 036	...	Région non spécifiée
Nepal	TFR						**Népal**
Total		385 297	375 398	383 926	526 705	500 277	Total
Africa		1 346	1 285	1 571	1 309	493	Afrique
Americas		29 791	26 385	27 991	41 348	42 080	Amériques
East Asia/Pacific		96 565	92 733	95 407	139 615	129 469	Asie de l'Est/Pacifique
Europe		131 999	112 341	108 166	157 505	146 590	Europe
Middle East		...	...	...	...	5 647	Moyen-Orient
South Asia		124 804	139 288	137 059	168 041	149 959	Asie du Sud
Region not specified		792	3 366	13 732	18 887	26 039	Région non spécifiée
Netherlands	TCER						**Pays-Bas**
Total		9 646 500	10 011 900	10 738 700	11 008 000	10 104 300	Total
Africa		117 300	101 100	92 700	91 900	83 800	Afrique
Americas		1 131 500	1 222 200	1 325 000	1 273 600	1 068 000	Amériques
East Asia/Pacific		753 700	748 700	722 600	738 500	667 700	Asie de l'Est/Pacifique
Europe		7 644 000	7 939 900	8 598 400	8 904 000	8 284 800	Europe
New Caledonia	TFR						**Nouvelle-Calédonie**
Total[9]		99 515	100 651	100 491	103 363	103 672	Total[9]
Africa		615	637	705	628	713	Afrique
Americas		1 676	1 785	1 854	1 918	2 707	Amériques
East Asia/Pacific		65 892	67 753	66 074	68 449	64 578	Asie de l'Est/Pacifique
Europe		29 992	30 268	31 850	32 252	35 636	Europe
Region not specified		1 340	208	8	116	38	Région non spécifiée
New Zealand	VFR						**Nouvelle-Zélande**
Total[9,40]		2 334 153	2 365 529	2 408 888	2 455 284	2 447 208	Total[9,40]
Africa		18 673	19 709	20 643	24 251	27 627	Afrique
Americas		275 699	275 616	294 450	289 860	295 075	Amériques
East Asia/Pacific		1 468 307	1 484 424	1 512 292	1 550 926	1 532 615	Asie de l'Est/Pacifique
Europe		488 674	521 267	515 716	517 080	518 666	Europe
Middle East		8 122	8 871	9 607	10 758	13 030	Moyen-Orient
South Asia		17 830	19 833	22 507	24 216	26 415	Asie du Sud
Region not specified		56 848	35 809	33 673	38 193	33 780	Région non spécifiée

Tourist/visitor arrivals by region of origin *(continued)*
Number

Arrivées de touristes/visiteurs par région de provenance *(suite)*
Nombre

Country or area of destination and region of origin[+]	Series[&] Série[&]	2004	2005	2006	2007	2008	Pays ou zone de destination et région de provenance[+]
Nicaragua	TFN						**Nicaragua**
Total		614 782[1]	712 444[2]	749 184[2]	799 996[2]	857 901[2]	Total
Africa		515	621	643	471	706	Afrique
Americas		552 846	619 305	623 470	671 603	714 212	Amériques
East Asia/Pacific		8 326	11 235	12 792	9 096	9 360	Asie de l'Est/Pacifique
Europe		52 564	58 964	58 319	52 525	57 649	Europe
Middle East		76	82	129	157	127	Moyen-Orient
South Asia		437	1 522	861	444	1 775	Asie du Sud
Region not specified		18	20 715	52 970	65 700	74 072	Région non spécifiée
Niger	TFN						**Niger**
Total		57 004	59 920	60 332	47 539	73 154	Total
Africa		38 000	35 952	36 199	23 770	39 680	Afrique
Americas		2 500	4 194	4 223	3 898	3 720	Amériques
East Asia/Pacific		1 500	2 996	3 017	1 778	2 656	Asie de l'Est/Pacifique
Europe		14 500	16 778	16 893	17 589	15 500	Europe
Middle East		...	...	...	504	444	Moyen-Orient
Region not specified		504	...	...	...	11 154	Région non spécifiée
Nigeria	VFN						**Nigéria**
Total		2 646 411	2 778 365	3 055 800	5 238 545	5 820 497	Total
Africa		1 825 312	1 916 246	2 107 870	3 613 664	4 014 981	Afrique
Americas		111 020	116 563	129 219	221 586	244 455	Amériques
East Asia/Pacific		153 020	160 666	177 001	302 260	337 587	Asie de l'Est/Pacifique
Europe		438 093	459 985	506 000	867 461	963 874	Europe
Middle East		47 714	50 095	55 104	94 756	105 357	Moyen-Orient
South Asia		61 714	64 796	72 000	123 627	137 364	Asie du Sud
Region not specified		9 538	10 014	8 606	15 191	16 879	Région non spécifiée
Niue	TFR						**Nioué**
Total[41]		2 550[3]	2 793[3]	3 008[3]	3 463[14]	4 748[3]	Total[41]
Americas		138	181	161	208	315	Amériques
East Asia/Pacific		2 217	2 272	2 588	3 026	3 881	Asie de l'Est/Pacifique
Europe		168	295	237	206	492	Europe
Region not specified		27	45	22	23	60	Région non spécifiée
Northern Mariana Islands	VFN						**Iles Mariannes du Nord**
Total		535 873	506 846	435 494	389 345	397 274	Total
Americas		37 334	37 989	32 582	28 082	31 361	Amériques
East Asia/Pacific		494 826	465 360	398 952	355 921	356 997	Asie de l'Est/Pacifique
Europe		666	1 300	2 324	4 676	7 742	Europe
Region not specified		3 047	2 197	1 636	666	1 174	Région non spécifiée
Norway	TFN						**Norvège**
Total[42]		3 628 000	3 824 000	4 070 000	4 377 000	4 440 000	Total[42]
Americas		176 000	146 000	163 000	177 000	134 000	Amériques
East Asia/Pacific		35 000	41 000	37 000	32 000	30 000	Asie de l'Est/Pacifique
Europe		3 307 000	3 508 000	3 698 000	3 939 000	4 056 000	Europe
Region not specified		110 000	129 000	172 000	229 000	220 000	Région non spécifiée
Occupied Palestinian Terr.	THSN						**Terr. palestinien occupé**
Total		56 011	88 360	122 616	264 168	387 143	Total
Africa		641	971	1 643	4 951	9 679	Afrique
Americas		10 649	13 735	18 728	32 440	39 453	Amériques
East Asia/Pacific		8 399	16 490	16 595	20 424	41 344	Asie de l'Est/Pacifique
Europe		35 210	55 324	83 178	203 468	293 659	Europe
Middle East		1 112	1 840	2 472	2 885	3 008	Moyen-Orient
Oman	THSN						**Oman**
Total		908 466	1 114 498	1 336 441	1 124 068	1 273 441	Total
Africa		28 266	18 307	15 108	15 550	17 606	Afrique
Americas		40 154	34 137	48 917	44 096	52 133	Amériques
East Asia/Pacific		54 971	69 310	80 346	78 974	94 402	Asie de l'Est/Pacifique
Europe		280 727	336 757	584 659	363 587	400 045	Europe
Middle East		249 285	198 577	237 835	193 121	220 955	Moyen-Orient
South Asia		130 565	127 104	139 162	177 739	170 654	Asie du Sud
Region not specified		124 498	330 306	230 414	251 001	317 646	Région non spécifiée

61 Tourist/visitor arrivals by region of origin *(continued)*

Number

Arrivées de touristes/visiteurs par région de provenance *(suite)*

Nombre

Country or area of destination and region of origin⁺	Series& Série&	2004	2005	2006	2007	2008	Pays ou zone de destination et région de provenance⁺
Pakistan	TFN						**Pakistan**
Total		647 993	798 260	898 389	839 500	822 828	Total
Africa		12 521	14 691	19 001	15 840	15 767	Afrique
Americas		103 104	146 548	160 722	160 615	155 870	Amériques
East Asia/Pacific		59 503	83 607	99 063	87 092	75 967	Asie de l'Est/Pacifique
Europe		280 877	356 804	394 209	386 751	389 207	Europe
Middle East		28 365	31 920	37 661	35 887	28 966	Moyen-Orient
South Asia		160 345	158 549	182 144	148 856	153 117	Asie du Sud
Region not specified		3 278	6 141	5 589	4 459	3 934	Région non spécifiée
Palau	TFR						**Palaos**
Total[43]		94 895	86 124	87 206	93 031	83 114	Total[43]
Americas		6 507	5 910	8 932	6 250	10 442	Amériques
East Asia/Pacific		84 381	75 501	73 714	82 297	67 293	Asie de l'Est/Pacifique
Europe		1 837	2 390	2 203	2 298	2 723	Europe
Region not specified		2 170	2 323	2 357	2 186	2 656	Région non spécifiée
Panama	VFR						**Panama**
Total[44]		498 415	576 050	703 545	948 946	1 136 079	Total[44]
Africa		335	390	477	646	766	Afrique
Americas		438 872	507 185	619 526	835 948	1 000 692	Amériques
East Asia/Pacific		13 919	16 095	20 041	27 001	32 476	Asie de l'Est/Pacifique
Europe		45 254	52 339	63 451	85 283	102 079	Europe
Middle East		35	41	50	68	66	Moyen-Orient
Papua New Guinea	TFR						**Papouasie-Nvl-Guinée**
Total		59 013	69 251	77 730	104 122	114 182	Total
Africa		241	353	500	725	947	Afrique
Americas		5 440	6 491	7 355	7 868	8 172	Amériques
East Asia/Pacific		47 963	57 516	63 325	85 026	93 542	Asie de l'Est/Pacifique
Europe		4 739	4 155	5 548	8 563	9 237	Europe
South Asia		630	736	1 002	1 940	2 284	Asie du Sud
Paraguay	TFN						**Paraguay**
Total[4,45]		309 287	340 845	388 465	415 702	428 215	Total[4,45]
Africa		211	253	358	484	301	Afrique
Americas		284 325	311 628	349 105	369 993	384 216	Amériques
East Asia/Pacific		4 718	5 466	8 058	9 174	8 390	Asie de l'Est/Pacifique
Europe		19 788	23 201	30 531	35 133	34 259	Europe
Middle East		96	97	184	377	642	Moyen-Orient
South Asia		148	200	229	427	393	Asie du Sud
Region not specified		1	...	...	114	14	Région non spécifiée
Peru	TFR						**Pérou**
Total[9]		1 349 959	*1 570 566	*1 720 746	*1 916 400	*2 057 620	Total[9]
Africa		2 760	3 435	3 130	3 819	3 511	Afrique
Americas		983 592	1 126 506	1 247 653	1 399 083	1 485 900	Amériques
East Asia/Pacific		64 572	76 852	84 847	94 271	108 953	Asie de l'Est/Pacifique
Europe		296 684	360 297	378 296	414 588	454 214	Europe
Middle East		155	229	185	249	314	Moyen-Orient
South Asia		1 245	1 831	1 965	2 755	3 785	Asie du Sud
Region not specified		951	1 416	4 670	1 635	943	Région non spécifiée
Philippines	TFR						**Philippines**
Total[2]		2 291 352	2 623 084	2 843 345	3 091 993	3 139 422	Total[2]
Africa		1 700	2 294	2 246	3 090	3 317	Afrique
Americas		545 867	604 793	651 705	674 921	685 427	Amériques
East Asia/Pacific		1 359 256	1 565 359	1 690 939	1 829 095	1 798 719	Asie de l'Est/Pacifique
Europe		212 305	246 449	264 353	300 372	322 864	Europe
Middle East		20 683	24 532	27 544	31 759	36 615	Moyen-Orient
South Asia		24 997	28 485	31 975	37 596	43 662	Asie du Sud
Region not specified		126 544	151 172	174 583	215 160	248 818	Région non spécifiée

Tourist/visitor arrivals by region of origin *(continued)*

Number

Arrivées de touristes/visiteurs par région de provenance *(suite)*

Nombre

Country or area of destination and region of origin+	Series& Série&	2004	2005	2006	2007	2008	Pays ou zone de destination et région de provenance+
Poland	VFN						**Pologne**
Total		61 917 759	64 606 085	65 114 865	66 207 767	59 935 000[46]	Total
Africa		11 114	13 217	14 914	16 861	15 000	Afrique
Americas		345 181	439 417	466 299	452 903	380 000	Amériques
East Asia/Pacific		123 114	163 414	193 899	228 844	220 000	Asie de l'Est/Pacifique
Europe		61 385 787	63 926 773	64 366 590	65 373 132	59 290 000	Europe
Middle East		6 471	7 636	8 265	9 507	10 000	Moyen-Orient
South Asia		11 710	13 219	15 246	19 721	20 000	Asie du Sud
Region not specified		34 382	42 409	49 652	106 799	...	Région non spécifiée
Poland	TCER						**Pologne**
Total		3 934 064	4 310 401	4 313 578	4 387 404	4 046 312	Total
Africa		5 483	5 637	6 969	6 657	6 538	Afrique
Americas		232 723	242 264	250 413	234 350	198 941	Amériques
East Asia/Pacific		98 239	110 944	117 857	121 185	121 129	Asie de l'Est/Pacifique
Europe		3 521 865	3 882 651	3 870 392	3 964 327	3 659 440	Europe
Middle East		4 403	3 648	5 742	5 288	5 024	Moyen-Orient
South Asia		8 659	8 293	7 093	10 504	12 564	Asie du Sud
Region not specified		62 692	56 964	55 112	45 093	42 676	Région non spécifiée
Portugal	TFR						**Portugal**
Total[9]		10 639 000[18]	10 612 000	11 282 000	12 321 000	...	Total[9]
Americas		367 000	413 000	499 000	600 000	...	Amériques
East Asia/Pacific		43 000	37 000	32 000	40 000	...	Asie de l'Est/Pacifique
Europe		9 343 000	9 271 000	9 831 000	10 693 000	...	Europe
Region not specified		886 000	891 000	920 000	988 000	...	Région non spécifiée
Puerto Rico	TFR						**Porto Rico**
Total[3,47]		3 541 000	3 685 900	3 722 000	3 687 000	3 894 300	Total[3,47]
Americas		2 754 400	2 847 400	2 929 900	2 886 700	3 046 600	Amériques
Region not specified		786 600	838 500	792 100	800 300	847 700	Région non spécifiée
Qatar	THSR						**Qatar**
Total[48]		732 454	912 997	945 970	963 573	1 404 850	Total[48]
East Asia/Pacific		145 974	159 279	180 543	203 465	216 742	Asie de l'Est/Pacifique
Europe		195 732	233 315	201 187	265 965	329 059	Europe
Middle East		295 335	364 977	413 523	361 139	628 440	Moyen-Orient
Region not specified		95 413	155 426	150 717	133 004	230 609	Région non spécifiée
Republic of Moldova	VFN						**République de Moldova**
Total[49]		26 045	25 073	14 239	14 722	8 710	Total[49]
Africa		71	15	9	7	...	Afrique
Americas		2 564	3 161	1 123	580	305	Amériques
East Asia/Pacific		307	277	243	293	188	Asie de l'Est/Pacifique
Europe		22 686	21 223	12 741	13 794	8 209	Europe
Middle East		392	362	114	27	4	Moyen-Orient
South Asia		25	35	9	21	4	Asie du Sud
Réunion	TFR						**Réunion**
Total		430 000	409 000	278 800	380 547	396 400	Total
Africa		26 222	24 815	20 109	33 245	20 800	Afrique
Americas		...	...	...	1 721	...	Amériques
East Asia/Pacific		...	...	...	2 491	...	Asie de l'Est/Pacifique
Europe		370 474	349 113	224 065	303 307	328 200	Europe
South Asia		...	...	...	418	...	Asie du Sud
Region not specified		33 304	35 072	34 626	39 365	47 400	Région non spécifiée
Romania	VFR						**Roumanie**
Total		6 600 115	5 839 374	6 036 999	7 721 741	8 862 119	Total
Africa		6 585	6 992	9 274	10 701	12 638	Afrique
Americas		139 463	154 244	171 930	188 807	191 709	Amériques
East Asia/Pacific		49 309	57 028	61 921	79 998	97 417	Asie de l'Est/Pacifique
Europe		6 360 587	5 580 091	5 751 503	7 394 449	8 506 343	Europe
Middle East		27 760	24 090	25 049	29 195	31 793	Moyen-Orient
South Asia		15 344	15 566	15 774	17 106	20 500	Asie du Sud
Region not specified		1 067	1 363	1 548	1 485	1 719	Région non spécifiée

61 Tourist/visitor arrivals by region of origin *(continued)*
Number
Arrivées de touristes/visiteurs par région de provenance *(suite)*
Nombre

Country or area of destination and region of origin⁺	Series& Série&	2004	2005	2006	2007	2008	Pays ou zone de destination et région de provenance⁺
Russian Federation	VFN						**Fédération de Russie**
Total		22 064 213	22 200 649	22 486 043	22 908 625	23 676 140	Total
Africa		29 217	26 909	28 288	29 964	35 734	Afrique
Americas		477 338	457 301	532 991	466 404	503 456	Amériques
East Asia/Pacific		1 313 669	1 315 480	1 345 870	1 381 412	1 477 644	Asie de l'Est/Pacifique
Europe		19 607 077	19 690 628	19 872 873	20 395 436	21 186 817	Europe
Middle East		31 765	33 405	33 029	23 998	38 839	Moyen-Orient
South Asia		62 927	68 421	71 917	100 150	96 376	Asie du Sud
Region not specified		542 220	608 505	601 075	511 261	337 274	Région non spécifiée
Rwanda	VFN						**Rwanda**
Total		...	...	...	826 375	980 577	Total
Africa		...	...	...	732 464	864 239	Afrique
Americas		...	...	...	23 349	35 843	Amériques
East Asia/Pacific		...	...	...	6 229	7 306	Asie de l'Est/Pacifique
Europe		...	...	...	39 707	50 137	Europe
Middle East		...	...	...	1 872	3 804	Moyen-Orient
South Asia		...	...	...	22 754	19 248	Asie du Sud
Saba	TFR						**Saba**
Total		11 012	11 462	11 012	11 673	12 043	Total
Americas		4 764	4 933	4 712	5 210	5 213	Amériques
Europe		4 628	5 097	4 776	4 884	5 605	Europe
Region not specified		1 620	1 432	1 524	1 579	1 225	Région non spécifiée
Saint Eustatius	TFR						**Saint-Eustache**
Total [50]		11 056	10 355	9 584	11 568	11 758	Total [50]
Americas		3 732	3 457	3 177	3 928	3 762	Amériques
Europe		5 505	5 400	4 851	5 893	6 201	Europe
Region not specified		1 819	1 498	1 556	1 747	1 795	Région non spécifiée
Saint Kitts and Nevis	TFR						**Saint-Kitts-et-Nevis**
Total [3]		117 638	140 504	139 268	124 181	121 380	Total [3]
Americas		103 093	125 031	123 530	107 263	107 699	Amériques
Europe		11 004	11 149	11 148	12 199	9 782	Europe
Region not specified		3 541	4 324	4 590	4 719	3 899	Région non spécifiée
Saint Lucia	TFR						**Sainte-Lucie**
Total [1]		298 431	317 939	302 510	287 407	295 761	Total [1]
Americas		197 433	214 621	214 463	192 018	197 750	Amériques
East Asia/Pacific		282	260	329	212	152	Asie de l'Est/Pacifique
Europe		96 793	101 790	85 565	89 647	93 601	Europe
Region not specified		3 923	1 268	2 153	5 530	4 258	Région non spécifiée
Saint Maarten	TFN						**Saint-Martin**
Total [51,52]		475 032	467 861	467 804	469 407	475 410	Total [51,52]
Americas		338 242	331 841	328 450	335 410	336 013	Amériques
Europe		96 403	93 821	97 058	96 365	102 713	Europe
Region not specified		40 387	42 199	42 296	37 632	36 684	Région non spécifiée
Saint Vincent-Grenadines	TFR						**Saint Vincent-Grenadines**
Total [3]		86 722	95 506	97 432	89 637	84 101	Total [3]
Americas		66 871	74 173	74 193	64 518	60 549	Amériques
Europe		18 652	19 928	21 961	23 454	22 302	Europe
Region not specified		1 199	1 405	1 278	1 665	1 250	Région non spécifiée
Samoa	TFR						**Samoa**
Total		98 155	101 807	115 882	122 352	122 163	Total
Americas		8 311	9 682	9 067	8 493	8 893	Amériques
East Asia/Pacific		84 882	87 217	101 915	109 130	107 580	Asie de l'Est/Pacifique
Europe		4 756	4 632	4 581	4 417	5 091	Europe
Region not specified		206	276	319	312	599	Région non spécifiée

61 Tourist/visitor arrivals by region of origin *(continued)*
Number

Arrivées de touristes/visiteurs par région de provenance *(suite)*
Nombre

Country or area of destination and region of origin+	Series& Série&	2004	2005	2006	2007	2008	Pays ou zone de destination et région de provenance+
San Marino	VFN						**Saint-Marin**
Total[53]		2 812 488	2 107 092[16]	2 135 589	2 164 419	2 111 736	Total[53]
Africa		...	111	140	193	188	Afrique
Americas		...	17 479	22 131	36 690	18 669	Amériques
East Asia/Pacific		...	53 328	36 340	26 475	17 411	Asie de l'Est/Pacifique
Europe		...	2 035 386	2 075 681	2 099 431	2 074 061	Europe
Middle East		...	270	88	696	272	Moyen-Orient
South Asia		...	436	...	693	379	Asie du Sud
Region not specified		...	82	1 209	241	756	Région non spécifiée
Sao Tome and Principe	TFN						**Sao Tomé-et-Principe**
Total		10 576	15 746	12 266	...	...	Total
Africa		2 076	4 361	2 751	...	...	Afrique
Americas		710	580	525	...	...	Amériques
East Asia/Pacific		...	156	...	...	...	Asie de l'Est/Pacifique
Europe		6 803	10 299	7 568	...	...	Europe
Middle East		...	35	...	...	...	Moyen-Orient
South Asia		...	23	...	...	...	Asie du Sud
Region not specified		987	292	1 422	...	...	Région non spécifiée
Saudi Arabia	TFN						**Arabie saoudite**
Total		8 599 430	8 036 613	8 620 465	11 530 834	14 757 444	Total
Africa		675 441	436 292	488 751	601 614	1 033 258	Afrique
Americas		53 190	70 196	66 464	235 900	297 143	Amériques
East Asia/Pacific		752 905	439 021	595 438	578 805	940 928	Asie de l'Est/Pacifique
Europe		424 297	340 310	484 575	656 937	1 185 068	Europe
Middle East		4 752 257	5 607 356	5 515 980	7 443 786	9 333 965	Moyen-Orient
South Asia		1 932 990	1 142 202	1 469 257	2 013 792	1 967 082	Asie du Sud
Region not specified		8 350	1 236	...	...	...	Région non spécifiée
Senegal	TFN						**Sénégal**
Total		666 616	769 489	866 154	874 623	...	Total
Africa		209 226	265 113	429 955	437 970	...	Afrique
Americas		24 686	26 274	25 921	26 004	...	Amériques
Europe		348 852	392 767	323 721	324 080	...	Europe
Region not specified		83 852	85 335	86 557	86 569	...	Région non spécifiée
Serbia	TCEN						**Serbie**
Total		391 826	452 679	468 842	696 045	646 494	Total
Americas		13 483	15 789	17 038	19 083	15 002	Amériques
East Asia/Pacific		4 879	5 675	6 402	7 433	7 826	Asie de l'Est/Pacifique
Europe		363 345	419 058	435 400	655 782	610 004	Europe
Region not specified		10 119	12 157	10 002	13 747	13 662	Région non spécifiée
Seychelles	TFR						**Seychelles**
Total		120 765	128 654	140 627	161 273	158 952	Total
Africa		12 598	12 478	13 408	16 847	19 117	Afrique
Americas		4 030	3 867	3 398	3 915	4 163	Amériques
East Asia/Pacific		2 135	2 647	2 996	3 793	3 486	Asie de l'Est/Pacifique
Europe		98 654	103 581	114 211	130 046	124 828	Europe
Middle East		1 911	4 458	4 731	4 930	5 489	Moyen-Orient
South Asia		1 437	1 623	1 883	1 742	1 869	Asie du Sud
Sierra Leone	TFR						**Sierra Leone**
Total[3]		43 560	40 023	33 704	32 223	35 670	Total[3]
Africa		24 446	21 798	10 122	10 846	11 915	Afrique
Americas		4 790	4 713	6 669	6 169	6 684	Amériques
East Asia/Pacific		2 257	2 343	4 898	2 916	3 142	Asie de l'Est/Pacifique
Europe		9 476	9 879	10 470	11 327	12 713	Europe
Middle East		2 591	1 290	1 545	965	888	Moyen-Orient
Region not specified		...	...	...	...	328	Région non spécifiée

61 Tourist/visitor arrivals by region of origin *(continued)*
Number
Arrivées de touristes/visiteurs par région de provenance *(suite)*
Nombre

Country or area of destination and region of origin+	Series& Série&	2004	2005	2006	2007	2008	Pays ou zone de destination et région de provenance+
Singapore	VFR						**Singapour**
Total[54]		8 328 720	8 943 029	9 751 141	10 284 545	10 116 054	Total[54]
Africa		70 626	78 803	87 132	93 600	86 023	Afrique
Americas		422 167	470 493	509 774	524 178	505 411	Amériques
East Asia/Pacific		6 072 703	6 445 012	7 012 238	7 322 529	7 070 353	Asie de l'Est/Pacifique
Europe		1 081 336	1 136 024	1 220 172	1 276 669	1 333 652	Europe
Middle East		55 450	56 165	65 923	78 353	87 690	Moyen-Orient
South Asia		626 165	751 437	849 808	968 389	1 026 576	Asie du Sud
Region not specified		273	5 095	6 094	20 827	6 349	Région non spécifiée
Slovakia	TCEN						**Slovaquie**
Total		1 401 189	1 514 980	1 611 808	1 684 526	1 766 529	Total
Africa		2 482	2 252	2 726	2 276	3 318	Afrique
Americas		38 712	42 100	39 118	43 697	41 456	Amériques
East Asia/Pacific		42 249	55 992	69 102	73 658	70 755	Asie de l'Est/Pacifique
Europe		1 316 705	1 412 628	1 499 394	1 558 688	1 647 872	Europe
Middle East		314	328	272	3 592	533	Moyen-Orient
South Asia		384	603	443	1 229	1 380	Asie du Sud
Region not specified		343	1 077	753	1 386	1 215	Région non spécifiée
Slovenia	TCEN						**Slovénie**
Total		1 498 852	1 554 969	1 616 650	1 751 332	1 771 237	Total
Africa		...	1 546	1 409	2 100	3 436	Afrique
Americas		45 880	59 303	67 159	66 900	61 010	Amériques
East Asia/Pacific		24 237	39 626	52 371	65 277	81 808	Asie de l'Est/Pacifique
Europe		1 410 671	1 454 494	1 495 711	1 617 055	1 624 983	Europe
Region not specified		18 064	...	...	...	...	Région non spécifiée
Solomon Islands	TFR						**Iles Salomon**
Total		5 558[55]	9 400[56]	11 482	13 748	16 264	Total
Americas		322	642	879	1 048	1 220	Amériques
East Asia/Pacific		4 864	8 128	9 755	11 628	13 772	Asie de l'Est/Pacifique
Europe		331	545	708	925	1 132	Europe
Region not specified		41	85	140	147	140	Région non spécifiée
South Africa	TFR						**Afrique du Sud**
Total[57]		6 677 844	7 368 742	8 395 833	9 090 881	9 591 828	Total[57]
Africa		4 638 371	5 370 137	6 280 500	6 862 105	7 343 765	Afrique
Americas		290 625	322 099	358 096	387 379	407 408	Amériques
East Asia/Pacific		238 829	238 885	257 666	281 567	270 657	Asie de l'Est/Pacifique
Europe		1 306 389	1 328 521	1 402 643	1 438 092	1 433 586	Europe
Middle East		16 037	17 194	19 806	20 954	23 412	Moyen-Orient
South Asia		36 172	36 045	44 337	51 823	51 929	Asie du Sud
Region not specified		151 421	55 861	32 785	48 961	61 071	Région non spécifiée
Spain	TFR						**Espagne**
Total		52 429 836	55 913 780	58 004 487	57 665 504	57 192 027	Total
Americas		2 079 065	2 232 851	2 377 824	2 312 514	2 397 783	Amériques
East Asia/Pacific		150 583	181 050	255 310	346 048	237 495	Asie de l'Est/Pacifique
Europe		49 238 605	52 189 873	54 312 755	53 926 639	53 512 157	Europe
Region not specified		961 583	1 310 006	1 058 598	1 080 303	1 044 592	Région non spécifiée
Sri Lanka	TFR						**Sri Lanka**
Total[1]		566 202	549 308	559 603	494 008	438 475	Total[1]
Africa		1 855	2 340	3 235	2 712	2 141	Afrique
Americas		30 500	47 162	36 098	32 317	28 050	Amériques
East Asia/Pacific		91 076	99 736	98 476	75 778	66 783	Asie de l'Est/Pacifique
Europe		298 776	236 481	242 666	222 669	199 223	Europe
Middle East		10 463	10 236	10 345	10 568	12 050	Moyen-Orient
South Asia		133 532	153 353	168 783	149 964	130 228	Asie du Sud
Sudan	TFN						**Soudan**
Total		60 577	245 798[9]	328 148[9]	436 295[9]	439 661[9]	Total
Africa		9 000	58 991	50 665	65 444	65 949	Afrique
Americas		...	20 751	11 607	15 526	15 388	Amériques
East Asia/Pacific		17 000	109 380	222 157	296 680	298 969	Asie de l'Est/Pacifique
Europe		17 000	55 796	43 719	56 718	57 156	Europe
Region not specified		17 577	880	...	1 927	2 199	Région non spécifiée

61 Tourist/visitor arrivals by region of origin *(continued)*

Number

Arrivées de touristes/visiteurs par région de provenance *(suite)*

Nombre

Country or area of destination and region of origin+	Series& Série&	2004	2005	2006	2007	2008	Pays ou zone de destination et région de provenance+
Suriname	TFR						**Suriname**
Total		137 808	160 022	152 895	162 509	...	Total
Africa		...	279	...	223	...	Afrique
Americas		44 802	56 338	48 627	50 857	...	Amériques
East Asia/Pacific		...	3 247	...	2 327	...	Asie de l'Est/Pacifique
Europe		86 913	99 265	98 292	108 134	...	Europe
Middle East		...	...	...	25	...	Moyen-Orient
South Asia		...	498	...	506	...	Asie du Sud
Region not specified		6 093	395	5 976	437	...	Région non spécifiée
Swaziland	VFR						**Swaziland**
Total		...	1 182 141	1 199 858	1 230 093	1 185 998	Total
Africa		...	1 043 248	1 056 388	1 075 005	1 041 211	Afrique
Americas		...	17 217	18 945	19 184	19 607	Amériques
East Asia/Pacific		...	9 699	9 642	12 009	11 779	Asie de l'Est/Pacifique
Europe		...	107 957	109 970	118 536	107 712	Europe
South Asia		...	4 020	4 913	5 359	5 689	Asie du Sud
Swaziland	THSR						**Swaziland**
Total[48]		352 040	311 656	316 082	299 226	...	Total[48]
Africa		151 879	134 456	167 347	176 417	...	Afrique
Americas		4 968	4 398	3 576	9 832	...	Amériques
East Asia/Pacific		3 485	3 085	5 423	8 044	...	Asie de l'Est/Pacifique
Europe		110 709	98 009	114 249	92 332	...	Europe
Region not specified		80 999	71 708	25 487	12 601	...	Région non spécifiée
Sweden	TCER						**Suède**
Total		4 675 923	4 883 202	4 729 088	5 223 655	4 728 323	Total
Americas		224 692	246 992	250 164	260 141	239 079	Amériques
East Asia/Pacific		148 113	182 979	191 324	199 248	214 571	Asie de l'Est/Pacifique
Europe		3 978 276	4 176 241	3 981 711	4 424 536	4 022 685	Europe
Region not specified		324 842	276 990	305 889	339 730	251 988	Région non spécifiée
Switzerland	THSR						**Suisse**
Total[58]		...	7 228 851	7 862 957	8 447 718	8 608 337	Total[58]
Africa		...	78 143	85 460	85 463	88 625	Afrique
Americas		...	829 551	933 715	954 115	878 356	Amériques
East Asia/Pacific		...	846 703	896 031	941 200	860 776	Asie de l'Est/Pacifique
Europe		...	5 304 949	5 747 455	6 225 587	6 520 802	Europe
Middle East		...	76 033	85 241	108 957	127 671	Moyen-Orient
South Asia		...	93 472	115 055	132 396	132 107	Asie du Sud
Syrian Arab Republic	VFN						**Rép. arabe syrienne**
Total[2,59]		6 334 106	5 858 791	5 681 751	5 434 253	6 950 852	Total[2,59]
Africa		89 664	92 585	81 136	77 526	85 242	Afrique
Americas		58 032	57 795	59 408	59 584	75 375	Amériques
East Asia/Pacific		36 852	35 088	35 155	34 998	41 021	Asie de l'Est/Pacifique
Europe		933 239	946 853	709 697	731 744	904 726	Europe
Middle East		3 956 642	3 456 403	3 445 033	3 123 927	4 390 535	Moyen-Orient
South Asia		217 947	268 952	289 658	355 530	388 819	Asie du Sud
Region not specified		1 041 730	1 001 115	1 061 664	1 050 944	1 065 134	Région non spécifiée
Syrian Arab Republic	TCEN						**Rép. arabe syrienne**
Total[2,59,60]		3 398 845	3 571 399	4 231 061	4 157 858	5 430 181	Total[2,59,60]
Africa		89 664	92 585	71 796	69 117	75 953	Afrique
Americas		58 032	57 795	54 583	54 738	69 575	Amériques
East Asia/Pacific		36 852	35 088	32 378	32 879	38 242	Asie de l'Est/Pacifique
Europe		313 956	430 120	467 151	486 063	618 272	Europe
Middle East		1 640 663	1 685 745	2 305 347	2 162 649	3 235 057	Moyen-Orient
South Asia		217 947	268 952	264 998	325 135	355 431	Asie du Sud
Region not specified		1 041 731	1 001 114	1 034 808	1 027 277	1 037 651	Région non spécifiée

61

Tourist/visitor arrivals by region of origin *(continued)*
Number

Arrivées de touristes/visiteurs par région de provenance *(suite)*
Nombre

Country or area of destination and region of origin+	Series& Série&	2004	2005	2006	2007	2008	Pays ou zone de destination et région de provenance+
Thailand	TFR						**Thaïlande**
Total		11 737 413[2]	11 567 341[2]	13 821 802[1]	14 464 228[1]	14 584 220[1]	Total
Africa		82 711	72 875	96 117	104 941	109 006	Afrique
Americas		692 792	739 703	825 079	817 564	853 348	Amériques
East Asia/Pacific		7 500 966	7 194 866	8 568 558	8 712 488	8 624 195	Asie de l'Est/Pacifique
Europe		2 706 062	2 778 693	3 439 010	3 812 782	3 963 326	Europe
Middle East		172 699	178 718	239 171	330 879	282 878	Moyen-Orient
South Asia		495 473	552 081	653 867	685 574	749 735	Asie du Sud
Region not specified		86 710	50 405	...	...	1 732	Région non spécifiée
TFYR of Macedonia	TCEN						**L'ex-R.Y. Macédoine**
Total		165 306	197 216	202 357	230 080	254 957	Total
Americas		8 362	8 439	9 181	8 947	9 632	Amériques
East Asia/Pacific		2 143	2 747	3 490	4 799	4 674	Asie de l'Est/Pacifique
Europe		151 215	182 534	186 519	212 365	236 122	Europe
Region not specified		3 586	3 496	3 167	3 969	4 529	Région non spécifiée
Togo	THSR						**Togo**
Total		82 686	80 763	94 096	86 165	73 982	Total
Africa		43 842	45 967	52 549	48 516	38 792	Afrique
Americas		2 738	2 633	3 314	2 928	2 405	Amériques
East Asia/Pacific		3 492	2 627	3 205	2 649	3 269	Asie de l'Est/Pacifique
Europe		30 018	27 092	33 266	31 181	29 376	Europe
Middle East		2 500	2 371	1 635	772	66	Moyen-Orient
Region not specified		96	73	127	119	74	Région non spécifiée
Tonga	TFR						**Tonga**
Total[3]		41 208	41 862	39 451	46 040	49 405	Total[3]
Americas		8 202	8 147	6 345	6 298	5 836	Amériques
East Asia/Pacific		28 972	30 424	29 634	36 524	37 754	Asie de l'Est/Pacifique
Europe		3 408	2 908	2 875	2 868	...	Europe
Region not specified		626	383	597	350	5 815	Région non spécifiée
Trinidad and Tobago	TFR						**Trinité-et-Tobago**
Total[3]		442 596	463 191	457 434	449 453	432 551	Total[3]
Africa		1 017	1 299	1 389	1 508	1 324	Afrique
Americas		347 181	365 311	364 888	356 177	359 997	Amériques
East Asia/Pacific		2 925	3 046	4 082	5 762	5 090	Asie de l'Est/Pacifique
Europe		89 512	91 424	84 243	82 495	63 170	Europe
Middle East		221	338	363	367	395	Moyen-Orient
South Asia		1 411	1 632	2 365	3 005	2 284	Asie du Sud
Region not specified		329	141	104	139	291	Région non spécifiée
Tunisia	TFN						**Tunisie**
Total[1]		5 997 918	6 378 430	6 549 549	6 761 906	7 049 000	Total[1]
Africa		984 538	993 378	1 010 195	1 045 637	1 043 121	Afrique
Americas		30 347	35 202	33 947	36 450	38 877	Amériques
East Asia/Pacific		10 784	13 710	15 442	16 702	16 472	Asie de l'Est/Pacifique
Europe		3 482 041	3 869 030	3 956 274	4 048 429	4 106 676	Europe
Middle East		1 471 752	1 440 387	1 507 155	1 581 512	1 807 656	Moyen-Orient
Region not specified		18 456	26 723	26 536	33 176	36 198	Région non spécifiée
Turkey	TFN						**Turquie**
Total		16 826 062	20 272 877	18 916 436	22 248 328	24 994 007	Total
Africa		131 148	154 489	152 983	166 883	203 522	Afrique
Americas		282 586	390 884	458 898	523 496	558 019	Amériques
East Asia/Pacific		288 326	421 643	471 280	585 706	567 663	Asie de l'Est/Pacifique
Europe		14 946 162	17 663 077	16 268 842	19 039 593	21 419 579	Europe
Middle East		498 095	625 686	630 140	787 561	1 009 759	Moyen-Orient
South Asia		660 787	994 620	917 360	1 124 724	1 212 330	Asie du Sud
Region not specified		18 958	22 478	16 933	20 365	23 135	Région non spécifiée

61 Tourist/visitor arrivals by region of origin *(continued)*
Number

Arrivées de touristes/visiteurs par région de provenance *(suite)*
Nombre

Country or area of destination and region of origin+	Series& Série&	2004	2005	2006	2007	2008	Pays ou zone de destination et région de provenance+
Turkmenistan	TFN						**Turkménistan**
Total		14 799	11 611	5 620	8 177	...	Total
Africa		...	1	...	13	...	Afrique
Americas		374	384	548	775	...	Amériques
East Asia/Pacific		1 053	753	872	943	...	Asie de l'Est/Pacifique
Europe		3 915	3 284	2 721	4 296	...	Europe
Middle East		32	4	...	7	...	Moyen-Orient
South Asia		9 425	7 185	1 479	2 143	...	Asie du Sud
Turks and Caicos Islands	TFR						**Iles Turques et Caïques**
Total		173 081	176 130	248 343	...	...	Total
Americas		148 736	156 773	221 650	...	...	Amériques
Europe		13 807	17 613	24 834	...	...	Europe
Region not specified		10 538	1 744	1 859	...	...	Région non spécifiée
Tuvalu	TFN						**Tuvalu**
Total		1 290	1 085	1 135	1 130	...	Total
Americas		79	101	63	65	...	Amériques
East Asia/Pacific		1 043	828	852	851	...	Asie de l'Est/Pacifique
Europe		108	104	120	87	...	Europe
Region not specified		60	52	100	127	...	Région non spécifiée
Uganda	TFR						**Ouganda**
Total		512 379	467 728	538 586	641 743	843 864	Total
Africa		405 706	337 188	397 031	479 802	624 352	Afrique
Americas		23 438	28 557	35 749	42 388	53 950	Amériques
East Asia/Pacific		8 150	10 046	12 003	14 466	14 687	Asie de l'Est/Pacifique
Europe		48 847	62 312	71 131	77 283	106 020	Europe
Middle East		3 133	3 766	4 111	4 971	9 720	Moyen-Orient
South Asia		12 139	13 879	14 339	14 803	18 845	Asie du Sud
Region not specified		10 966	11 980	4 222	8 030	16 290	Région non spécifiée
Ukraine	TFR						**Ukraine**
Total		15 629 213	17 630 760	18 935 775	23 122 157	25 449 078	Total
Africa		6 586	7 259	8 611	10 216	9 789	Afrique
Americas		99 135	95 540	142 519	167 103	163 371	Amériques
East Asia/Pacific		32 494	34 946	45 241	48 651	45 648	Asie de l'Est/Pacifique
Europe		15 450 129	17 442 407	18 679 863	22 825 500	25 163 875	Europe
Middle East		20 130	25 501	23 474	26 308	23 253	Moyen-Orient
South Asia		13 434	14 544	16 019	17 572	17 389	Asie du Sud
Region not specified		7 305	10 563	20 048	26 807	25 753	Région non spécifiée
United Arab Emirates	THSN						**Emirats arabes unis**
Total[61]		6 195 006	...	...	...	...	Total[61]
Africa		315 418	...	...	...	...	Afrique
Americas		285 627	...	...	...	...	Amériques
East Asia/Pacific		444 575	...	...	...	...	Asie de l'Est/Pacifique
Europe		2 007 600	...	...	...	...	Europe
Middle East		1 544 557	...	...	...	...	Moyen-Orient
South Asia		909 339	...	...	...	...	Asie du Sud
Region not specified		687 890	...	...	...	...	Région non spécifiée
United Kingdom	VFR						**Royaume-Uni**
Total		27 755 000	29 970 000	32 712 920	32 778 102	31 888 118	Total
Africa		639 000	659 000	701 468	653 917	644 718	Afrique
Americas		4 692 000	4 596 000	5 166 674	4 826 687	4 211 749	Amériques
East Asia/Pacific		2 086 000	2 231 000	2 310 449	2 315 607	2 146 669	Asie de l'Est/Pacifique
Europe		19 581 000	21 706 000	23 541 245	24 020 354	23 826 127	Europe
Middle East		386 000	384 000	471 856	489 559	537 585	Moyen-Orient
South Asia		371 000	394 000	521 228	471 978	521 270	Asie du Sud
United Rep. of Tanzania	VFR						**Rép.-Unie de Tanzanie**
Total		582 807	612 754	644 124	719 031	770 469	Total
Africa		256 455	275 718	293 440	305 748	373 053	Afrique
Americas		53 437	61 604	71 278	80 699	87 835	Amériques
East Asia/Pacific		22 928	24 714	28 222	29 760	32 442	Asie de l'Est/Pacifique
Europe		221 865	220 255	229 048	274 410	245 873	Europe
Middle East		11 594	10 528	6 815	11 444	10 377	Moyen-Orient
South Asia		16 528	19 935	15 321	16 970	20 889	Asie du Sud

Tourist/visitor arrivals by region of origin *(continued)*
Number

Arrivées de touristes/visiteurs par région de provenance *(suite)*
Nombre

Country or area of destination and region of origin+	Series& Série&	2004	2005	2006	2007	2008	Pays ou zone de destination et région de provenance+
United States	TFR						**Etats-Unis**
Total		46 086 257	49 205 528	50 977 290	55 979 277	57 937 451	Total
Africa		240 488	251 654	251 841	276 300	311 136	Afrique
Americas		29 195 830	31 178 408	33 128 495	36 463 985	37 128 338	Amériques
East Asia/Pacific		6 086 708	6 518 211	6 427 817	6 562 889	6 343 399	Asie de l'Est/Pacifique
Europe		10 055 657	10 701 847	10 530 566	11 839 074	13 249 818	Europe
Middle East		137 259	144 131	164 283	195 986	227 629	Moyen-Orient
South Asia		370 315	411 277	474 288	641 043	677 131	Asie du Sud
United States Virgin Is.	THSN						**Iles Vierges américaines**
Total		603 944	617 603	700 985	679 578	731 498	Total
Africa		289	162	59	115	72	Afrique
Americas		560 581	568 908	648 842	651 167	711 905	Amériques
East Asia/Pacific		379	501	350	351	375	Asie de l'Est/Pacifique
Europe		15 819	18 821	15 020	14 837	15 621	Europe
Region not specified		26 876	29 211	36 714	13 108	3 525	Région non spécifiée
Uruguay	VFN						**Uruguay**
Total [2]		1 870 858	1 917 049	1 824 340	1 815 281	1 997 884	Total [2]
Americas		1 457 944	1 497 756	1 402 957	1 406 790	1 544 086	Amériques
East Asia/Pacific		7 221	11 686	12 877	12 855	14 374	Asie de l'Est/Pacifique
Europe		97 223	119 553	124 215	132 636	139 282	Europe
Middle East		489	182	172	234	261	Moyen-Orient
Region not specified		307 981	287 872	284 119	262 766	299 881	Région non spécifiée
Uzbekistan	TFR						**Ouzbékistan**
Total		261 600	...	559 500	903 100	1 069 300	Total
Africa		1 000	...	2 000	2 000	2 500	Afrique
Americas		12 000	...	6 000	8 000	8 000	Amériques
East Asia/Pacific		140 000	...	295 900	442 700	578 600	Asie de l'Est/Pacifique
Europe		68 600	...	215 600	370 400	385 200	Europe
Middle East		30 000	...	30 000	50 000	55 000	Moyen-Orient
South Asia		10 000	...	10 000	30 000	40 000	Asie du Sud
Vanuatu	TFR						**Vanuatu**
Total		61 453	62 123	68 179[62]	81 344	90 654	Total
Americas		1 954	1 625	1 896	2 578	2 578	Amériques
East Asia/Pacific		55 027	55 894	61 023	73 214	81 162	Asie de l'Est/Pacifique
Europe		3 388	3 504	4 021	3 785	4 886	Europe
Region not specified		1 084	1 100	1 239	1 767	2 028	Région non spécifiée
Venezuela (Boliv. Rep. of)	TFN						**Venezuela (Rép. boliv. du)**
Total		486 401	706 103	747 930	770 567	744 709	Total
Africa		640	918	1 259	995	1 010	Afrique
Americas		217 699	374 460	411 772	420 056	408 219	Amériques
East Asia/Pacific		4 475	16 762	17 106	19 163	19 451	Asie de l'Est/Pacifique
Europe		258 178	296 310	297 601	316 041	301 579	Europe
Middle East		492	9 772	9 979	10 024	10 100	Moyen-Orient
South Asia		344	1 801	1 931	1 397	1 418	Asie du Sud
Region not specified		4 573	6 080	8 282	2 891	2 932	Région non spécifiée
Viet Nam	VFR						**Viet Nam**
Total [9]		2 927 873	3 467 757	3 583 488	4 243 626	4 253 741	Total [9]
Americas		326 286	396 997	459 398	508 202	417 198	Amériques
East Asia/Pacific		2 008 366	2 365 222	2 361 258	2 715 593	2 546 133	Asie de l'Est/Pacifique
Europe		354 735	425 774	480 585	634 461	...	Europe
Region not specified		238 486	279 764	282 247	385 370	1 290 410	Région non spécifiée
Yemen	THSN						**Yémen**
Total		273 732	336 070	382 332	379 390	404 497	Total
Africa		10 853	12 628	20 909	20 181	17 715	Afrique
Americas		17 099	18 253	18 771	17 615	18 118	Amériques
East Asia/Pacific		22 512	24 437	18 839	19 668	20 466	Asie de l'Est/Pacifique
Europe		28 608	26 456	32 789	33 079	36 099	Europe
Middle East		175 679	238 524	270 500	268 540	293 275	Moyen-Orient
South Asia		18 981	15 772	20 524	20 307	18 824	Asie du Sud

61 Tourist/visitor arrivals by region of origin *(continued)*
Number

Arrivées de touristes/visiteurs par région de provenance *(suite)*
Nombre

Country or area of destination and region of origin+	Series& Série&	2004	2005	2006	2007	2008	Pays ou zone de destination et région de provenance+
Zambia	TFR						**Zambie**
Total		515 000	668 862	756 860	897 413	811 775	Total
Africa		366 918	461 000	510 270	660 551	606 641	Afrique
Americas		29 053	37 580	52 457	50 606	47 360	Amériques
East Asia/Pacific		23 107	39 912	38 171	28 095	34 658	Asie de l'Est/Pacifique
Europe		91 863	121 712	143 304	145 729	109 182	Europe
South Asia		4 059	8 658	12 658	12 432	13 934	Asie du Sud
Zimbabwe	VFR						**Zimbabwe**
Total		1 854 488	1 558 501	2 286 572	2 508 255	1 955 596	Total
Africa		1 523 090	1 356 384	2 082 724	2 289 308	1 731 528	Afrique
Americas		75 161	43 976	44 746	40 388	43 412	Amériques
East Asia/Pacific		90 405	38 767	53 908	56 720	63 194	Asie de l'Est/Pacifique
Europe		155 767	112 608	96 849	109 119	108 161	Europe
Middle East		3 749	1 989	4 145	4 502	4 102	Moyen-Orient
South Asia		6 316	4 777	4 200	5 023	5 199	Asie du Sud
Region not specified		...	...	...	3 195	...	Région non spécifiée

Source:
World Tourism Organization (UNWTO), Madrid, UNWTO statistics database and the *Yearbook of Tourism Statistics*, 2010 edition.

+ For a listing of the Member States of the regions of origin, see Annex I, with the following exceptions:

Africa includes the countries and territories listed under Africa in Annex I but excludes Egypt and Libyan Arab Jamahiriya.
Americas is as shown in Annex I
Europe is as shown in Annex I, but also includes Armenia, Azerbaijan, Cyprus, Georgia, Israel, Kazakhstan, Kyrgyzstan, Tajikistan, Turkey, Turkmenistan and Uzbekistan.
East Asia and the Pacific includes the countries and territories listed under Eastern Asia, South-eastern Asia, and Oceania in Annex I except for Canton and Enderbury Islands, Christmas Island, Cocos Island, Johnston Island, Midway Islands, and Wake Island.
South Asia is as shown in Annex I under South-central Asia, but excludes Kazakhstan, Kyrgyzstan, Tajikistan, Turkmenistan and Uzbekistan.
Middle east is as shown in Annex I under Western Asia, but excludes Armenia, Azerbaijan, Cyprus, Georgia, Israel, and Turkey. The Western Asia group also includes Egypt and the Libyan Arab Jamahiriya.

& Series:

TFN: Arrivals of non-resident tourists at national borders (excluding same-day visitors), by nationality.
TFR: Arrivals of non-resident tourists at national borders (excluding same- day visitors), by country of residence.
TCEN: Arrivals of non-resident tourists in all types of accommodation establishments, by nationality.
TCER: Arrivals of non-resident tourists in all types of accommodation establishments, by country of residence.
THSN: Arrivals of non-resident tourists in hotels and similar establishments, by nationality.
THSR: Arrivals of non-resident tourists in hotels and similar establishments, by country of residence.
VFN: Arrivals of non-resident visitors at national borders (including tourists and same-day visitors), by nationality.
VFR: Arrivals of non-resident visitors at national borders (including tourists and same-day visitors), by country of residence.

Source:
Organisation mondiale du tourisme (OMT), Madrid, la base de données de l'OMT, et l'*Annuaire des statistiques du tourisme*, édition 2010.

+ On se reportera à l'Annexe I pour les États Membres classés dans les différentes régions de provenance, avec les exceptions ci-après :

Afrique – Comprend les États et territoires énumérés dans l'Annexe I, sauf l'Égypte et la Jamahiriya arabe libyenne.
Amériques – Comprend les États et territoires énumérés dans l'Annexe I.
Europe – Comprend les États et territoires énumérés dans l'Annexe I, mais comprend en revanche l'Arménie, l'Azerbaïdjan, Chypre, la Géorgie, l'Israël, le Kazakhstan, le Kirghizistan, le Tadjikistan, la Turquie, le Turkménistan, et l'Ouzbékistan.
L'Asie de l'Est et le Pacifique– Comprend les États et territoires énumérés dans l'Annexe I dans les Groupes Asie de l'Est, Asie du Sud-est et Océanie sauf les îles Canton et Enderbury, l'île Christmas, les îles Cocos, l'île Johnston, les îles Midway, Nauru, et l'île Wake.
Asie du Sud – Comprend les États et territoires énumérés dans l'Annexe I dans le groupe Asie centrale et du sud, sauf le Kazakhstan, le Kirghizistan, l'Ouzbékistan, le Tadjikistan et le Turkménistan.
Le Moyen-Orient – Comprend les États et territoires énumérés dans l'Annexe I dans le groupe Asie occidentale, sauf l'Arménie, l'Azerbaïdjan, Chypre, la Géorgie, Israël, la Turquie. Le Groupe comprend en revanche l'Égypte et la Jamahiriya arabe libyenne.

& Série :

TFN : Arrivées de touristes non résidents aux frontières nationales (à l'exclusion de visiteurs de la journée), par nationalité.
TFR : Arrivées de touristes non résidents aux frontières nationales (à l'exclusion de visiteurs de la journée), par pays de résidence.
TCEN : Arrivées de touristes non résidents dans tous les types d'établissements d'hébergement, par nationalité.
TCER : Arrivées de touristes non résidents dans tous les types d'établissements d'hébergement, par pays de résidence.
THSN : Arrivées de touristes non résidents dans les hôtels et établissements assimilés, par nationalité.
THSR : Arrivées de touristes non résidents dans les hôtels et établissements assimilés, par pays de résidence.
VFN : Arrivées de visiteurs non résidents aux frontières nationales (y compris touristes et visiteurs de la journée), par nationalité.
VFR : Arrivées de visiteurs non résidents aux frontières nationales (y compris touristes et visiteurs de la journée), par pays de résidence.

61 Tourist/visitor arrivals by region of origin *(continued)*

Number

Arrivées de touristes/visiteurs par région de provenance *(suite)*

Nombre

Footnotes on the totals also apply to the other regions.

1 Excluding nationals of the country residing abroad.
2 Arrivals of nationals residing abroad are included in the total and are all accounted for in "region not specified" only.
3 Air arrivals.
4 Excluding nationals residing abroad and crew members.
5 Including private accommodation.
6 Organized tourism.
7 Hotel establishments, camping areas, holiday centres, holiday villages and specific categories of accommodation.
8 International tourist arrivals in hotels of regional capitals.
9 Arrivals of nationals residing abroad are included in the total and are also accounted for in the individual regions.
10 For statistical purposes, the data for China do not include those for the Hong Kong Special Administrative Region (Hong Kong SAR), Macao Special Administrative Region (Macao SAR) and Taiwan Province of China.
11 Including arrivals by sea, land and by air.
12 Including stateless and Chinese people who do not have permanent residency in Hong Kong SAR, China.
13 Arrivals of foreign travellers at checkpoints of the Administrative Department of Security (DAS). Excluding cruise passengers and the foreign travellers arrived at terrestrial frontier points and that according to the Bank of the Republic were (in thousands): 2004: 777; 2005: 454; 2006: 992; 2007: 1,059; 2008: 1,097.
14 Air and sea arrivals.
15 Including arrivals in ports of nautical tourism.
16 New methodology.
17 Arrivals through all ports of entry.
18 Due to a change in the methodology, from 2004 the data are not comparable with those of previous years.
19 Non-resident visitor survey (EVE).
20 Charter tourists only.
21 Information based on administrative data.
22 Estimates for continental Guadeloupe (excluding Saint-Martin and Saint-Barthelemy).
23 Data based on a survey conducted at Guadeloupe airport.
24 Air arrivals at Conakry airport.
25 Arrivals at "Osvaldo Vieira" Airport.
26 Arrivals at Timehri airport only.
27 Departures.
28 The observation of the borders with the countries of the Schengen Area ceased from the year 2008.
29 Collective accommodation establishments.
30 Excluding seasonal and border workers.
31 Tarawa and Christmas Island.
32 Including crew members.
33 Data source: Department of Customs Control.
34 Excluding Syrian nationals, Palestinians and students.
35 Including Singapore residents crossing the frontier by road through the Johore Causeway.
36 Data based on departures by air and by sea.
37 Arrivals in the States of Kosrae, Chuuk, Pohnpei and Yap.
38 Change of methodology. Until 2007 the data correspond only to 12 border posts. From 2008, the data of all the border posts of the country are used.
39 Including tourist arrivals through border entry points to Yangon.
40 Data regarding short term movements are compiled from a random sample of passenger declarations. Source: Statistics New Zealand, External Migration.

Les notes sur les totaux s'appliquent aussi aux autres régions.

1 A l'exclusion des nationaux du pays résidant à l'étranger.
2 Les arrivées de nationaux résidant à l'étranger sont comprises dans le total, et sont toutes comptabilisées uniquement dans la catégorie Région non spécifiée.
3 Arrivées par voie aérienne.
4 A l'exclusion des nationaux du pays résidant à l'étranger et des membres des équipages.
5 Y compris l'hébergement privé.
6 Tourisme organisé.
7 Établissements hôteliers, terrains de camping, centres de vacances, villages de vacances et catégories spécifiques d'hébergement.
8 Arrivées de touristes internationaux dans les hôtels des capitales de département.
9 Les arrivées de nationaux résidant à l'étranger sont comprises dans le total, et comptabilisées aussi dans chacune des régions.
10 Pour la présentation des statistiques, les données pour la Chine ne comprennent pas la Région Administrative Spéciale de Hong Kong (Hong Kong RAS), la Région Administrative Spéciale de Macao (Macao RAS) et la province de Taiwan.
11 Y compris les arrivées par mer, terre et air.
12 Y compris les apatrides et les chinois qui ne résident pas de manière permanente à Hong-Kong SAR, Chine
13 Arrivées de voyageurs étrangers par des points de contrôle du Département Administratif de Sécurité (DAS). Exclus les passagers en croisière et les voyageurs étrangers arrivés par des points frontaliers terrestres et qui selon la Banque de la République ont été (en milliers) : 2004: 777; 2005: 454; 2006: 992; 2007: 1.059; 2008: 1.097.
14 Arrivées par voie aérienne et maritime.
15 Y compris les arrivées dans des ports à tourisme nautique.
16 Nouvelle méthodologie.
17 Arrivées à travers tous les ports d'entrée.
18 La méthodologie a été modifiée et pour cela, à partir de 2004 les données ne sont pas comparables avec celles des années précédentes.
19 Enquête auprès des visiteurs venant de l'étranger (EVE).
20 Arrivées en vols à la demande seulement.
21 Information tirée de données administratives.
22 Estimations pour la Guadeloupe continentale (sans Saint-Martin et Saint-Barthélemy).
23 Données tirées d'une enquête réalisée à l'aéroport de Guadeloupe.
24 Arrivées par voie aérienne à l'aéroport de Conakry.
25 Arrivées à l'aéroport "Osvaldo Vieira".
26 Arrivées à l'aéroport de Timehri seulement.
27 Départs.
28 La surveillance des frontières avec les pays de la zone Schengen a pris fin en 2008.
29 Etablissements d'hébergement collectif.
30 A l'exclusion des travailleurs saisonniers et frontaliers.
31 Tarawa et Ile Christmas.
32 Y compris les membres d'équipage.
33 Source d'information: Département du Contrôle douanier.
34 A l'exclusion des ressortissants syriens, palestiniens et sous-études.
35 Y compris les résidents de Singapour traversant la frontière par voie terrestre à travers le Johore Causeway.
36 Données tirées des départs par voies aérienne et maritime.
37 Arrivées dans les États de Kosrae, Chuuk, Pohnpei et Yap.
38 Changement de méthodologie. Jusqu'en 2007, les données correspondent seulement à 12 postes frontaliers. A partir de 2008, les données de tous les postes frontaliers du pays sont utilisées.
39 Comprenant les arrivées de touristes aux postes-frontières de Yangon.
40 Les données relatives aux mouvements de courte durée sont obtenues à partir d'un échantillon aléatoire de déclarations des passagers. Source : Statistiques de la Nouvelle Zélande, Immigration.

61 Tourist/visitor arrivals by region of origin *(continued)*
Number

Arrivées de touristes/visiteurs par région de provenance *(suite)*
Nombre

41	Including Niuans usually residing in New Zealand.	41	Y compris les nationaux de Niue résidant habituellement en Nouvelle-Zélande.
42	Figures are based on the guest survey carried out by Institute of Transport Economics.	42	Les chiffres se fondent sur "l'enquête auprès de la clientèle" de l'Institut d'économie des transports.
43	Air arrivals (Palau International Airport).	43	Arrivées par voie aérienne (Aéroport international de Palau).
44	Total number of visitors broken down by permanent residence who arrived in Panama at Tocumen International Airport.	44	Nombre total de visiteurs arrivés au Panama par l'aéroport international de Tocúmen.
45	E/D cards in the "Silvio Petirossi" airport and passenger counts at the national border crossings - National Police and SENATUR.	45	Cartes d'embarquement et de débarquement à l'aéroport Silvio Petirossi et comptages des passagers lors du franchissement des frontières nationales – Police Nationale et SENATUR.
46	Since Poland joined the Schengen area, precise counting of incoming traffic is not possible. Data presented here are based on surveys by the Institute of Tourism. Only approximate results for main countries can be given.	46	Depuis que la Pologne est entrée dans l'espace Schengen, le comptage précis du trafic entrant n'est pas possible. Les données présentées ici sont basées sur les enquêtes de l'Institut du Tourisme. Seuls des résultats approximatifs des principaux pays peuvent être fournis.
47	Fiscal year July to June.	47	Année fiscale de juillet à juin.
48	Arrivals in hotels only.	48	Arrivées dans les hôtels uniquement.
49	Visitors who received tourism services from licensed tourism agencies and tour operators. Excluding the left bank of the river Dniester and the municipality of Bender.	49	Visiteurs qui ont bénéficié des services touristiques des agences de tourisme et des voyagistes (titulaires d'une licence touristique). À l'exception de la rive gauche de la rivière Dniester et de la municipalité de Bender.
50	Excluding Netherlands Antillean residents.	50	A l'exclusion des résidents des Antilles Néerlandaises.
51	Arrivals at Princess Juliana International airport.	51	Arrivées à l'aéroport international "Princess Juliana".
52	Including visitors to Saint Martin (the French side of the island).	52	Y compris les visiteurs à Saint Martin (partie française de l'île).
53	Including Italian visitors.	53	Y compris les visiteurs italiens.
54	Excluding Malaysian citizens arriving by land.	54	Non compris les arrivées de malaysiens par voie terrestre.
55	Excluding the first and second quarters.	55	À l'exclusion des 1ers et 2èmes trimestres.
56	Excluding the first quarter.	56	À l'exclusion du 1er trimestre.
57	Excluding arrivals by work and contract workers.	57	À l'exclusion des arrivées par travail et les travailleurs contractuels.
58	Hotels and health establishments.	58	Hôtels et établissements de cure.
59	Survey of the incoming tourism in 2004, 2006 and 2007.	59	Enquête du tourisme récepteur en 2004, 2006 et 2007.
60	Excluding private accommodation.	60	À l'exclusion de l'hébergement chez des particuliers.
61	Domestic tourism and arrivals of nationals residing abroad are included in the total and are all accounted for in "Region not specified" only.	61	Les touristes nationaux et les arrivées de nationaux résidant à l'étranger sont compris dans le total, et sont tous pris en compte uniquement dans "Région non spécifiée" seulement.
62	From November 2006, including arrivals to Luganville.	62	À partir de novembre 2006, les arrivées à Luganville sont inclues.

Tourist/visitor arrivals and tourism expenditure

Thousands of arrivals and millions of US dollars

Arrivées de touristes/visiteurs et dépenses touristiques

Milliers d'arrivées et millions de dollars E.-U.

Country or area of destination	Series[&] Série[&]	2003	2004	2005	2006	2007	2008	Pays ou zone de destination
Albania								**Albanie**
Tourist/visitor arrivals [1]	THS	41	34	57	63	67	57	Arrivées de touristes/visiteurs [1]
Tourism expenditure		537	756	880	1 057	1 451	1 849	Dépenses touristiques
Algeria								**Algérie**
Tourist/visitor arrivals [2]	VF	1 166	1 234	1 443	1 638	1 743	1 772	Arrivées de touristes/visiteurs [2]
Tourism expenditure [3]		112	178	184	215	219	325	Dépenses touristiques [3]
American Samoa	TF							**Samoa américaines**
Tourist/visitor arrivals		...	...	24	25	...	...	Arrivées de touristes/visiteurs
Andorra	TF							**Andorre**
Tourist/visitor arrivals		3 138	2 791	2 418	2 227	2 189	2 059	Arrivées de touristes/visiteurs
Angola								**Angola**
Tourist/visitor arrivals	TF	107	194	210	121	195	294	Arrivées de touristes/visiteurs
Tourism expenditure		63	82	103	91	236	293	Dépenses touristiques
Anguilla								**Anguilla**
Tourist/visitor arrivals [4]	TF	47	54	62	73	78	68	Arrivées de touristes/visiteurs [4]
Tourism expenditure [5]		64	69	86	107	115	101	Dépenses touristiques [5]
Antigua and Barbuda								**Antigua-et-Barbuda**
Tourist/visitor arrivals [4]	TF	239	246[6]	245[6]	254[6]	262[6]	266[6]	Arrivées de touristes/visiteurs [4]
Tourism expenditure [5]		300	337	309	327	338	334	Dépenses touristiques [5]
Argentina [7]								**Argentine** [7]
Tourist/visitor arrivals	TF	2 995	3 457	3 823	4 173	4 562	4 665	Arrivées de touristes/visiteurs
Tourism expenditure		2 306	2 660	3 209	3 899	4 984	5 308	Dépenses touristiques
Armenia								**Arménie**
Tourist/visitor arrivals	TF	206	263	319	382	511	558	Arrivées de touristes/visiteurs
Tourism expenditure		90	188	240	307	343	377	Dépenses touristiques
Aruba								**Aruba**
Tourist/visitor arrivals	TF	642	728	733	694	772	827	Arrivées de touristes/visiteurs
Tourism expenditure		859	1 056[5]	1 094[5]	1 080	1 255	1 417	Dépenses touristiques
Australia								**Australie**
Tourist/visitor arrivals [8]	VF	4 746	5 215	5 499	5 532	5 644	5 586	Arrivées de touristes/visiteurs [8]
Tourism expenditure		16 647	20 453	22 566	23 729	26 633	28 470	Dépenses touristiques
Austria								**Autriche**
Tourist/visitor arrivals	TCE	19 078	19 374	19 952	20 269	20 773	21 935	Arrivées de touristes/visiteurs
Tourism expenditure		15 128	17 251	18 471	18 886	21 088	24 343	Dépenses touristiques
Azerbaijan								**Azerbaïdjan**
Tourist/visitor arrivals	TF	768	989	861	904	1 011	1 409	Arrivées de touristes/visiteurs
Tourism expenditure		70	79	100	201	317	381	Dépenses touristiques
Bahamas								**Bahamas**
Tourist/visitor arrivals	TF	1 510	1 561	1 608	1 601	1 528	1 463	Arrivées de touristes/visiteurs
Tourism expenditure		1 770	1 897	2 081	2 066	2 198	2 164	Dépenses touristiques
Bahrain								**Bahreïn**
Tourist/visitor arrivals	TF	2 955	3 514	3 914	4 519	4 935	...	Arrivées de touristes/visiteurs
Tourism expenditure		1 206	1 504	1 603	1 786	1 854	1 927	Dépenses touristiques
Bangladesh								**Bangladesh**
Tourist/visitor arrivals	TF	245	271	208	200	289	467	Arrivées de touristes/visiteurs
Tourism expenditure		59	76	79	80	76[5]	91[5]	Dépenses touristiques
Barbados								**Barbade**
Tourist/visitor arrivals	TF	531	552	548	563	575	568	Arrivées de touristes/visiteurs
Tourism expenditure		840	843	904	1 064	1 196	1 201	Dépenses touristiques
Belarus								**Bélarus**
Tourist/visitor arrivals [9]	TF	64	67	91	89	105	91	Arrivées de touristes/visiteurs [9]
Tourism expenditure		339	362	346	401	479	585	Dépenses touristiques
Belgium								**Belgique**
Tourist/visitor arrivals	TCE	6 690	6 710	6 747	6 995	7 045	7 165	Arrivées de touristes/visiteurs
Tourism expenditure		8 848	10 089	10 881	11 625	12 350	13 063	Dépenses touristiques
Belize								**Belize**
Tourist/visitor arrivals	TF	221	231	237	247	251	245	Arrivées de touristes/visiteurs
Tourism expenditure [5]		150	168	214	260	289	278	Dépenses touristiques [5]

Tourist/visitor arrivals and tourism expenditure *(continued)*
Thousands of arrivals and millions of US dollars

Arrivées de touristes/visiteurs et dépenses touristiques *(suite)*
Milliers d'arrivées et millions de dollars E.-U.

Country or area of destination	Series[&] Série[&]	2003	2004	2005	2006	2007	2008	Pays ou zone de destination
Benin								**Bénin**
Tourist/visitor arrivals [10]	TF	175	174	176	180	186	188	Arrivées de touristes/visiteurs [10]
Tourism expenditure		108	121	108	122	206	216	Dépenses touristiques
Bermuda								**Bermudes**
Tourist/visitor arrivals [6]	TF	257	272	270	299	306	264	Arrivées de touristes/visiteurs [6]
Tourism expenditure [5]		348[11]	426[11]	429[11]	495	569	431	Dépenses touristiques [5]
Bhutan								**Bhoutan**
Tourist/visitor arrivals	TF	6	9	14	17	21	28	Arrivées de touristes/visiteurs
Tourism expenditure [3]		8	13	19	24	30	39	Dépenses touristiques [3]
Bolivia (Plurin. State of)								**Bolivie (État plurinational de)**
Tourist/visitor arrivals	TF	427	480	524	521	573	594	Arrivées de touristes/visiteurs
Tourism expenditure		243	283	345	330	326	302	Dépenses touristiques
Bonaire								**Bonaire**
Tourist/visitor arrivals	TF	62	63	63	64	74	74	Arrivées de touristes/visiteurs
Tourism expenditure [5,12]		84	87	87	91	110	121	Dépenses touristiques [5,12]
Bosnia and Herzegovina								**Bosnie-Herzégovine**
Tourist/visitor arrivals	TCE	165	190	217	256	306	322	Arrivées de touristes/visiteurs
Tourism expenditure		404	507	557	658	810	920	Dépenses touristiques
Botswana								**Botswana**
Tourist/visitor arrivals	TF	1 406	1 523	1 474	1 426	1 455	1 500	Arrivées de touristes/visiteurs
Tourism expenditure		459	582	563	539	266	515	Dépenses touristiques
Brazil								**Brésil**
Tourist/visitor arrivals	TF	4 133	4 794	5 358	5 017	5 026	5 050	Arrivées de touristes/visiteurs
Tourism expenditure		2 673	3 389	4 168	4 577	5 284	6 109	Dépenses touristiques
British Virgin Islands								**Iles Vierges britanniques**
Tourist/visitor arrivals	TF	278	304	337	356	358	346	Arrivées de touristes/visiteurs
Tourism expenditure [3]		342	393	437	...	...	...	Dépenses touristiques [3]
Brunei Darussalam								**Brunéi Darussalam**
Tourist/visitor arrivals [6]	TF	...	119	126	158	179	226	Arrivées de touristes/visiteurs [6]
Tourism expenditure [5]		124	181	191	224	233	241	Dépenses touristiques [5]
Bulgaria								**Bulgarie**
Tourist/visitor arrivals	TF	4 048	4 630	4 837	5 158	5 151	5 780	Arrivées de touristes/visiteurs
Tourism expenditure		2 051	2 796	3 063	3 317	3 975	4 831	Dépenses touristiques
Burkina Faso								**Burkina Faso**
Tourist/visitor arrivals	THS	163	222	245	264	289	226	Arrivées de touristes/visiteurs
Tourism expenditure [13]		...	40[5]	45	55	57	...	Dépenses touristiques [13]
Burundi								**Burundi**
Tourist/visitor arrivals [2]	TF	74	133	148	201	...	...	Arrivées de touristes/visiteurs [2]
Tourism expenditure		1	2	2	2	2	2	Dépenses touristiques
Cambodia								**Cambodge**
Tourist/visitor arrivals [14]	VF	701	1 055	1 422	1 700	2 015	2 125	Arrivées de touristes/visiteurs [14]
Tourism expenditure		441	673	929	1 080	1 284	1 300	Dépenses touristiques
Cameroon								**Cameroun**
Tourist/visitor arrivals	THS	...	190	176	185	...	...	Arrivées de touristes/visiteurs
Tourism expenditure		266	212	229	231	254	165	Dépenses touristiques
Canada								**Canada**
Tourist/visitor arrivals [15]	TF	17 534	19 145	18 771	18 265	17 935	17 142	Arrivées de touristes/visiteurs [15]
Tourism expenditure		12 236	15 135	16 006	16 978	17 833	17 771	Dépenses touristiques
Cape Verde								**Cap-Vert**
Tourist/visitor arrivals	TF	150	157	198	242	267	285	Arrivées de touristes/visiteurs
Tourism expenditure		135	153	177	280	375	432	Dépenses touristiques
Cayman Islands								**Iles Caïmanes**
Tourist/visitor arrivals [6]	TF	294	260	168	267	292	303	Arrivées de touristes/visiteurs [6]
Tourism expenditure [3]		518	523	356	513	479	353	Dépenses touristiques [3]
Central African Rep.								**Rép. centrafricaine**
Tourist/visitor arrivals [16]	TF	6	8	12	14	17	31	Arrivées de touristes/visiteurs [16]
Tourism expenditure [17]		4[11]	8[11]	7	10	11	12	Dépenses touristiques [17]
Chad	TF							**Tchad**
Tourist/visitor arrivals		21	26	29	16	25	...	Arrivées de touristes/visiteurs

62 Tourist/visitor arrivals and tourism expenditure *(continued)*

Thousands of arrivals and millions of US dollars

Arrivées de touristes/visiteurs et dépenses touristiques *(suite)*

Milliers d'arrivées et millions de dollars E.-U.

Country or area of destination	Series[&] Série[&]	2003	2004	2005	2006	2007	2008	Pays ou zone de destination
Chile								**Chili**
Tourist/visitor arrivals	TF	1 614	1 785	2 027	2 253	2 507	2 699	Arrivées de touristes/visiteurs
Tourism expenditure		1 309	1 571	1 682	1 891	2 231	2 632	Dépenses touristiques
China[18]								**Chine**[18]
Tourist/visitor arrivals	TF	32 970	41 761	46 809	49 913	54 720	53 049	Arrivées de touristes/visiteurs
Tourism expenditure		18 707	27 755	31 842	37 132	41 126	44 130	Dépenses touristiques
China, Hong Kong SAR								**Chine, Hong Kong RAS**
Tourist/visitor arrivals	TF	9 676	13 655	14 773	15 821	17 154	17 319	Arrivées de touristes/visiteurs
Tourism expenditure[19]		9 004	11 893	13 628	15 541	18 234	20 413	Dépenses touristiques[19]
China, Macao SAR								**Chine, Macao RAS**
Tourist/visitor arrivals[10]	TF	6 309	8 324	9 014	10 683	12 942	10 605[20]	Arrivées de touristes/visiteurs[10]
Tourism expenditure		5 319	7 496	8 016	9 755	13 404	17 093	Dépenses touristiques
Colombia								**Colombie**
Tourist/visitor arrivals[21,22,23]	VF	668	840	981	1 104	2 242	2 396	Arrivées de touristes/visiteurs[21,22,23]
Tourism expenditure		1 191	1 369	1 574	2 009	2 262	2 499	Dépenses touristiques
Comoros								**Comores**
Tourist/visitor arrivals	TF	21	23	26	29	15	...	Arrivées de touristes/visiteurs
Tourism expenditure[24]		16	21	24	27	...	...	Dépenses touristiques[24]
Congo								**Congo**
Tourist/visitor arrivals	THS	23	31	35	43	...	...	Arrivées de touristes/visiteurs
Tourism expenditure		30	23	40[5]	45[5]	54[5]	...	Dépenses touristiques
Cook Islands								**Iles Cook**
Tourist/visitor arrivals	TF	78	83	88	92	97	95	Arrivées de touristes/visiteurs
Tourism expenditure[3]		69	72	91	90	107	105	Dépenses touristiques[3]
Costa Rica								**Costa Rica**
Tourist/visitor arrivals	TF	1 239	1 453	1 679	1 725	1 980	2 089	Arrivées de touristes/visiteurs
Tourism expenditure		1 424	1 586	1 810	1 865	2 221	2 526	Dépenses touristiques
Côte d'Ivoire								**Côte d'Ivoire**
Tourism expenditure		76	91	93	104	115	114[5]	Dépenses touristiques
Croatia								**Croatie**
Tourist/visitor arrivals	TCE	7 409	7 912	8 467	8 659	9 307	9 415	Arrivées de touristes/visiteurs
Tourism expenditure		6 513	6 945	7 625	8 296	9 601	11 668	Dépenses touristiques
Cuba								**Cuba**
Tourist/visitor arrivals[6]	TF	1 847	2 017	2 261	2 150	2 119	2 316	Arrivées de touristes/visiteurs[6]
Tourism expenditure[3]		1 999	2 114	2 399	2 414	2 415	2 548	Dépenses touristiques[3]
Curaçao								**Curaçao**
Tourist/visitor arrivals[6]	TF	221	223	222	234	300	409	Arrivées de touristes/visiteurs[6]
Tourism expenditure[12]		223	224	244	277	327	378	Dépenses touristiques[12]
Cyprus								**Chypre**
Tourist/visitor arrivals	TF	2 303	2 349	2 470	2 401	2 416	2 404	Arrivées de touristes/visiteurs
Tourism expenditure		2 325	2 552	2 644	2 691	3 108	3 222	Dépenses touristiques
Czech Republic								**République tchèque**
Tourist/visitor arrivals	TCE	5 076	6 061	6 336	6 435	6 680	6 649	Arrivées de touristes/visiteurs
Tourism expenditure		4 069	4 931	5 635	6 359	7 496	8 728	Dépenses touristiques
Dem. Rep. of the Congo	TF							**Rép. dém. du Congo**
Tourist/visitor arrivals		35[6]	36[6]	61	55	47[6]	50[6]	Arrivées de touristes/visiteurs
Denmark								**Danemark**
Tourist/visitor arrivals	TCE	3 474	4 421[25]	4 699	4 742[25]	4 770	4 503	Arrivées de touristes/visiteurs
Tourism expenditure[5]		5 271	5 652	5 293	5 587	6 218	6 686	Dépenses touristiques[5]
Djibouti								**Djibouti**
Tourist/visitor arrivals	THS	23	26	30	40	40	...	Arrivées de touristes/visiteurs
Tourism expenditure[5]		7	7	7	10	7	8	Dépenses touristiques[5]
Dominica								**Dominique**
Tourist/visitor arrivals	TF	73	80	79	84	81	...	Arrivées de touristes/visiteurs
Tourism expenditure[5]		52	61	57	72	74	81	Dépenses touristiques[5]
Dominican Republic								**Rép. dominicaine**
Tourist/visitor arrivals[2,6]	TF	3 282	3 450	3 691	3 965	3 980	3 980	Arrivées de touristes/visiteurs[2,6]
Tourism expenditure[5]		3 128	3 152	3 518	3 917	4 064	4 176	Dépenses touristiques[5]
Ecuador								**Equateur**
Tourist/visitor arrivals[4]	VF	761	819	860	841	937	1 005	Arrivées de touristes/visiteurs[4]
Tourism expenditure		408	464	488	492	626	745	Dépenses touristiques

62 Tourist/visitor arrivals and tourism expenditure *(continued)*

Thousands of arrivals and millions of US dollars

Arrivées de touristes/visiteurs et dépenses touristiques *(suite)*

Milliers d'arrivées et millions de dollars E.-U.

Country or area of destination	Series& Série&	2003	2004	2005	2006	2007	2008	Pays ou zone de destination
Egypt								**Egypte**
Tourist/visitor arrivals	TF	5 746	7 795	8 244	8 646	10 610	12 296	Arrivées de touristes/visiteurs
Tourism expenditure		4 704	6 328	7 206	8 133	10 327	12 104	Dépenses touristiques
El Salvador								**El Salvador**
Tourist/visitor arrivals	TF	720	951	1 127	1 279	1 339	1 385	Arrivées de touristes/visiteurs
Tourism expenditure		665	748	838	1 097	1 158	1 180	Dépenses touristiques
Eritrea								**Erythrée**
Tourist/visitor arrivals [2]	VF	80	87	83	78	81	70	Arrivées de touristes/visiteurs [2]
Tourism expenditure [19]		74	73	66	60	61	46	Dépenses touristiques [19]
Estonia								**Estonie**
Tourist/visitor arrivals [26]	TF	1 462	1 750[27]	1 917[27]	1 940[27]	1 900[27]	1 970[27]	Arrivées de touristes/visiteurs [26]
Tourism expenditure		883	1 111	1 229	1 361	1 416	1 662	Dépenses touristiques
Ethiopia								**Ethiopie**
Tourist/visitor arrivals [28]	TF	180	184	227	290	312	330	Arrivées de touristes/visiteurs [28]
Tourism expenditure		336	458	533	639	790	1 184	Dépenses touristiques
Fiji								**Fidji**
Tourist/visitor arrivals [4]	TF	431	504	545	549	540	585	Arrivées de touristes/visiteurs [4]
Tourism expenditure		496	588	722	684	725	840	Dépenses touristiques
Finland								**Finlande**
Tourist/visitor arrivals	TF	2 601	2 840	3 140	3 375	3 519	3 583	Arrivées de touristes/visiteurs
Tourism expenditure		2 678	2 975	3 070	3 509	4 287	4 861	Dépenses touristiques
France								**France**
Tourist/visitor arrivals [29]	TF	75 048	74 433[30]	74 988[30]	77 916[30]	80 853[30]	79 218[30]	Arrivées de touristes/visiteurs [29]
Tourism expenditure		43 406	52 607	52 150	54 415	63 653	66 821	Dépenses touristiques
French Guiana								**Guyane française**
Tourist/visitor arrivals	TF	...	...	95[31]	...	109	...	Arrivées de touristes/visiteurs
Tourism expenditure [3]		...	...	44	...	49	...	Dépenses touristiques [3]
French Polynesia								**Polynésie française**
Tourist/visitor arrivals [4]	TF	213	212	208	222	218	196	Arrivées de touristes/visiteurs [4]
Tourism expenditure		651	737	759	691	807	745	Dépenses touristiques
Gabon								**Gabon**
Tourist/visitor arrivals [32]	TF	222	244	269	296	325	358	Arrivées de touristes/visiteurs [32]
Tourism expenditure		84	74	13	...	...	...	Dépenses touristiques
Gambia								**Gambie**
Tourist/visitor arrivals [33]	TF	89	90	108	125	143	147	Arrivées de touristes/visiteurs [33]
Tourism expenditure		58	51	57	69	89	83	Dépenses touristiques
Georgia								**Géorgie**
Tourist/visitor arrivals	VF	313	368	560	983	1 052	1 290	Arrivées de touristes/visiteurs
Tourism expenditure		172	209	287	361	440	505	Dépenses touristiques
Germany								**Allemagne**
Tourist/visitor arrivals	TCE	18 399	20 137	21 500	23 569	24 421	24 884	Arrivées de touristes/visiteurs
Tourism expenditure		30 104	35 569	38 220	42 921	46 903	51 225	Dépenses touristiques
Ghana								**Ghana**
Tourist/visitor arrivals [2]	TF	531	584	429	497	587	698	Arrivées de touristes/visiteurs [2]
Tourism expenditure		441	495	867	910	990	970	Dépenses touristiques
Greece								**Grèce**
Tourist/visitor arrivals [34]	TF	13 969	13 313	14 765	16 039	16 165	15 939	Arrivées de touristes/visiteurs [34]
Tourism expenditure		10 842	12 809	13 453	14 495	15 687	17 586	Dépenses touristiques
Grenada								**Grenade**
Tourist/visitor arrivals	TF	142	134	99	119	130	130	Arrivées de touristes/visiteurs
Tourism expenditure [5]		104	86	71	94	108	105	Dépenses touristiques [5]
Guadeloupe								**Guadeloupe**
Tourist/visitor arrivals [6,35,36]	TCE	439[37]	456[37]	372[38]	393	408	...	Arrivées de touristes/visiteurs [6,35,36]
Tourism expenditure [3]		...	...	306	299	344	...	Dépenses touristiques [3]
Guam	TF							**Guam**
Tourist/visitor arrivals		910	1 160	1 228	1 212	1 225	1 140	Arrivées de touristes/visiteurs
Guatemala								**Guatemala**
Tourist/visitor arrivals	VF	880	1 182	1 316	1 502	1 628	1 715	Arrivées de touristes/visiteurs
Tourism expenditure		646	630[5]	791[5]	919[5]	1 055[5]	1 068[5]	Dépenses touristiques

Country or area of destination	Series& Série&	2003	2004	2005	2006	2007	2008	Pays ou zone de destination
Guinea								**Guinée**
Tourist/visitor arrivals	TF	44[39]	45	45[39]	46[39]	...	...	Arrivées de touristes/visiteurs
Tourism expenditure		...	...	...	...	1	2	Dépenses touristiques
Guinea-Bissau								**Guinée-Bissau**
Tourist/visitor arrivals [6]	TF	...	...	5	12	30	...	Arrivées de touristes/visiteurs [6]
Tourism expenditure		2	2	2[5]	3[5]	...	...	Dépenses touristiques
Guyana								**Guyana**
Tourist/visitor arrivals [40]	TF	101	122	117	113	131	133	Arrivées de touristes/visiteurs [40]
Tourism expenditure		28	27[5]	35[5]	37[5]	50[5]	59[5]	Dépenses touristiques
Haiti								**Haïti**
Tourist/visitor arrivals [6]	TF	136	96	112	108	386[2]	304[2]	Arrivées de touristes/visiteurs [6]
Tourism expenditure [5]		96	93	84	130	193	279	Dépenses touristiques [5]
Honduras								**Honduras**
Tourist/visitor arrivals	TF	611	641	673	739	831	899	Arrivées de touristes/visiteurs
Tourism expenditure		364	420	465	516	547	622	Dépenses touristiques
Hungary								**Hongrie**
Tourist/visitor arrivals [41]	TF	...	12 212	9 979	9 259	8 638	8 814	Arrivées de touristes/visiteurs [41]
Tourism expenditure		4 119	4 009	4 761	4 986	5 652	7 112	Dépenses touristiques
Iceland								**Islande**
Tourist/visitor arrivals	TCE	771	836	871	971	1 054	1 106	Arrivées de touristes/visiteurs
Tourism expenditure		486	558	630	702	848	881	Dépenses touristiques
India								**Inde**
Tourist/visitor arrivals [4]	TF	2 726	3 457	3 919	4 447	5 082	5 283	Arrivées de touristes/visiteurs [4]
Tourism expenditure		4 560	6 307	7 659	8 915	11 233	12 461	Dépenses touristiques
Indonesia								**Indonésie**
Tourist/visitor arrivals	TF	4 467	5 321	5 002	4 871	5 506	6 234	Arrivées de touristes/visiteurs
Tourism expenditure		4 461	5 226	5 094	4 890	5 831	8 150	Dépenses touristiques
Iran (Islamic Rep. of)								**Iran (Rép. islamique d')**
Tourist/visitor arrivals	TF	1 546	1 659	1 889	2 735	2 219	2 034	Arrivées de touristes/visiteurs
Tourism expenditure [42]		1 266	1 305	1 364	1 760	1 950	2 196	Dépenses touristiques [42]
Iraq								**Iraq**
Tourism expenditure		...	...	186	170	555	...	Dépenses touristiques
Ireland								**Irlande**
Tourist/visitor arrivals [43]	TF	6 764	6 953	7 333	8 001	8 332	8 026	Arrivées de touristes/visiteurs [43]
Tourism expenditure		5 206	6 075	6 780	7 664	9 263	9 953	Dépenses touristiques
Israel								**Israël**
Tourist/visitor arrivals [4]	TF	1 063	1 506	1 903	1 825	2 067	2 572	Arrivées de touristes/visiteurs [4]
Tourism expenditure [44]		2 473	2 847	3 343	3 294	3 748	4 807	Dépenses touristiques [44]
Italy								**Italie**
Tourist/visitor arrivals [45]	TF	39 604	37 071	36 513	41 058	43 654	42 734	Arrivées de touristes/visiteurs [45]
Tourism expenditure		32 591	37 870	38 374	41 644	46 144	48 793	Dépenses touristiques
Jamaica								**Jamaïque**
Tourist/visitor arrivals [46]	TF	1 350	1 415	1 479	1 679	1 701	1 767	Arrivées de touristes/visiteurs [46]
Tourism expenditure		1 621	1 733	1 783	2 094	2 142	2 222	Dépenses touristiques
Japan								**Japon**
Tourist/visitor arrivals [4]	VF	5 212	6 138	6 728	7 334	8 347	8 351	Arrivées de touristes/visiteurs [4]
Tourism expenditure		11 475	14 343	15 555	11 490	12 422	13 781	Dépenses touristiques
Jordan								**Jordanie**
Tourist/visitor arrivals [2]	TF	2 353	2 853	2 987	3 225	3 431	3 729	Arrivées de touristes/visiteurs [2]
Tourism expenditure		1 266	1 621	1 759	2 426	2 754	3 539	Dépenses touristiques
Kazakhstan								**Kazakhstan**
Tourist/visitor arrivals	TF	2 410	3 073	3 143	3 468	3 876	3 447	Arrivées de touristes/visiteurs
Tourism expenditure		638	803	801	973	1 213	1 255	Dépenses touristiques
Kenya								**Kenya**
Tourist/visitor arrivals	TF	927	1 193	1 536	1 644	1 783	...	Arrivées de touristes/visiteurs
Tourism expenditure		619	799	969	1 181	1 514	1 398	Dépenses touristiques
Kiribati [6,47]	TF							**Kiribati** [6,47]
Tourist/visitor arrivals		5	3	4	4	5	4	Arrivées de touristes/visiteurs
Korea, Republic of								**Corée, République de**
Tourist/visitor arrivals [48]	VF	4 753	5 818	6 023	6 155	6 448	6 891	Arrivées de touristes/visiteurs [48]
Tourism expenditure		7 005	8 226	8 290	8 508	8 947	12 783	Dépenses touristiques

Country or area of destination	Series[&] Série[&]	2003	2004	2005	2006	2007	2008	Pays ou zone de destination
Kuwait								**Koweït**
Tourist/visitor arrivals	VF	2 602	3 056	3 474	3 899	4 482	4 736	Arrivées de touristes/visiteurs
Tourism expenditure		328	398	413	508	530	610	Dépenses touristiques
Kyrgyzstan								**Kirghizistan**
Tourist/visitor arrivals [49]	TF	342	398	319	766	1 656	2 435	Arrivées de touristes/visiteurs [49]
Tourism expenditure		62	92	94	189	392	569	Dépenses touristiques
Lao People's Dem. Rep.								**Rép. dém. pop. lao**
Tourist/visitor arrivals	TF	196	407	672	842	1 142	1 295	Arrivées de touristes/visiteurs
Tourism expenditure [5,11]		87	119	147	173	233	276	Dépenses touristiques [5,11]
Latvia								**Lettonie**
Tourist/visitor arrivals [50]	TF	971	1 079	1 116	1 535	1 653	1 684	Arrivées de touristes/visiteurs [50]
Tourism expenditure		271	343	446	622	880	1 134	Dépenses touristiques
Lebanon								**Liban**
Tourist/visitor arrivals [51]	TF	1 016	1 278	1 140	1 063	1 017	1 333	Arrivées de touristes/visiteurs [51]
Tourism expenditure		6 782	5 931	5 969	5 457	6 046	7 690	Dépenses touristiques
Lesotho								**Lesotho**
Tourist/visitor arrivals	VF	329	304	304	357	300	293	Arrivées de touristes/visiteurs
Tourism expenditure [5]		28	42	26	27	43	34	Dépenses touristiques [5]
Liberia [5]								**Libéria [5]**
Tourism expenditure		...	59	67	124	135	158	Dépenses touristiques
Libyan Arab Jamah.								**Jamah. arabe libyenne**
Tourist/visitor arrivals	THS	...	43	81	42	38	34	Arrivées de touristes/visiteurs
Tourism expenditure		243	261	301	244	99	99	Dépenses touristiques
Liechtenstein	THS							**Liechtenstein**
Tourist/visitor arrivals		49	49	50	55	58	58	Arrivées de touristes/visiteurs
Lithuania								**Lituanie**
Tourist/visitor arrivals	TF	1 491	1 800	2 000	2 180	1 486	1 611	Arrivées de touristes/visiteurs
Tourism expenditure		700	834	975	1 077	1 192	1 406	Dépenses touristiques
Luxembourg								**Luxembourg**
Tourist/visitor arrivals	TCE	867	878	913	908	917	879	Arrivées de touristes/visiteurs
Tourism expenditure		3 149	3 880	3 612[5]	3 636[5]	4 030[5]	4 488[5]	Dépenses touristiques
Madagascar								**Madagascar**
Tourist/visitor arrivals [52]	TF	139	229	277	312	344	375	Arrivées de touristes/visiteurs [52]
Tourism expenditure		119	239	290	386	506	620	Dépenses touristiques
Malawi								**Malawi**
Tourist/visitor arrivals [53]	TF	424	427	438	638	735	742	Arrivées de touristes/visiteurs [53]
Tourism expenditure [54]		35	36	43	43	48	...	Dépenses touristiques [54]
Malaysia								**Malaisie**
Tourist/visitor arrivals [55]	TF	10 577	15 703	16 431	17 547	20 973	22 052	Arrivées de touristes/visiteurs [55]
Tourism expenditure		6 799	9 183	10 389	12 280	17 951	18 553	Dépenses touristiques
Maldives								**Maldives**
Tourist/visitor arrivals [6]	TF	564	617	395	602	676	683	Arrivées de touristes/visiteurs [6]
Tourism expenditure [5]		402	471	287	512	602	636	Dépenses touristiques [5]
Mali								**Mali**
Tourist/visitor arrivals [6]	THS	110	113	143	153	164	190	Arrivées de touristes/visiteurs [6]
Tourism expenditure		136	142	149	175	227	...	Dépenses touristiques
Malta								**Malte**
Tourist/visitor arrivals	TF	1 127	1 156[56]	1 171[56]	1 124[56]	1 244[56]	1 291[56]	Arrivées de touristes/visiteurs
Tourism expenditure		869	949	924	966	1 142	1 215	Dépenses touristiques
Marshall Islands								**Iles Marshall**
Tourist/visitor arrivals	TF	7[6]	9[58]	9[58]	6[6]	7[6]	6[6]	Arrivées de touristes/visiteurs
Tourism expenditure [3,57]		4	5	6	7	5	3	Dépenses touristiques [3,57]
Martinique								**Martinique**
Tourist/visitor arrivals	TF	453	471	484	503	501	481	Arrivées de touristes/visiteurs
Tourism expenditure [3]		247	291	280	306	299	...	Dépenses touristiques [3]
Mauritius								**Maurice**
Tourist/visitor arrivals	TF	702	719	761	788	907	930	Arrivées de touristes/visiteurs
Tourism expenditure		960	1 156	1 189	1 302	1 663	1 823	Dépenses touristiques
Mexico								**Mexique**
Tourist/visitor arrivals [2]	TF	18 665	20 618	21 915	21 353	21 370	22 637	Arrivées de touristes/visiteurs [2]
Tourism expenditure		10 058	11 610	12 801	13 329	13 988	14 647	Dépenses touristiques

Country or area of destination	Series[&] Série[&]	2003	2004	2005	2006	2007	2008	Pays ou zone de destination
Micronesia (Fed. States of)								**Micronésie (Etats féd. de)**
Tourist/visitor arrivals[59]	TF	18	19	19	19	21	26	Arrivées de touristes/visiteurs[59]
Tourism expenditure[3,57]		17	17	17	18	...	...	Dépenses touristiques[3,57]
Monaco	THS							**Monaco**
Tourist/visitor arrivals		235	250	286	313	328	324	Arrivées de touristes/visiteurs
Mongolia								**Mongolie**
Tourist/visitor arrivals[60]	TF	201	301	338	386	452	446	Arrivées de touristes/visiteurs[60]
Tourism expenditure		154	205	203	261	...	...	Dépenses touristiques
Montenegro								**Monténégro**
Tourist/visitor arrivals	TCE	142	188	272	378	984	1 031	Arrivées de touristes/visiteurs
Tourism expenditure[5]		...	...	...	...	629	755	Dépenses touristiques[5]
Montserrat								**Montserrat**
Tourist/visitor arrivals	TF	8	10	10	8	8	7	Arrivées de touristes/visiteurs
Tourism expenditure[5]		7	9	9	8	7	7	Dépenses touristiques[5]
Morocco								**Maroc**
Tourist/visitor arrivals[2]	TF	4 761	5 477	5 843	6 558	7 408	7 879	Arrivées de touristes/visiteurs[2]
Tourism expenditure		3 802	4 540	5 426	6 900	8 307	8 885	Dépenses touristiques
Mozambique								**Mozambique**
Tourist/visitor arrivals	TF	441[61]	470[61]	578[61]	664[61]	771[61]	1 815[62,63]	Arrivées de touristes/visiteurs
Tourism expenditure		106	96	138	145	182	213	Dépenses touristiques
Myanmar								**Myanmar**
Tourist/visitor arrivals[64]	TF	206	242	232	264	248	193	Arrivées de touristes/visiteurs[64]
Tourism expenditure		70	97	85	59	...	...	Dépenses touristiques
Namibia								**Namibie**
Tourist/visitor arrivals	TF	695	...	778	833	929	...	Arrivées de touristes/visiteurs
Tourism expenditure		383	426	363	473	542	382[5]	Dépenses touristiques
Nepal								**Népal**
Tourist/visitor arrivals[65]	TF	338	385	375	384	527	500	Arrivées de touristes/visiteurs[65]
Tourism expenditure		232	260	160	157	234	353	Dépenses touristiques
Netherlands								**Pays-Bas**
Tourist/visitor arrivals	TCE	9 181	9 646	10 012	10 739	11 008	10 104	Arrivées de touristes/visiteurs
Tourism expenditure		14 603	16 495	16 528	17 529	19 922	20 526	Dépenses touristiques
New Caledonia								**Nouvelle-Calédonie**
Tourist/visitor arrivals[2]	TF	102	100	101	100	103	104	Arrivées de touristes/visiteurs[2]
Tourism expenditure[5]		196	241	149	122	142	152	Dépenses touristiques[5]
New Zealand								**Nouvelle-Zélande**
Tourist/visitor arrivals	TF	2 086	2 325	2 353	2 390	2 434	2 411	Arrivées de touristes/visiteurs
Tourism expenditure[5]		4 201	5 035	5 176	4 765	5 379	5 030	Dépenses touristiques[5]
Nicaragua								**Nicaragua**
Tourist/visitor arrivals	TF	526	615	712[2]	749[2]	800[2]	858[2]	Arrivées de touristes/visiteurs
Tourism expenditure[5]		160	192	206	231	255	276	Dépenses touristiques[5]
Niger								**Niger**
Tourist/visitor arrivals	TF	55	57	60	60	48	73	Arrivées de touristes/visiteurs
Tourism expenditure		28	32	44	39	44	45[5]	Dépenses touristiques
Nigeria								**Nigéria**
Tourist/visitor arrivals	TF	924	962	1 010	1 111	1 212	1 313	Arrivées de touristes/visiteurs
Tourism expenditure		58	49	139	90	337	586	Dépenses touristiques
Niue								**Nioué**
Tourist/visitor arrivals[66]	TF	3	3	3	3	4	5	Arrivées de touristes/visiteurs[66]
Tourism expenditure[3]		1	1	1	1	2	2	Dépenses touristiques[3]
Northern Mariana Islands[6]	TF							**Iles Mariannes du Nord[6]**
Tourist/visitor arrivals		452	525	498	429	385	388	Arrivées de touristes/visiteurs
Norway								**Norvège**
Tourist/visitor arrivals[67]	TF	3 269	3 628	3 824	4 070	4 377	4 440	Arrivées de touristes/visiteurs[67]
Tourism expenditure		2 989	3 531	4 030	4 251	5 037	5 559	Dépenses touristiques
Occupied Palestinian Terr.								**Terr. palestinien occupé**
Tourist/visitor arrivals	THS	37	56	88	123	264	387	Arrivées de touristes/visiteurs
Tourism expenditure[5]		152	115	119	89	212	...	Dépenses touristiques[5]
Oman								**Oman**
Tourist/visitor arrivals	THS	630	908	1 114	1 336	1 124	1 273	Arrivées de touristes/visiteurs
Tourism expenditure		546	601	627	749	908	1 111	Dépenses touristiques

62 Tourist/visitor arrivals and tourism expenditure *(continued)*
Thousands of arrivals and millions of US dollars

Arrivées de touristes/visiteurs et dépenses touristiques *(suite)*
Milliers d'arrivées et millions de dollars E.-U.

Country or area of destination	Series[&] Série[&]	2003	2004	2005	2006	2007	2008	Pays ou zone de destination
Pakistan								**Pakistan**
Tourist/visitor arrivals	TF	501	648	798	898	840	823	Arrivées de touristes/visiteurs
Tourism expenditure		620	765	828	919	912	915	Dépenses touristiques
Palau								**Palaos**
Tourist/visitor arrivals [68]	TF	68	95	86	87	93	83	Arrivées de touristes/visiteurs [68]
Tourism expenditure [3]		76	97	97	90	...	...	Dépenses touristiques [3]
Panama								**Panama**
Tourist/visitor arrivals	TF	566	621	702	843	1 103	1 293	Arrivées de touristes/visiteurs
Tourism expenditure		804	903	1 108	1 425	1 806	2 223	Dépenses touristiques
Papua New Guinea								**Papouasie-Nvl-Guinée**
Tourist/visitor arrivals	TF	56	59	69	78	104	114	Arrivées de touristes/visiteurs
Tourism expenditure		4[5]	6	4	...	...	...	Dépenses touristiques
Paraguay								**Paraguay**
Tourist/visitor arrivals [8,69]	TF	268	309	341	388	416	428	Arrivées de touristes/visiteurs [8,69]
Tourism expenditure		81	87	96	112	121	128	Dépenses touristiques
Peru								**Pérou**
Tourist/visitor arrivals [70]	TF	1 136	1 350	1 571[71]	1 721[71]	1 916[71]	2 058[71]	Arrivées de touristes/visiteurs [70]
Tourism expenditure		1 023	1 232	1 438	1 782	2 222	2 396	Dépenses touristiques
Philippines								**Philippines**
Tourist/visitor arrivals [2]	TF	1 907	2 291	2 623	2 843	3 092	3 139	Arrivées de touristes/visiteurs [2]
Tourism expenditure		1 821	2 390	2 755	4 019	5 520	4 990	Dépenses touristiques
Poland								**Pologne**
Tourist/visitor arrivals	TF	13 720	14 290	15 200	15 670	14 975	12 960	Arrivées de touristes/visiteurs
Tourism expenditure		4 733	6 499	7 128	8 122	11 686	12 841	Dépenses touristiques
Portugal								**Portugal**
Tourist/visitor arrivals	TF	11 707[4]	#10 639[2]	10 612[2]	11 282[2]	12 321[2]	...	Arrivées de touristes/visiteurs
Tourism expenditure		7 634	8 858	9 009	10 438	12 917	14 047	Dépenses touristiques
Puerto Rico								**Porto Rico**
Tourist/visitor arrivals [52,72]	TF	3 238	3 541	3 686	3 722	3 687	3 894	Arrivées de touristes/visiteurs [52,72]
Tourism expenditure [3,73]		2 677	3 024	3 239	3 369	3 414	3 645	Dépenses touristiques [3,73]
Qatar								**Qatar**
Tourist/visitor arrivals [1]	THS	557	732	913	946	964	1 405	Arrivées de touristes/visiteurs [1]
Tourism expenditure [5,74]		369	498	760	874	...	...	Dépenses touristiques [5,74]
Republic of Moldova								**République de Moldova**
Tourist/visitor arrivals [75]	TF	21	24	23	13	13	7	Arrivées de touristes/visiteurs [75]
Tourism expenditure		79	112	138	148	225	289	Dépenses touristiques
Réunion								**Réunion**
Tourist/visitor arrivals	TF	432	430	409	279	381	396	Arrivées de touristes/visiteurs
Tourism expenditure [3]		351	390	384	282	401	448	Dépenses touristiques [3]
Romania								**Roumanie**
Tourist/visitor arrivals	VF	5 595	6 600	5 839	6 037	7 722	8 862	Arrivées de touristes/visiteurs
Tourism expenditure		523	607	1 325	1 676	2 065	2 627	Dépenses touristiques
Russian Federation								**Fédération de Russie**
Tourist/visitor arrivals	VF	22 521	22 064	22 201	22 486	22 909	23 676	Arrivées de touristes/visiteurs
Tourism expenditure		5 879	7 262	7 806	9 720	12 587	15 923	Dépenses touristiques
Rwanda								**Rwanda**
Tourist/visitor arrivals	VF	...	...	...	...	826	981	Arrivées de touristes/visiteurs
Tourism expenditure		30[5]	44[5]	49[5]	31[5]	66	202[5]	Dépenses touristiques
Saba	TF							**Saba**
Tourist/visitor arrivals		10	11	11	11	12	12	Arrivées de touristes/visiteurs
Saint Eustatius [76]	TF							**Saint-Eustache [76]**
Tourist/visitor arrivals		10	11	10	10	12	12	Arrivées de touristes/visiteurs
Saint Kitts and Nevis								**Saint-Kitts-et-Nevis**
Tourist/visitor arrivals [52]	TF	91	118	141	139	124	121	Arrivées de touristes/visiteurs [52]
Tourism expenditure [5]		75	103	121	132	126	122	Dépenses touristiques [5]
Saint Lucia								**Sainte-Lucie**
Tourist/visitor arrivals [4]	TF	277	298	318	303	287	296	Arrivées de touristes/visiteurs [4]
Tourism expenditure [5]		282	326	369	294	302	311	Dépenses touristiques [5]
Saint Maarten								**Saint-Martin**
Tourist/visitor arrivals [6,77]	TF	428	475	468	468	469	475	Arrivées de touristes/visiteurs [6,77]
Tourism expenditure [5,78]		538	626	659	651	662	663	Dépenses touristiques [5,78]

62

Tourist/visitor arrivals and tourism expenditure *(continued)*

Thousands of arrivals and millions of US dollars

Arrivées de touristes/visiteurs et dépenses touristiques *(suite)*

Milliers d'arrivées et millions de dollars E.-U.

Country or area of destination	Series[&] Série[&]	2003	2004	2005	2006	2007	2008	Pays ou zone de destination
Saint Vincent-Grenadines								**Saint Vincent-Grenadines**
Tourist/visitor arrivals [52]	TF	79	87	96	97	90	84	Arrivées de touristes/visiteurs [52]
Tourism expenditure [5]		91	96	104	113	111	90	Dépenses touristiques [5]
Samoa								**Samoa**
Tourist/visitor arrivals	TF	92	98	102	116	122	122	Arrivées de touristes/visiteurs
Tourism expenditure		54[5]	70	80	91	107	...	Dépenses touristiques
San Marino [79]	THS							**Saint-Marin** [79]
Tourist/visitor arrivals		41	42	50	50	69	115	Arrivées de touristes/visiteurs
Sao Tome and Principe								**Sao Tomé-et-Principe**
Tourist/visitor arrivals	TF	10	11	16	12	12	14	Arrivées de touristes/visiteurs
Tourism expenditure [5]		7	8	7	7	5	8	Dépenses touristiques [5]
Saudi Arabia								**Arabie saoudite**
Tourist/visitor arrivals	TF	7 332	8 599	8 037	8 620	11 531	14 757	Arrivées de touristes/visiteurs
Tourism expenditure		3 418[3]	6 916[3]	5 103	5 204	6 768	7 227	Dépenses touristiques
Senegal								**Sénégal**
Tourist/visitor arrivals	TF	495	667	769	866	875	...	Arrivées de touristes/visiteurs
Tourism expenditure		269	286	334	329	622	...	Dépenses touristiques
Serbia								**Serbie**
Tourist/visitor arrivals	TCE	339	392	453	469	696	646	Arrivées de touristes/visiteurs
Tourism expenditure		159[80]	220[80]	308[80]	398[80]	1 011	1 113	Dépenses touristiques
Seychelles								**Seychelles**
Tourist/visitor arrivals	TF	122	121	129	141	161	159	Arrivées de touristes/visiteurs
Tourism expenditure		258	256	269	323	366	...	Dépenses touristiques
Sierra Leone								**Sierra Leone**
Tourist/visitor arrivals [6]	TF	38	44	40	34	32	36	Arrivées de touristes/visiteurs [6]
Tourism expenditure [5]		60	58	64	23	22	34	Dépenses touristiques [5]
Singapore								**Singapour**
Tourist/visitor arrivals	TF	4 703	6 553	7 079	7 588	7 957	7 778	Arrivées de touristes/visiteurs
Tourism expenditure [5]		3 842	5 327	6 205	7 545	9 179	10 583	Dépenses touristiques [5]
Slovakia								**Slovaquie**
Tourist/visitor arrivals	TCE	1 387	1 401	1 515	1 612	1 685	1 767	Arrivées de touristes/visiteurs
Tourism expenditure		876	931	1 282	1 655	2 352	3 004	Dépenses touristiques
Slovenia								**Slovénie**
Tourist/visitor arrivals	TCE	1 373	1 499	1 555	1 617	1 751	1 771	Arrivées de touristes/visiteurs
Tourism expenditure		1 427	1 725	1 894	1 911	2 465	3 115	Dépenses touristiques
Solomon Islands								**Iles Salomon**
Tourist/visitor arrivals	TF	7	6[81]	9[82]	11	14	16	Arrivées de touristes/visiteurs
Tourism expenditure		2	4	8	10	4[5]	4[5]	Dépenses touristiques
South Africa								**Afrique du Sud**
Tourist/visitor arrivals [83]	TF	6 505	6 678	7 369	8 396	9 091	9 592	Arrivées de touristes/visiteurs [83]
Tourism expenditure		6 533	7 380	8 448	8 967	9 890	8 861	Dépenses touristiques
Spain								**Espagne**
Tourist/visitor arrivals	TF	50 854	52 430	55 914	58 004	58 666	57 192	Arrivées de touristes/visiteurs
Tourism expenditure		43 863	49 996	53 066	57 543	65 020	70 234	Dépenses touristiques
Sri Lanka								**Sri Lanka**
Tourist/visitor arrivals [4]	TF	501	566	549	560	494	438	Arrivées de touristes/visiteurs [4]
Tourism expenditure		709	808	729	733	750	803	Dépenses touristiques
Sudan								**Soudan**
Tourist/visitor arrivals	TF	52	61	246[2]	328[2]	436[2]	440[2]	Arrivées de touristes/visiteurs
Tourism expenditure [5]		17	21	89	167	262	331	Dépenses touristiques [5]
Suriname								**Suriname**
Tourist/visitor arrivals	TF	82[84]	138	160	153	163	...	Arrivées de touristes/visiteurs
Tourism expenditure		18	52	96	109	73	83	Dépenses touristiques
Swaziland								**Swaziland**
Tourist/visitor arrivals	THS	461	459	837	873	870	754	Arrivées de touristes/visiteurs
Tourism expenditure		70	75	77	75	32	...	Dépenses touristiques
Sweden								**Suède**
Tourist/visitor arrivals	TCE	4 268	4 676	4 883	4 729	5 224	4 728	Arrivées de touristes/visiteurs
Tourism expenditure		6 548	7 686	8 589	10 485	13 697	14 399	Dépenses touristiques

Country or area of destination	Series& Série&	2003	2004	2005	2006	2007	2008	Pays ou zone de destination
Switzerland								**Suisse**
Tourist/visitor arrivals	THS	6 530	...	7 229	7 863	8 448	8 608	Arrivées de touristes/visiteurs
Tourism expenditure		10 493	11 404	11 937	12 852	14 726	17 573	Dépenses touristiques
Syrian Arab Republic								**Rép. arabe syrienne**
Tourist/visitor arrivals [2]	TCE	2 598	3 399	3 571	4 231	4 158	5 430[85]	Arrivées de touristes/visiteurs [2]
Tourism expenditure		1 090	1 883	2 035	2 113	2 972	3 150[5]	Dépenses touristiques
Tajikistan								**Tadjikistan**
Tourism expenditure		7	9	10	11	16	24	Dépenses touristiques
Thailand								**Thaïlande**
Tourist/visitor arrivals	TF	10 082[86]	11 737[86]	11 567[86]	13 822	14 464	14 584	Arrivées de touristes/visiteurs
Tourism expenditure		10 456	13 054	12 102	16 614	20 623	21 980	Dépenses touristiques
TFYR of Macedonia								**L'ex-R.Y. Macédoine**
Tourist/visitor arrivals	TCE	158	165	197	202	230	255	Arrivées de touristes/visiteurs
Tourism expenditure		86	103	116	156	219	262	Dépenses touristiques
Togo								**Togo**
Tourist/visitor arrivals	THS	61	83	81	94	86	74	Arrivées de touristes/visiteurs
Tourism expenditure		26	25	27	23	38	...	Dépenses touristiques
Tonga								**Tonga**
Tourist/visitor arrivals [6]	TF	40	41	42	39	46	49	Arrivées de touristes/visiteurs [6]
Tourism expenditure		10[5]	13[5]	15[5]	16[5]	15	20[5]	Dépenses touristiques
Trinidad and Tobago								**Trinité-et-Tobago**
Tourist/visitor arrivals [6]	TF	409	443	463	457	449	433	Arrivées de touristes/visiteurs [6]
Tourism expenditure		437	568	593	517	621	615	Dépenses touristiques
Tunisia								**Tunisie**
Tourist/visitor arrivals [4]	TF	5 114	5 998	6 378	6 550	6 762	7 049	Arrivées de touristes/visiteurs [4]
Tourism expenditure		1 935	2 432	2 800	2 977	3 373	3 909	Dépenses touristiques
Turkey								**Turquie**
Tourist/visitor arrivals	TF	13 341	16 826	20 273	18 916	22 248	24 994	Arrivées de touristes/visiteurs
Tourism expenditure [87]		13 203[5]	15 888[5]	19 720	18 520	20 649	25 019	Dépenses touristiques [87]
Turkmenistan	TF							**Turkménistan**
Tourist/visitor arrivals		8	15	12	6	8	...	Arrivées de touristes/visiteurs
Turks and Caicos Islands	TF							**Iles Turques et Caïques**
Tourist/visitor arrivals		164	173	176	248	265	...	Arrivées de touristes/visiteurs
Tuvalu	TF							**Tuvalu**
Tourist/visitor arrivals		1	1	1	1	1	...	Arrivées de touristes/visiteurs
Uganda								**Ouganda**
Tourist/visitor arrivals	TF	305	512	468	539	642	844	Arrivées de touristes/visiteurs
Tourism expenditure		185	268	382	347	402	531	Dépenses touristiques
Ukraine								**Ukraine**
Tourist/visitor arrivals	TF	12 514	15 629	17 631	18 936	23 122	25 449	Arrivées de touristes/visiteurs
Tourism expenditure		1 204	2 931	3 542	4 018	5 320	6 722	Dépenses touristiques
United Arab Emirates								**Emirats arabes unis**
Tourist/visitor arrivals [1,88]	THS	5 871	6 195	7 126	...	...	...	Arrivées de touristes/visiteurs [1,88]
Tourism expenditure [3]		1 438	1 593	3 218	4 972	6 072	7 162	Dépenses touristiques [3]
United Kingdom								**Royaume-Uni**
Tourist/visitor arrivals	TF	22 787	25 678	28 039	30 654	30 870	30 142	Arrivées de touristes/visiteurs
Tourism expenditure		30 736	37 166	39 411	43 803	48 192	45 345	Dépenses touristiques
United Rep. of Tanzania								**Rép.-Unie de Tanzanie**
Tourist/visitor arrivals	TF	552	566	590	622	692	750	Arrivées de touristes/visiteurs
Tourism expenditure		654	762	835	986	1 215	1 358	Dépenses touristiques
United States								**Etats-Unis**
Tourist/visitor arrivals [89]	TF	41 218	46 086	49 206	50 977	55 979	57 937	Arrivées de touristes/visiteurs [89]
Tourism expenditure		99 207	112 957	123 039	128 941	145 416	166 530	Dépenses touristiques
United States Virgin Is.								**Iles Vierges américaines**
Tourist/visitor arrivals	TF	538	544	582	570	581	586	Arrivées de touristes/visiteurs
Tourism expenditure [3]		1 257	1 356	1 446	1 462	1 434	1 492	Dépenses touristiques [3]
Uruguay								**Uruguay**
Tourist/visitor arrivals	TF	1 420	1 756	1 808	1 749	1 752	1 938	Arrivées de touristes/visiteurs
Tourism expenditure		419	591	699	711	931	1 180	Dépenses touristiques

62 Tourist/visitor arrivals and tourism expenditure *(continued)*

Thousands of arrivals and millions of US dollars

Arrivées de touristes/visiteurs et dépenses touristiques *(suite)*

Milliers d'arrivées et millions de dollars E.-U.

Country or area of destination	Series& Série&	2003	2004	2005	2006	2007	2008	Pays ou zone de destination
Uzbekistan								**Ouzbékistan**
Tourist/visitor arrivals	TF	231	262	242	560	903	1 069	Arrivées de touristes/visiteurs
Tourism expenditure		48[3]	57[3]	28[5]	43[5]	51[5]	63[5]	Dépenses touristiques
Vanuatu								**Vanuatu**
Tourist/visitor arrivals	TF	50	61	62	68	81	91	Arrivées de touristes/visiteurs
Tourism expenditure		83	93	104	109	142	...	Dépenses touristiques
Venezuela (Boliv. Rep. of)								**Venezuela (Rép. boliv. du)**
Tourist/visitor arrivals	TF	337	486	706	748	771	745	Arrivées de touristes/visiteurs
Tourism expenditure		378	554	722	843	894	984	Dépenses touristiques
Viet Nam								**Viet Nam**
Tourist/visitor arrivals	VF	2 429	2 928	3 468	3 583	4 244	4 254	Arrivées de touristes/visiteurs
Tourism expenditure[3]		1 400	1 700	1 880	3 200	3 447	3 926	Dépenses touristiques[3]
Yemen								**Yémen**
Tourist/visitor arrivals	THS	155	274	336	382	379	404	Arrivées de touristes/visiteurs
Tourism expenditure[5]		139	139	181	181	425	886	Dépenses touristiques[5]
Zambia								**Zambie**
Tourist/visitor arrivals	TF	413	515	669	757	897	812	Arrivées de touristes/visiteurs
Tourism expenditure[5]		88	92	98	110	138	146	Dépenses touristiques[5]
Zimbabwe								**Zimbabwe**
Tourist/visitor arrivals	VF	2 256	1 854	1 559	2 287	2 508	1 956	Arrivées de touristes/visiteurs
Tourism expenditure[3]		61	194	99	338	365	294	Dépenses touristiques[3]

Source:
World Tourism Organization (UNWTO), Madrid, UNWTO statistics database and the *Yearbook of Tourism Statistics*, 2010 edition.

The majority of the expenditure data have been provided to the UNWTO by the International Monetary Fund (IMF). Exceptions are footnoted.

& Series:

- TF: Arrivals of non-resident tourists at national borders.
- VF: Arrivals of non-resident visitors at national borders.
- THS: Arrivals of non-resident tourists in hotels and similar establishments.
- TCE: Arrivals of non-resident tourists in all types of accommodation establishments.

1 Arrivals in hotels only.
2 Including nationals of the country residing abroad.
3 The expenditure figures are those provided by the country to UNWTO, which do not appear in the International Monetary Fund data.
4 Excluding nationals of the country residing abroad.
5 Excluding passenger transport.
6 Air arrivals.
7 Starting 2004, as a result of the importance of the "Survey on International Tourism", the estimates of the series of the "Travel" item of the Balance of Payments were modified. For this reason, the data are not rigorously comparable with those of previous years.
8 Excluding nationals residing abroad and crew members.
9 Organized tourism.
10 Country estimates.
11 Country data.
12 Source: Central Bank of the Netherlands Antilles.
13 Source: "Banque Centrale des Etats de l'Afrique de l'Ouest".
14 Arrivals by air. Visitor arrivals by all means of transportation.

Source:
Organisation mondiale du tourisme (OMT), Madrid, la base de données de l'OMT, et l'*Annuaire des statistiques du tourisme*, édition 2010.

La majorité des données sur les dépenses touristiques sont celles que le Fonds monétaire international (FMI) a fournies à l'Organisation mondiale du tourisme (OMT). Les exceptions sont signalées par une note.

& Série:

- TF : Arrivées de touristes non résidents aux frontières nationales.
- VF: Arrivées de visiteurs non résidents aux frontières nationales.
- THS: Arrivées de touristes non résidents dans les hôtels et établissements assimilés.
- TCE: Arrivées de touristes non résidents dans tous les types d'établissements d'hébergement touristique.

1 Arrivées dans les hôtels uniquement.
2 Y compris les nationaux du pays résidant à l'étranger.
3 Les chiffres de dépense sont ceux que le pays a fournis à l'OMT mais ils ne figurent pas dans les données du Fonds monétaire international.
4 A l'exclusion des nationaux du pays résidant à l'étranger.
5 Non compris le transport de passagers.
6 Arrivées par voie aérienne.
7 À partir de 2004, vu l'importance de l'« Enquête sur le tourisme international », des modifications ont été apportées aux estimations de la série du poste « Voyages » de la balance des paiements. C'est la raison pour laquelle les données ne sont pas rigoureusement comparables avec celles des années précédentes.
8 A l'exclusion des nationaux du pays résidant à l'étranger et des membres des équipages.
9 Tourisme organisé.
10 Estimations du pays.
11 Données du pays.
12 Source: "Central Bank of the Netherlands Antilles".
13 Source: Banque Centrale des Etats de l'Afrique de l'Ouest.
14 Arrivées par voie aérienne. Arrivées de visiteurs par tous les moyens de transport.

62 Tourist/visitor arrivals and tourism expenditure *(continued)*

Thousands of arrivals and millions of US dollars

Arrivées de touristes/visiteurs et dépenses touristiques *(suite)*

Milliers d'arrivées et millions de dollars E.-U.

15 Different types of methodological changes that affect the estimates for 2000 and 2001 for expenditures and characteristics of International Tourists to Canada have been introduced in 2002. Therefore, Statistics Canada advises not to compare the estimates for 2000 and 2001 with the years prior because of these methodological changes for the non-count estimates (one of the reasons average length of stay numbers are not provided).

16 Arrivals by air at Bangui only.

17 Source: "Banque des Etats de l'Afrique Centrale (B.E.A.C.)".

18 For statistical purposes, the data for China do not include those for the Hong Kong Special Administrative Region (Hong Kong SAR), Macao Special Administrative Region (Macao SAR) and Taiwan Province of China.

19 The expenditure figures used were the ones provided by the country to UNWTO, as this data series is more complete than that provided by the International Monetary Fund (IMF).

20 According to Statistics and Census Service, the visitor arrivals figures from year 2008 onward will not include other non-residents namely workers, students, etc.

21 Including cruise passengers.

22 Including the foreign travellers arrived at terrestrial frontier points and that according to the Bank of the Republic were (in thousands): 2007= 1,059, 2008= 1,097.

23 Arrivals of foreign travellers at checkpoints of the Administrative Department of Security (DAS).

24 Source: "Banque centrale des Comores".

25 New methodology.

26 Starting from 2004, border statistics are not collected any more.

27 Calculated on the basis of accommodation statistics and "Foreign Visitor Survey" carried out by the Statistical Office of Estonia.

28 Arrivals through all ports of entry. Including nationals residing abroad.

29 Estimated based on surveys at national borders.

30 Non-resident visitor survey (EVE).

31 2005 survey at Cayenne-Rochambeau airport on departure.

32 Arrivals of non-resident tourists at Libreville airport.

33 Charter tourists only.

34 Information based on administrative data.

35 Excluding the north islands (Saint Maarten and Saint Bartholemy).

36 Non-resident tourists staying in all types of accommodation establishments.

37 Non-resident tourists staying in hotels only

38 Data based on a survey conducted at Guadeloupe airport.

39 Air arrivals at Conakry airport.

40 Arrivals at Timehri airport only.

41 New series.

42 Source: Central Bank of Islamic Republic of Iran.

43 Including tourists from North Ireland.

44 Including the expenditures of foreign workers in Israel.

45 Excluding seasonal and border workers.

46 Arrivals of non-resident tourists by air. Including nationals residing abroad. E/D cards.

47 Tarawa and Christmas Island.

48 Including nationals residing abroad and crew members.

49 New data source: Department of Customs Control.

50 Non-resident departures. Survey of persons crossing the state border.

51 Excluding Syrian nationals.

52 Arrivals of non-resident tourists by air.

53 Departures.

54 Source: Reserve Bank of Malawi.

15 En 2002, il a été adopté différents types de changements méthodologiques qui ont eu des effets sur les estimations des dépenses et des caractéristiques des touristes internationaux ayant visité le Canada en 2000 et 2001. Pour 2000 et 2001, Statistique Canada conseille par conséquent de ne pas comparer les estimations ne reposant pas sur des comptages aux données des années précédentes (c'est une des raisons pour lesquelles les données durée moyenne de séjour ne sont pas fournies).

16 Arrivées par voie aérienne à Bangui uniquement.

17 Source: Banque des Etats de l'Afrique Centrale (B.E.A.C.).

18 Pour la présentation des statistiques, les données pour la Chine ne comprennent pas la Région Administrative Spéciale de Hong Kong (Hong Kong RAS), la Région Administrative Spéciale de Macao (Macao RAS) et la province de Taiwan.

19 Les données de dépense sont celles que le pays a fournies à l'OMT car il s'agit d'une série plus complète que celle obtenue du Fonds monétaire international (FMI).

20 D'après le Statistics and Census Service, à partir de 2008, les chiffres concernant les arrivées de visiteurs ne comprendront pas les autres catégories de non-résidents, à savoir les travailleurs, les étudiants, etc.

21 Y compris les passagers en croisière.

22 Y compris les voyageurs étrangers qui sont arrivés par les points frontaliers terrestres et qui selon la banque centrale ont été au nombre de 1 059 en 2007 et de 1 097 en 2008 (nombre: en milliers).

23 Arrivées de voyageurs étrangers aux points de contrôle établis par le Département administratif de la sécurité.

24 Source: Banque centrale des Comores.

25 Nouvelle méthodologie.

26 À partir de 2004, les statistiques de frontière ne sont plus collectées.

27 Calculé sur la base des statistiques d'hébergement et de la "Foreign Visitor Survey" menée par la "Statistical Office of Estonia".

28 Arrivées à travers tous les ports d'entrée. Y compris les nationaux résidant à l'étranger.

29 Estimations à partir d'enquêtes aux frontières.

30 Enquête auprès des visiteurs venant de l'étranger (EVE).

31 Enquête 2005 au départ de l'aéroport de Cayenne-Rochambeau.

32 Arrivées de touristes non résidents à l'aéroport de Libreville.

33 Arrivées en vols à la demande seulement.

34 Information tirée de données administratives.

35 Excluyant les îles du Nord (Saint Martin et Saint Barthélemy).

36 Arrivées de touristes non résidents dans tous les types d'établissements d'hébergement touristique.

37 Ne comprend que les touristes non résidents descendus dans des des hôtels.

38 Données tirées d'une enquête réalisée à l'aéroport de Guadeloupe.

39 Arrivées par voie aérienne à l'aéroport de Conakry.

40 Arrivées à l'aéroport de Timehri seulement.

41 Nouvelle série.

42 Source: "Central Bank of Islamic Republic of Iran".

43 Y compris les touristes en provenance d'Irlande du Nord.

44 Y compris les dépenses des travailleurs étrangers en Israël.

45 A l'exclusion des travailleurs saisonniers et frontaliers.

46 Arrivées de touristes non résidents par air. Y compris les nationaux qui résident a l'étranger. Cartes d'embarquement et de débarquement.

47 Tarawa et Ile Christmas.

48 Y compris les nationaux résidant à l'étranger et membres des équipages.

49 Nouvelle source d'information: Département du Contrôle douanier.

50 Départs de non-résidents. Enquête menée auprès de personnes franchissant la frontière de l'État.

51 A l'exclusion des ressortissants syriens.

52 Arrivées de touristes non résidents par voie aérienne.

53 Départs.

54 Source: "Reserve Bank of Malawi".

62 Tourist/visitor arrivals and tourism expenditure *(continued)*

Thousands of arrivals and millions of US dollars

Arrivées de touristes/visiteurs et dépenses touristiques *(suite)*

Milliers d'arrivées et millions de dollars E.-U.

55 Including Singapore residents crossing the frontier by road through the Johore Causeway.
56 Departures by air and by sea.
57 Fiscal years (October 1 to September 30).
58 Air and sea arrivals.
59 Arrivals in the States of Kosrae, Chuuk, Pohnpei and Yap. Excluding FSM citizens.
60 Excluding diplomats and foreign residents in Mongolia.
61 The data correspond only to 12 border posts.
62 The data of all the border posts of the country are used.
63 Change in methodology.
64 Including tourist arrivals through border entry points to Yangon.
65 Including arrivals from India.
66 Including Niueans usually residing in New Zealand.
67 Figures are based on the guest survey carried out by Institute of Transport Economics.
68 Air arrivals (Palau International Airport).
69 E/D cards in the "Silvio Petirossi" airport and passenger counts at the national border crossings - National Police and SENATUR.
70 From 2002, new estimated series including tourists with identity document other than a passport.
71 Preliminary data.
72 Source: "Junta de Planificacion de Puerto Rico".
73 Fiscal years (July-June).
74 Source: Qatar Central Bank.
75 Visitors who received tourism services from licensed tourism agencies and tour operators. Excluding the left bank of the river Dniester and the municipality of Bender.
76 Excluding Netherlands Antillean residents.
77 Including arrivals to Saint Maarten (the French side of the island).
78 Source: Central Bank of the Netherlands Antilles - Including the estimates for Saba and Saint Eustatius.
79 Including Italian tourists.
80 The expenditure figures are those provided by the country to UNWTO.
81 Excluding the first and second quarters.
82 Excluding the first quarter.
83 Excluding arrivals by work and contract workers.
84 Arrivals at Zanderij Airport.
85 The Iraqi nationals are included from 2008 only and they have been excluded in the previous years (from the beginning of 2008, they have to require a visa to enter Syria; if they arrived previously to this date, it is considered that they stayed for a period longer than a year, becoming residents).
86 Including arrivals of nationals residing abroad.
87 Including expenditure of the nationals residing abroad.
88 Including domestic tourism and nationals of the country residing abroad.
89 Including Mexicans staying one or more nights in the United States.

55 Y compris les résidents de Singapour traversant la frontière par voie terrestre à travers le Johore Causeway.
56 Départs par voies aérienne et maritime.
57 Années fiscales (du 1er octobre au 30 septembre).
58 Arrivées par voie aérienne et maritime.
59 Arrivées dans les États de Kosrae, Chuuk, Pohnpei et Yap. Excluant les citoyens de EFM.
60 Sont exclus les diplomates et les étrangers qui résident en Mongolie.
61 les données ne couvrent que 12 postes frontière.
62 Les données de l'ensemble des postes frontières du pays sont utilisées.
63 Changement de méthode.
64 Comprenant les arrivées de touristes aux postes-frontières de Yangon.
65 Y compris les arrivées à Inde.
66 Y compris les nationaux de Niue résidant habituellement en Nouvelle-Zélande.
67 Les chiffres se fondent sur "l'enquête auprès de la clientèle" de l'Institut d'économie des transports.
68 Arrivées par voie aérienne (Aéroport international de Palau).
69 Cartes d'embarquement et de débarquement à l'aéroport Silvio Petirossi et comptages des passagers lors du franchissement des frontières nationales – Police Nationale et SENATUR.
70 À partir de 2002, nouvelle série estimée comprenant les touristes avec une pièce d'identité autre qu'un passeport.
71 Données préliminaires.
72 Source : "Junta de Planificacion de Puerto Rico".
73 Années fiscales (juillet-juin).
74 Source: "Qatar Central Bank".
75 Visiteurs qui ont bénéficié des services touristiques des agences de tourisme et des voyagistes (titulaires d'une licence touristique). À l'exception de la rive gauche de la rivière Dniester et de la municipalité de Bender.
76 A l'exclusion des résidents des Antilles Néerlandaises.
77 Y compris les arrivées à Saint-Martin (la partie française de l'île).
78 Source : Banque centrale des Antilles néerlandaises. Comprend des estimations concernant Saint-Eustache et Saba.
79 Y compris les touristes touristes.
80 Les chiffres des dépenses sont ceux que le pays fournis à l'OMT.
81 Premier et deuxième trimestres.
82 À l'exclusion du 1er trimestre.
83 À l'exclusion des arrivées par travail et les travailleurs contractuels.
84 Arrivées à l'aéroport de Zanderij.
85 Les nationaux iraquiens ne sont pris en considérations que depuis 2008: depuis le début de 2008, ils doivent demander un visa pour se rendre en Syrie; s'ils sont arrivés avant cette date, on considère qu'ils sont restés dans le pays pendant une période dépassant une année et sont donc devenus des résidents.
86 Y compris les arrivées les nationaux résidant à l'étranger.
87 Y compris dépenses des nationaux résidant à l'étranger.
88 Y compris le tourisme interne et les nationaux résidant à l'étranger.
89 Incluyant Mexicains passant 1 nuit ou plus aux EU.

63 Outbound tourism

Departures in thousands; expenditure (total, travel and passenger transport) in million US dollars

Tourisme à l'étranger

Départs en milliers ; dépenses (total, voyage et transport de passagers) en millions de dollars E.-U.

Country or area	2004	2005	2006	2007	2008	Pays ou zone
Albania						**Albanie**
Departures (thousands)	1 694	2 097	2 616	2 979	3 716	Départs (milliers)
Total expenditure (millions $)	669	808	989	1 292	1 644	Dépenses totales (millions $)
Travel (millions $)	642	786	965	1 268	1 555	Voyage (millions $)
Passenger transport (millions $)	27	22	24	24	89	Transport de passagers (millions $)
Algeria						**Algérie**
Departures (thousands)	1 417	1 513	1 349	1 499	1 539	Départs (milliers)
Total expenditure (millions $) [1]	341	370	381	377	469	Dépenses totales (millions $) [1]
American Samoa						**Samoa américaines**
Departures (thousands)	...	35	41	...	...	Départs (milliers)
Angola						**Angola**
Total expenditure (millions $)	86	135	393	473	447	Dépenses totales (millions $)
Travel (millions $)	39	74	148	212	254	Voyage (millions $)
Passenger transport (millions $)	47	61	245	261	193	Transport de passagers (millions $)
Anguilla						**Anguilla**
Travel (millions $)	9	10	13	15	17	Voyage (millions $)
Antigua and Barbuda						**Antigua-et-Barbuda**
Departures (thousands)	...	...	...	...	434	Départs (milliers)
Travel (millions $)	38	40	45	52	55	Voyage (millions $)
Argentina						**Argentine**
Departures (thousands)	3 904	3 894	3 892	4 167	4 611	Départs (milliers)
Total expenditure (millions $)	3 208	3 554	4 038	5 063	5 971	Dépenses totales (millions $)
Travel (millions $) [2]	2 604	2 790	3 099	3 921	4 564	Voyage (millions $) [2]
Passenger transport (millions $)	604	764	939	1 142	1 407	Transport de passagers (millions $)
Armenia						**Arménie**
Departures (thousands)	221	269	329	468	516	Départs (milliers)
Total expenditure (millions $)	216	284	321	345	383	Dépenses totales (millions $)
Travel (millions $)	179	236	286	294	324	Voyage (millions $)
Passenger transport (millions $)	37	48	35	51	59	Transport de passagers (millions $)
Aruba						**Aruba**
Total expenditure (millions $)	248	240	255	300	345	Dépenses totales (millions $)
Travel (millions $)	218	216	232	281	323	Voyage (millions $)
Passenger transport (millions $)	30	24	23	19	22	Transport de passagers (millions $)
Australia						**Australie**
Departures (thousands)	4 369	4 756	4 941	5 462	5 808	Départs (milliers)
Total expenditure (millions $)	14 224	15 593	16 393	20 611	24 903	Dépenses totales (millions $)
Travel (millions $)	10 242	11 253	11 690	14 853	18 729	Voyage (millions $)
Passenger transport (millions $)	3 982	4 340	4 703	5 758	6 174	Transport de passagers (millions $)
Austria						**Autriche**
Departures (thousands) [3]	8 378	8 206	10 042	9 876	9 677	Départs (milliers) [3]
Total expenditure (millions $)	10 812	11 077	11 719	12 825	13 988	Dépenses totales (millions $)
Travel (millions $)	9 237	9 316	9 626	10 561	11 432	Voyage (millions $)
Passenger transport (millions $)	1 575	1 761	2 093	2 264	2 556	Transport de passagers (millions $)
Azerbaijan						**Azerbaïdjan**
Departures (thousands)	1 473	1 830	1 836	1 631	2 162	Départs (milliers)
Total expenditure (millions $)	140	188	256	381	454	Dépenses totales (millions $)
Travel (millions $)	126	164	201	264	341	Voyage (millions $)
Passenger transport (millions $)	14	24	55	117	113	Transport de passagers (millions $)
Bahamas						**Bahamas**
Total expenditure (millions $)	469	528	541	538	460	Dépenses totales (millions $)
Travel (millions $)	316	344	385	377	305	Voyage (millions $)
Passenger transport (millions $)	153	184	156	161	155	Transport de passagers (millions $)
Bahrain						**Bahreïn**
Total expenditure (millions $)	528	574	639	671	704	Dépenses totales (millions $)
Travel (millions $)	387	414	455	479	503	Voyage (millions $)
Passenger transport (millions $)	141	160	184	192	201	Transport de passagers (millions $)
Bangladesh						**Bangladesh**
Departures (thousands)	1 565	1 767	1 819	2 327	875	Départs (milliers)
Total expenditure (millions $)	442	375	444	530	918	Dépenses totales (millions $)
Travel (millions $)	161	136	140	156	184	Voyage (millions $)
Passenger transport (millions $)	281	239	304	374	734	Transport de passagers (millions $)

63 Outbound tourism *(continued)*
Departures in thousands; expenditure (total, travel and passenger transport) in million US dollars

Tourisme à l'étranger *(suite)*
Départs en milliers ; dépenses (total, voyage et transport de passagers) en millions de dollars E.-U.

Country or area	2004	2005	2006	2007	2008	Pays ou zone
Barbados						**Barbade**
Total expenditure (millions $)	163	153	166	177	154	Dépenses totales (millions $)
Travel (millions $)	108	96	104	99	80	Voyage (millions $)
Passenger transport (millions $)	55	57	62	78	74	Transport de passagers (millions $)
Belarus						**Bélarus**
Departures (thousands)	515	572	525	517	380	Départs (milliers)
Total expenditure (millions $)	500	516	675	724	812	Dépenses totales (millions $)
Travel (millions $)	450	448	586	606	668	Voyage (millions $)
Passenger transport (millions $)	50	68	89	118	144	Transport de passagers (millions $)
Belgium						**Belgique**
Departures (thousands)	8 783	9 327	7 852	8 371	8 887	Départs (milliers)
Total expenditure (millions $)	15 456	16 771	17 891	19 288	20 883	Dépenses totales (millions $)
Travel (millions $)	13 956	14 948	15 574	17 579	19 317	Voyage (millions $)
Passenger transport (millions $)	1 500	1 823	2 317	1 709	1 566	Transport de passagers (millions $)
Belize						**Belize**
Total expenditure (millions $)	47	45	43	46	44	Dépenses totales (millions $)
Travel (millions $)	43	42	41	43	41	Voyage (millions $)
Passenger transport (millions $)	4	3	2	3	3	Transport de passagers (millions $)
Benin						**Bénin**
Total expenditure (millions $)	59	58	71	107	130	Dépenses totales (millions $)
Travel (millions $)	29	27	34	72	60	Voyage (millions $)
Passenger transport (millions $)	30	31	37	35	70	Transport de passagers (millions $)
Bermuda						**Bermudes**
Departures (thousands)	156	161	170	181	192	Départs (milliers)
Total expenditure (millions $)	...	...	395	453	459	Dépenses totales (millions $)
Travel (millions $)	217[4]	239[4]	269	288	307	Voyage (millions $)
Passenger transport (millions $)	...	...	126	165	152	Transport de passagers (millions $)
Bolivia (Plurinational State of)						**Bolivie (État plurinational de)**
Departures (thousands)	346	386	472	526	589	Départs (milliers)
Total expenditure (millions $)	232	257	360	385	381	Dépenses totales (millions $)
Travel (millions $)	164	186	273	304	281	Voyage (millions $)
Passenger transport (millions $)	68	71	87	81	100	Transport de passagers (millions $)
Bonaire[5]						**Bonaire**[5]
Travel (millions $)	6	5	5	6	7	Voyage (millions $)
Bosnia and Herzegovina						**Bosnie-Herzégovine**
Total expenditure (millions $)	162	158	213	265	274	Dépenses totales (millions $)
Travel (millions $)	117	122	170	203	211	Voyage (millions $)
Passenger transport (millions $)	45	36	43	62	63	Transport de passagers (millions $)
Botswana						**Botswana**
Total expenditure (millions $)	280	301	285	449	490	Dépenses totales (millions $)
Travel (millions $)	276	282	277	446	488	Voyage (millions $)
Passenger transport (millions $)	4	19	8	3	2	Transport de passagers (millions $)
Brazil						**Brésil**
Departures (thousands)	3 701	4 667	4 625	4 823	4 936	Départs (milliers)
Total expenditure (millions $)	3 752	5 905	7 501	10 434	13 269	Dépenses totales (millions $)
Travel (millions $)	2 871	4 720	5 764	8 211	10 962	Voyage (millions $)
Passenger transport (millions $)	881	1 185	1 737	2 223	2 307	Transport de passagers (millions $)
Brunei Darussalam						**Brunéi Darussalam**
Travel (millions $)	382	374	408	430	458	Voyage (millions $)
Bulgaria						**Bulgarie**
Departures (thousands)	3 882	4 235	4 180	4 515	5 727	Départs (milliers)
Total expenditure (millions $)	1 935	1 858	2 099	2 593	3 380	Dépenses totales (millions $)
Travel (millions $)	1 363	1 309	1 478	1 826	2 380	Voyage (millions $)
Passenger transport (millions $)	572	549	621	767	1 000	Transport de passagers (millions $)
Burkina Faso[6]						**Burkina Faso**[6]
Total expenditure (millions $)	...	53	84	91	...	Dépenses totales (millions $)
Travel (millions $)	39	46	55	53	...	Voyage (millions $)
Passenger transport (millions $)	...	7	29	38	...	Transport de passagers (millions $)
Burundi						**Burundi**
Total expenditure (millions $)	29	62	126	106	98	Dépenses totales (millions $)
Travel (millions $)	23	60	125	104	91	Voyage (millions $)
Passenger transport (millions $)	6	2	1	2	7	Transport de passagers (millions $)

63 Outbound tourism *(continued)*

Departures in thousands; expenditure (total, travel and passenger transport) in million US dollars

Tourisme à l'étranger *(suite)*

Départs en milliers ; dépenses (total, voyage et transport de passagers) en millions de dollars E.-U.

Country or area	2004	2005	2006	2007	2008	Pays ou zone
Cambodia						**Cambodge**
Departures (thousands)	239	568	787	996	786	Départs (milliers)
Total expenditure (millions $)	80	138	176	194	191	Dépenses totales (millions $)
Travel (millions $)	48	97	122	123	108	Voyage (millions $)
Passenger transport (millions $)	32	41	54	71	83	Transport de passagers (millions $)
Cameroon						**Cameroun**
Total expenditure (millions $)	394	480	521	466	502	Dépenses totales (millions $)
Travel (millions $)	323	355	412	368	340	Voyage (millions $)
Passenger transport (millions $)	71	125	109	98	162	Transport de passagers (millions $)
Canada						**Canada**
Departures (thousands) [7]	19 595	21 099	22 732	25 163	27 037	Départs (milliers) [7]
Total expenditure (millions $)	19 267	22 734	26 075	31 199	34 007	Dépenses totales (millions $)
Travel (millions $)	15 524	18 017	20 620	24 716	27 306	Voyage (millions $)
Passenger transport (millions $)	3 743	4 717	5 455	6 483	6 701	Transport de passagers (millions $)
Cape Verde						**Cap-Vert**
Total expenditure (millions $)	93	82	106	123	143	Dépenses totales (millions $)
Travel (millions $)	78	67	82	107	133	Voyage (millions $)
Passenger transport (millions $)	15	15	24	16	10	Transport de passagers (millions $)
Central African Rep.						**Rép. centrafricaine**
Departures (thousands)	7	8	11	...	...	Départs (milliers)
Total expenditure (millions $) [8]	32	46	47	54	56	Dépenses totales (millions $) [8]
Travel (millions $) [8]	31	44	44	48	49	Voyage (millions $) [8]
Passenger transport (millions $) [8]	1	2	3	6	7	Transport de passagers (millions $) [8]
Chile						**Chili**
Departures (thousands)	2 343	2 651	3 005	3 234	3 061	Départs (milliers)
Total expenditure (millions $)	1 251	1 355	1 573	2 036	1 788	Dépenses totales (millions $)
Travel (millions $)	977	1 051	1 239	1 661	1 366	Voyage (millions $)
Passenger transport (millions $)	274	304	334	375	422	Transport de passagers (millions $)
China [9]						**Chine** [9]
Departures (thousands) [10]	28 853	31 026	34 524	40 954	45 844	Départs (milliers) [10]
Total expenditure (millions $)	21 360	24 715	28 242	33 264	40 987	Dépenses totales (millions $)
Travel (millions $)	19 149	21 759	24 322	29 786	36 157	Voyage (millions $)
Passenger transport (millions $)	2 211	2 956	3 920	3 478	4 830	Transport de passagers (millions $)
China, Hong Kong SAR						**Chine, Hong Kong RAS**
Departures (thousands)	68 903	72 300	75 812 [12]	80 682 [12]	81 911 [12]	Départs (milliers)
Travel (millions $) [11]	13 270	13 305	14 044	15 042	15 888	Voyage (millions $) [11]
China, Macao SAR						**Chine, Macao RAS**
Departures (thousands) [13]	212	295	272	212	229	Départs (milliers) [13]
Total expenditure (millions $)	357	428	452	537	621	Dépenses totales (millions $)
Travel (millions $)	332	358	378	463	554	Voyage (millions $)
Passenger transport (millions $)	25	70	74	74	67	Transport de passagers (millions $)
Colombia						**Colombie**
Departures (thousands)	1 405	1 553	1 768	2 041	2 042	Départs (milliers)
Total expenditure (millions $)	1 469	1 565	1 799	2 093	2 337	Dépenses totales (millions $)
Travel (millions $)	1 111	1 130	1 332	1 537	1 739	Voyage (millions $)
Passenger transport (millions $)	358	435	467	556	598	Transport de passagers (millions $)
Comoros						**Comores**
Total expenditure (millions $)	9	10	11	...	...	Dépenses totales (millions $)
Congo						**Congo**
Total expenditure (millions $)	176	...	...	...	...	Dépenses totales (millions $)
Travel (millions $)	103	112	132	168	...	Voyage (millions $)
Passenger transport (millions $)	73	...	...	...	...	Transport de passagers (millions $)
Cook Islands						**Iles Cook**
Departures (thousands)	12	13	13	13	13	Départs (milliers)
Costa Rica						**Costa Rica**
Departures (thousands)	425	487	485	577	519	Départs (milliers)
Total expenditure (millions $)	481	556	577	751	718	Dépenses totales (millions $)
Travel (millions $)	406	470	485	634	593	Voyage (millions $)
Passenger transport (millions $)	75	86	92	117	125	Transport de passagers (millions $)

63 Outbound tourism *(continued)*

Departures in thousands; expenditure (total, travel and passenger transport) in million US dollars

Tourisme à l'étranger *(suite)*

Départs en milliers ; dépenses (total, voyage et transport de passagers) en millions de dollars E.-U.

Country or area	2004	2005	2006	2007	2008	Pays ou zone
Côte d'Ivoire						**Côte d'Ivoire**
Total expenditure (millions $)	571	549	583	606	...	Dépenses totales (millions $)
Travel (millions $)	381	354	373	372	380	Voyage (millions $)
Passenger transport (millions $)	190	195	210	234	...	Transport de passagers (millions $)
Croatia						**Croatie**
Total expenditure (millions $)	881	786	770	1 025	1 152	Dépenses totales (millions $)
Travel (millions $)	848	754	737	985	1 109	Voyage (millions $)
Passenger transport (millions $)	33	32	33	40	43	Transport de passagers (millions $)
Cuba [14]						**Cuba** [14]
Departures (thousands)	124	162	199	194	202	Départs (milliers)
Curaçao [5]						**Curaçao** [5]
Total expenditure (millions $)	195	164	191	204	203	Dépenses totales (millions $)
Cyprus						**Chypre**
Departures (thousands)	743	781	789	932	1 042	Départs (milliers)
Total expenditure (millions $)	907	1 001	1 031	1 554	1 874	Dépenses totales (millions $)
Travel (millions $)	811	932	967	1 479	1 571	Voyage (millions $)
Passenger transport (millions $)	96	69	64	75	303	Transport de passagers (millions $)
Czech Republic						**République tchèque**
Total expenditure (millions $)	2 682	2 603	2 874	3 771	4 731	Dépenses totales (millions $)
Travel (millions $)	2 280	2 405	2 765	3 647	4 587	Voyage (millions $)
Passenger transport (millions $)	402	198	109	124	144	Transport de passagers (millions $)
Denmark						**Danemark**
Departures (thousands)	4 630	5 469	6 129	6 564	6 347	Départs (milliers)
Travel (millions $)	7 279	6 850	7 428	8 791	9 678	Voyage (millions $)
Djibouti						**Djibouti**
Total expenditure (millions $)	14	14	15	14	16	Dépenses totales (millions $)
Travel (millions $)	3	3	4	3	4	Voyage (millions $)
Passenger transport (millions $)	11	12	12	12	12	Transport de passagers (millions $)
Dominica						**Dominique**
Travel (millions $)	9	10	10	11	11	Voyage (millions $)
Dominican Republic						**Rép. dominicaine**
Departures (thousands)	368	419	420	443	413	Départs (milliers)
Total expenditure (millions $)	448	511	495	531	522	Dépenses totales (millions $)
Travel (millions $)	310	352	333	326	314	Voyage (millions $)
Passenger transport (millions $)	138	159	162	205	208	Transport de passagers (millions $)
Ecuador						**Equateur**
Departures (thousands)	603	664	733	801	815	Départs (milliers)
Total expenditure (millions $)	577	644	706	733	790	Dépenses totales (millions $)
Travel (millions $)	391	429	466	504	542	Voyage (millions $)
Passenger transport (millions $)	186	215	240	229	248	Transport de passagers (millions $)
Egypt						**Egypte**
Departures (thousands) [15]	5 210	5 307	4 531	...	...	Départs (milliers) [15]
Total expenditure (millions $)	1 543	1 932	2 156	2 886	3 390	Dépenses totales (millions $)
Travel (millions $)	1 257	1 629	1 784	2 446	2 915	Voyage (millions $)
Passenger transport (millions $)	286	303	372	440	475	Transport de passagers (millions $)
El Salvador						**El Salvador**
Departures (thousands)	1 079	1 239	1 242	1 012	...	Départs (milliers)
Total expenditure (millions $)	373	430	606	690	709	Dépenses totales (millions $)
Travel (millions $)	292	347	523	605	624	Voyage (millions $)
Passenger transport (millions $)	81	83	83	85	85	Transport de passagers (millions $)
Estonia						**Estonie**
Total expenditure (millions $)	486	530	706	804	938	Dépenses totales (millions $)
Travel (millions $)	399	439	586	670	808	Voyage (millions $)
Passenger transport (millions $)	87	91	120	134	130	Transport de passagers (millions $)
Ethiopia						**Ethiopie**
Total expenditure (millions $)	59	...	...	...	...	Dépenses totales (millions $)
Travel (millions $)	58	77	97	107	156	Voyage (millions $)
Passenger transport (millions $)	1	...	...	...	...	Transport de passagers (millions $)

Outbound tourism *(continued)*

Departures in thousands; expenditure (total, travel and passenger transport) in million US dollars

Tourisme à l'étranger *(suite)*

Départs en milliers ; dépenses (total, voyage et transport de passagers) en millions de dollars E.-U.

Country or area	2004	2005	2006	2007	2008	Pays ou zone
Fiji						**Fidji**
Departures (thousands)	94	109	121	120	124	Départs (milliers)
Total expenditure (millions $)	118	132	123	130	139	Dépenses totales (millions $)
Travel (millions $)	94	106	101	92	96	Voyage (millions $)
Passenger transport (millions $)	24	26	22	38	43	Transport de passagers (millions $)
Finland						**Finlande**
Departures (thousands) [16]	5 798	5 902	5 756	5 749	5 854	Départs (milliers) [16]
Total expenditure (millions $)	3 383	3 622	4 094	4 812	5 534	Dépenses totales (millions $)
Travel (millions $)	2 821	3 057	3 424	3 983	4 501	Voyage (millions $)
Passenger transport (millions $)	562	565	670	829	1 033	Transport de passagers (millions $)
France						**France**
Departures (thousands)	#21 131	24 800	25 080	25 139	23 347	Départs (milliers)
Total expenditure (millions $)	34 674	37 546	37 888	44 544	52 135	Dépenses totales (millions $)
Travel (millions $)	28 703	30 458	31 239	36 743	43 346	Voyage (millions $)
Passenger transport (millions $)	5 971	7 088	6 649	7 801	8 789	Transport de passagers (millions $)
French Polynesia						**Polynésie française**
Total expenditure (millions $)	425	430	256	408	412	Dépenses totales (millions $)
Travel (millions $)	311	312	122	159	159	Voyage (millions $)
Passenger transport (millions $)	114	118	134	249	253	Transport de passagers (millions $)
Gabon						**Gabon**
Total expenditure (millions $)	275	346	...	...	...	Dépenses totales (millions $)
Travel (millions $)	214	274	...	...	...	Voyage (millions $)
Passenger transport (millions $)	61	72	...	...	...	Transport de passagers (millions $)
Gambia						**Gambie**
Departures (thousands)	...	387	307	...	...	Départs (milliers)
Total expenditure (millions $)	6	7	8	9	...	Dépenses totales (millions $)
Travel (millions $)	4	5	6	7	8	Voyage (millions $)
Passenger transport (millions $)	2	2	2	2	...	Transport de passagers (millions $)
Georgia						**Géorgie**
Total expenditure (millions $)	196	237	257	277	338	Dépenses totales (millions $)
Travel (millions $)	147	169	167	176	204	Voyage (millions $)
Passenger transport (millions $)	49	68	90	101	134	Transport de passagers (millions $)
Germany						**Allemagne**
Departures (thousands)	72 300	77 400	71 200	70 400	73 000	Départs (milliers)
Total expenditure (millions $)	79 438	82 228	83 066	93 767	103 386	Dépenses totales (millions $)
Travel (millions $)	71 187	74 189	74 123	83 156	91 692	Voyage (millions $)
Passenger transport (millions $)	8 251	8 039	8 943	10 611	11 694	Transport de passagers (millions $)
Ghana						**Ghana**
Total expenditure (millions $)	270	472	575	816	870	Dépenses totales (millions $)
Travel (millions $)	186	303	345	558	542	Voyage (millions $)
Passenger transport (millions $)	84	169	230	258	328	Transport de passagers (millions $)
Greece						**Grèce**
Total expenditure (millions $)	2 880	3 045	3 004	3 430	3 946	Dépenses totales (millions $)
Travel (millions $)	2 872	3 039	2 997	3 423	3 930	Voyage (millions $)
Passenger transport (millions $)	8	6	7	7	16	Transport de passagers (millions $)
Grenada						**Grenade**
Travel (millions $)	9	10	16	16	13	Voyage (millions $)
Guatemala						**Guatemala**
Departures (thousands)	854	982	1 055	1 168	1 277	Départs (milliers)
Total expenditure (millions $)	488	531	654	736	750	Dépenses totales (millions $)
Travel (millions $)	385	420	528	597	606	Voyage (millions $)
Passenger transport (millions $)	103	111	126	139	144	Transport de passagers (millions $)
Guinea						**Guinée**
Total expenditure (millions $)	29	...	...	96	30	Dépenses totales (millions $)
Travel (millions $)	25	...	...	29	9	Voyage (millions $)
Passenger transport (millions $)	4	...	...	67	21	Transport de passagers (millions $)
Guinea-Bissau						**Guinée-Bissau**
Total expenditure (millions $)	22	18	...	...	...	Dépenses totales (millions $)
Travel (millions $)	13	10	16	...	...	Voyage (millions $)
Passenger transport (millions $)	9	8	...	...	...	Transport de passagers (millions $)

Outbound tourism *(continued)*

Departures in thousands; expenditure (total, travel and passenger transport) in million US dollars

Tourisme à l'étranger *(suite)*

Départs en milliers ; dépenses (total, voyage et transport de passagers) en millions de dollars E.-U.

Country or area	2004	2005	2006	2007	2008	Pays ou zone
Guyana						**Guyana**
Travel (millions $)	30	40	49	58	52	Voyage (millions $)
Haiti						**Haïti**
Total expenditure (millions $)	206	174	239	331	383	Dépenses totales (millions $)
Travel (millions $)	72	55	56	56	64	Voyage (millions $)
Passenger transport (millions $)	134	119	183	275	319	Transport de passagers (millions $)
Honduras						**Honduras**
Departures (thousands)	295	296	308	315	387	Départs (milliers)
Total expenditure (millions $)	300	321	425	467	421	Dépenses totales (millions $)
Travel (millions $)	244	262	355	370	344	Voyage (millions $)
Passenger transport (millions $)	56	59	70	97	77	Transport de passagers (millions $)
Hungary						**Hongrie**
Departures (thousands) [17]	17 558	18 622	17 612	18 471	...	Départs (milliers) [17]
Total expenditure (millions $)	2 482	2 826	2 565	3 487	4 637	Dépenses totales (millions $)
Travel (millions $)	2 421	2 382	2 126	2 949	4 037	Voyage (millions $)
Passenger transport (millions $)	61	444	439	538	600	Transport de passagers (millions $)
Iceland						**Islande**
Total expenditure (millions $)	699	991	1 084	1 336	1 107	Dépenses totales (millions $)
Travel (millions $)	697	980	1 076	1 326	1 103	Voyage (millions $)
Passenger transport (millions $)	2	11	8	10	4	Transport de passagers (millions $)
India						**Inde**
Departures (thousands) [18]	6 213	7 185	8 340	9 783	10 868	Départs (milliers) [18]
Total expenditure (millions $)	5 783	8 277	8 738	10 690	12 081	Dépenses totales (millions $)
Travel (millions $)	4 816	6 187	6 845	8 219	9 602	Voyage (millions $)
Passenger transport (millions $)	967	2 090	1 893	2 471	2 479	Transport de passagers (millions $)
Indonesia						**Indonésie**
Departures (thousands)	3 941	4 106	4 967	5 158	5 486	Départs (milliers)
Total expenditure (millions $)	4 569	4 740	5 458	6 578	8 547	Dépenses totales (millions $)
Travel (millions $)	3 507	3 584	4 030	4 904	5 397	Voyage (millions $)
Passenger transport (millions $)	1 062	1 156	1 428	1 674	3 150	Transport de passagers (millions $)
Iran (Islamic Rep. of) [19]						**Iran (Rép. islamique d')** [19]
Total expenditure (millions $)	4 402	4 560	5 767	7 335	9 482	Dépenses totales (millions $)
Travel (millions $)	4 093	4 202	5 315	6 809	8 685	Voyage (millions $)
Passenger transport (millions $)	309	358	452	526	797	Transport de passagers (millions $)
Iraq						**Iraq**
Total expenditure (millions $)	...	627	526	705	...	Dépenses totales (millions $)
Travel (millions $) [20]		439	395	639	...	Voyage (millions $) [20]
Passenger transport (millions $)	...	188	131	66	...	Transport de passagers (millions $)
Ireland						**Irlande**
Departures (thousands) [21]	5 409	6 113	6 848	7 713	...	Départs (milliers) [21]
Total expenditure (millions $)	5 291	6 186	6 978	8 785	10 551	Dépenses totales (millions $)
Travel (millions $)	5 177	6 074	6 862	8 656	10 425	Voyage (millions $)
Passenger transport (millions $)	114	112	116	129	126	Transport de passagers (millions $)
Israel						**Israël**
Departures (thousands)	3 614	3 687	3 713	4 147	4 207	Départs (milliers)
Total expenditure (millions $)	3 663	3 780	3 870	4 251	4 445	Dépenses totales (millions $)
Travel (millions $)	2 796	2 895	2 983	3 260	3 439	Voyage (millions $)
Passenger transport (millions $)	867	885	887	991	1 006	Transport de passagers (millions $)
Italy						**Italie**
Departures (thousands) [21]	23 349	24 796	25 697	27 734	28 284	Départs (milliers) [21]
Total expenditure (millions $)	24 064	26 774	27 437	32 754	37 728	Dépenses totales (millions $)
Travel (millions $)	20 460	22 370	23 152	27 329	30 839	Voyage (millions $)
Passenger transport (millions $)	3 604	4 404	4 285	5 425	6 889	Transport de passagers (millions $)
Jamaica						**Jamaïque**
Total expenditure (millions $)	318	290	315	340	312	Dépenses totales (millions $)
Travel (millions $)	286	249	273	298	268	Voyage (millions $)
Passenger transport (millions $)	32	41	42	42	44	Transport de passagers (millions $)
Japan						**Japon**
Departures (thousands)	16 831	17 404	17 535	17 295	15 987	Départs (milliers)
Total expenditure (millions $)	48 175	48 102	37 659	37 261	38 976	Dépenses totales (millions $)
Travel (millions $)	38 252	37 565	26 876 [22]	26 511	27 901	Voyage (millions $)
Passenger transport (millions $)	9 923	10 537	10 783	10 750	11 075	Transport de passagers (millions $)

Country or area	2004	2005	2006	2007	2008	Pays ou zone
Jordan						**Jordanie**
Departures (thousands)	1 420	1 523	2 139	2 094	2 288	Départs (milliers)
Total expenditure (millions $)	585	653	956	1 024	1 140	Dépenses totales (millions $)
Travel (millions $)	524	585	837	883	1 004	Voyage (millions $)
Passenger transport (millions $)	61	68	119	141	136	Transport de passagers (millions $)
Kazakhstan						**Kazakhstan**
Departures (thousands)	3 915	3 004	3 688	4 544	5 243	Départs (milliers)
Total expenditure (millions $)	997	940	1 060	1 355	1 305	Dépenses totales (millions $)
Travel (millions $)	844	753	821	1 041	1 022	Voyage (millions $)
Passenger transport (millions $)	153	187	239	314	283	Transport de passagers (millions $)
Kenya						**Kenya**
Travel (millions $)	108	124	178	265	266	Voyage (millions $)
Korea, Republic of						**Corée, République de**
Departures (thousands)	8 826	10 080	11 610	13 325	11 996	Départs (milliers)
Total expenditure (millions $)	13 507	16 924	20 989	23 359	19 512	Dépenses totales (millions $)
Travel (millions $)	12 350	15 406	18 851	20 890	17 125	Voyage (millions $)
Passenger transport (millions $)	1 157	1 518	2 138	2 469	2 387	Transport de passagers (millions $)
Kuwait						**Koweït**
Departures (thousands)	1 928	2 173	2 529	2 649	...	Départs (milliers)
Total expenditure (millions $)	4 147	4 997	6 074	7 267	8 341	Dépenses totales (millions $)
Travel (millions $)	3 701	4 532	5 573	6 636	7 570	Voyage (millions $)
Passenger transport (millions $)	446	465	501	631	771	Transport de passagers (millions $)
Kyrgyzstan						**Kirghizistan**
Departures (thousands)	239	201	454	559	1 521	Départs (milliers)
Total expenditure (millions $)	73	94	142	193	451	Dépenses totales (millions $)
Travel (millions $)	50	58	92	90	304	Voyage (millions $)
Passenger transport (millions $)	23	36	50	103	147	Transport de passagers (millions $)
Lao People's Dem. Rep.						**Rép. dém. pop. lao**
Travel (millions $)	15	16	9	8	16	Voyage (millions $)
Latvia						**Lettonie**
Departures (thousands)[23]	2 457	2 959	3 151	3 398	3 782	Départs (milliers)[23]
Total expenditure (millions $)	428	655	788	1 021	1 250	Dépenses totales (millions $)
Travel (millions $)	377	584	704	927	1 142	Voyage (millions $)
Passenger transport (millions $)	51	71	84	94	108	Transport de passagers (millions $)
Lebanon						**Liban**
Total expenditure (millions $)	3 719	3 565	3 783	3 914	4 297	Dépenses totales (millions $)
Travel (millions $)	3 170	2 908	3 006	3 114	3 564	Voyage (millions $)
Passenger transport (millions $)	549	657	777	800	733	Transport de passagers (millions $)
Lesotho						**Lesotho**
Total expenditure (millions $)	37	36	22	24	19	Dépenses totales (millions $)
Travel (millions $)	30	27	19	16	14	Voyage (millions $)
Passenger transport (millions $)	7	9	3	8	5	Transport de passagers (millions $)
Liberia						**Libéria**
Total expenditure (millions $)	29	33	41	48	58	Dépenses totales (millions $)
Travel (millions $)	14	16	17	21	30	Voyage (millions $)
Passenger transport (millions $)	15	17	24	27	28	Transport de passagers (millions $)
Libyan Arab Jamah.						**Jamah. arabe libyenne**
Total expenditure (millions $)	789	920	915	1 010	1 339	Dépenses totales (millions $)
Travel (millions $)	603	680	668	889	1 277	Voyage (millions $)
Passenger transport (millions $)	186	240	247	121	62	Transport de passagers (millions $)
Lithuania						**Lituanie**
Departures (thousands)	...	...	...	3 627	2 847	Départs (milliers)
Total expenditure (millions $)	643	757	931	1 168	1 533	Dépenses totales (millions $)
Travel (millions $)	636	744	909	1 144	1 497	Voyage (millions $)
Passenger transport (millions $)	7	13	22	24	36	Transport de passagers (millions $)
Luxembourg						**Luxembourg**
Total expenditure (millions $)	2 950	...	...	...	...	Dépenses totales (millions $)
Travel (millions $)	2 911	2 977	3 138	3 480	3 842	Voyage (millions $)
Passenger transport (millions $)	39	...	...	...	...	Transport de passagers (millions $)

63 Outbound tourism *(continued)*

Departures in thousands; expenditure (total, travel and passenger transport) in million US dollars

Tourisme à l'étranger *(suite)*

Départs en milliers ; dépenses (total, voyage et transport de passagers) en millions de dollars E.-U.

Country or area	2004	2005	2006	2007	2008	Pays ou zone
Madagascar						**Madagascar**
Total expenditure (millions $)	108	80	...	...	...	Dépenses totales (millions $)
Travel (millions $)	93	74	86	94	143	Voyage (millions $)
Passenger transport (millions $)	15	6	...	...	...	Transport de passagers (millions $)
Malawi [24]						**Malawi** [24]
Total expenditure (millions $)	59	75	75	84	...	Dépenses totales (millions $)
Travel (millions $)	50	65	65	73	...	Voyage (millions $)
Passenger transport (millions $)	9	10	10	11	...	Transport de passagers (millions $)
Malaysia						**Malaisie**
Departures (thousands) [25]	30 761	...	...	...	...	Départs (milliers) [25]
Total expenditure (millions $)	3 822	4 339	5 085	6 585	7 724	Dépenses totales (millions $)
Travel (millions $)	3 178	3 711	4 257	5 586	6 709	Voyage (millions $)
Passenger transport (millions $)	644	628	828	999	1 015	Transport de passagers (millions $)
Maldives						**Maldives**
Departures (thousands)	61	77	74	102	123	Départs (milliers)
Total expenditure (millions $)	75	94	106	127	148	Dépenses totales (millions $)
Travel (millions $)	56	70	78	93	109	Voyage (millions $)
Passenger transport (millions $)	19	24	28	34	39	Transport de passagers (millions $)
Mali						**Mali**
Total expenditure (millions $)	125	133	196	201	...	Dépenses totales (millions $)
Travel (millions $)	66	77	120	137	...	Voyage (millions $)
Passenger transport (millions $)	59	56	76	64	...	Transport de passagers (millions $)
Malta						**Malte**
Departures (thousands)	203	225	257	280	299	Départs (milliers)
Total expenditure (millions $)	291	311	362	420	482	Dépenses totales (millions $)
Travel (millions $)	255	268	320	376	431	Voyage (millions $)
Passenger transport (millions $)	36	43	42	44	51	Transport de passagers (millions $)
Mauritius						**Maurice**
Departures (thousands)	180	183	186	213	226	Départs (milliers)
Total expenditure (millions $)	277	295	347	384	489	Dépenses totales (millions $)
Travel (millions $)	255	275	327	357	452	Voyage (millions $)
Passenger transport (millions $)	22	20	20	27	37	Transport de passagers (millions $)
Mexico						**Mexique**
Departures (thousands)	12 494	13 305	14 002	15 083	14 450	Départs (milliers)
Total expenditure (millions $)	8 034	8 951	9 387	9 831	10 185	Dépenses totales (millions $)
Travel (millions $)	6 959	7 600	8 108	8 375	8 526	Voyage (millions $)
Passenger transport (millions $)	1 075	1 351	1 279	1 456	1 659	Transport de passagers (millions $)
Micronesia (Fed. States of) [1,26]						**Micronésie (Etats féd. de)** [1,26]
Total expenditure (millions $)	5	6	6	...	...	Dépenses totales (millions $)
Mongolia						**Mongolie**
Total expenditure (millions $)	207	173	212	...	...	Dépenses totales (millions $)
Travel (millions $)	193	157	188	...	...	Voyage (millions $)
Passenger transport (millions $)	14	16	24	...	...	Transport de passagers (millions $)
Montenegro						**Monténégro**
Travel (millions $)	...	...	...	37	43	Voyage (millions $)
Montserrat						**Montserrat**
Travel (millions $)	2	3	3	3	3	Voyage (millions $)
Morocco						**Maroc**
Departures (thousands)	1 603	2 247	2 135	2 669	3 058	Départs (milliers)
Total expenditure (millions $)	912	999	1 113	1 418	1 910	Dépenses totales (millions $)
Travel (millions $)	574	612	693	880	1 090	Voyage (millions $)
Passenger transport (millions $)	338	387	420	538	820	Transport de passagers (millions $)
Mozambique						**Mozambique**
Total expenditure (millions $)	140	187	205	209	241	Dépenses totales (millions $)
Travel (millions $)	134	176	179	180	208	Voyage (millions $)
Passenger transport (millions $)	6	11	26	29	33	Transport de passagers (millions $)
Myanmar						**Myanmar**
Total expenditure (millions $)	32	34	40	...	...	Dépenses totales (millions $)
Travel (millions $)	29	31	37	...	...	Voyage (millions $)
Passenger transport (millions $)	3	3	3	...	...	Transport de passagers (millions $)
Namibia						**Namibie**
Travel (millions $)	123	108	118	132	92	Voyage (millions $)

63

Outbound tourism *(continued)*

Departures in thousands; expenditure (total, travel and passenger transport) in million US dollars

Tourisme à l'étranger *(suite)*

Départs en milliers ; dépenses (total, voyage et transport de passagers) en millions de dollars E.-U.

Country or area	2004	2005	2006	2007	2008	Pays ou zone
Nepal						**Népal**
Departures (thousands)	286	373	415	469	561	Départs (milliers)
Total expenditure (millions $)	205	221	261	402	545	Dépenses totales (millions $)
Travel (millions $)	154	163	185	274	381	Voyage (millions $)
Passenger transport (millions $)	51	58	76	128	164	Transport de passagers (millions $)
Netherlands						**Pays-Bas**
Departures (thousands) [27]	17 130	17 039	16 695	17 556	18 458	Départs (milliers) [27]
Total expenditure (millions $)	16 937	16 621	17 453	19 477	22 212	Dépenses totales (millions $)
Travel (millions $)	16 348	16 140	17 087	19 110	21 825	Voyage (millions $)
Passenger transport (millions $)	589	481	366	367	387	Transport de passagers (millions $)
New Caledonia						**Nouvelle-Calédonie**
Departures (thousands) [28]	89	96	100	106	112	Départs (milliers) [28]
Travel (millions $)	167	122	129	149	168	Voyage (millions $)
New Zealand						**Nouvelle-Zélande**
Departures (thousands) [29]	1 733	1 872	1 861	1 978	1 965	Départs (milliers) [29]
Travel (millions $)	2 229	2 666	2 536	3 084	2 991	Voyage (millions $)
Nicaragua						**Nicaragua**
Departures (thousands)	701	740	773	949	1 100	Départs (milliers)
Total expenditure (millions $)	154	162	171	195	218	Dépenses totales (millions $)
Travel (millions $)	89	91	97	121	142	Voyage (millions $)
Passenger transport (millions $)	65	71	74	74	76	Transport de passagers (millions $)
Niger						**Niger**
Total expenditure (millions $)	42	42	42	48	...	Dépenses totales (millions $)
Travel (millions $)	22	30	28	29	49	Voyage (millions $)
Passenger transport (millions $)	20	12	14	19	...	Transport de passagers (millions $)
Nigeria						**Nigéria**
Total expenditure (millions $)	1 469	501	1 216	3 476	4 774	Dépenses totales (millions $)
Travel (millions $)	1 161	240	959	2 401	3 621	Voyage (millions $)
Passenger transport (millions $)	308	261	257	1 075	1 153	Transport de passagers (millions $)
Niue						**Nioué**
Departures (thousands)	2	2	2	2	2	Départs (milliers)
Norway						**Norvège**
Departures (thousands) [30]	2 960	3 166	3 236	3 395	...	Départs (milliers) [30]
Total expenditure (millions $)	8 894	10 591	12 072	...	...	Dépenses totales (millions $)
Travel (millions $)	8 489	10 111	11 586	14 043	15 932	Voyage (millions $)
Passenger transport (millions $)	405	480	486	...	...	Transport de passagers (millions $)
Occupied Palestinian Terr. [31]						**Terr. palestinien occupé** [31]
Total expenditure (millions $)	409	264	293	376	...	Dépenses totales (millions $)
Travel (millions $)	401	255	290	365	...	Voyage (millions $)
Passenger transport (millions $)	8	9	3	11	...	Transport de passagers (millions $)
Oman						**Oman**
Total expenditure (millions $)	823	863	894	952	1 199	Dépenses totales (millions $)
Travel (millions $)	644	668	712	752	858	Voyage (millions $)
Passenger transport (millions $)	179	195	182	200	341	Transport de passagers (millions $)
Pakistan						**Pakistan**
Total expenditure (millions $)	1 612	1 753	2 029	2 083	2 035	Dépenses totales (millions $)
Travel (millions $)	1 268	1 280	1 545	1 593	1 510	Voyage (millions $)
Passenger transport (millions $)	344	473	484	490	525	Transport de passagers (millions $)
Palau [1]						**Palaos** [1]
Total expenditure (millions $)	2	2	1	...	...	Dépenses totales (millions $)
Panama						**Panama**
Departures (thousands)	256	285	284	314	369	Départs (milliers)
Total expenditure (millions $)	294	388	403	457	560	Dépenses totales (millions $)
Travel (millions $)	239	271	271	307	366	Voyage (millions $)
Passenger transport (millions $)	55	117	132	150	194	Transport de passagers (millions $)
Papua New Guinea						**Papouasie-Nvl-Guinée**
Total expenditure (millions $)	72	56	...	...	...	Dépenses totales (millions $)
Travel (millions $)	71	56	...	...	...	Voyage (millions $)
Passenger transport (millions $)	1	1	...	...	...	Transport de passagers (millions $)

63 Outbound tourism *(continued)*

Departures in thousands; expenditure (total, travel and passenger transport) in million US dollars

Tourisme à l'étranger *(suite)*

Départs en milliers ; dépenses (total, voyage et transport de passagers) en millions de dollars E.-U.

Country or area	2004	2005	2006	2007	2008	Pays ou zone
Paraguay						**Paraguay**
Departures (thousands)	170	188	210	242	278	Départs (milliers)
Total expenditure (millions $)	121	130	144	184	210	Dépenses totales (millions $)
Travel (millions $)	71	79	92	109	124	Voyage (millions $)
Passenger transport (millions $)	50	51	52	75	86	Transport de passagers (millions $)
Peru						**Pérou**
Departures (thousands)	1 676	1 883	1 903	1 966	1 971	Départs (milliers)
Total expenditure (millions $)	852	970	1 034	1 274	1 353	Dépenses totales (millions $)
Travel (millions $)	643	752	789	1 007	1 067	Voyage (millions $)
Passenger transport (millions $)	209	218	245	267	286	Transport de passagers (millions $)
Philippines						**Philippines**
Departures (thousands) [32]	1 920	2 144	2 745	...	...	Départs (milliers) [32]
Total expenditure (millions $)	1 526	1 547	1 558	2 055	2 778	Dépenses totales (millions $)
Travel (millions $)	1 275	1 279	1 232	1 663	2 213	Voyage (millions $)
Passenger transport (millions $)	251	268	326	392	565	Transport de passagers (millions $)
Poland						**Pologne**
Departures (thousands) [33]	37 226	40 841	44 696	47 561	...	Départs (milliers) [33]
Total expenditure (millions $)	5 092	5 894	7 654	8 341	10 381	Dépenses totales (millions $)
Travel (millions $)	4 776	5 548	7 224	7 753	9 596	Voyage (millions $)
Passenger transport (millions $)	316	346	430	588	785	Transport de passagers (millions $)
Portugal						**Portugal**
Departures (thousands)	17 141	18 110	18 378	20 989	...	Départs (milliers)
Total expenditure (millions $)	3 369	3 744	4 142	4 864	5 283	Dépenses totales (millions $)
Travel (millions $)	2 763	3 050	3 340	3 937	4 328	Voyage (millions $)
Passenger transport (millions $)	606	694	802	927	955	Transport de passagers (millions $)
Puerto Rico						**Porto Rico**
Departures (thousands)	1 361	1 410	1 468	1 441	1 493	Départs (milliers)
Total expenditure (millions $) [1,34]	1 584	1 663	1 752	1 743	1 834	Dépenses totales (millions $) [1,34]
Travel (millions $) [1,34]	1 085	1 143	1 205	1 192	1 260	Voyage (millions $) [1,34]
Passenger transport (millions $) [1,34]	499	520	547	551	574	Transport de passagers (millions $) [1,34]
Qatar [35]						**Qatar** [35]
Travel (millions $)	691	1 759	3 751	...	...	Voyage (millions $)
Republic of Moldova						**République de Moldova**
Departures (thousands)	68	57	68	82	85	Départs (milliers)
Total expenditure (millions $)	135	170	224	271	345	Dépenses totales (millions $)
Travel (millions $)	113	141	190	214	274	Voyage (millions $)
Passenger transport (millions $)	22	29	34	57	71	Transport de passagers (millions $)
Réunion						**Réunion**
Departures (thousands)	385	395	409	410	...	Départs (milliers)
Romania						**Roumanie**
Departures (thousands)	6 972	7 140	8 906	10 980	13 072	Départs (milliers)
Total expenditure (millions $)	672	1 073	1 459	1 725	2 411	Dépenses totales (millions $)
Travel (millions $)	539	925	1 310	1 543	2 178	Voyage (millions $)
Passenger transport (millions $)	133	148	149	182	233	Transport de passagers (millions $)
Russian Federation						**Fédération de Russie**
Departures (thousands)	24 507	28 416	29 107	34 285	36 538	Départs (milliers)
Total expenditure (millions $)	16 082	18 305	19 478	24 164	28 122	Dépenses totales (millions $)
Travel (millions $)	15 285	17 314	18 112	22 133	24 890	Voyage (millions $)
Passenger transport (millions $)	797	991	1 366	2 031	3 232	Transport de passagers (millions $)
Rwanda						**Rwanda**
Total expenditure (millions $)	...	...	...	...	104	Dépenses totales (millions $)
Travel (millions $)	31	37	35	69	70	Voyage (millions $)
Passenger transport (millions $)	...	...	...	...	34	Transport de passagers (millions $)
Saint Kitts and Nevis						**Saint-Kitts-et-Nevis**
Travel (millions $)	10	11	14	12	13	Voyage (millions $)
Saint Lucia						**Sainte-Lucie**
Travel (millions $)	37	39	39	42	38	Voyage (millions $)
Saint Maarten [36]						**Saint-Martin** [36]
Travel (millions $)	80	94	86	85	88	Voyage (millions $)
Saint Vincent-Grenadines						**Saint Vincent-Grenadines**
Travel (millions $)	14	15	16	20	20	Voyage (millions $)

63 Outbound tourism *(continued)*

Departures in thousands; expenditure (total, travel and passenger transport) in million US dollars

Tourisme à l'étranger *(suite)*

Départs en milliers ; dépenses (total, voyage et transport de passagers) en millions de dollars E.-U.

Country or area	2004	2005	2006	2007	2008	Pays ou zone
Samoa						**Samoa**
Departures (thousands)	54	52	...	...	53	Départs (milliers)
Total expenditure (millions $)	12	17	16	14	...	Dépenses totales (millions $)
Travel (millions $)	5	9	6	5	...	Voyage (millions $)
Passenger transport (millions $)	7	8	10	9	...	Transport de passagers (millions $)
Sao Tome and Principe						**Sao Tomé-et-Principe**
Total expenditure (millions $)	2	1	1	1	...	Dépenses totales (millions $)
Travel (millions $)	1	^0	^0	^0	...	Voyage (millions $)
Passenger transport (millions $)	2	^0	1	1	...	Transport de passagers (millions $)
Saudi Arabia						**Arabie saoudite**
Departures (thousands)	3 811	4 403	2 000	4 126	4 087	Départs (milliers)
Total expenditure (millions $) [1]	4 600	9 290	13 491	21 570	16 666	Dépenses totales (millions $) [1]
Travel (millions $) [1]	4 428	9 087	12 979	20 171	15 129	Voyage (millions $) [1]
Passenger transport (millions $)	172	203	512	1 399	1 537	Transport de passagers (millions $)
Senegal						**Sénégal**
Total expenditure (millions $)	138	144	139	352	...	Dépenses totales (millions $)
Travel (millions $)	57	65	54	253	...	Voyage (millions $)
Passenger transport (millions $)	81	79	85	99	...	Transport de passagers (millions $)
Serbia						**Serbie**
Total expenditure (millions $)	208 [37]	260 [37]	322 [37]	1 194	1 435	Dépenses totales (millions $)
Travel (millions $)	...	...	...	1 042	1 251	Voyage (millions $)
Passenger transport (millions $)	...	...	...	152	184	Transport de passagers (millions $)
Seychelles						**Seychelles**
Departures (thousands)	48	52	55	58	54	Départs (milliers)
Total expenditure (millions $)	53	59	56	70	...	Dépenses totales (millions $)
Travel (millions $)	34	39	36	40	...	Voyage (millions $)
Passenger transport (millions $)	19	20	20	30	...	Transport de passagers (millions $)
Sierra Leone						**Sierra Leone**
Departures (thousands)	28	63	67	71	73	Départs (milliers)
Total expenditure (millions $)	30	34	15	17	24	Dépenses totales (millions $)
Travel (millions $)	30	32	12	14	24	Voyage (millions $)
Passenger transport (millions $)	^0	2	3	3	^0	Transport de passagers (millions $)
Singapore						**Singapour**
Departures (thousands)	5 165	5 159	5 533	6 024	6 828	Départs (milliers)
Travel (millions $)	9 291	10 070	11 116	12 477	14 189	Voyage (millions $)
Slovakia						**Slovaquie**
Departures (thousands) [17]	20 380	22 405	22 688	23 837	...	Départs (milliers) [17]
Total expenditure (millions $)	900	1 122	1 230	1 825	2 596	Dépenses totales (millions $)
Travel (millions $)	745	844	1 060	1 533	2 165	Voyage (millions $)
Passenger transport (millions $)	155	278	170	292	431	Transport de passagers (millions $)
Slovenia						**Slovénie**
Departures (thousands) [38]	2 800	2 660	2 680	2 496	2 459	Départs (milliers) [38]
Total expenditure (millions $)	937	1 019	1 058	1 260	1 567	Dépenses totales (millions $)
Travel (millions $)	868	950	974	1 144	1 314	Voyage (millions $)
Passenger transport (millions $)	69	69	84	116	253	Transport de passagers (millions $)
Solomon Islands						**Iles Salomon**
Total expenditure (millions $)	8	11	11	...	...	Dépenses totales (millions $)
Travel (millions $)	4	5	4	8	9	Voyage (millions $)
Passenger transport (millions $)	3	7	7	...	...	Transport de passagers (millions $)
South Africa						**Afrique du Sud**
Departures (thousands)	...	...	4 339	4 433	4 429	Départs (milliers)
Total expenditure (millions $)	4 237	4 811	5 229	6 103	6 792	Dépenses totales (millions $)
Travel (millions $)	3 157	3 373	3 384	3 927	4 291	Voyage (millions $)
Passenger transport (millions $)	1 080	1 438	1 845	2 176	2 501	Transport de passagers (millions $)
Spain						**Espagne**
Departures (thousands)	5 121	#10 464	10 678	11 276	11 229	Départs (milliers)
Total expenditure (millions $)	14 864	18 441	20 348	24 366	26 829	Dépenses totales (millions $)
Travel (millions $)	12 153	15 046	16 697	19 724	20 363	Voyage (millions $)
Passenger transport (millions $)	2 711	3 395	3 651	4 642	6 466	Transport de passagers (millions $)

Outbound tourism *(continued)*

Departures in thousands; expenditure (total, travel and passenger transport) in million US dollars

Tourisme à l'étranger *(suite)*

Départs en milliers ; dépenses (total, voyage et transport de passagers) en millions de dollars E.-U.

Country or area	2004	2005	2006	2007	2008	Pays ou zone
Sri Lanka						**Sri Lanka**
Departures (thousands)	680	727	757	862	966	Départs (milliers)
Total expenditure (millions $)	499	552	666	709	777	Dépenses totales (millions $)
Travel (millions $)	296	314	373	393	428	Voyage (millions $)
Passenger transport (millions $)	203	238	293	316	349	Transport de passagers (millions $)
Sudan						**Soudan**
Travel (millions $)	176	667	1 413	1 477	1 188	Voyage (millions $)
Suriname						**Suriname**
Total expenditure (millions $)	85	94	33	28	35	Dépenses totales (millions $)
Travel (millions $)	14	17	18	22	30	Voyage (millions $)
Passenger transport (millions $)	71	77	15	6	5	Transport de passagers (millions $)
Swaziland						**Swaziland**
Departures (thousands)	...	1 082	1 072	1 130	1 177	Départs (milliers)
Total expenditure (millions $)	54	60	54	63	...	Dépenses totales (millions $)
Travel (millions $)	48	49	49	51	...	Voyage (millions $)
Passenger transport (millions $)	6	11	5	12	...	Transport de passagers (millions $)
Sweden						**Suède**
Departures (thousands)	13 950	15 677	12 559	12 692	13 290	Départs (milliers)
Total expenditure (millions $)	11 088	11 844	12 837	15 749	17 310	Dépenses totales (millions $)
Travel (millions $)	10 165	10 771	11 529	13 975	15 432	Voyage (millions $)
Passenger transport (millions $)	923	1 073	1 308	1 774	1 878	Transport de passagers (millions $)
Switzerland						**Suisse**
Total expenditure (millions $)	9 924	10 579	11 199	12 300	13 407	Dépenses totales (millions $)
Travel (millions $)	8 104	8 782	9 252	10 116	10 973	Voyage (millions $)
Passenger transport (millions $)	1 820	1 797	1 947	2 184	2 434	Transport de passagers (millions $)
Syrian Arab Republic						**Rép. arabe syrienne**
Departures (thousands)	4 309	4 564	4 042	4 196	5 253	Départs (milliers)
Total expenditure (millions $)	688	584	585	710	...	Dépenses totales (millions $)
Travel (millions $)	650	550	540	645	800	Voyage (millions $)
Passenger transport (millions $)	38	34	45	65	...	Transport de passagers (millions $)
Tajikistan						**Tadjikistan**
Travel (millions $)	3	4	6	7	11	Voyage (millions $)
Thailand						**Thaïlande**
Departures (thousands)	2 709	3 047	3 382	4 018	4 038	Départs (milliers)
Total expenditure (millions $)	5 343	4 917	6 173	6 887	6 963	Dépenses totales (millions $)
Travel (millions $)	4 514	3 800	4 598	5 143	5 215	Voyage (millions $)
Passenger transport (millions $)	829	1 117	1 575	1 744	1 748	Transport de passagers (millions $)
TFYR of Macedonia						**L'ex-R.Y. Macédoine**
Total expenditure (millions $)	85	97	110	147	190	Dépenses totales (millions $)
Travel (millions $)	55	62	71	102	136	Voyage (millions $)
Passenger transport (millions $)	30	35	39	45	54	Transport de passagers (millions $)
Togo						**Togo**
Total expenditure (millions $)	38	42	42	59	...	Dépenses totales (millions $)
Travel (millions $)	8	8	5	17	...	Voyage (millions $)
Passenger transport (millions $)	30	34	37	42	...	Transport de passagers (millions $)
Tonga						**Tonga**
Travel (millions $)	6	4	8	11	10	Voyage (millions $)
Trinidad and Tobago						**Trinité-et-Tobago**
Total expenditure (millions $)	141	234	146	155	204	Dépenses totales (millions $)
Travel (millions $)	96	180	93	94	75	Voyage (millions $)
Passenger transport (millions $)	45	54	53	61	129	Transport de passagers (millions $)
Tunisia						**Tunisie**
Departures (thousands)	2 312	2 241	2 302	2 743	3 118	Départs (milliers)
Total expenditure (millions $)	427	452	498	530	555	Dépenses totales (millions $)
Travel (millions $)	340	374	410	437	458	Voyage (millions $)
Passenger transport (millions $)	87	78	88	93	97	Transport de passagers (millions $)
Turkey						**Turquie**
Departures (thousands)	7 299	8 246	8 275	8 938	9 873	Départs (milliers)
Total expenditure (millions $)	...	3 210	3 155	3 720	4 031	Dépenses totales (millions $)
Travel (millions $)	2 524	2 872	2 743	3 260	3 506	Voyage (millions $)
Passenger transport (millions $)	...	338	412	460	525	Transport de passagers (millions $)

63 Outbound tourism *(continued)*

Departures in thousands; expenditure (total, travel and passenger transport) in million US dollars

Tourisme à l'étranger *(suite)*

Départs en milliers ; dépenses (total, voyage et transport de passagers) en millions de dollars E.-U.

Country or area	2004	2005	2006	2007	2008	Pays ou zone
Turkmenistan						**Turkménistan**
Departures (thousands)	32	33	33	38	...	Départs (milliers)
Tuvalu						**Tuvalu**
Departures (thousands)	2	2	2	2	...	Départs (milliers)
Uganda						**Ouganda**
Departures (thousands)	231	189	254	272	337	Départs (milliers)
Total expenditure (millions $)	158	185	196	220	314	Dépenses totales (millions $)
Travel (millions $)	108	124	123	132	156	Voyage (millions $)
Passenger transport (millions $)	50	61	73	88	158	Transport de passagers (millions $)
Ukraine						**Ukraine**
Departures (thousands)	15 588	16 454	16 875	17 335	15 499	Départs (milliers)
Total expenditure (millions $)	2 660	3 078	3 202	4 022	4 585	Dépenses totales (millions $)
Travel (millions $)	2 463	2 805	2 834	3 569	4 023	Voyage (millions $)
Passenger transport (millions $)	197	273	368	453	562	Transport de passagers (millions $)
United Arab Emirates [1]						**Emirats arabes unis** [1]
Total expenditure (millions $)	4 472	6 186	8 827	11 273	13 288	Dépenses totales (millions $)
United Kingdom						**Royaume-Uni**
Departures (thousands)	64 194	66 494	69 536	69 450	69 011	Départs (milliers)
Total expenditure (millions $)	69 076	72 993	77 674	87 434	84 218	Dépenses totales (millions $)
Travel (millions $)	56 444	59 532	63 319	71 519	69 792	Voyage (millions $)
Passenger transport (millions $)	12 632	13 461	14 355	15 915	14 426	Transport de passagers (millions $)
United Rep. of Tanzania						**Rép.-Unie de Tanzanie**
Total expenditure (millions $)	470	577	571	616	746	Dépenses totales (millions $)
Travel (millions $)	445	554	534	595	721	Voyage (millions $)
Passenger transport (millions $)	25	23	37	21	25	Transport de passagers (millions $)
United States						**Etats-Unis**
Departures (thousands) [39]	61 809	63 503	63 662	64 028	63 684	Départs (milliers) [39]
Total expenditure (millions $)	94 344	99 469	104 450	109 954	117 969	Dépenses totales (millions $)
Travel (millions $)	69 626	73 320	76 949	81 517	85 372	Voyage (millions $)
Passenger transport (millions $)	24 718	26 149	27 501	28 437	32 597	Transport de passagers (millions $)
Uruguay						**Uruguay**
Departures (thousands)	569	658	666	635	734	Départs (milliers)
Total expenditure (millions $)	267	331	305	354	487	Dépenses totales (millions $)
Travel (millions $)	194	252	213	239	358	Voyage (millions $)
Passenger transport (millions $)	73	79	92	115	129	Transport de passagers (millions $)
Uzbekistan						**Ouzbékistan**
Departures (thousands)	455	572	893	1 248	1 150	Départs (milliers)
Vanuatu						**Vanuatu**
Departures (thousands)	13	14	15	16	19	Départs (milliers)
Total expenditure (millions $)	15	13	11	13	...	Dépenses totales (millions $)
Travel (millions $)	13	11	9	11	...	Voyage (millions $)
Passenger transport (millions $)	2	2	2	2	...	Transport de passagers (millions $)
Venezuela (Boliv. Rep. of)						**Venezuela (Rép. boliv. du)**
Departures (thousands)	816	1 067	1 095	1 410	1 745	Départs (milliers)
Total expenditure (millions $)	1 604	1 843	1 807	2 227	2 566	Dépenses totales (millions $)
Travel (millions $)	1 077	1 276	1 229	1 520	1 784	Voyage (millions $)
Passenger transport (millions $)	527	567	578	707	782	Transport de passagers (millions $)
Yemen						**Yémen**
Total expenditure (millions $)	183	224	225	247	246	Dépenses totales (millions $)
Travel (millions $)	126	167	162	184	183	Voyage (millions $)
Passenger transport (millions $)	57	57	63	63	63	Transport de passagers (millions $)
Zambia						**Zambie**
Total expenditure (millions $)	86	88	97	98	107	Dépenses totales (millions $)
Travel (millions $)	55	58	68	56	64	Voyage (millions $)
Passenger transport (millions $)	31	30	29	42	43	Transport de passagers (millions $)
Zimbabwe						**Zimbabwe**
Departures (thousands)	498	474	541	547	593	Départs (milliers)

63

Outbound tourism *(continued)*

Departures in thousands; expenditure (total, travel and passenger transport) in million US dollars

Tourisme à l'étranger *(suite)*

Départs en milliers ; dépenses (total, voyage et transport de passagers) en millions de dollars E.-U.

Source:
World Tourism Organization (UNWTO), Madrid, UNWTO statistics database and the *Yearbook of Tourism Statistics*, 2010 edition. The majority of the data have been provided to the UNWTO by the International Monetary Fund (IMF). Exceptions are footnoted.

1 The expenditure figures are those provided by the country to UNWTO, which do not appear in the International Monetary Fund data.
2 Starting 2004, as a result of the importance of the "Survey on International Tourism", the estimates of the series of the "Travel" item of the Balance of Payments were modified. For this reason, the data are not rigorously comparable with those of previous years.
3 Including leisure and business trips abroad with at least one overnight stay.
4 Country data.
5 Source: Central Bank of the Netherlands Antilles.
6 Source: "Banque Centrale des Etats de l'Afrique de l'Ouest".
7 Person-trips (one or more nights).
8 Source: "Banque des Etats de l'Afrique Centrale (B.E.A.C.)".
9 For statistical purposes, the data for China do not include those for the Hong Kong Special Administrative Region (Hong Kong SAR), Macao Special Administrative Region (Macao SAR) and Taiwan Province of China.
10 Including air crew members and other servicemen.
11 Source: Census and Statistics Department.
12 Including Hong Kong residents to Macao and Mainland China.
13 Package tours.
14 Including only tours authorized by the "Instituto de Turismo".
15 Travel for tourism and non-tourism purposes (more than 50% for work purpose).
16 Overnight trips abroad, including cruises abroad with overnight on board only.
17 The observation of the borders with the countries of the Schengen Area ceased from the year 2008.
18 Departures of nationals only, irrespective of purpose.
19 Source: Central Bank of Islamic Republic of Iran.
20 Source: Central Bank of Iraq.
21 Including same-day visitors.
22 The calculation method has been changed since January 2006.
23 Data by State Border Guard.
24 Source: Reserve Bank of Malawi.
25 Outgoing Peninsular Malaysians, including departures via the Johore Causeway by road.
26 Fiscal years (October 1 to September 30).
27 Holiday Departures of nationals.
28 Returning residents.
29 Departures of New Zealand residents abroad for a period of less than 12 months.
30 Holiday trips.
31 West Bank and Gaza.
32 Including overseas contract workers.
33 Outbound trips registered at frontiers.
34 Fiscal years (July-June).
35 Source: Qatar Central Bank.
36 Source: Central Bank of the Netherlands Antilles - Including the estimates for Saba and Saint Eustatius.
37 Figures provided by the country to the World Tourism Organisation (UNWTO).
38 Quarterly survey on travel of domestic population.
39 Including Americans staying one or more nights in Mexico.

Source:
Organisation mondiale du tourisme (OMT), Madrid, la base de données de l'OMT, et *l'Annuaire des statistiques du tourisme*, édition 2010. La majorité des données sont celles que le Fonds monétaire international (FMI) a fournies à l'Organisation mondiale du tourisme (OMT). Les exceptions sont signalées par une note.

1 Les chiffres de dépense sont ceux que le pays a fournis à l'OMT mais ils ne figurent pas dans les données du Fonds monétaire international.
2 À partir de 2004, vu l'importance de l'"Enquête sur le tourisme international", des modifications ont été apportées aux estimations de la série du poste "Voyage" de la balance des paiements. C'est la raison pour laquelle les données ne sont pas rigoureusement comparables avec celles des années précédentes.
3 Y compris les voyages de détente et les voyages d'affaires à l'étranger comportant au moins une nuitée.
4 Données du pays.
5 Source: "Central Bank of the Netherlands Antilles".
6 Source: Banque Centrale des Etats de l'Afrique de l'Ouest.
7 Personne-voyages (une ou plusieurs nuitées).
8 Source: Banque des Etats de l'Afrique Centrale (B.E.A.C.).
9 Pour la présentation des statistiques, les données pour la Chine ne comprennent pas la Région Administrative Spéciale de Hong Kong (Hong Kong RAS), la Région Administrative Spéciale de Macao (Macao RAS) et la province de Taiwan.
10 Y compris les membres de l'équipage des aéronefs et le personnel technique.
11 Source: "Département de recensement et statistiques".
12 Y compris les résidents de Hong Kong qui se rendent à Macao ou en Chine continentale.
13 Voyages organisés.
14 Ne comprend que les excursions autorisées par l'Isntituto de Turismo.
15 Voyages à des fins touristiques ou non touristiques (plus de 50% des Voyages sont liés au travail).
16 Voyages à l'étranger comprenant une nuitée, y compris les croisières à l'étranger avec nuitées à bord uniquement.
17 La surveillance des frontières avec les pays de la zone Schengen a pris fin en 2008.
18 Départs des nationaux seulement, quel que soit le but de leur voyage.
19 Source: "Central Bank of Islamic Republic of Iran".
20 Source: "Central Bank of Iraq".
21 Y compris les visiteurs qui ne restent qu'une journée.
22 La méthode de calcul a changé depuis janvier 2006.
23 Donnes émanant du Service des gardes-frontières.
24 Source: "Reserve Bank of Malawi".
25 Malaisiens vivant sur la partie péninsulaire qui sortent du pays, y compris les départs par la route, par le pont-jetée de Johor.
26 Années fiscales (du 1er octobre au 30 septembre).
27 Départs en vacances de nationaux.
28 Résidents de retour.
29 Départs de résidents néo-zélandais à l'étranger pour une période inférieure a 12 mois.
30 Voyages de détente.
31 Cisjordanie et Gaza.
32 Y compris les employés contractuels étrangers.
33 Voyages a l'étranger enregistrés aux frontières.
34 Années fiscales (juillet-juin).
35 Source: "Qatar Central Bank".
36 Source : Banque centrale des Antilles néerlandaises. Comprend des estimations concernant Saint-Eustache et Saba.
37 Chiffres fournis par le pays à l'Organisation mondiale du tourisme (OMT).
38 Enquête trimestrielle sur les voyages de la population nationale.
39 Y compris les Américains qui passent une ou plusieurs nuits au Mexique.

64 Civil aviation: scheduled airline traffic

Passengers carried (thousands); kilometres (millions)

Aviation civile : trafic aérien régulier

Passagers transportés (milliers) ; kilomètres (millions)

Country or area and traffic	Total traffic (domestic and international) Trafic total (intérieur et international)				International traffic Trafic international				Pays ou zone et trafic
	2006	2007	2008	2009	2006	2007	2008	2009	
Albania									**Albanie**
Kilometres flown	3	3	3	3	3	3	3	3	Kilomètres parcourus
Passengers carried	213	239	244	231	213	239	244	231	Passagers transportés
Passenger-kilometres	161	176	180	170	161	176	180	170	Passagers-kilomètres
Total tonne-kilometres	14	15	16	15	14	15	16	15	Tonnes-kilomètres totales
Algeria									**Algérie**
Kilometres flown	38	46	53	53	24	28	37	38	Kilomètres parcourus
Passengers carried	2 900	2 813	4 428	4 371	1 702	1 566	3 200	3 254	Passagers transportés
Passenger-kilometres	2 964	2 941	3 962	3 814	2 378	2 314	3 340	3 237	Passagers-kilomètres
Total tonne-kilometres	293	281	394	382	237	223	334	326	Tonnes-kilomètres totales
Angola									**Angola**
Kilometres flown	7	7	7	7	5	5	5	5	Kilomètres parcourus
Passengers carried	263	277	284	275	136	147	156	158	Passagers transportés
Passenger-kilometres	655	691	706	680	575	609	624	605	Passagers-kilomètres
Total tonne-kilometres	136	140	135	126	128	132	127	119	Tonnes-kilomètres totales
Antigua and Barbuda									**Antigua-et-Barbuda**
Kilometres flown	5	6	6	6	5	6	6	6	Kilomètres parcourus
Passengers carried	755	800	813	748	755	800	813	748	Passagers transportés
Passenger-kilometres	118	127	132	123	118	127	132	123	Passagers-kilomètres
Total tonne-kilometres	11	12	12	11	11	12	12	11	Tonnes-kilomètres totales
Argentina									**Argentine**
Kilometres flown	101	107	98	98	46	50	45	43	Kilomètres parcourus
Passengers carried	6 636	6 836	5 949	5 519	1 819	1 851	1 510	1 390	Passagers transportés
Passenger-kilometres	14 489	15 129	12 575	11 736	8 882	9 182	7 205	6 759	Passagers-kilomètres
Total tonne-kilometres	1 441	1 490	1 259	1 165	926	947	770	713	Tonnes-kilomètres totales
Armenia									**Arménie**
Kilometres flown	13	11	12	12	13	11	12	12	Kilomètres parcourus
Passengers carried	606	561	624	653	606	561	624	653	Passagers transportés
Passenger-kilometres	1 157	977	1 090	1 074	1 157	977	1 090	1 074	Passagers-kilomètres
Total tonne-kilometres	113	94	106	103	113	94	106	103	Tonnes-kilomètres totales
Australia									**Australie**
Kilometres flown	599	600	642	579	249	241	236	206	Kilomètres parcourus
Passengers carried	46 621	48 729	51 488	50 027	8 392	8 016	7 519	6 103	Passagers transportés
Passenger-kilometres	104 687	107 313	108 579	100 515	58 011	57 929	55 244	50 061	Passagers-kilomètres
Total tonne-kilometres	12 641	12 678	12 645	11 652	8 231	8 018	7 633	6 924	Tonnes-kilomètres totales
Austria									**Autriche**
Kilometres flown	170	160	159	145	166	156	155	141	Kilomètres parcourus
Passengers carried	8 785	9 141	9 141	8 521	8 289	8 627	8 626	8 044	Passagers transportés
Passenger-kilometres	19 921	17 408	16 465	14 775	19 790	17 271	16 324	14 644	Passagers-kilomètres
Total tonne-kilometres	2 696	2 291	2 155	1 893	2 682	2 277	2 140	1 879	Tonnes-kilomètres totales
Azerbaijan									**Azerbaïdjan**
Kilometres flown	15	17	17	15	12	14	15	13	Kilomètres parcourus
Passengers carried	1 253	1 441	1 294	840	607	752	810	621	Passagers transportés
Passenger-kilometres	1 519	1 767	1 777	1 274	1 146	1 373	1 492	1 148	Passagers-kilomètres
Total tonne-kilometres	153	171	171	122	114	135	144	110	Tonnes-kilomètres totales
Bahamas									**Bahamas**
Kilometres flown	8	8	8	8	4	5	5	5	Kilomètres parcourus
Passengers carried	1 033	1 090	1 089	979	456	483	491	452	Passagers transportés
Passenger-kilometres	276	294	301	276	176	189	196	184	Passagers-kilomètres
Total tonne-kilometres	25	27	28	25	16	18	18	17	Tonnes-kilomètres totales
Bahrain									**Bahreïn**
Kilometres flown	47	79	100	105	46	79	100	105	Kilomètres parcourus
Passengers carried	2 355	4 451	5 643	5 668	2 126	4 451	5 643	5 668	Passagers transportés
Passenger-kilometres	5 801	10 505	13 656	13 949	5 633	10 505	13 656	13 949	Passagers-kilomètres
Total tonne-kilometres	903	1 504	1 837	1 849	881	1 504	1 837	1 849	Tonnes-kilomètres totales

64

Civil aviation: scheduled airline traffic *(continued)*

Passengers carried (thousands); kilometres (millions)

Aviation civile : trafic régulier des lignes aériennes *(suite)*

Passagers transportés (milliers) ; kilomètres (millions)

Country or area and traffic	Total traffic (domestic and international) Trafic total (intérieur et international)				International traffic Trafic international				Pays ou zone et trafic
	2006	2007	2008	2009	2006	2007	2008	2009	
Bangladesh									**Bangladesh**
Kilometres flown	33	23	26	24	31	22	25	24	Kilomètres parcourus
Passengers carried	1 730	1 287	1 516	1 301	1 392	1 136	1 400	1 409	Passagers transportés
Passenger-kilometres	5 607	4 186	4 741	4 344	5 530	4 154	4 717	4 367	Passagers-kilomètres
Total tonne-kilometres	828	588	474	433	821	585	472	435	Tonnes-kilomètres totales
Belarus									**Bélarus**
Kilometres flown	7	8	8	7	7	8	8	7	Kilomètres parcourus
Passengers carried	307	365	351	333	307	365	351	333	Passagers transportés
Passenger-kilometres	414	487	463	438	414	487	463	438	Passagers-kilomètres
Total tonne-kilometres	39	45	42	40	39	45	42	40	Tonnes-kilomètres totales
Belgium									**Belgique**
Kilometres flown	132	163	154	144	132	161	153	143	Kilomètres parcourus
Passengers carried	3 641	5 614	5 288	4 859	3 641	5 614	5 288	4 859	Passagers transportés
Passenger-kilometres	5 312	7 859	7 690	7 158	5 312	7 859	7 690	7 158	Passagers-kilomètres
Total tonne-kilometres	1 205	1 695	1 763	1 543	1 205	1 686	1 744	1 534	Tonnes-kilomètres totales
Bhutan									**Bhoutan**
Kilometres flown	2	3	3	3	2	3	3	3	Kilomètres parcourus
Passengers carried	51	54	53	49	51	54	53	49	Passagers transportés
Passenger-kilometres	77	80	78	72	77	80	78	72	Passagers-kilomètres
Total tonne-kilometres	7	7	7	7	7	7	7	7	Tonnes-kilomètres totales
Bolivia (Plur. State of)									**Bolivie (État plur. de)**
Kilometres flown	17	10	21	20	11	4	13	13	Kilomètres parcourus
Passengers carried	1 443	979	1 718	1 537	424	180	568	523	Passagers transportés
Passenger-kilometres	1 413	746	2 050	1 895	1 034	432	1 596	1 497	Passagers-kilomètres
Total tonne-kilometres	136	53	190	175	100	25	147	138	Tonnes-kilomètres totales
Bosnia and Herzegovina									**Bosnie-Herzégovine**
Kilometres flown	...	...	2	3	...	...	2	3	Kilomètres parcourus
Passengers carried	...	...	56	80	...	...	56	80	Passagers transportés
Passenger-kilometres	...	...	115	111	...	...	115	111	Passagers-kilomètres
Total tonne-kilometres	...	...	10	9	...	...	10	9	Tonnes-kilomètres totales
Botswana									**Botswana**
Kilometres flown	4	4	4	4	2	3	3	3	Kilomètres parcourus
Passengers carried	214	228	236	234	153	165	174	177	Passagers transportés
Passenger-kilometres	110	116	118	113	79	84	86	83	Passagers-kilomètres
Total tonne-kilometres	10	10	11	10	7	7	8	8	Tonnes-kilomètres totales
Brazil									**Brésil**
Kilometres flown	478	524	601	680	111	136	152	151	Kilomètres parcourus
Passengers carried	40 945	53 111	58 763	67 946	3 121	5 631	6 660	6 620	Passagers transportés
Passenger-kilometres	49 218	56 741	66 144	74 049	17 824	16 816	20 774	20 649	Passagers-kilomètres
Total tonne-kilometres	5 879	6 072	6 798	7 364	2 523	2 091	2 458	2 464	Tonnes-kilomètres totales
Brunei Darussalam									**Brunéi Darussalam**
Kilometres flown	30	29	29	28	30	29	29	28	Kilomètres parcourus
Passengers carried	1 042	1 017	1 076	999	1 042	1 017	1 076	999	Passagers transportés
Passenger-kilometres	4 058	3 715	3 725	3 431	4 058	3 715	3 725	3 431	Passagers-kilomètres
Total tonne-kilometres	497	452	441	399	497	452	441	399	Tonnes-kilomètres totales
Bulgaria									**Bulgarie**
Kilometres flown	19	18	21	15	19	18	19	14	Kilomètres parcourus
Passengers carried	809	855	1 074	798	753	782	938	680	Passagers transportés
Passenger-kilometres	1 359	1 443	1 718	1 248	1 339	1 414	1 665	1 202	Passagers-kilomètres
Total tonne-kilometres	141	134	159	115	139	132	154	111	Tonnes-kilomètres totales
Burkina Faso									**Burkina Faso**
Kilometres flown	1	1	1	1	1	1	1	1	Kilomètres parcourus
Passengers carried	73	78	81	79	50	54	57	58	Passagers transportés
Passenger-kilometres	40	42	43	41	34	36	37	35	Passagers-kilomètres
Total tonne-kilometres	4	4	4	4	3	3	4	3	Tonnes-kilomètres totales
Cambodia									**Cambodge**
Kilometres flown	4	4	3	3	3	4	3	2	Kilomètres parcourus
Passengers carried	252	308	197	184	171	209	109	101	Passagers transportés
Passenger-kilometres	317	439	274	253	297	415	253	233	Passagers-kilomètres
Total tonne-kilometres	29	42	25	23	28	40	23	21	Tonnes-kilomètres totales

64 Civil aviation: scheduled airline traffic *(continued)*

Passengers carried (thousands); kilometres (millions)

Aviation civile : trafic régulier des lignes aériennes *(suite)*

Passagers transportés (milliers) ; kilomètres (millions)

Country or area and traffic	Total traffic (domestic and international) Trafic total (intérieur et international)				International traffic Trafic international				Pays ou zone et trafic
	2006	2007	2008	2009	2006	2007	2008	2009	
Cameroon									**Cameroun**
Kilometres flown	12	13	13	...	11	12	12	...	Kilomètres parcourus
Passengers carried	425	453	471	...	310	335	354	...	Passagers transportés
Passenger-kilometres	861	910	930	...	775	821	841	...	Passagers-kilomètres
Total tonne-kilometres	108	111	113	...	100	103	104	...	Tonnes-kilomètres totales
Canada									**Canada**
Kilometres flown	1 004	1 111	1 137	1 105	405	416	426	414	Kilomètres parcourus
Passengers carried	46 727	52 104	53 719	52 584	14 543	14 641	15 095	14 776	Passagers transportés
Passenger-kilometres	98 241	107 280	110 602	107 371	59 581	60 927	62 814	60 979	Passagers-kilomètres
Total tonne-kilometres	10 916	11 970	12 243	11 904	6 683	6 989	7 137	6 942	Tonnes-kilomètres totales
Cape Verde									**Cap-Vert**
Kilometres flown	12	12	12	12	8	9	9	9	Kilomètres parcourus
Passengers carried	754	793	808	777	341	368	389	396	Passagers transportés
Passenger-kilometres	1 165	1 232	1 259	1 216	1 065	1 129	1 156	1 121	Passagers-kilomètres
Total tonne-kilometres	110	114	119	115	101	104	109	107	Tonnes-kilomètres totales
Chile									**Chili**
Kilometres flown	120	139	150	136	75	85	87	81	Kilomètres parcourus
Passengers carried	6 017	7 191	8 022	8 097	2 659	3 095	3 143	3 040	Passagers transportés
Passenger-kilometres	13 858	16 056	17 427	17 523	10 108	11 498	12 111	11 822	Passagers-kilomètres
Total tonne-kilometres	2 272	2 752	2 891	2 769	1 882	2 290	2 357	2 204	Tonnes-kilomètres totales
China[1]									**Chine**[1]
Kilometres flown	2 009	2 301	2 430	2 718	370	465	460	400	Kilomètres parcourus
Passengers carried	158 013	183 613	191 001	227 849	13 659	16 430	14 785	13 091	Passagers transportés
Passenger-kilometres	234 505	275 593	285 295	330 243	51 329	60 493	56 380	50 831	Passagers-kilomètres
Total tonne-kilometres	30 091	36 062	37 169	41 188	9 976	12 741	12 554	11 651	Tonnes-kilomètres totales
Colombia									**Colombie**
Kilometres flown	142	155	162	158	85	92	99	97	Kilomètres parcourus
Passengers carried	10 616	11 631	12 339	12 115	2 275	2 677	2 880	2 833	Passagers transportés
Passenger-kilometres	10 478	12 114	14 025	14 534	5 131	6 165	7 784	8 629	Passagers-kilomètres
Total tonne-kilometres	2 022	2 457	2 524	2 530	1 457	1 830	1 879	1 944	Tonnes-kilomètres totales
Costa Rica									**Costa Rica**
Kilometres flown	26	28	28	27	21	23	24	23	Kilomètres parcourus
Passengers carried	943	1 017	1 024	933	726	770	782	719	Passagers transportés
Passenger-kilometres	2 216	2 373	2 467	2 312	2 193	2 346	2 440	2 289	Passagers-kilomètres
Total tonne-kilometres	150	161	168	156	148	158	165	154	Tonnes-kilomètres totales
Croatia									**Croatie**
Kilometres flown	13	13	15	15	11	12	13	13	Kilomètres parcourus
Passengers carried	1 389	1 545	1 753	1 679	942	1 056	1 209	1 188	Passagers transportés
Passenger-kilometres	1 005	1 084	1 217	1 151	861	926	1 043	998	Passagers-kilomètres
Total tonne-kilometres	93	101	112	106	80	86	96	92	Tonnes-kilomètres totales
Cuba									**Cuba**
Kilometres flown	22	24	25	23	19	20	21	20	Kilomètres parcourus
Passengers carried	812	857	861	781	508	538	547	503	Passagers transportés
Passenger-kilometres	2 337	2 499	2 594	2 425	2 219	2 374	2 469	2 316	Passagers-kilomètres
Total tonne-kilometres	254	271	282	261	237	254	264	246	Tonnes-kilomètres totales
Cyprus									**Chypre**
Kilometres flown	32	34	35	33	32	34	35	33	Kilomètres parcourus
Passengers carried	1 944	2 072	2 111	1 944	1 944	2 072	2 111	1 944	Passagers transportés
Passenger-kilometres	4 293	4 478	4 522	4 163	4 293	4 478	4 522	4 163	Passagers-kilomètres
Total tonne-kilometres	437	445	458	412	437	445	458	412	Tonnes-kilomètres totales
Czech Republic									**République tchèque**
Kilometres flown	74	73	76	76	73	72	75	74	Kilomètres parcourus
Passengers carried	4 922	4 870	4 975	5 048	4 814	4 757	4 857	4 942	Passagers transportés
Passenger-kilometres	6 652	6 311	6 297	6 334	6 624	6 282	6 267	6 307	Passagers-kilomètres
Total tonne-kilometres	644	606	601	597	641	603	598	594	Tonnes-kilomètres totales
Denmark									**Danemark**
Kilometres flown	108	42	110	97	82	36	102	90	Kilomètres parcourus
Passengers carried	10 373	2 624	10 398	8 880	5 902	1 795	8 805	7 462	Passagers transportés
Passenger-kilometres	10 581	4 314	10 222	8 781	8 636	4 132	9 857	8 476	Passagers-kilomètres
Total tonne-kilometres	1 259	569	1 169	960	1 065	553	1 135	932	Tonnes-kilomètres totales

64 Civil aviation: scheduled airline traffic *(continued)*

Passengers carried (thousands); kilometres (millions)

Aviation civile : trafic régulier des lignes aériennes *(suite)*

Passagers transportés (milliers) ; kilomètres (millions)

Country or area and traffic	Total traffic (domestic and international) Trafic total (intérieur et international) 2006	2007	2008	2009	International traffic Trafic international 2006	2007	2008	2009	Pays ou zone et trafic
Ecuador									**Equateur**
Kilometres flown	16	34	34	34	^0	18	18	18	Kilomètres parcourus
Passengers carried	2 505	3 465	3 801	3 829	14	586	608	646	Passagers transportés
Passenger-kilometres	1 083	3 693	3 796	3 947	6	2 496	2 577	2 783	Passagers-kilomètres
Total tonne-kilometres	102	472	456	452	1	360	342	344	Tonnes-kilomètres totales
Egypt									**Egypte**
Kilometres flown	84	90	110	113	78	82	104	108	Kilomètres parcourus
Passengers carried	4 954	5 829	6 689	6 216	3 525	4 104	5 040	5 225	Passagers transportés
Passenger-kilometres	10 336	12 001	14 266	14 801	9 683	11 213	13 537	14 344	Passagers-kilomètres
Total tonne-kilometres	1 360	1 429	1 631	1 670	1 295	1 350	1 557	1 624	Tonnes-kilomètres totales
El Salvador									**El Salvador**
Kilometres flown	35	37	33	29	35	37	33	29	Kilomètres parcourus
Passengers carried	2 289	2 537	2 280	1 997	2 241	2 495	2 245	1 971	Passagers transportés
Passenger-kilometres	3 808	4 282	3 775	3 516	3 799	4 275	3 769	3 512	Passagers-kilomètres
Total tonne-kilometres	365	407	358	332	364	407	358	331	Tonnes-kilomètres totales
Estonia									**Estonie**
Kilometres flown	9	10	10	6	9	10	10	6	Kilomètres parcourus
Passengers carried	598	651	686	396	598	651	683	383	Passagers transportés
Passenger-kilometres	682	754	758	359	682	754	758	357	Passagers-kilomètres
Total tonne-kilometres	63	69	70	33	63	69	70	33	Tonnes-kilomètres totales
Ethiopia									**Ethiopie**
Kilometres flown	61	69	75	82	57	66	72	78	Kilomètres parcourus
Passengers carried	1 954	2 290	2 715	2 914	1 642	1 977	2 361	2 509	Passagers transportés
Passenger-kilometres	6 640	7 947	9 303	9 746	6 504	7 810	9 147	9 562	Passagers-kilomètres
Total tonne-kilometres	888	1 041	1 399	1 478	876	1 029	1 384	1 460	Tonnes-kilomètres totales
Fiji									**Fidji**
Kilometres flown	25	6	27	26	19	...	21	20	Kilomètres parcourus
Passengers carried	932	305	1 231	1 147	625	...	931	865	Passagers transportés
Passenger-kilometres	2 506	52	3 861	3 549	2 455	...	3 809	3 501	Passagers-kilomètres
Total tonne-kilometres	346	5	424	386	342	...	419	381	Tonnes-kilomètres totales
Finland									**Finlande**
Kilometres flown	119	140	148	139	104	128	137	129	Kilomètres parcourus
Passengers carried	7 597	8 289	7 917	7 423	5 581	6 588	6 556	6 237	Passagers transportés
Passenger-kilometres	13 418	16 416	17 859	16 389	12 419	15 522	17 044	15 693	Passagers-kilomètres
Total tonne-kilometres	1 629	1 981	2 162	1 969	1 541	1 902	2 091	1 908	Tonnes-kilomètres totales
France [2]									**France** [2]
Kilometres flown	960	1 002	1 038	967	731	758	802	750	Kilomètres parcourus
Passengers carried	59 538	61 346	62 428	59 152	34 832	36 298	38 738	37 094	Passagers transportés
Passenger-kilometres	144 096	151 012	160 278	152 256	123 395	129 846	140 106	133 457	Passagers-kilomètres
Total tonne-kilometres	19 917	20 305	20 982	19 031	17 437	18 305	18 996	17 178	Tonnes-kilomètres totales
Gabon									**Gabon**
Kilometres flown	...	10	10	10	...	8	8	8	Kilomètres parcourus
Passengers carried	...	535	546	525	...	253	267	272	Passagers transportés
Passenger-kilometres	...	947	966	931	...	834	854	828	Passagers-kilomètres
Total tonne-kilometres	...	161	157	148	...	151	146	139	Tonnes-kilomètres totales
Georgia									**Géorgie**
Kilometres flown	7	9	9	9	7	9	9	9	Kilomètres parcourus
Passengers carried	231	304	310	294	231	304	310	294	Passagers transportés
Passenger-kilometres	505	612	627	594	505	612	627	594	Passagers-kilomètres
Total tonne-kilometres	48	56	58	55	48	56	58	55	Tonnes-kilomètres totales
Germany									**Allemagne**
Kilometres flown	1 397	1 484	1 548	1 425	1 268	1 348	1 413	1 300	Kilomètres parcourus
Passengers carried	98 717	105 911	107 942	103 397	77 969	84 011	86 142	82 887	Passagers transportés
Passenger-kilometres	204 118	214 655	220 759	205 371	194 717	205 010	211 126	196 382	Passagers-kilomètres
Total tonne-kilometres	28 091	29 670	30 074	27 097	27 176	28 740	29 156	26 243	Tonnes-kilomètres totales
Greece									**Grèce**
Kilometres flown	89	91	95	76	61	62	63	49	Kilomètres parcourus
Passengers carried	9 481	10 155	10 721	8 745	3 614	3 757	5 215	4 138	Passagers transportés
Passenger-kilometres	9 225	9 535	10 194	7 543	7 439	7 562	7 618	5 315	Passagers-kilomètres
Total tonne-kilometres	945	964	1 053	764	774	780	800	543	Tonnes-kilomètres totales

64 Civil aviation: scheduled airline traffic *(continued)*

Passengers carried (thousands); kilometres (millions)

Aviation civile : trafic régulier des lignes aériennes *(suite)*

Passagers transportés (milliers) ; kilomètres (millions)

Country or area and traffic	Total traffic (domestic and international) Trafic total (intérieur et international) 2006	2007	2008	2009	International traffic Trafic international 2006	2007	2008	2009	Pays ou zone et trafic
Hungary									**Hongrie**
Kilometres flown	57	58	54	50	57	58	54	50	Kilomètres parcourus
Passengers carried	3 073	3 134	3 112	2953	3 073	3 134	3 112	2953	Passagers transportés
Passenger-kilometres	4 140	4 435	4 062	3843	4 140	4 435	4 062	3843	Passagers-kilomètres
Total tonne-kilometres	401	430	381	360	401	430	381	360	Tonnes-kilomètres totales
Iceland									**Islande**
Kilometres flown	34	37	32	28	34	37	32	28	Kilomètres parcourus
Passengers carried	1 536	1 594	1 423	1 365	1 536	1 594	1 423	1 365	Passagers transportés
Passenger-kilometres	4 253	4 280	3 757	3 632	4 253	4 280	3 757	3 632	Passagers-kilomètres
Total tonne-kilometres	565	506	502	431	565	506	502	431	Tonnes-kilomètres totales
India									**Inde**
Kilometres flown	503	635	724	701	179	220	286	295	Kilomètres parcourus
Passengers carried	40 311	51 898	49 864	54 446	7 193	8 672	9 984	11 060	Passagers transportés
Passenger-kilometres	60 754	74 200	78 653	85 768	29 728	33 802	40 570	43 773	Passagers-kilomètres
Total tonne-kilometres	6 310	7 642	8 504	8 943	3 343	3 831	4 932	5 086	Tonnes-kilomètres totales
Indonesia									**Indonésie**
Kilometres flown	287	295	310	291	50	46	49	50	Kilomètres parcourus
Passengers carried	27 831	29 564	30 723	27 421	2 775	2 641	2 481	2 513	Passagers transportés
Passenger-kilometres	29 919	33 052	34 952	31 873	7 736	8 394	8 860	8 807	Passagers-kilomètres
Total tonne-kilometres	3 104	3 249	3 548	3 258	965	979	1 038	1 022	Tonnes-kilomètres totales
Iran (Islamic Rep. of)									**Iran (Rép. islamique d')**
Kilometres flown	107	113	104	114	40	43	44	45	Kilomètres parcourus
Passengers carried	13 507	13 916	12 029	13 053	2 944	3 286	3 298	3 056	Passagers transportés
Passenger-kilometres	12 620	13 394	12 292	12 818	5 204	5 843	5 909	5 482	Passagers-kilomètres
Total tonne-kilometres	1 190	1 265	1 175	1 205	522	584	601	546	Tonnes-kilomètres totales
Ireland									**Irlande**
Kilometres flown	350	442	525	573	350	442	525	573	Kilomètres parcourus
Passengers carried	50 738	60 098	69 447	77 747	50 738	60 098	69 447	77 747	Passagers transportés
Passenger-kilometres	54 272	67 667	79 498	87 475	54 272	67 667	79 498	87 475	Passagers-kilomètres
Total tonne-kilometres	5 026	6 223	7 292	8 008	5 026	6 223	7 292	8 008	Tonnes-kilomètres totales
Israel									**Israël**
Kilometres flown	108	111	104	103	103	105	99	98	Kilomètres parcourus
Passengers carried	4 384	4 663	4 627	4 606	3 408	3 602	3 590	3 547	Passagers transportés
Passenger-kilometres	17 098	18 180	17 404	17 251	16 800	17 857	17 088	16 931	Passagers-kilomètres
Total tonne-kilometres	2 696	3 099	2 683	2 362	2 668	3 070	2 654	2 333	Tonnes-kilomètres totales
Italy									**Italie**
Kilometres flown	428	441	392	387	294	298	285	285	Kilomètres parcourus
Passengers carried	35 894	37 855	31 758	33 195	14 922	15 347	16 790	17 714	Passagers transportés
Passenger-kilometres	50 040	50 486	41 217	39 811	37 909	37 426	32 338	31 366	Passagers-kilomètres
Total tonne-kilometres	6 343	6 450	5 364	4 329	5 192	5 249	4 486	3 494	Tonnes-kilomètres totales
Jamaica									**Jamaïque**
Kilometres flown	52	57	27	26	52	57	27	26	Kilomètres parcourus
Passengers carried	1 527	1 618	1 500	1 380	1 527	1 618	1 500	1 380	Passagers transportés
Passenger-kilometres	3 700	3 959	3 027	2 839	3 700	3 959	3 027	2 839	Passagers-kilomètres
Total tonne-kilometres	355	380	315	295	355	380	315	295	Tonnes-kilomètres totales
Japan									**Japon**
Kilometres flown	852	862	870	817	431	443	459	420	Kilomètres parcourus
Passengers carried	101 741	99 842	97 023	86 897	15 890	16 134	15 816	14 720	Passagers transportés
Passenger-kilometres	150 495	147 584	140 927	127 859	78 842	77 467	72 572	66 576	Passagers-kilomètres
Total tonne-kilometres	21 635	21 364	20 458	18 170	15 271	15 113	14 354	12 665	Tonnes-kilomètres totales
Jordan									**Jordanie**
Kilometres flown	50	54	55	56	50	54	55	56	Kilomètres parcourus
Passengers carried	2 047	2 288	2 355	2 324	1 998	2 249	2 298	2 262	Passagers transportés
Passenger-kilometres	5 589	6 446	6 400	6 363	5 576	6 436	6 384	6 346	Passagers-kilomètres
Total tonne-kilometres	769	756	719	687	768	755	718	685	Tonnes-kilomètres totales
Kazakhstan									**Kazakhstan**
Kilometres flown	39	49	40	39	19	26	20	19	Kilomètres parcourus
Passengers carried	1 283	2 132	1 276	1 193	411	737	425	395	Passagers transportés
Passenger-kilometres	2 722	4 452	2 758	2 570	1 575	2 725	1 610	1 483	Passagers-kilomètres
Total tonne-kilometres	264	447	268	249	157	282	160	146	Tonnes-kilomètres totales

64 Civil aviation: scheduled airline traffic *(continued)*

Passengers carried (thousands); kilometres (millions)

Aviation civile : trafic régulier des lignes aériennes *(suite)*

Passagers transportés (milliers) ; kilomètres (millions)

Country or area and traffic	Total traffic (domestic and international) Trafic total (intérieur et international) 2006	2007	2008	2009	International traffic Trafic international 2006	2007	2008	2009	Pays ou zone et trafic
Kenya									**Kenya**
Kilometres flown	51	57	61	64	48	52	57	60	Kilomètres parcourus
Passengers carried	2 548	2 858	2 881	2 949	2 007	2 226	2 291	2 353	Passagers transportés
Passenger-kilometres	7 269	7 952	8 047	7 925	7 045	7 694	7 812	7 695	Passagers-kilomètres
Total tonne-kilometres	953	1 023	1 022	987	933	999	1 000	966	Tonnes-kilomètres totales
Korea, Dem. P. R.									**Corée, R. p. dém. de**
Kilometres flown	1	1	1	1	1	1	1	1	Kilomètres parcourus
Passengers carried	105	111	109	101	105	111	109	101	Passagers transportés
Passenger-kilometres	43	45	44	41	43	45	44	41	Passagers-kilomètres
Total tonne-kilometres	6	7	7	6	6	7	7	6	Tonnes-kilomètres totales
Korea, Republic of									**Corée, République de**
Kilometres flown	425	488	516	513	381	446	473	475	Kilomètres parcourus
Passengers carried	35 298	36 655	36 078	34 169	18 861	21 263	21 140	21 224	Passagers transportés
Passenger-kilometres	74 187	81 387	83 192	82 264	67 850	75 494	77 435	77 276	Passagers-kilomètres
Total tonne-kilometres	14 592	16 404	16 283	16 059	13 970	15 835	15 753	15 589	Tonnes-kilomètres totales
Kuwait									**Koweït**
Kilometres flown	42	42	43	44	42	42	43	44	Kilomètres parcourus
Passengers carried	2 435	2 660	2 524	2 597	2 435	2 660	2 524	2 597	Passagers transportés
Passenger-kilometres	6 946	7 721	7 368	7 670	6 946	7 721	7 368	7 670	Passagers-kilomètres
Total tonne-kilometres	891	967	945	976	891	967	945	976	Tonnes-kilomètres totales
Kyrgyzstan									**Kirghizistan**
Kilometres flown	6	6	5	7	4	5	4	6	Kilomètres parcourus
Passengers carried	245	275	205	310	138	179	130	213	Passagers transportés
Passenger-kilometres	402	479	377	582	359	440	346	542	Passagers-kilomètres
Total tonne-kilometres	38	45	36	55	34	41	33	51	Tonnes-kilomètres totales
Lao People's Dem. Rep.									**Rép. dém. pop. lao**
Kilometres flown	4	4	4	4	1	1	1	1	Kilomètres parcourus
Passengers carried	327	328	323	303	81	85	84	78	Passagers transportés
Passenger-kilometres	141	144	142	133	50	52	51	47	Passagers-kilomètres
Total tonne-kilometres	14	15	14	13	6	6	6	5	Tonnes-kilomètres totales
Latvia									**Lettonie**
Kilometres flown	26	34	27	25	26	34	27	25	Kilomètres parcourus
Passengers carried	1 410	1 992	1 372	1 302	1 409	1 979	1 372	1 302	Passagers transportés
Passenger-kilometres	1 510	2 279	1 539	1 456	1 510	2 276	1 539	1 456	Passagers-kilomètres
Total tonne-kilometres	149	220	152	142	149	220	152	142	Tonnes-kilomètres totales
Lebanon									**Liban**
Kilometres flown	24	27	29	30	24	27	29	30	Kilomètres parcourus
Passengers carried	969	1 074	1 330	1 308	969	1 074	1 330	1 308	Passagers transportés
Passenger-kilometres	1 940	2 225	2 727	2 711	1 940	2 225	2 727	2 711	Passagers-kilomètres
Total tonne-kilometres	257	294	330	313	257	294	330	313	Tonnes-kilomètres totales
Libyan Arab Jamah.									**Jamah. arabe libyenne**
Kilometres flown	17	18	18	18	13	14	14	14	Kilomètres parcourus
Passengers carried	1 152	1 204	1 214	1 147	355	384	406	413	Passagers transportés
Passenger-kilometres	1 507	1 579	1 597	1 521	888	941	964	934	Passagers-kilomètres
Total tonne-kilometres	137	140	148	142	89	92	98	96	Tonnes-kilomètres totales
Lithuania									**Lituanie**
Kilometres flown	14	13	15	15	14	13	15	15	Kilomètres parcourus
Passengers carried	460	424	610	617	459	424	610	617	Passagers transportés
Passenger-kilometres	623	577	908	930	623	577	908	930	Passagers-kilomètres
Total tonne-kilometres	58	54	84	92	58	54	84	92	Tonnes-kilomètres totales
Luxembourg									**Luxembourg**
Kilometres flown	94	91	90	75	94	91	90	75	Kilomètres parcourus
Passengers carried	928	777	799	682	928	777	799	682	Passagers transportés
Passenger-kilometres	611	466	495	411	611	466	495	411	Passagers-kilomètres
Total tonne-kilometres	5 325	5 554	5 402	4 688	5 325	5 554	5 402	4 688	Tonnes-kilomètres totales
Madagascar									**Madagascar**
Kilometres flown	13	16	10	9	9	11	6	6	Kilomètres parcourus
Passengers carried	573	616	559	500	216	241	199	294	Passagers transportés
Passenger-kilometres	1 172	1 248	1 041	819	987	1 058	856	719	Passagers-kilomètres
Total tonne-kilometres	124	136	106	88	107	119	89	79	Tonnes-kilomètres totales

64 Civil aviation: scheduled airline traffic *(continued)*

Passengers carried (thousands); kilometres (millions)

Aviation civile : trafic régulier des lignes aériennes *(suite)*

Passagers transportés (milliers) ; kilomètres (millions)

Country or area and traffic	Total traffic (domestic and international) Trafic total (intérieur et international)				International traffic Trafic international				Pays ou zone et trafic
	2006	2007	2008	2009	2006	2007	2008	2009	
Malawi									**Malawi**
Kilometres flown	5	3	5	5	3	1	3	3	Kilomètres parcourus
Passengers carried	146	116	160	157	94	81	108	110	Passagers transportés
Passenger-kilometres	197	83	209	200	119	52	129	125	Passagers-kilomètres
Total tonne-kilometres	23	8	24	23	15	5	17	16	Tonnes-kilomètres totales
Malaysia									**Malaisie**
Kilometres flown	292	311	302	297	225	236	226	213	Kilomètres parcourus
Passengers carried	21 010	22 762	22 421	23 766	10 113	11 333	10 864	11 054	Passagers transportés
Passenger-kilometres	47 442	49 942	47 323	45 532	39 390	40 987	37 795	35 020	Passagers-kilomètres
Total tonne-kilometres	6 971	7 161	6 758	6 207	6 187	6 351	5 883	5 251	Tonnes-kilomètres totales
Maldives									**Maldives**
Kilometres flown	3	3	3	3	...	...	...	...	Kilomètres parcourus
Passengers carried	93	93	91	85	...	...	...	...	Passagers transportés
Passenger-kilometres	47	48	47	45	...	...	...	...	Passagers-kilomètres
Total tonne-kilometres	4	4	4	4	...	...	...	...	Tonnes-kilomètres totales
Malta									**Malte**
Kilometres flown	25	28	29	27	25	28	29	27	Kilomètres parcourus
Passengers carried	1 495	1 675	2 100	1 993	1 495	1 675	2 100	1 993	Passagers transportés
Passenger-kilometres	2 476	2 698	3 436	3 251	2 476	2 698	3 436	3 251	Passagers-kilomètres
Total tonne-kilometres	233	245	352	332	233	245	352	332	Tonnes-kilomètres totales
Marshall Islands									**Iles Marshall**
Kilometres flown	1	1	1	^0	^0	^0	^0	^0	Kilomètres parcourus
Passengers carried	30	30	30	1	1	1	1	1	Passagers transportés
Passenger-kilometres	42	43	42	1	1	1	1	1	Passagers-kilomètres
Total tonne-kilometres	4	4	4	^0	^0	^0	^0	^0	Tonnes-kilomètres totales
Mauritania									**Mauritanie**
Kilometres flown	1	1	1	1	1	1	1	1	Kilomètres parcourus
Passengers carried	149	155	154	142	20	22	23	23	Passagers transportés
Passenger-kilometres	65	68	68	64	23	25	25	25	Passagers-kilomètres
Total tonne-kilometres	6	6	7	6	2	2	3	2	Tonnes-kilomètres totales
Mauritius									**Maurice**
Kilometres flown	47	38	35	36	46	36	34	35	Kilomètres parcourus
Passengers carried	1 150	1 278	1 257	1 093	1 067	1 187	1 165	1 004	Passagers transportés
Passenger-kilometres	6 293	6 953	6 625	5 605	6 246	6 895	6 569	5 551	Passagers-kilomètres
Total tonne-kilometres	770	832	793	668	766	827	788	663	Tonnes-kilomètres totales
Mexico									**Mexique**
Kilometres flown	392	386	373	299	192	204	215	199	Kilomètres parcourus
Passengers carried	21 243	20 293	18 826	14 632	6 755	6 837	7 098	6 201	Passagers transportés
Passenger-kilometres	34 991	34 681	34 611	27 962	18 354	19 343	20 707	18 952	Passagers-kilomètres
Total tonne-kilometres	3 811	3 790	3 783	3 125	2 262	2 383	2 488	2 289	Tonnes-kilomètres totales
Monaco									**Monaco**
Kilometres flown	1	1	1	1	1	1	1	1	Kilomètres parcourus
Passengers carried	96	102	85	64	96	102	85	64	Passagers transportés
Passenger-kilometres	5	5	4	3	5	5	4	3	Passagers-kilomètres
Total tonne-kilometres ^	0	0	0	0	0	0	0	0	Tonnes-kilomètres totales ^
Mongolia									**Mongolie**
Kilometres flown	9	8	10	8	6	7	7	5	Kilomètres parcourus
Passengers carried	332	329	365	257	223	269	267	166	Passagers transportés
Passenger-kilometres	843	948	988	610	756	894	906	527	Passagers-kilomètres
Total tonne-kilometres	84	92	97	59	76	87	88	51	Tonnes-kilomètres totales
Morocco									**Maroc**
Kilometres flown	96	120	110	111	91	116	105	106	Kilomètres parcourus
Passengers carried	4 150	4 624	4 927	4 931	3 425	3 859	4 183	4 254	Passagers transportés
Passenger-kilometres	8 086	9 073	9 901	9 582	7 832	8 781	9 611	9 313	Passagers-kilomètres
Total tonne-kilometres	768	861	947	920	744	834	919	895	Tonnes-kilomètres totales
Mozambique									**Mozambique**
Kilometres flown	9	8	8	8	4	3	3	2	Kilomètres parcourus
Passengers carried	350	443	463	490	114	140	137	148	Passagers transportés
Passenger-kilometres	356	471	505	552	100	136	130	151	Passagers-kilomètres
Total tonne-kilometres	38	48	52	56	10	14	13	15	Tonnes-kilomètres totales

64

Civil aviation: scheduled airline traffic *(continued)*

Passengers carried (thousands); kilometres (millions)

Aviation civile : trafic régulier des lignes aériennes *(suite)*

Passagers transportés (milliers) ; kilomètres (millions)

Country or area and traffic	Total traffic (domestic and international) Trafic total (intérieur et international)				International traffic Trafic international				Pays ou zone et trafic
	2006	2007	2008	2009	2006	2007	2008	2009	
Myanmar									**Myanmar**
Kilometres flown	22	23	23	22	15	16	16	15	Kilomètres parcourus
Passengers carried	1 621	1 663	1 638	1 527	970	1 018	1 003	932	Passagers transportés
Passenger-kilometres	1 559	1 609	1 585	1 470	1 161	1 207	1 187	1 093	Passagers-kilomètres
Total tonne-kilometres	142	148	145	134	104	109	106	98	Tonnes-kilomètres totales
Namibia									**Namibie**
Kilometres flown	11	12	12	12	10	11	11	11	Kilomètres parcourus
Passengers carried	401	431	452	455	355	384	406	413	Passagers transportés
Passenger-kilometres	1 589	1 683	1 723	1 668	1 559	1 652	1 693	1 640	Passagers-kilomètres
Total tonne-kilometres	159	164	175	171	156	161	172	168	Tonnes-kilomètres totales
Nauru									**Nauru**
Kilometres flown	4	4	4	4	4	4	4	4	Kilomètres parcourus
Passengers carried	219	230	227	210	219	230	227	210	Passagers transportés
Passenger-kilometres	376	391	384	354	376	391	384	354	Passagers-kilomètres
Total tonne-kilometres	37	39	38	35	37	39	38	35	Tonnes-kilomètres totales
Nepal									**Népal**
Kilometres flown	10	11	11	10	8	9	9	8	Kilomètres parcourus
Passengers carried	510	528	520	484	392	412	406	377	Passagers transportés
Passenger-kilometres	911	947	931	858	892	928	912	840	Passagers-kilomètres
Total tonne-kilometres	86	90	88	80	84	89	86	79	Tonnes-kilomètres totales
Netherlands [3]									**Pays-Bas** [3]
Kilometres flown	503	521	573	537	502	521	573	537	Kilomètres parcourus
Passengers carried	27 455	28 857	30 946	29 109	27 411	28 807	30 906	29 072	Passagers transportés
Passenger-kilometres	86 833	90 915	95 190	90 185	86 826	90 906	95 183	90 178	Passagers-kilomètres
Total tonne-kilometres	13 710	14 108	14 306	13 112	13 709	14 107	14 305	13 111	Tonnes-kilomètres totales
New Zealand									**Nouvelle-Zélande**
Kilometres flown	195	208	212	203	128	142	145	136	Kilomètres parcourus
Passengers carried	12 382	12 598	12 951	12 104	4 790	4 738	4 870	4 524	Passagers transportés
Passenger-kilometres	27 032	27 281	28 045	25 924	23 586	23 736	24 400	22 473	Passagers-kilomètres
Total tonne-kilometres	3 621	3 679	3 772	3 429	3 255	3 303	3 385	3 062	Tonnes-kilomètres totales
Nigeria									**Nigéria**
Kilometres flown	21	18	24	23	11	9	12	12	Kilomètres parcourus
Passengers carried	1 308	1 365	1 461	1 365	296	427	346	352	Passagers transportés
Passenger-kilometres	1 767	1 528	1 978	1 873	754	956	898	870	Passagers-kilomètres
Total tonne-kilometres	161	143	179	169	69	89	82	80	Tonnes-kilomètres totales
Norway									**Norvège**
Kilometres flown	107	40	126	102	67	20	62	48	Kilomètres parcourus
Passengers carried	10 344	2 583	12 735	10 927	5 040	829	3 812	3 179	Passagers transportés
Passenger-kilometres	9 779	3 449	10 723	8 818	7 597	2 999	6 698	5 350	Passagers-kilomètres
Total tonne-kilometres	1 183	490	1 214	960	969	453	823	625	Tonnes-kilomètres totales
Oman									**Oman**
Kilometres flown	53	44	35	43	50	42	33	40	Kilomètres parcourus
Passengers carried	3 580	2 997	1 985	2 361	3 114	2 733	1 656	2 010	Passagers transportés
Passenger-kilometres	7 551	5 835	3 551	4 308	7 183	5 614	3 276	4 016	Passagers-kilomètres
Total tonne-kilometres	944	667	359	431	903	647	334	404	Tonnes-kilomètres totales
Pakistan									**Pakistan**
Kilometres flown	88	81	79	76	72	64	63	59	Kilomètres parcourus
Passengers carried	5 715	5 402	5 606	5 303	3 400	3 239	3 408	3 183	Passagers transportés
Passenger-kilometres	15 110	13 681	13 916	13 049	13 163	11 880	12 075	11 281	Passagers-kilomètres
Total tonne-kilometres	1 800	1 593	1 579	1 444	1 587	1 392	1 379	1 256	Tonnes-kilomètres totales
Panama									**Panama**
Kilometres flown	67	81	98	94	67	81	98	94	Kilomètres parcourus
Passengers carried	2 174	2 519	6 900	6 348	2 174	2 519	6 900	6 348	Passagers transportés
Passenger-kilometres	6 557	7 942	8 970	8 414	6 557	7 942	8 970	8 414	Passagers-kilomètres
Total tonne-kilometres	693	841	951	894	693	841	951	894	Tonnes-kilomètres totales
Papua New Guinea									**Papouasie-Nvl-Guinée**
Kilometres flown	14	14	14	14	5	5	5	5	Kilomètres parcourus
Passengers carried	919	919	905	847	154	161	159	148	Passagers transportés
Passenger-kilometres	771	791	780	728	410	426	419	386	Passagers-kilomètres
Total tonne-kilometres	100	104	102	94	61	65	62	56	Tonnes-kilomètres totales

64 Civil aviation: scheduled airline traffic *(continued)*

Passengers carried (thousands); kilometres (millions)

Aviation civile : trafic régulier des lignes aériennes *(suite)*

Passagers transportés (milliers) ; kilomètres (millions)

Country or area and traffic	Total traffic (domestic and international) Trafic total (intérieur et international) 2006	2007	2008	2009	International traffic Trafic international 2006	2007	2008	2009	Pays ou zone et trafic
Paraguay									**Paraguay**
Kilometres flown	7	8	8	8	7	8	8	8	Kilomètres parcourus
Passengers carried	433	459	466	429	429	455	462	425	Passagers transportés
Passenger-kilometres	481	514	535	502	480	513	534	501	Passagers-kilomètres
Total tonne-kilometres	43	46	49	46	43	46	48	46	Tonnes-kilomètres totales
Peru									**Pérou**
Kilometres flown	66	76	89	94	40	47	52	60	Kilomètres parcourus
Passengers carried	4 218	5 273	6 184	5 843	1 068	1 452	1 703	1 890	Passagers transportés
Passenger-kilometres	5 752	7 775	9 171	9 288	3 469	4 963	5 627	6 180	Passagers-kilomètres
Total tonne-kilometres	631	861	1 056	1 035	416	597	721	744	Tonnes-kilomètres totales
Philippines									**Philippines**
Kilometres flown	87	92	101	108	59	62	68	69	Kilomètres parcourus
Passengers carried	8 305	8 818	9 508	10 481	3 109	3 414	3 610	3 379	Passagers transportés
Passenger-kilometres	16 800	18 084	18 698	18 254	13 513	14 637	14 913	13 854	Passagers-kilomètres
Total tonne-kilometres	2 040	2 142	2 167	2 005	1 714	1 806	1 798	1 589	Tonnes-kilomètres totales
Poland									**Pologne**
Kilometres flown	81	92	97	89	74	84	90	82	Kilomètres parcourus
Passengers carried	3 701	4 270	4 635	4 279	2 844	3 277	3 749	3 496	Passagers transportés
Passenger-kilometres	6 720	7 288	7 854	7 169	6 469	6 997	7 593	6 939	Passagers-kilomètres
Total tonne-kilometres	735	786	785	700	714	762	764	681	Tonnes-kilomètres totales
Portugal									**Portugal**
Kilometres flown	171	185	203	195	147	161	179	172	Kilomètres parcourus
Passengers carried	9 449	9 815	10 158	9 904	6 449	6 798	7 350	7 185	Passagers transportés
Passenger-kilometres	19 010	20 900	23 182	22 820	16 603	18 515	20 909	20 600	Passagers-kilomètres
Total tonne-kilometres	2 050	2 245	2 462	2 385	1 800	2 000	2 231	2 161	Tonnes-kilomètres totales
Qatar									**Qatar**
Kilometres flown	145	184	219	241	145	184	219	241	Kilomètres parcourus
Passengers carried	7 071	8 879	9 703	10 211	7 071	8 879	9 703	10 211	Passagers transportés
Passenger-kilometres	24 032	32 438	36 203	40 408	24 032	32 438	36 203	40 408	Passagers-kilomètres
Total tonne-kilometres	3 068	4 237	4 922	5 621	3 068	4 237	4 922	5 621	Tonnes-kilomètres totales
Republic of Moldova									**République de Moldova**
Kilometres flown	5	6	7	6	5	6	7	6	Kilomètres parcourus
Passengers carried	270	314	401	402	270	314	401	402	Passagers transportés
Passenger-kilometres	363	434	530	532	363	434	530	532	Passagers-kilomètres
Total tonne-kilometres	40	47	58	56	40	47	58	56	Tonnes-kilomètres totales
Romania									**Roumanie**
Kilometres flown	41	51	55	55	38	47	51	50	Kilomètres parcourus
Passengers carried	2 048	3 004	3 253	3 268	1 804	2 622	2 729	2 716	Passagers transportés
Passenger-kilometres	2 430	3 695	3 980	3 960	2 343	3 563	3 795	3 762	Passagers-kilomètres
Total tonne-kilometres	234	355	380	378	226	343	363	359	Tonnes-kilomètres totales
Russian Federation									**Fédération de Russie**
Kilometres flown	749	868	931	836	279	323	363	305	Kilomètres parcourus
Passengers carried	28 837	34 212	37 940	34 403	9 634	11 429	13 307	11 992	Passagers transportés
Passenger-kilometres	69 499	82 332	91 096	83 828	29 332	34 747	40 943	37 143	Passagers-kilomètres
Total tonne-kilometres	8 242	9 707	10 669	9 918	4 061	4 770	5 551	5 168	Tonnes-kilomètres totales
Samoa									**Samoa**
Kilometres flown	6	6	6	6	4	5	5	4	Kilomètres parcourus
Passengers carried	288	295	291	271	170	179	176	163	Passagers transportés
Passenger-kilometres	384	399	393	362	370	385	378	348	Passagers-kilomètres
Total tonne-kilometres	36	38	37	34	35	37	36	33	Tonnes-kilomètres totales
Sao Tome and Principe									**Sao Tomé-et-Principe**
Kilometres flown	...	1	1	1	...	^0	^0	^0	Kilomètres parcourus
Passengers carried	...	50	52	51	...	31	33	33	Passagers transportés
Passenger-kilometres	...	21	21	20	...	10	10	10	Passagers-kilomètres
Total tonne-kilometres	...	2	2	2	...	1	1	1	Tonnes-kilomètres totales
Saudi Arabia									**Arabie saoudite**
Kilometres flown	154	179	191	196	88	103	117	120	Kilomètres parcourus
Passengers carried	16 831	17 141	16 708	17 508	5 914	6 403	6 902	7 196	Passagers transportés
Passenger-kilometres	25 314	26 904	27 736	28 891	16 545	18 147	19 451	20 248	Passagers-kilomètres
Total tonne-kilometres	3 353	3 659	3 888	3 746	2 487	2 799	3 071	2 902	Tonnes-kilomètres totales

64 Civil aviation: scheduled airline traffic *(continued)*

Passengers carried (thousands); kilometres (millions)

Aviation civile : trafic régulier des lignes aériennes *(suite)*

Passagers transportés (milliers) ; kilomètres (millions)

Country or area and traffic	Total traffic (domestic and international) Trafic total (intérieur et international)				International traffic Trafic international				Pays ou zone et trafic
	2006	2007	2008	2009	2006	2007	2008	2009	
Senegal									**Sénégal**
Kilometres flown	10	13	20	19	^0	12	20	19	Kilomètres parcourus
Passengers carried	501	539	567	573	463	500	529	538	Passagers transportés
Passenger-kilometres	937	993	1 017	985	927	982	1 006	975	Passagers-kilomètres
Total tonne-kilometres	94	97	103	101	93	95	102	100	Tonnes-kilomètres totales
Serbia									**Serbie**
Kilometres flown	10	17	17	15	10	17	17	15	Kilomètres parcourus
Passengers carried	716	1 118	1 135	927	560	1 118	1 135	927	Passagers transportés
Passenger-kilometres	715	1 137	1 146	947	668	1 137	1 146	947	Passagers-kilomètres
Total tonne-kilometres	67	106	107	89	63	106	107	89	Tonnes-kilomètres totales
Seychelles									**Seychelles**
Kilometres flown	16	17	17	17	15	16	16	16	Kilomètres parcourus
Passengers carried	545	575	586	565	258	279	295	300	Passagers transportés
Passenger-kilometres	1 359	1 440	1 474	1 428	1 346	1 427	1 461	1 416	Passagers-kilomètres
Total tonne-kilometres	163	168	171	165	162	166	170	164	Tonnes-kilomètres totales
Sierra Leone									**Sierra Leone**
Kilometres flown	2	2	2	2	2	2	2	2	Kilomètres parcourus
Passengers carried	19	20	21	22	19	20	21	22	Passagers transportés
Passenger-kilometres	101	108	110	107	101	108	110	107	Passagers-kilomètres
Total tonne-kilometres	19	19	19	18	19	19	19	18	Tonnes-kilomètres totales
Singapore									**Singapour**
Kilometres flown	444	453	469	419	444	453	469	419	Kilomètres parcourus
Passengers carried	19 566	20 671	21 050	18 428	19 566	20 671	21 050	18 428	Passagers transportés
Passenger-kilometres	90 126	93 685	96 711	84 514	90 126	93 685	96 711	84 514	Passagers-kilomètres
Total tonne-kilometres	15 902	16 279	15 902	12 973	15 902	16 279	15 902	12 973	Tonnes-kilomètres totales
Slovakia									**Slovaquie**
Kilometres flown	14	25	34	31	13	25	33	31	Kilomètres parcourus
Passengers carried	780	2 679	3 658	3 441	741	2 511	3 433	3 232	Passagers transportés
Passenger-kilometres	1 029	2 921	3 646	3 379	1 018	2 870	3 578	3 317	Passagers-kilomètres
Total tonne-kilometres	78	312	330	306	77	307	323	300	Tonnes-kilomètres totales
Slovenia									**Slovénie**
Kilometres flown	15	18	20	20	15	18	20	20	Kilomètres parcourus
Passengers carried	850	945	1 104	953	850	945	1 104	953	Passagers transportés
Passenger-kilometres	773	863	1 003	872	773	863	1 003	872	Passagers-kilomètres
Total tonne-kilometres	72	81	92	80	72	81	92	80	Tonnes-kilomètres totales
Solomon Islands									**Iles Salomon**
Kilometres flown	3	4	4	3	1	1	1	1	Kilomètres parcourus
Passengers carried	101	102	101	94	32	33	33	31	Passagers transportés
Passenger-kilometres	85	88	86	80	65	67	66	61	Passagers-kilomètres
Total tonne-kilometres	8	9	9	8	7	7	7	6	Tonnes-kilomètres totales
South Africa									**Afrique du Sud**
Kilometres flown	217	222	226	217	124	125	132	128	Kilomètres parcourus
Passengers carried	12 921	12 870	12 989	12 504	3 688	3 671	4 098	4 052	Passagers transportés
Passenger-kilometres	30 797	29 893	28 953	26 926	22 098	21 240	20 605	18 866	Passagers-kilomètres
Total tonne-kilometres	3 845	3 690	3 386	3 108	2 968	2 826	2 537	2 296	Tonnes-kilomètres totales
Spain									**Espagne**
Kilometres flown	575	639	627	560	330	380	386	357	Kilomètres parcourus
Passengers carried	53 114	60 665	55 214	49 289	17 417	21 766	21 765	20 634	Passagers transportés
Passenger-kilometres	77 100	88 404	87 100	80 134	53 057	62 406	63 991	59 821	Passagers-kilomètres
Total tonne-kilometres	8 093	9 247	9 011	8 279	5 811	6 790	6 849	6 361	Tonnes-kilomètres totales
Sri Lanka									**Sri Lanka**
Kilometres flown	45	47	47	38	45	47	47	38	Kilomètres parcourus
Passengers carried	3 101	3 207	2 952	2 418	3 101	3 207	2 952	2 418	Passagers transportés
Passenger-kilometres	9 271	9 773	9 071	7 750	9 271	9 773	9 071	7 750	Passagers-kilomètres
Total tonne-kilometres	1 164	1 227	1 155	988	1 164	1 227	1 155	988	Tonnes-kilomètres totales
Sudan									**Soudan**
Kilometres flown	9	9	9	9	7	8	8	8	Kilomètres parcourus
Passengers carried	563	598	618	607	365	394	417	424	Passagers transportés
Passenger-kilometres	1 072	1 132	1 154	1 111	908	963	986	956	Passagers-kilomètres
Total tonne-kilometres	142	146	148	140	124	127	127	121	Tonnes-kilomètres totales

64 Civil aviation: scheduled airline traffic *(continued)*

Passengers carried (thousands); kilometres (millions)

Aviation civile : trafic régulier des lignes aériennes *(suite)*

Passagers transportés (milliers) ; kilomètres (millions)

Country or area and traffic	Total traffic (domestic and international) Trafic total (intérieur et international) 2006	2007	2008	2009	International traffic Trafic international 2006	2007	2008	2009	Pays ou zone et trafic
Suriname									**Suriname**
Kilometres flown	6	4	6	6	5	4	6	5	Kilomètres parcourus
Passengers carried	307	156	330	303	299	156	322	296	Passagers transportés
Passenger-kilometres	1 676	843	1 865	1 749	1 675	843	1 864	1 749	Passagers-kilomètres
Total tonne-kilometres	205	95	229	212	205	95	229	212	Tonnes-kilomètres totales
Sweden									**Suède**
Kilometres flown	110	40	20	92	68	24	20	57	Kilomètres parcourus
Passengers carried	10 561	2 573	585	8 036	5 022	795	585	3 703	Passagers transportés
Passenger-kilometres	10 238	5 128	4 180	8 933	7 687	4 341	4 180	6 863	Passagers-kilomètres
Total tonne-kilometres	1 224	739	645	1 012	978	667	645	821	Tonnes-kilomètres totales
Switzerland									**Suisse**
Kilometres flown	165	181	220	216	162	178	219	213	Kilomètres parcourus
Passengers carried	10 849	12 157	14 353	14 701	10 096	11 551	13 757	14 083	Passagers transportés
Passenger-kilometres	22 140	25 150	30 268	29 560	21 987	25 017	30 140	29 423	Passagers-kilomètres
Total tonne-kilometres	3 282	3 660	4 225	4 023	3 267	3 647	4 211	4 009	Tonnes-kilomètres totales
Syrian Arab Republic									**Rép. arabe syrienne**
Kilometres flown	24	23	26	26	23	23	25	26	Kilomètres parcourus
Passengers carried	1 252	1 272	1 359	1 343	1 194	1 197	1 305	1 284	Passagers transportés
Passenger-kilometres	2 340	2 333	2 519	2 507	2 311	2 300	2 491	2 476	Passagers-kilomètres
Total tonne-kilometres	228	221	250	246	225	218	248	243	Tonnes-kilomètres totales
Tajikistan									**Tadjikistan**
Kilometres flown	8	9	13	16	7	7	10	14	Kilomètres parcourus
Passengers carried	394	501	683	765	239	321	490	591	Passagers transportés
Passenger-kilometres	708	966	1 458	1 778	645	891	1 375	1 701	Passagers-kilomètres
Total tonne-kilometres	69	91	136	167	63	84	128	160	Tonnes-kilomètres totales
Thailand									**Thaïlande**
Kilometres flown	246	270	259	249	215	238	228	215	Kilomètres parcourus
Passengers carried	20 102	21 192	19 993	19 619	14 154	14 551	12 931	12 009	Passagers transportés
Passenger-kilometres	56 378	62 479	57 185	53 478	52 863	58 505	52 948	48 885	Passagers-kilomètres
Total tonne-kilometres	7 259	8 156	7 509	6 970	6 928	7 785	7 112	6 539	Tonnes-kilomètres totales
TFYR of Macedonia									**L'ex-R.Y. Macédoine**
Kilometres flown	3	3	3	1	3	3	3	1	Kilomètres parcourus
Passengers carried	209	211	196	87	209	211	196	87	Passagers transportés
Passenger-kilometres	269	253	209	87	269	253	209	87	Passagers-kilomètres
Total tonne-kilometres	24	23	18	8	24	23	18	8	Tonnes-kilomètres totales
Trinidad and Tobago									**Trinité-et-Tobago**
Kilometres flown	27	29	30	29	27	29	30	29	Kilomètres parcourus
Passengers carried	1 024	1 086	1 103	1 014	1 013	1 074	1 091	1 004	Passagers transportés
Passenger-kilometres	2 976	3 184	3 312	3 106	2 976	3 184	3 311	3 106	Passagers-kilomètres
Total tonne-kilometres	315	337	351	325	315	337	351	325	Tonnes-kilomètres totales
Tunisia									**Tunisie**
Kilometres flown	31	34	37	35	31	34	37	35	Kilomètres parcourus
Passengers carried	2 014	2 055	2 275	2 279	2 014	2 055	2 275	2 279	Passagers transportés
Passenger-kilometres	2 976	2 960	3 357	3 220	2 976	2 960	3 357	3 220	Passagers-kilomètres
Total tonne-kilometres	308	303	343	326	308	303	343	326	Tonnes-kilomètres totales
Turkey									**Turquie**
Kilometres flown	227	281	322	375	168	198	252	304	Kilomètres parcourus
Passengers carried	19 361	25 157	28 132	31 339	8 341	10 412	14 514	17 150	Passagers transportés
Passenger-kilometres	27 890	36 308	42 561	49 529	21 145	26 559	34 251	40 682	Passagers-kilomètres
Total tonne-kilometres	3 256	4 011	4 709	5 669	2 619	3 126	3 924	4 855	Tonnes-kilomètres totales
Turkmenistan									**Turkménistan**
Kilometres flown	17	18	18	18	12	12	13	12	Kilomètres parcourus
Passengers carried	1 843	1 851	1 823	1 706	437	459	452	420	Passagers transportés
Passenger-kilometres	2 072	2 134	2 104	1 955	1 391	1 447	1 422	1 310	Passagers-kilomètres
Total tonne-kilometres	197	204	200	186	135	141	137	126	Tonnes-kilomètres totales
Uganda									**Ouganda**
Kilometres flown	3	3	3	3	3	3	3	3	Kilomètres parcourus
Passengers carried	55	60	63	64	55	60	63	64	Passagers transportés
Passenger-kilometres	327	346	355	344	327	346	355	344	Passagers-kilomètres
Total tonne-kilometres	61	63	61	58	61	63	61	58	Tonnes-kilomètres totales

Civil aviation: scheduled airline traffic *(continued)*

Passengers carried (thousands); kilometres (millions)

Aviation civile : trafic régulier des lignes aériennes *(suite)*

Passagers transportés (milliers) ; kilomètres (millions)

Country or area and traffic	Total traffic (domestic and international) Trafic total (intérieur et international)				International traffic Trafic international				Pays ou zone et trafic
	2006	2007	2008	2009	2006	2007	2008	2009	
Ukraine									**Ukraine**
Kilometres flown	62	35	68	71	50	29	56	58	Kilomètres parcourus
Passengers carried	2 770	1 736	3 456	3 428	1 951	1 150	2 420	2 436	Passagers transportés
Passenger-kilometres	4 929	2 623	6 532	5 959	4 472	2 307	5 945	5 366	Passagers-kilomètres
Total tonne-kilometres	491	256	655	595	450	227	602	541	Tonnes-kilomètres totales
United Arab Emirates									**Emirats arabes unis**
Kilometres flown	382	483	573	655	381	483	573	655	Kilomètres parcourus
Passengers carried	19 102	25 088	28 432	31 762	18 873	25 088	28 432	31 762	Passagers transportés
Passenger-kilometres	79 704	108 262	124 831	143 849	79 536	108 262	124 831	143 849	Passagers-kilomètres
Total tonne-kilometres	12 903	16 971	19 337	21 823	12 882	16 971	19 337	21 823	Tonnes-kilomètres totales
United Kingdom									**Royaume-Uni**
Kilometres flown	1 400	1 472	1 508	1 445	1 251	1 332	1 371	1 320	Kilomètres parcourus
Passengers carried	97 545	101 623	104 714	102 465	74 692	79 647	83 797	82 948	Passagers transportés
Passenger-kilometres	213 336	227 502	232 592	230 596	203 537	218 005	223 640	222 278	Passagers-kilomètres
Total tonne-kilometres	25 385	23 494	24 101	23 449	24 551	22 756	23 378	22 782	Tonnes-kilomètres totales
United Rep. of Tanzania									**Rép.-Unie de Tanzanie**
Kilometres flown	5	6	4	12	3	3	2	5	Kilomètres parcourus
Passengers carried	221	251	203	684	67	71	51	336	Passagers transportés
Passenger-kilometres	225	252	152	395	130	139	68	186	Passagers-kilomètres
Total tonne-kilometres	22	24	15	36	13	13	7	18	Tonnes-kilomètres totales
United States [4]									**Etats-Unis** [4]
Kilometres flown	12 228	12 490	11 910	11 312	2 518	2 648	2 747	2 619	Kilomètres parcourus
Passengers carried	724 054	744 302	703 035	680 596	84 822	89 027	90 751	86 043	Passagers transportés
Passenger-kilometres	1 270 646	1 316 774	1 278 997	1 227 573	357 431	379 670	393 773	372 738	Passagers-kilomètres
Total tonne-kilometres	156 679	161 500	157 072	147 819	55 086	57 759	58 958	54 372	Tonnes-kilomètres totales
Uruguay									**Uruguay**
Kilometres flown	8	8	9	8	8	8	9	8	Kilomètres parcourus
Passengers carried	569	524	613	564	569	524	613	564	Passagers transportés
Passenger-kilometres	940	926	1 047	982	940	926	1 047	982	Passagers-kilomètres
Total tonne-kilometres	89	83	99	93	89	83	99	93	Tonnes-kilomètres totales
Uzbekistan									**Ouzbékistan**
Kilometres flown	42	44	45	45	36	38	40	39	Kilomètres parcourus
Passengers carried	1 665	1 940	2 034	1 850	1 297	1 530	1 608	1 420	Passagers transportés
Passenger-kilometres	4 599	5 336	5 507	4 775	4 377	5 075	5 235	4 505	Passagers-kilomètres
Total tonne-kilometres	483	548	569	507	462	524	544	482	Tonnes-kilomètres totales
Vanuatu									**Vanuatu**
Kilometres flown	3	4	4	3	3	4	4	3	Kilomètres parcourus
Passengers carried	117	123	121	112	117	123	121	112	Passagers transportés
Passenger-kilometres	241	251	247	227	241	251	247	227	Passagers-kilomètres
Total tonne-kilometres	23	25	24	22	23	25	24	22	Tonnes-kilomètres totales
Venezuela (Boliv. Rep. of)									**Venezuela (Rép. boliv.du)**
Kilometres flown	61	64	65	59	20	21	22	21	Kilomètres parcourus
Passengers carried	5 226	5 495	5 767	5 121	844	895	909	836	Passagers transportés
Passenger-kilometres	2 635	2 803	2 947	2 649	945	1 011	1 052	987	Passagers-kilomètres
Total tonne-kilometres	236	250	265	239	87	93	98	92	Tonnes-kilomètres totales
Viet Nam									**Viet Nam**
Kilometres flown	68	69	91	99	48	45	55	54	Kilomètres parcourus
Passengers carried	6 631	7 482	9 991	11 074	2 989	2 905	3 378	3 090	Passagers transportés
Passenger-kilometres	11 717	12 468	15 762	16 473	8 923	8 870	10 152	9 530	Passagers-kilomètres
Total tonne-kilometres	1 297	1 363	1 716	1 792	980	962	1 114	1 065	Tonnes-kilomètres totales
Yemen									**Yémen**
Kilometres flown	22	22	24	24	22	22	24	24	Kilomètres parcourus
Passengers carried	978	1 039	1 065	1 051	952	1 007	1 040	1 024	Passagers transportés
Passenger-kilometres	2 815	3 041	3 029	3 015	2 771	3 020	2 987	2 969	Passagers-kilomètres
Total tonne-kilometres	291	344	315	307	287	341	311	303	Tonnes-kilomètres totales
Zambia									**Zambie**
Kilometres flown	2	2	2	...	1	1	1	...	Kilomètres parcourus
Passengers carried	59	62	63	...	23	25	26	...	Passagers transportés
Passenger-kilometres	19	20	20	...	8	9	9	...	Passagers-kilomètres
Total tonne-kilometres	2	2	2	...	1	1	1	...	Tonnes-kilomètres totales

64 Civil aviation: scheduled airline traffic *(continued)*

Passengers carried (thousands); kilometres (millions)

Aviation civile : trafic régulier des lignes aériennes *(suite)*

Passagers transportés (milliers) ; kilomètres (millions)

Country or area and traffic	Total traffic (domestic and international) Trafic total (intérieur et international)				International traffic Trafic international				Pays ou zone et trafic
	2006	2007	2008	2009	2006	2007	2008	2009	
Zimbabwe									**Zimbabwe**
Kilometres flown	10	11	11	11	9	10	10	10	Kilomètres parcourus
Passengers carried	239	255	264	262	171	185	196	199	Passagers transportés
Passenger-kilometres	671	711	727	703	642	681	697	676	Passagers-kilomètres
Total tonne-kilometres	76	78	81	79	73	75	78	76	Tonnes-kilomètres totales

Source:
International Civil Aviation Organization (ICAO), Montreal, the ICAO Integrated Statistical Database (ISDB), last accessed December 2010.

1 Including data for Hong Kong Special Administrative Region (Hong Kong SAR) and Macao Special Administrative Region (Macao SAR) but excludes Taiwan Province of China.

2 Including data for airlines based in the territories and dependencies of France.

3 Including data for airlines based in the territories and dependencies of the Netherlands.

4 Including data for airlines based in the territories and dependencies of the United States.

Source:
Organisation de l'aviation civile internationale (OACI), Montréal, la base de données statistique intégrée (ISDB), dernier accès décembre 2010.

1 Y compris les chiffres concernant la région administrative spéciale de Hong Kong (Hong Kong SAR) et la région administrative spéciale de Macao (Macao SAR) mais non compris ceux concernant la province chinoise de Taiwan.

2 Y compris les données relatives aux compagnies aériennes ayant des bases d'opérations dans les territoires et dépendances de France.

3 Y compris les données relatives aux compagnies aériennes ayant des bases d'opérations dans les territoires et dépendances des Pays-Bas.

4 Y compris les données relatives aux compagnies aériennes ayant des bases d'opérations dans les territoires et dépendances des Etats-Unis.

Technical notes: tables 61-64

The data on international tourism have been supplied by the United Nations World Tourism Organization (UNWTO) from detailed tourism information published in the *Yearbook of Tourism Statistics* and in the UNWTO statistics database available from http://www.unwto.org/statistics/index.htm.

For statistical purposes, the term "international visitor" describes "any person who travels to a country other than that in which he/she has his/her usual residence but outside his/her usual environment for a period not exceeding 12 months and whose main purpose of visit is other than the exercise of an activity remunerated from within the country visited".

International visitors include: (a) *tourists* (overnight visitors): "visitors who stay at least one night in a collective or private accommodation in the country visited"; and (b) *same-day visitors*: "visitors who do not spend the night in a collective or private accommodation in the country visited". The figures do not include immigrants, residents in a frontier zone, persons domiciled in one country or area and working in an adjoining country or area, members of the armed forces and diplomats and consular representatives when they travel from their country of origin to the country in which they are stationed and vice-versa. The figures also exclude persons in transit who do not formally enter the country through passport control, such as air transit passengers who remain for a short period in a designated area of the air terminal or ship passengers who are not permitted to disembark. This category includes passengers transferred directly between airports or other terminals. Other passengers in transit through a country are classified as visitors.

Tables 61 and 62: Data on arrivals of non-resident (or international) visitors may be obtained from different sources. In some cases data are obtained from border statistics derived from administrative records (police, immigration, traffic counts and other types of controls), border surveys and registrations at accommodation establishments.

Unless otherwise stated, table 61 shows the number of non-resident tourist/visitor arrivals at national borders classified by their region of origin. Totals correspond to the total number of arrivals from the regions indicated in the table. However, these totals may not correspond to the number of tourist arrivals shown in table 62. The latter excludes same day visitors except when indicated whereas they may be included in table 61.

When a person visits the same country several times a year, an equal number of arrivals is recorded. Likewise, if a person visits several countries during the course of a single trip, his/her arrival in each country is recorded separately. Consequently, arrivals cannot be assumed to be equal to the number of persons travelling.

Expenditure associated with tourism activity of visitors has been traditionally identified with the travel item of the Balance of Payments (BOP): in the case of inbound tourism, those expenditures in the country of reference associated with non-resident visitors are registered as "credits" in the BOP and refer to "travel receipts".

Notes techniques : tableaux 61 à 64

Les données sur le tourisme international ont été fournies par l'Organisation mondiale du tourisme (l'OMT) qui publie des renseignements détaillés sur le tourisme dans *l'Annuaire des statistiques du tourisme* et dans le la base de données de l'OMT en ligne au http://www.unwto.org/statistics/index.htm.

A des fins statistiques, l'expression "visiteur international" désigne "toute personne qui se rend dans un pays autre que celui où elle a son lieu de résidence habituelle, mais différent de son environnement habituel, pour une période de 12 mois au maximum, dans un but principal autre que celui d'y exercer une profession rémunérée".

Entrent dans cette catégorie: (a) *les touristes* (visiteurs passant la nuit), c'est à dire "les visiteurs qui passent une nuit au moins en logement collectif ou privé dans le pays visité"; et (b) *les visiteurs ne restant que la journée*, c'est à dire "les visiteurs qui ne passent pas la nuit en logement collectif ou privé dans le pays visité". Ces chiffres ne comprennent pas les immigrants, les résidents frontaliers, les personnes domiciliées dans une zone ou un pays donné et travaillant dans une zone ou pays limitrophe, les membres des forces armées et les membres des corps diplomatique et consulaire lorsqu'ils se rendent de leur pays d'origine au pays où ils sont en poste, et vice versa. Ne sont pas non plus inclus les voyageurs en transit, qui ne pénètrent pas officiellement dans le pays en faisant contrôler leurs passeports, tels que les passagers d'un vol en escale, qui demeurent pendant un court laps de temps dans une aire distincte de l'aérogare, ou les passagers d'un navire qui ne sont pas autorisés à débarquer. Cette catégorie comprend également les passagers transportés directement d'une aérogare à l'autre ou à un autre terminal. Les autres passagers en transit dans un pays sont classés parmi les visiteurs.

Tableaux 61 et 62: Les données relatives aux arrivées des visiteurs non résidents (ou internationaux) peuvent être obtenues de différentes sources. Dans certains cas, elles proviennent des statistiques des frontières tirées des registres administratifs (contrôles de police, de l'immigration, de la circulation et autres effectués aux frontières nationales), des enquêtes statistiques aux frontières et des enregistrements d'établissements d'hébergement touristique.

Sauf indication contraire, le tableau 61 indique le nombre d'arrivées de touristes/visiteurs non résidents aux frontières nationales par région de provenance. Les totaux correspondent au nombre total d'arrivées de touristes des régions indiquées sur le tableau. Les chiffres totaux peuvent, néanmoins, ne pas coïncider avec le nombre des arrivées de touristes indiqué dans le tableau 62, qui sauf indication contraire ne comprend pas les visiteurs ne restant que la journée, lesquels peuvent au contraire être inclus dans les chiffres du tableau 61.

Lorsqu'une personne visite le même pays plusieurs fois dans l'année, il est enregistré un nombre égal d'arrivées. En outre, si une personne visite plusieurs pays au cours d'un seul et même voyage, son arrivée dans chaque pays est enregistrée séparément. Par conséquent, on ne peut pas partir du postulat que les arrivées

The new conceptual framework approved by the United Nations Statistical Commission in relation to the measurement of tourism macroeconomic activity (the so-called Tourism Satellite Account) considers that "tourism industries and products" includes transport of passengers. Consequently, a better estimate of tourism-related expenditures by resident and non-resident visitors in an international scenario would be, in terms of the BOP, the value of the travel item plus that of the passenger transport item.

Nevertheless, users should be aware that BOP estimates include, in addition to expenditures associated with visitors, those related to other types of individuals.

The data published should allow international comparability and therefore correspond to those published by the International Monetary Fund (and provided by the Central Banks). Exceptions are footnoted.

Table 63: Outbound tourism includes departures (in thousands) as well as expenditure in million US dollars. Indicators on expenditure (in other countries) are equivalent to those for inbound tourism but are registered as "debits" in the BOP's *travel* and *passenger transport* items. The data published are also provided by the International Monetary Fund and the same previous warning is applicable.

More detailed tourism information from the United Nations World Tourism Organization is available in the *Compendium of Tourism Statistics* and from http://www.unwto.org/statistics/index.htm; information on the balance of payments is published by the International Monetary Fund in the *Balance of Payments Statistics Yearbook*.

Table 64: Data for total traffic cover both domestic and international scheduled services operated by airlines registered in each country. Scheduled services include supplementary services occasioned by overflow traffic on regularly scheduled trips and preparatory flights for newly scheduled services. The data are prepared by the International Civil Aviation Organization (see also www.icao.int).

The following terms have been used in the table:

- Kilometres flown - aircraft kilometres performed, which is the sum of the products obtained by multiplying the number of revenue flight stages flown by the corresponding stage distance.
- Passengers carried - the number of passengers carried is obtained by counting each passenger on a particular flight (with one flight number) once only and not repeatedly on each individual stage of that flight, with a single exception that a passenger flying on both the international and domestic stages of the same flight should be counted as both a domestic and an international passenger.
- Passenger-kilometres performed - a passenger-kilometre is performed when a passenger is carried one kilometre. Calculation of passenger-kilometres equals the sum of the products obtained by multiplying the number of revenue passengers carried on each flight stage by the stage distance. The resultant figure is equal to the number of kilometres travelled by all passengers.

sont égales au nombre de personnes qui voyagent.

Les dépenses associées à l'activité touristique des visiteurs sont traditionnellement identifiées au poste "Voyages" de la balance des paiements. Dans le cas du tourisme récepteur, ces dépenses associées aux visiteurs non résidents sont enregistrées dans la balance des paiements comme des "crédits" et il s'agit de "recettes au titre des voyages".

Le cadre conceptuel approuvé par la Commission de statistique de l'Organisation des Nations Unies concernant l'évaluation de l'activité touristique à l'échelle macroéconomique (cadre qu'il est convenu d'appeler compte satellite du tourisme) considère que la notion "industries et produits touristiques " englobe le transport de passagers. Par conséquent, une meilleure estimation des dépenses liées au tourisme international que font les visiteurs résidents et non résidents serait, sous l'angle de la balance des paiements, la somme des valeurs des postes "Voyages" et "Transport de passagers".

Néanmoins, les utilisateurs doivent être conscients que les estimations de la balance des paiements comprennent, outre les dépenses associées aux visiteurs, celles liées à d'autres types d'individus.

Les données publiées doivent permettre la comparabilité internationale et donc correspondre à celles publiées par le Fonds monétaire international (FMI) qui viennent des banques centrales. Les exceptions sont signalées par une note de pied.

Tableau 63: Tourisme à l'étranger comporte départs en milliers et dépenses en millions de dollars E.-U. Les indicateurs relatifs aux dépenses touristiques dans d'autres pays sont équivalents à ceux du tourisme récepteur mais ils sont enregistrés comme "débits" aux postes "Voyages" et "Transport de passagers" de la balance des paiements.

Les données publiées sont également fournies par le FMI. Il y a lieu de faire la même mise en garde que plus haut. On trouvera plus de renseignements publiés par l'Organisation mondiale du tourisme dans le *Compendium des statistiques du tourisme* et au http://www.unwto.org/statistics/index.htm; des renseignements sur la balance des paiements sont publiés par le Fonds monétaire international dans "*Balance of Payments Statistics Yearbook*".

Tableau 64: Les données relatives au trafic total se rapportent aux services réguliers, intérieurs ou internationaux des compagnies de transport aérien enregistrées dans chaque pays. Les services réguliers comprennent aussi les vols supplémentaires nécessités par un surcroît d'activité des services réguliers et les vols préparatoires en vue de nouveaux services réguliers. Les données sont préparées par l'Organisation de l'aviation civile internationale (voir aussi www.icao.int).

Les termes ci-après ont été utilisés dans le tableau:

- Kilomètres parcourus – le nombre de kilomètres parcourus équivaut à la somme des produits du nombre de vols payants effectués sur chaque étape par la longueur de l'étape.
- Passagers transportés – pour calculer le nombre de passagers transportés, on compte chaque passager d'un vol donné (correspondant à un numéro de vol) une seule

- Tonne-kilometres performed - a metric tonne of revenue load carried one kilometre. Tonne-kilometres performed equals the sum of the product obtained by multiplying the number of total tonnes of revenue load (passengers, freight and mail) carried on each flight stage by the stage distance. See http://www.icaodata.com/Terms.aspx for more information.

fois et non pour chacune des étapes de ce vol; toutefois, les passagers qui voyagent sur une étape internationale et sur une étape intérieure d'un même vol doivent être comptés à la fois comme passagers d'un vol intérieur et comme passagers d'un vol international.

- Passager-kilomètre réalisé – un passager-kilomètre est réalisé lorsqu'un passager est transporté sur une distance d'un kilomètre. Le nombre de passagers-kilomètres réalisés équivaut à la somme des produits du nombre de passagers payants transportés sur chaque étape par la longueur de l'étape. Le total obtenu est égal au nombre de kilomètres parcourus par l'ensemble des passagers.
- Tonnes-kilomètres réalisées – la tonne-kilomètre est une unité de mesure qui correspond au déplacement d'une tonne métrique de charge payante sur un kilomètre. Les tonnes-kilomètres réalisées sont la somme des produits du nombre de tonnes de charge payante (passagers, fret, envois postaux) transportées sur chaque étape par la longueur de l'étape. Pour plus de détails, voir http://www.icaodata.com/Terms.aspx.

65 Exchange rates

National currency per US dollar

Cours des changes

Valeur du dollar E.-U. en monnaie nationale

Country or area / Pays ou zone	2001	2002	2003	2004	2005	2006	2007	2008	2009
Afghanistan [1] (afghani) Afghanistan [1] (afghani)									
End of period Fin de période	47.259	47.263	48.865	48.220	50.410	49.850	49.720	52.140	48.740
Period average Moyenne sur période	47.500	47.263	48.763	47.845	49.495	49.925	49.962	50.250	50.233
Albania (lek) Albanie (lek)									
End of period Fin de période	136.550	133.740	106.580	92.640	103.580	94.140	82.890	87.910	95.810
Period average Moyenne sur période	143.485	140.155	121.863	102.780	99.870	98.103	90.428	83.895	94.978
Algeria (Algerian dinar) Algérie (dinar algérien)									
End of period Fin de période	77.820	79.723	72.613	72.614	73.380	71.158	66.830	71.183	72.731
Period average Moyenne sur période	77.215	79.682	77.395	72.061	73.276	72.647	69.292	64.583	72.647
Angola (kwanza) Angola (kwanza)									
End of period Fin de période	31.949	58.666	79.082	85.988	80.780	80.264	75.023	75.169	89.398
Period average Moyenne sur période	22.058	43.530	74.606	83.541	87.159	80.368	76.706	75.033	79.328
Anguilla (EC dollar) Anguilla (dollar des Caraïbes orientales)									
End of period Fin de période	2.700	2.700	2.700	2.700	2.700	2.700	2.700	2.700	2.700
Period average Moyenne sur période	2.700	2.700	2.700	2.700	2.700	2.700	2.700	2.700	2.700
Antigua and Barbuda (EC dollar) Antigua-et-Barbuda (dollar des Caraïbes orientales)									
End of period Fin de période	2.700	2.700	2.700	2.700	2.700	2.700	2.700	2.700	2.700
Period average Moyenne sur période	2.700	2.700	2.700	2.700	2.700	2.700	2.700	2.700	2.700
Argentina [2] (Argentine peso) Argentine [2] (peso argentin)									
End of period Fin de période	1.000	3.320	2.905	2.959	3.012	3.042	3.129	3.433	3.780
Period average Moyenne sur période	1.000	3.063	2.901	2.923	2.904	3.054	3.096	3.144	3.710
Armenia (dram) Arménie (dram)									
End of period Fin de période	561.810	584.890	566.000	485.840	450.190	363.500	304.220	306.730	377.890
Period average Moyenne sur période	555.078	573.353	578.763	533.451	457.687	416.040	342.079	305.969	363.283
Aruba (Aruban florin) Aruba (florin de Aruba)									
End of period Fin de période	1.790	1.790	1.790	1.790	1.790	1.790	1.790	1.790	1.790
Period average Moyenne sur période	1.790	1.790	1.790	1.790	1.790	1.790	1.790	1.790	1.790
Australia (Australian dollar) Australie (dollar australien)									
End of period Fin de période	1.958	1.766	1.333	1.284	1.363	1.264	1.134	1.443	1.115
Period average Moyenne sur période	1.933	1.841	1.542	1.360	1.309	1.328	1.195	1.192	1.282
Azerbaijan (manat) Azerbaïdjan (manat)									
End of period Fin de période	0.955	0.979	0.985	0.981	0.919	0.871	0.845	0.801	0.803
Period average Moyenne sur période	0.931	0.972	0.982	0.983	0.945	0.893	0.858	0.822	0.804
Bahamas [1] (Bahamian dollar) Bahamas [1] (dollar des Bahamas)									
End of period Fin de période	1.000	1.000	1.000	1.000	1.000	1.000	1.000	1.000	1.000
Period average Moyenne sur période	1.000	1.000	1.000	1.000	1.000	1.000	1.000	1.000	1.000
Bahrain (Bahrain dinar) Bahreïn (dinar de Bahreïn)									
End of period Fin de période	0.376	0.376	0.376	0.376	0.376	0.376	0.376	0.376	0.376
Period average Moyenne sur période	0.376	0.376	0.376	0.376	0.376	0.376	0.376	0.376	0.376
Bangladesh [1] (taka) Bangladesh [1] (taka)									
End of period Fin de période	57.000	57.900	58.782	60.742	66.210	69.065	68.576	68.920	69.267
Period average Moyenne sur période	55.807	57.888	58.150	59.513	64.328	68.933	68.875	68.598	69.039
Barbados (Barbados dollar) Barbade (dollar de la Barbade)									
End of period Fin de période	2.000	2.000	2.000	2.000	2.000	2.000	2.000	2.000	2.000
Period average Moyenne sur période	2.000	2.000	2.000	2.000	2.000	2.000	2.000	2.000	2.000
Belarus (Belarussian rouble) Bélarus (rouble bélarussien)									
End of period Fin de période	1 580.000	1 920.000	2 156.000	2 170.000	2 152.000	2 140.000	2 150.000	2 200.000	2 863.000
Period average Moyenne sur période	1 390.000	1 790.920	2 051.270	2 160.260	2 153.820	2 144.560	2 146.080	2 136.400	2 789.490
Belize (Belize dollar) Belize (dollar du Belize)									
End of period Fin de période	2.000	2.000	2.000	2.000	2.000	2.000	2.000	2.000	2.000
Period average Moyenne sur période	2.000	2.000	2.000	2.000	2.000	2.000	2.000	2.000	2.000
Benin (CFA franc) Bénin (franc CFA)									
End of period Fin de période	744.306	625.495	519.364	481.578	556.037	498.069	445.593	471.335	455.336
Period average Moyenne sur période	733.039	696.988	581.200	528.285	527.468	522.890	479.267	447.805	472.186
Bhutan (ngultrum) Bhoutan (ngultrum)									
End of period Fin de période	48.180	48.030	45.605	43.585	45.065	44.245	39.415	48.455	46.680
Period average Moyenne sur période	47.186	48.610	46.583	45.317	44.100	45.307	41.349	43.505	48.405
Bolivia (Plurinational State of) (boliviano) Bolivie (État plurinational de) (boliviano)									
End of period Fin de période	6.820	7.490	7.830	8.050	8.040	7.980	7.620	7.020	7.020
Period average Moyenne sur période	6.607	7.170	7.659	7.936	8.066	8.012	7.851	7.238	7.020
Bosnia and Herzegovina (convertible marka) Bosnie-Herzégovine (marka convertible)									
End of period Fin de période	2.219	1.865	1.549	1.436	1.658	1.485	1.329	1.405	1.358
Period average Moyenne sur période	2.186	2.078	1.733	1.575	1.573	1.559	1.429	1.335	1.408

65 Exchange rates *(continued)*

National currency per US dollar

Cours des changes *(suite)*

Valeur du dollar E.-U. en monnaie nationale

Country or area Pays ou zone	2001	2002	2003	2004	2005	2006	2007	2008	2009
Botswana (pula) Botswana (pula)									
End of period Fin de période	6.983	5.467	4.442	4.281	5.513	6.031	6.006	7.519	6.673
Period average Moyenne sur période	5.841	6.328	4.950	4.693	5.110	5.837	6.139	6.827	7.155
Brazil (real) Brésil (real)									
End of period Fin de période	2.320	3.533	2.888	2.654	2.340	2.137	1.771	2.336	1.740
Period average Moyenne sur période	2.350	2.920	3.077	2.925	2.434	2.175	1.947	1.834	1.999
Brunei Darussalam (Brunei dollar) Brunéi Darussalam (dollar du Brunéi)									
End of period Fin de période	1.851	1.737	1.701	1.634	1.665	1.534	1.442	1.440	1.403
Period average Moyenne sur période	1.792	1.791	1.742	1.690	1.664	1.589	1.507	1.417	1.455
Bulgaria (lev) Bulgarie (lev)									
End of period Fin de période	2.219	1.885	1.549	1.436	1.658	1.485	1.331	1.387	1.364
Period average Moyenne sur période	2.185	2.077	1.733	1.575	1.574	1.559	1.429	1.337	1.407
Burkina Faso (CFA franc) Burkina Faso (franc CFA)									
End of period Fin de période	744.306	625.495	519.364	481.578	556.037	498.069	445.593	471.335	455.336
Period average Moyenne sur période	733.039	696.988	581.200	528.285	527.468	522.890	479.267	447.805	472.186
Burundi (Burundi franc) Burundi (franc burundais)									
End of period Fin de période	864.200	1 071.230	1 093.000	1 109.510	997.780	1 002.470	1 119.540	1 234.980	1 230.500
Period average Moyenne sur période	830.353	930.749	1 082.620	1 100.900	1 081.580	1 028.680	1 081.870	1 185.690	1 230.180
Cambodia (riel) Cambodge (riel)									
End of period Fin de période	3 895.000	3 930.000	3 984.000	4 027.000	4 112.000	4 057.000	3 999.000	4 077.000	4 165.000
Period average Moyenne sur période	3 916.330	3 912.080	3 973.330	4 016.250	4 092.500	4 103.250	4 056.170	4 054.170	4 139.330
Cameroon (CFA franc) Cameroun (franc CFA)									
End of period Fin de période	744.306	625.495	519.364	481.578	556.037	498.069	445.593	471.335	455.336
Period average Moyenne sur période	733.039	696.988	581.200	528.285	527.468	522.890	479.267	447.805	472.186
Canada (Canadian dollar) Canada (dollar canadien)									
End of period Fin de période	1.593	1.580	1.292	1.204	1.165	1.165	0.988	1.225	1.047
Period average Moyenne sur période	1.549	1.569	1.401	1.301	1.212	1.134	1.074	1.067	1.143
Cape Verde (Cape Verde escudo) Cap-Vert (escudo du Cap-Vert)									
End of period Fin de période	125.122	105.149	87.308	80.956	93.473	83.728	74.907	79.234	76.545
Period average Moyenne sur période	123.228	117.168	97.703	88.808	88.670	87.901	80.567	75.279	79.377
Central African Rep. (CFA franc) Rép. centrafricaine (franc CFA)									
End of period Fin de période	744.306	625.495	519.364	481.578	556.037	498.069	445.593	471.335	455.336
Period average Moyenne sur période	733.039	696.988	581.200	528.285	527.468	522.890	479.267	447.805	472.186
Chad (CFA franc) Tchad (franc CFA)									
End of period Fin de période	744.306	625.495	519.364	481.578	556.037	498.069	445.593	471.335	455.336
Period average Moyenne sur période	733.039	696.988	581.200	528.285	527.468	522.890	479.267	447.805	472.186
Chile [1] (Chilean peso) Chili [1] (peso chilien)									
End of period Fin de période	656.200	712.380	599.420	559.830	514.210	534.430	495.820	629.110	506.430
Period average Moyenne sur période	634.938	688.937	691.398	609.529	559.768	530.275	522.464	522.461	560.860
China [1] (yuan) Chine [1] (yuan)									
End of period Fin de période	8.277	8.277	8.277	8.277	8.070	7.809	7.305	6.835	6.828
Period average Moyenne sur période	8.277	8.277	8.277	8.277	8.194	7.973	7.608	6.949	6.831
China, Hong Kong SAR (Hong Kong dollar) Chine, Hong Kong RAS (dollar de Hong Kong)									
End of period Fin de période	7.797	7.798	7.763	7.774	7.753	7.775	7.802	7.751	7.756
Period average Moyenne sur période	7.799	7.799	7.787	7.788	7.777	7.768	7.801	7.787	7.752
China, Macao SAR (Macao pataca) Chine, Macao RAS (pataca de Macao)									
End of period Fin de période	8.031	8.033	7.997	8.010	7.987	8.006	8.034	7.982	7.988
Period average Moyenne sur période	8.034	8.033	8.021	8.022	8.011	8.001	8.036	8.020	7.984
Colombia (Colombian peso) Colombie (peso colombien)									
End of period Fin de période	2 301.330	2 864.790	2 780.820	2 412.100	2 284.220	2 225.440	1 987.810	2 198.090	2 044.230
Period average Moyenne sur période	2 299.630	2 504.240	2 877.650	2 628.610	2 320.830	2 361.140	2 078.290	1 967.710	2 166.790
Comoros (Comorian franc) Comores (franc comorien)									
End of period Fin de période	558.230	469.122	389.523	361.183	417.028	373.552	334.195	353.501	341.502
Period average Moyenne sur période	549.779	522.741	435.900	396.214	395.601	392.168	359.450	335.854	354.140
Congo (CFA franc) Congo (franc CFA)									
End of period Fin de période	744.306	625.495	519.364	481.578	556.037	498.069	445.593	471.335	455.336
Period average Moyenne sur période	733.039	696.988	581.200	528.285	527.468	522.890	479.267	447.805	472.186
Costa Rica (Costa Rican colón) Costa Rica (colón costa-ricien)									
End of period Fin de période	341.670	378.720	418.530	458.610	496.680	517.895	498.100	555.470	565.240
Period average Moyenne sur période	328.871	359.818	398.662	437.935	477.787	511.302	516.617	526.236	573.288
Côte d'Ivoire (CFA franc) Côte d'Ivoire (franc CFA)									
End of period Fin de période	744.306	625.495	519.364	481.578	556.037	498.069	445.593	471.335	455.336
Period average Moyenne sur période	733.039	696.988	581.200	528.285	527.468	522.890	479.267	447.805	472.186

65

Exchange rates *(continued)*
National currency per US dollar

Cours des changes *(suite)*
Valeur du dollar E.-U. en monnaie nationale

Country or area Pays ou zone	2001	2002	2003	2004	2005	2006	2007	2008	2009
Croatia (kuna) Croatie (kuna)									
End of period Fin de période	8.356	7.146	6.119	5.637	6.234	5.578	4.985	5.156	5.089
Period average Moyenne sur période	8.342	7.872	6.705	6.034	5.949	5.838	5.365	4.935	5.284
Cyprus (Cyprus pound) Chypre (livre chypriote)									
End of period Fin de période	0.650	0.547	0.465	0.425	0.484	0.439	0.398	...	...
Period average Moyenne sur période	0.643	0.611	0.517	0.469	0.464	0.459	0.426	...	...
Czech Republic (Czech koruna) République tchèque (couronne tchèque)									
End of period Fin de période	36.259	30.141	25.654	22.365	24.588	20.876	18.078	19.346	18.368
Period average [1] Moyenne sur période [1]	38.035	32.739	28.209	25.700	23.957	22.596	20.294	17.072	19.063
Dem. Rep. of the Congo (Congo franc) Rép. dém. du Congo (franc congolais)									
End of period Fin de période	313.600	382.140	#372.520	444.088	431.279	503.430	502.986	639.320	902.660
Period average Moyenne sur période	206.739	346.688	#405.397	399.476	473.908	468.279	516.750	559.293	809.786
Denmark (Danish krone) Danemark (couronne danoise)									
End of period Fin de période	8.410	7.082	5.958	5.468	6.324	5.661	5.075	5.285	5.190
Period average Moyenne sur période	8.323	7.895	6.588	5.991	5.997	5.947	5.444	5.098	5.361
Djibouti (Djibouti franc) Djibouti (franc djiboutien)									
End of period Fin de période	177.721	177.721	177.721	177.721	177.721	177.721	177.721	177.721	177.721
Period average Moyenne sur période	177.721	177.721	177.721	177.721	177.721	177.721	177.721	177.721	177.721
Dominica (EC dollar) Dominique (dollar des Caraïbes orientales)									
End of period Fin de période	2.700	2.700	2.700	2.700	2.700	2.700	2.700	2.700	2.700
Period average Moyenne sur période	2.700	2.700	2.700	2.700	2.700	2.700	2.700	2.700	2.700
Dominican Republic [1] (Dominican peso) Rép. dominicaine [1] (peso dominicain)									
End of period Fin de période	17.149	21.194	37.250	31.109	34.879	33.797	34.342	35.458	36.210
Period average Moyenne sur période	16.952	18.610	30.831	42.120	30.409	33.365	33.263	34.624	36.027
Egypt [1] (Egyptian pound) Egypte [1] (livre égyptienne)									
End of period Fin de période	4.490	4.500	6.153	6.131	5.732	5.704	5.504	5.504	5.475
Period average Moyenne sur période	3.973	4.500	5.851	6.196	5.779	5.733	5.635	5.433	5.545
El Salvador [1] (Salvadoran colón) El Salvador [1] (cólon salvadorien)									
End of period Fin de période	8.750	8.750	8.750	8.750	8.750	8.750	8.750	8.750	8.750
Period average Moyenne sur période	8.750	8.750	8.750	8.750	8.750	8.750	8.750	8.750	8.750
Equatorial Guinea (CFA franc) Guinée équatoriale (franc CFA)									
End of period Fin de période	744.306	625.495	519.364	481.578	556.037	498.069	445.593	471.335	455.336
Period average Moyenne sur période	733.039	696.988	581.200	528.285	527.468	522.890	479.267	447.805	472.186
Eritrea (nakfa) Erythrée (nakfa)									
End of period Fin de période	13.798	14.309	13.788	13.788	15.375	15.375	15.375	15.375	15.375
Period average Moyenne sur période	11.310	13.958	13.878	13.788	15.368	15.375	15.375	15.375	15.375
Estonia (Estonian kroon) Estonie (couronne estonienne)									
End of period Fin de période	17.692	14.936	12.410	11.471	13.221	11.882	10.638	11.105	10.865
Period average Moyenne sur période	17.478	16.612	13.856	12.596	12.584	12.466	11.434	10.694	11.257
Ethiopia (Ethiopian birr) Ethiopie (birr éthiopien)									
End of period Fin de période	8.558	8.581	8.621	8.652	8.681	8.776	9.201	9.955	12.642
Period average Moyenne sur période	8.457	8.568	8.600	8.636	8.666	8.699	8.966	9.600	11.778
Euro Area [3] (euro) Zone euro [3] (euro)									
End of period Fin de période	1.135	0.954	0.792	0.734	0.848	0.759	0.679	0.719	0.694
Period average Moyenne sur période	1.118	1.063	0.886	0.805	0.804	0.797	0.731	0.683	0.720
Fiji (Fiji dollar) Fidji (dollar des Fidji)									
End of period Fin de période	2.309	2.065	1.722	1.645	1.745	1.664	1.551	1.764	1.929
Period average Moyenne sur période	2.277	2.187	1.896	1.733	1.691	1.731	1.610	1.594	1.958
Gabon (CFA franc) Gabon (franc CFA)									
End of period Fin de période	744.306	625.495	519.364	481.578	556.037	498.069	445.593	471.335	455.336
Period average Moyenne sur période	733.039	696.988	581.200	528.285	527.468	522.890	479.267	447.805	472.186
Gambia (dalasi) Gambie (dalasi)									
End of period Fin de période	16.932	23.392	30.960	29.674	28.135	28.047	22.539	26.542	26.941
Period average Moyenne sur période	15.687	19.918	27.306	30.030	28.575	28.066	24.875	22.192	26.644
Georgia (lari) Géorgie (lari)									
End of period Fin de période	2.060	2.090	2.075	1.825	1.793	1.714	1.592	1.667	1.686
Period average Moyenne sur période	2.073	2.196	2.146	1.917	1.813	1.780	1.670	1.491	1.670
Ghana [1] (cedi) Ghana [1] (cedi)									
End of period Fin de période	0.732	0.844	0.885	0.905	0.913	0.924	0.970	1.214	1.419
Period average Moyenne sur période	0.716	0.792	0.867	0.899	0.906	0.916	0.935	1.058	1.409
Grenada (EC dollar) Grenade (dollar des Caraïbes orientales)									
End of period Fin de période	2.700	2.700	2.700	2.700	2.700	2.700	2.700	2.700	2.700
Period average Moyenne sur période	2.700	2.700	2.700	2.700	2.700	2.700	2.700	2.700	2.700

65 Exchange rates *(continued)*

National currency per US dollar

Cours des changes *(suite)*

Valeur du dollar E.-U. en monnaie nationale

Country or area / Pays ou zone	2001	2002	2003	2004	2005	2006	2007	2008	2009
Guatemala (quetzal) Guatemala (quetzal)									
End of period Fin de période	8.000	7.807	8.041	7.748	7.610	7.624	7.631	7.774	8.347
Period average Moyenne sur période	7.859	7.822	7.941	7.947	7.634	7.603	7.673	7.560	8.162
Guinea (Guinean franc) Guinée (franc guinéen)									
End of period Fin de période	1 988.330	1 976.000	2 000.000	2 550.000	4 500.000	5 650.000	4 181.730	5 160.960	...
Period average Moyenne sur période	1 950.560	1 975.840	1 984.930	2 225.030	3 644.330	5 350.000	4 122.800	5 500.000	...
Guinea-Bissau (CFA franc) Guinée-Bissau (franc CFA)									
End of period Fin de période	744.306	625.495	519.364	481.578	556.037	498.069	445.593	471.335	455.336
Period average Moyenne sur période	733.039	696.988	581.200	528.285	527.468	522.890	479.267	447.805	472.186
Guyana [1] (Guyana dollar) Guyana [1] (dollar guyanais)									
End of period Fin de période	189.500	191.750	194.250	199.750	200.250	201.000	203.500	205.250	203.250
Period average Moyenne sur période	187.321	190.665	193.878	198.307	199.875	200.188	202.347	203.633	203.950
Haiti [1] (gourde) Haïti [1] (gourde)									
End of period Fin de période	26.339	37.609	42.085	37.232	43.000	37.591	36.784	39.818	42.019
Period average Moyenne sur période	24.429	29.251	42.367	38.352	40.449	40.409	36.861	39.108	41.198
Honduras [1] (lempira) Honduras [1] (lempira)									
End of period Fin de période	15.920	16.923	17.748	18.633	18.895	18.895	18.895	18.895	18.895
Period average Moyenne sur période	15.474	16.433	17.345	18.206	18.832	18.895	18.895	18.904	18.895
Hungary (forint) Hongrie (forint)									
End of period Fin de période	279.030	225.160	207.920	180.290	213.580	191.620	172.610	187.910	188.070
Period average Moyenne sur période	286.490	257.887	224.307	202.746	199.582	210.390	183.626	172.113	202.342
Iceland (Icelandic króna) Islande (couronne islandaise)									
End of period Fin de période	102.950	80.580	70.990	61.040	62.980	71.660	61.850	120.580	124.900
Period average Moyenne sur période	97.425	91.662	76.709	70.192	62.982	70.180	64.055	87.948	123.638
India (Indian rupee) Inde (roupie indienne)									
End of period Fin de période	48.180	48.030	45.605	43.585	45.065	44.245	39.415	48.455	46.680
Period average Moyenne sur période	47.186	48.610	46.583	45.317	44.100	45.307	41.349	43.505	48.405
Indonesia (Indonesian rupiah) Indonésie (roupie indonésien)									
End of period Fin de période	10 400.000	8 940.000	8 465.000	9 290.000	9 830.000	9 020.000	9 419.000	10 950.000	9 400.000
Period average Moyenne sur période	10 260.900	9 311.190	8 577.130	8 938.850	9 704.740	9 159.320	9 141.000	9 698.960	10 389.900
Iran (Islamic Rep. of) (Iranian rial) Iran (Rép. islamique d') (rial iranien)									
End of period Fin de période	1 750.950	#7 951.980	8 272.110	8 793.000	9 091.000	9 223.000	9 282.000	9 825.000	9 984.000
Period average Moyenne sur période	1 754.570	#6 907.130	8 193.890	8 613.990	8 963.960	9 170.940	9 281.150	9 428.530	9 864.300
Iraq [1] (New Iraqi dinar) Iraq [1] (nouveau dinar iraquien)									
End of period Fin de période	0.310	0.310	1 685.000	1 469.000	1 487.000	1 325.000	1 215.000	1 172.000	1 170.000
Period average Moyenne sur période	0.311	0.311	2 133.780	1 453.420	1 472.000	1 467.420	1 254.570	1 193.080	1 170.000
Israel (new sheqel) Israël (nouveau sheqel)									
End of period Fin de période	4.416	4.737	4.379	4.308	4.603	4.225	3.846	3.802	3.775
Period average Moyenne sur période	4.206	4.738	4.554	4.482	4.488	4.456	4.108	3.588	3.932
Jamaica (Jamaican dollar) Jamaïque (dollar jamaïcain)									
End of period Fin de période	47.286	50.762	60.517	61.450	64.381	67.032	70.397	80.217	89.328
Period average Moyenne sur période	45.996	48.416	57.741	61.197	62.281	65.744	69.192	72.756	87.894
Japan (yen) Japon (yen)									
End of period Fin de période	131.800	119.900	107.100	104.120	117.970	118.950	114.000	90.750	92.060
Period average Moyenne sur période	121.529	125.388	115.933	108.193	110.218	116.299	117.754	103.359	93.570
Jordan (Jordan dinar) Jordanie (dinar jordanien)									
End of period Fin de période	0.709	0.709	0.709	0.709	0.709	0.709	0.709	0.709	0.710
Period average Moyenne sur période	0.709	0.709	0.709	0.709	0.709	0.709	0.709	0.710	0.710
Kazakhstan (tenge) Kazakhstan (tenge)									
End of period Fin de période	150.200	154.600	144.220	130.000	133.980	127.000	120.300	120.790	148.460
Period average Moyenne sur période	146.736	153.279	149.576	136.035	132.880	126.089	122.554	120.299	147.497
Kenya (Kenya shilling) Kenya (shilling kényen)									
End of period Fin de période	78.600	77.072	76.139	77.344	72.367	69.397	62.675	77.711	75.820
Period average Moyenne sur période	78.563	78.749	75.936	79.174	75.554	72.101	67.318	69.175	77.352
Kiribati (Australian dollar) Kiribati (dollar australien)									
End of period Fin de période	1.958	1.766	1.333	1.284	1.363	1.264	1.134	1.443	1.115
Period average Moyenne sur période	1.933	1.841	1.542	1.360	1.309	1.328	1.195	1.192	1.282
Korea, Republic of (Korean won) Corée, République de (won coréen)									
End of period Fin de période	1 313.500	1 186.200	1 192.600	1 035.100	1 011.600	929.800	936.100	1 259.500	1 164.500
Period average Moyenne sur période	1 290.990	1 251.090	1 191.610	1 145.320	1 024.120	954.791	929.257	1 102.050	1 276.930
Kuwait (Kuwaiti dinar) Koweït (dinar koweïtien)									
End of period Fin de période	0.308	0.300	0.295	0.295	0.292	0.289	0.273	0.276	0.287
Period average Moyenne sur période	0.307	0.304	0.298	0.295	0.292	0.290	0.284	0.269	0.288

65

Exchange rates *(continued)*
National currency per US dollar

Cours des changes *(suite)*
Valeur du dollar E.-U. en monnaie nationale

Country or area Pays ou zone	2001	2002	2003	2004	2005	2006	2007	2008	2009
Kyrgyzstan (Kyrgyz som) Kirghizistan (som kirghize)									
End of period Fin de période	47.719	46.095	44.190	41.625	41.301	38.124	35.499	39.418	44.092
Period average Moyenne sur période	48.378	46.937	43.648	42.650	41.012	40.153	37.316	36.575	42.904
Lao People's Dem. Rep. (kip) Rép. dém. pop. lao (kip)									
End of period Fin de période	9 490.000	10 680.000	10 467.000	10 376.500	10 743.000	9 696.480	9 346.000	8 478.940	8 484.250
Period average Moyenne sur période	8 954.580	10 056.300	10 569.000	10 585.400	10 655.200	10 159.900	9 603.160	8 744.060	8 516.040
Latvia (lats) Lettonie (lats)									
End of period Fin de période	0.638	0.594	0.541	0.516	0.593	0.536	0.484	0.495	0.489
Period average Moyenne sur période	0.628	0.618	0.571	0.540	0.565	0.560	0.514	0.481	0.506
Lebanon (Lebanese pound) Liban (livre libanaise)									
End of period Fin de période	1 507.500	1 507.500	1 507.500	1 507.500	1 507.500	1 507.500	1 507.500	1 507.500	1 507.500
Period average Moyenne sur période	1 507.500	1 507.500	1 507.500	1 507.500	1 507.500	1 507.500	1 507.500	1 507.500	1 507.500
Lesotho[1] (loti) Lesotho[1] (loti)									
End of period Fin de période	12.127	8.640	6.640	5.630	6.325	6.970	6.810	9.305	7.380
Period average Moyenne sur période	8.609	10.541	7.565	6.460	6.359	6.772	7.045	8.261	8.474
Liberia[1] (Liberian dollar) Libéria[1] (dollar libérien)									
End of period Fin de période	49.500	65.000	50.500	54.500	56.500	59.500	62.500	64.000	70.500
Period average Moyenne sur période	48.583	61.754	59.379	54.906	57.096	58.013	61.272	63.208	68.287
Libyan Arab Jamah. (Libyan dinar) Jamah. arabe libyenne (dinar libyen)									
End of period Fin de période	0.650	1.210	1.300	1.244	1.352	1.284	1.223	1.255	1.233
Period average Moyenne sur période	0.605	1.271	1.293	1.305	1.308	1.314	1.263	1.224	1.254
Lithuania (litas) Lituanie (litas)									
End of period Fin de période	4.000	3.311	2.762	2.535	2.910	2.630	2.357	2.451	2.405
Period average Moyenne sur période	4.000	3.677	3.061	2.781	2.774	2.752	2.524	2.357	2.484
Madagascar (Malagasy ariary) Madagascar (ariary malgache)									
End of period Fin de période	1 326.240	1 286.950	1 219.620	1 869.400	2 159.820	2 013.950	1 786.690	1 860.360	1 954.640
Period average Moyenne sur période	1 317.700	1 366.390	1 238.330	1 868.860	2 003.030	2 142.300	1 873.880	1 708.370	1 956.210
Malawi (Malawi kwacha) Malawi (kwacha malawien)									
End of period Fin de période	67.294	87.139	108.566	108.943	123.781	139.343	140.316	140.600	145.995
Period average Moyenne sur période	72.197	76.687	97.433	108.898	118.420	136.014	139.957	140.523	141.167
Malaysia (ringgit) Malaisie (ringgit)									
End of period Fin de période	3.800	3.800	3.800	3.800	3.780	3.532	3.307	3.464	3.425
Period average Moyenne sur période	3.800	3.800	3.800	3.800	3.787	3.668	3.438	3.336	3.525
Maldives (rufiyaa) Maldives (rufiyaa)									
End of period Fin de période	12.800	12.800	12.800	12.800	12.800	12.800	12.800	12.800	12.800
Period average Moyenne sur période	12.242	12.800	12.800	12.800	12.800	12.800	12.800	12.800	12.800
Mali (CFA franc) Mali (franc CFA)									
End of period Fin de période	744.306	625.495	519.364	481.578	556.037	498.069	445.593	471.335	455.336
Period average Moyenne sur période	733.039	696.988	581.200	528.285	527.468	522.890	479.267	447.805	472.186
Malta (Maltese lira) Malte (lire maltaise)									
End of period Fin de période	0.452	0.399	0.343	0.319	0.363	0.326	0.292	...	...
Period average Moyenne sur période	0.450	0.434	0.377	0.345	0.346	0.341	0.312	...	...
Mauritania (ouguiya) Mauritanie (ouguiya)									
End of period Fin de période	264.120	268.710	265.600	257.190	270.610	270.610	252.880	261.500	261.990
Period average Moyenne sur période	255.629	271.739	263.030	...	265.528	268.600	258.587	238.203	262.366
Mauritius (Mauritian rupee) Maurice (roupie mauricienne)									
End of period Fin de période	30.394	29.197	26.088	28.204	30.667	34.337	28.216	31.756	30.291
Period average Moyenne sur période	29.129	29.962	27.902	27.499	29.496	31.708	31.314	28.453	31.960
Mexico[1] (Mexican peso) Mexique[1] (peso mexicain)									
End of period Fin de période	9.142	10.313	11.236	11.265	10.778	10.881	10.866	13.538	13.059
Period average Moyenne sur période	9.342	9.656	10.789	11.286	10.898	10.899	10.928	11.130	13.514
Micronesia (Fed. States of) (US dollar) Micronésie (Etats féd. de) (dollar des Etats-Unis)									
End of period Fin de période	1.000	1.000	1.000	1.000	1.000	1.000	1.000	1.000	1.000
Period average Moyenne sur période	1.000	1.000	1.000	1.000	1.000	1.000	1.000	1.000	1.000
Mongolia (togrog) Mongolie (togrog)									
End of period Fin de période	1 102.000	1 125.000	1 168.000	1 209.000	1 221.000	1 165.000	1 169.970	1 267.510	1 442.840
Period average Moyenne sur période	1 097.700	1 110.310	1 146.540	1 185.300	1 205.250	1 179.700	1 170.400	1 165.800	1 437.800
Montenegro (euro) Monténégro (euro)									
End of period Fin de période	...	...	...	...	...	0.759	0.679	0.719	0.694
Period average Moyenne sur période	...	...	...	...	...	0.797	0.731	0.683	0.720
Montserrat (EC dollar) Montserrat (dollar des Caraïbes orientales)									
End of period Fin de période	2.700	2.700	2.700	2.700	2.700	2.700	2.700	2.700	2.700
Period average Moyenne sur période	2.700	2.700	2.700	2.700	2.700	2.700	2.700	2.700	2.700

Country or area / Pays ou zone	2001	2002	2003	2004	2005	2006	2007	2008	2009
Morocco (Moroccan dirham) Maroc (dirham marocain)									
End of period Fin de période	11.560	10.167	8.750	8.218	9.249	8.457	7.713	8.098	7.860
Period average Moyenne sur période	11.303	11.021	9.574	8.868	8.865	8.796	8.192	7.750	8.057
Mozambique [1] (new metical) Mozambique [1] (nouveau metical)									
End of period Fin de période	23.320	23.854	23.857	18.899	24.183	25.970	23.820	25.500	29.190
Period average Moyenne sur période	20.704	23.678	23.782	22.581	23.061	25.401	25.840	24.301	...
Myanmar (kyat) Myanmar (kyat)									
End of period Fin de période	6.770	6.258	5.726	5.479	5.953	5.656	5.384	5.524	5.427
Period average Moyenne sur période	6.684	6.573	6.076	5.746	5.761	5.784	5.560	5.388	5.519
Namibia (Namibia dollar) Namibie (dollar namibien)									
End of period Fin de période	12.127	8.640	6.640	5.630	6.325	6.970	6.810	9.305	7.380
Period average Moyenne sur période	8.609	10.541	7.565	6.460	6.359	6.772	7.045	8.261	8.474
Nepal (Nepalese rupee) Népal (roupie népalaise)									
End of period Fin de période	76.475	78.300	74.040	71.800	74.050	71.100	63.550	77.650	74.650
Period average Moyenne sur période	74.949	77.877	76.141	73.674	71.368	72.756	66.415	69.762	77.545
Netherlands Antilles (Netherlands Antillean guilder) Antilles néerlandaises (florin des Antilles néerlandaises)									
End of period Fin de période	1.790	1.790	1.790	1.790	1.790	1.790	1.790	1.790	1.790
Period average Moyenne sur période	1.790	1.790	1.790	1.790	1.790	1.790	1.790	1.790	1.790
New Zealand (New Zealand dollar) Nouvelle-Zélande (dollar néo-zélandais)									
End of period Fin de période	2.407	1.899	1.538	1.392	1.468	1.417	1.292	1.729	1.386
Period average Moyenne sur période	2.379	2.162	1.722	1.509	1.420	1.542	1.361	1.423	1.600
Nicaragua [1] (córdoba) Nicaragua [1] (córdoba)									
End of period Fin de période	13.841	14.671	15.552	16.329	17.146	18.003	18.903	19.848	20.841
Period average Moyenne sur période	13.372	14.251	15.105	15.937	16.733	17.570	18.449	19.372	20.340
Niger (CFA franc) Niger (franc CFA)									
End of period Fin de période	744.306	625.495	519.364	481.578	556.037	498.069	445.593	471.335	455.336
Period average Moyenne sur période	733.039	696.988	581.200	528.285	527.468	522.890	479.267	447.805	472.186
Nigeria [1] (naira) Nigéria [1] (naira)									
End of period Fin de période	112.950	126.400	136.500	132.350	129.000	128.270	117.968	132.563	149.581
Period average Moyenne sur période	111.231	120.578	129.222	132.888	131.274	128.652	125.808	118.546	148.902
Norway (Norwegian krone) Norvège (couronne norvégienne)									
End of period Fin de période	9.012	6.966	6.680	6.040	6.770	6.260	5.410	7.000	5.780
Period average Moyenne sur période	8.992	7.984	7.080	6.741	6.443	6.413	5.862	5.640	6.288
Oman (rial Omani) Oman (rial omani)									
End of period Fin de période	0.385	0.385	0.385	0.385	0.385	0.385	0.385	0.385	0.385
Period average Moyenne sur période	0.385	0.385	0.385	0.385	0.385	0.385	0.385	0.385	0.385
Pakistan (Pakistan rupee) Pakistan (roupie pakistanaise)									
End of period Fin de période	60.864	58.534	57.215	59.124	59.830	60.918	61.221	79.098	84.263
Period average Moyenne sur période	61.927	59.724	57.752	58.258	59.515	60.271	60.739	70.408	81.713
Panama (balboa) Panama (balboa)									
End of period Fin de période	1.000	1.000	1.000	1.000	1.000	1.000	1.000	1.000	1.000
Period average Moyenne sur période	1.000	1.000	1.000	1.000	1.000	1.000	1.000	1.000	1.000
Papua New Guinea (kina) Papouasie-Nvl-Guinée (kina)									
End of period Fin de période	3.762	4.019	3.333	3.125	3.096	3.030	2.837	2.677	2.703
Period average Moyenne sur période	3.389	3.895	3.563	3.223	3.102	3.057	2.965	2.700	2.755
Paraguay (guaraní) Paraguay (guaraní)									
End of period Fin de période	4 682.000	7 103.590	6 114.960	6 250.000	6 120.000	5 190.000	4 875.000	4 945.000	4 610.000
Period average Moyenne sur période	4 105.930	5 716.260	6 424.340	5 974.580	6 177.960	5 635.460	5 032.720	4 363.240	4 965.390
Peru (new sol) Pérou (nouveau sol)									
End of period Fin de période	3.444	3.514	3.463	3.282	3.430	3.196	2.996	3.140	2.890
Period average Moyenne sur période	3.507	3.517	3.478	3.413	3.296	3.274	3.128	2.924	3.012
Philippines (Philippine peso) Philippines (peso philippin)									
End of period Fin de période	51.404	53.096	55.569	56.267	53.067	49.132	41.401	47.485	46.356
Period average Moyenne sur période	50.993	51.604	54.203	56.040	55.086	51.314	46.148	44.323	47.680
Poland (zloty) Pologne (zloty)									
End of period Fin de période	3.986	3.839	3.741	2.990	3.261	2.911	2.435	2.962	2.850
Period average Moyenne sur période	4.094	4.080	3.889	3.658	3.235	3.103	2.768	2.409	3.120
Qatar (Qatar riyal) Qatar (riyal qatarien)									
End of period Fin de période	3.640	3.640	3.640	3.640	3.640	3.640	3.640	3.640	3.640
Period average Moyenne sur période	3.640	3.640	3.640	3.640	3.640	3.640	3.640	3.640	3.640
Republic of Moldova (Moldovan leu) République de Moldova (leu moldove)									
End of period Fin de période	13.091	13.822	13.220	12.461	12.832	12.905	11.319	10.400	12.302
Period average Moyenne sur période	12.865	13.571	13.945	12.330	12.600	13.131	12.140	10.392	11.110

65

Exchange rates *(continued)*
National currency per US dollar

Cours des changes *(suite)*
Valeur du dollar E.-U. en monnaie nationale

Country or area Pays ou zone	2001	2002	2003	2004	2005	2006	2007	2008	2009
Romania [1] (Romanian leu) Roumanie [1] (leu roumain)									
End of period Fin de période	3.160	3.350	3.260	2.907	3.108	2.568	2.456	2.834	2.936
Period average Moyenne sur période	2.906	3.306	3.320	3.264	2.914	2.809	2.438	2.519	3.049
Russian Federation (ruble) Fédération de Russie (ruble)									
End of period Fin de période	30.140	31.784	29.455	27.749	28.783	26.331	24.546	29.380	30.244
Period average Moyenne sur période	29.169	31.349	30.692	28.814	28.284	27.191	25.581	24.853	31.740
Rwanda (Rwanda franc) Rwanda (franc rwandais)									
End of period Fin de période	457.900	511.854	580.280	566.860	553.719	548.650	544.220	558.898	571.240
Period average Moyenne sur période	442.992	475.365	537.655	577.449	557.823	551.710	546.955	546.849	568.281
Saint Kitts and Nevis (EC dollar) Saint-Kitts-et-Nevis (dollar des Caraïbes orientales)									
End of period Fin de période	2.700	2.700	2.700	2.700	2.700	2.700	2.700	2.700	2.700
Period average Moyenne sur période	2.700	2.700	2.700	2.700	2.700	2.700	2.700	2.700	2.700
Saint Lucia (EC dollar) Sainte-Lucie (dollar des Caraïbes orientales)									
End of period Fin de période	2.700	2.700	2.700	2.700	2.700	2.700	2.700	2.700	2.700
Period average Moyenne sur période	2.700	2.700	2.700	2.700	2.700	2.700	2.700	2.700	2.700
Saint Vincent-Grenadines (EC dollar) Saint Vincent-Grenadines (dollar des Caraïbes orientales)									
End of period Fin de période	2.700	2.700	2.700	2.700	2.700	2.700	2.700	2.700	2.700
Period average Moyenne sur période	2.700	2.700	2.700	2.700	2.700	2.700	2.700	2.700	2.700
Samoa (tala) Samoa (tala)									
End of period Fin de période	3.551	3.216	2.778	2.673	2.764	2.685	2.558	2.904	2.494
Period average Moyenne sur période	3.478	3.376	2.973	2.781	2.710	2.779	2.617	2.644	2.731
San Marino (euro) Saint-Marin (euro)									
End of period Fin de période	1.135	0.954	0.792	0.734	0.848	0.759	0.679	0.719	0.694
Period average Moyenne sur période	1.118	1.063	0.886	0.805	0.804	0.797	0.731	0.683	0.720
Sao Tome and Principe (dobra) Sao Tomé-et-Principe (dobra)									
End of period Fin de période	9 019.710	9 191.840	9 455.900	10 104.000	11 929.700	13 073.900	14 362.300	15 228.100	16 814.500
Period average Moyenne sur période	8 842.110	9 088.330	9 347.580	9 902.320	10 558.000	12 448.600	13 536.800	14 695.200	16 208.500
Saudi Arabia (Saudi Arabian riyal) Arabie saoudite (riyal saoudien)									
End of period Fin de période	3.750	3.750	3.750	3.750	3.745	3.745	3.750	3.750	3.750
Period average Moyenne sur période	3.750	3.750	3.750	3.750	3.747	3.745	3.748	3.750	3.750
Senegal (CFA franc) Sénégal (franc CFA)									
End of period Fin de période	744.306	625.495	519.364	481.578	556.037	498.069	445.593	471.335	455.336
Period average Moyenne sur période	733.039	696.988	581.200	528.285	527.468	522.890	479.267	447.805	472.186
Serbia (dinar) Serbie (dinar)									
End of period Fin de période	67.670	58.985	54.637	57.936	72.219	59.976	53.727	62.900	66.729
Period average Moyenne sur période	66.914	64.398	57.585	58.381	66.714	67.146	58.454	55.724	67.581
Seychelles (Seychelles rupee) Seychelles (roupie seychelloises)									
End of period Fin de période	5.752	5.055	5.500	5.500	5.500	5.796	7.998	#16.573	11.255
Period average Moyenne sur période	5.858	5.480	5.401	5.500	5.500	5.520	6.701	9.457	13.610
Sierra Leone (leone) Sierra Leone (leone)									
End of period Fin de période	2 161.270	2 191.730	2 562.180	2 860.490	2 932.520	2 973.940	2 977.600	3 042.240	3 855.680
Period average Moyenne sur période	1 986.150	2 099.030	2 347.940	2 701.300	2 889.590	2 961.910	2 985.190	2 981.510	3 385.650
Singapore (Singapore dollar) Singapour (dollar singapourien)									
End of period Fin de période	1.851	1.737	1.701	1.634	1.664	1.534	1.441	1.439	1.403
Period average Moyenne sur période	1.792	1.791	1.742	1.690	1.664	1.589	1.507	1.415	1.455
Slovakia (Slovak koruna) [1] Slovaquie (couronne slovaque) [1]									
End of period Fin de période	48.467	40.036	32.920	28.496	31.948	26.246	22.870	21.385	...
Period average Moyenne sur période	48.355	45.327	36.773	32.257	31.018	29.697	24.694	21.361	...
Slovenia (tolar) Slovénie (tolar)									
End of period Fin de période	250.946	221.071	189.367	176.243	202.430	181.931	...	...	...
Period average Moyenne sur période	242.749	240.248	207.114	192.381	192.705	191.028	...	...	...
Solomon Islands (Solomon Islands dollar) Iles Salomon (dollar des Iles Salomon)									
End of period Fin de période	5.565	7.457	7.491	7.508	7.576	7.616	7.663	8.000	8.065
Period average Moyenne sur période	5.278	6.749	7.506	7.485	7.530	7.609	7.652	7.748	8.055
South Africa [1] (rand) Afrique du Sud [1] (rand)									
End of period Fin de période	12.127	8.640	6.640	5.630	6.325	6.970	6.810	9.305	7.380
Period average Moyenne sur période	8.609	10.541	7.565	6.460	6.359	6.772	7.045	8.261	8.474
Sri Lanka (Sri Lanka rupee) Sri Lanka (roupie sri-lankaise)									
End of period Fin de période	93.159	96.725	96.738	104.605	102.117	107.706	108.719	113.140	114.384
Period average Moyenne sur période	89.383	95.662	96.521	101.194	100.498	103.914	110.623	108.334	114.945
Sudan [1] (Sudanese pound) Soudan [1] (livre soudanaise)									
End of period Fin de période	2.614	2.617	2.602	2.506	2.305	2.013	2.053	2.184	2.240
Period average Moyenne sur période	2.587	2.633	2.610	2.579	2.436	2.172	2.016	2.090	2.302

Exchange rates *(continued)*
National currency per US dollar

Cours des changes *(suite)*
Valeur du dollar E.-U. en monnaie nationale

Country or area / Pays ou zone	2001	2002	2003	2004	2005	2006	2007	2008	2009
Suriname (Surinamese dollar) Suriname (dollar surinamais)									
End of period Fin de période	2.179	2.515	2.625	2.715	2.740	2.745	2.745	2.745	2.745
Period average Moyenne sur période	2.178	2.347	#2.601	2.734	2.732	2.744	2.745	2.745	2.745
Swaziland (lilangeni) Swaziland (lilangeni)									
End of period Fin de période	12.127	8.640	6.640	5.630	6.325	6.970	6.810	9.305	7.380
Period average Moyenne sur période	8.609	10.541	7.565	6.460	6.359	6.772	7.045	8.261	8.474
Sweden (Swedish krona) Suède (couronne suédoise)									
End of period Fin de période	10.668	8.825	7.189	6.615	7.958	6.864	6.414	7.811	7.117
Period average Moyenne sur période	10.329	9.737	8.086	7.349	7.473	7.378	6.759	6.591	7.654
Switzerland (Swiss franc) Suisse (franc suisse)									
End of period Fin de période	1.677	1.387	1.237	1.132	1.314	1.220	1.126	1.064	1.031
Period average Moyenne sur période	1.688	1.559	1.347	1.244	1.245	1.254	1.200	1.083	1.088
Syrian Arab Republic (Syrian pound) [1] Rép. arabe syrienne (livre syrienne) [1]									
End of period Fin de période	11.225	11.225	11.225	11.225	11.225	11.225	11.225	11.225	11.225
Period average Moyenne sur période	11.225	11.225	11.225	11.225	11.225	11.225	...	...	...
Tajikistan (somoni) Tadjikistan (somoni)									
End of period Fin de période	2.550	3.000	2.957	3.037	3.199	3.427	3.465	3.452	4.371
Period average Moyenne sur période	2.372	2.764	3.061	2.971	3.117	3.298	3.442	3.431	4.143
Thailand (baht) Thaïlande (baht)									
End of period Fin de période	44.222	43.152	39.591	39.061	41.030	36.046	33.718	34.898	33.320
Period average Moyenne sur période	44.432	42.960	41.485	40.222	40.220	37.882	34.518	33.313	34.286
TFYR of Macedonia (TFYR Macedonian denar) L'ex-R.Y. Macédoine (denar de l'ex-R.Y. Macédoine)									
End of period Fin de période	69.172	58.598	49.050	45.068	51.859	46.450	41.656	43.561	42.665
Period average Moyenne sur période	68.037	64.350	54.322	49.410	49.284	48.802	44.730	41.868	44.101
Togo (CFA franc) Togo (franc CFA)									
End of period Fin de période	744.306	625.495	519.364	481.578	556.037	498.069	445.593	471.335	455.336
Period average Moyenne sur période	733.039	696.988	581.200	528.285	527.468	522.890	479.267	447.805	472.186
Tonga (pa'anga) Tonga (pa'anga)									
End of period Fin de période	2.207	2.229	2.020	1.912	2.060	2.000	1.887	2.134	1.904
Period average Moyenne sur période	2.124	2.195	2.146	1.972	1.943	2.026	1.971	1.942	2.034
Trinidad and Tobago (Trinidad and Tobago dollar) Trinité-et-Tobago (dollar de la Trinité-et-Tobago)									
End of period Fin de période	6.290	6.300	6.300	6.300	6.310	6.312	6.341	6.299	6.374
Period average Moyenne sur période	6.233	6.249	6.295	6.299	6.300	6.312	6.328	6.289	6.325
Tunisia (Tunisian dinar) Tunisie (dinar tunisien)									
End of period Fin de période	1.468	1.334	1.208	1.199	1.363	1.297	1.221	1.310	1.317
Period average Moyenne sur période	1.439	1.422	1.288	1.245	1.297	1.331	1.281	1.232	1.350
Turkey (new Turkish Lira) Turquie (nouveau livre turque)									
End of period Fin de période	1.450	1.644	1.397	1.340	1.345	1.409	1.171	1.525	1.491
Period average Moyenne sur période	1.226	1.507	1.501	1.426	1.344	1.428	1.303	1.302	1.550
Turkmenistan (Turkmen manat) Turkménistan (manat turkmène)									
End of period Fin de période	5 200.000	...	...	...	...	...	...	...	...
Period average Moyenne sur période	5 200.000	...	...	...	...	...	...	...	...
Uganda [1] (Uganda shilling) Ouganda [1] (shilling ougandais)									
End of period Fin de période	1 727.400	1 852.570	1 935.320	1 738.590	1 816.860	1 741.440	1 697.340	1 949.180	1 903.520
Period average Moyenne sur période	1 755.660	1 797.550	1 963.720	1 810.300	1 780.670	1 831.450	1 723.490	1 720.440	2 030.310
Ukraine (hryvnia) Ukraine (hryvnia)									
End of period Fin de période	5.299	5.332	5.332	5.305	5.050	5.050	5.050	7.700	7.985
Period average Moyenne sur période	5.372	5.327	5.333	5.319	5.125	5.050	5.050	5.267	7.791
United Arab Emirates (UAE dirham) Emirats arabes unis (dirham des EAU)									
End of period Fin de période	3.673	3.673	3.673	3.673	3.673	3.673	3.673	3.673	3.673
Period average Moyenne sur période	3.673	3.673	3.673	3.673	3.673	3.673	3.673	3.673	3.673
United Kingdom (pound sterling) Royaume-Uni (livre sterling)									
End of period Fin de période	0.689	0.620	0.560	0.518	0.581	0.509	0.499	0.686	0.617
Period average Moyenne sur période	0.695	0.667	0.612	0.546	0.550	0.543	0.500	0.544	0.642
United Rep. of Tanzania (Tanzania shilling) Rép.-Unie de Tanzanie (shilling tanzanien)									
End of period Fin de période	916.300	976.300	1 063.620	1 042.960	1 165.510	1 261.640	1 132.090	1 280.300	1 326.830
Period average Moyenne sur période	876.412	966.583	1 038.420	1 089.330	1 128.930	1 251.900	1 245.040	1 196.310	1 320.310
United States (US dollar) Etats-Unis (dollar des Etats-Unis)									
End of period Fin de période	1.000	1.000	1.000	1.000	1.000	1.000	1.000	1.000	1.000
Period average Moyenne sur période	1.000	1.000	1.000	1.000	1.000	1.000	1.000	1.000	1.000
Uruguay (Uruguayan peso) Uruguay (peso uruguayen)									
End of period Fin de période	14.768	27.200	29.300	26.350	24.100	24.400	21.500	24.350	19.627
Period average Moyenne sur période	13.319	21.257	28.209	28.704	24.479	24.073	23.471	20.949	22.568

65 Exchange rates *(continued)*

National currency per US dollar

Cours des changes *(suite)*

Valeur du dollar E.-U. en monnaie nationale

Country or area Pays ou zone	2001	2002	2003	2004	2005	2006	2007	2008	2009
Vanuatu (vatu) Vanuatu (vatu)									
End of period Fin de période	146.740	133.170	111.810	106.530	112.330	106.480	99.860	112.620	97.930
Period average Moyenne sur période	145.313	139.198	122.189	111.790	109.246	110.641	102.438	101.334	106.741
Venezuela (Boliv. Rep. of) (bolívar) Venezuela (Rép. boliv. du) (bolívar)									
End of period Fin de période	0.763	1.401	1.598	1.918	2.147	2.147	2.147	2.147	2.147
Period average Moyenne sur période	0.724	1.161	1.607	1.891	2.090	2.147	2.147	2.147	2.147
Viet Nam (dong) Viet Nam (dong)									
End of period Fin de période	15 084.000	15 403.000	15 646.000	15 777.000	15 916.000	16 054.000	16 114.000	16 977.000	17 941.000
Period average Moyenne sur période	14 725.200	15 279.500	15 509.600	15 746.000	15 858.900	15 994.300	16 105.100	16 302.300	17 065.100
Yemen (Yemeni rial) Yémen (rial yéménite)									
End of period Fin de période	173.270	179.010	184.310	185.870	195.080	198.500	199.540	200.080	207.320
Period average Moyenne sur période	168.672	175.625	183.448	184.776	191.509	197.049	198.953	199.764	202.847
Zambia (Zambia kwacha) Zambie (kwacha zambie)									
End of period Fin de période	3 830.400	4 334.400	4 645.480	4 771.310	3 508.980	4 406.670	3 844.810	4 832.260	4 640.560
Period average Moyenne sur période	3 610.940	4 398.590	4 733.270	4 778.880	4 463.500	3 603.070	4 002.520	3 745.660	5 046.110
Zimbabwe (Zimbabwe dollar) Zimbabwe (dollar zimbabwéen)									
End of period Fin de période	0.057	0.057	0.853	5.936	80.774	258.920	30 000.000	4.900[4]	...
Period average Moyenne sur période	0.055	0.055	0.697	5.069	22.364	164.361	9 675.780	6 715.420[4]	...

Source:

International Monetary Fund (IMF), Washington, D.C., database on International Financial Statistics, last accessed August 2010.

Source:

Fonds monétaire international (FMI), Washington, D.C., la base de données de Statistiques Financières Internationales, dernier accès août 2010.

1 Principal rate.

2 A unified floating exchange rate regime was introduced on 11 Feb. 2002, with the exchange rate determined by market conditions.

3 "Euro Area" is an official descriptor for the European Economic and Monetary Union (EMU). The participating member states of the EMU are Austria, Belgium, Cyprus (beginning 2008), Finland, France, Germany, Greece (beginning 2001), Ireland, Italy, Luxembourg, Malta (beginning 2008), Netherlands, Portugal, Slovakia (beginning 2009), Slovenia (beginning 2007), and Spain.

4 Figures in millions.

1 Taux principal.

2 Un régime de taux de change flottant unifié a été introduit le 11 février 2002, le taux de change étant déterminé par le marché.

3 L'expression "zone euro" est un intitulé officiel pour l'Union économique et monétaire (UEM) européenne. L'UEM est composée des pays membres suivants : Allemagne, Autriche, Belgique, Chypre (à partir de 2008), Espagne, Finlande, France, Grèce (à partir de 2001), Irlande, Italie, Luxembourg, Malte (à partir de 2008), Pays-Bas, Portugal, Slovaquie (à partir de 2009) et Slovénie (à partir de 2007).

4 Chiffres en millions.

66 International reserves minus gold

Millions of US dollars, end of period

Réserves internationales, moins l'or

Millions de dollars E.-U., fin de période

Country or area Pays ou zone	2000	2001	2002	2003	2004	2005	2006	2007	2008	2009
Albania Albanie										
Total reserves minus gold Rés. totale, moins l'or	615.6	739.9	838.8	1 009.4	1 357.6	1 404.1	1 768.8	2 104.2	2 319.8	2 313.9
Foreign exchange Devises étrangères	535.3	654.2	752.6	913.8	1 251.6	1 386.8	1 754.8	2 097.0	2 307.4	2 229.6
Algeria Algérie										
Total reserves minus gold Rés. totale, moins l'or	12 023.9	18 081.4	23 237.5	33 125.2	43 246.4	56 303.1	77 913.7	110 318.0	143 243.0	149 041.0
Foreign exchange Devises étrangères	11 910.0	17 963.0	23 108.0	32 942.0	43 113.0	56 178.0	77 781.0	110 180.0	143 102.0	147 221.0
Angola Angola										
Total reserves minus gold Rés. totale, moins l'or	1 198.2	731.9	375.5	634.2	1 374.1	3 196.9	8 598.6	11 196.8	17 869.4	13 664.1
Foreign exchange Devises étrangères	1 198.0	731.7	375.4	634.0	1 373.8	3 196.6	8 598.4	11 196.5	17 869.2	13 238.4
Anguilla Anguilla										
Total reserves minus gold Rés. totale, moins l'or	20.3	24.2	26.2	33.3	34.3	39.7	41.8	44.9	41.0	37.5
Foreign exchange Devises étrangères	20.3	24.2	26.2	33.3	34.3	39.7	41.8	44.9	41.0	37.5
Antigua and Barbuda Antigua-et-Barbuda										
Total reserves minus gold Rés. totale, moins l'or	63.6	79.7	87.6	113.8	120.1	127.3	142.6	143.8	138.0	127.9
Foreign exchange Devises étrangères	63.6	79.7	87.6	113.7	120.1	127.3	142.6	143.8	138.0	108.2
Argentina Argentine										
Total reserves minus gold Rés. totale, moins l'or	25 146.9	14 553.1	10 489.3	14 153.4	18 884.3	27 178.9	30 903.5	44 682.1	44 854.6	46 093.0
Foreign exchange Devises étrangères	24 414.4	14 542.4	10 395.1	13 144.8	18 007.5	22 742.0	30 420.9	44 175.1	44 360.4	42 922.3
Armenia Arménie										
Total reserves minus gold Rés. totale, moins l'or	302.0	317.2	415.6	502.0	547.8	669.5	1 071.9	1 659.1	1 406.8	2 003.6
Foreign exchange Devises étrangères	280.4	307.0	385.5	483.1	535.8	659.3	1 058.0	1 649.5	1 403.9	1 879.0
Aruba Aruba										
Total reserves minus gold Rés. totale, moins l'or	208.0	293.7	339.7	295.2	295.4	273.5	337.8	372.1	604.9	578.2
Foreign exchange Devises étrangères	208.0	293.7	339.7	295.2	295.4	273.5	337.8	372.1	604.9	578.2
Australia Australie										
Total reserves minus gold Rés. totale, moins l'or	18 118.1	17 955.3	20 688.5	32 188.7	35 802.5	41 941.2	53 448.1	24 768.5	30 690.9	38 950.2
Foreign exchange Devises étrangères	16 781.8	16 434.2	18 617.8	29 966.2	33 901.3	40 972.0	52 820.9	24 236.9	29 867.3	33 001.7
Austria Autriche										
Total reserves minus gold Rés. totale, moins l'or	14 318.6	12 509.1	9 683.2	8 470.0	7 858.4	6 839.1	7 010.0	10 688.5	8 912.0	8 114.3
Foreign exchange Devises étrangères	13 492.2	11 443.7	8 539.6	7 143.5	6 762.8	6 298.4	6 573.2	10 260.5	8 244.4	4 781.4
Azerbaijan Azerbaïdjan										
Total reserves minus gold Rés. totale, moins l'or	679.6	725.0	720.5	802.8	1 075.1	1 177.7	2 500.4	4 273.1	6 467.2	5 363.8
Foreign exchange Devises étrangères	673.0	722.5	719.8	784.8	1 060.5	1 163.8	2 484.9	4 262.9	6 465.5	5 125.7
Bahamas Bahamas										
Total reserves minus gold Rés. totale, moins l'or	349.6	319.3	380.6	491.1	674.4	586.3	461.3	464.5	567.9	1 009.8
Foreign exchange Devises étrangères	341.4	311.3	372.1	481.8	664.7	577.3	451.9	454.5	558.2	821.0

66 International reserves minus gold *(continued)*

Millions of US dollars, end of period

Réserves internationales, moins l'or *(suite)*

Millions de dollars des E.-U., fin de période

Country or area Pays ou zone	2000	2001	2002	2003	2004	2005	2006	2007	2008	2009
Bahrain Bahreïn										
Total reserves minus gold Rés. totale, moins l'or	1 564.1	1 684.0	1 725.8	1 778.4	1 940.5	...	...	...	...	...
Foreign exchange Devises étrangères	1 478.3	1 598.5	1 631.4	1 673.8	1 829.6	...	...	...	...	...
Bangladesh Bangladesh										
Total reserves minus gold Rés. totale, moins l'or	1 486.0	1 275.0	1 683.2	2 577.9	3 172.4	2 767.2	3 805.6	5 183.4	5 689.3	10 218.9
Foreign exchange Devises étrangères	1 485.3	1 273.6	1 680.7	2 574.4	3 170.9	2 766.0	3 803.9	5 182.2	5 686.7	9 499.9
Barbados Barbade										
Total reserves minus gold Rés. totale, moins l'or	472.7	690.4	668.5	737.9	579.9	603.5	636.1	839.4	738.5	871.1
Foreign exchange Devises étrangères	466.6	684.4	661.9	730.5	571.8	595.9	627.9	830.5	729.8	773.8
Belarus Bélarus										
Total reserves minus gold Rés. totale, moins l'or	350.5	390.7	618.8	594.8	749.4	1 136.6	1 068.6	3 952.1	2 687.0	4 831.4
Foreign exchange Devises étrangères	350.3	390.3	618.5	594.8	749.3	1 136.6	1 068.5	3 952.1	2 686.0	4 253.0
Belgium Belgique										
Total reserves minus gold Rés. totale, moins l'or	9 994.4	11 266.2	11 855.1	10 989.4	10 361.1	8 241.2	8 783.4	10 383.9	9 318.4	15 906.6
Foreign exchange Devises étrangères	7 988.3	8 743.4	8 908.7	7 651.3	7 714.9	6 815.1	7 618.9	9 297.8	7 767.1	7 800.9
Belize Belize										
Total reserves minus gold Rés. totale, moins l'or	122.9	112.0	114.5	84.7	48.3	71.4	113.7	108.5	166.2	213.7
Foreign exchange Devises étrangères	115.8	105.0	106.7	76.1	39.1	62.8	104.4	98.4	156.1	175.4
Benin Bénin										
Total reserves minus gold Rés. totale, moins l'or	458.1	578.1	615.7	717.9	640.0	656.8	912.2	1 209.2	1 263.4	1 229.8
Foreign exchange Devises étrangères	455.2	574.9	612.6	714.4	636.5	653.5	908.9	1 205.6	1 259.9	1 148.5
Bhutan Bhoutan										
Total reserves minus gold Rés. totale, moins l'or	317.6	323.4	354.9	366.6	398.6	467.4	545.3	699.0	764.8	...
Foreign exchange Devises étrangères	316.1	321.8	353.2	364.7	396.6	465.5	543.3	696.8	762.6	...
Bolivia (Plurinational State of) Bolivie (État plurinational de)										
Total reserves minus gold Rés. totale, moins l'or	926.4	886.4	580.5	716.8	872.4	1 327.6	2 614.8	4 554.0	6 927.4	7 583.8
Foreign exchange Devises étrangères	879.3	840.9	531.2	663.3	817.3	1 276.7	2 561.2	4 497.7	6 871.4	7 311.3
Bosnia and Herzegovina Bosnie-Herzégovine										
Total reserves minus gold Rés. totale, moins l'or	496.6	1 221.2	1 321.4	1 795.6	2 407.9	2 530.9	3 371.6	4 524.8	3 515.5	3 245.2
Foreign exchange Devises étrangères	485.9	1 215.1	1 318.2	1 792.2	2 407.4	2 530.5	3 371.3	4 524.5	3 515.3	3 240.9
Botswana Botswana										
Total reserves minus gold Rés. totale, moins l'or	6 318.2	5 897.3	5 473.9	5 339.8	5 661.4	6 309.1	7 992.4	9 789.7	9 118.6	8 704.0
Foreign exchange Devises étrangères	6 256.2	5 829.6	5 397.2	5 244.9	5 576.1	6 247.6	7 927.5	9 722.0	9 044.7	8 540.6
Brazil Brésil										
Total reserves minus gold Rés. totale, moins l'or	32 434.0	35 563.0	37 462.0	48 846.6	52 461.8	53 245.2	85 156.2	179 433.0	192 844.0	237 364.0
Foreign exchange Devises étrangères	32 433.6	35 552.5	37 187.3	48 844.3	52 457.6	53 216.4	85 147.8	179 431.0	192 842.0	231 888.0

66 International reserves minus gold *(continued)*

Millions of US dollars, end of period

Réserves internationales, moins l'or *(suite)*

Millions de dollars des E.-U., fin de période

Country or area Pays ou zone	2000	2001	2002	2003	2004	2005	2006	2007	2008	2009
Brunei Darussalam Brunéi Darussalam										
Total reserves minus gold Rés. totale, moins l'or	408.3	381.8	449.0	474.7	488.9	491.9	513.6	667.5	751.2	1 357.3
Foreign exchange Devises étrangères	355.8	329.6	369.1	376.5	384.7	431.2	459.8	625.5	710.5	996.7
Bulgaria Bulgarie										
Total reserves minus gold Rés. totale, moins l'or	3 154.9	3 290.8	4 407.1	6 291.0	8 776.3	8 040.5	10 943.0	16 477.9	16 815.5	17 127.3
Foreign exchange Devises étrangères	3 027.6	3 247.3	4 361.8	6 174.6	8 712.1	7 992.4	10 892.1	16 424.2	16 757.4	16 116.8
Burkina Faso Burkina Faso										
Total reserves minus gold Rés. totale, moins l'or	243.6	260.5	313.4	752.2	669.1	438.4	554.9	1 029.2	927.6	1 295.8
Foreign exchange Devises étrangères	233.8	250.9	303.1	741.1	657.6	427.7	543.7	1 017.4	916.1	1 208.8
Burundi Burundi										
Total reserves minus gold Rés. totale, moins l'or	32.9	17.7	58.8	67.0	65.8	100.1	130.5	176.3	265.7	322.0
Foreign exchange Devises étrangères	25.2	17.2	58.1	66.3	64.8	99.3	129.7	175.4	265.0	217.0
Cambodia Cambodge										
Total reserves minus gold Rés. totale, moins l'or	501.7	586.8	776.1	815.5	943.2	953.0	1 157.3	1 806.9	2 291.6	2 851.1
Foreign exchange Devises étrangères	501.5	586.3	775.6	815.3	943.1	952.7	1 157.1	1 806.7	2 291.4	2 743.7
Cameroon Cameroun										
Total reserves minus gold Rés. totale, moins l'or	212.0	331.8	629.7	639.6	829.3	949.4	1 716.2	2 906.8	3 086.4	3 675.5
Foreign exchange Devises étrangères	203.6	331.1	627.7	637.2	827.6	946.2	1 710.5	2 900.7	3 080.6	3 430.5
Canada Canada										
Total reserves minus gold Rés. totale, moins l'or	32 102.3	33 961.8	36 984.1	36 222.1	34 428.7	32 962.1	34 993.8	40 991.2	43 777.5	54 237.8
Foreign exchange Devises étrangères	29 019.0	30 484.0	32 685.0	31 537.0	30 166.0	30 664.0	33 198.0	39 314.0	41 537.0	42 602.0
Cape Verde Cap-Vert										
Total reserves minus gold Rés. totale, moins l'or	28.3	45.4	79.8	93.6	139.5	174.0	254.5	364.5	361.5	366.2
Foreign exchange Devises étrangères	28.2	45.4	79.8	93.6	139.5	173.9	254.4	364.3	361.2	353.3
Central African Rep. Rép. centrafricaine										
Total reserves minus gold Rés. totale, moins l'or	133.3	118.8	123.2	132.4	148.3	139.2	125.3	82.6	121.8	210.6
Foreign exchange Devises étrangères	133.1	118.6	123.1	132.2	145.6	138.9	124.4	81.6	121.5	205.9
Chad Tchad										
Total reserves minus gold Rés. totale, moins l'or	110.7	122.4	218.7	187.1	221.7	225.6	625.1	955.1	1 345.5	616.7
Foreign exchange Devises étrangères	110.3	122.0	218.3	186.7	221.2	225.1	624.6	954.5	1 344.9	612.0
Chile Chili										
Total reserves minus gold Rés. totale, moins l'or	15 034.9	14 379.0	15 341.1	15 839.6	15 993.8	16 929.2	19 392.0	16 836.8	23 072.4	25 283.5
Foreign exchange Devises étrangères	14 686.1	14 041.3	14 813.9	15 211.0	15 495.4	16 689.1	19 224.9	16 695.3	22 848.6	23 849.3
China[1] Chine[1]										
Total reserves minus gold Rés. totale, moins l'or	168 278.0	215 605.0	291 128.0	408 151.0	614 500.0	821 514.0	1 068 490.0	1 530 280.0	1 949 260.0	2 416 040.0
Foreign exchange Devises étrangères	165 574.0	212 165.0	286 407.0	403 251.0	609 932.0	818 872.0	1 066 340.0	1 528 250.0	1 946 030.0	2 399 150.0

66 International reserves minus gold *(continued)*

Millions of US dollars, end of period

Réserves internationales, moins l'or *(suite)*

Millions de dollars des E.-U., fin de période

Country or area Pays ou zone	2000	2001	2002	2003	2004	2005	2006	2007	2008	2009
China, Hong Kong SAR Chine, Hong Kong RAS										
Total reserves minus gold Rés. totale, moins l'or	107 542.0	111 155.0	111 896.0	118 360.0	123 540.0	124 244.0	133 168.0	152 637.0	182 469.0	255 768.0
Foreign exchange Devises étrangères	107 542.0	111 155.0	111 896.0	118 360.0	123 540.0	124 244.0	133 168.0	152 637.0	182 469.0	255 768.0
China, Macao SAR Chine, Macao RAS										
Total reserves minus gold Rés. totale, moins l'or	3 323.0	3 508.4	3 800.3	4 343.4	5 436.1	6 689.4	9 132.1	13 229.9	15 930.1	18 350.3
Foreign exchange Devises étrangères	3 323.0	3 508.4	3 800.3	4 343.4	5 436.1	6 689.4	9 132.1	13 229.9	15 930.1	18 350.3
Colombia Colombie										
Total reserves minus gold Rés. totale, moins l'or	8 916.0	10 153.7	10 732.4	10 783.9	13 393.8	14 787.0	15 296.2	20 767.3	23 478.8	24 747.7
Foreign exchange Devises étrangères	8 409.0	9 659.0	10 190.0	10 188.0	12 769.0	14 206.0	14 673.0	20 096.0	22 810.0	23 158.0
Comoros Comores										
Total reserves minus gold Rés. totale, moins l'or	43.2	62.3	79.9	94.3	103.7	85.8	93.5	117.2	112.2	...
Foreign exchange Devises étrangères	42.3	61.6	79.2	93.5	102.9	85.0	92.7	116.3	111.3	...
Congo Congo										
Total reserves minus gold Rés. totale, moins l'or	222.0	68.9	31.6	34.8	119.6	731.8	1 840.9	2 174.3	3 871.8	3 806.3
Foreign exchange Devises étrangères	221.3	68.0	27.7	33.4	111.5	728.6	1 839.9	2 173.2	3 870.7	3 695.5
Costa Rica Costa Rica										
Total reserves minus gold Rés. totale, moins l'or	1 317.8	1 329.8	1 501.7	1 839.2	1 921.8	2 312.7	3 114.6	4 113.6	3 798.7	4 066.2
Foreign exchange Devises étrangères	1 291.3	1 304.6	1 474.4	1 809.4	1 890.6	2 284.0	3 084.5	4 081.9	3 767.5	3 826.5
Côte d'Ivoire Côte d'Ivoire										
Total reserves minus gold Rés. totale, moins l'or	667.9	1 019.0	1 863.3	1 303.9	1 693.6	1 321.6	1 797.7	2 519.0	2 252.7	3 266.8
Foreign exchange Devises étrangères	666.2	1 017.9	1 861.5	1 302.7	1 692.5	1 320.0	1 795.7	2 517.3	2 250.3	2 838.1
Croatia Croatie										
Total reserves minus gold Rés. totale, moins l'or	3 524.4	4 703.2	5 884.9	8 190.5	8 758.2	8 800.3	11 487.8	13 674.5	12 957.3	14 894.5
Foreign exchange Devises étrangères	3 376.9	4 595.6	5 883.2	8 190.2	8 757.9	8 799.8	11 487.4	13 674.0	12 956.8	14 419.0
Cyprus Chypre										
Total reserves minus gold Rés. totale, moins l'or	1 741.1	2 267.8	3 022.1	3 256.7	3 910.0	4 191.1	5 646.8	6 118.6	#616.8	796.2
Foreign exchange Devises étrangères	1 694.0	2 221.9	2 953.2	3 154.5	3 832.7	4 155.9	5 621.5	6 100.1	#585.5	562.9
Czech Republic République tchèque										
Total reserves minus gold Rés. totale, moins l'or	13 019.2	14 341.2	23 555.6	26 770.6	28 259.3	29 330.4	31 181.7	34 549.6	36 654.5	41 156.6
Foreign exchange Devises étrangères	13 015.9	14 189.0	23 315.2	26 293.8	27 844.1	29 137.7	31 053.7	34 445.2	36 471.6	39 669.8
Dem. Rep. of the Congo Rép. dém. du Congo										
Total reserves minus gold Rés. totale, moins l'or	...	...	73.9	97.8	236.2	131.2	154.5	180.7	77.7	...
Foreign exchange Devises étrangères	...	...	65.5	89.8	230.7	129.8	154.2	177.4	71.8	...
Denmark Danemark										
Total reserves minus gold Rés. totale, moins l'or	15 108.2	17 110.2	26 985.7	37 105.0	39 083.7	#32 930.4	29 723.7	32 534.4	40 465.8	74 290.9
Foreign exchange Devises étrangères	14 469.0	16 117.0	25 901.0	36 004.0	38 196.0	#32 510.0	29 160.0	32 029.0	39 823.0	71 259.0

66

International reserves minus gold *(continued)*
Millions of US dollars, end of period

Réserves internationales, moins l'or *(suite)*
Millions de dollars des E.-U., fin de période

Country or area Pays ou zone	2000	2001	2002	2003	2004	2005	2006	2007	2008	2009
Djibouti Djibouti										
Total reserves minus gold Rés. totale, moins l'or	67.8	70.3	73.7	100.1	93.9	89.3	120.3	132.1	175.5	241.8
Foreign exchange Devises étrangères	66.0	68.8	71.2	98.4	91.2	87.7	117.8	130.3	173.7	219.6
Dominica Dominique										
Total reserves minus gold Rés. totale, moins l'or	29.4	31.2	45.5	47.7	42.3	49.2	63.0	60.5	55.2	75.5
Foreign exchange Devises étrangères	29.4	31.2	45.5	47.7	42.3	49.1	63.0	60.5	55.1	64.5
Dominican Republic Rép. dominicaine										
Total reserves minus gold Rés. totale, moins l'or	627.2	1 099.5	468.4	253.1	798.3	1 843.2	2 115.6	2 546.4	2 271.6	2 885.1
Foreign exchange Devises étrangères	626.8	1 099.0	468.1	253.0	796.7	1 842.6	2 091.2	2 447.8	2 235.6	2 609.5
Ecuador Equateur										
Total reserves minus gold Rés. totale, moins l'or	946.9	839.8	714.6	812.6	1 069.6	1 714.2	1 489.5	2 816.4	3 738.2	2 873.2
Foreign exchange Devises étrangères	924.3	815.9	689.4	786.1	986.9	1 667.9	1 456.1	2 764.9	3 685.5	2 819.8
Egypt Egypte										
Total reserves minus gold Rés. totale, moins l'or	13 117.6	12 925.8	13 242.4	13 588.7	14 273.2	20 609.1	24 461.6	30 187.7	32 216.1	32 253.0
Foreign exchange Devises étrangères	12 913.0	12 891.0	13 151.0	13 400.0	14 108.0	20 508.0	24 341.0	30 054.0	32 108.0	30 947.0
El Salvador El Salvador										
Total reserves minus gold Rés. totale, moins l'or	1 772.6	1 593.7	1 472.8	1 792.3	1 754.0	1 722.8	1 814.9	2 110.0	2 443.1	2 868.8
Foreign exchange Devises étrangères	1 740.0	1 562.3	1 438.9	1 755.2	1 715.2	1 687.1	1 777.3	2 070.5	2 404.6	2 612.0
Equatorial Guinea Guinée équatoriale										
Total reserves minus gold Rés. totale, moins l'or	23.0	70.9	88.5	237.7	945.0	2 102.5	3 066.7	3 845.9	4 431.2	3 251.9
Foreign exchange Devises étrangères	22.9	69.9	87.9	237.7	944.3	2 101.9	3 066.1	3 845.2	4 430.5	3 211.3
Eritrea Erythrée										
Total reserves minus gold Rés. totale, moins l'or	25.5	39.8	30.3	24.7	34.7	27.9	25.4	34.3	57.9	...
Foreign exchange Devises étrangères	25.5	39.7	30.3	24.7	34.7	27.9	25.3	34.3	57.9	...
Estonia Estonie										
Total reserves minus gold Rés. totale, moins l'or	920.6	820.2	1 000.4	1 373.4	1 788.2	1 943.2	2 781.2	3 262.7	3 964.9	3 971.9
Foreign exchange Devises étrangères	920.6	820.2	1 000.3	1 373.3	1 788.1	1 943.1	2 781.1	3 262.6	3 964.8	3 874.7
Ethiopia Ethiopie										
Total reserves minus gold Rés. totale, moins l'or	306.3	433.2	881.7	955.6	1 496.8	1 042.6	867.4	1 289.9	870.5	1 780.9
Foreign exchange Devises étrangères	297.1	424.1	871.9	944.8	1 485.1	1 032.1	856.3	1 278.1	859.0	1 741.7
Euro Area Zone euro										
Total reserves minus gold Rés. totale, moins l'or	242 854.0	235 147.0	247 460.0	223 507.0	212 291.0	184 917.0	197 193.0	215 444.0	218 766.0	282 824.0
Foreign exchange Devises étrangères	218 633.0	207 817.0	215 812.0	188 173.0	181 196.0	167 150.0	184 034.0	203 189.0	201 969.0	194 411.0
Fiji Fidji										
Total reserves minus gold Rés. totale, moins l'or	411.8	366.4	358.8	423.6	478.1	314.7	...	...	...	...
Foreign exchange Devises étrangères	386.5	341.5	331.5	393.3	446.1	284.9	...	...	...	...

66 International reserves minus gold *(continued)*

Millions of US dollars, end of period

Réserves internationales, moins l'or *(suite)*

Millions de dollars des E.-U., fin de période

Country or area Pays ou zone	2000	2001	2002	2003	2004	2005	2006	2007	2008	2009
Finland Finlande										
Total reserves minus gold Rés. totale, moins l'or	7 976.9	7 983.4	9 285.0	10 514.9	12 221.5	10 521.1	6 494.2	7 063.2	6 979.4	9 710.6
Foreign exchange Devises étrangères	7 340.7	7 197.6	8 436.8	9 544.5	11 425.3	10 075.8	6 134.6	6 689.2	6 492.3	7 403.2
France France										
Total reserves minus gold Rés. totale, moins l'or	37 039.2	31 749.1	28 365.3	30 186.5	35 314.0	27 752.9	42 651.6	45 709.7	33 617.5	46 633.5
Foreign exchange Devises étrangères	32 114.3	26 363.2	21 965.0	23 121.7	29 076.7	23 996.3	40 287.0	43 587.4	30 382.2	27 728.7
Gabon Gabon										
Total reserves minus gold Rés. totale, moins l'or	190.1	9.9	139.7	196.6	443.4	668.6	1 113.4	1 227.2	1 923.5	1 993.2
Foreign exchange Devises étrangères	189.8	9.6	139.4	196.3	436.9	668.1	1 112.2	1 226.0	1 922.3	1 784.2
Gambia Gambie										
Total reserves minus gold Rés. totale, moins l'or	109.4	106.0	106.9	59.3	83.8	98.3	120.6	142.8	116.5	224.2
Foreign exchange Devises étrangères	107.3	104.1	104.8	57.1	80.7	96.0	116.9	140.2	114.1	183.3
Georgia Géorgie										
Total reserves minus gold Rés. totale, moins l'or	116.0	161.9	202.2	196.2	386.7	478.6	930.8	1 361.2	1 480.2	2 110.3
Foreign exchange Devises étrangères	112.7	158.0	199.3	191.3	375.4	477.6	929.9	1 346.3	1 467.8	1 891.6
Germany Allemagne										
Total reserves minus gold Rés. totale, moins l'or	56 890.5	51 403.9	51 170.6	50 694.0	48 822.7	45 139.7	41 686.5	44 326.5	43 137.2	59 925.3
Foreign exchange Devises étrangères	49 667.3	43 709.8	42 495.4	41 095.5	39 898.6	39 765.3	37 718.9	40 768.3	38 557.0	36 928.3
Ghana Ghana										
Total reserves minus gold Rés. totale, moins l'or	232.1	298.2	539.7	1 352.8	1 626.7	1 752.9	2 090.3	...	...	...
Foreign exchange Devises étrangères	231.5	294.2	536.1	1 306.0	1 605.9	1 751.8	2 089.1	...	...	...
Greece Grèce										
Total reserves minus gold Rés. totale, moins l'or	13 424.3	#5 154.2	8 082.8	4 361.5	1 191.0	506.4	565.9	631.1	343.8	1 554.8
Foreign exchange Devises étrangères	13 115.5	#4 787.2	7 629.3	3 843.3	743.7	309.1	408.3	518.2	158.7	198.8
Grenada Grenade										
Total reserves minus gold Rés. totale, moins l'or	57.7	63.9	87.8	83.2	121.7	94.3	100.0	110.6	105.3	129.1
Foreign exchange Devises étrangères	57.7	63.9	87.8	83.2	121.7	94.2	99.8	110.4	104.1	112.4
Guatemala Guatemala										
Total reserves minus gold Rés. totale, moins l'or	1 746.4	2 292.2	2 299.1	2 833.2	3 426.3	3 663.8	3 915.0	4 129.9	4 461.9	4 963.6
Foreign exchange Devises étrangères	1 736.6	2 283.7	2 290.9	2 825.0	3 418.3	3 657.3	3 909.3	4 125.6	4 458.4	4 690.3
Guinea Guinée										
Total reserves minus gold Rés. totale, moins l'or	147.9	200.2	171.4	...	110.5	95.1	...	...	...	...
Foreign exchange Devises étrangères	147.6	199.3	169.6	...	110.4	94.9	...	...	...	...
Guinea-Bissau Guinée-Bissau										
Total reserves minus gold Rés. totale, moins l'or	66.7	69.5	102.7	32.9	73.1	79.8	82.0	112.9	124.6	168.6
Foreign exchange Devises étrangères	66.7	69.3	102.3	31.7	72.4	79.2	81.5	112.8	124.4	149.8

66 International reserves minus gold *(continued)*

Millions of US dollars, end of period

Réserves internationales, moins l'or *(suite)*

Millions de dollars des E.-U., fin de période

Country or area Pays ou zone	2000	2001	2002	2003	2004	2005	2006	2007	2008	2009
Guyana Guyana										
Total reserves minus gold Rés. totale, moins l'or	305.0	287.3	284.5	276.4	231.8	251.9	279.6	313.0	355.9	631.4
Foreign exchange Devises étrangères	295.8	284.8	279.8	271.5	224.7	251.4	278.0	312.5	355.9	627.5
Haiti Haïti										
Total reserves minus gold Rés. totale, moins l'or	182.1	141.4	81.7	62.0	114.4	133.1	253.1	452.0	541.4	788.6
Foreign exchange Devises étrangères	182.0	140.8	81.1	61.6	114.1	120.7	245.1	444.4	534.3	680.4
Honduras Honduras										
Total reserves minus gold Rés. totale, moins l'or	1 313.0	1 415.6	1 524.1	1 430.0	1 970.4	2 327.2	2 628.5	2 528.0	2 473.4	...
Foreign exchange Devises étrangères	1 301.7	1 404.4	1 511.9	1 417.1	1 956.9	2 314.6	2 615.5	2 514.3	2 460.0	...
Hungary Hongrie										
Total reserves minus gold Rés. totale, moins l'or	11 189.6	10 727.2	10 348.5	12 751.4	15 922.1	18 552.1	21 527.0	23 969.8	33 787.9	44 073.7
Foreign exchange Devises étrangères	10 915.0	10 302.0	9 721.0	12 029.0	15 326.0	18 296.0	21 316.0	23 773.0	33 620.0	42 479.0
Iceland Islande										
Total reserves minus gold Rés. totale, moins l'or	388.9	338.2	440.1	792.3	1 046.2	1 035.7	2 301.3	2 578.7	3 515.2	3 813.2
Foreign exchange Devises étrangères	364.6	314.8	414.7	764.6	1 017.3	1 009.1	2 273.2	2 549.1	3 486.2	3 638.7
India Inde										
Total reserves minus gold Rés. totale, moins l'or	37 902.2	45 870.5	67 665.5	98 937.9	126 593.0	131 924.0	170 738.0	266 988.0	247 419.0	265 182.0
Foreign exchange Devises étrangères	37 264.0	45 251.0	66 994.0	97 617.0	125 164.0	131 018.0	170 187.0	266 553.0	246 603.0	258 583.0
Indonesia Indonésie										
Total reserves minus gold Rés. totale, moins l'or	28 501.9	27 246.2	30 970.7	34 962.3	34 952.5	33 140.5	41 103.1	54 976.4	49 596.7	63 563.3
Foreign exchange Devises étrangères	28 280.4	27 047.5	30 754.3	34 742.4	34 724.1	32 925.5	40 866.0	54 737.3	49 338.9	60 572.0
Iraq Iraq										
Total reserves minus gold Rés. totale, moins l'or	...	...	...	...	7 824.1	12 104.1	19 931.9	31 297.6	50 042.5	46 255.4
Foreign exchange Devises étrangères	...	...	...	...	7 098.5	11 439.9	19 235.7	30 887.5	49 635.8	44 168.9
Ireland Irlande										
Total reserves minus gold Rés. totale, moins l'or	5 359.7	5 586.5	5 414.8	4 078.5	2 830.9	778.7	720.0	778.7	871.1	1 940.8
Foreign exchange Devises étrangères	4 982.7	5 195.5	4 879.4	3 425.2	2 323.7	514.4	493.8	590.8	609.2	516.7
Israel Israël										
Total reserves minus gold Rés. totale, moins l'or	23 281.2	23 378.6	24 082.9	26 315.1	27 094.4	28 059.4	29 153.2	28 518.5	42 513.2	60 611.4
Foreign exchange Devises étrangères	23 163.0	23 179.1	23 665.0	25 778.4	26 616.0	27 839.0	29 011.0	28 406.0	42 324.0	59 091.0
Italy Italie										
Total reserves minus gold Rés. totale, moins l'or	25 566.5	24 419.4	28 603.1	30 372.2	27 859.0	25 514.7	25 661.7	28 385.0	37 087.6	45 770.4
Foreign exchange Devises étrangères	22 423.2	20 905.3	24 587.8	26 062.0	24 011.1	23 527.9	24 413.2	27 319.2	35 306.0	34 521.1
Jamaica Jamaïque										
Total reserves minus gold Rés. totale, moins l'or	1 053.7	1 900.5	1 645.1	1 194.9	1 846.5	2 169.8	2 318.4	1 878.5	1 772.7	2 075.8
Foreign exchange Devises étrangères	1 053.6	1 899.0	1 644.2	1 194.8	1 846.4	2 169.8	2 318.2	1 878.2	1 772.6	1 729.4

66

International reserves minus gold *(continued)*
Millions of US dollars, end of period

Réserves internationales, moins l'or *(suite)*
Millions de dollars des E.-U., fin de période

Country or area Pays ou zone	2000	2001	2002	2003	2004	2005	2006	2007	2008	2009
Japan Japon										
Total reserves minus gold Rés. totale, moins l'or	354 902.0	395 155.0	461 186.0	663 289.0	833 891.0	834 275.0	879 682.0	952 784.0	1 009 360.0	1 022 240.0
Foreign exchange Devises étrangères	347 212.0	387 727.0	451 458.0	652 790.0	824 264.0	828 813.0	874 936.0	948 356.0	1 003 670.0	996 955.0
Jordan Jordanie										
Total reserves minus gold Rés. totale, moins l'or	3 331.3	3 062.2	3 975.9	5 194.3	5 266.6	5 250.3	6 722.0	7 542.0	8 561.6	11 689.3
Foreign exchange Devises étrangères	3 330.6	3 061.0	3 975.0	5 193.1	5 264.8	5 249.5	6 720.4	7 539.4	8 558.0	11 458.8
Kazakhstan Kazakhstan										
Total reserves minus gold Rés. totale, moins l'or	1 594.1	1 997.2	2 555.3	4 236.2	8 473.1	6 084.2	17 750.8	15 776.8	17 871.5	20 719.8
Foreign exchange Devises étrangères	1 594.1	1 997.2	2 554.3	4 235.0	8 471.9	6 083.0	17 749.5	15 775.4	17 870.1	20 179.6
Kenya Kenya										
Total reserves minus gold Rés. totale, moins l'or	897.7	1 064.9	1 068.0	1 481.9	1 519.3	1 798.8	2 415.8	3 355.0	2 878.5	3 849.0
Foreign exchange Devises étrangères	881.2	1 048.1	1 050.0	1 461.0	1 499.0	1 780.6	2 396.0	3 334.6	2 855.7	3 478.1
Korea, Republic of Corée, République de										
Total reserves minus gold Rés. totale, moins l'or	96 130.5	102 753.0	121 345.0	155 284.0	198 997.0	210 317.0	238 882.0	262 150.0	201 144.0	269 933.0
Foreign exchange Devises étrangères	95 855.1	102 487.0	120 811.0	154 509.0	198 175.0	209 968.0	238 388.0	261 771.0	200 479.0	265 202.0
Kosovo Kosovo										
Total reserves minus gold Rés. totale, moins l'or	...	...	...	...	...	...	...	951.7	892.1	830.2
Foreign exchange Devises étrangères	...	...	...	...	...	...	...	951.7	892.1	721.2
Kuwait Koweït										
Total reserves minus gold Rés. totale, moins l'or	7 082.4	9 897.3	9 208.1	7 577.0	8 241.9	8 862.8	12 566.0	16 660.0	17 112.8	20 267.5
Foreign exchange Devises étrangères	6 504.4	9 191.1	8 357.0	6 640.5	7 347.4	8 380.4	12 177.6	16 285.6	16 611.0	17 608.4
Kyrgyzstan Kirghizistan										
Total reserves minus gold Rés. totale, moins l'or	239.0	263.5	288.8	364.6	528.2	569.7	764.4	1 107.2	1 152.9	1 494.0
Foreign exchange Devises étrangères	238.3	262.2	288.2	354.3	508.3	564.5	731.1	1 093.4	1 097.6	1 331.9
Lao People's Dem. Rep. Rép. dém. pop. lao										
Total reserves minus gold Rés. totale, moins l'or	139.0	130.9	191.6	208.6	223.2	234.3	328.4	532.6	628.7	702.5
Foreign exchange Devises étrangères	138.9	127.5	185.5	189.5	207.9	220.2	313.7	517.1	613.6	622.5
Latvia Lettonie										
Total reserves minus gold Rés. totale, moins l'or	850.9	1 148.7	1 241.4	1 432.4	1 912.0	2 232.1	4 353.4	5 553.4	5 027.6	6 631.8
Foreign exchange Devises étrangères	850.8	1 148.6	1 241.3	1 432.2	1 911.7	2 231.9	4 353.1	5 553.1	5 027.2	6 445.0
Lebanon Liban										
Total reserves minus gold Rés. totale, moins l'or	5 943.7	5 013.8	7 243.8	12 519.4	11 734.6	11 887.1	13 376.4	12 909.9	20 244.5	29 102.9
Foreign exchange Devises étrangères	5 895.4	4 965.8	7 190.9	12 460.8	11 672.4	11 828.7	13 313.3	12 844.1	20 181.8	28 744.5
Lesotho Lesotho										
Total reserves minus gold Rés. totale, moins l'or	417.9	386.5	406.4	460.3	501.5	519.1	658.4	...	...	...
Foreign exchange Devises étrangères	412.6	381.5	401.0	454.4	495.3	513.5	652.7	...	...	...

66

International reserves minus gold *(continued)*
Millions of US dollars, end of period

Réserves internationales, moins l'or *(suite)*
Millions de dollars des E.-U., fin de période

Country or area Pays ou zone	2000	2001	2002	2003	2004	2005	2006	2007	2008	2009
Liberia Libéria										
Total reserves minus gold Rés. totale, moins l'or	0.3	0.5	3.3	7.4	18.7	25.4	72.0	119.4	160.9	...
Foreign exchange Devises étrangères	0.2	0.4	3.3	7.3	18.7	25.4	71.9	119.3	139.0	...
Libyan Arab Jamah. Jamah. arabe libyenne										
Total reserves minus gold Rés. totale, moins l'or	12 460.8	14 800.5	14 307.4	19 584.0	25 688.8	39 507.8	59 289.2	79 404.7	92 313.3	104 026.0
Foreign exchange Devises étrangères	11 407.7	13 749.0	13 159.4	18 309.8	24 336.3	38 235.2	57 907.3	77 897.5	90 803.4	100 917.0
Lithuania Lituanie										
Total reserves minus gold Rés. totale, moins l'or	1 311.6	1 617.7	2 349.3	3 372.0	3 512.6	3 720.2	5 654.4	7 565.8	6 281.5	6 453.2
Foreign exchange Devises étrangères	1 310.2	1 599.3	2 295.9	3 371.9	3 512.5	3 720.1	5 654.3	7 565.6	6 281.3	6 237.9
Luxembourg Luxembourg										
Total reserves minus gold Rés. totale, moins l'or	76.6	105.6	151.7	279.9	298.4	241.1	218.1	143.6	334.6	730.5
Foreign exchange Devises étrangères	0.1	0.1	0.2	88.9	143.9	166.7	156.0	93.8	258.4	267.5
Madagascar Madagascar										
Total reserves minus gold Rés. totale, moins l'or	285.2	398.4	363.3	414.3	503.5	481.3	583.2	846.7	982.3	1 135.5
Foreign exchange Devises étrangères	285.1	398.2	363.2	414.2	503.3	481.2	583.1	846.6	982.0	982.3
Malawi Malawi										
Total reserves minus gold Rés. totale, moins l'or	243.0	202.5	161.5	122.0	128.1	158.9	133.8	216.6	242.8	149.4
Foreign exchange Devises étrangères	239.6	198.8	158.3	118.2	123.3	154.6	129.6	212.9	239.1	143.6
Malaysia Malaisie										
Total reserves minus gold Rés. totale, moins l'or	28 329.8	29 522.3	33 360.7	43 821.7	65 881.1	69 858.0	82 132.3	101 019.0	91 148.8	95 431.7
Foreign exchange Devises étrangères	27 432.2	28 632.9	32 419.1	42 772.4	64 905.9	69 376.9	81 723.6	100 635.0	90 605.1	92 865.1
Maldives Maldives										
Total reserves minus gold Rés. totale, moins l'or	122.8	93.1	133.1	159.5	203.6	186.3	231.4	308.3	240.6	261.0
Foreign exchange Devises étrangères	120.5	90.8	130.6	156.7	200.7	183.6	228.5	305.3	237.6	246.4
Mali Mali										
Total reserves minus gold Rés. totale, moins l'or	381.3	348.9	594.5	952.5	860.7	854.6	969.5	1 087.1	1 071.6	1 604.5
Foreign exchange Devises étrangères	369.7	337.4	582.4	938.4	846.2	841.2	955.4	1 071.9	1 056.5	1 473.9
Malta Malte										
Total reserves minus gold Rés. totale, moins l'or	1 470.2	1 666.2	2 209.3	2 728.7	2 732.0	2 576.4	2 976.8	3 785.4	#368.3	532.1
Foreign exchange Devises étrangères	1 385.8	1 582.4	2 115.3	2 624.5	2 621.7	2 473.0	2 865.0	3 662.0	#288.3	329.7
Mauritania Mauritanie										
Total reserves minus gold Rés. totale, moins l'or	46.2	36.7	70.1	27.0	33.7	64.5	187.2	197.8	188.6	225.4
Foreign exchange Devises étrangères	45.9	36.5	69.9	26.9	33.7	64.3	187.1	197.8	188.5	225.2
Mauritius Maurice										
Total reserves minus gold Rés. totale, moins l'or	897.4	835.6	1 227.4	1 577.3	1 605.9	1 339.9	1 269.6	1 780.3	1 742.7	2 178.8
Foreign exchange Devises étrangères	857.1	796.3	1 184.5	1 519.2	1 544.7	1 289.2	1 226.3	1 739.9	1 693.4	2 001.5

66 International reserves minus gold *(continued)*

Millions of US dollars, end of period

Réserves internationales, moins l'or *(suite)*

Millions de dollars des E.-U., fin de période

Country or area Pays ou zone	2000	2001	2002	2003	2004	2005	2006	2007	2008	2009
Mexico Mexique										
Total reserves minus gold Rés. totale, moins l'or	35 508.8	44 740.7	50 594.4	58 955.6	64 140.7	74 054.1	76 270.5	87 109.2	95 126.1	99 589.2
Foreign exchange Devises étrangères	35 142.0	44 384.0	49 895.0	57 739.9	62 777.9	73 014.6	75 447.7	86 309.4	93 994.1	94 102.7
Micronesia (Fed. States of) Micronésie (Etats féd. de)										
Total reserves minus gold Rés. totale, moins l'or	113.0	98.3	117.4	89.6	54.8	50.0	46.6	48.5	40.0	55.7
Foreign exchange Devises étrangères	111.6	96.9	115.8	87.8	52.9	48.2	44.7	46.4	37.9	46.0
Mongolia Mongolie										
Total reserves minus gold Rés. totale, moins l'or	178.8	155.6	218.5	196.9	193.7	333.2	583.4	801.7	561.5	1 294.5
Foreign exchange Devises étrangères	178.7	155.5	218.4	196.7	193.5	332.9	583.2	801.5	561.2	1 217.8
Montenegro Monténégro										
Total reserves minus gold Rés. totale, moins l'or	...	...	58.2	63.7	81.8	204.0	432.7	688.8	435.7	572.6
Foreign exchange Devises étrangères	...	...	58.2	63.7	81.8	204.0	432.7	678.2	425.1	521.3
Montserrat Montserrat										
Total reserves minus gold Rés. totale, moins l'or	10.4	12.5	14.4	15.2	14.1	13.9	14.6	14.5	11.7	14.3
Foreign exchange Devises étrangères	10.4	12.5	14.4	15.2	14.1	13.9	14.6	14.5	11.7	14.3
Morocco Maroc										
Total reserves minus gold Rés. totale, moins l'or	4 823.2	8 473.9	10 132.7	13 851.1	16 336.6	16 187.4	20 340.7	24 123.3	22 103.8	22 797.3
Foreign exchange Devises étrangères	4 612.0	8 262.0	9 914.5	13 634.1	16 107.0	16 008.0	20 182.1	23 980.0	21 976.0	21 923.6
Mozambique Mozambique										
Total reserves minus gold Rés. totale, moins l'or	723.2	713.2	802.5	937.5	1 131.0	1 053.8	1 155.7	1 444.7	1 577.7	...
Foreign exchange Devises étrangères	723.1	713.2	802.4	937.4	1 130.9	1 053.6	1 155.5	1 444.5	1 577.6	...
Myanmar Myanmar										
Total reserves minus gold Rés. totale, moins l'or	223.0	400.5	470.0	550.2	672.1	770.7	1 235.6	...	...	...
Foreign exchange Devises étrangères	222.8	399.9	469.9	550.1	672.1	770.5	1 235.4	...	...	...
Namibia Namibie										
Total reserves minus gold Rés. totale, moins l'or	259.8	234.3	323.1	325.2	345.1	312.1	449.6	896.0	1 293.0	2 050.9
Foreign exchange Devises étrangères	259.8	234.2	323.0	325.1	344.9	312.0	449.4	895.9	1 292.8	1 846.4
Nepal Népal										
Total reserves minus gold Rés. totale, moins l'or	945.4	1 037.7	1 017.6	1 222.5	1 462.2	1 499.0	...	...	...	...
Foreign exchange Devises étrangères	937.9	1 030.4	1 009.8	1 213.1	1 452.5	1 490.2	...	...	...	...
Netherlands Pays-Bas										
Total reserves minus gold Rés. totale, moins l'or	9 642.5	9 034.3	9 563.3	11 167.0	10 654.8	8 986.0	10 802.4	10 269.7	11 476.4	17 870.5
Foreign exchange Devises étrangères	7 003.9	5 930.3	6 017.4	7 335.5	7 209.6	7 078.2	9 327.0	8 748.7	9 368.9	8 613.4
Netherlands Antilles Antilles néerlandaises										
Total reserves minus gold Rés. totale, moins l'or	260.7	301.1	398.9	372.9	415.4	545.4	495.0	660.9	818.9	867.0
Foreign exchange Devises étrangères	260.7	301.1	398.9	372.9	415.4	545.4	495.0	660.9	818.9	867.0

66 International reserves minus gold *(continued)*

Millions of US dollars, end of period

Réserves internationales, moins l'or *(suite)*

Millions de dollars des E.-U., fin de période

Country or area / Pays ou zone	2000	2001	2002	2003	2004	2005	2006	2007	2008	2009
New Zealand Nouvelle-Zélande										
Total reserves minus gold / Rés. totale, moins l'or	3 952.1	3 564.7	4 962.8	6 085.4	6 947.4	8 892.7	14 068.5	17 247.2	11 052.2	15 594.1
Foreign exchange / Devises étrangères	3 618.9	3 161.2	4 481.8	5 413.7	6 438.8	8 693.6	13 916.0	17 124.1	10 854.5	13 981.7
Nicaragua Nicaragua										
Total reserves minus gold / Rés. totale, moins l'or	488.5	379.9	448.1	502.1	668.2	727.8	921.9	1 103.3	1 140.8	1 573.1
Foreign exchange / Devises étrangères	488.4	379.6	448.1	502.0	667.7	727.5	921.5	1 103.2	1 140.7	1 408.6
Niger Niger										
Total reserves minus gold / Rés. totale, moins l'or	80.4	107.0	133.9	260.1	258.0	249.5	370.9	593.0	705.2	655.5
Foreign exchange / Devises étrangères	69.2	95.9	121.6	244.7	243.7	236.9	357.8	579.3	690.5	556.9
Nigeria Nigéria										
Total reserves minus gold / Rés. totale, moins l'or	9 910.9	10 456.6	7 331.3	7 128.4	16 955.6	28 279.6	42 298.7	51 334.2	53 001.8	44 762.7
Foreign exchange / Devises étrangères	9 910.4	10 455.8	7 331.0	7 128.0	16 955.0	28 279.0	42 298.1	51 333.1	53 000.4	42 382.5
Norway Norvège										
Total reserves minus gold / Rés. totale, moins l'or	27 597.4	23 277.5	31 999.8	37 220.0	44 307.5	46 985.9	56 841.6	60 839.6	50 949.8	48 859.3
Foreign exchange / Devises étrangères	26 706.9	22 197.5	30 692.1	35 890.2	43 078.2	46 377.4	56 181.4	60 294.1	50 214.1	45 718.6
Oman Oman										
Total reserves minus gold / Rés. totale, moins l'or	2 379.9	2 364.9	3 173.5	3 593.5	3 597.3	4 358.1	5 014.1	9 523.5	11 581.9	12 202.9
Foreign exchange / Devises étrangères	2 310.9	2 277.0	3 064.8	3 466.6	3 484.5	4 308.7	4 970.2	9 485.1	11 541.1	11 856.3
Pakistan Pakistan										
Total reserves minus gold / Rés. totale, moins l'or	1 513.4	3 640.0	8 078.3	10 941.0	9 799.0	10 032.8	11 543.1	14 044.0	7 194.2	11 318.2
Foreign exchange / Devises étrangères	1 499.0	3 636.0	8 076.0	10 693.0	9 554.0	9 817.0	11 327.6	13 829.0	7 011.5	9 937.6
Panama Panama										
Total reserves minus gold / Rés. totale, moins l'or	722.6	1 091.8	1 182.8	1 011.0	630.6	1 210.5	1 335.0	1 935.1	2 423.8	3 028.3
Foreign exchange / Devises étrangères	706.8	1 075.5	1 165.7	992.5	611.4	1 192.5	1 315.9	1 915.4	2 404.7	2 741.5
Papua New Guinea Papouasie-Nvl-Guinée										
Total reserves minus gold / Rés. totale, moins l'or	286.9	422.6	321.5	494.2	632.6	718.1	1 400.7	2 053.7	1 953.4	2 560.6
Foreign exchange / Devises étrangères	274.5	413.6	315.0	489.9	631.2	717.4	1 400.0	2 052.9	1 952.6	2 377.7
Paraguay Paraguay										
Total reserves minus gold / Rés. totale, moins l'or	762.8	713.5	629.2	968.9	1 168.1	1 297.1	1 702.2	2 461.5	2 844.6	3 838.6
Foreign exchange / Devises étrangères	632.6	584.3	486.8	811.2	1 001.1	1 140.3	1 532.0	2 383.9	2 767.3	3 632.0
Peru Pérou										
Total reserves minus gold / Rés. totale, moins l'or	8 374.0	8 671.9	9 339.1	9 776.8	12 176.4	13 599.4	16 733.3	26 856.5	30 271.5	32 012.6
Foreign exchange / Devises étrangères	8 372.5	8 670.1	9 338.3	9 776.4	12 176.1	13 598.9	16 732.4	26 852.7	30 262.5	30 999.8
Philippines Philippines										
Total reserves minus gold / Rés. totale, moins l'or	13 090.2	13 476.3	13 329.3	13 654.9	13 116.3	15 926.0	20 025.4	30 210.6	33 192.9	38 782.9
Foreign exchange / Devises étrangères	12 974.8	13 352.7	13 200.5	13 523.3	12 979.5	15 800.1	19 891.4	30 071.4	33 047.2	37 504.2

66

International reserves minus gold *(continued)*

Millions of US dollars, end of period

Réserves internationales, moins l'or *(suite)*

Millions de dollars des E.-U., fin de période

Country or area Pays ou zone	2000	2001	2002	2003	2004	2005	2006	2007	2008	2009
Poland Pologne										
Total reserves minus gold Rés. totale, moins l'or	26 562.0	25 648.4	28 649.7	32 579.1	35 323.9	40 863.7	46 371.1	62 966.8	59 305.6	75 923.3
Foreign exchange Devises étrangères	26 319.9	25 161.6	27 959.2	31 724.9	34 552.8	40 486.9	46 107.0	62 720.3	58 931.0	73 393.6
Portugal Portugal										
Total reserves minus gold Rés. totale, moins l'or	8 908.7	9 666.6	11 179.1	5 875.9	5 174.1	3 478.7	2 063.6	1 257.8	1 309.4	2 454.9
Foreign exchange Devises étrangères	8 539.2	9 228.2	10 655.8	5 248.8	4 631.2	3 173.4	1 835.3	1 044.4	1 022.0	811.4
Qatar Qatar										
Total reserves minus gold Rés. totale, moins l'or	1 158.0	1 312.7	1 566.8	2 944.2	3 395.9	4 542.4	5 382.7	9 416.4	9 649.5	18 369.7
Foreign exchange Devises étrangères	1 079.1	1 190.8	1 404.2	2 758.1	3 225.4	4 456.5	5 307.1	9 345.0	9 553.0	17 868.9
Republic of Moldova République de Moldova										
Total reserves minus gold Rés. totale, moins l'or	222.5	228.5	268.9	302.3	470.3	597.4	775.5	1 333.7	1 672.4	1 480.3
Foreign exchange Devises étrangères	222.1	227.8	268.6	302.2	470.2	597.4	775.3	1 333.5	1 672.3	1 476.7
Romania Roumanie										
Total reserves minus gold Rés. totale, moins l'or	2 469.7	3 922.5	6 125.3	8 040.0	14 616.4	19 872.1	28 066.2	37 194.1	36 868.4	40 756.6
Foreign exchange Devises étrangères	2 468.7	3 915.7	6 123.0	8 039.7	14 615.8	19 871.5	28 065.9	37 193.6	36 746.9	39 344.3
Russian Federation Fédération de Russie										
Total reserves minus gold Rés. totale, moins l'or	24 264.3	32 542.4	44 053.6	73 174.9	120 809.0	175 891.0	295 568.0	466 750.0	411 750.0	416 649.0
Foreign exchange Devises étrangères	24 262.6	32 538.1	44 050.8	73 172.1	120 805.0	175 690.0	295 277.0	466 376.0	410 695.0	405 825.0
Rwanda Rwanda										
Total reserves minus gold Rés. totale, moins l'or	190.6	212.1	243.7	214.7	314.6	405.8	439.7	552.8	596.3	742.7
Foreign exchange Devises étrangères	189.5	199.8	233.6	184.9	284.4	379.8	416.8	528.7	564.9	611.8
Saint Kitts and Nevis Saint-Kitts-et-Nevis										
Total reserves minus gold Rés. totale, moins l'or	45.2	56.4	65.8	64.8	78.5	71.6	88.7	95.8	110.4	136.4
Foreign exchange Devises étrangères	45.1	56.3	65.6	64.7	78.3	71.5	88.6	95.7	110.3	122.9
Saint Lucia Sainte-Lucie										
Total reserves minus gold Rés. totale, moins l'or	78.8	88.9	93.9	106.9	132.5	116.4	134.5	153.7	142.8	174.8
Foreign exchange Devises étrangères	77.0	87.1	91.9	104.7	130.2	114.2	132.2	151.2	140.3	150.6
Saint Vincent-Grenadines Saint Vincent-Grenadines										
Total reserves minus gold Rés. totale, moins l'or	55.2	61.4	53.2	51.2	75.0	69.5	78.7	87.0	83.7	87.8
Foreign exchange Devises étrangères	54.5	60.8	52.5	50.4	74.2	68.8	77.9	86.2	82.9	75.2
Samoa Samoa										
Total reserves minus gold Rés. totale, moins l'or	63.7	56.6	62.5	83.9	86.1	81.8	80.7	95.4	87.1	165.8
Foreign exchange Devises étrangères	59.8	52.8	58.3	79.3	81.3	77.3	75.9	90.2	81.9	145.0
San Marino Saint-Marin										
Total reserves minus gold Rés. totale, moins l'or	135.2	133.5	183.4	252.7	355.6	354.0	479.1	647.8	706.8	...
Foreign exchange Devises étrangères	129.6	127.9	177.3	245.9	348.3	347.2	471.8	639.8	698.7	...

International reserves minus gold *(continued)*

Millions of US dollars, end of period

Réserves internationales, moins l'or *(suite)*

Millions de dollars des E.-U., fin de période

Country or area Pays ou zone	2000	2001	2002	2003	2004	2005	2006	2007	2008	2009
Sao Tome and Principe Sao Tomé-et-Principe										
Total reserves minus gold Rés. totale, moins l'or	11.6	15.5	17.4	25.5	19.5	26.7	34.2	39.3	...	...
Foreign exchange Devises étrangères	11.6	15.5	17.3	25.4	19.5	26.7	34.1	39.3	...	...
Saudi Arabia Arabie saoudite										
Total reserves minus gold Rés. totale, moins l'or	19 585.5	17 595.7	20 610.4	22 620.0	27 290.9	#155 029.0[2]	226 035.0	305 455.0	442 249.0	409 694.0
Foreign exchange Devises étrangères	18 036.0	14 796.0	16 715.0	17 662.0	23 273.0	#152 573.0[2]	224 483.0	304 003.0	440 130.0	396 748.0
Senegal Sénégal										
Total reserves minus gold Rés. totale, moins l'or	384.0	447.3	637.4	1 110.9	1 386.4	1 191.0	1 334.3	1 660.0	1 602.2	2 123.2
Foreign exchange Devises étrangères	381.2	438.0	626.3	1 098.2	1 376.7	1 187.4	1 331.8	1 657.3	1 599.4	1 916.1
Serbia Serbie										
Total reserves minus gold Rés. totale, moins l'or	391.5	1 004.7	2 166.0	3 410.8	4 095.9	5 627.9	11 647.7	13 892.6	11 122.9	14 769.2
Foreign exchange Devises étrangères	371.7	996.1	2 165.0	3 410.4	4 095.8	5 597.7	11 638.9	13 891.8	11 120.7	14 749.9
Seychelles Seychelles										
Total reserves minus gold Rés. totale, moins l'or	43.8	37.1	69.8	67.4	34.6	56.2	112.9	40.8	63.8	190.5
Foreign exchange Devises étrangères	43.7	37.1	69.8	67.4	34.6	56.2	112.9	40.7	63.8	178.2
Sierra Leone Sierra Leone										
Total reserves minus gold Rés. totale, moins l'or	49.2	51.3	84.7	66.6	125.1	170.5	183.9	216.6	220.2	405.0
Foreign exchange Devises étrangères	43.9	50.9	60.6	32.1	74.1	137.7	154.7	185.8	189.7	215.3
Singapore Singapour										
Total reserves minus gold Rés. totale, moins l'or	80 170.3	75 677.0	82 221.2	96 245.5	112 579.0	116 172.0	136 260.0	162 957.0	174 193.0	187 803.0
Foreign exchange Devises étrangères	79 723.4	75 152.9	81 566.6	95 474.4	111 845.0	115 712.0	135 814.0	162 517.0	173 649.0	186 005.0
Slovakia Slovaquie										
Total reserves minus gold Rés. totale, moins l'or	4 022.3	4 141.0	8 808.7	11 678.1	14 417.5	14 900.7	12 646.6	18 032.1	17 854.2	#692.2
Foreign exchange Devises étrangères	4 021.8	4 140.3	8 807.5	11 676.8	14 416.1	14 899.4	12 645.2	18 025.8	17 804.9	#50.4
Slovenia Slovénie										
Total reserves minus gold Rés. totale, moins l'or	3 196.0	4 330.0	6 980.2	8 496.9	8 793.4	8 076.4	7 036.1	#979.8	868.1	966.1
Foreign exchange Devises étrangères	3 110.0	4 244.3	6 852.6	8 343.1	8 662.3	8 013.1	6 987.1	#942.0	809.9	589.5
Solomon Islands Iles Salomon										
Total reserves minus gold Rés. totale, moins l'or	32.0	19.3	18.2	37.2	80.6	95.4	104.4	119.1	89.5	146.0
Foreign exchange Devises étrangères	31.3	18.7	17.5	36.4	79.7	94.6	103.6	118.2	88.7	130.6
South Africa Afrique du Sud										
Total reserves minus gold Rés. totale, moins l'or	6 082.8	6 045.3	5 904.2	6 495.5	13 141.3	18 579.1	23 056.9	29 588.6	30 583.5	35 237.4
Foreign exchange Devises étrangères	5 792.7	5 765.1	5 600.8	6 163.7	12 794.3	18 259.6	22 720.1	29 234.2	30 237.8	32 431.8
Spain Espagne										
Total reserves minus gold Rés. totale, moins l'or	30 988.9	29 582.3	34 535.7	19 788.4	12 388.8	9 677.6	10 822.2	#11 480.2	12 413.7	18 205.1
Foreign exchange Devises étrangères	29 516.4	27 905.5	32 590.4	17 512.8	10 481.4	8 594.1	10 088.2	10 792.0	11 540.0	12 786.8

66 International reserves minus gold *(continued)*

Millions of US dollars, end of period

Réserves internationales, moins l'or *(suite)*

Millions de dollars des E.-U., fin de période

Country or area Pays ou zone	2000	2001	2002	2003	2004	2005	2006	2007	2008	2009
Sri Lanka Sri Lanka										
Total reserves minus gold Rés. totale, moins l'or	1 039.0	1 286.8	1 631.0	2 264.9	2 131.9	2 649.5	2 726.2	3 379.5	2 468.7	4 616.1
Foreign exchange Devises étrangères	976.4	1 225.9	1 563.6	2 193.2	2 057.4	2 579.6	2 651.5	3 297.1	2 393.0	4 521.0
Sudan Soudan										
Total reserves minus gold Rés. totale, moins l'or	137.8	49.7	248.9	529.4	1 338.0	1 868.6	1 659.9	1 377.9	1 399.0	1 094.2
Foreign exchange Devises étrangères	137.8	49.7	248.8	529.1	1 338.0	1 868.5	1 659.9	1 377.9	1 399.0	897.0
Suriname Suriname										
Total reserves minus gold Rés. totale, moins l'or	63.0	119.3	106.2	105.8	129.4	125.8	215.4	400.9	473.6	659.0
Foreign exchange Devises étrangères	52.7	109.6	95.9	94.7	118.0	115.5	204.9	390.4	463.6	522.9
Swaziland Swaziland										
Total reserves minus gold Rés. totale, moins l'or	351.8	271.8	275.8	277.5	323.6	243.9	372.5	774.2	751.9	958.9
Foreign exchange Devises étrangères	340.1	260.5	263.6	264.1	309.5	231.0	358.9	759.9	737.9	879.0
Sweden Suède										
Total reserves minus gold Rés. totale, moins l'or	14 862.6	13 976.9	17 127.4	19 681.1	22 157.7	22 090.1	24 777.8	27 044.4	25 896.4	42 859.6
Foreign exchange Devises étrangères	13 757.0	12 740.0	15 520.0	18 015.0	20 640.0	21 382.0	24 074.0	26 382.0	25 127.0	38 543.0
Switzerland Suisse										
Total reserves minus gold Rés. totale, moins l'or	32 272.1	32 005.6	40 154.7	47 652.5	55 496.6	36 297.3	38 093.7	44 474.2	45 060.9	98 199.4
Foreign exchange Devises étrangères	30 854.0	30 141.0	38 164.0	45 560.0	53 634.0	35 421.0	37 364.0	43 867.0	44 151.0	91 614.0
Syrian Arab Republic Rép. arabe syrienne										
Total reserves minus gold Rés. totale, moins l'or	...	...	...	...	...	17 346.9	16 467.4	17 013.0	17 061.9	17 397.7
Foreign exchange Devises étrangères	...	...	...	...	...	17 294.6	16 412.3	16 955.2	17 005.6	16 960.0
Tajikistan Tadjikistan										
Total reserves minus gold Rés. totale, moins l'or	92.9	92.6	89.5	111.9	157.5	168.2	175.1	...	...	...
Foreign exchange Devises étrangères	85.0	87.7	87.7	111.0	156.2	162.8	171.6	...	...	...
Thailand Thaïlande										
Total reserves minus gold Rés. totale, moins l'or	32 015.9	32 354.8	38 046.4	41 076.9	48 664.0	50 690.7	65 291.4	85 221.3	108 661.0	135 483.0
Foreign exchange Devises étrangères	31 933.2	32 349.5	38 042.2	40 965.1	48 497.5	50 502.0	65 147.1	85 110.1	108 317.0	133 599.0
TFYR of Macedonia L'ex-R.Y. Macédoine										
Total reserves minus gold Rés. totale, moins l'or	429.4	745.2	722.0	897.7	905.0	1 228.5	1 750.6	2 082.3	1 920.3	2 050.9
Foreign exchange Devises étrangères	428.7	742.9	715.9	897.4	904.2	1 227.7	1 747.6	2 080.8	1 919.0	1 959.9
Timor-Leste Timor-Leste										
Total reserves minus gold Rés. totale, moins l'or	...	...	43.5	61.3	182.4	153.3	83.8	230.3	210.4	249.9
Foreign exchange Devises étrangères	...	...	43.5	61.3	182.4	153.3	83.8	230.3	210.4	237.8
Togo Togo										
Total reserves minus gold Rés. totale, moins l'or	152.3	126.4	205.1	204.9	359.7	194.6	374.5	438.1	581.8	703.2
Foreign exchange Devises étrangères	151.9	125.8	204.4	204.2	359.2	194.1	373.9	437.5	581.2	609.8

66

International reserves minus gold *(continued)*

Millions of US dollars, end of period

Réserves internationales, moins l'or *(suite)*

Millions de dollars des E.-U., fin de période

Country or area Pays ou zone	2000	2001	2002	2003	2004	2005	2006	2007	2008	2009
Tonga Tonga										
Total reserves minus gold Rés. totale, moins l'or	24.6	23.8	25.1	39.8	55.3	46.9	48.0	65.2	69.8	95.7
Foreign exchange Devises étrangères	22.3	21.4	22.5	36.9	52.2	44.0	44.9	61.9	66.4	81.9
Trinidad and Tobago Trinité-et-Tobago										
Total reserves minus gold Rés. totale, moins l'or	1 386.3	1 907.1	2 027.7	2 451.1	3 168.2	4 960.8	6 585.7	6 693.7	9 442.6	9 177.9
Foreign exchange Devises étrangères	1 386.2	1 876.0	1 923.5	2 257.8	2 993.0	4 885.8	6 530.9	6 657.4	9 380.4	8 651.6
Tunisia Tunisie										
Total reserves minus gold Rés. totale, moins l'or	1 811.1	1 989.2	2 290.3	2 945.4	3 935.7	4 436.7	6 773.2	7 850.8	8 849.3	11 057.3
Foreign exchange Devises étrangères	1 780.9	1 962.2	2 260.2	2 912.9	3 895.0	4 405.6	6 741.4	7 816.8	8 812.9	10 646.5
Turkey Turquie										
Total reserves minus gold Rés. totale, moins l'or	22 488.4	18 879.2	27 068.6	33 991.0	35 669.1	50 579.0	60 891.9	73 383.9	70 428.1	70 873.7
Foreign exchange Devises étrangères	22 313.0	18 733.0	26 884.0	33 793.0	35 480.0	50 402.0	60 710.0	73 155.8	70 231.3	69 177.5
Uganda Ouganda										
Total reserves minus gold Rés. totale, moins l'or	808.0	983.4	934.0	1 080.3	1 308.1	1 344.2	1 810.9	2 559.8	2 300.5	2 994.5
Foreign exchange Devises étrangères	804.5	981.5	931.1	1 075.5	1 307.4	1 343.1	1 810.8	2 559.5	2 300.3	2 769.3
Ukraine Ukraine										
Total reserves minus gold Rés. totale, moins l'or	1 352.7	2 955.3	4 205.3	6 683.2	9 490.7	18 988.0	21 844.6	31 786.0	30 800.6	25 556.9
Foreign exchange Devises étrangères	1 103.6	2 704.3	4 177.0	6 662.0	9 489.5	18 987.0	21 843.2	31 783.2	30 791.9	25 493.3
United Arab Emirates Emirats arabes unis										
Total reserves minus gold Rés. totale, moins l'or	13 522.7	14 146.4	15 219.4	15 087.8	18 529.9	21 010.3	27 617.4	77 238.8	31 694.5	36 104.2
Foreign exchange Devises étrangères	13 303.9	13 918.2	14 897.2	14 731.5	18 209.0	20 867.7	27 511.9	77 161.9	31 556.6	35 070.4
United Kingdom Royaume-Uni										
Total reserves minus gold Rés. totale, moins l'or	38 773.6	34 188.7	37 549.9	35 348.5	39 942.3	38 467.2	40 697.8	48 958.1	44 348.3	55 702.4
Foreign exchange Devises étrangères	34 163.4	28 843.1	30 979.8	28 645.4	34 081.7	35 853.9	38 888.6	47 497.8	41 550.3	38 026.0
United Rep. of Tanzania Rép.-Unie de Tanzanie										
Total reserves minus gold Rés. totale, moins l'or	974.2	1 156.6	1 528.8	2 038.4	2 295.7	2 048.8	2 259.4	2 886.4	2 862.9	3 470.4
Foreign exchange Devises étrangères	961.1	1 143.6	1 515.2	2 023.1	2 280.1	2 033.8	2 244.2	2 870.4	2 847.5	3 205.9
United States Etats-Unis										
Total reserves minus gold Rés. totale, moins l'or	56 600.4	57 633.7	67 962.3	74 894.1	75 890.0	54 083.8	54 853.9	59 524.3	66 607.0	119 719.0
Foreign exchange Devises étrangères	31 238.3	28 981.0	33 818.0	39 721.8	42 718.3	37 838.1	40 943.5	45 803.8	49 583.6	50 519.9
Uruguay Uruguay										
Total reserves minus gold Rés. totale, moins l'or	2 478.9	3 097.1	769.1	2 083.2	2 508.5	3 074.1	3 085.3	4 114.3	6 352.8	8 028.6
Foreign exchange Devises étrangères	2 431.9	3 050.4	763.5	2 079.4	2 507.3	3 067.8	3 084.2	4 114.0	6 348.7	7 643.5
Vanuatu Vanuatu										
Total reserves minus gold Rés. totale, moins l'or	38.9	37.7	36.5	43.8	61.8	67.2	104.7	119.6	115.2	148.6
Foreign exchange Devises étrangères	34.8	33.5	32.0	38.8	56.5	62.2	99.3	113.8	109.4	142.2

66

International reserves minus gold *(continued)*
Millions of US dollars, end of period

Réserves internationales, moins l'or *(suite)*
Millions de dollars des E.-U., fin de période

Country or area Pays ou zone	2000	2001	2002	2003	2004	2005	2006	2007	2008	2009
Venezuela (Boliv. Rep. of) Venezuela (Rép. boliv. du)										
Total reserves minus gold Rés. totale, moins l'or	13 088.5	9 239.5	8 487.1	16 034.7	18 375.4	23 918.8	29 417.3	24 196.1	33 098.1	21 703.0
Foreign exchange Devises étrangères	12 633.0	8 825.0	8 038.0	15 546.0	17 867.0	23 454.0	28 933.0	23 686.0	32 581.0	17 687.0
Viet Nam Viet Nam										
Total reserves minus gold Rés. totale, moins l'or	3 416.5	3 674.6	4 121.1	6 224.2	7 041.5	9 050.6	13 384.1	23 479.4	23 890.3	16 447.1
Foreign exchange Devises étrangères	3 416.2	3 660.0	4 121.0	6 222.0	7 041.0	9 049.7	13 382.5	23 471.8	23 882.0	16 027.4
Yemen Yémen										
Total reserves minus gold Rés. totale, moins l'or	2 900.3	3 658.1	4 410.5	4 987.0	5 664.8	6 115.4	7 511.5	7 715.4	8 111.4	6 935.6
Foreign exchange Devises étrangères	2 815.6	3 639.6	4 365.6	4 982.0	5 613.5	6 096.6	7 504.4	7 715.4	8 110.9	6 622.0
Zambia Zambie										
Total reserves minus gold Rés. totale, moins l'or	244.8	183.4	535.1	247.7	337.1	559.8	719.7	1 090.0	1 095.6	1 892.1
Foreign exchange Devises étrangères	222.5	116.5	464.8	247.2	312.2	544.0	706.4	1 080.2	1 085.0	1 254.4
Zimbabwe Zimbabwe										
Total reserves minus gold Rés. totale, moins l'or	193.1	64.7	83.4	...	...	...	...	...	...	...
Foreign exchange Devises étrangères	192.5	64.3	82.9	...	...	...	...	...	...	...

Source:
International Monetary Fund (IMF), Washington, D.C., the database on International Financial Statistics, last accessed October 2010.

1 For statistical purposes, the data for China do not include those for the Hong Kong Special Administrative Region (Hong Kong SAR) and Macao Special Administrative Region (Macao SAR).

2 Prior to 2005, data on foreign exchange excluded investments and deposits abroad.

Source:
Fonds monétaire international (FMI), Washington, D.C., la base de données de Statistiques Financières Internationales, dernier accès octobre 2010.

1 Pour la présentation des statistiques, les données pour la Chine ne comprennent pas la Région Administrative Spéciale de Hong Kong (Hong Kong RAS) et la Région Administrative Spéciale de Macao (Macao RAS).

2 Avant 2005, les données sur le marché des changes ne comprenaient pas les investissements et les dépôts effectués à l'étranger.

Total external and public/publicly guaranteed long-term debt of developing countries

Millions of US dollars

Total de la dette extérieure et dette publique extérieure à long terme garantie par l'Etat des pays en développement

Millions de dollars des E.-U.

A. Total external debt [&] • Total de la dette extérieure [&]

Developing economies	2003	2004	2005	2006	2007	2008	2009	Economies en développement
Total long-term debt	**1 900 074**	**1 989 355**	**1 964 829**	**2 067 087**	**2 421 910**	**2 672 049**	**2 759 199**	**Total de la dette à long terme**
Public and publicly guaranteed	1 379 950	1 419 231	1 283 181	1 210 859	1 308 265	1 348 023	1 406 990	Dette publique ou garantie par l'Etat
Official creditors	794 731	812 190	714 294	636 047	666 297	707 661	764 061	Créanciers publics
Multilateral	374 135	385 970	373 417	347 610	372 517	393 444	438 044	Multilatéraux
IBRD	104 337	101 874	96 259	92 286	93 566	96 635	107 984	BIRD
IDA	113 825	124 576	121 077	99 005	107 675	111 269	116 903	IDA
Bilateral	420 596	426 220	340 876	288 437	293 780	314 217	326 017	Bilatéraux
Private creditors	585 220	607 041	568 887	574 812	641 968	640 361	642 929	Créanciers privées
Bonds	410 698	437 913	400 332	409 075	452 166	462 290	475 768	Obligations
Commercial banks	119 688	119 747	125 757	128 188	157 275	150 135	136 340	Banques commerciales
Other private	54 834	49 381	42 798	37 549	32 528	27 937	30 820	Autres institutions privées
Private non-guaranteed	520 123	570 124	681 648	856 227	1 113 645	1 324 026	1 352 210	Dette privées non garantie
Undisbursed debt	**236 029**	**235 766**	**223 516**	**218 595**	**234 941**	**247 265**	**275 941**	**Dette (montants non versés)**
Official creditors	178 126	189 467	190 684	189 309	203 529	217 469	250 673	Créanciers publics
Private creditors	57 902	46 299	32 832	29 287	31 412	29 796	25 268	Créanciers privées
Commitments	**137 040**	**132 718**	**157 350**	**140 021**	**189 986**	**172 739**	**216 731**	**Engagements**
Official creditors	48 925	53 327	65 946	59 633	71 058	79 348	131 864	Créanciers publics
Private creditors	88 115	79 391	91 404	80 389	118 929	93 571	84 864	Créanciers privées
Disbursements	**275 057**	**315 624**	**380 324**	**454 524**	**643 997**	**609 344**	**509 127**	**Versements**
Public and publicly guaranteed	123 679	136 196	142 528	140 018	181 983	171 783	190 191	Dette publique ou garantie par l'Etat
Official creditors	48 493	46 746	46 011	54 105	58 469	68 007	96 430	Créanciers publics
Multilateral	36 499	33 237	34 281	39 732	43 055	47 360	69 770	Multilatéraux
IBRD	10 905	10 039	9 178	11 933	10 498	13 608	22 125	BIRD
IDA	6 365	7 902	7 207	6 771	7 358	6 864	8 701	IDA
Bilateral	11 994	13 509	11 730	14 373	15 413	20 646	26 660	Bilatéraux
Private creditors	75 187	89 450	96 517	85 912	123 515	103 776	93 761	Créanciers privées
Bonds	51 690	61 034	61 066	56 972	72 216	72 936	68 909	Obligations
Commercial banks	17 099	24 328	31 732	24 160	47 941	28 446	19 047	Banques commerciales
Other private	6 397	4 088	3 718	4 781	3 358	2 394	5 805	Autres institutions privées
Private non-guaranteed	151 377	179 428	237 796	314 507	462 013	437 561	318 936	Dette privé non garantie
Principal repayments	**251 083**	**255 213**	**290 880**	**352 428**	**355 872**	**395 392**	**406 390**	**Remboursements du principal**
Public and publicly guaranteed	137 663	123 903	145 812	191 885	128 023	144 276	116 937	Dette publique ou garantie par l'Etat
Official creditors	62 822	56 152	69 878	96 994	53 328	50 130	46 503	Créanciers publics
Multilateral	36 971	30 388	26 634	36 465	26 480	26 972	25 471	Multilatéraux
IBRD	18 459	14 047	12 066	17 168	10 844	10 924	10 838	BIRD
IDA	1 343	1 526	1 621	1 779	1 836	2 296	2 250	IDA
Bilateral	25 851	25 764	43 243	60 529	26 848	23 158	21 032	Bilatéraux
Private creditors	74 841	67 750	75 935	94 891	74 695	94 145	70 435	Créanciers privées
Bonds	36 044	36 010	44 630	60 268	43 632	54 625	32 872	Obligations
Commercial banks	28 031	23 509	22 316	25 154	23 971	32 337	30 198	Banques commerciales
Other private	10 765	8 231	8 989	9 469	7 091	7 183	7 364	Autres institutions privées
Private non-guaranteed	113 420	131 310	145 067	160 543	227 849	251 117	289 453	Dette privée non garantie
Net flows	**23 974**	**60 411**	**89 444**	**102 096**	**288 124**	**213 952**	**102 737**	**Apports nets**
Public and publicly guaranteed	-13 984	12 293	-3 284	-51 867	53 960	27 508	73 254	Dette publique ou garantie par l'Etat
Official creditors	-14 329	-9 406	-23 866	-42 889	5 141	17 876	49 928	Créanciers publics
Multilateral	-472	2 849	7 647	3 267	16 575	20 388	44 300	Multilatéraux
IBRD	-7 502	-4 007	-2 886	-5 235	-346	2 684	11 287	BIRD
IDA	5 004	6 223	5 500	4 992	5 522	4 568	6 451	IDA
Bilateral	-13 858	-12 255	-31 513	-46 156	-11 435	-2 512	5 628	Bilatéraux
Private creditors	346	21 700	20 582	-8 978	48 819	9 631	23 326	Créanciers privés
Bonds	15 646	25 024	16 437	-3 296	28 584	18 311	36 037	Obligations
Commercial banks	-10 932	819	9 416	-994	23 970	-3 891	-11 151	Banques commerciales
Other private	-4 368	-4 143	-5 271	-4 688	-3 734	-4 789	-1 559	Autres institutions privées
Private non-guaranteed	37 958	48 117	92 729	153 963	234 164	186 444	29 483	Dette privée non garantie

67 Total external and public/publicly guaranteed long-term debt of developing countries *(continued)*

Millions of US dollars

Total de la dette extérieure et dette publique extérieure à long terme garantie par l'Etat des pays en développement *(suite)*

Millions de dollars des E.-U.

A. Total external debt [&] • Total de la dette extérieure [&]

Developing economies	2003	2004	2005	2006	2007	2008	2009	Economies en développement
Interest payments	**81 494**	**79 170**	**84 843**	**95 089**	**109 172**	**120 257**	**110 205**	**Paiements d'intérêts**
Public and publicly guaranteed	55 854	54 463	60 506	56 335	59 643	59 040	53 955	Dette publique ou garantie par l'Etat
Official creditors	23 395	21 512	23 904	19 694	20 163	18 960	16 885	Créanciers publics
Multilateral	11 931	10 709	10 572	11 659	12 859	12 287	10 422	Multilatéraux
IBRD	5 010	3 970	4 013	4 777	5 430	4 572	3 415	BIRD
IDA	706	893	897	811	758	908	798	IDA
Bilateral	11 464	10 803	13 332	8 035	7 303	6 674	6 463	Bilatéraux
Private creditors	32 459	32 951	36 602	36 641	39 481	40 080	37 071	Créanciers privées
Bonds	25 142	26 334	30 143	28 861	31 151	31 730	30 744	Obligations
Commercial banks	4 902	4 705	4 921	6 258	6 541	6 672	5 104	Banques commerciales
Other private	2 415	1 912	1 538	1 522	1 788	1 678	1 223	Autres institutions privées
Private non-guaranteed	25 641	24 707	24 337	38 755	49 529	61 217	56 250	Dette privée non garantie
Net transfers	**-57 520**	**-18 759**	**4 601**	**7 007**	**178 952**	**93 694**	**-7 468**	**Transferts nets**
Public and publicly guaranteed	-69 837	-42 169	-63 790	-108 202	-5 683	-31 533	19 299	Dette publique ou garantie par l'Etat
Official creditors	-37 724	-30 918	-47 771	-62 582	-15 022	-1 084	33 043	Créanciers publics
Multilateral	-12 403	-7 860	-2 925	-8 392	3 716	8 102	33 878	Multilatéraux
IBRD	-12 564	-7 977	-6 901	-10 012	-5 776	-1 888	7 873	BIRD
IDA	4 317	5 483	4 688	4 181	4 764	3 660	5 654	IDA
Bilateral	-25 321	-23 059	-44 845	-54 190	-18 738	-9 185	-835	Bilatéraux
Private creditors	-32 113	-11 251	-16 019	-45 619	9 339	-30 449	-13 744	Créanciers privées
Bonds	-9 496	-1 310	-13 706	-32 157	-2 568	-13 420	5 293	Obligations
Commercial banks	-15 834	-3 886	4 495	-7 252	17 428	-10 562	-16 256	Banques commerciales
Other private	-6 783	-6 056	-6 808	-6 210	-5 522	-6 467	-2 782	Autres institutions privées
Private non-guaranteed	12 317	23 411	68 391	115 209	184 636	125 227	-26 767	Dette privées non garantie
Total debt service	**332 577**	**334 383**	**375 723**	**447 517**	**465 044**	**515 650**	**516 595**	**Total du service de la dette**
Public and publicly guaranteed	193 517	178 365	206 318	248 219	187 667	203 316	170 893	Dette publique ou garantie par l'Etat
Official creditors	86 217	77 664	93 782	116 688	73 491	69 090	63 387	Créanciers publics
Multilateral	48 902	41 097	37 207	48 124	39 339	39 259	35 893	Multilatéraux
IBRD	23 469	18 017	16 079	21 945	16 274	15 496	14 252	BIRD
IDA	2 049	2 420	2 519	2 590	2 594	3 204	3 047	IDA
Bilateral	37 315	36 567	56 575	68 564	34 151	29 832	27 495	Bilatéraux
Private creditors	107 300	100 701	112 536	131 532	114 176	134 225	107 505	Créanciers publics
Bonds	61 187	62 344	74 772	89 128	74 784	86 355	63 616	Obligations
Commercial banks	32 933	28 214	27 237	31 412	30 513	39 009	35 303	Banques commerciales
Other private	13 180	10 143	10 526	10 991	8 880	8 861	8 587	Autres institutions privées
Private non-guaranteed	139 060	156 017	169 405	199 298	277 378	312 334	345 703	Dette privées non garantie

[&] The following abbreviations have been used in the table:
IBRD: International Bank for Reconstruction and Development
IDA: International Development Association

[&] Les abréviations ci-après ont été utilisées dans le tableau :
BIRD : Banque internationale pour la reconstruction et le développement
IDA : Association internationale de développement

Total external and public/publicly guaranteed long-term debt of developing countries

Millions of US dollars

Total de la dette extérieure et dette publique extérieure à long terme garantie par l'Etat des pays en développement

Millions de dollars des E.-U.

B. Public and publicly guaranteed long-term debt • Dette publique extérieure à long terme garantie par l'Etat

Country or area Pays ou zone	2000	2001	2002	2003	2004	2005	2006	2007	2008	2009
Afghanistan Afghanistan	...	...	...	...	...	...	910.8	1 893.8	1 984.6	2 202.5
Albania Albanie	921.3	970.9	994.8	1 231.9	1 402.7	1 378.7	1 601.0	1 828.7	2 264.2	2 829.2
Algeria Algérie	23 449.3	20 855.7	21 290.0	21 852.4	20 402.7	15 490.8	3 877.5	3 896.1	3 077.7	2 871.4
Angola Angola	8 084.8	6 982.7	7 530.9	7 620.0	8 166.1	9 506.5	7 337.3	9 246.7	12 712.7	13 721.8
Argentina Argentine	81 633.4	82 994.5	87 313.1	94 061.8	98 016.0	54 225.1	60 753.8	68 029.5	68 626.6	72 923.1
Armenia Arménie	675.1	715.6	818.5	877.2	960.7	922.5	1 037.3	1 282.4	1 445.7	2 376.3
Azerbaijan Azerbaïdjan	737.4	784.5	1 046.0	1 288.4	1 372.2	1 506.0	1 828.0	2 304.4	2 739.4	3 402.9
Bangladesh Bangladesh	14 985.0	14 355.6	15 926.1	17 624.9	18 643.4	17 384.6	18 377.8	19 425.7	20 307.0	21 206.4
Belarus Bélarus	688.9	664.3	748.6	710.0	744.4	785.6	841.9	2 337.9	3 751.6	4 757.7
Belize Belize	553.2	645.4	775.6	948.0	929.0	981.0	1 009.4	1 064.4	1 048.4	1 062.7
Benin Bénin	1 239.4	1 302.6	1 449.3	1 365.6	1 508.9	1 445.8	598.9	756.9	856.8	989.6
Bhutan Bhoutan	202.2	265.2	376.9	481.5	593.3	636.7	697.3	775.0	692.4	762.4
Bolivia (Plurinational State of) Bolivie (État plurinat. de)	4 136.5	3 126.2	3 517.2	4 159.8	4 557.1	4 568.2	3 175.4	2 194.0	2 402.7	2 544.7
Bosnia and Herzegovina Bosnie-Herzégovine	1 956.5	1 780.3	2 030.8	2 315.2	2 685.5	2 555.6	2 715.9	2 958.3	3 000.2	3 568.9
Botswana Botswana	437.8	378.9	472.4	484.7	488.0	412.3	358.2	391.1	390.8	1 388.3
Brazil Brésil	96 127.0	96 146.2	99 245.7	99 684.4	97 104.7	94 027.8	84 244.6	79 595.2	79 645.7	87 317.3
Bulgaria Bulgarie	7 671.4	7 386.6	7 479.9	7 676.2	7 413.7	5 075.2	5 065.9	5 241.5	4 397.2	4 772.3
Burkina Faso Burkina Faso	1 225.7	1 312.8	1 401.8	1 591.2	1 850.9	1 868.5	998.8	1 257.2	1 517.9	1 724.8
Burundi Burundi	1 036.0	985.6	1 104.3	1 251.9	1 326.8	1 229.6	1 291.4	1 343.7	1 308.0	419.8
Cambodia Cambodge	2 328.1	2 392.8	2 587.3	2 868.4	3 079.7	3 154.8	3 317.7	3 537.1	3 892.1	4 099.4
Cameroon Cameroun	8 547.1	8 125.2	8 634.5	9 567.5	8 784.5	6 075.3	2 243.4	2 113.4	2 054.6	2 127.9
Cape Verde Cap-Vert	312.6	339.6	378.5	429.5	451.0	461.9	508.4	564.0	610.8	694.7
Central African Rep. Rép. centrafricaine	797.3	758.4	984.0	911.8	934.9	877.5	868.5	849.0	817.2	250.4

67 Total external and public/publicly guaranteed long-term debt of developing countries *(continued)*
Millions of US dollars

Total de la dette extérieure et dette publique extérieure à long terme garantie par l'Etat des pays en développement *(suite)*
Millions de dollars des E.-U.

B. Public and publicly guaranteed long term debt • Dette publique extérieure à long terme garantie par l'Etat

Country or area Pays ou zone	2000	2001	2002	2003	2004	2005	2006	2007	2008	2009
Chad Tchad	986.6	977.5	1 138.8	1 405.5	1 527.7	1 494.7	1 627.5	1 712.5	1 704.8	1 711.2
Chile Chili	5 227.6	5 552.6	6 770.0	8 015.7	9 396.8	9 172.8	9 389.7	9 324.5	8 781.8	9 282.0
China Chine	94 841.5	91 759.3	88 595.1	85 308.3	89 751.3	85 227.0	88 216.6	87 791.0	89 282.4	93 125.2
Colombia Colombie	20 806.3	21 773.6	20 700.0	22 784.5	23 772.4	22 555.3	24 720.5	27 402.3	28 960.2	35 364.0
Comoros Comores	207.0	222.2	244.6	265.4	273.4	258.0	260.4	279.9	271.0	263.8
Congo Congo	3 682.0	3 584.9	3 919.8	4 360.7	5 761.8	5 413.5	5 749.4	5 247.0	5 504.4	4 785.2
Costa Rica Costa Rica	3 451.9	3 460.3	3 320.9	3 801.6	3 507.8	3 151.8	3 306.6	3 643.0	3 167.6	3 190.2
Côte d'Ivoire Côte d'Ivoire	9 063.5	8 589.6	9 098.4	9 689.8	11 082.1	9 965.2	10 822.7	11 646.2	10 621.9	10 979.0
Dem. Rep. of the Congo Rép. dém. du Congo	7 880.2	7 586.5	8 845.4	10 161.3	10 125.0	9 412.2	9 890.9	10 928.1	10 872.0	10 788.0
Djibouti Djibouti	238.3	236.6	301.3	361.6	389.5	378.9	423.6	634.9	666.6	731.9
Dominica Dominique	145.8	192.5	199.4	205.2	225.1	221.6	217.5	214.4	199.2	192.5
Dominican Republic Rép. dominicaine	3 311.3	3 798.4	4 053.1	5 464.9	5 981.0	5 772.1	6 223.4	6 275.2	6 847.6	7 714.2
Ecuador Equateur	10 874.6	10 777.6	10 901.7	11 068.6	10 860.7	10 850.2	10 304.0	10 709.9	10 043.1	6 910.3
Egypt Egypte	24 338.9	25 313.1	26 657.0	28 236.3	29 320.0	28 517.5	28 856.3	31 863.9	30 494.0	30 621.9
El Salvador El Salvador	2 710.1	3 217.8	4 414.8	4 842.2	4 974.9	4 786.3	5 589.2	5 435.2	5 742.6	6 131.0
Eritrea Erythrée	298.0	394.9	489.2	605.1	704.0	723.0	781.4	855.7	957.0	1 013.0
Ethiopia Ethiopie	5 338.8	5 572.6	6 337.1	7 049.9	6 350.7	5 928.0	2 200.9	2 571.4	2 829.1	4 812.4
Fiji Fidji	172.4	159.2	168.9	183.5	192.5	185.4	342.2	347.0	360.1	361.1
Gabon Gabon	3 457.2	3 044.4	3 212.3	3 366.0	3 777.1	3 562.5	3 696.8	2 599.5	2 055.5	2 022.1
Gambia Gambie	437.9	435.3	507.3	568.0	621.8	626.2	692.4	698.6	421.0	449.2
Georgia Géorgie	1 273.9	1 310.6	1 444.9	1 564.0	1 593.1	1 494.4	1 466.1	1 543.7	2 221.6	2 596.0
Ghana Ghana	4 994.4	5 253.5	5 755.7	6 418.7	5 878.8	5 727.7	1 882.5	3 032.3	3 418.2	4 125.8
Grenada Grenade	179.8	183.9	294.1	299.9	346.6	391.4	447.6	468.0	450.6	462.4
Guatemala Guatemala	2 539.7	2 928.4	3 097.7	3 426.6	3 794.5	3 687.5	3 920.8	4 188.6	4 352.1	4 930.9
Guinea Guinée	2 654.9	2 561.3	2 706.8	2 907.9	2 932.8	2 726.6	2 821.6	2 939.4	2 831.0	2 827.3
Guinea-Bissau Guinée-Bissau	822.1	779.8	837.6	914.2	968.2	880.8	901.7	925.3	930.5	949.7
Guyana Guyana	1 123.8	1 094.9	1 144.8	1 216.6	1 141.2	1 041.2	923.3	583.9	676.0	781.0

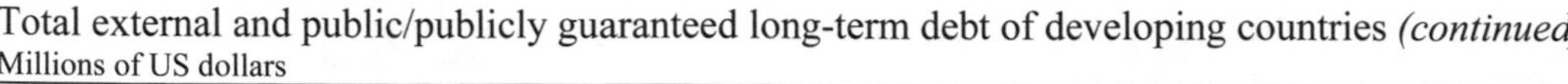

67 Total external and public/publicly guaranteed long-term debt of developing countries *(continued)*
Millions of US dollars

Total de la dette extérieure et dette publique extérieure à long terme garantie par l'Etat des pays en développement *(suite)*
Millions de dollars des E.-U.

B. Public and publicly guaranteed long term debt • Dette publique extérieure à long terme garantie par l'Etat

Country or area Pays ou zone	2000	2001	2002	2003	2004	2005	2006	2007	2008	2009
Haiti Haïti	1 043.0	1 031.3	1 065.9	1 210.1	1 225.0	1 277.9	1 346.1	1 524.6	1 841.7	1 077.5
Honduras Honduras	4 252.9	3 896.3	4 097.5	4 466.4	4 878.2	4 136.7	3 031.2	1 993.6	2 303.1	2 446.5
India Inde	81 194.9	78 976.9	82 052.2	63 672.6	64 879.5	54 728.7	60 034.9	69 719.4	74 966.5	76 530.9
Indonesia Indonésie	69 662.9	68 507.4	71 285.8	73 927.6	71 867.9	74 247.9	70 541.0	72 085.3	79 811.7	86 020.3
Iran (Islamic Rep. of) Iran (Rép. islamique d')	4 708.8	5 304.4	6 622.1	8 951.5	10 002.1	10 520.5	11 127.0	11 171.6	8 931.7	7 523.5
Jamaica Jamaïque	3 768.4	4 317.2	4 611.3	4 542.1	5 253.4	5 524.3	6 144.4	6 710.2	6 903.6	6 664.1
Jordan Jordanie	6 182.8	6 632.3	7 071.7	7 172.6	7 227.2	6 877.7	7 142.8	7 321.4	5 126.0	5 444.8
Kazakhstan Kazakhstan	3 622.5	3 450.2	3 210.4	3 469.4	3 232.9	2 176.8	2 136.2	1 697.7	1 915.0	2 486.9
Kenya Kenya	5 041.3	4 702.2	5 236.0	5 814.9	6 063.2	5 763.2	5 796.9	6 143.0	6 265.5	6 543.2
Kyrgyzstan Kirghizistan	1 220.3	1 256.8	1 397.3	1 584.5	1 742.4	1 664.8	1 830.8	1 897.9	1 962.8	2 319.5
Lao People's Dem. Rep. Rép. dém. pop. lao	2 458.6	2 455.4	2 619.7	1 892.0	2 033.6	1 989.4	2 259.2	2 515.1	2 720.5	2 922.8
Lebanon Liban	6 967.5	9 400.3	14 381.2	15 691.1	18 408.9	18 865.0	20 101.7	20 896.4	20 566.5	20 978.7
Lesotho Lesotho	656.7	578.5	628.5	672.6	721.6	618.9	613.5	642.2	659.2	681.1
Liberia Libéria	1 104.0	1 077.2	1 128.7	1 191.4	1 241.7	1 179.1	1 203.8	1 033.5	865.0	676.8
Lithuania Lituanie	2 206.4	2 382.5	2 499.9	2 129.5	3 067.7	1 990.9	4 576.8	5 866.4	5 334.6	9 059.1
Madagascar Madagascar	4 285.8	3 786.7	4 130.1	4 615.8	3 486.7	3 182.2	1 242.0	1 410.6	1 727.4	1 846.1
Malawi Malawi	2 544.1	2 468.8	2 670.1	2 934.5	3 295.6	3 061.8	788.9	804.9	834.7	899.4
Malaysia Malaisie	19 233.7	24 156.3	26 414.7	25 399.6	25 570.3	22 449.3	22 598.8	18 439.7	21 462.7	21 363.5
Maldives Maldives	184.7	180.7	223.0	260.7	333.3	329.7	383.6	444.4	497.3	569.4
Mali Mali	2 671.0	2 642.5	2 517.8	2 910.1	3 135.5	3 095.3	1 618.0	1 973.2	2 077.7	2 591.6
Mauritania Mauritanie	2 028.5	1 936.3	1 938.0	2 066.1	2 072.3	2 071.6	1 389.3	1 437.7	1 669.9	1 850.6
Mauritius Maurice	827.8	761.0	823.9	899.9	833.9	709.4	573.2	597.8	576.7	660.8
Mexico Mexique	81 488.2	94 159.8	99 434.0	106 660.0	108 507.0	108 482.0	96 029.4	105 376.0	113 950.0	99 373.6
Mongolia Mongolie	833.4	823.7	949.0	1 137.5	1 306.6	1 266.7	1 361.0	1 576.2	1 656.9	1 817.1
Montenegro Monténégro	...	...	...	...	...	...	828.6	848.1	855.3	1 093.0
Morocco Maroc	17 238.9	15 349.9	14 369.2	14 456.9	14 105.2	12 441.4	13 495.8	15 649.8	16 537.6	19 218.5
Mozambique Mozambique	4 740.5	2 582.8	2 903.4	3 188.5	3 435.5	3 430.9	2 109.4	2 424.2	2 844.8	3 354.3

67

Total external and public/publicly guaranteed long-term debt of developing countries *(continued)*
Millions of US dollars

Total de la dette extérieure et dette publique extérieure à long terme garantie par l'Etat des pays en développement *(suite)*
Millions de dollars des E.-U.

B. Public and publicly guaranteed long term debt • Dette publique extérieure à long terme garantie par l'Etat

Country or area Pays ou zone	2000	2001	2002	2003	2004	2005	2006	2007	2008	2009
Myanmar Myanmar	5 287.1	5 095.3	5 525.1	6 061.3	5 924.8	5 515.4	5 608.7	6 220.7	6 121.0	6 320.1
Nepal Népal	2 826.0	2 671.5	2 946.6	3 138.1	3 298.7	3 112.2	3 268.4	3 468.4	3 551.3	3 563.0
Nicaragua Nicaragua	5 380.2	5 335.0	5 448.3	5 758.5	3 993.9	3 898.6	3 195.9	2 146.7	2 230.4	2 460.6
Niger Niger	1 494.6	1 444.8	1 657.9	1 938.6	1 832.4	1 816.7	729.2	827.3	845.6	909.4
Nigeria Nigéria	30 019.9	29 218.1	28 057.1	31 267.1	32 521.1	20 197.8	3 743.6	3 509.1	3 877.7	4 156.5
Pakistan Pakistan	27 124.2	26 446.7	27 996.9	30 813.2	30 923.1	29 583.7	32 420.0	36 089.1	39 565.6	41 483.6
Panama Panama	5 696.4	6 320.0	6 398.1	6 475.1	7 209.0	7 486.9	8 682.5	9 175.0	9 609.8	11 281.9
Papua New Guinea Papouasie-Nvl-Guinée	1 454.0	1 370.2	1 438.8	1 504.5	1 445.1	1 261.7	1 207.9	1 126.2	1 063.9	1 036.9
Paraguay Paraguay	2 059.8	1 981.0	2 045.4	2 200.6	2 430.5	2 265.2	2 234.7	2 194.9	2 263.4	2 307.7
Peru Pérou	19 198.9	18 866.2	20 900.2	23 017.8	24 665.7	22 500.1	22 150.0	19 820.3	19 383.8	20 790.5
Philippines Philippines	33 744.5	29 210.2	32 318.6	36 146.7	35 981.2	35 364.1	36 750.8	37 959.2	39 077.2	41 738.4
Republic of Moldova République de Moldova	849.7	789.2	823.0	845.3	751.6	697.8	735.9	777.0	791.5	782.6
Romania Roumanie	6 583.0	7 028.7	9 028.7	11 723.6	13 661.9	13 329.6	14 184.5	15 200.3	14 987.8	17 904.1
Russian Federation Fédération de Russie	110 989.0	103 765.0	96 059.2	99 027.7	103 404.0	86 877.1	71 465.8	106 659.0	103 246.0	99 989.6
Rwanda Rwanda	1 146.6	1 161.9	1 303.4	1 414.2	1 540.2	1 414.5	380.1	542.8	627.4	725.5
Saint Kitts and Nevis Saint-Kitts-et-Nevis	153.1	215.1	264.8	314.2	312.6	292.0	289.2	270.9	246.6	222.3
Saint Lucia Sainte-Lucie	153.5	151.9	196.7	221.0	242.6	235.0	286.8	335.9	352.2	343.7
Saint Vincent-Grenadines Saint Vincent-Grenadines	163.3	162.4	172.8	194.0	223.0	246.3	241.0	198.3	202.4	201.7
Samoa Samoa	137.7	134.0	146.7	166.9	174.7	167.5	163.7	185.9	205.6	226.4
Sao Tome and Principe Sao Tomé-et-Principe	284.4	290.6	309.7	332.0	351.6	327.2	340.4	151.3	154.6	171.6
Senegal Sénégal	3 208.2	3 169.1	3 518.2	3 930.7	3 538.3	3 520.8	1 643.7	1 993.5	2 384.5	2 960.9
Serbia Serbie	6 178.0	6 177.6	7 538.9	8 130.6	8 124.2	7 622.9	7 631.1	8 313.6	8 311.5	8 725.5
Seychelles Seychelles	219.7	220.7	283.7	328.8	345.1	395.2	501.2	623.0	646.7	642.7
Sierra Leone Sierra Leone	972.8	1 033.6	1 175.6	1 334.6	1 410.4	1 327.1	1 220.0	270.4	336.4	370.9
Solomon Islands Iles Salomon	120.7	130.9	150.2	151.3	155.3	144.2	150.9	148.1	137.1	132.9
Somalia Somalie	1 825.1	1 794.7	1 859.9	1 936.1	1 949.1	1 881.5	1 922.6	1 978.8	1 982.8	1 987.5
South Africa Afrique du Sud	9 087.7	7 941.0	12 427.1	14 120.1	13 793.4	15 633.3	13 914.2	14 101.2	13 173.2	15 063.5

Total external and public/publicly guaranteed long-term debt of developing countries *(continued)*

Millions of US dollars

Total de la dette extérieure et dette publique extérieure à long terme garantie par l'Etat des pays en développement *(suite)*

Millions de dollars des E.-U.

B. Public and publicly guaranteed long term debt • Dette publique extérieure à long terme garantie par l'Etat

Country or area Pays ou zone	2000	2001	2002	2003	2004	2005	2006	2007	2008	2009
Sri Lanka Sri Lanka	7 876.5	7 437.3	8 348.8	9 119.4	9 805.9	9 611.9	10 295.5	11 835.6	12 608.8	13 646.8
Sudan Soudan	10 143.5	10 337.8	10 641.8	11 110.7	11 557.2	11 084.6	11 662.4	12 356.5	12 385.8	12 997.6
Swaziland Swaziland	262.9	262.2	311.3	355.1	365.3	362.2	364.7	368.6	355.0	390.8
Syrian Arab Republic Rép. arabe syrienne	16 464.0	16 111.5	...	...	...	...	...	...	4 737.0	4 480.4
Tajikistan Tadjikistan	755.1	761.6	901.1	908.8	804.1	825.6	839.8	1 063.1	1 374.4	1 603.1
Thailand Thaïlande	29 462.5	26 218.1	22 533.8	17 845.6	16 737.9	14 665.7	12 543.4	10 856.4	11 583.0	11 184.8
TFYR of Macedonia L'ex-R.Y. Macédoine	1 205.8	1 169.5	1 286.5	1 450.5	1 556.4	1 637.9	1 556.1	1 520.0	1 574.5	1 873.6
Togo Togo	1 227.6	1 201.8	1 333.3	1 494.5	1 600.2	1 444.8	1 551.3	1 652.3	1 479.1	1 501.5
Tonga Tonga	65.0	62.6	71.8	84.4	84.2	79.5	81.5	86.4	88.8	104.5
Tunisia Tunisie	8 884.3	9 109.0	10 974.5	13 235.2	14 488.9	12 999.5	13 438.1	14 507.8	14 437.7	14 836.6
Turkey Turquie	55 729.8	53 681.5	59 631.6	65 615.9	69 819.6	64 470.5	69 827.2	80 205.2	81 594.7	84 875.3
Turkmenistan Turkménistan	2 271.3	1 855.9	1 583.1	1 402.4	1 226.6	877.8	730.5	648.2	586.8	463.3
Uganda Ouganda	3 051.3	3 304.9	3 564.5	4 150.2	4 417.5	4 208.7	1 099.4	1 570.7	1 778.4	2 245.0
Ukraine Ukraine	8 141.8	8 098.6	8 272.1	8 890.9	9 882.0	9 750.9	9 754.8	10 847.5	11 121.6	10 449.0
United Rep. of Tanzania Rép.-Unie de Tanzanie	5 969.4	5 520.0	5 986.6	6 010.9	6 528.5	6 446.2	2 452.4	3 181.2	3 711.3	4 637.4
Uruguay Uruguay	5 550.6	6 061.9	6 707.1	7 478.6	7 828.1	7 734.4	9 083.0	10 328.0	9 980.5	10 954.7
Uzbekistan Ouzbékistan	3 761.7	3 896.0	4 005.5	4 149.0	4 107.2	3 619.1	3 289.0	3 133.3	3 143.6	3 237.9
Vanuatu Vanuatu	73.1	70.2	76.5	82.0	83.6	71.9	72.0	78.1	89.7	98.8
Venezuela (Boliv. Rep. of) Venezuela (Rép. boliv. du)	27 817.3	25 309.2	23 442.4	24 551.4	26 545.7	31 077.7	27 165.3	27 537.0	29 874.6	35 184.2
Viet Nam Viet Nam	11 583.9	11 433.6	12 159.5	14 342.6	15 574.5	16 257.2	16 002.6	17 943.4	20 564.1	23 403.4
Yemen Yémen	4 109.0	4 327.0	4 547.9	4 793.7	4 861.3	4 793.8	5 079.8	5 506.6	5 679.0	5 861.2
Zambia Zambie	4 443.7	4 826.6	5 255.6	5 572.6	5 842.9	3 944.9	967.3	1 115.9	1 166.8	1 210.1
Zimbabwe Zimbabwe	2 774.1	2 678.8	3 020.7	3 366.1	3 542.1	3 194.9	3 386.7	3 712.6	3 661.4	3 741.8

Source:
World Bank, Washington, D.C., the *Global Development Finance* (GDF) database, last accessed December 2010.

Source:
Banque mondiale, Washington, D.C., la base de données de "Global Development Finance" (GDF), dernier accès décembre 2010.

Technical notes: tables 65-67

Table 65: Foreign exchange rates are shown in units of national currency per US dollar. The exchange rates are classified into three broad categories, reflecting both the role of the authorities in the determination of the exchange and/or the multiplicity of exchange rates in a country. The *market rate* is used to describe exchange rates determined largely by market forces; the *official rate* is an exchange rate determined by the authorities, sometimes in a flexible manner. For countries maintaining multiple exchange arrangements, the rates are labelled *principal rate*, *secondary rate*, and *tertiary rate*. Unless otherwise stated, the table refers to end of period and period averages of market exchange rates or official exchange rates. For further information see *International Financial Statistics* and www.imf.org.

Table 66: Total Reserves Minus Gold is the sum of the items Foreign Exchange, shown in this table, as well as Reserve Position in the Fund, and the U.S. dollar value of SDR holdings by monetary authorities.

Foreign Exchange includes monetary authorities' claims on non-residents in the form of foreign banknotes, bank deposits, treasury bills, short- and long-term government securities, ECUs (for periods before January 1999), and other claims usable in the event of balance of payments need.

Table 67: The data on external debt for developing countries were extracted from *Global Development Finance*, published by the World Bank. In this table, developing countries are those in which 2009 GNI per capita was below $12,195.

The World Bank Debtor Reporting System (DRS) maintains statistics on the external debt of developing countries on a loan-by-loan basis. The estimated total external indebtedness of developing countries is a combination of DRS data and other information obtained from creditors through the debt data collection systems of other agencies such as the Bank for International Settlements (BIS) and the Organization for Economic Co-operation and Development (OECD), supplemented by market sources and estimates made by country economists of the World Bank and desk officers of the International Monetary Fund (IMF).

Long-term external debt is defined as debt that has an original or extended maturity of more than one year and that is owed to non-residents and is repayable in foreign currency, goods, or services. Long-term debt has three components: a) public debt, which is an external obligation of a public debtor, including the national government, a political subdivision (or an agency of either), and autonomous public bodies; b) publicly guaranteed debt, which is an external obligation of a private debtor that is guaranteed for repayment by a public entity; and c) private non-guaranteed external debt, which is an external obligation of a private debtor that is not guaranteed for repayment by a public entity. Public and publicly guaranteed long-term debts are aggregated.

All data related to public and publicly guaranteed debt

Notes techniques : tableaux 65 à 67

Tableau 65: Les taux des changes sont exprimés par le nombre d'unités de monnaie nationale pour un dollar des Etats-Unis. Les taux de change sont classés en trois catégories, qui dénotent le rôle des autorités dans l'établissement des taux de change et/ou la multiplicité des taux de change dans un pays. Par *taux du marché*, on entend les taux de change déterminés essentiellement par les forces du marché; le *taux officiel* est un taux de change établi par les autorités, parfois selon des dispositions souples. Pour les pays qui continuent à mettre en œuvre des régimes de taux de change multiples, les taux sont désignés par les appellations suivantes: "taux principal", "taux secondaire" et "taux tertiaire". Sauf indication contraire, le tableau indique des taux de fin de période et les moyennes sur la période, des taux de change du marché ou des taux de change officiels. Pour plus de renseignements, voir *Statistiques financières internationales* et www.imf.org.

Tableau 66 : Le total des réserves, déduction faite de l'or, correspond à la somme de tous les éléments de change figurant dans ce tableau, ainsi qu'à la situation des réserves du fonds, et à la valeur en dollars des États-Unis des droits de tirage spéciaux détenus par les autorités monétaires.

Les éléments de change comprennent les créances détenues par les autorités monétaires sur des non-résidents sous forme de billets de banque étrangers, de dépôts bancaires, de bons du Trésor, d'effets publics à court et à long terme, d'unités monétaires européennes (pour les périodes antérieures à 1999) et d'autres éléments utilisables si la situation de la balance des paiements l'exige.

Tableau 67: Les données concernant la dette extérieure des pays en développement sont tirées de *Global Development Finance*, publié par la Banque mondiale. Les pays en développement sont dans ce tableau ceux où le RNB par habitant était en 2009 inférieur à 12 195 dollars.

Le Système de notification de la dette de la Banque mondiale sert à tenir à jour prêt par prêt les statistiques de la dette extérieure des pays en développement. Le total estimatif de la dette extérieure des pays en développement a été calculé en combinant les données du Système de notification avec d'autres informations obtenues auprès des créanciers par le biais des systèmes de collecte de données d'autres organismes, tels que la Banque des règlements internationaux (BRI) et l'Organisation de coopération et développement économiques, ou de sources du marché, et avec des estimations des économistes chargés des pays à la Banque mondiale et au Fonds monétaire international (FMI).

La dette extérieure à long terme s'entend de celle dont la maturité d'origine (ou la maturité après prorogation) est à plus d'un an, contractée auprès de non-résidents et remboursable en devises, en biens ou en services. La dette à long terme comporte trois éléments : a) la dette publique, dette (ou administration relevant de l'un ou de l'autre), et adminis-

are from debtors except for those on lending by some multilateral agencies, in which case the data are taken from the creditors' records. These creditors include the African Development Bank, the Asian Development Bank, the Central Bank for Economic Integration, the Inter-American Development Bank, the International Bank for Reconstruction and Development (IBRD) and the International Development Association (IDA). (The IBRD and IDA are components of the World Bank.)

The data referring to public and publicly guaranteed debt do not include data for (a) transactions with the International Monetary Fund, (b) debt repayable in local currency, (c) direct investment and (d) short-term debt (that is, debt with an original maturity of less than a year).

The data referring to private non-guaranteed debt also exclude the above items but include contractual obligations on loans to direct-investment enterprises by foreign parent companies or their affiliates.

Data are aggregated by type of creditor. The breakdown is as follows:

Official creditors:

(a) Loans from international organizations (multilateral loans), excluding loans from funds administered by an international organization on behalf of a single donor government. The latter are classified as loans from governments;

(b) Loans from governments (bilateral loans) and from autonomous public bodies;

Private creditors:

(a) Suppliers: Credits from manufacturers, exporters, or other suppliers of goods;

(b) Financial markets: Loans from private banks and other private financial institutions as well as publicly issued and privately placed bonds;

(c) Other: External liabilities on account of nationalized properties and unclassified debts to private creditors.

A distinction is made between the following categories of external public debt:

– Debt outstanding (including undisbursed) is the sum of disbursed and undisbursed debt and represents the total outstanding external obligations of the borrower at year-end;

– Debt outstanding (disbursed only) is total outstanding debt drawn by the borrower at year-end;

– Commitments are the total of loans for which contracts are signed in the year specified;

– Disbursements are drawings on outstanding loan commitments during the year specified;

– Service payments are actual repayments of principal amortization and interest payments made in foreign currencies, goods or services in the year specified;

– Net flows (or net lending) are disbursements minus principal repayments;

– Net transfers are net flows minus interest payments or disbursements minus total debt-service payments.

The countries included in the table are those for which

trations publiques autonomes; b) la dette garantie par une administration publique, obligation extérieure d'un débiteur privé dont le remboursement est garanti par une entité publique; c) la dette extérieure privée non garantie, obligation extérieure d'un débiteur privé dont le remboursement n'est pas garanti par une entité publique. La dette extérieure publique et la dette extérieure garantie à long terme sont agrégées.

Toutes les données concernant la dette publique et la dette garantie par une entité publique proviennent des débiteurs, sauf celles concernant les prêts consentis par certains organismes multilatéraux, pour lesquels les données proviennent des dossiers des créanciers : il s'agit notamment de la Banque africaine de développement, de la Banque asiatique de développement, de la Banque centrale d'intégration économique, de la Banque interaméricaine de développement, de la Banque internationale de reconstruction et de développement (BIRD) et de l'Association internationale de développement (IDA) (la BIRD et l'IDA font partie du groupe de la Banque mondiale).

Les statistiques relatives à la dette publique ou à la dette garantie par l'Etat ne comprennent pas les données concernant: (a) les transactions avec le Fonds monétaire international; (b) la dette remboursable en monnaie nationale; (c) les investissements directs; et (d) la dette à court terme (c'est-à-dire la dette dont l'échéance initiale est inférieure à un an).

Les statistiques relatives à la dette privée non garantie ne comprennent pas non plus les éléments précités, mais comprennent les obligations contractuelles au titre des prêts consentis par des sociétés mères étrangères ou leurs filiales à des entreprises créées dans le cadre d'investissements directs.

Les données sont groupées par type de créancier, comme suit:

Créanciers publics:

(a) Les prêts obtenus auprès d'organisations internationales (prêts multilatéraux), à l'exclusion des prêts au titre de fonds administrés par une organisation internationale pour le compte d'un gouvernement donateur précis, qui sont classés comme prêts consentis par des gouvernements;

(b) Les prêts consentis par des gouvernements (prêts bilatéraux) et par des organisations publiques autonomes.

Créanciers privés:

(a) Fournisseurs: Crédits consentis par des fabricants exportateurs et autres fournisseurs de biens;

(b) Marchés financiers: prêts consentis par des banques privées et autres institutions financières privées, et émissions publiques d'obligations placées auprès d'investisseurs privés;

(c) Autres créanciers: engagements vis-à-vis de l'extérieur au titre des biens nationalisés et dettes diverses à l'égard de créanciers privés.

On fait une distinction entre les catégories suivantes de

data are sufficiently reliable to provide a meaningful presentation of debt outstanding and future service payments.

dette publique extérieure:

– L'encours de la dette (y compris les fonds non décaissés) est la somme des fonds décaissés et non décaissés et représente le total des obligations extérieures en cours de l'emprunteur à la fin de l'année;

– L'encours de la dette (fonds décaissés seulement) est le montant total des tirages effectués par l'emprunteur sur sa dette en cours à la fin de l'année;

– Les engagements représentent le total des prêts dont les contrats ont été signés au cours de l'année considérée;

– Les décaissements sont les sommes tirées sur l'encours des prêts pendant l'année considérée;

– Les paiements au titre du service de la dette sont les remboursements effectifs du principal et les paiements d'intérêts effectués en devises, biens ou services pendant l'année considérée;

– Les flux nets (ou prêts nets) sont les décaissements moins les remboursements de principal;

– Les transferts nets désignent les flux nets moins les paiements d'intérêts, ou les décaissements moins le total des paiements au titre du service de la dette.

Les pays figurant sur ce tableau sont ceux pour lesquels les données sont suffisamment fiables pour permettre une présentation significative de l'encours de la dette et des paiements futurs au titre du service de la dette.

Disbursements of bilateral and multilateral official development assistance and official aid to individual recipients

Versements d'aide publique au développement et d'aide publique bilatérale et multilatérale aux bénéficiaires

Country or area Pays ou zone	Year Année	Net disbursements (US $) - Versements nets ($E.-U.) Bilateral Bilatérale (millions)	Multilateral[1] Multilatérale[1] (millions)	Total (millions)	Per capita Par habitant
Total	**2004**	**79 855.0**	**20 532.8**	**100 387.9**	...
Total	**2005**	**107 830.0**	**24 490.3**	**132 320.3**	...
	2006	**104 823.7**	**27 388.1**	**132 211.8**	...
	2007	**104 181.1**	**29 603.3**	**133 784.4**	...
	2008	**122 296.0**	**34 034.1**	**156 330.1**	...
Afghanistan	2004	1 722.6	399.0	2 121.6	89.8
Afghanistan	2005	2 175.4	490.9	2 666.2	108.8
	2006	2 406.7	373.5	2 780.2	109.5
	2007	2 995.3	673.2	3 668.5	139.5
	2008	3 954.8	586.3	4 541.1	166.9
Albania	2004	172.2	98.2	270.3	87.2
Albanie	2005	178.2	116.2	294.4	94.6
	2006	193.8	94.2	288.0	92.3
	2007	205.1	102.6	307.7	98.2
	2008	267.9	110.9	378.7	120.5
Algeria	2004	234.8	92.1	326.9	10.1
Algérie	2005	266.6	94.2	360.7	11.0
	2006	206.4	69.8	276.2	8.3
	2007	291.9	105.8	397.7	11.8
	2008	244.7	101.3	346.0	10.1
Angola	2004	1 015.7	135.6	1 151.3	71.4
Angola	2005	247.7	196.0	443.7	26.7
	2006	-45.1	119.8	74.7	4.4
	2007	103.1	159.3	262.3	14.9
	2008	209.9	143.9	353.8	19.6
Anguilla	2004	1.4	1.2	2.6	193.5
Anguilla	2005	4.3	0.0	4.3	315.3
	2006	0.3	4.5	4.8	337.6
	2007	2.6	1.7	4.3	299.6
	2008	0.1	3.1	3.2	217.1
Antigua and Barbuda	2004	1.3	1.3	2.6	31.8
Antigua-et-Barbuda	2005	7.0	0.9	8.0	95.3
	2006	2.2	1.9	4.0	47.5
	2007	2.1	3.5	5.6	65.2
	2008	0.6	6.0	6.6	76.5
Argentina	2004	78.6	37.8	116.4	3.0
Argentine	2005	77.9	42.1	120.1	3.1
	2006	81.2	52.5	133.7	3.4
	2007	63.8	46.2	110.0	2.8
	2008	87.4	49.1	136.5	3.4
Armenia	2004	133.2	89.5	222.7	72.7
Arménie	2005	126.4	67.6	194.0	63.3
	2006	135.2	58.9	194.0	63.2
	2007	230.8	111.2	342.0	111.3
	2008	208.9	112.9	321.8	104.6
Azerbaijan	2004	92.4	61.7	154.1	18.4
Azerbaïdjan	2005	95.6	84.2	179.8	21.3
	2006	95.5	62.3	157.8	18.5
	2007	110.5	76.0	186.6	21.6
	2008	120.0	83.8	203.9	23.4
Bahrain Bahreïn	2004	1.5	0.4	1.9	2.6
Bangladesh	2004	656.2	605.2	1 261.5	8.4
Bangladesh	2005	580.3	721.5	1 301.8	8.5
	2006	478.5	493.7	972.2	6.3

68 Disbursements of bilateral and multilateral official development assistance and official aid to individual recipients *(continued)*

Versements d'aide publique au développement et d'aide publique bilatérale et multilatérale aux bénéficiaires *(suite)*

Country or area Pays ou zone	Year Année	Net disbursements (US $) - Versements nets ($E.-U.) Bilateral Bilatérale (millions)	Multilateral[1] Multilatérale[1] (millions)	Total (millions)	Per capita Par habitant
	2007	673.9	829.0	1 502.9	9.5
	2008	822.5	1 261.8	2 084.3	13.0
Barbados Barbade	2004	2.6	35.3	37.9	150.0
	2005	6.1	2.4	8.5	33.4
	2006	3.2	5.5	8.6	34.0
	2007	7.2	16.1	23.3	91.7
	2008	1.2	8.0	9.2	36.0
Belarus Bélarus	2005	33.8	16.5	50.3	5.1
	2006	38.2	29.7	67.9	7.0
	2007	48.8	23.0	71.8	7.4
	2008	58.3	30.2	88.5	9.1
Belize Belize	2004	3.9	2.4	6.3	22.8
	2005	7.5	5.9	13.4	47.5
	2006	4.2	6.7	10.8	37.6
	2007	8.5	12.4	20.9	71.1
	2008	4.4	15.8	20.2	67.3
Benin Bénin	2004	210.1	160.2	370.2	48.7
	2005	207.7	175.5	383.2	48.7
	2006	228.6	272.4	501.0	61.6
	2007	238.1	213.3	451.4	53.8
	2008	305.0	288.3	593.4	68.5
Bhutan Bhoutan	2004	53.3	23.0	76.2	120.3
	2005	57.2	37.3	94.5	145.4
	2006	51.3	32.6	83.9	126.4
	2007	43.7	45.1	88.7	131.3
	2008	49.1	34.2	83.3	121.2
Bolivia (Plurinational State of) Bolivie (État plurinational de)	2004	557.9	139.7	697.5	77.4
	2005	441.6	162.3	603.9	65.8
	2006	574.2	382.8	957.0	102.3
	2007	361.4	105.5	466.9	49.0
	2008	500.6	97.1	597.6	61.7
Bosnia and Herzegovina Bosnie-Herzégovine	2004	298.8	269.6	568.4	150.3
	2005	265.6	220.6	486.2	128.6
	2006	333.1	116.5	449.6	118.9
	2007	296.2	126.7	422.9	111.9
	2008	321.6	145.8	467.3	123.9
Botswana Botswana	2004	31.8	17.6	49.5	27.2
	2005	30.0	38.4	68.4	37.2
	2006	36.3	48.8	85.0	45.6
	2007	63.6	53.4	117.0	61.8
	2008	682.7	37.2	719.9	374.7
Brazil Brésil	2004	147.4	1 009.5	1 156.9	6.3
	2005	174.5	93.9	268.4	1.4
	2006	75.0	56.1	131.0	0.7
	2007	270.0	81.5	351.6	1.9
	2008	379.0	92.8	471.8	2.5
Burkina Faso Burkina Faso	2004	331.5	237.8	569.3	42.8
	2005	338.5	324.9	663.4	48.3
	2006	385.9	454.6	840.5	59.1
	2007	412.1	444.4	856.5	58.2
	2008	475.3	460.2	935.4	61.4
Burundi Burundi	2004	185.8	148.1	333.8	46.6
	2005	180.5	196.7	377.1	51.1
	2006	222.7	123.1	345.7	45.5
	2007	202.1	261.6	463.7	59.2
	2008	255.1	245.5	500.6	62.0
Cambodia Cambodge	2004	321.3	120.5	441.8	32.4
	2005	364.3	163.8	528.1	38.1

68 Disbursements of bilateral and multilateral official development assistance and official aid to individual recipients *(continued)*

Versements d'aide publique au développement et d'aide publique bilatérale et multilatérale aux bénéficiaires *(suite)*

Country or area Pays ou zone	Year Année	Net disbursements (US $) - Versements nets ($E.-U.) Bilateral Bilatérale (millions)	Multilateral[1] Multilatérale[1] (millions)	Total (millions)	Per capita Par habitant
	2006	361.3	141.8	503.1	35.7
	2007	452.5	189.9	642.5	44.9
	2008	459.7	210.5	670.2	46.0
Cameroon Cameroun	2004	572.7	162.0	734.7	42.2
	2005	332.1	140.6	472.7	26.5
	2006	1 505.6	348.2	1 853.7	101.6
	2007	1 697.1	200.7	1 897.8	101.7
	2008	298.4	202.6	501.0	26.3
Cape Verde Cap-Vert	2004	90.8	44.8	135.6	288.4
	2005	104.1	52.6	156.7	328.1
	2006	98.7	25.1	123.8	255.5
	2007	114.2	48.5	162.7	330.8
	2008	162.7	52.8	215.5	432.1
Central African Rep. Rép. centrafricaine	2004	54.8	56.8	111.6	27.7
	2005	60.5	51.7	112.2	27.4
	2006	65.3	69.8	135.1	32.3
	2007	118.0	102.6	220.5	51.8
	2008	128.5	127.7	256.2	59.0
Chad Tchad	2004	163.1	140.8	303.9	31.3
	2005	161.7	214.0	375.7	37.5
	2006	152.5	111.5	264.0	25.6
	2007	227.4	163.9	391.2	36.8
	2008	277.5	197.8	475.2	43.6
Chile Chili	2004	26.4	23.1	49.5	3.1
	2005	76.1	82.9	159.0	9.8
	2006	64.6	27.5	92.1	5.6
	2007	98.2	28.2	126.4	7.6
	2008	52.1	19.1	71.3	4.2
China Chine	2004	1 610.1	175.1	1 785.3	1.4
	2005	1 684.3	320.4	2 004.7	1.5
	2006	1 175.5	297.3	1 472.8	1.1
	2007	1 336.3	430.7	1 767.0	1.3
	2008	1 368.6	384.4	1 753.0	1.3
Colombia Colombie	2004	482.2	65.8	548.0	12.9
	2005	572.1	92.5	664.6	15.4
	2006	917.3	100.7	1 018.0	23.3
	2007	628.9	122.3	751.2	16.9
	2008	899.6	68.6	968.2	21.5
Comoros Comores	2004	13.9	11.4	25.3	42.0
	2005	15.1	18.2	33.2	53.9
	2006	19.9	17.3	37.3	59.1
	2007	19.6	32.9	52.5	81.3
	2008	20.8	20.5	41.3	62.6
Congo Congo	2004	47.8	51.8	99.6	29.8
	2005	1 344.0	79.5	1 423.5	416.6
	2006	169.4	83.1	252.5	72.4
	2007	48.6	82.8	131.4	37.0
	2008	382.6	96.5	479.1	132.5
Cook Islands Iles Cook	2004	5.9	2.2	8.1	430.8
	2005	7.0	0.8	7.7	405.6
	2006	31.0	3.1	34.1	1 761.4
	2007	9.0	1.9	10.9	558.6
	2008	4.4	1.4	5.8	295.2
Costa Rica Costa Rica	2004	11.9	13.8	25.7	6.0
	2005	25.5	23.6	49.0	11.3
	2006	20.8	19.2	40.0	9.1
	2007	50.1	16.3	66.4	14.9
	2008	61.9	16.0	77.9	17.2

Disbursements of bilateral and multilateral official development assistance and official aid to individual recipients *(continued)*

Versements d'aide publique au développement et d'aide publique bilatérale et multilatérale aux bénéficiaires *(suite)*

Country or area Pays ou zone	Year Année	Net disbursements (US $) - Versements nets ($E.-U.) Bilateral Bilatérale (millions)	Multilateral[1] Multilatérale[1] (millions)	Total (millions)	Per capita Par habitant
Côte d'Ivoire Côte d'Ivoire	2004	196.8	77.4	274.2	14.6
	2005	129.3	75.9	205.2	10.7
	2006	199.9	122.0	321.8	16.4
	2007	112.4	140.8	253.2	12.6
	2008	200.2	534.6	734.8	35.7
Croatia Croatie	2004	87.4	33.4	120.8	27.1
	2005	62.6	69.7	132.3	29.8
	2006	68.2	137.9	206.1	46.5
	2007	55.1	119.0	174.1	39.3
	2008	49.2	307.0	356.2	80.6
Cuba Cuba	2004	69.8	12.9	82.6	7.4
	2005	68.0	21.8	89.8	8.0
	2006	56.9	23.7	80.5	7.2
	2007	57.0	31.2	88.2	7.9
	2008	91.9	20.4	112.3	10.0
Dem. Rep. of the Congo Rép. dém. du Congo	2004	1 165.0	506.5	1 671.5	29.2
	2005	990.4	685.5	1 675.9	28.4
	2006	1 500.7	393.5	1 894.1	31.2
	2007	789.5	481.6	1 271.1	20.3
	2008	985.5	747.9	1 733.4	27.0
Djibouti Djibouti	2004	39.5	23.5	63.1	79.7
	2005	53.7	30.4	84.1	104.5
	2006	90.0	22.8	112.8	137.7
	2007	76.0	42.3	118.3	141.8
	2008	66.1	44.5	110.7	130.3
Dominica Dominique	2004	10.7	10.6	21.3	315.6
	2005	4.6	7.5	12.1	179.7
	2006	1.9	16.0	17.8	265.2
	2007	3.6	18.5	22.1	330.1
	2008	0.5	20.7	21.3	318.2
Dominican Republic Rép. dominicaine	2004	84.6	54.5	139.1	14.8
	2005	55.8	61.2	117.0	12.3
	2006	14.6	82.7	97.3	10.1
	2007	26.5	135.9	162.4	16.6
	2008	93.2	83.7	176.9	17.8
Ecuador Equateur	2004	158.0	33.2	191.2	14.8
	2005	192.2	77.0	269.2	20.6
	2006	170.8	63.0	233.8	17.7
	2007	183.8	67.8	251.6	18.9
	2008	196.0	58.8	254.8	18.9
Egypt Egypte	2004	1 177.8	312.3	1 490.1	19.7
	2005	667.2	311.5	978.7	12.7
	2006	542.4	323.0	865.4	11.0
	2007	792.8	278.0	1 070.9	13.4
	2008	967.3	301.1	1 268.4	15.6
El Salvador El Salvador	2004	202.1	31.9	234.0	38.8
	2005	164.6	66.5	231.1	38.2
	2006	151.0	36.5	187.4	30.8
	2007	72.6	44.5	117.1	19.2
	2008	205.8	43.5	249.3	40.6
Equatorial Guinea Guinée équatoriale	2004	23.1	8.7	31.8	53.6
	2005	29.8	20.4	50.2	82.4
	2006	18.9	22.4	41.3	66.1
	2007	25.8	14.5	40.3	62.7
	2008	18.5	16.5	35.0	53.1
Eritrea Erythrée	2004	177.5	65.2	242.7	56.4
	2005	226.0	124.1	350.1	78.3
	2006	63.2	58.7	121.9	26.3

Disbursements of bilateral and multilateral official development assistance and official aid to individual recipients *(continued)*

Versements d'aide publique au développement et d'aide publique bilatérale et multilatérale aux bénéficiaires *(suite)*

Country or area Pays ou zone	Year Année	Net disbursements (US $) - Versements nets ($E.-U.) Bilateral Bilatérale (millions)	Multilateral[1] Multilatérale[1] (millions)	Total (millions)	Per capita Par habitant
	2007	46.9	119.0	165.8	34.7
	2008	52.5	93.3	145.8	29.6
Ethiopia Ethiopie	2004	1 026.8	578.5	1 605.3	22.1
	2005	1 186.8	712.0	1 898.8	25.4
	2006	1 026.4	1 290.0	2 316.3	30.2
	2007	1 244.9	1 101.6	2 346.5	29.8
	2008	1 843.4	1 362.8	3 206.2	39.7
Fiji Fidji	2004	36.8	27.4	64.2	78.0
	2005	39.2	32.2	71.4	86.2
	2006	40.2	28.9	69.1	82.9
	2007	33.1	34.8	67.9	80.9
	2008	34.3	15.1	49.4	58.5
Gabon Gabon	2004	23.6	19.5	43.0	32.1
	2005	29.5	41.5	71.1	51.9
	2006	31.9	32.9	64.8	46.4
	2007	33.6	30.7	64.3	45.2
	2008	37.6	23.0	60.6	41.8
Gambia Gambie	2004	11.7	33.6	45.3	30.6
	2005	14.8	55.3	70.1	45.9
	2006	25.1	30.1	55.3	35.2
	2007	33.2	72.7	105.9	65.6
	2008	27.9	252.3	280.2	168.7
Georgia Géorgie	2004	209.1	96.2	305.3	67.6
	2005	183.3	114.5	297.7	66.7
	2006	210.5	94.8	305.3	69.2
	2007	244.4	141.5	385.9	88.6
	2008	578.5	271.3	849.8	197.3
Ghana Ghana	2004	928.5	347.2	1 275.7	59.5
	2005	615.3	503.0	1 118.2	51.0
	2006	594.9	1 023.2	1 618.1	72.3
	2007	709.8	390.6	1 100.4	48.1
	2008	725.7	537.2	1 262.9	54.1
Grenada Grenade	2004	10.6	4.8	15.3	149.7
	2005	26.1	20.0	46.2	450.5
	2006	3.5	16.1	19.5	189.7
	2007	4.6	13.8	18.4	177.9
	2008	1.4	18.5	19.8	191.5
Guatemala Guatemala	2004	204.6	34.5	239.0	19.3
	2005	220.5	59.2	279.8	22.0
	2006	447.4	61.0	508.4	39.0
	2007	415.2	64.4	479.6	35.9
	2008	469.7	78.1	547.8	40.0
Guinea Guinée	2004	178.3	102.2	280.5	31.0
	2005	126.0	104.8	230.8	25.0
	2006	102.9	67.7	170.6	18.1
	2007	124.5	146.7	271.1	28.2
	2008	209.9	148.0	358.0	36.4
Guinea-Bissau Guinée-Bissau	2004	28.6	47.4	76.0	52.9
	2005	26.8	56.1	82.9	56.3
	2006	39.4	61.0	100.4	66.6
	2007	43.6	99.7	143.3	93.0
	2008	52.9	86.4	139.2	88.4
Guyana Guyana	2004	70.3	25.0	95.3	124.9
	2005	40.1	66.8	106.9	140.0
	2006	46.6	93.0	139.6	182.7
	2007	40.6	49.1	89.7	117.4
	2008	41.9	86.2	128.1	167.8

Disbursements of bilateral and multilateral official development assistance and official aid to individual recipients *(continued)*

Versements d'aide publique au développement et d'aide publique bilatérale et multilatérale aux bénéficiaires *(suite)*

Country or area Pays ou zone	Year Année	Net disbursements (US $) - Versements nets ($E.-U.) Bilateral Bilatérale (millions)	Multilateral[1] Multilatérale[1] (millions)	Total (millions)	Per capita Par habitant
Haiti	2004	209.1	70.0	279.1	30.2
Haïti	2005	284.0	147.4	431.4	45.8
	2006	363.3	160.0	523.3	54.7
	2007	434.5	199.4	633.8	65.2
	2008	556.9	256.3	813.2	82.3
Honduras	2004	332.7	151.8	484.5	71.7
Honduras	2005	458.0	183.1	641.1	93.0
	2006	385.7	292.8	678.5	96.5
	2007	292.7	138.2	430.9	60.1
	2008	355.8	129.4	485.2	66.3
India	2004	15.4	898.9	914.3	0.8
Inde	2005	845.0	1 117.7	1 962.8	1.7
	2006	653.7	611.5	1 265.2	1.1
	2007	907.1	901.4	1 808.4	1.6
	2008	1 549.4	1 245.0	2 794.3	2.4
Indonesia	2004	-100.5	187.1	86.7	0.4
Indonésie	2005	2 260.4	279.0	2 539.4	11.6
	2006	620.9	426.1	1 047.0	4.7
	2007	391.4	436.3	827.7	3.7
	2008	593.3	625.1	1 218.4	5.4
Iran (Islamic Rep. of)	2004	140.2	43.8	184.1	2.6
Iran (Rép. islamique d')	2005	77.4	34.1	111.5	1.6
	2006	71.3	50.0	121.3	1.7
	2007	72.2	31.7	103.9	1.4
	2008	63.7	22.6	86.3	1.2
Iraq	2004	4 466.0	160.3	4 626.3	167.8
Iraq	2005	21 972.6	57.3	22 030.0	780.2
	2006	8 544.9	57.6	8 602.5	297.9
	2007	9 054.3	113.2	9 167.5	310.9
	2008	9 762.6	65.0	9 827.7	326.5
Jamaica	2004	13.4	74.7	88.1	33.3
Jamaïque	2005	11.4	46.0	57.4	21.5
	2006	-0.5	64.8	64.3	24.0
	2007	-16.9	61.5	44.6	16.5
	2008	-4.2	90.5	86.3	31.9
Jordan	2004	434.7	107.9	542.5	100.5
Jordanie	2005	441.5	100.8	542.2	97.4
	2006	365.1	103.2	468.2	81.5
	2007	291.7	118.6	410.3	69.1
	2008	428.6	165.0	593.6	96.7
Kazakhstan	2004	206.4	23.5	229.9	15.2
Kazakhstan	2005	149.9	24.9	174.8	11.5
	2006	98.7	33.7	132.4	8.7
	2007	183.0	30.7	213.7	13.9
	2008	233.1	38.3	271.3	17.5
Kenya	2004	470.3	204.3	674.6	19.3
Kenya	2005	520.9	298.0	818.9	22.9
	2006	775.6	236.4	1 012.0	27.5
	2007	826.7	465.8	1 292.5	34.2
	2008	953.2	445.4	1 398.6	36.1
Kiribati	2004	10.1	5.2	15.3	169.5
Kiribati	2005	21.4	8.6	30.0	325.8
	2006	19.7	7.9	27.6	294.9
	2007	22.7	7.1	29.8	313.5
	2008	20.1	5.9	26.1	269.9
Korea, Dem. P. R.	2004	102.2	48.1	150.3	6.4
Corée, R. p. dém. de	2005	39.5	50.4	89.9	3.8
	2006	28.9	37.5	66.3	2.8

68 Disbursements of bilateral and multilateral official development assistance and official aid to individual recipients *(continued)*

Versements d'aide publique au développement et d'aide publique bilatérale et multilatérale aux bénéficiaires *(suite)*

Country or area Pays ou zone	Year Année	Net disbursements (US $) - Versements nets ($E.-U.) Bilateral Bilatérale (millions)	Multilateral[1] Multilatérale[1] (millions)	Total (millions)	Per capita Par habitant
	2007	71.7	38.2	109.8	4.6
	2008	189.6	28.5	218.1	9.2
Kyrgyzstan Kirghizistan	2004	110.0	87.0	197.0	38.1
	2005	125.3	87.5	212.9	40.8
	2006	124.2	65.2	189.4	35.9
	2007	118.8	96.8	215.6	40.3
	2008	142.4	142.6	285.0	52.7
Lao People's Dem. Rep. Rép. dém. pop. lao	2004	179.7	80.7	260.4	45.0
	2005	168.6	126.5	295.1	50.2
	2006	201.2	98.8	299.9	50.1
	2007	239.6	129.0	368.7	60.5
	2008	225.2	139.0	364.3	58.7
Lebanon Liban	2004	129.7	104.3	234.0	58.1
	2005	129.7	77.1	206.8	50.7
	2006	389.3	254.2	643.5	156.0
	2007	469.7	115.6	585.2	140.6
	2008	749.1	163.6	912.8	217.7
Lesotho Lesotho	2004	35.1	47.4	82.5	41.7
	2005	39.9	43.8	83.6	41.9
	2006	38.5	35.5	73.9	36.7
	2007	62.3	83.2	145.5	71.6
	2008	66.0	87.3	153.3	74.8
Liberia Libéria	2004	163.0	56.8	219.7	68.1
	2005	143.9	109.5	253.4	76.0
	2006	187.4	96.4	283.8	81.8
	2007	229.1	364.1	593.1	163.5
	2008	819.2	227.2	1 046.4	275.9
Libyan Arab Jamah. Jamah. arabe libyenne	2005	16.8	6.7	23.5	4.0
	2006	33.5	6.6	40.1	6.6
	2007	15.6	5.2	20.8	3.4
	2008	52.2	7.4	59.5	9.5
Madagascar Madagascar	2004	684.7	391.1	1 075.8	62.8
	2005	497.7	392.1	889.7	50.5
	2006	261.1	701.6	962.6	53.2
	2007	386.6	452.1	838.7	45.1
	2008	274.5	495.6	770.1	40.3
Malawi Malawi	2004	308.3	177.6	485.9	36.6
	2005	325.4	286.9	612.3	44.8
	2006	398.0	593.5	991.5	70.6
	2007	400.7	346.6	747.3	51.8
	2008	432.0	403.1	835.1	56.3
Malaysia Malaisie	2004	294.1	1.5	295.6	11.7
	2005	18.5	13.5	32.0	1.3
	2006	231.1	15.0	246.2	9.4
	2007	192.4	15.2	207.6	7.8
	2008	153.3	10.0	163.3	6.1
Maldives Maldives	2004	8.9	8.6	17.5	60.7
	2005	42.8	25.9	68.7	234.9
	2006	16.1	24.8	40.9	137.9
	2007	18.1	26.5	44.6	148.3
	2008	20.7	8.9	29.6	97.0
Mali Mali	2004	327.6	235.9	563.5	48.8
	2005	370.8	329.3	700.1	59.2
	2006	398.4	554.0	952.5	78.6
	2007	557.6	396.0	953.7	76.9
	2008	531.4	367.8	899.2	70.8
Marshall Islands Iles Marshall	2004	49.5	1.0	50.4	907.7
	2005	55.8	1.5	57.3	1 010.1

68 Disbursements of bilateral and multilateral official development assistance and official aid to individual recipients *(continued)*

Versements d'aide publique au développement et d'aide publique bilatérale et multilatérale aux bénéficiaires *(suite)*

Country or area Pays ou zone	Year Année	Net disbursements (US $) - Versements nets ($E.-U.) Bilateral Bilatérale (millions)	Multilateral[1] Multilatérale[1] (millions)	Total (millions)	Per capita Par habitant
	2006	55.0	1.2	56.3	970.6
	2007	51.5	2.5	54.0	910.7
	2008	50.5	2.5	53.0	874.4
Mauritania Mauritanie	2004	83.8	106.7	190.5	65.5
	2005	105.4	88.9	194.3	65.1
	2006	93.8	232.0	325.8	106.4
	2007	133.4	183.9	317.3	101.1
	2008	139.1	132.2	271.3	84.4
Mauritius Maurice	2004	14.8	23.2	38.0	30.6
	2005	21.5	23.7	45.2	36.1
	2006	8.5	28.2	36.7	29.1
	2007	43.6	40.8	84.4	66.4
	2008	16.1	96.2	112.3	87.7
Mayotte Mayotte	2004	208.6	0.0	208.6	1 231.5
	2005	201.9	0.2	202.1	1 158.2
	2006	337.5	0.3	337.8	1 882.4
	2007	406.9	0.6	407.5	2 209.9
	2008	474.7	0.7	475.4	2 511.8
Mexico Mexique	2004	80.5	70.3	150.8	1.5
	2005	161.1	54.8	215.9	2.1
	2006	209.2	55.3	264.5	2.5
	2007	79.3	85.8	165.1	1.5
	2008	105.3	42.1	147.5	1.4
Micronesia (Fed. States of) Micronésie (Etats féd. de)	2004	85.2	0.7	85.8	788.1
	2005	104.4	2.4	106.8	976.4
	2006	106.0	2.3	108.3	986.4
	2007	110.7	3.7	114.3	1 038.3
	2008	86.6	5.5	92.1	834.0
Mongolia Mongolie	2004	149.3	73.5	222.8	88.5
	2005	131.4	61.3	192.7	75.6
	2006	132.0	50.5	182.5	70.7
	2007	153.2	64.4	217.6	83.3
	2008	177.5	62.2	239.7	90.8
Montenegro Monténégro	2006	60.3	22.3	82.6	133.0
	2007	45.3	45.0	90.3	145.3
	2008	60.7	34.0	94.7	152.1
Montserrat Montserrat	2004	37.4	7.5	44.8	8 374.1
	2005	27.0	1.0	28.0	4 968.0
	2006	24.9	7.5	32.4	5 603.7
	2007	32.5	3.9	36.4	6 192.3
	2008	32.3	1.8	34.1	5 771.4
Morocco Maroc	2004	396.0	240.1	636.1	21.1
	2005	288.3	334.7	623.0	20.4
	2006	569.1	368.2	937.3	30.4
	2007	630.8	356.1	986.9	31.6
	2008	614.4	458.1	1 072.5	33.9
Mozambique Mozambique	2004	731.3	403.8	1 135.1	55.9
	2005	760.3	484.0	1 244.3	59.7
	2006	938.4	654.4	1 592.8	74.6
	2007	1 073.4	623.2	1 696.6	77.6
	2008	1 341.3	598.2	1 939.5	86.7
Myanmar Myanmar	2004	84.4	43.4	127.9	2.7
	2005	85.8	104.4	190.1	3.9
	2006	100.5	80.3	180.8	3.7
	2007	129.8	104.1	233.9	4.8
	2008	421.8	112.9	534.7	10.8
Namibia Namibie	2004	124.0	44.0	168.0	85.2
	2005	88.1	47.3	135.4	67.4

68 Disbursements of bilateral and multilateral official development assistance and official aid to individual recipients *(continued)*

Versements d'aide publique au développement et d'aide publique bilatérale et multilatérale aux bénéficiaires *(suite)*

Country or area Pays ou zone	Year Année	Net disbursements (US $) - Versements nets ($E.-U.) Bilateral Bilatérale (millions)	Multilateral[1] Multilatérale[1] (millions)	Total (millions)	Per capita Par habitant
	2006	105.7	64.9	170.7	83.3
	2007	143.5	98.1	241.6	115.7
	2008	150.0	59.5	209.5	98.3
Nauru Nauru	2004	13.6	0.0	13.6	1 347.6
	2005	9.0	0.4	9.4	929.7
	2006	17.3	0.8	18.0	1 777.9
	2007	25.1	0.9	26.0	2 563.0
	2008	29.0	1.5	30.5	2 997.0
Nepal Népal	2004	320.2	128.8	448.9	16.8
	2005	347.3	134.3	481.5	17.7
	2006	319.5	175.6	495.1	17.8
	2007	388.9	234.6	623.5	22.0
	2008	455.8	261.0	716.7	24.9
Nicaragua Nicaragua	2004	856.6	168.7	1 025.3	190.4
	2005	510.2	167.9	678.1	124.3
	2006	391.1	335.7	726.8	131.6
	2007	503.0	189.8	692.8	123.8
	2008	540.3	115.3	655.6	115.7
Niger Niger	2004	305.7	192.3	498.1	39.4
	2005	254.4	245.4	499.7	38.1
	2006	235.3	398.2	633.5	46.6
	2007	232.8	275.5	508.3	36.0
	2008	269.1	292.6	561.7	38.2
Nigeria Nigéria	2004	313.7	257.7	571.4	4.2
	2005	5 930.5	436.3	6 366.8	45.2
	2006	10 820.0	381.2	11 201.2	77.6
	2007	1 384.8	514.3	1 899.1	12.9
	2008	637.2	618.5	1 255.7	8.3
Niue Nioué	2004	13.8	^0.0	13.9	8 195.3
	2005	20.1	2.0	22.1	13 461.1
	2006	8.6	1.7	10.2	6 381.3
	2007	14.0	1.3	15.3	9 807.3
	2008	16.4	1.5	17.9	11 812.8
Occupied Palestinian Terr. Terr. palestinien occupé	2004	609.0	308.6	917.6	252.4
	2005	570.6	316.3	887.0	235.8
	2006	755.6	367.5	1 123.2	288.8
	2007	833.9	693.1	1 526.9	380.1
	2008	1 350.3	718.2	2 068.5	498.8
Oman Oman	2004	2.1	3.4	5.5	2.1
	2005	3.7	4.6	8.3	3.2
	2006	-14.5	4.0	-10.5	-3.9
	2007	9.7	3.8	13.4	4.9
	2008	4.0	0.9	4.9	1.7
Pakistan Pakistan	2004	383.3	751.0	1 134.3	7.0
	2005	790.1	729.4	1 519.5	9.2
	2006	1 149.0	493.5	1 642.5	9.7
	2007	979.7	1 044.9	2 024.6	11.7
	2008	918.5	624.5	1 542.9	8.7
Palau Palaos	2004	19.5	...	19.5	971.9
	2005	23.4	0.3	23.7	1 175.7
	2006	37.2	0.6	37.8	1 868.5
	2007	21.8	0.5	22.3	1 098.3
	2008	40.6	1.4	42.0	2 062.5
Panama Panama	2004	25.7	112.5	138.2	43.5
	2005	17.9	14.8	32.6	10.1
	2006	19.7	25.1	44.8	13.6
	2007	-137.5	20.6	-116.9	-35.0
	2008	27.3	10.6	37.9	11.1

Disbursements of bilateral and multilateral official development assistance and official aid to individual recipients *(continued)*

Versements d'aide publique au développement et d'aide publique bilatérale et multilatérale aux bénéficiaires *(suite)*

Country or area Pays ou zone	Year Année	Net disbursements (US $) - Versements nets ($E.-U.) Bilateral Bilatérale (millions)	Multilateral[1] Multilatérale[1] (millions)	Total (millions)	Per capita Par habitant
Papua New Guinea Papouasie-Nvl-Guinée	2004	249.4	30.7	280.1	46.9
	2005	244.9	52.0	296.9	48.5
	2006	247.8	51.3	299.1	47.7
	2007	288.1	60.5	348.7	54.3
	2008	263.0	54.3	317.3	48.3
Paraguay Paraguay	2004	27.5	7.4	34.9	6.0
	2005	57.3	13.0	70.3	11.9
	2006	64.1	11.2	75.2	12.5
	2007	88.6	33.4	122.0	19.9
	2008	102.5	34.4	136.9	21.9
Peru Pérou	2004	442.4	64.6	507.0	18.4
	2005	391.5	102.7	494.2	17.8
	2006	379.3	104.6	483.9	17.2
	2007	181.5	113.7	295.2	10.4
	2008	393.4	79.6	472.9	16.4
Philippines Philippines	2004	421.3	60.3	481.6	5.7
	2005	532.3	85.2	617.4	7.2
	2006	526.5	88.0	614.5	7.1
	2007	575.6	131.3	706.9	8.0
	2008	-4.9	98.2	93.4	1.0
Republic of Moldova République de Moldova	2004	76.6	30.4	107.0	28.0
	2005	84.5	77.4	161.9	43.1
	2006	83.5	59.8	143.3	38.7
	2007	93.1	151.6	244.8	66.7
	2008	114.2	134.2	248.4	68.4
Rwanda Rwanda	2004	216.9	210.0	427.0	48.4
	2005	281.4	297.2	578.6	64.3
	2006	321.5	400.0	721.5	78.3
	2007	374.7	324.5	699.2	74.0
	2008	451.6	427.6	879.1	90.4
Saint Helena Sainte-Hélène	2004	26.1	0.1	26.2	5 473.2
	2005	22.5	0.3	22.7	4 819.7
	2006	23.1	5.0	28.1	6 046.5
	2007	40.6	4.0	44.5	9 727.0
	2008	56.0	8.8	64.8	14 344.6
Saint Kitts and Nevis Saint-Kitts-et-Nevis	2004	-0.1	0.8	0.7	13.4
	2005	1.8	1.5	3.2	65.5
	2006	3.6	4.8	8.4	169.4
	2007	3.6	2.6	6.3	124.6
	2008	33.3	12.4	45.7	894.0
Saint Lucia Sainte-Lucie	2004	-23.7	3.8	-19.9	-121.7
	2005	6.6	6.0	12.6	76.3
	2006	2.4	7.7	10.1	60.7
	2007	7.6	10.0	17.6	104.3
	2008	-0.3	18.7	18.4	108.0
Saint Vincent-Grenadines Saint Vincent-Grenadines	2004	7.3	5.3	12.6	116.2
	2005	5.8	1.7	7.5	68.5
	2006	2.3	3.9	6.3	57.5
	2007	48.0	19.1	67.1	615.2
	2008	10.0	16.3	26.2	240.5
Samoa Samoa	2004	24.7	7.1	31.8	178.1
	2005	30.1	19.9	49.9	278.9
	2006	38.4	12.6	51.0	284.7
	2007	29.3	13.2	42.5	237.6
	2008	26.4	15.1	41.5	232.1
Sao Tome and Principe Sao Tomé-et-Principe	2004	21.8	10.9	32.7	217.7
	2005	18.4	21.8	40.2	263.7
	2006	18.3	15.7	34.0	219.1

68 Disbursements of bilateral and multilateral official development assistance and official aid to individual recipients *(continued)*

Versements d'aide publique au développement et d'aide publique bilatérale et multilatérale aux bénéficiaires *(suite)*

Country or area Pays ou zone	Year Année	Net disbursements (US $) - Versements nets ($E.-U.) Bilateral Bilatérale (millions)	Multilateral[1] Multilatérale[1] (millions)	Total (millions)	Per capita Par habitant
	2007	31.1	61.1	92.2	584.8
	2008	26.4	20.1	46.6	290.7
Saudi Arabia Arabie saoudite	2004	8.7	95.6	104.3	4.5
	2005	13.2	2.4	15.6	0.7
	2006	11.2	7.1	18.3	0.8
	2007	-144.0	4.0	-139.9	-5.7
Senegal Sénégal	2004	755.9	246.0	1 001.8	91.2
	2005	444.1	261.3	705.5	62.5
	2006	510.0	529.8	1 039.8	89.8
	2007	453.2	315.5	768.6	64.6
	2008	554.4	404.2	958.6	78.5
Serbia Serbie	2004	584.0	496.7	1 080.7	109.2
	2005	766.5	249.0	1 015.5	103.0
	2006	1 169.5	381.5	1 551.0	157.7
	2007	476.4	347.9	824.4	83.9
	2008	541.3	419.3	960.6	97.6
Seychelles Seychelles	2004	6.1	1.9	8.0	97.0
	2005	7.9	6.8	14.8	178.9
	2006	7.2	8.3	15.5	186.6
	2007	1.5	5.4	6.9	83.1
	2008	5.0	6.7	11.7	139.8
Sierra Leone Sierra Leone	2004	162.7	147.6	310.2	63.0
	2005	129.3	212.5	341.8	66.9
	2006	179.5	137.4	317.0	60.1
	2007	380.9	484.3	865.2	159.6
	2008	174.9	172.1	347.0	62.4
Solomon Islands Iles Salomon	2004	116.8	11.4	128.1	277.5
	2005	172.3	31.6	203.9	430.4
	2006	179.0	29.9	208.9	429.8
	2007	237.0	12.4	249.5	500.7
	2008	219.1	7.8	226.9	444.4
Somalia Somalie	2004	139.7	56.6	196.3	24.0
	2005	145.1	117.5	262.6	31.4
	2006	263.2	149.6	412.8	48.3
	2007	256.7	156.0	412.7	47.3
	2008	565.6	178.8	744.3	83.4
South Africa Afrique du Sud	2004	459.3	158.1	617.3	13.0
	2005	466.0	247.7	713.7	14.9
	2006	560.8	180.3	741.1	15.2
	2007	594.2	250.5	844.7	17.2
	2008	881.7	222.3	1 104.0	22.2
Sri Lanka Sri Lanka	2004	342.5	162.1	504.6	26.1
	2005	858.1	262.8	1 120.9	57.4
	2006	507.8	189.5	697.3	35.4
	2007	331.2	271.6	602.7	30.3
	2008	406.1	338.1	744.1	37.1
Sudan Soudan	2004	849.4	129.8	979.2	25.8
	2005	1 455.5	350.1	1 805.6	46.7
	2006	1 517.9	451.4	1 969.3	49.8
	2007	1 665.4	361.6	2 027.0	50.1
	2008	1 820.9	387.8	2 208.7	53.4
Suriname Suriname	2004	15.8	6.8	22.6	45.7
	2005	33.6	12.4	46.0	92.0
	2006	55.7	7.3	63.0	124.6
	2007	123.9	29.1	152.9	299.7
	2008	74.0	24.1	98.1	190.4
Swaziland Swaziland	2004	7.3	25.5	32.8	29.4
	2005	21.0	45.0	65.9	58.6

Disbursements of bilateral and multilateral official development assistance and official aid to individual recipients *(continued)*

Versements d'aide publique au développement et d'aide publique bilatérale et multilatérale aux bénéficiaires *(suite)*

Country or area Pays ou zone	Year Année	Net disbursements (US $) - Versements nets ($E.-U.) Bilateral Bilatérale (millions)	Multilateral[1] Multilatérale[1] (millions)	Total (millions)	Per capita Par habitant
	2006	12.3	40.1	52.5	46.2
	2007	12.5	46.6	59.1	51.3
	2008	17.8	58.6	76.4	65.5
Syrian Arab Republic Rép. arabe syrienne	2004	15.9	134.5	150.4	8.1
	2005	5.8	67.6	73.4	3.8
	2006	-10.4	55.3	44.9	2.3
	2007	9.4	86.7	96.2	4.7
	2008	54.7	78.0	132.7	6.3
Tajikistan Tadjikistan	2004	92.1	85.7	177.9	27.6
	2005	105.0	106.1	211.1	32.3
	2006	91.9	101.5	193.4	29.2
	2007	106.2	91.3	197.4	29.4
	2008	143.4	121.4	264.8	38.7
Thailand Thaïlande	2004	-1.2	39.6	38.3	0.6
	2005	-210.5	74.1	-136.4	-2.1
	2006	-290.7	115.1	-175.6	-2.6
	2007	-394.1	136.4	-257.7	-3.9
	2008	-698.8	91.8	-607.0	-9.0
TFYR of Macedonia L'ex-R.Y. Macédoine	2004	162.2	99.0	261.1	128.5
	2005	165.4	73.5	238.9	117.4
	2006	131.0	83.1	214.1	105.1
	2007	134.1	78.2	212.2	104.0
	2008	141.0	77.6	218.6	107.1
Timor-Leste Timor-Leste	2004	141.4	20.8	162.1	170.5
	2005	160.4	34.4	194.9	196.5
	2006	174.3	43.0	217.2	211.1
	2007	227.6	60.6	288.2	270.8
	2008	230.3	44.8	275.1	250.4
Togo Togo	2004	52.4	15.3	67.8	11.6
	2005	58.8	38.9	97.6	16.3
	2006	54.9	44.0	98.9	16.1
	2007	65.2	84.6	149.8	23.8
	2008	176.0	236.6	412.6	63.9
Tokelau Tokélaou	2004	8.4	0.0	8.4	6 637.7
	2005	15.9	0.2	16.2	13 314.1
	2006	10.7	0.8	11.5	9 688.0
	2007	12.6	1.0	13.5	11 447.9
	2008	21.4	0.0	21.4	18 053.9
Tonga Tonga	2004	14.9	4.9	19.9	196.3
	2005	24.8	9.5	34.3	336.4
	2006	18.7	5.1	23.7	231.3
	2007	26.6	6.4	33.0	319.9
	2008	23.4	2.7	26.1	252.1
Trinidad and Tobago Trinité-et-Tobago	2004	7.3	13.5	20.7	15.8
	2005	6.1	8.7	14.8	11.3
	2006	4.1	22.9	27.0	20.4
	2007	7.0	21.5	28.5	21.5
	2008	3.9	8.6	12.5	9.4
Tunisia Tunisie	2004	232.1	107.3	339.4	34.7
	2005	268.2	131.4	399.6	40.5
	2006	286.0	178.9	465.0	46.6
	2007	193.6	163.9	357.5	35.5
	2008	250.6	229.8	480.4	47.2
Turkey Turquie	2004	-17.0	324.8	307.8	4.4
	2005	-9.4	448.0	438.6	6.2
	2006	147.1	426.8	573.9	8.0
	2007	240.6	592.0	832.6	11.4
	2008	659.7	1 228.3	1 888.0	25.5

68 Disbursements of bilateral and multilateral official development assistance and official aid to individual recipients *(continued)*

Versements d'aide publique au développement et d'aide publique bilatérale et multilatérale aux bénéficiaires *(suite)*

Country or area Pays ou zone	Year Année	Net disbursements (US $) - Versements nets ($E.-U.) Bilateral Bilatérale (millions)	Multilateral[1] Multilatérale[1] (millions)	Total (millions)	Per capita Par habitant
Turkmenistan Turkménistan	2004	11.4	4.7	16.1	3.4
	2005	11.9	7.9	19.8	4.1
	2006	5.4	9.0	14.4	2.9
	2007	1.4	9.3	10.6	2.1
	2008	-1.1	9.7	8.6	1.7
Turks and Caicos Islands Iles Turques et Caïques	2004	1.2	1.5	2.7	93.0
	2005	3.1	1.8	4.9	159.5
	2006	0.1	0.1	0.1	4.1
	2007	2.6	13.2	15.9	489.9
Tuvalu Tuvalu	2004	5.4	2.6	7.9	814.7
	2005	5.9	3.4	9.3	951.7
	2006	12.7	2.9	15.6	1 592.4
	2007	9.0	2.8	11.8	1 195.5
	2008	14.7	1.1	15.8	1 600.9
Uganda Ouganda	2004	684.1	421.1	1 105.1	39.8
	2005	690.8	507.1	1 197.8	41.7
	2006	938.4	958.1	1 896.5	64.0
	2007	1 002.7	633.6	1 636.3	53.4
	2008	1 005.7	620.7	1 626.4	51.4
Ukraine Ukraine	2005	236.0	144.0	380.0	8.1
	2006	281.4	190.2	471.6	10.1
	2007	245.0	170.8	415.8	9.0
	2008	286.3	271.7	558.0	12.1
United Rep. of Tanzania Rép.-Unie de Tanzanie	2004	1 029.9	579.6	1 609.5	42.4
	2005	860.7	666.4	1 527.0	39.2
	2006	995.6	1 193.5	2 189.1	54.6
	2007	1 839.0	844.2	2 683.2	65.0
	2008	1 372.9	916.0	2 288.9	53.9
Uruguay Uruguay	2004	10.1	13.6	23.7	7.1
	2005	3.0	17.1	20.1	6.0
	2006	10.8	18.5	29.4	8.8
	2007	19.9	20.8	40.7	12.2
	2008	12.8	20.1	32.9	9.8
Uzbekistan Ouzbékistan	2004	208.1	24.5	232.6	8.9
	2005	123.5	38.2	161.7	6.1
	2006	96.8	44.6	141.3	5.3
	2007	105.5	53.7	159.2	5.9
	2008	113.2	50.8	164.0	6.0
Vanuatu Vanuatu	2004	34.6	3.5	38.1	181.0
	2005	33.4	11.0	44.4	205.2
	2006	41.4	12.9	54.3	244.4
	2007	52.2	9.6	61.8	270.8
	2008	89.1	4.2	93.3	399.0
Venezuela (Boliv. Rep. of) Venezuela (Rép. boliv. du)	2004	28.4	43.6	72.0	2.7
	2005	21.0	34.4	55.4	2.1
	2006	33.0	29.9	62.9	2.3
	2007	44.8	31.9	76.6	2.8
	2008	46.6	13.7	60.3	2.2
Viet Nam Viet Nam	2004	1 216.2	446.9	1 663.1	20.0
	2005	1 268.1	513.7	1 781.8	21.2
	2006	1 316.4	266.2	1 582.6	18.6
	2007	1 513.0	712.3	2 225.3	25.8
	2008	1 649.4	796.2	2 445.6	28.1
Wallis and Futuna Islands Iles Wallis et Futuna	2004	71.5	1.3	72.8	4 901.7
	2005	71.7	0.4	72.1	4 830.4
	2006	102.0	0.5	102.4	6 827.3
	2007	117.0	0.1	117.1	7 754.3
	2008	129.8	0.6	130.4	8 574.2

Disbursements of bilateral and multilateral official development assistance and official aid to individual recipients *(continued)*

Versements d'aide publique au développement et d'aide publique bilatérale et multilatérale aux bénéficiaires *(suite)*

Country or area Pays ou zone	Year Année	Net disbursements (US $) - Versements nets ($E.-U.) Bilateral Bilatérale (millions)	Multilateral[1] Multilatérale[1] (millions)	Total (millions)	Per capita Par habitant
Yemen Yémen	2004	154.0	120.1	274.1	13.4
	2005	156.9	164.8	321.7	15.3
	2006	142.7	104.0	246.7	11.4
	2007	169.0	141.0	310.0	13.9
	2008	207.0	190.1	397.1	17.3
Zambia Zambie	2004	745.8	291.6	1 037.4	90.4
	2005	822.6	459.0	1 281.6	109.2
	2006	1 115.4	742.3	1 857.7	154.6
	2007	713.8	286.7	1 000.5	81.3
	2008	703.9	402.9	1 106.7	87.7
Zimbabwe Zimbabwe	2004	166.6	55.0	221.6	17.7
	2005	186.9	166.3	353.2	28.3
	2006	200.0	100.6	300.6	24.1
	2007	371.9	132.6	504.5	40.5
	2008	532.4	78.8	611.2	49.0

Source:
Organization for Economic Co-operation and Development (OECD), Paris, the OECD Development Assistance Committee database, last accessed December 2010. Per capita calculated by the United Nations Statistics Division from the *World Population Prospects: The 2008 Revision*, mid-year population data.

1 As reported by OECD/DAC, covers agencies of the United Nations family, the European Commission, IDA and the concessional lending facilities of regional development banks. Excluding non-concessional flows (i.e., less than 25% grant elements).

Source:
Organisation de coopération et de développement économiques (OCDE), Paris, la base de données du comité d'aide au développement de l'OCDE, dernier accès décembre 2010. Les données par habitant ont été calculées par la Division de statistiques de l'ONU de "World Population Prospects: The 2008 Revision," d'après les données de la population au milieu de l'année.

1 Communiqué par le Comité d'aide au développement de l'OCDE, comprend les institutions et organismes du système des Nations Unies, la commission européenne, l'Association internationale de développement, et les mécanismes de prêt à des conditions privilégiées des banques régionales de développement. Les apports aux conditions du marché (élément de libéralité inférieur à 25) en sont exclus.

Net official development assistance from DAC countries to developing countries and multilateral organizations

Net disbursements: millions of US dollars and as a percentage of gross national income (GNI)

Aide publique au développement nette des pays du CAD aux pays en développement et aux organisations multilatérales

Versements nets: millions de dollars E.-U. et en pourcentage du revenu national brut (RNB)

Country or area Pays ou zone	2004 $ millions	2004 % of GNI % du RNB	2005 $ millions	2005 % of GNI % du RNB	2006 $ millions	2006 % of GNI % du RNB	2007 $ millions	2007 % of GNI % du RNB	2008 $ millions	2008 % of GNI % du RNB	2009 $ millions	2009 % of GNI % du RNB
Total **Total**	**79 855**	**0.25**	**107 830**	**0.32**	**104 823**	**0.30**	**104 181**	**0.27**	**122 296**	**0.30**	**119 681**	**0.31**
Australia Australie	1 460	0.25	1 680	0.25	2 123	0.30	2 669	0.32	2 954	0.32	2 761	0.29
Austria Autriche	678	0.23	1 573	0.52	1 498	0.47	1 808	0.50	1 714	0.43	1 142	0.30
Belgium Belgique	1 463	0.41	1 963	0.53	1 977	0.50	1 951	0.43	2 386	0.48	2 610	0.55
Canada Canada	2 599	0.27	3 756	0.34	3 683	0.29	4 080	0.29	4 795	0.33	4 013	0.30
Czech Republic République tchèque	108	0.11	135	0.11	161	0.12	179	0.11	249	0.12	...	...
Denmark Danemark	2 037	0.85	2 109	0.81	2 236	0.80	2 562	0.81	2 803	0.82	2 810	0.88
Finland Finlande	680	0.37	902	0.46	834	0.40	981	0.39	1 166	0.44	1 286	0.54
France France	8 473	0.41	10 026	0.47	10 601	0.47	9 884	0.38	10 908	0.39	12 431	0.46
Germany Allemagne	7 534	0.28	10 082	0.36	10 435	0.36	12 291	0.37	13 981	0.38	12 079	0.35
Greece Grèce	321	0.16	384	0.17	424	0.17	501	0.16	703	0.21	607	0.19
Hungary Hongrie	70	0.07	100	0.11	149	0.13	103	0.08	107	0.08	...	...
Iceland Islande	21	0.18	27	0.18	41	0.27	48	0.27	48	0.47	...	...
Ireland Irlande	607	0.39	719	0.42	1 022	0.54	1 192	0.55	1 328	0.59	1 006	0.54
Italy Italie	2 462	0.15	5 091	0.29	3 641	0.20	3 971	0.19	4 861	0.22	3 297	0.16
Japan Japon	8 922	0.19	13 126	0.28	11 136	0.25	7 679	0.17	9 579	0.19	9 480	0.18
Korea, Republic of Corée, République de	423	0.06	752	0.10	455	0.05	696	0.07	802	0.09	816	0.10
Luxembourg Luxembourg	236	0.79	256	0.79	291	0.89	376	0.92	415	0.97	415	1.04
Netherlands Pays-Bas	4 204	0.73	5 115	0.82	5 452	0.81	6 224	0.81	6 993	0.80	6 426	0.82
New Zealand Nouvelle-Zélande	212	0.23	274	0.27	259	0.27	320	0.27	348	0.30	309	0.28
Norway Norvège	2 199	0.87	2 786	0.94	2 954	0.89	3 728	0.95	3 963	0.88	4 086	1.06
Poland Pologne	118	0.05	205	0.07	297	0.09	363	0.10	372	0.08	...	...
Portugal Portugal	1 031	0.63	377	0.21	396	0.21	471	0.22	620	0.27	513	0.23
Slovakia Slovaquie	28	0.07	56	0.12	55	0.10	67	0.09	92	0.10	...	...
Spain Espagne	2 437	0.24	3 018	0.27	3 814	0.32	5 140	0.37	6 867	0.45	6 571	0.46

Net official development assistance from DAC countries to developing countries and multilateral organizations *(continued)*

Net disbursements: millions of US dollars and as a percentage of gross national income (GNI)

Aide publique au développement nette des pays du CAD aux pays en développement et aux organisations multilatérales *(suite)*

Versements nets: millions de dollars E.-U. et en pourcentage du revenu national brut (RNB)

Country or area Pays ou zone	2004 $ millions	2004 % of GNI % du RNB	2005 $ millions	2005 % of GNI % du RNB	2006 $ millions	2006 % of GNI % du RNB	2007 $ millions	2007 % of GNI % du RNB	2008 $ millions	2008 % of GNI % du RNB	2009 $ millions	2009 % of GNI % du RNB
Sweden Suède	2 722	0.78	3 362	0.94	3 955	1.02	4 339	0.93	4 732	0.98	4 548	1.12
Switzerland Suisse	1 545	0.40	1 772	0.43	1 646	0.39	1 685	0.38	2 038	0.44	2 305	0.47
Turkey Turquie	339	0.11	601	0.17	714	0.18	602	0.09	780	0.11	...	...
United Kingdom Royaume-Uni	7 905	0.36	10 772	0.47	12 459	0.51	9 849	0.36	11 500	0.43	11 505	0.52
United States Etats-Unis	19 705	0.17	27 935	0.23	23 532	0.18	21 787	0.16	26 842	0.19	28 665	0.20

Source:
Organisation for Economic Co-operation and Development (OECD), Paris, the OECD Development Assistance Committee database, last accessed December 2010.

Source :
Organisation de coopération et de développement économiques (OCDE), Paris, la base de données du Comité d'aide au développement de l'OCDE, dernier accès décembre 2010.

70 Socio-economic development assistance through the United Nations system

Development grants: thousands of US dollars, 2008

Assistance en matière de développement socioéconomique fournie par le système des Nations Unies

Subventions au développement : en milliers de dollars des E.-U., 2008

Region, country or area Région, pays ou zone	UNDP PNUD	UNFPA FNUAP	UNHCR HCR	UNICEF	WFP PAM	IFAD FIDA	Specialized agencies[a] Institutions spécialisées[a]	Other UN funds and programmes[b] Autres fonds et programmes des NU[b]	Total development grants Total subventions au développ.
Total Total	**4 269 797**	**436 455**	**1 597 473**	**2 808 339**	**3 535 746**	**450 077**	**3 762 977**	**1 641 788**	**18 630 532**
Regional programmes Totaux régionaux	**455 456**	**0**	**0**	**169 525**	**3 234**	**0**	**2 172 108**	**388 210**	**3 286 235**
Africa Afrique	2 672	0	0	21 145	1 307	0	509 994	41 355	591 705
Americas Amériques	9 108	0	0	12 245	1 851	0	101 327	11 628	149 779
Asia and the Pacific Asie et le Pacifique	2 537	0	0	24 087	55	0	304 393	18 584	365 212
Europe Europe	10 404	0	0	4 348	0	0	122 587	5 524	155 263
Western Asia Asie occidentale	431	0	0	2 749	21	0	257 143	11 999	276 508
Global/Interregional Global/Interrégional	173 810	0	0	104 951	0	0	873 885	299 121	1 488 420
Other countries Autres pays	256 494	0	0	0	0	0	2 778	0	259 357
Not elsewhere classified Non-classé ailleurs	**0**	**6 421**	**285 077**	**0**	**175 185**	**...**	**660 747**	**102 502**	**1 234 824**
Total all countries Total, tous pays	**3 814 341**	**430 034**	**1 312 397**	**2 638 814**	**3 357 327**	**450 077**	**930 122**	**1 151 076**	**14 109 464**
Afghanistan Afghanistan	405 825	8 067	74 514	74 967	204 841	0	39 091	37 792	845 096
Albania Albanie	6 011	737	728	6 270	0	2 147	1 882	1 001	18 776
Algeria Algérie	1 294	308	9 560	1 473	22 776	0	1 830	376	37 617
Angola Angola	35 196	2 702	4 570	60 052	3 503	531	5 336	740	112 631
Antigua and Barbuda Antigua-et-Barbuda	561	0	0	0	0	0	337	0	898
Argentina Argentine	164 816	636	4 002	4 835	0	3 065	15 398	774	194 178
Armenia Arménie	6 278	984	2 556	1 237	3 824	4 281	2 604	262	22 027
Aruba Aruba	0	0	0	0	0	0	38	0	38
Australia Australie	0	0	1 093	0	0	0	42	0	1 135
Austria Autriche	0	0	984	0	0	0	115	0	1 099
Azerbaijan Azerbaïdjan	9 029	1 285	3 773	2 468	1 473	4 254	1 730	94	24 107
Bahamas Bahamas	0	0	0	0	0	0	47	0	47
Bahrain Bahreïn	1 516	0	0	0	0	0	221	-194	1 543
Bangladesh Bangladesh	96 116	8 279	6 863	68 237	94 938	13 411	13 665	2 443	303 952

70

Socio-economic development assistance through the United Nations system *(continued)*

Development grants: thousands of US dollars, 2008

Assistance en matière de développement socioéconomique fournie par le système des Nations Unies *(suite)*

Subventions au développement : en milliers de dollars des E.-U., 2008

Region, country or area Région, pays ou zone	UNDP PNUD	UNFPA FNUAP	UNHCR HCR	UNICEF	WFP PAM	IFAD FIDA	Specialized agencies[a] Institutions spécialisées[a]	Other UN funds and programmes[b] Autres fonds et programmes des NU[b]	Total development grants Total subventions au développ.
Barbados Barbade	3 904	0	0	0	86	0	592	273	4 855
Belarus Bélarus	10 483	453	1 333	869	0	0	521	109	13 768
Belgium Belgique	0	0	3 806	0	0	0	0	0	3 806
Belize Belize	1 431	0	0	1 383	50	0	369	23	3 256
Benin Bénin	6 398	3 088	1 529	17 653	4 627	2 633	1 742	698	38 369
Bhutan Bhoutan	4 391	1 138	0	3 164	2 210	1 840	254	682	13 680
Bolivia (Plurin. State of) Bolivie (État plurin. de)	35 396	2 495	0	17 123	11 391	3 500	7 172	1 451	78 564
Bosnia and Herzegovina Bosnie-Herzégovine	23 072	474	6 130	3 818	0	2 353	1 043	-5	36 885
Botswana Botswana	8 152	1 713	2 827	3 279	0	0	1 091	361	17 422
Brazil Brésil	154 984	2 718	3 785	17 395	0	12 056	118 160	16 253	325 930
Brunei Darussalam Brunéi Darussalam	0	0	0	0	0	0	0	3	3
Bulgaria Bulgarie	9 700	257	893	1 407	0	0	1 165	44	13 466
Burkina Faso Burkina Faso	17 756	5 115	0	31 970	14 182	7 924	6 223	710	83 880
Burundi Burundi	33 432	8 770	34 747	19 678	31 845	6 300	8 869	1 130	144 871
Cambodia Cambodge	35 415	6 328	1 222	21 381	20 187	4 146	9 265	2 229	121 960
Cameroon Cameroun	5 487	2 382	10 673	14 722	8 752	3 205	2 484	870	48 575
Canada Canada	0	0	1 584	0	0	0	35	0	1 619
Cape Verde Cap-Vert	4 581	1 437	0	741	673	1 026	1 352	753	10 563
Central African Rep. Rép. centrafricaine	16 831	3 787	4 566	22 314	36 160	0	4 065	2 894	90 617
Chad Tchad	6 733	8 132	93 214	33 926	94 714	3 609	6 471	4 914	251 714
Chile Chili	17 706	209	0	1 160	0	20 772	1 579	120	41 949
China Chine	62 697	6 762	7 771	38 642	402	5 686	20 852	2 285	145 099
China, Macao SAR Chine, Macao RAS	0	0	0	0	0	0	565	0	565
Colombia Colombie	105 324	3 698	16 957	11 302	19 658	90	8 782	46 984	213 263
Comoros Comores	3 034	841	0	3 597	0	90	218	0	7 780
Congo Congo	11 970	2 587	6 014	6 868	3 411	2 798	1 543	413	35 603
Cook Islands Iles Cook	280	0	0	0	0	0	249	0	529
Costa Rica Costa Rica	4 889	608	3 149	882	0	0	1 764	174	11 480

Socio-economic development assistance through the United Nations system *(continued)*

Development grants: thousands of US dollars, 2008

Assistance en matière de développement socioéconomique fournie par le système des Nations Unies *(suite)*

Subventions au développement : en milliers de dollars des E.-U., 2008

Region, country or area Région, pays ou zone	UNDP PNUD	UNFPA FNUAP	UNHCR HCR	UNICEF	WFP PAM	IFAD FIDA	Specialized agencies[a] Institutions spécialisées[a]	Other UN funds and programmes[b] Autres fonds et programmes des NU[b]	Total development grants Total subventions au développ.
Côte d'Ivoire Côte d'Ivoire	30 981	7 585	8 376	34 072	16 543	1 056	6 054	6 103	110 770
Croatia Croatie	8 525	0	3 513	1 411	0	439	653	84	14 625
Cuba Cuba	19 331	1 023	278	2 671	4 134	0	3 300	11	30 748
Cyprus Chypre	15 519	0	862	0	0	0	46	0	16 427
Czech Republic République tchèque	0	0	427	0	0	0	118	0	545
Dem. Rep. of the Congo Rép. dém. du Congo	188 313	12 585	62 373	151 629	101 323	2 361	34 719	12 698	566 002
Djibouti Djibouti	1 564	848	4 446	6 350	8 227	828	654	0	22 917
Dominica Dominique	300	0	0	0	0	0	1 081	5	1 386
Dominican Republic Rép. dominicaine	9 674	1 710	0	1 907	3 057	106	2 677	319	19 555
Ecuador Equateur	36 490	1 359	7 252	6 141	79 284	543	2 614	223	133 929
Egypt Egypte	64 504	2 857	10 514	10 762	4 536	12 817	10 506	2 870	119 366
El Salvador El Salvador	13 307	1 448	0	2 190	3 837	4 905	4 503	143	30 334
Equatorial Guinea Guinée équatoriale	2 168	1 708	0	1 557	0	0	330	0	5 762
Eritrea Erythrée	14 074	2 105	4 496	16 081	137	2 771	2 159	758	42 580
Estonia Estonie	0	0	0	0	0	0	1 682	0	1 682
Ethiopia Ethiopie	46 971	9 535	37 290	128 345	287 404	6 573	18 545	5 380	540 043
Fiji Fidji	11 618	0	0	0	0	0	381	339	12 338
Finland Finlande	0	0	0	0	0	0	50	0	50
France France	0	0	2 805	0	0	0	565	0	3 369
Gabon Gabon	4 161	991	2 233	1 493	0	0	2 822	411	12 110
Gambia Gambie	3 999	1 169	75	2 969	3 849	2 731	910	101	15 803
Georgia Géorgie	11 175	1 995	21 706	7 544	9 510	2 883	1 698	376	56 887
Germany Allemagne	0	0	2 467	0	0	0	537	0	3 004
Ghana Ghana	13 857	3 915	6 458	24 635	9 209	5 930	3 085	506	67 596
Greece Grèce	0	0	1 156	0	0	0	714	0	1 870
Grenada Grenade	338	0	0	0	0	699	324	0	1 361
Guatemala Guatemala	82 747	4 327	0	6 956	8 165	4 756	9 874	425	117 250
Guinea Guinée	16 327	2 978	7 870	11 374	19 733	4 000	2 511	1 587	66 379

Socio-economic development assistance through the United Nations system *(continued)*
Development grants: thousands of US dollars, 2008

Assistance en matière de développement socioéconomique fournie par le système des Nations Unies *(suite)*
Subventions au développement : en milliers de dollars des E.-U., 2008

Region, country or area Région, pays ou zone	UNDP PNUD	UNFPA FNUAP	UNHCR HCR	UNICEF	WFP PAM	IFAD FIDA	Specialized agencies[a] Institutions spécialisées[a]	Other UN funds and programmes[b] Autres fonds et programmes des NU[b]	Total development grants Total subventions au développ.
Guinea-Bissau Guinée-Bissau	10 325	2 714	0	6 903	3 316	0	1 529	981	25 768
Guyana Guyana	502	0	0	2 280	0	365	431	315	3 892
Haiti Haïti	20 796	5 381	0	21 565	59 523	9 502	10 783	2 725	130 275
Honduras Honduras	53 152	2 711	0	5 163	-983	7 047	4 833	574	72 496
Hungary Hongrie	0	0	2 681	0	0	0	219	0	2 900
Iceland Islande	0	0	0	0	0	0	49	0	49
India Inde	42 615	9 162	4 204	106 233	19 128	15 890	11 977	5 181	214 391
Indonesia Indonésie	66 816	5 465	2 479	116 013	26 025	4 868	31 532	7 818	261 017
Iran (Islamic Rep. of) Iran (Rép. islamique d')	9 183	1 512	15 563	2 752	1 238	0	1 949	2 229	34 427
Iraq Iraq	86 356	3 610	50 707	40 292	45 388	0	36 561	13 311	276 225
Ireland Irlande	0	0	724	0	0	0	0	0	724
Israel Israël	0	0	1 753	0	0	0	223	0	2 041
Italy Italie	0	0	3 915	0	0	0	1 143	0	5 058
Jamaica Jamaïque	2 911	0	0	3 117	1	0	1 155	555	7 738
Japan Japon	0	0	2 895	0	0	0	2 814	1 023	6 732
Jordan Jordanie	16 405	509	45 556	6 762	138	6 662	2 466	131 801	210 300
Kazakhstan Kazakhstan	11 910	718	2 030	2 029	0	0	377	602	17 667
Kenya Kenya	39 066	6 905	66 462	44 695	162 293	11 170	5 804	3 971	340 365
Kiribati Kiribati	4	0	0	0	0	0	50	0	54
Korea, Dem. P. R. Corée, R. p. dém. de	-10	3 623	0	15 015	73 026	2 290	3 574	0	97 519
Korea, Republic of Corée, République de	8 136	0	749	0	0	0	1 275	206	10 351
Kosovo Kosovo	14 244	883	0	3 670	0	0	718	1 720	21 235
Kuwait Koweït	3 226	0	0	0	0	0	400	116	3 742
Kyrgyzstan Kirghizistan	17 284	869	1 716	2 654	69	0	1 432	1 441	25 465
Lao People's Dem. Rep. Rép. dém. pop. lao	13 126	1 571	0	14 348	9 436	5 149	3 805	2 494	50 103
Latvia Lettonie	1 125	0	0	0	0	0	524	0	1 649
Lebanon Liban	40 112	1 448	8 806	9 297	0	7	12 210	124 096	195 976
Lesotho Lesotho	2 773	1 272	0	6 558	10 927	1 621	3 372	469	26 993

70

Socio-economic development assistance through the United Nations system *(continued)*
Development grants: thousands of US dollars, 2008

Assistance en matière de développement socioéconomique fournie par le système des Nations Unies *(suite)*
Subventions au développement : en milliers de dollars des E.-U., 2008

Region, country or area Région, pays ou zone	UNDP PNUD	UNFPA FNUAP	UNHCR HCR	UNICEF	WFP PAM	IFAD FIDA	Specialized agencies[a] Institutions spécialisées[a]	Other UN funds and programmes[b] Autres fonds et programmes des NU[b]	Total development grants Total subventions au développ.
Liberia Libéria	49 727	5 971	26 555	32 294	31 980	0	7 800	14	154 342
Libyan Arab Jamah. Jamah. arabe libyenne	3 203	0	1 888	0	194	0	3 028	2 345	10 659
Lithuania Lituanie	946	0	0	0	0	0	903	75	1 924
Madagascar Madagascar	9 207	4 386	0	32 512	13 120	6 368	10 153	536	76 375
Malawi Malawi	26 207	14 169	2 241	38 785	28 858	3 465	6 566	660	120 951
Malaysia Malaisie	4 759	408	5 652	1 444	0	0	676	0	12 939
Maldives Maldives	4 381	513	0	4 040	0	0	152	-10	9 076
Mali Mali	19 698	3 679	76	27 120	13 577	5 266	5 144	981	75 541
Malta Malte	0	0	112	0	0	0	321	0	433
Marshall Islands Iles Marshall	0	0	0	0	0	0	93	0	93
Mauritania Mauritanie	7 312	3 765	8 549	6 623	27 659	5 980	2 925	610	63 423
Mauritius Maurice	6 318	83	0	0	0	31	657	233	7 322
Mexico Mexique	23 582	2 717	2 231	6 746	314	6 304	11 098	911	54 307
Micronesia (Fed. States of) Micronésie (Etats féd. de)	0	0	0	0	0	0	55	0	55
Mongolia Mongolie	4 453	2 523	169	3 259	0	2 192	2 797	411	15 804
Montenegro Monténégro	6 210	0	2 642	934	0	0	594	0	10 381
Montserrat Montserrat	3	0	0	0	0	0	0	0	3
Morocco Maroc	15 285	2 228	1 620	4 449	0	9 762	5 294	653	39 292
Mozambique Mozambique	16 435	13 810	3 411	64 540	42 055	6 604	12 105	4 256	163 217
Myanmar Myanmar	25 356	6 720	13 742	79 540	81 165	0	10 896	4 599	222 018
Namibia Namibie	8 288	1 918	2 516	5 135	3 313	0	1 720	523	23 413
Nauru Nauru	0	0	0	0	0	0	61	0	61
Nepal Népal	25 485	6 695	10 958	26 365	44 388	2 467	4 574	2 909	123 842
Nicaragua Nicaragua	29 266	5 176	0	6 286	15 893	5 608	6 211	79	68 563
Niger Niger	14 805	5 386	0	40 127	31 382	2 601	6 645	1 311	102 256
Nigeria Nigéria	35 803	12 458	3 230	110 657	0	8 881	5 649	11 481	188 160
Niue Nioué	271	0	0	0	0	0	53	0	324
Norway Norvège	0	0	0	0	0	0	32	0	32

70

Socio-economic development assistance through the United Nations system *(continued)*
Development grants: thousands of US dollars, 2008

Assistance en matière de développement socioéconomique fournie par le système des Nations Unies *(suite)*
Subventions au développement : en milliers de dollars des E.-U., 2008

Region, country or area Région, pays ou zone	UNDP PNUD	UNFPA FNUAP	UNHCR HCR	UNICEF	WFP PAM	IFAD FIDA	Specialized agencies[a] Institutions spécialisées[a]	Other UN funds and programmes[b] Autres fonds et programmes des NU[b]	Total development grants Total subventions au developp.
Occupied Palestinian Terr. Terr. palestinien occupé	0	4 953	0	20 970	52 244	0	6 500	502 167	586 833
Oman Oman	0	845	0	1 218	0	0	414	0	2 477
Pakistan Pakistan	30 993	7 719	31 988	84 413	46 792	11 251	18 969	11 124	243 319
Palau Palaos	0	0	0	0	0	0	10	0	10
Panama Panama	187 194	951	1 233	1 424	55	3 824	6 750	191	201 660
Papua New Guinea Papouasie-Nvl-Guinée	6 173	1 638	913	7 227	0	0	240	332	16 523
Paraguay Paraguay	20 224	1 552	0	1 935	0	1 024	654	0	25 394
Peru Pérou	103 022	8 628	0	9 522	52 375	5 565	9 209	4 604	192 953
Philippines Philippines	12 343	5 014	213	15 867	8 327	6 056	3 971	578	52 369
Poland Pologne	4 240	16	873	0	0	0	710	502	6 341
Portugal Portugal	0	0	86	0	0	0	431	0	517
Qatar Qatar	0	0	0	0	0	0	1 016	1 308	2 324
Republic of Moldova République de Moldova	17 826	669	703	3 698	0	13 139	2 462	644	39 142
Romania Roumanie	5 884	478	954	2 713	0	0	1 316	1 335	12 680
Russian Federation Fédération de Russie	11 595	1 430	14 841	11 255	6 185	0	3 250	6 101	54 656
Rwanda Rwanda	27 094	4 715	8 779	17 537	19 343	9 929	3 536	1 122	92 054
Saint Kitts and Nevis Saint-Kitts-et-Nevis	27	0	0	0	0	0	434	0	461
Saint Lucia Sainte-Lucie	256	0	0	0	0	0	185	0	441
Saint Vincent-Grenadines Saint Vincent-Grenadines	289	0	0	0	0	0	421	117	827
Samoa Samoa	1 780	0	0	0	0	0	311	0	2 091
Sao Tome and Principe Sao Tomé-et-Principe	2 224	653	0	1 146	635	1 025	274	0	5 957
Saudi Arabia Arabie saoudite	8 757	0	3 155	1 145	0	0	16 659	0	29 716
Senegal Sénégal	13 894	3 360	13 372	11 770	8 559	7 400	5 010	252	63 617
Serbia and Montenegro Serbie-et-Monténégro	17 629	158	23 393	3 281	0	0	5 444	1 627	51 532
Seychelles Seychelles	0	87	0	0	0	0	586	0	673
Sierra Leone Sierra Leone	39 190	5 949	6 620	23 505	14 803	654	2 827	1 176	94 724
Singapore Singapour	0	0	0	0	0	0	176	0	176
Slovakia Slovaquie	0	0	443	0	0	0	154	183	780

70 Socio-economic development assistance through the United Nations system *(continued)*

Development grants: thousands of US dollars, 2008

Assistance en matière de développement socioéconomique fournie par le système des Nations Unies *(suite)*

Subventions au développement : en milliers de dollars des E.-U., 2008

Region, country or area Région, pays ou zone	UNDP PNUD	UNFPA FNUAP	UNHCR HCR	UNICEF	WFP PAM	IFAD FIDA	Specialized agencies[a] Institutions spécialisées[a]	Other UN funds and programmes[b] Autres fonds et programmes des NU[b]	Total development grants Total subventions au développ.
Slovenia Slovénie	0	0	98	0	0	0	316	0	413
Solomon Islands Iles Salomon	347	0	0	0	0	0	55	0	402
Somalia Somalie	60 661	2 604	20 245	79 639	178 781	5	23 468	9 475	374 878
South Africa Afrique du Sud	5 044	1 603	12 443	10 946	67	0	4 635	3 001	37 739
Spain Espagne	0	0	1 356	0	0	0	548	0	1 904
Sri Lanka Sri Lanka	12 723	1 726	20 124	37 040	51 702	5 636	9 379	8 014	146 344
Sudan Soudan	198 234	30 212	89 996	180 082	635 316	13 109	51 014	25 119	1 223 083
Suriname Suriname	0	0	0	0	0	0	145	0	145
Swaziland Swaziland	1 949	1 267	0	9 569	9 432	2 217	1 818	577	26 828
Sweden Suède	0	0	1 630	0	0	0	0	0	1 630
Switzerland Suisse	0	0	675	0	0	0	121	0	796
Syrian Arab Republic Rép. arabe syrienne	8 046	3 357	108 123	16 783	19 753	6 166	5 256	57 516	225 000
Tajikistan Tadjikistan	26 025	979	905	8 616	16 685	0	9 166	2 788	65 163
Thailand Thaïlande	14 520	1 627	13 980	9 123	0	292	3 140	555	43 236
TFYR of Macedonia L'ex-R.Y. Macédoine	8 917	155	3 064	1 998	0	122	1 355	40	15 652
Timor-Leste Timor-Leste	21 579	2 264	214	8 075	8 123	0	6 243	788	47 286
Togo Togo	18 479	1 708	379	8 963	4 034	0	2 251	303	36 137
Tokelau Tokélaou	162	0	0	0	0	0	0	0	162
Tonga Tonga	0	0	0	0	0	0	379	0	379
Trinidad and Tobago Trinité-et-Tobago	4 215	0	0	0	0	0	728	433	5 375
Tunisia Tunisie	2 060	514	639	1 149	0	8 838	1 180	77	14 458
Turkey Turquie	21 909	4 480	8 380	5 737	0	6 781	1 619	1 012	49 917
Turkmenistan Turkménistan	3 173	797	899	1 894	0	0	43	547	7 353
Tuvalu Tuvalu	2	0	0	0	0	0	32	0	72
Uganda Ouganda	20 408	7 864	36 830	59 996	117 827	12 004	14 981	4 230	274 139
Ukraine Ukraine	23 585	2 098	2 938	3 853	0	0	2 410	755	35 639
United Arab Emirates Emirats arabes unis	1 642	0	2 133	0	0	0	411	230	4 416
United Kingdom Royaume-Uni	0	0	1 742	0	0	0	82	0	1 824

70

Socio-economic development assistance through the United Nations system *(continued)*

Development grants: thousands of US dollars, 2008

Assistance en matière de développement socioéconomique fournie par le système des Nations Unies *(suite)*

Subventions au développement : en milliers de dollars des E.-U., 2008

Region, country or area Région, pays ou zone	UNDP PNUD	UNFPA FNUAP	UNHCR HCR	UNICEF	WFP PAM	IFAD FIDA	Specialized agencies[a] Institutions spécialisées[a]	Other UN funds and programmes[b] Autres fonds et programmes des NU[b]	Total development grants Total subventions au développ.
United Rep. of Tanzania Rép.-Unie de Tanzanie	26 217	5 062	50 881	33 936	29 233	17 000	10 181	1 848	174 359
United States Etats-Unis	0	0	3 424	0	0	0	473	0	3 897
Uruguay Uruguay	18 399	1 663	0	1 622	0	2 138	4 593	75	28 546
Uzbekistan Ouzbékistan	15 943	1 162	136	4 764	0	0	708	549	23 262
Vanuatu Vanuatu	0	0	0	0	0	0	192	2	194
Venezuela (Bol. Rep. of) Venezuela (Rép. Bol. du)	29 093	1 180	3 575	2 673	0	5 697	2 438	133	44 790
Viet Nam Viet Nam	18 973	7 307	855	16 952	0	11 514	7 620	2 192	65 500
Yemen Yémen	10 903	3 709	15 671	15 230	12 842	6 239	2 863	193	67 650
Zambia Zambie	15 327	4 268	11 515	18 501	26 529	3 135	6 024	912	86 211
Zimbabwe Zimbabwe	11 484	8 527	2 704	71 945	155 610	99	12 235	3 153	265 757

Source:
United Nations, *Comprehensive statistical analysis of the financing of operational activities for development of the United Nations system for 2008, Report of the Secretary-General* (A/65/79).

The following abbreviations have been used in the table:
- IFAD: International Fund for Agricultural Development
- UNDP: United Nations Development Programme
- UNFPA: United Nations Population Fund
- UNHCR: United Nations High Commissioner for Refugees
- UNICEF: United Nations Children's Fund
- WFP: World Food Programme

[a] Expenditures by FAO, IAEA, ICAO, ILO, IMO, ITU, UNESCO, UNIDO, UPU, WIPO, WHO, WMO and the World Tourism Organization.
[b] Expenditures by ITC, UNAIDS, UNCTAD, UNEP, UN-Habitat, UNODC, UNRWA and the Office for the Coordination of Humanitarian Affairs.

Source:
Nations Unies, *Analyse statistique globale du financement des activités opérationnelles de développement du système des Nations Unies pour 2008, Rapport du Secrétaire général* (A/65/79).

Les abréviations ci-après ont été utilisées dans le tableau :
- FIDA : Fonds international de développement agricole
- PNUD : Programme des Nations Unies pour le développement
- FNUAP : Fonds des Nations Unies pour la population
- HCR : Haut Commissariat des Nations Unies
- UNICEF : Fonds des Nations Unies pour l'enfance
- PAM : Programme alimentaire mondial

[a] Dépenses engagées par la FAO, l'AIEA, l'OACI, l'OIT, l'OMI, l'UIT, l'UNESCO, l'ONUDI, l'UPU, l'OMPI, l'OMS, l'OMM et l'Organisation mondiale du tourisme.
[b] Dépenses engagées par le CCI, ONUSIDA, la CNUCED, le PNUE, ONU/Habitat, UNODC, l'UNRWA et le Bureau de la coordination des affaires humanitaires.

Technical notes: tables 68-70

Table 68 presents estimates of flows of financial resources to individual recipients either directly (bilaterally) or through multilateral institutions (multilaterally).

The multilateral institutions include the World Bank Group, regional banks, financial institutions of the European Union and a number of United Nations institutions, programmes and trust funds.

The source of data is the Development Assistance Committee of OECD to which member countries reported data on their flow of resources to developing countries and territories, countries and territories in transition, and multilateral institutions.

Additional information on definitions, methods and sources can be found in OECD's *Geographical Distribution of Financial Flows to Aid Recipients* and www.oecd.org.

Table 69 presents the development assistance expenditures of donor countries. This table includes donors' contributions to multilateral agencies; therefore, the overall totals differ from those in table 68, which include disbursements by multilateral agencies.

Table 70 includes data on expenditures on operational activities for development undertaken by the organizations of the United Nations system. Operational activities encompass, in general, those activities of a development cooperation character that seek to mobilize or increase the potential and capacity of countries to promote economic and social development and welfare, including the transfer of resources to developing countries or regions in a tangible or intangible form.

Expenditures on operational activities for development are financed from contributions from governments and other official and non-official sources to a variety of funding channels in the United Nations system. These include United Nations funds and programmes such as contributions to the United Nations Development Programme, contributions to funds administered by the United Nations Development Programme, and regular (assessed) and other extra budgetary contributions to specialized agencies.

Data are taken from the 2008 report of the Secretary-General to the General Assembly on operational activities for development.

Notes techniques : tableaux 68 à 70

Le *tableau 68* présente les estimations des flux de ressources financières mises à la disposition des pays soit directement (aide bilatérale) soit par l'intermédiaire d'institutions multilatérales (aide multilatérale).

Les institutions multilatérales comprennent le Groupe de la Banque mondiale, les banques régionales, les institutions financières de l'Union européenne et un certain nombre d'institutions, de programmes et de fonds d'affectation spéciale des Nations Unies.

La source de données est le Comité d'aide au développement de l'OCDE, auquel les pays membres ont communiqué des données sur les flux de ressources qu'ils mettent à la disposition des pays et territoires en développement et en transition et des institutions multilatérales.

Pour plus de renseignements sur les définitions, méthodes et sources, se reporter à la publication de l'OCDE, *la Répartition géographique des ressources financières de aux pays bénéficiaires de l'Aide* et www.oecd.org.

Le *tableau 69* présente les dépenses que les pays donateurs consacrent à l'aide publique au développement (APD). Ces chiffres incluent les contributions des donateurs à des agences multilatérales, de sorte que les totaux diffèrent de ceux du tableau 68, qui incluent les dépenses des agences multilatérales.

Le *tableau 70* présente des données sur les dépenses consacrées à des activités opérationnelles pour le développement par les organisations du système des Nations Unies. Par "activités opérationnelles", on entend en général les activités ayant trait à la coopération au développement, qui visent à mobiliser ou à accroître les potentialités et aptitudes que présentent les pays pour promouvoir le développement et le bien-être économiques et sociaux, y compris les transferts de ressources vers les pays ou régions en développement sous forme tangible ou non.

Les dépenses consacrées aux activités opérationnelles pour le développement sont financées au moyen de contributions que les gouvernements et d'autres sources officielles et non officielles apportent à divers organes de financement, tels que fonds et programmes du système des Nations Unies. On peut citer notamment les contributions au Programme des Nations Unies pour le développement, les contributions aux fonds gérés par le Programme des Nations Unies pour le développement, les contributions régulières (budgétaires) et les contributions extrabudgétaires aux institutions spécialisées.

Les données sont extraites du rapport annuel de 2008 du Secrétaire général à la session de l'Assemblée générale sur les activités opérationnelles pour le développement.

Annex I

Country and area nomenclature, regional and other groupings

A. Changes in country or area names

In the periods covered by the statistics in the *Statistical Yearbook*, the following changes in designation have taken place:

Bolivia (Plurinational State of) was formerly listed as Bolivia;

Cambodia was formerly listed as Democratic Kampuchea;

Czech Republic, Slovakia: Since 1 January 1993, data for the Czech Republic and Slovakia, where available, are shown separately under the appropriate country name;

Democratic Republic of the Congo was formerly listed as Zaire;

Hong Kong Special Administrative Region of China: Pursuant to a Joint Declaration signed on 19 December 1984, the United Kingdom restored Hong Kong to the People's Republic of China with effect from 1 July 1997; the People's Republic of China resumed the exercise of sovereignty over the territory with effect from that date;

Macao Special Administrative Region of China: Pursuant to the joint declaration signed on 13 April 1987, Portugal restored Macao to the People's Republic of China with effect from 20 December 1999; the People's Republic of China resumed the exercise of sovereignty over the territory with effect from that date;

Myanmar was formerly listed as Burma;

Saint Kitts and Nevis was formerly listed as Saint Christopher and Nevis;

Serbia, Montenegro: As of 1992, data provided for Yugoslavia refer to the Federal Republic of Yugoslavia which was composed of the two republics of Serbia and Montenegro. On 4 February 2003, the official name of the "Federal Republic of Yugoslavia" was changed to "Serbia and Montenegro". On 3 June 2006, Serbia and Montenegro formally dissolved into two independent countries. When data are available separately for Montenegro and/or Serbia, they are shown under the respective heading.

Timor-Leste was formerly listed as East Timor;

Venezuela (Bolivarian Republic of) was formerly listed as Venezuela;

Yemen: On 22 May 1990 Democratic Yemen and Yemen merged to form a single State. Since that date they have been represented as one Member with the name "Yemen".

It should be noted that unless otherwise indicated, for statistical purposes, the data for China exclude those for Hong Kong Special Administrative Region of China, Macao Special Administrative Region of China and Taiwan province of China.

Annexe I

Nomenclature des pays ou zones, groupements régionaux et autres groupements

A. Changements dans le nom des pays ou zones

Au cours des périodes sur lesquelles portent les statistiques, dans l'*Annuaire Statistique* les changements de désignation suivants ont eu lieu:

Le Bolivie (État plurinational de) apparaissait antérieurement sous le nom de Bolivie ;

Le Cambodge apparaissait antérieurement sous le nom de la Kampuchéa démocratique;

République tchèque, Slovaquie: Depuis le 1er janvier 1993, les données relatives à la République tchèque, et à la Slovaquie, lorsqu'elles sont disponibles, sont présentées séparément sous le nom de chacun des pays;

La République démocratique du Congo apparaissait antérieurement sous le nom de Zaïre;

Hong Kong, région administrative spéciale de Chine: Conformément à une Déclaration commune signée le 19 décembre 1984, le Royaume-Uni a rétrocédé Hong Kong à la République populaire de Chine, avec effet au 1er juillet 1997; la souveraineté de la République populaire de Chine s'exerce à nouveau sur le territoire à compter de cette date;

Macao, région administrative spéciale de Chine: Conformément à une Déclaration commune signée le 13 avril 1987, le Portugal a rétrocédé Macao à la République populaire de Chine, avec effet au 20 décembre 1999; la souveraineté de la République populaire de Chine s'exerce à nouveau sur le territoire à compter de cette date;

Le Myanmar apparaissait antérieurement sous le nom de Birmanie;

Saint-Kitts-Et-Nevis apparaissait antérieurement sous le nom de Saint-Christophe-et-Nevis;

Serbie, Monténégro: Les données fournies pour la Yougoslavie à partir de 1992 se rapportent à la République fédérale de Yougoslavie, qui était composée des deux républiques de la Serbie et du Monténégro. Le 4 février 2003, la "République fédérale de Yougoslavie", ayant changé de nom officiel, est devenu la "Serbie-et-Monténégro". Le 3 juin 2006, la Serbie-et-Monténégro s'est officiellement dissoute pour former deux États indépendants. Lorsque des données sont disponibles séparément pour la Serbie et le Monténégro, elles sont présentées dans leurs catégories respectives.

Timor-Leste: apparaissait antérieurement sous le nom de Timor oriental;

Le Venezuela (République bolivarienne du) apparaissait antérieurement sous le nom de Venezuela ;

Yémen: Le Yémen et le Yémen démocratique ont fusionné le 22 mai 1990 pour ne plus former qu'un seul Etat, qui est depuis lors représenté comme tel à l'Organisation, sous le nom 'Yémen'.

Il convient de noter que sauf indication contraire, les données statistiques relatives à la Chine ne comprennent pas celles qui concernent la région administrative spéciale de Hong Kong, la région administrative spéciale de Macao et la province chinoise de Taiwan.

B. Regional groupings

The scheme of regional groupings given below presents seven regions based mainly on continents. Five of the seven continental regions are further subdivided into 21 regions that are so drawn as to obtain greater homogeneity in sizes of population, demographic circumstances and accuracy of demographic statistics. This nomenclature is widely used in international statistics and is followed to the greatest extent possible in the present *Yearbook* in order to promote consistency and facilitate comparability and analysis. However, it is by no means universal in international statistical compilation, even at the level of continental regions, and variations in international statistical sources and methods dictate many unavoidable differences in particular fields in the present *Yearbook*. General differences are indicated in the footnotes to the classification presented below. More detailed differences are given in the footnotes and technical notes to individual tables.

Neither is there international standardization in the use of the terms "developed" and "developing" countries, areas or regions. These terms are used in the present publication to refer to regional groupings generally considered as "developed": these are Europe and the former USSR, the United States of America and Canada in Northern America, and Australia, Japan and New Zealand in Asia and Oceania. These designations are intended for statistical convenience and do not necessarily express a judgement about the stage reached by a particular country or area in the development process. Differences from this usage are indicated in the notes to individual tables.

B. Groupements régionaux

Le système de groupements régionaux présenté ci-dessous comporte sept régions basées principalement sur les continents. Cinq des sept régions continentales sont elles-mêmes subdivisées, formant ainsi 21 régions délimitées de manière à obtenir une homogénéité accrue dans les effectifs de population, les situations démographiques et la précision des statistiques démographiques. Cette nomenclature est couramment utilisée aux fins des statistiques internationales et a été appliquée autant qu'il a été possible dans le présent *Annuaire* en vue de renforcer la cohérence et de faciliter la comparaison et l'analyse. Son utilisation pour l'établissement des statistiques internationales n'est cependant rien moins qu'universelle, même au niveau des régions continentales, et les variations que présentent les sources et méthodes statistiques internationales entraînent inévitablement de nombreuses différences dans certains domaines de cet *Annuaire*. Les différences d'ordre général sont indiquées dans les notes figurant au bas de la classification présentée ci-dessous. Les différences plus spécifiques sont mentionnées dans les notes techniques et notes de bas de page accompagnant les divers tableaux.

L'application des expressions "développés" et "en développement" aux pays, zones ou régions n'est pas non plus normalisée à l'échelle internationale. Ces expressions sont utilisées dans la présente publication en référence aux groupements régionaux généralement considérés comme "développés", à savoir l'Europe et l'ex-URSS, les Etats-Unis d'Amérique et le Canada en Amérique septentrionale, et l'Australie, le Japon et la Nouvelle-Zélande dans la région de l'Asie et du Pacifique. Ces appellations sont employées pour des raisons de commodité statistique et n'expriment pas nécessairement un jugement sur le stade de développement atteint par tel ou tel pays ou zone. Les cas différant de cet usage sont signalés dans les notes accompagnant les tableaux concernés.

Africa

Sub-Saharan Africa

Eastern Africa

Burundi
Comoros
Djibouti
Eritrea
Ethiopia
Kenya
Madagascar
Malawi
Mayotte
Mauritius
Mozambique
Réunion
Rwanda
Seychelles
Somalia
Uganda
United Republic of Tanzania
Zambia
Zimbabwe

Middle Africa

Angola
Cameroon
Central African Republic
Chad
Congo
Democratic Republic of the Congo
Equatorial Guinea
Gabon
Sao Tome and Principe

Afrique

Afrique subsaharienne

Afrique orientale

Burundi
Comores
Djibouti
Erythrée
Ethiopie
Kenya
Madagascar
Malawi
Maurice
Mayotte
Mozambique
Ouganda
République-Unie de Tanzanie
Réunion
Rwanda
Seychelles
Somalie
Zambie
Zimbabwe

Afrique centrale

Angola
Cameroun
Congo
Gabon
Guinée équatoriale
République centrafricaine
République démocratique du Congo
Sao Tomé-et-Principe
Tchad

Southern Africa

Botswana
Lesotho
Namibia
South Africa
Swaziland

Western Africa

Benin
Burkina Faso
Cape Verde
Côte d'Ivoire
Gambia
Ghana
Guinea
Guinea-Bissau
Liberia
Mali
Mauritania
Niger
Nigeria
Saint Helena
Senegal
Sierra Leone
Togo

Northern Africa

Algeria
Egypt
Libyan Arab Jamahiriya
Morocco
Sudan
Tunisia
Western Sahara

Americas

Latin America and the Caribbean

Caribbean

Anguilla
Antigua and Barbuda
Aruba
Bahamas
Barbados
British Virgin Islands
Cayman Islands
Cuba
Dominica
Dominican Republic
Grenada
Guadeloupe
Haiti
Jamaica
Martinique
Montserrat
Netherlands Antilles
Puerto Rico
Saint Kitts and Nevis
Saint Lucia
Saint Vincent and the Grenadines
Trinidad and Tobago
Turks and Caicos Islands
United States Virgin Islands

Central America

Belize
Costa Rica
El Salvador
Guatemala
Honduras
Mexico
Nicaragua
Panama

South America

Argentina
Bolivia (Plurinational State of)
Brazil
Chile
Colombia
Ecuador
Falkland Islands (Malvinas)
French Guiana
Guyana
Paraguay
Peru
Suriname
Uruguay
Venezuela (Bolivarian Republic of)

Afrique australe

Afrique du Sud
Botswana
Lesotho
Namibie
Swaziland

Afrique occidentale

Bénin
Burkina Faso
Cap-Vert
Côte d'Ivoire
Gambie
Ghana
Guinée
Guinée-Bissau
Libéria
Mali
Mauritanie
Niger
Nigéria
Sainte-Hélène
Sénégal
Sierra Leone
Togo

Afrique septentrionale

Algérie
Egypte
Jamahiriya arabe libyenne
Maroc
Sahara occidental
Soudan
Tunisie

Amériques

Amérique latine et Caraïbes

Caraïbes

Anguilla
Antigua-et-Barbuda
Antilles néerlandaises
Aruba
Bahamas
Barbade
Cuba
Dominique
Grenade
Guadeloupe
Haïti
Iles Caïmans
Iles Turques et Caïques
Iles Vierges américaines
Iles Vierges britanniques
Jamaïque
Martinique
Montserrat
Porto Rico
République dominicaine
Sainte-Lucie
Saint-Kitts-Et-Nevis
Saint-Vincent-et-les Grenadines
Trinité-et-Tobago

Amérique centrale

Belize
Costa Rica
El Salvador
Guatemala
Honduras
Mexique
Nicaragua
Panama

Amérique du Sud

Argentine
Bolivie (État plurinational de)
Brésil
Chili
Colombie
Equateur
Guyana
Guyane française
Iles Falkland (Malvinas)
Paraguay
Pérou
Suriname
Uruguay
Venezuela (République bolivarienne du)

Northern America [a]

Bermuda
Canada
Greenland
Saint Pierre and Miquelon
United States of America

Asia

Eastern Asia

China
China, Hong Kong Special Administrative Region
China, Macao Special Administrative Region
Democratic People's Republic of Korea
Japan
Mongolia
Republic of Korea

South-central Asia

Afghanistan
Bangladesh
Bhutan
India
Iran (Islamic Republic of)
Kazakhstan
Kyrgyzstan
Maldives
Nepal
Pakistan
Sri Lanka
Tajikistan
Turkmenistan
Uzbekistan

South-eastern Asia

Brunei Darussalam
Cambodia
Indonesia
Lao People's Democratic Republic
Malaysia
Myanmar
Philippines
Singapore
Thailand
Timor-Leste
Viet Nam

Western Asia

Armenia
Azerbaijan
Bahrain
Cyprus
Georgia
Iraq
Israel
Jordan
Kuwait
Lebanon
Occupied Palestinian Territory
Oman
Qatar
Saudi Arabia
Syrian Arab Republic
Turkey
United Arab Emirates
Yemen

Europe

Eastern Europe

Belarus
Bulgaria
Czech Republic
Hungary
Poland
Republic of Moldova
Romania
Russian Federation
Slovakia
Ukraine

Northern Europe

Åland Islands
Channel Islands
Denmark
Latvia
Lithuania
Norway

Amérique septentrionale [a]

Bermudes
Canada
Etats-Unis d'Amérique
Groenland
Saint-Pierre-et-Miquelon

Asie

Asie orientale

Chine
Chine, Hong Kong, région administrative spéciale
Chine, Macao, région administrative spéciale
Japon
Mongolie
République de Corée
République populaire démocratique de Corée

Asie centrale et du Sud

Afghanistan
Bangladesh
Bhoutan
Inde
Iran (République islamique d')
Kazakhstan
Kirghizistan
Maldives
Népal
Ouzbékistan
Pakistan
Sri Lanka
Tadjikistan
Turkménistan

Asie du Sud-est

Brunei Darussalam
Cambodge
Indonésie
Malaisie
Myanmar
Philippines
République démocratique populaire lao
Singapour
Thaïlande
Timor-Leste
Viet Nam

Asie occidentale

Arabie saoudite
Arménie
Azerbaïdjan
Bahreïn
Chypre
Emirats arabes unis
Géorgie
Iraq
Israël
Jordanie
Koweït
Liban
Oman
Qatar
République arabe syrienne
Territoire palestinien occupé
Turquie
Yémen

Europe

Europe orientale

Bélarus
Bulgarie
Fédération de Russie
Hongrie
Pologne
République de Moldova
République tchèque
Roumanie
Slovaquie
Ukraine

Europe septentrionale

Danemark
Estonie
Finlande
Irlande
Îles d'Åland
Islande

Estonia
Faeroe Islands
Finland
Guernsey
Iceland
Ireland
Isle of Man
Jersey
Svalbard and Jan Mayen Islands
Sweden
United Kingdom of Great Britain and Northern Ireland

Southern Europe

Albania
Andorra
Bosnia and Herzegovina
Croatia
Gibraltar
Greece
Holy See
Italy
Malta
Montenegro
Portugal
San Marino
Serbia
Slovenia
Spain
The former Yugoslav Republic of Macedonia

Western Europe

Austria
Belgium
France
Germany
Liechtenstein
Luxembourg
Monaco
Netherlands
Switzerland

Oceania

Australia and New Zealand

Australia
New Zealand
Norfolk Island

Melanesia

Fiji
New Caledonia
Papua New Guinea
Solomon Islands
Vanuatu

Micronesia-Polynesia

Micronesia

Guam
Kiribati
Marshall Islands
Micronesia (Federated States of)
Nauru
Northern Mariana Islands
Palau

Polynesia

American Samoa
Cook Islands
French Polynesia
Niue
Pitcairn
Samoa
Tokelau
Tonga
Tuvalu
Wallis and Futuna Islands

C. Other groupings

Following is a list of other groupings and their compositions presented in the *Yearbook.* These groupings are organized mainly around economic and trade interests in regional associations.

Guernesey
Ile de Man
Iles Anglo-Normandes
Iles Féroé
Iles Svalbard et Jan Mayen
Jersey
Lettonie
Lituanie
Norvège
Royaume-Uni de Grande-Bretagne et d'Irlande du Nord
Suède

Europe méridionale

Albanie
Andorre
Bosnie-Herzégovine
Croatie
Espagne
Ex-République yougoslave de Macédoine
Gibraltar
Grèce
Italie
Malte
Monténégro
Portugal
Saint-Marin
Saint-Siège
Serbie
Slovénie

Europe occidentale

Allemagne
Autriche
Belgique
France
Liechtenstein
Luxembourg
Monaco
Pays-Bas
Suisse

Océanie

Australie et Nouvelle-Zélande

Australie
Ile Norfolk
Nouvelle-Zélande

Mélanésie

Fidji
Iles Salomon
Nouvelle-Calédonie
Papouasie-Nouvelle-Guinée
Vanuatu

Micronésie-Polynésie

Micronésie

Guam
Iles Mariannes septentrionales
Iles Marshall
Kiribati
Micronésie (Etats fédérés de)
Nauru
Palaos

Polynésie

Iles Cook
Iles Wallis-Et-Futuna
Nioué
Pitcairn
Polynésie française
Samoa
Samoa américaines
Tokélaou
Tonga
Tuvalu

C. Autres groupements

On trouvera ci-après une liste des autres groupements et de leur composition, présentée dans l'*Annuaire*. Ces groupements correspondent essentiellement à des intérêts économiques et commerciaux d'après les associations régionales.

Andean Common Market (ANCOM)
- Bolivia (Plurinational State of)
- Colombia
- Ecuador
- Peru

Marché commun andin (ANCOM)
- Bolivie (État plurinational de)
- Colombie
- Equateur
- Pérou

Asia-Pacific Economic Cooperation (APEC)
- Australia
- Brunei Darussalam
- Canada
- Chile
- China
- China, Hong Kong Special Administrative Region
- Indonesia
- Japan
- Malaysia
- Mexico
- New Zealand
- Papua New Guinea
- Peru
- Philippines
- Republic of Korea
- Russian Federation
- Singapore
- Taiwan Province of China
- Thailand
- United States of America
- Viet Nam

Coopération économique Asie-Pacifique (CEAP)
- Australie
- Brunei Darussalam
- Canada
- Chili
- Chine
- Chine, Hong Kong, région administrative spéciale
- Etats-Unis d'Amérique
- Fédération de Russie
- Indonésie
- Japon
- Malaisie
- Mexique
- Nouvelle-Zélande
- Papouasie-Nouvelle-Guinée
- Pérou
- Philippines
- Province chinoise de Taiwan
- République de Corée
- Singapour
- Thaïlande
- Viet Nam

Caribbean Community and Common Market (CARICOM)
- Antigua and Barbuda
- Bahamas (member of the Community only)
- Barbados
- Belize
- Dominica
- Grenada
- Guyana
- Haiti
- Jamaica
- Montserrat
- Saint Kitts and Nevis
- Saint Lucia
- Saint Vincent and the Grenadines
- Suriname
- Trinidad and Tobago

Communauté des Caraïbes et Marché commun des Caraïbes (CARICOM)
- Antigua-et-Barbuda
- Bahamas (membre de la communauté seulement)
- Barbade
- Belize
- Dominique
- Grenade
- Guyana
- Haïti
- Jamaïque
- Montserrat
- Sainte-Lucie
- Saint-Kitts-Et-Nevis
- Saint-Vincent-et-les Grenadines
- Suriname
- Trinité-et-Tobago

Common Market for Eastern and Southern Africa (COMESA)
- Burundi
- Comoros
- Democratic Republic of the Congo
- Djibouti
- Egypt
- Eritrea
- Ethiopia
- Kenya
- Libyan Arab Jamahiriya

Marché commun de l'Afrique de l'Est et de l'Afrique australe (COMESA)
- Burundi
- Comores
- Djibouti
- Egypte
- Erythrée
- Ethiopie
- Kenya
- Jamah. arabe libyenne
- Madagascar
- Malawi

Madagascar
Malawi
Mauritius
Rwanda
Seychelles
Sudan
Swaziland
Uganda
Zambia
Zimbabwe

Commonwealth of Independent States (CIS)

Armenia
Azerbaijan
Belarus
Kazakhstan
Kyrgyzstan
Republic of Moldova
Russian Federation
Tajikistan
Turkmenistan
Ukraine
Uzbekistan

Euro Area

Austria
Belgium
Cyprus
Finland
France
Germany
Greece
Ireland
Italy
Luxembourg
Malta
Netherlands
Portugal
Slovakia
Slovenia
Spain

European Union (EU)

Austria
Belgium
Bulgaria
Cyprus
Czech Republic
Denmark
Estonia
Finland
France
Germany
Greece
Hungary
Ireland
Italy
Latvia
Lithuania

Maurice
Ouganda
République démocratique du Congo
Rwanda
Seychelles
Soudan
Swaziland
Zambie
Zimbabwe

Communauté d'Etats indépendants (CEI)

Arménie
Azerbaïdjan
Belarus
Fédération de Russie
Kazakhstan
Kirghizistan
Ouzbékistan
République de Moldova
Tadjikistan
Turkménistan
Ukraine

Zone euro

Allemagne
Autriche
Belgique
Chypre
Espagne
Finlande
France
Grèce
Irlande
Italie
Luxembourg
Malte
Pays-Bas
Portugal
Slovaquie
Slovénie

Union européenne (UE)

Allemagne
Autriche
Belgique
Bulgarie
Chypre
Danemark
Espagne
Estonie
Finlande
France
Grèce
Hongrie
Irlande
Italie
Lettonie
Lituanie
Luxembourg

Luxembourg
Malta
Netherlands
Poland
Portugal
Romania
Slovakia
Slovenia
Spain
Sweden
United Kingdom of Great Britain and Northern Ireland

Least developed countries (LDCs)

Afghanistan
Angola
Bangladesh
Benin
Bhutan
Burkina Faso
Burundi
Cambodia
Central African Republic
Chad
Comoros
Democratic Republic of the Congo
Djibouti
Equatorial Guinea
Eritrea
Ethiopia
Gambia
Guinea
Guinea-Bissau
Haiti
Kiribati
Lao People's Democratic Republic
Lesotho
Liberia
Madagascar
Malawi
Mali
Mauritania
Mozambique
Myanmar
Nepal
Niger
Rwanda
Samoa
Sao Tome and Principe
Senegal
Sierra Leone
Solomon Islands
Somalia
Sudan
Timor-Leste
Togo
Tuvalu
Uganda
United Republic of Tanzania

Malte
Pays-Bas
Pologne
Portugal
République tchèque
Roumanie
Royaume-Uni de Grande-Bretagne et d'Irlande du Nord
Slovaquie
Slovénie
Suède

Pays les moins avancés (PMA)

Afghanistan
Angola
Bangladesh
Bénin
Bhoutan
Burkina Faso
Burundi
Cambodge
Comores
Djibouti
Erythrée
Ethiopie
Gambie
Guinée
Guinée équatoriale
Guinée-Bissau
Haïti
Iles Salomon
Kiribati
Lesotho
Libéria
Madagascar
Malawi
Mali
Mauritanie
Mozambique
Myanmar
Népal
Niger
Ouganda
République centrafricaine
République démocratique du Congo
République démocratique populaire lao
République-Unie de Tanzanie
Rwanda
Samoa
Sao Tomé-et-Principe
Sénégal
Sierra Leone
Somalie
Soudan
Tchad
Timor-Leste
Togo
Tuvalu
Vanuatu

Vanuatu
Yemen
Zambia

Mercado Común Sudamericano (MERCOSUR)
Argentina
Brazil
Paraguay
Uruguay

North American Free Trade Agreement (NAFTA)
Canada
Mexico
United States of America

Organisation for Economic Cooperation and Development (OECD)
Australia
Austria
Belgium
Canada
Chile
Czech Republic
Denmark
Estonia
Finland
France
Germany
Greece
Hungary
Iceland
Ireland
Israel
Italy
Japan
Luxembourg
Mexico
Netherlands
New Zealand
Norway
Poland
Portugal
Republic of Korea
Slovakia
Slovenia
Spain
Sweden
Switzerland
Turkey
United Kingdom of Great Britain and Northern Ireland
United States of America

Organization of Petroleum Exporting Countries (OPEC)
Algeria
Iran (Islamic Republic of)
Iraq
Kuwait

Yémen
Zambie

Marché commun sud-américain (Mercosur)
Argentine
Brésil
Paraguay
Uruguay

Accord de libre-échange nord-américain (ALENA)
Canada
Etats-Unis d'Amérique
Mexique

Organisation de coopération et de développement économiques (OCDE)
Allemagne
Australie
Autriche
Belgique
Canada
Chili
Danemark
Espagne
Estonie
Etats-Unis d'Amérique
Finlande
France
Grèce
Hongrie
Irlande
Israël
Islande
Italie
Japon
Luxembourg
Mexique
Norvège
Nouvelle-Zélande
Pays-Bas
Pologne
Portugal
République de Corée
République tchèque
Royaume-Uni de Grande-Bretagne et d'Irlande du Nord
Slovaquie
Slovénie
Suède
Suisse
Turquie

Organisation des pays exportateurs de pétrole (OPEP)
Algérie
Arabie saoudite
Emirats arabes unis
Iran (République islamique d')
Iraq
Jamahiriya arabe libyenne
Koweït
Nigéria

Libyan Arab Jamahiriya
Nigeria
Qatar
Saudi Arabia
United Arab Emirates
Venezuela (Bolivarian Republic of)

Southern African Customs Union (SACU)
Botswana
Lesotho
Namibia
South Africa
Swaziland

a The continent of North America comprises Northern America, Caribbean and Central America.

Qatar
Venezuela (République bolivarienne du)

Union douanière d'Afrique australe
Afrique du Sud
Botswana
Lesotho
Namibie
Swaziland

a Le continent de l'Amérique du Nord comprend l'Amérique septentrionale, les Caraïbes et l'Amérique centrale.

Annex II

Conversion coefficients and factors

The metric system of weights and measures is employed in the *Statistical Yearbook*. In this system, the relationship between units of volume and capacity is: 1 litre = 1 cubic decimetre (dm^3) exactly (as decided by the 12th International Conference of Weights and Measures, New Delhi, November 1964).

Section A shows the equivalents of the basic metric, British imperial and United States units of measurements. According to an agreement between the national standards institutions of English-speaking nations, the British and United States units of length, area and volume are now identical, and based on the yard = 0.9144 metre exactly. The weight measures in both systems are based on the pound = 0.45359237 kilogram exactly (Weights and Measures Act 1963 (London), and *Federal Register announcement of 1 July 1959: Refinement of Values for the Yard and Pound* (Washington D.C.)).

Section B shows various derived or conventional conversion coefficients and equivalents.

Section C shows other conversion coefficients or factors which have been utilized in thc compilation of certain tables in the *Statistical Yearbook*. Some of these are only of an approximate character and have been employed solely to obtain a reasonable measure of international comparability in the tables.

For a comprehensive survey of international and national systems of weights and measures and of units' weights for a large number of commodities in different countries, see *World Weights and Measures*.

Annexe II

Coefficients et facteurs de conversion

L'*Annuaire statistique* utilise le système métrique pour les poids et mesures. La relation entre unités métriques de volume et de capacité est: 1 litre = 1 décimètre cube (dm^3) exactement (comme fut décidé à la Conférence internationale des poids et mesures, New Delhi, novembre 1964).

La section A fournit les principaux équivalents des systèmes de mesure métrique, britannique et américain. Suivant un accord entre les institutions de normalisation nationales des pays de langue anglaise, les mesures britanniques et américaines de longueur, superficie et volume sont désormais identiques, et sont basées sur le yard = 0.9144 mètre exactement. Les mesures de poids se rapportent, dans les deux systèmes, à la livre (pound) = 0.45359237 kilogramme exactement (*Weights and Measures Act 1963* (Londres), et *Federal Register Announcement of 1 July 1959: Refinement of Values for the Yard and Pound* (Washington, D.C.)).

La section B fournit divers coefficients et facteurs de conversion conventionnels ou dérivés.

La section C fournit d'autres coefficients ou facteurs de conversion utilisés dans l'élaboration de certains tableaux de l'*Annuaire statistique.* Certains coefficients ou facteurs de conversion ne sont que des approximations et ont été utilisés uniquement pour obtenir un degré raisonnable de comparabilité sur le plan international.

Pour une étude d'ensemble des systèmes internationaux et nationaux de poids et mesures, et d'unités de poids pour un grand nombre de produits dans différents pays, voir *World Weights and Measures*.

A. Equivalents of metric, British imperial and United States units of measure

A. Equivalents des unités métriques, britanniques et des Etats-Unis

Metric units Unités métriques	British imperial and US equivalents Equivalents en mesures britanniques et des Etats-Unis		British imperial and US units Unités britanniques et des Etats-Unis	Metric equivalents Equivalents en mesures métriques	
Length — Longueur					
1 centimetre – centimètre (cm)	0.3937008	inch	1 inch	2.540	cm
1 metre – mètre (m)	3.280840	feet	1 foot	30.480	cm
	1.093613	yard	1 yard	0.9144	m
1 kilometre – kilomètre (km)	0.6213712	mile	1 mile	1609.344	m
	0.5399568	international nautical mile	1 international nautical mile	1852.000	m
Area — Superficie					
1 square centimetre – (cm^2)	0.1550003	square inch	1 square inch	6.45160	cm^2
1 square metre – (m^2)	10.763910	square feet	1 square foot	9.290304	dm^2
	1.195990	square yards	1 square yard	0.83612736	m^2
1 hectare – (ha)	2.471054	acres	1 acre	0.4046856	ha
1 square kilometre – (km^2)	0.3861022	square mile	1 square mile	2.589988	km^2
Volume					
1 cubic centimetre – (cm^3)	0.06102374	cubic inch	1 cubic inch	16.38706	cm^3
1 cubic metre – (m^3)	35.31467	cubic feet	1 cubic foot	28.316847	dm^3
	1.307951	cubic yards	1 cubic yard	0.76455486	m^3
Capacity — Capacité					
1 litre (l)	0.8798766	British imperial quart	1 British imperial quart	1.136523	l
	1.056688	U.S. liquid quart	1 U.S. liquid quart	0.9463529	l
	0.908083	U.S. dry quart	1 U.S. dry quart	1.1012208	l
1 hectolitre (hl)	21.99692	British imperial gallons	1 British imperial gallon	4.546092	l
	26.417200	U.S. gallons	1 U.S. gallon	3.785412	l
	2.749614	British imperial bushels	1 imperial bushel	36.368735	l
	2.837760	U.S. bushels	1 U.S. bushel	35.239067	l

Metric units Unités métriques	British imperial and US equivalents Equivalents en mesures britanniques et des Etats-Unis		British imperial and US units Unités britanniques et des Etats-Unis	Metric equivalents Equivalents en mesures métriques	
Weight or mass — Poids					
1 kilogram (kg)	35.27396	av. ounces	1 av. ounce	28.349523	g
	32.15075	troy ounces	1 troy ounce	31.10348	g
	2.204623	av. pounds	1 av. pound	453.59237	g
			1 cental (100 lb.)	45.359237	kg
			1 hundredweight (112 lb.)	50.802345	kg
1 ton – tonne (t)	1.1023113	short tons	1 short ton (2 000 lb.)	0.9071847	t
	0.9842065	long tons	1 long ton (2 240 lb.)	1.0160469	t

B. Various conventional or derived coefficients

Air transport

1 passenger-mile = 1.609344 passenger kilometre
1 short ton-mile = 1.459972 tonne-kilometre
1 long ton-mile = 1.635169 tonne kilometre

Electric energy

1 Kilowatt (kW) = 1.34102 British horsepower (hp)
1.35962 cheval vapeur (cv)

C. Other coefficients or conversion factors employed in *Statistical Yearbook* tables

Roundwood

Equivalent in solid volume without bark.

Sugar

1 metric ton raw sugar = 0.9 metric ton refined sugar

For the United States and its possessions:
1 metric ton refined sugar = 1.07 metric tons raw sugar

Energy

1 metric ton peat = .325 metric ton of coal oil equivalent
1 ton oil equivalent = .4186 GJ or 11.63 MWh

B. Divers coefficients conventionnels ou dérivés

Transport aérien

1 voyageur (passager) – kilomètre = 0.621371 passenger-mile
1 tonne-kilomètre = 0.684945 short ton-mile
0.611558 long ton-mile

Energie électrique

1 British horsepower (hp) = 0.7457 kW
1 cheval vapeur (cv) = 0.735499 kW

C. Autres coefficients ou facteurs de conversion utilisés dans les tableaux de l'*Annuaire statistique*

Bois rond

Equivalences en volume solide sans écorce.

Sucre

1 tonne métrique de sucre brut = 0.9 tonne métrique de sucre raffiné

Pour les États-Unis et leurs possessions:
1 tonne métrique de sucre raffiné = 1.07 tonne métrique de sucre brut

Energie

1 tonne métrique d'équivalent charbon = 3.08 tonnes métrique de tourbe
1 GJ = 2.39 tonne d'équivalent pétrol or 1 MWh = .086 tonne métrique d'équivalent pétrol

Annex III

Tables added and omitted

A. Tables added

The present issue of the *Statistical Yearbook* includes the following tables which were not presented in the previous issue:

Table 8: Population in urban and rural areas, rates of growth and largest urban agglomeration population
Table 18: Implicit price deflators
Table 25: Employment by economic activity
Table 32: Livestock
Table 33: Fertilizers
Table 35: Meat

B. Tables omitted

The following tables which were presented in previous issues are not presented in the present issue. They will be updated in future issues of the *Yearbook* when new data become available:

- Daily newspapers
- Fabrics
- Government final consumption expenditure by function in current prices
- Household consumption expenditure by purpose at current prices
- Index numbers of industrial production (regional)
- Industrial production indices
- Machine tools
- Oil crops
- Patents
- Selected indicators of life expectancy, childbearing and mortality
- Summary of balance of payments
- Trucks
- Wages in manufacturing

The following table has been discontinued:

- Sulphuric acid

Annexe III

Tableaux ajoutés et supprimés

A. Tableaux ajoutés

Dans ce numéro de l'*Annuaire statistique*, les tableaux suivants n'ont pas été présentés dans le numéro antérieur, et ont été ajoutés :

Tableau 8: Population urbaine, population rurale, taux d'accroissement et population de l'agglomération urbaine la plus peuplée
Tableau 18: Déflateurs implicites des prix
Tableau 25: Emploi par activité économique
Tableau 32: Cheptel
Tableau 33: Engrais
Tableau 35: Viande

B. Tableaux supprimés

Les tableaux suivants qui ont été repris dans les éditions antérieures n'ont pas été repris dans la présente édition. Ils seront actualisés dans les futures livraisons de l'*Annuaire* à mesure que des données nouvelles deviendront disponibles:

- Journaux quotidiens
- Tissus
- Dépenses de consommation finale des administrations Publiques par fonction aux prix courants
- Dépenses de consommation des ménages par fonction aux prix courants
- Indices de la production industrielle (régionaux)
- Indices de la production industrielle
- Machines-outils
- Cultures oléagineuses
- Brevets
- Choix d'indicateurs de l'espérance de vie, de la maternité et de la mortalité
- Résumé des balances des paiements
- Camions
- Salaires dans les industries manufacturières

Le tableau suivant a été discontinué :

- Acide sulfurique

Statistical sources and references

A. Statistical sources

1. Carbon Dioxide Information Analysis Center (CDIAC) of the Oak Ridge National Laboratory, *database on national CO_2 emission estimates*; http://cdiac.esd.ornl.gov.
2. Food and Agriculture Organization of the United Nations (Rome), *FAO Statistical Yearbook*; http://faostat.fao.org.
3. ________, *FISHSTAT Dataset*; http://www.fao.org/fishery/statistics/software/fishstat/en.
4. ________, *Global Forest Resources Assessment 2010*; http://www.fao.org/docrep/013/i1757e/i1757e00.htm.
5. International Civil Aviation Organization (Montreal), *Integrated Statistical database (ISDB).*
6. International Labour Organization (Geneva), *the ILO labour statistics database*; http://laborsta.ilo.org.
7. ________, *Yearbook of Labour Statistics*; http://laborsta.ilo.org.
8. International Monetary Fund (Washington, D.C.), *International Financial Statistics database*; http://www.imfstatistics.org/imf.
9. International Parliamentary Union (Geneva), *Women in National Parliaments, PARLINE database*; http://www.ipu.org/wmn-e/world.htm.
10. International Sugar Organization (London), *Sugar Yearbook 2009.*
11. International Telecommunication Union (Geneva), *Yearbook of Statistics 2010.*
12. ________, *World Telecommunication/ICT Indicators 2009.*
13. ________, *ITU database*; www.itu.int.
14. Organisation for Economic Co-operation and Development (Paris), *OECD Development Assistance Committee database*; http://stats.oecd.org/qwids.
15. ________, *Geographical Distribution of Financial Flows to Aid Recipients,* 2004-2008; www.oecd.org.
16. United Nations, *Demographic Yearbook 2008* (United Nations publication, Sales No. 11.XIII.1).
17. ________, *Energy Statistics database*, http://unstats.un.org/unsd/energy/edbase.htm.
18. ________, *Energy Statistics Yearbook 2007* (United Nations publication, Sales No. 10.XVII.8).
19. ________, *Industrial Commodity Statistics Yearbook 2007* (United Nations publication, Sales No. 10.XVII.12, vols. I and II).
20. ________, *Industrial Commodity Statistics database*, http://unstats.un.org/unsd/industry/ics_intro.asp.
21. ________, *International Trade Statistics Yearbook 2009*, (United Nations publication, Sales No. 11.XVII.2).
22. ________, *International Trade Statistics database*; http://comtrade.un.org.

Sources statistiques et références

A. Sources statistiques

1. “Carbon Dioxide Information Analysis Center (CDIAC)”, *la base de données des estimations nationales des émissions de CO_2*; http://cdiac.esd.ornl.gov.
2. Organisation des Nations Unies pour l’alimentation et l’agriculture (Rome), *Annuaire statistique de la FAO*; http://faostat.fao.org.
3. ________, *les données des pêches de FISHSTAT*; http://www.fao.org/fishery/statistics/software/fishstat/en.
4. ________, *Evaluation des ressources forestières mondiales 2010*; http://www.fao.org/docrep/013/i1757e/i1757e00.htm.
5. Organisation de l’aviation civile internationale, (Montréal); *la base de données statistiques intégrée (ISDB).*
6. Bureau international du Travail (Genève), *la base de données du BIT*; http://laborsta.ilo.org.
7. ________, *Annuaire des statistiques du Travail*; http://laborsta.ilo.org.
8. Fonds monétaire international (Washington, D.C.), *la base de données de Statistiques Financières Internationales*; http://www.imfstatistics.org/imf/.
9. Union interparlementaire (Genève), *les femmes dans les parlements, la base de données PARLINE*; http://www.ipu.org/wmn-e/world.htm.
10. Organisation internationale du sucre (Londres), *Annuaire du sucre 2009.*
11. Union Internationale des télécommunications (Genève), *l’Annuaire statistique 2010.*
12. ________, “*World Telecommunication/ICT Indicators 2009*”.
13. ________, *la base de données de l’UIT*; www.itu.int.
14. Organisation de Coopération et de Développement Economiques (Paris); *la base de données du comité d’aide au développement de l’OCDE*; http://stats.oecd.org/qwids.
15. ________, *la Répartition géographique des ressources financières de aux pays bénéficiaires de l’aide*, 2004-2008 ; www.oecd.org.
16. Nations Unies, *Annuaire démographique 2008* (publication des Nations Unies, No de vente 11. XIII.1).
17. ________, *la base de données pour les statistiques de l'énergie*; http://unstats.un.org/unsd/energy/edbase.htm.
18. ________, *Annuaire des statistiques de l'énergie 2007* (publication des Nations Unies, No. de vente 10.XVII.8).
19. ________, *Annuaire des statistiques industrielles par produit 2007,* (publications des Nations Unies, No. de vente 10.XVII.12, vols. I et II).
20. ________, *la base de données pour les statistiques industrielles*;

23. ________, *Monthly Bulletin of Statistics Online;* http://unstats.un.org/unsd/mbs.
24. ________, *National Accounts Statistics: Main Aggregates and Detailed Tables, 2008* (United Nations publication, Sales No. 11.XVII.5).
25. ________, *the National Accounts database*; http://unstats.un.org/unsd/snaama/Introduction.asp.
26. ________, *Comprehensive statistical analysis of the financing of operational activities for development of the United Nations system for 2008, Report of the Secretary-General* (A/65/79).
27. ________, *World Population Prospects: The 2008 Revision* (United Nations publication Sales No. 09.XIII.5).
28. ________, *World Urbanization Prospects: The 2009 Revision* (United Nations publication, Sales No. POP/DB/WUP/Rev. 2009), CD-ROM.
29. United Nations Environment Program, Ozone Secretariat (Nairobi), http://ozone.unep.org/Data_Reporting/Data_Access.
30. United Nations Educational, Scientific and Cultural Organization, Institute for Statistics (Montreal), *UIS database*; www.uis.unesco.org.
31. United Nations World Tourism Organization (Madrid), *Yearbook of Tourism Statistics, 2010 edition*; www.world-tourism.org.
32. World Bank (Washington, D.C.), *Global Development Finance*, vols. I and II; www.worldbank.org.
33. World Conservation Union (IUCN) / Species Survival Commission (SSC) (Gland, Switzerland and Cambridge, United Kingdom), *IUCN Red List of Threatened Species*, 2006, 2008 and 2010; www.iucnredlist.org.
34. World Health Organisation (WHO) and United Nations Children's Fund (UNICEF), *the WHO/UNICEF Joint Monitoring Programme for the Water and Sanitation database*; http://www.wssinfo.org/en/124_dataProcess.html.

http://unstats.un.org/unsd/industry/ics_intro.asp.
21. ________, *Annuaire statistique du commerce international 2009*, (publication des Nations Unies, No. de vente 11.XVII.2).
22. ________, *la base de données pour les statistiques du commerce extérieur*; http://comtrade.un.org.
23. ________, *Bulletin mensuel de statistique* ; http://unstats.un.org/unsd/mbs.
24. ________, "*National Accounts Statistics: Main Aggregates and Detailed Tables, 2008*" (publication des Nations Unies, No. de vente 11.XVII.5).
25. ________, *la base de données sur les compte nationaux*; http://unstats.un.org/unsd/snaama/Introduction.asp.
26. ________, *Analyse statistique du financement des activités opérationnelles de développement du système des Nations Unies pour 2008, Rapport du Secrétaire général* (A/65/79).
27. ________, "*World Population Prospects: The 2008 Revision*" (publication des Nations Unies, No. de vente 09.XIII.5).
28. ________, "*World Urbanization Prospects: The 2009 Revision*" (publication des Nations Unies, No. de vente POP/DB/WUP/Rev. 2009), CD-ROM.
29. Secrétariat de l'ozone du programme des Nations Unies pour l'environnement (Nairobi), centre de communication de données; http://ozone.unep.org/Data_Reporting/Data_Access.
30. Organisation des Nations Unies pour l'éducation, la science et la culture (UNESCO) Institut de statistique (Montréal), *la base de données de l'Institut de statistique de l'UNESCO*; www.uis.unesco.org.
31. Organisation mondiale du tourisme (OMT) (Madrid), *l'Annuaire des statistiques du tourisme, édition 2010*; www.world-tourism.org.
32. Banque mondiale (Washington, D.C.), "*Global Development Finance*", Vols. I et II ; www.worldbank.org.
33. Union mondiale pour la nature (UICN) / Commission de la sauvegarde des espèces (Gland, Suisse, et Cambridge, Royaume-Uni), *La liste rouge des espèces menacées de l'UICN*, 2006, 2008 et 2010; www.iucnredlist.org.
34. Organisation mondial de la santé (OMS) et Fonds des Nations Unies pour l'enfance (UNICEF), *la base de données de la Programme commun OMS/UNICEF de surveillance de l'eau et de l'assainissement*; http://www.wssinfo.org/en/124_dataProcess.html.

B. References

35. International Labour Office, *International Standard Classification of Occupations, Revised Edition 1968* (Geneva, 1969); revised edition, 1988, *ISCO-88* (Geneva, 1990), revised edition, 2008, *ISCO-08* (Geneva, 2007).
36. United Nations Statistics Division, Classifications of Expenditure According to Purpose: Classification of the Functions of Government (COFOG), Classification of Individual Consumption According to Purpose (COICOP), Classification of the Purposes of Non-Profit Institutions Serving Households (COPNI), Classification of the Outlays of Producers According to Purpose (COPP), Series M, No. 84 (United Nations publication, Sales No. E.00.XVII.6).
37. ________, *Energy Statistics: Definitions, Units of Measure and Conversion Factors*, Series F, No. 44 (United Nations publication, Sales No. E.86.XVII.21).
38. ________, *Energy Statistics: Manual for Developing Countries*, Series F, No. 56 (United Nations publication, Sales No. E.91.XVII.10).
39. ________, *Handbook of Vital Statistics Systems and Methods*, vol. I, *Legal, Organization and Technical Aspects*, Series F, No. 35, vol. I (United Nations publication, Sales No. E.91.XVII.5).
40. ________, *Handbook on Social Indicators*, Studies in Methods, Series F, No. 49 (United Nations publication, Sales No. E.89.XVII.6).
41. ________, *International Recommendations for Industrial Statistics 2008*, Series M, No. 90 (United Nations publication, Sales No. E.08.XVII.8).
42. ________, *International Standard Industrial Classification of All Economic Activities*, Statistical Papers, Series M, No. 4, Rev. 2 (United Nations publication, Sales No. E.68.XVII.8); Rev. 3 (United Nations publication, Sales No. E.90.XVII.11).
43. ________, *International Trade Statistics: Concepts and Definitions*, Series M, No. 52, Rev. 2 (United Nations publication, Sales No. 98.XVII.16).
44. ________, *Methods Used in Compiling the United Nations Price Indexes for External Trade*, volume 1, Statistical Papers, Series M, No. 82 (United Nations Publication, Sales No. E.87.XVII.4), volume 2 (United Nations publication, sales No. E.91.XVII.8).
45. ________, *Principles and Recommendations for Population and Housing Censuses*, Statistical Papers, Series M, No. 67 (United Nations publication, Sales No. E.80.XVII.8).
46. ________, *Provisional Guidelines on Statistics of International Tourism*, Statistical Papers, Series M, No. 62 (United Nations publication, Sales No. E.78.XVII.6).

B. Références

35. Organisation internationale du Travail, *Classification internationale type des professions, édition révisée 1968* (Genève, 1969); édition révisée 1988, *CITP-88* (Genève, 1990). édition révisée 2008, *CITP-08* (Genève, 2007).
36. Division de statistique de Nations Unies, "Classifications of Expenditure According to Purpose: Classification of the Functions of Government (COFOG), Classification of Individual Consumption According to Purpose (COICOP), Classification of the Purposes of Non-Profit Institutions Serving Households (COPNI), Classification of the Outlays of Producers According to Purpose (COPP)", Série M, No.84 (publication des Nations Unies, No. de vente E.00.XVII.6).
37. ________, *Statistiques de l'énergie: définitions, unités de mesures et facteurs de conversion*, Série F, No. 44 (publication des Nations Unies, No. de vente F.86.XVII.21).
38. ________, *Statistiques de l'énergie: Manuel pour les pays en développement*, Série F, No. 56 (publication des Nations Unies, No. de vente F.91.XVII.10).
39. ________, "*Handbook of Vital Statistics System and Methods*, Vol. 1, *Legal, Organization and Technical Aspects*", Série F, No. 35, Vol. 1 (publication des Nations Unies, No. de vente E.91.XVII.5).
40. ________, *Manuel des indicateurs sociaux*, Série F, No. 49 (publication des Nations Unies, No. de vente F.89.XVII.6).
41. ________, *Recommandations internationales concernant les statistiques industrielles 2008*, Série M, No. 90 (publication des Nations Unies, No. de vente F.08.XVII.8).
42. ________, *Classification internationale type, par industrie, de toutes les branches d'activité économique*, Série M, No. 4, Rev. 2 (publication des Nations Unies, No. de vente F.68.XVII.8); Rev. 3 (publication des Nations Unies, No. de vente F.90.XVII.11).
43. ________, *Statistiques du commerce international: Concepts et définitions*, Série M, No. 52, Rev. 2 (publication des Nations Unies, No. de vente 98.XVII.16).
44. ________, Méthodes utilisées par les Nations Unies pour établir les indices des prix des produits de base entrant dans le commerce international, Série M, No. 82, Vol. 1 (publication des Nations Unies, No. de vente F.87.XVII.4), Vol. 2 (publication des Nations Unies, No. de vente F.97.XVII.8).
45. ________, Principes et recommandations concernant les recensements de la population et de l'habitation, Série M, No. 67 (publication des Nations Unies, No. de vente F.80.XVII.8).

47. _______, *Standard International Trade Classification Rev. 4,* Series M, No. 34/Rev. 4 (United Nations publication, Sales No. E.06.XVII,10), *Revision 3*, Statistical Papers, Series M, No. 34, Rev. 3 (United Nations publication, Sales No. E.86.XVII.12), *Revision 2*, Series M, No. 34, Rev. 2 (United Nations publication), *Revision*, Series M, No. 34, Revision (United Nations publication, Sales No. E.61.XVII.6).
48. _______, *Supplement to the Statistical Yearbook and the Monthly Bulletin of Statistics, 1977,* Series S and Series Q, Supplement 2 (United Nations publication, Sales No. E.78.XVII.10).
49. _______, *System of National Accounts, Studies in Methods*, Series F, No. 2, Rev. 3 (United Nations publication, Sales No. E.69.XVII.3).
50. _______, *System of National Accounts 2008,* Series F, No. 2/Rev. 5, (United Nations publication, Sales No. 08.XVII.29), *System of National Accounts 1993*, Studies in Methods, Series F, No. 2, Rev. 4 (United Nations publication, Sales No. E.94.XVII.4).
51. _______, *Towards a System of Social and Demographic Statistics, Studies in Methods*, Series F, No. 18 (United Nations publication, Sales No. E.74.XVII.8).
52. _______, *World Weights and Measures* (United Nations publication, Sales No. E.66.XVII.3).
53. World Tourism Organization, Methodological Supplement to World Travel and Tourism Statistics (Madrid, 1985).
54. _______, *Recommendations on Tourism Statistics*, Statistical Papers, Series M, No. 83 (United Nations publication, Sales No. E.94.XVII.6).

46. _______, Directives provisoires pour l'établissement des statistiques du tourisme international, Série M, No. 62 (publication des Nations Unies, No. de vente 78.XVII.6).
47. _______, Classification type pour le commerce international (troisième version révisée), Standard International Trade Classification Rev. 4, Series M, No. 34/Rev. 4 (publication des Nations Unies , No. de vente E.06.XVII,10), Révision 3, Série M, No. 34, Rev. 3 (publication des Nations Unies, No. de vente F.86.XVII.12), Révision 2, Série M, No. 34, Rev. 2 (publication des Nations Unies), Révision, Série M, No. 34, Révision (publication des Nations Unies, No. de vente F.61.XVII.6).
48. _______, *Supplément à l'Annuaire statistique et au bulletin mensuel de statistique, 1977,* Série S et Série Q, supplément 2 (publication des Nations Unies, No. de vente F.78.XVII.10).
49. _______, *Système de comptabilité nationale*, Série F, No. 2, Rev. 3 (publication des Nations Unies, No. de vente F.69.XVII.3).
50. _______, *Système de comptabilité nationale 2008,* Series F, No. 2/Rev. 5, (United Nations publication, Sales No. 08.XVII.29), *Système de comptabilité nationale 1993*, Série F, No.2, Rev. 4 (publication des Nations Unies, No. de vente F.94.XVII.4).
51. _______, *Vers un système de statistiques démographiques et sociales, Etudes méthodologiques,* Série F, No. 18 (publication des Nations Unies, No. de vente F.74.XVII.8).
52. _______, "*World Weights and Measures*" (publication des Nations Unies, No. de vente E.66.XVII.3).
53. Organisation mondiale du tourisme, Supplément méthodologique aux statistiques des voyages et du tourisme mondiaux (Madrid, 1985).
54. _______, "*Recommendations on Tourism Statistics*, Statistical Papers", Série M, No. 83 (publication des Nations Unies, No. de vente E.94.XVII.6).

Country and area index

Indice de pays et zones

	Population		Gender / Femms			Education		Communication			National accounts / Compatibilités nationale					
Table	**7**	**8**	**9**	**10**	**11**	**12**	**13**	**14**	**15**	**16**	**17**	**18**	**19**	**20**	**21**	**Tableau**
Afghanistan	•	•	•	•	•	•		•	•	•	•	•	•	•		Afghanistan
Albania	•	•	•	•	•	•		•	•	•	•	•	•	•		Albanie
Algeria	•	•	•	•	•	•		•	•	•	•	•	•	•	•	Algérie
American Samoa	•	•		•	•			•	•							Samoa américaines
Andorra	•	•	•	•	•	•	•	•	•	•	•	•	•	•		Andorre
Angola	•	•	•		•	•	•	•	•	•	•	•	•	•	•	Angola
Anguilla	•	•		•	•	•	•				•	•	•	•	•	Anguilla
Antigua and Barbuda	•	•	•	•	•	•		•	•	•	•	•	•	•		Antigua-et-Barbuda
Argentina	•	•	•	•	•	•	•	•	•	•	•	•	•	•	•	Argentine
Armenia	•	•	•	•	•	•	•	•	•	•	•	•	•	•	•	Arménie
Aruba	•	•		•	•	•	•	•	•	•	•	•	•	•	•	Aruba
Ascension	•															Ascension
Australia	•	•	•	•	•	•	•	•	•	•	•	•	•	•	•	Australie
Austria	•	•	•	•	•	•	•	•	•	•	•	•	•	•	•	Autriche
Azerbaijan	•	•	•	•	•	•	•	•	•	•	•	•	•	•	•	Azerbaïdjan
Bahamas	•	•	•	•	•	•		•	•	•	•	•	•	•	•	Bahamas
Bahrain	•	•	•	•	•	•		•	•	•	•	•	•	•	•	Bahreïn
Bangladesh	•	•	•	•	•	•	•	•	•	•	•	•	•	•	•	Bangladesh
Barbados	•	•	•	•	•	•	•	•	•	•	•	•	•	•	•	Barbade
Belarus	•	•	•	•	•	•	•	•	•	•	•	•	•	•	•	Bélarus
Belgium	•	•	•	•	•	•	•	•	•	•	•	•	•	•	•	Belgique
Belgium-Luxembourg																Belgique-Luxembourg
Belize	•	•	•	•	•	•	•	•	•	•	•	•	•	•	•	Belize
Benin	•	•	•	•	•	•	•	•	•	•	•	•	•	•	•	Bénin
Bermuda	•	•		•	•	•	•	•	•	•	•	•	•	•	•	Bermudes
Bhutan	•	•	•	•	•	•	•	•	•	•	•	•	•	•	•	Bhoutan
Bolivia	•	•	•	•	•	•	•	•	•	•	•	•	•	•	•	Bolivie
Bonaire																Bonaire
Bosnia and Herzegovina	•	•	•	•	•	•		•	•	•	•	•	•	•		Bosnie-Herzégovine
Botswana	•	•	•	•	•	•	•	•	•	•	•	•	•	•	•	Botswana
Brazil	•	•	•	•	•	•	•	•	•	•	•	•	•	•	•	Brésil
British Indian Ocean Terr																Terr. brit. de l'océan Indien
British Virgin Islands	•	•		•	•	•	•				•	•	•	•	•	Iles Vierges britanniques
Brunei Darussalam	•	•		•	•	•		•	•	•	•	•	•	•		Brunéi Darussalam
Bulgaria	•	•	•	•	•	•	•	•	•	•	•	•	•	•	•	Bulgarie
Burkina Faso	•	•	•	•	•	•	•	•	•	•	•	•	•	•	•	Burkina Faso
Burundi	•	•	•	•	•	•	•	•	•	•	•	•	•	•	•	Burundi
Cambodia	•	•	•	•	•	•	•	•	•	•	•	•	•	•	•	Cambodge
Cameroon	•	•	•	•	•	•	•	•	•	•	•	•	•	•	•	Cameroun
Canada	•	•	•	•	•	•	•	•	•	•	•	•	•	•	•	Canada
Cape Verde	•	•	•	•	•	•	•	•	•	•	•	•	•	•	•	Cap-Vert
Cayman Islands	•	•		•	•	•	•	•	•	•	•	•	•	•	•	Iles Caïmanes
Central African Rep.	•	•	•	•	•	•	•	•	•	•	•	•	•	•		Rép. centrafricaine
Chad	•	•	•	•	•	•	•	•	•	•	•	•	•	•	•	Tchad
Channel Islands		•														Iles Anglo-Normandes
Chile	•	•	•	•	•	•	•	•	•	•	•	•	•	•	•	Chili
China	•	•	•	•	•	•		•	•	•	•	•	•	•	•	Chine
China, Hong Kong SAR	•	•		•	•	•	•	•	•	•	•	•	•	•	•	Chine, Hong Kong RAS
China, Macao SAR	•	•		•	•	•	•	•	•	•	•	•	•	•		Chine, Macao RAS
Christmas Is.																Ile Christmas
Cocos (Keeling) Islands																Iles des Cocos (Keeling)
Colombia	•	•	•	•	•	•	•	•	•	•	•	•	•	•	•	Colombie
Comoros	•	•	•		•	•		•	•	•	•	•	•	•	•	Comores
Congo	•	•	•	•	•	•	•	•	•	•	•	•	•	•	•	Congo
Cook Islands	•	•		•		•					•	•	•	•		Iles Cook
Costa Rica	•	•	•	•	•	•	•	•	•	•	•	•	•	•	•	Costa Rica
Côte d'Ivoire	•	•	•		•	•	•	•	•	•	•	•	•	•	•	Côte d'Ivoire
Croatia	•	•	•	•	•	•		•	•	•	•	•	•	•		Croatie
Cuba	•	•	•	•	•	•	•	•	•	•	•	•	•	•	•	Cuba
Curaçao																Curaçao
Cyprus	•	•	•	•	•	•	•	•	•	•	•	•	•	•	•	Chypre
Czech Republic	•	•	•	•	•	•	•	•	•	•	•	•	•	•	•	République tchèque
Dem. Rep. of the Congo	•	•	•	•	•	•		•	•	•	•	•	•		•	Rép. dém. du Congo
Denmark	•	•	•	•	•	•	•	•	•	•	•	•	•	•	•	Danemark
Djibouti	•	•	•	•	•	•	•	•	•	•	•	•	•	•	•	Djibouti
Dominica	•	•	•	•	•	•	•	•	•	•	•	•	•	•	•	Dominique
Dominican Republic	•	•	•	•	•	•	•	•	•	•	•	•	•	•	•	Rép. dominicaine

	Finance		Labour, wages and prices Main d'œuvre, salaires et prix				Agriculture, forestry and fishing Agriculture, forêts et pêche						Manufacturing Industries manufacturières			
Table	**22**	**23**	**24**	**25**	**26**	**27**	**28**	**29**	**30**	**31**	**32**	**33**	**34**	**35**	**36**	**Tableau**
Afghanistan		•					•	•	•	•	•	•	•	•		Afghanistan
Albania	•	•		•		•	•	•	•	•	•	•	•	•	•	Albanie
Algeria	•	•		•		•	•	•	•	•	•	•	•	•	•	Algérie
American Samoa						•	•		•	•	•					Samoa américaines
Andorra						•										Andorre
Angola	•					•	•	•	•	•	•	•	•	•	•	Angola
Anguilla	•	•		•		•				•						Anguilla
Antigua and Barbuda	•	•		•			•			•	•			•	•	Antigua-et-Barbuda
Argentina		•		•	•	•	•	•	•	•	•	•	•	•	•	Argentine
Armenia		•		•	•	•	•	•	•	•	•	•	•	•	•	Arménie
Aruba	•	•		•		•				•						Aruba
Ascension																Ascension
Australia		•		•	•	•	•	•	•	•	•	•	•	•	•	Australie
Austria			•	•	•	•	•	•	•	•	•	•		•	•	Autriche
Azerbaijan	•	•		•		•	•	•	•	•	•	•	•	•	•	Azerbaïdjan
Bahamas	•	•		•		•	•			•	•		•	•		Bahamas
Bahrain		•		•		•	•		•	•	•	•		•		Bahreïn
Bangladesh	•			•	•	•	•	•	•	•	•	•	•	•		Bangladesh
Barbados	•	•					•			•	•	•	•	•	•	Barbade
Belarus	•				•		•	•	•	•	•	•	•	•	•	Bélarus
Belgium		•	•	•	•	•	•	•	•	•	•			•	•	Belgique
Belgium-Luxembourg								•								Belgique-Luxembourg
Belize	•	•		•		•	•	•	•	•	•	•	•	•	•	Belize
Benin	•	•					•	•	•	•	•		•	•	•	Bénin
Bermuda				•		•	•	•		•	•		•			Bermudes
Bhutan				•		•	•	•	•	•	•	•		•		Bhoutan
Bolivia	•	•		•	•	•	•	•	•	•	•	•	•	•	•	Bolivie
Bonaire																Bonaire
Bosnia and Herzegovina						•	•	•	•	•	•	•	•	•	•	Bosnie-Herzégovine
Botswana	•			•	•	•	•	•	•	•	•		•	•	•	Botswana
Brazil	•	•		•	•	•	•	•	•	•	•	•	•	•	•	Brésil
British Indian Ocean Terr										•						Terr. brit. de l'océan Indien
British Virgin Islands						•	•			•	•					Iles Vierges britanniques
Brunei Darussalam				•		•	•	•	•	•	•	•	•	•		Brunéi Darussalam
Bulgaria	•	•	•	•	•	•	•	•	•	•	•	•	•	•	•	Bulgarie
Burkina Faso	•	•				•	•	•	•	•	•	•	•	•	•	Burkina Faso
Burundi	•	•				•	•	•	•	•	•	•	•	•	•	Burundi
Cambodia				•		•	•	•	•	•	•	•	•	•		Cambodge
Cameroon	•					•	•	•	•	•	•	•	•	•	•	Cameroun
Canada	•	•		•	•	•	•	•	•	•	•	•	•	•	•	Canada
Cape Verde	•	•				•	•	•		•	•		•	•		Cap-Vert
Cayman Islands				•		•	•			•	•					Iles Caïmanes
Central African Rep.	•					•	•	•	•	•	•		•	•	•	Rép. centrafricaine
Chad	•					•	•	•	•	•	•		•	•		Tchad
Channel Islands										•						Iles Anglo-Normandes
Chile	•	•		•	•	•	•	•	•	•	•	•	•	•	•	Chili
China	•			•		•	•	•	•	•	•	•	•	•	•	Chine
China, Hong Kong SAR	•	•			•	•				•			•		•	Chine, Hong Kong RAS
China, Macao SAR		•		•		•				•			•			Chine, Macao RAS
Christmas Is.																Ile Christmas
Cocos (Keeling) Islands																Iles des Cocos (Keeling)
Colombia	•	•		•	•	•	•	•	•	•	•	•	•	•	•	Colombie
Comoros	•						•	•		•	•		•	•		Comores
Congo	•					•	•	•	•	•	•	•	•	•	•	Congo
Cook Islands						•	•			•	•			•		Iles Cook
Costa Rica	•			•		•	•	•	•	•	•	•	•	•		Costa Rica
Côte d'Ivoire	•	•					•	•	•	•	•	•	•	•		Côte d'Ivoire
Croatia	•	•	•	•	•	•	•	•	•	•	•	•	•	•	•	Croatie
Cuba						•	•	•	•	•	•	•	•	•	•	Cuba
Curaçao																Curaçao
Cyprus	•	•	•	•	•	•	•	•		•	•	•	•	•	•	Chypre
Czech Republic	•	•	•	•	•	•	•	•	•	•	•	•	•	•	•	République tchèque
Dem. Rep. of the Congo	•	•					•	•	•	•	•	•	•	•		Rép. dém. du Congo
Denmark	•	•	•	•	•	•	•	•	•	•	•	•		•	•	Danemark
Djibouti							•			•	•		•	•		Djibouti
Dominica	•	•				•	•		•	•	•	•		•	•	Dominique
Dominican Republic		•		•		•	•	•	•	•	•		•	•	•	Rép. dominicaine

	Manufacturing Industries manufacturiès												
Table	**37**	**38**	**39**	**40**	**41**	**42**	**43**	**44**	**45**	**46**	**47**	**48**	**Tableau**
Afghanistan			•		•								Afghanistan
Albania	•		•	•	•		•						Albanie
Algeria			•	•	•		•		•		•		Algérie
American Samoa													Samoa américaines
Andorra	•												Andorre
Angola			•		•		•						Angola
Anguilla													Anguilla
Antigua and Barbuda													Antigua-et-Barbuda
Argentina	•		•	•	•		•	•	•	•	•	•	Argentine
Armenia	•	•	•	•	•								Arménie
Aruba													Aruba
Ascension													Ascension
Australia			•	•	•		•	•		•	•	•	Australie
Austria			•	•	•	•	•	•					Autriche
Azerbaijan	•	•	•	•	•		•	•	•	•	•	•	Azerbaïdjan
Bahamas			•										Bahamas
Bahrain				•	•			•					Bahreïn
Bangladesh	•		•	•	•	•			•	•			Bangladesh
Barbados				•	•								Barbade
Belarus	•	•	•	•	•		•		•	•	•	•	Bélarus
Belgium	•		•	•	•	•	•						Belgique
Belgium-Luxembourg			•	•									Belgique-Luxembourg
Belize	•		•										Belize
Benin			•		•								Bénin
Bermuda													Bermudes
Bhutan			•	•	•								Bhoutan
Bolivia	•	•	•	•	•								Bolivie
Bonaire													Bonaire
Bosnia and Herzegovina	•		•	•	•		•	•					Bosnie-Herzégovine
Botswana		•											Botswana
Brazil	•	•	•	•	•	•	•	•	•	•	•	•	Brésil
British Indian Ocean Terr													Terr. brit. de l'océan Indien
British Virgin Islands													Iles Vierges britanniques
Brunei Darussalam			•		•								Brunéi Darussalam
Bulgaria	•	•	•	•	•	•	•	•	•				Bulgarie
Burkina Faso			•		•								Burkina Faso
Burundi	•		•										Burundi
Cambodia			•		•								Cambodge
Cameroon	•		•		•			•					Cameroun
Canada	•		•	•	•	•	•	•					Canada
Cape Verde													Cap-Vert
Cayman Islands													Iles Caïmanes
Central African Rep.			•										Rép. centrafricaine
Chad			•										Tchad
Channel Islands													Iles Anglo-Normandes
Chile	•	•	•	•	•	•	•			•	•	•	Chili
China	•	•	•	•	•	•	•	•			•	•	Chine
China, Hong Kong SAR	•	•			•								Chine, Hong Kong RAS
China, Macao SAR	•	•											Chine, Macao RAS
Christmas Is.													Ile Christmas
Cocos (Keeling) Islands													Iles des Cocos (Keeling)
Colombia	•		•	•	•		•			•			Colombie
Comoros													Comores
Congo	•		•										Congo
Cook Islands													Iles Cook
Costa Rica			•	•	•								Costa Rica
Côte d'Ivoire			•		•								Côte d'Ivoire
Croatia	•	•	•	•	•	•	•	•					Croatie
Cuba	•	•	•	•	•	•	•		•		•	•	Cuba
Curaçao													Curaçao
Cyprus	•	•	•		•	•							Chypre
Czech Republic		•	•	•	•	•	•	•	•				République tchèque
Dem. Rep. of the Congo			•	•	•		•						Rép. dém. du Congo
Denmark	•	•	•	•	•	•	•	•	•	•	•		Danemark
Djibouti													Djibouti
Dominica			•										Dominique
Dominican Republic	•		•	•	•	•	•						Rép. dominicaine

	Energy		Environment					Science and technology		International merchandise trade			
	Energie		Environnement					Science et technologie		Commerce nternational des marchandises			
Table	**49**	**50**	**51**	**52**	**53**	**54**	**55**	**56**	**57**	**58**	**59**	**60**	**Tableau**
Afghanistan	•	•	•	•	•	•	•			•			Afghanistan
Albania	•	•	•	•	•	•	•			•			Albanie
Algeria	•	•	•	•	•	•	•	•	•	•			Algérie
American Samoa		•	•			•				•			Samoa américaines
Andorra	•	•	•	•		•	•			•			Andorre
Angola	•	•	•	•	•	•	•			•			Angola
Anguilla	•	•	•	•		•	•			•			Anguilla
Antigua and Barbuda	•	•	•	•	•	•	•			•			Antigua-et-Barbuda
Argentina	•	•	•	•	•	•	•	•	•	•	•		Argentine
Armenia	•	•	•	•	•	•	•	•	•	•			Arménie
Aruba	•	•	•	•		•	•			•			Aruba
Ascension													Ascension
Australia	•	•	•	•	•	•	•	•	•	•	•	•	Australie
Austria	•	•	•	•		•	•	•	•	•	•	•	Autriche
Azerbaijan	•	•	•	•	•	•	•	•	•	•			Azerbaïdjan
Bahamas	•	•	•	•	•	•	•			•			Bahamas
Bahrain	•	•	•	•	•	•	•			•			Bahreïn
Bangladesh	•	•	•	•	•	•	•			•			Bangladesh
Barbados	•	•	•	•	•	•	•			•			Barbade
Belarus	•	•	•	•	•	•	•	•	•	•			Bélarus
Belgium	•	•	•	•		•	•	•	•	•	•	•	Belgique
Belgium-Luxembourg													Belgique-Luxembourg
Belize	•	•	•	•	•	•	•			•			Belize
Benin	•	•	•	•	•	•	•	•		•			Bénin
Bermuda	•	•	•	•		•			•	•			Bermudes
Bhutan	•	•	•	•	•	•	•			•			Bhoutan
Bolivia	•	•	•	•	•	•	•		•	•	•		Bolivie
Bonaire													Bonaire
Bosnia and Herzegovina	•	•	•	•	•	•	•	•		•			Bosnie-Herzégovine
Botswana	•	•	•	•	•	•	•	•	•	•			Botswana
Brazil	•	•	•	•	•	•	•	•	•	•	•		Brésil
British Indian Ocean Terr						•							Terr. brit. de l'océan Indien
British Virgin Islands	•	•	•	•		•	•						Iles Vierges britanniques
Brunei Darussalam	•	•	•	•	•	•		•	•	•			Brunéi Darussalam
Bulgaria	•	•	•	•	•	•	•	•	•	•	•		Bulgarie
Burkina Faso	•	•	•	•	•	•	•	•	•	•			Burkina Faso
Burundi	•	•	•	•	•	•	•			•			Burundi
Cambodia	•	•	•	•	•	•	•	•	•	•			Cambodge
Cameroon	•	•	•	•	•	•	•	•		•			Cameroun
Canada	•	•	•	•	•	•	•	•	•	•	•	•	Canada
Cape Verde	•	•	•	•	•	•	•	•		•			Cap-Vert
Cayman Islands	•	•	•	•		•	•			•			Iles Caïmanes
Central African Rep.	•	•	•	•	•	•	•	•		•			Rép. centrafricaine
Chad	•	•	•	•	•	•	•			•			Tchad
Channel Islands			•										Iles Anglo-Normandes
Chile	•	•	•	•	•	•	•	•	•	•			Chili
China	•	•	•	•	•	•	•	•	•	•			Chine
China, Hong Kong SAR	•	•		•		•		•	•	•	•	•	Chine, Hong Kong RAS
China, Macao SAR	•	•		•		•		•	•	•			Chine, Macao RAS
Christmas Is.						•							Ile Christmas
Cocos (Keeling) Islands						•							Iles des Cocos (Keeling)
Colombia	•	•	•	•	•	•	•	•	•	•	•		Colombie
Comoros	•	•	•	•	•	•	•			•			Comores
Congo	•	•	•	•	•	•	•			•			Congo
Cook Islands	•	•	•	•	•	•	•			•			Iles Cook
Costa Rica	•	•	•	•	•	•	•	•	•	•			Costa Rica
Côte d'Ivoire	•	•	•	•	•	•	•	•		•			Côte d'Ivoire
Croatia	•	•	•	•	•	•	•	•	•	•			Croatie
Cuba	•	•	•	•	•	•		•	•	•			Cuba
Curaçao													Curaçao
Cyprus	•	•	•	•	•	•	•	•	•	•			Chypre
Czech Republic	•	•	•	•	•	•	•	•	•	•	•		République tchèque
Dem. Rep. of the Congo	•	•	•	•	•	•	•	•	•	•			Rép. dém. du Congo
Denmark	•	•	•	•		•	•	•	•	•	•	•	Danemark
Djibouti	•	•	•	•	•	•	•			•			Djibouti
Dominica	•	•	•	•	•	•	•			•	•		Dominique
Dominican Republic	•	•	•	•	•	•	•			•			Rép. dominicaine

	International tourism and transport Tourisme international et transport				International finance Finances internationales			Development assistance Aide au développement			
Table	61	62	63	64	65	66	67	68	69	70	Tableau
Afghanistan					•		•	•		•	Afghanistan
Albania	•	•	•	•	•	•	•	•		•	Albanie
Algeria	•	•	•	•	•	•	•	•		•	Algérie
American Samoa	•	•	•								Samoa américaines
Andorra	•	•									Andorre
Angola	•	•	•	•	•	•	•	•		•	Angola
Anguilla	•	•	•		•	•		•			Anguilla
Antigua and Barbuda	•	•	•	•	•	•		•		•	Antigua-et-Barbuda
Argentina	•	•	•	•	•	•	•	•		•	Argentine
Armenia	•	•	•	•	•	•	•	•		•	Arménie
Aruba	•	•	•		•	•				•	Aruba
Ascension											Ascension
Australia	•	•	•	•	•	•			•	•	Australie
Austria	•	•	•	•		•			•	•	Autriche
Azerbaijan	•	•	•	•	•	•	•	•		•	Azerbaïdjan
Bahamas	•	•	•	•	•	•				•	Bahamas
Bahrain	•	•	•	•	•	•		•		•	Bahreïn
Bangladesh	•	•	•	•	•	•	•	•		•	Bangladesh
Barbados	•	•	•		•	•		•		•	Barbade
Belarus	•	•	•	•	•	•	•	•		•	Bélarus
Belgium	•	•	•	•		•			•	•	Belgique
Belgium-Luxembourg											Belgique-Luxembourg
Belize	•	•	•		•	•	•	•		•	Belize
Benin	•	•	•		•	•	•	•		•	Bénin
Bermuda	•	•	•								Bermudes
Bhutan	•	•		•	•	•	•	•		•	Bhoutan
Bolivia	•	•	•	•	•	•	•	•		•	Bolivie
Bonaire	•	•	•								Bonaire
Bosnia and Herzegovina	•	•	•	•	•	•	•	•		•	Bosnie-Herzégovine
Botswana	•	•	•	•	•	•	•	•		•	Botswana
Brazil	•	•	•	•	•	•	•	•		•	Brésil
British Indian Ocean Terr											Terr. brit. de l'océan Indien
British Virgin Islands	•	•									Iles Vierges britanniques
Brunei Darussalam	•	•	•	•	•	•				•	Brunéi Darussalam
Bulgaria	•	•	•	•	•	•	•			•	Bulgarie
Burkina Faso	•	•	•	•	•	•	•	•		•	Burkina Faso
Burundi	•	•	•		•	•	•	•		•	Burundi
Cambodia	•	•	•	•	•	•	•	•		•	Cambodge
Cameroon	•	•	•	•	•	•	•	•		•	Cameroun
Canada	•	•	•	•	•	•			•	•	Canada
Cape Verde	•	•	•	•	•	•	•	•		•	Cap-Vert
Cayman Islands	•	•									Iles Caïmanes
Central African Rep.	•	•	•		•	•	•	•		•	Rép. centrafricaine
Chad	•	•			•	•	•	•		•	Tchad
Channel Islands											Iles Anglo-Normandes
Chile	•	•	•	•	•	•	•	•		•	Chili
China	•	•	•	•	•	•	•	•		•	Chine
China, Hong Kong SAR	•	•	•		•	•					Chine, Hong Kong RAS
China, Macao SAR	•	•	•		•	•				•	Chine, Macao RAS
Christmas Is.											Ile Christmas
Cocos (Keeling) Islands											Iles des Cocos (Keeling)
Colombia	•	•	•	•	•	•	•	•		•	Colombie
Comoros	•	•	•		•	•	•	•		•	Comores
Congo	•	•	•		•	•	•	•		•	Congo
Cook Islands	•	•	•					•		•	Iles Cook
Costa Rica	•	•	•	•	•	•	•	•		•	Costa Rica
Côte d'Ivoire		•	•		•	•	•	•		•	Côte d'Ivoire
Croatia	•	•	•	•	•	•		•		•	Croatie
Cuba	•	•	•	•				•		•	Cuba
Curaçao	•	•	•								Curaçao
Cyprus	•	•	•	•	•	•				•	Chypre
Czech Republic	•	•	•	•	•	•			•	•	République tchèque
Dem. Rep. of the Congo	•	•			•	•	•	•		•	Rép. dém. du Congo
Denmark	•	•	•	•	•	•			•		Danemark
Djibouti	•	•	•		•	•	•	•		•	Djibouti
Dominica	•	•	•		•	•	•	•		•	Dominique
Dominican Republic	•	•	•		•	•	•	•		•	Rép. dominicaine

	Population		Gender / Femms			Education		Communication			National accounts / Compatibilités nationale					
Table	**7**	**8**	**9**	**10**	**11**	**12**	**13**	**14**	**15**	**16**	**17**	**18**	**19**	**20**	**21**	**Tableau**
Ecuador	•	•	•	•	•	•	•	•	•	•	•	•	•	•	•	Ecuador
Egypt	•	•	•	•	•	•	•	•	•	•	•	•	•	•	•	Egypte
El Salvador	•	•	•	•	•	•	•	•	•	•	•	•	•	•	•	El Salvador
Equatorial Guinea	•	•	•	•	•	•		•	•	•	•	•	•	•		Guinée équatoriale
Eritrea	•	•	•		•	•	•	•	•	•	•	•				Erythrée
Estonia	•	•	•	•	•	•	•	•	•	•	•	•	•	•	•	Estonie
Ethiopia	•	•	•	•	•	•	•	•	•	•	•	•	•	•	•	Ethiopie
F. R. Germany																R. f. Allemagne
Faeroe Islands	•	•		•				•	•	•						Iles Féroé
Falkland Is. (Malvinas)	•	•														Iles Falkland (Malvinas)
Fiji	•	•	•	•	•	•		•	•	•	•	•	•	•	•	Fidji
Finland	•	•	•	•	•	•	•	•	•	•	•	•	•	•	•	Finlande
France	•	•	•	•	•	•	•	•	•	•	•	•	•	•	•	France
French Guiana	•	•		•				•	•	•			•	•	•	Guyane française
French Polynesia	•	•		•				•	•	•	•	•	•	•		Polynésie française
Gabon	•	•	•		•	•		•	•	•	•	•	•	•	•	Gabon
Gambia	•	•	•	•	•	•		•	•	•	•	•	•	•	•	Gambie
Georgia	•	•	•	•	•	•	•	•	•	•	•	•	•	•	•	Géorgie
Germany	•	•	•	•	•	•	•	•	•	•	•	•	•	•	•	Allemagne
Ghana	•	•	•	•	•	•	•	•	•	•	•	•	•	•	•	Ghana
Gibraltar	•	•		•		•		•	•	•						Gibraltar
Greece	•	•	•	•	•	•	•	•	•	•	•	•	•	•	•	Grèce
Greenland	•	•		•				•	•	•	•	•	•		•	Groenland
Grenada	•	•	•		•	•		•	•	•	•	•	•	•	•	Grenade
Guadeloupe	•	•		•									•	•	•	Guadeloupe
Guam	•	•		•				•	•	•						Guam
Guatemala	•	•	•	•	•	•	•	•	•	•	•	•	•	•	•	Guatemala
Guernsey	•	•						•	•	•						Guernesey
Guinea	•	•	•		•	•	•	•	•	•	•	•	•	•		Guinée
Guinea-Bissau	•	•	•	•	•	•		•	•	•	•	•	•	•	•	Guinée-Bissau
Guyana	•	•	•	•	•	•	•	•	•	•	•	•	•	•	•	Guyana
Haiti	•	•	•	•	•			•	•	•	•	•	•		•	Haïti
Holy See	•	•														Saint-Siège
Honduras	•	•	•	•	•	•		•	•	•	•	•	•	•	•	Honduras
Hungary	•	•	•	•	•	•	•	•	•	•	•	•	•	•	•	Hongrie
Iceland	•	•	•	•	•	•	•	•	•	•	•	•	•	•	•	Islande
India	•	•	•	•	•	•	•	•	•	•	•	•	•	•	•	Inde
Indonesia	•	•	•	•	•	•	•	•	•	•	•	•	•	•	•	Indonésie
Iran (Islamic Rep. of)	•	•	•	•	•	•	•	•	•	•	•	•	•	•	•	Iran (Rép. islamique d')
Iraq	•	•	•	•	•	•		•	•	•	•	•	•	•	•	Iraq
Ireland	•	•	•	•	•	•	•	•	•	•	•	•	•	•	•	Irlande
Isle of Man	•	•														Ile de Man
Israel	•	•	•	•	•	•	•	•	•	•	•	•	•	•	•	Israël
Italy	•	•	•	•	•	•	•	•	•	•	•	•	•	•	•	Italie
Jamaica	•	•	•	•	•	•	•	•	•	•	•	•	•	•	•	Jamaïque
Japan	•	•	•	•	•	•	•	•	•	•	•	•	•	•	•	Japon
Jersey	•							•	•	•						Jersey
Jordan	•	•	•	•	•	•		•	•	•	•	•	•	•	•	Jordanie
Kazakhstan	•	•	•	•	•	•	•	•	•	•	•	•	•	•	•	Kazakhstan
Kenya	•	•	•	•	•	•	•	•	•	•	•	•	•	•	•	Kenya
Kiribati	•	•	•	•	•	•		•	•	•	•	•	•	•	•	Kiribati
Korea, Dem. P. R.	•	•	•	•				•	•		•	•				Corée, R. p. dém. de
Korea, Republic of	•	•	•	•	•	•	•	•	•	•	•	•	•	•	•	Corée, République de
Kosovo											•	•	•	•		Kosovo
Kuwait	•	•	•		•	•	•	•	•	•	•	•	•	•	•	Koweït
Kyrgyzstan	•	•	•	•	•	•	•	•	•	•	•	•	•	•	•	Kirghizistan
Lao People's Dem. Rep.	•	•	•	•	•	•	•	•	•	•	•	•		•		Rép. dém. pop. lao
Latvia	•	•	•	•	•	•	•	•	•	•	•	•	•	•	•	Lettonie
Lebanon	•	•	•		•	•	•	•	•	•	•	•	•	•	•	Liban
Lesotho	•	•	•		•	•	•	•	•	•	•	•	•	•	•	Lesotho
Liberia	•	•	•	•	•	•	•	•	•	•	•	•	•	•	•	Libéria
Libyan Arab Jamah.	•	•	•	•	•	•		•	•	•	•	•	•	•	•	Jamah. arabe libyenne
Liechtenstein	•	•	•	•	•	•		•	•	•	•	•	•		•	Liechtenstein
Lithuania	•	•	•	•	•	•	•	•	•	•	•	•	•	•	•	Lituanie
Luxembourg	•	•	•	•	•	•		•	•	•	•	•	•	•	•	Luxembourg
Madagascar	•	•	•	•	•	•	•	•	•	•	•	•	•	•	•	Madagascar
Malawi	•	•	•	•	•	•		•	•	•	•	•	•	•	•	Malawi
Malaysia	•	•	•	•	•	•	•	•	•	•	•	•	•	•	•	Malaisie

	Finance		Labour, wages and prices / Main d'œuvre, salaires et prix				Agriculture, forestry and fishing / Agriculture, forêts et pèche						Manufacturing / Industries manufacturières			
Table	**22**	**23**	**24**	**25**	**26**	**27**	**28**	**29**	**30**	**31**	**32**	**33**	**34**	**35**	**36**	**Tableau**
Ecuador	•			•	•	•	•	•	•	•	•	•	•	•	•	Equateur
Egypt	•	•		•	•	•	•	•	•	•	•	•	•	•	•	Egypte
El Salvador		•		•		•	•	•	•	•	•	•	•	•		El Salvador
Equatorial Guinea	•					•	•		•	•	•					Guinée équatoriale
Eritrea							•	•	•	•	•	•	•	•		Erythrée
Estonia		•		•		•	•	•	•	•	•	•	•	•	•	Estonie
Ethiopia		•		•		•	•	•	•	•	•	•	•	•	•	Ethiopie
F. R. Germany																R. f. Allemagne
Faeroe Islands						•	•			•	•			•		Iles Féroé
Falkland Is. (Malvinas)						•	•			•	•			•		Iles Falkland (Malvinas)
Fiji	•	•				•	•	•	•	•	•	•	•	•	•	Fidji
Finland		•		•	•	•	•	•	•	•	•	•		•	•	Finlande
France		•	•	•	•	•	•	•	•	•	•	•		•	•	France
French Guiana						•	•	•	•	•	•			•		Guyane française
French Polynesia				•		•	•			•	•	•		•		Polynésie française
Gabon	•					•	•	•	•	•	•	•	•	•	•	Gabon
Gambia	•					•	•	•	•	•	•	•	•	•		Gambie
Georgia		•		•	•	•	•	•	•	•	•	•	•	•	•	Géorgie
Germany		•	•	•	•	•	•	•	•	•	•	•		•	•	Allemagne
Ghana	•	•				•	•	•	•	•	•	•	•	•	•	Ghana
Gibraltar						•							•			Gibraltar
Greece		•		•	•	•	•	•	•	•	•	•		•	•	Grèce
Greenland						•	•			•	•					Groenland
Grenada	•	•				•	•			•	•			•		Grenade
Guadeloupe						•	•			•	•			•		Guadeloupe
Guam						•	•			•	•					Guam
Guatemala		•		•	•	•	•	•	•	•	•	•	•	•	•	Guatemala
Guernsey																Guernesey
Guinea	•					•	•	•	•	•	•	•	•	•		Guinée
Guinea-Bissau	•	•				•	•	•	•	•	•		•	•		Guinée-Bissau
Guyana	•	•		•		•	•	•	•	•	•	•	•	•	•	Guyana
Haiti						•	•	•	•	•	•		•	•		Haïti
Holy See																Saint-Siège
Honduras						•	•	•	•	•	•	•	•	•		Honduras
Hungary	•	•	•	•		•	•	•	•	•	•	•	•	•	•	Hongrie
Iceland	•	•		•		•	•			•	•	•	•	•	•	Islande
India	•	•			•	•	•	•	•	•	•	•	•	•	•	Inde
Indonesia	•	•		•	•	•	•	•	•	•	•	•	•	•	•	Indonésie
Iran (Islamic Rep. of)				•	•	•	•	•	•	•	•	•	•	•	•	Iran (Rép. islamique d')
Iraq	•	•		•		•	•	•	•	•	•	•	•	•		Iraq
Ireland		•	•		•	•	•	•	•	•	•	•		•	•	Irlande
Isle of Man						•				•						Ile de Man
Israel	•	•			•	•	•	•	•	•	•	•	•	•		Israël
Italy		•	•		•	•	•	•	•	•	•	•		•	•	Italie
Jamaica		•				•	•	•	•	•	•	•	•	•	•	Jamaïque
Japan	•	•			•	•	•	•	•	•	•	•	•	•	•	Japon
Jersey						•										Jersey
Jordan	•	•			•	•	•	•	•	•	•	•	•	•	•	Jordanie
Kazakhstan	•	•				•	•	•	•	•	•	•	•	•	•	Kazakhstan
Kenya		•				•	•	•	•	•	•	•	•	•	•	Kenya
Kiribati						•	•			•	•			•		Kiribati
Korea, Dem. P. R.							•	•	•	•	•		•	•		Corée, R. p. dém. de
Korea, Republic of	•	•			•	•	•	•	•	•	•	•	•	•	•	Corée, République de
Kosovo						•										Kosovo
Kuwait	•	•			•	•	•	•		•	•	•	•	•		Koweït
Kyrgyzstan		•				•	•	•		•	•	•	•	•	•	Kirghizistan
Lao People's Dem. Rep.	•	•				•	•	•	•	•	•		•	•	•	Rép. dém. pop. lao
Latvia	•	•			•	•	•	•	•	•	•	•	•	•	•	Lettonie
Lebanon	•	•				•	•	•	•	•	•	•	•	•		Liban
Lesotho	•	•				•	•	•	•	•	•			•	•	Lesotho
Liberia							•	•	•	•	•		•	•		Libéria
Libyan Arab Jamah.	•	•					•	•	•	•	•	•	•	•		Jamah. arabe libyenne
Liechtenstein							•		•		•					Liechtenstein
Lithuania	•	•		•	•	•	•	•	•	•	•	•	•	•	•	Lituanie
Luxembourg			•	•	•	•	•	•	•		•	•		•	•	Luxembourg
Madagascar		•		•		•	•	•	•	•	•	•	•	•	•	Madagascar
Malawi	•	•				•	•	•	•	•	•	•	•	•	•	Malawi
Malaysia	•	•		•	•	•	•	•	•	•	•	•	•	•		Malaisie

	Manufacturing Industries manufacturières												
Table	**37**	**38**	**39**	**40**	**41**	**42**	**43**	**44**	**45**	**46**	**47**	**48**	**Tableau**
Ecuador	•		•	•	•	•	•				•		Equateur
Egypt	•		•	•	•		•	•			•	•	Egypte
El Salvador		•	•	•	•	•	•						El Salvador
Equatorial Guinea			•										Guinée équatoriale
Eritrea					•								Erythrée
Estonia		•	•	•	•	•	•						Estonie
Ethiopia	•		•	•	•								Ethiopie
F. R. Germany													R. f. Allemagne
Faeroe Islands													Iles Féroé
Falkland Is. (Malvinas)													Iles Falkland (Malvinas)
Fiji	•		•		•								Fidji
Finland	•	•	•	•	•	•	•	•	•	•	•	•	Finlande
France	•	•	•	•	•	•	•	•	•	•	•	•	France
French Guiana			•		•								Guyane française
French Polynesia													Polynésie française
Gabon	•		•		•								Gabon
Gambia			•										Gambie
Georgia	•	•	•	•	•								Géorgie
Germany	•	•	•	•	•	•	•	•	•	•	•	•	Allemagne
Ghana	•		•		•		•	•					Ghana
Gibraltar													Gibraltar
Greece	•	•	•	•	•	•	•	•			•	•	Grèce
Greenland													Groenland
Grenada													Grenade
Guadeloupe			•		•								Guadeloupe
Guam													Guam
Guatemala	•		•	•	•		•						Guatemala
Guernsey													Guernesey
Guinea			•		•								Guinée
Guinea-Bissau			•										Guinée-Bissau
Guyana			•										Guyana
Haiti			•		•								Haïti
Holy See													Saint-Siège
Honduras	•		•	•	•								Honduras
Hungary	•	•	•	•	•	•	•	•	•	•	•	•	Hongrie
Iceland					•			•					Islande
India	•		•	•	•	•	•	•	•	•	•	•	Inde
Indonesia			•	•	•	•	•	•			•	•	Indonésie
Iran (Islamic Rep. of)	•	•	•	•	•	•	•	•	•	•	•	•	Iran (Rép. islamique d')
Iraq	•	•	•	•	•				•				Iraq
Ireland	•	•	•	•	•	•	•		•	•	•		Irlande
Isle of Man													Ile de Man
Israel				•	•		•						Israël
Italy	•	•	•	•	•		•	•			•	•	Italie
Jamaica	•		•		•								Jamaïque
Japan	•	•	•	•	•	•	•		•	•	•	•	Japon
Jersey													Jersey
Jordan	•	•		•	•	•	•					•	Jordanie
Kazakhstan	•	•	•	•	•	•	•		•	•	•	•	Kazakhstan
Kenya	•	•	•	•	•	•	•			•			Kenya
Kiribati													Kiribati
Korea, Dem. P. R.			•	•	•		•						Corée, R. p. dém. de
Korea, Republic of	•		•	•	•	•	•	•	•	•	•	•	Corée, République de
Kosovo													Kosovo
Kuwait		•		•	•			•					Koweït
Kyrgyzstan	•	•	•	•	•				•				Kirghizistan
Lao People's Dem. Rep.	•		•		•								Rép. dém. pop. lao
Latvia	•	•	•	•	•	•	•					•	Lettonie
Lebanon	•		•	•	•								Liban
Lesotho		•											Lesotho
Liberia			•		•								Libéria
Libyan Arab Jamah.			•	•	•		•						Jamah. arabe libyenne
Liechtenstein			•										Liechtenstein
Lithuania	•	•	•	•	•	•					•		Lituanie
Luxembourg			•	•	•		•						Luxembourg
Madagascar	•		•	•	•								Madagascar
Malawi	•		•		•								Malawi
Malaysia	•		•	•	•		•		•	•	•		Malaisie

	Energy Energie		Environment Environnement					Science and technology Science et technologie		International merchandise trade Commerce international des marchandises			
Table	**49**	**50**	**51**	**52**	**53**	**54**	**55**	**56**	**57**	**58**	**59**	**60**	**Tableau**
Ecuador	•	•	•	•	•	•	•	•	•	•	•		Equateur
Egypt	•	•	•	•	•	•	•	•	•	•			Egypte
El Salvador	•	•	•	•	•	•	•	•	•	•			El Salvador
Equatorial Guinea	•	•	•	•	•	•	•			•			Guinée équatoriale
Eritrea	•	•	•	•	•	•	•						Erythrée
Estonia	•	•	•	•	•	•	•	•	•	•	•		Estonie
Ethiopia	•	•	•	•	•	•	•	•	•	•			Ethiopie
F. R. Germany													R. f. Allemagne
Faeroe Islands	•	•	•	•		•				•			Iles Féroé
Falkland Is. (Malvinas)	•	•	•	•		•							Iles Falkland (Malvinas)
Fiji	•	•	•	•	•	•	•			•			Fidji
Finland	•	•	•	•		•	•	•	•	•	•	•	Finlande
France	•	•	•	•		•	•	•	•	•	•	•	France
French Guiana	•	•	•	•		•	•						Guyane française
French Polynesia	•	•	•	•		•	•			•			Polynésie française
Gabon	•	•	•	•	•	•	•	•		•			Gabon
Gambia	•	•	•	•	•	•	•	•		•			Gambie
Georgia	•	•	•	•	•	•	•	•	•	•			Géorgie
Germany	•	•	•	•		•	•	•	•	•	•	•	Allemagne
Ghana	•	•	•	•	•	•	•			•			Ghana
Gibraltar	•	•	•	•		•				•			Gibraltar
Greece	•	•	•	•		•	•	•	•	•	•	•	Grèce
Greenland	•	•	•	•		•				•			Groenland
Grenada	•	•	•	•	•	•	•			•			Grenade
Guadeloupe	•	•	•	•		•	•						Guadeloupe
Guam		•	•			•	•			•			Guam
Guatemala	•	•	•	•	•	•	•	•	•	•			Guatemala
Guernsey	•	•				•							Guernesey
Guinea	•	•	•	•	•	•	•			•			Guinée
Guinea-Bissau	•	•	•	•	•	•	•			•			Guinée-Bissau
Guyana	•	•	•	•	•	•	•			•			Guyana
Haiti	•	•	•	•	•	•	•			•			Haïti
Holy See						•							Saint-Siège
Honduras	•	•	•	•	•	•	•	•		•	•		Honduras
Hungary	•	•	•	•	•	•	•	•	•	•	•		Hongrie
Iceland	•	•	•	•	•	•	•	•	•	•	•	•	Islande
India	•	•	•	•	•	•	•	•	•	•	•	•	Inde
Indonesia	•	•	•	•	•	•	•	•	•	•	•		Indonésie
Iran (Islamic Rep. of)	•	•	•	•	•	•	•	•	•	•			Iran (Rép. islamique d')
Iraq	•	•	•	•	•	•	•	•					Iraq
Ireland	•	•	•	•		•	•		•	•	•	•	Irlande
Isle of Man	•	•	•			•							Ile de Man
Israel	•	•	•	•	•	•	•		•	•	•	•	Israël
Italy	•	•	•	•		•	•	•	•	•	•	•	Italie
Jamaica	•	•	•	•	•	•	•		•	•			Jamaïque
Japan	•	•	•	•	•	•	•	•	•	•	•	•	Japon
Jersey	•	•				•							Jersey
Jordan	•	•	•	•	•	•	•	•	•	•	•		Jordanie
Kazakhstan	•	•	•	•	•	•	•	•	•	•			Kazakhstan
Kenya	•	•	•	•	•	•	•			•	•		Kenya
Kiribati	•	•	•	•	•	•	•			•			Kiribati
Korea, Dem. P. R.	•	•	•	•	•	•	•						Corée, R. p. dém. de
Korea, Republic of	•	•	•	•	•	•	•	•	•	•	•	•	Corée, République de
Kosovo													Kosovo
Kuwait	•	•	•	•	•	•	•	•	•	•			Koweït
Kyrgyzstan	•	•	•	•	•	•	•	•	•	•			Kirghizistan
Lao People's Dem. Rep.	•	•	•	•	•	•	•	•	•	•			Rép. dém. pop. lao
Latvia	•	•	•	•	•	•	•	•	•	•	•		Lettonie
Lebanon	•	•	•	•	•	•	•			•			Liban
Lesotho	•	•	•		•	•	•	•	•	•			Lesotho
Liberia	•	•	•	•	•	•	•			•			Libéria
Libyan Arab Jamah.	•	•	•	•	•	•	•	•		•	•		Jamah. arabe libyenne
Liechtenstein			•		•	•							Liechtenstein
Lithuania	•	•	•	•	•	•		•	•	•	•		Lituanie
Luxembourg		•	•	•		•	•	•	•	•			Luxembourg
Madagascar	•	•	•	•	•	•	•	•	•	•			Madagascar
Malawi	•	•	•	•	•	•	•			•			Malawi
Malaysia	•	•	•	•	•	•	•	•	•	•	•		Malaisie

	International tourism and transport Tourisme international et transport				International finance Finances internationales			Development assistance Aide au développement			
Table	**61**	**62**	**63**	**64**	**65**	**66**	**67**	**68**	**69**	**70**	**Tableau**
Ecuador	•	•	•	•		•	•	•		•	Equateur
Egypt	•	•	•	•	•	•	•	•		•	Egypte
El Salvador	•	•	•	•	•	•	•	•		•	El Salvador
Equatorial Guinea					•	•		•		•	Guinée équatoriale
Eritrea	•	•			•	•	•	•		•	Erythrée
Estonia	•	•	•	•	•	•				•	Estonie
Ethiopia	•	•	•	•	•	•	•	•		•	Ethiopie
F. R. Germany											R. f. Allemagne
Faeroe Islands											Iles Féroé
Falkland Is. (Malvinas)											Iles Falkland (Malvinas)
Fiji	•	•	•	•	•	•	•	•		•	Fidji
Finland	•	•	•	•		•			•	•	Finlande
France	•	•	•	•		•			•	•	France
French Guiana	•	•									Guyane française
French Polynesia	•	•	•								Polynésie française
Gabon		•	•	•	•	•	•	•		•	Gabon
Gambia	•	•	•		•	•	•	•		•	Gambie
Georgia	•	•	•	•	•	•	•	•		•	Géorgie
Germany	•	•	•	•		•			•	•	Allemagne
Ghana	•	•	•		•	•	•	•		•	Ghana
Gibraltar											Gibraltar
Greece	•	•	•	•		•			•	•	Grèce
Greenland											Groenland
Grenada	•	•	•		•	•	•	•		•	Grenade
Guadeloupe	•	•									Guadeloupe
Guam	•										Guam
Guatemala	•	•	•		•	•	•	•		•	Guatemala
Guernsey											Guernesey
Guinea	•	•	•		•	•	•	•		•	Guinée
Guinea-Bissau	•	•	•		•	•	•	•		•	Guinée-Bissau
Guyana	•	•	•		•	•	•	•		•	Guyana
Haiti	•	•	•		•	•	•	•		•	Haïti
Holy See											Saint-Siège
Honduras	•	•	•		•	•	•	•		•	Honduras
Hungary	•	•	•	•	•	•			•	•	Hongrie
Iceland	•	•	•	•	•	•			•	•	Islande
India	•	•	•	•	•	•	•	•		•	Inde
Indonesia	•	•	•	•	•	•	•	•		•	Indonésie
Iran (Islamic Rep. of)		•	•	•	•		•	•		•	Iran (Rép. islamique d')
Iraq		•	•		•	•		•		•	Iraq
Ireland	•	•	•	•		•			•	•	Irlande
Isle of Man											Ile de Man
Israel	•	•	•	•	•	•				•	Israël
Italy	•	•	•	•		•			•	•	Italie
Jamaica	•	•	•	•	•	•	•	•		•	Jamaïque
Japan	•	•	•	•	•	•			•	•	Japon
Jersey											Jersey
Jordan	•	•	•	•	•	•	•	•		•	Jordanie
Kazakhstan	•	•	•	•	•	•	•	•		•	Kazakhstan
Kenya	•	•	•	•	•	•	•	•		•	Kenya
Kiribati	•	•			•			•		•	Kiribati
Korea, Dem. P. R.				•				•		•	Corée, R. p. dém. de
Korea, Republic of	•	•	•	•	•	•			•	•	Corée, République de
Kosovo						•				•	Kosovo
Kuwait	•	•	•	•	•	•				•	Koweït
Kyrgyzstan	•	•	•	•	•	•	•	•		•	Kirghizistan
Lao People's Dem. Rep.	•	•	•	•	•	•	•	•		•	Rép. dém. pop. lao
Latvia	•	•	•	•	•	•				•	Lettonie
Lebanon	•	•	•	•	•	•	•	•		•	Liban
Lesotho	•	•	•		•	•	•	•		•	Lesotho
Liberia		•	•		•	•	•	•		•	Libéria
Libyan Arab Jamah.	•	•	•	•	•	•		•		•	Jamah. arabe libyenne
Liechtenstein	•	•									Liechtenstein
Lithuania	•	•	•	•	•	•	•			•	Lituanie
Luxembourg	•	•	•	•		•			•		Luxembourg
Madagascar	•	•	•	•	•	•	•	•		•	Madagascar
Malawi	•	•	•	•	•	•	•	•		•	Malawi
Malaysia	•	•	•	•	•	•	•	•		•	Malaisie

	Population	Gender / Femms			Education		Communication			National accounts / Compatibilités nationale					
Table	**7**	**8**	**9**	**10**	**11**	**12**	**13**	**14**	**15**	**16**	**17**	**18**	**19**	**20**	**21**	**Tableau**
Maldives	•	•	•	•	•	•	•	•	•	•	•	•	•		•	Maldives
Mali	•	•	•	•	•	•	•	•	•	•	•	•	•	•	•	Mali
Malta	•	•	•	•	•	•		•	•	•	•	•	•	•	•	Malte
Marshall Islands	•	•	•		•	•		•	•	•	•	•		•		Iles Marshall
Martinique	•	•		•									•	•	•	Martinique
Mauritania	•	•	•	•	•	•	•	•	•	•	•	•	•	•	•	Mauritanie
Mauritius	•	•	•	•	•	•	•	•	•	•	•	•	•	•	•	Maurice
Mayotte	•	•														Mayotte
Mexico	•	•	•	•	•	•	•	•	•	•	•	•	•	•	•	Mexique
Micronesia (Fed. States of)	•	•	•		•	•		•	•	•	•	•	•			Micronésie (Etats féd. de)
Monaco	•	•	•	•		•					•	•				Monaco
Mongolia	•	•	•	•	•	•	•	•	•	•	•	•	•	•	•	Mongolie
Montenegro	•	•	•	•				•	•	•	•	•	•	•		Monténégro
Montserrat	•	•			•	•					•	•	•	•		Montserrat
Morocco	•	•	•	•	•	•	•	•	•	•	•	•	•	•	•	Maroc
Mozambique	•	•	•	•	•	•	•	•	•	•	•	•	•	•	•	Mozambique
Myanmar	•	•		•	•	•		•	•	•	•	•	•	•	•	Myanmar
Namibia	•	•	•	•	•	•	•	•	•	•	•	•	•	•	•	Namibie
Nauru	•	•	•		•	•		•			•	•				Nauru
Nepal	•	•	•	•	•	•	•	•	•	•	•	•	•	•	•	Népal
Netherlands	•	•	•	•	•	•	•	•	•	•	•	•	•	•	•	Pays-Bas
Netherlands Antilles	•	•		•	•			•	•	•	•	•	•	•	•	Antilles néerlandaises
New Caledonia	•	•						•	•	•	•	•	•	•		Nouvelle-Calédonie
New Zealand	•	•	•	•	•	•	•	•	•	•	•	•	•	•	•	Nouvelle-Zélande
Nicaragua	•	•	•	•	•	•		•	•	•	•	•	•	•	•	Nicaragua
Niger	•	•	•	•	•	•	•	•	•	•	•	•	•	•	•	Niger
Nigeria	•	•	•	•	•	•		•	•	•	•	•	•	•	•	Nigéria
Niue	•	•		•	•	•										Nioué
Norfolk Island	•															Ile Norfolk
Northern Mariana Islands	•	•		•				•	•							Iles Mariannes du Nord
Norway	•	•	•	•	•	•	•	•	•	•	•	•	•	•	•	Norvège
Occupied Palestinian Terr.	•	•		•	•	•		•	•	•	•	•	•	•	•	Terr. palestinien occupé
Oman	•	•	•	•	•	•	•	•	•	•	•	•	•	•	•	Oman
Pakistan	•	•	•	•	•	•	•	•	•	•	•	•	•	•	•	Pakistan
Palau	•	•	•	•	•	•		•	•	•	•	•		•		Palaos
Panama	•	•	•	•	•	•	•	•	•	•	•	•	•	•	•	Panama
Papua New Guinea	•	•	•	•	•	•		•	•	•	•	•	•	•	•	Papouasie-Nvl-Guinée
Paraguay	•	•	•	•	•	•		•	•	•	•	•	•	•	•	Paraguay
Peru	•	•	•	•	•	•	•	•	•	•	•	•	•	•	•	Pérou
Philippines	•	•	•	•	•	•	•	•	•	•	•	•	•	•	•	Philippines
Pitcairn	•	•														Pitcairn
Poland	•	•	•	•	•	•	•	•	•	•	•	•	•	•	•	Pologne
Polynesia																Polynésie
Portugal	•	•	•	•	•	•	•	•	•	•	•	•	•	•	•	Portugal
Puerto Rico	•	•		•				•	•	•	•	•	•	•	•	Porto Rico
Qatar	•	•	•	•	•	•	•	•	•	•	•	•	•	•	•	Qatar
Republic of Moldova	•	•	•	•	•	•	•	•	•	•	•	•	•	•	•	République de Moldova
Réunion	•	•		•									•	•	•	Réunion
Romania	•	•	•	•	•	•	•	•	•	•	•	•	•	•	•	Roumanie
Russian Federation	•	•	•	•	•	•	•	•	•	•	•	•	•	•	•	Fédération de Russie
Rwanda	•	•	•	•	•	•	•	•	•	•	•	•	•	•	•	Rwanda
Saba																Saba
Saint Eustatius																Saint-Eustache
Saint Helena	•	•		•												Sainte-Hélène
Saint Kitts and Nevis	•	•	•		•	•	•	•	•	•	•	•	•	•	•	Saint-Kitts-et-Nevis
Saint Lucia	•	•	•	•	•	•	•	•	•	•	•	•	•	•	•	Sainte-Lucie
Saint Maarten																Saint-Martin
Saint Pierre and Miquelon	•	•														Saint-Pierre-et-Miquelon
Saint Vincent-Grenadines	•	•	•		•	•	•	•	•	•	•	•	•	•	•	Saint Vincent-Grenadines
Samoa	•	•	•	•	•	•		•	•	•	•	•		•		Samoa
San Marino	•	•	•	•		•		•	•	•	•	•	•		•	Saint-Marin
Sao Tome and Principe	•	•	•		•	•		•	•	•	•	•	•	•		Sao Tomé-et-Principe
Saudi Arabia	•	•	•	•	•	•		•	•	•	•	•	•	•	•	Arabie saoudite
Senegal	•	•	•	•	•	•	•	•	•	•	•	•	•	•	•	Sénégal

	Finance		Labour, wages and prices / Main d'œuvre, salaires et prix				Agriculture, forestry and fishing / Agriculture, forêts et pèche						Manufacturing / Industries manufacturières			
Table	**22**	**23**	**24**	**25**	**26**	**27**	**28**	**29**	**30**	**31**	**32**	**33**	**34**	**35**	**36**	**Tableau**
Maldives	•	•		•		•	•			•			•			Maldives
Mali	•	•		•		•	•	•	•	•	•	•	•	•	•	Mali
Malta	•	•	•	•		•	•	•		•	•	•	•	•		Malte
Marshall Islands						•	•			•						Iles Marshall
Martinique						•	•			•	•			•		Martinique
Mauritania	•	•				•	•	•	•	•	•		•	•		Mauritanie
Mauritius		•		•		•	•	•		•	•	•	•	•	•	Maurice
Mayotte										•						Mayotte
Mexico		•		•	•	•	•	•	•	•	•	•	•	•	•	Mexique
Micronesia (Fed. States of)							•			•	•			•		Micronésie (Etats féd. de)
Monaco										•						Monaco
Mongolia	•	•		•		•	•	•	•	•	•	•	•	•		Mongolie
Montenegro		•		•	•			•	•	•	•			•	•	Monténégro
Montserrat	•	•					•		•	•	•			•		Montserrat
Morocco	•	•		•	•	•	•	•	•	•	•	•	•	•		Maroc
Mozambique	•	•				•	•	•	•	•	•	•	•	•	•	Mozambique
Myanmar	•					•	•	•	•	•	•	•	•	•		Myanmar
Namibia	•	•		•		•	•	•		•	•	•	•	•	•	Namibie
Nauru							•			•	•					Nauru
Nepal	•	•		•		•	•	•	•	•	•	•	•	•	•	Népal
Netherlands			•	•	•	•	•	•	•	•	•	•		•	•	Pays-Bas
Netherlands Antilles	•	•		•		•	•			•	•		•			Antilles néerlandaises
New Caledonia						•	•	•		•	•	•		•		Nouvelle-Calédonie
New Zealand	•	•		•	•	•	•	•	•	•	•	•	•	•	•	Nouvelle-Zélande
Nicaragua				•		•	•	•	•	•	•	•	•	•		Nicaragua
Niger	•	•				•	•	•	•	•	•	•	•	•	•	Niger
Nigeria	•	•		•		•	•	•	•	•	•	•	•	•	•	Nigéria
Niue						•	•			•	•					Nioué
Norfolk Island						•										Ile Norfolk
Northern Mariana Islands						•				•						Iles Mariannes du Nord
Norway	•	•	•	•	•	•	•	•	•	•	•	•	•	•	•	Norvège
Occupied Palestinian Terr.				•	•	•	•	•		•	•			•		Terr. palestinien occupé
Oman	•	•		•	•	•	•	•		•	•	•		•		Oman
Pakistan	•	•			•	•	•	•	•	•	•	•	•	•		Pakistan
Palau				•						•						Palaos
Panama		•		•	•	•	•	•	•	•	•	•	•	•	•	Panama
Papua New Guinea	•	•		•		•	•	•	•	•	•	•	•	•		Papouasie-Nvl-Guinée
Paraguay	•	•		•		•	•	•	•	•	•	•	•	•		Paraguay
Peru	•	•		•	•	•	•	•	•	•	•	•	•	•	•	Pérou
Philippines	•	•		•	•	•	•	•	•	•	•	•	•	•		Philippines
Pitcairn										•						Pitcairn
Poland	•	•	•	•	•	•	•	•	•	•	•	•	•	•	•	Pologne
Polynesia																Polynésie
Portugal			•	•	•	•	•	•	•	•	•	•		•	•	Portugal
Puerto Rico						•	•	•		•	•			•	•	Porto Rico
Qatar	•	•		•		•	•	•		•	•	•		•		Qatar
Republic of Moldova		•		•		•	•	•	•	•	•	•	•	•	•	République de Moldova
Réunion						•	•	•		•	•			•		Réunion
Romania		•		•	•	•	•	•	•	•	•	•	•	•	•	Roumanie
Russian Federation	•	•	•	•	•	•	•	•	•	•	•	•	•	•	•	Fédération de Russie
Rwanda	•	•				•	•	•	•	•	•	•	•	•		Rwanda
Saba																Saba
Saint Eustatius																Saint-Eustache
Saint Helena				•		•				•	•					Sainte-Hélène
Saint Kitts and Nevis	•	•		•		•				•	•		•		•	Saint-Kitts-et-Nevis
Saint Lucia	•	•		•		•	•			•	•			•		Sainte-Lucie
Saint Maarten																Saint-Martin
Saint Pierre and Miquelon						•	•									Saint-Pierre-et-Miquelon
Saint Vincent-Grenadines	•	•		•		•	•	•		•	•			•		Saint Vincent-Grenadines
Samoa				•		•	•		•	•	•		•	•		Samoa
San Marino				•		•										Saint-Marin
Sao Tome and Principe	•					•	•	•		•	•			•		Sao Tomé-et-Principe
Saudi Arabia				•		•	•	•		•	•	•	•	•		Arabie saoudite
Senegal	•	•		•		•	•	•	•	•	•	•	•	•		Sénégal

	Manufacturing Industries manufacturières												
Table	37	38	39	40	41	42	43	44	45	46	47	48	Tableau
Maldives													Maldives
Mali	•		•		•								Mali
Malta													Malte
Marshall Islands													Iles Marshall
Martinique			•		•								Martinique
Mauritania			•	•	•		•						Mauritanie
Mauritius	•		•										Maurice
Mayotte													Mayotte
Mexico	•	•	•	•	•	•	•		•	•	•	•	Mexique
Micronesia (Fed. States of)													Micronésie (Etats féd. de)
Monaco													Monaco
Mongolia			•		•		•						Mongolie
Montenegro	•	•	•				•						Monténégro
Montserrat													Montserrat
Morocco			•	•	•		•						Maroc
Mozambique	•	•	•		•	•		•					Mozambique
Myanmar	•		•	•	•		•						Myanmar
Namibia													Namibie
Nauru													Nauru
Nepal	•	•	•	•	•	•			•				Népal
Netherlands			•	•	•		•	•					Pays-Bas
Netherlands Antilles													Antilles néerlandaises
New Caledonia			•		•								Nouvelle-Calédonie
New Zealand	•		•	•	•		•	•					Nouvelle-Zélande
Nicaragua	•		•		•								Nicaragua
Niger			•		•								Niger
Nigeria	•	•	•	•	•		•		•	•	•		Nigéria
Niue													Nioué
Norfolk Island													Ile Norfolk
Northern Mariana Islands													Iles Mariannes du Nord
Norway		•	•	•	•	•	•	•			•		Norvège
Occupied Palestinian Terr.					•								Terr. palestinien occupé
Oman					•								Oman
Pakistan	•		•	•	•		•						Pakistan
Palau													Palaos
Panama	•		•		•								Panama
Papua New Guinea			•										Papouasie-Nvl-Guinée
Paraguay			•	•	•		•						Paraguay
Peru	•	•	•	•	•	•	•				•		Pérou
Philippines			•	•	•		•						Philippines
Pitcairn													Pitcairn
Poland	•	•	•	•	•	•	•	•	•	•	•	•	Pologne
Polynesia													Polynésie
Portugal	•	•	•	•	•	•	•		•	•	•		Portugal
Puerto Rico					•								Porto Rico
Qatar					•		•						Qatar
Republic of Moldova	•	•	•	•	•		•		•			•	République de Moldova
Réunion			•	•	•								Réunion
Romania	•	•	•	•	•	•	•	•		•	•	•	Roumanie
Russian Federation	•	•	•	•	•	•	•	•	•	•	•	•	Fédération de Russie
Rwanda			•		•								Rwanda
Saba													Saba
Saint Eustatius													Saint-Eustache
Saint Helena													Sainte-Hélène
Saint Kitts and Nevis													Saint-Kitts-et-Nevis
Saint Lucia													Sainte-Lucie
Saint Maarten													Saint-Martin
Saint Pierre and Miquelon													Saint-Pierre-et-Miquelon
Saint Vincent-Grenadines													Saint Vincent-Grenadines
Samoa			•										Samoa
San Marino													Saint-Marin
Sao Tome and Principe			•										Sao Tomé-et-Principe
Saudi Arabia				•	•		•						Arabie saoudite
Senegal			•		•								Sénégal

	Energy Energie		Environment Environnement					Science and technology Science et technologie		International merchandise trade Commerce international des marchandises			
Table	**49**	**50**	**51**	**52**	**53**	**54**	**55**	**56**	**57**	**58**	**59**	**60**	**Tableau**
Maldives	•	•	•	•	•	•	•			•			Maldives
Mali	•	•	•	•	•	•	•	•		•			Mali
Malta	•	•	•	•	•	•	•	•	•	•			Malte
Marshall Islands	•	•	•	•	•	•	•						Iles Marshall
Martinique	•	•	•	•		•	•						Martinique
Mauritania	•	•	•	•	•	•	•			•			Mauritanie
Mauritius	•	•	•	•	•	•	•		•	•	•		Maurice
Mayotte			•			•							Mayotte
Mexico	•	•	•	•	•	•	•	•	•	•	•		Mexique
Micronesia (Fed. States of)			•	•	•	•	•						Micronésie (Etats féd. de)
Monaco					•	•	•	•	•	•			Monaco
Mongolia	•	•	•	•	•	•	•	•	•	•			Mongolie
Montenegro	•	•	•		•		•	•	•	•			Monténégro
Montserrat	•	•	•	•		•	•			•			Montserrat
Morocco	•	•	•	•	•	•	•	•	•	•	•		Maroc
Mozambique	•	•	•	•	•	•	•	•	•	•			Mozambique
Myanmar	•	•	•	•	•	•	•	•	•	•			Myanmar
Namibia	•	•	•	•	•	•	•			•			Namibie
Nauru	•	•	•	•	•	•	•	•					Nauru
Nepal	•	•	•	•	•	•	•	•		•			Népal
Netherlands	•	•	•	•		•	•	•	•	•	•	•	Pays-Bas
Netherlands Antilles	•	•	•	•		•				•			Antilles néerlandaises
New Caledonia	•	•	•	•		•				•			Nouvelle-Calédonie
New Zealand	•	•	•	•	•	•	•	•	•	•	•	•	Nouvelle-Zélande
Nicaragua	•	•	•	•	•	•	•	•	•	•			Nicaragua
Niger	•	•	•	•	•	•	•	•		•			Niger
Nigeria	•	•	•	•	•	•	•	•		•			Nigéria
Niue	•	•	•	•	•	•	•			•			Nioué
Norfolk Island			•			•							Ile Norfolk
Northern Mariana Islands			•			•	•						Iles Mariannes du Nord
Norway	•	•	•	•	•	•	•	•	•	•	•	•	Norvège
Occupied Palestinian Terr.	•	•	•	•		•	•	•		•			Terr. palestinien occupé
Oman	•	•	•	•	•	•	•			•			Oman
Pakistan	•	•	•	•	•	•	•	•	•	•	•	•	Pakistan
Palau	•	•	•	•	•	•	•						Palaos
Panama	•	•	•	•	•	•	•	•	•	•	•		Panama
Papua New Guinea	•	•	•	•	•	•	•			•	•		Papouasie-Nvl-Guinée
Paraguay	•	•	•	•	•	•	•	•	•	•			Paraguay
Peru	•	•	•	•	•	•	•	•	•	•	•		Pérou
Philippines	•	•	•	•	•	•	•	•	•	•	•		Philippines
Pitcairn			•			•							Pitcairn
Poland	•	•	•	•	•	•	•	•	•	•	•		Pologne
Polynesia													Polynésie
Portugal	•	•	•	•		•	•	•	•	•	•	•	Portugal
Puerto Rico	•	•	•										Porto Rico
Qatar	•	•	•	•	•	•	•			•			Qatar
Republic of Moldova	•	•	•	•	•	•	•	•	•	•	•		République de Moldova
Réunion	•	•	•	•		•							Réunion
Romania	•	•	•	•	•	•	•	•	•	•	•		Roumanie
Russian Federation	•	•	•	•	•	•	•	•	•	•	•		Fédération de Russie
Rwanda	•	•	•	•	•	•	•			•			Rwanda
Saba													Saba
Saint Eustatius													Saint-Eustache
Saint Helena	•	•	•	•		•							Sainte-Hélène
Saint Kitts and Nevis	•	•	•	•	•	•	•			•			Saint-Kitts-et-Nevis
Saint Lucia	•	•	•	•	•	•	•		•	•			Sainte-Lucie
Saint Maarten													Saint-Martin
Saint Pierre and Miquelon	•	•	•	•		•							Saint-Pierre-et-Miquelon
Saint Vincent-Grenadines	•	•	•	•	•	•	•	•	•	•			Saint Vincent-Grenadines
Samoa	•	•	•	•	•	•	•			•			Samoa
San Marino			•			•							Saint-Marin
Sao Tome and Principe	•	•	•	•	•	•	•			•			Sao Tomé-et-Principe
Saudi Arabia	•	•	•	•	•	•	•	•		•			Arabie saoudite
Senegal	•	•	•	•	•	•	•	•	•	•			Sénégal

	International tourism and transport				International finance			Development assistance			
	Tourisme international et transport				Finances internationales			Aide au développement			
Table	**61**	**62**	**63**	**64**	**65**	**66**	**67**	**68**	**69**	**70**	**Tableau**
Maldives	•	•	•	•	•	•	•	•		•	Maldives
Mali	•	•	•		•	•	•	•		•	Mali
Malta	•	•	•	•	•	•				•	Malte
Marshall Islands	•	•		•				•		•	Iles Marshall
Martinique	•	•									Martinique
Mauritania				•	•	•	•	•		•	Mauritanie
Mauritius	•	•	•	•	•	•	•	•		•	Maurice
Mayotte								•			Mayotte
Mexico	•	•	•	•	•	•	•	•		•	Mexique
Micronesia (Fed. States of)	•	•	•		•	•		•		•	Micronésie (Etats féd. de)
Monaco	•	•		•							Monaco
Mongolia	•	•	•	•	•	•	•	•		•	Mongolie
Montenegro	•	•	•		•	•	•	•		•	Monténégro
Montserrat	•	•	•		•	•		•		•	Montserrat
Morocco	•	•	•	•	•	•	•	•		•	Maroc
Mozambique	•	•	•	•	•	•	•	•		•	Mozambique
Myanmar	•	•	•	•	•	•	•	•		•	Myanmar
Namibia	•	•	•	•	•	•		•		•	Namibie
Nauru				•				•		•	Nauru
Nepal	•	•	•	•	•	•	•			•	Népal
Netherlands	•	•	•	•		•			•		Pays-Bas
Netherlands Antilles					•	•					Antilles néerlandaises
New Caledonia	•	•	•								Nouvelle-Calédonie
New Zealand	•	•	•	•	•	•			•		Nouvelle-Zélande
Nicaragua	•	•	•		•	•	•	•		•	Nicaragua
Niger	•	•	•		•	•	•	•		•	Niger
Nigeria	•	•	•	•	•	•	•	•		•	Nigéria
Niue	•	•	•					•		•	Nioué
Norfolk Island											Ile Norfolk
Northern Mariana Islands	•	•									Iles Mariannes du Nord
Norway	•	•	•	•	•	•			•	•	Norvège
Occupied Palestinian Terr.	•	•	•					•		•	Terr. palestinien occupé
Oman	•	•	•	•	•	•		•		•	Oman
Pakistan	•	•	•	•	•	•	•	•		•	Pakistan
Palau	•		•					•		•	Palaos
Panama	•	•	•	•	•	•	•	•		•	Panama
Papua New Guinea	•	•	•	•	•	•	•	•		•	Papouasie-Nvl-Guinée
Paraguay	•	•	•	•	•	•	•	•		•	Paraguay
Peru	•	•	•	•	•	•	•	•		•	Pérou
Philippines	•	•	•	•	•	•	•	•		•	Philippines
Pitcairn											Pitcairn
Poland	•	•	•	•	•	•			•	•	Pologne
Polynesia											Polynésie
Portugal	•	•	•	•		•			•	•	Portugal
Puerto Rico	•	•	•								Porto Rico
Qatar	•	•	•	•	•	•				•	Qatar
Republic of Moldova	•	•	•	•	•	•	•	•		•	République de Moldova
Réunion	•		•								Réunion
Romania	•	•	•	•	•	•	•			•	Roumanie
Russian Federation	•	•	•	•	•	•	•			•	Fédération de Russie
Rwanda	•	•	•		•	•	•	•		•	Rwanda
Saba	•	•									Saba
Saint Eustatius	•	•									Saint-Eustache
Saint Helena								•			Sainte-Hélène
Saint Kitts and Nevis	•	•	•		•	•	•	•		•	Saint-Kitts-et-Nevis
Saint Lucia	•	•	•		•	•	•	•		•	Sainte-Lucie
Saint Maarten	•	•	•								Saint-Martin
Saint Pierre and Miquelon											Saint-Pierre-et-Miquelon
Saint Vincent-Grenadines	•	•	•		•	•	•	•		•	Saint Vincent-Grenadines
Samoa	•	•	•	•	•	•	•	•		•	Samoa
San Marino	•	•			•	•					Saint-Marin
Sao Tome and Principe	•	•	•	•	•	•	•	•		•	Sao Tomé-et-Principe
Saudi Arabia	•	•	•	•	•	•		•		•	Arabie saoudite
Senegal	•	•	•	•	•	•	•	•		•	Sénégal

	Population	Gender Femms			Education		Communication			National accounts Compatibilités nationale					
Table	**7**	**8**	**9**	**10**	**11**	**12**	**13**	**14**	**15**	**16**	**17**	**18**	**19**	**20**	**21**	**Tableau**
Serbia	•	•	•	•	•	•		•	•	•	•	•	•	•	•	Serbie
Serbia and Montenegro			•										•	•		Serbie-et-Monténégro
Seychelles	•	•	•		•	•	•	•	•	•	•	•	•	•	•	Seychelles
Sierra Leone	•	•	•	•	•	•	•	•	•	•	•	•	•	•	•	Sierra Leone
Singapore	•	•	•	•		•	•	•	•	•	•	•	•	•	•	Singapour
Slovakia	•	•	•	•	•	•	•	•	•	•	•	•	•	•	•	Slovaquie
Slovenia	•	•	•	•	•	•	•	•	•	•	•	•	•	•	•	Slovénie
Solomon Islands	•	•	•		•	•		•	•	•	•	•	•	•	•	Iles Salomon
Somalia	•	•	•	•	•			•	•	•	•	•	•	•	•	Somalie
South Africa	•	•	•	•	•	•	•	•	•	•	•	•	•	•	•	Afrique du Sud
Spain	•	•	•	•	•	•	•	•	•	•	•	•	•	•	•	Espagne
Sri Lanka	•	•	•	•	•	•		•	•	•	•	•	•	•	•	Sri Lanka
Sudan	•	•	•	•	•	•		•	•	•	•	•	•	•	•	Soudan
Suriname	•	•	•	•	•	•		•	•	•	•	•	•	•	•	Suriname
Svalbard and Jan Mayen Is.	•															Svalbard et îles Jan Mayen
Swaziland	•	•	•		•	•	•	•	•	•	•	•	•	•	•	Swaziland
Sweden	•	•	•	•	•		•	•	•	•	•	•	•	•	•	Suède
Switzerland	•	•	•	•	•		•	•	•	•	•	•	•	•	•	Suisse
Syrian Arab Republic	•	•	•	•	•	•	•	•	•	•	•	•	•	•	•	Rép. arabe syrienne
Tajikistan	•	•	•	•	•	•	•	•	•	•	•	•	•	•	•	Tadjikistan
TFYR of Macedonia	•	•	•	•	•	•		•	•	•	•	•	•	•	•	L'ex-R.Y. Macédoine
Thailand	•	•	•	•	•	•	•	•	•	•	•	•	•	•	•	Thaïlande
Timor-Leste	•	•	•	•	•	•	•	•	•	•	•	•	•	•		Timor-Leste
Togo	•	•	•	•	•	•	•	•	•	•	•	•	•	•	•	Togo
Tokelau	•	•		•	•	•										Tokélaou
Tonga	•	•	•		•	•		•	•	•	•	•	•	•	•	Tonga
Trinidad and Tobago	•	•	•	•	•	•		•	•	•	•	•	•	•	•	Trinité-et-Tobago
Tristan da Cunha	•															Tristan da Cunha
Tunisia	•	•	•	•	•	•	•	•	•	•	•	•	•	•	•	Tunisie
Turkey	•	•	•	•	•	•		•	•	•	•	•	•	•	•	Turquie
Turkmenistan	•	•	•	•				•	•	•	•	•	•	•		Turkménistan
Turks and Caicos Islands	•	•		•	•	•	•				•	•	•	•		Iles Turques et Caïques
Tuvalu	•	•	•	•	•	•		•	•	•	•	•	•	•		Tuvalu
Uganda	•	•	•	•	•	•	•	•	•	•	•	•	•	•		Ouganda
Ukraine	•	•	•	•	•	•	•	•	•	•	•	•	•	•	•	Ukraine
United Arab Emirates	•	•	•	•	•	•	•	•	•	•	•	•	•	•	•	Emirats arabes unis
United Kingdom	•	•	•	•	•	•	•	•	•	•	•	•	•	•	•	Royaume-Uni
United Rep. of Tanzania	•	•	•	•	•	•		•	•	•	•	•	•	•	•	Rép.-Unie de Tanzanie
United States	•	•	•	•	•	•	•	•	•	•	•	•	•	•	•	Etats-Unis
United States Virgin Is.	•	•						•	•	•						Iles Vierges américaines
Uruguay	•	•	•	•	•	•	•	•	•	•	•	•	•	•	•	Uruguay
Uzbekistan	•	•	•	•	•	•		•	•	•	•	•	•	•		Ouzbékistan
Vanuatu	•	•	•	•	•	•	•	•	•	•	•	•	•	•	•	Vanuatu
Venezuela (Bolivarian Rep.of)	•	•	•	•	•	•	•	•	•	•	•	•	•	•	•	Venezuela (Rép. bolivarienne du)
Viet Nam	•	•	•	•		•	•	•	•	•	•	•	•	•		Viet Nam
Wallis and Futuna Islands	•	•														Iles Wallis et Futuna
Western Sahara	•	•														Sahara occidental
Yemen	•	•	•	•	•	•	•	•	•	•	•	•	•	•	•	Yémen
Zambia	•	•	•	•	•	•	•	•	•	•	•	•	•	•	•	Zambie
Zanzibar											•	•		•		Zanzibar
Zimbabwe	•	•	•	•	•	•		•	•	•	•	•	•	•	•	Zimbabwe

	Finance		Labour, wages and prices / Main d'œuvre, salaires et prix				Agriculture, forestry and fishing / Agriculture, forêts et pèche						Manufacturing / Industries manufacturières			
Table	**22**	**23**	**24**	**25**	**26**	**27**	**28**	**29**	**30**	**31**	**32**	**33**	**34**	**35**	**36**	**Tableau**
Serbia	•	•		•	•	•		•	•	•	•	•	•	•	•	Serbie
Serbia and Montenegro							•	•	•	•	•	•		•	•	Serbie-et-Monténégro
Seychelles	•	•				•	•			•	•			•	•	Seychelles
Sierra Leone		•		•		•	•	•	•	•	•		•	•	•	Sierra Leone
Singapore		•		•	•	•	•			•	•	•	•	•		Singapour
Slovakia	•	•	•	•	•	•	•	•	•	•	•	•	•	•	•	Slovaquie
Slovenia	•	•	•	•	•	•	•	•	•	•	•	•	•	•	•	Slovénie
Solomon Islands		•				•	•	•	•	•	•			•		Iles Salomon
Somalia							•	•	•	•	•		•	•		Somalie
South Africa	•	•		•	•	•	•	•	•	•	•	•	•	•		Afrique du Sud
Spain		•	•	•	•	•	•	•	•	•	•	•		•	•	Espagne
Sri Lanka	•	•		•		•	•	•	•	•	•	•	•	•	•	Sri Lanka
Sudan							•	•	•	•	•	•	•	•		Soudan
Suriname				•		•	•	•	•	•	•	•	•	•		Suriname
Svalbard and Jan Mayen Is.																Svalbard et îles Jan Mayen
Swaziland	•	•				•	•	•	•	•	•		•	•		Swaziland
Sweden	•	•		•	•	•	•	•	•	•	•	•		•	•	Suède
Switzerland	•	•		•	•	•	•	•	•	•	•	•	•	•		Suisse
Syrian Arab Republic	•			•	•	•	•	•	•	•	•	•	•	•	•	Rép. arabe syrienne
Tajikistan	•			•			•	•	•	•	•	•	•	•	•	Tadjikistan
TFYR of Macedonia	•			•	•	•	•	•	•	•	•	•	•	•	•	L'ex-R.Y. Macédoine
Thailand	•	•		•	•	•	•	•	•	•	•	•	•	•	•	Thaïlande
Timor-Leste							•	•	•	•	•			•		Timor-Leste
Togo	•	•		•		•	•	•	•	•	•	•	•	•	•	Togo
Tokelau							•			•	•					Tokélaou
Tonga				•		•	•			•	•	•		•		Tonga
Trinidad and Tobago	•	•			•	•	•	•	•	•	•	•	•	•	•	Trinité-et-Tobago
Tristan da Cunha																Tristan da Cunha
Tunisia		•			•	•	•	•	•	•	•	•	•	•	•	Tunisie
Turkey	•	•	•	•	•	•	•	•	•	•	•	•	•	•	•	Turquie
Turkmenistan							•	•		•	•		•	•	•	Turkménistan
Turks and Caicos Islands				•						•						Iles Turques et Caïques
Tuvalu						•	•			•	•					Tuvalu
Uganda	•	•		•		•	•	•	•	•	•	•	•	•	•	Ouganda
Ukraine	•	•		•	•	•	•	•	•	•	•	•	•	•	•	Ukraine
United Arab Emirates				•		•	•			•	•	•	•	•		Emirats arabes unis
United Kingdom		•		•	•	•	•	•	•	•	•	•		•	•	Royaume-Uni
United Rep. of Tanzania	•	•		•		•	•	•	•	•	•	•	•	•	•	Rép.-Unie de Tanzanie
United States	•	•	•	•	•	•	•	•	•	•	•	•	•	•	•	Etats-Unis
United States Virgin Is.							•			•	•			•		Iles Vierges américaines
Uruguay	•	•		•	•	•	•	•	•	•	•	•	•	•	•	Uruguay
Uzbekistan							•	•		•	•		•	•	•	Ouzbékistan
Vanuatu	•	•				•	•	•	•	•	•			•		Vanuatu
Venezuela (Bolivarian Rep.of)	•	•	•		•	•	•	•	•	•	•	•	•	•		Venezuela (Rép. bolivarienne du)
Viet Nam	•	•		•	•	•	•	•	•	•	•	•	•	•	•	Viet Nam
Wallis and Futuna Islands							•			•	•					Iles Wallis et Futuna
Western Sahara							•	•			•			•		Sahara occidental
Yemen		•		•		•	•	•	•	•	•	•	•	•		Yémen
Zambia	•	•				•	•	•	•	•	•	•	•	•		Zambie
Zanzibar						•				•						Zanzibar
Zimbabwe	•	•				•	•	•	•	•	•	•	•	•	•	Zimbabwe

	Manufacturing Industries manufacturières												
Table	**37**	**38**	**39**	**40**	**41**	**42**	**43**	**44**	**45**	**46**	**47**	**48**	**Tableau**
Serbia	•	•	•	•	•	•	•	•		•			Serbie
Serbia and Montenegro	•		•	•	•	•	•	•			•	•	Serbie-et-Monténégro
Seychelles	•												Seychelles
Sierra Leone			•		•								Sierra Leone
Singapore			•	•	•		•						Singapour
Slovakia		•	•	•	•	•	•	•		•	•		Slovaquie
Slovenia		•	•	•	•	•	•			•			Slovénie
Solomon Islands			•										Iles Salomon
Somalia			•										Somalie
South Africa			•	•	•	•	•	•	•		•	•	Afrique du Sud
Spain	•	•	•	•	•	•	•	•	•	•	•	•	Espagne
Sri Lanka	•		•	•	•	•	•						Sri Lanka
Sudan			•	•	•					•	•		Soudan
Suriname			•		•			•					Suriname
Svalbard and Jan Mayen Is.													Svalbard et îles Jan Mayen
Swaziland			•										Swaziland
Sweden	•	•	•	•	•	•	•	•	•	•	•	•	Suède
Switzerland	•		•	•	•		•	•					Suisse
Syrian Arab Republic	•		•	•	•		•				•	•	Rép. arabe syrienne
Tajikistan	•	•			•			•			•		Tadjikistan
TFYR of Macedonia	•	•	•	•	•	•	•	•			•		L'ex-R.Y. Macédoine
Thailand	•		•	•	•		•		•	•	•	•	Thaïlande
Timor-Leste													Timor-Leste
Togo			•		•								Togo
Tokelau													Tokélaou
Tonga			•										Tonga
Trinidad and Tobago	•		•		•		•						Trinité-et-Tobago
Tristan da Cunha													Tristan da Cunha
Tunisia	•		•	•	•		•						Tunisie
Turkey	•		•	•	•	•	•	•			•	•	Turquie
Turkmenistan					•								Turkménistan
Turks and Caicos Islands													Iles Turques et Caïques
Tuvalu													Tuvalu
Uganda	•		•	•	•		•						Ouganda
Ukraine	•	•	•	•	•	•	•	•	•	•	•	•	Ukraine
United Arab Emirates				•	•		•	•					Emirats arabes unis
United Kingdom	•	•	•	•	•	•	•	•		•	•	•	Royaume-Uni
United Rep. of Tanzania	•	•	•	•	•	•							Rép.-Unie de Tanzanie
United States	•		•	•	•		•	•			•	•	Etats-Unis
United States Virgin Is.													Iles Vierges américaines
Uruguay	•	•	•	•	•	•	•						Uruguay
Uzbekistan	•			•	•		•				•	•	Ouzbékistan
Vanuatu			•										Vanuatu
Venezuela (Bolivarian Rep. of)			•	•	•		•	•		•			Venezuela (Rép. bolivarienne du)
Viet Nam	•	•	•	•	•	•	•		•	•	•	•	Viet Nam
Wallis and Futuna Islands													Iles Wallis et Futuna
Western Sahara													Sahara occidental
Yemen	•			•	•								Yémen
Zambia			•	•	•								Zambie
Zanzibar													Zanzibar
Zimbabwe	•		•	•	•		•						Zimbabwe

	Energy		Environment					Science and technology		International merchandise trade			
	Energie		Environnement					Science et technologie		Commerce international des marchandises			
Table	**49**	**50**	**51**	**52**	**53**	**54**	**55**	**56**	**57**	**58**	**59**	**60**	**Tableau**
Serbia		•	•		•		•	•	•	•	•		Serbie
Serbia and Montenegro	•			•						•			Serbie-et-Monténégro
Seychelles	•	•	•	•	•	•	•	•	•	•	•		Seychelles
Sierra Leone	•	•	•	•	•	•	•			•			Sierra Leone
Singapore	•	•	•	•	•	•	•	•	•	•	•	•	Singapour
Slovakia	•	•	•	•	•	•	•	•	•	•	•		Slovaquie
Slovenia	•	•	•	•	•	•	•	•	•	•	•		Slovénie
Solomon Islands	•	•	•	•	•	•	•			•			Iles Salomon
Somalia	•	•	•	•	•	•	•						Somalie
South Africa	•	•	•	•	•	•	•	•	•	•	•	•	Afrique du Sud
Spain	•	•	•	•		•	•	•	•	•	•	•	Espagne
Sri Lanka	•	•	•	•	•	•	•	•	•	•	•		Sri Lanka
Sudan	•	•	•	•	•	•	•	•	•	•			Soudan
Suriname	•	•	•	•	•	•	•			•			Suriname
Svalbard and Jan Mayen Is.						•							Svalbard et îles Jan Mayen
Swaziland	•	•	•	•	•	•	•			•			Swaziland
Sweden	•	•	•	•		•	•	•	•	•	•	•	Suède
Switzerland	•	•	•	•	•	•	•	•	•	•	•	•	Suisse
Syrian Arab Republic	•	•	•	•	•	•	•			•			Rép. arabe syrienne
Tajikistan	•	•	•	•	•	•	•	•	•	•			Tadjikistan
TFYR of Macedonia	•	•	•	•	•	•	•	•	•	•			L'ex-R.Y. Macédoine
Thailand	•	•	•	•	•	•	•	•	•	•	•		Thaïlande
Timor-Leste	•	•	•	•	•	•	•						Timor-Leste
Togo	•	•	•	•	•	•	•	•		•			Togo
Tokelau			•			•	•						Tokélaou
Tonga	•	•	•	•	•	•	•			•			Tonga
Trinidad and Tobago	•	•	•	•	•	•	•	•	•	•			Trinité-et-Tobago
Tristan da Cunha													Tristan da Cunha
Tunisia	•	•	•	•	•	•	•	•	•	•			Tunisie
Turkey	•	•	•	•	•	•	•	•	•	•	•	•	Turquie
Turkmenistan	•	•	•	•	•	•	•			•			Turkménistan
Turks and Caicos Islands	•	•	•	•		•				•			Iles Turques et Caïques
Tuvalu		•	•		•	•	•			•			Tuvalu
Uganda	•	•	•	•	•	•	•	•	•	•			Ouganda
Ukraine	•	•	•	•	•	•		•	•	•			Ukraine
United Arab Emirates	•	•	•	•	•	•	•			•			Emirats arabes unis
United Kingdom	•	•	•	•		•	•	•	•	•	•	•	Royaume-Uni
United Rep. of Tanzania	•	•	•	•	•	•	•			•			Rép.-Unie de Tanzanie
United States	•	•	•	•	•	•	•	•	•	•	•	•	Etats-Unis
United States Virgin Is.		•	•			•							Iles Vierges américaines
Uruguay	•	•	•	•	•	•	•	•	•	•	•		Uruguay
Uzbekistan	•	•	•	•	•	•	•			•			Ouzbékistan
Vanuatu	•	•	•	•	•	•	•			•			Vanuatu
Venezuela (Bolivarian Rep. of)	•	•	•	•	•	•	•	•		•	•		Venezuela (Rép. bolivarienne du)
Viet Nam	•	•	•	•	•	•	•	•	•	•			Viet Nam
Wallis and Futuna Islands	•	•	•	•		•	•						Iles Wallis et Futuna
Western Sahara	•	•	•	•		•							Sahara occidental
Yemen	•	•	•	•	•	•	•			•			Yémen
Zambia	•	•	•	•	•	•	•	•		•			Zambie
Zanzibar													Zanzibar
Zimbabwe	•	•	•	•	•	•	•			•			Zimbabwe

	International tourism and transport Tourisme international et transport				International finance Finances internationales			Development assistance Aide au développement			
Table	**61**	**62**	**63**	**64**	**65**	**66**	**67**	**68**	**69**	**70**	**Tableau**
Serbia	•	•	•	•	•	•	•	•			Serbie
Serbia and Montenegro										•	Serbie-et-Monténégro
Seychelles	•	•	•	•	•	•	•	•		•	Seychelles
Sierra Leone	•	•	•	•	•	•	•	•		•	Sierra Leone
Singapore	•	•	•	•	•	•				•	Singapour
Slovakia	•	•	•	•	•	•			•	•	Slovaquie
Slovenia	•	•	•	•	•	•				•	Slovénie
Solomon Islands	•	•	•	•	•	•	•	•		•	Iles Salomon
Somalia							•	•		•	Somalie
South Africa	•	•	•	•	•	•	•	•		•	Afrique du Sud
Spain	•	•	•	•		•			•	•	Espagne
Sri Lanka	•	•	•	•	•	•	•	•		•	Sri Lanka
Sudan	•	•	•	•	•	•	•	•		•	Soudan
Suriname	•	•	•	•	•	•		•		•	Suriname
Svalbard and Jan Mayen Is.											Svalbard et îles Jan Mayen
Swaziland	•	•	•		•	•	•	•		•	Swaziland
Sweden	•	•	•	•	•	•			•	•	Suède
Switzerland	•	•	•	•	•	•			•	•	Suisse
Syrian Arab Republic	•	•	•	•	•	•	•	•		•	Rép. arabe syrienne
Tajikistan		•	•	•	•	•	•	•		•	Tadjikistan
TFYR of Macedonia	•	•	•	•	•	•	•	•		•	L'ex-R.Y. Macédoine
Thailand	•	•	•	•	•	•	•	•		•	Thaïlande
Timor-Leste						•		•		•	Timor-Leste
Togo	•	•	•		•	•	•	•		•	Togo
Tokelau								•		•	Tokélaou
Tonga	•	•	•		•	•	•	•		•	Tonga
Trinidad and Tobago	•	•	•	•	•	•		•		•	Trinité-et-Tobago
Tristan da Cunha											Tristan da Cunha
Tunisia	•	•	•	•	•	•	•	•		•	Tunisie
Turkey	•	•	•	•	•	•	•	•	•	•	Turquie
Turkmenistan	•	•	•	•	•		•	•		•	Turkménistan
Turks and Caicos Islands	•	•						•			Iles Turques et Caïques
Tuvalu	•	•	•					•		•	Tuvalu
Uganda	•	•	•	•	•	•	•	•		•	Ouganda
Ukraine	•	•	•	•	•	•	•	•		•	Ukraine
United Arab Emirates	•	•	•	•	•	•				•	Emirats arabes unis
United Kingdom	•	•	•	•	•	•			•	•	Royaume-Uni
United Rep. of Tanzania	•	•	•	•	•	•	•	•		•	Rép.-Unie de Tanzanie
United States	•	•	•	•	•	•			•	•	Etats-Unis
United States Virgin Is.	•	•									Iles Vierges américaines
Uruguay	•	•	•	•	•	•	•	•		•	Uruguay
Uzbekistan	•	•	•	•			•	•		•	Ouzbékistan
Vanuatu	•	•	•	•	•	•	•	•		•	Vanuatu
Venezuela (Bolivarian Rep. of)	•	•	•	•	•	•	•	•		•	Venezuela (Rép. bolivarienne du)
Viet Nam	•	•		•	•	•	•	•		•	Viet Nam
Wallis and Futuna Islands								•			Iles Wallis et Futuna
Western Sahara											Sahara occidental
Yemen	•	•	•	•	•	•	•	•		•	Yémen
Zambia	•	•	•	•	•	•	•	•		•	Zambie
Zanzibar											Zanzibar
Zimbabwe	•	•	•	•	•	•	•	•		•	Zimbabwe

Index

Note: References to tables are indicated by **boldface** type.